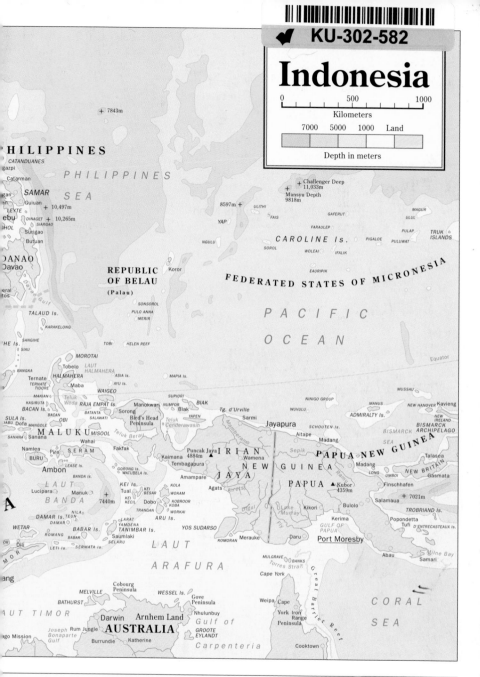

Indonesia

0   500   1000
Kilometers

7000   5000   1000   Land
Depth in meters

The Republic of Indonesia, with 190 million people, is the world's fourth largest country. Originally controlled by several Hindu and Islamic kingdoms, these 18,508 islands attracted the interest of European spice traders beginning in the 16th century. By the 19th century, the East Indies were a colony of Holland. Nationalist sentiment grew in the early 20th century, and after World War II and a difficult Japanese occupation, Sukarno, who was to be Indonesia's first president, declared independence on August 17, 1945. The Dutch were ousted five years later. The Indonesian language is a variant of Malay, long the region's lingua franca. The largest Islamic nation in the world, 88 percent of Indonesians are Muslims. In the more remote parts of the archipelago, traditional lifestyles are still practiced.

DIVING
INDONESIA

KAL MULLER

Edited by David Pickell

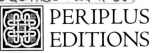

PERIPLUS
EDITIONS

WITHDRAWN

The Periplus Guide Books

SUMATRA

JAVA

BALI

EAST OF BALI
From Lombok to Timor

KALIMANTAN
Indonesian Borneo

SULAWESI
The Celebes

MALUKU
Indonesia's Spice Islands

IRIAN JAYA
Indonesian New Guinea

DIVING INDONESIA

WEST MALAYSIA
and Singapore

SABAH & SARAWAK
with Brunei Darussalam

The name PERIPLUS, meaning "voyage" or "journey," derives from the Greek. One of the earliest classical texts to mention Southeast Asia was the *Periplus of the Erythrean Sea*, an Alexandrian sailing manual dating from the first century of the common era. Periplus Editions, founded in 1988 by Eric Oey, specializes in the arts, cultures and natural history of the Malay archipelago—making authoritative information on the region available to a wider audience.

© 1996 by Periplus Editions (HK) Ltd.
ALL RIGHTS RESERVED
Printed in Singapore
ISBN 962-593-145-7

Publisher: Eric Oey
Design, Production and Cartography:
David Pickell

Distributors:

Australia: (New South Wales) R & A Book Agency, Unit 1, 56-72 John Street Leichhardt 2040 (Victoria, SA & Tasmania): Ken Pryse & Associates, 156 Collins Street, Melbourne 3000 (Western Australia) Edwards Book Agencies, 70 Jersey Street, Jolimont WA 6014

Germany: Brettschneider Fernreisebedarf, Hauptstrasse 5, D-85586 Poing

Hong Kong & Taiwan: Asia Publishers Services Ltd., 16/F, Wing Fat Commercial Building, 218 Aberdeen Main Road, Aberdeen, Hong Kong

Indonesia: C. V. Java Books, Jl. Gading Kirana Timur, Blok A13 No. 23, Jakarta 14240

Japan: Charles E Tuttle Inc., 21-13, Seki 1-Chome, Tama-ku, Kawasaki, Kanagawa 214

Singapore & Malaysia: Berkeley Books Pte. Ltd., 5 Little Road, #08-01 Singapore 536983

Thailand: Asia Books Co. Ltd., 5 Sukhumvit Soi 61, Bangkok 10110

The Netherlands: Nilsson & Lamm bv, Postbus 195, 1380 AD Weesp

UK: GeoCentre U.K. Ltd., The Viables Centre, Harrow Way, Basingstoke, Hampshire RG22 4BJ

USA (Action Guides only): Fielding Worldwide, Inc, 308 South Catalina Ave, Redondo Beach, CA 90277

USA (Adventure Guides only): NTC Publishing Group, 4255 West Touhy Ave, Lincolnwood, IL 60646-1975

South Africa: Verbatim Distributors, 23 Bergendal Road, Constantia Hills, S Africa 7800

Pages 4–5: A reef whitetip shark, *Triaenodon obesus,* snatches some food on a reef in the Bunaken group, North Sulawesi. Photograph by Ed Robinson/IKAN.

Frontispiece: Bunaken Island, Sulawesi. Photograph by Ed Robinson/IKAN.

Contents

See page 46

See page 119

See page 141

See page 149

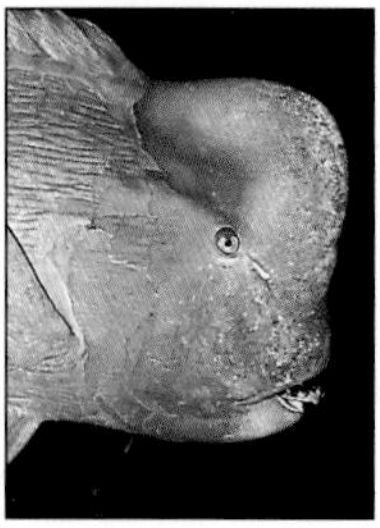

See page 66

Nusa Tenggara

Sulawesi

See page 51

See page 69

See page 63

Author's Dedication

To my editor, David Pickell
He missed out on the fun part of this effort—the diving—and instead struggled behind his computer to whip the book into shape from the mess of my manuscripts.

Essential to this book were the many dive operators, guides and dive buddies who contributed their time and knowledge, and who made certain I stayed out of trouble underwater (and sometimes above). Very special thanks to **Easy Ed Donohue**, who kept a close watch over me in my PC (Pre-Computer) days. Also to **Cody Shwaiko**, a close friend and my most frequent dive buddy, who traveled across Indonesia from his home in Bali several times to join me during the research for this book. And to **Wally Siagian**, who stands head and shoulders above all dive guides, who took me to all the right sites in Bali, and found me a cold beer whenever I could not live without one. And to **Loky Herlambang**, pioneer dive operator, founder of Nusantara Diving Centre, and conservation prize-winner, who did the same in Manado. And to **Edi Frommenwieler**, operator of the *Pindito* and **Peter**, the dive master, for the best dive series of my life. And to **Graeme** and **Donovan Whitford** for their sense of humor and never ending enthusiasm, along with truly world-class diving on Alor. And to **Larry Smith**, the most professional of instructors/guides, over 11,000 dives under his weight belt, the best of buddies if anything should go wrong. And to my most recent dive buddy, my son **Kalman**, in the hopes that his interest in marine biology may quickly surpass my own.

Editor's Acknowledgements

Any book of this scope represents the sweat and talent of many people, and an awful lot of both have gone into this one.

The fieldwork for this volume—hundreds of dives, thousands of kilometers of airplane and boat travel, sometimes weeks at a time without a cold beer—was conducted by Kal Muller, a Hungarian-born photographer and writer who has spent some 20 years tromping around the archipelago with his cameras and notebook. Kal is an old friend and probably the most tireless and good-humored person I know. Others who have contributed to this volume:

Dr. Charles Anderson, a marine biologist with the Marine Research Section of the Ministry of Fisheries of the Republic of the Maldives, provided an excellent introduction to the marine life of Indonesia. For this edition, he updated the practical section for Sumatra.

Cody Shwaiko, an experienced diver living in Bali, provided the Kangean Islands section, parts of the Banda dive narrative, the section on Sumba, and the section on Sangihe–Talaud. Cody has also recently taken up underwater photography, and several of his pictures are included in this volume.

Dive guide **Wally Siagian** not only kept Kal out of trouble while he was researching the Bali section of this book, but also provided detailed sketch maps of the Bali and Banda Islands sites, and to this edition, several photographs. Wally, who has an instinct for finding underwater life that is second to none, also pioneered all the best sites around Komodo Island.

Helmut Debelius, founder of the IKAN agency, provided us with his own photographs, as well as those of agency photographers **Ed Robinson**, **Jan Post** and **Lionel Pozzoli**. Helmut also provided a nice anecdote about discovering the beautiful reef lobster that now bears his name.

Photographer **Mike Severns**, who runs a dive operation in Maui with his wife, marine biologist **Pauline Fiene-Severns**, provided us with some of his very fine work from North Sulawesi. Mike's most recent book of photographs, *Sulawesi Seas*, co-authored with Pauline, has garnered widespread praise from both journalists and fellow professionals.

Rudie Kuiter is an experienced underwater photographer and the author of one of the best fish identification guides to the region: *Tropical Reef-Fishes of the Western Pacific*. Rudie provided an essay on discovering new species and a series of very interesting photographs.

Mark V. Erdmann, a coral reef ecologist who has conducted research in Indonesia for four years, provided the section on South Sulawesi. Mark's primary concern is marine conservation and development, and he has authored several articles on destructive fishing techniques in the archipelago.

Janet Boileau and **Debe Campbell**, both freelance writers living in Jakarta, wrote the Java section, and Debe helped update the practical section for Bali in this edition.

Andy Udayana, a student at the National Tourism University in Bali also helped update the practical section for Bali in this edition.

— **David Pickell**
Singapore 1996

Introducing the Indonesian Islands

The islands of Indonesia spread in a wide arc, more than 5,000 kilometers long, from mainland Southeast Asia to Papua New Guinea. Dotted with volcanoes, covered with thick tropical vegetation and bright green rice fields, and surrounded by coral reefs, the Indonesian archipelago is one of the world's most beautiful places.

No one really knows how many islands there are in Indonesia. The most commonly offered figure is 13,677, with some 6,000 of these named and 1,000 inhabited. A more thorough recent survey, however, came up with 18,585—but at what season and tidal stage this count was taken has not been listed.

What can be said reliably is this: Indonesia is the largest archipelagic nation in the world, with more than 80,000 kilometers of coastline (more than any other nation) and 3.1 million square kilometers of territorial waters.

Indonesia is the world's fourth-largest country, with 200 million inhabitants. Most are Muslims, but there are significant Christian and Hindu minorities. Racially the majority of Indonesians are Malayo-Polynesian, with Chinese and Papuan minorities. The capital and largest city is Jakarta, in West Java.

The Indonesian language is a variant of Malay, which, in this nation of hundreds of languages, has long served as the lingua franca of trade.

Seafaring Empires

Indonesians refer to their country as *tanah air kita*—"our land and water"—and have always considered the seas as an integral part of their country. The ancestors of the great majority of Indonesians—the Austronesians—arrived in the archipelago by boat. The invention of the outriggered canoe some 5,000 years ago was as essential a development to seafarers as the wheel was to land-locked people.

Spreading first from the Asian mainland to Taiwan, and then—about 3,000 B.C.—through the Philippines and into the larger islands of western Indonesia, the Austronesians brought with them rice and domesticated animals, and thrived on the rich volcanic soil of the Sunda Islands.

But seafaring skills were not forgotten. Starting in the 4th century, Indonesians from south Kalimantan (Borneo) sailed across the Indian Ocean to settle in uninhabited Madagascar, just off the coast of Africa.

The first great Indonesian empire, the Buddhist Srivijaya, was a maritime empire based around the port of Palembang in southeast Sumatra. The Srivijaya controlled the Straits of Malacca, the key to the crucial China–India trade route, from the 7th to the 13th centuries.

Influences from the Asian subcontinent continued to reach the archipelago, which became increasingly Indianized in culture and religion.

From A.D. 1294 to the 15th century, most of western Indonesia was controlled by the powerful East Java kingdom of Majapahit, the most famous of the archipelago's ancient kingdoms. Majapahit is thought to have exacted tribute from islands as far away as New Guinea.

Above: *Many of Indonesia's 18,508 islands are graced with beautiful, palm-lined beaches. This is the south coast of Bali.*

Overleaf: *A porcelain crab,* Neopetrolisthes ohshimai, *in Merten's carpet anemone,* Stichodactyla mertensii. *The porcelain crab is a shy filter-feeder that uses the stinging tentacles of the anemone for protection. Photo by Mike Severns.*

Opposite: *A snapper,* Macolor macularis, *and a cloud of peach anthias and lyretail anthias,* Pseudanthias dispar *and P.* squammipinnis, *at Mike's Point, on the northwest corner of Bunaken Island in Sulawesi. This site was named after the photographer. Photograph by Mike Severns.*

Above: *A fisherman tries his luck off the dock at Ampenan, Lombok.*

Islam and the Europeans

Beginning in the mid–13th century, Indonesian traders and rulers began converting to Islam, for both political and religious reasons. The biggest boost to Islamization of the archipelago came with the conversion of the ruler of Malacca, which sat in a very strategic position on the strait between Sumatra and peninsular Malaysia.

Most of these conversions were peaceful—the Sufi doctrine offering a theologically smooth transition for the Hinduized kingdoms—but Majapahit, past its prime, fell by force to the neighboring Islamic kingdom of Demak in the early 16th century.

This was also about the time the Portuguese, seeking spices, arrived in the archipelago, conquering Malacca in 1511. Soon after, the Spanish and English also sought Indonesia's valuable spices, but it was a century later that Holland, newly independent of the Holy Roman Empire, ruled from Spain, succeeded in controlling the market in cloves, nutmeg and pepper. During much of the 17th and 18th centuries, the Dutch East India Company held a virtual monopoly.

The company went broke in 1799, and in the 19th century, the Dutch concentrated their colonial efforts on Java, leading to a huge increase in the population of this island.

During World War II, the Japanese quickly swept through the Dutch Indies, evicting the colonialists in 1942. At the end of the war, Indonesian nationalist leaders declared independence —on August 17, 1945—but it took four more years to oust the Dutch. Irian Jaya, the western part of New Guinea, was transferred to Indonesia in the 1960s; the former Portuguese colony of East Timor was annexed in 1976.

Lush Islands

The "Ring of Fire" runs through Sumatra, Java, the Lesser Sundas, and then up through the Moluccas. These islands are marked by jagged volcanoes, and the rich, black soil that produces the great rice crops of Java and Bali. Some of the islands—for example, Timor, Seram and Biak—are formed of uplifted coral limestone. Here the soil is poor, and some areas—particularly parts of Timor—exhibit dry grassland that is more reminiscent of Australia than the tropics.

Two seasons of wind sweep through Indonesia each year. The northwest monsoon, usually starting (depending on the area) between late October and late November and ending between March and April, brings rain and wind. The southeast monsoon, with wind but much less rain, begins around late April to late May, and ends in early September. The *pancaroba*—between monsoons—brings generally calm seas and good weather, and falls just about everywhere in the archipelago in October and April.

The worst of the rainy season in most of Indonesia is in the months of December and January. The weather in the eastern province of Maluku is the most out of step with the rest of the country, and the worst comes in July and August. Some islands—such as Bali—have mountains that block the rains, creating a dry rain shadow in their lee.

Fantastic Diving, but Kafkaesque Transport

Indonesia is the least known of the world's best dive locations. The introduction of scuba gear and the beginning of dive operations here are barely a decade old, and new locations are still being explored and opened, albeit slowly.

It will be many years before diving in Indonesia reaches its full potential, which has both great advantages and serious drawbacks. Experienced divers will be excited by the possibility of diving clear, rich waters without being surrounded by hordes of human beings. It is still very possible to dive areas where no one has yet gone underwater. This will be a refreshing change from sites like the Caribbean, Hawaii, the Great Barrier Reef, the Maldives and the popular spots in the Pacific Islands.

In all of the huge Indonesian archipelago, containing 10–15 percent of the world's coral reefs, there are few locations with dive services, and a handful of year-round live-aboard boats.

The diving is excellent, inexpensive (averaging around $75 a day for two dives) and uncrowded. This does not come without a cost, however: flights can be unceremoniously cancelled, the quality of guides is variable, and the weather is sometimes fickle.

Live-aboards are the obvious solution to diving in Indonesia, with its thousands of islands and huge area. Some of the boats are luxurious and expensive but take you to the top dive locations in Indonesia. A few are more basic.

Indonesia's Dive Sites

The sites listed below are the main ones in Indonesia, with compressors, equipment and other facilities for diving. They appear here in the order they appear in this book, roughly west to east across the archipelago.

West Java. The Pulau-Pulau Seribu—"Thousand Islands"— dive area is quite close to the capital of Indonesia, Jakarta, and many efficient dive clubs provide all the necessary transportation and services to these islands. There is some interesting diving here, but in general coral and fish life is quite limited, and visibility poor. The clubs will also take you diving off the islands

Above: *Although it makes a heroic effort to connect the archipelago's far-flung islands, Merpati Airlines is often the bane of travelers to Indonesia. Above is one of the airline's rugged Twin Otters in Karubaga, in the highlands of Irian Jaya.*

Below: *A diver in the waters off Bali peers into a large barrel sponge, Petrosia testudinaria.*

Above: *Beautiful Bali cattle wander the rocky beach at Tulamben, Bali, one of the most popular dive sites in Indonesia. These placid animals are a domesticated form of the wild cow or banteng.*

around the famous Krakatau volcano, and off the Ujung Kulon Nature Reserve on the tip of southwest Java.

If your plans will take you through Jakarta, these dives might be worthwhile, but the diving is much better at points east. If you are coming all the way to Indonesia expressly to dive, your destination should not be Java.

Sumatra. Just an hour's ferry ride from Singapore, north Bintan Island has opened for diving. Visiblity is limited, but there's a wealth of life to see, especially at night. On the opposite side of the island, offshore Padang and the Mentawai Islands promise great diversity—shipwrecks and fringing reefs to wall dives. And much of it is still relatively unexplored.

Bali. Bali has more tourist services than anywhere else in Indonesia. It is a beautiful island, and the diving is excellent. There are many different sites here, from the clear water and steep walls of Menjangan to the famous Tulamben wreck to the 4-knot currents and cold water of Nusa Penida. The visibility is usually very good, and the fish and coral life are excellent. One caveat: almost 1 million tourists a year visited Bali at last count, and here is one of the few places where you might find a crowd.

The *Spice Islander* of Spice Island Cruises, with regular runs to Komodo and Kupang, offers diving on their normal

cruises as well as special dive charters both in the Lesser Sundas as well as the Banda Sea.

Lombok. The only diving available on this island, just a cheap ferry ride or short flight from Bali, is on the Gilis, three tiny islands off Lombok's west coast. Gili Trawangan and Gili Air have quite good reefs, but even these are far from Indonesia's best. But the Gili islands have fine white beaches and a get-away-from-it-all kind of appeal, and the diving is just offshore. You can find luxury accommodations in Senggigi beach on the mainland, an hour's ride from the islands. The dive businesses are all based there. With prior arrangements for pickup, it's better to rough it at the small places on the beach in the Gilis, with the young frisbee-tossers and sunbathers.

Komodo Island. The waters between Komodo Island (home of the fabled "dragon," a large monitor lizard) and Labuhanbajo, Flores are speckled with small islands ringed with coral. It is also swept by fierce currents. There are several places in Labuhanbajo which sometimes offer day trips for diving.

For the best locations, try the inexpensive live-aboard, the *Komodo Plus.* The boat does not offer luxury, but their chart shows all the best locations in this world-class area, all pioneered by the outfit.

Maumere, Flores. Maumere Bay is slowly recovering from a triple whammy: earthquake, tidal waves and a cyclone. Much of the underwater life has been devastated, but there are still a few good locations. Life is returning to the area and diving can be interesting from this perspective. Services could be improved, but all the essentials are there.

Sumba. It's no piece of cake to get there, but the south coast of Sumba offers a top location, dubbed Magic Mountain. It's an undersea mound, teeming with large fishes. The resort on land has been bought by the internationally acclaimed Oberoi chain.

Kupang, West Timor, and Roti and Alor. This area provides the closest diving for North Australia–based divers. The marine life is plentiful, and the Aussie operators are very good, experienced and enthusiastic. The only drawback to Kupang is the visibility, which is poor to just fair by Indonesian standards: 6–12 meters. Roti is better.

For the best diving, the operators have pioneered Alor Island, where a couple of dozen spots, along with some in the Banda Sea, top our best-of-the-best in Indonesia list. Currents can be strong and the dive boat could be improved, but for hard core divers, Alor gets our highest recommendation.

Sulawesi. The steep coral walls ringing the islands off Manado are some of the very best in the world. The visibility is very good, and the variety of marine life is superb. Some of the dive operators could use more reli-

able dive boats, and English-speaking dive masters with international certification. Bangka Island offers excellent spots, without the crowds at Bunaken. A new dive center, quiet and luxurious, offers very good diving from just north of Bitung, on the other side of the peninsula from Manado. The waters of the Lembeh Strait are very rich, and hold interesting WW II wrecks.

The *Serenade* and its daughter ship *Arlena,* both operated by Murex, and the liveaboard operated by Liburan Adventure Diving Tours, all run out of Manado to the Sangihe-Talaud Islands. The Spermonde archi-pelago off Ujung Pandang, Selayar island just off the southwest peninsula, the Tukang Besi archipelago off the southeast tip, and the Togian islands tucked away in Tomini Bay in central Sulawesi all offer exciting exploratory diving opportunities.

East Kalimantan. Manta rays and a salt-water inland lake are the top drawing cards here. World-famous Borneo Divers, the folks who pioneered Sipandan diving, started operations in

Below: *A school of pennant butterfly-fish,* Heniochus diphreutes. *Swarms of these beautiful butterflyfish are a common sight on Indonesian reefs.*

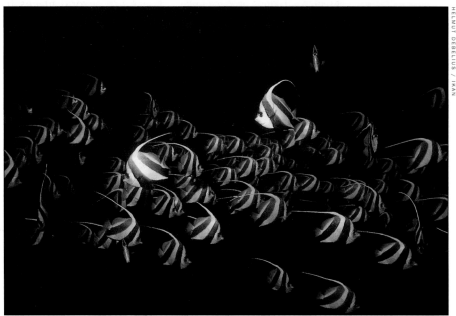

Sangalaki. After a period of suspended operations, they have reopened their dive business with a new Indonesian partner. A dive business, locally run, also offers diving on Sangalaki, but not nearly on the same level as Borneo Divers.

Ambon. Dive operations in Ambon and the Lease Islands are smoothing out. Operators now have adequate boats, with all the essentials. The diving here is very good and there will be no crowds at all. But the quality of dive personnel varies greatly. New sites here are still waiting to be discovered.

Our favorite live-aboard, the wooden *Pindito,* operates out of Ambon. Most of the year, it covers the Banda Sea. When the weather gets bad there, it runs dive cruises to Irian Jaya. The *Pindito* has pioneered most of the best dive spots in the Banda Sea and they know the area well. With the deepest seas in Indonesia and islands jutting up from abyssal depths, this is truly spectacular diving, second to none.

Banda Islands. The Banda Islands are a tiny group rising incongruously out of the middle of the wide Banda Sea—the Hawaii of Indonesia. Some of the dive sites here are fantastic, and large pelagics are commonly seen. There's not always someone around with formal dive training, although recently a European divemaster has taken up residence in Banda. The real problem is getting to these beautiful islands, however. They are really out of the way, and the bottleneck is the final leg on a small plane from Ambon.

Irian Jaya. Abundant reef life and little-explored ship and aircraft wrecks make diving in the Raja Ampat islands and Cenderawasih Bay on the north coast of Irian Jaya exciting adventures.

Exploratory dives

In addition to the few locations in Indonesia where compressors, tanks, weights and guides are available, dozens of others have been prospected, and await investment to be opened. To this list, add hundreds of sites—a few "discovered" but most unexplored—accessible only by the live-aboards.

You can also simply charter a large enough boat, and head off to a location of your own choosing. The problem, of course, is finding a compressor. This may be possible in Bali, however, which would open up locations such as the Kangean Islands, Taka Bone Rate and the Bonerate group. This is territory for real explorers, and if you have the time, patience, and self-sufficiency, this could provide a once-in-a-lifetime experience.

Scuba Guides: Variable

Dive services and guides in Indonesia are, to be polite, "variable." Most of these guides have spent more time underwater than their customers, accumulating thousands of dives, and are excellent scuba divers. But this does not make them good guides. They usually fall short in emergency training and organization.

It best to dive with the foreknowledge that you probably can not expect any help from your guide. Many guides may even have had some theoretical training in emergency procedures. But we have only rarely seen a first-aid kit on any of the local dive boats, let alone oxygen. Do not expect your guide to rescue you if you get into trouble.

This is not much of a problem for well-trained, experienced divers, particularly those who are traveling as a group. In fact, if you fall into this category, Indonesia is going to be a paradise for diving—no crowds, virgin reefs, and a lot of underwater time for your buck.

Beginners, on the other hand, are advised to use extreme caution—especially those who take a resort course after arrival here. Indonesian certification is administered by POSSI, which although under the auspices of the Paris-based CMAS—Confederation Mondiale des Activites Subaquatiques—is not as rigorous or as well-organized as the American or European agencies.

Many of the resort course instructors are not even certified by POSSI. Instructors' command of English is usually incomplete and safety procedures are often neglected. Being "certified" in Indonesia does not make you a competent diver. If a resort course here is your only diving experience, stick to the easy locations, and be very particular in choosing a guide.

In all cases be extremely wary of rental gear. This equipment is very expensive to buy with Indonesian rupiah, and operators use it to within an inch of its life. If maintenance were regularly scheduled and carried out properly, this wouldn't be a problem. But spare parts are expensive and very hard to get here, and training in repair and diagnostics of dive equipment is basically non-existent.

In most places, dive guides and assistants will ready your gear for you, but we suggest you do this yourself. If you are in the habit of just looking at the pressure gauge to make sure you have a good fill, you better change your way of thinking in Indonesia. Test *everything*—regulator, gauges, BC valves and straps. You should infer from this advice that we highly recommend you bring your own gear.

Indonesia is not the place to push your limits as a diver. We discourage dives below 30 meters, especially if decompression stops are required. Take your dive tables (better yet, a computer) and follow them scrupulously. Don't even think about a decompression cham-

bers being available—they are too few and too far away.

Dive-tour operators, particularly in Europe, are reluctant to send their clients to Indonesia because of the poor training of local guides. This situation will be remedied only when more dive guides receive adequate instruction in dive planning, emergency procedures and language skills.

Transportation: Kafkaesque

Marine tourism in Indonesia is also stalled by the archipelago's transportation infrastructure. Bali, Java and Sulawesi are easy to get to, but particularly at the height of the tourist seasons, July–August and December–January, travel to Maumere, Banda, and other points in eastern Indonesia can be an exercise in frustration. Delays, overbooked

Above: *Since most of the Indonesian dive sites are the steep outer walls of fringing reefs, access is usually just a matter of a short ride by outboard-powered canoe. This is the fringing reef off Bunaken Island in northern Sulawesi.*

Above: *Tulamben in Bali is famous for the World War II* Liberty *shipwreck, lying just 30 meters from the beach. This dive location is also noted for its remarkable diversity of marine life.*

flights, and broken computers will make a mess of your schedule. The guilty airport is Ujung Pandang in South Sulawesi. This is the main hub to eastern Indonesia, but too few planes fly there to and from Bali.

The scene at the ticket counters of the Indonesian government airlines—Garuda and Merpati—often produces a strange mix of Kafkaesque angst and hilarity.

It's not always this bad. Things are better in the off-peak months, and even during the middle of the tourist rush, only perhaps 25 percent of the confirmed passengers have problems. The basic problem is that Merpati—the main internal carrier—has too few airplanes, lacks organization, and owns a computer reservation system that is, in fact, often worse than useless.

Start with the obvious—it can't hurt. Ask the travel agent with whom you made your original booking if the company has a local correspondent. Many have agents in Bali who can re-check confirmations. Even before you arrive, try to obtain something tangible from this agent and/or Merpati airlines, such as a fax or telex showing your confirmed dates. As soon as you get to Bali, re-check your bookings.

As soon as you make it to your destination, confirm your return booking. The dive resorts and many hotels are quite effi-

cient at doing this—they will usually ask you for your plane details right away—but still make sure that it's been done.

If you do all this, it's likely—but not guaranteed—that things will work out as planned. But, just in case, keep some flexibility in your schedule in case there is a day or two of delay. If you have to sit in Bali for a day or two, there are plenty of good day-trips for diving. Unless you are traveling in a large group, go to the airport and try to get on your desired flight, even if you have been told that it's full. We've been on many of these over-booked flights where half or more of the seats are empty.

If you don't get a seat on the plane, forget about lodging an official complaint, getting mad, or punching somebody. If you throw a fit, you will provide a great deal of entertainment to the people waiting around the counter, but such unsavory behavior will inevitably lead to more delays. Sometimes—but not always—it might help to offer to pay "something extra" to get on your flight. It is not unknown that even someone with a confirmed reservation has been "bumped" due to a shady deal.

Are all these potential hassles worth it? You bet. Chances are you won't have problems. We just wanted to warn you—not scare you away. Remember: the diving is great out there. If you can schedule your visit from April through June, or September through early November, planes will be less crowded and everything will be much easier.

When planning your visit, don't try to visit too many places. If you have a week, go just to one place. Otherwise, you can spend much of your precious vacation time contending with the difficulties mentioned above.

Coral Growth and the Formation of Reefs

Diving over a tropical coral reef has been compared to stepping into a time machine. You find yourself in a strange place, 10 million years out of sync with the land. The reef is a reminder of a time when all the life on earth existed in shallow, tropical seas, the original soup of creation.

The myriad fish and invertebrates that shelter among and encrust the rugged surfaces provided by the clumps, shelves and branches of coral are overwhelming in their numbers, shapes and colors. Nowhere else is there such a diversity of animal forms.

Clear tropical seawater is nutrient poor, an aquatic desert. The strange and varied forms of the members of coral reef communities allow each to fill a niche in a complex nutrient cycle, beginning with the fixing of nutrients by the photosynthesis of algae, and working up to the barracuda that snatches an aging fish from the school. The ammonia and feces secreted by the predator are cycled right back into the reef ecosystem.

Over 240 million years, when scleractinian coral reefs first formed, this community has made a remarkable geological impact. The stony coral skeletons become overgrown and compacted into rock, eventually building up a prodigious thickness of limestone. When forced upward by the buckling of the earth's crust, this old reef rock forms islands.

Distribution of Coral Reefs

Reef-building corals require large amounts of sunlight, and thus are only found in the trop-ics, and even there only in shallow water. The effective limit of coral growth is usually given as 100 meters, although in Indonesia coral usually stops at half this depth. Corals, even hard corals, are found as deep as 6,000 meters, but these grow slowly and do not form the diverse communities of tropical coral reefs.

The Indo-Pacific region, centered around the islands of Indonesia, harbors most of the world's coral reefs. Of the total area covered by coral reefs, 55 percent is in southeastern continental Asia, Indonesia, the Philip-

Below: *The presence of large gorgonians, crinoids and schools of planktivores like these anthias indicates plankton-rich waters, which can provide a spectacular concentration of marine life. Mike's Point, Bunaken Island, Sulawesi.*

MIKE SEVERNS

pines, North Australia and the Pacific islands; 30 percent is in the Indian Ocean and the Red Sea; 14 percent is in the Caribbean; and 1 percent is in the North Atlantic. In variety, central Indonesia is the richest in the world: 76 genera, 350 species.

Reef-building corals grow only in water from 18°C (65°F) to 33°C (91°F). And the extremes of this range can only be tolerated for very short periods.

This explains why reefs are generally found only on the eastern coasts of large continents. The wind patterns caused by the rotation of the earth create currents that bring an upwelling of cold water (14°C [57°F]) from the depths at least part of the year to the western coasts of the Americas, Europe and Africa. Thus the Indian Ocean side of Africa has extensive reefs, and the Atlantic side almost none.

No cold currents flow through Indonesia, but even temporary rises in sea temperatures can devastate reefs. In 1983 sea temperatures around the Pulau Seribu islands off western Java rose to 33°C (91°F), killing much of the shallow reef coral there. Most has now recovered.

Turbid waters, those carrying a great deal of suspended sediment, deter reef formation. This is a very important in South and Southeast Asia, where rivers dump 70 percent of all sediments delivered to the ocean worldwide. (The Ganges is the champion, carrying almost 1.7 billion tons a year to the Bay of Bengal.) In Indonesia, the larger rivers in Kalimantan and Sumatra produce enough sediment to discourage reef formation a significant distance from their mouths.

The Biology of Corals

True reef-building or hermatypic corals are animals grouped in the phylum Cnidaria, order Scleractinia. They all have an indispensable symbiotic relationship with dinoflagellate algae called zooxanthellae. (see "Zooxanthellae and Corals," opposite.) These algae are essential for respiration and nutrient uptake, and the vigorous deposition of calcium.

Coral skeletons are made of aragonite, a very soluble form of calcium carbonate. The material is secreted as a way of disposing of excess ionic calcium.

Grazing and predation of fish and invertebrates causes portions of the coral skeletons to die, and these are immediately encrusted with algae, sponges, soft corals, or any of a myriad forms of small invertebrates. Over time, these too are grazed, silted over by coral sand, or outcompeted by other organisms, and their remains become part of another compacted layer.

The lithification of coral rock is not well understood, but a fine-grained carbonate cement seems to form in the pores of the old coral, turning it into dense coral rock. This is thought perhaps to result from bacterial action.

The buildup of limestone on the reef is not a simple process of accumulation. It is a cycle just like the nutrient cycle. Scientists studying a 7-hectare reef in the Caribbean measured an annual production of 206 tons of calcium carbonate; they also measured an annual loss of 123 tons. The greatest part of this erosion was produced by boring sponges, and the rest by grazing fishes and echinoderms.

Not all the limestone produced is created by corals, either. In some areas, particularly where there is very strong wave action, calcareous algaes are the primary producers of carbonate, forming algal ridges at the outer edge of the reef.

Coral Reef Architecture

Coral reefs are generally defined as falling into three main types: fringing reefs, barrier reefs and atolls. In a sense, these types also

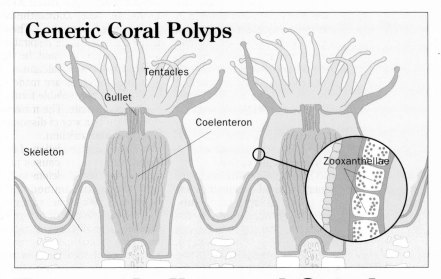

Generic Coral Polyps

Tentacles

Gullet

Coelenteron

Skeleton

Zooxanthellae

Zooxanthellae and Corals

Reef-building corals have evolved an indispensable, symbiotic relationship with a type of yellow-brown algae called zooxanthellae, which is "farmed" in the tissues of the coral polyp. The relationship is mutually beneficial: the coral receives oxygen and nutrients, and the algae receives carbon dioxide and "fertilizer" in the form of animal waste.

The presence of zooxanthellae is so important to the health of the coral that scientists speculate the symbiotic algae must have been present in the polyp tissue almost throughout modern coral's 50–100 million years of evolution.

The zooxanthellae alga has been dubbed *Symbiodinium microadriaticum,* part of a "supergenus" of marine dinoflagellate algas, but recent research suggests there are more than one species. These algas are dinoflagellates, which have whip-like processes giving them some limited ability to move. This is probably how the cells initially enter the corals, although once they are there they divide vegetatively, and take on a simpler structural form.

Corals are not the only reef animals to have zooxanthellae. Sea anemones and other cnidarians host the algae, as do some molluscs, most famously the giant clams (*Tridacna*). Because zooxanthel-

lae is a yellow-brown algae, and the host tissues are generally colorless—to pass the greatest amount of light to the algae—zooxanthellae-containing animals are usually a dull color: beige, brown, olive green. There are exceptions, however, including some of the giant anemones and *Tridacna* clams, which can be richly hued. As a general rule, however, the most brightly colored invertebrates—such as some of the soft corals—do not harbor zooxanthellae.

Coral nutrition

Corals derive their food energy from three sources: plankton captured by their tentacles, organic nutrients absorbed directly from the water, and organic compounds provided by the zooxanthellae. For the reef-building corals, the latter is by far the most important.

In the presence of sunlight, the zooxanthellae produce oxygen and photosynthetically fix nutrients—glycerol, glucose and amino acids—which are "leaked" to the surrounding tissues of the coral polyp. The raw materials for this process are the waste products of the coral animal: carbon dioxide, ammonia, nitrates and phosphates. It is a very efficient, almost self-sustaining partnership.

— *David Pickell*

form a historical progression. As a fringing reef grows outward, a boat channel forms behind. As the reef widens, the boat channel becomes a lagoon, and the fringing reef graduates to a barrier reef. If the fringing reef began around an island, and the island subsequently sinks or the sea level rises, the final result is an atoll, a near circular reef surrounding a central lagoon.

These are not the only forms, and scientists studying reef topography offer many more types. For example, bank reefs, reefs that grow up more or less in patches in open water where the depths are relatively shallow, are an important type in the Coral Sea off Australia. These reefs often form at the edge of undersea plates, and appear when geologic activity causes an uplifting of the bottom. If the bottom is pushed up high enough that sunlight can reach it, a bank reef will form.

Fringing reefs. Most of the reefs a diver will be exploring in Indonesia are fringing reefs, coral formations that grow right up to the edge of an island.

These reefs can take many forms. The steep coral walls for which Indonesian diving is famous are fringing reefs, with sometimes just a few meters of reef flat, and a reef edge that has an almost vertical slope.

Walls, or drop-offs, fascinate divers because these are where deeper dwelling animals come closest to the surface. Semi-precious black coral (*Antipathes* sp.) usually grows far below sport diving depths, but on Indonesian walls can be found at 30 meters. Some of the deep-dwelling dwarf angelfish (*Centropyge* spp.), damsels, and anthias (e.g., *Pseudanthias pleurotaenia*) can be found at comfortable depths only along steep drop-offs.

Generally, a fringing reef consists of a reef edge of stout corals, which absorb the brunt of the waves and current; a reef flat, a shallow area exposed at the lowest spring tide; and perhaps a boat channel or back reef, deeper than the reef flat and quite calm.

The reef edge, and the fore-reef area towards the open sea, are the most rewarding areas for the diver. Here the current is

Below: On the steep walls of Indonesian reefs, normally deep-dwelling species can be seen at relatively shallow depths. This is a male square-spot anthias, Pseudanthias pleurotaenia.

HELMUT DEBELIUS / IKAN

strong, bringing plankton and fresh water from the open sea. Here also is where divers will see larger reef fish, and occasional pelagic visitors to the reef. Sometimes the reef edge is indistinct, marked by pinnacles or other formations. And sometimes the area just back of the reef edge will not immediately become part of the reef flat, but instead, protected from the full force of the current, will be rich in more delicate corals and animals.

The reef flat is shallow, and usually light brown with sediment. This is an area of coral sand and detritus, with small boulders of hardy massive corals and clusters of branching *Acropora* coral, growing in pools. Usually there are fewer than a handful of very hardy coral species on the reef flat.

Most divers will walk or wade across this area (wearing a pair of dive boots, of course) without even looking down. Here there are echinoderms—particularly brittle stars, which sometimes occur in great numbers—small fish, a variety of molluscs and soft algaes. Sometimes there will be meadows of the calcareous alga *Halimeda*.

The back reef or boat channel is a deeper area, between the reef flat and the shore. Although often deep enough for swimming, the coral growth here is poor because of sediment run-off from the shore. Resistant *Porites, Acropora* or *Goniastrea* grow in the boat channel in patches. Further inland, there may be beds of turtle grass, a rich habitat for juvenile fishes and many crustaceans.

Barrier reefs. The most famous barrier reefs are the Great Barrier Reef off Queensland, Australia, which is 2,000 kilometers long and 150 kilometers wide, and the large barrier reef off the coast of Belize in the Gulf of Honduras. A barrier reef is a fringing reef where the back

Trepang drying on a dock in Pagimana, Sulawesi

Trepang Fishing

The lowly sea cucumber, a lumbering, inoffensive detritus feeder, hardly looks like something you would want to touch, much less eat. But this homely animal is the target of small-scale fishermen all over Indonesia, and for many it serves as a major source of cash income.

Plucked from the shallow reefs of Indonesia, the sea cucumbers are dried, cleaned and sold in small lots to local businessmen, who ship them to Ujung Pandang, the center of the trade. There they are graded, and sold to the Asian market where this trepang becomes the key ingredient in a Chinese soup.

Most of the collectors are young boys. Wearing homemade goggles made of circles of glass fitted with pitch into carved sections of bamboo, the trepang collectors scan the shallows for their foot-long quarry.

Although the animals are not dangerous, they have a tendency to eject their Cuvierian tubules—long, sticky white strands—when disturbed. Collectors invariably get this goo, designed to immobilize a predator, all over their hands.

Some 30 species—generally *Holothuria*—are collected. The inferior, small black ones are sold to the Chinese market, where they fetch up to $2.40 a kilo for the wholesalers in Ujung Pandang. The real prize, however, is *H. aculeata,* fat and whitish when dried. These are saved for the more lucrative Hong Kong market, where they sell for up to $17/kilo wholesale.

Trepang, a Malay word, is also called bêche-de-mer, a pseudo-French word derived from an old English word, derived from the Portuguese *bicho do mar,* "sea worm." The original Latin, however, is more evocative: "little sea beast."
— *David Pickell*

Biak Fish Bomb Industry

Fish bombing and dynamite fishing are unfortunately widespread in Indonesia. The practice began in earnest after World War II, as wartime construction brought dynamite to Indonesia, the Philippines, and the Pacific Islands. In Indonesia, a flourishing cottage industry has developed to remove the cordite from surplus Allied shells—dumped in the sea at war's end—and distribute it to markets across the archipelago for fish bombs.

Fish bombing is a simple process. A likely spot is located and staked out by a fisherman. A small bomb, usually powder packed into a beer bottle, is stuffed into a cored papaya and thrown overboard. After the explosion, the stunned

Padaido Islands

and killed fish are scooped up with nets as fast as possible. The papaya helps the bomb sink and muffles the blast; one doesn't want any unsolicited "helpers" when the fish start floating upward.

To a fisherman, who works a long, hard day to bring a few fish to market, the appeal of bombing is obvious. Unfortunately, the impact on the reef is disastrous. Not all the dead fish float, of course, and method is very wasteful. But the most damage is caused by the destruction of the coral by the blast. Fish will essentially reproduce to fill the environment. Coral *is* the environment.

Flourishing Cottage Industry

According to a report by Stephen Nash of the World Wildlife Fund for Nature, an old Allied ammo dump in the Padaido Islands has been the source of a cottage industry supplying the fish bombs used in Biak and the Cenderawasih Bay, and may supply powder to markets as far away as western Indonesia. The report was written several years ago, and at the time the supply of easily-found shells was running out. But the author feared that scuba gear, brought to Biak to equip collectors of tropical marine fish, would make accessible new supplies of bombs.

The Padaido islanders are masters of the very delicate art of live bomb recovery. The shells are found by dragging the sandy bottom with a piece of iron tied to a rope. When it is felt to hit something hard, a diver puts on goggles and dives to the bottom—18 meters—ties the bomb to the rope, and returns to the surface. Then the bomb is hauled up. Once on land, the bomb is carefully opened, and the priming mixture and cordite are extracted for packaging and sale.

The trickiest part of building the fish bombs is constructing the fuse, which is made of the flat, malleable aluminum from a tube of toothpaste. Priming mixture is "diluted" with crushed matchheads and the aluminum sheet is rolled around it like a cigaret. The aluminum makes the fuse waterproof; heat and combustion gases keep the water from rushing in the open end. Different lengths of this waterproof fuse are used depending on how deep the fisherman wants the bomb to go before exploding.

The fuse is attached to a standard beer bottle—or a large ale bottle, or a small medicine bottle—with coconut husk rope and pitch. The whole package is stuffed into a papaya, and thrown overboard. According to the report, fish bombers off the south coast of Biak near the airport time their bombs with the noisy arrival of the Garuda flight, which effectively masks the explosion.

Today, the supply of cordite and gunpowder has for the most part disappeared. Unfortunately, the clever fishermen have now discovered how to make bombs using ingredients found in widely available chemical fertilizers.

— *David Pickell*

reef or boat channel has become a large lagoon. In the case of the Great Barrier Reef, this "lagoon" is in places 100 kilometers wide.

A barrier reef that forms around an island is sometimes called an "almost atoll." There can be multiple barrier reefs, extending outward like ripples, and the large lagoon behind a barrier reef can harbor small patch reefs and sandy cay reefs.

Atolls. Some 425 of these characteristic circular reefs, with a large central lagoon, have been recorded throughout the tropics. The vast majority (more than 300) are in the Indo-Pacific. The largest is Kwajalein in the Marshall Islands, which forms an oval 120 by 32 kilometers.

The largest atoll in Indonesia—and the third-largest in the world, just 20 percent smaller than Kwajalein—is Taka Bone Rate, in the Flores Sea south of Sulawesi. Taka Bone Rate (called Tijger in older texts) stretches 72 by 36 kilometers, covers 2,220 square kilometers, and includes 22 sandy islands. "Taka,"probably a Bugis word, is a generic term for atoll or bank reef.

The lagoon of an atoll, because it is so thoroughly cut off from the open ocean, forms a unique environment, and is often much richer in life than the lagoon side of, say, a small barrier reef. The level of organic matter in the water inside the atoll's lagoon is considerably higher than outside, allowing it to support as much as 10 times the biomass as the outer reef edge. And, because it is not adjacent to a large land mass, problems caused by run-off and turbidity are eliminated.

The richness of the lagoon water is thought to be the result of deep ocean water percolating through the walls of the basement structure of the reef, bringing with it nutrients that previously had been locked away in geological storage.

KAL MULLER

The Formation of Reefs

Darwin's theory. British naturalist Charles Darwin first published his theory of coral reef formation in 1842, and it is still the dominant theory today. Darwin, investigating atolls in the South Pacific, suggested that a fringing reef around the edges of an island would gradually grow outward, leaving a lagoon in its wake, and evolving into a barrier reef. If the island, over geological time, subsided, then what would be left would be an atoll:

"Now, as the island sinks down, either a few feet at a time or quite insensibly, we may safely infer from what we know of the conditions favourable to the growth of coral, that the living masses bathed by the surf on the margin of the reef, will soon regain the surface...

"Let the island continue sinking, and the coral-reef will continue growing up its own foundation, whilst the water gains inch by inch on the land, until the last and highest pinnacle is covered, and there remains a perfect atoll." (See diagram at right.)

This, like natural selection, was pure speculation on Darwin's part. Atoll-formation was a phenomenon of history, and not something that he could "prove" with 19th century technologies. In fact, it was not until the 1950s, when the U.S. Geologic Survey conducted an extensive drilling

Above: *In the clear waters of Indonesian reefs, ultraviolet radiation can penetrate several meters underwater. Pigments made up of amino acids shield the delicate growing tips of shallow-water corals such as this* Acropora sp.

Step 1. *A fringing reef forms around an island.*

Step 2. *The island sinks, and the fringing reef grows into a barrier reef.*

Step 3. *The island sinks below the surface, and only an atoll remains.* (After Darwin, 1842)

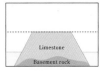

Step 1. *Limestone is exposed by geological forces.*

Step 2. *Rainfall erodes exposed limestone.*

Step 3. *Water level rises, and eroded limestone is colonized by coral. (After Purdy, 1974)*

Below: *The emperor angelfish,* Pomacanthus imperator.

program on Pacific atolls, that Darwin's theory was confirmed: deep down, below the layer of coral in the atoll lagoons, the core samples revealed the volcanic rock of a former island.

However, this still did not explain the mechanism for Darwin's "subsistence" of the island. We now know, for example, that the Ice Ages, by locking up much of the earth's water into ice, brought about large changes in the level of the earth's oceans. At the peak of the last Ice Age, 15,000 years ago, the sea level stood almost 130 meters lower than it does today. In some cases, particularly in Indonesia, it has probably been the rising of the oceans and not the sinking of the island that has created atolls.

Karstic saucers. Darwin's is not the only theory of reef formation, and there are some areas where geological evidence does not accord well with his speculations. A newer explanation has been offered, called the karstic saucer theory. "Karst" is the name given to the formations caused by the action of rainwater on exposed limestone—caves,

sinkholes and underground channels. (The name comes from the type region around the Dinaric Alps, near the Adriatic coast of Yugoslavia.)

This theory proposes that an area of exposed limestone, acted upon by the weak carbonic acid produced by rainfall, would take the shapes Darwin's theory attributes to reef growth. When the water level subsequently rose, corals would colonize the already shaped and eroded limestone. (See illustration at left.)

One of the great appeals of this theory to scientists is that it can be tested in the laboratory. Weak acid applied to a flat-topped block of calcareous rock will tend to erode it into the shape of a saucer, the acid acting to a greater degree in the center than at the edges.

Products from the Sea

Indonesians have always been sea-farers, and for an archipelagic nation, the ocean is still its greatest resource. Fish provides the main source of protein to Indonesia's 90 million people. The waters off Indonesia are

thought to be able to support a fishing industry of 5 million tons a year, with actual catches just 20 percent of this.

Commercially valuable sea products also provide some cash to people living on sandy islands with little or no resources, save perhaps copra from coconuts. Ujungpandang, the capital of Sulawesi, is the Indonesian leader in the export of sea products, shipping several thousand tons a year. These include pearl oysters, mother-of-pearl or *Trochus* shells, other shells and dried sea cucumbers. The sea cucumbers, or *trepang,* are used in Chinese soup. (See "Trepang Fishing," page 27.)

Although collecting these animals provides necessary income to the islanders, over-harvesting by itinerant Bugis and Bajo fishermen has all but wiped out certain species in some areas. Particularly hard-hit are the giant clams (*Tridacna*). The meat is canned and then sold at considerable prices in places like Taiwan, and the shells are made into floor tiles in factories in Surabaya, Java. These clams used to grow in huge "fields" in the reefs of eastern Indonesia. You can now dive in the same areas and not see a single one.

Triton shells (*Charonia tritonis*), helmet conchs (*Casis cornuta*) and turban shells (*Turbo marmoratus*), which are sold as trinkets, have also disappeared from some areas.

Future of Coral Reefs

Although Indonesia has some of the most untouched coral reefs in the world, even in the remote parts of the archipelago, where industrialization has not yet reached, the reefs are not free of danger. According to officials of the World Wildlife Fund for Nature in Irian Jaya, the Indonesian half of the island of New Guinea, it is predominantly the reefs, and not the great forests of

that island, that are most at risk.

Even the fastest-growing corals can add new growth only at the rate of 3–4 centimeters a year; and, much like the rain forests, reefs are subject to succession. A diverse, well-populated reef does not just spring from the sandy bottom. Once a reef is wiped out, unprotected wave action and current may prevent regrowth from taking place.

In the more developed areas of Indonesia, dredging of channels, harvesting of coral for construction materials, and filling of estuarial waters has had a devastating impact on the reefs. The Bay of Ambon, in the central Moluccas, once had a reef that moved naturalist Alfred Russel Wallace to write: "There is perhaps no spot in the world richer in marine productions, corals, shells and fishes, than the har-

Above: *Giant clams like this* Tridacna gigas *were once common on Indonesian reefs. But a market for the canned meat in Asia, and the use of giant clam shells in making terazzo in Surabaya, Java have decimated the population in many areas.*

bour of Amboyna." During the post-war building boom, the coral was dragged up for building material in Ambon town. Today, the bay is a wasteland.

Also damaging is the continuing practice of fish bombing, in which small powder charges are thrown overboard to stun fish so they can be easily captured for market. (See "The Biak Fish Bomb Industry," page 28). The bombs don't just kill the fish. They create lifeless craters in the reef, deserts where all the coral and the life it supported have been destroyed. In some places this practice has reduced all the nearshore reef to barren rubble.

In the long run, however, the greatest damage to reefs will probably be a result of bad land use: poor farming practices, including overgrazing, public works projects that expose the thin tropical soil to erosion, and deforestation through timbering.

These practices increase run-off and erosion, loading rivers up with silt, which is then carried out to sea. Silt chokes off coral growth, and leads to eutrophication, a great increase in nutrients in the water. This, in turn, causes an algae bloom, which robs the water of oxygen and can form a lethal mat over the coral.

Divers in Indonesia also have a responsibility to keep the country's reefs, many of which truly are in pristine condition, in a continued state of health. This means taking no souvenirs, developing good diving habits so as not to break off or damage fragile corals, and not harassing larger animals like sea turtles. In some areas, careless placement of dive boat anchors has already caused noticeable damage.

In many places diving programs are rudimentary, and the guides are not educated in reef conservation. I have been served fresh giant clam after a dive by a guide who took the animal while diving on an Indonesian reef that was a protected marine reserve. He couldn't at first understand why we were upset. As visitors—and customers—divers are in an excellent position to help dive operators develop good conservation habits. I think we owe it to the people and reefs of Indonesia to do at least this much.

Below: *A gorgonian goby (*Bryaninops *sp.) on an antipatharian wire coral. This little animal is no more than 4 centimeters long. Many fishes rely on invetebrates for food, shelter, and protection, but few are as particular as the gorgonian gobies. Some species of* Bryaninops *live and lay their eggs on only a single species of gorgonian or antipatharian.*

The Varied Inhabitants of Indonesia's Reefs

The waters surrounding the islands of Indonesia form the richest marine habitat on earth. Indonesia lies at the epicenter of species diversity for the entire tropical Indo-Pacific region, which stretches from Madagascar and the Comoros islands in the west to the easternmost of the Pacific islands—a vast 12,000-mile sweep through the Indian and Pacific Oceans.

Perhaps 3,000 species of fish, and several hundred species of coral populate the reefs off the larger Indonesian islands. A 19th century Dutch ichthyologist cataloged 780 species of marine fish just in Ambon Bay alone, almost as many as can be found in all the rivers, lakes and seas of Europe. (Alas, this reef has been destroyed, dredged after World War II to provide building materials for booming Ambon town). Even the healthiest Caribbean reef has just 10–20 percent of the species diversity of a comparable Indonesian reef.

The islands that now make up Indonesia are likely to have been the genetic "source" of Indo-Pacific marine life. This region has remained tropical for 100 million years, exposed to the strong sunlight that makes tropical waters so much richer than temperate waters, giving the animals a long time to diversify.

Although ocean currents distribute fish widely, the further across the Pacific one goes from Indonesia, the fewer species will be found. For example, 123 species of damselfish are found in Indonesia.* (see note at right.) In the Philippines, 118. In Papua New Guinea, 100. In Fiji, 60. In the Society Islands, 30. In the

Galapagos, just 18. The entire Caribbean holds just 16 species.

One million years ago the Ice Ages began, periodically tying up much of the earth's water in ice. This lowered sea levels by as much as 130 meters, reducing the tropical Atlantic to a small refuge in the south Caribbean, decimating the animal population. The Indo-Pacific never suffered such an extinction.

But volcanism and continental drift caused similar disruptions in Indonesia, and it is probably because the islands provide such a wide variety of habitats— deep sea trenches, rocky shores, sand and mud flats, sea grass beds, mangrove swamps and, of course, coral reefs—that the fauna here is so diverse.

While muddy turtle grass beds, mangrove swamps and estuarial waters are of immense interest to the biologist, divers usually find little in these shallow, turbid waters to hold their attention. When divers talk about tropical water diving, they mean coral reefs.

A Compendium of Reef Life

There are so many species present on the Indonesian reefs that even specialists can not give an exact tally of their numbers here. With this in mind, the aim of this chapter is to provide an introduction to the major groups of animals that will be seen when diving on Indonesian reefs. No attempt at comprehensive coverage is made.

Algae

Although people often mistakenly think of many of the reef animals—corals, gorgonians, sea

Above: *A long-nosed hawkfish,* Oxycirrhites typus, *sitting among the lacy gorgonians encrusting a wreck, just off Molas beach near Manado, Sulawesi.*

*Australia, chiefly because it includes both tropical and colder-water habitats, hosts the most damselfish species, 132.

Above: *Turtle grass, Thalassia sp., is one of the very few true marine plants. Although not found on reefs, back-reef areas may have beds of turtle grass, which nourish crustaceans and juvenile fishes as well as the green turtle.*

Below: *The marine algas* Udotea *(top) and* Halimeda *can both be occasionally found on the reef.* Udotea *is only lightly calicified, but the calcium carbonate disks of* Halimeda *are in some areas a major component of the reef substrate.*

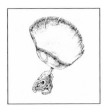

"anemones"—as plants, what is perhaps most striking about the coral reef is the apparent lack of plant life. Other rich coastal marine environments, for example the kelp forests off California or the sea-grass beds and mangrove swamps off some of the Indonesian islands, are obviously based on the photosynthetic production of oxygen and nutrient-fixing by algae or higher plants.

On the reef, however, despite its teeming life, plants seem absent. In fact, plants are the primary producers on the reef, just like every other environment. Most of the algae found on the reef grows as a short "turf," a fine carpet of hairs that is a mix of dozens or hundreds of species of brown, red and green algaes. While diving, look closely at an area of bare coral rock and you will probably see a fine carpet of "hairs" growing on it.

The algal turf grows at a prodigious rate, but a herd of grazers—tangs, parrotfish, damselfish, sea urchins, snails and many others—keeps it clipped short. If an area of reef were caged off to prevent the entry of herbivores, the turf would quickly sprout into a thicket. The farmerfish damsel (*Stegastes lividus*) does just this, by force of personality keeping out all intruders from his own luxurious green patch of hair algae.

Some reef algaes, the so-called coralline algaes, are calcified, providing them with protection both from grazers and physical damage by surge. These appear as small pink "trees," or flat, encrusting pink or lavender growths on old chunks of coral. Some of the coralline algaes grow in areas of very high wave action, indeed preferring areas that are too turbulent for even corals to survive.

On reefs facing the open ocean, it is a ridge of coralline red algae that receives the full force of the crashing ocean

waves, dissipates their energy, and allows less robust organisms including corals to thrive. Other varieties of coralline algae grow deep on the reef, below the level at which reef-building corals can survive, where they contribute significantly to reef growth and sand production.

One recognizable green macro-alga that can sometimes be seen on shallower reefs is *Halimeda,* a heavily calcified alga made up of chains of green disks, each the size of a small button. These disks are calcium carbonate, like coral, and in some areas *Halimeda* rubble is a major component of the reef substrate.

Sometimes an inshore reef will merge with shallow beds of turtle grass, one of the very few true marine plants. These grassy beds provide an environment for seahorses, pipefish, damselfish, wrasses, and the young of some reef fishes, including butterflyfish, as well as small crustaceans, mollusks and worms. The sea grass also provides forage for the rare dugong (*Dugong dugon*), or sea cow, which ranges across Indonesian waters.

Plankton

The diver will rarely *see* plankton, and if he or she does, it will usually be apparent as a cloudiness of the water, or an irritating backscatter in photographs. But plankton is an important link in the reef food chain. Reef areas rich in plankton will be characterized by an abundance of filter-feeders, animals that have evolved methods of sifting or snaring plankton from the current—including soft corals, mussels and oysters, anemones, crinoids, gorgonians and sponges.

Plankton consists of both "plants"—phytoplankton—and "animals"—zooplankton, and the larger zooplankters are predatory on the diatoms and algae of the phytoplankton. The plankton also contains some temporary

members, the meroplankton, which consists of the larval stages of fish and invertebrates. As these grow, they settle out of the plankton stream to become part of the swimming nekton (fish, jellyfish) or the crawling or fixed benthos, or bottom dwellers (sea urchins, gorgonians).

Sponges

Indonesian reef sponges vary in size from tiny to huge, from the small patches of color provided by encrusting sponges (family Clionidae) to the meter-high barrel sponges (*Petrosia*). All sponges are members of the phylum Porifera, "the hole-bearers," and their porous, "spongy" nature is crucial to their mode of feeding. Sponges are the archetypal filter-feeders, straining plankters from the water through myriad microscopic pores.

A cross-section of a sponge shows a very sophisticated system for moving water. Small intake pores lead to an internal system of tiny canals and chambers lined with cells bearing whip-like processes. Beating constantly, these cells create a current through the sponge that moves its own volume of water every 4–20 seconds. Even a relatively small sponge can circulate as much as 5,000 liters a day. The chimney or barrel shape of many larger sponges helps increase surface area and the water flow through the animal.

Sponges are notoriously difficult to identify. Colors vary and even the shape or size of a sponge does not necessarily mark its species; sometimes shape is just a response to local conditions. Scientists would call this new form an "ecomorph."

Scientists rely on detailed examination of the internal "skeleton" to identify sponges. Sponges are made of a proteinaceous secretion called spongin. This fibrous net forms the useful part of the bath sponges (*Spongia* and *Hippospongia*) harvested in the Mediterranean and Caribbean. Many sponges also contain spicules of silica or calcium carbonate, or both, bound together with spongin.

There are an estimated 830 species of sponges in Indonesia. The giant barrel sponges are

Above: *A school of sapphire damsels,* Pomacentrus pavo, *takes shelter in a sponge. Halmahera, Maluku.*

Below. *Marine dinoflagellate plankters, top to bottom:* Gymnodinium, Gonyaulax, Peridinium, Ceratium.

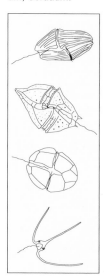

most impressive to divers, but the smaller tube sponges and vase sponges also create colorful and aesthetically pleasing forms.

Like many invertebrates, sponges can grow to a remarkable age. Experiments with commercial farming of bath sponges in the Caribbean have led researchers to estimate that larger specimens are at least 50 years old, and maybe much older.

Reef sponges create an environment that is exploited by a variety of other creatures. Small crabs and shrimps and even fish hide in the tubes and cavities. Crinoids perch on upright sponges to filter plankton from the current. And sea cucumbers and other detritus feeders graze on the organic material that collects on the sponge's surfaces.

Corals and their relatives

Corals, soft corals, sea anemones, gorgonians, hydroids, jellyfish and the other members of the phylum Cnidaria (formerly Coelenterata) cause a great deal of confusion for the diver trying to identify the teeming mass of branched and tentacled life he sees attached to the reef. Taxonomists identify these animals by their stinging cells, nematocysts, and simple coelenteron, from the Greek *koilos,* "hollow," and *enteron,* "gut." All have the form of a polyp at some stage in their lives. Other than these shared characteristics, the form of these animals varies widely.

Aristotle considered them an intermediate form between plants and animals, and they were first placed by taxonomists in a group called Zoophyta, "animal-plants." Only in 1723 were corals properly identified as animals, and Jean André Peyssonel, the naturalist who proposed this to the French Academy of Sciences, was laughed at and quit science in disgrace.

Phylum Cnidaria is usually divided into four classes: Hydro-

zoa, hydroids and fire corals; Anthozoa, corals and anemones; Cubozoa, box jellies; Scyphozoa, jellyfish. Anthozoa, in turn, is split into three sub-classes: Alcyonaria (Octocorallia), containing the soft corals and gorgonians; and Zoantharia (Hexacorallia), containing the stony corals and anemones; and Ceriantipatharia, including the black corals and cerianthids, or tube anemones.

The Stony Corals

The stony or hard corals are the reef-builders. They are in the order Scleractinia, and are sometimes called scleractinian or "true" corals. The skeletons these animals secrete range in shape from the massive, smooth boulders of *Porites* and stout-branched *Pocillipora* that take a pounding at the reef edge to the finely foliated needle coral *Seriatopora histrix.*

These corals are colonies, comprised of thousands of individual coral animals, or polyps. Each polyp, upon close examination, will be seen to have much the same shape as a sea anemone, with tentacles ringing a central mouth. What makes the stony coral polyp distinctive, and so ecologically important, is that it deposits calcium carbonate around its lower part, forming a

Right: *The presence of whip coral gorgonians often indicates very clean water and plenty of plankton. Bunaken group, Sulawesi.*

skeletal cup. The skeleton is essentially formed of repeated casts of the tiny polyp.

Most reef-building corals are nocturnal. During the day, the polyps are retracted, drawn down into the skeletal cup. At night, these corals are transformed from dead-looking lumps of rock into miniature forests thick with polyps, which expand to feast on the abundant night plankton. Tiny plankters are snared by the polyp's tentacles, which are armed with stinging nematocysts. Although they feed on plankton, the vast majority of the nutrition of reef-building corals is provided by the symbiotic zooxanthellae in their tissues. (See sidebar, "Zooxanthellae and Corals," page 25.)

Corals, like other reef animals, also spawn at night, releasing pink clouds of sperm and eggs. To increase the chances of fertilization, corals of the same species tend to coordinate the release of their eggs and sperm. Many reef animals spawn around the time of the full moon, when tidal currents are strongest, to ensure wide dispersal of the larvae. On the Great Barrier Reef of Australia the majority of corals spawn 4–5 days after the November full moon. Some corals in Indonesia spawn at this time too, but the full pattern of coral spawning has not yet been determined here.

According to travel brochure clichés, corals are supposed to be "kaleidoscopic" with color. Divers, of course, know that at least for the reef-building corals, this is not at all the case. Most shallow water corals are a dull brown color, a consequence of the pigments in their zooxanthellae. Still, some are blessed with subtle pastel tints. In particular, the growing tips of *Acropora* can be colored with a pinkish or purplish pigment, a group of amino acids called S-320 which serves as an ultraviolet filter to protect

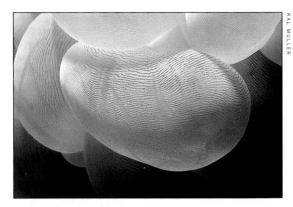

KAL MULLER

Above: *A detail of the eponymous vesicles of the bubble, or grape coral,* Plerogyra sinuosa. *These sacs, called acrorhagi, possess stinging nematocysts. During the day they are inflated with water and protect the polyp tentacles. At night they shrivel, and the polyps are extended to snare plankton. The acrorhagi also discourage other corals from overgrowing* Plerogyra, *blocking its sunlight and supply of plankton.*

the still-young polyps.

The shape of stony corals, rather than their color, is their most salient characteristic. The form the coral will take is strongly influenced by wave action and currents, and even the same species may take different forms under different conditions. A specimen of the distinctive palmate Caribbean elkhorn coral (*Acropora palmata*) placed in a research ecosystem at the Smithsonian Institute in Washington, D.C. sent up new growth in the bushy form of *A. prolifera*. This, it would seem, further complicates the already difficult project of stony coral identification.

Massive forms. In general, massive, boulder-like forms grow in shallow water where light is plentiful, and along the reef edge where the current is strong. These include the common *Monastrea, Pocillopora,* and *Porites.* In the shallow, often turbid water of the back reef, the more robust branching forms (*Acropora*) can out-compete the massive forms, which are more vulnerable to siltation.

Massive corals sometimes form "micro-atolls" in relatively calm backreefs and reef flats. These are flat-topped forms in which the center has been killed by excessive siltation or regular exposure by low tides. The sides continue to grow outward, demonstrating Darwin's theory in miniature.

Goniopora is an unusual massive coral that extends its polyps during the day. These are also usually large, reaching 20–30 centimeters in length. The effect is of a round stone, covered with little brown flowers.

Branching forms. Deeper in the reef, or in protected parts of the shallows, the diver will encounter finely branched and "leafy" forms. These more delicate structures cannot withstand strong wave action, and the added surface area of their shapes serves to better expose their zooxanthellae to the diminished sunlight of deeper waters.

The most common is the fast-growing and ubiquitous *Acropora*. This genus (there are some 100 species) takes a variety of forms, ranging from branching thickets to table-like formations. The tables are considered to be a defense mechanism, as the *Acropora* quickly grows outward, shading any other corals that might try to overgrow it.

Another branching coral often recognized by divers is the needle coral *Seriatopora hystrix,* sending up delicate, pointed branches of cream, blue or pink. *Seriatopora* is usually found in quiet, rather shallow water.

Smaller corals. Some of the smaller coral colonies have distinct, interesting shapes. These corals are not primary reef builders, but colonize already established areas of the reef.

The mushroom corals (family Fungiidae) are common in Indonesia. These form carbonate skeletons that are flat and oval-shaped, perhaps 15–30 centimeters inches long, with fine, radial structures reminiscent of the "gills" of a mushroom. The skeletons are not attached to the reef, and particularly on drop-off reefs, are often knocked upside down by currents. These corals are capable of limited movement, and can usually right themselves eventually. The long-tentacled

Heliofungia actiniformis is often mistaken for a sea anemone.

The flower corals (*Euphyllia*) are not as common as *Fungia,* but can be quite beautiful. They form a maze of flat plates that stick up vertically 10–20 centimeters and cover an area 50 centimeters or even much more in diameter. These corals have long, colorful tentacles, which they extend during the day. *Euphyllia* tolerates turbid water, and can be found growing on patch reefs in back reef channels.

The very bright orange polyps of the coral *Tubastrea* (or the similar *Dendrophyllia*) can be seen in small clusters, usually in low-light areas such as deep on the reef or under overhangs. These finger-sized polyps can easily be mistaken for anemones. They are true scleractinian corals, however, and secrete a very fragile internal skeleton. *Tubastrea* contains no zooxanthellae and receives all its nutrition by capturing plankton. At night, you can watch the polyps feeding by using your light to attract the plankton within reach of the polyps' tentacles. (If your light is very bright, shade it so the polyps won't retract.)

Anemones

Despite their soft and fleshy appearance, sea anemones (order Actinaria) are more closely related to stony corals than soft corals. The giant anemones commonly encountered in Indonesia contain symbiotic algae and are most abundant in relatively shallow areas. They can be seen growing in sand, or tucked into the coral rock in the shallows or at the lip of drop-off reefs.

Like the corals, color and even shape varies widely in the giant anemones, and they are often very difficult to identify. In Indonesia, one can find the long-tentacled *Heteractis*, the short-tentacled carpet anemone, *Stichodactyla*, and the unusual

Discovering New Species

For the diving scientist, Indonesian waters are the most exciting in the world. Not only can "new" species be found on just about every dive, but so much of the behavior of these animals is still unknown that underwater observations are full of surprises.

Scuba has radically changed the way scientists study marine animals. No longer is it necessary to collect everything to study in an aquarium, an artificial environment that often produces artificial behavior, or to collect species the old way—netting, trapping, or even poison. A diver can collect very selectively, and make observations without interfering with the animals' ways of life.

Innumerable small crustaceans and other benthic creatures living in the cracks and crevices of Indonesian reefs go undescribed by science. Even among the best-known reef animals—the fishes—new discoveries are made regularly.

The Grandfather of Ichthyology

To find new species of fish, a good eye and thorough knowledge of the literature serves one better than an academic degree. The grandfather of Indonesian ichthyology was Pieter Bleeker, a Dutch army doctor with a keen interest in fishes. He arrived in Jakarta in 1842, and over the following 30 years produced some 500 papers that became the foundation of his famous, nine-volume *Atlas Ichthyologique* (1862–78).

Unlike many 19th century scientists, who were for the most part simple taxonomists, Bleeker had a very modern understanding of the inter-relationship of species. His work is highly respected by today's scientists.

Finding New Species

Bleeker's work was so good that species described 100 years ago are still waiting to be "re-discovered." It is amazing how many deep-water fishes were collected in those days and never seen again. But scientists tend to concentrate on these, and the intertidal areas are often overlooked.

Above: *The red-headed wrasse,* Halichoeres *sp., is sexually dichromic (the male is at top). This beautiful wrasse was discovered by Kuiter in 1986 in Maumere Bay. Common there, it has not been seen anywhere else.*

A knowledgeable diver, with sharp powers of observation, has a very good chance of finding an unknown animal on just about any dive in Indonesia.

I have been visiting the Flores Sao Resort on a regular basis since 1986, photographing and observing the animal life of Maumere Bay. Despite my many dives in these waters, new species turn up on every trip. Often a "new" species looks very similar to a well-known one, and thus has been overlooked. But in other cases the new species is so spectacular one wonders how it could possibly have ever gone unnoticed.

I started underwater photography 20 years ago, and even among my first dives with a camera, I photographed things that I have never seen since. I always take the picture first, and try to sort out the story later. The underwater world is so diverse you may never see it again.

—*Rudie Kuiter*

Entacmaea quadricolor, with bulbous-tipped tentacles. These anemones are large, sometimes growing to half a meter or more in diameter, although what at first seems to be one anemone is sometimes a group of several.

Giant anemones are easy to spot because they nearly always host a pair, or small group of clownfish *(Amphiprion* and *Premnas).* (See "Clownfishes and their Sea Anemone Hosts," page 46.) These fish are not the only animals to take advantage of the security of the anemone's stinging tentacles. Porcelain crabs *(Neopetrolisthes)* and shrimps are also anemone commensals.

Corallimorphs. These animals (order Corallimorpharia) have some of the characteristics of anemones, and others of corals. In fact, however, they look like small anemones. They are mostly colonial, and consist of flat disks, 2–4 inches in diameter, with a smooth, napped or tentacled surface. One genus, *Discosoma,* is particularly colorful, overgrowing rocks with its bright blue, purple or red disks.

Soft corals and gorgonians

These animals (subclass Alcyonaria) are among the loveliest of the cnidarians. In the clean, plankton-rich waters of Indonesia, soft corals and gorgonians—sea whips or sea fans—are common. Some contain zooxanthellae, but many frequent the deeper parts of the reef, where they filter plankton from the water. Semi-precious pink "coral" is a gorgonian *(Corallium),* harvested from deep waters off Japan and in the Mediterranean.

Soft corals. Soft corals, as the name suggests, lack the hard limestone skeletons of their reef-building relatives. Instead, the numerous polyps that make up the colony are supported by a fleshy central "body"; in some cases strengthened by spicules, spines of silica or calcium.

Soft corals (order Alcyonacea) have few obvious defense mechanisms, and might seem to be vulnerable to attack by predators and parasites, or to fouling by overgrowth. The animals avoid these problems by secreting various bioactive substances, a kind of chemical defense. Substantial efforts are being made by biochemists and pharmaceutical companies to identify compounds in soft corals—and also sponges—that may have properties useful in medicine. Since many of these compounds have evolved to prevent alien growths, they are receiving attention as potential anti-cancer drugs.

A very common group of soft corals in Indonesia are the leather corals *(Lobophytum, Sarcophyton* and *Sinularia)* so-named because of their color and texture. These corals grow as wrinkled lobes in well-lit, shallow areas of reef. Because of their symbiotic zooxanthellae, they are a dull brown, sometimes with a slightly green or yellow tinge. When their white polyps are extended for feeding they are easy to identify as soft corals, but when their polyps are retracted they could be mistaken for sponges. The leather corals, however, have a much smoother surface than sponges.

Perhaps the most beautiful of the soft corals is *Dendronephthya,* a soft coral with fuzzy branches of vivid pink, white, orange, red, red-and-white, and a variety of other colors. The main "stem" is normally translucent and contains numerous white spicules, which offer some structural support. Most of the color comes from the polyps, which also contain sharp spicules to deter browsing by fishes. *Dendronephthya* grows deeper on the reef and in areas of low light, and always where currents can provide it with abundant plankton.

Xenia, particularly common in Indonesia, has perhaps the

largest individual polyps of any soft coral, each 6–8 centimeters long. The white (also tan, or light blue) polyps grow in clusters, and the tentacles at the end of each are feathery. These continually open and close, like numerous grasping hands. In *Xenia* one can easily count eight tentacles, which is one feature that distinguishes soft corals (Octocorallia) from hard corals and anemones (Hexacorallia) which have six, or multiples of six, tentacles.

Gorgonians. Gorgonians (order Gorgonaceae) have a strong, horny skeleton, which gives strength and support without sacrificing flexibility. They tend to grow on the deeper parts of the reef, away from strong wave action. They live by filter feeding, and to maximize the water flow across their surfaces always grow at right angles to the prevailing current. Where the tidal current flows along the reef, gorgonians grow with their long axis vertical. Sometimes, however, particularly on some of the big walls in Indonesia, large sea fans can be seen growing horizontally out from the reef wall, to take advantage of the current upwelling.

There are many species of these animals. Some have a twig-like structure, like a branch from a delicate tree. Many are brightly colored. The sea fans (Melithaeidae and Plexauridae) are flat nets, growing in some cases to three meters across. The skeleton of a sea fan is coated with a kind of "rind," which is sometimes a delicate shade. When you see a big gorgonian it is worth spending a few moments looking closely at its surface because they often host an assortment of small symbiotic animals.

Sea pens. These animals (order Pennatulacea) are filter-feeders related to the gorgonians. Their common name comes from their resemblance to the old-fashioned quill pen. Although common in Indonesia, they are not really reef dwellers, and will usually only be seen by night divers who venture out over mud or sand bottoms. Sea pens, sometimes growing in large fields, rotate gently back and forth with the current, their "feathers" sifting plankton from the current.

Below: *Closeup of the lovely soft coral* Dendronephthya. *In this photograph the strengthening spicules are clearly visible in the animals' transparent tissue.*

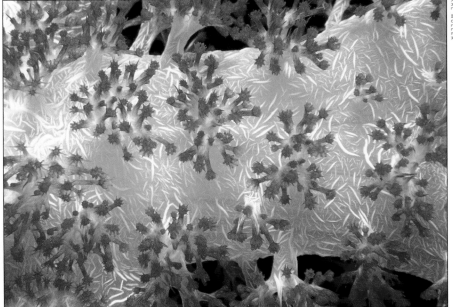

KAL MULLER

Black corals. Black coral (subclass subclass Ceriantipatharia, order Antipatharia) looks to the diver like a gorgonian, although it is more closely related to the stony corals and anemones. In Indonesia, on deeper dives, one can see wire corals (*Cirrhipathes*) and bushy black coral trees (*Antipathes*).

The polished skeleton of the latter, particularly the thicker branches, is the precious black coral. Black coral is scarce, and its export from Indonesia and import into many other countries is prohibited by laws.

Cerianthids. In some areas, particularly with sandy bottoms, one can find cerianthids (subclass Ceriantipatharia, order Ceriantharia) or tube anemones. These are quite different from true anemones. Cerianthids have very fine tentacles arranged in two concentric bands, and secrete a horny tube into which they can retract if disturbed.

ED ROBINSON / IKAN

Fire coral and hydroids

All cnidarians have stinging cells on their tentacles with which they can defend themselves and immobilize their prey. In most cases, however, these are rather weak and are usually not capable of penetrating human skin. One group, class Hydrozoa, which includes the fire corals and their relatives, has members capable of inflicting very painful stings.

The notorious Portuguese-man-of-war (*Physalia physalis*) is a hydrozoan, and not, despite its appearance, a jellyfish. Fortunately for divers this animal is more of an open ocean dweller.

Stinging hydroids. A far greater nuisance to divers in Indonesia are the hydroids *Aglaophenia* and *Lytocarpus*. Despite their delicate, fern-like appearance, these colonial animals can deliver a burning sting that raises a welt on bare skin. They are fairly common on many Indonesian reefs, and their presence prompts divers to wear Lycra or thin neoprene suits even in the warmest of conditions. The stinging hydroids are sometimes called sea ferns, or sea nettles.

Fire corals. Somewhat less virulent are the fire corals of the genus *Millepora*, but as their name suggests they too should be treated with respect. These hydrozoans are members of a group called hydrocorals for their superficial resemblance to the true corals. Hydrocorals secrete a limestone skeleton, and form colonies that are usually a dull-yellow brown in color (*Millepora*) although some species (*Distichopora, Stylaster*) can be brightly colored.

The unusual blue coral (*Heliopora coerulea*), is a fire coral which has a skeleton that when dried displays a light blue tint. It is taxonomically distinct, however and has been placed in class Anthozoa with the octocorals.

Some hydrocorals are important reef-builders, particularly *M. platyphylla,* which can be found growing with massive scleractinian corals at the pounding edge of the reef.

Jellyfish

These familiar animals (class Scyphozoa) are characterized by a dominant medusa stage. Like all cnidarians they form a polyp for part of their lives, but for the

INTRODUCTION

jellyfish, this is just temporary. Occasionally, large jellyfish can be seen while diving in Indonesia, particularly in areas of rich plankton. These can be quite beautiful to observe. More bothersome are the cubomedusae, or sea-wasps, tiny jellyfish that can have an irritating sting. Members of the genus *Chironex* have even been responsible for human fatalities in Australia. Because they tend to inhabit the surface layer during the day, they are more of a bother for snorkelers. The lights of night divers, however, can often attract an unwelcome swarm of these creatures.

Worms

Although the word conjures up a dull, and faintly repulsive animal to many people, the worms found on the reefs of Indonesia show a diversity of form and color that often astounds the observer.

There are many different sorts of worms, but most likely to be seen by divers on Indonesian reefs are those in the following phyla: the flatworms (phylum Platyhelminthes); the ribbonworms (phylum Nemertina); the tongueworms (phylum Echiura); and the segmented worms (phylum Annelida).

Flatworms. Flatworms often have the strikingly beautiful colors divers associate with nudibranchs (which are molluscs). The species seen on Indonesian reefs rarely grow longer than 10 centimeters, and feed on sessile animals such as tunicates and sponges. Flatworms move by gliding over the bottom, or by muscular undulations. This latter waving action is characteristic, and mimicked by the juveniles of several species of fish. This mimicry and the bright colors suggest the presence of a noxious chemical to deter predators.

Ribbonworms. These animals are longer than flatworms, and not as showy. Many are white, with dark stripes or bands.

They tend to live under rocks and corals or in the sand, and are most likely to be seen by divers at night. Some can grow to astonishing sizes, as much as several meters. They feed on molluscs and other worms.

Tongueworms. The tongueworm *Bonellia* can be seen on reef slopes. However, it hides its sac-like body in a crevice, with only a forked proboscis protruding, is easily overlooked. These

animals have an unusual sex life. All the fully formed *Bonellia* are females; if a larva settles into an area where there are no worms, it becomes a female. If there are already *Bonellia* established in the area, the larva passes into the body of an adult, becoming a dwarf male, which lives like a parasite on the female "host."

Segmented worms. The segmented worms are the most abundant and diverse of all the

Above: *Two dorid nudibranchs,* Notodoris citrina *(top) and* Nembrotha sp. *Nudibranchs tend to be very prey-specific.* Nembrotha, *as is shown here, feeds only on hydroids.* Notodoris *was photographed in Halmahera, Maluku;* Nembrotha *in Flores.*

groups of reef worms. Divers are familiar with the feathery feeding parts of the tiny Christmas tree worms (*Spirobranchus*) which extend from lumps of living coral. The body of the worm is hidden in a tube within a *Porites* coral head. The similar, but larger fanworm, or feather duster worm (*Protula, Sabellastarte*), secretes a tube of flexible parchment to protect its soft body. From its tube, it periodically extends a crown of colorful "feathers" to collect plankton. These worms make good subjects for macrophotography, but any sudden movement will cause them to withdraw their crowns.

Some of the segmented worms have evolved unusual reproductive strategies, perhaps the most famous being that of the palolo worms, (*Eunice aphroditois*). Called *nyale* in parts of Indonesia, these worms spend their lives in coral crevices, but one night a year, their tail parts metamorphose into a sexual form, containing either eggs or sperm.

These sexual forms, called epitokes, break off and swarm to the surface. The timing of the event is set by the moon, and in parts of Indonesia, most notably western Sumba and southern Lombok, the appearance of the epitokes is an important event in the ritual or cultural calender. It is also a great culinary event, as the rich-tasting epitokes are highly prized for eating.

Molluscs

Molluscs are one of the largest and most familiar groups of invertebrate animals, and thousands of species live in Indonesian waters. The phylum is organized into either five or eight classes, the main ones found on Indonesian reefs being: Gastropoda (univalves—single shells), including snails, cowries and conches, as well as the shell-less sea slugs; Pelecypoda (bivalves—two-part shell),

Above: *The triton shell,* Charonia tritonis. *This gastropod preys on crown-of-thorns starfish.*

Above: *The helmet conch,* Casis cornuta. *Indonesians call this shell* kima kepala kambing, *the "goat's head."*

including clams, oysters and mussels; and the Cephalopoda, including octopi, squid and cuttlefish. Despite their differences, animals in these three groups all possess a soft, fleshy body (mollusc means "soft") and most—octopi and nudibranchs are exceptions—have the ability to produce a calcareous shell.

Nudibranchs and snails

Gastropods are abundant on Indonesian reefs, but they are easily overlooked because most are small, many are nocturnal, and some are very well camouflaged. Nevertheless the diver who develops the habit of carefully scrutinizing the reef surface will soon find many of these delightful creatures.

Nudibranchs. Nudibranchs, the "naked gilled" sea slugs, are the most interesting to the diver. Like common garden slugs, they are snail-like animals that have lost their shells. Nudibranchs are often strikingly colored.

In some species the coloration is clearly cryptic, allowing them to blend in with their chosen prey. Nudibranchs are carnivorous, and most are very prey specific, feeding for example only on particular types of soft coral or sponges. Since these prey animals are often very colorful, so are the nudibranchs.

In other species, it seems certain that coloration serves as a warning to would-be predators that the animals are foul-tasting or poisonous. Nudibranchs are known to produce some very concentrated toxins. Some even have nematocysts, which they obtain from their cnidarian prey and concentrate in the outer layers of their own skin.

Most nudibranchs are small, although a few mainly nocturnal forms grow to 20 centimeters or more in length. One of the largest and certainly the most spectacular nudibranch found in Indonesia is the Spanish dancer,

Hexabranchus sanguineus, a beautiful, crimson-colored animal. This nudibranch only wanders out at night, and if it is found and gently picked up, it will begin its "dance." The wild undulations of its body and surrounding skirt are thought to serve as part of a warning display. Like many nudibranchs, Spanish dancers lay their eggs in huge numbers, in spiral ribbons that can look like flowers.

Rock shells. The rock shells or murex (*Murex* spp.) feed heavily on small bivalve molluscs such as oysters. This is not an easy task, because the bivalves clamp their shells shut when attacked. A murex shell overcomes this resistance by chipping away at the edge of the oyster with its sharp radula or mouthpart, and then pokes its proboscis into this opening to feed on the fleshy tissues within. Another species, with similar tastes in prey, is the drill (*Thais*). This small gastropod literally drills a hole through the oyster's shell. The large number of bivalve shells with neat holes drilled in them that are washed up on Indonesian beaches testifies to the efficiency of this feeding method.

Tritons. The triton shell (*Charonia tritonis*) is famous as a predator of the troublesome crown-of-thorns starfish, which has devastated Australian reefs. This large shell (to more than 30 cm.) is a popular souvenir, and over-harvesting has been blamed for population explosions of the crown-of-thorns. The helmet conch (*Casis cornuta*) is another large, predatory gastropod found in Indonesia. Because of collectors, both the triton and helmet conch are endangered in parts of Indonesia.

Cone shells. Cone shells (*Conus* spp.) are even more rapacious predators. Their radulas are modified as barbs, with which they stab their victims. They then immobilize their prey by injecting a neurotoxic poison. Most cone shells eat worms, although a few are piscivorous. The poison of some of the fish-eating *Conus* species is powerful enough to kill a human, so treat them with respect.

Cowries. Cowries (*Cypraea*

Above: Tridacna gigas *is the largest of the seven species of giant clams. It can be distinguished by its size and the pebbly texture of its mantle. Scientists believe these to be among the longest-lived animals, some surviving as long as 200 years. A speciman as large as the one pictured here is probably well over 50 years old.*

Above: *A predatory gastropod prying open a bivalve.*

HETERACTIS MAGNIFICA

Above: The colorful magnificent anemone, one of the largest clownfish anemones.

Clownfish and their Sea Anemone Hosts

There is perhaps no sight more charming than a pair of bright clownfishes nestled in one of the colorful giant reef anemones. Although known to possess powerful stinging cells, the anemones clearly don't harm the clownfishes, which look downright snug tucked into the soft tentacles of their host.

The relationship between the fish and the actinian is commensal; the anemonefishes clearly benefit, receiving protection for themselves and their offspring. They even pluck at the tentacles and oral disk of the anemone, eating the organic material that has collected there.

The benefit to the anemone is less clear. The constant prodding, cleaning and stimulation provided by the fishes certainly *seems* enjoyable, but this maybe just to us. Anemonefishes are never found without anemones;

Below: Juvenile Clark's anemonefish, in the distinctive bulb-tentacled anemone. 15 meters, Bunaken Island, Sulawesi.

anemones, however, are sometimes found without the fish.

A Delicate Operation

It had been thought that clownfishes were somehow immune to the anemone's stinging nematocysts. Close observations, however, have shown this not to be the case. The fish, through a series of brief—and careful— encounters with the actinian, picks up a substance in its mucous that the anemone recognizes as its own. The nematocysts don't fire when touched by the fish for the same reason one tentacle doesn't sting another.

Some cold-hearted experimenters tested this theory by scraping the mucous off a clownfish and placing it back with its anemone. The hapless fish was immediately and unceremoniously stung.

Clownfishes are protandrous

AMPHIPRION CLARKII   ENTACMAEA QUADRICOLOR

hermaphrodites; that is, all mature as males, and then a few sex-reverse to females. A typical anemone will contain a pair of clownfish, and perhaps a few young ones.

The largest fish in the group is the female. If she should die, the reigning male sex-reverses, and the dominant juvenile becomes the functional male. Juveniles sharing an anemone with an adult pair are hormonally stunted, and remain small.

Although clownfish are the only fishes to require an anemone host, other small damsels will opportunistically occupy anemones as juveniles, especially various species of *Dascyllus*.

Sea Anemones

Some of the giant reef anemones can reach a meter in diameter. All have zooxanthellae, and are thus found in relatively shallow water. They derive most of their nutrition from the algae, but also consume plankton and any other small animal unlucky enough to blunder into their tentacles.

Anemones can live to a ripe old age. In the 19th century, British naturalist John Dalyell kept a coldwater *Actinia* sp. anemone for 66 years. Over this period, it produced 750 young (by budding), 150 of these after the age of 50. The anemone eventually outlived the scientist.

Some 10 species of Indonesian anemones, in three families, host clownfish. The systematics of this group was in some confusion until Dr. Daphne Fautin reorganized it in 1981.
Cryptodendrum adhaesivum. Lies flat; very short tentacles. Hosts only Clark's anemonefish.
Entacmaea quadricolor. The bubble anemone. (See photo at left.) Hosts 11 species.
Macrodactyla doreensis. Very long, widely spaced tentacles.

AMPHIPRION CLARKII   HETERACTIS AURORA

Left: *Young Clark's anemonefish,* Amphiprion clarkii, *in the distinctive sand anemone,* Heteractis aurora.

PREMNAS BIACULEATUS   ENTACMAEA QUADRICOLOR

Left. *The spine-cheek anemonefish, in the bulb-tentacled anemone. The spine-cheeked anemonefish varies from red to almost black.*

AMPHIPRION OCELLARIS   STICHODACTYLA HADDONI

Left: *A pair of common anemonefish, in Haddon's anemone.*

Usually dull color, buries column in sand. Hosts 2 species.
Heteractis aurora. Dull color, buries column in sand. Distinctive tentacle shape (see top photo above.) Hosts 7 species.
H. crispa. Long, thin, almost pointed tentacles that often seem tangled. Hosts 11 species.
H. magnifica. Brightly colored column, blunt tentacles. Often photographed. (See small photo opposite.) Hosts 10 species.
H. malu. Buries column in sand, fairly short tentacles, limited range. Hosts only Clark's.
Stichodactyla haddoni. Haddon's carpet anemone. Short-tentacles. Grey, with white radial stripes. Hosts 6 species.
S. gigantea. Bludru anemone. Longer tentacles, larger than Haddon's. Hosts 6 species.
S. mertensii. Merten's anemone. Colorful; largest carpet anemone, to 1m across. (See bottom photo above.) Hosts 10 species.
— *David Pickell*

Above: *One of the piscivorous cone shells (*Conus *sp.) devouring a small goby. Most cone shells eat worms, but the relatively few fish-eating species are very dangerous.*

Below: *The octopus has highly developed eyes and a very sophisticated nervous system. It is thus considered "intelligent," and people find it hard to believe that it is a mollusc.*

spp.) are common, small (most just a few cm.) gastropods with a smooth shell that is completely covered by the animal's fleshy mantle. Both the shells and mantles can be beautifully marked, often with very different patterns. The cowries are omnivorous, feeding on algae as well as a variety of sedentary animals such as soft corals.

Trochus. Top shells (*Trochus* spp.) are relatively large (6–8 cm.), and conical. Before the advent of plastics they were widely collected for the manufacture of buttons. Removing the grubby outer layer of shell reveals the lustrous nacre, or mother-of-pearl beneath. Until the invention of Bakelite, and the many plastics that followed, shell nacre for buttons was an important business in Indonesia. Today they are still collected, most to be used in souvenirs and to supply the small market for "real" buttons.

Clams and Oysters

The bivalves include such familiar forms as clams, oysters, mussels and scallops. All have two articulated shell halves that can

be closed with a large muscle. It is this muscle that makes bivalves so prized as seafood. With a very few exceptions, bivalves cannot move, like gastropods, and thus most have adapted to filter-feeding. They draw water in through one tube or "siphon" and pass it out through another. This stream of water passes through the animal's gills, which serve the dual purpose of respiration and filtering out food particles.

All bivalves must hold their shell halves at least slightly ajar to maintain water circulation through their bodies. But when danger threatens they are clamped shut. Some Indonesian bivalves gain further protection by boring into corals and reef rock, so that predators cannot reach them. The boring is achieved by a combination of chemical action and rasping with the two shell haves. Eventually, reef bivalves become so encrusted with sponges, coralline algae, bryozoans and cnidarians that they are barely visible.

Giant clams. The giant reef clams, *Tridacna* spp., have a dif-

ED ROBINSON / IKAN

ferent means of feeding. Like reef-building corals, *Tridacna* clams harbor zooxanthellae in their fleshy mantles, and can thus "manufacture" most—or perhaps all—of their own food. Like corals, they require lots of light, and tend to be found in the shallows. They grow with the hinge of their shells down, and their rippled gape facing the sun.

There are seven species of *Tridacna,* of which the giant clam, *T. gigas,* is the most dramatic. These animals can reach a meter and a half in diameter. An animal that big could be a century old. Although smaller than *T. gigas, T. squamosa* has a beautiful ruffled shell. The fleshy mantles of *Tridacna* clams are beautiful, varying in color from brown to yellow to green to blue, with contrasting spots or mottling.

Tridacna clams are a great delicacy in Asia, particularly in Taiwan, and their shells are made into terrazzo in factories in Surabaya. Over-harvesting has greatly reduced their numbers throughout Indonesia. Shallow reefs in Eastern Indonesia that used to support literally fields of giant clams have been stripped in just the past few years. There is fear that the population in many areas is no longer at a self-sustaining level.

Recently, however, researchers at the Micronesian Mariculture Demonstration Center in Palau, headed by Gerald Heslinga, have discovered a method of "farming" giant clams by inoculating the veliger larvae with zooxanthellae. Once the symbiotic algae is in place, the clams need only a good supply of seawater and plenty of light to thrive. The farming operation requires little room, and the clams reach 10 centimeters across in just two years. Because of the commercial potential for these clams, a number of pilot farms have recently been established in the Pacific region.

Oysters. A number of oysters can be found on the reef, in many cases so well camouflaged with encrusting growths that they are at first invisible. The cock's comb oyster (*Lopha cristagalli*) has a distinctive sharp, zig-zag opening, and is often covered by encrusting sponges.

The colorful mantle of the thorny oyster (*Spondylus* spp.) stands out, although its rough shell is usually overgrown with algae, sponges, and small cnidarians.

In many parts of Indonesia, Japanese operators seed pearl oysters (*Pinctata*) and hang them in the shallows to grow pearls. The oysters are purchased from local collecters, and the "seed" comes from a freshwater mussel found in the Mississippi basin. Security on these "farms" is high, and divers are unwelcome.

Cephalopods

These animals, despite their close relationship to the snails and clams, are active, "intelligent" predators with highly developed eyes and sophisticated behaviors. The octopus has eight suckered arms, while squid and cuttlefish have an additional two grasping tentacles. Both octopi and squids have a hard, chitinous beak. The nautilus—of which only one genus is extant— differs markedly from the other cephalopods. It has 90 arms,

Above: *The thorny oyster (*Spondylus sp.*) is often so encrusted with sponges, algae, tunicates and other organisms that only when it is agape with its bright mantle showing (as here) can it be seen. Halmahera, Maluku.*

without suckers, and a well-developed shell. Unlike other cephalopods, the nautilus has very primitive eyes, lacking a lens and open to the water.

Octopi. These familiar animals can be found on the reef, although they normally hide in small caves or crevices. They have no internal skeleton so are able to squeeze into surprisingly small spaces.

Chromatophores on their skin give octopi remarkable abilities to change color, which they do either to blend in with their surroundings or to display emotion. Some species can also change their surface texture, from smooth to lumpy and back, producing very believable imitations of shells, and even lionfish.

Octopuses are particularly fond of eating crabs and other crustaceans, and a pile of shells often marks a hole where one is resident. Normally an octopus crawls rather slowly across the reef, but it can also swim by contractions of its legs, much like an umbrella opening and closing. If disturbed, it can produce a short burst of speed by squirting water out of its large gill cavity through a muscular siphon.

Beware of the common, small blue-ringed octopi (*Hapalochlaena*) which can be found under rocks on the reef flats in Indonesia. Do not pick one up. They possess a very virulent poison.

Squid. Squid are free-swimming animals, usually seen in groups in shallow lagoon areas or along the reef edge. They have perfected the mode of jet-propelled movement. While stationary they maintain position with gentle undulations of their lateral fins. Movement, either forward or backward, is achieved by the highly maneuverable water jet. Like the octopus, squids can change their coloration, adopting a sparkling array of brilliant colors and patterns.

Squid have a rudimentary

internal "shell," actually a non-calcareous strengthening device called a pen. It is of a clear, flexible substance that looks and feels like a piece of plastic.

Although you will never see one on the reef, the largest cephalopods by far are the giant squids (*Architecteuthis*), which can reach a length of 18 meters. These animals frequent very deep water, and little is known of their habits. They are the preferred prey of the sperm whale.

Cuttlefish. Cuttlefish (*Sepia*) superficially resemble squid, but can be distinguished by their generally larger size and more robust shape. Unlike squid, which often travel in large groups, lone cuttlefish can often be seen foraging on the reef slope, and are the most frequently encountered cephalopods.

Like the other cephalopods, cuttlefish can squirt out a blob of ink if threatened. The shape of this blob, roughly the size of the animal that ejected it, and its strong smell, distracts the would-be predator while the cuttlefish jets away. In earlier times, this ink was used for writing, as is suggested by the cuttlefish's genus name, *Sepia*.

Instead of the squid's flexible pen, cuttlefish have a "cuttlebone," a calcareous structure perhaps most familiar for its use as a dietary supplement for cage birds. Although it provides some stiffness, the most important use of the porous "bone" is for buoyancy control, balancing the animal's vertical movements across the reef face.

Nautilus. These animals, with their distinctive spiralled shell, are the most unusual of the living cephalopods. The chambered shell serves as a form of buoyancy control, like the cuttlefish bone, but much more sophisticated. This control is necessary as the animals undergo a considerable daily vertical migration. During the daylight hours, the

Opposite: A mantis shrimp, Odontodactylus scyllaris. *These animals are fierce predators, using their modified front claws to seize or bludgeon prey in the manner of their namesake, the praying mantis.* Odontodactylus *is the most colorful and one of the larger mantis shrimps—it is said to be able to smash a four-inch crab with one strike. Some divers call these animals "thumb-splitters" and with good reason. Do not try to touch one! Tulamben, Bali.*

HELMUT DEBELIUS / IKAN

nautilus stay at 1,000–1,500 meters, and only rise into relatively shallow water at night. Only very rarely are they found in depths a sport diver could reach. In this way they avoid predators, and perhaps also are able to more easily find their food—carrion and, particularly, the molts of crustaceans.

There are several species, but the most common on Indonesian reefs is the pearly nautilus (*Nautilus pompilius*).

Crustaceans

The jointed-foot animals—Arthropoda—is the single most successful phylum of animals. On land, the insects and spiders dominate; in the water, the subphylum Crustacea is king, with almost 40,000 species. Crustaceans—crabs, shrimp and lobsters—are very abundant on Indonesian coral reefs, but many keep themselves well-hidden, particularly during the day. They are most likely to be seen by night divers.

The largest commonly seen crustaceans are the spiny lobsters, *Panulirus*. By day spiny lobsters hide in caves and crevices, often in small groups, with only their long antennae protruding. But at night they venture out of their retreats in search of food. If surprised out in the open, spiny lobsters can swim backwards with great speed using powerful flicks of their tail.

These lobsters, of course, make very fine eating, but visiting divers should resist the temptation of trying to catch a lobster for the table. Removal of animals from a dive site is short-sighted, and lobster catching is quite a skilled operation. An unpracticed diver who attempts it is likely to be left only with painful cuts and a handful of antennae.

Shrimps

On night dives large shrimps can sometimes be spotted out in the open where their reflective eyes catch the light and stand out as two bright red spots. But even by day the careful observer should be able to spot several species of small shrimp.

Commensals. A variety of sometimes colorful shrimp associate with anemones, coral and echinoderms for protection, making them easy to spot. The tiny bumble-bee shrimps (*Gnathophyllum*) associate with sea urchins. Various species of *Periclimenes*, some quite colorful, associate with anemones, gorgonians, and echinoderms. One, *P. imperator*, lives in the folds of the Spanish dancer nudibranch.

Cleaner shrimps. Also easy to see are the cleaner shrimps, protected from predation by the services they offer. These cleaners pick parasites and bits of dead tissue from fish, and can all

Below: *A dispute developed between these two prawn gobies,* Mahidolia mystacina, *when the yellow goby and its shrimp wandered into the grey goby's territory. When the grey fish came out of its burrow, the sand started to fly. Both of these gobies are females. Tulamben, Bali.*

RUDIE KUITER

be recognized by long, white antennae.

The candy shrimps (*Lysmata*) are beautiful red striped or spotted cleaners. The coral shrimps (*Stenopus*) live in pairs in small caves or holes extending their large white antennae to attract the attention of passing fish.

The common banded coral shrimp, *Stenopus hispidus,* has well-developed front claws, and is sometimes called the boxer shrimp. Various species of *Periclimenes* also serve as cleaners.

Cleaner shrimp often set up a "station," that fish visit repeatedly. It is quite a sight to watch a tiny shrimp crawl into the mouth and gills of a grouper or large angelfish. If approached slowly enough cleaner shrimps will climb onto a diver's outstretched hand, to see if it too needs cleaning, or even into his mouth.

Pistol shrimp. These animals (*Alpheus* and *Synalpheus*) have well-developed pincers, one much larger than the other. By some means that is not well understood, the pistol or snapping shrimp is able to create an audible clicking sound with its large claw.

Some of the blind or near-blind pistol shrimp have developed interesting relationships with small gobies. In lagoons and on sandy patches around the reef you can see these small fish sitting up on their fins outside a small burrow. Next to the fish will be one or more pistol shrimps. The shrimps rely on the gobies, with which they keep in contact by their long antennae, to warn them of the approach of any danger. The gobies benefit from this relationship by having a safe burrow dug for them.

Crabs

Many species of crabs live on Indonesian reefs, but they are not always easy to find. Crabs would soon be eaten by strong-jawed fish such as wrasses if they ventured out boldly by day. Many species are therefore only seen at night when they come out under the cover of darkness to feed. If you look closely at a well-protected coral thicket, however, you will likely see a few small crabs safely wedged in.

Hermit crabs. These familiar, and comical creatures use the discarded shells of gastropods as portable refuges. Some of these small animals are very colorful, particularly *Aniculus* and the demon hermit crabs, *Trizopagurus*. A few species of hermit crabs go one stage further, carrying small sea anemones on their shells as additional discouragement to potential predators.

The large terrestrial coconut or robber crab (*Birgus latro*), a delicacy in the Moluccas and other parts of Indonesia, is actually a hermit crab that abandons its shell when it reaches adulthood. Small land hermit crabs (*Coenobita*) are common along the high tide line on some Indonesian beaches.

Decorator crabs. These are types of spider crabs that protect themselves by sticking live sponges, gorgonians or other material onto their fuzzy or spiny backs as camouflage. Small decorator crabs may be spotted at any time on sea fans or black coral trees. But look out for the large nocturnal species that carry massive chunks of soft coral or sponge on their backs, held on with their last pair of legs.

The small and colorful boxer crab, *Lybia tesselata,* grasps a pair of tiny sea anemones in its claws which it then uses for both defense, and to collect food.

Porcelain crabs. The porcelain crabs (*Neopetrolisthes*), so-named for their smooth, colorful shells, are sometimes called "half-crabs," for they are structurally similar to prawns and lobsters. They are commensals on the giant anemones where, protected from predators, they strain plankton from the water with mouthparts that have been modified for filter-feeding.

Echinoderms

Everyone is familiar with the common starfish or sea star. But starfishes are only one of five groups that together form the Echinodermata, "hedgehog-skinned" animals. The others are the sea urchins, the brittle stars, the feather stars and the sea cucumbers. Most echinoderms have a skeleton of spiny plates—most developed in the sea urchins, and least developed in the sea cucumbers—and five-sided symmetry.

Starfish. The five-sided symmetry of the echinoderms is clearly displayed in the starfishes. Most Indonesian species have five arms, although some individuals may have one arm more or less. The common cobalt-blue starfish *Linckia laevigata* is particularly variable in this regard. Some of the larger starfishes may have a great number of arms.

Starfishes are predators, feeding on a wide variety of bottom-dwelling animals, or detritivores. A feeding starfish envelops its prey with its arms, then actually pushes part of its stomach out through its mouth over the victim, digesting it externally. Starfishes are able to hang on to even actively struggling prey with their myriad tube feet, tiny suckers that cover the undersides of their arms. The gripping power of these animals is considerable, and over time they can even overpower the strong muscle of a bivalve. The tube feet are also used for locomotion.

Some starfish have very thick arms, particularly the pincushion starfish (*Culcita* spp.) common on Indonesian reefs. These animals can inflate their bodies to the point where they become almost spherical. *Culcita* normally have tiny symbiotic shrimps living on their lower surfaces.

The most notorious starfish in Indonesian waters is the crown-of-thorns, *Acanthaster plancii,* which is found throughout the tropical Indian and Pacific Oceans. This animal feeds exclusively on coral polyps.

Normally the crown-of-thorns, large, multi-armed and bristly, occurs in very low numbers on coral reefs—divers usually see perhaps one per dive. But population densities have occasionally reached plague proportions, and at these times whole reefs can be destroyed. Some of the greatest damage has been on the Great Barrier Reef of Australia and on the reefs of southern Japan, but *Acanthaster* outbreaks have occurred throughout its range, including Indonesia.

These plagues have been the subject of a long and heated debate by reef scientists. Some argue that over-fishing, over-harvesting of predators like the triton conch, and agricultural runoff have contributed to the disastrous outbreaks. Huge coral heads, hundreds of years old, have been destroyed by the ravages of the starfish. These scientists argue that control measures are necessary, and advocate the removal of *Acanthaster* whenever seen by divers. (Note: The crown-of-thorns is spiny, and some people have a toxic reaction to its thorns. Do not touch one unprotected.)

Another opinion suggests that the outbreaks are a natural phenomenon, and point to core samples taken on the Great Barrier reef that show periodic accumulations of *Acanthaster* spines. These scientists say the outbreaks remove dominant coral species, and may be necessary to increase the species diversity of tropical reefs. They note that the reefs have recovered relatively rapidly from the outbreaks, and suggest removal of crown-of-thorns would in the long run be counter-productive.

Brittle stars. Brittle stars are quite similar in appearance to starfish, but have thin, flexible arms. These arms are easily broken off, hence the name. While starfish move mainly by the action of the tiny tube feet on the underside of their arms, brittle stars move by movements of the whole arm.

Many brittle stars have spines on their arms which are very sharp and can give the unwary diver a nasty sting. Despite these spiny defences and their unappetizing appearance, brittle stars are preyed upon by several species of fish, and thus tend to remain well-hidden.

On the shallow reef flats one can sometimes find literal "fields" of brittle stars, their bodies flat on the bottom and their arms wriggling in the water, filtering plankton and debris. On deeper areas of the reef, these animals are less bold, and extend just an arm or two from the safety of their crevices.

Serpent stars are brittle stars with smooth arms, and often very striking colors. These animals can sometimes be seen with their arms coiled in tight loops around gorgonians.

Basket stars are the most highly developed filter-feeding brittle stars. They only come out to feed at night, when they extend their branched arms to capture planktonic animals drifting past. Basket stars are beautiful creatures to watch, and they are particularly common on Indonesian reefs, where they can grow to over a meter across.

Crinoids. The crinoids or feather stars are survivors of the sea lilies, animals that once were among the most common in the seas. Although there are still some stalked crinoids extant, those seen on Indonesian reefs are unstalked. They perch on the edge of sponges or gorgonians with a set of small clasping legs, and deploy their delicate arms— of which they have 30 or more— to strain plankton from the water. Feather stars can also walk on these long arms, and if dislodged may swim with them in a beautiful but rather inefficient manner.

Food filtered from the current

Below: *Many species of shrimps act as cleaners. This is a* Leandrites *sp. at work on the mouth of a coral grouper,* Cephalopholis miniata.

by the fine hairs on the crinoid's arms are passed down a channel to the central mouth. Crinoids sit "upside-down" compared to the starfish, and the mouth is on top the animal.

Some feather stars are nocturnal and hide by day in reef crevices. As night falls they come out of hiding and climb up onto prominent blocks of coral or other high points where they are exposed to the strongest current flow. Crinoids are particularly abundant in plankton-rich areas.

Sea urchins. Sea urchins are important and abundant grazers on Indonesian coral reefs. Even the spiniest of urchins may be attacked if they venture out into the open by day, so they tend to confine their activities to the night. By day they wedge themselves into crevices or hollows to avoid the attentions of predatory fish. Sea urchins have a very sophisticated feeding apparatus which they use to scrape at the reef, removing not only algae but

also quantities of coral rock. In fact, some small species actually excavate their own daytime hiding places out of the soft coral rock by the constant scraping of their jaws and spines.

On shallow, quiet reefs in Indonesia one can often see the black, long-spined urchin *Diadema,* so-named for the cluster of glistening "jewels" set into its upper body. This urchin has very

long and brittle spines, and stepping on one would be a real disaster. In harbors and other disturbed areas of reef, very large numbers of these animals can be found. Shrimpfish and urchin clingfish hide among their spines.

The rarely seen slate pencil urchin (*Heterocentrotus mamillatus*) is a distinctive species, with thick, pink spines. No longer used as chalk, the unfortunate animals' attractive spines are in some areas now being made into wind chimes.

The bodies of most sea urchins seem roughly spherical, but in fact they are made up of five radial segments, in typical echinoderm fashion. Sea urchins develop a calcareous skeleton or test, which contains the feeding apparatus, the intestines, and the gonads. Prior to reproduction the gonads expand to fill the whole shell, and it is this rich substance that make sea urchins so attractive to hungry fish despite their spiny defenses.

The ripe gonads of the sea urchin *Hemicentrotus pulcherrimus* are prized in Japan for sushi; the taste of this *uni* is strong, but delicious.

Sea cucumbers. Though at first they look just like loose sacks, or large worms, sea cucumbers (class Holothuria) are constructed with the same five-sided symmetry typical of the echinoderms. Because they are so elongate, they have a "head" and a "tail," unlike the starfish or urchins. The head of a sea cucumber is not, however, particularly well developed, consisting of little more than a ring of tentacles around the mouth. Sea cucumbers are an important trade item in Indonesia. (See "Trepang Fishing," page 27.)

Most species are detritus feeders, the tentacles being used to pick up sand and pass it into the mouth. Organic matter is digested and the undigested remains are passed out through the anus. Sea cucumbers have to eat a lot of sand in order to obtain enough food, so they often leave a continuous trail of sandy feces behind them. A few species are filter feeders. They hide their bodies in reef crevices and hold their tentacles up in to the water current to feed. The tentacles are rapidly withdrawn if disturbed.

Sea cucumbers appear as elongated and somewhat flaccid forms lying among coral rubble or sea grass, moving slowly in a worm-like way by contractions of their bodies. These are usually black or dull-colored. A few species, such as the sea apple (*Pseudocolochirus*), are very colorful, however.

Many sea cucumbers are active by day. Since they are not attacked by predatory fish it would seem that they must have some efficient means of defense. Some species can discharge sticky white threads if molested, and most tropical sea cucumbers contain toxins.

Tunicates

The tunicates or sea squirts are an entirely marine group of animals, and are unfamiliar to many people. Despite their unimpressive appearance, they are chordates, and—technically—are more closely related to human beings than to any of the invertebrates listed above. They have a notochord, a primitive backbone, only in their larval form. Once they settle out of the plankton and become sessile filter-feeders, the backbone is unceremoniously shed. (So much for the vaunted evolutionary superiority of "higher order" forms.)

The tunicates seen on Indonesian reefs are all in the class Ascidiacea, a name derived from the ancient Greek word for leather bottle. They are rather like little bottles, with (usually) two openings rather than just one. Water is drawn in through the uppermost of these siphons,

filtered through a basket-like arrangement internally, and then passed out through the lower siphon. Peer into the opening of a large tunicate and you may be able to make out the fine sieving apparatus within. Many tunicates have stout spikes projecting from the inner wall of their siphons, to thwart small fish or other unwanted intruders.

One of the most common and

conspicuous tunicates on Indonesian reefs is the beautiful white, purple and yellow *Polycarpa aurata*. These creatures are about the size of a man's thumb, and have a tough leathery outer coating, or tunic. *Polycarpa* is a solitary and very distinctive animal and easy to identify underwater. But many tunicates are colonial, and can easily be mistaken for sponges. If the siphons

Above: *A cluster of tunicates,* Rhopalaea crassa. *Water enters through the uppermost opening, is filtered of plankton and nutrients, and then passed out the lower opening. Bunaken group, Sulawesi.*

Above: *The blue ribbon eel,* Rhinomuraena quaesita, *is one of the most attractive moray eels. Young eels are black, and don't turn electric blue until they reach a bit over a half-meter in length. Bunaken group, Sulawesi.*

of a sea-squirt are touched (gently so as not to harm the animal) they will squeeze shut. Sponges do not react to touch. If a tunicate is lifted out of the sea this same contraction will cause water to be squirted out of its siphon—hence the common name sea squirt.

Most colonial tunicates are overlooked because they tend to be tucked away in dark corners. An exception are the marble-sized, white-and-green grape ascidians, *Diademnum molle,* a common compound tunicate on shallow reefs in Indonesia. Diademnid tunicates have a single large inhalent opening, and many small exhalent openings around their globular tunics.

Their green color comes from a symbiotic algae living within its tissues, much like the zooxanthellae of stony corals. The relationship between this tunicate and its algae is one of mutual dependency, neither party being able to survive alone. *Diademnum* larvae even carry samples of the algae with them to ensure that the relationship is continued in the next generation.

The Fishes

Corals and other invertebrate animals can provide a lifetime of interest for a diver in Indonesia, but the fish are what really grabs one's attention. On most reefs, brightly colored and beautifully patterned fish are everywhere,

darting among the corals or lying sedately in mid-water. It would be impossible in the space available here to offer a complete description of the thousands of fish species found on Indonesian reefs, so all that will be attempted is a brief survey. Consult "Further Readings" page 321 for more complete resources.

Elasmobranchs

Sharks and rays are elasmobranchs, and differ from true bony fishes by having a cartilaginous skeleton, only parts of which are calcified (e.g., the jaws of a shark). Gill structure—elasmobranch means "plate-gilled"—and other physical features differ between bony fish and sharks and rays, which are considered a more primitive form.

Sharks. There are many species of sharks in Indonesian waters, but those most commonly seen by divers are the reef white-tip shark (*Triaenodon obesus*), the gray reef shark (*Carcharhinus amblyrhynchos*), and the reef black-tip shark (*C. melanopterus*).

The reef white-tip shark grows to 1.7 meters, and is a thin, gray fish with white tips to its dorsal and tail fins. This is the most commonly seen shark on the Indonesian reefs. This small shark can be often be found hiding under overhangs.

The gray reef shark grows up to 2.3 meters, and has a very dark trailing edge to its tail. Although this animal is known to be aggressive in some areas, it is not considered dangerous in Indonesia.

The reef black-tip shark grows to 1.8 meters, and is pale gray or brown with distinct black tips on all its fins. This shark sometimes comes up into very shallow water on reef flats and in lagoons to look for food.

The largest fish extant is the whale shark (*Rhincodon typus*), a harmless animal that strains krill and small fish from the water. Growing to more than 12 meters in length (although specimens of 5–7 meters are more common), the whale shark is not a reef fish, although it can be found seasonally off some reefs in Indonesia.

The only really dangerous sharks a diver might encounter on an Indonesian reef are the tiger shark (*Galeocerdo cuvieri*), a large—up to 5.5 meters—scavenger that sometimes comes up onto the reefs at night or in the late afternoon.These sharks, however, are very rarely seen.

Rays. Structurally, rays are essentially flattened sharks. The stingrays have one or two stout spines at the base of their tail, which are their main means of defence. They will not normally be used against divers, although you should always take care to avoid stingrays while walking in shallow water.

Stingrays are bottomfish, and have strong teeth which they use to crush shellfish. In areas where stingrays are common you may see large craters in the bottom, caused by their feeding activities. Perhaps the most common stingrays in Indonesia are two species of blue-spotted stingray: *Taeniura lymma*, which frequents coral rich areas, and *Dasyatis kuhlii,* which lives in sandy areas of disturbed reef, or between patch reefs. A much larger animal is the grey reef ray (*Taeniura melanospilos*).

Not all rays are bottom-dwellers. The spotted eagle ray (*Aetobatis narinari*) cruises the reef edge looking for crustaceans. Eagle rays can reach 2.3 meters across.

The largest ray, however, is the manta (*Manta birostris*). Like the whale shark, mantas are essentially open water fish, but they are regularly seen by divers in Indonesia. The manta ray, growing up to 6.7 meters across and weighing 1,400 kilos, is a planktivore. Both whale sharks

and mantas occur only seasonally in different parts of the country, as they migrate to the areas where the plankton is thickest.

Because they are found in areas dense with plankton, mantas tend to be seen at times when visibility is relatively low. This, however, is a small inconvenience when weighed against the pleasure of swimming with such magnificent creatures.

Sometimes seen in the same places that attract mantas are the smaller, but very similar devil rays (*Mobula*). These animals travel in groups and sometimes large schools.

Bony Fishes

Eels. The moray eels (family Muraenidae) are common both in folklore and on the Indonesian reef. Although not as dangerous as Hollywood would have us

Below: *The ornate ghost pipefish,* Solenostomus para-doxus. *This strange animal is a relative of the seahorses and pipefishes, however in* Solenosto-mus *the female broods the eggs. Although this juvenile stands out here against the brilliant red crinoids, the coloration and growths are probably cryptic. Tulamben, Bali.*

RUDIE KUITER

believe, they have sharp teeth and should not be provoked. The largest species, the giant moray (*Gymnothorax javanicus*), can reach more than two meters in length, and weigh 35 kilos. Many morays are nocturnal hunters, resting in holes by day and prowling the reef by night. They feed on dozing fish which they detect by smell.

A very beautiful eel, related to the morays but more delicately built, is the blue ribbon eel (*Rhinomuraena quaesita*). The adult coloration of this animal is electric blue and yellow, and adult females turn bright yellow. Juveniles are black.

Several species of the unusual garden eels (a subfamily of the conger eels) can be found on sandy bottoms in Indonesia. They live in burrows in often large groups, and the sight of all their thin bodies waving in the current gives them their common name. They have small mouths, and pluck plankton from the current. If you swim over the "garden" the eels will slip back down into their burrows, disappearing in a wave before you.

Although garden eels are usually found in deeper water, particularly the sandy channels between reefs, they can sometimes be seen in very shallow sand patches on the reef. There is a colony of garden eels in shallow water on the approach to the popular wreck at Tulamben, Bali.

Seahorses and pipefish. These fishes (family Syngnathidae) are generally slow-moving and secretive, and are not often easy to find. They are planktivores, and can be found in sea grass beds and estuaries as well as in coral reefs. In fact, their fins are poorly developed, and they shun areas of high current or surge. Seahorses (*Hippocampus*) can be highly camouflaged, some exactly matching a single species of gorgonian.

The master of camouflage, however, is the ghost pipefish (*Solenostomus cyanopterus*), an animal whose shape and color precisely duplicate a blade of turtlegrass. A strikingly colored relative is the ornate ghost pipefish, *S. paradoxus*.

Pipefish are long and thin, and superficially appear quite dif-

Below: *A school of shrimpfishes,* Aeloiscus strigatus. *The shrimpfishes always swim with their noses pointed downward. In the process of evolution their dorsal, tail and anal fins have migrated to a position on the side fo the body, where they can produce lateral motion while the animal is oriented vertically.*

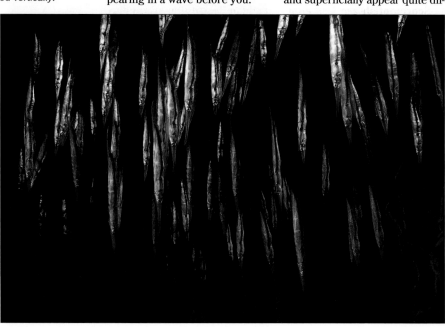

ferent from seahorses. In fact, structurally they are quite similar, the pipefish just being a stretched-out version. The male incubates the eggs in a pouch on its stomach, and the young are born "live."

The large trumpetfish (*Aulostomus chinensis*) looks like a pipefish on steroids (these can be a half-meter or longer) and feeds on small fish. It has the curious habit of hiding behind larger fishes until it comes within range of its prey. One color morph is bright yellow.

Scorpionfish. The most commonly seen of this family (Scorpaenidae) are the lionfishes (*Pterois* and *Dendrochirus*). During the day these lavishly colored fish can be seen perching on coral heads. Perhaps because of their poisonous fin rays, they are relatively unperturbed by the presence of divers.

Lionfishes feed mainly at night on shrimps and small fishes. They use their elaborate fins to shepherd their prey into a suitable position, whereupon they shoot forward and inhale it whole into their large mouths.

Scorpionfish are less commonly seen, chiefly because they are so well camouflaged. Covered with folds and flaps of skin, they blend right in with the algae and other growths.

The scorpionfishes and lionfishes have a row of poisonous spines along their backs. So, despite their usually benign behavior these fish should be treated with some respect. More than one underwater photographer has been stuck by a lionfish while trying to encourage it into position for that perfect photograph. Lionfish poison is not strong enough to kill an adult, but it will certainly give you many hours of acute pain.

Some victims have required hospitalization. The best treatment is to immerse the affected part in very hot water, as heat breaks down the venom.

Much more dangerous is the stonefish (*Synanceia verrucosa*), which carries a toxin responsible for several well-publicized deaths. These animals are masters of disguise, and encrusting algae and bryozoans actually grow onto their skin. When a small fish or crustacean absently wanders within range, it is engulfed by the animal's formidable mouth.

Groupers. The groupers (family Serranidae), are a common family on Indonesian reefs, ranging in size from more than a meter to the tiny dottybacks or pseudochromids, colorful planktivores no larger than a man's little finger.

Most of the larger groupers are plainly marked, but some, most notably the bright red and blue-spotted coral grouper (*Cephalopholis miniata*) and the flagtail grouper (*C. urodeta*) are exceptions. One of the largest fish on the reef is the giant grouper (*Ephinephelus lanceolatus*), which can reach 2 meters and weigh 400 kilos.

The fairy basselets or anthias (subfamily Anthiinae) are also groupers. Anthias, which hover in large schools around coral heads and soft coral colonies, picking plankton from the water, are very beautiful, and staples of underwater photography. Their names—the peach fairy basslet (*Pseudanthias diaspar*), the purple queen (*P. pascalus* and *P. tuka*) and the square spot anthias (*P. pleurotaenia*)—hint at their lovely colors.

Anthias are protogynous hermaphrodites, meaning that the fish all mature as females, and then a few undergo a terminal sex-change to male. These terminal males exhibit distinct, and very striking colors.

The dottybacks (Pseudochromidae), also among the real jewels of the reef, are small, secretive fishes that hide in caves and under ledges.

Another unique member of the grouper family is the comet (*Calloplesiops altivelis*). This small fish has long, black fins covered with a multitude of white spots. Because of the ocelli on the fins, and the fish's movements, it is thought to be a Batesian mimic of the juvenile spotted moray eel (*Gymnothorax meleagris*). A Batesian mimic uses its

---

Ciguatera Poisoning

Ciguatera is a toxin produced by a tiny dinoflagellate alga, *Gambierdiscus toxicus*. The alga itself is harmless enough, living around rocks, seagrass and filamentatious algae. The quantities of poison in each organism are minute.

But the dinoflagellates are eaten along with the algae in which they live by herbivorous fish and invertebrates. These herbivores are then eaten by larger, carnivorous fishes, and these are in turn are eaten by even larger, and more voracious predators. Since the ciguatera is not broken down, it concentrates in the tissues of these higher order predators.

A human being who eats a ciguatoxic fish will experience numbness in hands and feet, disorientation, weakness, vomiting, diarrhea, shortness of breath and even cardiac arrest. The poison is very serious. People have died from ciguatera and there is no available cure.

The greatest danger comes from fish at the highest levels of the food chain: snappers, groupers, large jacks, barracuda, some triggerfish and moray eels. For reasons not well understood, certain species are more frequently ciguatoxic than others: particularly the red snapper (*Lutjanus bohar*), and also the giant moray (*Gymnothorax javanicus*), the saddleback grouper (*Plectropomus laevis*) and the giant grouper (*Epinephelus lanceolatus*).

Open-water fish (tuna, mackerel, etc.) are not part of the same food chain and are not affected, but any large, predatory reef fish is a candidate.

— *David Pickell*

---

resemblence to a known dangerous animal to discourage predation.

Hawkfish. Hawkfishes (family Cirrhitidae) get their name from their predatory habits. These small fish (6–10 cm.) perch on coral heads or sponges—anything that gives them a good lookout—and when a small crustacean or fish comes within range, they swoop down on it like a hawk. Because they are so sedentary, they make very easy photo subjects. Some species are also quite colorful—particularly the large Forster's hawkfish (*Paracirrhites forsteri*)—and the long-nosed hawkfish (*Oxycirrhitus typus*) has an interesting, pointed "beak."

Jacks. The jacks or trevallies (family Carangidae) are often seen patrolling the upper reef slope in small groups. They are among the most active predators on the reef. Jacks are always on the lookout for a meal, and groups regularly interrupt their steady cruising with powerful bursts of speed as they chase unwary smaller reef fish. Sometimes a few jacks will make a sortie into a lagoon in search of prey. If they find and attack a school of fish the sea surface erupts as the hunted fish desperately try to escape, sometimes throwing themselves onto the beach in the attempt.

Snappers and sweetlips. Snappers (*Lutjanus*) are common predatory fish around deeper reefs, and are an important food fish. The red snapper (*Lutjanus bohar*), although delicious, is in some areas one of the most frequently ciguatoxic fishes (see "Ciguatera Poisoning," at left.)

Perhaps the most commonly seen reef fish in Indonesia is the yellow-backed fusilier (*Caesio teres*), a streamlined, 20–30 centimeter fish marked with bright blue and yellow. These planktivores, related to snappers, travel in large aggregations that provide a measure of protection against predators such as jacks.

Sweetlips (*Plectorhinchus*) are medium-sized, strikingly marked fish related to the snappers. They are common in Indonesia, where they can often be seen in mixed schools. The juveniles are especially attractive, with bold stripes and dots of white against a brown or black background.

Batfishes. The batfishes (*Platax*) are common inhabitants of Indonesian reefs. As adults, these animals take the shape of a large, silvery platter, as much as half a meter in length, with two or three broad black vertical bands. Traveling about the reef in small groups, they have a reputation for being very "intelligent," and seem to regard divers with curiosity.

There are three species commonly seen in Indonesia, the orbiculate (*Platax orbicularis*), the round-faced (*P. tiera*) and the pinnate (*P. pinnatus*). As adults, orbiculate and round-faced batfish are almost impossible to distinguish. The pinnate batfish can be recognized by its long snout.

As juveniles, the fish are very different in shape, with greatly elongated dorsal and ventral fins. Juvenile orbiculate batfish are mottled brown and have a transparent tail, which—together with their habit of floating on their sides in the shallows—allows them to match a dead leaf. Juvenile round-faced batfish are black and white and have long fins.

The most beautiful as a juvenile is *P. pinnatus*, which has a band of electric orange all around its body and fins. This juvenile, sometimes called the orange-rimmed batfish, is thought to mimic a toxic flatworm.

Butterflyfishes. The butterflyfishes (family Chaetodontidae) are beautiful, delicate looking fish that feed on small benthic animals. Some species feed heavily on coral polyps. They have laterally compressed bodies, and snouts and teeth adapted to their particular feeding habits, enabling them to pick up their preferred prey deftly. In particularly, the long-nosed butterflyfishes (*For-*

cipiger) have long, thin mouths perfect for snatching small animals from cracks and crevices in the reef. These bright yellow fish will be seen hovering under overhangs in the reef, sometimes even upside down.

Some species, occur singly or in pairs, e.g. *Forcipiger*. Others are schooling fish. The black, white, and yellow pyramid butterflyfish (*Hemitaurichthys*

HELMUT DEBELIUS / IKAN

polylepsis), for example, occurs in massive aggregations along the walls in Manado and other parts of eastern Indonesia. Common schooling butterflyfish include the bannerfish (*Heniochus*), the most distinctive of which is the pennant bannerfish (*Heniochus diphreutes*), which has a very elongated dorsal fin and bright yellow, white and black markings.

Angelfish. The angelfishes

Above: *The twinspot lionfish, Dendrochirus biocellatus, is one of the most attractive of the dwarf lionfishes. It is much smaller than* Pterois *sp., growing to just 8 centimeters. Halmahera, Maluku.*

(family Pomacanthidae) probably make it onto more postcards than any fish other than the Moorish idol. They browse the reef for sponges, algae and occasional small crustaceans. Adult angelfish, some of which can reach 30 centimeters, are truly magnificent animals.

In Indonesia, one can often see emperor angelfish (*Pomacanthus imperator*), with thin, horizontal stripes of blue and yellow; blue-girdled angelfish (*P. [Euxiphipops] navarchus*), with a deep blue "girdle" against bright orange; and regal angelfish (*Pygoplites diacanthus*), the most shy of the bunch, with vertical stripes of yellow, white and blue.

All *Pomacanthus* species have very similar juvenile coloring, a series of thin white or light blue stripes against a dark blue background. Two fish with dramatically different adult coloration, for example the blue-girdled and emperor angelfish, look so similar as juveniles that only an expert could tell them apart.

Damselfish. These small, ubiquitous fish (family Pomacentridae) are members of one of the largest groups of tropical reef fish. In addition to the reef itself, they occur along rocky shores, algal flats, and even in silt-choked harbors. The damselfish feed on plankton and algae, some even setting up small territories from which they aggressively keep all herbivores away, "farming" the algal turf that then grows on the coral rock.

The black and white three-striped damselfish (*Dascyllus aruanus*), the blue devil (*Chrysiptera cyanea*), and the blue damsels (*Pomacentrus*) are common among the coral heads and rubble of the shallow reef. The pugnacious black farmer fish (*Stegastes lividus*) also defends its patch of algae in the shallows.

Deeper on the reef, the planktivorous blue-green chromis (*Chromis viridis*) is common, occurring in large schools like anthias, which it superficially resembles. Along rich drop-offs, the pugnacious yellow Golden sergeant (*Amblygliphidodon aureus*) is often seen. A single good Indonesian reef can host more than 100 species.

Favorites among divers are the anemonefish (*Amphiprion* and *Premnas biaculaeatus*). These beautiful and plucky little fish will even nip a diver to defend their anemone home. (See "Clownfish and their Sea Anemone Hosts," page 46.)

Wrasses. The wrasses (family Labridae) are a large and successful family on the coral reefs. Most are small, elongated fishes, with a distinct swimming style that depends more on the pectoral fins than the tail. Many are colorful, and inhabit the shallow parts of the reef and reef flats, although some (such as the hogfishes) are characteristic of the deep reef.

Wrasses undergo sometimes dramatic color changes as they pass from juveniles to adults. Many of these predators on worms and small crustaceans bury in the sand at night to sleep, or dive into the sand to escape predators.

Most familiar to divers is the blue-streak cleaner wrasse (*Labroides dimidiatus*), which set up stations to clean small parasites and pockets of decay from the skin, mouth and gills of larger reef fish. Some wrasse act as cleaners only when young (for example, the colorful lyretail hogfish, *Bodianus anthoides*).

The largest of the family is the Napoleon wrasse (*Cheilinus undulatus*), which can reach 1.8 meters. This is one of the largest fish a diver will see on many dives. These stately animals, also called the humphead wrasse, have a prominent forehead and formidable-looking snout and cruise the outer edge of the reef in loose groups, with one large

male and a few smaller females.

Parrotfish. The parrotfishes (family Scaridae) are among the most important herbivores on the reef. They get their name from their bright colors, curious flapping "flight" (much like wrasses), and their strong, bird-like beaks, which they use to scrape algae and other living matter from rocky surfaces. In so doing they inevitably take in great quantities of coral rock. This is ground down by powerful sets of teeth in the throat so that the organic material can be more easily digested. The waste product of the feeding activities of parrotfish is coral sand—a major component of Indonesian beaches especially on the offshore islands.

Parrotfishes are protogynous hermaphrodites that undergo a series of color changes with age and sexual status. Primary phase parrotfish—whether males or females—are exceedingly difficult to identify, all being relatively drab grey or rust-colored. The terminal males are striking, however, usually green with bright markings, particularly around the cheeks and eyes. In most species the primary phase is made up of mixed males and females (diandric); in others the primary phase is all females (monandric).

One notable exception to this pattern is the bumphead parrotfish (*Bolbometopon muricatum*). All bumphead parrotfish (males, females and juveniles) are a dull green in color. Although parrotfish have popularly been considered coral-eaters, they are chiefly herbivores, scraping the reef surface to extract the algal turf, not to eat coral polyps. The bumphead parrotfish is an exception, and feeds for the most part on living coral. They are massive beasts which grow to over a meter in length and travel along the reef in groups looking for all the world like squadrons of army tanks, leaving clouds of coral sand in their wakes. Sometimes their crunching can be heard underwater.

They should not to be confused with the Napoleon wrasse (see above), a superficially similar fish. The bumphead parrotfish has a more rounded head.

Above: *The Napoleon wrasse, or humphead wrasse, Cheilinus undulatus, is the largest wrasse and—at up to two meters— often the largest fish of any kind one will see on a given dive. This predator on crustaceans, gastropods, fishes and echinoderms is usually a solitary rover, but sometimes a pair or a small "squad" will be seen. Australians call this fish the Maori wrasse.*

At night, parrotfish secrete a transparent cocoon of mucus in which to sleep. At first glance such a fragile structure would seem to offer little protection against predators, but at night, most predators hunt with their sense of smell, not their eyes, and the cocoon is an effective defense against this.

Barracudas. These familiar fish (family Sphyraenidae) are

ED ROBINSON / IKAN

Above: *The bump-head parrotfish,* Bolbometopon muriaticum. *This, the largest parrotfish, is also one of the few true coral feeders. With its impressive fused "beak" it can crunch on corals like they were pretzels. It is sometimes confused with the Napoleon wrasse, but a comparison of this photo with the one on the previous page should make clear the physical differences between them.*

one of the most important predators on the reef, but their reputation for ferociousness is exaggerated. Despite their formidable teeth, in Indonesia they are not known to attack divers. Smaller species of barracuda often gather in schools during the day, sometimes numbering many hundreds of individuals. In contrast, large barracudas (which may grow up to 1.7 meters) tend to be solitary. Such giants may be quite old, so are less likely to be seen near heavily populated areas where there is a lot of fishing pressure.

Blennies. These little fishes (family Blenniidae) often go unnoticed by divers. They are most abundant in the shallows, and can also be found on back-reefs and in murky estuarial waters. Most are not very colorful. Some have interesting "faces," although these are only really visible to the macro lens.

The mimic blenny (*Aspidontus taeniatus*) mimics the color

and even the movements of the blue-streak cleaner wrasse *Labroides dimidiatus.* However, instead of cleaning parasites from the larger fish, the mimic blenny bites off a tender chunk of scales and flesh, and then beats a hasty retreat.

Dartfishes. One group the diver will notice, because of their striking colors and their habit of hovering in small groups above the coral sand, are the firefishes (*Nemateleotris* spp.), particularly *N. magnifica,* a beautiful fish with a greatly elongated dorsal fin which it flicks in nervous little movements.

Gobies. These fish (family Gobiidae) are small, usually dull-colored, and often remain hidden in crevices and the branches of coral. There are many hundreds of species and perhaps 100 genera in the Indo-Pacific, making them the single most successful family on the coral reefs. Identifying these fishes is very difficult, and there are probably hundreds still undescribed.

Although not reef-dwellers, the curious mudskippers (*Periophthalmus*), which can be found in Indonesia on the brackish mudflats around mangrove swamps, are also gobies. As long as their gills and skin remain wet, these small brown fish can hop about on land.

Related to the gobies are the little dragonets. These are found in weedy areas and sea grass beds as well as the reef itself. Perhaps the most spectacular is the mandarinfish (*Synchiropus splendens*), with a pattern that could have come off a bright paisley silk tie.

Surgeonfish. The surgeonfishes and tangs (family Acanthuridae) are a particularly important group of herbivores. They are sometimes seen singly, in shallow water over coral flats. Since single grazers are often chased by damselfishes protecting their territories, surgeonfishes sometimes form large feeding aggregations.

Despite their apparently destructive feeding habits, herbivorous fish are of immense value to the coral reef community. By breaking down hard-to-digest plant material they make the nutrients in it available to other animals. Furthermore, by limiting the growth of plants they may actually enhance that of corals. Without grazing, the plants would grow to such an extent that they would soon cover the reef, making new coral settlement virtually impossible.

The surgeonfish family includes some of the most exquisitely patterned and colored of all reef fishes. But one feature that is common to all is that they all have one or two pairs of scalpel-like blades on the sides of their tails. These give the family its name and can inflict serious cuts if the fish are handled carelessly.

The orangespine unicornfish (*Naso lituratus*) with its bright orange spots warning of its spines; the hepatus tang (*Paracanthurus hepatus*) with its electric blue and black body, and the clown surgeonfish (*Acanthurus lineatus*), orange-and-blue striped, are just a few examples.

Moorish idol and Rabbitfishes. The Moorish idol (*Zanclus cornutus*) and the rabbitfishes (*Siganus*) are close relatives of the surgeonfishes. The Moorish idol is for many people the quintessential reef fish; with its bright, contrasting yellow, white and black color, prominent snout, and long, thin dorsal fin, it is indeed an elegant-looking animal. They are fairly common grazers, and can be found all the way from the east coast of Africa to the west coast of Central America.

The rabbitfishes look much like surgeonfish or Moorish idols, although with the exception of the foxface (*Siganus volpi-*

nus) and the coral rabbitfish (*S. corallinus*), not as brightly colored. They have no "scalpels," but they do have a strong venom in the short spines of their fins, and should not be handled.

Tuna and Mackerels. Although one or two members of the family Scombridae patrol reefs—particularly the dogtooth tuna (*Gymnosarda unicolor*)—most are true pelagics, living in

the open sea, and will only occasionally be seen on the outer reef edge. When traveling by boat between islands or to offshore dive sites it is not unusual to see big schools of tuna splashing at the surface, often with attendant flocks of seabirds overhead. These schools are usually composed of skipjack tuna, although there are several other species found in Indonesia.

Above: *A school of pyramid butterflyfishes,* Hemitaurichthys polylepsis. *These plankton feeders gather in large groups around the lip of drop-off reefs in eastern Indonesia. The Bunaken group, Sulawesi.*

ED ROBINSON / IKAN

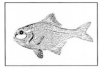

Above: *Indonesian flashlight fishes.* Anomalops katoptron, *top, is the more common of the two.* Photoblepheron palpebratus *tends to be found in smaller groups in rather deep caves. Both species are easy to see in Tulamben Bali:* Anomalops *on the wreck, and* Photoblepheran *on the wall. Both grow to about 10 centimeters long.*

Skipjack (*Katsuwonis pelamis*) grow to just under a meter in length, and are plump and streamlined, with a characteristic series of about five black lines on their bellies. They will not be seen on the reef itself, however, although there will be plenty in the fish market.

Triggerfish. Triggers (family Balistidae) are common fish at moderate depths on the reefs, where they hunt spiny crustaceans and echinoderms. Shaped like a compressed football and often exquisitely marked, they use powerful jaws to dispatch their hard-shelled prey. Large schools of the black triggerfish (*Odonus niger*), which is actually more blue in color, can be seen hovering off the reef walls, swimming with characteristic undulations of their fins. This fish is sometimes called the red-toothed trigger, although you have to look very closely to see that its teeth are, indeed, red.

Some distinctively marked triggers include the Picasso trigger (*Rhinecanthus aculeatus*), so-named for its cubist markings, and the undulate trigger (*Pseudobalistes fuscus*), covered with wavy markings. The largest trigger you will see on the Indonesian reefs is the Titan triggerfish (*Balistoides viridescens*), a loopy-eyed and sometimes aggressive animal that grows to more than 60 centimeters.

The most dramatic of the family is the clown triggerfish (*Balistoides conspicullum*), with its bright orange snout, blue body, and white-spotted belly. The clown trigger is very territorial, and will patrol the same area of reef. When threatened, a clown trigger will wedge its body head-first into a crack in the coral wall, and extend its dorsal spine. The first spine, once raised, is locked in place by the second, making it impossible to pull the fish out of his hole. A diver who knows what he is doing can reach in and

gently push back the second spine, unlocking the fin. He can then extract the irritated fish.

Puffers. The curious pufferfishes (family Tetraodontidae) are solitary omnivores, often seen wandering about the reef in their slow, almost clumsy way and plucking at algae, crustaceans, molluscs, worms and sponges. When threatened they inflate themselves with large quantities of water, which either locks them into a coral crevice, or makes it impossible for a predator to swallow them. In addition to this protection, the skin and most of the internal organs of puffers contain a deadly poison. This poison is absent from the flesh, which in Japan is the highly prized *fugu*.

A common puffer on Indonesian reefs is the dog-faced or black-spotted puffer (*Arothron nigropunctatus*), which exhibits a great deal of color variability, from the usual dull brown to bright yellow, always with many small black spots.

The related porcupinefishes (family Diodontidae) possess the same defenses as the puffers, with the addition of numerous spines, which become erect when the animal is inflated. The common porcupinefish (*Diodon hystrix*) is often seen. Boxfishes (family Ostraciontidae) are similar to puffers, except their protection comes in the form of a hard, roughly cubical external covering.

Nocturnal fish. At night the schools of day active species break up and the fish take refuge in holes in the reef. They are replaced by nocturnal species such as the cardinalfishes (family Apogonidae), bigeyes (family Priacanthidae), and squirrelfishes or soldierfishes (family Holocentridae), which feast on the abundant night plankton.

One of the most interesting families of fish to come out at night are the flashlight fishes (family Anomalopidae). These delightful little black fish have special organs under their eyes which contain millions of light-producing bacteria. The fish are able to cover and uncover these organs to produce characteristic flashes of blue-green light. The function of these lights is not fully understood, but they are probably used to communicate, to see by, and perhaps to confuse predators.

Two species of flashlight fish are found in Indonesia. The most often seen is *Anomalops kataptron*, a 6–8 centimeter fish that forages for plankton in shallow reef waters, often in large schools. (*Anomalops* also occurs in a much larger—27 centimeters—deepwater form that lives in up to 400 meters of water.) *Photoblepharon palpebratus* is rare and tends to occur in relatively small groups in deep caves.

Marine Reptiles

Sea turtles. One of the most delightful experiences a diver can have is swimming with turtles, and in Indonesia such encounters are quite common.

Six species of marine turtles are found in Indonesian waters, but the two most likely to be seen by divers are the hawksbill turtle (*Eretmochelys imbricata*) and the green turtle (*Chelonia mydas*).

They are not always easy to distinguish underwater, although the hawksbill has a distinct beak, and the trailing edge of its shell is jagged. The hawksbill is also generally smaller, and is tortoiseshell brown (instead of olive green) although such relatively minor color differences are very hard to determine underwater. A third species that may be seen by divers is the loggerhead (*Caretta caretta*), which is much like the green turtle, except it has a massive head.

The green turtle feeds almost entirely on sea grass, while the hawksbill and loggerhead are both largely carnivorous. The shell of the hawksbill is covered with large horn-like scales, the source of "tortoiseshell." Tortoiseshell products—and even stuffed and varnished hawksbill turtles—are offered in Indonesian markets, although import into most Western countries is

Below: *A bluestreak cleaner wrasse,* Labroides dimidiatus *picks at the eye of a bright, terminal male purple queen,* Pseudanthias tuka. *The little cleaners provide an essential service and are never molested by their "customers."* Manado, Sulawesi.

strictly prohibited.

Marine turtles spend nearly all their lives at sea, but their eggs have to be laid on land. At certain secluded beaches females regularly emerge at night to deposit their eggs above the high water mark.

Sea snakes. Most sea snakes (family Hydrophiidae) never come onto land at all, even giving birth at sea. There are some 60 species of sea snakes in the world, over half of which are found in Indonesia. They tend to be patchily distributed, very common in some areas and absent from others. As reptiles, they must come up for air, although they have a very large lung and can stay under for many hours.

Sea snakes can be seen underwater poking their small heads into cracks and crevices, searching for small fish and crustaceans. The head of a sea snake is often difficult to distinguish from the tail, as both are blunt, although the head is always smaller, and the tail is laterally flattened, to aid in swimming.

Sea snakes are equipped with extremely toxic venom which can be delivered through two short fangs on the upper jaw. The venom is used to subdue prey such as spiny fish or moray eels, which could cause the snake considerable damage if not killed very quickly. Since fish are quite resistant to most toxins, it is not surprising that sea snake venom is so strong.

Sea snakes are rarely aggressive towards divers, however, and unprovoked attacks are virtually unknown. They are sometimes inquisitive, however, and may inspect a diver.

The grey-and-black banded colubrine or amphibious sea snake (*Laticauda colubrina*) is common in Indonesia. This animal—collected in huge numbers in the Philippines for its skin—It is an inoffensive creature, and slow to anger. Guides often catch the animals for their clients to pose with. We don't suggest you try this, however.

The yellow-bellied sea snake (*Pelamis platurus*) is the most numerous reptile on earth. This colorful animal is so completely adapted to an aquatic life that, if washed ashore, it will die. It cannot even crawl back to the water.

Crocodiles. One marine reptile that is truly dangerous is the salt water crocodile (*Crocodylus porosus*). These monsters can grow to many meters in length, although real giants are very rare these days. Fortunately for divers they usually live in murky estuarine areas, not on coral reefs. Saltwater crocodiles are found in Irian Jaya, and in scattered locations in Maluku.

Marine Mammals

While common enough in Indonesian waters, sea mammals are rarely seen while diving, and swimming with whales or dolphins is a rare occasion indeed for a diver.

Dolphins. Schools of dolphins are a frequent sight while traveling out to dive sites by boat. Sometimes their "whistling" can be heard during a dive (a sound that is sometimes uncannily like a leaking air cylinder) but they will normally stay well beyond the range of visibility. The best way to see them underwater is to snorkel from the dive boat when a school is encountered in deep water. Usually they will move away, but you could get lucky.

There are several dolphin species in Indonesia and identifying them at sea is a far from easy task. Common species here include the spinner dolphin (*Stenella longirostris*), so-called because of its characteristic high, spinning jumps; the common dolphin (*Delphinus delphis*), which has a black-tipped snout, and a crisscross pattern on its flanks; and the spotted dolphin, with a pattern of fine spots on its sides.

Whales. Several species of large whales also occur in Indonesia, some arriving seasonally from polar regions, others being year-round residents. Like dolphins they are best watched from a boat rather than the water. Some whales breed in Indonesian waters, so it is very important not to harass them by chasing them in boats.

Most of the species seen are plankton-eating baleen whales which have vertical spouts and a small, but distinct, dorsal fin. They might be distinguished on the basis of size, but this requires some experience. The blue whale (*Balaenoptera musculus*) is known in Indonesian waters, as are several smaller but very similar species, including the fin whale (*B. physalus*) and minke whale (*B. acutorostrata*). The humpback, (*Megaptera novaeangliae*), is easier to identify.

The sperm whale (*Physeter catodon*), of *Moby Dick* fame, is a very different animal. These are toothed whales, which feed on giant squid and fish snatched from great depths. The sperm whale has a characteristic forward pointing spume and humplike ridges rather than a dorsal fin on its back. Pygmy and dwarf sperm whales (*Kogis*) also inhabit Indonesian waters.

Dugong. It is very unlikely that a diver will see this rare animal. The dugong or sea cow (*Dugong dugon*) is a slow-moving animal, up to 2.5 meters long, that looks like a walrus without the tusks. There are only three other members of order Sirenia, manatees from Florida, the Amazon basin and West Africa.

The dugong is the only herbivorous marine mammal, and is strictly aquatic. The animals can eat 10 percent of their body weight a day in sea grasses, and are found mainly in sheltered bays where these plants grow.

Dugongs are threatened throughout their range, because they are slow-moving, easy targets for hunters—their tusks are used for cigaret holders—and because they take so long to reproduce. Calving takes place only once every 3–7 years, and dugongs take 15 years to mature.

—*Charles Anderson and David Pickell*

Introducing the Island of Java

Lush and populous Java—together with Bali the most familiar of Indonesia's many islands—is the political, cultural and industrial heart of the island nation. Some 115 million people live on Java, almost two-thirds of Indonesia's total population on just 7 percent of the nation's land area.

The island is rugged and volcanic, and its rich soil makes it one of the world's most productive agricultural regions. In Dutch colonial times, Java was called "The Garden of the East."

Jakarta

The Ibu Kota—literally "Mother City"—of Indonesia is Jakarta, on the northwest coast of Java. With more than 10 million inhabitants, it is one of the world's biggest cities. Jakarta is the fourth most densely populated city in the world, more dense, even, than Bombay. This richness of humanity—or crush, depending on your outlook—is essential to Jakarta's bustling (and hustling) charm.

History of Java

Java, which until 20,000 years ago was connected together with Sumatra and Borneo to the southeast Asian mainland, is one of the world's earliest populated spots. In 1894, Dutch naturalist Eugène Dubois announced that he had discovered a "Java ape-man," the first known fossil remains of what scientists now call *Homo erectus*.

Between "Java Man," who lived more than 1 million years ago, and the first Bronze Age Javanese, who lived 2,000 years ago, there is little surviving archaeological record on Java.

The ancestors of modern-day Melanesians and the Australian aboriginals are thought to have passed through Java some 50,000 years ago. But the ancestors of today's Javanese were the Austronesians, the region's great seafarers and most successful settlers, who moved into Java about 5,000 years ago.

Java is most famous for her great Indianized kingdoms, which developed out of trading contacts with India, beginning in the first millennium A.D. The Hindu and Buddhist kingdoms of central Java produced the largest Buddhist stupa extant, Borobudur on the Kedu plain, and the many Hindu monuments of Prambanan, including the 47-meter high Loro Jonggrang.

East Java's Majapahit, which lasted through the 14th and 15th centuries, was the most successful of the early Javanese kingdoms. According to an old manuscript, Majapahit claimed an area under its control greater than that of present day Indonesia.

By the 16th century, Islam had displaced the old Indianized kingdoms and at the same time, European traders seeking spices began arriving. The Portuguese were first, but it was the Dutch East India Company, the Vereenigde Oostindische Compagnie, that established a chokehold on the spice trade. After the V.O.C. went bankrupt in 1799 the Dutch government ran Indonesia as a colony.

With the imposition of the "Cultivation System" in Java, Dutch planters grew wealthy, and the Javanese worked as near slaves growing export crops like coffee and sugar. Resentment

Overleaf: *A school of sleek unicornfish, Naso hexacanthus. Photograph by Ed Robinson of IKAN. Manado, Sulawesi.*

Opposite: *A pair of maroon, or spine-cheeked anemone-fish,* Premnas biaculeatus, *in their host anemone,* Entacmaea quadricolor. *Photograph by Helmut Debelius of IKAN. Flores.*

grew and nationalism boiled at the turn of the 20th century.

After World War II and a cruel Japanese occupation, the nationalists declared independence on August 17, 1945. The Dutch were unwilling to relinquish their colony, however, and it took five years of fighting and mounting international opposition to the Dutch to drive them out. The Dutch signed sovereignty to the Republic of Indonesia in December 1949.

People and Culture

The great majority of the Javanese—88 percent—are Muslims, and in fact Indonesia is the largest Muslim country in the world. Still, older threads of Hinduism, Buddhism and many regional ethnic cultures are deeply woven into Javanese culture. Hindu epics, the *Mahabharata* and *Ramayana,* are still the chief source of material for the very popular shadow puppet theater, *wayang kulit*, and drama, *wayang orang.*

Javanese music, played on the famous gamelan orchestra of metallophones, drums, gongs and other mostly percussion instruments, is a holdover from the days of the Hindu courts.

Batik, fabric that has been patterned through repeated dyeings over a wax resist, is sometimes considered a Javanese invention, although it is perhaps more likely that the techniques came from India. Whatever the source, Javanese batik is today very popular.

Geography

Several of Java's volcanoes are still active, and Merapi erupted in November 1994, killing more than 60 people. Java's most famous eruption occurred in 1883, when Krakatau exploded.

The Java Sea to the north of the island is quite shallow, less than 200 meters. But to the island's south is the Java trench, where the Indian Ocean reaches its deepest point, 7,450 meters.

Much of the island's forest has been given up to cultivated land. The last wilderness area is Ujung Kulon National Park on Java's westernmost peninsula.

— *Janet Boileau and Debe Campbell*

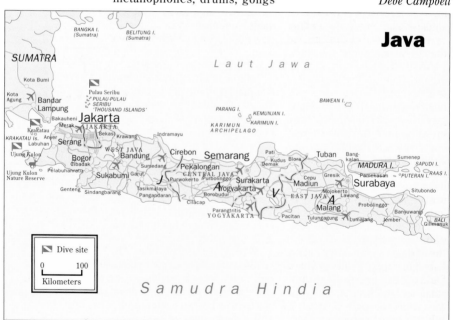

Diving Krakatau and Ujung Kulon Park

Diving in the waters off Krakatau, the rocky islands forming the crater of an underwater volcano in the Sunda Strait off West Java, or in the waters around the Ujung Kulon peninsula in southwest Java, is not the best to be found in Indonesia. But the seascape of cracked volcanic rock around Krakatau, and the caves and tunnels around Ujung Kulon provide an interesting underwater experience.

Reaching either of these sites requires some patience and initiative. There is little chance of making a day of it from Jakarta. One must overland to Anyer or Labuhan, and then take a boat to the dive sites.

Recent road repairs make the trip from Jakarta to Anyer quite pleasant. From there, a boat will take you the 50 kilometers to the Krakatau group, a 4-hour crossing (see map page 78). To reach Ujung Kulon, one can go either by train or car to Labuhan, and then by boat to Ujung Kulon.

We strongly suggest that you organize your jaunt with a Jakarta dive outfit. (See "Java Practicalities" page 273). You can either go with your own group, or hook up with one of the many weekend dive excursions. It can be a challenge to find a seaworthy boat, and strong and unpredictable winds in the strait could prove quite troublesome to an inexperienced captain.

If our warning does not deter you, you can charter a boat through the ranger stations at Labuhan, Carita, or Ujung Kulon Park, or through one of the many small hotels scattered along the way. Alternately, a tour agent in Jakarta could arrange a boat

charter for you. In any case, do not expect a purpose-built dive boat with an attached Zodiac. What you will likely find is an older wooden *pinisi,* a traditional sailing craft that has been converted to diesel power.

Krakatau

The famous eruption of Krakatau on August 26, 1883 sent up a plume of ash and pumice 26 kilometers high and 6,000 kilometers wide, and the explosion could be heard from Myanmar to Australia. The huge tsunamis created by the blast destroyed some 165 villages in Sumatra and Java, and killed more than 36,000 people.

The original caldera collapsed in on itself, leaving three islands remaining of its rim: Sertung, Panjang and Rakata. In 1928, Anak Krakatau—"Child of Krakatau"—appeared. This still active daughter cone continues to eject tephra and lava, growing

---

AT A GLANCE
Krakatau and Ujung Kulon

Reef type:	Volcanic rock slabs and formations, some reef
Access:	4 hrs from Anyer by boat for Krakatau; Ujung Kulon sites 15–30 min from ranger station
Visibility:	Fair to good, 10–20 meters
Current:	Gentle, to 1 knot; swells and 1.5 knot current at Ujung Kulon sites
Fish:	Fair to good variety
Highlights:	Underwater landscape at Krakatau; rock tunnels at Karang Copong; good coral at Tg. Jajar

---

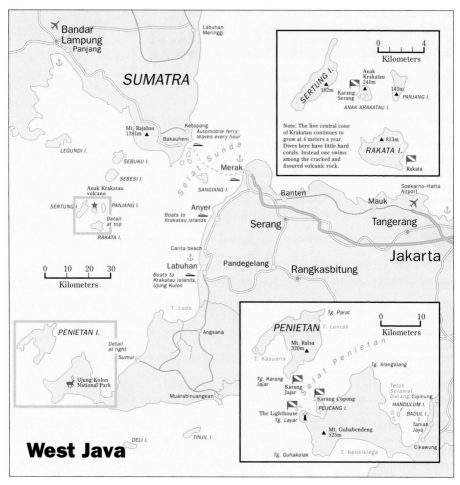

West Java

at the rate of 4 meters each year, now having reached 240 meters.

A rocky, wide skirt of black sand rings the island. Being so new, Anak Krakatau has provided a perfect laboratory for scientists studying early colonization of islands by plant and animal life. So far, 120 species of plants have found their way to the little island. The shoreline is dominated by feathery casuarinas, and a few tough succulents have found a niche further up the slope.

It takes just 20 minutes to climb the 150 or so meters to the rim of the new crater. Inside, the steaming cone is surrounded by a lunar landscape of fumaroles. Looking outward, one can see the surrounding island remains of the once-massive original Krakatau. The descent is easy, and is best finished with a refreshing swim along the black sand beach.

Karang Serang Rocks

These rocks, painted white by the sea birds, mark the site of a dive off Anak Krakatau. The underwater scenery consists of large blocks of volcanic rock, seemingly sheered off by the blast. The cracked and sharp-edged rocks make a west-facing submarine cliff look like the ruin of an ancient Greek temple. In the crevices of the rock, coral growth is beginning.

The visibility is fair to good, 10 to 20 meters. Schools of Moorish idols and other reef fish inhabit the area, and one occasionally sees reef whitetip sharks. The bright colors of emperor angelfish stand out starkly against the background of dark rock.

On the south end of the site, the slab scenery is interrupted by growths of staghorn and table *Acropora,* some with blue-tinted tips. Around the rocks to the east grow an astonishing number of orange fan coral gorgonians. The smallest covered three square meters, and the largest, five square meters. The visibility drops here, because of the sandy bottom. Reef blacktip sharks patrol this area.

Rakata

This site, off the southeast end of Rakata, offers a nice drift dive. The steep sides of the island prevent access. The depths here are modest, to just 25 meters, and the gentle current carries you east. The underwater scenery is, again, slabs of volcanic rock.

A decent variety of small reef fish populates the shallower depths, and some of the crevices have been claimed by moray eels. Green turtles are numerous at this site. In the 19th century, before it exploded, Krakatau island was a common stop for sailors, who loaded up on turtles.

An unusual feature of this dive are the many underwater trees, which have been cast from the island cliffs by landslides. These attract large schools of fusiliers and jacks.

Ujung Kulon

This park, covering the peninsula at the southwest tip of Java and Penietan Island (the Krakatau group is also part of the park), is a rich area of lowland tropical rainforest. On these 420 square kilometers are hornbills and mynahs, wild boar and rusa deer, macaques and monitor lizards. The most famous inhabitants,

however, are the last wild Javan rhinos. These animals, of which only 57 are still believed to exist, are so elusive that even some park rangers have not seen one.

Accommodations at the Pulau Peucang ranger station, Taman Jaya, and Pulau Handeuleum run $10–$80 a night. There is even a new restaurant at the ranger station on Peucang. The station's 16 units attract surfers, who frequent the peninsula's south side, known for its great waves. Peucang Island also has some beautiful beaches, but beware of the nosey macaques. They will rummage through unattended bags and take to the trees with whatever strikes their fancy.

The Lighthouse

Tanjung Layar lighthouse on the tip of Ujung Kulon is the landmark for triangulating a rocky

Above: *The common lionfish,* Pterois volitans. *Although the dorsal and pectoral spines of this fish carry a potent venom, it is not an aggressive creature. The lionfish's lavish finnage and lazy disposition make it a favorite with photographers. Maumere Bay, Flores.*

island. The highlight of this shallow (to 12 meters) dive are tunnels in the rock that lead to caves in the island. Seeing schools of fish swimming in and out of these tunnels is a surprisingly breathtaking experience. Visibility is 20 meters.

The surge here is quite strong, and you are rocked back and forth as the prevailing current carries you from the tunnels across some sandy mounds, where the sea life is abundant—including some nice soft corals—but visibility is quite reduced, to less than 10 meters. This site makes a fine night dive.

Karang Jajar

This site is on the rocks off large Penietan Island's Karang Jajar cape. It is an hour by boat from the ranger station at Peucang. If conditions are right, a drift dive off the south stretch offers a good, and very colorful growth of coral. You drop to 15 meters, and then drift east with a gentle current to a maximum of 20 meters. Below you, the wall plunges to past 40 meters. Turtles frequent the area, and we saw too many stingrays to count.

Badul Island

Tunggal Jaya is a sleepy community on the northern side of the isthmus of the Ujung Kulon peninsula. Just offshore here is a tiny, sandy island, Badul, which is surrounded by a good reef. You enter the water from about 15 meters off Badul's west shore, and an easy drift dive takes you about 3/4 of a kilometer before your air runs out.

Coral growth around the island is not spectacular, but the variety of both hard and soft corals was good. Visibility during our dive was less than 8 meters. Schools of bannerfish and fusiliers inhabit the reef, and we saw some bright nudibranchs.

—Janet Boileau and
Debe Campbell

Above: *The Thousand Islands archipelago is very close to Jakarta, Indonesia's largest city, and many of the islands, such as this one, have been developed into fancy resorts providing weekend getaways for rich city dwellers.*

dive location off the west point of the peninsula. Expect swells to rock your dive boat, heavy surface current, and unusually cool water temperatures.

Beneath the surface, however, the sea is surprisingly calm. The visibility is quite good, around 20 meters. The rocks that jut just above the water plunge underneath the surface to 30 meters, looking just like submerged mountains. Coral is scarce, but in the underwater valleys there were large barracuda, schools of fusiliers and other medium-sized fish, and platoons of bumphead parrotfish. We also saw turtles circling the submerged rocks and a fat, nosey reef whitetip shark.

Karang Copong

This is a small island within sight of the northwest tip of Peucang

Diving on Java's 'Thousand Islands'

Pulau-Pulau Seribu

While not noted for Indonesia's best diving, Pulau-Pulau Seribu —the "Thousand Islands"—can be a good choice because of its proximity to Jakarta, and because of the great number of available sites. The islands, which actually number about 110, are scattered in a vertical group north from Jakarta in the shallow Java Sea.

Some 12,000 people live on Pulau-Pulau Seribu, more than half of them on the island of Pulau Kelapa.

With some advance planning, it is quite easy to get to the islands from Jakarta. Boats, ranging from inter-island shuttles to large cabin cruisers, ferry passengers to and from the various islands for $3.50 to $50, depending on the comfort of the craft and the distance to the island. The nearest islands are just 10 minutes from shore; the furthest can take nearly two hours by speedboat.

Accommodations on the islands also vary dramatically. International standards accommodations that cater to divers can be found on the islands of Putri, Pelangi, Sepa, Kotok, Pantara (Barat and Timur) and Matahari. Each of these also has a shop offering dive equipment rentals and compressors.

Transportation, and bookings for accommodations and dive trips, may be made at the departure pier in Ancol Marina, or through Jakarta travel agents or certified dive centers, such as the Jakarta Hilton's Dive Masters. Also check the English language daily newspaper, the *Jakarta Post,* for trips and special offers. Mid-week diving and accommodations are usually easy to arrange, but be aware that Pulau Seribu is very popular among Jakartans for weekend jaunts.

Popular Resorts

Some of the islands have resort type accommodations, and they may provide some music or a bar at night. On the less "civilized" islands, nighttime entertainment might be limited to the buzzing of mosquitoes.

Upmarket resorts, built in cooperation with Japan Airlines, have gone up on Pantara Timur and Pantara Barat islands. These are very posh, with all the comforts one might expect from a fine hotel in Singapore or Hawaii.

Pelangi and Putri islands offer somewhat less toney accommodations. Putri has small bungalows, a restaurant and bar, and sailboats and sailboards can be rented. Pelangi is a larger resort, and boasts fancy cottages, tennis courts, and a popular restaurant out over the water. Shops here

---

AT A GLANCE

Pulau-Pulau Seribu

Reef type: Coral slopes

Access: 45 min to 2 hrs by boat, depending on location and type of vessel

Visibility: Poor to fair, 8–15 meters

Current: Quite gentle

Coral: In places, good

Fish: Good varieties and numbers

Highlights: Wooden shipwreck at Pulau Piniki; excellent coral at Pulau Kotok and Pulau Gosonglaga

---

Pulau-Pulau Seribu

Reef

Dive site

0   5   10
Kilometers

DUA ISLANDS
DUA BARAT I.
DUA TIMUR I.

PETELORAN Kcl. I.
PETELORAN Bsr. I.
PENJALIRAN TIMUR I.
PENJALIRAN BARAT I.
JAGUNG I.

NYAMPLUNG I.
RINGIT I.
ALIMAN I.
SEBARU Bsr. I.
BUNDER I.
SEBARU Kcl. I.
HANTU Bsr. I.
HANTU Kcl. I.
GOSONGLAGA Kcl. I.
YU Bsr. I.
YU Kcl. I.
GOSONGLAGA Bsr. I.
SATU I.
JUKUNG I.
CINA I.
MALINJO I.
SEPA Kcl. I.
MELINTANG Bsr. I.
SEPA Bsr. I.
MELINTANG Kcl. I.
SEMU Is.
TONDAN ISLANDS
PETAK I.
PAPA THEO (TONDAN TIMUR) I.
PANJANG I.
PELANGI (TONDAN BARAT) I.
TANGKIN I.
PUTRI TIMUR I.
MACAN Kcl. I.
PUTRI BARAT I.
MACAN (MATAHARI) I.
PUTRI GUNDUL I.
BIRA Bsr. I.
GENTENG Bsr. I.
GENTENG Kcl. I.
BIRA Kcl. I.
PANJANG Kcl. I.
PEMEGARAN I.
PANJANG Bsr. I.
RAKITTIANG I.
PALEMPARAN I.
KALIAGEH Bsr. I.
KALIAGEH Kcl. I.
OPAK Bsr. I.
SEMUT I.
OPAK Kcl. I.
KOTOK Kcl. I.
KARANGBONGKOK I.
PINIKI I.
KOTOK Bsr. I.
KARANG PANDAN I.
GOSONGCONGKAK I.
SEMPIT I.
SEMADAUN I.
KARYA I.
LAYAR I.
PANGGANG I.
PRAMUKA I.
AIR I.
SEKATI I.
KARANGBERAS I.

TIDUNG Bsr. I.
TIDUNG Kcl. I.

AIR BESAR Is.
PAYUNG Kcl. I.
PAYUNG Bsr. I.
TIDUNG ISLANDS
JONG I.
TIKUS I.
PARI I.
TENGAH I.

DAPUR I.

LANCANG Bsr. I.

BOKOR I.
LANCANG Kcl. I.
LAKI I.
RAMBUT I.
UTUNGJAWA I.
UBI Kcl. I.
Tg. Kait
UBI Bsr. I.
Tg. Pasir
Tanjungpasir
ONRUS I.
Karangserang
CIPIR I.
Mauk
Kramat
Fish
Ponds

J A V A
Teluk Naga

Soekarno–Hatta
International Airport

and at the other resorts offer basic items like toothpaste and suntan lotion.

Resorts on some of the nearest islands have been in use since Dutch colonial times, and some of the islands have historical interest. Pulau Onrust, just off Tanjung Pasir and 1/2 hour from Ancol by ferry, is where Jan Pieterszoon Coen, the head of the Dutch East India company, planned his final, successful attack on the town of Jayakarta in 1619. Afterward, he named the town Batavia, which it was to be called until 1942, when the invading Japanese renamed it "Jakarta," a name the Indonesians kept.

Diving Pulau Seribu

The dive possibilities are almost countless here. The reefs around many of the 110 islands are excellent in terms of coral growth and fish life. What makes the diving here just fair by Indonesian standards is the visibility, which usually hovers around 10–15 meters. It sometimes improves, but even then only reaches 20 meters.

Daily rainfall here determines how good the visibility will be, but it is generally best in the middle of the dry season, typically May through September.

With few exceptions, the marine life at most Pulau Seribu locations will include an abundant variety of hard and soft corals, a good variety of reef fish and some pelagics, turtles and an occasional shark.

Unfortunately, at some sites the deterioration of marine life is increasingly noticeable. Like the dwindling reef in the Florida Keys, Pulau-Pulau Seribu has suffered for its proximity to a large population center. Pollution, and in some cases, mismanagement, is killing off the coral.

Pulau Piniki

This is an oblong island (see map opposite), oriented along a north–south axis. A few people live here, and the island is marked by a transmission antenna. There is an interesting reef off the western side of Piniki. The reef starts at 5 meters, but has its best coral growth and fish life at around 20 meters.

At the southwest point is the wreck of a 20-meter wooden cargo ship. The ship's cargo of cement has solidified, but the weakened wooden structure is not safe to enter.

Schools of barracuda, batfish, large parrotfish and moray eels have made the wreck their home. There is also a particularly large number of anemones and anemonefish here.

Pulau Papa Theo

This island, formerly called Pulau Tondan Timur, was renamed when the *Papa Theo,* a cargo vessel, sank on the reef here in 1982. The vessel, about 20 meters long, rests now with its port side facing the reef. The bow is at 20 meters, and the stern at 30 meters.

Until April 1991, the ship stood almost upright, but then its stern collapsed, spilling its until then intact cargo of paper products and pharmaceuticals, including condoms.

Until the cargo spilled, the beautiful reef was a favorite dive spot with Jakarta residents. Once the debris has been washed away, the reef may again become a popular spot. All the fittings and other items of value have been removed from the *Papa Theo.*

It is a simple wreck dive, with lots of marine life and an occasional shark in the deeper waters at the stern end. There are parrotfish, some resident groupers, many morays and a particular abundance of stingrays. The north reef is often chosen for night dives.

Papa Theo island is a very pleasant island hideaway, even for non-divers. The simple huts are clean and comfortable, and a basic Indonesian *mandi* or splash bath is provided. The generator shuts down at dark, and then one hears only the sound of the waves through the thatch walls. A candle-lit restaurant serves very fresh fish and standard Indonesian dishes.

Below: *A juvenile pinnate batfish,* Platax pinnatus, *examines a diver in an underwater grotto off Maumere, Flores. At right is a regal angelfish,* Pygoplites diacanthus.

KAL MULLER

Above: *A hawksbill turtle,* Eretmochelys imbricata. *Hawksbills, the smallest of the sea turtles, are also the most commonly seen on Indonesian reefs. Their shells provide the raw material for tortoiseshell, although the importation of such products is banned in many countries, including the United States. In Indonesian markets, one can see small hawksbill turtles, stuffed and varnished, offered as souvenirs, and even live ones, which are destined for the stew pot.*

Kuburan Cina

This very small island is among the best diving sites in Pulau-Pulau Seribu. The good reef begins due west of the island, continues around the south, then east. There is a small bit of reef at the north tip. Excellent coral growth provides the backdrop for a good drift dive in 8–20 meter depths. In areas, the coral is good to almost 30 meters.

Low tide exposes a wide expanse of reef flat. At high tide, the island shrinks dramatically, with only a sand bank showing.

Pulau Malinjo

A very good reef extends from the west around to the north, and along the south–southwest edge of the island. The best diving is at 8–12 meters.You can find lobsters here up to 30 centimeters long. The reef is also home to a great number of moray eels.

Pulau Kotok

This island sits on the western edge of the Pulau-Pulau Seribu group, and thus offers some of the best coral growth. The undamaged reef here is good for snorkeling as well as diving. Pulau Kotok is the best in the islands for snorkeling and off-the-beach diving. The west, north and east reefs are good to 20 meters.

Because it faces the open sea, Kotok is the place to see schools of sweetlips, turtles and sharks. Small manta rays have been seen here. The area is abundant in gorgonians and soft corals.

Pulau Gosonglaga

This island is basically a small sandbank surrounded by an immense reef. The entire circumference of the reef is good, and in areas good coral growth extends down to more than 20 meters. Since the island is on the fringe of the Pulau-Pulau Seribu group, it is one of the best places to see larger reef fish and occasional pelagics.

*— Janet Boileau and
Debe Campbell*

Note: The authors would like to thank PADI Dive instructor Vimal Lekhraj of Dive Masters, Jakarta for his invaluable help in preparing this section.

Good, Shallow Diving Close to Singapore

Who says that there's no decent diving near Singapore? How about this, folks: four nurse sharks taking an afternoon siesta, indecently close together, under boulders with several peek-holes; seahorses on two successive dives, tails tightly wrapped around staghorn coral branches; a crocodile fish lying without the slightest twitch, waiting for lunch to come within leaping-range; an absolutely huge banded sea snake, slithering around rocks and sand; a most unusual fish, the comet, showing us its rear end, impersonating an aggressive white-spotted moray; a fat, meter-plus mottled grouper, resting under a ledge.

This was in north Bintan island, forty-five minutes' ferry ride from Singapore's Tanah Merah Ferry Terminal. Visability and the underwater structure here is nothing to brag about, but there's certainly plenty to see.

Our general assessment of diving off Bintan is quite positive in spite of the restricted visibility which ranged from a close to awful 3 meters (but still a lot better than Singapore) to a passable 7 meters. The water clarity was disturbed by fine sediment, and we are not sure if it is just a seasonal aberration. Currents are just about non-existent and the bottom is shallow, a perfect area for beginners.

There is plenty to keep the attention of more advanced divers. Nudibranchs and flatworms—unusual and colorful—are abundant, and we counted at least three dozen species, all competing for the prize in the "small-is beautiful" category.

We saw Tridacna clams—with their hallucinogenic patterns and colors—in the 25–60 centimeter range. Anemones and their spunky clownfish guests (at least three species) enliven most locations. We encountered two species of jellyfish—a large pinkish one, and a smaller-belled, cream-colored one with long, graceful tentacles. Both pulsated beautifully. A fine group of fishes—big, medium and small—also riveted our attention. Hard corals are abundant, in many areas in surprisingly good shape.

Night dives are particularly rewarding here, in fact the vari-

AT A GLANCE
Bintan

Reef type: Shallow fringing reefs

Access: 15 min–1 hr by boat, depending on location

Visibility: Poor, 3–7 meters

Current: Almost none

Coral: In places, quite good

Fish: Good varieties and numbers

Highlights: Nudibranchs by day; crustaceans by night

ety of life is excellent. Sea urchins of several species, including a couple of exuberantly colorful ones, teach careful underwater movements. Gaudy shrimp and crabs come out of their lairs to scavenge; some bright red, and others imaginatively camouflaged.

Exploring Bintan

An old Mexican saying goes: "So far from God, but so close to the United States" and divers think-

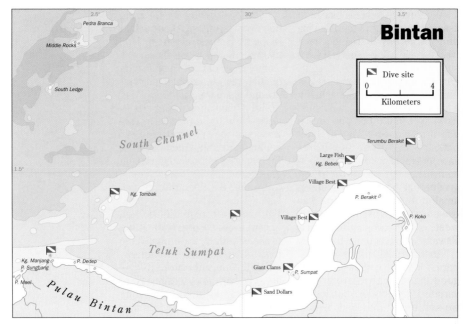

Dive site

0 ⊢———⊣ 4
Kilometers

Pedra Branca

Middle Rocks

South Ledge

2.5°

30°

3.5°

South Channel

1.5°

Kg. Tombak

Terumbu Berakit

Large Fish
Kg. Bebek

Village Best

P. Berakit

P. Koko

Village Best

Teluk Sumpat

Kg. Manjang
P. Sungbang

P. Dedep

P. Maoi

Pulau Bintan

Giant Clams

P. Sumpat

Sand Dollars

ing about Bintan could well be forgiven for giving this their own spin: "So far from eastern Indonesia (scuba heaven), but so close to Singapore (lousy diving)." But being close to Singapore gives distinct advantages to Bintan (we're not sure about Mexico): funds for infrastructure, including resort development, and developing professionally run diving programs.

One of these resorts, the Mana-Mana Beach Club, a water sports complex, offers—among many other aquatic activities—scuba diving under the professional supervision of a well-qualified, personable instructor, Jonathan Ho.

Just before the October 1994 opening of the Mana-Mana resort, Jon conducted a last-minute survey of dive sites around north Bintan. We dove off the Singapore-based power cruiser and dive live-aboard, the *Seri Delima,* owned and operated by Capt. Tan.

We covered a dozen sites, day and night. The Banda Sea it ain't. But to those divers used to Singapore waters and popular and

crowded Tioman, diving on Bintan will be a pleasant surprise: we had a fine dive series, in spite of restricted visibility (3–4 meters) at some sites. Our visibility never exceeded 7 meters, but during our week-long trip (in May), several storms whipped up the sediments. Calmer seas should increase the clarity of the shallow waters.

There are no deep dives here: our computers barely touched the 10 meter mark a couple of times. So there's plenty of time for checking out the underwater scene. It was a real treat to dive 60–70 minutes and still have half a tank remaining. And no decompression stops. In addition, there are plenty of dive locations along the 30-odd kilometer stretch of north Bintan.

Our team included Biologist Carsten Huettche, a young German tropical ecologist, who was then working for Bintan Resort Management as its Conservation Management Executive, a position from which he hoped to do something to help preserve the natural ecosystem of north Bintan Island.

We dove at several places to assess the diving potential. Visibility generally increased from west to east. But two of the better sites were towards the western end of Bintan's north shore. At Tanjung Tondang we were hit by a fairly strong current and visibility was lousy, but the coral growth was surprisingly good, both in variety and health. We saw several fish traps on the bottom, one with a good sized grouper, along with a half dozen smaller species. Coral life was even better a short way to the west, off a small island called Rawa.

As we proceeded west, the hard coral cover remained quite good but the fish life was very variable. Around Pulau Sumpat we saw large spreads of sea dollars, unusual for Indonesia. Invertebrate and fish life were also excellent at Sumapt. But both hard and soft corals, as well as the variety and numbers of fishes improved as we dove towards a place called "Black Rock" on our charts. We saw the most schooling fishes here and consider it the best site on Bintan Island.

The best diving in the area, however, is off an island called Mapor, northeast of Bintan. This marked the top of our dive series from every point of view: visibility, invertebrates and fishes, variety and absolute numbers of animals. Only the night dives here—which are excellent— were not noticeably better than our dives near the north shore of Bintan. The variety of life is staggering.

Fish life

The single largest fish we saw was a huge grouper, which we found sleeping in a crevice at night. Sensing us, it woke up, swam like mad, then settled down between two vertical rocks. Other biggies included normal-sized groupers in the 20 to 40 centimeter range, a school of jacks, several individual queen-fish (*Scomberoides*) and blue-spotted stingrays.

During another night dive, an incredibly long banded sea snake slithered into view. It fled in panic as we tried to approach it, but then returned a few minutes later to check up on our activi-

Below: *A large Semaeostome jelly-fish (perhaps Cyanea) off Bintan. The waters off north Bintan, though not particularly clear, are rich in life.*

ties. After we swam back to our boat and clambered on, the snake came by again, brightly lit by the ship's lights. It was followed by two smaller relatives. Other night camp followers, basking in our ship's lights, included a flock of gracefully undulating flatworms, mini magic carpets. We were also treated to visiting wide-eyed squid.

During an afternoon dive, We spotted a couple of sleeping sharks. A closer look revealed two more, the biggest one with a sharksucker tightly fastened to its back. The sharks, packed like sardines in a can, did not seem to mind our peeking through several openings between rock slabs. Only one, whose head was fairly close to a peek-hole, kept a wary eye on the struggling photographer trying to squeeze one of his giant flash units into a tight hole to throw light on the resting beasts.

Keen-eyed Jonathan spotted the unusual comet, a rarely encountered fish. When alarmed, this fish, a relative of the groupers, sticks its head in a crack, displaying the rear of its body and its flowing fins. In this way its head is protected and, because of its spotted pattern and a prominent false eye, the back end of the comet looks convincingly like the head of a lurking white-spotted moray eel. Few carnivorous fish are nervy enought to mess around with this fearsome customer.

Jonathan also came up with a prize reserved for only the best-behaved divers: a pair of sea horses. In just over 1,000 dives in Indonesia, these interesting animals have always kept well out of my sights. The pair of yellow seahorses that Jonathan found hid inside a protective tangle of branching corals, stubbornly refusing to come out for a portrait. The next day, however, one of the two obliged, swimming out from the coral far enough to pose for my camera.

Unusual species

Also common in this area are beaked coralfish, long-snouted butterflyfish with bright coppery orange bands. This fish uses its long "beak" to pluck invertebrate

Below: *A beautiful, unidentified soft coral (perhaps Telesto). The photographer, who has dived extensively in Indonesia, has seen this only once, in Bangka island off North Sulawesi.*

snacks from tiny hard coral cracks. An false eye spot near the back of its body helps to confuse predators. The little juveniles, always in pairs, are curious, checking out buoyancy-controlled divers who make no brusque, threatening gestures. Members of this genus (*Chelmon*) frequent reefs adjacent to large land masses with mangrove—for example, Sumatra—and are never seen on the smaller, more isolated Indonesian islands.

Another colorful species, the majestic blue-ring angelfish, also enlivens the reef with its crazy blue stripes on a yellow body. This is another fish that is common here, but not often seen at some of the more dramatic sites in eastern Indonesia. At one dive site, several adults and their camp followers hung around us, perhaps wanting to play tag, but almost always staying just outside of decent camera range.

Schooling fishes included the ever-present yellow-and-blue fusiliers, sea chubs, rabbitfish, and snappers. Parrotfish and damsels were common. We encountered several large groups of shrimpfish, swimming in their characteristic head down position.

Several other noteworthy denizens of the fish world were spotted. A crocodile fish, confident of his camouflage, allowed us to approach to within a few centimeters. We saw at least one species of shrimp goby, and the banded combtooth blenny, complete with square head and bulging eyes. An occasional harlequin sweetlips, black spots all over its yellow body, finned by quickly to check us out.

We also found a tiny fan-bellied leatherjacket, a filefish that could change its pattern and coloration in a wink, chameleon-like. Fascinating.

We also saw numerous eight-banded butterflyfish, a species that lives strictly on coral polyps, and thus whose presence on a reef has been taken by scientists as a general indicator of stony coral growth and condition. When these "canaries" become scarce, enviornmental biologists become worried about the health of the reefs.

Below: *A black-spotted puffer (Arothron nigropunctatus) shelters in a barrel sponge (Petrosia testudinaria).*

KAL MULLER

Introducing The Island of Bali

KAL MULLER

The tiny volcanic island of Bali is one of the most physically beautiful and culturally rich places in the world. The balmy climate, lush, green ricefields and lavish productions of the Hindu-Balinese cultural calendar never fail to charm visitors. Although writers continue to flatter Bali with adjectives, none has surpassed Indian prime minister Pandit Nehru, who called the island "the morning of the world."

Much of the mythology erected around this "paradise" is more revealing of its western authors than of the island itself—*South Pacific*'s silly "Bali-Hai" comes most immediately to mind—but visitors persistently find themselves drawn here. Today, over 1 million tourists a year visit Bali.

Balinese Culture

Indonesia is the largest Islamic country in the world, but the 2.5 million Balinese are overwhelmingly Hindu. *Agama Hindu Dharma* as practiced in Bali is a philosophy, religion and cultural organizing principal that has resulted from Buddhist and Hindu doctrines and practices arriving from India—partly through Java—between the 8th and 15th centuries. It is a uniquely Balinese meld.

Balinese cultural life cycles according to the Pawukon, a complex 210-day ritual calendar. Holiday celebrations—New Year, temple anniversaries, Galungan—and rites of passage—tooth filings, weddings, cremations—are scheduled according to the Pawukon. These ceremonial events, marked by bright costumes, lavish offerings of food, and dance performances, leave visitors with some of their fondest memories of Bali.

Bali has been famous for her art since the arrival of the first European tourists in the early 20th century. Balinese masks are now almost *de rigueur* on the walls of fashionable apartments in uptown Manhattan. The island's artists turn out painted Hindu icons like Garuda, whimsical animals, and unfinished abstract and surrealistic figures. Most of Bali's painters work in watercolor, producing intricate and detailed group scenes.

Balinese dance ranges from stately processionals to wild leaping and posturing. In general it is more lively than the very refined Javanese court dances, which are considered ancestors to Balinese dance. Some of the most popular forms—such as the monkey dance or *kecak*—are purely secular events, hybrids of old court dances and modern, western-influenced sensibilities.

Dance is accompanied by the *gamelan,* an all-percussion orchestra of metallophones, gongs and cymbal-like instruments. Rhythm is everything in gamelan music, and the musicians' overlapping runs on their bright-sounding instruments create an unforgettable sound.

History of Bali

Before about the 9th century, when writing and other Indian influences made their way to Bali, little is known of the island's history. Stone altars and sarcophagi, dating back to several centuries B.C. have been found on the island, and these suggest a Bronze Age culture of herders and farmers who practiced a

Above: *Rangda, the antagonist in Bali's famous Barong drama. Rangda is a powerful sorceress.*

Overleaf: *An orange skunk anemonefish (Amphiprion sandaracinos) in Merten's anemone (Stichodactyla mertensii). Photo by Cody Shwaiko.*

Opposite: *Divers on the wreck at Tulamben, perhaps Bali's single most popular dive site. Photo by Kal Muller.*

form of ancestor worship.

From the 9th century onward, Bali had regular contact with Java, at the time being influenced by Indian cultural practices. During the 14th and 15th centuries, East Java was dominated by the Majapahit empire, of which Bali became a colony in 1365.

This event and date—though by no means certain, as its source, the *Negarakertagama,* is something of a panegyric—marks the point when the Hindu caste system, court culture, performing arts, and other Javanese influences came to Bali.

For the next several centuries Bali was ruled by a single court, but factions developed, and by the time the Dutch arrived in the 19th century, Bali was made up of nine realms: Badung, Gianyar, Bangli, Klungkung, Karangasem, Buleleng, Mengwi, Tabanan and Jembrana.

Although they had been in the archipelago since the turn of the 17th century, the Dutch avoided Bali at first. The Balinese had a reputation of being quite fierce, and the fractious internal politics of the little island were considered too great an obstacle to Dutch rule there. Besides, the only important trade item the Balinese offered were slaves.

The Dutch finally subjugated Buleleng (now Singaraja) on the north coast and established a colonial center there in 1849. Then, some 50 years later, a Dutch ship ran aground on the reef off Sanur. The disappearance of the cargo to freelance salvage operators served as a pretext for an armed invasion of the south. The Badung court expired in 1906 in a *puputan,* a ritual mass suicide.

Geography and Climate

The island of Bali was shaped by the action of volcanoes, which produced the rich, black soils that nourish Bali's beautiful and productive rice paddies.

Just 8°–9° south of the equator, Bali is always warm—a mean 27.2°C, although the highlands are about 6° cooler. Humidity is an almost constant 75 percent. Most of Bali's annual 2,500–3,000 millimeters of rain falls from November through March.

—*David Pickel*

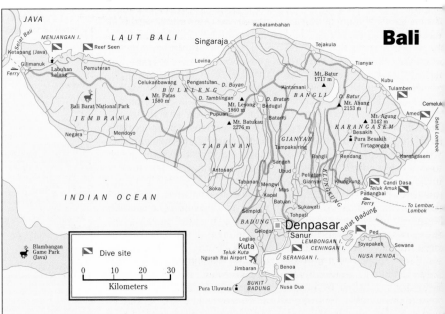

Splendid Wreck, Fine Walls and Varied Sites

Bali is one of Indonesia's most beautiful islands, and always a favorite with tourists. Although it looks small on the map, Bali's winding and narrow roads can eat up a lot of your underwater time. So, before arriving, think a bit about how much time you want to spend diving, and how much sight-seeing.

Most tourist accommodations are in the south, in the Kuta—Nusa Dua—Sanur triangle. (See map opposite.) If you stay here, there is one interesting, undemanding dive nearby, on the reef off Tanjung (Cape) Benoa, that can give you an introduction—but no more—to Bali's underwater world. The best dive sites require several hours driving from the southern tourist center.

Serious divers should find accommodations close to the best dive spots: at Candi Dasa, Tulamben, or Pemuteran. None of these has the range of *losmen,* restaurants, tourist services and shops as does Kuta Beach or the other resort areas of the south, but they are much closer to the good diving.

Where to Stay

Candi Dasa, in the old Karangasem Regency on the island's east coast, is the best compromise between comfort and proximity to good diving: Cemeluk and Tulamben are within an hour's drive, the little islands of Tepekong and Mimpang are just offshore, Padang Bai is just across the bay, and Nusa Penida is a fairly short boat trip away. Only Menjangan Island, off the far western tip of Bali, is distant.

And Candi Dasa, particularly in recent years, has become quite a bustling little town. There are plenty of accommodations and good restaurants. People have compared it to Kuta beach before the big boom in tourism.

For diving on the *Liberty* wreck off Tulamben, we suggest staying in Tulamben itself—if you can get a room. There are few accommodations, and these are often booked up, especially during the two high seasons, July–August and around Christmas and New Year.

For the dives off Menjangan Island, stay at Pemuteran, a short drive away. There is a very comfortable bungalow style resort there, and an affiliated dive operation offers diving just offshore as well as at Menjangan.

Dive Operators

Unless you are planning just a few, casual dives in Bali, contact one of the dive operators before you arrive and plan a series of dives with them. They can book a hotel for you in your price range, and plan a diving program that matches your interest and experience. (See Dive Operators in "Bali Practicalities," page 277.)

At this same time—well before your arrival—request a good, English-speaking dive guide. Don't wait until you arrive to do this, or you may end up with someone you will be giving English lessons to. The very best guide in our experience is Wally Siagian of Wally's Special Tours. There are other competent guides as well, but if you wait until the last minute, the best will be booked up.

If you have made plans with an operator, an itinerary will be worked out for you ahead of

Wally's Rankings

Beginning in this section, will be offering dive guide Wally Siagian's rankings of the various sites in Bali and elsewhere. They will be presented as a gloss in the margins.

Basically, Wally's system evaluates sites based on 1) How interesting the bottom is; 2) How good the visibility is; 3) How rich the fish life is; 4) How rich the coral cover is; and 5) Whether there is anything special about the site.

According to this system, the hypothetical best dive in the world would get a 10 as follows:

Best Site

Bottom formation	3
Visibility	2
Coral variety	2
Fish variety	2
Special	1
Total:	**10**

Note that not all categories are weighted the same, e.g. bottom formation, which is unchanging, is considered more important than fish life, which can change with seasons and local conditions

1. The best sites to do your open water certification are Cemeluk and Tulamben.

2. Your most memorable night dive will be on a full moon at Tulamben wreck.

3. When the wind is from the north, it is difficult to dive Cemeluk, Tulamben and Menjangan.

4. During the rainy season (November through March), the visibility at Nusa Dua, Padang Bai and Cemeluk will be reduced. Your best diving will be at Nusa Penida and Menjangan in these months.

—*Wally Siagian*

Water temperature

Water temperature in Bali is normally quite comfortable, from 24° to 26°C (75°–79°F).

During July and August, the temperature drops to 21°C (70°F), and sometimes as low as 19°C (66°F) at the following sites: Nusa Dua, Nusa Penida, Padang Bai and Tepekong.

—*Wally Siagian*

time. If not, contact the operators when you arrive—at hotel counters, or at their office. You will be diving with whomever else signs up. Pickups at your hotel are fairly early in the morning, and drop-offs late in the afternoon.

The tours are usually all-inclusive, including tanks and weights, guides and lunch. If you need other equipment, such as a BC and regulator, check to make sure that they are available. It is also a very good idea to take a close look at the equipment the day before the dive.

Bali's Dive Sites

There are five main areas for diving in Bali, working counter-clockwise around the island from the airport in the south: Nusa Dua and Sanur; Nusa Penida; Padang Bai and Candi Dasa; Cemeluk and Tulamben; and Pemuteran and Menjangan.

Each area offers dive locations for novice, intermediate and advanced divers—except for Nusa Dua and Sanur, where no location requires more than a little experience. (Diving is also available at Lovina. It is not really worth a special trip, but if you are passing through you might want to take a look. See "Bali Practicalities," page 280.)

At most sites, you can plan a dive to match your degree of experience—just try to be with divers whose level is similar to yours. It is no fun for either beginners or experts to be lumped together just to convenience the tour operator. Currents of 2–2.5 knots are not going to disturb an experienced diver, but for your first drift dive a half a knot is quite sufficient.

We found very little of interest on Bali's reefs beyond the safe sport diving limit. The best diving in Bali lies between 5 and 40 meters.

Nusa Dua and **Sanur.** The dives here are along the outer edge of a reef that runs from below Nusa Dua to Sanur. Operators ferry their clients over wide, shallow reef flat to the dive site. The passage is difficult or impossible at low tide. The dives are drop-offs, but to only about 15 meters. Coral cover is poor but fish life is fair to good.

Nusa Penida. The dive sites off Nusa Penida, and nearby Ceningan and Lembongan islands, require the longest boat rides and strong currents and surge make conditions tricky, although a good guide can usually find an alternate site. These are drop-off dives, and the fish life and coral variety is excellent. The water can be quite cold because of upwelling.

Candi Dasa and **Padang Bai.** The coastal sites in Amuk Bay are shallow and undemanding, with only occasional, mild currents. Visibility can be quite poor. The islands in front of Candi Dasa—Tepekong, Gili Mimpang, and Gili Likuan—offer excellent diving with a great variety of fish life, including many larger species. Temperatures are usually low, and a 3mm wet suit is almost essential. Currents can be strong and unpredictable, including downdrafts and surge.

Cemeluk and **Tulamben.** These areas have excellent coral walls with many species of fish. Some sites also have a great diversity of corals. The Tulamben shipwreck is the area highlight, offering unlimited photo opportunities at shallow depths. There is very little current here. The beach entry over rocks at the wreck dive site can be difficult if the surf is high.

Pemuteran and **Menjangan Island.** Pemuteran offers a variety of rich bank reefs, just offshore or a short boat ride away. Menjangan is an undemanding dive with excellent walls and very clear water—up to 50 meters visibility. There is also an old wreck at 40 meters, and superb coral gardens in just 5–7 meters.

Convenient and Undemanding Dives

The dives just beyond the reef line east of the northern part of Tanjung Benoa peninsula, or in front of Sanur, are not the best in Bali. But the sites are easy to get to, and there is quite a good variety of reef fish to see. These dives serve perfectly as a quick refresher if you haven't dived in a while, or as your first dive if you have just completed a dive course. (See map page 98.)

An outboard-powered outrigger canoe takes you the few hundred meters from the beach to the dive location, just beyond where the waves break. The only way out is over very shallow reef flat, so the tide must be in to make the trip. Be prepared for a bit of spray during the ride out or back and when crossing the (usually low) breaking waves.

On the reef face off Tanjung Benoa, we dropped down to 8–9 meters on a slightly sloping bottom with scattered coral formations. Visibility (late September) was just 6–8 meters, but we were told that it is usually twice this. The majority of the fish were at

---

AT A GLANCE
Nusa Dua and Sanur

Reef type: Drop-off to moderate depth

Access: 5 minutes by small boat

Visibility: Low, 6–8 meters (can reach 15 meters on occasion)

Current: Very gentle

Coral: Limited coverage, few species

Fish: Surprisingly good variety

Highlights: Feeding frenzy on a fresh spawn

Other: Nusa Dua has slightly better coral cover than Sanur

Below: *A swarm of anthias, mostly red-cheeked fairy basslets,* Pseudanthias huchtii. *Nusa Penida, Bali.*

HELMUT DEBELIUS / IKAN

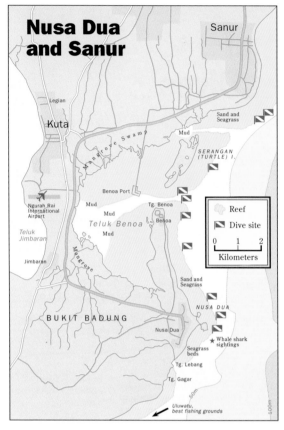

Nusa Dua and Sanur

Fairy basslets hovered over almost every coral outcrop. Damsels were present in a variety of species. The butterfly fish were well-represented, but the only schooling species we saw was a small group of masked bannerfish (*Heniochus monoceros*). Groupers were common, especially the white-lined grouper (*Anyperodon leucogrammicus*), which we saw in both color morphs: white, and brown-green.

Parrotfish were present in good variety, but the only species we noticed more than once was the blue-barred parrot (*Scarus ghobban*). The only angelfish we saw were the dwarf bicolor angel (*Centropyge bicolor*) and several big emperor angels. Surgeonfish were common, particularly the spotted unicorn fish (*Naso brevirostris*). We saw pairs of rabbitfish of at least three species, and a single pair of Titan triggerfish.

A Feeding Frenzy

The highlight of the dive came when we saw a furious cloud of several dozen fish of various species whirling around what looked like a bare patch of dark, reddish coral. Caught up in a feeding frenzy, the small fish allowed us to approach as close as we wished. We could even touch them, they were so intent on their meal. We never did identify what it was they were eating, although it is likely it was a fresh spawn of some kind.

Dives off Nusa Dua will probably not offer such a show very often, but are still worth making for the variety of fish here. The reef to the north, off the Sanur coast, is similar—wide tidal flats behind the reef front—and access is also impossible at the lowest tide. The variety of fishes is quite good in Sanur, but there is even less coral cover than at Nusa Dua. If you are a serious diver, either of these dives will just whet your appetite for more challenging locations.

8–10 meters. We made a couple of quick dips to 14 meters, and saw nothing.

Good Variety of Fish

The coral cover here is not fantastic, but the few mini-pinnacles drew plentiful fish life with a good variety of species. We saw several 50–75 centimeter fish glide by, but visibility was too restricted to make an identification. Our guide found a giant moray and pointed him out to us. This big fellow lives in a coral cave with several openings, and for a while he played hide and seek, popping his head out of three different holes.

We saw a fairly large group of yellowtail fusiliers, a nicely compacted hovering mass of blue-lined snappers, a few red bigeyes and several small aggregations of bigeye soldierfish.

Nusa Dua/Sanur

Bottom formation	1
Visibility	.5
Coral variety	1
Fish variety	1
Special	0
Total:	**3.5**

Some sites do better, earning perhaps a 6, but recent dredging of the Benoa harbor has ruined visibility and the Nusa Dua and Sanur sites are average at best.

—Wally Siagian

Abundant Pelagics, Some Fierce Currents

Nusa Penida, across the Badung Strait from Bali's southern tip, offers some of the best diving to be found anywhere. But conditions around Penida and its two small sister islands—Nusa Lembongan and Nusa Ceningan—can sometimes be difficult, with unpredictable currents reaching four or more knots. This is not a place for beginning divers, inexperienced boatmen, or engines in less than perfect condition. Also, upwellings from the deep water south of Bali, which keep visibility here clear, can also make the water uncomfortably cold.

Even if you are an expert diver, contract with one of Bali's well-organized diving services to dive Nusa Penida, and make sure that you get a reliable boat and a guide with plenty of experience. The currents in this area can usually be predicted from the tide tables, but they can increase, decrease or shift direction with no advance notice, and vary dramatically with depth. We recommend that your guide bring a buoy, and that you do not wander off by yourself. The dive locations are all close together, and an experienced guide can easily shift you to an alternate site if the conditions at your planned location are unsatisfactory.

Dive boats to Nusa Penida leave from Nusa Dua or Sanur, or from Padang Bai. (See map page 101.) From either of the resorts the 34-kilometer (18-nautical-mile) trip takes 1.5 hours; from Padang Bai, just 17 kilometers (9 nautical miles) from Penida, it takes 45 minutes to 1 hour, depending on the boat. You can also rent a speedboat at Padang Bai (about $110 round-trip) to shave trip time to the minimum, but if you do, make sure your dive guide knows the boatman. The chap could fall asleep while you're under and be out of whistle range when you come up with the current. It has happened.

Coral Walls and Pelagics

Most of the dive spots are around the channel between Nusa Penida and Nusa Ceningan. The standard reef profile here has a terrace at 8–12 meters, then a wall or steep slope to 25–30 meters, then a fairly gentle slope to the seabed at 600 meters. Pinnacles and small caves are often encountered. At 35–40 meters, long antipatharian wire corals are common, spiraling outward more than 8 meters.

Pelagics are the main attraction here, and you have a good chance to see jacks, mackerel and tuna. Reef sharks are so

Getting to Nusa Penida

The quickest transfer to Nusa Penida is from Padang Bai, using the "Express" ferry, which has twin 85hp engines. This takes 26 minutes to Toyapakeh.

—*Wally Siagian*

Caution!

Tidal currents between Nusa Penida and Ceningan will get *very* strong to the south.

—*Wally Siagian*

AT A GLANCE
Nusa Penida

Reef type:	Drop-offs, steep slopes
Access:	45 min to 1.5 hrs by boat
Visibility:	Good, 15 meters
Current:	Moderate to very strong (4+ knots)
Coral:	Very good variety of hard corals; excellent stand of soft corals
Fish:	Excellent variety; many pelagics
Highlights:	Large school of sweetlips, very large hawksbill turtle. Site also hosts sharks, mantas, and even *Mola mola*
Other:	Can be *very* cold; currents are unpredictable and often fierce

and southwest coasts of Penida, but these areas, swept by tricky currents, require an experienced guide and more time than is available in a daytrip to reach.

A Dive off Penida

We were staying at Baruna's Puri Bagus Beach Hotel in Candi Dasa when the opportunity came to dive Nusa Penida. One of the hotel's minibuses picked us up early, and after a 15-minute ride dropped us off at Padang Bai, where the large diesel-powered *Baruna 05* dive boat was already waiting for us. We waded through waist-high water to load our gear, and were soon on our way for the hour-and-a-half trip.

The boat anchored off the Ped/S.D. area, and we dropped into a practically currentless sea. From an initial 7 meter depth, we followed the slope of 45 degrees down to 37 meters. There was good hard coral cover, and an occasional pinnacle reared up 5–6 meters from the slope. We crossed a big school of black triggerfish mixed with a few sleek unicornfish.

A small cave in one of the coral knolls held a densely packed school of pygmy sweeps (*Parapriacanthus ransonetti*). These greenish, semi-transparent fish feed at night on small plankton attracted by the bioluminous organs located just in back of their pectoral fins.

Early in the dive we crossed paths with a large black-spotted stingray. He allowed us to approach to within just over a meter, but after just one photo flew off to his next appointment. Shortly after we met the ray, we saw a hawksbill turtle, one of the largest we have ever seen. This 1.3–1.5 meter animal flippered off before I could approach within decent camera range.

The rest of our dive passed through busy schools of yellow-tailed and lunar fusiliers, and occasional schools of longfin ban-

Above: *Two clown anemonefish,* Amphiprion ocellaris, *in the host anemone* Heteractis magnifica. *Bali.*

S.D.

Bottom formation	1
Visibility	1.5
Coral variety	1.5
Fish variety	1.5
Special	0
Total:	**5.5**

Malibu Point

Bottom formation	2.5
Visibility	1.5
Coral variety	2
Fish variety	1.5
Special	1
(Sharks, big pelagics, Mola mola)	
Total:	**8.5**

—Wally Siagian

common that after a while you stop noticing them. Mantas are frequently sighted. Perhaps the most unusual pelagic visitor to Nusa Penida is the weird mola-mola or oceanic sunfish (*Mola mola*), a mysterious large, flattened fish with elongate dorsal and ventral fins, and a lumpy growth instead of a tail fin.

Dive guide Wally Siagian says he has seen a mola-mola here about once every 15 dives. On two occasions he has been able to swim up and touch the bizarre, up to 2-meter-long animals.

The most common dive spots are just south of the dock at Toyapakeh, or a bit further east, at Ped, the site of an important temple of the same name, Sampalan Point, and "S.D.," named for the *sekolah dasar* or primary school there. There are other dive spots down the northeast

nerfish. We saw several groupers and even more sweetlips, and an occasional clown or Titan triggerfish. A good-sized barracuda observed us from above. Visibility was good, in the 15-meter range.

When we ascended we noticed the surface current had increased markedly since we began our dive. Wally complained that we had not spotted any big sharks, which are common in this area.

Toyapakeh

We motored a bit further west along the coast of Nusa Penida, and dropped anchor a few hundred meters from the dock at Toyapakeh. We descended through a slight current (less than 1 knot) into veritable clouds of peach fairy basslets (*Pseudanthias dispar*), each the exact color of a blue-eyed Nordic tourist who had done too much time in the sun. The anthias were mixed with large aggregations of firefish, which are more often seen in pairs or small groups.

A long stretch of our dive route—this at 25–30 meters—consisted of an almost unbroken thicket of pastel-tinted *Dendronephthya* soft corals. A school of two dozen or more greater amberjacks swam several lazy circles around our group, mixing sometimes with a larger school of bigeye jacks. As we started upwards, we saw a huge black-

Toya Pakeh

Bottom formation	1.5
Visibility	2
Coral variety	1.5
Fish variety	1.5
Special	1
(Mantas, Mola mola)	
Total:	**7.5**

Gamat

Bottom formation	2
Visibility	2
Coral variety	1.5
Fish variety	1
Special	1
(Turtles, marlin, mantas, Mola mola)	
Total:	**7.5**

—Wally Siagian

Nusa Penida

Reef
Dive site
0 1 2 3 4 5
Kilometers

Malibu Point. This is guide Wally Siagian's favorite spot in Bali. Visibility is 20m, and there is always strong current, up to 4 knots. The area is small, and the conditions are tricky, but one can see big pelagics, tuna, mantas, turtles, and a wide variety of sharks.

Gamat Bay

Mouth of bay has coral outcrops, crevices and grottos

Inside of bay is shallow and full of coral; good for snorkeling

WALLY SIAGIAN
The Best Dive Guide in Bali

Take a group of the most experienced divers in Indonesia and ask them who they think is the best dive guide in the islands. Wilhelm Siagian—"Wally," to one and all—will be at the top of the list, every time.

Wally has shown off his Balinese reefs to top underwater pros, including Gerald R. Allen, Rudie Kuiter, John E. Randall, and Roger Steene—the leading authorities on the archipelago's marine life and some of the world's top underwater photographic professionals. As a result, Wally has become an informal student of Allen, Kuiter and Steene, learning the Latin names of the fish with which he is so familiar.

Wally was born in Bandung, Java in 1960 of Sundanese, Batak and German blood-lines. He was 16 when he first started diving, with a CMAS certificate from Jakarta's Ganesha Diving Club. After some 200 dives around Pulau Seribu and about 30 off Ujung Kulon, he left for a bit of travel. Stints of working and diving around Sorong, Irian Jaya and Balikpapan, East Kalimantan led Wally to decide that diving was all that really mattered in life. (It was while diving near an oil rig off Balikpapan that Wally saw the biggest barracuda of his career—more than 2 meters and fa-a-a-t.)

After Kalimantan, Wally decided to settle with his Swiss wife in Bali. Times were difficult for a while, until he landed a miserably paying job with Baruna Watersports in 1985. Since then, he has made thousands of dives around Bali, pioneering new sites and working his way up the diving ranks: Dive Master rating in 1988 from CMAS, Open Water Instructor from SSI in 1990, and SSI Advanced Open Water Instructor with Dive Control speciality, awarded in Australia, in 1991.

Though training is important, it is his experience and motivation that makes Wally a superior guide. He knows the Latin and English common names of hundreds of fish in the reefs around Bali. He really knows the dive locations, and can set up a sequence of dives to suit the interest and level of competence of any divers in his charge. If necessary, he can cure wounds with traditional medicine and even deliver an excellent massage. A true Renaissance Man.

He has an open personality, a sense of humor and an infectious enthusiasm for diving—and he'll find a cold beer in the most unlikely places. He is my friend, drinking buddy and, of course, my favorite dive guide. — *Kal Muller*

spotted moray, with about 1 meter of its snaky body sticking out of its lair.

We surfaced just at funnel mouth of the channel between Nusa Penida and Nusa Ceningan. The local fishermen were unfurling the sails of their *jukung*s, and we climbed back on board just as the current began to pick up speed.

The *Baruna 05* tied up to the dock at Toyapakeh, and Wally borrowed a bystander's bicycle to go fetch us some food. While he was gone, a fisherman pulled up in his outrigger, and we bought a just-caught 20-kilo yellowfin tuna for dinner.

Sunset Show

Just before sunset, the current picked up to 5–6 knots. We watched the *jukung*s literally shoot through the channel on their way out for a night's fishing. Others, taking advantage of the wind and a back current headed for "mainland" Bali in the direction of towering Gunung Agung. This was one of the finest sunset shows I had ever admired in Indonesia.

The tuna we bought ended up as sashimi and charcoal-grilled tuna steaks, and combined with a lobster Wally had snatched from a grotto on our first dive, we had a splendid supper. We then spread our mattresses on the top deck, and settled down to drinking beer. A few little boats fished around us with bright pressure lamps, and we drifted off to sleep.

The night was surprisingly cool, and I woke up at midnight to a sky full of stars. I quickly discarded all thoughts of a night dive as I heard the current rushing by the boat. The beer had taken its usual route, and I relieved myself overboard, creating swirling bioluminescence on the water's surface.

Another Dive at S.D.

The next morning, after the sun

ad warmed us thoroughly, we headed back east along Nusa Penida's coast to begin our next and last dive where we had ended the previous morning: in front of the long, red-roofed elementary school.

This was a drift dive, in a 1.5 to 2 knot current that occasionally "gusted" to 3 knots. The fish hovered effortlessly in the current as we sped by. Swimming diagonally, we approached two large map puffers, and several smaller, but exquisitely patterned cube trunkfish. We also took a closer look at a hallucinogenic scribbled filefish.

Between two coral knolls we came on an aggregation of some 40 sweetlips. The fish were split into four groups, all facing the current. The sight of these attractively patterned fish was too much to just pass by, so we carefully grabbed onto some hard corals and crawled along the bottom for a closer look at the sweetlips show.

Perhaps feeling there was safety in numbers, these magnificent animals allowed us to approach to within 2 meters before they drifted off to find a new spot just a bit further away. While we watched our sweetlips, a turtle rose up just ahead and, with no effort at all, swam off straight into the current.

Then, a huge grouper, well over a meter long, appeared out of nowhere, buzzing one of our group before disappearing just as suddenly. Consulting the fish books later, we came to a consensus that our visitor was likely to have been a blotchy grouper (*Epinephelus fuscogattus*).

We later saw triggerfish, a barracuda and a reef white-tip shark; still, it was anticlimactic.

Above: *The comet,* Calloplesiops altivelis. *When alarmed this fish ducks its head into a crevice and displays its long fins and tail, mimicking a moray eel. These unusual fish can be found at the Tulamben drop-off, S.D. on Nusa Penida, and Tepekong.*

Below: *Guide Wally Siagian gets his teeth cleaned by the shrimp* Lysmata amboinensis.

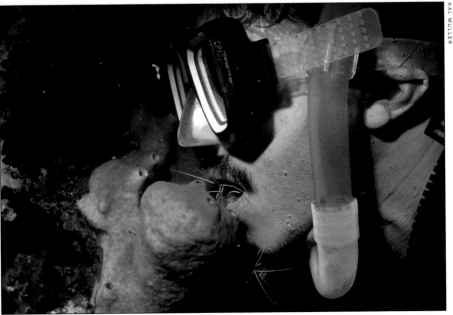

Padang Bai

Fair Diving Along the Coast of Amuk Bay

Blue Lagoon

Bottom formation	1
Visibility	.5
Coral variety	1
Fish variety	1
Special	.5

(Some rare species can be found here)

Total: **4**

Note: This is soon to be a site for a Pertamina oil storage facility

Pura Jepun

Bottom formation	1
Visibility	.5
Coral variety	.5
Fish variety	.5
Special	.5

(Flying gurnards here, also jewel anemones)

Total: **3**

—*Wally Siagian*

There are two main dive spots at Padang Bai: Pura Jepun and Tanjung Bungsil. We rate these sites as slightly better than those off Nusa Dua or Sanur, but a damn sight colder. Bring a wet suit if you're going to dive this area. A good, deep chill can take the pleasure out of any dive.

The ride to Padang Bai from the Kuta–Nusa Dua–Sanur triangle is a long, traffic-clogged 60 kilometers. Padang Bai is the port for the five-times-a-day Lombok ferry run, and things can always get a bit congested near the dock area. It's far more convenient to dive this spot from Candi Dasa, just 15 minutes away.

Before diving, you will suit up on the beach, at the restaurant favored by your dive operator. Most small dive groups are taken to the site in little local outriggered fishing canoes powered by small outboard motors. It's usually just two divers per craft, so if you have a large group, the little armada plays follow-the-leader to the site. There will probably be some spray just as you leave the harbor, and it may follow you further on if the wind is up. Both dive sites are a short 10–15 minutes away. (See map page 106.)

Pura Jepun

We started our first dive about 50 meters from shore, just opposite a small temple shrine (*pura*) called Pura Jepun, after the Balinese word for frangipani, although no flowers were in evidence along the stretch of coast leading to our entry point. (The shrine sits on a little cape, also called Jepun, so the site is sometimes called Tanjung Jepun.)

After leaving the harbor, we headed northeast along the coast, passing Blue Lagoon Bay with an idyllic white sand beach at its back. A rocky point, against which some pretty large waves crashed, marked the end of Blue Lagoon, and from there to the Pura Jepun site the steep hills ended in small cliffs. These look like they drop straight down to the depths, but unfortunately continue only 2–3 meters underwater. At this point the bottom levels off quickly to a wide terrace at 6–10 meters.

We jumped overboard and began our drift dive, pushed back the way we came by a slight, less than one-knot current. Further out from the initial, 6–10 meter terrace, a slight slope eases down to 15–20 meters, followed by flat sand at 40 meters.

After a very quick look in the deeper areas, we restricted ourselves to 6–12 meters, where we had determined most of the animal life was to be found. Coral formations were scattered, although there were quite a num-

---

AT A GLANCE
Padang Bai

Reef type:	Flat-bottomed mixed reef and sandy bottom, some wall
Access:	10–15 min by small canoe
Visibility:	Variable; poor to good, 6–15 m
Current:	Usually gentle, but up to 3 knots
Coral:	Scattered outcrops, fair variety
Fish:	Good variety and numbers
Highlights:	Large feeding Titan triggerfish, blue-spotted stingrays

ber of giant anemones, crinoids of varying colors, odd clumps of tunicates and a few sponges. The bottom remained quite flat across our "flight path" until we reached the rocky point that marks the entrance to Blue Lagoon Bay, where a sheer wall drops close to 40 meters. Visibility throughout the dive was a decent enough 10–12 meters.

Since we remained in quite shallow water during most of the dive, we were treated to several schools of elongated surface feeders: silvery, pencil-thin keeled needlefish (*Platybelone platyura*) and halfbeaks (*Hemiramphus* sp.), and only slightly more substantial arrow barracuda (*Sphyraena novaehollandiae*).

I disturbed a peacock flounder (*Bothus manchus*), delicately patterned to blend in with the sand, quite unlike its namesake. It is only when the fish swims slowly that one can appreciate its colorful back pattern and strangely positioned eyes. The dive's other highlights included a playful few minutes with a cuttlefish, and two small lionfish cowering in a vase sponge. Two blue-spot-

ted stingrays also made a brief appearance but disappeared quickly.

Otherwise, the dive was basically average for Indonesia, which is to say not bad at all. We saw lizardfish, hawkfish, a bright yellow trumpetfish, the odd small grouper, a few oriental sweetlips, goatfish, parrotfish, wrasses, butterflies, emperor and blue-faced angelfish, damselfish—especially plucky sargeant-majors—foxface and lined rabbitfish, a cubefish, a dog-faced puffer, Moorish idols, surgeonfish—including clown surgeonfish and a single electric-blue hepatus tang—and several species of triggerfish. Although the hard coral was not plentiful, we saw a fair number of anemones, crinoids and sponges. Even though I was not carrying a macro set-up, and was looking for overview shots, I noticed a very beautiful nudibranch.

Blue Lagoon

When we arrived off the wall below the rocky point at the end of Blue Lagoon, we dipped down just far enough (25 meters) to see a few larger predatory jacks:

Above: *Photographer Rudie Kuiter caught this moray eel at night in the act of snatching a cardinalfish. The eel is the undulate moray,* Gymnothorax undulatus; *the cardinalfish is an unidentified* Apogon *sp. Tulamben, Bali.*

Seahorses

In the shallows, just off Padang Bai beach (at the end of the road) is an extensive growth of several different kinds of *Caulerpa* algae. If you are patient, and have good eyes, you can find seahorses here.

—*Wally Siagian*

rainbow runners, a couple of black jacks, and blue-lined sea breams. There are said to be occasional strong down-currents towards the base of this wall, but we felt no pull whatever.

When we were almost out of air, we surfaced and, not seeing our boat around, snorkeled to the beach at Blue Lagoon, stopping along the way to check out a few coral outcrops in the sandy bottom. When we clambered out of the surf in our gear, we were the sunbathers' center of attention. These included four very pretty Italian girls, but unfortunately our boatman showed up immediately, apologizing profusely for the delay. Arivaderci.

Tanjung Bungsil

After a quick lunch, we headed for Tanjung Bungsil, on the south side of Padang Bai harbor. This dive was to be even shallower than the morning's—at the end my computer showed a maximum depth of 10.2 meters. The very slightly sloping bottom was a bit rockier here than at Tanjung Jepun, with corals growing to within a few meters of the surface. Some large carpet anemones grew here in the shallows. In places the visibility dropped to a very poor 5–6 meters.

The good variety of fish life here was similar to the morning's dive. We also saw several six-banded angelfish, and a little group of the curious, headstanding shrimpfish. As I tried (unsuccessfully) to sneak up on a clown triggerfish, a very attractively marked ringtail wrasse (*Cheilinius unifasciatus*) swam up and insisted on posing for a portrait.

The dive's highlight was a Titan triggerfish, doing a headstand while furiously snapping away with its strong teeth at a patch of coral rubble, apparently trying to dislodge an irresistible hors d'oeuvre.

This big boy's energetic activities attracted a host of camp followers looking for a free snack: angelfish, butterflyfish, wrasses, goatfish and even a pair of Moorish idols.

Unfortunately, the triggerfish did not allow human beings into his circle of friends, and abandoned his activities as soon as we approached to within 3 meters.

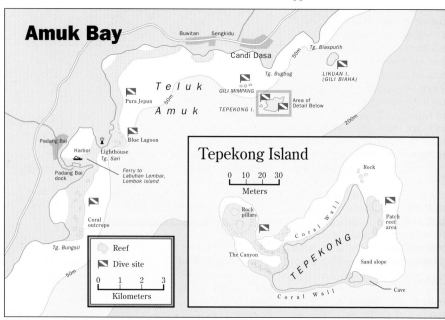

Swirling with the Fish in Tepekong's Canyon

Candi Dasa

Just offshore from Candi Dasa is tiny Tepekong, a little outcrop that offers some spectacular diving. The coral walls are steep, the water is cold, and the current can be strong. But for an experienced diver, drifting with a 3-knot current through The Canyon offers an unforgettable underwater experience.

You can reach Tepekong from anywhere along the southeast coast, but access is easiest from Candi Dasa. There are actually three dive sites here: Tepekong (sometimes called Kambing—"Goat"—Island); Gili Mimpang (three mini-islands sometimes called Batu Tiga, "Three Rocks"); and Biaha Island, sometimes called Likuan Island. (See map opposite.)

Your ride to the dive site is a fishing boat or *jukung,* fitted with a tiny outboard. Two or three divers at most will fit in a *jukung.* The boats must cross the edge of a fringing reef about 75 meters offshore. This will give you a thorough soaking, the skills of your boatmen notwithstanding. When the tide is low, you might even have to get out of the *jukung* to help push it over the reef flat. Once across the reef, you are 10–15 minutes from Mimpang or Tepekong.

Tepekong has the best diving. It is also the coldest—occasionally a bone-chilling 19°C—and most difficult. Tiny Tepekong is just 100 meters long and 50 meters wide. There are no beaches. The sides of the island plunge straight into the sea.

Diving the Canyon

With Wally Siagian as my dive buddy and guide, we twice tried to dive his favorite spot, the southside Canyon, but the combination of over 4 knot current and undertow from swell and waves crashing into Tepekong's western side defeated our attempts. On the third try, however, it worked.

We dropped in about halfway along the western side of Tepekong, descending in a slight current to a sloping bottom at 9 meters, near the vertical underwater continuation of Tepekong's above-water cliff. We were just nearing the bottom when a large Napoleon wrasse appeared at the edge of our 10 meter visibility. He drifted out of sight, as did a school of 30-odd roundfaced batfish (*Platax teira*). We followed the slope, dotted with coral knolls, to 24 meters, then dropped down into a canyon. The Canyon was lined with huge boulders, and bottomed out at 32 meters.

**The Canyon
(a.k.a. The Toilet)**

Bottom formation	3
Visibility	1.5
Coral variety	1
Fish variety	2
Special	1
Total:	**7.5**

—Wally Siagian

AT A GLANCE
Candi Dasa

Geography: Steep coral walls; underwater canyon

Access: 20–30 min by small outboard

Visibility: Variable; poor to very good; 6–20 meters

Current: Can be extremely strong, more than 5 knots

Coral: Excellent coverage and variety

Fish: Literally teeming with fish

Highlights: Tepekong's Canyon, good chance to see pelagics

Other: Very tricky currents, strong surge; uncomfortably cold

---

East Tepekong

Bottom formation	1
Visibility	1
Coral variety	1
Fish variety	2
Special	0
Total:	**4**

Gili Mimpang

Bottom formation	2
Visibility	1.5
Coral variety	1
Fish variety	1.5
Special	1
(Lots of sharks)	
Total:	**7**

—Wally Siagian

RUDIE KUITER

Above: *The little galatheid crab above was first found in 1985 by Wally Siagian at Tulamben, diving with Roger Steene at the time, at 30 meters on the slope past the wreck. A specimen was sent to Dr. Keiji Baba at Kumamoto University in Japan, and he described it—only the second discovered member of its genus—in 1993. It has been named after Wally:* Lauriea siagiani. *These attractive crabs can be found at a number of sites, always living in the outer folds of the barrel sponge* Petrosia testudinaria.

Here, visibility increased to close to 20 meters and the fish life also increased considerably. So did the current, to 2.5–3 knots. Sometimes the current here swirls around the Canyon with a downward pull, leading to Wally's nickname for the place: "The Toilet."

The conditions that produce this unforgettable experience are usually strong swell from the north or northeast. If these are the conditions on the surface, do not dive the Canyon. Unless you want to be sucked down in a swirling current.

As soon as we entered the Canyon we saw a huge aggregation of sweetlips, 50 or 60 of them, hovering next to a pinnacle: Goldman's sweetlips, oriental sweetlips, and yellow ribbon sweetlips. Then we saw a very healthy looking grouper, well

over a meter in length. Wally thought the fish we saw was an Australian potato cod (*Epinephelus tukula*), perhaps north for a quick vacation.

Groups of schooling fish hung in the current, which "gusted" occasionally to such speeds that I almost felt my mask was going to tear off. We hung on to outcrops, watching schools of rainbow runners, bigeye trevally, sleek unicornfish and little packs of Moorish idols. We occasionally shifted our position, disturbing a resident whitetip shark at one point, and a cubefish at another.

Each coral-covered pinnacle hosted firefish, which flicked their long dorsal spines in the current, and clouds of lyretail coralfish (*Pseudanthias squammipinnis*). These were all at our 5-meter decompression stop.

This dive was one of the best I have experienced in Indonesia. But it was far from easy. Conditions could well have postponed this dive until my time in the area had run out. And even for an experienced diver, this is a tricky dive. Wally doesn't call it "The Toilet" for nothing.

The teeming fish life makes it well worth whatever effort it takes, however. It is particularly easy here to get very close to normally wary fish. You might even see an oceanic sunfish, the strange *Mola mola*. Wally has seen one on three occasions in his more than 100 dives here.

East Tepekong

After one of our aborted attempts on the Canyon, Wally directed our *jukung* to the far eastern end of the island. We dropped into surging, cold water, and shivered as we descended. Visibility was restricted by the water movement to around 8 meters. And the surge was too strong to allow us to peer into the many caves—between 16 and 32 meters—as well as a 10-meter-long passage between several huge boulders that appear to have fallen from the topside cliff.

We spotted a tuna, a fairly big grouper and a cuttlefish after we made our way down the slope to about 25 meters. The coral cover was good, including both stony corals and soft corals, and several blunt pinnacles sheltered reef fish in shallow pockets.

Fish huddled between overlapping layers of table coral, each irregular "shelf" holding several species. All this was fine, but the strong continuing surge, lack of visibility and cold water led us to surface before our air ran out.

Gili Mimpang

These same conditions plagued our dive on Gili Mimpang, a cluster of three little exposed rocks between Tepekong and the coast of Bali. Despite our wet suits, we were freezing. Descending to the 12-meter bottom, we disturbed a small blue-spotted stingray, and a much larger black-spotted ray. We swam against a slight current to the top of a wall around 30 meters, working our way around detached clumps of coral. About 10 minutes into the dive I was ready to quit, mainly because of the cold, but also because of the increasing current and the restricted visibility. I signalled to Wally and we headed up.

Around 18 meters we hit a thermocline, and life took a very definite turn for the better. Almost instantaneously, the water temperature increased 6°C. Fish life improved considerably as well, beginning with a docile star puffer, three easily spooked (as usual) reef white-tip sharks and several blue-finned trevally. A school of blue-lined snappers buzzed us from above.

As we stopped on top of a pinnacle at around 7–8 meters, a school of bignose unicornfish parted just enough to afford us a glimpse of a Napoleon wrasse on one side and several bumphead parrotfish on the other. A small school of longfin bannerfish accompanied us, from a safe distance, almost to the surface.

Back in the *jukung,* Wally said that had we not turned back, we could well have seen lots of large pelagics ahead. But I was well satisfied, and very happy to be warm and dry.

Below: *A yellow-headed moray eel* (Gymnothorax rueppelliae) *nestled among tube sponges. Bali.*

Outstanding Variety of Fishes and Corals

Below: *A black-spotted puffer,* Arothron nigropunctatus, *has found the perfect resting place in the leather coral* Sarcophyton trocheliophorum. *Bali.*

Divers on a tight schedule could dive Cemeluk in the morning, and the Tulamben wreck—just a few kilometers away—in the afternoon. But these are both excellent dive spots, so why rush? Cemeluk—sometimes called Amed—offers the best variety of fish life we have seen in all of Bali. In this regard it matches even the teeming reefs of Manado and eastern Indonesia.

Cemeluk is just off Bali's main east coast highway. From the resort areas of the south, the highway passes through Klungkung, then Candi Dasa, then

swings inland past Karangasem, skirting 1,175-meter Mt. Seraya, Bali's easternmost mountain. Just before it reaches the coast again, about 10 kilometers before Tulamben, a paved side road from the little town of Culik drops directly to the coast at Amed, 3 kilometers away.

From Amed, the paved road turns right and passes a long stretch of traditional salt works. Two kilometers from Amed, you're in Cemeluk, a fairly small bay with a beach of black, volcanic sand, crowded with dozens of colorful *jukung,* local outrigger fishing canoes powered by sails or small outboards.

Diving Cemeluk

The reef off Cemeluk curves around a rock outcropping just east of town. We took a *jukung* out into the bay, and dropped into a very slight current pushing us southeast along the reef. At about 8 meters we came down on an extensive spread of staghorn *Acropora* teeming with damselfishes and cardinalfishes. A short slope led to a coral wall, where we dropped to 43 meters, hanging there about 8–10 meters above the sandy bottom. The wall was magic.

Schools of fish of several species cascaded down the wall or took the electric stairs back up in orderly, two-way traffic. The numbers were staggering, the best we have seen in Bali and only rarely matched or surpassed to the east. The schools included black triggerfish, lots of banner-fish, black snappers, humpback snappers, pyramid butterflies, and countless others. Further off from the wall, the usual school of

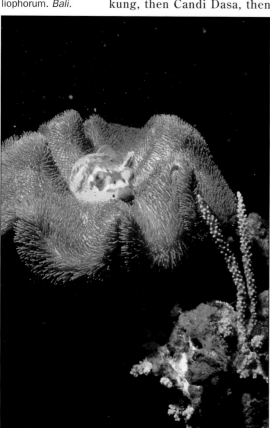

HELMUT DEBELIUS / IKAN

Cemeluk

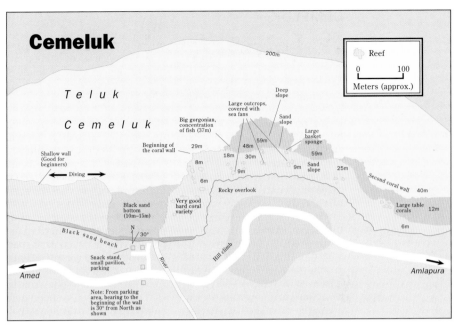

yellowtail fusiliers kept an eye on proceedings.

According to Wally Siagian, my stellar dive guide, by beginning our dive towards the southeast part of Cemeluk Bay we left the best coral formations behind, although there were still impressive outcrops along our 200-odd-meter journey, covered with sponges, sea fans and crinoids. One sponge sheltered a small lionfish, and in another a well-camouflaged tassled scorpionfish would have passed unnoticed except for Wally's sharp eyes.

Towards the end of the dive, the dense growth of sponges and gorgonians created a tunnel between two of the outcrops. Inside, it was wall-to-wall with life. Large barrel sponges poked out from clearings in this forest. A couple of mean-looking Titan triggerfish eyed us with undisguised hate, but refrained from charging. A clown triggerfish approached, then fled. On a small sandy patch next to an outcrop, a little juvenile blue ribbon eel (the juveniles are black) stood his ground bravely.

The larger fish included a longnose emperor, a patrolling giant trevally, and several bluefin trevallys. Two very large tuna, both over a meter and in the 30–40 kilo range, shot by quickly. As we finished the dive, we saw a mismatched pair of Napoleon wrasse: a very large adult and a very small juvenile. Wally often sees reef white-tip sharks here, although we saw none on this day. Our visibility was around 10 meters, but can double under the right conditions. The area is calm year around with only very occa-

No Anchors!

Please remind your guide not to anchor at Cemeluk. It is easy enough for boats to wait without anchoring, and the coral cover here is so rich there is no place to put down an anchor without causing damage.

—*Wally Siagian*

AT A GLANCE
Cemeluk

Reef type: Coastal reef; flats, slope and wall

Access: Beach; 5 min by small boat

Visibility: Fair to very good, 10–20 meters

Current: Mild

Coral: Excellent; best hard coral variety in Bali

Fish: Excellent numbers, superb variety

Highlights: Density of fish on the deep wall; coral species just off beach

sional surge and high current conditions.

A Dive from the Beach

A dive directly from the black sand and pebble beach at Cemeluk gave a very different perspective: smaller fish, but a great number and variety of corals. We had barely donned our fins and dropped to the less than two-meter depth when we saw a scattered group of orange-band surgeonfish (*Acanthurus olivaceous*), some 15 strong. Their bright orange marks are distinctive, and we had seen very few in previous dives.

Neon blue devils darted around, two parrotfish paddled furiously, and a graceful pair of Moorish idols swam into view. Two yellow-margined triggerfish were doing headstands while furously blowing at the sand hoping to uncover some worm or spiny thing to eat. A dozen striped convict tangs (*Acanthurus triostegus*), which we had not seen in Bali before, swam across our path. All this within 15 meters of shore!

Just a bit further out (we were

Below: *An undulate or orange-striped triggerfish,* Balistapus undulatus, *takes shelter in a sponge. This speciman is a male. Bali.*

heading due north) all life stopped, the sloping grey sand offering nothing until we saw crate-like enclosures holding bits of coral, an experiment conducted to determine coral growth in this environment. A few dozen meters beyond the crates, several scattered coral outcrops jutted up from the sand, little oases in the sandy desert.

From the outcrops we headed east at about 20 meters, crossing a stretch of grey sand bottom until we came to the reef wall, which follows the coast from this point. About 10 meters from the surface, the irregular wall started sprouting fan gorgonians and pastel trees of *Dendronephthya*. Tube sponges were numerous.

The reef here is topped by a relatively flat area, just 2–5 meters deep and 30 or more meters from the rocky shore.

The relatively small area between here and the sandy beach holds the greatest variety of corals we have seen in Bali, and they are swarming with fish.

Perhaps the area's stable conditions and clear waters are responsible for this abundance.

The *Liberty* Wreck, Bali's Most-visited Site

At first sight, the little village of Tulamben is rather uninviting. Its beach is a spread of black sand covered by smooth, fist-size rocks, the waterworn remains of rubble cast here by Gunung Agung's 1963 eruption. In the dry season, the countryside assumes a nondescript shade of brown.

Like all the north coast villages, there are no lush rice fields here—Gunung Agung and the other mountains steal the rain, which comes from moisture-laden air that blows in from the south. Thus South Bali is the island's rice bowl.

What brings people to Tulamben is not visible from above water, however. People wake up early, fight the snarled traffic from the tourist centers of the south and emerge from their *bemos,* groggy and cross, for only one reason: to dive the wreck of the *Liberty* at Tulamben.

The Liberty

Just 30 meters from the beach at Tulamben is a World War I–era cargo ship, broken up but impressively large, stretching along more than 100 meters of steeply sloping sand. The top of the wreck is just 3 meters underwater; the bottom is at 29 meters. (See map page 114.)

On January 11, 1942, this ship was hit by torpedoes from a Japanese submarine while crossing the Lombok Strait (See note at right). The damage was critical, but two destroyers hitched up to the ship and tried to tow it to the port at Singaraja. The wounded cargo ship was taking on too much water, however, and her crew ran the vessel up on the beach at Tulamben. There she

stayed there until 1963. Local entrepreneurs stripped the boat of its cargo—one source says raw rubber and railroad parts—and were in the process of cutting her up for scrap when Gunung Agung exploded in 1963. The explosion was disasterous, killing thousands and destroying vast tracts of fertile

riceland to the south. It also pushed the *Liberty* off the beach to its present location, in the process splitting the hull in two.

Welcoming Committee

Divers simply walk out from the beach, spit in their masks, and go. Sometimes the waves are up, churning up the sand and turning a suited-up diver into an ungainly creature. And the big smooth stones that serve as a beach are always hard on the feet—bring diving boots! Never mind these small indignities, however. This dive is most decidedly worth it. Wave action is

Tulamben Wreck

Bottom formation	2
Visibility	1.5
Coral variety	1.5
Fish variety	2
Special	1
Total:	**8**

AT A GLANCE
Tulamben

Reef type: *Liberty* wreck; wall

Access: Beach; ship is 30 meters offshore

Visibility: Fair to good, 12–15 meters

Current: None or moderate, 1 knot

Coral: Good growth of encrusting animals on wreck; fine coral on wall

Fish: Superb variety, excellent numbers

Highlights: Full moon night dive on wreck

Other: Fish on wreck are regularly fed and quite tame; during midday, wreck can be crowded

Some notes on the Liberty

The Liberty *was a U.S. Army cargo ship built in 1918 by the Federal Ship Building Company in Kearny, New Jersey. She was 395 ft. (120 m.) long, 55 ft. wide, and grossed 6211 tons. Despite her early date of manufacture, the ship had a turbine engine.*

The Liberty *is not, as is sometimes* (Continued next pg.)

suggested, a Liberty class ship, which are piston-engined ships built during World War II.

At the time the Liberty was torpedoed, 4:15 a.m. on January 11, 1942, the ship was carrying materiél from Australia to the Philppines. The Japanese sub that torpedoed the Liberty, I-166, was itself sunk by the British submarine Telemachus off Penang, Malaysia, on July 17, 1944.

—Research by Bruce Watkins

strongest during the southeast monsoon, late June through August and again—but somewhat less—from late November through January.

As soon as you dump the air out of your BC and drop to the black sandy bottom, you know that you've made the right move. Right away you meet a colony of spotted garden eels (*Heteroconger hassi*), heads and bodies swaying in the current like plants in a breeze. Their tails remain in the sand as they snap plankton from the current. As you get closer the eels shoot back into their burrows, disappearing into the sand like an illusion. At this disturbance, goatfishes hit the sand, searching for juicy tidbits.

You look up and here comes the welcoming committee: several species of snubnose chubs, sweetlips, parrotfishes and a small army of fearless sergeant-majors, not so numerous elsewhere in Bali. These plucky little damselfishes swim right up to your face, to the point where you can even touch them. If you've brought a camera, excercise restraint. If you don't watch out, you'll shoot your whole roll before even reaching the wreck.

Electric blue neon damsels, darting around with a seeming inexhaustible store of energy, stand out vividly against the black sand and rocks. As I watched, their happy antics were interrupted. A hawkfish pounced,

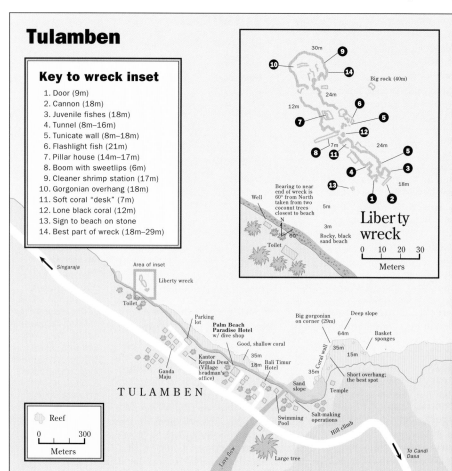

Tulamben

Key to wreck inset

1. Door (9m)
2. Cannon (18m)
3. Juvenile fishes (18m)
4. Tunnel (8m–16m)
5. Tunicate wall (8m–18m)
6. Flashlight fish (21m)
7. Pillar house (14m–17m)
8. Boom with sweetlips (6m)
9. Cleaner shrimp station (17m)
10. Gorgonian overhang (18m)
11. Soft coral "desk" (7m)
12. Lone black coral (12m)
13. Sign to beach on stone
14. Best part of wreck (18m–29m)

snatching a small damsel in a flash. A sudden jerk, the damsel's head disappeared, and the hawkfish resumed its motionless posture, looking for his next meal. Small groupers, cornetfish and trumpetfish, the odd parrotfish and a few morays inhabited patches of coral along our route.

The black sand bottom around the wreck makes an excellent background for fish photos—but be careful with auto-exposure cameras, as the meter will want to overexpose your shots. On and around the ship, carefully monitor your buoyancy. Bumping the wreck could lead to a nasty burn from a stinging hydroid, or even a more serious sting from a lionfish or scorpionfish. More likely, however, you will just damage the fragile organisms encrusting the ship. Move slowly and carefully. This is also the best way to get close to the fish.

On to the Wreck

The wreck of the *Liberty* lies parallel to shore on a steep sand slope. Part of the superstructure is within snorkeling distance from the surface. The hulk is broken into large chunks, and there are lots of big holes in the hull, making it easy to explore the vessel's innards. Don't expect to find any interesting mementoes inside, however. Remember, this ship was stripped while still on the beach.

The treasures of Tulamben are swimming in and around the wreck: hundreds of species of fish in good numbers, most having become semi-tame and used to divers. We saw several fairly large—a meter or so—specimens, but it is the huge numbers of medium-sized fish—30–80 centimeters—that make the wreck such an interesting dive. If you planned just one or two dives here, we guarantee you will regret not having more time.

Unfortunately, not everything

is perfect in Tulamben. When we dove there in late June, visibility was just 12–15 meters, and this seldom improves much.

Expert underwater photographers and marine biologists, men like Rudie Kuiter, John E. Randall and Roger Steene, dive Tulamben over and over, coming up with great shots and even new species. Australian Rudie Kuiter, author of the definitive guide to Indonesian reef fishes, estimates that some 400 species of reef fishes live on the wreck, which is also visited by perhaps 100 species of pelagics. These are remarkable numbers for an area just 100 meters long.

On our dives we never saw any sharks or other really big fish at Tulamben. There were a few good sized tuna, bonito, several 80-centimeter plus emperors, and jacks, Napoleon wrass-

Above: *A school of lunar fusiliers,* Caesio lunaris, *at the Tulamben wreck. Tulamben, Bali.*

Other Dives

Just off the beach in front of the Palm Beach Paradise Hotel and dive shop are some excellent shallow water corals, a site Wally calls Coral Gardens.

Coral Gardens

Bottom formation	1
Visibility	1
Coral variety	1.5
Fish variety	1.5
Special	1
(Easy beach dive)	
Total:	**6**

es pushing the meter mark, and one huge 80-centimeter scribbled filefish. On the sandy bottom next to the wreck, where I thought rays would abound, I saw only one small eagle ray, and a very large blue-spotted stingray. Both ducked for cover before I could say "Glenfiddich." We also saw a meter-long barracuda, but one of my dive partners, Wolfgang Bresigk of Baruna Water Sports, says a 1.5 meter barracuda regularly forages on the wreck.

Another dive buddy, Wally Siagian, saw a huge oceanic sunfish (*Mola mola*) close to the wreck, four times in a one-week span. On one of these occasions, he saw this most unusual fish being cleaned by several singular bannerfish (*Heniochus singularis*). Off to one side of the wreck Wally took us to visit a colorful black-spotted moray eel (*Gymnothorax melanospilos*), a beautifully marked animal with a yellow body and black markings. The eel lives at the base of a barrel sponge at about 40 meters.

A Swarm of Beggars

Arriving at the wreck, we stayed shallow and settled near the upper edge of one of the ship's large holds. The top of the open hold lies at around 5 meters, with its bottom at around 14 meters. The superstructure reaches to couple of meters of the surface.

It took a good ten minutes before the swarms of sergeant-majors, a couple of insistent crescent wrasses, and a dozen large bignose unicornfish all understood that we had no food for them and stopped bothering us. Fish here are often fed by divers or their guides, which is why they allow divers to get so close. Bananas, strange as this may seem, are their standard fare. Clearly nonplussed that we had not brought any food, the fish finally left us alone—but not before the sergeant-majors gave

us a few nips.

Once the beggars left us alone, we were able to look over the swarms of fishes living on and around the wreck. Schools of several dozen golden and lined rabbitfishes hung almost motionless in 6–7 meters of water. Standing out like a sore thumb in this group, was an occasional big-eye emperor, or large red snapper. Below this group were bright pairs of coral and foxface rabbitfishes. These beauties were a bit nervous, and it took patience to get within good camera range.

Lone snappers and mixed schools of sweetlips also inhabited the shallow areas near the northeast corner of the wreck. We identified five species of sweetlips: clown sweetlips, Sulawesi sweetlips, striped sweetlips, Goldman's sweetlips, and, most numerous of all, the oriental sweetlips. These fish allowed us to approach to one meter.

Surgeonfishes were common, and inhabited various depths. We frequently saw yellowfin surgeonfish, orangeband surgeonfish, Thompson's surgeonfish, and clown surgeonfish. We saw a few orangespine unicornfish, with their curious mandrill-like faces, and a few male spotted unicornfish. Bignose unicornfish wandered the wreck in large schools, mostly consisting of drab females, but with an occasional bright blue courting male, his magnificent tail filaments undulating with each flip. These fish allowed us to get very close, and we saw them on every dive.

A variety of fairly large parrotfishes (40–75 centimeters) added color to every dive. With a bit of patience we could get to within a meter of the blue-barred parrotfishes, but the others—mostly palenose parrotfish and bullethead parrotfish—were more shy.

Small damsels were common, in particular golden damselfish.

These bold little animals frequently nipped us if we got too close to their home turf.

Butterflyfishes are not present here in overwhelming numbers. Perhaps the dearth of hard corals is responsible for this, as many butterflyfishes are polyp feeders, some relying completely on this source of nutrition. The vaguaries of memory have reduced the list to six: lined butterflyfish, raccoon butterflyfish, threadfin butterflyfish, Bennett's butterflyfish, spotnose butterflyfish and the Pinocchio-like longnose butterflyfish.

I had seen Titan triggerfish—a sometimes nasty animal with a distinctive "mustache" and loopy eyes—on many previous dives in eastern Indonesia, sometimes as many as a half-dozen in a single dive. They had always been very wary, never allowing me to get close. On the wreck, however, they were much more relaxed, allowing me to get within 1.5 meters. These were also among the largest I had seen, doing justice to the name "Titan."

Angelfishes were not particularly abundant on the wreck, but those that I saw here were among the largest specimens I have seen. We spotted blue-faced angels, blue-girdled angels, emperor angels and regal angels. None of these fellows shamelessly coddled up to divers to beg for food or out of curiosity, but kept a healthy distance from the human visitors. Moorish idols here shared the same trait; none was as bold as the similarly marked longfin bannerfish.

Groupers prowled around on every dive, including red-mouth groupers and white-lined groupers, although the real stars were the aptly named peacock grouper, and its even more colorful relatives: the coral grouper, the flagtail grouper, and the black-tipped grouper. The largest groupers we saw were the blotchy grouper, and the saddleback grouper, sometimes called the giant coral trout.

Sea Fans and Sponges

The encrusted wreck is mostly a community of opportunists: soft corals, sponges, gorgonians, hydroids, bryozoans, tunicates, bivalves and crinoids. It is still

Above: *An emperor angelfish,* Pomacanthus imperator, *on the wreck at Tulamben. Although the steel structure has not yet been much colonized by hard corals, it is heavily encrusted with soft corals, gorgonians and hydrozoans.*

Enoplometopus debelius: A Reef Lobster of One's Own

It was night, and 15 meters down I glided along the sloping reef in pitch black water. I could hear the noise of my bubbles much more clearly than during the day. A pair of cardinalfish swam into the beam from my lamp and, startled, fled at high speed. I had learned to find my way around this beautiful reef off Tulamben during the afternoon, and I was now looking for reef lobsters and other big crustacea as I always do on night dives.

I shone my light into every crevice and cave. Here it fell on dancing shrimps, and there on a marbled shrimp. I saw the brightly colored common reef lobster, *Enoplometopus occidentalis,* and snapped two pictures before it could hide. Suddenly the beam of my light came to rest on a patch of violet. I looked again, and made out the shape of a reef lobster, crouching in the coral rubble.

I could scarcely breathe as I adjusted the focus of the camera, for this species looked completely new to me. The entire body of the little 10-centimeter lobster

Above: *A gravid female* Enoplometopus debelius. *Author and photographer Helmut Debelius is a skilled aquarist, and has succeeded in spawning the lobsters in captivity.*

was sprinkled with small violet dots, an enchanting sight in the bright light. I snapped off three shots as the animal slowly backed up.

Quickly, I laid my camera aside and took a small net from my wetsuit and placed it behind the lobster. With my free hand I gently touched its pincers and, as I had expected, the animal dashed backwards into the net. "A shame for you," I muttered to the lobster, but when it comes to scientific aims, I have no mercy.

Later, my suspicions were confirmed: Dutch crustacean expert Prof. L.B. Holthuis examined the animal and said that it was a new species. He named it after me: *Enoplometopus debelius.*

The Reef Lobsters

Reef lobsters are beautiful, but rarely seen inhabitants of the holes and crevices of Indonesian reefs. In size and shape they resemble freshwater crayfish more than the common spiny lobsters of Indo-Pacific reefs. These omnivorous creatures emerge only at night, to feed on carrion, worms and anything else they can catch—even a sleeping fish.

—*Helmut Debelius*

Left: Enoplometopus debelius *in one of the author's tanks in Germany.*

much too soon for a really large accumulation of hard corals. In less than 30 years, however, great sections of the wreck's iron hull have been smothered in a bright encrustation of life.

Great sea fans, gorgonians up to 2 meters across, jut from the bow section. Several large trees of black coral (*Antipathes* sp.) grow here safe from the jeweler. Sponges, tunicates and hydroids crowd each other for a holdfast. In places, there are great aggregations of thorny oysters, their bright "lips" visible through parted shells. Crinoids cling to every stable growth—a sponge, a gorgonian—and unfurl their arms to the current. In one of the the shallower spots, a growth of hard plate coral has already reached over 3 meters.

The many "cleaner stations" around the wreck offer a great show. Fish line up to be cleaned by one of the small cleaner wrasses (*Labroides*). We saw both bluestreak and bicolor cleaner wrasses at work here. Some divers have actually succeeded in having the fish pick bits of food out from between their teeth—although this requires holding one's breath from a minute or so.

Night Dive on the Wreck

Daytime dives are extraordinary on the wreck, but a night dive, especially around full moon, will be among the most memorable dives you will make.

As we walked along the beach to the entry point, three local fishing outriggers sailed silently by in the moonlight. We waded out, took our bearings, and headed toward the wreck. As we approached the ship, we extinguished our lights. The large hulk loomed above us, a massive ghostly presence with the bright moon a distant pinpoint of light.

We kept our lights off for a bit. Each fin-stroke stirred up a twinkling trail of biolumines-

cence. Peering into the dark hold of the wreck, we saw a magical show of zigzagging lights. These were the curious flashlight fishes (*Anomalops*), each possessed of a bioluminescent organ beneath its eye.

Many sections of the wreck provide the overhangs preferred by the large, bright orange polyps of *Tubastraea* and *Dendrophyllia*. These corals are best appreciated at night. At night one can also see crinoids crawling about in search of a new holdfast, or perhaps even swimming, their feathery legs opening and closing in the manner of a octopus. Sometimes when we trained our lights on the wreck, hundreds of red shrimp eyes stared back.

Here again, however, the fish are the real stars of the show. We saw a couple of unconcerned common lionfish, and a stunning spotfin lionfish. A large red parrotfish slept, secure in its mucous cocoon, under a shallow overhang. We approached a big map puffer, and several groggy unicornfish.

The most interesting fish we came upon was an absolutely huge barred filefish (*Cantherhines dumerilii*). I spotted the big fella at least 10 meters above me, sleeping under a large lacy plate of coral growing horizontally from the wreck.

My computer screamed its warning just as I made for this animal, but I paid it no heed. My

Above: *Closeup of a soft coral. Note the small goby in the background.*

Tulamben Wall

Bottom formation	2
Visibility	1.5
Coral variety	1.5
Fish variety	1
Special	1
Total:	**7**

subject was sleeping in a tilted position. After a few shots, I pushed him a bit to correct his posture. He didn't particularly appreciate this, but obliged me anyway. I moved him into the open water. A few more shots, and he had had enough, charging straight for me. We photographers really are a pain.

A Popular Site

Tulamben is probably the most popular dive spot in Indonesia (and justifiably so), and during the daily rush, from about 11:30 a.m. to 4 p.m., an average of three or four groups of about a dozen divers each visit the wreck. The ship is big, however, and most of the groups just zip by. But serious divers seldom appreciate crowds, and novice divers, not having mastered buoyancy control, have the unfortunate habit of thrashing up clouds of sand with their fins.

Some of our best dives on Tulamben were in the early morning and late afternoon, before and after the crowds. The only way to do this is to overnight in Tulamben (see "Bali Practicalities" page 280, 285).

Staying overnight also takes a lot of the logistical headaches out of night dives, but be sure to stash a towel on the beach. The 10-minute walk back can be chilly. For day trippers, there's a shower at the toilet block on the beach, next to the dive site, but sometimes there is no water, and there can be long lines.

The Tulamben Wall

Should you want to take a break from wreck diving, there is a good coral wall beginning just off the eastern end of the beach. The rocky knoll southeast of town plunges straight down into the sea, and coral grows along its face. Be careful who you dive with—or what group you follow—as the fine gray sediment here is easily stirred up.

Just as we began our dive, heading down over sloping grey sand, a good sized barracuda cruised by—but that was the only big fish we saw during the dive. We soon found our wall: it has a nice overhang around the 18 meter mark, and drops to a sand bottom at just over 60 meters. We explored only to the 30 meter mark, following the ridge to its furthest extension. This wall does not host huge numbers of fish, but like the wreck has a tremendous variety.

At one point along the dive, Wally stopped at a shrimp cleaning station, manned by the candy-striped cleaner shrimp *Lysmata amboinensis*. Taking out his regulator and opening his mouth, he soon had two of the fellows working on the remains of his lunch. Others were eager for leftovers, but there are limits to Wally's breath-holding capabilities.

Large barrel sponges sprouted from the slope, and sponges in general were abundant here—tube sponges, vase sponges, and encrusting sponges. Once we left the wall, the coral grew only in small knolls.

The final part of the dive was a short glide over black sand. This environment, though it at first appears featureless, is home to many interesting animals, including skeleton shrimp, ornate ghost pipefish, and juvenile scorpionfish. If you have air left, take a close look.

The Tulamben Wall is known for rare species, including the comet (*Calloplesiops altivelis*), a beautiful fish with elaborate finnage and a false eye-spot. The posture and coloration of the comet mimics the spotted moray eel (*Gymnothorax meleagris*).

For the keen-eyed observer, new species are waiting here to be discovered. A few years ago science added a new fairy basslet to its list, *Pseudoanthias bimaculeatus,* first discovered here.

Good Diving and a Comfortable Resort

It's a long drive from the Nusa Dua/Sanur/Kuta area to Menjangan, which adds up to a lot of time on the road for just a couple of dives. But there is an excellent alternative: stay at the Taman Sari Beach Bungalows in Pemuteran, which has a professionally-run dive operation, Reef Seen Aquatics, which offers very good diving. Pemuteran is located just a few kilometers east of Menjangan on the north coast, on a little bay.

Reef Seen runs its own boat to Menjangan, but divers often prefer the closer locations. The latter are all just a few minutes away. There are five main dive spots, well explored by the operator, each worth several dives.

The dive center caters to small groups of divers, especially to those staying for several days, for whom discounts are available. Independent divers, not requiring a guide, can save a bundle on both day and night dives from shore. We highly recommend this dive business, developed by PADI instructor Chris Brown, a pro in all senses of the term, who also takes concrete measures to preserve the marine ecology.

The atmosphere in Pemuteran is quiet and pleasant, and the Taman Sari Beach Bungalows are very nicely designed: The rooms are spare and decorated with natural woods and clean white sheets on the beds; the bathrooms are open to the sky, and feature dripping Japanese bamboo pipes and smooth black river pebbles. A very comfortable, and romantic place.

All the sites Chris Brown has pioneered off Pemuteran are small *takas,* or bank reefs. He is constantly investigating new sites, however.

The diving here is generally good year-round, with very occasional rough seas during the southeast monsoon, May–July. The very best times are from March to early May, and September through January. The rainy season, during the northwest monsoon from January to early March, usually brings heavy rain only in the late afternoon ar at night. Water temperatures almost always are around 28°–32°C. Visibility is good, but not as clear as Menjangan under the best of conditions. There is hardly any current, and this is a good site for beginners.

Napoleon Reef

"Napoleon Reef," is a flat-topped, underwater mound, about the size of a football field. At its shallowest, to bottom rises to about 5–10 meters of the surface. The reef is covered with sponges and corals, including great table-top

---

AT A GLANCE
Pemuteran

Reef type:	Near shore banks and mounds
Access:	Shore, or a few min by boat
Visibility:	Good, 10–15 meters
Current:	Very slight
Coral:	Good numbers and variety; abundant soft corals
Fish:	Good number, good variety
Highlights:	Deep end of Napoleon Reef, occasional mantas
Other:	Convenient dives, operator is pioneering new sites.

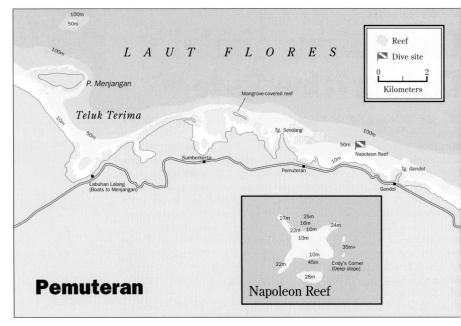

Pemuteran

Napoleon Reef

Acropora reaching a diameter of 5 meters. From the top, the profile follows a gentle slope to 35 meters, with very good invertebrate life. Two enormous barrel sponges serve as landmarks. Fish life is quite good. Large cuttlefish are often seen. Occasionally, manta rays appear to feed across the reeftop.

The southeastern point of Napoleon drops down to 35 meters, where there is an excellent deep reef with soft corals and whip corals, dubbed "Cody's Corner."

Close Encounters

"Pertamuan Dekat" (literally "Close Encounters") takes its name from the big fish here which allow—and even initiate—close encounters with divers: reef sharks, tuna, mackerel, barracuda and jacks, and an occasional large grouper or Napoleon wrasse. Even whale sharks have been seen here on occasion

Lebar Reef

At Lebar (literally "wide") Reef, steep slopes drop to flat sand at about 25 meters. Out over the

sand, coral outcrops appear at 25 meters and again at 35 meters. Both the reeftop and sides of the *taka* are covered with thickets of staghorn *Acropora*, some with colorful blue tips, interspersed with tabletops *Acropora* and fan gorgonians.

Kebun Batu

Kebun Batu ("Rock Garden") is just a 5-minute snorkel from shore. Here a huge boulder rises vertically from about 18 meters to just 3 meters from the surface. The rock, full of crevices and small, shallow caves, serves as a hotel to many fish. Elsewhere, the substrate shows a mixture of sponges, hard and soft corals. This is a very good night dive.

Kebun Chris

Kebun Chris ("Chris's Garden") is the dive operators current favorite site. Diving begins just 20 meters from his back door, with hard corals starting at less than a meter's depth and continuing on down to about 10 meters. This reef spreads continues for about 300 meters, parallelling the shoreline.

Clear Water off Bali's Distant 'Deer' Island

Menjangan Island—the name means "deer"—hangs just off-shore of the mountainous point in far northwestern Bali. Because the island is in a protected position, currents and wind-generate waves are rarely a bother, and the reefs here offer fine diving, particularly for beginning and intermediate divers. Occasionally, the water can be crystal clear—a snorkeler, distinct, 50 meters above you—and the rest of the time visibility seldom drops to less than 25 meters.

The island is part of Bali Barat National Park, a protected reserve area that encompasses much of Bali's little-populated western end. (See map page 125.) The drive from the resort areas of the south is at least three hours, the first hour through the thick traffic that envelops Denpasar like a fog.

Craggy Walls

The coral walls around Menjangan are vertical down to 30–60 meters, and then slope outward. The reef surface is particularly rugged: caves, grottoes, crevasses and funnel-like splits break up the coral wall, and the surface is textured with little nooks and crannies. Gorgonians of many kinds reach large sizes here, and huge barrel sponges are abundant. Soft corals blanket the colorful walls all the way down.

We found the variety of fish here to be somewhat inferior to other dive sites—we ask for a lot!—but the numbers are good and some of the fish are quite bold, as guides feed them regularly. We were blessed with a curious pack of half a dozen fully grown roundfaced batfish, and

two aggregations of bignose uni-cornfish. A few individuals from a large school of longfin banner-fish approached us, but the majority kept a discreet distance, as did the yellowback fusiliers, which accompany almost every dive in Indonesia.

Small boats ferry divers from the Nature Reserve dock at

AT A GLANCE
Menjangan

Reef type:	Walls, particularly rugged; wreck
Access:	30 min by boat from Labuan Lalang post
Visibility:	Excellent to superb, 25–50 meters
Current:	Very slight
Coral:	Very good numbers and variety; abundant soft corals
Fish:	Good number, only average variety
Highlights:	"Anker" wreck
Other:	Past 60 meters, can find the rare *Genicanthus bellus* here

Labuhan Lalang to Menjangan's small beach, where gearing up takes place in the sandy-bottomed shallows. The edge of the reef terrace is at 1–5 meters, and a V-shaped delta of sand points the way out to the edge.

Guides usually take their groups to the east (left) on their first dive—keep an eye out for a huge gorgonian at 18 meters—and down to 15–30 meters, and then back through the shallows (5–10 meters) on the way back. After a lunch on the beach, the group goes west (right). Here the wall has much more relief, and the guides send their boat to pick up divers at the end of their dive, returning them directly to the Nature Reserve dock at Labuhan Lalang.

On the second dive, we saw a couple of names carved into sponges. Please don't join the ranks of the morons.

The Anchor Wreck

Menjangan's western tip holds a deeper, but more interesting dive on an old wreck. The so-called "Anker" wreck is just off the coast, near a small dock and guardpost maintained by the Park Service (PHPA). (See map opposite.) The guardpost—"Pos II"—is about a 30-minute boat ride; our craft anchored about 75 meters from the beach at a point designated by our guide. (Note: few guides know the location of this wreck.)

We entered the water near the reef edge, and dropped some 5 meters through very clear water (more than 20 meters visibility) right onto the large coral-encrusted anchor of our sunken ship. Dropping over the reef edge, we followed a fairly steep slope with bits and pieces of wreckage and anchor chain down to 30 meters where the ship was resting, prow shoreward. Along the way, we saw a reef white-tip shark (sharks and rays are common here) and a few lizardfishes.

It seems obvious that the craft, probably a copper-sheathed sailor from the last century, tried to anchor just off the reef, broke the anchor chain, sunk and slid back to its resting place on the sloping sand bottom. It's a small ship, just 25 meters long, and its stern sits in 45 meters of water.

Flat rectangular sheets, perhaps copper sheathing material, lay in what had been the hold, which also contains an assortment of ceramic and glass bottles. These perhaps had contained *arak,* a powerful local booze distilled from palm wine that had been a major trade item of the last century. Miraculously, previous divers have not stolen all the bottles—yet.

There were fewer fish on the wreck than usual, according to my guide, but this was because a group of divers had just passed through. We saw several snap-

Below: *A dive boat off Menjangan Island.*

Menjangan Island

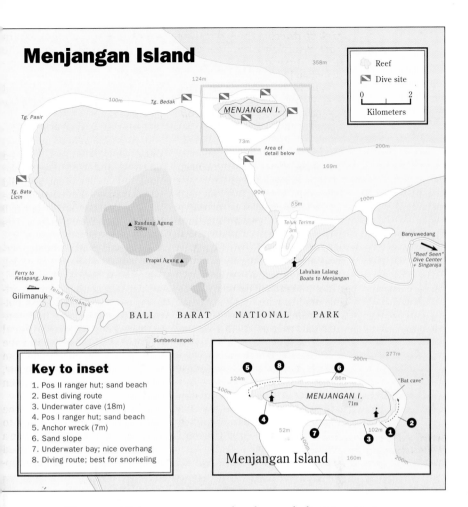

Reef

Dive site

0   2

Kilometers

358m

124m

100m

Tg. Bedak

MENJANGAN I.

Tg. Pasir

73m

Area of
detail below

169m

200m

Tg. Batu
Licin

90m

55m

100m

▲ Randung Agung
338m

Teluk Terima
3m

Banyuwedang

"Reef Seen"
Dive Center
+ Singaraja

Prapat Agung ▲

Ferry to
Ketapang, Java

Labuhan Lalang
Boats to Menjangan

Gilimanuk

Teluk Gilimanuk

BALI   BARAT   NATIONAL   PARK

Sumberklampek

Key to inset

1. Pos II ranger hut; sand beach
2. Best diving route
3. Underwater cave (18m)
4. Pos I ranger hut; sand beach
5. Anchor wreck (7m)
6. Sand slope
7. Underwater bay; nice overhang
8. Diving route; best for snorkeling

200m

277m

124m

86m

"Bat cave"

100m

MENJANGAN I.
71m

52m

102m

160m

200m

Menjangan Island

---

pers, sweetlips, goatfishes, wrasses and Moorish idols. In the vicinity of the wreck, visibility dropped to just 10 meters, again perhaps because of the last group. Large gorgonians grow on the wreck as well as on the slope leading to it. The wreck and the area around it was dominated by soft corals. The sandy slope beyond the wreck was largely bare.

After less than 10 minutes, we decided to ascend a bit, partially because of the depth, but mostly because my guide had said earlier that the reef life was most abundant above, and a bit south of the wreck. He was certainly right. On our slow upward progress, diagonally to the slope,

we crossed a slow, orderly cascade of surgeonfish, broken up by two bright, terminal male filament-finned parrotfish, chasing each other at top speed.

Here, and in the shallows above, were more species of parrotfish than we have ever seen on a single dive. There were also many unicornfish, with the bluespine unicornfish being the most numerous. Several large and colorful bignose unicornfish tried hard to keep their harems under control, but on our approach, the ladies beat a hasty retreat into nearby minicaves. A large, spread-out school of longfin bannerfish was much less concerned with our presence.

The butterflyfishes were well

Menjangan

Wally Siagian rates the various sites around Menjangan Island from 6 to 7.

He figures the cave along the south coast (#3 on the map above) has perhaps the most interesting structure of any of the sites.

represented, especially the masked bannerfish (*Heniochus monoceros*). We saw a large pinnate batfish, and several small roundfaced batfish. Rabbitfishes, fairy basslets and damselfish were abundant. Perched on coral knobs and gorgonians were two species of hawkfishes, tiny falco hawkfish, and curious longnose hawkfish. From 20 meters on up, stretches of the coral face were cut with caves and narrow, vertical funnels. These offered refuge to soldierfishes and medium-sized groupers, including a couple of clownish polkadot groupers (*Cromileptes altivelis*). A pair of longnose emperors appeared against the dark blue sea background.

Back in the shallows—5–7 meters—our visibility returned to its original 20+ meters. Here we saw two red snappers, and a small school of blackspotted snappers. A pair of Clark's anemonefish, living in a beautiful green-tentacled anemone, challenged us to a brawl. The tentacles of this anemone (*Entactmaea quadricolor*) have strange, bulbous tips. Nearby, a tassled

scorpionfish did not defy anyone secure with the power of its venom. Moorish idols were unusually abundant, but shy.

Colorful Picasso triggerfish played hide and seek amidst the coral, and a large scribbled file fish seemed unconcerned as we closed in on him to within a half a meter for a photo. Two Titan triggerfish, intent on each other, took little notice of us, nor did a small patrol of bumphead parrot fish, following their meter-plus leader. But a school of black triggerfish seemed almost to wish us Godspeed. We reluctantly left our fantasy playground, out of film and almost out of air.

Getting to Menjangan

Most of the people who dive Menjangan sleep in the Kuta-Nusa Dua–Sanur tourist triangle. They are picked up around 7:30 a.m. by one of the dive operators, with filled tanks, weights, any rented gear and box lunches already packed in the minivan. For the first hour or so of the three-hour ride, you might as well catch up on your sleep as the driver maneuvers out of the

Below: *Two arrow crabs* (Chirostylus) *on a gorgonian*

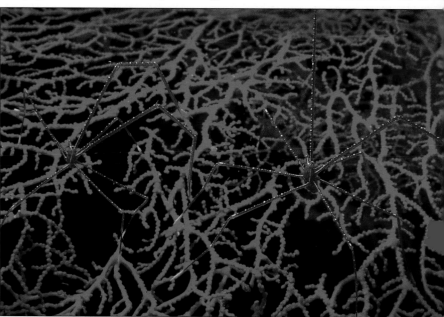

heavy traffic surrounding Denpasar and continuing past the town of Tabanan. The next hour and a half are worth opening your eyes for, with wide spreads of terraced rice fields reaching to the sea on the left.

The road is a good one (it's the main Java–Bali highway) and the drivers are quite aggresive—if you get nervous at such things, stay out of the front seat. As you approach the town of Negara, the land becomes drier, and there are lots of coconut plantations producing copra. Past Negara, it's a half hour to Cekek, the headquarters of the Bali Barat (West) National Park, just 3 kilometers short of Gilimanuk, the ferry crossing to Java. Macaques, looking for handouts, line the road a bit before Cekik, and after the turnoff for the 12-kilometer stretch to Labuhan Lalang. Labuhan Lalang is a total of 125 kilometers from Denpasar.

At the boat landing, while you register with the park service—name, nationality, passport number—all your gear is unloaded from the minivan into a boat, big enough for six divers and all their accompanying gear.

While driving through west Bali, keep your eyes out for an unusual bird, endemic to this area. The Bali starling, or Rothschild's myna, (*Leucopsar rothschildi*) is a crested, snow-white bird with black on its wing-points and the tip of its tail, and a bright blue patch of skin around its eyes. Unfortunately, you will almost certainly not see one, as fewer than 100 are thought to remain here.

As a cage bird, Rothschild's myna fetches a very high price; there are many more now in captivity than in the wild. Do not be fooled if you see a white, crested myna with a black tail and wings. This is the black-winged starling (*Sturnus melanopterus*). It has much more black on it than the Bali starling, and the skin patch around its eyes is yellow.

It's just short of a half-hour ride to Menjangan, and on the way you can see three of Java's eastern-most volcanoes. As you approach Menjangan, keep a lookout for dolphins. Menjangan island is uninhabited—except, of course, by deer.

Below: *A troupe of common lionfish (Pterois volitans). These animals sometimes seem to travel in packs, lurking particularly around vertical formations like coral outcrops or shipwrecks.*

WALLY SIAGIAN

Exploratory Dives on Islands North of Bali

We left the port of Benoa, in Bali, at 2 o'clock in the afternoon, after a long wait for port clearance. We had chartered a boat and were bound for the Kangean archipelago, a cluster of small islands that lies 130 kilometers due north of Bali. These were to be exploratory dives, as there is no organized diving in the Kangean group. Our air would be provided by an on-board compressor.

Beneath the Kangean islands are huge reservoirs of natural gas that are expected to supply the energy needs of Surabaya, Indonesia's second-largest city.

Although north of Bali, the islands are part of the province of Madura, Java. Construction on the 130-kilometer pipeline has started, but the Kangean islands are still undeveloped, and as such, an idyllic destination for a small group of divers.

Leaving from eastern Bali our course took us through the Lombok Strait, a particularly fickle stretch of water. We knew the strait was subject to strong currents, but we weren't prepared for the persistent monster our craft had to battle the first night—at sunrise, we were still within sight of Bali. Soon, however, our speed improved, and in another few hours we could see the islands ahead.

Arriving at Sepankur

Three waving men, balancing on what looked from our still distant position like a log, welcomed us to Sepankur island, right in the middle of the group. (See map opposite.) As they paddled closer, we realized they were in a small canoe. The men were hunting sea turtles, and one of the divers still wore his goggles.

Below: *A swarm of purple queens, Pseudanthias tuka, hovers over a very healthy section of Indonesian reef.*

These were homemade: disks of glass cut from the bottom of soda bottles fitted with pitch into sections of bamboo. The strap came from an old inner-tube.

We dropped anchor in a sheltered bay on the north of Sepankur. There were holding nets here filled with thousands of live sea bass, awaiting their fortnightly shipment to Hongkong. This was an unexpected bonus, as dinner was only a matter of swimming over to the nets, and choosing a fish from the keeper.

This was only one of many beautiful anchorages we discovered in the next four days as we sailed from island to island in this shallow sea. The dozens of small islands are inhabited by Muslim fishermen and their families, and in the evenings we would invite them aboard for conversation. The first night we found out about the crocodiles.

Apparently, a fellow villager who was poaching teak logs from the nearby Kangean Reserve had recently been attacked by a very large saltwater crocodile and severely mauled, dying of blood loss before proper medical attention could be found. We were also told that during the rainy season the crocodiles have been known to swim across to Sepankur and enter the holding nets, helping themselves to the Hongkong delicacies.

(Back in Bali a few months later, we heard that the crocodiles had been particularly active since our visit—there were reports of 10 deaths.)

Diving Sepankur

Our first dive at the southwest point of Sepankur was understandably a nervous one. Unfortunately, however, it was disappointingly uneventful. The greater part of the sea here is shallow, no deeper than 25 meters. On our first dive we explored a shallow (8.5 meter) sandy bottom with coral outcrops

Kangean Islands

around which we found blue-spotted stingrays, angelfish, goatfish and butterflyfish.

On our way back to the boat on the Zodiac, we met a fishing boat with more divers. These men were rigged in hookah outfits, with the air delivered by a hand pump on deck. They had had a successful day fishing for trepang and lobster, which they would sell on Kangean, the largest island of the group.

After this uninspiring beginning to our diving trip, we decided to snorkel any potential diving spots first. We headed for Saebus, a green, palm-fringed island surrounded by white sand beaches and inhabited by more friendly fishermen.

We took the Zodiac to the southwest "corner" of this elongated island and jumped in to snorkel the sandy slopes only 20–30 meters off the shore, immediately coming face to face with a group of four bumphead parrotfish, and a turtle.

We rushed back to the Zodiac, geared up, and descended. As we entered the channel between Saebus and Saur, the sandy bottom gave way to a fine white clay which, owing to the half-knot current, produced poor visibility—at times only five meters.

Huge coral knolls, each with dozens of different types of corals, and terraces of table corals were abundant. Again we saw many rays, angelfish, butterflyfish, parrotfish and wrasse. We gently drifted through the canyons made by the coral bommies. Our maximum depth was 20 meters and the gentle current made for an effortless drift back to the yacht.

Diving a Submerged Reef

We dived early the next day before the swell picked up and disturbed the sediment. We had gone back to the submerged reef we had navigated around the day before, on our way to Saebus, between Sepankur and Saur.

This bank reef was approximately 140 meters by 40 meters, and the local fishermen called it a "taka." At low tide it was only a meter below the surface, and extended down to a sandy bottom, ten meters below.

Coral cover was quite good, although we saw some evidence of bombing by the fishermen. As we descended, we frightened away a reef whitetip shark, and saw a large school of snappers. The variety and numbers of fish were amazing—butterflyfish, angelfish, surgeonfish and more.

Pangerang Island

On our navigational maps, the north coast of Pangerang Island was the next spot that had looked like potential diving. The visibility was great—25–30 meters. A sandy bottom at 18 meters rose to coral slopes alive with fish: firefish, blackspot snapper, fusiliers, bream, humphead bannerfish, six-banded angelfish and emperor angelfish. We swam close to a school of large bumphead parrotfish, came across numerous blue-spotted rays nestled under the edges of coral outcrops, and found a medium-sized turtle.

Sakala Island

Our time was running out, but we had just enough left to dive off the island of Sakala, the most easterly of the Kangean group.

Here we were on the edge of the Sunda shelf, and our dive site was once again on a bank, but much deeper than the others. Its top was at 16 meters, and its sandy slopes descended out of sight. This dive was quite different from our previous dives.

Visibility was 20 meters or more, and we saw many pelagic fish, particularly sharks—at least a dozen reef whitetip sharks, reef black-tips, and even a couple of gray whalers. Schools of mackerel and trevally patrolled the area. The reef was flat with few pinnacles, and very little live coral, other than a few gorgonians. We surmised that it was unprotected, and swept clean by currents.

Coming back from Sakala we hugged the coast of Sepanjang, hoping for another quick dive, but we could only manage an exploratory snorkel as the water was too rough to take the loaded Zodiac out. We discovered a sight not unlike our first dives, only much deeper, perhaps 20 meters. The bottom formation was a flat sand terrace gently sloping out of sight, interspersed with low coral knolls at intervals of 20–30 meters. The knolls were alive with myriad reef fish, and we sighted an enormous spotted eagle ray, and two reef whitetip sharks. The visibility here was very good—25 to 30 meters.

A Wild Storm

We left the Kangean islands and headed back to Bali. Our trip was smooth and uneventful until sunset, when we sighted Bali. Then, a strong wind blew up. We didn't reach land until dawn the following morning, 20 kilometers off course and drenched through by the waves that continually swamped our decks. It wasn't until we were well and truly out of the rough water that Eric, our captain, admitted it was the worst storm he had ever experienced in the Lombok Strait.

—*Cody Shwaiko*

Luxury Live-Aboards for Genteel Diving

The 37-meter *Spice Islander,* operated by Spice Island Cruises, represents perhaps the most luxurious dive option available in Indonesia. This large catamaran was outfitted to take small groups of well-heeled travelers through the islands of Nusa Tenggara, and is not a purpose-built dive boat. It features large cabins for two people and five-star meals.

Passengers can dive during the normal one-week cruises between Benoa, Bali and Kupang, West Timor along the northern route, or the one-week return from Kupang to Bali along the southern route. One can also book a two-week round-trip from either port.

Don't expect three dives a day, however. Diving is only one activity in an overall program of sight-seeing and watersports, including snorkeling, waterskiing, sailing, windsurfing, and glass-bottomed boat exploration. There is only a cruise director to handle all clients— divers and non-divers alike.

Dive Charters

Serious divers should sign on for one of the special two-week dive charters. These are held several times a year, and almost always include Komodo, Kupang, Banda and Ambon. On these trips, internationally certified dive masters run the show, and three dives a day are scheduled, with night dives thrown in here and there. Dive sites include "secret" locations, considered among the best in Indonesia, including Penyu Island and Gunung Api, way out in the middle of the Banda Sea.

Lecturers on these dive charters have included Ron and Valerie Taylor, Dr. Eugene Clark (world famous deep sea scientist), and the late Peter Scott (renowned ichthyologist and son of the polar explorer). These are very well-run charters, and space on them evaporates quickly. Contact Spice Island Cruises for information on scheduling and availability (see "Bali Practicalities," page 281.)

When we finally had the opportunity to participate in one of Spice Island's dive charters, we found that it was a world of difference from the casual diving offered during the normal cruises. While there was no dive master on board, the ship took us to excellent locations and allowed unlimited diving. Some of the fanatics actually dove six times in a single day. In addition to this there was a night dive.

Not all dive locations were tops. Since the boat began in Bali, we had some traveling east before we reached the best diving. So we stopped for a couple of plunges a day in the beginning wherever we happened to be.

Island Explorer

There is no question that it is great to bask in the lap of luxury between dives. And the *Spice Islander* is quite well equipped from a diver's point of view. Zodiacs zip divers from the mother ship to the dive sites, which are always nearby. The ship has good compressors, plenty of tanks and weight belts, and some spare BCs. The suiting up area is large, and includes a big freshwater barrel for cameras and other sensitive gear, and a place for a quick post-dive shower.

Above: *The Island Explorer, a luxury catamaran, anchored off Komodo Island.*

The dive coordinator and crew are most helpful with dive preparations and exits. The boatmen in the Zodiacs are alert, and ready to pick up divers within a minute of surfacing.

A few improvements could be made, however. The water level platform, used for getting into and out of the Zodiacs, is right next to one of the exhaust ports. A dose of fumes is not an ideal way to start a dive. And, perhaps most importantly, on our dives during non-dive charter cruises, the dive coordinator did not have a good command of English. He never announced a dive plan. It was the follow-me-if-you-want school of leadership. In his defense, he was very good underwater at finding and pointing out unusual animals.

The great advantage of a live-aboard is that it gives you access to isolated dive sites. Some of the places I dove off the *Island Explorer* can be reached by other means, and they are described elsewhere in this book. Others, however, can at the time of this writing, be reached no other way.

Taka Bone Rate

Spread over 2,220 square kilometers in the Flores Sea south of Sulawesi, Taka Bone Rate is the largest atoll in Indonesia, and the third-largest in the world. Only Kwajalein in the Marshall Islands (2,850 sq. km.) and Suvadiva in the Maldives (2,240 sq. km.) are larger. The 21 small islands of Taka Bone Rate offer nesting areas for sea turtles, which thrive on the huge seagrass meadows.

The atoll rises sharply from the side of a submerged ridge, 2,000 meters down. Once a huge volcano, it has since subsided, leaving a wide ring of coral. The waters inside the atoll are magnificent turquoise, surrounded by the deepest blue imaginable. And they are rich: a survey found 158 coral species here.

Our dive started at 2–3 meters over the reef top, and then we swam out over the outer wall of the atoll. Visibility was well over 30 meters, and the wall seemed to extend downward forever. The growth of coral and gorgonians was excellent, and schools of jacks cruised the wall. In the huge cuts and crevasses in the wall, we saw three giant groupers, Napoleon wrasse, turtles, lionfish and moray eels.

Unfortunately, as an overall dive site, Taka Bone Rate suffers from having been extensively fish-bombed by itinerate fisherman. Only the outer edge of the atoll offers good diving, particularly in the north.

Moyo Island

This large island, blocking the mouth of Saleh Bay north of Sumbawa Besar in west Sumbawa, is surrounded by a beautiful wall that starts at 12 meters and descends to infinity. The wall was cut through by some of the largest crevasses I have ever seen. We saw sharks, giant groupers, moray eels, stingrays, puffers, Moorish idols and large schools of foraging surgeonfish.

Komodo Island

The Komodo area features prominently on Spice Island's dive charters. On a normal cruise, the short trek to see the dragons is normally followed by a half day at Pantai Merah (Red Beach). While snorkeling is excellent there, diving is not so good—although it can get exciting when the tidal currents rip through.

For dive charters, there are several excellent locations in the area, with sharks, large schools of fishes and some of the most prolific invertebrate life found anywhere. We also tried some exploration dives. One of these was my shortest dive ever: four minutes in a washing machine current before surfacing.

Hantu Island

Just off the south-west corner of Lembata Island, a bit east of Flores, is Hantu Island, basically just a rock outcrop about 200 meters from Lembata. Visibility was best during the earliest dives, but there was enough excitement (*very* big fishes) to dive all day.

The island offers a wide, swim-through archway, sometimes a bit difficult when going against the current, but always worth it: we saw several manta rays, some big tuna, schools of jacks and sharks galore. Only Spice Island brings divers here.

Below: *A school of yellow-backed fusiliers* (Caesio teres)*, one of the most common schooling fishes seen in Indonesia.*

KAL MULLER

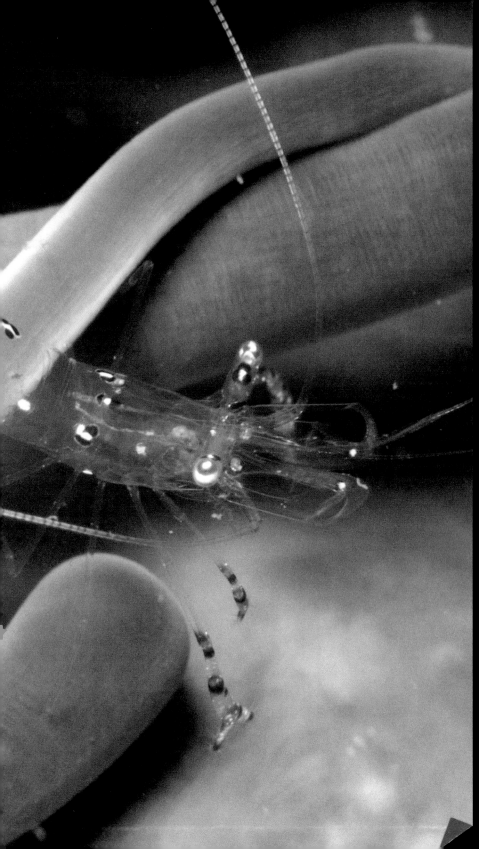

Introducing Nusa Tenggara

The islands east of Bali, running from Lombok in the west to Timor in the east, are called Nusa Tenggara, the "Southeastern Islands." These rough, dry and sometimes volcanic islands support a culturally diverse population of 10 million people.

Stretching 1,300 kilometers east to west, the islands lie just a few degrees south of the equator. One count yielded 566 islands, 246 of which were named and 42 inhabited. (See map page 138.)

The region is divided into three provinces: Nusa Tenggara Barat ("West"), including Lombok and Sumbawa, Nusa Tenggara Timur ("East"), including Sumba, Flores and West Timor, and Timor Timur (East Timor), which is a special province all by itself. The three provinces together cover 82,161 square kilometers, a little over 4 percent of Indonesia's total land area

Diversity of Cultures

Nusa Tenggara remained for the most part outside the great historical changes that swept through Indonesia, including the period of Indianization, from the 8th through the 15th centuries, and the later spread of Islam and European colonialism.

Only Timor had a trade product of interest: fragrant white sandalwood. For hundreds of years, the wood of the sandalwood tree (*Santalum album*) has been used in China, India and the Middle East for incense. The Portuguese were the first Europeans to reach Timor in 1515, but a century later the Dutch took over control of the trade.

Languages in at least 50 distinct groups are spoken by the people of Nusa Tenggara. The populations of Lombok and Sumbawa are Muslim, and because of a relatively long history of Portuguese colonial involvement in eastern Flores and Timor, the people of these areas are Roman Catholics. But in much of the rest of the region—and even in the areas where one of the modern religions holds sway—community religious life takes the form of animism and ancestral spirit worship.

The most spectacular cultural event in the region is the yearly Pasola in Sumba. In this dangerous celebration, the seasonal spawning of sea worms triggers a ceremonial, but very real spear fight between hundreds of mounted horsemen.

Volcanoes and Chalk Cliffs

Two geologically distinct island arcs make up Nusa Tenggara. The northern islands—Lombok through Flores and Alor—are volcanic, with jagged coastlines and rich soil. The southern islands—Sumba, Savu, Roti and Timor—were formed from uplifted coral limestone and sediment, and are dry and relatively barren.

Some 40 volcanoes have been identified in Nusa Tenggara, 25 of which are still active. The greatest eruption in modern history took place when Mt. Tambora, on Sumbawa Island, exploded on April 5, 1815. The blast produced 150 cubic kilometers of ash, far greater than that produced by the better-known explosion of Krakatau in 1883 (See "West Java" page 77).

The largest volcano in the islands is Mt. Rinjani in Lombok, which stands 3,726 meters, one

Overleaf: *An anemone shrimp,* Periclemenes holthuisi, *in the anemone* Heteractis magnifica. *Ambon, Maluku. Photograph by Jan Post, IKAN.*

Opposite: *A snorkeler with a whale shark,* Rhincodon typus. *These harmless, krill-feeding giants can be found seasonally at some sites in Indonesia. Indonesian fisherman call the whale shark ikan hiu bodoh, literally "stupid shark," because the animal has so little fight in it. Maumere, Flores. Photograph by Lionel Pozzoli, IKAN.*

of the highest points in Indonesia. Perhaps the most beautiful of Nusa Tenggara's volcanoes is Keli Mutu in south-central Flores, a trio of craters, each containing a differently colored lake.

The southern islands have no dramatic volcanoes, and are covered in dry scrub. The terrain of parts of Timor looks like Australian savannah. Limestone cliffs and beautiful white beaches ring some of these islands.

Most of the people of Nusa Tenggara, particularly in the western islands, subsist on rice, which is grown in wet "paddies" or *sawah*. But in the drier areas, corn, manioc and various tuber crops are grown. On Roti and Savu, among the driest parts of Indonesia, islanders depend on the drought-resistant *lontar* palm to give them nourishment through the dry season.

Rainfall patterns in Nusa Tenggara are quite complicated, and determined as much by local geographical conditions as by the seasonal monsoon winds. In general, southeast winds from May to July tend to bring wind and some rain to the south coasts of islands, and northwest winds from December to March bring rain to the north coasts. Prolonged rainfall is rare.

Plant and Animal Life

The islands of Nusa Tenggara form a biogeographical transition zone between the animals of Asia and those of Australia. This region is called Wallacea, in honor of Alfred Russel Wallace, a British naturalist who discovered the transition in types of wildlife here when he explored the islands in 1854–1862.

These dry islands are less rich in plant and animal life than the more densely forested islands of Borneo, Java and Sumatra to the west. Offshore, however, the islands teem with life, supporting some of the archipelago's richest reefs.

The region's most famous endemic species is the Komodo dragon (*Varanus komodoensis*), a huge monitor lizard found only on the tiny islands of Komodo, Rinca and a bit of west Flores. These fierce predators are the size of crocodiles.

—David Pickell

Nusa Tenggara

Diving on Lombok's Three Islands Resort

The Gilis

The three Gilis—Trawangan, Meno and Air—just off the west coast of Lombok, are beautiful little sandy islands that have become a favorite destination for sun-bathing, frisbee tossing and other low-impact seashore sports. The Gilis are close to Bali, and are particularly popular with young, European tourists.

Although all three islands are ringed by coral, the diving here is not exactly world class. The reef slope peters out into sand at a maximum of 25 meters, and the visibility hovers around 15 meters, just fair by Indonesian standards. Still, we saw a quite good assortment of fish life, including large trevally and sharks. Mantas are said to make an appearance here as well, albeit not often.

The coral is generally quite healthy around the Gilis, but unfortunately the authorities have not yet been able to put a complete stop to fish bombing. Still, the practice—which has lit-

erally destroyed some Indonesian reefs—is now quite uncommon here.

AT A GLANCE
Gili Islands

Reef type: Coral slopes and sandy bottom, some wall

Access: 15 min by boat

Visibility: Fair, 15 meters

Current: Gentle, occasionally to 2 knots

Coral: Good variety and fair amount, some bombing damage

Fish: Fair to good variety and numbers

Highlights: Reef whitetip sharks and giant trevally at Takat Malang

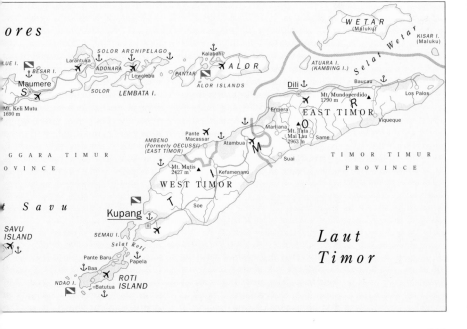

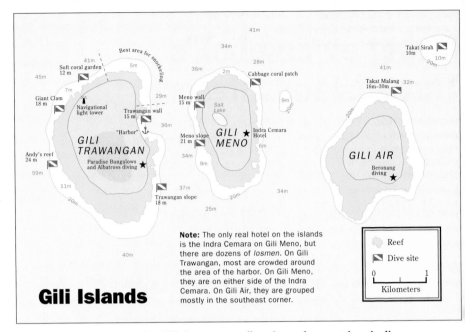

Map labels:
- 41m
- 34m
- Takat Sirah 10m
- 20m / 10m
- Best area for snorkeling
- Soft coral garden 12 m
- 5m
- 41m
- 36m
- 28m
- 2m
- Cabbage coral patch
- 41m
- Takat Malang 16m–30m / 32m
- 45m
- 7m
- 29m
- Meno wall 15 m
- Salt Lake
- 9m
- 20m
- Giant Clam 18 m
- Navigational light tower
- Trawangan wall 15 m
- 36m
- GILI TRAWANGAN
- "Harbor"
- Meno slope 21 m
- GILI MENO
- Indra Cemara Hotel
- 6m
- GILI AIR
- Andy's reef 24 m
- Paradise Bungalows and Albatross diving
- 34m
- 9m
- Beronang diving
- 59m
- 11m
- 37m
- 34m
- 20m
- Trawangan slope 18 m
- 25m
- 40m
- 20m

Note: The only real hotel on the islands is the Indra Cemara on Gili Meno, but there are dozens of *losmen*. On Gili Trawangan, most are crowded around the area of the harbor. On Gili Meno, they are on either side of the Indra Cemara. On Gili Air, they are grouped mostly in the southeast corner.

Reef
Dive site
0 — Kilometers — 1

Gili Islands

The Gili sites are excellent for less experienced divers: most dives were in very calm water, no deeper than 18 meters. During two of our dives the current was slight, and in one it approached 2 knots, a little unsettling perhaps for a novice.

Much of the credit for the good diving here should go to Albatross diving, which pioneered five sites off Gili Trawangan, and Baronang Divers, which takes divers to sites north of Gili Air. Other operators take divers to the Gilis as well, but we recommend these two, which are headquartered on the islands themselves. In 1990 we had a series of really awful dives here arranged by other companies.

The best time to dive the Gilis is from late April to late August. We dove in late September, when the mid-day and late afternoon winds created some fairly choppy conditions—however the water was always smooth during the morning hours. Visibility averaged 15 meters. At the height of the northwest monsoon, late December–late February, big waves discourage all but

the most fanatic divers.

Gili Trawangan

Trawangan is the furthest west, and at 3.5 square kilometers, the largest of the three islands. Some 700 people live here, and the island is very popular with tourists. We found the best diving off the west coast, at two contiguous sites called, by Albatross, Andy's Reef and Giant Clam. (See map, this page.) While there were neither the absolute numbers of fish or species we have seen elsewhere in Indonesia, the marine life here was quite enough to make for interesting dives. And we can substantiate Albatross' claim of (almost) guaranteeing sharks in this area. We saw three reef whitetip sharks in one dive and five in another, with remoras in attendance. We were able to approach them to within 4–5 meters before our bubbles sent them off in a lazy retreat.

Andy's Reef and Giant Clam required just a 15-minute boat ride. We entered at some 100 meters from shore, dropped some 6–7 meters to spreads of staghorn coral, checked out the slope to 24 meters where flat sand began, then spent the bulk of the dive between 18 and 20 meters. Visibility was 15 meters.

The hard coral cover was decent, with tables, small domes and occasional pinnacles. One stretch showed heavy dynamite damage but elsewhere we saw only a few small bombed out spots. There was a very slight current, less than half a knot. Small channels of low coral and sand, cut parallel to the shoreline, were the favorite haunts of reef whitetip sharks. One dive ended conveniently on a coral pinnacle swarming with fish, just 5 meters from the surface. Another offered us a view of dead coral for our usual 3-minutes-at-5-meters stop before surfacing.

At Giant Clam, our guide took us to see the site's namesake, a *Tridacna gigas* more than a meter long. Such a large specimen is very unusual in this part of Indonesia. Our guide said that he has seen manta rays at this site on two occasions. We had to be satisfied with the mundane blue-spotted lagoon stingrays, plus a fair variety of reef fish.

We saw two quite impressive schools of fish: a packed mass of at least 200 blue-lined snappers (*Lutjanus kasmira*) in the shallows, and a bit deeper, a loose gathering of some 15 Goldman's sweetlips. We also saw schools of surgeonfish, small groups of bronze soldiers, and a very friendly cuttlefish.

Soft Coral Garden

This site is a drift dive along the north coast of Trawangan. The reef slopes to 25 meters where the coral gives way to grayish sand. We saw a lone tuna cruising this depth. During our dive, the current swept us along at a very healthy 1.5–2 knot clip.

There is little hard coral growth here, but the many gorgonians, sea fans and lacy soft corals well justify the area's underwater name.

Trawangan Slope

We sampled the east coast of Trawangan at night, drifting along the Trawangan Slope in a moderate current. This was definitely not a dive for beginners. At both entry and exit points we had to make our way from the beach over a low, wide, coral ledge. Boots are essential, and a steadying hand from a member of the Albatross staff was much appreciated. Albatross staffers, who had previously checked the strength and direction of the current, followed our progress from shore, and were helpfully on hand at our exit point.

The reef slope became flat sand at 20 meters, and the fish life—whether asleep, somnambulent or alert—was best at about 15 meters.

Below: *A young clown triggerfish,* Balistoides conspicillum. *This plucky species is among the most wildly patterned fishes on the reef.*

FIONA NICHOLS

Gili Meno Wall

Gili Meno, the middle island, is home to about 350 people, and has the only real hotel of the three, the Indra Cemara. There is no fresh water here, and drinking water must be shipped in from Lombok.

The Gili Meno Wall is on the west coast, and is quite a nice reef, marred only by more than occasional fish bomb craters. The variety of reef fishes justified this site's claim as a good destination for beginning divers—easy and plenty to see.

From a shallow spread of staghorn *Acropora*, the terrain sloped to sand at 20–23 meters. A few isolated coral knolls rose from the slope, each harboring a mini-world of fish and invertebrate life. As one descended along the slope, more massive and thick-fingered hard coral gave way to carpets of soft corals, sponges and gorgonians. Two short sections of the wall were pocked with ledges and overhangs sheltering fish.

Gili Air

This island is the closest to Lombok, and the most populous, with 1,000 inhabitants. The beach circles the entire island, as does the coral, but the west coast in particular is quite barren. Just north of the island, however, at a site called Takat Malang, we had our best dive in the Gilis, better even than the West Trawangan dives. We counted 9 reef whitetip sharks, and 3 absolutely huge giant jacks (*Caranx ignobilis*).

The bottom is flat and featureless, but following some channels down around 30 meters, we found plenty of whitetip sharks.

Takat Sirah, our second dive, was anticlimactic. Some 15 minutes from Takat Malang, we dropped anchor and descended about 10 meters onto a dome-like bank of coral. Staghorn *Acropora*

forms large thickets on this coral bank that rises from the 20–25 meter sandy bottom. We saw anthias and hordes of damsels, but except for one Titan triggerfish, nothing bigger.

Dive Operators

Albatross, on Gili Trawangan, is the best outfit for dives off that island and nearby Meno. We found the guides reliable, knowledgeable and familiar with local conditions. Albatross's Bauer compressor is well-maintained, and while the guides do not use computers, they know their tables. Six regulator and BC sets are available for rent, along with basic snorkeling equipment.

Prior to dives, tanks and all gear are taken by cart the 500 meters or so to the dive boat's anchorage, so you have nothing to lug. Depending on the water conditions and the number of clients, Albatross uses one of three boats—a small speedboat, a long outriggered canoe, and a wide-hulled fiberglass.

All have 40hp outboards and plenty of space to suit up. A metal ladder provides easy exits. Boats and engines are well-maintained, and the helmsmen are capable.

During the short rides to the dive sites, if you like, the crew will assemble your gear for you. Two-way radios keep the boats in touch with the office on Trawangan and, from there, Lombok. The guide uses a buoy on all drift dives. Our boat was always close-by when we surfaced.

Our dives off Gili Air were arranged by Baronang Divers, named after the locally common rabbitfish. Baronang is basically a one-man show, run by Pak Sjahral Nasution. Nasution, a Batak from Sumatra, is a strong, well-trained diver who inspires confidence. Nasution spent 11 years in France, and speaks fluent French. He has a Bauer compressor, 30 tanks and 6 regulator and BC sets.

Little-Explored Reefs around Dragon Island

Komodo

Out of the corner of my eye, I caught sight of a shape moving steadily towards us. A *huge* shape. For a split second I thought: a tiger shark! Fear of this species—aggressive, and a known man-killer—lurks in the subconscious of every tropical diver. Then the apparition veered, displaying its side, decorated by a reassuring pattern of white spots.

This was a whale shark, the world's largest fish, and as gentle and peaceful as a whale. Suspended 20 meters down in the rich seas south of Komodo Island, this glorious, 6-meter-long animal glided by just a few meters from my face mask. Wow. My first sighting of this magnificent species ranks among the greatest thrills I have experienced in more than 1,000 dives in Indonesia.

World class diving

I saw this whale shark while diving in front of a sheer cliff on the south face of Kode Island, which almost fills a wide bay on the southernmost extension of Rinca Island, between Komodo and Flores. The north side of Kode faces a protected channel; the south faces the deep strait between Flores and Sumba.

Even without the whale shark, diving in the area around Komodo and Rinca is among the most exciting in the world. The boat halts just off great cliffs of black basalt, relentlessly pounded by sheets of blue water. Scattered rocks and outcroppings lie just offshore. Some of the pinnacles have an almost eerie look. Black and angular, and undercut at the base by the action of the

seas, they look just like the statues at Easter Island. The surge and swirl of current visible at the surface is a bit daunting, but once you are down about 10 meters, things calm down considerably.

Underwater, the black cliffs continue, cut by huge chasms and in places split into huge, rectangular blocks, like undersea buildings. The black rock provides a dramatic backdrop to the colorful encrusting growth of gorgonians and soft corals, and the rugged terrain is unlike just about any other tropical reef in the world.

Healthy growths of hard corals—boulders, the tangled branches of staghorn coral, table corals and many other forms—decorate the occasional protected coves and the shallow tops of the undersea cliffs. On the sheer drop-offs, and in the caves and crevasses, the rock is covered by a solid mat of bright yellow cup corals, multi-colored gorgonians and countless varieties of soft

---

AT A GLANCE

Komodo

Reef type:	Sloping reef, takas and walls
Access:	Liveaboard, speedboat
Visibility:	Variable, 2–30 meters; usually quite good
Current:	From gentle to wicked (8+ knots), often around 2 knots
Coral:	Excellent at the best sites
Fish:	Very good to excellent
Highlights:	Whale sharks, mantas, great underwater formations, profusion of interesting invertebrates

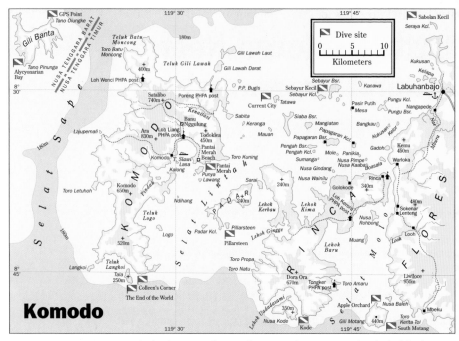

coral. A photographer trying to steady himself with his left hand cannot find enough unoccupied space for even a single finger.

Dragons and Fierce Currents

Komodo island is most famous as the habitat of the Komodo dragon, the largest lizard extant. *Varanus komodoensis* is a varanid or monitor lizard—what the Australians call a "goanna"—an alert and agile predator and scavenger that can reach 2.5 meters in length and 125 kilos. Locally called *ora,* about 2,000 of the dragons inhabit Komodo and about 600 live on Rinca island. There are reports of a small population on Flores.

Komodo village is a stop-over on the ferry from Sape, Sumbawa to Labuhanbajo, Flores, and has become a very popular tourist destination. In the past, tourists would visit this dry, rocky island to watch the great beasts tear apart goats that have been hung at carefully monitored sites by the Indonesian Parks service. Today, the service has stopped the organized feeding, and the impressive animals can be seen from a watering hole blind.

Labuhanbajo is a quiet little Muslim fishing village of about 3,000 people on an attractive harbor in northwest Flores. Because of tourist interest in Komodo's dragons, Labuhanbajo has enjoyed a small boom of late, with more *losmen* being built.

Geologically, Komodo and Rinca are part of Flores, separated from Sumbawa to the west by the Sape Strait. In the middle of the strait, the bottom drops to almost 300 meters. The many islands and relatively shallow seas between Flores and Komodo's west coast mean very fast currents at tidal changes.

By "fast" we mean more than 8 knots, which is a problem no matter how experienced a diver you are. Because of upwellings, it can also get very, very cold. Don't dive here with a super-thin, high-tech, pantyhose type suit. Bring a proper, thick suit. Even a hood wouldn't hurt.

Biological riches

The Komodo area offers just about every imaginable type of

diving, from current-swept sea mounds patrolled by groups of sharks, tuna and other big fish to dead-calm, colorful reefs alive with invertebrates and hundreds of colorful reef fishes. The water temperature varies from a chilly, upwelling-induced 22° C to 30°C bath water. Visibility ranges from a clear 25 to 30 meters in the horizontal plane, to a dismal 3 meters, where clouds of tiny fish and plankton allow only macro photography.

The underwater relief varies just as much: sheer walls, one of which we checked out to 70 meters, and it just kept going; caves, cracks and overhangs; slopes of varying angles; sea mounds; sand and mud bottoms.

The variety of marine life in the Komodo area rivals the world's best. There are deep seas both north and south of the narrow straits running between the little islands, and strong currents and upwellings bring nutrients and plankton, keeping everything well-fed, from tiny polyps right up to the sharks.

Unlike other areas of Indonesia, the reefs around the southern area of Komodo have suffered relatively little damage from the use of dynamite for fish bombing. Much of the area lies within the Komodo National Park, and local fishermen may only use lines and nets.

The shallow reefs between Labuhanbajo and north Komodo, extensively bombed in the past, are in the process of slowly recovering. This damaged sector covers perhaps 15 percent of the Komodo archipelago, and even here steep drop-offs and current-swept points offer good diving.

Exploration Diving

The Komodo area is not well explored, and we picked our dives based on a marine chart, advice from pearl divers and fishermen, and a good look at the above-water structure and water movement. These were real exploration dives, and in most places we jumped into water that nobody had ever dived before. Although this is exciting—and the kind of diving we like the best—it means that you have to take the good with the bad.

Some of our dives dropped us into water churned up by the winds and current, or over reefs that were empty of fish or had poor coral growth. Occasionally we miscalculated the current, and were swept in the wrong direction, over bare sand. One has to make the best of these experiences. There is almost always some redeeming feature.

For example, based on some information from local fishermen and our charts, we chose a lone rock in an island group just north of Rinca for a dive. When we descended, however, we found a sparse reef with very poor fish life. The visibility was okay, but there was nothing to see.

We were about to scrub the dive due to lack of enthusiasm when a flight of at least a dozen stingrays flapped off gracefully when we approached their sandy lair. Then we began to look at the bare sand, and found graceful sea pens, beautifully tentacled cerianthids, and a variety of other interesting animals.

In most of this area, however, particularly in the south, it is hard to go wrong. The whale sharks off both Kode and Motang Islands were the highlights of the trip, but even our typical dives in this area were excellent.

Diving the South

Conventional wisdom has it that December is the wrong time to visit Komodo, but in our experience this is not so. Although the rainy season is well on its torrential way in the western part of Indonesia, around Komodo the skies are usually blue and the tanning sun beats down. The seas are calm at this time, and there is enough of a breeze to cool down sunburnt bodies.

Because of the prevailing winds, in the middle of the summer when most people travel, the southern islands in the Komodo and Rinca area are inaccessible. The seas are just too rough. This is the time to dive the north. But in the winter, when wind and waves are stirring up the water

ED ROBINSON / IKAN

Above: *A spotted eagle ray,* Aetobatis narinari. *Unlike other reef-dwelling rays, these large animals—the wingspan can reach 2.3 meters—swim well above the bottom, and do not bury themselves in the sand.*

at the northern sites, head south.

In December—as well as late November and January—visibility is as good as it can get in such plankton-rich seas, 10–15 meters, and the coral growth and fish life in the south are nothing short of excellent.

Tala Island

Tala, a tiny, angular island in Langkoi Bay, just south of the

southernmost part of Komodo Island, offers several excellent sites. The inner passage between Tala and Komodo proper is shallow, and ripping with current, but the southern point of the island has two adjacent sites: to the west, "The End of the World," a sheer wall of black rock that goes down well past 100 meters; to the east, "Colleen's Corner," a reef slope through rugged blocks of rock leading to a deepwater grove of wire coral.

On our first dive off Tala, the current at the point broke east, so we dropped in and went that way. We descended along a steep slope, full of coral-encrusted chunks of black rock, ending up in a strange forest of spiral whip coral on a sand bottom at 40 meters.

We were immediately greeted by a group of white-tip reef sharks, including one large and friendly individual who acted as if he had never seen a diver before.

We also encountered a turtle, and a very large reef ray finally got tired of our attentions and lifted slowly off the bottom. As we worked our way back up, we entered an area of reef that was very rich with damsels, anthias, butterflyfishes, and other colorful reef fishes.

At a point where a short tunnel led through a coral boulder, a large school of boldly patterned sweetlips gathered. We passed snappers, and several large schools of surgeonfish.

The rocky reef surface was everywhere covered with extensive carpets of bright cup corals. We surfaced near a little cove, graced by an incongruously white beach about the size of an apartment kitchen.

West of the point is a sheer wall of rock, broken up by some nice cuts, overhangs, and sandy shelves down to about 40 meters, and from there on a flat, black plane. Here we saw sharks, rays, morays and rich coral growth in

the cuts and shelves. On one dive, a strange group of pelagic puffers conducted an elaborate series of maneuvers in the open water just off the wall.

The flat areas of the wall are covered with vast fields of orange cup corals, a beautiful effect against the dark rock. On one dive we followed the wall down to 70 meters, and although visibility was good, we never saw the bottom.

Pillarsteen

This site is identified by a tiny pinnacle, just off the southern tip of a small island east of Padar's southern point. In honor of its designation on our old Dutch map we call it "Pillarsteen"; on the British Admiralty chart, it is identified as "Pillar Rock."

The best plan—conditions willing—is to drop of the southernmost point of the pinnacle and head west. The structure here is wonderful, with huge chunks of rock broken up by caves and channels, canyons, and chimneys. The rugged underwater topography continues to 50–60 meters. There are good caves at about 40 meters, and at 16 meters. Visibility, in the winter, averaged about 10–12 meters here.

The fish life is first rate, with large groups of medium-sized schooling fish, such as fusiliers, sweetlips and surgeonfish, as well as sharks, and a big *Mobula* ray. In areas, antipatharian wire corals grow out horizontally 4–5 meters from the rock, and the variety of soft corals and gorgonians here is excellent.

In places we saw sea apples, squat, plankton-feeding sea cucumbers that are unbelievably bright red and purple. This is a world-class site.

Heading east from the point, the structure is not as interesting, but there is a nice shallow area that makes a good safety or decompression stop.

Nusa Kode

Off Kode, we followed the coral-covered ridges down to 50 meters—this was our limit, as we were diving three times a day to explore as many sites as possible. The water was cold, a result of the upwelling of deep water

Above: *The scribbled filefish,* Aluterus scriptus. *This large (to 71 cm.) and weirdly marked fish can occasionally be seen on reefs throughout Indonesia.*

that also gives the area is biological richness. Visibility was 15 meters horizontal.

The shallows were very rich in fish life, particularly plankton feeders. Fork-tailed fairy basslets swarmed around the drop-offs in great orange and purple schools. Pairs of colorful butterflyfish foraged in the reef crannies for small crustaceans or coral polyps. Clown triggerfish, perhaps the most distinctively marked of all the reef fishes, staked out their territory along the face of the reef.

As soon as we got into the deeper waters a couple of white tip reef sharks swung around to give us a closer look. Sharks tend to be wary animals, but these approached us quite closely. Then we encountered a huge grouper, weighing perhaps 90 kilos. Red snappers, with bright yellow eyes, kept a wary distance. A highly esteemed food fish, the snapper has a right to be careful around mankind. Then a green turtle rowed by, soon followed by a huge school of narrow banded batfish, a rare sight.

And of course, at 20 meters, the whale shark. Only one thing kept this dive from being perfect: when the giant cruised by, I was working with my macrophotography set-up. I also dive with a Nikonos and 15mm lens, but I had already used up my film.

(On the next dive, off nearby Gili Motang, I was prepared when a whale shark cruised by. Unfortunately, even though I finned with all my might, I could not close in on the big fellah as much as I wanted. I squeezed off a few shots anyway.)

Gili Motang

The south face of Gili Motang, which sits between Flores and southern Rinca, blocking the Molo Strait, offers sites with good coral growth, nice bommies and chunks of rock, and seasonal pelagics like whale sharks and mantas. But our favorite site is in the north: "Apple Orchard."

This spot is literally covered with the colorful filter-feeding sea cucumbers called sea apples (*Pseudocolchirus violaceus*). These beautiful animals—deep blood-red or purple, and with contrasting white or yellow radial stripes—are rarely seen, and nowhere have we seen so many in one place.

The other invertebrates here—unusual nudibranchs, plentiful soft corals, strange, bright-blue compound stalked tunicates—rival temperate waters in their color intensity.

The site, working west from the tip of Motang's small northern peninsula, offers rich coral growth in the shallows at top, and then a nice rock slope down to about 25–30 meters. Visibility, like most of the area, varies, but is usually around 12 meters or so, plenty for the up-close experience the site offers. This is an excellent place for macrophotography.

The rugged Komodo Plus

In 1992 we did our first dives off the *Komodo Plus,* a 18-meter wooden boat designed to ferry tourists to Komodo Island. At that time, we had six tanks and rented a rough-looking but still functioning compressor from a defunct *trepang* gathering operation in Bima, Sumbawa. Short of lead for our weight belts, we fashioned serviceable weights from steel pipe fittings and bits of chain. Not particularly fashionable, but they worked.

While there are a few local pearl-diving boats taking clients to locations close to Labuhanbajo, most of the best dive spots were pioneered by the *Komodo Plus*, including those mentioned above.

The *Komodo Plus* is a newly built craft, designed and constructed in traditional Bugis style but with an interior fixed up for western tastes. Cruising speed, with a 105-horsepower engine, is up to 11 knots, depending on the mood of the seas, of course. As of this writing, the boat is the only live-aboard currently operating in this area. It is definitely not luxurious—there is no air-conditioning, for example—but it's comfortable enough. The six small double and six single bunks can accommodate a dozen or more people, but for divers, particularly those wielding cameras, six or eight is much better. The boat has two modern shower-toilets. The food is delicious, varied and plentiful.

When we last checked, diving equipment included two compressors, 30 tanks, weights, but only 1 complete set of rental gear. Divers should bring their own basic gear, but with sufficient notice, rentals for six sets can be arranged. Entry consists of a giant leap from the mother ship, and pickup is either by the *Komodo Plus* itself, or by a fiberglass dinghy powered by a 25hp motor.

The boat is operated by Grand Komodo Tours, based in Bali, and you should contact them for booking information (See Komodo Practicalities page 290.) The *Komodo Plus*'s home port is Sape, Sumbawa, because until the airport in Labuanbajo gets lengthened, Bima airport is a far more reliable way to get to the area.

Diving the North

The first dive we made in the area, some years ago, was off Komodo Island's Pantai Merah, literally "Red Beach." This site is very near the old dragon feeding station, and snorkeling and lunch here was a regular stop on most tour operators' schedules.

The snorkeling is excellent, over a healthy, shallow reef. Where we dove, however, was at the reef edge, where the bottom

drops down to 20 meters or so.

When we hit the water, the current was like a raging river. Out of the dozen divers in my group, half came right out and into the Zodiac. My partner and I headed straight down, where the current was a bit less strong and we could grab coral outcrops.

By the time we had the situation more or less under control and could take a look around, we were surrounded by thousands

Below: *The spotfin lionfish,* Pterois antennata, *displaying the eponymous spots on its pectoral fins. Bali.*

of fish of every color and shape, against a beautiful background of corals, gorgonians and sponges. Although worth the struggle, this was not a dive for someone who has just completed a resort course.

We dove in August, but the best weather for diving should be around late March through early May, and again from late September to early November, but there is often current here.

Above: *A pair of firefish,* Nemateleotris magnifica. *Firefish are skittish plankton-feeders that hover in pairs or small groups near the reef bottom. Flores.*

Below: *A pair of fimbriated moray eels, Gymnothorax fimbriatus, curled in their lair. This relatively small (to 80 cm.) moray is primarily nocturnal.*

Banta Island

Perhaps the best site in the North Komodo area, and dive guide Wally Siagian's personal favorite, is "GPS Point," a small bank reef just off the point of the easternmost of Banta Island's two north-facing peninsulas. The reef is most easily located using a Global Positioning Satellite receiver.

The top of this sea mound lies just 6–14 meters underwater, and it attracts lots and lots of fish. This is one of the very best sites to see sharks, and five species can be identified in a single dive. GPS Point is also often swarming with jacks, dogtooth tuna, and big schools of barracuda and surgeonfish.

Unfortunately, this site seems to have been discovered by shark fin hunters. On his last dive on the mound, Wally Siagian found several shark carcasses, sad dead bodies with their fins rudely hacked off. This is a common practice among shark-fin fishermen, who often pull in a shark, cut off its fins, and throw the still living animal back, as there is just not enough space on the boat to keep the rest of the animal. The fins are dried, but there is no easy way to preserve the rest of the animal.

The soft coral growth at GPS Point in particular is excellent, and the entire surface of the sea mound is richly overgrown with sessile invertebrates.

Strong currents often sweep the top of the mound, "gusting" to 3 knots or more. Things settle down around 25 meters or so, but this is not really a beginners' dive. Visibility here is variable, and can drop below 10 meters because of plankton in the water. It is usually clearer at depth.

Banta offers several other sites, including a protected bay in the southwest, "Alcyonarian Bay," which is quiet and rich with interesting soft corals and delicately structured hard corals, and "Banta Bommies"

Sabolan Kecil

Sabolan Kecil ("Little Sabolan") and its partner island, Sabolan Besar ("Big Sabolan") are north of Labuhanbajo, just a bit west of the large island of Seraya Besar.

Just east of Sabolan Kecil, heading toward Sabolan Besar, are two sea mounds, a site called "Wally's Shark Bank." The first—and larger—of the two starts about 18 meters, and continues down to a sand bottom at 35 meters. The second is much smaller, and rises just 5–10 meters from the bottom.

Hard coral cover here is minimal, but there are lots of soft corals, and some very large gorgonians. The reason to dive here, however, is for the fish life, particularly sharks. Work your way down to the valley between the two mounds and pause for a while to watch the white-tips, silver-tips and black-tips.

The most exciting, particularly when the visibility is marginal, are the constantly circling and usually slightly irritated grays. If you don't make too much commotion—there is a large sponge you can hide behind—look out across the sand bottom here, and you will see a very large colony of garden eels.

Like just about everywhere around Komodo, conditions here vary widely, and visibility, especially near the top of the first mound, can be absolutely soupy from plankton. It always clears out as you get deeper, and once the visibility at depth was more than 25 meters.

Tatawa Island

A bit south and slightly west of Tatawa Island is a rocky islet called Batu Besar, literally "Big Stone," the location of a site called "Current City." East of the islet, as the name suggests, currents can regularly top 3 knots, making diving a bit of a headache. If the current is this strong along the East face, however, it is usually fairly calm along the West.

The west face of Batu Besar offers a series of steep drops to about 30 meters, and several nice coral caves. The soft coral cover is very good, and there are lots of fish, including large schools of sweetlips. Sharks are common here, as are turtles, and we have seen very large reef rays here.

Sebayur Kecil

We had another top rated dive off the north coast of Sebayur Kecil Island. Our entry point was 25 meters off a white sand beach. The beach is marked by a clump of three trees, and is next to the highest point on the island.

The reef top sits just 4–5 meters from the surface, and from here a nice wall, covered with corals and sponges, drops to a sandy bottom at 25–30 meters.

Underwater we headed east, then followed the reef as it curved south. Visibility was excellent, more than 25 meters. (Note: We also tried this site in the winter, and found visibility reduced to 1.5 meters). As we began our descent, we met a group of 5 Napoleon wrasse, and schools of striped bristletooth tangs. Reef fishes—puffers, butterflyfish, and others—were plentiful. We also spotted a very large giant grouper, but it quickly hid in a deep cave.

At one point we surprised an absolutely beautiful juvenile pinnate batfish, fringed with bright orange. This bright coloration is thought to mimic a toxic flatworm, affording the young fish some protection from predators. This one was not very confident, however, and peered out at us from a coral niche.

Another interesting site in this area is off a rock outcrop just west of about the middle of Sebayor Besar called Barusa Saha. The bottom here is just sand and coral rubble, but there are more stingrays here than just about anywhere else we have seen. A one point, a synchronized flight of more than a dozen of the animals took off from the sand, a very dramatic sight indeed.

MAUMERE

Diving North Flores After the Earthquake

Until December of 1992, Maumere was universally considered one of Indonesia's best dive spots. But then, disaster struck: an earthquake, followed by tsunami waves and then, shortly afterwards, a cyclone.

Is it still worth it to dive Maumere? Opinions are definitely divided. Several divers, familiar with the area, state that the underwater damage is immense. On the other hand, author, biologist and underwater photographer Rudie Kuiter writes: "Little has changed and in a way it is even more interesting."

Kuiter, who organizes the yearly underwater photo competition at the Flores Sao Resort, and who has done more diving and research here than just about anyone else, continues: "I would say that perhaps 10 percent of the outer drop-offs have suffered bad damage, but little on the coastal reefs."

Yet, contrary opinions abound. And after a relatively short series of dives there in

early September 1993, our own opinion is, at best, divided.

Tsunami, cyclone

The Bay of Maumere, with its two dive resorts, was devastated by an earthquake in December 1992. Some 2500 people died. Tsunamis in some areas reached over coconut trees. The epicenter of the quake was offshore to the north. The worst damage was on Babi Island, just north east of Maumere Bay, where the tsunamis killed well over 1000 people. And if that wasn't enough, a cyclone swept the area a month after the earthquake.

When we visited a year later there was little evidence of damage on land. Massive infusions of aid and rebuilding have wiped out just about all evidence of devastation. There are very few piles of rubble left in town and all along the coast, vegetation does not seem affected. But what about underwater?

Marcos, the local dive master at the Sao Wisata, told me that 11 of the previous 45-odd dive sites were still worthwhile. He is the guide with the most experience in these waters, and I followed his suggestions as to where the best dive spots remained. After all, he sets up the dives for the guests, so these locations are where you will likely be diving.

Pamana Kecil

Our first dive, off the Pamana Kecil, was the best for big fellows. Even before beginning our descent, just as I peered below, two large dogtooth tuna cruised by some ten meters beneath me. We descended in very good 15–20 meter horizontal visibility.

AT A GLANCE
Maumere

Reef type:	Mostly steep walls, some vertical
Access:	Up to 2 hrs by boat
Visibility:	Good to very good, 10–20 m
Current:	Gentle at the coastal sites, can be strong (to several knots) around the islands
Coral:	Good at some sites
Fish:	Very good numbers of big fish at the best sites
Highlights:	Sharks and dogtooth tuna

Maumere Bay

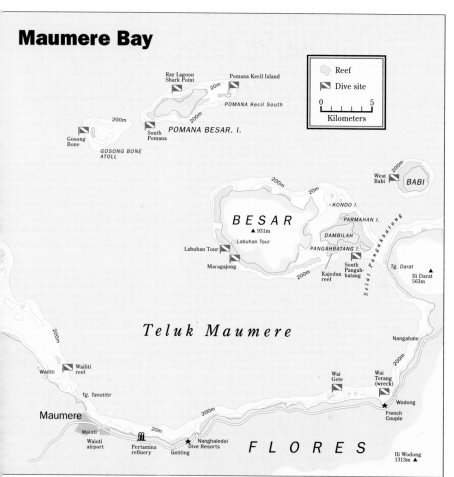

Reef
Dive site

0 — 5
Kilometers

Ray Lagoon Shark Point
20m
Pomana Kecil Island
POMANA Kecil South
200m
200m
South Pomana
POMANA BESAR. I.
Gosong Bone
GOSONG BONE ATOLL

200m
West Babi
BABI
200m
20m
KONDO I.
PARMAHAN I.
B E S A R
▲ 931m
DAMBILAH
PANGAHBATANG I.
Labuhan Tour
Labuhan Tour
Maragajong
South Pangah-batang
Kajodan reef
Selat pangahbatang
Tg. Darat
Ili Darat 563m

T e l u k M a u m e r e
Nangahale
200m
Wailiti reef
Wailiti
Tg. Tanotitir
Wai Gete
Wai Terang (wreck)
Wodong
French Couple
Maumere
200m
Waioti
Waioti airport
Pertamina refinery
Geliting
20m
Nanghaledoi Dive Resorts
F L O R E S
Ili Wodong 1313m ▲

down a sheer vertical wall which bottoms out around 60 meters.

Several white tip sharks checked us out from a respectful distance and a couple of gray sharks looked us over from a bit closer. A large school of good-sized jacks were hardly disturbed by our passage, remaining in a disciplined swirl within a meter or two away. Several white tips were resting on a ledge around 55 meters and I dropped for a closer look. Not far off, a large hammerhead cruised by.

Coming up under the admonishment of my computer, a large Napoleon wrasse headed the other way. At around 30 meters, we spotted a group of a half dozen large dogtooth tuna. Another pair of these toothy

blokes followed us for the rest of the dive, often coming to within 4–5 meters. A guide spotted and grabbed a medium-sized green turtle, showing off the distressed beast until I took his photo so he would let it go.

While the big fish were exciting enough for anyone, the wall was disappointing: little coral growth and few reef fishes. Much of it was covered with a layer of sand, a condition we noted at other dive sites here. Our decompression step was enlivened by one of our guides spotting four small nurse sharks under a clump of large rocks.

Gosong Bone

The day's second dive, near the leading light buoy on Gosong

Bone atoll, was disappointing. There were very few fish, coral growth was poor, and invertebrate life was almost absent. A couple of medium-sized schools of fusiliers and a large, wary puffer were the most interesting fish we saw on the dive.

We checked the vertical wall to 40 meters, especially along the 35 and 20 meter levels, but saw few reef fishes, even inside interesting-looking shallow caves and a swim-through passage. Visibility was quite good, in the 12–15 meter range, but the teeming life we remembered from previous years' dives was gone.

West Babi

Marcos recommended good diving off Babi Island. This struck me as odd, because Babi bore the brunt of the tsunami, and was the single most devastated spot. We dove at the outer edge of the reef fringing the western coast of the island. Visibility was 7–12 meters, and current was slight. We dropped down a wall to about 40 meters (the wall continued to 50 meters) where the visibility improved to about 15 meters. A couple of giant fan gorgonians marked the 40 meter level.

Heading south, we saw a good cover of soft corals and sponges, along with medium to small gorgonians and patches of hard corals. Fish life was concentrated in several areas with good numbers and variety of snappers, along with a few emperors, damsels, parrotfishes and schools of yellow-tail fusiliers.

The underwater structure here used to be full of caves and depressions, and although a few of these remained, most had collapsed. Some areas were covered with the sandy deposit seen on other dives, but by and large, the scenery and life here was pretty much as I remembered from previous years. Only the top 10 meters was dead, and showed little evidence of regeneration. According to Marcos, the other dive spots off Babi have simply been washed away.

Two dives off the south side of the islands blocking northeast Maumere Bay showed Maumere diving like its old, glorious, pre-earthquake days.

Maragajong

At Maragajong we anchored on the reef flat and swam against a fairly strong current over dead coral rubble to reach a vertical, 40 meter wall with good invertebrate cover, especially small soft coral trees and sponges, overhangs and small, shallow caves. Visibility was none too good, fluctuating from 6 to 10 meters. The current gusted to two knots, but most of the time it was a manageable, less than a knot.

The good growth lasted but about 100 meters before an underwater landslide marked our turnaround point. On the way back, rounding an outcrop we were greeted with strong gusts of current and a plethora of fish: large, colorful parrotfish (*Scarus festivus*), a huge cloud of sergeant majors, an unusual school of emperors and the usual fusiliers. The mass of fish life was impressive but the current forced us to hang on to rocks to watch the show.

South Pangahbatang

Another dive to the east, of south Pangahbatang also started in a strong current. But here the reeftop was in top shape, the growth dominated by large leather corals. Visibility was no great (less than 10 meters) and the current gusted to 1.5 knots as we dropped along a slope to sand bottom at 27 meters, the maximum for this dive.

A good-sized white tip shark was curious enough to come in fairly close, but there were too many of us (six) for its careful nature. Other white tips hovered

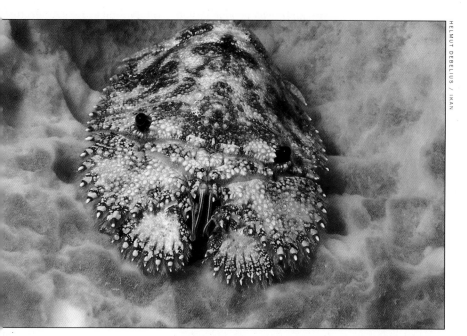

n the current further off along with a couple of 2-meter grays and a black tip. While the shark aggregation was impressive, so were the soft coral trees, among the largest, most colorful and splendid we have ever seen.

We crossed a white sand trough, spotting a couple of good-sized tuna, a crocodilefish, several blue-spotted rays, a Napoleon and a lumbering bumphead parrotfish, perhaps part of a shadowy pack, at the very edge of visibility. At one edge of the sand, a mini-forest of garden eels disappeared during our approach, cautiously slithering out heads and part of their bodies after our passage.

One rocky area was speckled with many small bright yellow sea cucumbers (*Pentacta*), the only place we have seen them in a concentration outside of Kupang. A splendid dive indeed, in spite of the strong finning required by the current.

Wailiti Reef

On the far west side of Maumere Bay, where the full force of the tsunamis hit, diving was said to be good only below the 20 meter level, to where the slope stops at around 30 meters and blends into an almost flat sand bottom. We found the contrary to be true.

Except for a couple of blue spotted stingrays fish life was better further up: fairly good numbers and variety, but nothing outstanding by Indonesian standards. We noticed the common yellow-eyed black snappers (*Macolor macularis*), several *Phyllidia* nudibranchs covered with yellow-tipped bumps as well as a couple of nudibranchs.

The invertebrate scene was dominated by several fairly large gorgonians decorated with crinoids. The dive's highlight was a friendly cuttlefish, which allowed a very close encounter for several minutes before drifting off backwards, gently undulating. The reeftop was in very good condition at snorkeling depths.

Labuhan Tour

Labuhan Tour, off west Besar Island, also offered good shallow

Above: *A slipper lobster,* Scyllarides, *lodged in a small barrel sponge. In these small lobsters, the foremost pair of appendages have evolved into small, flat plates rather than the thorny antennae of the more familiar spiny lobster.*

diving, to about 15 meters. On our way down the vertical wall, we saw a large Napoleon wrasse at about 15 meters, then very little life from 15 meters to the bottom, at 45 meters. On the return to the boat, between 10 and 15 meters, we found two large, colorful nudibranchs and a clown triggerfish, along with a good sized puffer hovering in a cave.

In the top 15 meters, coral

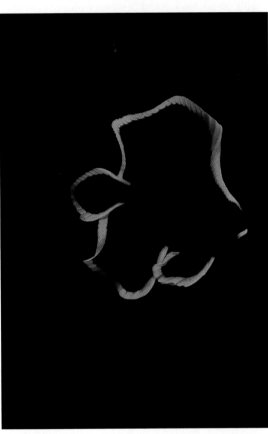

MIKE SEVERNS

octopus. Below, small soft corals grew well, along with sponges and a variety of tunicates, but except for a school of the common yellow-tailed fusiliers, fish life was poor.

We did not try three of the 11 spots which Marcos said still offered good diving. These were Ray Lagoon/Shark Point where, Marcos says, the coral is all gone and there is strong current, but big fish are often encountered. At Pamana Selatan, the topside coral is gone, but the lower levels are worthwhile, Marcos says. This site also often has current, and choppy seas.

Wai Terang

At Wai Terang, where a sunken Japanese freighter from World War II lies close to the beach, the coral growth on the wreck is unaffected, according to Marcos. Some parts of the wreck collapsed, but the fish life is the same as before.

When we dove there before, it was a difficult but excellent spot. Nowhere else have we seen so many lionfish (all *Pterois volitans*), in groups of four, six and even up to a dozen, including some huge old fellas. The wreck lies on its side, almost completely turned over, on a slope. Although depths range from 12 to 24 meters, there is no reason to use up your air on the deeper part of the wreck, as there is more than enough to see near the top. The ship is less than 100 meters from the beach.

The substrate here is a fine, gray sand that produces an instant smoke screen as soon as someone gets a fin within two meters of its surface—this is not a dive on which one wants to invite neophytes still struggling with their buoyancy control. On our first visit, we were in a group of a dozen divers who cut the 10–15 meter visibility to zero within five minutes. For our second dive on the wreck, we came

Above: *A juvenile pinnate batfish (Platax pinnatus). This is a particularly young individual, and it has not yet developed long dorsal and ventral fins. The coloration is thought to mimic a toxic flatworm. Lembeh Strait.*

growth, both hard and soft, was quite good. As we decompressed at 5 meters, a fat saddleback grouper (*Pletropomus laevis*) swam by below. This one must have been of record length.

Other Sites

We stopped at Waigete, on the coast due south of eastern Besar, but we saw little life down to 15 meters, except for a couple of

s a group of three more sea-
oned divers, and carefully mon-
:ored our movements.

The silty bottom restricts
oral growth, and there is none
round the wreck. On the hull
:self, however, we found small
lumps of branching hard coral
rotecting tiny fish. A few
ponges and lots of clams cling
o the side of the hull, along with
unches of grassy whip coral.
everal fat sea cucumbers
rawled along the ship. Juvenile
hree-spot dascyllus (*Dascyllus
rimaculatus*) found protection
ear the beautiful stinging sacs
r acrorhagi of bubble coral, *Pler-
gyra* sp.

Although far from over-
helming, we found the fish life
ere quite adequate. In addition
o the remarkable number of
onfish, a small cloud of anthias
ecorated the top of the lower
ull and fat goatfish rooted in the
ilt. A dozen adult pinnate batfish
ppeared from the wreck, swam
ff into the haze, and then
eturned, as if they had forgotten
omething.

We also found a beautiful little
lue and white juvenile emperor
ngelfish. Several groupers and
rasses wandered in and out of a
irge hole in the hull. The silt
iside, however, prevented
uman exploration.

My dive buddies startled a
irge cuttlefish, and saw two
ioray eels posturing at each
ther with open mouths. Was it
erritorial defense or love?

ea World

)iving in Maumere began in the
arly 1970s, when an Italian cou-
le began operating Sea World.
he original owners gave up the
usiness, which was taken over
y a local Roman Catholic foun-
ation. Sea World still runs dive
iurs, but only about 15 percent
f their clients dive.

Sea World owns a well-main-
iined Bauer compressor, but
ie operation has frequent trou-

RUDIE KUITER
Photographer and Author

Rudie Kuiter's knowledge of Pacific reef fishes
and underwater photography is equaled by few
others. At first, he comes across as a more handsome Charles Bronson, with a long lion's mane of
hair and clear blue eyes. But there is nothing
gruff or closed about this man—he is willing to
share his endless knowledge of Indonesia's reef
animals with peers and beginners alike.

After logging hundreds of dives in Indonesia—mostly in Maumere Bay and Bali—Kuiter
authored *Tropical Reef-Fishes of the Western Pacific: Indonesia and Adjacent Waters*. His interest in
this project began in 1985 with an invitation to survey the fishes of Maumere Bay for the Flores Sao
Resort. In the process, he catalogued over 1,200
species, including a half dozen new to science.
From 1990 to 1993, Kuiter organized the yearly
underwater photo competition at the Sao Resort.

Kuiter's interest in fishes began in 1948, when
at the mature age of five he started catching river
fish with cotton and worm lures in his native Holland. His father built him a fish pond where
Kuiter raised local species. After training in electronics and a two year stint in the army, he
moved to Australia, his home since 1964. Today,
he lives with his wife and children in Melbourne.

Within a month of his arrival in Australia,
Kuiter was already taking a scuba course. A few
years later, he began taking underwater photographs, using a housed Nikon F with a 55
macro. Kuiter's knowlege of electronics, with
which he supported himself until 1979 (and on a
self-employment basis since) has served him well
in putting together his underwater gear and keeping it in working shape in the field.

Today, Kuiter works with 60 mm and 105 mm
macro lenses mounted in an F4. The whole is
contained in a custom housing which he has
modified. He also tore apart two Nikon SB24
flashes—sophisticated units with active links to
the camera's built-in computer and light meter—
and rebuilt them according to his requirements.
It is a one-off, state-of-the-art setup.

According to Alison, Kuiter's wife and the
mother of red-haired Hendrik and blond Steven,
Kuiter's success is due to his unbelievable powers of observation and endless patience as much
as his technical skill. Alison Kuiter was already a
keen diver and underwater photographer when
she met Rudie in 1976.

— *Kal Muller*

bles with their dive boat, and
their rental equipment could
stand to be upgraded.

New rooms have been added
but unfortunately, these are
rather unattractive, motel-style
buildings. The existing beachside cottages are pleasant,
although they certainly need
some fixing up.

My sleep in one was dis-
turbed by a scampering rat (I can
handle that) and a huge spider
by the light switch (not han-
dleable, absolutely horrible). The
food and service at the restaurant
was excellent, however, and the
staff is helpful and friendly.

While Sea World has no
swimming pool, their beach is
much better than at the more
expensive resort next door. They
also have a less restrictive policy
on locals who try to make contact
with the guests, trying out their
limited English.

Flores Sao Resort

The best place in Maumere fo
divers is the Flores Sao Resor
While not exclusively a div
operation, almost half of the
guests are divers. Their boat
reliable, is equipped with a tw
way radio, and staffed by a cre
well trained in assisting diver
There is new scuba equipment i
the pipeline—BCs, regulator
wet suits and dive computers-
plus the expertise to servic
them properly. Divers who re
their gear have it rinsed by th
staff at the end of each day's div
and re-packed the followin
morning.

Guests with their own ge
have large individual concret
tubs at their disposal, with ru
ning water, at the beachside div
house. After rinsing, open woo
en compartments are availab
for drying, next to the tubs, con
plete with hangers for wet suit
An airy well-planned space fo
post-dive equipment care.

Morning departures ar
around 8:30 am, after a very bri
briefing as to dive location an
what can be expected. Marco
who runs the show, speaks goo
English but he does not usuall
accompany the divers. The div
guides, pleasant enough chap
hardly communicate with th
guests, due to their very limite
English. They also stay very sha
low on the dives, keeping an ey
on the divers below.

As the best dive sites are 1
to 2 hours out, it's a long rid
both ways and the seas ca
become quite choppy for th
return trip in the afternoon, wit
spray on the forward part of th
deck where the guests sit. Whil
motoring from the first site to th
second location, lunch is serve
in well-designed plastic contai
ers. Passable but nothing to wri
home about. The second dive
followed by lukewarm tea, coff
and cookies. Try to get an earl
start and cut down on the surfac

nterval (if possible) or return before the wind raises the waves n the afternoon.

Still Worth It?

Is it still worthwhile to travel to Maumere just for the diving? The answer depends on your interests, level of experience, time available in Indonesia and a host of other factors. With other Indonesian dive sites in mind, we would give good marks to only three locations: Pamana Kecil, with its many sharks and tuna which, according to Marcos, are almost always there; Maragaong, which despite the restricted visibility and gusting current, we still recommend for its teeming fish life; and Pangabatang, with its huge soft coral trees, sharks and stingrays. The other sites, however, we would grade just fair to poor.

To balance our relatively negative assessment, we quote from a report by Rudie Kuiter:

"The damage is very localized. Earthquake damage is restricted to the drop-offs facing the epicenter and most coastal reefs show no damage at all. The hurricane affected many reef flats but this is short term ... the place now has a special interest to see how reefs are formed and regrown. It is now obvious that the caves and crevices which Babi is known for were formed by previous earthquakes."

Kuiter's opinion is that by the earthquake's 1994 anniversary a lot of soft coral will be back and in 4–5 years things will be the same as before. It will be interesting to see if this is the case. Scientists have noticed elsewhere that for some reason, reef recovery from natural disasters seems to take place much more quickly than recovery from damage caused by man. In fact, cycles of storm damage in some areas seem to have a relationship to coral diversity, clearing monotypic stands of fast-growing branching corals, and giving other species a chance to take their place on the reef.

For the time being, however, unless you have a special interest in reef succession and recovery, we feel that you should dive elsewhere in Indonesia.

We can still recommend Maumere if you are also interested in visiting the colored volcanic lakes of Keli Mutu and ikat-weav-

KAL MULLER

ing villages. Otherwise, we suggest diving at Komodo or the newly developed sites around Kupang, very easily reached from Bali, along with nearby Roti and the just-opened dive sites at Alor, among the very best in Indonesia.

Above: One of the Sao Resort's dive boats, out on the water in Maumere Bay, Flores.

Magic
Mountain

A Rich Sea Mound Swarming with Sharks

We were a kilometer off the western shore of Sumba Island, anchored in 15 meters of water atop a submarine mound. The green murky water was not at all inviting. The word 'ominous' even comes to mind. This mound is a famous fishing site, but the stories of easy strikes when trolling across the mound are always qualified with a caution about a second run—subsequently hooked fish are invariably eaten by sharks before they can be landed.

With this in our minds, we quickly descended the anchorline, and hugged the bottom as we accustomed ourselves to the 6–8 meter visibility. Following the contour of the plateau in a southerly direction, we dropped

of conflict and carnage, and hosted three obviously well-fed remoras. We were shadowed for an interminable five minutes before they relaxed and left us alone. Either we had moved outside their territory, or they had come to accept that we weren't a threat. With a collective exhalation of relief we turned our attention to the passing parade.

Magic Mountain

We've only rarely witnessed a concentration and density of fish life as found on the site we dubbed Magic Mountain. In other areas of Indonesia, rich fishing grounds such as these would have been exploited and fishbombed to oblivion by local fisherfolk. But Sumba lacks the population demands of western Indonesia; neither does it have much of a fishing tradition.

The technology used here is primitive: fishermen paddle small dugout canoes no further than a kilometer offshore and fish with handheld lines. More organized exploitation is limited to the sporadic visits of turtle or shark boat.

The waters around Magic Mountain are rich in plankton and consequently, in fish life. Schooling fish here are profuse fusiliers, bannerfish, unicornfish and triggerfish literally engulf a diver. Big predatory fish prowled the sea mound, jacks, dogtooth tuna and wahoo. Mackerel scad, smaller jacks, and rainbow runners swept by in schools.

Most impressive were the vast schools of barracuda, which in the daytime hover in groups of hundreds or thousands as a form of protection. Their giant

---

AT A GLANCE
Sumba

Reef type:	Sea mound, some slopes
Access:	15 min by boat
Visibility:	Poor to good, 6–15 m
Current:	Can be strong across the mound
Coral:	Good at some sites
Fish:	Very good numbers of big fish at the best sites
Highlights:	Lots of sharks, huge schools of barracuda, profuse fish life

---

onto a saddle at 20 meters and continued descending along the eastern wall.

There they were: five grey whalers swimming away, and then circling back, and these fellows were agitated! The leader of the pack was a plump, 2-meter-plus beast with a tatooed history

Magic Mountain

Schooling barracudas — 15m

27m

60m — Cave

Barracudas, bigeyes

10m

40m

Lobsters (25m)

8m — Top

Moray (15m)

Canyon (grey whalers)

20m

0 — 50
Meters

Detail at left — Magic Mountain

S U M B A

Tg. Karoka

cousins, the great barracuda, were also around. While fewer in number, they definitely grabbed our attention.

At the top of the chain were the sharks, including the whalers, grey reef sharks, white-tips, and a solitary hammerhead shark.

The mound itself was rich in invertebrate life, including big barrel sponges, table corals, and bright soft corals. Much of the area was covered with orange cup corals, and green trees of *Tubastrea micrantha*. The variety of smaller reef fishes was excellent. We also saw the biggest sea snake we have seen anywhere: more than two meters long.

Sumba Reef Lodge

Magic Mountain can be explored easily in a morning of diving from Sumba Reef Lodge, on Tanjung Karoka about 20 kilometers south of Waikabubak, West Sumba. Sumba Reef Lodge is not solely a dive operation—it is a luxury resort that emphasizes outdoor activities. In addition to diving, horseback riding, trekking, sea kayaking, and deep sea fishing are also offered. But

whatever you do, don't neglect to spend a few relaxing hours in the gigantic free-form pool whose edge leads to the horizon between heaven and the sea.

Meloba Bay

Sumba Reef also offers dive safaris to Meloba Bay, east of Tanjung Karoka. These are an adventure in their own right. Camp is pitched on a expansive white sand beach in a secluded bay with good snorkeling.

The diving in Meloba is not as exceptional as Magic Mountain. We found hard coral only in areas completely protected from the walls of water generated by the southeast tradewinds in July and August. The typical underwater profile was silty clay bottom covered with tough leather corals and coralline algae. The visibility was generally poor, and the bottom is quite shallow.

The pinnacles at the entrance to Meloba Bay were the exception to the norm. Here we found good visibility, depths to 30 meters, wonderful craggy rock formations, and lots of fish.

—*Cody Shwaiko*

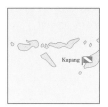

Kupang

Big Fish, Top Service, and Great Night Dives

Kupang, located near the southwest tip of Timor Island in Indonesia, has started to acquire a well-deserved reputation in diving circles the world around. Other places in Indonesia also offer great diving, but in Kupang the business is well-run by two Australians, and there are none

of the language problems that can get in the way elsewhere.

The two men are well qualified. Donovan Whitford holds a PADI instructor's license, and his father is a dive-master. They have dived the area for the past four years, establishing dozens of proven dive locations, all within an hour's boat ride from Kupang. The operation has also pioneered Roti Island, as well as Alor.

While there is no specific dive "season" here, wind conditions put some of the locations out of reach from mid-January to early March and sometimes in the

June to August period. Visibility varies considerably, usually from 5 to 15 meters, but the suspended planktonic matter sustains a great diversity of both invertebrates and fishes. Little and medium sized chaps support the big fellas: sharks, Napoleon wrasses and big groupers (cod to Aussies), along with mantas, other rays and turtles.

It is very likely that you will see one or more of these on any one dive—and, with a bit of luck, all of them in a dive series. If the heavens really smile on you—as they did once on us—you could, on a single dive, see manta rays and a ride on a whale shark. No guarantees on this one, of course.

Diving in Kupang

The Whitfords had developed 22 dive sites when we last visited in mid-1994, some of which are worth several repeats. Plans were to check out other spots, including sites where there are Japanese ships sunk by the Allies during World War II.

At least one of these wrecks lies in Teluk Pelikaan (Pelican Bay) on Semau Island. This is a Japanese fuel barge that was sunk by Beaufighters out of Drysdale on April 6, 1944, exploding in a "great ball of fire" according to one of the pilots. Visibility around the wreck is limited, but it is enough to see the encrusted barge. So far, nobody has been brave enough to enter.

For a variety of practical reasons, dives from Kupang are restricted to the area around the harbor, the northeast coast of Semau Island, and Kera Island, a

---

AT A GLANCE
Kupang

Reef type: Slopes and walls, some nicely pocked with caves

Access: 45 min by boat from Kupang

Visibility: Variable, 5–15 meters; rarely exceeds 12 meters

Current: Gentle or none; occasionally to 2 knots

Coral: Generally good coverage and varieties

Fish: Generally good numbers and varieties, particularly big fish

Highlights: Night dives at Donovan's Delight were fantastic; no day dives without at least one big fish

---

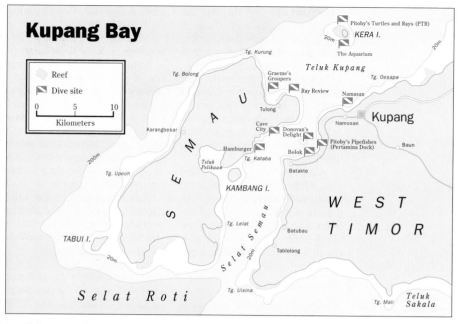

Kupang Bay

Reef

Dive site

0	5	10

Kilometers

Pitoby's Turtles and Rays (PTR)

KERA I.

20m

20m

Tg. Kurung

The Aquarium

Teluk Kupang

Tg. Bolong

Graeme's Groupers

Tg. Oesapa

Ray Review

Namasan

Tulong

Kupang

Cave City

Donovan's Delight

Namosan

Karangbesar

Hamburger

Bolok

Pitoby's Pipefishes (Pertamina Dock)

Baun

200m

Teluk Pelikaan

Tg. Kataba

Batakte

Tg. Upeoh

KAMBANG I.

W E S T

Tg. Lelat

Batubau

T I M O R

TABUI I.

20m

Tablolong

S e l a t   R o t i

Tg. Uisina

Tg. Mali

Teluk Sakala

---

low-lying, sand fringed island north of Kupang (see map above). It takes about 45 minutes to reach any of the locations on the *Pitoby Sport,* a beamy 13-meter wooden craft powered by a 40hp outboard. The boat has a high tarp roof, and tanks are stored in an out-of-the-way spot. The boat draws very little water, so there could be a bit of spray bouncing around, depending on the wind.

The *Pitoby Sport* picks up clients at Tenau, the main harbor, at the bottom of a wide flight of stairs. Getting on and off can be a bit tricky somtimes, but there are always plenty of helping hands. The crew will get your dive bag aboard. On the way to the dive site, divers can either sit in the shade under the awning, or work on their tans out in the bow area. Fishing gear is usually available, if you want to troll on the way to the dive site.

Pulau Kera

Pulau Kera ("Monkey Island"), circled by a brilliant white sand beach, lies at the entrance of Kupang Bay. Pitoby's has a long-

term lease on this little piece of paradise, and plans on building cottages here, and making it the base of their water sports operations, which include, in addition to snorkeling and diving, windsurfing, waterskiing, surfing, fishing and sailing.

"The Aquarium," a site off Kera's south coast, offers good diving, particularly for beginning divers. A shallow (2 meters) offshore sandbank ends at a coral wall that extends to about 12 meters before becoming a gently sloping sand bottom. Visibility varies considerably, but there are fair numbers and varieties of reef fish here.

"PTR," short for Pitoby's Turtles and Rays, is a site on the far side of Kera, and offers just what its name suggests. With the boat anchored offshore, we dropped some 20 meters and landed at the edge of the scattered coral formations that slope up to the island. We were right where the sandy bottom began in earnest, and it sloped gently into infinity. As soon as I neared the bottom, a startled blue-spotted stingray flew off, the first of at least a half

NOTE
Freshwater Caves

Pitoby's also offers diving in large freshwater caves just behind the ferry terminal at Bolok. (Two of four caves have been explored.) The water is crystal clear and wonderfully refreshing, but good buoyancy control and careful finning are required to keep from turning the water into soup. Depths are to 15 meters, and usually divers are taken 50 meters from the entrance.

—Kal Muller

dozen we spotted during the dive. We also discovered a very large black-spotted stingray, (*Taeniura melanospilos*), wedged under a maze of hard coral.

Some four or five turtles shot out of our way as we worked along at 20 meters. Then, just off our flight path, we caught another turtle, this one napping, with two striped remoras firmly attached to its back.

About halfway through the dive, a school of perhaps a dozen bumphead parrotfish rumbled in formation at the very edge of visibility. Our safety stop took place along a colorful spread of corals dense with small reef fish, right at the 5-meter level.

Semau Island

"Graeme's Groupers" lies about 100 meters off the beach at Semau where Teddy's and the Flobamor's cottages are located. The name comes from the unusual number of varieties of groupers (cod to the Aussies) that inhabit this reef. The reef extends from the shore in a very gradual slope, reaching 4–9 meters before the edge of a coral wall, which drops sharply to a sandy bottom at 30 meters.

Much of the hard coral growth here has been destroyed by extensive fish bombing here, but soft corals are present in fair numbers. The wall is pocked with shallow depressions and caves, some reaching back a meter or two.

True to the site's name, we identified a half-dozen species of groupers: blotchy, coral, flagtail, polkadot, saddleback and whitelined. These were all 20–30 centimeters, with an occasional fat 40-centimeter specimen. Cleaner wrasses worked their stations along the wall, servicing the groupers as well as longnose emperors, black-and-white snappers, sweetlips, dogface puffers and roundfaced batfish. We saw several large emperor and six-banded angelfish. Visibility never exceeded 10 meters.

"Ray Review" is a short distance east of Graeme's Groupers. The reef here is also wide and flat, dropping unevenly to a slightly sloping sandy bottom at 22 meters. Several detached coral pinnacles jut upward. Close to the sand bottom, we saw a half-dozen blue-spotted stingrays, which appear first as a pair of eyes, the rest of their bodies covered with fine sand.

Few fish inhabited the area except for schools of black triggerfish. We also swam over a small forest of garden eels (*Heteroconger*) which disappeared at our approach.

"Cave City" is on the east coast of Semau, around the northeast tip and past the skeleton of the Japanese pier. The site is a coral wall more than a kilometer long, with at least a dozen good sites. The caves are the distinguishing feature here, some reaching back more than 5 meters. The reeftop, covered by 2–5 meters of water, drops off very close to shore to a sandy bottom, 20–40 meters below.

Hard coral growth is good and we saw lots of gorgonians, some of them reaching several meters across. Soft corals grew in white tufts like wind-blown snow. On the very deepest sections of wall, we encountered bushy growths of antipatharian black corals.

In one cave we saw a school of yellow ribbon sweetlips, in another a large hawksbill turtle and in others several species of groupers. Some of the animals swam back to the far dark corners of their homes before we could make an identification. Smaller caves were guarded by detachments of soldierfish.

We spotted two large, but skittish Napoleon wrasse (they are frequently sighted here). The waters near the wall were dominated by schools of black triggerfish, and we also spotted several gaudy clown triggerfish and small Picasso triggers. The six-banded angelfish we saw here were among the largest and fattest we had ever seen. As we ascended, we crossed paths with a school of tank-like bumphead parrotfish.

Visibility in the shallower waters was reduced to almost zero by hazy clouds of tiny fish. Below 20 meters, it was about average for this area.

Donovan's Delight

While flying into Kupang a while back, Graeme Whitford noticed a large, relatively shallow area in the Semau channel, fairly close to the main port. This looked promising to his trained eyes. His son Donovan embarked on a series of exploratory dives here, and was delighted after each one.

The site, marked by a navigational buoy, is now featured in all of Pitoby's dive series, and makes an especially good night dive. This is fine, fascinating diving indeed—with the usual caveat of poor to fair visibility. In our five dives here, it never surpassed 8 meters, and once it dropped to a really miserable 2–3 meters.

"Donovan's Delight" covers an irregular, oval shaped rise, more than 200 meters along its long axis. The reef top is 3–9 meters below the surface, and a vertical coral wall partially encircles the rise, dropping to a sandy bottom at 25–40 meters.

A fair variety and number of hard corals cover the top of the dome (there is some fish bomb damage, but it is not extensive) and soft corals are plentiful. The wall features several shallow caves.

During several dives here we saw sharks, both reef whitetips and reef blacktips, a number of large hawksbill turtles, and groupers up to 90 centimeters. Blue-spotted lagoon rays hide under table coral in the shallows or in the sandy bottom. Towards the ragged bottom of the wall, we saw clusters of sweetlips, emperor fish and puffers.

Groups of 10 to 20 roundfaced batfish patrolled the walls, and pairs of very large six-banded and blue-girdled angelfish wan-

Below: *A common lionfish (Pterois volitans) taking refuge in a sponge. Note that at least eight differently colored crinoids grip the edge of the sponge.*

HELMUT DEBELIUS / IKAN

Above: *A crown-of-thorns starfish (Acanthaster plancii). Outbreaks of this large, voracious coral-eating animal have occasionally proved ruinous for entire reefs. Do not handle these starfish, as their thorns can cause a toxic reaction.*

dered the reef face. Lionfish hovered near the top of the wall, including black morphs of *Pterois volitans.*

The wide, relatively flat reef top was ideal for safety stops. Several times we saw cuttlefish that would allow us to handle them gently. Large clusters of bright red anemones held their aggressive little guests.

There was, however, a strange absence of butterflyfish and damselfish here. In several areas we found small (5–8 cm.) bright yellow feather sea cucumbers (*Pentacta*), spread in a carpet over several square meters. We have seen these colorful animals in only a few other places, and nowhere in such numbers.

One afternoon dive, thanks to Donovan's keen eyes, we spotted more than a dozen species of nudibranchs.

Night Dive at Donovan's

A night dive at Donovan's Delight was one of the most fascinating hours of my life. I had hardly reached the shallow reef top and Donovan was already playing with an indignant puffer. Then he spotted three Spanish dancer nudibranchs (*Hexabranchus*), one of them with a silvery diamond pattern on its back.

The crinoids were hard at work, waving their feathery tentacles through the water. Following us around was the longest trumpetfish I have ever seen.

This fellow was so intent in participating in our fun that he kept bumping into me.

Sea urchins ambled around, some looking like World War II mines, others fuzzy balls, and still others with long, banded spines. Basket stars, creeping little bushes with agitated branches, clung to the high ground on coral and sponges, wherever there was a bit of room.

Ever alert Donovan spotted a large hawksbill turtle, tugged the sleepy giant out of its lair and tried to go for a joyride—but by then our turtle was wide awake and shot away at breakneck speed. In contrast, several cuttlefish and a squid were in a playful mood, allowing us to gently pet them. Our attentions caused one to change colors unbelievably fast, from a brownish red to barely spotted white and back again.

A fimbriated moray eel (*Gymnothorax fimbriatus*) nestled in the crack of a spread of red sponge, and the lionfish were out in force.

A great non-stop show all around—the only things we missed were the slipper lobsters and large bailer shells often seen on night dives here. Topside, a couple of swigs of Glenfiddich capped my best night dive ever.

Pitoby's Pipefishes

Just 10–15 minutes by boat from Donovan's Delight is Pitoby's Pipefishes, a shallow dive off the Pertamina dock. The very irregular coral slope drops to 12–14 meters, but most of the action is above 10 meters. In addition to the pipefishes, we saw a good variety of small reef fish. A fine dive for beginners.

The namesake pipefishes are fascinating little creatures, much like seahorses with the kinks ironed out. We saw several network pipefish (*Corythoichthys flavofasciatus*), and several scribbled pipefish (*C. intestinalis*) in just 4–6 meters of water.

Manta Rays and still Little-Explored Diving

The western tip of Roti offers a fine underwater show. Walls of bright soft corals grow amid the rugged limestone formations of the island's coast. Fish life, particularly large and medium-sized species, is very good. Only the restricted visibility we encountered (8–10 meters) keeps the site from being world-class.

Roti is a small, dry island just off Timor's southwestern tip. In some areas dramatic white cliffs line the rugged coastline. Perhaps 100,000 people live here, tending small farms and fishing. The staple food of Roti—and Savu, further west—is the rich sap of the draught-resistant *lontar* palm, which is made into syrup, sugar and even a mild toddy.

The island capital is Ba'a, a town of 3,000 midway along the island's northern coast. (See map page 168.) Here, passable accommodations are available for visitors. Graeme and Donovan Whitford of Pitoby Water Sports in Kupang, the pioneers and only operators here, took us to Roti.

Batu Termanu

Batu ("Stone") Termanu is just a half-hour northeast of Ba'a. We puttered along coastline of mixed beaches and rugged chunks of raised coral in an open fishing boat, 8 meters long and powered by a 25 hp outboard. There are two sites at Batu Termanu, each marked by differently shaped stone pinnacle.

The closest and largest one, with a tip of sculpted limestone with two holes cut through it, is locally dubbed Batu Termanu Mai, the "female." Some 15 minutes further east, Batu Termanu Jantan, the "male," is less impressive: a low, rounded rock with a detached, oval pinnacle. At high tide, only the pinnacle shows.

The vertical rock face of "Lady" Termanu continues a few meters underwater, and then a flat reef begins that slopes gently to a wall just 100 meters offshore. This wall drops vertically to 25–27 meters. It is almost completely covered with bright and pastel soft corals, yielding at the deeper end to green soft corals and stands of black coral.

As we began to explore the small caves in the wall, we were distracted by a large school of surgeonfish, followed by a quite large shark, heading down the wall. Just as the big fellow disappeared, a smaller reef whitetip appeared out of the gloom. He would not allow us to get within four meters, but he stuck around for at least 10 minutes.

Fish cascaded down and up the wall: schools of surgeonfish and unicornfish, groups of pinnate batfish, and big parrotfish.

AT A GLANCE

Roti

Reef type:	Slopes and drop-offs, often amid rocky outcrops
Access:	30 min to 4 hrs from Ba'a
Visibility:	Poor to fair, 8–10 meters
Current:	Generally mild
Coral:	Good growth and variety, particularly soft corals
Fish:	Variable; sharks and rays relatively common
Highlights:	Manta rays and good wall at Batu Termanu

Yellowtail fusiliers flashed by traveling horizontally. Below, sweetlips hung in small groups, and a large barracuda shot off into the darkness. Prides of lionfish—including a group of nine!—patrolled the reef wall. We drifted along the slight current, one-half to one knot, until our air was finished.

The seaward dive path from Batu Termanu Jantan—Christened "The Cathedral" by the Whitfords—leads through narrow passages between rocky outcrops. The bottom deepened gradually to 25–30 meters, the limit of our journey.

A reef whitetip shark monitored out our progress, but the highlight of the dive was a school of blackfin barracuda (*Sphyraena genie*). Discovered in the shallows, these 50–75 centimeter fish were almost friendly. During the deeper part of the dive, we saw two schools of jacks. We barely noticed the groupers, lobster and rainbow-hued parrotfish.

Termanu beach

The Whitfords have also pioneered another dive in the area of Termanu Mai, beginning from the beach. The reef starts close to shore, and soon one encounters a series of craters, 2–4 meters across, and 5–6 meters into the rock. The current turns these into swirling funnels, which are sometimes full of fish trapped by the outgoing tide. Further out from shore, great chunks of rock covered with soft corals lead to the near side of Termanu.

In this channel, at around 12 meters, I saw the grand spectacle of two manta rays, at least two meters across, gliding overhead. Later, at similar depth, a single manta cruised by overhead. Gently flapping his wings, he banked directly overhead. As he reached the limit of visibility, around 8–10 meters, he turned sharply and made another overhead passage, just two meters away. Two little remoras stuck to his smooth, wide belly. Donovan Whitford, who has dived here in April, May and August, has seen mantas every time.

Ndao Island

On a special arrangement basis, Pitoby's offers a two-day, one-

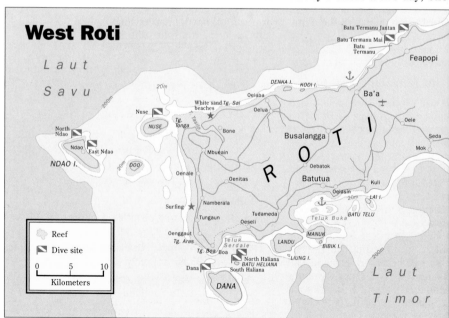

night trip from Ba'a to Ndao Island, a tiny island off the tip of Roti about 4 hours by boat from Ba'a. This is neither for fanatical divers, nor for tourists hungry for cultural events. It is a casual mix of interesting diving and contact with friendly people who seldom see foreigners in their midst.

Ndao Island is a dry, poor island that is the home of itinerant silver and goldsmiths. These men spend from March to November in Roti, Sumba, Flores and Timor, making jewelry out of old coins with simple tools.

We made the trip in August, but we recommend that you do so between September and May, as the June–August period has the strongest winds and worst waves. It was unseasonably calm when we went, but we were still drenched with spray on several occasions. We followed Roti's coast, past Nuse Island, and then out to the pristine beaches of Ndao. We checked in with the local authorities and walked around the village of thatch- and tin-roofed huts, all laid out on neatly swept sand.

Diving Ndao

Our marine chart showed a contour line at 50 meters just off Ndao's deserted northwest coast, so we decided to try a pioneer dive there. Despite the chart, the underwater profile turned out to be quite different. We descended to about 8 meters, then swam far out on a strong current over a very slight slope. The bottom reached only 25 meters, with detached outcroppings of coral rock covered with hard and soft corals, and the usual complement of reef fish. A couple of small reef whitetip sharks vanished as soon as we saw them, and a school of ringtail surgeonfish (*Acanthurus blochii*) drifted by. A large group of longnose emperors followed us for much of the dive. Visibility was poor, just 7–8 meters.

Our marine chart proved wrong again on our second dive, just in front of Ndao village. Instead of an 8 meter bottom, dropping very gradually to 16 meters, we went right down on a steep sand slope to 35 meters. The slope just kept going into the gloom. After a few patches of seagrass, the bottom was bare sand. Scattered here and there we saw cerianthids and strange-looking sea urchins sheltering tiny fish in their spines. In the shallows, we saw sea pens and several fat, long worms. Neither I nor my buddy had ever experienced such a dive—almost pure sand below, and menacing gloom ahead and on either side.

An Evening on Ndao

As dusk settled on Ndao, we bucket-bathed in the back of our host's house, then settled in to enjoy our home-stay. A supper of rice, vegetables and salted fish was followed by singing and dancing in the living room. An elderly gentleman played the *sasando,* a Rotinese string instrument made from bamboo and folded *lontar* palm leaves. While we were drinking *tuak,* the juice of the *lontar* palm, three little girls danced for us, decked out in beautiful wrappings of locally woven *ikat* cloth.

Although the people of Ndao originally came from Sawu, much of their culture—weaving styles, the *sasando*—has been borrowed from their near neighbors, the Rotinese. Very little of original Ndao culture is left, except gold and silver smithery.

After a night in very comfortable beds, complete with (unnecessary) mosquito netting, we woke to hot coffee, followed by a breakfast of rice, vegetables and chicken curry. We left early on the outgoing tide.

Nuse Island

Our boat cruised past Doo Island, deserted, and lined with

Above: *A terminal phase pale-nose parrotfish,* Scarus psittacus, *asleep in its mucous cocoon. This covering, which is secreted from the skin, is thought to block the parrot- fish's scent from night predators. Mapia atoll, Irian Jaya.*

white beaches. We decided against a dive there. Continuing to Nuse Island, we motored past a small hamlet of Ndao fisher- men and anchored off the north coast to try a dive. Just then we saw a manta ray breaching. Our crew said the large rays are often hooked by local fishermen.

Things didn't look too promis- ing at first, however, as we dropped to scattered patches of coral. We went along a slope to 40 meters, where all life ceased. Returning to shallower depths, and more life, we spotted a large, light brown stingray keeping a wary eye on us. We approached carefully, however, and got to within an arm's length before it slowly drifted away.

Just about then my buddy grabbed me and pointed up. Holy cow! A huge manta ray hovered over us, turned slowly, and, with exquisite grace, flew out of our range of visibility. We came up in ecstasy, ready for the long tan- ning haul back to Ba'a.

Batu Heliana

The Whitfords have also pio- neered some dive sites off south- west Roti, the southernmost extremity of Indonesia. We dove off both sides of Batu Heliana, a jagged pinnacle rearing up from the sea a short (15–20 minute) boat ride from Oeseli village. The sheer sides of the rock unfortu- nately do not continue underwa- ter. There is no wall, only slop-

ing bottom, well-covered by soft corals. Here and there, detached coral blocks—at 10–15 meters— support good populations of reef fish and invertebrates. We saw two small reef sharks, a turtle and a stingray.

Off the southwest face of the rock, the only large fish we saw was a single golden trevally. We descended to 20 meters, but saw nothing of interest. The visibility was lousy, less than 8 meters. In the shallows, we discovered a good number of *Tridacna* clams, and the largest spreads of carpet anemones we had ever seen.

As we motored away, the engine's racket flushed out hun- dreds of flying foxes. These large fruit-eating bats are the only per- manent inhabitants of the "island." Birds nest here as well, but only seasonally.

Large Dana Island has an inviting beach, but no one lives here. Its inhabitants were massa- cred several centuries ago, and their spirits keep out everyone except occasional deer hunters (the island teems with deer.) We worked our way around the island's northwest tip to a spot beyond the big waves, which broke in perfect tubes, enough to make any surfer drool.

We dropped 8 meters to the reef top, which was cut through with narrow surge channels. The reef sloped to 12 meters, then dropped sharply to 25 meters. Visibility was about 10 meters.

We saw a spotted grouper, a hawksbill turtle, and a 1.5 meter reef whitetip shark. Along the wall we saw a school of a dozen or more pinnate batfish, and a couple of large schools of fusi- liers. A shadowy mass of sur- geonfish, distinguishable only by the silhouette they cast, passed by at the limit of visibility. On other occasions, the Whitfords have seen huge specimens of almost every kind of tropical fish here, all in excellent visibility. On this day I was not so lucky.

Eastern Indonesia's Dream Dive Sites

Experienced sports divers, a tough lot to satisfy, dream about this. Whence the site name: "Kal's Dream." We had it right in front of us, with ringside seats. Four good sized grey sharks circling us, then cruised back-and-forth while a black tip and a white tip made a brief appearance. At the same time two groups of tuna, each following by an absolutely huge leader cruised by just overhead, drifting off, returning for a closer look, then coming back again.

To one side a mere few hundred jacks swirled around our dive guide. A small group of yellowtail barracuda were dwarfed by one well qualified for its name of "great" barracuda. None of us had ever seen so many big fishes at the same time. We hung on in the gusting current, living a diver's dream.

Welcome to Alor, a small island north of West Timor, at the end of a little archipelago east of Flores. The dive locations here, just pioneered, are absolutely world class. But for those divers who are concerned about creature comforts, better wait while. There is nothing here even close to star-rated accommodations, and it's going to be a long time before a luxury hotel rises on the shore of the long, narrow bay where Kalabahi, the district capital, is located.

And the food is also strictly Indonesian: no burgers, juicy steaks or junk food. The dive boat, rented locally, usually runs native passengers and freight between nearby islands. For those not adapted to third world travel conditions, the toilet—a hole in the planks at the stern—is a very bad joke. Worse are the occasional gusts of diesel fumes from the rough engine, usually timed to clear out your lungs, just before a dive. Never mind. The roof is big and warm, a perfect place to warm your body and soul between plunges.

Alor is still pretty much in the middle of nowhere, and getting there takes an effort. The three scheduled weekly flights from Kupang, the district capital, are often cancelled. The throbbing ferry is reliable, but takes 14 hours to get there from Kupang.

The bright spot, of course, is that there won't be any crowds. The pioneer, and currently the only operator in the area is Pitoby Watersports, based in Kupang. Based on solid bookings, Pitoby's sends out a compressor and tanks on the ferry, and organizes one of the small flights for their clients. Pitoby's is not a large outfit, and as they also run diving around Kupang, and to Roti, advance bookings are essential.

AT A GLANCE
Alor

Reef type: Banks and walls

Access: 15 min–2 hrs by boat

Visibility: Generally good, 12–20 meters

Current: At some sites, 2 knots or more

Coral: Very good coverage and varieties

Fish: Superb numbers and varieties, particularly big fish

Highlights: Sharks, giant grouper, sheer richness of fish life

The Alor locations—actually a series of sites in the Pantar Strait between western Alor and smaller Pantar Island—were pioneered in April 1993 by Pitoby's Donovan Whitford, who took a small group there from Perth, West Australia. Graeme, Donovan's father, had looked over the place when planning a pearl farm and thought that diving could be excellent. The Perth group, which had dived with Pitoby's in Kupang and Roti, wanted to try a new location on their island hopping trip to Bali. Alor was their first stop. Boy did they get lucky.

Kal's Dream

All the hassles are forgotten when you finally make the giant leap into the underwater world. At The Dream, aside from the big fellows, we also saw an incredibly huge mass of fish, either schooling or in loose aggregations: fusiliers, triggerfish, unicorns and surgeons and at least three species of snappers, all in the 40–70 cm range.

This giant, species-rich mass moved around the quiet leeward side of the sea, dominated by the big fellows. Aside from an unusually large concentration of large, eye-catching imperial angelfish, we did not even bother to look at the usual reef fishes.

What we did notice was that the surfaces of the substrate were completely covered with invertebrates, so grabbing a handhold in the current—which gusted up to two knots—always presented our ecologically oriented conscience with a dilemma. As we let go, with our air running low, a huge Napoleon wrasse passed by, seeing off his guests. We drifted fast during the decompression stop, but our boat was nearby when we surfaced, physically and emotionally drained.

Of course we could not leave well enough alone, and returned the next day for another dive at the same site. The current was even faster this time, and we lost an anchor trying to hook up the boat. We put in just a bit too far downcurrent, and had to kick hard to reach the sea mound, whose top portion comes to 8–10 meters of the surface.

A couple of gray sharks watched our struggles, but only with passing interest. By the time we grabbed hold and looked around, we saw that the previous day's show had changed, and we could not crawl over the top of the sea mound to the calmer side. There were no tuna around, and the 7 or 8 sharks which appeared throughout the dive quickly drifted out of sight.

But just ahead and above us, four absolutely huge yellowtail barracuda faced into the current, with barely a tail flick necessary remain in place. Hand over hand we managed to approach them to within a couple of meters before they moved off a bit.

We began an only partially controlled drift along the current-swept side of the sea mound, between 25 and 35 meters down, past a group of Napoleon wrasse, which eyed us curiously. There were at least eight of them of varying sizes, from 50 cm juveniles to huge grand-daddies, the largest concentration of these fish we had ever seen.

A school of at least 50 batfish flickered by, swam out of sight and returned twice for a closer look. One of our party spotted a sea snake heading for the depths from 35 meters and Moorish idols appeared in large numbers. Clouds of the two-hued blue triggerfish hovered over the outer edge of the mound.

With the current occasionally gusting to a mask-and-regulator–wrenching three knots, and no bare rock to hold on to, there was time to look over the invertebrate life, none of which managed to struggle to any height above 20 centimeters. The most

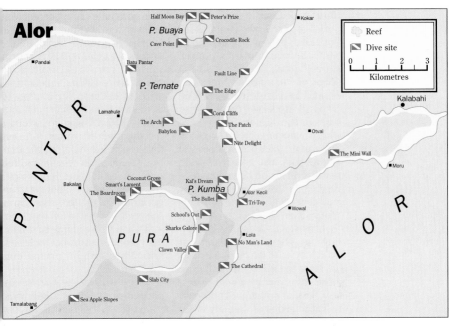

Alor

Half Moon Bay — Peter's Prize
Kokar
P. Buaya
Cave Point — Crocodile Rock
Pandai
Batu Pantar
Fault Line
P. Ternate — The Edge
Kalabahi
Lamahule — Coral Cliffs
The Arch — The Patch
Babylon — Otvai
Nite Delight
The Mini Wall
Moru
Coconut Grove — Kal's Dream
Smart's Lament — P. Kumba
Bakalan — Alor Kecil
The Boardroom — The Bullet — Tri-Top
School's Out — Wowal
P U R A
Sharks Galore — Lola
Clown Valley — No Man's Land
The Cathedral
Slab City
Sea Apple Slopes
Tamalabang

P A N T A R

A L O R

Reef
Dive site
0 1 2 3
Kilometres

abundant species we remember were small sponges, soft coral trees and small, tightly packed colonial cup corals, normally nigh feeders but a few open ones with tiny yellow tentacles, searching for plankton.

Monster Grouper

On our third Dream dive we managed to get over the sea mound, found a quiet ringside seat at about 25 meters, and again witnessed the greatest show in the sea. If we missed the circling grey-shark formation of the first dive, others were bold enough to approach us closer than previously.

There were more big barracuda this time, and a breath-taking formation of four tuna, all over 1.5 meters, followed by a dozen or more smaller ones. But all of this paled when the main attraction showed up on the scene: an absolute giant, the mother of all groupers, 2 meters long if it was an inch, with a dark head and light grayish midsection.

These monster groupers are a tough lot, said to swallow whole spiny lobsters, sharks and possibly even pearl divers. The one we saw certainly looked capable of bullying just about anything it encountered, and could certainly swallow us for dessert. Even the largest gray shark gave it a wide berth. He checked us out from 3–4 meters, drifted off a bit, and returned for another look.

While we were holding still and keeping a wary eye on our fat monarch, three of the giant-sized tuna cruised around, often coming into close range, probably just curious, over and over. Deciding that the noisy intruders into his kingdom posed no threat, the grouper drifted off.

We left with our fish-story and bodies intact except for a few coral scrapes. Out of my 1000-odd dives, the three on the Dream are all in the top five. Nowhere else comes even close to the variety of huge fish: barracuda, tuna, shark, grouper.

The strong current that almost continuously sweeps the area brings nutrients to the invertebrates and small fishes, fodder for medium-sized fishes which in turn are gobbled by the big ones. Don't miss this show.

Sharks Galore

For those put off by strong current, there's almost as good a show a quick ride away, off the coast of Pura Island, across a short stretch of sea from The Dream. Here we dove at the edge of the "Clown Valley" site where a previous group had spotted a giant grouper and several sharks. But instead of following our dive plan and heading north, we decided to go with the flow and drift south, in a gentle current, along the sloping profile.

Less than a minute after hitting the water, we were greeted by at least a dozen great barracuda, all in the meter-range. These were followed by a half dozen long, sleek barracuda. They were still at the edge of visibility when a swirling school of bigeye jacks surrounded us, finning rapidly with no apparent purpose. Later in the dive we were shadowed by even larger jacks.

About half way into the dive, at about 30 meters, we came to a ledge and stopped there for most of our remaining bottom time. In front of us was the shark show,

with an occasional appearance by a giant-sized dogtooth tuna.

The dogtooth tuna, (*Gymnosorda unicolor*), is a sharp-toothed coral reef marauder which moves with a characteristic jerky tail beat. It can grow to over two meters in length and weigh 125 kg. Unlike most tunas, the dogtooth is primarily a reef dweller, preferring rough, current-swept areas which are also home to fast-moving, aggressive, requiem sharks. In Alor, you can get close enough to these tuna to see their large, conical teeth, set in a single row along each jaw. Also look for short pectoral fins, dark finlets and a prominent, wavy lateral line.

These tuna are voracious predators of fishes, especially planktivores. The body is without scales and the white flesh is of high quality. Due to this latter factor, the dogtooth tuna has been fished out under regular pressure in much of the Indo-Pacific. We hope you get to see them in Alor before they get fished out from there also.

While at any one time we saw "only" nine sharks, there must

KAL MULLER

have been well over a dozen of them, all of very respectable size except for a couple of reef whitetips which seemed somewhat more at ease than usual, perhaps feeling a degree of protection from their bigger brothers. And some of the brothers were big indeed. Taking into account the hard fact that everything looks 30 percent bigger underwater, plus human beings' natural tendency to exaggerate—especially when telling shark stories—the 4 or 5 grey sharks in front of us were a good 2 meters long, and there were several reef blacktips almost the same size. The reef whitetips were a manageable 1.25 meters.

The show lasted a good while as we anxiously glanced at our computers and air gauges. Just before our instruments told us to get out of there, a curious pair of sharks appeared. They seemed joined in the forward-section of their bodies, like Siamese twins. As all of us confirmed this—it was unlikely to be a narcosis-produced vision. Perhaps it was the shark version of sexual foreplay.

The anti-climatic decompression stop was held in an almost solid carpet of anemones, interspersed with orange sponges and, in the shallower portion, with hydroids. Strangely, we saw no clownfish in any of the anemones. Back on board, excitely matching sightings and numbers, we dubbed the location "Sharks Galore."

Soon, we had something else to talk about. As we were motoring to Ternate Island from the south, a huge number of pilot whales broke the surface, some leaping and frolicking, accompanied by dolphins. We never came very close to the seething mass, but on another occasion Donovan led a group of snorkelers who were rewarded by underwater sightings of a half-dozen pilot whales which approach to within 5 or 6 meters. Our guide also snorkeled with these whales just off the entrance to Kalabahi Bay.

The Mini Wall

Tired from too much input and three-dive days, we had time only for one night dive. This was along the southern edge of Kalabahi Bay, about 10 kilometers from town. We entered off a peb-

Above: *This young Alorese fisherman wears homemade goggles made of wood, pitch and salvaged glass chipped into circles.*

bled beach, and headed parallel to the coast over rubble covered with an almost continuous carpet of crinoids. Some 30 meters of this, then a small wall, cracked in several places and pocked with shallow holes. The "Mini Wall" bottomed in sand at 7 meters.

Soft corals, sponges and invertebrates covered the wall, a solid, multi-hued mass of life. Several reef fishes were still swimming, but others slept, oblivious to the humans. The keen eyes of Donovan, my dive guide, picked out three exquisite little shrimp, along with several decorator crabs and two other species of colorful crabs, unidentified. A tiny cuttlefish, just 7–8 centimeters long, allowed us to play with it until it became tired of games and shot off in a cloud of ink, surprisingly large given its tiny body.

We saw nothing big, but there was plenty of that in the day dives. However, all the locals admired our bravery for diving at this location. The entry area is considered haunted, as access to it is by a path across a cemetery.

And there are many stories, unconfirmed, of a huge snake living in one of the caves under the wall. We checked carefully but no monster snake eyes were reflected in our lights. Just as well.

Walls and Sea Mounds

The dive locations explored up till now in this area are concentrated around the three islands lying between Alor and Pantar: Pulau Buaya in the north, Pulau Ternate in the middle, and Pulau Pura to the south. Most of the sites show an excellent wall profile, dropping to 50 or more meters and with a topside ledge perfect for the decompression stop. Many of the walls are pocketed with caves. Invertebrate life and reef fishes compare favorable—both in absolute numbers and species diversity—other top dive locations in Indonesia.

Some of the sites are "takas," or sea mounds, generally coming to about 8 meters or so of the surface. The steeply sloping bottom prevents convenient, up-current anchorage. There's no other choice: giant leap and down fast, finning like hell at an angle to the current to reach the nearest part of the sea-mound. Then it's hand-over-hand to the far side, and down to 25 meters for a ring-side seat. We can't really say how rich these mounds are in invertebrate and small fish life, as we were always too busy watching all the big ones. In general, however, on both walls and *takas*, the Pantar Strait is very rich.

Of the normally seen tropical reef fishes, we saw unusual concentrations of longnose emperors, red-tooth triggers, surgeonfish and unicorns, emperor angels, and snappers. The latter two species showed up several times in close to unbelievable concentrations. Of the larger fellows, sharks showed up on almost every dive, usually the harmless, and rather skittish reef whitetip. Less frequent but still common are the great barracuda, Spanish mackerel and schools of big eyed jacks.

Visibility varied from a good 12 meters to—rarely—an excellent 40 meters in the horizontal plane. Most locations are suitable for even neophyte divers, with no current and plenty of action. However, the best spot to see really big fish, Kal's Dream, requires some experience, because of the strong current usually encountered.

Pitoby Water Sports

The only way to dive in the Alor area is through Pitoby Water Sports in Kupang, the capital of Nusa Tenggara Timur Province. Access to Kupang is easy, via several daily flights from Bali. Pitoby's arranges everything from airport pickup to seeing your final flight off back to Bali or to Darwin, Australia. Donovan Whitford, a PADI dive instructor with Pitoby's, is the only dive guide available. Young but with plenty of experience, always cheerful and pleasant, he can adapt dive series to match experience and interest.

We hope that a more suitable dive boat will be found in the future as those suiting up on the engine exhaust side sometimes clear their lungs with fumes just before diving. A ladder, which appeared—thankfully—on the second day of diving, disappeared the next day. We had to haul ourselves up after dives on rubber tires which normally keep the boat from scraping against the dock or another vessel.

For those who are not professional gymnasts, this is a bit of a struggle, especially when you are tired after fighting currents. Answering calls of nature is not too bad for males—when no ladies are present. Otherwise manners require you to use the joke of a toilet.

The usual dive routine calls for leaving the hotel after break-fast, around 8 am, and riding about a half hour in a minibus from Kalabahi to Alor Kecil, some 20 kilometers away. The road follows the north coast of Kalabahi Bay, with pretty panoramas villages, yells of "Hello Meeester!" from the kids and young hotbloods showing of their English skills. At Alor Kecil, a swaying canoe or small outrigger takes divers and gear to the boat, which is anchored about 50 meters out.

This transfer is no problem in calm waters, but in choppy seas it's not recommended for those prone to heart attacks—especially those carrying several thousand dollars worth of above-water camera gear.

Dive sites are 15 minutes to two hours from Alor Kecil. The first dive is followed by a box lunch, and wet suits dry a bit as the boat heads for the second site. Hot tea, coffee and snacks rewards the second dive. If it has been planned and the weather permits, there could be a third dive before returning to Alor Kecil, then overland to Kalabahi. The days are tiring, but exciting.

Below: *The fish and invertebrate life of Indonesia is still little-explored. The cardinalfish below, living in a very shallow area of disturbed reef in Sulawesi, is new to science. According to Gerald R. Allen, an expert on Indo-Pacific fishes who is currently at work on a comprehensive book on the cardinalfishes, it will be the third known species in the genus* Sphaeramia. *Around the time of this writing, Allen and author and photographer Kal Muller—who discovered the fish—had planned an expedition to collect it.*

KAL MULLER

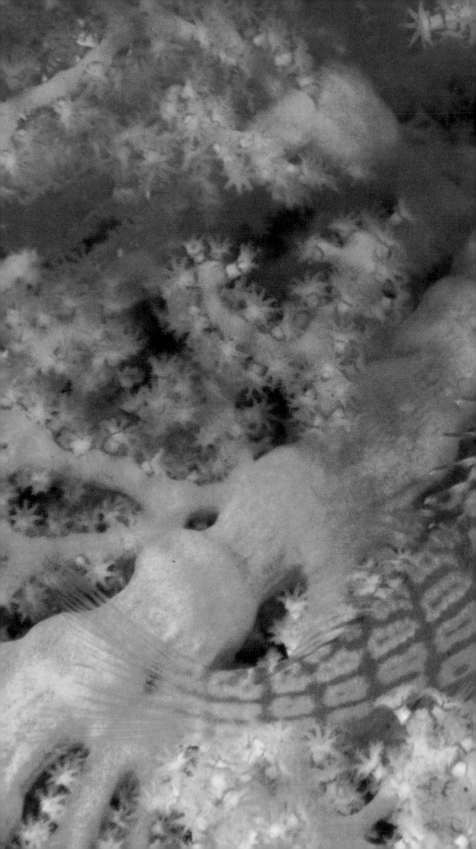

Introducing Sulawesi

Siau Island
Manado

The contorted island of Sulawesi lies in the middle of the archipelago's sweep, north of Flores and reaching almost to the Philippines. Formerly—and on some maps, still—called the Celebes, the island offers some of the most stunning scenery in all of Indonesia, both above and below water.

The people of Sulawesi are culturally diverse, ranging from the cosmopolitan Bugis of Ujung Pandang, Sulawesi's largest city and the hub of eastern Indonesia, to the traditional Toraja of the highlands.

Shaped by Fire

The island took its unusual shape about 3 million years ago, when a chunk of land that had split from western New Guinea and drifted eastward (Sulawesi's eastern and southeastern peninsulas) collided with a volcanic island that had formed along a fault line east of Borneo (the south and the northern peninsula). The force of collision spun the two islands and left them joined in the middle.

The great majority of Sulawesi's 227,000 square kilometers is higher than 500 meters. The province has 17 active volcanoes, concentrated in North Sulawesi and in the Sangihe Islands. In the past few years, Lokon near Manado and Siau Island's Karangetang have been the most active.

Exquisite Reefs

Because of its unique shape, no part of the island is more than 100 kilometers from the sea, and Sulawesi has a whopping 6,000 kilometers of coastline. More than 110 small offshore islands are also part of the Sulawesi

group. Most of this coastline is ringed with reef.

Although too disturbed to be of interest to divers, the 16,000 square kilometers of reef off Ujung Pandang supports one of the most productive fisheries in the world. In the north, the near pristine reefs off Manado are famous for their sheer walls and abundance of fish life.

Perhaps the best diving in the island remains inaccessible: the Togian Islands in Tomini Bay, famous for displaying in a very small area every known type of coral reef; Taka Bone Rate, southeast of Selayar Island in the south and the third-largest atoll in the world (see map page 182); and the Tukang Besi Islands off southeast Sulawesi, rumored to have moved Jacques Cousteau—who recently passed through Indonesia—to declare them the finest diving site in the world.

Because it straddles the Asian and Australian biogeographical zones and offers a wide range of habitats, Sulawesi has a great number of endemic species. Discounting bats, fully 98 percent of the island's mammals are found nowhere else. Among the most unusual of these are the babirusa—literally "pig deer"—a wild pig with huge, curving tusks; the rare anoa, a water buffalo the size of a dog; and the tiny tarsier, a big-eyed primate the size of a hamster. Some 34 percent of the non-migratory birds—88 species—are endemic.

Famous Entrepôt

Although the Gowanese and Bugis developed their own writing systems, adapted from an Indian alphabet, the early texts

Overleaf: A long-nosed hawkfish, Oxycirrhites typus, in a gorgonian. This little predator keeps a lookout from its perch, and then swoops down and 'hawks' small crustaceans. Bunaken group, Sulawesi. Photograph by Mike Severns.

Opposite: A colubrine sea snake, Laticauda colubrina, pokes its head (lower right) behind a sponge in search of food. Too slow to snatch a swimming fish, these snakes must corner their prey in tight crevices or feed on spawn. This species, with leather much smoother than its terrestrial brethren, is heavily collected in the Philippines, where it supports a very large snakeskin industry. Though not in the least aggressive, the colubrine sea snake is quite venomous and should not be harassed. Bunaken group, Sulawesi. Photograph by Mike Severns.

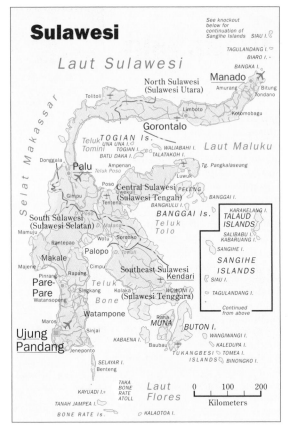

Sulawesi

Laut Sulawesi

See knockout below for continuation of Sangihe Islands SIAU I.

TAGULANDANG I.
BIARO I.
BANGKA I.

North Sulawesi (Sulawesi Utara)
Manado
Amurang Bitung
Tondano
Tolitoli
Limboto
Kotamobagu
Gorontalo

Selat Makassar

Donggala
Teluk TOGIAN Is.
Tomini UNA UNA I.
TOGIAN I. WALIABAHI I.
BATU DAKA I. TALATAKOH I.
Laut Maluku

Palu
Ampenan
Teluk Poso
Poso
Central Sulawesi PELENG
Uwekuli
(Sulawesi Tengah)
Tentena
Tg. Pangkalaseang
Luwuk
BANGGAI I.

Gimpu
BANGKULU I.
South Sulawesi
D. Poso
(Sulawesi Selatan) D. Matano
Mamuju
Wotu Soroako
BANGGAI Is.
Teluk
Tolo
KARAKELANG I.
TALAUD
ISLANDS
SALIBABU I.
KABARUANG I.
SANGIHE I.

Rantepao
Palopo D. Towuti
Makale
Cimpu
Majene
Rapang
Pinrang
Southeast Sulawesi
Kendari
SANGIHE
ISLANDS
SIAU I.

Pare-Pare
Singkang
Kolaka
WOWONI I.
Teluk
Bone
(Sulawesi Tenggara)
TAGULANDANG I.
Watansopeng
Watampone
Continued from above

Maros
Rana
MUNA
Ujung Pandang
Sinjai
BUTON I.
WANGIWANGI I.
KABAENA I.
KALEDUPA I.
Jeneponto
Baubau
TUKANGBESI TOMEA I.
ISLANDS BINONGKO I.
SELAYAR I.
Benteng

TAKA
BONE
RATE
ATOLL
Laut Flores
KAYUADI I.
0   100   200
Kilometers
TANAH JAMPEA I.
BONE RATE Is.
KALAOTOA I.

The Dutch arrived at this time, and quickly muscled the Portuguese out of the spice trade. Although Holland used force of arms to insist that sellers accept low prices, spices continuted to "escape" to Makassar, where sellers got a fair return. To save their monopoly, the Dutch fought the famous "Battle of Makassar," defeating Gowa by allying with the Bugis.

The People of Sulawesi

Among the 11.5 million people living on Sulawesi are dozens of ethnic groups, of which the Bugis, Makassarese and Mandarese of the south, the Minahasans of the north, and the Torajans of the interior are the best known.

The Muslim Bugis have always been famous seafarers, and their distinctive wooden *pinisi*—schooner-shaped boats now fitted with diesel engines—still serve as the vehicles for much of the inter-island cargo carried around the archipelago.

The people of Manado and the Minahasa region in the north are predominantly Christians, having converted during the early 19th century. Good relations with the Dutch led to the region being blessed with schools and other perquisites of colonial favor.

The most famous of Sulawesi's ethnic groups among visitors are the Toraja, who live in the beautiful highlands north of Makale. The Torajans' tall, sway-backed *tongkonan,* or ancestral houses, graced by huge stacks of water buffalo horns, are the archipelago's most distinctive architectural feature.

Even Torajans working in the big cities of western Indonesia return home for an important funeral of one of their kinsmen. At these grand events, in which the entire community participates, hundreds of very valuable water buffalo are slaughtered.

---

are concerned chiefly with myths of origin and royal genealogies. Until the Europeans arrived in the 16th century, little is known of the island's history.

The Portuguese pioneered the European trade route to the Spice Islands, and Makassar (now Ujung Pandang) was a regular stop on the route from Malacca to the nutmeg and clove islands of Maluku. At the time, the Gowanese and Bugis sailed the monsoon winds as far as Australia in search of trepang and other sea products.

The king of Gowa petitioned the Portuguese for missionaries, but these never arrived. The proselytizers of Islam were more responsive, however, and by the early 17th century South Sulawesi—both the Gowanese and the Bugis—had become a Muslim stronghold.

World-Class Walls and Outstanding Fish Life

Divers, from neophytes to those who have dived all the world-famous spots, have nothing but praise for the reefs surrounding the small islands in Manado Bay. These are very steep, pristine coral walls. In good weather, visibility on Bunaken Island's drop-offs is typically around 25 meters, very good for Indonesian waters. At some sites, and when the current is up a bit, this can drop to 12 meters because of plankton in the water.

The reefs here are basically untouched. Little damage from fish bombing is visible, in part because the reefs are steep, and drop off so near the shore. Nor have there been enough divers here to tear up the sites. In 1989, thanks to the efforts of Hanny Batuna and Loky Herlambang, co-founders of Nusantara Diving Centre (NDC), the pioneering dive operator here, 75,265 hectares of underwater area around Bunaken, Manado Tua, Siladen, Montehage and Nain islands became a national marine reserve: Taman Nasional Laut Bunaken–Manado Tua.

North Sulawesi and the islands in the Bunaken group face the Sulawesi Sea, which reaches more than 6 kilometers. Even on the short boat rides to the dive sites, one passes over more than a kilometer of water covering a trench that separates the islands from the mainland. Nutrient-rich water from these depths sweeps across the islands' reefs.

The variety of marine life here is excellent; the surfaces of the walls are crowded with hard and soft corals, whip corals, sponges, and clinging filter-feeders like crinoids and basket stars. Huge schools of pyramid butterflyfish (*Hemitaurichthys polylepsis*) and black triggerfish (*Odonus niger*), and clouds of anthias swarm around the reef edge and the upper part of the wall. Sharks, schools of barracuda, rays, moray eels and sea snakes—particularly the black-and-grey–banded colubrine sea snake (*Laticauda colubrina*)—are relatively common here.

Beginners like the ease of the conditions. There is usually very little current, and the boats

AT A GLANCE
Manado

Reef type:	Steep coral walls
Access:	45 min to 1.5 hr by boat
Visibility:	Fair to very good; 12–25 meters
Current:	Usually gentle; at some sites to 2 knots or more
Coral:	Excellent condition and variety, particularly soft corals
Fish:	Good numbers and excellent variety
Highlights:	Pristine walls; sheer number of species; interesting wreck

anchor right on the edge of the walls. Experts appreciate the fact that most operators keep groups small: four to seven people.

The Bunaken–Manado Tua reserve features some dozen-and-a-half dive sites. Most are concentrated off the south and west coasts of Bunaken, a low, crescent-shaped coral island completely surrounded by a steep fringing reef. Adjacent Manado Tua—"Old Manado"—

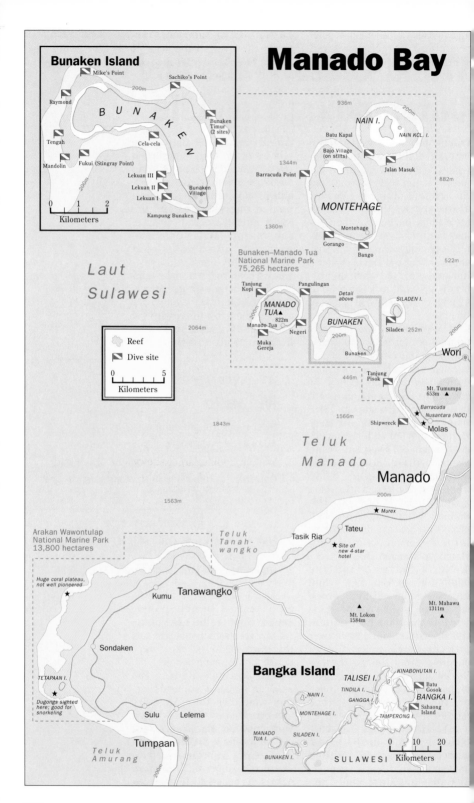

Manado Bay

Bunaken Island

Mike's Point
Sachiko's Point
Raymond
200m
B U N A K E N
Bunaken Timur (2 sites)
Tengah
Cela-cela
Mandolin
Fukui (Stingray Point)
Lekuan III
Lekuan II
Lekuan I
Bunaken Village
Kampung Bunaken

0 1 2
Kilometers

Laut
Sulawesi

Reef
Dive site

0   5
Kilometers

936m
NAIN I.
200m
Batu Kapal
NAIN KCL. I.
Bajo Village (on stilts)
Jalan Masuk
1344m
Barracuda Point
882m
MONTEHAGE
Montehage
1360m
Gorango
Bango
522m

Bunaken–Manado Tua
National Marine Park
75,265 hectares

2064m

Tanjung Kopi
Pangulingan
Detail above
SILADEN I.
MANADO TUA▲
200m
822m
Manado Tua
Negeri
BUNAKEN
Siladen 252m
Muka Gereja
200m
Bunaken
Wori
200m

Mt. Tumumpa 653m ▲
446m
Tanjung Pisok
Barracuda Nusantara (NDC)
1566m
Shipwreck
Molas

1843m

Teluk
Manado

Manado
200m

1563m
★ Murex

Arakan Wawontulap
National Marine Park
13,800 hectares

Teluk
Tanah-
wangko
Tasik Ria
Tateu
★ Site of new 4-star hotel

Huge coral plateau, not well pioneered
★
Kumu
Tanawangko

Mt. Mahawu 1311m ▲
▲ Mt. Lokon 1584m

Sondaken

TETAPAAN I.
★ Dugongs sighted here; good for snorkeling

Sulu
Lelema

Tumpaan

Teluk
Amurang

Bangka Island

KINABOHUTAN I.
TALISEI I.
TINDILA I.
Batu Gosok
BANGKA I.
NAIN I.
GANGGA I.
MONTEHAGE I.
Sahaong Island
TAMPERONG I.
MANADO TUA I.
SILADEN I.
BUNAKEN I.
0 10 20
SULAWESI
Kilometers

is a volcano, a well-shaped cone reaching 822 meters. Three other islands complete the group: tiny Siladen, a stone's throw northeast of Bunaken; Montehage, the largest of the islands, north of Bunaken; and Nain, a tiny island north of Montehage surrounded by a large barrier reef. (See map at left.)

Bunaken Island

The reef is good all the way around Bunaken, and the 6-kilometer-long island features no fewer than 13 dive sites. Bunaken is the centerpiece of the reserve, and with careful observation, on this one island you could probably see the majority of coral reef fishes found in Indonesia.

All the sites are similar in that they feature steep walls of coral, pocked with small caves, and buzzing with small and medium-sized reef fish. Good coral growth usually extends down to 40–50 meters, and in the deeper parts of the wall one can see sharks, large rays and Napoleon wrasse. The current is usually gentle, perfect for a slow drift along the face of the wall, although it can occasionally come up in the afternoon.

Lekuan I, II and III. The most frequented site on Bunaken is a three-pronged coral wall in front of Lekuan Beach. Here your chances are very good of seeing Napoleon wrasse, turtles, bumphead parrotfish, scorpionfish and lionfish, and on the reef edge, swarms of anthias.

The Lekuan sites offer little current and clear water, and are perfect for beginners. They are popular for night dives as well. Here—and everywhere else in the Manado Bay area—watch out for the stinging hydroid *Aglaophenia*. This "sea nettle" looks like a pinkish or brownish fern, and when brushed by unprotected skin causes a burning sensation.

Kampung Bunaken. This site, in front of Kampung ("Village") Bunaken on the island's southeastern tip, offers much the same underwater scenery as the Lekuan sites. However, the shallow reef flat here has suffered the most damage of any around the island, thanks to its proximity to the village.

Bunaken Timur. The two sites called "East Bunaken," barely separated from each other, feature a more sloping profile than the sites on the south and west of the island. Here we discovered turtles, Napoleon wrasse, and some sleeping reef whitetip sharks.

Sachiko's Point. Named after a Japanese tour leader, this steep wall is prowled by big fish, including large tuna, and turtles. The soft coral growth here is particularly good, and there are nice caves around 30 meters. The current is often quite strong at Sachiko's Point.

Mike's Point. Named for photographer Mike Severns (whose work appears in these pages), the profile here features wall and a pinnacle. The coral growth—including large, showy gorgonians—is very good. This site is particularly rewarding at depths of 30 meters or more. The point is sometimes swept by strong currents, and one can occasionally see sharks, and large schools of jacks. Pelagic visitors such as yellowtail tuna also call on Mike's Point.

Raymond. This is a wall, with good hard and soft coral growth and some nice whip corals. Fish life is good, including Napoleon wrasse. Colubrine sea snakes are particularly common here, both on the reef flats and in the reef itself. *Laticauda colubrina* is sometimes called the amphibious sea snake, and it spends more time ashore than most of its brethren. Although not aggressive, the snakes are poisonous and should not be harassed, although the guides

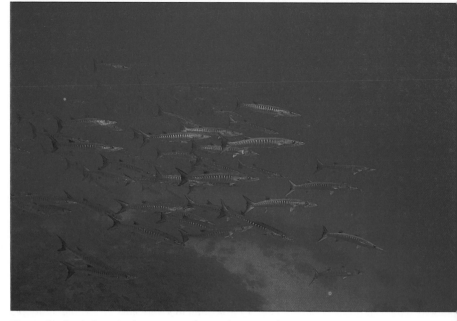

Above: A school of blackfin barracuda (Sphyraena genie). Groups of these swift predators can be seen at several locations around the Bunaken group.

and crew members often round one or two up for photographs. Strong "gusts" of current can sometimes be felt here, both horizontal and vertical. Don't panic, just hang onto the coral rock if necessary until it passes.

Tengah. This site, which means "middle" or "midway," is about in the middle of Bunaken's western reef face. This spot and nearby Mandolin are known for large schools of yellowtail fusiliers. One can also see an occasional turtle or shark here.

Mandolin. Just south of Tengah, this site also offers schooling fusiliers, and good coral growth. The wall here is best at depths of 30–35 meters.

Fukui Point. This site, also called Stingray Point, has a stepped profile: the reef top is at 2–4 meters, and then slopes down with several short, but steep, drops. It is known for its rays, of course, as well as turtles, barracuda and a couple of good-sized *Tridacna* clams.

Cela-Cela. This site, in the crook of the reef along the south face, offers many of the same charms as the popular Lekuan

sites. Good coral growth and fish, and mild currents.

Siladen. There is one regular site off the small island of Siladen, just 2 kilometers northeast of Bunaken. The wall is steep down to about 35 meters, and coral growth—particularly soft corals—is good. Siladen is a good place to see big pelagic fish, and the largest stingrays in the reserve.

Manado Tua

"Old Manado" is a dormant volcano jutting up just west of Bunaken. The two best sites are wall dives, on the west coast.

Muka Gereja. This site, in front of the church, is a steep wall with vertical canyons cut into it. Coral growth is good, and there is a nice cave at 20 meters. Sharks, barracuda and Napoleon wrasse are common.

Tanjung Kopi. "Coffee Cape" is also a wall, and offers sharks—usually reef whitetips, but with an occasional hammerhead—and barracuda. The cape is often swept by strong currents.

Negeri. A decent wall, with caves and good soft corals.

Pangulingan. This site, on the northeast of the island, has a sloping profile. There are nice shelf corals here, but the current can be very strong and there are few fish. It is best at 35 meters.

Montehage and Nain

Montehage is a large, flat island north of Bunaken. A community of Bajo fishermen has built a village on stilts in the shallow estuarial back reef area north of the island. The dive sites are off the west and south, which is fringed with a wide, shallow reef flat, much of it exposed at low tide.

Bango. The profile here is slope, then wall. Soft coral growth is good, and there are some caves. Scorpionfish are easy to find here, and Napoleon wrasse and sharks are common.

Gorango. The name of this site means "shark" in the local dialect, and these can usually be seen here. The reef profile is a steep wall to about 40 meters.

Barracuda Point. This is a steep slope from 5 meters to about 20 meters, then a sheer wall to more than 30 meters. Schools of barracuda can be seen here, as well as sharks—at a shallower depth than at most sites—Napoleon wrasse, and bumphead parrotfish. Occasionally, huge tuna appear here.

Nain is a tiny island, but is surrounded by a wide lagoon filled with patches of reef, and a barrier reef. The people living on the island have cut a path through the reef just wide enough for their canoes. The island features two dive sites, both on the outer edge of the barrier reef.

We didn't dive Jalan Masuk ("Entryway"), but were told the scenery was the same as Batu Kapal, which we dove twice.

Batu Kapal. This site, literally "Stone Boat," is a slope down to 42 meters to a coral outcrop shaped like a boat (hence the name). A narrow canyon begins here that plunges way, way down. A couple of European dive instructors in our group went down to 90 meters (on a single tank) into the canyon to look at some big jacks under an overhang. A light and a depth gauge exploded. (This is not recommended for beginners. These

Below: *A red-spotted blenny* (Istiblennius chrysospilos) *pokes its clownish face out of a hidey hole. This fish is relatively common in quite shallow water, but only the sharp-eyed will see it, as the red-spotted blenny grows to just 10 centimeters and rarely shows more than its head.*

MIKE SEVERNS

two were used to diving in the Mediterranean, where dives to 60 meters are common.)

There is some bomb damage on the reef flat, but the rest of the coral is pristine. We saw sharks, big tuna and Napoleon wrasse. We also saw large groups of parrotfish, and at the reef top one of the guides found a couple of the strange crocodile fish (*Cymbacephalus beauforti*).

Below: *Soft corals. Rooted in the substrate, these animals strain the water for plankton.*

Tanjung Pisok

HELMUT DEBELIUS / IKAN

HELMUT DEBELIUS / IKAN

Above: *Spiral wire coral* (Cirrhipathes spiralis). *Bunaken group.*

The dive at Cape Pisok is just off the mainland, some 15 minutes motoring from Molas Beach. The profile begins with a gentle slope, and then becomes a wall. Tanjung Pisok is one of the best places to see blue ribbon eels (*Rhinomuraena quaesita*), slender and gaudy relatives of the morays. The animals are quite shy, and guides and a great deal of tact are required to see them. One can also see blue ribbon eels

in relatively shallow depths at some of the Bunaken sites. There are barracuda at Pisok, including an occasional big one, and—particularly in the afternoon—squid and sharks.

The Manado Wreck

A steel-hulled German merchant ship, which sank on February 22 1942, lies in the mud just 5 minutes from Molas beach. The wreck makes a fine break from wall diving. It might take the crew a few minutes to find it, as there is no buoy—if the local fishermen knew its location, they would soon catch all its fish.

Loky Herlambang of NDC found the wreck in 1980 while diving for trepang to try to make ends meet at his fledgling diving club. The harbormaster's office has no records of the ship. It has been discovered to be German, and when Loky first found it there was a machine gun and belts of ammunition on the foredeck. (Long gone now.)

Once the wreck is found, the crew drops anchor and you follow the line down, as visibility is usually lousy here. The wreck lies on a sandy slope, at 25–40 meters. The twin screws of the 60-meter ship are still intact.

The hull is largely undamaged, but you can enter the wreck through several openings on the deck. Bring good underwater lights! Most of the cargo space is easily accessible, but the engine room is tricky. Following the ladder (towards the stern) down the first couple of meters is easy, but to get through the narrow passage, you must remove your BC and tank. The engines and pistons are in good shape, as is one of the two electrical gauges. Move very slowly: perhaps a half-meter of fine sand and mud fill the compartment. A few careless strokes of your fins and you won't be able to see your hand in front of your face.

Because of the depth and the

generally murky water (8–10 meters at best), there is little hard coral growth here. But there are plenty of giant black coral bushes, and some gorgonians and feather stars. Fish are not normally abundant. We saw a reef whitetip shark, a bright yellow trumpetfish, a large puffer, angelfish, some butterflyfish, Moorish idols, and small schools of sweetlips and snappers.

Our favorites were a beautiful and shy juvenile pinnate batfish (*Platax pinnatus*), and an adult roundfaced batfish (*P. tiera*) that seemed to be living in the wheelhouse. If you ask your guides ahead of time, they might find and point out to you two unusual species in the wreck: banded pipefish (*Doryrhamphus dactyliophorus*) and the longsnout flathead (*Platycephalus chiltonae*).

As this is a fairly deep dive, be aware of your depth times or check your computer, and keep a close watch on your air supply to allow for a decompression stop. Usually the crew will hang a spare tank and regulator at 5 meters, but this is really a precaution, and you shouldn't count on it. If you want to have a look inside the ship, we suggest you make two dives: one to get acquainted with the wreck, and one to explore inside.

Nusantara Diving Centre

North Sulawesi's reefs are becoming internationally famous, and credit can only go to two men: Hanny Batuna and Loky Herlambang. Hanny was free-diving with the Bajo as a young man, which began his interest in the underwater world. He wanted to join the navy, but his father forced him to study medicine. Loky was studying biology at Bandung, Java when he read Jules Verne's *20,000 Leagues Under the Sea*.

Loky was in Manado collecting marine ornamentals and pursuing a girlfriend when he met Hanny. They quickly became associates. Hanny bought the land and put up the capital, while Loky ran the new buisiness: Nusantara Diving Centre (NDC).

NDC was founded in 1975, and in 1977 their choice of locations was confirmed by a visit from John E. (Jack) Randall, Curator of Ichthyology at the Bernice P. Bishop Museum in Hawaii. Randall encouraged the

HELMUT DEBELIUS / IKAN

men's efforts to promote recreational diving in the Bunaken Island group.

They started a program of conservation among the local fishermen. In 1982, the local government declared the Bunaken–Manado Tua area a protected zone (as well as the Arakan–Wawontulap area southwest of Manado), and the federal government made them both marine

Above: A half-grown pinnate batfish, Platax pinnatus, *in the wreck just off Molas Beach. The ship, which sunk during World War II, lies on a soft bottom, 25–40 meters underwater.*

Guide Larry Smith

Folks, meet Larry Smith. He has been in the business for more than 25 years, and has 12,500 dives under his weight belt. He has a deep bass voice, a red beard, and almost always a smile. Larry is built like a linebacker, the kind of man you want with you on a dark night in a dark alley—or underwater in an emergency.

Larry, from Longview, Texas, learned scuba diving under Doctor Blood—a.k.a. Captain Blood—a Ph.D. in chemistry, sea captain, inventor of polypropylene rope, and generally a figure of legend. During the next decade, Larry fueled his passion by opening a dive shop, combining teaching, commercial scuba work, and organizing dive trips to Mexico and Central America. He helped his good friend, gourmet chef Gladys Howard, set up a dive resort in the Caribbean's best dive location, Little Cayman.

After many years in the Caribbean, Larry became the dive director of the *Tropical Princess,* Indonesia's first live-aboard, cruising out of Biak, Irian Jaya. He fell in love with the country. He trained the *Princess's* crew from scratch, treating them like brothers, sharing the hard work and meals, and even the occasional drinking binge.

Not satisfied with the dive locations close to Biak, Larry looked at the charts and found Mapia atoll, 18 hours away. During the tidal change, Mapia's reef channel came alive with sharks, rays and other big fish, and it became a world-class dive location. He eventually left the *Princess,* and it has also stopped operation.

While working on the *Princess* Larry met Dewi, a pretty young woman from Central Java. The two married, and Larry passed to his wife his passion for diving.

Following his stint in the eastern part of the archipelago, Larry became the divemaster of the *Cehili,* a dive boat that ran seasonally along the Sangihe–Talaud islands north of Sulawesi, and the Banda Sea. The *Cehili* stopped operations a year ago, leaving Larry without a job.

This proved a stroke of luck for Kungkungan Bay Resort on the eastern side of Sulawesi's northern peninsula (see page 192) and they took advantage of Larry's prodigious talents. Since then, Larry has led divers to the rich reefs and shipwrecks of the Lembeh Strait.

No hardcore diver could but admire Larry at work. He knows the charts, he knows the tides and conditions, and most of all, he knows the animals. He is, simply, the best.

parks in 1989. In recognition of his conservation efforts, President Soeharto awarded Loky the prestigious Kalpataru Environmental Award in 1985.

In the early '80s, business suffered as an unscrupulous French dive agent sent numerous clients to dive, but refused to pay NDC. With the business at this low point, Hanny lost interest, but Loky stayed on. From a trickle of clients in the early '80s, he slowly built the business to the thriving state it is in today.

In 1980, Hanny bought a seaside property south of Manado as a weekend family house, and a fish farm. He continued to dive with many expatriate friends, who eventually convinced him to get back into the dive business. He had moved his family house to the location in 1987, and in the same year started Murex, short for Manado Underwater Explorations.

Diving Bunaken

There are three main dive operations in the area: NDC, which is the oldest; Murex, which many divers consider to be the best managed; and Barracuda, which also has its partisans, although some consider the service to be inconsistent. Some newer operations have sprung up as well, most of them associated with new resort hotels.

The dive process is similar at all three of the main dive resorts. Divers depart around 9 am, and reach Bunaken or the other sites in the area in 30 minutes to an hour and a half, depending on the remoteness of the site and the boat's engine.

Bungalows have been built on Bunaken Island itself, and this operator offers convenient shore diving. We think that building even a small operation in the middle of a nature reserve is, at best, misguided, and do not recommend divers encourage this by staying here.

Good Diving and a Fine Boat Ride North

Divers, snorkelers or just visitors interested in a scenic boat ride will enjoy the day trip to Bangka Island, on Sulawesi's northernmost tip. Scuba diving off Bangka was pioneered by Dr. Hanny Batuna of Murex and this outfit offers a delightful trip to Bangka—with the option of going or returning overland.

As you leave mainland Sulawesi from Murex, just north of Manado, Lokon and Mahawu volcanoes are at your back, and the island of Manado Tua looms large, often cloud-wreathed, with low-lying Bunaken in the foreground. The dive boat cruises past several scenic islands, and the mainland looks fine too.

Soft Coral Gardens

Bangka Island, of contorted bays and hills, has a few white-sand beaches, but mostly the tropical vegetation grows right down to the sea. Jagged pinnacles stick out of the waters off southern and southeastern Bangka, and it is here that Dr. Batuna, the owner of Murex, pioneered some outstanding dive locations.

The rugged scenery continues underwater. The tips of some of the jagged pinnacles don't make it to the surface, while others shoot a few meters into the air. The spread and variety of soft corals here is truly outstanding and at some drop-off points, the swarms of fish cascade about as in a wind-driven snowstorm.

There are also a few big fellas around: we spotted a decent sized shark, several hefty Napoleon wrasse and a dozen large barracuda with unusual yellow tails. Some small sharks hid under the table coral. Visibility was good, 10–15 meters, but because the current often picks up here—to 2 knots or more—the site is best for more experienced divers.

Fish for Hong Kong

We took lunch under a shelter on a sandy beach in a deep bay. There was good snorkeling here as well. But dismaying was the sight of a floating house in the bay with large attached nets. This operation used nets and lines to capture live groupers—particularly *Cromileptes altivelis*—and Napoleon wrasse. These were kept in a live well, and periodically shipped to Hong Kong, where they command a very high price at the table. When we revisited the site in 1996, the operation was thankfully shut down. Uncommon and beautiful animals like the Napoleon wrasse should be left alone.

For the way back to Manado, you have a choice: a scenic one-hour drive back from the mainland village of Likupang, or the boat ride back the way you came.

AT A GLANCE
Bangka

Reef type:	Pinnacles, coral slope
Access:	1.5 hr by boat
Visibility:	Fair to good; 10–15 meters
Current:	Usually some, occasionally to 2 knots or more
Coral:	Good; outstanding soft corals
Fish:	Good numbers and excellent variety
Highlights:	Sharks, barracuda, soft corals

Diving the Rich Waters of the Lembeh Strait

The busy port of Bitung, the main shipping harbor for north Sulawesi, seems an unlikely choice for a dive center. Yet just north of the port, in the straight formed by Lembeh Island, is some of the finest diving in North Sulawesi.

Lembeh Island—long, narrow and parallel to the coast of Sulawesi—creates a calm channel, protected from both the northeast and southwest monsoons. Prevailing currents through the area are also concentrated by the strait, bringing a rich supply of plankton, and since Lembeh Island and the coast of Sulawesi offer many different habitats—sandy bays, craggy volcanic outcrops, and mangrove—a wide variety of animals settle out of the plankton stream here. As a result, the waters are unusually rich, both in numbers of animals and in diversity.

Because they are so full of plankton, the waters here are not particularly clear, with visibility generally ranging around 10–15 meters. And there are no pow-

dery white sand beaches here the protection of the island and the volcanic rock yielding only gravelly black strips of sand. But for divers interested in rare and unusual animals—sea horses, mandarinfish, squid and octopus, sea spiders, snake eels, strange crabs and shrimp, nudibranchs, scorpionfish—this is one of the best sites in the world.

As testimony to the richness and uniqueness of this area, in 1994 a National Geographic Explorer film crew chose the area to shoot a special on venomous reef animals.

. The only dive operator here is Kungkungan Bay Resort, a U.S.-operated hotel on a little bay of the same name in the village of Tanduk Rusa, five kilometers by twisty road north of Bitung. The site—a former coconut plantation—is quiet, and isolated, and the tasteful cottages are constructed of the attractive grainy wood of coconut trees.

The divemaster is Larry Smith (see profile page 190), one of the most capable men working in the area. Most of the sites were first found by local boat captain Engel Lamakeki, and in the past year Larry has added several more, including two new wrecks. None of the strait's top sites is more than about 30 minutes away by boat.

Batu Angus

Batu Angus, at the northern end of the strait on the Sulawesi side, is the site of an old lava flow, hence the name, which literally means "burnt rock." Here rough chunks of black, volcanic rock enclose a quiet area that looks like the mouth of a river.

AT A GLANCE
Bitung

Reef type:	Slopes, pinnacles, wreck
Access:	5–30 min by boat
Visibility:	Fair to good, 10–15 meters
Current:	Very little inside the strait
Coral:	Very good, especially soft and black corals
Fish:	Good numbers, excellent variety
Highlights:	Wreck, sheer richness of species

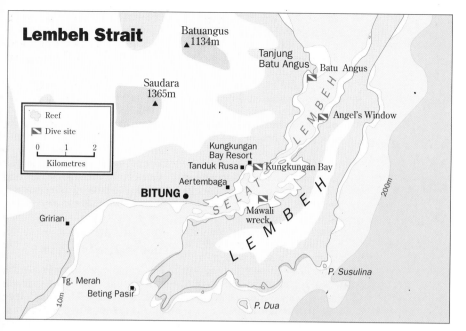

Batuangus
▲1134m

Tanjung
Batu Angus
Batu Angus

Saudara
1365m
▲

Angel's Window

Reef

Dive site

0   1   2
Kilometres

Kungkungan
Bay Resort
Tanduk Rusa
Kungkungan Bay

Aertembaga

BITUNG

SELAT

Mawali
wreck

LEMBEH

Gririan

P. Susulina

Tg. Merah

Beting Pasir

P. Dua

10m

200m

Underwater, the site is a large bowl, just 10 meters deep and about 50 meters across. The entire area, completely protected from current, is covered in finely branched and thin leafy corals. There is literally not a single square inch that isn't covered.

There are no big fish in here, but the variety of smaller species is very good. And this is one of the few places where one can easily see the reclusive and beautifully patterned mandarinfish (*Synchiropus splendens*) as well as tiny, colorful coral gobies. Batu Angus is also a fine spot for snorkeling.

Mawali Wreck

This wreck, a sunken Japanese freighter from World War II, lies just across the strait from Kungkungan Bay, a ten-minute boat ride away. The coral-encrusted ship lies on its side between 17 and 30 meters. This wreck is in very good condition,

The wreck is beautifully encrusted with crinoids, black coral trees and soft corals. The boom sticks straight out sideways, and in this area huge schools of fish gather. On one dive we saw a group of at least a hundred full-grown batfish, and schools of small silversides the size of a house.

Moray eels hide in iron crevices, and it seems at times that every encrusted lump is a scorpionfish of one species or another. Within the groove of an overgrown iron spool we found two large octopus, perhaps interrupted in a private moment.

The owners of the wreck, however, are a pride of lionfishes. Groups of 6 or 10 are always out, and at times as many as 40 of these calmly majestic animals gather together.

Kungkungan Bay

Some of our favorite dives were right out in front of the resort itself, beginning under the pier at the southern end of the beachfront, and working our way north. Night dives are especially nice here, and no cold boat ride to get between a tired diver and his or her glass of whisky.

The richness of the waters here can be seen beginning right under the dock, where you can see Henshaw eels, buried in sand up to their evil-looking teeth, several species of *Actinodendron* anemones, some with their commensal shrimp, cerianthids, sea spiders, crabs, cuttlefish and octopus. How often, for example, does one find beautiful red gorgonians growing on a wooden dock pier, or crinoids in—literally—six inches of water?

Working our way along the good coral in just 2–4 meters of water, we saw scorpionfish, octopus, strange little cuttlefish like big green bumblebees, nudibranchs, and crabs, including the beautiful demon hermit crab *Trizopagurus*, whose striking red-and-yellow–striped body is flattened so it can take advantage of cast-off cone shells, with their long, narrow openings.

Angel's Window

This is the one dive location where Larry Smith will guarantee all guests a frogfish (anglerfish to our Aussie mates). Sure enough when I dove there, Larry found one for me within about twenty minutes. The beast's black, globular body was sprinkled with silvery sand-like specks as it waited, motionless, propped on its pectoral fins between two sponges. The frogfish was not camouflaged by color, but by holding perfectly still, it was difficult to see.

The site's name comes from a swim-through, at about 25 meters. The passageway, about four or five meters long, is festooned with gorgonian fans. With careful buoyancy control, so as not to bust up the scenery, I finned through. On the other side—surprise—four Napoleon wrasse greeted me.

Kungkungan Bay Resort

The Kunkungan Resort's luxurious, but tasteful bungalows opened in late 1994. An architecturally interesting two-tiered lobby-cum-dining room, built out over the water, offers western cuisine and a few local dishes, although the latter are invariably underspiced.

Although they're all still working on their English, the staff are friendly, and a joy to be around. The setting is quiet and breezy, and, well, salubrious.

Below: *A frogfish and a scorpionfish share an encrusted pinnacle on the Mawali wreck in the Lembeh Strait.*

Sangihe-Talaud Islands

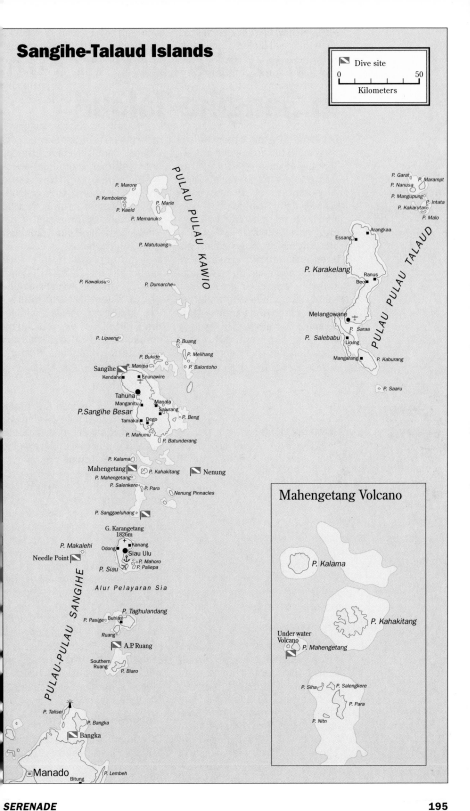

Dive site

0   50
Kilometers

PULAU PULAU KAWIO

P. Marore
P. Kemboleno
P. Kaeld
P. Marie
P. Memanuko
P. Matutuang

P. Kawalusu
P. Dumarche

P. Lipaeng
P. Buang
P. Bukide
P. Melihang
P. Manipa
P. Balontoho
Sangihe
Kendahe
Enunawire
Tahuna
Manganitu
Manala
Salurang
P.Sangihe Besar
Tamaka
Dego
P. Beng
P. Mahumu
P. Batunderang

P. Kalama
Mahengetang
P. Kahakitang
Nenung
P. Mahengetang
P. Salenkere
P. Para
Nenung Pinnacles

P. Sanggaeluhang

G. Karangetang
1826m
P. Makalehi
Odong
Kanang
Needle Point
Siau Ulu
P. Mahoro
P. Siau
P. Paliepa

Alur Pelayaran Sia

P. Taghulandang
P. Pasige
Buhias
Ruang
A.P Ruang
Southern
Ruang
P. Biaro

PULAU-PULAU SANGIHE

P. Talisei
P. Bangka
Bangka

Manado
Bitung
P. Lembeh

P. Garat
P. Marampt
P. Nanusa
P. Mangupung
P. Intata
P. Kakarutano
P. Malo
Essang
Arangkaa
P. Karakelang
Ranus
Beo
Melangowane
PULAU PULAU TALAUD
P. Saraa
P. Salebabu
Lirung
Mangarang
P. Kaburang

P. Saaru

Mahengetang Volcano

P. Kalama

P. Kahakitang

Under water
Volcano
P. Mahengetang

P. Siha
P. Salengkere
P. Para
P. Nitn

Serenade

SERENADE

Diving the Ring of Fire in Sangihe-Talaud

It looked like any other midwater reef, until we dropped onto it. The top of the reef was flat and featureless with a telltale yellow cast—and it was steaming with strings of tiny bubbles.

The coral substrate was covered in yellow and yellow and brown algae, strange colors not often encountered beneath sea. We dropped over the reef edge and descended down a rocky rubble slope following a cleft in the structure to a sandy bottom 40 meters below. This sandy plain was alive with a forest of black coral in every color imag-

---

AT A GLANCE
Serenade

Reef type: Slopes, pinnacles, walls
Access: Liveaboard
Visibility: Variable; 8–15 meters
Current: Often tricky, and strong
Coral: Usually very good
Fish: Excellent numbers and variety
Highlights: Underwater volcano, sheer profusion of life at most sites

---

inable. This was a cruise unlike any other I had ever been on.

MV Serenade

We were abroad the *MV Serenade,* a 25-meter wooden motor vessel operating in the seas to the north of Sulawesi, between Manado and Mindanao in the Philippines. It is one of two liveabroad dive boats operating in this area (See "Cehili" page 195). The *Serenade* was built locally in 1992, is manned by a local crew and is capable of a cruising speed

of 9 knots. There are four air-conditioned double cabins on the top deck and four additional cabins with shared facilities down below. The optimal dive group is ten, but larger groups can be accommodated if required.

We had boarded the *Serenade* the evening before in Manado and motored all night to our anchorage at Makalehi Island, near Siau Island in the Sangihe group. Dawn broke while we were still at sea, and we awoke to the sight of a volcano belching smoke ahead of us, dolphins breaching to starboard and a rainbow billowing to port.

Needle Point

The first dive was on the southeastern point of the island: three finger rocks pointed the way to the coral outcrop—underwater, a vertical wall dropped 65 meters to a white sand bottom. This dive—and all our dives in the area—were marked by very capricious current, one minute flowing in one direction and the next completely reversing itself, or worse, sucking unwary divers down. My dive buddy said he didn't remember much about the wall—he was too busy watching his bubbles go down!

We dubbed this site "Needle Point" as it was literally covered in bushes of white needle coral (*Seriatopora hystrix*). The fish life was prolific, featuring schools of unicornfish, snappers, fusiliers and butterflyfish.

Mahengetang

Due north was Mahengetang, the site of the submerged volcano. Some 200 meters west of the island, separated by a shallow saddle, are two cones at just four meters depth. Though the surface was at the mercy of wild currents—our boat spun around the anchorline in a 180-degree arc twice, in just 10 minutes—we encountered little current below. The undersea panorama was captivating. Everything was tinged in sulphurous tones of yellow, hard and soft coral included.

Everything seemed larger than it should have been, or more numerous. It was a magical landscape. There might be better diving in Indonesia, but surely nothing quite like this.

Drowned Village

The most mysterious site was on on Sangihe, north of the capital of Tahuna. The weather had turned overcast and misty, the perfect backdrop for our search for a lost village.

The information we received was scanty and anecdotal. We surmised that the village had slipped into the sea in a landslide associated with the cataclysmic earthquakes that occured in 1963 throughout Indonesia.

A rainstorm had made the waters murky, and we descended the anchorline to a clay bottom at 40 meters. Black corals were abundant, but this wasn't what we were looking for. We ascended along silt-covered terraces, reminiscent of rice paddies. It was beginning to look like a wild goose chase and then, at 25 meters, we found a horizontal tunnel, then a makeshift door, then some obviously fabricated stone blocks. A strange scene.

Nenung Pinnacles

The port of Tahuna, nestled in a deep and narrow bay, was our anchorage until just before dawn of the following day, when we motored to the pinnacles of Nenung. The setting was dramatic: craggy rocks riddled with caves and veined with the telltale rust of iron oxides; hillcrests cov-

ered in tenacious scrub; swarms of terns startled into flight by the sound of our engine.

The dive site at the southernmost of the pinnacles is named after Michael Aw, a photographer and our guide on this trip. Currents were strong, and we had to circle the southernmost of the pinnacles repeatedly, in opposition to the current, to drop divers in squads on the south face. The strategy was to empty BCs, drop fast, and grab hold.

We found two plateaus, then a gentle slope to white sand at 50 meters. There was good soft coral growth, and around the northeast, where the current picked up, huge schools of fish.

Ruang Island

We were wondering how the diving could possibly get any better, and then we went to Ruang, a dormant volcano that last erupte in 1956. The southern coast is a intriguing mosaic of verdant greens contrasting with the black bleakness of volcanic rock.

After a series of dives off south Ruang, we baptized site "Basilica," as its structure and carpeting of life inspired the wonder and awe of a baroque cathedral. Sponges were arrayed in all shapes, sizes and colors; crinoids came in every color. The fish life was fantastic: sharks, a giant grouper, dogtooth tuna, and huge schools of barracuda.

—Cody Shwaiko

Above: *A bubbling vent of the underwater volcano at Mahengetang in the Sangihe group.*

Atolls, Wrecks and a Diversity of Corals

Although not as famous or well-developed as the North Sulawesi sites, South and Central Sulawesi offer a trove of little-explored diving gems. Among the more notable are the Spermonde Archipelago off Ujung Pandang, Tanjung Bira and Selayar, the Tukang Besi Archipelago in Southeast Sulawesi, and the Togian Islands, nestled in Tomini Bay. The infrastructure for mass or luxury diving in these areas is not yet developed, but for those interested in exploratory diving, these are the places to go.

AT A GLANCE
South & Central Sulawesi

Reef types: Fringing reef slopes and walls, atolls, wrecks
Access: Speedboats, fishing boats
Visibility: Fair to excellent
Current: Moderate to strong, particularly during tidal flush
Coral: Excellent
Fish: Variable numbers, great diversity
Highlights: Kapoposang, Tukang Besi atolls, Taupun (Togians)

Ujung Pandang

The 16,000-square-kilometer Spermonde Archipelago off Ujung Pandang offers over 150 reefs within easy reach of the capital city of South Sulawesi. Home of the famous Makassarese and Bugis seafaring peoples, this archipelago, although heavily fished, ranks at the top of marine biodiversity surveys for eastern Indonesia.

The Spermonde offers a wide range of exciting dive possibilities— among them numerous fringing reefs with average to spectacular coral formations in 5–20 meter depths, three under-explored WWII wrecks in 20–40 meter depths and world-class wall diving along the shelf edge at Kapoposang Island, which has recently been gazetted as a marine park .

Although the fish life here has been heavily exploited, the reefs are generally in good shape and they boast over 300 species of hard coral, easily one of the highest diversity counts in the world for an area of this size. Coral buffs in particular should check out the west side of Bone Tambung, a tiny fishing village 14 kilometers offshore Ujung Pandang. This particular reef has an unusually well-developed reef flat with luxuriant coral growth in 2–6 meters depth. The very gradual western reef slope is interrupted by several sand terraces which are frequented by spotted eagle rays; huge cuttlefish are also commonly spotted here. Other mid-shelf reefs which afford similar diving possibilities include LumuLumu, Badi, and Bone Lola.

Wreck-diving enthusiasts will not be disappointed as this area was the site of numerous WW II skirmishes between Japanese and American forces, and the Makassar Dive Center offers trips to three of the better-preserved wrecks: a Japanese destroyer, a Japanese supply vessel, and an American fighter plane. Other wrecks rumored to exist in the area include a WW II bomber and a minesweeper.

For those who require sharks

for an adrenalin rush, deep dives along the shelf edge at Lanyukang Island (a wall which starts at 30 meters) or the wall at Kapoposang are guaranteed thrillers. The Makassar Dive Center has pioneered numerous dive sites along the extensive 200-meter-plus dropoff at Kapoposang. This is one of the few sites in the Spermonde where large fish are still relatively common—large grouper, Napoleon Wrasse and bumphead parrotfish on the wall nearest the island, and giant trevally and Spanish mackerel on the seaward side of the dropoff. The lagoon on the northwest side of the island is a true jewel. The protected waters have nurtured delicate coral formations which are absoutely stunning.

The best months for diving are April–June and September–November. Try to avoid the northwest monsoon (November–March), as the weather and seas can be very rough.

There is only one dive operator in Ujung Pandang—the Makassar Diving Center, locally known as POPSA—however, several travel agents and hotels offer day and overnight trips to the islands for snorkelling/picnicing. If you are of an independent mindset and can speak Indonesian reasonably, you can rent gear/tanks from the Makassar Diving Center and arrange a trip of your own by chartering a wooden speedboat from Pak Laut (literally, "Mr. Ocean") on the beach across from Fort Rotterdam. Talk to Pak Laut to arrange Sahid as your boatman, who has extensive knowledge of the reefs.

Bira/Selayar

At the southeastern tip of the southwest leg of Sulawesi lies Tanjung (Cape) Bira, and below it, the long narrow island of Selayar. This area, which has been slated for major tourism development, offers enthusiasts some

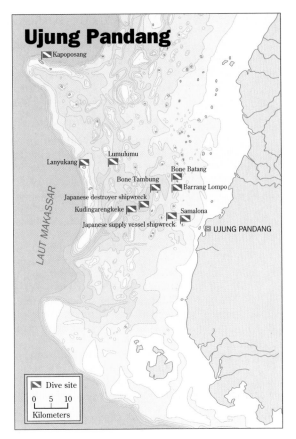

excellent exploratory diving.

Tanjung Bira is a very dry peninsula of uplifted fossil coral, with no freshwater river input. This feature, combined with the very deep waters of the Makassar Strait, makes for outstanding visibility year-round, and a plethora of marine life, including dolphins, mantas, large pelagics, and the ever-present sharks.

The diving around Bira itself is on nice fringing reefs, but most outstanding by far are the sheer walls of Pulau Kambing (Goat Island), a stark slab of rock rising out of the ocean between Bira and Selayar. The coral cover and fish life here can be fantastic.

The east coast of Selayar is said to have some of the most stunning beaches in Indonesia, with diving to match. A glance at the nautical charts for the area would seem to affirm this: the mountains plunge abruptly to the beach, creating spectacular waterfalls which cascade into white sand coconut groves, with further drop-offs into the deep blue only a couple of meters from the shore.

Tukang Besi Archipelago

Just off the southeastern tip of Sulawesi lies one of the undiscovered jewels of Indonesian diving, the Tukang Besi islands.

Named for the ironsmiths on the southernmost island of Binongko, this remote archipelago had Jacques Cousteau and members of the *Calypso* raving during their visit in the mid-1980's. Rising deep out of the Banda Sea, these islands boast all three of the major coral reef formations — atolls, fringing reefs, and a single barrier reef off the island of Wangi.

In addition, the four major islands of Wangi, Kaledupa, Tomea, and Binongko ("WaKa-ToBi") are very interesting in that they have been formed by geologic uplift of fossil coral terraces, evident in the step-like appearance of these islands from afar. A stroll through any of these islands reveals fascinating fossil reef formations, including the occasional giant clam or nautiloid shell.

The four big islands are populated, inland by the Butonese and at the ocean edge by the Bajo people ("sea gypsies"). The Bajo have thinned the fish populations on the fringing reefs, but there is still some excellent diving near the islands, especially the steep dropoffs around Binongko and Hoga.

But the real draw of this area are the many scattered atolls, most of which are inaccessible to the Bajo's dugout canoes for seven months of the year. Standouts include the Ndaa, Kapota, Koromaha, Moromaho, and Koka atolls. The fish populations here are as dense as any in Indonesia. The corals, both hard and soft, are fantastic.

The entire area serves as a cetacean thoroughfare, and night dives along the walls here are absolutely breathtaking. The entire wall bursts into vivid color as the Tubastrea and soft corals "bloom", and the diversity of in-

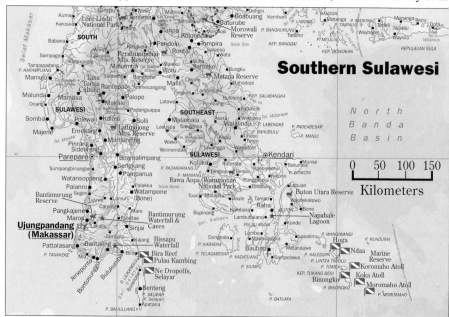

Southern Sulawesi

vertebrates (crustaceans, nudi-branchs, pencil urchins, etc) is bewildering. During two months of diving there, we encountered dugongs, sperm and pilot whales, spinner and bottlenose dolphins, coconut crabs, maleo birds, and orcas.

Currently, this area is completely inaccessible to divers except through expeditions with **Operation Wallacea**, a non-profit venture supported by Hong-kong Bank and the Indonesian government. The Tukang Besi archipelago is now slated for development as a National Marine Park, but the area is mostly unknown.

The concept behind Operation Wallacea is to bring in experienced dive volunteers, train them in coral reef rapid ecosystem assessment techniques, and then take them on two to four-week expeditions around the archipelago to assess the status of the reefs and fish populations. This data will then be used to help formulate a management plan for the park and zone it appropriately.

Togian Islands

For those who are interested in true exploration diving and are prepared to endure a tough journey to find it, the Togians are a must. These islands located in Tomini Bay in Central Sulawesi are well worth the journey.

Tomini Bay, reputedly the calmest bay in the world, is almost completely surrounded by the spidery arms of Sulawesi, which means relatively flat seas almost year-round and spectacular cyan-blue visibility. The islands are renowned for displaying all major reef formations (fringing, barrier, and atoll) and the corals here, safe from the threat of heavy wave damage, grow into beautifully delicate underwater forests.

Large schools of barracuda, big-eyed jacks and other pelagics are common around the outer reefs of Taupun, Taipi and the southeast of Batudaka and Togian. Hawksbill turtles and even dugongs are spotted among the many islands.

Of the six dives we did here, Taupun was unquestionably our favorite. The dropoff here is quite topographically complex and offers numerous small caves and crevices teeming with cryptic fish and crustaceans. Two large dog-toothed tuna continually buzzed us during the dive, and a huge eagle ray, apparently lulled into a dreamy glide by the bath-calm water, literally bumped into us before shooting off into the deep. A platoon of 20 large long-toms in flank formation hovered motionless near the surface, and butterfly-like clouds of anthias alternately swam into the slight current to feed, and then darted back into the reef framework for shelter. The ocean was so flat that the dense coral gardens of the reef flat were reflected down to us from the surface, creating the surreal impression of being surrounded by coral above, below and to the side. A banded sea krait kept us company during our safety stop, rounding out a truly unforgettable dive.

The Togian islands themselves are stunning. Scores of densely-forested rocky islands rise out of the placid water to create endless idyllic bays; a sea-kayaker's dream. Small pods of dolphins cruise the channels between these islands, and the sound of their spouting is one of the few disturbances to the mountain lake tranquility of the place. Reefs fringing the islands in these bays are poorly developed, but interesting for their abundance of gorgonians and soft corals. Avoid diving the reefs outside of the bay mouths during ebb tide, as quite strong currents flush the bays and temporarily reduce visibility drastically.

—*Mark Erdmann*

Mantas, Turtles, and a Strange Jellyfish Lake

The outline of a huge shape slowly emerged from the gloom. A shot of adrenaline whacked me as I made out a set of slowly flapping wings. At five meters the manta snapped into focus, enormous and black all over. Normal mantas are dark on top with a white belly. The black mantas are the largest of the many that hang around Sangalaki Island, off the east coast of Kalimantan, Indonesian Borneo.

The mantas around Sangalaki seldom reach their maximum 6 meter size; the larger ones averaging some 3.5 meters across.

AT A GLANCE
Sangalaki

Reef type:	Walls and slopes
Access:	1 hr by boat from Derawan
Visibility:	Seasonal; 5–15 meters
Current:	Modest
Coral:	Very good
Fish:	Excellent numbers and variety
Highlights:	Mantas, jellyfish lake at Kakaban Island

But what they lack in size, they make up in numbers—on a clear, sunny day, during the April–October season, up to a hundred have been seen on a single dive. They tend to feed near the surface in currents of about 1.5 knots, so to enjoy this show divers only have to descend 5 meters and go with the flow.

Since Sangalaki opened for sports diving in April 1993, every client has seen mantas, with the exception of three members of a small group who were there in early January. Others, in the same group did see some, so very occasionally manta sightings could be a matter of luck. During the local rainy season, which starts around November–December and ends around late March, the visibility sometimes falls to 5–8 meters, but it does not stay this lousy all the time during the wet season—all it takes is a few days of sunshine for visibility to improve.

Even in restricted visibility, there's plenty to see. Circumstances brought me to Sangalaki in mid-January for five days' diving—not the ideal time for clear waters. But the diving was still so good that I wanted to extend my stay a few more days which, unfortunately, was impossible.

Diving Sangalaki

Every dive at Sangalaki was worthwhile, revealing something unusual for me. One of my guides, Yien-Yien, has identified over 40 species of nudibranchs along with at least six colorful flatworms. She pointed out couple of dozen nudis and four flatworms during our dives. My other guide, Jon, spotted three species of barracuda during one of our night dives, along with sleeping flounders, a nesting Titan triggerfish (about the only marine organism I fear—but only in daytime) and lots more. One day dive brought a huge grouper into view, on another we found a pair of unusual pink leaf-fish. Friendly cuttlefish abound. Polka-dot groupers (*Chromileptes altavelis*) are common, as are scorpionfishes.

By top-Indonesian standards, we found fish life somewhat lack-

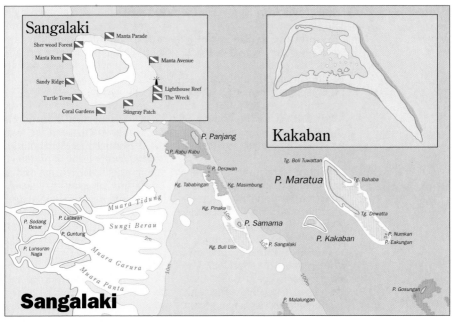

Sangalaki

Sher wood Forest | Manta Parade
Manta Rum | Manta Avenue
Sandy Ridge |
Turtle Town | Lighthouse Reef / The Wreck
Coral Gardens | Stingray Patch

P. Panjang
P. Rabu Rabu

Kakaban

Tg. Boli Tuwattan
P. Derawan
Kg. Tababingan   Kg. Masimbung   P. Maratua
Tg. Bahaba

Kg. Pinaka
Tg. Dewatta
P. Sodang Besar   P. Lajawan   Sungi Berau
P. Guntung   2m   P. Samama   P. Kakaban
Kg. Buli Ulin   P. Sangalaki   P. Numkan / P. Eakungan
P. Lunsuran Naga

Muara Tidung
Muara Garura
Muara Panta

10m   100m

P. Malalungan
P. Gosungan

Sangalaki

ing—good but not excellent. Schooling fish were only occasionally seen: spotted rabbitfish, batfish, snappers, fairy basslets, glassfish and cardinals. On the other hand, both hard and soft coral cover is excellent, showing no dynamite damage. A few overturned blocks of table coral were perhaps due to careless diving by the abundant green turtles.

Development of Sangalaki

Borneo Divers' building of a 5-star PADI facility on Sangalaki deserves unstinted praise. This top-rated dive operator opened the island of Sipadan several years ago, after an extensive program of explorations searching for a world-class location. Sipadan surpassed all expectations and, with extensive marketing, drew demanding clients from the USA and Europe. But the superb diving also drew other operators to Sipadan with now far too many bodies — divers and support staff — for the small island's fragile ecology.

So Borneo Divers' search began all over for another dive location. It took a couple of years to find Sangalaki and to check out its potential. Then, having learned their lesson from Sipadan, Borneo Divers, along with their Indonesian partners, obtained the exclusive rights to develop the island's potential: no other operators allowed. Following the strictest ecological guidelines possible, ten two-bed wood bungalows were built with all the required support facilities.

After scarcely a year of operation Borneo Divers' Indonesian partners, who were loosing money in other businesses, were forced to pull out. The dive operation shut down, but after a year and a half, Borneo Divers found another partner and reopened diving on Sangalaki.

Derawan Island

Derawan Island, about an hour's boat ride from Sangalaki, also offers diving and tourist facilities—and at the time of this writing, the only access to Sangalaki. Just over 1,000 people live on 2.5-square-kilometer Derawan, most of them of the Bajau ethnic group. These former sea nomads and occasional pirates started settling down in the area in the late 19th century.

While the diving is not as good on Derawan as it is at Sangalaki, the scuba facilities, a part of the Bhumi Manimbora complex, seem well run by two PADI-trained dive masters from Bali. (We didn't have the chance to dive with them). The compressor and rental equipment looked well looked-after.

The nearby dive spots are passable and, although the boat ride is a bit long, the operator can take you diving on Sangalaki, Kakaban, and other sites.

For diving with this outfit, you make reservations at their dive shop, the Derawan, at the Benakutai Hotel in Balikpapan, then fly on a small Merpati plane to Tanjung Berau via Samarinda. The operator will pick you up at Tanjung Berau and whiz you over to Derawan by speedboat. (See Practicalities page 291).

Tourism started on Derawan in 1987 and most foreign visitors, usually Europeans, visit the island in July and August. But so far, no crowds, so it's unlikely that accommodations will be full.

A new resort with cottage-style rooms facing the white-sand beach should be open by the time you read this, and there are two inexpensive *losmen* on the island. There is also the possibility of homestays.

A newly started yearly Pesta Laut ("Sea Festival") starts on November 4 and runs for four days. Featured events include: diving, competition swimming, spear and line fishing and a "marathon" around the island. During the evening, songs and traditional dances entertain guests—who so far are few indeed, due to a lack of publicity.

Sea Turtles

Green sea turtles love, breed and lay their eggs on several of the small islands off the northeast coast of Kalimantan. Sangalaki is their island of choice, a genetically imprinted home turf, programmed when the baby turtles hatch and make that first mad dash for the sea. About 20 years after birth, the green turtles (*Chelonia mydas*) return to their home island measuring well over a meter in length, and weighing

Below: *The pier on Derawan Island.*

some 90 kilograms.

They breed just off the island, then the females crawl ashore at night, laboriously dig a large hole in the sand, lay an average of 70 fertilized eggs, cover the nests with sand and drag themselves back into the sea. This procedure is repeated three to five times during the female's fertile season, which occurs every two or three years after sexual maturity.

Depending on the ambient temperature, the eggs hatch in 50 to 65 days. The baby's sex is also temperature-determined: if the nest temperature is above 27°C, all the eggs develop as females, if colder, all males. Most of the babies perish in that first clumsy run to the sea, as birds and other predators gobble up the helpless little fellows. Estimates of the hatchlings' survival rate suggest that perhaps 2 percent make it to adulthood.

Until Borneo Divers developed the site, Sangalaki was a famous turtle egg gathering site. In 1991, some 1.5 million eggs were taken from the nests on the various islands, about half of these from Sangalaki. Using the 2 percent survival estimate, that meant 30,000 fewer adult turtles every year.

When they opened Sangalaki, Borneo Divers found the perfect way to stop the collecting. The turtle egg concessions are awarded through a bidding process, and Borneo Divers simply bought the concession for Sangalaki. This was a rather expensive solution, however, and on April 1, 1993, they paid $50,000 to insure that not more eggs would be taken from the island.

Even better, the dive outfit hired the men who had previously made their living by robbing the nests. One of these men, Pak Tambuli, the doyen of turtle-egg gatherers, had been at this job since before World War II. Now well into his 70s, (he doesn't know exactly how old he is) the still vigorous old man gathers data on the turtles. Walking around the island each day, guided by the turtle tracks in the sand, he counts the number of nests made the previous night. He keeps track on a long leaf or piece of scratch paper. He also tracks how many nests hatch each day. This information is entered into the resort's computer to build a long-term record.

Borneo Divers further helped the laying mother turtles by following a minimum necessary electric light policy at night to prevent the disorientation of the females when they return to the ocean. The technique works. During my five nights on Sangalaki, when some 50 nests were dug every night, anywhere from one to four nests were made within a few meters from my cabin—with one nest just outside my front porch.

Be sure to bring a flashlight to prevent stumbling into a nest when returning at night from the central lobby to your cabin, or when you have to answer a call of nature. Watching the turtles dig their nest and lay their eggs is a unique experience for Sangalaki's visitors.

And, of course, you will see them underwater. The turtles here are not as diver-friendly as those on Sipadan, a well-known dive site north of Sangalaki, off the coast of Sabah, Malaysian Borneo, which have had several years to get used to the human bubble-machines. But we had several brief but intimate encounters with the green turtles during our dives.

Kakaban Island

Less than a half hour away in one of the dive boats, Kakaban Island offers an excellent wall dive with a vertical, cave-pocked drop to a bit over 50 meters. There might be some current here, but basically this is an easy dive for expe-

Above: *Sangalaki is one of the most favored green turtle (Chelonia mydas) nesting areas in the region. Unfortunately, a taste for their eggs and—in Bali—a market for the meat threatens these animals.*

rienced divers.

We saw many schooling surgeons and snappers, along with barrel sponges and, at depth, large gorgonian fans. Other divers here have spotted reef white-tip sharks, grays and—on one occasion—a bone-chilling 5-meter hammerhead. The topside decompression stop alone is worth the dive, with excellent coral cover, swarming with colorful fairy basslets.

But Kakaban has a much more unusual dive site. A brackish lake fills much of the central part of the island, slightly above sea level, with a salt concentration only about two-thirds that of the ocean. The lake holds many species of marine life, some very new to science. There are hundreds of stingless jellyfish, of four different species, pulsating along on the surface and at various depths. (See "Kakaban" opposite.)

There are just eight species of fish, all of them small, but they are unusually unafraid of divers. We watched some fish dive into the soft muck at the lake bottom for what we supposed were tasty

tidbits. Others would follow some of the divers who, with less than perfect buoyancy control and careless finning technique, stirred up great clouds which settle very slowly. Fish enter these clouds, we suppose for mini-morsels.

We also saw tunicates, small, colonial bivalves, nudibranchs, a land snake, the unusual jellyfish-eating white Kakaban anemone, at least three species of sea cucumbers, sponges, and two kinds of crabs, These crabs were the only animals in the lake which we could call skittish.

The lake is ringed by thickly encrusted mangrove roots, and the slopes at the lake edge are covered in Vegetation includes heavily encrusted mangrove roots at the lake's edge and a thick, bushy growth of *Caulerpa* on the slopes and covering some sections of the bottom profile.

It's an easy, 10-minute walk to the lake along a wide trail hacked out of the vegetation. The trail leads past a hut used by some copra makers, who temporarily live on the island to gather and dry coconuts.

Kakaban: A Biological Paradise

Kakaban, a low, limestone island off the coast of eastern Borneo, holds a fascinating surprise: a brackish lake literally alive with jellyfish.

"The lake is totally unique—a biological paradise," said Canadian marine ecologist Dr. Thomas Tomascik, who together with his wife Anmarie has been studying Kakaban. "It teems with jellyfish and other marine creatures, yet is isolated from the sea. You really must see it for yourself to appreciate it."

According to Tomascik, the famous jellyfish lake in the Palau Islands—the only other known example—is a biological desert compared to Kakaban.

Kakaban Island is a coral atoll that has been uplifted by geological forces, turning the lagoon into a land-locked lake. The 5-square-kilometer lake, surrounded by a 50-meter ridge, occupies most of the interior of this uninhabited island, which has been declared a government nature reserve.

The Tomasciks hope to solve the mystery of how the lake's plants and animals are able to survive in this isolated system. The lake has no outlets, but fresh saltwater continually seeps in from below, mixing with trapped rainwater. The salinity averages 24–26 parts per thousand, considerably less salty than normal sea water.

The seepage from outside seems insufficient to sustain the abundance of life in the lake, and most likely the lake operates as a more or less closed system, with nutrients being produced and recycled in its own waters.

From the surface Kakaban looks like a typical freshwater lake, but below there is an abundance of colorful marine life. The shoreline is fringed with a tangle of mangroves. Their sturdy roots, as thick as a human arm, are cloaked with sponges, seaweeds and tunicates. Visibility is around 10–12 meters, and the lake is at most 11 meters deep.

Although not a particularly diverse ecosystem, the lake's unique ecology and the unusual associations between organisms make it a fascinating subject.

The dominant animals in the lake are jellyfishes, of which two species are particularly abundant. In the deeper areas, a species of rhizostome jelly forms such dense concentrations that it's like swimming in a kettle of jellyfish soup. Fortunately they do not usually sting. Another species, the upside-down jelly, literally carpets the bottom in parts of the lake.

One of the most unusual animals in the lake is an as yet undescribed species

ROGER STEENE

of pure white anemone which, in the absence of more usual planktonic prey, feeds on jellyfish. Jellyfish that blunder into its tentacles are immobilized and summarily devoured.

Eight species of fish have been identified here. A cardinalfish (*Apogon lateralis*) and goby (*Exyrias puntang*) are by far the most abundant, and in the absence of large fish predators these are totally fearless. Another of the lake's five gobies is a new species of *Cristatagobius* with an unusual cock's comb.

—*Gerald R. Allen*

Introducing Maluku

The islands of the Moluccas—Maluku in modern Indonesian—were the first in the archipelago to capture the imagination of the Europeans. Not for their beauty, although these thousand-odd islands, with powder-white beaches, swaying coconut palms, and constant, lazy sunshine certainly fit most northerners' definition of paradise. The Europeans came in search of one of the world's most coveted commodities—spices.

The Spice Islands

In the 16th century, cloves, nutmeg and mace were literally worth their weight in gold in Europe. When the 18 men aboard the *Victoria,* the only survivors of Ferdinand Magellan's original expedition of 230 men and five ships, hobbled home with their load of just over a ton of cloves, they all became rich men.

From the beginning of the spice trade—Chinese sources make reference to cloves as early as the beginning of the common era—until the Dutch planted cloves on Ambon Island, every clove in the world came from the tiny islands of Ternate and Tidore, just off the west coast of Halmahera (see map page 212). All the world's nutmeg—and the even more precious mace, which comes from the bright red aril that surrounds the nutmeg "nut"—came from the tiny, and isolated, Banda Islands.

Today, Indonesia grows more cloves in Sulawesi than in Ternate or Tidore, and nutmeg and mace is produced in Grenada, in the Caribbean. The early European explorers would no doubt be shocked to find out where most of the world's cloves end up today: in *kretek,* the ubiquitous Indonesian clove cigarets.

The People of Maluku

Maluku no longer attracts much attention. The old Dutch forts sit crumbling, and ancient Portuguese armor and gold pieces have become heirlooms to be passed down by families through the generations. Other than Ambon—a city of 275,000 and the center for communications in the three provinces of Maluku—and Ternate, the islands have only scattered small population centers.

Most Moluccans are fishermen and farmers. Because many of the sandy islands do not support rice, they rely on manioc, taro and sweet potatoes as staples, with fresh fish for protein.

In the interiors of Seram, Halmahera and some of the other large islands, people who trace their genealogies back further even than the arrival of the first Malays live lives relatively untouched by the modern world.

Two Island Arcs

The islands of Central and South Maluku are made up of two parallel, but differently formed, island chains. The outer arc of islands—continuing from Timor through Leti, the Babar Islands, the Tanimbars, the Kei Islands and then around through Seram and Buru—is made of calcareous rock, the remainder of ancient reefs. The inner arc—continuing from Flores and the Alor archipelago to Wetar, the Damar Islands, and ending in the isolated Banda archipelago—is part of Indonesia's "Ring of Fire," a string of volcanic islands that

Overleaf: *A view of Gunung Api in the Banda Islands, sitting in splendid isolation in the middle of the Banda Sea. Photograph by Kal Muller.*

Opposite: *Pearl oysters hanging from an underwater fence. The oysters are cultivated in this way until they are large enough to form pearls. Then they are shipped off to one of the many Japanese-run pearl farms where they are seeded and left to grow pearls. This is Bobale Island, off the east coast of Halmahera's north peninsula. Photograph by Helmut Debelius, IKAN.*

mark the edge of a crustal plate.

North Maluku is quite separate. Halmahera Island, shaped like a miniature Sulawesi, was formed, like its larger neighbor, when two long islands were joined together by the forces of continental drift. The western side of the island, including tiny Ternate and Tidore, is volcanic; the eastern side is a mixture of limestone and other rock.

Underwater Riches

The sea was never low enough to allow land crossings between all the islands of Maluku, and the animal life of the islands reflects this: although there are few mammals, birds and insects have done well on the islands. The birds are varied and beautiful—kingfishers, lories, parrots and in the Aru Islands, the legendary birds of paradise.

According to 19th century naturalist Alfred Russel Wallace the fishes of Maluku are "perhaps unrivaled for variety and beauty by those of any one spot on earth."

Unfortunately, diving in the region is currently limited to the Banda Islands and a very new operation in Ambon. One can only dream of what the diving is like in the Gorom and Watubel Islands, or the small islands in the Kei group, seasonally washed by rich upwellings from the depths of the Banda Sea.

—*David Pickell*

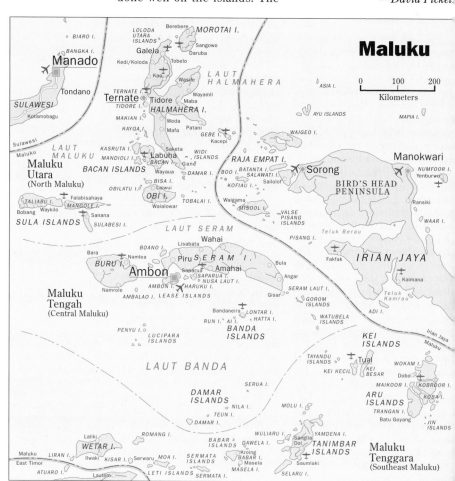

Fine Diving in the Central Moluccas

In the Ambon and Saparua areas, aficionados can find dive sites that are truly world-class. Scuba has just begun here, and the divers who have experienced the area have been trying hard to keep it secret. Sorry chaps, here is the lowdown.

Our summer dives off Ameth village on Nusa Laut island rate the very highest marks, particularly for the number of big fish seen there. Divers have asked Tony Tomasoa, currently the only dive operator in the area, not to spread the word. But you can't blame Tony. He is a businessman, and has no objections to more clients.

Nusa Laut

In just one and one-half hours underwater off Nusa Laut, we saw: three gray reef sharks of 1.5 meters; three large turtles, including one of over a meter; a dozen enormous Napoleon wrasse, including one school of four; two very impressive giant groupers; two large dogtooth tuna; two black-spotted rays; a barracuda of more than a meter; a dozen longnosed emperors; and two huge reef lobsters.

In addition to the big fellows, we were enveloped at one point by a huge school of fearless longfin bannerfish (*Heniochus diphreutes*). We saw a school of black jacks (*Caranx lugubris*) and a few giant jacks (*C. ignoblis*); several large schools of unicornfish; and a school of Thompson's surgeonfish.

The colorful crowd of reef fish were out in force. We counted 12 species of butterflyfish, six species of angelfish, and saw Moorish idols, snappers, rainbow runners, and more. This is really a rich site. Some divers have reported spotting the rare, lumbering dugongs here.

But the big ones are not guaranteed at this location. Our initial dives at Nusa Laut were in May, when visibility was nothing to brag about, around 10–15 meters. As a very general rule, the top visibility in the Ambon/Lease area lasts from September through November.

The northwest monsoon blows on and off from May through August, bringing occasional showers and rough seas for a few days. The southeast monsoon lasts from May through August, with long, heavy rains and wind-driven seas which can go on for weeeks. But during this time, the north shores are still diveable.

June is the area's wettest month, averaging some 650 millimeters over 24 rainy days. Diurnal tides are between 2.2 and 2.3 meters. Usually (but not always) the fish life is best seen during the rising tide.

AT A GLANCE
Ambon and Lease

Reef type: Walls and slopes

Access: 30 min to 1 hr by speedboat

Visibility: Fair to excellent, 10–13 meters; depending on the season

Current: Moderate or none

Coral: Some areas quite good

Fish: Excellent at the best sites

Highlights: Huge arches, possibility of large fish at several sites

Lease Islands Diving

Although we found our initial dives at Ameth village the very best in the Ambon/Saparua vicinity, this was probably due to plain dumb luck. There are many other excellent locations. For diving around Saparua, Nusa Laut and Molana islands, it is the most convenient to stay at the Mahu Diving Lodge on the east shore of Tuhana Bay, north Saparua Island. The center is owned and operated by Tony Tomasoa's Daya Patal Tour and Travel, based in Ambon. This travel agency can handle all your logistics and diving.

While the dive operation on Mahu was not a professional one, help was on its way in early 1994. The dive guides speak very little English but the capable boatmen know the locations well. Speedboats powered by twin 40 hp outboards whisk divers to sites.

Ameth and Akon

Ameth village on Nusa Laut faces a small bay filled with sand and coral that is exposed at low tide. The reefs off this village, as well as those off Akon, further south along coast of Nusa Laut, offer fine diving. (See map below.)

The people of Ameth and Akon take good care of their reefs, allowing no fish bombing. Before diving here, the operator must ask the villagers' permission, which is easily obtained upon payment of a very reasonable users' fee. (This is included in the package prices already paid by the guests.)

Dives at Ameth begin off the reef edge, which drops vertically to sloping sand at 40–60 meters. The far ends of the site are coral and sand slopes. (See map page 218). Corals—both hard and soft—are abundant in areas, but not overall. But sponges grow here in unusual numbers.

During some dives in May and July, the big fish life here was tremendous. But dives off Ameth in late January offered nothing big except for a panic-stricken reef white-tip shark, a couple of Napoleons, a few barracuda and the odd tuna. Of course, this wouldn't have been too bad if we had not remembered the previous dives here.

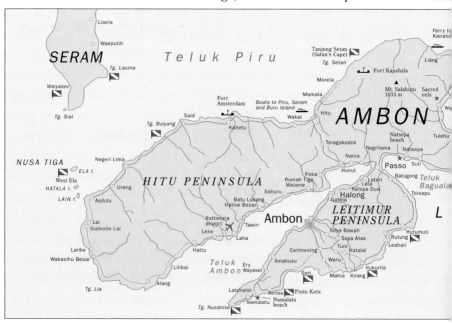

Also, January visibility was much better, in the 25–30 meter range.

The next time we dove we stuck to the areas marked 5 and 6 on the map on page 218, and at slack tide. Here we found a large (well over 100) mixed aggregation of snappers and chubs, drifing along at 15–20 meters near a huge school of surgeons. Sand flats at 15 meters sprouted mini-forests of garden eels, patrolled by Titan triggerfish.

The coral knoll (6 on the map) was decorated by two very large soft coral trees at its base which, from the seaward side, opens into a swim-through featuring two schools of cardinal-fishes. A long decompression stop was rewarded by excellent coral cover at 3–5 meters, with many damselfish and outrageously colorful small wrasses.

During our two dives off Akon we encountered visibility of more than 30 meters. The wall drops from the fringing reeftop, at 2–6 meters, straight down to 50–60 meters. The wall is full of shallow caves and has several ledges.

A huge arch marks the end of the dive—one could also start here, depending on the current. The top of this arch forms a continuation of the reef edge, at about 6 meters. At its highest, the inner arch reaches to about 12 meters below the surface, with a width varying between 6 and 12 meters.

The arch encloses an approximately oval-shaped opening, 5 meters high and 15 meters wide. The bottom profile slopes through the arch, then drops vertically in ledges from to more than 40 meters. The body of the arch, especially the underside of the "roof," is full of small pockets, along with thickets of soft coral trees, barrel sponges growing at crazy angles and daisy cup corals. Try it at night, when the polyps open to feed.

The bulk of the wall section that we dove off Akon had the usual invertebrates and reef fishes. With one notable exception: a cape-like projection into the sea, at about 20 meters, where the current picked up from 1/4 knot to occasional gusts of one knot. From the sheltered side of the cape we observed a very large aggregation of curious

The Lease Islands

Selat Seram

Forts Niew Hoorn and New Zeeland (both in ruins)
Ferry landing
Pelau
Kulor
Pia
Nolot
Itawaka
Teluk Tuhaha
Iha
Ferry landing
Iha-Mahu
Mahu
Tuhaha

Kabau
Hulahu
Tiou
SAPARUA
Fort Duurstede
Sirisore Saran
Sirisore Islam

HARUKU
Porto Haria
Saparua
Waisisil beach
Ouw

Haruku
Wesu
Aburu
Paperu
Booi
Teluk Saparua
Pombo Booi
Pottery making
Fort Beverwijk

Northwest Molana
East Molana
MOLANA I.
Nalahia
Ameth
Ameth

South Molana
Tenitu
Sila
NUSA LAUT
Akon & Arch

E I S L A N D S
Titawai
Akon
Abubu

Laut Banda

Dive site
0   5   10
Kilometers

medium-sized fishes, mostly snappers and unicorns.

Molana Island

South Molana is a good dive, off a flat reef which extends south of the island. The reef slops very gradually from 3-4 meters to the drop-off at 10-20 meters. From this edge, a wall drops vertically to flat sand at 40 meters. The wall face is full of caves, ledges and large depressions, with soft corals and a few gorgonian fans.

Reef fish variety was quite good, highlighted by three humphead parrots. The topside deco stop offered spreads of staghorn coral. A few snappers came up from their normal, slightly deeper habitants and several small schools of yellow-striped goatfish. Our dive here offered 25–30 meters visibility, and no currents, although a slight downcurrent often runs from the reeftop to the depths. We saw none of the sharks said to be present in numbers according to locals.

The profile at Southeast Molana is similar to that on the island's south side, but the reeftop is higher, 2–6 meters, and less extensive. The wall, with less relief, bottoms out to sand at 30 meters. Fish life was slightly better here than on the other sides of Molana, with schooling fusiliers, a large school of bannerfish near the lower end of the wall and a big, lonely barracuda patrolling the shallows. The topside showed good cover of hard and soft corals.

Pombo Booi

A small islet just east of the southwest peninsula of Saparua Island goes by the name of Pombo (local name for pigeon) Booi (the name of the nearest village. The site is also sometimes called Mamala.

We found the fish life here better than Molana—excellent species variety and very good

numbers. The most noticeable species included painted sweet-lips, snappers, yellow- and blue-streak fusiliers, long-nosed emperors, angels and Titan trig-gerfish. And a fair-sized black-tipped reef shark, along with a large Napoleon wrasse.

There were lots of tunicates and spreads of leather corals, along with a normal variety of soft corals. We dove in a slight current, and reached a sand bottom at 35 meters. The dive spot has many outcrops, some with caves and swim-thoughts.

We had an excellent night dive in Saparua Bay at a nearby location. Highlights include numerous Spanish Dancers, hermit crabs, and octopus. Depths vary from 4 to 12 meters. We also saw many urchins—at least five different species—all with mean sets of spines, so be careful at night. This location is only known to and dived during the cruises of the live-aboard *Pindito*. (See page 228.)

Nusa Tiga

The three tiny islands at the westernmost end of Ambon Island are called, simply enough, Nusa Tiga ("Three Islands"). We anchored for the night at Asilu-lu, on the far western tip of Ambon's Hitu Peninsula, and after obtaining permission from the traditional ruler of the area, headed out to dive the area.

We started both dives off the west coast of Ela Island, following the reef north on the first dive, south on the second one. The reef profile was a slope of 45 degrees, well-covered in diverse species of coral. Several large schools of black triggerfish (*Odonus niger*) checked us out, and moray eels weaved menacingly out of several holes.

We saw fusiliers, a very large aggregation of unicornfish (at least 70 individuals) and a small group of sweetlips. Clown and Titan triggerfish patrolled the

reef, and we counted a dozen species of butterflyfish.

At depths of 15 to 25 meters we saw several large bamboo fish traps, belonging to the Butonese fishermen who maintain a few huts and a prayer house on Ela Island.

Diving Ambon

The Ambon Dive Centre, which opened in early 1994, seems like a good bet to see the best of the nearby underwater world. The operator has two NAUI dive masters, one Indonesian, the other English. Sony, with hundreds of dive around Ambon, knows the best dive spots and guarantees good, year-round dives, shifting locations according to weather conditions. Laura handles walk-in clients and promotions as well as escorting guests. It is a professionally run outfit.

The Centre is based in Namalatu, near the Leitimur Peninsula's southwest tip. Namalatu is about a half-hour's drive, along the shore of Ambon Bay, from the city. It is a pleasant trip once you're out of city traffic. From there, the operator's 9-meter fiberglass dive boat, powered by twin 40 hp outboards, whisk divers to various locations.

During the northwest monsoon, from around September to March diving is generally along the south coast; during the southeast winds, about May through August, diving is better on Ambon's northern areas, along with west Seram.

The maximum length of the boat rides is two hours, usually much less. If the seas are a bit rough for the speedboat ride from Namalatu to the north, clients are taken overland to Hilu, where the operator maintains a base camp and the speedboat waits. The Centre plans to buy a 15-meter wooden ship, with a rubber dingy, for diving at further out locations.

There are a wealth of attractions among the Centre's 30-odd tried-and-true dive spots. The sites feature a variety of profiles, some with spectacular underwater formations: arches, caves, bubbling sand, chimneys, and vertical walls.

Fish life is always good, but it takes luck to see the area's most

Above: *Cuttlefish can sometimes be coaxed into allowing a diver to touch them. Although molluscs, they have a very large repertoire of behaviors, and like their relatives, squid and octopus, can be among the most entertaining animals encountered on the reef. The cuttlefish's "cuttlebone" is a porous calcareous structure that helps the animal with buoyancy control.*

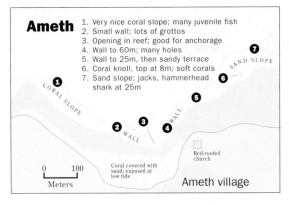

Ameth
1. Very nice coral slope; many juvenile fish
2. Small wall; lots of grottos
3. Opening in reef; good for anchorage
4. Wall to 60m; many holes
5. Wall to 25m, then sandy terrace
6. Coral knoll, top at 8m; soft corals
7. Sand slope; jacks, hammerhead shark at 25m

CORAL SLOPE

SAND SLOPE

WALL

WALL

0   100
Meters

Coral covered with sand; exposed at low tide

Red-roofed church

Ameth village

spectacular denizens: big tuna, sharks, manta and eagle rays, Napoleon wrasses, schools of humphead parrots, barracuda. The real show-stoppers, according to the guides, are absolutely huge groupers, described to us as "VW Beetle–sized."

Of course, none of these can be guaranteed on any one dive. But in one of the locations, several species of big morays are always lurking in their caves. A strange blue-colored dart goby (a species which is usually red) can be occasionally spotted. Octopus sightings are frequent.

Night diving, just in front of the Centre's base at Namalatu, can be rewarding indeed, with Spanish dancer nudibranchs and lots more. It can be so good in fact, that the liveaboard *Cehili*'s divemaster, Larry Smith, says he has had his best night dive ever here. (And Larry Smith has more than 11,000 dives).

Amboina Diving Club

If you speak at least some Indonesian, and you want to dive with the locals try the Amboina Diving Club. The club was founded in 1988 and has 20 active members. Most are businessmen, so they practice their sport only on Sundays and holidays. But the club owns two dive boats and there are guides—who speak minimal English—available with a bit of advance notice.

The club offers two-dive day trips to 11 locations off the outer periphery of Ambon, with the cost depending on the distance from the harbor. While none of the dive spots are world-class, most are quite decent, and the club knows the area very well. We tried two locations with one of their guides.

Waimahu, off the southwest tip of Leitimur, looked good—it si on the cape and there was current flowing—but turned out to be quite ordinary. It was a beach entry and we swam out by following long, narrow gaps in the dead reef.

At first we dipped into a half-knot current, following a slope to about 30 meters, then returned in shallower water. Visibility was fair at 15 meters, and the coral was undamaged by fish-bombing. But fish life was rather scarce: sharks, sometimes sighted here, kept well out of sight when we dove.

Our second dive, at Pintu Kota ("City Gate") was much better. We followed the dive boat's anchor line to about 25 meters and a Napoleon wrasse was waiting to greet us. Following the sea bed at the lower edge of a ridge, we soon arrived at a huge arch some 10 meters high and 15 meters wide: the City Gate.

Two species of jacks, including some big ones, came by to check us out, the more curious approaching to within a meter. A school of surgeonfish and a bunch of fusiliers guarded one side of the arch, and a white-tip shark patrolled the far side.

We ascended up a couple of submerged ridges sprouting an almost-solid carpet of small tapering orange sponges covered with bumps and interspersed with purple-laced *Polycarpa* tunicates. A moray slithered out of its lair, curious but not aggressive. Stopping at 8 meters on the ridge-top, we hung on in a half-knot current to decompress a bit. An excellent dive.

Pristine Reefs and Many Pelagic Fish

The Banda Islands are one of Indonesia's top destinations for divers. Both experts and beginners will enjoy themselves here, as the diving ranges from the shallow lagoon between Banda Neira and Gunung Api to the vertical walls of Hatta Island, the most easterly in the group.

The variety and numbers of fish are both excellent; the chances here are always good to see several big animals of a meter or more: reef sharks, Napoleon wrasse, turtles, rays and groupers. Schools of medium sized fish, and the usual kaleidoscope of small reef fish in the shallows are all here in abundance. The reefs we saw were pristine, with no signs of fish bombing damage. Currents were negligible at the sites and times we dove.

Banda has two dive seasons—one centered around April, the other in October. The months before and after these are usually quite good also, but any more than that is a matter of luck. The off seasons bring high waves and relatively turbulent seas, usually December/January during the northwest monsoon, and early June through August for the southeast monsoon.

But, with enough time and patience, one can enjoy good diving even off-season, as there are always breaks in the weather. Visibility, however, remains restricted to 10–20 meters off season, reaching 30–40 meters only around the ideal months.

Staying in Banda

Diving is available only to guests staying at one of Des Alwi's hotels, although this is hardly a problem. Des Alwi is Banda's most famous son, and a tireless promoter of his islands. While Mohammed Hatta and Sutan Sjahrir—two of the leaders of Indonesian independence—were exiled in Banda, they became mentors to the young Des Alwi, who later entered the world of diplomacy and business.

AT A GLANCE

Banda

Reef type:	Vertical walls, and some slopes
Access:	5 min to 1.5 hrs by speedboat
Visibility:	Fair to excellent, 10–20 meters in the off season; up to 40 meters during the best months
Current:	None or moderate, to 1.5 knots
Coral:	Excellent, undamaged reefs
Fish:	Excellent numbers and varieties at the best sites
Highlights:	Pristine, sheer walls and great number of fish off Ai and Hatta

---

After a quarter of a century, he returned to his native islands, and there applied himself to building up the infrastructure and the economy, and raising the profile of the little islands in the Indonesian nation and in the world. He is extremely knowledgeable about the history and culture of his islands.

The cost of diving—boat, tanks, weight belts—is quite reasonable, and if there are just two people diving, there are good spots near Banda Neira to keep boat costs down. For trips further out, it's easier on the wallet to form groups of 4 to 6 divers.

Although there are a few BCs and regulators for rent, we suggest, as always, that you bring your own equipment, including lights for night dives. The boatmen know the good dive spots, but there are no dive masters.

Non-divers need not worry about boredom: the snorkeling is good in the lagoon right off Banda Neira, there are tennis courts, and jaunts can easily be arranged to ruined forts and nutmeg plantations. Although the Bandas are not the ideal place for children, attentive hotel staffers will look after them as they jump off seaside diving boards, swim in calm waters, or watch the sharks, fish and turtles in two coral enclosures in the lagoon.

Sonegat

You could start diving the day you get to Banda, as the flight from Ambon arrives in the early morning. The nearest site for a decent dive is just five minutes by boat from the hotels. It is in the *sonegat*—"sea arm"—between Banda Neira and Gunung Api, just offshore from a little seaside house owned by Des Alwi.

The dropoff here is steep, and the wall extends down 25 meters to a grey, sandy bottom. The wall is cut by vertical clefts, and is overgrown with huge patches of cabbage coral. There were few fish around, but a good-sized dogtooth tuna cruised by, and we saw some of the beautiful blue-girdled and emperor angelfish.

Keraka Island

Pulau Keraka—"Crab Island"— is just a few minutes further out, and protects the north entrance of the Neira–Gunung Api sea passage. A nice sandy stretch on the north coast is perfect for a picnic. We started our dive just off the south shore, descending some 18 meters down a mini-wall covered with hundreds of large blue-and-yellow tunicates (*Polycarpa* sp.).

Swimming to the east, we rounded Keraka's tip, where there is a lighthouse, and started along the north face. Just as we turned the corner, we met a huge grouper, who examined us unhurriedly. At 10 meters we encountered a good assortment of reef fish, and a school of half-

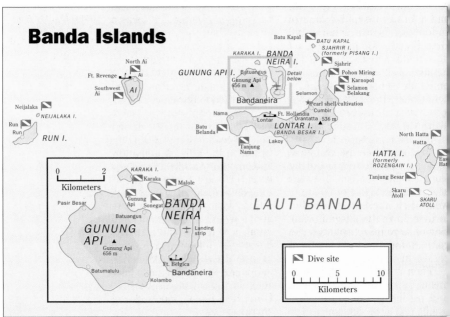

neter-long barracudas, hanging
out like hoodlums deciding on
their next move.

Sjahrir and Batu Kapal

Just off the northern tip of Lontar
Island is Sjahrir (formerly Pulau
Pisang, "Banana Island"), recently renamed for Sutan Sjahrir, one
of Des Alwi's childhood mentors
and a former Prime Minister of
Indonesia. Sjahrir Island, and
Batu Kapal—"Boat Stone"—off
its northern point, are just 20
minutes by boat from the hotels
on Banda Neira. These two sites
combine well for a morning dive,
a picnic on the beach, and an
afternoon dive.

Our first dive was off the
north edge of Batu Kapal, and at
first we encountered a boring
slope leading to a sandy trench
at 25 meters. This did not auger
well for an interesting dive. But
further down the slope a profusion of large barrel sponges, fan
coral and a good variety of soft
corals cheered us up.

Then a meter-long grouper
met us just off the sandy bottom,
and we swam into a cloud of
bright reef fish, notable for the
profusion of butterflyfish. The
best was just ahead: two enormous, rounded coral pinnacles,
reaching to around 10 meters of
the surface. From 30 meters
depth, the bottom dropped down
out of our range of vision. The
variety and number of fish swimming around or lurking in the
caves in these towers of coral
was overwhelming. This was a
superb dive, marred only by
restricted visibility, 10–12
meters. (This was early June.)

The afternoon dive, off the
south coast of Sjahrir, started
well. A steep coral slope dropped
us down to a resting black-spotted stingray at 22 meters. He let
us approach quite close before
trying to hide under a shallow
ledge. As we started our ascent, a
large spotted eagle ray, well over
a meter across, buzzed us, flapping by just two or three meters
away. We also saw an unusual
number of triggerfishes, including several Titan triggerfish, and
at least six species of butterflyfish in good numbers, including
schools of pennant bannerfish.
Other divers have reported reef
sharks in this area.

Above: *The strange
crocodile fish,
Cymbacephalus
beauforti. This crea-
ture, which here
looks a perfect
match for the algae-
covered coral boul-
ders, lies in wait for
any small fish or
crustacean to wan-
der within range of
its prodigious
mouth. Mapia atoll,
Irian Jaya.*

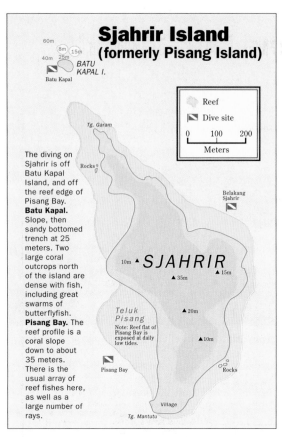

Sjahrir Island
(formerly Pisang Island)

60m
8m 15m
40m 25m
BATU KAPAL I.
Batu Kapal

Reef
Dive site
0   100   200
Meters

Tg. Garam

Rocks

Belakang
Sjahrir

The diving on Sjahrir is off Batu Kapal Island, and off the reef edge of Pisang Bay. **Batu Kapal.** Slope, then sandy bottomed trench at 25 meters. Two large coral outcrops north of the island are dense with fish, including great swarms of butterflyfish. **Pisang Bay.** The reef profile is a coral slope down to about 35 meters. There is the usual array of reef fishes here, as well as a large number of rays.

10m ▲ S J A H R I R

▲35m   ▲15m

Teluk Pisang   ▲20m
Note: Reef flat of Pisang Bay is exposed at daily low tides.

▲10m

Pisang Bay

Rocks

Village

Tg. Mantutu

Gunung Api

The last major explosion, in May 1988, killed of most of the offshore coral formations around Gunung Api, but amazingly spared many sponges. Some corals are beginning to grow back, but by and large the seascape remains bleak. There are no walls off Gunung Api. The bottom slopes gradually to 30–35 meters, where life peters out.

It is startling to see bright reef fishes in such a barren seascape. We saw a fair number of colorful individual species, including clown triggerfish, a bright yellow trumpetfish and some sweetlips. Huge schools of fusiliers cruised the area, and we spotted a few small dogtooth tuna. The stars of the show were a fat, 90-centimeter-long grouper, and an eagle ray a meter-and-a-half across.

Lontar Island

The outer edge of Lontar Island which represents part of the rim of a sunken caldera, offers several good dive sites, of which we visited two.

Selamon Belakang. We dove off Selamon Belakang (*belakang* means behind), so named because it lies across the island from Selamon village. The dive was superb from the start as we descended down a steep dropoff split by a vertical cleft and covered with coral. The wall extended down to 45 meters.

We stopped at 30 meters finding an unusual barrel sponge—huge, and with three openings. We encountered gorgonians and black coral trees. The wall held an unusually large concentration of lionfish, including a black-and-white juvenile who seemed very interested in the intruders. Visibility was 20 meters, very good for this time of year.

We swam north through a good variety of reef fish, with unusual numbers of Vlaming's unicornfish and schools of black triggerfish. The wall was interrupted here and there by sand falls. The dive's highlight was a bumphead parrotfish, a crusty old giant of almost a meter.

Batu Belanda. This site—literally "Dutchman's Stone"—is at the opposite end of Lontar Island. Here we found a good wall, this one ending with sloping sand at 30–35 meters. The drop featured many barrel and tube sponges, and small caves and cracks which offered refuge to abundant fish. The fish were varied and plentiful: a school of snappers, large emperor and blue-girdled angelfish, wrasses by the dozen, a large pinnate batfish, and numerous bannerfish.

Hatta Island

We rode in the newest of the Hotel Maulana's 8-meter open

Ai, Hatta and Run Islands

Hatta Island
(formerly Rozengain)

Hatta village

Tg. Kenari
Tg. Salamasa
Mt. Hari 140m ▲
Tg. Pulu

HATTA

Tg. Pohon Pinang
Tg. Besar
Tg. Buton

SKARU ATOLL

1. Vertical wall to 60m; many grottoes
2. Wall to 30m–40m; soft corals on 5m shelf
3. Wall to 30m–40m
4. Coral slope; very good hard corals plus lots of fish, including sharks, if the current is strong.
5. Wall to 40m; distinctive formations, many gorgonians—most anywhere in Banda
6. Very nice overhang at 27m; gorgonians
7. Coral terrace at 10m; coral knolls to 10m; huge schools of fish
8. Wall to 35m
9. Sandy slope with terrace at 20m; pinnacles
10. Wall to 30m–40m
11. Many pelagics at point; current picks up
12. Sandy slope at 12m; coral outcrops to 6m

Ai Island

Tg. Kelip
Parigi
Fort Revenge
Ai Village
Tg. Nama
Nama
Tg. Keli
Tg. Besar

A I

136m ▲
Batu Dua

0 ___ 1
Kilometers

Tg. Batu Udang
Tg. Goranga

1. Wall to 70m; caves at 25m and 35m; schools of jacks, sharks sometimes; after bare of fish
2. Wall to 45m; large gorgonians; terrace at 7m–12m with coral outcrops
3. Wide terrace to edge, wall to 45m; barrel sponges, soft corals
4. Wall continues, terrace narrows; fishermen here
5. Wall to 50m; clefts, cracks, overhang at 35m; huge gorgonians—largest seen in Banda
6. Wall breaks up; spurs and sand falls

Banda Islands

BANDA NEIRA I.
BATU KAPAL
SJAHRIR I.
Batuangus
Ai
AI
GUNUNG API I.
Lontar
Bandaneira
NEIJALAKA I.
Run
RUN I.
Nama
LONTAR (BANDA BESAR)
Hatta
HATTA I.

0 __ 5 __ 10
Kilometers

LAUT BANDA

NEIJALAKA I.
Tg. Timbal
Tg. Tenusan

Sand and coral exposed at low tide
Tg. Robin

Run Island

Reef exposed at low tide
Tg. Soawor
Tg. Cincin Seleman
Tg. Tuledan

1. Coral slope to 35m; many coral spurs, clefts and overhangs, all dusted with white sand
2. Sand slope, 45°, with coral knolls; good dive for beginners

Run Village

R U N

Tg. Lenore
Tg. Sehee
Tg. Nuret
Mt. Tanah Merah ▲
▲ 188m
Waynero beach
Tg. Waynero
Tg. Gandulang
Reef always submerged

0 ___ 1
Kilometers

fiberglass dive boats—powered by twin 40hp outboards—to Hatta Island, about 25 kilometers by sea from Banda Neira. Because of the calm seas, usual for October and November, the trip took just 50 minutes.

Hatta is a recent name for the island, bestowed in honor of Mohammed Hatta, one of the founding fathers and the first vice-president of Indonesia. History buffs will recall the island's

Above: *Nudi-branchs,* Polycera *sp. (above) and* Chromodoris bullocki. *Polycera was photographed in Bali, and Chro-modoris, Flores.*

old name, Rosengain, a British possession at the time when control of the Banda spice trade was still disputed.

Skaru Atoll. Our first stop was the Skaru atoll, a barely submerged reef a few hundred meters off the southern point of Hatta. (See map page 223.) The atoll is completely underwater, and is only visible from a distance because of the waves breaking over it.

The sea was milky with a whitish sediment more commonly found here during the *pance roba* season in July and August. The conditions lingered because of an errant weather pattern associated with the El Niño effect, which irregularly every few years brings warmer water temperatures to the East Pacific off the coast of South America. The promised visibility of 30–40 meters usual in October and November has thus eluded us.

We began our first dive at the western end of the north edge of the atoll, as the site provided protection from the southeast swell and took advantage of a slight current running east. We dropped onto a coral slope that quickly became a wall, ending in a sandy bottom 35 meters below. During the first part of the dive we encountered many sandy terraces at around 20 meters, and the wall reached 45 meters before ending at the eastern reach of the north edge.

At the point, the current quickened to 1.5 knots, and we encountered a multitude of schooling fish. We perched on a coral outcrop and watched the passing parade of unicornfish, fusiliers, jacks and rainbow runners for a good ten minutes. In the course of the dive, we also saw some giants: a reef whitetip shark almost two meters long, two dogtooth tuna, a Napoleon wrasse, and a hawksbill turtle.

At this point the wall ended and we passed over a sloping terrace of fine white sand, here and there broken up by coral knolls. In this area we found colonies of garden eels (*Heteroconger hassi*) and a prolific assortment of butterflyfish, angelfish (including the blue-faced angel, *Pomacanthus xanthometapon,* which has a very spotty distribution and is not often seen), triggerfish and schools of sergeant-majors.

Tanjung Besar. Our next dive was off the south coast of

Hatta itself, east of a point called Tanjung Besar ("Big Cape"). The wall was sheer, and ended in white sand at 40 meters. Its surface was honeycombed with small grottos and overhangs—at times we felt ourselves in a hanging garden, due to the unusual variety of soft coral dangling from the roof of the grottoes. We saw more gorgonians here than anywhere else in Banda.

This was a perfect environment for moray eels, and we found them in abundance. No sooner would we find one, but another would slither out—invariably right next to our faces!

A gentle current bore us east, past large schools of fish riding thermoclines up and down the wall. We decompressed on a coral terrace at 12 meters. This flat was studded with huge coral outcrops, each reaching almost to the surface. The "plain" was swarming with schools of snapper, fusiliers and unicornfish. The colors and variety of forms of the hard and soft corals here were outstanding.

Northeast Hatta. Our third dive was off the island's north coast, near Hatta village. Although the reef formation was virtually the same on every dive, this area is different in that we encountered many coral spurs, interspersed with falls of fine, white sand. The deepest wall here extended down 60 meters.

Halfway through our dive we encountered a very strange sight: a white object that looked like one of the margarine sculptures one finds in the restaurant of a fancy hotel. We descended to a sand terrace at 30 meters to investigate, and what we found was the whitened corpse of a Napoleon wrasse. Closer inspection revealed that a chunk of flesh was missing from behind the cranial hump. We surmised that this individual had been bested in a territorial dispute.

Just then, two enormous Napoleons buzzed us, an unusual display for such normally shy creatures. We were amazed that the corpse was intact, especially as we had seen two sharks earlier in the dive. From its white color, we judged the body had lain here for at least three days. It was fascinating to observe this monster at leisure, and at such close proximity. The strong teeth are intimidating, and combined

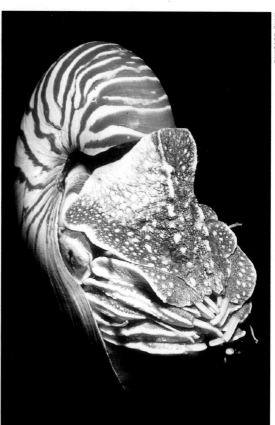

with the animal's thick lips, one can see how it so easily dispatches the hard-shelled and thorny crustaceans and echinoderms that are its preferred prey.

Later, we told Des Alwi what we saw, and he had another explanation. There is, he said, a small green shrimp capable of poisoning the Napoleon wrasse.

For our second dive, we continued along the same formation,

Below: The pearly nautilus (Nautilus pompilius). These animals spend the day at near abyssal depths, and only rise to a few hundred meters of the surface at night. Ascending some 1,000 meters is a tedious process, and can take sever-

MIKE SEVERNS

al hours. Because their tentacles are not equipped with suckers, nautilus are poor predators and feed on carrion and the molts of crustaceans. This specimen was captured in a trap set at 100 meters, released, and then photographed.

but heading east from the northwest corner of the island. We found a 45 degree coral slope that continued down to 30 meters. Here we spent a few minutes playing with a large stingray, and then explored the reef.

Twenty minutes into the dive, the reef profile once again changed into a wall. We were back into the earlier formation, and found the dive to be much the same. There was an abundance of semi-pelagic predators, including dogtooth tuna, a giant jack and a school of bluefin jacks (*Caranx melampygus*), and kingfish (*Carangoides*).

Ai Island

Together with Hatta, this island offers Banda's best diving. Both the north coast and the southwest of Ai are ringed with flawless coral walls, dropping in one place to 70 meters. The walls are rugged and full of caves, just the kind of habitat that harbors fish. Some of the gorgonians are the biggest we have seen.

The highlights go on and on: a fat grouper, pushing a meter-and-a-half; a school of more than 300 Heller's barracuda; a couple of meter-long chevron barracuda; a lobster with a body the size of a man's thigh; endless schools of fusiliers; a longnosed emperor close to a meter, the maximum for its species; a group of spotted sweetlips, with one close to its maximum 70 centimeters; many unicornfish; an abundance of clown triggerfishes, and Titan triggerfishes within sight the entire dive; a large school of pyramidal butterflyfish; turtles; and moray eels.

North Ai. Along the north coast, the wall drops to 50 meters at the northwest point—where there is a large overhang—and then to 30–40 meters until it breaks up near Ai village. At this point, coral ridges alternate with sand filled clefts, and huge swarms of fish congregated. Perhaps it was the shifting warm and cold currents flowing here that attracted the fish.

Southwest Ai. The southwest area features perhaps the best wall in all of Banda, with good growth to 70 meters. Growing on wide terrace on the west coast were tube and barrel

Below: *Smaller species of barracuda such as these* (Sphyraena genie) *often school during the day as a form of protection. The shifting shapes of these schools—balls, spirals, rings—are fascinating. At night the fish separate, and prowl the reef individually.*

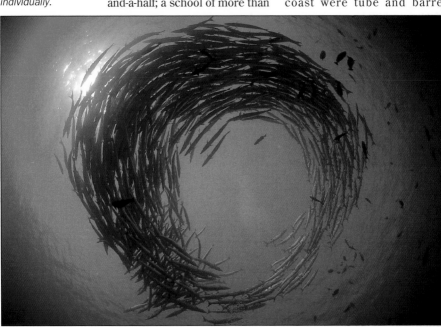

sponges, and great quantities of soft coral in red, beige, purple and orange hues.

This site gets a perfect 10 from dive guide Wally Siagian, which is high praise indeed. The richness of fish life, the sheer drop-off, the caves and fissures in the rock, and the overwhelming richness of life here compares only to the very best sites in South Komodo, in the Pantar Strait, and a few dive sites on the isolated islands of the Banda Sea, reachable only by live-aboard.

Run Island

The furthest dives from Banda Neira are off Run Island and tiny Neijalaka, a companion island off its northern point. In moderately choppy seas, it took an hour-and-a-half to reach Run.

The British once claimed Run Island, and it remained a hold-out against the Dutch, who controlled the rest of the archipelago, until 1667. In this year the Dutch and the British tried to consolidate their holdings. Britain gave the Dutch Run, and the Dutch gave the British New Amsterdam—or, as it is now called, Manhattan.

Run. The coral wall on the coast off Run village was somewhat disappointing. While there were shallow caves and clefts in the wall, the coral spreads were poor and covered in a layer of fine white sand. Reef fish were moderately abundant at 15–25 meters, and we spotted one turtle and a couple of fairly large barracuda. The best of the dive came at 3–5 meters, snorkeling depth: two big barracuda, a 90-centimeter Napoleon wrasse, and four huge parrotfish.

Neijalaka. We followed with a dive off the north coast of this tiny island, attached to Run by a wall of coral exposed at low tide. The gently slope had only isolated coral heads, and the fish were notable for their scarcity. Only a pair of barracuda, some 80 centimeters each, saved this dive from total disappointment.

We even surfaced early for lack of enthusiasm. We had been told that Japanese divers favored this site, which we found very strange indeed.

—*Kal Muller and Cody Shwaiko*

Above: *A school of lunar fusiliers,* Caesio lunaris. *Fusiliers are among the most common schooling fish seen in Indonesia.*

Pindito

Luxury Diving in the Wilds of the Banda Sea

One of the huge groupers had been expected sooner or later—two top dive masters had assured me that four of these beasts regularly patrolled the reef off tiny Koon Island at the far eastern edge of the Banda Sea. Yet, even with forewarning, the first sight of the chap sent a rousing rush of adrenaline through my system.

For the past few minutes, a huge school of big-eyed jacks—well over a thousand of them—had welcomed me as one of their own. A cautious approach had been rewarded by the school opening up slightly to allow me in their midst. Thousands of unconcerned eyes stared at me as the fish slowly finned by, within touching distance.

I took a few photos, and enjoyed the dream-like spectacle for a while, then drifted slowly out of the school to observe them from the nearby reef. As they shifted away, the huge grouper appeared just behind them, a shepherd keeping a close eye on its flock.

A full two meters long and with the bulk to match, the giant grouper clearly dominated this kingdom. As it slowly vanished into the sea, my second rush of adrenaline of the past quarter hour slowly subsided.

Diving off a Pinisi

With a group from Switzerland, we had been diving off the *Pindito,* a beautiful, well-designed, wooden boat built along the lines of a *pinisi,* traditional Sulawesi-style trading schooners which, for the past three centuries, have dominated the inter-island trade in Indonesia.

Today, the *pinisi* no longer set sail with holds full of exotic products like bird-of-paradise feathers, pearls, sandalwood, tortoise shell, damar pitch (for fine varnish) or trepang. They are now all equipped with diesel engines, and they move more mundane bulk cargo: lumber, cement, packaged foods, and household utensils.

The schooners retain the handsome, classical lines of the sailing ships, however, which is why the *Pindito*'s builders stuck to the traditional design. The few modifications were to allow for eight air-conditioned double cabins, and all the other creature comforts required by demanding clients. And, of course, a professional setup for scuba diving. Indeed, the ship's name is an acronym created from the phrase: *pinisi* dive tourism.

Built in South Kalimantan, part of Indonesian Borneo, the 40-meter, 230-ton ship is the pride and joy of its Swiss designer and general manager, Edi

---

AT A GLANCE

Pindito

Reef type: Vertical walls and steep slopes

Access: Live-aboard

Visibility: Good to very good, 15–25 meters

Current: Variable, usually some

Coral: Rich, pristine reefs

Fish: Superb numbers and varieties at the best sites

Highlights: Sheer mass of schooling fish, huge groupers, curiosity and tameness of the fish at the most isolated sites

---

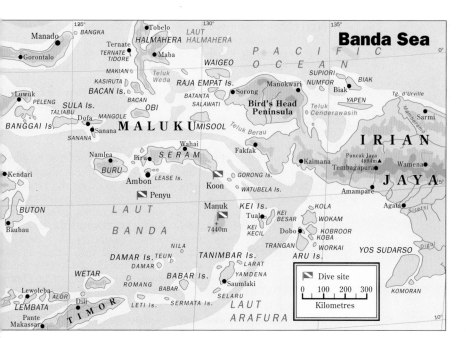

Frommenwiler.

Since April 1992 Frommenwiler has taken divers and adventurers into the most remote part of the Moluccas. He has settled into his adopted country, marrying a pretty Javanese woman and becoming the proud father of a baby boy.

The *Pindito* takes divers to sites in the Banda Sea, and when the weather shifts, to the Raja Empat Islands off Irian Jaya's Bird's Head Peninsula. We accompanied the ship during a Banda Sea run.

Cruises to Raja Empat take divers to sunken World War II Japanese fighter aircraft in the Sorong area, some excellent dives off tall offshore pinnacles, and—from April to September— some lucky clients are taken to one of the very few known nesting beaches of the giant leatherback sea turtles.

Koon Island

During our 10-day dive cruise on the *Pindito,* we checked out a couple of dozen locations pioneered by Peter, the on-board dive instructor, and Frommen- wiler. Visibility was generally good, but not really excellent due to the plankton in the water, ranging from 15–25 meters. Most of the reefs were drop-offs and steep slopes around isolated islands. All were top spots, but the best of the best was, undisputedly, Koon Island.

Giant groupers are really something to see, but it was a combination of underwater spectacles that made our dives on Koon among the very best among more than 1,000 dives in Indonesia. Never have we seen so many huge schools and aggregations of various fish species.

In addition to the big-eye jacks, we saw large groups of batfish, bright yellow sailfin snappers and yellow-eyed midnight snappers, barracuda, longnose emperors, bannerfish, blue-fin jacks, unicornfish, painted sweetlips, and blue triggerfish. While on other dives I have seen one or two of these species in schools or large, loose groups—except for the sailfin snappers and the painted sweetlips—at Koon the diversity and numbers were overwhelming.

Reef sharks were conspicuous by their absence—except for a string of five (or was it six?) large white-tips, swimming by in single file, heads and tails almost touching, a formation I had never before witnessed. Other unusual marine life included many large groupers of a half-dozen species, all in the 60 centimeter to 1 meter range. And, of course, plenty of reef fishes of various kinds and the occasional turtle and sea snake.

Our next plunge was one of those once-in-a-lifetime experiences, reserved by Neptune only for divers who are patient and extremely well behaved (or are lucky enough to have booked on the Pindito). Visibility was nothing to brag about, around 15 meters at the surface and a bit better further down. My buddy and I had decided to go deep at first, take a quick look and then come up to where the fish life is more abundant.

We dropped in near the edge of the sloping reef and quickly made our way to where the vertical wall began. Right then we froze: one of the giant groupers decided to check us out. Slowly finning back and forth just out of decent photo range, the big fella must have decided that we were a harmless curiosity and drifted in for a closer look, stopping just a couple meters away. This was one big, big fish.

Video whirling and camera clicking like mad, our giant grouper seemed happy enough to pose until we had our visual fill. By then, we had spotted a huge school of batfish below and dropped a bit for a closer look. We needn't to have bothered—apparantly we piqued their curiosity, too, and they came up to check *us* out.

With our computers ready to edge into decompression mode, which is strongly discouraged by the *Pindito*'s divemaster, we slowly ascended to around 15 meters. This turned out to be the perfect ringside seat for the upcoming show.

From this vantage point, we watched schools of at least seven species, plus small groups of individuals of a dozen more species, a combined mass of fish that was truly breathtaking.

Night Diving

The walls turn into a night-time fish hotels, many species sleeping off their daytime labors, relatively safe from nocturnal predators—but not from the lights and gazes of divers. Species that would never allow a close-up daytime look blissfully sleep with open eyes, unaware of divers being far inside their private territory and zone of comfort.

One of these, a high-bodied grouper close to a meter in length, had put on impossibly colorful pajamas, bright and strongly patterned, but we could not even find it in any of the fish identification books on board the *Pindito*.

Our lights also brought out the bright yellow and orange polyps of the cup corals, along with the strong colors of soft coral trees. And crustaceans, seldom seen in daytime, were busy foraging: a slipper lobster here, several hermit crabs there, unconcerned by our bright lights.

It is probably tiny Koon Island's position which accounts for its almost incredible mass of fish life. It is the southernmost and final island in the little archipelago connected by very shallow waters to the southeast tip of large Seram Island.

These shallows end in a very extensive reef flat, about 15 kilometers long and 3–4 kilometers wide. Koon perches near the edge of this reef, very close to the Gorong Islands, but separated from them by deep waters: over 600 meters.

The eastern extremity of

Koon's reef, where we dove, is wide and flat. Its shallow areas, from 3 to 10 meters, are dotted with coral outcrops reaching close to the surface, each a wonderland of fish and invertebrates.

Sand flats alternate with the outcrops, and the rest of the underwater landscape is filled with hard and soft corals. We saw almost no fish-bombing damage on this reef.

The gently sloping reef leads to a wall, which begins at 10 to 30 meters. After that, a sheer drop to 50–70 meters. The wall is full of small and medium-sized caves, some reaching way back into the reef—and large ledges and overhangs. Upwellings and currents bring plankton and necessary nutrients to the bottom of the food chain, which sustains the great mass of fish found here.

The Pindito

The *Pindito* operates most efficiently, but the dive schedule is flexible in the face of unforseen circumstances: unseasonal weather, lost baggage, guests hitting the bottle a bit too hard, something new in a dive location. The normal routine—if tremendous, world-class dives can be called normal—calls for two daytime dives plus one at night.

The suiting-up routine has been well thought out, and there's plenty of space for it. The crew brings filled tanks from the compressor area in the stern of the boat to the wide front deck where large open baskets hold the clients' dive gear. Everyone puts on his or her own BC and regulator, then the crew carries the tanks down wide ladders—one on the port side, the other on starboard—to the three waiting Zodiacs.

After a briefing by the divemaster, the clients step down the ladders for the short ride (usually 5 to 10 minutes) to the dive site. Two safety rules apply: no diving deeper than 40 meters, and a maximum of 60 minutes bottom time. The ship always anchors far enough away from the reefs to prevent damage.

Our cruise on the *Pindito* was one of the most exciting and enjoyable ones we have ever taken. The all-wood ship looks

Below: *A pair of Holthuis's shrimps (Periclimenes holthuisi) in a strange, unidentified anemone.*

CODY SHWAIKO

and feels great. Solid, top-quality ironwood below the waterline, *meranti* for the deck, and fine wood paneling elsewhere.

The crew of 15, while speaking little English, is as cheerful and efficient as we had sailed with in Indonesia. The ever-varied meals were healthy and delicious. The atmosphere in the dining-room and lounge area was always cordial. With the main

MIKE SEVERNS

Above: *Jacks sweeping past a gorgonian. The best of the Banda Sea sites are famous for huge schools of jacks and other fish.*

engine well muffled, and electric motors on the compressors, noise was never a problem.

The only weakness in the boat's design is that, since the *Pindito* is engine-powered, she draws only 2.7 meters, resulting in more pitching and rolling in heavy seas than deeper-keeled craft. But because the ship's routes are planned with monsoon winds in mind, wave-

induced rocking should not be a problem.

Manuk Island

The shark just appeared all of a sudden in my camera frame. Focus, shoot. Focus, shoot. Exultation. Yahoo! It was a common white-tip reef shark, notoriously difficult to photograph, unless baited, which some of us consider grossly unsportsmanlike.

White-tips barely qualify as sharks, and normally flee in panic at the sight of a diver. But not this one; curious and fearless, that's all. And not dangerous at all. Only divers unused to sharks try to swallow their regulators when they see the beasts.

Eyes glued to the viewfinder, I had tried to keep calm and concentrate on technical matters. This was not easy: the viewfinder kept filling with fish species which usually have a fear of strange, burbling creatures in their vicinity.

But off Manuk Island, some inbred, genetic molecules seemed to be missing, resulting in fearless fishes, and not just fearless, but downright curious. Not all species—the angelfish in the shallows were a bit flighty, and a group of jacks, heading straight for us, turned back after getting to within a few meters.

But the rest—focus, and click. The golden rule for underwater photography is "the closer, the better" and it was all too easy to follow here. In fact, the damn things kept getting *too* close. Now that's a complaint you don't often hear from underwater photographers.

The Galapagos Islands are the best known of those few rare places that are so isolated that the animals have no mortal fear of man. It is unlikely that more than a handful of humans visited the Galapagos before the mid 19th century, when Charles Darwin put these Ecuadorian islands on the map of general human knowledge.

Now, the presence of too many tourists threatens the ecology of the Galapagos. That's definitely not the case for Manuk Island. Occasionally, a few fishermen from the Banda Islands spend several weeks here, catching and salting tuna and snapper. But the often rough seas, and lack of freshwater on the island severly limits their stay.

Manuk is quite isolated. The closest landfall—and just another tiny island—is Serua, almost 100 kilometers to the southwest. Serua, together with Nila and Teun, were evacuated by the Indonesian government in the 1970s because of unpredictable volcanic activity.

The closest inhabited island, Hatta of the Banda group, lies over 110 kilometers to the northwest. The seas around Manuk are deep: just 10 nautical miles from the island the bottom drops to 3,000–4,000 meters; a bit further it drops to 6 kilometers.

An Isolated Volcano

Manuk Island is the easternmost active volcano in a long chain that sweeps through Indonesia, beginnning in Sumatra and including Java, Bali, Lombok, Sumbawa and Flores, before reaching the southwestern edge of the Banda Sea.

Here, beginning at Wetar Island, the volcanic chain of small islands sweeps through deep waters in a graceful arc, including Romang, Damar, Teun, Nila, Serua and Manuk, then heading northwest to end at Gunung Api in the tiny Banda group. This volcanic chain marks the boundary of a tectonic plate.

Aside from a bit of smoke, we saw little volcanic activity on Manuk during our visit. A few of us climbed the island volcano, reaching the 285-meter peak. Two fishermen led the way, hacking through patches of tropical vegetation with *parangs* (the Indonesian machete). The bare suggestion of a trail swept steeply upward, forcing us to pause several times to catch our breath. We caught occasional glimpses of large rats, common on the island.

As we left the line of vegetation, the sky filled with birds, mocking our laborious, sweaty progress. Light blue sky and dark blue ocean filled the rest of the breath-taking panorama, making the climb worth every drop—and there were many—of sweat.

We saw two species of boobies, one with a dark head and yellow feet, the other blue-beaked with a white head and reddish feet, and frigate birds, including a few breeding males with huge swollen red necks.

Frigate birds are the pirates of the air. Terrible fishermen themselves, they wait until a boobie catches a fish, and then, in mid-air, force it to regurgitate its catch.

The top of Manuk, covered with volcanic rocks, showed several very hot fissures, some with yellow sulfur deposits. A large, deep, but inactive crater and a broken rim, face south. Eventually we had had enough. Delicious showers and cold beer were waiting on the *Pindito*. We descended in record time.

Our fishermen guides were also happy. Aside from an unexpected tip, they had gathered a couple of dozen bird eggs for supper. Occasionally, they also eat the birds, which are easy enough to catch: walk up to them, grab one, and wring its neck. We preferred the meal waiting for us on the *Pindito*.

Diving North Manuk

Our first dive, off north Manuk, was good but not really spectacular. We saw lots of sea snakes, many of them coming to within a few centimeters of us, then loosing interest. They are of no dan-

ger to divers. While their venom is very strong, and can easily kill a man, they rarely bite. And when they do, they often don't deliver their venom. (Apparently the venom takes some time to produce, thus the snakes don't use it unless they really have to.)

The only human fatalities we have heard of from sea-snakes are fishermen who net their catch, then sort through the writhing mass, bare-handed. The banded sea-snakes of Manuk displayed a pattern and coloration we had not seen elsewhere in Indonesia.

The coral formations were good, showing no fish-bomb damage. Lots of large barrel-sponges dotted the seascape, but we only saw one large school of fish. This was the only hint of the tremendous second dive, described above, which is definitely one of the best single dives of my career.

The highlights of that night's dive were the still foraging sea snakes, and several interesting gastropods, including a rare cowry and a seldom-seen tun shell (*Tonna perdix*) of unusual size. This latter was, as is its habit, moving at break-neck speed (seeking other gastropods) but over hard coral, not usual sandy preying grounds.

Karang Pekelo

The fish show at Karang Pekelo, a site off southcentral Seram Island, was almost overwhelming. Even as we were descending we were greeted by a couple dozen long, sleek rainbow runners, a lone torpedo mackerel (*Scomberoides lysan*) and several good-sized tunas.

At about 12 meters, just above the reef top, we were mobbed by a huge school of big-eye jacks, dashing about with no apparent purpose, stopping, and then darting off again at breakneck speed. Visibility was a very good 20–25 meters.

A few couples, one the normal silvery color, the other completely dark except for a small white dot at the very tip of its dorsal fin, around the school with quick gyrations of their own, in perfect unison and often in physical contact with one another—a frantic mating dance, perhaps. The school vanished quickly but returned several times during the course of the dive.

We dropped down the reef face to sand at 30–35 meters, with a few scattered coral outcrops on the flat substrate. Upon arrival, a school of unicorn filefish (*Acanthurus monoceros*) finned by, a species we had never seen before.

Then, some 20 meters away, we distinguished a familiar species, the yellow-eyed puffer (*Arothon immaculatus*) but instead of just one we were looking at a most unusual school of about 50 individuals.

Warned by our computers that bottom time was up, we rose to the 20 meter level and settled in for a ringside seat at the fish parade: big-nosed unicornfish, surgeonfish, yellow- and blue-streak fusiliers, and red snappers. We never identified the fish in the biggest school, which kept parading back and forth. They were snappers of some kind, but with dirty-looking, mottled gray-brown bodies in need of a good scrubbing.

A couple of very obvious, and big, black jacks (*Corax lugubris*) finned by, but our attention was riveted on a giant grouper: 2 meters long of it was an inch. Other big boys included several very large Napoleon wrasses, and a couple of bumphead parrotfish.

But for one of our dive companions, none of these was the dive's highlight. At one point in the dive, a big gray reef shark made straight for her, fast, stopping only at the cardiac-arrest distance of a meter. There it took a good hard look at her, turned around, and left behind one very upset lady. A stiff drink back on board miraculously restored her powers of speech.

Schooling fishes of many species enliven all of Indonesia's better dive locations. During a typical dive, two or three schools put in a brief appearance, and quickly vanish. But only a very few dive locations literally swarm with masses of fish. Karang Pekelo, discovered only in late 1993, is one of these fantastic places.

Other Sites

While we have seen the highlights of a single *Pindito* cruise, other routes also feature exceptional diving. This includes a small group smack in the middle of the Banda Sea and well over 200 kilometers away from the Banda Islands.

These "lost" mini islands are divided into two small groups, and are so little known they go under various names, either the Lucipara Islands or Pulau Tujuh ("Seven Islands").

Four islands close to each other are shown on maps as Maisel; just a bit off, three more are called Shilpad or Penyu (this last means "turtle"). The northernmost of the tiny dots is referred to as Bingkudu or sometimes as Penyu.

Nesting turtles can be found throughout the group. the Lucipara Islanders catch green turtles, and sell them to traders who take them to Bali, where the meat is very popular, particularly in a ritual dish called *ebat,* in which raw turtle meat is pounded together with many spices into a paste. Turtles are expensive, and ironically, it's the new, tourist-derived wealth in Bali that is threatening sea turtles throughout Indonesia. South Bali's appetite for sea turtles is said to now reach 40,000 a year.

Underwater in Lucipara, there are fine dropoffs with excellent hard corals and black corals. There is nothing unusual in the fish life there, except that common species grow much larger than normal, close to or surpassing record lengths.

Introducing Irian Jaya

Irian Jaya is one of the last really wild places on earth. Although a few roads have been laid that lead a bit inland from some of the population centers on the coast, parts of the interior of the western half of New Guinea, an almost continent-sized island, are still shrouded in mystery. Even today, the flight maps used by pilots working the highlands for Protestant missions and mineral exploration contain large areas marked: Relief Data Incomplete.

Fewer than 2 million people live in Irian Jaya's 410,660 square kilometers. The largest city and capital of the province is Jayapura, a buzzing town of 170,000 on the north coast near the border with Papua New Guinea, which neatly cuts the island in half. Modern Jayapura boomed after World War II, based on infrastructure laid by U.S. General Douglas MacArthur, who began his famous island-hopping strategy from here.

Irian Jaya was not relinquished by Holland at the same time as the rest of the former Dutch East Indies, and did not formally become part of Indonesia until 1969. The territory was dubbed Irian Jaya—"Victorious Irian"—in the early 1970s.

The transition was far from smooth, and local rebellions by spear-wielding warriors and an independence movement, the Organisasi Papua Merdeka (OPM) —"Free Papua Movement"—haunted the changeover. There is little OPM activity today, but the government keeps a large military presence in the province, and many areas are still off-limits to tourism.

Linguists do not agree on how many unique languages are spoken in Irian, although most estimates hover around 250. The island's indigenous people, dark-skinned and kinky-haired—hence "Papua," Malay for kinky hair—trace their ancestry back to before the expansion of the Malays through Indonesia.

An Impenetrable Island

The interior of Irian is craggy and mountainous—Puncak Jayakesuma, at 4,884 meters, is the highest point between the Himalayas and the Andes—and to reach it from the coast one must cross thick swamps and forests. The rivers of the north are so full of oxbows that running them doubles or triples the overland distance to the interior. In the south, treacherous tides—changing the water level in rivers even 100 kilometers inland—conspired against explorers.

Until American explorer Richard Archbold flew over the Baliem Valley in 1938, and saw the neat little compounds and sweet potato fields of the Dani, these people had lived in their valley isolated from contact with any outsiders for some 10,000 years. Today, the Dani are Irian's most famous ethnic group. Their numbers have grown to about 70,000, and Wamena, a small town in the Baliem Valley and the de facto capital of Dani country, has been attracting several hundred visitors a month.

Farmers and Artists

Famous warriors in the past, today the Dani are simply farmers, living in thatch and wood huts and raising their staple sweet potatoes and pigs in the

Overleaf: An undersea ledge, encrusted with cup corals. These corals extend their bright yellow tentacles to snare plankton only at night. Mapia atoll. Photograph by Kal Muller.

Opposite: *A pink clownfish,* Amphiprion perideraion, *in front of its host anemone,* Heteractis magnifica. *Because the anemone is partially contracted, its bright column is visible. Bunaken Island, 3 meters. Photograph by Mike Severns.*

salutary climate of the 1,500-meter-high Baliem Valley. Despite 40 years of Protestant missionaries, many Dani are unregenerate in wearing their *kotekas,* or penis gourds.

If the Dani are the most famous of Irian's peoples, the Asmat are the most notorious. Living in the hostile tidal swamps of the south coast, ritual head-hunting had in the past been the centerpiece of Asmat culture.

This fact made international headlines in 1961, when Michael Rockefeller, the young son of then-governor of New York Nelson Rockefeller, disappeared after trying to swim ashore when his boat capsized. Whether or not Rockefeller was actually eaten by the people of Otsjanep has fueled many speculations, but has never been determined.

Rockefeller was visiting the Asmat to collect their art, among the most powerful and respected in the world. Huge war shields, canoe prows and several-meters-long *bisj* poles, decorated with abstract and heavily expressionistic figures, display the kind of raw energy that modernist Euro-pean painters treasured in their collections of "primitive" art.

Rich, Unexplored Waters

Cenderawasih—"Bird-of-Paradise"—Bay and the islands off New Guinea's western tip hold some stunning, unexplored reefs. Currently, only Irian Diving in Sorong (see "Irian Jaya Practicalities" pg. 307) operates in the region. The outfit takes divers to World War II–era wrecks and other fine sites in the Sorong area, in the Raja Ampat islands, and in Dore Bay.

South of Irian is the shallow Arafura Sea, which until perhaps just 18,000 years ago connected New Guinea to Australia. The coast here is silty, and fringed with brackish rivers and stands of mangrove and casuarina.

Bintuni Bay, cut deep into the Bird's Head Peninsula, offers one of the largest and most unmolested mangrove swamps in the world. Athough such habitats are not a paradise for divers, they play an important ecological role in developing the larval stages of fish and crustaceans.

—*David Pickell*

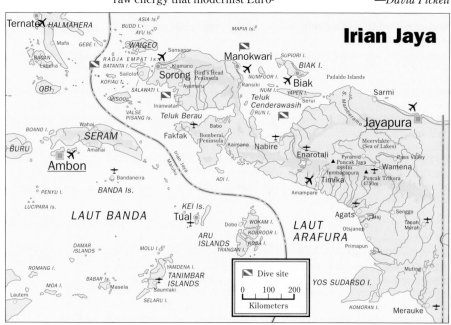

World-Class Wreck and Pioneer Diving

A wide range of diving possibilities are offered through the dozens of locations from which to choose. New locations are also listed, so divers who want to pioneer dive can check out any of the dozens of unconfirmed stories about reported wrecks and fabulous dive sites. The areas are so extensive that even a life time of diving would not be enough to really know what is there.

Irian Diving is a newly established diving operation founded in 1995 by Anita E. Matahari and Max Ammer. After pioneering diving off Irian Jaya for six years, Sorong was chosen as home base for the new diving operation which specializes in wrecks, drift, reef, and adventurous pioneer diving in both the Sorong-Radja Empat Islands and Manokwari-Cenderawasih Bay areas.

The dives are almost always boat dives and care is taken not to unload everyone at the same spot. At drift dives, intervals of five minutes or more, and in reef diving, buddy pairs are dropped off half a kilometer or more, apart from the following pair. The boat always returns to pick up divers, so they do not need to swim against the current. Generally, there are three dives a day, the atmosphere is always relaxed, anything is possible, and nothing is a must.

Diving the Sorong-Radja Empat Area

Sorong, home base of Irian Diving and central to the Radja Empat Islands, is one of Irian Jaya's biggest towns, located on the west cape of Irian's Bird's Head peninsula. At present, a new land-based airport is under construction, however, until its completion (estimated mid-1998), the Jefman Airfield, situated on Jefman Island (just a few meters longer than the runway) is used. Approaching Jefman by air provides a beautiful view of some of the Radja Empat islands and their surrounding reefs. The island is well worth a walk around, as there are still many remnants of WW II.

To reach Sorong from Jefman, one can take either the

AT A GLANCE
Irian Diving

Reef type: Vertical walls, lagoon channels, caves, platform reefs, etc.

Access: By boat from base camps

Visibility: Very good, 20–45 meters

Current: Moderate, excellent for drift diving

Coral: Excellent – abundant & diverse

Fish: Variety & abundance guaranteed

Highlights: Snorkeling with dolphins near the Wai base camp (5 m); white-tip sharks under a P47B wing; finding new wrecks untouched/complete

---

local ferry ($2 for a one hour ride) or charter a long boat ($22 for a one-half hour ride).

The roughest seas and decreased visibility in the Radja Empat area are from mid-June until the end of August. During the rest of the year, the sea is mostly very smooth with good visibility. January and December have less visibility and millions of very small jellyfish, however, this does not really affect diving. To compensate, there are many

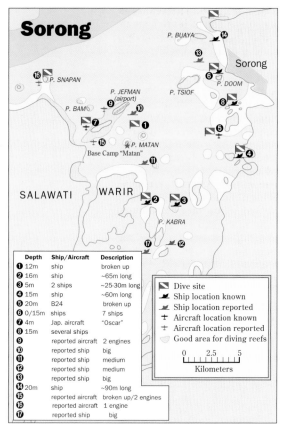

Sorong

P. BUAYA ⓮
⓭
Sorong
⑯ P. SNAPAN
⑥ P. DOOM
P. JEFMAN (airport)
P. TSIOF
P. BAM
⑨ ⑩
⑧
⑦ ❶
⑤
⑮ P. MATAN
Base Camp "Matan" ⑪ ❹
SALAWATI WARIR ❷ ❸
P. KABRA
⑰ ⑫

Depth	Ship/Aircraft	Description
❶ 12m	ship	broken up
❷ 16m	ship	~65m long
❸ 5m	2 ships	~25-30m long
❹ 15m	ship	~60m long
❺ 20m	B24	broken up
❻ 0/15m	ships	7 ships
❼ 4m	Jap. aircraft	"Oscar"
❽ 15m	several ships	
⑨	reported aircraft	2 engines
⑩	reported ship	big
⑪	reported ship	medium
⑫	reported ship	medium
⑬	reported ship	big
⑭ 20m	ship	~90m long
⑮	reported aircraft	broken up/2 engines
⑯	reported aircraft	1 engine
⑰	reported ship	big

◤ Dive site
◣ Ship location known
◣ Ship location reported
✛ Aircraft location known
✛ Aircraft location reported
  Good area for diving reefs

0   2.5   5
Kilometers

whales during this time, sometimes swimming alongside the boats.

The Passage: Recently discovered, "The Passage" is an extraordinary site, not only underwater, but also above. It is a ravine-like crack disconnecting the hilly landscape of Waigeo Island from Gam Island. The entrance of the crack is difficult to spot because of the numerous small rocky islands in that part of Kaboei Bay.

The approach to the passage appears like a river gorge entrance. It is only 15–20 meters wide, with walls on both sides towering 10–15 meters high and covered with thick jungle vegetation. "The Passage" curls itself through the rocks for approximately 4 km before opening into the sea again.

The landscape is even stranger underwater. White sand with lots of big rocks, many caves, overhangs, and walls covered with lush growth of soft coral in great varieties. Great quantities of fish abound, including white-tip sharks, humphead parrotfish, Napoleon wrasses, barracuda, turtles, rays, etc., etc. You name it, it's there! On a rating of 1 to 10, with 10 being the very best, comments on this dive were: "11 plus!" "Where is my second tank?" "You can leave me here!" This is definitely a place not to be missed.

The Garden: Just north of Batanta Island are two small islands covered with pine trees. The islands are fringed by a huge reef along the north side. There is always something special to see here in the white sand, hilly landscape dotted with surreal coral pinnacles of exceptional height. One can just sit and admire the scenery— overwhelming fish life, sponges over two-and-one-half meters high, and a great abundance of hard corals. Large groups of batfish, schools of trevally, as well as solo giant trevally, schools of snappers, surgeon fishes, big tunas and mackerels, white-tip, black-tip and grey reef sharks, eagle and manta rays. Every dive brings new discoveries.

Permanent residents of this reef are a family of potato cods. One is 2 meters long, for sure (grandpa cod), while the rest of the family is in the one-and-a-half meter range. They are all monsters. While other fish are generally shy, these cods are not; they approach divers easily. This is another place you wouldn't want to miss.

Mike's Point: "Mike's Point" is a small rock island approximately 30 meters in diameter, a 15-minute boat ride north from base camp "Mansuar" near Mansuar Island. "Mike's Point" rises straight up from a 35-meter depth. There are overhangs, walls and caves, as well as the sloping platform-like area covered with lots of soft corals and some snow white anemones with their colorful clown fish residents. Barracudas and other schooling fish are plentiful, while in shallow depths one finds epaulette sharks and wobbegongs. This is a great site for macro photography. As the current around the island can be very fierce, the dives must be planned very carefully to make use of slack tide.

Dofior Island: Just 200 meters off the shore from Sorong sits tiny Dofior Island. Despite its closeness to the harbor, quite unexpectedly, it houses a myriad of soft corals. Starting at just 3 meters to approximately 10 meters deep, one can find a rainbow of color options in soft corals and gorgonian fans of 4-meter diameters. Fish life is good, though not exceptional. Lionfish are abundant and wobbegongs and crocodile fish are often seen.

This is also a good wreck area. It is said that the Dutch dumped equipment here when they retreated from Irian, but this is unconfirmed. The reality is that there are at least 7 small boats, trucks, parts of a crane, and a tractor-like vehicle. The area is littered with all sorts of stuff. Presently, everything is very beautifully overgrown with soft coral, primarily red and light pink. Although visibility can be very poor due to rain and the close location to town, it is still the best spot in the area for soft coral.

The P47B Aircraft Wrecks: The reefs off the northwest side of Wai Island are especially rewarding. Two huge giant clams exceeding one-and-one-half meters are the center of an area crowded with fish. But what makes this little island unique is the fact that on its sloping reef edges there are three WWII aircraft remains. One is located to the northeast side of the island, on a reeftop approximately 250 meters from the beach in only 3 meters of water. The aircraft broke up during landing, leaving the wings with part of the hull in good shape. One can easily identify the eight .50 caliber machine guns in its wings and the engine

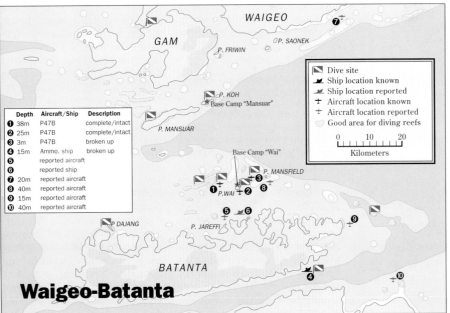

Depth	Aircraft/Ship	Description
❶ 38m	P47B	complete/intact
❷ 25m	P47B	complete/intact
❸ 3m	P47B	broken up
❹ 15m	Ammo. ship	broken up
❺	reported aircraft	
❻	reported ship	
❼ 20m	reported aircraft	
❽ 40m	reported aircraft	
❾ 15m	reported aircraft	
❿ 40m	reported aircraft	

◥ Dive site
⚓ Ship location known
⚓ Ship location reported
+ Aircraft location known
+ Aircraft location reported
◯ Good area for diving reefs

0   10   20
Kilometers

Waigeo-Batanta

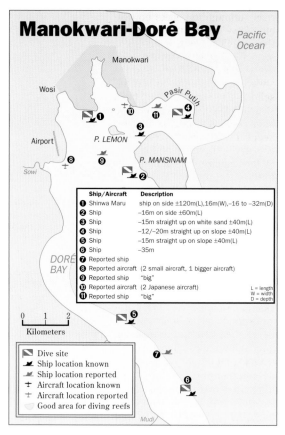

Manokwari-Doré Bay

Pacific Ocean

Manokwari

Wosi

Pasir Putih

Airport

P. LEMON

Sowi

P. MANSINAM

DORÉ BAY

Ship/Aircraft	Description
1 Shinwa Maru	ship on side ±120m(L),16m(W),–16 to –32m(D)
2 Ship	–16m on side ±60m(L)
3 Ship	–15m straight up on white sand ±40m(L)
4 Ship	–12/–20m straight up on slope ±40m(L)
5 Ship	–15m straight up on slope ±40m(L)
6 Ship	–35m
7 Reported ship	
8 Reported aircraft	(2 small aircraft, 1 bigger aircraft)
9 Reported ship	"big"
10 Reported aircraft	(2 Japanese aircraft)
11 Reported ship	"big"

L = length
W = width
D = depth

0 1 2
Kilometers

Dive site
Ship location known
Ship location reported
Aircraft location known
Aircraft location reported
Good area for diving reefs

Mudi

lying nearby. The two other aircrafts are situated on the southwest side on a reef slope approximately 100 meters from the beach. Both aircraft are complete and in very good condition.

Diving the Manokwari-Cenderawasih Bay Area

Manokwari is a pleasant little town with colonial atmosphere, nestled on the shores of Doré Bay, on the east cape of Bird's Head peninsula. Built on a hill, it overlooks Doré Bay, Mansinam and Lemon Islands, as well as the Arfak Mountains which stretch across the opposite side of the bay. Doré Bay is the final resting place of many Japanese warships. The Cenderawasih Bay area doesn't have any rough sea period; June to August are very good. The Doré Bay wreck site is protected in all seasons.

Merpati flies daily to Manokwari from Biak. The Cenderawasih Bay area is reached either by local wooden ferry or newly re-surfaced road to Ransiki.

The Cross Wreck: Mansinam Island is the larger of the two islands in front of Manokwari. The landing spot of the first two Christian missionaries who introduced Christianity to Irian Jaya is marked with a large concrete cross on the north coast of Mansinam Island. Approximately 200 meters off the beach, directly in front of the cross, is one of our favorite wreck dive sites. The vessel stands perfectly upright on a patch of white sand in only 18 meters of water, and is beautifully overgrown by both hard and soft corals. Shallow depth, great visibility, diverse fish life, and coral growth make this a great dive. The ship's lamps still stand in place or lay on deck, blown down by the explosion. On the rear of the ship one can see two rows of depth charges. There is so much to see, one dive is just not enough time to discover everything.

Wreck-certified divers can penetrate into the engine room, where a giant moray eel has made its home. It's the biggest moray eel I've seen, or maybe it was because of the confined space and the creature eyeballing me from less than 10 inches away!

Already a world-class dive during the day, the wreck's true wonders can only be seen during a night dive. The many corals show their beautiful colors by night, fully expanding their polyps, and the wreck becomes even more colorful. Perhaps most astonishing is the fact that this wreck has been chosen by both Napoleon wrasse and humphead parrotfish as resting spots. The lowest count has been three humphead parrotfish and one Napoleon wrasse, but it's more likely to be two *huge* Napoleon wrasses of two meters and 10 humphead parrotfish ranging 1–1.25 meters in length. While the humphead parrotfish choose to lay around on the decks or on the white sandy bottom next to the hull of the ship, the Napoleon wrasse prefer to find a place to sleep somewhere inside the wreck. These fishes can be approached—with caution—close enough to touch, making the dive an especially rewarding experience.

The Shinwa Maru: The final resting place of the *Shinwa Maru*, a Japanese warship, is approximately 200 meters from the beach, southwest of Tanjung Sanggeng. The ship is very impressive, lying on its left side from 30–32 meters, measuring over 120 meters in length. The width of the ship (16 meters) makes this a good dive for divers who do not want to go deeper than 20–25 meters. Although there is bomb damage at the front starboard—a hole big enough for a train—the rest of the wreck is intact. Part of the cargo (cables, construction mate-rials, ammunition, sake bottles, etc.) have fallen out because of the wreck's position. A huge school of big-eyed trevally keep the ship as their home and it's always a great sight to see the school move around the ship's structures. The ship also holds a huge cod, but so far, the monster keeps its distance. Several kinds of parrotfish, surgeon and big puffers can also be seen, and frequently humphead parrotfish sleep in the ship. The surrounding sandy bottom is a good place to look for big mollusks, such as the sea triton and queen conch. A night dive here is also very rewarding.

Cenderawasih Bay: The bay features world-class diving sites too numerous to mention. On just one dive, we encountered 3 dugong, 5 manta rays, several turtles, a school of barracudas, one white-tip reef shark, and at the end of the dive, a mako shark who was particularly interested in circling us and coming back several times to investigate. It made us want to go back and investigate further too.

—*Max Ammer*

Below: *The decorated dartfish,* Nemateleotris deco-ra. *Pairs of these beautiful little dartfish can be found hovering over sandy patches, where they pluck plankters and small crustaceans from the water. Bunaken Island, 40 meters.*
Overleaf: *A swarm of striped eel catfish,* Plotosus lineatus, *on a shalliw reef at Manado, Sulawesi. Photograph by Ed Robinson, IKAN.*

MIKE SEVERNS

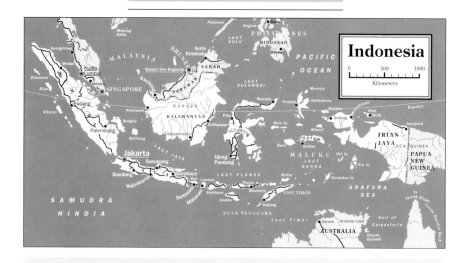

Indonesia At A Glance

The Republic of Indonesia is the world's fourth largest country, with 190 million people. The vast majority (88%) is Muslim, making this the world's largest Islamic country. More than 400 languages are spoken, but Bahasa Indonesia, a variant of Malay, is the national language.

The nation is a republic, headed by a strong President, with a 500-member legislature and a 1,000-member People's Consultative Assembly. There are 27 provinces and special territories. The capital is Jakarta, with 9 million people. The archipelago comprises just over 2 million square km of land. Of 18,508 islands, about 6,000 are named, and 1,000 permanently inhabited.

Indonesia's $175 billion gross national product comes from oil, textiles, lumber, mining, agriculture and manufacturing, and the country's largest trading partner is Japan. Per capita income is $850. Much of the population still makes a living through agriculture, chiefly rice. The unit of currency is the rupiah, which trades at approximately 2,300 to $1 (1996).

Historical overview. The Buddhist Sriwijaya empire, based in southeastern Sumatra, controlled parts of western Indonesia from the 7th to the 13th centuries. The Hindu Majapahit kingdom, based in eastern Java, controlled even more from the 13th to the 16th centuries. Beginning in the mid-13th century, local rulers began converting to Islam.

In the early 17th century the Dutch East India Company (VOC) founded trading settlements and quickly wrested control of the Indies spice trade. The VOC was declared bankrupt in 1799, and a Dutch colonial government was established.

Anti-colonial uprisings began in the the early 20th century, when nationalism movements were founded by various Muslim, communist and student groups. Sukarno, a Dutch-educated nationalist, was jailed by the Dutch in 1930.

Early in 1942, the Dutch Indies were overrun by the Japanese army. Treatment by the occupiers was harsh. When Japan saw her fortunes waning toward the end of the war, Indonesian nationalists were encouraged to organize. On August 17, 1945, Sukarno proclaimed Indonesia's independence.

The Dutch sought a return to colonial rule after the war. Four years of fighting ensued between nationalists and the Dutch, and full independence was achieved in 1949.

During the 1950s and early 1960s, President Sukarno's government moved steadily to the left, alienating western governments. In 1963, Indonesia took control of Irian Jaya and began a period of confrontation with Malaysia.

On September 30, 1965, the army put down an attempted coup attributed to the communist party. Several hundred thousand people were killed as suspected communists.

In the following years, the powers of the presidency gradually shifted away from Sukarno and General Suharto became president in 1968. His administration has been friendly to Western and Japanese investment and the nation has enjoyed three decades of solid economic growth.

MISS YOUR LOVED ONES BACK HOME?
PUT YOURSELF IN THE PICTURE WITH 001

When you're far away from home, nothing brings you closer to loved ones than a phone call. And it's so easy with 001. Indosat offers International Direct Dial to over 240 countries. Plus, you save 25% during discount hours on weekends*, and around the clock on national holidays and weekends. Call today, and share the good times!

IDD = **001** | COUNTRY CODE | AREA CODE | TELEPHONE NUMBER

From Hotel = HOTEL ACCESS CODE | **001** | COUNTRY CODE | AREA CODE | TELEPHONE NUMBER

 NUMBER ONE **INDOSAT**

1 Java
2 Sumatra
3 Bali
4 Nusa Tenggara
5 Sulawesi
6 Maluku
7 Irian Jaya

Practicalities

TRAVEL ADVISORY, TRANSPORTATION, PRACTICALITIES

The following sections contain all the practical information you need for your journey. **Travel Advisory** provides background about traveling in Indonesia, from the economy and health precautions to bathroom etiquette. **Transportation** is concerned exclusively with transportation: getting to and traveling around Indonesia. It is followed by a handy **Language Primer** and a list of **Indonesian Dive Terms**.

The **Area Practicalities** sections focus on each destination and contain details on transport, accommodations, dive operators, dining and services. These sections are organized by area and correspond to the first half of the guide.

Java 1

Sumatra 2

Bali 3

Nusa Tenggara 4

Sulawesi 5

Maluku 6

Irian Jaya 7

Travel Advisory

TOURIST INFORMATION

Overseas, you can contact the Indonesian embassy or consulate, or one of the following **Indonesia Tourist Promotion Board** offices: **ASEAN & Southeast Asia**, 10 Collyer Quay #15–07, Ocean Building, Singapore 0104. ☎ (65) 5342837, 5341795, fax: (65) 5334287. **Australia & New Zealand,** Level 10, 5 Elizabeth Street, Sydney NSW 2000, Australia. ☎ (61 2) 2333630, fax: (61 2) 2333629, 3573478. **Europe**, Wiesenhuttenstrasse 17, D-6000 Frankfurt/Main 1, Germany. ☎ (49 169) 233677, fax: (49 169) 230840. **Japan & Korea**, Sankaido Building, 2nd Floor, 1-9-13 Ahasaka, Minatoku, Tokyo 107. ☎ (81 3) 35853588, fax: (81 3) 35821397. **North America** , 3457 Wilshire Boulevard, Los Angeles, CA 90010-2203. ☎ (213) 3872078, fax: (213) 3804876. **Taiwan & Hong Kong**, 66 Sung Chiang Road, 5th Floor, Taipei, Taiwan. ☎ (886 2) 5377620. fax: (886 2) 5377621. **United Kingdom, Ireland, Benelux & Scandinavia**, 3-4 Hanover Street, London W1R 9HH. ☎ (44 171) 4930334, fax: (44 171) 4931747.

The **Directorate General of Tourism** in Jakarta has brochures and maps on all Indonesian provinces: Jl. Kramat Raya 81, PO Box 409, Jakarta 10450. ☎ (021) 3103117/9, fax: (021) 3101146.

Local government tourism offices, *Dinas Pariwisata*, are generally only good for basic information. More useful assistance is often available from privately run (but government approved) **Tourist Information Services**. Be aware that many offices calling themselves "Tourist Information" are simply travel agents.

VISAS

Nationals of the following 45 countries do not need visas, and are granted visa-free entry for 60 days upon arrival.

Argentina	Iceland	Philippines
Australia	Ireland	Saudi Arabia
Austria	Italy	Singapore
Belguim	Japan	South Korea
Brazil	Kuwait	Spain
Brunei	Liechtenstein	Sweden
Canada	Luxembourg	Switzerland
Chile	Malaysia	Taiwan
Denmark	Maldives	Thailand
Egypt	Malta	Turkey
Finland	Mexico	United Arab
France	Monaco	Emirates
Germany	Morocco	United Kingdom
Greece	Netherlands	United States
Hungary	New Zealand	Venezuela
	Norway	

Be sure to check your passport before leaving for Indonesia. You must have at least one empty page to be stamped upon arrival and the passport must be valid for at least six months after the date of arrival. For visa-free entry, you must also have proof of onward journey, either a return or through ticket. Employment is strictly forbidden on tourist visas or visa-free entry.

Visa-free entry to Indonesia cannot be extended beyond two months (60 days) and cannot be converted to any other kind of visa.

A visa is required in advance for all other nationals or arrivals at minor ports.

Upon arrival you will be given a white embarkation/disembarkation card to fill out. Keep this card with your passport as you must present it when leaving the country.

Other Visas

The 2-month, non-extendable tourist pass is the only entry permit that comes without a great deal of paperwork.

A social visa, usually valid initially for 4–5 weeks, can be extended for up to 3 months. You must have a good reason for spending time in Indonesia (relatives, language study) and you must have a sponsor who will assume financial responsibility for you. The process can take weeks and extensions are at the discretion of the immigration office where you apply.

A business visa requires a letter from a company stating that you are performing a needed service for a company in Indonesia. It is valid for up to one year, but you must leave the country every 4 months. This is not intended as an employment visa, but is for investors, consultants, or other business purposes. You are not to earn money in Indonesia on a business visa.

Two other types of visas are available: the temporary residence card (KITAS) for research, formal study or employment, and the permanent residence card (KITAP). Both are difficult to get.

When dealing with the authorities, be on your best behavior and dress appropriately.

Customs

Narcotics, firearms and ammunition are strictly prohibited. The standard duty-free allowance is: 2 liters of alcoholic beverages, 200 cigarettes, 50 cigars or 100 grams of tobacco.

There is no restriction on import and export of foreign currencies in cash or travelers checks, but there is an export limit of 50,000 Indonesian rupiah.

All narcotics are illegal in Indonesia. The use, sale or purchase of narcotics results in long prison terms, huge fines and death, in some cases. Once caught, you are immediately placed in detention until trial, and the sentences are stiff, as demonstrated by Westerners currently serving sentences as long as 30 years for possession of marijuana.

FOREIGN EMBASSIES & CONSULATES

All foriegn embassies are in Jakarta:
Australia Jl. H.R. Rasuna Said, Kav. C/15-16, ☎ 5227111.
Austria Jl. P. Diponegoro No. 44, ☎ 338090.
Belgium Jl. Jend. Sudirman, Kav. 22-23, ☎ 5712180.
Brunei Darussalam Jl. Jend. Sudirman, Kav. 22-23, ☎ 5712180.
Canada Wisma Metropolitan I, 15th Floor, Jl. Jend. Sudirman, Kav. 29, ☎ 5250709.
China Jl. Jend. Sudirman, Kav. 69, ☎ 714596.
Denmark Bina Mulia Bldg., 4th Floor, Jl. H.R. Rasuna Said, Kav. 10, ☎ 5204350.
Finland Bina Mulia Bldg., 10th Floor, Jl. H.R. Rasuna Said, Kav. 10, ☎ 516980.
France Jl. M.H. Thamrin No. 20, ☎ 3142807.
Germany Jl. Raden Saleh 54-56, ☎ 3849547.
Greece Jl. Kebon Sirih No. 16, ☎ 360623.
India Jl. H.R. Rasuna Said No. S-1, ☎ 5204150.
Italy Jl. Diponegoro 45, ☎ 337445.
Japan Jl. M.H. Thamrin No. 24, ☎ 324308
Malaysia Jl. H.R. Rasuna Said Kav. X/6/1-3, ☎ 5224947.
Myanmar Jl. H. Agus Salim No. 109, ☎ 3140440.
Mexico Wisma Nusantara, 4th Floor, Jl. M.H. Thamrin No. 59, ☎ 337479.
Netherlands Jl. H.R. Rasuna Said, Kav. S-3, ☎ 511515.
New Zealand Jl. Diponegoro No. 41, ☎ 330680.
Norway Bina Mulia Bldg. I, 4th Floor, Jl. H.R. Rasuna Said, Kav. 10, ☎ 5251990.
Pakistan Jl.Teuku Umar No. 50, ☎ 3144009.
Papua New Guinea Panin Bank Centre 6th Floor, Jl. Jend. Sudirman No. 1, ☎ 7251218.
Philippines Jl. Imam Bonjol No. 6-8, ☎ 3149329.
Singapore Jl. H.R. Rasuna Said, Block X Kav. 2, No. 4, ☎ 5201489.
South Korea Jl. Gatot Subroto, Kav. 57-58, ☎ 5201915.
Spain Jl. Agus Salim No. 61, ☎ 331414.
Sweden Bina Mulia Bldg. I, Jl. H.R. Rasuna Said,

Kav. 10, ☎ 5201551.
Switzerland Jl. H.R.Rasuna Said B-1, Kav. 10/32, ☎ 516061.
Thailand Jl. Imam Bonjol No.74, ☎ 3904055.
United Kingdom Jl. M.H. Thamrin No.75, ☎ 330904.
United States of America Jl. Medan Merdeka Selatan No. 5, ☎ 360360.
Vietnam Jl. Teuku Umar No. 25, ☎ 3100357.

Passport Loss

If you lose your passport, it will be difficult to get new documents to leave the country unless you have the proper official forms from the police. Always keep a photocopy of your passport, visa and driver's license separate from the originals. You can then prove your identity in case of theft or loss.

When theft occurs, report to your consulate. Verification of your identity and citizenship takes two or three weeks and involves going to the local immigration office.

WHAT TO BRING ALONG

When packing, keep in mind that you will be in the tropics, but that it can get cold in the mountains. Bring wash and wear, light cotton clothes that absorb perpiration. (Synthetic fabrics are really uncomfortable in the tropics.) A medium-weight sweater or wind breaker is also a must, as is a light rain jacket with a hood. Don't bring too much, as you will be tempted by the great variety of inexpensive clothes available here. If you visit a government office, men should wear long trousers, shoes and a shirt with collar. Women should wear a neat dress, covering knees and shoulders, and shoes.

For those wanting to travel light, a *sarong* purchased upon arrival in Indonesia ($5–10) is one of the most versatile items you could hope for. It serves as a wrap to get to the bath, a beach towel, pajamas, bed sheet, fast drying towel, etc.

Indonesians are renowned for their ability to sleep anytime, anywhere; so they are not likely to understand your desire for peace and quiet at night. Sponge rubber **earplugs** are available from pharmacies in the West or from the in-flight airline toiletry kit. Many consider them the most important 4 grams they carry.

Tiny **padlocks** for use on luggage zippers are a handy deterrent to pilfering hands. Some come with combination locks. **Flashlights** may come in handy, although these can be easily purchased locally.

Bring along some **pre-packaged alcohol towelettes** (swabs). These are handy for disinfecting your hands before eating, or after a trip to the *kamar kecil* (lavatory).

Rural Indonesia may not have Western-style department stores, so for things like **contact lens solutions, dental floss, tampons, sun-**

screen, and insect repellent, if you think you might need them, pack them.

Passport photos may come in handy for applications/permits (for parks) or even as gifts.

On your travels you will meet people who are kind and helpful, yet you may feel too embarrassed to give money. In this kind of situation a small gift is appropriate. Chocolates, biscuits, pens, stationery from your hotel, even your T-shirt with foreign designs are appreciated.

CLIMATE

In general, Indonesia experiences two yearly seasons of monsoon winds: the southeast monsoon, bringing dry weather (musim panas—dry season), and the northwest monsoon, bringing rain (musim hujan—rainy season). Often the changing seasons can bring the time of high waves (musim ombak).

The rainy season is normally November to April, with a peak around January/February, when it rains for several hours each day. The rain is predictable, however, and always stops for a time, when the sun may come out. Before it rains, the air gets very sticky; afterwards it is refreshingly cool. Some areas are inaccessible during the rainy season and flights are even more unreliable.

The dry season, May to October (especially June to August), is, generally, a better time to come. Humidity is down and nights can be cool. This is the time to climb mountains or visit nature reserves; when wild bulls go in search of water and sea turtles lay eggs more often.

This nice, neat picture is interrupted in Maluku province, where local effects alter weather patterns, and in areas where the rain shadow of mountains changes seasonal patterns. We have tried to give the best local times for diving in each relevant section.

The seas are more predictable. July and August are the best times to navigate off the north coast. January to March and June to October are the dangerous months for sailing off the south coast.

Tides in Indonesia average between one and three meters. The only place in the country with really big tidal fluctuations is the south coast of Irian Jaya, where the shallow Arafura Sea rises and falls 5 meters or more.

TIME ZONES

There are three time zones in Indonesia. The westernmost time zone, Western Indonesia Standard Time (including Sumatra and Java), is Greenwich Mean Time (GMT) +7 hours. Central Indonesia time (Bali, Nusa Tenggara and Sulawesi) is GMT +8, and Eastern Indonesian time (Maluku and Irian Jaya) is GMT +9.

MONEY

Prices quoted in this book are intended as a general indication. They are quoted in US dollars because the rupiah is being allowed to devalue slowly, so prices stated in US dollars are more likely to remain accurate.

Standard currency is the Indonesian rupiah: Notes come in 50,000, 20,000, 10,000, 5,000, 1,000, 500 and 100 denominations. Coins come in denominations of 1,000, 500, 100, 50, 25, 10 and 5 rupiah. Unfortunately, the new coins are very similar in size, so look carefully.Coins below Rp50 are rarely available. In stores small change is often replaced by candies.

Banking

It is best to carry travelers' checks of two leading companies as sometimes, for mysterious reasons, a bank won't cash the checks of a company as well known as, say, American Express. U.S. dollars—checks and cash—are accepted in all banks which deal in foreign exchange, as are Australian dollars and (usually) Japanese yen, Deutsche marks, French and Swiss francs. Carrying cash is not a good idea. Aside from the possible loss, banks won't take the bills unless they are in perfect condition.

Moneychangers and banks accepting foreign currency are found in most tourist areas. State banks are open from 8am–3pm, Monday to Friday. Private banks open also on Saturday until 11am. The bank counters at major airports offer competitive rates. Bank lines in town can be long and slow; the best way around it is to arrive promptly at opening time.

Get a supply of Rp1,000 and Rp500 notes when you change money, as taxi drivers and vendors often have—or claim to have— no change for big bills. When traveling in the countryside, Rp100 notes are also useful.

Carrying cash (US$) can be a handy safety precaution as it is still exchangeable should you lose your passport, but Indonesian banks only accept foreign currency that is crisp and clean.

Major credit cards may be accepted in some shops and hotels, but they often add a 3% surcharge. Most cities have at least one bank at which cash advances can be made—look for Bank Duta, BCA and Danamon. Visa and MasterCard are the most frequently accepted.

There are no exchange controls and excess rupiah (bills only) can be freely reconverted at the airport.

Tax, service and tipping

Most larger hotels and restaurants charge 21% tax and service on top of your bill. Tipping is not a custom here, but it is appreciated for special services. Rp500 per bag is considered a good tip for roomboys and porters. Taxi drivers will want to round up to the nearest Rp 500 or Rp 1,000. When tipping the driver of your rental car or a *pembantu* (housekeeper) of the house in which you've been a guest, fold the money and give it with the right hand only.

OFFICE HOURS

Many government offices have converted to a five-day work week and are officially open Monday to Friday, 8 am to 4 pm, but if you want to get anything done, be there by 11 am. In large cities most private businesses are open 9 am to 5 pm. Shops from 9 am to 9 pm. In smaller towns shops close for a siesta at 1 pm and reopen at 6 pm.

COMMUNICATIONS

Mail

Indonesia's postal service is reliable, if not terribly fast. *Kilat* express service is only slightly more expensive and much faster. *Kilat khusus* (domestic special delivery) will get there overnight. International express mail gets postcards and letters to North America or Europe in about 7 days from most cities.

Kantor pos (post offices) are in every little village, generally open Mon–Thurs 8am–2pm, Fri until 11, Sat until 1pm. Main post office in bigger cities are open daily (except Sunday) 8am–8pm.

Hotels will normally sell stamps and post letters for you, or you can use private postal agents to avoid hassles. Look for the orange *Agen Kantor Pos* (postal agency) signs.

Telephone and Fax

Long distance phone calls, both within Indonesia and international, are handled by satellite. Domestic long distance calls can be dialed from most phones. To dial your own international calls, find an IDD (International Direct Dial) phone and dial "001" or "008," otherwise you must go via the operator, which is far more expensive.

A magnetic debit (*kartu telpon*) phone card can be purchased at hotels, post offices and many other outlets. This is used on card phones which are increasing in popularity, eliminating the need for small change.

If your hotel has no IDD link you have to go to the main telephone office (*kantor telepon*), use a silver card phone (*kartu telpon*) and pay an uninflated rate or use a private postal and telephone service: *Wartel (warung telekommunikasi)/warpostel/warparpostel*. These small "telecom shops" are all over Indonesia and fast becoming the most convenient way to call international (you avoid hotel price hikes). They are often run by well-trained, efficient staff and offer fast IDD services at near standard rates. Open daily from 8am to 10pm or 11pm. Prices per minute are about $2.30 to the Americas and $3.10 to most European countries. Night rates are lower.

International calls via MCI, Sprint, ATT, and the like can be made from IDD phones using the access code for your calling card company. Recently, special telephones have been installed in Indonesia's airports with pre-programmed buttons to connect you via these companies to various countries.

Faxes and can be sent and received at *wartel* offices and most main post offices.

Courier Services

Some of the big international courier outfits operate in Indonesia, along with some domestic ones. DHL Worldwide Express and LTH Worldwide Courier Service are probably the most reliable here.

ELECTRICITY

Most of Indonesia has converted to 220 volts and 50 cycles, though a few places are still on the old 110 lines. Ask before you plug in if you are uncertain. Power failures are common in smaller cities and towns. Voltage can fluctuate considerably so use a stabilizer for computers and similar equipment. Plugs are of the European two-pronged variety.

HEALTH

Before You Go

Check with your physician for the latest news on the need for malaria prophylaxis and recommended **vaccinations** before leaving home. Frequently considered vaccines are: Diphtheria, Pertusis and Tetanus (DPT); Measles, Mumps and Rubella (MMR); and oral Polio vaccine. Gamma Globulin every four months for Hepatitis A is recommended. For longer stays many doctors recommend vaccination to protect against Hepatitis B requiring a series of shots over the course of 7 months. Vaccinations for smallpox and cholera are no longer required, except for visitors coming from infected areas. A cholera vaccination is recommended for travel in outlying areas, but it is only 50% effective.

Find out the generic names for whatever prescription medications you are likely to need as most are available in Indonesia but not under the same brand names as they are known at home. Get copies of doctors' prescriptions for the medications you bring into Indonesia to avoid questions at the customs desk. Those who wear spectacles should bring along prescriptions.

First Aid Kit

A basic first aid kit should consist of aspirin and multivitamins, a decongestant, an antihistamine, disinfectant (such as Betadine), antibiotic powder, fungicide, an antibiotic eyewash, Kaopectate or Lomotil, and sunscreen. Also good strong soap, perhaps Betadine or other antiseptic soap. Avoid oral antibiotics unless you know how to use them. For injuries, make up a little kit containing Band-aids and ectoplast strips, a roll of sterile gauze and treated gauze for burns, surgical tape, and an elastic bandage for sprains. Also very important are Q-tips, tweezers, scissors, needles and safety pins. Keep your pills and liquid medicines in small unbreakable plastic bottles, clearly labeled with indelible pen.

Hygiene

Hygeiene cannot be taken for granted in Indonesia. Away from the tourist areas few places have running water or sewerage. Most water comes from wells, and raw sewerage goes into the ground or the rivers. Tap water is not potable and must be boiled.

Most cases of stomach complaints are attributable to your system not being used to the strange foods and stray bacteria. To make sure you do not get something more serious, take the following precautions:

☛ Never drink unboiled water from a well, tap or bak mandi (bath tub). Brush your teeth only with boiled or bottled water, never with water from the tap or bak mandi. Bottled water is available everywhere and usually called "Aqua", which is the most popular and reliable brand name.

☛ Ice is made in government regulated factories and is deemed safe for local immunities. Confirm that the ice is made from boiled water before relaxing with an ice drink.

☛ Plates, glasses and silverware are washed in unboiled water and need to be completely dry before use.

☛ Fruits and vegetables without skins pose a higher risk of contamination. To avoid contamination by food handlers, buy fruits in the market and peel them yourself.

☛ To mandi (bathe) two or three times a day is a great way to stay cool and fresh. But be sure to dry yourself off well and you may wish to apply a medicated body powder such as Purol to avoid the nastiness of skin fungus, especially during the rainy season from November to April.

Exposure

Many visitors insist on instant sun tans, so overexposure to the heat and sun are frequent health problems. Be especially careful on long boat rides where the roof gives a good view. The cooling wind created by the boat's motion disguises the fact that you are frying like an egg.

Telephone Codes

From outside Indonesia, the following cities may be reached by dialing 62 (the country code for Indonesia) then the city code, then the number. Within Indonesia, the city code must be preceded by a 0 (zero).

City	Code	City	Code
Ambon	911	Mataram	364
Balikpapan	542	Medan	61
Banda Aceh	651	Merauke	971
Bandar		Metro	725
Lampung	721	Mojokerto	321
Bandung	22	Nusa Dua	361
Banjarmasin	511	Padang	751
Banyuwangi	333	Palangkaraya	514
Batam	778	Palembang	711
Belawan	619	Palu	451
Bengkulu	736	Pare-Pare	421
Biak	961	Pasuruan	343
Binjai	619	Pati	295
Blitar	342	Pekalongan	285
Bogor	251	Pekanbaru	761
Bojonegoro	353	Pematang-	
Bondowoso	332	siantar	622
Bukittinggi	752	Ponorogo	352
Cianjur	263	Pontianak	561
Cilacap	282	Parapat	625
Cipanas	255	Probolinggo	335
Cirebon	231	Purwakarta	264
Cisarua	251	Purwokerto	281
Denpasar	361	Sabang	652
Gadog	251	Salatiga	298
Garut	262	Samarinda	541
Gresik	31	Sekupang	778
Jakarta	21	Semarang	24
Jambi	741	Serang	254
Jember	331	Sibolga	731
Jombang	321	Sidoarjo	319
Kabanjahe	628	Sigli	653
Karawang	267	Situbondo	338
Kebumen	287	Solo	271
Kediri	354	Sorong	951
Kendal	294	Sukabumi	266
Kendari	401	Sumbawa	
Klaten	272	Besar	371
Kota Pinang	624	Sumedang	261
Kotabaru	518	Surabaya	31
Kutacane	629	Tangerang	21
Kuala Simpang	641	Tapak Tuan	656
Kudus	291	Tarakan	551
Kupang	391	Tasikmalaya	265
Lahat	731	Tebing Tinggi	
Lhok Seumawe	645	Deli	621
Lumajang	334	Ternate	921
Madiun	351	Tulung Agung	355
Magelang	293	Ujung Pandang	411
Malang	341	Wates	274
Manado	431	Wonosobo	286
Manokwari	962	Yogyakarta	274

Wear a hat, loose-fitting, light-colored, long-sleeved cotton clothes, pants, and use a good-quality sunscreen (bring a supply with you). Do not wear synthetic fibers that do not allow air to circulate. Tan slowly—don't spoil your trip. Drink plenty of fluids and take salt.

Cuts and Scrapes

Your skin will come into contact with more dirt and bacteria than it did back home, so wash your face and hands more often. Cuts should be taken seriously and cleaned with an antiseptic like Betadine or Dettol, available from any pharmacy (*apotik*). Once clean, antibiotic powder (*Sulfanilamide*) or ointment, both available locally, should be applied. Cover the cut during the day to keep it clean, but leave it uncovered at night and whenever you are resting so that it can dry. Constant covering will retain moisture in the wound and only encourage an infection. Repeat this ritual after every bath. Areas of redness around the cut indicate infection and a doctor should be consulted. At the first sign of swelling it is advisable to take broad spectrum antibiotics to prevent a really nasty infection.

Not every mosquito bite leads to malaria, but in the tropics a scratched bite or small abrasion can quickly turn into a festering ulcer. You must pay special attention to these things. Apply calamine solution or Tiger Balm—a widely available camphorated salve—or some imitation thereof to relieve the itching. For light burns, use Aristamide or Bioplacenteron.

Diarrhea

A likely traveling companion. In addition to the strange food and unfamiliar micro-fauna, diarrhea is often the result of attempting to accomplish too much in one day. Taking it easy can be an effective prevention. Ask around before leaving about what the latest and greatest of the many remedies are and bring some along. Imodium is locally available as are activated carbon tablets (Norit) that will absorb the toxins giving you grief.

When it hits, it is usually self-limiting to two or three days. Relax, take it easy and drink lots of fluids, perhaps accompanied by rehydration salts such as Servidrat (local brands are Oralit and Pharolit). Especially helpful is water from the young coconut (*air kelapa muda*) or strong, unsweetened tea. The former is an especially pure anti-toxin. Get it straight from the coconut without sugar, ice or food color added. When you are ready, bananas, papayas, plain rice, crackers or dry biscuits, and *bubur* (rice porridge) are a good way to start. Avoid fried, spicy or heavy foods and dairy products for a while. After three days without relief, see a doctor.

Not all bouts of diarrhea mean dysentery. If you contract the latter, which is much more se-rious, you must seek medical help. Do this if your stools are mixed with blood and pus, are black, or you are experiencing severe stomach cramps and fever. If no medical help is available, try tetracycline and Diatab, effective for bacillary dysentery. If you feel no relief in a day or two, you have the more serious amoebic dysentery which requires additional medication.

To prevent stomach problems, try to eat only thoroughly cooked foods, don't buy already peeled fruit, and stay away from unpasteurized dairy products. For constipation, eat a lot of fruit.

Intestinal Parasites

It is estimated that 80 to 90 percent of all people in Indonesia have intestinal parasites and these are easily passed on by food handlers. Prevention is difficult, short of fasting, when away from luxury hotel restaurants and even these are no guarantee. It's best to take care of parasites sooner rather than later, by routinely taking a dose of anti-parasite medicine such as *Kombatrin* (available at all *apotik*) once a month during your stay and again when you get on the plane home.

If you still have problems when you get back, even if only sporadic, have stool and blood tests. Left untreated, parasites can cause serious damage.

Mosquito-Borne Diseases

Malaria is a problem in some parts of Indonesia. The disease accounts for a sizeable percentage of the country's total mortality, and is nothing to be irresponsible about.

Malaria is caused by a protozoan, *Plasmodium*, which affects the blood and liver. The vector for this parasite is the *Anopheles* mosquito. After contracting malaria, it takes a minimum of six days—or up to several years—before symptoms appear.

If you are visiting rural Indonesia, you *must* take malaria pills. Do not think that pills offer complete protection, however, as they don't. A virulent strain of malaria has recently become dominant particularly in Nusa Tenggara. If you are pregnant, have had a splenectomy or have a weak immune system, or suffer from chronic disease, you should weigh carefully whether the trip is worth the risk.

Chloroquine phosphate is the traditional malaria prophylactic, but in the past 10–15 years, the effectiveness of the drug has deteriorated. Deciding on an appropriate anti-malarial is now more complicated. There are actually four forms of malaria: *Plasmodium vivax*, which is unpleasant and can lie dormant for 50 years or more, but is rarely fatal to healthy adults; *P. melariae*, which is the least serious variant; *P. ovale*, which is rare in Indonesia; and *P. falciparum*, which can be quickly fatal. *P. falciparum* is dominant in parts of Indonesia.

Malaria pills. As a prophylactic for travel, take two tablets of Chloroquine (both on the same day) once a week, and one tablet of Maloprim (pyrimethamine) once a week. Maloprim is a strong drug, and not everybody can tolerate it. If you are planning on taking Maloprim for more than two months, it is recommended that you take a folic acid supplement, 6 mg a day, to guard against anemia. [**Note**: The anti-malarial drugs only work once the protozoan has emerged from the liver, which can be weeks after your return. You should continue on the above regimen for one month after returning.]

There is now widespread resistance to Chloroquine in Irian. Mefloquin (such as Larium) seems to be the most commonly used prophylaxis now. It has been shown effective, although unpleasant side effects have been demonstrated for it as well. Mefloquine is also very expensive, about $3 a tablet. However, it can be a lifesaver in cases of resistant *falciparum* infection.

These drugs are not available over-the-counter in most western countries (or, indeed, even behind the counter at most pharmacies), and if you visit a doctor, you may have trouble convincing him of what you need. Doctors in the temperate zones are not usually familiar with tropical diseases, and may even downplay the need to guard against them. Do not be persuaded. Try to find a doctor who has had experience in these matters.

You can also buy Chloroquine and Maloprim over-the-counter in Indonesia, for very little (a few dollars for a month's supply). Maloprim, however, may still be difficult to find. [**Note**: there is a non–chloroquine based drug sold in Indonesia called Fansidar. This drug is not effective against the resistant strains of *P. falciparum* and not for use as a prophylaxis.]

The antibiotic Doxycycline can also be used as a prophylaxis for short-term stays (2-6 weeks): 100 mg. once a day with food, starting 2 days before arrival and continued through 4 days after departure of the malarious area.

Treatment. Malaria in the early stages is very hard to distinguish from a common cold or flu. A person infected may just suffer from headache and nausea, perhaps accompanied by a slight fever and achiness, for as long as a week until the disease takes hold. When it does, the classic symptoms begin:

1) Feeling of intense cold, sometimes accompanied by shaking. This stage lasts from 30 minutes to two hours.

2) High fever begins, and victim feels hot and dry, and may vomit or even become delirious. This lasts 4–5 days.

3) Sweating stage begins, during which the victim perspires very heavily, and his body temperature begins to drop.

The classic fever/chill pattern is more likely to occur with people who are not taking prophylaxis. Those on a prophylaxis will have stronger "flu" symptoms (aches, nausea, headache).

If you think you have malaria, you should call on professional medical help immediately. A good medical professional is your best first aid. Only if you cannot get help, initiate the following treatment:

1) Take 4 Chloroquine tablets immediately.

2) 6 hours later, take 2 more Chloroquine tablets.

3) The next day, take 2 more.

4) The following day, take 2 more.

Note: If the Chloroquine treatment does not cause the fever to break within 24 hours, assume the infection is the very dangerous *P. falciparum* and begin the following treatment immediately:

1) Take 3 tablets (750 mg) of Mefloquine (Larium)

2) Six hours later, take 2 more tablets (500 mg) of Mefloquine.

3) After 12 hours—and only if you weigh 60 kg (130 lbs) or more—take one more tablet (250 mg) of Mefloquine.

The other mosquito concern is **dengue fever**, spread by the morning-biting *Aedes aegypti*, especially during the rainy season. The most effective prevention is not getting bitten (there is no prophylaxis for dengue). Dengue fever symptoms are headache, pain behind the eyes, high fever, muscle and joint pains and rash appearing between the third and fifth days of illness. Within days, the fever subsides and recovery is seldom hampered with complications. The more serious variant, dengue haemorrhagic fever (DHF), which can be fatal, may be the reaction of a secondary infection with remaining immunities following a primary attack.

Cases of **Japanese encephalitis**, a viral infection affecting the brain, have occured recently and are added cause to take protective measures against mosquito bites.

Prevention. Malaria, dengue fever, and Japanese encephalities are carried by mosquitos. If you don't get bit, you don't get the diseases.

1) While walking around, use a good quality mosquito repellent, and be very generous with it, particularly around your ankles. Wear light-colored, long-sleeved shirts or blouses and long pants. (Effective insect repellent may be hard to find, so bring some from home.) Any chemical repellent container deet (diethyl toluamide) should be applied with caution and never to the face. Application to clothing can be more effective. A local non-chemical solution is citronella mixed with eucalyptus oil (*minyak gosok, cap tawon*).

2) While eating or relaxing in one spot, burn mosquito coils. These are those green, slightly brittle coils of incense doped with pyrethrin that were banned in the United States some years ago. They last 6-8 hours and are quite effective. You will get used to the smell. (If you

are worried about inhaling some of the poison they contain, re-read the classic symptoms of malaria above.) In Indonesia, the ubiquitous coils are called *obat nyamuk bakar*. Double Rabbit is one of the more relizble brands. (There are brands which do not contain pyrethum, so are ineffective.) In some places where there is electricity, there is a smokeless repellent with a similar ingredient that is inserted into a unit plugged into the wall.

3) While sleeping, burn *obat nyamuk* and use a mosquito net. Some hotels have nets, but not many, and you should bring your own. If you set a couple of *obat nyamuk* coils going in strategic places when you go to sleep you will be protected. Remember that mosquitos like damp bathrooms—where few people bother to light a mosquito coil.

AIDS & Hepatitis B

Surprise! **Safe sex** is also a good idea. Documentation, awareness and education is just beginning. Another area of concern is the Hepatitis B virus which affects liver function and is only sometimes curable and can be fatal. The prevalence of Hepatitis B in Indonesia is the basis for international concern over the ominous possibilities for the spread of HIV virus, which is passed on in the same ways.

Medical Treatment

Pharmacies—*apotik*—carry just about everything you might need. You can readily get malaria pills here, and an excellent anti-bacterial ointment called Bacitran. Tiger Balm is available everywhere in Asia, and it is excellent for itching bites and muscles pains. Mycolog is a brand of fungicide sold in Indonesia. Oral rehydration salts are usually sold in packets to be mixed with 200 ml of (clean) water. Outside the larger cities, it's nearly impossible to purchase medicines or first aid supplies.

In the larger towns there are decent government hospitals (*rumah sakit*) and medicines are widely available. Smaller villages only have government clinics (*puskesmas*), which are not equipped to deal with anything serious. Your hotel or losmen will probably be able to find you doctor who speaks English.

Doctors and health care are quite inexpensive by western standards, but the quality leaves much to be desired. (At least they're familiar with the symptoms and treatment of tropical diseases, however, which is something your family doctor might have a real tough time recognizing back home.)

Consultations with doctors are very cheap in Indonesia, usually about $5–$8 for general practitioners, $8–$15 for specialists. If you check into a hospital, get a VIP room ($20–$30 for everything—including doctors' fees—but

not medicines) or a somewhat cheaper "Klas I" room. The cheaper hospital rooms and wards tend to get less attention from the medical staff. Government hospitals, at provincial capital and district level, have improved considerably since the late 1980s.

Misuse of antibiotics is still a concern in Indonesia. They should only be used for bacterial diseases and then for at least 10 to 14 days to prevent developing antibiotic resistant strains of your affliction. If an injection or antibiotics are prescribed, be sure it's necessary. Ensure syringes have never been used before or better yet, buy your own disposable from an *apotik* (pharmacy) and take it to the clinic.

Emergency Medical Assistance

Even in the big cities outside of Jakarta, emergency care leaves much to be desired. Your best bet in the event of a life-threatening emergency or accident is to get on the first plane to Jakarta or Singapore. Contact your embassy or consulate by phone for assistance (see below). Medivac airlifts are very expensive ($26,000) and most embassies will recommend that you buy insurance to cover the cost of this when traveling extensively in Indonesia.

Insurance

Check your health insurance before coming to make sure you are covered. Travel insurance should include coverage of a medical evacuation to Singapore and a 24-hour worldwide phone number as well as some extras like luggage loss and trip cancellation.

AEA International Asia Emergency Assistance offers insurance packages for travelers and expatriates living in Asia. This well-respected outfit is considered to have the best response time and operation in Indonesia. AEA maintains 24-hour alarm centers in Jakarta, Bali, Singapore, Sydney, Bangkok, Hong Kong, Seoul, Beijing, and Ho Chi Minh City. Premium for one-year (approx. $125) is available for travelers and covers the cost of medical evacation to Singapore and repatriation if recommended by the AEA doctor. Contact: **AEA International Pte. Ltd.**,331 North Bridge Road, 17th Floor, Odeon Towers, Singapore 0718. ☎ (65) 338 2311, fax: (65) 338 7611.

International SOS Assistance Asia Pacific Regional Head Office: 10 Anson Road, #21-08/A International Plaza, Singapore 0207. ☎ (65) 221 3981, fax: (65) 226 3937, telex: 24422 SOSAFE. Offers a range of emergency services worldwide. Numerous large corporate clients. Contact them for rates and types of coverage

FOOD AND DRINK

Drink lots of fluids. The equatorial sun takes out a lot from you and dehydration can be a serious problem. Symptoms are infrequent urination, deep yellow/orange urine, headaches.

Tap water in Indonesia is not potable and it should be brought to a full boil for ten minutes before being considered safe. Indonesians are themselves fussy about drinking water, so if you're offered a drink it is almost certainly safe.

Most Indonesians do not feel they have eaten until they have eaten rice. This is accompanied by side dishes, often just a little piece of meat and some vegetables with a spicy sauce. Other common items include *tahu* (tofu), *tempe* (soybean cake) and salted fish. Crispy fried tapioca crackers flavored with prawns and spices (*krupuk*) usually accompany a meal.

No meal is complete without *sambal*—a fiery paste of ground chili peppers with garlic, shallots, sugar, and sometimes soy sauce or fish paste. Fruit, especially pineapple and papaya provide quick relief for a chili-burned mouth.

Cooking styles vary greatly from one region to another. The Sundanese of West Java are fond of raw vegetables, eaten with chili and fermented prawn paste (*lalab/sambal trasi*). Minihasan food in North Sulawesi is very spicy, and includes some interesting specialties: fruit bat wings in coconut milk, *sambal* rat, and dog. In the more isolated parts of the archipelago, the food can be quite plain, and frankly, quite dull.

In most Indonesian restaurants there is a standard menu of *satay* (skewered barbequed meat)—most common are *ayam* (chicken) and *kambing* (goat), *gado-gado* or *pecel* (boiled vegetables with spicy peanut sauce) and *soto* (vegetable soup with or without meat). Also common are Chinese dishes like *bakmie goreng* (fried noodles), *bakmie kuah* (noodle soup) and *cap cay* (stir-fried vegetables).

In most larger towns you can also find a number of Chinese restaurants on the main street. Some have menus with Chinese writing, but usually the cuisine is very much assimilated to local tastes. Standard dishes, in addition to the *bakmie* and *cap cay* mentioned above, are sweet and sour whole fish (*gurame asem manis*), beef with Chinese greens (*kailan/caisim ca sapi*), and prawns sauteed in butter (*udang goreng mentega*).

Indonesian fried chicken (*ayam goreng*) is common and usually very tasty—although the local -grown chicken can be a bit stringy. Then there is the ubiquitous *nasi goreng* (fried rice); the "special" (*istimewa*) comes with an egg on top and is often served for breakfast.

There are restaurants everywhere in Indonesia that specialize in food from **Padang**, West Sumatra. This spicy, and very tasty cuisine has a distinctive way of being served. As many as 15-20 different dishes are displayed in the glass case in front of the restaurant. You tell the waiter what you want and he sets a whole stack of the little dishes in front of you. At the end of the meal, you are charged for what you have eaten and any untouched plates are put back in the case.

As tempting as fresh vegetables may be, avoid eating garnishes or raw salads unless the veggies are air-flown/imported.

The beers available in Indonesia are Bintang and Anker, both brewed under Dutch supervision and rather light (perhaps appropriately for the tropics). With electricity such a precious commodity, however, in out-of-the-way places the only way to quaff it cold is to pour it over ice.

Fruits

Tropical fruits are plentiful and delicious. Amongst the more unusual and tastiest are *salak*, which has a brown snakeskin covering three segments, two of which contain a large brown seed and tastes like a cross between an apple and a walnut, and *manggis* (mangosteen), which is pure heaven hidden within a thick purple-brown cover. The juicy white segments almost melt away. *Rambutan*, a relative of lychee, has soft spiny "hairs" (*rambut*) on its soft shell. All of these juicy delights are in season between November and March. Bananas, apples, tangerines, papaya, pineapples, pomelos (*jeruk Bali*), starfruit (*blimbing*), guava (*buah biji*), and watermelon are found year round.

Warung (Street Stalls)

Restaurant kitchens do not necessarily have healthier food preparation procedures than roadside *warung*. The important thing at a *warung* is to watch and judge whether or not the cooks inspire confidence. Beware: *warung* rarely have a supply of running water.

The first portion may not fill you up, so a second portion can be ordered by saying "Tambah separuh" (add half portion). But only the price is halved. The amount of food is more like three-quarters. Finish off with a banana and say "Sudah" (I've had plenty, thank you). The seller will total up the prices of what was served you and ask you how many *krupuk, tempe,* etc. you added; so keep track. The total will come to between Rp1000 and Rp2,500 (50¢–$1.25).

Vegetarianism

Say "*saya tidak makan daging*" (I don't eat meat), "*tidak pakai ayam*" (without chicken) or "*tidak pakai daging*" (without meat). Dietary restrictions are very acceptable and common due to the various religious and spiritual practices involving food. However, finding food that truly has no animal products is a problem. Often meals which appear to be made exclusively of vegetables will have a chunk of beef or chicken in them to add that certain oomph. Tempe (fermented soy bean cake) and *tahu* (tofu) are common sources of protein.

SECURITY

Indonesia is a relatively safe place to travel and violent crime is almost unheard of, but petty crime is on the upswing. Pay close attention to your belongings, especially in big cities. Use a small backpack or moneybelt for valuables: shoulderbags can be snatched. Bags have been snatched by thieves on motorbikes, so be vigilant. Be especially wary on crowded *bemos*, buses and trains; this is where **pick-pockets** lurk. They usually work in groups and are very clever at slitting bags and extracting valuables without your noticing anything.

Be sure that the door and windows of your hotel room are locked at night, including those in the bathroom, as thieves are adept at sneaking in while you are asleep. Big hotels have **safety boxes** for valuables. If your hotel does not have such a facility, it is better to carry all the documents along with you. Make sure you have a photocopy of your passport, return plane ticket and travelers' check numbers and keep them separate from the originals.

ADDRESSES

The Indonesian spelling of geographical features and villages varies considerably as there is no form of standardization that meets with both popular and official approval. We have seen village names spelled three different ways, all on signboards in front of various government offices. In this guide, we have tried to use the most common spellings.

There are three overlapping and concurrent address systems for any given location: old street name and number, new street name with new numbers, and *kampung* (neighborhood) name with block numbers. Every town now has its street named after the same national heroes, so you will find Jalan Jendral Sudirman (General Sudirman Street) in every city throughout the archipelago.

The names with the new house numbers are the preferred designations for postal purposes. However, when tracking down a hotel address you may find that the old street names, the *kampung* names, or local landmarks more helpful. You will also find number 38 next to number 119 and the streets referred to by different names, such as Jalan Diponegoro (an Indonesian hero), Jalan Abdi Dongo (from local history) or Gajahan Gang II (the *kampung* name and alley number).

Finding Your Way

Westerners are used to finding things using telephone directories, addresses, and maps. But in Indonesia, phone books are incomplete, addresses can be confusing and maps little understood. The way to find something is to ask.

To ask for directions, it's better to have the name of a person and the name of the *kampung*. Thus "Bu Murni, Jetis" is a better address for asking directions even though "Jalan Kaliwedas 14" is the mailing address. Knowing the language helps here but is not essential. Immediately clear answers are not common and you should be patient. You are likely to get a simple indication of direction without distance or specific instructions. The assumption is that you will be asking lots of people along the way. Begin by asking three people. Usually two point toward the same general vicinity. Proceed, then ask again.

Maps are useful tools for you, but introducing them into discussions with Indonesians may cause more confusion than clarity. More than likely the north arrow on the map will be turned to real north before a reading. Periplus Travel Maps provide detailed and accurate maps of all major tourist destinations.

CALENDAR

The Indonesian government sets national holidays every year, both fixed and moveable dates.The fixed national holidays on the Gregorian calendar are the International New Year, Jan. 1; Independence Day, Aug. 17; and Christmas, Dec. 25. The Christian Good Friday, Easter Day, and Ascension Day, the Balinese new year, Nyepi, and the Buddhist Waisak are also national holidays. These holy days and all the Muslim holy days are based on the moon, so confusion results in attempting to extrapolate several years ahead.

Official Muslim holidays in Indonesia (the dates are for 1996):

Idul Fitri February 20-21. The end of the Muslim fasting month, Ramadan, also called Lebaran.

Idul Adha April 28. The day of Abraham's sacrifice and the day that the haji pilgrims circle the Kaaba in Mecca.

Hijryah May 19. The Islamic New Year, when Muhammad traveled from Mecca to Medina.

Maulud Nabi Muhammad SAW July 28. Muhammad's birthday.

Isra Mi'raj Nabi Muhammad SAW. December. 8. When Muhammad ascended on his steed Bouraq.

The 12 lunar months of the Muslim calendar are, in order: Muharram, Safar, Rabiul Awal, Rabiul Ahir, Jumadil Awal, Jumadil Ahir, Rajab, Sa'ban, Ramadan, Sawal, Kaidah, Zulhijja.

Note: The Muslim calendar begins with the Hijriah, Muhammad's flight to Median, in A.D. 622 according to the Gregorian calendar. Early A.D. 1996 corresponds to A.H. 1416. The Muslim calendar is a lunar calendar (354 or 355 days) and gains 10 or 11 days on the Gregorian calendar (365 days) each year.

ETIQUETTE

In the areas of Indonesia most frequented by Europeans, many are familiar with the strange ways of Westerners. But it is best to be aware of how certain aspects of your behavior will be viewed. You will not be able to count on an Indonesian to set you straight when you commit a *faux pas*. They are much too polite. They will stay silent or even reply *tidak apa apa* (no problem) if you ask if you did something wrong. So here are some points to keep in mind:

☛ The left hand is considered unclean as it is used for cleaning oneself in the bathroom. It is inappropriate to use the left hand to eat or to give or receive anything with it. When you do accidentally use your left hand then say *"ma'af, tangan kiri"* (please excuse my left hand).

☛ The head is considered the most sacred part of the body and, hence, the feet the least sacred. Avoid touching people on the head. Go for the elbow instead. Never step over food or expose the sole of your foot toward anyone.

☛ As it is impolite to keep one's head higher than others, it is appropriate to acknowledge the presence of others by stooping (extending the right arm, drooping the right shoulder, and leaning forward) while passing closely by someone who is sitting.

☛ Pointing with the index finger is impolite. Indonesians use their thumbs (palm turned upward, fingers curled in) or open palms instead.

☛ Summoning people by crooking the forefinger is impolite. Rather, wave downward with a flat palm face down.

☛ Alcohol is frowned upon in Islam, so take a look around you and consider taking it easy.

☛ Hands on hips is a sign of superiority or anger.

☛ Indonesians don't blow their noses. Keep a handkerchief handy.

☛ Take off your shoes when you enter someone's house. Often the host will stop you, but you should go through the motions until he does.

☛ Don't drink or eat until invited to, even after food and drinks have been placed in front of you. Sip your drink and don't finish it in one gulp. Never take the last morsels from a common plate.

☛ You will often be invited to eat with the words *makan, makan* ("eat, eat") if you pass somebody who is eating. This is not really an invitation, but simply means "Excuse me as I eat."

☛ If someone prepares a meal or drink for you it is most impolite to refuse.

Some things from the west filter through to Indonesia more effectively than others and stories of "*free sek*" (free sex) made a deep and lasting impression in Indonesia. Expect this topic to appear in lists of questions you will be asked in your cultural exchanges. It is best to explain how things have changed since the 1960s and how we now are stuck with "*saf sek*."

Keeping Your Cool

At government offices like immigration or police, talking loudly and forcefully doesn't make things easier. Patience and politeness are virtues that open many doors in Indonesia. Good manners and dress are also to your advantage.

ACCOMMODATIONS

A hierarchy of lodgings and official terminology has been set by the government. A "hotel" is an up-market establishment catering to businessmen, middle- to upper-class travelers and tourists. A star-rating (one to five stars) is applied according to the range of facilities. Smaller places with no stars and basic facilities are not referred to as hotels but as *losmen* (from the French *logement*), *wisma* (guesthouse) or *penginapan* (accommodation) and cater to the masses and budget tourists.

Prices and quality vary enormously. In the major cities that don't have many tourists, such as Jakarta, Surabaya and Medan, there is little choice in the middle ranges and you have to either pay a lot or settle for a room in a *losmen*. In areas where there are a lot of tourists, such as Bali and Yogya, you can get very comfortable and clean rooms with fan or air-conditioning for less than $20 a night. In small towns and remote areas, you don't have much choice and all accommodations tend to be very basic.

It's common to ask to see the room before checking in. Shop around before deciding, particularly if the hotel offers different rooms at different rates. Avoid carpeted rooms, especially without air-conditioning, as usually they are damp and this makes the room smell.

Advance bookings are necessary during peak tourist seasons (July to August and around Christmas and New Year). Popular resorts near big cities are always packed on weekends and prices often double, so go during the week when it's cheaper and quieter.

In many hotels, discounts of up to 50% from published rates are to be had for the asking, particularly if you have a business card. Booking in advance through travel agencies can also result in a lower rate. Larger hotels always add 21% tax and service to the bill.

Bathroom Etiquette

When staying in *losmen*, particularly when using communal facilities, don't climb in or drop your soap into the tub of water (*bak mandi*). This is for storing clean water. Scoop and pour the water over yourself with the ladle/dipper provided.

If you wish to use the native paper-free cleaning method, after using the toilet, scoop water with your right hand and clean with the left. This is the reason one only eats with the right hand—the left is regarded as unclean. Use soap and a fingernail brush (locals use a rock) for cleaning hands. Pre-packaged alcohol towelettes may make you feel happier about opting for this method. But don't throw the towelletes down the toilet.

Bring along your own towel and soap (although some places provide these if you ask).

Staying in Villages

Officially, the Indonesian government requires that foreign visitors spending the night report to the local police. This is routinely handled by losmen and hotels, who send in a copy of the registration form you fill out when you check in. Where there are no commercial lodgings, you can often rely on local hospitality. But when staying in a private home, keep in mind the need to inform the local authorities. One popular solution is to stay in the home of the local authority, the village head (*kepala desa*).

Carry photocopies of your passport, visa stamp and embarkation card to give to officials when venturing beyond conventional tourist areas. This saves time, and potential hassles, for you and your host.

Keep in mind that people in many rural parts of Indonesia have had limited experience with foreigners to date and are still learning how to share their homes with you. Villagers in rural Indonesia do not routinely maintain guest rooms. Things like soft beds, cold drinks and electricity are luxury items, and it is not guaranteed you will find someone who speaks anything other than Indonesian or the local language. They will, however, offer you the best they have and you should graciously return that respectful treatment. Paying a modest fee ($5) for a meal and a bed is appropriate and polite.

If a cash arrangement has not been pre-arranged, you should leave a gift appropriate to local needs—sugar, salt, biscuits, mirrors, small clasp-knives, clothing, cigarettes, or D-cell batteries for radios in remote villages. These gifts will be deeply appreciated. Send prints of any photos you take of your hosts.

SHOPPING

Be extremely cautious when buying antiques, works of art or other expensive objects, especially in the tourist areas. Most are reproductions, though very good ones and cheap to boot!

Handicrafts are produced all over Indonesia, and even if a good selection is available in hotels and tourist areas, it can be fun to seek out craftsmen in the villages (though often it's not cheaper unless you are very good at bargaining).

Bargaining

The secret here is not to care, or at least appear not to care. Some merchants are very upfront about giving prices that are about the minimum of what they want to sell an item for (*harga pas:* fixed price), but the trader who expects the buyer to bargain is more commonplace. A general rule of thumb is to aim for half the asking price by opening with an offer lower than that. The 50% rule is by no means universal and many sellers will only come down by 20%. On the other hand, in tourist areas, vendors will often ask 10 times or more the reasonable selling price, so don't feel shy about offering them 10% of the asking price.

More often than not the deal is closed in a ritual in which you cheerfully thank the merchant for their time and take steps towards the next stall or the door as the case may be. At this point keep your ears pricked for the *real* final offer of the seller and either thank them again and move on or return and claim your prize. If your final price is accepted it is a major breach of etiquette not to consummate the purchase.

In any event, staying cheerful and good humored will not only be more fun but can make a huge difference in the final price. This isn't just about money; it's also the nature of the interaction. And, yes, you should pay a bit more than an Indonesian would. That's the way it works.

Souvenirs

The best place for souvenir-shopping is Bali. The traveler's problem is how to lug around what is brought for the rest of the trip. While the most common souvenir items, hand-woven traditional cloths, are relatively light, they do take up some space. Carvings and other handicrafts are available in many areas, but Indonesia is not, as it is sometimes imagined, rich in craft everywhere. Particularly in some of the areas where divers frequent—coastal and lightly populated—the villages are populated by fishermen and copra farmers who do almost no craftwork.

SHIPPING & FREIGHT

Shipping goods home is relatively safe and painless. Items under one meter long and 10 kg in weight can be sent via most postal agents. All the packing will be done for you at minimal charge, although it's always advisable to keep an eye on how it's done. Buy insurance.

Larger purchases are best sent by air or sea cargo. Fowarders will handle the whole process for a price, from packing to customs. Some retailers may also prepared to send goods if purchased in quantity.

Air cargo is charged by the kilogram (10 kg min), and can be costly. Sea cargo (min. one cubic meter) is around $350 to the US or Europe and takes about 60 days. Insure your shipment: sea insurance is about 2.75% of the claimed value.

When shipping cargo, you are responsible for clearing customs back home and for the transportation from the port of entry to your destination. This can cost up to $500 so cargo is only economical for large purchases.

PHOTOGRAPHY

Indonesians generally enjoy being photographed. However, if you are in doubt or the situation seems awkward, it is polite to ask. Some religious activities, eating, and bathing are inappropriate subjects.

Beware of the strong shadows from the equatorial sun. Late afternoon and, especially, early morning, provide the most pleasing light and the richest colors. The only way to deal with the heavy shadows in midday is to use a fill flash.

The heat and humidity of the tropics is hard on camera equipment. Be particularly careful when moving equipment from an air-conditioned room to the muggy outdoors. Moisture will condense on the inside and outiside of the camera, Wait until it evaporates; don't be tempted to wipe it off. Also, watch the location of your camera bag and film. Temperatures in hot cars or on boats can be searing.

In general, stick with reliable equipment you are familiar with and bring extra batteries.

Photographic Supplies

Some 35mm Fuji and Kodak film is widely available in Indonesia, including color print film from ASA 100 to 400 and Ektachrome and Fujichrome 100 ASA daylight transparency film. In larger towns you can buy Fuji Neopan 100 ASA black-and-white negative film and Fuji Velvia.

PROTECTED SPECIES

Indonesia is home to more than 500 animal species—more than anywhere else in the world. It also has the greatest number of endangered species in the world. Establishing an effective environmental conservation program is a formidable project. The government with the help of private conversation agencies, such as the World Wide Fund for Nature and the Nature Conservancy, is working to create a viable network of national parks and nature reserves where fragile ecosystems and threatened species can be protected. Two of these national parks, Ujung Kulon in West Java (home to the world's most endangered large mammal, the Javan rhino) and Komodo in the Lesser Sundas (home to the Komodo dragon) have been declared World Heritage Sites by the World Conservation Union.

There are strict laws and severe penalties for trade in endangered species. The appendices of the Convention on International Trade in Endangered Species (CITES) lists more than 200 protected species of Indonesian mammals, birds, reptiles, insects, fish, and mollusks—including orangutan, parrots, cockatoo, crocodiles, tortoises and turtles, birdwing butterflies, and black coral. Visitors should be aware of the fragility of Indonesia's natural environment and not contribute to any further degradation of it.

TOURS AND TRAVEL AGENTS

Hiring your own vehicle for a private tour naturally allows you much more flexibility. An AC vehicle with a driver/guide costs anywhere from $30 up to $60 per day, all inclusive. The guides on both types of tours do expect tips, however be aware that they also get a 20%–40% commission on any of your purchases in the large souvenir shops along the way.

Travel agencies offer a variety of tours with knowledgeable, multilingual guides. If your time is limited, it may be best to entrust your schedule to an agency and let them handle all the arrangements.

Refer to area practicalities for local tours.

Transportation

GETTING AROUND IN INDONESIA

This advisory gives you an overview of the wide range of travel options available during your stay in Indonesia. A comprehensive run-down of travel services enables you to plan your way around the island according to time and budget. More specific details for each area you will be visiting can be found in the relevant Practicalities sections. Prices are in US dollars, unless otherwise stated. Prices and schedules are given as an indication only as they change frequently according to the season. Check with a travel agent prior to departure for the most up-to-date information.

GETTING TO INDONESIA

You can fly direct to Indonesia from just about anywhere. Most people traveling from Europe and the US arrive on direct flights to Jakarta, while those coming from Australia usually go first to Bali. The main international entry points are Soekarno-Hatta airport in Jakarta, Ngurah Rai airport in Bali, and Polonia airport in Medan. There are also non-stop flights from several Asian cities, including Singapore, Hong Kong, Taipei, Seoul, Nagoya, Fukuoka and Osaka.

Jakarta's Soekarno-Hatta airport is served by many international airlines, with over a dozen flights a day from Singapore alone. A cut-price alternative from Europe or the US may be to get a cheap flight to Singapore and buy an onward discount ticket to Jakarta from there: the cost of these can be as low as $75 single, $150 return. An excursion fare return ticket from Singapore to Bali with stops in Jakarta and Yogyakarta, good for a month, is available in Singapore for around $300. Buy through travel agents—check the classified section of the *Straits Times*. [**Note**: an onward ticket ensures visa-free entry upon arrival in Indonesia.]

Direct flights also connect Jakarta with many major cities in Asia and Europe. Air fares vary depending on the carrier, the season and the type of ticket purchased. A discount RT fare from the US costs from $1,000-1,200 and from Europe costs $800-1,200; about half that from Australia or East Asian capitals. Garuda Airlines now has a direct flight from Los Angeles that flies non-stop via Honolulu to Denpasar.

Air tickets from Batam and Bintan are also inexpensive. These Indonesian islands just off the coast of Singapore can be reached via short ferry hops from Singapore's World Trade Centre (Batam) and the Tanah Merah Ferry Terminal (Bintan). Ferries to Batam cost $13 single, $21 return, and to Bintan $35 single, $45 return.

Garuda offers a visit pass to foreigners purchasing outside of Indonesia. A minimum of three coupons can be purchased for $300. Additional coupons are $100 each, up to 10 coupons. One coupon is valid for one flight and you can not return to a destination already covered. If the flight is not directly to your intended destination, you are charged one coupon per stop. This program is good value for long-haul travel within Indonesia, Medan to Jakarta for instance or Bali to Biak, which otherwise is quite costly.

TRAVELING IN INDONESIA

Having arrived in Indonesia, your choices for onward travel depend, as always, on time and money. In many ways, Indonesia is an easy place to get around. Indonesians are, as a rule, hospitable, good-humored, and willing to help a lost or confused traveler. The weather is warm, the pace of life relaxed, and the air is rich with the smells of clove cigarettes, the blessed durian fruit and countless other wonders.

However, the nation's transportation infrastructure does not move with the kind of speed and efficiency that Western travelers expect, which often leads to frustration. Bookings are often difficult to make; flights and reservations are sometimes mysteriously canceled.

It is best to adjust your pace to local conditions. What seems like nerve-wracking inefficiency is really so only if one is in a hurry. If you have to be somewhere at a particular time, allow plenty of time to get there. Check and double-check your bookings. Otherwise just go with the flow. You can't just turn off the archipelago's famous *jam karet*—"rubber time"—when it's time to take an airplane and turn it on again when you want to relax. You will get there eventually.

Peak periods around the Christmas/New Year holidays and during the June to August tourist season are the most difficult. It is imperative to book well in advance and reconfirm your bookings at every step along the way. Travel anywhere in Indonesia during the week

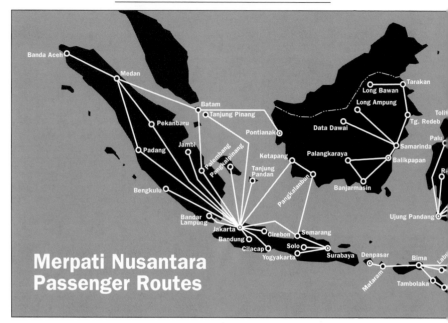

Merpati Nusantara Passenger Routes

prior to the Islamic Lebaran holiday is practically impossible. Find a nice spot and sit it out.

The golden rule is: things will sort themselves out. Eventually. Be persistent, of course, but relax and keep your sense of humor. Before you explode, have a *kretek* cigarette, a cup of sweet coffee, or a cool glass of *kelapa muda* (young coconut water). Things might look different.

Planning an Itinerary

The first thing to do to be easy on yourself andn ot to plan an impossibly tight schedule. Things happen slowly here, so adjust yourself to the pace. Better to spend more time in a few places and see them in a leisurely way, than to end up hot, hassled, and hurried. You'll see *more* this way, not less.

Wherever you are, keep in mind that the tropical heat takes its toll and you should avoid the midday sun. Get an early start, before the rays become punishing (the tropical light is beautiful at dawn). Retreat to a cool place after lunch and go out again in the afternoon and early evening, when it's much more pleasant.

AIR TRAVEL

The cardinal rule is book early, confirm and reconfirm often. If you are told a flight is fully booked, go to the airport anyway and stand in line. While Garuda's booking system is computerized, the other local airlines' are not, and bookings evaporate at the last minute all the time. However it is rare that flights are completely full. Always keep the following points in mind:

✈ It's practically impossible to get a confirmed booking out of a city other than the one you're in. You can buy a ticket and it may say you have a booking, but don't believe it until you reconfirm with the airline in the city of departure.

✈ Reconfirm bookings directly with the airline office in the city of departure between 24 and 72 hours before your flight, particularly during peak tourist seasons and Indonesian holidays. Your seat may be given away if you reconfirm either too early or too late (or not at all).

✈ Make bookings in person, not by phone.

✈ Get written proof or computer printout of bookings. Note the name of the person who gives it to you so you can hold them responsible if you're later told you don't have one.

✈ Note the computer booking code or PRN (passenger record number). Names have a tendency to go astray or be misspelled. Concrete proof of your booking is essential.

✈ If your name isn't on the computer try looking under your first or middle names as these are frequently mistaken for surnames.

✈ If you are told a flight is full, ask to be put on the waiting list, then go to the airport about two hours before departure and check the waiting list. Hang around the desk and be friendly to the staff and you will probably get on the flight. A tip will sometimes, but not always, help.

✈ There are usually alternate ways of getting from point A to B. Search them out.

✈ Generally, students (12-26 years old) receive a discount of 10-25% (show an international student ID card) and children between the ages of 2–10 pay 50% of the regular fare. Infants not occupying a seat pay 10% of the reg-

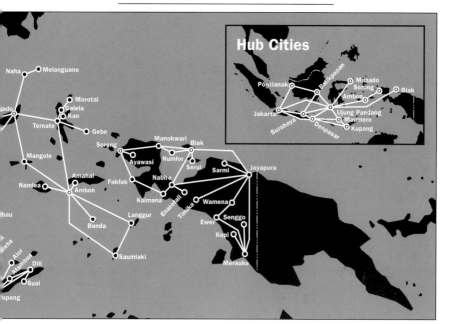

ular fare. Ask the airlines or travel agent.

Garuda Indonesia's flagship airline has been in business since 1946. It serves all major cities in Indonesia and at least 38 international destinations. They fly only jets, mainly wide-bodies, and the service is reasonably good.

Head office is at the BDN Building, Jl. MH Thamrin, No. 5 (☎ [021] 2300925, fax: [021] 334430). Sales counters also at the Borobudur Hotel (☎ [021] 2310023, fax: [021] 2310448, Hotel Indonesia (☎ [021] 2300568, fax: [021] 2300870, and the ITC Building, Blok D 1-5, Jl. Arteri Mangga Dua (☎ [021] 2600238, fax: [021] 2600244). A small Garuda office at Wisma Dharmala Sakti, Jl. Sudirman 32, is open 24 hours (☎ [021] 2512286, fax: [021] 2512276).

Merpati A Garuda subsidiary, with a domestic network serving more than 160 airports throughout Indonesia. Merpati (literally "pigeon") flies smaller jets and turboprops (McDonnell Douglas DC-9s, Fokker F-28s) as well as turbo-props (Fokker F-27s, Canadian DeHavilland DHC-6 "Twin-Otters," the Indonesian built Casa Nusantara CN-235s and CN-212s, and Boeing B-737 jets).

Merpati is not known for its punctuality, its service or its safety, but the airline does at least connect towns and villages across the archipelago, in some cases landing on a grass airstrip in a highland village of only 100 people that would take days to reach by any other means. Consider yourself lucky that you can even fly to these places.

Merpati's standard baggage allowance is 20 kg. for economy class, but some of the smaller aircraft permit only 10 kg. (after which excess baggage charges of $1/kg. apply)

Main office: Jl. Angkasa 2, Jakarta. ☎ (021) 4243608, 6548888; fax: (021) 4246616, 6540609.

Sempati A privately-owned competitor, with quality service and a growing network inside and outside of Indonesia. Sempati flies new Fokker F-28s and F-100s to several cities in Asia, such as Singapore, Kuala Lumpur, Taipei, and Perth.

Domestically it flies between major cities such as Jakarta, Yogyakarta, Surabaya, Ujung Pandang, Jayapura, and Denpasar. Sempati has also added destinations previously difficult to reach, such as Balikpapan, Banjarmasin, Tarakan, Palangkaraya, Palu, Padang, and Manado.

Head office: Ground floor terminal building, Halim Perdana Kusuma Airport, Jakarta. ☎ (021) 8094407, 8011612; fax: (021) 8094420.

Bouraq A small, private company, flying mainly older planes and a few newer B-737s linking secondary cities in Java, Bali, Kalimantan, Nusa Tenggara, Sulawesi, and other remote destinations. Main office: Jl. Angkasa 1–3, Jakarta. ☎ (021) 65955179; fax: (021) 6008729.

Mandala Operates a few prop planes and B-737s to out-of-the-way airstrips in Sumatra, Sulawesi, Kalimantan. Main office: Jl. Garuda 76, Jakarta. ☎ (021) 4246100; fax: (021) 4243480.

NOTE: Travel agents often give cheaper fares than airline offices and are easily found. The best for ticketing are **Pacto** Jl. Surabaya 8, Menteng, Jakarta, ☎ (021) 3487447 and **Vayatour** Jl. Batutulis 38, Jakarta, ☎ (021) 3800202, fax: (021) 3455252.

Departure Tax

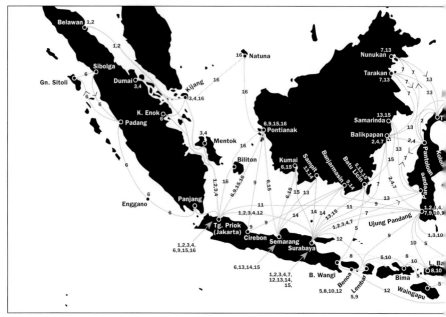

Airport tax for departing passengers is Rp17,000 for international routes and Rp8,800 for domestic flights.

SEA TRAVEL

There is four times as much sea in Indonesia as land, and for many centuries transportation among the islands has been principally by boat. Tiny ports are scattered all over the archipelago, and the only way to reach many areas is by sea.

To travel by boat, you need plenty of time. Most ships are small, and are at the mercy of the sea and the seasons. Think of it as a romantic journey, and don't be in a hurry.

Pelni (Pelayaran Nasional Indonesia) the national passenger line, has 10 large ships (some 70 ships total) criss-crossing the archipelago carrying up to 1,500 passengers each. These boats travel on fixed schedules and the first and second class cabins are comfortable.

Many of the older vessels look like floating trash cans, but the new German-built passenger ships are modern and comfortable. (See route map previous page for destinations served.) Fares are fixed, and there are up to 5 classes, with different numbers of people sharing each cabin, and different service.

Head office: 5th floor, Jl Gajah Mada 14, Jakarta 10130. ☎ (021) 384 4342, 384 4366; Fax: (021) 385 4130. Main ticket office: Jl Angkasa 18, Kemayoran ☎ 421 1921. Open in the mornings.

There are a myriad of other options. Rusty old **coastal steamers** ply the eastern islands, stopping at tiny ports to pick up copra, seaweed and other cash crops and deliver commodities like metal wares, fuel and the occasional outboard motor. You can book deck passage on one of these ships in just about any harbor, for very little money. If you do, stock up on food—you will quickly tire of the rice and salt fish that the crew eat. Bring a waterproof tarpaulin and a bag to protect your gear. You can often rent bunks from the crew, to get a comfortable night's sleep.

Crowded **overnight ferries** connect smaller islands. Use your luggage to stake out a spot early, and bring a straw mat to lie on. It is usually best to stay on deck, where the fresh sea breezes keep your spirits up. Below deck tends to be noisy, verminous and smelly.

Small **perahu** can be rented in many areas for day trips upriver, around the coast, or to neighboring islands. These can be hired by the hour or by the trip, to take you snorkeling, sightseeing or birdwatching. Outboard motors are expensive in Indonesia, and tend to be small. Inspect any boat carefully before hiring it, as some craft are only marginally seaworthy. See if the boatman can rig up a canopy to block the blazing sun or the occasional cloudburst.

TRAVEL OVERLAND

By Train

Train travel (across Java and Sumatra) can be very cheap, depending on the class. The problem is that first class trains travel at night (you don't see much), and anything less than first class on long journeys is crowded, noisy, hot, and uncomfortable. Still, you can stretch your

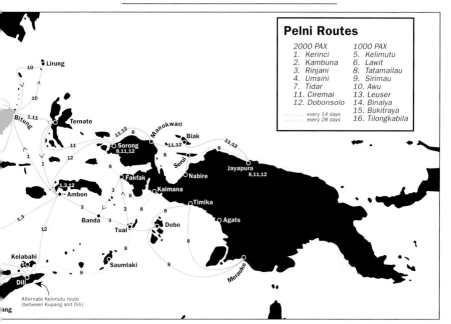

Pelni Routes

2000 PAX	1000 PAX
1. Kerinci	5. Kelimutu
2. Kambuna	6. Lawit
3. Rinjani	8. Tatamailau
4. Umsini	9. Sirimau
7. Tidar	10. Awu
11. Ciremai	13. Leuser
12. Dobonsolo	14. Binalya
	15. Bukitraya
——— every 14 days	16. Tilongkabila
-------- every 28 days	

Alternate Kelimutu route
(between Kupang and Dili)

legs, walk through the train, sit on the back step and watch the tracks stream out from under you.

First class is good, but first class tickets do not always guarantee a seat when you get on the train. (In this case, see the station master for a hassle and eventual refund.) If your budget requires economy travel, purchase a second or third class ticket, spread a *sarong* out and sleep under the seats, not in the aisles, as vendors will tread over or spill things on you.

Tickets normally have to be bought at the station on the day of departure (go early in the morning!) or in the case of night express trains, the day before. Authorized agents also sell tickets. During major Indonesian holiday periods, better forget it: take a plane or a bus, or better still, stay put.

Between major cities there is only a single line, dating from Dutch times, and delays are common as a result. Trains traveling in opposite directions have to wait for one another; if one is late or breaks down, the whole system is thrown out of whack, which happens often.

On the Road

Road conditions in Indonesia have improved dramatically over the past years, but traffic has also increased and driving is a slow and hazardous affair.

Fully loaded trucks, with marginal brakes and drivers going for broke anyway; full-size buses, one and three-quarters lanes wide; small public minivans, stopping anywhere and with no warning for passengers; the occasional private car; scores of motorcycles, most of them small two-stroke affairs, usually piled with goods or,

at the hands of a young hotshot, screaming along at full throttle; horse-drawn passenger carts; *becaks*, bicycle rigs that carry passengers in a cart in front; bicycles, with perhaps some children fore and aft, and almost always piled with produce, or perhaps fighting cocks in their cages; and, of course, pedestrians of all ages, all compete in what is at times a crazy battle for tarmac, where the biggest and fastest rule.

Rental cars and motorcycles are available in many major cities, and a number of different types of buses run cheap and regular services.

Night Express Buses—*bis malam*

The preferred mode of transportation for Indonesians, these buses operate only at night. Available in a wide variety of classes: from the public *patas* air-conditioned with reclining seats (crowded, run by the army) to the ultra-luxurious "Big Top" buses that run from Jakarta (these have seats like business class airline seats).

The better buses have a bathroom and arctic air-conditioning: the other reason you brought a sweater. The key to successful *bis malam* trips is sleep.

Most buses are fitted with televisions and show movies whether you want them or not, often followed by music. You are likely to be the only one who is annoyed by the volume, but a cheerful suggestion that the music be turned off (*dimatikan*) will at least get it turned down to the point where earplugs can block out the rest.

These buses leave in late afternoon and go all night, and often well into the next day. When *bis malam* cross from island to island, they go on the ferry. Tickets are sold at the bus terminal, or by agents, and there are usually a number of different buses going your way. Shop around, to see what you are getting.

Local Buses

The major advantages of these rattling buses is that they are extremely cheap, run every few minutes between major towns, and can be picked up at the terminals or any point along their routes. This is also their biggest disadvantage: they stop constantly.

The seats are very small, both in terms of leg room and width. You and your bag may take up (and be charged for) two seats. This is fair. But be sure you're not being overcharged for not knowing any better. The key is to know better. Ask someone what the proper fare is before getting on. A few words of Indonesian are indispensable to be able to ask for directions.

Larger towns have city buses charging nominal fares, usually Rp300 (15¢). Flag them down wherever you see them. The catch is knowing which one to take as there are no maps or guides.

Express Minibuses—"travel" or "colt"

These come in two varieties: old and hot (sit by a window and keep it open) and the newer, much revered, L300 van with air-conditioning. Even the L300 gets a lot of engine heat, and at midday can still be sauna-like: especially if the air-conditioning is broken and the windows shut.

These 8 to 11 passenger vans connect major cities and deliver you right to your destination. They sometimes also pick you up. They usually travel during the day, though on longer routes they travel at night like the *bis malam.*

Local Minibuses—*bemo*

These non air-conditioned vans ("colt" or "bemo") are the real workhorses of the transport network, going up and down even relatively impassable mountain tracks to deliver villagers and produce all over the island. Regular seats are supplemented by wooden benches, boosting the capacity of these sardine cans to 25. And there is *always* room for more.

There are standard fares but these are flexible to account for how much room you and your bag are taking up. Ask someone before flagging one down if you are concerned by the potential Rp100 price gouging. Flag one down on any roadside. You can also charter one to most destinations. Just say "charter" and where you want to go, then bargain for the fare in advance.

Chartering a Car or Minibus

This can be the best way to handle a land tour as you have the freedom to stop whenever things look interesting and the flexibility to try out some less traveled routes. This can also be an economical alternative if you can fill up a van. The minibus can take up to 7, but you need extra space if you are to be in it for a few days, so 5 passengers is generally maximum.

Some asking around will quickly give you an idea of where to hire a driver and what the local going rates are for a specific excursion or longer itinerary. A full day of driving one-way will cost from $50 to $80 and a five-day trip around $300. Much of this is for fuel, so distance is a major factor. Most of the rest goes to the owner of the vehicle, and only a tiny percentage left for the driver. It is understood that you will pay for the driver's meals and accommodation both while he is with you and on his journey back home. A tip of Rp5,000 per day is also appreciated if the driver is good.

The quality of both the driver and the vehicle will figure heavily in the enjoyability of your trip so don't be shy about checking both out before striking a deal.

Metered Taxis

Metered taxis are becoming increasingly common in major cities, not just Jakarta. If the taxi is equipped with an argometer, then the driver should be using it. Insist on this when you get in the taxi. Otherwise, you may end up paying twice the metered amount. If the driver claims that the meter is broken, then get out and flag down another one.

Driving On Your Own

Driving in Indonesia is not for the faint-hearted. At first glance the unwritten driving rules of Indonesia seem like a maniacal free-for-all. It is only later that the subtle hierarchy (truck vx. car: you lose) and finesse (2-centimeter tolerances) become evident. Vehicles and creatures of every size, shape and description charge onto the road out of nowhere. The traffic is horrendous on the main highways. Drive slowly and carefully. Road construction sites are not marked and few cyclists have relectors for use at night. The condition of road networks has considerably improved in recent years, however, and driving off the beaten track is one of the best ways to explore the territory. check your fuel gauge regularly as there are few gas stations away from the main roads. Small roadside fuel shops indicated by a "premium sign, sell gasoline for the bit more than the Pertamina stations.

A valid international license is required for driving cars and motorbikes. Insurance is not compulsory, but strongly recommended. You can get a policy from most of the rental companies and travel agents. Check the condition of the car before signing the contract. Beware: vehicles are usually rented with an empty tank. More important than the agency you rent from is to check and test-drive the car before renting.

Indonesian Language Primer

Personal pronouns

I   *saya*
we   *kita* (inclusive), *kami* (exclusive)
you   *anda* (formal), *saudara* (brother, sister),
   kamu (for friends and children only)
he/she   *dia*   they   *mereka*

Forms of address

Father/Mr   *Bapak ("Pak")*
Mother/Mrs   *Ibu ("Bu")*
Elder brother   *Abang ("Bang" or "Bung")*
         Mas (in Java only)
Elder sister   *Mbak* (in Java only)
Elder brother/sister   *Kakak ("Kak")*
Younger brother/sister   *Adik ("Dik")*
Note: These terms are used not just within the family, but generally in polite speech.

Basic questions

How?   *Bagaimana?*
How much/many?   *Berapa?*
What?   *Apa?*   What's this?   *Apa ini?*
Who?   *Siapa?*   Who's that?   *Siapa itu?*
What is your name?   *Siapa namanya?*
(Literally: Who is your name?)
When?   *Kapan?*
Where?   *Di mana?*
Why?   *Kenapa? Mengapa?*
Which?   *Yang mana?*

Civilities

Welcome   *Selamat datang*
Good morning (7–11am)   *Selamat pagi*
Good midday (11am–3pm)   *Selamat siang*
Good afternoon (3–7pm)   *Selamat sore*
Goodnight (after dark)   *Selamat malam*
Goodbye (to one leaving)   *Selamat jalan*
Goodbye (to one staying)   *Selamat tinggal*
Note: Selamat is a word from Arabic meaning "May your time (or action) be blessed."
How are you?   *Apa kabar?*
I am fine.   *Kabar baik.*
Thank you.   *Terima kasih.*
You're welcome.   *Kembali.*
Same to you.   *Sama sama.*
Pardon me   *Ma'af*
Excuse me   *Permisi*
(when leaving a conversation, etc).

Numbers

1	*satu*	6	*enam*
2	*dua*	7	*tujuh*
3	*tiga*	8	*delapan*
4	*empat*	9	*sembilan*
5	*lima*	10	*sepuluh*
11	*sebelas*	100	*seratus*
12	*dua belas*	600	*enam ratus*
13	*tiga belas*	1,000	*seribu*
20	*dua puluh*	3,000	*tiga ribu*
50	*lima puluh*	10,000	*sepuluh ribu*
73	*tujuh puluh tiga*		
1,000,000	*satu juta*		
2,000,000	*dua juta*		
half	*setengah*		
first	*pertama*	third	*ketiga*
second	*kedua*	fourth	*ke'empat*

Time

minute   *menit*
hour   *jam*
(also clock/watch)
day   *hari*

Sunday   *Hari Minggu*
Monday   *Hari Senin*
Tuesday   *Hari Selasa*
Wednesday   *Hari Rabu*

Pronunciation and Grammar

Vowels

a   As in f**a**ther
e   Three forms:
   1) Schwa, like th**e**
   2) Like **é** in touch**é**
   3) Short **è**; as in b**e**t
i   Usually like long **e** (as in Bal**i**); when bounded by consonants, like short **i** (h**i**t).
o   Long **o**, like g**o**
u   Long **u**, like y**ou**
ai   Long **i**, like cr**i**me
au   Like **ow** in **ow**l

Consonants

c   Always like **ch** in **ch**urch
g   Always hard, like **g**uard
h   Usually soft, almost unpronounced. It is hard between like vowels, e.g. *ma***h***al* (expensive).
k   Like **k** in **k**ind; at end of word, unvoiced stop.
kh   Like **k**ind, but harder
r   Rolled, like Spanish **r**
ng   Soft, like fli**ng**
ngg   Hard, like ti**ngg**le
ny   Like **ny** in So**ny**a

Grammar

Grammatically, Indonesian is in many ways far simpler than English. There are no articles (a, an, the).

The verb form "to be" is usually not used. There is no ending for plurals; sometimes the word is doubled, but often number comes from context. And Indonesian verbs are not conjugated. Tense is communicated by context or with specific words for time.

week	*minggu*	Thursday	*Hari Kamis*
month	*bulan*	Friday	*Hari Jum'at*
year	*tahun*	Saturday	*Hari Sabtu*
today	*hari ini*	later	*nanti*
tomorrow	*besok*	yesterday	*kemarin*

What time is it?   *Jam berapa?*
(It is) eight thirty.   *Jam setengah sembilan*
  (Literally: "half nine")
How many hours?   *Berapa jam?*
When did you arrive?   *Kapan datang?*
Four days ago.   *Empat hari yang lalu.*
When are you leaving?
  Kapan berangkat?
In a short while.   *Sebentar lagi.*

Useful words

yes   *ya*   no, not   *tidak, bukan*
Note: *Tidak* is used with verbs or adverbs; *bukan*
with nouns.

and	*dan*	better	*lebih baik*
with	*dengan*	worse	*kurang baik*
for	*untuk*	this/these	*ini*
from	*dari*	that/those	*itu*
good	*baik*	same	*sama*
very good	*bagus*	different	*lain*
more	*lebih*	here	*di sini*
less	*kurang*	there	*di sana*
to be	*ada*	to be able to	*bisa*
to buy	*membeli*	correct	*betul*
to know	*tahu*	wrong	*salah*
big	*besar*	small	*kecil*
to need	*perlu*	to want	*ingin*
to go	*pergi*	to stop	*berhenti*
slow	*pelan*	fast	*cepat*
to wait	*tunggu*	to continue	*terus*
to	*ke*	at	*di*
old	*tua, lama*	new	*baru*
full	*penuh*	empty	*kosong*
quiet	*sepi*	crowded, noisy	*ramai*
few	*sedikit*	many	*banyak*
cold	*dingin*	hot	*panas*
clean	*bersih*	dirty	*kotor*
entrance	*masuk*	exit	*keluar*

Small talk

Where are you from?   *Dari mana?*
I'm from the US.   *Saya dari Amerika.*
How old are you?   *Umurnya berapa?*
I'm 31 years old.
  Umur saya tiga pulu satu tahun.
Are you married?   *Sudah kawin belum?*
Yes, I am.   *Yah, sudah.*
Not yet.   *Belum.*
Do you have children?   *Sudah punya anak?*
What is your religion?   *Agama apa?*
Where are you going?   *Mau ke mana?*
I'm just taking a walk.   *Jalan-jalan saja.*
Please come in.   *Silahkan masuk.*
Please sit down.   *Silahkan duduk.*

Hotels

room	*kamar*	bed	*tempat tidur*
towel	*handuk*	bedsheet	*sprei*
bathe	*mandi*	bathroom	*kamar mandi*
hot water	*air panas*		

Where's a losmen?   *Di mana ada losmen?*

cheap losmen   *losmen yang murah*
good hotel   *hotel yang baik*
Please take me to...   *Tolong antar saya ke...*
Are there any empty rooms?
  Ada kamar kosong?
Sorry there aren't any.   *Ma'af, tidak ada.*
How much for one night?
  Berapa untuk satu malam?
One room for two people.
  Dua orang, satu kamar.
I'd like to stay for 3 days.
  Saya mau tinggal tiga hari.
Here's the key to the room.
  Ini kunci kamar.
Please call a taxi.
  Tolong panggilkan taksi.
Please wash these clothes.
  Tolong cucikan pakaian ini.

Restaurants

to eat   *makan*   to drink   *minum*
drinking water   *air putih, air mimun*
breakfast   *makan pagi, sarapan*
lunch   *makan siang*   dinner   *makan malam*
Where's a good restaurant?
  Di mana ada rumah makan yang baik?
Let's have lunch.   *Mari kita makan siang.*
May I see the menu?
  Boleh saya lihat daftar makanan?
I want to wash my hands.
  Saya mau cuci tangan.
Where is the toilet?   *Di mana kamar kecil?*
fish, squid, goat, beef, chicken
  ikan, cumi-cumi, kambing, sapi, ayam
salty, sour, sweet, spicy (hot)
  asin, asam, manis, pedas

Shopping

cheap   *murah*   expensive   *mahal*
Please, speak slowly.
  Tolong, berbicara lebih pelan.
I want to buy...   *Saya mau beli...*
Where can I buy...   *Di mana saya bisa beli...*
How much does this cost?   *Berapa harga ini?*
2,500 Rupiah.   *Dua ribu, lima ratus rupiah.*
That cannot be true!   *Masa!*
That's still a bit expensive.   *Masih agak mahal*
May I bargain?   *Boleh tawar?*
Is there a discount?   *Ada diskon?*
Thanks, I already have one/some...
  Terima kasih, saya sudah punya ...

Directions

here	*di sini*	there	*di sana*
near	*dekat*	far	*jauh*
inside	*di dalam*	outside	*di luar*
map	*peta*	street	*jalan*
north	*utara*	south	*selatan*
east	*timur*	west	*barat*
central	*pusat*	middle	*tengah*
left	*kiri*	right	*kanan*
straight	*terus*	turn	*belok*

I am looking for this address.
  Saya cari alamat ini.
How far is it?   *Berapa jauh dari sini?*
Which area?   *Daerah mana?*

Java PRACTICALITIES

Jakarta, with its 9.5 million people, is the center of Indonesia's government and commerce. It is beyond the scope of this book to give a complete description of all the lodging and transportation possibilities there. If you are going to be in Jakarta, you will need a good guidebook. Instead, this section offers practical information relating to diving Pulau Seribu and West Java.

Prices in US dollars.

Telephone code for Jakarta is 021.

DIVE OPERATORS

There are many dive operators in Jakarta who take divers to Pulau Seribu and the West Java sites. Here are a few of the most reliable:

Aquasport Jl. Bangka Raya, No. 39A, Kel. Pela, Jakarta 12720. ☎ 7199045; fax: 7198974.

Active PADI 5-Star IDC Center located in new premises, with a large retail area, 3 classrooms and their own 4m deep swimming pool. A very professional, reliable full-service facility (as is their affiliate, Divemasters Indonesia), offering snorkeling and diving equipment sales, rentals and servicing. They offer the full range of PADI courses—evening and daytime—in five languages (English, French, Dutch, German, Indonesian), including a host of specialities, such as wreck diver and underwater photographer, and at least twice a year, PADI Instructor Development Courses with related instructor-level training. Also stockist of PADI materials. They offer dive trips to Pulau Seribu nearly every weekend and special charters throughout the year.

Divemasters Indonesia Jakarta Hilton International Hotel, Indonesian Bazaar Shop 31, Jl. Jend. Gatot Subroto, Jakarta 10002 Indonesia. ☎ 5703600 ext. 9037, 9006; fax: 7198974, 4204842. Contact: Vimal Lekhraj

This highly recommended outfit is the country's largest dive specialist. They are a PADI 5-Star Dive Center; a professional, reliable, full-service facility. Apart from offering a full range of PADI courses, they are Indonesia's largest equipment retailer, handling US Divers, Seaquest, Tabata, Underwater Kinetics, Bauer, Poseidon, Sea and Sea and others. Snorkeling and diving equipment sales rentals, servicing, and diving equipment repair seminars. They offer dive trips to Pulau Seribu nearly every weekend and special charters throughout the year. They can also tailor-make dive trips to your needs. They have their own custom built catamaran dive boat, which is available for charter.

Jakarta Dive School and Pro Shop Jakarta Hilton International Hotel, Indonesia Bazaar Shop 32, Jl. Jend. Gatot Subroto, Jakarta 10002 Indonesia. ☎ 5703600 ext. 9008, 9010, fax: 4204842; Telex: 46673, 46698 HILTON IA. Contact: Andre Pribadi

They organize dive trips to Pulau Seribu, Bali, Manado, Flores and Ambon. PADI 5-star training facility. Also fills, equipment sales, rentals and repairs, and u/w photography.

Laut Dive Indo Club House Cilandak Sport Centre, Jl. Tb. Simatupang Arteri Cilandak, Jakarta 12014. ☎ 7504963 ext. 109, 129; fax: 7504969. Contacts: Jono Sugiyanto or Slamet.

This is a new business, and comes recommended by Jakarta expats as offering reliable service and very competitive rates. While they specialize in dive trips around the Jakarta area, especially Pelabuhan Ratu—where you really need a dive-master familiar with the currents—Laut Dive Indo also runs trips to Indonesia's top dive locations. Young, enthusiastic owner. Certification available, including PADI and SSI.

Stingray Dive Centre Gedung Mangal Wanabakti, Wisma Rimabawan 2d floor, room 4, Jl. Jend. Gatot Subroto, Jakarta Indonesia. ☎ 5703245, 5703264; ☎/fax: 5700272. Contact: Andy or Hendro

PADI instruction, dive equipment sales and servicing and rentals. They are familiar with many dive spots throughout Indonesia, and have several scheduled departures every month to dive locations near and far. Contact them for a very extensive list of dive trips.

WEATHER

Diving is generally best during the dry season, which varies but generally takes place March through November. The very best time is from May to September.

Pulau Seribu

These islands are a favorite place for Jakartans to spend a relaxing weekend, so you should definitely book ahead. Ferries depart daily around 7 am from the Ancol Marina, usually without prior booking. The trip takes about 2.5 hours—depending on the island—and the return ferry leaves the islands around 2:30 pm. By speedboat and hydrofoil, the same trip can take one hour. Inquire at Putri Pulau Seribu Paradise office in Djakarta Theatre building.

DIVE CHARTERS

It is far less complicated to book your entire trip with one of the above listed dive outfits. Dive weekends to sites in Pulau Seribu average $110–$150. This includes round trip transportation, 4 boat dives, and one night in basic, air-conditioned, twin-share accommodations. Afternoon meals are included, although full board may be extra.

West Java

Travel to Krakatau or Ujung Kulon is more of an effort than Pulau Seribu. It requires an overland journey to Anyer or Labuhan, and then a fairly long boat ride. Again, it is much better to organize such a trip with a reliable Jakarta dive outfit.

Krakatau

Boats can be chartered from Labuhan or Carita beach, just 8 kilometers north of Labuhan. A forestry official in either town can help arrange boats for up to 20 people—about $100—or local fisherman can be contacted to charter a smaller vessel, about $50. It is impossible to determine the seaworthiness of these boats, or just how reliable are their motors. Remember, this is a 4-hour crossing over rather unpredictable seas. Too many stories circulate of foreigners adrift on crippled boats for days or even weeks for them all to be apocryphal.

Ujung Kulon

The peninsula can be reached only by boat, or by a lengthy hike—good for seeing wildlife, but not practical for diving. You can arrange a boat at Labuhan, but again, it is best to organize the whole thing with a Jakarta dive agency. A government forestry boat at Labuhan will run about $100 for the 9-hr. trip to Peucang Island or Taman Jaya. To reach the actual dive sites, figure on some intense bargaining with local fishermen.

— Janet Boileau,
Debe Campbell
and Kal Muller

Sumatra PRACTICALITIES

Diving is still in its infancy on Sumatra. Spectacular sea life and unspoiled beaches await the adventurous. Much of the diving activity on the island is from either Singapore or Thailand.

Prices in US dollars. S = Single; D = Double; T = Triple; AC = Air-conditioning.

Bintan and Riau

Batuta Resort Mapor Island, Riau Indonesia. Agent in Singapore: Yacht Construction (SEA) Pte. Ltd., #50, Track 24, Punggol Road, Singapore 1954. ☎ (65) 3833036; fax: (65) 3833037. This outfit runs divers to Mapor island, north of Bintan. The trip begins and ends at the World Trade Centre dock in Singapore. Passengers are taken by ferry to Tanjung Pinang on Bintan Island, driven across Bintan, where they board the *Mapor I.* The trip to Mapor takes about an hour.

Round-trip to Mapor, $100; cottage accommodations, $40D, additional bed, $13 ; lunch or dinner, $8. Boat dives: single tank, $28; 2 tanks, $42. Rental equipment: regulator and BC, $18; mask, snorkel and fins, $12; skin suit, $4; whole kit, $26.

Reclaim II Marsden Bros (Pte) Ltd., 32 Cassia Drive, Singapore. ☎ (65) 4622915, fax: (65) 4664910. Operating out of Singapore, the *Reclaim II* is a 56' motor yacht beautifully equipped for cruising and diving. Sleeps eight passengers. One of the pioneers of the underwater world of the eastern Riau islands, it is the only company to frequent the waters on a regular basis. Liveaboard trips can be scheduled to the Riau archipelago can be scheduled between April and October. The crew are British zoologists and PADI master scuba diver trainers who specialize in marine research and scuba diving training.

North Sumatra

The oldest established outfit is on We island, off the northernmost tip of Sumatra (Sabang, the biggest town on the island, is better known than the island itself). This is as far east as you can get and still be in Indonesia. **Stingray Divers** (see Jakarta practicalities) have a small dive center there. Check with them for details.

Padang

Diving in Padang, in central Sumatra on the Andaman Sea side, is said to be good year-round, with the best season being April–September.

Merpati has direct 45-minute flights between Singapore and Padang. The city is well connected to the rest of the islands through Jakarta.

Padang Diving Wisata Jl. Batang Arau No. 88 B/6, Padang 25001, West Sumatra. ☎ (0751) 25876; fax: (0751) 28121. Shore-based diving. Efficient family run business, down by the river. Operates 2 x 9m boutboard boats for day dives near Padang. Has a very basic 20m wooden vessel for more extended lie-aboard trips. Day dives, including 2 full tanks, transport, diving guide, weights, and lunch, $98 (one diver)— $63 (4 divers). Equipment available for rent, but better to bring your own. PADI open water diving course, $375.

Live-aboard Charters, Inc. P.O. Box 22, Patong Beach, Phuket, Thailand. ☎ (6676) 340088; fax: (6676) 340309. Fantasea Divers of Phuket are planning to operate their live-aboard M.B. Fantasea in the Mentawai Islands, based out of Padang. Superb diving on the equator. 9-day/10-night cruise, $1,999.

Pusako Island Resort on Pulau Sikuai. Jl. Muara No. 38B, Padang, West Sumatra. ☎ 35311, fax: (0751) 22895. 21 cottages. Luxury beach resort on an otherwise uninhabited island, just south of Padang. Good and varied snorkelling. $90–$110S, $100–$120D. Boat transfer round-trip, $15/person.

Dipo Hotel ☎ 34261; fax: 34265. Owner, Osman Iskander, is the local contact for Fantasea Diver Live-aboard. $20–$30.

Pengaran Beach Hotel Jl. Ir. H. Juanda 79, Padang. ☎ 51333; fax: 54613. North of town; full service beach resort. $64–$88 standard, $150–$375 suite.

—Charles Anderson

3 **Bali** PRACTICALITIES

INCLUDES LIVE-ABOARDS

Bali, a verdant, volcanic island with nearly 3 million people, is the tourist center of Indonesia. The Balinese are themselves not especially focused toward the sea, but the waters off Bali are very rich. It is not the best diving in Indonesia, but it is very good, and the combination of beautiful surroundings, convenient diving, plenty of tourist services, and colorful and interesting culture is hard to beat.

Prices in US dollars. S = Single; D = Double; T = Triple; AC = Air-conditioning.

Telephone code for southern Bali (Kuta, Sanur, Nusa Dua) is 0361; north Bali (Tulamben, Lovina, Menjangan) is 0362, east Bali (Candi Dasa, Amlapura) is 0363.

GETTING THERE

The best way to arrive in Bali is at the Ngurah Rai International Airport which, despite its often being referred to as "Denpasar" is actually on the isthmus connecting the Bukit Badung peninsula to Bali, much nearer to Kuta Beach than Bali's capital city. Daily Garuda flights from Jakarta, Yogyakarta, and many other Indonesian cities connect to Ngurah Rai, and a growing number of international flights—including those from Australia, Hong Kong, Japan, the Netherlands, Singapore and the United States—land here as well.

By Air

Flights from the Soekarno-Hatta International Airport in Jakarta are frequent, and if you land in Jakarta before 5 pm you can usually get a connection to Bali. (Although in peak season, these 90-min flights are almost always full. Book your flight all the way to Bali.) From the airport, hire a taxi to the place you intend to stay.

Domestic airline offices:

Bouraq Jl. Sudirman 7A, Denpasar, ☎ 223564.
Garuda Jl. Melati 61, Denpasar, ☎ 235139.
Merpati Jl. Melati 51, Denpasar, ☎ 235358.
Sempati Jl. Diponegoro, Komplek Diponegoro Megah, Blok B/No. 27, ☎ 237343.

The following international airlines have offices in the Grand Bali Beach in Sanur, ☎ 288511. Direct phone lines are: Air France, ☎ 755523; Ansett Australia, ☎ 289636; Cathay Pacific, ☎ 753942; Continental-Micronesia, ☎ 287065/287774; Garuda, ☎ 288243; Japan Airlines and Japan Asia Airways, ☎ 287476/287577; Lufthansa, ☎ 286952; Malaysia Air Service, ☎ 288716/288511; Qantas, ☎ 288331; Sempati Air, ☎ 288824; Singapore Airlines, ☎ 287940; Thai International, ☎ 285071/3.

Wisti Sabha Building at the Airport houses: Air New Zealand, ☎ 756170/751011 ext. 1116; China Airlines, ☎ 754856/757298; EVA Air, ☎ 298935; KLM, ☎ 756127; Korean Air Lines, ☎ 754856/757298, fax: 757275; Royal Brunei, ☎ 757292.

By Train

One can also take a train from Jakarta (slow, and a nightmare with scuba gear) which connects to Surabaya (12 hrs on Bima, $43 Executive; 8 hrs. on the new Express, $44 Executive class), then a train to Bayuwangi (4 hrs, $7.50 Business class), then a bus to and across the Ketapang, Java–Gilimanuk, Bali ferry ($3) and on to Denpasar (4 hrs, $2).

By Bus

Taking a night bus the entire way is probably a better option (24 hrs, Jakarta–Denpasar, $30.) From Ubung Terminal outside Denpasar, where you are dropped off, a minibus to the tourist triangle of Kuta–Sanur–Nusa Dua runs $3–$5. All in all, best to arrive by plane.

LOCAL TRANSPORTATION

Airport taxis One-way fares from Ngurah Rai airport to the tourist centers are fixed. You pay a cashier inside, and receive a coupon which you surrender to your driver. (Of course, there will be plenty of touts and free-lancers offering you their services. These are never a better deal.) Fares range from $3 to nearby Kuta Beach to $17 to Ubud, far inland.

Minibuses All hotels have *bemos* for hire with a driver or with an English-speaking driver/guide. Rates run $3–$5/hr, with a 2-hr minimum. Day rates run $30–$40, more for an air-conditioned vehicle.

Bemos Public minibuses in Bali are called

"*bemos*," a compression of *becak* (bicycle-like pedicabs) and *mobil*. This is the way the Balinese travel and the cheapest way to get around the island. Fares are very inexpensive and you could probably get all the way across the island for less than $2, but you will need to know some Indonesian or be very good at charades to make sense of the routes and drop-off points. Public *bemos* can be rented for the day, usually for $20–$30. Still, it's probably better to get one through your hotel.

For a diving visitor to Bali, *bemos* are most useful for short day trips around the area or to hop locally around town. Get one of your diving guides or someone at the hotel to explain the ins and outs of the local routes.

Vehicle rental In almost all cases, it is best to leave the driving in Bali to someone who knows how to negotiate the roads and traffic. The roads are narrow, twisting, and full of hazards: unmarked construction sites, chickens, dogs, children, Vespas as wide as cars due to huge baskets of produce, and tough, unflinching truck drivers, to name just a few. You can rent a small (100cc–125cc) motorcycle for $5–$7/day if you have an international motorcycle driver's license, but you better know how to ride.

Renting a car—particularly since you will be carrying diving gear—is perhaps a more practical solution. These run $25–$35/day for little Suzuki jeeps; more for larger, more comfortable Toyota Kijangs. Rent through an agency (even Avis has outlets) or from numerous local rental companies. Ask at your hotel or comb the streets where there's an agent on nearly every block. Be sure your rental includes insurance for loss and damage.

MEDICAL

Emergency Care

Call the Bali Hyatt for emergency evacuation services—☎ 288271 ext. 8160 (Bali Hyatt), 281127 (house clinic). The affiliated clinic is an SOS member of the international evacuation service and on 24-hr standby. The clinic is associated with Dr. Darmianti & Associates, which has clinics in the Nusa Dua Beach and Sanur Beach hotels. Set fees. Open 24 hours daily. (See page 258 for information on medical evacuation insurance.)

The two largest hospitals (*rumah sakit*) in Bali are in Denpasar. Both have emergency units with English-speaking doctors on duty 24 hrs, but they are not terribly well equipped:

General Hospital Sanglah Jl. Kesehatan Utara 6, ☎ 227914.

General Hospital Wangaya Jl. Kartini 109, ☎ 222141.

Hyperbaric Emergencies

The only recompression chamber in the general area is an Indonesian Navy–run unit in Surabaya, East Java. The doctor who runs the unit, Dr. Suharsono, was trained in Australia by Dr. Carl Edmonds and speaks English very well. Some statistics on the Surabaya chamber:

Volume is 75 cubic meters with a capacity of 4–5 "bent" divers at a maximum working pressure of 6 atmospheres. The unit was built in 1981 by Aqualogistics International, St. Helena, UK. Other instrumentation includes spirometry, audiometery, EKG, and chromatography.

LAKESLA Direktorat Kesehatan TNI-AL, Lembaga Kesehatan, Keangkatan Lautan, Jl. Gadung No. 1, Surabaya, Java. ☎ (031) 45750, 41731

General

Doctor Dr. Handris Prasetya hasa private practice on Jl. Sumatra No. 21 in Denpasar, open Mon–Sat 5–8 pm. He speaks English well and is accustomed to treating foreigners.

Dentist For dental treatment, Dr. Indra Guizot's private practice is on Jl. Pattimura 19, Tel: 222445, Mon–Fri 10 am–8 pm.

PHOTOGRAPHIC SUPPLIES

P.T. Modern Foto This outfit is the local Fuji agent, with a huge showroom in Kuta just opposite the gas station and Gelael supermarket. They have the best E-6 processing in Bali and the freshest film. For prints, there are many instant mini-labs in all the larger towns and tourist centers offering while-you-wait service. You cannot buy Kodachrome film in Bali.

The biggest range of photographic equipment and supplies can be found in Denpasar at **Tati Photo**, Jl. Sumatra 72, ☎ 226912, and **Prima Photo**, Jl. Gajah Mada 14, ☎ 222505.

Dive Operators

Diving tour operators in Bali are concentrated in the tourist triangle—Kuta, Nusa Dua and Sanur—and in two places close to good dive spots—Candidasa on the east coast and Lovina, between the Tulamben wreck and Menjangan Island, in the north. The bigger outfits maintain desks at the major hotels, or at least keep brochures at the desk.

Almost all the local dive guides speak some English (and/or Japanese) and dive very well. Where many fall short, however, is in dive planning—particularly tailoring a dive for your specific needs—and emergency assistance.

Bali 3

Most outfits, chiefly for financial reasons, offer "initial" introductory dive courses to non-divers (we highly discourage this). These courses vary widely in price, $65–$100. Operators also offer 4–5 day "resort courses" with CMAS (French), PADI (U.S.), PAUI (Australian), or POSSI (Indonesian) certification. These course range in price from $250 to $400. If the course is advertised for less than $370, find out if it includes manuals, dive tables and certification—sometimes a cheap initial price sucks in customers, but you may end up paying more in the long run by the time all the "extras" are factored in.

With scuba diving currently booming on Bali, new operators spring out of thin air almost daily. Horror stories abound: young local kid, barely knows how to dive himself, buys two tanks, fills them god knows how, sets himself up as dive operator. Cheap prices. Inexperienced client dies after surfacing too fast.

While more and more Indonesians are qualified dive instructors/guides, we suggest checking the operator to see if there are any foreigners on the staff. Indonesian certification, CMAS or POSSI, can be lax. Try to find PADI- or PAUI-trained guides or instructors.

A resort course will give you some of the basics, but definitely does not make you at ease in currents, caves or at night. A graduate of a resort course is not an experienced diver. We suggest that after taking a resort course, you accumulate at least 20–30 dives before diving some of the potentially more difficult sites. Always stay above the 25-meter mark and plan your dives well.

Experienced divers should request, if at all possible, that their group does not include beginners. All outfits require a minimum of two passengers per trip (you need a buddy anyway). Some offer the possibility of a third day dive or one at night. All offer snorkeling for non-divers. Serious divers should take time to plan a dive series with the operator, taking into consideration time available, budget and weather.

Prices are fairly standard: $40–$85 (depending on location) inclusive of guides, transportation, and lunch, for a two-dive visit and $35–$45 for a one-tank night dive. Operators have equipment for rent for casual divers. Rates per day: BC and regulator, $10–$12; mask/snorkel/ fins, $3–$5; wet suit $5–$7; flashlight $5.

At last count, there were over 30 dive operators in Bali, mostly around the Kuta/Sanur/Nusa Dua area. Five of these cater only to the Japanese market. Of those remaining, we can recommend the following. Prices are roughly similar, but the quality of the instruction, facilities and dive guides vary considerably, as does the English proficiency of the guides and instructors. At least you can expect clean air and reliable transportation from these operators.

KUTA AND LEGIAN

Bali International Diving Service Jl. Kuta Raya, Kuta 16M (in front of the Gelael Supermarket and gas station). ☎ 751342; fax 752956. Seven instructors, five dive masters, all CMAS-certified. Some 2–3 day dive packages available.

Baruna Water Sports Head office: Jl. Bypass Ngurah Rai 300B, Kuta (in back of gas station) Mailing address: P.O. Box 419 Denpasar 80001, Bali. ☎ 753820, 753821; fax: 753809.

Baruna, named after the Balinese water deity, is Bali's oldest and largest scuba diving operator. They operate two outriggered speedboats and a larger diesel-powered boat.

Baruna organizes tours for divers, individuals or groups, to all of Bali's dive sites, and anywhere else in Indonesia. This includes obtaining airplane reservations and tickets, which can be quite difficult to do on your own for remote places. They also run special-interest diving tours, fixed program tours and can arrange yacht charters (with on-board compressor) for groups of two to six.

Baruna owns a very attractive 50-room, bungalows-style hotel, the Puri Bagus Beach, beachside, at the extreme eastern end of Candi Dasa. The architecture, grounds and pool are all in good taste and well maintained. Although you can make bookings from elsewhere, it is best to stay here if you are diving in the area, especially if you are on one of Baruna's package tours, as their dive operations for eastern Bali are run from here.

Pineapple Divers Jl. Raya Kuta No. 382, P.O. Box 308, Kuta. ☎ 757567/754855; fax: 755891. A reputable outfit, specializing in Japanese clients.

Wally's Special Tours Dive guide Wally Siagian (see profile, page 102) is really in a category of his own. Wally caters to small groups (2–6 clients) whose special interests include marine life and photography. He offers a special 10-day/9-night tour of all of Bali's best dive spots and can arrange yacht charters for diving near or far. Wally handles his groups according to diving ability: novice, intermediate and expert. For the last group, there are night dives, deep dives, and dives in up to 3-knot currents.

Wally gives a briefing before every dive, a short de-briefing afterwards, and nights are spent going over the day's dives and talking about the client's special interests over cold beer. We cannot recommend these tours highly enough—but give yourself plenty of time. Optionals include shopping (Wally doesn't commissions and even helps you bargain for the lowest possible prices), sightseeing, and even bar- or disco-hopping. It's up to you—Wally's schedule is flexible and interests wide-ranging.

Wally can be contacted through Rudy's Business Centre, fax: 730354, 730555, or through Grand Komodo Tours in Sanur, ☎ 287166; fax: 287165.

SANUR

Ambisi Dive Center Jl. Tukad Pakerisan 98, Sanur. Mailing address: P.O. Box 3734, Denpasar 80228. ☎ 241428; fax: 241421. Formerly Oceana. Has changed management along with the name and location. Osanu Okuno is manager-instructor and caters to Japanese-speaking divers.

Bali Marine Sports Jl. Bypass Ngurah Rai, Belanjong, Sanur. ☎ /fax: 287872. Good organization, equipment and guides. Basic and advanced dive courses. A PADI International Dive Center, run by very professional westerners. They own three 12-person dive boats with radio communications to the dive center. All divers insured. Cross-certification and specialty courses offered. Various all-inclusive dive tours of Bali, ranging from $160 (2 days, 1 night) to $570 (7 days, 6 nights). Highly recommended if the same people stay on staff.

Dive and Dives Jl. Bypass Ngurah Rai 23, Sanur. ☎ 288052; fax: 289309. Probably the best outfit in Bali at the time of this writing. Highly recommended. Dive shop with gear for sale and rent, small cafe, nice diver ambiance. They can arrange multi-day dive tour packages and safaris around Bali or anywhere elsewhere in Indonesia.

ENA Diver Centre Jl. Tirta Ening 1, Sanur. ☎ 288829, 287945; fax: 287945. On a back street in Sanur, not easy to find, but they'll pick you up at your hotel. This operator owns the Saya Resort in Tulamben. Various all-inclusive dive safaris around Bali, ranging from $240 (4 days, 3 nights) to $950 (14 days, 13 nights).

Pro Dive Bali Jl. Sekarwaru No. 13, Sanur. ☎ /fax: 288756. Australian-operated company offering PADI open water dive courses for $345 and continuing education programs in advanced open water diving, rescue diving, divemaster and specialty courses. The 10m *Explorer II*, 115 hp motor boat speeds divers to sites so you can spend more time in the water instead of on the water. Boat dives include two tanks, land and/or sea transportation, dive guide, all equipment, and lunch.

NUSA DUA

Barrakuda Bali Dive At the Bali Tropic Palace Hotel, Jl. Pratama 34A, Nusa Dua. ☎ 772130, ext. 731; fax 772131. Located at the hotel. One instructor and two guides, all CMAS-certified. Also has counters in Candi Dasa and Lovina.

YOS Diving Centre & Marine Sports Jalan Pratama, Tanjung Benoa, Nusa Dua, Bali, Indonesia. ☎ 773774, 752005; fax 752985.

CANDIDASA

Balina Diving About 4 km west of Candi Dasa, just off the main road, in the hotel by the same name. ☎ (0363) 41001/3. This outfit could use better organization. Their outriggered dive boat has a 25 hp engine. Single dive, minimum two clients, including dive master, transportation and equipment: Nusa Penida ($50), Gili Tepekong ($35), Cemeluk ($40), Tulamben ($40), Menjangan ($65). Second dive at same location, $15 extra—this also includes lunch. Night dive at same location, including underwater light rental, $15. Introductory course, theory plus one dive ($50). Three-day all-inclusive package (meals, accommodations, diving) with 5 dives at Cemeluk, Tulamben and Menjangan ($210).

Sea Lion Diving Club (Stingray Dive Service) Bali Samudra Indah Hotel. ☎ (0363) 41062, 41181. Inclusive, two-dive tours (all gear included): Nusa Penida ($70), Padang Bai Blue Lagoon ($50), Gili Tepekong ($55), Tulamben ($55), Menjangan, minimum 4 persons ($70). Night dive at Tulamben ($40), Padangbai ($35). Two dives at any location, with accommodation ($90). Five-day course, with CMAS certification ($250). Introductory dive ($85).

TULAMBEN

Dive Paradise Tulamben Attached to the Paradise Palm Beach Hotel, PO Box 31, Amlapura 80811, Bali. No phone yet, but they can be contacted through the Friendship Shop in Candi Dasa, ☎ (0361) 29052. Their dive guide, Nengah Putu, holds an "advanced diver" rating. One wreck dive with instructor-guide ($30), two dives ($50). The dive shop also organizes dives at other spots around Bali. Prices include transportation from Tulamben, dive guide, two dives, and all equipment. Nusa Penida ($85), Padang Bai ($60), Gili Tepekong ($65), Cemeluk ($55), Menjangan ($75). Night dive off Tulamben or Cemeluk ($35). For snorkelers at Tulamben, the Dive Paradise has 10 sets of fins, masks and snorkels, $1.50/day.

LOVINA

This is a very good spot for beginning divers, with shallow depths and often excellent visibility (15–30 meters). The reef has a good variety of hard corals, sponges, crinoids and anemones, and abundant small reef fish: damsels, butterflyfish, wrasses, and even a few angelfish. The dive operators take experienced divers to Menjangan Island and to Tulamben, each a bit over an hour's drive away, the first to the west, the second to the east.

Spice Dive On the south side of the main coastal road. Contact through the pleasant Angsoka Home Stay, ☎ (0362) 41841. Dive instructor, Iin, a friendly young man, heads this small, well-run operation. Introductory dives available. 4–5 day courses with POSSI or CMAS certification, ($285). Two dives, all-inclusive, including all gear: Tulamben ($65), Lovina ($45), Menjangan ($65). Knock off 10% if you bring your own gear. Menjangan package requires a minimum of two clients. You can also arrange day dives at Nusa Penida, Padang Bai and Gili Tepekong (however, because of distance, just one dive per day).

Barrakuda At Bali Lovina Beach Cottages in Singaraja. ☎/fax: (0362) 41385, 21836. In Sanur, ☎/fax: 233386, 287694. This dive operator's head office is in Sanur. Prices and conditions similar to those at Spice Dive.

PEMUTERAN (MENJANGAN AREA)

Reef Seen Aquatics Associated with Taman Sari Beach Bungalows, Desa Pemuteran, Gerokgak, Singaraja, 8115, Bali. ☎/fax: (0362) 92339. ☎ (0362) 289031; fax: (0362) 289285. Two dives at the Pemuteran sites, just offshore, from boat, $55. Shore dives $10, with guide, $20; shore night dives $10, with guide, $25. The dive prices include tanks and weight belts. Trips to Menjangan, including 2 dives, buffet lunch and soft drinks, $65/person, plus $20/person for equipment, minimum of four divers.

Reef Seen's dive boat is a 12-meter, custom made wooden craft dedicated to diving. It is powered by twin 40 hp outboards and carries 7–8 divers in comfort. Oxygen and a good first aid kit kept on board.

The well-maintained rental gear is expensive, so better bring your own. Charges *per dive*: regulator $5, skin suit $3, mask/snorkel/ fins $3, or, for everything, one dive $10, full day $20, plus $3.50 for flashlight. If desired, well-qualified, English-speaking guides are available. Film and 110V or 220V charging facilities, multi-system video playback, separate freshwater rinse tanks for photo and video gear. Snorkeling, temple visits and nature walks in Bali Barat National Park are options.

Dive-master Chris Brown has pioneered more than a dozen sites within a few minutes by boat from Taman Sari and is continuing his explorations.

LIVE-ABOARDS

The Spice Islander ☎ 286283; fax: 286284. This luxury catamaran, based in Bali, offers occasional special dive charters throughout the year. Formerly operated by P & O Cruises, now operated by Spice Island Cruises. Although not cheap, the boat is very well-run and the trip is almost guaranteed to be great. The ship-board food is tops, the service excellent, the accommodations comfortable. All the most modern navigation gear and safety equipment is present on the 400-ton, 37-meter long steel catamaran, which, powered by twin 400 hp engines, cruises easily at 10 knots. While she bucks a bit during the occasionally rough seas, the sailing is usually smooth over tropical waters. **Spice Island Cruises** Jl. Padang Galak 25, Sanur. ☎ 286283; fax: 286284. General sales agent in the US: Esplanade Tours, 581 Boylston Street, Boston, MA. 02118. ☎ (817) 2667485 or (800) 4265492; fax: (617) 2629829. Japan agent: Cruise Vacation, Shuwa Nishigotanda Building 1F5-2-4, Nishigotanda, Shingawa-Ku, Tokyo 141. ☎ (3) 54870901; fax: (3) 54870905.

Space on the dive charters is always snapped up quickly. In Indonesia, contact **Aquasport** (in Jakarta), ☎ (021) 7199045; fax: 7198974.

YACHT CHARTERS

For a unique dive experience, you can charter a boat and head off to explore on your own. A Bauer compressor ($25/day) and tanks ($5/day) can be arranged. Yachts range from $290/day plus $15/day for meals, to $1,500/day. Up to 15 people can be accommodated. **Rasa Yacht Charters** ☎ 71571. 2 fine yachts, the 14-meter steel-hulled ketches *Rasa III* and *Rasa V*, which have state-of-the-art electronics and twin, 100 hp engines.

Grand Komodo Tours P.O. Box 477, Denpasar Bali 80001. ☎ 287166; fax: 287165. Runs *Wyeema* (14 meters, 6 persons for short trips) for $290/day; *Electric Lamb* (18 meters, 6 persons) for $350/day. Captained by owner David Plant (English).

Tourdevco Bali Benoa Port, ☎ 31591; fax: 31592. Their Jakarta office is at Jl. Johar Menteng 2A, Menteng, Jakarta 10340, ☎ (021) 3805011, fax: (021) 7200756. Eight boats, various sizes and prices. Currently the biggest operator in Bali.

PERIPLUS ADVENTURE GUIDES
The complete guidebook series on Indonesia

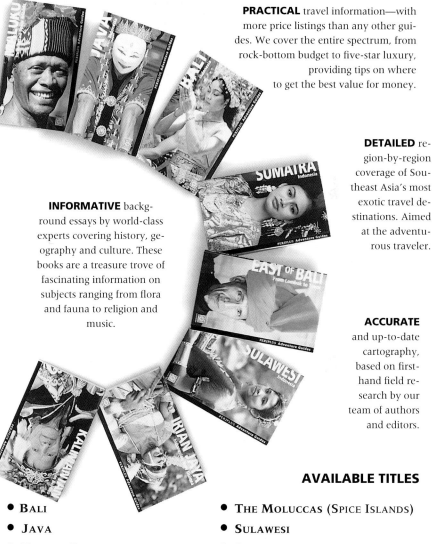

PRACTICAL travel information—with more price listings than any other guides. We cover the entire spectrum, from rock-bottom budget to five-star luxury, providing tips on where to get the best value for money.

DETAILED region-by-region coverage of Southeast Asia's most exotic travel destinations. Aimed at the adventurous traveler.

INFORMATIVE background essays by world-class experts covering history, geography and culture. These books are a treasure trove of fascinating information on subjects ranging from flora and fauna to religion and music.

ACCURATE and up-to-date cartography, based on first-hand field research by our team of authors and editors.

AVAILABLE TITLES

- BALI
- JAVA
- EAST OF BALI
- IRIAN JAYA (NEW GUINEA)
- KALIMANTAN (BORNEO)

- THE MOLUCCAS (SPICE ISLANDS)
- SULAWESI
- SUMATRA
- WEST MALAYSIA & SINGAPORE
- EAST MALAYSIA & BRUNEI

Distributed by:
Berkeley Books Pte. Ltd. (Singapore & Malaysia)
5 Little Road, #08-01, Singapore 536983 Tel: (65) 280 3320 Fax: (65) 280 6290
C.V. Java Books (Indonesia)
Jl. Gading Kirana Timur Blok A13 No. 23, Jakarta 14240
Tel: (021) 453 4988 Fax: (021) 453 4987

Accommodations

Bali has a very wide range of accommodations, from 5-star hotels to modest *losmen*. You can spend $1,200/night in a lavish suite at Nusa Dua or $3/night at a friendly little *losmen* in Candi Dasa. It's your choice.

Bali, the land of 10,000 temples, has more than that number of hotel rooms and it would be impossible for us to list all the available lodgings here. We keep the list short in popular areas, such as the Kuta–Sanur–Nusa Dua triangle, and concentrate on those places divers might have a special interest in staying, particularly Candi Dasa and Lovina. All the more up-market hotels charge 21% government tax and service on top of the listed prices.

KUTA AND LEGIAN

A town has grown up around the beach here that has become the tourist center of Bali. Robert and Louise Koke, surfers from southern California, first built their Kuta Beach Hotel here in 1936. Still, it wasn't until the late '60s and early '70s, when a generation of hippies and other western drop-outs "discovered" Bali, that Kuta exploded.

Today, the town, which now extends north up to Legian, bustles with activity, its streets and tiny *gangs* (alleyways) lined with shops, restaurants, discos, and *losmen*. It is even an international fashion center with a distinct, colorful style falling somewhere between neon sporting wear and a Grateful Dead T-shirt. Although it is currently fashionable to malign Kuta, the place does have an irrepressible, youthful charm.

Budget (under $20)

Blue Ocean south of Jl. Double Six. 29 rooms. A popular hangout for locals and surfers, right on Legian Beach. $9–$10.

Rita's House, Gang Poppies I, Kuta. ☎ 751760, 222390; fax: 236021. 13 rooms. Very quiet, clean, well-kept, and friendly; right in the center of Kuta. Rooms with shower and toilet. $4.50–$7 fan, $11–$16 AC, incl. breakfast.

Sorga Beach Inn Gang Menuh, between Jl. Melasti and Jl. Padma, Legian. ☎ 751609. 10 rooms. Fan only. Walk to the beach. $8–$10.

Yulia Beach Inn Jl. Pantai Kuta 43. ☎ 751893; fax: 751055. 48 rooms. One of the original Kuta places near the beach, where you have an ample choice of rooms. $3 w/o private bath, up to $30 for AC.

Intermediate ($25–$75)

Asana Santhi Willy Jl. Tegalwangi 18, Kuta. ☎ 751281, 752641. 10 rooms. In the heart of Kuta. Pleasant, newly renovated with antique furnishings and semi-open bathrooms, swimming pool. Willy II (14 rooms) next door has large rooms, but no character. $30–$35.

Bali Niksoma Beach Cottages Jl. Padma, Legian. ☎ 751946; fax: 753587. 52 rooms. A quiet beachfront place in Legian. Rooms with fan $21–$25, AC $45–$55,deluxe $65–$80, suites $95.

Bruna Beach Inn Jl. Pantai Kuta. ☎ 751565. 36 rooms. Across the road from Kuta beach. Attached or bungalow style, AC and non-AC. $12, $30–$35. Family room for $65 sleeps 5.

Garden View Cottages Jl. Padma Utara 4, Legian. ☎ 751559; fax: 753265. 56 rms. Secluded, on a Legian backlane. Short walk to beach. $38–$45.

Kuta Beach Club Jl. Bakung Sari, Kuta. ☎ 751261; fax: 752896. 100 rooms. A tranquil setting with garden and bungalows, right in the center of Kuta. $38–$40.

Poppies Cottages I Gang Poppies I, Jl. Legian, Kuta (behind Jl. Pantai Kuta). ☎ 751059; fax: 752364. 20 rooms. Well-designed cottages in a beautiful garden. Refrigerator in every room. 300 metres from the beach and always filled to capacity; reservations a must. $65–$70.

Poppies Cottages II Poppies Lane II, Kuta. ☎ 751059; fax: 52364. 4 rooms with fans, showers and fridges. $23–$28, $5 extra for a private kitchen.

Sandi Phala Jl. Kartika Plaza, Kuta. ☎ 753042; fax: 754889. 12 rooms. Two-story bungalows overlooking the beach in a big compound with pool and beachfront restaurant. $30–$45.

First Class ($75 and up)

Bali Oberoi Jl. Kayu Aya, Petitenget. ☎ 730361; fax: 730791. 75 rms. Tucked between ricefields and the sea at the northern end of the beach; bungalows of coral rock scattered tastefully about landscaped grounds. Beds are hand-carved 4-posters and the baths have open-air gardens. $225–$850 for a beachside villa with private pool.

Bali Intan Cottages Jl. Melasti 1, Legian. ☎ 751770; fax: 751891. 150 rms. Across the road from Legian beach. Standard $80–$90, superior $90–$100, cottage $100–$110, suite $180.

Bali Mandira Jl. Padma, Legian. ☎ 751381; fax: 752377. 120 rooms. Rows of cottages clustered around tidy courtyards. Tennis and squash. $80–$100, suites $135–170.

Intan Bali Village Spa & Club Jl. Petitenget ☎ 730777; fax: 730778. 311 rooms. Past the Oberoi at the quiet, northern end of the beach. Soothing views from the beachfront bar. Extensive facilities include a gym. $80–$90, up to $525 for the presidential suite.

Jayakarta Bali Jl. Pura Bagus Teruna, Legian. ☎ 751433; fax: 752074. 281 rooms. Right on the beach; rooms are in large, two-story blocks. Standard $95–$100, up to $250 for a suite.

Kuta Beach Hotel Jl. Pantai Kuta. PO Box 3393. ☎ 751361; fax: 751362. 137 rooms right on Kuta Beach. $80–$90, bungalow $90–$100, suite $135–$300.

Patra Jasa Bali Jl. Kuta Beach, Tuban. ☎ 751161, 752810; fax: 752030. 206 rooms. Just five minutes from the airport, on the beach at the southern end of Kuta. Tennis courts, golf course, badminton and watersports. $130, up to $800 for a suite.

Pesona Bali Jl. Kayu Aya, Petitenget. ☎ 753914, 753915. 160 rms, 7 2-room bungalows. Near the beach. Kitchenettes in every 2-story bungalow. $180–$1000 (sleeps 4). Extremely quiet and remote.

NUSA DUA

This resort offers luxury, and isolation from touts, peddlers, stray dogs, cold-water showers and other indignities. It's also quite antiseptic. Preferred by the international jet set. There are no cheap lodgings here.

Bualu Village P.O. Box 6, Denpasar. ☎ 771310; fax: 771313. 50 rms. Sports activities are free and the hotel has a PADI-certified diving instructor. The beach is five minutes away by foot or horsecart. $69–$112.

Club Mediterranée Nusa Dua P.O. Box 7, Denpasar. ☎ 771521, 771523; fax: 771831. 350 rooms. Looks more like a traditional luxury hotel than other Club Meds around the world. A fun place; attractive international staff. No room service, TVs or telephones. Packages including airfare, meals and entertainment through your travel agent.

Melia Bali Sol P.O. Box 1048, Tuban. ☎ 771410, 771510; fax: 771362, 771360. 496 rooms. Recently renovated; managed by the Spanish Sol Melia chain, the Bali Sol reflects a certain Spanish ambience, including a replica of the Alhambra fountain at the entrance. Popular with Japanese tourists. Indoor pool and spa, outdoor pool with sunken bar. $176–198 superior, up to $1,100 for the deluxe suite.

Nusa Dua Beach Hotel P.O. Box 1028, Denpasar. ☎ 771210; fax: 771229. 380 rooms. Recently renovated with luxury Nusa Dua Spa added. The spectacular Balinese *candi bentar* gate at the entrance is a Nusa Dua landmark. Elaborately decorated with stone carvings in the manner of a Klungkung palace. Where then-U.S. President and Mrs. Ronald Reagan stayed. Gym and squash courts. $165 superior, $3,200 for a suite with private pool and entrance.

Putri Bali P.O. Box 1, Denpasar. ☎ 771020; fax: 771139. 384 rooms. Managed by the Hotel Indonesia chain. Book the cottages for more privacy. $120–$155 superior, $155–175 cottages, $210–$600 suites.

TANJUNG BENOA

This is a recently established resort just north of Nusa Dua. The beach hotels here are small and cozy, although there are some newly opened larger hotels. The nice, white-sand beach here is popular for water sports: parasailing, windsurfing, waterskiing and, of course, snorkeling and diving. All the accommodations are intermediate or budget, and provide a nice complement to nearby Nusa Dua's deluxe digs. All lodgings are on Jl. Pratama.

Matahari Terbit Bungalows ☎ 771018; fax: 772027. 8 rooms. Overlooking pool, restaurant in center. $60.

Puri Joma Bungalows ☎ /fax: 771526. 10 rooms. For people who like staying in a small hotel away from the crowds. Very relaxing beachfront pool. $55–$60.

SANUR

Sanur was Bali's first resort town and is, in a sense, the grey eminence of the tourist triangle. Compared to Kuta, it is quiet and dignified (or just dull, depending on your point of view and, inescapably, your age) and compares to Nusa Dua as old wealth does to new. The town is very quiet at night and the beach here, protected by the reef flat, is very calm. People who intend to spend a long time on Bali often stay in Sanur.

Budget (under $25)

Sanur Plaza Jl. Bypass Ngurah Rai. ☎ 288808. 40 rooms. Spacious bungalows with thatched roof and hot water. A pool is available. They also have a family room. $12–$20.

Taman Agung Beach Inn Jl. Danau Tamblingan 146, Batujimbar. ☎ 289161, 288549; fax: 289161. 24 rooms. One of the best *losmen* in Sanur. Pleasant atmosphere. Five minutes from the beach. $25 fan, $50 suite.

Intermediate ($25–$75)

Baruna Beach Inn Jl. Sindhu 17, Sindhu. ☎ 288546; fax: 289629. 8 rooms. Pleasant old bungalows on the beach with lots of character, furnished with antiques and opening onto a courtyard bordering the sea. Cozy, very popular. $35–$40 with fridge. $65 suite. Breakfast, tax and service included. Credit cards not accepted. There is a house nearby for long stays.

Bali Sanur Besakih Beach Bungalows Jl. Danau Tamblingan 45, Batujimbar. ☎ 288424; fax: 286059. 50 rooms. Set in a garden leading to the sea. $65–$75.

Palm Garden Jl. Kesumasari No. 3, Semawang. ☎ 287041; fax: 289571. 23 rooms, all with living room. $100 standard, $200–$300 suite. **Sindhu Beach Hotel** at the beach end of Jl. Sindhu. Mailing address: Jl. Danau Tondano 14, Batujimbar. ☎ 288351; fax: 289268. 104 rooms in beachside bungalows. Owned by Natour chain. $40–$100.

First Class ($75 and up)

Bali Hyatt Jl. Danau Tamblingan, Semawang. ☎ 288271; fax: 287693. 390 rooms. With thatched-roof and terra-cotta-tiled lobby, open, relaxed reel, and magnificently landscaped garden, this is not your typical luxury chain hotel. For years, this has been *the* place to stay in Bali. Renovations completed in 1994 returned it to its classical Balinese roots. Several indoor and outdoor restaurants. Complete sports facilities. One pool has a replica of the famous Goa Gajah—plus waterfall, Jacuzzi and cold dip. $140–$185 superior/deluxe, $165–$185 executive/king, $180–$215 Regency Club, $400–$685 suite.

La Taverna Bali Jl. Tanjung Sari. ☎ 288387, 288497; fax: 287126. 34 rooms. Noted for its unique blend of Mediterranean and Balinese architecture combining thatched roofs and stucco. Tasteful antique-furnished rooms set in a tropical garden. Excellent beachside restaurant serves a variety of Italian and Indonesian specialities. $120–$160 standard, $195–$260 suite.

Sanur Bali Travelodge Jl. Mertasari, P.O. Box 9476, Semawang. ☎ 288833, 287301/2; fax: 287303. 194 rooms. Located at the southern end of Sanur's beach strip. $110–$140 superior to luxury, $170 beachfront, $350 suite.

Sanur Beach Hotel Jl. Mertasari, Semawang; P.O. Box 279, Sanur. ☎ 288011; fax: 287566. 425 rooms. This four-story block is one of the older beachfront hotels in Sanur. Known for its friendly service.$125–$135 standard, $145–$170 deluxe, $200–$425 Studio, $350–$900 suite. Super-deluxe bungalow with marbled bathroom and private swimming pool $850. Group rates: $85–$95/person. Garuda office on 2nd floor.

Sativa Sanur Cottages off Jl. Mertasari, Semawang, ☎ /fax: 287881. 50 rooms. Shaded by coconut trees, this well-managed hotel is one of the coziest places to stay in Sanur, but it is away from the beach. The restaurant is excellent. $74–$184.

Segara Village Hotel Jl. Segara Ayu, Sindhu. ☎ 288407, fax: 287242. 120 rooms. Mini-villages of private bungalows by the sea, "rustic Balinese" (some look like *lumbung*, traditional rice granaries). Efficient, friendly staff. Balinese dance classes, a children's recreation room, gym, sauna. $65–$135, suite $210.

Tandjung Sari Hotel Jl. Tanjung Sari. ☎ 288441; fax: 287930. 26 rooms. Built in 1962, this remains the top choice for many visitors. Charming decor, tranquil, elegant. The bungalows are reminiscent of those found in the pleasure gardens of the Balinese *rajas*. Caters to a celebrity clientele. The restaurant is highly recommended. $200–$1,250 standard, $300–$380 suites.

The Grand Bali Beach (formerly Hotel Bali Beach) Jl. Hang Tuah. ☎ 288511; fax: 287917. The first large luxury hotel in Bali. Offers the most complete hotel facilities in Bali. One of its restaurants is a rooftop supper club with panoramic views. The golf course may be the reason why lots of Japanese groups stay here. Bowling alleys, tennis courts, local banks, American Express TRS office, and airline offices. $165–185.

CANDI DASA

This town is quiet and relatively uncrowded compared to Kuta and Sanur to the south. There are at least 50 hotels, *losmen,* and homestays, and plenty of restaurants. The availability of services and its location—between Nusa Penida and Padang Bai to the south and Cemeluk and Tulamben to the north—make it, probably, the best place for serious divers to settle.

Accommodations

There is a wide range of prices and quality of accommodations here, from small, practically windowless cement block cells to large suites overlooking the ocean. Prices vary accordingly.

Bayu Paneeda Beach Inn ☎ (0363) 41104. 14 rooms. West of town. Medium-sized twin huts set in a huge tract of land. A large, grassy lawn makes this a favorite spot for families with kids. Blankets, reading lights and towels are supplied. Some hot water units with fans and screens. $9–$16.

Candi Beach Cottage Desa Sengkidu, kecamatan Manggis. ☎ (0363) 41234; fax: (0363) 41111. 64 rooms. Hotel and cotage rooms with satellite TV, mini-bar, verandah. Also has a pool, spa, open water diving school, fitness center, and tennis court. $75–$100.

Candi Dasa Beach Bungalows II ☎ (0363) 41536; fax: (0363) 41537. 69 spacious rooms overlooking the sea. A large two-story block of rooms. Swimming pool and open-air bar. Some rooms have refrigerators and TVs. $60–$85, bungalow $100, suite $150.

Homestay Pelangi 9 rooms. West of town in a quiet oceanside setting. Private garden. Decent-sized bamboo rooms, bathrooms with open-air garden. The owner, Pak Gelgel, is very friendly. Often a pair of bamboo gamelans with flute lull one to sleep. $7–$9, breakfast included. You can join organized treks to Tenganan via Kestala for as little as $5/person.

Ida Homestay Jl. Raya Candi Dasa. ☎ (0363) 41096. 6 rooms. East of town on the beach.

Private thatched bamboo bungalows in a large, grassy coconut grove. Two-story houses provide upstairs bedrooms with wide ocean views. Beautiful open-air bathrooms. Carved furniture in some units. No hot water. $9–$23.

Losman Geringsing 15 rms. The best bargain in town. This friendly place offers small bamboo and brick bungalows in a banana grove on the beach. One of the few places to have any beach left, though only at low tide. $9–$14, includes breakfast, but not tax and service.

Puri Bagus Beach Hotel Jl. Raya Candi Dasa. P.O. Box 129, Amlapura. ☎ (0363) 41291/2; fax: (0363) 41290. 50 rms. Clean, spacious bungalows with semi-open bathroom and minibar. Pool and restaurant overlooking the ocean. $65–$125. Ocean view/front room surcharge $10–$15.

Puri Pundak ☎ (0363) 33978. 17 rooms. In the banana groves east of town, near the homes of local fishermen. Large bamboo rooms, Western bathrooms, some with bathtubs. Overlooks the bay. $7–$23.

Rama Ocean View Bungalows Balina. ☎ (0363) 33974; fax: (0363) 233975. 74 rms. West of Candi Dasa, away from the noise and bustle. A beachside enclave with a pool, restaurant, mini bar, and satellite TV. Fitness center, sauna, tennis court, and games rooms. $75–$90, suite $250–$350.

Serai Desa Buitan, Manggis. P.O. Box 13, Karangasem 80871. ☎ (0363) 41011/2; fax: (0363) 41015. 58 rooms. Just west of Candi Dasa. Secluded beachfront hotel with swimming pool, restaurant. $90 superior, deluxe $105, $175 suite.

The Water Garden ☎ (0363) 41540; fax: (0363) 41164. 12 rooms. This hotel venture of TJ's Restaurant in Kuta has been designed with their usual attention to detail and quality. Gorgeous bungalows set in a network of cascading streams, pools and elegant gardens. Mountain bikes, hiking maps and information about local events and places of interest available. Swimming pool. $60–$65.

Dining

There are lots of restaurants in Candi Dasa. The typical menu will contain salads, Indonesian and Chinese standards and a few basic western dishes. Prices are very reasonable, averaging $4–$5/person, with drinks. Seafood, though delicious, can be considerably more expensive. Most restaurants close up by 10 pm. Breakfast and lunch are available everywhere.

Arie Bar and Restaurant 8 tables. Down-to-earth, family-run establishment with a good selection of Balinese, Chinese and Western dishes. Good quality and prices that are hard-to-beat.

Kubu Bali ☎ (0363) 41532. 36 tables. Serves a bit of everything, but excels in seafood—grilled, steamed or fried. Their open kitchen is fun to watch. Finish up with peach melba, chilled fruit or a cognac.

Lotus Sea View Larger and more formal than the neighboring Toke Cafe, but it has great seafood and its location near the water gives it a Venetian flavor.

Pandan Restaurant ☎ (0363) 41541. 30 tables. By the beach. Well-known for its Balinese buffet of *babi guling* (roast pork), chicken, fish, vegetables, noodles and salads. Experience this feast or sample one of the many other delicious local or Chinese dishes.

Rama Bungalow and Restaurant Has added Swiss dishes, such as *Roschti*, *Kartoffel* and *Puffer Mitgemuse* to an already good menu.

TJ's Cafe ☎ (0363) 41540. 22 tables. The best grilled fish, stuffed baked potatoes and salads around. Elegant open pavilions overlook a carp pond. Popular western music and the delicious desserts.

Toke Cafe Near the bend in the road, beachside. Wonderful combination of Balinese ambience and Western intimacy. Great welcoming drink and good pasta, all of this just for a couple of dollars.

Warung Ibu Rasmini The best *nasi campur* (mixed vegetables, *tempe*, and chicken over rice) in town for under $1, plus a range of other simple Indonesian dishes.

TULAMBEN

Most divers travel to Tulamben (or nearby Cemeluk) on a package tour from Kuta, Sanur, Nusa Dua, or Candi Dasa, but independent-minded divers can make their way by rented car or, if not carrying gear, by motorcycle. It's about 4 hrs from Kuta or Nusa Dua, 30 min. less from Sanur. The traffic through Candi Dasa will likely be heavy, and only the last hour of the trip—from Candi Dasa onward—could be called pleasant. From Tulamben to Menjangan takes about 3.5 hrs.

There are several places in Tulamben which offer tanks, weights, and equipment rental, along with guides for independent divers who arrive on their own. There are several accommodations in both the Tulamben area as well as Cemeluk for multi-day dive programs.

Accommodations

Ganda Mayu ("Fragrant Flower") 7 rooms. Simple beachfront accommodations. Near dive entry point to wreck site. Bali Coral Dive Center in front of bungalows. $7–$14.

Mimpi Resort Sales office: Kawasan Bukit Permai, Jimaran, Denpasar 80361. ☎ (0361) 701070; fax: (0361) 701074. 16 new bungalows. Swimming pool, restaurant, and Bukit Kencana Dive Center on beachfront grounds. Fan and AC. $75–$125. Minibuses of day-

Bali 3

divers park next to this *losmen.*

Paradise Palm Beach PO Box 31, Amlapura 80811. ☎ (0363) 41032. 22 nice, thatched bungalows, each with two beds, fan and toilet. Beach restaurant, souvenir shop and Tulamben Dive Center attached. Reserve in high season. Inexpensive meals, although they aren't great and the service can be slow. Cold beer and some liquor available. $11–$16. Two rooms with AC and hot water, $35.

From the Paradise, it's about 300 m to the entry point on the beach for the wreck. You can hire someone to carry your gear for about $1.50 for two dives ($1.75 at night.) There is a government tax of 25¢ per diver per day.

Saya Resort 5 AC rooms, mini-bar, private balconies. Attached restaurant. Snorkeling and dive excursions with hotel's Ena Dive Center. $35–$50, American breakfast included.

Dining

Sunrise Next to the Paradise, away from the wreck, on the beach. Chicken or fish ($2), also —less expensive—vegetables, *gado-gado,* and sandwiches. Soft drinks and beer.

Equipment Rental

Bali Dive has a branch office on the main road, at the turnoff to the parking area near the entry point for the wreck. Has tanks, regulators and BCs for rent.

Dive Paradise Tulamben Attached to the Paradise Palm Beach. This outfit maintains a good Bauer compressor. Tank fills $4, full tank and weight belt rental, $10/day. They have a few well-maintained BCs and regulators and sets of snorkeling equipment ($1.50).

Tulamben Dive Center P.O. Box 31, Amlapura 80811. ☎ (0363) 41032. Next to the Paradise on the main road. Has a compressor, tanks and rental gear. Same prices as the Paradise. Associated with the *losmen* Tulamben Beach Pondok Wisata, 4 rooms $5–$10.

CEMELUK

There is no compressor or rental gear in the immediate vicinity of this dive site. Bring your own from Tulamben, Candi Dasa or wherever, or join a group from Kuta/Sanur/Nusa Dua for a day trip. Past Cemeluk, on the way to Karangasem, there are a few *losmen,* on the bad, but paved and spectacular road which follows the coast around Bali's easternmost peninsula.

Coral View. New resort with 19 thatched bungalows, swimming pol, bar, and restaurant. Motorboat available for dolphin cruises. All rooms with hot water. $29 economy with fan, $40 standard with fan, $52 AC, $104 suite.

Good Karma Dusun Selang, Amed. 10 bamboo bungalows on the beach. Small, friendly, quiet

place favored by young Europeans. $9–$11.

Hidden Paradise Cottages Lipah, Bunutan, Abang, Amed. ☎ (0361) 431273; fax: (0363) 21044, (0361) 423820. 16 rooms. Hot water, fan and AC. Complete facilities: swimming pool, bicycles and watersports. Snorkeling equipment, boat available. $35–$87, including American breakfast.

Kusuma Jaya Beach Inn Jemuluk village, 12 km from Amlapura. ☎ (0363) 21250. 12 rooms. On a steep hill above the pool with wonderful vistas. Beautiful sunrises and sunsets. Take the steep steps on the left past the bridge. Snorkeling gear available for guests. $13–$16, including breakfast.

Vienna Cottage P.O. Box 112, Lipah, Amed. 12 bungalows. Watersports facilities: diving, snorkeling, fishing, sailing. $11–$21, including breakfast.

Note: there's a small sunken wooden boat in shallow (snorkelable) depth at Banyuning/ Waru, close to the beach, between the Vienna and the Good Karma.

SAMBIRENTENG

Alam Anda Sambirenteng. Contact Astawa Enterprises, c/o Nyumpene, Jl. Legian Tengah 436N, Legian. ☎ /fax: (0361) 752296. 9 bungalows, 4-room house. Unique, new seaside resort devoted to relaxation. Organizes trips through unspoilt landscapes, as well as sailing, snorkeling, and dive trips to Amed, Tulamben, Menjangan, and Nusa Penida. They have an experienced dive master in residence and diving equipment in top condition for rent. $24–$29 rooms, $39–$44 bungalows, including breakfast.

LOVINA

Lovina is the generic name for a cluster of villages spread along Bali's north coast. They are, from east to west: Tukad Munggah, Anturan, Kalibukbuk (Lovina), and Temukus. The beach is shiny black sand and the surf is calm. It is a quiet town.

If you are going to dive at Menjangan and if you don't stay at the Taman Sari in Pemuteran, then Lovina is the next best place to stay. (See "Dive Operators," page 280 for more on dive tours from Lovina.)

Accommodations

Most lodgings here are budget *losmen* or intermediate lodgings. Prices are a bargain compared to the tourist towns in the south.

Aditya Jl. Seririt. P.O. Box 35, Lovina. ☎ 41059; fax: 41342. 75 rooms. Some spacious new suites with AC, hot water, tub, and phone are available. $$20–$25 fan, $35–$45

AC, including Continental breakfast.

Agung Homestay, Bar & Restaurant P.O. Box 124, Anturan. 5 rooms. One of the first hotels in Lovina, the building uses bamboo throughout. Very friendly atmosphere. No private baths. $3–$4.50. Reservations are needed.

Angsoka Kalibukbuk. ☎ 41841. 26 rooms. Comfortable two-story bungalows, some with hot water. $4–$7.50 fan, $20–$25 AC.

Angsoka Seaside Cottages Jl. Lovina. ☎ 41841; fax: 41023. 26 rooms. Special facilities for bungalows include split AC, bathtub and hot water. $7–$18 fan, $12 open Bali-style baths.

Astina Kalibukbuk. 8 km west of Singaraja, PO Box 141, Singaraja 81151. ☎ 41803 (c/o Ayodya). 12 rooms, 5 cottages. On the beach. Bamboo-walled rooms around a nice garden. $5.50–$7 with common bath, $8–$9 with private bath $11–$12.50 cottages with fan, mosquito net, private bath.

Awangga Tukad Munggah, Banjar Banyualik, Desa Kalibukbuk. ☎ 41561. 8 clean and spacious rooms, close to the beach. $7, including American breakfast.

Ayodya Kalibukbuk. ☎ 41803. 5 bamboo-walled rooms in a well-kept old house. Despite its location on the main road, pleasantly calm. No private bathrooms. $3–$4.

Bali Lovina Beach Cottage Jl. Seririt, Singaraja, Lovina. PO Box 186. ☎ /fax: 41285; fax: 41478. 34 bungalow-style rooms. $30–$35 fan, $40–$45 AC, $50–$60 superior, including a generous breakfast, with bacon eggs and toast. $30S, $35D, $35F, $40D w/AC.

Bali Taman Beach Hotel Jl. Raya Seririt, Desa Tukad Mungga, PO Box 99. ☎ 41126; fax: 41478. 18 bungalow-stlye rooms. Tennis court, fridge and TV available. $22.50–$27.50 fan, $45–$55 AC and hot water. Continental breakfast included.

Banyualit Beach Inn Jl. Singaraja, P.O. Box 116, Kalibukbuk. ☎ 41789; fax: 41563. 20 rooms. Simple to newly renovated AC with hot water. Some of the verandahs are literally on the water's edge. Friendly and helpful staff. Ask for a room close to the beach. $12–$15 fan, $16–$23 AC.

Baruna Beach Cottages Desa Temaron. P.O. Box 149, Lovina. ☎ 41746; fax: 41252. 42 rooms. Several cottages overlooking the beach. All rooms with private bath. $17 budget w/fan, $24–$32 cottages w/fan, $40–$52 AC. Excluding tax, service and breakfast.

Janur's Dive Inn Kalibukbuk, Tukad Mungga. P.O. Box 100, Singaraja. ☎ 41056. 5 rooms with fans. Friendly family place run by Janur and Rose and Gede, who live in the same compound. Very simple accommodations, but special and cozy. Ask Janur to guide you around. $4.50.

Jati Reef Bungalows P.O. Box 52, Tukad Mungga. ☎ 41052. 16 rooms in four separate bungalows, with a short walk through the rice-fields to get to your room. $7 fan.

Kalibukbuk Beach Inn Jl. Lafiana, Desa Kalibukbuk. ☎ 41701. 25 rooms. At the end of Banyualit lane, just a few steps from the beach. $9 budget, $11–$14 fan, $16–$20 AC.

Nirwana Desa Kalibukbuk, Lovina. ☎ 41288; fax: 41090. 32 rooms. Spacious, clean, right on the beach. The largest room can sleep four. Two-story bungalows with bamboo trim spread set in a lush garden. $14–$18, family suite $23.

Palma Hotel Jl. Raya Lovina-Singaraja. P.O. Box 131. ☎ 41775, 41658; fax: 41659. 45 rooms, standard and cottages, AC, hot showers. Other facilities include meeting room tennis court and recreation facilities, including boat sailing, push bikes. $72–$81 standard, $94–$102 cottages, $192–$210 suites, including American breakfast.

Perama Jl. Lovina, Anturan. ☎ 41161. 10 rooms very close to one another and right on the main road, so it can be rather noisy. $4.50 for rooms with private shower, $3.60 without.

Puri Tasik Madu/Tama ☎ 41376. 12 rooms. This was one of the first hotels in the area. Rooms are newly-renovated. Pleasant staff and a very friendly atmosphere. $8.50–$17.

Rini Kalibukbuk. ☎ 41386. 20 rooms. Clean,all rooms with private bath. No breakfast. $15–$30.

Samudra Beach Cottage Jl. Seririt, Desa Temukus. P.O. Box 142, Temukus. ☎ 41751. 24 rooms. At the western end of the beach. Very quiet. $7–$11 fan, $9–$16 AC, including Continental breakfast.

Simon's Seaside Cottage Jl. Semit, Desa Anturan. P.O. Box 151, Tukad Mungga. ☎ 41183. 16 rooms in four two-story bungalows. Clean and roomy. Great upper rooms with verandahs front and back overlooking the beach and rice-fields $11–$14.

Sri Homestay Jl. Singaraja, Seririt, Desa Anturan. ☎ 41135. 12 bamboo rooms by the beach. Bathrooms are not the cleanest around, but where else can you look over ricefields while taking a shower? Has a narrow veranda in front. The owner, Sri, is helpful and friendly. $11–$15.

Most hotels can arrange watersports, not only for the Lovina area, but for Pulau Mejangan to the west (around $18). The usual rates are as follows: snorkeling: $3–$4/ person (a bargain). Trip to the dolphins: $5/person. Fishing trip: $5/person. It may be cheaper to bargain with local fishermen.

Dining

Nearly all hotels in the area have restaurants. **Janur's Dive Inn** has one that is great value for money. Very pleasant atmosphere, serving standard favorites like *cap cay* (mixed vegetables) for $1.

The most famous restaurant is **Khi Khi** in Lovina. If the food is to your liking, go to their open-air kitchen and takes notes on the recipes. Grilled fish and fried prawns are the favorites here. Another popular restaurant is the **Kakatua**, near Lovina beach. Try their fried fish for $2. Oryou can go to **Srikandi** for fried rice, which you eat sitting on a mat. For those who want live music, go to **Wina** or **Malibu**. The latter turns into a disco on Fridays.

PEMUTERAN/MENJANGAN

Boats from Labuhan Lalang to Menjangan, carrying up to 10 passengers (perhaps 6 divers with full gear): $20 for the first 4 hrs, $3 extra for each additional hr. (Note: If you come on a package tour, the boat fare is included.) Leave your valuables in a safe place.

Matahari Beach Resort, Pemuteran, Singaraja. ☎ 92312; fax: 92313. 32 rooms. New, exclusive 5-star resort, quite unexpected in this environment. Built in Balinese style with German management, spacious bungalows, each with two rooms with marble terraces, living room, AC, and outdoor baths. Full facilities include tennis, watersports, mountain biking, and a dive center, David's Sport Center. Airport transfer

for $30 is a luxury with dive gear. $140–$160 garden view, $170–$190 sea view, $220–$240 deluxe, $330–$350 super deluxe. All prices plus 20% tax and service.

Pondok Sari Beach Bungalows Desa Pemuteran, Gerokgak, Singaraja. ☎ /fax: 92337. 20 rooms in 10 bungalows. The predecessor of Taman Sari Beach Bungalows. $18 fan, $29 AC, plus 15% tax and service.

Pulau Menjangan Inn 3 km from the boat landing. 8 rooms, strictly basic accommodation. Simple meals ($1.25–$2). $5.

Taman Sari Beach Bungalows Desa Pemuteran, Gerokgak, Singaraja. ☎ (0362) 92623, (0361) 289031, (0361) 288096 c/o Putu Tini; fax: (0361) 289285. These bungalows are very clean and comfortable, and the setting is very peaceful. The tasteful room furnishings and the open-air bathrooms with Japanese touches—smooth river pebbles, dripping bamboo—are very nice. The restaurant on the premises offers good western and Indonesian cuisine, plus cold beer. $$18 fan, $35 AC, plus 15% tax and service.

—updated by Debe Campbell/Andy Udayana

4 Nusa Tenggara PRACTICALITIES

Most of Nusa Tenggara is not yet part of the standard Indonesian tourist circuit, although the infrastructure is developing rapidly. If you schedule ahead of time, most dive operators will meet you at the airport. The islands here are rugged and—in the northernmost part of the chain—volcanic. This is one of the best parts of Indonesia for traditional cloth, and in some areas, particularly Sumba and Flores, old animist religions are still followed.

Prices in US dollars. S = Single; D = Double; T = Triple; AC = Air-conditioning.

Gili Islands

Lombok, Nusa Tenggara Barat (NTB)
Telephone code 0364

These islands, because they are so close to Bali, have become a very popular destination. The simplest way to get here is to take the ferry from Padangbai, Bali (3.5 hrs). There are ferries daily every two hours, beginning at 6 am. Fare: $2.50 economy, $4 VIP. The ferry reaches Lombok at Labuhan Lembar. From Lembar, minibuses head to any of a number of destinations, including Mataram (the island's capital and largest city) and Senggigi Beach.

A more luxurious alternative is the Mabua Intan Express, a 40 m catamaran that speeds at 60 kn/h between Benoa and Lambar in just 2 hours. Reclining seats, overhead lockers, a bar, and even videos make this a luxury. In rough weather the cat literally jumps over the waves, causing a lot of upset stomachs. Departures from Benoa are at 8 am and 2:30 pm, from Lembar at 11:30 am and 5:30 pm. Economy class $12.50, middle class $17.50 and first class $25, including snack and beverage. ☎ (0361) 772521 on Bali or (0364) 37224 on Lombok.

You can also fly from Bali to Lombok's Selaparang airport. Merpati Nusantara and Sempati Air have several flights daily ($27, 25 min).

The jump off point for the Gili Islands is Bangsal, north of Senggigi. You can take a public minibus to Pemenang ($1.50), and then hire a *cidomo,* a horse-drawn cart, for the short remaining trip to Bangsal harbor (35¢). Or you can just charter a minibus to take you directly to Bangsal (maybe $8–$15).

At the harbor, book your passage at the official ticket booth on one of the regular 20-seat boats to Gili Air (50¢), Gili Meno (60¢), or Gili Trawangan (75¢). These leave regularly in the early morning and late afternoon, and at other times when they fill up. You can also buy a one-way charter to Gilis Air (20 min, $6); Meno (30 min, $7); or Trawangan (45 min, $9).

DIVE OPERATORS

While there are several dive operators on Gili Trawangan and a couple on Gili Meno, they are not particularly reliable. We suggest taking a good look at their compressors and filters before diving with any of these outfits. It's not worth it to pay less and get bad or questionable air, along with unreliable rental gear. We also strongly discourage taking a dive course from any of the operators on the islands: we have encountered instructors with fake certifications who were unqualified.

It's much better to book with one of the operators from Senggigi, even if it's more expensive and requires a fairly long boat ride (an hour or so).

Albatross Jl. Raya Senggigi, near the Lina Hotel. PO Box 1066, Mataram 83010, Lombok. ☎ 93399; fax: 93388. This is currently the best dive operator on Lombok, under the direction of owner-manager Andy Chan. He has found several new dive locations just north of the Gilis, so ask about those.

Plan your dive itinerary with Andy, who will come up with spots for your level of experience. All-inclusive two-dive trips to the Gilis, $55 (min 2 people, price includes BC and regulator, if needed), night dive $35.

Baronang Divers Pak Sjahrul Nasution, P.O. Box 24, Mataram, Lombok. ☎ 27793. He keeps his dive boat at Teluk Nara, just off the main road from Senggigi going north along the coast and shortly before Bangsal. The man might be hard to find, but he gives good service at very reasonable prices.

Baruna A branch of this large, Bali-based diving operator is located at the Senggigi Beach

Hotel. ☎ 93210, ext. 8412. Two dives in the Senggigi area, $50, two dives off the Gilis, $65. To both prices add $10 for BC and regulator, plus $5 for a wet suit, the latter usually not necessary.

Rinjani Divers At Senggigi's Lombok Intan Laguna Hotel. ☎ 93090; fax: 93185. Two-dive day trips to Gili Air, Trawangan, Tanjung Bonita $65 (2 people minimum); further away, to Gili Petangan or Pantai Karibu, $75.

Komodo

Nusa Tenggara Timur (NTT)

There are two ways of diving this relatively unexplored region; either by live-aboard vessels based outside of the immediate Komodo area, or by shore-based diving through one of the two dive operators in Labuanbajo. Live-aboard trips are best arranged in Bali, with the best known operation being **Grand Komodo Tours and Travel.** Their 20m *Komodo Plus* specializes in Komodo diving and pioneered many sites in the area (for other Bali-based live-aboards, see "Diving Operators" page 273). The other option is to make your own way to Labuanbajo and dive with either the **Bajo Beach Diving Club** or **Komodo Kalypso Dive Center.**

Theoretically, you can fly from Bali to Labuanbajo, via Bima (eastern Sumbawa), every day at 9:20am ($98). In practice, however, the Bima-Labuanbajo air connection is very unreliable, and you would be better off debarking in Bima ($70 one way), taking a minibus to Sape (2 hrs, $1 public bus, $18 charter), and then boarding the ferry to Komodo and Labuanbajo (9–11 hours to Labuanbajo, departs daily from Sape at 8am, $6). To make this early morning connection, one can either overnight in Sape ($5 for very basic room at one of the local *losmens*) or spend the night in Bima and catch the 5am minibus to Sape.

A much more comfortable, quicker, and less expensive alternative is to board one of the Pelni oceanliners which service Labuanbajo from Bali, Ujung Pandang or Kupang/Waingapu. 1st and 2nd class cabins on the brand-new *Tilongkabila* are as comfortable as any hotel room, the meals excellent, and divers carrying heavy gear needn't worry about overweight baggage. The *Tilongkbila* makes the 14 hour voyage to Labuanbajo from Ujung Pandang every other Sunday ($48 first class, $30 second) and from Denpasar to Labuanbajo every other Wednesday (24 hours, $78 first class, $60 second). The Pelni ships *Kelimutu* (from Denpasar, every other Tuesday and from Kupang every other Friday) and *Tatamailau* (from Denpasar, every third Tuesday) also service Labuanbajo. Check with any Pelni office for schedules and tickets.

Although diving is possible in Komodo year-round, the best visibility is during the dry season, April to October.

DIVE OPERATORS

Grand Komodo Tours & Travel Main office: Jl. Bypass Ngurah Rai 9, Sanur. P.O. Box 3477, Denpasar 80034, Bali. ☎ (0361) 287166; fax: (0361) 287165. In Bima: Jl. Sukarno Hatta, Bima NTB. ☎ (0374) 42018; fax: 42812.

This experienced outfit runs diving around Komodo on two newly-built live-aboards, the *Komodo Plus I* and *II*, both 20m traditional boats built in the Bugis style. Accomodations on the ship are simple, but comfortable. The *Komodo Plus I* sleeps up to 18 people in a large central cabin (non-private bunks), while the *KP II* has private cabins for 12 divers. Groups fly directly from Bali to Bima, Sumbawa, where they are met by Grand Komodo and driven overland to Sape, where the boats are docked.

The minimum dive package available is 6 days/5 nights and costs $900/person, which covers everything except airfare to Bima and drinks. Additional days run $130. Either boat can also be chartered ($400-450/day for boat only-food, guides,transfers extra), and an excellent combination for a small group is to charter the *Komodo Plus* (*I* or *II*) and hire Bali-based dive guide Wally Siagan—who did much of the initial pioneering for Grand Komodo, and who currently is familiar with almost 50 sites in the Komodo area—to come along as a guide. Contact Grand Komodo for details.

Grand Komodo also runs shorter tours to Komodo/Rinca for dragon-viewing. 3 day tour, all inclusive: $290/person (from Bima), 4 day tour: $330/person.

Komodo Kalypso Dive Center (Varanus Tours and Travel). Main office: Jl. Yos Sudarso 10, P.O. Box 3, Labuanbajo 86554 Flores, NTT. ☎ (0385) 41007, fax: 41202. In Jakarta: Varanus Tours and Travel, Jl. Pulonangka Timur III C/3 Jakarta 13260. ☎ /fax: (021) 4716360.

Owner/guide Pak Linus has been running dive tours in the Komodo area since 1992, and is very knowledgeable about diving in the area. This is a small, but safe and friendly operation, with 2 compressors, 26 tanks, 7 sets of rental gear and a twin-engined fiberglass speedboat (the fastest in Labuanbajo).

Day trips, including full gear, 2 dives, guide and lunch box run from $75/person for the closer reefs (Sabolan, Bididari, etc) up to $100/person for diving around Komodo and Rinca (using local wooden boats instead attracts a discount of $10/person). Expect a discount for multiple-day diving as well. Pak Linus is very flexible with his packages.

A highly recommended option is to charter either the speedboat or a local boat for several days, rent a compressor, and explore this exciting region, which boasts an amazingly diverse array of marine habitats. If you choose this adventure, consult with Pak Subianto or Pak Yitno at the PHPA Komodo National Park Office in Labuanbajo first. They both have extensive knowledge of the area and can recommend not only dive sites, but secluded, inviting bays in which to overnight.

Pak Linus can also arrange night dives and land-based tours to Komodo/Rinca or Western Flores. He requires 4-5 hours to fully arrange dive trips or you can book ahead.

Bajo Beach Diving Club Hotel Bajo, Jl. Yos Sudarso, Labuanbajo, Flores, NTT. ☎ (0385) 41008; fax: 41009. Owner Pak Hendrik Chandra runs a similar operation and is located just down the road from Varanus. His dive packages (2 person minimum) include gear, 2 tanks, guide and lunch, and also vary in cost depending on distance: Bidadari, $50/person; Sabolan/Sebayur, $60/person; Komodo/Rinca, $75/person. His package prices are based on local diesel boat transport, although for a slight price increase he can arrange for a speed boat.

The club has at its disposal 2 compressors, 30 tanks and 10 full sets of dive gear. Large groups of 10 persons or more receive complimentary meals and lodging at the Hotel Bajo, otherwise, expect to pay $36D, (AC, no meals). Pak Hendrik requires a full day to arrange dive trips, so it is best to book ahead.

Should you want to take a break from diving, Pak Hendrik has land-based tour packages. One includes a cave (*Batu Cermin*), a whip fight and an area where there is petrified wood. $50–$125/person depending on group size.

PHPA Komodo National Park Office Labuanbajo. Although not a dive operator, the rangers at the PHPA office, especially Pak Yitno, are very familiar with the area and are a great source of information regarding unknown dive sites, dangerous current areas, places to camp, etc. Two sites within the park have developed camping facilities with a cafeteria and night-time electricity: Loh Buaya on Rinca and Loh Liang on Komodo (both $5S, $7D, $10T). PHPA plans to award a single dive concession to a yet-to-be determined dive operator to run expeditions out of the park itself in the near future.

—updated by Mark Erdmann

Maumere

Flores, Nusa Tenggara Timur (NTT)

Maumere is the visitor's center of Flores, offering the best accommodations and infrastructure for tourists. Both of the dive clubs are close to each other, 12 km east of Maumere town and 10 km east of the airport. At the airport you can buy taxi coupons (approx. $5 to the resorts) while you wait for your luggage. The Sao Resort has transportation for guests with reservations.

Merpati schedules daily flights between Maumere and Bali ($97); Bima, Sumbawa ($52); and Kupang ($33). Flights to Ujung Pandang, Sulawesi ($60) run three days/week. Connections to Surabaya and Jakarta through Bali.
Merpati Jl. Don Thomas 18, ☎ (0382) 21342.

DIVE OPERATORS

Flores Sao Resort (Sao Wisata) Jl. Sawista, Maumere, ☎ (0382) 21555; fax: (0382) 21666. (Neither phone nor fax is particularly reliable.) For bookings and arrangements, contact their Jakarta office: Sao Wisata, Room 6B, 2nd Floor, Hotel Borobudur Inter-Continental, Jl. Lapangan Banteng Selatan, Jakarta 10710. ☎ (021) 370333 or 3805555, ext. 78222 or 78223; fax: (021) 359741.

This resort is a two-star hotel with a dive operation. All inclusive (including accommodations) 4 night/3 day (2 diving days) packages, $260–$320 S; $465–$530 D; extension days $80-$100 S; $150–$170 D, prices varying with type of room. 7 day/6 night packages $480–$630 S, $940–$1,100 D, extension days $75–$95 S, $145–$165 D. Full equipment rental $30. For guests at the resort, $55 for a two-dive day, including boat use. Four-day dive courses $400 with CMAS certification. The operation has 5 compressors, 94 tanks and 20 sets of rental gear. Marcus Koli Tolang, the man in charge of diving, plans to start the Panca Sila Dive Club for expats and locals.

Land tours: Half day to weaving village, $23–$35; full day to Keli Mutu $35–$45; Kelimutu overnight tour $65–$75, prices per person, depending on total number joining tour. (Add 15.5% tax and service to all prices).

Seaworld Club (Waiara Cottages) P.O. Box 3, Maumere, Flores, NTT, ☎ (0382) 21570. 38 rooms and bungalows. Lunch ($4), dinner ($5) available. $10–$25S, $15–$30D including breakfast.

Daily dive rates, with accommodations, $70–$80 S, $75–85 D; diving only, $60 for two-tank day with boat. 6 day/6 night dive packages, $420–$480S, $390–$450 D. BC/regulator rental, $15/day. Seaworld's one dive boat was out of order when we checked in 1993 (as it was when we checked in 1990 and 1991) so we could not assess their operation.

Various land tours available, including Kelimutu (minimum, 4 persons) $15 per head.

Sumba

Nusa Tenggara Timur, NTT

Currently, the only diving available on Sumba is through a luxury resort on the southwest coast, due south of the West Sumba capital of Waikabubak. **Sumba Reef Lodge** P.T. Indonesia Adventure Sport, P.O. Box 1018, Tuban, Bali. ☎/fax: (0361) 731172. When completed, this luxury resort will have 23 villas, 7 of them with private swimming pools! (There is a quite wonderful, large pool already). The average room rate is $250/night.

Current prices for diving: two boat dives, unlimited tanks for beach diving, accommodation and food runs $250/person per day. Game fishing is the same, and surfing runs $125/person per day. For trips south to the camp at Rua Nature Reserve, including two dives, accommodation and food, $150/person per day.

Kupang, Roti, Alor

Nusa Tenggara Timur (NTT)
Telephone code 0391

Kupang is a large town, the capital of the Nusa Tenggara Timur province, and has four one-star hotels and a good range of more moderately priced accommodations. English is spoken at most places.

Kupang's El Tari airport is 15 km east of downtown Kupang. A taxi from the airport costs $4. Try to get one to yourself or you could end up running all over town while others are dropped off.

Kupang receives daily Merpati flights from Jakarta ($200), Bali ($103), Ujung Pandang ($85), and Maumere ($40) among other cities in the region. Also, international flights from Darwin, Australia, land here. **Merpati** Jl. Kosasih No. 2. ☎ (0391) 32662, 33654, 33205.

Pitoby Water Sports Jl. Eltari No. 19, Kupang, Timor. Mailing address: P.O. Box 1120, Kupang NTT. Diving hotline, 24-hr, ☎/fax: 24833.

This operation is part of Pitoby Travel Agency, an efficient agency and the biggest in this part of Indonesia. Diving operations—"Dive Kupang"—are run by an Australian father and son team, divemaster Graeme Whitford and PADI-certified dive instructor Donovan Whitford. The Whitford's offer all-inclusive packages, beginning with a pick-up at El Tari airport.

Dive Kupang several basic packages, ranging from 4 days/3 nights to 11 days/10 nights. Here's a sample:

Kupang Bay 4 days/3 nights (5 dives), $245; 6 days/5 nights (9 dives) $345; 8 days/7 nights (11 dives) $595.

Roti 5 days/4 nights (3 dives) $375; 7 days/6 nights (7 dives) $575.

Kupang and Roti 8 days/7 nights (10 dives) $645; 11 days/10 nights (15 dives), $895.

Alor 8 days/7nights, 10 dives, $645 (Note: This does not include the round-trip Merpati flight to Kalabahi, Alor, which runs $100.)

All packages include one night dive. 10% discount for divers who bring their own gear. Accommodations and full board (at the Pitoby Lodge for Kupang diving, see below) included, only extra is booze.

These prices are based on a group of four divers (add 50% for fewer in the group), but if you arrive only with your dive buddy Dive Kupang will likely (but it's not guaranteed) find another couple to join you. All tours include a "cultural show," two if you go to Roti. The agency takes care of everything, beginning with picking you up at the airport and ending with seeing you on your plane back home.

Client-booked or "walk-ins" can have two day dives, including transfers and lunch, for $75 ($50 w/own gear); single day dive, $45 ($30 w/own gear). Group discounts possible. There are also non-diving tours for snorkelers.

Pitoby Lodge Jl. Kosasih 13, ☎ 32910. 12 twin rooms and 3 shared bathrooms. One "suite" has its own bathroom. Downtown location, clean and pleasant atmosphere, lots of nice woven cloths and terrible wood carvings for sale. A good restaurant features seafood, Italian and Indonesian food. Lobster ($12.50/kilo) is available with notice. The western food is excellent, the Indonesian dishes, so-so. Room rates (if you're not on a package): $7.50–$15 S, $10–$20 D.

5 Sulawesi PRACTICALITIES

Sulawesi is a rugged, forested volcanic island in north-central Indonesia. The island sends one of its strange, flailing peninsulas reaching northeast, and this is where the developed dive sites are: the Bunaken group near Manado, the capital of North Sulawesi, the Lembeh Strait on the east coast of the peninsula, north of the port town of Bitung, and the Sangihe and Talaud island groups, stretching to the north. Still unexplored sites off Selayar and the Tukang Besi archipelago, and the Togian Islands in south and central Sulawesi remain to be explored.

Prices in US dollars. S = Single; D = Double; T = Triple; AC = Air-conditioning.

Manado Area

Telephone code 0431

Manado—the entry point to diving North Sulawesi—is a large city and is well-connected by air to the rest of Indonesia. The Dr. Sam Ratulangi airport Airport is 7 km outside of town, and taxi coupons to just about anywhere in town cost $3–$4. If you reserve ahead with one of the dive operators, they will meet you at the airport. Airport information, ☎ 52117 or 60865.

GETTING THERE

Because of the Garuda/Merpati monopoly on flights, in the past it was a long and expensive proposition to get to Manado. But this is now changing. First Bouraq opened its flight to Manado, followed by Sempati. But still no international flights were allowed to land, except for a short-lived and mysteriously ended series of flights from Guam.

Then Manado began to open its skies to international flights with Bouraq's flights to Davao City (Philippines), being the first step. Now there is a direct, twice a week, 3.5-hour run from/to Singapore by SilkAir, the daughter airline of Singapore Airlines. There were also rumors of flights from Taiwan, Japan, and Korea. If these come to pass, the attractions of North Sulawesi will be appreciated by many more visitors.

Garuda Jl. Diponegoro 15, ☎ 64535, 52154; fax: 62242. Open 8am to 4pm weekdays, Sat. 7:30am–12:30pm, Sun. 8am–12 noon. Airbus flights daily to Ujung Pandang ($153), Denpasar ($254) and Jakarta ($345).

Merpati Jl. Sudirman 132, ☎ 64027, 64028, 81512. Same hours as Garuda. Ambon, 4 weekly flights ($167); Bali, daily ($254) continuing to Jakarta ($414); also daily to Gorontalo, ($70) and Ternate ($73); four flights weekly to Naha, near Tahuna, Sagihe Besar ($79); twice weekly to Sorong ($158); twice weekly to Mangole ($90); twice weekly to Melanguane on Karakelong Island in the Talaud group ($107); once weekly to Palu ($108); and once weekly to Poso ($120).

Bouraq Jl. Sarapung 27, ☎ 62675, 62757. Daily flights to Balikpapan ($143), Banjarmasin ($192), Jakarta ($324), and Palu ($108); four times weekly to Gorontalo ($50) and Tarakan ($222); three times a week to Ujung Pandang ($144); twice weekly to Ternate ($48); and twice weekly to Davao City, ($240 one-way, $480 RT, or $180 one-way, $314 RT with advance purchase).

Sempati Kawanus City Hotel, Jl. Sam Ratulangi 1. ☎ 51612; fax: 61205. Open 8am to 6pm, Sun. 9 am to 4 pm. Six weekly flights to Surabaya ($314) continuing to Jakarta ($414) and ($186 extra) to Singapore. Also flies to Ujung Pandang ($184), Medan $528), and Balikpapan ($221).

SilkAir Jl. Sarapung No. 5. ☎ 63744, 63844; fax: 53841. The direct singapore lfight route is welcome particularly by divers, as it is more convenient, less time-consuming and less exhausting than transferring through Jakarta. Punctual flight schedule, reliable reservations and bookings, and proficient service. Twice weekly to Singapore ($445 one-way, $742 RT).

LOCAL TRANSPORTATION

Any of the dive resorts will be able to arrange some kind of transport for you if you want to sightsee or travel anywhere. There are also several forms of public transportation around Manado.

Oplet. Travel around the city is by *oplet*, tiny minivans one enters by the rear. They run regular routes, and the destination is displayed on a sign in the front. The driver will stop for you anywhere along the route, just flag them down as you would a taxi. When you get to your stop, pull the cord inside (or bang on the window behind the driver if the cord is broken, as it often is) and the vehicle will stop sharply. The fare is Rp250 (10¢). Larger minibuses (*mikrolet*) also run regular routes. These cost the same, but carry more people and one enters on the side.

The problem with this form of transportation (in addition to the fact that they are cramped) is making sure you get in the right one. If you are confident you have gotten past this hurdle, don't be overly alarmed if the little truck veers off the main road and starts heading down a tiny back alley somewhere. Passengers often make special requests to be dropped off at their doorsteps.

Taxis. Two types of *taksi* operate in Manado. One is unmarked with no meter, and you must negotiate a price to your particular destination. The other type are metered white sedans with signs on their roofs. The four taxi companies are: **Indra Kelana Taxi Company,** ☎ 52033, **Dian Taksi,** ☎ 51010, **Merit** ☎ 61195, 61465, and **Cender** ☎ 64422. The Merit fare for the first km is Rp900 and Rp450 for subsequent kms; Dian taxis run Rp 700 for the first km and Rp400 for each additional km. Indra and Cender fares vary considerably, depending on who's driving and what adjustments have been made on the meters—if there is one in the taxi. Your best bet is to negotiate the fare before you get into the car. Some drivers will try to take advantage of visitors, especially on night tours of the town, so be on your guard!

Charters. One can charter any of the above forms of transport. Empty *oplets* can be chartered for around $1.60/hr (no minimum), and *mikrolets* for a bit more. Taxis can be hired by the hour, around $2.75/hr (3-hr minimum around town, 5-hr minimum out of town).

TOURIST SERVICES

Communications

Post office (*Kantor Pos*) Jl. Sam Ratulangi 23, 5 minutes walk south of Kawanua City Hotel: 8am–8pm, Mon.–Fri.; to 6 pm, Sat. and Sun. **Telephone office** (*Perumtel*) Jl. Sam Ratulangi between the Kawanua City Hotel and the post office (opposite side of the street). Open 24 hrs.

Photo Processing

There are many shops in Manado and the dive outfits can take your film in for you. If you are taking care of this yourself, we recommend these three services: **Angkasa Color Photo Service** Jl. Yos Sudarso 20, ☎ 62467. One-day slide service. **Fuji Star Plaza** Jl. Sam Ratulangi 203. ☎ 63469. Probably the most proficient in photo procesing in Manado. Good color reproduction and a professional choice of camera equipment. **Modern Photo Film Co** Fuji Image Plaza, Jl. Wenang Permai, Bl. J/4, between Jumbo Supermarket and the central square. ☎ 68226.

Bookstores

Borobudur has a resonable choice of English, and German dictionaries, English language Indonesia travel books, and a good selection of postcards. **Jumbo Supermarket,** Jl. Letjen. Suprapto 1 (☎ 63236) gets regular supplies of *Asian Diver* magazine and has a good stock of Rudie Kuiter's *Tropical Reef-Fishes of the Western Pacific—Indonesia And Adjacent Waters,* Periplus postcards, and the English-language daily, *Jakarta Post.* **President,** located in the center of town (in the theater complex) has a selection of regional maps. The **Kawanua City Hotel** receives Time magazine, although a bit late.

PT Serimpi–Divex, located in the Wenang district, about 50m from the Plaza complex are the regional distributors for *Asian Diver* magazine and stocks Periplus postcards. Free magazine delivery within Manado. The first *Manado Diver's Log* is now available. The log book is designed for usage with PADI dive tables, good for 100 dives, $10. Contact Deby, ☎ 51123, 52123, fax: 67667.

Tours and Guides

These can be arranged through the dive clubs, or at a travel agency or some of the hotels. Tours available include the popular day trip through the Minahasa area ($30), Tomohon and the crater lake of the Mahawu volcano ($25), and the much less frequent jaunt, with 4-wheel-drive vehicle, through a section of the Tangkoko–Batuangus–Dua Saudara Nature Reserve ($45). Prices based on a minimum of two clients. **North Sulawesi Tourism Office** Easy to find, just beyond the Garuda Indonesia office on Jl. Diponegoro. ☎ 51723, 51835, fax: 52730. Open 7am–2pm, Mon-Fri. Drs. Gromang and his staff will be happy to attend to any traveller or visitor seeking assistance, information or advice concerning tourism in Sulawesi. Maps and brochures of the North Sulawesi region are available upon request.

DIVE OPERATORS

Currently, there are several dive operators taking divers to the Bunaken group. For serious diving, we suggest booking a package—including accommodations and board—with one of the dive clubs.

Barracuda Molas Beach, Dusun II, about 10 kms

north of Manado. ☎ 54288, 54279; fax: 64848.

Barracuda, established in 1989, offers chalet-type accommodations on a small hill, the only one of the three resorts that has a view. It has the same quiet charm as Murex. They also have a glass-bottom boat, on-boat dive pro-files; the larger craft are equipped with radio. They also carry oxygen onboard during their longer trips or for the shipwreck dives. Their boats are new, and in good shape: three large dive boats, and 6 dive boats, each with a 80 hp engine. They also have a glass-bottom sight-see-ing and dive boat—which carries up to 28—with two 80 hp engines. PADI courses available include (training and certification): open water ($395), advanced ($145), rescue ($300), divemaster ($450).

Day rate (2 dives, tanks, weights, boat, lunch)—$65, min. 2 persons. Sightseeing, $30; snorkeling, $40. Package rate, including full room and board and two dives, $80–$95/day. Night dive, $20 extra. 6 dive masters, 10 dive guides, 2 instructors. 100 tanks, 30 BCs, 25 regulators, and 8 UW lights. Barracuda offers dives off Bangka Island, at no extra charge. They take you there by catamaran (2.5 hrs) and bring you back overland from Likupang (1.5 hrs).

Accommodations: 21 double rooms$25–$35 bungalow with fan, $35–$42 bungalow with AC. Good seafood restaurant.

Murex (Manado Underwater Explorations). Jl. Sudirman 28. P.O. Box 236, Manado 95123. ☎ 66280, ☎/fax: 52116. European representative: DIVEX Indonesia, P.O. Box 5352, 30053 Hannover, Germany. ☎ (49 511) 647-6129; fax: (49 511) 647-6120. About 10 km south of Manado.

This is the smallest, quietest and most "intimate" of the resorts, with very nice land-scaping featuring lotus pools. It has the best boats, and the only dive guides to use computers and safe second stages. It is also located fur-thest from the dive sites. Murex is run by a per-sonal medical doctor and dive instructor, who divides his time between several occupations. Dr. Hanny Batuna, the owner, pioneered diving in the area, and has the only live-aboard, the *Serenade*, which runs regular cruises to the Sangihe–Talaud Islands.

Quite good, wide diving boats. The ride from here to Bunaken is a bit longer than that from the Molas-based clubs, and the boats cut through more open water (thus waves and spray). Good use of space on boats for tank and equipment storage and suiting up.

Sulawesi 5

Accommodations: 19 rooms in both old-fashioned and modern cottages $25–$30 fan, $30–$35 standard AC, $35–$40 superior AC. Day rate (2 dives, tanks, weights, boat, lunch), $70/person, minimum 3 in group. Package rate (double occupancy room, meals, 2 dives)—$100/person. Dives to the Lembeh Strait or Bangka Island, $20 extra, as it's a lot further from this site. 60 tanks, 6 BCs, 12 regulators. Medical doctor and NAUI instructor Hanny Batuna offers a 40-hour dive course leading to NAUI certification ($250). 8 dive guides, 5 divemasters, and 2 instructors.

Manado Diving Center (MDC) Jl. Bethesda 75. P.O. Box 11, Manado 95115. ☎ 62880, 66622, 65001; fax: 63857.

MDC has been around for several years and offers dive tours, hotel accommodations, as well as national and international package tours. They have bungalow accommodation on Bunaken Island at reasonable rates. 3 PADI divemasters, 5 dive guides and 1 instructor for an open-water dive course.

Accommodations: 15 rooms. $17.50–$21 standard, $47.50 suite.

Dive packages (2 dives, tanks, weights, boat, dive guide, full board)—$86S, $75D standard; $120S, $100D suite. All rooms with AC, TV and phone. Additional third dive or night dive, $20. Snorkeling tour for min. 3 people, $35. Tour of Bunaken island for min. 4 people, $25; Minahasa land tour, $50.

Nusantara Diving Centre (NDC) Molas Beach. P.O. Box 1015, Manado 95242. ☎ 63988, 60638; fax: 60368, 63688.

Run by Loky Herlambang, who with Hanny Batuna pioneered diving here. Devoted staff, some of whom have been working for NDC for 15 years. New rental equipment, BCs and regulators, plus trained personnel to service there. Located close to the sea, but the beach is mangrove and mud. NDC has 11 boats, 12 outboards (40 hp), 25 guides, and 140 tanks.

Accommodations: 43 rooms. $7.50–$10 economy, $115–$20 standard fan, $35–$40 AC.

Day rate (2 dives, tanks, weights, boat, lunch), min. two persons, $60. Package rates—2 dives, room, meals—$70–$100, depending on room. 6 BCs available for rent ($7.50/ day), and 6 regulators ($7.50/day). Night dive (after two day dives) $20 extra. Snorkeling or sightseeing available. Open water dive course (PADI-SSI), $500. No pool, all beginning underwater instruction takes place on a shallow reef.

Reservations recommended, especially for July and August. Mastercard, Visa and American Express accepted, with at least one day's notice before checkout.

Novotel Manado Jl. Sam Ratulangi No. 22. ☎ 51245, 51174; fax: 63545. All marine activities operate under the supervision of two Australian dive professionals with PADI Instructor ratings. Novotel will operate 8 high-powered

fiberglass dive boats, each with a capacity of 20 divers, plus two large passenger vessels (one for 100 passengers, the other for 200 passengers) for sightseeing cruises around the marine park. The largest vessel is ideal for special functions, banquets, and parties. A semi-submersible viewer boat, Aqua Scoop, with a capacity of 40, affords tours around the marine park. 5 divemasters, 30 dive guides, 2 instructors. Open water, advance, rescue, divemaster, and specialty courses offered.

Accommodations: Four-star hotel with all the amenities, including a swimming pool with a magnificent view of Bunaken Island, fitness center and cauna, and seafood restaurant. Jet-ski and windsurfing rentals, daily trips on semi-submersible viewer, fishing trips, and land excursions and sightseeing tours available. $105 standard, $120 superior.

Dive packages: 4 nights in four-star hotel, 4 days buffet breakfast, 3 days diving (2 dives/day), 1 night dive optional—$379, tanks, weights, boat, dive guide, airport transfer. Other dive package arrangements are available upon request. Additional third dive/night dive, $40. Glassbottom boat tour, $38.

Paradise Beach Hotel & Resort Desa Maen, Likupang. ☎ 68200, 68868, 68222, 68880; fax: 62200, 64888. 32 km from Sam Ratulangi International Airport at the northern tip of North Sulawesi. Opened in March 1996, Paradise Beach Hotel promises to integrate 5-star comfort and service with a philosophy to protect and enhance the environment. Set in 450 hectares of unspoiled tropical jungle with 2.5 kms of white sand beaches, clear seas and unique sea gardens.

The hotel runs joint ventures with Eurodivers. The PADI-affiliated dive operator is run by instructor, Jason, who has just stocked his dive shop with 40 tanks, 2 new Bauer compressors, Scubapro wetsuits, 20 Sea Quest jackets, 30 sets of regulators, and several Aladdin pro-dive computers. Jason has surveyed the area and has added 30 new dive sites on the map around the Likupang, Bangka and Pulau Lembeh area.

An impressive, tidy and well-organized outfit. Dive courses available: open water ($425), advanced ($325), rescue ($340), divemaster ($883), assistant instructor ($904).

Accommodations: 320 rooms and luxury suites. 3 restaurants, business center, tennis courts, watersports, diving center and golf course. $130–$150 standard, $250 deluxe, $350–$550 suite.

Day rate (includes tanks, weights, dive guide for lagoon and house reef dives): Single dive, $45; 5 dives, $210; 10 dives, $400; 15 dives, $550; six day no limit (including night dive), $420. Group rate for a minimum of 6 divers available, but must register 30 days before arrival. Fishing tour, $400.

Tirta Satwa Diving Center P.O. Box 1082, Manado. ☎ 56954, 56314; fax: 65164. Offers CMAS courses. Scuba dive tour for minimum 2 divers, 2 dives plus boat, tanks, weights, and guide, $50. Additional third dive or night dive, $30. Economy bungalows on Bunaken, $25S, $30D. Bungalows on Siladen, $10S, $20D.

LIVE-ABOARDS

Liburan Adventure Diving Tours P.O. Box 1449, Manado 95001. ☎ /fax: 69849. European reservations through DIVEX Indonesia, P.O. Box 5352, 30053 Hanover, Germany, ☎ /fax: (49) 5043-3459.

This new live-aboard boat started operations in June 1995 and offers dive tour cruises throughout the North Sulawesi and Maluku areas. This 16m boat has a cruising speed of 13 knots and offers accommodations for 10 divers. The boat is equipped with marine radio, sonar GPS, Bauer compressor, a new range of equipment (US Divers & Sea Quest), and 12 liter aluminium dive tanks. There are two toilets andshowers, a small conveniently equipped kitchen and a spacious upper deck. The food on board is excellent and there's always plenty of it. Cold beer and other beverages are available at moderate prices.

All diving activities are under the supervision of Henry Maulany, a master scuba diver who can tailor your diver excursions in these areas.

Package rates per person per day (all including tanks, weights, divemaster, and hotel/airport transfer): Bunaken Marine Park—3 dives, lunch, $85 (min. 2 divers); extra dive $20. Bunaken Marine Park with accommodation on the Liburan—no limit diving, all meals, $110 (min. 4 divers); Sangihe–Talaud Islands, Biaro, Siau, Togian Islands, or Maluku (Halmahera, Ternate, Ambon, Banda Naira, Saparua)—7 days, accommodation and all meals on board, no limit, additional land/island excursions, $145 (min. 6 divers).

Serenade Contact Murex for information and reservations. The *Serenade* is fully air-conditioned and has 7 twin sharing rooms. She has a depth sounder and radar, carries 35–40 tanks, and has two Bauer compressors on board. She is good for 8–10 knots. Tours the North Sulawesi district, including Bunaken Marine Park, Bangka, Biaro, Taliwei, and features spectacular dive sites around the remote Sangihe-Talaud islands. The package rates per person per day $165, includes accommodations in a twin-shared cabin, full board meals, no limit diving, airport pick-up, tanks, weights, and guides.

New in Dr. Batuna's program is a smaller craft called the *Arlena,* which accommodates 4 divers, and has a cabin shower and an outdoor shower. Tour operations are similar to those of the *Serenade*, and rates are somewhat cheaper, about $125/person per day. Chartering the *Arlena* is more of a bargain for a smaller group.

ACCOMMODATIONS

Bastiaano's Island Cottages Bunaken Island Jl. Kol. Sugiono 31, Manado. ☎ 63417, 67648, 53566; fax: 63629. Any diver taking a lunch break on the Liang Beach of Bunaken Island will surely "discover" these cottages. Located in the heart of the marine park, all cottages are sited at the beachfront with an exceptional view of the lagoon and Manado Tua volcano on the horizon. Conveniently equipped, carefully landscaped. Sightseeing tours, open sea tuna fishing, and boat charter can be arranged. Diving rates are $65–$80/person, including 2 dives, tanks, weights, boat, and guide, minimum 2 divers. $20 for room, full board, coffee and tea. For guests wishing to stay more than 4 nights, free boat transportation from Manado to Bunaken can be arranged.

Small local passenger boats motor to Bunaken, usually in the early morning or late afternoon, with passage costing about $1.50. These boats leave from Kuala Jenkey, between the bridge and the mouth of the Tondano River and occasionally from the harbor area near the fish-auction market.

Manado Beach Hotel Tasik Ria. ☎ 67001; fax: 67007. This four-star hotel lies 20 km south of Manado, just beyond Mokupa. An Australian-managed dive center and marina have just set up shop next door and will run joint diving operations with the hotel beginning in June. $110–$650.

Mokupa Palace Cottages Jl. Trans-Sulawesi, Mokupa, Kec. Tombariri, Minahasa, Manado. ☎ 54277, 54272, fax: 54277. Reservations in Europe: DIVEX Indonesia, see Murex above. 14 rooms. Small resort located 20 km south of Manado with an overwhelming view of the Minahasa mountains in the back and a small beach cove sheltered by mangroves and palm trees in the front. Several small lotus ponds, scenic beach front with view over Manado Bay. Fully AC, spacious bathrooms, plus separate tiled room for storing and rinsing dive equipment. The house reef is excellent for beginning divers and snorkeling, and there are still several unexplored reefs in the vicinity. Swimming pool, tennis court. sightseeing and snorkeling tours available; diving operations commence during the course of the high season. $40–$50 standard, $55–$65 superior.

Ranopaso Cottages, Restaurant & Hot Springs Koya Tondano, Minahasa 95618. ☎ (0436) 21585, 21600; fax: (0436) 21585. For a refreshing change from dive touring adventures. Ranopaso is located approximately 3 km from the Minahasan town of Tondano, in the midst of traditional rice fields. Because of the altitude, the climate is quite cool, so it may be advisable to bring along some extra T-shirts and long sleeves for the evenings. The hot water springs are renown for their healing effect of skin diseases, rheumatism and similar illnesses. For the healthy diver, it revitalizes the circulatory system. However, it is not recommended to take a hot bath after diving, and divers should consider going to Ranopaso the day after diving because of the altitude. A hot bath costs $1.50/person/hour.

The resort location is an ideal starting point for Minahasa excursions. Lake Tondano is just a walk around the corner and offers a spectacular view of the former volcanic lake, traditional fishing villages, and a neverending plateau of rice fields. $15–$40, not including tax and service.

Tagaroa Seaside Cottages c/o Mrs. Gerry Lolong, P.O. Box 1068, Manado. ☎ /fax: 61100, fax: 67667. 6 rooms. This resort is probably one of the smallest of its kind in the Manado area, however, it is amongst the top ranking for landscaping, innovative bungalow design and resort location. Tucked away behind the Tanawangko hills, approximately 28 km south of Manado, the resort offers an intimate atmosphere and one of the most captivating scenic views of the surrounding rain forests and the Bunaken National Marine Park. Located virtually on top of the Arakan Wawontulap Marine Park, divers and snorkelers can encounter a vivacious underwater environment and a good variety of hard and soft corals.

Diving tours range between $75–$100, depending on location and distance, and include 2 dives, tanks, weights, divemaster, and boat, minimum 4 divers. Land tours can be arranged for 3 participants to Minahasa, $30/person, and Tangkoko, $40. Good food and service is standard. $50S, $60D, includes room, full board, airport transfers.

Bitung

Telephone code 0438

Bitung, on the other side of the peninsula from Manado, is North Sulawesi's busiest port. The long, narrow island of Lembeh blocks the weather, protecting the port year-round. Kungkungan Bay Resort is the only dive operator on the east coast of North Sulawesi, and the pioneer of most of the Lembeh Strait sites. There are a few *losmen* in Bitung, but Kungkungan is a self-contained resort, and is not set up for walk on dive customers. If you want to dive the Lembeh Strait, book with Kungkungan.

Kungkungan Bay Resort On a bay of the same name in the village of Tanduk Rusa, about 5 kilometers north of Bitung. Mailing address: P.O.

Box 16, Bitung, Sulawesi Utara, Indonesia. ☎ 30300; fax: 31400. Make reservations through the U.S. office: Staples Ecenbarger, Inc., P.O. Box 5577, Concord, CA 94524. ☎ (510) 8251939, fax: (510) 8250105.

This quiet, beautifully designed resort sits on the site of an old coconut plantation, facing a small bay north of Bitung, in the protected waters of the Lembeh Strait. The suites are spacious, all face the water, and have comfortable porches. A large lobby/restaurant, built out over the water, is the center of activities. The operation has one dive boat, several dozen tanks and a new Bauer compressor.

Accommodations only: $120S, $140D, plus tax and service charge. Day rate for 2 dives, lunch, boat, tanks, weights, and guide, $80. Additional third dive/night dive, $45.

Packages: 7 nights/8 days ($1,565S, $1156D/person; 3 nights/4 days ($631S, $455D/person); additional days ($$233S, $175D/person). Prices include beach-front suite, 2 boat dives a day, all meals, taxes, service charges and transfers. Beach dives are included, at the discretion of the divemaster.
—updated by Michael Smith

Ujung Pandang

Telephone code 0411

DIVE OPERATORS

Makassar Diving Center Jl. Ujung Pandang 3, opposite Fort Rotterdam, ☎ 326056; fax: (c/o Shogun Restaurant) 319842. The manager of MDC, Pak Jeffrey, is also an excellent dive guide and runs a very professional operation.

One day dive trips to any of the dive sites in the Spermonde archipelago range from $50–75/person, depending on distance (minimum 2 divers, including 2 tanks, weight belt, boat, guide and lunch box). The 2 day/1 night trip to Kapoposang (4 dives) are $150/person (3 person minimum, all meals included), with 3 day/2 night trips (6 dives) costing $200/person. Accomodation on this beautiful coconut-fringed island is in a spacious traditional cottage.

Half-day snorkelling/island sightseeing trips run $25/person (minimum 4 people, including snorkel gear, snack box and transportation). For all above packages, a discount of 10–20% is given for larger groups. MDC's well-maintained gear includes, per day, mask, snorkel, fins ($5), BC ($7), regulator ($7). Pak Jeffrey speaks good English.

Caraka Travel Indo Jl. Samalona 12, Ujung Pandang 90174 Sulawesi. ☎ 318877; fax: 318889. Dutch general manager Jan Wezendonk and his assistant Andrea can arrange a wide variety of quality, unique tours throughout Indonesia, including snorkelling/island hopping trips within the Spermonde. They specialize in Sulawesi and can arrange trips anywhere within this little-explored island.

Makassar Gate Beach Hotel Jl. Pasar Ikan 10, Ujung Pandang. ☎ 325791; fax: 316303. The general manager of this hotel, Australian Robert Hotson, is knowledgeable on the reefs of the area and can arrange boat trips to any of the local islands. He also has jet skiis for hire.

Bira/Selayar

There are no organized dive tours of the area at this time, so your best bet is to rent gear and several tanks from the **Makassar Diving Center** in Ujung Pandang, take the 4 hour minibus ride to Bira ($4 public bus, $35 charter), and then charter a wooden boat at Bira ($20-$50/day, depending on size of boat and distance of journey). There are a number of charming little homestays in Bira, and David at **Anda Bungalows** is especially helpful in setting up boat charters (including week-long sailboat voyages around Selayar). On your way back to Ujung Pandang, be sure to stop at Tana Beru (25 km from Bira) to observe the amazing craftsmanship displayed in traditional Pinisi boatbuilding.

Tukang Besi

DIVE OPERATORS

Operation Wallacea Contact: Marine director, Operation Wallacea, 6A Robin Drive, Lew Mansions, Singapore 258264. ☎ (65) 7347693 fax: (65) 7389945. Operation Wallacea offers 2 and 4 week expeditions for divers with a minimum of 20 hours diving experience. No scientific experience necessary. 2 week expeditions cost $1550/person, including boat transfer from Kendari, accomodation,food, and all diving (group discounts available). 4 week expeditions, $2800/person.

Fly to Kendari from Ujung Pandang on board Sempati or Merpati, daily morning flights ($58). Diving platforms include wooden speedboats and the 22m live-aboard *MV Empress,* a very comfortable vessel. In the future, Operation Wallacea may offer day trip diving packages to those intrepid travellers who have made their own way to the Tukang Besi for a few days. Contact the director for more information.

Togian Islands

Getting to the Togians is no small task. One possibility is to hire a minivan with driver from Caraka Travel Indo in Ujung Pandang ($40/day, see Ujung Pandang Practicalities) and make the 20 hour drive to Ampana (the jump-off point for Togian trips), perhaps stopping in Tana Toraja or the Bada Valley in the Sulawesi highlands for sleep and/or cultural sightseeing. From Ampana, catch one of the medium-sized ferries which cross Tomini Bay between Poso and Gorontalo, stopping in the Togians ($5, 4-6 hrs). If coming from Manado,fly ($60, 1 hr) or bus ($10, 12 hrs) to Gorontalo and catch these same ferries to the Togians on their return journey. You can also fly from Ujung Pandang to Palu ($66 one way, daily flights at 9:30 am), and then catch a bus to Ampana ($10, 10 hrs).

The Tomini Bay ferries have several ports of call in the Togians; Wakai is perhaps the best for diving. Local businessman Edi Yusuf and his charming wife Huntje run the Togian Islands Hotel there, and they arrange flexible snorkelling/diving trips throughout the Togians for very reasonable rates. Pak Edi can suggest good dive sites (and warn you of the areas that are damaged from blast fishing) or simply consult the detailed bathymetric chart they have at the hotel and explore your own best hunches—its hard to go wrong.

You can also debark at Ketupat, rumoured to have a small dive operation as well, or try the island of Melenge-the Indonesian nature NGO YABSHI has a station there and may be willing to rent their dive gear.

DIVE OPERATORS

Togian Islands Hotel Wakai, Kabupaten Poso, Sulawesi Tengah. Owner Pak Edi has 4 sets of dive gear, 7 tanks, a compressor and a twin-engined speedboat. He has a standard 1 day diving package that includes gear, 2 tanks, lunchbox and transport by local wooden boat ($32/person, minimum 2 people), but a far better option is to rent the speedboat for the day ($120, driver, fuel and lunch included) , rent gear if necessary, and explore these islands, stopping at your whim.

Rooms in this charming wooden hotel over the water are $8-22D, breakfast included. Ibu Huntje can give you suggestions for nice day walks through the island's forests, home of the elusive *babirusa* (pig-deer).

—*updated by Mark Erdmann*

Donggala

There is a little-known piece of tropical paradise, at Donggala near Palu, in Central Sulawesi—Prinz John's Dive Resort. The setting is idyllic: well-built wood-and-thatch cottages, excellent meals, no electricity or TV, white sand beach, and year-round water sports, including scuba diving. Expert divers can explore the wrecks just off Donggala Harbor. The best one, recently discovered and completely unmolested since it sank, lies on her side at 32–50 meters. The boatman at the Prinz John's can find it.

Prinz John's Dive Resort Just before the end of the road to Tanjung Karang, off a right turn. Booking via the Hotel Central in Palu. 3 bungalows plus 10 rooms. Owner Peter Meroniak is almost always there on weekends. $8–$12.50S, $15–$17.50D, meals included.

All inclusive dive package, $50/day. Wind surfing, $2.50/hour; sailing local traditional boat, $3 for half day, including free fishing with local gear—good chance for tuna. Mask and snorkel rental, $2 per day, fins $2 per day.

Sangalaki

At the time of this writing, Borneo Divers, the pioneers of Sangalaki, had ended their operations there. They may try to restart, however, so if you are interested in diving Sangalaki or Kakaban you might try to contact them.

Borneo Divers Head office: Rooms 401–409 4th Floor, Wisma Sabah, Kota Kinabalu, Sabah Malaysia. ☎ 60 (88) 222226 (5 lines), fax: (88) 221550; Tlx: MA 81644 BDIVER; Cable: BORNEODIVE. Dive shop is on the ground floor of the Wisma Sabah.

Derawan Island

Currently, the only way to dive Sangalaki and Kakaban is with Bhumi Manimbora, a dive resort on Derawan Island.

Bhumi Manimbora Derawan Island. Head office at Jl. Durian 2 in Tanjung Redeb. Mailing address: P.O. Box 170, Tanjung Redeb, Berau 77311, Kalimantan Timur. ☎ (0554) 21770. They also work with a dive shop called Derawan, at the Benakutai Hotel in Balikpapan, East Kalimantan (☎ 542 23522, fax: 542 23893) where clients can make arrangements for travel to and staying at the resort. You can also make reservations from the following places:

Bali: Bali Mandira Cottages Jl. Padma Legian, Kuta, ☎ (0361) 51381.

Surabaya: Jl. Rungkut Industri Raya 10, Wisma Sier Lt. 3, ☎ /Fax: (031) 831189

Tarakan, East Kalimantan: Jl. Karang Anyar Dalam No. 10C. ☎ (0551) 21972, fax: 21793.

Diving: Around Derawan, $75 for two dives. To either Sangalaki or Kakaban, $120 for two dives plus $40 for the boat, to be split among the divers. Night dive, $35. Regulator and BC rental, $15/day. Two PADI certified dive masters, both from Bali.

Accommodations: 11 completed cottages (the rest of the cottages and the restaurant, at the end of a long pier, were not yet completed) some with AC and attached toilet, some with shared facilities. $30S, $50D, meals $7.50.

Maluku PRACTICALITIES

6

Maluku consists of three island-strewn provinces, the most spread-out and lightly populated part of Indonesia. Maluku, with thousands of islands, seems a natural for diving. The fish and invertebrate life here is rich, and little disturbed, but in all but a few areas access is difficult. In some of the areas where diving has been developed for a while, such as the Bandas, the airplanes are small, have limited weight allowance, and and are still rather irregular. It is certainly worth any effort to dive here, however.
Prices in US dollars. S = Single; D = Double; T = Triple; AC = Air-conditioning.

Ambon

Telephone code 0911

Pattimura Airport is on Ambon Island's Hitu Peninsula across the bay from Ambon City—37 kilometers and 45 minutes by road. A vehicle and passenger ferry runs every few minutes between Poka and Galala, where the bay narrows, which cuts the traveling distance in half. Sometimes a long queue of vehicles waits at the ferry, so it might be faster to take the long way around. In either case, the airport taxis charge either $9 or $10 (air-conditioned cars) for the trip.
Merpati Jl. A. Yani. ☎ 42480; fax: 52572.
Mandala Airlines Jl. A. Y. Pattimura #19. ☎ 42377, 42551.
Sempati Air Jl. Wem Reawaru SK 1/14 No. 9B, Ambon 97124. ☎ 56601, 51612; fax: 56600

GETTING THERE

Mandala airlines has three weekly flights on the route from Ambon to Ujung Pandang, Surabaya and Jakarta. Sempati flies daily to Ujung Pandang, Surabaya and Jakarta. Bouraq flies four times weekly to Ternate and once a week to Manado. Merpati flies daily to Ujung Pandang and Jakarta; four times weekly to Denpasar; four times weekly to Tual (Kei Islands); three times weekly to Banda; six times weekly to Ternate and once a week to Manado.

As the government sets flight prices, the airlines can only compete on the basis of scheduling and service. From Ambon to/from Ujung Pandang, $138; Jakarta $282; Surabaya $246; Denpasar (Bali) $204; Manado $200; Ternate $96; Tual $180 and Banda $60.

LOCAL TRANSPORTATION

Taxis and public minibuses (and *becaks*, three-wheeled bicycle carts) provide transportation in and around Ambon town. Taxis run about $3/hr, sometimes with a two-hour minimum. The main transportation center is in the Mardika market.
Private taxis out of town run about $3/hr ($5/hr w/AC). For a round-trip to Hila, including waiting time, a non-AC taxis would cost $20–$30. For a run to Liang, stopping at Natsepa and Waai (to see the eels) on the way, figure about $30–$35 w/AC, $18 w/o AC.
Crowded minibuses go everywhere around the island, more often in the early morning and late afternoon. Fares run from 15¢ to nearby Galala (6 km) to $ 1.25 to Asilulu (70 km). You can charter one of these for about $5–$7.50/hr.

DIVE OPERATORS

P.T. Daya Patal Tour and Travel Jl. Said Perintah 53, Ambon 97126. ☎ 53344, 52498, 41136, 41821; fax: 54127. Contact: Tony Tomasoa.
P.T. Daya Patal is at present one of two dive operators (and one new club) in Ambon. They specialize in diving around Saparua and nearby islands. (See below for their resort on Saparua.) They can arrange boats, tanks, guides, food, and, if needed, a compressor. While there are no certified dive guides yet, staff members can show you where the good spots are located. We had superb diving with this outfit, with all arrangements running as planned. See below, under Saparua, for prices, including pickup at the Ambon airport and transfer direct to Saparua.
Ambon Dive Centre Jl. Pantai Namalatu, Latuhalat, Ambon 97118 Maluku. ☎ 62101; fax: 62104. Contacts: Sonny and Carol.
Two dives with lunch, tanks, weights, guide, and boat, $70. Gear for rent : mask/snorkel/fins,

$5; regulators, $5; BC, $5; wetsuit, $5; or full set for $15. Video playback, all systems, at the operator's base. Planned E6 slide processing. NAUI courses available, as well as Easy Scuba Experience for non divers, $50.

Amboina Diving Club Jl. A.J. Patty 50. ☎ 52528; fax: 41364. Also: Jl. Skip SK27/4. ☎ 42275. Ask for Wempy Sietolus or Robert Chandra.

Two-dive day trips with tanks and weight belts, cost from $45–$100, depending on distance. The Pintu Kota/Seri locations, at $50, are a good value-for-money. Equipment for rent: mask, snorkel, fins $5/day; BC $10/day; regulator with gauges $13. Nikonos V, with macro and wide angle adapters, plus SB102 flash, $95/day. Sony F340 video in housing with one light, $125/day. Nikon 801s in housing with SB 103 flash, $110/day. Both of their dive boats, one 8 meters, the other 10 meters, are powered by twin 40hp Yamaha outboards.

Maulana Ambon Hotel At the roadside, a short way before reaching Tulehu from Ambon City. For inquiries and reservations, contact their Jakarta office: Maulana Hotels, Jl. Bangka Raya 85, Pela Mampang, Jakarta 12720. ☎ (021) 7994885.

Due to open shortly after this writing. A new hotel offering diving in the area. With large swimming pool, bar and restaurant. Room prices $35–$65. Dive packages (min. 2 persons), first dive, $55, then $35 per additional dives. (4 to 6 persons, 20% discount). Additional charges for "intermediary zone" $10/diver plus $40 boat charge; for the "outer zone," $10/person, plus $80 boat charge. PADI dive instruction available.

LAND TOURS

The **Daya Patal** agency also runs non-diving tours to Banda, Ternate, Tanimbar and elsewhere in the Moluccas. Contact Hans Rijoly or Karole, they both speak excellent English. Other operators offering tours:

Sumber Budi Tour and Travel Jl. Mutiara 2/16, ☎ 51744; fax: 53205

Pedoman Pratama Tours Jl. Dr. Soetono SK 3/2 #65, ☎ 51703, 53905; fax: 54761.

Lorihua Tropis Jl. Pattimura 12. ☎ 53075; fax: 72324.

Novita Sari Jl. Mutiara 79. ☎ 41866; fax: 51444.

ACCOMMODATIONS

We recommend the following hotels and *losmen* in Ambon:

Amboina Jl. Kapitan Ulupaha. ☎ 41725. 38 rooms. Restaurant, bar, shops, conference room, and TV room. $21S, $32D. New rooms will be 20%–30% more expensive.

Ambon Manise Jl. Pantai Mardika 53A, Ambon 97123. ☎ 53888, 54888, 55888; fax: 54492,

54493. 99 rooms. A large, new hotel, hosting tourist groups and businessmen, with restaurant, bar, and conference facilities. $40 economy, $50 standard, $60 deluxe, $70 executive, $80–$125 suite. All prices for single occupancy. Add $5 for double; $10 for extra bed.

Beta Jl. Wim Reawaru, ☎ 53463. 26 rooms. One of the best of the cheaper hotels. $5–8S, $8–$10D.

Cenderawasih Jl. Tulukabessy. ☎ 52487. 18 rooms with TV. Restaurant. $41S, $45D.

Game Jl. A. Yani. 14 rooms. One of the best of the cheaper hotels. $12.

Manise Jl. W.R. Spratman. ☎ 42905. 56 rooms. A businessman's hotel. $25–$40S, $30–$45D. Add 20% service charge.

Mutiara Jl. Raya Pattimura, ☎ 53075, 53076. 31 rooms, all with TV and AC. Pleasant staff, nice atmosphere; many interesting people stay here. Restaurant and bar. English language *Jakarta Post* newspaper available in the lobby for guests. Discount possible if staying more than a couple of days. $29S, $49D.

Santai Beach Resort Contact: Ambon Dive Centre, Pantai Namalatu. ☎ 62101, fax: 62104. Relaxing, friendly, overlooking the beach.10 minutes walk from Ambon Dive Centre. $26 standard, $42 deluxe.

DINING

The traditional cuisine of Ambon is not one of the archipelago's most exciting. The staples—such as sago cakes—are generally bland. The fruit, however, is excellent, and lobsters ($6–$10 each, best at the Hotel Manise) can often be obtained. We recommend the following:

Amboina Jl. A. Y. Pattimura 63. Best bakery in town, locally-made ice cream. A nice place for a quick meal. Makes a good *roti saucise,* a hot dog in a bun.

Kakatoa Jl. Said Perintah 20. European cooking, run by Belgian couple, the only place in town for a real change from Asian cooking. Very pleasant atmosphere, well run. Count an about $4–$10 per person per meal.

Pondok Asri Next to the Hotel Manise. Features Chinese and Indonesian dishes, as well as Japanese meals ($12–$14), imported US beef ($11–$12) and lots of seafood. Nice decor and quiet setting.

TOURIST SERVICES

Banks and Money-changing

There are plenty of banks around Ambon for money-changing, and credit cards are becoming more popular—the best are Visa and the card issued by Bank Central Asia.

6 Maluku

PERIPLUS TRAVEL MAPS
Detailed maps of the Asia Pacific region

This five-year program was launched in 1993 with the goal of producing accurate and up-to-date maps of every major city and country in the Asia Pacific region. About 12 new titles are published each year, along with numerous revised editions. Titles in **BOLDFACE** are already available (32 titles in mid-1996). Titles in *ITALICS* are scheduled for publication in 1996.

INDIVIDUAL COUNTRY TITLES

Australia	ISBN 962-593-150-3
Burma	ISBN 962-593-070-1
Cambodia	ISBN 0-945971-87-7
China	ISBN 962-593-107-4
Hong Kong	ISBN 0-945971-74-5
Indonesia	ISBN 962-593-042-6
Japan	ISBN 962-593-108-2
Malaysia	ISBN 962-593-043-4
Singapore	ISBN 0-945971-41-9
Thailand	ISBN 962-593-044-2
Vietnam	ISBN 0-945971-72-9

AUSTRALIA REGIONAL MAPS

Sydney	ISBN 962-593-087-6
Melbourne	ISBN 962-593-050-7
Cairns	ISBN 962-593-048-5
Brisbane	ISBN 962-593-049-3

CHINA REGIONAL MAPS

Beijing	ISBN 962-593-031-0
Shanghai	ISBN 962-593-032-9

INDONESIA REGIONAL MAPS

Bali	ISBN 0-945971-49-4
Bandung	ISBN 0-945971-43-5
Batam	ISBN 0-945971-69-9
Bintan	ISBN 962-593-139-2
Jakarta	ISBN 0-945971-62-1
Java	ISBN 962-593-040-X
Lombok	ISBN 0-945971-46-X
Surabaya	ISBN 0-945971-48-6
Tana Toraja	ISBN 0-945971-44-3
Yogyakarta	ISBN 0-945971-42-7

JAPAN REGIONAL MAPS

Tokyo	ISBN 962-593-109-0
Osaka & Kyoto	ISBN 962-593-110-4

MALAYSIA REGIONAL MAPS

Kuala Lumpur	ISBN 0-945971-75-3
Malacca	ISBN 0-945971-77-X
Johor Bahru	ISBN 0-945971-98-2
Penang	ISBN 0-945971-76-1
West Malaysia	ISBN 962-593-129-5
Sabah	ISBN 0-945971-78-8
Sarawak	ISBN 0-945971-79-6

NEPAL REGIONAL MAPS

Kathmandu	ISBN 962-593-063-9

THAILAND REGIONAL MAPS

Bangkok	ISBN 0-945971-81-8
Chiang Mai	ISBN 0-945971-88-5
Phuket	ISBN 0-945971-82-6
Ko Samui	ISBN 962-593-036-1

Distributed by:

Berkeley Books Pte. Ltd.
(Singapore & Malaysia)
5 Little Road, #08-01, Singapore 536983
Tel: (65) 280 3320 Fax: (65) 280 6290

C.V. Java Books (Indonesia)
Jl. Gading Kirana Timur
Blok A13 No. 23, Jakarta 14240
Tel: (021) 453 4988 Fax: (021) 453 4987

Medical

Kantor Kesehatan Wilayah (District Health Office). ☎ 52861, 52392. Three doctors—Dr. Krishna (clinic telephone: 52715), Dr. Polanunu and Dr. Ristianto (home phone: 53411, 51526)—speak English.
Rumah Sakit Umum (Public Hospital). ☎ 53438 ext. 118 or 348.
Pelita Farma pharmacy Jl. Setia Budi. Open 24-hours.

Communications

Telephone Office Jl. Raya Pattimura. In general, phone connections are good, both nationally and internationally. Fax and telex machines are available as well as telephones.

Like everywhere else in the world, hotels in Ambon take a cut on long distance telephone calls and can charge a bundle for fax and telex services. Ask before making a call. Much cheaper to go to one of the several *wartel* mini-offices around town for international phone calls (via satellite) where you pay just about the same as a direct-dialed. Not much English spoken but easy enough to make yourself understood.

Photography

Union Photo Jl. A.Y. Pattimura No. 3, Ambon. ☎ 53569. In-store print processing, $1 for negatives, 15¢ for each print. Kodacolor and Fuji-color negative films; Ektachrome 100 slide film, but no slide processing. No Fuji Velvia or other specialized films.

AMBON UNDERWATER FESTIVAL

A yearly underwater festival in Ambon began in 1993. The week-long event, usually held in late October, features 4 days of diving with 10 plunges, including two night dives.

The highlight is an underwater photo competition, with $10,000 prize money split among three categories—wide angle, macro and animal behavior. Fuji from Jakarta provides film and processing. There is lots of local entertainment, including traditional song and dance.

The festival package is almost incredibly cheap: $750/person, which includes all diving, six days room and full board plus round-trip ticket from Bali. Information, reservations and registration through the Ambon Dive Centre (see above).

DIVE SEASON

As a general rule, the best diving in the Ambon and Lease area is between September and December. During this period, all areas are available for diving, and visibility is at its greatest.

From April through August, diving is limited to the north coast of Ambon and the Lease Islands, and the nearby south coast of Seram. From January through March, diving is best along the south, with occasional journeys to the north, if weather permits.

Saparua

GETTING THERE

Regular boats leave from Tulehu on Ambon Island's east coat to the bigger villages on Haruku and Saparua. The regular boat from Tulehu to Pelau, on the north coast of Haruku and the island's largest village, costs $1.50. A regular ferry leaves for Saparua at 9am and 2pm, Mon–Sat and at 11 on Sun, and stops at Tuhaha ($5) on the east coast of Tuhaha Bay in the north. Another boat goes to Saparua Town ($2) and then continues on to Amahai on Seram Island to the north (another $2 and 2.5 hours).

Regular boats from Saparua Town head to Nusa Laut only on Wednesdays and Saturdays, when they have lots of business ferrying people back and forth to Saparua's market. If you want to go to the little island on another day, you will have to charter a boat.

Chartering speedboats. You can also charter a speedboat—able to carry 3–6 passengers—from Ambon to various villages on Haruku and Saparua. Prices vary, depending on distance, traffic and your bargaining ability, approx. $80.

LAND TRANSPORTATION

On the two big islands, buses wait for passengers in the morning at the ferry terminals. Fares range from 15¢ to 75¢ from the ferry terminal on either Haruku or Saparua to anywhere else on the islands. Charters run $5–$7.50/hour.

DIVE OPERATORS

Tony Tomasoa (of P.T. Daya Patal in Ambon, see above) operates a resort on Saparua, near Mahu Village. Two compressors and dive gear are kept on the premises. Although you can dive with Daya Patal from a base in one of the hotels in Ambon City, it is much more pleasant and convenient on Saparua, as you don't have to take the long boat ride in the morning and returning in the afternoon to Ambon.
Mahu Diving Lodge Desa Mahu, Saparua. All bookings through Daya Patal Tours, Jl. Said Perintah SK II / 27A, Ambon. ☎ 53344, 41136; fax: 54127, 53287.

The resort consists of attractive bungalows

facing mangrove trees at the sea's edge in a coconut plantation. The resort is locally called "Kelapa Indah" ("Beautiful Coconut"). Dugongs have been occasionally seen feeding in the shallow beds of sea grass not far from the resort. The cottages are spacious, airy, thatch-roofed structures with showers and flush toilets. Electricity (220/240 volts) available.

The diving just in front of the resort is not good, but the coral on the other side of the bay is fine for snorkeling, in 2–3 m depths. The resort has "self-paddle" outrigger canoes to make the short cross-bay run. Light tackle available for fishing trips with boat and pilot/ guide. In August and September, black marlin and also tuna in the 50–100 kg range hit regularly.

Two dives to Nusa Laut or Maulana Island, $55; Moloth, Itawaka or Kulor, $45; two divers minimum. Package (room, meals, 2 dives, boat, guide, tanks and weights) $85–$100, depending on distance, two diver minimum. Regulator rental $10/day, BC $10/day. Extra (third) dive $15, night dive $20.

Accommodations at the Mahu Resort Lodge only: $45S, $55D, includes full board. Airport pickup $20 per person to Tulehu. Speedboat charter, round trip to Mahu, $80 for up to 6 people. Normal ferry boat to Saparua (two departures daily) $5. Payment possible by Visa or Mastercard or travelers' cheques; 3% surcharge if credit card payment.

OTHER ACCOMMODATIONS

Losmen Siri Sore In Siri Sore Saram, on the east shore of Saparua Bay. 12 clean rooms, breakfast included. Land and sea excursions can be organized. $12–$14S; $13–$18D.

On Haruku and Nusa Laut, travelers must negotiate for a place to stay with a family.

Pindito

The live-aboard *Pindito* is based in Ambon. Trips—around the Banda Sea and the Islands off Western Irian Jaya, depending on the season—are usually of 12 days, with all but one day for diving. Rate: $220/day, all-inclusive (even beer, liquor, equipment rental). Note: we still recommend divers bring their own, recently checked dive gear. The ship can also be chartered, for $3,000/day, with a capacity of up to 16 divers. As the *Pindito* is a busy ship, we advise bookings well ahead of time (6 months or even a year) for confirmed space. However, one or two beds are often available on short notice, but, of course, not guaranteed. So far, marketing has been aimed at Germany and Switzerland. There are two places for booking. The

Pindito's main office can also arrange flights, hotel bookings, and extensions to other parts of Indonesia.

Pindito Main office: Pindito Reisen Ag, Regensdorferstr. P.O. Box CH-8105 Watt Regensdorf, Switzerland. ☎ (411) 8700207; fax: (411) 8700215. In Ambon: Pondok Permai RT 18/RW 03, Hative Kecil, Ambon, Maluku, Indonesia. ☎ /fax: 51569. Contact: Ambon-based manager, Edi Frommenwiler.

Banda

Telephone code is 0910.

Merpati flies one of its 18-passenger Twin Otters to Bandaneira from Ambon on Mondays, Wednesdays and Saturdays (1 hr, $50). The possibility of cancellations (weather or technical problems) is very real and should always be taken into account.

A local passenger ship makes the Banda–Ambon run on a semi-regular basis or when too many flights have been canceled or there are too many air passengers. Inter-island mixed freighters or large Pelni passenger liners also make the trip about every three weeks (see Travel Advisory, page 266.) You can easily walk from the airstrip to the Bandaneira hotels, but not with dive gear. Hop into one of the mini-buses that will be waiting.

DIVE OPERATORS

Diving is available to guests at the Maulana Inn or the Laguna Inn. For reservations, contact: Hotel Maulana, P.O. Box 3193, Jakarta. ☎ (021) 360372; fax: 360308. In Banda: ☎ (0910) 21022 or 21023; fax: 21024.

Laguna Inn 12 rooms. Three meals $22. $25–$60S, $29–$70D. Some bungalows at $15 on twin-share basis. All plus 10% tax.

Maulana Inn 50 rooms. The best rooms in Bandaneira. The hotel offers a nice view of Gunung Api across the lagoon. Three meals $22/person + 10%. Cold beer, small can $2. Bottle of *arak* $3. Meals are okay, but boring. The *sushi*, however, is great when available (order one day ahead; $4.50 for a big plate of *sashimi* tuna). $60–$87S; $70–$140D, plus 10% tax.

Diving for people staying at either of these hotels (min of 4 people): To Ai, Hatta and Run, $60 (with your own gear); $75 (regulator and BC provided), $80 (all gear provided). The ride to the dive sites takes 60–70 minutes by speedboat. For other, nearby locations, the rates are: $50, $65, $70, with a two-person minimum. 5–30 minutes by speedboat. Night dives, $30.

For snorkeling off Bandaneira, the near coast of Lontar, and Gunung Api, a boat can drop you off and pick you up at predetermined time for $6/person (6 persons or more). The same arrangement to Sjahrir Island and the far side of the Lontar, $10/person.

For a special trip to Manukang (Suangi) Island or Manuk Island (lots of birds), contact the manager of the Maulana Hotel. It is, essentially, the cost of the boat charter—to Manukang, 4 hours each way by diesel, 1.5 to 2 hours by speedboat; to Manuk, about 11 hours each way (diesel only).

Other watersports Windsurfing, mid June to September, January to March, $2/hr; water-skiing $30/hr; fishing is included in price of boat rental. May to September, the yellowtail tuna, sailfish, swordfish, and Spanish mackerel run; from October to June, it's barracuda. Jacks are caught all year round.

OTHER ACCOMMODATIONS

Aside from the above places owned by Des Alwi, there are some simple *losmen*: the **Delfika** with 8 rooms, all enclosed facilities, $9.50/person including tax and three meals; the **Selecta** with 7 rooms, also offering full board, $10 with attached toilet facilities, $8.50 for rooms with shared facilities.

These *losmen* are all quite close to the main mosque and its blaring loudspeakers. All accommodations on Banda tend to fill during the last two weeks of December as well as most of October. Make sure to reserve ahead during these times.

DINING

Best at the Maulana and the Laguna, where you usually are served two kinds of fish and a vegetable. There are many little restaurants in Bandaneira town where the simple meals of rice or noodles with chicken cost about 75¢. We found the **Selecta II** the most pleasant of these—there is cold beer available here (sometimes) for a $1.40 per can.

TOURIST SERVICES

Excursions

Sunset cruise Two-hour cruise around Gunung Api by boat, and a stop at Sambayang to visit a cinnamon plantation and to snorkel in the sea and in hot water springs. $6 (6 person minimum). **Climbing Gunung Api** It takes one to three hours to climb the 656-meter-high volcano. One day's notice is required. Guide $5.50 per person (whether he carries anything or not) and round-trip boat $5. Upon returning, you obtain a certificate declaring you an honorary citizen of Banda. This document requires a $2 donation

to the museum.

Lontar Village This is a trip to Lontar island to see a nutmeg plantation, sacred wells and Fort Hollandia, this last reached by climbing 360 steps. The tour starts at 4 pm, and takes about two hours. $6/person, minimum of two; if guide needed, extra $5.

Cultural Events

In April and October, 37-man *kora-kora* (war canoe) races are held. The rest of the year, you can commission a demonstration: $150 for one *kora-kora* and crew. A *cakalele* war dance costs $350 and requires 10-day's notice.

Banks and Money-changing

There are no banks on Banda, so bring all the rupiah you will need from Ambon.

DIVING SEASON

The best diving is March through June, and October through November. From July/August to mid-September, diving is usually restricted to locations close to Bandaneira, due to heavy seas. December to February is supposed to be Banda's driest period, but in 1993 and 1994 there were heavy rains at this time.

7 Irian Jaya PRACTICALITIES

Irian Jaya, the Indonesian province that covers the western half of the large island of New Guinea, is one of the world's last unknown expanses, especially underwater. Diving is excellent—diverse coral, stunning fish life, turtles, dugongs, sharks, rays, whales are common sights, not to mention an abundance of ship and aircraft wrecks just now being discovered.

Prices in US dollars. S = Single; D = Double; T = Triple; AC = Air-conditioning. Telephone code for Sorong 0951.

Currently, aside from the *Pindito's* seasonal trips to the Raja Ampat islands, the only way to dive Irian is with Irian Diving, which operates out of Sorong on the Bird's Head peninsula. Divers will be met by this outfit in either Sorong to dive in the Raja Ampat Islands, or Manokwari, departure point for dives in Dore and Cenderawasih Bays.

GETTING THERE

Merpati flights connect Sorong (departure point for the Raja Ampat Islands) with other diving centers throughout the country:

Ambon	Daily	$ 67
Denpasar	Daily (via Ambon, U.P.)	$236
Jakarta	Daily (via Ambon, U.P.)	$296
Manado	Th,Su	$110
Ujung Pandang	Daily (via Ambon)	$176
Jayapura	M,W,Th,Su (via Biak)	$152
Manokwari	W,F,Sa	$ 79

For diving in Cenderawasih Bay, head for Manokwari on the north coast:

Ambon	M,T,W,Th,Su (via Biak)	$172
Manado	Sa	$175
Ujung Pandang	F (3 stops)	$265
Jayapura	Tu,Th,F,Su	$120

Both cities are stopovers for Pelni Lines' two passenger boats, the *Dobonsolo* and the *Ciremai* every two weeks on their way from Jakarta to Jayapura and the *Tatamailau* (Denpasar–Jayapura) calls monthly.

DIVE OPERATOR

Irian Diving Jl. Gn. Gamalama No. 3, Kampung Baru, Sorong, Irian Jaya. ☎ /fax: (0951) 25274. Mailing address: P.O. Box 187, Sorong. Contact in the Netherlands: Irian Diving. ☎ /fax: (31 38) 4478293, (31 183) 443430. Contact: Max Ammer.

Can arrange day trips from Sorong and Manokwari (Dore Bay), and more day trips from one of their base camps in the Raja Ampat Islands and Cenderawasih Bay areas. Specializes in tailor-made diving trips. Their base camps on uninhabited islands in the Raja Ampat Islands and Cenderawasih Bay consist of 3 or 4 traditionally built huts for accommodations, plus 1–2 more for kitchen and equipment storage. Outboard powered boats transfer divers from the camps to the reefs and wrecks.

Equipment includes 1 wooden boat, 2 fiberglass dive boats, 1 long boat, GPS navigation used to locate wreck and dive sites, a generator to charge batteries, 3 Bauer compressors, 60 tanks, and 8 complete sets of diving equipment.

All trips are guided by Max Ammer, who, with more than 6 years diving experience in Irian Jaya, has located more than 60 ship and 30 aircraft wrecks. Small groups (6–12 divers) only, accompanied by 3 or 4 Irianese staff and one diving instructor/guide. All of our staff are certified divers.

Day trips from Sorong or Manokwari, including 2 tanks, boat, weights, lunch, and dive guide, $65. Unlimited diving from one of the base camps, including accommodations, meals, tanks, weights, boat, dive guide, $115/day. Pioneer dive expeditions, $1,400 (2 weeks), $2,000 (3 weeks). Add $120 for Manokwari area. Airport transfers can be arranged.

Diving trips offered all year round, as there are good dive sites in all seasons. Diving is conducted 6 days/week, no activity on Saturday. Contact them as early as possible, as they work on with small groups and are often booked far in advance. Additional information in English, Dutch, German, or Indonesian available upon request.

Underwater Hazards

We have all heard far too many shark attack stories. There is a remote possibility of a shark attack of course, but the odds are against it. You are far safer diving in Indonesian waters than riding around Bali on a motorcycle.

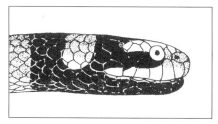

Above: *The colubrine sea snake,* Laticauda colubrina.

The biggest hazards are currents and cold water, and cuts and scrapes on coral. Still, there are a number of dangerous animals on Indonesia's reefs, and they should not be toyed with. In 1991, a diver died from trying to ride a large reef stingray. He must have thought it was a manta, and climbed on its back.

In almost 300 dives in Indonesia, my problems have been few. I brushed stinging hydroids with my exposed wrists, and small jellyfish stung the area around my throat. And I was once attacked by a Titan triggerfish (*Balistoides viridescens*), although all he got were a few clumps of hair.

My biggest problem in the beginning was cold. I had a 1mm suit, but this left me shivering in some of the cold water off Bali. Later, I added a 3mm shorty on top when we encountered cold water. A few times, I wished I had a hood as well.

ANIMALS THAT BITE

Sharks

Of the hundreds of species of sharks, only 12 have been known to attack humans, and another 28 are considered capable of such an act. The great white shark (*Carcharodon carcharias*), reaching 6.5 meters, is probably the most fearsome of these. This animal prefers cool waters, and sticks to Australia and the west coast of the United States. We only know of one great white sighting, off Bali. The diver held still, stuck to the coral wall and prayed (he's an atheist) as he watched the monster cruise by. Jacques Cousteau considers the oceanic whitetip (*Carcharhinus longimanus*)—a chiefly pelagic species almost never seen by divers in Indonesia—to be the most unpredictable and dangerous species.

The only really dangerous species one is likely to see diving off Indonesia's reefs is the tiger shark (*Galeocerdo cuvier*), a large deepwater fish that sometimes comes up onto the reefs to feed, particularly in the late afternoon and at night. It is probably not worth tempting fate with this animal, which is occasionally sighted by divers.

The common reef sharks you will see in Indonesia are not considered dangerous, and one never hears of attacks. (In fact, your big problem will be that they're so shy it's hard to get good photos.) But still, don't harass them, and spearfishing always dramatically increases the risk of attack.

Sharks are very highly developed predators, with a very keen sense of smell, and a lateral line sensitive to the vibrations given off by a wounded or distressed fish. Since there is easier prey around—smaller, more familiar and less menacing—sharks very seldom attack humans. When they do, it is more likely to be a territorial defense than an attempt at getting a meal.

Prior to a territory related attack, sharks will warn divers with a "dance" display: the circling animals shake their heads back and forth, arch their backs, and point their pectoral fins downward. It is very distinctive (much like a big dog defending his territory) and even without this description you would probably get the message.

The classic shark feeding behavior consists of circling the prey, gradually increasing in speed and moving in closer. Sharks are more cautious than you might think they need to be, and the animals often test their potential prey's defenses by brushing against it with their abrasive skin.

Should either of these behaviors develop while you are underwater, it is best to get out of there as soon as possible. Stay calm, stick to your buddy, and back up against the reef wall. Work your way steadily up and get back to the beach or the dive boat. If one or more of the animals comes too close, try banging it on its sensitive nose with your camera, a dive light, or your fist—whichever is most handy.

Barracuda

Barracuda are far less dangerous than sharks, but have sharp teeth and the great barracuda (*Sphyraena barracuda*) grows to 2 meters. These fish are sometimes drawn to flashy jewelry (and speared fish). Dive lights occasionally attract them at night, and if temporarily blinded, they could become disoriented and dangerous. For some reason, Atlantic Ocean barracuda are much more likely to attack than their Pacific Ocean brethren.

Sea snakes

Sea snakes carry some of the most deadly poison known (they are the most poisonous of snakes). The species seen in Indonesia, however, are not aggressive. Sea snakes are sometimes inquisitive, and don't panic if one should explore your face underwater. Remember: they have very short teeth, very rarely bite, and even if they do bite, often they do not inject their venom. It seems that it takes the snakes a day or more to regenerate their venom supply, and they are loath to use it unless faced with a real emergency. Do not make them feel they are facing an emergency.

If bitten (with poison), restrict circulation from the affected limb, and get the victim to a doctor. There is little pain at first, but paralysis and death can follow hours later.

Others

Sea turtles, and even small reef fish, particularly triggers and puffers, have powerful jaws and strong teeth that can do damage. It may seem silly to run from a foot-long fish, but better that than a painful wound.

STINGING FISH

Stingrays

These common animals use their tail stinger when stepped on or startled. They frequent sandy areas, and are sometimes practically invisible. A good habit if walking in the shallows is to shuffle your feet giving them time to get out of your way. When diving, don't try to sneak up on a stingray. Approach slowly, from in front. The sting from a ray is rarely fatal to an adult, although it is extremely painful. (Note: in the example cited above, the stinger literally pierced the victim's heart.)

Scorpionfish

All scorpionfish carry poison in their dorsal, anal and pelvic fins. The pain from most can be excruciating, but only the stonefish (*Synanceia*

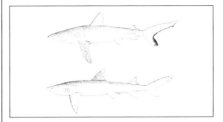

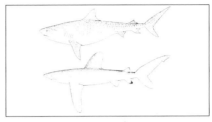

Above: *(Top to bottom)* Grey reef shark, Carcharhinus amblyrhynchos*; reef whitetip shark,* Triaenodon obesus*; tiger shark,* Galeocerdo cuvier*; oceanic whitetip shark,* Carcharhinus longimanus.

verrucosa) has been responsible for human fatalities. The stonefish is the world's most venomous fish, and being stung by one is a real disaster—at best you can expect local tissue death and perhaps the loss of your toes; at worst, a painful death. Be careful! Many scorpionfish are masters of camouflage, making it easy to step on or brush one.

Lionfish (*Pterois* spp.) are more conspicuous. They sometimes travel in packs, however, and particularly at night, when they are attracted to the small fish stunned by your lights, you could accidentally bump one.

A sting from a ray or scorpionfish causes excruciating pain, which can bring on unconsciousness. Get the victim topside immediately. Remove any spine still stuck in the skin, and wash and slightly bleed the puncture area. As quickly as possible, immerse the wound in hot water, up to 50°C (use tea if you have some on the boat), or use hot compresses. If attended to quickly enough, good results are likely from this method. Treat for shock, and take the victim to a doctor.

PRICKS AND CUTS

Sea urchins

The long, black spines of the *Diadema* spp. sea urchins are not something one would voluntarily bump against. But it happens. These animals are found more often in harbors, lagoons and rather eutrophic back-reef areas than on the fore-reef where divers spend their time. Be careful walking out, particularly through cloudy water! Other urchins are not as dramatic, but can still be a real irritation, and some are venomous.

Try to remove the spines with a tweezers, but if this is impossible, try crushing them: use a shoe or a weight from your belt. This will relieve the pain somewhat, and the spines will eventually be absorbed.

Coral scrapes

Infected coral cuts are the divers' most frequent problems in Indonesia. Do not neglect any broken skin in the tropics. A festering, pus-filled sore will develop, possibly swelling your lymph glands and starting real trouble.

Don't let things get this far. Clean and disinfect the wound as soon as you are finished diving. Keep a loose open bandage on it and change it frequently.

ANIMALS THAT 'BURN'

The hazard presented by these animals can usually be prevented by even a thin suit. Often it is the areas around the face or the wrist where you can get stung.

Jellyfish

The most dangerous jellyfish is the sea wasp (*Chironex fleckeri*). It is a problem in Australia, and swimming is prohibited in the Darwin area when the mature animals are about. Children and adults with cardio-respiratory problems are the most at risk from this transparent, 20-centimeter creature. A coma and death can result. Remove the victim from the water, and gently remove any still-adhering tentacles. Vinegar may reduce further discharge of nematocysts, or use local anaesthetic sprays or ointments. Resuscitation may be required. Other jellyfish are more unpleasant than dangerous, but vinegar or creams may help with them as well.

Stinging hydroids

The stinging hydroid *Aglaophenia* is common in Indonesia, looking like a beige or pinkish fern. Fire coral (*Millepora*) grows as smooth, wrinkled sheets (brownish or greenish) or as encrusting forms. Gloves and even Lycra suits offer protection, but a brush against it with bare skin will burn, and leave an itchy, bumpy rash. This is irritating, but not enough to make you abort a dive.

Indonesian Reef Fishes

WITH ENGLISH, LATIN, INDONESIAN AND LOCAL LANGUAGES

Family name (Latin family name) English common name (*Genus species*); standard length (does not include tail)	Indonesian; Bajo (Ba); Bugis (Bu); Manado dialect (M); Ambon dialect (A) —In Indonesian, almost all fish names begin with "ikan" (*fish*) which we omit below.

Sharks (Rhincodontidae, whale shark; Orectolobidae, nurse and zebra sharks; Hemigaleidae, reef whitetip; Sphyrnidae, hammerheads; Alopiidae, thresher sharks; Carcharhinidae, requiem shark)	Ikan hiu; cucut (*kiss, suck*); kareo (Ba); mengihang (Bu); gorango (M); kalayu (A); also bengiwang
Whale shark (*Rhincodon typus*); 12m, perhaps more	Hiu Abu-abu (*ashes*) Hiu gender (*gamelan instrument*), cucut lintang, ikan hiu bodoh (*stupid*)
Nurse shark (*Nebrius concolor*); 3.2m	Hiu buta (*blind*); kareo bisu (*deaf*) (Ba)
Leopard shark (*Stegastoma varium*); 2.3m	Hiu kembang (a *flower*), cucut tokek
Reef whitetip shark (*Triaenodon obesus*); 1.7m	Hiu sirip putih (*white fin*); kareo batu (Ba)
Silvertip shark (*Carcharhinus albimarginatus*); 2.8m	
Grey reef shark (*C. amblyrhynchos*); 2.3m	
Oceanic whitetip shark (*C. longimanus*); 2.7m	Hiu samudera (*ocean*), berujung (*top*), putih Hiu sirip putih laut dalam (*deep sea white fin*); kareo pansa (Ba)
Reef blacktip shark (*C. melanopterus*); 1.8m	Hiu sirip hitam (*black fin*); kareo mengali (Ba), hiu karang berujung hitam
Tiger shark (*Galeocerdo cuvier*); 5.5m, perhaps more	Hiu macan (*tiger*)
Hammerhead shark (*Sphyrna sp.*); perhaps 5m	Hiu ronggeng (*Javanese dancer/bar girl*), cucut rongceng, ikan hiu martil (*ham- mer*); kareo bingkoh (Ba); gorango martelu (M)
Thresher shark (*Alopias pelagicus*); 3.3m	Hiu penebah

Rays in general (Rajidae)	Ikan pari; pari luncur

Guitarfishes (Rhinobatidae)	Cucut biola (*violin*), cucut panrong
White-spotted guitarfish (*Rhynchobatus djiddensis*); 3m	

Stingrays (Dasyatididae)	Pari sengat (*sting*)
Leopard ray (*Himantura uarnak*); 1.8m width	Pari, Pareh; Pai (Ba); Pari, Nyoa (*bird*) (Bu)
Blue-spotted stingray (*Taenura lymma*); 1m width	Pari macan (*tiger*), pari kembang Pari pasir bintik biru (*blue spotted sand ray*); pai kiam (Ba); nunang, nyoa pasir (*sand*) (Bu)
Black-spotted stingray (*T. melanospilos*); 1.7m width	Pari pasir; pai kikir (Ba)

Eagle rays (Myliobatidae)	
Spotted eagle ray (*Aetobatis narinari*); 2.3m width	Pari burung (*bird*), pari ayam (*chicken, for the taste*); pai mano (Ba); pari mano, nyoa burung (Bu)

Manta rays (Mobulidae)	
Manta ray (*Manta alfredi*); 6.7m width; usually to 3m	Pari hantu (*ghost*), pari manta Pari jurig, pari satan (Sundanese); pai saranga (Ba); pari pangka (Bu); bele-

lang, bou, moku (*Lamalera dialect*)

Moray eels (Muraenidae)
Snowflake moray (*Echidna nebulosa*); 75cm
Fimbriated moray (*Gymnothorax fimbriatus*); 80cm
Yellow-margined moray (*G. flavimarginatus*); 1.2m
Giant moray (*G. javanicus*); 2.4m, maybe 3m
Spotted moray (*G. meelagris*); 1.2m
Black-spotted moray (*G. melanospilos*); 1m
Zonipectis moray (*G. zonipectis*); 46cm
Blue ribbon eel (*Rhinomuraena quaesita*); 1.2m

Sidat morena/Sidat moa
Ladu (*lava*), morea, kerundung (*veil*); ndoh (Ba); lado (M). [Note: belut for "eel" in Indonesian; belut (usually means freshwater species) of the Synbranchiformes order]

Garden eels (Congridae; subfamily Heterocongridae)
Spotted garden eel (*Heteroconger hassi*); 35cm

Sidat conger
Sidat kebun (*garden*)

Snake eels (Ophichthidae)
Banded snake eel (*Myrichthys colubrinus*); 88cm
Spotted snake eel (*M. maculosus*); 1m

Milkfishes (Chanidae)
Milkfish (*Chanos chanos*); 50cm, rarely to 1.8m

Ikan bandeng
Gelondongan (*adult*), nener (*fry*) [Note: these are farmed in fishponds]

Eel catfishes (Plotosidae)
Striped eel catfish (*Plotosus lineatus*); 30cm

Sembilang karang (*coral catfish*); titinagan (Ba)

Anchovies (Engraulididae)
Anchovies (*Stolephorus* spp.); 5–10cm

Teri; puri (A); ikan bilis (Malay)

Herrings (Clupeidae)
Sprats (*Dussumieria* spp. and *Spratelloides* spp.); 10cm
Herrings (*Herklotsichthys* spp.); 15cm

Ikan haring
Japuh [also terubuk (*Clupes toli*), tembang and lemuru (*Sardinella* sp.)]

Lizardfishes (Synodontidae)
Graceful lizardfish (*Saurida gracilis*); 31cm
Nebulous lizardfish (*S. nebulosa*); 17cm
Twin-spot lizardfish (*Synodus binotatus*); 13cm
Reef lizardfish (*S. englemani*)
Black-blotch lizardfish (*S. jaculum*); 14cm
Variegated lizardfish (*S. variegatus*); 20cm

Ikan kadal
Beloso, gabus, ikan kepala busok (*fish with depraved expression*); taropatau (Ba); gosi cina (M)

Frogfishes (Antennariidae)
Painted frogfish (*Antennarius pictus*); 16cm
Sargassumfish (*Histrio histrio*); 14cm

Needlefishes (Belonidae)
Keeled needlefish (*Platybelone argalus platyura*); 37cm
Reef needlefish (*Strongylura incisa*); 1m
Crocodile needlefish (*Tylosaurus crocodilis*); 1.3m

Cendro, ikan julung-julung (*unlucky*); timbaloah (Ba); sori (Bu); sako (M)

Halfbeaks (Hemirhamphidae)
Island halfbeack (*Hemiramphus archipelagicus*); 25cm
Spotted halfbeak (*H. far*); 40cm

Ikan kacang-kachang (*beans*), ikan julung-julung (*unlucky*); pipilangan (Ba); cado-cado (Bu); sako (M)

Flashlightfishes (Anomalopidae)
Flashlightfish (*Anomalops katoptron*); 9cm
Flashlightfish (*Photoblepheron palpebratus*); 9cm

Ikan leweri air, ikan leweri bau; oho (Ba)

Soldierfishes and Squirrelfishes (Holocentridae)
Bronze soldierfish (*Myripristis adusta*); 25cm
Bigscale soldierfish (*M. berndti*); 24cm

Ikan tupai (*squirrel*)
Karoo, kabakok, ikan mata bulan (*moon-eyed*), ikan mata besar (*big-eyed*);

Red soldierfish (*M. murdjan*); 22cm
Fine-lined squirrelfish (*Sargocentron microstoma*); 16cm
Soldierfishes (in general) (*Myrptis sp*)

karango (Ba); susunu, gora (Bu)

Serdadu (*soldier*)

Trumpetfishes (Aulostomidae)
Trumpetfish (*Aulostomus chinensis*); 62cm

Mulut (*mouth*), pipa (*pipe*)
Manok, ikan terompet; tarigonoh (Ba)

Cornetfishes (Fistulariidae)
Flutemouth cornetfish (*Fistularia commersonii*); 1m

Seruling, tangkur, moncong (*snout, muzzle*);
ikan terompet; teligonoh (Ba); malo (Bu)

Shrimpfishes (Centriscidae)
Shrimpfish (*Aeoliscus strigatus*); 15cm

Ikan udang, piso-piso;
Ikan pisau-pisau (*knife*); barbadisamo (Ba)

Ghost pipefishes (Solenostomus)
Ghost pipefish (*Solenostomus cyanopterus*); 16cm
Ornate ghost pipefish (*S. paradoxus*)

Ikan hantu (*ghost*)

Pipefishes and Seahorses (Syngnathidae)
Thorny seahorse (*Hippocampus histrix*); 15cm
Common seahorse (*H. kuda*); 30cm
Crowned seahorse (*H. planifrons*); 15cm
Network pipefish (*Corythoichthys flavofasciatus*); 11cm
Scribbled pipefish (*C. intestinalis*); 16cm
Double-headed pipefish (*Trachyramphus bicoarctata*);
   39cm

Tangkur kuda (*javanese*)
Tangkur, tangkur buaya (*crocodile*), ikan
   kuda (*horse*); pipilando (Ba)
Pipilando samo (Ba)
Tangkur kuda; pipilando jarang (Ba)

Dragonfishes (Pegasidae)
Sea moth (*Pegasus sp*)

Ikan ngengat (*moth*) laut

Flatheads (Platycephalidae)
Crocodilefish (*Cymbacephalus beauforti*); 50cm
Longsnout flathead (*Platycephalus chiltonae*); 20cm

Ikan kepala (*head*), pipih (*flat, thin*)
Papangao (Ba)

Scorpionfishes (Scorpaenidae)

Devil scorpionfish (*Scorpaenopsis diabolus*); 19cm
Tassled scorpionfish (*S. oxycephala*); 19cm
Weedy scorpionfish (*Rhinopias frondosa*); 19cm
Stonefish (*Synanceia verrucosa*); 35cm

Devilfish (*Inimicus didactylus*); 15cm
Twinspot lionfish (*Dendrochirus biocellatus*); 8cm
Shortfin lionfish (*D. brachypterus*); 15cm
Zebra lionfish (*D. zebra*); 25cm
Spotfin lionfish (*Pterois antennata*); 19cm
Tailbar lionfish (*P. radiata*); 20cm
Lionfish (*P. volitans*); 30cm

Ikan pipi-perisai (*cheek-shield*)
Ikan kalajengking
Lepu (*fish with toxic spines*), ikan anjing
   (*dog fish*), pangaten, ikan suanggi
   (*witch doctor*); kelopo (Ba)
Ikan tembaga (*copper*); laroh (Ba)
Lepu batu

Lepu ayam (*chicken*)—all lionfishes

Lepu

Lepu ayam (*chicken*)

Perciformes: Bangsa Kerapu (Grouper clan)

Fairy Basslets and Groupers (Serranidae)
Magenta slender basslet (*Luzonichthys waitei*); 5cm
Peach fairy basslet (*Pseudanthias dispar*); 8cm
Red-cheeked anthias (*P. huchtii*); 8cm
Lyretail coralfish (*P. squammipinnis*); 10cm
Purple queen (*P. pascalus*); 12cm
Pink-square anthias (*P. pleurotaenia*); 10cm
Purple queen (*P. tuka*); 8cm
White-lined grouper (*Anyperodon leucogrammicus*); 41cm
Peacock grouper (*Cephalopholis argus*); 42cm
Leopard grouper (*C. leopardus*); 20cm

All fairy basslets: Nona manis (*sweet girl*),
   ikan pisang-pisang (*bananas*); daya-
   suboh (Ba)
All groupers: kerapu, garupa; kiapu (Ba);
   suno (Bu)

Argus bintik (*spot, stain*), biru (*blue*)
Kiapu tongko, kiapu geang (Ba)

Coral grouper (*C. miniata*); 30cm
Flagtail grouper (*C. urodeta*); 19cm
Polkadot grouper, pantherfish (*Cromileptes altivelis*); 70cm
Black-tipped grouper (*Ephinephelus fasciatus*); 29cm
Blotchy grouper (*E. fuscogattatus*); 89cm
Honeycomb grouper (*E. merra*); 23cm
Giant grouper (*E. lanceolatus*); 3m total length, 400 kg
Saddleback grouper (*Plectropomus laevis*); 1m
Lyretail grouper (*Variola louti*); 56cm

Kiapu mirah (Ba)
Kiapu pedi betah (Ba); loong (Bu)
Kerapu bebek (*duck*), Geris Keli (*Grace Kelly!*)

Kerapu macan (*tiger*)

Kerapu lumpur; kiapu lohong (Ba)
Suno Bendera (Bu)
Suno enro (Bu)

Soapfishes (Grammistidae)
Lined soapfish (*Grammistes sexlineatus*); 27cm

Cantik jelita (*lovely, usually to girls*)

Prettyfins (Plesiopidae)
Comet (*Calloplesiops altivelis*); 11cm
Argus comet (*C. argus*); 11cm

Dottybacks (Pseudochromidae)
Paccagnalle's dottyback (*Pseudochromis paccagnallae*); 6cm
Magenta dottyback (*P. porphyreus*); 5cm

Ikan jentung

Hawkfishes (Cirrhitidae)
Falco hawkfish (*Cirrhitichthys falco*); 5cm
Pixy hawkfish (*C. oxycephalus*); 7cm
Longnose hawkfish (*Oxycirrhites typus*); 8cm
Arc-eye hawkfish (*Paracirrhites arcatus*); 11cm
Forster's hawkfish (*P. forsteri*); 17cm

Cardinalfishes (Apogonidae)
Cardinalfishes (*Apogon* spp.); av. 5–8cm
Pajama cardinalfish (*Sphaeramia nematoptera*); 6cm

Serinding, ikan sang karang; bebeseh (Ba)

Bigeyes (Priacanthidae)
Glasseye (*Heteropriacanthus cruentatus*); 23cm
Goggle-eye (*Priacanthus hamrur*); 26cm

Gora suanggi (*witch doctor*), serinding tembako (*tobacco cardinalfish*)

Remoras (Echeneididae)
Striped sharksucker (*Echeneis naucrates*); 90cm
Remora (*Remora remora*); 40cm

Kutu (*louse*); keluyu
Gemih
Gemih besar (*big*)

Jacks and Trevallies (Carangidae)

Kuwe or kuweh, bubara (*jacks*), selar (*Selar* sp. *scads*), ikan layang (*scads*), tetengkek (*hardtail scads*); pipili (Ba) (*jacks*)

Slender scad (*Decapterus macrosoma*); 35cm
Bigeye scad (*Selar crumenophthalmus*); 30cm
Threadfin pompano (*Alectis ciliaris*); 65cm
Indian threadfish (*A. indicus*); 1.5m
Golden trevally (*Gnathanodon speciosus*); 1.1m
Giant trevally (*Caranx ignobilis*); 1.7m
Black jack (*C. lugubris*); 91cm
Bluefin trevally (*C. melampygus*); 80cm
Bigeye jack (*C. sexfasciatus*); 85cm
Leatherback (*Scomberoides lysan*); 70cm

Ikan layang
Selar bentong
Kuwe rambut (*hair*)
Kuwe rambut (*hair*)
Kuwe macan (*tiger*)

Dayah nyumbah (Ba)

Lasi (*forbidden eating*), lima jari (*five fingers*); manok (Ba)

Rainbow runner (*Elagatis bipinnulatus*); 1.2m
Greater amberjack (*Seriola dumerili*); 1.9m
Silver pompano (*Trachinotus blochii*); 1.1m

Sunglir; uroh-uroh (Ba); suru (Bu)
Bangaya (Ba)

Mojarras (Gerreidae)
Common mojarra (*Gerres argyreus*); 19cm

Ikan kapas-kapas (*cotton*)

Snappers (Lutjanidae)
Blue-lined sea bream (*Symphorichthys spilurus*); 50cm
Black-and-white snapper (*Macolor macularis*); 50cm
Black snapper (*M. niger*); 60cm
River snapper (*Lutjanus argentimaculatus*); 70cm
Red snapper (*L. bohar*); 80cm

Blackspot snapper (*L. ehrenbergi*); 26cm
Flametail snapper (*L. fulvus*); 35cm
Humpback snapper (*L. gibbus*); 42cm
Bluelined snapper (*L. kasmira*); 26cm
Onespot snapper (*L. monostigmus*); 45cm

Bambangan, gerot-gerot; sulayasa (Ba)
Dayah sangai (Ba)
Kakap
Ikan tanda-tanda (*signs, markers*)

Ikan merah (*red fish*), jenaha, kakap;
ahrang (Ba)

Dapa

Fusiliers (Caesionidae)
Yellowtail fusilier (*Caesio cuning*); 23cm
Lunar fusilier (*C. lunaris*); 26cm
Yellowback fusilier (*C. teres*); 27cm
Bluestreak fusilier (*Pterocaesio tile*); 22cm
Three-striped fusilier (*P. trilineata*); 13cm

Pisang-pisang, lalosi
Ekor kuning (*yellowtail*); bulek kuneh (Ba)

Sweetlips and Grunts (Haemulidae)

Slatey sweetlips (*Diagramma pictum*); 78cm
Sulawesi sweetlips (*Plectorhinchus celebecus*); 41cm
Clown sweetlips (*P. chaetodonoides*); 60cm
Goldman's sweetlips (*P. goldmanni*); 60cm
Oriental sweetlips (*P. orientalis*); 72cm
Spotted sweetlips (*P. picus*); 70cm
Yellow-ribbon sweetlips (*P. polytaenia*); 70cm

Ikan gerot-gerot, raja bau (*smell*), raja caci,
pepondok.
Kerong-kerong (Ba); kokoreh (Bu)

Laundung (Ba)
Balekeh (Ba)
Balekeh (Ba)
Lepeh (Ba)
Gaiji

Threadfin breams (Nemipteridae)
Black-and-white spinecheeks (*Scolopsis lineatus*); 20cm
Redfin mid-water bream (*Pentapodus macrurus*); 30cm

Suelala (Ba)

Emperors (Lethrinidae)
Yellowspot emperor (*Gnathodentex aurolineatus*); 21cm
Bigeye emperor (*Monotaxis grandoculus*); 45cm
Ambon emperor (*Lethrinus amboinensis*); 57cm
Blackspot emperor (*L. harak*); 50cm
Longnose emperor (*L. olivaceus*); 84cm

Lencam, ketambak, asunan
Lalanga (Ba)

Sikuda; lausa (Ba); anduping (Bu)

Goatfishes (Mullidae)
Yellowstripe goatfish (*Mulloides flavolineatus*); 36cm
Yellowfin goatfish (*M. vanicolensis*); 31cm
Dash-dot goatfish (*Parupeneus barberinus*); 50cm
Multibarred goatfish (*P. multifasciatus*); 24cm

Biji nangka (*jackfruit seed*), jangut kuniran
(*yellow beard*), ikan kambing (*goat
fish*); jajango (Ba); salmoneti,
matadung (Bu)

Sweepers (Pempheridae)
Pigmy sweep (*Parapriacanthus ransonneti*); 6cm

Chubs (Kyphosidae)
Snubnose chub (*Kyphosus cinerascens*); 37cm

Batfishes (Ephippidae)
Orbiculate batfish (*Platax orbicularis*); 47cm
Pinnate batfish (*P. pinnatus*); 37cm
Round-faced batfish (*P. tiera*); 41cm

Kalong (*fruit-eating bat/flying fox*)
Gebel, ikan bawal, ikan bendera (*flag*)
Gebel bunder
Gebel asli (*native*)
Gebel biasa (*ordinary*)

Butterflyfishes (Chaetodontidae)
Threadfin butterflyfish (*Chaetodon auriga*); 15cm
Baroness butterflyfish (*C. barronessa*); 11cm
Bennett's butterflyfish (*C. bennetti*); 15cm
Saddleback butterflyfish (*C. ephippium*); 17cm
Klein's butterflyfish (*C. kleinii*); 11cm
Lined butterflyfish (*C. lineolatus*); 24cm
Raccoon butterflyfish (*C. lunula*); 16cm
Meyer's butterflyfish (*C. meyeri*); 14cm
Ornate butterflyfish (*C. ornatissimus*); 15cm
Spotnape butterflyfish (*C. oxycephalus*); 17cm
Raffles' butterflyfish (*C. rafflesii*); 11cm
Red-finned butterflyfish (*C. trifasciatus*); 12cm
Vagabond butterflyfish (*C. vagabundus*); 16cm
Copperband butterflyfish (*Chelmon rostratus*); 18cm
Longnose butterflyfish (*Forcipiger flavissimus*); 18cm
Big longnose butterflyfish (*F. longirostris*); 18cm
Pyramid butterflyfish (*Hemitaurichthys polylepis*); 13cm
Bannerfish (*Heniochus acuminatus*); 20cm
Bannerfish (*H. diphreutes*); 19cm
Pennant bannerfish (*H. chrysostomus*); 13cm
Masked bannerfish (*H. monoceros*); 18cm
Singular bannerfish (*H. singularis*); 24cm
Humphead bannerfish (*H. varius*); 15cm

Kepe-kepe, ikan kupu-kupu (*butterfly*),
ikan daun-daun (*leaves*), kiper laut
[Note: Colorful reef fishes in general, butterflyfish, angelfish, damselfish: ikan karang (*coral*), ikan prong or ikan hias (*ornamental*), ikan cincin (*ring*)]

Kepe-kepe monyung asli (*native, true*)
Kepe-kepe monyung palsu (*false*)

Angelfishes (Pomacanthidae)
Three-spot angelfish (*Apolemichthys trimaculatus*); 26cm
Bicolor angelfish (*Centropyge bicolor*); 14cm
Dusky angelfish (*C. bispinosus*); 10cm
Lemonpeel angelfish (*C. flavissimus*); 8cm
Keyhole angelfish (*C. tibicen*); 15cm
Pearlscale angelfish (*C. vrolikii*); 8cm
Blackspot angelfish (*Genicanthus melanospilos*); 15cm
Regal angelfish (*Pygoplites diacanthus*); 21cm
Blue-ring angelfish (*Pomacanthus annularis*); 30cm
Emperor angelfish (*P. imperator*); 30cm

Blue-girdled angelfish (*P. navarchus*); 20cm
Semicircle angelfish (*P. semicirculatus*); 29cm
Six-banded angelfish (*P. sextriatus*); 38cm
Blue-faced angelfish (*P. xanthometopon*); 32cm

Injel ("*angel*"), ikan kupu-kupu (*butterfly*);
edo (Ba)
Injel biru-kuning (*blue and yellow*)

Injel hitam (*black*)

Injel lurik (*type of striped cloth*)

Kambing (*goat*), raja (*king*)
Kaiser, beluston, betman ("*batman*")
Injel piyama (*yes, "pyjamas"*)
kambing (*goat*), koran (*Muslim holy book*)

Beluston, beluboran

Damselfishes (Pomacentridae)
Sergeant-major (*Abudefduf vaigiensis*); 17cm
Golden damsel (*Amblygliphidodon aureus*); 10cm
Staghorn damsel (*A. curacao*); 9cm
Skunk anemonefish (*Amphiprion akallopisos*); 9cm
Orange-fin anemonefish (*A. chrysopterus*); 13cm
Clark's anemonefish (*A. clarkii*); 10cm
Red saddleback anemonefish (*A. ephippium*); 11cm
Tomato anemonefish (*A. frenatus*); 11cm
Dusky anemonefish (*A. melanopus*); 9cm
Clown anemonefish (*A. ocellaris*); 8cm
Pink anemonefish (*A. perideraion*); 8cm
Saddleback anemonefish (*A. polymnus*); 10cm
Orange anemonefish (*A. sandaracinos*); 11cm
Reef chromis (*Chromis agilis*); 8cm
Yellow-speckled chromis (*C. alpha*); 9cm
Ambon chromis (*C. amboinensis*); 6cm
Yellow chromis (*C analis*); 14cm
Black-axil chromis (*C. atripectoralis*); 9cm

Asan, giru
Bonang-bonang, sersan major

For all anemonefishes: Klon ("*clown*"),
klon asan, giru prong, gemutu, ikan
jamur (*mushroom*); kinsang (Ba)

For all *Chromis* spp.: Gucia, betok laut,
kapas-kapas (*cotton fleece*)

Bicolor chromis (*C. margaritifer*); 6cm
Blue-green chromis (*C. viridis*); 7cm
Blue devil (*Chrysiptera cyanea*); 6cm
Blue-spot damsel (*C. oxycephala*); 7cm
Three-striped dascyllus (*Dascyllus aruanus*); 7cm
Black-tailed dascyllus (*D. melanurus*); 7cm
Reticulated dascyllus (*D. reticulatus*); 6cm
Three-spot dascyllus (*D. trimaculatus*); 11cm
Black damsel (*Neoglyphidodon melas*); 13cm
Java damsel (*N. oxyodon*); 12cm
Behn's damsel (*N. nigroris*); 9cm
Neon damsel (*Pomacentrus coelestis*); 7cm
Lemon damsel (*P. moluccensis*); 6cm
Peacock damsel (*P. pavo*); 9cm
Spine-cheek anemonefish (*Premnas biaculeatus*); 17cm
Farmerfish (*Stegastes lividus*); 13cm
Dusky farmerfish (*S. nigricans*); 12cm

Dakocan (*black puppet*), giru bolong (*pierced*), giru gete-gete

Wrasses (Labridae)
Lyretail hogfish (*Bodianus anthoides*); 24cm
Axilspot hogfish (*B. axillaris*); 16cm
Red-breasted wrasse (*Cheilinus fasciatus*); 28cm
Napoleon wrasse; humphead wrasse (*C. undulatus*);
   1.8m; total length to 2.3m
Ringtail wrasse (*C. unifasciatus*); 38cm
Slingjaw wrasse (*Epibulus insidiator*); 30cm
Clown coris (*Coris aygula*); 1m
Yellowtail coris (*C. gaimard*); 35cm
Bird wrasse (*Gomphosus varius*); 18cm
Two-tone wrasse (*Thalassoma amblycephalum*); 12cm
Lunar wrasse (*T. lunare*); 18cm
Bicolor cleaner wrasse (*Labroides bicolor*); 10cm
Bluestreak cleaner wrasse (*L. dimidiatus*); 9cm

Keling (*small wrasses*). Babi (*pig*) or Nuri-nuri (*a type of parrot*) (*large wrasses*). Gigi anjing (*dog's tooth*) (*tuskfishes*). Lamboso; lampah (Ba) (*hogfishes*).
Besiparai (Ba)
Napoleon; langkoeh, angkeh (Ba)

Keling merah putih (*red-white*)

Ikan doktor (*doctor fish*)
Ikan doktor (*doctor fish*)

Parrotfishes (Scaridae)
Bumphead parrotfish (*Bolbometopon muricatum*); 1m
Bicolor parrotfish (*Cetoscarus bicolor*); 60cm
Filament-finned parrotfish (*Scarus altipinnis*); 41cm
Blue-chin parrotfish (*S. atropectoralis*); 42cm
Bleeker's parrotfish (*S. bleekeri*); 39cm
Festive parrotfish (*S. festivus*); 34cm
Yellowfin parrotfish (*S. flavipectoralis*); 21cm
Blue-barred parrotfish (*S. ghobban*); 57cm
Java parrotfish (*S. hypselopterus*); 26cm
Pale-nose parrotfish (*S. psittacus*); 27cm
Rivulated parrotfish (*S. rivulatus*); 34cm
Redlip parrotfish (*S. rubroviolaceus*); 48cm
Bullethead parrotfish (*S. sordidus*); 26cm

Ikan kakatua (*cockatoo*); pelo, mogoh (Ba)
Ankeh (Ba); Loong (Bu)
Mogoh (Ba)

Mullets (Mugilidae)
Fringelip mullet (*Crenimugil crenilabis*); 50cm
Engel's mullet (*Valamugil engeli*); 15cm
Mullet (*V. speigleri*)

Mul abu-abu (*ashes*)
Belanak, tikus-tikus (*mice*), kuro, sumbal
Ikan janggut (*beard*); depoh (Ba)
Bunteh (Ba)

Barracudas (Sphyraenidae)
Great barracuda (*Sphyraena barracuda*); 1.7m
Blackfin barracuda (*S. genie*); 1.5m
Arrow barracuda (*S. novaehollandiae*); 50cm

Senuk, alu-alu, barakuda
Pangaluang (Ba), barakuda besar

Sandperches (Pinguipedidae)

Sandperches (*Parapercis* spp.); approx. 14cm

Blennies (Blenniidae)
Bicolor blenny (*Ecsenius bicolor*); 8cm
Red-spotted blenny (*Istiblennius chrysospilos*); 11cm
Cleaner mimic blenny (*Aspidontus taeniatus*); 10cm
Scale-eating blenny (*Plagiotremus tapienosoma*); 12cm

Ikan tembakul

Dragonets (Callionymidae)
Mandarinfish (*Synchiropus splendidus*); 5cm

Dartfishes (Microdesmidae)
Zebra dartfish (*Ptereleotris zebra*); 10cm
Decorated dartfish (*Nemateleotris decora*); 7cm
Firefish (*N. magnifica*); 5cm

Gobies (Gobiidae)
Prawn gobies (various); ave. 7cm
Gorgonian goby (*Bryaninops amplus*); 5cm
Coral gobies (*Gobiodon* and *Paragobiodon* spp.); ave.
    4cm
Mudskipper (*Periophthalmus kalolo*); 10cm

Beladok cina; belosoh

Belosoh karang (*coral*)

Beladok, glodok

Surgeonfishes (Acanthuridae)
Ringtail surgeonfish (*Acanthurus blochii*); 32cm
Clown surgeonfish (*A. lineatus*); 24cm
Whitecheek surgeonfish (*A. nigricans*); 16cm
Powder-blue surgeonfish (*A. leucosternun*); 20cm
Orangeband surgeonfish (*A. olivaceus*); 25cm
Mimic tang (*A. pyroferus*); 19cm
Thompson's surgeonfish (*A. thompsoni*); 19cm
Convict tang (*A. triostegus*); 21cm
Yellowfin surgeonfish (*A. xanthopterus*); 43cm
Striped bristletooth tang (*Ctenochaetus striatus*); 20cm
Goldring surgeonfish (*C. strigosus*); 14cm
Tomini surgeonfish (*C. tominiensis*); 10cm
Hepatus tang (*Paracanthurus hepatus*); 20cm
Brown tang (*Zebrasomas scopas*); 15cm
Sailfin tang (*Z. veliferum*); 30cm
Whitemargin unicornfish (*Naso annulatus*); 1m
Humpback unicornfish (*N. brachycentron*); 90cm
Spotted unicornfish (*N. brevirostris*); 60cm
Sleek unicornfish (*N. hexacanthus*); 75cm
Orangespine unicornfish (*N. literatus*); 31cm
Humpnosed unicornfish (*N. tuberosus*); 60cm
Bluespine unicornfish (*N. unicornis*); 70cm
Bignose unicornfish (*N. vlamingii*); 50cm

Surgeonfishes—Gron, Botana; kadodoh
    (Ba). Unicornfishes—Gutana; kumai
    (Ba).
Botana kasur (*mattress*)

Kecamata (*eyeglasses*)

Gron Lorek (*stripe*), Lima (*five*)

Angka enam (*the numeral 6*)
Tetpai tambako (*makes you "drunk"*) (Ba)

Kumai tandoh (Ba)

Moorish Idol (Zanclidae)
Moorish Idol (*Zanclus cornutus*); 14cm

Ikan bendera (*flag*), gayam, moris idol

Rabbitfishes (Siganidae)

Foxface (*Siganus [Lo] volpinus*); 18cm
Seagrass rabbitfish (*S. canaliculatus*); 23cm
Coral rabbitfish (*S. corallinus*); 23cm
Pencil-streaked rabbitfish (*S. doliatus*); 20cm
Golden rabbitfish (*S. guttatus*); 33cm
Lined rabbitfish (*S. lineatus*); 34cm
Scribbled rabbitfish (*S. spinus*); 23cm
Double-barred rabbitfish (*S. virgatus*); 20cm

Baronang, bihang, masadar; uhi, bulawis
    (Ba); belawis (Bu); bete-bete (M)
Berah (Ba)
Lingkis, bulawis samo

Kea-kea
Baronang lada; berah (Ba)

Bulawis jantang (Ba)

Tunas and mackerels (Scombridae)

Frigate mackerel (*Auxis thazard*)
Double-lined mackerel (*Grammatorcynos bilineatus*); 60cm
Dogtooth tuna (*Gymnosarda unicolor*); 2m
Striped mackerel (*Rastrelliger kanagurta*); 35cm
Narrow-barred king mackerel (*Scomberomorus commersoni*); 2.2m
Skipjack tuna (*Katsuwonus pelamis*)
Albacore (*Thunnus alalunga*)
Yellowfin tuna (*T. albacares*)

Southern bluefin tuna (*T. maccoyii*)
Bigeye tuna (*T. obesus*)
Longtail tuna (*T. tonggol*)

Tuna (*tunas and billfish*), tongkol (*little tunas, makerels*), tenggiri (*makerels*)
Tongkol, makelel fregat
Andeh-andeh (Ba)

Bambuloh (Ba); pakukul (Bu)
Kembung lelaki
Tenggiri

Cakalang
Albakor
Madidihang, pane, tuna sirip (*fin*) kuning (*yellow*)
Tuna sirip biru (*blue-fin*)
Tuna mata besar (*big-eye*)
Abu-abu (*ashes*), tuna ekor panjang (*longtail*)

Flounders (Pleuronectiformes)

Ikan sebelah (*one-half*)

Flatfishes (Bothidae)
Peacock flounder (*Bothus mancus*); 40cm
Black-spotted sole (*Aseraggodes melanostictus*); 5cm

Kalankan, ikan lidah (*tongue*)

Triggerfishes (Balistidae)

Orange-striped triggerfish (*Balistapus undulatus*); 23cm
Clown triggerfish (*Balistoides conspicillum*); 25cm

Titan triggerfish (*B. viridescens*); 63cm
Grey triggerfish (*Melichthys niger*); 28cm
Black triggerfish, red-tooth triggerfish (*Odonus niger*); 29cm
Yellow-margined triggerfish (*Pseudobalistes flavomarginatus*); 53cm
Undulate triggerfish (*P. fuscus*); 41cm
Picasso triggerfish (*Rhinecanthus aculeatus*); 20cm
Rectangular triggerfish (*R. rectangulus*); 18cm
Blackbelly Picasso triggerfish (*R. verrucosa*); 19cm

Triger, ikan tato, ikan tatul (*wound*); ampala (Ba); pogo (Bu); sunga (M)
Kauk; popogo batu (Ba); kau (Bu)
Triger kembang (*flower*), triger ceplok (*polkadot*); ampala bulunti (Ba)
Triger sisir (*comb*); ampala gila (*crazy*) (Ba)

Triger abu-abu (*ashes*)

Triger liris (*batik pattern*)
Triger matahari (*sun*)
Triger segi tiga (*triangle*)

Filefishes (Monacanthidae)
Scribbled filefish (*Aluterus scriptus*); 71cm
Barred filefish (*Cantherhines dumerili*); 25cm
Wire-net filefish (*C. pardalis*); 20cm
Longnose filefish (*Oxymonacanthus longirostris*); 10cm
Blackbar filefish (*Pervagor janthinosoma*); 11cm

Bulusan babi (*pig*), hayam

Trunkfishes (Ostraciidae)

Longhorn cowfish (*Lactoria cornuta*); 30cm

Cubefish (*Ostracion cubicus*); 31cm
Spotted trunkfish (*O. meleagris*); 15cm
Reticulate boxfish (*O. solorensis*); 10cm

Ikan buntel kotak (*swelled box*); pogo, lumis, kepe (Ba)
Ikan buntel tanduk (*horn*); cocoring (Ba); kabila, tatumbu (Bu)

Puffers (Tetradontidae)
Whitespotted puffer (*Arothron hispidus*); 45cm
Map puffer (*A. mappa*); 54cm
Guineafowl puffer (*A. melagris*); 40cm
Dog-faced puffer, black-spotted puffer (*A. nigropunctatus*); 27cm

Ikan buntal (*swollen, bloated*)

Gurisang (Ba)

Star puffer (*A. stellatus*); 90cm
Ambon sharpnose puffer (*Canthigaster amboinensis*);
   10cm
Crowned sharpnose puffer (*C. cornata*); 10cm
Spotted sharpnose puffer (*C. solandri*); 9cm
Valentini's sharpnose puffer (*C. valentini*); 8cm

Porcupinefishes (Diodontidae)	Ikan duren (*spiky, delicious fruit*); konkeh
Porcupinefish (*Diodon hystrix*); 80cm	(Ba); landah (Bu), landak (*porcupine*)

Boxfishes (Ostraciidae)	
Cowfish (*Lactoria cornuta*)	Buntal lembu (*ox, cow, bull*)
Boxfish (*Ostrocion sp.*)	Buntal kotak (*box*)
	Buntal tanduk (*horns*)

Other animals	Ular laut

Sea snakes (famlly Hydrophiidae)
Colubrine sea snake (*Laticauda colubrina*)
Yellow-bellied sea snake (*Pelamis platurus*)

Sea turtles (order Chelonia)	Penyu (*any kind of turtle*)
Loggerhead (*Caretta caretta*)	Penyu tempayan (*large water jar*)
Green turtle (*Chelonia mydas*)	Penyu hijau (*green*), penyu daging (*meat*)
Leatherback turtle (*Dermochelys coriacea*)	Penyu belimbing (*like a starfruit*)
Hawksbill turtle (*Eremochelys imbricata*)	Penyu sisik (*tortoiseshell*), penyu kembang
Flatback turtle (*Natator depressus*)	Penyu pipih
Olive ridley turtle (*Lepidochelys olivacea*)	Penyu lekang

Dugong (order Sirenia)	Dugung
Dugong (*Dugong dugon*)	

Whales (order Cetacea)	Ikan paus (*pope fish*)
Shortfin pilot whale (*Globicephala macrorhynchus*)	Temu bela (*Lamalera*)
Great killer whale (*Orcinus orca*)	Seguni
Pygmy killer whale (*Feresa attenuata*)	

Striped dolphin (*Stenella coeruleoalba*)	Lumba-lumba (*all dolphins*)
Spinner dolphin (*S. longirostris*)	Timu kira (*Lamalera language*)
Common dolphin (*Delphinus delphis*)	
Bottlenose dolphin (*Tursiops truncatus*)	Lumba-lumba berhidung botol (*bottlenose*)

Pygmy sperm whale (*Kogis* spp.)	
Sperm whale (*Physeter catodon*)	Lodan, kotal lema

Minke whale (*Balaenoptera acutorostrata*)	Kararu
Sei whale (*B. borealis*)	Kararu
Bryde's whale (*B. edeni*)	Kararu
Blue whale (*B. musculus*)	Ikan paus biru (*blue*)
Fin whale (*B. physalus*)	Kararu
Humpback whale (*Megaptera novaeangliae*)	

Indonesian Dive Terms
WITH ENGLISH, GERMAN AND FRENCH

ENGLISH	INDONESIAN	GERMAN	FRENCH
Dive	Selam	Tauchgang	Plonger
Flipper/fin	Sepatu bebek ("duck shoe")	Flosse	Palmes
Regulator	Regulator	Lungenautomat	Détendeur
Mask	Masker or Kacamata Selam	Maske or Taucherbrille	Masque or Combinaison
Snorkel	Snorkel	Schnorchel	Tuba
BC	Pelampung	Tarierweste	Bouée
Weight	Timbah or pemberat	Gewicht	Plomb
Weight belt	Ikat pinggang	Bleigurt	Ceinture
Tank	Tenki or tabung	Pressluftflasche	Bouteille
O-ring	Oli sel or karet	Dichtung/O Ring	Joint thorique
Flashlight	Senter	Taschenlampe	Pile
Compressor	Kompresor	Kompressor	Compresseur
Air	Angin	Luft	Air
Follow	Ikut	Befolgen	Suivre
Bubble	Gelembung udara	Luftblase	Bulle
The air is no good (oily)	Angin kurang baik (rasa oli)	Die Luft ist nicht gut (ölig)	Mauvais air (huile)
Current	Arus	Strömung	Courant
Strong current	Arus kuat	Starke Strömung	Courant fort
Fast	Cepat	Schnell	Vite
Slow	Palan-palan	Langsam	Lentement
Danger	Berbahaya	Gefahr	Dangereux
Look out!	Awas!	Pass auf!	Attention!
Careful	Hati-hati	Vorsichtig	Attention
Water	Air	Wasser	Eau
High tide	Air pasang	Flut	Marée haute
Low tide	Air surut	Ebbe	Marée basse
Wave	Ombak	Welle	Vague
Big wave	Ombak besar	Grosse Welle	Grosse vague
Little wave	Ombak kecil	Kleine Welle	Petite vague
East	Timur	Osten	Est
West	Barat	Westen	Ouest
North	Utara	Norden	Nord
South	Selatan	Süden	Sud
Full moon	Purnama	Vollmond	Pleine lune
Deep	Dalam	Tief	Profond
How deep?	Berapa dalam?	Wie tief?	Quelle profondeur?
Shallow	Dankal	Seicht	Peu profond
Sand	Pasir	Sand	Sable
Coral	Karang	Koralle	Corail
Sea urchin	Bulu babi (*pig bristle*)	Seeigel	Oursin
Boat	Kapal	Boot	bateau
Canoe	Prahu	Kanu	Pirogue
Outrigger	Tangah (also *ladder*)	Ausleger	Echelle
Outboard	Jonson (Johnson)	Aussenborder	Horsbord
Horsepower	P.K.	Pferdestärken, PS	Chevaux
How much horsepower?	Berapa P.K.	Wieviel PS?	Quelle puissance?
How long?	Berapa panjang?	Wie lang?	Quelle longueur?
Rent, charter	Carter, sewa	Mieten, chartern	Louer
How much?	Berapa?	Wieviel?	Combien?
	Per jam, per hari	Pro Stunde, pro Tag	Par heure, par jour

Further Reading

In addition to a good guide, a diver is probably most interested in a fish identification book, to help make some order out of the more than 2,500 species swimming around the reefs of Indonesia. Two excellent resources recently became available.

TROPICAL REEF-FISHES

Tropical Reef-Fishes Of The Western Pacific— Indonesia And Adjacent Waters, by Rudie H. Kuiter is the first extensive guide to the reef fishes of Indonesia.

This compact, handsome book is a manageable 300 pages long, and includes 1,300 excellent color photographs, illustrating 1,027 species including males, females and juveniles, where color or morphological differences exist. *Tropical Reef-Fishes* covers more than 50 families of reef fishes, just about every species you are likely to see around Indonesia's reefs down to about 30 meters.

Each family receives a brief description, headed by a large photo and followed by several smaller ones, usually six to the page. The common names are Australian usage (Kuiter lives in Australia). Kuiter is one of the world's leading authorities on Pacific reef fishes, being the principal author of the description of a half-dozen new species and associate author for a dozen more. Some of these new species are included in this book. Because of space constraints, however, not all families are listed. In particular, there is nothing on sharks, rays and some of the roving lagoon species, and pelagic species are skipped over lightly. Some of these, of course, are of great interest to the diver. Still, it is an indispensable work.

MICRONESIAN REEF FISHES

Micronesian Reef Fishes: A Practical Guide to the Identification of the Inshore Marine Fishes of the Tropical Central and Western Pacific, 2d ed., by Robert F. Myers, also belongs in the library of every diver in Indonesia. While Myers has not sought to write a book about Indonesian species, there is a great deal of overlap in the faunas of the two regions, and well over 90 percent of the species discussed can be found in Indonesia.

Myers' book is a model of accuracy and detail, with clear color photos of more than 1,000 species, complete meristics, and a dense 50–100 word description of the habitat and behavior of each species. A large number of black-and-white photos of preserved specimens and line drawings are particularly useful, showing such details as the location of cirri and mouth shapes where it is important in identification.

Myers covers the sharks and rays, and a number of other families Kuiter leaves out. Still, Kuiter's book describes 15–20 more butterflyfish, and 30 more damsels. The best solution is to get both.

OTHER WORKS OF INTEREST

The grandfather of all Indonesian fish guides is of course Bleeker's Atlas Ichthyologique. It is still very accurate, although not even close to being portable, or even available. Another very valuable book that became available as we were in production is Gerald R. Allen's *Damselfishes of the World*. This fine book describes and illustrates some 321 damselfish, all that are currently known, including 16 new species. Full meristics, and range and habitat descriptions of all the species are included.

The most available series of books on Indo-Pacific reef life in the United States are those put out by Tropical Fish Hobbyist publications in New Jersey. Unfortunately, however, these books are almost universally awful. They are really badly edited, with misidentified photos and poor organization.

Unfortunately, we were unable to find any books on the rich invertebrate life of Indonesian reefs as thorough and compact as the above-mentioned fish books. We have listed some below, however, that may prove helpful.

FISHES

Allen, Gerald R. *Butterfly And Angelfishes Of The World.* New York: Wiley Interscience, 1979.

——*Damselfishes of the World.* Hong Kong: Mergus, 1991. (Distributed in the United States by Aquarium Systems, 8141 Tyler Blvd., Mentor OH 44060.)

Allen, Gerald R. and Roger C. Steene. *Reef Fishes Of The Indian Ocean* (Pacific Marine

Fishes, Book 10). Neptune, N.J.: T.F.H. Publications, 1988.

Bleeker, Pieter. *Atlas Ichthyologique des Indes Orientales Neerlandaises* (9 volumes). Amsterdam, 1877. (Dr. Bleeker's classic "Atlas." Out of print and very valuable. Look for it at a good library.)

Burgess, Warren E. *Atlas Of Marine Aquarium Fishes*. Neptune, N.J.: T.F.H. Publications, 1988. (Full of inaccuracies and misidentified photos; no scientific value.)

Burgess, Warren E. and Herbert R. Axelrod. *Fishes of the Great Barrier Reef* (Pacific Marine Fishes, Book 7). Neptune, N.J.: T.F.H. Publications. 1975.

——*Fishes of Melanesia* (Pacific Marine Fishes Book 7). Neptune, N.J.: T.F.H. Publications, 1975.

Carcasson, R. H. *A Guide To Coral Reef Fishes Of The Indian And West Pacific Regions*. London: Collins, 1977. (Out of date, hard to recognize fishes from the drawings.)

Kuiter, Rudie H. *Tropical Reef-Fishes Of The Western Pacific—Indonesia And Adjacent Waters*. Jakarta: Gramedia, 1992. (Excellent, see above.)

Myers, Robert F. *Micronesian Reef Fishes: A Practical Guide to the Identification of the Inshore Marine Fishes of the Tropical Central and Western Pacific*, 2d ed. Guam: Coral Graphics, 1991. (Excellent, see text above. Order through Coral Graphics, P.O. Box 21153, Guam Main Facility, Barrigada, Territory of Guam 96921.)

Nelson, J.S. *Fishes Of The World*. New York: John Wiley and Sons, 1984.

Piesch, Ted and D.B. Grobecker. *Frogfishes Of The World*. Stanford, CA: Stanford University Press, 1987.

Randall, John E., Gerald R. Allen and Roger Steene. *Fishes of the Great Barrier Reef and the Coral Sea*. Bathhurst, Australia: Crawford House Press, University of Hawaii Press, 1990.

Sawada, T. *Fishes in Indonesia*. Japan International Cooperation Agency, 1980.

Schuster W.H. and R.R. Djajadiredja. *Local Common Names For Indonesia Fishes*. Bandung, Java: N.V. Penerbit W. Van Hoeve, 1952.

Weber, M. and de Beaufort, L.F. *The Fishes Of The Indo- Australian Archipelago* (11 volumes, 404–607 pages each). Leiden, E.J. Brill. 1913–1962.

INVERTEBRATES

Debelius, Helmut. *Armoured Nights of the Sea*. Kernan Verlag, 1984.

Ditlev, Hans A. *A Field-Guide to the Reef-Building Corals of the Indo-Pacific*. Klampenborg: Scandinavian Science Press, 1980. (Good, compact volume.)

Randall, Richard H. and Robert F. Myers. *Guide to the Coastal Resources of Guam, vol. 2: the Corals*. Guam: University of Guam Press, 1983.

Usher, G.F. "Coral Reef Invertebrates In Indonesia." IUNC/WWF Report, 1984.

Walls, Jerry G., ed. *Encyclopedia of Marine Invertebrates*. Neptune, N.J.:T.F.H. Publications, 1982. (The text of this 700-page book is often good. There are the usual mistakes with photos, however, and many of the names have not kept up with recent changes. A preponderance of the illustrations are Caribbean.)

Wells, Sue, *et al*, eds. *The IUNC Invertebrate Red Data Book*. Gland, Switzerland: International Union for Conservation of Nature and Natural Resources, 1983.

Wood, Elizabeth M. *Corals of the World*. Neptune, N.J.: T.F.H. Publications, 1983.

REEF ECOLOGY

Darwin, Charles. *The Structure and Distribution of Coral Reefs*. Tucson, AZ: University of Arizona Press, 1984.

——*The Voyage of the Beagle*. New York: Mentor (Penguin), 1988.

George, G. *Marine Life*. Sydney: Rigby Ltd, 1976 (also: New York: John Wiley & Sons).

Goreau, Thomas F., Nora I. Goreau and Thomas J. Goreau. "Corals and Coral Reefs," *Scientific American* vol. 241, 1979.

Henry, L.E. *Coral Reefs of Malaysia*. Kuala Lumpur: Longman, 1980.

Randall, Richard H. and L.G. Eldredge. "A Marine Survey Of The Shoalwater Habitats Of Ambon, Pulau Pombo, Pulau Kasa and Pulau Babi." Guam: University of Guam Marine Laboratory, 1983.

Salm, R.V. and M. Halim. *Marine Conservation Data Atlas*. IUNV/WWF Project 3108, 1984.

Soegiarto, A. and N. Polunin. "The Marine Environment Of Indonesia." A Report Prepared for the Government of the Republic of Indonesia, under the sponsorship of the IUNC and WWF, 1982.

Umbgrove, J.H.F. "Coral Reefs of the East Indies," *Bulletin Of The Geological Society of America,* vol. 58, 1947.

Wallace, Alfred Russel. *The Malay Archipelago*. Singapore: Oxford University Press, 1986.

Wells, Sue, *et al*. *Coral Reefs Of The World* (3 volumes). Gland, Switzerland: United Nations Environmental Program, 1988.

Whitten, Anthony J., Muslimin Mustafa and Gregory S. Henderson. *The Ecology of Sulawesi*. Yogyakarta, Java: Gadjah Mada University Press, 1987. (Though not exclusively or even particularly marine in focus, a very interesting work.)

Wyrtri, K. "Physical Oceanography of the Southeast Asian Waters, Naga Report Vol. 2." La Jolla, CA: University of California, Scripps Institute of Oceanography, 1961.

Index

Map Index

Canada

THE ROUGH GUIDE

written and researched by

Tim Jepson, Phil Lee and Tania Smith

with additional contributions by

Kirk Marlow

THE ROUGH GUIDES

TRAVEL GUIDES • PHRASEBOOKS • MUSIC AND REFERENCE GUIDES

 We set out to do something different when the first Rough Guide was published in 1982. Mark Ellingham, just out of university, was travelling in Greece. He brought along the popular guides of the day, but found they were all lacking in some way. They were either strong on ruins and museums but went on for pages without mentioning a beach or taverna. Or they were so conscious of the need to save money that they lost sight of Greece's cultural and historical significance. Also, none of the books told him anything about Greece's contemporary life – its politics, its culture, its people, and how they lived.

So with no job in prospect, Mark decided to write his own guidebook, one which aimed to provide practical information that was second to none, detailing the best beaches and the hottest clubs and restaurants, while also giving hard-hitting accounts of every sight, both famous and obscure, and providing up-to-the-minute information on contemporary culture. It was a guide that encouraged independent travellers to find the best of Greece, and was a great success, getting shortlisted for the Thomas Cook travel guide award, and encouraging Mark, along with three friends, to expand the series.

The Rough Guide list grew rapidly and the letters flooded in, indicating a much broader readership than had been anticipated, but one which uniformly appreciated the Rough Guide mix of practical detail and humour, irreverence and enthusiasm. Things haven't changed. The same four friends who began the series are still the caretakers of the Rough Guide mission today: to provide the most reliable, up-to-date and entertaining information to independent-minded travellers of all ages, on all budgets.

We now publish 100 titles and have offices in London and New York. The travel guides are written and researched by a dedicated team of more than 100 authors, based in Britain, Europe, the USA and Australia. We have also created a unique series of phrasebooks to accompany the travel series, along with an acclaimed series of music guides, and a best-selling pocket guide to the Internet and World Wide Web. We also publish comprehensive travel information on our Web site:

www.roughguides.com

HELP US UPDATE

We've gone to a lot of effort to ensure that this new edition of The Rough Guide to Canada is accurate and up to date. However, things change – places get "discovered", opening hours can be fickle, restaurants and rooms raise prices or lower standards, extra buses are laid on or off. If you feel we've got it wrong or left something out, we'd like to know, and if you can remember the address, the price, the time, the phone number, so much the better.

We'll credit all contributions, and send a copy of the next edition (or any other Rough Guide if you prefer) for the best letters. Please mark letters: "Rough Guide Canada Update" and send to:
Rough Guides, 62–70 Shorts Gardens, London WC2H 9AB, or Rough Guides, 375 Hudson St, 9th floor, New York NY 10014.
Or send email to: mail@roughguides.co.uk
Online updates about this book can be found on Rough Guides' Web site www.roughguides.com

THE AUTHORS OF THE ROUGH GUIDE TO CANADA

Phil Lee first experienced Canada as a bartender in an Ontario water-ski resort. Subsequent contacts have been less chaotic and have given him an abiding interest in the country. Phil has worked as a freelance author with the Rough Guides for the last ten years. Previous titles include Mallorca & Menorca, Norway, Belgium & Luxembourg, and the Pacific Northwest. He lives in Nottingham, where he was born and raised.

Tania Smith joined the Rough Guides' squad shortly after returning from a trip to watch the World Cup in Italy, then missed a season after giving birth to a daughter. She returned to the team for this edition of the Canada guide, and took the opportunity to introduce young Saba to the delights of Québec and Ontario. Tania Smith lives in Brighton, but is a Liverpool supporter.

Tim Jepson's career began with street busking and work in a slaughterhouse. Having acquired fluent Italian, he went on to better things as a Rome-based journalist and a leader of walking tours in Umbria. He is also co-author of the Rough Guide to Tuscany & Umbria, and the Rough Guide to Pacific Northwest.

READERS' LETTERS

Our thanks to everyone who has contributed letters, comments, accounts and suggestions over the years, and especially to this 1998 edition. In particular:

Nigel Bradley, David & Monica Martyn, Margaret McDonnell & Elliott Anderson, Michael Lilley, David Perrott, Karen Vosmer, Jon Hart & Sarah Pascoe, Valter Di Girolamo, Jill & David Spear, Ray Wood, Mike Daschuk, Peter K Smith, Allison & Chris Ewan, Rose Lindsay-Smith, Dr MO Pritchard, Dr Robert J Young, Matthew Gorman, Stephen & Kathi Quinn, Charles Paxton, PJ Smith, Larry J Geller, Anton Visser & Marissa Koster, Nicholas Hunt, ESJ Deards, Lucia Calland, Terrence Sakamoto, Rachel Allen, Diane Penttila, Peter Skeggs, Hazel Orchard, RV Somers Cocks, O Smith, Drs Roger & Di Gaubert, Jerry Al, Edson & Vagner Castilho, Mike Boyer, Matthew Young, Peter Wiltmann, Nobby Norman & Rhys Lewis, Shahriar Esfandiari, SM O'Garra, D Bowden.

CONTENTS

PART THREE   CONTEXTS   861

LIST OF MAPS

MAP SYMBOLS

———	Railway		✦	Airport
═══	Road		◉	Subway station
-----	Path		⍭	Lighthouse
– – –	Ferry route		⬩	Waterfall
———	Waterway		ⓘ	Tourist office
———	Chapter division boundary		⊠	Post office
▪▪▪▪	International borders		▪	Building
▬▬ ··	Province / Territory borders		✚	Church
Λ	Campsite		▒	Park
◉	Accommodation		▒	National park
⛩	Picnic area		░	Glacier
▲	Peak		▒	Alpine area
⋀⋀	Mountains			

INTRODUCTION

Canada is almost unimaginably vast. It stretches from the Atlantic to the Pacific and from the latitude of Rome to beyond the Magnetic North Pole. Its archetypal landscapes are the Rocky Mountain lakes and peaks, the endless forests and the prairie wheatfields, but Canada holds landscapes that defy expectations: rainforest and desert lie close together in the southwest corner of the country, while in the east a short drive can take you from fjords to lush orchards. What's more, great tracts of Canada are completely unspoiled – ninety percent of the country's 28.5 million population lives within 100 miles of the US border.

Like its neighbour, Canada is a spectrum of cultures, a hotchpotch of immigrant groups who supplanted the continent's many native peoples. There's a crucial difference, though. Whereas citizens of the United States are encouraged to perceive themselves as Americans above all else, Canada's concertedly multicultural approach has done more to acknowledge the origins of its people, creating an ethnic mosaic as opposed to America's "melting-pot". Alongside the French and British majorities live a host of communities who maintain the traditions of their homelands – Chinese, Ukrainians, Portuguese, Indians, Dutch, Polish, Greek and Spanish, to name just the most numerous. For the visitor, the mix that results from the country's exemplary tolerance is an exhilarating experience, offering such widely differing environments as Vancouver's huge Chinatown and the austere religious enclaves of Manitoba. Canadians themselves, however, are often troubled by the lack of a clear self-image, tending to emphasize the ways in which they are different from the US as a means of self-description. The question "What is a Canadian?" has acquired a new immediacy with the interminable and acrimonious debate over Québec and its possible secession, but ultimately there can be no simple characterization of a people whose country is not so much a single nation as a committee on a continental scale. Pierre Berton, one of Canada's finest writers, wisely ducked the issue; Canadians, he quipped, are "people who know how to make love in a canoe".

The typical Canadian might be an elusive concept, but you'll find there's a distinctive feel to the country. Some towns might seem a touch too well-regulated and unspontaneous, but against this there's the overwhelming sense of Canadian pride in their history and pleasure in the beauty of their land. Canada embraces its own clichés with an energy that's irresistible, promoting everything from the Calgary Stampede to maple syrup festivals and lumberjacking contests with an extraordinary zeal and openness. As John Buchan, writer and Governor-General of Canada, said, "You have to know a man awfully well in Canada to know his surname".

Where to go

The time and expense involved in covering Canada's immense distances means that most visitors confine their explorations to the area around one of the main cities – usually Toronto, Montréal, Vancouver or Calgary for arrivals by air. The attractions of these centres vary widely, but they have one thing in common with each other and all other Canadian towns – they are within easy reach of the great outdoors.

Canada's most southerly region, south **Ontario**, contains not only the manufacturing heart of the country and its largest city, **Toronto**, but also **Niagara Falls**, Canada's premier tourist sight. North of Toronto there's the far less packaged scenic attraction of **Georgian Bay**, a beautiful waterscape of pine-studded islets set against crystal blue waters. Like the forested Algonquin park, the bay is also accessible from the capital city of **Ottawa**, not as dynamic a place as Toronto, but still well worth a stay for its art galleries and museums, and for the nightlife over the Ottawa River in Hull.

Québec, set apart from the rest of the continent by the profundity of its French tradition, focuses on its biggest city, **Montréal**, which is for many people the most vibrant place in the country, a fascinating mix of old-world style and commercial dynamism. The pace of life is more relaxed in the historic provincial capital, **Québec City**, and more easy-going still in the villages dotted along the St Lawrence lowlands, where glittering spires attest to the enduring influence of the Catholic Church. For something more bracing, you could continue north to **Tadoussac**, where whales can be seen near the mouth of the splendid **Saguenay** fjord – and if you're really prepared for the wilds, forge on through to **Labrador**, as inhospitable a zone as you'll find in the east.

Across the mouth of the St Lawrence, the pastoral **Gaspé** peninsula – the easternmost part of Québec – borders **New Brunswick**, a mild-mannered introduction to the three **Maritime Provinces**, whose people have long been dependent on timber and the sea for their livelihood. Here, the tapering **Bay of Fundy** boasts amazing tides – rising and falling by nine metres, sometimes more – whilst the tiny fishing villages characteristic of the region are at their most beguiling near **Halifax**, the bustling capital of **Nova Scotia**. Perhaps even prettier, and certainly more austere, are the land and seascapes of **Cape Breton Island**, whose rugged topography anticipates that of the island of **Newfoundland** to the north. Newfoundland's isolation has spawned a distinctive culture that's at its most lively in the capital, **St John's**, where the local folk-music scene is the country's best. The island also boasts some of the Atlantic seaboard's finest landscapes, particularly the flat-topped peaks and glacier-gouged lakes of **Gros Morne National Park**.

Back on the mainland, separating Ontario from Alberta and the Rockies, the so-called prairie provinces of **Manitoba** and **Saskatchewan** have a reputation for dullness that's somewhat unfair: even in the flat southern parts there's the diversion of **Winnipeg**, whose traces of its early days make it a good place to break a trans-Canadian journey. To the north, the myriad lakes and gigantic forests of the provinces' wilderness regions offer magnificent canoeing and hiking, especially within **Prince Albert National Park**. Up in the far north, beside Hudson Bay, the settlement of **Churchill** – remote but accessible by train – is famous for its polar bears, who gather near town from the end of June waiting to move out over the ice as soon as the bay freezes.

Moving west, **Alberta's** wheatfields ripple into ranching country on the approach to the **Canadian Rockies**, whose international reputation is more than borne out by the reality. The provincial capital, **Edmonton**, is overshadowed by **Calgary**, a brash place grown fat on the region's oil and gas fields, and the most useful springboard for a venture into the mountains. **British Columbia** embodies the popular picture of Canada to perfection: a land of snow-capped summits, rivers and forests, pioneer villages, gold-rush ghost towns, and some of the greatest hiking, skiing, fishing and canoeing opportunities in the world. Its urban focus, **Vancouver**, is the country's third city, known for its spectacular natural setting and a laid-back West Coast hedonism. Off the coast lies **Vancouver Island**, a microcosm of the province's immense natural riches, and home to **Victoria**, a devotedly anglophile little city.

North of British Columbia, wedged alongside Alaska, is the **Yukon Territory**, half grandiose mountains, half sub-arctic tundra, and full of evocative echoes of the Klondike gold rush. **Whitehorse**, its capital, and **Dawson City**, a gold-rush relic, are virtually the only towns here, each accessed by dramatic frontier highways. The **Northwest Territories**, arching over the provinces of Alberta, Saskatchewan and Manitoba, are an immensity of stunted forest, lakes, tundra and ice, the realm of Dene and Inuit native bands whose traditional way of life is being threatened as oil and gas exploration reaches up in to the Arctic. Roads are virtually non-existent in the deep north, and only **Yellowknife**, a bizarre frontier city, plus a handful of ramshackle villages, offer the air links and resources necessary to explore this wilderness.

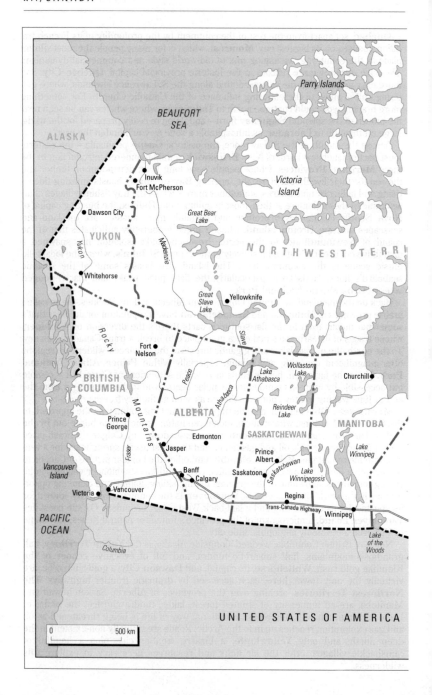

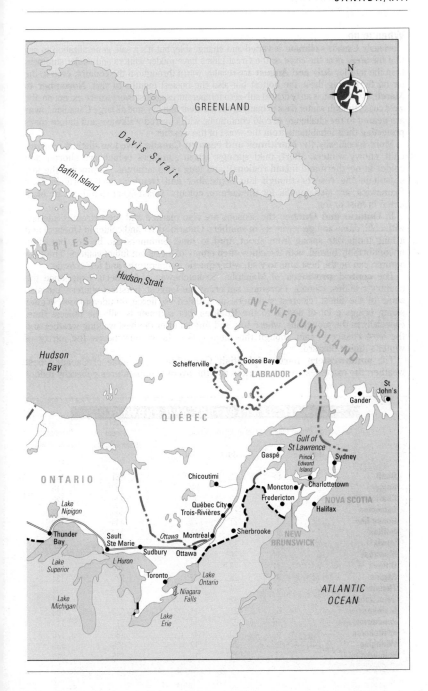

When to go

Obviously Canada's **climate** is varied and changeable, but it's a safe generalization to say that the areas near the coast or the Great Lakes have milder winters and cooler summers than the interior. **July and August** are reliably warm throughout the country, even in the far north, making these the hottest but also the busiest months to visit. **November to March**, by contrast, is an ordeal of sub-zero temperatures almost everywhere except on the west coast, though winter days in many areas are clear and dry, and all large Canadian towns are geared to the challenge of cold conditions, with covered walkways and indoor malls protecting their inhabitants from the worst of the weather.

More specifically, the **Maritimes and eastern Canada** have four distinct seasons: chill, snowy winters; short, mild springs; warm summers (which are shorter and colder in northern and inland regions); and long crisp autumns. Summer is the key season in the resorts, though late September and October, particularly in New Brunswick, are also popular for the autumn colours. Coasts year-round can be blanketed in mist or fog.

In **Ontario and Québec** the seasons are also marked and the extremes intense, with cold, damp and grey winters in southern Ontario (drier and colder in Québec) and a long temperate spring from about April to June. Summers can be hot, but often uncomfortably humid, with the cities often empty of locals but full of visitors. The long autumn can be the best time to visit, with equable temperatures and few crowds.

The **central provinces** of Manitoba, Saskatchewan and Alberta experience the country's wildest climatic extremes, suffering the longest, harshest winters, but also some of the finest, clearest summers, punctuated by fierce thunderstorms. Winter skiing brings a lot of people to the **Rockies**, but summer is still the busiest time, especially in the mountains, where July and August offer the best walking weather and the least chance of rain, though this often falls in heavy downpours, the mirror of winter's raging blizzards.

The **southwestern parts of British Columbia** enjoy some of Canada's best weather: the extremes are less marked and the overall temperatures generally milder

CLIMATE: TEMPERATURE AND SNOWFALL						
Average daily max. temperatures in degrees Celsius					Annual snowfall (cm)	Duration of cover (days)
	Jan	April	July	Oct		
Banff	-7	8	22	10	251	149
Calgary	-6	9	23	12	153	116
Charlottetown	-3	7	23	12	275	122
Edmonton	-17	9	22	11	136	133
Goose Bay	-12	3	21	7	445	188
Halifax	-1	9	23	14	217	99
Inuvik	-25	-8	19	-5	177	232
Montréal	-6	11	26	13	243	116
Ottawa	-6	11	26	13	206	121
Regina	-13	9	26	12	87	134
Thunder Bay	-9	8	24	11	213	132
Saint John	-3	8	22	12	224	104
St John's	0	5	21	11	322	109
Vancouver	5	13	22	14	51	11
Whitehorse	-16	6	20	4	78	170
Winnipeg	-14	9	26	12	126	135
Yellowknife	-25	-1	21	1	135	210

than elsewhere. Much of the province, though, bears the brunt of Pacific depressions, so this is one of the country's damper regions – visiting between late spring and early autumn offers the best chance of missing the rain.

Across the **Yukon and Northwest Territories** winters are bitterly cold, with temperatures rarely above freezing for months on end, though precipitation year-round is among the country's lowest. Summers, by contrast, are short but surprisingly warm, and spring – though late – can produce outstanding displays of wild flowers across the tundra.

PART ONE

THE
BASICS

GETTING THERE FROM BRITAIN

The only economical way to get to Canada from Britain is to fly. The main gateways into the country are Montréal and Toronto, but there are also scheduled non-stop flights from Britain to Calgary, Edmonton, Halifax, Ottawa, St John's, Winnipeg and Vancouver, and connecting services to a number of other destinations. You can fly non-stop to Canada from Heathrow, Gatwick, Stansted, Birmingham, Newcastle, Manchester, Edinburgh and Glasgow.

Competition between the big two **Canadian carriers**, Air Canada and Canadian Airlines, keeps scheduled rates reasonable, and **charter flights** to the more popular destinations, especially Toronto and Montréal, throw up even more low-cost options. Canada 3000, an international carrier, has return flights from London and Manchester to Calgary from £316 and can be booked

---

Typical **midweek Apex return fares** (low season/high season) from London are as follows:

Toronto, Montréal, St John's or Halifax
£374/550.

Calgary, Edmonton, Vancouver or Winnipeg
£484/660.

Seat sale fares, where available, are usually slightly cheaper than this; standard returns, with fewer restrictions, are considerably more expensive.

---

only via Canadian Affair, Bluebird, First Choice and Pioneer (see "Flight agents" box on p.5). It may also be worth considering a cheap flight **to the US**, as the greater competition between airlines on the US routes can produce fares to New York as low as £180 return; from the US it's easy to get into Canada cheaply by bus or train (see "Getting there from the US", on p.8).

For a precise picture of all the available options at any given time, contact an **agent** specializing in low-cost flights (see box on p.5) which may – especially if you are under 26 or a student – be able to undercut the regular Apex fares. These agents also offer cut-price seats on charter flights, though these tend to be of limited availability during the summer. Package operators can also be a source of cheap one-off flights, as they sell off any unsold seats at the last moment. Finally, be sure to check the travel ads in the Sunday papers, and, in London, in *Time Out* and the *Evening Standard*.

FARES AND ROUTES

The best-value airfares are the **Apex** (advance purchase) fares; however, there are a variety of restrictions on these tickets to be aware of. The cheapest from Air Canada has to be booked 21 days in advance with a minimum stay of 7 nights and a maximum of one month. Alternatively you can book 14 days in advance with a maximum stay of three months or 7 days in advance with a maximum stay of six months; both have a minimum stay of seven nights. Canadian Airlines offers Apex deals with seven- and fourteen-day advance booking, both with a minimum stay of seven nights, maximum of one to six months. British Airways has 7-, 14- and 21-day advance booking with minimum stays of 7 nights, and maximum of 6 months', 3 months' and 1 month's stay respectively. **Seat sale** fares, which cost about the same as 21-day Apex deals, are available on both Canadian majors and must be completely paid for within 7 days of booking. Generally these require a minimum stay of a week and a maximum of 30 days.

Most agents also offer **"open-jaw"** deals that enable you to fly into one Canadian city and back from another – a useful idea if you want to make your way across the country; fares are calculated

Air Canada, 7–8 Conduit St, London W1R 9TG (☎0990/247226).
Non-stop services from London, Heathrow to Calgary (daily), Edmonton (daily, with touchdown in Calgary), Halifax (3 weekly), Montréal (daily), Ottawa (5 weekly), St John's (4 weekly), Toronto (daily) and Vancouver (daily). Connections are available to London (Ontario), Regina, Saskatoon, Thunder Bay, Windsor and Winnipeg from Toronto; to Charlottetown, Deer Lake, Fredericton, Gander, Goose Bay, Moncton, Saint John and Sydney from Halifax; and to Victoria from Vancouver. Non-stop, too, from Manchester to Toronto (daily); and daily connections to Calgary, Edmonton, London, Ontario, Montréal, Ottawa, Vancouver and Winnipeg from Toronto. From Glasgow, non-stop flights to Toronto (daily), with connections to Calgary (daily), Edmonton (daily), Halifax (daily), Montréal, (daily), Ottawa (daily), St John's (4 weekly), Vancouver (daily) and Winnipeg (daily).

Air India, 55 Berkeley Square, London W1X 5DB (☎01753/684828).
Twice weekly non-stop to Toronto from Heathrow.

American Airlines, 15 Berkeley St, London W1 (☎0345/789789).
Daily flights to Toronto via Chicago or New York from Heathrow; Toronto via Dallas or Chicago from Gatwick; Calgary via Chicago from Heathrow, or via Dallas or Chicago from Gatwick; Halifax via Boston from Heathrow; Montréal via New York from Heathrow, or via Chicago from Gatwick; Ottawa via Chicago from Heathrow or Gatwick; and Vancouver via Chicago from Heathrow, or via Dallas from Gatwick.

British Airways, 156 Regent St, London W1R 5TA (☎0345/222111).
Daily non-stop flights from Heathrow to Toronto, Montréal and Vancouver; also, via London, daily flights from Birmingham, Edinburgh, Glasgow, Manchester and Newcastle to Toronto, Montréal and Vancouver. There's also a daily service from Birmingham to Toronto via New York.

Canadian Airlines International, 15 Berkeley St, London W1X 6ND (☎0345/616767).
Non-stop flights from Heathrow to Calgary (daily), Toronto (4 daily) and Vancouver (2 daily), Montréal (daily). Flights to Halifax (daily), London, Ontario (daily), Ottawa (daily) and Winnipeg (daily) all go via Toronto. Flights to Saskatoon (daily) and Regina (daily) go via Calgary or Vancouver. Flights to Victoria (daily) and Whitehorse (daily) stop at Vancouver. Edmonton (daily) flights go via Calgary.

Canada 3000, no telephone or address but available through Canadian Affair, Bluebird Holidays, First Choice and Ilkeston Co-op Travel flight agents.

Icelandair, 172 Tottenham Court Rd, London W1P 0LY (☎0171/388-5599).
Twice-weekly service to Halifax via Reykjavik from Heathrow and Glasgow.

KLM, KLM Building, 8 Hanover St, London W1R 9HF (☎0990/750900).
Flights to Halifax, Ottawa, Montréal, Calgary and Vancouver via Amsterdam from Heathrow, Manchester, Birmingham, Cardiff, Bristol and Southampton and numerous other UK airports, via connecting flights on KLM's partner, AIR UK.

Northwest Airlines, Northwest House, Tinsley Lane, Crawley, West Sussex RH10 2TP (☎01293/561000).
Flights to Toronto, Montréal, Calgary, Vancouver, Saskatoon, Ottawa, Halifax and Winnipeg via Minneapolis and/or Detroit, Edmonton via Minneapolis, Detroit or Seattle from Gatwick.

United Airlines 7–8 Conduit St, London W1R 9TG (☎08458/444777).
Flights to Toronto via Chicago or Washington, Calgary via Chicago or Denver and Vancouver via San Francisco or Chicago from Heathrow.

---

by halving the return fares to each destination and adding the two figures together.

Generally, **high season** (and thus the most expensive time to fly) is between early July and mid-September and around Christmas. Mid-May to early July and mid-September to mid-October – the "shoulder" seasons – are slightly less pricey, leaving the rest of the year as low season. Make sure of the exact season dates observed by your operator or airline, as you might be able to make major savings by shifting your departure by as little as a day. Whatever time of year you fly, **midweek flights** tend to cost around £15 less than weekend ones, and airport taxes of around £32 are usually added to the quoted price. Return **flights from regional airports** cost around £100 more than flights from London, though some shuttles are free.

FLIGHT AGENTS

Airtours, Wavell House, Holcombe Rd, Helmshore, Rossendale, Lancashire BB4 4NB (☎01708/260000).

A.T. Mays, 12 Terminus Rd, Eastbourne, East Sussex BN21 3LP (☎01323/411500).

Bluebird Holidays, Vanguard House, 277 London Rd, Burgess Hill, West Sussex RH15 9QU (☎0990/320000).

Bridge the World, 1–2 Ferdinand St, London NW1 8AN (☎0171/916–0990).

Campus Travel, 52 Grosvenor Gardens, London SW1W 0AG (☎0171/730-2101); 541 Bristol Rd, Selly Oak, Birmingham (☎0121/414-1848); 39 Queen's Rd, Clifton, Bristol (☎0117/929-2494); 5 Emmanuel St, Cambridge (☎01223/324283); 53 Forest Rd, Edinburgh (☎0131/668-3303); 166 Deansgate, Manchester (☎0161/833-2046); 105–105 St Aldates, Oxford (☎01865/242067); 3 Market Place, Reading (☎0118/9567356); Nelson Mandela Building, Pond St, Sheffield (☎0114/275-8366); 14 High St, Southampton (☎01703/236868); Wulfruna St, Wolverhampton (☎01902/23863).

Canadian Affair, 591 Fulham Rd, London, SW6 5UA (☎0171/385-4400). *They have cheap charter flights' fares.*

Council Travel, 28a Poland St, London W1V 3DB (☎0171/437-7767).

CTS Travel, 220 Kensington High St, London W88 7RG (☎0171/937-3388).

Destination Group, 41–45 Goswell Rd, London EC1V 7EH (☎0171/253-9000).

First Choice Holidays and Flights Ltd, First Choice House, London Rd, Crawley, West Sussex RH10 2GX (☎01293/560777).

Globeair Travel, 93 Piccadilly, London W1 (☎0171/493-4343).

Ilkeston Co-op Travel, 12 South St, Ilkeston, Derbyshire DE7 5SG (☎0115/932-3546). Biggest in East Midlands/South Yorkshire.

Jetsave, Sussex House, London Rd, East Grinstead, West Sussex RH19 1LD (☎01342/327711).

Jetset, Amadeus House, 52 George St, Manchester M1 4HF (☎0990/555757).

STA Travel, 6 Wrights Lane, London W8 6TA (☎0171/361-6262); University of West England, Coldharbour Lane, Bristol (0117/929-4399; 38 Sidney St, Cambridge (☎01223/366966); 75 Deansgate, Manchester (☎0161/834-0668); 36 George St, Oxford (01865/792800); and personal callers at 117 Euston Rd, London NW1; 88 Vicar Lane, Leeds; 9 St Mary's Place, Newcastle-upon-Tyne; and offices at the universities of Birmingham, Kent, Strathclyde, Durham, Sheffield, Nottingham, Warwick, Coventry and Loughborough and at King's College, Imperial College, LSE, Queen Mary's and Westfield College in London.

Trailfinders, 42–50 Earl's Court Rd, London W8 6EJ (☎0171/938-3366). *Branches nationwide.*

Travel Bug, 597 Cheetham Hill Rd, Manchester M8 5EJ (☎0161/721-4000).

Vacation Canada, Cambridge House, 8 Cambridge St, Glasgow G2 3DZ (☎0141/332-1511).

Courier flights can be a good option for those on a tight budget, but you'll be given strict restrictions on dates and can be limited to hand luggage only. Furthermore, few companies operate a courier service to Canada – it's actually far easier to reach the USA on a courier flight. Try Bridges Worldwide (☎01895/465465) or check the Yellow Pages.

PACKAGE HOLIDAYS

Package holidays – whether fly-drive, flight-accommodation, flight-guided tours or a combination of all three – can work out cheaper than arranging the same trip yourself, though they do have drawbacks: chiefly loss of flexibility and the fact that you'll probably have to stay in relatively expensive chain hotels.

Short-stay **city packages** start from around £400 per person for a transatlantic return flight and accommodation in a downtown Montréal or Toronto hotel for three nights – seven nights for more like £600. **Fly-drive** deals, which give cut-price car rental when buying a transatlantic ticket from an airline or tour operator, are always cheaper than renting on the spot and give great value if you intend to do a lot of travelling: a return flight to Vancouver and a fortnight's car rental might cost as little as £500 per person.

A typical **flight-guided tour** might comprise a fourteen-day trans-Canadian holiday taking in Toronto, Niagara Falls, Ottawa, Montréal, Calgary, the Rockies and Vancouver, including an outbound flight to Toronto, a domestic flight, coach trips,

TOUR OPERATORS

Air Canada Vacations, 525 High Rd, Wembley, London HA0 2DH (☎0990/747100). *Canada-wide packages and tours at reasonable rates.*

All Canada Travel & Holidays, Sunway House, Raglan Road, Lowestoft, Suffolk NR32 2LW (☎01502/585825). *Holidays in all provinces.*

British Airways Holidays, Astral Towers, Betts Way, London Road, Crawley, West Sussex RH10 2XA (☎01293/722727). *Bargain packages and tours of most descriptions. Primarily Québec, Ontario, Alberta and BC.*

Canada West Holidays, 1 Sawston Close, Radbrook Green, Shrewsbury, Shropshire SY3 6AY (☎01743/366415). *Holidays in Alberta and BC.*

Canada's Best, 7 Derwent Rd, York, North Yorkshire YO1 4HQ (☎01904/658436). *All types of holiday Canada-wide.*

Canadian Connections, 10 York Way, Lancaster Road, High Wycombe, Buckinghamshire HP12 3PY (☎01494/473173). *Canada-wide.*

Canadian Travel Service, 16 Bathurst Rd, Folkestone, Kent CT20 2NT (☎01303/249000).

Contiki Holidays, Wells House, 15 Elmfield Rd, Bromley, Kent BR1 1LS (☎0181/290-6422). *Holidays to Western Canada.*

Experience Canada, 14 Terminus Rd, Eastbourne, East Sussex BN21 3LP (☎01323/416699). *Tours and tailor-made holidays in all the provinces except Saskatchewan.*

Kuoni Travel Ltd, Kuoni House, Deepdene Avenue, Dorking, Surrey RH5 4AZ (☎01306/742888). *Tailor-made and guided tours to Québec, Ontario, Yukon, Alberta and BC, and city breaks.*

Leisurail, PO Box 113, Peterborough PE3 8YH (☎01733/335599). *VIA Rail, Rocky Mountaineer rail tours, Brewsters coach tours and Atlantic tours.*

Maple Leaf Tours, PO Box 435, Belfast, Co Antrim BT13 2JE (☎01252/313122). *Holidays in Alberta, Ontario and BC.*

Travelbag, 12 Hugh St, Alton, Hampshire GU34 1BN (☎01420/88380); 373–375 The Strand, London WC2R 0JF (☎0171/287-5559); 52 Regent St, London W1R 6DX (☎0171/240-3669). *Tailor-made trips, car hire, flights and itineraries to suit all budgets.*

Vacation Canada, Cambridge House, 8 Cambridge Rd, Glasgow G2 3DZ (☎0141/332-1511). *Skiing, city tours, guided coach tours, rail journeys, etc across Canada.*

Virgin Holidays, The Galleria, Station Road, Crawley, West Sussex RH10 1WW (☎01293/617181). *Bargain packages and tours with the emphasis on Québec, Alberta and BC.*

Accessible Isolation Holidays, 44 Downing

ADVENTURE AND SPECIAL-INTEREST HOLIDAYS

St, Farnham, Surrey GU9 7PH (☎01252/718808).

Action Canada, 368 Kingston Rd, Ewell, Epsom, Surrey (☎0500/226232).

Agritour, 13 Central Chambers, The Broadway, London W5 2NB (☎0181/840-8131).

AmeriCan Adventures, 45 High St, Tunbridge Wells, Kent TN1 1XL (☎01892/511894); 64 Mount Pleasant Ave, Tunbridge Wells, Kent TN1 1QY (☎01892/512700).

Arctic Experience 29 Nork Way, Banstead, Surrey SM7 1PB (☎01737/218800).

Greyhound International, Sussex House, London Road, East Grinstead, West Sussex RH19 1LD (☎01342/317317).

Go Fishing Canada, 6 Barons Gate, 33–35 Rothschild Rd, London W4 5HT (☎0181/742-3700).

Great Rail Journeys, 71 The Mount, York YO32 2AX (☎01904/679961).

Headwater Holidays, 148 London Rd, Northwich, Cheshire (☎01606/486099).

Mountain and Wildlife Ventures, Compston Road, Ambleside, Cumbria (☎015394/33285).

Ramblers Holidays Ltd, Box 43, Welwyn Garden City, Hertfordshire AL8 6PQ (☎01707/331133).

The Polar Travel Company, Wydemeet, Hexworthy, Yelverton, Devon PL20 6SF (☎01364/631470).

Wildlife Worldwide, 170 Selsdon Rd, South Croydon, Surrey CR2 6PJ (☎0181/667-9158).

middle-range hotel accommodation and some sightseeing tours, at a cost of around £1800.

To see a chunk of Canada's great outdoors without being hassled by too many practical considerations, you could take a specialist **touring** or **adventure package**, which usually includes transport in Canada, accommodation, food and a guide – but not flights. Some of the more adventurous carry small groups around on minibuses and use a combination of budget hotels and camping, providing all equipment. These deals are not cheap, however – a typical package of five days' hiking in the Yukon will cost around £900 and prices are far higher in areas that require detailed planning and outfitting. Operators offering a range of Canadian adventure holidays are listed in the box opposite; local companies specializing in the more extreme locations – for example, Labrador – are given in the appropriate sections of the Guide.

GETTING THERE FROM IRELAND

There are no non-stop direct flights from Ireland to Canada, though British Airways, Air Canada and Canadian Airlines will quote you through-fares from Dublin to most major Canadian destinations, including the gateway cities of Toronto and Montréal. Surprisingly, Aer Lingus does not fly to Canada.

All flights **from Dublin** to Canada are via London. Air Canada offers flights to Toronto via London, and their fourteen-day Apex return fare costs from IR£485, or from IR£593 if you're heading to Vancouver. **From Belfast** with Air

---

AIRLINES

Air Canada, no offices in Northern Ireland or the Republic (reservations ☎0990/247246).

British Airways, 9 Fountain Centre, College Street, Belfast BT1 6ET (reservations ☎0345/222111, bookings and travel agency services ☎0345/326566). BA doesn't have a Dublin office but Aer Lingus acts as their agents (reservations ☎1-800/626747).

British Midland, Northern Ireland (☎0345/554554); Nutley, Merrion Road, Dublin 4 (☎01/283-8833).

Canadian Airlines, Northern Ireland ☎0345/616767 or ☎0990/247226; the Republic ☎1-800/709900.

FLIGHT AGENTS

American Holidays, Lombard Street, Belfast (☎01232/238762) and Pearse St, Dublin 2 (☎01/679-8800 or 679-6611).

Apex Travel, 59 Dame St, Dublin 2 (☎01/671-5953).

Chieftain Tours Ltd, Twin Spires Centre, 155 Northumberland St, Belfast (☎01232/247795).

CIE Tours International, 35 Lower Abbey St, Dublin 1 (01/703-1888).

Corporate Travel, 10 Portland Ave, Glengormley, Newtownabbey, Co. Antrim (☎01232/833789).

Shandon Travel Ltd, 84 Oliver Plunkett St, Cork (☎021/277094).

Trailfinders, 4–5 Dawson St, Dublin 2 (☎01/677-7888).

Thomas Cook, 11 Donegal Place, Belfast (☎01232/242341); 118 Grafton St, Dublin 2 (☎01/677-1721).

USIT, Aston Quay, O'Connell Bridge, Dublin 2 (☎01/677-8117); Fountain Centre, College St, Belfast BT1 6ET (☎01232/324073); 10–11 Market Parade, Patrick St, Cork (☎021/270900); 33 Ferryquay St, Derry (☎01504/371888); 19 Aston Quay, Dublin 2 (☎01/602-1777 or 677-8117, Europe and UK ☎01/602-1600 or 679-8833, long-haul ☎01/602-1700); Victoria Place, Eyre Square, Galway (☎091/565177); Central Buildings, O'Connell St, Limerick (☎061/415064); 36–37 George's St, Waterford (☎051/872601).

Canada a 21-day Apex to Toronto via London costs from £497 return; to Vancouver, £607 return.

Students and under-26s should consult USIT, which can usually offer the best deals – their return fares from Dublin or Belfast to Toronto are priced from £281 and from £383 to Vancouver.

It's often possible to save money by **flying independently** from Dublin to London on a domestic carrier – British Midland, for example, runs seven flights daily from Dublin to Heathrow with a Super Saver return at IR£69, and an Apex return at IR£109 – to link into the Heathrow network.

GETTING THERE FROM THE US

Crossing the longest undefended border in the world is straightforward. Many visitors from the northern US just drive, as the major Canadian cities – Montréal and Toronto in the east, Winnipeg and Calgary in the middle and Vancouver in the west – are all within an hour's drive of the border. However, if you're coming from Florida or southern California, or want to go from New York to British Columbia, flying is obviously a lot quicker. Travelling by train is another alternative, at least if you're not in a hurry and want to see something of the landscapes along the way, and there are a few bus and ferry options too.

BY CAR

The US highway system leads into Canada at thirteen points along the border. The busiest cor-

ridors are Blaine, WA–White Rock, British Columbia; Detroit–Windsor, Ontario; Buffalo–Fort Erie, Ontario; and Niagara Falls. You may encounter traffic jams at the border and long lines, particularly at the weekends, in the summer months and on US or Canadian holidays. From New York to Montréal (383 miles), count on eight hours' driving; from San Francisco to Vancouver (954 miles), around nineteen hours. For route advice in the US, call the AAA. They have offices in most major cities, but you probably won't find them much help unless you're a member. For more detailed route enquiries within Canada, call the Canadian Automobile Association (see "Getting around", p.27).

At customs you will probably be asked to declare your citizenship, place of residence and proposed length of stay. Vehicle insurance, with minimum liability coverage of US$200,000, is compulsory and it is also advisable to obtain a yellow Non-Resident Inter-Province Motor Vehicle Liability Card from your insurance company before you go. Make sure you have your driver's licence, documents establishing proof of insurance and proof of vehicle ownership with you at all times while driving in Canada. If you are renting a car in the US you should mention that you intend to travel to Canada, though this is rarely a problem. Fill the car with gas before going, as US prices are still less than those over the border.

BY BUS

The **Greyhound** (☎1-800-231-2222) bus network extends into Canada from three points on the East Coast and one each from the West and middle America. The buses run from New York to Montréal (7 daily; 7hr–8hr 30min; US$72 one-way or US$91 return); Buffalo to Toronto (approximately 17 daily; 2hr 30mins–3hr; US$16.20 one-way or

US$28.85/32.40 return); Burlington (Vermont) to Montréal (5 daily; 2hr 30min–3hr; US$23 one-way or $46 return); Seattle to Vancouver (6 daily; 3hr 30min-4hr 30min; US$25 one-way or US$42 return); and Fargo (North Dakota) to Winnipeg (1 daily; 6hr 10min; US$43.25 one-way or US$83.50 return). Be sure to arrive at the terminal one hour before departure.

The alternative to long-distance bus hell, **Green Tortoise** (494 Broadway, San Francisco, CA 94133, ☎1-800-227-4766), with its foam cushions, bunks, fridges and rock music, no longer runs a regular service into Canada, but it does still offer a 28–30 day-trip from San Francisco north to Alaska, which includes a ferry ride along the Inside Passage and side-trips into the Canadian Rockies (US$1500, plus US$250 for food).

BY AIR

There are plenty of non-stop **flights** on the prime national carriers, Air Canada and Canadian Airlines, and most US airlines offer regular flights between the US and Canada: Montréal, Toronto and Vancouver are the most popular destinations, but there are also services to Halifax, Calgary, Winnipeg and many others. Connecting flights within Canada serve some 75 additional places.

Sample budget **return** fares quoted by the major airlines are: New York to Toronto US$195; New York to Montreal US$225; New York to Halifax: US$275; Chicago to Winnipeg US$310; LA to Calgary US$260; LA to Vancouver US$220. If you only plan a long weekend trip, there are often NY/Toronto fares for US$120 or Chicago/Winnipeg for US$190.

Even more so than with other international connections, you really need to **shop around** to get the very best deals on the busy US/Canada routes. In addition to fares with the usual Apex restrictions (21-day advance booking, Saturday night stay, midweek travel, etc), you might find special offers which require you to book before a particular date, limit your stay, fly at a certain time of day, or, perversely, allow you more flexibility than on a higher fare. Your best bet is to first try a discount agent like Council or STA, who may be able to dig up scheduled return fares for as little as US$90 (New York/Toronto), US$155 (New York/Montréal) or US$199 (LA/Vancouver); always be sceptical of any alleged rock-bottom fares quoted by telephone booking agents for the major carriers.

Domestic flights wholly within the US or Canada generally cost somewhat less than flights

FLIGHT TIMES

Flying north/south between the US and Canada is reasonably quick: from New York to Montréal takes around 1hr 15min; New York to Toronto 1hr 30min; New York to Halifax 1hr 50min; Chicago to Winnipeg 2hr 10min; LA to Vancouver 2hr 45min; LA to Calgary 3hr. **Flying east/west** is fairly painless, too (New York–LA or Montréal–Vancouver takes around 5hr). However, flying east/west between countries usually involves a stopover or onward connection, so New York–Vancouver can take 7–8hr.

between the two countries, so you may make savings by crossing the border before or after your flight. If you're willing to sacrifice convenience for economy it might be worth your while flying from New York to Buffalo and taking the bus across the border and on up to Toronto, for instance, rather than flying New York to Toronto direct. This is especially true of long-haul flights: a transcontinental flight from New York to Seattle can be considerably cheaper than a similar flight to Vancouver, only a hundred miles north. Sample budget return fares within Canada are Toronto to Montréal, C$235; Montréal to Vancouver, C$379; Vancouver to Winnipeg, C$350 and Winnipeg to Toronto, C$279. If your main destination is somewhere upcountry you can often save money by buying a separate, domestic flight from the nearest major Canadian destination, rather than treating that leg of the journey as part of an international itinerary.

BY TRAIN

Three Amtrak routes from the northeastern US have direct connections with VIA Rail, Canada's national rail company: the Maple Leaf from New York to Toronto via Buffalo and Niagara Falls (1 daily; 12hr; US$65 in low season US$99 in high season, one-way); the Adirondack from New York to Montréal via Albany and Plattsburgh (1 daily; 9hr 30min; US$49/62 one-way) and the International from Chicago to Toronto (1 daily; 14hr; US$98 one-way). Sleeping cars have recently been discontinued on these trains, but they may well be reintroduced sometime in the future. In the northwest, the Mount Baker International runs from Seattle to Vancouver (1 daily; 4hr; US$19/31 one-way). All the above fares are for

AIRLINES

Air Canada from US call ☎1-800-776-3000; from Canada call ☎1-800-555-1212 for various local toll-free numbers.

American Airlines (☎1-800-433-7300).

British Airways from US call ☎1-800-247-9297; from Canada call ☎1-800-426-7000.

Canadian Airlines from US call ☎1-800-426-7000; from Canada call ☎1-800-665-1177.

Continental Airlines (☎1-800-231-0856).

Delta Airlines (☎1-800-241-4141).

Northwest Airlines (☎1-800-447-4747).

Trans World Airlines (☎1-800-892-4141).

United Airlines (☎1-800-538-2929).

US Airways (☎1-800-428-4322).

DISCOUNT FLIGHT AGENTS, TRAVEL CLUBS & CONSOLIDATORS

Council Travel, *Head office:* 205 E 42nd St, New York, NY 10017 (☎1-800/226 8624; 1-888 COUNCIL; 212/822-2700). *Other offices at:* 530 Bush St, Suite 700, San Francisco, CA 94108 (☎415/421-3473); 10904 Lindbrook Drive, Los Angeles, CA 90024 (☎310/208-3551); 1138 13th St, Boulder, CO 80302 (☎303/447-8101); 3300 M St NW, 2nd Floor, Washington, DC 20007 (☎202/337-6464); 1153 N Dearborn St, Chicago, IL 60610 (☎312/951-0585); 273 Newbury St, Boston, MA 02116 (☎617/266-1926). *Nationwide US organization. Mostly, but by no means exclusively, specializes in student travel.*

Educational Travel Center, 438 N Frances St, Madison, WI 53703 (☎1-800-747-5551). *Student/youth discount agent.*

Encore Travel Club, 4501 Forbes Blvd, Lanham, MD 20706 (☎1-800-444-9800). *Discount travel club.*

Last Minute Travel Club, 100 Sylvan Rd, Suite 600, Woburn, MA 01801 (☎1-800-LAST MIN). *Travel club specializing in standby deals.*

New Frontiers/Nouvelles Frontières, *Head offices:* 12 E 33rd St, New York, NY 10016 (☎1-800-366-6387); 1001 Sherbrook E, Suite 720, Montréal H2L 1L3 (☎514/526-8444). *French discount travel firm. Other branches in LA, San Francisco and Québec City.*

Now Voyager, 74 Varick St, Suite 307, New York, NY 10013 (☎212/431-1616). *Courier flight broker.*

STA Travel, ☎1-800-777-0112. *Offices at:* 10 Downing St, New York, NY 10014 (☎212/627-3111); 7202 Melrose Ave, Los Angeles, CA 90046 (☎213/934-8722); 51 Grant Ave, San Francisco, CA 94108 (☎415/391-8407); 297 Newbury St, Boston, MA 02115 (☎617/266-6014); 429 S Dearborn St, Chicago, IL 60605 (☎312/786-9050); 3730 Walnut St, Philadelphia, PA 19104 (☎215/382-2928); 317 14th Ave SE, Minneapolis, MN 55414 (☎612/615-1800). *Worldwide specialist in independent travel.*

TFI Tours International, 34 W 32nd St, New York, NY 10001 (☎1-800-745-8000 or 212/736-1160).*Consolidator; other offices in Las Vegas, San Francisco, Los Angeles and Miami.*

Travel Avenue, 10 S Riverside, Suite 1404, Chicago, IL 60606 (☎1-800-333-3335). *Discount travel agent.*

Travelers Advantage, 3033 S Parker Rd, Suite 900, Aurora, CO 80014 (☎1-800-548-1116). *Discount travel club.*

Worldtrek Travel, 111 Water St, New Haven, CT 06511 (☎1-800-243-1723). *Discount travel agency.*

Worldwide Discount Travel Club, 1674 Meridian Ave, Miami Beach, FL 33139 (☎305/534-2082). *Discount travel club.*

travel in economy (the cheapest) class, where pillows are provided for overnight journeys.

For specific journeys, the train is usually more expensive than the bus (and often the plane), though special deals, especially in off-peak periods, can bring the round-trip cost down considerably. There are discounts available on trains for "Student Advantage" pass-holders, senior citizens and travellers with disabilities. Children from 2 to 15 who are accompanied by an adult go for half-fare; children under 2 travel free.

You should always reserve as far as possible in advance, as it is compulsory to have a seat and some of the eastern seaboard trains in particular get booked up solid. Amtrak information and reservations are available on ☎1-800-USA-RAIL.

BY FERRY

There are five US–Canada **ferry services**: three on the West Coast and two on the East. Quite apart from the enjoyment of the ferry ride, the services can save you hours of driving on some cross-country routes.

WEST COAST FERRIES

On the West Coast, the Victoria Clipper catamaran for foot passengers runs between Seattle and Victoria on Vancouver Island, three times daily from mid-June to mid-September and once daily in spring and fall (2hr 30min; US$54/58 one-way; reservations ☎206/448-5000).

Further north, Alaska Marine Highway ferries link several Alaskan towns with Prince Rupert. The Juneau service, for instance, operates on alternate days from May to late September (24hr; US$104 one-way, cars US$240; reservations in US ☎1-800-642-0066, in Yukon and BC ☎1-800-478-2268).

However, the most useful West Coast ferry is the Washington State Ferries service from Anacortes on the Washington mainland to Sidney, on Vancouver Island. The ferry travels twice daily in summer, once in winter via Washington's beautiful San Juan archipelago (average-sized vehicle with driver $35.65 each way, extra adult passengers $6 each; 3hr; reservations essential, ☎1-206-464-6400; 1-800-84-FERRY Washington State

TOUR OPERATORS

Adventure Center, 1311 63rd St, Suite 200, Emeryville, CA 94608 (☎1-800-227-8747). *Adventure and hiking holidays. Their 8 day "Newfoundland, Naturally" package runs from $1895 (land only). The 15 day "Rocky Mountains and the Pacific" starts at $985 (land only).*

American Airlines Vacations, 9933 E 16th St, Tulsa, OK 74128 (☎1-800-321-2121). *City breaks and more extensive packages. 5 nights in Québec City, with 3 star hotel accommodation, car rental and return flight out of New York would cost from around $855.*

Backroads, 801 Cedar St, Berkeley, CA 94710 (☎1-800-462-2848). *Camping/cycling holidays from $798 (6 days; land only).*

Contiki Holidays, 300 Plaza Alicante, Suite 900, Garden Grove, CA 92840 (☎1-800-CONTIKI). *Travel specialists for 18–35s.*

Different Strokes Tours, 1841 Broadway, New York, NY 10023 (☎1-800-668 3301). *Customized tours for gay/lesbian travellers.*

Globus and Cosmos, 5301 South Federal Circle, Littleton, CO 80123 (☎1-800-556-5454). *2 weeks or more motorcoach sightseeing tours.*

Holidaze Ski Tours, 810 Belmar Plaza, Belmar, NJ 07719 (☎1-800-526-2827). *Ski holidays at Lake Louise from $282 (4 nights).*

Kemwel's Premiere Selections, 106 Calvert St, Harrison, NY 10528 (☎1-800-234-4000). *10 day transcontinental rail excursion from $2078 (most meals and train/hotel accommodation included).*

Maupintour, 1515 St Andrews Drive, Lawrence, KS 66046 (☎1-800-255-4266). *Fully escorted*

group tours (land only): 7 day "Rocky Mountain Escape" from $1550; 12 day "Trans Canada by Train" from $3265.

Questers Worldwide Nature Tours, 381 Park Ave S, New York, NY 10016 (☎1-800-468-8668). *Nature tours to Newfoundland and the Yukon.*

Rod and Reel Adventures, 3507 Tully Rd, Suite B6, Modesto, CA 95356 (☎1-800-356-6982). *Fishing holidays.*

Saga Holidays, 222 Berkeley St, Boston, MA 02116 (☎1-800-343-0273). *Specialists in group travel for seniors, with a variety of Canada tours.*

Suntrek, 77 W 3rd St, Santa Rosa, CA 95401 (☎1-800-292-9696). *Hiking and walking tours from $779 (2 weeks, May to October) .*

Trek America, PO Box 189, Rockaway, NJ 07866 (☎1-800-221-0596). *Camping, hiking, canoeing, horseback-riding, white-water rafting, etc. Their 21-day "Frontier Canada" trip, which departs from Seattle or New York and spans the continent, costs around $1180.*

United Vacations Ski, PO Box 1460, Milwaukee, WI (☎1-800-328-6877). *Ski trips to Whistler or Banff from $888 (return flights from New York, 3 nights 2 star accommodation, transfers).*

Worldwide Quest International, 36 Finch Ave W, Toronto, Ontario M2N 2G9 (☎1-800-387-1483 or 416-221-3000). *A wide range of exotic nature tours: Arctic Expedition Cruises (from $1995, 9 days); Algonquin Park in the fall ($1195, 12 days).*

only). Disabled travellers and senior citizens can get discounts of around twenty percent; children from 5 to 11 pay half-fare; under-5s travel free. There are no student discounts.

EAST COAST FERRIES

In the east, from early May to mid-October a car ferry, the *Scotia Prince*, runs almost nightly from Portland, Maine to Yarmouth, Nova Scotia. The travel time is approximately eleven hours. The price varies seasonally: US$58/78 per person one-way; cars US$80/98; cabins US$20–60/32–95. Five- to 14-year-olds pay half one-way fare and under-5s travel free. Also worth looking into are the return discount packages for two adults and car: the Spring Supersaver, the Summer Getaway and the Indian Summer (reservations ☎1-800-482-0955 in Maine, ☎1-800-341-7540 elsewhere).

In addition, the *Blue Nose* ferry runs from Bar Harbor in Maine to Yarmouth, Nova Scotia daily from May to October. Travel time is roughly six hours. Prices vary seasonally: US$27.25/41.50 one-way; cabins cost an extra US$36/40; cars US$50/55; senior citizens US$24.50/37.25; children from 5 to 12 US$13.75/20.75; children under 5 travel free. Some discounts are offered in conjunction with local hotels (reservations ☎1-888-249-7245). Advance reservations are strongly recommended on both the East Coast services.

PACKAGES

US **tour operators** offer a variety of options from all-inclusive packages (combining plane tickets, bus or train travel, hotel accommodation, meals, transfers and sightseeing tours) to land-only deals based around a single specialized activity (bird-watching, for instance).

These kind of holidays may not sound too appealing to an independent traveller, but one reason why a package could be your best bet – unless you're an expert survivalist – is if you're travelling into the wilderness for backcountry adventure. Local guides and training (for example, in white-water canoeing) are commonly available as well as the normal flights/lodgings, etc. If you live on the west coast, one of the cheapest options is to take a Green Tortoise bus to Canada, with included excursions around the Canadian Rockies (see p.9).

ENTRY, ID AND CUSTOMS

If you're a United States citizen, you don't need a visa to enter Canada as a tourist. All you need is one **ID card** with your photo, plus proof of US citizenship. This can be a valid US passport, an original US birth certificate, certified copy thereof, or original US naturalization papers. Note that a US driver's licence alone is insufficient proof of citizenship. Visitors with **children** must show identification for each child similar to that required by adults and a letter of permission from the parents of any children for whom they don't have legal custody. Divorced parents with shared custody rights should carry legal documents that establish their status. Unaccompanied children should have a letter of permission from their parents or a legal guardian.

Contrary to expectations, since the signing of the North American Free Trade Agreement (NAFTA), entering and exiting Canada has become a particularly sensitive issue – on both sides of the border. You would be well advised, where documentation is involved, to always err on the side of caution.

All US citizens wishing to **work** in Canada, including those exempted from the validation process by the terms of NAFTA, must obtain employment authorization from a Canadian embassy or consulate before entering the country. **Students** who are US citizens, permanent residents of the US, or Green Card holders, who have already been accepted by a school in Canada and have sufficient funds to cover all expenses, must apply for student authorization at a port of entry or a Canadian consulate four months before entering the country.

Bear in mind that if you cross the border in your car, trunks and passenger compartments are subject to spot searches by the **customs** personnel of both the US and Canada. Officers at the more obscure entry points on the border can be real sticklers, so expect to be delayed. Americans who visit Canada for at least 48 hours and haven't made an international trip in thirty days can bring back goods to the value of US$400. Gifts valued at less than C$60 that do not contain tobacco or alcohol can be brought into Canada; those valued at more than C$60 are subject to regular import duty on the excess amount. The US Customs Service (☎202/927-6724) can help with any queries.

GETTING THERE FROM AUSTRALIA & NEW ZEALAND

Travelling **from Australia and New Zealand**, there are **daily direct flights** to Vancouver, Canada's western point of entry, on Qantas and Air New Zealand from A$1629/NZ$1899 with other onward destinations being well served by Canadian Airlines and Air Canada. You can expect to pay around A/NZ$420 on top of your main ticket to the eastern cities of Toronto and Montréal and around A/NZ$250 to Edmonton and Calgary. However, if you intend to do a fair amount of flying around, you'd be better off taking advantage of some of the **coupon deals** that can be bought with your main ticket. Canadian Airlines' passes, available only with Qantas and Air New Zealand tickets, are C$450 for the first three and C$60 for subsequent ones (maximum of eight in total) while Air Canada's are a little more: C$499 for three and C$70 for extras, but not restricted. A number of flights stop off in Honolulu, Hawaii; where you can usually stay over for as long as you like for no extra charge. Alternatively, if you don't mind going via Asia, JAL and Korean Airlines fares to Vancouver include a night's accommodation in their home cities and start from around A$1500/NZ$1799.

Seat availability on most international flights out of Australia and New Zealand is often limited, so it's best to book at least three weeks ahead. Tickets purchased direct from the airlines tend to be expensive and you'll get much better deals on fares from your local travel agent, as well as the latest information on limited specials, fly-drive, accommodation packages, stopovers en route and round-the-world fares. The best discounts are through **Flight Centres** and **STA** (for students and under-26s), who can also advise on visa regulations.

Airfares are seasonally adjusted: low season from mid-January to end February, and October to November; high season from mid/end May to August, December and January; and shoulder seasons the rest of the year. Seasons vary slightly depending on the airline.

FROM AUSTRALIA

Fares from eastern Australian capitals are generally the same (airlines offer a free connecting service between these cities), whereas fares from Perth and Darwin are about A$400 less via Asia and more via the US.

Canadian Airlines code-sharing with Qantas (sharing the same flight) offer the best through-service to destinations beyond Vancouver. For example, you can expect to pay around A$1929 low season and A$2279 high season to Edmonton and Calgary, and A$2099/2449 to Montréal and Toronto. United Airlines also has services to Calgary and Edmonton from Sydney via LA for slightly more (around A$1949/2299) and to Toronto and Montréal for A$2119/2469. Air New Zealand and Canadian Airlines offer the lowest fares: A$1629/1979 to Vancouver and A$2049/2399 to Toronto via Auckland and Honolulu. To Vancouver, Qantas and United Airlines start at A$1699. A slightly cheaper option is via Asia with either JAL (A$1499/1799) or Korean Airlines (A$1559/1899), and often includes a night's stopover accommodation in their respective cities of Tokyo and Seoul.

FROM NEW ZEALAND

Canadian Airlines–Air New Zealand, via Honolulu and United Airlines, via LA provide daily connections to Vancouver (NZ$1899 in low season and NZ$2299 in high season), Edmonton and Calgary (NZ$2299/2499) and Toronto and Montréal (NZ$2399/2599) as well as other major cities in Canada. Qantas can get you to Vancouver via Sydney

AIRLINES

☎800 and ☎300 numbers are toll-free, but only apply if dialled outside the city in the address. ☎13/ numbers are charged at the local rate nationwide.

Air Canada, Australia ☎1-800-221-015; New Zealand ☎09/703-3793. *Coupons for extended travel in the US.*

Air New Zealand, Australia ☎13/2476; New Zealand ☎09/357-3000. *Daily flights to Vancouver and Toronto from major Australasian cities via Auckland and Honolulu with onward connections to other cities with Canadian Airlines.*

Canadian Airlines, Australia ☎1-300-655-767 or 02/9299-7843; New Zealand ☎09/3090-3620. *Code-share with Qantas and Air New Zealand to major cities in Canada from Sydney and Auckland several times a week via Vancouver; onward connections to other destinations in Canada.*

JAL Japan Airlines, Australia ☎02/9272-1111;

New Zealand ☎09/379-9906. *Several flights a week to Vancouver with either a transfer or an overnight stopover in Tokyo.*

Korean Airlines, Australia ☎02/9262-6000; New Zealand ☎09/307-3687. *Several flights a week from Sydney and Brisbane to Vancouver via an overnight stopover in Seoul.*

Qantas, Australia ☎13/1211; New Zealand ☎09/357-8900 or 0-800/808-767. *Daily to Vancouver from major Australasian cities either direct or via Honolulu, with onward connection to other destinations with Canadian Airlines.*

United Airlines, Australia ☎13/1777; New Zealand ☎09/379-3800. *Daily to Vancouver, Edmonton, Calgary, Montréal and Toronto from Sydney and Auckland via a transfer in LA.*

DISCOUNT TRAVEL AGENTS

Anywhere Travel, 345 Anzac Parade, Kingsford, Sydney (☎02/9663-0411).

Brisbane Discount Travel, 260 Queen St, Brisbane (☎07/3229-9211).

Budget Travel, 16 Fort St, Auckland, plus branches around the city (☎09/366-0061 and 0800/808040).

Destinations Unlimited, 3 Milford Rd, Auckland (☎09/373-4033).

Flight Centres, Australia: 82 Elizabeth St, Sydney, plus branches nationwide (☎13/1600). New Zealand: 205 Queen St, Auckland (☎09/309-6171), plus branches nationwide.

Northern Gateway, 22 Cavenagh St, Darwin (☎08/8941-1394).

STA Travel, Australia: 702 Harris St, Ultimo, Sydney; 256 Flinders St, Melbourne; other offices in state capitals and major universities (for nearest branch ☎13/1776; fastfare telesales ☎1300/360960). *New Zealand:* 10 High St, Auckland (☎09/309-0458; fastfare telesales ☎09/366-6673), plus branches in Wellington, Christchurch, Dunedin, Palmerston North, Hamilton and at major universities. World Wide Web site: *www.statravelaus.com.au*; email: *traveller@statravelaus.com.au*

Thomas Cook, Australia: 175 Pitt St, Sydney; 257 Collins St, Melbourne; plus branches in other state capitals (for local branch ☎13/1771, Thomas Cook Direct telesales ☎1800/063-913); New Zealand: 96 Anzac Ave, Auckland (☎09/379-3920). *Travellers' cheques, rail and bus passes.*

SPECIALIST AGENTS AND OPERATORS

Adventure Specialists, 69 Liverpool St, Sydney (☎02/9261-2927). *Overland and adventure tour agent offering a variety of trips throughout Canada.*

Adventure World, 73 Walker St, North Sydney (☎02/9956-7766 or 1800/221-931), plus branches in Brisbane and Perth; New Zealand: 101 Great South Rd, Remuera, Auckland (☎09/524-5118). *Agents for a vast array of international adventure travel companies that operate a variety of trips in Canada.*

Peregrine Adventures, 258 Lonsdale St, Melbourne (☎03/9663-8611), plus offices in Brisbane, Sydney, Adelaide and Perth. *Offer a variety of active holidays, from short camping, walking and sea kayaking trips in British Columbia to longer overland adventures.*

Snow Bookings Only, 1141 Toorak Rd, Camberwell, Melbourne (☎1800/623-266). *Skiing and snowboarding holidays in British Columbia and Alberta.*

Sydney International Travel, 75 King St, Sydney (☎02/9299-8000). *Extensive range of Canadian tours and accommodation including short city-stays.*
Topdeck Travel, 8th Floor, 350 Kent St, Sydney. (☎02/9299-8844 or 1-800-800-724). *Agents for*

Exodus's extended small-group camping trips tracing the gold rush days through the Rockies and Yukon.
Wiltrans, Level 10, 189 Kent St, Sydney (☎02/9255-0899). *Fully escorted cultural tours staying in famous hotels through Canada.*

for around NZ$1999/2499, but the best deals are out of Auckland with JAL, with either a transfer or stopover in Tokyo for NZ$1799/2149. Add about NZ$100 for Christchurch and Wellington departures.

ROUND-THE-WORLD

If you intend to take in Canada as part of a world trip, a **round-the-world** ticket offers the best value for money, working out just a little more than an all-in ticket. Cathay Pacific–UA's "Globe-

trotter", or Air New Zealand–KLM–Northwest's "World Navigator" and Qantas–BA's "Global Explorer" all offer six stopovers worldwide, limited backtracking, and additional stopovers (around $120 each), from A$2499/NZ$3089 to A$3199/NZ$3599. More US-oriented, but only available in Australia, is Singapore–TWA's "Easyworld" fare, allowing unlimited stopovers worldwide with a maximum of eight within the US, and limited backtracking within the US (flat rate A$3023).

RED TAPE AND VISAS

Citizens of the EU, Scandinavia and most Commonwealth countries travelling to Canada do not need an entry visa: all that is required is a full valid passport. United

States citizens simply need some form of identification; see below for more details.

All visitors to Canada have to complete a **waiver form**, which you'll be given on the plane

CANADIAN HIGH COMMISSIONS, CONSULATES AND EMBASSIES ABROAD

AUSTRALIA AND NEW ZEALAND

Auckland 9th Floor, Jetset Centre, 44–48 Emily Place, Auckland 1 (☎09/309-3690).

Canberra Commonwealth Avenue, Canberra, ACT 2600 (☎06/273-3844).

Sydney Level 5, Quay West Building, 111 Harrington St, Sydney, NSW 2000 (☎02/9364-3000).

EUROPE

Germany Prinz-Georg-Strasse 126, 40479 Düsseldorf (☎0211/172170); Friedrich-Wilhelm-Strasse 18, 53113 Bonn (☎049/228-9680).

Ireland 65 St Stephen's Green, Dublin 2 (☎01/478-1988).

Netherlands Sophialaan 7, 251 4JP, The Hague (☎070/311-1600).

Norway Oscars Gate 20, Oslo 3 (☎022/466955).

Sweden Tegelbacken 4, 7th Floor, Stockholm (☎08/613-9900).

United Kingdom Macdonald House, 1 Grosvenor Square, London W1X 0AB (☎0171/258-6600).

UNITED STATES

Chicago Suite 2400, 2 Prudential Plaza, 180 N Stetson Ave, Chicago, IL 60601 (☎312/616-1860).

Los Angeles 9th Floor, 550 South Hope St, Los Angeles, CA 90071-2627 (☎213/346-2700).

New York 16th Floor, Exxon Building, 1251 Ave of the Americas, New York, NY 10020-1175 (☎212/596-1600).

Washington 501 Pennsylvania Ave NW, Washington, DC 20001 (☎202/682-1755).

There are also consulates in **Atlanta, Boston, Buffalo, Dallas, Detroit, Miami, Minneapolis** and **Seattle**. Check the phone book for details.

or at the US–Canada border. On the form you'll have to give details of where you intend to stay during your trip. If you don't know, write "touring", but be prepared to give an idea of your schedule and destinations to the immigration officer.

At the point of entry, the Canadian **immigration** officer decides the length of stay permitted up to a **maximum of six months**, but not usually more than three. The officers rarely refuse entry, but they may ask you to show them how much **money** you have: a credit card or $300 cash per week of the proposed visit is usually considered sufficient. They may also ask to see a return or onward ticket. If they ask where you're staying

and you give the name and address of friends, don't be surprised if they check.

For visa and immigration enquiries, visits of more than six months, study trips and stints of temporary employment, contact the nearest Canadian embassy, consulate or high commission for authorization prior to departure (see p.15). Inside Canada, if an extension of stay is desired, written application must be made to the nearest **Canada Immigration Centre** well before the expiry of the authorized visit.

The **duty-free** allowance if you're over 19 (18 in Alberta, Manitoba and Québec) is 200 cigarettes and 50 cigars, plus 1.4 litres of liquor or 24 355ml-sized bottles of beer.

INFORMATION AND MAPS

Few countries on earth can match the sheer volume of tourist information as that handed out by the Canadians. The most useful sources of information before you go are the various provincial tourist departments in Canada. The box opposite provides their addresses; if you contact them well in advance of your departure, and are as specific as possible about your intentions, they'll be able to provide you with everything you need to know.

Outside Canada, the consulates, embassies and high commissions (see "Red tape and visas", p.15) usually have tourist departments, though these cannot match the specific detailed advice dispensed in Canada. One or two Canadian

provinces maintain offices or brochure line numbers in London (see overleaf), though these serve mainly as clearing houses for free publicity material. Most of Canada's provinces have at least one **toll-free visitor information number** for use within mainland North America. The toll-free numbers are staffed by tourist office employees trained to answer all manner of queries and to advise on room reservations.

LOCAL INFORMATION

In Canada, there are often seasonal **provincial tourist information centres** along the main highways, especially at provincial boundaries and along the US border. The usual **opening hours** for the seasonal centres are daily 9am–9pm in July and August and weekdays 9am–5 or 6pm in May, June, September and October. These dispense all sorts of glossy material and, most usefully, have details of local provincial and national parks. The parks themselves (see "Outdoor pursuits") have offices that sell fishing and backcountry permits and give help on the specifics of hiking, canoeing, wildlife watching and so forth. At the country's **airports** general information is harder to come by, though there's usually a city tourist desk or a free phone which will help arrange accommodation.

All of Canada's large cities have their own **tourist bureaux**, with the services of the main branch complemented by summertime booths, kiosks and offices. Smaller towns nearly always

PROVINCIAL TOURIST OFFICES IN CANADA

Alberta, Travel Alberta, Visitor Sales and Service, 3rd Floor, 101–102nd St Edmonton, Alberta T5J 4G8 (☎403/422-1725).
Toll-free: within Canada and mainland USA ☎1-800-661-8888.

British Columbia, Tourism British Columbia, Box 9830, Parliament Buildings, Victoria, BC V8V 1X4 (☎604/387-1642).
Toll-free: within Canada and mainland USA ☎1-800-663-6000.

Manitoba, Travel Manitoba, 7th Floor, 155 Carlton St, Winnipeg, Manitoba R3C 3H8 (☎204/945-3796).
Toll-free: within Canada and mainland USA ☎1-800-665-0040.

New Brunswick, New Brunswick Department of Tourism, PO Box 6000, Fredericton, New Brunswick E3B 5C3 (☎506/789-2050).
Toll-free: within Canada and mainland USA ☎1-800-561-0123.

Newfoundland and Labrador, Newfoundland and Labrador Department of Tourism, Culture and Recreation, PO Box 8700, St John's, Newfoundland A1B 4JB (☎709/729-2830).
Toll free: within Canada and mainland USA ☎1-800-563-6353.

Northwest Territories, Northwest Territories Department of Tourism, PO Box 1320 Yellowknife, Northwest Territories X1A 2L9 (☎403/873-7200).
Toll-free: within Canada and mainland USA ☎1-800-661-0788.

Nova Scotia, Nova Scotia Tourism and Culture, PO Box 130, Halifax, Nova Scotia B3J 2R5 (☎902/424-4207).
Toll-free: within Canada ☎1-800-565-0000; within mainland USA ☎1-800-341-6096.

Nunavut, Nunavut Tourism, PO Box 1450, Iqaluit, NT X0A 0H0 (☎867/979-6551).
Toll-free: within Canada ☎1-800-491-7910.

Ontario, Ontario Travel, Queen's Park, Toronto, Ontario M7A 2E5 (☎416/314-0944).
Toll-free: within Canada and mainland USA ☎1-800-668-2746.

Prince Edward Island, Tourism PEI, West Royalty Industrial Park, Charlottetown, PEI (☎902/368-5540).
Toll-free: within Canada and mainland USA ☎1-800-463-4734.

Québec, Tourisme Québec, PO Box 20000, Québec, Québec G1K 7X2 (☎514/873-2015).
Toll-free: within Canada and mainland USA ☎1-800-363-7777.

Saskatchewan, Tourism Saskatchewan, 500-1900 Albert St, Regina, Saskatchewan S4P 4L9 (☎306/787-2300).
Toll-free: within Canada and mainland USA ☎1-800-667-7191.

Yukon, Tourism Yukon, PO Box 2703, Whitehorse, Yukon Y1A 2C6 (☎403/667-5340).
Toll-free: within Canada and mainland USA ☎1-800-661-0788.

TOURIST OFFICES

AUSTRALIA AND NEW ZEALAND

Australia *Tourist offices are usually sections of a consulate or embassy, so refer to these for further information.*

New Zealand, 33a Portland Rd, Remuera, Auckland (☎9/522-0921).

NETHERLANDS

Netherlands *Tourist offices are usually sections of a consulate or embassy, so refer to these for further information.*

UK

Alberta Brochure line only: ☎0171/924-5050.

British Columbia British Columbia House, 1 Regent St, London SW1Y 4NS (☎0171/930-6857).

Québec Brochure line only: ☎0990/561705.

Ontario Postal enquiries only: PO Box 157, Tunbridge, Kent TN12 9XI.

Visit Canada Centre, 62–65 Trafalgar Sq, London WC2N 5DY. *Open weekdays.*

Visit Canada Telecentre ☎0891/715000.

US

Tourist offices are usually sections of a consulate or embassy, so refer to these for further information.

CANADA ON THE INTERNET

Air Canada
http://www.aircanada.ca/home.html
Details of flight times, fares and reservations.

Bed and Breakfast
http://www.bbcanada
An extensive online source, with over 1900 colour listings of B&Bs across the country.

Canada's Most Wanted
http://www.rcmp-grc.gc.ca/html/graphics/wanted/list.htm
A few people to avoid on your trip. A site reserved by the Royal Canadian Mounted Police for their favourite villains.

Canadian Airlines
http://www.cdnair.ca/
Schedules, fares and reservations.

Canadian Parks
http://parkscanada.pch.gc.ca/parks/main_e.htm
A good site by Canadian Heritage detailing opening times, camping facilities and how to get there, to all major Canadian parks.

Canadian Tourism Commission
http://xinfo.ic.gc.ca/Tourism/Canada/index.html
Excellent site answering almost any query you care to think of concerning travel within Canada.

The Globe and Mail
http://www.theglobeandmail.com/index2.html
Canada's premier paper online.

Greyhound Buses
http://www.greyhound.ca/
Provides schedules and prices for a ream of destinations.

Infospace
http://in-101.infospace.com/info/cansvcs.htm
Exhaustive Yellow Pages-like listings. If you want to find a vet in Labrador or a body piercer in Prince Albert, this will have it.

MacLean's
http://www.macleans.ca
Top stories and the editor's pick from past issues of Canada's premier news magazine.

Maps on the Net
http://www.mapquest.com/
Maps from all over the world, including all major Canadian cities and towns.

Skiing
http://www.skinetcanada.ca/
Latest ski conditions, weather, prices, facts and figures from Canada's ski resorts.

Slam! Sport
http://www.canoe.ca/Slam/
A very thorough Canadian site on all matters sporting.

Tickets
http://www.ticketmaster.ca/
Ticket booking service for shows, gigs and sporting events across Canada.

Trains
http://www.viarail.ca
VIA Rail's page with times and tickets for Canada's train services.

Yahoo!: Canada
http://www.yahoo.ca/
The canuck section of the useful Web directory provides good avenues of investigation.

---

have a seasonal **tourist office, infocentre** or **visitors' centre**, frequently operated by the municipal chamber of commerce, holding local maps and information. The usual opening hours in summer are daily 9am–6pm; in winter, tourist information is often dispensed from the city hall or chamber of commerce (Mon–Fri 9am–5pm). Many larger towns have a **free newspaper** or broadsheet, carrying local reviews and entertainment listings.

MAPS

The **free maps** issued by each province, and available at all the outlets listed opposite, are excellent for general driving and route planning,

especially as they provide the broad details of ferry connections. The best of the commercially produced maps are those published by Rand McNally, also available bound together in their Rand McNally Road Atlas of North America.

In the case of **hiking** and **canoe** routes, all the national and most of the provincial parks have visitors' centres, which provide free parkland maps indicating hiking and canoe trails. Many of them also sell proper local survey maps, as do lots of outfitters and some of the provincial parks' departments, whose details are given in the Guide or can be obtained through the toll-free numbers.

MAP OUTLETS IN BRITAIN

London
National Map Centre, 22–24 Caxton St, SW1H 0QU (☎0171/222-4945).

Stanfords, 12–14 Long Acre, WC2 9LP (☎0171/836-1321).

Edinburgh
Thomas Nelson and Sons Ltd, 51 York Place, EH1 3JD (☎0131/557-3011).

Glasgow
John Smith and Sons, 57–61 St Vincent St (☎0141/221-7472).

Maps by **mail or phone order** are available from *Stanfords* (☎0171/836-1321).

MAP OUTLETS IN NORTH AMERICA

Chicago
Rand McNally, 444 N Michigan Ave, IL 60611 (☎312/321-1751).

Montréal
Ulysses Travel Bookshop, 4176 St-Denis (☎514/843-9447).

New York
British Travel Bookshop, 551 5th Ave, NY 10176 (☎1-800-448-3039 or 212/490-6688).

The Complete Traveler Bookstore, 199 Madison Ave, NY 10016 (☎212/685-9007).

Rand McNally, 150 East 52nd St, NY 10022 (☎212/758-7488).

Traveler's Bookstore, 22 W 52nd St, NY 10019 (☎212/664-0995).

San Francisco
The Complete Traveler Bookstore, 3207 Fillmore St, CA 92123 (☎415/923-1511).

Rand McNally, 595 Market St, CA 94105 (☎415/777-3131).

Santa Barbara
Map Link, Inc, Unit 5, 30 S La Patera Lane, CA 93117 (☎805/692-6777).

Seattle
Elliot Bay Book Company, 101 S Main St, WA 98104 (☎206/624-6600).

Toronto
Open Air Books and Maps, 25 Toronto St, M5R 2C1 (☎416/363-0719).

Vancouver
World Wide Books and Maps, 1247 Granville St. (☎604/687-3320).

Washington DC
Rand McNally, 1201 Connecticut Ave NW, Washington, DC 20036 (☎202/223-6751).

Note that *Rand McNally* have numerous stores across the US; phone ☎1-800-333-0136 ext 2111 for the address of your nearest store, or for **direct mail** maps.

MAP OUTLETS IN AUSTRALIA AND NEW ZEALAND

Auckland
Specialty Maps, 58 Albert St (☎09/307-2217).

Adelaide
The Map Shop, 16a Peel St, Adelaide, SA 5000 (☎08/231-2033).

Brisbane
Worldwide Maps and Guides 187 George St, Brisbane (☎07/3221-4330).

Melbourne
Bowyangs, 372 Little Bourke St, Melbourne, VIC 3000 (☎03/9670-4383).

Perth
Perth Map Centre, 891 Hay St, Perth, WA 6000 (☎08/9322-5733).

Sydney
Travel Bookshop, 20 Bridge St, Sydney, NSW 2000 (☎02/9241-3554).

If you want to be absolutely sure of getting the maps you need for independent wilderness travel, contact the **Canada Map Office**, 130 Bentley Ave, Ottawa, Ontario K1A 0E9 (☎613/952-7000). It supplies map indexes, which will identify the map you need; it also produces two useful brochures entitled *How to Use a Map* and *Maps and Wilderness Canoeing*, and publishes two main series of maps, 1:250 000 and 1:50 000.

TRAVELLERS WITH DISABILITIES

Canada is one of the best places in the world to travel if you have mobility problems or other physical disabilities. All public buildings are required to be wheelchair-accessible and provide suitable toilet facilities, almost all street corners have dropped kerbs, and public telephones are specially equipped for hearing-aid users. Though wheelchair users will probably encounter problems when travelling on city public transport, main population centres are gradually introducing suitable buses.

INFORMATION

The Canadian Paraplegic Association can provide a wealth of **information** on travelling in specific provinces, and most of its regional offices produce a free guide on the most easily accessed sights. Provincial tourist offices are also excellent sources of information on accessible hotels, motels and sights. Some also supply special free guides, like *Montréal – Useful Information for the Handicapped*, available from Québec House. You may also want to get in touch with Kéroul in Montréal, an organization that specializes in travel for mobility-impaired people, and publishes the bilingual guide *Accès Tourisme* ($15 plus $3 postage). Twin Peaks Press also publishes three useful guides: the *Directory of Travel Agencies for the Disabled* ($19.95), which lists more than 370 agencies worldwide, *Travel for the Disabled* ($19.95) and the *Directory of Accessible Van Rentals and Wheelchair Vagabond* ($14.95), both of which are loaded with handy tips.

TRANSPORT AND FACILITIES

Most **airlines**, both transatlantic and internal, will do whatever they can to ease your journey, and will usually allow attendants of more seriously disabled people to accompany them at no extra charge – Air Canada is the best-equipped carrier.

The larger **car-rental** companies, like Hertz and Avis, can provide cars with hand controls at no extra charge, though these are only available on their most expensive models; book one as far in advance as you can – Hertz insists on the request being made five days before the car is needed and supplies are limited. A wheelchair-accessible **coach** with hydraulic lift and on-board accessible toilet can be rented from National Motor Coach Systems, Box 3220, Station B, Calgary, Alberta T2M 4L7 (☎403/240-1992). In order to obtain a **parking privilege permit**, disabled drivers must complete the appropriate form from the province in question. Contact addresses and organizations vary from province to province, though the permit, once obtained from one province, is valid across Canada. Contact provincial tourist offices for details. In British Columbia you should contact the Social Planning and Research Council of British Columbia, 106-2182 W 12th Ave, Vancouver, BC V6K 2N4 (☎604/736-8118, fax 736-8697). Their conditions are typical: enclose a letter with name, address, phone number and date of birth; the medical name of the disabling condition; a letter from a doctor with original signature (*not* a photocopy) stating the disability that makes it difficult for a person to walk more than 100m and whether the prognosis is temporary or permanent. You should also include date of arrival and departure in Canada (BC), a contact address if known, a mailing address for the permit to be sent to, date and signature, and a cheque or money order for $15 to cover processing.

All VIA Rail **trains** can accommodate wheelchairs that are no larger than 81cm by 182cm and weigh no more than 114kg, though 24 hours notice is required for the Québec–Windsor corridor and 48 hours on other routes. They offer an excellent service, including served meals, roomettes at no extra charge for blind people travelling with a guide dog, as well as help with boarding and disembarking. Those who need attendants can apply for a two-for-one fare certificate under the **"Helping Hand"** scheme; it's available from the Canadian Rehabilitation Council for the Disabled, if you submit a medical certificate and an application signed by a doctor.

Although **buses** are obliged to carry disabled passengers if their wheelchairs fit in the luggage compartment, access is often difficult. However, nearly all bus companies accept the two-for-one

CONTACTS FOR TRAVELLERS WITH DISABILITIES

AUSTRALIA AND NEW ZEALAND

ACROD (Australian Council for Rehabilitation of the Disabled), PO Box 60, Curtin, ACT 2605 (☎02/6282-4333).

Barrier Free Travel, 36 Wheatly St, North Bellingen, NSW 2454 (☎066/551733).

Disabled Persons Assembly, 173–175 Victoria St, Wellington (☎04/811-9100).

UK

Holiday Care Service, 2nd Floor, Imperial Buildings, Victoria Road, Horley, Surrey RH6 7PZ (☎01293/774535, fax 784647).
Information on all aspects of travel.

RADAR, Unit 12, City Forum, 250 City Rd, EC1U 8AF (☎0171/250-3222).
A good source of advice on holidays and travel abroad.

Tripscope, The Courtyard, Evelyn Road, London W4 5JH (☎0181/994-9294, fax 994-3618).
Offers advice and information on travel for sick, elderly and disabled people.

CANADA

BC Coalition of People with Disabilities, 204–456 W Broadway, Vancouver, BC (☎604/875-0188).
Offers advice and assistance for travellers in BC.

Canadian Paraplegic Association. Their main office is at Suite 320, 1101 Prince of Wales Drive, Ottawa, Ontario K2C 3W7 (☎613/723-1033, fax 613/723-1060, and there are offices in every province: 520 Sutherland Drive, Toronto M4G 3V9 (☎416/422-5644); 780 SW Marine Drive, Vancouver, BC V6P 5YT (☎604/342-3611); 825 Sherbrook St, Winnipeg, Manitoba (☎204/786-4753).

Kéroul 4545 Pierre-de-Courbetin, CP 1000, Montréal (☎514/252-3104).

VIA Rail information and reservations for the speech- and/or hearing-impaired are available on ☎416/368-6406 from Toronto, ☎1-800-268-9503 from elsewhere.

Western Institute for the Deaf, 2125 W Seventh Ave, Vancouver, BC V6K 1X9 (☎604/736-7391 or 736-2527).
Gives advice for the hearing-impaired.

USA

Directions Unlimited, 720 N Bedford Rd, Bedford Hills, NY 10507 (☎1-800-533-5343).
Tour operator specializing in custom tours for people with disabilities.

Mobility International USA, Box 10767, Eugene, OR 97440 (voice and TDD ☎541/343-1284).
Information, access guides, tours and exchange programmes. Annual membership $25 (includes quarterly newsletter).

Society for the Advancement of Travel for the Handicapped (SATH), 347 5th Ave, New York, NY 10016 (☎212/447-7284).
Information on suitable tour operators and travel agents.

Travel Information Service, Moss Rehabilitation Hospital, 1200 W Tabor Rd, Philadelphia, PA 19141 (☎215/456-9600).
Telephone information service and referral.

"Helping Hand" certificates, and drivers are usually extremely helpful.

Larger **hotels** like *Holiday Inn* often have specially designed suites for disabled guests, and major motel chains like *Best Western* and *Journey's End* have full access – but it is always worth checking with the tourist offices (and the particular hotel) to confirm facilities.

INSURANCE, CRIME AND PERSONAL SAFETY

It's essential to have travel insurance to cover loss of possessions and money as well as the cost of all medical and dental treatment. Many bank and charge accounts include some form of travel cover, and insurance is also sometimes offered if you pay for your trip with a credit card. In all cases, you must make sure you keep all medical bills and, if you have anything stolen, get a copy of the crime report number when you report the incident – otherwise you won't be able to claim.

Remember that certain activities, like **scuba diving**, **mountain climbing** and other risky sports, are unlikely to be covered by most policies, although by paying an extra premium you can usually get the additional cover required. Also note that few insurers will arrange on-the-spot payments in the event of a major expense or loss; you will usually be reimbursed only after going home – though most credit card and travellers' cheque companies will reimburse or replace pretty much immediately.

INSURANCE POLICIES

Among **British** insurers, Endsleigh (97–107 Southampton Row, London WC1B 4AJ; ☎0171/436-4451) are about the cheapest, offering a month's cover from around £50, which includes medical and dental treatment as well as theft and loss of possessions. Similar policies are available from most youth/student travel specialists like Campus Travel or STA (see p.5 for addresses), or from low-cost **insurers** Columbus

Travel Insurance (17 Devonshire Square, London EC2B 4SQ; ☎0171/375-0011). Almost all UK banks and travel agents issue reasonably priced policies too. For trips of **up to four months**, or for several shorter trips within one year, you will be better off with a **frequent traveller policy**, which offers twelve months of cover for around £130 – details from the outlets mentioned above.

In **Australia**, CIC Insurance, offered by Cover-More Insurance Services (Level 9, 32 Walker St, North Sydney; ☎02/202-8000; branches in Victoria and Queensland), has some of the widest cover available and can be arranged through most travel agents. A typical policy for Canada will cost: A$130/NZ$145 for two weeks, A$190/NZ$210 for one month, A$280/NZ$310 for two months.

Travellers from the **US** should carefully check any existing insurance policies before taking out a new one. You may discover that you're covered already for medical and other losses while abroad. Holders of **ISIC** cards are entitled to be reimbursed for $3000 worth of accident coverage and sixty days of inpatient benefits up to $100 a day for the period the card is valid – though this isn't going to go far in the event of a serious setback. If you do want a specific travel insurance policy, there are numerous kinds to choose from: short-term combination policies covering everything from baggage loss to broken legs are the best bet. The policy offered by STA comes with or without medical cover. Rates are $110/85 for one month, $165/120 for two, and rise by $55/35 for each extra month. Other companies you might try are Travel Guard, 1145 Clark St, Stevens Point, WI 54481 (☎1-800-826-1300), Carefree Travel Insurance, PO Box 9366, 100 Garden City Plaza, Garden City, NY 11530 (☎1-800-323-3149), Travel Assistance International, 1133 15th St NW, Suite 400, Washington, DC 20005 (☎1-800-821-2828) or Travel Insurance Services, Suite 200, 2930 Camino Diablo, Walnut Creek, CA 94596 (☎1-800-937-1387).

Travel insurance is available from most travel agents or direct from insurance companies for periods ranging from a few days to a year or even longer. Most policies are similar in premium and coverage – but if you plan to indulge in high-risk activities check the policy carefully to make sure you'll be covered.

POLICE AND TROUBLE

There's little reason why you should ever come into contact with the **Royal Canadian Mounted Police** (RCMP), who patrol Canada in the form of provincial and metropolitan forces. In contrast to the US, there's very little street crime and even in Toronto, Vancouver and Montréal you shouldn't have any problems in terms of **personal safety** if you stick to the main parts of town, though it's obviously advisable to be cautious late at night. However, if you're drinking in one of the country's many rough-and-ready bars, don't be too surprised if there's a fight, though the males (very rarely females) involved will almost always be too busy thumping people they know to bother with a stranger – and hitting a woman (in this context) is almost unheard of. **Theft** is also uncommon, though it's obviously a good idea to be on your guard against petty thieves: always keep an eye on your luggage at bus and train stations, secure your things in a locker when staying in hostel accommodation, and avoid leaving valuables on a beach or in a tent or car.

Canadian officials are notorious for coming down hard if you're found with **drugs** – especially on non-Canadians. Stiff penalties are imposed, even when only traces of any drug are found, so don't even think about it.

If you are unlucky enough to be attacked or have something stolen, phone the police on ☎**911**. If you're going to make an **insurance claim** or **travellers' cheque refund application**, ensure the crime is recorded by the police and make a note of their crime report number.

Should you lose your **passport**, contact the nearest consulate (see box below) and get them to issue a **temporary passport**, which is basically a sheet of paper saying you've reported the loss. This will get you home, but if you were planning to travel on from Canada, you'll need a new passport – a time-consuming and expensive process.

Another possible problem is **lost airline tickets**. On scheduled and most charter flights, the airline company will honour their commitment on the lost ticket (especially if they can contact the issuing agent), but you may have to pay for a new ticket and wait a period (often as long as six months) for reimbursement once the airline is satisfied the ticket has not been used. Whatever happens, it's bound to involve hassle at the airport and afterwards. With some bargain-basement tickets, airlines will also make you pay again unless you can produce the lost ticket's number. Similarly, if you lose your travel insurance policy document, you won't be able to make a claim unless you quote its number. To avert both calamities, keep a copy of the numbers or documents at home. For **lost travellers' cheques**, if you've followed the issuer's suggestion and kept a record of the cheque numbers separate from the actual cheques, all you have to do is ring the issuing company on their given toll-free number to report the loss. They'll ask you for the cheque numbers, the place you bought them, when and how you lost them and whether it's been reported to the police. All being well, the missing cheques should be reissued within a couple of days – and you may get an emergency advance to tide you over.

CONSULATES AND EMBASSIES

UNITED KINGDOM

Edmonton, Suite 1404, 10025 Jasper Ave (☎403/428-0375).

Halifax, 1 Canal St, Dartmouth, Nova Scotia B2Y 3Y9 (☎902/461-1381).

Montréal, 1155 Université (☎514/866-5823).

Ottawa, 80 Elgin St (☎613/237-1530).

St John's, 113 Topsail Rd (☎709/579-2002).

Toronto, Suite 1910, College Park, 777 Bay St (☎416/593-1267).

Vancouver, Suite 800, 1111 Melville St (☎604/683-4421).

Winnipeg, 111 Aldershot Building (☎204/896-1380).

UNITED STATES

Calgary, Suite 1050, 615 MacLeod Trail SE (☎403/266-8962).

Halifax, Suite 910, Cogswell Tower, Scotia Square (☎902/429-2480).

Montréal, Complex Desjardins, South Tower (☎514/281-1468).

Ottawa, 100 Wellington St (☎613/238-5335).

Québec City, 2 Terrasse Dufferin (☎418/692-2095).

Toronto, 360 University Ave (☎416/595-1700).

Vancouver, 1095 W Pender St (☎604/685-4311).

COSTS, MONEY AND BANKS

Most basic items cost less than in Britain and a bit more than they do in the US; more specific details are given below and throughout the Guide. Generally, if you're sticking to a very tight budget – camping and buying food from shops – you could squeeze through on £14–18/US$25–30 a day. You're not going to last long living like this, though, and a more comfortable average daily budget, covering a motel room, bus travel, a museum or two and a restaurant meal would work out at around £40–45/US$65–75. Naturally, once you upgrade your accommodation, eat out two or three times a day, and take in the city nightlife, this figure can easily double.

CURRENCY

Canadian **currency** is the dollar ($), made up of 100 cents (¢) to the dollar. Coins are issued in 5¢ (nickel), 10¢ (dime), 25¢ (quarter), $1 and $2 denominations: the $1 coin is known as a "loonie" after the bird on one face; no one's come up with a suitable name for the newer $2 coin – "twoonie" has been tried but hasn't really caught on. Paper currency comes in $2, $5, $10, $50, $100, $500 and $1000 denominations. Although US dollars are widely accepted, it's often on a one-for-one basis, and as the US dollar is usually worth slightly more than its Canadian counterpart, it makes sense to exchange US currency. There's no limit to the amount of money you can take into or out of Canada.

CURRENT EXCHANGE RATE

£1 = C$2.34	C$1 = US$0.70
C$1 = £0.42	A$1 = C$0.98
US$1 = C$1.40	C$1 = A$1.01

CREDIT CARDS, ATMs, CHEQUES AND BANKS

One of the quickest and easiest ways of obtaining money in Canada is through an **ATM**, particularly if your home bank ATM card is on the Cirrus or Delta networks. It's also virtually essential to have at least one **credit card** to reserve and pre-pay for hotels or car rental, where otherwise you're likely to be asked for a big cash deposit: Visa, MasterCard, American Express and Diners are widely accepted. Credit cards can also be used to obtain **cash advances** over the counter in most banks but there will invariably be a minimum amount you can draw and you'll pay credit card rates of interest on the cash from the date of withdrawal. If you have a PIN you can also obtain cash from ATMs with your credit card. With other credit cards, state bank cards and ATM cards, you should check with your bank before leaving home.

While it's a good idea to have some Canadian cash from the outset, a good way to carry the bulk of funds is in **travellers' cheques**, available from banks and building societies, usually with a one percent commission on the amount ordered. (Exchange costs are usually waived if you have a bank-issued travel insurance policy.) Buy **cheques in Canadian dollars** and try to take American Express or Visa cheques, which are accepted as cash in virtually every shop, garage, restaurant and bar throughout Canada. Using travellers' cheques in this way is a better option than trying to cash them in a bank – a surprising number of major banks in Canada will not change travellers' cheques, and when they do you'll usually have to pay a commission.

If you run out of money abroad, or there is some kind of emergency, the quickest way to get **money sent out** is to contact your bank at home and have them wire the cash to the nearest bank. You can do the same thing through Thomas Cook or American Express (free to card holders) if there is a branch nearby, and can also have cash sent out through Western Union (☎1-800-235-0000 in Canada; ☎0800/833833 in UK; ☎1-800-325-6000 in US) to a bank, post office or local agent – a process that takes just minutes but will be expensive.

Banking hours are Monday to Thursday 10am to 3pm, and until 6pm on Fridays; the trend is increasingly to longer hours and Saturday morning opening. But don't rely on finding a bank open outside these core weekday hours. The main nationwide banks include the Toronto Dominion, the Royal Bank of Canada, the National Bank of Canada, the Bank of Montréal and the Canadian Western Bank.

AVERAGE COSTS

Canada is generally good value, a fact which becomes evident from the minute you wake up: cheap Canadian breakfasts are the stuff of legend, dishing up coffee, bacon, eggs and toast for around $8 or less, while healthier snacks like soups and salads cost from about $5.

Bus fares are reasonable, the twelve-hour journey from Vancouver to Calgary, for instance, costing about $102. **Trains** cost a good deal more – $211 for the 24-hour trip from Vancouver to Edmonton – but usually much less than internal flights, though charter companies like Canada 3000 are bringing prices of these flights down: Vancouver to Calgary, an hour's flight, will cost around $120 excluding tax on an early-morning or late-evening charter.

Room rates start at around $15 for a hostel dorm, and about $35 for a double in the grottier hotels. In most parts of the country, you should find perfectly good motel rooms from around $45. Basic town **campgrounds** are never expensive, and provincial and national sites start from as little as $10; in fully serviced commercial places it's rare to pay more than $25. Accommodation prices are higher from June to early September, and throughout the more remote areas of the north, particularly the Yukon and NWT.

TIPS AND TAXES

There are several hidden costs to take into account when travelling round Canada. **Tips and service** are generally not added to restaurant bills; it's usual to leave fifteen percent, even after the cheapest meals. More importantly, though, virtually all prices in Canada for everything from bubblegum to hotel rooms is quoted **without tax**.

> Unless stated otherwise, all **accommodation prices** in this book are for high-season doubles, not including taxes; the majority of **entry charges** are the full adult ticket price – the majority of museums and similar attractions give at least fifty percent **discounts** for children and seniors, as well as **student reductions**.

This means the price you see quoted is rarely the price you pay, and round-figures prices of things costing, say, $5 or $55, end up being ludicrous sums like $5.63 or $59.94.

There are both national and provincial taxes. The dreaded **Goods and Services Tax** (GST) – the equivalent of VAT in Europe – is a nationwide seven percent charge levied on most goods and services, including hotel and restaurant bills. All provinces except Alberta, the Yukon and NWT levy a **Provincial Sales Tax** (PST) of five to ten percent on most goods and services, including hotel accommodation; only visitors to Québec (where it's called TVQ), and Manitoba, Nova Scotia and Newfoundland can currently apply for a rebate – claim forms are supplied by tourist offices (the rebate situation changes from time to time, and some other provinces may start to offer rebates to keep their visitors sweet). A so-called **Harmonized Sales Tax** (HST), a fifteen percent combination of GST and PST, applies in Nova Scotia, New Brunswick, Labrador and Newfoundland. Most provinces also have a **hotel rooms' tax** of up to ten percent. The net result is that you can end up paying something like seventeen per cent over the listed price for hotel rooms in some parts of the country.

As a small mercy, visitors can claim a **rebate** of GST on certain goods over the value of $3.50 if they're for use outside Canada and removed from the country within sixty days. More significantly, a GST rebate is available for **accommodation expenditure** over $100 during a maximum period of one month. Claim forms are available at many hotels, shops and airports or from any Canadian embassy. Return them, with **all original receipts**, to the address given on the form. People leaving by land to the USA can claim their rebate at selected border duty-free shops. The amounts can add up, so it's worth thinking about. For more information call ☎902/432-5608 (outside Canada) or ☎1-800-668-4748.

HEALTH MATTERS

It is vital to have travel insurance (see Insurance, crime and personal safety" on p.22) against potential medical expenses. Canada has an excellent health service, but it costs non-residents anything between $50 to $1000 a day to use. There is no free treatment to non-residents, and in some provinces doctors and hospitals add a surcharge to treatment meted out to foreigners. If you have an accident, medical services will get to you quickly and charge you later.

Doctors can be found listed in the Yellow Pages, and ambulance services are usually displayed on the inside cover. In emergencies call ☎911. If you are bringing medicine prescribed by your doctor, bring a copy of the prescription; first, to avoid problems at customs and immigration and, second, for renewing medication with Canadian doctors. Pharmacies are often well equipped to advise on minor ailments and to distinguish between unfamiliar brand names. Most larger towns and cities should have one open 24 hours, and many chemists stay open late as a matter of course.

SPECIFIC HEALTH PROBLEMS

Canada requires no specific vaccinations, but problems can start when you're walking or camping in the backcountry. Tap water is generally safe to drink, though at campgrounds water is sometimes good for washing only – ask if in doubt. You should always boil backcountry water for at least ten minutes to protect against the *Giardia* parasite (or "beaver fever"), which thrives in warm water, so be careful about swimming in hot springs – if possible, keep nose, eyes and mouth above water. Symptoms are intestinal cramps, flatulence, fatigue, weight loss and vomiting, all of which can appear up to a week after infection. If left untreated, more unpleasant complications can arise, so see a doctor.

Blackfly and mosquitoes are notorious for the problems they cause walkers and campers, and are especially bad in areas near water and throughout most of northern Canada. Horseflies are another pest. April to June is the blackfly season, and the mosquito season is from July until about October. Before you go, take three times the recommended daily dosage of Vitamin B complex for two weeks, and take the recommended dosage while you're in Canada – this cuts down bites by up to 75 percent. Once you're there, repellent creams and sprays may help: the best repellents are those containing DEET – the ointment version of Deep-Woods Off is the best brand, with 95 percent DEET. If you're camping or picnicking you'll find that burning coils or candles containing allethrin or citronella can help (but watch those smells – they'll attract the bears; see pp.598–599). If you're walking in an area that's rife with pests, it's well worth taking a gauze mask to protect your head and neck; wearing white clothes and no perfumed products also makes you less attractive. Once bitten, an antihistamine cream like phenergan is the best antidote. On no account go anywhere near an area marked as a blackfly mating ground – people have died from bites sustained when the monsters are on heat.

If you develop a large rash and flu-like symptoms, you may have been bitten by a tick carrying lyme borreliosis (or "lyme tick disease"). This is easily curable, but if left can lead to nasty complications, so see a doctor as soon as possible. It's spreading in Canada, especially in the more southerly and wooded parts of the country. Check on its prevalence with the local tourist authority – it may be advisable to buy a strong tick repellent and to wear long socks, trousers and sleeved shirts when walking. Whether ticks give you anything or not, they're nasty on their own, burying into your skin, often after spending time moving surreptitiously over your body to find a nice warm soft spot.

In backcountry areas look out for poison ivy, which grows in most places, but particularly in a belt across southern Ontario and Québec, where poison ivy ointment is widely available. If you're likely to be walking in affected areas, ask at tourist offices for tips on where it is and how to

The nationwide emergency number for police, fire or ambulance is ☎911, but in some remoter areas you will still have to call ☎0 for the operator.

recognize the plant. It causes itchy open blisters and lumpy sores up to ten days after contact. Wash body and clothes as soon as possible after contact, smother yourself in calamine lotion and try not to scratch. In serious cases, hospital emergency rooms can give antihistamine or adrenalin jabs. Also keep an eye open for **snakes** in certain western areas; pharmacists and wilderness outfitters can advise on snakebite kits, and park wardens can give useful preventive advice. Should you get bitten without an antidote on you, get a good look at the culprit so that the doctor can identify the species and administer the right medicine.

If walking or climbing, go properly equipped and be prepared for sudden changes of weather. Watch out for signs of **exposure** – mild delirium, exhaustion, inability to get warm – and on snow or in high country during summer take a good **sun block**. Finally, of course, take the same precautions against **HIV** infection as you would back home – use a condom and don't share needles.

GETTING AROUND

It's essential to plan carefully how you'll get around. With VIA Rail services becoming more skeletal each year, province-wide bus companies provide the main surface links between major cities, though in isolated areas you may be thrown back on more sporadic local services. Flying is of course more expensive, but competition in the skies can lead to some decent bargains.

On most forms of public transport there are **discounted fares** for children under 12, for youths between 13 and 21, and over-60s. It has to be said, however, that things are always easier if you have a **car**: even if a bus can take you to the general vicinity of a provincial park, for example, it can prove impossible to explore the interior without your own vehicle.

BY BUS

If you're travelling on your own, **buses** are by far the cheapest way to get around. Greyhound Canada runs most of the long-distance buses west of Toronto, including a service along the Trans-Canada Highway from Toronto to Vancouver. The major centres in the east of the country are served by a network of smaller lines and by a wide range of different companies. **Long-distance buses** run to a fairly full timetable (at least during the day), stopping only for meal breaks and driver changeovers. Nearly all are non-smoking, have toilets and coffee-making facilities and are less uncomfortable than you might expect – it's feasible to save on a night's accommodation by sleeping on the bus, though you may not feel up to much the next day.

Any sizable community will have a main bus station, but in smaller places a gas station or restaurant will double as the bus stop and ticket office – though often they are inconveniently situated on the edge of town. Seats can be reserved but this is rarely necessary: only those services between nearby cities like Montréal and Québec are likely to get booked out, and even then you'll only have to wait an hour or so for the next departure. Out in the less populated areas, buses are fairly scarce, sometimes only appearing once or twice a week, and here you'll need to plot your route with care.

Fares are pretty standard from company to company: as an example, Toronto to Winnipeg, a distance of 2100km, costs $150 one-way. The free *Official Canadian Bus Guide,* containing all Canadian bus **timetables,** is produced bimonthly but is not made readily available to travellers. Consequently you'll need to rely on free individual timetables from the major bus stations or local tourist offices. Always double-check routes and times by phoning the local terminal (we've included telephone numbers for most cities), or the companies (see box below). For Greyhound Canada, reservations are not necessary; if a bus is full, another is automatically laid on. However, an increasing number of services can make "seat selection" for a small fee which guarantees a specfic seat on the first bus out (useful for window-seat sightseeing).

PASSES

Travellers intending to explore Canada by bus can save a lot of money by purchasing one of two **passes** before leaving home. The **Greyhound Canada Pass** allows unlimited travel within a fixed time limit on all Greyhound Canada lines (Toronto–Vancouver on the Trans-Canada; throughout Alberta and mainland British Columbia; New York–Montréal; New York–Toronto) plus Voyageur Colonial services in parts of Québec and Ontario. Prices are seven days £99; fifteen days £135; thirty days £175; sixty days £230.

The **Canada Pass Plus** covers the same routes as well as the services of Orleans Express in Québec, Acadian Bus Lines in Nova Scotia and SMT Lines in New Brunswick and PEI for fifteen days (£165), thirty days (£215), and sixty days (£265). **Go Canada Budget Travel Pass** offers fifteen or thir-

---

CANADA'S PRINCIPAL BUS COMPANIES

Acadian Lines, 6040 Almon St, Halifax, Nova Scotia (☎902/454-9321). *Nova Scotia services.*

Alaskon Express-Grayline of Yukon (☎403/668-3225 or 1-800-780-6652). *Skagway, Whitehorse, Fairbanks and other Alaskan destinations.*

Brewster Transportation ☎403/762-6767 or 1-800-661-1152. *Services Calgary, Calgary airport, Banff, Lake Louise and Jasper.*

Dempster Highway Bus Service ☎403/979-4100 or 1-800-661-0721. *Services within the Yukon and from Dawson City to Inuvik, NWT.*

DRL Coachlines, Suite 103, Scotia Centre, 235 Water St, St John's, Newfoundland (☎709/738-8088). *Island-wide carrier.*

Frontier Coach Lines, 16 102nd St, Big River, NWT (☎403/874-2566). *Principal service links Hay River and Yellowknife.*

Go Transit, 20 Bay St, Suite 600, Toronto, Ontario (☎416/869-3200). *Suburban services around metropolitan Toronto.*

Greyhound Canada, 877 Greyhound Way SW, Calgary, Alberta (☎403/265-9111 or 1-800-661-8747). *Long-distance buses in western Canada.*

Intercar, 505 blvd Maisonneuve, Montréal, Québec (☎514/842-2281). *Québec routes.*

Laidlaw, 700 Douglas St, Victoria, British Columbia (☎250/385-4411 or 1-800-318-0818). *Services on Vancouver Island.*

Limocar, 4129 rue Lavoisier, Boisbriand, Québec (☎514/435-6767). *Services within the Laurentians.*

Mackenzie Bus Lines, PO Box 249, 210 York St, Bridgewater, Nova Scotia (☎902/543-2491). *Serves the southwest shore of Nova Scotia.*

Norline Coaches (Yukon) Ltd, 34 MacDonald Rd, Whitehorse, Yukon (☎403/668-3864). *Services from Whitehorse to Dawson City in the Yukon.*

Ontario Northland, 555 Oak St E, North Bay, Ontario (☎705/472-4500). *Serves northern Ontario.*

Orléans Express, 420 rue McGill, 2nd Floor, Montréal (☎514/395-4000). *Services across the province of Québec.*

Pacific Coachlines ☎604/662-8074 or 250/385-4411. *Services in and around Vancouver, Vancouver Island and on the Sunshine Coast.*

Penetang-Midland Coach Lines, 475 Bay St, Midland, Ontario (☎705/526-0161). *Local Ontario services north of Toronto around Georgian Bay.*

Rival Highway Tours, Suite 1, Berner Heritage Building, 342 3rd Ave W, Prince Rupert, BC (☎250/624-6124). *Services along the Cassiar Hwy, between Prince Rupert and Whitehorse.*

Saskatchewan Transportation Company, 2041 Hamilton St, Regina, Saskatchewan (☎306/787-3340 or 1-800-663-7181). *Provincial carrier.*

SMT (Eastern) Ltd, 100 Midland Drive, Dieppe, New Brunswick (☎506/859-5100). *Buses within New Brunswick, plus services from New Brunswick to New York and Charlottetown, PEI.*

Trentway-Wagar, PO Box 1017, 791 Webber Ave, Peterborough, Ontario (☎705/748-6411). *Wide range of services within southern Ontario, plus routes into the US and Québec.*

Voyageur Colonial, 265 Catherine St, Ottawa, Ontario (☎613/238-5900). *Québec and Ontario routes.*

ty nights in eighty hostels across Canada available from Greyhound but has to be bought in conjunction with Greyhound or All Canada Pass. The Go Canada Budget Travel Pass *with* Greyhound Canada Pass for fifteen days/nights is £310 and for thirty days/nights is £455. The Go Canada Budget Travel Pass *with* Canada Pass Plus for fifteen days/nights is £340 and for thirty days/nights is £495.

In the UK the passes are available from Campus Travel (North American enquiries on ☎0171/730-2101; *www.campustravel.co.uk*), or from *Greyhound's* office at Sussex House, London Road, East Grinstead, West Sussex RH19 1LD (☎01342/317317; *www.greyhound.com*).

If you are exploring just **Ontario and Québec** it could be worth investing in a **Route-Pass**. Available from mid-April to late November from major bus terminals in the two provinces, it costs $212 for fourteen consecutive days and is valid on nearly all bus lines. Two additional days can be purchased for $21.

If you are coming in from the US, note that Greyhound's **Ameripass** is not valid for travel in Canada except for the **Seattle to Vancouver** route.

BY TRAIN

The railway may have created modern Canada but passenger trains are now few and far between – at the beginning of 1990 more than half the **VIA Rail** services were eliminated at a stroke and fares were increased dramatically. Services are notoriously slow and delays common as passenger trains give way to freight, though the city links between Montréal and Toronto are still speedy and efficient. However, rail travel can still be a very rewarding experience, especially on trains with special "dome cars" that allow an uninterrupted rooftop view of the countryside.

One of the saddest losses of the VIA cutbacks was the legendary Canadian train which followed the old Canadian Pacific lines daily from Montréal to Vancouver. Today's Canadian departs three times a week from Toronto and uses the more northerly old Canadian National lines, through the monotonous muskeg of northern Ontario, stopping at Winnipeg, Saskatoon and Edmonton before hitting Jasper. However, the scenery between there and Kamloops, the last big station before Vancouver, is some of the Rockies' best. The trip is scheduled to take three nights but usually runs late; it costs a minimum of $430 per person one-way in low season, $570 in high.

The other major VIA trains still running are the **Western Canada** services from Winnipeg to Churchill, Jasper to Prince Rupert, and Victoria to Courtenay; **Ontario** has services linking Toronto with Windsor, Ottawa and Niagara Falls; **Québec** has trains between Montréal and Québec City – as well as Ottawa; and the **Eastern Canada** network runs between Montréal, Halifax and the Gaspé.

FARES AND PASSES

One-way fares from Toronto to Winnipeg give an idea of the cost of rail travel. **Coach** (or economy) class, the Canadian equivalent of second class, with reclining seats, costs $210 in low season, $275 in high (prices given respectively below), while **sleeper** class comes in three categories: **double berths**, with large seats that become curtained bunks at night, costing $870/1200 for two – and you can, of course, share with a stranger; **roomettes**, private single rooms with a toilet and a bed that folds out from the wall, costing $610/823; and **bedrooms**, which are spacious cabins with two armchairs, large windows, a table, toilet, wardrobe and bunk bed, costing $1218/1646, again for two. Meals are included in the price of all three sleeper class categories.

Ten percent **reductions** are available for the over-60s, and 2- to 15-year-olds pay half-fare. In the Windsor/Québec City and Montréal/Halifax corridors, **off-peak fares** – on every day except Friday, Sunday and holidays – are often forty percent less than the standard rate, though discounted seats are limited and seven-day advance purchase is obligatory. Between the Maritimes and Ontario or Québec, the standard rate is reduced by forty percent on "Coach" travel all year except from mid-June to early September and from mid-December to early January, with the requirement of five days' advance purchase. In western Canada, a 25 percent (and sometimes even forty percent) reduction applies on "Coach" travel from November to mid-December and early January to late April; again a week's advance purchase is necessary.

Non-North American visitors can cut fares greatly by buying a **Canrailpass** ($395; $610 from June to mid-Oct), which allows unlimited "Coach" class travel for twelve days within a thirty-day period. There are discounts on passes for the under-25s, students and the over-60s. For further details, VIA can be reached on the Internet

VIA RAIL AGENTS

UK
Leisurail, PO Box 113, Peterborough PE3 8HY (☎01733/335599).

Australia
Asia Pacific-Walshes World, 4 Davies St, Surry Hills, NSW, 2010 (☎02/9319-66240).

New Zealand
Walshes World Ltd, 2nd Floor – Dingwall Building, 87 Queen St, Private Bag 92136, Auckland 1 (☎09/379-3708).

VIA RAIL TOLL-FREE INFORMATION

☎1-800-561-3926 in Newfoundland.

☎1-800-561-3952 in Prince Edward Island, Nova Scotia and New Brunswick.

☎1-800-361-5390 in Québec.

☎1-800-361-1235 (in area codes 519, 613, 705, 905) or ☎1-800-561-8630 (area code 807) in Ontario.

☎1-800-561-8630 from Manitoba, Saskatchewan, Alberta, British Columbia, Yukon and NWT.

(*www.viarail.ca*) and they also have an international network of ticket agents. Canrailpasses can be purchased in Canada from any VIA Rail station, but are slightly more expensive if you don't buy seven days in advance.

PRIVATE RAIL LINES

Other than VIA Rail, various private companies operate passenger trains that travel through otherwise inaccessible wilderness. Most spectacular is the **Rocky Mountaineer** from Vancouver to Banff and then on to Calgary, or to Jasper, which is best experienced through a package from Rocky Mountaineer Railtours (☎1-800-665-7245). These tours, which are swiftly booked out, run from May to September and cost $640 ($100 less in the shoulder season) one-way to Jasper or Banff, plus a supplement of $70 per person for one-way travel between Banff and Calgary. Rates do not include tax but do include light meals, and a night's hotel accommodation in Kamloops. Another west Canada option is BC Rail service from Vancouver to Prince George. In Ontario, shorter trips can be made on the **Polar Bear Express** from Cochrane to Moosonee (see p.172) and the **Algoma Central Railway** from Sault Ste Marie to Hearst (see pp.183–184).

BY AIR

The complexity of Canada's **internal flight network** is immense, and throughout this guide we have given indications of which services are most useful. Canadian Airlines offers the most prolific domestic service, with planes serving more than 125 destinations, while both Air Canada and Canadian Airlines link up with numerous minor lines – like Labrador Airways in Labrador – to reach the farthest-flung recesses of Canada. One

company to look out for is Canada 3000, an economical, international carrier that also serves Canada's big cities and links Whitehorse with Vancouver. However, no one could pretend that flying around Canada is, in general terms at least, a low-budget option. For special bargains, look in the travel sections of local newspapers, especially on Sundays, or splash out on one of the many varieties of air pass (see below), each of which brings hefty discounts. If you're set on exploring the deep north, there is no alternative to air transport, as these zones are unpenetrated by rail line or road, with a few rare exceptions, such as Churchill in Manitoba.

PASSES

A multitude of **air passes** provide internal air travel at special rates. The passes have to be bought before taking a transatlantic (or transpacific) flight, and are available in the UK from Air Canada, Canadian Airlines, British Airways, Canadian Regional Airlines and Horizon Air. All are also available from Airpass Sales (☎01737/ 555300).

All air-pass deals are broadly similar, involving the purchase of at least three coupons for around £200 (with a maximum purchase of eight) extra coupons costing around £30 each. Every coupon is valid for a flight of any duration within the continent. Canadian Airlines, with the strongest domestic connections, has a good variety of passes; study the possibilities carefully before committing yourself. The main **unlimited** pass within Canada is the **Canadian Regional Airpass NationalPass**, allowing unlimited travel between seventeen destinations throughout the country, plus Seattle and Portland in the US. It's available from UK travel agents before departure and costs £199 for seven days, £249 for fourteen

MAJOR AIRLINE NUMBERS IN CANADA

Air Canada
British Columbia ☎1-800-661-3936.
Manitoba ☎1-800-542-8940.
New Brunswick and Nova Scotia ☎1-800-565-3940.
Newfoundland ☎1-800-563-5151.
Northwest Territories ☎1-800-663-9100.
Ontario ☎1-800-268-7240.
Prince Edward Island ☎1-800-776-3000.
Québec ☎1-800-361-8620.
Saskatchewan ☎1-800-665-0520.

Canada 3000
Calgary ☎403/221-1870.
Edmonton ☎403/890-4590.
Halifax ☎902/873-3030.
Montréal ☎514/476-9500.
St John's ☎709/576-0555.
Toronto ☎416/674-0257.
Vancouver ☎604/273-4883.
Winnipeg ☎204/784-0500.

Canadian Airlines
Canada-wide ☎1-800-665-1177.

days, £299 for 21 days. If you're travelling only in the east, you could consider the **Canadian Regional EastPass**, covering the area east of Winnipeg (£145 for 7, £195 for 14, £245 for 21 days). The **WestPass** costs the same and allows travel from Winnipeg to destinations west. The Canadian Regional Airpass sales office in the UK is at Enterprise House, 4 Station Parade, Chipstead, Surrey CR5 3TE (☎01737/555330).

BY CAR

Travelling by **car** is the best way to see Canada, even though a vehicle can be a bit of a liability in the big cities, with their stringent parking areas and rush-hour tailbacks. Any US and UK national over 21 with a full driving licence is allowed to drive in Canada, though rental companies may refuse to rent to a driver who has held a full licence for less than one year, and under-25s will probably get lumbered with a higher insurance premium. Car rental companies will also expect you to have a credit card; if you don't have one they may let you leave a hefty deposit (at least $300) but don't count on it.

Most of Canada's vehicles – and almost every rental car – run on unleaded fuel, which is sold by the litre; prices vary, but are generally around 70–80¢ per litre. **Fuel** is readily available – there are literally hundreds of gas stations, though they thin out markedly in the more remote regions, where you should exercise some caution by checking locally about the distance to the next one.

CAR RENTAL

Often the least expensive way to **rent a car** is either to take a fly-drive package (see p.5) or book in advance with a major rental company like Avis, Budget, Hertz, Thrifty or Tilden (a Canadian outfit). Specialist agents can also offer economical deals – in the UK, Holiday Autos (☎0990/300400) are particularly good. Bear in mind also that at the height of the season in popular tourist areas it's a good idea to book ahead. Amongst the big car rental companies competition is fierce and, as you might expect, special deals are more commonplace in the shoulder - and low season when there are scores of vehicles lying idle. It's always worth ringing round to check rates – Budget and Thrifty usually have competitive tariffs. Finally, if you take a transatlantic flight, check to see if your airline offers discounted car rental for its passengers.

In Canada itself, expect to pay from around $200 a week for a two-door economy saloon in low season to $350 for a four-door medium car in high season, though throughout the year special promotions are offered by the major companies, which can get rates down to as low as $150 per week. Provincial **taxes** and GST or HST (see p.25) are not included in the rates, but the biggest **hidden surcharge** is often the **drop-off charge**, levied when you intend to leave your car in a different place from where you picked it up. This is usually equivalent to a full week's or more rental, and can go as high as $500. Also be sure to check if **unlimited mileage** is offered; an important consideration in a country where towns are so widely dispersed: the usual free quota is 150–200km per day – woefully inadequate if you're contemplating some serious touring – after which an extra charge of around 20¢ per kilometre is standard.

You should also check the policy for the excess applied to claims and ensure that, in general terms, it provides adequate levels of financial cover. Additionally, the **Loss Damage Waiver** (LDW), a form of insurance that isn't included in the initial rental charge, is well worth the expense. At around $14 a day, it can add substantially to the total cost, but without it you're liable for every scratch to the car – even if it wasn't your fault.

For **breakdown** problems, there'll be an emergency number attached to the dashboard or stored in the glove compartment. If you're stranded on a major highway, you could do as well to sit tight and wait for the **RCMP** (the police) who cruise by fairly regularly. An extra safety option is to rent a **mobile telephone** from the car rental agency – you often only have to pay a nominal amount unless you actually use it. Having a mobile can be reassuring at least,

and a potential life-saver for trips into the northern wilderness.

If you take a rental car **across the US–Canada border**, be sure to keep a copy of the contract with you. It should bear an endorsement stating that the vehicle is permitted entry into the US.

DRIVEAWAYS

A variation on car rental is a **driveaway**, whereby you drive a car from one place to another on behalf of the owner. The same rules as for renting apply, but you should look the car over before taking it as you'll be lumbered with any repair costs and a large fuel bill if the vehicle's a gas guzzler.

Most driveaway companies will want you to give a personal reference as well as a deposit in the $200–400 region. The most common routes are along the Trans-Canada Highway and between Toronto or Montréal and Florida in the autumn and winter, although there's a fair chance you'll find something that needs shifting more or less to where you want to go. You needn't drive flat out, although not a lot of leeway is given – around eight days is the time allowed for

---

MAJOR CAR RENTAL COMPANIES

AUSTRALIA
Avis ☎1800/225 533.
Budget ☎13/2727.
Hertz ☎13/3039.

CANADA
Avis ☎1-800-387-7600 from Ontario and Québec; ☎1-800-268-2310 from elsewhere.
Budget ☎1-800-268-8970 from Québec; ☎1-800-268-8900 from elsewhere.
Dollar ☎1-800-421-6868.
Hertz ☎1-800-620-9620 from Toronto; ☎1-800-263-0600 from elsewhere.
Rent-a-Wreck ☎1-800-535-1391.
Thrifty ☎1-800-367-2277.
Tilden ☎1-800-361-5334.

NEW ZEALAND
Avis ☎09/526-2847.
Budget ☎09/375-2222.
Hertz ☎09/309-0989.

UK
Avis ☎0990/900500.
Budget ☎0800/181181.
Eurodollar ☎01895/233300.
Hertz ☎0990/996699.
Thrifty ☎0990/168238.
Holiday Autos ☎0990/300400.

USA
Alamo ☎1-800-354-2322.
Avis ☎1-800-331-1212.
Budget ☎1-800-527-0700.
Dollar ☎1-800-421-6868.
Hertz ☎1-800-654-3131.
National ☎1-800-227-7368.
Rent-a-Wreck ☎1-800-535-1391.
Thrifty ☎1-800-367-2277.

driving from Toronto to Vancouver. Driveaway companies are included in some city listings, or check under "Automobile driveaways" in the telephone directory.

RENTING AN RV

Recreational vehicles (RVs) can be rented through most travel agents specializing in Canadian holidays. It's best to arrange rental before getting to Canada, as RV rental outlets are not too common there, and travel agents here will often give cheap rates if you book a flight through them as well. You can rent a huge variety of RVs right up to giant mobile homes with two bedrooms, showers and fully fitted kitchens. A price of around $1200 in low and $1900 in high season for a five-berth van for one week is fairly typical, and on top of that you have to take into account the cost of fuel (some RVs do less than 25km to the litre), drop-off charges, and the cost of spending the night at designated trailer parks, which is what you're expected to do. Canada also has strict regulations on the size of vehicle allowed; in Ontario, for example, the maximum length for a trailer is 48 feet, 75 feet for trailer plus car – so if you are coming in from the US check that your RV isn't over the limit. The best UK-based rental company is Hemmingways Ltd, 56 Middle St, Brockham, Surrey RH3 7HW (☎01737/842735), with various packages and pick-up points throughout Canada.

ROADS, RULES AND REGULATIONS

The best **roads** for covering long distances quickly are the straight and fast multi-lane highways that radiate for some distance from major population centres. These have a maximum of six lanes divided by a central causeway and are marked on maps with thick lines and shields that contain the highway number. Outside populated areas, highways go down to one lane each way and, though paved, the hard shoulder consists of gravel – which you must on all accounts avoid hitting at speed as this will throw you into a spin, a potentially lethal experience. Up in the north and off the beaten track, highways may be entirely of gravel – broken windscreens are an occupational hazard on some stretches of the Alaska Highway, for example. Note also that after rain gravel and dirt roads are especially treacherous and indeed if you're planning a lot of dirt-road driving, you'd be well advised to rent a

four-wheel drive. The Trans-Canada Highway (TCH) travels from coast to coast and is marked by maple leaf signs at regular intervals along its length. Different sections of the TCH do, however, carry different highway numbers and in some places the TCH forks to offer more than one possible routing. Lesser roads go by a variety of names – county roads, provincial routes, rural roads or forest roads. Out in the wilds rural and forest roads are rarely paved.

Canadians drive on the **right-hand** side of the road. In most **urban areas** streets are arranged on a grid system, with traffic lights at most intersections; at junctions without lights there will be either yellow triangular "Yield" signs or red octagonal "Stop" signs ("Arrêt" in Québec) at all four corners. In the latter case, **priority** is given to the first car to arrive, and to the car on the right if two or more cars arrive at the same time. Except in Québec, you can turn right on a red light if there is no traffic approaching from the left. Traffic in both directions must stop if a yellow school bus is stationary with its flashing lights on, as this means children are getting on or off. Roundabouts or rotaries are almost unknown.

Exits on multi-lane highways are numbered by the kilometre distance from the beginning of the highway, as opposed to sequentially – thus exit 55 is 10km after exit 45. This system works fine, but gets a little confusing when junctions are close together and carry the same number supplemented by "A", "B", etc. Rural **road hazards** include bears, moose and other large animals trundling into the road – particularly in the summer, and at dawn and dusk, when the beasts crash through the undergrowth onto the highway to escape the flies, and in spring, when they are attracted to the salt on the roads. Warning signs are posted in the more hazardous areas. Headlights can dazzle wild animals and render them temporarily immobile.

Driving laws are made at provincial level, but the uniform **maximum speed limit** is 100kph on major highways, 80kph on rural highways and 50 kph or less in built-up areas – though there has been some provincial tinkering with the maximum limit on the highways, experiments which may result in permanent change. Canadians have a justifiable paranoia about speed traps and the traffic-control planes that hover over major highways to catch offenders – if you see one, slow down. On-the-spot fines are standard for speeding violations, for failing to carry your **licence**

DRIVING DISTANCES IN KILOMETRES

The figures shown on this chart represent the total distances in kilometres between selected cities in the Canada and the US. They are calculated on the shortest available route by road, rather than straight lines drawn on a map. One kilometre equals five-eighths of a mile.

	Calgary	Chicago	Edmonton	Halifax	Montréal	New York	Ottawa	Regina	St John's	Seattle	Toronto	Vancouver	Whitehorse	Winnipeg	Yellowknife
Calgary	—														
Chicago	2760	—													
Edmonton	299	2750	—												
Halifax	5042	2603	5082	—											
Montréal	3743	1362	3764	1318	—										
New York	4294	1280	4315	1270	610	—									
Ottawa	3553	1220	3574	1508	190	772	—								
Regina	764	2000	785	4297	2979	2789	3534	—							
St John's	6183	3950	6212	1349	2448	2619	2638	5427	—						
Seattle	1204	3200	1352	5828	4585	4478	4334	1963	7200	—					
Toronto	3434	825	3455	1857	539	880	399	2670	2987	4050	—				
Vancouver	1057	3808	1244	6119	4801	5382	4611	1822	7248	230	4492	—			
Whitehorse	2385	4854	2086	7168	5850	6427	5660	2871	8298	2796	5528	2697	—		
Winnipeg	1336	1432	1357	3726	2408	2966	2218	571	4855	2548	2099	2393	3524	—	
Yellowknife	1811	4240	1511	6593	5275	5800	5086	2297	7723	2500	4966	2411	2704	2868	—

with you, and for having anyone on board who isn't wearing a **seat belt**.

Canadian law also requires that any alcohol be carried unopened in the boot of the car, and it can't be stressed enough that **drunk driving** is a very serious offence. Bars in some provinces now have **designated driver schemes** whereby the driver of a group gives the keys to the head barperson and is then given free soft drinks all night; if the driver is spotted taking a sip of alcohol, he or she must pay for all the soft drinks consumed and leave their keys in the bar until the following morning. On the road, spot checks are frequently carried out, particularly at the entrances and exits to towns, and the police do not need an excuse to stop you. If you are over the limit your keys and licence will be taken away, and you may end up in jail for a few days.

In cities **parking meters** are commonplace, charging 25¢–$1 or more per hour. Car parks charge up to $30 a day. If you park in the wrong place (such as within 5m of a fire hydrant) your car will be towed away – if this happens, the police will tell you where your car is impounded and then charge you upwards of $150 to hand it back. A minor parking offence will set you back around $25; clamps are also routinely used in major cities, with a fine of between $100 and $150. Also, when parking, ensure you park in the same direction as the traffic flows.

If you're using your own vehicle – or borrowing a friend's – get the appropriate insurance and make sure you're covered for free **breakdown service**. Your home motoring organization will issue an appropriate insurance and breakdown policy with all the appropriate documentation. The Canadian Automobile Association, Suite 200, 1145 Hunt Club Rd, Ottawa, Ontario K1V OY3 (☎613/820-1890), is the biggest recovery and repair company in Canada, and has offices in most major cities.

RIDE-SHARING

Ride-sharing is an established means of travel within the more heavily populated parts of Canada. Organizations coordinating ride-share travel come and go – local tourist offices will have the latest details – but Allo-Stop, with main offices in Montréal and Toronto, is well established. With them, all you pay is a nominal registration fee and a share of the fuel costs – Toronto to Ottawa will set you back about $30, less if you are with other people. Rides are also routinely advertised on university and youth hostel notice boards.

BY BIKE

Cyclists are reasonably well catered for in environment-friendly Canada: most cities have cycling lanes and produce special maps for cyclists, and long-distance buses and trains will allow you to transport your bike, perhaps for a small fee. The Canadian Cycling Association *(CCA)*, 1600 James Naismith Drive, Gloucester, Ontario K1B 5N4 (☎613/748-5629; Web site *www.canadiancycling.com*), can offer information on cycling throughout the country and publishes several books, including the invaluable *Complete Guide to Cycling in Canada* ($24 including postage and packing). Standard **bike rental** costs are around $15 per day, plus a sizable cash sum or a credit card as deposit; outlets are listed throughout the Guide.

ACCOMMODATION

Accommodation isn't hugely expensive in Canada, but is still likely to take a good portion of your budget. The least expensive options are camping and dormitory beds in hostels, where prices start at around $12 but be aware that campgrounds and hostels in cities are heavily used. In hotels and motels, double rooms start at around $45; less in rural areas away from the big sights. People on their own pay relatively more, but for travellers in pairs or groups motels and hotels can work out costing little more than hostels.

Canada is big and empty. If you're heading into remote parts of the country, always check the availability of accommodation before setting off. Places that look large on the map often have few facilities at all, and US visitors will find motels far scarcer than in similar regions back home. Wherever you intend to stay, it's best to try to **book a room** well before you arrive, particularly in summer and especially in big national parks like Banff and popular major cities such as Montréal, Québec, Toronto and Vancouver. Also look out for local events and festivals such as the Calgary Stampede, when accommodation is always at a premium. If you're arriving late, stress the fact, as **reservations** are generally held only until 6pm, or even 4pm in major resorts. Reservations can be made over the phone by credit card. Wherever possible take advantage of **toll-free numbers**, but note that some are accessible only in restricted areas, typically a single province, or in Canada or North America only. It can also be worth confirming check-in/check-out times, particularly in busy areas, where your room may not be available until late afternoon. Check-out times are generally between 11am and 1pm. Be certain to **cancel** any bookings you can't make, otherwise the hotel

or motel is within its right to deduct a night's fee using your credit card details. Most places have a 24-hour-notice cancellation policy, but in places like Banff it can be as much as three days.

Also be prepared to pay for at least the first night in advance, and be ready for a fifteen per cent **surcharge** to a room's advertised price, the result of provincial sales and federal taxes. **Costs** can be kept down if you're in a group – most places will set up a third bed in a double room for around $15 – though single travellers have a hard time of it, for single rooms are usually double rooms let out at only marginally reduced rates. **Costs** also come down outside high season, typically mid-May to early September (Labour Day) when the country's smartest hotels often offer especally large discounts. Also be on the lookout for weekend rates, or last-minute deals offered by hotels trying to fill empty rooms.

Local tourist information offices can often help out with accommodation if you get stuck: most offer free advice and will book a place free of charge, but few are willing to commit themselves to specific recommendations. Some large resorts, like Banff and Jasper in the Rockies, have a privately run central reservations agency that will find rooms for a small fee. Before going to Canada it's worth picking up the full accommodation and camping listings put out by the provinces (see p.17 for office addresses); they all give details of prices, size and facilities.

HOTELS

It is consistently easy to find a plain room in all but Canada's more remote backwoods. Drivers approaching any significant town or city are confronted by ranks of motels on prominent highways, neon signs advertising their presence, room rates and room availability. In-town **hotels** tend to fall into one of two categories: high-class five-star establishments or grim downtown places, often above a bar. Middle-ground spots are thin on the ground, their role often being filled by motels, which are basically out-of-town hotels by another name.

Top-of-the-range hotels can be very grand indeed, for instance particularly those run by Canadian Pacific in busy tourist spots like Québec City, Banff and Lake Louise. In the cities, the emphasis is on the business traveller rather more than the tourist. Topnotch hotels charge anywhere between $150 and $500, though $250 would get you a fairly luxurious double in most places. It's always worth enquiring about midweek reductions and out-of-season discounts, as these can reduce rates to as low as $100 a night. If you are going to treat yourself, think whether you want the sort of old-style comfort and building offered by traditional hotels or the high-tech polish provided by the new breed of luxury hotel: most cities and some resorts have both types.

Mid-price hotels are often part of a chain, such as *Holiday Inn* or *Best Western*, and usually offer a touch more comfort than middling motels. You should be able to find a high-season double in such places from around $90; more if you're in a well-known resort or the downtown area of a major city.

Bottom-bracket hotels – those costing anything from $25 to $45 – are mostly hangovers from the days when liquor laws made it difficult to run a bar without an adjoining restaurant or hotel. Found in most medium- and small-sized towns, they usually have the advantage of being extremely central – often they've been there since the town first sprang to life – but the disadvantage is that the money-generating bars usually come first, with the rooms mostly an afterthought. Many have strip joints or live music likely to pound until the small hours, and few pay much attention to their guests, many of whom are long-stay clients as seedy as the hotel itself. Rooms are mostly battered but clean, but probably won't have much in the way of facilities beyond a washbasin and TV. Basic meals are often on hand in the bar, though you'd usually do better to eat in a nearby café or restaurant.

MOTELS

Motels may be called inns, lodges, resorts or motor hotels, but they all amount to much the same thing: driver-friendly, reasonably priced and reliable places on the main highways almost always on the edge of town. The simplest rooms start at around $45, with the **average** price nearer $60 – though in resorts and more remote areas it's not unusual to find well over $100 being charged for what are fairly basic rooms. As a rule of thumb, prices drop in the larger centres the further you move from downtown. Many offer **off-season rates**, usually between October and

April, some have triple- or quadruple-bedded rooms, and most are fairly relaxed about introducing an extra bed into "doubles" for a nominal charge. Many also offer a **Family Plan**, whereby youngsters sharing their parents' room stay free. You may also be able to negotiate cheaper deals if you're staying more than one night, and especially if you're staying a week – many places advertise weekly rates.

In all but the most basic motels you can expect a remarkably good standard: a good-sized double bed, a private bathroom, TV and phone, while in smarter places there may be frills like free coffee and the use of saunas, Jacuzzis, sun beds and swimming pools. Often there's not much to be gained in paying extra for motels: you don't get a much better deal or better facilities by paying, say, $75 instead of $50. Some places, though, have rooms with **kitchenettes** for self-catering, or basic cooking facilities, either included in the room price or available for a few dollars more. More ritzy spots may also have a small restaurant, but generally you can expect nothing in the way of **food and drink** except for a soft-drinks machine and coffee-maker in the room. What they all have is good parking, often right in front of the door to your room.

BED AND BREAKFAST

In recent years there has been a dramatic increase in the number of **B&Bs/Gîtes du Passant** both in the big cities and in the towns and villages of the more popular resort areas. Standards in B&B homes or guesthouses are generally very high, and prices are around $50 and upwards per couple including breakfast. There are no real savings over cheaper hotels and motels. This said, you may wind up with a wonderful – if often over-homely – room in a heritage building in a great location, with the chance to meet Canadians on closer terms. There are, however, things to watch out for and ask about when making a booking. There's an increasing tendency to provide a light continental breakfast rather than a cooked meal with all the trimmings that'll set you up for the day. Establishments are often keen to indicate whether they have a private guest entrance, useful if you're likely to be staggering in late or simply don't particularly want to mix with your hosts. Another trend is for smaller hotels to advertise themselves as a "Bed and Breakfast Inn", or something similar, meaning simply that they're privately owned

ACCOMMODATION PRICE CODES

Throughout this book, accommodation prices have been graded with the symbols below, according to the cost of the least expensive double room throughout most of the year.

However, with the exception of the budget motels and lowliest hotels, there's rarely such a thing as a set rate for a room. A basic motel in a seaside or mountain resort may double its prices according to the season, while a big-city hotel in Québec or Vancouver that charges $200 per room during the week will often slash its tariff at the weekend when all the business visitors have gone home. The high and low seasons for tourists vary widely across the country, but as a general rule **high season** refers to July and August, **shoulder season** is May, June, September and October, and **low season** refers to the rest of the year.

Local and federal taxes will also add around fifteen per cent to rates. Only where we explicitly say so do the room rates we've indicated include local taxes.

① up to $40	③ $60–80	⑤ $100–125	⑦ $175–240
② $40–60	④ $80–100	⑥ $125–175	⑧ $240+

rather than in the hands of a chain. These are usually intimate but rather expensive places and not B&Bs in the accepted sense. B&B establishments have a quite rapid turnover, so to find one it's often best to visit tourist offices, many of which have bulging catalogues and photographs of what's available, or in the big cities contact one of the many private agencies who can line you up with something suitable. Take careful note of an establishment's location: in cities and larger towns they're often out in the suburbs and inconvenient for transport and downtown sights, though some hosts will pick you up from the airport or bus station on your arrival.

HOSTELS

Canada has about eighty **Hostelling International** (HI) hostels affiliated to what was formerly known as the International Youth Hostels Federation (IYHF), and many more non-affiliated minihostels (also known as Homes or Backpackers' Hostels), which may or may not figure in HI literature. Reports suggest certain non-affiliated hostels are slipping in standard as their cheap beds are appropriated by long-stay clients rather than by genuine visitors on a budget. Some are downright unsafe. These sorts of places are also often shoestring operations and may close at short notice. Similarly, new ones appear each year. Try to check local reputations at tourist offices or by word of mouth.

HI hostels are graded in four categories (basic, simple, standard and superior), and accommodation is mostly in single-sex dorms, which cost $10–25

for members, depending on category and location, though family and private double rooms are becoming more prevalent. In theory you're supposed to be an HI member to use hostels; in practice you can usually join the HI on the spot, or rely on most hostels making a higher charge for non-members ($12–28). However, most hostels will generally give preference to members, which is an important consideration in some of the more popular locations. Most hostels offer communal recreation areas and all have cooking facilities, plus pillows and blankets, though you're expected to provide, or rent, your own sheet sleeping bag and towels; normal sleeping bags are generally not allowed.

Many hostels have improved beyond recognition in the past few years: premises have been renovated, hostels are open longer and later, cafeterias have been introduced, and the booking system has been partly computerized. You can now book up to six months in advance at the bigger, or gateway, hostels; notably those in the Rockies, where hostels at Banff and Calgary act as central booking agents for a number of smaller hostels around the region. Most major hostels now accept credit card bookings, with **reservations** strongly recommended in summer for city hostels and most of the Rockies' hostels (toll-free across North America ☎1-800-444-6111). Most HI offices around the world stock the comprehensive *Hostelling North America* handbook, as do many of Canada's larger hostels.

Mini-hostels tend to be private homes or tiny commercial hotels with breakfast included. Prices are about $10–20, with a surcharge for non-members, and you must have your own sheet sleeping bag. A full current list is available from most larger youth hostels.

YS AND STUDENT ACCOMMODATION

Both the **YMCA** and **YWCA** – often known as "Ys" – have establishments in most Canadian cities. In many cases the quality of accommodation is excellent, matching that of the cheaper hotels, and invariably exceeding that of most other hostel-type lodgings. Often the premises have cheap **cafeterias** open to all, and sports facilities, gymnasium and swimming pools for the use of guests. **Prices**, however, reflect the comforts, and though you can usually find bunks in shared dorms from about $15, the trend is increasingly for single, double and family units (with or without private bathrooms), ranging between $30 and $100 depending on private or shared bathroom. This still reflects excellent value, especially in cities, where Ys are usually in central downtown locations. As Ys become more like hotels, so you need to treat them as such, with credit card **reservations** in advance virtually essential to secure private singles and doubles in high summer. Most places keep a number of rooms and dorm bunks available each day for walk-in customers, though in places like Banff it's not unknown for queues for these to develop

around the block first thing in the morning. The old demarcation of the sexes is also breaking down, though many YWCAs will only accept men if they're in a mixed-sex couple. Some YWCAs accept women with children, others only in emergencies.

In Canada's university cities it's possible to stay in **student accommodation** during vacations. Anyone can use the facilities, though priority is usually given to other students. Often the accommodation is adequate and functional, if soulless, and you'll have access to the campus's sports facilities; on the downside, most places are a good distance from city centres. Prices for single and double rooms start from about $35. Most campuses have a special office to handle such accommodation, and it's a good idea to call well ahead to be sure of a room.

FARM VACATIONS

Farm vacations, on which you spend time as a paying guest on a working farm, give you the chance to eat well, sleep cheaply – and even work (if you want) – as well as mingle with your hosts. There are often a wide range of outdoor activities on tap. Most places offer daily and weekly accommodation, either on rough campsites from as little as $5 per day, bed and breakfast from $20, or room and full board from $35

YOUTH HOSTEL INFORMATION

Australia
Australian Youth Hostels Association, Level 3, 10 Mallett St, Camperdown, NSW (☎02/565-1325).

Canada
Hostelling International (*HI*), Room 400, 205 Catherine St, Ottawa, Ontario K2P 1C3 (☎613/237-7884 or 1-800-663-5777 in Canada).

England and Wales
Youth Hostel Association (*YHA*), Trevelyan House, 8 St Stephen's Hill, St Albans, Herts AL1 (☎017278/45047). London shop and information office: 14 Southampton St, London WC2E 7HY (☎0171/836-1036).

Ireland
An Oige, 39 Mountjoy Square, Dublin 1 (☎01/363111).

New Zealand
Youth Hostels Association of New Zealand, PO Box 436, Christchurch 1 (☎03/799970).

Northern Ireland
Youth Hostel Association of Northern Ireland, 56 Bradbury Place, Belfast BT7 1RU (☎01232/324733).

Scotland
Scottish Youth Hostel Association, 7 Glebe Crescent, Stirling FK8 2JA (☎01786/51181). There's also an outlet at 161 Warrender Park Rd, Edinburgh EH9 1EQ (☎0131/229-8660, fax 0131/229-2456).

USA
Hostelling International – American Youth Hostels (*HI-AYH*), 733 15th St NW, Suite 840, PO Box 37613, Washington DC 20005 (☎202/783-6161).

daily. Most provinces now have farm vacation associations to prepare lists of farms and inspect facilities. For further details, consult tourist offices or provincial accommodation guides or call Farm Tours (☎01509/261810) 16a Swan St, Loughborough, Leicestershire, LE11 0BL.

CAMPING

Few countries offer as much scope for **camping** as Canada. Many urban areas have a campground; all national parks and the large proportion of provincial parks have outstanding government-run sites, and in most wilderness areas and in the vast domain of Canada's federally owned Crown Lands you can camp rough more or less where you please, though you should ask permission where possible and – for your own safety and the sake of the environment – adhere strictly to all rules and recommendations that apply to camping in the backcountry. If you're travelling with a tent, check a campground's small print for the number of **unserviced** (tent) sites, as many places cater chiefly for **recreational vehicles** (RVs), providing them with **full or partial hook-ups** for water and electricity (or "serviced sites"). Anywhere described as an "RV Park" ought to be avoided completely (unless, of course, you have an RV).

During July and August campgrounds can become as busy as all other types of accommodation in cities, and particularly near mountain, lake or river resorts. Either aim to arrive early in the morning or book ahead – we've given phone numbers wherever this is possible. Generally reservations can only be made at private campgrounds, not – crucially – at national park or provincial park campgrounds, where access is mostly on a first-come, first-served basis. This state of affairs is, however, slowly changing, with places at a selection of provincial and national park campgrounds now reservable through a reservation phone number. Finally, check that your chosen site is open – many campgrounds only open seasonally, usually from May to October.

CAMPGROUND TYPES

At the bottom of the pile are **municipal camp-grounds**, usually basic affairs with few facilities, which are either free or cost only a few dollars – typically $5 per tent, $10 per RV, though many often have tent places only. **Private camp-grounds** run the gamut: some are as basic as their municipal cousins, others are like huge outdoor pleasure domes with shops, restaurants, laundries, swimming pools, tennis courts, even saunas and Jacuzzis. As for **price**, private campgrounds have several ways of charging. Some charge by the vehicle; others per couple; comparatively few on a tent or per-person basis. Two people sharing a tent might pay anything between $2.50 and $25 each, though an average price would be nearer $7–11. You can book places in private campgrounds but there's often no need outside busy areas as most are obliged to keep a certain number of pitches available on a first-come, first-served basis.

Campgrounds in **national and provincial parks** are run by Parks Canada and individual provincial governments respectively. All are immaculately turned out and most, in theory, are **open** only between May and September. In practice most are available all year round, though key facilities are offered and fees collected only in the advertised period: off season you may be expected to leave fees in an "honesty box". You'll usually find at least one site serviced for **winter camping** in the bigger national parks, particularly in the Rockies. **Prices** vary from about $8.50 to $19 per tent depending on location, services and the time of year – prices may be higher during July and August. See "Outdoor pursuits", p.50, for more details.

Sites in the **major national parks**, especially close to towns, usually offer a full range of amenities for both tents and RVs, and often have separate sites for each. As a rule, though, provincial sites and more remote national park campgrounds tend to favour tents and offer only water, stores of firewood and pit toilets. Hot showers, in particular, are rare. But both national park and provincial sites, of course, invariably score highly on their scenic locations. Both types of park campground fill most of their pitches on a **first-come, first-served** basis, but a growing number of parks are setting up reservation services.

PRIMITIVE CAMPING

Camping rough – or **primitive camping** (or backcountry camping) as it's known in Canada – has certain rules that must be followed. Check that fires are permitted before you start one – in large parts of Canada they aren't allowed in summer because of the risk of **forest fire.** If they are permitted, use a fire pit (if provided), or a stove in preference to local materials. In wilderness areas, try to camp on previously used sites.

Be especially aware of the precautions needed when in bear country (see pp.589–599). Where there are no toilets, bury human waste at least 10cm into the ground and 30m from the nearest water supply and campsite. Canadian parks ask for all rubbish to be carried away; else-

where burn rubbish, and what you can't burn, carry away.

Never drink from rivers and streams, however clear and inviting they may look. If you have to drink **water** that isn't from taps, you should boil it for at least ten minutes, or cleanse it with an iodine-based purifier (such as Potable Aqua) or a *Giardia*-rated filter, available from camping or sports shops.

EATING AND DRINKING

Canada's sheer number of restaurants, bars, cafés and fast-food joints is staggering, but at first sight there's little to distinguish Canada's mainstream urban cuisine from that of any American metropolis: the shopping malls, main streets and highways are lined with pan-American food chains, trying to outdo each other with their bargains and special offers.

However, it's easy to leave the chain restaurants behind for more interesting options – increasingly so, as the general standard of Canadian cooking has improved dramatically in the last few years. In the big cities there's a plethora of ethnic and speciality restaurants, on either seaboard the availability of fresh fish and shellfish enlivens many menus, and even out in the country – once the domain of unappetizing diners – there's a liberal supply of first-rate, family-run cafés and restaurants, especially in the more touristy areas. Non-smokers may also be relieved

to know that almost every café and restaurant has a non-smoking area and increasing numbers don't allow smoking at all.

BREAKFAST

Breakfast is taken very seriously all over Canada, and with prices averaging between $7 and $10 it's often the best-value and most filling meal of the day. Whether you go to a café, coffee shop or hotel snack bar, the breakfast menu, on offer until around 11am, is a fairly standard fry-up – eggs in various guises, ham or bacon, streaky and fried to a crisp, or skinless and bland sausages (except for Nova Scotia's famous Lunenburg sausage, a hot spicy version pioneered by settlers from Europe). Whatever you order, you nearly always receive a dollop of fried potatoes (called hash browns or sometimes home fries). Other favourite breakfast options include English muffins or, in posher places, bran muffins, a glutinous fruitcake made with bran and sugar, and **waffles** or **pancakes**, swamped in butter with lashings of maple syrup. Also, because the breakfast/lunch division is never hard and fast, mountainous meaty **sandwiches** are common too.

Whatever you eat, you can wash it down with as much **coffee** as you can stomach: for the price of the first cup, the waiters/waitresses will – in most places – keep providing free refills until you beg them to stop. The coffee is either **regular** or **decaf** and is nearly always freshly ground and very tasty, though lots of the cheaper places dilute it until it tastes like dishwater. In the big cities, look out also for specialist coffee shops, where the range of offerings verges on the bewildering. As a matter of course, coffee comes with cream or

half-and-half (half-cream, half-milk) – if you ask for skimmed milk, you're often met with looks of disbelief. **Tea**, with either lemon or milk, is also drunk at breakfast, and the swisher places emphasize the English connection by using imported brands – or at least brands that sound English.

LUNCH AND SNACKS

Between 11.30am and 2.30pm many big-city restaurants offer special **set menus** that are generally excellent-value. In Chinese and Vietnamese establishments, for example, you'll frequently find rice and noodles, or dim sum feasts for $7 to $10, and many **Japanese** restaurants give you a chance to eat sushi very reasonably for under $15. **Pizza** is also widely available, from larger chains like *Pizza Hut* to family-owned restaurants and pavement stalls. Favourites with white-collar workers are **café-restaurants** featuring wholefoods and vegetarian fare, though few are nutritionally dogmatic, serving traditional meat dishes and sandwiches too; most have an excellent selection of daily lunch specials for around $7.

For quick **snacks**, many **delis** do ready-cooked food, including a staggering range of sandwiches and filled bagels. Alternatively, shopping malls sometimes have **ethnic fast-food stalls**, a healthier option (just about) than the inevitable burger chains, whose homogenized products have colonized every main street in the land. Regional snacks include **fish and chips**, especially in Newfoundland; Québec's traditional thick, yellow pea soup, smoked meat sandwiches and *poutine*, fries covered in melted mozzarella cheese or cheese curds and gravy; and the Maritimes' ubiquitous **clam chowder**, a creamy shellfish and potato soup.

Some city **bars** are used as much by diners as drinkers, who turn up in droves to gorge themselves on the free **hors d'oeuvres** laid out between 5pm and 7pm from Monday to Friday in an attempt to grab commuters. For the price of a drink you can stuff yourself with pasta and chilli. **Brunch** is another deal worth looking out for; a cross between breakfast and lunch served up in bars at the weekend from around 11am to 2pm. For a set price ($10 and up) you get a light meal and a variety of complimentary cocktails or wine.

MAIN MEALS

Largely swamped by the more fashionable regional European and ethnic cuisines, traditional **Canadian cooking** relies mainly on local game and fish, with less emphasis on vegetables and salads. In terms of price, meals for two without wine average between $25 and $45.

Newfoundland's staple food is the cod, usually in the form of fish and chips, supplemented by salmon, halibut and hake and more bizarre dishes like cod tongues and cheeks, scruncheons (fried cubes of pork fat), smoked or pickled caplin and seal flipper pie. The island's restaurants are not usually permitted to sell moose or seal meat, but many islanders join in the annual licensed shoot and, if you befriend a hunter, you may end up across the table from a hunk of either animal.

In the **Maritimes**, lobster is popular everywhere, whether it's boiled or broiled, chopped up or whole, as are oysters, clams, scallops and herrings either on their own or in a fish stew or clam chowder. **Nova Scotia** is famous for its blueberries, Solomon Gundy (marinated herring), Annapolis Valley apple pie, fat archies (a Cape Breton molasses cookie) and rappie pie (an Acadian dish of meat or fish and potatoes). **New Brunswick** is known for its fiddleheads (fern shoots) and dulse (edible seaweed). Fish are **Ontario**'s most distinctive offering – though the pollution of the Great Lakes has badly affected the freshwater catch. Try the whitefish, lake trout, pike and smelt, but bear in mind that these are easier to come by in the north of the province than in the south. Pork forms a major part of the **Québec** diet, both as a spicy pork pâté known as *creton*, and in *tourtière*, a minced pork pie. There are also splendid thick pea and cabbage soups, beef pies (*cipâte*), and all sorts of ways to soak up maple syrup – *trempette* is bread drenched with it and topped with fresh cream. And, of course, Québec is renowned for its outstanding French-style food.

Northern **Saskatchewan and Manitoba** are the places to try fish like the goldeye, pickerel and Arctic char, as well as pemmican (a mixture of dried meat, berries and fat) and fruit pies containing the Saskatoon berry. The **Arctic** regions feature caribou steak, and Alberta is also noted for its beef steaks. Finally, **British Columbia** cuisine features Pacific fish and shellfish of many different types, from cod, haddock and salmon to king crab, oysters and shrimp. Here and there, there's also the odd native people's restaurant, most conspicuously at the **Wanuskewin Heritage Park** in Saskatoon, Saskatchewan, where the restaurant serves venison, buffalo and black-husked wild rice.

Although there are exceptions, like the Ukrainian establishments spread across central Manitoba, the bulk of Canada's **ethnic restaurants** are confined to the cities. Here, amongst dozens of others, Japanese restaurants are fashionable and fairly expensive; Italian food is popular and generally cheap, providing you stick to pizzas and basic pasta dishes; and there's the occasional Indian restaurant, mostly catering for the inexpensive end of the market. East European food is a good, filling standby, especially in central Canada, and cheap Chinese restaurants are common throughout the country. French food, of course, is widely available – though, except in Québec, it's nearly always expensive.

DRINKING

Canadian bars, like their American equivalents, are mostly long and dimly lit counters with a few customers perched on stools gawping at the bartender, and the rest of the clientele occupying the surrounding tables and booths. Yet, despite the similarity of layout, bars vary enormously, from the male-dominated, rough-edged drinking holes concentrated in the blue-collar parts of the cities and the resource towns (dealing in mining and oil) of the north, to more fashionable city establishments that provide food, live entertainment and an inspiring range of cocktails. Indeed, it's often impossible to separate restaurants from bars – drinking and eating are no longer the separate activities they mostly were up until the 1960s.

The **legal drinking age** is 18 in Alberta, Manitoba and Québec and 19 in the rest of the country, though it's rare for anyone to have to show ID, except at the government-run liquor stores (closed Sun), which exercise a virtual monopoly on the sale of alcoholic beverages of all kinds direct to the public; the main exception is Québec, where beer and wine are sold at retail grocery stores.

BEER

By and large, Canadian beers are unremarkable, designed to quench your thirst rather than satisfy your palate. Everywhere they're served ice-cold, and light, fizzy beers rule the roost. The two largest Canadian brewers, **Molson** and **Labatts**, market a remarkably similar brew under all sorts of names – Molson Canadian, Molson Export, Labatts Ice, Labatts Blue – that inspire, for reasons that elude most foreigners, intense loyalty. The tastier **Great Western Beer** is made by the country's third largest brewer, based in Saskatoon, Saskatchewan, while the heavily marketed **Moosehead** beer, despite its Arctic image, is produced in Saint John, New Brunswick. There's also a niche market for foreign beers, although **Heineken**, the most popular, is made under licence in Canada; American beers like **Budweiser** and **Coors** are common, too. A welcome trend is the proliferation of independent small breweries, or microbreweries, whose products are sold in a pub on the premises, but as yet these remain pretty much confined to the bigger cities.

Drinking bottled beer in a bar works out a good deal more expensive than the draught, which is usually served by the 170ml glass; even cheaper is a pitcher, which contains six or seven glasses.

WINE AND SPIRITS

Once something of a joke, **Canadian wines** are fast developing an excellent reputation, particularly those from Ontario's Niagara-on-the-Lake region, which are subject to the stringent quality control of the Vintners Quality Alliance, the VQA (see p.102). However, if you don't want to experiment, **imported wines** from a wide range of countries are readily available and not too pricey.

Copying its giant neighbour, Canada excels with its **spirits**. Even in run-of-the-mill bars there are startling arrays of gins and vodkas, and usually a good selection of rums. In the more traditional places, the most popular liquor is **whiskey** – either Scottish and Irish imports or the domestically made Canadian Club and VO rye whiskey. In the smarter places, you can experiment with all sorts of **cocktails**, costing anywhere between $4 and $10.

COMMUNICATIONS, POST, PHONES AND THE MEDIA

POSTAL SERVICES

Post office opening hours are Monday to Friday 8.30am to 5.30pm, though a few places open on

Saturday between 9am and noon. Offices are sometimes found inside larger stores, so look out for Canada Post signs. **Stamps** can also be bought from automatic vending machines, the lobbies of larger hotels, airports, train stations, bus terminals and many retail outlets and newsstands. Within Canada, letters and postcards up to 30g cost 45¢, to the USA 52¢ for under 30g, and international mail up to 20g is 92¢. If you're posting letters to Canadian addresses, always include the postcode or your mail may never get there.

Letters can be sent **poste restante** to any Canadian main post office by addressing them c/o General Delivery or c/o Poste Restante in Québec. Make a pick-up date if known, or write "Hold for 15 days", the maximum period mail will usually be held. After that time the post is returned to sender, so it's a good idea to put a return address on any post. Take some ID when collecting. Letters will also be held by hotels; mark such mail

USEFUL TELEPHONE NUMBERS AND CODES

DIRECTORY ENQUIRIES

Canada's nationwide number for telephone information is ☎555-1212. If you need a number in another province, dial the area code (see below) + 555-1212. In most cities you can also dial ☎411 for local information. The operator's number is ☎0.

EMERGENCY

☎911; ask for the appropriate emergency service: fire, police or ambulance. In smaller towns and rural areas, you may need to dial 0 for an operator, who will connect you to the police or other emergency services.

PROVINCE CODES

Alberta ☎403.

British Columbia ☎604 (Vancouver) ; ☎250 (rest of BC).

Manitoba ☎204.

New Brunswick ☎506.

Northwest Territories ☎403/819.

Nova Scotia ☎902.

Newfoundland and Labrador ☎709.

Ontario ☎416 (Toronto region); ☎705 (central and northeast); ☎519 (southwest peninsula); ☎613 (Ottawa region); ☎807 (northwest).

Prince Edward Island ☎902.

Québec ☎514 (Montréal region); ☎819 (north); ☎418 (east).

Saskatchewan ☎306.

Yukon ☎867.

INTERNATIONAL CODES

For direct international calls from Canada, dial the country code (see below), the area code minus its first 0, and then the subscriber's number.

Australia ☎011 61.	Ireland ☎011 353.	Sweden ☎011 46.
Denmark ☎011 45.	Netherlands ☎011 31.	UK ☎011 44.
Germany ☎011 49.	New Zealand ☎011 64.	

SWIFTCALL NUMBERS

London ☎0171/488-2001.
Manchester ☎0161/245-2001.
Glasgow ☎0141/616-2001.

Dublin ☎01/671-0457.
Belfast ☎01232/314524.

CALLING CANADA FROM ABROAD

Calling Canada from the UK, dial 001 + province code + subscriber number.
Calling Canada from the US, dial province code + subscriber number.
Calling Canada from Australia dial 0011 + country code.
Calling Canada from New Zealand dial 00 + country code.

"Guest Mail, Hold for Arrival". If you have an American Express card or travellers' cheques, you can have mail marked "Client Mail Service" sent to Amex offices throughout Canada. Others can pick up mail from Amex for a small fee.

INTERNATIONAL CALLS

In Britain, it's possible to obtain a free **BT charge card** (☎0800/800838), with which all calls from overseas can be charged to your quarterly domestic account, but they are expensive. To use these cards in Canada, call ☎1-800-408-6420 and you will be asked for your account number and PIN.

British visitors who are going to be making a number of calls to Canada, and who want to be able to call ☎1-800 numbers, otherwise inaccessible from outside North America, should take advantage of the **Swiftcall** telephone club. You need a touch-tone phone. Call ☎0800/769-0800 or 0000 24 hours a day; once you've paid, by credit card, for however many units you want, you are given a PIN. Any time you want to get an international line, simply dial ☎1488 from BT phones or 0800/769-8000 from any phone, punch in your PIN, and then dial as you would were you in Canada, putting a 1 before the area code, followed by the number. Calls to Canada – including ☎1-800 calls – cost about 16p per minute, a saving of over fifty percent.

In the **US** you can get telephone calling/bank credit cards from the companies listed below, who can also supply long-distance phone cards and "prepaid" debit phone cards: AT&T (☎800-CALL-ATT) or Sprint (☎800-PIN-DROP).

Australia's Telstra Telecard (application forms available from Telstra offices) and **New Zealand** Telecom's Calling Card (contact ☎04/382-5818) can be used to make calls charged to a domestic account or credit card.

TELEPHONES AND TELEGRAMS

Coin-operated telephones are available in most public places. Whenever you are dialling a number outside the telephone region of the call box you are using, you have to prefix the number with 1; this puts you through to the operator, who will tell you how much money you need to get connected. The operator asks for an amount (about $2.50) to cover the initial time period, which even within a province is fairly brief. Thereafter you'll be asked to shovel money in at regular intervals, so unless you're making a reverse-charge/collect call you need a stack of coins – usually quarters (25¢). Some connections within a single telephone area are charged at the long-distance rate, and thus need the "1" prefix; a recorded message will tell you if this is necessary as soon as you dial the number. Local calls cost 25¢ from a public phone and are dialled direct; private subscribers pay nothing for these, so you'll find that shops often don't mind you using their phone for local calls.

Long-distance calls are cheapest from 11pm to 8am daily, and most expensive from 8am to 6pm Monday to Saturday. From 6pm to 11pm on Monday to Saturday and from 8am to 11pm on Sunday, charges are more economical. Detailed rates are listed at the front of the **telephone directory**.

Needless to say, using pocketfuls of money is an inconvenient way of making **international calls**. Pay phones taking major credit cards, however, are increasingly common, especially in transport and major tourist centres. In some cities there are Bell offices that enable you to make your call and pay afterwards. Special **phone debit cards** are increasingly common; Bell, which operates in Québec and Ontario, issues the HELLO or ALLO, cards which have PIN numbers so they can be used from any phone in the country. Their Quickchange or LaPuce smart cards can only be used in some public phones that are common only in Québec and Ontario.

Various companies produce **long-distance calling cards**. Cardcaller Canada (☎416/733-2163) cards are sold in various outlets in $10, $20 and $50 denominations and charge 60¢ a minute. AT&T have two types of long-distance calling card: a prepaid card (☎1-888-240-3295) and one that is debited straight from your credit card.

More upmarket hotels and motels have **direct-dial** phones where the call is automatically charged to your bill. Elsewhere, the hotel switchboard operator will place a call for you, or you'll be linked to an operator who will ask for the room number to which to charge the call – but be warned that virtually all hotels will levy a service charge in the region of 65–95 percent.

Many hotels, tourist offices and transport companies have **toll-free numbers** (prefixed by ☎1-800). Some of these can only be dialled from phones in the same province, others from anywhere within Canada, a few from anywhere in North America – as a rough guideline, the larger the organization, the wider its toll-free net.

To send a **telegram** either within Canada or abroad, ask at your hotel or tourist office for the nearest CN/CP Public Message Centre. At any time, day or night, you can also phone in **Telepost** messages, a guaranteed next-day or sooner service in Canada and the US; billing arrangements are made at the time of giving the message. **Intelpost** is an international fax service available at main post offices, and paid for by cash.

Most major cities now have cybercafés, where you can **email**. They tend to charge around $2–5 an hour for use of their computers, and you can generally sup on cappuccinos and sandwiches. You can also access email at most large, corporate hotels.

THE MEDIA

Canada has no truly national **newspaper**. The closest thing is the *Globe and Mail*, a Toronto broadsheet also published in a western edition and available more or less throughout the country. Most cities have a quality paper, like the *Toronto Star*, *Calgary Herald* or *Vancouver Sun*, which is also available throughout their province – though in rural areas you're more likely to find small-town tabloids on newsstands. The weekly, and dull but worthy, *Maclean's* is the most widely read news magazine, and *Chatelaine* is the principal general-interest mag.

To low-budget travellers, watching cable **television** in a motel room may well be the commonest form of entertainment. Bar local stations, the Canadian Broadcasting Corporation (CBC), Canadian Television Corporation (CTV) and one or two public-broadcasting channels, Canada's TV is effectively the TV of mainstream America. Most US stations can be picked up.

The majority of Canadian **radio** stations, too, stick to a bland commercial format. Most are on the AM band and display little originality – though they can be good sources of local nightlife and entertainment news, and road and weather reports. On FM, on the other hand, the nationally funded CBC channels provide diverse, listenable and well-informed programmes. Although some of the large cities boast good specialist music stations, for most of the time you'll probably have to resort to skipping up and down the frequencies. Driving through rural areas can be frustrating, as for hundreds of kilometres you might only be able to receive one or two very dull stations. With this in mind, it's worth asking your car rental agency if their cars are fitted with cassette players.

OPENING HOURS, TIME ZONES AND HOLIDAYS

Most **shops and supermarkets** open from about 9am to 5.30pm Monday to Saturday, though in bigger towns and cities supermarkets and **malls** may open as early as 7.30am and close around 9pm. Enforced Sunday closing of shops, bars and restaurants operates over much of the country, but a growing number of provinces now have limited Sunday hours, usually 9am to 5pm, particularly in touristy areas. As a general rule, between BC and Québec there are limited Sunday opening hours; and east of Québec shops will be shut on Sunday. Many retail shops open late on Thursday and Friday evenings. In cities you usually find a pharmacist open 24 hours and there's often a convenience store like Mac's or 7–11 that's open around the clock.

Time of year makes a big differance to opening times of **information centres, museums** and other attractions, most of which, particularly in remote areas, have shorter winter hours or close altogether from late September to mid-May. In cities, more upmarket **restaurants** usually open from around noon to 11pm, longer at weekends; many diner-type places, however, close around 8pm, and small-town restaurants tend to close early too. Opening regulations for **bars** – often part of a hotel or restaurant – vary tremendously from province to province; most open daily from 10am to 1am, but in certain areas all bars except a few hotel lounges are shut on Sunday.

TIME ZONES

Canada has six time zones, but only 4.5hrs separate Newfoundland from British Columbia. Newfoundland is on Newfoundland Standard Time (3hr 30min behind GMT); the Maritimes and Labrador are on Atlantic Standard Time (4hr behind GMT); Québec and most of Ontario are on Eastern Standard Time (5hr behind GMT); Manitoba, the northwest corner of Ontario and eastern Saskatchewan are on Central Standard Time (6hr behind GMT); west Saskatchewan, Alberta and a slice of northeast British Columbia are on Mountain Standard Time (7hr behind GMT), and the Yukon and the bulk of British Columbia are on Pacific Standard Time (8hr behind GMT). The Northwest Territories run from Eastern to Mountain Standard Time. Daylight saving – when the

NATIONAL HOLIDAYS

New Year's Day (January 1).
Good Friday.
Easter Monday.
Victoria Day (third Monday in May).
Canada Day (July 1).

Labour Day (first Monday in September).
Thanksgiving (second Monday in October).
Remembrance Day (November 11).
Christmas Day (December 25).
Boxing Day (December 26).

PROVINCIAL HOLIDAYS

Alberta Family Day (third Monday in February); Alberta Heritage Day (first Monday in August).

British Columbia British Columbia Day (first Monday in August).

New Brunswick New Brunswick Day (first Monday in August).

Newfoundland and Labrador St Patrick's Day (March 17); St George's Day (third Monday in April); Discovery Day (penultimate Monday in June); Memorial Day (first Monday

in July); Orangeman's Day (third Monday in July).

Nova Scotia, Manitoba, NWT, Ontario and Saskatchewan Civic Holiday (first Monday in August).

Québec Epiphany (January 6); Ash Wednesday; Ascension (forty days after Easter); Saint-Jean-Baptiste Day (June 24); All Saint's Day (November 1); Immaculate Conception (December 8).

Yukon Discovery Day (third Monday in August).

FESTIVALS AND EVENTS

For further details of the selected festivals and events listed below, including more precise dates, see the relevant page of the Guide, or contact the local authorities direct. The provincial tourist boards listed on p.17 can provide free calendars for each area.

JANUARY

Polar Bear Swim, Vancouver, BC. A New Year's Day swim in the freezing waters of English Bay Beach – said to bring good luck for the year.

FEBRUARY

Winterlude, Ottawa, Ontario. Winter–warming activities like ice sculpting, snowshoe races, ice boating and skating for all on the canal.

Winter Carnival, Québec City, Québec. Eleven-day festival of winter-sports competitions, ice-sculpture contests and parades. Includes the Canadian ski marathon when skiers race between Lachute and Gatineau.

MARCH

Pacific Rim Whale Festival, Vancouver Island, BC. Celebrating the spring migration of grey whales with lots of whale-spotting expeditions as well as music and dance events.

APRIL

TerrifVic Jazz Party, Victoria, BC. Dixieland, and other jazz bands, from around the globe.

Shaw Festival, Niagara-on-the-Lake, Ontario. Highly regarded theatre festival featuring the work of George Bernard Shaw and his contemporaries. Performances from April to late October.

MAY

Apple Blossom Festival, Annapolis Valley, Nova Scotia. Community-orientated festival held in the small towns and villages of the apple-producing Annapolis Valley.

Stratford Festival, Stratford, Ontario. The small town of Stratford is well-known for its first-class Shakespeare Festival. Runs from May to early November.

Canadian Tulip Festival, Ottawa, Ontario. Three million tulips in an orgy of colour all over the city.

JUNE

Jazz City International Festival, Edmonton, Alberta. Ten days of jazz concerts, free outdoor events and workshops.

Banff Festival of the Arts, Banff, Alberta. Young-artist showcase – music, opera, dance, drama, comedy and visual arts.

International Blues Festival, Halifax, Nova Scotia. Big musical event showcasing the best of US and Maritime blues.

Metro International Caravan, Toronto, Ontario. Nine-day multiethnic celebration with some fifty pavilions dotted across the city.

International Jazz Festival, Montréal, Québec. 2000 jazz acts, including the world's top names, and 75 percent of the performances are free.

JULY

Pow-wows. Traditional native Canadian celebrations that take place on reserves across the country in July and August.

Calgary Stampede, Calgary, Alberta. One of the biggest rodeos in the world: all the usual cowboy trappings, plus hot-air-balloon races, chuckwagon rides, craft exhibitions, native dancing and a host of other happenings. Billed as the "Greatest Outdoor Show on Earth".

---

clocks are put forward one hour – is in effect in all regions except Saskatchewan and northeast British Columbia from the first Sunday in April to the last Saturday in October.

Train, bus and plane **timetables** are always given in local time; something it's worth bearing in mind if you're making long journeys across several zones. Most timetables use the 24-hour clock; those that do not, notably Greyhound bus schedules, use light type for am, bold for pm.

Daylight saving time takes effect in Canada in all regions except Saskatchewan and the northeast corner of British Columbia. Clocks go forward one hour on the first Sunday of April, and back one hour on the last Sunday in October.

Klondike Days, Edmonton, Alberta. Pioneer era in Edmonton revisited with gold panning, raft races, pancake breakfasts and gambling.

Loyalist City Festival, Saint John, New Brunswick. Celebration of the city's loyalist heritage with parades in period costume.

Antigonish Highland Games, Antigonish, Nova Scotia. All sorts of traditional Scottish sports and activities recall the settlement of the area by Highlanders.

Atlantic Jazz Festival, Halifax, Nova Scotia. First-class jazz festival pulling in big names from round the world.

Canada Day, Ottawa, Ontario and throughout Canada. Fireworks, parades and a day off for patriotic shenanigans.

Caribana Festival, Toronto, Ontario. Large-scale West Indian carnival with music, dance and a flamboyant parade.

Festival d'Été, Québec City, Québec. Arts performances, live bands and other shows on and off the sun-filled streets and parks of Québec City.

Juste Pour Rire, Montréal, Québec. The funniest festival in Canada. Internationally acclaimed comic get-together with comedians from around the world performing in theatres and outdoor stages.

AUGUST

Fringe Theatre Festival, Edmonton, Alberta. One of North America's most prestigious alternative-theatre festivals.

Squamish Days Loggers Sports Festival, Squamish BC. A lumberjacks' convention with impressive logging competitions.

Acadian Festival, Caraquet, New Brunswick. Celebration of Acadian culture in the northeast of New Brunswick.

Miramichi Folk Song Festival, Newcastle, New Brunswick. New Brunswick's prestigious

folk festival, featuring many of the finest fiddlers in the Maritimes.

Nova Scotia Gaelic Mod, South Gut, St Ann's, Nova Scotia. Seven-day Scottish heritage knees-up with all traditional sports, crafts and contests featured. One of the biggest and best of many similar events in Nova Scotia.

World Film Festival, Montréal, Québec. Eclipsed by Toronto's new film festival, but still a good showcase for new movies.

SEPTEMBER

Toronto International Film Festival, Toronto, Ontario. Internationally acclaimed film festival spread over ten days, inundated with Hollywood stars.

OCTOBER

Vancouver International Film Festival, Vancouver, BC. Another of Canada's highly rated film fests.

Okanagan Wine Festival, Okanagan, BC. One of the many wine events in this vine-growing region.

Oktoberfest, Kitchener-Waterloo, Ontario. Alcohol and cultural events in honour of the twin towns' roots.

NOVEMBER

Royal Agricultural Winter Fair, Toronto, Ontario. The world's largest agricultural indoor fair, apparently.

DECEMBER

Coral Ships, Vancouver, BC. When carol singers sail around Vancouver harbour in sparkly boats.

New Year Eve, throughout Canada, but celebrated in style in St John's, Newfoundland, where everyone heads from the pub to the waterfront for a raucous midnight party.

HOLIDAYS

Banks, schools and government buildings all over the country close on Canada's **national holidays**, and within specific regions on the **provincial holidays** that fall on certain – often movable – days throughout the year. Many shops, restaurants, museums and sights remain open, however. Campgrounds, smaller information centres, B&Bs and many resort hotels often use Victoria Day and Labour Day or Thanksgiving as markers for their open and closed seasons. University students have their holidays from May to early September (plus a one- or two-week break in March), while schoolchildren take theirs from the end of June to Labour Day.

OUTDOOR PURSUITS

Canada's mountains, lakes, rivers and forests offer the opportunity to indulge in a vast range of outdoor pursuits. We've concentrated on hiking, skiing and canoeing – three of Canada's most popular activities – and on the national parks, which have been established to preserve and make accessible the best of the Canadian landscape.

Other popular activities such as whale-watching, horseriding, fishing and rafting are covered in some detail in the main text, but whatever activity interests you, be certain to send off to the provincial tourist offices for information before you go. Once in Canada you can rely on finding outfitters, equipment rental, charters, tours and guides to help you in most areas; tourist offices invariably carry full details or contact numbers. Also make a point of visiting Canadian bookshops – most have a separate outdoor pursuits section with a wide variety of specialist guides.

THE NATIONAL PARKS

Canada's thirty or so **national parks** are administered by Parks Canada, a federal body, with information provided locally by **park information centres** (though the terminology may vary from park to park). Visit these to pick up special **permits** if you intend to fish or camp in the backcountry, and for information and audiovisual displays on flora, fauna and outdoor activities. Many offer talks and nature walks presented by park naturalists, as well as reports on snow, weather and recent bear sightings. **Regulations** common to all national parks include a total ban on firearms, hunting, snowmobiles or off-road vehicles, the feeding of wildlife, and the removal or damaging of any natural objects or features.

Note that most national park regulations relating to the care of the environment and campground behaviour are usually applicable to **provincial parks**. Entry to these parks is free but you'll have to pay for fishing and hunting permits – though specifics vary from province to province. Where provincial parks provide facilities or contain a specific attraction, you can also expect to pay a modest admission fee and, naturally, you have to pay to use provincial park campgrounds.

PERMITS

At national parks all motor vehicles, including motorbikes, require a **park permit** before entering, usually from a roadside booth at the point where the road crosses the park boundary. In the past people entering on foot, bicycle, boat or horseback have been exempt, as have vehicles passing straight through certain parks without stopping overnight. This is no longer the case and a permit based on a per-person usage of the park is now required. This costs around $5 to $10 per person per day with the customary concessions for the young and old. If you intend to visit a number of national parks, it's worth investing in either a regional or national pass – details from any park information centre. As an illustration, an annual pass providing admission to the dozen or so western parks costs around $35. For more on passes in the Rockies and surrounding parks, see p.567. Additional permits are also required to **fish** in national parks (over and above any provincial permits; see "Fishing", p.52). These are available from park centres, wardens or park administration buildings, and cost around $13 annually, $6 weekly or $5 daily. There may well be quotas on the types and numbers of fish you can catch, which you can find out when you buy a permit; in all parks there's an extra surcharge to fish for salmon.

CAMPING IN THE PARKS

Most parks have large, well-run campgrounds close to the park's main settlement; some for tents or RVs only, others mixed. Fees depend on facilities, and currently run from $8.50 per tent or per vehicle for semi-primitive sites (with wood, water and pit toilets) up to about $20 for those with electricity, sewage, water and showers. Park permits do not cover campground fees. Some park campgrounds have also introduced another fee (around $3) for use of firewood.

Most parks also have **primitive campgrounds**, which are basic backcountry sites providing, as a rule, just fire pits and firewood. Regulations for **rough camping** vary enormously. Some parks, like Jasper in the Rockies, allow backcountry camping only in tightly defined sites; others, like Banff, have a special **primitive wildland** zone where you can pitch a tent within a designated distance of the nearest road or trail-head. Simply ask at park centres or tourist offices for latest details. Whether you want to use a primitive campground or camp rough in parks, however, the one thing you must do is obtain an **overnight permit** from the park centre (either free or just a few dollars), which enables the authorities to keep a check on people's where-abouts and regulate numbers in the backcountry.

HIKING

Canada boasts some of North America's finest **hiking**, and whatever your abilities or ambitions you'll find a walk to suit you almost anywhere in the country. All the national and many of the provincial parks have well-marked and -main-tained trails, and a visit to any park centre or local tourist office will furnish you with ade-quate **maps** of local paths. Park trails are usual-ly sufficiently well marked not to need more detailed maps for short walks and day hikes. This applies to virtually all the hikes described in features in this guide. If you're venturing into backcountry, though, try to obtain the appropri-ate 1:50 000 (or 1:250 000) sheet from the *Cana-dian Topographical Series*. For key hiking areas we've given a brief summary of the best trails in the appropriate parts of the Guide, though with over 1500km of paths in Banff National Park alone, recommendations can only scratch the surface of what's on offer. Park staff can advise on other good walks, and **trail guides** are wide-ly available for most of the country's prime walk-ing regions.

It's essential, of course, to be **properly equipped** if you're walking in high or rough coun-try: good boots, waterproof jacket and spare warm clothing. Be prepared for sudden changes of weather and the sort of health problems asso-ciated with the Canadian backcountry (see "Health matters", p.26). Outdoor clothing can be bought easily in most towns, and in walking areas there's a good chance of being able to **rent** tents, specialized cold-weather gear and all manner of other minor outdoor gear.

MAIN HIKING AREAS

In picking out the country's prime walking areas we've usually chosen the parks that are accessi-ble by road, where maps are available and the trail system developed, and where you can turn up without too much planning or special wilder-ness training.

Best known and most developed of these are the **Rockies national parks** of Alberta and British Columbia. Thousands of kilometres of well-kept and well-tramped paths crisscross the "big four parks"– Banff, Jasper, Yoho and Koote-nay – as well as the smaller enclaves of Glacier, Revelstoke and Waterton lakes. Scope for hiking of all descriptions is almost limitless.

More modest areas dotted all over British Columbia boast walking possibilities out of all proportion to their size: we pay less attention to these, but by most relative standards hiking here is still among the best in North America. All the following provincial parks offer a variety of day hikes, short strolls and longer trails that could keep you happy for a week or more: **Wells Gray**, north of Kamloops; **Kokanee Glacier**, near Nel-son: **Manning**, east of Vancouver; **Garibaldi**, north of Vancouver; and **Strathcona**, on Vancou-ver Island. Walking guides are available for all these regions in local bookstores: tourist offices, as ever, will also offer guidance.

In Manitoba, the **Riding Mountain National Park** offers about thirty hiking trails, but though there's plenty of upland walking to be had in the so-called prairie provinces, you have to move east to Québec's **Mauricie, Forillon** and **Gatineau** parks for a taste of mountains comparable to the western provinces. In Ontario, **Lake Superior Provincial Park** and the **Algonquin Park** are the most challenging terrains. New Brunswick's **Fundy National Park** offers coastal walks, while Newfoundland's hiking centres on its two national parks: **Terra Nova** on the east coast, and the high plateau and fjords of the west coast's **Gros Morne**. For the truly bold, however, nothing can match the Arctic extremes of **Baffin Island**, whose principal trail lies over an icecap that never melts.

LONG-DISTANCE FOOTPATHS

In areas with highly developed trail networks, sea-soned backpackers can blaze their own **long-distance footpaths** by stringing together several longer trails. Recognized long-haul paths, however, are relatively rare, though more are being designat-ed yearly. One of the best is the Chilkoot Trail from Dyea in Alaska to Bennett in British Columbia, a 53-kilometre hike that closely follows the path of prospectors en route to the Yukon during the 1898 gold rush (see pp.818–819). The most popular is probably Vancouver Island's demanding West Coast Trail, which runs for 80km along the edge of the Pacific Rim National Park (see pp.729–730).

More far-reaching walks include the **Rideau Trail**, which follows paths and minor roads for 386km from Kingston to Ottawa; the 690-kilometre **Bruce Trail** from Queenston, on the Niagara River to Tobermory on the Bruce Peninsula; and the **Voyageur Trail** along the north shores of lakes Superior and Huron, which is the longest and most rugged route in the province.

Before you set out on any long-distance trail, however, it is vital to seek local advice from either the nearest tourist or park office, or from a local adventure-tour operator.

SKIING

Wherever there's hiking in Canada, there's also usually **skiing**. The increasingly popular resorts of the Rockies and British Columbia are the main areas, followed by Québec, but there's also skiing in Newfoundland and the Maritimes, and even a few runs in Manitoba and Saskatchewan. We've provided special features on the country's leading resorts at Whistler, Banff, Lake Louise and Jasper. Most **cities** are close to excellent downhill and cross-country runs: Vancouver is a ninety-minute drive from Whistler, one of the world's top three resorts; Calgary is the same distance from the Rockies' six big centres; Ottawa lies just half an hour from Camp Fortune and Mont Cascade; and Montréal is around an hour from three hundred runs in the Laurentians and one hundred-plus slopes in L'Estrie (the Eastern Townships).

Canadian **ski packages** are available from most UK and US travel agents, but it's perfectly feasible to organize your own trips, as long as you book well ahead if you're hoping to stay in some of the better-known resorts. **Costs** for food, accommodation and **ski passes** are still fairly modest by US and European standards – a day's pass in one of the Rockies' resorts, for example, costs around $40. Tourist offices in skiing areas are open in winter to help with practicalities, and many nearby towns have ski shops to buy or rent equipment. Companies and hotels in some cities even organize their own mini-packages to nearby resorts. Skiing provinces publish regional ski and winter sports directories, all available in the UK and US from state or provincial tourist offices.

FISHING

Canada is fishing nirvana. While each region has its specialities, from the Arctic char of the Northwest Territories to the Pacific salmon of British Columbia, excellent fishing can be found in most of the country's superabundant lakes, rivers and coastal waters. Most towns have a fishing shop for equipment, and any spot with fishing possibilities is likely to have companies running boats and charters. As with every other major type of outdoor activity, most provinces publish detailed booklets on everything that swims within the area of their jurisdiction.

Fishing is governed by a range of **regulations** that vary from province to province. These are baffling at first glance, but usually boil down to the need for a **non-resident permit** for freshwater fishing, and another for saltwater fishing. These are obtainable from most local fishing or sports shops for about $30 and are valid for a year. Short-term (one- or six-day) licences are also available in some provinces. In a few places you may have to pay for extra licences to go after particular fish, and in national parks you need a special additional permit (see above). There may also be quotas or a closed season on certain fish. Shops and tourist offices always have the most current regulations.

CANOEING

Opportunities for **canoeing** are limited only by problems of access and expertise – some of the rapids and portages on the country's more challenging routes are for real pros only. The most straightforward regions to canoe are in **Ontario**, with its estimated 250,000 lakes and 35,000km of waterways, some 25,000km of which have been documented as practical canoe routes. The key areas are the Algonquin, Killarney and Quetico provincial parks, though the single most popular run is the 190-kilometre **Rideau Canal**, a tame run from Kingston to Ottawa.

The rivers of **British Columbia** offer generally more demanding white-water routes, though the lake canoeing – in the Wells Gray Provincial Park, for example – is among the country's most beautiful. One of the province's other recognized classics is the 120-kilometre trip near Barkerville on the Cariboo River and the lakes of the Bowron Lakes Provincial Park. More challenging still are the immense backcountry lakes and rivers of the

Mackenzie system and the barren lands of the Northwest Territories, where you can find one of the continent's ultimate river challenges – the 300-kilometre stretch of the **South Nahanni River** near Fort Simpson. Growing in popularity, partly because of improved road access, are trips on and around the **Yukon River system**, particularly the South Macmillan River east of Pelly Crossing. Other areas that will test the resources of any canoeist are to be found in Manitoba and Labrador – all detailed in the Guide.

Once you've decided on an area, provincial tourist offices can send you full lists of outfitters and rental agencies whose brochures pro-vide a good idea of what you can expect in their various regions. When you arrive, **outfitters** are available in most centres to rent equipment, organize boat and plane drop-offs, and arrange provisions for longer trips. Typical **costs** are in the region of $80 for weekly canoe rental, $25 daily for a wet suit. Most also supply **maps**, but for longer trips you should obtain maps from the Canada Map Office, 130 Bentley Ave, Ottawa, Ontario K1A 0E9 (☎613/952-7000). Specialist canoe **guides** are also widely available in Canadian bookshops, many giving extremely detailed accounts of particular river systems or regions.

SPECTATOR SPORTS

Canadians are sports-mad – ice hockey, baseball and Canadian football matches are all extremely popular, both the professional games, and the intercollegiate competitions, the intensity of whose rivalries are notorious. Interestingly, lacrosse is the "official" national sport but, unsurprisingly, the unofficial one is ice hockey.

ICE HOCKEY

The sport that really ignites the passions of all Canadians is **ice hockey**. With players hurtling around at nearly 50kph and the puck clocking speeds of over 160kph, this would be a high-adrenaline sport even without its relaxed attitude to combat on the rink – as an old Canadian adage has it, "I went to see a fight and an ice-hockey game broke out." Players, especially in the minor leagues, are as adept at a right hook as they are at skating, and a few years ago the national team waged such a battle against the Soviet Union that the fight only stopped when officials turned all the lights off.

The North American **National Hockey League (NHL)** consists of 25 teams, of which six are from Canada: the Montréal Canadiens,

---

NHL TEAMS AND VENUES

EASTERN CONFERENCE

Northeast Division

Montréal Canadiens, Centre Molson, 1260 de la Gauchitiere, Montréal (☎514/790-1245).

Ottawa Senators, Corel Centre, 1000 Palladium Drive, Kanata (☎1-800-444-SENS).

WESTERN CONFERENCE

Central Division

Toronto Maple Leafs, Maple Leaf Gardens, 60 Carlton St, Toronto (☎416/872-5000).

Pacific Division

Calgary Flames, Canadian Airlines Saddledome, Calgary (☎403/777-0000).

Edmonton Oilers, Edmonton Coliseum, 7424 118th Ave, Edmonton (☎403/471-2191).

Vancouver Canucks, General Motors Place, 800 Griffiths Way, Vancouver (☎604/280-4400).

Ottawa Senators, Toronto Maple Leafs Vancouver Canucks, Calgary Flames and the Edmonton Oilers. There are two conferences – **Western** and **Eastern** – both divided into two divisions. The Montréal Canadiens and the Ottawa Senators meet teams from Buffalo, Boston, Carolina and Pittsburgh in the Northeast division of the Eastern conference and the Toronto Maple Leafs face Chicago, Dallas, Detroit, St Louis and Phoenix in the Central division of the Western conference. The other Canadian teams play in the Pacific division of the Western conference, where they face the Los Angeles Kings.

Teams have six players and perpetual substitutions are allowed during the game – some players rarely spend more than a few minutes on the ice at one time. There are three twenty-minute periods in a match, but the clock is frequently stopped for a variety of reasons so play usually goes on for three hours. Each team plays over ninety games a **season**, which lasts from October to May, and on alternate weeks will play two and then three games. At the end of the season the top three teams in each league go on into the play-offs for the **Stanley Cup**, ice hockey's most prestigious title. The two most successful teams are the Montréal Canadiens, who have won the Stanley Cup 23 times, and the Toronto Maple Leafs, who have eleven victories under their belt.

Ticket prices range from around $15 for ordinary games to hundreds of dollars for a Stanley Cup final – indeed, you can forget about getting into this event unless you have high-level political or sporting contacts. For nearly all matches you have to buy a ticket in advance.

Other than the NHL there are also numerous **minor league** clubs composed of **farm teams**, so called because they supply the top clubs with talent. Ontario and Québec both have their own minor leagues; the rest of the country plays in the Western league, all with play-offs for a variety of awards. For **college hockey**, the University of Toronto and York in Toronto, Concordia in Montréal, St Mary's in Halifax and the University of Alberta in Edmonton all have good teams.

CANADIAN FOOTBALL

Professional **Canadian football**, played under the aegis of the **Canadian Football League (CFL)**, is largely overshadowed by the National Football League in the US, chiefly because the best home-grown talent moves south in search of better money while NFL castoffs move north to fill the ranks. The two countries' football games vary slightly, but what differences do exist tend to make the Canadian version more exciting. In Canada the playing field is larger and there are twelve rather than eleven players on each **team**. There is also one fewer **down** in a game – ie after kickoff the attacking team has three, rather than four, chances to move the ball forward ten yards and score a first down en route to a **touchdown**. Different rules about the movement of players, and the limited time allowed between plays, results in a faster-paced and higher-scoring sport, in which ties are often decided in overtime or in a dramatic final-minute surge.

Despite the sport's potential, the CFL has suffered a blight of media and fan indifference, which has caused immense financial problems,

CFL TEAMS

WEST DIVISION

BC Lions, BC Place Stadium, 777 Pacific Blvd S, Vancouver (☎604/930-5466).

Calgary Stampeders, McMahon Stadium, 1817 Crowchild Trail NW, Calgary (☎403/289-0258).

Edmonton Eskimos, Commonwealth Stadium, 11000 Stadium Rd, Edmonton (☎403/448-ESKS).

Saskatchewan Roughriders, Taylor Field, 2940 10th Ave, Regina (☎306/525-2181).

EAST DIVISION

Hamilton Tiger-Cats, Ivor Wynne Stadium, 75 Balsam Ave N, Hamilton (☎905/527-1508 or 1-800-714-ROAR).

Montréal Alouettes, Olympic Stadium, Av Pierre de Courbetin, Montréal (☎514/252-4668).

Toronto Argonauts, Skydome, 1 Blue Jays Way, Toronto (☎416/341-5151).

Winnipeg Blue Bombers, Winnipeg Stadium, 1465 Maroons Rd, Winnipeg (☎204/780-7328 or 1-800-465-7328).

though recently the crisis seems to be easing, with high-profile celebrity investment. The CFL has tried to expand into the US over the past couple of years, but all the expansion teams folded at the end of the 1995–96 season. The **season**, played by two divisions of eight teams, lasts from June to November, each team playing a match a week – 72 matches in all. At the end of the season are the play-offs, which culminate with the hotly contested Grey Cup – which the Toronto Argonauts have won twenty times, most recently in 1996. Tickets are fairly easy to come by, except for important games, and vary in cost from $10 to a Grey Cup final price of over $100.

BASEBALL

Baseball, with its relaxed summertime pace and byzantine rules, is generally considered an exclusively American sport, but the **Toronto Blue Jays** and the **Montréal Expos** perform in the US's two leagues, the National and the American respectively. In 1993 and 1994, the Toronto Blue Jays became national heroes when they won the World Series twice in a row, beating America at their own game. Historically a lowlier bunch, the Expos are now in financial trouble and gunning for a new downtown stadium to boost ticket sales. However, it was they who became the first non-US team to play in a US league in 1968, eight years before the Blue Jays.

Even if you don't understand what's going on, a game can be a pleasant day out, drinking beer and eating burgers and popcorn in the sun, with friendly family-oriented crowds. Moreover, the home ground of each team is a vast, wondrous

modern stadium – the Skydome in Toronto and, for the moment at least, the Olympic Stadium in Montréal. With six teams in each division, there are 81 home games each season, played from April to late September, with play-offs continuing through October; there is no set match day and games are either played in the afternoon or evening. Lasting for anything from two to three hours, baseball games never end in a tie: if the scores are level after nine innings, extra innings are played until one side wins.

Tickets for the Blue Jays are hard to come by and it's easier to get in for games in Montréal. Nothing can match the glitz of the big two, but there are other minor league **farm teams**, including the Edmonton Trappers, Calgary Cannons and Vancouver Canadians.

BASKETBALL

Basketball was invented by a Canadian, Dr James A. Naismith, in 1891. What began with a bunch of his students and a peach basket suspended in the air has become a fast-paced exciting sport with the world's tallest athletes. After a 48-year absence two Canadian teams have joined the now misnamed National Basketball Association in 1995, the Toronto Raptors and the Vancouver Grizzlies, who did about as well as could be expected in their first season. Toronto is gutting the old Postal Delivery Building and turning it into the Air Canada Centre to make a new home for the Raptors by February 1999.

The NBA consists of 29 teams divided into two conferences, Eastern and Western, which are further divided into two divisions. The Toron-

BASEBALL TEAMS

AMERICAN LEAGUE

Toronto Blue Jays, Skydome, 277 Front St W, Toronto (☎416/341-1234 or 1-800-GO-JAY outside Toronto).

NATIONAL LEAGUE

Montréal Expos, Olympic Stadium, Av Pierre-de-Coubertin, Montréal (☎514/253-3434).

PACIFIC COAST LEAGUE

Calgary Cannons, McMahon Stadium, 1817 Crowchild Trail NW, Calgary (☎403/284-1111).

Edmonton Trappers, John Ducey Park, 10233 96th Ave, Edmonton (☎403/429-2934).

Vancouver Canadians, Nat Bailey Stadium, 4601 Ontario St, Vancouver (☎604/872-5232).

INTERNATIONAL LEAGUE

Ottawa Lynx, Ottawa Stadium, 300 Coventry Rd, Ottawa (☎613/747-5969).

NY/PENN LEAGUE

St Catherines Stompers, Community Park, 4 Seymour Ave, St Catherines, Ontario (☎905/641-5297).

to Raptors play in the Central division of the Eastern conference (along with the Chicago Bulls, Michael Jordan's team) and the Vancouver Grizzlies compete in the Midwest division of the Western conference. Teams play an 82-game season with 41 home games in a season that lasts from November to April – tickets cost from $5 to $100.

BASKETBALL TEAMS

Toronto Raptors, Skydome, 1 Blue Jays Way, Toronto (☎416/872-5000).

Vancouver Grizzlies, General Motors Place, 800 Griffiths Way, Vancouver (☎604/899-4667).

DIRECTORY

ADDRESSES Generally speaking, roads in built-up areas in Canada are laid out on a grid system, creating "blocks" of buildings. The first one or two digits of a specific address refer to the block, which will be numbered in sequence from a central point, usually downtown. For example, 620 S Cedar Ave will be six blocks south of downtown. It is crucial, therefore, to take note of components such as "NW" or "SE" in addresses; 3620 SW King St will be a very long way indeed from 3620 NE King St. Where a number is prefixed to the street number, this indicates an apartment or suite number in a block at the same street address.

BEARS Be aware of the dangers posed by bears. Most people blow a whistle while walking in bear country to warn them off. If confronted don't run, make loud noises or sudden movements, all of which are likely to provoke an attack. Leave the animal an escape route and back off slowly. If you

have a pack, leave it as a distraction. If attacked, climbing a tree or playing dead may save you from a grizzly, but not from black bears. Fighting back only increases the ferocity of an attack. For more on bears, see pp.598–599.

ELECTRIC CURRENT Electricity in Canada is supplied at an alternating current of 110 volts and at a frequency of 60Hz, the same as in the US. Visitors from the UK will need transformers for appliances like shavers and hair dryers, and a plug converter for Canada's two-pin sockets.

FLOORS The *first* floor in Canada is what would be the ground floor in Britain; the *second* floor would be the first floor, and so on.

ID Should be carried at all times. Two pieces should suffice, one of which should have a photo; a passport and credit card are your best bet.

MEASUREMENTS Canada officially uses the metric system, though many people still use the imperial system. Distances are in kilometres, temperatures in degrees Celsius, and foodstuffs, petrol and drink are sold in grams, kilogrammes or litres.

PUBLIC TOILETS Rare even in cities, but bars, fast-food chains, museums and other public buildings invariably have excellent facilities.

SENIOR TRAVELLERS For many senior citizens, retirement brings the opportunity to explore the world in a style and at a pace that is the envy of younger travellers. As well as the advantages of being free to travel during the quieter, less expensive seasons, and for longer periods, anyone over the age of 65, often 60, can enjoy the tremendous variety of discounts on offer to those who can produce suitable ID. VIA Rail and

Greyhound, for example, offer (smallish) percentage reductions on fares to older passengers; while the majority of museums and similar attractions give at least fifty percent discounts for seniors.

VIDEOS If you purchase a prerecorded video in Canada, make sure it's been recorded on the PAL system, or else it will be useless back in Europe. Blank videos can be used in either continent without any problem.

METRIC CONVERSIONS

1 centimetre (*cm*) = 0.394in
1 inch (*in*) = 2.54cm
1 foot (*ft*) = 30.48cm
1 metre (*m*) = 100cm
1 metre = 39.37in
1 yard (*yd*) = 0.91m
1 kilometre (*km*) = 1000m
1 kilometre = 0.621 miles
1 mile = 1.61km
1 hectare = 10,000 square metres
1 hectare = 2.471 acres

1 acre = 0.4 hectares
1 litre = 0.22 UK gal
1 UK gallon (*gal*) = 4.55 litres
1 litre = 0.26 US gal
1 US gallon (*gal*) = 5.46 litres
1 gramme (*g*) = 0.035oz
1 ounce (*oz*) = 28.57g
1 kilogramme (*kg*) = 1000g
1 kilogramme = 2.2lb
1 pound (*lb*) = 0.454kg

CHAPTER ONE

ONTARIO

The one million square kilometres of **Ontario,** Canada's second-largest province, stretch all the way from the St Lawrence River and the Great Lakes to the frozen shores of Hudson Bay. Some two-thirds of this territory – all of the north and most of the centre – is occupied by the forests and rocky outcrops of the Canadian Shield, whose characteristically flat, lake-studded landscapes the Iroquois called Ontario, literally "glittering waters". **Algonquian** and **Iroquoian** natives were the first to cultivate the more hospitable parts of southern Ontario, a fertile flatland in which the vast majority of the province's ten million people are now concentrated.

The first **Europeans** to make regular contact with these peoples were the **French explorers** of the seventeenth and eighteenth centuries, most famously the intrepid Brulé and Champlain, but these early visitors were preoccupied with the fur trade, and it wasn't until the end of the American War of Independence and the immigration of the **United Empire Loyalists** that mass settlement began. Between 1820 and 1850 a further wave of migrants, mostly English, Irish and Scots, made Upper Canada, as Ontario was known until Confederation, the most populous and prosperous Canadian region. This pre-eminence was reinforced towards the end of the nineteenth century by the industrialization of its larger towns, a process underpinned by the discovery of some of the world's richest mineral deposits – in the space of a few years nickel was found near Sudbury, silver at Cobalt, gold in Red Lake and iron ore at Wawa.

Nowadays, a highly mechanized timber industry, massive hydroelectric schemes and thousands of factories – making more than half the country's manufactured goods – keep Ontario at the top of the economic ladder. However, this industrial success has created massive **environmental problems**, most noticeable in the wounded landscapes around Sudbury and the heavily polluted waters of lakes Erie and Ontario. Furthermore, despite the diversity of its economy and its tremendous natural resources, Ontario in the 1980s experienced a slump that contributed to the electoral success of the New Democratic Party (NDP) in 1990, an upset in a province that had long been dominated by the Progressive Conservative Party, commonly known as the "Big Blue Machine". NDP control was short-lived, but the Conservatives, sucked increasingly into the flinty politics of the right, have failed to re-establish their domination, creating a new volatility in provincial politics that has been marked by an increasingly deep rural–urban split.

With more than three million inhabitants, **Toronto** is Canada's biggest city, a financial and industrial centre that might lack a certain grace and elegance but compensates in terms of museums, restaurants and nightlife. To the south of the metropolis, **Lake Ontario** is ringed by nondescript suburbs and ugly industrial townships that culminate in the steel city of **Hamilton**, a few kilometres from Canada's premier tourist spot, **Niagara Falls** – best visited on a day-trip from Toronto or from colonial **Niagara-on-the-Lake**. Most of the rest of southern Ontario, sandwiched between lakes Huron and Erie,

TOLL-FREE INFORMATION NUMBER

Ontario Travel ☎1-800-668-2746.

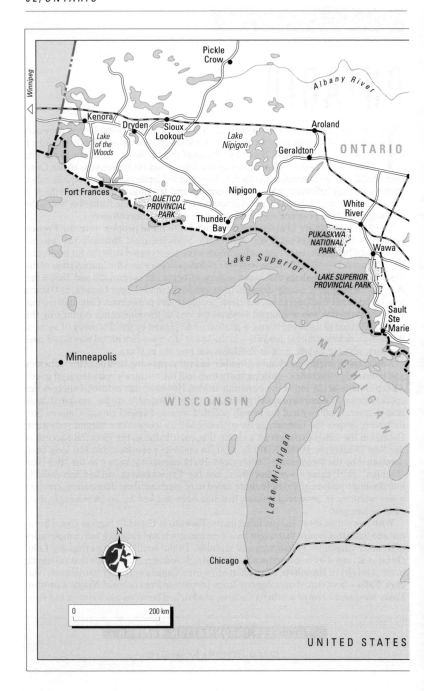

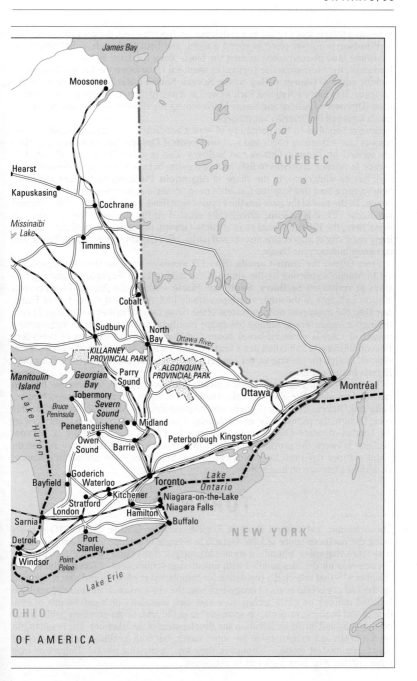

is farming terrain that's as flat as a Dutch polder. Nevertheless, the car-producing town of **Windsor** is a lively place to spend a night, and both **Goderich** and **Bayfield** are charming little places tucked against the bluffs along the Lake Huron shoreline. For landscape, the most attractive regions of southern Ontario are the **Bruce Peninsula** and the adjacent **Georgian Bay**, whose **Severn Sound** is the location of the beautiful Georgian Bay Islands National Park as well as a pair of topnotch historical reconstructions, Discovery Harbour and Sainte-Marie among the Hurons – no wonder the area is much favoured by Ontarian vacationers.

Severn Sound is on the periphery of what Canadians call **cottage country**, a vast tract of land extending north and east over **central Ontario**, approximately the triangle formed by Toronto, Ottawa and Sudbury. This is where the province's city folk escape to isolated lakesides to fish, boat and swim, but even this largely domesticated idyll has its wilderness, in the shape of **Algonquin Park**, where beavers and black bears roam a land that inspired Canada's most prestigious art movement, the Group of Seven. To the east of the park lies the Loyalist heartland, centred on the militaristic and handsome city of **Kingston**, strategically situated on the shores of the St Lawrence. From here, the **Rideau Canal** runs north to **Ottawa**, the nation's capital but a surprisingly small city of impeccable streets and parks, high-class museums and galleries, and incessant bureaucratic bustle.

From Ottawa the **Trans-Canada** (Hwy 17) wends its way west through endless forest to Manitoba, passing by the shore of the mighty **Lake Superior**; a journey that takes in revitalized **Sudbury**, **Sault Ste Marie** – where the **Agawa Canyon** train affords a glimpse of the otherwise inpenetrable hinterland – and the sprawl of **Thunder Bay**, the major port on the greatest of the Great Lakes. Further north, Hwy 11 cuts through a region whose mining towns are moribund testimony to the extraordinary impact of Canada's mineral-based boom and the subsequent ravages of recession. Beyond this line of habitation lies a brutal country where hunters are the only regular visitors, though the passing tourist can get a taste of the terrain on board the *Polar Bear Express* from **Cochrane**.

Toronto is at the heart of Ontario's **public transport** system, with regular bus and rail services along the shore of Lake Ontario and the St Lawrence between Niagara Falls and Ottawa, from where there are frequent links to Montréal. Away from this core, though, the picture is far more sketchy. There are fairly regular bus services on the London–Windsor–Detroit route and along the Trans-Canada and Hwy 11, but connections between the province's smaller towns are few and far between – reckon on about one per day even for prominent places, though in some cases (for instance, Goderich) there are no buses at all.

TORONTO

The economic and cultural focus of English-speaking Canada, **TORONTO** sprawls along the northern shore of Lake Ontario in a jangle of satellite townships and industrial zones that cover a hundred square kilometres. The country's largest metropolis, Toronto was for decades saddled with unflattering soubriquets – "Toronto the Good", "Hogtown" – that reflected a reputation for complacent mediocrity and greed. Spurred by the bad press into years of image-building, the city's postwar administrations have lavished millions on glitzy architecture and slick museums, on a careful mix of residential and business projects, on sponsorship of the arts, on an excellent public transport system, and on the reclamation and development of the lakefront. The result might be too brash and metamorphic for some tastes, but with justifiable pride its people maintain a modest motto – Toronto is, they say, "a city that works". Detractors may point out that it is "New York run by the Swiss".

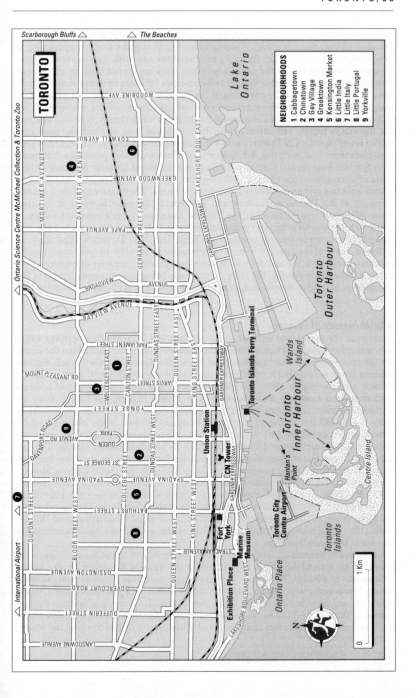

NEIGHBOURHOODS
1 Cabbagetown
2 Chinatown
3 Gay Village
4 Greektown
5 Kensington Market
6 Little India
7 Little Italy
8 Little Portugal
9 Yorkville

Huge new shopping malls reflect the economic successes of the last two or three decades, a boom that has attracted immigrants from all over the world, transforming an overwhelmingly anglophone city into a cosmopolitan one, with some sixty significant minorities. And its thoughtful multiculturalism goes far deeper than an extravagant diversity of restaurants and a slightly self-conscious ethnicity of street signs ("Chinatown", "Little Italy", etc): the city schools, for instance, have extensive "**Heritage Language**" programmes, positively encouraging the maintenance of the immigrants' first cultures. Getting the feel of Toronto's diversity is one of the great pleasures of a stay, but the city is replete with attention-grabbing sights as well, of which the most celebrated is perhaps the **CN Tower**, the world's tallest free-standing structure. Other prestige attractions lead with the **Art Gallery of Ontario**, which possesses a first-rate selection of European and Canadian painting, and the **Royal Ontario Museum**, where pride of place goes to the Chinese collection, but it's the pick of Toronto's smaller, less-visited galleries and period homes that really charms. There are exquisite Canadian paintings at the **Thomson Gallery** and a wonderful range of footwear at the **Bata Shoe Museum**, not to mention the Toronto Dominion Bank's eclectic **Gallery of Inuit Art,** the mock-Gothic extravagances of **Casa Loma**, and the replica of the colonial settlement where Toronto began, **Fort York**. That said, Toronto's sights illustrate different facets of the city, but in no way crystallize its identity. In this sense, the city remains opaque, too big and diverse to allow for a general character to emerge – very much a modern metropolis, the icing on the cake being an extravagant range of fine restaurants and what is one of Canada's most energetic rock and performing arts scenes.

A brief history of Toronto

Situated on the slab of land separating Lake Ontario and Georgian Bay, **Toronto** was on one of the three early portage routes to the northwest, its name taken from the Huron for "place of meeting". The first European to visit the district was the French explorer Étienne Brulé in 1615, but it wasn't until the middle of the eighteenth century that the French made a serious effort to control the area with the development of a simple settlement and stockade, **Fort Rouillé**. The British pushed the French from the northern shore of Lake Ontario in 1759, but then chose to ignore the site for almost forty years until the arrival of hundreds of Loyalist settlers in the aftermath of the American Revolution. In 1791 the British divided their remaining American territories into two, Upper and Lower Canada, each with its own legislative councils. The first capital of Upper Canada was Niagara-on-the-Lake, but this was too near the American border for comfort and the province's new lieutenant-governor, **John Graves Simcoe**, moved his administration to the relative safety of Toronto in 1793, calling the new settlement **York**. Simcoe had grand classical visions of colonial settlement, but even he was exasperated by the conditions of frontier life – "the city's site was better calculated for a frog pond . . . than for the residence of human beings". Soon nicknamed "Muddy York", the capital was little more than a village when, in 1812, the Americans attacked and burnt the main buildings.

In the early nineteenth century, effective economic and political power lay in the hands of an anglophilic oligarchy christened the **Family Compact** by the radical polemicists of the day. Their most vociferous opponent was a radical Scot, **William Lyon Mackenzie**, who promulgated his views both in his newspaper, the *Colonial Advocate*, and as a member of the Legislative Assembly. Mackenzie became the first mayor of Toronto, as the town was renamed in 1834, but the radicals were defeated in the elections two years later and a frustrated Mackenzie drifted towards the idea of

The Toronto area telephone code is ☎416.

armed revolt. In 1837, he staged the **Upper Canadian insurrection**, a badly organized uprising of a few hundred farmers, who marched down Yonge Street, fought a couple of half-hearted skirmishes and then melted away. Mackenzie fled across the border and two of the other ringleaders were executed, but the British parliament, mindful of their earlier experiences in New England, moved to liberalize Upper Canada's administration instead of taking reprisals. In 1841, they granted Canada responsible government, reuniting the two provinces in a loose confederation, prefiguring the final union of 1867 when Upper Canada was redesignated Ontario. Even Mackenzie was pardoned and allowed to return, arguably giving the lie to his portrayal of the oligarchs as hard-faced reactionaries; indeed, this same privileged group had even pushed progressive antislavery bills through the legislature as early as the 1830s.

By the end of the nineteenth century Toronto had become a major manufacturing centre dominated by a conservative mercantile elite who were exceedingly loyal to British interests and maintained a strong Protestant tradition. This elite was sustained by the working-class Orange Lodges, whose reactionary influence was a key feature of municipal politics – no wonder Charles Dickens had been offended by the city's "rabid Toryism". That said, these same Protestants were enthusiastic about public education, just like the Methodist-leaning middle classes, who also spearheaded social reform movements, principally Suffrage and Temperance. The trappings, however, remained far from alluring: well into this century Sunday was preserved as a "day of rest" – Eaton's store even drew its curtains to prevent Sabbath window-shopping. Indeed, for all its capital status, the city was strikingly provincial by comparison with Montréal until the 1950s, when the opening of the St Lawrence Seaway in 1959 gave the place a kick, and the complexion of Toronto changed completely with the arrival of immigrant communities. More recently, Toronto was an indirect beneficiary of the assertion of francophone identity in Québec, as many of Montréal's anglophone-dominated financial institutions and big businesses transferred their operations to the Ontario capital.

Arrival, information and city transport

Toronto's main **airport**, Lester B. Pearson International, is about 25km northwest of the city centre. There are three terminals – terminals 2 and 3 are where most international flights arrive, Terminal 1 handles the majority of domestic flights. At both terminals 2 and 3, a volunteer-run **Travellers' Aid desk** will telephone to book accommodation at no charge, and can often get hotel discounts of up to fifteen percent. From outside each of the airport's three terminals, an express **bus** service takes about forty minutes to reach downtown (6am–12.30am; every 20min), dropping passengers at all the major hotels. Most of the drivers are also prepared to stop near less obvious destinations – just ask. Tickets can be purchased either at the kiosk by the bus stop or from the driver. A one-way fare costs $12.50, a return $21.50, valid for one year. There's also a **limo** service to the centre leaving from beside the bus platform, a shared taxi system that costs about $25 per person; limos only leave when they're full. **Taxis** charge about $40.

Air Ontario (☎925-2311) flights from Montréal, Ottawa and London, Ontario, land at the smaller **Toronto City Centre Airport**, which is on one of the islands in Toronto's harbour, close to downtown. From here, there's a free minibus service to the *Royal York Hotel*.

Well connected to most of the major towns of eastern Canada, Toronto's **bus station** is conveniently situated downtown at Bay and Dundas St West. The nearest subway station is five minutes' walk east at Yonge and Dundas. The **Union Railway Station** is also in the downtown core, at the junction of Bay Street and Front St West, with regular services from the larger cities of Ontario and Québec, supplemented by more occasional trains from the Maritime Provinces, the Prairies and Vancouver. Union Station is at the heart of Toronto's public transport system.

Information

Tourism Toronto operates a **Visitor Information Centre** (daily: May–Sept 8am–8pm; Oct–April 9am–6pm) in the city's Convention Centre at 255 Front St West – a couple of minutes' walk west from Union Station. The centre provides a comprehensive range of free information, including average-quality city maps, a *Ride Guide* to the transport system, accommodation listings in the *Annual Visitor's Guide*, and entertainment details in the monthly magazine *Where*. Tourism Toronto's **main office** is on the fifth floor of the Queen's Quay Terminal building, 207 Queen's Quay West – by the lakeshore at the foot of York Street – but they are geared up to handle telephone enquiries rather more than walkins (Mon–Fri 8.30am–5pm; phone hours Mon–Fri 8.30am–5pm, Sat 9am–5pm, Sun 9.30am–5pm; ☎203-2500 or 1-800-363-1990 toll-free within North America). In addition, the **Ontario Travel Centre** (Mon–Fri 10am–9pm, Sat 9.30am–6pm, Sun noon–5pm), inside the Eaton shopping centre at Yonge and Dundas, will usually help with Toronto enquiries, but they are more at home with provincial matters, stocking an excellent range of information on all of Ontario's major attractions. They also provide free Ontario road maps and a comprehensive camping and RV guide, and issue a series of trip planner booklets dealing with different parts of the province in detail, though the accommodation and attraction listings are far from exhaustive: presumably you have to pay to be listed.

Orientation and transport

Toronto's downtown core is sandwiched between Front Street to the south, Bloor to the north, Spadina to the west and Jarvis to the east. **Yonge Street** is the main north–south artery: principal street numbers start and names change from "West" to "East" from here. To appreciate the transition between the different downtown neighbourhoods, it's best to **walk** round the centre – Front to Bloor is about 2km, Spadina to Jarvis 1km. In an attempt to protect shoppers from Ontario's climate, there's also an enormous sequence of pedestrianized shopping arcades called the **PATH Walkway**, which begins beneath Union Station, twisting up as far as the Eaton centre – the Visitor Information Centre has free maps.

Fast, frequent and efficient, the city's **public transport** is run by the Toronto Transit Commission (TTC) and is pivoted on a simple **subway** system. One line crosses from east to west along Bloor and the other forms a loop heading north from Union Station, along both University Avenue and Yonge. The immediate area around each subway station is serviced by complementary **buses** and **streetcars**. There's also a small **Light Railway Transit** (LRT) that heads south and west from Union Station to points on the lakeshore as far as the southern end of Spadina.

Main services operate from 6am to around 1am (9am on Sundays), with a limited night-time operation. You can buy single **tickets** from bus and trolley drivers and single metallic **tokens** from subway stations for $2. More economically, a batch of ten tickets or tokens can be bought for $16 at any subway station and many convenience stores and newsagents. Students and seniors get a 33 percent discount. Each ticket or token entitles passengers to one complete journey of any length on the TTC system. If this involves more than one sort of transport, it's necessary to get a paper **transfer** at the point of entry; there are automatic machines providing transfers at subway stations. A **day pass** costs $6.50 and provides one adult with unlimited TTC travel all day on Saturdays and after 9.30am on weekdays. On Sundays, the same pass covers two adults. For the physically disabled, TTC has a special door-to-door service, **Wheel-Trans** (☎393-4111).

As far as **sightseeing tours** are concerned, Gray Line (☎594-3310) operate several different types of city tour daily from April through to October, with the two-hour version, a quick zip round the main attractions, costing $25; they pick up from major downtown hotels. Alternatively, the double-decker buses and old trolleys of Olde Town Toronto Tours (☎798-2424) shuttle round the downtown area, visiting many of the sights. You can hop on and off as you please, buses appear at regular intervals and a day's ticket costs $25.

Accommodation

Toronto has no shortage of **places to stay**, and only during major festivals and exhibitions is there any difficulty in finding somewhere reasonably convenient. The Visitor Information Centre, 255 Front St West, will help in finding a hotel room, or you can telephone Tourism Toronto down at the Queen's Quay Terminal building instead. The *Annual Visitor's Guide* contains a comprehensive list of the city's accommodation.

Most of Toronto's **hotels** occupy modern skyscrapers and although the degree of luxury does vary there is much stylistic uniformity in the standardized chain-hotel fittings and furnishings. The range of charges scrupulously reflects floor space. Prices are fairly high, but there's considerable seasonal variation and some hotels will offer discounts if you stay for a few days and are prepared to haggle. Toronto has surprisingly few **motels**, but there's a cluster on the west side of town out along Lake Shore Boulevard West, near Humber Bay Park, and these benefit from cool lake breezes in summer. If you're strapped for cash, it's best to contact one of the **Bed and Breakfast** places – or B&B agencies – we've listed, or try a hostel, or – from mid-May to August – one of the university colleges. For longer stays – say a fortnight or more – you could also consider one of the city's **apartment hotels,** where the rates are reasonable and you get a bedroom and kitchenette. There are no **campgrounds** near downtown Toronto and without your own transport the sites on the outskirts are virtually impossible to reach.

Hotels

Best Western Primrose Hotel, 111 Carlton St (☎977-8000, fax 977-4874). Big, modern high-rise hotel in a dreary part of downtown, a short walk from the Gay village. Reasonably priced doubles. Outdoor pool. Five minutes' walk east of College subway. ③.

Bond Place Hotel, 65 Dundas St East (☎362-6061, fax 360-6406). Popular with package-tour operators and ideally located, just a couple of minutes' walk from the Eaton Centre; simple, unassuming doubles; some weekend reductions. Dundas subway. ③.

Clarion Essex Park Hotel, 300 Jarvis St (☎977-4823 or 1-800-CLARION, fax 977-4830). Comfortable, convenient high-rise hotel in busy Jarvis Street. Good facilities – indoor swimming pool, sauna, etc. Five minutes' walk east of Yonge along Gerrard Street; College subway. ⑥.

Days Inn Toronto Downtown, 30 Carlton St (☎977-6655 or ☎1-800-DAYS-INN, fax 977-0502). Routine modern hotel with competitively priced rooms. Occupies a chunky tower block metres from College subway. ⑤.

Delta Chelsea Inn, 33 Gerrard St West (☎595-1975 or 1-800-243-5732, fax 585-4366). Near the Eaton Centre, this is the biggest hotel in town with excellent leisure facilities, including swimming pool, gym, sauna and childcare. The comfortable, attractively furnished rooms are a comparative bargain, with substantial weekend discounts. Dundas subway. ⑥.

Four Seasons Hotel, 21 Avenue Rd (☎964-0411, fax 964-2301). Luxurious modern hotel in the wealthy and fashionable district of Yorkville. A particularly pleasant place to stay with all mod cons – but it's pricey. Just off Bloor Street and a 5min walk north of Museum subway. ⑨.

Novotel Toronto Centre, 45 The Esplanade (☎367-8900 or 1-800-NOVOTEL, fax 360-8285). In a splendidly converted old building, with an elegant arcaded facade and other Art Deco flourishes, this polished hotel has all conveniences. Next door to one of the city's most striking skyscrapers – a bright-white triangle of glass and stone. Metres east of Union Station. ⑥.

The Royal York Hotel, 100 Front St West (☎368-2511, fax 368-2884). On completion in 1927, the *Royal York* was the largest hotel in the British Empire and retains much of its original grandeur. Rooms aren't as pricey as you'd expect, particularly at weekends. Union subway. ⑥.

Strathcona Hotel, 60 York St (☎363-3321, fax 363-4679). It doesn't look much from the outside, but this hotel occupies a handy downtown location a couple of minutes' walk from Union Station, and its air-conditioned rooms are perfectly adequate. ③.

Town Inn Suites, 620 Church St at Charles St East (☎964-3311, fax 924-9466). Large, downtown apartment hotel and hotel with good facilities. ④.

The Westin Harbour Castle, One Harbour Square (☎869-1600, fax 869-3682). An extremely plush modern hotel, with over 900 rooms, perched on the waterfront at the foot of Yonge. It has an indoor pool, saunas, jogging track, and a revolving rooftop restaurant with great views; offers good weekend discounts. Queen's Quay subway on the LRT. ⑥.

Motels

Beach Motel, 2183 Lake Shore Blvd West, near Humber Bay Park (☎259-3296). Standard-issue motel with forty comfortable rooms. ③.

Executive Motor Hotel, 621 King St West (☎504-7441, fax 504-4722). This cheap, motel-like establishment, near Bathurst and King, is near the bottom end of its price category. ③.

Shore Breeze, 2175 Lake Shore Blvd West, near Humber Bay Park (☎ & fax 251-9613). No-frills motel with seventeen rooms. ②.

Bed and Breakfast agencies

Bed and Breakfast Homes of Toronto, PO Box 46093, College Park Post Office, 444 Yonge St, Toronto, Ontario M5B 2L8 (☎363-6362). Agency for eighteen private homes dotted around town. Will readily accept last-minute bookings. Brochure on request. ②.

Bed and Breakfast Association of Downtown Toronto, PO Box 190, Station B, Toronto, Ontario M5T 2W1 (☎368-1420, fax 368-1653). Rooms in renovated downtown Victorian homes; non-smokers only. Telephone for brochure. ②.

Toronto Bed and Breakfast Inc, Box 269, 253 College St, Toronto, Ontario M5T 1R5, (☎588-8800, fax 690-5089). The city's longest-established agency representing a variety of B&Bs, most of which are downtown. Brochure on request. ③.

Bed and Breakfasts

Beverley Place B&B, 235 Beverley St (☎977-0077, fax 599-2242). Appealing and attractively restored three-storey Victorian house, kitted out with antique furnishings. A 10min walk west of Queen's Park subway along College Street. ③.

Casa Loma Inn, 21 Walmer Rd (☎924-4540, fax 259-7017). A non-smoking Victorian guesthouse in a residential area with 23 nicely decorated rooms. Dupont subway. ③.

Clarence Square, 13 Clarence Square (☎598-0616, fax 598-4200). Just a couple of blocks from the Skydome, this trim B&B occupies a nineteenth-century building and has three guest rooms. Reservations advised. ③.

Palmerston Inn B&B, 322 Palmerston Blvd (☎920-7842, fax 960-9529). On a leafy avenue, this well-maintained old house has eight guest rooms, all with air conditioning. Just off College, two blocks west of Bathurst. ③.

Hostels and college rooms

Hostelling International Toronto, 223 Church St (☎971-4440, fax 368-6499). In the heart of the city at Dundas and Church, three blocks east of the main entrance to the Eaton Centre. The 150 beds are in dorm rooms; it has a laundry and kitchen. Dundas subway. Book ahead in summer or all year for groups of six or more. Members $20, non-members $24. ②.

Marigold International Travellers' Hostel, 2011 Dundas St West (☎536-8824, fax 588-2678). Basic dormitory accommodation for $22 per person. No cooking facilities, but you get free coffee and a doughnut in the morning. Linen provided; coin laundry. Open 2pm daily. If you telephone ahead, they will collect you from the train and bus station, or even the airport. Well to the west of downtown, just over the railway bridge beyond Lansdowne Avenue. #505 streetcar west along Dundas.

The Neill Wycik College Hotel, 96 Gerrard St East (☎977-2320, fax 977-0296). The 300 rooms here are small and basic, but the location – by Ryerson Polytechnic – is very convenient. College subway. Available early May to late Aug. ②.

University of Toronto at the St George Campus, 45 Willcocks St, off Spadina Avenue (☎978-8735, fax 978-1081). Single, twin and apartment-style rooms in several college buildings dotted across the University's pleasant, downtown campus. Advance booking advised. Mid-May to late Aug. ③.

Victoria University, 140 Charles St (☎585-4522, fax 585-4530). 600-room residence, one block south of Bloor; includes breakfast. Museum subway. Mid-May to late August. Near the bottom of its price range. ③.

YWCA, 80 Woodlawn Ave East (☎923-8454, fax 923-1950). Off Yonge Street, north of downtown near Summerhill subway. 115 rooms for women only. Near the bottom of its price range. ③.

Campground

Indian Line Tourist Campground, 7625 Finch Ave West, north of the airport off Hwy 427 (☎905/678-1233, fax 678-1305). Closest campground to the centre, in the leafy Claireville Conservation Area. Water and electrical hook-ups, laundry and showers. Mid-May to mid-Oct. From $16.

Downtown Toronto

Toronto evolved from a lakeside settlement, but its growth was sporadic and often unplanned, resulting in a cityscape that can strike the visitor as a random mix of the run-down and the new. This apparent disarray, combined with the city's muggy summers, means that, rather than walking the streets, most newcomers to Toronto spend their time hopping from sight to sight on the efficient public transport system and there's no doubt that if you've only got a day or two to spare this is the way to get a grip on the city.

However, if you've the time to get below the surface, the best thing to do is stroll through **DOWNTOWN TORONTO**, and the logical place to start is the **CN Tower**, from where you can take in the lie of the land for kilometres around. Nearby **Union Station**, hub of the city's public transport system, lies on the edge of the **business** district, whose striking skyscrapers march up Yonge as far as Queen Street, where they give way to the main **shopping** area, revolving around the enormous Eaton Centre. To the west of this commercial zone there's **Chinatown** and the **Art Gallery of Ontario**; to the northwest, along University Avenue, there's the most obviously English-influenced area of town around **Queen's Park**, incorporating the Ontario Parliament building, the University of Toronto and the **Royal Ontario Museum**. On the periphery of central Toronto the key attractions are **Casa Loma** and the **Bata Shoe Museum** in the north and **Old Fort York** to the west, while the redeveloped **Harbourfront** south of Union Station offers flashy shops, the Power Plant Gallery of modern art, and the jetty from where ferries make the short hop over to the **Toronto Islands**.

The CN Tower and around

The obligatory start to a Toronto visit is to take your place in the queue at the foot of the minaret-thin **CN Tower** (daily: late May to early Sept daily 8am–11pm; early Sept to late May 9am–10pm; $12), which tapers to a point 553.33m above the waterfront just off Front St West. Tourists are whisked up its outside in leg-liquefying glass-fronted elevators to the first viewing platforms – the Indoor and Outdoor Observation Levels – at 342m, from where it's another 100m to the Space Deck (an extra $3) and views as far

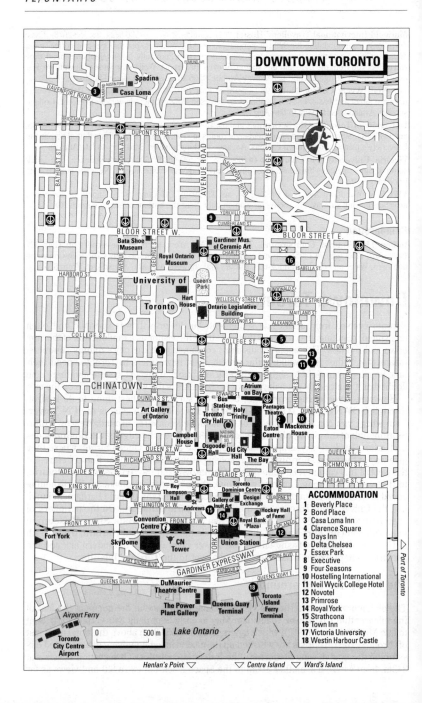

DOWNTOWN TORONTO

ACCOMMODATION

1 Beverly Place
2 Bond Place
3 Casa Loma Inn
4 Clarence Square
5 Days Inn
6 Delta Chelsea
7 Essex Park
8 Executive
9 Four Seasons
10 Hostelling International
11 Neil Wycik College Hotel
12 Novotel
13 Primrose
14 Royal York
15 Strathcona
16 Town Inn
17 Victoria University
18 Westin Harbour Castle

Spadina
Casa Loma

EDMUND AVE
DAVENPORT ROAD
BRIDGMAN AVE
AUSTIN TERR.
WALMER RD

DUPONT STREET
DAVENPORT ROAD
YONGE STREET
AVENUE ROAD
SPADINA AVE
BATHURST ST

YORKVILLE AVE
CUMBERLAND ST.
BLOOR STREET W.
BLOOR STREET E.
ISABELLA ST.

Bata Shoe Museum
Gardiner Mus. of Ceramic Art
Royal Ontario Museum
CHARLES ST.
ST. MARYS ST.
IRWIN AVE
HAYDEN ST

HARBORD ST.
University of
Queen's Park
DUNDONALD ST.
WELLESLEY STREET E.

Hart House
Toronto
Ontario Legislative Building
WELLESLEY STREET W.
MAITLAND ST.
GROSVENOR ST.
ALEXANDER ST.

COLLEGE ST.
COLLEGE ST.
CARLTON ST.

CHINATOWN
Atrium on Bay
EDWARD ST
Bus Station
Holy Trinity
Pantages Theatre
Mackenzie House

Art Gallery of Ontario
DUNDAS ST. W.
Toronto City Hall
Eaton Centre
DUNDAS ST. E.

Campbell House
NATHAN PHILLIPS SQ.
Osgoode Hall
Old City Hall
The Bay
QUEEN ST. W.
QUEEN ST. E.

RICHMOND ST. W.
RICHMOND ST. E.
ADELAIDE ST. W.
ADELAIDE ST. E.

Roy Thompson Hall
Toronto Dominion Centre
KING ST. W.
KING ST. E.

St Andrews
Gallery of Inuit Art
Design Exchange
WELLINGTON ST. W.

Hockey Hall of Fame
Royal Bank Plaza
FRONT ST. W.
THE ESPLANADE

Convention Centre
Union Station
Fort York
SkyDome
CN Tower
LAKE SHORE BLVD. W.

GARDINER EXPRESSWAY
QUEENS QUAY W.
QUEENS QUAY E.
Port of Toronto

Airport Ferry
DuMaurier Theatre Centre
Toronto Island Ferry Terminal

The Power Plant Gallery
Queens Quay Terminal

Toronto City Centre Airport

0   500 m

Lake Ontario

Henlan's Point   Centre Island   Ward's Island

TORONTO'S NEIGHBOURHOODS

One of Toronto's most striking features is its division into distinct **neighbourhoods**, many of them based on ethnic origin, others defined by sexual preference or income. Bilingual street signs identify some of these neighbourhoods, but architecturally they are often indistinguishable from their surroundings. The following rundown will help you get the most from the city's demographic mosaic, whether you want to shop, eat or just take in the atmosphere. But bear in mind that there is a certain artificiality in the nomenclature – Chinatown has hundreds of Vietnamese residents, Little Italy many Portuguese.

The Beaches, lying along and south of Queen St East between Woodbine and Victoria, is a prosperous suburb with chic boutiques and a sandy beach trimmed by a popular boardwalk.

Cabbagetown, just to the east of Yonge Street, roughly bounded by Gerrard St East on its south side, Wellesley to the north and Sumach to the east, is renowned for its Victorian housing, now occupied by a mixture of *haut bourgeois* and urban poor. Its name comes from the district's nineteenth-century immigrants, whose tiny front gardens were filled with cabbages.

Chinatown is concentrated along Dundas between Bay and Spadina, and along Spadina to King. It's one of Toronto's most distinctive neighbourhoods, with numerous busy restaurants and stores, selling anything from porcelain and jade to herbs and pickled seaweed.

The Gay and Lesbian Village, with its bars, restaurants and bookshops, is around Church and Wellesley.

Greektown, a burgeoning neighbourhood, along Danforth Avenue, between Pape and Woodbine.

Kensington Market, just north of Dundas between Spadina and Augusta, is the most ethnically diverse part of town,

combining Portuguese, West Indian and Jewish Canadians, who pack the streets with a plethora of tiny shops and open-air stalls.

Little India is along Gerrard St East, running one block west from Coxwell Avenue.

Little Italy – the *Corso Italia* – runs along St Clair Ave West between Bathurst and Lansdowne. One of Toronto's liveliest neighbourhoods.

Little Portugal lies between Dundas and College, west of Bathurst.

Queen St West, between University and Spadina, has one of the highest retail rents in the city and is home to all things trendy and expensive. The students and punks who once hung around here have moved on to what is known as Queen West west, between Spadina and Bathurst and beyond.

Yorkville, just above Bloor between Yonge and Avenue Road, was "alternative" in the 1960s, with appearances by figureheads of the counterculture, like Gordon Lightfoot and Joni Mitchell. Today, it houses some of Toronto's most expensive clothes shops and art galleries.

as Niagara Falls and Buffalo. Dispiritingly, the tower has also been equipped with a string of tacky attractions, the worst being the incongruous "ecological" area, the most enjoyable the glass floor of the Outdoor Observation Level.

Next door to the CN Tower is the home of the Blue Jays baseball team – the magnificent **Skydome** complex, which houses a colossal *McDonald's* and hosts major concerts. Hour-long Skydome **tours** (daily 9am–5pm; $9.50) give you a chance to marvel at the retractable roof – taking twenty minutes to cover no less than eight acres of turf and terrace – and the world's largest video-replay screen, but there's not much point in going if you're not getting some action for your money. The same goes for the **Roy Thompson Hall** (tours most weekdays; ☎593-4822 for schedule), just north of the CN Tower at 60 Simcoe St. Home of the Toronto Symphony Orchestra, it was finished in 1982 to a design by Arthur Erickson; by day it looks like an upturned soup bowl, but at night it's transformed as the glass-panelled walls cast light over the pavements.

In contrast, **St Andrew's Presbyterian Church**, across the street at Simcoe and King, is a reminder of an older Toronto, its Romanesque Revival towers, gables and galleries given a vaguely Norman appearance by the rose window and triple-arched entrance. Built in 1876 for a predominantly Scottish congregation, the church has a delightful interior, its cherrywood pews and balcony sloping down towards the chancel, dappled light filtered by the stained-glass windows. More importantly, St Andrew's has an admirable history of social action: the city's churches have played a leading role campaigning against poverty and homelessness since the very earliest days of settlement, and they continue to do so today.

The banking district

To the east of the CN Tower, the beaux-arts splendour of **Union Railway Station** and the matching **Royal York Hotel** mark the boundary of the banking district, whose bizarre juxtapositions of old buildings and high-rises are due to one of Toronto's stranger city ordinances. Toronto's buildings have been decreed to have a notional maximum altitude; owners of historic properties are not allowed to extend their buildings, but they are permitted to sell the empty space between their roofs and this notional maximum to the builders of new structures, who may add this volume of air to that maximum, thereby creating the skyscrapers that the ordinance would seem to forbid. The arrangement enhances neither the old nor the new, but some of the high-rises are undeniably impressive, such as the colossal twin towers of the **Royal Bank Plaza**, at Bay and Wellington, and the four reflective black blocks of the **Toronto Dominion Centre**, along Wellington St West between Bay and York. Just one of these four blocks is on the south side of Wellington and here you'll find the **Gallery of Inuit Art** (Mon–Fri 8am–6pm, Sat & Sun 10am–4pm; free), which boasts an exquisite collection of Inuit sculpture. The exhibits are owned by the Dominion Bank, who commissioned a panel of experts to collect the best of postwar Inuit art in 1965. Exhibited on two levels, their haul features some simple and forceful stonecarvings by Johnny Inukpuk, whose impressionistic style contrasts with the precision of the *Migration* by Joe Talirunili, in which the rowers crane forward in eagerness and anxiety. Even more detailed is the incised caribou antler from Cape Dorset, on which natural dyes pick out a cartoon strip of Inuit life.

Around the corner at 234 Bay St, the old **Toronto Stock Exchange** has been mutilated by its incorporation within a skyrise that imitates – but doesn't match – the sober black blocks of the adjacent Toronto Dominion Centre. Nevertheless, the facade has survived, its stone lintel decorated with muscular carvings of men at work, a frieze given a political twist by the top-hatted figure – the capitalist – who dips his hand into a worker's pocket, a subversive subtext by an unknown stonemason. The interior of the Stock Exchange now accommodates the temporary exhibitions of the **Design Exchange** (Tues–Fri 10am–6pm, Sat & Sun noon–5pm; $5), the DX, whose purpose is to foster innovative design.

From the DX, it's a short stroll to the old Bank of Montréal building, a solid Neoclassical edifice of 1885 that houses the **Hockey Hall of Fame**, 30 Yonge St at Front (late June to Aug Mon–Sat 9.30am–6pm, Sun 10am–6pm; Sept to late June Mon–Fri 10am–5pm, Sat 9.30am–6pm, Sun 10.30am–5pm; $9.50). The place is stuffed with ice hockey memorabilia, has a replica of the Montréal Canadiens' dressing room and proudly exhibits the sport's most important trophy, the Stanley Cup.

City Hall and around

One of the most distinctive of Toronto's landmarks lies across Queen Street, to the north of the banking zone – **Nathan Phillips Square**. Laid out by the Finnish architect Viljo Revell, the square is overlooked by his **City Hall**, whose curved glass and concrete towers bracket a sort of central mushroom, in turn fronted by *The Archer*, a Henry Moore sculpture that resembles a giant kidney. Revell won all sorts of awards for this project, which seemed the last word in thrusting dynamism but has faded into a desolate symbol of 1960s urban planning. On a positive note, it is at least associated with political change – its sponsor, Nathan Phillips, was Toronto's first Jewish mayor. Had Phillips's grand scheme been carried out fully, the city would have lost the **Old City Hall**, on the east side of the square, a flamboyant pseudo-Romanesque building, whose front is a hectic jangle of towers, columns and arches beneath a copper-green roof. Completed in 1899, it was designed by E.J. Lennox who had a fractious relationship with his paymasters on the city council and took his revenge by carving gargoyle-like representations of the city fathers on the arches at the top of the front steps.

Immediately to the west of Nathan Phillips Square, along Queen Street, stands **Osgoode Hall**, a Neoclassical pile built for the Law Society of Upper Canada early in the nineteenth century. Looking like a cross between a Greek temple and an English country house, it's protected by a wrought-iron fence and gates, designed to keep cows and horses off the lawn. The elegant Georgian mansion on the opposite side of University Avenue is **Campbell House** (late May to mid–Oct Mon–Fri 9.30am– 4.30pm, mid-Oct–late May Mon–Fri only; Sat & Sun noon–4.30pm; $3.50), built on Adelaide Street for Sir William Campbell, Chief Justice and Speaker of the Legislative Assembly – it was transported here in 1972. There are regular guided tours of the period interior and these provide a well-researched overview of early nineteenth-century Toronto, in which Campbell was a leading figure, and a progressive one too, eschewing the death penalty whenever feasible and even awarding the radical William MacKenzie damages when his printing press was wrecked by a mob of Tories in 1826.

The Eaton Centre and the Thomson Gallery

A couple of minutes' walk from the Old City Hall, the **Eaton Centre** stretches south from its main entrance at Dundas and Yonge all the way to Queen Street, its four-storey assortment of shops and restaurants spread out underneath a glass-and-steel arched roof. Timothy Eaton, an Ulster immigrant, opened his first store here in 1869, and his cash-only, fixed-price, money-back-guarantee trading revolutionized the Canadian market. Soon a Canadian institution, Eaton kept a grip on the pioneer settlements in the west through his mail-order catalogue, known as the "homesteader's bible" – or the "wish book" amongst native peoples. The company runs department stores in all of Canada's big cities, and has tried to keep ahead of the competition by investing heavily in shopping complexes like this one, but recently it has struggled to keep afloat.

At the southern end of the Eaton Centre, a first-floor walkway crosses Queen Street into The Bay store, where, on the eighth floor, you'll find the crystal chandeliers and Greco-Roman decor of the *Arcadian Court Restaurant*. Up above, on the ninth floor, is the **Thomson Gallery** (Mon–Sat 11am–5pm; $2), which offers an outstanding introduction to many of Canada's finest artists, especially the Group of Seven (see p.79). Highlights include an impressive selection of paintings by Lawren Harris, like his almost surrealistic *Lake Superior*, and a small selection of paintings by J.E.H. MacDonald, whose *Rowan Berries* of 1922 stands out. Tom Thomson, the main inspiration of the Seven, is represented by the vivid *Maple Saplings* and his heated *Autumn's Garland,* blotchy contrasts with A.Y. Jackson's smooth-flowing *Road to Chicoutimi* and the wriggling spirals of his *Yellowknife Country*, in which the trees swirl above a heaving, purplish earth. Franklin Carmichael, the youngest original member of the Group, also

GLENN GOULD

In the 1970s, anyone passing the Eaton department store around 9pm on any day of the year might have seen the door unlocked for a distracted-looking figure swaddled in over-coat, scarves, gloves and hat. This character, making his way to a recording studio set up for his exclusive use inside the shop, was perhaps the most famous citizen of Toronto and the most charismatic pianist in the world – **Glenn Gould**.

Not the least remarkable thing about Gould was that very few people outside the CBS recording crew would ever hear him play live. In 1964, aged just 32, he had retired from the concert platform, partly out of a distaste for the accidental qualities of any live performance, partly out of hatred for the cult of the virtuoso. Yet no pianist ever provided more material for the mythologizers. He possessed a memory so prodigious that none of his acquaintances was ever able to find a piece of music he could not instantly play perfectly, but he loathed much of the standard piano repertoire, dismissing romantic composers such as Chopin, Liszt and Rachmaninoff as little more than showmen. Dauntingly cerebral in his tastes and playing style, he was nonetheless an ardent fan of Barbra Streisand – an esteem that was fully reciprocated – and once wrote an essay titled "In Search of Petula Clark". He lived at night and kept in touch by phoning his friends in the small hours of the morning, talking for so long that his monthly phone bill ran into thousands of dollars. Detesting all blood sports (a category in which he placed concert performances), he would terrorize anglers on Lake Simcoe by buzzing them in his motorboat. He travelled everywhere with bags full of medicines and would never allow anyone to shake his hand, yet soaked his arms in almost scalding water before playing in order to get his circulation going. At the keyboard he sang loudly to himself, swaying back and forth on a creaky little chair made for him by his father – all other pianists sat too high, he insisted. And even in a heatwave he was always dressed as if a blizzard were imminent. To many of his colleagues Gould's eccentricities were maddening, but what mattered was that nobody could play like Glenn Gould. As one exasperated conductor put it, "the nut's a genius".

Gould's first recording, Bach's *Goldberg Variations*, was released in 1956, became the best-selling classical record of that year, and has remained available ever since. Soon after, he became the first Western musician to play in the Soviet Union, where his reputation spread so quickly that for his final recital more than a thousand people were allowed to stand in the aisles of the Leningrad hall. On his debut in Berlin, the leading German critic described him as "a young man in a strange sort of trance", whose "technical ability borders on the fabulous". The technique always dazzled, but Gould's fiercely wayward intelligence made his interpretations controversial, as can be gauged from the fact that Leonard Bernstein, conducting Gould on one occasion, felt obliged to inform the audience that what they were about to hear was the pianist's responsibility, not his. Most notoriously of all, he had a very low opinion of Mozart's abilities – and went so far as to record the Mozart sonatas in order to demonstrate that Wolfgang Amadeus died too late rather than too soon.

Gould's legacy of recordings is not confined to music. He made a trilogy of radio documentaries on the theme of solitude: *The Quiet in the Land*, about Canada's Mennonites; *The Latecomers*, about the inhabitants of Newfoundland; and *The Idea of North*, for which he taped interviews with people who, like himself, spent much of their time amid Canada's harshest landscapes. Just as Gould's Beethoven, Bach and Mozart sounded like nobody else's, these were documentaries like no others, each a complex weave of voices spliced and overlaid in compositions that are overtly musical in construction. However, Gould's eighty-odd piano recordings are the basis of his enduring popularity, and nearly all of them have been reissued on CD, spanning Western keyboard music from Orlando Gibbons to Arnold Schoenberg. One of the most poignant is his second version of the *Goldberg*, the last record to be issued before his sudden death in 1982 at the age of 50 – the age at which he had said he would give up playing the piano entirely.

developed a flowing, harmonious technique, a beautiful example being his *Cranberry Lake* of 1931. Finally, a contemporary of the Group of Seven, Emily Carr, was famous for her paintings of west coast Indian villages and the totemic figures she developed as a symbol of native culture. *Thunderbird, Campbell River BC* and *Thunderbird* are good examples of her later style, a marked progression from the fastidiousness of the early *Gitwangak, Queen Charlotte Islands*.

The gallery's assortment of early and mid-nineteenth century Canadian and Canada-based artists is less distinguished, but there are some fine canvases, such as the curiously unflattering *Portrait of Joseph Brant* by William Berczy and the winter scenes typical of the work of Cornelius Krieghoff (see p.153). Interesting in a different way is the series by the artist-explorer **Paul Kane**, whose paintings show a conflict of subject and style that highlights the achievement of the Group of Seven in finding an indigenous manner: Kane's *Landscape in the Foothills with Buffalo Resting*, for example, looks more like a placid German valley than the prairies. Born in Ireland in 1810, Kane first emigrated to Toronto in the early 1820s, but returned to Europe at the age of 30, where, ironically enough, he was so impressed by an exhibition of paintings on the American Indian that he promptly decided to move back to Canada. In 1846, he finally wangled himself a place on a westward-bound fur-trading expedition and started an epic journey – travelling from Thunder Bay to Edmonton by canoe, crossing the Rockies by horse, and finally returning to Toronto two years after setting out. During his time away Kane made some seven hundred sketches, which he then proceeded to paint onto canvas, paper and cardboard, and in 1859 published *Wanderings of an Artist among the Indian Tribes of North America*, the story of his journey. It includes this account of Christmas dinner at Fort Edmonton: "At the head, before Mr Harriett, was a large dish of boiled buffalo hump; at the foot smoked a boiled buffalo calf . . . one of the most esteemed dishes among the epicures of the interior. My pleasing duty was to help a dish of mouffle, or dried moose nose [while] the worthy priest helped the buffalo tongue and Mr Randall cut up the beaver's tails. The centre of the table was graced with piles of potatoes, turnips and bread conveniently placed, so that each could help himself without interrupting the labours of his companions. Such was our jolly Christmas dinner at Edmonton."

At the back of the Eaton Centre, the appealing nineteenth-century brick **church of the Holy Trinity** and its surrounding square were only just saved from the developers. It was here, with the church set against the skyscrapers that crowd in on it, that the Canadian director David Cronenberg filmed the last shot of *Dead Ringers*. Interestingly Cronenberg was responsible for a classic quote in fending off criticism of his subject matter – "I don't have a moral plan. I'm a Canadian."

It's hardly an essential visit, but the **Mackenzie House** (daily except Mon: winter noon–4pm; summer noon–5pm; $3.50), a five-minute walk east from the Eaton Centre at 82 Bond St and Dundas, is of some interest as the home of William Lyon Mackenzie. Born in Scotland, Mackenzie moved to Toronto where he scraped a living publishing *The Colonial Advocate*, a radical anti-Tory newspaper. Frustrated by the clique who ran the colony, Mackenzie was one of the leaders of the Rebellion of 1837, after which he was obliged to spend twelve years in exile in the US until he was pardoned. Mackenzie lived in these premises on Bond Street for just a couple of years (1859–61), and the house has been restored to an approximation of its appearance at that time, complete with a print shop of 1845 whose workings are demonstrated by costumed guides..

The Art Gallery of Ontario

Just west of University Avenue along Dundas St West, hemmed in by the bustle of **Chinatown**, looms the home of the **Art Gallery of Ontario** – or AGO (mid-May to mid-Oct Tues–Fri noon–9pm, Sat & Sun 10am–5.30pm, mid-Oct to mid-May Wed–Fri noon–9pm, Sat & Sun 10am–5.30pm; recommended donation $5) – a place renowned both for its excellent temporary exhibitions and for its extensive collection of international art. A recent refurbishment has also softened the lines of what was originally a harsh, lumpen exterior, and inside all is light, space and harmony.

On the ground floor, the central Walker Court is surrounded on three sides by the **European art** of the seven Old Masters galleries, covering the Italian Renaissance to French Impressionism. Early works include some rather pedestrian Italian altarpieces, but pick up with the Northern Schools in which Pieter Bruegel the Younger's incident-packed *Peasants' Wedding* is a particular highlight. There's also a fifteenth-century *Expulsion of the Money Changers* by the Master of the Kress Epiphany, featuring Christ dispelling the uglies with a length of knotted rope, and nearby an *Adam and Eve* by Lucas Cranach creates a disconcerting set of colour contrasts. Other **Flemish** painters represented include Van Dyck, Cuyp, Frans Hals, Goyen and Carel Fabritius, whose exquisite *Portrait of a Lady with a Handkerchief* is one of the few of his works to have survived the powder-magazine explosion that killed him and destroyed most of his paintings at Delft in 1654. **French** painters are much in evidence too, from the seventeeth century onwards; look out for *St Anne with the Christ Child* by Georges de la Tour, with its distinctive handling of candlelight illuminating the faces, and Poussin's *Venus Presenting Aeneas with Arms*. The **Impressionist** pictures include Degas's archetypal *Woman Drying Herself after a Bath*, Renoir's screaming-pink *Concert* of 1918, and Monet's wonderful *Vétheuil in Summer*, with its hundreds of tiny jabs of colour. The fourth side of Walker Court is bordered by the 20th Century European Art gallery, where pride of place goes to Picasso's classically cubist *Seated Woman*, Marc Chagall's *Over Vitebsk*, a whimsical celebration of his Russian birthplace, and Paul Gauguin's evocative *Hina and Fatu*, a wooden stump carved with Polynesian figures. Other neighbouring galleries are used for temporary exhibitions.

On the first floor, the strong suit of the **Canadian Historical Art** section is the cross-section of work from the **Group of Seven** (see box opposite) and their contemporaries, with the key paintings accompanied by a wealth of background information. One of the most distinctive artists of the Group of Seven was **Lawren Harris**, whose *Above Lake Superior* of 1922 is a pivotal work – nothing he had done before had the same clarity of conception, with its bare birch stumps framing a dark mountain beneath Art Deco clouds. Nearby, his large and brilliant *Lake and Mountains* has a mass of frosty ice spitting into the sky above deep-green mountains and a silvery green lake, an ejaculatory image if ever there was one.

Fred Varley, another founder member, preferred softer images and subtler colours, exemplified by the sticky-looking brushstrokes of *Moonlight after Rain*, whereas his friend **J.E.H. MacDonald** was fond of dynamic, sweeping effects, his panoramic *Falls, Montréal River* setting turbulent rapids beside hot-coloured hillsides. A sample of **A.Y. Jackson**'s work includes the characteristically carpet-like surface of *Algoma Rocks, Autumn, 1923*, while **A.J. Casson**'s bright and rather formal *Old Store at Salem* offers a break from the scenic preoccupations of the rest of the Seven – though Varley's soft-hued portraits break the mould too. **Emily Carr**, represented by several works here, was a great admirer of the Seven, but she was never accepted as a member despite her obvious abilities. Perhaps the most famous of all Canadian paintings is here as well – *The West Wind* by the greatly influential **Tom Thomson**, who was the first to approach wilderness landscapes with the determination of an explorer. It accompanies several of his less familiar (but no less powerful) works, including a moody *Northern Lake* and a Cubist-influenced preparatory painting, *Autumn Foliage 1915*.

The Canadian Historical Art section also features the work of earlier leading figures – most notably Paul Kane (see p.153) and Cornelius Krieghoff (see p.153) – and there's a small gallery of Inuit art too, but most of the rest of the first floor is given over to temporary exhibitions and the AGO's permanent collection of **Contemporary Art,** show-

THE GROUP OF SEVEN

In the autumn of 1912, a commercial artist by the name of **Tom Thomson** returned from an extended trip to the Mississauga country, north of Georgian Bay, with a bag full of sketches that were to add a new momentum to Canadian art. His friends, many of them fellow employees of the art firm of Grip Ltd in Toronto, saw Thomson's naturalistic approach to native subject matter as a pointer away from the influence of Europe, declaring the "northland" as the true Canadian "painter's country". World War I and the death of Thomson – who drowned in 1917 – delayed these artists' ambitions, but in 1920 they formed the **Group of Seven**: Franklin H. Carmichael, Lawren Harris, A.Y. Jackson, Arthur Lismer, J.E.H. MacDonald, F.H. Varley and Frank Johnston (later joined by A.J. Casson, L.L. Fitzgerald and Edwin Holgate). Working under the unofficial leadership of Harris, they explored the wilds of Algoma in the late 1910s, travelling around in a converted freight car, and later foraged even further afield, from Newfoundland and Baffin Island to BC.

They were immediately successful, staging forty shows in eleven years, a triumph due in large part to Harris's many influential contacts. However, there was also a genuine popular response to the intrepid frontiersman element of their aesthetics. Art was a matter of "taking to the road" and "risking all for the glory of a great adventure", as they wrote in 1922, whilst "nature was the measure of a man's stature" according to Lismer. Symbolic of struggle against the elements, the Group's favourite symbol was the lone pine set against the sky, an image whose authenticity was confirmed by reference to the "manly" poetry of Walt Whitman.

The legacy of the Group of Seven is double-edged. On the one hand, they rediscovered the Canadian wilderness and established the autonomy of Canadian art. On the other, their contribution was soon institutionalized, and well into the 1950s it was difficult for Canadian painters to establish an identity that didn't conform to the Group's precepts. Among many practising artists the Group is unpopular, but the Ontario artist Graham Coughtry is generous: "They're the closest we've ever come to having some kind of romantic heroes in Canadian painting."

casing works by European, British and American artists. In particular, watch out for Warhol's *Elvis I* and *II*, Mark Rothko's powerful *No.1 White and Red* and Claes Oldenburg's quirky if somewhat frayed *Hamburger* of 1962. The contemporary art culminates in the **Henry Moore Sculpture Gallery**, the world's largest collection of pieces by Moore, which includes a representative range of his work in different media from woodcuts and etchings to bronze and plaster casts. Look out for the charming series of pen-and-ink drawings of sheep.

On the south side of the AGO, and accessible from the ground-floor galleries, is **The Grange**, an early nineteenth-century house that was the original home of the gallery. The interior has been restored as a gentleman's house of the 1830s, with the usual costumed guides on hand to answer questions.

The Ontario Legislative Assembly Building and Toronto University

University Avenue cuts north from Dundas to College lined by gleaming tower blocks and overlooked by the pink sandstone mass of the **Ontario Legislative Assembly Building** (summer daily 9am–4.30pm; winter Mon–Fri 9am–3.30pm; frequent free guided tours), which was completed in 1892. No one could say this Romanesque Revival edifice was elegant, but its ponderous symmetries speak volumes of the bourgeois assertiveness that drove the provincial economy, whilst the long hallways of the interior sport some enjoyable Canadian paintings. Incidentally, accusations of political corruption have always been ten-a-penny in Ontario, but even so the choice of architect was a surprise, for Richard Waite, the chairman of the appropriate committee, selected himself.

Behind the Legislative Building, at the centre of modest **Queen's Park**, stands a heavyweight equestrian statue of King Edward VII in full-dress uniform, an imperial leftover that was originally plonked down in Delhi – and you can't help but feel the Indians must have been pleased to off-load it. Bordering the park are the various faculties of the **University of Toronto**, opened in 1843 and the province's most prestigious academic institution. Its older buildings, with their quadrangles, ivy-covered walls and Gothic interiors, deliberately evoke Oxbridge: **Hart House**, on the west side of the park, at the end of Wellesley Street, is the best example, attached to the **Soldier's Tower**, a neo-Gothic memorial to those students who died in both world wars. The arcaded gallery abutting the tower lists the dead of World War I and is inscribed with the Canadian John McCrae's *In Flanders Fields*, arguably the war's best-known Canadian poem.

The Royal Ontario Museum and the Gardiner Museum of Ceramic Art

The **Royal Ontario Museum** (ROM), by the Museum subway at Queen's Park and Bloor (Mon & Wed–Sat 10am–6pm, Tues till 8pm, Sun 11am–6pm; $10, free Tues after 4.30pm), contains one of the country's most ambitious collections of fine and applied art, albeit a collection whose intended scope sometimes overstretches its physical resources. It's basically a jumble of disparate private collections, but there's more than enough first-rank stuff here to fill an afternoon – longer if you want to examine the Chinese material; a particular highlight. The museum is spread over four floors and a free map is available at reception; a ticket entitles visitors to a same-day discount at the the **McLaughlin Planetarium**, next door.

The ROM starts with two colossal **totem poles** from British Columbia, bolted into the stairwells just beyond the domed entrance hall. Amazing elemental objects, they're decorated with stylized carvings representing the supernatural animals and birds that were associated with their owners and their particular clan. The best known of native art forms, totem poles were a by-product of European trade – imported metal tools enabled the Indians to increase the size of their carvings, while the fur trade brought both economic prosperity and intense rivalry, from which the totem pole emerged as a symbol of clan status. Production peaked on the Pacific coast in the 1860s, but, mirroring the collapse of the local economy, the art had virtually disappeared by the turn of the century.

Beyond the totem poles, the **street level** of the ROM holds an extraordinary range of exhibits from the **Far East**, including fine Hindu and Buddhist sculptures and a sample of Imperial Chinese applied art, notably a collection of ceramic head cushions and an extraordinary number of snuff bottles made from quartz, bronze, silver, glass – even tangerine skin. However, the star turn here is the monumental Ming Tomb, the only complete example on display in the West – though it is a conglomerate version. Thought to date from the seventeenth century, the tomb and its archways are guarded by beautifully carved animals and servants. The **second level** deals with the **Life Sciences**, featuring several sections on evolution, innumerable stuffed animals, an "interactive" mock-up of a bat cave, and a magnificent set of dinosaur skeletons recovered from the Alberta badlands. Moving on, the **third level** concentrates on the ancient Mediterranean, whilst in the basement – called **One Below** – lurks the Canadian Heritage section, which is largely devoted to the rather uninspiring Sigmund Samuel collection of furniture and decorative arts. That said, the intimate wood-panelled Belanger room, carved in the 1820s and transported here from St-Jean-Port-Joli in Québec, is a delight. This section also stages some interesting semi-permanent exhibitions on topics such as native peoples and refugees in Canada.

Across the road from the ROM, the **Gardiner Museum of Ceramic Art** (Mon & Wed–Sat 10am–5pm, Tues till 8pm, Sun 11am–5pm; free, donation requested) is the purpose-built home of the stunning ceramics collection of George Gardiner, local businessman-turned aesthete. Well presented, labelled and described, the collection focuses on four specialisms: Pre-Columbian pottery; Italian majolica (brightly coloured, tin-glazed earthenware of the Italian Renaissance); English Delftware; and eighteenth-century European porcelain. The most popular section is devoted to the tiny porcelain figures inspired by the commedia dell'arte and placed on dinner tables by the aristocracy to amuse their guests; perhaps the most unusual is the series of Delftware serving plates – or chargers – that bare crude but somehow rather whimsical portraits of English monarchs.

Bata Shoe Museum

Within easy walking distance of the ROM, the **Bata Shoe Museum**, 327 Bloor St West at St George (Tues, Wed, Fri & Sat 10am–5pm, Thurs 10am–8pm, Sun noon–5pm; closed Mon; $6), was designed by Raymond Moriyama, the much-lauded, Vancouver-born architect whose other prestigious creations include the Ontario Science Centre and Toronto's Reference Library. This particular structure was built for Sonja Bata, of the Bata shoe manufacturing family, to house the fabulous assortment of footwear that she has spent a lifetime collecting. There's everything imagineable on display here, from antique French chestnut-crushing boots and Chinese silk shoes for binding women's feet through to sixteenth-century platform shoes from Venice. Celebrity footwear includes Elvis Presley's blue-and-white patent-leather loafers, Queen Victoria's ballroom slippers and Robert Redford's cowboy boots – not to mention Pierre Trudeau's hiking sandals and Louis Riel's snowshoes. An imaginative and fascinating museum: it's well worth a visit.

Casa Loma and Spadina

A couple of minutes' walk north of Dupont subway station, along Spadina to Davenport Road, a flight of steps leads to Toronto's most bizarre attraction, **Casa Loma** (daily 9.30am–4pm; $8), an enormous towered and turreted mansion built to the instructions of Sir Henry Pellatt between 1911 and 1914. Every inch the self-made man, Pellatt made a fortune by pioneering the use of hydroelectricity, harnessing the power of Niagara Falls to light Ontario's expanding cities. Determined to construct a house no one could ignore, Sir Henry gathered furnishings from all over the world and even imported Scottish stonemasons to build the wall around his six-acre property. He spent more than $3million fulfilling his dream, but business misfortunes and the rising cost of servants forced him to move out in 1923, earning him the nickname of "Pellatt the Plunger". His legacy is a strange mixture of medieval fantasy and early twentieth-century technology: secret passageways and an elevator, claustrophobic wood-panelled rooms confused by gargantuan pipes and plumbing.

Free diagrams of the layout of the house are available at reception – taped commentaries along the suggested route elucidate such mysteries as why Sir Henry took to dressing up in a costume that combined a British colonel's uniform with the attire of a Mohawk chief. The main entrance is on the first floor, near Sir Henry's favourite room, the study, with secret passageways leading to the wine cellar and his wife's suite. Nearby, the Great Hall is a pseudo-Gothic extravagance with a eighteen-metre high, cross-beamed ceiling and enough floor space to accommodate several hundred guests. In a touch worthy of Errol Flynn, the hall is overlooked by a balcony at the end of Pellatt's second-floor bedroom; in a typically odd contrast, the bathroom behind the bedroom is 1910s white-marble high-tech, featuring an elaborate multinozzled shower.

Next door, **Spadina House** (tours Tues–Sun noon–5pm; closes 4pm winter weekdays; $5) is an elegant Victorian property whose modesty is in striking contrast to the pretensions of its neighbour. Until 1980, it was the residence of the Austin family, the descendants of the Irish founder of the Toronto Dominion Bank, and as a result nearly all the contents are genuine antiques. Particular highlights include an inventive and delicate Art Nouveau decorative frieze in the billiard room, an assortment of period chairs designed to accommodate the largest of bustles, and a trap door in the conservatory that allowed the gardeners to come and go unseen by their employers. The open fanlights above the doors were inspired by Florence Nightingale, whose much-publicized experiences of sickness in the Crimea had convinced her of the need for a good flow of air.

The Harbourfront and the Toronto Islands

In recent years, an ambitious and massively expensive redevelopment programme has transformed **the Harbourfront**, the zone extending west from the foot of Yonge, into one of the more fashionable parts of the city. It's best reached from Union Station by the LRT, which brings you within a few metres of the **Harbourfront Centre**, at the southern end of York, which incorporates the du Maurier Theatre Centre, Molson Place, an outside performance area, and the **Power Plant Contemporary Art Gallery** (Tues & Thurs–Sun noon–6pm, Wed till 8pm; $4). Beyond, a pleasant lakeside walkway extends west as far as Bathurst, passing restaurants, lakeside condominiums, office suites and marinas.

Several operators run lake cruises from the Harbourfront, but you can get just as good a view more cheaply from the ferry ride over to the **Toronto Islands**, the low-lying, crescent-shaped sandbanks that protect the city's harbour. From the late nineteenth century, the islands were popular with day-tripping Torontonians, who rowed across to enjoy the cool lake breezes and sample some rather odd attractions – including J.W. Gorman's "diving horses", who would jump into the lake from a high-diving board. Today, the islands are maintained by the Toronto Parks Department, who keep the islands spotless and car-free. There are three main islands, connected by bridges: to the east is **Ward's Island**, a quiet residential area with parkland and wilderness; in the middle, **Centre Island** is the busiest and the most developed; and to the west, **Hanlan's Point**, edging Toronto's tiny City Centre Airport, has the best sandy beach – though Lake Ontario is too polluted for swimming. Some 6km from one end to the other, the islands are readily explored on foot or by bike – there are cycle rental places on Centre Island – and make sure to drop by the Centreville Amusement Park; there's nothing garish here, instead the children's rides are delightfully folksy with paddle boats shaped as swans and suchlike.

Ferries to the islands leave from the foot of Yonge Street, next door to the *Westin Harbour Castle Hotel*; they take ten minutes to make the crossing and cost $4 return (Ward's Island daily: June–Sept 6.35am–11.15pm at least hourly; Oct–May 6.35am–11pm at least every 2hr; Hanlan's Point June–Sept daily 8am–9.30pm at least hourly; Oct–May Mon–Fri 4 daily; Centre Island June–Sept daily 9am–10.30pm hourly).

West of the Harbourfront: Fort York and Exhibition Place

Modern Toronto improbably traces its origins to the ill-starred **Fort York** (July & Aug daily 10am–5pm; Sept–June closed Mon; $5), built to reinforce British control of Lake Ontario in 1793. It was never properly fortified, partly through lack of funds and partly because it was too remote to command much attention, and within ten years the stockade was in a state of disrepair, even though the township of York had become the capital of Upper Canada. In 1811 the deterioration in Anglo-American relations prompted a refortification, but its main military achievement was entirely accidental. Forced to evacuate the fort in 1813, the British blew up the gunpowder magazine, but underestimated the force of the explosion. They killed ten of their own number and 250 of the advancing enemy, including the splendidly named American general, Zebulon Pike. After the war, Fort York was refurbished and its garrison – the largest local consumer of supplies – made a considerable contribution to the development of Toronto, as York was renamed in 1834.

Fort York is situated in the shadow of the Gardiner Expressway, a fifteen-minute walk west from Union Station: follow Front St West to the end, turn left down Bathurst and, after crossing the railway bridge, take the signposted footpath on the right that leads to the fort's rear entrance. The site was opened as a museum in 1934, and is now staffed by guides who provide informative and free tours that take about an hour, or you can wander around under your own steam. The meticulously restored ramparts enclose a sequence of log, stone and brick buildings, notably the attractive **Officers' Quarters** and a stone **powder magazine**, built with two-metre-thick walls and sparkproof copper and brass fixtures. The **Blue Barracks**, or junior officers' quarters, have an absorbing exhibition on the various military crises that afflicted nineteenth-century Canada, including the War of 1812 and the curious affair of the Fenian raids launched from the US in the 1860s. During the American Civil War, the British had continued to trade with the Confederacy, much to the chagrin of the North. After the war, many believed that the US was itching for the opportunity to seize Canada, no one more so than the **Fenian Brotherhood**, formed by Irish exiles in New York in 1857. Their tactics were simple: believing that an unofficial international incident would push Washington into action, they organized a series of cross-border raids, the most serious of which, in 1866, involved 1000 men. In the event, British regulars drove the Fenians out and Congress didn't take the bait.

From the front entrance of Fort York, it's a ten-minute walk along Garrison Road to busy Strachan Avenue, where Princes' Gate is the grandiose gateway to **Exhibition Place**, a huge complex trapped between Lake Shore Boulevard and the Gardiner Expressway, and reached on the Bathurst streetcar (#511). Used for trade fairs, concerts and sports events, the complex also contains a moderately diverting **Marine Museum** (summer: Tues–Fri 10am–5pm, Sat & Sun noon–5pm; winter: Tues–Fri 10am–4pm; $3.50), located in an old barracks close to Princes' Gate and concentrating on the development of local shipping, complete with a 1930s tug, the *Ned Hanlan*.

From beside the Marine Museum, a footbridge crosses Lake Shore Boulevard to **Ontario Place**, a theme-park-cum-entertainment-complex built on three artificial islands.

Greater Toronto

The satellite suburbs and industrial areas that make up most of **GREATER TORONTO** are of little appeal, a string of formless settlements sprawling over a largely flat and dreary landscape that extends from Scarborough in the east to Mississauga in the west and north as far as the districts around Steeles Avenue. In all this area, there's only one really distinctive geographic feature: the cliffs that make up the **Scarborough Bluffs**. Yet the region is home to several impressive attractions, notably the **Ontario Science Centre**, which comes complete with dozens of interactive science displays, the **McMichael Collection** of the Group of Seven's paintings, and the garish extravagance of Paramount's **Wonderland**.

Ontario Science Centre

Opened in 1969, the **Ontario Science Centre**, 11km from downtown at 770 Don Mills Rd, North York (daily: July & Aug 10am–8pm; Sept–June 10am–5pm, Wed till 8pm, Fri till 9pm; $8), bills itself as a "vast playground of science" and draws more than one million visitors a year. The centre traces the development of technology through some seven hundred exhibits, many of which invite participation – staring at strangely coloured Canadian flags until you go dotty, piloting a spacecraft, or having your hair raised by a Van der Graaf generator, and there's a massive Omnimax Theatre too, with a 24-metre dome screen ($8; combined ticket with the Centre $13). You could spend a day here on your own, though it's much more enjoyable with kids. To get there, take the Bloor Street subway east to Pape, transfer to the Don Mills bus and get off right in front on the Don Mills Road at St Dennis Drive.

Paramount Canada's Wonderland
Located at Vaughan, 30km from downtown and immediately east of Hwy 400 at the Rutherford Road exit, **Paramount Canada's Wonderland** (days of opening and closing times vary – call ☎905/832-7000 for information) is Toronto's Disneyworld, a theme park featuring over fifty different rides spread across several different themed areas such as "Hanna Barbera Land". Wonderland's roller-coaster rides are enough to make the strongest stomachs churn, if the kitsch doesn't do it first. By public transport, catch the Wonderland Express GO bus from Yorkdale or York Mills subway station; buses leave every hour and take forty minutes.

Toronto Zoo
Toronto Zoo (daily: summer 9am–7.30pm; winter 9.30am–4.30pm; $12), 40km from downtown near Hwy 401 at Meadowvale Road in Scarborough, covers no less than 710 acres and has over 5000 animals exhibited in re-creations of their natural habitats – which in the case of the African species means enormous wood and glass pavilions. The North American animals are kept in the Rouge River Valley surrounding the main part of the zoo, and they can be visited by monorail.

For access from the city, take the Bloor subway to Kennedy then transfer to bus #86A.

The McMichael Canadian Art Collection
The **McMichael Canadian Art Collection** (late May to mid-Oct daily 10am–5pm; mid-Oct to late May Tues–Sat 10am–4pm, Sun 10am–5pm; $7) is situated in the commuter township of Kleinburg, roughly 40km northwest of downtown, off Hwy 400. The collection, housed in a series of handsome log and stone buildings in the wooded Humber River valley, was put together by Robert and Signe McMichael, devoted followers of the Group of Seven, and given to the province in 1965. Of particular interest is the Tom Thomson Gallery, featuring many of the small panels the artist painted on location in preparation for the full-sized canvases he worked on back in his studio. Gallery 5, The Spirit of the Land, is of similar interest as it concentrates on the early work of the Group as they explored their country from coast to coast. Three other exhibition areas are devoted to Canada's native peoples, including contemporary Indian art and Inuit soapstone carvings and lithographs.

From downtown Toronto, it's just about possible to make a day-trip visit to the McMichael by subway and bus, but effectively you need your own transport.

Eating and drinking

To get the best from Toronto's kitchens, head for any one of the city's **ethnic neighbourhoods**, where there's an abundance of good **restaurants**, or go to one of the many downtown **cafés**, **café-bars** or **restaurants** that have carefully nurtured a good reputation. Toronto's shopping malls are dominated by chain restaurants, most of which offer bland and basic fare, and a similar criticism also applies to many of the city's hotels, whose café-restaurants serve mundane food at prices that roughly parallel the hotel's tariff. Many of the city's restaurants emphasize their use of Canadian ingredients – fish and wild-animal meat especially – but there's no real distinctive local cuisine: if there is a Toronto dish, it's hamburger, fries and salad.

Prices range from the deluxe, where a meal will set you back upwards of $60, to the cheap fast-food chains, where a decent-sized snack or sandwich works out at about $9. The majority of Toronto's restaurants fall somewhere in between – a $25 bill per person for a two-course meal, excluding drinks, is a reasonable average. Most of the city's popular restaurants feature bargain daily specials from about $7 upwards and serve food till about 10pm, drinks till 1am.

For **drinking**, many of Toronto's neighbourhood bars are rough-and-ready places that look and feel like beer halls. Dominated by men – until fairly recently, it was common for them to have one entrance for men accompanied by women, the other for men only – the beer halls remain popular with many of the city's blue-collar workers, but are being replaced by the combined **restaurant/bar**, whose development has made the traditional distinction between eating and drinking houses redundant.

Cafés and café-bars

The Artful Dodger, 12 Isabella St, just off Yonge south of Bloor. English-style pub with darts and British beer. Reasonable steak-and-kidney and shepherd's pies from $7.50.

Bellair Café, 100 Cumberland St, in Yorkville. Good pasta and salads; pleasant, relaxed setting with smart clientele; snacks from about $14.

Bistretto, 133 Yorkville Ave, Yorkville. Flashy bistro with massive windows and a lively French-influenced menu.

College St Bar, 574 College St. Pasta, fish and R&B combine to make this a vibrant spot.

Duncan Street Grill, 20 Duncan St, One block from University at Queen St West. Busy café-bar with tasty grilled meats.

Epicure Café, 512 Queen St West. Animated café-bar with an inventive, medium-price menu.

La Fenice Pasta Bar, 317 King St West. Amiable café-bar serving up all sorts of pastas with fancy sauces.

Peter Pan, 373 Queen St West. Good Italian menu and whopping portions, all at affordable prices.

Pints, 518 Church St at Maitland. Lively café-bar with a pleasing patio area. Filling portions of tasty food from a varied menu.

Queen Mother Café, 206 Queen St West. Popular spot with a good range of basic, well-prepared dishes – the chicken is perhaps the best. Snacks from about $9.

Shopsy's Delicatessen, 33 Yonge St at Front St East. One of Toronto's oldest delis, with attractive wood partitions separating the booths. Opposite the Hummingbird Centre. Large, inexpensive sandwiches with piles of meat, plus traditional stuff like corned-beef hash and meat platters. Justifiably popular. Also at 284a King St West.

Strathcona Hotel, 60 York St. Good, cheap breakfasts and lunches served in the hotel's ground-floor restaurant in the centre of the business district. Packed at lunch times. (Mon–Fri).

Taro Grill, 492 Queen St West. Broadly Italian meals with oodles of vegetables are served up here in this cleverly decorated café-restaurant.

Restaurants

With its large immigrant population, Toronto prides itself on the diversity of its cuisine. The city has more than four thousand eating establishments offering a spectacular range of foods from all over the world and is one of Canada's few cities where you can eat high-quality food of almost any ethnic origin. One cautionary note is that many restaurants are closed on Sundays and sometimes Mondays too – telephone ahead before you start a major excursion.

Chinese

Champion House, 480 Dundas St West. Famous for its Peking duck, this restaurant also does a tasty line in bean curd side dishes.

Happy Seven, 358 Spadina Ave. Topnotch Chinese restaurant offering Cantonese and Szechwan dishes.

Lee Garden, 331 Spadina Ave. Cantonese with an exceptionally varied menu; the seafood is a treat.

Ethiopian

Ethiopian House, 4 Irwin Ave. Off Yonge north of Wellesley, close to the University of Toronto campus. Inexpensive place, popular with students, where the pulses, spices, vegetables and beef of traditional Ethiopian cooking are put through their paces.

French and French Canadian

Arlequin, 134 Avenue Rd (☎928-9521). One of the best French restaurants in town, offering imaginative bistro-style cuisine with hints of the Middle East. Reservations advised.

Le Papillon, 16 Church at Front St East. French-Canadian food and delicious crêpes. Closed Mon.

Scaramouche Restaurant, 1 Benvenuto Place (☎961-8011). Off Edmund Avenue, which is itself off Avenue Road, north of Yorkville. One of Toronto's premier restaurants; magnificent French cuisine at high prices. Dinner only. Reservations recommended. Closed Sun.

Le Select Bistro, 328 Queen St West. Standard French-style menu; slick decor; jazz and classical background music. Meals from $20 per person.

Zola, 162 Cumberland St, Yorkville (☎515-1222). Chic and fashionable restaurant where the onion soup is a dream – but then most of the main courses are as well. Arm-and-a-leg prices. Reservations advised.

Greek

Astoria Shish Kebab House, 390 Danforth Ave, near Chester subway. In Greektown; good-quality shish kebabs and souvlakis; moderate prices.

Omonia, 426 Danforth Ave, near Chester subway. First-class, authentic Greek restaurant in Greektown.

Pappas Grill, 440 Danforth Ave, near Chester subway. Good Greek food; reasonable prices..

Indian

Gujurat Durbar, 1386 Gerrard St East at Coxwell. Outstanding vegetarian restaurant serving up Gujurat cuisine. Inexpensive. East of downtown.

The Madras Durbar, 1435 Gerrard St East at Coxwell. Tamil vegetarian dishes from $10. East of downtown.

Italian

Biagio Ristorante, 155 King St East. Expensive and excellent Italian restaurant located in the nineteenth-century elegance of St Lawrence Hall. Certainly one of the best restaurants of its type in the city, it also benefits from an extensive Italian wine list.

Centro, 2472 Yonge St at Eglinton (☎483-2211). Smart, first-class restaurant offering the best of Italian cuisine, overlaid with French technique and Canadian ingredients. North of downtown. Reservations advised.

Il Fornello, 486 Bloor St West and 214 King St West. Tasty clay-oven pizzas from $12; arguably this is the best pizza chain in the city.

Giovanna, 637 College St. A classy Italian restaurant serving complicated and sophisticated new-wave Italian dishes. Light and airy dining room with tables spilling outside.

P.J. Mellons, 489 Church St. Tasty food in the heart of the Gay Village. Fine pasta selection; excellent daily specials from $10. Very busy.

Spinello, 53 Colborne St, off Church near King St East. Fashionable, reasonably priced restaurant specializes in pizzas, pastas and grilled meats.

Japanese

Masa, 205 Richmond St West (☎977-9519). Mouth-watering Japanese food, with part of the restaurant equipped with mats and partitions. All the old favourites – such as eel, seaweed and teriyaki. Reservations advised at weekends.

Nami, 55 Adelaide St East (☎362-7373). One of the finest Japanese restaurants in Toronto. Quite reasonably priced. Reservations advised.

Seafood

Chiado, 864 College St. An expensive and exuberant Portuguese restaurant serving the freshest of fish imaginatively cooked.

Filet of Sole, 11 Duncan St, just west along Queen from University. Extensive range of seafood served in lively warehouse-style surroundings. Quantity rather more than quality cuisine.

The Fish House, 144 Front St West. Unassuming restaurant offering a reasonable variety of well-prepared fish dishes.

Old Fish Market, 12 Market St, next to St Lawrence Market. Wide selection of fish, but sauces are rather discordant – stick to the more straightforward dishes.

La Pêcherie, 133 Yorkville Ave, Yorkville. Fashionable café-restaurant with a first-rate range of daily seafood specials.

Rodney's Oyster House, 209 Adelaide St East. Oysters and an extraordinary variety of sauces are the deal here, in what regulars claim as the best oyster restaurant in the province.

Spanish

Segovia, 5 St Nicholas St. Traditional Spanish restaurant right down to the bullfighting trinkets. Go for the paella – it's fab. Off Yonge north of Wellesley St West.

Tapas Bar, 226 Carlton St. Delicious tapas washed down by Spanish wine on two floors of an old Cabbagetown house. An inexpensive treat.

Steaks

Carman's, 26 Alexander St, off Yonge north of Carlton. Good quality charcoal-broiled steaks. Pricey.

Senator, 253 Victoria St. Expensive but superb steaks at arguably the best steakhouse in Toronto. Behind Pantages Theatre, just one block east of Yonge at Dundas.

Vegetarian

Health Haven, 4 Dundonald St, east of Yonge and one block north of Wellesley. One of the few specifically vegetarian establishments in the city, with inexpensive and tasty food. Vegan dishes and an all-you-can-eat buffet.

Living Well Café, 692 Yonge St. Competent veggie food at inexpensive prices.

Nightlife and entertainment

Toronto is the cultural centre of English-speaking Canada and has gone to great expense to maintain a wide-ranging programme of highbrow performance, from **theatre** and **opera** to **ballet** and Brahms. Prices vary from $8 to around $30, but T.O. Tix (Tues–Sat noon–7.30pm, Sun 11am–3pm; ☎596-8211), 208 Yonge St just north of Queen, sells spare dance and theatre tickets at half-price for that day's performances. The city of the Cowboy Junkies obviously has some life in its **music** scene, and though many local bands who hit the big time move to the States, the city does have its fair share of venues, especially for **jazz**. Several bars and clubs sponsor a range of modern and traditional jazz, and there are free open-air jazz concerts at various downtown locations throughout the summer. Four local **bands** to look out for are Rusty (alternative), the Rheostatics (alternative folk rock), Big Rude Jake (lounge) and I Mother Earth (rock). Toronto's mainstream **cinemas** show Hollywood releases long before they reach the UK and, as you'd expect from a university city, it has good outlets for arthouse stuff.

For **listings and reviews** check out either of the city's main free newspapers, *eye* and *Now*. Tourism Toronto's Visitor Information Centre (daily 8am–8pm), in the city's Convention Centre near Union Station at 255 Front St West, has two other free publications, an *Annual Visitors' Guide* and *Where*, which also have listings sections, but their reviews are bland and uncritical. For happenings in the Gay Village, see *Xtra*, the city's third free newspaper.

Venues, music bars and clubs

The Black Bull, 298 Queen St West. Local rock groups.

Cameron House, 408 Queen St West. Showcase for local bands of varying abilities and styles.

C'est What, 67 Front St East. Avant-garde jazz and folk.

The Docks, 11 Polson St. An enormous waterfront bar on the edge of the Port of Toronto dockyards. Features a wide range of music, from Latino to House, with the occasional live act too.

Grossman's, 379 Spadina Ave. R&B venue.

Horseshoe, 370 Queen St West. For good-quality and better-known bands.

Lee's Palace, 529 Bloor St West. Hosts some of the best up-and-coming bands from punk through to folk. Upstairs is the **Dance Cave**, a lively alternative dance bar.

El Mocambo, 464 Spadina Ave, just south of College. Has seen the likes of Elvis Costello and the Rolling Stones, and still has appearances by big names.

Montreal Jazz, 65 Sherbourne St. Well-established spot offering traditional and modern jazz.

The Pilot, 22 Cumberland St. High-quality modern jazz.

The 360, 326 Queen St. Busy place where many local bands get their first gig.

Top O' the Senator, 294 Yonge St. Showcases some of the biggest names in jazz and blues.

Discos

Bamboo, 312 Queen St West. Regular live acts, but is best for its ska, reggae and salsa discos.

The Joker, 318 Richmond St West. Huge, upmarket club offering a good mixture of dance music.

Whiskey Saigon, 250 Richmond St West. Big nightspot with three floors and a wide range of music – rock and funk through House and disco.

Performing arts

Du Maurier Theatre at the Harbourfront Centre, 231 Queens Quay West (☎954-5199). Renovated from a 1920s ice house, this new theatre puts on theatrical and musical shows in a lakeshore setting.

Ford Centre for the Performing Arts, 5040 Yonge St (☎733-9388). This three-theatre venue stages classical concerts in its acoustically impressive Recital Hall as well as mainstream musicals.

Hummingbird Centre for the Performing Arts, 1 Front St East at Yonge (☎393-7469). Home of the Canadian Opera Company and the National Ballet of Canada.

Pantages Theatre, 263 Yonge St (☎872-2222). Splendidly restored Victorian auditorium, where *The Phantom of the Opera* has been playing for donkey's years.

Poor Alex Theatre, 296 Brunswick Ave (☎923-1644). One of the city's best venues for inventive and engaging modern drama.

Princess of Wales Theatre, 300 King St West (☎872-1212). Built especially to stage *Miss Saigon* and opened in early 1994, this multimillion dollar venue has already recouped its investment.

Roy Thomson Hall, 60 Simcoe St at King St West (☎872-4255). Base of the highly regarded Toronto Symphony Orchestra.

Royal Alexandra Theatre, 260 King St West (☎872-1212). Refurbished nineteenth-century theatre, concentrating on top-drawer transfers from London and Broadway.

St Lawrence Centre for the Performing Arts, 27 Front St East (☎366-7723). Home to the Canadian Stage Company, which produces modern Canadian plays and is responsible for a classical music programme, and Theatre Plus, the city's only resident acting ensemble, whose contemporary international and Canadian season runs from April to September.

Tarragon Theatre, 30 Bridgeman Ave (☎531-1827). Specializes in new Canadian plays.

Cinema

Bloor Cinema, 506 Bloor St West (☎532-6677). A student favourite, with an excellent programme of international and arthouse films; mostly two shows daily.

Carlton Cinema, 20 Carlton St at College subway (☎598-2309). Toronto's best mainstream cinema, with ten screens and four shows daily.

Cinémathèque Ontario, Jackman Hall, Art Gallery of Ontario, 317 Dundas St West (☎923-FILM). Eclectic mix of English-language and subtitled films.

Eaton Centre, Dundas Street at Yonge (☎593-4536). Fifteen mainstream films and frequent showings.

The Revue, 400 Roncesvalles Ave (☎531-9959). First-rate selection of arthouse and key mainstream films.

Festivals

One of the biggest of Toronto's many festivals is the **International Caravan**, a nine-day multiethnic celebration held from mid- to late June, with some fifty pavilions dotted across the city representing Toronto's different communities. In late June, the outstanding **du Maurier Downtown Jazz Festival** usually overlaps with the week-long **Toronto Gay & Lesbian Pride Celebration**, which culminates in a whopping Pride Day Parade. Late July and early August sees the **Caribana**, a West Indian carnival with a fantastic parade plus music and dance, as well as the **Beaches International Jazz Festival**. In early September, the widely acclaimed **Toronto International Film Festival** is a ten-day showing of new films from around the world. The most sedate annual event is perhaps the **International Festival of Authors**, held at the Harbourfront Centre in early October.

Listings

Airlines Air Canada (☎925-2311); Canadian Airlines (☎798-2211). Air Ontario (☎925-2311) has regular, bargain deals from Toronto City Centre Airport to London, Montréal and Ottawa and also operates flights to more obscure destinations within Ontario; for flights to the States try American Airlines (☎1-800-433-7300) and USAir (☎1-800-428-4322).

Airport enquiries Pearson International (☎247-7678); Toronto City Centre (☎203-6942).

Algonquin Park Call of the Wild, 23 Edward St, Markham, Ontario (☎416/200-9453, fax 905/472-9453), organize first-class, camping, canoeing and hiking trips to Ontario's Algonquin Park (see p.128). They last from three to seven days and the price covers food, equipment, guides and transportation from Toronto. A three-day canoe and hiking trip costs around $300.

Bike rental Cyclepath, 2106 Yonge St (☎487-1717), and Wheel Excitement Inc, south of the Skydome at 5 Rees St (☎260-9000), who also hire out rollerblades.

Bookshops Best of the general bookshops is The World's Biggest Bookshop, 20 Edward St, near Yonge and Dundas. Lichtman's is good for best sellers and newspapers, with outlets at Yonge and Richmond, and in the Atrium on Bay shopping mall, Bay and Dundas. For travel books, try Open Air Books and Maps, downtown at 25 Toronto St, or Ulysses Travel Bookshop, 101 Yorkville. There's also the excellent Smith Books in the Eaton Centre.

Bus information General, automated bus information line (☎393-7911). Individual companies: PMCL (☎695-1867) for Midland, Penetang and Owen Sound; Trentway-Wagar (☎393-7911) for Niagara Falls, Kitchener, US destinations and Montréal; Greyhound (☎367-8747) both for long-distance buses – Montréal, Ottawa, Sault Ste Marie, Winnipeg and points west – and a handful of domestic flights. Toronto Transit Commission (daily 7am–10pm; ☎393-INFO).

Camping equipment Mountain Equipment Co-op, 41 Front St East (☎363-0122); Trail Head, 61 Front St East (☎862-0881).

Car rental Budget, 1319 Bay at Davenport (☎961-3932) and at the airport (☎676-0522); Discount, 20 Bloor St East at Yonge (☎921-1212) and 132 Front St East at Jarvis (☎864-0550); Hertz, 128 Richmond St East (☎363-9022) and at the airport (☎674-2020); Thrifty Car Rental at the *Sheraton Centre Hotel*, 123 Queen St West (☎862-7262) and at the airport (☎673-9308); Tilden, beside Union Station (☎364-4191) and at the airport (☎905/676-2647).

Consulates Australia, 175 Bloor St East (☎323-3919); Belgium, 2 Bloor St West (☎944-1422); Netherlands, Suite 2106, 1 Dundas St West (☎598-2520); Norway, 2600 South Sheridan Way, Mississauga (☎822-2339); Sweden, 2 Bloor St West (☎963-8768); UK, 777 Bay St (☎593-1267); US, 360 University Ave (☎595-1700).

Emergencies Assaulted Women's Helpline and Rape Crisis (☎597-8808).

Hospital Wellesley Central Hospital, 160 Wellesley (24hr general line ☎926-7014; 24hr emergency line ☎929-7037).

Laundry Bloor Laundromat and Dry Cleaners, 598 Bloor St West at Bathurst; Dundas Coin Laundry, 345 Dundas St East.

Lost property GO transit (☎869-3200); TTC, Bay subway (☎393-4100); VIA Rail (☎366-8411).

Newspapers Toronto has two first-rate newspapers, the *Toronto Star* and the *Globe and Mail*, which is sold all over Canada.

Pharmacies There are Shoppers Drug Marts all over town; for the nearest location and late-night opening, call the company's information line on ☎363-1020.

Post offices Postal facilities at most Shoppers Drug Marts with downtown locations including 360 Bloor St West, 725 College St and 69 Yonge at King. There are post offices downtown at 36 Adelaide St East, 50 Charles St East off Yonge and in the Atrium, at the corner of Bay and Dundas.

Rail GO Transit (☎869-3200); VIA Rail enquiries (☎366-8411).

Rideshare Allo-Stop (☎975-9305).

Sports The Toronto Maple Leafs, of the National Hockey League, play home fixtures in Maple Leaf Gardens at Carlton and Church, College subway (☎977-1641). The Blue Jays, of the American Baseball League, play in the Skydome (☎341-1234); the Argonauts, of the Canadian Football League, also play there (☎341–5151).

Weather For up-to-date bulletins, call ☎661-0123.

Winter sports Ring Metro Parks (☎392-1111) for information on outdoor rinks and cross-country ski routes. Ski hire available at Trail Head, 61 Front St East (☎862-0881).

SOUTHERN ONTARIO

The chain of towns to the east and west of Toronto, stretching 120km along the edge of Lake Ontario from Oshawa to Hamilton, is often called the **Golden Horseshoe**, a misleadingly evocative name that refers solely to their geographic shape and economic success. This is Ontario's manufacturing heartland, a densely populated strip whose principal places of interest are in the steel-making city of **Hamilton**, the home of both the Royal Botanical Gardens and the delightful mansion of Dundurn Castle. Further round the lake are the famous **Niagara Falls**, undoubtedly Canada's most celebrated sight, though the Falls adjoin the uninspiring town of the same name – and it's best to use the charming, colonial village of **Niagara-on-the-Lake** as a base for a visit. At neighbouring Queenston the **Niagara Escarpment** begins its rambling journey across the region to the Bruce Peninsula, the major interruption in a generally flat terrain. To the west of this limestone ridge the main attractions lie on the coast, most notably **Point Pelee National Park**, the vigorous town of **Windsor**, and the small-town pleasures of **Goderich** and leafy **Bayfield**. The **Bruce Peninsula** itself boasts dramatic coastal scenery and incorporates two outstanding national parks, which make for some great walking, climbing and scuba diving. To the east of the Niagara Escarpment, along the southern shore of **Severn Sound**, there's a string of lethargic ports, the most amiable of which is **Penetanguishene**, located a few kilometres from the sturdy palisades of the replica Jesuit mission of **Sainte-Marie among the Hurons**. The eastern shore of the Sound boasts the lion's share of the stunningly beautiful **Georgian Bay Islands National Park**, an elegiac land and waterscape of rocky, pine-dotted islets and crystal-blue lake. The islands are best approached by boat from the tourist resort of **Honey Harbour** or on the summer island cruises from the town of **Midland**.

There are fast and frequent **buses** and **trains** between Toronto and Niagara Falls, and a similarly efficient service between the region's other major settlements, like Windsor, London and Kitchener. But if you're visiting the smaller towns things are much more patchy: Hamilton, Penetanguishene and Midland, for instance, have reasonably good bus connections, but you can only reach Niagara-on-the-Lake via Niagara Falls and there are no buses along the east shore of Lake Huron (Goderich and Bayfield) and up the Bruce Peninsula – where Tobermory has a **ferry boat** service to South Baymouth on Manitoulin Island, a useful short cut to northern Ontario.

Kitchener, Elora and Stratford

The industrial city of **Kitchener** is southern Ontario at its most mundane, but amid the prevailing architectural gloom it does have a couple of sights that are worth an hour or so. In marked contrast, **Elora**, 30km north of Kitchener, is a pleasant little village of old stone houses and mills on the periphery of the **Elora Gorge**, a narrow limestone ravine that's a popular spot for a day's walk and picnic. Fifty kilometres west of Kitchener, **Stratford** is different again, a modest country town that hosts one of Canada's most prestigious cultural events, the **Shakespeare Festival**.

Kitchener

Just off Hwy 401 about 80km west of downtown Toronto, **KITCHENER** lies at the centre of an industrial belt whose economy is based on rubber, textiles, leather and furniture. The town was founded as Sand Hills in 1799 by groups of **Mennonites**, a tightly knit Protestant sect who came here from the States, where their pacifist beliefs had incurred the wrath of their neighbours during the Revolution. Soon after, German farmers began to arrive in the area, establishing a generally good-humoured trading relationship with the Mennonites. The new settlers had Sand Hills renamed Berlin in 1826, but during World War I it was thought prudent to change the name yet again, to prove their patriotism: they chose "Kitchener" after the British field marshal. Today around sixty percent of Kitchener's inhabitants are descendants of German immigrants, a heritage celebrated every year during **Oktoberfest**, nine days of alcoholic stupefaction when even the most reticent men can be seen wandering the streets in lederhosen. The Mennonites have drifted out of Kitchener itself, and are concentrated in the villages north and west of Waterloo, Kitchener's glum neighbour.

Kitchener's centre is marked by the **Farmers' Market**, open on Saturdays from 6am to 2pm – be sure to sample the delicious German sausages. The Mennonite traders are unmistakable, with the men wearing traditional black suits and broad-brimmed hats, or deep-blue shirts and braces, the women ankle-length dresses and matching bonnets. The Ontario Mennonites are, however, far from being an homogeneous sect – over twenty different groups are affiliated to the Mennonite Central Committee (MCC) and although they all share certain religious beliefs reflecting their Anabaptist origins – the sole validity of adult baptism being crucial – precise practices and dress codes vary from group to group. Members of the traditional wing of the Mennonite movement, sometimes called **Amish** or Ammanites after the seventeenth-century elder Jakob Ammann, own property communally and shun all modern machinery, travelling to the market and around the back lanes on spindly horse-drawn buggies. To explain their history and faith, the MCC runs **The Meeting Place** (May–Oct Mon–Fri 11am–5pm, Sat 10am–5pm, Sun 1.30–5pm; Nov–April Sat 11am–4.30pm, Sun 2–4.30pm; donation), a small tourist-office-cum-interpretation-centre in the village of **St Jacobs**, just north of Waterloo on Hwy 86, where there's also a popular Mennonite craft shop.

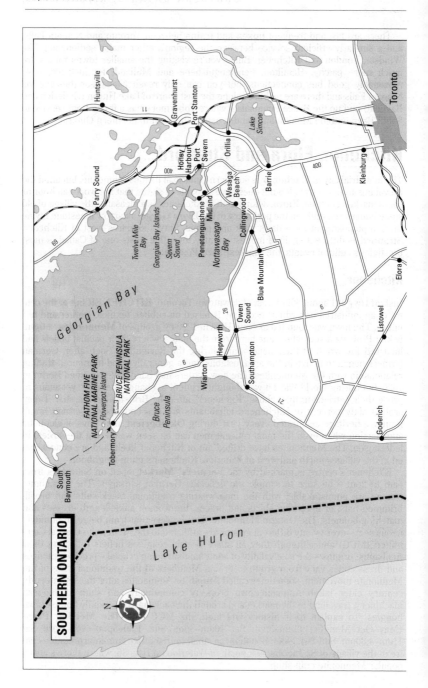

SOUTHERN ONTARIO

Toronto

Huntsville

Gravenhurst

Port Stanton

Lake Simcoe

Orillia

Honey Harbour

Port Severn

Parry Sound

Twelve Mile Bay

Georgian Bay Islands

Severn Sound

Penetanguishene

Midland

Wasaga Beach

Nottawasaga Bay

Barrie

Kleinburg

Collingwood

Blue Mountain

Elora

Georgian Bay

Owen Sound

Listowel

Hepworth

FATHOM FIVE NATIONAL MARINE PARK

Flowerpot Island

BRUCE PENINSULA NATIONAL PARK

Wiarton

Southampton

Goderich

Bruce Peninsula

South Baymouth

Tobermory

Lake Huron

N

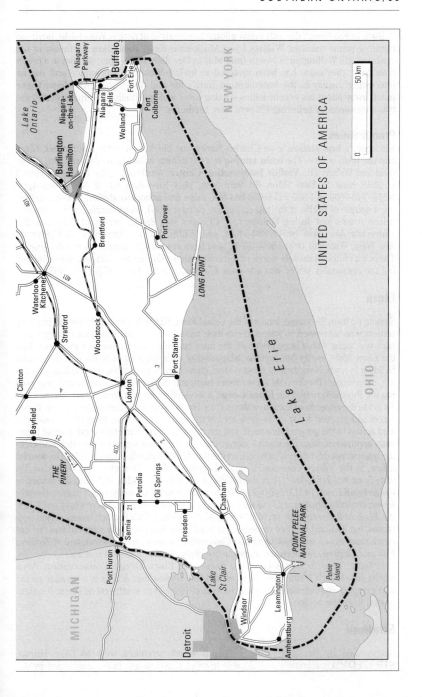

Back in Kitchener, the only conventional tourist sight of note is **Woodside**, boyhood home of prime minister William Lyon Mackenzie King, about 1km northeast of the centre at 528 Wellington St North (mid-May to Dec daily 10am–5pm; $2). Set in a pretty little park, the house has been restored to its late-Victorian appearance and has an interesting display in the basement on King's life and times, though it doesn't give much away about his eccentricities – a dog lover and spiritualist, he amalgamated the two obsessions by believing his pets were mediums.

Practicalities

Kitchener's **bus station** is on Charles Street, one block west of the main street, King, and the town centre. The **train station** is a ten-minute walk north of downtown, at Victoria and Weber. The **Visitor Information Centre**, southeast of the centre off Hwy 8 at 2848 King St East (Mon–Fri 9am–5pm, plus June–Aug Sat & Sun 10am–4pm; ☎519/748-0800 or 1-800-265-6959) has free maps and **accommodation** listings, including a couple of B&Bs at the top end of the category (①); many families offer similarly priced rooms just during Oktoberfest. Cheaper still, the University of Waterloo, 200 University Ave West (☎519/884-5400), and Wilfrid Laurier University, 75 University Ave West, Waterloo (☎519/884-1970), also have rooms (①), from May to mid-August. There's a clutch of **motels** north of the centre along Kitchener's Victoria Street, including the reasonably priced and adequate *Mayflower*, at no. 1189 (☎519/745-9493; ①).

Elora

Sloping up from the craggy banks of the Grand River, **ELORA** was founded in the 1830s by settlers who harnessed its waters to run their mills. Some of their limestone cottages have survived, along with a large grist mill, the main landmark, which has been converted into the *Elora Mill Country Inn*, a clever adaptation of what has long been the most important building in town. Nonetheless, most visitors come here to gaze at the waterfalls beside the inn, even though they're only a few metres high, and then stroll on to viewpoints overlooking the three-kilometre-long **Elora Gorge**, a forested ravine with limestone cliffs close by. To get to the gorge from the inn, walk up Price Street to the top of the hill, turn left on James Street and proceed as far as the park area at the end of Henderson, from where footpaths lead across to the gorge. Elora itself, just ten minutes' walk from end to end, is most pleasantly approached from the south – along Route 21 – across a narrow bridge that leads into the main street, Metcalfe, which cuts across tiny Mill Street, adjoining the falls. The **tourist office**, in the Village Common, a small shopping mall on Metcalfe (June–Aug Mon–Fri 9am–5pm; ☎519/846-9841), has the details of a handful of **B&Bs**, including the attractive *Gingerbread House* (☎519/846-0521; $80), just by the bridge, and the much plainer *Hornsby Home*, centrally situated at 231 Queen Street (☎519/846-9763; $45). There's only one hotel, the *Elora Mill Country Inn,* on Mill Street (☎519/846-5356; $135), which boasts period bedrooms, log fires and beamed ceilings. The hotel has a first-rate restaurant, but you can **eat** much more economically at *Leyanders Café*, footsteps away on Mill Street, and at *Tiffany's Fish and Chiperie*, 146 Metcalfe, opposite the *Dalby House*, Elora's liveliest bar.

If you're keen to see more of the gorge, the **Elora Gorge Conservation Area** (daily: Jan–March 10am–5pm; May to mid-Oct 10am–dusk; $3.25) is a popular picnic and camping spot spread out along the Grand River 2km southwest of Elora: it's signposted from the bridge.

Stratford

Surrounded by flat and fertile farmland which stretches west to Lake Huron, **STRATFORD** is a homely and likeable town of 27,000 people that's brightened by the

Avon River trimming the centre and by the grandiose city hall, a brown-brick fiesta of cupolas, towers and limestone trimmings. More importantly, the town is also the home of the **Shakespeare Festival**, which started in 1953 and is now one of the most prestigious theatrical occasions in North America, attracting no fewer than half a million visitors from May to early November. Although the core performances are still Shakespearean, the festival has broadened its appeal to include other drama, from Racine to O'Casey and Beckett.

The **Festival Box Office** at the Festival Theatre (late Feb–April daily 9am–5pm; May to early Nov Mon–Sat 9am–8pm, Sun 9am–5pm; ☎1-800-567-1600 or 519/273-1600) accepts applications in person, by letter (PO Box 520), by phone or by fax (☎519/273-6173). Tickets cost between $40 and $60, and from $21 to $40 for students and seniors at matinée performances. Many plays are sold out months in advance, but the box office does set aside a limited number of rush tickets for two of the three main theatres – the Festival and the Avon, but not the Tom Patterson) – at about $25. These are for sale from 9am on the day of the performance, but the seats are the worst in the house. The box office also organizes a number of **discount packages** with savings upwards of ten percent for various categories of performance, plus accommodation ranging from hotels down to guesthouses.

Practicalities

Stratford **bus** and **train stations** are on Shakespeare Street, a fifteen-minute stroll from the town centre. There are two **tourist offices**: a main Visitors' Information Centre (early to late May Mon & Sun 9am–3pm, Tues–Sat 9am–5pm; June–Aug Mon & Sun 9am–5pm, Tues–Sat 9am–8pm; Sept to mid-Nov Tues–Sat 9am–5pm, Sun 10am–2pm; ☎1-800-561-7926 or 519/273-3352), by the river on York Street, immediately northwest of the central Erie–Downie–Ontario intersection; and Tourism Stratford, 88 Wellington St (Mon–Fri 9am–4.30pm; ☎519/271-5140), which is off Downie on the west side of the Market Place.

Stratford has over 250 guesthouses and a dozen or so hotels and motels, but **accommodation** can still be hard to find during the Festival's busiest weekends in July and August. The walls of the Information Centre are plastered with pictures and descriptions of many of the town's **guesthouses** and **B&Bs**, mostly first-rate places with prices starting in category ①. There are several comfortable **hotels** near the centre, including the *Stone Maiden Inn*, 123 Church St (☎519/271-7129; ⑤); the *Queen's Inn*, 161 Ontario St (☎519/271-1400; ④); and the *Albert Place Twenty Three*, 23 Albert St (☎519/273-5800; ④).

Stratford has plenty of excellent **cafés** and **restaurants**, with one of the best being *Fellini's Italian Café & Grill*, 107 Ontario St, which offers a good range of fresh pizzas and pastas at reasonable prices. There are also tasty snacks and light meals at *Let Them Eat Cake*, by the Market Place at 90 Wellington St, and pastries and gourmet coffees at *Balzac's*, 149 Ontario St. *Rundles*, 9 Coburg St, is arguably the classiest restaurant in town, serving up imaginatively prepared French-style cuisine at finger-burning prices.

Hamilton and around

Some 70km from Toronto, **HAMILTON** lies at the extreme western end of Lake Ontario, focus of a district first surveyed by George Hamilton, a Niagaran storekeeper-turned-landowner who moved here in 1812 to escape the war between America and Britain. Strategically located, the town was soon established as a trading centre, but its real growth began with the development of the farm-implements industry in the 1850s. By the turn of the century, Hamilton had become a major steel producer and today its mills churn out sixty percent of the country's output.

The city

For a city of half a million people, Hamilton is not overendowed with attractions. The finest building in the centre is **Whitehern** (June–Aug daily 11am–4pm; Sept–May Tues–Sun 1–4pm; $2.50), a couple of minutes' walk east of the city hall at 41 Jackson St West. A good example of early Victorian architecture, it has an overhauled interior with an eccentric mix of styles ranging from a splendid mid-nineteenth-century circular stairway to a dingy wood-panelled 1930s basement, the garbled legacy of the McQuestern, family who lived here from 1852 until the 1960s.

About twenty minutes' walk west of the town centre, straight down York Boulevard from James, you come to the much more entertaining **Dundurn Castle** (June–Aug daily 10am–4pm; Sept–May Tues–Sun noon–4pm; $5), a Regency villa built in the 1830s for Sir Allan Napier MacNab, a soldier, lawyer and land speculator who became one of the leading conservative politicians of the day. He was knighted for his loyalty to the Crown during the Upper Canada Rebellion of 1837, when he employed bands of armed Indians to round up supposed rebels and loot their property. Carefully renovated, Dundurn is an impressive broadly Palladian building with an interior that easily divides into "upstairs" and "downstairs": the former filled with fine contemporaneous furnishings, the latter a warren of poorly ventilated rooms for the dozens of servants. Nearby, the gatekeeper's cottage has been turned into a small **military museum** (June–Aug daily 1–5pm; Sept–May Tues–Sun 1–5pm; free admission with castle), detailing local involvement in the War of 1812 and in the Fenian (Irish–American) cross-border raids of the 1860s.

From Dundurn Castle, York Boulevard crosses the four-kilometre-long isthmus that spans the west end of Hamilton harbour before heading into the neighbouring city of Burlington. The **Royal Botanical Gardens** cover some 3000 acres around the northern end of the isthmus, their several sections spread over 15km of wooded shoreline. There are no public transport connections from either Hamilton or Burlington, so it's difficult to get around without a car. The displays are gorgeous, though – especially the Hendrie Park Rose Garden (best June–Oct), the Laking Garden with its irises and peonies (May & June) and the Lilac Dell (late May to mid-June). Admission to the outdoor gardens (daily 9.30am–6pm) is $6 and there's a further charge of $2 to visit the conservatory which accommodates the Mediterranean Garden (daily 9am–5pm), beside the RBG centre.

Practicalities

Hamilton **bus station** is at the corner of Hunter and James streets, three blocks south of Main Street which, together with King, one block further to the north, forms the downtown core. The **tourist information office**, 127 King St East at Catherine (daily 9am–5pm), can supply you with brochures on the city and its surroundings, plus restaurant and hotel lists. There's very little cheap downtown **accommodation** to be had, except the YMCA, 79 James St South (☎416/529-7102; ①); and the YWCA, 75 MacNab St South (☎416/522-9922; ①). The major hotel chains have branches in Hamilton, with rooms starting from around $60; one of the most comfortable is the centrally located *Ramada Hotel*, 150 King St East (☎905/528-3451; ④).

Brantford and the Bell Homestead

The modest manufacturing town of **BRANTFORD**, to the west of Hamilton beside the Grand River, takes its name from Joseph Brant, who led a large group of Loyalist Iroquois here after the American War of Independence, then worked to form a confederation of Iroquois to keep the United States out of Ohio. His dream was undermined by jealousies amongst the Indian nations, whereupon he withdrew to Burlington, where he lived the life of an English gentleman. The town was later the birthplace of ice-hockey's greatest player, Wayne Gretzky, but no one's built a museum yet.

The only thing to see in the town itself is the **Brant County Museum**, 57 Charlotte St (Tues–Fri 9am–5pm, Sat & Sun 1–4pm; $2), where there's a reasonable collection of Iroquois artefacts. However, 6km southwest of Brantford, in the low wooded hills overlooking the river, stands the much more diverting **Bell Homestead**, 94 Tutela Heights Rd (Tues–Sun 9.30am–4.30pm; $2.50). **Alexander Graham Bell** left Edinburgh for Ontario in 1870 at the age of 23, a reluctant immigrant who came only because of fears for his health after the death of two close relatives from tuberculosis. Soon afterwards he took a job as a teacher of the deaf, motivated by his mother's loss of hearing and, in his efforts to discover a way to reproduce sounds visibly, he stumbled across the potential of transmitting sound along an electrified wire. The consequence was the first long-distance call, made in 1876 from Brantford to the neighbouring village of Paris. The Homestead consists of two simple, clapboard buildings. The first, moved here from Brantford in 1969, housed Canada's original Bell company office and features a series of modest displays on the history of the telephone. The second, the cosy family home, fronts a second small exhibition area devoted to Bell's life and research. There's no public transport from Brantford to the site.

Niagara Falls and the Niagara River

In 1860 thousands watched as Charles Blondin walked a tightrope across **NIAGARA FALLS** for the third time; at the midway point he cooked an omelette on a portable grill and then had a marksman shoot a hole through his hat from the *Maid of the Mist* tug boat, 50m below. As attested by Blondin's subsequent career, by the antics of innumerable lunatics and publicity seekers, and by several million waterlogged tourist photos, the Falls simply can't be beaten as a theatrical setting. Yet the stupendous first impression of the Niagara doesn't last long, especially on jaded modern palates, and to prevent each year's twelve million visitors becoming bored by the sight of a load of water crashing over a 52-metre cliff, the Niagarans have ensured that the Falls can be seen from every angle imaginable – from boats, viewing towers, helicopters, cable cars and even tunnels in the rock face behind the cascade. The **tunnels** and the **boats** are the most exciting, with the entrance to the first right next to the Falls and the second leaving from the bottom of the cliff at the end of Clifton Hill, 1500m downriver. Both give a real sense of the extraordinary force of the waterfall, a perpetual white-crested thundering pile-up that had Mahler bawling "At last, fortissimo" over the din.

Trains and **buses** from Toronto and most of southern Ontario's larger towns serve the **town of Niagara Falls** (see below), 3km to the north of the action; the availability of discount excursion fares makes a day-trip to see the Falls a straightforward proposition, although, if you do decide to spend the night, quaint **Niagara-on-the-Lake**, 26km downstream beside Lake Ontario, is a much better option than the crassly commercialized town of Niagara Falls itself. Niagara-on-the-Lake can be reached from the Falls by shuttle bus (see p.100), but note that accommodation there is extremely tight in high season, when you'd be well advised to book up a couple of days in advance. Both the **Niagara Parkway** road and the **Niagara River Recreation Trail**, a jogging and cycle path, stretch the length of the Niagara River from Fort Erie to Niagara-on-the-Lake.

The Falls

Though you can hear the growl of the **Falls** kilometres away, nothing quite prepares you for the spectacle; the fearsome white arc shrouded in clouds of dense spray, with

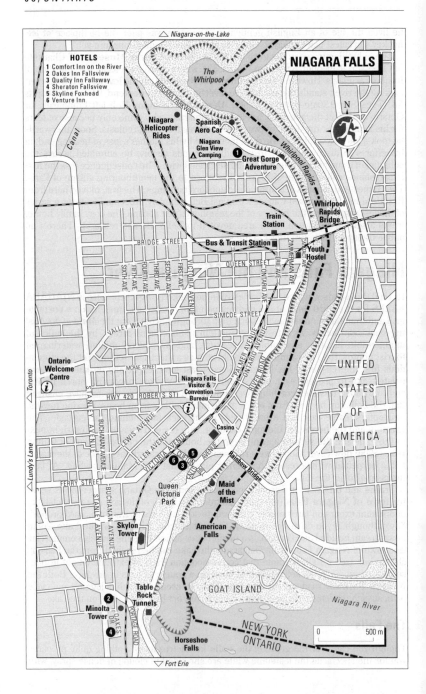

HOTELS
1 Comfort Inn on the River
2 Oakes Inn Fallsview
3 Quality Inn Fallsway
4 Sheraton Fallsview
5 Skyline Foxhead
6 Venture Inn

NIAGARA FALLS

△ Niagara-on-the-Lake

The Whirlpool

NIAGARA PARKWAY

Canal

Niagara Helicopter Rides

Spanish Aero Car

Niagara Glen View Camping

Great Gorge Adventure

Whirlpool Rapids

Train Station

Bus & Transit Station

ZIMMERMAN AVE

Youth Hostel

BRIDGE STREET

VICTORIA AVENUE

FIRST AVE
SECOND AVE
THIRD AVE
FOURTH AVE
FIFTH AVE
SIXTH AVE

QUEEN STREET

ERIE AVE

ONTARIO AVE

Whirlpool Rapids Bridge

SIMCOE STREET

VALLEY WAY

PALMER AVENUE

ONTARIO AVENUE

UNITED

Ontario Welcome Centre

MCRAE STREET

Niagara Falls Visitor & Convention Bureau

RIVER ROAD

STATES

HWY 420 (ROBERTS ST)

OF

AMERICA

Casino

LEWIS AVENUE

ELLEN AVENUE

VICTORIA AVENUE

FALLS AVENUE

6 5
3

Rainbow Bridge

FERRY STREET

Queen Victoria Park

Maid of the Mist

BUCHANAN AVENUE

STANLEY AVENUE

Skylon Tower

American Falls

MURRAY STREET

Table Rock Tunnels

GOAT ISLAND

Niagara River

Minolta Tower

2

PORTAGE ROAD

NEW YORK

4

Horseshoe Falls

ONTARIO

0   500 m

△ Toronto

△ Lundy's Lane

▽ Fort Erie

N

the river boats struggling below, mere specks against the surging cauldron. There are two cataracts, the accelerating water being sliced into two channels by tiny Goat Island: on the far side, across the frontier, the river slips over the precipice of the **American Falls**, 320m wide but still only one half of the width of the **Horseshoe Falls** on the Canadian side. If anything, it's an even more amazing scene in winter, with snow-covered trees edging a jagged armoury of freezing mist and heaped ice blocks. It looks like a scene of untrammelled nature, but it isn't. Since the 1910s, successive hydroelectric schemes have greatly reduced the water flow, and all sorts of tinkering has spread what's left of the Niagara more evenly over the crest line. As a result, the process of erosion, which has moved the Falls some 11km upstream in 12,000 years, has slowed down from 1m per year to 30cm. This obviously has advantages for the tourist industry, but the environmental consequences of training this deluge for decades on one part of the Niagara riverbed are unclear. At least the cardsharps and charlatans who overran the riverside in Blondin's day are long gone – the Niagara Parks Commission, which controls the area along the river and beside the Falls, ensures that the immaculately tended tree-lined gardens and parkland remain precisely so.

Beside the Horseshoe Falls, **Table Rock House** has a small, free observation platform and elevators which travel to the base of the cliff, where **tunnels**, grandiosely named the Journey Behind the Falls (all year; $5.75), lead to points behind the waterfall. For a more panoramic view, a pint-sized Incline Railway ($1) takes visitors up the hill behind Table Rock House to the **Minolta Tower**, 6732 Oakes Drive (daily: June–Sept 9am–midnight; Oct–May 9am–11pm; $7), which has three observation platforms, though the views are rather better from the Skylon tower (see below).

From Table Rock House, a wide and crowded path leads north along the cliffs beside the river, with the manicured lawns of Queen Victoria Park to the left and views over to the American Falls to the right. After a few minutes, turn left up Murray Street to visit the **Skylon** tower (daily 8/9am–11pm; $6.95), at 5200 Robinson; or continue along the path to the foot of Clifton Hill – the main drag linking the riverside area with Niagara Falls town – where **Maid of the Mist boats** edge out into the river and push up towards the Falls, an exhilarating and extremely damp trip (May to late June & mid-Sept to late Oct Mon–Fri 10am–5pm, Sat & Sun 10am–6pm; late June to mid-Aug daily 9am–8pm; mid-Aug to early Sept daily 9am–7.30pm; at least every 15min in high season, otherwise every 30min; $10.10 including waterproofs). **Clifton Hill** itself is a tawdry collection of fast-food joints and bizarre attractions, from the innocuous House of Frankenstein to the grotesque voyeurism of the Guinness World of Records Museum and the absurdity of the Believe It or Not Museum, where, amongst other wonders, you can spy a dog with human teeth and a Chinese chap with double the normal number of eye pupils. Actually, if you stick to the riverside you can, by courtesy of the Niagara Parks Commission, avoid this unattractive side of Niagara altogether, as well as the area's second-biggest crowd puller, the brand new **casino** just off Clifton Hill, near the Rainbow Bridge leading over to the States.

Continuing north along the riverside from Clifton Hill, it's a further 3km to the **Great Gorge Adventure** ($4.75), where an elevator and then a tunnel lead to a boardwalk beside the Whirlpool Rapids, and a further 1km to the brightly painted **Spanish Aero Car** ($5), a cable-car ride across the gorge that's as near as you'll come to emulating Blondin's antics. From here, it's 1.5km downstream to **Niagara Helicopter Rides**, 3731 Victoria Ave (☎905/357-5672), who offer a nine-minute excursion over the Falls

The **Explorer's Passport Plus**, a combined ticket covering three of the main attractions – the Journey Behind the Falls (the tunnels at Table Rock), the Great Gorge Adventure and the Spanish Aero Car – and public transport between them, is available at each of these sights and costs $17.75. The Maid of the Mist is available as a single ticket costing $10.10.

for $80 per person. You don't need to book, as the six-seater helicopters whiz in and out with unnerving frequency from 9am until sunset – weather permitting.

Practicalities

Unless you're travelling by public transport, you're unlikely to catch sight of the surprisingly low-key centre of **NIAGARA FALLS town**, 3km north of the Falls themselves. It's here you'll find the **train station** directly opposite the **bus terminal**, 420 Bridge St at Erie. Next door to the bus station, the **Niagara Transit** depot is the starting point for town and suburban services, including the **Falls Shuttle** (mid-May to early Oct daily 9am–1am), which runs to the Maid of the Mist departure point, the Skylon tower and Clifton Hill hourly – every thirty minutes at peak periods; this service travels along Lundy's Lane, the main motel strip, too. A single ticket costs $2.25 and an all-day pass is $4. The Shuttle also connects with the Niagara Parks' **People Mover System** (daily: late April to mid-June & Sept to early Oct 10am–6pm, often later; mid-June to Aug 9am–7pm, often later), whose buses travel 30km along the riverbank between Queenston Heights Park, north of the Falls, and the Rapids' View car park to the south. People Movers appear at twenty-minute intervals and an all-day **pass** costs $4.25.

As for **information**, the **Ontario Welcome Centre** (mid-June to Aug daily 8am–8pm; mid-May to mid-June & Sept Mon–Thurs & Sun 8.30am–6pm, Fri & Sat 8am–8pm; Oct–March daily 8.30am–4.30pm) is located beside Hwy 420 – the main road to the Falls from the QEW – at Stanley Avenue, and is reasonably well stocked with literature on the whole of the province. Also beside Hwy 420, but nearer the Falls at Victoria Avenue, is the official **Niagara Falls Visitor and Convention Bureau** (daily: mid-May to Aug 8am–8pm; Sept to mid-May 9am–6pm; ☎905/356-6061 or 1-800-563-2557). Confusingly, both outlets have privately run rivals close by – and these are best avoided. There are also a number of official tourist kiosks close to the Falls, the most comprehensive being at the Maid of the Mist departure point and at the Table Rock complex.

Sightseeing tours run by Double Decker leave from beside the ticket office at the bottom of Clifton Hill several times daily from mid-May to mid-October, travelling north as far as Queenston Heights. Passengers can get on and off the bus when they wish; the $33 ticket (for Tour Package A) is valid for two days and includes admission to the river's major attractions.

Accommodation

Niagara Falls is billed as the "Honeymoon Capital of the World", which means that many of its motels and hotels have an odd mix of cheap, basic rooms and gaudy suites with heart-shaped bathtubs, waterbeds and the like. Out of season it's a buyer's market, so it's well worth trying to haggle – but if you want the easy option, assistance is available from the **Niagara Falls Visitor and Convention Bureau** (☎905/356-6061 or 1-800-563-2557). For the most part, the least expensive choices are either out along **Lundy's Lane**, an extremely dispiriting motel strip that extends west of the Falls for several kilometres, or in the uninteresting centre of **Niagara Falls town**. Neither area is much fun (especially Lundy's Lane) and you're much better off spending a little more to stay either in the **Clifton Hill area**, which has – once you've adjusted to it – a certain kitsch charm, or on leafy **River Road** – running north from the foot of Clifton Hill – which holds a string of good B&B places. If you want a room with a decent view of the Falls, you'll be paying premium rates: the premier hotels near the **Minolta Tower** offer some of the best views but you should always check the room before you shell out: descriptions can be fairly elastic and some rooms claiming to be in sight of the Falls require minor gymnastics for a glimpse.

HOTELS

Comfort Inn on the River, 4009 River Rd (☎905/356-0131 or 1-800-565-0035, fax 356-3306). Although part of a standard-issue hotel chain, this inn does possess a particularly attractive location, flanked by parkland down on River Road near the Spanish Aero Car. ④.

Oakes Inn Fallsview, 6546 Buchanan Ave (☎905/356-4514, fax 356-3651). Near the Minolta Tower with views of the Falls, this smart modern high-rise hotel features all mod cons from pool to whirlpool. ②–⑤.

Quality Inn Fallsway, 4946 Clifton Hill (☎905/358-3601 or 1-800-263-7137, fax 358-5738. Comfortable, pleasantly furnished motel-style rooms just off Clifton Hill. ②–④.

Sheraton Fallsview Hotel, 6755 Oakes Drive (☎905/374-1077 or 1-800-267-8439, fax 374-6224). Big, lavish hotel and conference centre overlooking the Falls. Near the Minolta Tower. ②–⑧.

Skyline Foxhead Hotel, 5875 Falls Ave (☎905/374-4444 or 1-800-263-7135, fax 357-4804). At the foot of Clifton Hill, this is one of Niagara's older hotels, a tidy tower block whose upper storeys have views over the American Falls. ⑥–⑧.

Venture Inn, 4960 Clifton Hill (☎905/358-3293 or 1-800-263-2557, fax 358-3818). Functional but perfectly adequate motel rooms just off Clifton Hill. ②–④.

BED AND BREAKFASTS, HOSTELS AND CAMPING

Butterfly Manor B&B, 4917 River Rd (☎ & fax 905/358-8988). In a large house set back from the road, this B&B has six air-conditioned bedrooms and also operates as a reservations agency for other Niagara B&Bs. ②.

Glen Mhor B&B, 5381 River Rd (☎905/354-2600). Pleasant B&B with four air-conditioned bedrooms. ③.

Eastwood Tourist Lodge, 5359 River Rd (☎905/354-8686). Four commodious, air-conditioned bedrooms in an attractive, old villa with elegant balconies. ③.

Niagara Falls Youth Hostel, 4549 Cataract Ave (☎905/357-0770 or 1-888-749-0058). HI hostel a 5min walk from the bus and train station in Niagara Falls town. Two-storey brick building in a dreary location: Cataract Avenue is a narrow sidestreet off Bridge Street as it approaches the Whirlpool Rapids Bridge over to the States. There are laundry facilities, bicycle rental, a kitchen and a lounge; discounts on local attractions; dormitory beds cost in the region of $17.

Niagara Glen-View Tent and Trailer Park (☎905/358-8689 or 1-800-263-2570). There are several campgrounds out along Lundy's Lane, but this site, along the river about 4.5km north of Clifton Hill, occupies a far more agreeable location at the corner of Victoria Avenue and the Niagara Parkway. It has two hundred sites starting at around $20.

Eating

There are literally dozens of cheap chain **restaurants** and fast-food bars along and around Clifton Hill. Most of them are unremarkable, though the *Fallsway Restaurant*, in the *Quality Inn* at 4946 Clifton Hill, has a good basic menu with main courses from around $8. Other possibilities include Italian pizzas and snacks at both *Mama Mia's*, 5719 Victoria Ave at Clifton Hill, and *Big Anthony's*, 5685 Victoria Ave, a family-run place owned by a well-known ex-professional wrestler, pictures of whom decorate the windows. Further afield, the *Ponderosa Steak House*, 5329 Ferry St, is good at what it does, whilst the Skylon tower has a revolving restaurant 236m up and, although dinner here will cost you $33, breakfast (from 8am) is more feasible, at $12.

Downstream from the Falls

Downstream from the Falls, the **Niagara Parkway** road follows the river parallel to the **Niagara River Recreation Trail**, a combined cycle and walking track. The road and trail loop round the treacherous waters of the Whirlpool, just beyond the Spanish Aero Car (see p.99), before continuing to the **Niagara Glen Nature Reserve**, where paths lead down from the clifftop to the bottom of the gorge, a hot and sticky trek in the height of the summer. Nearby, a little further downstream, lie the spick-and-span **Nia-**

ONTARIO'S WINES

Until the 1980s **Canadian wine** was something of a joke. The industry's most popular product was a sticky, fizzy concoction called Baby Duck and other varieties were commonly called block and tackle wines after a widely reported witticism of a member of the Ontario legislature: "If you drink a bottle and walk a block, you can tackle anyone." This state of affairs has, however, been transformed by the **Vintners Quality Alliance**, the VQA, who have, since 1989, come to exercise tight control over wine production in Ontario, which produces eighty percent of Canadian wine. The VQA's appellation system distinguishes between – and supervises the quality control of – two broad types of wine. Those bottles carrying the Provincial Designation on their labels (ie Ontario) must be made from 100 percent Ontario-grown wines from an approved list of European varieties of grape and selected hybrids; those bearing the Geographic Designation (ie Niagara Peninsula, Pelee Island or Lake Erie North Shore), by comparison, can only use *Vitis vinifera*, the classic European grape varieties, such as Riesling, Chardonnay and Cabernet Sauvignon. As you might expect from a developing wine area, the results are rather inconsistent, but the **Rieslings** have a refreshingly crisp, almost tart, flavour with a mellow, warming aftertaste – and are perhaps the best of the present Canadian range, white or red.

Over twenty **wineries** are clustered in the vicinity of Niagara-on-the-Lake and most are very willing to show visitors round. Local tourist offices carry a full list with opening times, but one of the most interesting is **Inniskillin**, Line 3 (Service Road 66), just off the Niagara Parkway, about 5km south of Niagara-on-the-Lake (daily: May–Oct 10am–6pm; Nov–April 10am–5pm; ☎905/468-3554), where you can follow a twenty-step self-guided tour. Inniskillin have produced a clutch of award-winning vintages and have played a leading role in the improvement of the industry. They are also one of the few Canadian wineries to produce **ice wine**, a sweet dessert wine made from grapes that are left on the vine till December or January, when they are hand-picked at night when frozen. The picking and the crushing of the frozen grapes is a time-consuming business and this is reflected in the price – about $50 per 375ml bottle.

gara Parks Botanical Gardens**, whose splendid **Butterfly Conservatory** (daily 9am–5/6pm; $6) attracts visitors in droves.

About 3km further on, **Queenston Heights Park** marks the original location of the Falls, before the force of the water – as it adjusts to the hundred-metre differential between the water levels of lakes Erie and Ontario – eroded the riverbed 11km upstream. Soaring above the park, there's a grandiloquent monument to Sir Isaac Brock, the Guernsey-born general who was killed here in the War of 1812, leading a head-on charge against the Americans. From beside the park, the road begins a curving descent down to the pretty little village of **QUEENSTON**, whose importance as a transit centre disappeared when the Welland Canal was completed in 1829, creating a placid waterway between lakes Erie and Ontario. In the village, on Partition Street, the **Laura Secord Homestead** (June–Aug daily 10am–6pm; $2) is a reconstruction of the house of Massachusetts-born Laura Ingersoll Secord, whose dedication to the imperial interest was such that she ran 30km through the woods to warn the British army of a surprise attack planned by the Americans in the War of 1812.

Niagara-on-the-Lake

One of the most charming places in Ontario, **NIAGARA-ON-THE-LAKE**, 26km downstream from the Falls, boasts lines of elegant clapboard houses surrounded by well-kept gardens, all spread along tree-lined streets. The town, much of which dates from the early nineteenth century, was originally known as Newark and became the first capital of Upper Canada in 1792. But four years later it lost this distinction in favour of York

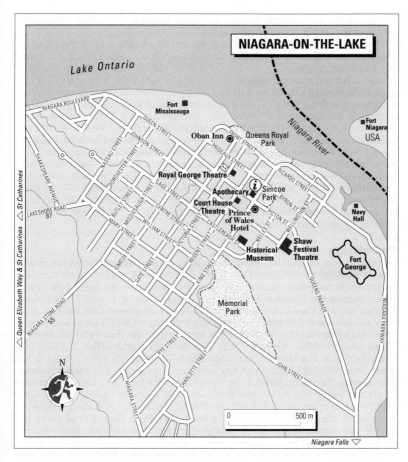

Niagara Falls ▽

(Toronto) because of its proximity to the frontier – a wise decision, for the Americans crossed the river and destroyed the place in 1813. It was rebuilt (and renamed) immediately afterwards, and has managed to avoid all but the most sympathetic of modifications ever since. This period charm attracts a few too many day-trippers for the town's own good, but the crowds are rarely oppressive, except on weekends in July and August.

The charm of Niagara-on-the-Lake lies in the whole rather than in any particular sight, but **Queen Street**, the main drag, is the setting for the **Apothecary** (June–Aug daily noon–6pm), which is worth a look for its beautifully carved wooden cabinets and porcelain jars, while the **Niagara Historical Museum**, 43 Castlereagh St (Jan & Feb Sat & Sun 1–5pm; March, April, Nov & Dec daily 1–5pm; May–Oct daily 10am–5pm; $2.50), has a mildly interesting collection of local artefacts. Niagara-on-the-Lake is also the location for one of Canada's more acclaimed theatrical seasons, the Shaw Festival (April to late Oct), featuring the work of George Bernard Shaw and his contemporaries. There are three main theatres and tickets cost between $20 and $65 – half that for Rush seats which are, when they're on offer, available from 9am on the day of the performance. Contact the **Shaw Festival box office** (☎1-800-511-SHAW or 905/468-2172) for further details.

There were so many desertions from the British military post of **Fort George** (April–Oct daily 10am–5pm; $6), 1km southeast of Niagara-on-the-Lake, that it eventually had to be garrisoned by the Royal Canadian Rifle Regiment, a force consisting mostly of married men approaching retirement who were unlikely to forfeit their pensions by hightailing it down south. If they did try and were caught, they were branded on the chest with the letter "D" and then either lashed or transported to a penal colony – except in wartime, when they were shot. The fort, part of a line of stockades slung across the waterways of the Great Lakes, was destroyed during the War of 1812, and today's site is a splendid reconstruction. The palisaded **compound** holds ten buildings, among them three pine blockhouses and the powder magazine, its inside finished in wood and copper to reduce the chances of an accidental explosion – and the soldiers who worked here wore shoes with no metal fastenings. There are also lantern-light **ghost tours** (May & June Sat 8.30pm; July & Aug Mon, Thurs & Sun 8.30pm; $5) of Fort George – good fun with or without an apparition. Tours begin at the *Queen's Landing Inn*, 155 Byron St; tickets in advance from the shop at Fort George, or from the guide at the beginning of the tour.

Practicalities

The easiest way to reach Niagara-on-the-Lake by **public transport** is on the **Shuttle bus** (☎358-3232) from Niagara Falls. From mid-April to October there are three services daily in each direction, one daily in winter, and the return fare is $15. Pick-up points include the *Sheraton Fallsview* and *Skyline Foxhead* hotels. There's also a minibus service, Van-Go, linking Niagara Falls with Niagara-on-the-Lake four times daily and this – at $12.50 return – costs a little less; ring ☎295-5167 for pick-up points.

In Niagara-on-the-Lake, the Shuttle bus stops outside the *Prince of Wales Hotel*, on Picton Street, a couple of minutes' walk from the main **tourist office**, 153 King St at Prideaux (Jan & Feb Mon–Fri 9am–5pm; March–Dec Mon–Fri 9am–5pm, Sat & Sun 10am–5pm; ☎905/468-4263), which has town maps and operates a free **room reservation service**. This is invaluable, as the town's hotels are frequently booked up months in advance – especially on summer weekends – and your only chance of a room may well be in one of the town's hundred odd **B&Bs** (③–④). This is scarcely a hardship, however, as many of these B&Bs occupy lovely old villas in the centre of town – just specify your requirements with the tourist office and they will make every effort to meet them. Incidentally, if you arrive after the office has closed, note that they display a list of last-minute vacancies in their window. Niagara-on-the-Lake also possesses some of the province's most appealing **hotels and inns**, amongst which the *Oban Inn*, 160 Front St (☎905/468-2165; ⑤), is, with its splendid gardens, quite outstanding.

It only takes a few minutes to stroll from one end of the town to the other, but to venture further afield – especially to the Falls – it's worth considering hiring a **bicycle** from Niagara Printer's & Sportswear, 92 Picton St (☎905/468-0044). For **food**, the *Buttery Restaurant*, 19 Queen St, has tasty home-made pies on its imaginative and reasonably priced menu, while *The Olde Angel Inn,* 224 Regent St just off Queen St, sells worthwhile bar snacks and is a good place for a drink – it's kitted out in the style of a British pub. Alternatively, the *Shaw Café and Wine Bar*, 92 Queen St, offers a pleasant range of pasta dishes.

Upstream from the Falls: Fort Erie

The 32km of the **Niagara Parkway** south of the Falls are less appealing than the stretch to the north, even though the road sticks close to the riverbank and gives some pleasant views over to the States. Beyond dreary Chippawa the river is wide and quiet, divided into two channels by Grand Island, just downstream of **Fort Erie**, a small industrial town at the end of the Queen Elizabeth Way (QEW) that sits opposite the American city of Buffalo. Roughly 2km south of the town, **Historic Fort Erie** (mid-May to mid-Sept daily 10am–5pm; $4.25) overlooks the lake from the mouth of the Niagara River. It's a reconstruction of the third fort the British built on the site, which was razed by the Americans in 1814, and is entered across a wooden drawbridge that leads to a central compound, where there's the usual array of army buildings and a tiny museum of military equipment.

London

The citizens of **LONDON** are proud of their clean streets, efficient transit system and neat suburbs, but to the outsider the main attractions are the leafiness of the centre and the city's two **music festivals** in late June and July – the Big Band Festival and the three-day Home County Folk Music Festival. London owes its existence to the governor of Upper Canada, **John Graves Simcoe**, who arrived in 1792 determined to develop the wilderness north of Lake Ontario. Because of its river connections to the west and south, he chose the site of London as his new colonial capital and promptly renamed its river the Thames. Unluckily, Simcoe's headlong approach to his new job irritated his superior, Governor Dorchester, who vetoed his choice with the wry comment that access to London would have to be by hot-air balloon. When York (present-day Toronto), was chosen as capital instead, Simcoe's chosen site lay empty until 1826, yet by the 1880s London was firmly established as the economic and administrative centre of a prosperous agricultural area. With a population of some 350,000, it remains so today.

The City

London's **downtown core** is laid out as a grid on either side of its main east–west axis, Dundas Street. At the west end of Dundas, close to the river, the **Art Gallery**, 421 Ridout St North (Tues–Sun noon–5pm; free), was designed by Raymond Moriyama of Toronto, a once fashionable architect whose dramatic concrete buildings are characterized by a preference for contorted curves and circles rather than straight lines. The gallery's permanent collection features a somewhat indeterminate mix of lesser eighteenth- and nineteenth-century Canadian painters and there's a modest local history section too, but the temporary modern art exhibitions – some of which come here straight from Toronto – are usually excellent.

London's oldest residence, **Eldon House** (Tues–Sun noon–5pm; $3) is a couple of minutes' walk north from the gallery, at 481 Ridout St North. Built by John Harris, a retired Royal Navy captain, in the 1830s, the house is a graceful clapboard dwelling, whose interior has been returned to its mid-nineteenth-century appearance. The British influence is also easy to pick out in the nearby **St Paul's Anglican Cathedral** – take Fullarton from the Eldon House as far as Richmond. A simple red-brick structure built in the English Gothic Revival style in 1846, it's in marked contrast to its rival cathedral, **St Peter's Catholic Cathedral**, just to the north at Dufferin and Richmond, a flamboyant, high-towered, pink stone edifice, in the French Gothic style that was so popular amongst Ontario's Catholics in the late nineteenth century.

About 8km northwest of downtown London, the **London Museum of Archaeology** (May–Aug daily 10am–5pm; Sept–Nov Tues–Sun 10am–5pm; $3.50), 1600 Attawandaron Rd, has a careful but somehow rather dreary reconstruction of a Neutral Indian village that stood here five hundred years ago – cedar palisades and elm long houses. Next door to the reconstructed village, inside the museum building, the history of these local Iroquois-speaking bands is traced through audiovisual displays and a ragbag of archeological finds. To get to the site, take bus #9 from Wharncliffe at Kensington, near the western end of Dundas; get off on Wonderland Road and follow the signs.

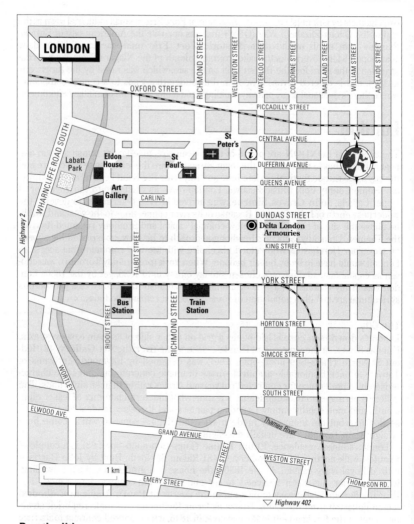

Practicalities

London's **train station** is centrally situated at York and Richmond, a couple of minutes' walk east of the **bus depot** at York and Talbot. The most central **tourist office** is in the city hall at 300 Dufferin and Wellington (Mon–Fri 8.30am–4.30pm; ☎519/661-5000 or 1-800-265-2602). As far as accommodation is concerned, the best **hotel** in town is the *Delta London Armouries Hotel*, 325 Dundas St and Waterloo (☎519/679-6111 or 1-800-668-9999; ⑤), part of which occupies an old Edwardian drill hall with a robust, crenellated facade. There's a cluster of inexpensive **motels** east of the centre along Dundas Street, including the *Motor Court*, no. 1883 (☎519/451-2610; ①); the *White Village*, no. 1739 (☎519/451-5840; ①); and the *Maple Glen*, no. 1609 (☎519/451-8300; ①). Incidentally, the cheapest hotels in town are in the vicinity of the bus station, but these are little more than flophouses that are best avoided. London also has around fifteen **B&Bs**, some of which are in fetching Edwardian villas (②) – details from the tourist office or direct from the London B&B Association, 2 Normandy Gardens (☎519/641-0467).

In recent years, **eating out** in London has become much more enjoyable, with the opening of a string of café-restaurants along and around Richmond Street, with the majority offering a broadly Mediterranean cuisine. Tempting choices include *Extra Virgin*, 374 Richmond at King, where a wide range of dishes is prepared in a variety of olive oils; the cosy *Capsaicin Café*, 432 Richmond St, with its emphasis on the use of chili peppers – capsaicin is the hot-tasting part of the plant; the *Bon Appétit*, 476 Richmond, which serves up Italian meals and has a pleasant patio area; and the inexpensive *Sunflower Café*, 646 Richmond, serving up everything from soups and sandwiches to pastas and muffins. There's a music scene, too: try the *Old Chicago Speakeasy & Grill*, on Carling, a short sidestreet off Richmond just north of Dundas, where quality R&B and blues bands sometimes perform.

Windsor and around

"I'm going to Detroit, Michigan, to work the Cadillac line" moans the old blues number, but if the singer had crossed the river he'd have been equally at home amongst the car plants of **WINDSOR**. The factories are American subsidiaries built as part of a complex trading agreement which, monitored by the forceful Canadian United Automobile Workers Union, has created thousands of well-paid jobs. Living opposite Detroit makes the "Windsors" feel good in another way too: they read about Detroit's problems – the crime and the crack – and the dire difficulties involved in rejuvenating that city, and shake their heads in disbelief and self-congratulation. A robustly working-class place, Windsor has a handful of good restaurants, a lively café-bar nightlife, and is also a good base for visiting both the remains of the British **Fort Malden** in Amherstburg, 25km to the south, and **Point Pelee National Park**, some 50km away to the southeast. The main Windsor shindig is the International Freedom Festival with all sorts of folksy events spread over an eighteen-day period in late June and early July.

The Town

Windsor itself has few specific sights, but **Dieppe Gardens**, stretching along the waterfront from the junction of Ouellette and Riverside, is a good place to view the audacious Detroit skyline. It's also overlooked by both parts of the fantastically popular Windsor **casino** – the tower block and the replica paddlesteamer, the *Northern Belle*. One block south of the riverfront, you could also drop by **Windsor's Community Museum**, 254 Pitt St West (Tues–Sat 10am–5pm, Sun 2–5pm; free), which has a small and mildly diverting local-history display. The museum occupies a pretty brick house built in 1812 by François Baby (pronounced *Baw-bee*), scion of a powerful French-Canadian clan who proved consistently loyal to the British interest after the fall of New France, an example of the money going with the power. Further afield, some 3km east of the casino, free tours of Hiram Walker & Sons' **Canadian Club Distillery**, 2072 Riverside Drive at Walker Road (all year; 1hr; times on ☎519/254-5171 ext 499) explain how whiskey is manufactured. Windsor boomed during Prohibition from the proceeds of its liquor industry, with bootleggers smuggling vast quantities of whiskey across the border into the US.

Some 6km south of the casino, in temporary accommodation until it returns to a prime riverside spot, the **Art Gallery of Windsor**, in the Devonshire Mall, 3100 Howard Ave (Tues–Fri 10am–7pm, Sat 10am–5pm, Sun noon–5pm; free), has a well-

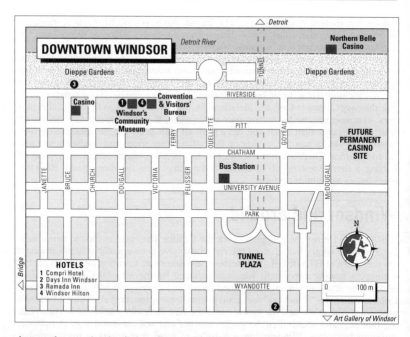

DOWNTOWN WINDSOR

△ Detroit

Detroit River

Northern Belle Casino

Dieppe Gardens **❸**

Dieppe Gardens

RIVERSIDE

Casino

❶■**❹**■

Windsor's Community Museum

Convention & Visitors' Bureau

FERRY

OUELLETTE

PITT

GOYEAU

FUTURE PERMANENT CASINO SITE

CHATHAM

Bus Station ■

UNIVERSITY AVENUE

JANETTE

BRUCE

CHURCH

DOUGALL

VICTORIA

PELISSIER

McDOUGALL

PARK

N

◁ Bridge

HOTELS
1 Compri Hotel
2 Days Inn Windsor
3 Ramada Inn
4 Windsor Hilton

TUNNEL PLAZA

WYANDOTTE

0   100 m

❷

▽ Art Gallery of Windsor

deserved reputation for the excellence of its temporary exhibitions. The permanent collection is first-rate too, and includes some good examples of the work of the Group of Seven – including Lawren Harris's skeletal *Trees and Snow* and the dramatic perspectives of Arthur Lismer's *Incoming Tide, Cape Breton Island*. Also on display is a splendid sample of Inuit art, with a particular highlight being *Hunters and Polar Bear*, a dark and elemental soapstone carving by Juanasialuk.

Practicalities

Well connected to London, Toronto and Niagara Falls, Windsor's **bus station** is right in the centre of town on Chatham, just east of the main street, Ouellette, which runs south from the river. From the bus station, Transit Windsor (☎519/944-4111) runs a shuttle service (1–3 hourly) over to Detroit via the tunnel whose entrance is bang in the middle of town at Goyeau and Park; traffic bypassing Windsor en route to Detroit uses the Ambassador Bridge, on Hwy 3. Windsor **train station** is some 3km east of the city centre, near the waterfront at 298 Walker Rd and Wyandotte; to get into the centre from here, either take a taxi ($9) or catch the Crosstown 2 bus (every 20min), which runs west along Wyandotte. The Windsor **Convention and Visitors' Bureau**, Suite 103, City Centre Mall, 333 Riverside Drive West (Mon–Fri 8.30am–4.30pm; ☎519/255-6530 or 1-800-265-3633), is located just west of Ouellette and has free maps and glossy local brochures.

The city's **downtown core** is surprisingly compact, with most of the action focused on Ouellette from the river to Wyandotte – merely five minutes' stroll from top to bottom. If you're staying the night, convenient options near the river include several chain **hotels** like the *Days Inn Windsor*, 675 Goyeau St (☎519/258-8411 or 1-800-325-2525; ③), and *Quality Suites by Journey's End*, 250 Dougal Ave (☎519/977-9707 or 1-800-228-5151; ③). The best rooms in the city are to be found in the plush, central and modern hotels overlooking the river and the Detroit skyline: the *Compri*, 333 Riverside Drive West (☎519/977-9777 or 1-800-267-9777; ⑥); the *Ramada Inn*, 480 Riverside Drive West (☎519/253-4411; ⑤); or the *Windsor Hilton*, 277 Riverside Drive West (☎519/973-5555 or 1-800-463-6655; ⑦).Otherwise, the Convention and Visitors' Bureau has the details of a handful of **B&Bs** (②–③), though most of their addresses are a good way from the centre, whilst there are several **motels** out on Hwy 2: the *Ivy Rose Motor Inn*, 2885 Howard Ave (☎ & fax 519/966-1700 or 1-800-265-7366; ③), has all mod cons including an outside swimming pool.

Amongst a bevy of busy **café-bars** dotted on and around Ouellette, try *Plunketts*, 28 Chatham St East, which specializes in pasta and grilled meats; the chic *Pitt for Pasta*, 56 Pitt St West, where they serve a good range of Italian dishes; or the stylish *Ground Zero*, 110 Chatham St West, for coffee and snacks. There are light meals at the *Coffee Exchange*, 339 Ouellette, whilst *Ye Olde Steak House*, 46 Chatham St West, and the Italian restaurant *Casa Bianca*, 345 Victoria at University, are two of the town's more established and traditional eateries.

The *Room*, available at downtown cafés and record stores, is a free monthly news sheet with **listings** of gigs and clubs, a service also provided by the local evening newspaper, the *Windsor Star*. In the city centre, the *Aar'd'vark Blues Café*, 89 University Ave West at Pelissier, has R&B and blues five nights a week and showcases the cream of the Detroit crop.

Amherstburg and Fort Malden

Highway 18 runs south from Windsor, slicing through the industrial region that edges the Detroit River, whose murky waters form the border with the US. The enmity of the Americans prompted the British to build a fort here near the mouth of the river at **AMHERSTBURG** in 1796, but it proved difficult to supply and they were forced to abandon the stockade during the War of 1812. Reoccupied after the war, the British made half-hearted attempts to improve the fort's defences and it probably would have been abandoned had it not been for the Upper Canada Rebellion of 1837. In a panic, the colonial powers rebuilt what was now called Fort Malden and garrisoned it with four hundred soldiers, stationed here to counter the efforts of the insurgents and their American sympathizers. The last troops left in 1859 and the fort was handed over to the province, who turned it into a lunatic asylum.

Today, the early nineteenth-century ditches and corner bastions of **Fort Malden** (Jan–April Mon–Fri 1–5pm, Sat & Sun 10am–5pm; May–Dec daily 10am–5pm; $3) are easy to pick out: a sequence of grassy defensive lines surrounding the excavated foundations of several buildings and a single-storey brick **barracks** of 1819. The interior of the barracks, complete with British army uniforms, is deceptively neat and trim for, as the guides explain, conditions were appallingly squalid. Across from the barracks, the asylum's old laundry and bakery has been turned into an **interpretation centre** with intriguing accounts of the various episodes of the fort's history, including the War of 1812 and the Rebellion of 1837. Original artefacts are few and far between, but it's here you'll find the powder horn of the Shawnee chief and staunch British ally, Tecumseh, one of the most formidable and renowned of the region's leaders. Born in present-day Ohio in 1769, Tecumseh spent the better part of his life struggling to keep the American settlers from spreading west into Shawnee territory. To this end he allied himself to the British, who were, he felt, less of a territorial threat, and managed by the sheer force of his personality to hold together a Native Canadian army of some size. He was killed in the War of 1812 at Moraviantown and his army promptly collapsed.

Leamington

About 400km long, the largely flat and often tedious northern shoreline of **Lake Erie** is broken up by a string of provincial parks and a handful of modest port-cum-resorts, such as Port Stanley, whose popularity declined when the more beautiful landscapes around Georgian Bay became accessible. **LEAMINGTON**, 50km southeast of Windsor, is the largest agricultural centre in this highly productive region and the nearest town to the north shore's most distinctive attraction, the elongated peninsula of **Point Pelee National Park** (see below). The main drag is Erie Street, which runs up from the harbour to the town centre at Talbot, where the **tourist office** (daily: May–Aug 9am–5pm; Sept & Oct 10am–4pm) is sited in a large plastic tomato, a reminder that Leamington is billed as the "tomato capital of Canada": there's a massive Heinz factory here.

A once-daily **bus** service runs from Toronto to the centre of Leamington, but without your own transport you'll be struggling to get round this sprawling town – and there are no connections on to Point Pelee Park, which begins 8km to the south. Neither does Leamington have anything in the way of sights – it's actually rather dull – so you're much better visiting Point Pelee on a day-trip from Windsor rather than staying the night. That said, Leamington does have a handful of reasonably priced **motels**, including a cluster along Talbot St East including the *Wigle's Colonial Motel* at no. 133 (☎519/326-3265; ③) and the *Town and Country Motor Inn*, no. 200 (☎519/326-4425; ③).

Point Pelee National Park

Occupying the southernmost tip of Canada's mainland and on the same latitude as Rome and Barcelona, **Point Pelee National Park** (daily 6am–10pm; cars $3.25; no camping) fills the southern half of a twenty-kilometre sandspit. The park boasts a variety of habitats unequalled in Canada, including marshlands and open fields, but most remarkably it is one of the few places where the ancient **deciduous forest** of eastern North America has survived: one-third of its area is covered by jungle-like forest, packed with a staggering variety of trees, from hackberry, red cedar, black walnut and blue ash to vine-covered sassafras. The park's mild climate and its mix of vegetation attract thousands of **birds** on their spring and fall migrations, and in the latter season – in September – the sandspit also funnels thousands of southward-moving **monarch butterflies** across the park, their orange and black wings a splash of colour against the greens and the browns of the undergrowth.

From the **park entrance**, it's a three-kilometre drive down behind the shore to the start of the **Marsh Boardwalk** nature trail, where there's a restaurant and bikes and canoes can be rented during the summer. It's a further 4km to the **visitor centre** (daily 10am–6pm), at the beginning of the Tilden's Wood Trail and the Woodland Trail. From April to October, propane-powered "trains" shuttle the last 3km from the visitor centre to the start of the short footpath leading to the tip of the peninsula. However, the tip itself is merely a slender wedge of coarse brown sand that can't help but seem a tad anticlimactic – unless, that is, a storm has piled the beach with driftwood.

Sarnia and around

The land south and east of **SARNIA**, a border town 100km from London, was one of the last parts of southern Ontario to be cleared and settled, as its heavy clay soil was difficult to plough and became almost impassable in rain. Established as a lumber port in 1863, Sarnia is a negligible place in itself, but offers the nearest accommodation to a couple of the region's minor sights.

With connecting services to London, Toronto, Port Huron in Michigan, and Chicago, Sarnia's **train station** is on the southern edge of town, at the end of Russell Street, an $8 taxi ride from the workaday grid iron that serves as the town centre. The **bus depot** is much more convenient – located close to the riverside on Christina at the foot of Cromwell – but both local and long-distance services are few and far between. The muncipal **tourist office** is ten minutes' walk west from the bus depot at 224 Vidal St North and George (Mon–Fri 9am–5pm), a couple of blocks back from the waterfront. There's also an **Ontario Travel Information Centre** on the northern side of the centre, beside the approach road to the Bluewater Bridge over to the States (mid-May to mid-June Mon–Thurs & Sun 8.30am–6pm, Fri & Sat 8am–8pm; late June to Aug daily 8am–8pm; Sept to mid-May daily 8.30am–4.30pm). Both offices have details of local **accommodation**, which includes a handful of B&Bs (from around $40) and a reasonable selection of chain motels strung out along London Road, one of the main drags running south of (and parallel to) Hwy 402. There's not much in the centre itself, though the garish mock-Gothicism of the *Drawbridge Inn*, 283 Christina St North (☎519/337-7571; ③), has a certain garish appeal.

Petrolia and Oil Springs

The grand stone buildings of tiny **PETROLIA**, just off Hwy 21 about 35km southeast of Sarnia, speak volumes about the sudden rush of wealth that followed the discovery of oil round here in 1855. This was Canada's first oil town and as the proceeds rolled in so the Victorian mansions and expansive public buildings followed. Several have survived, dotted along and around the main drag, Petrolia Street. Three prime examples are **Nemo Hall**, 419 King at Victoria, an impressive brick building decorated by splendid wrought-iron trimmings, **St Andrew's Presbyterian church**, close by at Petrolia and Queen, which is awash with neo-Gothic gables and towers, and the similarly ambitious **Municipal Offices**, at Petrolia and Greenfield. To emphasize the town's origins, its streetlamps are cast in the shape of oil derricks, but really, once you've had a scout round the architecture there's no reason to hang round.

Some 10km to the south along Hwy 21, the hamlet of **OIL SPRINGS** once formed the nucleus of a rough-and-ready frontier district whose flat fields were packed with hundreds of eager fortune-seekers and their hangers-on. The first prospectors were attracted to the area by patches of black and sticky oil that had seeped to the surface through narrow fissures in the rock. These **gum beds** had long been used by local native peoples for medicinal and ritual purposes, but it was not until Charles and Henry Tripp of Woodstock incorporated their oil company in 1854 that serious exploitation began. Four years later, James Miller Williams dug North America's first commercial oil well, and in 1862 a certain Hugh Shaw drilled deeper than anyone else and, at 49m, struck the first gusher. The shock of seeing the oil fly up into the trees prompted Shaw, a religious man, to use the words of his Bible – "And the rock poured me out rivers of oil" (Job 29:6). Shaw became rich, but his luck ran out just one year later when he was suffocated by the gas and sulphur fumes of his own well. At the height of the boom, the oilfields produced about 30,000 barrels of crude a day, most of it destined for Sarnia, transported by stagecoach and wagon along 45km of specially built plank road.

Just 1km south of Oil Springs, signposted off Hwy 21, the **Oil Museum of Canada** (May–Oct daily 10am–5pm; Nov–April Mon–Fri only; $3) has been built next to the site of James Williams' original well. Highlights of the open-air display area include a nineteenth-century blacksmith's shop, with some fascinating old sepia photos taken during the oil boom, and an area of gum bed. The inside of the museum has a motley collection of oil-industry artefacts and background geological information. Oil is still produced in the fields around the museum, drawn to the surface and pushed on into an underground system of pipes by some seven hundred low-lying pump jacks.

THE UNDERGROUND RAILROAD

The Underground Railroad – the UGRR – started in the 1820s as a loose and secretive association of abolitionists dedicated to smuggling slaves from the southern states of America to Canada. By the 1840s, the UGRR had become a well-organized network of routes and safe houses, but its real importance lay not so much in the number of slaves rescued – the total was small – but rather in the psychological effect it had on those involved in the smuggling. The movement of a single runaway might involve hundreds of people, if only in the knowledge that a neighbour was breaking the law. To the extent that white Americans could be persuaded to accept even the most minor role in the Railroad, the inclination to compromise with institutional slavery was undermined, though the psychology of racism remained intact: like Beecher Stowe's Uncle Tom, the freed negroes were supposed to be humble and grateful, simulating childlike responses to please their white parent-protectors.

Uncle Tom's Cabin

Some 25km south of Oil Springs, Hwy 21 slips through the agricultural town of **DRESDEN**, which is itself just 2km from **Uncle Tom's Cabin Historic Site** (mid-May to June & Sept to mid-Oct Tues–Sat 10am–4pm, Sun noon–4pm; July & Aug Mon–Sat 10am–4pm, Sun noon–4pm; $5), where a handful of old wooden buildings incorporates a simple church and the clapboard house that was once the home of the **Reverend Josiah Henson**. A slave who fled from Maryland to Canada in 1830 by means of the Underground Railroad (see box), Henson and a group of abolitionist sympathizers subsequently bought 200 acres of farmland round Dresden and founded a vocational school for runaway slaves known as the "British American Institute". Unable to write, Henson dictated his life experiences and in 1849 these narrations were published as *The Life of Josiah Henson – Formerly a Slave*. It's a powerful tract, unassuming and almost matter-of-fact in the way it describes the routine savagery of slavery – and it was immediately popular. One of its readers was **Harriet Beecher Stowe**, who met Henson and went on to write the most influential abolitionist text of the day, *Uncle Tom's Cabin* (1852), basing her main character on Henson's accounts. Most of the Dresden refugees returned to the States after the Civil War, but Henson stayed on, accumulating imperial honours that must have surprised him greatly. He was even presented to Queen Victoria and, in commemoration of this royal connection, his tombstone, which stands outside the complex, is surmounted by a crown. He died in 1883.

Henson's book is hard to get hold of, but copies ($6) are sold here at the **interpretive centre**, where there's also a small museum on slavery and the UGRR plus an intriguing video giving more details on Henson's life and times.

Bayfield and Goderich

A popular summer resort area, the southern section of the **Lake Huron shoreline** is trimmed by sandy beaches and a steep bluff that's interrupted by the occasional river valley. The water is much less polluted than Lake Ontario, the sunsets are fabulously beautiful, and in Bayfield and Goderich the lakeshore possesses two of the most appealing places in the whole of the province. Of the two, the more southerly is **BAYFIELD**, a wealthy and good-looking village whose handsome timber villas nestle amongst well-tended gardens beneath a canopy of ancient trees about 80km north of London. The villagers have kept modern development at arm's length – there's barely a neon sign in sight, never mind a concrete apartment block – and almost every old house has been beautifully maintained: look out for the scrolled woodwork, the fanlights and the graceful verandas. Historical plaques give the lowdown on the older buildings that line Bayfield's short Main Street, and pint-sized Pioneer Park on the bluff overlooking the lake is a fine spot to take in the sunset, but it's the general appearance of the place that appeals rather than any particular sight. If you've the time, you should also venture down to the harbour on the north side of the village and from there ramble up along the banks of the Bayfield River where, in season, you can pick wild mushrooms and fiddleheads – details and directions from the tourist office. In winter there's ice fishing and skating to enjoy.

There are no **buses** to Bayfield – the nearest you'll get is **CLINTON**, on the London–Owen Sound bus route (1 daily) about 15km inland on Hwy 4. If you pre-book hotel accommodation in Bayfield, the hotelier may be willing to pick you up – though such a request may be seen as being somewhat eccentric. Bayfield's **tourist office** (May–Sept Wed, Thurs, Sat & Sun 10am–6pm, Fri noon–8pm; ☎519/565-2021), in the village hall beside the green at the end of Main Street, has a full list of local **accommodation** and they will help you find a room, though their assistance is only really necessary in July and August when most places – including the B&Bs – are fully booked. At other times of the year, it's easy enough to find a place yourself. The best **hotel** for kilometres around is the outstanding *Little Inn of Bayfield*, Main St (☎519/565-2611 or 1-800-565-1832; ④), a tastefully modernized nineteenth-century timber and brick building with a lovely second-floor veranda and delightfully furnished rooms, most of which have whirlpool baths. The hotel has an annexe just across the street and once again the rooms here are simply splendid. Other options include the pleasant *Albion Hotel*, on Main Street (☎519/565-2641; ②), and several charming **B&Bs**: try beside the village green at either the *Clifton Manor*, 19 The Square (☎519/565-2282; ④; reservations required), or *Clair on the Square*, 12 The Square (☎519/565-2135; ③). Just outside of the centre, the *Camborne House* occupies the old rectory at 23 Main St South (☎519/565-5563; ③). There's **camping** at **Pinery Provincial Park** (☎519/243-8575), a popular chunk of forested sand dune beside Lake Huron about 40km south of Bayfield.

Bayfield has several great places to **eat**, but it's hard to beat the restaurant of the *Little Inn of Bayfield*, which is the best place to sample fish from Lake Huron – perch, white fish, pickerel or steelhead. Footsteps away, the *Red Pump Restaurant* is similarly classy, whilst the *Albion Hotel* has more routine, but appetizing and less costly bar food and meals. *Spago's Pizza*, just north of the village green on Hwy 2, is popular with locals and serves up a good line in pizzas, burgers and soups.

Goderich

Situated just 20km north of Bayfield at the mouth of the Maitland River, **GODERICH** is a delightful country town of eight thousand inhabitants that's saved from postcard prettiness by its working harbour. It began life in 1825, when the British-owned Canada Company bought two and a half million acres of southern Ontario – the **Huron Tract** – from the government at the ridiculously low rate of twelve cents an acre, amid rumours of bribery and corruption. Eager to profit on their investment, the company pushed the **Huron Road** through from Cambridge in the east to Goderich in the west, an extraordinary effort that was witnessed by a certain Mr Moffat – "The trees were so tall, the forest was eternally dark and with the constant rains it was endlessly damp . . . Clearing the centuries of undergrowth and tangled vines was only the beginning, the huge rotted deadfalls of hardwood had to be hauled deeper into the bush, already piled high with broken pine. Since each man was responsible for cooking his own food after a hard day's work, the men sometimes ate the fattest pork practically raw . . . To make up for such fare, a barrel of whiskey with a cup attached always stood at the roadside." Completed in 1828, the road attracted the settlers the company needed. Indeed, within thirty years, the Huron Tract had two flourishing towns, Stratford and Goderich, and was producing large surpluses of grain for export, as it continues to do today.

The Town

The wide tree-lined avenues of the geometrically planned centre of Goderich radiate from a grand octagonal circus dominated by the white-stone courthouse. From here, the four main streets follow the points of the compass.

A couple of minutes' walk up North Street, the compendious **Huron County Museum** (May–Aug Mon–Sat 10am–4.30pm, Sun 1–4.30pm; Sept–April Mon–Fri 10am–4.30pm, Sun 1–4.30pm; $3) concentrates on the district's pioneers. Highlights include a fantastic array of farm implements, from simple hand tools to gigantic, clumsy machines like the steam-driven thresher. There's also a beautifully restored Canadian Pacific steam engine and intriguing displays on the history of Huron County and the Canada Company, as well as exhibition areas featuring furniture, transportation and military memorabilia, and reconstructed rooms.

A ten-minute walk up to the far end of North Street and right along Gloucester brings you to the **Huron Historic Jail** at 181 Victoria St (April & Oct daily 1–4.30pm; May–Sept Mon–Sat 10am–4.30pm; $3), which was constructed as a combined courthouse and jail between 1839 and 1842. The tour begins on the third floor of the main block, whose claustrophobic courtroom and council chamber were originally situated next to a couple of holding cells. The design was most unpopular with local judges, who felt threatened by the proximity of those they were sentencing. The other problem was the smell: several judges refused to conduct proceedings because of the terrible odour coming from the privies in the exercise yard below. In 1856, the administration gave way and built a new courthouse in the town centre. On the second and first floors, there's the original jailer's apartment and a string of well-preserved prison cells, reflecting various changes in design between 1841 and 1972, when the prison was finally closed. The worst is the leg-iron cell for "troublesome" prisoners, where unfortunates were chained to the wall with neither bed nor blanket. The final part of the tour is through the Governor's House, with its pleasantly restored late Victorian interior.

Back in the centre, **West Street** leads the 1km through a cutting in the bluffs to the Lake Huron shoreline, just south of the harbour and salt workings. A footpath leads north round the harbour to the **Menesetung Bridge**, the old CPR railway bridge that now serves as a pedestrian walkway crossing high above the Maitland River. On the north side of the river, you can pick up the Tiger Dunlop Heritage Trail, which forms part of the longer Maitland Trail that's suitable for hikers, mountain bikers and cross-country skiers. In the opposite direction – south from the harbour – the shoreline has been tidied up to create a picnic area, but although the sunsets are spectacular the beach is unenticingly scrawny.

Practicalities

There's no **public transport** to Goderich – the nearest bus service passes through **Clinton**, about 20km inland, on its way between London and Owen Sound (1 daily). Goderich's **Tourist Information Booth** (mid-May to Aug Mon–Sat 9am–7pm, Sun 10am–7pm; Sept to early Oct Mon–Fri 9am–4pm; ☎519/524-6600) is at Nelson and Hamilton, a couple of minutes' walk northeast of the central circus, and it has details of the town's twenty-odd **B&Bs**. These average out at about $45 per double per night. Two of the more appetizing options are the *Parsonage*, 40 Victoria St South (☎519/524-6927; ②), located in a restored manse southeast of the central circus, and – on the opposite side of the circus – the *Colborne B&B*, 72 Colborne St (☎519/524-7400; ③). The **hotel** scene is less varied, but the reasonably priced *Hotel Bedford*, right in the centre at 92 The Square (☎519/524-7337; ②), is certainly distinctive. Built in 1896, the *Bedford* has an enormous open stairwell fitted with a grandiose wooden staircase just like a saloon in a John Ford movie – though the modernized rooms beyond are a bit of a disappointment. There's **camping** near town, too, just 7km north along the lakeshore at *Point Farms Provincial Park* (☎519/524-7124).

For **food**, the *West Side Restaurant*, 42 West, serves up tasty, standard dishes at reasonable prices, as does the *Park House Tavern & Eatery*, 168 West, which also offers views of the lake and is popular with the town's teenagers. Moving upmarket, *Robindale's*, in a Victorian house across from the tourist booth at 80 Hamilton St, has a more imaginative menu, but it's far more expensive.

The Bruce Peninsula

Dividing the main body of Lake Huron from Georgian Bay, the **BRUCE PENINSULA** boasts two of Ontario's most impressive national parks: the **Bruce Peninsula National Park**, whose magnificent cliff-line walks cross the best part of the east shore, and the **Fathom Five Marine National Park**, at the northern tip of the peninsula, where extraordinary rock formations, plentiful shipwrecks and limpid waters provide wonderful sport for divers. There's a reasonable choice of hotel and motel accommodation at either end of the peninsula – in **Owen Sound** and **Tobermory** – and both parks have campsites. You'll need a car to visit, though – the peninsula has no bus services.

Owen Sound

Just under 200km northwest from Toronto, **OWEN SOUND** lies in the ravine around the mouth of the Sydenham River, at the base of the Bruce Peninsula. In its heyday, Owen Sound was a rough and violent port packed with brothels and bars, prompting the Americans to establish a consulate whose main function was to bail out drunk and disorderly sailors. For the majority it was an unpleasant place to live, and the violence spawned the Women's Christian Temperance Organization, whose success was such that an alcohol ban was imposed in 1906 and only lifted in 1972. The town was in decline long before the return of the bars, its port facilities undercut by the railways from the 1920s, but it's managed to reinvent itself and is now an amiable sort of place, with three central sights of some interest: the **Marine-Rail Museum**, overlooking the harbour in the old railway station at 1165 1st Ave West (June–Sept Tues–Sat 10am–noon & 1–4.30pm, Sun 1–4.30pm; admission by donation), with photos of old sailing ships and their captains; the **Tom Thomson Memorial Art Gallery**, 840 1st Ave West (July & Aug Mon–Sat 10am–5pm, Sun noon–5pm; Sept–June Tues–Sat 10am–5pm, Sun noon–5pm; admission by donation), which has temporary exhibitions by Canadian artists and a clutch of Thomson's less familiar paintings; and the **Billy Bishop Museum**, 948 3rd Ave West (July & Aug daily 1–4pm, otherwise by appointment; admission by donation), concentrating on the military exploits of Canada's VC-winning air ace.

Owen Sound **bus station** is at 10th St East and 3rd Ave East, ten minutes' walk from the **tourist office**, which is next door to the Marine-Rail Museum at 1155 1st Ave West (Mon–Fri 9am–4.30pm June–Aug also Sat & Sun noon–4pm; ☎519/371-9833). They have a list of local accommodation, including details of a dozen **B&Bs** (①–②). There's also a handful of **motels** a couple of kilometres east of the town centre along 9th Ave East (Hwy 6/10): both the *Diamond*, no. 713 (☎519/371-2011 or 1-800-461-7849; ③), and the *Pinecrest*, no. 896 (☎519/376-3510; ②), are spick, span and modern, and have outside pools. Incidentally, **orientation** in Owen Sound is a tad difficult, but the main rules to remember are that *Avenues* run one way, *Streets* the other, while the river, which bisects the compact town centre, separates Avenues and Streets *East* from those marked *West*.

For downtown **food**, try *Green's Deli*, 261 9th St East, for excellent, cheap snacks including home-made *latke*, a potato pancake, and *beef knish*; or *Larry's Place Fish and Chips*, 791 1st Ave East and 8th St East, which serves good fish and seafood.

The Bruce Peninsula National Park

Most of the Bruce Peninsula's villages are inconclusive affairs, little more than a few shops and restaurants surrounded by second homes, and the first place worth stopping is **Cyprus Lake**, signposted off Hwy 6 just 10km south of Tobermory. With its trio of campgrounds, Cyprus Lake is the headquarters of the **BRUCE PENINSULA NATIONAL PARK** (all year; ☎519/596-2233), a magnificent mixture of limestone cliff, rocky beach, wetland and forest that's best visited in June when the wildflowers are in bloom and it's not too crowded. Four walking tracks start at the northern edge of Cyprus Lake; three of them connect with (one of the most dramatic portions of) the **Bruce Trail**, the 700-kilometre hiking trail from Queenston to Tobermory.

Tobermory

Sitting on the northern tip of the peninsula, **TOBERMORY** is an unpretentious fishing village fanning out from a sheltered double harbour – known as Big Tub and Little Tub. Many motorists pass straight through, making use of the **car ferry** to South Baymouth on Manitoulin Island (mid-June to Aug 4 daily; mid-May to mid-June & Sept–Oct 2–3 daily; 2hr; $11 single, $25 cars; ☎1-800-265-3163), but quite a few hang around to explore the Fathom Five Marine Park (see below), calling in first at the **National Park Visitor Centre** right on the Little Tub waterfront (June & Sept Mon–Fri 9am–4.30pm; July & Aug daily 9am–9pm).

There are a dozen or so **hotels** and **motels** in and around the village, with most of the less expensive establishments in category ③, though there are considerable seasonal variations. Convenient choices include the *Blue Bay Motel* (☎519/596-2392; ③), *Bruce Anchor* (☎519/596-2555; ③), the *Harbourside* (☎519/596-2422; ③) and the *Tobermory Lodge* (☎519/596-2224 or 1-800-572-2166; ③) – the last also owns some **cottages** and **chalets** overlooking Little Tub (①–②). The village has a couple of **restaurants** specializing in seafood – try the whitefish and ocean perch at the *Lighthouse*, just up from the ferry.

Prospective divers need to book in at the **Registration Centre** (mid-May to Oct daily 8am–4.30pm), beside the Little Tub, and diving gear can be hired round the corner at G&S Watersports (☎519/596-2200). **Boat rental** is available along the waterfront, working out at about $55 per day. For less immediate exploration of the waters and shipwrecks of the Fathom Five, a multitude of **boat trips** begin at Little Tub; the longer, more worthwhile excursions stop at Flowerpot Island (see below) and average out at about $15.

THE BRUCE TRAIL

Ontario's oldest and most popular long-distance footpath, the **Bruce Trail** follows the route of the Niagara Escarpment from Queenston to Tobermory. The path is maintained by the **Bruce Trail Association**, PO Box 857, Hamilton, Ontario (☎416/529-6821 or 1-800-665-HIKE), who produce a detailed hiking guide, *The Bruce Trail Guidebook* – essential reading if you're planning anything more than a day's walk. The guidebook is available from the Association and at major bookshops across southern Ontario.

Fathom Five Marine National Park

One of the Bruce Peninsula's main attractions is the **Fathom Five Marine National Park**, whose nineteen uninhabited islands are enclosed within a boundary drawn round the waters off the end of the peninsula, just north of Tobermory. To protect the natural habitat, only **Flowerpot Island**, 4km from the mainland, has any amenities, with six tiny campgrounds and five marked walking trails of roughly two hours each. A delightful spot, Flowerpot takes its name from two pink-and-grey rock pillars that have been eroded away from its eastern shore and are best seen from the Flowerpot Loop Trail.

Surprisingly, there are usually vacancies at the **campgrounds** – places can be booked at the Park Visitor Centre in Tobermory, which also provides a good guide to the island's fauna and flora. Flowerpot is accessible from Tobermory by water taxi, with a going rate of around $25 for a return. Make sure you arrange a collection time with the pilot and pack your own food and drink.

Lake Simcoe: Orillia

Highway 400 north from Toronto, the obvious route to the southern shore of Georgian Bay and Algonquin Park, runs through Barrie, a mundane industrial and commuter town beside a western arm of **Lake Simcoe**, with nothing much to recommend it except its good bus connections to the north and south.

A far more pleasant stop along Hwy 11, the road to Algonquin, is **ORILLIA**, half an hour's drive from Barrie. The town lies close to the narrow channel that connects the northern tip of Lake Simcoe with Lake Couchiching, a waterway that was once a centre of Huron settlement. When **Samuel de Champlain** arrived here in 1615, he promptly handed out muskets to his Huron allies, encouraging them to attack their Iroquois rivals in order to establish French control of the fur trade – an intervention that was to lead to the destruction of the Jesuit outpost at Sainte-Marie in 1649 (see p.123). Two hundred years later, a second wave of Europeans cleared the district's forests, and today Orillia is a trim town of 23,000 citizens; part lakeside resort, part farming centre.

Orillia **town centre** spreads out on either side of the main drag, Mississaga Street, which runs west from Lake Couchiching. At the foot of Mississaga, **Centennial Park** incorporates a marina and a boardwalk that runs north to **Couchiching Beach Park**, complete with an Edwardian bandstand and a bronze statue of Champlain. Centennial Park is the embarkation point for sightseeing **cruises** of lakes Simcoe and Couchiching on board the *Island Princess*, a replica of a paddle-boat steamer. The main non-aquatic attraction is some 3km southeast of the town centre, signposted off Hwy 12B and on the edge of a modern housing estate – the **Stephen Leacock House** (mid-June to Aug daily 10am–7pm; Sept to mid-June Mon–Fri 10am–2pm; $7). Built in 1928 in the colonial style, with symmetrical pitched roofs and an ornate veranda, this was the summer home of the humourist and academic Stephen Leacock until his death in 1944. His most famous book, *Sunshine Sketches of a Little Town*, gently mocks the hypocrisies and vanities of the people of Mariposa, an imaginary town so clearly based on Orillia that it caused great local offence. Some of the rooms contain furnishings and fittings familiar to Leacock, others shed light on his career, interests and attitudes. The books may be engagingly whimsical, but you can't help but wonder about a man who had concealed spyholes in his library so that he could watch his guests and, perhaps worse, carefully positioned his favourite living-room chair so that he could keep an eye on his servants in the pantry via the dining-room mirror. After you've explored the house, take a few minutes for the easy stroll out along the adjacent wooded headland and drop by the gift-shop, which sells almost all of his works.

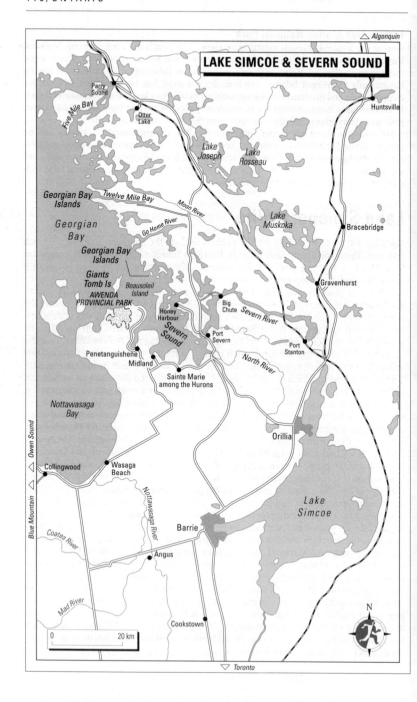

LAKE SIMCOE & SEVERN SOUND

△ Algonquin

Parry Sound

Otter Lake

Huntsville

Five Mile Bay

Lake Joseph

Lake Rosseau

Georgian Bay Islands

Twelve Mile Bay

Moon River

Georgian Bay

Go Home River

Lake Muskoka

Bracebridge

Georgian Bay Islands

Giants Tomb Is

Beausoleil Island

AWENDA PROVINCIAL PARK

Honey Harbour

Big Chute

Severn River

Gravenhurst

Severn Sound

Port Severn

Port Stanton

Penetanguishene

Midland

North River

Sainte Marie among the Hurons

Nottawasaga Bay

Orillia

◁ Owen Sound

Collingwood

Wasaga Beach

◁ Blue Mountain

Lake Simcoe

Coates River

Nottawasaga River

Barrie

Angus

Mad River

Cookstown

0   20 km

N

▽ Toronto

Practicalities

Orillia's **bus station** occupies the old railway station at the southern end of the town centre off Front St South. From here, it's a ten-minute walk along Front St South to the seasonal **tourist information centre** (☎705/326-6314) right on the harbour; the Chamber of Commerce all-year **Visitor and Convention Bureau** is at 150 Front St South (Mon–Fri 9am–5pm; ☎705/326-4424). Both have the details of local **accommodation** including several B&Bs (②), which they will book on your behalf. More pleasant than these, though, is the *Lakeside Inn*, 86 Creighton St (☎705/325-2514; ③), an unassuming modern place overlooking Lake Simcoe, about 5km southeast of town – drive across the narrows on Hwy 12 and take the signposted turning immediately after the bridge. The town's **youth hostel** (☎705/325-0970) is located at 198 Borland St East, six blocks north of Mississaga.

For **food**, *Weber's*, 16 Front St North, has a good range of burgers, steaks and sandwiches, and the *Blue Anchor Brewpub*, 47 West St South at Mississaga, serves tasty lunches. *John Dory Seafoods*, 318 Memorial Green, has a wide selection of shellfish and fresh fish, or you can head for the first-rate Italian restaurant *Cosmo's*, at 90 Mississaga St East.

Nottawasaga Bay: Wasaga Beach and Blue Mountain skiing

East of Owen Sound the southern curve of Georgian Bay forms **Nottawasaga Bay**, one of the province's most popular holiday areas. In summer, the focus of attention is the crowded resort of **Wasaga Beach**, where a seemingly endless string of chalets and cottages fringe the several kilometres of protected sand that make up **Wasaga Beach Provincial Park**. With its amusement parks and fast-food joints, there's nothing subtle about the place, but the beach is of fine golden sand, the swimming excellent and you can rent out all manner of watercraft from jet skis through to canoes. There's also one historical curiosity at the **Nancy Island Historic Site** (mid-May to late June Sat & Sun 10am–6pm; late June to Aug daily 10am–6pm; free, but parking charge), on the main drag – Mosley Street – behind Beach Area 2. In the War of 1812, the Americans managed to polish off the few British ships stationed in the upper Great Lakes without too much difficulty, and the last Royal Navy vessel, the supply ship *Nancy*, hid out here, just beyond the bay at the mouth of the Nottawasaga River. The Americans tracked down and sunk the *Nancy*, but silt subsequently collected round the sunken hull to create Nancy Island. In 1927, the hull was raised from the silt and today it forms the main exhibit of the island's museum, whose imaginative design resembles the sails of a schooner.

Wasaga Beach makes for a good day's swimming and sunbathing, but if you do decide to stay the night there are lots of reasonably priced **motels** to choose from as well as cottages and campsites – just drive along Mosley Street until somewhere takes your fancy. The seasonal **tourist office** near the Nancy Island Historic Site will help you find accommodation, as will the local Chamber's all-year **information centre** at 35 Dunkerron St and 18th, in Beach Area 3 (Mon–Fri 9am–5pm; ☎705/429-2247).

Collingwood and Blue Mountain

The small-time port of **COLLINGWOOD**, 20km west along the bayshore from Wasaga Beach, has a clutch of fine early twentieth-century buildings dotted along its main street, Hurontario – red-brick facades decorated with geometric designs and roughly dressed sandstone sills. More importantly, the town is also the gateway to the **Blue Mountain**, a segment of the Niagara Escarpment whose steepish slopes are now a major winter sports area, mainly for Alpine skiing though several cross-country trails have also been developed. To get there from Collingwood, take the Blue Mountain Road which reaches – after about 10km – the **downhill ski slopes** at the *Blue Mountain Inn* (☎705/445-0231; ③), a large and modern lodge that is the centre of wintertime activity. This is not, however, the best place to stay: instead continue along the Blue Mountain Road for another kilometre as far as the *Blue Mountain Auberge* (☎705/445-1497; ②), an informal and attractive lodge, built in Alpine style with a dozen rooms, sauna, kitchen and barbecue area, that's tucked into the wooded slopes of the Blue Mountain. It's a great location and reservations are advised both in the winter and summer, when hikers use the *Auberge* as a jumping-off point for the Bruce Trail (see p.116) which passes close by. The *Auberge* doesn't hire out ski gear, but this is readily available from outlets nearby. In total, the Blue Mountain has 33 downhill ski slopes of varying difficulty, with a maximum vertical drop of 219m and length of 1219m; the ski lifts rarely gets crowded. Toronto–Owen Sound PMCL **buses** stop in Collingwood and at the *Blue Mountain Inn* at least a couple of times a day, sometimes more.

Severn Sound

Severn Sound, the southeastern inlet of Georgian Bay, is one of the most beautiful parts of Ontario, its sheltered southern shore lined with tiny ports and its deep-blue waters studded by the outcrops of the **Georgian Bay Islands National Park**, whose glacier-smoothed rocks and wispy pines were celebrated by the Group of Seven painters. In **Discovery Harbour**, on the edge of **Penetanguishene**, and **Sainte-Marie among the Hurons**, outside Midland, Severn Sound also possesses two of the province's finest historical reconstructions – the first a British naval base, the second a Jesuit mission. Getting round the southern shore by **bus** is fairly feasible – there's a reasonably good network of local bus services, operated by PMCL and running up from Toronto via Barrie.

Penetanguishene

The most westerly town on Severn Sound, homely **PENETANGUISHENE** – "place of the rolling white sands" – was the site of one of Ontario's first European settlements, a Jesuit mission founded in 1639, then abandoned in 1649 following the burning of Sainte-Marie (see p.119). Europeans returned some 150 years later to establish a trading station where local Ojibwa exchanged pelts for food and metal tools. However, the settlement remained insignificant until just after the War of 1812, when the British built a naval dockyard that attracted shopkeepers and suppliers from both French and British communities. Today Penetanguishene is one of the few places in southern Ontario that maintains a bilingual tradition.

As is so often the case, it's the atmosphere and bayshore setting that please rather than any individual sight, though the long main drag, **Main Street**, is a pleasant enough place for a stroll, its bars and shops installed behind sturdy red-brick facades. While you're here, take a peek at the **Centennial Museum**, 13 Burke St (mid-May to mid-Oct Mon–Sat 9.30am–4.30pm, Sun noon–4.30pm; $2.50), a couple of minutes' walk east of Main Street along bayside Beck Boulevard. The museum has a reconstruction of an old fire hall, a lumber office and a general store, and features a good collection of old photos and postcards illustrating the town's early history. From the jetty at the north end of Main Street, there are also three-hour **cruises** of the southern stretches of Georgian Bay and its Thirty Thousand Islands (late June to Aug, 1 afternoon sightseeing cruise daily; $14; ☎1-800-363-7447).

Finally, 5km north of the town centre — follow the blue-and-white ship signs – is **Discovery Harbour** (late May to June & early Sept to early Oct Mon–Fri 10am–5pm, Sat & Sun 11am–4pm; July to early Sept daily 10am–5pm; $6), an ambitious and first-class reconstruction of the important British base that was established here in 1817. It was the War of 1812 against the States that gave the British the impetus to develop a naval station at Penetanguishene, primarily to keep an eye on American movements on the Great Lakes, and between 1820 and 1834 up to twenty Royal Navy vessels were stationed here, protecting the imperial interest by showing the flag and supplying the military outposts to the west. Lieutenant Henry Bayfield, who undertook the monumental task of surveying and charting the Great Lakes, used it as his winter quarters, informing his superiors of his determination "to render this work so correct that it shall not be easy to render it more so" – an ambition he achieved to such a degree that his charts remained in use for decades. The naval station was more short-lived: by 1834, relations with the US were sufficiently cordial for the Navy to withdraw and the base was turned over to the Army, who maintained a small garrison until 1856.

Staffed by enthusiastic costumed guides, the sprawling site spreads along a gentle hillside above a tranquil inlet, its green slopes scattered with accurate reconstructions of everything from a sailors' barracks, saw-pit and blacksmith's through to several period houses, the prettiest of which is the Keating House, named after the base's longest-serving adjutant, Frank Keating. Only one of the original buildings survives – the dour limestone Officers' Quarters, at the far end of the site, which dates from the 1840s. However, pride of place goes to the working-harbour-cum-dockyard where a brace of fully rigged sailing ships, the HMS *Bee* and HMS *Tecumseth*, have been rebuilt to the original nineteenth-century designs. Manned by volunteers, both schooners are used for sailing trips with the active participation of fee-paying passengers – telephone ☎705/549-8064 for times and reservations, though sailings are only definite in July and August when you can expect the *Tecumseth* (Wed, Thurs & Fri afternoons; 3.5hr; $20) and the *Bee* (Tues, Thurs & Sat evenings; 4hr; $22) to sail three times weekly. Discovery Harbour also accommodates the King's Wharf Theatre, which offers a summer season of plays as well as concerts and musicals.

Well connected to Midland and Toronto, Penetanguishene **bus station** is beside the town's principal intersection at Main Street and Robert, a ten-minute walk south of the harbour, where the **tourist office** (Mon–Fri 9am–5pm plus summer weekends 10am–6pm; ☎705/549-2232) has the details of about a dozen **B&Bs** (mostly ①) in and around town. Amongst them, the *Jury Drive B&B*, 1 Jury Drive (☎705/549-6851; ②; May–Oct), is a pleasant villa out near Discovery Harbour, while the *Chesham Grove B&B*, 72 Church St (☎705/549-3740; ②), is central and a tad less expensive. As for eating, *Memories Roadhouse*, 32 Main St, has an excellent café menu, and the *Blue Sky Family Restaurant*, 48 Main St, is an agreeable small-town diner offering good-quality snacks and meals. Incidentally, if you decide to use Penetanguishene as a base, you can zip off to other local attractions with Union Taxi (☎705/549-7666), next door to the bus station.

Awenda Provincial Park

Awenda Provincial Park (☎705/549-2231), just 11km northwest of Penetanguishene, is one of Ontario's larger parks, its delightful mainland portion dominated by a dense deciduous forest that spreads south from the Nipissing Bluff on the edge of Georgian Bay. The other section lies offshore, around Giants Tomb Island, but you'll need to bring your own boat to get there. Awenda has a few small rock-and-pebble beaches, four good **campgrounds** (May to late Sept), and a handful of hiking trails starting near the park office, which has trail guides and maps. A recommended route is to take the Bruce Trail through the forest to connect with the Dune Trail, which leads to a vantage point above the bay – 5km in all.

Midland

MIDLAND, southeast of Penetanguishene, has suffered badly from recurrent recession, losing its engineering plants in the 1930s, its shipyards in 1957 and much of its flour-mill capacity in 1967. But it has bounced back, shrugging off these setbacks with the help of provincial and federal grants, and nowadays the town has a sprightly air, its main street – King Street – an amenable parade of shops and cafés with the occasional mural to brighten up the sturdy brick buildings. Efforts to cash in on the tourist industry have included the construction of a marina and the redevelopment of the harbourfront, where sightseeing **cruises** of the Thirty Thousand Islands leave from mid-May to mid-October (1–4 daily; $14; reservations on ☎705/526-0161).

Sooner or later, every schoolkid in Midland gets taken to the **Huronia Museum** and **Huron Indian Village** (May–Aug Mon–Sat 9am–5.30pm, Sun 10am–5.30pm; Sept–April Mon–Sat 9am–5pm, Sun 10am–5pm; $5), a twenty-minute walk south of the harbour along King Street. Highlights of the museum include a large number of Huron artefacts and a series of photos tracing the pioneer settlement of Midland. The adjacent Indian Village is a replica of a sixteenth-century Huron settlement, its high palisade encircling storage pits, drying racks, a sweat bath, a medicine man's lodge and two long houses. These characteristic Huron constructions, with their bark-covered walls of cedar poles bent to form a protective arch, contain tiers of rough wooden bunks draped with furs, whilst herbs, fish, skins and tobacco hang from the roof to dry. It's all very interesting and feels surprisingly authentic, but still lags far behind the comparable section of Sainte-Marie among the Hurons up the road.

Midland **bus station** is close to the waterfront on Bay Street, metres from Deluxe Taxi (☎705/526-2217) and a couple of minutes' walk east of the **Tourist Information Centre**, at the foot of King Street (June–Aug Mon–Fri 8.30am–5pm, Sat & Sun 10am–6pm; Sept–May Mon–Fri 9am–5pm; ☎705/526-7884). The centre has the details of local and regional **accommodation** – anything from cottage rental through to a handful of downtown **B&Bs** (②), amongst which two perfectly adequate options are the *Midland B&B*, in a good-looking Victorian house at 670 Hugel Ave (☎705/526-4441; ②), and the plainer *Kylemore*, 427 King St (☎705/526-6063; ②), also occupying Victorian premises. Alternatively, there are several reasonably priced **motels** on Yonge Street, which cuts across King about 500m south of the harbourfront, as well as a chain *Comfort Inn* (☎705/526-2090; ④), on the outskirts of town at King Street and Hwy 12.

For **food**, the *Daily Perk*, 292 King St, serves first-class deli-style sandwiches and meals; *Midland Fish & Chips*, 311 King, does what it does rather well; and the *Midland Boatworks*, by the town dock, is a popular, boisterous bar, where you can also get a reasonable meal.

Sainte-Marie among the Hurons

One of Ontario's most arresting historical attractions is **Sainte-Marie among the Hurons** (mid-May to mid-Oct daily 10am–5pm; $7.25), the carefully researched and beautifully maintained site of a crucial episode in Canadian history. It's 5km east of Midland beside Hwy 12 – there are no buses, but the taxi fare from Midland is only $6.

In 1608, **Samuel de Champlain** returned to Canada convinced that the only way to make the fur trade profitable was by developing alliances with the native hunters. The Huron were the obvious choice, as they already acted as go-betweens in the exchange of corn, tobacco and hemp from the bands to the south and west of their territory, for the pelts collected to the north. In 1611, having participated in Huron attacks on the Iroqouis, Champlain cemented the alliance by a formal exchange of presents. His decision to champion one tribe against another – and particularly his gifts of firearms to his allies – was to disrupt the balance of power entirely amongst the native societies of the St Lawrence and Great Lakes area.

Social cohesion within the Huron community itself was undermined after 1639, when the **Jesuits** established their centre of operations at **Sainte-Marie**, where they succeeded in converting a substantial minority of the native people, by then enfeebled by three European sicknesses: measles, smallpox and influenza. In 1648 the Dutch on the Hudson River began to sell firearms to the Iroquois, who launched a full-scale invasion of Huronia in March 1649, slaughtering their enemies as they moved in on Sainte-Marie. Fearing for their lives, the Jesuits of Sainte-Marie burnt their settlement and fled. Eight thousand Hurons went with them; most starved to death on Christian Island, in Georgian Bay, but a few made it to Québec. During the campaign two Jesuit priests, fathers Brébeuf and Lalemant, were captured at the outpost of Saint-Louis, near present-day Victoria Harbour, where they were bound to the stake and tortured, as per standard Iroquois practice: the image of Catholic bravery and Indian cruelty lingered in the minds of French-Canadians long after the sufferings of the Hurons had been forgotten.

A visit to Sainte-Marie starts in the impressive reception centre. An audiovisual show provides some background information, ending with the screen lifting dramatically away to reveal the painstakingly restored **mission** site. The 22 wooden buildings are divided into two sections: the Jesuit area with its watchtowers, chapel, forge, farm buildings complete with pigs, cows and hens, living quarters and well-stocked garden; and the native area, including a hospital and a pair of bark-covered long houses – one for Christian converts, the other for heathens. Fairly spick and span today, it takes some imagination to see the long houses as they appeared to Father Lalemant, who saw ". . . a miniature picture of hell . . . on every side naked bodies, black and half-roasted, mingled pell-mell with the dogs . . . you will not reach the end of the cabin before you are completely befouled with soot, filth and dirt". Costumed guides act out the parts of Hurons and Europeans with great gusto, answering questions and demonstrating crafts and skills, though they show a certain reluctance to eat the staple food of the region, *sagamite*, a porridge of cornmeal seasoned with rotten fish. The grave in the simple wooden church between the Christian and native areas is believed to have been the place where the remains of Brébeuf and Lalemant were interred.

A path leads from the site to the excellent **museum**, which traces the story of the early exploration of Canada with maps and displays on such subjects as fishing and the fur trade, seen in the context of contemporary European history. This leads into a section on the history of the missionaries in New France, with particular reference to Sainte-Marie. Information on the archeology of the site follows: its whereabouts was always known as the Jesuits had all the documentation in Rome, even though local settlers helped themselves to almost every chunk of stone – from what was known locally as "the old Catholic fort" – during the nineteenth century. Excavations began on the site in the 1940s and work continues today.

Overlooking Sainte-Marie, the twin-spired church of the **Martyrs' Shrine** (mid-May to mid-Oct daily 9am–9pm; $2) was built in 1926 to commemorate the eight Jesuits who were killed in Huronia between 1642 and 1649. Blessed by Pope John Paul II in 1984 – when he bafflingly remarked that it was "a symbol of unity of faith in a diversity of cultures" – the church, along with the assorted shrines and altars in its grounds, is massively popular with pilgrims. The latter have left a stack of discarded crutches in the transept in sight of the reliquaries that claim to be from the bodies of the murdered priests.

Port Severn and Honey Harbour

Sitting on the northern shore of Severn Sound at the mouth of the Severn River, tiny **PORT SEVERN** is the gateway to the **Trent–Severn Waterway**, a 400-kilometre canalized route that connects Georgian Bay with Lake Ontario. With a minimum depth of only 2m, it's of little commercial importance today, but until the late nineteenth century it was one of the region's principal cargo routes. It's open from the middle of May to the middle of October and takes about a week to travel from one to the other. If you've the inclination for a serious boating trip, your first line of enquiry should be to the waterway's free **Cruise Planning Service** (☎1-800-663-2628); for a taster, two-hour **cruises** (May to mid-Oct 1 daily; $13) leave from Lock #45 in Port Severn, travelling as far as the **Big Chute Marine Railway**, where boats are lifted over the eighteen-metre drop between the upper and lower levels of the river. Frankly, the Big Chute is something of a yawn, but it certainly attracts its share of visitors, most of whom drive here – just follow the signs off Hwy 400 north of Port Severn.

It's 13km northwest from Port Severn across the mouth of the river and down Route 5 to **HONEY HARBOUR**, the nearest port to the Georgian Bay Islands National Park. Little more than a couple of shops, a liquor store and a few self-contained hotel resorts, the village achieved some notoriety in the 1970s when the bar of the *Delawana Inn* was the site of violent confrontations between Toronto's Hell's Angels and local Ojibwa families. The feud ended with the Angels walking home after their bikes had been dynamited. Things are much more civil today, but Honey Harbour is still a lively place in summer, with motorboats whizzing in and out as cottagers drop by to collect supplies.

There's no doubt that the beauty of Severn Sound's islet-shredded shoreline is best appreciated by boat, preferably with an island cottage as a base. This does, however, require some preplanning either in Midland or even better Toronto, where a wide range of cottage rentals are advertised. Failing that, the Georgian Bay Islands National Park has some smashing **campsites** (see below), whilst Honey Harbour's lakeshore *Delawana Inn* (☎1-800-627-3387; ⑧ for full board in high season, with discounts on package deals; late June to early Sept) has spacious chalet cabins dotted round its extensive, pine-forested grounds. Guests also have use of the resort's canoes, kayaks and windsurfers. More modestly, Honey Harbour has a couple of **B&Bs** – try the *Elk's Hideaway* (☎705/756-2993; ②), right in the centre of the village opposite the national park office. As for other practicalities, the Gray Coach **bus** service from Toronto to Sudbury passes through Port Severn, but there are no connections on to Honey Harbour; **restaurants** are few and far between – your best bet is to eat at one of the resorts; and don't forget the insect repellent.

The Georgian Bay Islands National Park

A beautiful area to cruise, the **Georgian Bay Islands National Park** consists of a scattering of about sixty islands spread between Twelve Mile Bay and Honey Harbour, a distance of about 50km. The park's two distinct landscapes – the glacier-scraped rock of the Canadian Shield and the hardwood forests and thicker soils of the south – meet at the northern end of the largest and most scenic island, **Beausoleil**, a forty-minute boat ride west of Honey Harbour. The most-visited and scenically diverse part of the park, Beausoleil has eleven short **hiking trails**, including two that start at the **Cedar Spring landing stage**, on the southeastern shore – the Treasure Trail, which heads north behind the marshes along the edge of the island, and the Christian Trail, which cuts through beech and maple stands to the balsam and hemlock groves overlooking the rocky beaches of the western shoreline. At the northern end of Beausoleil, within comfortable walking distance of the **Little Dog** and **Chimney jetties**, the Cambrian and Fairy trails are two delightful routes through the harsher Canadian Shield scenery, while, just to the west, the Dossyonshing Trail tracks through a mixed area of wetland, forest and bare granite that covers the transitional zone between the two main landscapes. The **national park** office in Honey Harbour (June–Aug Mon–Fri 8am–6pm, Sat 10am–6pm; Sept–May Mon–Fri 9am–4.30pm; ☎705/756-2415) provides a full range of information on walking trails, flora and fauna, and in winter a visit is essential as the wardens will advise on where it's safe to ski across the ice to the islands.

The park has fifteen **campgrounds**, thirteen on Beausoleil and one each on Island 95B and Centennial Island; the charge is about $10 a night and all operate on a self-registration, first-come, first-served basis; with the exception of Cedar Spring, where the visitor's centre (☎705/756-5909) takes reservations on half the 89 sites for an additional $10 fee. For everywhere else, ask about availability at the park office before you set out. Three Honey Harbour operators run a **water taxi** service over to Centennial Island, Island 95B and Beausoleil with a one-way trip costing around $28; Honey Harbour Boat Club (☎705/756-2411), about 600m from the park office, is as good as any. There are no set times, but in summer boats leave for Beausoleil every hour or so. Fares to the park's other islands are negotiable, but make sure there's an agreed pick-up time wherever you go. If you want to head southwest, a one-way water-taxi trip to Midland costs around $70.

CENTRAL ONTARIO

Lying between Lake Ontario's north shore and the Ottawa Valley border with Québec, **central Ontario** is a region that now relies on the lumber industry and tourism, but until the late eighteenth century this was the hunting ground of the Ojibwa, Cree and Ottawa tribes. This native population was squeezed out by the arrival of United Empire Loyalists escaping from the newly independent United States, a group who initially settled along the St Lawrence Valley then spread north in parallel with the construction of the **Rideau Canal** from Kingston to Ottawa. Once the economic potential of the vast interior had been realized, rail lines were laid down and the **Trent-Severn** waterway was opened up from Trenton to Georgian Bay, to serve the farmers, merchants and timber barons who rushed to populate the wilderness.

With Ontario's industries using road transport, most of the traffic on the Rideau Canal and Trent-Severn is now recreational boats, and the lakelands of the **Muskokas** and **Kawarthas** also attract vanloads of anglers and canoeists. However, the wondrous expanse of **Algonquin Park** is the best reason for visiting central Ontario, giving a glimpse of the state of this region before the white invaders got at it. Apart from the road into Algonquin, there are three other broad routes through this region: from Toronto to Ottawa, either directly via **Peterborough** and Hwy 7 or the longer route via the Loyalist towns of Lake Ontario's north shore, past historic **Kingston** and along a broad sweep of the St Lawrence; and from Port Severn along Hwy 69 towards Sudbury, following the beautiful east coast of the vast **Georgian Bay**.

Parry Sound and around

PARRY SOUND, 225km north of Toronto, is the principal resort on the shore of Georgian Bay. Named after the Arctic explorer Sir William Edward Parry, it earned the nickname of "Parry Hoot" because the log-drivers on the river chose this as the place to get drunk in. These days the town has become a popular stopover for boats roaming the Thirty Thousand Islands, of which you can get a taster by taking a **cruise** from the Government Wharf at the end of Bay Street. Canada's largest sightseeing cruise ship – the *Island Queen* – just manages to squeeze through the Thirty Thousand Islands in a spectacular and hair-raising trip (June & Sept to mid-Oct daily 2pm; also July–Aug daily 10am; $16). Seaplanes and skiplanes are a more exciting option, from $25 for twenty minutes in the air; contact Parry Sound Air Service (☎705/389-3793). The **Festival of Sound** is a well-respected classical music event that livens up the town in summer with concerts. For more **information**, try the Parry Sound Area Chamber of Commerce, in town at 70 Church St (May–Aug Mon–Thurs 8am–4pm, Fri 8am–6pm; Sept–April Mon–Fri 8am–4pm), or the tourist office 10km south of town on Hwy 69 (Mon–Thurs 9am–5pm, Fri 9am–7pm, Sat & Sun 9am–6pm). Should you want to **stay**, the best idea is to contact the Parry Sound and District Bed and Breakfast Association (☎705/746-5399; average rooms ②). Parry Sound's eateries are nothing to get excited about, but most are along James Street in the south end of town.

Nearby, Parry Island is the residence of a few hundred Ojibwa and is one of the largest Georgian Bay islands (18km long, 59km around), linked to the mainland by a swing bridge. You can rent canoes here for $2 an hour and go cove-exploring with great views of the nearby islands thrown in.

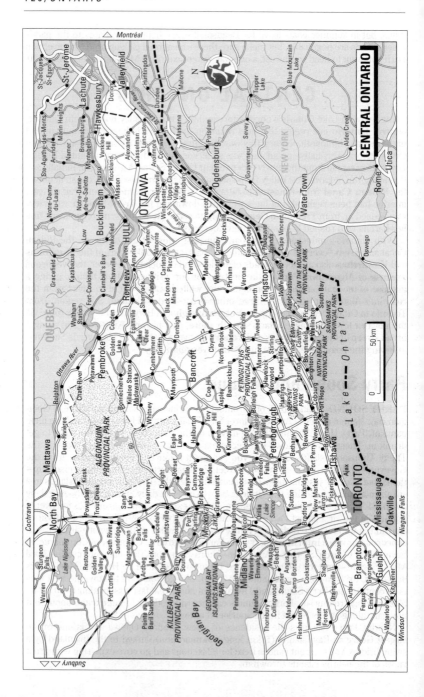

CENTRAL ONTARIO

Killbear Provincial Park

The wild Georgian Bay shoreline, formed by glaciers that scoured the rock and dumped mighty boulders onto its long beaches, is seen at its finest in **Killbear Provincial Park** (May to mid-Oct; $7), reached by driving 18km north from Parry Sound on Hwy 69 then 20km southwest on Hwy 559. Along the shore, windswept, crooked cedars and black spruce cling precariously to the Canadian Shield's southern pink granite outcrops, whilst the interior of this peninsular park is a forest of maple, beech and yellow birch. The 3.5-kilometre loop of the **Lookout Point Trail**, which starts about 1.5km east of the park office and heads to a lookout across Parry Sound, is the best of the park's three short hiking trails. Killbear gets very busy in July and August, if you're camping at any of the six **campgrounds**, some by the water, others in the forest and all costing between $14.75 and $18, you need to preregister at one of the two campground offices, situated on the park's only road (☎705/342-5227; early May to Aug). (For some peace check out those that are radio-free.) For **canoe rental** the nearest outlet is Killbear Park Mall Ltd (☎705/342-5747) in Nobel, about 5km south of the Hwy 559 turnoff.

The Muskokas

Served by Gray Coach buses and VIA trains as far as Huntsville, the route to Algonquin from Toronto passes through the **Muskokas**, a region of more than 1500 lakes and hundreds of urbanite cottage retreats. Named after an Ojibwa chief, Mesqua-Ukee, who settled here with his people after aiding the British in their defence of Little York during the War of 1812, the area was opened to tourism in 1860, when two hikers made the two-day trek from Toronto to a small Ojibwa settlement where Gravenhurst now stands. By the 1890s this had become the in place to holiday for the wealthy families of southern Ontario, and it's still primarily the preserve of city folks with lots of loot.

Gravenhurst

The gateway to Muskoka is **GRAVENHURST**, sited at the southern end of Lake Muskoka 163km north of Toronto. A favourite with painters ever since the Group of Seven painted here, Gravenhurst is also host in late February to the **Muskoka Winter Carnival**, when all manner of events are held from demolition derbies to delicate ice-sculpture competitions. Outside of carnival time, the main attraction is the **Bethune Memorial House**, 235 John St North (mid-May to late Oct daily 10am–noon & 1–5pm; late Oct to mid-May Mon–Fri only; $2.25), the birthplace of Norman Bethune, a doctor who introduced Western medicine to the Chinese in the 1930s and invented mobile blood-transfusion units. During his lifetime even Chairman Mao dedicated an essay to him. The house has been restored to how it looked in 1890 and has displays on Bethune's accomplishments – detailed in English, French and Chinese for the benefit of the Chinese leaders who make frequent pilgrimages to the house. Having surveyed the good doctor's career, you could hop aboard RMS *Segwun*, a 105-year-old steamship (the oldest still operating in North America) that cruises up Lake Muskoka from the town wharf (June to early Oct daily; $17.25–29.95 depending on length of cruise), giving a fine view of the hills and the summer mansions of Ontario's plutocrats.

The **information centre** at 295 Muskoka Rd South (Mon–Fri 8.30am–4.30pm) offers an **accommodation** service and in summer there's a kiosk at the Opera House (July–Aug daily 8.30am–4.30pm). For **B&B** you could also contact the Muskoka Bed and Breakfast Association (☎705/687-4511; average rooms ③). *Pinedale Inn*, 200 Pinedale Lane (☎687-2822; ③) is a good **motel** on the shore of Lake Gull surrounded by pine trees with rooms that have kitchenettes and bathrooms. KOA (☎705/687-2333) has a campground with full facilities on Hwy 11, 6km north of town.

For very posh food, try *Ascona Place*, 1 Bethune Drive (☎705/687-5906), possibly the best **restaurant** in the Muskokas – stick to a modest bottle and the bill should not exceed $50 each; a good alternative is *Sloanes*, 155 Muskoka St, which has been here as long as Gravenhurst, and serves a divine blueberry pie.

Bracebridge

Situated 25km north of Gravenhurst, pretty **BRACEBRIDGE** prides itself on being "Halfway to the North Pole" – the powers that be have decided this is the summer home of Santa Claus, decorating the town with all-year banners of the jolly soul and building a horrendous **Santa's Village** just west of town (mid-June to Aug daily 10am–6pm; adults and children $15.15, 2–4s $9.30, under 2s free). Admission price includes unlimited use of rides like Rudolf's Roller Coaster Sleigh Ride, Elves' Island and the Christmas Ball Ferris Wheel, as well as a meeting with Santa Claus so the kids can get their orders in nice and early. If you want to spoil the children (or yourself) some more, **Maple Orchard Farms**, 14 Gray Rd (Mon–Fri 10am & 2pm; free), runs sticky tours of its maple sugar shack and chocolate house, explaining just how maple syrup is turned into sweets.

In Bracebridge itself, **Woodchester Villa** (July & Aug Tues–Sun 9am–5pm; donation) with its **Chapel Gallery** (Tues–Sat 10am–1pm & 2–5pm; donation), is an unusual octagonal building dating from 1882 that is now a venue for arts and crafts exhibitions. The town's **information centre**, 9–1 Ontario St (Mon–Fri 9am–5pm) has details on **accommodation** in the area and can book for you, plus information on the whole Muskoka area. Good, cheap food is available at the *Muskokan*, on the corner of Kimberley and Manitoba, and the *Forget-Me-Not* tearoom, 30 Ontario St (closed Sun), which has fine teas, an awesome selection of home-made jams, and light lunches.

Huntsville

The main attraction of **HUNTSVILLE** – 35km beyond Bracebridge – is that it's as near as the buses and trains get to Algonquin Park, though it does have a Festival of the Arts in July and the pleasant **Muskoka Pioneer Village** on Brunel Road (museum daily 11am–4pm; village mid-May to June & early to mid-Oct Sat & Sun 11am–4pm; July–Sept daily 11am–4pm,; $5), where costumed staff demonstrate mid-nineteenth-century cooking and the like. If you need a place to stay before heading into Algonquin, cheap **motels** are located along King William Street – check out *Huntsville Motor Court Motel* at no. 19 (☎705/789-4431; ②), *King William Motel* at no. 23 (☎705/789-9661; ②), or the *Comfort Inn by Journey's End* at no. 86 (☎705/789-1701 or 1-800-668-4200; ③).

Algonquin Park

Created in 1893, **ALGONQUIN PARK** is Ontario's oldest provincial park and for many people is the quintessential Canadian landscape. Located on the southern edge of the Canadian Shield, the park straddles a transitional zone, with the hilly two-thirds to the west covered in a hardwood forest of sugar maple, beech and yellow birch, whilst in the drier eastern part jack pines, white pines and red pines dominate. Throughout the park, the lakes and rocky rounded hills are interspersed with black spruce bogs, a type of vegetation typical of areas far further north. Canoeing is very popular here and with an astounding 2400km of routes there's a good chance of not bumping into anybody.

Wildlife is as varied as the flora – any trip to Algonquin is characterized by the echo of birdsong, from the loons' ghostly call to the screech of ravens. Beavers, moose, black bears and racoons are all resident, as are white-tailed deer, whose population thrives on the young shoots that replace the trees felled by the park's loggers. Public "howling parties" – which can attract up to 2000 people – set off into the wilderness during August in a search of **timber wolves** and their howling – each expedition takes a park

THE BEAVER

The beaver is the national animal of Canada – it appeared on the first postage stamp issued by the Colony of Canada in 1851, and now features on the back of the current 5¢ piece. Once so vital to Canada's economy, the creatures are now viewed with affection and are largely protected.

Beavers are actually aquatic rodents, which grow to around 750cm long and weigh about 35kg. Their importance to the Canadian economy was due to their thick soft pelts, composed of long guard hairs and a dense undercoat, which was used by the native peoples for clothing long before the arrival of the Europeans. Early fur traders quickly realized the value of beaver-skins, particularly for the manufacture of felt, for which there was a huge demand for hat-making. To keep up with demand the beaver was extensively trapped, and the *voyageurs* pushed further and further west along the lake and river systems in pursuit of it, thus opening up more and more of present-day Canada. The beaver population was decimated to the point of extinction in some areas of the east, but after beaver hats went out of fashion in the nineteenth century the species rapidly recovered and outside the cities signs of the beaver are extensive.

Bark (for food) and water (in which to escape from danger) are two vital elements for beavers. They build a **dam** to create a large pond in which to escape from their enemies and to serve as a winter food store. Beavers start their dams, which can be up to 700m wide, by strategically felling one tree across a stream. This catches silt and driftwood and the beaver reinforces it with sticks, stones, grass and mud, which is laboriously smoothed in as a binding element. The **lodge** is constructed simultaneously; sometimes it forms part of the dam and sometimes it is fixed to the shore or an island in the pond. It is about 2m in diameter and has two entrances: one accessible from land and one from underwater. Lodges are topped with grass thatch and a good layer of the indispensable mud, which freezes in winter, making them virtually impenetrable. During the fall, the beaver stocks the pond formed by the dam with large numbers of young soft-bark trees and saplings; it drags these below the water line and anchors them to the mud at the bottom. It then retires to the lodge for the winter, only emerging to get food from the store or repair the dam in case of emergency. Beaver lakes are not always the tree-fringed paradises portrayed by nature-film makers; a mud-banked pond, surrounded by untidily felled trees and with a bedraggled-looking domed heap of sticks and sludge somewhere along its banks is often nearer the mark. If you spot an untidy-looking lake anywhere in northwest Ontario, the chances are that a beaver's lodge will be close by, though you're unlikely to see the ubiquitous creature itself.

ranger who knows exactly where to head, as the movements of the packs are charted with radio transmitters. If you don't have your own transport, enquire at the information centres in case there's a spare seat.

Access to the park is via either the **West Gate**, 45km from Huntsville on Hwy 60, or the less convenient **East Gate**, 56km away through the park's southern end. The well-signposted main **visitor centre**, 43km from the West Gate on Hwy 60 (late April to Oct & Christmas daily 8am–6pm; Nov to late April Sat & Sun 9am–5pm), was opened in 1993 for the park's centennial and, besides the usual gift shop, has a series of dioramas explaining the general and natural history of the Algonquin; there's also a life-size moose on display. Because Algonquin is the most popular of Ontario's parks, the park operates a **permit system** that allows a limited number of cars through each entrance every day; to avoid being turned away, either arrive early or book your $10 day permit by credit card (☎705/633-5538, fax 633-5581). Away from Hwy 60 – or the Parkway Corridor as it's known within the park boundary – walking and canoeing are the only means of transport. Before striking off into the interior, it's worth investing in *Backpacking Trails of Algonquin Provincial Park* ($1.95) and *Canoe Routes of Algonquin Provincial Park* ($4.95), both available at the information centres.

The Parkway Corridor

Accommodation along the **Parkway Corridor** is provided by eight lakeside **campgrounds**, whose location is indicated by distances from the West Gate (eg km 10). The less popular sites are those that prohibit motorboats – namely Canisbay Lake (km 23), Coon Lake (km 40) and Kearney Lake (km 37); all are open from mid-June to August. All-year camping is available at Mew Lake (km 30), which costs $9.75 off season. In summer, sites cost $15.75 without showers, $17.75 with showers. It's almost essential to **reserve** (☎705/633-5538; $6 fee). On the same number you can reserve Algonquin's **cabins** ($30–60 per night) and **yurts** ($40 per night), which are your best bet if you don't have a tent. Though meagre **food** supplies are available near Canoe Lake (km 14), Two Rivers (km 31) and Opeongo Lake (about 6km north of km 45), you are best advised to bring your own.

Of the ten **day treks** from Hwy 60, the two-kilometre **Beaver Pond Trail** (km 45) is a rugged but easy trail that takes you past huge beaver dams, while the equally short but steeper **Lookout Trail** (km 39) gives a remarkable view of the park. For a longer trail with greater chances of spotting wildlife, the eleven-kilometre **Mizzy Lake Trail** (km 15) is recommended. Other points of interest in the Parkway Corridor include two small **museums**: the Park Museum at km 20 (mid-May to mid-June Sat & Sun 9am–5pm; mid-June to early Oct daily 9am–5pm) and a Pioneer Logging Exhibit (late May to mid-Oct daily 9am–5pm) at the East Gate. A totem pole at Canoe Lake marks the spot where Tom Thomson, the artist who inspired the Group of Seven, died by drowning – the mystery of whether the expert canoeist died accidentally or was killed has never been solved.

The Park Interior

The depths of the **Park Interior** are best explored by **canoe**, and there are several outfitters in the small towns around the park's periphery, and in the Parkway Corridor itself from May to mid-October – the Portage Store at Canoe Lake and the Opeongo Store at Opeongo Lake. The latter also runs a useful water-taxi service and shuttle into the Park Interior. Because of Algonquin's popularity, two weeks' advance reservation for canoe rental is recommended (☎705/635-2243). Given Algonquin's immense popularity, canoeing is best avoided at holiday weekends: horror stories abound of three-hour jams of canoeists waiting their turn to tackle the portages between the lakes.

If you don't want to embark on the 1500km of canoe routes you can experience the Park Interior via two long-distance hiking trails from Hwy 60. The **Western Uplands Hiking Trail** (km 2.5) is composed of a series of loops that allow you to construct a hike of up to 71km, while the equally challenging **Highland Hiking Trail** (km 29) has loops of up to 35km. **Campgrounds** in the interior are limited to nine people at a time; permits ($6.50 per person per night) must be obtained from the information offices.

If you want all the organizing done for you, Call of the Wild, 23 Edward St, Markham, Ontario (☎416/200-9453 or 1-800-776-9453, fax 905/472-9453) run half-day ($35), three-day ($295), four-day ($365) and five-day ($465) personalized and relaxed adventure canoe trips in Algonquin. Price includes all meals, permits, equipment and transport from Toronto. It's essential to book in advance – mention the *Rough Guides* and you'll receive a ten percent discount. To escape the boys, Women in Wilderness, 24 Brock St West, Uxbridge, Ontario (☎705/765-3158 or 905/771-7802, fax 905/852-0416) run two- and three-day guided tours for women only.

Peterborough and around

Though it has one of Ontario's major universities, Trent University, for most people **PETERBOROUGH** is worth a call only for its access to the Kawartha Lakes and a couple of Ontario's more diverting ancient sites. Outside of the older downtown buildings and gardens, it does have one strange sight – the largest hydraulic **lift lock** in the world. The star turn on the **Trent–Severn Waterway**, the lock operates by counter-balancing two watertight boxes, each large enough to hold several vessels – an ingenious piece of engineering explained in the neighbouring interpretive centre on Hunter Street (daily: April–June, Sept & Oct 10am–5pm; July–Aug 9am–6pm; donation), where it's possible to watch the lock in action from May to September daily. If you want to experience being lifted and lowered 20m in a boat, a lift-lock **cruise** sets off from the marina (mid-May to June & Sept to mid-Oct Sat & Sun 1.30pm; July & Aug daily 1.30pm; $15).

Peterborough's newest attraction is the **Canadian Canoe Museum**, 910 Monaghan Rd (Mon–Fri 10am–5pm; donation). The museum has the world's largest collection of canoes and kayaks. Not all six hundred or so crafts are displayed at one time, but you may see the splendid Nootka whaling dugout from BC, made from one red cedar log; the Guinness world-record-holding canoe that was paddled from Winnipeg to the Amazon; the world's largest birch-bark canoe and the unusual odeyak (half-canoe, half-kayak) that the Crees–Inuit paddled from Hudson Bay to New York to protest against Hydro-Québec's James Bay II project in 1990. (Hydro-Québec were about to build a number of dams and divert rivers flowing into James Bay, which would have flooded traditional hunting areas of the Cree and Inuit.) Construction materials cover every type of wood, bark, animal skin, cloth and synthetic substance including, unbelievably, an experimental craft made of concrete. The **Peterborough Centennial Museum and Archives**, near the lift lock at 300 Hunter St East (Mon–Fri 9am–5pm, Sat & Sun noon–5pm; $2.50), is dull in comparison, though its section on the immigrant experience is interesting. Once you've done that there's just the **Hutchinson House** at 270 Brock St (Jan–March Sat & Sun 1–5pm; May–Dec Tues–Sun 1–5pm; $2), celebrating local physician Dr John Hutchinson, an Irish immigrant who died in 1847 after contracting typhus from one of his patients. The house and gardens, restored in the style of the 1840s, include a museum with exhibits pertaining to Hutchinson's second cousin Sandford Fleming, the originator of standard time, adopted across the continent in 1883, and responsible for the design of Canada's first postage stamp. They also do a fine line in teas in July and August (Tues–Sun 1–4pm).

Peterborough's Voyageur Bus Terminal is in the middle of town at 202 King St. For **tourist information**, the extremely helpful Peterborough Kawartha Tourism and Convention Bureau, 175 George St (mid-May to mid-Sept daily 8am–8pm; mid-Sept to mid-May Mon–Fri 9am–5pm) is in the now-defunct train station. Cheap **rooms** are best sought via the *Kawartha Lakes B&B* (☎1-800-574-3664 or 705/743-4101; starting from ①). For **restaurants** the best deal is at *The India Food House*, 217 Hunter St West, which offers superb Indian food at incredibly low prices, the funky *Hot Belly Mama's*, on the corner of Simcoe and Water, or *The Electric Clove*, 25 George St West, which serves Thai and Chinese food as well as the odd alligator. A favourite with students for light lunches (the home-made fries are great) is *Charlotte Anne's*, 303 Queen St. George Street is a good stamping ground for cheap **coffee shops**, including the *George Street Café* at no. 241, with a wide selection of muffins and snacks, and *Häaselton* at no. 394, which has great cappuccinos.

The Kawartha Lakes

Stretching northwards to the Canadian Shield, the drumlin terrain of the **Kawartha Lakes** is prime fishing country, most of whose visitors arrive laden with maggots and rods. Of the area's villages, one of the most attractive is **LAKEFIELD**, off Hwy 28 on the shores of Lake Katchewanooka, famous as the home of sister pioneer authors Catherine Parr Traill and Susanna Moodie. Moodie emigrated to Canada in 1832 with her new husband, a half-pay officer, and, as she explained in her most famous book

Roughing it in the Bush, regarded emigration "as a severe duty performed at the expense of enjoyment". Needless to say she detested her life in the New World, living in constant fear of the remoteness and wildlife, and finding it impossible to sustain any level of gentility in the pioneer environment. Her sister, however, was fascinated by life in Upper Canada – her *Backwoods of Canada* relishes the flora and fauna like a trained botanist, and envisages the full potential of the emergent nation.

Further north on Hwy 50, **BUCKHORN**'s **Gallery on the Lake**, on Gallery Road (daily 9am–5pm; free) exhibits works by more than twenty artists, including potters, in a hexagonal building built of knotty pine. If you want to explore the Kawarthas by canoe, Buckhorn is a good base – Club Whitesands (☎705/657-8432) rents canoes and supplies partial outfitting. If you're planning to stay, there's a concentration of reasonably priced (②) lakeside cottage resorts by the supermarket on Hwy 23 – the approach from Peterborough.

Serpent Mounds Park

From 100 to 300 AD the peoples of the so-called Point Peninsula culture conducted their ceremonial burials at the site now given over to the **Serpent Mounds Park** (late April to late Oct), 20km southeast of Peterborough (Hwy 7 east for 9km to the turnoff for Keene, then south for 11km). The park has recently been handed back to the Hiawatha band (part of the Iroquois tribe) and is no longer a provincial park. The largest of the burial mounds – 60m in length and up to 2m high – would be a compound grave: high-status individuals were interred in pits beneath the mound, while the remains of others were scattered throughout the mound fill. The rituals of burial and the development of pottery distinguish this culture from its contemporaries, and they evidently had also established extensive trade networks: this site has yielded copper from Lake Superior, silver from northern Ontario, and a conch shell from the Gulf of Mexico. An activity centre located near the mounds has displays on the exploration of the site; opening times vary but a free video presentation on the outside of the building explains the origins of the mounds. You can **camp** in the park from mid-May to mid-Oct (☎705/295-6879).

Petroglyphs Provincial Park

To the Ojibwa the sacred land of the **Petroglyphs Provincial Park** (mid-May to mid-Oct daily 10am–5pm; $6 per vehicle), 55km northeast of Peterborough, is known as Kinomagewapkong, meaning "the rocks that teach". Etched into the white crystalline limestone surface between 900 and 1400 AD, this is Canada's largest array of petroglyphs, including over nine hundred figures of spirits, people, animals, boats, weapons and other objects recounting the aboriginal story of life. Whenever a male Ojibwa entered adolescence, the elders would lead him to this site by a secret route marked by rocks that only they could decipher. The boy was then left alone in the forest, refraining from food, drink or sleep until a vision of his guardian spirit appeared, when he would be told of the particular powers he was to receive later in life – in hunting, warfare or shamanism.

The Ojibwa carvings teach that humans must coexist with nature, a lesson squandered on later settlers – a specially designed building now protects the carvings from acid rain. However, despite being beset by the socioeconomic problems that many of Canada's native peoples suffer, the Ojibwa are determined that their culture will survive. Though the traditional initiation is no longer observed, many Ojibwa make the pilgrimage to the site, where they are forced to stand with tourists to look at the petroglyphs from behind barriers. An excellent film at the site fills in the cultural background.

Prince Edward County

East from Toronto, Hwy 401 zips straight along the north shore of Lake Ontario to Québec, paralleled by the slower Hwy 2, which cuts right through the heart of most of the communities in this mainly agricultural locale. From Oshawa, the roads pass the pretty towns of Port Hope and Cobourg to Trenton, which has been all but ruined by motels and fast-food chains catering for the crews of pleasure boats on the Trent-Severn Waterway. Here and at humdrum Belleville there's a road link to **Prince Edward County**, essentially a backwater of winding lanes and isolated farms, despite the popularity of its long sandy beaches.

Referred to by its residents as **Quinte's Isle** – after the Mohawk settlement of Kente, once situated on the site now occupied by Belleville – the island has been occupied since 1000 BC, but it wasn't until the exodus of United Empire Loyalists in the late eighteenth century that any towns grew up. After the War of 1812, when the US government slapped a tax on whiskey and Americans switched to drinking beer, Prince Edward County became Ontario's major barley producer to the breweries of the US, but nowadays the farmers concentrate their efforts on fresh fruit and veg, of which they are among Ontario's largest producers.

Picton and around

PICTON is the main hub of the island and the terminus for long-distance buses, but it's no more than a peaceful, laid-back village with some impressive nineteenth-century buildings – with a wacky diversion in the shape of **Birdhouse City** to the south of the centre, a collection of 92 birdhouse replicas of local public buildings and landmarks. The **information** centre is located next to the war monument at 116 Main St (Mon–Fri 9am–5pm) and has details on the whole island. Their lists of **farm vacations** are excellent value and give a chance to sample real Ontarian cooking.

There are two **motels** in Picton itself – the *Picton Bay Inn*, 33 Bridge St (☎613/476-2186 or 1-800-678-7906; ③), and *Tip of the Bay Motor Hotel*, 35 Bridge St (☎613/476-2156; ②). Alternatively, cheap **B&Bs** can be obtained anywhere on the island through the B&B of Prince Edward County (☎613/399-1299; starting from ②).

A good, reasonably priced place to **eat** is *Daffodils*, the dining lounge of the *Tip of the Bay Motor Hotel*, but the island's best is the pricey *Waring House Restaurant*, 1.5km west of Picton on the intersection of County Road 1 and Hwy 33 (☎613/476-7492). Further west, the village of **BLOOMFIELD**, with its red-brick houses, 6km from Picton, has a renowned **restaurant**, *Angelines*, 433 Main St, with inventive food that costs a fortune but the table d'hôte is reasonable at $25. They also have a nice **motel** (☎613/393-3301; ③). Nearby the *Painted Garden Café* at no. 106 is good for snacks and ice cream. Another place to check out is the *Milford Coffee Gallery*, on the intersection of County Roads 9 and 10 south of Picton, housed in an 1886 general store, it serves delicious soups, pasta, coffees and homemade scones. Moving on from Picton to the mainland, Hwy 33 is connected by the Glenora free ferry to Aldophustown (mid-May to Oct 2–4 hourly; Nov to mid-May at least every 30min), where the bulk of the first Loyalists landed in this part of Ontario in 1794.

Lake on the Mountain Provincial Park

On an eastern finger of the island, 9km from Picton, **Lake on the Mountain Provincial Park** (early May to mid-Oct; $5 per car) preserves an extraordinary sight – a lake on top of a mountain above the Bay of Quinte. The Mohawks believed this was inhabited by powerful spirits, and European settlers were mystified by the lake's lack of an apparent source – despite recent scientific studies geologists can only guess that the sixty-metre-deep basin is replenished by ground water from neighbouring marshy grounds. An outlet flows to the Bay of Quinte, but no one has been able to explain how the lake's fluctuations exactly replicate those of Lake Erie, 200km away.

Sandbanks Provincial Park

The **Sandbanks Provincial Park** (April to late Oct; $8 per car), about 20km southwest of Picton, is the location of the island's most spectacular sand bars and dunes – the West Lake formation is the largest freshwater sand-dune system in the world (8km long, 2km wide), and the smaller East Lake side is almost as impressive. The once-straight West Lake Road is now a meandering route, evidence of the distance the dunes have moved. When barley became the staple crop of Prince Edward County, the cattle that had formerly occupied the fields were moved to the dunes, where they ate the stabilizing grasses and shrubs; it wasn't until government assistance in the 1950s and 1960s that the drift was halted. Today the sand is all but swamped by people on summer days, with an atmosphere reminiscent of Australian beach life, but without the surf. Reserved **campgrounds** are available from May to August (☎613/969-8368; April $9.75, May, June, Sept & Oct $16.75, July & Aug $17.75).

North Beach Provincial Park

Located 35km west of Picton on the south side of the island, **North Beach Provincial Park** (late June to early Sept; $7 per car) boasts a three-kilometre sandy beach that becomes absolutely packed in summer. The North Bay side of the sand bar is usually less crowded because the beach is steep there, and visitors are advised to keep children on the Lake Ontario side.

Kingston

Birthplace of Bryan Adams and self-proclaimed Limestone City, **KINGSTON** is the finest-looking and largest of the communities along this stretch of coast, even though it now has to import limestone from Niagara. Located on the Cataraqui River where Lake Ontario begins to narrow into the St Lawrence, the city's roots go back to Champlain's initiation of the fur trade with the Iroquois of Cataraqui village. By 1673 the French, under the governorship of Comte de Frontenac, had built a fortified trading post here, but its beginnings were disastrous. During Frontenac's absences the acting governor, Denonville, pursued a policy of trading the Iroquois rather than fur, inviting natives to attend conferences at the fort then shipping them back to France as slaves. Denonville was eventually forced to abandon the fort, but when it reopened in 1696 it was caught in the midst of hostilities between the Huron and Iroquois, whose long enmities were intensified by the European traders.

In 1758 the fort fell to a force of British-Americans and Iroquois, a victory soon followed by an influx of United Empire Loyalists who equipped the scrubby wooden town of Kingston with Ontario's first gristmill. By the War of 1812 Kingston had become a shipbuilding centre and the construction of the mighty *St Lawrence* ensured that no enemy ship ventured near the place. With the completion of the **Rideau Canal**, Kingston's population was swelled by the now unemployed navvies, whose ranks included a fair number of Scottish masons. These masons built limestone houses for themselves, following the model of the homes they had left behind, transformed the city and are still its greatest aesthetic asset.

Short-lived capital of Canada from 1841 to 1844, Kingston retains a wealth of links with the nineteenth century, and the scenic Thousand Islands, nearby, further enhance its appeal. Yet Kingston's main importance lies not in its tourist potential but in its military and educational institutions: **Queen's University** is one of the best known in the country, and the city is also home to Canada's equivalent of Sandhurst and West Point.

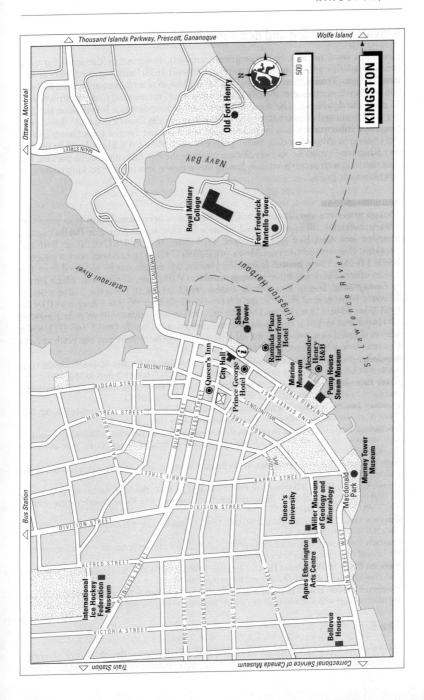

KINGSTON

Thousand Islands Parkway, Prescott, Gananoque

Wolfe Island

N

500 m

Ottawa, Montréal

MAIN STREET

Old Fort Henry

Navy Bay

Royal Military College

Fort Frederick Martello Tower

Cataraqui River

LA SALLE CAUSEWAY

Kingston Harbour

St Lawrence River

Shoal Tower

Ramada Plaza Harbourfront Hotel

Queen's Inn

City Hall

Prince George Hotel

Marine Museum

Alexander Henry B&B

Pump House Steam Museum

WELLINGTON ST

RIDEAU STREET

MONTREAL STREET

WELLINGTON ST

KING STREET EAST

ONTARIO STREET

BAGOT STREET

QUEEN STREET

PRINCESS STREET

RAGLAN ROAD

BARRIE STREET

BARRIE STREET

COURT STREET

Murney Tower Museum

Macdonald Park

DIVISION STREET

DIVISION STREET

Queen's University

Miller Museum of Geology and Mineralogy

KING STREET WEST

Bus Station

ALFRED STREET

PRINCESS STREET

BROCK STREET

JOHNSON STREET

EARL STREET

UNION STREET

Agnes Etherington Arts Centre

International Ice Hockey Federation Museum

VICTORIA STREET

Bellevue House

Train Station

Correctional Service of Canada Museum

Arrival, information and accommodation

Kingston's small **airport**, in the southeast outskirts, is served by Canadian Partners (☎613/384-7072) and Voyageur Airways (☎1-800-461-1636), with regular flights to and from Toronto. **Trains** from Toronto, Ottawa and Montréal terminate at the VIA Rail station on Hwy 2, northeast of the city at the junction of Princess and Counter streets; bus #1 goes into downtown. The terminus for Voyageur long-distance **buses** is on the corner of Division and Counter streets in the north of the city; bus #2 goes into downtown. Maps and **information** can be picked up at the Kingston Tourist Information Office, 209 Ontario St (May–Aug daily 9am–7pm; Sept–April Mon–Fri 9.30am–4pm), in the former Kingston-Pembroke Railway Station opposite the city hall. It's usually packed, but they can help with accommodation and, in the summer, provide free parking passes for downtown car parks.

Accommodation

Though prices are usually steep, much of Kingston's **accommodation** is in attractive historic buildings, all of which need advance booking in summer. For **B&Bs** contact Kingston and Area Bed and Breakfast, 47 William St (☎613/542-0214) or Bed and Breakfast Registry, 39 Glenaire Mews (☎613/545-1741), who can both book a range of B&Bs (②–③). A new **hostel** is opening shortly; full details can be obtained from the tourist office. There are three **campgrounds** in the vicinity of Kingston: *Hi-Lo Hickory Campground*, Hogan Road, Wolfe Island (☎613/385-2430; $16 a site), is at a beach location, 12km east of Wolfe Island's ferry berth off Hwy 96; *KOA Kingston*, Hwy 38 (☎613/546-6140; $18 a site; mid-May to mid-Oct) is a five-minute drive from Kingston off Hwy 401 at exit 611; and *Rideau Acres Campground*, Hwy 15 (☎613/546-2711; $16 a site) is situated 8km from the city, off Hwy 401. In the town itself you can pitch at *Lake Ontario Park,* King Street (☎613/542 6574).

Alexander Henry Bed and Breakfast, Marine Museum, 55 Ontario St (☎613/542-2261). A moored ice-breaker provides a unique B&B right downtown. Closed early Sept to May. ②.

Hotel Belvedere, 141 King St East (☎613/548-1565 or 1-800-559-0584, fax 546-4692). Beautifully decorated rooms, and rates include a delicious continental breakfast. ⑤.

Comfort Inn by Journey's End, 1454 Princess St (☎613/549-5550 or 1-800-424-6423, fax 549-1388). Three-star accommodation in Canada's budget motel chain. ③.

Hochelaga Inn, 24 Sydenham St (☎ & fax 613/549-5534). A quiet Victorian red-brick inn furnished with antiques and completed with a lovely veranda and garden. All rooms are en suite and continental breakfast is offered. ④.

Kelly's House Bed and Breakfast, 35 Wellington St (☎613/548-4796). An old oak home within walking distance of downtown. ②.

Prince George Hotel, 200 Ontario St (☎613/547-4451 or 1-800/308-8284, fax 547-4451). A beautiful 1809 heritage hotel, opposite the tourist information centre, with Victorian-style rooms, some of which overlook Lake Ontario. ④.

Queen's Inn, 125 Brock St (☎613/546-0429). One of Canada's oldest hotels (1839), now with four stars and seventeen rooms. ④.

Queen's University, various locations (☎613/545-2223, fax 545-6624). Summer accommodation in the halls of residence. ③ includes breakfast.

Ramada Plaza Harbourfront Hotel, 1 Johnson St (☎613/549-8100). Newly renovated posh hotel with pool and views of Lake Ontario and the marina. ⑥.

Western Fireside Inn, 1217 Princess St (☎613/549-2211 or 1-800-567-8800, fax 549-4523). A building made of logs with Canadian country decor. Includes whirlpools and fitness centre. ③–⑤.

The City

To get a real feel of what Kingston is all about, wander down **Brock Street**, the original main throughfare that winds up from the waterfront through the downtown core, flanked by limestone buildings that have been left to grow old gracefully. Many of the shops remain unchanged – *Cooke's Old World Shop* at no. 61 is worth popping into, not least to sample the coffee and the outrageously good smells.

At the end of Brock Street at no. 216 stands the domed **City Hall** (June–Aug Mon–Fri 8.30am–4.30pm; self-guided tours; free), billed by the tourist office as "British Renaissance Tuscan Revival-style architecture". Intended as the Parliament buildings but completed too late to fulfil that function, it has housed shops and saloons, and now contains municipal offices. Canada's first farmers' market, next door in **Market Square**, still specializes in fresh fruit and veg, but there are also excellent craft stalls and an antiques market on Sundays.

For many years Kingston's main function was a shipbuilding port responsible for the construction of warships; the first ship of the Great Lakes was built here in 1678. Kingston is still a water-orientated city and, opposite the city hall, **Confederation Park** runs the length of the waterfront, where there is a modern marina crammed with fancy yachts in the summer.

Cruises of the Thousand Islands depart from the Crawford Dock at the foot of Brock Street – take your pick between the *Island Queen Showboat*, a paddle wheeler with live vaudeville acts (May to mid-June & early Sept to early Oct, 1 daily; mid-June to early Sept, 4 daily; 3hr; $15.95) or the modern catamaran *Sea Fox II* (May to mid-June & Sept–Oct 4 daily; mid-June to Aug, 5 daily; 2hr; $12). The ferry to **Wolfe Island** just across from the harbour offers a far less scenic and very brief view of the islands (hourly 6.15am–2am; free). Tranquil Wolfe Island, with its small-town atmosphere, market gardens and clapboard houses, is worth a peek; if you're driving south, it provides an alternative route to the US border and New York State. For a different type of aquatic experience you could take the **Governor's Canoe**, a replica of a voyager's canoe that leaves from the marina below the tourist office, exploring the backwaters and islands around the town (May–Sept 4 daily; $15).

On the site of the old shipyard in the western area of the park is the **Marine Museum** of the Great Lakes, 55 Ontario St (Jan–March Mon–Fri 10am–4pm; April to mid-Dec daily 10am–5pm; $3.75), which has a nineteenth-century engine house containing the machinery to pump out the dry dock. Close by at 23 Ontario St, **The Pump House Steam Museum** (June–Aug daily 10am–5pm; $3.75) is best visited between June and early September, when the Victorian municipal water-pumping station is in action; otherwise you'll have to content yourself with model trains.

West Kingston: Queen's University and around

West from downtown along Union Street lies **Queen's University**, whose small art gallery, the **Agnes Etherington Art Centre**, on the corner of University Avenue and Queen's Crescent (Tues–Fri 10am–5pm, Sat & Sun 1–5pm; $2), has an excellent reputation both for its changing exhibitions and its permanent collection of Canadian art. Major pieces include Tom Thomson's painterly *Autumn, Algonquin Park*, and Inuit prints by Kenojuak, Pitseolak and Lucy – some of the best-known Inuit artists of modern times. Other interesting items are the heritage quilts from eastern Ontario, which date back to 1820, a comprehensive collection of West African sculptures, Canadian costume from the 1790s to the 1960s, and some seventeenth-century Dutch and Flemish paintings. Nearby in Miller Hall there's a free **Museum of Geology and Minerology** (Mon–Fri 9am–5pm) with a collection of rocks, minerals, fossils and a dinosaur exhibition.

Sir John A. Macdonald, Kingston's most famous past resident, lived as a child at 110 Rideau St and later at **Bellevue House**, 35 Centre St, on the western borders of the campus (daily: April–May & Sept–Oct 10am–5pm; June–Aug 9am–6pm; $2.50). Macdonald rented this bizarrely asymmetrical, pagoda-type house in the 1840s in the hope that the country air would improve the ill health of his wife, whose headaches were made worse by the treatment – opium. Both the house and gardens have been restored to the period of the late 1840s.

In nearby Macdonald Park, on the corner of Barrie and King St East, the **Murney Tower** (mid-May to Aug daily 10am–5pm; $2) is the most impressive of four such towers built during the Oregon Crisis of 1846–47 to defend the city's dockyards against the anticipated US attack. Displays inside elucidate the military principles, spiced with social artefacts from nineteenth-century Kingston. On Christmas Day 1885, members of the Royal Canadian Rifles regiment took their field hockey sticks and a lacrosse ball onto the frozen lake at Kingston, thereby inventing a sport that has become a national passion. In the **International Ice Hockey Federation Museum**, on the corner of York and Albert streets in the grounds of the Kingston Memorial Centre (mid-June to mid-Sept daily 10am–5pm; $2), the history of the game is illustrated by a mass of memorabilia, from the square puck used in an 1896 match between Queen's and the Royal Military College, through to the number nine sweater and gloves of Gordie Howe, who was the oldest player in the history of the professional game when he retired at the age of 52. An old National Hockey Association contract values Alf Smith of Ottawa at $500 a year; a facsimile of the million-dollar cheque awarded to prolific goal-scorer Bobby Holst in the early 1970s shows how the popularity of the game has rocketed in the last century.

Nowadays Kingston's prisons are among the most civilized in North America, enabling people to spend weekends with their jailed spouses for what are known as "trailer weekends". Things have come a long way since 1850, when members of the public paid to watch the torture of prisoners, and warden Henry Smith allowed his son to chase inmates around the yard with a bow and arrow – Smith was finally taken to court, where he was represented by none other than John A. Macdonald. Housed in the 1873 warden's residence, the **Correctional Service of Canada Museum** (just past the women's prison and opposite the men's prison) at 555 King St West (mid-May to Aug Wed–Fri 9am–4pm, Sat & Sun 10am–4pm; free) dwells on the penitentiary's darker days with a collection of torture instruments, inmate art and primitive escape devices up to the current focus on interactive counselling and education.

East Kingston: Old Fort Henry and around

Over the La Salle Bridge on a finger of land just east of the Cataraqui River stands **Old Fort Henry** (late May to early Oct daily 10am–5pm; $9.50), built to repel American invaders during the War of 1812. Though it never saw a shot fired in anger, the fort was used as a British garrison up to 1870 and as a Canadian garrison for the next twenty years until, as a mark of respect to those across the border, it was allowed to fall into disrepair.

The vast parade ground comes to life in summer, when students fill the fort with the smoke of muskets and cannons and the racket of bugles, drums and fifes (daily 2pm). Everything on offer is aimed at families, and there's masses for kids to do, from parading for drill in miniature uniforms and helping with the gun salute, to participating in lessons in a Victorian schoolroom and doing the laundry. If this doesn't appeal you can explore the ramparts, with their vistas of Lake Ontario and the Thousand Islands, as well as the magazines, kitchens and officers' quarters, and the fort's collection of firearms, medals and military equipment.

On the opposite side of Navy Bay stands the **Royal Military College**, training academy for officers of all three services. Within the beautiful grounds, the **Fort Frederick Martello Tower** (July & Aug daily 10am–5pm; free) houses a museum outlining the history of the college, the exploits of its graduates, and an arms collection that once belonged to General Porfirio Diaz, president of Mexico at the turn of the century.

Eating, drinking and nightlife

For a city its size, Kingston has a large number of excellent places to eat: for those on a tight budget there are several **cafés** worth checking out, and many of the **restaurants** are reasonably priced as well. Kingston also has several decent English-style pubs and bars that often feature live music sessions. **Nightlife** outside of the bar scene is limited to a few disco-clubs populated in the main by Queen's students, and a couple of small theatres. For **listings**, see the monthly *Key to Kingston*, available from major hotels, restaurants and the tourist office.

Cafés and snacks

The Chinese Laundry Café, 291 Princess St. Trendy café with home-made bagels and bread. Outdoor patio in the summer.

Delightfully Different Café, 118 Sydenham St. Home-made muffins and cakes, as well as salads, soups and sandwiches. Open Mon–Fri 7am–4pm.

Ghetto House Café, 506 Princess St. Friendly, large restaurant/café with big portions.

The Sleepless Goat, 91 Princess St. A bakery-cum-café serving good sandwiches, delicious breads and rolls, and great desserts.

Tara Natural Foods, 340 King St East. A huge, laid-back health-food store with great drinks and vegetarian carry-outs.

Tea and Company, 237 Brock St. Basic home-made foods, like steak-and-vegetable pie and Cornish pasties. Open Tues–Sat 7am–4pm.

White Mountain Ice-Cream, 176 Ontario St. Seriously rich home-made ice-cream and waffle cones. Try the White Mountain special – vanilla dotted with chocolate, pecan and maple brittle.

Windmill Café, 184 Princess St. Amazing cakes and a varied menu. There's a takeout deli round the side. Live music on Wednesday, Thursday and Sunday.

Restaurants

The Bistro Delight, 308 Bagot St. Czech beer and sausages and other eastern European delights.

Café Max, 39 Brock St and King St. Very popular with a cheap evening table d'hôte.

Le Caveau, 354 King St East. Cosy restaurant with fish specialities.

Chez Piggy, 68 Princess St. Kingston's best-known restaurant is housed in a restored stable dating from 1810. The patio is packed in summer and the interior has handcrafted pine and limestone walls. The menu has Thai, Vietnamese, South American, African and standard North American influences, with good lunch-time specials at $7. Closed Mon.

Clark's by the Bay, 4085 Bath Rd (☎613/384-3551). One of eastern Canada's best restaurants, with prices to match but a reasonable prix fixe. Booking essential.

The Curry Village, 169a Princess St (☎613/542-5010). Popular, reasonably priced Indian restaurant; reservations recommended.

Darbar, 478 Princess St. Moderately priced Indian place with great tandooris and breads from a traditional oven.

River Mill, 2 Cataraqui St (☎613/549-5759). Beautifully situated overlooking the inner harbour, this is another one for a splurge. Canadian specialities and delicious fish; reservations recommended.

Stoney's, 189 Ontario St. Lakeside restaurant with terrace serving pizzas, ribs, seafood, salads and steaks.

Bars, pubs and clubs

A.J.'s Hangar, 360 Princess St. A favourite with the student population, you can dance to live bands and play pool; the decor includes a complete aeroplane.

Cocamo's, 178 Ontario St. Disco with the usual lights, screens and bopping bodies, apparently based on New York's Limelight.

Duke of Kingston, 331 King St East. The best of Kingston's English pubs, with darts and pool tables. Live bands on Thursdays and Sundays.

Kingston Brewing Company, 34 Clarence St. A brew pub serving natural ales and lagers brewed on the premises. The brewery is open to the public and there is also a beer garden.

The Sports, 125 Brock St. Excellent sports bars with big screens and free popcorn. It is rumoured that the Ontario Hockey Association was formed here.

Stages, 380 Princess St. Popular nightclub on three levels, with laser shows and live entertainment. $3 admission. Open until 3am on Fridays and Saturdays.

TirNanÓg, 200 Ontario St. Opposite the tourist information office, the Irish pub was handcrafted in Ireland and the ceiling was swiped from a century-old Irish nunnery. The Guinness is good and there's live Celtic music on Wednesday & Sunday nights.

Toucan–Kirkpatrick's, 76 Princess St. Student pub with excellent live music from blues to traditional Irish. Thursday is underground night with alternative music, which can produce some surprises.

The Wellington, 207 Wellington St. Always packed, noisy and fun; live bands and an occasional admission charge.

Kingston to Ottawa: the Rideau Canal

The **Rideau Canal**, which cuts through 200km of coniferous and deciduous forest, bogs, limestone plains and granite ridges, was completed in 1832 after a mere six years' work, but at the cost of the lives of scores of workers, many of whom had immigrated from Scotland and Ireland to dig the canal. Though intended to provide continental transport with a safer route than the St Lawrence, which after the War of 1812 was considered vulnerable to American attack, the canal never became anything more than an artery for regional commerce – albeit one that led to the development of Canada's capital and attracted more settlers to eastern Ontario. The introduction of the railways in the 1850s further diminished its significance, and by the end of the last century pleasure boats were already plying the route regularly. Today the holiday traffic is thicker than ever. The route can also be walked along the waymarked **Rideau Hiking Trail** – information from the Rideau Trail Association in Kingston (☎613/545-0823). There are campgrounds near all 24 lock-stations.

The upper St Lawrence

Heading east from Kingston along the shore of the St Lawrence, the first sixty or so kilometres are dominated by the **Thousand Islands** – the meandering Hwy 2 is known as the Thousand Islands Parkway, and the towns along it have little interest other than as jumping-off points for island cruises. Beyond the islands, the river was an eighty-kilometre sequence of rapids until, in the 1950s, the US and Canadian governments created the **St Lawrence Seaway** – the world's longest artificial shipping lane. The project made the waters navigable to the massive ocean-going freighters and created power plants to harness the river's hydroelectric potential, most notably at **Cornwall**, Ontario's easternmost town and site of the biggest dam in the northern hemisphere. On a negative note, the Seaway necessitated the destruction of many riverside towns, a process at which one local newspaper scribe bewailed, "once again another patch of Ontario is sicklied o'er with the pale cast of progress". One threatened patch has survived by transplantation to the **Upper Canada Village**, near Morrisburg, the region's most popular and worthwhile sight (see p.142).

The Thousand Islands

The **Thousand Islands** – the 1768 chunks of Canadian land that have inspired a salad dressing – were called Manitouana "Garden of the Great Spirit" by the native population, who believed they were created when petals of heavenly flowers were scattered on the mighty river. Part of the Frontenac axis, a ridge of million-year-old rock that stretches down into New York State, the islands are mostly pink granite covered in pine, birch and poplar trees, and in spring they become a wonderful show of white when the provincial flower, the trillium, blooms.

The populated islands range from **Wellesley Island**, with its *Millionaire's Row*, right down to **Just Room Enough Island**, with its single tiny home. Along with Irving Berlin and Jack Dempsey, the most famous resident of the islands was George Boldt, owner of New York's *Waldorf Astoria*, who in 1899 bought one of the islands and reshaped it into a heart as a tribute to his wife – hence the name **Heart Island**. He spent $2 million building the huge turreted **Boldt Castle** (mid-May to early Oct daily 10am–6pm; $5) with material from around the world, then abandoned it when his wife died, taking his new salad-dressing recipe back to New York. The Thousand Islands Bridge Authority purchased the castle for $1 in 1978, and it can be explored on a trip from Gananoque (see below) – take your passport, as it's in American waters. Other sights you might pick out from the boat are the island of **St Helena**, which has a house built in the shape of Napoleon's hat, and Canada's shortest international bridge between the two Zavikon Islands.

Gananoque

GANANOQUE, 29km beyond Kingston, offers the best trips to the Thousand Islands from this side of the border and gets packed in summer, of which the most rewarding is the cruise to Boldt Castle (early May to mid-Oct, 2–9 daily; 3hr; $15). In the Mitchell–Wilson building on the waterfront **Dinosaurs in Gananoque** (July & Aug daily 10am–9pm; $4) has full-cast dinosaur skeletons and fleshed-out models to scare the kids. And if that's not enough you can really scare them at the **House of Haunts** on Water and Main streets across from the boat dock (mid-May to mid-Oct daily 9am–6pm; July & Aug 9am–9pm; $4) for a ghoulish tour of a house built in 1883. There are masses of **motels** around Gananoque – most convenient for the cruises is the *Blinkbonnie Motor Lodge*, 50 Main St (☎613/382-7272; ②), one block from the dock, or, for a nicer inn, carry on down Main Street to *The Victoria Rose*, 279 King St West (☎613/382-3368; ③). The **information centre** at 2 King St East (July & Aug daily 8.30am–7pm; Sept–June Mon–Fri 8.30am–5pm; ☎613/382-3250) has details of other vacancies.

Brockville

The industrial city of **BROCKVILLE**, 80km from Kingston, is a nice-looking but rather dull community, founded in 1785 by the Loyalist William Buell, and once claiming more millionaires per capita than anywhere else in Canada. You get some idea of the level of excitement in modern Brockville from the fact that its chief sight is the oldest **railway tunnel** in the country, disused since 1954 and now home to a 1954 CP caboose which holds a museum (mid-June to Aug Tues–Sun 10am–5pm; 50¢). Tunnel Bay, opposite, is the departure point of Thousand Island **cruises** on a replica of a St Lawrence steamboat (mid-May to mid-Oct, 2 daily; $9–13), passing St Helena, Heart and Wellesley islands. From Tunnel Bay, a walk through the Armagh S. Price Park brings you to one of the town's oldest homes, **Brockville Museum**, 5 Henry St (mid-May to mid-Oct Mon–Sat 10am–5pm, Sun 1–5pm; mid-Oct to mid-May Mon–Fri 10am–4.30pm; $1.50), which illustrates the history of the town. Nearby, William Buell's village green, at the end of Broad Street, is dominated by the 1842 county courthouse and jail (Mon–Fri 8am–4pm; free), and the four churches that mark each corner.

Fulford Place, 287 King St West (Wed, Sat & Sun 1–5pm; $2.50) is a vast mansion built at the turn of the century for Senator George Taylor Fulford, who made his fortune with a cure-all remedy brilliantly marketed as "Pink Pills for Pale People".

Information is available from the Tourist Office in City Hall, 1 King St (mid-June to Aug daily 8am–8pm; Sept to mid-June Mon–Fri 9am–4.30pm). Head north along Stewart Boulevard for reasonably priced **motels** – try the *Queen's Grant Motor Hotel* at no. 325 (☎613/345-1437; ③).

Prescott

The deep-water port of **PRESCOTT** – rather eclipsed since the opening of the St Lawrence Seaway – was founded in 1810 by General Prescott with land granted to him in thanks for his efforts during the American Revolution. Though now tied to the US by the bridge to Ogdensburg, New York, the people of Prescott raucously celebrate their Loyalist origins in the third week of July, when the ten-day Loyalist Days Festival includes the largest military pageant in Canada.

The pageant takes place at **Fort Wellington National Historic Site** on Hwy 2 east (mid-May to Sept daily 10am–6pm; Oct to mid-May by reservation Mon–Fri 10am–5pm; ☎613/925–2896; $2.25), which was built, like Kingston's Fort Henry, to protect the vulnerable St Lawrence frontier during the War of 1812. It was completed in 1814 and was never attacked, though its garrison captured two American fortifications in Ogdensburg. After the completion of the Rideau Canal the fort fell into disrepair and it wasn't until 1837 that the British rebuilt it as a guard against the Canadian rebels and their American sympathizers. The subsequent bloody four-day engagement known as the Battle of the Windmill was the last action seen by the troops of Fort Wellington, apart from the short-lived Irish-American Fenian raids of 1865. The four original 1813 structures are surrounded by artillery-resistant earthworks, while the 1838 stone blockhouse contains a guardroom, armoury, powder magazine and barracks, all refurnished as of the mid-nineteenth century.

There's a seasonal **tourist office** in the lighthouse on Water Street (June–Aug daily 10am–5pm).

Upper Canada Village

During the construction of the St Lawrence Seaway the villages of **Iroquois** and **Morrisburg** were relocated to escape the river's rising waters, and are now situated 18km and 31km respectively from Prescott. The finest of the endangered buildings were painstakingly reconstructed 11km west of Morrisburg to form the **UPPER CANADA VILLAGE** (late May to early Oct daily 9.30am–5pm; late May to Aug $9.50, Sept to early Oct $8.75), situated on Hwy 2 in Crysler Farm Battlefield Park. This is an entirely self-sufficient settlement, whose inhabitants are skilled at producing cheeses, quilts, brooms, bread and cloth in exactly the same way as their pioneer ancestors – not one nail is machine-made. The site is easily accessible by public transport, as the Colonial Montréal–Toronto and Ottawa–Cornwall buses both serve the village.

A nice place to stay hereabouts is the *Upper Canada Migratory Bird Sanctuary Nature Awareness Campsite*, 14km east of Morrisburg on Hwy 2 (☎613/543-3704).

Cornwall

The largest town on the St Lawrence, **CORNWALL** has little to recommend it. Founded in 1784 by Scottish Loyalists, it is now a rather ugly industrial city of just over 47,000, who rely on pulp, paper, hydroelectric dams and cotton. The town is right on the border, and has a bridge to New York State in the US.

If you do decide to stop, the **Inverardan Regency Cottage Museum** on Montréal Road (April–Nov Tues–Sat 11am–5pm, Sun 2–5pm; free) is a beautiful house on the banks of the St Lawrence. Built for fur merchant John Macdonald in 1816, it is replete with period furniture. There's also a small attraction, the **Wood House Museum**, 731 Second St (April–Nov Tues–Sat 11am–5pm, Sun 1–5pm), which has a collection of Canadian art and local artefacts. The **information** office is also on Montréal Road at no. 1302 (Mon–Fri 8.30am–4.30pm). The *Gemini Café*, 241 Pitt St, has quality food or there are fast-food outlets on Vincent-Massey Street; for accommodation, there are a string of **motels** on the same street.

OTTAWA

OTTAWA has three major claims to fame: it's the capital of the second biggest country on the planet, it's the Western world's coldest capital, and popular opinion holds that it is one of the world's dullest. The Canadian government, all too aware of the third, have spent lashings of dollars to turn Ottawa into "a city of urban grace in which all Canadians can take pride". The grid-planned streets virtually sparkle. Buggies guzzle up the litter even in pouring rain, snow is whisked off the pavements as soon as it hits the deck, and because Ottawa's main industry is chinwagging, pollution is almost non-existent. Ottawa has been painstakingly groomed to impress visitors and stimulate its population of just over 313,000 with parks and gardens, bicycle and jogging paths, national museums, cultural facilities like the National Arts Centre and a downtown farm – just in case the four-kilometre-wide green belt isn't close enough.

This investment is resented by many Canadians, an attitude that has been almost constant since Queen Victoria, inspired by some watercolours of the **Gatineau Hills**, declared Ottawa the capital, leaving Montréal and Toronto smarting at their rebuff. Once Victoria had made her momentous decision things started to happen in Ottawa – it changed from a brawling, boozy lumbering town to a place where Canada's future would be decided. As nineteenth-century pundit Goldwin Smith curtly pointed out, Ottawa was "a subarctic lumber village converted by royal mandate into a political cockpit".

Yet, despite the promotion in status, the capital has a small-town atmosphere and an easily manageable size. It is divided by the Rideau Canal into Upper and Lower Town: to the west, on the steep banks of the Ottawa River, the Gothic-inspired **Parliament Buildings** are the high point of Upper Town, whilst in Lower Town the focal point is the boulevard of Sussex Drive, which curves along the river to the posh locale of Rockcliffe in the northeast, passing the glasshouse of the **National Gallery** and several other smaller museums on the way. To the south, beyond the Lower Town, the **National Museum of Science and Technology** is the main draw.

As Parliament Hill resounds to politicians debating the complexities of Québec nationalism, exemplary Canadian diplomacy has ensured that the national capital is not an anglophone bastion. The Québécois town of **Hull**, just across the Ottawa River in a region known as the Outaouais, is linked to Ottawa by five bridges and is fast becoming an integrated part of the city, though Hull is still very proud of its French heritage – after the introduction of Québec's language laws one local shopkeeper was fined $1000 for displaying an English "Merry Christmas" poster. Federal investment has created Hull's wonderful **Musée Canadien des Civilisations**, and the marriage of the two settlements is confirmed by the five-kilometre tourist route called **Confederation Boulevard**, which links the main attractions on both sides of the river.

Various immigrant communities – including Italians, Lebanese and Chinese – have enriched the atmosphere of Ottawa in recent years, bringing international **restaurants** and numerous festivals to the scene. Renovations of historic districts such as the **Byward Market** in Lower Town have paved the way for the development of trendy boutiques, eateries and open-air markets – finding a ready market among the students from Carleton University and the University of Ottawa. A city dubbed too perfect for excitement is at last reforming its reputation.

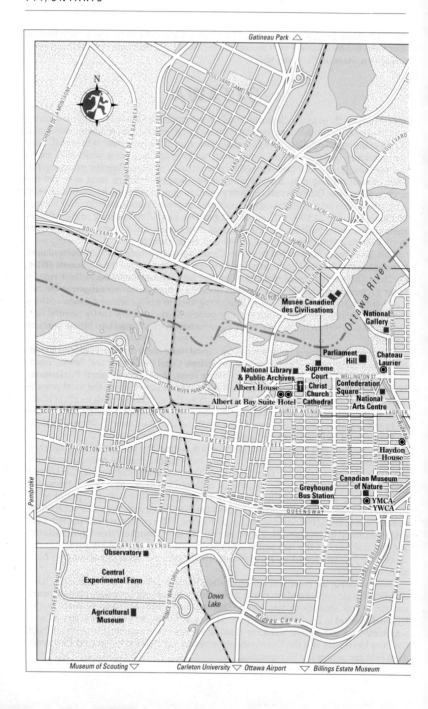

Gatineau Park △

N

CHEMIN DE LA MONTAGNE

PROMENADE DE LA GATINEAU

PROMENADE DU LAC DES FÉES

BOULEVARD GAMELIN

BOULEVARD ST-JOSEPH

BOUL MONTCLAIR

BOULEVARD

ST-RÉDEMPTEUR

BOUL SACRÉ-CŒUR

LAURIER

LAURIER

MONTCALM

ST-LAURENT

MAISONNEUVE

BOULEVARD TACHÉ

Ottawa River

PROM DU PORTAGE

OTTAWA RIVER PARKWAY

Musée Canadien
des Civilisations

National
Gallery

SUSSEX DRIVE

Parliament
Hill

Chateau
Laurier

National Library
& Public Archives

Supreme
Court

WELLINGTON ST

Confederation
Square

Albert House

Christ
Church
Cathedral

National
Arts Centre

Albert at Bay Suite Hotel

PARKDALE AVENUE

SCOTT STREET

WELLINGTON STREET

LAURIER AVENUE

WELLINGTON STREET

SOMERSET STREET

LAURIER

Rideau

GLADSTONE AVENUE

BAYSWATER AVENUE

PRESTON STREET

BOOTH STREET

BRONSON AVENUE

BAY STREET

KENT STREET

BANK STREET

O'CONNOR STREET

METCALFE STREET

ELGIN STREET

Haydon
House

Canadian Museum
of Nature

Greyhound
Bus Station

YMCA-
YWCA

QUEENSWAY

Pembroke △

FISHER AVENUE

CARLING AVENUE

Observatory

Central
Experimental Farm

*Dows
Lake*

Agricultural
Museum

PRINCE OF WALES DRIVE

Rideau Canal

QUEEN ELIZABETH DRIVEWAY

COLONEL BY DRIVE

MAIN STREET

Museum of Scouting ▽   Carleton University ▽ Ottawa Airport   ▽ Billings Estate Museum

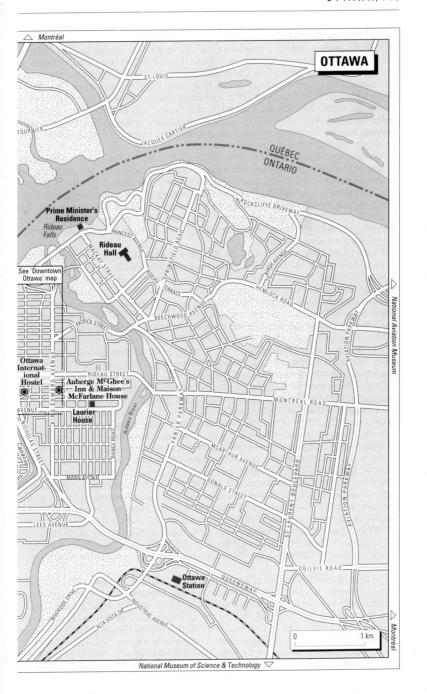

OTTAWA

△ Montréal

ST-LOUIS

FOURNIER

JACQUES CARTIER

QUÉBEC
ONTARIO

ROCKCLIFFE DRIVEWAY

Prime Minister's Residence
Rideau Falls

PRINCESS AVENUE

SPRINGFIELD ROAD

BIRCH AVENUE

Rideau Hall

MACKAY STREET

RIDEAU TERRACE

HEMLOCK ROAD

See 'Downtown Ottawa' map

BEECHWOOD AVENUE

ST PATRICK STREET

AVIATION PARKWAY

National Aviation Museum ▷

Ottawa International Hostel

RIDEAU STREET

Auberge McGhee's Inn & Maison McFarlane House

KING EDWARD AVENUE

RIDEAU RIVER

MONTREAL ROAD

Laurier House

AVENUE

NICHOLAS STREET

RANGE ROAD

VANIER PARKWAY

MCARTHUR AVENUE

ST LAURENT BOULEVARD

AVIATION PARKWAY

MANN AVENUE

DONALD STREET

LEES AVENUE

RIVERSIDE DRIVE

Ottawa Station

QUEENSWAY

OGILVIE ROAD

INDUSTRIAL AVENUE

ALTA VISTA DR

△ Montréal

0   1 km

National Museum of Science & Technology ▽

A brief history of Ottawa

OTTAWA's earliest history is much like that of every other logging town in Ontario. The Outaouais, a tribe of Algonquian Indians, hunted in this area for thousands of years. Then in 1613 Samuel de Champlain pitched up, paused to watch his Indian guides make sacrifices of tobacco to the misty falls which he christened **Chaudière** (French for "cauldron") and took off in search of more appealing pastures. Later, when Champlain established Canada's fur trade with Europe, the **Ottawa River** became a major transportation route, but the area where Ottawa now stands remained just a camping stop for the voyagers, Jesuit missionaries and European explorers who trickled slowly into this newly discovered wilderness.

Permanent settlement began in 1800 on the north side of the river, when **Philemon Wright** snowshoed up the frozen Ottawa River from Massachusetts. Wright called the small settlement Wrightstown, a name he later changed to **Hull** in honour of his parents' birthplace in England. At this time Britain was embroiled in the Napoleonic Wars and desperate for shipbuilding wood, and it didn't take long for Wright to realize the economic potential of the pine that grew all around him. He had soon worked out a way of shifting the tall trees by squaring them off, tying them together and floating them as rafts down the river to Montréal.

It wasn't until the construction of the **Rideau Canal** in 1826 that development shifted from the north to the south side of the river. The area was then settled by a mixed workforce of Irish, Scottish and French workers, army engineers and British veterans from the Napoleonic and American wars, all of them under the command of **Lieutenant-Colonel John By** and the Royal Engineers. **Bytown**, as the new town was called, became the centre for not only the canal workers and military personnel, but also a rush of immigrants from Ireland escaping the potato famine, and a seasonal population of raftsmen from winter logging camps. The loggers drank most of their earnings in the taverns of Bytown, while the English, Irish, Scottish and French did not leave their political differences in Europe: the result was that nights in Bytown were characterized by drunken brawls and broken bones.

Despite these raucous goings-on, a group of American lumber barons were attracted to the area: the workers were already there, the Ottawa River and Rideau Canal provided perfect access, and wood was plentiful. By the mid-1830s, Wrightsville and Bytown were the centre of the Ottawa River Valley's squared-timber trade.

In 1855 Bytown became **Ottawa** in a bid to become the capital of the Province of Canada, hoping that a change of name would relieve the town of its sordid reputation. In order to secure the title the community stressed its attractive location conveniently between Upper and Lower Canada, its remoteness from America, and its industrial prosperity. Queen Victoria's decision in 1857 upset the other contenders, but an American newspaper noted that it was an easily defended capital, as any "invaders would inevitably be lost in the woods trying to find it". America may have been able to see the wisdom in the queen's choice, but the politicians sent to work in the capital did not – Sir Wilfred Laurier, prime minister from 1896, found it "hard to say anything good" about the place. Nonetheless, this did not stop him and his successor Mackenzie King trying to convert Ottawa from the "Westminster in the wilderness" to the "Washington of the North".

For all their efforts it remained a rough-and-ready town until the late 1940s, when the Paris city planner, Jacques Greber, was commissioned to beautify the city with a profusion of parks, wide avenues and tree-lined pathways. A decade later the railway and its associated noise and dirt were removed from the city centre, and the huge green belt was established to prevent urban sprawl. For many years there was a law against building structures higher than the Parliament Buildings Peace Tower, which is 89.5m high. Later changes in the regulations paved the way for the construction of high-rise office buildings and apartments, transforming but not engulfing a capital that is now a showpiece for the nation.

Arrival, information and transport

The **Ottawa International Airport** is a twenty-minute drive south of the city. An airport bus run by Carleton Bus Lines links the airport to various downtown hotels and leaves every half-hour at a cost of $9. The cheaper local bus #96 from outside the airport travels to Billings Bridge at the south end of the city, where you can pick up a transfer and change to bus #1 for Elgin in downtown (for fares, see "City transport", below). A taxi from or to downtown will set you back about $18.

Ottawa's spanking new **train station** is on the southeastern outskirts at 200 Tremblay Rd, about 5km from Parliament Hill. There are direct VIA Rail trains to and from Belleville, Brockville, Kingston, Montréal and Toronto, but they are frequently late, especially in the winter, and massive cuts in the services occur every year. Local bus #95 goes downtown; a taxi fare to the centre is approximately $15.

Long-distance **buses** arrive at and depart from the Voyageur bus station at 265 Catherine St on the corner of Kent just off the Queensway. Take local bus #4 to get further downtown.

Information

The **Capital Infocentre**, 90 Wellington St (daily: mid-May to Aug 8.30am–9pm; Sept to mid-May 9am–5pm), is the slick new centre for information right opposite the Parliament Buildings. It's a busy place but the staff can help you to find accommodation as well as a mass of info about the city – they have a scale model of Ottawa that really helps to get your bearings – and there's even a computer terminal outside if the centre is closed. Information on the capital can also be obtained by phoning ☎1-800-465-1867.

City transport

Downtown Ottawa, incorporating parts of both Upper and Lower towns, is an extremely compact area and can be crossed by foot in a little over half an hour. To make the most of the entire capital, the best idea is to hire a **bicycle** and take advantage of Ottawa's 150km of safe and scenic pathways (see "Listings"), but if you'd prefer to roam without effort, there's the **bus** service run by OCTranspo on the south side and STO on the north side of the river. The buses from both companies interconnect along Rideau and Wellington streets in Ottawa, and around the Portage Bridge area and at Place d'Accueil in Hull. All routes in downtown Ottawa meet at the Rideau Transit Mall on Rideau between Nicolas and Sussex and the Mackenzie King Bridge. Buses run from 6am to around midnight. In Ottawa, fares are $1.85 ($2.80 for express services), and in Hull tickets cost $2.60 ($3.10 for express services). Tickets can be bought at corner stores, or on the bus itself if you have the correct change. If you need to change buses to complete your journey, ask for a transfer (at no extra cost) – they are valid for both systems for up to an hour.

It is only really necessary to take a **taxi** after midnight, when most of the buses have finished. All are metered and start with $2.60 on the clock, charging $1 per kilometre, with a tip of ten to fifteen percent average. Taxis can only be boarded at ranks, which are located outside major hotels and nightspots: central ones include *Chateau Laurier* and *The Novotel* on Nicolas, and during the small hours fleets of taxis wait outside Promenade de Portage in Hull to return revellers to Ottawa.

The Ottawa telephone code is ☎613. The Hull telephone code is ☎819.

Accommodation

With all the business conferences in Ottawa, there is no shortage of rooms in the city, but average **hotel** prices tend to be quite high. On the other hand, even the poshest hotels knock a good chunk off their price tags in the summer, when Parliament is in recess, and special weekend rates are also widely available – make sure you ask about these, as some places might neglect to mention them. The best bet for a low-cost room in downtown Ottawa, though, is **B&B**; the number of these increases every year and they offer one of the few ways to stay in a heritage building – and most have free parking. Should the places we've listed be booked up, try one of Ottawa's three referral services, all of whom have B&Bs in and around the capital starting in price from category ②: Capital Bed and Breakfast, 2071 Riverside Drive (☎737-4129); Ottawa Bed and Breakfast Association, 488 Cooper St (☎563-0161); or Ottawa Centretown Bed and Breakfast Association, 253 McLeod St (☎234-7577).

Of course the other way drivers can avoid Ottawa's mob of traffic wardens is to stay in a **motel**; the majority are located to the east and west of town, but there are a couple downtown too. The cheapest beds in town are at the official HIC **hostel**, which is open all year round and is right downtown. There are also **campgrounds** close to the heart of the city, with a single reservation service (☎456-3016).

Hotels

Albert at Bay Suite Hotel, 435 Albert St (☎238-8858). Smart and roomy self-catering suites in downtown, that can sleep up to six comfortably. ⑥.

Capital Hill Hotel and Suites, 88 Albert St (☎235-1413 or 1-800-463-7705, fax 235-6047). A few blocks from Parliament Hill, this 158-year-old hotel has been around almost as long as Ottawa and has recently been completely renovated. Hotel ④, suites ⑤.

Chateau Laurier, 1 Rideau St (☎241-1414 or 1-800-441-1414, fax 786-8030). Slap bang next to the Parliament Buildings, this 500-room hotel is reminiscent of a stocky Disney castle. It's a favourite drinking hole of politicians: dress up to check in, or risk being thrown out. ⑦.

Doral Inn, 486 Albert St (☎230-8055 or 1-800-26-DORAL, fax 237-9660). Five minutes from the Parliament Buildings, next to the Bay Mall. A restored 1879 inn, this is one of the few reasonable Ottawa hotels with a touch of character and it offers special weekend rates. It has a coffee shop, pool and Spanish restaurant. ③–⑤.

Lord Elgin Hotel, 100 Elgin St (☎235-3333 or 1-800-267-4298, fax 235-3223). This Ottawa landmark has all the pomp of a classy hotel but has reasonable prices, including weekend and summer rates. ④.

Somerset House Hotel, 352 Somerset St West (☎233-7762). Downtown's cheapest hotel which is above a pub. Apartments and rooms with basic facilities. ③.

Quality Hotel by Journey's End, 290 Rideau St (☎789-7511 or 1-800-424-6423, fax 789-2434). Part of a chain, right downtown, with full facilities and comfort. ④.

Motels

Parkway Motel, 475 Rideau St (☎789-3781 or 1-800-263-0649, fax 789-0207). Rather characterless, despite its good downtown location. Three-star motel with a cheap coffee shop, free parking, air conditioning and TVs in all rooms. ③.

Richmond Plaza Motel, 238 Richmond St (☎722-6591, fax 764-5539). A small, low-budget west Ottawa motel. ②.

Town House Motor Hotel, 319 Rideau St (☎789-5555, fax 789-6196). Dull, three-star motel in a good location. ③.

Traveller's Inn, 2098 Montréal Rd (☎745-1531). Out of downtown but well priced, with a pool. ②.

WelcomINNs, 1220 Michael St (☎748-7800 or 1-800-387-4381, fax 748-0499). Part of a chain across Canada, this very modern motel is situated in east Ottawa. Rates include continental breakfast. ②–③.

Bed and Breakfasts

Albert House, 478 Albert St (☎236-4479 or 1-800-267-1982, fax 237-9079). Seventeen-bedroomed heritage mansion which has been well restored to include bathrooms en suite. ③–⑤.

L'Auberge du Marché, 87 Guiges Ave (☎241-6610 or 1-800-465-0079). In the heart of Byward Market. Often full, and very popular; only four bedrooms. ②.

Auberge McGee's Inn, 185 Daly Ave (☎237-6089, fax 237-6201). A restored Victorian mansion with fourteen bedrooms, some with Jacuzzis. ②–⑥.

Australis Guest House, 35 Marlborough Ave (☎235-8461). Rooms with fireplaces in this three-room heritage home, 20min walk from Parliament Hill; price includes full delicious breakfast. Pick-up from train or bus stations. ②.

Beatrice Lyon Guest House, 479 Slater St (☎236-3904). Another three-bedroomed place right downtown, just off Bank Street; price includes full breakfast. ②.

Foisy House, 188 St Andrew St (☎562-1287). Close to downtown with a pool and just three rooms. ②.

Gasthaus Switzerland Inn, 89 Daly Ave (☎237-0335 or 1-800-267-8788). Swiss-style B&B with muesli for breakfast. 22 rooms with private bathrooms. Smoke-free. ②.

Haydon House, 18 The Driveway (☎230-2697). Victorian home with antiques and Canadian art. Free parking and breakfast. ②.

Laurier Guest House, 329 Laurier Ave East (☎238-5525). Well located, cheap, but no breakfast. ①.

Maison McFarlane House, 201 Daly Ave (☎341-0095). Three air-conditioned bedrooms and full breakfast. The most expensive room has a jacuzzi. ②.

Natures Choice, 263 McLeod St (☎563-4399, fax 230-3043). Vegetarian, non-smoking B&B with massage ($62) and aromatherapy sessions ($40). ③.

O'Connor House, 172 O'Connor St (☎236-4221). Claims to be Ottawa's most centrally located B&B. Rates include all-you-can-eat breakfast, free bicycles and skates. Parking is free but limited. ②.

Ottawa House, 264 Stewart St (☎789-4433). Small friendly guesthouse supplying filling breakfasts. ②–③.

Paterson House, 500 Wilbrod St (☎565-2030). The poshest B&B in town in a beautiful Queen Anne mansion with its own health centre. ⑥.

Robert's Bed and Breakfast, 488 Cooper St (☎563-0161). A heritage home with three rooms. ②.

Hostels and college rooms

Carleton University Residence, 223 Commons Building, 1233 Colonel Broadway (☎788-5609). South of the central core, but with air conditioning, Olympic-sized swimming pool, saunas and a whirlpool. Open May to Aug. ②, but reductions with student card.

Ottawa International Hostel, 75 Nicholas St (☎235-2595). Stay in cells complete with bars on the windows in Ottawa's nineteenth-century jail now converted into a hostel. The solitary confinement area is now a laundry but Death Row remains the same with its 1m-by-2m cells and gallows. Dorm beds are available, but reservations can only be made for family rooms; curfew is 1am. From the bus station take bus #4 to the corner of Rideau and Nicolas; from the train station take bus #95 and get off at Rideau Shopping Mall; buses from Montréal will drop you at Laurier and Elgin. ①.

Ottawa YMCA-YWCA, 180 Argyle Ave (☎237-1320). Slightly less convenient than the hostel, but a better standard of accommodation with a pool, gym and cafeteria. ②.

University of Ottawa, 100 University St (☎564-5400). Student dorms are available at Stanton residence off Nicolas Street. The reception is at 100 Hastey on the west side of the university buildings. Open May to Aug. ①.

Campgrounds

Le Breton Camping, corner of Fleet and Booth (☎943-0467). Just west of Parliament Hill right in the heart of downtown with 200 sites; $7.50 per person.

Camp Hither Hills, Bank St (☎822-0509). Ten kilometres south on Hwy 31. 200 sites, some with electrical hook-ups. Camp includes heated pool, shop, restaurant and bar next door; $13 for a site.

The City

The National Capital Region officially spans thousands of square kilometres along the Ottawa Valley encompassing several separate communities. The major sights, however, lie within a small area around the Ottawa River in the downtown centres of Ottawa and its French neighbour **Hull**: once on **Parliament Hill**, the symbolic and topographical apex of the city, a short walk brings you to all the major sights.

Parliament Hill

Ottawa's *raison d'être*, the **Parliament Buildings**, are dramatically situated on the limestone bluff of **Parliament Hill** overlooking the Ottawa River, the geographic high point originally used by the British military as barracks during the building of the Rideau Canal. In summer (late June to late Aug) the Governor General's Foot Guards and Grenadier Guards march onto the Hill for the 10am **Changing of the Guard**; Ottawa's winters are too cold for stationary guards. The white Infotent (mid-May to late June daily 9am–5pm; late June to Aug Mon–Fri 9am–8pm, Sat & Sun 9am–5pm), situated between the Centre and West blocks, has tickets for all the tours and the latest on what's going on – a massive renovation plan over the next decade will cause upheaval for tourists and politicians alike. Try to avoid the tours after the Changing of the Guard – the busiest time.

The entrance to the Hill through the south gate from Wellington Street leads past the **Centennial flame**, lit in 1967 to commemorate a century of Confederation. In front stand the three Parliament Buildings – begun in 1860 – which, like Britain's Houses of Parliament, are built along mock-Gothic lines, but unlike the London version it's the acreage of copper roofing that catches the eye, rather than fiddly stonework.

Recently relaid, the copper shines bright again on the **Centre Block** (daily: mid-May to Aug Mon–Fri 9am–8.30pm, Sat & Sun 9am–5.30pm; Sept to mid-May 9am–4.30pm; free) – the original workmen reputedly urinated on the roof to speed up the oxidization process. In 1916 a fire destroyed the Centre Block and the present building, which contains the Senate and the House of Commons, dates from 1920 when it was built along the original plans but increased to one and a half times the size. From the centre of the facade rises the **Peace Tower**, which was added in 1927 as a memorial to Canadians who served in World War I – the floor is paved with stone brought from the battlefields of Europe. From the top, nearly 90m above the river, you can see 65km in all directions.

To get into the Centre Block itself, go through the Peace Tower entrance, which leads to **Confederation Hall** and the **House of Commons**, where the Speaker's chair is made of English oak from Westminster Hall and from Nelson's ship *Victory*. The red-carpeted **Senate** is far more impressive, though, with its murals of scenes from World War I surmounted by a beautiful gilded ceiling. Adjoining the Centre Block is the **Library**, the only part of the building to survive the fire of 1916; the circular design and the richly carved wooden galleries make this the most handsome of the buildings, but it will be closed from 1998 to 2001 as part of the renovation programme.

The **West Block** is closed, but the **East Block** (July & Aug daily 9am–5pm) has four rooms open to the public – the original Governor General's office, the offices of Sir John A. Macdonald and Sir George Étienne Cartier, and the Privy Council Chamber. More like a museum, with an interior restored to look like the 1870s, the costumed guides endeavour to relate the politics of a century ago to today's Parliament.

More entertaining than the buildings themselves are the **debates** in the House of Commons (Mon, Tues & Thurs 11am–1pm & 2–6.30pm, Wed 2–6pm, Fri 11–1pm & 2–5pm) and the Senate (Tues 8pm, Wed & Thurs 2pm), both of which are open to the public – a white light at the top of the Peace Tower indicates when Parliament is in session. For **Question Period** in the House of Commons you'll certainly have to queue

(☎992-4793 for information on dates and times), but watching the Right Honourable ladies and gentlemen rant and rave can be the best show in town.

Of the buildings' lawny surroundings, the most interesting part lies on the Ottawa River side of the Hill, where there are excellent views from a paved pavilion. The grounds themselves are formally laid out with various statues of Canada's greater statesmen, with one of Queen Victoria thrown in for good measure. Almost $2.5 million has been spent to bring more attention to what is considered to be Canada's symbol of freedom and democracy, with a free summer-evening **sound and light show**, poetically titled "Reflections of Canada – A Symphony of Sound and Light", illustrating Canada's history (May–Sept French and English performances nightly; they alternate which goes first).

Wellington Street and around

Practically next door to the Parliament Buildings stands the **Supreme Court of Canada** (Mon–Fri 9am–5pm; free), a rather austere Art Deco building, beyond which you'll find the **National Archives of Canada** (daily 9am–9pm); both feature regular free exhibitions. The western area of Wellington Street leads to Ottawa's business district, with tall, modern office blocks and streets crowded with the bureaucrats for which Ottawa is infamous.

Sparks Street Mall, parallel to Wellington Street, was once the site of a pioneer farm and is now an expensive open-air shopping zone. In the thick of the boutiques, at 245 Sparks, the **Currency Museum** (Mon–Sat 10.30am–5pm, Sun 1–5pm; $2) is housed in the old HQ of the Bank of Canada – when they expanded their premises they encased the original 1937 stone building in two green glass towers with an indoor jungle garden court. Within the garden, in front of the museum, is a huge Yap stone, a symbol of wealth in the South Pacific; such stones usually remain at the bottom of the sea, their possession simply changing hands among the islanders by agreement. Inside the museum the stress is on Canadian currencies, from the small beads and shells known as wampum through to playing cards, beaver pelts and modern banknotes.

Confederation Square and the Rideau Canal

The eastern end of Sparks Street Mall meets the triangular **Confederation Square**, site of the **National Arts Centre** (tours May–Aug daily noon, 1.30pm & 3pm; Sept–April Tues, Thurs & Sat noon, 1.30pm & 3pm), a complex of low hexagonal buildings housing an opera hall, theatres and the main information centre. The free tours are very popular with tourist groups and last a bit too long – far better to visit as part of an audience and to appreciate the excellent design and acoustics of the place.

The National Arts Centre hugs the side of the **Rideau Canal**, which in winter becomes the world's longest skating rink, with hot chocolate and muffin stands providing sustenance for the skaters, many of whom use the route to get to work. The canal joins the river at the foot of Parliament Hill, where a flight of locks lowers pleasure boats into the river. Beside the locks you'll find the **Bytown Museum** (April to mid-May, Oct & Nov Mon–Fri 10am–4pm; mid-May to Sept Mon–Sat 10am–5pm, Sun 1–5pm; $2.50), Ottawa's oldest building, where military supplies were stored during the construction of the canal. The history of the waterway is shown in a short video display, while the rest of the museum contains assorted Ottawan memorabilia, including some of Colonel By's belongings.

On the other side of the canal and next door to the *Château Laurier* hotel in a reconstructed railway tunnel, the **Canadian Museum of Contemporary Photography** (May–Aug Mon, Tues & Fri–Sun 11am–5pm, Wed 4–8pm, Thurs 11am–8pm; Sept–April Wed & Fri–Sun 11am–5pm, Thurs 11am–8pm; donation). The collection numbers around 158,000 photographs, which are used for research as well as being displayed in changing exhibitions.

Sussex Drive and Major's Hill Park

Crossing the canal beside the locks takes you past Ottawa's most ostentatious hotel, the *Château Laurier*, to **Sussex Drive**, whose southern section is one of Ottawa's oldest streets: the buildings between George and St Patrick might seem brand-new, but they date from Ottawa's pioneer days. The general stores that once lined the city's busiest throughfare have been gutted and their fronts restored to house expensive shops and galleries. The most excessive renovation has been carried out on the east side of the street in **Tin House Court**; for example, the entire facade of a tinsmith's house has been hung on the side of a stone building. On the opposite side of the road, **Major's Hill Park** is the area chosen by Colonel By as the site of his home so he could overlook the progress of the canal; the park has a beautiful setting, its peace disturbed only by the **Noon Day Gun** (except Sundays, so as not to disturb churchgoers), a tradition introduced in 1869 to regulate the postal service. Major's Hill Park merges with

Nepean Point, an area of land that juts out into the Ottawa River, with excellent views of the Chaudière Falls, Hull and the Laurentian Mountains.

The National Gallery of Canada

In the area between Nepean Point and Sussex Drive rises the magnificent **National Gallery of Canada** (May to mid-Sept daily 10am–6pm, Thurs till 8pm; mid-Sept to April Wed–Sun 10am–5pm, Thurs till 8pm; free), designed by Moshe Safdie to reflect the circular design of the Parliament Library. The collection was founded in 1880 by the Marquis of Lorne, the governor general of the time, who persuaded members of the Royal Canadian Academy to donate a work to the government. Over the next century artworks were gathered from all over the world, resulting in a collection that now contains more than 25,000 pieces. The gallery also holds world-class temporary exhibitions.

The Canadian Galleries

Predictably, the **Canadian Galleries**, laid out in roughly chronological succession on level one, are the finest in the building, following the history of Canadian painting from the mid-eighteenth century to the mid-twentieth. They begin with religious art from Québec and the gilded high altar by Paul Jourdain from Longueuil, followed by a room showing the emergence of secular art in the early nineteenth century, with paintings by immigrant artists trained in Europe. The most notable of these was Joseph Légaré, who was not only a painter but also a politician and nationalist – his *Cholera Plague, Québec*, is a fine example of his work. For popularity, though, none could match Cornelius Krieghoff, who could turn his hand to anything requested by his patrons from the emerging middle classes – as illustrated by his *Winter Landscape* and *White Horse Inn by Moonlight*. Next comes the gallery's most intriguing exhibit, the Rideau Street Convent Chapel, rebuilt piece by intricate piece after it was threatened by demolition in 1972. Designed in 1887 by the architect and priest Canon Georges Bouillon for a convent school in Ottawa, it has slender cast-iron columns supporting a fan-vaulted ceiling – one of the few examples of its kind in North America. Contained in the chapel is a collection of silver and wooden church sculptures from Québec.

The growth of the Maritimes and Upper Canada during the nineteenth century is depicted in the room that follows. John Poad Drake's *The Port of Halifax* and John O'Brien's dramatic depictions of storm-tossed frigates illustrate the importance of the Atlantic provinces in this period, while the effects of colonization in Upper Canada on the native population are shown in the forceful portraits by Paul Kane, Canada's first artist-explorer. At the centre of the Kane gallery is the unique Croscup room from Nova Scotia. Once the living room of a shipping family, it is covered in murals that juxtapose images from nineteenth-century North America and Europe – portraits of Micmac Indians next to Queen Victoria and family, for example.

The construction of the railroads enabled artists to explore the wilder zones of Canada, a development encapsulated in Lucius O'Brien's *Sunrise on Saguenay*. However, painters of this period were still in thrall to European masters – the Royal Canadian Academy of Arts sent its students to Paris to complete their training – and the influence of Europe remained unshakable right into this century, as shown by the impressionistic work of Cullen and Suzor-Côte, and the sombre rural scenes of Morris, Williamson, Watson and Walker, inspired by the Dutch and Barbizon school.

However, with the **Group of Seven** a purely Canadian style emerged, which aimed to capture the spirit of the northern landscape, rather than trying to depict vast vistas in the European style. The Group was inspired by the work of contemporary Scandinavian painters, who were wrestling with similar problems of scale on the other side of the Atlantic (see box on p.79). The first room dedicated to their works concentrates on their apprenticeship under Tom Thomson, whose startling *The Jack Pine* could be taken as the Group's clarion call – trees, often windswept or dead, are a constant symbol in the Group's paintings of Canada's *terre sauvage*. Using rapid, brash, often brutal brushstrokes, their works are faithful less to the landscape itself than to the emotions it evoked – Lawren Harris's *North Shore, Lake Superior* and J.E.H. Macdonald's *The Solemn Land* are good awestruck examples.

Following Macdonald's death in 1932, the Group of Seven formed the Canadian Group of Painters, embracing all Canadian artists of the time whatever their style. Initially landscape remained the predominant genre, but the effects of the Depression forced sociopolitical subjects to the fore – *Ontario Farm House* by Carl Schaefer turns a landscape into a social statement, while Jack Humphrey, Miller Brittain and Sam Borenstein depict the harsh reality of urban environments.

Emily Carr's mystical, monumental paintings dominate the room given over to pictures of BC's landscape, a section followed by works produced in 1940s, Montréal, the most cosmopolitan arts centre in the country. Abstraction was first explored by the Montréal Automatistes, whose emphasis on the expressive qualities of colour was rejected by the Platiciens, with whom geometrical and analytical forms were a preoccupation. Both groups are represented here, as are postwar artists from Vancouver and Toronto – like William Ronald, known for aggressive images such as *The Hero*. The last rooms contain temporary exhibitions of works from the 1950s.

The Contemporary Art Collection

The **Contemporary Art Collection**, on the same level as the Canadian Galleries, spans the years between 1960 and 1980, and again shows Canadian artists looking for a lead outside their country. The shadow of New York's Abstract Expressionists falls over Charles Gagnon's *Cassation/Open/Ouvert*, while the genealogy of mixed-media pieces like Jeff Wall's *The Destroyed Rooms* becomes clearer when you get to the collection of American contemporary art. Highlights here include Andy Warhol's *Brillo* sculpture, George Segal's life-size assemblage *The Gas Station* and Carl Andre's minimalist *Lever* – a line of firebricks.

The European and American galleries

The **European and American galleries**, situated on level two, begin with pieces from the workshops of Duccio in Siena and Giotto in Florence, accompanied by Filippino Lippi's *Triumph of Mordecai* and *Ester at the Palace Gate*, painted for chests that contained a bride's dowry, as well as a fine Bronzino *Portrait of a Man*. Northern European art in the fifteenth and sixteenth centuries is also represented primarily by religious art – note Quentin Matys's *Crucifixion*, with Jerusalem looking decidedly like a Flemish town circled by ramparts.

The collection of works from seventeenth-century Europe is particularly impressive: apart from Bernini's sculpture of his patron Pope Urban VIII, there's Claude Lorrain's *Landscape with a Temple of Bacchus*, an *Entombment* by Rubens, Rembrandt's sumptuous *Heroine from the Old Testament* and Van Dyck's *Suffer the Little Children to Come Unto Me*, an early work that includes portraits thought to be of Rubens and his family. Venetian genre paintings include Canaletto's *Campo di Rialto* and Guardi's *Santa Maria Della Salute*. From Britain in the eighteenth century there are portraits by Reynolds and Gainsborough, and Romney's *Joseph Brant (Thayendanegea)*, a portrait of a Mohawk chief on a visit to London to discuss the native involvement in the American Revolution with George III. Also here is *The Death of General Wolfe* by Benjamin West, an American who became George III's official painter.

The nineteenth-century selection is ottawa: basically a show of minor paintings by great artists: Delacroix's romantic *Othello and Desdemona*, Corot's orderly *The Bridge at Narni*, Constable's *Salisbury Cathedral from the Bishop's Grounds* and Turner's *Mercury and Argus*, with a sunset that anticipates his future masterpieces. In stark contrast, the realist strain of the nineteenth century is represented by Courbet's *The Cliffs at Étretat* and Millet's *The Pig Slaughter*, though tranquillity is soon restored by Monet's *Waterloo Bridge: The Sun through the Fog*, beautifying London's notorious fog, and two canvases by Pissarro. Van Gogh's *Iris* and Cézanne's *Forest* are the only worthy Post-Impressionist works.

American art takes over in the following room, residence of Barnet Newman's *Voice of Fire*, the very mention of which causes some Canadians to break out in a cold sweat – not because of its artistic significance but because it cost $1.76 million. The artist intended the 5.5-metre-high piece to give the viewer a "feeling of his own totality, of his own separateness, of his own individuality, and at the same time of his connection to others, who are also separate"; unfortunately the purchase of the painting caused a furore, with one Manitoba Tory MP ranting that it could have been "done in ten minutes with two cans of paint and two rollers". The same room contains work by Jackson Pollock and Mark Rothko.

The final galleries have works from twentieth-century Europe, a diverse and high-class assembly that includes the disturbing *Hope I* by Gustav Klimt, Matisse's *Nude on a Yellow Sofa*, Francis Bacon's macabre *Study for Portrait No. 1*, and pieces by Picasso, Léger, Epstein, Mondrian, Dali and Duchamp.

Inuit and Photograph galleries

On the same level are the Asian art, prints, drawings and photograph galleries. The **Inuit art** section, on ground level, includes *The Enchanting Owl* by Kenojuak, whose flamboyant depictions of fantasy birds are the most famous of Inuit works. The **Photograph Gallery** displays a changing selection from the gallery's 17,000 photographs, covering the entire history of photography from its invention in 1835 to today.

The Canadian War Museum, Notre-Dame and around

Next door to the gallery, surrounded by tanks and cannons, is the **Canadian War Museum** (May–Aug Mon–Wed & Fri–Sun 9.30am–5pm, Thurs 9.30am–8pm; Sept–April closed Mon; $2.50, free on Thurs 5–8pm), the largest military collection in the country. One of the main exhibits is "Hitler's car" – the museum acquired it as Goering's car but the vehicle was renamed in the hope that it would encourage more visitors. The windscreen has bullet holes in it, added by the previous owner to fool people into thinking the Nazis had driven the Merc into battle. Other exhibits include a mock-up of a World War I trench, a gallery of medals and insignias, an intricate frigate constructed out of matchsticks by a bored sailor, and an arsenal of weapons from Indian clubs to machine guns.

Opposite the National Gallery is the capital's Catholic cathedral, the plain-looking **Notre Dame Basilica**. Completed in 1890, it took fifty years to build and is Ottawa's oldest church. Inside, the altar is surrounded by over one hundred wooden sculptures – some with a kitschy marble finish – many of which were created by the sculptors who worked on the Parliament Buildings.

Along Sussex, at no. 457a, is the **Canadian Ski Museum** (Tues–Sun noon–4pm; $1), one of the few museums in Ottawa that has failed to squeeze any money out of the NCC. Amid the haphazard collection of skis, photos and paraphernalia, check out the 5000-year-old cave drawing of men on skis.

Byward Market and the Laurier House

Since the 1840s the **Byward Market**, just east of Sussex and north of Rideau Street, has been a centre for the sale of farm produce, but in the last few years it has become Ottawa's hippest district. The 1927 Byward Market building has been renovated to house the **Ottawa Arts Exchange**, whose arts and crafts merchandise spills out onto the streets to merge with market stalls selling a variety of wares from ethnic gear to fresh fruit and veg. Most of Ottawa's best restaurants and bars are located here and during the day the area is busy with shoppers and buskers; at night it's buzzing until 2am, closing time at the bars.

Northeast of here, closer to the Rideau River in the upmarket area of Sandy Hill, is the **Laurier House**, 335 Laurier Ave East (April–Sept Tues–Sat 9am–5pm, Sun 2–5pm; Oct–March Tues–Sat 10am–5pm, Sun 2–5pm; $2.25), former home of prime ministers Sir Wilfred Laurier and William Lyon Mackenzie King. Laurier, Canada's first French-speaking prime minister, served from 1896 to 1911; Mackenzie King, his self-proclaimed "spiritual son", was Canada's longest-serving (1921–30 and 1935–48). Notoriously pragmatic, he enveloped his listeners in a fog of words through which his political intentions were barely discernible, as exemplified by his most famous line, "Not necessarily conscription, but conscription if necessary" – supposedly a clarification of his plans at the onset of World War II, which most Québécois viewed as a European imperialist conflict. Even more famous than his obfuscating rhetoric was his personal eccentricity. His fear that future generations would view him as the heir of his grandfather William Lyon Mackenzie – who in the 1830s led rebellions in Upper Canada – eventually led him into spiritualism: he held regular seances to tap the advice of great dead Canadians, including Laurier, who allegedly communicated to him through his pet dog.

The house is dominated by King's possessions, including his crystal ball and a portrait of his obsessively adored mother, in front of which he placed a red rose every day. Other mementoes include the programme Abraham Lincoln held the night of his assassination and a guest book signed by Churchill, Roosevelt, de Gaulle, Nehru, the Dionne quintuplets and Shirley Temple. The house also contains a reconstruction of a study belonging to prime minister Lester B. Pearson, who was awarded the Nobel peace prize for his role in the 1956 Arab–Israeli dispute. Laurier Avenue East eventually meets the **Rideau River**, which is escorted by walkways and bicycle paths to the **Rideau Falls**, whose twin cataracts are separated by Green Island – the site of the Ottawa City Hall, an unattractive building built in the 1950s. The Falls themselves were once enveloped in an industrial complex, which has now been cleared away to allow excellent views across the river to Hull.

Rockcliffe

North of the Falls lies **Rockcliffe**, Ottawa's Beverly Hills, a tranquil haven colonized by parliamentary bigwigs and diplomats – and in the evening by local lovers, who canoodle in the pavilions on the river shore, looking across to the Gatineau Hills. The prime minister resides in a stately mansion barely visible through the trees at 24 Sussex, while the stately **Rideau Hall**, at no. 1 (guided tours July & Aug Sat & Sun 10am–4pm; free), has been the home of Canada's governors general since Confederation. The Hall's gardens of maples and fountains are open to the riffraff for hourly guided tours (April to late May Sat & Sun 10am–3pm; late May to late June Wed–Sun 10am–3pm; late June to late Aug daily 10.15am–5.15pm; mid to late Oct Sat & Sun 10am–3pm; free).

At the east end of Rockcliffe, 4km from downtown, is the huge hangar of the **National Aviation Museum** (daily: May–Aug 9am–5pm, Thurs 9am–8pm; Sept–April 10am–5pm, Thurs 10am–8pm; $5, free Thurs 5–8pm) – served by bus #198. Highlights include a replica of the *Silver Dart*, which made the first powered flight in Canada in

1909; it flew for a full nine minutes, a major achievement for a contraption that seems to be made out of spare parts and old sheets. There are also bombers from both world wars and some excellent videos, including a programme to simulate a helicopter flight and a virtual reality hang-glider.

South Ottawa

Of **south Ottawa**'s straggle of attractions, the most central is the **Canadian Museum of Nature**, installed in a fortress-like building on the corner of McLeod and Metcalfe, just one block south of Gladstone (daily: May–Aug 9.30am–5pm, Thurs till 8pm; Sept–April 10am–5pm, Thurs till 8pm; $4, Thurs $2 till 5pm, afterwards free). Covering the evolution of the natural world from the beginning of life on the planet, the museum contains a couple of million zoological specimens, including a good collection of dinosaur skeletons. The dioramas of present-day Canadian wildlife are the most interesting – everything you ever wanted to know about the moose and grizzly. You can also descend into a "working" gold mine and "walk" along a cliff face.

Following the canal south along Queen Elizabeth Driveway brings you to Dows Lake, which before the building of the canal was known as Dow's Great Swamp. Surrounding the lake is the arboretum of the **Central Experimental Farm** (daily 9am–5pm; $2, family $5; bus #31), among whose 2000 tree species are many non-native to Canada. The farm itself, covering 1235 acres on the other side of Prince of Wales Driveway, began in 1886 as an attempt by the government to improve existing farm practices and help pioneers get the most from the wilderness. Now one of five such farms, it is still primarily concerned with agricultural experimentation and the study of how flora survive in Canada's harsh climate. Beside the information building at the junction of Maple Drive and the Driveway, the **Agricultural Museum** (daily 9am–5pm; $3) has a collection of turn of the century farming equipment and special shows on such riveting subjects as "Haying in Canada", "The Amazing Potato" and "A Barn in the 1920s". Although the farm has various livestock herds, the Clydesdale horses are the only animals put to work, pulling wagonloads of visitors along the lanes from outside the museum. Other than animals the farm also has a varied collection of plants – the Tropical Plant Greenhouse has over 500 tropical plants including orchids and banana trees. At the intersection of Carling Avenue and Maple Drive, still within the bounds of the farm, the now redundant **Observatory** (Mon–Fri 8.30am–4pm) houses a collection of instruments used to measure earthquakes.

East of the farm lies the **Billings Estate Museum** at 2100 Cabot St (May–Oct Mon–Thurs & Sun noon–5pm; $2.50; bus #149), home of Bradish Billings and his wife – the first white settlers to take up land on the south side of the Rideau River. The grounds have great views, and the house contains exhibits on Ottawa's growth from wilderness to capital.

About 3km further east, a lighthouse from Cape North in Nova Scotia marks the site of the **National Museum of Science and Technology**, 1867 St Laurent Blvd (May–Aug daily 9am–6pm, Fri till 9pm; Sept–April Tues–Sun 9am–5pm; $6, family $12, free Thurs 5–9pm; bus #85). Surrounding the museum is the so-called Technology Park, whose steam locomotive and other vehicles indicate the museum's main thrust. For, although the museum has a fair showing of hands-on exhibits on scientific topics from agriculture to astronomy – you can make your own paper, see chicks hatch in an incubator and queue for a peek through Canada's largest refracting telescope – the main draws are the hardware of land, sea and space transportation. The cars section has vintage vehicles as well as the popemobile used on John Paul II's 1984 tour of Canada; old cruisers and models of ships fill out the story of marine transport; and the pristine Apollo 7 space capsule sits beside the burnt-out chunk of a Soviet satellite that landed in northern Canada in 1978.

Hull

Hull, though recognized as part of Canada's capital region in 1969, remains distinctly separate and predominantly francophone. For years it was a paper-milling town, an industrial, working-class area removed from the rat-race atmosphere on the south side of the river. However, pressure on the government has led to the building of a number of high-rise administration buildings and the capital's finest national museum, the Musée Canadien des Civilisations, which now dominates the waterfront. At the moment, though, Hull is still best known as Ottawa's nightlife spot and receives its heaviest tourist influx after dark.

The Musée Canadien des Civilisations

The **Musée Canadien des Civilisations**, right by the foot of the Alexander Bridge, is the one museum in the capital region not to be missed (May & Sept to early Oct daily 9am–6pm, Thurs till 9pm; July–Aug Mon–Wed, Sat & Sun 9am–6pm, Thurs & Fri 9am–9pm; early Oct to April Tues–Sun 9am–5pm, Thurs till 9pm; $5, family $12, children $1, free Sun 9am–noon). The building itself is an amazing sight – undulating over 24 acres, it was designed by Douglas Cardinal, an Indian architect, to represent the landscape created by the meeting of the rocky Canadian Shield and the snow and ice of the deep north. Inside, the museum is a state-of-the-art presentation of the human history of Canada, from the native populations, through European domination to today's immigrants.

In the **Grand Hall** the world's largest collection of totem poles is displayed outside five native houses from Pacific coast tribes. The interiors have displays of native ceremonies and their present-day relevance, and excellent videos that present a balanced view of the plight of the native peoples today. **Canada Hall** – still being completed – illustrates Canada's history from 1000 AD to the present day, its exhibits taking the form of life-size reconstructions of historical environments. Beginning with Norsemen embarking on Newfoundland's shores, the early history concentrates on the Basques who crossed the Atlantic to trawl the fertile Gulf of St Lawrence and Labrador Sea. Permanent settlement by the French on the Atlantic coast is re-created with an Acadian settlement, focusing on the dyke-making techniques that enabled them to turn salt marshes into arable land. The farming communities of New France, which by the eighteenth century were strung along the St Lawrence, are represented by farmhouses, a cooperage, a pub and a hospital. A separate section deals with the fur trade that opened up Canada – a fur trading post and Métis camp are followed by the wagons of the new immigrants from America. A mock-up of a British officers' quarters, based on a painting by Cornelius Krieghoff, illustrates the military's expansion of Canada's transport and communication lines in the nineteenth century, while a full-scale section of a schooner gives a sharp insight into the maritime life at the time. The liveliest part of the show is the Ontarian main street of the turn of the century, populated by the resident theatre company in the summer. Future exhibits will include sections on the Prairies, the west coast and the Arctic, with special emphasis on the effects of modern development on the Inuit. In the meantime, elsewhere in the museum you'll find changing exhibitions of Indian and Inuit art, the **Canadian Postal Museum** with changing exhibits on all things mail, and a **Children's Museum** whose interactive displays include a "world tour" bus that takes children on an imaginary journey through eight different countries including a desert and a bazaar. Outside, a mighty dragon leads to **Adventure World** where children can play on the tug boat featured on the old $1 bill. The recently opened **First Peoples Hall** has been put together in collaboration with the First Nations to present the art, crafts, legends, history and way of life of Native Canadians and is one of the finest features of this unmissable museum.

In addition to all this, there's the **Cineplus** (adults $7, children $5), a space-age cinema with a huge Imax screen that virtually engulfs the audience. Canadian-made films on natural wonders and human skills like skiing, ballet and rock climbing take full advantage of the immense size of the screens – indeed the effects are so overwhelming that before performances a guide advises the audience to close their eyes should they feel any motion sickness. Films are shown at regular intervals during the day.

Gatineau Park

Ottawa's playground in the wilderness, the 88,000-acre **Gatineau Park** was founded in 1934 when the government purchased the land to stop the destruction caused by the need for cheap firewood during the Depression. It's located on Hull's western borders, about a fifteen-minute drive from Parliament Hill, and there is no public transport except during the Fall Festival, when a bus operates from outside the Musée Canadien des Civilisations. Alternatively, there's a bicycle path from opposite the National Gallery – a lengthy but pleasant ride.

Other than the standard hiking and cross-country ski trails – where you may be lucky enough to spot a few beavers – the main attraction is **Mackenzie King Estate** (late May to late June Wed–Sun noon–5pm; late June to early Oct daily noon–5pm; $5.50 per car), in the southern sector of the park. King retreated here to escape the rigours of public life and in a characteristically eccentric manner strewed the grounds with various architectural fragments – chunks of the old Parliament Buildings, Corinthian columns and blocks of the British House of Commons retrieved after the Blitz. The summerhouse tearoom is open in summer and serves a decent cup.

Eating

Eating out is not an aspect of the average Ottawan day, and despite the relatively recent explosion in the numbers of **restaurants** – ethnic eateries in particular – the capital is not on the list of the world's best cities to eat in. Moreover, keeping track of the best places is tricky, as restaurants come and go in Ottawa faster than in anywhere else in Canada – eighty percent of establishments change hands in the first five years, due largely to the Ottawan habit of eating in and going to bed early. The trendiest joints are in the Byward Market area, but there are also a number of good places along Elgin and Bank, and a small Chinatown on Somerset West and Bronson. Considering the majority of eateries are located in the centre of a capital city, the price tags are extremely reasonable – a decent meal with a drink can be had for around $20.

Snack and fast-food outlets seem to have most staying power, probably because they don't take up too much of the workaholics' time and get a lot of their custom from the more relaxed blue-collar workers. Chip vans have become an Ottawa institution; be sure to try their mouthwatering *poutine* – fries covered in gravy and chunks of mozzarella. Other excellent places for cheap food are the numerous Lebanese establishments, where kebabs and vegetarian falafels are both reasonable and delicious.

Cafés and snacks

Bagel Bagel, 92 Clarence St. Nine different types of bagel with an assortment of fillings from $2.25. Open 24hr Sat & Sun.

Boko Bakery, 87 George St. Mini-pizza, croissants and *pain au chocolat*, pricey but worth every cent. Open 7am–6pm.

Café Bohemian, 89 Clarence St. A well-established market eatery. Simple decor and imaginative food from cognac pâté to strawberry pancakes. The biggest *café au lait* in Ottawa and great food too.

Café Nostalgia, 603 Cumberland St. Big breakfasts, vegetarian lunches and a big terrace.

Café Wim, 537 Sussex Drive. Traditional Dutch "brown" café, the kind of place you can hang in for hours.

Cyber-Perk Café, 347 Dalhousie St. The place to log on with coffee and snacks.

Glebe Café, 840 Bank St. Good hang-out with Middle Eastern food.

Hooker's All Canadian Beavertails, Sparks St Mall and on the corner of York and William (Byward Market). Specializes in the Ottawan snack that is half-pizza, half-doughnut, covered either in garlic butter and cheese or home-made jam.

Lois 'n' Frima's, 361 Elgin St. Probably the finest ice cream in the country. No artificial colours or flavourings. The real thing.

Nate's, 316 Rideau St. At $1.75, the cheapest full breakfast in the capital's most popular deli.

The Painted Potato, 167 Laurier Ave. Cheap place to get stuffed; various fillings for baked potatoes.

Pasticceria Gelateria Italiana, 200 Preston St. Pastries, espressos and cappuccinos to die for.

Restaurants

Allegro, Preston Street. Inexpensive Italian dishes.

Ben Ben, 697 Somerset St. Szechwan and Cantonese food in Chinatown with good vegetarian dishes and takeout.

La Bottega, 64 George St. This Italian restaurant offers wholesome food with home-made sauces at a good price.

Café Crepe de France, 76 Murray St. Divine crêpes from $5 in an distinctive French-style café.

Casablanca Resto, 41 Clarence St. Wonderful Moroccan cuisine and delicious coffees.

Chez Jean Pierre, 210 Somerset St West (☎235-9711). The best French restaurant in town from the US Embassy's ex-chef, with prices to match. Reservations essential.

Courtyard, 21 George St (☎241-1516). In a cobblestone courtyard, this pretty place has a summer terrace and on Sundays brunch is accompanied by live classical music. Advisable to reserve at weekends.

Coriander Thai, 282 Kent St. The best Thai in Ottawa. Amazing satays, rich green and red curries, lemongrass tea and other classic dishes at fair prices.

Domus Café, 87 Murray St. In the Domus houseware store, this is a bright place with excellent cooking that uses produce from the Farmers Market. Good for breakfast and brunch on a Sunday.

Flippers, corner of Bank Street and Fourth Avenue. A cosy fish restaurant, usually filled with locals tucking into a varied and good-value menu.

Good Morning Vietnam, 323 Richer St. Lively, non-smoking Vietnamese place with plain decor and delicious food.

The Green Door, Main Street. Organic vegetarian buffet that is sold by weight.

Haveli, Market Mall, George Street. Elegant Indian restaurant of dark wood and brass. The all-you-can-eat lunch buffet is one of the best buys in Ottawa. Good vegetarian food.

Icho Restaurant, 87 George St. Expensive Japanese food and beer.

Kamal's, 683 Bank St. A budget restaurant but serving good, hearty Lebanese food.

Mama Teresa, 300 Somerset St West (☎236-3023). Home-made pasta, fresh parmesan, filtered water, fresh olives and real Italian coffee. Very popular, so booking is advisable. Most pasta dishes around $10.

Mandarin Ogilvy, 137 Ogilvy Rd. It's way out of Ottawa but serves the area's finest dim sum.

Mekong, 637 Somerset St. A wide offering of Vietnamese and Chinese food in the heart of Chinatown.

Maple Leaf Café, 529 Richmond Rd (☎722-5118). Probably Ottawa's most elegant restaurant with prices to match. Set in a gorgeous old stone house (1831), the bistro/bar part of the "café" is more reasonably priced.

Mexicala Rosa's, 895 Bank St. Moderately priced Mexican restaurant with a good atmosphere. One of four in the city.

Newfoundland Pub and Restaurant, on the corner of Hochelage and Montréal Road. A long way from downtown, but if you're going east it offers a good chance to try such Newfie delicacies as cod cheeks and tongues. Bus #2.

Oregano's, corner of William and George streets. Good-value pasta dishes, soup and salads and a great brunch on Sunday.

The Ritz, 15 Clarence St, 274 Elgin St, 375 Queen Elizabeth Driveway, 1665 Bank St and 226 Nepean St. The best place in Ottawa for a bit of a splurge. There are five *Ritzes*, all varying slightly. The one on Clarence is an old brick house with brick-oven pizzas and home-made bread; the original and the best *Ritz* is on Elgin; the Canal *Ritz*, on Queen Elizabeth Drive, has Ottawa's best location. Closed Sun lunch times.

La Ronde, Radisson Hotel, 100 Kent St (☎238-1122). Ottawa's only revolving restaurant. The food is expensive but worth it for the ultra-friendly service and all-round views (especially at sunset).

Las Palmas, 111 Parent Ave. Inexpensive Mexican fare with hefty portions and feisty margaritas to wash it all down with.

Sam's Falafel Tabouleh Garden, 464 Rideau St. Well-priced Lebanese food in a nice atmosphere.

The Siam Kitchen., Bank Street. Excellent Thai food, especially the noodle and squid dishes.

Silk Roads Café, 47 William St. Delicious Afghan cuisine with funky art displayed.

Something Fishy in Bells Corner, Village Mews Plaza, 194 Robertson St. Fish shop/café with the freshest of fish dishes and a good wine list. There's nearly always a queue.

Suisha Gardens, Slater Street. Tasty sushi, tempura, sukiyaki and teriyaki that is cheaper at lunch time. There's also a tatami room where you can sit on rush mats and eat Japanese-style.

Wringer's Laundromat-Restaurant, 151 Second Ave. Tuck into a hamburger while your clothes spin.

Zak's Diner, 16 Byward Market. A 1950s-style time warp with chrome decor, rock'n'roll blaring from the jukebox and good all-American food. Open daily until midnight.

Drinking and nightlife

Most **bars and pubs** depend on a student crowd to fill the tills, and during the week most places are pretty dead. Beer does not come cheap either – tax is heavy and the policy of tipping the bartender soon empties your wallet. It is illegal to sell drink in Ottawa without providing food, so all the pubs and bars sell finger foods – the current fads are Mexican snacks and spicy chicken wings. Ottawa's **nightlife** used to be in Hull but now that bars on both sides of the river close at 2am you may as well stay in Ottawa for a night out. Hull's bars are quite clubby, with dance floors and loud music, though few charge an entrance fee, but the happy hours and ladies' nights can get a bit childish ("Ladies without bras" nights, etc), but there may be something worth the trip across the river – take bus #8 or a taxi, costing $6.50 from downtown Ottawa. On both sides of the river the clubs and **discos** tend to be your average Top 40 boppy music and good old-fashioned rock'n'roll though some are a bit more experimental. As for **live music**, Ottawa has a good selection of venues, but decent bands are few and far between. Big names from the Eagles to Pavarotti play at the Corel Centre, twenty minutes from downtown on the #183 bus (☎599-0123). Live **jazz**, however, is extremely popular and there is a Jazzline (☎829-5428) with the latest info on gigs.

For **listings** on events of all sorts, there's the free bilingual *WHERE Ottawa-Hull*, a monthly promotional magazine designed for tourists. On Fridays the *Ottawa Citizen* prints a list of current entertainment, but for gig details as well as other more objective listings and information the weekly *Xpress* newspaper is the capital's trendiest and most comprehensive source.

Bars and pubs

Chateau Lafayette, 42 York St. A dark, dingy dive as old as Ottawa itself. See the city's life beneath its comfy veneer, as the old-timers add salt to their beer. Try to avoid the inevitable fights – and leave a tip if you want to leave in one piece.

The Mayflower, 247 Elgin St and 201 Queen St. Two English pubs; on Queen, there's a better buzz.

Molly McGuire's, 130 George St. Boisterous pub with live rock'n'roll on the weekends.

On Tap, 160 Rideau St. Ottawa's trendiest bar has pitchers of beer for $6.95 and big screens for sport. Live music at the weekends.

Rasputin's, 696 Bronson Ave. Small, packed pub and folk venue to the west of downtown.

Royal Oak, 779 Bank St, 318 Bank St and 161 Laurier Ave East. Three British-style pubs, all serving draught and bottled beers and inexpensive food, including ploughman's lunch and fish and chips. All branches have rock bands several times a week.

Tramps, 53 William St. The best bar in the Market, with good finger foods; try the deep-fried zucchini and chicken wings at weekends. The sports bar upstairs has table ice hockey and basketball.

Music bars and venues

Barrymore's Music Hall, 323 Bank St (☎237-5301). Commercial, mainstream and local bands play live here every night except Sunday. Both U2 and Tina Turner have played in this huge seven-level venue.

Downstairs Club, 307 Rideau St. Small, smoky venue with excellent free blues on Tuesday and live bands with a cover charge of $4–5 on the weekends.

Irene's Pub Restaurant, 885 Bank St. Live Celtic and folk music and imported beers.

Rainbow Bistro, 76 Murray St. Atmospheric blues club with jam sessions on Sunday.

Tucson's, 2440 Bank St. A variety of blues is played at this downtown venue.

Vineyard's Wine Bar, 54 York St. Hot jazz spot with an awesome wine cellar.

Zaphod Beeblebrox, 27 York St. The whole spectrum of live bands from C&W to alternative.

Zoe's, Château Laurier. Elegant piano and classical music bar.

Dance bars, discos and clubs

Atomic, 137 Bressener St. Ottawa's coolest club with occasional all-nighters. Most nights are free but others are $5 before 1am, $7 after.

Le Bistro, 115 Promenade de Portage, Hull. The best bar in Hull, with grunge and assorted disco as the fare. Monday and Tuesday are promotion nights, with a beer and a shot for $4.

Le Bop, 180 Promenade de Portage, Hull. A loud, heaving dance bar. Promotions on Monday and Tuesday (rock'n'roll night), when all beers are $3.

The Cave, 63 Bank St. Ambient on Sunday, disco on Monday and popular Retro 1980s on Tuesday and Thursday. $1.

Mercury Lounge, 56 Byward Ave. Big loft with great Martinis and vinyl couches. Acid-jazz, House and techno with DJs from all over Canada along with weird and wacky live acts.

Stoney's, 62 York St. Open-air disco that attracts a young studenty crowd.

Zap, 75 Promenade de Portage, Hull. Nightclub with impressive laser show.

Gay venues

Camp 8, 3836 Bank St. Gay and lesbian pub.

Centretown Pub, 340 Somerset St. Leather cruise joint.

Central Park & Zipper Club, 340 Somerset St West. Popular gay-male venue – during the day for its below-stairs café, at night for its dance bar.

Le Club, 77 Wellington St, Hull. Ottawa's longest-established gay nightclub.

Coral Reef Club, 30 Nicholas St. Lesbian bar on Friday nights.

Market Station Bar-Bistro, 18 George St. Stylish gay hang-out with artworks and funky music.

The New Le Pub, 175 Promenade de Portage, Hull. Gay/mixed/alternative crowd. Rooftop patio that looks over Hull's nightlife street. Drag shows on Saturday. Open til 3am.

P.R.I.D.E., 363 Bank St. Mixed crowd. Techno and drum-and-bass sounds. $5 at weekends.

Shadows, 433 Cooper St. Ottawa's sole women-only club.

Performing arts and cinema

Ottawa's focus of culture, the National Arts Centre, 53 Elgin St (☎755-1111), presents **plays** by the resident company and touring groups, **concerts** by the resident orchestra, **operas** with simultaneous French and English subtitles, and **dance** from (among others) the National Ballet of Canada and the Royal Winnipeg Ballet. As a further attraction, the Canadian Film Institute also presents **films** here. Tickets begin at $12.50 and wherever you sit the acoustics are outstanding.

Quality **theatre** is also presented by The Great Canadian Theatre Company, 910 Gladstone St (☎236-5192), which presents avant-garde Canadian plays with strong social or political overtones; Ottawa Little Theatre, 400 King Edward (☎233-8948), an amateur group who perform a variety of popular plays, usually comedies; and Hull's Théâtre l'Île, 1 Wellington St (☎819/595-7455), on an island in the Ottawa River. Hull also has its own **opera house** at Le Théâtre Lyrique, 109 Wright (☎770-8031). For other visual and performing arts, check out the programme at the Arts Court, 2 Daly Ave (☎564-7240).

Free **concerts** are held during the summer at Astrolobe, a 1500-seat open-air amphitheatre in Nepean Point Park behind the *Chateau Laurier Hotel*; while the Nepean Symphony Orchestra sometimes gives free concerts at parks in and around the capital.

Ottawa has a good selection of **cinemas**, with Thursday as cheap night at most venues. The Bytowne Cinema, 325 Rideau, is the capital's most popular repertory cinema. The Canadian Film Institute, 395 Wellington, shows arty programmes arranged by theme. Rideau Centre Cinemas, 50 Rideau, has the latest releases, as does the Mayfair Theatre, 1074 Bank.

For **comedy**, Yuk Yuks, at the *Capital Hill Hotel,* 88 Albert (☎236-5233), features stand-up comedians from Canada, the States and Europe; Wednesday is "New Talent Night".

Festivals

Ottawa uses every excuse in the book to put on **festivals**, and its munificence is evident at every jamboree. Public holidays like Canada Day are celebrated here with the sort of spectacle that other cities muster, but with extra dollars to boost the show, while seasonal festivals like the Winterlude and the Canadian Tulip Festival are as lavish as any in the country. Other than these large bashes, ethnic festivals embracing Canada's diverse population are smaller but equally entertaining and fun affairs – with the Franco-Ontarien Festival becoming more popular every year. The list below is arranged chronologically.

Winterlude. A ten-day snow-and-ice extravaganza, usually scheduled at the beginning of February. Concentrated around the frozen Rideau Canal, it includes ice sculptures at Confederation Park – renamed the Crystal Garden for the duration – and snow sculptures around Dows Lake. Other events include speed skating, bed races and dog-sled races.

Odawa Powwow. Held in May at Nepean Tent and Trailer Park. Ottawa's powwow is less spectacular than others in the country, but there are competitions in dancing, drumming and singing as well as stalls selling crafts and food.

Canadian Tulip Festival. Held in mid-May, this is the oldest of Ottawa's festivals – it began in 1945 when the Dutch sent 100,000 tulip bulbs to the capital to thank the Canadian soldiers who helped liberate the Netherlands. More bulbs arrived the following year from Queen Juliana, who had taken refuge in Ottawa when the Netherlands were occupied. The transformation of the city didn't meet with universal approval at first – Mackenzie King thought the planting of tulips around the Parliament Buildings was "undignified", but his staff planted thousands in secret anyway. Nowadays the bulbs are planted around Parliament, along the canal and around Dows Lake, an outbreak of colour that's accompanied by concerts, parades, fireworks and a huge craft show. The major events take place in Major's Hill Park and Dows Lake – but few are free, and the festival has a reputation for being rather upmarket and touristy.

Children's Festival. June. Children-oriented performances in mime, dance, music and theatre.

Italian Week. June. A celebration of the Italian contribution to Canadian life, with Italian films, outdoor concerts and expensive gala performances.

Franco-Ontarien Festival. Mid-June. This celebration of French culture has built up a reputation as being the party that brings a bit of wildness to conservative Ottawa. Dalhousie Street is closed off to traffic for up to ten days, so the bands and street dancers can take over.

Canada Dance Festival. End of June. Dance troupes from around the country rock and roll, tap and generally swing their pants in various locations across the capital, including a barge on the canal.

Bluesfest. July. Canada's largest fest of blues including international crooners with concerts in various venues and free shows in Confederation Park.

Donnie Gilchrist Festival. July. Traditional fiddling and step-dancing competitions.

Festival Canada. July. Based around the National Arts Centre, a weekend of vocal artists and cabaret with over seventy performances of opera, concerts, choral works, jazz, English and French theatre, cabaret and workshops.

Ottawa Fringe Festival. July. Small-scale but fun fringe-theatre week.

Cultures Canada. July. This government-backed programme of the performing arts attracts entertainers from all over the country to celebrate the "diverse ethnic and regional character of Canada". The performances take place along Confederation Boulevard in Ottawa and Hull with outdoor concerts at the Astrolobe. Many of the performances are free and those that require ticket purchase are rarely more than $5.

Ottawa International Jazz Festival. Mid-July. One of Ottawa's most popular festivals, with more than 400 musicians performing. The main stage is in Confederation Park with concerts at noon, 6.30pm and 8.30pm ($5); however, local bands play all around Byward Market and Sparks Street Mall.

Pride. July. Small, serious gay and lesbian parade.

Ottawa Chamber Music Festival. Late July to early August. North America's largest classical music festival, with concerts in venues and churches across the city.

Gatineau Hot Air Balloon Festival. August. From Gatineau Park, strange and wonderfully shaped hot-air balloons drift over the city.

Taste of Ottawa. August. A weekend of gluttony with free samples from Ottawa's restaurants.

Ottawa Folk Festival. August. Traditional folk festival backed up with craft shows.

International Buskers Festival. August. Jugglers, mime acts and whacky weirdness along Sparks Street Mall.

Festival of the Arts. Mid-September. Includes video and film presentation, visual art exhibits, crafts and concerts.

Japan Fest. October. Hosted by the Japanese Embassy, with art exhibitions, theatre, dance and martial arts demonstrations.

Lebanorama. November. Music, song, dance, cuisine and crafts from the Lebanon at Festival Plaza. There are also parades and special guests from the Lebanon.

Listings

Airlines Air Canada, Air Alliance, Air Nova and Air Ontario, 275 Slater St (☎247-5000); British Airways (☎1-800-247-9297); Canadian Airlines International, 50 O'Connor St (☎237-1366); First Air, Carp Airport, Carp, Ontario (☎738-0200).

Airport enquiries ☎998-3151.

Babysitters Quickcare ☎(233-8280).

Baseball The Ottawa Lynx, a farm team (minor league) of the Montréal Expos, play at the Ottawa Stadium, Coventry Rd (☎747-5969). The season runs from mid-April to late September.

Bike rental Rent-a-Bike, Mackenzie Ave, behind Château Laurier (April to Thanksgiving daily 9am–6pm; ☎241-4140).

Bookshops Books Canada, 71 Sparks St, has a fine selection of Canadian literature and non-fiction. The Book Market on the corner of Dalhousie and Rideau streets buys and sells secondhand books. The Nicolas Goal Hostel and the Canadian Hostelling Association, 18 Byward Market, sell travel books, as does World of Map and Travel Books, 118 Holland St.

Bus information Local: STO (Hull ☎770-3242); OC Transpo (Ottawa ☎741-4390). Long-distance: Voyageur Colonial and Greyhound (☎238-5900).

Camping equipment The Expedition Shoppe, 43 York St; Trailhead, 101 Clarence St.

Car parks The most central car parks are by the National Gallery on Sussex Drive and beside the National Arts Centre in Confederation Square.

Car rental Budget, 443 Somerset St West (☎729-6666); Hertz, 30 York St (☎1-800-263-0600); Tilden, 226 Queen St (☎232-3536); Rent-a-wreck, 77 Richmond St (☎722-6650).

Dental emergencies Ottawa ☎(523-4185); Hull ☎(568-3368).

Embassies Australia, 50 O'Connor St (☎236-0841); UK, 80 Elgin St (☎237-1530); Ireland, 170 Metcalfe St (☎233-6281); Netherlands, 350 Albert St (☎237-5030); NZ, 729 Bank St (☎238-5991); US, 100 Wellington St (☎238-5335).

Gay Ottawa Gays of Ottawa, 318 Liskeard St, operate an excellent information service (Mon–Fri 7.30–10.30pm, Sat & Sun 6–9pm; ☎238-1717) and publish GO Info, which is available free from most bars. For books and magazines, check out Mags and Fags at 286 Elgin St.

Hospitals Ottawa General, 501 Smythe Rd (☎737-7777; bus #85).

Ice hockey From September to April the Ottawa Senators play NHL games at the new 18,500-capacity Corel Centre, 1000 Palladium Drive, Kanata (☎1-800-444-SENS), 20min from downtown, bus #183.

Laundry Rideau Coinwash, 436 Rideau St; and several along Bank and dotted around the city.

Left luggage There are lockers at the train and bus stations; downtown, the Nicolas Gaol Hostel charges a nominal fee for left luggage.

Pharmacy Rideau Pharmacy, 390 Rideau St (daily 9am–9pm).

Post office 59 Sparks St Mall.

Rideshare Allo-Stop (☎778-8877).

Soccer Ottawa Intrepid play at Lansdowne Park, 1015 Bank (bus #7 or #1) or the Terry Fox Stadium, Riverside Drive (bus #96). Tickets cost around $10.

Taxis A-1 (☎746-1616); Blondeau (☎749-5838); Blue Line (☎238-1111).

Ticket agency Ticketmaster ☎(735-1111).

Train information ☎(244-8289).

Travel agencies Algonquin Travel, 90 Sparks St (☎237-9200); Club Adventure, 115 Parent Ave, Byward Market (☎236-5006); Ottawa Travel, 197 Sparks St (☎563-0744); Voyageur Travel, 300-161 Laurier Ave West (☎237-2700).

Weather For up-to-date weather details, call ☎998-3439.

Women's Ottawa The Ottawa Women's Bookstore, 380 Elgin St, is the best place to go for contacts (Mon–Sat 10am–6pm, Thurs & Fri till 9pm). Useful in emergencies are the Ottawa Distress Centre (☎238-3311), the Sexual Assault Support Centre (☎234-2266) and the Rape Crisis Centre (☎729-8889).

NORTHERN ONTARIO

Stretching from the north shores of lakes Huron and Superior to the frozen reaches of Hudson Bay, **NORTHERN ONTARIO** is a land of sparse population and colossal distances, summed up thus by Canadian humorist Stephen Leacock: "The best that anyone could say of the place was that it was a 'sportsman's paradise', which means a good place to drink whiskey in." Attracted by the exploitable skills of the nomadic Ojibwa, Cree and Algonquian natives and by the strategic waterways, European fur traders were the first people to establish permanent settlements here, though sizable communities began to develop only at the end of the last century, with the rise of the lumber industry. Later, mineral strikes brought prospectors flooding in, but now that most of the mines have closed or dwindled and the timber industry is declining through ill-planned replanting and the switch to recycling, towns are having to rely on the passing trade of lorry drivers, freight trains and tourists. Most of the visitors who linger here tend be equipped with rod or gun, for, despite the poisons from local pulp industries, the wildlife is abundant and the thousands of lakes and rivers well stocked. However, an increasing number of non-hunting clientele are attracted by **Lake Superior Provincial Park** and by the **tour trains** from Sault Ste Marie and Cochrane – convenient ways of reaching the wilderness.

Northern Ontario's two main thoroughfares – highways 11 and 17 – diverge on **North Bay**, 345km north of Toronto. The older Hwy 11, which runs 1896km from Toronto to Rainy River on the Ontario–Minnesota border, heads north through the mining towns that made Ontario's fortune, passing through **Cochrane**, from where a lone rail line strikes north to **Moosonee** on the shores of James Bay. The more scenic

Hwy 17 heads west via **Sudbury**, historic **Sault Ste Marie** and along the shore of the magnificent **Lake Superior** to the inland port of **Thunder Bay**. Most towns on both highways are served by regular buses (passenger train connections diminish every year), but all the provincial parks require private transport.

North Bay and Highway 11

At **North Bay**, the transport nexus of northern Ontario, **Highway 11** begins a thousand-kilometre loop to Nipigon, passing though a region which, far from the moderating effects of Lake Superior, has a climate as savage as any in the world. The long winters are so cold that inhabitants who die in the winter cannot be buried until the spring. Though the highway's infrequent towns are served by Greyhound, Grey Goose and Ontario Northland buses, this is definitely a region where a car is needed – you don't want to be hanging around too long for a connection. Note also that food and drink are more expensive in this region than elsewhere in Ontario; your best bet is to eat where you sleep.

North Bay

Despite being a city since 1935, **NORTH BAY** is not much more than a small dull town, handy as a springboard for points north or west. Ontario Northland **trains** from Cochrane and Toronto and all long-distance **buses** terminate at the Intermodal station at 100 Station Rd, to the east of town (☎705/495-4200). To get to Main Street walk through the shopping mall opposite, and take a bus from the front of the mall to the local bus terminal on Oak Street, one block from Main Street – the fare is $1.

The #4 bus goes to North Bay's only interesting museum, the **Dionne Quints Museum**, on the corner of Seymour where Hwy 11 hits the south side of town by the information centre (daily: mid-May to June & Sept to mid-Oct 9am–5pm; July–Aug 9am–7pm; $2.75). The museum is housed in the small log cabin from Corbeil, just west of North Bay, where the Dionne quintuplets were born on May 28, 1934 – to this day the world's only identical quintuplets. Kept alive with drops of whiskey, the quins were considered miracle children by the economically depressed nation, and at the age of three months the government took custody of them, removing them from their parents and five brothers and sisters. Until they were 9 years old the quins were put on display in a glassed-in playground, to the delight of up to 6000 sightseers who turned up each day to watch them – and to pay for souvenirs such as "birth-promoting" stones picked up from the North Bay area. The girls were educated in a synthetic "normal school atmosphere" provided by ten classmates, five of whom were English to help the quins with their second language. This bizarre childhood eventually caused a highly publicized estrangement between the quins and their parents, and doubtless contributed to the unhappiness of their later lives – a story dominated by illness, depression and failed marriages. The three surviving quints – Yvonne, Annette and Cécile – now live in Québec and recently published a biography accusing their father of sexual abuse, their mother of verbal abuse and the Ontario government of exploitation; they are currently trying to sue for damages. The small museum contains dresses, toys, photographs, advertising hoardings and souvenirs of the quins' childhood, including the bed they were born in.

Practicalities

The **information centre** is by the Dionne Homestead Museum at 1375 Seymour St (daily: mid-June to Aug 8.30am–8.30pm; Sept to mid-June 9am–5pm). North Bay's glut of **accommodation** is concentrated along Lake Nipissing on Lakeshore Drive, served regularly by the Marshall and Lakeshore buses. Cheap **motel** rooms are available at the *Bayshore* at no. 566 (☎705/472-5350; ①). If you prefer **B&B** *Grandview House on* *the Lake*, 1177 Premier Rd (☎705/474-5531; ③), has a shallow beach, sunbathing deck and blueberries for breakfast. The **campground** *Camp Conewango* (☎705/776-2320; $15) is 18km northwest of town; take Hwy 63 to Songis Road, then continue for 14km.

For **eating**, **drinking** and **nightlife**, head for the area around Main Street. The *Windmill Café*, 168 Main St, is a decent, family-run greasy spoon with all the usuals on offer. For soup and sandwiches, *The Magic Kettle*, 407 Ferguson St, is cheap and delicious. *Mike's Seafoods*, 406 Lakeshore Drive, serves reasonably priced fish dishes, while *Churchill's*, at 631 Lakeshore Drive, has the best ribs in the province. Students keep the bars along Main Street alive; check out the popular dance **bars** like *Waves* at no. 134. *The Lion's Heart*, 147 Worthington East, is a British-style pub with good brews.

Temagami

The beautifully located resort village of **TEMAGAMI**, 97km past North Bay, started as a rest stop on the long portage from Snake Lake into Lake Temagami. With its hundreds of bays and islands, Lake Temagami has been attracting tourists since the turn of the century, when it built the region's first grand hotel and introduced a steamship company and rail line to transport the holiday-makers. Now it's a tranquil place, though it does attract the overflow from Algonquin Park. Just before you hit town, the **Temagami Tower** allows visitors to climb 30m up the old fire tower for a stunning view of the area; you may even spot a peregrine falcon, a victim of the toxic pesticide DDT; they were reintroduced here in 1997.

Beneath the tourism and tranquillity, Temagami is a focus of intense controversy and you may find many of its campsites booked out by protesters in the summer. Temagami's old-growth **red and white pines** are complicated ecosystems that support thousands of species of plant and animal life, but since the 1920s ninety percent of the forest has been cut down, leaving fifty-metre-wide buffer zones around the rivers, lakes and roads to mask the extent of the destruction. Local people were compromised by the need to conserve jobs, but when the provincial government began an illegal extension of a logging road deep in the forest they were galvanized into campaigning for the preservation of this unique habitat. It wasn't until May 1989 that the Ontario Ministry of Natural Resources acknowledged that only a quarter of the trees had been replanted in the 1980s and that forty percent of the replanted forests "do not have enough surviving trees to support future logging". As a consequence the mill was closed, but no legislation was made to prevent other lumber companies clear-cutting or harvesting the old-growth pines.

The issue is made more complicated by the fact that much of the land is an Ojibwa reservation whose occupants have distanced themselves from the whole battle, because this is a provincial not a federal issue and Native Canadians come under federal jurisdiction. Both the Native Canadians and the locals favour multi-use of the land, combining recreation, hunting, fishing, mining and logging, whilst environmentalists from other parts of the country want the area left totally untouched. After years of meetings a stalemate still exists at the time of going to press, but it is hoped that a renewed investment in tourism will jump-start the village's economy.

Finlayson Point and Lady Evelyn Smoothwater provincial parks

Although Temagami's provincial parks preserve the surrounding countryside, **Finlayson Point** (mid-May to Sept; $7; ☎705/569-3205), 1km south of Temagami, is rather a disappointment if you're looking for unspoilt wilderness. It's primarily a campsite, and contains some old-growth pine within its boundaries, but the effect is rather ruined by being under a flight path. However, it is a good embarkation point for canoe trips and within easy walking distance of the village for supplies. Of the park's hundred or so

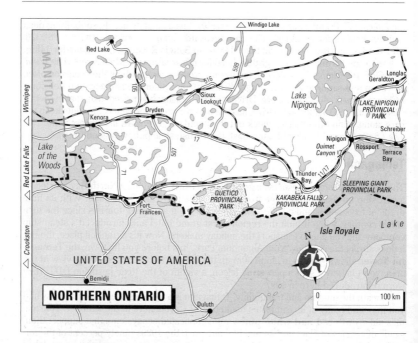

NORTHERN ONTARIO

sites, a third of them have hook-ups. There are good facilities and sites cost from $14.75 to $16.25 and need to be booked in advance.

In contrast, **Lady Evelyn Smoothwater** is an unmanaged park and covers most of the lake area. This is serious backcountry – there's nothing out there but the beauty of the bush. You need to know what you're doing, take everything you need with you and leave nothing behind – remember to dig your own latrine, as some of the campsites are left in a pitiful state.

Practicalities

Both **trains** and **buses** terminate at the station on Hwy 11 opposite the **Welcome Centre** on Lakeshore Boulevard (July & Aug daily 8am–8pm; Sept–June Mon–Fri 9am–5pm); the centre has details on accommodation, most of which is in tourist camps that cater for hunters and fishermen. Temagami is not suitable for novice canoeists and the backcountry campsites are as basic as they come. It's a good idea to invest in Temagami Canoe Routes ($7), available locally. For complete **canoe outfitting**, Smoothwater Outfitters (☎705/569-3539) can provide everything from first-aid kits to frying pans; the Temagami Wilderness Centre (☎705/569-3733), 22km south on the highway, also organizes canoe trips at reasonable rates. You can fly in and canoe out with Lakeland Airways (from $180; ☎705/569-3455), whose float planes take off by the Welcome Centre. They also do sightseeing packages for $40 per person.

Cobalt

Less than a century ago it was neither Toronto nor Ottawa that brought visitors to Ontario – it was **COBALT**, the town that silver built and silver destroyed. Local legend contends that it all started when a blacksmith named Fred LaRose threw a hammer at

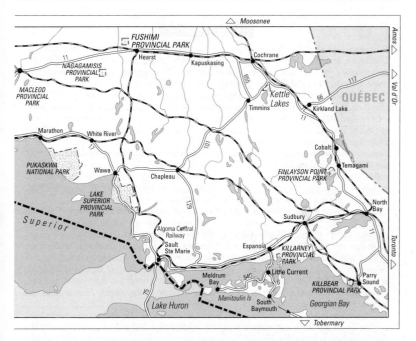

a fox and hit a rock instead, uncovering the silver vein. In fact the first strike was by two lumberjacks called McKinley and Darraugh, but in the summer of 1903 both the McKinley-Darraugh mine and the LaRose mine began operating, changing the landscape of the area almost overnight.

New mine shafts were dropped every few weeks and by 1911 the haphazard collection of tents, log cabins and huts had become a community of seven thousand. As output burgeoned, Cobalt merged with nearby Haileybury and New Liskeard to form the "tritowns", the miners living in Cobalt, the managers living on the Lake Temiskaming waterfront in Haileybury, and the mine owners and investors keeping their distance in New Liskeard. Life in Cobalt was perilous: typhoid, smallpox and flu were common and many of the homes were built from wooden dynamite boxes, and so were regularly wrecked by fires. Yet Cobalt survived the slumps caused by enlistment in World War I and by the Depression, only to be killed off by the recent world reduction in silver prices. The last mine closed in 1990, and every year the blue population signs at the entrance to the town are repainted. At one time twelve thousand people lived here; now the number is less than one thousand, all living in the hope that Cobalt's boom will come again.

The Town and mines

On Cobalt's main street, Silver Street, only one shop – a pet shop – remains. Just up the road, an old head frame (top of the mine shaft) protrudes from the roof of what was once the grocery store (the store used the disused shaft as a refrigerator); opposite, a small park has a large painted sign listing the 104 mines operating in 1908. At no. 24, Canada's oldest **Mining Museum** (June–Sept daily 9am–5pm; Oct–May Mon–Fri 1–4pm; $3.25) is housed in a converted newspaper office, with a vast collection of ores from the mines, including a collection of luminous stones. A block away stands Cobalt's grandest building, the former train station; renovated in 1990, it contains the **Bunker**

GREY OWL

Temagami was once the domain of one of Canada's most colourful characters – Wah-Sha-Quon-Asin, or **Grey Owl**, as he was more commonly known. One of the world's first conservationists, he travelled Canada, Britain and the US spreading the Indian message of respect for the flora and fauna of the wilderness, publishing articles in such magazines as *Country Life,* and turning out books that became best sellers. In 1938, at the age of 50, Grey Owl died. It was only then that it became known just how extraordinary his life had been.

Grey Owl was in fact **Archie Belaney**, an Englishman from Hastings who had emigrated at the age of 17 to escape his authoritarian aunt. Arriving in Canada, Belaney made his way to the silver strike in Cobalt, but on a sudden whim got off the train at Temagami. There he worked as a guide in the tourist camps and became fascinated with the Ojibwa population of the reserve on Lake Temagami's Bear Island. He learned the native stories and customs, and eventually married a young Ojibwa named **Angele**, with whom he produced a daughter. Prone to drinking and causing trouble, Belaney was finally run out of town after a brawl that ended in bloodshed.

Archie moved to Biscotasing and became a forest ranger, but soon his arrest warrant caught up with him and he had to leave town again – though not before impregnating another Indian woman, **Marie Girard**. She died of consumption shortly after giving birth to their child. During World War I, Belaney temporarily abandoned his Indian ways to fight with the army in Flanders, where he was wounded by shrapnel. During his convalescence in England he met and married his nurse, thereby adding bigamy to his many accomplishments. The call of the Canadian wilderness proved this marriage's undoing, and Belaney returned to Biscotasing, stopping en route to see Angele for four days and inevitably conceiving another child.

Since his departure Biscotasing had been taken over by the whites, who were busy cutting down the trees and scaring away the wildlife that Archie had grown to love. His determination to renounce his European roots now became even stronger, and his anarchic attitude made his persona as a "drunken Injun" the more convincing to the locals. In 1925, Belaney – by this time almost exclusively known as Grey Owl – returned to Temagami to live with Angele and their two children and resume work as a guide. It was there that he met **Anahereo**, a 19-year-old Iroquois. Angele was duly dumped as Anahereo and Grey Owl eloped to a hut in northern Québec, where their only companions were two beavers, McGinnis and McGinty. It was these two animals and Jelly Roll, a later addition, that inspired much of Grey Owl's writing and prompted him to start a beaver colony to prevent the extinction of Canada's national animal. To raise money for the project Grey Owl began writing and lecturing about his life as a Canadian native, a publicity campaign that also secured him the post of warden of Riding Mountain National Park and later Prince Albert National Park.

Grey Owl's long absences and the days spent writing led to the break-up of his relationship with Anahereo, but it didn't take long for him to marry someone else, this time a French-Canadian who adopted the Indian name of Silver Moon. Grey Owl made a final lecture tour of Britain and America in 1938, which included an audience with King George and the princesses Elizabeth and Margaret. The tour left Grey Owl suffering such exhaustion that he died later that same year. Only then did his wives, friends and family find out about his charade.

Military Museum (June to mid-Sept daily 9am–5pm; mid-Sept to May Sat & Sun 1–4pm; $2), one man's immense collection of military artefacts and uniforms.

In the surrounding area, where abandoned head frames have become the homes of red squirrels, skunks and birds, huge holes appear regularly as shafts give way. A fire in 1977 destroyed all records of the shafts' locations, so the Geological Society constantly combs the wilderness marking the areas that are about to collapse. It's unwise to go out into this region unaccompanied, so the Ontario Ministry of Northern Development and Mines have laid out a six-kilometre **Heritage Silver Trail Tour**. It begins at the Mining Museum. To take the tour, your own vehicle is preferable, but if you are without a car enquire at the Mining Museum, as it may be possible to join a tour – provided on demand – that actually goes down the old mine shafts, left unchanged since the early days.

If you're running short of things to read, call in at the **Highway Bookshop** (daily 9am–10pm), 8km south of the town on Hwy 11. This huge warehouse in the middle of nowhere has 10,000 secondhand and new books piled from floor to ceiling on incredibly rickety shelves.

Practicalities

Information is available from 18 Silver St (Mon–Fri 9am–5pm). For services, head for New Liskeard – connected by the Tritown Trolley, a regular bus service costing $1.30 – which has **motels** along Hwy 11: the *Quality Inn* (☎705/647-7357 or 1-800-228-5151; ③), or the *Husky* (☎705/647-6721; ②). In Haileybury, also served by the bus, the *Haileybury Motel*, 462 Farr Ave (☎705/672-3354; ②), has fine views of the lake. For **camping**, there's *Sharpe Lake Park* (☎649-8241), just outside Cobalt, and *Bucke Park* near Devil's Rock on Hwy 567, off Hwy 11B. The liveliest time to be in Cobalt is for the five days around the August Civic Holiday weekend, when **Cobalt's Miners' Festival** features mining contests (including drilling holes, operating machinery and throwing hammers), a flea market and an industrial amount of drinking.

Timmins

Fourteen kilometres north of the Hwy 11 and Hwy 66 junction, about 105km from Cobalt, Hwy 11 passes through the **Arctic Watershed**, or Height of Land, an elevation in the Canadian Shield that divides the flow of water in the province. North of this area, all water flows to James and Hudson bays, and south of here it flows to the Great Lakes and the St Lawrence. Just north of the watershed, 61km west along Hwy 101, lies **TIMMINS**, home to the richest silver-zinc mine in the world and once one of the largest gold-mining camps in North America – with the highest number of bars per capita on the continent. The numerous small mining communities of this region have now been subsumed into the city, making Timmins the second largest municipality in Canada, with an area in excess of 3100 square kilometres and a population of just under 50,000. Boom time came just after World War I – in 1914 the population was 935, by 1929 it was 13,000. More on the town's history can be seen at **Timmins Museum**, 70 Legion Drive (Mon–Fri 9am–5pm, Sat & Sun 1–5pm; $2).

The well-signposted **Timmins Underground Gold Mine Tour** (mid-May to June, 2 daily; July & Aug 5 daily; Sept & Oct call ☎705/267-6222 for bookings; surface tour $7, underground tour $17, family $50) is worth a go, particularly for families. It takes around two hours and features simulated explosions, gold pouring and earblasting mining demonstrations, as well as a chance to pan for gold and keep what you find. The mine also has another genuine relic from Timmins boom era: a **Hollinger House**, moved here from downtown Timmins. It used to be one of row upon row of identical tiny wooden shacks covered in red and green tar paper that housed the mine's employees, mainly immigrants from all over Europe, in particular Croats, Finns, Italians, Poles, Scots and Ukrainians. If you're not too fed up with mines there's another one, **Kidds Creeks Mines**, 26km east of the city on Hwy 101 (tours July & Aug Wed 1pm; $3, family $6), which is the world's richest zinc plant, and has the added attraction of a herd of buffalo who regularly graze near the complex.

For **information**, the Chamber of Commerce, 76 McIntyre Rd, is helpful (July & Aug daily 8.30am–8.30pm; Sept–June Mon–Fri 9am–noon & 1–5pm). Timmins' **accommodation** consists of a series of motels concentrated along Algonquin Boulevard – try *Bon*

Air at no. 355 (☎705/264-1275 or 1-800-461-9832; ③), or the *Comfort Inn by Journey's End* at no. 939 (☎705/264-9474 or 1-800-228-5100; ②). The *Porcupine Danté Club* on Cedar Street has well-priced Italian food.

Kettle Lakes Provincial Park

Kettle Lakes Provincial Park technically lies within the boundaries of Timmins, but is actually 40km east of the centre on Hwy 101 and can only be reached by car. The park's twenty small glacial lakes – known to geologists as "kettles" because they have no inlets or outlets – are surrounded by jack pine and aspen, the species that recovered best from a forest fire that devastated this area in 1911. The two campgrounds ($14.50) in the park are located by the park entrance and by Island Lake in the south of the park and cannot be reserved in advance. Of the park's hiking trails the best goes via Mud Lake, a popular spot for moose, who submerge themselves to escape the flies.

Cochrane

COCHRANE, 50km from the junction of Hwy 101 and Hwy 11, grew up as a repair and turntable station for the railroad companies serving the north. Most of the workshops have closed down but this is still the departure point for the Ontario Northland railway's *Polar Bear Express* to James Bay and into the land of the Cree. That's really the only attraction of this workaday town, but if you have time to spare check out the railcars and native crafts in the **Cochrane Railway & Pioneer Museum** on 13th Avenue, across from Cochrane Station (mid-June to Aug daily 10am–8pm; $1.50). The **information centre** (July & Aug daily 9am–8.30pm; Sept–June Mon–Fri 9am–4.30pm) is by "Chimo", the huge white polar bear at the entrance to Cochrane on the junction of Hwy 11 and 2nd Street. The *Station Inn*, 200 Railway St (☎705/272-3500 or 1-800-265-2356; ③), is your best bet if you're catching the *express* – or there's a mass of motels on the highway west of town. The *JR Ranch BBQ*, 63 3rd Ave, is good for meaty North American meals.

The Polar Bear Express and the Little Bear

The summer-excursion train journey from Cochrane to Moosonee, known as the **Polar Bear Express** (late June to Aug daily except Fri; departs Cochrane 8.30am, arrives Moosonee 12.50pm; departs Moosonee 6.15pm, arrives Cochrane 10.05pm; $49 return), traverses a region where there are in fact no polar bears, but the train goes as far north as anyone can easily go in Ontario and is increasingly popular as a tourist excursion. The tourist bumph promises that on arrival at Moosonee the traditional Cree greeting "Watchi" will resound around the station and you'll have a unique view of Crees and non-natives living and working together in harmony. The reality is different: the government administrators live in pleasant homes in Moosonee, while the 2000 Cree are confined to shacks on the reserve on Moose Factory Island just offshore in the Moose River. Nonetheless, it's a remarkable 300-kilometre trip across the tundra line.

All year round the **Little Bear** (departs Cochrane Mon, Wed & Fri 11.15am, arrives Moosonee 4.15pm; departs Moosonee Tues, Thurs & Sat 9am, arrives Cochrane 2.30pm; $80.90 return), one of Canada's last remaining flagstop trains, takes freight and stops along the way to pick up trappers, fishers, hunters and Crees, whose ancestors first arrived here 10,000 years ago. Europeans arrived somewhat later – in 1673 the first English-speaking settlement in Ontario was established at Moose Factory by the Hudson's Bay Company, and Moosonee itself was founded in 1903 by Révillon Frères, a French fur-trading company. In those days the journey from Cochrane took ten days of hard graft on snowshoes or canoe, but since 1932 the two towns have been connected by rail, which remains the only way – bar flying – of reaching the settlement.

KIRKLAND LAKE AND SIR HARRY OAKES

About 100km north of Cobalt on Hwy 66 lies the mining community of **Kirkland Lake**, producer of one-fifth of Canada's gold. The main street, Government Road, is actually paved with gold – the construction crew used the wrong pile of rocks to construct the road, resulting in a main street made from gold ore instead of waste rock. There's no real reason to head off this way, but the town featured prominently in one of the most sensational stories of Canada's recent past – the story that Nic Roeg made into the film *Eureka* with Gene Hackman and Rutger Hauer.

In the summer of 1911, **Sir Harry Oakes** arrived in Swastika, close to Kirkland Lake, with $2.65 in his pocket. He left in 1934 with $20 million, the largest fortune ever gained through mining in Canada. Oakes began his quest for gold in 1898, his search taking him to Alaska, where his vessel was blown into the Bering Strait and then captured by Cossacks. He escaped under rifle fire and continued his explorations in the relatively safer regions of Australia, West Africa, Mexico and California until, on the run from a revolution in South America, he joined the budding gold rush in northern Canada. In 1912 he founded a mine in what was to become known as Kirkland Lake, where the narrow vein produced $100,000-worth of gold a month, and in 1928 opened up the Lake Shore mine, the most lucrative ore ever discovered in Canada. Oakes, obsessed with keeping his wealth from the revenue services, then emigrated to the tax-free Bahamas.

Around midnight on July 8, 1943, Oakes was murdered in his bed in Nassau, a crime that knocked World War II off the front pages of the newspapers. Detectives immediately arrested Alfred de Marigny, a handsome playboy who had eloped with Oakes's daughter, Nancy, two years previously. The case against him was thin, resting on the presence of a single fingerprint in Oakes's bedroom and the motive of money – with Oakes dead his daughter would inherit a fortune. During the trial it became obvious that the detectives had planted the fingerprint and de Marigny was acquitted. The case was never reopened, but the murder of Sir Harry Oakes has prompted a variety of theories. Alfred de Marigny implicated Oakes's debt-ridden friend Harold Christie, who had defrauded Oakes in a property deal that was about to be exposed by the auditors. Rumours of voodoo and Mafia involvement were rife at the time, but more intriguing is a possible cover-up involving Oakes's confidant, the Duke of Windsor. It has come to light that the Duke and Oakes were involved in a money-laundering operation with a Swedish industrialist and alleged Nazi agent; the suggestion is that the Duke, terrified that the scam would come to light in the course of a prolonged police investigation, might have wanted de Marigny's quick arrest in order to throw people off the scent.

Oakes's 1919 Frank-Lloyd-Wright-style chateau is now the **Museum of Northern History** (Mon–Sat 10am–4pm, Sun noon–4pm; $3), which is off Hwy 66 near the west end of Kirkland Lake. The museum details his climb from rags to riches and displays antique mining equipment, ores, minerals and stuffed animals. One room also highlights the famous hockey players from the town – it's produced 51 NHL stars!

Moosonee

A couple of museums in **MOOSONEE** outline its history: the **Révillon Frères Museum** (late June to Aug daily 9am–5pm; free), in one of the original company buildings, explores the bloody conflicts between the British and French over the area's fur trade. More worthwhile, though, is to hop into a Cree canoe to **Moose Factory Island**, or – if you plan to stay – take the Polar Princess cruise boat, which leaves from the dock opposite the museum (late June to early Sept daily except Sat 9am–3pm; $42.50 including lunch), which goes via James Bay, the Island Bird Sanctuary and Tidewater Provincial Park to Moose Factory for a bus tour. Alternatively, freighter canoes (late June to early Sept daily 1pm; $6) visit Moose Factory or Fossil Island (late June to early Sept daily except Fri; $15.50), 10km up the river where 350-million-year-old fossils have been found. **Moose Factory Centennial Museum Park** (late June to early Sept; free) shows the history of the settlement, the original blacksmith's shop (1740), graveyard, the old powder magazine (the island's only stone building), and a teepee where the locals sell bannock (freshly baked bread) and crafts. South of here, **St Thomas Anglican Church**, built in 1860, has an altar cloth of beaded moose hide, prayer books written in Cree, and removable floor plugs to prevent the church floating away in floods. To the north of the park up Riverside Drive, the **Cree Cultural Organisation** has displays on Cree history, lifestyle and present situation. No driving licence is required on the island and the trucks are pretty reckless – so take care.

If you want to stay longer than the time allowed by the return train (5hr 10min), make sure you reserve your **accommodation** in advance, either at the *Moosonee Lodge* (☎705/336-2351; ③), the *Polar Bear Lodge* (☎705/336-2345; ③), or the *Osprey Country Inn* on Ferguson Road (☎705/336-2226; ④). **Camping** is available at *Tidewater Provincial Park* (☎705/336-2987; $18) on Charles Island. Ontario Northland also offer three- to five-day packages from Cochrane ($255–435 per person, $170–298 if there are three of you), which include accommodation in Cochrane and Moosonee, the *Polar Bear Express*, most meals and some tours.

Kapuskasing and beyond

Kapuskasing marks the halfway point between North Bay and Thunder Bay, beyond which the highway continues west through a stark land of stunted spruce and balsam. The towns have very little of interest and the provincial parks, though often deserted compared to their more southern counterparts, are not really worth the detour.

Kapuskasing

Once known as the model town of the north, **KAPUSKASING**, locally known as the Kap, began as MacPherson Siding in 1913 on the newly completed National Transcontinental Railway, but it was when the community turned to forestry in the 1920s, utilizing the hydroelectric potential of the falls on the Kapuskasing River, that Kap really developed. The Ontario government financed the building of a planned town, with Tudor-style buildings and a layout like a cartwheel whose hub is now marked by a monstrous concrete "K". The town hit the skids in the early 1990s, when uneconomical forestry management by the main employer, Spruce Falls Power and Paper Company, nearly forced the loss of over a thousand jobs. The town's jobs were saved when the employees bought 52 percent of the company, and by 1997 Spruce Falls Inc had been sold on at a lucrative profit.

There's precious little to do here, but a pleasant day out can be spent by taking a boat from the town dock to nearby Beaver Falls, where an hour-and-a-half stopover allows you to explore the area (June–Aug daily 1pm; $10).

For **accommodation**, the rail hotel of *Kapuskasing Inn*, 80 Riverside Drive (☎705/335-2261; ②), is as old as Kap itself and makes a nice change from the clutch of modern motels along Government Road, the cheapest of which is *Prestige Motel* at no. 430 (☎705/335-4505; ②). **Campgrounds** are located at *Rene Brunelle Provincial Park*, just off Government Road, and at Remi Lake, 13km to the north. For **eating**, *Dante's Tavern*, 9 Lang Ave, has a wonderful Italian meal for two for $14.95, and also offers the usual pasta and pizza. The Friday noon buffet and the Sunday brunch will satisfy the largest appetite.

Hearst and Fushimi

Linked by the Algoma Central Railway to Sault Ste Marie, **HEARST** has a statue of a moose outside the information centre which translates as meaning "Welcome to huntsville". Yet this largely French-speaking lumber centre is also a university town, with comparatively chic boutiques and restaurants reflecting a self-confidence that many northern towns are sadly lacking. The helpful **information centre** (Mon–Fri 9am–5pm), on the highway east of town, has information on the whole of northern

THE HUDSON'S BAY COMPANY

In 1661 two Frenchmen, **Medard Chouart des Groseilliers** and **Pierre-Esprit Radisson**, reached the southern end of Hudson Bay overland and realized it was the same inland sea described by earlier seafaring explorers. They returned to the St Lawrence with three hundred canoes packed with superb furs, upon which the French governor arrested them for trapping without a licence. Understandably peeved, in 1665 they turned to the English for financial support and Charles II's cousin, Prince Rupert, persuaded the king and others to finance and equip two ships, the *Eaglet* and the *Nonsuch*. The *Nonsuch* returned with a fantastic cargo of furs, which led to the incorporation of the **Hudson's Bay Company** by Charles II on May 2, 1670. The Company was granted wide powers, including exclusive trading rights to the entire territory traversed by the rivers flowing into Hudson Bay, to be called **Rupert's Land**.

The HBC was a joint-stock company, the shareholders annually electing a governor and committee to hire men, order trade goods and arrange for fur auctions and shipping. By 1760, **trading posts** had been built at the mouths of the major rivers flowing into the bay; these were commanded by factors, or land agents, who took their policy orders from London. The orders were often unrealistic and based on the concept of native trappers bringing furs to the posts – the direct opposite to the Montréal-based North West Company, whose mainly francophone employees spent months in the wilderness working with the natives. Unsurprisingly, the NWC undercut the Company's trade considerably and there was intense competition between the rival concerns right across the Northwest to the Pacific, occasionally resulting in physical violence. By 1821 a compromise was reached and the two companies **merged**, keeping the name Hudson's Bay Company and with the monopoly privileges confirmed by the British parliament extended to include the whole of the Northwest Territories.

The administrative structure of the Company changed and a North American governor was appointed whose councils dealt increasingly with local trading concerns, though the London governor and committee continued to have the last say. The monopoly rights were fiercely resented by the local traders, and after 1849 when the Meti trader Sayer was convicted but not punished for trading with the Indians, the Company's stranglehold on trading competition gradually eroded. Additionally, the HBC became increasingly involved in government as the west was settled. **James Douglas**, a company official, was appointed governor of Vancouver and when British Columbia was created in 1858 the British government forced him to resign from the HBC before becoming governor of the new province. This marked the beginning of the end of the Company's colonial role.

These changes were of little concern to the majority of shareholders, who were more interested in real-estate speculation than the fur trade. In 1870 the HBC sold Rupert's Land to Canada. In return it received a cash payment, but, more importantly, retained the title to the lands on which the trading posts had been built and one-twentieth of the fertile land open to settlement. Given that the trading posts occupied land that was the nucleus of the burgeoning western cities, the Company became a major **real-estate developer** in western Canada, a position it still holds today. By the 1920s it had become involved in oil and gas exploration and production; it finally disposed of its oil interests in 1982. As the west was settled, the fur posts were gradually transformed into **retail shops** and the Company set up its own wholesale division. Today the HBC controls three retail chains and is Canada's largest retailer and a major wholesaler. The Company still retains offices in London, though its official headquarters are now in Winnipeg.

Ontario, while Hearst & Area Bed and Breakfast Association (☎705/362-4442) can fix up cheap **accommodation** in local **B&Bs** (①).

If you want to see moose, head for **Fushimi Lake Provincial Park** (mid-May to Sept; $5), 35km from Hearst and 13km north of Hwy 11, or **Nagagamisis Provincial Park** (mid-May to Sept; $5), on Hwy 631 about 100km southwest of Hearst. The former, named after Prince Fushimi of Japan who visited the area in 1907, is a favourite breeding ground of the bloodsucking blackfly, so stock up on repellent if you're heading for one of its half-dozen **campgrounds** ($14.50). The park is an ancient Algonquian hunting ground, where many thousand-year-old relics have been found – it is possible to canoe to two ancient burial sites from the campground.

Longlac and Geraldton

LONGLAC, 213km west from Hearst, is a lumber and sawmill town that's home to the largest Ojibwa reserve in northern Ontario. It's also the only town in the area that has not banned buck nights, the Canadian equivalent of a stag night. Ontarian buck nights involve trailing the bridegroom around the streets to be subjected to indignities such as pelting with eggs – the missiles are sold to passers-by in aid of charity.

The first thing anyone notices when arriving in **GERALDTON**, 35km further west, are the wide streets, a reminder of Geraldton's glory days during the mining boom. *The Geraldton Hotel*, 100 First Ave (☎807/854-0660; ①), is another local landmark which still looks like you should park your horse outside. The **Macleod Provincial Park** (June to mid-Sept; $2), 6km south of Geraldton, is your best bet if you are under canvas ($12).

Sudbury

SUDBURY, the economic centre of northeastern Ontario, is parked on the edge of the Sudbury Basin, a pit created either by a volcano or, the preferred theory, by a giant meteor. Whatever did the damage, the effect was to throw one of the world's richest deposits of nickel and copper towards the surface. It was the nickel – used to temper steel – that made Sudbury's fortune, but its by-products caused devastation. Most of the damage was done by a smelting method known as heap roasting, used until the 1920s, which spread clouds of sulphurous fumes over forests already ravaged by lumber firms and mineral prospectors, who often started fires to reveal the traces of metal in the bare rocks. Likened to Hell or Hiroshima, the bleak landscape had only one advantage: in 1968 it enabled Buzz Aldrin and Neil Armstrong to practise their great leap for mankind in a ready-made lunar environment.

Having continued to produce sulphur-laden smoke from the stacks of their nickel smelters, the mining companies were finally forced to take action when a whole community of workers from Happy Valley, just northeast of Sudbury, were evacuated in the 1970s because of the number of sulphur-induced illnesses, particularly lung cancer. Pollutants in the immediate environs of the city have been reduced, albeit by means such as building the world's tallest superstack, which now belches poisons out half a kilometre above the city, where they drift off to contaminate areas way to the north. But, with a regreening programme that was internationally recognized at the UN's Earth Summit in Rio, thousands of acres have spluttered back to life, and the thirty lakes in the vicinity, including one in the middle of town, are no longer stagnant pools of vinegar. Sudbury's multinational population of 160,000 – over half of them French-speaking – are fiercely proud of a city that has received nothing but lousy publicity for decades. Though it can seem that the main effect of the recent redevelopment has been an efflorescence of shopping malls, the city can boast two of north Ontario's most impressive tourist sights, Science North and Big Nickel Mine. And it gets warmer than any other of Ontario's other industrial cities – the pollution-blackened rocks retain the heat of the sun.

The City

Sudbury is a sprawling city with a small central core that offers very little except the opportunity to browse through the **Farmer's Market** (May–Oct Sat & Sun 7am–5pm)

Moose

Beaver

Lake of Two Rivers, Algonquin National Park, Ontario

CN Tower, Toronto, Ontario

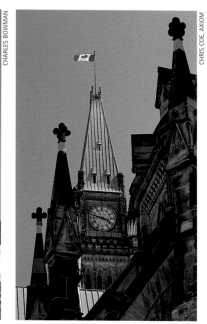
Parliament Buildings, Ottawa, Ontario

Niagara Falls and the *Maid of the Mist*, Ontario

Château Frontenac, Québec City, Québec

Art stalls in Vieux Montréal, Québec

The Illuminated Crowd, Montréal, Québec

A harbour in Nova Scotia

Vieux Québec at night, Québec

A catch of cod in Newfoundland

On the dock of the bay, Newfoundland

Fishing boats iced in at Rose Blanche, Newfoundland

on Shaughnessy Street, a limp imitation of Ottawa's Byward Market; or check out the offbeat art exhibitions at the **Art Gallery of Sudbury** housed in the coach house and former home of lumber magnate W.J. Bell at 251 John St, just off Paris (Tues–Sun noon–5pm; donation).

The main attractions of Sudbury are located to the south of the central core. In trying to change it from a black hole into a resort, the powers that be have made the most out of the city's unusual geology, and most of the exhibits in **Science North** (daily: May to late June & Sept to mid-Oct 9am–5pm; late June to Aug 9am–6pm; mid-Oct to April 10am–4pm; $8.95, children $6.50; bus #500), a huge snowflake-shaped structure on Ramsey Lake Road, are installed in a cavern blasted into the rock of the Canadian Shield. The hands-on displays enable you to simulate a miniature hurricane, gauge your fitness, lie on a bed of nails, learn to lip-read, call up amateur radio hams worldwide, tune in to weather-tracking stations and try different sensory tests, all under the guidance of students from Laurentian University. The museum also has a collection of insects and animals, most of which can be handled. The flying squirrels give exhibitions of their prowess, sailing effortlessly 25m through the air, and there's a rather smelly and somnulent porcupine of considerable charm called Ralf.

The underground theatre shows a combination 3-D and laser film on the evolution of the Sudbury basin; the special effects are impressive but it's marred by a dreadful story line and wooden acting. You'd be better to take in a show at the new $5-million **Imax Theatre** (daily; adults $8, children $6.50) with its 22-metre-wide screen – the film shot on board the space shuttles was described by astronauts as "the next best thing to being there". Double bills are shown in the evening (adults $11.25, children $8.50). By the Imax entrance, the **Virtual Voyage** ($6.50) is a virtual-reality roller-coaster journey to Mars.

The town's symbol, a nine-metre-high steel replica of a five-cent piece, imaginatively known as the Big Nickel, stands by the Trans-Canada on the western approach to town. You can get here on the infrequent #940 bus or take a $9 taxi ride from Science North. The nickel marks the entrance to the **Big Nickel Mine** (daily: May to late June & Sept to mid-Oct 9am–5pm; late June to Aug 9am–6pm; $8.50), where you can take a less than enthralling tour of a replica mine and mail a card from the underground postbox to let the folks back home know you've travelled 20m below the earth's surface. Worth a glance is the subterranean tree nursery; humidity and constant temperature provide ideal conditions for raising different species.

Various **combination tickets** save money on the above attractions. All-day passports (adults $24.95, children $15.95) give admission to Science North, up to three Imax films, two Virtual Voyages and the Big Nickel.

Believe it or not, one of the most spectacular sights in this area is **slag-pouring**, which you can watch from **Copper Cliff**, the workers' estate beneath the slag heaps to the west, beyond the Big Nickel. At the end of the smelting process the red-hot slag is poured into hopper cars, which are pulled by an electric train to the top of huge slag piles, from where it's poured like volcanic lava down the hill. The best view is from the Lasalle Boulevard bypass, reached by bus #940 (information on times ☎705/682-6666).

Bus #940 continues to a hilltop west of Copper Cliff, site of **Little Italy**, a quarter built by Italian miners at the turn of the century to re-create the hillside villages of their home country. Italian is still more commonly spoken than English here, and it's one of the more atmospheric parts of the city.

Practicalities

Sudbury's **train** station, the terminus of trains from the east, is about 20km northeast of town, near the airport in Falconbridge; local buses from outside go to the downtown terminus on the junctions of Elm and Cedar – the flat fare, payable on board, is $1.50. The Greyhound **bus** depot is at 854 Notre Dame; some long-distance buses also stop at

Science North. For **information**, the Sudbury Welcome Centre (May–Aug daily 8.30am–8.30pm; Sept–April Mon–Wed 9am–6pm, Thurs & Fri 9am–8pm, Sat 10am–6pm) is to the south of town on Hwy 69.

Accommodation

During the summer, **student rooms** are also available at Laurentian University, Ramsey Lake Road (☎705/673-6597; ①). For **B&B**, there are four centrally located establishments (②): *Avenue d'Youville B&B*, 216 d'Youville (☎705/673-7967); *By the Lake*, 65 Nepahuin Ave (☎705/522-3803); *Lafleur B&B*, 5073 Croatia Rd (☎705/522-5799); and *Serendipity B&B*, 556 Brenda Drive (☎705/523-8626). The two central budget **hotels** in town are grotty and usually full with transient workers; most hotels have a policy of only renting out for the week. For posher accommodation, try: *The Days Inn Sudbury*, 117 Elm St West (☎705/674-7517 or 1-800-325-2525; ③), a three-star place right in the middle of town; the *Travelway Inn*, 1200 Paris St (☎705/522-1122 or 1-800-461-4883; ③); or the nearby *Travelodge*, 1401 Paris St (☎705/522-1100 or 1-800-578-7878; ③), part of a chain and with lots of facilities. Many of the larger hotels offer packages that include tickets to Science North. The proliferation of **motels** west of town on Lorne Street are all pretty characterless; it's best to head for Pioneer Road south of town – *The Brockdan Motor Hotel* at no. 1222 (☎705/522-5270; ③) is cheap, with air-conditioned rooms.

For **camping**, *Carol's Campsite* (☎705/522-5570 or 1-800-887-5570; $12 a site) and *Mine Mill Campground* (☎705/522-5076; $12–18) are 8km south on Hwy 69 in a pretty wilderness area; you need to reserve at both.

Eating, drinking and nightlife

To **eat** cheaply, *Frank's Delicatessen*, 112 Durham, is good for light meals, and upstairs at the City Centre Mall there is an adequate food court with the usual selection of bargain fast-food outlets. Fresh pickerel from the lakes in the vicinity can be sampled at *The Red Lobster*, 1600 Lasalle, or the more expensive *Teklenburg's* at no. 1893. Italian food is cheap at *Mingle's*, 762 Notre Dame, a studenty pizza and pasta restaurant, whilst comfortable *Pasta e Vino*, 118 Paris St, has delicious home-made pasta.

For Indian food, *Taste of India*, 1873 Kingsway, is worth a try, while the *Jade Garden*, 1875 Paris St, and the *Peking Gazebo*, 1716 Regent St, both offer good Chinese food at reasonable prices. The reliable chains also have branches here – *Beef and Brand* in the City Centre Mall; *Swiss Chalet*, 1349 Lasalle, for chicken; and *Buzzy Brown's* for Mexican and Canadian fare.

The best **bars** are the *Coulson* on the corner of Larch and Durham; the popular *Trevi Tavern*, 1837 Lasalle; *Cactus Pete's*, 187 Shaugnessy; and *The Pub* at Laurentian University. The busiest **nightclubs** are *Studio 4* in Brady Street and the C&W *Rock and Rodeo* in the *Seranto Hotel* at 1400 Kingsway. *Yuk Yuk's* **comedians** perform on Thursday, Friday and Saturday evenings at the *Ramada Inn*, 85 Ste Anne Rd.

Killarney Provincial Park

Located on the north shore of Georgian Bay, 100km southwest of Sudbury, is the so-called crown jewel of Ontario's provincial parks, **Killarney Provincial Park**. Dominated by the white quartzite ridges of the La Cloche mountains, this was a popular haunt of the Group of Seven – Franklin Carmichael even had a cottage here and was reported to find the park "the most challenging and gratifying landscape in the province".

Driving south from Copper Cliff, you will pass the park entrance 10km before the tiny village of **Killarney**, close to the southern tip of the park. In the summer Manitoulin Transport runs a daily bus that stops at the park gates en route to Sudbury, call

☎705/287-2507 or 677-5108 for details. The village is the closest community to the park, and has **accommodation** at the *Sportsman's Inn*, 37 Channel St (☎705/287-2411 or 1-800-461-1117; doubles ③). Killarney Outfitters, 3 Commissioner St (May–Oct; ☎705/287-2828 or 1-800-461-1117, fax 287-2828), located on Hwy 637, 5km east of Killarney, offers complete outfitting for canoe trips ($49 per day).

Places in the campgrounds around **George Lake** ($6; mid-June to Aug), close to the park gate, must be reserved far in advance at the nearby park office (☎705/287-2900); canoeists and hikers heading into the interior must obtain permits from the office and also register a route plan that does not allow for any detours. Camping is allowed from May to mid-October, with midweek permits easier to obtain than weekend ones. The three short **hiking trails** from the George Lake campground can often be crowded with day-trippers, but the interior hiking is unsurpassable. **La Cloche Silhouette Trail** across the north ridges of the La Cloche mountains requires a week to ten days of hiking and is not for the unfit – the campgrounds along the way are primitive and you need to be self-sufficient for the whole trip. The highlight of the trail is **Silver Peak**, 543m above sea level, where views over Georgian Bay are awe-inspiring. Off-trail hiking is also permitted but needs to be well organized and is strictly for experienced hikers.

The **canoe routes** have well-marked portages and are generally suitable for beginners as well as experienced canoeists. The waters are sparkling and beautiful, but don't drink them – acid rain coupled with the natural acidity of the quarzite has all but wiped out the fish population. It is also possible to canoe into Georgian Bay, but this is not advised for beginners, as the weather on the coast is unpredictable.

Manitoulin Island

The Ojibwa believe that when Gitchi Manitou (the Great Spirit) created the world he reserved the best bits for himself and created **MANITOULIN** (God's Island) – the world's largest freshwater island – as his own home. A continuation of the limestone Niagara Escarpment, Manitoulin is beautifully different from the harsh grey rocks of the Canadian Shield, with its white cliffs skirting lakes and woodland that's home to a substantial population of white-tailed deer. For the time being, despite the popularity of the ferry link with Tobermory on the Bruce Peninsula as a route between the south and north of the province, this is a place of solitary villages and quiet lanes that wind past hundreds of lakes and acres of farmland neatly divided by unique fences. This may soon change, however – the farms, unable to keep up with the levels of production in more southern regions, are changing into cottage resorts and campgrounds for the rapidly expanding tourist industry, and Manitoulin may not much longer present a contrast with the overloaded rural retreats on the other side of Georgian Bay.

Over a quarter of the island's 11,000 population are native peoples, descendants of groups believed to have arrived over 10,000 years ago, leaving some of the oldest human traces on the continent. An Iroquois invasion in 1652 – two years after Champlain arrived here – forced the island's natives to flee, and it wasn't until the early nineteenth century that the Ojibwa, Odawa and Pottawatomi people were brought back by missionaries. In 1838 the government sponsored an establishment at Manitowaning, legendary home of the Great Spirit, to "instruct the Indians in the ways of civilization", a lamentable experiment that collapsed in 1861, when the natives were persuaded to cede their land to white settlers instead. It was only the Ojibwa band living on the eastern tip of the island at Wikwemikong who refused the treaty, and today the majority of Manitoulin's Indians still live on this unceded reserve, which is officially not a part of Canada. During the August Civic Weekend, Wiky – as it's always known – holds the largest **powwow** in the country.

Getting there

There are no scheduled air, bus or train services to Manitoulin and most people arrive on the island via the MS *Chi-Cheemaun*, the **car ferry** that travels between Tobermory on the Bruce Peninsula and South Baymouth on the south side of the island (May to late June & Sept to mid-Oct, 2–3 daily; late June to Aug, 4 daily; 1hr 45min; $11 single, $24 cars; ☎1-800-265-3163). From northern Ontario Hwy 6 connects Espanola on Hwy 17 with the north shore of Manitoulin – if you're in your own car it is worth taking a detour to the tiny village of Willisville for stunning views of the whole island and the La Cloche mountains. The island is linked to mainland Ontario by a swing bridge at Little Current that still opens for fifteen minutes every hour to allow boats through. The nearest **long-distance bus** station is at Espanola, a $50 taxi ride from Manitoulin's Little Current. There are **information centres** in Gore Bay, Manitowaning, South Baymouth and Little Current, all of which close from September to May.

East Manitoulin: South Baymouth to Little Current

First sight of Manitoulin for most visitors is **SOUTH BAYMOUTH**, a pleasantly situated if nondescript village that grew on its fish-salting factories. Your best advice is to keep moving once you're off the ferry. If you're heading north along Hwy 6 to the mainland, your route runs through **MANITOWANING**, fifteen minutes away on the southwestern shore of Manitowaning Bay, where the **Assignack Museum** (daily: June–Aug 9am–5pm; Sept 11am–4pm; $1), in the 1850s limestone jail, details the history of the Manitowaning Experiment in "civilizing" the native peoples.

Midway between South Baymouth and Manitowaning, *Happy Acres B&B* (☎705/859-3453; ②; summer only) is a pleasant farm if you need a place to stay.

Wikwemikong

At Manitowaning a branch road runs east to the reserve of **WIKWEMIKONG**, 14km from Hwy 6 on the western shore of Smith Bay. Home to 2500 people of the Three Fire Tribes – Odawa, Ojibwa and Pottawatomi – this is the only unceded reserve in North America, but it looks much like every other run-down reserve in Canada with its gravel track flanked by wooden yellow shacks and, like so many of them, it's generally a sad place of massive unemployment and alcoholism. Every August Civic Weekend, though, Wiky is transformed by the country's largest **powwow**, which brings in the best of the continent's performers and is packed with stalls selling native foods and crafts. Amongst the programme of traditional dances and ceremonies, the local theatre group De-Ba-Jeh-Mu-Jig retell native legends and perform contemporary plays by native playwrights; during the rest of the summer they perform at various venues in Wiky from the school to the ruins of the 1888 Holy Cross Mission that burnt down in 1954 – call ☎705/859-2317 for play dates.

The reserve's new interpretive/heritage centre located upstairs in the Wikwemikong Bay Marina has historical artefacts, photos, artworks and regalia, as well as a tourist information office that can help find local accommodation. *Wiky Bed and Breakfast* (☎705/859-2955) is the only official place to stay here, and *The Coffee Shop* provides a great sub sandwich if you're hungry.

Sheguiandah and Little Current

A few kilometres beyond the amazing **Ten Mile Point Lookout**, which overlooks the waters of Lake Huron as they funnel into the North Channel, you come to **SHEGUIANDAH** and the **Little Current-Howland Museum** (April–Oct daily

10am–4.30pm; $3). It was in this woodland setting that archeologists found pieces of local quartzite that had been fashioned into tools 30,000 years ago, allegedly the oldest evidence of human habitation in North America. Yet the museum makes little reference to the prehistoric discoveries, instead housing the normal run-of-the-mill tools and furnishings of early Victorian settlers.

Though it's the largest community on Manitoulin and the only all-year gateway to the island, **LITTLE CURRENT** is a drowsy place that can make a pleasant stopover; *Little Current Motel*, 18 Campbell St (☎705/368-2882; ②), is the most central **accommodation**, or try *Ruth's B&B*, 73 Campbell St (☎705/368-3891; ②). *The Olde English Pantry* opposite the waterfront has some delicious cream teas, while *Farquhar's Dairy*, next door to the information centre on Hwy 6, turns out a mean ice cream.

North Manitoulin: Little Current to Meldrum Bay

Highway 540 stretches the length of Manitoulin along the shore of the North Channel, one of Ontario's foremost areas for folks with boats and the route with the remotest villages and the most interesting of Manitoulin's **hiking trails**. The six-kilometre **Cup and Saucer** is the best-known trail, located 18km west of Little Current at the junction of Hwy 540 and Bidwell Road, just east of West Bay; the trail reaches the highest point of the island (460m) and involves climbing ladders through natural rock chimneys. Several short hikes lead from behind *Abby's Dining Lounge* at the Ojibwa reserve at **WEST BAY**, 30km southwest of Little Current – the eight-kilometre **M'Chigeeng** trail is accompanied by signs retelling local folklore and legends.

Midway between West Bay and Gore Bay is **KAGAWONG**, approached by turning off Hwy 540 at Billings Co Store and following the nineteenth-century streetlamps into the village. Just before Kagawong, **Bridal Veil Falls** are the place for cool dips on hot days – you can even walk behind the water cascade. A leaflet from the information centre provides a good walking tour of this pleasant village if you have time to kill. *Bridal Veil B&B* (☎705/282-3300; ②) has **rooms** for the night in a century-old home by the beach (by reservation only in the winter) or there's *Bayview B&B*, another Victorian house in the middle of the village, with home-made bread for breakfast (☎705/282-0741; ②).

Another 15km west brings you to **GORE BAY**, an attractive village right on the shore, worth visiting if only to stay in the beautifully situated *Hill House*, 6 Borron St (☎705/282-2072; ①–②) – the best **B&B** on the island.

Highway 540 continues west through hamlets that you'll miss if you blink, passing back roads that lead to bays deserted enough for skinny-dipping. The road peters out at the most westerly point of the island marked by **MELDRUM BAY**, a tiny settlement of white wooden buildings. Twelve kilometres beyond stand the red roofs of the century-old **Mississagi Lighthouse** (mid-May to June Sat & Sun 10am–4pm; July & Aug daily 9am–9pm; $1), now converted into a museum and restaurant with pioneer food, soups, beans and bread. You can **camp** here in the adjoining heritage park (☎283-3011).

Southern Manitoulin

Though **south Manitoulin** is less impressive than the north, its proximity to the Bruce Peninsula has led to more tourist development. The most worthwhile part is **PROVIDENCE BAY**, about 40km west of South Baymouth, which boasts the island's longest sand beach plus the unique attraction of the "burning boat", a glowing apparition that appears on the horizon around 3am on nights with a full moon. *The School House* (☎705/377-4055) is the island's best eatery – a frilly **restaurant** in the former school. Nearby *Huron Sands* (☎705/377-4616; ④) is an upmarket motel/resort and the outlet for delicious Hawberry Jams, the jams, chutneys, sauces and relishes that are on sale throughout Manitoulin. **Camping** on the beach is available at *Providence Bay Tent and Trailer Park* (☎705/377-4650; May–Oct).

Sault Ste Marie

Strategically situated on the rapids of St Mary's River, the link between lakes Superior and Huron, **SAULT STE MARIE** – more popularly called the Soo – sits opposite an American town of the same name and sees constant two-way traffic: tourists flow over the International Bridge to experience Canada's wilderness, while a stream of Canadians heads across to the States for cheaper groceries and petrol. The river is bordered by an American and a Canadian **canal**, each constructed in the nineteenth century, when the relationship between the halves of the continent was not the reciprocal one of today. These waterways enabled the Soo to graduate from a major pulp-and-paper producer to the province's second largest producer of steel. For years the freighters have travelled exclusively via the four American locks on what is one of the busiest sections of the Great Lakes, however recently the Canadian locks have finally reopened after overcoming a catalogue of engineering difficulties.

Northern Ontario's oldest community, the Soo was originally settled by fishing parties of the Ojibwa called *Saulteux* – "people of the falls" – by the French. In 1667 Jesuit missionaries renamed the town, a prelude to its development as a fur-trading post; it was here that Sieur de St Lusson proclaimed France's lawful claim to the whole of America in 1671. The following centuries present a steady tale of economic growth, and the only significant event of recent years was the Soo's declaration of English as its official language, a symbolic protest that duly caused a furore in Québec. Despite the Soo's industrial make-up it is a cosy, well-tended town with handsome red sandstone buildings and the added unmissable attraction of the **Algoma Central Railway**.

The City

The Soo's agreeable downtown area is centred on Queen's Road, parallel to the waterfront, which contains all of the Soo's sights in a pleasant renovated area. Of the designated historic sites the most impressive is the **Ermantinger Old Stone House**, 831 Queen St East (mid-April to May Mon–Fri 10am–5pm; June–Sept daily 10am–5pm; Oct & Nov Mon–Fri 1–5pm; $2), built in 1814 and originally home to the fur trader Charles Ermantinger, his Ojibwa princess wife Manonowe – who was unceremoniously renamed Charlotte – and their thirteen children. Since then the house has served as a hotel, the sheriff's house, a meeting hall for the YWCA and a social club. Restoration has returned it to the look of 1814–30, and the period-costumed staff bake tasty cakes in the summer. Across the road in the old post office, the **Sault Ste Marie Museum** (Mon–Sat 9am–4.30pm, Sun 1–4.30pm; $2) has various exhibits on the Soo's history, from a birchbark Ojibwa house to a re-creation of Queen Street in 1910. Nearby, the **Great Lakes Forestry Centre**, 1219 Queen St (Mon–Fri 8.30am–4.30pm; free), Canada's largest forest research complex, is open for tours through the labs and greenhouses.

Soo's waterfront, just a block south of the museum, is a good area to wander for a couple of hours, and its recent rebuilding includes the better-than-average **Art Gallery of Algoma**, 10 East St (Mon–Sat 9am–5pm, Thurs till 9pm, Sun 1.30–4.30pm; donation), whose exhibitions of Canadian art often feature local artists inspired by the Algoma countryside. Five minutes' walk west from here you'll find the **Roberta Bondar Pavilion**, a huge tent-like permanent structure named after Canada's first astronaut, who came from the Soo. It's used for concerts and exhibitions and locals are proud of the murals running round its exterior, which show aspects of the area painted inside wigwam shapes; subjects range from shipping and lake scenes to fall colours, pictographs and winter landscapes. From May to October on Wednesdays and Saturdays, a great Farmer's Market, selling fruit and veg, is held here. The Soo is also the home, since 1876, of **Northern Breweries**, 503 Bay St (☎1-800-461-2258), which has tours for over-19s to get you thoroughly acquainted with the art of brewing beer. At the waterfront hangar at the end of Bay Street, the **Canadian Bushplane Heritage Centre** (daily: mid-May to Oct 10am–7pm; Nov to mid-May 10am–4pm; $3) is an interesting diversion that tells the story of the bushplane and the forest firefighting crews that manned them.

There are two-hour **cruises** through the **Soo lock** system (June to mid-Oct, 3–4 daily; $16), which handles more tonnage than the Suez and Panama put together. Unless you are crazy about cruises it is far better to view the locks and the traffic from the boardwalk of the **Sault Canal National Historic Site** (mid-May to mid-Oct daily 10am–5pm; mid-Oct to mid-May Mon–Fri 8.30am–4.30pm; free), which leads through a wooded area to the edge of the St Mary's Rapids from the south end of Huron Street.

The Algoma Central Railway

The main attraction of the Soo is as the departure point for the **Algoma Central Railway** (ACR), a 500-kilometre rail line constructed in 1901 to link the factories to the vital timber resources further north. It was first used for recreational purposes by the Group of Seven, who shunted up and down the track in a converted boxcar which they used as a base to canoe into Canada's wilds. The ACR now offers everyone an opportunity to journey into the Algoma fastnesses, where the train snakes through a vista of deep ravines and countless secluded lakes, hugging the hillsides and crossing gorges on skeletal trestle bridges. To see everything, sit on the left-hand side – otherwise your window will look out onto a wall of rock.

Three tours now depart from the Algoma Central Railway Terminal, 129 Bay St. The **Agawa Canyon Train Tour** takes the whole day (June to mid-Oct departs 8am, returns 5pm; June–Aug $49, Sept to mid-Oct $55; ☎705/946-7300 or 1-800-242-9287), and its popularity with the Americans means that it is always necessary to book, often two days in advance. A two-hour stop within the canyon's 180-metre walls allows for a lunch break and a wander around the well-marked nature trails, which include a lookout post from where the rail line is a thin silver thread far below. Unless you are properly equipped don't miss the train back – the canyon gets very cold at night, even during the summer, and the flies are merciless.

During the winter when the lakes are frozen and the country is laden with snow, the **Snow Train** (late Dec to mid-March Sat & Sun departs 8am, returns 4.10pm; $49; ☎705/946-7300 or 1-800-242-9287) travels right through the canyon to the dramatic exit, where the walls are only 15m apart, before returning to the Soo.

The third and longest trip is the **Tour of the Line** (mid-May to mid-Oct Wed & Fri–Sun departs 9.40am, arrives 6.45pm; mid-Oct to mid-May Fri–Sun departs 9am, arrives 6.05pm; $125 return, accommodation extra; ☎705/946-7300 or 1-800-242-9287), a return trip that takes two days with one overnight stay in Hearst, at the end of the line (see p.174). North of the canyon the scenery of low coniferous forest can be flat and dreary – though you'll probably spot a few moose – and Hearst is no great shakes, but if you are heading west anyway and are sick of travelling by Greyhound, the journey is worth considering.

In addition to these tourist-oriented expeditions, every day from mid-May to mid-October you can jump on board the ACR's so-called "moose meat special", which picks up the hunters and trappers at various points along the track, allowing you to simply step out into the great unknown alone. The cost is 23¢ per km, which makes it more expensive than the tour train (to get to the canyon from the Soo costs $29.55 one-way), and because it stops all the time it takes longer; but camping in this kind of country is as far away from civilization as you can get, with the security of knowing that you can always flag down the next train if you get completely sick of the flies. There are several lodges en route, most of which are located beside clear, silent lakes; information about them is available at the terminal in the Soo, though the staff there seem more interested in the well-heeled American travellers.

Practicalities

The Soo's **bus** station is at 73 Brock St. Because the Soo receives so many American tourists, the **Ontario Travel Information Centre**, 261 Queen St West (daily: mid-May to early Sept 8am–8pm; early Sept to mid-Oct 8.30am–6pm; mid-Oct to mid-May 8.30am–4.30pm), a five-minute walk from the bus station, is an excellent source of information on the whole province.

Accommodation

As ever, the cheapest **accommodation** is in the **youth hostel**, housed in the old *Algonquin Hotel*, 865 Queen St East (☎705/253-42311; ①; open 24hr a day all year). The cheapest **B&Bs** are at 99 Retta St (☎705/253-8641; ①) and 345 Elizabeth St (☎705/253-2349; ①). For elegant B&B try the pet- child- and smoke-free *Brockwell Chambers B&B*, 183 Brock St (☎ & fax 705/949-1076; ②). Others worth considering are *Top o' the Hill*, 40 Broos Rd (☎705/253-9041; ②), and *Hillsview Bed and Breakfast*, 406 Old Garden River Rd (☎705/759-8819; ②), the latter for non-smokers only.

The *Bay Front Quality Inn*, 180 Bay St (☎705/945-9264 or 1-800-228-5151; ④), with all mod cons including an indoor pool, is right opposite the ACR train station, and the *Diplomat Motel*, 844 Queen St East (☎705/254-4371; ②), is a motel-style place, centrally located, near the waterfront. Of the profusion of motels, the *Algoma Cabins and Motel*, 1713 Queen St East (☎705/256-8681; ②), is a good bet; or try the *Bel-Air*, 398 Pim St (☎705/256-2285; ②), or the *Skyline*, 232 Great Northern Rd (☎705/942-1240 or 1-800-461-2624; ③).

Camping is available in various locations just out of town – KOA have a campground with hook-ups at 501 Fifth Line, 8km north of the Soo off Hwy 17, and *Blueberry Hill Tent and Trailer Park* is 2km further north on Hwy 17.

Eating and drinking

Sault Ste Marie has an excellent variety of eateries to suit all budgets and tastes. The proliferation of American-style **diners** with chrome bars and low bar stools provide huge amounts of grub for low prices, though most close early. *Ernie's Coffee Shop*, 13 Queen St East (Tues–Sat 7am–7pm), is the best and most popular of these, with lengthy queues for its non-stop coffee, breakfast specials for $2.95, and jukeboxes on each table. Operating since 1932, *Mike's Quick Lunch*, 518 Queen St East (closed Sun), is equally popular, while nearby *Mary's Lunch*, 663 Queen St East, has breakfast specials all day.

The Soo's proximity to vast expanses of water has yielded a good set of fish restaurants: *Gino's*, 1076 Great Northern Rd, has local lake trout for $6 and the *Sea Buoy*, 265 Bruce St, has good English-style fish and chips; the pricier *Aurora's*, 384 McNabb, has a reputation for great lobster. Top of the tree, though, is *A Thymely Manner*, 531 Albert St (☎705/759-3262; open Tues–Sun), which, despite the hideous name, is one of Canada's top restaurants, famed for its lamb from nearby St Joseph's Island and its great Caesar salad; it'll cost you around $40 a head, and reservations are a must.

Nightlife is pretty thin on the ground, but local youth swear by the *Club Princess*, 945 Gore St, housed in an old cinema complete with screen, where you can watch yourself dancing to raucous local bands, or head for *The River Rock* at 2 Queen St East, another popular nightclub.

Listings

Airlines Air Ontario, at the airport (☎1-800-268-7240).

Bike rental Vernes's Hardware, 51 Great Northern Rd (☎705/254-4901).

Bus information Local: (☎705/759-5438). Long-distance: Greyhound, (☎705/949-4711).

Canoe rental Oskar's Heyden Crafts Company, RR 2 (☎705/777-2426).

Car rental Avis, 95 Second Line East (☎705/254-4349); Budget, 100 Queen St East (☎705/942-1144); Thrifty, 680 Great Northern Rd (☎705/759-0120); Tilden, 440 Pim St (☎705/949-5121).

Festivals The Bon Soo Carnival in February and the Algoma Fall Festival in September are both littered with fun and cultural events, with family-orientated celebrations and fireworks.

Ice hockey The Soo Greyhounds of the Ontario Hockey League play at the 3500-seater rink, Memorial Gardens, 269 Queen St East (§8; ☎705/759-5251). Tickets §8.

Hiking Over 400km of Ontario's longest hiking trail, the Voyageur Trail, has been completed – it now reaches the Soo from Manitoulin, passing through the La Cloche Mountains via the rocky shore of Lake Superior. For more information and a detailed guidebook, contact the Voyageur Trail Association, Box 66, Sault Ste Marie, Ontario P5A 5L2 (☎705/759-2480).

Laundry Station Mall Laundromat, 293 Bay St (daily 8am–9pm).

Pharmacy Medical Centre Pharmacy, 974 Queen St East.

Post office 451 Queen St East.

Weather For up-to-date bulletins, call ☎705/789-8983.

The north shore of Lake Superior

With a surface area of 82,000 square kilometres, **Lake Superior** is the largest freshwater lake in the world, and one of the wildest. The **north shore**, stretching for nearly 700km from Sault Ste Marie to Thunder Bay, is a windswept, forested, rugged region formed by volcanoes, earthquakes and glaciers, its steep forested valleys often overhung by a steely canopy of grey sky. In 1872 Reverend George Grant wrote of Superior: "It breeds storms and rain and fog, like a sea. It is cold . . .wild, masterful and dreaded." The native Ojibwa also lived in fear of the storms that would suddenly break on the lake they knew as Gitche Gumee, the Big-Sea-Water, and propitiated their gods to placate it. With icy waters that cause its many victims to sink like stones, Lake Superior is hauntingly known as the lake that never gives up its dead.

The highlights of this region are the vast **parks of Lake Superior** and **Pukaskwa**, whose innumerable waterways and treks are a challenging route into some of Ontario's most dramatic wilderness, and the **Sleeping Giant** provincial park, between **Nipigon** and Thunder Bay – which is also close to the wonderful canyon of **Ouimet**. With few exceptions, the small towns are humdrum places based on railroading, mining, lumber and the endless stream of truckers and tourists who motor through on the Trans-Canada. Though passenger trains only serve White River, nearly all the other communities are regularly served by Greyhound buses.

Lake Superior Provincial Park

Stretching on either side of the Trans-Canada, its southern border 124km from Sault Ste Marie, the **Lake Superior Provincial Park** (May to late Oct) is an awesome yet easily accessible portion of Superior's granite shoreline and its hinterland. Fall is perhaps the best time to visit, when the blackflies have abated and the forests of sugar maples and yellow birch are an orgy of colour, but the scenery and wildlife are enthralling throughout the year. Moose, chipmunks and beavers are the commonest mammals, sharing their habitat with more elusive species including white-tailed deer, woodland caribou, coyote, timber wolves and black bears, as well as myriad migratory and resident birds. The **Park Office** (May–Oct daily 9am–6pm; ☎705/856-2284), beside the highway about 194km from the Soo, provides maps of the park's outstanding **hikes** and canoe routes, and information on vacancies at the park's three major **campgrounds** – located at quiet **Crescent Lake** ($13–14.50; Aug & Sept) on the southern boundary popular **Agawa Bay** ($13–17.75; mid-May to Sept), 8km further north right on Lake Superior and at **Rabbit Blanket Lake** ($13–14.50; May–Oct) just north of the Park Office. A camping permit must be purchased from the office or the campgrounds if you plan to stay overnight. You must also register at the office or at the trail entrances before embarking on any of the long-distance hikes, and interior camping costs $5; the staff will warn you if weather conditions look perilous, but always expect the worst – the park receives more rain and snow than any other area in Ontario.

Agawa Rock

For thousands of years the Ojibwa used the park area for hunting, a single hunter's territory sometimes extending for as much as 1300 square kilometres. Their sacred rock carvings, created at inaccessible sites in order to heighten their mystery, are best seen on **Agawa Rock**, where the pictures represent a crossing of the lake by Chief Myeegn and his men, during which they were protected by Misshepexhieu, the horned lynx demigod of Lake Superior. To reach Agawa Rock, take the short access road west of Hwy 17 about 16km from the southern border of the park; from here a 400-metre trail leads to a rock ledge from where the pictographs can be viewed.

The Coastal Trail

The finest of the park's trails – the **Coastal Trail** – begins some 140km from Sault Ste Marie at Sinclair Cove by the pictographs, and runs north to Chalfont Cove, a challenging route of high cliffs, sand and cobbled beaches, sheltered coves and exposed granite ledges. There are numerous designated campsites on the route, though the burnt-out fires on the beaches indicate where most people choose to pitch. The entire trek takes about five to seven days but access points enable you to do shorter sections of the trail; the southern part of the trail is not as demanding, with fewer climbs and easier going on sand rather than cobbled beach.

Wawa to Nipigon

Past the park's northern border, the mixed deciduous–coniferous forest gives way to a boreal forest of balsam fir, white birch, trembling aspen, and white and black spruce. From Wawa to Marathon the highway travels inland, losing sight of Lake Superior behind a continuous screen of conifers before resuming the panoramic stint along the lake, whose white fringe of beaches looks like a frigid Caribbean. There is little to stop for other than to take a few snaps, but if you are after a rest stop, **Rossport** is your best bet.

Wawa

The inconsequential iron-mining town of **WAWA**, just north of the park, was named by the natives after the cry of the Canadian geese and was developed as a Mormon camp at the end of the nineteenth century, when gangs of Seventh-Day Adventists were hired to work on the CPR. However, the present population stems from the workers brought here during the Depression, when deposits of low-grade iron ore were developed. There is nothing to keep you here, but as it is less than 10km from Lake Superior Provincial Park's northernmost point, it's a good embarkation point or recovery station.

The **tourist information centre** (mid-May to early Oct daily 9am–7pm), situated on Pinewood Drive just off the highway, is marked by a massive but daft statue of a goose. Long-distance buses stop at the Esso garage, 95 Broadway. Naturally Superior Adventures (☎705/856-2939) rent out canoes ($30), sea kayaks ($35) and a superb fibreglass replica of an eleven-metre Voyageur canoe. They are 5km southeast of Wawa at the mouth of the Michipictoen River, but provide a useful shuttle service. If you're very serious about tackling the wilds of this area, there's the opportunity to go heli-hiking with Wilderness Helicopters, 36 Montréal Ave (☎705/856-1660). Several **motels** in Wawa offer a comfortable bed for the night, including the *Wawa Motor Inn*, 100 Mission Rd (☎705/856-2278 or 1-800-561-2778; ③), and the older *Lakeview Hotel*, 28 Broadway Ave (☎705/856-2625; ①), opposite the lake in town. The *Wawa Motor Inn* is also the best place for **food**, with Lake Superior trout and walleye for dinner, and excellent muffins and home-made soups for snacks. The *Cedar Hof*, just south of Wawa (☎705/856-1136; May–Oct) is the finest place hereabouts to try Lake Supeior trout – dinner for two will set you back around $50.

White River

The next settlement of any size is **WHITE RIVER**, 90km north of Wawa, which has billed itself as the coldest spot in Canada since the winter of 1935, when temperatures dropped to -72°F. Another odd claim to fame is that this was the original home to Winnie the Pooh, a small bear cub named Winnipeg who was exported to London Zoo in 1914. In 1992, White River won the rights from Disney to erect a statue of the tubby honey-lover – and a monstrously hideous fibreglass statue has appeared near the huge thermometer that symbolizes the big freeze. Things get busy here during **Winnie's Hometown Festival** on the third weekend of August, when masses of teddy-bear enthusiasts (of which Canada seems to have a high proportion) get down at various parades and family frolics. White River is linked to Sudbury by **train**; the station is on Winnipeg Road, about four blocks from the Trans-Canada. If you need to stay here, try the *Continental Motel* (☎807/822-2500; ②) and the *White River Motel* (☎807/822-2333; ①–②), both located on the Trans-Canada near the junction with Hwy 631. Just to the west of town, the waste disposal site is a good place to see bears at dusk.

West from Pukaskwa National Park to Terrace Bay

Pukaskwa National Park, 1878 square kilometres of hilly boreal forest and stunning coastline, can only be reached by car via the well-marked Hwy 627, a turnoff from the Trans-Canada 85km west of White River. Campgrounds, parking facilities, a visitor information centre and a park office (early June to Sept daily 8.30am–6.30pm; ☎807/229-0801) are located at Hattie Cove in the northwest corner of the park, from where the **Coastal Hiking Trail** travels 60km south through the boreal forest and over the ridges and cliffs of the Canadian Shield. Open throughout the year, but best visited between early June and September, it is not an easy trail and should only be embarked upon after gaining permission at the park office. In the summer tug boats are available to drop you off at various points so you can then just hike one way back to Hattie Cove. Along the way, campgrounds are 3km apart.

    MARATHON, 7km beyond the junction with Hwy 627, would be a perfect jumping-off point for Pukaskwa National Park if it wasn't for the fact that a newly opened mine has filled every motel with migratory workers. Marathon has long had a reputation for being the Trans-Canada's most inhospitable spot – one believable tale tells of a hitchhiker who was thumbing for so long that he ended up marrying a local girl. Now that rooms are nonexistent, Marathon is best avoided altogether.

    If you're heading to or from Pukaskwa, you may want to stop in **TERRACE BAY**, an hour or so's drive further west, which has everything you need in the way of services and accommodation. It's a planned town, built originally because of the local pulp mill, and is now the service centre for a large area. The name comes from the glacial terraces formed as the lake line receded during the last ice age; the surrounding landscape and eight offshore islands were a source of inspiration for the ubiquitous Group of Seven. The 48-kilometre **Casques Isles Trail** runs east from here along the coast to Schreiber; you can camp anywhere along the way, or hike different sections; there are numerous points where you can join the trail signposted off the highway.

The **tourist information centre** (daily: May & June 9am-5pm; July–Sept 9am–9pm) is right beside the highway and can help with **accommodation**. Two good bets are the *Norwood Motel* (☎807/825-3282; ②) and the modern, more upmarket *Red Dog Inn* (☎807/825-3285; ③), which has a good restaurant specializing in lake fish.

Rossport

ROSSPORT is one of the most picture-perfect and friendly little towns along the Trans-Canada, and makes an ideal stopover for a couple of nights on the monotonous trek west. Originally a Hudson's Bay Company trading post, the settlement's natural island-fringed harbour made it an obvious fishing centre as soon as the railway arrived in 1884. The good years lasted until the 1960s, when a combination of over-fishing and a lamprey attack on the lake trout led to the industry's decline. Nowadays the village is making a concerted effort to attract tourists in search of tranquillity.

The best place to stay is the nineteenth-century *Rossport Inn* on Bowman Street (☎807/824-3213; rooms ③, cabins ②): it has six bedrooms; ten wooden cabins, with double beds, in the garden; a wood-fired sauna; and a well-priced fish-based menu in its restaurant. Alternatively, try *The Willows Bed and Breakfast* (☎807/824-3389; ④), an upmarket outfit opposite the dock in Rossport's old schoolhouse; or for campersthere's Rossport **campground** (☎807/824-2298; $14.50; May–Sept), part of Rainbow Falls Provincial Park, a beautiful site just west of town on the shore of Lake Superior. Superior Outfitters (☎807/824-3314) rent canoes and kayaks on a daily or weekly basis, and give tuition.

Nipigon

NIPIGON, where the northern Hwy 11 meets the Trans-Canada, is a typical northern pulpwood town and fishing centre. Located at the mouth of the Nipigon River, the site was occupied by Ojibwa for hundreds of years until the fur trade ousted the natives and made Nipigon the first white community on the north shore of Lake Superior. Essentially a centre for anglers, Nipigon has **accommodation** at the several resorts and motels, but unless you can't face another inch of tarmac press on to Thunder Bay, just over 100km west.

Directly north of town, the fabulously undeveloped **Lake Nipigon** is, at 4480 square kilometres, the largest lake wholly within Ontario's boundaries. The sixty-kilometre drive from Nipigon to **Lake Nipigon Provincial Park** (June–Aug; $7) is a stunner, bordered by the lake on the left and the sheer cliffs of the Pijitawabik Canyon on the right. The park itself has eighty campsites ($13–14.50; no hook-ups) and black-sand beaches. The only other place to stay on the 1050km of lake shoreline is at *Poplar Lodge Park*, a municipal park with awesome sunsets. It's located 12km along Hwy 580, which runs west from Hwy 11 from the village of Beardmore.

Ouimet Canyon Provincial Park – and the amethyst mines

Some 45km west of Nipigon and 11km north of the Trans-Canada is one of Ontario's most spectacular and curiously ignored sights – the **Ouimet Canyon Provincial Park** (mid-May to mid-Oct daily; free). The canyon was formed during the last ice age, when a sheet of ice 2km thick crept southward, bulldozing a fissure 3km long, 150m wide and 150m deep. Nearly always deserted, the canyon has two lookout points that hang over the terrifyingly sheer sides looking down to the permanently dark base – an anomalous frozen habitat whose perpetual snow supports some very rare arctic plants. The vistas are particularly awe-inspiring in the fall, when the forests become bunches of red, orange and yellow. Unfortunately there is no public transport to the canyon, but Bay-way Tours, 308 Memorial St in Thunder Bay (☎807/345-3678), runs the odd bus tour to Ouimet during the summer.

The mines

The twenty-kilometre stretch of the Trans-Canada beyond Ouimet gives access to several **amethyst mines**, source of Ontario's official mineral, a purple-coloured variety of quartz first discovered in this area in the 1800s. The first is some 40km west of Nipigon, the **Ontario Gem Amethyst Mine** (May–Sept daily 9am–6pm) and 25km further is the busier **Thunder Bay Amethyst Mine Panorama** (daily: July & Aug 10am–7pm; May & June & Sept to mid-Oct 10am–5pm; $1) – you just walk in, pick up a bucket and digging tool, gather as many lumps of rock as you want, and pay for your booty on the way out. Closer to Thunder Bay, the **Thunder Bay Agate Mine** (June–Sept daily 10am–6pm), along Hwy 527 (Spruce River Road/Armstrong Road), is located on one of only two or three vein formations of this semi-precious gemstone – you can mine your own and check out South and North America's largest agate.

The Sleeping Giant Provincial Park

Leaving the Trans-Canada 69km west of Nipigon, Hwy 587 runs the 42-kilometre length of **Sibley Peninsula**, whose entire area is given over to the dramatically scenic **Sleeping Giant Provincial Park**, so named because of the recumbent form of the four mesas that constitute its backbone. Established in 1944 to protect what the logging companies had left of the red and white pines, the park covers 243 square kilometres of high, barren rocks and lowland bogs, crisscrossed with 100km of trails. Acting as a sort of catch net for animals, the peninsula is inhabited by beaver, fox, porcupine, white-tailed deer and moose, though the moose are becoming scarce. There are also wolves in the more remote areas – on a still night you can hear their howls.

Highway 587 enters the park about 6km south of the village of Pass Lake, and driving into the park will set you back $7. The park office (May–Aug Mon–Fri 8am–4.30pm; ☎807/977-2526) is situated at the south end of Lake Marie Louise, about 20km from the park entrance; it's advisable in summer to pay the $6 fee to book a place at the nearby **campgrounds** ($14.75–16.25); if you intend to camp in the park interior, a permit from the office costs $6. The gatehouse beside the office (May–Aug daily 10am–10pm) provides maps and leaflets on the hiking trails. Of the park's hikes, the forty-kilometre **Kaybeyun Trail** is the most spectacular and the hardest. Beginning at the southern end of Hwy 587, it runs around the tip of the peninsula via the rock formation known as the **Sealion** to the **Chimney**, at the Sleeping Giant's knees, then on to **Nanabijou Lookout** at the chest of the Giant, and finally to the Thunder Bay Lookout. You have to be fit – the walk to the Chimney takes about nine hours of hard graft up rugged pathways, where the boulders are the size of cars, and in 1km you go up 244m.

For those who can't take the pace there are two far easier trails – the **Talus** and the **Sawyer** – which leave the Kabeyun at Sawyer Bay on the southwest side of the peninsula. Easier still are the **Joe Creek Trail** and the **Pinewood Hill Trail**, both of which are situated in the northern end of the park near Hwy 587; the latter leads to a fine viewpoint over Joeboy Lake – a favourite spot for moose escaping the flies. The brief **Sibley Creek Trail**, which passes a number of beaver dams, begins near Lake Louise, so you're likely to share the wilderness with a number of other walkers.

At the most southern end of Hwy 587, the unusual sight of **Silver Islet** is worth a visit, particularly in the cooler months when it is less crowded. A century ago this was one of Canada's greatest silver towns, but now all that remains are fifty houses, a customs house, a log jail, a weathered general store with rusted Pepsi signs, and a population of just two. The settlement was begun in 1872 by mining magnate Alexander Sib-

---

TERRY FOX

West of Nipigon, highways 17 and 11 merge to become the **Terry Fox Courage High-way,** named after Terrance Stanley Fox, one of modern Canada's most remarkable figures. At the age of 18 Terry developed cancer and had to have his right leg amputated. Determined to advance the search for a cure, he planned a money-raising run from coast to coast and on April 12, 1980, he set out from St John's in Newfoundland. For 143 days he ran 26 painful miles a day, covering five provinces by June and raising $34 million. In September, at mile 3339, just outside Thunder Bay, Terry was forced by lung cancer to abandon his run; he returned home to Port Coqitlam in British Columbia, where he died the following summer. More than $85 million has now been raised for cancer research in his name.

On the eastern outskirts of Thunder Bay, the end of the Terry Fox Courage Highway is marked by the **Terry Fox Monument,** erected in June 1982 at the Scenic Lookout, and recently relocated to the opposite side of the highway to stand by the new Terry Fox Centre, Thunder Bay's information centre. Great views of the Sleeping Giant and Lake Superior ensure a constant crowd of people with cameras.

---

ley and engineer William Frue, who built a wall to keep Lake Superior's tempestuous waters from a silver deposit by the tiny islet that's visible just offshore. Over the years the town exhausted the local firewood supply and had to rely on coal for fuel. One winter, the coal boat was caught in frozen waters – the last straw for the miners, who had already seen many lives lost when the damp shafts collapsed.

Thunder Bay

The inland port of **THUNDER BAY** is much closer to Winnipeg than to any of the other large urban centres of Ontario, and the population of just over 114,000 refer to themselves as Westerners. Economics as well as geography define this self-image, for this was until recently Canada's largest grain-handling port, and the grain, of course, is harvested in the Prairies. Established as a fur-trading depot, Thunder Bay boomed as the great Canadian lake head, shipping grain and ore through the Great Lakes and down the St Lawrence Seaway to the sea 3200km away. The grain elevators dominate the harbourfront, but with federal legislation favouring Canada's Pacific ports their significance has been drastically cut – eleven years ago they handled sixty percent of Canada's wheat exports and employed 1700 workers, against today's figure of less than four hundred. Thunder Bay is now concentrating its efforts on attracting tourists year-round with the summer attractions of provincial parks and several ski areas for winter visitors.

Thunder Bay is actually the amalgamation of two towns, Fort William and Port Arthur, which were united in January 1970. **Fort William**, established in 1789 by the British, became the upcountry headquarters of the Northwest Company, which was displaced in 1816 by the Hudson's Bay Company, five years before the two companies united. When the beaver hat went out of fashion in the old country, the main industry of the fort declined, but in the mid-nineteenth century a rumour that a huge silver lode lay close to **Port Arthur** drew prospectors to the area. The boom was not to last, and the Port Arthur, Duluth and Western railway (PD&W), built to link the silver mines, was nicknamed "the Poverty, Distress and Welfare" as the effects of the depression set in the silver market. The Canadian Northern Railway, which took over the abandoned PD&W lines, did much to rescue the local economy but did not bring Fort William and Port Arthur closer together. Rudyard Kipling noted that "The twin cities hate each other with the pure, passionate, poisonous hatred that makes cities grow. If Providence wiped out one of them, the other would pine away and die." Even today, residents will immediately inform you which area they live in, and moving from one to the other is viewed as an act of betrayal.

Scarred by industrial complexes and crisscrossed by rail lines, Thunder Bay is not an attractive city, and the five-kilometre waterfront between Fort William and Port Arthur – officially Thunder Bay South and Thunder Bay North – is a wasteland of fast-food chains, motels and garages. But it has a unique atmosphere, since the industry that has carved up the town has attracted workers from all over the world. Over forty ethnic groups have chosen to settle in Thunder Bay, and many of them have retained their language and culture. Thunder Bay is thus the nearest you'll find to a cosmopolitan city in hicksville northern Ontario, and can make a pleasant stopover on the Greyhound trans-Canada journey – it is, after all, a long way to Winnipeg.

Arrival and transport

Thunder Bay Airport is a fifteen-minute drive from town in the western suburbs; local bus #4 departs at least every forty minutes for the Brodie Street **bus terminal** in Fort William. The long-distance **bus** station is at 815 Fort William Rd, and is the terminal for Greyhound buses arriving from Sault Ste Marie, Winnipeg (via Kenora) and Duluth, as well as the Grey Goose services from Winnipeg via Fort Frances. The local bus #1, which connects the Brodie Street terminal with the east end of Port Arthur, runs past this long-distance terminal.

The new **information centre**, the Terry Fox Centre (daily: mid-May to Aug 8.30am–8.30pm; Sept to mid-May 9am–5pm), is on Hwy 11/17, 1km east of town by the Terry Fox Monument. In summer there's also a pagoda with local info on the corner of Red River and Water streets in Port Arthur (May–Sept daily 9am–5pm).

City transport
The public transport service run by **City Transit** has two bus depots useful for getting around this spread-out city: the Northward terminal, serving Port Arthur, is in Water Street by the CN information centre; the Southward terminal, serving Fort William, is at Brodie St South, opposite the Paterson Park information centre. The flat fare is $1.30; ask for a transfer if you need more than one bus to complete your journey, and be warned that services are fairly infrequent and the routes circuitous and slow. Most buses run from 6am to midnight during the week and often don't run at weekends.

Accommodation

Campers with a vehicle are well catered for in Thunder Bay, and budget accommodation is not a problem as, although the HIC-approved **hostel** is a long way out of town, it is reachable via Greyhound buses, and North of Superior B&B Association has places in and around town. Other than those alternatives there's a profusion of characterless but well-priced motels. If you are **camping**, there are several campgrounds, but most are situated some distance from Thunder Bay proper without any public transport links.

Hotels and Bed and Breakfasts
Airplane Hotel, 698 West Arthur St and Expressway (☎577-1181 or 1-800-465-5003, fax 475-4852). Within easy reach of Old Fort William, this new hotel has all mod cons and three restaurants. ⑤.

Archibald Arbor, 222 South Archibald St (☎622-3386, fax 622-4471). Downtown, cheap bed and breakfast. ①–②.

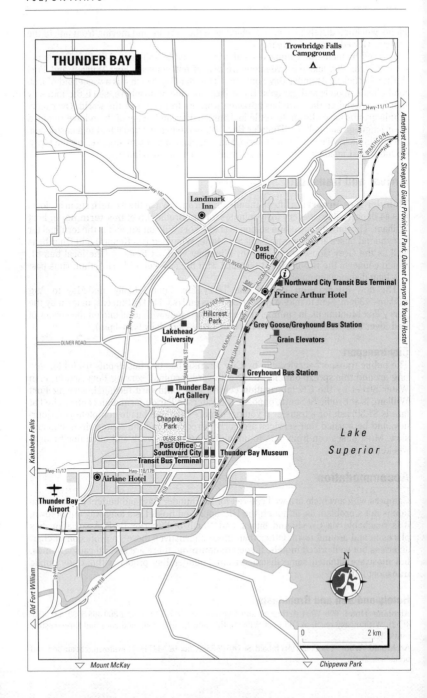

THUNDER BAY

Trowbridge Falls
Campground

Hwy-11/17

Hwy-11B/17B

STRATHCONA

Amethyst mines, Sleeping Giant Provincial Park, Ouimet Canyon & Youth Hostel

Hwy-102

Landmark
Inn

COURT ST

WATER ST

Post
Office

RED RIVER RD

BAY ST

ALGOMA ST

Northward City Transit Bus Terminal

Prince Arthur Hotel

OLIVER RD

Hillcrest
Park

Hwy-11/17

Lakehead
University

MEMORIAL ST

FORT WILLIAM RD

Grey Goose/Greyhound Bus Station

Grain Elevators

OLIVER ROAD

BALMORAL ST

Greyhound Bus Station

Thunder Bay
Art Gallery

MAY ST

Chapples
Park

BRODIE ST

DEASE ST

*Lake
Superior*

Post Office

Southward City
Transit Bus Terminal

Thunder Bay Museum

Hwy-11/17

Hwy-11B/17B

Airlane Hotel

Thunder Bay
Airport

Kakabeka Falls

Old Fort William

Hwy-61B

N

0   2 km

▽ *Mount McKay*

▽ *Chippewa Park*

Landmark Inn, 1010 Dawson Rd (☎767-1681 or 1-800-465-3950, fax 767-1439). Thunder Bay's top hotel, with four stars. ②.

Prince Arthur Hotel, 17 Cumberland St North (☎345-5411 or 1-800-267-2675, fax 345-8565). Large, centrally located hotel with all mod cons and a swimming pool. ③.

Sleeping Giant Cambrian Place, 532 Cambrian Crescent (☎475-3105). Great garden and Danish pancakes for breakfast. Lunch and dinner on request. ②.

Valhalla Inn, 1 Valhalla Inn Rd (☎577-1121 or 1-800-964-1121, fax 475-4728). The largest hotel in town, with 275 well-equipped rooms. ⑤, weekend rates ③.

Venture Inn, 450 Memorial St (☎345-2343 or 1-800-387-3953, fax 345-3246). Over ninety Canadian-style rooms with air conditioning and an indoor pool; rates include breakfast. ③.

Motels

Old Country Motel, 500 Cumberland St North (☎344-2511 or 1-800-454-7638). One of the cheapest motels in town. ②.

Ritz Motel, 2600 Arthur St East (☎623-8189). Three-star accommodation with reasonable rates. ②.

Strathcona Motel, 573 Hodder Ave (☎683-8136). A six-bedroomed motel near the lakefront. ②.

Hostel and student accommodation

Lakehead University, 953 Oliver Rd (☎343-8612). Dorm beds or single rooms available in summer. Buses #2 and #16 and the faster cross-town bus run here from Water Street terminal. ①.

Thunder Bay Backpackers International Hostel (Longhouse Village), 1594 Lakeshore Drive (☎983-2042, fax 983-2914). Run by a knowledgeable husband-and-wife team, who were once missionaries in Borneo, the hostel is the first home of many immigrants and has a friendly commune-like atmosphere, a beautiful setting and no curfew. However, it's 20km northeast of Thunder Bay and not served by city buses. The eastbound Greyhound bus will drop you off at the end of Mackenzie Station Road on Hwy 11/17, which is a 20min walk from the hostel – it's worth it, this is without doubt the best place to stay. Camping is available outside the hostel for a small fee. ①.

Campgrounds

Chippewa Park, City Road (☎623-3912). On junction of Hwy 61 and Hwy 61B, 8km south of Thunder Bay. From $11; also has eighteen log cabins for up to six people, from $24 per cabin.

KOA Thunder Bay, Hwy 11/17 at Spruce River Road turnoff (☎683-6221). The largest campground, 2.5km east of the Terry Fox Lookout on the Trans-Canada. There is also a restaurant and grocery store. From $12.75. Mid-May to mid-Oct.

Trowbridge Falls Campground, Copenhagen Road (.☎683-6661). Near the junction of Hwy 11/17 and Hodder Avenue, and within walking distance of Centennial Park. From $11. Mid-May to mid-Sept.

Fort William

The tourist industry is concentrating its attentions on **Fort William**, the more depressed area of the city, but frankly most of its "sights" might well make *you* a depressed area. The **Thunder Bay Museum**, 425 Donald St East (mid-June to Aug daily 11am–5pm; Sept to mid-June Tues–Sun 1–5pm; $2, free on Sat), in the stately-looking old courthouse and police station, has the usual collection of local antiquities and mock-ups of Victorian businesses, but the Indian beadwork is worth a look, as are the displays about local oddities White Otter Castle and Silver Islet. Two blocks north, the **Amethyst Gift Centre**, 400 East Victoria Ave (Mon–Fri 8.30am–6pm; free), has tours showing the production of various tacky souvenirs and some gorgeous amethysts.

> The telephone code for Thunder Bay is ☎807.

Further north across Chapples Park, on Confederation College campus off Balmoral, is the **Thunder Bay Art Gallery** (Tues–Thurs noon–8pm, Fri–Sun noon–5pm; donation), whose collection includes works by local-born Norval Morisseau, one of Canada's most famous native artists, who came to public attention in the 1960s. Known as the originator of the Cree-Ojibwa art style usually referred to as "Woodlands art", he initially came into conflict with his elders by using Ojibwa legends as his subject matter – in Ojibwa tradition it is taboo for anyone other than a shaman to depict legendary figures. The Woodlands art movement is now one of the main vehicles of native identity amongst the Cree and Ojibwa. The gallery also has a knack of getting native art exhibits on loan from major national and international museums and galleries.

Mount McKay, southwest of the Kaministikwia River on City Road, is the tallest mountain in the Northwestern chain, rising 488m above sea level and 305m above the city. This massive mesa is the reservation of the Mission Indians,who charge a fee of $5 for car parking; it is possible to see the whole of Thunder Bay from the top, but you'll get more scenic views free of charge from Hillcrest Park in Port Arthur (see below).

Old Fort William

Thunder Bay's *tour de force* is the reconstructed fur-trading post of **Old Fort William** (mid-May to mid-Oct daily 10am–5pm; $10), about 15km west of Fort William centre and 13km upriver from its original site. Inside the fort is a new **visitors' centre**; a film is shown here that provides an introduction to the fort as it looked in 1815, when it was the inland headquarters of the North West Company and their major shipment base. The 42 impeccably researched buildings and Ojibwa camp are staffed by students dressed as merchants, workers, servants and natives. Look out for the fur warehouse, festooned with the pelts of beaver, lynx and arctic fox, and the canoe workshop, where exquisite birch-bark canoes are made to traditional designs for museums all over Canada. There are demonstrations of contemporary trades and crafts, as well as a working kitchen, kitchen garden and a farm complete with sheep, pigs and cows.

Old Fort William is particularly enjoyable in July, when there is a ten-day re-enactment of the **Great Rendezvous**, an annual gathering of the North West Company employees, attended nowadays by enthusiastic fur-trade re-enactors from all over Canada and the US. If you miss this, there's a smaller shindig in August, the **Ojibwa Keeshigun**, which celebrates the native contribution to the fur trade. To get to the fort, local bus #10 goes from Fort William every hour.

Port Arthur

Thunder Bay North, still obdurately called **Port Arthur**, is the more upbeat side of town, and its most attractive enclave is the Finnish district of **Little Suomi**, stretching from Oliver Road to Pearl Street and from Hillcrest Park to the waterfront. Arriving in Thunder Bay in 1872, the Finns created the world's largest Finnish community outside their homeland, and as you wander the streets you will still hear more Finnish spoken than English – even the signs are bilingual. The most pleasant area is the intersection of Bay and Algoma, which is dotted with good restaurants and older buildings.

Port Arthur has some good city parks. On the High Street **Hillcrest Park** has panoramic views of the harbour and the Sleeping Giant. **Waverley Park**, on the corner of Waverley and Red River Road, holds free open-air concerts in the summer – from Sinatra-type crooners to rap artists from Toronto. Finally, along the shores of Current River 9km out of town, the more natural-looking **Centennial Park** features a 1910 bush camp (mid-June to Aug daily 10am–8pm), a small logging-history museum and a farm for the city kids, with rabbits, sheep and pigs.

Eating, drinking and nightlife

The best place to **eat** is in Little Suomi, at the junction of Bay and Algoma, where you can sample tasty Finnish food in healthy portions. The majority of the area's eateries close early, and for late eating there's little on offer except the standard burgers and pizzas. **Nightlife** is restricted to a few decent bars and nightclubs – most bars serve finger foods and have a dance floor and the occasional live band, usually churning out the rehashed Top 40 numbers.

Snacks and restaurants

Boston Pizza, 217 Arthur St and 505 Memorial Ave. Average pizzas, ribs and pasta with the advantage of being open until 3am on Fri and Sat.

Calabria Restaurant, 287 Bay St (☎344-9376). Southern Italian food including spaghetti with dandelion roots and anchovies for $6.95. Advisable to book at the weekends.

Hoito Restaurant, 314 Bay St. Established in 1918, Thunder Bay's best-known Finnish restaurant is always full and the specials on the board should not be missed. Open daily until 8pm.

Kangas Sauna, 379 Oliver Rd. Previously a small counter service for the sauna users, now a larger restaurant with delicious home-made soups, omelettes and sweet berry pies. Closed Sun & Mon.

Scandinavian Homemade, 147 Algoma South. A friendly, cosy café with full breakfasts for $5 and delicious Finnish pancakes. Open Mon–Sat 7am–4pm.

Thunder Bay Restaurant, 188 Bay St. Billed as "the working man's place to eat", this greasy spoon has generous helpings and a fine collection of the baseball caps that are the uniform of this area. Non-stop coffee and full breakfast for $2.99. Open daily until 7pm.

Bars, clubs and live music

Coyotes, 920 Tungsten St. Very popular country bar.

Brasserie, 901 Red River Rd. Trendy American-type pub with pricey beer; packed at weekends.

Casey's, *Venture Inn*, 450 Memorial Ave. Small dance bar, popular with thirty-something singles.

Inntowner, corner of Arthur and Brodie streets. Leather jackets and hard rock; entry fee for live bands.

The Office, 215 Red River Rd. Features live blues bands.

Stages, 37 Cumberland St South. Live bands, two levels, pool tables, lots of drinking – this place heaves on a Saturday night.

The Wayland, 1019 Gore St West. Free pizza for groups of six or more at this popular bar.

The Westfort, 1408 Brown St. An old fire station converted into a bar.

Listings

Airlines Air Canada, airport (☎623-3313); Canadian Air, airport (☎577-6461).

Bus information Local: City Transit (☎344-9666). Long-distance: Greyhound (☎345-2194); Grey Goose (☎345-8231).

Camping equipment Wildwaters Wilderness Shop & Expeditions, 119 Cumberland St North (☎345-0111); Gear Up For Outdoors, 894 Alloy Place (☎345-0001).

Car rental Avis, 330 Memorial Ave (☎345-9929) and 1475 Walsh St West (☎577-5766); Budget, 899 Copper Crescent (☎345-2425); Thrifty, 899 Tungsten St (☎345-7111); Tilden, 556 Arthur St West (☎577-5783).

Hospital Port Arthur General, 460 Court St North (☎343-6621).

Laundry Algoma Home Style Laundry, 213 Algoma St South (daily 8am–11pm); Honey's Washeteria, 230 Leland South (Mon–Sat 8.30am–10pm, Sun 10am–10pm).

Pharmacy Medical Centre Pharmacy, 63 Algoma St.

Post office 321 Archibald St North and 33 Court St South.

Ski information Ski Thunder Bay, 520 Leith Ave (☎1-800-667-8386).

Taxis Diamond-Amber (☎622-6001).

Weather For up-to-date bulletins, call ☎345-9111.

West of Thunder Bay

Heading west from Thunder Bay, the nearest attraction that might make you stop is **Kakabeka Falls Provincial Park**, a pleasant spot if not quite the most enthralling aquatic spectacle in the country. Some 39km further, the Trans-Canada splits into Hwy 11 and Hwy 17 – the latter the more frequented and faster route to Winnipeg via the attractive lakeshore-based **Kenora**; the former running past the border crossing at Fort Frances, where the relatively secluded Hwy 71 turns north to rejoin Hwy 17 via the east shore of the beautiful and vast **Lake of the Woods**. All three highways are served by regular long-distance buses. Remember that time goes back one hour 20km or so west of where the highway splits.

Kakabeka Falls Provincial Park

Thirty kilometres west of Thunder Bay, close to Hwy 11/17, the Kaministikwia River plunges nearly 40m into a gorge, creating the **Kakabeka Falls** (mid-May to mid-Oct; $5–7), taking its name from the Ojibwa word for "thundering waters". Local legend has it that Greenmantle, the daughter of an Ojibwa chief, promised to guide the fearsome Sioux to the Ojibwa camp in return for her own life, and then steered the Sioux to their deaths in the cataract. It is said she sometimes appears in the mist of the falls, but these days she doesn't have too many opportunities, as a hydroelectric dam now controls the flow to such an extent that locals jokingly refer to the "Only on a Sunday Falls". In summer there's usually just a yellow trickle here, but during the spring and fall the river flows at full force if the dam allows it – which is usually at the weekends. Now with provincial park status, the area has been adapted for family outings with picnic tables, viewing posts and a spanking new information centre. Camping is available from mid-May to mid-Oct (☎807/473-9231; $9.75–16.25).

Quetico Provincial Park – and on to Kenora

Quetico Provincial Park, 161km west of Thunder Bay on Hwy 11, is a wild but well-organized park located between the highway and the border with Minnesota. A perfect destination for canoeists, it presents a landscape typical of the region, with its rocky cliffs and forests of black spruce and jack pine laced with countless waterways. As well as an impressive array of animal and bird life – including wolves, black bears, lynx, bald eagles and ospreys – the park has the additional attraction of the thirty or so cliff faces decorated with miniature pictographs whose origins and age still remain uncertain.

The service town for the park is **Atikokan**, 48km west of the park gate, which is the nearest you can get to the park by bus. If you need to stay here, your best bet is the *Radisson Motel*, located on the main street into town at 310 Mackenzie Ave (☎807/597-2766; ③). There are several outfitters in Atikokan, but none is as convenient as the Quetico Trading Post (☎807/929-2177), 5km west of the park entrance, which rents out canoes for $35 a day – it is best to reserve in advance. For total outfitting, transportation and even park permits, contact Quetico Discovery Tours, 18 Birch Rd (☎807/597-2621) with four-day trips from $250. Right by the entrance the **Quetico Information Pavilion** provides maps of the park's extensive canoe routes and details of the pictograph sites, which are visible only from the water; camping ($9.75–14.50) and vehicle permits ($5–10) are also issued here. **Campgrounds** can be reserved by phone from mid-May to the end of August, for a $6 fee (Mon–Fri 8am–4.30pm; ☎807/597-2735 or 597-2737).

Lake of the Woods

Some 400km west of Thunder Bay, segmented by the provincial and international borders, lies the **LAKE OF THE WOODS**, whose 14,000 islands gave rise to the Ojibwa name "Min-es-tic" (Lake of the Islands) – which the French settlers misinterpreted as "Mis-tic", the native word for "woods". Today's Ojibwa live on scruffy reserves, some located on the lake's remoter islands. Fierce prejudice, which seems to stem from the fact that their native status allows them to catch as many fish as they like, prevents their employment in the region's main town of Kenora. Their situation has worsened since 1974, when the Ojibwa, sick of the slow pace of land-claims negotiations, staged an armed but bloodless protest that prompted a local backlash whose effects can still be felt.

For the visitor, this is principally an area for boating and fishing, but even for landlubbers the lake is impressive, its myriad islands a refreshing change from the usual unbroken expanses of water. The echoing sound of the loons is all that breaks the stillness of the area, while fantastic sunsets change the water into a kaleidoscope of colour.

Kenora

The Lake of the Woods' reputation as an angler's paradise is indicated by "Husky the Muskie", a twelve-metre statue of a fish at **KENORA**, a town that used to be known as Rat Portage until a flour company refused to build a mill here, arguing that the word "rat" on sacks of their product would not do much for sales. Nowadays the permanent population of 9000 quadruples in the summer, when droves of Americans hit the lake – a fortunate boost to the town's economy since the main employer, the newsprint-paper mill, is threatened with closure as the continent switches to recycled paper. Renting a boat costs over $1000 for a week, so unless you are loaded you will probably be land-based, but it's an enjoyable spot – especially in summer when there's a really laid-back feel to this beautifully located town. The murals that decorate the place are added to each summer by young artists, who you may see working. They reflect aspects of the town and its history – sports, fur trade, mining, the railroad, and so on.

The impressive **Lake of the Woods Museum**, 300 Main St (July & Aug daily 10am–5pm; Sept–June Tues–Sat 10am–5pm; $2), relates the history of the area with a fine selection of native ceremonial pipes and clothing, including a sacred jingle dress that is thought to have healing properties – its design came as a vision to a chief whose sick daughter was cured when she wore it.

At the foot of Main Street the MS *Kenora* **cruises** the Lake of the Woods' islands and channels for two hours (mid-May to mid-Sept Mon–Sat, 4 daily, Sun, 1 daily; $13), offering an opportunity to see **Devil Gap's Rock** at the entrance to Kenora harbour. In 1884 the rock's resemblance to a human face was emphasized with paint and it has been repainted ever since, but this is not a gimmicky attraction – it's an Ojibwa spirit rock, to which food and tobacco sacrifices were made in order to propitiate the supernatural giant known as Windigo – the personification of winter. His powers could only be controlled by powerful shamen, and when hunters disappeared in the bush they were thought to have been eaten by Windigo. When winter food shortages drove starving Ojibwas to develop a craving for human flesh they would request execution rather than be taken over by Windigo. Passing vacationers still throw the odd cigarette at the rock.

Kenora's **bus terminus** is across the bay in neighbouring **Keewatin**, from where local buses run to Kenora itself. The Lake of the Woods **Tourism Centre** is located on Hwy 17 east of town (mid-May to June daily 9am–5pm; July & Aug daily 9am–8pm; Sept to mid-May Mon–Fri 9am–5pm).

First choice for **accommodation** is the *Kenricia Hotel*, 155 Main St (☎807/468-6461; ③), which has been around as long as Kenora. It's now rivalled by the eight-storey *Best Western Lakeside Inn & Convention Centre*, 470 1st Ave South (☎807/468-5521 or 1-800-465-1120; ⑤), with great views. There's the usual string of **motels** stretching along the highway just outside town, all of which require reservations in the summer: *Lake-Vu Motel*, 740 Lakeview Drive (☎807/468-5501; ②), is a moderately priced three-star place. For **food**, the renowned steaks in the *Kenrilia Hotel* dining room cost $11.95, while the *Plaza Restaurant*, 135 Main St, is a friendly Greek place that serves sandwiches as well as full meals.

travel details

Trains

Cochrane to: Moosonee (5 weekly in summer, 3 weekly in winter; 5hr 15min).

Kingston to: Belleville/Cobourg/Port Hope/Toronto (1 daily; 40min/1hr 10min/1hr 20min/2hr 20min).

Ottawa to: Brockville/Kingston/Cobourg/Toronto (1–2 daily; 1hr 10min/1hr 45min/3hr/4hr 12min); Brockville/Gananoque/Kingston/Port Hope/Toronto (1 daily; 1hr 10min/1hr 35min/1hr 45min/3hr 10min/4hr 15min); Brockville/Kingston/Belleville/Toronto (1 daily; 1hr 15min/1hr 40min/2hr 30min/4hr 7min); Dorval/Montréal (2–4 daily; 2hr/2hr 20min).

Sault Ste Marie to: Hearst (3–4 weekly; 9hr).

Sudbury to: White River (3 weekly; 8hr 20min).

Toronto to: Buffalo, NY (1 daily; 4hr); Chicago, IL (1 daily; 11hr); Cobalt (6 weekly; 7hr); Cochrane (6 weekly; 10hr); Gravenhurst (6 weekly; 2hr); Hearst (6 weekly; 13hr 45min); Huntsville (6 weekly; 2hr 45min); Kapuskasing (6 weekly; 12hr 25min); Kingston (7 daily; 2hr); Kitchener (2 daily; 1hr 45min); London (7 daily; 3hr); Montréal (4–6 daily; 4hr 45min; express daily except Sat; 4hr); New York, NY (1 daily; 12hr); Niagara Falls (2 daily; 2hr); North Bay (6 weekly; 4hr 40min); Ottawa (3–4 daily; 4hr); Parry Sound (3 weekly; 4hr 15min); Sarnia (2 daily; 4hr 15min); Stratford (2 daily; 2hr 10min); Sudbury Junction (3 weekly; 7hr 15min); Temagami (6 weekly; 6hr 20min); Windsor (4 daily; 4hr); Winnipeg (3 weekly; 29hr 45min).

Buses

Kenora to Fort Frances (1 daily; 3hr); Winnipeg (5 daily; 2hr 30min).

Kingston to: Belleville/Trenton/Cobourg/Port Hope/Peterborough (3 daily; 45min/1hr 15min/2hr/2hr 15min/2hr 50min); Cornwall/Montréal (2 daily; 1hr 50min/3hr 25min); Ottawa (4 daily; 2hr 45min).

London to: Hamilton (2 daily; 2hr); Kitchener (2 daily; 2hr); Niagara Falls (2 daily; 3hr 45min); Owen Sound (1 daily; 3hr 45min); Stratford (2 daily; 1hr); Windsor (1 daily; 3hr).

North Bay to: Kirkland Lake/Cochrane/Kapuskasing/Hearst (3 daily; 4hr/7hr/8hr 30min/9hr 30min); Sudbury (3 daily; 2hr); Temagami/Cobalt/New Liskeard/Kirkland Lake/Timmins/Cochrane/Kapuskasing/Hearst (2 daily; 1hr 10min/1hr 50min/2hr 15min/3hr 15min/5hr 20min/6hr 15min/8hr 20min/9hr 30min); Temagami/Cobalt/Haileybury/New Liskeard/Kirkland Lake/Timmins (2 daily; 1hr 10min/1hr 50min/2hr/2hr 15min/3hr 50min/6hr).

Ottawa to: Brockville (1 daily; 2hr 10min); Cornwall (1 daily; 1hr 20min); Kingston (4 daily; 2hr 45min); Montréal (11 daily; 2hr 20min); North Bay (3 daily; 2hr 30min); North Bay/Sudbury (3 daily; 4hr 50min/6hr 45min); Toronto (6 daily; 5hr 30min); Upper Canada Village/Cornwall (summer only 1 daily; 1hr 30min/2hr).

Sault Ste Marie to: Pancake Bay/Wawa/White River/Marathon/Terrace Bay/Schreiber/Nipigon/Thunder Bay/Kenora/Winnipeg (1–3 daily; 1hr/3hr/4hr/5hr 30min/7hr/7hr 30min/8hr 30min/10hr/16hr/19hr); Toronto (3 daily; 10hr 50min); White River/Marathon/Nipigon/Thunder Bay/Winnipeg (1 daily; 4hr/5hr/7hr 40min/9hr/18hr 30min).

Sudbury to: North Bay/Pembroke/Ottawa/Montréal (3 daily; 2hr/5hr/7hr 30min/11hr); Sault Ste Marie (4 daily; 4–5hr); Timmins (1 daily; 4hr 10min); Toronto (4 daily; 5hr 30min).

Thunder Bay to: Atitokan/Fort Frances (1 daily; 1hr 50min/3hr 30min); Dryden/Kenora/Winnipeg (3 daily; 3hr 30min/5hr/8hr); Hearst (3 daily; 6hr 30min).

Timmins to: Cochrane (6 daily; 1hr–1hr 50min); Cochrane/Kapuskasing/Hearst (2 daily; 1hr 10min/3hr 20min/4hr 30min).

Toronto to: Cobourg (3 daily; 2hr 30min); Collingwood (4 daily; 2hr 50min); Cornwall (7 daily; 5hr 15min); Espanola (4 daily; 6hr); Gravenhurst (4 daily; 3hr); Hamilton (every 15min–hourly; 1hr); Hunstsville (3 daily; 4hr); Kingston (7 daily; 3hr); Kitchener (8 daily; 1hr 45min); London (8 daily; 2hr 20min–3hr); Midland (3 daily; 2hr 35min); Montréal (10 daily; 7hr); New York, NY (express 7 daily; 12hr); Niagara Falls (hourly; 1hr 30min–2hr); Nipigon (4 daily; 18hr 15min); North Bay (1 daily; 4hr 45min); Ottawa (10 daily; 5hr–8hr); Owen Sound (3 daily; 3hr 15min); Parry Sound (6 daily; 2hr–4hr 15min); Penetanguishene (3 daily; 2hr 45min); Peterborough (4 daily; 2hr 40min); Port Hope (3 daily; 2hr 10min); Sault Ste Marie (4 daily; 10hr 50min); Sudbury (4 daily; 5hr); Thunder Bay (4 daily; 21hr 30min); Trenton (3 daily; 3hr 25min); Wawa (4 daily; 13hr 50min); Wasaga Beach (2–3 daily; 2hr 15min); White River (4 daily; 17hr); Windsor (8 daily; 4hr 30min); Winnipeg (3 daily; 30hr 30min).

Planes

Ottawa to: Calgary/Banff (5–9 daily; 3hr 40min); Halifax/Dartmouth (3–6 daily; 2hr); Montréal (7–16 daily; 30min); Québec City (6–18 daily; 1hr); Vancouver (8 daily; 5hr 20min); Winnipeg (6–7 daily; 2hr 20min).

Toronto to: Calgary (5–7 daily; 4hr 15min); Edmonton (5–7 daily; 1hr 40min); Fredericton (5–6 daily; 1hr 45min); Halifax (7–9 daily; 2hr); Moncton (5 daily; 2hr); Montréal (15–26 daily; 1hr 15min); Ottawa (11–22 daily; 1hr); Québec City (8–19 daily; 1hr 45min); Saint John (4–5 daily; 1hr 45min); Saskatoon (2–3 daily; 3hr 30min); St John's (6–7 daily; 3hr); Thunder Bay (2–5 daily; 1hr 30min); Vancouver (6–7 daily; 5hr); Winnipeg (5 daily; 2hr 45min).

CHAPTER TWO

QUÉBEC

As the only French-speaking enclave in North America, **Québec** is totally distinct from the rest of the continent – so distinct, in fact, that it seems to be moving inexorably towards independence. The genesis of this potential political separation of Québec from its English-speaking neighbours tracks back to France's ceding of the colony to Britain in 1760. At first this transfer saw little change in the life of most Québécois. Permitted to retain their language and religion, they stayed under the control of the Catholic Church, whose domination of rural society – evident in the huge churches of Québec's tiny villages – resulted in an economically and educationally deprived subclass, but a subclass whose huge families preserved the demographic domination of the province by French-speakers – the so-called *revanche du berceau (revenge of the cradle)*.

The creation of Lower and Upper Canada in 1791 served to emphasize the inequalities between anglophones and francophones, with the French-speaking majority in Lower Canada ruled by the so-called **Château Clique**, an assembly of francophone priests and seigneurs who had to answer to a British governor and council appointed in London. Rebellions by French *Patriotes* in 1837 against this hierarchy led to an investigation by Lord Durham, who concluded that French-Canadians had "peculiar language and manners" and should be immersed in the English culture of North America. The establishment of the Province of Canada in 1840 was thus a deliberate attempt to marginalize francophone opinion within an English-speaking state.

French-Canadians remained insulated from the economic mainstream until twentieth-century **industrialization**, financed and run by the better-educated anglophones, led to a mass francophone migration to the cities. Here, a French-speaking middle class soon began to articulate the grievances of the workforce and to criticize the suffocating effect the Church was having on francophone opportunity. The shake-up of Québec society came with the so-called **Quiet Revolution** of the 1960s, when the provincial government, led by the newly elected Liberals, took over the control of welfare, health and education from the Church, as well as instigating the creation of state-owned industries to reverse the financial domination of the anglophones.

In order to implement such legislation, Québec needed a disproportionate share of the nation's taxes, and the Liberals, despite being staunchly federalist, were constantly at loggerheads with Ottawa. Encouraged and influenced by other nationalist struggles, the Québécois's desire for cultural recognition and political power intensified, reaching a violent peak in 1970 with the terrorist actions of the largely unpopular **Front de Libération du Québec** (FLQ) in Montréal. Six years later a massive reaction against the ruling Liberals brought the separatist **Parti Québécois** (PQ) to power in Montréal. Led by René Lévesque, the Parti Québécois accelerated the process of social change with the *Charte de la langue française*, better known as **Bill 101**, which established French as the official language of the province. With French now dominant in the workplace and the classroom, the Québécois thought they had got as close as possible to cultural and social independence. Still reeling from the terrorist activities of the FLQ and scared that Lévesque's ultimate objective of separatism would leave Québec economically adrift, the 6.5-million population voted 60:40 against sovereignty in a 1980 referendum. And, in 1985, the Liberals were returned to provincial power.

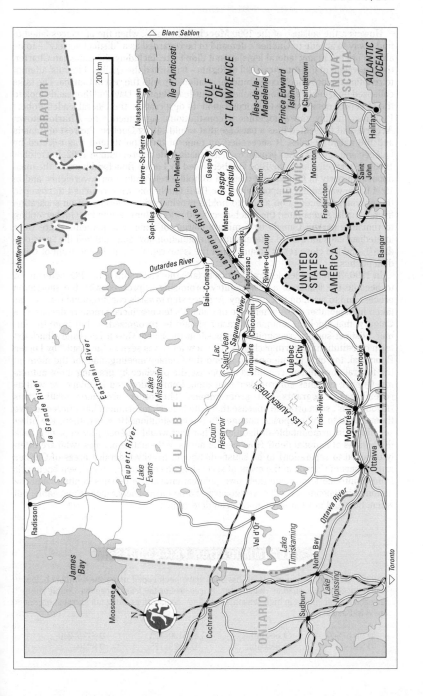

However, the collapse of the 1990 **Meech Lake** talks, when the provinces failed to find a way to accede to Québec's demand to be regarded as a "distinct society" – to be able to opt out of any federal legislation it didn't like, including the Canadian Charter, the equivalent of the American Bill of Rights – frustrated the Québec Liberals' attempt to redefine the province's constitutional relationship with the rest of Canada. The talks collapsed on Québec's national holiday, Saint-Jean-Baptiste Day, and thousands took to the streets to demonstrate their frustration. In desperation, the Liberal leader, Robert Bourassa, hastily threw together a constitutional agreement, the **Charlottetown Accord**, and presented it as a package that would satisfy Québec, the rest of Canada and the native peoples. It succeeded on none of these points and was rejected by Québec and several other provinces in a Canada-wide referendum in 1992. In October 1993's federal elections, the Bloc Québécois led by Lucien Bouchard became the main opposition party in Ottawa and pledged to hold a referendum on sovereignty, and in 1994 there was added support when the Parti Québécois were returned to power in the provincial elections on a vow to hold a province-wide referendum on separation from Canada. A year later, the much-discussed referendum resulted in Québec opting to remain a part of Canada by a minute margin of under one percent. There were immediate calls for a third referendum (the situation now aptly dubbed the "neveren-dum"), and the close result ensured that the issue remained at the forefront of Canadian politics.

In 1996, Bouchard left federal politics to take the leadership of the PQ, determined to become the leader of a new country, promising to proceed with the separation process and to work on the economy. Another step towards constitutional reform was taken in September 1997, when nine of Canada's ten provincial premiers declared, in Calgary, that Québec's unique character should be recognized, a shift from the former "distinct society" recognition proposal in the failed Meech Lake and Charlottetown constitutional reform packages. The new term was seen as "an insult" by Lucien Bouchard, the only premier not to attend the Calgary meeting, and for the moment the federal government continues to appease the province by granting more autonomy. Québec now has control over education, immigration and language, as well as receiving extra grants and programmes. The other provinces dislike this "favouritism", so in order to appease them the federal government has offered to give them a veto to any proposed changes to the constitution. However, there are other seemingly insurmountable difficulties. What part would Québec play in paying back the billions of national debt? How are the needs of the native peoples (who are utterly opposed to separation) to be satisfied? Should heavily federalist areas of Québec remain part of Canada in the event of secession? Recently, there have even been calls from Montréalers to create their own political entity. The debates continue and the notion of independence will never go away. Some form of separation is inevitable, but when, how and in what form no one can determine.

ACCOMMODATION PRICE CODES

All the accommodation prices in this book have been coded using the symbols below, corresponding to Canadian dollar rates. Prices are for the least expensive double room in each establishment in high season, excluding special offers. For a full explanation, see p.38 in Basics.

① up to $40   ③ $60–80   ⑤ $100–125   ⑦ $175–240
② $40–60   ④ $80–100   ⑥ $125–175   ⑧ $240+

NATIVE CANADIANS

Francophone–anglophone relations may be the principal concern of most Québécois – eighty percent of them have French as their mother tongue – but the province's population also includes ten nations of Native Canadians, the majority of whom live on reservations "granted" them by the early French settlers. Resentment and racism are as rife here as elsewhere in Canada – as shown by the fact that it was only a decade ago that the name above a portal of the National Assembly in Québec City was changed from "Les Portes de Sauvage" to "Les Portes de la Famille Amerindienne". Native grievances are particularly acute in Québec because most of the province's tribes are English-oriented, and until recently most learned English if they spoke any language other than their native tongue – the Mohawks near Montréal even fought on the side of the British during the conquest. Relations are bad between the authorities and French-speaking groups as well. The Hurons (see pp.264–265) near Québec City battled for eight years, all the way to the Supreme Court of Canada, to retain their hunting rights, while around James Bay the Crees are still fighting to block the expansion of Québec's hydroelectric network, which if completed would cover an area the size of Germany. Begun in 1971, the project is only one-third finished but has already resulted in the displacement of Crees and Inuits, due to flooded lands as well as the pollution of rivers that have not been safely channelled. Native peoples have categorically voted against separation and have used peaceful methods to register their land claims, which amount to 85 percent of the province's area, but there has been violence (at the Mohawk uprising at Oka near Montréal in 1990 (see p.235)), which, though condemned by most Canadians and natives at the time, drew attention to the concerns of Native Canadians. This has led to a nationwide government examination of the issues at stake – The Royal Commission on Aboriginal Peoples, which has become the largest and, at $60 million, the most expensive commission, in Canadian history. In November 1996, the Commission recommended a revamping of the native welfare system, greater self-government and a settlement of land-claims negotiations. All of this needs a vast amount of government spending, which in the present climate is unlikely to be forthcoming.

The cities and landscapes

Should Québec secede, Canada will lose its largest province – accounting for a sixth of the country's territory; its 1.5 million square kilometres are capable of enclosing Portugal, Spain, Germany, France, Belgium and Switzerland. Of this vast expanse, sixty percent is forest land peppered with more than a million lakes and waterways and, though some mining towns dot the interior, the majority of the population is concentrated in the rich **arable lands** along the southern stretches of the mighty St Lawrence.

The Gallic ancestry of most Québécois is clear in their attitude to hedonistic pleasures – they eat and drink in a style that combines the simplicity of the first settlers with the rich tastes of the French. Nowhere is this more evident than in the island metropolis of **Montréal**, premier port of the province and home to a third of all Québécois. Montréal's skyscrapers and nightlife bear witness to the economic resurgence of French-speaking Canada, whereas in **Québec City** the attraction lies more in the ancient streets and architecture. Beyond these centres, the **Gaspé Peninsula**, poking into the eastern side of the Gulf of the St Lawrence, is the most appealing area with its inspiring mountain scenery and rocky coastline, some of which is protected as parkland, providing sanctuary for a variety of wildlife, from moose to herons. Here, a score of once-remote fishing villages have become mini-resorts, the most attractive of which is **Percé**.

The toll-free information number is ☎01-800-363-7777.

Along the opposite shore of the St Lawrence, the agricultural – and intermittently industrial – settlements that dot the landscape north of Montréal thin out past Québec City, giving way to the bleak desolation of a coastal road that stretches as far as **Havre-St-Pierre**. On the way, you'll pass through the delightful resort of **Baie-Saint-Paul** and through **Tadoussac**, which offers magnificent opportunities to go **whale-watching**, while nearby the contrasting landscapes of Saguenay fjord and the northerly **Mingan Archipelago** are among Québec's most dramatic sights. Beyond the regions covered in this guide, Québec's inhospitable and largely roadless **tundra** is inhabited only by pockets of Inuits and other native peoples; it's a destination only for those travellers who can afford an expensive bushplane and the equipment needed for survival in the wilderness.

Transport

Train services within the province serve Montréal, Gaspé, Québec City and Jonquière, and there are also services to Ontario, New Brunswick and the United States – with Montréal very much the pivot. Buses are your best bet for getting around, with the major places connected by Voyageur services, supplemented by a network of smaller local lines. However, distances between communities in the outlying areas can be immense, and in order to reach remoter parks and settlements on secondary roads a car is pretty much essential. Around Montréal and Québec City the shores of the St Lawrence are linked by bridges, and towards the north a network of ferries links the Gaspé with the Côte Nord. In the far north the supply ship *Nordik Express* serves the Île d'Anticosti and the roadless lower north shore as far as the Labrador border – the ultimate journey within Québec.

MONTRÉAL

MONTRÉAL, Canada's second largest city, is geographically as close to the European coast as to Vancouver, and in look and feel it combines some of the finest aspects of the two continents. Its North American skyline of glass and concrete rises above churches and monuments in a medley of European styles, a medley as complex as Montréal's social mix. This is also the second largest French-speaking metropolis outside France, but only two-thirds of the city's two million people are of French extraction, the other third being a cosmopolitan mishmash of *les autres* – including eastern Europeans, Chinese, Italians, Greeks, Jews, South Americans and West Indians. The result is a truly multi-dimensional city, with a global variety of eateries, bars and clubs, matched by a calendar of festivals that makes this the most vibrant place in Canada.

Montréal has long been the dynamo behind Québécois **separatism**, the tension between the two main language groups culminating in the terrorist campaign that the Front de Libération du Québec focused on the city in the 1960s. The consequent political changes affected Montréal more than anywhere else in the province: in the wake of the "francization" of Québec, English-Canadians hit Hwy 401 in droves, tipping the nation's economic supremacy from Montréal to Toronto. However, though written off by Canada's English-speaking majority, the city did not sink into oblivion – rather it reached its 350th year in 1992 on a peak of resurgence.

Everywhere you look there are the signs of civic pride and prosperity. In the historic quarter of **Vieux-Montréal**, on the banks of the St Lawrence, the streets and gracious squares are flanked by well-tended buildings, from the mammoth **Basilique de Notre-Dame** and steepled **Chapelle de Notre-Dame-de-Bonsecours**, to the sleek and stately commercial and public buildings. Old houses have been converted into lively restaurants and shops, abandoned warehouses into condos and the disused **Vieux-Port** into a summer playground with state-of-the-art exhibitions in the old hangars. Beneath the forested rise of **Mont Royal**, the grid of downtown boulevards and leafy squares is alive from the morning rush hour right through to the early hours, when revellers return from Montréal's clubland — centred on **Ste-Catherine** and the Bohemian **Latin Quarter**. Below ground, the walkways of the **Underground City** and the outstanding **Métro** system link the nodal points of the city, while towards the eastern outskirts the **Olympic Stadium** was completed by the addition of a leaning tower that overshadows the vast **Jardin Botanique**, second in international status only to London's Kew Gardens.

To mark Montréal's 350th anniversary, its **museums** were transformed. The **Centre Canadien d'Architecture**, one of the continent's most impressive specialist collections, was matched by the splendid new wing of the **Musée des Beaux Arts**, and many other projects were also realized: the **McCord Museum of Canadian History** reopened after a multi-million-dollar expansion, there is a modern art gallery in the **Place des Arts**, a new **Musée d'Archéologie et d'Histoire de Montréal** at Pointe-à-Callière in Vieux-Montréal, and the **Biodôme**, a unique museum of the environment, out at the Parc Olympique.

Beyond the city limits, Montréalers are blessed with superb vacation regions, most within an hour or two of the metropolis. To the north, the fertile banks of the St Lawrence and the lake-sprinkled mountains of the **Laurentians** offer a reprieve from muggy summer temperatures, while in winter the mountain ski resorts are among the busiest in the country. To the east the charm of **Les Cantons-de-l'Est** lies in the acres of farmlands, orchards, maple woods and lakeshore hamlets. En route to Québec City, the **Mauricie** valley, the province's smallest national park, is a glorious summer haven, with a web of waterways and lakes amidst a landscape of mountainous forest.

Some history

The island of Montréal was first occupied by the St Lawrence **Iroquois**, whose small village of Hochelaga ("Place of the Beaver") was sited at the base of Mont Royal. European presence began in October 1535 when Jacques-Cartier was led here while searching for a northwest route to Asia. However, even after the arrival of Samuel de Champlain the French settlement was little more than a small garrison, and it wasn't until 1642 that the colony of Ville-Marie was founded by the soldiers of **Paul de Chomedey**, Sieur de Maisonneuve. They were on orders from Paris to "bring about the Glory of God and the salvation of the Indians", a mission that predictably enough found little response from the natives. Bloody conflict with the Iroquois, fanned by the European fur trade alliances with the Algonquins and Hurons, was constant until a treaty signed in 1701 prompted the growth of Ville-Marie into the main embarkation point for the fur and lumber trade.

When Québec City fell to the British in 1759, Montréal briefly served as the capital of New France, until the Marquis de Vaudreuil was forced to surrender to General Amherst. The ensuing **British occupation** suffered a seven-month interruption in 1775, when the Americans took over, but after this hiatus a flood of Irish and Scottish immigrants soon made Montréal North America's second largest city. It was not a harmonious expansion, however, and in 1837 there was an uprising of the French against the British ruling class, an insurgence followed by hangings and exiles.

With the creation of the **Dominion of Canada** in 1867, Montréal emerged as the new nation's premier port, railroad nexus, banking centre and industrial producer. Its population reached half a million in 1911 and doubled in the next two decades with an influx of émigrés from Europe. It was also during this period that Montréal acquired its reputation as Canada's "sin city". During Prohibition in the US, Québec province became the main alcohol supplier to the entire continent: the Molsons and their ilk made their fortunes here, while prostitution and gambling thrived under the protection of the authorities. Only in the wake of World War II and the subsequent economic boom

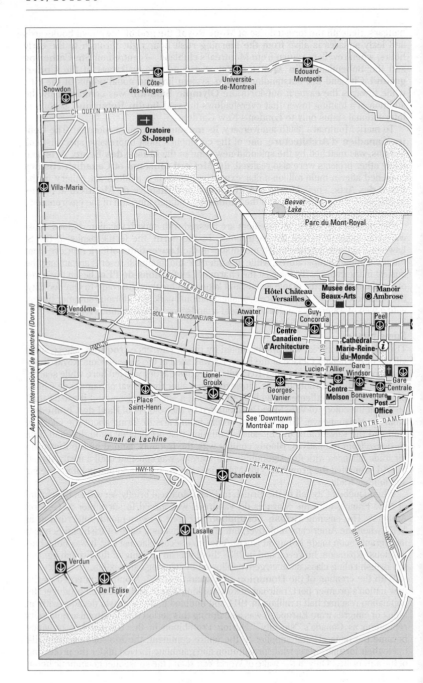

Snowdon

Côte-des-Nieges

Université-de-Montréal

Edouard-Montpetit

CH QUEEN MARY

Oratoire St-Joseph

CH DE LA CÔTE-DES-NIEGES

Villa-Maria

Beaver Lake

Parc du Mont-Royal

AVENUE SHERBROOKE

Hôtel Château Versailles

Musée des Beaux-Arts

Manoir Ambrose

Vendôme

BOUL DE MAISONNEUVE

Atwater

Guy Concordia

Peel

Centre Canadien d'Architecture

Cathédral Marie-Reine-du-Monde

Lionel-Groulx

Lucien-l'Allier

Gare Windsor

Gare Centrale

Place Saint-Henri

Georges-Vanier

Centre Molson

Bonaventure

Post Office

See 'Downtown Montréal' map

NOTRE-DAME

Canal de Lachine

Aeroport International de Montréal (Dorval)

HWY-15

ST-PATRICK

Charlevoix

Lasalle

Verdun

De l'Eglise

BRIDGE

HWY-10

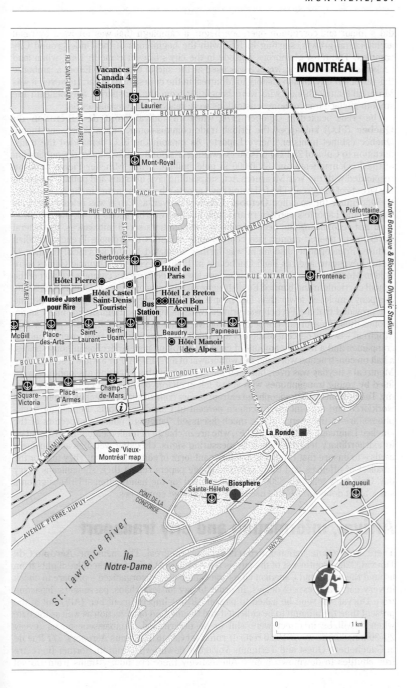

did a major anti-corruption operation begin, a campaign that was followed by rapid architectural growth, starting in 1962 with the beginnings of the Underground City complex. The most glamorous episode in the city's face-lift came in 1967, when land reclaimed from the St Lawrence was used as the site of the **World Expo**, a jamboree that attracted fifty million visitors to Montréal in the course of the year. However, it was Montréal's anglophones who were benefiting from the prosperity, and beneath the smooth surface francophone frustrations were reaching dangerous levels.

The crisis peaked in October 1970, when the radical **Front de Libération du Québec** (FLQ) kidnapped the British trade commissioner, James Cross, and then a Québec cabinet minister, Pierre Laporte. As ransom the FLQ demanded the transportation to Cuba of 25 FLQ prisoners awaiting trial for acts of violence, the publication of the FLQ manifesto and $500,000 in gold bullion. Prime Minister Pierre Trudeau responded with the War Measures Act, suspending civil liberties and putting troops on the streets of Montréal. The following day Laporte's body was found in the boot of a car. By December the so-called **October Crisis** was over, as Cross was released and his captors and Laporte's murderers arrested, but the reverberations shook the nation.

At last recognizing the need to redress the country's social imbalances, the federal government poured money into country-wide schemes to promote French-Canadian culture. Francophone discontent was further alleviated by the provincial election of **René Lévesque** and his Parti Québécois in 1976, the year the Olympic Games were held in Montréal. The consequent language laws made French a compulsory part of the school curriculum and banned English signs on business premises in Québec unless the company employed fewer than fifty people, in which case bilingual signs were permitted, provided that the French was printed twice as big as the English. For many anglophones these measures were pettily vindictive, and nearly 100,000 English speakers left Montréal – twenty percent of the city's population. They took with them over a hundred companies and a massive amount of capital, provoking a steep decline in house prices, a halt on construction work and the withdrawal of investment. For a while it seemed that Montréal's heyday was over, but soon the gaps left by the departing anglophones were filled by young francophones who at last felt in charge of their own culture and economy. Today Montréal's francophone entrepreneurs control sixty percent of the province's workforce and account for seventeen percent of Canada's exports. Remaining anglophones are at the mercy of the much-discussed "language police", inspectors of the Québec Language Federation (QLF), who are in charge of implementing Bill 101 and go to extraordinary lengths – such as measuring signs, checking websites and business cards – to ensure that French is the dominant form of communication. They fine for the smallest of offences and the English-language papers report their shenanigans every day. One story tells of a $200 fine implemented for the handwritten "PUSH" sign on a stuck toilet door, for the sole use of the anglophone employees.

Arrival, information and city transport

There are two international **airports** serving Montréal. The main one, **Aéroport de Dorval**, 22km southwest of the city, is the new arrival point for scheduled flights from around the world and Canadian cities and can be very disorganized – prepare to check in very early, and expect delays. In order to pay for less chaos, passengers departing from Dorval will soon be asked to pay an Airport Improvement Fee (AIF) but at the present time the amount to be collected and the method of collection as well as the date when it will be in effect were still to be determined. Connaisseur buses (every 20–30min; $9 one way, $16.50 return) run a service to Terminus Aéroport, 777 Rue de la Gauchetiére Ouest and Terminus Voyageur downtown. From the former there are free shuttles to downtown hotels. Alternatively there are hourly trains from Dorval

> The Montréal area telephone code is ☎514.

train station to Gare Centrale which take twenty minutes and cost $5 one way. Ask for a transfer (*une correspondance*) from the ticket seller, which allows you to complete your journey by bus or Métro for no extra cost. Several local buses also connect Dorval to downtown but they take ages. A taxi into downtown works out at around $25.

Montréal's second airport, **Aéroport de Mirabel**, 55km northwest of the city, is used solely by charter flights. From Mirabel to the same locations downtown takes about 45 minutes and costs $14.50 one way, $20.50 return on the bus, $50 by taxi.

Montréal's main **train station**, Gare Centrale, is below the *Queen Elizabeth* hotel on the corner of René-Lévesque and Mansfield. The station is the major terminus for Canada's VIA Rail trains from Halifax, Toronto, Ottawa, Québec and the Gaspé as well as US Amtrak trains from Washington and New York. The Bonaventure Métro station links it with the rest of the city.

Long-distance **buses** arrive and depart from Terminus Voyageur on Boulevard de Maisonneuve Est. The Berri-UQAM Métro is right in the station.

Information

Montréal's main **information** centre, Infotouriste (daily: June–Labour Day 9am–7pm; Labour Day–May 9am–5pm; ☎873-2015), is on the corner of Metcalfe and Square-Dorchester at 1001 Square-Dorchester. The nearest Métro is Peel, from where painted footprints lead you to the information centre. In addition to masses of useful free information – including the *Montréal* booklet and an excellent guide to walks in Vieux-Montréal – it offers an accommodation service, which will make any number of free calls to find out vacancies for you. Other than the small information offices at Montréal's **airports** (daily: Dorval noon–2.30pm & 3–8pm; Mirabel 1–8pm), there's also a branch in **Vieux-Montréal** on the corner of Place Jacques-Cartier, at 174 Notre-Dame Est (daily: June–Labour Day 9am–7pm; Labour Day–May 9am–5pm).

Transport

The **public transport** system is one of the city's greatest assets, linking the 65-station Métro to 118 bus routes. The clean, speedy, convenient, reliable and cheap **Métro** system has four colour-coded lines, the major interconnecting stations being Berri-UQAM (which links the orange, green and yellow lines), Lionel-Groulx (green and orange), Snowdon and Jean-Talon (blue and orange). Coloured signs indicate the direction of each line by showing the name of the terminus; maps of the system can be picked up at stations and information centres. One-way fares are a flat $1.85, or 90¢ for under-18s, students and over-65s; a book of twelve – a *carnet de tickets* – costs $16. A *correspondance*, available from machines at the Métro stations, is valid for an hour and allows you to complete your journey by bus at no extra cost. The transfer system also works in reverse from buses to Métro – ask the driver for one as you board. Most **buses** stop running at 12.30am, shortly before the Métro, though some run all through the night; they have the same fare system as the Métro, but only exact change is accepted.

An **STCUM** tourist card allows unlimited travel on the subway and bus routes; it costs $5 a day or $12 for three consecutive days. Available from the information centres, Berri–UQAM Métro station and from April to October from all downtown Métro stations plus Pie-IX, Viau, Jean-Talon and Longueuil stations.

It is rarely necessary to take a **taxi**, though they are not too expensive if you're in a group; they cost $2.50 plus $1 per kilometre, and a 10–15 percent tip is normal. Taxis can be boarded at ranks outside hotels and transport terminals, although if you flag madly they usually stop.

Accommodation

Much of Montréal's **accommodation** is geared towards expense-account travellers in the downtown hotels. However, **hotel** rooms in categories ③–⑥ are conveniently concentrated around the Voyageur bus terminal or the livelier St-Denis area, and a growing number of **B&B** places offer budget accommodation in Vieux-Montréal. Rock-bottom prices are charged in the city's **hostels** and **university residences**. For campers the outlook is not so good, as the **campgrounds** are at least twenty minutes' drive out of town, with no public transport. The peak season is from May to the end of October, with July and August especially busy.

Hotels

Hôtel l'Appartement in Montréal, 455 Rue Sherbrooke Ouest (☎284-3634 or 1-800-363-3010, fax 287-1431). Apartments with kitchenettes, bathrooms, air conditioning, phones and TVs. Free use of outdoor pool and sauna, though parking is extra; discounts for longer stays. ④.

Hôtel Bon Accueil, 1601 Rue St-Hubert (☎527-9655, fax 527-8004). Aptly named, central red-brick hotel near the bus station. All rooms have private bathrooms. ③.

Hôtel Le Breton, 1609 Rue St-Hubert (☎524-7273, fax 527-7016). Near the bus station, this clean, air-conditioned hotel has rooms with TVs, and friendly reception; some rooms accommodate four at $9 per extra person. ③.

Hôtel Castel Saint-Denis Touriste, 2099 Rue St-Denis (☎842-9719, fax 843-8492). One of the best budget hotels in Montréal, right in the trendy St-Denis area, but quiet. ①.

Hôtel Château Versailles, 1659 Rue Sherbrooke Ouest (☎933-3611 or 1-800-361-7199, fax 933-7102). A unique, beautifully furnished hotel in four stone buildings downtown. Book well in advance, as it's one of the city's most popular hotels; family discounts and cheap winter weekend rates also available. ⑤.

Hôtel Louisbourg, 1649 Rue St-Hubert (☎598-8544, fax 524-8796). Cheap hotel with sparse facilities, near the bus station. ①.

Hôtel Manoir des Alpes, 1245 Rue St-André (☎845-9803 or 1-800-465-2929, fax 845-9886). Next to the bus station, this Victorian house is now a two-star hotel with tacky Swiss overtones; rates include breakfast and parking. ③.

Hôtel de Paris, 901 Sherbrooke Ouest (☎522-6861 or 1-800-567-7217, fax 522-1387). An excellent old mansion near Rue St-Denis with a balcony café to hang out in. All rooms are en suite with TVs, telephone and air con. ②–④. Cheap dormitory accommodation in basement; ①.

Hôtel Pierre, 169 Rue Sherbrooke Est (☎288-8519). Nine-bedroom bargain hotel with free parking. ②.

Manoir Ambrose, 3422 Rue Stanley (☎288-6922, fax 288-5757). A couple of blocks from the heart of downtown. Cheap rooms, some with air conditioning and bathrooms. ③.

Hôtel la Residence du Voyageur, 847 Sherbrooke Est (☎527-9515, fax 526-1070). Excellent-value, immaculately clean family-run hotel with lots of personal touches; rates include breakfast. ③.

Bed and Breakfast

A Montréal Oasis, 3000 Rue de Breslay (☎935-2312). Most B&Bs at this agency are centrally located with the emphasis on gorgeous breakfasts. ②–⑤.

Bed & Breakfast Downtown Network, 3458 Rue Laval (☎289-9749 or 1-800-267-5180). Almost always has a vacancy, in one of their hundred or so homes downtown or in Vieux-Montréal, starting in category ② and ranging from quaint Victorian homes to modern apartments.

Welcome Bed & Breakfast, 3950 Rue Laval (☎844-5897 or 1-800-227-5897). Offers moderately priced rooms in Victorian homes located around Rue St-Denis, starting in category ②.

Hostels and student accommodation

Auberge Alternative du Vieux Montréal, 358 Rue St-Pierre (☎282-8069). Rooms for six to sixteen people and some doubles. You don't need to be a member to stay here. ①.

Auberge de Jeunesse Internationale de Montréal, 1030 Rue Mackay (☎843-3317 or 1-800-663-3317, fax 934-3251). Check-in 9.30am–2am. 246 beds, air con, showers in every room. Single, family or shared rooms. Free parking. Advisable to reserve from June to September. Lucien L'Allier Métro. ①.

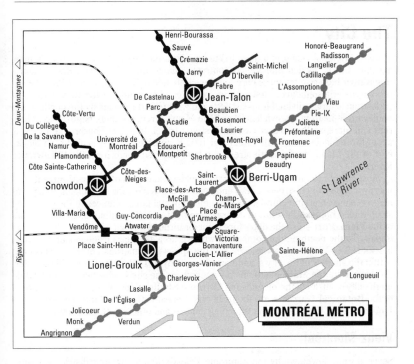

MONTRÉAL MÉTRO

Auberge de Paris, 874 Rue Sherbrooke Ouest (☎522-6861 or 1-800-567-7217, fax 522-1387). A brand-new youth hostel conversion opposite the *Hôtel de Paris*. Cooking facilities, laundry, café, garden and TV room. ①. The second floor has a few rooms if you fancy more privacy. ②–④.

Downtown YMCA, 1450 Rue Stanley (☎849-8393). Expensive, mixed YMCA with a floor for women only, and a swimming pool and cafeteria. Peel Métro. ②.

McGill University Residences, 3935 Rue Université (☎398-6367). Popular residence for visiting anglophones and consequently often full. Good weekly rates. ①.

Université Concordia, 7141 Rue Sherbrooke Ouest (summer only; ☎848-4755, fax 848-4780). ①.

Vacances Canada 4 Saisons, 5155 Rue de Gaspé (☎495-2581, fax 278-7508). 200 beds available all year, and 550 in July and August. Accommodation in Collège Français residences, popular with school groups so often booked up. Rooms have one to seven beds. Open till 2am. One-bedroom studios are available for $130 a week. Gym in the summer. Laurier Métro. ①.

The Women's Y of Montréal, YWCA, 1355 René-Lévesque Ouest (☎866-9941). Women-only, near the station. Laundry facilities as well as swimming pool and cafeteria. Lucien L'Allier Metro. ②.

Camping

Camping Alouette, 3449 Rue de l'Industrie, St-Mathieu-de-Belouil (☎464-1661). Exit 105 off Route 20. With 250 sites this is the largest of the city's campgrounds with a store, washing machines, hook-ups and outdoor swimming pool. Sites $17.

Camping St-Claude, 415 Montée St-Claude, St-Philippe (☎659-3389). Hwy 30 west, Exit 104, Route 104 East. Big, charmless campground with hook-ups, playground, showers, washing machines and restaurant. Sites $13.

Koa Montréal Sud, 130 blvd Monette, St-Philippe-de-la-Prairie (☎659-8626 or 1-800-562-8636). About 20km west of downtown; take exit 38 off Hwy 15, turn left, and it's 3km on. Full facilities at well-kept campground. Sites $18.

The City

Though Montréal island is a huge 51km by 16km, the heart of the city is very manageable, and is divided into Vieux-Montréal – along the St Lawrence River – and a **downtown** high-rise business core, on the south side of the hill of Mont Royal. Sherbrooke, de Maisonneuve, Ste-Catherine and René-Lévesque are the main east–west pedestrian arteries, divided into east (*est*) and west (*ouest*) sections by the north–south boulevard St-Laurent, known locally as "The Main". Street numbers begin from St-Laurent and increase the further east or west you travel: thus 200 Sherbrooke Ouest is about three blocks west of the Main and 1000 René-Lévesque Est is about ten blocks east of the Main. North–south street numbers increase north from the St Lawrence River.

Most visitors to Montréal sample first the old-world charm of **Vieux-Montréal**. The narrow cobblestoned streets, alleys and squares are perfect for strolling, at every corner revealing an architectural gem, from monumental public edifices to the city's first steep-roofed homes. Close by, in contrast, are the futuristic exhibitions in the hangars of the **Vieux-Port** – also the departure point for thrilling jet boat trips down the Lachine Rapids. To the north, in the compact downtown area, the glass frontages of the office blocks reflect Victorian row houses and the spires of numerous churches, clustered within the shadow of the city's landmark, **Mont Royal**. To the east of the hill the eateries and bars of the **Main** make this the spot where the city's pulse beats fastest, while on the city's outskirts the magnificent **Olympic Stadium** complex and the vast green of the **Botanical Gardens** are the main pull. Beneath street level the passages of the **Underground City** link hotels, shopping centres and offices with the Métro.

Vieux-Montréal

Severed from downtown by the Autoroute Ville-Marie, the gracious district of **Vieux-Montréal** was left to decay until fairly recently, when the developers stepped in with generally tasteful renovations that brought colour and vitality back to the area. The continent's greatest concentration of seventeenth-, eighteenth- and nineteenth-century buildings has its fair share of tourists, but it's just as popular with Montréalers too – formerly as a symbolic place to air francophone grievances; more recently as a spot to while away the hours in a café or restaurant.

Place d'Armes and around

The focal point of Vieux-Montréal is the **Place d'Armes**, its centre occupied by a century-old statue of Maisonneuve, whose missionary zeal raised the wrath of the displaced Iroquois. The mutt among the luminaries represents the animal who warned the French of an impending attack in 1644; legend has it that the ensuing battle ended when the unarmed Maisonneuve killed the Iroquois chief on this very spot.

Despite the addition of an ugly skyscraper on its west side, the square is still dominated by the twin-towered, neo-Gothic **Basilique Notre-Dame** (daily 7am–8pm), the cathedral of the Catholic faithful since 1829. Its architect, the Protestant Irish-American James O'Donnell, was so inspired by his creation that he converted to Catholicism. The western of the two towers, named Temperance and Perseverance, holds the ten-tonne Jean-Baptiste bell, whose booming can be heard 25km away. The breathtaking gilt and sky-blue interior, flooded with light from three rose windows in the ceiling and flickering with multicoloured night-lights, was designed by Montréal architect Victor Bourgeau and some talented craftsmen. Most notable of the detailed furnishings are Louis-Philippe Hébert's fine wooden carvings of the prophets on the pulpit and the awe-inspiring main altar by French sculptor Bouriché. Imported from Limoges in France,

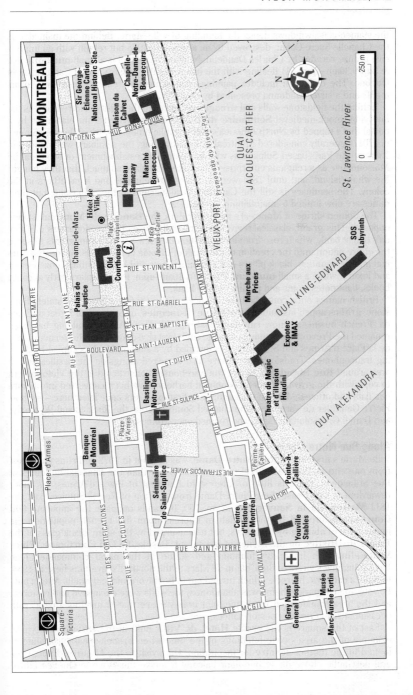

the stained-glass windows depict the founding of Ville-Marie. Behind the main altar is the Chapelle Sacré-Coeur, destroyed by an arsonist in 1978 but rebuilt with an impressive bronze reredos by Charles Daudelin. Next to the chapel is a small **museum** (Sat & Sun 9.30am–4pm; $1) dealing with the history of the basilica and of Catholicism in Québec. The collection includes paintings and sculptures, church vestments, ornaments and a silver Madonna presented by Louis XV.

Behind the fieldstone walls and wrought-iron gates to the right of Notre-Dame is the low-lying, mock-medieval **Séminaire de Saint-Sulpice**, saved from blandness by a portal that's topped by North America's oldest public timepiece, which began chiming in 1701. Generally considered Montréal's oldest building, the seminary was founded in 1685 by the Paris-based Sulpicians, who instigated the establishment of Montréal by Maisonneuve as a religious enterprise. They liked the place so much that they bought the whole island, and until 1854 were in charge of religious and legal affairs in the colony. The seminary is still the Canadian headquarters of the Sulpicians, but their duties are now limited to maintaining the basilica.

The domed shrine of Montréal's financial rulers, the **Banque de Montréal**, stands opposite. This grand, classical-revival building still houses the headquarters of Canada's oldest bank, which rose from its foundation by a few Scottish immigrants to serve the entire nation until the creation of the Bank of Canada in the 1930s. Inside, the original marble counters, black pillars and gleaming brass and bronze fittings ooze wealth and luxury, while a small **museum** (Mon–Fri 10am–4pm; free) displays early account books, banknotes, coins and pictures of the bank.

British names once controlled the finances of the continent from the stately limestone, griffin-capped institutions along **Rue St-Jacques**, once the Wall Street of Canada. French businesses now rule the roost: the Art Deco Aldred Building has been renamed the Prévoyance Building, and the city's first skyscraper – on the corner of côte de la Place d'Armes and St-Jacques – is dwarfed by a soaring block occupied by thriving francophones. Transformations have also occurred alongside the basilica, in the area around **Rue St-Sulpice**, where the warehouses constructed in the Victorian era to cope with the growing trade of Montréal harbour have been converted into luxurious flats and offices. Many of the continent's first explorers once lived here – such as Pierre Gaulthier de Varennes, who charted South Dakota, the Rockies and Wyoming, and Daniel Greysolon du Luth, who roamed over Minnesota.

Along Rue Notre-Dame

Ville-Marie's first street, **Rue Notre-Dame**, was laid out in 1672 and runs east–west from one end of Vieux-Montréal to the other. Other than the financial buildings of Rue St-Jacques, there is little of interest to the west of Place d'Armes; it's more rewarding to head east along Notre-Dame from the top of Rue St-Sulpice, past the 1811 **Maison de la Sauvegarde** at no. 160. It stands opposite the imposing **Old Courthouse**, erected by the British to impress upon the French population the importance of abiding by their laws, but now usurped by the shiny black glass of the **Palais de Justice** on the corner of St-Laurent. Beside the Old Courthouse, **Place Vauquelin**, with its pretty fountain and statue of the naval commander Jean Vauquelin, gives views of the Champ de Mars to the north. Excavations here in 1984, to build a car park, hit rock, which turned out to be the original city walls. After a public vote, the car park scheme was abandoned, the walls were excavated and restored, and the area transformed into a pleasant grassy space that is used as a park, with occasional *son et lumière* performances.

East of the square is the ornate **Hôtel de Ville**, built in the 1870s and a typical example of the area's civic buildings of the time when French-speaking architects looked to the mother country for inspiration. On a visit to the Montréal Expo, General de Gaulle chose its second-floor balcony to make the "Vive le Québec Libre" speech. This speech left the anglophones reeling at the thought that Québec was on its way to independent status and infused the francophones with a fervour that culminated in the October Crisis.

Opposite is the long, low fieldstone manor house of the **Château Ramezay** (June–Sept daily 10am–6pm; Oct–May Tues–Sun 10am–4.30pm; $5), looking much as it did in 1756, the only addition being an incongruous tower, which hoisted the building into "chateau" status in the 1800s. One of the oldest buildings in North America, Château Ramezay was built by the Compagnie des Indes as offices and storage space and then became residence for the French governors, before passing into the hands of the British. During the fleeting American invasion Benjamin Franklin stayed here in an attempt to persuade Montréalers to join the United States, but he lost public and church support by not promising the supremacy of the French language in what would have been the fourteenth state. Nowadays, after a variety of other uses, it's a historical **museum**, displaying oil paintings, domestic artefacts, tools, costumes and furniture from the eighteenth and nineteenth centuries. The most impressive room is a reconstruction of the Grande Salle of the Compagnie des Indes, the fur-trading company that built the chateau and had a monopoly on beaver pelts until the coming of the British. Though the company used the chateau as their headquarters, the ornately carved wood panelling is an import from Nantes in France, donated to Montréal during the Expo. Other rooms are furnished in the bourgeois style of New France, while in the deep stone vaults the life of the native peoples before European settlement is the subject.

At the intersection of Notre-Dame and Berri, the **Sir George-Étienne Cartier National Historic Site** (May–Sept daily 10am–6pm; Oct–April Wed–Sun 10am–5pm; $3.25) comprises two adjoining houses that were inhabited by the Cartier family from 1848 to 1871. The cocky Sir George-Étienne Cartier was one of the fathers of Confederation, persuading the French-Canadians to join the Dominion of Canada by declaring "We are of different races, not for strife but to work together for the common welfare." Today leaders of French-Canadian nationalism decry Cartier as a collaborator, and the displays in the east house diplomatically skirt over the issue of whether he was right or wrong and emphasize instead his role in the construction of Canada's railways. The rooms in the west house have been furnished with over a thousand original artefacts to evoke the period when Sir George lived here, and there are thematic exhibitions and seasonal theatre to explain his achievements.

Place Jacques-Cartier

Sloping down to the river from Place Vauquelin, the cobbled **Place Jacques-Cartier** is one of Montréal's favourite hangouts, its buzz generated at the restaurants and cafés that spill out of the square's historic buildings and by the buskers and horse-drawn calèches that serve the tourist crowds. Just off the square, the narrow Rue St-Amable is choked with struggling artists who produce pastel sketches of Madonna and oils of Burt Reynolds for the same audience.

At the top of the square itself the empty plinth has now been stripped of a controversial **Monument to Nelson** that until recently stood above the flower stalls that are the only reminders that this was once Montréal's main marketplace. The monument, only a third of the size of its more famous London counterpart but a few years older, was funded by anglophone Montréalers delighted with Nelson's defeat of the French at Trafalgar in 1805. Québec separatists adopted it as a rallying point in the 1970s – ironically the anglophones never liked it much either, because it faced away from the water. In 1997, it was officially removed to acquire a more favourable position, but it is unlikely to return in francophone Montréal. The most notable buildings on the square are Maison Vandelac, Maison del Vecchio and the Maison Cartier, showing the architectural features typical of Montréal architecture in the 1800s with pitched roofs to shed heavy snowfalls and small dormer windows as a defence against the cold.

Rue St-Paul

Running parallel to Rue Notre-Dame along the southern end of Place Jacques-Cartier, **Rue St-Paul** is one of Montréal's most attractive thoroughfares, lined with nineteenth-century commercial buildings and Victorian lampposts. Though the buildings differ little from when Charles Dickens stayed here, they now house restaurants and specialist shops selling everything from Inuit crafts to kites.

A block from Place Jacques-Cartier is the silver-domed **Marché Bonsecours**, with its long facade of columns. For years this elegant building was used as municipal offices, but for the city's 350th in 1992 is was restored and transformed to house a farmers' market, designer boutiques, expensive artworks and special exhibitions.

Mark Twain noted that in Montréal "you couldn't throw a brick without hitting a church", and just past Marché Bonsecours is Montréal's favourite, the delicate and profusely steepled **Chapelle de Notre-Dame-de-Bonsecours** (daily: May–Oct 9am–5pm; Nov–April 10am–3pm), or the Sailors' Church. The outstretched arms of the Virgin on the tower became a landmark for ships on the St Lawrence and, once safely landed the mariners would endow the chapel with wooden votive lamps in the shape of ships, many of which are still here. The chapel dates back to the earliest days of the colony, when Maisonneuve helped cut the wood for what was Ville-Marie's first church, under the instigation of Marguerite Bourgeoys, who had been summoned to Ville-Marie to teach the settlement's children. The devout Bourgeoys also founded the nation's first religious order and was in charge of the *filles du Roi* – orphaned French girls sent to marry bachelor settlers and multiply the colony's population. She was canonized in 1982, becoming Canada's first saint. Today's chapel, postdating Bourgeoys by some seventy years, contains a small **museum** devoted to her life (May–Oct daily 9am–4.30pm; Nov–April Tues–Sun 10.30am–2.30pm; $2). Be sure to climb the narrow stairs leading to the summit of the tower above the apse, known as **Le Monument**, for excellent views.

Opposite the chapel is the three-storeyed, high-chimneyed **Maison du Calvet**, built in 1725 and one of Montréal's best examples of French domestic architecture. Photographed, painted and admired more than any other house in the district, it was the home of a Huguenot draper called Pierre Calvet, a notorious turncoat who changed his allegiances from the French to the British and then to the Americans. When the British returned to power after the American invasion, they threw their former justice of the peace into prison. On his release three years later, he discovered that the Americans had no intention of paying for the services he had rendered, then drowned at sea before his claims for compensation reached court. The house is now a café.

Rue Bonsecours, which links Rue St-Paul to Notre-Dame, is another typical Vieux-Montréal street. The **Maison Papineau** at no. 440 was home to four generations of the Papineau family, including Louis-Joseph who, as Speaker of the Assembly, championed the *habitants* of the St Lawrence farmland against the senior Catholic clergy, the British government and the Montréal business class. Calling for democratic election of the executive officers of church and government, he fuelled the rage of the *Patriotes* – the leaders of Lower Canada reform – but deserted the scene as the 1837 rebellion reached a bloody climax.

Vieux-Port

At the southern end of Bonsecours lies the **Vieux-Port** of Montréal, once the import and export conduit of the continent. When the main shipyards shifted east in the 1970s they left a vacant lot, which has been renovated for public use, with biking, cross-country skiing and jogging paths and excellent exhibitions in the quayside hangars.

The King Edward quay has a small information centre on Promenade de Minster. Walking down you'll pass the **Marché aux Puces,** in hangar 8, selling everything from chipped crockery to local art (May–Sept Tues–Sun 11am–8pm), but now threatened with closure. Opposite, the **Magic and Illusion Houdini Theatre** has a mad one-hour show of levitation, metamorphosis and extrasensory perception – a good spot for rainy days (late June to mid-Aug daily 2–9.30pm; English show Sat & Sun 4pm; adults $9.95, children $7.95, family $28). Another good family shelter from the weather is the ever impressive **IMAX** cinema (daily: mid-April to early Sept 10.15am–10.15pm; early Sept to mid-April closed on Mon; adults $11.95, children $7.35, family $33.95; ☎496-IMAX) which takes full advantage of the seven-storey screen, with eye-popping films scanning vast panoramas and launching into the odd sickening plunge.

At the end of the quay, **SOS Labyrinthe** (April to mid-June Sat & Sun noon–8pm; mid-June to Aug Mon noon–10.30pm, Tues–Sun 10am–10.30pm; Sept to mid-Oct Sat & Sun 11am–5pm; adults $7.70, children $6) has converted hangar 10 into a Mystery Cargo Ship. This strange maze, which changes every week, has 2km of dark corridor with obstacles, dead ends and twisting tunnels.

To recover from all that, there's a great lookout at the tip of the quay with views of Vieux-Montréal framed by the downtown skyline.

The Vieux-Port is also the departure point for various **boat trips** and tours. The best by far is the **Jet Boat** from the Clock Tower Pier (May–Oct daily 9am–7pm; $45). Scooting through the Lachine Rapids, the trip is wet, exhilarating and terrifying. For those who like to take things at a more leisurely pace, take the **amphibus** (May–Oct daily, times vary; $18) from in front of the IMAX cinema. In true James Bond style, it sails on water and drives along the streets of Vieux-Montréal.

Place Royale to Place d'Youville

Once the site of duels, whippings and public hangings amidst the pedlars and hawkers who sold wares from the incoming ships, **Place Royale** is dominated by the neat classical facade of the **Old Customs House**, fronted by the Founder's Obelisk, a monument to the founders of the city. After a nine-day journey from Québec City, Maisonneuve and his posse moored their boats at nearby **Pointe-à-Callières**, now landlocked after the changes in the Vieux-Port. At the extremity of the point stands a monument to **John Young**, who was responsible for enlarging Montréal's port in the seventeenth century, an act that enabled the city to expand as a trading centre.

The **Musée d'Archéologie et d'Histoire de Montréal** (July & Aug Tues–Fri 10am–6pm, Sat & Sun 11am–6pm; Sept–June Tues–Fri 10am–5pm, Sat & Sun 11am–5pm; $8) occupies a splendid new building on the Pointe, and spreads underground through the Place Royale as far as the Old Customs House. The theme of this $27-million centre is the development of Montréal as a meeting and trading place, told through the archeological remains excavated here at the oldest part of the city. A high-tech audiovisual presentation in a theatre, which incorporates part of the dig, is an excellent introduction to the museum, to archeology generally, and to that of Montréal in particular. Early remnants of the city include a cemetery from 1648, eighteenth-century water conduits and sewage systems, and walls dating from different centuries. Guides are on hand and there are many well-displayed exhibits, including models of the site development and state-of-the-art videos and quizzes. The underground sections emerge into the Old Customs House, which holds a permanent exhibition on Montréal's history, as well as temporary shows, all with an archeological theme. Children are invited to leave something for future archeologists and have their photos automatically stored in the archives.

Rue de la Commune – in the nineteenth century a morass of taverns and brothels – continues past the **Old Docks** to Rue d'Youville. From here, turn right into Rue St-Pierre for the **Musée Marc-Aurèle Fortin** at no. 118 (Tues–Sun 11am–5pm; $4), a small gallery dedicated to a Québec painter whom the proprietors seem to believe was the greatest artist since the Impressionists. Unfortunately Fortin's directionless experiments with various styles do nothing to justify the praise. His twee oils of pastoral Laurentian scenes convey no real depth of feeling and, though his paintings were bought by French-Canadians, they were hung in Montréal homes as decoration, not as great statements. Fortin became increasingly frustrated with what he took to be the misunderstandings of the public, and his later works – completed just before he went blind – are both sombre and frantic.

Continuing north takes you past the renovated wing of the **Grey Nuns' General Hospital**, where the sick, old and orphaned of Ville-Marie were first cared for. In the centre of the adjacent square, **Place d'Youville**, the red-brick fire station, has been converted into the **Centre d'Histoire de Montréal** (mid-May to mid-Sept daily 10am–5pm; mid-Sept to mid-May Tues–Sun 10am–5pm; $4.50), with dioramas of the city's history from its days as an Iroquois settlement to its present expansions under and above ground. Nothing goes into great depth but it is fine for a sketchy overview; an English booklet is available free from reception for translations of the displays. Usually more stimulating are the temporary exhibitions upstairs, highlighting unusual aspects of the city from its back alleys to prominent citizens.

On the south side of the square, the **Youville Stables**, with its shady courtyard, gardens, restaurants and offices, was one of the first of the area's old buildings to be yuppified. The complex was in fact a warehouse – the stables were located next door. Dating from 1825, the courtyard layout is a throwback to a design used by the earliest Montréal inhabitants as a protection against the hostilities of the Iroquois.

Downtown Montréal

Even if you're not staying in one of the area's hotels, you'll spend at least some time in **downtown Montréal**, as it's here that you'll probably arrive – either at the train stations or the Voyageur bus station. Though the main sights are the high-rises and shopping complexes, the area is dotted with old churches and museums, and Montréal is also one of the cities that has a downtown business area as alive at night as during the day.

Square Dorchester and around

People tend to gravitate towards **Square Dorchester**, originally a Catholic cemetery and now a leafy spot right in the centre of downtown. In the summer the office blocks around the square empty their personnel onto the park benches for a snack and a chat, while tourists mill around the Art Deco-inspired **Infotouriste** building – starting point for various guided tours in summer. The oldest building here is the Victorian **St George's Anglican Church** (May–Sept Tues–Sun 8.30am–5.30pm), with an impressive tapestry from Westminster Abbey used at the Queen's coronation.

The adjacent **Place du Canada** was bought in 1840 by Thomas Phillips, who insisted that the buildings around the square should be the most beautiful in Montréal. Most of the resulting edifices still stand. Dwarfed by its high-rise neighbours, the **Cathédrale Marie-Reine-du-Monde** (daily: Mon 7am–8pm, Tues–Fri 7am–7.15pm, Sat 8am–8pm, Sun 9.30am–7.15pm; free), is a quarter-size replica of St Peter's in Rome. It was commissioned in 1870 by Bishop Ignace Bourgeau as a reminder that Catholicism still dominated the largest city in the new Dominion of Canada. Inside it's not as opulent as one would expect, though the high altar of marble, onyx and ivory is surmounted by a gilded copper reproduction of Bernini's baldachin over the altar in St Peter's. To your right on entering is the **Chapelle des Souvenirs**, which contains various relics, including the wax-encased remains of the immensely obscure St Zoticus.

Opposite the cathedral is the grey granite **Sun Life Building**, built in 1918 and for a quarter of a century the largest building in the British Commonwealth.

In the spring of 1996 the city's world-class ice-hockey team, the Montréal Canadiens, moved into their new home, a 21,000-seater amphitheatre billed as the most modern in North America – **Centre Molson**, right in downtown at 1250 Rue de la Gauchetière

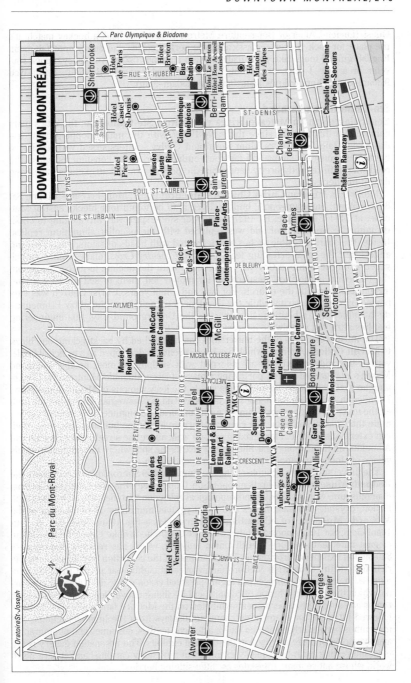

Ouest (Lucien-L'Allier or Bonaventure Métro). When there isn't a hockey match, it's the place for rock concerts, classical music performances and family entertainment. English guided tours take place daily at 11am and 2pm ($7). If you fancy a puck souvenir or a new T-shirt, check out, The Canadiens' Souvenir Boutique (Mon–Wed 9.30am–6pm, Thurs & Fri 9.30am–9pm, Sat 9.30am–5pm).

Ste-Catherine and around

Continuing north up Metcalfe brings you to **Rue Ste-Catherine**, the city's main commercial throughfare since the early 1900s, with the main shopping centres – Eaton, La Baie, Les Cours Mont Royal and Ogilvy – interspersed with exclusive boutiques, souvenir shops and fast-food outlets. For all its consumerist gloss the road was until recently pretty seedy, but the peepshows and strip clubs have been driven further east.

Montréal's Anglican **Christ Church Cathedral** (daily: Mon–Fri 8am–5.45pm, Sat 8am–4.30pm, Sun 8am–5pm), built in 1859, is to be found four blocks east of Metcalfe, at 1444 Union Ave. By 1927 its slender stone spire was threatening to crash through the wooden roof and was replaced with the peculiar aluminium replica. Inside, the soaring Gothic arches are decorated with heads of saints, gargoyles and angels, but the most arresting feature is the *Coventry Cross*, made from nails salvaged from the bombed Coventry Cathedral. With the decline in its congregation, the cathedral authorities' desperation for money led them to sell off all the land around and beneath the church. For two and a half years, Christ Church was supported on concrete struts while the developers tunnelled out the glitzy Promenade de la Cathédrale, a boutique-lined part of the Underground City; this engineering feat has attracted worldwide interest.

The most prestigious of the universities can be reached by backtracking one block to **McGill College Avenue**, which has been recently redeveloped as a principal boulevard – the wide pavements are adorned with sculptures, most notably Raymond Mason's *Illuminated Crowd*, portraying a mass of larger-than-life Montréalers. Continuing up McGill College Avenue brings you to the leafy campus of **McGill University**. Founded in 1813 from the bequest of James McGill, a Glaswegian immigrant fur trader, the university is now world-famous for its medical and engineering schools, and has more than 20,000 students. The campus of ornate limestone buildings and their modern extensions is perfect for relaxing or for a walk above the street level of downtown. A boulder on the campus near Sherbrooke marks the spot where the original Iroquois village of Hochelaga stood before European penetration.

The university boasts a couple of fine museums. At 859 Sherbrooke Ouest there's the **Redpath Museum** (Mon–Fri 9am–5pm, Sun 1–5pm; free), the first custom-built Canadian museum, with an eclectic anthropological collection that includes a rare fossil collection, crystals, dinosaur bones and two Eygptian mummies. Better known is the **McCord Museum of Canadian History** (Tues–Fri 10am–6pm, Sat & Sun 10am–5pm; Sat 10am–noon $8, otherwise free), 690 Sherbrooke Ouest, housed in the elegant nineteenth-century McGill Union building, which has recently undergone a $20-million expansion progamme. The main part of the collection was amassed by the rich and worthy Scots-Irish McCord family over an eighty-year period from the mid-nineteenth century; it represents a highly personal vision of the development of Canada, which they saw as a fusion of colonial and declining native elements. The first few rooms are devoted to a permanent exhibition on the McCord family and their history, followed by space for six-monthly changing displays from the huge collections. The museum is particularly strong on native artefacts, textiles, costumes and photographs, and examples of these are used in the themed exhibits. The first-nation gallery is the most interesting, with high-quality examples of furs, ivory carvings and superb beadwork, whose native name translates as "little shining berries".

Nearby, right next to the Place des Arts at 185 Ste-Catherine Ouest, the **Musée d'Art Contemporain de Montréal** (Tues–Sun 11am–6pm, Wed till 9pm; $6) is the city's foremost showcase for work by living Québécois artists, and also stages major international exhibitions. It has a terrace often filled with live music, a sculpture garden and usually some exciting works.

Rue Sherbrooke and around

Rue Sherbrooke crosses half of Montréal island, but other than the Olympic Stadium far out east its most interesting part is the few blocks from the university to Rue Crescent, an elite stretch of private galleries, exclusive hotels and outlets for the likes of Saint-Laurent, Ralph Lauren and Armani. At the corner of Drummond is the **Ritz Carlton Hotel**, Montréal's most ornate hotel – Elizabeth Taylor married Richard Burton here. Inside, the **Claude Lafitte Art Gallery** (Mon–Fri 10am–6pm, Sat 10am–5pm) is a small gallery with works by Picasso, Miro, Chagall and Canadian artists Riopelle, Fortin, Lemieux, Borduas and Pallan. The hotel remains a symbol of what was once known as the Golden Square Mile, the area between Sherbrooke, Mont Royale, Côte des Neiges and Avenue de Parc. From the late nineteenth century to World War II it is estimated that seventy percent of Canada's wealth was owned by a few hundred people who lived here. Known as the Caesars of the Wilderness, the majority were Scottish immigrants who made their fortunes in brewing, fur trading and banking, and who financed the railways and steamships that contributed to Montréal's industrial growth.

Almost opposite the *Ritz* stands Montréal's **Musée des Beaux Arts** (Tues–Sun 11am–6pm, Wed till 9pm; $10), Canada's oldest museum. Recently extended for a second time, the building can at last do justice to its permanent collection, much of which used to be displaced whenever one of the museum's prestigious temporary exhibitions was on. The Canadian art collection is one of the country's most impressive, covering the spectrum from the devotional works from the days of New France, through paintings of the local landscape by, among others, James Wilson Morrice, Maurice Cullen and Clarence Gagnon, to the more radical canvases by the Automatistes – Paul Émile Borduas and Jean-Paul Riopelle – who transformed Montréal's art scene in the 1940s. Predictably enough, the Group of Seven get a showing too, but the most accomplished paintings are in the European section, where many of the canvases – by such masters as El Greco, Rembrandt and Memling – were donated by the merchants of Montréal's heyday. Their contributions are supplemented by equally high-class later acquisitions by Rodin, Picasso, Henry Moore and other twentieth-century luminaries.

To the left of the museum is another reminder of the Scottish roots of this neighbourhood – the **Church of St Andrew and St Paul**, the regimental church of the Black Watch, the Highland Regiment of Canada. Though the Gothic Revival building is not particularly impressive, Burne-Jones' stained-glass windows are worth a quick peek.

The Centre Canadien d'Architecture

Continue west on Sherbrooke to St-Marc then walk down to Baile, and you'll come face to face with the gigantic **Centre Canadien d'Architecture** (June–Sept Tues–Sun 11am–6pm, Thurs till 8pm; Oct–May Wed & Fri–Sun 11am–6pm, Thurs 11am–8pm; $5, Thurs 6–8pm free). A wonderfully sleek building with a curiously windowless facade and vast glass doors that open smoothly with the least amount of effort, the centre was heaped with accolades when it opened in 1989. The Peter Rose design incorporates the beautifully restored Shaughnessy Mansion (the former residence of a president of the CPR) and its Art Nouveau conservatory, while the light-filled galleries display the museum's vast collection of prints, drawings and books in exhibitions that range from individual masters to whole movements from all cultures and periods.

Behind the museum on boulevard Rene Lévesque, on an area known as the Dorchester Plateau, are the **CCA Sculpture Gardens** (free). This whole area, once full of rambling villas like the Shaughnessy Mansion, was ripped apart in 1969 for the construction of the Autoroute Ville-Marie, and the gardens have restored pride in what was until recently a derelict area. Designed by prominent Montréal artist and architect Melvin Charney, the sculptures are a wacky mishmash of architectural references, arranged in a way reminiscent of ancient stone circles.

Underground City

From the CCA it's about a ten-block walk east back to Dorchester Square and nearby **Place Ville-Marie**, the beginning of Montréal's famous **Underground City**, planned as a refuge from weather that is outrageously cold in the winter and humid in the summer. The underground network began with the cruciform Place Ville-Marie in the 1960s. Montréalers flooded into the first climate-controlled shopping arcade, and the Underground City duly spread. Today its 31km of passages provide access to the Métro, major hotels, shopping malls, transport termini, thousands of offices, apartments and restaurants, and a good smattering of cinemas and theatres. Everything underground is well signposted, but you're still likely to get lost on your first visit, unless you pick up a map of the ever-expanding system from a tourist office.

The Main and East Montréal

Boulevard St-Laurent – the **Main** – leads all the way up from Vieux-Montréal to the northern extremities of the city. North of Sherbrooke is the most absorbing episode along the way, a district where Montréal's cosmopolitan diversity is evident in distinct enclaves of immigrant neighbourhoods. Crossed by **Rue St-Denis**, the heart of the upbeat studenty Latin Quarter, this zone is where the most fun can be had in Montréal, with a huge array of ethnic food outlets and bars spilling out onto the streets. If the party atmosphere is too much, you can head for the landscaped expanse of **Mont Royal** or the overwhelming **Olympic Stadium** and the vast **Botanical Gardens** further east.

Boulevard St-Laurent and Mont Royal Plateau

Traditionally **Boulevard St-Laurent** divided the British in the west from the French in the east of the city. Montréal's immigrants, first Russian Jews, then Greeks, Portuguese, Italians, east Europeans and, more recently, South Americans, settled in the middle and, though many prospered enough to move on, the area around the Main is still a cultural mix where neither of the two official languages dominates. Delis, bars, nightclubs, hardware stores, bookshops and an increasing number of trendy boutiques provide the perfect background to a wonderful jumble of sights, sounds and smells.

At no. 2111, **Musée Juste Pour Rire** (March, April, Sept & Oct Tues–Sun 9am–5pm; May–Aug daily 9am–6pm, $7.95) was opened as an offshoot of the phenomenally successful Montréal comedy festival of the same name. Unfortunately, it has not been able to draw anywhere near the same crowds. It's Humour Hall of Fame looks at Québécois comedy – the first part of a permanent exhibition intended to honour Québec humour. Comics, cartoons, live performances and other bits and bobs do raise a giggle or two.

Wandering north from downtown will bring you onto one of Montréal's few pedestrianized streets, **Prince Arthur**, thronged with buskers and caricaturists in the summer. Turning right leads to the beautiful **Square St-Louis**, the city's finest. Designed in 1876, the square was originally the domain of rich corporate Montréalers, but the magnificent houses are now occupied by artists, poets and writers – including Leonard Cohen. During the winter the square's pathways are converted into skating rinks.

The east side of the square divides the lower and upper areas of **St-Denis**, a relaxed, bohemian district of balconied red-brick houses and a wealth of cafés, bars and clubs. The part of St-Denis back towards downtown has long had a rather grubby reputation, but though this is still a favourite haunt of drug pushers it is becoming increasingly colonized by terrace cafés crammed with students well into the early hours. Further north lies the stamping ground of the francophone intellectual set, where a different yet equally heady atmosphere pervades the sidewalks.

Mont Royal

Little more than a hill to most tourists but a mountain to Montréalers, **Mont Royal** reaches a less than lofty height of 225m but its two square kilometres of greenery are visible from anywhere in the city. Mont Royal holds a special place in the history of the city – it was here that the Iroquois established their settlement and that Maisonneuve declared the island to be French – but for centuries the mountain was privately owned. Then, during an especially bitter winter, one of the inhabitants cut down his trees for extra firewood. Montréalers were outraged at the desecration and in 1875 the land was bought by the city for the impressive sum of $1million. Frederick Law Olmsted, designer of New York's Central Park and San Francisco's Golden Gate Park, was hired to landscape the hill, which now boasts 56km of jogging paths and 20km of skiing paths to keep the city's inhabitants happy all year round.

The city has steadfastly refused any commercial developments on this lucrative site, the only construction being **Beaver Lake**, built in the 1930s as a work creation scheme for the unemployed. In the 1950s, protection of the mountain reached a puritanical extreme when a local journalist revealed that young couples were using the area for amatory pursuits and, even worse, that people were openly drinking alcohol. Consequently all the underbush was uprooted, which only succeeded in killing off much of the ash, birch, maple, oak and pine trees. Within five years Mont Royal was dubbed Bald Mountain and a replanting campaign had to be instigated.

From avenue Mont Royal you can turn left onto avenue du Parc to the **George-Étienne Cartier monument**, where every Sunday buskers and people of all ages congregate until the sun goes down. Paths lead up to the summit via an illuminated cross marking the spot where Maisonneuve placed his cross in 1642. Olmsted Road, which leads up to the summit from downtown, has various lookout points for views of the city.

Oratoire St-Joseph

On the west side of the mountain the awesome **Oratoire St-Joseph** (daily: May–Sept 6.30am–10pm; Oct–April 6.30am–5pm) rises from its green surroundings on Montréal's highest point. If you don't want to walk across the summit, the nearest Métro is Côte des Neiges, from where the oratory is signposted.

In 1904 a certain Brother André built a small chapel here to honour St Joseph, Canada's patron saint. Before long André's ability to heal people had earned him the soubriquet "The Miracle Man of Montréal", and huge numbers of delighted patients donated so much money that in 1924 he could afford to begin work on this immense granite edifice. It was completed in 1967, thirty years after Brother André's death, and is topped by a dome that is second in size only to St Peter's in Rome. The interior of St Jo's – as it's known locally – does not live up to the splendour of the Italianate exterior, though the chapel in the apse is richly decorated with green marble columns and a gold-leaf ceiling. The roof terrace, above the portico, has excellent views of the city and the St Lawrence beyond. A small **museum** in the basement displays items relating to Brother André's life, including the room in which he died, which was shifted here from a local hospice. Even stranger is Brother André's heart enclosed in a glass case; the devout believe it quivers occasionally.

Outside, the **Way of the Cross** has some particularly beautiful sculptures in smooth white Carrara marble and Indiana buff stone by Montréal artist Louis Parent – a tranquil site used as the setting for Canada's most famous film, *Jesus of Montreal*. On the other side of the oratory the original chapel and Brother André's tiny room can be visited.

The Parc Olympique and around

It's best to take the Métro to Viau in order to view Montréal's most infamous architectural construction, the **Parc Olympique**. The main attraction, the **Olympic Stadium**, is known by Montréalers as The Big O for three reasons: its name, its circular shape and the fact that the city owes so much money for its construction – some call it the Money Pit. The main facilities for the 1976 Olympics were designed by Roger Taillibert, who was told that money was no object with Mayor Jean Drapeau declaring "It is as unlikely that Montréal will incur a debt as for a man to bear a child." The complex ended up costing $1.4 billion (of which $300 million are *still* outstanding), and was not even completed in time for the event. It's now the most heavily used stadium in the world, in a desperate attempt to pay the debts: the ceaseless schedule features everything from Pink Floyd concerts to regular baseball games played by the Expos, though they are now vying for a downtown ground. Daily **guided tours** are available (June to Aug 9am–5pm; Sept–May 12.40–3.40pm; $5.25) and you can opt for an extra multimedia, multiscreen show called Montréal...Voilà! ($8)

The stadium's 168-metre **tower** is a major engineering feat: the highest inclining tower in the world, its main function was to hold a retractable 65-tonne roof. But the 45-minute process never really worked properly so in 1998 the stadium is having to fork out $50 million for a new immovable roof. The latest attraction here is a **shuttle ride** up the tower to an observation deck, with eighty-kilometre views and displays on the history of the complex (daily: May–Sept 10am–10pm; Oct–April 10am–5pm; $7.25).

Close by is the **Biodôme** (daily: May to mid-Sept 9am–8pm; mid-Sept to April 9am–6pm; $9.50, children $4.75), housed in a globe-shaped building that started life as a venue for cycling events during the Olympics. Now it's a stunning environmental museum comprising four ecosystems: tropical, Laurentian forest, maritime and polar. You can wander freely through the different zones, which are planted with appropriate flourishing vegetation and are inhabited by the relevant birds, animals and marine life. Watch out for the sloths in the tropical section; they move so slowly that their fur grows mould, unlike the lively monkeys that swing through the trees. You can look at a beaver dam and a take a televised peek inside its lodge, then move on to an impressive rock pool complete with foaming waves and a multicoloured population of anemones, crabs, lobsters and starfish. Gulls fly overhead and puffins bob and dive, while next door, in the Arctic zone, temperatures drop so low that penguins can slide down snow-covered slopes into the water. It's all highly educational and good fun; but try to avoid visiting on Sundays, when the entire population of Québec and its children head there.

Near the stadium and linked by a free shuttle bus from mid-May to mid-September is the **Jardin Botanique de Montréal**, 4101 Sherbrooke Est (daily: mid-June to early Sept 9am–8pm; early Sept to mid-June 9am–6pm; peak season $8.75, off season $6.75). Covering 73 hectares, they comprise some thirty different types of gardens from medicinal herbs to orchids. Highlights include a Japanese garden designed by the landscape architect Ken Nakajima, its ponds of water lilies bordered by greenish sculpted stone and crossed by delicate bridges. In 1991 the Japanese garden was joined by the Chinese garden, the largest of its kind outside China – over 1500 tonnes of materials from China were used to reproduce a replica of the Ming Gardens of fifteenth-century Shanghai. Other attractions in the gardens include the **Insectarium** (daily 9am–6pm; entry included in garden admission fee), a bug-shaped building containing insects of every shape and size. The museum is mainly geared towards children, but adults will learn a fascinating thing or two – like the fact that the housefly has more than five thousand muscles.

The "Get an Eyeful" ticket ($20.75, children $11.75) is a one-day pass that allows entry to the Biodôme, Olympic tower, Jardin Botanique and Insectarium.

Near the southwest corner of the gardens, on the junction of Pie-IX and Sherbrooke, is the stately mansion of the **Château Dufresne** (Wed–Sun 11am–5pm; $3), built in the 1910s for the Dufresne brothers – one an engineer, the other an industrialist – who were both instrumental in Montréal's expansion. Its impressive Edwardian interior houses post-1935 *objets d'art*, plus occasional special decorative-arts exhibitions.

Montréal's other attractions

The islands of Montréal, Île Ste-Hélène and Île Notre-Dame and their environs, offer various slightly-out-of-the-way sights, all well served by public transport but mostly worth the trip only if you have time to kill. Lying just south of Montréal, the combined 2.7 square kilometres of the **smaller islands** were the main venue for Expo '67 and have been developed as playgrounds for the city's inhabitants, with **La Ronde** amusement park the main draw. The **Maison St-Gabriel** is included in this section as it is a bit of a hike from central Montréal. The fur-trading centre of **Lachine** is located on the western shore of Montréal island, about the same distance from downtown as the art museum in the suburb of **St-Laurent**, while the **Musée Ferroviaire Canadien** (the Canadian Railway Museum) is located off the island on the south shore of the St Lawrence.

Cosmodôme, Space Camp Canada, 2150, Autoroute des Laurentides, Laval (late June to Aug daily 10am–6pm; Sept to late June Tues–Sun 10am–6pm). A voyage through the solar system in a moving theatre, where you can walk on the moon, see a real moon rock, take control of the space shuttle Endeavour and become a cosmonaut. Henri-Bourassa Métro, bus #60.

Musée Stewart, Old Fort, Île Ste-Hélène (daily 10am–5pm; $6). Located in the fortified arsenal commissioned by the Duke of Wellington, the museum contains a collection of weapons and assorted domestic and scientific artefacts. The fort is also the summer venue for the re-enactment of seventeenth- and eighteenth-century military manoeuvres by the Fraser Highlanders and Compagnie Franche de la Marine.

Écomusée du Fier Monde, 2050 Amherst St (Wed 11am–8pm, Thurs–Sun 10.30am–5pm). Housed in a wonderful former public bathhouse, this museum focuses on the history of Montréal's industrialization.

Leonard & Bina Ellen Art Gallery, 1400 Maisonneuve blvd West (Mon–Fri 11am–7pm, Sat 1–5pm). Canadian art by both established and emerging artists. Guy-Concordia métro.

Maison St-Gabriel, 2146 Place Dublin (guided tours mid-April to mid-Dec Tues–Sat 1.30–3pm, Sun 1.30–3.30pm; donation). Dating from 1698, this stone farmhouse was the home of Marguerite Bourgeoys (see p.155); antique furniture and the restored kitchen are the main attractions. Bus #61 from Square Victoria Métro.

Musée d'Art de St-Laurent, 615 Ste Croix blvd, Ville St-Laurent (Tues–Fri & Sun noon–5pm; free). A small museum in the former neo-Gothic chapel of St-Laurent college, featuring early arts and crafts from Québec. Du Collège Métro.

Musée Ferroviaire Canadien, 122a St-Pierre, St-Constant (May–Aug daily 9am–5pm; Sept to late Oct Sat & Sun 9am–5pm; $2.25). Special buses connect Longueuil and Angrignon Métros to Canada's largest collection of railway, tramway and steam locomotives.

Musée de Lachine, 110 chemin LaSalle, Lachine (Wed–Sun 11.30am–4.30pm; closed Jan & Feb; free). This seventeenth-century fur-trading post contains a humdrum collection of contemporaneous artefacts and a display on the history of the Lachine canal. Bus #110 from Angrignon Métro.

National Historic Site – The Fur Trade in Lachine, 1255 St Joseph blvd, Lachine (April to mid-Oct Mon 1–6pm, Tues–Sun 10am–12.30pm & 1–6pm; mid-Oct to Nov Wed–Sun 9.30am–12.30pm & 1–5pm; ☎637-7433; $2.50). On the shore of Lac St-Louis, the old Lachine warehouse houses an exhibition on the fur trade; the staff wear the costumes of natives, *coureurs des bois*, and the Scottish merchants who worked here in the eighteenth and early nineteenth centuries. Bus #191 from Lionel-Groux Métro.

Palais de la Civilisation, Île Notre-Dame (mid-May to Sept daily 10am–8pm; admission varies). Originally the French pavilion for the Expo, this now holds exhibitions on subjects from clothing to archeology. Bus #167 from Île Ste-Hélène Métro.

Planétarium de Montréal, 1000 St Jacques Ouest (several performances daily; ☎872-4530; $5.50). Shows include "guided tours" of the solar system and more distant galaxies, while various performances explain eclipses, sunspots and the movement of the planets.

La Ronde, Île Ste-Hélène (early May to late June daily 10am–9pm; late June to Aug Mon–Thurs & Sun 11am–11pm, Fri & Sat 11am–midnight; adults $23, children $11, families $50.90). Ticket gives unlimited access to every ride in the amusement park and admission to the nearby Aqua Parc, a waterslide park. La Ronde is the venue for various celebrations throughout the year, including the annual Fireworks Competition from June to July. Île Ste-Hélène Métro.

Eating

Montréalers conduct much of their business and their social lives in the city's **eating places**, and Montréal food is as varied as its population, ranging from the rich meat dishes of typical Québécois cuisine to bagels bursting with cream cheese. Masses of restaurants line the area around **Ste-Catherine** downtown, though American fast-food chains seem to be taking over, while **Vieux-Montréal** has an ever-expanding number of places to eat, though here most are touristy and slightly overpriced. The best for food, and upbeat atmosphere, is around the **Latin Quarter** and further east in the more French area of the metropolis. Montréal comes a close second to New York as the **bagel** capital of the world, and they are sold everywhere from grimy outlets to stylish cafés – particularly delicious when fresh, white and crammed with cream cheese and lox (smoked salmon).

For those on a **tight budget** the delis, diners and cafés are perfect and if you're really broke the so-called pizza war downtown has got slices of pizza down to 49¢. *Apporter son vin* establishments, of which there are many on Prince Arthur and Duluth, are the cheaper restaurant alternatives. Remember when checking the menu that the present federal and provincial **taxes** will add just under sixteen percent to the meal, and tips are a further fifteen percent.

Snacks and cafés

Ambiance, 1874 Rue Notre Dame Ouest. Tearoom and antique shop in Vieux-Montréal.

Bagel Etc., 4320 Rue St-Laurent. Trendy New York-type diner. Excellent bagels from the simple cream cheese to caviar. Open Tues–Fri until 3.30am, Sat & Sun until 6am.

Beauty's, 93 av du Mont-Royal Ouest. The best bargain eatery in this area and a brunch favourite with Montréalers. Wonderful 1950s decor and typical diner fare on the menu.

Ben's Delicatessen, 1475 Rue Metcalfe. Lithuanian Ben Kravitz opened his deli in 1908 and his sons and grandsons still run this Montréal institution. Around 3am the gaudy 1930s interior is packed with customers, from truckers to jewellery-adorned theatregoers, and the wall of fame is constantly being added to. The speciality Big Ben Sandwich ($8.50) is 2.5cm thick and the equally famous strawberry cheese cake ($5) is exceptional. Open Mon–Thurs & Sun 7am–4am, Fri & Sat 7am–5am.

La Binerie Mont-Royal, 367 av du Mont-Royal. Four tables and a chrome counter seat the hundreds of people who visit this well-known café daily. The menu consists of beans, beans and more beans with ketchup, vinegar or maple syrup. Also served is pork, beef, *tourtière* (a minced pork pie) or Binerie's famous stew.

Le Breakfast Plus, 1439 blvd René-Lénisque Ouest. Tiny all-day breakfast joint serving imaginative egg dishes with lots of fruit and freshly squeezed juice.

Briskets, 4006 chemin de Ste-Catherine Ouest, 1073 Beaver Hall and 2055 Bishop. Plain decor with wooden tables, popular with students. Smoked meat to eat in or take away. Closed Sun.

Café Ciné-Lumière, 5163 Rue St-Laurent. Antique Parisian decor, cheap French food and continuous movies, which you listen to through headsets.

Café El Dorado, 5226 Rue St-Laurent. Coffees from all over the world, and fine desserts.

Café Santropol, 3990 Rue St-Urbain. Vegetarian café on the corner of Duluth. Popular with health-conscious anglophones having midlife crises – known locally as "granolas" because they munch health-food snacks. Huge sandwiches, quiches and salads as well as various herbal teas and coffees.

Café Toman, 1421 Rue Mackay. A quiet Czech coffee shop in downtown. The cakes are great but soups and salads are also available. Popular with students from nearby Concordia. Closed Sun & Mon.

Café La Tulipe Noire, 2100 Rue Stanley. Good pastries, excellent cheesecake and a daily special.

Le Café Mondial d'Internet, 5173 chemin de la Côte-des-Neiges. Get online and wired on coffee at this simple Internet café.

La Chartreuse, 3439 Rue St-Denis. Upmarket café with delicious cakes. Closed Mon.

CyberParc, 5316 av du Parc. Another computer hangout. Much larger, and with special rates for students.

Le Daphnée, 3808 Rue St-Denis. Hyper-civilized and expensive *salon de thé*.

La Desserte, 5258 Rue St-Laurent. Creating the most divine cakes, particularly the cheesecake, this patisserie is expensive but worth every cent. Serves discounted specials for cinema-goers on some nights – keep your tickets. Open until 1am at weekends.

Dunn's, 892 Chemin de Ste-Catherine Ouest. An excellent deli with great jars of pickles in the window and a wealth of smoked meats. Frantic atmosphere and friendly service. A favourite with local business types, and thus packed at lunch times. Open 24hr.

Fairmount Bagel Bakery, 74 av Fairmount Ouest. Possibly the best bagel outlet in Montréal, offering a huge variety of bagels. There is nowhere to sit, but arm yourself with a bag of bagels, a pot of cream cheese and some smoked salmon (lox), sit on the nearest kerb and you'll soon be in bagel heaven. Open daily 24hr.

Faubourg Ste-Catherine, 1616 Rue Ste-Catherine Ouest. A gigantic restored building on the corner of Guy. Downstairs is a wealth of food stalls from cookies to fresh veg; upstairs a fast-food mall to surpass all others – everything from fresh salmon to crêpes and cookies.

Le Petit Peu, 318 Rue Ontario Est. Very cheap vegetarian and health-food café. Closed Sat.

Maison Pierre du Calvet, 401 Rue Bonsecours. Coffee, home-made soup and sandwiches in one of the sights of Vieux-Montréal.

Schwartz's Montréal Hebrew Delicatessen, 3895 Rue St-Laurent. A small, narrow deli serving colossal sandwiches. *Schwartz* tends to stay at the top of the word-of-mouth "Who does the best smoked meat?" competition more often than its competitors.

Wilensky's Light Lunch, 5167 Rue Clark. Used for countless filmsets because the decor hasn't changed since 1932 and that includes the till, the grill and the drinks machine. The Wilensky Special includes four types of salami and costs around $4. Closed weekends.

Restaurants

Montréal's ethnic diversity is amply displayed by the variety of **cuisines** available and Montréalers try to outdo each other by indulging in exotic fare from Japanese rotis to earthy Portuguese grub. The city has its own **Chinatown** just north of Vieux-Montréal, a **Little Italy** around Jean-Talon Métro, a **Greek** community whose cheaper restaurants are concentrated along Prince Arthur – but for more traditional Greek cuisine head further north along Avenue du Parc where a number of Greek-Canadians live. Most prominent of the ethnic eateries are the **eastern European** establishments dotted around the city. Opened by immigrants who came to work in the garment factories, their speciality is **smoked meat**, which has become a Montréal obsession, served between huge chunks of rye bread with pickles on the side.

Asian

Azuma, 901 Rue Sherbrooke Est (☎525-5262). A popular Japanese restaurant with a reasonable $20 a head menu. Reserve if possible.

Copacabana, 3928 Rue St-Laurent. Very cheap and delicious Malaysian place with wonderful samosas.

Hong Kong, 1019–23 Rue St-Laurent. Vast menu at this Chinese food place, packed with Chinese-Canadians.

Katsura, 2170 Rue de la Montagne. Large and popular downtown Japanese restaurant. Fairly reasonable.

The Elysée Mandarin, 1221 Rue Mackay. A beautifully decorated, moderately priced Chinese restaurant.

Maison Kam Fung, 1008 Rue Clark. This is Montréal's vast temple to dim sum, right in the heart of Chinatown. Well-priced menu but not dirt-cheap. There are often long queues so get there early. "Dim sum" is *élan du coeur* in Québécois.

Le Pique Assiette, 2051 Rue Ste-Catherine Ouest. Cheap, Indian, vegetarian and meat buffet.

French

Au Petit Extra, 1690 Rue Ontario Est. Large, lively and inexpensive bistro with amazing food and authentic French feel.

Le Bonaparte, 443 Rue St-François-Xavier. Moderately priced, well-situated French restaurant in Vieux-Montréal. The fish is good and there are tables on the balconies.

Le Caveau, 2063 Rue Victoria. Red-and-white tablecloths, dripping candles and great French food in this three-floored restaurant in a twee downtown house. Very pricey but worth the splurge.

L'Express, 3927 Rue St-Denis (☎845-5333). Fashionable Parisian-style bistro, with hectic service. Pretty expensive, and reservations essential.

Laloux, 250 Rue des Pins Est. East of the city, this Parisian-style bistro serves pricey *nouvelle cuisine*.

La Maison Pierre du Calvet, 401 Rue Bonsecours. Probably Montréal's finest French restaurant; pricey but excellent.

Mediterranean

Arahova Souvlaki, 256 Rue St-Viateur Ouest. Superb, yet inexpensive choice for authentic Greek cuisine.

La Casa Greque, 200 Rue Prince Arthur Est. One of numerous cheap Greek establishments in this area, all of much the same standard.

Eduardo, 404 av Duluth Est. Crowded cheap Italian with huge portions. Bring your own alcohol and expect a queue.

Euro Deli, 3619 Rue St-Laurent. Busy deli where you can get stuffed for about $5 on sandwiches, calzone, pasta and veggie food.

Milos, 5357 av du Parc. Expensive, but the finest Greek restaurant in the city.

Modigliani, 1251 Rue Gilford. Lots of plants and a pianist. Reasonable prices for great Italian food.

La Pizzaïolle, 5100 Rue Hutchison. Thick-crusted pizzas straight out of a brick oven. Pricey but worth every cent.

Pizzédélic, 3509 Rue St-Laurent. Modern decor and experimental pizzas.

Pizzeria Napoletana, 189 Rue Dante, Little Italy. Very cheap; take your own alcohol and expect to queue at the weekend.

North American

Bar-B-Barn, 1201 Rue Guy, just off Ste-Catherine. Brilliant ribs served in Western "Yeee-Ha" decor; a favourite with the local "cowboy" business world – hundreds of business cards are stuck in the log rafters. Always packed to the hilt.

Bio Train, 310 Rue St-Jacques. Self-serve health-food restaurant.

Chez Claudette, 351 Rue Laurier Est. Cheap family bistro which is great for a big breakfast fry-up.

Chez Delmo, 211 Rue Notre-Dame Ouest. Popular with anglophones and workers from the nearby stock exchange in Vieux-Montréal. Eat in the first room with its two long oyster bars. Fish and seafood dishes are the speciality, and the chowder is excellent. Closed Sun.

Le Commensal, 1204 Rue McGill College, 3715 chemin Queen Mary and 2115 Rue St-Denis. Cheap vegetarian with hot or cold buffet; unlicensed. The St-Denis location has the best atmosphere. Open daily until late.

Il Était une Fois, 600 Place d'Youville. Old train station converted into a hamburger restaurant. One of the best deals in Vieux-Montréal.

Laurier BBQ, 381 Rue Laurier Ouest. Great hunks of Québec-style barbecued chicken and huge salads; a Montréal favourite for half a century.

Moishe's, 3961 Rue St-Laurent (☎845-3509). Favourite haunt of Montréal's business community. Excellent steaks, but very expensive, with notoriously bad-tempered service. Reservations recommended.

PatatiPatata, 4175 Rue St-Laurent. Small place with excellent and cheap home-made food.

La Paryse, 302 Rue Ontario Est. Delicious home-made hamburgers and chips in a 1950s-style diner. Highly recommended.

Shed Café, 3515 Rue St-Laurent and 1333 Ste-Catherine Est. Hamburger, salad and sandwich joint where trendy Montréalers come to see and be seen. Avant-garde, wacky interior. Open until 5am Fri & Sat.

Bars and nightlife

Montréal's **nightlife** keeps going into the small hours of the morning, and its bars and clubs cater for everyone – from the students of the Latin Quarter and the punks who hang out on the corner of Ste-Catherine and St-Denis, to the anglophone yuppies of Crescent Street. The places listed here are the best of the bunch and are open until 3am unless stated otherwise. Always tip the bar staff – the perks constitute the main whack of their wages. Many of the bars have regular music nights, with **jazz** being especially popular. Other than the bars, there are numerous venues in the city, with top-name touring bands playing at the new Centre Molson and the Olympic Stadium.

For up-to-date **information**, the *Mirror* and the *Hour* are free English weekly news-papers with an excellent listings section. The English-language daily *The Montréal Gazette* also carries comprehensive listings – the Friday weekend guide is particularly good. *Montréal Scope*, available in tourist information offices and the better hotels, is primarily for mainstream tourists.

Bars

Angels, 3604 Rue St-Laurent. Young, university hangout, with the atmosphere of the average common room.

Bar Salon St-Laurent, 3874 Rue St-Laurent. Popular student bar with loud South American and West Indian music.

Les Beaux Esprits, 2073 Rue St-Denis. Local blues and jazz artists can be seen here for free.

La Bibliothèque, 1647 Rue St-Denis. Quiet bar with outside terrace, which is decorated like a library. The terrace overlooks the goings-on on Rue St-Denis. Two drinks for one on Friday and Saturday nights.

Café Campus, 57 Rue Prince Arthur Est. The original *Café Campus* was known for its great atmos-phere and free popcorn, but it has now moved to a new venue.

Le Central, 4479 Rue St-Denis. Unpretentious, old jazz bar. Another student hangout, as the drinks are cheap and admission is free.

Le Cheval Blanc, 809 Rue Ontario Est. Old-style Montréal pub, with the same decor as when it opened in the 1940s. They brew their own beer.

Futenbulle, 273 av Bernard Ouest. Probably the largest selection of beers in Montréal.

Le Grand Café, 1720 Rue St-Denis. Loud bar that spills out into trendy St-Denis in the summer. Live jazz and blues from Wednesday through Saturday. Free entry.

Hurley's Irish Pub, 1225 Rue Crescent. Very popular Irish pub with smooth Guinness on tap.

Île Noire, 342 Rue Ontario Est. Sophisticated Scottish-type bar with warming whiskeys.

Isart, 263 Rue St-Antoine Ouest. Bar/club with fun-loving crowd. Hip-hop on Saturday nights.

Jello Bar, 151 Rue Ontario Est. Enjoy live jazz and blues at this bar furnished with 1960s and 1970s novelties. Martini cocktails a speciality.

Le Pub . . . de Londres à Berlin, 4557 Rue St-Denis. Excellent atmosphere with the trendiest of Montréal's young Bohemian crowd – particularly up-and-coming actors, comedians and artists. Big sacks of free popcorn, numerous draught beers and pool tables. Open till 2am Sat & Sun.

Roy Bar, 351 Rue Roy Est. Restored old tavern popular with students.

Le St-Sulpice, 1682 Rue St-Denis. A three-floored beautifully decorated fashionable bar in the heart of Montréal's Latin Quarter. Terrace at the back and front, perfect for people-watching.

Pub Sir Winston Churchill, 1459 Rue Crescent. Known locally as *Winny's*, this English-style pub attracts local and visiting anglophone professionals. Pool tables and a small dance floor. Prime pick-up joint.

Pub le Vieux-Dublin, 1219 Rue Université. Irish pub with Celtic music and a massive choice of draught beers. Popular with everyone.

Swimming, 3643 Rue St-Laurent. In a bizarre turn-of-the-century building, this is a massive pool hall and happening bar.

Whisky Café, 3 Rue Bernard Ouest. Elegantly decorated with a young wealthy clientele.

Yoda's Den, 258 Rue Roy. Couches and cool but friendly crowd. After-hours drink, chat and ambient, ultra-chilled DJs.

Venues, clubs and discos

L'Air du Temps, 194 Rue St-Paul Ouest (☎842-2003). The most famous of Montréal's jazz spots. In the heart of Vieux-Montréal with ornate antique interior. Admission $7, but arrive early to get a decent seat. Live acts from 10pm Thursday–Sunday; closed Mon–Wed.

Aux Deux Pierrots, 104 Rue St-Paul Ouest. Québécois folk singers are the mainstay of this club. There's usually a good crowded atmosphere but don't expect to understand a word unless your French is excellent. Outside terrace in the summer. Admission from $3.

Le Balattou, 4372 Rue St-Laurent. Montréal's only African nightclub. Dark, smoky, crowded, hot, loud and friendly. Live acts every night; entrance $5 on weekdays, $7 at weekends (includes one drink).

Le Belmont, 4483 Rue St-Laurent. Yuppie disco dance bar. Admission Thurs $3, Fri & Sat $4, Sun free. Closed Mon–Wed

Le Bifteck, 3702 Rue St-Laurent. Studenty, cheap beer bar/venue with music from grunge to hip-hop.

Club Soda, 5240 av du Parc. One of Montréal's most popular venues. Attracts good acts, especially during the comedy and jazz festivals.

Les Foufounes Électriques, 87 Rue Ste-Catherine Est. A bizarre name ("The Electric Buttocks") for a bizarre and wonderful bar/club/venue. Known fondly as *Les Foufs* it's the best place in Québec for alternative bands, attracting all of Montréal's young crowd from ravers to students. Has a huge outside terrace perfect for summer evenings. Tickets for bands from $10, otherwise admission is free and pitchers of beer are cheap.

Le Grand Café, 1720 Rue St-Denis. Jazz and blues bands play at this busy bar in the midst of throbbing Rue St-Denis.

Groove Society, 1288 Amherst. Inspired by NY's *Lava Lounge* with waterfall, fun-fur walls and club kids. Gay on Thursdays.

Jailhouse Rock Café, 30 Rue Mont-Royal Ouest. On the corner of St-Laurent with eclectic live bands from punk to ska and spoken-word events.

Jungle, 4177 Rue St-Denis. On the third floor with great music – drum and bass, reggae, hip-hop and R&B.

Le Loft, 1405 Rue St-Laurent. Indigo techno decor and the odd arty exhibition attracts trendy under-25s.

Le Métropolis, 59 Rue Ste-Catherine. A huge converted theatre that's now Montréal's largest disco. No jeans. Admission weekdays $5, Saturday $8.

Le Passeport, 4156 Rue St-Denis. Small dance-music club with long queues at weekends. Frequented by Québec's rich and famous; drinks are overpriced. Admission Thursday to Saturday $3.50, free the rest of the week.

Purple Haze, 3699a Rue St-Laurent. Goth stuff.

Sona, 1439 Rue de Bleury. Weekend all-nighters (until 10am) for ecstatic kids. Psychedelic lights and loud, loud, loud music. $25 and expect a long queue.

The performing arts and cinema

Montréal's most prestigious centre for the **performing arts** is the Place des Arts, 1501 Jeanne Mance (information ☎285-4200, tickets ☎842-2112), a four-hall complex with a comprehensive year-round programme of dance, music and theatre. The Théâtre de Verdure in Lafontaine Park is an outdoor theatre with a summer-long programme of free plays, ballets and concerts. Another eclectic venue is the Théâtre St-Denis, 1594 St-Denis (☎849-4211), which presents blockbuster musicals and other shows. The Saidye

Bronfman Centre, 5170 chemin de la Côte Ste-Catherine (☎739-2301), contains an exhibition centre and a three-hundred-seater venue for music, dance, film and theatre.

The city's foremost French-language **theatre** is the Théâtre du Rideau Vert, 4664 St-Denis (☎845-0267), which gives prominence to Québec playwrights, while the Théâtre du Nouveau Monde, 84 Ste-Catherine Est (☎866-8667), presents a mix of contemporary and classic plays in French. Montréal's main English-language theatre is the Centaur Theatre, housed in the former stock exchange at 453 St-François-Xavier (☎288-3161).

Montréal has more than ten excellent **dance** troupes from the internationally acclaimed Les Grandes Ballets Canadiens (☎849-8681) and Ballets Classiques de Montréal to the avant-garde LaLaLa Human Steps and Tangente, who perform at various times at the Place des Arts, Théâtre de Verdue and during the festivals. The continent's premier contemporary dance festival is the **Festival International de Nouvelle Danse**, held at various city locations every two years from late September to early October.

There are two well-known **orchestras** based in the city, the Montréal Symphony Orchestra (☎842-9951) and the Orchestre Métropolitain (☎598-0870), each of whom holds regular concerts at Place des Arts and the Basilique Notre-Dame. The city also has a programme of free summer concerts in various city parks (information ☎842-3402). L'Opéra de Montréal (☎985-2258) produces five bilingually subtitled productions a year at Place des Arts.

Films in English, usually the latest releases from the States, can be caught at nearly all the city's cinemas, as they are shown for about a fortnight before the dubbed versions are available. Central ones include Eaton, 705 Ste-Catherine Ouest; Centre Ville, 2001 Université; and Palace, 698 Ste-Catherine Ouest. The city's only English rep cinema is the Rialto Cinema, 5723 du Parc; French rep cinemas include the Ouimetoscope, 1204 Ste-Catherine Est, and Cinéma de Paris, 896 Ste-Catherine Ouest. For Québécois film-makers, check out Cinématique Québécoise, 335 de Maisonneuve Est (Tues–Sun 11am–9pm) which has screening and exhibition programmes that bring together the history, events and future of cinema, TV and new media.

Festivals and other events

The **Montréal International Jazz Festival** is North America's largest jazz festival, with over 400 shows, most of them free. From late June to early July, more than 2000 international musicians descend on the city, including the likes of B.B. King, Etta James, Al Jarreau, Dave Brubeck, Ben E. King and Branford Marsalis. Continuing the superlatives, there's the mid-July **Juste pour Rire** ("Just For Laughs"), which is the world's largest comedy festival, with past headliners including Tim Allen, Rowan Atkinson, Jim Carrey, John Candy and Lily Tomlin. Theatres host 650 comedians from 14 countries performing in over 1000 shows.

Noisiest of the city shindigs is the **International Fireworks Competition**, whose participants are competing to get contracts for the July 4 celebrations in the States. Held from June to July, the music-coordinated pyrotechnics are a breathtaking sight. The action takes place at La Ronde and tickets are around $20, but across the water and on the Jacques-Cartier Bridge the spectacle is free, and the music for the displays is broadcast live on local radio. Firework concerts are staged every Sunday at 10pm throughout the summer at La Ronde even when the main competition is over; same conditions apply as during the competition and it's well worth catching.

In June, **Beer Mundial** in the Vieux-Port offers the opportunity to get legless on over 250 brands of beer from around the world, and later in the month you can recover with the **Worldwide Kite Rendez-Vous,** which takes place at Parc Therrien in Verdun.

In winter, the **Fête des Neiges** takes place in early February, with costumed characters warming up the place in a fun carnival.

Montréal has **film festivals** practically every month; some thematic, some devoted to individuals. The most notable is the **Montréal World Film Festival** in late August, the city's answer to Cannes, Berlin and Venice.

Finally, the **Cirque du Soleil** (information ☎522-2324) is a fantastic circus company that travels all over the world, but every year has a big-top season in its home city. Refusing to exploit animals, the circus's acrobats, trapeze artists, clowns, jugglers and contortionists present an incredible show, with original music scores, extravagant costumes and mind-blowing stunts. The annual publication, *Les Événements Ro-na*, lists all these events and many more; it's available free from the tourist office.

Gay Montréal

Montréal has an excellent **gay** scene, with the action concentrated in the area known as the **Village** – roughly located on Ste-Catherine Est between Amherst Street and the Papineau Métro station. There are two English **information lines** for up-to-date news on the latest events in the city: Gay-Info (Fri & Sat 7.30–10.30pm; ☎768-0199) is bilingual, The Gayline (daily 6–10pm; ☎990-1414) is in English and Gai-Écoute (☎521-1508) provides a similar service for French-speakers. For contacts L'Androygyne, 3636 St-Laurent, is a gay and lesbian bookshop, and *RG* and *Fugues* magazines are the city's monthly French gay and lesbian mags (there's usually a small English section hidden among the ads and pictures). In July **Parade de la Fierté Gaie et Lesbienne** ("Gay and Lesbian Pride Parade") is the event of the year, held along Ste-Catherine, ending with shows in Campbell Park.

Cafés and restaurants
Most of the restaurants and hangouts in the Village cater to a lesbian, bisexual and gay crowd.

L'Amorican, 1550 Rue Fullum. Excellent French eatery.

L'Anecdote, 801 Rue Rachel Est. Small, cosy hamburger and sandwich joint.

La Paryse, 302 Rue Ontario Est. Extraordinary and exotic range of burger fillings.

Le Planète, 1541 Plessis. Food from around the planet. Massive portions.

Saloon, 1333 Rue Ste-Catherine Est. Pizzas, burgers and salads. Mixed crowd of young and old, gay and straight.

Bars, clubs and discos
Biliti's, 2017 Fountenac. Women-only disco.

Bistro Four, 4040 Rue St-Laurent. Male gay bar.

Cabaret l'Entre Peau, 1115 Rue Ste-Catherine Est. The best (and outrageously worst) of Montréal's drag shows, with a mixed fun-loving clientele.

Club Date, 1218 Rue Ste-Catherine Est. Piano bar with older male patrons.

Club Home, 1450 Rue Ste-Catherine Est. Massive dance floor with loud House music, laser shows and the rest. Very cruisey. Mixed gay/straight on Fridays.

L'Exit II, 4297 Rue St-Denis. Women-only, with a mostly older francophone crowd. Pool and dance floor.

Sisters, 1450 Rue Ste-Catherine Est. Mainly women, but men with women are welcome. Has a casual atmosphere with dance music, pool and a bar on Thursdays from 11am to midnight.

Sky, 1474 Rue Ste-Catherine Est. Dance-club nirvana. Two dance floors (the music is generally more technofied upstairs), two pool rooms and a bar/restaurant. Thursday is for women only but is usually mixed, student night is Friday and drag shows are on Saturday nights.

La Track, 1584 Rue Ste-Catherine Est. Men-only gay bar and disco. Cruisey male leather crowd. Very cheap on Wednesdays.

Listings

Airlines British Airways, 1021 blvd de Maisonneuve (☎287-9282); Air Canada, Air Alliance, Air Nova and Air Ontario, 2020 blvd Université (Canada and USA ☎393-3333); Air France, 2000 Rue Mansfield (☎847-1106); Canadian Airlines, 999 blvd de Maisonneuve (☎847-2211); Swiss Air, 1253 av McGill College (☎879-9154).

Airport enquiries Dorval ☎633-3105; Mirabel ☎476-3010; both airports ☎1-800-465-1213.

Baseball The Montréal Expos' home ground is the Olympic Stadium, 4141 av Pierre-de-Coubertin (Pie-IX Métro). Tickets cost $1–13.50 (information ☎252-8687). The team are putting serious pressure on the city for a new downtown arena, which they may well get very soon.

Bike rental Bicycletterie JR, 151 Rue Rachel Est (☎843-6989), bikes for rent from $20 per day, with credit card needed as deposit; La Cordée, 2159 Rue Ste-Catherine Est rents bikes from $35 a day (☎524-1515); Vélo Aventure Montréal, King Edward Dock, Old Port (☎847-0666) rents bikes from $20 a day and rollerblades from $8.50 an hour.

Bookshops English books can be bought from most major bookshops, specifically. W.H. Smith, Place Ville-Marie and Place de la Cathédrale and Paragraphs Books and Café, 2065 Rue Mansfield. Double Hook, 1235a av Greene, specializes in English-Canadian authors. A decent selection of travel books in English and French are available from Ulysses Travel Bookshop, 4176 Rue St-Denis, 560 av du President-Kennedy, and downstairs at Ogilvy on the corner of Rue Ste-Catherine and blvd de la Montagne.

Bus infomation Local: ☎288-6287, long-distance: Orléans Express ☎842-2281, Adirondack Trailways (to New York) ☎914/339-4230.

Camping equipment You can hire or buy all you need for the outdoors at Altitude, 1472 Peel (☎288-8010).

Car rental Alamo, Montréal Airport (☎633-1222); Avis, 1225 Rue Metcalfe (☎866-7906); Budget, 1240 Guy (☎938-1000); Discount Car & Truck Rentals, 607 blvd du Maisonneuve Ouest (☎286-1554); Hertz Canada, 1073 Rue Drummond (☎938-1717); Sako Location, 2350 Rue Manella (☎735-3500); Thrifty, 1076 Rue de la Montagne (☎989-7100).

Consulates Belgium, 999 blvd Maisonneuve Ouest (☎849-7394); Denmark, 1 Place Ville-Marie (☎871-8977); Finland, 800 Carré Victoria (☎397-7600); Germany, 3455 Rue de la Montagne (☎286-1820); Great Britain, Suite 901, 1155 Rue Université (☎866-5863); Netherlands, 1002 Rue Sherbrooke Ouest (☎849-4247); Norway, 1155 blvd René-Lévesque Ouest (☎874-8087); Sweden, 800 Carré Victoria (☎866-4019); Switzerland, 1572 Dr Penfield (☎932-7181); USA, 1155 Rue St Alexandre (☎398-9695).

Dental emergencies 24hr dental clinic, 3546 Van Horne St (☎342-4444).

Driveaway Auto Drive-Away, 1117 Rue Ste-Catherine Ouest (☎844-1033); Montréal Drive-Away, 4036 Rue Ste-Catherine Ouest (☎937-2816). Expect to pay $200-400 deposit plus petrol.

Exchange Banque Nationale du Canada, 1001 Rue Ste-Catherine Ouest and 600 Rue de la Gauchetière Ouest. Thomas Cook, 625 blvd René-Lévesque Ouest. Automatic teller machines that exchange money are located at Dorval and Mirabel airports and downtown at Complexe Desjardins on Rue Ste-Catherine Ouest between Jeanne-Mance and St-Urbain (daily 6am–2am).

Hospital Montréal General Hospital, 1650 av Cedar (☎937-6011).

Ice-hockey Canada's most successful ice-hockey team, the Montréal Canadiens, play in the fall at their brand-new amphitheatre, the Centre Molson, 1250 Rue de la Gauchetière (☎932-CLUB). Métro: Lucien L'Allier or Bonaventure.

Information MTL-INFO (☎685-4736). Up-to-the-minute information on shows, restaurants, clubs, recreational activities and exhibitions, as well as weather reports and train and bus schedules. This free service can also be used to make reservations for restaurants and shows.

Laundry Le Nettoyeur, 1001 Rue Université, 1447 Rue Drummond and 4090 Rue Ste-Catherine (Mon–Fri 8am–6pm, Sat 8am–noon).

Left luggage There are $1 lockers at the Gare Central and Terminus Voyageur.

Métro information General (☎280-5666); timetable information (☎288-6287); lost and found (☎280-4637).

Pharmacy Pharmaprix Drug Store, 5122 ch de la Côte des Neiges and 901 Rue Ste-Catherine Est; open 24hr.

Post offices The main post offices are Station B, 1250 Rue Université (Mon–Fri 8am–5.45pm, Sat 8am–noon) and Station C, 1250 Rue Ste-Catherine Est (Mon–Fri 8am–5.45pm). The city's poste restante is located at Station A, 285 Rue St-Antoine Ouest (Mon–Fri 8am–5.45pm, Sat 8am–noon).

Ridesharing Allo-Stop, 4317 Rue St-Denis (☎985-3032 or 985-3044). Membership for a passenger costs $6 per year plus you pay the share of petrol. For a driver it's $7 per year and you receive about sixty percent of the fees paid by the passenger. Typical prices are: Ottawa $14, Toronto $26, Québec $15, New York $40.

Sexual Assault Centre Bilingual, 24hr crisis line (☎934-4504).

Taxis Co-op (☎725-9885); Diamond (☎273-6331); Lasalle (☎277-2552). $2.50 minimum fare, then 75¢ per kilometre.

Telephones Bell-Canada, Bureau Public, 700 Rue de la Gauchetière Ouest on the corner of Université (Mon–Fri 9am–5pm).

Train information Via Rail (☎989-2626); Amtrak (☎1-800-USA-RAIL).

Travel agencies La Billeterie, 800 Place Victoria (☎282-1022), offers good prices on air tickets and sells bus and train tickets. Tourbec, 535 Ontario Est (☎288-4455), is excellent for budget travellers.

Weather information (☎636-3302); road conditions (☎673-4121).

White-water rafting The Rivière Rouge offers the best white-water rafting in the Montréal vicinity. Adventures en Eau Vive, R. R., 2 chemin Rivière Rouge, Calumet (☎242-6084 or 1-800-567-6881), runs rafting trips for $67 at the weekend, $63 during the week for groups of over eight people; a smaller group costs more.

Around Montréal

The lake-dotted countryside **around Montréal** offers a range of recuperative pleasures for the city-dweller, from the peaks of the **Laurentian Mountains** north of the metropolis to the lush farmland of **Cantons-de-l'Est** (formerly L'Estrie), east towards the US border. Where the Lower Laurentians meet the St Lawrence's north shore, historic agricultural and religious settlements give an insight into the early days of New France. Further north, the more dramatic Upper Laurentians have sprouted ski resorts by the dozen, but brief hikes from the main centres – all linked by bus to Montréal – will soon get you into a seemingly never-ending forest, patched with deserted lakes and waterways. The developers are also moving in on Cantons-de-l'Est, but lakeside hamlets, tranquil farms and apple orchards still present an enticing rural escape.

Don't expect dramatic, jagged peaks when exploring the Laurentians – five hundred million years of erosion have moulded one of the world's oldest ranges into a rippling landscape of undulating hills and valleys. The mountains extend all the way along the north side of the St Lawrence from the Ottawa River to the Saguenay, with the zone closest to Montréal one of the more accessible. Immediately north of Montréal, the Lower Laurentians are dotted with whitewashed farm cottages and manor houses, but settlement in the Upper Laurentians did not begin until the 1830s, when the construction of the P'tit Train du Nord let in the mining and lumber industries. When the decline in both industries left the area in a depression, salvation came in the form of the recreational demands of the growing populace of Montréal. The region is now one of North America's largest ski areas, with the number of resorts multiplying annually.

Finally, if you are heading for Québec City, consider breaking your journey in the small town of **Trois-Rivières** – an excellent jumping-off point for the beautiful interior of the **Mauricie** Valley.

The Lower Laurentians (Les Basses Laurentides)

Once the domain of various native groups, the **Lower Laurentians** were granted by Ville-Marie's governors to the colony's first seigneurs who, using a modified version of the feudal land system of the motherland, oversaw the development of the land by their tenants, or *habitants*. As the St Lawrence was the lifeline of the colony, these tenant farms were laid out perpendicular to the river in long, narrow rectangular seigneuries. Typical of these is the **Seigneurie de Terrebonne** (late June to Aug Tues–Sun

10am–8pm; free) on the Île des Moulins, a twenty-minute drive via Hwy 25 (exit 17 Est). This was a seigneury from 1673 to 1883, and the restored nineteenth-century buildings – including the manor house of the area's last seigneur and Canada's first francophone millionaire, Joseph Masson – powerfully evoke life under the long regime.

A forty-minute drive northwest of Montréal, via Hwy 13 or 15 then Hwy 640, lies the town of **ST-EUSTACHE**, also served by the slow Montréal-to-Ottawa Voyageur bus. It was here that the frustrations of the *habitants* with the British occupancy met a tragic end in the 1837 Rebellion. In the early 1800s British immigrants to Lower Canada were offered townships (*cantons*) while the francophones were not allowed to expand their holdings, exacerbating the resentment caused by the favouritism extended to the English-speaking businesses in Montréal. The situation was worsened by high taxes on British imports and a savage economic depression in 1837. Wearing Canadian-made garments of *étoffe du pays* as a protest against British imports, the leaders of Lower Canada reform – known as the *Patriotes* – rallied francophones to rebel in Montréal. As Louis-Joseph Papineau, the seigneur whose speeches in the Assembly had encouraged the rebellions, fled the city, fearful that his presence would incite more rioting, the government sent out military detachments to the countryside, the hotbed of the *Patriotes*. Two hundred *Patriotes* took refuge in St-Eustache's church, where eighty of them were killed by British troops, who went on to raze much of the town.

Today, over thirty of the period buildings that survived the battle are still intact – the **church**, at 123 St-Louis, still bears the scars. Rue St-Eustache has the main concentration of sights, with the wedding-cake **Manoir Globensky** at no. 235 (Mon–Fri 9am–noon & 1.15–4.30pm; free) and the eighteenth-century **Moulin Légaré** at no. 232 (late April to mid-Nov Mon–Fri 9am–noon & 1–4.30pm, Sat & Sun 12.30–4.30pm; free), the oldest water-powered flourmill in Canada. If you have time, you could drop by at **La Maison Jean-Hotte**, 405 Grand Côte (May to mid-Oct daily 10am–5pm; $5), a hotchpotch collection of old cars, trains and antique toys.

Oka

Southwest of here, on Hwy 344, lies the small lakeside town of **OKA**, which can also be reached by taking the commuter train from Montréal's Gare Windsor to Hudson on the opposite shore, then catching the free ferry over the river Outaouais. Until recently a quiet resort, Oka achieved national prominence in the summer of 1990 when it became the stage for a confrontation between **Mohawk** warriors and the provincial government. The crisis began when Oka's town council decided to expand its golf course onto a sacred burial ground, a provocation to which the Mohawks responded by arming themselves and barricading Kanesataka, a small reserve near Oka. Although the Native Affairs Minister for Québec was close to reaching an agreement with the Mohawks, the mayor of Oka sent in the provincial police to storm the barricades. In the ensuing fracas a policeman was killed – no one knows by whom, but the autopsy established it was not by a police bullet. Hostilities now reached a new pitch and the two sides became ever more polarized: as the Mohawks set up barricades across the Mercier Bridge, one of Montréal's main commuter arteries, groups of white Québécois attacked them with stones, while sympathetic groups of native people sprang up all over Canada and the USA. The federal government then offered to buy the land for the natives on the condition that they surrender, but the standoff continued as negotiators failed to agree on terms. In the end the crisis lasted 78 days, until the core of fifty Mohawks was encircled by 350 Canadian army soldiers and forced to give up. The fate of the disputed land, along with hundreds of other similar claims, is still being negotiated. However, many believe that the natives went too far at Oka, and the existing distrust between Native Canadians and other Canadians seems to have deepened. As George Erasmus, former national chief of the Assembly of First Nations, said: "Our demands are ignored when we kick up a fuss – but they are also ignored if we do not."

In complete contrast, one of North America's oldest monasteries, the **Abbaye Cistercienne d'Oka**, 1600 chemin d'Oka (Mon–Sat 4–5pm; gardens Mon 1–4.30pm, Tues–Fri 9.30–11.30am & 1–4.30pm, Sat 9am–4pm), commands a spectacular site just outside town, its century-old bell tower rising amidst enveloping hills. The Trappists arrived here from France in 1880, their life in Canada beginning in a miller's house that's now totally overshadowed by the rest of the complex and the landscaped gardens of the abbey. The monastery shop sells a wealth of organic Trappist products, from maple syrup and chocolates to variations on the famed Oka cheese. The nearby **Calvaire d'Oka** with its mid-eighteenth-century chapels is best visited on September 14, when native pilgrims hold the Feast of the Holy Cross along the banks of the Lac des Deux Montagnes. The Calvaire is set in the **Parc d'Oka**, which has 45km of hiking trails: two lead up Colline d'Oka for views of the region, one is 5.5km and goes past the Calvaire, the other is 7.5km and leads to a wonderful viewing area. The only other **place to stay** in Oka itself is the *La Clos des Lilas*, 14 Rue Ste-Anne (☎514/479-8216; ②).

The Upper Laurentians (Les Hautes Laurentides)

The slopes of the **Upper Laurentians**, a vast sweep of coniferous forests dotted with hundreds of tranquil lakes and scored with rivers, was once Montréal's "wilderness back yard". Nowadays the huge silence is shattered in the winter as Québécois take to the slopes at over 25 ski resorts, yet much of the land has been left relatively untouched – like in the **Parc du Mont Tremblant** – and the area is a must when the colours of fall take over.

The Upper Laurentians really cater for families on a week's sporty vacation, and much of the **accommodation** is pricey, as it includes gyms, tennis courts, golf courses and the like. However, a smattering of B&Bs and numerous motels offer an alternative to those on a tight budget, as does the youth hostel, *Le Chalet Beaumont,* in Val-David (see opposite). You could also check out travel agents in Montréal – weekend packages can be a bargain. There's a free telephone accommodation service for the region too (☎1-800-561-6673). **Information** on the resorts is available from the main tourist office in Montréal and offices in the majority of Laurentian towns – pick up the useful *Laurentides* booklet. During the ski season, SkiLine (☎514/875-7558) reports ski conditions as does "The Snow Report" column printed in *The Montréal Gazette.*

Two **roads** lead from Montréal to this area of the Laurentians: the Autoroute des Laurentides (Hwy 15) and the slower Hwy 117. Limocar Laurentides offer regular services from the Voyageur **bus** station in Montréal to most of the towns. In winter the slightly more expensive Aerocar offers a ski bus from Dorval and Mirabel airports to various resorts. Express ski-bus services are also run by Limocar, Murray Hill and Tour Autocar from various downtown hotels and the Voyageur bus station. Rates for **ski passes** are around $30 a day in the decent areas, a few dollars more at weekends.

St-Sauveur-des-Monts

The ski resorts start at **ST-SAUVEUR-DES-MONTS**, 60km from Montréal. Boasting a total of 42 pistes in the immediate vicinity and an ever-increasing number of condominium complexes, its resident population of just four thousand is boosted to a peak-season maximum of thirty thousand. The main drag, Principale, is packed with every type of restaurant, separated by designer boutiques and craft shops competing for the charge cards. Night-time sees numerous flash clubs and discos boogieing till the early hours.

For those with money, this is *the* place to be seen, and hotel prices reflect the fact – the excellent and luxurious *Auberge St-Denis*, 61 St-Denis (☎514/227-4602; ⑥), leads the way for class with a pool and beautifully decorated rooms. Cheaper options are *Dentelle et Café*, 100 Lafleur Nord (☎514/227-7279; ②) or *Auberge de la Vallée*, 520 Rue

Principale (☎514/227-5998; ③). Budget travellers will be pretty well limited to the **food** at Dunns, a branch of Montréal's famous smoked meat deli, located on chemin Lac Milette. **Information** on shopping and skiing is available from the Bureau Touristique, 3rd Floor, 100 Rue Guindon (daily 9am–5pm; ☎514/227-2564).

Val-David
Further north, **VAL-DAVID** is the Bohemian resort of the Laurentians, chosen by artists and craftspeople as a haven from the yuppie developments elsewhere in this beautiful region: the main street, Rue de l'Église, has various galleries and craft shops run by the artisans themselves. Val-David's excellent **youth hostel**, *Le Chalet Beaumont*, 1451 Beaumont (☎819/322-1972; ①), is the only one in the region, a massive chalet with roaring fires in the winter, and great views all year. Located a twenty-minute walk from the bus station, the hostel offers a pick-up service. Other **accommodation** in Val-David is fairly expensive: *Auberge Parkers*, 1340 Lac Pacquin (☎819/322-2026; ⑤), is in the shadow of the ski slopes of Vallée Bleue and its rooms are about as cheap as they come. The swishest ski lodge is *La Sapinière*, by Mont Alta at 1244 chemin de la Sapinière (☎819/322-2020; ⑦), which is built of logs and serves some of the most highly regarded cuisine in the area. Nearby at no. 1267, *La Chaumière aux Marguerites* (☎819/322-2043; ②) is a B&B place. There is one **campground** along Hwy 117 – *Camping Laurentien* (☎819/322-2281) – with pitches from $16. Rue de l'Église has a selection of decent, well-priced **restaurants**, including the friendly, *La Grand Pa*, at no. 2481, and *Le Continent*, at no. 2301, which is good value.

Ste-Agathe-des-Monts
Nearby, on the shores of Lac des Sables, is **STE-AGATHE-DES-MONTS**, a luxurious resort since the 1850s and now the largest town in the Laurentians. Located 97km from Montréal and not entirely quashed by tourism, it is a good base for exploring the less developed towns and the wildlife reserves further north. The **bus** from Montréal arrives at the shopping mall on Hwy 117, across the road from the **information** centre.

The cheapest **accommodation** is above a rowdy bar at the *Auberge du Coin*, 55 Préfontaine Est (☎819/326-4901; ①), a couple of blocks from the main drag. A quieter but pricier stay can be had at the *Auberge de la Tour-du-Lac*, 173 chemin du Tour du Lac (☎819/326-1276; ③), one of the town's most beautiful historic homes with its pointed roof and wraparound veranda; or the duller *Motel Clair de Lune*, 30 Morin (☎819/326-3626; ③). **B&B** is available at *Auberge des Mets*, 242 Rue St-Venant (☎819/326-7692; ②-③), where some rooms have private bathrooms, and *La Villa Verra*, 246 Rue St-Anne (☎819/326-0513; ③), a sweet place with delicious food. The nearest **campground** is *Parc des Campeurs* (☎1-800-561-7360; from $21), 15km from town (follow signs for *"Camping Ste Agathe")*, accessible via exit 53 of Hwy 15, an enormous place with a beach on Lac des Sables.

Most of Ste-Agathe's **restaurants and bars** are concentrated on the lakefront, the most attractive part of town: try *Chez Girard*, at 18 Principale Ouest, for reasonably priced, delicious French cuisine; or *Sauvagine*, 1592 rte 329 nord (☎819/326-7673 or 1-800-767-7172), which is a chapel converted into a French restaurant; they also have **rooms** upstairs; (②–④).

St-Jovite-Mont-Tremblant
Situated some 130km north of Montréal, **ST-JOVITE-MONT-TREMBLANT** is the Laurentians' oldest and most renowned ski area, focused on the range's highest peak, **Mont Tremblant** (960m), so called because the native population believed it was the home of spirits that were capable of moving the mountain. There are 34 slopes on the

mountain for all levels, with a maximum vertical drop of more than 640m – the longest ski run in Québec. One-day ski passes cost $35. In 1997, the company that developed Whistler announced they were pumping some $50 million in Mont-Tremblant over the next five years, so expect a number of major developments in the near future – though no amount of money will stop this being one of the most bitterly cold places to ski in Canada.

St-Jovite is the commercial centre of the area, while Mont-Tremblant (10km north) is a tiny village with only the most basic services. In and around the two are a variety of lodges, including the most glamorous in the Laurentians: *Club Mont-Tremblant*, by Lac Tremblant at the base of the mountain (☎1-800-467-8341; ⑦), and *Auberge Gray Rocks*, near St-Jovite (☎819/425-2771 or 1-800-567-6767; ⑦). Less pricey rooms are available at *Hôtel Mont Tremblant*, 1900 Rue Principale (☎819/425-3232; ④ including breakfast). **Information** is available from Bureau Touristique St-Jovite/Mont-Tremblant, 305 chemin Brébeuf in St-Jovite (daily: June–Sept 9am–7pm; Oct–May 9am–5pm). For **eating** in St-Jovite, there's a cheap French restaurant, *La Darguse*, 889 Rue Ouimet, and a bargain café, *La Brunch Café*, at no. 816.

The **Parc du Mont Tremblant**, a wilderness area of over 1000 square kilometres spreading northwards from the villages, is a favourite with Québécois. Skiing, snowmobiling and snowshoeing are the sports in winter; in summer the park attracts campers, canoeists, hunters and hikers – in the more remote areas you may see bears, deer and moose. The park's three lakeside **campsites** need to be reserved in advance (☎819/688-2281; $14–21). There's no public transport, but hitching is possible.

Cantons-de-l'Est (The Eastern Townships)

Beginning about 80km southeast of Montréal and extending to the US border, **Cantons-de-l'Est** was once Québec's best-kept secret, but its nineteenth-century villages are fast becoming no more than shopping arcades fringed with condominium complexes for Montréal commuters. A growing ski industry – concentrated around Mont Sutton, just north of the Vermont border – is making its mark on the land too. However, the region's agricultural roots are still evident, especially in spring, when the maple trees are tapped for syrup. At this time of year remote *cabanes à sucre* offer sleigh rides and Québec fare such as "Taffy" – strips of syrup frozen in the snow.

The land, once the domain of scattered groups of natives, was first cultivated by United Empire Loyalists hounded out of the United States after the American Revolution. Their loyalty to the crown resulted in land grants from the British, and townships with very English names like Sherbrooke and Granby were founded at this time. In the mid-nineteenth century the townships opened up to industry, which attracted an influx of French Canadians seeking work: today, 95 percent of the 400,000 population are francophone. The area's new French name, L'Estrie, was abandoned only recently for the name Cantons-de-l'Est, a direct translation of the area's original English name of the Eastern Townships.

Cantons-de-l'Est can be reached from Montréal by the Autoroute de Cantons-de-l'Est (Hwy 10), which has a useful information centre for the whole region at exit 68 (daily: June–Sept 10am–6pm; Oct–May 9am–5pm; ☎1-800-355-5755) or the more picturesque Hwy 112. Most of the villages and towns are served regularly by Voyageur **buses** from Montréal, and VIA Rail runs a Montréal-to-Sherbrooke **train**, which continues on to New Brunswick and Nova Scotia.

Granby

Coming from Montréal, Cantons-de-l'Est begins at the sprawling and mundane city of **GRANBY**, renowned for the **Zoo de Granby** (mid-May to Aug daily 10am–5pm; Sept Sat & Sun 10am–5pm; adults and over-4s $16) – Québec's best-known zoo and an absolute nightmare. The animals are kept in terrible conditions without a blade of grass in sight and most look suicidal. The town redeems itself with the **Centre d'Interpretation de la Nature du Lac Bolvin**, 700 Drummond (daily 6.30am–4.30pm; free) where observation towers allow a terrific vantage point for watching birds peck and preen on the marsh. Granby's **information centre**, at 650 Principale (June–Sept daily 10am–6pm; Oct–May Mon–Fri 9am–5pm; ☎372-7273 or 1-800-567-7273), can supply a copy of the *Eastern Townships* booklet, which has up-to-date listings of the region's accommodation and activities. There are several motels along Principale, should you get stuck here.

Magog and around

The summer resort town of **MAGOG**, less than 60km further east, gets its name from a corruption of a native word meaning "great expanse of water". The expanse of water in question is one of the township's largest lakes, **Lac Memphremagog**, which reaches right into the town and is unremarkable except for the fact that Sylvester Stallone and Donald Sutherland have homes on its shore and a strange beast known as Memphré apparently lurks in its waters (the subject of various fishy tales since 1798). A cruise boat plies the lake daily in summer and at weekends in September and October (1hr 45min; $12). There's also the option of a ride to Newport in the US (June–Aug 2–3 weekly; $45 including meals); call ☎843-8058 for reservations. To explore the area by bike, on the numerous well-kept trails, Ski-Vélo Vincent Richard, 49 Sherbrooke, can provide you with wheels for around $10 a day. The other draw is **Mont Orford Park**, accessed via Hwy 141, where you can ski on Mount Orford (859m) in winter (daily 8.30am–4pm; day ski passes $32.75) or hike in the summer – the chair lift operates year-round ($7.95).

The **bus** stops on Sherbrooke; turn right and right again to reach the main drag, Principale. The Magog **information centre** is located at 55 rue Cabana, access by Hwy 112 (June–Sept daily 10am–6pm; Oct–May Mon–Fri 9am–5pm). In the event that you decide to stay, there's a huge number of places to choose from. The century-old houses converted into **B&Bs** are the best option for atmosphere: try *La Vieille Chapelle Ramsay*, 193 chemin des Pères (☎819/847-0120; ③), where bizarre murals offer the opportunity to sleep with angels; *Au Coeur du Magog*, 120 Merry Nord (☎819/868-2511; ②), is a fine old house with home-made breakfasts, and *La Belle Victorienne*, 142 Merry Nord (☎819/847-0476; ②), has beautiful gardens and comfy rooms. For **hotels**, *Auberge Orford*, 20 Merry Sud (☎819/843-9361; ②), is a cheap but noisy option with its own pub; *Auberge du Grand Lac*, 40 Merry Sud (☎819/843-4039; ⑤ including breakfast), is the pink house near the lake with a rooftop terrace for sunsets, offering full facilities, comfortable rooms and a basic breakfast. Several **bars and restaurants** can be found along Principale: *Aux Plaisirs des Dieux* is a teashop at no. 468, and is cake heaven, and you can get veggie food at *Bonjour Santé* at no. 351. Most people hang out at the bistro/bar *La Grosse Pomme* at no. 276 in the evening.

ORFORD, 5km north of Magog, is a less hectic base for the park. *Le Gîte de la Tour*, 1837 Alfred-Desrochers (☎819/868-0753; ②), is a charming inn or, in the summer, there's a great **youth hostel**, *La Grand Fugue,* 3165 chemin du Parc (Hwy 141) (☎819/843-8595 or 1-800-567-6155; ①), actually in the park. For more luxury, *Auberge Au Lion d'Or*, 2240 chemin du Parc (☎819/843-6000; ⑤), has a health spa and a heated outdoor pool.

Near the northwest corner of the park, a twenty-minute drive from Magog, are the unusual **Kebec Crystal Mines**, located near the village of **Bonsecours** off Hwy 243 (June–Sept daily 10am–5pm; guided tours at the weekends – phone ahead to book an English-speaking tour, on ☎514/535-6550; $6). This small operation is the only quartz crystal mine in Canada, and it's a peaceful place that just mines enough to sell in the shop. North America's largest crystal, a whopping great smoky quartz from Brazil, is here, and there are regular quartz-crystal-bowl "concerts", when extraordinary singing harmonies are produced.

About 25km south of Magog, just off the road to Austin, is the **Abbaye St-Benoît-du-Lac**, its presence signalled by its white granite turrets. Occupied by about sixty Benedictine monks (many of them under a vow of silence) and a small number of nuns, it's renowned as a refuge for flustered politicians and prominent figures who need a time of contemplation, but the abbey's doors are open to anyone who wants to stay, in accordance with the order's tradition of hospitality. Food and **accommodation** are free, though a donation is expected. There is no public transport to the abbey; a taxi costs about $25 from Magog.

On the lake's opposite shore lies **GEORGEVILLE**, accessible via Hwy 247 from Magog. A totally unspoilt hamlet, its clapboard buildings, which include an old general store, are set around a village green on the lake border. There's one **hotel**, the *Auberge Georgeville*, 71 chemin Channel (☎819/843-8683; ⑥).

Sherbrooke and around

The 100,000-strong university town of **SHERBROOKE**, 147km east of Montréal, revels in the title "Queen of the Eastern Townships", a strange accolade for the town with the lowest average wage in Canada. To be fair, it doesn't feel overly impoverished, but it's no great shakes, with just two mild attractions in the shape of the **Musée des Beaux Arts de Sherbrooke**, 174 Palais (Tues–Sun 1–5pm, Wed till 9pm; $2), a display of local work that includes a fairly impressive collection of Naive painters and the **Musée du Séminaire de Sherbrooke**, 222 Frontenac (May–Aug daily 10am–5pm; Sept–April Tues–Sun 12.30–4.30pm; $4), which consists of the dusty **Musée de la Tour** up in the seminary's tower, with row upon row of glass cases displaying a collection that includes pickled toads, stuffed bison heads, shells, crystals and mocassins. Around the corner, the other part of the museum, **Centre d'Exposition Léon-Marcotte**, has changing, interactive displays on the natural sciences.

The **bus** station, with connections to and from Montréal, Québec City and various local towns, is at 20 King Ouest. The **information** centre is located in the **train** station at 48 Dépôt (daily: June–Sept 9am–6pm; Oct–May 9am–5pm).

The cheapest **accommodation** in summer is the student residence at 2500 blvd Université Sherbrooke (☎819/821-7000; ②). Otherwise there are numerous modern motels along King Street Ouest: the cheapest are the three-star *L'Ermitage* at no. 1888 (☎819/569-5551; ②) and *Motel la Réserve* at no. 4235 (☎819/566-6464; ④). For a more expensive stay, the brand-new *Delta Hotel*, 2685 King Ouest (☎819/822-1989 or 1-800-268-1133; ⑤), is probably the plushest in town.

Restaurants, **bars** and **cafés** are also concentrated along King Street Ouest and the cross-streets of Wellington, just by the bus station, and Belvédère, four blocks further west. Try the well-priced bistro *Bla-Bla Café*, 2 Wellington, or *Au Four à Bois*, 3025 King Ouest, for a sound pizza. *King Hall*, 286 King Ouest, is good for a beer or lunch-time meal. Award-winning local specialities are served at *La Falaise Saint-Michel* at 100 Webster.

The region south of Sherbrooke holds its Loyalist connections dear, and this is one of the few areas in Québec where you'll encounter vestiges of the snobbish anglophone attitudes that once pervaded the whole province. **NORTH HATLEY**, a ten-minute drive from Sherbrooke, is a veritable anglophone bastion, with boutiques selling Lipton teas, Liberty products, tweeds and Aran jumpers – and a population that steadfastly refuses to have their home's name changed to Hatley Nord. Situated right on the shore of Lake Massawippi, with clapboard houses painted in pastel shades, the hamlet is primarily a resort for rich Canadians and Americans, who first adopted the area for vacations during Prohibition. The village boasts two of Québec's classiest inns: the romantic turn-of-the-century five-star *Manoir Hovey* (☎819/842-2421 or 1-800-661-2421; ⑧) and *Auberge Hatley* (☎819/842-2451; ⑥). If you can afford to **stay**, book rooms early. The cuisine in the inns is also renowned, but those on a tight budget will be limited to *Le Pilsen*, 55 Main, an English-style **pub** with locally brewed draught and basic meals.

Montréal to Québec City

There are two **autoroutes** covering the 270km between Montréal and Québec City: the boring Hwy 20 along the south shore, and Hwy 40 along the north shore, which is flanked by the farms of the seigneurial regime. The slower Hwy 138 meanders along the north shore, giving a closer look at rural Québec. VIA Rail **trains** and Voyageur **buses** connect the two cities with regular services, the slower buses stopping at various towns en route.

Trois-Rivières

The major town between the two cities is **TROIS-RIVIÈRES**, straddling the three channels of the St Maurice River midway between Montréal and Québec. European settlement dates from 1634, when the town established itself as an embarkation point for the French explorers of the continent and as an iron-ore centre. Lumber followed, and today Trois-Rivières is one of the world's largest producers of paper, the delta chockfull of logs to be pulped. It's often dismissed as an industrial city and little else, but its shady streets of historic buildings – neither as twee as Québec City, nor as monumental as Vieux-Montréal – are well worth a wander, and the town is a good starting point for exploring the Mauricie Valley.

Trois-Rivières's compact downtown core is centred on the small square of Parc du Champlain. Rue Bonaventure runs from near the bus station to the square and the neo-Gothic **Cathédrale de l'Assomption** (daily 7–11.30am & 2–5.30pm; free), with its Florentine stained-glass windows. One of the town's oldest buildings, now the **information centre** (summer daily 9am–5pm; winter Mon–Fri only), is close by at 168 Rue Bonaventure: the **Manoir Boucher-de-Niverville** is a pretty white manor hosting a small collection of eighteenth-century Québécois furniture and dating from 1730, when it was the home of the local seigneur. Further down Bonaventure, a left turn leads into the narrow and ancient Rue des Ursulines, where at no. 864 the three-storey **Manoir de-Tonnancour** (Tues–Fri 1.30–5pm, Sat & Sun 1–6pm; free) holds temporary exhibitions on various themes from stamps to sculpture. Local art is on display at **Maison Hertel-de-la-Fresnière** at no. 802 (Tues–Thurs 9.30am–4.30pm, Fri 9.30am–9pm, Sat 9.30am–5pm; free), which also serves as a Maison des Vins and an exhibition space for local artists. Dominating the street is the slender silver dome of the **Musée-des-Ursulines**, established by a small group of Ursuline nuns who arrived from Québec City in 1697. The chapel, though badly damaged by fire in 1897, has attractive frescoes and gilt sculptures, whilst the nunnery's treasures are displayed in a little museum in the old hospital quarters (May–Sept Tues–Fri 9am–5pm; Nov–April Wed–Sun 1.30–5pm; closed Oct; free).

On the nearby, rather characterless waterfront, the **Centre d'Exposition sur l'Industrie des Pâtes et Papiers**, 800 Parc Portuaire (June–Aug daily 9am–6pm; Sept Sat & Sun 11am–5pm; $2.50), has an informative if unthrilling exhibition on the industry that's the backbone of the community. Finally, the ruined buildings of **Les Forges du St-Maurice**, which put the town on the map as a supplier to the farmers and arsenals of Québec and Europe, is now a national historic park, linked to downtown by bus #4 (May–Oct daily 9am–5pm; $3).

The bureau de Tourisme, in the Manoir Boucher (see above), has **information** on all the town's activities and sights. For **accommodation**, the cheapest option is the clean and comfortable **youth hostel**, *Auberge la Flottille*, in the heart of downtown at 497 Radisson (☎819/378-8010; ①). **B&B** is available at the ten-roomed *Gîte du Huard*, 42 rue St-Louis (☎819/375-8771; ②–④), in the old part of the city, one of the rooms has a kitchenette. Centrally located **hotels** include the high-rise *Delta*, 1620 Notre-Dame (☎819/376-1991; ⑥), and *Des Gouverneurs*, 975 Hart (☎819/379-4550; ④), which are both modern hotels with full facilities. For **food**, try *Creperie des Korrigans*, blvd des Forges, for pancakes; the *Gaspard* restaurant, 475 blvd des Forges (☎819/691-0679), serves the best seafood and beef dishes; whilst *Le Bolvert*, 1556 Rue Royale, offers excellent healthy fare; and *Le Zenob*, 171 Bonaventure, is a bar with a small terrace that also sells sandwiches.

The Mauricie

North of Trois-Rivières lies the mountainous area of the St-Maurice valley – the **Mauricie** – where the best of the landscape is demarcated by the **Parc National de la Mauricie** (May–Nov), over 500 square kilometres of soft-contoured hills, lakeland, rivers, waterfalls, sheer rock faces and breathtaking views. There is no public transport to the park, but a Voyageur bus leaves Trois-Rivières for Grand-Mère (45km) daily at 12.15pm, returning at 6.35pm. Hitching the 20km from Grand-Mère to the park's southeast entrance should not take too long, so this allows for an afternoon in the park. Information centres at the park's entrances have excellent maps and booklets about the park's well-maintained hiking trails, canoe routes and bike paths, and also provide canoe rental. **Camping** places are allocated at the centres on a first-come, first-served basis, though the hundreds of available places are rarely filled.

QUÉBEC CITY

Spread over Cap Diamant and the banks of the St Lawrence, **QUÉBEC CITY** is Canada's most beautifully located and most historic city. Vieux-Québec, surrounded by solid fortifications, is the only walled city in North America, a fact that prompted UNESCO to classify it as a World Heritage Treasure in 1985. In both parts of the Old City – Haute and Basse – the winding cobbled streets are flanked by seventeenth- and eighteenth-century stone houses and churches, graceful parks and squares, and countless monuments. Although some districts have been overly renovated to give the tourists as seductive an introduction to Québec as possible, this is an authentically and profoundly French city: 96 percent of its 500,000 population are French-speaking, and it is often difficult to remember which continent you are in as you tuck into a croissant and a steaming bowl of coffee in a café full of the aromas and sounds of Paris. Moreover, despite the fact that the city's symbol is a hotel, the **Château Frontenac**, the government remains the main employee, not tourism, and some of the more impressive buildings remain government-run and off limits.

Arriving from Montréal you're immediately struck by the differences between the province's two main cities. Whilst Montréal is international, dynamic and forward-thinking, Québec City is more than a shade provincial, often seeming too bound up with its religious and military past – a residue of the days when the city was the bastion of the Catholic Church in Canada. On the other hand, the Church can claim much of the credit for the creation and preservation of the finest buildings, from the quaint **Église Notre-Dame-des-Victoires** to the decadently opulent **Basilique Notre-Dame de Québec** and the vast **Seminary**. In contrast, the austere defensive structures, dominated by the massive **Citadelle**, reveal the military pedigree of a city dubbed by Churchill as the "Gibraltar of North America", while the battlefield of the **Plains of Abraham** are now a national historic park. Of the city's rash of museums, two are essential visits – the modern **Musée de la Civilisation**, in Vieux-Québec, expertly presenting all aspects of French-Canadian society, and the recently expanded **Musée du Québec**, in the Haute-Ville, west of Vieux-Québec, which has the finest art collection in the province.

Outside the city limits, the town of **Lévis** and the Huron reservation, **Wendake**, make worthwhile excursions, whilst the churches and farmland of the **Côte-de-Beaupré** and the **Île d'Orléans** hark back to the days of the seigneurs and *habitants*. The gigantic **Basilique de Ste-Anne-de-Beaupré**, attracting millions of pilgrims annually, is one of the most impressive sights in Québec, and for equally absorbing natural sights there are the spectacular waterfalls at **Montmorency** and **Sept-Chutes**, and the wildlife reserve in the **Laurentians**.

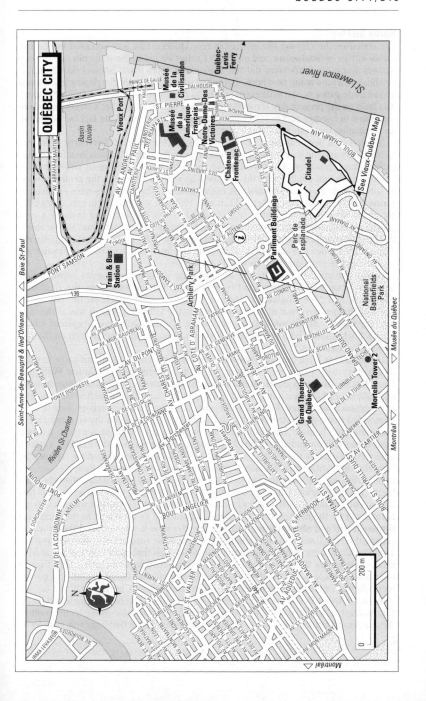

QUÉBEC CITY

St Lawrence River

Québec-Levis Ferry

Musée de la Civilisation

Musée de la Amérique Français

Notre-Dame-Des Victoires

Vieux Port

Basin Louise

Château Frontenac

See Vieux-Québec Map

BOUL CHAMPLAIN

Citadel

Parliment Buildings

Parc de l'esplanade

Train & Bus Station

Artillery Park

National Battlefields Park

△ Musée du Québec

△ Montréal

Grand Theatre de Québec

Mortello Tower 2

Rivière St-Charles

Saint-Anne-de-Beaupré & Ile d'Orleans △ △ Baie St-Paul

BOUL LANGELIER

200 m

N

△ Montreal

Some history

For centuries the cliff-top site of what is now Québec City was occupied by the **Iroquois** village of **Stadacona**, and although Cartier visited in the sixteenth century permanent European settlement did not begin until 1608, when Samuel de Champlain established a fur-trading post here. To protect what was rapidly developing into a major inland trade gateway, the settlement shifted to the cliff-top in 1620 when Fort St-Louis was built on the present-day site of the Château Frontenac. Québec's steady expansion was noted in London, and in 1629 Champlain was starved out of the fort by the British, an occupation that lasted just three years.

Missionaries began arriving in 1615, and by the time Bishop Laval arrived in 1659 Québec City and the surrounding province were in the grip of Catholicism. In the city's earliest days, however, the merchants of the fur trade wielded most power and frequently came into conflict with the priests, who wanted a share in the profits in order to spread their message amongst the native peoples. The wrangles were resolved by **Louis XIV**, who assumed power in France in 1661 and was advised to take more interest in his kingdom's mercantile projects. By 1663 New France had become a royal province, administered by a council appointed directly by the crown and answerable to the king's council in France. Three figures dominated the proceedings: the governor, responsible for defence and external relations; the intendant, administering justice and overseeing the economy; and, inevitably, the bishop.

Before the century was out, the long-brewing European struggles between England and France spilled over into the colony with French attacks on the English in New York and New England in 1689 and a foiled naval attack on the city by Sir William Phipps, governor of Massachusetts, in the following year. It was at this time that the **Comte de Frontenac**, known as the "fighting governor", replaced Champlain's Fort St-Louis with the sturdier Château St-Louis, and began work on the now famous fortifications.

In September 1759, during the Seven Years' War, the most significant battle in Canada's history took place here, between the British under general **James Wolfe** and Louis Joseph, **Marquis de Montcalm**. The city had already been under siege from the opposite shore for three months and Montcalm had carefully protected the city from any approach by water. Finally, Wolfe and his four thousand troops heard of an unguarded track, scaled the cliff of Cap Diamant and crept up on the sleeping French regiment from behind. The twenty-minute battle on the Plains of Abraham left both leaders mortally wounded and the city of Québec in the hands of the English, a state of affairs confirmed by the Treaty of Paris in 1763. Madame de Pompadour commented: "It makes little difference; Canada is useful only to provide me with furs."

In 1775 – the year after the Québec Act of 1774 allowed French-Canadians to retain their Catholic religion, language and culture – the town was attacked again, this time by the Americans, who had already captured Montréal. The battle was won by the British and for the next century the city quietly earned its livelihood as the centre of a **timber-trade** and **shipbuilding** industry. By the time it was declared the provincial capital of Lower Canada in 1840, though, the accessible supplies of timber had run out. The final blow came with the appearance of steamships that could travel as far as Montréal, while sailing ships had found it difficult to proceed beyond Québec City. Ceasing to be a busy seaport, the city declined into a centre of small industry and local government, its way of life still largely determined by the Catholic Church.

With the Quiet Revolution in the 1960s and the rise of Québec nationalism, Québec City became a symbol of the glory of the French heritage – for example, the motto *Je me souviens* ("I remember") above the doors of its parliament buildings was transferred

The Québec area telephone code is ☎418.

to the licence plates of Québec cars, to sweep the message across Canada. Though the city played little active part in the changes, it has grown with the upsurge in the francophone economy, developing a suburbia of shopping malls and convention centres as slick as any in the country.

Arrival, information and city transport

Québec City's **airport**, 20km west of the city, caters almost exclusively for domestic flights, primarily those of Air Canada and Canadian Airlines: most international flights arrive at Montréal. A bus leaves for downtown at 8am and 5pm every day, or a shuttle connects the airport with several downtown hotels ($7.50 to Vieux-Québec). The twenty-minute trip by taxi will cost you about $30.

Trains from Montréal arrive at the central Gare du Palais in Basse-Ville, whereas services from the Atlantic provinces arrive at Lévis, across the St Lawrence, from where there's a regular ferry. **The long-distance bus** terminal is at 320 Abraham-Martin, adjoining the Gare du Palais (see "Listings" on pp.263 and 264 for bus and train information numbers). **Parking** downtown can be a real pain: it's best to leave your vehicle outside the centre, off Grande Allée (for parking details, see "Listings" on p.264).

Information

For **information** about Québec City's sights and events and an accommodation service, the main information centre is near Porte St-Louis at 60 d'Auteuil (mid-March to June Mon–Fri 8.30am–5.15pm; June–Aug daily 8.30am–7.45pm; Sept to mid-Oct daily 8.30am–5.15pm; mid-Oct to mid-March Mon–Fri 9am–4.45pm; ☎692-2471). An information centre for the city has recently opened at 835 av Wilfred-Laurier. Information on the whole province is available at the central Maison du Tourisme de Québec on the other side of Place d'Armes from Château Frontenac at 12 Ste-Anne (daily: early June to Aug 8.30am–7.30pm; Sept to early June 9am–5pm; ☎641-2280 or 1-800-363-7777). Both centres provide an adequate free map and a booklet, *Greater Québec Area*, which lists the latest opening hours and entrance fees.

Transport

Québec City's sights and hotels are packed into a small area, so walking is the best way of getting around. Motorcycles are banned from Vieux-Québec. For sights further out, like the Musée du Québec, STCUQ **local buses** are efficient and run from around 6am to 1am. Fares are a standard $1.50 per journey by pre-paid ticket, available at newsstands, grocery stores and supermarkets across town, as are one-day passes ($4); the cash fare per journey is $1.85, exact fare only. If you need more than one bus to complete your journey, pick up a transfer (*une correspondance*) from the driver, which enables you to take the second bus for no extra charge. The main bus stop in Vieux-Québec is on the west side at Place d'Youville, near Porte St-Jean. The terminus for all STCUQ buses is at Place Jacques-Cartier, reachable by buses #3, #5, #7, #8 and #30 from Place d'Youville.

Accommodation

The **accommodation** in Québec City is perfect for budget travellers. In the Vieux-Québec quarter there are three **youth hostels**, and the **budget hotels** are as well located as those at the top end. However, the city is one of Canada's most frequented tourist destinations, so try to reserve in advance, particularly during the summer months and the Carnaval in February. Even at those times, though, you're not likely to find the city completely full, as the suburbs have masses of motels, all of them just a local bus ride away.

The hotels in Vieux-Québec are usually renovated town houses with the rooms fitted to provide a variety of accommodation. For cheaper rooms, in category ①, head for the area around rues St-Louis and Ste-Ursule, streets that are lined with budget hotels; the posher places are around the Jardin des Gouverneurs in the shadow of the prestigious Château Frontenac and in the Latin Quarter. In Basse-Ville, hotel accommodation is surprisingly more expensive and options are limited to a couple of special places mentioned here or a mass of run-of-the-mill motels.

All of Québec City's **campgrounds** are around 20km outside town, which means they are only convenient for those with their own transport; the ones recommended below are the closest.

Basse-Ville

Auberge Sainte-Antoine, 10 Rue Saint-Antoine (☎692-2211 or 1-888-692-2211, fax 692-1177). Close to the Musée de la Civilisation. Cosy hotel divided into two buildings with a wonderful wooden hall. Some rooms have views of the river and all are tastefully decorated. ⑧.

Le Priori, 15 Rue du Saul-au-Matelot (☎522-8108, fax 692-0883). Tastefully renovated old house; an excellent place to stay. ⑥.

Avenue Ste-Geneviève

Hôtel Cap-Diamant, 39 Ste-Geneviève (☎694-0313). Two-star, nine-bedroom guesthouse with Victorian furnishings near Jardin des Gouverneurs. Rooms all have bathrooms. ③.

Hôtel au Château Fleur de Lys, 15 Ste-Geneviève (☎694-1884). Just off the Jardin, on the corner of Laporte. Air-conditioned rooms. ⑤.

Hôtel le Château de Pierre, 17 Ste-Geneviève (☎694-0429, fax 694-0153). An 1853 mansion with plush rooms also just off the Jardin. Two stars. ⑤.

Maison du Fort, 21 Ste-Geneviève (☎692-4375, fax 692-5253). Another small guesthouse near Jardin des Gouverneurs with air-conditioned rooms. ⑤.

Hôtel Manoir Ste-Geneviève, 13 Ste-Geneviève (☎ & fax 694-1666). Sitting in the shadow of the Château Frontenac, this charming four-star hotel dating from 1880 has beautiful Victorian rooms. ⑤.

Hôtel Manoir sur le Cap, 9 Ste-Geneviève (☎694-1987, fax 667-6395). Cheapest hotel overlooking the Jardin des Gouverneurs. Some rooms have air conditioning and all have TVs. ⑦.

Rue St-Louis

Auberge St-Louis, 48 St-Louis (☎692-2424, fax 692-3797). The cheapest two-star inn in the St-Louis area. Basic furnishings but comfy, and with an excellent location. ④.

Hôtel le Clos St-Louis, 71 St-Louis (☎694-1311 or 1-800-461-1311, fax 694-9411). Another two-star with simple, clean rooms with TVs. ⑤.

Jardin des Gouverneurs and around

Hôtel Château Bellevue, 16 Rue Laporte (☎692-2573 or 1-800-463-2617, fax 692-4876). Modern hotel in an old building, with views of the Jardin and the Château Frontenac. Free parking. ⑤.

Hôtel Château de Léry, 8 Rue Laporte (☎692-2692 or 1-800-363-0036, fax 692-5231). One of the less pricey hotels right on the Jardin des Gouverneurs and recently renovated. Two-star rooms. ④.

Hôtel Château de la Terrasse, 6 Terrasse Dufferin (☎694-9472, fax 694-0055). The better rooms have the best views in town, overlooking the St Lawrence. ④.

Le Château Frontenac, 1 Rue de la Carrières (☎692-3861 or 1-800-441-1414, fax 692-1751). This opulent Victorian "castle", built for William Van Horne, president of CP Railways, in 1893, has accommodated such dignitaries as Churchill, Roosevelt, Madame Chiang Kai-shek and Queen Elizabeth II. It's the most expensive place in town, with splendid rooms, and even offers its own guided tours. ⑧.

Hôtel au Jardin du Gouverneur, 16 Rue Mont-Carmel (☎692-1704, fax 692-1713). On the corner of Mont-Carmel and Laporte, next to the Château Frontenac. Seventeen rooms all with adjoining bathrooms. ⑤.

Rue Ste-Ursule

Hôtel l'Ermitage, 60 Ste-Ursule (☎694-0968, fax 694-2234). Quality hotel with ten bedrooms, all of which have bathrooms and air conditioning. Free parking. ⑥.

Hôtel Maison Acadienne, 42 Ste-Ursule (☎694-0280 or 1-800-463-0280, fax 694-0458). Three ancestral dwellings with cosy rooms and shared bathrooms. ④.

Hôtel la Maison Demers, 68 Ste-Ursule (☎692-2487 or 1-800-692-2487). Parking and breakfast included in the price; the more expensive rooms have bathrooms en suite. ③.

Maison Ste-Ursule, 40 Ste-Ursule (☎ & fax 694-9794). Built in 1780, with green shutters, tiny doors and bare-bones furnishing. ②.

Manoir la Salle, 18 Ste-Ursule (☎682-9953). Small red-brick hotel that is typical of Quebec's first houses. Only one of the nine rooms is en suite. ②.

Rue Ste-Anne and Rue d'Auteuil

Auberge la Chouette, 71 d'Auteuil (☎694-0232). In the road running parallel to Ste-Ursule, in the shadow of the city walls; all rooms have bathrooms. ③.

Auberge du Trésor, 20 Ste-Anne (☎694-1876). Modern rooms with private bathrooms in a house built in 1676. ④.

Auberge de la Place d'Armes, 24 Ste-Anne (☎694-9485, fax 694-1315). Perfectly located opposite the Anglican Cathedral, on the pedestrianized part of Ste-Anne. ④.

Hôtel Clarendon, 57 Ste-Anne (☎692-2480 or 1-800-463-5250, fax 692-4052). Québec City's oldest hotel, dating from 1870. Renovated in the 1930s, it has a classic Art Deco reception area. ⑤.

Hôtel la Maison Doyon, 109 Ste-Anne (☎694-1720, fax 694-1164). Well situated near the Latin Quarter with a helpful landlord. ④.

Hôtel le Manoir d'Auteuil, 49 d'Auteuil (☎694-1173, fax 694-0081). Lavish 1835 town house by the city walls, with three-star rooms. ⑥.

Elsewhere in Vieux-Québec

Hôtel Belley, 249 Rue St-Paul (☎692-1694, fax 692-1696). Eight-bedroomed, slickly designed hotel near the Gare du Palais. Three-star rooms, with off-season price reductions. ③.

Hôtel Manoir des Remparts, 3.5 Rue des Remparts (☎692-2056, fax 692-1125). At the north end of Vieux-Québec on the ramparts, near the Latin Quarter, with views of the St Lawrence. Simple hotel with some en-suite rooms and TVs and telephones. ③.

Hôtel Manoir Victoria, 44 côte du Palais (☎692-1030 or 1-800-463-6283, fax 692-3822). A four-star hotel, off St-Jean. Rambling manor with pool, sauna, gym and modern rooms. ⑧.

Au Petit Hôtel, 3 Ruelle des Ursulines (☎694-0965, fax 692-4320). Located in a peaceful cul-de-sac just off Ste-Ursule, parallel to St-Louis. ③.

Motels, hostels and student accommodation

Auberge de la Paix, 31 Rue Couillard (☎694-0735). Situated in the Latin Quarter, this is by far the best hostel in Québec City. Bike rental is available, and the rate includes breakfast. ①.

Centre International de Séjour de Québec, 19 Rue Ste-Ursule (☎694-0755 or 1-800-461-8585, fax 694-2278). The official youth hostel, located in a former boarding school, is often full and is very impersonal, though it offers laundry facilities, bike rental, luggage lockers and tourist information. Curfew is 11pm and discounts are offered in winter. ①.

Motel Doyon, 1215 Rue Ste-Foy (☎527-4408). One of the cheapest motels around, in the University suburb of Ste-Foy. Basic but clean, with free parking. 10min bus ride to Vieux-Québec. ①.

Services des Residences de l'Université Laval, Pavillion Alphonse-Marie-Parent, Room 1643, Cité Universitaire, Ste-Foy (☎656-5632). Single and double rooms are available in the student residences, a ten-minute bus ride from Haute-Ville. Early May to mid-Aug. ①.

YWCA, 855 av Holland (☎683-2155, fax 663-5526). Chiefly for women only, though couples are allowed in the summer. Located just off chemin St-Louis, about a 15min bus ride from the Old Town. ②.

Campgrounds

Camping Aéroport, 2050 Route de l'Aéroport (☎871-1574, fax 877-0739). Take exit 305 off Hwy 440 onto Route de l'Aeroport – the campsite is around 5km north of the airport itself. $18 for a party of four.

Camping Base de Plein Air Ste-Foy, Rue Laberge, Ste-Foy (☎654-4641, fax 654-4162). Exit 305 off Hwy 440 leads to this park-set campsite. Reservations recommended. $20 for a party of four.

Camping Municipal de Beauport, 95 Rue Serenité, Beauport, off Boulevard Rochette (☎666-2228, fax 656-2360). Take exit 322 off Hwy 40. Bus #800 to Beauport, then #50 or #55. June–Sept. $20 for a party of four.

The City

Québec City spreads from its historic heart into a bland suburbia but the highlights lie beside the St Lawrence, with main attractions being evenly distributed between the upper and lower portions of what is known as **Vieux-Québec** (Old Québec). On the Cap Diamant, **Haute-Ville** (Upper Town) spreads along the St Lawrence from the old city walls and the furthest you need to wander from here is to the Musée du Québec, set in the extensive parkland of the Plains of Abraham. As the oldest part of the city this area comprises some of the main sights of interest, including the magnificent Citadelle. The Terrasse Dufferin is also worth a stroll to watch street entertainers, café life, unproductive students, or the views over the river. The second part of the city, the **Basse-Ville** (or Lower Town) is connected to Haute-Ville by funicular from Terrasse Dufferin or by several windy streets and stairs. One of the main pleasures of the area, beside the wonderful old houses and small museums, is the Musèe de la Civilisation.

This itinerary begins at Vieux-Québec's **Place d'Armes** and then explores the upper part of Vieux-Québec and the Haute-Ville as far west as the Musée du Québec. To finish the tour, you can explore Vieux-Québec's compact Basse-Ville, which can be reached directly from Place d'Armes. Strapped between the cliffs and the St Lawrence, this district is of considerable interest and is a pleasant area to wander around.

Place d'Armes and around

The ten square kilometres of Vieux-Québec, encircled by the city walls, form the Québec City of the tourist brochures. Its centre of gravity is the main square, the **Place d'Armes**, whose central fountain serves in the summer as a resting place for weary sightseers. It was here that Champlain established his first fort, on the site now occupied by the gigantic **Château Frontenac**, probably Canada's most photographed building. Commissioned by the Canadian Pacific Railway in 1893, New York architect Bruce Price drew upon the French-Canadian style of the surroundings to produce a pseudo-medieval red-brick pile crowned with a copper roof – an over-the-top design to make the most of the stupendous location atop Cap Diamant. Numerous celebrities, including Queen Elizabeth II have stayed here, and the hotel has hosted one pair or more of newlyweds every night since it opened. The hotel has guided tours (May to mid-Oct daily 10am–6pm; mid-Oct to April Sat & Sun 1–5pm; $5.50; reservations on ☎691-2166).

The cape's cliff top is fringed by the wide boardwalk of the **Terrasse Dufferin**, which runs alongside the chateau to the fortifications of the Citadelle overlooking the narrowing of the river that was known to the natives as the *kebec* – the source of the province's name. At the beginning of the walkway – which offers charming views of the river – stands a romantic statue of Champlain and, beside it, a modern sculpture symbolizing Québec's status as a UNESCO site. From here the steep Frontenac steps and a funicular descend to Vieux-Québec's Basse-Ville (see p.257).

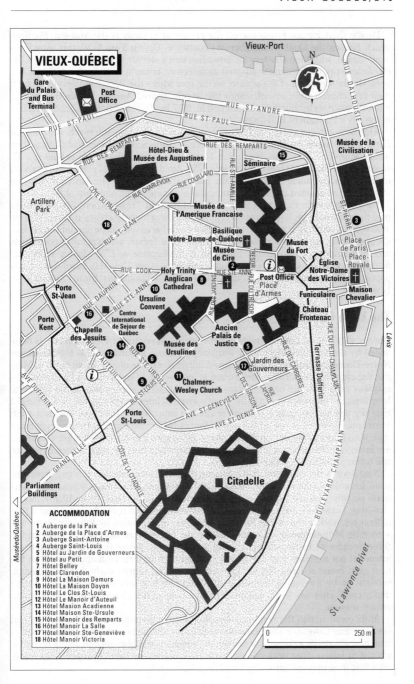

VIEUX-QUÉBEC

Vieux-Port

N

Gare du Palais and Bus Terminal

Post Office

RUE ST-ANDRE

RUE ST-PAUL

RUE ST-PAUL

RUE DES REMPARTS

Musée de la Civilisation

RUE DES REMPARTS

Hôtel-Dieu & Musée des Augustines

Séminaire

RUE COUILLARD

RUE CHARLEVOIX

RUE STE-FAMILLE

CÔTE DU PALAIS

RUE ST-PIERRE

Artillery Park

Musée de l'Amerique Francaise

RUE ST-JEAN

Basilique Notre-Dame-de-Québec

Musée du Fort

Place de Paris / Place-Royale

Musée de Cire

RUE COOK

Holy Trinity Anglican Cathedral

RUE STE-ANNE

RUE DU TRÉSOR

Église Notre-Dame des Victoires

Porte St-Jean

RUE DAUPHIN

RUE STE-ANNE

RUE DES JARDINS

Post Office

Place d'Armes

Funiculaire

Maison Chevalier

Ursuline Convent

Centre International de Sejour de Québec

Château Frontenac

Porte Kent

Chapelle des Jesuits

Musée des Ursulines

Ancien Palais de Justice

RUE D'AUTEUIL

Jardin des Gouverneurs

RUE DES CARRIÈRES

RUE DES GRISONS

RUE ST-URSULE

RUE ST-LOUIS

Chalmers-Wesley Church

RUE LAPORTE

Terrasse Dufferin

Porte St-Louis

AVE ST-GENEVIÈVE

AVE ST-DENIS

GRAND ALLÉE

CÔTE DE LA CITADELLE

Citadelle

BOULEVARD CHAMPLAIN

Parliament Buildings

St. Lawrence River

Lévis

Musée du Québec

ACCOMMODATION

1 Auberge de la Paix
2 Auberge de la Place d'Armes
3 Auberge Saint-Antoine
4 Auberge Saint-Louis
5 Hôtel au Jardin de Gouverneurs
6 Hôtel au Petit
7 Hôtel Belley
8 Hôtel Clarendon
9 Hôtel La Maison Demurs
10 Hôtel La Maison Doyon
11 Hôtel Le Clos St-Louis
12 Hôtel Le Manoir d'Auteuil
13 Hôtel Masion Acadienne
14 Hôtel Maison Ste-Ursule
15 Hôtel Manoir des Remparts
16 Hôtel Manoir La Salle
17 Hôtel Manoir Ste-Geneviève
18 Hôtel Manoir Victoria

0   250 m

Beside the Château Frontenac on the corner of St-Louis is the **Maison Maillou**, which houses the Québec chamber of commerce. Dating from 1736, this grey limestone house, with blue shutters for insulation and a steeply slanting roof, displays the chief elements of the climate-adapted architecture brought over by the Norman settlers. On the west side of the square, on the spot where the Récollet missionaries built their first church and convent, stands the largely ignored **Ancien Palais de Justice**, a Renaissance-style courthouse designed in 1887 by Eugène-Étienne Tâché, architect of the city's Parliament Buildings.

On the northeast corner of Place d'Armes, where Ste-Anne intersects with Rue du Fort, is the **Musée du Fort** (spring & fall daily 10am–5pm; summer daily 10am–6pm; winter Mon–Fri 11am–3pm, Sat & Sun 11am–5pm; $5.50), whose sole exhibit is a 37-square-metre model of Québec City circa 1750. Amid the streets of plastic, the city's six major battles, including the battle of the Plains of Abraham and the American invasion of 1775, are re-enacted in an entertaining thirty-minute sound and light show.

Parallel to Rue du Fort is the narrow alley of **Rue du Trésor** where French settlers paid their taxes to the Royal Treasury; nowadays it is a touristy artists' market. Visitors who want to take home a portrait rather than a saccharine cityscape should shuffle into the pedestrianized section of Ste-Anne to the west of Trésor, which is full of portraitists and their subjects. At no. 22 Rue Ste-Anne, in the impressive 1732 Maison Vallée, the **Musée de Cire de Québec** (daily: June–Sept 9am–11pm; Oct–May 10am–5pm; $5) is populated by unrealistic wax figures of Québécois luminaries from Champlain to Lévesque.

The Latin Quarter

Québec City's small **Latin Quarter**, in the northeast section of Vieux-Québec, is dominated by the seventeenth-century seminary in whose grounds stands the **Basilique Notre-Dame de Québec** (daily 6.30am–5.30pm; free). The oldest parish north of Mexico, the church was burnt to the ground in 1922 – one of many fires it has suffered – and was rebuilt to the original plans of 1647. Absolute silence within the cathedral heightens the impressiveness of the rococo-inspired interior, culminating in a ceiling of blue sky and billowy clouds. The silver chancel lamp, beside the main altar, was a gift from Louis XIV and is one of the few treasures to survive the fire. In the crypt more than nine hundred bodies, including three governors and most of Québec's bishops, are interned. Champlain is also rumoured to be buried here, though archeologists are still trying to work out which body is his.

Next door to the cathedral, in the Maison du Coin, is the entrance to – and departure point for guided tours of – the **Musée de l'Amérique Française**, whose three sections occupy a small part of the old **Séminaire** (June–Sept daily 10am–5.30pm; Oct–May Tues–Sun 10am–5pm; $3). The Séminaire, which recently underwent a $30-million renovation and is due for more changes, was founded by the aggressive and autocratic **Monseigneur François-Xavier de Laval-Montmorency** in 1663. In the three decades of his incumbency Laval secured more power than the governor and intendant put together and any officer dispatched from France found himself on the next boat home if Laval did not care for him. Laval retired early due to ill health, brought on by a religious fervour that denied him blankets and proper food. Death finally came after his feet froze on the stone floor of the chapel during his morning prayer session.

At its construction the seminary was the finest collection of buildings the city had seen, leaving Governor Frontenac muttering that the bishop was now housed better than him. Primarily a college for priests, the seminary was also open to young men who wanted to follow other professions, and in 1852 it became Laval University, the country's first francophone university.

The Welcome Pavillion in the Maison du Coin has a small exhibition centre upstairs and adjoins the Roman-style chapel, housing Canada's largest collection of relics – bones, ashes and locks of hair, a few of which are on display. Laval's memorial chapel contains his ornate marble tomb, but not his remains, which were moved to the Basilica when the chapel was deconsecrated in 1993.

The wrought-iron gates just down the street from the Pavillon d'Accueil (follow the white footprints) lead into a vast courtyard flanked by austere white buildings with handsome mansard roofs. Here, the **Pavillon Jérôme-Demers** (same opening hours as the museum) displays mostly well-presented, historical, temporary exhibitions, based on the eclectic items gathered by Québec's bishops and academics at Laval: scientific instruments, an Egyptian mummy – with a remarkably well-preserved penis – a diverting collection of European and Canadian paintings from the art historians, as well as a wealth of silverware and some of Laval's personal belongings.

Parc Montmorency

To the east, between the upper and lower parts of the old city, lies **Parc Montmorency**, its monuments recalling the historic figures of the area. This land was granted by Champlain to Canada's first agricultural settler and seigneur, Louis Hébert, and was later the meeting place of Québec's first legislature in 1694. The park gives wonderful views of Québec's port and its massive grain elevators, as does the flanking Rue des Remparts, where the cannons that once protected the city still point across to Lévis.

Hôtel-Dieu and Artillery Park

Rue des Remparts circles round to the **Hôtel-Dieu du Précieux Sang**, which dates from the seventeenth century, making it the oldest hospital in North America. The stone buildings are still occupied by the Augustinian order of nuns, who founded the hospital in 1637. Turning left up Côte du Palais and first left again leads to the **Musée des Augustines de l'Hôtel-Dieu de Québec**, 32 Charlevoix (daily: Tues–Sat 9.30am–noon & 1.30–5pm, Sun 1.30–5pm; free), where the artworks include some of Québec's oldest paintings – including the earliest known portrayal of the city in the background of the portraits of the Duchess of Auguillon and her uncle Cardinal Richelieu, who together funded the hospital. Another notable painting is the *Martyrdom of the Jesuits*, a gruesome tableau showing the torture of Jesuit missionaries in southern Ontario by the Iroquois in 1649. Each section shows a different missionary undergoing trial and punishment by baptism with boiling water, wearing a collar of red-hot hatchets and other forms of excruciating pain. Grateful patients also donated a fine collection of antique furniture, copperware and ornaments. Many of the items are French, as the first settlers usually found themselves interned in the hospital to recover from the diseases rife on the ocean crossing. Ancient medical instruments of the early settlement are also displayed. On request the Augustines offer free guided tours of the chapel where Catherine de St Augustin, their first mother superior, is buried, and the cellars where the nuns sheltered from the British in 1759.

Artillery Park

Backtracking, Rue des Ramparts leads to the northwest corner of Vieux-Québec and **Artillery Park**, whose immense defensive structures were raised in the early 1700s by the French, in expectation of a British attack from the St Charles River. After the fall of Québec the British added to the site, which was used primarily as a barracks for the Royal Artillery Regiment. Under the Canadians a foundry and cartridge factory provided the army with ammunition in both world wars, but was finally closed in 1964. The massive Dauphin Redoubt, named after Louis XIV's son, typifies the changes of fortune here: used by the French as the barracks for their garrison, it became the officers' mess under the British and then the residence of the superintendent of the Canadian Arsenal. The jumble of fortifications is well explained at the reception and **interpretation centre** (April–Oct Mon 1–5pm, Tues–Sun 10am–5pm; Nov–March Mon–Fri 10am–noon & 1–5pm; $3) in the former foundry beside Porte St-Jean. The centre has displays on the military pedigree of the city, including a vivid model of Québec City in 1808. The nearby Officers' Quarters, where the British officers lived until 1871, is now a military museum for children, with costumed guides providing a prettified version of events.

Beyond Porte St-Jean, the steep Rue d'Auteuil running alongside the park rises to Porte Kent, next to the **Chapelle des Jésuites**, 20 Rue Dauphine (daily 10am–5pm; free). The church's delicately carved altar and ecclesiastical sculptures are by Pierre-Noel Levasseur, who was one of the most illustrious artists to work on the early Québec parish churches.

Around the Jardins de l'Hôtel de Ville

Rue Dauphin continues to Rue Cook, which leads to the **Jardins de l'Hôtel de Ville**, scene of numerous live shows in the summer. The park is overlooked by the Hôtel de Ville, which dates from 1883, and the far more impressive Art Deco buildings of the **Hôtel Clarendon** and the **Édifice Price** (the city's first skyscraper), at nos. 57 and 65 Ste-Anne respectively.

By the corner of Ste-Anne and Rue des Jardins stands the first Anglican cathedral built outside the British Isles, the **Holy Trinity Anglican Cathedral** (daily: May & June 9am–6pm; July & Aug 9am–8pm; Sept–Nov 10am–6pm; free guided tours). The site was given by the king of France to the Récollet Fathers but their church burnt down in the late eighteenth century. Its replacement was constructed in 1800–04 on orders from King George III, following the lines of London's church of St Martin-in-the-Fields. The simple interior houses the 1845 bishops' throne, reputedly made from the wood of the elm tree under whose branches Samuel de Champlain used to confer with the Iroquois. Many of the church's features came from London, including the silverware from George III and the wood for the pews from Windsor's royal forest. The golden bars on the balcony denote the seats for the exclusive use of British sovereigns. In the courtyard is the *L'Atelier Plein Air*, a small crafts and clothes market that avoids selling tourist tack.

The Chapelle des Ursulines and around

Heading back south along Rue des Jardins brings you to the narrow Rue Donnacona and the **Chapelle des Ursulines**, built by a tiny group of Ursuline nuns who arrived in Québec in 1639 calling themselves "the Amazons of God in Canada". Their task was to bring religion to the natives and later to the daughters of the settlers, a mission carried out in the classrooms of North America's first girls' school – the buildings still house a private school. They also cared for the *filles du roi*, marriageable orphans and peasant girls imported from France to swell the population. These girls were kept in separate rooms in the convent for surveillance by the local bachelors, who were urged to select a wife within fifteen days of the ship's arrival – a fine of three hundred livres was levied on any man who failed to take his pick within the period. Fat girls were the most desirable, as it was believed they were more inclined to stay at home and be better able to resist the winter cold.

The Ursulines' first mother superior, Marie de l'Incarnation, was widowed at the age of 19 and left a son behind in France. Her letters to him give some sharp insights into the early days of the city: "It would be hard to live here an hour without having the hands protected and without being well covered. Although the beds are covered well with quilts or blankets, scarcely can one keep warm when lying on them." Her likeness can be seen in a replica of a posthumous portrait by Pommier in the interesting little **museum** (Feb–Nov Tues–Sat 9.30am–noon & 1–4.30pm, Sun 12.30–5pm; free), housed in the former home of one of the first nuns. Documents, paintings and household items testify to the harshness of life in the colony, but lace-work and embroidery are the highlights, particularly the splendid ornamental gowns produced by the Ursulines in 1739. As a grisly counterpoint, Montcalm's skull and one of his bones are also on display.

Montcalm himself is buried in the **chapel** (May–Oct Tues–Sat 10–11.30am & 1.30–4.30pm, Sun 1.30–4.30pm; free), rebuilt in 1902 but retaining the sumptuous eighteenth-century interior by sculptor Pierre-Noel Levasseur. A painting by Frère Luc, though executed in France, pictures a Canadian version of the Holy Family: Joseph is shown presenting a Huron girl to Mary, while through the window one can glimpse Cap Diamant and the St Lawrence flowing past wigwams and campfires. Next to the museum is the **Centre Marie-de-l'Incarnation** (Tues–Sat 10–11.30am & 1.30–4.30pm, Sun 1.30–4.30pm; free), which sells religious and historical books, and has a few of Marie's personal effects on show.

Maisons Jacquet and Kent

On the corner of Rue des Jardins and Rue St-Louis – the main restaurant strip in Vieux-Québec – stands **Maison Jacquet**, occupied by the restaurant *Aux Anciens Canadiens*. The name comes from Québec's first novel, whose author, Philippe Aubert de Gaspé, lived here for a while in the middle of the last century. Dating from 1677, the house is another good example of seventeenth-century New France architecture, as is the blue-and-white **Maison Kent** at no. 25 on St-Louis, which was built in 1649. Once home of Queen Victoria's father, the Duke of Kent, it's best known as the place where the capitulation of Québec was signed in 1759.

Jardin des Gouverneurs and around

Rue Haldimand, beside Maison Kent, leads to the **Jardin des Gouverneurs**, whose wonderful prospect of the St Lawrence was once the exclusive privilege of the colonial governors who inhabited Château St-Louis. The garden's Wolfe-Montcalm obelisk monument, erected in 1828, is rare in paying tribute to the victor and the vanquished. Converted merchants' houses border this grandiose area, and the nearby streets are some of the most impressive in Vieux-Québec – check out Rue Laporte and the parallel Rue des Grison on the park's west side, which boasts some fine eighteenth-century homes, the most outstanding example being the **Maison Allaire-Langan** at no. 12.

From the Jardin des Gouverneurs, avenue Ste-Geneviève runs west towards Porte St-Louis. En route turn right onto Rue Ste-Ursule for the **Chalmers-Wesley United Church** at no. 78 (July & Aug Mon–Fri 10am–3pm; free), which was built in 1852 and is one of the most beautiful in the city. Its slender, Gothic Revivalist spires are a conspicuous element of the skyline, and inside the stained-glass windows are worth a look. Opposite, the 1910 **Sanctuaire Notre-Dame-du-Sacré-Coeur** (daily 7am–8pm; free) also has impressive stained-glass windows.

A left turn onto Rue St-Louis leads to the Porte St-Louis, one of the four gates in the city wall. It's surrounded by **Parc de l'Esplanade**, the main site for the Carnaval de Québec, and departure point for the city's smart horse-drawn calèches. The park's **Poudrière de l'Esplanade**, 10 St-Louis (mid-May to June Mon–Fri 10am–5pm; July & Aug daily 10am–5pm; Sept & Oct daily 1–5pm; free), a powder house constructed in 1810, has a dull exhibition on the fortifications of Vieux-Québec, but it's here that most visitors start their 4.5-kilometre stroll around the city wall.

The Citadelle

Dominating the southern section of Vieux-Québec, the massive star-shaped **Citadelle** is the tour de force of Québec City's fortifications. Occupying the highest point of Cap Diamant, 100m above the St Lawrence, the site was first built on by the French, but the majority of buildings were constructed by the British under orders from the Duke of Wellington, who was anxious about American attack after the War of 1812.

The complex of 25 buildings covers forty acres and is the largest North American fort still occupied by troops – it's home to the Royal 22nd Regiment, Canada's only French-speaking regiment. Within the courtyard are ranged various monuments to the campaigns of the celebrated "Van-Doos" (*vingt-deux*), encircled by the summer residence of Canada's governor general and two buildings dating back to the French period: the 1750 powder magazine, now a mundane museum of military artefacts, and the Cap Diamant Redoubt, built in 1693 and thus one of the oldest parts of the Citadelle.

In addition to entertaining hour-long **guided tours** around the Citadelle (daily: mid-March to April 10am–3pm; May & June 9am–4pm; July & Aug 9am–6pm; Sept & Oct 9am–4pm; $4), other activities include the colourful **Changing of the Guard** (mid-June to Aug daily 10am) and the **Beating of the Retreat** tattoo (July & Aug Tues, Thurs, Sat & Sun 7pm).

The Parliament Buildings

Sweeping out from Porte St-Louis and flanked by grand Victorian mansions, the tree-lined boulevard of **Grande-Allée** is proclaimed the city's equivalent of the Champs Élysées, with its bustling restaurants, hotels and bars. Adjacent to the *Loews Le Concorde* hotel, Place Montcalm has a monument to Montcalm and a more recent statue of Charles de Gaulle, the French president who declared "Vive Québec" back in the 1960s, much to the separatists' delight. This area is now known as Parliament Hill, a new name that caused a lot of controversy, as Canada's Parliament area in Ottawa has the same title and anglophones thought it presumptious of Québec City to label itself like a capital city. However, there is indeed a hill here, and upon it, at the eastern end of Grande-Allée, stand the stately buildings of the **Hôtel Parliament** (late June to Aug 9am–4.30pm daily; Sept to late June Mon–Fri 9am–4.30pm; free CD tours), designed by Étienne Taché in 1877 in imitation of the Louvre. The ornate facade includes niches for twelve bronze statues by Québec sculptor Louis-Philippe Hébert of Canada's and Québec's major statesmen, while finely chiselled and gilded walnut panels in the entrance hall depict important moments in Québec's history, coats of arms and other heraldic features. From here the corridor of the President's Gallery, lined with portraits of all the Legislative Assembly's speakers and presidents, leads to the Chamber of the National Assembly, where the 122 provincial representatives meet for debate.

National Battlefields Park

Westward of the Citadelle are the rolling grasslands of the **National Battlefields Park**, a sizable chunk of land stretching along the cliffs above the St Lawrence. The park encompasses the historic Plains of Abraham, which were named after Abraham Martin, the first pilot of the St Lawrence River in 1620. The Plains were to become the site on which Canada's history was rewritten. In June 1759 a large British force led by **General Wolfe** sailed up the St Lawrence to besiege **General Montcalm** in Québec City. From the end of July until early September the British forces shuttled up and down the south side of the river, raking the city with cannon fire. Montcalm and the governor, Vaudreuil, became convinced that Wolfe planned a direct assault on the citadel from Anse de Foulon (Wolf's Cove), the only handy break in the cliff face – opinion confirmed when lookouts observed a British detachment surveying Cap Diamant from across the river in Lévis. Montcalm thus strengthened the defences above Anse de Foulon, but made the mistake of withdrawing the regiment stationed on the Plains themselves. The following night the British performed the extraordinary feat, which even Wolfe had considered "a desperate plan", of scaling the cliff below the Plains via Anse de Foulon, and on the morning of September 16 Montcalm awoke to find the British drawn up a couple of kilometres from the city's gate. The hastily assembled French battalions, flanked by native warriors, were badly organized and rushed headlong at the British, whose volleys of gunfire mortally wounded Montcalm. On his deathbed Montcalm wrote a chivalrous note of congratulations to Wolfe, not knowing that he too was dead. Québec City surrendered four days later.

The dead of 1759 are commemorated by a statue of Joan of Arc in a beautifully maintained sunken garden just off Laurier at Place Montcalm by the Ministry of Justice. More conspicuous, standing out amid the wooded parklands, scenic drives, jogging paths and landscaped gardens, are two Martello towers, built between 1805 and 1812 for protection against the Americans. During the summer, **Martello Tower 2**, on the corner of Laurier and Taché, has astronomical displays (early June to early Sept Mon noon–5.30pm, Tues–Sun 9.30am–5.30pm; free), whilst **Martello Tower 1** (same hours), further south in the park, has superb views of the St Lawrence from its rooftop lookout. Further west, outside the Musée du Québec, there's a monument to General Wolfe, whose body was shipped back to England for burial, pickled in a barrel of rum. Beyond the park's western peripheries, the Côte Gilmour climbs down the cliffs at Anse de Foulon.

The Musée du Québec

Canadian art had its quiet beginnings in Québec City three hundred years ago, and the full panoply of subsequent Québécois art is displayed in the **Musée du Québec**, whose bright, glassy entrance is at 1 Wolfe-Montcalm (June to early Sept daily 10am–5.45pm, Wed till 9.45pm; early Sept to May Tues–Sun 11am–5.45pm, Wed till 8.45pm; $5.75, free on Wed except early Sept to May): the main building is to the right, and the renovated Victorian prison, renamed the Baillairgé building, is to the left. If you don't fancy walking, bus #11 connects Vieux-Québec to avenue Wolfe-Montcalm along Grande-Allée.

The Church was the first patron of the arts in Canada, and the work produced under the sponsorship of Bishop Laval was enriched by the 1670 arrival of the Récollets, who included in their number the painter **Frère Luc**, a former assistant to Poussin. His influential output is represented here by the *Guardian Angel*, depicting the story of Tobias and the archangel Raphael. Secular art began with the fashion for portraiture among Québec City's upper classes: **François Malepart de Beaucourt's** portraits of the affluent Eustache-Ignace Trottier and his wife (1793) are the earliest examples of this genre, and his approach is far from servile – bonneted Madame is shown as the perfect hostess, but her husband is shown frittering away the family's fortune at the gaming table.

Nineteenth-century art

One of Québec's most prolific artists was the travelling portraitist **Jean-Baptiste Roy-Audy**, whose primitive style, heavily influenced by his artisan background as the son of a woodworker, is best seen in his *Monsigneur Rémi Gaulin* (1838) with its ivory-like surface. Roy-Audy's modest roots are reflected in the inconspicuous placement of his signature on the spine of the meticulously painted books in the background.

The most favoured portrait painter of the bourgeoisie was **Antoine Plamondon**, who had trained in Paris under Charles X's court painter Guérin, himself a pupil of the classicist David – a lineage evident in Plamondon's poised *Madame Tourangeau* (1842).

Plamondon was a very quarrelsome man, described as being unable to find "excellence but in himself", and having railed against anyone who threatened to establish themselves in Québec he finally sulked out of the scene altogether to manage a farm. **Théophile Hamel**, a pupil of Plamondon, combined what he learned from his tour around Europe in the 1840s – the palette of Rubens and the draughtsmanship of the Flemish masters – in his *Self-Portrait in the Studio*, painted soon after his return. A successful career painting Canada's leading citizens lay ahead of him, and he was to influence a whole generation of post-Confederation painters.

The first artist to depict Canadian scenes for their own sake was the Québec-born **Joseph Légaré**, whose sympathy with radical French-Canadians led to his imprisonment after the 1837 Rebellion. His *Fire in the Saint-Jean Quarter* – depicting the 1845 conflagration that made 10,000 homeless – is one of his many paintings recording local scenes and events. His counterpart in Montréal was the Irish immigrant **James Duncan** who worked mainly in watercolour but is represented here by the only oil painting he signed, *Montréal from the Mountain* (1845), a classical view of the city with its spires lit by the rays of the sun. Another contemporary, **Cornelius Krieghoff**, emigrated to America in 1836 from Amsterdam, and worked as a sign painter in Montréal before moving to Québec City in 1853, the year of his *Québec Seen from Pointe-Lévis*. His romanticized works were a major hit and he became one of the country's best-known artists.

Of the **sculptures** dotted around these galleries – all of them taken from Québec's churches – the most notable are by just two dynasties. Brothers Pierre-Noel and François-Noel Levasseur dominated the beginning of the eighteenth century, then three generations of Baillairgés took over in the second half.

The collections of **modern art** begin with the works of artists disparagingly termed the "fossil school" – for reasons made plain by the lifeless children in **Napoléon Bourassa's** *The Little Fishermen* (1870). The more emotive work of **Horatio Walker** is typified by his painting of mighty oxen ploughing. Walker was born in Ontario but moved to Québec in the 1880s and became completely engrossed in the lives of the French-Canadian *habitants*. Though his work recalls Millet in its subject matter, he lacks the sociological dimension: Millet's peasants are bent by labour; Walker's *habitants* simply love every minute of it.

Early twentieth-century art

Canada's art scene was rejuvenated by the impact of Impressionism and Post-Impressionism, first seen in the work of Newfoundlander **Maurice Cullen** – the rich orange and green hues of his *L'Anse-des-Mères* (1904) show the touch of Gauguin. Cullen's compatriot, the rich anglophone **James Wilson Morrice**, hobnobbed with the likes of Whistler in Paris and London, an acquaintance that shows in his *The Citadelle of Québec* (1897), showing the fortification covered in snow, a theme that was to occur over and over again in the coming decades. A more colourful winter scene appears in **Clarence Gagnon's** *Laurentian Village* (1915) – he used to grind his own colours to achieve greater intensity.

The works of the Group of Seven are more usually associated with the remote wilds of Ontario, but **Arthur Lismer**, one of the founders of the Group, visited Charlevoix many times, producing pieces such as *Québec Village, Ste-Hilarion* (1925). Urban life at the time is admirably recorded by **Adrien Hébert**, son of sculptor Louis-Philippe Hébert: his *Port of Montréal* (1924) is one of many canvases dominated by grain elevators, steamers and harbour installations, symbolically dwarfing the men in the foreground. The contemporaneous **Marc-Aurèle Fortin's** best works were his impressionistic renditions of trees, as seen in *Elm at Pont-Viau* (1935), where one gigantic tree of numerous intense greens dominates the entire riverscape.

The modernism of Matisse and Picasso was introduced to Canada by **Alfred Pellan**, who returned from Paris in 1940 to teach at Montréal's École des Beaux-Arts. Pellan's comparative radicalism – represented here by his *Young Woman with a White Collar* (1932) – caused confrontations with his bosses, the clash reaching its peak with a semi-riot at the 1945 degree show, precipitated by the conservative director's removal of controversial items produced by Pellan's students.

Sculpture underwent a similar process of European-led development, beginning with the production of religious votary objects. Secular art flourished in the nineteenth century, when one of the most prolific sculptors was **Louis-Philippe Hébert**, whose classical works grace most of Québec's buildings and parks. He is represented here most strikingly by *The Halt in the Forest*, a copy of which graces the Parliament Buildings as a tribute to the province's native peoples. By the 1920s and 1930s the influence of Rodin had become overwhelming, as is evident in **Suzor-Côte's** *Women of Chaughnawaga* and **Aldred Laliberté's** *The Spirit of Marble*, in which a smooth nude emerges from a block of hewn marble.

Contemporary art

Contemporary art is dominated by the work of Montréal's Automatistes, who held their first exhibition in 1947 and were greatly influenced by the Abstract Expressionists in New York. This is clear in the splashy work of **Paul-Émile Borduas**, whose 1948 manifesto *Refus Global* was adopted as a general manifesto for disgruntled young French-Canadians. Other strands of abstraction appear in **Ferdinand Leduc's** *L'Alphiniste* (1957), a work indebted to Mondrian, and the monochrome grey canvas of **Yves Gaucher's** *R-M-III N/69* (1969). Extremely simplified forms spilled over into the sculpture of the period, as is evident in Louis Archambault's scarcely detailed *Head* (1948) and Vaillancourt's massive *Tree on Rue Durocher*. On the same floor there's a gallery showcasing avant-garde paintings and sculptures from Québec.

The red brick of the adjoining former jail has been spruced up to create a warm interior far removed from the sombre outside. Montréal sculptor David Moore has created a unique two-storey sculpture in the prison's tower with huge torsos and legs of wood scaling the walls and a central figure diving from the summit. As well as a variety of prestigious temporary exhibitions, this part of the museum houses the impressive drawing and print collection, and a hi-tech interpretation centre outlining the history of the Plains of Abraham.

Basse-Ville

The birthplace of Québec City, **Basse-Ville**, can be reached from Terrasse Dufferin by either the steep **escalier casse-cou** (Breakneck Stairs) or by the **funicular** alongside, which turned out, in October 1996, to be far more dangerous than the stairs when a cable snapped and it plummeted – two people were killed and a dozen others injured. As a result it is closed until the summer of 1998. Until then a shuttle bus ($1) links the upper and lower parts of the city. The Basse-Ville station of the funicular is the 1683 **Maison Louis-Jolliet**, 16 Petit-Champlain, built for the retired discoverer of the Mississippi, Louis Jolliet, the first Québécois to make history. It now houses a second-rate souvenir shop, a ghastly introduction to this interesting area.

Dating back to 1685, the narrow cobbled **Rue du Petit-Champlain** is the city's oldest street, and the surrounding area – known as **Quartier du Petit-Champlain** – is the oldest shopping area in North America. The boutiques and art shops in the quaint seventeenth- and eighteenth-century houses are not too overpriced and offer an array of excellent crafts, from weird and wonderful ceramics to Inuit carvings. Older artefacts can be seen closer to the harbour, on the corner of boulevard Champlain and Rue du Marché Champlain, where three merchant houses – **Maison Chanaye-de-la-**

Garonne, **Maison Fréot** and the **Maison Chevalier** – are now used by the Musée de la Civilisation for changing exhibits of period furniture, costumes, toys, folk art and domestic objects (mid-May to early Oct daily 10am–5pm; free).

Place-Royale

From here it's a short walk along Rue Notre-Dame to **Place-Royale**, where Champlain built New France's first permanent settlement in 1608, to begin trading fur with the native peoples. The square – known as Place du Marché until the bust of Louis XIV was erected here in 1686 – remained the focal point of Canadian commerce until 1759, and after the fall of Québec the British continued using the area as a lumber market, vital for shipbuilding during the Napoleonic Wars. After 1860 Place-Royale was left to fall into disrepair, a situation reversed as recently as the 1970s, when the scruffy area was renovated. Its pristine stone houses, most of which date from around 1685, are undeniably photogenic, with their steep metal roofs, numerous chimneys and pastel-coloured shutters, but it's a Legoland townscape, devoid of the scars of history. Fortunately the atmosphere is enlivened in summer by entertainment from classical orchestras to juggling clowns.

In Maison Thibaudeau, an old warehouse, the **interpretation centre** at 215 Marché-Finlay (May–Sept daily 10am–6pm; free), outlines the stormy past of Place-Royale, the mercantile aspects and the changes in the look of the square from the days when it was inhabited by the Iroquois to its recent renovation. Listings of the square's up-and-coming events are also available here.

The **Église Notre-Dame-des-Victoires** (daily 9am–4.30pm), on the west side of the square, nearly always has a wedding in progress during the summer. It was instigated by Laval in 1688 but has been completely restored twice – after being destroyed by shellfire in 1759 and after a fire in 1969. Inside, the fortress-shaped altar alludes to the two French victories over the British navy that gave the church its name: the destruction of Admiral Phipp's fleet by Frontenac in 1690 and the sinking of Sir Hovenden Walker's fleet in 1711. Above the altar, paintings depicting these events hang by copies of religious paintings by Van Dyck, Van Loo and Boyermans, gifts from early settlers to give thanks for a safe passage. The model ship suspended in the nave has a similar origin.

The Musée de la Civilisation

Rue de la Place leads to **Place de Paris**, where a modern sculpture called *Dialogue with History* marks the disembarkation place of the first settlers from France. Close by, the *Batterie Royal*, trimly restored in the 1970s, was used to defend the city during the siege of 1759. The **ferry to Lévis** (see p.268) leaves from one block south, while a walk north along Rue Dalhousie brings you to Québec City's most impressive and dynamic museum, the **Musée de la Civilisation**, 85 Rue Dalhousie (mid-June to early Sept daily 10am–7pm; early Sept to mid-June Tues & Thurs–Sun 10am–5pm, Wed 10am–9pm; $6, free on Tues Sept–June). Designed by Canada's top-rank modern architect, Moshie Safdie, the building reflects the steeply pitched roofs of Québec's earliest architecture and has won numerous awards for the way it blends with the historic surroundings. It actually incorporates three historic structures, including the two-storey merchant's house called the Maison Estèbe, whose arched cellars now contain an excellent gift shop.

Concentrating primarily on Canada but also diversifying into a wider perspective, the museum presents various changing exhibitions ranging from soap operas to immigration. Other than the foyer sculpture, Astri Reusch's *La Débâcle*, which symbolizes the break-up of the ice in the spring thaw, there are two permanent exhibitions: "Memories", a labyrinth that expertly displays life in Québec from the early days of the settlers to the present, and "Objects of Civilization", antique artefacts selected from the museum's collection including *La Barque*, the remains of a 250-year-old boat found on the site of the museum.

Vieux-Port and around

To the east, at the confluence of the St Charles and the St Lawrence, lies the **Vieux-Port de Québec**, the busiest harbour in the province until its eclipse by Montréal. Much of the harbour has been renovated as a recreational area, with theatres, yuppie flats, sheltered walkways, restaurants and a marina packed with pleasure boats and yachts. A remodelled cement plant bordering the Louise Basin at 100 St-André now hosts an **interpretation centre** for the Vieux-Port (March, April to mid-May & Sept–Nov Tues–Fri 10am–noon & 1–4pm, Sat & Sun 11am–5pm; mid-May to June Mon 1–4pm, Tues–Fri 9am–4pm, Sat & Sun 10am–5pm; July & Aug Mon 1–5pm, Tues–Sun 10am–5pm), housing a display on the lumber trade and shipbuilding in the nineteenth century. Nearby, along the basin, the **Marché du Vieux-Port** (March–Nov daily from 8am) is a throwback to how the port used to be – its busy market stalls selling fresh produce from the local area.

Also on the south side of the Louise Basin, the next street down from St-André is Rue St-Paul, heart of Québec's **antiques district**. Numerous cluttered antique shops, art galleries, cafés and restaurants now occupy warehouses and offices abandoned after the demise of the port. From Rue St-Paul the steep Côte Dambourges leads to Rue des Remparts on the northern borders of the Latin Quarter.

The Cartier-Brébeuf National Historic Site

West of Quebec, on the banks of the Saint-Charles River (bus #3 or #4), the **Cartier-Brébeuf National Historic Site**, 175 de l'Espinay (April–Sept daily 10am–5pm; Oct–March Mon–Fri 10am–noon & 1–5pm; free) has a double claim to fame. It marks the spot where Jacques Cartier spent the winter of 1535-36 in friendly contact with the people of the surrounding Iroquoian villages – a cordial start to a relationship that Cartier later soured by taking a local chief and nine of his men hostage. It is also where Jean de Brébeuf, with his Jesuit friends, built his first Canadian residence in 1626: Brébeuf is best known for his martydom near today's Midland in Ontario (see pp.121–122). The **interpretation centre** features an excellent account of Cartier's voyages and of the hardship he and his crew endured during the winter. On the site, there's also a mock-up of an Iroquian longhouse and, most impressive of all, a full-size replica of Cartier's flagship *La Grande Hermine*.

Eating

It is when you start **eating** in Québec City that the French ancestry of the Québécois hits all the senses: the eateries of the city present an array of culinary delights adopted from the mother country, from beautifully presented gourmet dishes to humble baguettes.

Whether you are on a tight budget or not, Québec's lively **cafés** are probably where you will want to spend your time, washing down bowls of soups and croutons (toasted baguettes dripping with cheese) with plenty of coffee. Decked out in a variety of decors, from the traditional to the stylish, they are always buzzing with activity, as students and workers drop in throughout the day. As you might expect, Vieux-Québec is home to most of the gourmet **restaurants** and cafés, but other areas – notably along St-Jean and Grande-Allée, just outside the city walls – have their fair share.

Snacks and cafés

Bouche Bée, 383 Rue St-Paul. Cheap café in Vieux-Québec, serving sandwiches, quiches, soups, etc.

Café Buade, 31 Rue Buade. In a central location, with good light and simple breakfasts. Open from 7.30am.

Les Couventines, 1124 Rue St-Jean. Mouthwatering crêpes and ice cream; a must.

Croissant Plus, 50 Rue Garneau. One of a chain of fast-food croissant places; cheap, but not that tasty.

L'Esplanade, 1084 Rue St-Jean. Plain and simple, but cheap, serving sandwiches and the like.

La Garonnelle, 297 Rue St-Jean. A wonderful café with great desserts.

Café Loft, 49 Rue Dalhousie. Sleek yuppie café, which serves good bagels in a converted warehouse.

Café du Monde, 57 Rue Dalhousie. Fairly pricey and chic bistro.

L'Omelette, 66 Rue St-Louis. Reasonable tourist joint with omelette specialities; breakfast from 7am.

Café Retro, 1129 Rue St-Jean. Well priced if touristy; serves everything from sandwiches to T-bone steaks.

Café Ste-Julie, 865 Rue Zouaves. Simple café popular with students with a background of rock music.

Café Taste-Vin, 32 Rue St-Louis. Centrally located café, with set meals for around $20.

Chez Temporal, 25 Rue Couillard. Bowls of steaming *café au lait*, croissants and *chocolatines* make this Latin Quarter café, a few doors from the *Peace Hostel*, a perfect place for breakfast. Soups and sandwiches are also available throughout the day and night.

Chez Victor, 145 Rue St-Jean. Popular scruffy café serving superior hamburgers and salads.

Restaurants

In Québec's finer **restaurants** high-quality French cuisine is easy to come by and, although prices tend to be rather high, even the poshest restaurants have cheaper lunch-time and table d'hôte menus. For a change of taste, the dishes of other countries are also represented, including Italian, Greek, Swiss, Thai – as well as the good old hamburger. Strangely though, typical French-Canadian cooking – game with sweet sauces followed by simple desserts with lashings of maple syrup – is available at a very few places in town.

On and around Rue St-Jean

À la Table de Serge Bruyère, 1200 St-Jean (☎694-0618). Probably the best restaurant in Canada, serving fresh produce, beautifully prepared and presented. Dinner for two comes to around $150 and reservations are standard. Closed Sun & Mon.

Au Petit Coin Breton, 1029 St-Jean. A pretty good and reasonably priced specialist creperie, where servers wear traditional Breton costume – it may put you in the mood.

Casse-Croute Breton, 1136 St-Jean. Diner-style resturant where crêpes are made in front of you with two or three fillings, costing $5.

La Crémaillière, 21 Rue St-Stanislas (☎692-2216). Superior European cuisine at reasonable prices; advance booking advised.

Couventines, 1124 St-Jean. Organic crêpes and yummy ice cream. Wicked restaurant.

Les Frères de la Côte, 1190 St-Jean. Fairly cheap, very friendly eatery with snails, smoked salmon and great pizzas on the menu.

Le Hobbit, 700 St-Jean (☎647-2677). One of the best bargains around, with great vegetarian food and a good studenty atmosphere; advance booking advised.

Le Mykonos, 1066 St-Jean. Well-priced Greek restaurant. A full meal will set you back around $15.

Piazzetta, 707 St-Jean. There's always a queue outside this trendy pizzeria – the pizzas come close to perfection and are dead cheap.

Pizzeria d'Youville, 1014 St-Jean. Variety of brick-oven pizzas in the heart of the Latin Quarter.

Le Saint-Stanislas, 29 Rue St-Stanislas (☎694-9260). Recommended as one of the best steakhouses in Vieux-Québec with an Art Deco interior; advance booking advised.

On and around rue St-Louis

L'Apsara, 71 Rue d'Auteuil. Cambodian, Vietnamese and Thai food in Vieux-Québec near Porte St-Louis. Three-course lunch is around $10, dinners in the $30 region.

Aux Anciens Canadiens, 34 Rue St-Louis (☎694-0253). This expensive (around $50 a head) and touristy restaurant is located in one of the oldest homes in Québec City. It serves typical Québécois food like duck glazed with maple, turkey in hazelnut sauce, and lamb in blueberry wine sauce. As a side dish, baked beans gain a whole new meaning, and for pudding there's blueberry tart or maple-syrup pie.

Le Continental, 26 St-Louis. Old-fashioned place down the street from the Château Frontenac. Their three-course table d'hôte is $26–30.

Café de la Paix, 44 Rue des Jardins. The desserts in the front window taste as good as they look – and the rest of the menu is equally delicious. Approximately $40 per person. Closed Sun.

Primavera, 73 St-Louis. The specialities here include pizzas from a wood-burning oven and mouth-watering mussels.

Restaurant au Parmesan, 38 St-Louis. Bland Italian and French food, but popular with tourists because of its central Haute-Ville location and reasonable prices.

Le Saint-Amour, 48 Rue Ste-Ursule (☎694-0667). Romantic French restaurant, with excellent food at around $80 for two.

Vieux-Québec's Basse-Ville

Le Cochon Dingue, 46 Rue Champlain. Fun and reasonably priced pasta-and-burger bistro.

Le Délice du Roy, 33 Rue St-Pierre. Around the corner from Place-Royale, this canteen-style place dishes up traditional Québécois food at reasonable prices – table d'hôte $5.95–10.95.

Le Lapin Sauté, 52 Petit-Champlain. Very popular, informal restaurant specializing in rabbit.

Laurie Raphael, 117 Dalhousie (☎692-4555). Warm and relaxed atmosphere in a resturant that is very popular and needs reservations. The food is beautifully presented with the fish being a speciality.

Le Marie Clarisse, 12 Petit-Champlain (☎692-0857). Fine fish restaurant in Basse-Ville, serving a four-course meal for around $45; advance booking advised.

On and around Place d'Armes

Charles Baillargé, *Hôtel Clarendon*, 57 Ste-Anne. Opened in 1870, this is supposedly Canada's oldest restaurant and serves classic French cuisine. Expensive, and dress is formal.

Gambrinus, 15 du Fort (☎692-5144). Excellent Italian and French food in the shadow of Château Frontenac, with seafood specialities. Menu of the day is around $35; advance booking advised.

Le Poisson d'Avril, 36 Côte-de-la-Fabrique. Next to City Hall, this friendly little restaurant, dripping with fishing tackle and nets, serves quality seafood and pasta.

Restaurant au Café Suisse, 32 Rue Ste-Anne. Touristy fondue place, which is good for people-watching, as the restaurant spills out onto the pedestrian-only part of Ste-Anne in the heart of Vieux-Québec.

On and around bvld René-Lévesque

L'Astral, 1225 Place Montcalm (☎647-2222). Rotating restaurant on the top floor of the *Hôtel Loews le Concorde*. The food is generally expensive but the views can't be beaten. On Saturday nights the all-you-can-eat Buffet Royal costs an extremely reasonable $35.

Le Cochon Dingue, 46 blvd René-Lévesque. Near the Parliament Buildings, sister joint to the branch in Basse-Ville.

Bars and nightlife

Nightlife in Québec City is far more relaxed than in Montréal: an evening spent in an intimate bar or a jazz or blues soiree is more popular than a big gig or disco. Few major bands tour here, except during the Festival d'Été, when everyone lets their hair down. Québec City's main bar and nightclub strip is around St-Jean, outside the city walls. For up-to-date **information** on the goings-on, check out the listings section in the French daily newspapers *Le Soleil* and *Journal de Québec* and the free weekly newspaper *Voir*. The quarterly bilingual magazine for tourists *Voilà Québec* also carries information, as does the English *Québec Chronicle Telegraph*, published every Wednesday.

Bars and live music

L'Acropole, 217 Rue St-Paul. Video bar with billiard tables.

L'Amour Sorcier, 789 Côte Ste-Geneviève. Popular, intimate gay bar with cheap beers, soft music and roof terrace.

Bar Chez Son Pére, 24 Rue St-Stanislas. Just off St-Jean in Haute-Ville, above street level. Québécois folk singers create a great thigh-slapping atmosphere. Free admission.

Le d'Auteuil, 35 Rue d'Auteuil. Cheap bar with blues, folk and jazz bands.

Dorchester Taverne, 251 Rue Dorchester. True Québécois inn with cheap beer and bar games.

Ecuador, 889 Côte Ste-Geneviève. A salsa, reggae pick-up joint.

L'Emprise, *Hôtel Clarendon*, 57 Rue Ste-Anne. Art Deco surroundings attract a sophisticated touristy crowd to evenings of smooth jazz and blues.

Le Fou Bar, 525 Rue St-Jean. Trendy, packed student bar.

Fourmi Atomik, 33 Rue d'Auteuil. The trendiest bar in Haute-Ville, with cheap beers, snacks, pool tables and loud music.

L'Inox, 37 Rue St-André. The only brew pub in Québec City; the ales are a lot better than the food.

Le Pape Georges, 8 Rue Cul-de-Sac, near Place Royale. Small wine bar with traditional folk singing.

Le Pub Saint Alexandre, 1987 St-Jean. Over 170 beers in this yuppie English-style pub.

Tango, 63 Rue St-Paul. Bar/café/art gallery with friendly punters and jazz.

Taverne Le Drague, 804 Rue St-Augustin. A gay bar, café and nightclub, with cheap imported beers. Popular with Québec's small transvestite population.

Clubs and discos

Le Ballon Rouge, 811 Rue St-Jean. Gay male disco, with loud, good music and free entry.

Chez Dagobert, 600 Grande-Allée Est. A huge club in a renovated warehouse, with its dance floor on the first floor and a stage for mainly rock bands downstairs. Free unless a band is playing.

Maurice, 575 Grande-Allée Est. Happening club with different DJs each night.

Merlin, 1175 Rue Cartier. Young, chic Québécois disco hangout.

Studio 157, 157 Ste-Foy. Disco/bar for gays and lesbians, which is known locally as the *Venus*.

Le Vogue, 1170 Rue d'Artigny. Trendy dance-music club, at the top of the hip list.

Entertainment and festivals

Québec City is not especially renowned for its high culture, but from May to September there are **dance**, **theatre** and **music** events at various outdoor venues, and throughout the year performances can be caught at the city's theatres. The liveliest periods are in February and July, when the entire city is animated by its two principal **festivals**: the excellent Carnaval and the equally frenzied Festival d'Été. Tickets for most events can be purchased through the Admission agency (☎1-800-361-4585 or 691-7211).

Theatre

Québec City has a fair smattering of **theatres**, all producing plays in French only. The city's main theatre for the performing arts is the Grand Théâtre de Québec, 269 René-Lévesque Est (☎643-8131), which has a sound programme of drama, as well as dance shows and classical music concerts. Other main theatres include Le Palais Montcalm, 995 Place d'Youville (☎670-9011), and Salle Albert Rousseau, 2410 Ste-Foy (☎659-6710). For small-scale dramatic productions, check out the Théâtre de la Bordée, 1143 St-Jean (☎694-9631), and Théâtre Capitole, 972 St-Jean (☎694-4444).

Open-air **summer theatres** are particularly popular in Québec. The largest is the Agora, in the Vieux-Port at 120 Dalhousie (☎648-4370), a huge amphitheatre used for a range of productions from comedies to classical music. Théâtre du Bois du Coulonge

(☎681-0088), set near the Musée du Québec in Battlefields Park, is a perfect venue for a summer theatre. A summer-long programme of activities is also enacted on open stages in the Jardins de l'Hôtel-de-Ville; at the Pigeonnier beside Grande-Allée, just beyond the Parliament Buildings; and in the Place d'Youville.

Music
Canada's oldest symphony orchestra, L'Orchestre Symphonique de Québec, performs at the Grand Théâtre. Other classical concerts can be caught at the Bibliothèque Gabrielle-Roy, 350 Rue St-Joseph (☎529-0924). In Place d'Youville and Place Royale, there are various free classical **music** concerts in the summer, and the Agora is used for summer concerts too.

Cinema
The city has a smattering of **cinemas**, mostly out in the suburbs. The most convenient is the popular Cinéma de Paris, Place d'Youville (☎694-0891), which sometimes features undubbed English films when they first come out, as well as Québécois and French movies. Cinéma le Clap, 2360 Rue Ste-Foy (☎650-2527; bus #7), is the city's rep cinema. Canada's largest cinema screen is at the Theatre IMAX, 5401 blvd des Galeries (☎627-4629; bus #60) with films that take full advantage of the immense visuals and wraparound sound.

Festivals
Québec City is renowned for its two large annual **festivals**, the first of which is the eleven-day **Carnaval de Québec** in freezing early February, when large quantities of the lethal but warming local brew, *caribou*, are consumed amid parades and ice-sculpture competitions, all presided over by the mascot snowman called Bonhomme Carnaval. In early July, the ten-day **Festival d'Été** is an equally cheery affair, especially as the provincial law prohibiting drink on the streets is temporarily revoked. The largest festival of francophone culture in North America attracts hundreds of artists, and everyone is roped into the celebration, with restaurants offering discounts and all of Québec's major performers pitching up to dance, make music and lead the party from massive open-air stages.

It is also worth being in the city on **St-Jean Baptiste** Day on June 24, the provincial holiday, when an outpouring of Québécois pride spills onto the streets in a massive parade, with the entire city decked with thousands of fleur-de-lis flags.

Listings

Airlines Air France, 610 Place Québec (☎529-0663 or 1-800-667-2747); Air Canada and Air Alliance, Aéroport de Québec (☎692-0770 or 1-800-361-5373); British Airways, Aéroport de Québec (☎1-800-668-1059); Canadian Airlines, Aéroport de Québec (☎692-1031 or 1-800-665-1177).

Banks and exchange American Express, 46 Garneau; Banque Royale, 700 Place d'Youville and 160 Grande-Allée Est; Caisse Populaire des Jardins du Vieux-Québec, 19 Rue des Jardins (summer daily 9am–6pm; winter Mon, Tues & Fri 9.30am–3pm, Wed & Thurs 9.30am–6pm) has exchange facilities and a cashpoint (ATM) in Vieux-Québec.

Bike rental Location Petit-Champlain, 92 Rue du Petit-Champlain, and at the youth hostel *Auberge de la Paix* (☎692-2817).

Bookshops English books can be purchased at Librairie Garneau, 5 Place Québec; La Maison Anglaise, 2600 Rue Laurier, Rue Ste-Foy; and at Pantoute, 1100 Rue St-Jean. For travel books, Librairie Ulysse, 4 blvd René Lévesque.

Bus enquiries Long-distance: bus terminal, 320 Rue Abraham-Martin (☎525-3000). Local: STCUQ, Place Jacques-Cartier, 325 du Roi (☎627-2511).

Car parks Hôtel-de-Ville, Chauveau (near Hôtel-de-Ville), Haldimand (near Jardin des Gouverneurs), Complex "H" and "J" outside Porte St-Louis, "D" Youville (off Dufferin), Dalhousie,

Vieux-Port.

Car rental Avis, *Hôtel Hilton* (☎523-1075) and at the airport (☎872-2861); Budget, 380 Rue Wilfred-Hamel (☎687-4220) and at the airport (☎872-9885); Discount, 12 Rue Ste-Anne (☎692-1244); Hertz, airport (☎871-1571), 44 Rue du Palais (☎694-1224) and 580 Grande Allée Est (☎647-4949); Thrifty, *Holiday Inn,* 395 Rue de la Couronne (☎523-0099) and at the airport (☎877-2870).

Consulate US, 2 Terrasse Dufferin (☎692-2095).

Dentists For dental emergencies, ring ☎653-5412 (Mon–Wed 8am–8pm, Thurs 8am–6pm, Fri 8am–4pm) or ☎656-6060 at the weekend.

Hospitals Hôtel-Dieu Hospital, 11 Rue du Palais (☎691-5042); Jeffrey Hale Hospital, 1250 Rue Ste-Foy (☎683-4471).

Ice hockey The Rafales, who are not in the NHL, play at 350 blvd Wilfred-Hamel (tickets ☎691-7211 or 1-800-900-SHOW; season is mid-Sept to April).

Laundry Lavoir la Lavandière, 625 Rue St-Jean and 17 av Ste-Ursule (Mon–Sat 9am–9pm); Lavoir Côte Ste-Geneviève, 684 Rue Ste-Geneviève.

Left luggage Both the train and bus stations have $1 luggage lockers.

Medical advice 24hr medical service (☎648-2626).

Pharmacy 24hr service: Pharmacie Brunet, 4266 av 1ère, in the westerly suburb of Charlesbourg.

Post office 300 Rue St-Paul (Mon–Fri 8am–5.45pm).

Rape crisis line ☎692-2252.

Ridesharing Allo-Stop, 467 Rue St-Jean (☎522-0056).

Road conditions For 24hr information, call ☎643-6830 (Nov to mid-April).

Taxis Taxi Coop (☎525-5191); Taxi Québec (☎525-8123); Taxi de la Capitale (☎527-0530).

Train enquiries VIA Rail (☎692-3940 or 1-800-361-5390); Gare du Palais, 450 Rue de la Gare du Palais (☎524-4161); Gare de Lévis, 5995 Rue St-Laurent, Lévis (☎833-8056); Gare de Ste-Foy, 3255 Chemin de la Gare (☎658-8792).

Weather information For 24hr bulletins (☎848-7766).

Around Québec City

If you're staying in Québec City for a while, there are various options for a swift or protracted trip out from the city. In **Wendake**, west of the city, the past and present crafts of Canada's only surviving Huron community can be seen, while to the east the **Côte-de-Beaupré**, though something of a city annexe, boasts the spectacular waterfalls of **Montmorency** and **Sept-Chutes**. Just offshore, the **Île d'Orléans** has a tranquil charm, its agricultural landscapes dotted with gîtes and auberges, and the homes of the well heeled. For those in search of wilderness, the **Réserve Faunique des Laurentides** is within easy reach also. **Lévis**, on the opposite shore of the St Lawrence, is less inundated by visitors than Québec City and has great views of its more illustrious neighbour.

Buses run to Chute Montmorency, Wendake and **Ste-Anne-de-Beaupré**, while a quick **ferry** trip lands you in Lévis. The only places for which your own transport is essential are the Île d'Orléans and Sept-Chutes.

Wendake

Just to the west of Québec City lies **WENDAKE**, the only **Huron reserve** in Canada. Its name is derived from the Hurons' own name for their people – *Wendat*, meaning "people of the peninsula". In 1650, French Jesuit missionaries led three hundred Huron from Ontario's Georgian Bay to the shores of the St Lawrence around today's Vieux-Québec, thereby saving them from extermination at the hands of the Iroquois. As more French settlers arrived, so the Hurons were successively relocated, ending up here beside the St-Charles River in 1697. Today, with a population of two thousand, the central village core of the reserve retains typical Québécois wooden houses with sloping and gabled roofs, but the main reason tourists visit is to shop for Huron crafts – moccasins, mittens, beaded belts, jewellery and embroidered duffel coats.

The STCUQ #801 runs from Place d'Youville to its terminus at Charlesbourg, from where the #72 goes to Wendake; get a transfer *(une correspondance)* and the forty-minute or so journey will set you back $1.85. The bus arrives at the red-roofed chapel of **Notre-Dame-de-Lorette** (May–Oct Mon–Fri 9am–8pm, Sat & Sun 9am–6pm; Nov–April Mon–Wed 10am–6pm, Thurs & Fri 10am–7pm; free), which is now a small museum containing old manuscripts and religious objects. Opposite the chapel, one of the early wooden houses, the **Maison Arouanne** (July & Aug daily 10am–6pm; Sept–June Mon–Fri 8am–4pm; free), displays an interesting collection of Huron cultural objects, including ceremonial attire beaded with pearls and porcupine quills, drums of moose hide and feathered headdresses used for festive occasions.

Every summer the replica Huron village **Onhoüa Chetek8e** (mid-May to mid-Oct daily 9am–6pm; $3) is constructed for the benefit of tourists. It consists of wooden longhouses, Hurons in traditional garb and delicious native foods. August is the best time to visit, for the local powwow celebrations. Of the village's numerous artisan shops, Le Huron and Petit Huron Moc on Maurice-Bastien are recommended.

The Réserve Faunique des Laurentides

The zone of the Laurentians to the northwest of Québec City is considerably more wild than the mountains near Montréal, thanks to the creation of the 8000-square-kilometre **Réserve Faunique des Laurentides**. The vast wooded terrain, with summits of more than 1000m towards the east, was once a hunting ground of the Montagnais, until the Hurons, supplied with arms by the French, drove the small population further north. The area became a park in 1895 to protect the caribou herds, an intervention that was not a great success – very few exist today. However, though it allows controlled moose-hunting, the park's main function is still to preserve native animals such as the beaver, moose, lynx, black bear and deer, all of which you may see in the remoter areas.

The best way to see the park is to drive through it via Hwy 175 to Chicoutimi (see p.297); halfway through the park Hwy 169 branches off to Alma on Lac St-Jean (see p.301); Autocars Fournier, 5675 des Tournelles (☎627-9108), runs a bus service through the park from Québec City to Alma. If you want to stop off in the park, the **Camp Mercier** reception centre, near the reserve's southern perimeter, gives out **information** and there's **camping** beside Lac Jacques-Cartier at *Camping la Loutre* (☎846-2201; $14), about 25km south of the Hwy 175/169 junction. Skiing for a day costs $9 and chalets are available for $75 for two.

The Côte-de-Beaupré

Dubbed the "coast of fine meadows" by Jacques Cartier, the **Côte-de-Beaupré** stretches along the St Lawrence to the **basilica of Ste-Anne-de-Beaupré**, 40km from Québec City. There are two roads along the coast: the speedy Dufferin–Montmorency autoroute (Hwy 440, then Hwy 138) and the winding avenue Royale (Hwy 360), which is served by local buses. The latter gives a far better introduction to the province's rural life, with ancient farmhouses and churches lining the way.

Chute Montmorency

Nine kilometres northeast of Québec City the waters of the Montmorency River cascade 83m down from the Laurentians into the St Lawrence, which makes the **Chute Montmorency** one and a half times the height of Niagara, though the volume of water is considerably less. The falls, which were named by Champlain in honour of the governor of New France, were the site of Wolfe's first attempt on the colony. However, Wolfe and his men were driven off by Montcalm's superior forces. In those days – before a hydroelectric dam cut off much of the flow – the falls were a far more spectacular sight, but it remains an awesome spectacle, especially in winter, when the water and spray become a gigantic cone of ice, known locally as the "sugar loaf". Inevitably, the falls attract droves of tourists, especially now that the site has been thoroughly developed: from the main car park ($6), a cable car ($4) shoots up to the **interpretation centre**, from where a cliffside walkway leads to the bridge over the falls and onto the zigzag path down the other side. Local STCUQ bus #53 stops at the bottom of the falls, #50 at the top; both buses leave from Place Jacques-Cartier in Québec and take around fifty minutes, each costing $1.45.

Ste-Anne-de-Beaupré

Québec's equivalent of Lourdes, the **Basilique de Ste-Anne-de-Beaupré**, 39km from Québec City (1hr by STCUQ bus #50 from Place Jacques-Cartier; $1.45), dominates the skyline, its twin spires soaring proudly above the St Lawrence shore. The legend of its foundation has it that some Breton sailors were caught in a storm on the St Lawrence in 1650 and vowed to build a chapel to St Anne if she saved them. The sailors survived and building began in 1658 on the spot where they came ashore. The first miracle occurred when a crippled peasant was cured so that he could help build the chapel, and from then on everyone caught in the St Lawrence's frequent storms prayed to St Anne and donated *ex votos* to the shrine. In the early days the devout came to this site on their knees from the beach or walked shoeless from Québec City; now, one and a half million pilgrims flock to the site every year in comfortable coachloads.

The neo-Romanesque granite cathedral with lofty symmetrical spires is the fourth church to stand here, fires and floods having destroyed the first three. It has a capacity of 10,000, and most of its decoration – countless stained-glass windows and massive murals – depict the miraculous powers of St Anne, though the wooden pews bear delightful animal carvings. Behind the ornate golden statue of St Anne, depicted holding her daughter Mary, is a chapel containing a portion of Anne's forearm, donated by the pope in 1960. Those who have been cured by her intervention have left a vast collection of crutches and wooden limbs hanging on the basilica's back pillars. The **information booth** in front of the basilica (early May to mid-Sept daily 8.30am–5pm) runs pious, free, guided tours daily at 1pm.

Several little chapels cringe in the basilica's shadow. The simple **Chapelle Souvenir** (early May to mid-Sept daily 8am–8pm), across the street, was built in the nineteenth century using the stones of the first chapel; some of its paintings date from the shrine's earliest days. The fountain in front is the apparent agency through which Anne performs her healing. Nearby, the small white chapel of the **Scala Santa** (same times) is the container for a set of holy stairs that replicate those climbed by Christ on his meeting with Pontius Pilate. Lumps of earth from various holy places are contained in glass boxes embedded in each stair, and the devout accomplish the ascent on their knees. Another obligatory part of the penitential route is the nearby **Way of the Cross**, which curves steeply up the hillside; on summer evenings torchlit processions wend their way through each station. Less athletic visitors can pay their respects to the basilica's collection of *ex votos* and treasures in the **Historial** (May–Oct daily 9am–7.30pm; $2.50), which also contains a missable wax museum depicting scenes from the life of St Anne.

Sept-Chutes

Just off Hwy 138 some 10km east of Ste-Anne-de-Beaupré, the falls at **Sept-Chutes** (daily: late May to late June & early Sept to mid-Oct 10am–5pm; late June to early Sept 9am–7pm; $5) can only be reached by car, which takes about thirty minutes from Québec City. The tourist bumph describes the gorge created by the river as a "Grand

Canyon", which is pushing the hyperbole a little far, but the area is spectacular; the water tumbles more than 130m in a series of waterfalls flanked by a chasm fringed with woodlands and crisscrossed by short nature trails. Over the falls a precarious rope bridge allows for splendid and terrifying views, whilst other, (sturdier) lookout points cling to crevices on the side of the gorge.

Île d'Orléans

From just north of Québec City to a short distance beyond Ste-Anne-de-Beaupré, the St Lawrence is bottlenecked by the **Île d'Orléans**, a fertile islet whose bucolic atmosphere and handy location have made it a popular spot for holiday-making Québécois. More than most places on the mainland, Île d'Orléans, with its old stone churches, little cottages and seigneurial manors, has kept a flavour of eighteenth-century French Canada. This is largely because it was cut off from the mainland until 1932, when a suspension bridge was constructed from Hwy 440, about 10km out of the city, to the west end of the island.

To its first inhabitants, the **Algonquins**, the island was known as Minigo, which means "enchanting place". Jacques Cartier christened it Île de Bacchus because the vines he saw here were "such as we had seen nowhere else in the world". (He was soon to change the name to Île d'Orléans in honour of the son of the king.) Agriculture is still the mainstay for the population of seven thousand: roadside stalls heave under the weight of fresh fruit and vegetables, jams, dairy products, home-made bread and maple syrup, and the island's restaurants and B&Bs are some of the best in the province, thanks to the supplies from local farms.

Encircling the island, the 67-kilometre chemin Royal (route 368) dips and climbs over gentle slopes and terraces past acres of neat farmland and orchards, passing through the six villages on the island's periphery. The island's **information office** (☎828-9411) is situated on the right just after the bridge at 490 côte du Pont. Nearly all the information is in French, except the *Île d'Orléans* booklet ($2), which has an adequate map and accommodation listings.

From here it's best to head west towards Ste-Pétronille in the region known locally as the "end of the island", a district still characterized by the grand homes of the merchants who made their fortunes trading farm produce with Québec City.

Ste-Pétronille

In the eighteenth century rich anglophones spent their leisure time in **STE-PÉTRON-ILLE**, the island's oldest and most beautifully situated settlement, with the noble rise of Québec City dominating the skyline – Wolfe used this spot to observe the city before his bombardment. The white **Maison Gourdeau-de-Beaulieu** at no. 137 Royal was the island's first permanent dwelling, built in 1648 and still home to the Beaulieu family. Some of the best views can be had from rue Horatio Walker, where the home of landscape painter **Horatio Walker** stands at no. 13. Known unofficially as the grand seigneur of Ste-Pétronille, Walker lived here from 1904 until his death in 1938. He despised his English heritage, continually emphasizing a French branch in his ancestry and refusing to speak English. His subject matter was almost entirely based on the Île d'Orléans, which he viewed as a "sacred temple of the muses and a gift of the gods". Though most of his paintings now grace Canada's larger galleries, some of his lesser-known works and sketches can be viewed in his studio (late May to Oct; reservations only ☎828-2275).

Budget **accommodation** in the village is limited to three often booked-out **B&Bs**: *Gîte la Vieille École*, 25 du Bout de l'Île (☎828-2737; ②), *B&B Horatio Walker*, 13 Horatio Walker (☎829-1078; ④) and the *Gîte du Bout de l'Île*, 91 du Bout de l'Île (☎828-2678; ②). A pricier stay can be had at the delightful *Auberge la Goéliche*, 22 du Quai (☎828-2248 or 1-800-463-1568; ⑤), a wooden waterside Victorian inn with delicious French/Québécois cuisine and great views. For home-made food, *Café Belle Rive* makes a great stop.

St-Laurent and St-Jean

The south shore of the island was once the domain of sailors and navigators, with the village of **ST-LAURENT** being the island's supplier of "chaloupes", the long rowing boats that were the islanders' only means of getting to the mainland before the bridge was built.

Continuing along the shore, **ST-JEAN** was similarly nautical, with the cemetery of its hull-shaped local church containing the gravestones of numerous mariners. St-Jean has a museum of antique furniture and domestic objects housed in the stately **Manoir Mauvide-Genest**, 1451 Royal (late May to early Sept daily 10am–5pm; $3), the one-time home of Louis XV's surgeon; its metre-thick walls withstood the impact from Wolfe's bombardment. Nearby, at no. 1477, *La Maison sur la Côte* (☎829-2971; ②) has **B&B** and offers a filling table d'hôte for around $10, or try the *Mansarda* at no. 1403, an old balconied house with simple rooms and close to the marina (☎828-2780).

St-François, Ste-Famille and St-Pierre

From St-Jean, the road continues to the island's easterly tip and the village of **ST-FRANÇOIS**, where a precarious observation tower is the only attraction since a suicidal driver recently wrecked the 1734 church. If you intend to **camp**, try the lovely and conveniently located *Camping Orléans*, near the village jetty at 357 chemin Royal (☎829-2953; $19 for two people). For a roof over your head, the rural *Auberge Chaumont*, 425 chemin Royal (☎829-2735; ③; summer only) is a quiet place for the night.

However, you're probably better off turning north at St-Jean to cross the interior along the Route du Mitan to **STE-FAMILLE**. Among its wealth of French-regime stone buildings, the **Maison Canac-Marquis**, 4466 chemin Royal, is a particularly fine example, and the richly decorated **church**, built in 1743, includes a painting of the Holy Family by Québec's foremost early painter, Frère Luc. The local *boulangerie*, G.H. Blouin, is one of the island's oldest and best, with mouthwatering bread and local fare. Another of the village's Normandy manors is now the highly recommended **restaurant** *L'Âtre*, 4403 chemin Royal (☎829-2474), where delicious French/Québécois food is served from around $15 for a main course. Nearby, at 3879 chemin Royal, *Au Toit Bleu* (☎829-1078; ②) offers **B&B** in three comfortable rooms.

The remaining village, **ST-PIERRE**, to the west of Ste-Famille, is notable for its **church**; constructed in 1718, it has pews with special hot-brick holders for keeping bottoms warm on seats. *Gîte de la Colomba*, 1501 chemin Royal (☎828-2417; ②) is a pleasant four-bedroomed **B&B** if you need a place to stay.

Lévis

It's hard to think of any commuters who have as pleasant a morning trip as those who cross the St Lawrence from **LÉVIS** to Québec City. Lévis itself is an attractive Victorian town, but it's really the views of Québec that make the visit a treat. The regular ferry leaves day and night from near Place Royale, and costs $1.25 for the fifteen-minute crossing – and no extra for the return if you stay on the boat.

Most tourists stay on the ferry for the free return trip, but those dauntless enough to scale the staircase to the Terrasse on the heights of Lévis are rewarded with an even greater panorama. The Terrasse runs through a landscaped park whose centrepiece is a statue of Father Joseph David Déziel, founder of Lévis. The main street of Lévis, Carré Déziel, is a couple of blocks north from the Terrasse and runs parallel to the river. The streets leading off it are as narrow and steep as those in Québec City – on Notre-Dame, Wolfe and Guenette streets, look out for examples of elaborate brickwork and ornate roof lines that are as fine as those across the water. The **Maison Alphonse-Desjardins**, at 6 Mont-Marie, is a particular delight with its icing-cake facade.

Along Hwy 132: towards the Gaspé Peninsula

Heading east from Lévis **towards the Gaspé Peninsula**, the most scenic route to take is **Hwy 132**, which sticks religiously to the St Lawrence shoreline as opposed to the Trans-Canada (Hwy 20) that zips along to just past Rivière-du-Loup. The road twists across a flat agricultural landscape, whose long, narrow fields are remnants of the old seigneurial system (see below), and passes through a string of quiet villages overshadowed by their oversized Catholic churches. The two stops worth making on the 180-kilometre trip between Lévis and Rivière-du-Loup, which is effectively the start of the Gaspé Peninsula, are at the woodcarving centre of **St-Jean-Port-Joli** and at pretty **Kamouraska**, with its quaint architecture.

St-Jean-Port-Joli

The first settlement of any note along Hwy 132, some 80km east of Lévis, is **ST-JEAN-PORT-JOLI**, where the long main street accommodates the galleries of the region's most popular woodcarvers. A traditional Québécois folk art, woodcarving flourished in the eighteenth and nineteenth centuries, but had almost expired by the 1930s, when the Bourgault brothers established their workshop here. Initially religious statuary was their main source of income, but their folksy style and francophile themes were adopted and popularized by the nationalists in the 1960s.

Along the main road, on the west side of the village, the ugly **Musée des Anciens Canadiens**, 332 av de Gaspé Ouest (daily: mid-May to June 9am–5pm; July & Aug 8.30am–9pm; Sept & Oct 9am–6pm; $4), has an interesting collection of monumental woodcarvings cut in white pine and Canadian walnut, many of which are the work of the Bourgaults. The most impressive piece is the giant *Les Patriotes*, a tribute to the Québec rebels of 1837 who, under the leadership of Louis-Joseph Papineau, tried to drive out the British; however, the studied romance of the woodcarving bears little relation to the actual rebellion which was badly organized and easily suppressed.

A few doors down the same road at no. 322, the **Maison Médard-Bourgault** (mid-June to Aug 10am–5pm; $2) concentrates on the life and work of Médard Bourgault, the most talented of the brothers – he even carved the walls and furniture – while the delicate and ornate interior of the village church, **Église St-Jean Baptiste** at no. 2, celebrates the work of an earlier generation of Québécois woodcarvers from the 1770s, the Baillarge Brothers. Any of the dozen or so galleries along the main road sell woodcarvings; the shop adjoining the museum is one of the best.

At nearby no. 377, housed in an octagonal barn, is the **Centre d'Art Animalier Faunart** (daily: May & June, Sept & Oct 9am–6pm; July & Aug 9am–9pm; $4) displays artworks inspired by nature and animals – a good intro to Canadian wildlife, though the taxidermy exhibits might make stomachs churn. You can chat to sculptors as they work in Galerie des 8.

St-Roch-des-Aulnaies and La Pocatière

Fourteen kilometres east of St-Jean is the village of **ST-ROCH-DES-AULNAIES**, where a water mill and manor house have survived from the old nineteenth-century seigneurial estate. Now offering a fascinating glimpse into that era, **La Seigneurie des Aulnaies** (daily: mid-June to Aug 10am–6pm; Sept & early Oct 9am–4pm; $5), once the estate of a rich merchant, is named after the alder trees that grow along the banks of the Ferrée River. The river powered Québec's largest bucket wheel in the estate's three-storey communal grist mill. Now refurbished and in full working order, the mill has frequent flour-grinding displays and mouthwatering muffins and pancakes in the café. Just upstream from the mill, the verandaed villa has period rooms, guides in costume and diverting interactive displays on the seigneurial system.

THE SEIGNEURIAL SYSTEM

In the seventeenth century, the agricultural settlement of New France – now Québec – was conceived as an extension of European-style feudalism with the granting of **seigneuries** to religious orders, nobleman, merchants and, in a break from tradition, others of humble birth. The average seigneury covered around fifty square kilometres and part of the land was owned by the seigneurs, the rest rented by **habitants**, who were secure in their tenancy (they could sell the land and pass it on to their children) provided they met certain obligations: they had to pay a yearly tithe for the upkeep of the parish church, pay rent in kind (usually grain, as the seigneurs had a monopoly on milling), work on the roads and make themselves available for the militia.

In the early days the waterways provided the easiest form of transportation and so each of the *habitants*'s farms had a riverfrontage of around a couple of hundred metres in length, with the rest of their land extending back in a narrow strip. One result of this was that *habitants* lived near their neighbours and, content with this decentralized way of life, long resisted the development of nuclear settlements. You can still see these ribbon farms and villages, which are very much in evidence along the St Lawrence today.

The seigneurial system was abolished in Ottawa in 1854 by legislation that passed land ownership rights to the *habitants*.

A few minutes' drive from St-Roch, agricultural **LA POCATIÈRE** sits on a ridge above the coastal plain, overawed by its vast modern cathedral, dating from 1969, and surrounded by ribbon farms characteristic of the region (see below). It is now home to the factory that produces most of Montréal's and New York's metro trains. Beside the cathedral is the **Musée Francoise-Pilote**, 100 4th Ave (Mon–Sat 9am–noon & 1–5pm, Sun 1–5pm; Oct–May closed Sat; $3), which has an enjoyable exhibition about the country parish as of 1990. For a moderately priced meal with all the trimmings, visit *Chez Denis*, 421 4th Ave in a wonderful old villa.

On Hwy 132 the **information centre** for the whole Bas St-Laurent region that stretches from here to Rimouski is located at exit 439 (daily: mid-May to mid-June & Sept to mid-Oct 9am–5pm; mid-June to Aug 9am–8pm).

Kamouraska

Some 40km further along the St Lawrence is **KAMOURASKA**, a pretty village, whose cramped centre, right next to the river, abuts the enormous Victorian **Palais de Justice** (early June to early Sept daily 10am–noon & 1–5pm; $3). The village boasts many examples of the Bas-St-Laurent's most distinctive architectural feature, the Kamouraska roof. Extended to keep the rainwater off the walls, the arched and rounded eaves project from the houses in a design borrowed from the shipyards. You may also spot the eel traps in the river – these are rows of wooden stakes that ensnare the eels, traditionally the village's economic mainstay. The **site d'interpretation de l'anguille**, 205 av Morel (mid-may to mid-Oct daily 9am–6pm; $4), provides an insight into the eel-fishing industry.

Manoir Taché at 4 av Morel (mid-June to mid-Sept daily 9am–10pm; $2.50) was the scene of a crime passionnel in 1839 when the wife of the local seigneur, Achille Taché, planned with her lover and his friend, Doctor Holmes, to kill her husband and run away. The doctor did murder him and managed to inspire *Kamouraska* by Anne Hébert, one of Québec's best-known novels, and a subsequent film by Claude Jutra. Today the manor is now centre stage for the villainy and sexploits of a popular TV series, *Cormoran*, whose fans flock to check the place out. It is possible to stay here, but call well in advance (☎492-3768; ②).

Kamouraska has two seasonal **motels**: the *Motel au Relais*, 253 Morel (☎492-6246; ②), and the more attractive *Motel Cap Blanc* (☎492-2919; ②). There are also three **B&Bs** along avenue Morel: one at no. 81 (☎492-2921; ②), one at no. 92 (☎492-2916; ②) and one at no. 124 (☎492-2973; ②).

THE GASPÉ PENINSULA AND ÎLES-DE-LA-MADELEINE

The scenic **Gaspé Peninsula** is approached from Québec City via the trim villages of the Chaudière-Appalaches and Bas-St-Laurent regions along the St Lawrence's south shore. The peninsula has always been sparsely inhabited and poor, its remote communities eking out an existence from the turbulent seas and the rocky soil. In recent years it's become a major summer holiday spot and can get very busy; if you're travelling in summer, be sure to book your accommodation in advance. However, the influx of holiday-makers and new service-industry jobs have failed to dent the high rate of unemployment.

The people of the peninsula are predominantly and proudly Québécois, though there are pockets of long-established English-speaking settlement, particularly in and around Gaspé town, while Carleton and **Bonaventure** are centres of Acadian culture, established in 1755 in the wake of the British deportation of some 10,000 Acadians from the Bay of Fundy in Nova Scotia (see p.335). Neither of these communities has created visually distinctive villages or towns, however, and the Gaspé looks as French as the heartlands of rural Québec.

Bounded by the Gulf of St Lawrence to the north and west, and by the Baie des Chaleurs to the south and east, the peninsula is roughly 550km long, with a chain of mountains and rolling highlands dominating the interior and the northern shore – providing some wonderful scenery of forested hills, deep ravines and craggy mountains tumbling to a jagged coastline. This landscape makes the coastal drive along Hwy 132 a delight, though the principal towns strung along this shore – **Rimouski**, **Matane** and **Gaspé** – are in themselves less appealing than smaller villages like **Marsoui**, **Mont-Saint-Pierre** and busy **Percé**.

The Gaspé also has two outstanding parks: the extravagantly mountainous **Parc de la Gaspésie**, inland from **Sainte-Anne-des-Monts**, and the **Parc National de Forillon**, at the tip of the peninsula, with its mountain and coastal hikes and wonderfully rich wildlife. Just to the south of the Forillon park, the village of Percé is famous for the offshore **Rocher Percé**, an extraordinary limestone monolith that has been a magnet for travellers for more than a hundred years. East of here, stuck out in the middle of the Gulf of St Lawrence, the **Îles-de-la-Madeleine** are most easily reached by ferry from Prince Edward Island. This windswept archipelago has empty, treeless landscapes, fringed by fine beaches and crazily eroded sandstone cliffs, and appeals particularly to cyclists and walkers.

The **south coast** of the Gaspé is, for the most part, flatter and duller than the north but the resort of **Carleton**, where the mountains return to tower over the coast, is an agreeable place to break your journey, especially as it's near the extraordinary fish and plant fossils of the **Parc de Miguasha museum**.

The Gaspé is well served by **bus**, with regular services travelling both the north and south coasts from Rimouski, Rivière-du-Loup and Québec City. The interior and the peninsula's parks are, however, difficult to explore without a car. VIA Rail links Halifax, Moncton, Lévis (Québec City) and Montréal with the Gaspé's southern coast as far as Gaspé town – but there's a gap between Gaspé and Rimouski on the northern coast. Be warned, though, that some of the stations (like Percé) are miles from the towns they serve.

Rivière-du-Loup

Whether you're coming up from the heartlands of Québec or crossing over from New Brunswick on the Trans-Canada Highway via Cabano (see below), **RIVIÈRE-DU-LOUP** is to all intents and purposes the beginning of the Gaspé Peninsula. The town is a prosperous-looking place, whose hilly centre, complete with broad streets and hand-

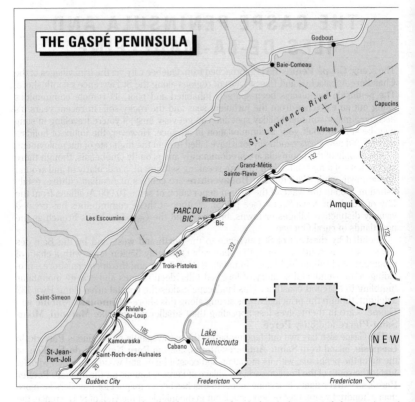

THE GASPÉ PENINSULA

Godbout

Baie-Comeau

Capucins

St. Lawrence River

Matane

132

Grand-Métis

Sainte-Flavie

Rimouski

PARC DU
BIC

Amqui

Les Escoumins

Bic

132

232

Trois-Pistoles

Saint-Siméon

Rivière-
du-Loup

185

Lake
Témiscouta

NEW

Kamouraska

Cabano

St-Jean-
Port-Joli

Saint-Roch-des-Aulnaies

20

▽ Québec City   Fredericton ▽   Fredericton ▽

some Victorian villas, owes its development to the timber industry and the coming of the railway in 1859, which established Rivière-du-Loup as a crossroads for traffic between the Maritimes, the peninsula and the rest of the province. Its significance as an administrative and commercial centre has grown accordingly and today it has a population of around 16,000.

Bisecting the town, the river, which gives the place its name, crashes down a thirty-metre drop close to the centre, at the top of Rue Frontenac. However, although the **waterfall** generates a lot of noise and spray, even the specially built platform fails to make the view enthralling. Similarly modest, the town has two museums: the central **Musée du Bas-Saint-Laurent**, 300 Rue St Pierre (June–Aug daily 10am–5pm; Sept–May Mon–Fri 10am–noon & 1–5pm, Sat & Sun 1–5pm; $3.50), which combines ethnological displays of the region with historical exhibits and works of modern art by local artists; and the **Musée des Carillons**, on the eastern edge of town at 393 Rue Témiscouata (June–Oct daily 9am–9pm; $3), which displays bells of all types and sizes.

If you're interested in the architectural heritage of the place, you could pick up the interpretive booklet from the tourist office and take a stroll round the centre: there's nothing special, but it's a pleasant way to while away an hour. You may want to check out **Le Manoir Fraser**, 32 Rue Fraser (June–Aug daily 10am–5pm; $4), the newly opened home of Seigneur Fraser where, instead of costumed guides, a computer-

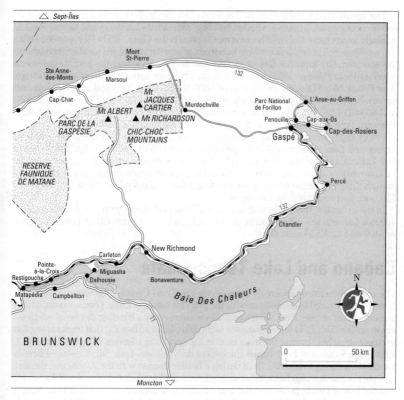

animated seigneur introduces you to his life and time. The red-brick manor also has a fancy tearoom and garden – don't miss the masterful slide show on Rivière-du-Loup, which makes the town and local area look gorgeous.

Rivière-du-Loup is a good place for **boat trips** on the St Lawrence River. Beginning at around $35 per person per trip, these excursions are not cheap, but they are well organized and there's a good chance of seeing beluga, minke and finback whales throughout the summer. Croisières AML by the marina, at 200 Rue Hayward (☎867-3361 or 1-800-563-4643), specializes in **whale-watching** trips; alternatively, **La Société Duvetnor,** at the same address (☎867-1660), has cruises to various midstream sea-bird and mammal sanctuaries, with overnight stops ($135 per person) a possibility. Sailings depart daily between mid-May and late September; reservations are advised. There's also a **car ferry** service over to Saint-Siméon, on the north shore (April–Dec 2–5 daily; 1hr; passengers $11.65, cars $34.85).

Practicalities

Highway 132 runs right through the centre of Rivière-du-Loup. The town's **bus station** is on boulevard Cartier, beside the junction of Hwys 132 and 20, about ten minutes' walk northeast of the centre. The **tourist office** at 89 Rue Hôtel-de-Ville (May–Sept daily 8.30am–8.30pm; Oct–April Tues–Sun 9am–5pm), will help you get your bearings and provide accommodation listings.

The **youth hostel** (☎862-7566 or 1-800-461-8585; ①; April–Oct), on the same street at no. 46, occupies an attractive wooden building with ornate banisters and balustrades. A similarly inexpensive and equally convenient option is the *Cégep*, 325 St Pierre (☎862-6903; ①), a college hall of residence where hundreds of spartan rooms are on offer throughout the summer. The town has lots of **motels** and **hotels**, including the bargain-basement *Motel au Vieux Piloteux*, 185 Fraser (☎867-2635; ②). More agreeably, the seasonal *Auberge de la Pointe*, 10 bvld Cartier (☎862-3514 or 1-800-463-1222; ③), has comfortable rooms and its own health spa, or try the similarly priced *Motel Lévesque*, 171 Rue Fraser (☎862-6927 or 1-800-463-1236; ③), which has gorgeous gardens. The municipal **campground**, Rue Hayward (☎862-4281; mid-May to Sept), is off Hwy 132, near the harbour.

Pricey high-class **restaurants** abound in the centre of town – *Le St-Patrice*, 169 Rue Fraser and *Chez Antoine*, 433 Rue Lafontaine being two of the best – but a walk down Rue Lafontaine, near the river, reveals some less expensive alternatives. Best value is *La Gourmande* at no. 120, where salads and vegetarian meals average out at about $11, though things get more pricey in the evenings; also well priced is *Café de la Cour* at no. 110, with fish and rabbit on the menu.

In the evenings, the bright young things of Rivière-du-Loup gather at *Le Nouveau*, at 409 Rue Lafontaine – a **bar** with beer and loud music, or the mainstream clubs *Le Jet* at no. 409 and *Le Kojak* next door.

Cabano and Lake Témiscouata

The area southeast of Rivière-du-Loup, along the Trans-Canada Highway towards New Brunswick, is saved from mediocrity by the graceful sweep of **Lake Témiscouata**, where a combination of lake, river, woods and hills is adorned by a dazzling display of wildflowers in spring. The TCH offers glimpses of the lake, but it's Hwy 232 that tracks along the prettiest stretches, leaving the main road at the sprawling lakeside village of **CABANO**. This is the location of **Fort Ingall** (June–Sept daily 9.30am–6pm; $6), a restored British fortification dating from 1839. Built during a border dispute with the Americans, the fort was part of a series of schemes that strengthened the land link between the St Lawrence and the Bay of Fundy, protecting the area's timber resources. Abandoned in 1842, having seen no action, Ingall has been painstakingly reconstructed, its high stockade surrounding a squat wooden barracks, blockhouse and officers' quarters. Inside the officers' quarters are enjoyable displays on the background to the fort's construction, contemporaneous army life and local archeological finds. There's also a section on Archie Belaney, aka **Grey Owl**, the British conservationist turned native, who settled in the area in the 1920s (see p.170). From Cabano, Hwy 232 follows the shore of the lake before snaking back to the St Lawrence at Rimouski – or you can take the more direct Hwy 293 from the lake's northern extremity to Trois-Pistoles (see below).

There are several **campgrounds** along the shores of Lake Témiscouata, the nearest to Cabano being the *Témilac*, 33 Rue de la Plage, near the junction of Highway 232 and the TCH (☎854-7660; $18; mid-May to mid-Oct). For more comfortable **accommodation**, the campground adjoins the unpretentious *Hébergement Témilac* (same number; ③). Alternatively, you could try the *Motel Royal*, 19 Rue St-Louis (☎854-2307; ②), a decent and inexpensive place to stay.

Trois-Pistoles

Heading northeast from Rivière-du-Loup along the St Lawrence, with the far bank clearly visible, the coastal highway passes through a succession of farming and fishing villages on its way to **TROIS-PISTOLES**, named after a silver goblet worth three pistoles (gold coins), which a French sailor once lost here. It is now popular among Québécois as the home of scriptwriter and novelist Victor-Lévy Beaulieu, who has created several *téléromans* – a distinctly Québécois genre which is part soap opera, part drama – which are set in the area. His house and studio at 23 rue Petellier (June to mid-Sept daily 9am–5pm; $7) are nothing special unless you're a fan of such hits as *Bouscette*. The town is dominated by the enormous church of **Notre-Dame-des-Neiges-de-Trois-Pistoles** (mid-May to mid-Sept daily 9am–6pm), built in 1887. From a distance it looks like something out of Disneyland, as the roof, surmounted by four pinnacles, is painted silver. Inside, the vaulted Italianate ceiling is supported by massive trompe-l'oeil-marble columns with ornate gilded capitals, while the walls are dotted with nineteenth-century devotional paintings.

The **Musée Saint-Laurent**, 552 rue Notre-Dame Ouest (late June to mid-Sept daily 8.30am–6pm; free) has a great ensemble of cars, with vehicles from the 1930s to the 1970s and an eclectic collection ranging from old packs of cigarettes to harpoons.

A **ferry** service crosses from here to Les Escoumins (mid-May to mid-Oct 1–3 daily; 1hr 15min; passengers $9.65, cars $24.75), and 3.5-hour excursions are also available to the **Île aux Basques**, a bird sanctuary that lies a couple of kilometres offshore (mid-June to mid-Oct daily; ☎851-1202; $12). As early as the sixteenth century, the island was used as a whaling station by Basque sailors, who built huge stone furnaces to render the blubber into whale oil; the scant remains of these can still be seen. Other Basque artefacts, and the bone remains of whales found on the island, are now on display in Trois-Pistoles at **Parc de l'Aventure Basque en Amérique** near the ferry wharf (daily: late June to mid-July & mid- to late Aug 10am–5pm; mid-July to mid-Aug 10am–8pm; $5, children $2.50, family $13), a new interactive exhibition that explores Basque culture complete with a reconstruction of a *pelote* court – a type of Basque racquetball.

Information on the town is available at the office on the highway with the miniature windmill and lighthouse outside (June–Sept daily 9am–7pm). Should you want to break your journey here, try *Le Motel Trois-Pistoles*, 64 Route 132 Ouest (☎851-2563; ②), which has 32 comfortable rooms, some with views of the river. For **B&B**, *Gîte Coucher de Soleil* at 175 rang 2 est (☎851-3626; ②) is worth a try. Just outside town, *La Ferme Paysagée*, Route 293 (☎963-3315; ③), is a farm with llamas as well as the more usual sheep and goats. For **snacks**, *Le Quidam*, on the corner opposite the church door, is a brashly cheerful bar, while *L'Ensoleille*, at 158 Rue Notre-Dame Est, has vegetarian and fish dishes.

Bic and Rimouski

North from Trois-Pistoles the main road crosses a comparatively tedious landscape of fertile agricultural land, until it reaches the rocky wooded hummocks of the shoreline's **Parc du Bic**. This is naturalists' paradise whose headlands push up tight against the river, where it's possible to see herds of grey seals. The park has a series of short hiking trails, a beach, a visitors' centre (mid-June to Sept daily 10am–5pm) and an excellently situated **campground**, *Camping Bic* (☎736-4711; $16 a pitch; early June to early Sept). From late June to early September, there are also daily two-hour **boat trips** along the park's shoreline ($25 per person) – ask at the visitors' centre for details – or **sea-kayak** along with Kayak Aventure (☎723-0160; $27 per person).

Just beyond the park along Route 132, the elongated village of **BIC**, perched on a low ridge above its snout-shaped harbour, is a handsome medley of old and modern architectures. Here you'll find the charming *Auberge du Mange Grenouille*, 148 rue Ste-Cécile (☎736-5656; ②), with a superb **restaurant** (reservations advised) and attractively furnished double **rooms**. The *Auberge du Vieux Bicois*, 134 Ste-Cécile (☎736-5317; ①), is a far more modest alternative.

Rimouski

Some 20km northeast of Bic lies **RIMOUSKI**, the administrative capital of eastern Québec. It's an unremarkable town of 30,000 souls, best visited during the **Jazz Festival** at the end of August or the **Film Festival** in late September. There's not much else to see here, but you could pop into the **Galerie Basque** (late June to Aug daily 10am–noon & 1–5pm; Sept–May Tues, Wed, Sat & Sun 1–5pm, Thurs–Fri 1–5pm & 7–9pm; free), on the western edge of town at 1402 blvd St-Germain Ouest. This is an eclectic commercial art gallery of some renown, featuring work by modern French-Canadian painters. A few kilometres northeast of town, along Hwy 132, the **Musée de la Mer** (early June to mid-Oct daily 9am–6pm; $3.75) has an interesting series of displays on the *Empress of Ireland*, a luxury liner that sank just offshore with the loss of over a thousand lives in 1914. The staff here will also unlock the door of the adjoining **Pointe-au-Père Lighthouse**, which marks the point at which the St Lawrence River becomes the Gulf of St Lawrence.

Rimouski's **tourist office**, 50 Rue St-Germain Ouest (June–Sept daily 8am–8pm; Oct–May Mon–Fri 8.30am–4.30pm; ☎723-2322) is right in the centre of town, on the waterfront. They have **accommodation** listings, including college rooms which are available during the summer vacation, at *Logis Vacances*, 320 Rue Potvin (☎723-4636; ②). There's also a **youth hostel** – *Auberge La Voile* at 58 St-Germain Est (☎722-8002; ①). The town's cheapest motel is the *Motel-Chalets Belle Vue*, 1038 blvd St-Germain Ouest (☎723-0034; ①), or you could try the *Motel Colonial*, at no. 438 (☎723-8960; ②). For **camping**, *La Bocage*, 124 Route 132 (☎739-3125; $15), is near a lake. Rivi-Air Aventure (☎735-2383) are a good outfit to go **white-water rafting** with.

Rimouski has one of the province's best budget **restaurants** in *La Vieille Demoiselle*, 11 Rue St-Denis, for fresh game and fish, as well as a couple of student hangouts that make good places to eat: *Café la Bohème*, 31 Rue d'Éveche for down-to-earth grub, and the slightly pricier *La Forge du Père Cimon*, 35 Rue St-Germain Est. You can eat by weight at the organic restaurant *La Nature* at 208 blvd St-Germain Est and *Le Mix* at no. 50. On the same street is the best **bar**, along with *Bar Country Chez Dallas* at no. 134, for line-dancing and yee-has. For onward **transport**, the Orléans Express bus station is at 90 av Léonidas (☎723-4923), the VIA Rail station at 57 de L'Évêché Est (☎722-4737 or 1-800-361-5390), and the rideshare outfit Allo-Stop at 106 Rue St-Germain Est (☎723-5248).

Rimouski to Matane

From Rimouski to Matane there are only two places worth stopping. The first is the **Gaspésie Regional Tourist Office**, 357 rte de la Mer beside Hwy 132 at Sainte-Flavie (daily: mid-June to Aug 8am–8pm; Sept to mid-June Mon–Fri 8.30am–5pm), which has armfuls of literature on the whole of the peninsula and operates a free room-reservation service. Nine kilometres further east along the highway, in Grand-Métis, are the **Jardins de Métis** (early June to Sept daily 8.30am–8pm; $6), the creation of Elsie Reford, who was given the estate in 1919 by her uncle, Lord Mount Stephen, first president of the Canadian Pacific Railway. These wonderful gardens, subdivided into eight distinct areas, boast species and varieties of plants not usually seen this far north; the azaleas, lilies and rhododendrons are especially lush. In the centre of the gardens stands **L'Historique Villa Reford** (daily 10am–6pm) with panelled rooms of Australian red gum. Here guides give the lowdown on the life of the Victorian gentry, with knick-knacks from Elsie Reford's day and mock-ups of the local church, shop and school to get a feel of her era. You can feed on veggies from the garden, fresh fish and regional cuisine in the overpriced restaurant, or buy gardening gear and gifts at the artisan boutique.

At first sight, **MATANE**, 56km further east, appears to be dominated by oil refineries and cement works, but in fact fishing and forestry have long been the mainstays of the local economy. The town is bisected by the Matane River, which is spanned by a duo of bridges – one beside the harbour (part of Hwy 132), the other a shorter affair a few hundred metres upstream; the shorter bridge sits next to the fish ladder, which was built to help the salmon head upstream to spawn. Matane's main claim to fame is its **Festival de la Crevette**, held during the last week in June. It takes its name from the prawn harvest but, in fact, celebrates the entire range of local seafood – all the town's restaurants and bars participate. There are more fishy happenings from the dam **Barrage Mathieu-D'Amours** where an observation area allows visitors to watch salmon battling to get upstream on the river.

Matane's **tourist office** is beside Hwy 132, just west of the centre, in the lighthouse at 968 av du Phare Ouest (late June to mid-Sept daily 8am–8pm; mid-Sept to late June Mon–Fri 8.30am–5pm; ☎562-1065). Simple institutional **accommodation** can be rented at *Cégep de Matane*, 616 av St-Rédempteur (☎562-1240; ①), and there's a comfortable **B&B** called *Auberge la Seigneurie*, near the centre on the west side of the river, at 621 av St-Jérôme (☎562-0021; ②). Most of Matane's **hotels** and **motels** are pricey; *Belle Plage*, 1310 rue Matane-sur-Mer (☎562-2562 or 1-888-244-2333; ③; summer only) has a good restaurant and is right on the sea. There's a municipal **campground**, south of the centre of town at 150 Route Louis-Félix Dionne (☎562-3414; $11 for four-person site; mid-June to Aug). Sandwiches and other **snacks** are available at the cheap *Café aux Delices*, 109 rue St-Jean in town. For seriously good pizza, check out *La Pizzeria Italia*, on the corner of rues St-Pierre and St-Jérôme, and for some of Québec's finest food there's the **restaurant** in the *Hôtel des Gouverneurs*, 260 av du Phare Est and the expensive *La Maison sous la Vent* at no. 1014 down the road (☎562-7611).

From Matane, a ferry runs to Godbout (early June to early Sept 1–3 daily; early Sept to early June 1 daily except Sat) and Baie-Comeau (Jan–March 4 weekly; April–Dec 1–2 daily) on the north side of the St Lawrence. For both destinations, the journey takes around two and a half hours and costs $10 per passenger, $24.50 per car; information on ☎562-2500.

Around Matane: the wildlife reserve

About an hour's drive from the town along Hwy 195 lies the **Réserve Faunique de Matane** (☎562-3700), a chunk of wooded hills and mountains interspersed with lakes and rivers that are noted for salmon fishing. Beside the road, the park's **Reception Centre** has the details of various hiking routes and there's a well-established **campground** close by, *Camping John* (☎224-3345; sites from $11.50; early June to Aug).

Sainte-Anne and the Gaspésie park

East of Matane the highway hugs the shoreline, passing through an increasingly rugged scenery where the forested hills of the interior push up against the fretted, rocky coast. A string of skimpy fishing villages breaks up this empty landscape – places like Capucins, with its fine headland setting, and **Cap Chat**, just west of which the **Éolienne de Cap-Chat** (mid-June to Aug daily 8.30am–5pm; $6) is visible for miles around. At 100m, it's the tallest and most powerful vertical-axis wind tower in the world.

Just 16km beyond Cap-Chat, unenticing **SAINTE-ANNE-DES-MONTS** sprawls along the coastline, its untidy appearance only offset by its relaxed atmosphere and its convenience – it's an easy place to break your journey before heading on to the cape, or inland to the Parc de la Gaspésie. For **accommodation**, try the *Motel Manoir sur*

Mer, 475 1ère av Ouest (☎763-7844; ②), where the rooms back onto the beach, or the **B&B** *Chez Marthe-Angéle*, on the same road at no. 268 (☎763-2692; ②). The terraced Victorian *Auberge Chateau Lamontagne*, 170 1ère av Est (☎763-2589; ③), once the home of Québec poet Blanche Beauregard–Lamontagne, is the finest place to stay. For a tasty bite to eat, try the reasonably priced *Le Café la Détente*, 63 1ère Avenue Ouest.

The Parc de la Gaspésie

As you travel south from Ste-Anne-des-Monts on Hwy 299, the snowcapped **Chic-Choc Mountains** – which make up most of the **Parc de la Gaspésie** – can be spotted in the distance, a stark and forbidding backdrop to the coastal plain. The Chic-Chocs are the most northerly protrusions of the Appalachian Ridge, which extends deep into the USA, and the serpentine road reveals the full splendour of their alpine interior. The sequence of valleys framed by thickly wooded slopes culminates in the staggering ravine that lies at the foot of the towering **Mont Albert**. In this ravine, 40km from Sainte-Anne-des-Monts, the park's **Reception and Interpretation Centre** (June to early Sept daily 8am–8pm; ☎763-3301) has details and maps of half a dozen well-signposted **hiking trails**, each of about a day's duration; prospective hikers should come fully equipped and log their intended route at the centre. These mountain trails ascend to the summits of the area's three highest mountains – Mont Jacques-Cartier, Mont Richardson and Mont Albert – and are remarkable in that they climb through three distinctive habitats. Herds of **Virginia deer** thrive in the rich vegetation of the lowest zone, while **moose** live in the boreal forest, and **caribou** in the tundra at the peaks. This is the only place in Québec where the three species exist in close proximity.

The park has two **campgrounds**, one of which, the *Camping du Mont Albert* (☎763-2288; $15 for four-person site), is conveniently situated near the Interpretation Centre. Close by, too, is the smart and modern *Auberge Gîte du Mont Albert* (☎763-2288 or 1-800-463-0860; ③), which offers the only fixed **lodgings** in the park; room prices rocket during the summer and skiing seasons, but you couldn't wish for a handier location. The *Auberge* also controls a number of **chalets** (③) around the park, offering simple but reliable facilities.

Sainte-Anne to the Forillon park

Heading east from Sainte-Anne-des-Monts towards the tip of the Gaspé Peninsula, the road often squeezes between the ocean and the sheer rock faces of the mountains, its twists and turns passing tumbling scree and picturesque coves. Aim to be hungry by the time you reach **MARSOUI**, a tiny fishing village 34km east of Ste-Anne with a remarkable **restaurant**, *La Couquerie* – very reasonably priced and one hundred per-cent French Canadian. It started life in 1937 as the refectory of the defunct local lumber mill, and the interior remains functional, with simple hard benches beside six long tables. However, the daily specials here are glorious – try the salmon or the meat and vegetable stew (*cipaille*), real bargains at around $10. **Accommodation** is available at the *Hôtel Marsoui* (☎288-5677; ①); the village also has a sheltered shingly beach.

The view as you approach **MONT-SAINT-PIERRE** is majestic, the curving seashore and the swelling mountains together framing this little community set at the mouth of a wide river valley. Mont-Saint-Pierre is a low-key resort, dedicated to bathing and sea fishing, except during the **hang-gliding festival** at the end of July. During the rest of the summer you can fly in tandem for $100 with the Centre de Renseignments sur le Vol Libre et d'Acceuil Touristique, 116 Prudent-Cloutier (☎797-2222). The *Auberge de Jeunesse les Vagues* **youth hostel**, on the waterfront at 84 rue Prudent Cloutier (☎797-2851; ①), is the cheapest place to stay, or there are several cheap-and-cheerful **motels** along the same street: try the *Hôtel Motel Mont-*

Saint-Pierre at no. 60 (☎797-2202; ②) or the *Motel Restaurant au Délice* at no. 100 (☎797-2850; ③). For **camping**, try the *Du Pont* on Hwy 132 (☎797-2951; four-person sites $12; June–Sept).

The Parc National de Forillon

Lying at the very tip of the peninsula, the **PARC NATIONAL DE FORILLON** is the scenic culmination of the Gaspé, encompassing some 250 square kilometres of thick forest and mountain, crossed by hiking trails and fringed by stark cliffs along a deeply indented coastline. The splendour of the landscape is complemented by the **wildlife**: black bears, moose, beavers, porcupines and foxes are all common, and over two hundred species of birds have been seen, ranging from sea birds like gannets, cormorants and guillemots to songbirds such as the skylark and chaffinch. From the coastal paths around Cap Gaspé itself, **whales and porpoises** can also be spotted between May and October. As Thomas Anburey, a British soldier, observed in the 1770s, "They cause most beautiful fire works in the water: for being in such abundance, and darting with amazing velocity, a continued stream of light glides through the water, and as they cross each other, the appearance is so picturesque that no description can reach it."

Roughly triangular in shape, the park is sandwiched between the Gulf of St Lawrence and the Baie de Gaspé and encircled by Hwys 197 and 132, the former crossing the interior to delineate the park's western limits, the latter mostly keeping to the seashore to connect the park's facilities and attractions. Highway 132 also threads through a series of tiny coastal villages, but these are desultory affairs set just outside the park's boundary – and you're far better off staying within the park.

There are **visitors' centres** at the two road entrance points both on Hwy 132: one is on the northern shore, at **L'Anse-au-Griffon** (daily: early June to Aug 8.30am–9.30pm; Sept to mid-Oct 9am–4pm; ☎368-5505 or 1-800-463-6769); the other on the south coast at **Penouille** (same hours; ☎892-5661). The **interpretation centre** (daily: early June 1–4pm; mid-June to early Sept 9am–6pm; early Sept to mid-Oct 9am–4pm; ☎892-5572), close to the lighthouse near the village of Cap-des-Rosiers on the north shore, is, however, the best place to start a visit. Here, the natural and human history of the area is imaginatively presented, with a wealth of suggestions as to how to spend your time.

Perhaps the best **hike** is to the tip of **Cap Gaspé**. This ninety-minute return trip starts a few kilometres to the south of the interpretation centre from the end of the paved road beyond Grande-Grave, a pleasant, restored small fishing village founded by immigrants from Jersey – the inhabitants were relocated as recently as 1970 when the park was established. The trail follows the southern coast of the cape, rising and falling until it makes the final steep ascent to the **lighthouse**, which is set on a 150-metre cliff with the ocean on three sides. On a clear day, you can see the rock at Percé, 40km to the south. More leisurely pursuits include two-hour **boat trips** along the northern shore from near the interpretation centre (mid-June to mid-Sept every 2hr from 9am; 1hr 55min; $15) and **whale-watching** excursions from Grande-Grave (June–Oct 10am–1.30pm & 4.30pm; 2hr 30min; $30).

Also on the south side of the park, along the road west of Cap-aux-Os, lie the remains of **Fort Péninsule**, the bay's World War II coastal gun battery, located in an underground bunker whose history is detailed by a series of explanatory plaques. The fort was built to protect Gaspé town and harbour from German U-boats, who ventured as far as Matane in search of victims. It was a particularly important defence, as Gaspé town, along with Shelburne in Nova Scotia, was scheduled to be the base for the Royal Navy in the event of a successful German invasion of Great Britain. Nearby, the small tongue of land called **Penouille** pokes out into the bay, its woods and sand dunes making it ideal for swimming, sunbathing and picnicking.

Park practicalities

There are half a dozen **campgrounds** in the park and all of them are pleasantly situated and well maintained; call ☎368-8050 for reservations ($11.85 for six-person site). *Camping Cap Bon-Ami* (early June to early Sept) has a particularly delightful setting just south of the interpretation centre. The visitors' centres and interpretation centre have details of all sites, and can arrange accommodation in **chalets** (③) around the park, which are cheaper if booked by the week. Cars are charged $5 a day to enter the park. Alternatively, the villages edging the park offer a smattering of plain accommodation that includes Anse-au-Griffon's *Motel le Noroit*, 589 blvd Griffon (☎892-5531; ②), and *Le Gîte du Parc* (☎892-5864; ②), in Cap-aux-Os, which also has a **youth hostel**, at 2095 blvd Grande-Grève (☎892-5153; ①). The hostel has a café, laundry facilities and a **mountain-bike rental** shop (☎892-5952; around $20 a day).

Gaspé

The town of **GASPÉ**, straddling the hilly estuary of the York River, is a disappointment after the scenic drama of the national park, a humdrum settlement of about 17,000 people whose hard-pressed economy is reliant on its deep-water port. This is the spot where the French navigator and explorer **Jacques Cartier** landed in July 1534, on the first of his three trips up the St Lawrence. He stayed here for just eleven days, time enough to erect a wooden cross engraved with the escutcheon of Francis I, staking out the king's – and Christianity's – claim to this new territory. Cartier's first aim was to find a sea route to the Orient, but he also had more extensive ambitions – to acquire land for himself and his men, exploit the Indians as fur gatherers and discover precious metals to rival the loot the Spaniards had taken from the Aztecs. Naturally, Cartier had to disguise his real intentions on the first trip and his initial contacts with the Iroquois were cordial. Then, in the spring of 1536, on his second visit, he betrayed their trust by kidnapping a local chief and nine of his men, and taking them back to Francis I. None of the captives ever returned, and when Cartier made his third trip in 1541 the Iroquois were so suspicious that he was unable to establish the colony he had been instructed to found. Desperate to salvage his reputation, Cartier sailed back to France with what he thought was a cargo of gold and diamonds. They turned out to be iron pyrites and quartz crystals.

Just to the east of the town centre, at 80 blvd Gaspé, the **Jacques Cartier Monument** looks out over the bay from the grounds of the town museum. It consists of six striking bronze dolmens carved in relief with a record of Cartier's visit supplemented by some anodyne homilies on the nature and unity of humankind. The **museum** itself (late June to Aug daily 8.30am–8.30pm; Sept to mid-Oct Mon–Fri 9am–5pm, Sat & Sun noon–5pm; mid-Oct to late June Mon–Fri 9am–noon & 1–5pm; $3.50) illuminates the social issues that have confronted the inhabitants of the peninsula to the present – isolation from the centres of power, depopulation and, more recently, unemployment. There are also interesting temporary displays, most of which concentrate on local subjects, like the peninsula's artists and musicians.

A good ten minutes' walk away, near the top of Rue Jacques-Cartier, stands the controversial **Gaspé cathedral**. Built in 1934 to commemorate the fourth centennial of Cartier's landing, it's the only cathedral in North America to be built of wood, and from the outside it has an extraordinarily dour and industrial appearance. The interior is completely different: the nave – all straight lines and symmetrical simplicity – is bathed in warm, softly coloured light that pours in through an enormous stained-glass window in the style of Mondrian. Directly in front of the cathedral stands a massive granite **cross**, also erected in 1934 in honour of the explorer.

Just outside town, next door to the white **Sanctuaire Notre-Dame des Douleurs**, a popular pilgrimage site, is the **Site Historique Micmac de Gespeg** (June–Sept daily

9am–5pm; $3), an exact replica of the original native village that stood at *Gespeg* ("the end of the land" in the Micmac language) in the seventeenth century.

Practicalities

Buses to Gaspé stop on the main street, Rue Jacques-Cartier, at the *Restaurant Hotel Adams*. The **tourist office** (mid-June to Aug daily 8am–8pm) is on the far side of the river from the town centre along Hwy 132; it has accommodation listings and maps of the town. **College rooms** are available during the summer at the Cégep de la Gaspésie et des Îles at 94 Rue Jacques-Cartier (☎368-2749; ①). The central *La Normande*, 19 Rue Davis (☎368-5468; ②), *La Canadienne*, 201 Mgr Le Blanc (☎368-3806; ②), and the *Gîte Baie Jolie*, 270 montée Wakeham (☎366-2149; ②) are the only registered **B&Bs**. There's bargain-basement **motel** accommodation at *Motel Plante*, 137 Rue Jacques-Cartier (☎368-2254; ②), and Motel Fort Ramsay, 254 blvd Gaspé (☎368-5094; ②; summer only); *L'Auberge des Commandants*, 178 Rue de la Reine (☎ & fax 368-1702; ③), has far more comfortable rooms.

Le Bourlingueur, next to the Jacques-Cartier Mall opposite the main bridge at 207 de la Reine, is recommended for **breakfast** at around $4, though the Chinese and Canadian dishes on the evening menu are rather pricey, with main courses at around $13. Otherwise, *Brize-Brize*, 2 Côte Carter, is a great café and a swinging bar at night. Nearby *Café à Grain*, 76 rue Jacques-Cartier, is a natural-foods store, good for stocking up if you're heading for the parks. *Mastro Pizzeria*, at the bottom of Rue Jacques-Cartier, has competent Italian **food** for about $9, and there's also a decent café-bar in the bus depot. If you're feeling flush, check out *La Quatre Temps*, 135a Rue de la Reine (☎368-1455) – it's one of the best restaurants on the peninsula for French cuisine. *Bacalao del Castillo*, 4 Rue du Chantier-Maritime, is a cheaper option for traditional fare.

Percé

Once a humble fishing community, **PERCÉ** is a prime holiday spot, thanks to the tourist potential of the gargantuan limestone rock that rears up from the sea here facing the reddish cliffs of the shore. One of Canada's most celebrated natural phenomena, the **Rocher Percé** is nearly 500m long and 100m high, and is an almost surreal sight at dawn, when it appears bathed in an eerie golden iridescence. The town is now replete with tourist facilities, like gift shops, private art galleries, restaurants and bars. Despite this it still makes for a pleasant overnight stop and, off season, when much of the resort closes down, Percé maintains a delightfully relaxed and sleepy feel.

At low tide it's possible, if you hurry, to walk round most of the rock, accompanied by the overpowering screams of the sea birds that nest in the cliffs. One of the most spectacular longer-range views of the monolith is from the top of **Mont Sainte-Anne**, which rises directly behind Percé town; the path is signposted from behind the church on avenue de l'Église and the walk takes about an hour each way, or you can drive up there.

Apart from the rock, there's precious little else to see in Percé, though the **Centre d'Interprétation du Parc de l'Île-Bonaventure-et-du-Rocher-Percé** (early June to mid-Oct daily 9am–5pm; free), some 2km to the south of the centre off Hwy 132 at Route des Failles and left along Route d'Irlande, has some enjoyable displays on the area's flora and fauna. In the middle of town, in the old Charles-Robin-Company building used for processing and storing fish, the **Musée la Chafaud**, 145 Route 132 (June–Sept daily 10am–10pm; $2), displays traditional and contemporary art. Otherwise, Percé makes a useful base for visiting several natural attractions, including the **Great Crevasse**, a volcanically formed split in a rocky outcrop that's just a few millimetres wide but several hundred metres deep. The clearly marked path takes about an hour to walk in each direction and begins behind the *Auberge de Gargantua*, a first-class restaurant on Route des Failles.

From the wharf in the centre of Percé, there are frequent boat trips (1hr 30mins–3hr; $15–30) round the nearby Île Bonaventure bird reserve (daily: June & Sept to mid-Oct 8.15am–4pm; July & Aug 8.15am–5pm), whose precipitous cliffs are favoured by gannets in particular, as well as kittiwakes, razorbills, guillemots, gulls, cormorants and puffins. You can also arrange to disembark at the island's tiny jetty, where all of the several-hour-long walking trails lead to the cliff tops above the gannet colonies, but be sure to book your return in advance. The return trip costs around $15.

The wharf is also the departure point for **whale-watching** excursions – between mid-April and December, the blue and humpback whales are often in the area, and you may also see porpoises, seals and the rarer white-sided dolphins. Zodiacs speed out with Observation Littoral Percé (☎782-5359), or you can go on a larger boat with Les Croisières Duval (☎782-5001). Trips last from two to three hours and cost around $25. If you feel like even more adventure, rent a sea kayak from Cours de Kayak (June–Sept; ☎782-5403) for guided tours that last from two hours ($30) to a day ($40–65).

Practicalities

Highway 132 bisects Percé and passes just to the north of the main wharf, close to the **tourist office** (mid-June to Aug daily 8am–8pm), which has a comprehensive list of accommodation, operates a free room-reservation service and keeps a variety of boat and tide timetables. Arriving from Carleton or Gaspé, **buses** drop passengers in the centre of Percé at the Petro-Canada service station, but the VIA Rail station is 10km south of town on Hwy 132.

Some of the cheapest **rooms** in town are at the seasonal *Maison Avenue House* guesthouse, 38 av de l'Église (☎782-2954; ①; summer only) and there's a new *Auberge de Jeunesse*, 167 Route Principale (☎782-2122; ①), that has a good location. Alternatively, there are lots of **motels** dotted along Hwy 132 and, although there's little to distinguish them, advance bookings are advised in July and August. Some of the less expensive options include the *Bleu Blanc Rouge*, no. 103 (☎782-2142; ③; summer only); *Motel Bellevue*, no. 183 (☎782-2182; ②; summer only); *Le Macareux*, no. 262 (☎782-2414; ②; summer only); and no. 288, *Le Mirage du Rocher* (☎782-5151 or 1-800-463-9011; ②; summer only). Rather more upmarket, the *Hôtel la Normandie*, 221 Hwy 132 Ouest (☎782-2112 or 1-800-463-0820; ⑤; summer only), has a clutch of brightly modern bedrooms with superb views along the coast. The south end of town is where you'll find the **campgrounds**: try the shoreline's *Camping Côte Surprise* on Hwy 132 (☎782-5443; four-person sites from $17.50), where there are great views of the rock.

La Maison du Pêcheur, just up from the wharf, has fine **seafood** dishes; the *Restaurant Biard*, on the main street at no. 99, has an enjoyable set-price buffet for $12. Substantial **snacks**, coffees and vegetarian dishes are best in the faintly Bohemian atmosphere of *Les Fous de Bassan*, also in the centre on the main street. For very fine food, dine at *L'Auberge Gargantua*, 222 Rue des Failles (☎782-2852), with gourmet French cuisine and great panoramas over town, or *La Normandia*, 221 Hwy 132 Ouest (☎782-2112), for such delights as lobster baked in champagne.

The Baie des Chaleurs

Along the coastal road to the southwest of Percé, the dramatic mountains that dominate the north and east of the peninsula are replaced by a gently undulating landscape of wooded hills and farmland. **Chandler**, the first town of any size on this route, is an ugly lumber port notable solely for the wreck of the Peruvian freighter *Unisol* in the mouth of the harbour. It ran aground in a gale in 1983, allegedly because its captain, unable to negotiate entry into the port for his cement-laden vessel, got drunk and allowed the vessel to run onto the sandbank where it remains today. Beyond Chandler lies the **Baie** des Chaleurs, the long wedge of ocean that separates the heart of the Gaspé from New Brunswick. As its name implies, this sheltered inlet has relatively warm waters, and the bay is dotted with seaside resorts-cum-fishing-villages and farming communities, all connected by the coastal highway.

Bonaventure

The most easterly resort on the bay is **BONAVENTURE**, whose tiny centre, beside Hwy 132, edges the marshy delta and man-made lagoon of the river that sports its name. The town is, uniquely, a centre for the production of fish-leather products, such as purses and wallets, but it's usually visited for its salmon fishing and sandy beach. Bonaventure is also a stronghold of **Acadian culture**, whose traditions and heritage are celebrated at the **Musée Acadien du Québec**, 95 av Port-Royal (late June to Aug daily 9am–8pm; Sept to late June Mon–Fri 9am–noon & 1–5pm, Sat & Sun 1–5pm; $3.50), set in an imposing blue and white wooden building, once the church hall, in the town centre. Highlights of the collection include some delightful handmade furniture dating from the eighteenth century and a whole range of intriguing photographs that encapsulate something of the hardship of Acadian rural life.

Next door, Bonaventure's **tourist office**, 91 av Port-Royal (mid-June to Aug daily 9am–6pm), has background information on the town and **accommodation** lists. The latter includes the *Motel le Bocage*, 173 av Port-Royal (☎534-3430; ②; summer only); *Motel Grand Pré*, 118 av Grand-Pré (☎534-2053 or 1-800-534-2053; ⑥) and the B&Bs, *Chez Arsenault*, at 188 Rang Thivierge (☎534-2697; ①) and *Gîte au Bord de l'Eau*, 199 av Port-Royal (☎534-4040; ②). *CimeAventure* on chemin A (☎534-2333) has tepees (①) to sleep in and runs adventure trips into the local area (3hr – 6 days; prices vary). *Camping Beaubassin*, 154 av Beaubassin (early June to Aug) is a municipal **camp-ground** on the spit of land between the lagoon and the bay. Close by, with its name emblazoned in whitewash on the roof, the excellent *Café Acadien* serves imaginative French-Canadian **food** – try the home-baked bread and the fiddlehead soup, made from fern shoots. *Gourmet de la Rose*, 119 av Grand-Pré, has the more usual bagels, sandwiches and salads.

New Richmond

NEW RICHMOND, 30km from Bonaventure, has only one worthy attraction, the **British Heritage Centre of the Gaspésie**, located beside the bay towards the west end of town, 7km from the highway, at 351 blvd Perron Ouest (mid-June to Aug daily 9am–6pm; $4). Set in wooded parkland around the old lighthouse at Duthie's Point, near the mouth of the Cascapédia River, it's a kind of Loyalist theme park, made up of a collection of wooden buildings assembled from the surrounding region, all restored to their nineteenth- or early twentieth-century appearance. None of the buildings is outstanding, but the historical displays on the three most influential groups amongst the region's English-speaking colonists – the Irish, the Scots and the Loyalist Americans – are diverting, and the Centre is spacious enough for a pleasant stroll along the shore. It even has its own tiny beach.

If you're **staying** in New Richmond, try the *Motel Francis*, 210 chemin Pardiac (☎392-4485; ④), the cheaper *Hôtel New Richmond*, 138 av Cyr (☎392-4825; ②), or **camp** at *Camping Parc de la Rivière Cascapédia*, 410 blvd Perron (☎392-5631), but frankly there's nothing to keep you here.

Carleton and around

Just to the west of New Richmond, Hwy 299 runs north along the banks of the Cascapédia towards the Parc de la Gaspésie (see p.278), while the coastal Hwy 132 continues on to the popular bayside resort of **CARLETON**, where the mountains of the interior return to dominate the landscape. Founded in 1756 by Acadian refugees, Carleton is an unassuming little place that stands back from the sea behind a broad lagoon, linked to the narrow coastal strip by a couple of long causeways. The town has a bird sanctuary – a favourite haunt of wading species like the sandpiper and plover – and several possible bathing beaches, but what makes it special is the contrast between the coastal flatlands and the backdrop of wooded hills that rise up behind the town. At 594m, **Mont Saint-Joseph** is the highest of these, ascended by a three-kilometre maze of steep footpaths that slip past streams and waterfalls before they reach the summit, where there are splendid panoramic views over the bay and across to New Brunswick. You can also take the less adventurous (but easier) option and drive up.

Carleton is a good place for an overnight stay and, while you're here, the hilly **Miguasha Peninsula**, some 20km to the west off Hwy 132, makes a pleasant excursion. Famous for its fossils, this tiny peninsula is home to the **Parc de Miguasha**, where the cream of the fossil crop is displayed at the combined research centre and **museum** (June to late Sept daily 9am–6pm; free). Frequent and free guided tours include the museum, the research area and a walk along the beach and cliffs. Also on the peninsula, about 800m from the museum, is the jetty for the little **car ferry** (hourly 7.30am–7.30pm; 20min; $12 one way for driver and car) that crosses over to Dalhousie in New Brunswick, a short cut that avoids the tip of the Baie des Chaleurs.

Carleton's six **motels** are dotted along the main street, Perron. The cheaper choices include: *Auberge la Vieille Surprise*, no. 527 (☎364-6553; ②); *L'Abri*, no. 360 (☎364-7001; ③); *Manoir Belle Plage*, no. 474 (☎364-3388 or 1-800-463-0780; ②); and the *Motel Carleton*, no. 1751 (☎364-3288; ②). The town has a good **campground**, the *Carleton*, on the causeway, banc de Larocque (☎364-3992; $16 for four persons; mid-June to Aug).

Bistro Entre-Nous serves delicious bagels and crêpes in the centre of town at 681 blvd Perron, while more substantial **seafood meals** are available just down the road to the west at *Restaurant le Héron*, no. 561 (where the bus stops), and at *La Maison Monti*, back east at 840 blvd Perron.

Pointe-à-la-Croix and around

Some 50km to the west of Carleton, humdrum **Pointe-à-la-Croix** is the site of the interprovincial bridge over to Campbellton, New Brunswick. During the summer, a **tourist booth** in the tiny wooden house by the turning for the bridge on Hwy 132 (daily 8am–8pm) offers a full range of information on the Gaspé Peninsula. Just before the bridge, a right turn leads to the little waterside community of **RESTIGOUCHE**, at the heart of a Micmac Indian reservation which, oddly enough, functions on New Brunswick time because all the children go to school in Campbellton. The village is home to the Micmacs, an Algonquian-speaking people who spread across the Atlantic seaboard from Nova Scotia through to the Gaspé and east Newfoundland. Their history is a familiarly sad one: trading furs for European knives, hatchets and pots, the Micmacs quarrelled with other native groups over hunting grounds until there was a state of perpetual warfare. In later years, the Micmacs proved loyal allies to the French military cause, but, like all the other native groups, their numbers were decimated by European diseases and they remain a neglected minority. However, the reserve is self-governing and one of the five richest in Canada (there are 800-odd reserves). On your right as you enter the reserve, the locals have reconstructed **Fort Listugui** (mid-June to Oct daily 10am–7pm; $5), based on a 1760 Acadian fort. Built entirely of cedar with a tepee circle in the centre, the fort is staffed by costumed guides and the atmosphere is entertaining and laid-back with traditional singing, drumming, storytelling, craft making and incredible food – try the local bread (*lusgnign*), baked in the outside ovens or the Acadian-style smoked fish. It's possible to stay in the tepees on a bed of fir (①) and in the bunks of the soldiers' cabins (①) – warm bedding is provided. Opposite the fort's entrance the **Listugui Arts and Cultural Centre** (May–Sept daily 9am–5pm; $3) is another new venture that displays traditional crafts and buildings from before European contact. The clothing, canoes and porcupine quill boxes have all been made locally in the last few years to rekindle Micmac interest and skills.

A couple of kilometres west of the bridge, back along Hwy 132, the **Parc Historique National de La Bataille-de-la-Ristigouche** commemorates the crucial naval engagement of 1760, which effectively extinguished French hopes of relieving their stronghold in Montréal, the year after the fall of Québec City. The French fleet, which had already taken casualties in evading the blockade of Bordeaux, was forced to take refuge in the mouth of the Restigouche River and then, despite assistance from local Micmacs and Acadians, was overpowered by superior British forces. The site's excellent **Interpretive Centre** (daily: June–Aug 9am–5pm; Sept to early Oct 9am–noon & 1–4pm; free) contains relics of the French fleet, especially the frigate *Le Machault*, which has been partly reconstructed. There's also an audiovisual display providing a graphic account of the battle and of its strategic significance.

You wouldn't want to stay in Pointe-à-la-Croix, but if you're marooned there's a **youth hostel**, *Auberge de Jeunesse* (☎788-2048; ①), in Pointe-à-la-Garde, some 6km east of the bridge signposted off Hwy 132. It's partly located in an eccentrically Renaissance-style wooden castle, Château Bahia; breakfast is included – and the food is excellent.

Matapédia

Located at the western tip of the Baie, beside the confluence of the Ristigouche and Matapédia rivers, the tiny village of **MATAPÉDIA** is attractively surrounded by steep green hills and lies at the centre of an excellent salmon-fishing region. Not a lot else happens here, but there is an excellent and reasonably priced **restaurant**, *La Belle Époque*, right in the centre, which serves fine seafood dishes for around $12. Close by, the smart *Hôtel Restigouche*, 3 rue du Saumon (☎865-2155; ③ including breakfast), is the **place to stay** if you're here fishing, or for budget travellers there's the *Auberge de Jeunesse* (☎865-2100; ①) just behind the highway's petrol station. From Matapédia, Hwy 132 cuts north across the interior of the peninsula through Amqui, a dreary little town that serves as a ski resort in the winter.

The Îles-de-la-Madeleine

The archipelago of the **Îles-de-la-Madeleine** (Magdalen Islands), scattered in the middle of the Gulf of St Lawrence some 200km southeast of the Gaspé Peninsula and 100km east of Prince Edward Island, consists of twelve main islands of which seven are inhabited and six of these are connected by narrow sand spits, crossed by paved and gravel roads. Together these dozen islands form a crescent-shaped series of dunes, lagoons and low rocky outcrops that measures 65km from end to end, with the main village and ferry port roughly in the middle at **Cap-aux-Meules**. The islands lie in the Gulf Stream, which makes the winters warmer than those of mainland Québec, but they are subject to almost constant winds, which have eroded the red sandstone cliffs along parts of the shoreline into an extraordinary array of arches, caves and tunnels. These **rock formations**, the archipelago's most distinctive attraction, are at their best on the central **Île du Cap-aux-Meules** and the adjacent **Île du Havre-aux-Maisons**.

In 1534, **Jacques Cartier** stumbled across the Îles-de-la-Madeleine on his way west to the St Lawrence River. Cartier, always keen to impress his sponsors with the value of his discoveries, wrote with characteristic exaggeration, "The islands are full of beautiful trees, prairies, fields of wild wheat, and flowering pea plants as beautiful as I've ever seen in Brittany." Despite Cartier's eulogy, the islands attracted hardly any settlers until the Deportations of 1755, when a few Acadian families escaped here to establish a mixed farming and fishing community. Remote and isolated, the **Madelinots,** as the islanders came to be known, were unable to control their own economic fortunes, selling their fish at absurdly low prices to a series of powerful merchants who, in turn, sold them tackle and equipment at exorbitant rates. One of the most notorious of these men was a certain **Isaac Coffin**, who developed a classically colonial form of oppression in the 1790s when he forced many of the islanders to sell their lands to his company. Only in 1895 did a provincial statute allow the Madelinots to buy them back. Today the 15,000 inhabitants are largely dependent on fishing in general, and the lobster catch in particular. Lobster, herring, mackerel, scallops and halibut are the island's mainstay and most of the people work at local companies that freeze, can, smoke, ship or market their catch. Until recently, when international pressure brought it to an end, the annual seal hunt supported many islanders (in March, the seals can be easily spotted on the ice floes). Other sectors of the fishery are now suffering because of fish stock depletion and the community's future livelihood revolves around tourism. This has many residents worried about preserving their way of life and the fragile ecology of their beautiful islands.

For, although the archipelago's tiny villages are rather drab and desultory, it has become a popular tourist destination, mostly visited for its wide-open landscapes and sense of isolation – it's easy to find a dune-laden beach where you can be alone with the sea. Bear in mind, though, that throughout the islands powerful currents and changeable weather conditions make sea bathing dangerous.

Every month except February and March there's a daily car **ferry** to Cap-aux-Meules from Souris, on Prince Edward Island (Souris ☎902/687-2181; Cap-aux-Meules ☎418/986-6600 or 1-888-936-3278); a return costs $258 for a car with two passengers and it's a five-hour trip. Reservations are advised in July and August. There's also a cargo and fifteen-passenger ship, the *CTMA Voyageur*, that leaves Montréal for the islands every Sunday and takes 48 hours to sail down the St Lawrence (Montréal ☎514/937-7656; Cap-aux-Meules ☎418/986-6600; $436 one way including meals). During February and March, the ferry operates from Matane. In July and August another ferry run by Croisières Carleton-les-Îles links Carleton on the Gaspé Peninsula with the islands; departures are every other day and the trip takes fourteen and a half hours (☎418/364-6207). There are daily scheduled flights to Havre-aux-Maisons on Inter-Canadian (☎418/969-2771 or 1-800-665-1177) from Montréal, Québec City, Ottawa, Toronto and Mont Joli. Air Alliance (bookings via Air Canada; ☎418/969-2888 or 1-800-361-8620) also offers daily flights from Gaspé town, Mont Joli, Québec City and Montréal. Book a fortnight in advance for discount flights.

There are just 21 **inns**, **motels** and **hotels** on the Magdalens, so it's a good idea to book a bed before you fly or sail here. The tourist office at Cap-aux-Meules also has details of the islands' many **B&B** addresses (mostly ②) and a substantial number of **cottage** and **apartment** rentals, starting at roughly $250 per week. In addition to the official places detailed below, it is possible to **camp** just about anywhere – though make sure you ask permission first.

Île du Cap-aux-Meules

In the middle of the archipelago, **Île du Cap-aux-Meules** boasts the islands' largest community – **CAP-AUX-MEULES**, on the eastern shore, a useful base for exploring the other islands. Just a couple of kilometres west of the village, there are fine views of the entire island chain from the **Butte du Vent**, the area's highest hill. Further west,

The Gaspé and Îles-de-la-Madeleine telephone code is ☎418.

on the other end of the island near the fishing port of **L'Étang-du-Nord**, you'll find some particularly extravagant coastal rock formations. In the opposite direction, the main road skirts the southern tip of the islands' longest lagoon before heading on across the Île du Havre-aux-Maisons.

Île du Havre-aux-Maisons

Île du Havre-aux-Maisons' smooth green landscapes contrast with the red cliffs of its southern shore. Crisscrossed by narrow country roads and littered with tiny straggling villages, this island is arguably the most appealing of the group, and the weird shapes of the coastal rocks around **Dune-du-Sud** are well worth a visit.

North of here, across the sand spit and along Hwy 199, the hamlet islet of **Pointe-aux-Loups** is edged by two long and deserted beaches. Should you want to **stay**, the *Auberge la P'tite Baie*, 187 Hwy 199 (☎969-4073; ③), with its lovely rooms and sea vistas is your best bet; alternatively you could try the restored convent *Au Vieux Couvent*, 292 route 199 (☎969-2233; ②), which also has a lively **bar** that gets packed every night and serves great **food**.

Grosse-Île and Île de la Grande-Entrée

At the far end of the archipelago, the twin islets of anglophone **Grosse-Île** and francophone **Île de la Grande-Entrée** border the wildlife reserve of the **Pointe-de-l'Est**, whose entrance is beside the main road. On its south side, the reserve is edged by the enormous sandy expanse of the Plage de la Grande Échouerie, whose southern end is framed by yet more splendid rock formations at Old Harry's Point. This is where Europeans first came to the islands in order to slaughter walruses (sea cows). Nowadays the ten-kilometre walk down the beach is a good chance to spot seals. A kilometre past the wharf at **Old Harry** there's a pretty white church with beautifully sculpted doors with the islands as backdrop for biblical tales. A little further, the old red schoolhouse is now the Council for Anglophone Magdalen Islanders, with a museum (June–Sept Mon–Sat 9am–4pm, Sun 11am–4pm; free) telling the history of the anglophone population, most of whom are of Scottish descent.

The lobster port of Grande-Entrée, the last of the islands to be inhabited, has a couple of **accommodation** options – open in summer, *L'Émergence*, 122 chemin des Pealey (☎985-2801; ②), is run by a singer/poet and is a basic but peaceful B&B with great views and use of the kitchen. *Club Vacances "Les Îles"*, 377 Route 199 (☎985-2833; ③) is open all year and has camping space as well as rooms. The food is expensive but it's possible to pay for full board. There are also various activities on offer – they run trips to the caves of Île Boudreau – and seal spotting in the summer.

Île du Havre-Aubert

To the south of the Île du Cap-aux-Meules, **Île du Havre-Aubert** has one significant community, **HAVRE-AUBERT**, that's edged by round sloping hills. It's a picturesque location and its undoubtable charm attracts a lot of visitors. It is situated around **La Grave**, a pebbly beach flanked by a boardwalk and wooden buildings once used by sailors and fishermen and now transformed into bars, cafés, restaurants, souvenir shops and an art gallery for the island's new trade in tourists. Here, the **Musée de la Mer** (daily: late June to late Aug Mon–Fri 9am–6pm, Sat & Sun 10am–6pm; late Aug to late June Mon–Fri 9am–noon & 1–5pm, Sat & Sun 1–5pm; $3.50) has a series of displays on local fishing techniques and the history of the islands – especially the many shipwrecks. At Les Artisans du Sable all sorts of things from lampshades to decorations are made out of sand by a special Madelinot technique. The **sandcastle contest** held on the beach in mid-August (weather permitting) produces some awesome creations.

Centre Nautique de l'Istorlet, 100 chemin de l'Isorlet (☎937-5266) rents out **sea and surf kayaks**, a fun way to explore the cliffs and caves of the coast; it also has cheap **rooms** (①). Alternatively you can stay in La Grave at *Chez Charles Painchaud*, 930 Route 199 (☎937-2227; ③), or the seasonal *Le Berceau des Îles*, 701 chemin principal in Havre-Aubert (☎937-5614; ④). Both are B&Bs and the latter can arrange for pick-ups from the airport or ferry as well as organizing winter and summer activities – they even rent out cars.

Eating places are good quality in Havre-Aubert: try the seafood at *Auberge Chez Denis à François*, 404 chemin d'en Haut – they even have seal on the menu. *La Saline*, 1009 Route 199 in La Grave, is open for delicious evening fare in one of the traditional buildings – there's also live music in the adjoining bar. The much more expensive *La Marée Haute*, 25 chemin des Fumoirs, is also only open at night and serves up some of Canada's finest, including sea urchins and smoked seal. For chunky sandwiches, head for *Café de la Grave* in the old general store at La Grave or *Le Petit Mondrain* on chemin de la Grave, which is popular with locals and possibly has the islands' cheapest seafood.

Île d'Entrée

To the southeast, tiny anglophone **Île d'Entrée** is the only inhabited island that's not linked by land to the rest of the archipelago. This grassy hillock is encircled by footpaths and makes a pleasant day out, providing the sea is calm on the **ferry** trip from Cap-aux-Meules (Mon–Sat 2 daily; $18 return; information ☎986-5705). The islands' highest point, Big Hill (174m), is here – from the port take chemin Main and then chemin Post Office, then follow the path across the fields to the top for a view of the whole archipelago. If you're staying here you'll probably end up in someone's home – call ☎986-2245 for more information. For food, there's a bar-restaurant and a grocery.

Practicalities

The islands' **airport** is inconveniently situated at the north end of Île du Havre-aux-Maisons, some 20km from Cap-aux-Meules. Some of the flights have connecting buses to Cap-aux-Meules, but otherwise you'll have to take a Lafrance taxi (☎986-6649; about $35), or **hire a car** from the Tilden (☎969-2590 or 986-2409) or Budget (☎985-4825) at the airport. The **ferry terminal** at Cap-aux-Meules is near the **tourist office**, 128 chemin du Débarcadère (late June to Aug daily 7am–9pm; Sept to late June Mon–Fri 9am–noon & 1–5pm; ☎986-2245). They have masses of free leaflets and operate a free room reservation service with a special emphasis on B&B.

The best way to tour the principal islands is by **bike**, which are available for rent at Le Pédalier, 365 chemin Principal, Cap-aux-Meules (☎986-2965) and **mopeds** can be rented from Cap-aux-Meules Honda, route 199 at La Vernière, southwest of Cap-aux-Meules (☎986-4085). **Boat** and **fishing trips** leave from near the ferry terminal throughout the summer (information ☎986-4745); the cliff and cave excursions are best, at around $30 per person.

More reasonably priced **accommodation** options include the *Motel Boudreau*, 280 chemin Principal (☎986-2391; ④); the *Motel Bellevue*, 40 chemin Principal (☎986-4477; ④); and the *Auberge du Village*, 205 chemin Principal (☎986-3312; ③). Alternatively, the overlarge *Château Madelinot*, 323 Hwy 199 (☎986-3695 or 1-800-661-4537; ⑤), offers fine sea views, great food and comfortable rooms, whilst *Auberge Chez Sam*, in L'Étang-du-Nord (☎986-5780; ②; summer only), has more modest accommodation in an equally relaxing setting.

There are two **campgrounds**: the peaceful *Le Barachois*, chemin du Rivage, Fatima (☎986-6065-5678; $18 for two-person site; May–Sept) and *Camping la Martinique*, 37 chemin du Radar, L'Étang du Nord (☎986-3076; $15 for four-person site; May–Sept) situated in a forest. You can also camp on Île de la Grande-Entrée at *Club Vacances "Les Iles"* (☎985-2833) where there's a dorm, should you need to escape from the rain. They also organize excursions and have a great cafeteria.

For outstanding but pricey **food**, you should try the seafood at *La Table des Roy*, 1188 Hwy 199 (closed Mon) in La Vernière just west of Cap-aux-Meules, but dinner will cost over $50. The *Petit Café* in the *Château Madelinot* is open all year, with a menu that ranges from hamburgers to lobsters; evening specials cost $25. Less expensive options include sandwiches and submarines at *Café le Bistrot*, and wonderful ice cream at *Bar Laitier au Cornet*, both in Cap-aux-Meules.

NORTH QUÉBEC

Québec's true north is a mighty, inhospitable tundra inhabited only by mining communities, groups of Inuits, and the hardy characters who staff the hydroelectric installations with which so many of the rivers are dammed. This section deals with the only readily accessible region, along the north shore of the St Lawrence and its main tributary, the Saguenay, covering an area that changes from trim farmland to a seemingly never-ending forest bordering the barren seashore of the St Lawrence.

Immediately northeast of Québec City is the beautiful **Charlevoix** region of peaceful villages and towns that bear the marks of Québec's rural beginnings – both in the architecture of the seigneurial regime and in the layout of the land. Often the winding highways and back roads pass through a virtually continuous village, where the only interruptions in the chain of low-slung houses are the tin-roofed churches. The beguiling hills and valleys give way to dramatic ravaged rock just beyond the Charlevoix borders, where the **Saguenay River** crashes into the immense fjord that opens into the St Lawrence at the resort of **Tadoussac**.

Inland, **Lac Saint-Jean** – source of the Saguenay – is an oasis of fertile land in a predominantly rocky region, and its peripheral villages offer glimpses of native as well as Québécois life. The adventurous can head beyond Tadoussac to **Havre-St-Pierre** through a desolate, sparsely populated region where the original livelihoods of fishing and lumber have largely given way to ambitious mining and hydroelectric projects. The remoteness of northern islands such as the **Île d'Anticosti** and the sculptured terrain of the **Mingan archipelago** – as a national park, well served by boats from Havre-St-Pierre – is matched by the isolation of the unmodernized fishing communities along the **Lower North Shore,** where no roads penetrate and visits are possible only by supply ship.

Charlevoix

Stretching along the north shore of the St Lawrence east of Québec City, from the Beaupré coast to the Saguenay River, the area of Charlevoix, named after the Jesuit historian Francois Xavier de Charlevoix, is the world's only inhabited UNESCO World Biosphere Reserve. Species like the arctic caribou and great wolf, not usually associated with such southerly latitudes, can be seen in the more remote areas, and because the ice age that shaped the rest of eastern Canada missed this breathtaking portion of the Canadian Shield, numerous pre-glacial plants still thrive here. Its 6000 square kilometres consist of gently sloping hills, sheer cliffs and vast valleys veined with rivers, brooks and

The telephone code for North Québec is ☎418.

waterfalls; a landscape that Québec's better known artists – Clarence Gagnon, Marc-Aurèle Fortin and Jean-Paul Lemieux – chose for inspiration. Though Charlevoix has been a tourist destination for years, the land has been carefully preserved, and quaint villages and tin-roofed churches still nestle in an unspoiled countryside.

Highway 138, the main route through Charlevoix, travels 225km from Québec City to Baie-Ste-Catherine on the Saguenay. The main towns along this highway are served by Intercar buses from Québec City, but many of the quintessential Charlevoix villages – in particular those along the coastal Hwy 362 – are not served by public transport. Be prepared to rent a car or bike – the expense is well worth it.

Baie-Saint-Paul

One of Charlevoix's earliest settlements and long-time gathering place for Québec's landscape painters, the picture-perfect **BAIE-SAINT-PAUL** is tucked into the Gouffré valley at the foot of the highest range of the Laurentian mountains. Dominated by the twin spires of the church, the streets wind from the centre of town flanked by houses that are more than two hundred years old – and just wandering around Baie-Saint-Paul is the main attraction. For an overview of the works of art produced in Charlevoix, visit the **Centre d'Art de Baie-Saint-Paul**, behind the church at 4 Fafard (daily: late June to Aug 9am–7pm; Sept to late June 9am–5pm; free), which has excellent exhibitions of paintings and sculptures mostly inspired by the surrounding countryside; the Centre's boutique also sells local crafts. Opposite, the plush **Centre d'Exposition** (same times; $3), opened in 1992, has established an international reputation for the excellence of its temporary exhibitions, with the emphasis on contemporary French-Canadian art. Also every June to September, a symposium is held here, when the public can watch young Canadian and European artists at work.

From beside the church, the Rue St-Jean-Baptiste slips through the commercial heart of the town edged by numerous quaint cottages characteristic of Québec's earliest houses, with curving roofs and wide verandas, many converted into commercial galleries. At no. 58 Rue St-Jean-Baptiste, **Maison René Richard** (daily 10am–6pm; $2.50) offers an insight into the works of René Richard, an associate of the Group of Seven. The 1842 house has been left exactly the same since Richard died in 1983; bilingual guided tours take you around his studio and living quarters, a rare glimpse at the Charlevoix of the 1940s when some of Québec's finest painters hung out here.

At no. 41 on the same street, **Randonnées Nature-Charlevoix** (☎435-6275) runs excellent tours of the environs either on foot, ski or bus (late June to Sept 1 daily; 2hr; $15) around the Charlevoix Crater – one of the planet's largest craters and made by a meteorite – or by bike (2hr; $6 including bike rental). There's even the opportunity to take a canoe tour of the salmon stream, Rivière du Gouffre.

Baie-Saint-Paul's nearest park is the **Parc des Grands-Jardins** (daily: late May to mid-June & late Aug to late Oct 9am–5pm; mid-June to late Aug 8am–8pm), 42km away on Hwy 381 but with no public transport. Within the forests and lakes of the park, the 900-metre Mont du Lac des Cygnes gives the best of all Charlevoix panoramas; it's a four-hour climb there and back from the trailhead just beyond the **Thomas-Fortin reception centre** (June–Aug daily 9am–5pm; ☎457-3945) at the park entrance on Hwy 381. Hwy 381 continues to Chicoutimi on the Saguenay River (see p.297). Skiing for a day here costs around $5. **Chalets** are available but must be reserved in advance (☎1-800-665-6527).

In the winter months Husky Charlevoix, 145 Rang 5 (☎435-6520), organizes **dog-sled** excursions. They cost $150 per person per day, including meals, a guide and a lot of fun.

Practicalities

The **information centre** for Baie-Saint-Paul and the whole Charlevoix area is in the Centre d'Art, 4 Ambroise-Fafard (daily: Sept to mid-June 9am–5pm; mid-June to Aug

9am–9pm; ☎665-4454 or 1-800-667-2276); there is also a seasonal office on Hwy 138 (mid-June to Aug daily 9am–9pm).

For a town its size, Baie-Saint-Paul has an excellent variety of **accommodation**, from luxurious historic hotels to an outstanding youth hostel. The best **hotels** are the 1840 *Auberge la Maison Otis*, 23 St-Jean-Baptiste (☎435-2255; ⑧), and the *Auberge la Pignoronde*, 750 Mgr-de-Laval (☎435-5505 or 1-800-463-5250; ⑨), both of which are very expensive. Next door to each other on the waterfront, the *Auberge Domaine Belle-Plage*, 192 Ste-Anne (☎435-3321; ④), and the *Auberge le Cormoran* at no. 196 (☎435-6030; ④), both have comfortable doubles. **B&Bs** are located along the winding St-Jean-Baptiste – the best is *La Muse* at no. 39 (☎435-6839; ②); slightly cheaper is the *Gîte la Tourterelle*, 77 St-Jean-Baptiste (☎435-2441; ①). The town's best bargain is the **hostel/campsite** *Le Balcon Vert*, Hwy 362 (☎435-5587; mid-May to early Oct), about 3km out on the road to Malbaie, with four-berth cabins (①), camping – $20 for four-person site – and a restaurant and bar on site. **Camping** is also available during the summer at the riverside *Camping du Gouffré*, 439 St-Laurent ($16 for four-person site) or the larger *Camping le Genévrier*, 1175 Mgr-de-Laval ($21.50 for two-person site).

The cheapest **food** is at *L'Oasis*, 1 Fafard, a trendy café with great sandwiches and smoked meat or, for a light meal, you could try any one of several excellent patisserie-cafés along St-Jean-Baptiste. For country cooking, the award-winning *Le Mouton Noir*, 43 Ste-Anne, serves hearty fare; check out the smoked sausages with maple syrup. On the same street at no. 29, *Pasta l'Eden* is good for an Italian bite. The restaurant of the *Belle-Plage* also has an excellent reputation.

Hwy 362

From Baie-Saint-Paul the main route onwards is Hwy 138, but if you have your own transport you should opt for the coast-hugging detour of **Hwy 362**, which twists and turns its way through a succession of cliff-top villages.

The first settlement out of Baie-Saint-Paul is **LES ÉBOULEMENTS**, which means "landslides" – after the massive earthquake of 1663, one of many that shaped this region. Just west of the village at nos. 157–159 Principale are the well-kept grounds of the eighteenth-century **Manoir de Sales-Laterrière** (daily 9–11am & 2–4pm; free), whose farmhouse and operating mill (June–Sept daily 10am–5pm; $2) atop a pretty waterfall are among the few intact structures left from the seigneurial regime of New France. At the entrance to the grounds is a charming chapel (1840) built of wood and relocated here from St-Nicholas, a village on the St Lawrence. The manor is not actually open to the public, as it's used as a school, but it can be seen from the mill. Further down the road, in the village itself, the **Centre d'Interpretation de la Forge Tremblay** (May to mid-Oct daily 10am–5pm; $2), dating from 1891, is still used by blacksmiths and there's refreshment in the tearoom next door.

From Les Éboulements a steep secondary road that has been paved only in recent years leads to the pretty village of **SAINT-JOSEPH-DE-LA-RIVE**, a once-important shipyard whose maritime connections are reduced now to the hourly free ferry to Île aux Coudres. Pop into the local **church** (June–Oct daily 9am–8pm; free) on chemin de l'Église, where the altar is propped up by anchors and the font is a huge seashell from Florida. *La Loup-Phoque*, 188 Rue Félix-Antoline Savard, is good for **food** and views.

Île aux Coudres

The ferry takes fifteen minutes to reach the sixteen-kilometre-long island of **Île aux Coudres**, which is said to have been formed when an earthquake shook it from the escarpment at Les Éboulements. Cartier celebrated Canada's first Mass here in 1535 and named the island after its numerous hazelnut trees. Missionaries were the first permanent settlers, arriving in 1748, and the growing population came to depend on shipbuilding and beluga whale hunting for their livelihoods. Ship- and canoe-building still takes place here, but the main industry of its 1600 inhabitants is harvesting peat moss from the bogs in the centre of the island.

The island's stone manors and cottages nowadays attract huge numbers of visitors, who drive and cycle around the 26-kilometre peripheral road that connects – in a clockwise direction – the three villages of **ST-BERNARD, LA BALEINE** and **ST-LOUIS**. Of the incidental attractions along the way, the only real diversions are the restored wind and adjacent water mills – **Les Moulins** (mid-May to late June & Sept to mid-Oct daily 10am–5pm; late June to Aug daily 9am–6.45pm; $2.50) – in the southwest corner of the island, both of which are in full working order churning out buckwheat and wheat flours. There is an **information centre** (mid-June to Aug daily 9am–9pm) near the ferry dock in St-Bernard, with maps of the island. Bikes can be rented from either Gérard Desgagnees, near the jetty at 34 Rue du Port (☎438-2332), or from Vél 'O'-Coudres, 743 des Coudriers in La Baleine, 15km from the dock (☎438-2118), which has all kinds of bikes from tricycles to tandems.

Most **hotels** are located in La Baleine – the best deals are the *Motel la Baleine*, 140 Principale (☎438-2453; ②), and *Motel Écumé*, at 808 Principale (☎438-2733; ③). There's also an ever-expanding number of **B&Bs**, but the island's best bargain is the splendidly located *Motel l'Islet*, 10 l'Islet (☎438-2423; ③; summer only) in an isolated spot near St-Louis, on the west tip of the island. The island's **campgrounds** are *Camping Leclerc*, 183 Principale, La Baleine ($15 for two-person site) and *Camping Sylvie*, 191 Royale, St-Bernard ($17 for four-person site).

T-Coq, near the ferry wharf in St-Bernard, does reasonable burgers while *La Quenouille*, the restaurant of the *Motel l'Islet* in St-Louis, has good local **meals**, as does the nearby *La Mer Veille*, 160 des Coudriers. The island's posh hotel, the *Cap-aux-Pierres* at 246 Principale in La Baleine, serves good-value lunch-time buffets.

From La Malbaie to Saint-Siméon

Highways 362 and 138 converge about 50km from Baie-Saint-Paul, at **LA MALBAIE** – "Bad Bay", so called because Champlain ran aground here in 1608. Situated at the mouth of the Malbaie River, the town sprawls along the riverfront with little to detain you, though the **Maison du Tourisme**, beside the main road at 630 blvd de Comporté (daily: mid-June to Sept 9am–9pm; Oct to mid-June 9am–5pm), has a full range of regional tourist info; the bus arrives on the same road. *Motel Murray Bay*, 40 Laure-Conan (☎665-2441; ②) is a good **accommodation** option. If you have the equipment, head for Charlevoix's oldest and most beautifully situated **campground**, *Camping des Chutes Fraser*, 500 de la Vallée (☎665-2151; sites $20 for four persons; mid-May to mid-Oct), located by the falls of the same name about 3km north from Malbaie.

Adjoining La Malbaie – back along Hwy 362 – is the ritzy resort of **POINTE-AU-PIC**, where you'll find the luxurious chateau-like pile that is the *Manoir Richelieu*, 181 av Richelieu (☎665-3703 or 1-800-463-2613; ⑥). Built in the late 1920s for the Canadian Steamship Line, who ferried tourists here from New York and Montréal, the hotel, now part owned by the provincial government, makes for a delightful overnight **stay** – and there's a brand-new casino next door. Also in Pointe-au-Pic on Hwy 362, the *Auberge des Trois Canards*, 49 côte Bellevue (☎665-3761 or 1-800-461-3761; ⑤), has motel rooms and one of the finest restaurants in Québec – with prices to match. *Auberge Vacances-Santé au Petit Berger,* 1 côte Bellevue (☎665-4428; ③), offers the opportunity to stay in a health spa.

The Hautes-Gorges

One sight that should not be missed in the Charlevoix region is the **Parc Régional des Hautes-Gorges-de-la-Rivière-Malbaie**, a network of valleys that slice through a maze of lofty peaks 45km west of La Malbaie. To get there take Hwy 138 to **St-Aimé-des-Lacs**, from where a stunning thirty-kilometre unpaved forest road leads to the park's **information centre**, Chalet l'Écluse (June to mid-Oct daily 9am–6pm), beside the Malbaie River. On all sides the cliff faces rise over 700m, constituting Canada's deepest canyon east of the Rockies, formed by a slip in the earth's crust 800 million years ago. The uniqueness of the park lies not just in this astounding geology but also in the fact that all Québec's forest species grow in this one comparatively small area. From the Chalet l'Écluse a tiring but rewarding five-kilometre **hike** leads to the canyon's highest point, passing through a Laurentian maple grove on the way to the arctic-alpine tundra of the 800-metre summit – it's a good idea to take food, water and a jacket as protection against the mountain breezes. Other shorter trails offer less strenuous alternatives, and from the l'Écluse dam, beside the information centre, leisurely river cruises depart regularly in summer ($20.50). As well as free maps, the centre has **canoes to rent** ($8 an hour, $18 a day) for the six-kilometre paddle along the calm "Eaux Mortes" of the river, and mountain bikes ($15 a day). The park has just one **campground**, *Camping du Pin Blanc* (☎439-4402; $10; June–Aug).

Cap-à-l'Aigle and Port-au-Persil

Leaving La Malbaie en route to Saint-Siméon you'll pass by a couple of peaceful Québécois villages worth a stop for their vistas of the St Lawrence: **CAP-À-L'AIGLE**, 2km down the road, an agricultural village with a hideous modern church, and the harbour community of **PORT-AU-PERSIL**, 25km further. The former has an excellent **B&B**, *Claire Villeneuve*'s, at 215 St-Raphael (☎665-2288; ①), with a thatched grange that is one of the best examples of Québécois rural architecture.

Saint-Siméon

The hillside village of **SAINT-SIMÉON** marks the junction of Hwy 138 to the Côte Nord and Hwy 170 to the awesome Parc du Saguenay and Lac Saint-Jean (see p.299) – public transport serves only the former. Saint-Siméon also has a ferry service across to Rivière du Loup (2–5 daily; see p.271). Missing the last boat is about the only eventuality that will make you want to **stay**: should it arise, *Chez Éliette*, 166 Rue du Quai (☎638-2228; ①), is a cheap and convenient option.

The Parc du Saguenay

A stupendous expanse of rocky outcrops, sheer cliffs and thick vegetation, the **Parc du Saguenay** perches above both sides of one of the world's longest fjords, which cuts through the Canadian Shield from Tadoussac to Lac Saint-Jean. Coming from the south, the best approach is to drive along the wriggling Hwy 170 from Saint-Siméon, a road that strikes the fjord about 50km from Saint-Siméon, close to **L'ANSE-ST-JEAN**. The only village on the Saguenay when it was founded in 1838, L'Anse-St-Jean is famous now for its Pont du Faubourg, the covered bridge featured on the back of the Canadian $1000 note, which managed to survive the flood of 1996 (see p.297) though the rest of the village was badly affected. There are two-hour **boat cruises** out on the fjord, and they leave from the marina in L'Anse-St-Jean (June–Sept 2 daily; $29.95). The village has a **B&B**, the *Gîte l'Anjeannoise*, 289 St Jean-Baptiste (☎272-3437; ①), and cliff-top cottages and condos at *Gîtes du Fjord*, 344 St Jean-Baptiste (☎272-3430 or 1-800-561-

8060; ③), as well as a couple of **campgrounds** – *Camping de l'Anse* (☎272-2554; $25 for four-person site) is in a good position close to the fjord and has excellent facilities. L'Anse-St-Jean also boasts a particularly fine view of the Saguenay from the La Tabatière lookout – the half-kilometre trail begins at the lookout's car park. An alternative trip is to hike the 10km east from L'Anse-St-Jean through the Parc du Saguenay to **PETIT SAGUENAY**, where the *Auberge du Jardin*, 71 Dumas (☎272-3444 or 1-888-272-3444; ③), offers good-quality **accommodation**.

Continuing along the fjord, **RIVIÈRE-ÉTERNITÉ**, 83km from Saint-Siméon and 59km east of Chicoutimi (see p.297), is the main gateway to the Parc du Saguenay (free, but parking $5.50). The park's **information centre** (mid-May to mid-Oct daily 9am–5pm), 8km from the village, has free maps of hiking trails, exhibitions on the flora and fauna, and expert naturalists on hand. A smaller information post is 1.5km from the village, on the park's border. A word of warning about the park's only unpleasant feature – arm yourself with anti-bug cream and long-sleeved tops and trousers, as the blackflies love this place.

Hikes and cruises

From the main information centre, two short hikes and a long one are laid out through the park. Of the short hikes, the **statue hike** is a four-hour round trip up the massive bluff of Cap Trinité, which – with the equally intimidating Cap Éternité – flanks the deep blue water of the Baie Éternité. The summit is topped by a huge statue known as Our Lady of the Saguenay, erected in 1881 by Charles-Napoléon Robitaille after he was saved from drowning in the river. The easier **interpretation hike** (1.6km in total) winds along the banks of the Éternité River; various panels along the way explain the wildlife and geographical phenomena of the area. The park's long-distance hike (25km) follows the bay of the Éternité River back to L'Anse-St-Jean via massive plateaus, ravines, waterfalls and stunning views. The hike takes about three days and there are wilderness campgrounds and a couple of refuges along the way; registration with the information centre is a must (☎272-3008).

If you don't want to hike, one-hour **cruises** of the Baie Éternité (mid-May to mid-Oct daily; $16) leave from near the information centre. Alternatively, in July and August, there's the occasional longer cruise to Chicoutimi ($30), sometimes via **La Baie** on the Baie des Ha! Ha!, which is linked by CITS buses #50 and #51 to Chicoutimi.

Tadoussac to Lac Saint-Jean

The "gateway to the Kingdom of the Saguenay", **Tadoussac** lies some 40km north of Saint-Siméon, at the confluence of the St Lawrence and the Saguenay, whose source – the vast **Lac Saint-Jean** – sits 200km inland. Traffic along Hwy 138 crosses the neck of the Saguenay fjord by a free **car ferry** to Tadoussac, which runs 24 hours a day. The area around Tadoussac and along the fjord is protected by park status, to the benefit of the migratory whale population, which can be observed here at their southern limit. Closer to the lake a glut of aluminium and paper plants using the river as a power source has resulted in the growth of characterless industrial towns, the largest of which is **Chicoutimi**. Further west, the lake's farmland periphery is still relatively untouched and offers the opportunity to stay on the Montagnais reserve at **Pointe-Bleue** near Roberval, a unique **zoo** at **Saint-Félicien** and the strange sight of **Val-Jalbert**, Québec's most accessible ghost town.

Tadoussac

One of Canada's oldest villages, **TADOUSSAC** is beautifully situated beneath the rounded hills that gave the place its name – it comes from the Algonquian word *tatoushak*, meaning "breasts". Basque whalers were the first Europeans to live here and by the time Samuel de Champlain arrived in 1603 Tadoussac was a thriving trading post. The mid-nineteenth century saw Tadoussac evolve into a popular summer resort for the anglophone bourgeoisie: the first hotel opened in 1846 and by the 1860s steamerloads of rich anglophones were arriving every summer to escape the heat of the city. Nowadays it's the best place in Québec for **whale-watching**, especially the rare belugas, the white whale. Late June is a good time to be here, when every outlet with a venue, from the poshest hotels to the smallest bars, have concerts featuring a range of talent; traditional Québécois folk singers, jazz pianists, rock guitarists all play a part in the popular **Festival de la Chanson**.

The waterfront Bord de l'Eau is dominated by the red roof and green lawns of the *Hôtel Tadoussac*, a landmark in Tadoussac since 1864 and the focus of the historic quarter. Next door is the oldest wooden church in Canada, the tiny **Chapelle de Tadoussac** (mid-June to mid-Sept daily 9am–9pm; $1), built by the Jesuits in 1747; inside there are displays of clothing and icons. Tucked on the other side of the hotel, the steep-roofed wooden **Poste de Traite Chauvin** (daily: May, June & Oct 9am–noon & 3–6pm; July–Sept 9am–8.30pm; $2.75) exactly replicates – right down to the handmade nails – the first trading post on the north shore of the St Lawrence as described in Champlain's 1603 diary; it houses a small museum of beaver pelts and bits and pieces pertaining to the fur trade. Also small, but informative, is the **Musée Maritime de Tadoussac** (July–Sept; $2.75), which has exhibits on the history of shipbuilding and navigation in the area.

Following the waterfront towards the harbour brings you to the modern **Centre d'Interprétation des Mammifères Marins**, 108 de la Cale-Sèche (daily: mid-May to late June, Oct & Nov noon–5pm; late June to Sept 9am–8pm; $4.75), which is a must if you intend to go whale-watching, as its excellent documentary films and bilingual displays explain the life cycles of the whales in the St Lawrence and the efforts being made to save their ever-diminishing numbers.

The Tadoussac sector of the **Saguenay National Park** offers some easy **hikes** around the village; an **information office** (mid-June to Sept daily 9am–5pm) in the car park just after the ferry terminal supplies free maps of the trails. To the northeast of Tadoussac are the long terraced **sand dunes** on the Baie du Moulin-à-Baude, known locally as *le désert*. To reach the dunes, follow chemin du Moulin-à-Baude 5km northeast to the **interpretation centre**, the Maison des Dunes (mid-June to Sept daily 9am–5pm; free). The 112-metre-high dunes are popular with sand-skiers, and skis can be rented from the youth hostel (see below).

Practicalities

The **bus** terminus is at 443 Bateau-Passeur on Hwy 138 by the campground (☎235-4653). The excellent **information** centre for the entire Côte-Nord is in the smart red-brick manor at 197 des Pionniers (daily: late June–Aug 8am–10pm; Sept to late June 9am–5pm; ☎235-4744); they have a load of leaflets, an accommodation service and next door you can watch videos of the area. The pick of Tadoussac's wealth of **accommodation** is the *Hôtel Tadoussac*, 165 Bord de l'Eau (☎235-4421 or 1-800-463-5250; ⑨). Cheaper is the *Motel le Jaseur*, 414 Rue du Bateau-Passeur (☎235-4737; ③), or the *Motel l'Anse-à-l'Eau*, 173 des Pionniers (☎235-4958; ③), which does a fine breakfast. As does *Le Mer Veilleuse*, 113 Coupe-de-L'Islet (☎235-4396; ②). For a bargain-basement stay check in to *Chez Jocelyne* (☎235-4370; ①). **B&Bs** are situated along des Pionniers: *Maison Clauphi* at no. 188 (☎ & fax 235-4303; ④) is a B&B-cum-motel, or try *Gîte de la Baleine*, no. 161 (☎235-4870 or 235-4283; ②; June–Sept). *Maison Hovington,* no. 285 (☎235-4466; ③; June–Oct), is a century-old B&B with five beautifully decorated rooms – and the bilingual owners will pick you up from the bus station. To lodge in a **family home**, call ☎235-4744.

The **youth hostel** *Maison Majorique*, 154 Bateau-Passeur (☎235-4372; ①), is one of the best youth hostels in Québec. Bikes, skis for sand-skiing, canoes, skidoos and snowshoes are all available for rent, and various activities such as guided hikes, snowshoe excursions and dog-sleigh trips are organized in their relative seasons. Suppers for $7 and all-you-can-eat breakfasts for $3.50 are optional, and camping ($3) is available in the hostel grounds. Family-style **camping** away from the hostels is available in summer at *Camping Tadoussac*, 428 Bateau-Passeur (☎235-4501; $24 for two-person site), 2km from the ferry terminal on Hwy 138.

Eating possibilities include: *La Bateau*, 246 des Forgerons, is a popular place that churns out an all-you-can-eat buffet of Québécois food; *Le Gibard* is cosy, cheap and has a fun atmosphere with music; *Café Fjord*, 154 Bateau-Passeur near the youth hostel, is a young hangout with good music and a great atmosphere is kicking throughout the summer – they also have food; *Chez Georges*, 135 Bateau Passeur, is in Tadoussac's oldest house with simple food and a table d'hôte for $21, *La Bolée*, 164 Morin, is a pricey place with crêpes, salads and a takeaway deli underneath with delicious breads; and the *Hôtel Tadoussac*, which has a vast dining room and a reasonably priced set menu. Great evenings of **drinking** can be had at the bar of *Le Gibard*, which stays open until 3am.

The Saguenay Marine Park

The **Saguenay Marine Park**, in Tadoussac's immediate vicinity, contains six different ecosystems supporting hundreds of marine species. This region is part of the hydrographic basin of the St Lawrence and the Great Lakes, and the toxic waste tipped into the St Lawrence once made this the most polluted waterway in Canada. Since the creation of the park, the federal government has promised to reduce ninety percent of the pollutants from fifty industrial plants in the immediate vicinity. The damage has already been done, though – the number of **St Lawrence beluga whales** is down from five thousand to five hundred, placing them on Canada's list of endangered species. That said, the area continues to attract the whales because the mingling of the cold Labrador sea waters with the highly oxygenated freshwater of the Saguenay produces a uniquely rich crop of krill and other plankton. The white St Lawrence beluga lives in the area all year round, and from May to October it is joined by six species of migratory whales including the minke, finback and the blue whale, the largest mammal on earth.

Every season more and more companies offer **whale-watching trips** from Tadoussac from mid-May to mid-October, charging around $30 for a trip of up to three hours with qualified bilingual naturalists on board. Officially they are not allowed to approach the protected belugas or to stay within 300m of these peaceful creatures, but the whales don't know that and often come close to the crafts – a magical sight. Pop into *La Croisière*, 231 des Pionniers, who have full information and sell tickets (at the same price as the companies) for all the available trips. Sunset is a wonderful time to go. The smaller dinghy boats can get really close to the whales and only carry a dozen people – contact Les Accent Croisières Express, 161 des Pionniers (☎235-4771 or 1-888-235-6842), they also have *L'ExploraTHOR Express*, a new Zodiac-type boat that holds 48. Smaller boats are provided by La Compagnie de la Baie de Tadoussac, 145 Bord de l'Eau (☎235-4548), and they get really close to the whales; dry suits are provided but it's unlikely that you'll end up in the icy depths. You can view the fjord and check out whales on a catamaran with Croisières 2001 (☎659-5489 or 1-800-694-5489), whilst Croisière Hôtel Tadoussac, 165 Bord de l'Eau (☎235-4421 or 1-800-463-5250), offer whale safaris aboard a catamaran, a whaler or the more sedate 1922 schooner *Marie Clarisse*. If you can't afford a boat trip take the short hike around the Pointe de l'Islet from the marina, which has lookout points for whale-watching. At the other end of the scale, Aviation du Fjord, 231 des Pionniers (☎235-4640), take you up in a seaplane for $45, so you can watch whales from the air.

THE FLOOD OF 1996

In July 1996, the Saguenay–Lac St-Jean region was devastated by one of the biggest catastrophes in Canada's recent past – a major flood that wiped out homes and businesses in several towns. As you travel the area, construction work is still being carried out and a dramatic video of the tragic scenes that gripped the country is available at nearly every outlet in the area.

The events leading to the flood are still under enquiry but what is known for sure is that, unusually for July, 150–280mm of rain fell on the area – that's equivalent to the amount of water that passes over Niagara Falls in four weeks. Lac Kénogami, just upstream from Chicoutimi, was already full and the dam operators appealed to their bosses in Québec City to open the first of the four dams on the Chicoutimi River, but permission was refused until it was too late. When the dam was finally opened the water surged down the river, passing 2m over the dam in downtown Chicoutimi. By that time, the authorities knew a disaster was in the making and 16,000 people were given a few hours to get out of the area, many of whom had to be evacuated by helicopter.

In all 39 municipalities were affected, with 596 houses destroyed and 1953 damaged. Hardest hit were Chicoutimi, La Baie, L'Anse St-Jean, Jonquière, Ferland-Boileau and Lattière. La Baie suffered $165 million of damage and Chicoutimi $67 million. As the flood was an "act of God" no one received insurance, but those who lost their homes were helped out by donations from across the country. However, many are still in inadequate, temporary housing hurriedly constructed on the edge of the towns – the mobile homes are from Florida and unsuitable for Canada's winters. The flood also took the lives of seven people, including two children who were killed after the deluge when a landslide wiped out their home in La Baie.

Ste-Rose-du-Nord

The daily Intercar bus from Tadoussac to Chicoutimi follows Hwy 172 parallel to the fjord, a dramatic route that gives occasional panoramas over the water. About 40km along the way is the turnoff for **STE-ROSE-DU-NORD**, a tiny village of white houses crammed beneath the precipitous walls of the fjord, 3km from the main road. The **Musée de la Nature**, 199 de la Montagne (daily 8.30am–9pm; $3), is a small but surprisingly informative museum housing an eclectic range of exhibits from stuffed animals to knotty roots, all found in the local region. The church of **Ste-Rose-de-Lima**, with its interior of wood, birch bark, branches and roots, is also worth a peek. If you intend to visit Lac Saint-Jean, you could continue your journey by a two-hour **cruise** to Chicoutimi with *Croisières la Marjolaine* (☎1-800-363-7248; $30), along the most stunning stretch of the fjord. Sometimes there's a boat connection with Tadoussac; enquire at the information centre for details.

Should you want to **stay** over, you could try the award-winning *Auberge le Presbytère*, 136 du Quai (☎675-2503; ②; summer only), which has an outstanding restaurant, with full menus at around $30. Rooms are also available above the *Musée de la Nature* (☎675-2348; ①), while *Camping la Descente des Femmes* (☎675-2500) has sites from $17 for four persons.

Chicoutimi

Since its founding by a Scottish immigrant in 1842, the regional capital of **CHICOUTIMI** has grown from a small sawmill centre into one of the province's largest towns and as such is not a particularly enticing place. In 1996 it was on all of Canada's front pages, as the Chicoutimi River, which along with the Saguenay and Moulin rivers crosses the town, surged through its centre leaving one house standing. The house is now a shrine and stands amidst bare rock near the dam. Opposite, the church displays photographs and details of the flood that devastated the area.

Nearby, Chicoutimi's main attraction is **La Pulperie** at 300 Dubuc (mid-May to June & Aug to mid-Oct daily 9am–6pm; July daily 9am–8pm; mid-Oct to Nov Mon–Fri noon–4pm; $8.50), five austere brick buildings raised on the rapids by the Chicoutimi Pulp Company, which was founded in 1896 and quickly became Canada's largest producer of paper pulp. Left to rot in 1930, these gigantic ghosts of Chicoutimi's industrial past had been restored to prime condition but the flood caused $1 million damage and the site lost its restaurant and summer theatre.

Relocated to the 1921 mill of the pulperie in 1994 is the strange **Maison du Peintre Arthur Villeneuve**. The former home of Naive painter Arthur Villeneuve, the house is in effect one big painting, with murals of Canadian scenes covering inside and out. The subject matter is somewhat unadventurous, but the artist's work is bright and cheery while scenes of 1950s Chicoutimi – when Villeneuve started his project after retiring as a barber – are intriguing. Tours, in French, are given on the half-hour. The **Musée du Saguenay-Lac Saint-Jean** is currently closed and being prepared for relocation to the La Pulperie, ready for unveiling in 1999.

Practicalities

Chicoutimi's **bus station** (☎543-1403) is on the corner of Tessier and Racine, right in the centre of town. Buses from Montréal, Québec City, Lac Saint-Jean, Tadoussac and Charlevoix all connect here. The CITS local bus link with Jonquière's **train station** (arrival point for trains from Montréal) runs at least hourly from 7.15am to 9.45pm. There's a municipal **tourist office** at 2525 blvd Talbot, where Hwy 175 meets Hwy 170 (Mon–Fri 8.30am–noon & 1.30–4.30pm), a regional branch at 198 Racine Est (same times) and a small seasonal office in the Port (mid-June to Aug daily; 8.30am–noon & 1.30–4.30pm).

Accommodation is readily available in Chicoutimi, as the town hosts a variety of business conferences all year round. Budget rooms can be obtained through CÉGEP, 534 Jacques-Cartier (☎549-9520; ①), in the summer. *Auberge Centre-Ville*, 104 Jacques-Cartier (☎543-0253; ②), is a small, central **hotel** with cheap rates, *Hôtel-Motel le Montagnais*, 1080 blvd Talbot (☎543-1521 or 1-800-463-9160; ③), is a new hotel with an equally good location. On the main drag, *Hotel Chicoutimi*, 460 Racine (☎549-7111 or 1-800-463-7930; ⑥), has air-conditioned rooms with all mod cons.

There are numerous **fast-food** places and little **restaurants** on Racine. Recommended are *La Cuisine Café-Resto* at no. 387, which has French food in the $10–20 range and great cakes; *Le Salon de Thé Jalouise* at no. 460 and *Le Croissant Chic* at no. 400 are good for light lunches. For a better class of meal, *La Bourgresse*, 260 Riverin (☎543-3178), serves French cuisine for $20–40 and the grilled grub is renowned at *Georges Steak House* at no. 433. Most **nightlife** is also located on Racine – the **bar** *Pile ou Face* at no. 383 and the **disco** *Le Caméléon* at no. 460 are both young, lively spots.

Croisières la Marjolaine (☎543-7630, 543-7631 or 1-800-363-7248) offer once-daily summer **cruises** ($30) on the Saguenay as far as Ste-Rose-du-Nord (see p.297). Finally, the town is host to one of the best of Québec's **festivals**. For the ten-day **Carnaval Souvenir** in mid-February, what seems like the entire population dresses in costumes from circa 1890; lumber camps, can-can clubs, operetta shows, and the period authentic heavy drinking, augment the pioneer atmosphere.

Jonquière

Fifteen kilometres west of Chicoutimi, Jonquière thrives due to its Alcan aluminium smelter, one of the largest in the world, and its two paper mills. The smelter brought many eastern European immigrants to the area when it was first opened in 1925, and the industry overtook the Price sons and their wood empire as the largest employer.

A modern town with wide avenues, it can make a good stop for budget travellers because of its youth hostel, an Allo-Stop and train connections with Montréal – it also has a better nightlife than Chicoutimi.

During the day, there are tours of the Art Deco **Shipshaw Hydroelectric Power Plant**, 1471 Route du Pont (June–Aug Mon–Fri 1.30–4.30pm; free), which supplies electricity to the aluminium plants. Nearby, the **Aluminium Bridge** which you cross on your way into downtown was built in 1948 to show that aluminium was good for construction – it weighs a third of its equivalent in steel.

Up Mont Jacob at 4160 rue du Vieux Pont, the **Centre National d'Exposition** (Mon & Fri 8.30am–4.30pm, Tues–Thurs 8.30am–8.30pm, Sat & Sun 1–6pm; $2) has history, art and science exhibitions if you have time to kill.

PRACTICALITIES

The **bureau du tourisme**, 2665 blvd du Royaume in the Centre des Congrès (daily: mid-May to Aug 8am–8pm; Sept to mid-May 8am–noon & 1.30–4.30pm; ☎548-5691), has information on the town, and in summer there's a smaller office at 3885 blvd Harvey (same hours). **Buses** terminate at 2249 Rue St-Hubert (☎547-2167) and **trains** arrive at the VIA Rail station (☎1-800-361-5390). Allo-Stop is located at 2017 Rue Price (☎543-3992).

If you decide to **stay**, the **youth hostel** *Auberge du Vieux Saint-Pierre*, 387 Saint-Pierre (☎547-0848 or 1-888-547-0845; ①), is not far from the bus and train stations, with fifty beds, some in private rooms. You can also camp outside. *Hôtel Jean Dequen*, 2841 blvd du Royaume (☎548-7173; ②), is cheap and reasonable, but all amenities are available at *Hôtel Roussillon Saguenay* at no. 2675 on the same street (☎548-3124; ③). Lists of **gîtes** are available at the bureau du tourisme.

For **eating**, *Le Puzzle*, 2497 Saint-Dominique, is a young place with cool decor; *Les Pâtes Amato*, 2655 blvd de Royaume, has coffees, pasta and Italian desserts to die for; and, more expensive, *L'Amandier*, 5213 chemin Saint-Andre (☎542-5396), is out of town but worth the trip for the bizarre dining room of carved plaster and wood. Wander along Saint-Dominique for **bars** and **clubs** – *Le Puzzle*, *L'Audace*, *L'Envoi* and *Le Singapour* are all a good laugh.

Lac Saint-Jean

To the west of Chicoutimi, around **Lac Saint-Jean**, stretches a relatively untouched area whose tranquil lakeshore villages are linked by the circular route of Hwy 169. Named after Father Jean Duquen, the first European to visit the region in 1647, the huge glacial lake is fed by most of the rivers of northeastern Québec and – unusually for an area of the rocky Canadian Shield – is bordered by sandy beaches and a lush, green terrain that has been farmed for over a century. A bike route encircles the whole lake. The local cuisine, especially the delicious coarse meat pie called a *tourtière* and the thick blueberry pie, are renowned throughout the province. Further bonuses for budget travellers are the lake's two excellent youth hostels and its **public transport**: there's a daily bus service between Chicoutimi and both Alma and Dolbeau, the latter running round the south side of the lake; during the winter and spring a bus runs on Fridays and Sundays from Dolbeau to Alma via the villages on the north shore, and on Fridays only there's a service in the opposite direction.

Val-Jalbert

From Chicoutimi, Hwy 170 runs 50km west to Hwy 169, which continues to one of the main tourist attractions of the region, **VAL-JALBERT** (daily: mid-May to mid-June & Sept to mid-Oct 9am–5pm; mid-June to Aug 9am–7pm; $8.50). The seventy-metre Ouiatchouan waterfall, which dominates the town, led to the establishment of a pulp mill here at the turn of the century, and by 1926 the village had around 950 inhabitants, with a convent serving the educational needs of the community. In the following year, though, the introduction of chemical-based pulping made the mill redundant, and the village was closed down. Val-Jalbert was left to rot until 1985, when the government decided to renovate it as a tourist attraction.

From the site entrance a bus (with on-board French commentary) runs around the main sights of the village, ending at the mill at the base of the falls. You can then wander around whatever catches your eye along the way – the abandoned wooden houses, the convent (now a museum) or the general store (now a souvenir shop). From the mill – itself converted into an excellent crafts market and cafeteria – a cable car ($3.75) leads to the top of the falls, from which there are stunning views of the village and Lac Saint-Jean beyond. It is possible to stay in Val-Jalbert's renovated **hotel** above the general store (☎275-3132; ④), in apartments in the converted houses on St-George Street ($44–88 for one to six people), or in the **campground** (☎275-3132; $22 for four-person site) just outside the village. In fall and winter, when the site is officially closed, you can still gain access for free and it is a beautifully tranquil place to spend some time.

Mashteuiatsh

Ten kilometres west, at Roberval, a turnoff leads to the Montagnais reserve of **MASH-TEUIATSH**, also known as **Pointe-Bleue**. Before European contact the Montagnais were a migratory people who split into small family groups for summer hunting, often directed to new grounds by a shaman who would locate the animals by "reading" the cracks on burnt animal bones. When the Europeans arrived they found the Montagnais in bitter conflict with the Iroquois, an enmity that Champlain intensified by allying himself with the Montagnais for trade. By the late seventeenth century their population had been greatly weakened by warfare, European diseases, depletion of game, and displacement from their lands. This reserve was created in 1856, and today around 1500 of eastern Québec's 10,000 Montagnais live here. Like many Canadian reserves, Mashteuiatsh is dry in an attempt to reduce alcoholism and its attendant problems, yet the Montagnais suffer a great deal of prejudice from the surrounding white communities – so much so that there's no bus service, because Québécois bus drivers refuse to go there.

The village is situated right on the lake, and has an **information centre** on the main street at 1516 Ouiatchouan (mid-June to Sept daily 8am–8pm). Up the hill from the information office, at 407 Amishk, is **Musée Amérindien**, the only Montagnais museum in Canada, which is currently undergoing extensive renovation and is due to reopen in 1998. At the end of July a **powwow** is held on the waterfront by the four concrete tepee sculptures that represent the seasons.

The only place to stay is the log-house **youth hostel**, the *Auberge Kukum*, 241 Ouiatchouan (☎275-0697; ①). The *Kukum,* which means "grandmother" in Montagnais, is no mere hostel – it is an introduction to the life of the native peoples of Canada, with nightly discussions of Montagnais issues over a communal supper of local dishes. Traditional music fulls the auberge and documentary films are shown regularly.

From August to September, *Ilnu-Tepiskau*, 2202 Ouiatchouan (☎679-8242 or 1-800-679-8242), organizes **adventure trips** into the bush where you are completely submerged in the traditional way of life, relying on the resources of the surrounding woodlands and rivers to build shelters, make fires and prepare food (from $40 per person per day).

Saint-Félicien, Dolbeau and Mistassini

Situated on the western extremity of the lake on the Ashuapmushuan River, **SAINT-FÉLICIEN** is the site of Québec's best zoo, the **Jardin Zoologique de Saint-Félicien** (late May to late Sept daily 9am—5pm, open till 7pm in July; $17), located on Chamouchouane Island. The 130 mainly Canadian species roam free all over the site — the humans are the ones in cages, hauled around on the back of a mini-train. The brand-new Arctic environment for the polar bears allows you to see the magnificent beasts swim underwater. The zoo also has a historical angle, with mock-ups of an Indian village, trading post, loggers' camp and settlers' farm. The **information office** is located at 1209 Sacré-Coeur (Mon–Fri 8.30am–noon & 1.30–4.30pm). For **accommodation**, check out the cheap *Hôtel Bellevue*, 1055 Sacré-Coeur (☎679-0162; ②), or the **B&B** – one of four – *Auberge Centre Ville*, 1245 Sacré-Coeur (☎679-1882; ②).

Continuing clockwise around the lake from Saint-Félicien brings you to **DOLBEAU**, 39km further on. It's at its best during mid-July's ten-day **Western Festival**, with rodeos and people wandering around in stetsons and spurs. If you get stranded, the *Hôtel du Boulevard*, 1610 blvd Wallberg (☎276-8207; ②), is passable.

Nearby **MISTASSINI**, the region's blueberry capital, hosts a better feast in early August, the **Festival du Bleuet** — one big blowout on blueberries dipped in chocolate, blueberry pie, blueberry cheesecake and an extremely potent blueberry wine. Over the Mistassini River the **Monastère des Pères Trappistes** sells its own organic produce – a large quantity of the berries are on offer in season.

Continuing east, 5km beyond the settlement of Péribonka on Hwy 169, is the **Musée Louis-Hémon** (June–Sept daily 9am–5.30pm; Oct–May Mon–Sat 9am–4pm, Sun 1–5pm; $4.50), which pays tribute to the Brittany-born novelist Louis Hémon. The author arrived in Péribonka in 1912 and his experiences as a farmhand here inspired his most famous (in French-speaking Canada at least) book, *Maria Chapdelaine*, a folksy, frontier tale of young love. Unfortunately, Hémon didn't have much time to enjoy his royalties – he was flattened by a train a year after the book's publication.

Sainte-Monique and Alma

Another 16km round the shore is the village of **SAINTE-MONIQUE**, on whose outskirts you'll find an island-based **youth hostel** and **campground**: the *Auberge de l'Île du Repos de Péribonka* (☎347-5649; ①, camping from $9). Bikes can be rented for $25 a day, useful for an excursion to **Pointe-Taillon park**. Occupying a finger of land that juts into Lac Saint-Jean, the park is bordered by long and often deserted beaches.

From Sainte-Monique, it's 29km to the dull aluminium-producing city of **Alma**, useful only for its **buses** to Chicoutimi and Québec City.

The Côte Nord

The **St Lawrence River** was the lifeline of the wilderness beyond Tadoussac (see p.294) until the 1960s, when Hwy 138 was constructed along the **Côte Nord** to Havre-St-Pierre, 625km away. In 1996, the road was extended to Natashquan, a further 145km. The road sweeps from high vistas down to the rugged shoreline through the vast regions of Manicouagan and Duplessis, the few distractions offered in the villages and towns en route being supplemented by panoramas of spruce-covered mountains, the vast sky and the mighty river. **Bears** and **moose** often lumber out of the stunted forest onto the highway, and in the summer the shiny backs of **whales** are frequently spotted arching out of the water.

Basque whalers were the first Europeans to penetrate this chilly shore in the sixteenth century, but later, when they began to trade fur with the native Montagnais, Naskapi and Inuit, they were ousted by French merchants. After the British conquest the fur trade continued but fishing remained the main industry until this century, when mining, lumber and hydroelectric projects led to the growth of a few settlements into fair-sized towns. Despite this, the region has a population density of just five people per square mile, and the distances between communities become longer and longer the further you travel, overwhelming the visitor with the sense of Canada's vastness.

The Québec City to Tadoussac Intercar **bus** serves the North Shore as far as Baie-Comeau, from where Autobus du Littoral travels to Sept-Îles and onwards to Havre-St-Pierre. At the time of writing there is no public transport to Natasquan, but a bus service is expected – ask at tourist information for details. At Natasquan the highway gives out altogether and the only onward transport is by supply **ship** from Sept-Îles and Havre-St-Pierre, which serves the wildlife haven of Île d'Anticosti and undertakes a breathtaking journey along the inlets of the windswept coastline of the Lower North Shore. Other ferries link various points to the south shore and the Gaspé, which means you can plot a varied return trip.

Tadoussac to Port-Cartier

The craggy terrain is the chief attraction of the 200km of highway from Tadoussac to Baie-Comeau, though within the first half of the route the communities of **Berg-eronnes** and **Les Escoumins** (22km and 31km from Tadoussac) have regular half-day **whale-watching** trips (May–Oct 1–10 daily; $25). Bergeronne's **Centre d'Inter-prétation et d'Observation de Cap-de-Bon-Désir**, 166 Hwy 138 (mid-June to mid-Sept daily 9am–8pm; $3), built around the Cap Bon Désir lighthouse, has displays on the whale's life and a lookout post by a popular whale-feeding ground – but you may well have a fruitless wait. A less thankless task is to visit the **Centre d'Interpretation Archéo-Topo**, 498 Rue de la Mer (May–Oct daily 8am–6pm; $2), to check out the findings from archeological digs in the area. From Les Escoumins there's a ferry across the St Lawrence to Trois-Pistoles (see p.274). At the Montagnais reserve, **Essipit**, just past the village there's a whale-watching tower and a few craft shops.

Baie-Comeau

The road into **BAIE-COMEAU** passes a monstrous newsprint mill plant that churns out poisonous emissions 24 hours a day. Established in 1936 by Colonel Robert R. McCormick, the publisher of the *Chicago Tribune*, Baie-Comeau has done nothing but boom ever since – with a population of 26,000, it dwarfs the communities around it. There's no real reason to hang around here, but if you have time to kill while waiting for a northward bus or a ferry to Gaspé's Matane you might stroll through the **quarti-er Sainte-Amélie** in the eastern Marquette sector, where the streets are lined by grand American houses dating from the 1930s. The **Sainte-Amélie Church**, 37 av Marquette (Mon–Fri 8am–7.30pm; free), is worth a quick peek for its stained-glass windows, designed by Italian artist Guido Nincheri.

The *Maison Régionale du Tourisme*, 871 Rue de Puyjalon (Mon–Fri 9am–noon & 1–5pm) and the *Bureau des Congrès et du Tourisme de Baie-Comeau* (same hours) have **information** on the entire region. **Buses** terminate at 330 blvd Lasalle (☎296-6921); the departure point for the **car ferry** to Matane and Godbout is at the western end of boulevard Lasalle (April–Dec; 1–2 daily; 2hr 30min; $10.90 single, cars $26.50; ☎294-8593).

Accommodation is available at the rambling brick hotel *Le Manoir*, 8 Cabot (☎296-3391; ⑥), which overlooks the St Lawrence. Less expensive **motels** are located along boulevard Lasalle; try the modern *Hôtel-Motel la Caravelle*, at no. 202 (☎296-4986; ③). The cheapest place in town is *Motel Lasalle*, 196 blvd Lasalle (☎296-6601; ②). For **camping**, *Camping Manic 2* on Hwy 389 has six-person sites for $12.50. *La Manoir Hôtel* is pricey for **eating** but has an excellent reputation. For down-to-earth eats, *Les 3 Barils*, 200 blvd Lasalle is convenient and *Les Deux Fours*, 1257a blvd Laflèche, has a varied menu. There are various fast-food places, including the major chains, on Lasalle and Laflèche boulevards.

The Manic Dams

One of the few roads to penetrate the bleak terrain north of the St Lawrence is the partly paved Hwy 389 (Manic Road), which runs 215km into the forest from the east end of Baie-Comeau. The road was built as a supply route for the hydroelectric company who built the colossal **dam system** on the Manicouagan River, the only artificial site to rival the landscape in these parts. The Hydro-Québec **information** kiosk at 135 blvd Comeau (mid-June to Aug daily 8am–3pm), where Hwy 389 branches off from Hwy 318, offers a cheap **bus** service to the two massive dams that are open to visitors along the Manic Road on request.

The first dam in the system, **Manic 2**, is a half-hour drive from Baie-Comeau, a journey that takes in great views of the rocky Canadian Shield. A free guided tour of the dam takes you inside the massive wall (mid-June to Aug daily 9am, 11am, 1pm & 3pm), but an even more stupendous structure awaits two and a half hours' drive further north at the end of the road – the awesome **Manic 5** or Daniel Johnson dam. Constructed in 1968, it is named after the premier of Québec who died here on the morning of the opening ceremony. With a length of 1314m and a central arch of 214m, the dam is the world's largest multiple-arch structure. Free guided tours take visitors to the foot of the dam (mid-June to Aug daily 9am, 11am, 1.30pm & 3.30pm) and across the top, giving panoramic views of the Manicouagan Valley and the 2000-square-kilometre reservoir. There's **accommodation** right by the Manic 5 at the *Motel de L'Énergie* (☎584-2301; ④).

Franquelin

The old logging town of **FRANQUELIN**, midway between Baie-Comeau and Godbout, is the site of Village Forestier d'Antari, 27 rue des Erables (May–Oct daily 9am–6pm; $5), an interesting centre, set in historic buildings used by the loggers. It explains the forestry activities of the region and serves hearty bushcamp meals. The village also has a **youth hostel**, *Auberge Sieur de Franquelin,* on the highway (☎296-6839; ①), which offers a host of well-priced activities from sea kayaking to snowmobiling, depending on the season.

Godbout

The attractive fishing village of **GODBOUT**, situated on a crescent-shaped bay 54km from Baie-Comeau, is not just the most pleasant place hereabouts – it also has an excellent **Musée Amérindien et Inuit**, 134 Rue Pascal-Comeau (late June to Sept daily 9am–10pm; $2.50). The museum was founded by Claude Grenier, who spent ten years in the frozen north in the 1970s on a government scheme to boost the Inuit economy by promoting native culture. Consequent commercialism has diluted the output since then, but the private collection of the Greniers features nothing but genuine pieces, from the characteristic soapstone carvings to domestic artefacts. Just down the road, the old general store (June–Aug daily 9am–5pm) is worth a peek. The village is linked to Matane on the south shore by a daily **ferry** (2hr 30min; $10 single, $25 for cars). For **accommodation**, try the *Motel Chantal*, 111 Hwy 138 (☎568-7511; ②), or, for **B&B,** there's *Aux Berges*, at 180 Pascal-Comeau (☎568-7748; ①; summer only). There's **camping** at *Camping l'Estuaire* (☎568-7737) on the highway, with pitches from $15 for four people.

Pointe-des-Monts and Port-Cartier

Situated where the St Lawrence River merges into the Gulf of St Lawrence, **POINTE-DES-MONTS**, 24km from Godbout (via a gravel turning off the highway), has not changed since the nineteenth century. Mind you, there's not a lot to change – all that stands on this rocky outcrop is Canada's oldest **lighthouse** dating from 1830 and a small missionary **chapel** built in 1898. The lighthouse, listed as a historical monument, now contains a small **museum** (late June to mid-Sept daily 9am–7pm; $1.50), a fairly expensive seafood **restaurant** and a **B&B** (☎939-2332; ②; June–Aug). From mid-May to mid-October there are also **whale-watching** excursions from the lighthouse (2/4hr; $18/45); the boats are small and need to be reserved in advance at the B&B.

From here it's an uneventful journey over the 113km to Sept-Îles, passing through Pointe-aux-Anglais and, 63km further, the lumber and iron-ore centre of **PORT-CARTIER**. The town's only attraction is as the entrance to the **Réserve Faunique de Sept-Îles-Port-Cartier**, a wilderness park popular with hunters, anglers and experienced canoeists, who ride the rapids on the Rochers River.

Sept-Îles

The largest ore-exporting port in eastern Canada, **SEPT-ÎLES** is a good base for trips further north, owing to its rail links with Labrador. With its alphabetically named streets of dull prefab houses, the town itself has as much character as a pile of iron ore, but it's pleasantly located on the St Lawrence shore and you could spend an enjoyable day here – especially in August, when one of Québec's foremost native music festivals is held nearby.

An interesting overview of local history is offered by the **Vieux Poste**, located on boulevard des Montagnais, west of the centre (late June to late Aug daily 9am–5pm; $3.25). Prior to the British conquest, when the Hudson Bay Company took over the trade here, Sept-Îles was leased by the French crown to merchant traders. Settlements like these opened up Québec for the Europeans but practically destroyed the lives of the native Montagnais. Converted to Christianity and overwhelmed by their desire for and subsequent need of European goods – particularly firearms, which aided them in their battles against the feared Iroquois – the Montagnais were forced by market pressure to hunt more and more fur-bearing animals. The resulting depletion of game was worsened so much by the later lumber and mining industries that the Montagnais were obliged to live on official reserves in order to become eligible for state hand-outs. The reconstructed Vieux Poste, with its small chapel, store and postmaster's house, presents an absorbing portrayal of the Montagnais culture and is staffed by local Montagnais who produce crafts and food, which are sold at a decently priced handicrafts store.

In town, the modern white block of the **Musée Régional de la Côte Nord**, 500 blvd Laure (daily: late June to Aug 9am–5pm; Sept to late June Mon–Fri 9am–noon & 1–5pm, Sat & Sun 1–5pm; $3.25), is a venue for archeological finds of ethnological interest from the Côte Nord, Amerindian objects and modern works by Canadian and local artists.

The name of the town comes from the archipelago just offshore, whose largest island, **Grande Basque** – where there are easy walking trails and picnic spots – is served by a **ferry** from the Parc du Vieux-Quai (1–8 daily; 20 min; $13). A **cruise** boat, run by *Crosiere Archipal des Sept-Îles*, also tours the islands from the same departure point (late June to early Oct daily; 3hr; $24); whales and a sea-bird sanctuary are the main attractions. **Fishing trips**, around $20 for half a day, are also available if you fancy cod for dinner.

The Innu Nikamu Festival

One of the more offbeat Canadian chart successes of recent years has been the local native group Kashtin, the only nationally known band to perform in a native tongue. Their appearance is now a highlight of the excellent **Innu Nikamu Festival** of song and music (information ☎927-2985), held every August, 14km east of Sept-Îles in the Montagnais reserve of Maliotenam. Inspired by Kashtin's success, numerous other groups travel to the festival to produce some of the best of Canada's contemporary and traditional native music. As well as the music, the festival includes native food and craft stalls – despite the reserve's alcohol ban, there is always a good buzz. There is no public transport to the reserve: by car, take Hwy 138 towards Havre-St-Pierre and turn right at the Moisie intersection for the Maliotenam entrance. Tickets cost around $5 and are available from the Sept-Îles tourist information kiosk.

Practicalities

There's a seasonal **tourist office,** 516 au Arnaud (late June to Aug daily 9am–6pm) down by the waterfront in the Parc du Vieux-Quai, and a **maison du tourisme** on the outskirts of town at 1401 blvd Laure (late June to Aug daily 9.30am–9pm; Sept to late June Mon–Fri 8.30am–5pm). The *Le Tangon* **youth hostel,** 555 Cartier (☎962-8180 or 1-800-461-8585; ①; June-Sept), is very cheap but grotty and characterless, with a midnight curfew; camping is allowed in the grounds for $8. Alternatively, try the luxurious *Hôtel les Gouverneurs,* 666 Laure (☎962-7071 or 1-800-463-2820; ④), the uneventful but more affordable *Motel Comfort Inn,* 854 Laure (☎968-6005 or 1-800-267-3837; ③), or the *Motel Mingan,* 665 Laure (☎968-2121; ②).

For **eating** Sept-Îles has great sea food restaurants: the best value are *Café du Port,* 495 av Brochu, and nearby *Chez Omer* at no. 372. At no. 588, *Le Bistroquet* is a new addition to the town in an old house – the seafood is outstanding.

The **bus** station, 126 Rue Monseigneur-Blanche (☎962-2126), has buses north to Havre-St-Pierre; the **train** station, with weekly trains to Labrador City ($100 return) and Schefferville ($137 return), is to the north of town (☎968-7808 or 968-7538). There is also an **Allo-Stop** office here (☎962-5035). The *Nordik Express* supply **ship** (☎1-800-463-0680) leaves Sept-Îles every Wednesday morning except during February and March, arriving at Port-Menier on the Île d'Anticosti ($59.80) that evening and Havre-St-Pierre ($89.31) early the next morning, before continuing along the Lower North Shore almost as far as Labrador.

Havre-St-Pierre and offshore

There is little of interest along the blackfly-ridden stretch of shore known as the Mingan Coast until you reach **HAVRE-ST-PIERRE**, where the stunning islands of the Mingan Archipelago offer a unique environment of sculpted rock formations and profuse wildlife. The community of Havre-St-Pierre would have remained a tiny fishing village if it hadn't been for the discovery in the 1940s of a huge deposit of ilmenite, the chief source of titanium. The quarries are 45km north of the town itself, where fishing and tourism provide employment for the non-miners, the latter industry having received a major boost when the forty islands of the **Mingan Archipelago** were made into a national park in 1983. Before setting off to the park, check out the **Centre d'Accueil et d'Interprétation, Réserve du Parc National de l'Archipel de Mingan,** 975 de l'Escale (mid-June to early Sept 9am–6pm, till 9pm mid-season; free), with photographic displays and info on the flora, fauna and geology of the islands.

Havre-St-Pierre's **information centre** is at 1081 Rue de la Digue (June–Aug daily 10am–10pm). The *Auberge de la Minganie* **youth hostel** (☎538-2944; ①; May–Nov) is inconveniently located 15km west of town, but the bus from the south will let you off early. An old fishing camp with minimum renovations and lots of bugs, the hostel serves substantial $3 breakfasts. In town, you could try the *Hôtel-Motel du Hâvre,* 970 de l'Escale (☎538-2800; ④), but the cheapest accommodation is in the **B&B** *Le Gîte Chez Louis,* 1045 Boréal (☎538-2799; ②). Alternatively, the tourist office runs a network of **private homes** that offer cheap rooms to visitors (☎538-2512); or *Camping Municipal* is on Hwy 138 ($15). For good seafood, and smoked salmon pizza, try the **restaurant** *Chez Julie,* 1023 Dulcinée. The **bus station** is located at 1023 Rue de la Digue (☎538-3590). The wharf is the departure point for the *Nordik Express* (see above).

The Mingan Archipelago

Immediately offshore from Havre-St-Pierre, the **Mingan Archipelago National Park Reserve** offers some of the weirdest and most beautiful landscapes in Québec. Standing on the islands' white-sand shorelines are innumerable eight-metre-high rocks like ancient totem poles, with bright orange lichen colouring their mottled surfaces and bonsai-sized trees clinging to their crevices. These formations originated as underwater sediment near the equator, which was thrust above sea level over 250 million years ago and then covered in an icecap several kilometres thick. As the drifting ice melted, the islands emerged again, seven thousand years ago, at their present location. The sea and wind gave the final touch by chipping away at the soft limestone to create the majestic monoliths of today.

Bizarre geology isn't the archipelago's only remarkable feature. The flora constitutes a unique insular garden of 452 arctic and rare alpine species, which survive here at their most southern limit due to the limestone soil, long harsh winters and cold Gulf of Labrador current. As for **wildlife**, other than the Gulf's whale populations, the permanent inhabitants of the national park include puffins, who build nests in the scant soil of three of the islands from early May to late August, and 199 other species of birds.

From June to September various **boat tours** around portions of the archipelago are available from Havre-St-Pierre, but they need to be booked in advance: *La Relève II* operates from 925 Babouin (3 daily; $25; ☎538-2865), and the *Perroquet de Mer* (3 daily; $25) and *Le Calculot* (2 daily; $25) are run by La Tournée des Îles Inc, 1155 de la Digue (☎538-2547). Free **camping** is allowed on six of the islands but the only transport is the more expensive water taxis, available from Bateau-Bus, 879 Acara (☎538-3427). Permits must be obtained from the interpretation centre.

Information is available from three visitor centres – 30 Rue du Bord-de-la-Mer in Longue-Pointe-de-Mingan and the others in Havre-St-Pierre at 975 Rue de l'Escale and 1010 Rue de la Promenade des Anciens.

Île d'Anticosti

Situated in the Gulf of St Lawrence between the Jacques Cartier and Honguedo Straits, the remote 220-kilometre-long **Île d'Anticosti** was once known as the "Graveyard of the Gulf", as more than four hundred ships have been wrecked on its shores, including Admiral Phipp's fleet, retreating from Québec City in 1690. Its 7770-square-kilometre expanse is made up of windswept sea cliffs and forests of twisted pine, crisscrossed by turbulent rivers and sheer ravines.

Known as Notiskuan – "the land where we hunt bears" – by the natives, and a walrus- and whale-fishing ground for the Basques, Île d'Anticosti became the private domain of Henri Menier, a French chocolate millionaire, in 1873. He imported white-tailed Virginia deer, red fox, silver fox, beaver and moose to his domain in order to gun them down at his leisure. Nowadays a less exclusive horde of hunters and fishers comes here to blast the deer from the back of their four-wheel-drives and to hoist the salmon from the rivers, which now fall under the jurisdiction of the province. For other travellers it presents an opportunity to explore an area that's untamed and still practically deserted, with a population of just 340.

Menier established the tiny village of Baie Ste-Claire on the western tip in 1873; less than thirty years later the settlers moved to **PORT-MENIER** on the south side of this tip, and Baie-Ste-Claire's homes were left to the ravages of the salt air. The human population is now concentrated in the blue-roofed houses of Port-Menier, where the weekly *Nordik Express* from Havre-St-Pierre or Sept-Îles comes in. A small museum in Port-Menier, the **Écomusée d'Anticosti** (late June to late Aug daily 10am–8pm; free), has small displays on the history and ecology of the island with century-old photos, while moccasins, gloves and other objects made of Virginia-deer leather are readily available in the handicraft stores of the village.

Port-Menier edges the westerly portion of the **Réserve Faunique de l'Île d'Anti-costi** whose protected landscapes are continued further east in the reserve's two other sectors – one deep in the interior, the other covering the island's eastern tip. The twist-ing, potholed road that crosses the island, jokingly called the "Trans-Anticostian", pro-vides access to the central and eastern portions of the reserve. Driving is the only way of getting there – you can hire a car in Port-Menier at Location Georges Lelièvre Anti-costi. En route, a rough track leads from the "main" road to Québec's largest cave. Dis-covered as recently as 1982, the glacial **Caverne de la Rivière à la Patate**, has a mod-est opening that leads into a cathedral-like chamber and a warren of 500-metre-long passages. A few kilometres further on you can glimpse the impossible canyon of the **Observation river**, whose bleak walls rise to over 50m. The reserve's scenery is equally impressive and a good basis for its attempt to encourage adventure tourism dur-ing the summer months. La Réserve d'Anticosti runs ecologically sound packages which, although pricey (around $500 a week), include transport, meals, accommoda-tion and four-wheel-drive vehicles (information ☎1-800-463-0863).

The *Nordik Express* from Havre-St-Pierre costs $33.07 (or $59.80 including meals) from Sept-Îles; the return trip from Sept-Îles to Port-Menier and back to Havre-St-Pierre costs $80.31 per person. **Accommodation** is available in Port-Menier at a **youth hos-tel** *Au Vieux Menier*, 26 chemin de la Faure, Port-Menier (☎535-0111; ①; mid-June to mid-Oct) and *Auberge Port Menier* (☎535-0122; ②).

The Lower North Shore

Until 1996, Hwy 138 terminated at Havre-St-Pierre, leaving the dozen or so villages along the rugged **Lower North Shore** cut off from the rest of Québec for centuries – to such an extent that most of the inhabitants speak only English. Now a new section of Hwy 138 links Havre-St-Pierre with **Natashquan** and three other villages on the 145-kilometre stretch. If you make the lonely journey by car – as yet there is no bus – you will receive a welcome unique to a people that have only just been connected by road to the rest of Canada.

The original inhabitants of the area were Montagnais, Naskapi and Inuits, who were invaded by Vikings in the year 1000. Cartier saw the coast in 1534 but did not register it as a discovery because it was already seasonally occupied by Basque, Spanish and Portuguese fishermen, and fishing is still the only industry on this desolate coast. The current 6500 inhabitants are descendants of fishermen from the Channel Islands and Newfoundland.

To Natashquan

The first settlement 65km east of Havre-St-Pierre is the 100-strong village of **BAIE-JOHAN-BETZ**. It is named after painter and sculptor Johan-Betz, whose extraordinary and enormous house is open for free tours, but book 24 hours in advance (☎539-0137; May–Oct). Afterwards you can head straight for the fishing village of Natashquan, pass-ing through **Aguanish** and **Île-à-Michon**, the tiny hamlets en route. At the end of the road, a small church, wooden houses and the old fishing huts are all there is to see in **NASTASHQUAN**, the one-time home of poet Gilles Vigneault. **Accommodation** is available in the ten rooms of *Auberge la Cache*, 163 chemin d'en Haut (726-3347; ③), which also serves Québécois cooking. Nearby is the Montagnais reserve of **Pointe-Parent** – the locals run canoeing and snowmobiling expeditions; contact Expédition Grande Natashquan for details (☎726-3750).

Beyond Natashquan

When the road peters out, the only access further along the coast is by boat. The trip by **Nordik Express** from Havre-St-Pierre affords stunning views of a rocky, sub-arctic landscape, which is so cold that icebergs float past the ship even in the height of summer. During the day, whales, dolphins and a wealth of sea birds are a common sight, and at night during the fall and winter the northern lights present an unforgettable display. At each stop the village inhabitants surround the boat, as its weekly arrival is about all that happens here.

Chief stops include the village of **Kegaska**, whose roads are covered with white seashells and whose pavements are made of wood, and **Vieux-Fort**, where you can always see seals sunning themselves on the rocks surrounding the bay.

To visit the roadless Lower North Shore, the Nordik Express leaves Havre-St-Pierre on Wednesday night and arrives in **Blanc-Sablon**, Québec's most easterly village, on Friday evening. The boat then returns, arriving back in Havre-St-Pierre on Sunday night. The price is pretty hefty but includes meals and a cabin berth: Havre-St-Pierre to Blanc-Sablon is $438.23 return. **Accommodation** in Blanc-Sablon is available at the *Motel Anse-aux-Cailloux* (☎461-2112; ③).

From Blanc-Sablon it is possible to get a ferry across to Newfoundland (May–Dec 2 daily; 1hr 30min) or drive along the coast into Labrador (see p.418).

travel details

Trains

Montréal to: Québec City (3–5 daily; 3hr); Dorval / Toronto (6 weekly; 20min/4hr); Lévis/Rivière-du-Loup / Trois-Pistoles / Rimouski / Mont Joli / Amqui / Matapédia / Carleton / New Richmond / Bonaventure / Grande-Rivière / Percé / Gaspé (3 weekly; 3hr 20min / 5hr 30min / 6hr 10min / 7hr / 7hr 40min / 8hr 40min / 9hr 45min / 11hr 30min / 12hr 15min / 12hr 45min / 15hr 15min / 15hr 30min / 17hr); Lévis / Rivière-du-Loup / Trois-Pistoles / Rimouski / Mont Joli / Amqui / Matapédia (6 weekly; 3hr 20min / 5hr 30min / 6hr 10min / 7hr / 7hr 40min / 8hr 40min / 9hr 45min); Jonquière (3 weekly; 9hr); Dorval / Ottawa (2–4 daily; 20min / 2hr); Dorval / Cornwall / Brockville / Kingston / Toronto (6 weekly; 20min / 1hr / 1hr 45min / 2hr 30min / 4hr 45min); Dorval / Cornwall / Brockville / Kingston / Belleville / Trenton / Cobourg / Toronto (1 daily; 20min / 1hr 15min / 2hr / 2hr 50min / 3hr 30min / 3hr 50min / 4hr 20min / 5hr 40min); Dorval / Kingston / Toronto (6 weekly; 20min / 2hr 15min / 4hr 30min); Dorval / Cornwall / Kingston / Toronto (6 weekly; 20min / 1hr / 2hr 30min / 4hr 15min); Dorval / Cornwall / Prescott / Brockville / Kingston / Belleville / Cobourg / Toronto (1 daily; 20min / 1hr / 1hr 45min / 2hr / 2hr 35min / 3hr 15min / 3hr 50min / 5hr); New York, USA (2 daily; 11hr 30min).

Sept-Îles to Labrador City (1–2 weekly; 8hr); Schefferville/Labrador City (1 weekly; 14hr/19hr).

Buses

Baie-Comeau to: Godbout/Baie-Trinité / Port-Cartier / Sept-Îles (1 daily; 45min / 2hr 10min / 2hr 40min / 3hr 50min).

Chicoutimi to: Jonquière / Alma (1–3 daily; 20min / 1hr); Jonquière / Alma / Val-Jalbert / Roberval / Saint-Félicien / Dolbeau (2 daily; 30min / 1hr 15min / 2hr 10min / 2hr 25min / 2hr 50min / 3hr 60min).

Dolbeau to: Mistassini / Péribonka / Alma (1 weekly; 5min / 30min / 1hr 15min).

Montréal to: Cornwall / Kingston (2 daily; 1hr 35min / 3hr 25min); Cornwall / Kingston / Toronto / Niagara Falls (5 daily; 1hr 30min / 3hr 20min / 6hr 20min / 9hr 20min); Granby (1–3 daily; 1hr); Granby / Bromont / Mt Orford / Magog / Sherbrooke (1–2 daily; 1hr 30min / 2hr / 2hr 30min / 2hr 45min / 3hr 15min); Kingston (2 daily; 3hr 15min); Kingston / Toronto/Niagara Falls (3 daily; 3hr 15min / 6hr 20min / 10hr); Lévis / Rivière-du-Loup (5 daily; 2hr 20min/4hr); North Bay (3 daily; 8hr); Magog / Sherbrooke (5–8 daily; 1hr 40min / 2hr 15min); Ottawa (11 daily; 2hr 20min); Ottawa / North Bay (3 daily; 3hr / 5hr 30min); Québec City (19 daily; 3hr 5min); Québec City / Alma/Val-Jalbert / St-Félicien / Dolbeau (2 daily except Sun; 4hr / 6hr 45min / 8hr 20min / 9hr / 10hr); Québec City / Baie-Saint-Paul / La Malbaie / Cap-à-l'Aigle / Saint-Siméon / Baie St-Catherine / Tadoussac / Grandes Bergeronnes / Les Escoumins / Baie-Comeau (2 daily; 3hr 30min / 4hr 45min / 5hr 30min / 5hr 40min / 6hr / 7hr 10min / 7hr 35min / 7hr 55min / 8hr 10min / 10hr 15min); Québec City / Chicoutimi / Jonquière (4–5 daily; 3hr 5min / 6hr / 6hr 30min); St-Sauveur / Ste-Adèle / Val-David / Ste-Agathe / St-Jovite / Mont-Tremblant (1–3 daily; 1hr 15min / 1hr 30min / 1hr 35min / 1hr

45min / 2hr 15min / 2hr 40min); Toronto (10 daily; 6hr 10min); Trois-Rivières / Québec City (3 daily; 1hr 30min / 3hr 15min).

Québec City to: Rivière-du-Loup / Rimouski (5 daily; 2hr 20min / 4hr); Sherbrooke (2–4 daily; 3hr).

Rimouski to: Carleton / New Richmond / Bonaventure / Chandler / Grande-Rivière / Percé / Gaspé (1 daily; 4hr / 4hr 30min / 5hr / 6hr 30min / 6hr 45min / 7hr 10min / 8hr); Mont Joli / Matane / Sainte-Anne-des-Monts (1 daily; 30min/1hr 30min /3hr); Mont Joli / Amqui / Matapédia / Campbellton / Carleton (1 daily; 35min / 1hr 45min / 3hr / 3hr 25min / 4hr 25min); Mont Joli/Amqui / Matapédia / Campbellton / Carleton / New Richmond / Bonaventure / Chandler / Grande-Rivière / Percé / Gaspé (1 daily; 30min / 1hr 40min / 2hr 50min / 3hr 20min / 4hr 15min / 5hr 30min / 6hr / 7hr 30min / 7hr 50min / 8hr 20min / 9hr 10min); Mont Joli / Matane / Ste-Anne-des-Monts / Gaspé (1 daily; 30min / 1hr 30min / 3hr/6hr 55min).

Rivière-du-Loup to: Edmundston (3 daily; 2hr 30min).

Sept-Îles to: Havre-St-Pierre (5 weekly; 3hr 10min).

Sherbrooke to: Trois-Rivières (5 weekly; 2hr 10min); Québec City (2–4 daily; 3hr).

Tadoussac to: Sacré-Coeur / Ste-Rose-du-Nord / Chicoutimi (daily except Sat; 15min / 55min / 1hr 40min).

Trois-Rivières to: Grand-Mère (2 daily; 1hr).

Ferries

Baie-Ste-Catherine to: Tadoussac (1–3 hourly; 10min).

Blanc-Sablon to: St Barbe, Newfoundland (2 daily; 1hr 30min).

Matane to: Baie-Comeau (2–6 daily; 2hr 30min); Godbout (2–6 daily; 2hr 15min).

Québec City to: Lévis (1–3 hourly; 15min).

Rimouski to: Sept-Îles / Port-Menier / Havre St-Pierre / Natashquan / Kegaska / La Romaine / Harrington Harbour / Tête-à-la-Baleine / La Tabatière / St-Augustin / Vieux-Fort / Blanc-Sablon (1 weekly; 11hr 30min / 25hr 15min / 32hr 45min / 40hr 15min / 46hr / 50hr 30min / 58hr 15min / 62hr 15 min / 65hr 45min / 70hr 15min / 75hr / 79hr 15min).

Rivière-du-Loup to: St-Siméon (April–Jan 2–5 daily; 1hr 15min).

St-Joseph-de-la-Rive to: Île-aux-Coudres (hourly to 11 daily; 15min).

Trois-Pistoles to: Les Escoumins (May–Oct 2–3 daily; 1hr 15min).

Flights

Montréal to: Bagotville (Chicoutimi) (1–4 daily; 1hr 5min); Bathurst (6 weekly; 1hr 40min); Calgary (1–2 daily; 4hr 20min); Fredericton / St John's / Halifax (1 daily; 1hr 5min / 1hr 35min / 2hr 20min); Halifax (4–5 daily; 1hr 20min); Moncton (3–5 daily; 1hr 20min); Ottawa (7–10 daily; 40min); Québec City (10–14 daily; 45min); Québec City / Mont Joli (Rimouski)/Baie-Comeau (6 weekly; 45min / 1hr 45min / 2hr 5min); Québec City / Mont Joli / Gaspé / Îles-de-la-Madeleine (2 daily; 45min / 1hr 35min / 2hr 25min / 3hr 40min); Québec City / Sept-Îles / Wabush (1 daily; 45min / 2hr / 2hr 50min); St John's (1 daily; 2hr 20min); Toronto (36–40 daily; 1hr 15min); Winnipeg (1 daily; 2hr 50min).

Québec City to: Ottawa (5 weekly; 1hr 5min); St John's/Halifax (1 daily; 1hr 10min / 1hr 50min); Toronto (2–3 daily; 1hr 30min).

Sept-Îles to: Québec City / Montréal / Ottawa (2–3 daily; 1hr 30min / 2hr 20min / 3hr).

CHAPTER THREE

THE MARITIME PROVINCES

The **MARITIME PROVINCES** – Nova Scotia, New Brunswick and Prince Edward Island – are Canada's three smallest provinces, and their combined population of around one and a half million has been largely confined to the coasts and river valleys by the thin soils of their forested interiors. Even today, the bulk of the region remains intractable – 84 percent of New Brunswick, for example, is covered by pine, maple and birch forests – and this rough-and-ready wilderness combines with a ruggedly beautiful coastline to form one of Canada's most scenic regions. Of some appeal too are the chunks of fertile land that punctuate the forests, principally in the undulating fields of PEI (Prince Edward Island) and the lowlands around New Brunswick's Grand Falls, both of which produce massive crops of potatoes, and in Nova Scotia's Annapolis Valley, a major fruit-producing area.

Most visitors to the Maritimes come for the coastal scenery and the slow pace of the "unspoilt" fishing villages, but the Maritimes were not always as sleepy as they appear today. When the three provinces joined the Dominion in the middle of the nineteenth century, their economies were prospering from the export of their fish and timber and the success of their shipyards. But, as opponents of the confederation had argued, the Maritimers were unable to prevent the passage of protectionist measures favouring the burgeoning industries of Ontario and Québec. This discrimination, combined with the collapse of the shipbuilding industry as steel steamers replaced wooden ships, precipitated a savage and long-lasting recession that, within the space of thirty years, transformed most of the Maritimes from a prosperous, semi-industrialized region to a pastoral backwater dependent on the sale of its raw materials – chiefly wood and fish. In recent years, tourism has helped to keep the region's economy afloat and the tourist industry hereabouts is extremely well-organized, though out of season – before mid-May and after mid-October – many attractions and B&Bs are closed.

Bypassed economically, many of the region's villages still retain their nineteenth-century appearance, with pastel-shaded clapboard houses set around rocky coves and bays. However, the Maritimes offer more variety than this old-fashioned image suggests. In **Nova Scotia**, the southwest coast does indeed have a clutch of quaint fishing ports, but it also harbours the busy provincial capital of **Halifax**, whilst **Annapolis**

ACCOMMODATION PRICE CODES

All the accommodation prices in this book have been coded using the symbols below, corresponding to Canadian dollar rates. Prices are for the least expensive double room in each establishment in high season, excluding special offers. For a full explanation, see p.38 in Basics.

① up to $40	③ $60–80	⑤ $100–125	⑦ $175–240
② $40–60	④ $80–100	⑥ $125–175	⑧ $240+

TOLL-FREE INFORMATION NUMBERS

The Nova Scotia Department of Tourism operates an information and accommodation reservation service on ☎1-800-565-0000 from anywhere within Canada and the
USA. **Tourism New Brunswick** ☎1-800-561-0123 from anywhere in Canada and
mainland USA. **PEI Department of Tourism** ☎1-800-463-4734 from anywhere in
Canada and mainland USA.

Royal, with its genteel mansions, is but a few kilometres from **Port Royal** and its
reconstruction of the fort Samuel de Champlain built in 1605. Further east, **Cape
Breton Island**, connected to the mainland by a causeway, is divided into two by **Bras
d'Or Lake**: the forested plateaus around industrial **Sydney** is unremarkable, but in
the west the elegiac hills and lakes flanking the resort of **Baddeck** lead into the mountainous splendour of **Cape Breton Highlands National Park** – a rare chunk of
mountain in a region that is relatively flat. Moving on, **New Brunswick** has urban
pleasures in the shape of its cosy capital **Fredericton** and the gritty, revitalized port
of **Saint John** (never "St John") – but its star turn is the **Bay of Fundy**, whose taper
creates tidal variations of up to 12m, a phenomenon observable right along the shoreline and at the beautiful **Fundy National Park**. The tides churn the nutrient-rich
waters down near the ocean bed towards the surface and this draws an abundance of
marine life into the bay – including several species of **whale**, beginning with finback
and minkes in late spring, and humpbacks from mid-to late June. By the middle of July
all three species are frequently sighted and they usually stay around till late summer
and fall, which is when the rare North Atlantic right whale is seen too. Whale-watching trips leave from a string of Fundy ports in both Nova Scotia and New Brunswick –
those from Westport, near **Digby**, and **Grand Manan Island**, are among the best.
Last but certainly not least is **PEI**, linked to the mainland by the whopping Confederation Bridge in 1997. The island possesses one of the region's most amenable towns
in leafy, laid-back **Charlottetown**, well worth at least a couple of days especially as it's
but a short hop from the magnificent sandy beaches of the **Prince Edward Island
National Park**.

NOVA SCOTIA

The character of **NOVA SCOTIA** has been conditioned by the whims of the North
Atlantic weather, a climate so harsh in wintertime that the seaboard Nova Scotian
colonists of the eighteenth century earned the soubriquet Bluenoses for their ability to
stand the cold. The descendants of these hardened sailors do not typify the whole
province, however. The farmers of the **Annapolis Valley** and their Acadian neighbours
were quite distinct from the mariners of the Atlantic coast, and different again were the
mixed bag of emigrants who came to work the coal mines and steel mills of central Nova
Scotia and Cape Breton Island from the 1880s – differences that remain noticeable today.
    To get the full sense of Nova Scotia you have to do a tour, and the logical place to
start is the capital, **Halifax**, which sits on a splendid harbour on the south coast. With
its excellent restaurants, lively nightlife and handful of historic attractions, the city can
easily fill a couple of days. To continue the tour, it's best to take in the beguiling fishing villages of the southwest shore, turning inland at **Liverpool** for the remote forests
and lakes of **Kejimkujik National Park**, then on to **Annapolis Royal**, the old capital
of Acadia, and Champlain's habitation at **Port Royal**. Heading east along the Annapolis Valley, it's a further 100km to the pleasant college town of **Wolfville** and another
90km back to Halifax.

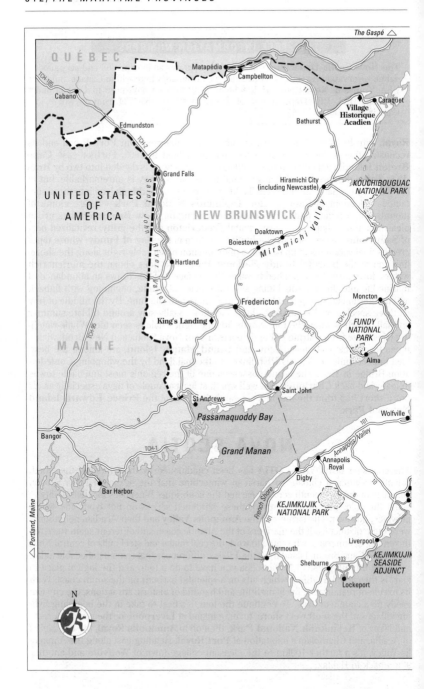

The Gaspé △

QUÉBEC

TCH 185

Cabano

Matapédia

Campbellton

11

Caraquet

Village
Historique
Acadien

Bathurst

Edmundston

TCH-2

Grand Falls

Hiramichi City
(including Newcastle)

KOUCHIBOUGUAC
NATIONAL PARK

8

11

UNITED STATES
OF
AMERICA

NEW BRUNSWICK

Doaktown

Boiestown

Miramichi Valley

Hartland

8

Moncton

TCH-2

Fredericton

FUNDY
NATIONAL
PARK

TCH-2

King's Landing

Alma

MAINE

TCH-95

1

1

3

Saint John

St Andrews

Passamaquoddy Bay

Wolfville

101

Annapolis Valley

Bangor

TCH-1

Grand Manan

Annapolis
Royal

Digby

10

8

△ Portland, Maine

Bar Harbor

French Shore

KEJIMKUJIK
NATIONAL PARK

Liverpool

KEJIMKUJIK
SEASIDE
ADJUNCT

Yarmouth

Shelburne

103

Lockeport

N

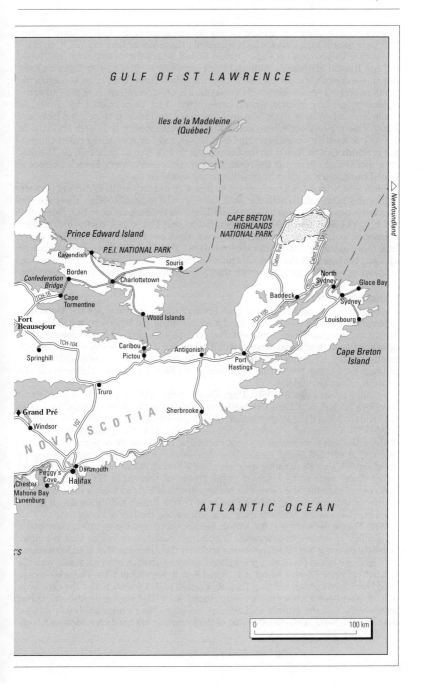

Nova Scotia's other outstanding circular tourist route is the **Cabot Trail**. Named after the explorer John Cabot, who is supposed to have landed here in 1497, it encircles the northern promontory of **Cape Breton Island**, where the mountainous landscapes of **Cape Breton Highlands National Park** constitute some of eastern Canada's most stunning scenery. Cape Breton Island – and the strip of Nova Scotia coast bordering the Northumberland Strait – attracted thousands of Scottish highlanders at the end of the eighteenth century, mostly tenant farmers who had been evicted by Scotland's landowners when they found sheep-raising more profitable than renting farmland. Many of the region's settlements celebrate their Scots ancestry and Gaelic traditions in one way or another – museums, Highland Games and bagpipe-playing competitions – and in **South Gut St Ann's**, on the Cabot Trail, there's even a Gaelic college. The final attraction of Cape Breton is the reconstructed eighteenth-century French fortress of **Louisbourg**, stuck in splendid isolation on the southeast tip.

Southwest Nova Scotia is well served by **bus**, with daily connections running between Halifax and Yarmouth via both the south shore and the Annapolis Valley. There are also frequent buses from Halifax to Sydney and Truro, for connections on to New Brunswick and PEI. **VIA Rail** services run between Halifax and Truro, then continue on to New Brunswick and Québec. Elsewhere, however, you'll need a **car**, particularly if you're keen to see anything of the wilder sections of the Cabot Trail. **Car ferries** link Yarmouth with Bar Harbour and Portland in Maine; North Sydney with Newfoundland; Caribou, near Pictou, with PEI; and Digby with Saint John, which often makes a useful short cut.

A brief history of Nova Scotia

The original inhabitants of the Maritime Provinces were the **Micmacs** and **Malecites**, Algonquian-speaking peoples who lived a semi-nomadic life based on crop cultivation, fishing and hunting. Never numerous, both groups were ravaged by the diseases they contracted from their initial contacts with Basque and Breton fishermen in the late sixteenth century. Consequently, they were too weak to contest European colonization, although the Micmacs were later employed by the French to put the frighteners on the colonists of northern Maine.

Founded by the French in 1605, **Port Royal**, on the south shore of the Bay of Fundy, was Nova Scotia's first European settlement, but it was razed by Virginian raiders in 1613 and abandoned the following year. In 1621, James I, King of England and Scotland, granted "**Nova Scotia**" – as New Scotland was termed in the inaugural charter – to William Alexander, whose colony near Port Royal lasted just three years. The French returned in the mid-1630s, establishing themselves on the site of today's Annapolis Royal and this time designating the region as the French colony of **Acadie**. These competing claims were partly resolved by the **Treaty of Utrecht** in 1713 – when Britain took control of all the Maritimes except Cape Breton Island and today's PEI – and finally determined after the fall of New France in 1759, a British victory tarnished by the cruel expulsion of the Acadians from their farms along the Bay of Fundy.

With France defeated and the British keen to encourage immigration, there was a rapid influx of settlers from Ireland, England and Scotland as well as United Empire Loyalists escaping New England during and after the American War of Independence. This increase in the population precipitated an administrative reorganization, with the creation of Prince Edward Island in 1769 and New Brunswick in 1784. The new, streamlined Nova Scotia prospered from the development of its agriculture and the expansion of its fishing fleet. Further profits were reaped from shipbuilding, British-sanctioned privateering, and the growth of Halifax as the Royal Navy's principal North Atlantic base. In 1867 Nova Scotia became part of the Dominion of Canada confident of its eco-

The Nova Scotia telephone code is ☎902.

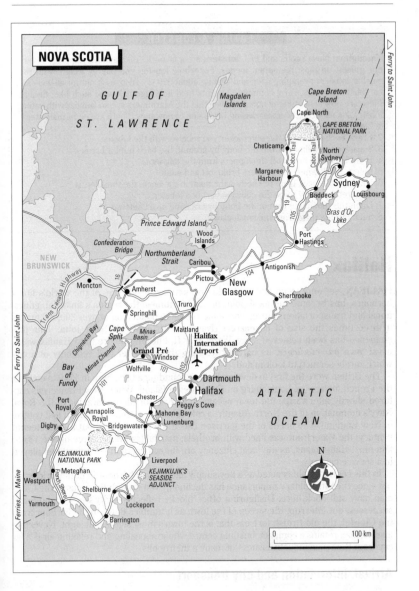

nomic future. However, the province was too reliant on shipbuilding and, when this industry collapsed, Nova Scotia experienced a dreadful recession, whose effects were only partly mitigated by the mining of the province's coalfields and the industrialization of Cape Breton's **Sydney**, which became a major steel producer. Most of the pits and steel mills were closed in the 1950s, and the province is now largely dependent on farming, fishing and tourism.

EATING A LOBSTER

Throughout Nova Scotia and PEI, **lobsters** are a favourite dish and they appear, in various guises, on most restaurant menus. For whole lobster, you pay by weight with the smaller lobsters averaging 450g and costing about $20–25. Also, look out for all-you-can-eat lobster suppers, rural community events held in village halls and such like, though these are now something of a rarity. Given that the Maritimers are so familiar with eating lobster, it's particularly embarrassing if you don't know how. There are eight main steps:

1. Twist off the claws.
2. Crack each claw with the nutcracker you receive with the lobster.
3. Separate the tailpiece from the body by arching the back until it breaks.
4. Bend back and break off the flippers from the tailpiece.
5. Insert a fork where the flippers broke off and push.
6. Unhinge the back from the body – the meat in the back, the tomalley, is considered by many to be the choicest part of a lobster.
7. Open the remaining part of the body by cracking apart sideways.
8. Suck out the meat from the small claws.

Halifax

HALIFAX, set on a steep and spatulate promontory beside one of the world's finest harbours, has become the focal point of the Maritimes, the region's financial, educational and transportation centre, whose metropolitan population of over 300,000 makes it three times the size of its nearest rival, New Brunswick's Saint John. This preeminence has been achieved since World War II, but long before then Halifax was a naval town *par excellence*, its harbour defining the character and economy of a city which rarely seemed to look inland.

The British were the first to develop Halifax, founding a base here in 1749 to counter the French fortress of Louisbourg on Cape Breton Island. When New France was captured shortly afterwards, the town became a heavily fortified guarantor of the Royal Navy's domination of the North Atlantic, a role reinforced when the British lost control of New England. The needs of the garrison called the tune throughout the nineteenth century: the waterfront was lined with brothels; martial law was in force till the 1850s; and most Haligonians, as the local citizenry are known, were at least partly employed in a service capacity.

In this century Halifax acted as a key supply and convoy harbour in both world wars, but since then its military importance has declined, even though the ships of the Canadian navy still dock here. Disfiguring office blocks reflect the city's new commercial successes, but interrupt the sweep of the town as it tumbles down to the harbour from the **Citadel**, the old British fortress that is the town's most significant sight. Nevertheless, Halifax retains a compact, bustling centre whose appealing and relaxing air is a far cry from the tense industriousness of many a metropolis.

Arrival, information and city transport

Halifax International Airport is located 35km northeast of the city centre and has its own **tourist information office** (daily 9am–10pm). Airbus runs a bus **shuttle** service from the airport to the classier downtown hotels (daily: hourly 7.30am to 10pm; 1hr 15min; $12 single, $20 return). If you're not staying at one of these, ask the driver how near to your destination he will let you off; for downtown get off at the *Delta Barrington Hotel*, which is on Barrington Street at Duke, right in the centre. The **taxi** fare from the

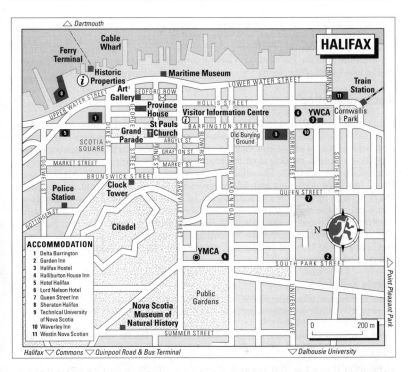

△ Dartmouth

Cable Wharf

Ferry Terminal

Historic Properties

HALIFAX

Maritime Museum

LOWER WATER STREET

Train Station

Art Gallery

BEDFORD ROW

UPPER WATER STREET

HOLLIS STREET

Province House

Visitor Information Centre

YWCA

Cornwallis Park

St Pauls

BARRINGTON STREET

Church

Grand Parade

ARGYLE ST.

Old Burying Ground

SCOTIA SQUARE

PRINCE ST.

GRAFTON ST.

SPRING GARDEN ROAD

MORRIS STREET

SOUTH STREET

MARKET STREET

MARKET ST.

BRUNSWICK STREET

COGSWELL ST.

GOTTINGEN ST

Police Station

Clock Tower

SACKVILLE STREET

QUEEN STREET

Citadel

YMCA

N

ACCOMMODATION
1 Delta Barrington
2 Garden Inn
3 Halifax Hostel
4 Halliburton House Inn
5 Hotel Halifax
6 Lord Nelson Hotel
7 Queen Street Inn
8 Sheraton Halifax
9 Technical University of Nova Scotia
10 Waverley Inn
11 Westin Nova Scotian

SOUTH PARK STREET

Point Pleasant Park

Public Gardens

UNIVERSITY AVE.

Nova Scotia Museum of Natural History

SUMMER STREET

0   200 m

Halifax ▽ Commons ▽ Quinpool Road & Bus Terminal   ▽ Dalhousie University

airport to the centre is around $40. The Acadian Lines terminal, 6040 Almon St, about 4km northwest of the centre just off Robie St, houses the long-distance bus station and also McKenzie Buses (for Yarmouth and the South Shore): transit bus #7 connects the terminal with downtown. The VIA Rail station, Hollis Street at Cornwallis Park, handles just six **trains** in and out per week, connecting Halifax with Truro, New Brunswick, the Gaspé and Montréal. From the train station it's a fifteen-minute walk into the centre down Barrington Street, or else catch the #9 bus (every 30min during the week, hourly on the weekend).

Information

Both of Halifax's main **tourist offices** cover the city and province, and are centrally situated. The **International Visitor Information Centre** (June–Aug daily 8.30am–7pm; Sept–May Mon–Fri 9am–5pm; ☎490-5946) at 1595 Barrington and Sackville, will gladly fix up accommodation in town and across the whole of Nova Scotia, advise on tours and provide you with armfuls of maps, brochures and leaflets including the comprehensive *Halifax Visitor Guide*. Five minutes' walk away, just off the waterfront in the area known as the Historic Properties, the **Nova Scotia Visitor Information Centre** (June–Aug daily 9am–7pm; Sept–May Mon–Fri 9am–5pm; ☎424-4247) offers a similar service. At both, the room reservation service is free.

City transport

The best way to see **downtown** Halifax is on foot, but for outlying attractions and accommodation **Metro Transit** (☎490-6600) bus services are reliable and efficient, though they are sharply curtailed in the evenings and on weekends. There's a flat fare of $1.50 in the Halifax area – exact fare only. If you need to change buses on the same journey, ask for a free transfer ticket at the outset. Free Metro Transit route maps and schedules are available from the International Visitor Information Centre and the information desk on the lower level of the Scotia Square shopping mall at Barrington and Duke.

Accommodation

Finding **accommodation** in Halifax is rarely a problem and the International Visitor Information Centre is especially helpful in emergencies. To get a flavour of the city your best bet is to stay in – or at least close to – downtown. Here you'll find a number of modern skyrise **hotels**, ranging from the comfortable to the luxurious, as well as several more distinctive offerings. These include a couple of stylish hotels with Art Deco flourishes, two **inns** occupying tastefully converted old town houses and the occasional **B&B**, though most of the city's B&Bs are far from downtown. Halifax's **motels** are stuck out on the peripheries of town too, inconveniently concentrated about 10km northwest of the centre along Bedford Highway (Hwy 2), beside Bedford Basin bay. The main budget alternatives are the **college rooms** offered by several city universities between mid-May and mid-August, and the pleasant, centrally located youth hostel. There is no city campground.

Hotels and inns

Delta Barrington, 1875 Barrington St (☎429-7410 or 1-800-268-1133, fax 420-6524). Modern luxury, bang in the middle of downtown, with weekend discounts of up to 30 percent. Attached to one of the city's larger shopping malls. ⑤.

Hotel Halifax, 1990 Barrington St (☎425-6700 or 1-800-441-1414, fax 425-6214). Large, modern downtown hotel occupying a concrete and glass tower block with attractive, spacious rooms that are discounted at weekends. ⑤.

Halliburton House Inn, 5184 Morris St (☎420-0658, fax 423-2324). Near the railway station off Barrington Street, this attractively restored Georgian town house with garden offers good value and includes breakfast. Thirty rooms. ⑤.

Lord Nelson Hotel, 1515 South Park St (☎423-6331 or 1-800-565-2020, fax 423-7148). Opposite the Public Gardens at the corner of Spring Garden Road. The lobby of this popular brown-brick hotel is spacious and elegant, with Art Deco details dating from its 1920s construction. The 200-odd rooms do not quite live up to the lobby, but they are comfortable and still compare well with those of their rivals. ④.

Queen Street Inn, 1266 Queen St at Morris (☎422-9828). Southwest of downtown this charmingly renovated Victorian villa has just six rooms but doesn't include breakfast. No children. ③.

Sheraton Halifax, 1919 Upper Water St (☎421-1700 or 1-800-325-3535, fax 422-5805). One of the city's grandest hotels, built in a broadly retro style to blend in with the adjacent Historic Properties. Overlooks the waterfront and has casino, saunas, swimming pool and whirlpool. ⑥.

Twin Elms Hotel, 5492 Inglis St at Queen (☎423-8974, fax 423-4140). This modest hotel has around twenty basic rooms, only a handful of which are en suite. It occupies a prewar property about 1.5km from the city centre, out towards Point Pleasant Park. Rates include continental breakfast. ②.

Waverley Inn, 1266 Barrington St (☎423-9346 or 1-800-565-9346, fax 425-0167). Elegant Victorian mansion, with thirty rooms, that's been delightfully refurbished with period furnishings. Oscar Wilde stayed here on a North American lecture tour, apparently turning up in green velvet pantaloons – outlandish gear which only seems to have added to his notoriety amongst the locals. The inn is situated about 5min walk from the train station; reservations advised. Rates include breakfast. ④.

Westin Nova Scotian, 1181 Hollis St (☎421-1000 or 1-800-228-3000, fax 422-9465). Massive, luxurious hotel with all mod cons in the upgraded premises of the old railway hotel, which – with its Art Deco touches – is next door to the new train station. 15min stroll along Barrington or Hollis Street from the centre. ⑥.

Bed and Breakfast, hostels and college rooms

Dalhousie University, west end of University Avenue (☎494-8840, fax 494-1219). Located 2km southwest of the centre with facilities that include swimming pool and sports halls. Single and double rooms available, usually with shared bathrooms, but breakfast is included. ②.

Garden Inn Bed and Breakfast, 1263 South Park St (☎492-8577). No-frills rooms in fairly central B&B, 1km southwest of downtown. ②.

Halifax Heritage House Hostel, 1253 Barrington St (☎ & fax 422-3863). Only 500m from the train station, this clean and agreeable hostel with family rooms (doubles $36) and dorm beds ($15) has a laundry, kitchen, patio and parking. ①.

St Mary's University, 923 Robie St (☎420-5485, fax 420-5511). About 2km southwest of the centre, on the way to Point Pleasant Park; singles and doubles available; shared bathrooms. ①.

Technical University of Nova Scotia, O'Brien Hall, 5217 Morris St (☎420-7780, fax 420-2628). Off Barrington Street, 10min walk south of the centre, this hostel has singles and doubles available with a shared bathroom and rates include breakfast. ①.

Virginia Kinsfolks, 1722 Robie St (☎ & fax 423-6687). About 1.5km west of downtown, opposite Halifax Infirmary. Plain B&B with three en-suite rooms. ③.

YMCA, 1565 South Park St at Sackville (☎423-9622, fax 425-0155). Opposite the Public Gardens, this YMCA, for men and women, has fifty rooms, none of which are en suite but there's a gym. ②.

YWCA, 1239 Barrington St (☎423-6162; fax 423-7761). Near the Halifax hostel by the train station this women-only hostel has facilities that include kitchen, gym and sauna. ②.

The City

With its shopping malls and brusque tower blocks, the commercial and social heart of modern Halifax clambers up the steep hillside from the harbourfront, its narrow streets dotted with scores of bustling bars and restaurants. The city's main attractions – most notably the **Art Gallery**, with its eclectic collection of modern Canadian paintings, the **Maritime Museum** and the **Georgian Province House** – all huddle close together in the lower part of town beneath Halifax's star turn, the Vaubanesque **Citadel**. On a sunny day, a pleasant diversion is a trip to see a couple of the **outer fortifications** built to defend Halifax harbour, and you can also catch the ferry over to neighbouring **Dartmouth**, home of the old **Quaker House**.

The Citadel

The distinctively bright Georgian **Clock Tower**, a solitary landmark sitting at the top of George Street beside the path up to the Citadel, looks somewhat confused, its dainty balustraded tower set on top of the dreariest of rectangular shacks. Completed in 1803, the tower is a tribute to the architectural tastes of its sponsor, Edward, Duke of Kent, the father of Queen Victoria, who was sent here as military commandant in 1794. The Duke insisted the tower had a clock on each of its four faces so none of the garrison had an excuse for being late, a preoccupation typical of this unforgiving martinet.

Up above the Clock Tower, the present fortifications of the **Citadel National Historic Site** (mid-May to mid-June & Sept to mid-Oct daily 9am–5pm, $3.50; mid-June to Aug daily 9am–6pm, $5.75; limited opening hours mid-Oct to mid-May, free) were completed in 1856, the fourth in a series dating from Edward Cornwallis's stockade of 1749. The star-shaped fortress, constructed flush with the crest of the hill to protect it from artillery fire, seems insignificant until you reach the massive double stone and earth walls flanking the deep encircling ditch, a forbidding approach to one of Britain's most important imperial strongholds. Despite their apparent strength, however, the walls, faced with granite and ironstone, were a source of worry to a succession of British engineers. The sunken design simply didn't suit the climate – in winter the water in the mortar and earth froze and the spring melt came with regular collapses.

A slender footbridge spans the ditch and leads into the fort, whose vast **parade ground** is flanked by stone walls, within which a string of storehouses hides a diverse collection of military bric-a-brac. Here you'll find a couple of reconstructed powder magazines and the **Communications Exhibit**, which explains the niceties of the Admiralty's signalling system. Dominating the parade ground is the three-storey **Barracks**, whose long, columned galleries house a barrack room as of 1869 and an **Army Museum** (recommended donation $1), which adopts an earthy soldier's outlook in the labelling of its wide collection of small arms. Ancient and sometimes rare photos track the Canadian army through its various imperial entanglements – from the Boer War onwards – and there's an interesting section tracing Canadian involvement with the Anglo-French attack on Bolshevik Russia after World War I.

Free and entertaining half-hour **guided tours** of the Citadel leave the information office in the Barracks building at regular intervals, while close by in the theatre an hour-long film, *The Tides of History*, details the development of Halifax and its military past. Throughout the summer, bagpipe bands and marching "soldiers" perform on the parade ground in period uniform and one of the cannons is ceremoniously fired every day at noon. If militarism leaves you cold, the Citadel is still worth a visit for the grand view from its ramparts over the city and harbour.

Downtown

If you retrace your steps past the Clock Tower and head down George Street, you'll hit the tree-lined, elongated square known as the **Grand Parade**, the social centre of the nine-teenth-century town. For the officer corps, this was the place to be seen walking on a Sunday, when, as one obsequious observer wrote, "their society generally [was] sought, frequently courted, and themselves esteemed" – a judgement rather different from that of the radical journalist Joseph Howe, who hated their "habits of idleness, dissipation and expense". The southern edge of the parade borders the handsome **St Paul's Church** (Mon–Fri 9am–4.30pm; free), whose chunky cupola and simple timber frame date from 1750, making it both the oldest building in town and the first Protestant church in Canada. Inside, the church's simple symmetry – with balcony and sturdy pillars – is engaging, an unpretentious garrison church enlisting God to the British interest; look out, too, for the piece of wood embedded in the plaster above the inner entrance doors, a remnant of the 1917 Halifax Explosion (see p.323). Following the disaster, the vestry was used as an emergency hospital and the bodies of hundreds of victims were laid in tiers around the walls.

Charles Dickens, visiting in 1842, described the graceful sandstone **Province House**, a couple of minutes' walk from Grand Parade down George Street at Hollis (July & Aug Mon–Fri 9am–5pm, Sat & Sun 10am–4pm; Sept–June Mon–Fri 9am–4pm; free), as "a gem of Georgian architecture" whose proceedings were "like looking at Westminster through the wrong end of a telescope". Highlights of the free guided tour include a peek into the old upper chamber, with its ornate plasterwork and matching portraits of Queen Caroline and her father-in-law, George I. She should have been pictured with her husband, George II, of course, rather than her father-in-law, but no one has ever bothered to rectify this costly decorative error. The present legislature meet in the Assembly Room, a cosy chamber that partly resembles a Georgian bedroom rather than Nova Scotia's seat of government.

Across the road from the Province House, the **Art Gallery of Nova Scotia**, 1741 Hollis St (Tues–Fri 10am–5pm, Sat & Sun noon–5pm; June–Aug open till 9pm on Thurs; $3, free on Tues), occupies an imposing Victorian building that has previously served as a courthouse, police headquarters and post office. The gallery's two lower floors accommodate temporary exhibitions of modern sculpture and painting, have a section for children and hold a small but enjoyable selection of the work of modern Canadians drawn from the permanent collection: the egg tempera on Masonite *Island in the Ice* by the Nova Scotian artist Tom Forrestall is perhaps the most striking painting here (in Gallery 5), its sharp, powerful colours and threatening ice- and seascape are enhanced by a tight control of space.

Up above, the mezzanine level features local folk art – largely naive and boldly painted woodcarvings and panel paintings – as well as a small sample of Inuit work. On the second floor there's an excellent collection of **Canadian Art**, whose earlier canvases are distinguished by four intriguing views of Halifax in the 1760s produced by Dominic Serres in the minutely observed Dutch land- and seascape tradition (Gallery 9); surprisingly Serres never actually visited Canada, but painted Halifax while in Europe, from drawings produced by a camera obscura. In the same gallery, there's Joshua Reynolds' flattering *Portrait of George Montagu Dunk, 2nd Earl of Halifax*. As the man responsible for colonial trade, Dunk permitted his recently acquired title to be used in the naming of "Halifax" – quite what would have happened but for his timely ennoblement (Dunk Town?) is anyone's guess. Moving on, Gallery 13 holds several canvases by Cornelius Krieghoff (see p.153) and outstanding contributions by members of the **Group of Seven** (see p.79). In particular, look out for A.Y. Jackson's *Little Fox River* and *Houses of Prospect*, both typical of Jackson's later (post-Group) style of softly coloured landscapes. Next door, Gallery 14 is devoted to modern Nova Scotian painters. Forrestall makes another appearance here, but it's his mentor, **Alex Colville**, who takes pride of place, with several characteristically disconcerting works, a sort of Magic Realism of passive, precisely juxtaposed figures caught, cinema-like, in mid-shot. Finally, there's a tiny selection of British and European paintings, and – a real surprise – an assortment of ribald Hogarth engravings.

The waterfront

One block south of the bottom of George Street stands the **Maritime Museum of the Atlantic**, 1675 Lower Water St (June to mid-Oct Mon & Wed–Sat 9.30am–5.30pm, Tues 9.30am–8pm, Sun 1–5.30pm; mid-Oct to May Tues–Sat 9.30am–5pm, Sun 1–5pm; $4.50), which houses a fascinating exhibition covering all aspects of Nova Scotian seafaring from colonial times to the present day. By the entrance, there's a reconstruction of a nineteenth-century chandlery, stocked with everything from chains, ropes, couplings and barrels of tar through to ships' biscuits and bully beef. Other displays include a collection of small boats and cutaway scale models illustrating the changing technology of shipbuilding, a feature on the history of the schooner *Bluenose* (see below) and a number of gaudy ships' figureheads: look out for the turbaned Turk once attached to the British barque *Saladin*. In 1844, the *Saladin*'s crew mutinied in mid-Atlantic, killed the captain and ran the boat aground near Halifax, where they were subsequently tried and hanged. There's also a feature on the Halifax Explosion, illustrated by a first-rate video, *One Moment in Time*, and don't miss the section on the *Titanic*, which sank east of Halifax in 1912. Several pieces of fancy woodwork found floating in the ocean after the sinking have ended up in the museum, a pathetic epitaph to the liner's grand Edwardian fittings. Docked outside the museum are an early twentieth-century steamship, the CSS *Acadia*, and a World War II corvette, HMCS *Sackville*. The first is part of the museum, the second is a (free) attraction in its own right; both can only be boarded in the summer.

The much-vaunted **Historic Properties** comprise an area of refurbished wharves, warehouses and merchants' quarters situated below Upper Water Street, 400m north of the Maritime Museum. The ensemble has a certain urbane charm – all bars, boutiques and bistros – and the narrow lanes and alleys still maintain the shape of the waterfront during the days of sail, but there's not much to see unless the schooner **Bluenose II** is moored here, as it often is during the summer. The original *Bluenose*, whose picture is on the 10¢ coin, was famed throughout Canada as the fastest vessel of its kind in the 1920s, although she ended her days ingloriously as a freighter, foundering off Haiti in 1946. The replica has spent several years as a floating standard-bearer, representing Nova Scotia at events such as the Montréal Expo, but it's now on its last sea legs and its future is uncertain. Pressure groups are campaigning to have it berthed permanently here at Halifax or at its home port of Lunenburg.

The Old Burying Ground and the Nova Scotia Museum

Mysterious and spooky at dawn and dusk, the **Old Burying Ground**, ten minutes' walk south of Grand Parade at Barrington Street and Spring Garden Road, looks something like the opening shot of David Lean's *Great Expectations* – though the over-blown memorial by the gates in honour of a brace of Canadian officers killed in the Crimean War does somewhat undermine the effect. Many of the tombstones are badly weathered, but enough inscriptions survive to give an insight into the lifes (and early deaths) of the colonists and their offspring. The oldest tomb is that of a certain John Connor, who ran the first ferry service over to Dartmouth before dying in 1754.

Walking west up Spring Garden Road from the Burying Ground, it's about 800m to the edge of the city's **Public Gardens**, off South Park Street (May–Oct 9am–sunset; free), whose sixteen acres were first planted in the 1870s. Meticulously maintained, the exotic shrubs and trees flank ornamental statues, water fountains and a brightly painted bandstand – a pleasant interlude on the way to the **Nova Scotia Museum of Natural History**, to the rear of the old grassy commonland at the back of the Citadel, at 1747 Summer St (June to mid-Oct Mon–Sat 9.30am–5.30pm, Wed open till 8pm, Sun 1–5.30pm; mid-Oct to May Tues–Sat 9.30am–5pm, Wed till 8pm, Sun 1–5pm; $3). The best of the museum's wide-ranging exhibits are those depicting the region's marine and land-based wildlife and the displays of local and traditional furniture and furniture-making. Other galleries cover a variety of subjects ranging from blow-up representations of pubic and head lice to ceramic mushrooms and the Micmacs.

The outer fortifications

In the eighteenth century the British navy protected the seven-kilometre-long sea passage into **Halifax harbour**, and the Bedford Basin behind it, with coastal batteries strung along the shore between the city and the Atlantic. Two of these are worth a visit, though more for their commanding views than the ragbag of military remains. There's one at **Point Pleasant**, at the tip of the Halifax peninsula about 3km south of the city; the other is on McNab's Island, sitting in the middle of the main seaway, 4km south of the city.

At the end of South Park Street and its continuation, Young Avenue, **Point Pleasant Park** (bus #9 from Barrington Street) incorporates the remains of four gun batteries and the squat **Prince of Wales Martello Tower** (July–Aug daily 10am–6pm; free), which was built at the end of the eighteenth century as a combined barracks, battery and storehouse. One of the first of its type, the design was copied from a Corsican tower (at Martello Point) which had proved particularly troublesome to the British. The self-contained, semi-self-sufficient defensive fortification with its thick walls and protected entrance proved so successful that Martello towers were built throughout the empire, only becoming obsolete in the 1870s with advances in artillery technology. The surrounding park, 200 acres of wooded hills and shoreline crisscrossed by paths and trails, boasts thousands of butterflies and birds, and is one of the few places in North America where heather grows, supposedly originating from seeds shaken from the bedding of Scots regiments stationed here.

McNab's Island, 5km long and 2km wide, contains the remnants of five different fortifications, dating from the middle of the eighteenth century to the establishment of Fort McNab in 1890. The island, half of which is parkland, is laced with hiking trails and dotted with picnic spots, making a relaxing retreat from the city. To reach McNab's Island take a **ferry** from the downtown jetty on Cable Wharf at the bottom of George Street (June–Sept 2 daily; 20min; $11 return).

THE HALIFAX EXPLOSION

Nothing in the history of the Maritimes stands out like the **Halifax Explosion** of 1917, the greatest human-caused cataclysm of the pre-atomic age. It occurred when Halifax was the departure point for convoys transporting troops and armaments to Europe. Shortly after dawn on December 6, a Norwegian ship called the *Imo*, a vessel carrying relief supplies to Belgium, and a French munitions carrier called the *Mont Blanc* were manoeuvring in Halifax harbour. The Norwegian ship was steaming for the open sea, while the *Mont Blanc*, a small, decrepit vessel, was heading for the harbour stuffed with explosives and ammunition, including half a million pounds of TNT – though it flew no flags to indicate the hazardous nature of the cargo. As the ships approached each other, the *Imo* was forced to steer into the wrong channel by a poorly positioned tugboat. With neither ship clear about the other's intentions and each attempting to take evasive action, they collided, and the resulting sparks caused the ignition of the drums of flammable liquid stored on the *Mont Blanc*'s deck. A fire took hold, and the crew abandoned their vessel, which drifted under the force of the impact towards the Halifax shore.

A large crowd had gathered on the waterfront to witness the spectacle when the TNT exploded. The blast killed 2000 people instantly and flattened over 300 acres of north Halifax, with fire engulfing much of the rest. Windows were broken in Truro over 80km away and the shock-wave was felt in Cape Breton. Nothing remained of the *Mont Blanc*, and part of its anchor, a piece of metal weighing over half a ton, was later found more than 4km away. To make matters worse, a blizzard deposited 40cm of snow on Halifax during the day, hampering rescue attempts. The bodies of many victims were not recovered until the spring.

It's hard to appreciate today the vision of Armageddon that haunted Halifax after the explosion, but haunt the city it did, as the poignant newspaper cuttings in the Maritime Museum show.

Dartmouth

Gritty **DARTMOUTH**, across the harbour from Halifax, is often ignored by visitors as it lacks the more obvious appeal of its neighbour. Nevertheless, it is the province's second largest town, with 70,000 inhabitants, and although it's primarily an industrial centre the ferry ride over provides wide views of the harbour and the Halifax waterfront, and there are a couple of minor attractions to further justify a sortie.

From Dartmouth ferry terminal a footpath curves across a harbourside park before skirting the edge of a couple of tiny shipyards on its way to the **Shubenacadie Canal Interpretive Centre**, at 140 Alderney Drive (June–Aug Mon–Fri 9am–5pm, Sat & Sun 1–5pm; free) – a five-minute walk. The centre commemorates the ill-fated ninety-kilometre canal that linked the Bay of Fundy to Dartmouth. Begun in 1826, this monumental feat of engineering, linking a dozen existing lakes with new watercourses and locks, was completed in 1860, but the canal only made a profit for ten years before it was superseded by the railways – and then left to rot.

After the American War of Independence, several Quaker whaling families emigrated from Nantucket Island, off Cape Cod, to Dartmouth. One of their dwellings has survived, the charming **Quaker House** at 57 Ochterloney St (June–Aug Wed–Sat 9.30am–1pm & 2–4pm; free), a small, grey clapboard residence sitting three blocks up the hill from the ferry dock – or ten minutes' walk across town from the Canal Centre by heading back along the footpath and taking the first right up King Street. The interior has been painstakingly restored to its late eighteenth-century appearance, its spartan fittings reflecting Quaker values. Among the exhibits are a two-hundred-year-old pair of shoes found under the floorboards during renovations in 1991, and the eye of a Greenland whale preserved in formalin – though the staff won't show you this if they think you're squeamish. Don't miss the herb garden behind the house.

The Dartmouth **ferry** leaves the Halifax waterfront from beside the Historic Properties at the foot of George Street (Mon–Sat 6.30am–11.30pm; every 15–30min, plus June–Sept Sun noon–5.30pm; $1.50). The twin cities are also connected by two road bridges: the Mac-Donald, running just to the north of both city centres, and the Mackay, part of the outer ring road. Metro Transit bus #1 uses the MacDonald.

Eating and drinking

It's easy to **eat** well and cheaply in Halifax. There's a host of **downtown** cafés, café-bars and restaurants within easy walking distance of Grand Parade and at most of them a substantial meal will only set you back about $15–20, excluding drinks. Seafood is the leading local speciality, with **lobster** being a particular favourite and served in the tourist season at quite a few places on a fixed-price, all-you-can-eat basis from around $25. Bear in mind also that most kitchens start to finish off at around 9.30–10pm.

They say Halifax has more **bars** per head than anywhere in Canada, except St John's Newfoundland, and though many of them are eminently forgettable those we've listed rise well above the general standard and many offer a reasonable menu as well. Bars and restaurants sometimes occupy different floors of the same premises, which can be a little confusing.

Cafés, café-bars and restaurants

The Bluenose Restaurant, 1824 Hollis at Duke Street. Something of an institution, this long-established diner serves filling and fairly tasty meals until 10pm. Lobster, in various guises, is a speciality.

La Cave, 5244 Blowers at Grafton. Tiny bistro serving French cuisine and great cheesecakes. Tucked away in a basement; live jazz one or two nights a week.

Cinnamon Café, 1673 Barrington St. Straightforward, agreeable downtown café serving tasty snacks and light meals.

Economy Shoe Shop, 1663 Argyle St. Everything here is imaginative – from the name and the decor through to the menu, offering *tapas* to Italian. One of a cluster of fashionable café-bars on Argyle.

Five Fishermen, 1740 Argyle St (☎422-4421). One of Halifax's best restaurants, with an excellent menu, specializing in superb seafood. The mussel bar and the lobster are both highly recommended; very expensive but well worth the extravagance. Reservations advised.

Grabbajabba Fine Coffee, 5475 Spring Garden Rd. About 1.5km west of downtown between Queen and South Park and also at 1791 Barrington. One of several speciality coffee shops that also serves delicious pastries.

The Green Bean Coffee House, 5220 Blowers St. Lively, informal café with good snacks and speciality coffees. Open 9am–9pm.

McKelvie's, 1680 Lower Water St (☎421-6161). Big and popular restaurant-bar with a wide range of seafood, though the fish tends to be cooked without much artistry. Reservations advisable on the weekend.

Mediterraneo, 1571 Barrington St. Inexpensive downtown café serving tasty Lebanese and Canadian dishes.

Midtown Tavern and Grill, at Prince and Grafton. One of the most enjoyable places in town, this blue-collar favourite serves up mouthwatering steaks at amazingly reasonable prices. It's a far cry from the tourist-industry niceties down on the waterfront, and none the worse for it.

Momoya Restaurant, 1671 Barrington St at Prince. Unassuming but first-rate Japanese restaurant right downtown.

Salty's, Historic Properties. On the waterfront, this busy restaurant with its large patio area heaves with tourists, who feast on the lobster – generally reckoned to be as well prepared as anywhere.

Satisfaction Feast, 1581 Grafton St. Vegetarian restaurant, with vegan options available. Open daily from early morning until mid-evening.

Bars

Granite Brewery, 1222 Barrington St at South. Advertises itself as a genuine English pub. Of course it's not, but it's still charmingly intimate and they brew most of the ale on the premises. Try their "Peculiar", a fair approximation of the sultry grandeur of the legendary British Theakston's. Also at 1660 Barrington and Prince.

Lawrence of Oregano, 1726 Argyle St. Cavernous and chaotic pick-up spot beside Grand Parade. Avoid the food. Shares its premises with **My Apartment**, which has a large dance floor.

Maxwell's Plum, 1600 Grafton. Large selection of imported draught beers and Scotches. Popular spot, though lacking in atmosphere.

Peddlers' Pub, Granville Street at Duke. Occupying part of an old commercial block at the pedestrianized northern end of Granville Street, this pub has a pleasant outside area and a big and breezy bar.

Split Crow, 1855 Granville Street at Duke. Another supposedly English pub. Very central, often featuring live Maritime fiddle music.

Your Father's Moustache, 5686 Spring Garden Rd at South Park. Good range of ales with frequent live acts – blues a speciality.

Nightlife and entertainment

If you want to go out and rave, Halifax has a vibrant **live music scene** with around fifty of its café-bars and bars offering everything from blues and jazz through to indie and techno. Many of these places have live music on just a couple of nights a week, and detailed entertainment listings, along with reviews, are given in a free weekly newssheet, *The Coast*, which is available at record shops, bars and the tourist office. The local newspaper *The Chronicle-Herald* carries reviews and listings on Thursdays, and *Where*, a free magazine supplied by the tourist office, has a useful section describing the city's most popular bars and giving their opening hours. The venues listed below are places where you can expect to see live music on most nights of the week. The main musical **event** is the nine-day *duMaurier Atlantic Jazz Festival*, held towards the end of July and featuring many of the biggest international names. Halifax, as the provincial capital, also attracts major live acts in key **classical** and theatrical performances and has a fairly prestigious **theatre** scene.

Folk, jazz and blues

Birmingham Bar and Grill, 5657 Spring Garden Rd at South Park Street. Wide range of wine and beers with nightly jazz.

Blues Corner, 1565 Argyle St. Popular downtown bar featuring jazz and blues acts.

Lower Deck, in the Privateer's Warehouse, one of the Historic Properties. Traditional Maritime folk music.

Market Street Jazz Café, Market and George Streets. Modern jazz nightly.

Contemporary

Bearly's Bar & Grill, 1269 Barrington St. Out near the youth hostel, this low-key bar has regular local acts supplying a wide range of sounds.

Café Mokka Ultrabar, 1588 Granville St. Fashionable downtown spot showcasing up-and-coming local bands plus jazz and blues.

Granville Hall, 1544 Granville St. Good local talent and promising imports from surf rock to indie.

New Palace, 1721 Brunswick St. Massive, brash and noisy nightclub where Halifax's young more than get acquainted; open till 3.30am nightly.

Tickle Trunk, 5680 Spring Garden Rd. Wide range of music featuring local bands.

Cinemas

Oxford Theatre, 6408 Quinpool Rd at Oxford (☎422-2022). Mainstream cinema.

Park Lane 8, 5657 Spring Garden Rd (☎423-4598). Mainstream cinema in the Park Lane Mall.

Wormwood's Dog and Monkey, 2112 Gottingen St at Cogswell (☎422-3700). The city's main arthouse cinema; named after a vaudeville show which brought the first moving pictures to Halifax.

Theatre and classical music

Neptune Theatre, 1593 Argyle St (☎429-7070). The doyen of Halifax's live theatres, offering a wide range of mainstream dramatic productions; closes for three months in summer.

Scotia Festival of Music, at the Dalhousie Arts Centre, 6101 University Ave (☎429-9467). A fortnight of classical music, usually in late May or early June, featuring chamber works and master classes.

Symphony Nova Scotia, Suite 301 Park Lane, 5657 Spring Garden Rd (☎421-1300). Professional orchestra that usually performs at the Dalhousie Arts Centre, 6101 University Ave. Concert season from October to May.

Listings

Airlines Air Canada, Scotia Square, Barrington Street and Duke (☎429-7111); Air St Pierre, Halifax airport (☎873-3566); Canadian Airlines, Scotia Square, Barrington Street and Duke (☎427-5500).

Banks Bank of Novia Scotia, Scotia Square, Barrington Street and Duke; Toronto Dominion, 1785 Barrington.

Bike rental Cycledelics, 1678 Barrington at Prince (☎425-7433); The Trail Shop, 6210 Quinpool Rd (☎423-8736).

Bookshops There are several good bookshops in the city centre, both new and secondhand. The Book-Room, 1546 Barrington at Blowers, originated in 1839 (Canada's oldest) and makes for compulsive browsing. Trident, 1570 Argyle at Blowers, offers secondhand books with coffee and cakes. The chain bookshop Smithbooks, with an outlet at Scotia Square, is more mainstream.

Car rental Budget, 1588 Hollis (☎492-7500) and at the airport (same number); Discount, 1240 Hollis St (☎423-6446); Dollar, 1960 Brunswick inside the *Citadel Halifax Hotel* (☎429-1892) and at the airport (☎860-0203).

Consulates Netherlands, 1959 Upper Water St (☎422-1485); Norway, 11 Morris Drive (☎468-1330); Sweden, 115 Chain Lake Drive (☎450-5252); USA, Cogswell Tower (☎429-2480).

Emergencies Main police station on the corner of Rainnie Drive and Gottingen Street. General emergency number ☎911.

Hospital Halifax Infirmary, 1335 Queen St (☎496-2781).

Laundry Bluenose Laundromat, 2198 Windsor at Cunard (daily 7.30am–9pm). Self-service and service washes, with dry-cleaning too.

Post office Central office at 1680 Bedford Row.

Taxis Yellow Cab (☎422-1551).

Transport Acadian Bus Lines (☎453-8912); Halifax Metro Transit (☎490-6600); Mackenzie Bus (to South Shore and Yarmouth; ☎453-8912); *VIA Rail* (☎429-8421).

Weather For up-to-date bulletins, call ☎426-9090.

Southwest Nova Scotia

The jagged coastline running southwest of Halifax to **Yarmouth**, a distance of 300km, boasts dozens of tiny fishing villages glued tight against the shore by the vast forest that pours over the interior. Most were founded by Loyalists, whose dedication to the British interest both during and after the American War of Independence obliged them to hotfoot it out of the USA, often as penniless refugees. Today, the most beguiling of these villages are **Peggy's Cove**, an incredibly picturesque smattering of higgledy-piggledy clapboard houses dotted along a wild shore, and lesser-known **Lockeport**, with its old-fashioned air and fine sandy beaches. Equally diverting are the towns of **Lunenburg**, with its stunning Victorian architecture, and ritzy, leafy **Chester**, both of which derived their former prosperity, like their coastal neighbours, from the now- defunct shipbuilding business and from privateering.

Travelling the shoreline is the **Lighthouse Route**, a tourist trail that details everything of any possible interest: you're better off sticking to the main road, Hwy 103, and dropping down to the coast for the highlights. At workaday **Liverpool**, there's a choice of routes: you can stick to the coast, passing the seashore section of Kejimkujik National Park and Lockeport on the way to Yarmouth, where the **Evangeline Route** continues on to Annapolis Royal. Or – and this is probably the better option, unless you've bags of time – you can cut across the peninsula to Annapolis Royal on Hwy 8, past the wilderness splendours of the main portion of **Kejimkujik National Park**.

The area is popular with tourists, but not oppressively so, and almost every settlement has at least a couple of fine old Victorian mansions that have been converted into **inns** or **B&Bs**. These provide first-rate accommodation at reasonable prices and reservations are only essential in the height of the season and on holiday weekends. In terms of **restaurants**, seafood is the big deal around here – usually simply prepared and quite delicious. For **public transport**, Mackenzie Bus, based in the Halifax bus station, operate a daily service (except on Sat) between Halifax and Yarmouth along the southern shore, and Acadian Bus Lines connect Halifax with Yarmouth five times weekly via the Annapolis Valley, Digby and the **French Shore**.

Peggy's Cove

Highway 333 leaves Hwy 103 a few kilometres west of Halifax to make its slow progress through the forested hinterland that so successfully confined the region's early settlers to the coast. Once at the shoreline, the road slips through ribbon fishing villages, past glacial boulders and round rocky bays to reach tiny **PEGGY'S COVE**, 45km from Halifax. Founded in 1811, the hamlet, with a resident population of just sixty, surrounds a rocky slit of a harbour, with a spiky timber church, a smattering of clapboard houses and wooden jetties on stilts. It's a beautiful spot, the solitary lighthouse set against the sea-smoothed granite of the shore, and it attracts swarms of tourists; try to visit at sunrise or sunset, when the coach parties leave the village to its residents. Behind the lighthouse, *The Sou'wester* dispenses mundane meals, while the three-roomed *Peggy's Cove B&B,* overlooking the harbour from the end of Church Road (☎823-2265; ③; May–Oct), provides simple but perfectly adequate accommodation – advance reservations are advised.

Beyond Peggy's Cove Hwy 333 sticks closely to the coastline, meandering through a magnificently desolate landscape of stunted firs and cumbersome seashore boulders. There are several places to pull in for a stroll along the shore or you can press on north through the gentler scenery that leads back to Hwy 103.

Chester

It's a thirty-minute drive north from Peggy's Cove to Hwy 103 and a further 40km west to **CHESTER**, a handsome and prosperous-looking town tumbling over a chubby little peninsula. Founded by New Englanders in 1759, the town, with its fine old trees and elegant frame houses, has long been the favoured resort of yachting enthusiasts whose principal shindig is the race-week regatta held in mid-August. In July and August, Chester also hosts an excellent summer festival of contemporary music and Canadian-orientated drama at the **Chester Playhouse**, right in the middle of town (information and reservations ☎275-3933 or 1-800-363-7529; tickets around $14). Finally, out in the bay and reached from Chester jetty by **passenger ferry** (Mon–Fri 4 daily, Sat & Sun 2 daily; 45min; $5 return) are two tiny islets, **Big** and **Little Tancook**, whose quiet country roads and benign scenery are popular with walkers, who pop across for a day's ramble. Big Tancook is the prettier of the two and there's somewhere to eat here too – *Carolyn's Café,* opposite the jetty.

Chester **tourist office** (June & Sept Mon–Sat 10am–5pm, Sun noon–5pm; July & Aug Mon–Sat 9am–7pm, Sun 10am–5pm; ☎275-4616) is located in the old train station on the northern edge of town, beside Hwy 3. They have town maps, issue a historic walking tour leaflet and will help arrange **accommodation**, but even so you'll be lucky to find anywhere during the festival. The rest of the year, things are easier – especially on weekdays – and the town has a reasonable range of inns and B&Bs. Best of the lot is the *Captain's House Inn*, a pleasantly refurbished nineteenth-century villa at 29 Central St (☎275-3501; ③), followed by the four-roomed *Mecklenburgh Inn*, a B&B in a Victorian house at 78 Queen St (☎275-4638; ③; June–Oct). Failing these two, try the three-roomed *Hemlock House B&B*, 71 Central St (☎275-3854; ③; May–Oct). For delicious **seafood**, head for the *Rope Loft* by the jetty, or the more informal *Sea Deck* on the floor below.

Mahone Bay

In 1813, the wide waters of **Mahone Bay** witnessed the destruction of the splendidly named American privateer the *Young Teaser*, which had been hounded into the bay by a British frigate. On board was a British deserter who knew what to expect if he was captured, so he blew his own ship up instead – a tribute to the floggers of the Royal Navy. Legend has it that the ghost of the blazing vessel reappears each year. Neither is this the only strange story attached to the area. In 1795, three boys discovered the top of an underground shaft on tiny **Oak Island**, a low-lying, offshore islet a few kilometres west of Chester. The shaft, or "Money Pit", soon attracted the attentions of treasure hunters, who were convinced that this was where a vast horde of booty had been interred. At first the betting was on Drake, Kidd or Morgan, but present favourites include the Templars and even the Rosicrucians. No treasure has ever been found, but the diggings became so dangerous that the island's owners have closed it to the public; if you go, you can only get to the chain at the start of the causeway.

Just 25km west of Chester lies the **village of MAHONE BAY**,whose waterfront is dominated by three adjacent church towers, which combine to create one of the region's most famous views. There's not much else to the place, though you could drop by the **Settlers' Museum**, 578 Main St (mid-May to Aug Tues–Fri 10am–5pm, Sat & Sun 1–5pm; free), for a look at its period furniture and early nineteenth-century ceramics and have a bite to eat: the *Market at Mahone Bay*, beside the crossroads that forms the centre of the village, sells fresh local produce and superb sandwiches, whilst *Mimi's Ocean Grill*, a five-to ten-minute walk south along Main Street, serves up tasty lunches in attractive waterfront surroundings. Nearby, the four-roomed *Sou'Wester Inn*, 788 Main St (☎624-9296; ③), in a large and well-tended Victorian shipbuilder's house, is an agreeable spot to overnight.

Lunenburg

Comely **LUNENBURG**, 10km south of the village of Mahone Bay, perches on a narrow bumpy peninsula, its older central streets, sloping steeply down to the southward-facing harbourfront, decorated by brightly painted wooden houses. Dating from the late nineteenth century, the most flamboyant of these mansions display an arresting variety of architectural features varying from Gothic towers and classic pillars to elegant verandas, high gables and peaked windows, all decorated with intricate scrollwork. Amidst the virtuousity, a distinctive municipal style is noticable in the so-called "Lunenburg Bump", where overhanging window dormers are surmounted by triple-bell cast roofs – giving the town a vaguely European appearance appropriate to its original settlement. Lunenburg was founded in 1753 by German and Swiss Protestants, who of necessity soon learned to mix the farming of their homeland with fishing and shipbuilding. They created a prosperous community with its own fleet of trawlers and scallop-draggers, although nowadays the town earns as much from the tourist industry as from fishing.

Lunenburg's pride and joy is the **Fisheries Museum of the Atlantic** (mid-May to mid-Oct daily 9.30am–5.30pm; mid-Oct to mid-May Mon–Fri 8.30am–4.30pm; $7), housed in an old fish-processing plant down by the quayside. It has an excellent aquarium, a room devoted to whales and whaling, and displays on fishing and boat-building techniques.

Another section features the locally built 1920s schooner *Bluenose* and its replica *Bluenose II* (see p.321), whilst the *August gales* display has wondrous tales of mountainous seas and helmsmen tied to the mast to stop being swept overboard. Moored by the jetty, there's a trawler and a scalloper, but the real high spot here is the *Theresa E. Connor*, a saltbank fishing **schooner** launched in 1938. Superbly restored, the schooner was one of the last boats of its type to be built, a two-masted vessel constructed to a design that has changed little since the early eighteenth century: if you read *Treasure Island* as a child and were confused by the layout of the boat, all is revealed. The main change in schooner design came with the installation of engines in the early 1900s: the helmsman no longer needed to keep an eagle-eye on the sails and so he could be moved aft. Further protection was provided by a wheelhouse, though there were teething problems with these and initially an alarming number were lost at sea. With or without engines, fishing schooners worked in the same way: each carried several **dories**, small row boats that were launched at the fishing grounds. The men rowed the dories away from the schooner, fanning out to trail long hand-lines with baited hooks over the ocean – line-fishing. At the end of the day, the catch would be brought back to the schooner. Dory-fishing was a dangerous business – the transfer of the catch was especially risky and there was always the chance of being caught in the dory by a sudden squall. Not surprisingly, therefore, local fishermen did not need much persuading to abandon their schooners and dories for the larger **trawlers** that replaced them in the 1950s. The *Theresa E. Connor* soldiered on, but her last voyage was an ignominious failure: in 1963 she sailed out of Lunenburg, bound for Newfoundland to raise the rest of her 25-man crew. No one turned up and the schooner had to return home empty-handed.

There's more of maritime interest down along the harbourfront at the **Dory Shop**, where they make wooden boats in traditional style and hire out sail and row boats. If you haven't the confidence/experience to sail out on your own, regular boat trips leave the jetty near the museum throughout the summer. Theere are also two- to three-hour **whale-watching** trips operated daily during the summer by *Lunenburg Whale Watching Tours* (☎527-7175).

Lunenburg **tourist office** (May–Oct daily 9am–8pm; ☎634-3656) occupies an imitation lighthouse on Blockhouse Hill Road, above the hilly gridiron that comprises the town centre. It operates a free room reservation service, has a book with illustrations of local accommodation, and supplies a leaflet detailing the town's architectural highlights – though their $7 guidebook is far more interesting and informative. Many of the town's historic houses have been turned into first-class **inns** and **B&Bs**. Pick of the bunch are the delightful shingle-clad *1826 Maplebird House B&B*, 36 Pelham St (☎634-3863, fax 634-9415; ②; June–Sept), with its outside pool, garden and patio area overlooking the harbour; the beautifully maintained *Hillcroft Guest House*, 53 Montague St (☎634-8031; ③; May–Dec); the grand Victorian *Bluenose Lodge*, a couple of minutes' walk from the central gridiron at Dufferin Street and Falkland Avenue (☎ & fax 634-8851; ③); and the salmon-pink *Kaulbach House Inn*, an ornate villa at 75 Pelham St (☎1-800-568-8818, fax 634-8818; ③; mid-March to mid-Dec). The municipal **campground** (☎634-8100; mid-May to Oct) is next door to the tourist office.

Eating places abound in the centre. The moderately priced *Magnolia's Grill*, just off the waterfront at 128 Montague St, is a small café with a good atmosphere and tasty snacks, while the *Hillcroft Café*, 53 Montague St, offers delicious meals from a wide-ranging and imaginative menu. If you're crying out for lobster or seafood generally, there's no better place than Lunenburg: both the *Grand Banker Seafood Bar & Grill*, by the harbour on Montague St, and the *Old Fish Factory Restaurant*, next to the museum, serve a splendid range of mouthwatering seafood dishes. The other local culinary delights are the **Lunenburg sausage**, traditionally served at breakfast, which is made of lean pork and beef, flavoured with coriander and allspice, and the **Solomon Gundy**, marinated herring with sour cream or occasionally mustard.

Liverpool

Like its British namesake, **LIVERPOOL**, 150km from Halifax along Hwy 103, skirts the mouth of a Mersey River and has a strong seafaring tradition, but there the similarities end. Nova Scotia's Liverpool was founded by emigrants from Cape Cod in 1759, who established a fearsome reputation for privateering during both the American Revolution and the War of 1812, when their most famous ship, the *Liverpool Packet,* claimed a hundred American prizes. These piratical endeavours were cheekily celebrated in a local broadsheet of the time as upholding "the best tradition of the British Navy". Nowadays, Liverpool is a minor fish-processing and paper-making town, a desultory settlement only cheered by the fine old houses grouped around the eastern end of Main Street. One of these, the **Perkins House** (June to mid-Oct Mon–Sat 9.30am–5.30pm, Sun 1–5.30pm; free), has been restored to its late eighteenth-century condition, when it was the home of Simeon Perkins, who moved here from New England in 1762. A local bigwig, Perkins was a shipowner, a merchant, a colonel in the militia and a justice of the court, but he still had time to keep a detailed diary from 1766 until his death in 1812. The diaries provide an insight into the life and times of colonial Nova Scotia and they show Perkins as a remarkably unflappable man: in 1780 Liverpool was attacked by Americans, who Perkins outwitted and drove off, describing the dangerous emergency as just a "dubious and difficult affair". Copies of the four-volume diary are on display at the house, whilst the adjacent **Queens County Museum** (June to mid-Oct Mon–Sat 9.30am–5.30pm, Sun 1–5.30pm; mid-Oct to May Mon–Sat 9am–5pm; free) sometimes sells excerpts ($2) – and also possesses a diverting collection of early local photographs.

Liverpool has one good **B&B**, the *Taigh Na Mara*, 58 Main St (☎354-7194; ②), in an attractive, creeper-clad building overlooking the bay from near the Perkins House. For simple sustaining meals, try the *Liverpool Pizzeria*, 155 Main St, or *Lane's Privateer Inn*, just across the bridge from the centre, at 27 Bristol Ave.

Kejimkujik National Park

There's no better way to experience the solitude and scenery of the southwest Nova Scotian hinterland than to head north 70km from Liverpool along Hwy 8 to Maitland Bridge, the entrance to the **Kejimkujik National Park**. This magnificent tract of rolling wilderness has a rich variety of forest habitats – both hardwood and softwood – interrupted by rivers and brooks linking about a dozen lakes. The park is a riot of wildflowers in the spring and fall and provides cover for an abundance of porcupines, white-tailed deer and beavers, as well as three sorts of turtle – the Painted, the Snapping and, rarest of all, the Blanding's turtle, a green and yellow amphibian that grows to around 25cm.

Hiking trails crisscross Kejimkujik, but the easiest way to explore the park and its flat-water rivers and lakes is by canoe. These can be rented for $20 a day – plus $30 deposit – from **Jakes Landing** (☎682-2196; reservations recommended), roughly 10km by road from the entrance to the park. A couple of clearly defined, day-long **canoe trips** begin here, the delightful paddle amongst the islets of Kejimkujik Lake and an excursion up the Mersey River beneath a canopy of red maples. For overnight trips, the park has around fifty primitive **campgrounds** dotted along both canoe routes and hiking trails, which are a better bet than the large year-round campground (☎682-2772) at **Jeremys Bay**, also 10km by road from the main entrance. A park entrance fee of $3 per adult per day is levied from mid-May to October. For backcountry camping, you must register at the **information centre** (mid-June to Aug daily 8.30am–9pm; Sept–May usually 8.30am–4.30pm; ☎682-2772), near the entrance, where you can also pick up detailed maps and trail advice. The best time to visit is in the spring and fall, when the insects aren't too troublesome: the blackfly peak between mid-May and late June. The nearest **beds** are at the tiny *Whitman Inn* (☎682-2226; ②) in **Kempt**, 4km south of Maitland Bridge on Hwy 8; the nearest town is Annapolis Royal (see p.334), 40km to the north.

Kejimkujik's Seaside Adjunct

Back on Hwy 103, about 25km west of Liverpool, is the hard-to-find **Seaside Adjunct of Kejimkujik National Park**, a parcel of pristine coastline that provides an ideal half-day's hike. The Adjunct straddles the tip of a beautiful but inhospitable peninsula where the mixed forests and squelchy bogs of the interior back onto the tidal flats, lagoons, headlands and beaches of the coast. If you're lucky, you'll catch sight of the rare piping plover, which nests here between May and early August. Two wet and rough hiking trails provide the only access into the park, of which the more convenient is the three-kilometre hike down to the shore along an old cart track on the park's west side: there are no signs off Hwy 103 to the park, but turn down **St Catherine's Road**, a six-kilometre-long dirt road leading off the highway to the combined parking lot and trailhead.

Lockeport

Well off the beaten track, 65km west of Liverpool, lies **LOCKEPORT**, a sleepy fishing port sitting on a tiny island that's approached across a 1.5-kilometre-long causeway, fringed by the white sands of **Crescent Beach**. The beach is never crowded, the sea is deep and clear, and the village features a row of five contrasting houses built by the prosperous Locke family over a forty-year period in the nineteenth century. It's a lovely, relaxing spot, where nothing much seems to happen except for the comings and goings of the odd fishing smack. It also boasts one of the most delightful **B&Bs** on the coast in *Seventeen South*, 17 South St (☎656-2512; ②), a tastefully modernized Cape Cod house with three guest rooms perched on a wooded knoll in sight of the seashore, not far from the harbour. If it's full, the seasonal tourist office (☎656-3123), in the brash building at the end of the causeway, has details of a few other local B&Bs and beachside cottages. Lockeport has a good restaurant too, in *Locke's Island Dining*, 18 North St.

Shelburne

Used as the backdrop to the much-scoffed-at 1994 film version of Nathaniel Hawthorne's classic *The Scarlet Letter*, **SHELBURNE**, 70km west of Liverpool, has a vaguely disconsolate air, despite the well-kept shingle and clapboard houses that string down from Water Street, the main drag, to Dock Street and the waterfront. Both Dock and Water streets run parallel to the third largest harbour in the world, after Halifax and Sydney – easily big enough, so the plan went, to accommodate the British fleet if Hitler managed to launch a successful invasion. The British would have been welcome: Shelburne has been intensely anglophile ever since thousands of Loyalists fled here in the 1780s – including two hundred free blacks, ancestors of the town's present black community.

Shelburne is home to the **Nova Scotia Museum Complex**, centred on Dock Street, which has three distinct elements. The **Shelburne County Museum** (mid-May to mid-Oct daily 9.30am–5.30pm; mid-Oct to mid-May Mon–Sat 9.30am–noon & 2–5pm; $2) provides a broad overview of the town's history and its maritime heritage; the adjacent **Ross-Thomson House** (June to mid-Oct daily 9.30am–5.30pm; free) is a Loyalist merchant's store and home, pleasingly restored to its appearance circa 1800; and the nearby **Dory Shop** (mid-June to mid-Sept daily 9.30am–5.30pm; free) comprises a waterfront boat factory/museum. Rarely more than 5m long and built to ride the heaviest of swells, the flat-bottomed **dory** was an integral part of the fishing fleet during the days of sail. Each schooner carried about six of them: manned by a crew of two, they were launched from the deck when the fishing began, fanning out to maximize the catch. The Dory Shop produces three a year, but only for private use for hand-fishing – the few dories used today in the offshore fishery are steel-hulled. Allow about an hour to visit the three sites – and while you're here take a peek at the handful of heavyweight shingle buildings left over from the filmset, just off Dock Street.

There's no real reason to stay in Shelburne, but the **tourist office** (summer daily 9am–7pm), at the north end of Dock Street, does operate a free room reservation service. The most agreeable **hotel** in town is the *Cooper's Inn*, which occupies a lavishly refurbished old shingle house at 36 Dock St (☎875-4656; ③; April–Oct). Wooded, lakeside **camping** is available 5km west round the bay at the *Islands Provincial Park* ($10; ☎875-4304; mid-May to August). There's inexpensive and unpretentious **food** at *Claudia's Diner*, 149 Water St; wholesome meals at *Charlotte Lane Café*, down an alley off Water Street; and first-rate cuisine at the *Cooper's Inn* restaurant.

Barrington

There's not much to delay you on the 130-kilometre journey west from Shelburne to Yarmouth, but you should make a brief stop at minuscule **BARRINGTON**, where the **Old Meeting House** (mid-June to Sept Mon–Sat 9.30am–5.30pm, Sun 1–5.30pm; free), with its simple wooden pews and severe pulpit, reflects the intellectual rigour of the Nonconformist settlers who migrated here from New England in the mid-eighteenth century. In its simplicity, it's a beautiful building, which is more than can be said for the adjacent **Lighthouse Museum** (same hours; free), where a smattering of lightkeepers' memorabilia is housed in a replica of the lighthouse that once stood on remote Seal Island – though this version stands on a hillside apropos of nothing in particular.

Yarmouth

Arriving by ferry from Maine, many American visitors get their first taste of Canada in **YARMOUTH**, and most of them leave immediately. And indeed it is a mundanely modern place, though gallant efforts have been made to freshen up the waterfront and the town's deep tidal bay provides a modicum of scenic interest. It's also a good place for tourist information with the **Nova Scotia Visitor Centre**, just uphill from the ferry terminal (daily: May, June & Sept, Oct 9am–5pm; July & Aug 8am–7pm), issuing bucketloads of free leaflets and brochures. If you're stuck here for the night, there's a comfortable B&B right opposite the visitors' centre, the *Murray Manor*, 225 Main St (☎ & fax 742-9625; ②). Alternatively, the *Midtown Motel*, 13 Parade St (☎742-5333; ②), offers simple but adequate rooms a ten-minute walk north along Main Street from the ferry terminal.

From Yarmouth, Bay Ferries (☎1-888-249-SAIL) operate **car ferries** to Bar Harbour, Maine (June to mid-Oct 1 daily; 6hr; passengers $34–52, vehicles $62–68). And Scotia Prince (☎742-6460 or 1-800-341-7540) sail to Portland, Maine (May to late Oct 1 daily; 11hr; passengers $58–78, cars $80–100, cabins from $20–95; up to forty percent discounts for returns).

The French Shore

North from Yarmouth, Hwy 101 and the far slower Hwy 1 slip across the flat littoral of the 100km **FRENCH SHORE**, whose straggling villages house the largest concentration of Acadians in the province. Their gold-starred red, white and blue flags are everywhere, but there's nothing worth stopping for – **Meteghan**, the main town, is strikingly ugly – until you reach **Church Point**. Here, right next to the sea, is the massive church of **St Mary's** (July to mid-Oct daily 9.30am–5pm; free), whose stolid tower and steeple, finished in 1905, reach a giddy 56m. The fastidiously clean interior has some of the worst religious paintings imaginable, nineteenth-century dross with none of the medievalism suggested by the reliquaries beside the altar, which includes the ubiquitous wooden shards from the Holy Cross. Ten kilometres further north is the church of **St Bernard**, a cumbersome granite pile that took 32 years to complete (1910–42) – and is, if nothing else, certainly a tribute to the profound Catholicism of local Acadians.

Digby and Brier Island whale-watching

It's around 30km from St Bernard to the fishing port of **DIGBY**, whose workaday centre spreads over a hilly headland protruding into the Annapolis Basin. A narrow channel known as the Digby Gut connects the Basin with the Bay of Fundy, thereby subjecting Digby harbour to the swirling effects of the Fundy tides – and it's the harbour, with its rickety wooden piers, which is the most appealing part of town. The low-lying bluff extending from the harbour fronts Water Street and its continuation, Montague Row, where there's a line of restaurants, inns and B&Bs. Otherwise, Digby is notable for two things: its delicious scallops, which you can sample at the popular *Fundy Restaurant*, 34 Water St, and its smoked herrings known as "Digby chicks" – chewy, dark and salty delicacies on sale beside the harbour at the Royal Fundy Seafood Market.

Digby **tourist office**, also on Water Street (early June to mid-Oct daily 9am–8pm; ☎245-5714), runs a room reservation service and can give information on **whale-watching trips**. The best of these leave from **WESTPORT** on Brier Island at the far end of the eighty-kilometre-long **Digby Neck**, a narrow finger of land that runs west from town into the Bay of Fundy, with its far reaches broken into two little islands. A pair of car ferries shuttle across the narrow channels between the islands hourly, 24 hours a day, charging just $2 for the return trip, and they make it possible to complete the whole excursion – including the whale-watching trip – comfortably in a day: allow two hours for the drive and ferry rides down from Digby to Westport. Amongst a bevy of Westport whale-watching companies, two of the more established are Brier Island Whale & Seabird Cruises (☎839-2995 or 1-800-656-3660) and Whale Watch (☎839-2467 or 1-800-952-0225). There are daily whale-watching trips from June to early October and they are heavily subscribed, so advance reservations are highly recommended; if the weather is poor, check to see if sailings have been cancelled before you set out. Trips usually lasts about three hours and cost around $35. To state the obvious, no one can guarantee you'll spy a whale, but there's every chance, beginning with finback and minkes in late spring, and humpbacks from mid-to late June. By the middle of July all three species are sighted and usually hang around the Bay of Fundy till late summer and fall, which is when the rare north Atlantic right whale is seen too. (See p.877 in "Contexts" for information about whales.)

There's no particular reason to stay **overnight** on Brier Island, but if you do Westport's *Brier Island Lodge* (☎839-2300 or 1-800-662-8355; ③; April–Dec), set high above the seashore, provides the best accommodation. Back in Digby, there's much more choice, beginning with the agreeable *Thistle Down Inn*, an old two-storey house with a motel-style annexe overlooking the Annapolis Basin at 98 Montague Row (☎245-4490 or 1-800-565-8081; ③; mid-May to Oct). Just along the waterfront at no. 90 are the cheery toytown-like chalets of the *Seawinds Motel* (☎245-2573; ②; April–Dec), while the *Bayside B&B*, at no. 115 (☎245-2247; ②; all year), occupies an old timber house and has a pleasant patio.

From the ferry port 5km outside of Digby, Bay Ferries (☎1-888-249-7245) runs regular **ferries** across the Bay of Fundy to Saint John, saving a long drive if you're heading north (Jan to early June & mid-Oct to Dec 1–2 daily; early June to mid-Oct 2–3 daily; 3hr; passengers $18–23 single, cars $42–50, bicycles $11). **Buses** to Digby stop at the Irving gas station, just off Montague Row; a five- to ten-minute stroll from the harbour.

The Annapolis Valley

The **Annapolis Valley**, stretching 136km northeast from Annapolis Royal to Windsor, is sheltered by ranges of gently undulating hills from the winds and fog that afflict much of the central part of the province. This factor, combined with the fertility of the soil, makes the valley ideal for fruit growing, and the brief weeks of apple-blossom time, from late May to early June, are the subject of much sentimental and commercial exploitation – as well as the communal knees-ups of the **Apple-Blossom Festival**. The valley's string of modest towns were settled by Loyalists from New England after the expulsion of the Acadians, but the only one worth a second look, apart from delightful **Annapolis Royal**, with its extravagant Victorian mansions and proximity to the historic site of Port Royal, is **Wolfville**, an amiable university town of some charm. Wolfville is also within easy striking distance of **Grand Pré National Historic Site**, the harsh scenery of **capes Blomidon** and **Split**, and **Windsor**, site of the Haliburton House Museum, once the home of the nineteenth-century humorist Thomas Haliburton.

Annapolis Royal

With a population of just seven hundred, the township of **ANNAPOLIS ROYAL**, 114km north of Liverpool, spreads across a podgy promontory tucked between the Annapolis River and the Allain River, its tributary. The long main drag, St George Street, part of Hwy 8, sweeps through the leafy southern outskirts to reach the end of the promontory, where it turns right to run parallel to the waterfront through the commercial heart of town. Here, the merchants and shipwrights of yesteryear have been replaced by restaurants and shops, and there's a tourist-oriented boardwalk near the jetty, but the town maintains a relaxed and retiring air that's hard to resist.

Edging St George Street just before it swings right are the remains of **Fort Anne** (open access), whose grass-covered ramparts surround the old parade ground. A few military remains are encased within the ramparts – namely a couple of powder magazines – but the only significant remaining building, in the middle of the compound, is the officers' quarters, which were completed by the British during the Napoleonic Wars; surmounted by three outsize chimney stacks, they house a small **museum** (mid-May to mid-Oct daily 9am–6pm; $2.50) comprising a ragbag of military memorabilia, a reconstruction of an Acadian domestic interior and an outline of the fort's development. There's also a contemporaneous copy of the original charter by which James I incorporated "Nova Scotia" in 1621, and a cheerful community tapestry tracing the town's history. The view downriver from Fort Anne is simply delightful and it's a lovely peaceful spot, but it wasn't always so. Both colonial powers, France and England, neglected the fort and its garrison, and when a new military governor arrived at the fort in 1708 he told his superiors in Paris that the officers stationed here were "more in need of a madhouse than a barracks". If you want more of the flavour of early Annapolis Royal, ask at the museum for details of their candlelight tours of the **old graveyard** (summer 3 weekly) next to the fort – good fun, and a snip at $3.

Five minutes' walk from the fort back along St George Street, lie the ten-acre **Historic Gardens** (mid-May to mid-Oct daily 8am–dusk; $4), which feature a string of "theme gardens", from the fussy formality of a Victorian garden to an extensive rose collection in which the different varieties are arranged broadly in chronological order. The whole site slopes gently down towards the Allain River, with a dykewalk offering views of mud flats and salt marshes and also twisting through elephant grass, a reed imported by the Acadians to thatch their cottages.

Practicalities

One **bus** a day stops in the centre of town on the Acadian Lines route between Halifax and Yarmouth – but note that there are only five buses weekly from Yarmouth. The **tourist office** is inside the generating station on the bridge on Hwy 1, just 1km to the north of town (daily: late May to June & Sept to mid-Oct 10am–5pm; July & Aug 8am–8pm; ☎532-5454). They can arrange accommodation. Best are the **B&Bs**, several of which are in immaculately maintained heritage

THE ACADIANS

Acadia – *Acadie* in French – has at different times included all or part of Maine, New Brunswick and Nova Scotia. The etymology of the name is as vague as the geographical definition, derived from either the local Micmac word *akade*, meaning "abundance", or a corruption of *Arcadia*, an area of Greece that was a byword for rural simplicity when transient French fishermen arrived here in the early 1500s.

Whatever the truth, the origins of Acadian settlement date to 1604, when a French expedition led by Pierre Sieur de Monts and Samuel de Champlain built a stockade on the islet of **Saint-Croix**, on the west side of the Bay of Fundy. It was a disaster: with the onset of winter, the churning ice floes separated the colonists from the fresh food and water of the mainland, and many died of malnutrition. The following spring the survivors straggled over to the sheltered southern shore of the bay, where they founded **Port Royal**, considered Canada's first successful European settlement.

However, Champlain and Sieur de Monts soon despaired of Port Royal's fur-trading potential and moved to the banks of the St Lawrence, leaving Acadia cut off from the main flow of French colonization. Port Royal was **abandoned** in 1614 and, although it was refounded on the site of present-day Annapolis Royal in 1635, there were few immigrants. Indeed, the bulk of today's Acadians are descendants of just forty French peasant families who arrived in the 1630s. Slowly spreading along the **Annapolis Valley**, the Acadians lived a semi-autonomous existence in which their trade with their English-speaking neighbours was more important than grand notions of loyalty to the French Empire. When the British secured control of Port Royal under the Treaty of Utrecht in 1713, the Acadians made no protest.

But then, in the 1750s, the tense standoff between the colonial powers highlighted the issue of Acadian loyalty. In 1755, at the start of the Seven Years' War, government officials attempted to make the Acadians swear **an oath of allegiance** to the Crown. They refused, so Governor Lawrence decided – without consultation with London – to **deport** them en masse to other colonies. The process of uprooting and removing a community of around 13,000 was achieved with remarkable ruthlessness. As Lawrence wrote to a subordinate, "You must proceed with the most vigorous measures possible not only in compelling them to embark, but in depriving those who should escape of all means of shelter or support, by burning their houses and destroying everything that may afford them the means of subsistence in the country."

By the end of the year over half the Acadians had arrived on the American east coast, where they faced a cold reception – the Virginians even rerouted their allocation to England. Most of the rest spread out along the north Atlantic seaboard, establishing communities along New Brunswick's Miramichi Valley, on Prince Edward Island and in St-Pierre et Miquelon. Many subsequently returned to the Bay of Fundy in the 1770s and 1780s, but their farms had been given to British and New England colonists and they were forced to settle the less hospitable lands of the **French Shore**, further west. For other deportees, the expulsion was the start of wider wanderings. Some went to Louisiana, where they were joined in 1785 by over 1500 former Acadian refugees who had ended up in France – these were the ancestors of the **Cajuns**, whose name is a corruption of "Acadian".

The Acadian communities of the Maritime Provinces continued to face discrimination from the English-speaking majority and today they remain firmly planted at the bottom of the economic pile. Nevertheless, the Acadians have resisted the pressures of assimilation and have recently begun to assert their cultural independence, most notably in New Brunswick, where Moncton University has become their academic and cultural centre.

properties. The *Hillsdale House Inn*, 519 St George St (☎532-2345; ③; mid-May to mid-Oct), and the *Queen Anne Inn*, opposite at no. 494 (☎ & fax 532-7850; ③), are the finest choices – the former occupying an elegant villa of 1849, the latter a grand turreted and towered extravagance of the 1860s. Alternatively, try the *Turret*,

372 St George St (☎532-5770; ②), in another old but rather more modest house, or the well-tended *Bread and Roses Inn*, a spiky late Victorian mansion at 82 Victoria St (☎532-5727; ③; March–Oct). The *Dunroamin* **campground** (☎532-2808; mid-April to Oct), just beyond the tourist office on the far side of the Annapolis River, occupies a wooded position by the riverside.

Eating well and in style is easy here, and prices are reasonable. *Newman's*, 218 St George St, has a brisk and pleasant atmosphere and offers delicious seafoods and salads. Next door, *Leo's Café* serves first-rate snacks and lighter meals, while the inexpensive *Fort Anne Café*, opposite the entrance to the fort, sells tasty and substantial meals from a traditional Canadian menu – don't be put off by the downbeat decor.

For **entertainment**, *Ye Olde Towne* at 9 Church St serves good draught beer and the King's Theatre, 209 St George St (☎532-5466), showcases all sorts of enjoyable acts from folk music through to storytellers, comedians and mime artists. Films are shown here too and there's often live theatre, mostly with a local theme.

Port Royal

Port Royal National Historic Site (mid-May to mid-Oct daily 9am–6pm; $2.75), 12km west of Annapolis Royal on the opposite side of the Annapolis River, was where Samuel de Champlain and Pierre Sieur de Monts first set up camp in 1605 after their dreadful winter on the Île Saint-Croix. Their scurvy-ridden men, scared of English attack, hastily constructed a *habitation* similar in design to the fortified farms of France, where a square of rough-hewn, black-painted timber buildings presented a stern, partly stockaded face to any enemy. The stronghold dominated the estuary from a low bluff, as does today's replica, a painstaking reconstruction relying solely on the building techniques of the early seventeenth century.

The *habitation* was captured by roving Virginians in 1613 and passed over to the British, who, led by Sir William Alexander, settled the district in 1629 with the enthusiastic support of King James I, who wished to found a New Scotland – in the Latin of the deeds, "Nova Scotia" – near Port Royal. After three years of hardship and starvation, the Scots settlers were forced to return, like their French predecessors.

For both French and Scot settlers alike, the problem of survival was compounded by acute boredom during the months of winter isolation. To pass the time Champlain constituted the **Order of Good Cheer**, whose "entertainments programme" starred the poet Marc Lescarbot – though the role hardly filled him with colonial zeal, to judge from a poem he wrote for a gang of departing buddies:

We among the savages are lost
And dwell bewildered on this clammy coast
Deprived of due content and pleasures bright
Which you at once enjoy when France you sight.

There are **no bus services** from Annapolis Royal to the *habitation*.

Wolfville

The well-heeled university town of **WOLFVILLE**, 110km northeast from Annapolis Royal, was originally called Mud Creek until the daughter of a local dignitary, Justice DeWolf, expressed her embarrassment at the hick-sounding name. He modestly had it renamed after himself, but the mud flats around the forlorn little harbour, off Main

Street, remain the town's most distinctive feature. They are the creation of the **Fundy tides**, which rush up the Cornwallis River from the Minas Basin to dump the expanse of silt that's become home to hundreds of herons and waders, with thousands of sandpipers arriving in late summer on their annual migration from Arctic breeding grounds. From Wolfville harbour, two short and easy loop walking trails lead out along the causeway that encircles a portion of the wetland and its enclosing dykes. The more westerly route, the Wolfville Dyke Trail – running from the harbour to Cherry Lane – is the one to take as it also provides pleasant views of Wolfville, its skyline punctured by the sedate lines of **Acadia University**, whose three thousand students double the resident population.

Wolfville's other curiosity is the **Robie Tufts Nature Centre**, down Elm Avenue from Main Street, which is best visited an hour before sunset on a summer's evening (usually from the second or third week in May till late August), when there's an amazing performance by an enormous flock of brown-grey **chimney swifts**. After a long day hunting for insects, the birds fly in ever-decreasing circles above the centre, which is no more than a wooden shelter built around an old chimney, then suddenly swoop en masse into the chimney to roost for the night.

Practicalities

Wolfville is on the Acadian Bus Lines **bus** route connecting Halifax and Yarmouth. Buses stop on the Acadia University campus, on the west side of the tiny town centre, which consists of Main Street and a few subsidiary side streets. The **tourist office** is located on the east side of the town centre, just off Main Street on Willow Avenue (daily: May–June & Sept to mid-Oct 9am–5pm; July & Aug 9am–7pm; ☎542-7000), and has information on the whole of the Annapolis Valley as well as local accommodation lists. The town has several splendid **inns** and **B&Bs**, the pick of the bunch in attractively renovated old mansions. Tempting choices include the *Blomidon Inn*, 127 Main St (☎542-2291 or 1-800-565-2291; ④), an elegant sea captain's mansion with 26 guest rooms and four acres of carefully maintained gardens; the plush and rather formal Victoriana of the *Tattingstone Inn*, 434 Main St (☎542-7696 or 1-800-565-7696; ④); and the more modest but perfectly comfortable *Seaview House B&B*, just off Main Street at 8 Seaview Ave (☎542-1436; ②).

For **food**, there are good snacks, cakes and coffee at *The Coffee Merchant*, Elm at Main; everything from pizzas through to burgers and sandwiches at inexpensive *Joe's*, just down the street; and delicious salads and seafood at the smart *Acton's Café*, 268 Main St. The restaurant *Chez la Vigne*, 17 Front St, offers exquisite French regional cuisine, and the *Front Street Café*, metres away at no. 10, is a laid-back spot with great coffee and tasty food.

Grand Pré

In 1847, Henry Wadsworth Longfellow chose **GRAND PRÉ**, 5km east of Wolfville along Hwy 1 and beside the dykelands of the Minas Basin, as the setting for his epic poem *Evangeline – A Tale of Acadie*, which dramatized the deportations through the star-crossed love of Evangeline for her Gabriel. Horribly sentimental and extremely popular, the poem turned the destruction of this particular community into a symbol of Acadian suffering and British callousness. The **Grand Pré National Historic Site** (mid-May to mid-Oct daily 9am–6pm; free), with its trim lawns, planted trees and statues of Longfellow and Evangeline, is a strangely antiseptic tribute to the Acadians. The chapel standing on the site of the original church has a modest Acadian display, but there's nothing very insightful and the Acadian blacksmith's shop and garden at the end of the site seem very much an afterthought.

Capes Blomidon and Split

The rugged, hook-shaped peninsula north of Wolfville encompasses the dramatic scenery of **Cape Split** and of **Cape Blomidon**, which, local legend has it, takes its name from the sailors' phrase "Blow me down". To reach the peninsula from Wolfville, take Hwy 101 west for 6km then turn north at exit 11 for the ten-kilometre drive along Hwy 358 to **CANNING**, where there's a choice of routes depending on the cape you're aiming for: a signposted thirteen-kilometre-long minor road leads down to **Blomidon Provincial Park**, a narrow slice of seashore where steep sea cliffs back onto a lush, coastal forest of maple, birch, fir and beech, laced by some 14km of footpath. It's a popular spot and the park has a shaded **campground** (☎582-7319; mid-June to mid-Oct). The more impressive journey, though, is to continue north on Hwy 358 from Canning, climbing steeply for 4km to the highest point of the peninsula, the **Look-off**, where the view over the Annapolis Valley and the Minas Basin is truly spectacular. Behind the café here is the *Look-off Campground* (☎582-3022; mid-May to mid-Oct), one of the best-sited in the province.

From the Look-off, it's a further 17km to the end of the road, where one of the region's most popular and not-too-difficult hiking trails leads the 7km to the tip of Cape Split; the Wolfville tourist office has maps. The trail passes sheer towering cliffs, heavily eroded rock formations and precipitous waterfalls, before ending up on a small beach of eccentrically shaped boulders – keep an eye out for amethysts and agates.

Windsor

Pint-sized **WINDSOR**, sloping along the shore of an inlet of the Minas Basin 25km from Wolfville, was originally settled by Acadians and it was here in 1750 that the British built a fort to overawe them. The stockade was subsequently used to hold Acadians during the deportations, but all that remains today is a sorry-looking timber blockhouse conserved as the **Fort Edward National Historic Site** (daily: July & Aug 10am–4pm; Sept 11am–3pm; free), which, complete with musket loopholes and cannon portholes, perches on a grassy, treeless hill overlooking Hwy 101 and the tidal mud flats that stretch out towards the basin. On the other side of town, set in its own leafy grounds on a hillside 1km west of the centre, is the **Haliburton House Museum** (June to mid-Oct Mon–Sat 9.30am–5.30pm, Sun 1–5.30pm; free), one-time home of Thomas Chandler Haliburton, a mid-nineteenth-century judge and humorist. The house has been returned to something akin to its appearance when Haliburton lived here, writing the short stories that made him famous – cuttingly sarcastic tales whose protagonist, the itinerant Yankee clock pedlar, **Sam Slick of Slickville**, travels Nova Scotia meanly defrauding its gullible, unenterprising inhabitants. Immensely popular at the time, the stories are interesting as literary history, but leave a nasty High-Tory taste, although it was through Slick that Haliburton coined a bucketload of epigrams that remain in use: "six of one and half a dozen of the other"; "facts are stranger than fiction"; "raining cats and dogs"; "the early bird gets the worm"; and "as quick as a wink" – and many more – all came from his pen. Most of Haliburton's work is out of print, but the museum has a small supply and, if you're keen to sample his stories, begin with *The Clockmaker* ($7.50).

Central Nova Scotia

Most visitors hurry through **central Nova Scotia**, the chunk of forested land north and east of Halifax, on their way to Cape Breton Island, PEI or New Brunswick. By and large they're right to do so, but there is the odd pleasant diversion en route, and a couple of places make for a convenient overnight stay. One place it's difficult to avoid is workaday **Truro**, the region's largest town, situated at the east end of the Minas Basin and so subject to the Bay of Fundy tides. The most appealing parts of the bay are well to the west, but if time is tight there are dramatic (and very wet) three-hour, $65 raft rides upriver with the tidal bore from **Maitland**, 25km west of Truro – ring ☎902/752-0899 for the schedule. Heading northwest from Truro, the Trans-Canada Highway heads off to New Brunswick's Fort Beauséjour, scooting past the old coal-mining centre of **Springhill**, home town of the singer Anne Murray. In the opposite direction, the highway travels just inland from the **northeast shore**, whose gently rolling countryside was a centre of Scottish settlement from the end of the eighteenth century. The Scots first landed in **Pictou**, near New Glasgow, and this is the pick of the fishing, lumber and agricultural communities round here – especially as it's conveniently close to the PEI ferry terminal.

An alternative route between Halifax and Cape Breton is along the **southeast shore**, an isolated region of skinny bays and the tiniest of fishing villages connected by a tortuous 320-kilometre road. The coastal scenery is often quite delightful, but the villages don't deserve their redolent names – Spanish Ship Bay, Ecum Secum, Mushaboom – and the only place worthy of attention is **Sherbrooke**, where around thirty old buildings have been preserved to create an enjoyable village museum. Sherbrooke lies some 200km east of the capital on the coastal road, but is more rapidly reached from the Trans-Canada Highway, east of New Glasgow.

Acadian Bus Lines operates a four times daily **bus** service from Halifax to Truro, with three buses daily continuing either northeast to New Glasgow and Cape Breton Island, or northwest to New Brunswick's Moncton. **VIA Rail**'s Halifax–Montréal **trains** pass through Truro en route to Moncton. There's no public transport to either Pictou or Sherbrooke.

Springhill

Just off the Trans-Canada, 200km from Halifax and 30km from New Brunswick, **SPRINGHILL**, a town of 4000 people, has had more than its share of tragedies, mostly associated with the coal mine that was sunk here in 1872: 125 miners perished in a subterranean disaster in 1891; 39 died in a gas explosion in 1956; and a tunnel collapse in 1958 accounted for 76 more. In addition, two fires in 1957 and 1975 wiped out the town's commercial district. The collieries are closed now, but the mining tradition is kept alive at the **Springhill Miners' Museum**, on Black River Road, 3km out of town off Hwy 2 (mid-May to mid-Oct daily 9am–5pm; $4.50). There you can see the wash house and lamp room, looking exactly as they did in the 1950s; but the real highlight is the trip down to a coalface in the company of retired pitmen. Yet it's the **Anne Murray Centre**, 36 Main St (mid-May to mid-Oct daily 9am–5pm; $5.50), that pulls the crowds – an exercise in organized sycophancy to the Springhill-born balladeer who shot to fame with her sugary song *Snowbird* in 1970.

In the unlikely event you decide to **stay**, your choice of lodgings is confined to the *Rollways Motel*, 9 Church St (☎597-3713; ②).

Pictou

Signs proclaim **PICTOU**, 170km from Halifax, as the "Birthplace of New Scotland" on the basis of the arrival in 1773 of the ship *Hector*, loaded with settlers from Rosshire, the advance guard of the subsequent Scots migrations. To maintain the connection, the town has its own middle-of-August **Hector Festival**, featuring Scottish traditional dancing and the playing of the bagpipes. Pictou is also having a replica of the *Hector* built in the harbour, an expensive and time-consuming project because they're sticking to the original shipbuilding techniques. Visitors can inspect progress from close quarters via the adjacent **Hector Heritage Quay Interpretative Centre** (June to mid-Oct Mon–Sat 9am–6pm, Sun noon–6pm; $3), which gives the historical lowdown on the voyage – complete with nautical sound effects. It's all excellently done and spruces up

Pictou's unassuming centre, where the narrow streets slope up from the harbour dotted with stone buildings of Scottish appearance.

Located near the PEI ferry terminal and halfway between Halifax and Cape Breton, Pictou is a convenient place to spend the night, and there are several quality **inns** and **hotels**. The best is the *Consulate Inn*, 157 Water St (☎485-4554 or 1-800-424-8283; ③-④), housed in an elegant early nineteenth-century mansion that once served as a US consulate. There's also the modern and comfortable *Braeside Inn*, on a hillside above the harbour at 126 Front St (☎485-5046 or 1-800-613-7701; ③), and the *Walker Inn*, 34 Coleraine St (☎485-1433 or 1-800-370-5553; ③), a pleasantly renovated Victorian house metres from the Hector Quay. For **food**, the best restaurant in Pictou is at the *Consulate Inn*. Amongst several rather average town-centre cafés, try the filling snacks of the *Stone House Café*, 11 Water St.

Pictou is 8km south of **Caribou**, where there are frequent **car ferries** over to Prince Edward Island most of the year (May to mid-Dec; 1hr 15min; $9.50 return, $30.50 for cars; schedules ☎1-888-249-7245).

Sherbrooke

Developed as a timber town in the early nineteenth century, **SHERBROOKE** boomed when gold was found near here in 1861, the start of a short-lived gold rush that fizzled out within the space of twenty years, though a handful of mines struggled on until the 1940s. Most of the population checked out after the gold rush, and Sherbrooke returned to the lumber trade but without much success: the decline of the industry gradually whittled the population down to 400 today. One result has been the creation of the open-air museum of **Sherbrooke Village** (June to mid-Oct daily 9.30am–5.30pm; $6), which encompasses those late nineteenth- and early twentieth-century buildings that are, for the most part, now surplus to requirements. It's a large site, several streets situated beside St Mary's River just beyond the modern part of the village, and costumed "interpreters" preside. Amongst the thirty-odd buildings highlights include the Neoclassical lines of the surprisingly grand 1850s Court House and the Victorian luxury of the high-gabled Greenwood Cottage nearby. Also of special note are the assorted baubles and throne-like chairs of the Masonic Lodge, which still meets on the second floor of the Masonic Hall; the Temperance Hall of 1892; Cummings Bros General Store; and the jail, where jailer and prisoner lived cheek by jowl right up until the 1960s. Finally, a replica nineteenth-century water-powered sawmill has been built about 600m outside the village. Allow two to three hours to do the place justice.

There are three main ways to reach Sherbrooke: from the west along Nova Scotia's southeast shore, and from the north by turning off Hwy 104 (the Trans-Canada) either along Hwy 347 just east of New Glasgow or down Hwy 7 about 50km further east still. The most agreeable of the five places to **stay** in Sherbrooke is *Vi's B&B* (☎522-2042; ②; June-Sept), in the centre of the village. The tiny *Riverside Campground* (☎522-2913; mid-May to Oct) is near the sawmill. There's not much choice about where to eat, but fortunately the central *Bright House* is an excellent **restaurant** – be sure to try the seafood casserole. The *Main Street Café* sells competent snacks and pizzas.

Cape Breton Island

"I have travelled the globe. I have seen the Canadian and American Rockies, the Andes and the Alps and the Highlands of Scotland: but for simple beauty Cape Breton outrivals them all." With these words Alexander Graham Bell summed up a part of Nova Scotia whose scenery continues to attract its share of hyperbole. From the lakes and hills of the southwest to the wild and inhospitable promontory of the north, **Cape Breton Island** – or at least its more westerly half – offers the most exquisite of landscapes, reaching its melodramatic conclusion along the stark coast of the **Cape Breton Highlands National Park**. Encircling the park and some of the adjacent shore is the **Cabot Trail**, a 300-kilometre loop that is reckoned to be one of the most extraordinary drives on the continent.

By contrast, the more easterly half of Cape Breton – east, that is, of **Bras d'Or Lake** and its subsidiary channels – was once a busy coal-mining and steel-milling region, centred on the town of **Sydney**. It was here in the early 1920s that the struggles of the miners against the pit companies grabbed national headlines. The worst of several disputes began when the owners, the British Empire Steel Corporation (BESCO), decided to cut the men's wages by a third. The miners went on strike and the dispute escalated until BESCO persuaded prime minister King to send in the militia – and the colliers were forced back to work. Today the area's industries have largely collapsed and a deindustrialized sprawl blotches the landscape, only relieved by the splendid reconstruction of the French fortress town of **Louisbourg**, stranded out on the coast.

Yet Cape Breton is not just about scenery and sights: the Scottish Highlanders who settled much of the island in the late eighteenth and early nineteenth centuries brought with them strong cultural traditions and today these are best recalled by the island's **musicians**, especially the **fiddle players**. Names to watch out for include Buddy Mac-Master, Ashley MacIsaac, Natalie MacMaster and the Rankin family, not to mention Glenn Graham and Jackie Dunn – though it's impossible to pick out "the best" as each fiddler has their own particular style. Local tourist offices will gladly advise you on **gigs**, whether it be a ceilidh, concert or square dance, and during the summer there's something happening almost every day. That said, both the Saturday night Family Square Dances at West Mabou and the Wednesday night ceilidhs at neighbouring Mabou are highly regarded – and take place all year.

The scenic delights of Cape Breton attract thousands of summer tourists and consequently, although there's a liberal sprinkling of **accommodation** across the island – especially in the west – it's still a good idea to make a reservation a day or two beforehand. Failing that, all the island's tourist offices offer a free room reservation service. There's no obvious place to aim for on Cape Breton and most visitors stay in the tiny villages that dot the island, but two of the most enjoyable spots are undoubtedly the busy resort of **Baddeck** and the quieter coastal community of **Chéticamp**.

Without your own transport, getting around much of Cape Breton is a struggle. **Buses** from Halifax, Fredericton and Moncton bomb along Hwy 105 via Baddeck and **North Sydney** – the departure port for **ferries to Newfoundland** – en route to Sydney, still the island's largest town. All traffic has to cross the **Strait of Canso** by the causeway as this is the only road route onto the island. There are no buses to either Louisbourg or the Cape Breton Highlands National Park, though a couple of companies do offer minibus excursions, beginning at either Sydney or Baddeck. Look out also for ferries from PEI or the Îles-de-la-Madeleine (see p.285) to Chéticamp – there are none at present, but negotiations are in progress.

Finally, note that Cape Breton's **weather** is notoriously unpredictable, even in summer, and the Cabot Trail is pretty miserable in mist and rain.

The Cabot Trail

Just up the hill from the Canso causeway is the **Port Hastings Visitor Information Centre** (daily: mid-May to June & Sept to mid-Oct 9am–5pm; July & Aug 8.30am–8.30pm; ☎625-4201), where you can get your bearings and make advance room reservations on all of Cape Breton Island. From here it's about 50km on Hwy 105 (the Trans-Canada) through low forested hills to the hamlet of **IRON MINES**, overlooking a small inlet at the western limit of Bras d'Or Lake – a pleasant foretaste

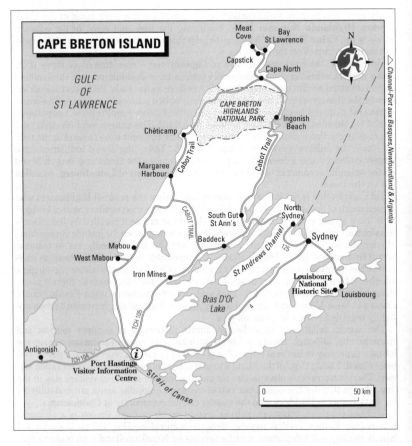

of the splendours beyond. From Iron Mines, it's a further 35km to the **Cabot Trail**, which begins by slipping the 50km northwest across the island's spartan interior to enter the Margaree River Valley, reaching the windswept seashore at **MARGAREE HARBOUR**.

Chéticamp

North from Margaree Harbour, the Cabot Trail offers lovely views of land and sea as it cuts past the scattered dwellings that are home to an Acadian community that was founded by returning deportees in the 1780s. After 26km, the road runs into the main village hereabouts, **CHÉTICAMP**, where the towering Catholic church of **St-Pierre**, with its soaring silver steeple, was built in 1893 of stones lugged across the ice from the Île-de-Chéticamp, just offshore. Inside, the frescoes and stained-glass windows were added in the 1950s and, even though they're awfully sanctimonious, they do have a certain cheery kitsch charm. Below the church – a couple of hundred metres back down the road – is the **Co-operative Artisanale** (May to mid-Oct), where a tiny Musée Acadien features a selection of the crudely patterned hooked rugs that are a characteristic craft of the area. The display is hardly spellbinding, but the unassuming *Restaurant Acadien* upstairs is excellent – the *poulet fricot* (chicken stew) is mouthwatering. There's a rather better exhibition of Acadian crafts at the north end of the village in **Les Trois Pignons** (May–Oct Mon–Fri 9am–5pm; $3), a cultural centre that proudly displays the tapestries of Elizabeth LeFort, an artist of some local renown.

Just north of the church along the main road, Chéticamp's pocket-sized jetty has a **tourist office** (July–Sept) where you can get the latest details on a variety of boat trips. Options include **deep-sea fishing** on board the *Danny Lynn* (July & Aug 3 daily, June, Sept & Oct 1–3 daily; 3–4hr; $25; ☎224-3606 or 1-800-813-3376); and **whale-watching** with the highly reputable *Whale Cruisers Ltd* (mid-May to June & mid-Sept to mid-Oct 2 daily, July to mid-Sept 3 daily; 3hr; $25; ☎224-3376 or 1-800-813-3376). Indeed, summer whale-watching cruises are big business in these parts and they are available at almost every significant settlement – usually three-hour trips for about $25. There are around twenty **motels** and **B&Bs** in and around Chéticamp. Amongst them, the well-maintained *Ocean View Motel* (☎224-2313; ②; mid-April to mid-Nov) sits by the seashore on the main road, as does the equally pleasant and slightly larger *Acadian Motel* (☎224-2640; ③; May–Oct). Above the main road on the south side of the village is *L'Auberge Doucet Inn* (☎224-3438 or 1-800-646-8668; ③; May to mid-Nov), which offers great sea views and has large and comfortable rooms. For **food** – apart from the *Restaurant Acadien*, as above – try inexpensive *Laurie's*, on the main road near the jetty, where they have everything from hamburgers to seafood.

Cape Breton Highlands National Park

The 950 square kilometres of **Cape Breton Highlands National Park**, immediately north of Chéticamp, offer some of the most gorgeous scenery anywhere in the country – a mix of mountain passes, steep hairpin descents, undulating forestland, long-range valley and mountain views, and rocky coastal headlands. Although visitors get a sniff of the park travelling by car – 120km of highway trimming all but its southern edge – the essence of the place is only revealed on foot: thirty **hiking trails** are signposted from the road, some of them the easiest of woodland strolls, others striking deep into the interior to the small lakes and wetlands of the central plateau. One of the most popular is the seven-kilometre **Skyline loop trail** which clambers up the coastal mountains north of Corney Brook, a few kilometres up the coast from Chéticamp. Another good trail is the seven-kilometre **Franey loop trail**, a steep walk up through the mountains and lakes north of Ingonish Beach. Most of the wildlife inhabits the inner reaches of the park – garter snakes, red-backed salamanders, snowshoe hares and moose are common; bald eagles, black bear and lynx are rare. The only artificial sight is the **Lone Sheiling**, a replica of a Highland crofter's cottage, set near the road on the northern perimeter of the park.

The park has two **information centres**, one just beyond Chéticamp on the west coast (daily: mid-May to late June & Sept to late Oct 9am–5pm; late June to Aug 8am–8pm; ☎224-3403), the other at Ingonish Beach on the east (same times; ☎285-2691). Both have 1:50,000-scale maps, guides to local flora and fauna, and exhaustive details of the hiking trails, which are in peak condition from July to September. They also levy an entrance fee of $3.50 per day per adult, and issue backcountry camping permits. The park has six serviced **campgrounds**, all within easy reach of the road, and two **wilderness campsites** – Fishing Cove and Lake of Islands – along the more arduous trails.

Cape North

Beyond the northern perimeter of the National Park is **Cape North**, a jagged slab of land jutting out into the sea where the Gulf of St Lawrence meets the Atlantic Ocean.

The Cabot Trail skirts the periphery of the cape, passing through the tiny **village of CAPE NORTH**, no more than a few lonely buildings straggling along the road. There are, however, several **places to stay** round here, including the handy *Macdonald's Motel* (☎383-2054; ②; mid-May to Oct), at the main intersection near the excellent *Morrisson Pioneer Restaurant*, and the rustic *Oakwood Manor B&B* (☎ & fax 383-2317 or 1-800-565-0000; ②; May–Oct), on a farm just north of the village – take the Bay St Lawrence road for 1.5km, then turn left down Northside Road.

Pushing on up the North Cape, away from the Cabot Trail, it's 17km to the much prettier hamlet of **BAY ST LAWRENCE**, where the small, white church is set against the most photogenic of harbours. **Captain Cox's whale-watching** cruises depart from here in the summer (June, Sept & Oct 1-3 daily, July & Aug 3 daily; 2–3hr; $25; ☎383-2981) and, amongst a handful of **B&Bs**, the *Highlands by the Sea* (☎383-2537; ②; mid-June to Oct) occupies a nineteenth-century rectory, 3km back down the road in **ST MARGARET'S VILLAGE**. This neighbouring settlement is itself close to the start of the gravel byroad leading northwest to **Capstick** – famous for its dramatic cliff-top sunsets – and **Meat Cove**, at the end of the road, where the small **campsite** (☎383-2379; June–Oct) is full of the roar of the ocean.

The Gaelic Coast

Leaving the National Park at Ingonish Beach, the Cabot Trail slips down the eighty-kilometre **Gaelic Coast** – named after the Scottish Highlanders who first settled here – passing through **SOUTH GUT ST ANN'S**, the location of the **Gaelic College of Celtic Arts and Crafts**. Standing on its own campus in the hills, the college looks like a small university, and it offers courses in the Gaelic language and all manner of Highland activities – bagpiping, tartan-weaving, dancing and Scots folklore. The main focus of a visit here is the **Great Hall of the Clans** (July to early Oct daily 8.30am–5pm; $2), which provides an amateurish depiction of the nineteenth-century Nova Scotian migrations. The seven-day **Gaelic Mod**, one of the province's principal Scottish festivals, takes place here during the first full week in August, with all traditional sports, crafts and contests featured.

Baddeck

The resort and yachting town of **BADDECK**, some 20km southwest of South Gut St Ann's along Hwy 105, enjoys an attractive lakeside setting on St Patrick's Channel, an inlet of the Bras d'Or Lake, and is home to the fascinating **Alexander Graham Bell Museum** (daily: June & Sept 9am–7pm; July & Aug 9am–8pm; Oct–May 9am–5pm; $3.75), which overlooks the waterfront from a tiny park and whose excellent exhibits do full justice to the fertility of Bell's mind. The museum is a mine of general biographical information about Bell, as well as giving detailed explanations of all his inventions – both successful and unsuccessful. Most famous for the invention of the telephone, Bell also made extraordinary advances in techniques for teaching hearing-impaired children, in animal husbandry and in the development of aircraft and boats – his nautical adventures culminated in 1919 with the launch of the world's first hydrofoil, the HD-4 (of which there's a full-scale replica in the museum), which reached a speed of 70mph on the lake right in front of town. Bell (1847–1922) spent his last 37 years in Baddeck, working away at **Beinn Bhreagh** (no public access), the family mansion that still stands amongst the trees across the bay from the museum. Otherwise, there's not much else to Baddeck, though in July and August the local Lion's Club runs a free shuttle-boat service from the town's jetty to **Kidston Island**, a couple of hundred metres offshore, where you can go for a stroll in the woods.

Baddeck is on the main Acadian Bus Lines **bus** route between Halifax and Sydney, with two buses daily in each direction stopping at the Irving gas station 3.5km west of town. The **tourist office** (summer daily 9am–8pm; ☎295-1911) has lots of useful local information and sits by the side of the resort's main intersection – at the top of the short main street, Chebucto Street. Baddeck is a popular holiday spot, so there's a wide range of **accommodation**, but it fills up fast in the height of the season. Downtown choices include the motel-style rooms of the agreeable *Telegraph House*, on Chebucto Street (☎295-1100; ③), and the *Duffus Inn* (☎295-2172; ④; mid-May to mid-Oct), which occupies a well-renovated Victorian town house by the waterfront. More appealing still are the smarter resort-hotels that string along Shore Road, south of the town centre – especially the *Silver Dart Lodge* (☎295-2340 or 1-800-565-8439; ④–⑤), whose spacious chalets spread over a hillside in view of the lake. If your budget doesn't stretch that far, the *Restawyle B&B* (☎295-3253; ②; mid-May to mid-Dec), also on Shore Road, is perfectly adequate and a good deal cheaper. The nearest **campground** is the *Bras d'Or Lakes* (☎295-2329; mid-May to Sept), about 6km west on Hwy 105.

Considering the resort's popularity, Baddeck's **restaurants** are something of a disappointment, with the emphasis seemingly on quantity rather than quality: the *Bell Buoy*, on Chebucto Street, is as good as any. The best **café** in town is Chebucto Street's *High Wheeler*, which serves up a good range of wholefood snacks and salads.

Based in Baddeck, both Island Highlight Tours (☎295-2510) and Bannockburn Tours (☎295-3310) run day-long **excursions** during the season along the Cabot Trail to the Cape Breton Highlands National Park – reckon on about $50–60 per person. Bannockburn Tours also operates a shuttle minibus service to Louisbourg costing $35 for the return trip. Island Eco-Adventures (☎295-3303 or 1-800-707-5512), just 300m west of the tourist office, hire out camping equipment, mountain bikes and canoes in the summer, and cross-country ski equipment and snowmobiles in winter; they also run guided backcountry tours. **Car hire** is available in Sydney (see below), though Hertz (☎1-800-263-0600) may be prepared to deliver a vehicle to Baddeck.

Sydney and around

Poor old **SYDNEY**, sprawling along the east bank of the Sydney River 430km from Halifax and 85km from Baddeck, was once the industrial dynamo of eastern Canada. From the late nineteenth century to the 1950s its steel mills processed Newfoundland iron ore with Nova Scotian coke, but as gas and oil came on stream this arrangement became uneconomic and the subsequent decline has been severe and long-lasting: the city regularly records an unemployment rate twice the national average. It's hardly surprising, therefore, that the town lacks charm, though brave efforts have been made to reinvigorate the **North End** waterfront, along and around the **Esplanade**, downtown between Prince and Amelia streets. This is the district to head for and it's here you'll find Sydney's oldest buildings, including the early nineteenth-century **St Patrick's Church**, 87 Esplanade, a broadly Gothic structure that now holds a local history museum (mid-June to Sept daily 9.30am–5.30pm; free). Nearby, the **Cossit House**, 75 Charlotte St (June to mid-Oct daily 9.30am–5.30pm; free), was built for the town's first Anglican minister in 1787.

Arriving from Baddeck and Halifax, long-distance Acadian Lines buses pull in to the **bus station** at 99 Terminal Rd off Prince Street, a good ten- to fifteen-minute walk from the Esplanade. There are several **hotels** along the Esplanade, with two good options being the *Delta Sydney* (☎562-7500 or 1-800-268-1133; ④), a large and well-equipped chain hotel at no. 300, and the more basic *Pauls Hotel* (☎562-5747; ②), in an old building on the corner of Pitt Street. The **tourist office** (☎539-9876), on the edge of town beside Hwy 125 (exit 6), has the list of all the town's accommodation and can also advise on local minibus services to the Cabot Trail. The leading company is Cape Breton Tours, 24 Kings Rd (☎564-6200), who also shuttle visitors out to Louisbourg for $25 return. For **car hire**, both Hertz (☎1-800-263-0600) and Avis (☎1-800-879-2847) have Sydney branches.

Sydney's airport offers the shortest and least expensive (1–3 weekly; $280 return) flights from the mainland to St-Pierre et Miquelon (see p.403): for details, contact Air St-Pierre (☎562-3140) or Canadian Airlines, its international partner. Finally, **NORTH SYDNEY**, 21km west of Sydney along Hwy 125, is the harbour for the **Newfoundland ferry** (☎794-5254 or 1-800-341-7981; also see pp.420–421). Acadian Lines buses drop passengers near the ferry terminal on their way to and from Sydney and usually run to meet sailing times. Inside the ferry terminal building, there's a **Newfoundland tourist office**, which operates a room reservation service for the province and has armfuls of free literature. North Sydney is itself unremarkable, but if for some reason you get stuck here there's a comfortable chain hotel, the *North Star Inn*, on the hill next to the ferry terminal at 39 Forrest St (☎794-8581; ④).

Louisbourg

Beginning work in 1719, the French constructed the coastal fortress of **LOUISBOURG**, 37km southeast of Sydney, to guard the Atlantic approaches to New France and salvage their imperial honour after the humiliation of the Treaty of Utrecht. The result was a staggeringly ostentatious stronghold covering a hundred acres and encircled by ten-metre-high stone walls; it took so long to build and was so expensive that Louis XV said he was expecting its towers to rise over the Paris horizon. However, Louisbourg was wildly ill-conceived: the humid weather stopped the mortar from drying, the fort was overlooked by a score of hillocks, and developments in gunnery had already made high stone walls an ineffective means of defence. As Charles Lawrence, the British governor, confirmed "the general design of the fortifications is exceedingly bad and the workmanship worse executed and so disadvantageously situated that . . . it will never answer the charge or trouble". And so it proved: Louisbourg was only attacked twice, but it was captured on both occasions, the second time by Wolfe, on his way to Québec in 1758.

A visit to the **Louisbourg National Historic Site** (daily: June & Sept 9.30am–5pm July & Aug 9am–7pm; $11; rest of year by prior arrangement on ☎733-3548) begins just 2km beyond the modern village at the Reception Centre, where there's a good account of the fort's history and its reconstruction in the 1960s. From here, a free shuttle bus runs to the fort, whose stone walls rise from the sea to enclose more than four dozen restored buildings, a mid-eighteenth-century fortress town set beneath a soaring church spire and including powder magazines, forges, guardhouses, warehouses, barracks and the chilly abodes of the soldiers, all accompanied by costumed guides to provide extra atmosphere. It's an extraordinary reconstruction in a lovely coastal setting and particular care has been taken with the **governor's apartments**, which have been splendidly furnished according to the inventory taken after the death of Governor Duquesnel here in 1744. It's amazing the man hadn't died before: already minus a leg from early in his military career, Duquesnel's body was buried under the chapel floor and when it was exhumed in the 1960s the remains showed him to have been suffering from a bewildering variety of ailments from arthritis and arteriosclerosis through to dental abscesses.

Allow at least a couple of hours to look round the fortress and sample the authentic refreshments that are available at the taverns and eating houses; the most sustaining food of all is the soldiers' bread (wheat and rye wholemeal), sold by the loaf at the King's Bakery.

Stringing along the seashore down the bay from the fortress, the modern **village of Louisbourg** has a cheerful setting and several good **places to stay**. Choices include the *Stacey House B&B*, 7438 Main St (☎733-2317; ②; May–Oct), an attractive, high gabled old home with just four guest rooms; the fiercely pink *Cranberry Cove Inn*, 1 Wolfe St (☎733-2171; ④), a lavishly refurbished old house on the edge of the village on the way out towards the fort; and the *Manse B&B*, 10 Strathcona St (☎733-3155; ②; April–Oct), which occupies a pleasant Victorian house down an alley just off Main

Street, though its waterfront location is spoilt by an abandoned fish factory. There's a no-frills **campground**, the *Louisbourg Motorhome Park* (☎733-3631; June-Sept), down by the harbour in the centre of the village. The **tourist office**, in the old train station at the east end of Main Street (June & Sept Mon–Fri 9am–5pm; July & Aug daily 8am–8pm), has the complete lodgings list.

Amongst several **cafés** and **restaurants**, the *Grubstake*, 1274 Main St, is recommended for its fish platters and home-baked pastries, whilst the *K&M Café*, 1152 Main Street, serves filling snacks. Both the breakfast and dinner at the *Cranberry Cove Inn* are excellent.

NEW BRUNSWICK

The province of **NEW BRUNSWICK**, roughly 320km long and 240km wide, attracts less tourist attention than its Maritime neighbours, and it's hard to understand quite why. It's true that the forested upland that makes up the bulk of the province is a trifle repetitious, but the long river valleys that furrow the landscape compensate and the funnel-shaped **Bay of Fundy**, with its dramatic tides and delightful coastline, is outstanding. Equally, in **Fredericton**, the capital, the province has one of the regions most appealing towns, a laid-back easy sort of place which, besides offering the bonus of the Beaverbrook Art Gallery, also possesses strings of fine old villas and a good-looking cathedral. Handsome scenery is within easy reach too – it's a short trip south to scenic **Passamaquoddy Bay**, an island-studded inlet of the Bay of Fundy that's home to the likeable resort of **St Andrews.** Southeast of Fredericton, the Saint John River snakes a tortuous route to the Bay of Fundy at the busy port of **Saint John**. Along with most of the settlements of southern New Brunswick, Saint John was founded by United Empire Loyalists, whose descendants, mingled with those of British colonists, account for around sixty percent of the province's 725,000 inhabitants. Some 130,000 people live here in Saint John, making this the province's big city – it's much larger than Fredericton – and although hard times have left the place frayed at the edges the city boasts a splendid sample of Victorian architecture and a lively nightlife. Also, although industry has scarred the Fundy coast hereabouts, there's still no denying the rugged charms of Saint John's setting, and within easy reach are the more pristine land- and seascapes of **Fundy National Park**.

The remaining third of New Brunswick's population are French-speakers, the descendants of those Acadians who settled in the region after the deportations of 1755. To avoid further persecution, these refugees clustered in the remote northern parts of the province, though since the 1960s they have become more assertive – following the example set by their Québecois cousins – and have made **Moncton**, in southeast New Brunswick, the effective capital of modern Acadia, with a French-speaking university as their cultural centre. Moncton is, however, of limited interest – it's a modern, somewhat characterless place – and is chiefly appealing for its proximity to Fundy National Park and the beautifully remote remains of **Fort Beauséjour**. As for the other Acadian districts, they are best visited on the way to Québec. Two main roads link Fredericton with its northern neighbour. The first – which is both more scenically diverting and more direct – slices up the western edge of the province along the St John River Valley to French-speaking **Edmundston**, en route to Rivière-du-Loup (see p.271). The second cuts northeast for the long haul up the **Miramichi River Valley** to the cluster of small towns that are known collectively as **Miramichi City**. Near here are the untamed coastal marshes of the **Kouchibouguac National Park** and, in the northeast corner of the province, the **Acadian Peninsula**, whose pride and joy is the recreated **Village Historique Acadien**, near the fishing village of **Caraquet.**

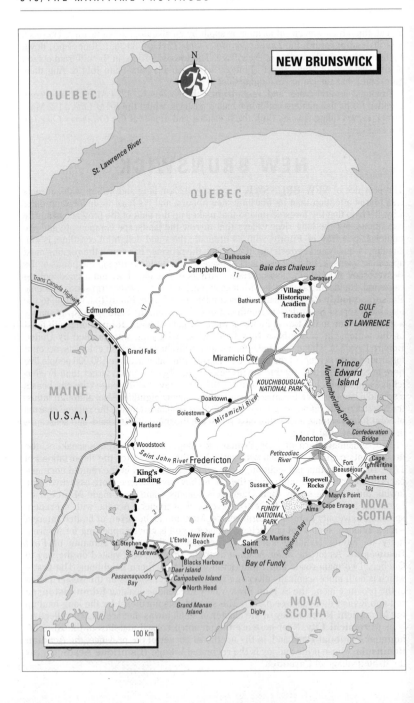

SMT **buses** run a reasonable province-wide network of services, with daily connections along the Saint John River Valley and up the east coast from Moncton to Campbellton. There are also regular buses from Fredericton, Saint John and Moncton over to Charlottetown on PEI, via the Confederation Bridge. The Saint John to Digby **car ferry** is a useful short cut if you're heading down to southwest Nova Scotia.

A brief history of New Brunswick

Administered as part of the British colony of Nova Scotia until 1784, **New Brunswick** was created to cope with the sudden arrival of thousands of Loyalists in the early 1780s. The New Englanders were concentrated in Saint John, which they expected to be the new provincial capital. However, they were outmanoeuvred by the governor's aristocratic claque who managed to get Fredericton chosen as the seat of government. This unpopular decision led to an unusual separation of functions, with Fredericton developing as the province's political and administrative capital, whereas Saint John became the commercial centre. Throughout the nineteenth century conservative Fredericton stagnated whilst liberal Saint John boomed as a shipbuilding centre, its massive shipyards, dependent on the vast forests of the New Brunswick interior, becoming some of the most productive in the world. By 1890 the province was Canada's most prosperous region, but within the space of twenty years its economy had collapsed as wooden ships were replaced by steel steamers. The recession was long-lasting, ultimately reflecting New Brunswick's inability to develop a diversified industrial economy, and this remains the problem today. The province splutters along on the profits from its raw materials, principally timber, fish and potatoes, plus zinc, lead and copper from the northeast around Bathurst, but – like its Maritime neighbours – it exercises no control over price-setting mechanisms, and sharp boom-and-bust economic cycles continue.

Fredericton

Situated 100km inland from the Bay of Fundy on the banks of the Saint John River, **FREDERICTON**, the capital of New Brunswick, has a well-padded air, the streets of its tiny centre graced by well-established elms and genteel villas. There's scarcely any industry here and the population of 47,000 mostly work for the government or the university, at least partly fulfilling the aims of one of the town's aristocratic sponsors, who announced in 1784: "it shall be the most gentlemanlike place on earth". Fredericton has few specific sights; just the odd building left from the **Military Compound** that once housed the garrison, and the **Beaverbrook Art Gallery**, the gift of that crusty old reactionary Lord Beaverbrook.

Arrival and information

The SMT **bus** terminal is at 101 Regent St at King, about five minutes' walk south of the river and one block south of the main drag, Queen Street. There are no **trains** to Fredericton: the nearest service is to Moncton. Both Air Canada and Canadian Airlines provide a wide range of domestic and a few international flights into Fredericton **airport**, 16km southeast of town; the taxi fare into the centre will cost you around $25.

Fredericton has a downtown **Visitors' Information Centre** in City Hall on the corner of Queen and York streets (mid-May to mid-June & Sept to early Oct daily 8am–5pm; mid-June to Aug daily 8am–8pm; mid-Oct to mid-May Mon–Fri 8.15am–4.30pm; ☎452-9616), and another out on the Trans-Canada, next to exit 289 (daily: mid-May to mid-June & Sept to early Oct 9am–6pm; mid-June to Aug 9am–8pm; ☎458-8331). Both will ring ahead for accommodation.

Accommodation

Finding a **place to stay** in Fredericton is rarely a problem, though you should try to avoid the humdrum motels on the outskirts in favour of the downtown area, where the choice is limited to just two hotels and an inn, but these are easily the most tempting options. If you're strapped for cash, the university hires out student rooms in the summer, and there are several **campgrounds** out of town along the Saint John River Valley.

Hotels and inns

Carriage House Inn, 230 University Ave at George (☎452-9924, fax 458-0799). This ten-room inn, on the east side of the city centre occupies a grand Victorian house, with big verandas, in one of the older residential areas, though the interior is a bit too formal for comfort. ③.

Comfort Inn by Journey's End Motels, 255 Prospect St (☎453-0800 or 1-800-668-4200). Routine chain motel south of the town centre – take exit 289 off the Trans-Canada, Hwy 2. One of several motels on Prospect Street. ③.

Lord Beaverbrook Hotel, 659 Queen St (☎455-3371 or 1-800-561-7666, fax 455-1441). Polished downtown hotel with Art Deco flourishes; overlooks the river. All facilities including an indoor pool. Often has weekend discounts of up to 25 percent. ④.

Sheraton Fredericton Hotel, 225 Woodstock Rd (☎457-7000 or 1-800-325-3535, fax 457-4000). Modern high-rise hotel in an attractive retro style with dormer windows and stone finishings. Luxurious suites and posh doubles with views of the river; located a few blocks west of the centre. ④–⑥.

College rooms and campground

Mactaquac Provincial Park Campground, near Mactaquac (☎363-4747). Large, popular and well-equipped campground some 20km west of Fredericton, on the north side of the Saint John River off Hwy 105. ①.

UNB Tourist Hostel, University of New Brunswick campus (☎453-4891). Over a thousand single ($18) and double ($30) rooms for rent, at the south end of University Avenue just beyond Beaverbrook Street, about 2km south of the river. Mid-May to mid-Aug. ①.

The City

The **Saint John River**, running from northern Maine to the Bay of Fundy, was for a long time the fastest way to reach Fredericton, whose early streets, bounded by Brunswick Street to the south and York Street to the west, were laid out close to a curve of the south bank. Here the provincial administration set up shop and the garrison, stationed to counter the threat of American attack, paraded on the **Officers' Square**, at the foot of Regent Street. Mostly grassed over, the square still has space for the Changing of the Guard, a re-enactment of British drill that takes place during the summer (July & Aug Tues–Sat 11am & 7pm). If you miss it, the sentry changes every hour on the hour, a brief march between the square and City Hall just along the street.

The square forms the eastern perimeter of the **Military Compound**, which once stretched over to York Street between Queen Street and the river. It was a large garrison for such a small place and, once Canada–US relations were on a secure footing, the attitude of the local citizenry towards the antics of the military hardened. They could put up with the grog shops and brothels discreetly located on the other side of the river, but they were infuriated by a huge brawl between soldiers and sailors that swept right across town – and when the British regulars finally departed in 1869 many were relieved. One reminder of the British presence is the elegant three-storey **Officers' Quarters**, on the square's west side, whose symmetrical columns and stone

The New Brunswick telephone code is ☎506.

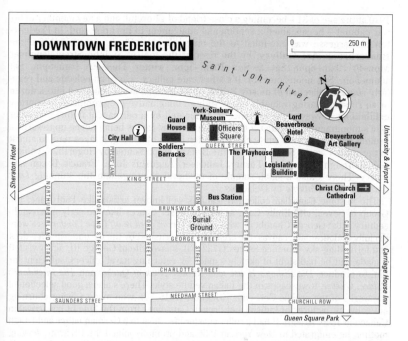

arches follow a design much used by the Royal Engineers of the nineteenth century. Inside, the **York-Sunbury Historical Museum** (May & June Tues–Thurs & Sat 10am–6pm; July & Aug Mon & Fri 10am–9pm, Tues–Thurs & Sat 10am–6pm, Sun noon–6pm; Sept to mid-Oct Mon–Fri 9am–5pm, Sat noon–4pm; mid-Oct to April Mon, Wed & Fri 11am–3pm; $2) possesses an intriguing assortment of local bygones, which fills every nook and cranny of this warren-like building. There are old ski shoes, sepia photographs, a rawhide and birch-bark "call" for luring moose, needlework samplers, irons, washing machines and all sorts of domestic knick-knacks on the first floor; military uniforms, armaments and a reconstruction of a World War I trench on the second floor; and, up above, a couple of Native-Canadian rooms as well as the stuffed remains of the twenty-kilo "Coleman Frog", a giant-sized amphibian of dubious origins. It's not known whether the creature is real or not, but the local innkeeper, who produced it in the 1880s, claimed to have fed it on beer and buttermilk. Allow an hour or so for the museum; perhaps less, as recent efforts to systematize the exhibits threaten to undermine its jumble-like charm.

A few metres west along Queen, at the foot of Carleton Street, is the **Guard House** (June–Aug daily 10am–6pm; free), where guides in period British uniforms show you round a restored orderly room, a guardroom and detention cells that create a fearsome picture of military life in the middle of the nineteenth century – the guardroom is not too different from the airless cells where villains were locked up waiting to be flogged, branded or transported. Directly opposite, with its back to Queen Street, is the **Soldiers' Barracks** (same times) a sturdy three-storey block that at one time accommodated more than two hundred squaddies. Most of the building now houses offices, but one room has been restored to its appearance in the early 1800s.

Lord Beaverbrook, the newspaper tycoon and champion of the British Empire, was raised in New Brunswick's Newcastle, and although he moved to England in

1910 at the age of 31 – becoming a close friend of Churchill and a key member of his war cabinet – he sustained a sentimental attachment to his homeland. In Fredericton his largesse was extended to the university, the Playhouse theatre and the **Beaverbrook Art Gallery**, by the river at the foot of St John Street (summer Mon–Fri 9am–6pm, Sat & Sun 10am–5pm; winter Tues–Fri 9am–5pm, Sat 10am–5pm, Sun noon-5pm; $3). It's a first-rate gallery, where an eclectic and regularly rotated collection of mostly British and Canadian art is squeezed into a dozen or so rooms, sharing valuable space with an imaginative programme of temporary exhibitions. However, the entrance is dominated by a permanent fixture, Salvador Dali's monumental *Santiago el Grande* depicting St James being borne up towards a vaulted firmament on a white charger. After Dali's blitzkrieg, it takes time to adjust to the subtler works beyond, where the Brits are represented by Hogarth, Reynolds, Gainsborough, Constable, Turner, Landseer, Augustus John, Francis Bacon and Lowry. There's also a small sample of medieval paintings and the stunning *Lady Macbeth Sleep-Walking* by Delacroix.

The fulsome Canadian collection features well-known artists like Paul Kane, the Group of Seven, and Emily Carr, as well as lesser figures like the early nineteenth-century artist George Chambers, whose *The "Terror" Iced in off Cape Comfort* is a wonderfully melodramatic canvas, the creaking ship crushed by the ice underneath a dark and forbidding sky. Dominic Serres (1722–93), a favourite of George III, never visited Canada, but he had sight of sketches made by returning naval officers, sufficient for him to produce *The Bishop's House with Ruined Town of Québec* and *The Intendant's Palace, Québec*, townscapes in the Italian vedute style. There's also a good selection of the works of the prolific Cornelius Krieghoff (1815–72), who made a living churning out souvenir pictures of Indians and French Canadians from the time of his arrival in Canada in 1840. Krieghoff had a roller-coaster life. Born to a German father and Dutch mother, he emigrated to New York in 1836 and promptly joined the US army, serving in the Second Seminole War down in Florida. Discharged in 1840, Krieghoff immediately re-enlisted, claimed three months' advance pay and deserted, hotfooting it to Montréal with the French-Canadian woman he had met and married in New York. Montréal was a disaster – no one would buy his paintings – but when he moved to Québec City he found a ready market for his work amongst the British officers of the garrison and their well-heeled friends. This was Krieghoff's most productive period and the finely detailed, carefully composed anecdotal scenes of French-Canadian life he painted during these years are his best – and two of the finest, *Merrymaking* and *Coming Storm at the Portage*, can be seen here.

The **Legislative Assembly Building** (guided tours June–Aug Mon–Fri 9am–6pm, Sat & Sun 10am–5pm; Sept–May Mon–Fri 9am–4pm; free), the home of New Brunswick's parliament, stands opposite the art gallery, its robust and imposing exterior topped by a ponderous tower and cupola. The interior is graced by a splendid oak and cherry spiral staircase, which leads to the sumptuously decorated Assembly Chamber, adorned with portraits of George III and Queen Charlotte by Joshua Reynolds. The pictures were rescued from the previous parliament building, which burnt down in 1880.

The Legislature occupies the grandest building in Fredericton, but the nearby **Christ Church Cathedral**, King Street and Church (mid-June to Aug Mon–Fri 9am–8pm, Sat 10am–5pm, Sun 1–5pm; Sept to mid-June Mon–Sat 9am–5pm; free guided tours from mid-June to Aug), comes a close second. A mid-Victorian copy of the fifteenth-century parish church of Snettisham, in Norfolk, England, it's distinguished by the elegance of its tapering spire and the intricate grace of its red pine hammerbeam ceiling. The church also marks the beginning of the smartest part of town, whose leafy streets, lined by handsome Victorian mansions complete with gingerbread scrollwork and expansive verandas, stretch south towards tiny **Queen Square Park**.

Eating and drinking

Downtown Fredericton offers a reasonable range of informal **cafés** and **restaurants** and there are enough **bars** to entertain for a night or two. In the summer there's free outdoor theatre and live music down on Officers' Square. The Playhouse (☎458-8344), beside the Legislative Assembly Building, puts on a good variety of shows and is home to the province's only professional English-speaking **theatre** company, Theatre New Brunswick. The tourist office has the details of all up-and-coming events.

Cafés and restaurants

Bar-B-Q-Barn, 540 Queen St opposite Officers' Square. Cosy, family restaurant noted for chicken and ribs. Inexpensive.

Bruno's Seafood Café, at the *Sheraton Fredericton Hotel*, 225 Woodstock Rd (☎457-7000). One of the most popular spots in town, this first-rate café-restaurant is noted for its lavish help-yourself buffets where the emphasis is on pasta and seafood. Eat either inside the hotel or outside on the large riverside patio and watch the sunset.

Café du Monde, 610 Queen at Regent Street. Enjoyable, bistro-style café serving from a wide menu that includes delicious vegetarian and seafood dishes.

Dimitri's, Pipers' Lane, 349 King St. Standard-issue Greek restaurant amongst the café-bars crowding Pipers Lane, in between King and Queen streets, just west of York.

M & T Deli, 602 Queen at Regent Street. Arguably Fredericton's best deli, specializing in New York-style bagels and Montréal smoked meat. (Mon–Fri 7.30am–4pm, Sat 10am–2pm).

Molly's Coffee Shop, 554 Queen St opposite Officers' Square. Fine coffee and tasty snacks in this little café.

Bars

Dolan's Pub, Pipers' Lane, 349 King St. Bustling bar with imported and domestic beers on draught. Some live folk music.

Lunar Rogue Pub, 625 King St. Busy pub serving British and Maritime ales as well as hearty bar food. Live, usually folk, music on most weekends.

Rockin' Rodeo, 546 King St. Fredericton's only C&W pub-cum-club, with occasional live acts.

Passamaquoddy Bay

In the southwest corner of New Brunswick, abutting the state of Maine, lies **Passamaquoddy Bay**, a deeply indented inlet of the Bay of Fundy whose sparsely populated shoreline is a bony, bumpy affair of forest, rock and swamp. Easily the prettiest of the region's coastal villages is **St Andrews**, a Loyalist settlement turned seaside resort, 135km south of Fredericton. The other main attraction is the **Fundy Islands** archipelago at the mouth of Passamaquoddy Bay. Here, accessible from the US by road and by ferry from mainland New Brunswick (via **Deer Island**), lies **Campobello Island**, the site of Franklin Roosevelt's immaculately maintained country home. Finally, stuck out in the bay two hours by ferry from the Canadian mainland, the far larger **Grand Manan Island** is a much wilder and more remote spot noted for its imposing sea cliffs and variety of bird life.

St Andrews

ST ANDREWS was once a busy fishing port and trading centre but is now a leafy resort with a laid-back, low-key air that makes for a restful place to spend a night. The town is at its prettiest amongst the antique clapboard houses flanking King Street – which leads up the hill from the busy little pier – while Water Street, the main drag, tracks along the waterfront lined with cafés and craft shops. The only sights as such are the **Horticultural**

Garden on the crest of King Street and the squat, minuscule **St Andrews Blockhouse**, a replica of the original wooden fort built in 1813 to protect the area from the Americans. It's at the west end of Water Street, and at low tide you can scramble around the reefs and rock pools just below. The pier is packed with boat tour companies. Amongst several, Quoddy Link Marine (☎529-2600) operate first-class **whale-watching** cruises (late May to September; 3hr; $42), each of which has a naturalist on board; and Seascape runs regular **kayak** trips from $55 per half-day (☎529-4866).

Of particular interest also are the guided tours of **Minister's Island** (June to mid-Oct 1–2 daily; 2hr; $5; ☎529-5081), whose undulating farmland is reached by car along a tidal causeway. The island was once the property of William Van Horne, the Victorian railway baron, who built a grand stone mansion here as well as a clutter of farm buildings. Highlights of the two-hour tour include a romp round the dilapidated mansion and inspection of the windmill, with its kerosene-powered reserve engines; the tidal bathhouse down on the seashore; and the magnificent, state-of-the-art livestock barn, where Horne pampered his horses and cattle – treating them, according to local legend, rather better than his workforce.

St Andrews is accessible by SMT **bus** from Saint John (1 daily; 1hr 30min) and passengers are dropped on Water Street, a couple of blocks east of the pier. The **tourist office** is on Hwy 127 as you enter the town (May to late Oct daily 9am–8pm; ☎529-3000). They issue free tide tables and town maps, supply information on local bicycle hire, have the schedule for visits to Minister's Island, and will happily help you with accommodation, though advance bookings are a good idea during the height of the season. Most illustrious of all the **hotels** is the *Algonquin* (☎529-8823 or 1-800-441-1414; ④–⑦), a sprawling and well-equipped resort complex whose turrets and gables, dating from 1915, dominate the northwest of town, about 1.5km from the waterfront on Prince of Wales Street. Even more unusual – and almost in the shadow of the *Algonquin* – is the *Pansy Patch B&B*, 59 Carleton St (☎529-3834 or 1-888-726-7972; ⑤–⑥), where nine quaint guest rooms, each with a sea view, occupy a charming country home, built in a variation of the French Normandy style in 1912; the food here is excellent too and the garden is beautiful. Other less expensive **B&Bs** within a few minutes' walk of the pier include the *Hanson House*, in a trim and well-cared-for old house at 62 Edward St (☎529-4947; ②); the *Harris Hatch Inn*, 142 Queen St (☎529-4713; ④; May–Oct), in an elegant, broadly Georgian mansion with shutters, fanlight and Neoclassical columns; and the *Garden Gate*, whose wide verandas and lovely garden are in a quiet part of town at 364 Montague St (☎529-4453; ③; May–Sept). The *St Andrews Motor Inn*, 111 Water St (☎529-4571; ④), is a spick and span modern motel on the seashore. The popular *Passamaquoddy Park Campground* (☎529-3439; May–Oct) has a great seaside location just over 1km east of the town centre along Water Street.

St Andrews has an excellent range of **cafés** and the occasional good **restaurant**. The *Chef's Café*, 180 Water St, offers reliably priced fish platters as part of a wide-ranging menu and occupies an old-fashioned diner decked out with all sorts of retro bits and bobs. Nearby, the inexpensive *Gables Restaurant Bar & Patio*, 143 Water St, is a funky little place, serving tasty food from its bayshore location, while the nearby *Lobster Bay Eatery*, at no. 113, is a family-orientated restaurant offering up delicious lobsters – though many regular visitors swear by the lobsters at the *Algonquin*. For a special meal in fairly formal surroundings, head for *L'Europe Dining Room*, an expensive restaurant at 48 King St (☎529-3818).

Deer Island

The only way to reach Campobello Island from the rest of New Brunswick is by ferry from adjacent **Deer Island**, a pocket-sized member of the Fundy archipelago containing straggling ribbon villages and low forested hills. **Ferries to Deer Island** (summer every 30min 7am–7pm, then hourly till 9pm; less frequent in winter; 25min;

free) leave from **L'Etete** on the southeast shore of Passamaquoddy Bay, 14km south of the village of St George, beside Hwy 1. They dock at the island's northern shore, from where it's 16km south to the **Deer Island–Campobello ferry** (June to Sept 6–7 daily; 35min; car & driver $13, foot passengers $2). Ferries also sail from this jetty to Maine's Eastport (late June to mid-Sept, hourly 9am–7pm; 20min). Metres from the jetty, at the southern tip of the island, is **Deer Island Point Park**, which overlooks a narrow sound where it's sometimes possible to hear the whirlpool known as the Old Sow. It's caused by the Fundy tides as they sweep round the island and is at its peak three hours before high tide. There's a well-appointed seashore **campground** in the park (☎747-2423; June–Sept).

Campobello Island

Franklin D. Roosevelt loved **Campobello Island,** 16km long by 5km wide, for its quiet wooded coves, rocky headlands and excellent fishing. Those sleepy days are long gone, but although the island is sprinkled with second homes and is busy with day-trippers – who come here by ferry from Deer Island (see opposite) or over the bridge from Lubec in Maine – the southern half is protected as the **Roosevelt Campobello Internation-al Park**. Here, mixed forests, marshes, tidal flats, beaches and gullies are explored by 24km of gravel road, which themselves give access to a variety of gentle hiking trails. Several of these – including the enjoyable, 1.5-kilometre-long walk over to Friar's Head – begin beside the island's star turn, the red and green **Roosevelt Cottage** (late May to mid-Oct daily 10am–6pm; free), set amongst the woods by the seashore about 3km south of the landing stage. One look at the place and you'll see that "cottage" is an understatement – it's a 35-room mansion built in a Dutch colonial style and packed with memorabilia, from the great man's childhood potty to the Christmas list he made when he was knee-high and the megaphone with which the children were summoned to dinner. It was at the cottage in 1921 that Roosevelt contracted polio and, poignantly, the stretcher on display was the one used to carry him off the island.

Campobello is easily seen in a day, but if you decide to stay the night head for *Lupine Lodge* (☎752-2555; ②-⑤; June–Oct), whose delightful log cabins, with their Art Deco lines, occupy a clearing in the woods, in sight of the sea about 500m north of Roosevelt Cottage. The lodge itself dates from 1915 and holds a first-class restaurant.

Grand Manan Island

Poking into the Bay of Fundy, **Grand Manan Island**, 30km from tip to toe, has a scat-tered population of around 2500, who are largely dependent on fishing and tourism. The ferry arrives at the tiny settlement of **North Head**, from where footpaths lead to the cliffs of the truncated north shore and its brace of lighthouses. The main road begins at North Head too, then slips down the east coast past rocky coves and harbours to reach the main settlement, **Grand Harbour**, where tourist information is available at the museum (mid-June to Sept; ☎662-3524). En route, a rougher road cuts west across the island to the ninety-metre sea cliffs and battered beach of **Dark Harbour**, famous for its dulse (edible seaweed) and periwinkles. Marking the island's southern tip are yet more precipitous sea cliffs and a third lighthouse. Grand Manan has long been noted for its sea birds – the celebrated naturalist and painter, John James Audubon, visited in 1831 – and puffins, gannets, guillemots, stormy petrels and kitti-wakes are just some of the three hundred species that gather in their thousands on the coastal cliffs. The best birdwatching times are in the spring migratory period (early April to early June), the summer nesting season and during the fall migration (late August through September).

To get to Grand Manan, catch the car **ferry** from Black's Harbour, 10km from Hwy 1 between St Andrews and Saint John (July & Aug 5–6 daily, Sept–June 3 daily; 1hr 30min–2hr; foot passengers $8.50 return, cars $25.50; ☎662-3724). Spaces are allocated on a first-come, first-served basis and you should be prepared for lengthy delays in the height of the summer. Amongst a number of Grand Manan boat tour companies, *Sea Watch Tours* (☎662-8552), based in the south part of the island at Seal Cove, offer bird-watching trips from mid-June to August and whale-watching from mid-July to mid-September – reckon on $40 per adult per trip. North Head's Adventure High Sea Kayaking & Cycling (reservations required: ☎662-3563 or 1-800-732-5492) organizes guided excursions and also does **bike rental**.

For **accommodation**, Grand Manan has a handful of inns as well as a wide selection of B&Bs and cottages, but things still get tight in the height of the summer, when advance booking is recommended. In North Head, good choices include the comfortable, harbourside *Compass Rose Inn* (☎662-8570; ②; May–Oct) and the arty *Aristotle's Lantern B&B* (June–Sept; ☎662-3788; ②). Another tempting option is *McLaughlin's Wharf Inn* (June–Sept; ☎662-8760; ③), which occupies a converted post office at Seal Cove on the southern shore.

Saint John

At first sight **SAINT JOHN** seems a confusing hotchpotch of industrial and residential zones spread over the bluffs, valleys and plateaus where the Saint John River empties into Fundy Bay, 100km southeast of Fredericton. In fact, the downtown area is squeezed onto a chubby peninsula immediately east of the river mouth and focused on the short main drag, **King Street**, to form a surprisingly compact centre for a city of 130,000 people. In 1877 a fire wiped out most of the town, but Saint John was sufficiently wealthy, as a major shipbuilding centre, to withstand the costs of immediate reconstruction, so almost all the city's older buildings – at their most resplendent along and around **Prince William Street** – are late Victorian. Most of the shipyards have now gone and the place survives as a modest seaport and manufacturing town, with a bustling nightlife and a good range of restaurants. Apart from its outstanding Victorian architecture, Saint John's leading attractions are the **New Brunswick Museum** and the **Reversing Falls Rapids**; the latter a good place to see the effects of the Fundy tides. The town's most famous son is Donald Sutherland; its most celebrated product, Moosehead beer.

Arrival, information and city transport

Saint John **bus station**, 300 Union St at Carmarthen, ten minutes' walk east of Market Slip, is where SMT buses arrive from – and depart to – all of New Brunswick's major settlements. There are no **rail** services to Saint John; the nearest you'll get is Moncton. Saint John's **ferry terminal**, 5km west of the centre across the mouth of the Saint John River, is served by Bay Ferries (☎1-888-249-7245), who sail across Fundy Bay to Digby, in Nova Scotia (Jan to early June & mid-Oct to Dec 1–2 daily, early June to mid-Oct 2–3 daily; 3hr; passengers $18–23 single, cars $42–50, bicycles $11). There are no buses direct to the centre from the terminal, but Saint John Transit (☎658-4700) operates an East–West bus (#1, #2, #3 and #4) that picks up on Woodville Street, about ten minutes' walk away. Most transit buses, including the East–West bus, start and finish downtown at King's Square. The main **tourist office** is in the Market Square mall, beside Market Slip at the foot of King Street (daily: early June to Aug 9am–8pm; Sept to early June 9am–6pm; ☎658-2855 or 1-888-364-4444). They will help with accommodation and have a wide range of local and provincial information. This is also the best place to get the latest details of local **boat trips**, the two most appealing being jet-boat rides up the Reversing Falls Rapids and Fundy Bay whale-watching excursions. Of particular note, too, are the three, excellent and free walking-tour leaflets the tourist office issues; one each for the Loyalist, Victorian merchants' and residential Victorian trails.

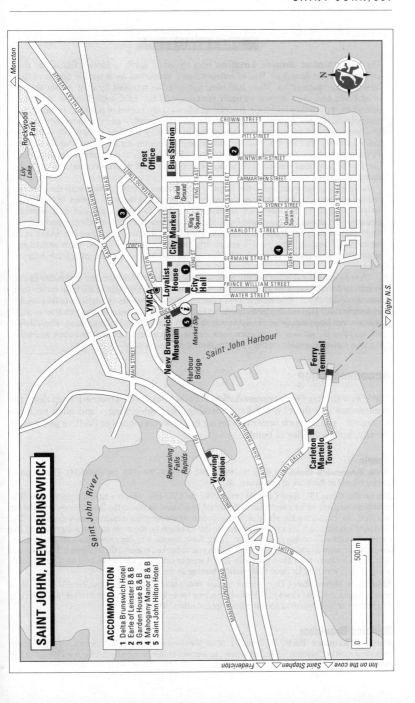

SAINT JOHN, NEW BRUNSWICK

ACCOMMODATION
1 Delta Brunswick Hotel
2 Earle of Leinster B & B
3 Garden House B & B
4 Mahogany Manor B & B
5 Saint John Hilton Hotel

Saint John River

Rockwood Park

Lily Lake

△ Moncton

CROWN STREET
PITT STREET
WENTWORTH STREET
CARMARTHEN STREET
SYDNEY STREET
CHARLOTTE STREET
GERMAIN STREET
PRINCE WILLIAM STREET
WATER STREET

KING STREET EAST
LEINSTER STREET
PRINCESS STREET
DUKE STREET
QUEEN STREET
BROAD STREET

CITY ROAD
WATERLOO STREET
UNION STREET
DORCHESTER
CARLETON
KING ST
DOCK ST
MAIN STREET

SAINT JOHN THROUGHWAY

Bus Station
Post Office
Burial Ground
King's Square
Queen Square
City Market
Loyalist House
City Hall
YMCA
New Brunswick Museum
Market Slip

Saint John Harbour

Harbour Bridge

Reversing Falls Rapids

Viewing Station

SAINT JOHN THROUGHWAY

BRIDGE ROAD

MANAWAGONISH ROAD

Ferry Terminal

Carleton Martello Tower

WOODVILLE ST
FUNDY DRIVE
BLEURY

△ Digby N.S.

Inn on the cove ▷   Saint Stephen ▷   Fredericton ▷

0   500 m

THE LOYALISTS

The 40,000 **United Empire Loyalists** who streamed north to British Canada in the aftermath of the American War of Independence accounted for a sizable chunk of the New England population. Many had been subjected to reprisals by their revolutionary neighbours and most arrived virtually penniless. All but 8000 settled in the Maritime provinces, where they and their descendants formed the kernel of powerful commercial and political cliques. As a result, the Loyalists have frequently – and not altogether unfairly – been pilloried as arch-conservatives, but in fact they were far from docile subjects: indeed shortly after their arrival in Canada they were pressing the British for their own elective assemblies. Crucially, they were also to instil in their new country an abiding dislike for the American version of republican democracy – and this has remained a key sentiment threading though Canadian history.

Before their enforced exile, the Loyalists conducted a fierce debate with their more radical compatriots, but whereas almost everyone today knows the names of the revolutionary leaders, the Loyalists are forgotten. The Loyalist argument had several strands – loyalty to Britain, fear of war, the righteousness of civil obedience and rather more subliminally the traditional English Tory belief that men are most free living in a hierarchical society where roles are clearly understood. One of their most articulate spokesmen was Daniel Leonard, who during his epistolary debate with John Adams wrote:

"A very considerable part of the men of property in this province, are at this day firmly attached to the cause of government . . . [and will . . . if they fight at all, fight under the banners of loyalty . . . And now, in God's name, what is it that has brought us to this brink of destruction? Has not the government of Great Britain . . . been a nursing mother to us? Has she not been indulgent almost to a fault? . . . Will not posterity be amazed, when they are told that the present destruction took its rise from a three penny duty on tea, and call it a more unaccountable frenzy . . . than that of the witchcraft?"

Accommodation

There's no shortage of **accommodation** in Saint John. Budget motels line up along the main routes into the city, but for something more interesting – and often no more expensive – you're much better off staying in a downtown hotel or B&B, or just west of the city, beside the Bay of Fundy.

Hotels

Delta Brunswick Hotel, 39 King St (☎648-1981 or 1-800-268-1133, fax 658-0914). Comfortable, modern hotel in the thick of downtown. ⑤.

Inn on the Cove, 1371 Sand Cove Rd (☎672-7799, fax 635-5455). This is a fabulous place to stay. The mainly modern inn, with its five ornately furnished bedrooms, overlooks the Bay of Fundy from the top of a bluff. You can survey the whole of the seashore from the splendid breakfast-cum-dining room. The food is as inventive as it is mouthwatering, with the emphasis on the freshest of local ingredients. The owner-chefs do a TV cookery programme, *Tide's Table*. Needless to say, reservations are pretty much essential and anyway you won't get dinner unless you've booked at least 24hr in advance. It takes about 10min to drive there from downtown: take Hwy 1 west to exit 107A, where you turn off to travel south along Bleury, watching for Sand Cove Road, a turning on the right. ③–⑤.

Saint John Hilton Hotel, One Market Square (☎693-8484 or 1-800-561-8282, fax 657-6610). Most rooms have waterfront views at this plush, modern tower block right beside Market Slip. Check at the Market Square tourist office for Hilton special offers. ⑥.

Bed and Breakfast

Earle of Leinster B&B, 96 Leinster St at Wentworth (☎652-3275). Seven, en-suite guest rooms in a rather solemn Victorian house, in a down-at-heel area, about 15min walk east of the Market Slip. ②.

Garden House B&B, 28 Garden St (646-9093). Comfortable, downtown B&B with just three guest rooms occupying a Victorian timber house. To get there, walk east along Union, turn left at Charlotte, right on Coburg and keep straight. ②.

Mahogany Manor B&B, 220 Germain St at Queen (☎636-8000). This is the pick of the town's B&Bs, just three en-suite guest rooms in an elegant Victorian villa with high gables and wraparound veranda. Located in a quiet, leafy part of town about 10min walk southeast of Market Slip. ②.

Campground

Rockwood Park Campground (☎652-4050). Popular campground located near the southern entrance of Rockwood Park about 2km east of the city centre. Take exit 113 off Hwy 1. Late May–Sept. $15 per-tent site with electricity.

The City

The tiny rectangular harbour at the foot of King Street, known as the **Market Slip**, witnessed one of the more dramatic Loyalist migrations, when three thousand refugees disembarked here in 1783. They were not overly impressed by their new country; one recorded that it was "the roughest land I ever saw . . . such a feeling of loneliness came over me that I sat down on the damp moss with my baby in my lap and cried". The Slip no longer functions as a port, but it's still at the heart of Saint John and is next to its most entertaining "shop" (really a museum), **Barbour's General Store** (mid-May to mid-Oct 9am–6pm), a refurbished emporium stuffed with Victorian paraphernalia from formidable-looking sweets to an old barber's chair. The opposite side of the Slip has been gentrified, the old brick wharf warehouses converted into wine bars, restaurants and boutiques fronting the modern Market Square shopping mall behind. Inside the mall, the gleaming **New Brunswick Museum** (Mon–Fri 9am–9pm, Sat 10am–6pm, Sun noon–5pm; $6) is devoted to the province's human, natural and artistic life and has a particularly revealing section on the Age of Sail as well as a fine collection of Chinese decorative and applied art. In addition, there's much on the region's marine life, including the skeleton of a rare North Atlantic right whale in the "Hall of Great Whales" and a thirteen-metre-high tidal tube constructed to illustrate the rise and fall of the Bay of Fundy tides.

A five-minute walk up King Street and left along Germain, the white wooden **Loyalist House**, at 120 Union St (June to early Sept daily Mon–Sat 10am–5pm, Sun 1–5pm; $3), was erected in 1810 for merchant David Merritt, whose family lived here for six generations. Inside, the early nineteenth-century furnishings and fittings include a fine, sweeping staircase, cleverly worked curved doors and hand-carved mouldings; costumed guides give the lowdown on Loyalist life. Just down the hill, back along Germain, is the entrance to the lively **City Market** (Mon–Thurs 7.30am–6pm, Fri 7.30am–7pm, Sat 7.30am–5pm), heaped with the characteristic foods of New Brunswick – *fiddleheads*, a succulent fern tip that tastes rather like asparagus, and *dulse*, a dried seaweed that enlivens the chowders hereabouts. Behind the market are the Union Jack paths and fanciful Edwardian bandstand of **King's Square**.

After the fire of 1877, the city's merchant class funded a rebuilding programme that would, they believed, properly reflect Saint John's status as a major seaport and shipbuilding centre. Blissfully unaware of the hard years ahead, they competed with each other in the construction of grand offices and banks, brimmingly self-confident structures that line up along **Prince William Street**, south of the Market Slip. There's an extraordinary attention to detail here, the careful symmetries of each red-brick facade patterned with individualistic designs – everything from angular stone trimmings and dog-tooth window ledges through to hieroglyphic insets and elaborately carved window arches. Amongst the predominate red-brick are the grandiose Neoclassical and Second Empire facades of the Old Post Office at no. 113, the Old City Hall at no. 116, and the Nova Scotia Bank's Palatine Building at no. 124. These finely worked stone extravagances, with their columns, pediments and arcades, were built as institutional confirmation of the city's excellent prospects. To the middle class of the time this was all in good taste, but there were limits. The Chubb's Corner building, at 111 Prince William St, was decorated by a singular series of mini-gargoyles: "We trust no more of our buildings will be adorned by such buffoonery," thundered the local newspaper.

The outskirts

Like just about every other place along the shores of the Bay of Fundy, Saint John is proud of its tides. What you have here are the **Reversing Falls Rapids**, created by a sharp bend in the Saint John River about 3km west of the centre. At low tide the river – still some 60m deep – flows quite normally, but the incoming tide forces it into reverse, causing a brief period of equilibrium when the surface of the water is totally calm, before a churning, often tumultuous, surge upstream. You need to stick around for a couple of hours to see the complete process, and there's a **viewing station** (late May to mid-Oct daily 8am–8pm; free) high above the river at the far end of the bridge on Hwy 100 – take the East–West transit bus (#1, #2, #3 and #4) from King's Square. The attached **information centre** shows a film ($1.25) telescoping a day's tidal flow into fifteen minutes. There are also a couple of mini-parks beneath the bridge where you can view the phenomenon from near the river bank – one upstream in eyeshot of the noxious paper mill, the other downstream and reached via a short, steep path from the car park. Better still, Reversing Falls Jet Boat operates trips through the Reversing Falls during the summer from their jetty near the bridge (May to mid-Sept; 20min; $20; ☎634-8987).

When you've finished with the river, it's another short transit ride west to the **Carleton Martello Tower** on Fundy Drive (June to mid-Oct daily 9am–5pm; $2.50). This stone tower was raised as part of a projected series to protect the Fundy coast from American attack, its squat design – and that of several hundred others dotted across the empire – copied from a Corsican tower that had previously proved especially troublesome to the British navy. Completed in 1815, too late to be of much use in the struggle against the States, the tower was soon abandoned, though it was eventually recycled as a detention centre for deserters in World War I and as the focal point of the coastal defence system protecting Saint John harbour in World War II – hence the ungainly concrete structure plonked on top. Inside, there's a reconstruction of a nineteenth-century barrack room and displays on World War II – and splendid views over town and bay. Beyond the ferry terminal just 1km out in the bay, you'll spy **Partridge Island**, the first quarantine station in North America. A lighthouse was built on this 24-acre islet in 1791, but by the middle of the nineteenth century no fewer than thirteen hospitals had been placed here as well, with teams of doctors separating the healthy from the sick immigrants. The busiest period was during the Irish famine and a Celtic cross commemorates the many Irish who died on the island. After a hundred years, the quarantine site was closed in 1938. The island bristles with World War II ruins and holds six cemeteries, where over one thousand unfortunate would-be immigrants are buried. It's uninhabited now but there are occasional boat trips out to the island – check the tourist office for details.

Eating, drinking and nightlife

Saint John is a boisterous, lively place to **eat and drink**. *Reggie's*, a well-lived-in diner near the city market at 26 Germain St, serves up superb chowders, all sorts of sandwiches and whopping breakfasts. Inside the market, the *Wild Carrot Café* provides wholesome snacks, and *Billy's Seafood Company* has fine fresh seafood and an oyster bar. Down by the Market Slip, amongst a string of bars and cafés, are *Maxamoré*, whose speciality is enormous Italian sandwiches, and *Grannan's Seafood Restaurant* (☎634-1555), where the catch of the day is a treat. For something a little spicier, try *Taco Pica*, a Mexican-Guatemalan restaurant at 96 Germain St. Nearby is *Incredible Edibles*, 42

Princess St (closed Sun), which has a wide-ranging menu specializing in simply pre-pared and thoughtfully presented seafood and vegetarian dishes. *Vito's Restaurant*, at 1 Hazen Ave at Union, specializes in Greek and Italian food or alternatively there's *Beatty and the Beastro*, a café/restaurant next door to the Imperial Theatre on King Street, which has crêpes, pasta and seafood through to delicious New Brunswick lamb.

After dark, the rollicking *3 Mile Tavern,* 1 Golden Grove Rd, north of the centre off Rothesay Avenue near McAllister Drive (☎634-1983), puts on all sorts of live shows and dances but is best for C&W. More convenient is *O'Leary's*, 46 Princess St, which has draught imported and domestic beers and features live music towards the back end of the week – mostly folk, Irish or Maritime. *Tapps Brewpub & Steakhouse*, 78 King St, the city's first microbrew pub, offers several especially tasty light ales, as well as live music Thursday to Saturday. *Nipper's Pub*, 43 Princess St, is a popular nightspot, with frequent live music, especially blues, R&B and Maritime. For **performance arts**, the city's lead-ing venue is the Imperial Theatre, an attractively refurbished Edwardian theatre at 24 King's Square (☎633-9494).

Fundy National Park to Moncton

One of the most beautiful portions of New Brunswick's shoreline has been protected as the **Fundy National Park**, where the rugged sea cliffs, bays and coves are pat-terned with superb hiking trails. Highway 114 cuts a scenic diagonal through the park, branching off the Trans-Canada east of Saint John to provide access to its trails and campgrounds. It emerges at the seaside hamlet of **Alma**, the only sizable settlement hereabouts and a handy spot to break your journey. East of Alma, a lovely coastal drive along minor roads passes by turnings for tide-battered **Cape Enrage** and the curious-ly-shaped **Hopewell Rocks** on the way to **Moncton**, the province's third city. Beyond Moncton, the isthmus linking New Brunswick with Nova Scotia lies beside Chignecto Bay, at the east end of the Bay of Fundy. Of brief strategic significance after the Treaty of Utrecht, with the British in control of Nova Scotia and the French in Québec, the isth-mus and its surrounding shoreline has long been a sleepy backwater of tiny fishing vil-lages and Acadian-style marshland farming, though past imperial disputes are recalled by the beguiling, windswept remains of **Fort Beauséjour**.

Fundy National Park and its environs are a popular holiday spot, so it's a good idea to book accommodation ahead of time. Also, pick up a tide timetable at any local tourist office – the tides rise and fall by about 9m, making a spectacular difference to the shore-line – and be prepared for patches of pea-soup fog: the Bay of Fundy is notoriously prone to them. There's no public transport along Hwy 114.

Fundy National Park

Bisected by Hwy 114, **Fundy National Park** encompasses a short stretch of the Bay of Fundy shoreline, whose jagged cliffs and tidal mudflats edge the forested hills, lakes and river valleys of the central plateau. This varied scenery is crossed by more than 100km of hiking trails, most of which are short, easy walks taking no more than three hours to complete – though the fifty-kilometre Fundy Circuit links several of the trails and takes between three and five days. The pick of the hiking trails are, however, along the Fundy shore and it's here you'll find both the spectacular Point Wolfe Beach trail, a moderately steep, 300-metre hike down from the wooded headlands above the bay to the beach below, and the 4.5-kilometre loop of the Coppermine trail, which meanders through the forests with breathtaking views out along the seashore.

All the park's trails are described in booklets available at either of the two **informa-tion centres** beside Hwy 114 – one at the west entrance near Lake Wolfe, about 25km south of the Trans-Canada (mid-May to mid-June & Sept to early Oct Mon–Fri 8.15am–4.30pm, Sat & Sun 10am–6pm; mid-June to Aug daily 8am–10pm; mid-Oct to mid-May Mon–Fri 8.15am–noon & 12.45–4.30pm, plus weekends from early Jan to late March 9am–4pm), the other about 20km to the east, on the coast next door to **Alma** (mid-May to mid-June Fri–Sun 10am–6pm; mid-June to Aug Mon–Thurs & Sat 10am–6pm, Fri 8am–9pm). Entrance to the park costs $3.50 per adult. The park is well equipped for **camping**, with four serviced grounds and a string of wilderness sites. The serviced grounds largely operate on a first-come, first-served basis, though reservations are taken for two of the four on ☎1-800-213-7275. Wilderness sites require reservations (☎506/887-6000); backcountry permits are available from either information centre. Two of the serviced campgrounds – *Chignecto* (mid-May to mid-Oct) and *Headquarters* (mid-June to Aug) – are located near Alma along with most of the park's tourist facilities. For a greater degree of isolation, take the ten-kilometre byroad southwest from Alma to **Point Wolfe**, where a medium-sized, unserviced campground (late June to mid-Aug) is tucked in amongst the wooded hills above the coast – and near the starting point of the Point Wolfe Beach and Coppermine trails.

If you're after a roof over your head, there are a couple of modern chalet complexes just inside the park near Alma – those at Fundy Park Chalets (☎887-2808; ②–③) come with kitchenettes – and there's also an extremely basic HI **youth hostel** (reception 8.30–10am & 5–10pm; ☎887-2216; ①; June–Aug) on Devil's Half Acre Road, some 2km from the Alma information centre; hidden away amongst the woods, the hostel overlooks the bay and its beds are in simple cabins. Much more enticing **accommodation** is on offer at **Alma**, which is pleasantly located in the right angle between Fundy Bay and the Salmon River. Here, Main Street is bordered by a string of motels and hotels, including the pleasant *Alpine Motor Inn* (☎887-2052; ②; May–Sept); the trim, timber *Captain's Inn* (☎887-2017; ③); and the bayshore's *Parkland Village Inn* (☎887-2313; ②; April–Oct). For **food**, the *Parkland* has a competent restaurant and great pancakes. Kelly's Bake Shop nearby is well-known for its sticky buns – enormous, delicious things that look rather like brains.

East of Alma: Cape Enrage and the Cape Hopewell Rocks

Just east of Alma, Local Hwy 915 branches off Hwy 114 to stick close to the coast, threading through a gentle valley of isolated farmsteads sheltering behind rugged sea-cliffs. Here and there the coast comes into view – wide vistas of beach and cliff – but the most dramatic scenery is at **Cape Enrage**, 6km down a sideroad off Hwy 915, where the lighthouse is glued to a great shank of rock soaring high above the sea. It's actually quite remarkable that you can drive down to the Cape at all. When the lighthouse was automated in 1988, the keepers moved away, abandoning their old house to the elements. Offended by the neglect, a Moncton schoolteacher – from Harrison Trimble High – initiated an ambitious plan to protect and develop the site with the enthusiastic help of his students. In the last five years, they've transformed the place. There's now a wooden walkway up to the foot of the lighthouse and the old keepers' house has been converted into a pleasant café – try the fish chowder. The students staff the cape in the summer and help run a programme of adventurous pursuits, principally sea-kayaking (May–Oct; 4hr; $50) and abseiling (May–Oct; 2–3hr; $40); bookings on ☎887-2273. Returning to Hwy 915, it's a further 11km east to the first of two gravel byroads that lead down to the tidal mud flats and sands of **Mary's Point**, where thousands of migrating Semipalmated Sandpipers appear in late July and early August, tearing round in formation, the greyish white of their undersides flashing in the sun. It's an extraordinary sight and the birds usually stay for three weeks, but check locally to see if they've arrived or moved on. Beyond these two turnings, it's a short drive back to Hwy 114, which travels east passing through farmland and offering attractive views of headlands and tidal flats on its way to Hopewell Cape, where the Petitcodiac River flows into the bay. The cape is the site of the red-sandstone **Hopewell Rocks** ($4), gnarled pinnacles rising up to 15m above the beach and snared within a tiny park that attracts too many visitors for its own good. At high tide the rocks resemble stark little islands covered in fir trees, but at low tide look like enormous termite hills. The rocks were pushed away from the cliff face by glacial pressure during the ice age, and the Bay of Fundy tides have defined their present, eccentric shape. Steps lead down to the beach and you can safely walk round the rocks two hours either side of low tide (tide times and advisory notices are posted), or you can paddle round them at high tide by hiring a kayak at the visitors' centre. From the Hopewell Rocks, it's 35km along the west bank of the Petitcodiac River to Moncton.

Moncton

MONCTON, 80km from Alma, was named after colonel Robert Monckton [sic], though the Acadians had originally called the place **Le Coude** ("the elbow"), which at least hinted at its setting on a sharp bend of the Petitcodiac River. Indeed, the river provides Moncton with its only attraction, the tidal bore, which sweeps up from the Bay of Fundy, 35km downstream. Otherwise, Moncton is a minor commercial centre and major transport junction surrounded by marshy flatlands, which may sound unpromising, but the downtown area has recently been spruced up and there are now enough bars and good restaurants to make an overnight stay enjoyable. In part this rejuvenation reflects the increasing confidence of local Acadians: Moncton hosts the province's only French-speaking university and boasts of its bilingualism – the result of Acadian ex-deportees settling here in the 1790s. It also lies conveniently near the Confederation Bridge over to PEI.

Moncton's **tidal bore** is a wave that varies from a few centimetres to a metre in height, depending on weather conditions and the phase of the moon. At low tide you'll be in no doubt as to why the locals called the Petitcodiac the "chocolate river" – but the mud flats disappear after the bore arrives, when the river level rises by up to 8m. Tiny **Tidal Bore Park**, downtown at Main and King streets, has information plaques on the tide times and a small grandstand so you can watch the phenomenon in comfort.

Practicalities

Moncton's **bus station** is about 2km west of Tidal Bore Park, at 961 Main St. SMT buses arrive here from all major settlements in New Brunswick and they also operate three buses daily to and from PEI's Charlottetown; SMT and Acadian Bus Lines combine to link Moncton with Halifax in Nova Scotia. Moncton's **train station** is nearby – behind the Eaton Centre, a couple of blocks further west along Main Street – with services running to Halifax and Montréal. Moncton's main **tourist office** is in the gleamingly modern City Hall, at 655 Main St (Jan–May & July–Dec Mon–Fri 9am–5pm, June–Aug also Sat & Sun 8.30am–6.30pm; ☎853-3590). They'll book accommodation for no charge, provide free city maps, and give information on forthcoming events.

Moncton has a good supply of convenient **accommodation**. Amongst several downtown **hotels** on Main Street, the *Hotel Beauséjour*, at 750 Main St (☎854-4344 or 1-800-441-1414; ⑥), is the most lavish, a big modern high-rise bang in the middle of town, though the motel-style rooms of the much more modest *Travelodge*, beside Tidal Bore Park, at 434 Main St (☎382-1664 or 1-800-578-7878; ③), are perfectly adequate if rather plain. Alternatively, several pleasant **B&Bs** are dotted amongst the leafy residential avenues to the north of Main Street. The pick of the bunch is the *Bonaccord House*, 250 Bonaccord St (☎388-1535; ②), north of the bus station in an attractive Victorian villa with picket fence and portico. A good reserve is the gracious *Park View*, beside the park to the north of Main Street's Eaton Centre at 254 Cameron St (☎382-4504; ②).

For **food**, *Le Château à Pape*, 2 Steadman St (☎855-7273), serves the finest of Acadian cuisine from its premises in a big old house a couple of minutes' walk west along the river bank from Tidal Bore Park, whilst the *Brass Vine Bistro*, 589 Main St, features delicious crêpes and tasty stir-fries. Less expensive places include *Rye's Deli & Pub*, 785 Main St, where the bagels and the daily specials are excellent, and the *Café Robinson*, off Main at 187 Robinson St, for quality snacks and coffee. *Jean's Diner*, 369 St George St, about three blocks north of Main Street, is worth a trip at lunch time for the clams.

For **nightlife**, *Fat Tuesday's*, 720 Main St, is a lively brewpub; *Ziggy's Bar*, 730 Main St, is a brash, noisy place open till 2am; and the *Club Cosmopolitan*, 700 Main St, showcases local rock bands.

Fort Beauséjour

Stuck on a grassy treeless hill, with the wide sweep of Chignecto Bay and its flattened foreshore in full view, **Fort Beauséjour National Historic Site** (June to mid-Oct daily 9am–5pm; $2.50) lies about 55km south of Moncton, just 2km from the junction of Trans-Canada Hwy 2 – to Nova Scotia – and TCH 16 to PEI. The French built the first fort here in 1750 to inhibit incursions from the south, but after a two-week siege in 1755 it fell into the hands of the British, who refortified the site initially to deter resistance from the local Acadian population, and later – until its abandonment in 1835 – as a defence against the Americans. Flush with the brow of the hill, the remains of the star-shaped fort include much of the original earthwork, the concentric ditches and mounds typical of the period, as well as a couple of deeply recessed casements, used for general storage. The site also has a delightful **museum** with excellent displays on the history of the fort and of the Acadian farmers who settled the region in the 1670s – some of the most interesting exhibits, like ancient clogs and farm tools, were recovered when the fort was repaired and restored in the 1960s. The Acadians enclosed and drained the marshes below the fort to produce hay, grain crops and vegetables – and the lines of their dykes and ditches are still visible from the hill.

The Saint John River Valley

The **Saint John River Valley** between Fredericton and **Edmundston**, a distance of 275km, is not consistently beautiful but does have its moments, when it weaves through maple and pine forests or, to the north, where its low-lying hills and farmland are finally replaced by more mountainous, heavily forested terrain. The valley towns, dotted along the Trans-Canada, are not especially memorable, but the restored pioneer village of **King's Landing** is first-rate and well worth at least a couple of hours, as is the waterfall at **Grand Falls**.

SMT operates a twice-daily **bus** between Fredericton and Edmundston, with services continuing on to Montréal.

King's Landing

Some 25km west of Fredericton on the Trans-Canada lies the **Mactaquac Dam**, part of a hydroelectric project whose reservoir stretches 75km up the valley. **King's Landing Historical Settlement** (June to mid-Oct daily 10am–5pm; $8.75), 10km west of the dam, exists because of the project. Making a virtue of necessity, several nineteenth-century buildings were carefully relocated to form the nucleus of a fictitious agricultural community as of 1850. Further judicious purchases added to the housing stock and, supplemented by a handful of replicas, there are now no less than thirty buildings spread out amidst the delightful waterside woods and fields. Like similar reconstructions, King's Landing aims to provide a total experience to its visitors, with its "inhabitants" engaged in bread-making, horseshoeing, logging, milling, weaving, cattle-driving and so on. Perhaps it is a bit daft, but it all works very well and several of the buildings are fascinating in their own right – particularly the Jones House, a stone dwelling built into the hillside in a manner typical of this area; the Ingraham House, once the property of a well-to-do farmer; and the fully operational sawmill.

Hartland and Grand Falls

Surrounded by forest, **HARTLAND**, some 90km from King's Landing, advertises itself exclusively on the size of its wooden **bridge**, which at 391m is by far the longest covered bridge in the world. It was completed in 1901, the idea being to protect the timbers of the bridge from the elements by means of a long shed-like affair built in the manner of a barn. It's not graceful – but it is long.

North of Hartland, the scenery changes as the maples give way to the beginning of a great undulating belt of potato fields. This is really dreary, but a surprise lies in store at **GRAND FALLS**, 105km from Hartland. Here, right in the centre of an otherwise nondescript town, a spectacular weight of water squeezes through hydroelectric barriers to crash down a 23-metre pitch. Even if the diversion of water through nearby turbines has deprived the falls of their earlier vigour, they're still impressive, as is the two-kilometre gorge they've carved downstream, a steep-sided ravine encircling half the town. There are two short walks into the gorge: one leads to near the base of the falls themselves, the other to the bottom of the gorge, where, amid the pounding of the water and the sheer faces of the rock, it's hard to believe you're still in the middle of town.

There's nothing else to see in Grand Falls, and the **visitors' centre** on the bridge (May–Sept daily 9am–9pm) is preoccupied with the river too, though it does have a mildly diverting section outlining the history of the town. In emergencies, there's simple **accommodation** right by the gorge (and its thunderous waterfall!) at the *Hill Top Motel*, 131 Madawaska Rd (☎473-2684; ②).

Edmundston

Lying at the confluence of the Saint John and Madawaska rivers, wood-pulping **EDMUNDSTON** is the largest town in the north of New Brunswick, with a population of nearly twelve thousand. It's a brash, modern place, a profusion of flashing neon signs and ranks of old-style American cars proclaiming the proximity of the USA, which lies just over the biggest of the town's three bridges. Edmundston is mainly French-speaking and, curiously, regards itself as the capital of the enclave known as the **Republic of Madawaska**, the snout-shaped tract of Canadian territory jutting out into the state of Maine. While the idea of an independent state here is preposterous, the "Republic" is more than a publicity stunt: it signifies the frustration of a people over whom the British and Americans haggled for thirty years until 1842, and who still feel ignored by Fredericton. Yet the town packages the Republic frivolously, with Ruritanian touches such as a coat of arms, a flag, honorary knights and a president, (otherwise the mayor).

There's a seasonal **tourist office** adjoining the dreary municipal museum just off the Trans-Canada (exit 18) at the top of Boulevard Hébert, which runs downtown. SMT **buses** pull in at 169 Victoria St, just off Boulevard Hébert before the Fournier Bridge over the Madawaska River into the town centre. Nearby, at 127 Victoria St, is the admirably cheap and snazzy *Hotel Praga* (☎735-5567; ①), with bargain-priced double rooms.

The Miramichi Valley

Running northeast of Fredericton, Hwy 8 traverses the **Miramichi River Valley**, passing endless stands of timber en route to the **City of Miramichi**, an amalgamation of the six tiny logging ports that flank the mouth of the river – and amongst which **Newcastle** is easily the most diverting. The 180-kilometre trip takes three to four hours;

longer if you pause at the one sight of any real interest, the Woodmen's Museum in **Boiestown**. The river valley is, however, much more famous for its salmon fishing, which draws anglers from all over the world. The season begins anywhere between April and July, depending on the waters to be fished, and every angler has to buy a licence, with non-residents charged between $30 and $110. A veritable raft of regulations control the sport but any local tourist office will have the details. The other big deal hereabouts is the **Miramichi Folksong Festival**, held the first week of August in Miramichi City and generally reckoned to be one of the best of its kind, with fiddle music its forte. Look out for two big local names, Ned Landry and Winston Crawford.

SMT **buses** ply Hwy 8 daily, and at Chatham, (part of Miramichi City), there are connecting services north to Montréal and south to Moncton and Halifax.

Boiestown and Doaktown

Some 70km from Fredericton, **BOIESTOWN** was once a rowdy loggers' settlement whose drunken "goings-on" inspired the region's balladeers – "If you're longing for fun and enjoyment, or inclined to go out on a spree, come along with me to Boiestown, on the banks of the Miramichi." The **Woodmen's Museum**, beside Hwy 8 (daily: June–Aug 9.30am–5.30pm; Sept 9am–5pm; $5), recalls these rougher days beginning with a pair of large huts jam-packed with loggers' artefacts, from all sorts of strange-looking tools to fascinating photographs of the men floating the logs downstream. There are more intimate exhibits too: the loggers collected resin from spruce trees, chewed it until it was smooth and sweet and then placed it in "gumbooks", a couple of which are on display, to give to their kids back home. After the huts, it only takes a few minutes to wander the rest of the site, where there's an incidental assortment of old lumber-industry buildings, including a sawmill, pitsaw, an earthy bunkhouse and cookhouse and a fire tower. For some obscure reason, an old and well-built fur-trapper's cabin has ended up here as well, and a small train, the *Whooper* ($2), runs round the edge of the museum.

DOAKTOWN, 20km further down the valley, is a favourite spot for fishermen, who congregate here to catch the **Atlantic salmon** as it struggles up the Miramichi, one of its major spawning rivers, on the last leg of its complex life cycle. Early each spring, thousands of tiny Atlantic salmon emerge from pea-sized orange eggs deposited in the riverbed the previous fall. These young fish – or fry – soon acquire dark markings and are then known as parr. The parr remain in the river for two to six years (determined by water temperature and the availability of insects and other aquatic food) before a springtime transformation when their internal systems adapt for saltwater life and they turn silver, becoming smolt. It seems that the odours of the smolt's native river are imprinted in its memory before it heads out to sea, to be recalled when it returns to spawn. Some fish, the grilse, return to spawn after a year, but the majority, the salmon, swim back after two years or more, entering the Miramichi between April and November and weighing anywhere between 4kg and 20kg. Once they're back in the fresh water, the salmon stop feeding and their bodies deteriorate in favour of egg or sperm production, with the male developing a hooked lower jaw or kype. After they spawn in late fall, the adults (now known as kelt, or black salmon) return to the ocean to begin the cycle again – unlike their Pacific cousins, all of whom die after their first and only spawning. Incidentally, the kelt are nowhere near as tasty as the smolt. Doaktown's **Atlantic Salmon Museum** (early June to Sept daily 10am–5pm; $4; ☎365-7787), beside Hwy 8, illustrates the salmon's arduous life cycle, has a small aquarium and looks at different fishing techniques – but you're much better off having a go at fishing yourself: there are lots of outfitters and guides in and around town; ask for information at the museum.

Newcastle and around

Recently incorporated within the City of Miramichi, the old shipbuilding centre of **NEWCASTLE** sits on the north bank of the Miramichi River as it nears the sea. Its compact centre is cheered by a pleasant little park at Ritchie Wharf and by the trim town square which, with its Italian gazebo and English garden seats, was spruced up at the whim of local-lad-made-good Max Aitken, otherwise Lord Beaverbrook, whose bust sits in the square too. There's nothing much else to the place, but it is a convenient stopping point on the long drive north to Québec's Gaspé Peninsula and there are a couple of reasonable **places to stay**: the modern, motel-like *Wharf Inn*, near the bridge at 1 Jane St (☎622-0302 or 1-800-561-2489; ③), and the *Comfort Inn*, 201 Edward St (☎622-1215 or 1-800-228-5150; ③). Alternatively, across the river from Newcastle in **Nelson**, the HI *Beaubear Manor Youth Hostel* (☎622-3036; ①) occupies an attractive Victorian mansion and offers dormitory beds and family rooms. If you're here for the **Miramichi Folksong Festival**, the **visitors' centre**, in the Lighthouse on Ritchie Wharf (mid-May to early Sept daily 9am–9pm; ☎622-9100), has gig details.

Kouchibouguac National Park

From Chatham on the eastern edge of Miramichi City, Hwy 11 slices off down the coast for the fifty-kilometre trip to the coastal forests, bogs, salt marshes, lagoons and sandy beaches of the **Kouchibouguac** ("Koo-she-boo-gwack") **National Park**. Near the park's main entrance (admission $3.50) is the **visitors' centre** (daily: mid-May to mid-June 10am–6pm; mid-June to Aug 8am–8pm; Sept to mid-Oct 9am–5pm), where displays explore the area's complex ecology and the habits of some of its rarer inhabitants. From here, it's a few kilometres' drive, past the trailheads of several short woodland walks, to the turning down to the sandy expanse of **Kellys beach** – the park's main attraction. The seawater here is, you're assured, the warmest north of Virginia, with temperatures between 18° and 24°C. Further on, past the turning, there's a restaurant as well as bike, kayak and canoe rental at **Ryans Rental Centre** (early June to Aug daily 8am–9pm), on the south bank of the Kouchibouguac River. Just upriver is the trailhead of the longest track, the fourteen-kilometre **Kouchibouguac River Trail**, which wriggles west along the river bank passing one of the park's few wilderness campgrounds. Another and much shorter option is the 1.2-kilometre Cedar Trail loop, which offers wide views over lagoons and sand dunes. If you're planning to hike, don't forget the insect repellent.

The park has two serviced and three wilderness **campgrounds**. One of the wilderness campgrounds is open all year, the rest are seasonal. Easily the biggest serviced campground is the South Kouchibouguac (mid-May to mid-Oct), near Ryans Rental Centre. The park fills up fast, so either arrive early in the day or take advantage of the reservation system (☎1-800-213-7275). If you're not camping, the park is easily visited on a day-trip from Newcastle, or you can stay in one of the villages nearby. The modern *Habitant Restaurant and Motel*, 213 Main St (☎523-4421 or 1-800-561-7666; ③), is in **Richibucto** – roughly 20km south of the park entrance on Hwy 134.

The Acadian Peninsula

The **Acadian Peninsula**, which protrudes some 130km into the Gulf of St Lawrence in the northeast corner of New Brunswick, is promoted as a part of the province where the twentieth century has yet to gain a foothold. For the Acadians who fled here to avoid the deportations, the isolation was a life-saver, and more than anywhere else in the Maritimes this is where they have maintained their traditional way of life, based on fishing and marshland farming – though frankly there's precious little actually to see: the countryside is uniformly dull and the ribbon villages are hardly enticing. The mundane port of **Caraquet**, on the north shore, serves as the peninsula's cultural focus and is the best base for a visit to the replica **Village Historique Acadien**, the one sight of any note.

Caraquet

Heading east from the mining town of Bathurst, Hwy 11 bobs along the Acadian Peninsula's northern shore, trimming the edge of the rolling countryside as it makes its way the 40km to **CARAQUET**. This sprawling fishing port was founded by Acadian fugitives in 1758 and now spreads for some 13km along the seafront. The **Musée Acadien de Caraquet**, at 15 blvd St-Pierre East (June–Aug Mon–Sat 10am–8pm, Sun 1–6pm; $3), chronicles the hardships of those early settlers and has a small gallery devoted to the work of local artists, while, at the west end of town, the shrine of **Ste-Anne-du-Bocage** was built to commemorate the founding families' trials and tribulations. Caraquet is the setting for the region's most important **Acadian Festival**, a ten-day programme of music and theatre held in early August, which begins with the blessing of the fishing fleet by a local bishop.

The **Village Historique Acadien** (daily: June–Aug 10am–6pm; Sept 10am–4pm; $8), 11km west of Caraquet along Hwy 11, consists of around two dozen old Acadian buildings relocated from other parts of New Brunswick – only the church was purpose-built. Costumed "inhabitants" emphasize the struggles of the settlers and demonstrate traditional agricultural techniques as well as old methods of spinning, cooking and so on – all in a rustic setting.

Amongst several simple and inexpensive **motels**, **inns** and **B&Bs** in Caraquet, the *Hotel Paulin*, 143 blvd St-Pierre West (☎727-9981; ②), is a comfortable place and offers genuine Acadian meals on request. A second and slightly more expensive choice is *Le Pignon Rouge*, a B&B at 338 blvd St-Pierre East (☎727-5983; ②).

PRINCE EDWARD ISLAND

The freckly face and pert pigtails of Anne of Green Gables are emblazoned on much of **PRINCE EDWARD ISLAND**'s publicity material, and her creator, local-born novelist Lucy Maud Montgomery, was the island's most gushing propagandist, depicting the place floating "on the waves of the blue gulf, a green seclusion and haunt of ancient peace . . . invested with a kind of fairy grace and charm". Radical William Cobbett, who soldiered here in the 1780s, was not so dewy-eyed, and saw instead "a rascally heap of sand, rock and swamp . . . a lump of worthlessness [that] bears nothing but potatoes". Each had a point. The economy may not be quite as uniform as Cobbett suggested, but PEI does remain thoroughly agricultural – Million-Acre Farm, as it's sometimes called. On the other hand, the country's smallest province – a crescent-shaped slice of land separated from Nova Scotia and New Brunswick by the Northumberland Strait – can be beguiling. The 220-kilometre shoreline is serrated by dozens of bays and estuaries, where the ruddy soils and grassy tones of the rolling countryside are set beautifully against the blue of the sea.

Charlottetown, the capital and only significant settlement, sits on the south coast beside one of these inlets, the tree-lined streets of the older part of town occupying a chunky headland that juts out into a wide and sheltered harbour. With its graceful air, wide range of accommodation and good restaurants, this is easily the best base for exploring the island, especially as almost all of PEI's villages are formless affairs whose houses string out along the island's roads. One exception is **Victoria**, a tiny old seaport southwest of Charlottetown, which makes a peaceful overnight stay. Otherwise,

The Prince Edward Island telephone code is ☎902.

Orwell Corner Historic Village, just to the east of the capital, is an agreeable attempt to recreate an island village as of 1890; **Cavendish**, on the north coast, boasts the house that Montgomery used as the setting for her books; and, close by, **Prince Edward Island National Park** has kilometres of magnificent sandy beach. Further east is the rough-and-ready township of **Souris**, also worth a peek and located just down the coast from the delightful fishery museum at **Basin Head**. In the west, the chief interest is social: descendants of PEI's **Acadian** settlers – once the majority of the population – today constitute some fifteen percent of its inhabitants, many of them living on the wedge of land that runs down from the village of Wellington to Cap-Egmont.

PEI is a major holiday spot, so there's plenty of **accommodation** to choose from with B&Bs, inns, cottages and campgrounds liberally sprinkled across the whole of the island – though it's still a good idea to make advance reservations during July and August. Note, also, that although it's easy to reach Charlottetown by bus the rest of PEI has hardly any **public transport**. On a culinary note, PEI has a reputation for the excellence of its **lobsters**, which are trapped on the west side of the island during August and September and in the east from June to July. A number of restaurants specialize in lobster dishes, but keep a look out for local posters advertising lobster suppers, inexpensive buffet meals served in some church and community halls during the summer.

Getting to the island

There are regular domestic **flights** to Charlottetown airport from most cities in eastern Canada, but the majority of visitors arrive via the fourteen-kilometre-long **Confederation Bridge** spanning the Northumberland Strait between New Brunswick's Cape Tormentine and Borden, 60km west of Charlottetown. There's a toll of $35 per vehicle for using the bridge and this is collected on the way off the island. Cyclists aren't allowed on the bridge, but are transported across in a free shuttle bus – ring ☎902/437-7300 for further details. The bridge is used by the twice-daily SMT **bus** service connecting Fredericton, New Brunswick, with Charlottetown via Saint John and Moncton.

You can also reach the island by **ferry**: Northumberland Ferries take 75 minutes to cross from **Caribou**, Nova Scotia, to **Wood Islands**, 61km east of Charlottetown ($45 return for car and passengers; ☎902/566-3838 or ☎1-888-249-7245 in North America), with fares collected when you leave the island – but not when you arrive. This is a far more scenic approach to the island's capital than the drive in from the bridge. Ferries run every one and a half hours from June to November and every three hours in May and early December. There's no ferry from late December to April. Ferries operate on a first-come first-served basis and queues are common in high season – arrive about an hour and a half before departure to be safe.

A second ferry does the five-hour hop between **Cap-aux-Meules** on the Îles-de-la-Madeleine and **Souris**, 81km northeast of Charlottetown (Feb & March no ferries; summer & fall 6–14 weekly; winter 3–5 weekly; $33.75 single, $64.25 per car; schedules ☎902/687-2181, reservations ☎418/986-3278 or 1-888-986-3278).

A brief history of Prince Edward Island

Jacques Cartier claimed Prince Edward Island for France on the first of his voyages across the Atlantic, naming it the Île-St-Jean in 1534. However, the French and the Acadian farmers he brought with him from the Bay of Fundy made little impact on the island until they were reinforced in 1720 by three hundred French colonists, who founded a tiny capital at **Port La Joye**, near the site of present-day Charlottetown. In 1754, there were about three thousand settlers, but their numbers doubled the following year with the arrival of refugees from the deportations (see p.335), a sudden influx with which the island was unable to cope. After the capture of Louisbourg in 1758, the British army turned its attention to Île-St-Jean and its starving, dispirited population. **Lord Rollo**

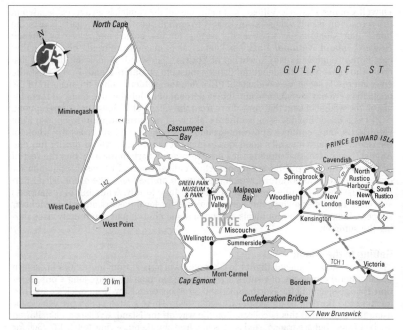

▽ New Brunswick

rounded up and shipped out all but three hundred of the Acadians and the colony was subsequently renamed the Island of St John in 1763, and **Prince Edward Island** in 1799.

After the expulsion of the Acadians, the island was parcelled out to wealthy Englishmen on condition that they organized settlement, but few did. Consequently, when the island's population climbed from around seven thousand to eighty thousand in the first half of the nineteenth century, the majority of the colonists were tenant farmers or squatters, victims of an absentee landowning system that was patently unjust and inefficient. Although most of these immigrants were drawn from the poor of the Scottish Highlands and Ireland, the new citizens had come here in the hope of owning land. Their ceaseless petitioning eventually resulted in the compulsory **Land Purchase Act** of 1875, and within a decade PEI became a land of freeholders.

With the agricultural, fishing, shipbuilding and logging industries buoyant, the late 1870s marked the high point of the island's fortunes, but this prosperity was short-lived. The Canadian government's protectionist **National Policy** discriminated in favour of the manufactured goods of Ontario and Québec and the result was a long-lasting recession that helped precipitate a large-scale emigration, which left PEI a forgotten backwater, derisively nicknamed **Spud Island**. Depopulation remains a problem to this day, though the successful exploitation of the island's tourist potential has brought much relief, as has the modernization of its agriculture and fishery. Many islanders also argued that the construction of a bridge between PEI and the mainland would provide a further economic boost, whilst their opponents asserted that the island would be swamped by outsiders, its farms bought up as second homes and its closely knit communities overwhelmed. Those in favour of the bridge won the day (if not the argument) and the **Confederation Bridge** was completed in 1997; locals await the consequences with mixed feelings – and lots of jokes about islanders heading for the mainland hurrying to "catch the bridge".

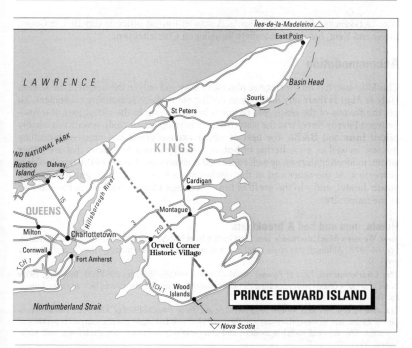

Charlottetown

Tiny **CHARLOTTETOWN**, the administrative and business centre of PEI, is the most urbane spot on the island, its comfortable main streets – Grafton and Kent – hemmed in by leafy avenues of clapboard villas, the most opulent of which spread west of the centre towards **Victoria Park**. But although these well-disposed streets give the place a prosperous and sedate appearance, this is not the whole truth: Charlottetown has a high rate of unemployment and you'll glimpse the poverty here and there, particularly in the abject stuff on show in its cheaper department stores – a contrast with the up-market touristy shops on the snazzily developed harbourfront. That said, Charlotte-town is a pleasant place to spend a couple of days and it also has, in small-island terms, a reasonable **nightlife**, with a handful of excellent restaurants and a clutch of good bars.

Arrival and information

Connected with all of Canada's major cities, Charlottetown **airport** is located 8km north of the town centre. There's no public transport from here to town, but the **taxi** fare costs just $8. What few **buses** there are all arrive centrally: the SMT depot is at 330 University Ave.

Inside the airport there's a **tourist information** free phone (mid-June to mid-Sept daily 8am–8pm), which provides accommodation advice and a room reservation service. PEI's main **Visitor Information Centre** is on the harbourfront, a couple of minutes' walk from the town centre at the foot of Hillsborough Street (daily: Sept–May 9.30am–5pm; June & mid Aug 8am–8pm; July to mid-Aug 8am–10pm; ☎368-4444); its free literature includes a comprehensive *Visitors' Guide,* town maps and leaflets on the island's B&Bs and farm vacation spots. A smaller **tourist office** in City Hall, at Queen Street and Kent, has racks of leaflets focusing on Charlottetown.

Accommodation

Charlottetown has no shortage of **places to stay** and only in the height of the season (July & Aug) is there any difficulty in finding somewhere reasonably convenient. To get the flavour of the place, you're much better staying in the oldest part of town – between Fitzroy Street and the waterfront – where options include several reasonably priced **inns** and **B&Bs**, the best of which occupy grand late nineteenth-century houses, as well as a smattering of **hotels** – mostly expensive places that are either smart, modern high-rises or well-conceived conversions of some of the town's oldest properties. At the other end of the market are a handful of small **guesthouses**, a **youth hostel**, and – to the north of town – **college rooms**, available in the summer at the university.

Hotels, inns and bed & breakfasts

Best Western MacLauchlan's Inn, 238 Grafton St at Hillsborough (☎892-2461 or 1-800-463-2378, fax 566-2979). Although this chain hotel has routine furnishings and fittings – they're at the luxury level. ⑤.

The Charlottetown, Kent at Pownal (☎894-7371 or 1-800-565-7633, fax 368-2178). Imposing 1930s hotel (part of a chain) with appealing Art Deco flourishes, though the rooms lack a certain intimacy. ④.

Dundee Arms Inn and Motel, 200 Pownal St at Fitzroy (☎892-2496, fax 368-8532). The inn occupies a flashy, late nineteenth-century timber mansion and has eight guest rooms with period furnishings. The adjacent motel is modern and comparatively mundane, but attractively well maintained. Motel ④; inn ⑤.

Fitzroy Hall, 45 Fitzroy St at Pownal (☎368-2077, fax 894-5711). This lavishly restored Victorian mansion with pillars, portico, dormer windows and wrought ironwork has six well-appointed, ensuite guest rooms, one of which has a Jacuzzi. Excellent place to stay. ④.

Hillhurst Inn, 181 Fitzroy St at Hillsborough (☎ & fax 894-8004). Classily renovated Georgian Revival mansion with finely carved interior. Nine large guest rooms, each with ornate antique furnishings. It is open year-round, but by advance reservation only from late November to March. ④.

The Inns on Great George, Great George Street (☎892-0606 or 1-800-361-1118, fax 628-2079). Bang in the centre of town, opposite St Dunstan's, a row of old timber houses has been carefully renovated to hold this smart hotel. All the rooms are comfortable and tastefully decorated – the most appealing overlook the Basilica. ④.

Prince Edward Hotel, 18 Queen St (☎566-2222 or 1-800-441-1414, fax 566-2282). Charlottetown's plushest hotel, in a high-rise overlooking the harbour; luxurious rooms with superb facilites including pool and health centre. ⑥.

Guesthouses, college rooms and the hostel

Aloha Tourist Home, 234 Sydney St at Prince (☎892-9944). Plain and simple guesthouse with three furnished rooms; kitchenettes and a shared bathroom. ①.

Blanchard Tourist Home, 163 Dorchester at Hillsborough (☎894-9756). Modest but quite well-tended place in an old shingle and clapboard dwelling with just three guest rooms. May–Oct. ①.

Charlottetown Youth Hostel, 153 Mount Edward Rd (☎237-7884, fax 628-6424). Inconveniently situated 3km from the town centre, behind the university campus; there's no bus. Facilities include bike rental and kitchen. June–Aug. ①.

University of Prince Edward Island, 550 University Ave (☎566-0442, Sept–May ☎566-0362, fax 628-4319). Single and double rooms as well as apartments available on the university campus, 3km north of town. Rooms available May to late Aug. Double rooms ①.

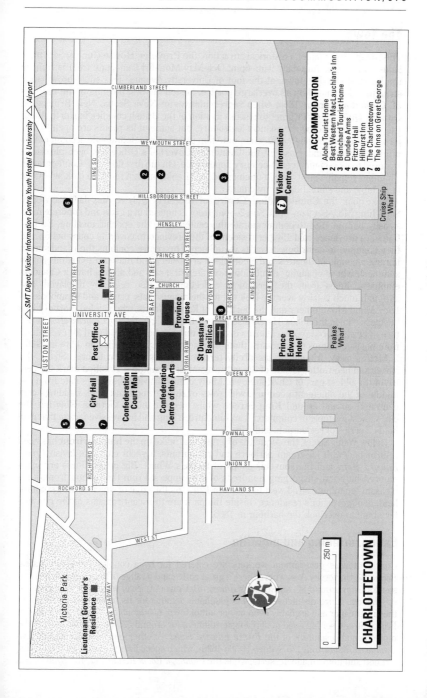

CHARLOTTETOWN

ACCOMMODATION

1 Aloha Tourist Home
2 Best Western MacLauchlan's Inn
3 Blanchard Tourist Home
4 Dundee Arms
5 Fitzroy Hall
6 Hillhurst Inn
7 The Charlottetown
8 The Inns on Great George

The Town

The island's most famous historical attraction, the **Province House** (June & Sept daily 9am–5pm; July & Aug daily 9am–6pm; Oct–May Mon–Fri 9am–5pm; free) is right in the heart of Charlottetown, at the foot of University Avenue. This squat brownstone structure, dominated by its overlarge portico, hosted the first meeting of the **Fathers of Confederation** in 1864, when representatives of Nova Scotia, New Brunswick, Ontario, Québec and PEI met to discuss a union of the British colonies in North America. Today it's used by the island's legislature, but some of its rooms are open to visitors. On the ground floor, a fifteen-minute film provides a melodramatic account of that original meeting and, close by, the Lieutenant Governor's Office has been pleasantly restored to its mid-nineteenth-century appearance. On the first floor, the Confederation Chamber remains pretty much unchanged, but frankly it's not much to look at – just a large table and some heavy-duty chairs.

Next door, the **Confederation Centre of the Arts** (July & Aug daily 9am–8pm; Sept–June Mon–Sat 9am–6pm, Sun 2–5pm; free) is housed in a glass and concrete monstrosity built in 1964 to commemorate the centenary of the epochal meeting. Each of Canada's provinces paid 15¢ per resident of the province to cover its construction and they continue to contribute towards its upkeep. The centre contains the island's main library, a couple of theatres and a combined art gallery and museum ($3 admission in summer), whose changing exhibitions are often first-rate and always have a Canadian emphasis. Items from the permanent collection are also regularly displayed, and although much is fairly average look out for the manuscripts, papers and scrapbooks of Lucy Maud Montgomery and the portraits of Robert Harris, who painted most of PEI's business elite in the 1880s. Harris also painted the iconic *Fathers of Confederation*, a picture of bewhiskered representatives in debate that has been reproduced for everything from postage stamps to postcards, though in fact the original was lost in a fire in 1916.

Metres away, fringed by the pretty terraced houses of Great George Street, the spires and neo-Gothic facade of the extravagant **St Dunstan's Basilica** mark the centre of the oldest part of Charlottetown. Many of this district's buildings date from the middle of the nineteenth century, with rows of simple wood and brick buildings concentrated on and around **King Street**, whilst pedestrianized **Victoria Row** has the city's finest example of commercial architecture, a long and impressive facade that now holds a series of restaurants and bars.

Below Water Street, the sequence of jetties that make up the **harbourfront** has been refurbished with ice-cream parlours and restaurants, a yacht club, the lavish *Prince Edward Hotel* and the souvenir shops of Peake's Wharf. Big cruise liners are often moored here too, disgorging hundreds of day-trippers. From the harbourfront, it's a pleasant ten-minute stroll west to **Victoria Park**, on the edge of which is the grandiose lieutenant-governor's residence. Inside the park are the scant remains of the gun battery built to overlook the harbour in 1805.

Eating, drinking and nightlife

Charlottetown's government workers are catered for by a couple of first-rate **cafés**: *Beanz*, 38 University Ave, where there's great coffee and a range of tasty sandwiches and snacks from around $8; and *Cedar's Eatery*, 81 University Ave, which serves Lebanese specialities. More distinctively, PEI is justifiably famous for its **lobsters** and, although they're cheaper and arguably even tastier out of town, *Lobster on the Wharf*, at the foot of Prince Street, serves good-quality lobster dinners for around $25 per pound, as does the more formal restaurant of the *Prince Edward Hotel*. Another option is the superb *Off-Broadway Restaurant*, 125 Sydney (☎566-4620), which specializes in exotic crêpes, steaks, seafood and home-made desserts, while the *Claddagh Room Restaurant*, 131 Sydney, has a delicious selection of reasonably priced seafood – even more lobster – and beef dishes. It's also attached to the busy *Olde Dublin Pub*, where there's often live **folk music**. Close by, behind the Confederation Centre, are the assorted bars-cum-restaurants of Victoria Row; the row is the town's liveliest spot after dark – both the *Island Rock Café*, no. 132, and *Kelly's*, with its high ceilings and heavy woodwork at no. 34, fill up fast with drinkers, especially on the weekend, and each has a pleasant patio area. There's another cluster of bars and restaurants on Kent Street between University and Prince. Here you'll find *D'Arcy McGee's* bar, as well as *Myron's*, 151 Kent (☎892-4375), which puts on a wide range of live music and club nights. Every summer, it also hosts performances of *Annekenstein*, a comedy revue that parodies – obviously enough – *Anne of Green Gables*, though the long-running show has itself become something of an institution.

The programme of events at the **Confederation Centre of the Arts** (☎566-1267) encompasses an extensive variety of acts, from rock and jazz through to comedians, magicians, theatre, opera and ballet. The centre is also the home of the main show of the annual **Charlottetown Festival** (mid-June to Sept), which – surprise, surprise – is a musical adaptation of *Anne of Green Gables*. The musical has been running for years, though modifications are made every year to freshen it up. During festival time in particular, Charlottetown offers all sorts of comedy revues and shows. The *Buzz*, a free monthly newssheet available all over town and at the tourist office, carries comprehensive listings and reviews.

Listings

Airlines Air Canada (☎892-1007) has an office at the airport, where Canadian Airlines enquiries are handled by Air Atlantic (☎1-800-665-1177).

Bike rental MacQueen's, 430 Queen St (☎368-2453); the *Charlottetown Youth Hostel* (June–Aug); and Smooth Cycle, 172 Prince St at Kent (☎566-5530 or 1-800-310-6550).

Bus companies The Shuttle, connects Charlottetown with Cavendish (☎566-3243); SMT, 330 University (☎628-6432).

Car rental Avis, at the airport and at the corner of University and Euston (both ☎892-3706); Budget, at the airport and 215 University Ave (both ☎566-5525); Rent-a-Wreck, 57a St Peter's Rd (☎566-9955); Tilden, downtown at the *Prince Edward Hotel*, 18 Queen St (☎368-2228) and at the airport (☎628-6990). All these companies do good deals on short-term rentals.

Ferry companies Northumberland Ferries, 94 Water St (☎566-3838 or 1-888-249-7245).

Hospital Queen Elizabeth Hospital, Riverside Drive (☎894-2111).

Ice cream Something of an island institution, Cows produces delicious ice cream; there are outlets down on the harbourfront and on the corner of Grafton and Queen, opposite the Confederation Centre.

Laundries Midtown Laundromat and Café, 236 University Ave at Bishop (☎628-2329).

Newspapers The main local daily is *The Guardian*, which makes an enjoyable read; its motto is likeable too – "covers PEI like the dew".

Pharmacy Shoppers Drug Mart, 128 Kent (☎566-1200) and 390 University Ave (☎892-3433).

Police 450 University Ave (☎368-2677). General emergency number (☎911).

Post office 135 Kent St.

Taxis City Cab, 168 Prince (☎892-6567); Ed's Taxi, 73 University Ave (☎892-6561).

The rest of the island

Prince Edward Island is divided into three counties: in the middle, **Queens County** incorporates the province's most popular tourist attractions and has some of its prettiest scenery and best beaches, the pick of which are protected within the **Prince Edward Island National Park**; to the east, **Kings County** covers two broad geographical areas, the tree-dotted farmland and estuary townships of the south giving way to wilder scenery further north; and to the west, **Prince County** makes up the flattest part of PEI, its broad-brimmed, sparsely populated landscapes curving round a handful of deep bays. The provincial government has worked out three **scenic drives** covering each of the counties: Lady Slipper Drive (287km) to the west, Blue Heron Drive (191km) in the centre, and the Kings Byway Drive (367km) to the east. However, although these drives visit everything of interest, they are frequently dreary, so unless you really love driving it's better to be more selective.

PEI's **public transport** system is rudimentary, but from early June to August there is a **Shuttle** (2–4 daily; $14 return; ☎566-3243) linking Charlottetown's visitors' centre and youth hostel with Cavendish visitors' centre, at the junction of Hwys 6 and 13. Alternatively, several Charlottetown companies operate **sightseeing tours**, with two of the best being Abegweit, 157 Nassau St (☎894-9966), and Prince Edward Tours, 18 Queen St (☎566-5466). The island is also excellent for **cycling** and there are several **cycle tour operators**, though it's a good deal cheaper (and entirely straightforward) to plan your own route: both Smooth Cycle, 172 Prince St at Kent (☎566-5530 or 1-800-310-6550), and MacQueen's, 430 Queen St (☎368-2453), rent out all the necessary gear and sell the comprehensive *PEI Cycling Guide* ($15).

Queens County

The north shore's **Prince Edward Island National Park**, some 40km from end to end and mostly no more than one or two hundred metres wide, is **Queens County's** – if not the island's – main attraction, its gorgeous sandy beaches drawing thousands of visitors every summer. It's an ideal place to swim and sunbathe, especially as the beaches are protected by a sliver of low red cliff and marram-covered sand dune, a barrier that is only interrupted by slender inlets connecting the ocean with a quartet of chubby little bays. A narrow road runs behind the shoreline spanning these inlets, with the exception of the widest, the main channel into Rustico Bay, which divides the park into two. The smaller, more westerly portion runs from Cavendish – the site of Green Gables House – to North Rustico Harbour; the other (and more enjoyable section) from Rustico Island to Dalvay. In either section, it's easy enough to drive along behind the beach until you find a place to your liking.

There's a seasonal **visitors' centre** or **information kiosk** at every entrance to the park and from June to August they levy an entrance fee of $3 per adult per day. On arrival, you're issued with a free and comprehensive guide and out of season this is available at the park's headquarters in Dalvay (Mon–Fri 8.15am–4.30pm; ☎672-6350). The park has eight short **hiking trails**, easy strolls that take in different aspects of the coast from its tidal marshes and farmland through to its woodlands. The most strenuous is the five-kilometre-long Woodlands Trail, up through a red pine plantation near Dalvay. It doesn't take long to cycle to the park from Charlottetown and **bicycle hire** is available amongst the many tourist facilities on the park's peripheries.

The park has three **campgrounds**. The largest is the well-equipped *Cavendish* (early June to late Sept), where there's a supervised sandy beach that's great for swimming. The *Stanhope* (mid-June to Aug), a short walk from the beach in the eastern section, is similarly well equipped and appointed, while *Rustico Island* (early July to mid-Aug) occupies a more remote location, a lovely spot amongst the wooded dunes beside Rustico Bay. Most sites are allocated on a first-come, first-served basis, but some can be reserved (☎1-800-213-7275).

The fastest route from Charlottetown to the eastern section of the park is the half-hour thump along Hwy 15, which branches off Hwy 2 on the north side of town. This takes you past long ranks of chalet-style second homes and, as you approach the park entrance, the delightful *Dunes Studio Gallery and Café*, a combined pottery shop, art gallery and restaurant that serves mouthwatering and reasonably priced snacks and meals from an imaginative menu of seafood and vegetarian dishes. Close by are all sorts of resorts and cottages – one of the best is the rustic *Shaw's Hotel and Cottages* (☎672-2022; ③; for full board; June–Sept), whose chalets, cottages and guest rooms are just off Hwy 15, about ten minutes' walk from the park; *Shaw's* also does **bike rental**.

Inside the park, at the end of Hwy 15, you turn left along the seashore for the causeway over to **Rustico Island** and right for **Stanhope beach**, the setting for a string of seaside cottage-motel resorts. These include *Del-Mar Cottages* (☎883-1290 or 1-800-699-2582; ③ for up to 4 people; late May to Sept) and *Surf Cottages* (☎672-2233; ③ for up to 4; June to mid-Sept). Just 6km further east, at the end of the beach road, is **Dalvay**, whose most conspicuous asset is the high-gabled *Dalvay-by-the-Sea Hotel* (☎672-2048; ⑥ including breakfast and dinner; early June to Sept), a Victorian mansion with a magnificent wraparound veranda and wood-panelled and -balconied foyer.

New Glasgow

The forty-kilometre journey from Charlottetown to the western portion of the National Park at Cavendish covers some of PEI's prettiest scenery – take Hwy 2 west from the capital and turn north along Hwy 13. This country road wends over hill and dale, passing brightly painted timber homesteads before threading through the tiny settlement of **NEW GLASGOW**, whose matching pair of black and white clapboard churches sit on opposite sides of an arm of Rustico Bay. In the centre of the village, the Prince Edward Island Preserve Company is a great place to buy local jams, mustards and maple syrups, and the attached coffee bar has superb breakfasts and evening meals – try the Atlantic salmon. There are **lobster suppers** available in the village, too, at *New Glasgow Lobster Suppers*, on Hwy 258 (June to early Oct daily 4–8.30pm; reservations ☎964-2870), though those at **Saint Ann's Church**, in the hamlet of the same name, about 5km west of New Glasgow along Hwy 224, are generally considered better (June–Oct Mon–Sat 4–9pm; reservations ☎621-0635); at both, reckon a 450-gramme lobster in its shell will set you back between $20 and $25.

From New Glasgow, Hwy 13 cuts a straight course to the coast at Cavendish.

Cavendish

Clumped around the junction of Hwys 6 and 13, the inconsequential hamlet of **CAVENDISH** is not much more than a stone's throw from long sandy beaches, but the busloads of visitors who descend on the place are mostly headed for **Green Gables House** (daily: mid-May to late June, Sept & Oct 9am–5pm; late June to Aug 9am–8pm; $2.50), situated in a little dell just 500m from the crossroads. Part of a tourist complex, with a gift shop and visitors' centre, the two-storey wooden farmhouse that pulls in the crowds was once occupied by the cousins of Lucy Maud Montgomery, one of Canada's best-selling authors. In 1876, when Montgomery was just two years old, her mother died and her father migrated to Saskatchewan, leaving her in the care of her grandparents in Cavendish. Here she developed a deep love for her native island and its people and, although she spent the last half of her life in Ontario, PEI remained the main inspiration for her work. Completed in 1905 and published three years later, *Anne of Green Gables* was her most popular book, a tear-jerking tale of a red-haired, pigtailed orphan girl that Mark Twain dubbed "the sweetest creation of child life ever written". The mildly diverting period bedrooms and living rooms – supposedly the setting for *Anne* – are worth a quick look, though you may think twice when you see the crowded car park. Surprisingly, many of the tourists are Japanese – the book has been on school curriculums there since the 1950s and remains extremely popular. If you decide to **stay** in Cavendish, go for the *Anne Shirley Motel and Cottages* (☎963-2224 or 1-800-561-4266; ③; June–Sept) by the crossroads – where the gas station rents out bikes.

Green Gables House is about 1.5km from the most westerly of the the park's beaches – **Cavendish Beach East** and **West** – and Cavendish campground. From here, the park's coastal byroad travels east, sticking close to the beach and its swelling dunes on the way to the scrawny fishing port of **North Rustico Harbour**, the home of the seasonal *Fisherman's Wharf Restaurant*, (☎963-2669), a good place to sample the island's lobsters. Beyond the harbour, Hwy 6 leaves the park, slipping round the peaceful waters of Rustico Bay on its way to meet Hwy 15 from Charlottetown.

West of Cavendish

West of Cavendish, Hwy 6 passes through the most commercialized part of the island, an unappealing tourist strip stretching as far as New London. Here, Hwy 20 branches north along the coast and you'll soon see signs to PEI's most bizarre sight, the large-scale reproductions of famous British buildings that make up **Woodleigh** (daily: June & Sept to mid-Oct 9am–5pm; July & Aug 9am–7pm; $6.50). Built by a certain Colonel Johnston, who developed an obsessional interest in his ancestral home in Scotland, it features models of such edifices as the Tower of London, York Minster and Anne Hathaway's cottage. Some of the structures are even big enough to enter and their interiors have been painstakingly recreated, right down to the Crown Jewels in the Tower.

South Queens County

The **southern reaches of Queens County** are split into west and east by the deep inlet of Charlottetown harbour. In the west, the **Confederation Bridge** has become a major attraction in its own right and the tourist facilities of the adjoining Gateway Village take a stab at introducing visitors to the island. Elsewhere, the **Fort Amherst/Port-La-Joye National Historic Site** (late June to Aug daily 10am–6pm; $2.25), on an isolated promontory across the bay from Charlottetown, marks the spot where the Acadians established their island headquarters, Port-La-Joye, in 1720. The British subsequently built Fort Amherst here, but all that survives today is a scattering of grass-covered earthworks. Much more diverting is the old seaport of **VICTORIA**, overlooking the Northumberland Strait. There's nothing remarkable among its unpretentious streets and nineteenth-century timber houses, but it's a pretty spot and a relaxing place to while away a couple of hours. Victoria has a lovely old **hotel**, the *Orient* (☎658-2503; ③; mid-May to mid-Oct), and is also home to the Victoria Playhouse (☎658-2025), where a good range of modern plays and musical evenings are performed during July and August.

Some 30km east of Charlottetown along the Trans-Canada Highway lies the delightfully rustic **Orwell Corner Historic Village** (mid-May to late June Mon–Fri 10am–3pm; late June to Aug Tues–Sun 9am–5pm; Sept to late Oct Tues–Sun 10am–3pm; $3), which was originally settled by Scottish and Irish pioneers in the early nineteenth century, taking its name from Sir Francis Orwell, an English government official. At first, the village prospered as an agricultural centre, but by the 1890s it was undermined by the expansion of Charlottetown and mass emigrations to the mainland. Orwell was finally abandoned in the 1950s, but the historical graveyard and a handful of buildings remained, principally the main farmhouse-cum-post-office-cum-general-store and the church. In recent years, these have been restored and supplemented by replicas of some of the early buildings, like the blacksmith's shop, barns, shingle mill and the school, and the village hosts a wide variety of special events. Close by, the **Sir Andrew Macphail Homestead** (June & Sept Tues–Sun 10am–5pm; July–Aug Tues 10am–5pm, Wed–Sun 10am–8pm; donation) holds the comfortable nineteenth-century house from where MacPhail ran his farm, wrote as a journalist and dabbled in medical research. The period furnishings and fittings have a real sense of Victorian gentility, albeit in what was then backcountry, and the veranda accommodates a pleasant tearoom.

Kings County

Near Orwell Corner Historic Village, **Hwy 210** turns off the Trans-Canada to snake its way east across the rich farmland bordering the Montague River before reaching **Hwy 4**, **Kings County**'s principal north–south road. This leads to PEI's northeast corner, where **SOURIS**, curving round the shore of Colville Bay, has a busy fishing port and harbour with a regular ferry service to the Magdalens (Îles-de-la-Madeleine; see p.285). The docks are a few hundred metres from the town centre, and the stretch of shoreline between the two is the most elegant part of Souris, a sequence of Victorian mansions that includes the excellent *Matthew House Inn*, on Breakwater Street (☎687-3461; ④; mid-May to mid-Oct). Souris's main drag, on the other hand, is a grimy affair edged by cheap and tatty snack bars, its grittiness only partly redeemed by the graceful lines of several older buildings tucked away down the sidestreets.

The **Basin Head Fisheries Museum** (mid- to late June & most of Sept Mon–Fri 10am–3pm; July & Aug daily 10am–7pm; $3), a few minutes' drive up the coast from Souris, has a gorgeous setting, lodged on a headland overlooking sand dunes and a fine sandy beach that's trapped between the sea and a narrow, gurgling stream that runs out from an elongated lagoon. Too isolated and barren for any settlement, Basin Head was never more than a fishermen's outpost, and the museum details the lives of these men with displays of equipment, photographs of boats, and miniature dioramas showing the fishing techniques they employed.

From here, it's possible to drive right round the island's northeast corner along Hwy 16 but, with the possible exception of the mid-nineteenth-century lighthouse at **East Point**, there's nothing much to see.

Prince County

Some 50km west of Charlottetown, Hwy 2 crosses the **Prince County** boundary, from where it's another 10km to **SUMMERSIDE**, PEI's second largest settlement, a sprawling and uninspiring bayside city of fourteen thousand people that was once the island's main port. If you're in town, pop into the curious **International Fox Museum and Hall of Fame**, a couple of blocks from the harbourfront at 286 Fitzroy St (June–Sept Mon–Sat 9am–6pm; free). This traces the history of the island's fox-ranching industry from its beginnings in 1894 to its heyday in the 1920s, when fox-fur collars reached the height of their popularity in the cities of Europe and the States. There are potted biographies of the leading fox-ranchers, some of whom grew extremely rich from the furs of the silver fox, a rare variety of the common red fox, whose pelts reached astronomical values – up to $20,000 each. At one time, indeed, fox pelts became PEI's leading export.

Heading west from Summerside, it's a few minutes' drive along Hwy 2 to Miscouche, where the **Acadian Museum** (mid-June to Aug daily 9.30am–5pm; Sept to mid-June Mon–Fri only; $2.75) is devoted to the island's French-speaking community. Miscouche was the site of the second Acadian Convention in 1884, when the assembled representatives boldly chose their own flag – the French tricolour with a gold star, the *Stella Maris* ("Star of Mary"), inserted onto the blue stripe. The museum's exhibits are, however, rather paltry – a series of modest displays outlining Acadian historical development, from pioneer days and deportation through to today – and it's the interesting fifteen-minute video that (partly) saves the day. There are around 17,000 Acadians on PEI, of whom only 7000 speak French as their first language, a state of linguistic affairs that has made community leaders apprehensive of the future. The museum aims to support the Acadian identity and holds an Acadian Research Centre, complete with a library and extensive archives.

Continuing west, the headland south of the village of **Wellington** is a centre of Acadian settlement, but it doesn't look any different from the surrounding districts until you reach **Mont-Carmel**. This tiny coastal village is dominated by the hulking red-brick mass and mighty spires of the **Église Notre-Dame**, whose fantastically ugly appearance is made bizarre by a series of peculiarly sentimental statues and statuettes dotted around the entrance.

After the church, there's nothing else of any real interest around here, and it's a time-consuming drive north before you leave the flattened farmland of this part of Prince County for the slightly hillier scenery along the west shore of Malpeque Bay. The bay's reedy waters were once fringed by tiny shipbuilding yards and the scant remains of one of them have been conserved as part of the **Green Park Shipbuilding Museum** (early June to Aug daily 9am–5pm; $3), which also incorporates an interpretation centre, focusing on PEI's shipbuilding industry, and the **James Yeo house**. The most successful of the island's shipbuilders, the Canadian Yeos maintained close contacts with their Cornish cousins and the two branches of the family combined to develop a prosperous transatlantic shipping business. Some of the proceeds went on the Yeo House, whose slender gables and mini-tower date from the 1860s. The interior, with its fetching Victorian furnishings and fittings, is a real delight – look out for the beautiful wax fruit in the parlour.

There's no real reason to hang around once you've visited the museum, but there is a bayshore **campground** in the Green Park Provincial Park next door (☎831-2370; late June to Aug), whilst the minuscule village of **Tyne Valley**, 4km away, is home to a pleasant **B&B**, the *Doctor's Inn B&B* (☎831-3057; ②), which occupies a big old house and has just a couple of guest rooms. The owners run the adjoining three-acre organic garden, whose produce is well-known hereabouts, and you can have dinner at the inn providing you make an advance booking.

It's about 70km from Green Park to the southwest corner of the island – follow the signs from Hwy 2 along Hwy 14 – where the remote and windswept **West Point Lighthouse** (daily: early June, Sept & Oct 8am–8pm; mid-June to Aug 8am–9.30pm) contains a small collection of photographs and memorabilia portraying the lives of the lighthouse keepers. Next door, the *West Point Lighthouse Inn* (☎859-3605 or 1-800-764-6854; ③; June–Sept), with its nine en-suite guest rooms, makes the most of a great seaside location, overlooking a long sandy beach. The lighthouse and inn are surrounded by the **Cedar Dunes Provincial Park**, which has a **campground** about 500m down the coast (☎859-8785; late June to Aug).

travel details

Trains

Campbellton to: Halifax (6 weekly; 9hr 30min); Matapédia, Québec (6 weekly; 1hr); Moncton (6 weekly; 4hr); Montréal (6 weekly; 9hr 45min).

Halifax to: Moncton (6 weekly; 4hr 40min); Montréal (6 weekly; 19hr); Truro (6 weekly; 1hr 30min).

Moncton to: Halifax (6 weekly; 4hr 40min); Montréal (6 weekly; 14hr).

Buses

Campbelltown to: Chatham (1 daily; 3hr); Moncton (1 daily; 5hr 30min); Québec City (1 daily; 6hr 30min); Saint John (1 daily; 9hr 30min).

Charlottetown to: Fredericton (2 daily; 7hr); Halifax (2 daily; 7hr); Moncton (2 daily; 3hr); Saint John (2 daily; 5hr 50min); Sydney (1 daily; 13hr).

Edmundston to: Fredericton (2 daily; 3hr); Halifax (2 daily; 9hr 30min); Québec City (3 daily; 5hr 30min); Rivière-du-Loup, Québec (3 daily; 2hr 45min).

Fredericton to: Charlottetown (2 daily; 7hr); Edmundston (2 daily; 3hr); Halifax (2 daily; 6hr); Moncton (2 daily; 2hr); Montréal (2 daily; 12hr); Newcastle (1 daily; 3hr); Saint John (2 daily; 1hr 30min).

Halifax to: Annapolis Royal (1 daily; 3hr 20min); Charlottetown (2 daily; 7hr); Fredericton (2 daily; 6hr); Liverpool (1 daily; 3hr); Lunenburg (1 daily;

1hr 30min); Moncton (3 daily; 3hr 30min-4hr); Montréal (2 daily; 19hr); Sydney (4 daily; 6–7hr); Truro (4 daily; 1hr 30min); Yarmouth, via the Annapolis Valley (1 daily; 5hr 15min), and via the southwest shore (1 daily; 6hr).

Moncton to: Charlottetown (2 daily; 3hr); Fredericton (2 daily; 2hr); Chatham (1 daily; 3hr); Saint John (2 daily; 2hr 45min); Halifax (2 daily; 6hr 45min); Newcastle (1 daily; 5hr); St Andrews (1 daily; 1hr 20min).

Sydney to: Charlottetown (1 daily; 13hr); Halifax (4 daily; 6–7hr); North Sydney (2 daily; 25min).

Yarmouth to: Annapolis Royal (1 daily; 2hr 30min); Chester (1 daily; 4hr); Halifax, via the Annapolis Valley (1 daily; 5hr 15min), and via the southwest shore (1 daily; 6hr); Liverpool (1 daily; 3hr).

Ferries

Cap-aux-Meules, Îles-de-la-Madeleine, to: Souris, PEI (April to mid-June & late Sept 1 daily except Mon; late June to early July & mid-Aug to mid-Sept 1 daily; mid-July to mid-Aug 2 daily; Nov–Jan 3–5 weekly; no ferries in Feb & March; 5hr).

Caribou, Nova Scotia, to: Wood Islands, PEI (June–Nov every 90min, May & early Dec every 3hr; no service from late Dec to April; 1hr 15min). Ferries operate on a first-come, first-served basis, and queues are common in high season.

North Sydney, Nova Scotia, to: Argentia, Newfoundland (late June to early Sept 2–3 weekly; 14hr); Channel-Port-aux-Basques, Newfoundland (June–Oct 1–2 daily; 6hr).

Saint John, New Brunswick, to: Digby, Nova Scotia (Jan to early June & mid-Oct to Dec 1–2 daily; early June to mid-Oct 2–3 daily; 3hr).

Yarmouth to: Bar Harbour, Maine (June to mid-Oct 1 daily; 6hr); Portland, Maine (May to late Oct 1 daily; 11hr).

Flights

Halifax to: Charlottetown (8 daily; 35min); Fredericton (3 daily; 1hr 20min); Montréal (3 daily; 1hr 40min); St John's, Newfoundland (5 daily; 2hr); Toronto (7 daily; 2hr 20min).

Newcastle to: Fredericton (1 daily; 3hr); Saint John (1 daily; 5hr).

Saint John to: Charlottetown (2 daily; 5hr 50min); Fredericton (2 daily; 1hr 30min).

CHAPTER FOUR

NEWFOUNDLAND AND LABRADOR

In 1840 an American clergyman named Robert Lowell described Newfoundland as "a monstrous mass of rock and gravel, almost without soil, like a strange thing from the bottom of the deep, lifted up, suddenly, into sunshine and storm", an apt evocation of this fearsome island, which is still referred to – by Newfoundlanders and mainlanders alike – as "The Rock". Its distant position between the Atlantic Ocean and the Gulf of St Lawrence has fostered a distinctive, inward-looking culture that has been unfairly carica-tured by many Canadians in the stereotype of the dim "Newfie" – a term coined by ser-vicemen based here in World War II. This ridicule can be traced to the poverty of the islanders, the impenetrability of their dialect – an eclectic and versatile mix of Irish and English – and even to their traditional food. Fish and chips, the favourite dish, is reason-able enough in the eyes of most people, but many stomachs churn at stand-bys such as cods' tongues, fried bread dough with molasses ("toutons"), and seal flipper pie.

Isolated from the rest of the country, Newfoundland is also a place of great isolation within its own boundaries. Only in recent years have many of the **outports** – the ancient **fishing settlements** that were home to the first Europeans – been linked by road to the solitary highway, the Trans-Canada, which sweeps 900km from the south-west corner of the island to the **Avalon Peninsula**, where **St John's**, the capital, sits on the northeast shore. Ferries from Nova Scotia touch the southwest and the Avalon, but most visitors fly straight to St John's, the island's only significant town and the obvi-ous place to start a visit, for its museums, its flourishing **folk music** scene and its easy access to the **Witless Bay** sea-bird reserve. Yet there are more delightful spots than this: tiny **Trinity**, on the **Bonavista Peninsula** north of the Avalon isthmus, is easily the most beguiling of the outports; the French-owned archipelago of **St-Pierre et Miquelon** is noted for its restaurants; **Gros Morne National Park**, in the west, fea-tures wondrous mountains and glacier-gouged lakes; and at the far end of the **North-ern Peninsula** you'll find the scant but evocative remains of an eleventh-century Norse colony at **L'Anse aux Meadows**, the only such site in North America.

The definition and control of **Labrador** is the subject of a seemingly interminable dis-pute between Québec and Labrador, a row so intense that a Newfoundland senator, Alexander Baird, was once roused to declare, "We Newfoundland-Canadians don't want to

ACCOMMODATION PRICE CODES

All the accommodation prices in this book have been coded using the symbols below, corresponding to Canadian dollar rates. Prices are for the least expensive double room in each establishment in high season, excluding special offers. For a full explanation, see p.38 in Basics.

① up to $40	③ $60–80	⑤ $100–125	⑦ $175–240
② $40–60	④ $80–100	⑥ $125–175	⑧ $240+

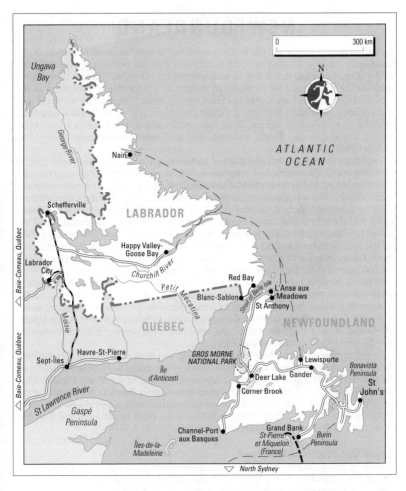

fight, but, by jingo, if we have to, then I say we have the ships, the money and the men", to which Québecois senator Maurice Bourget added sneeringly – "and the fish". The major point of contention was the establishment of the massive **Churchill Falls** hydro-electric project, whose completion was a boost to the Newfoundland-Labrador economy, yet despite the last few years of industrial development and the construction of a few incongruous planned towns, Labrador remains a scarcely explored wilderness, boasting some of Canada's highest mountains, wonderful fjords, crashing rivers, a spectacular shoreline with minuscule coastal settlements, and a forested hinterland teeming with wildlife. A trip to Labrador is not something to be undertaken lightly, but its intimidating landscapes are the nearest thing eastern Canada can offer to the challenge of the deep north.

The Newfoundland and Labrador telephone code is ☎709.

NEWFOUNDLAND

The inhospitable interior and the fertile ocean kept the first European settlers on **Newfoundland** – most of English and Irish extraction – glued to the coast when they founded the outports during the sixteenth and seventeenth centuries. Though they hunted **seals** on the winter pack ice for meat, oil and fur, they were chiefly dependent on the codfish of the **Grand Banks**, whose shallow waters, concentrated to the south and east of the island, constituted the richest fishing grounds in the world. It was a singularly harsh life, prey to vicious storms, dense fogs and the whims of the barter system operated by the island's merchants, who exercised total control of the trade price of fish until the 1940s in some areas.

To combat the consequent **emigration**, various populist premiers have attempted to widen the island's economic base, sometimes with laughable ineptitude – as in the case of a proposed rubber factory, sited ludicrously far from the source of its raw materials. Furthermore, efforts to conserve the fisheries, primarily by extending Canada's territorial waters to two hundred nautical miles in 1977, have failed to reverse the downward spiral, and the overfished Grand Banks are unable to provide a livelihood for all the reliant Newfoundlanders. The federal government in Ottawa spent $39 million bailing out the Atlantic fishery in 1992 alone, but there is one bright spot – profits from the offshore Hibernia gas and oilfield, which was completed in 1997 and produces about 125,000 barrels of oil daily, have slowly begun to transform the economy.

Home to lively **St John's** and a sprawl of ribbon villages, the **Avalon Peninsula** is easily the most populated portion of Newfoundland, but here, as elsewhere, it's the rocky, craggy coast that makes a lasting impression – no less than 10,000km of island shoreline, dotted with the occasional higgledy-piggledy fishing village of which **Trinity** and **Grand Bank** are the most diverting, especially if the weather holds: even in summer, Newfoundland can be wet and foggy.

To get anything like the best from this terrain you need a car, for Newfoundland's **public transport** is thin on the ground. There are no trains and only one daily long-distance **bus**, DRL Coachlines, which travels the length of the Trans-Canada. Elsewhere, Viking Express runs a limited service from Corner Brook to St Anthony, at the top of the Northern Peninsula, and a number of **minibus** companies connect St John's with various destinations, principally Argentia for the Nova Scotia ferry and **Fortune** for the boat to **St-Pierre et Miquelon**.

A brief history of Newfoundland

Numerous Europeans may have seen the island before him, but it was **John Cabot**, sailing from Bristol for Henry VII in 1497, who stirred a general interest in Newfoundland when he reported back that "the sea is swarming with fish, which can be taken not only with the net, but in baskets let down with a stone". This was the effective start of the **migratory ship fishery**, with boats sailing out from France and England in the spring and returning in the fall, an industry that was soon dominated by the merchants of the English West Country, who grew fat on the profits.

In the early 1700s the English fishery began to change its modus operandi, moving towards an offshore **bank fishery** based in the harbours of the eastern coast. This encouraged greater permanent settlement, with the British concentrated in **St John's** and the French around **Placentia**, their main fishing station since the 1660s. Mirroring the wars of Europe, these rival nationalities fought a series of desultory campaigns until the **Treaty of Utrecht** in 1713, when France gave up her claims to the island in return for the right to catch, land and dry fish on the northwest coast, the so-called **French Shore** – an arrangement that lasted until 1904. In 1763 the French also swapped Labrador for St-Pierre et Miquelon.

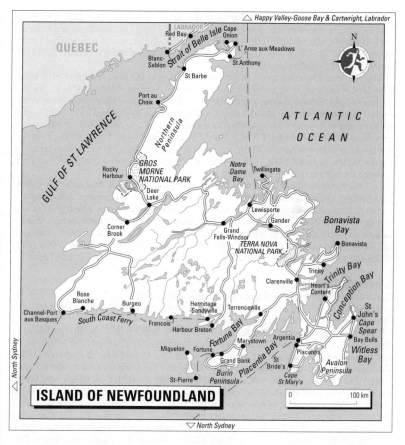

△ Happy Valley-Goose Bay & Cartwright, Labrador

ISLAND OF NEWFOUNDLAND

0   100 km

▽ North Sydney

Meanwhile, in 1729 the British government had introduced a bizarre system, whereby the commanders of the naval convoy accompanying the fishing fleet became the temporary **governors** of Newfoundland, even though they returned home in the fall. Largely left to their own devices, the English and Irish settlers, who numbered about thirty thousand by 1790, spread out along the coasts, massacring the native **Beothuks** who, by 1829, had completely died out. A permanent governor was eventually appointed in 1817; the island was recognized as a colony in 1824; and representative, ultimately **responsible government** followed shortly after.

Struggling through a period of sectarian violence, Protestant English against Irish Catholic, Newfoundlanders decided not to join newly formed Canada in the 1860s, opting instead for self-governing **dominion** status. However, by the 1910s class conflict had replaced religious tension as the dominant theme of island life, reflecting the centralization of the economy in the hands of the bourgeoisie of St John's – a process that impoverished the outports and fuelled the growth of the trade unions. The biggest of these, the **Fishermen's Protective Union**, launched a string of hard-fought campaigns that greatly improved the working conditions of the deep-sea fishermen and sealers. Newfoundland's export-orientated economy collapsed during the Great

Depression of the 1930s, and the bankrupt dominion turned to Great Britain for help. The legislative chamber was suspended and replaced by a London-appointed commission. However, almost before they could start work, the economy was revived by the boom created by World War II, which also saw Newfoundland garrisoned by 16,000 American and Canadian servicemen.

Though a narrow majority voted for **confederation** in the referendum of 1949, many islanders remain at least suspicious of the rest of Canada, blaming Ottawa for the decline of the fishing industry and the high levels of unemployment. Many more regard Québec's claims to distinct status with a mix of contempt and incredulity – after all, they argue, no one's as distinctive as themselves and anyway it's their fellow fishermen on St-Pierre et Miquelon who should be respected as proper "Parisian French", not the charlatan Québecois. These sentiments underlie the assertive stance taken by **Clyde Wells**, premier from 1989 to 1996, in the constitutional wranglings that have become a constant feature of Canadian politics.

In 1997 Newfoundland celebrated the 500th anniversary of its **discovery** by Cabot, who landed at Cape Bonavista, and – in an effort to boost the **tourist economy** – a series of festivals and special events was held throughout the year. The highlight was the landing, in Bonavista, of a replica of Cabot's ship, the *Matthew*, complete with sailors and deckhands in late fifteenth-century dress. The ship then travelled around the island and to Labrador, beginning at Bonavista and stopping at sixteen other ports on its course, at each place re-enacting Cabot's landing on the "New Founde Lande".

Getting to Newfoundland

There are regular domestic **flights** to St John's from all of Canada's major cities and frequent services onward across the island to several smaller settlements; most usefully Deer Lake, for Gros Morne National Park.

Marine Atlantic operates two **ferries** from North Sydney, on Cape Breton Island in Nova Scotia. One goes to **Channel-Port aux Basques**, 900km west of St John's (early Jan to mid-Jan 1–2 daily except Mon & Tues; mid-Jan to mid-June & mid-Sept to Dec 1–2 daily; mid-June to mid-Sept 1–3 daily; 5–7hr; $19 per person one way, $59 for cars, cabins $42–90; reservations ☎902/794-5700), from where DRL Coachlines **bus** leaves for St John's (1 daily at 8am; 13hr 55min; $90). The other serves **Argentia** (mid-June to Aug 3 weekly; early Sept to mid-Sept 2 weekly; 14hr; $52.50 per person one way, $118 for cars, cabins $100–125; reservations ☎902/794-5700), on the Avalon Peninsula 131km southwest of St John's, where Newhook's **minibuses** connect with the capital, a two-hour drive away, for $17. A third Marine Atlantic ferry connects Goose Bay, Labrador, with **Lewisporte** (mid-June to early Sept 2 weekly; 38hr; $97 per person one way, $160 for cars, cabins $37.50–150; arrivals and departures ☎709/896-0137, reservations ☎1-800-341-7981). If you're telephoning from the USA, there's a toll-free reservation line for all three ferries (☎1-800-341-7981).

St John's and around

For centuries, life in **ST JOHN'S** has focused on the harbour. In its heyday it was crammed with ships from a score of nations, but today – although its population is about 105,000 – it's a shadow of its former self, with just the odd oil tanker or trawler creeping through the 200-metre-wide channel of The Narrows into the jaw-shaped inlet. Once a rumbustious port, it's become a far more subdued place, the rough houses of the waterfront mostly replaced by shops and offices, its economy dominated by white-

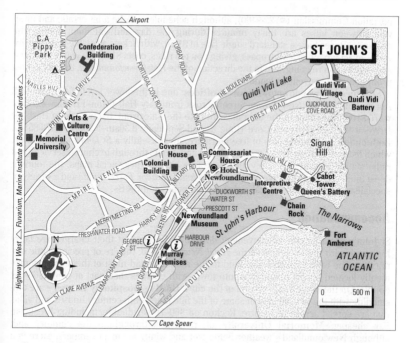

collar workers who are concentrated in a string of downtown skyscrapers and in the Confederation Building, the huge government complex on the western outskirts.

Yet although the city's centre of gravity has begun to move west, the waterfront remains the social centre, home of lively bars that feature the pick of Newfoundland **folk music** – the best single reason for visiting. Almost all of the older buildings were destroyed by fire in the nineteenth century or demolished in the twentieth, so although St John's looks splendid from the water, with tier upon tier of pastel-painted houses rising from the harbour, there are not a lot of major sights, with the notable exception of the grand **basilica**, and the **Newfoundland Museum**, which provides an excellent introduction to the history of the island and its people. Elsewhere, **Signal Hill National Historic Site**, overlooking The Narrows, has great views back over the city and out across the Atlantic, while the drive out to the rugged shoreline of **Cape Spear**, the continent's most easterly point, makes for a pleasant excursion, as does the trip to the **Witless Bay Ecological Reserve**.

Arrival and information

St John's **airport** is about 6km northwest of the city centre and there's a seasonal **tourist information desk** inside (May to Oct Mon–Sat 9am–midnight, Sun 10am–midnight; ☎772-0011). There's no public transport from the airport to the centre, and **taxis** charge around $14; should there not be a taxi in sight when you arrive, use the direct free phone to Co-op Taxi in the arrivals concourse. Oddly enough, for a city of its size, St John's has no **bus station**. Travellers come into the city from towns along the Trans-Canada with DRL Coachlines and are dropped off at either the airport or at Memorial University (see "Listings", p.397). From the university you can take bus #3 to the city centre. To get around the city itself, you'll use the **Metrobus**, run by St John's Transportation Commission (☎722-9400), although schedules can be a bit erratic and intervals between buses are thirty minutes during the day and one hour during the evenings. Buses have a standard single fare of $1.50, with tickets available from the drivers – exact fare only; a Metropass, giving you ten rides, costs $12.50. If you're not quite sure where you're going, aim in the direction of the *Hotel Newfoundland*, the city's most prominent and convenient landmark.

St John's has two downtown **tourist offices**: one in the lower level of the City Hall Annex building, on New Gower Street across from City Hall (Mon–Fri 9am–4.30pm; ☎576-8106), the other in the old railcar next to the waterfront, halfway along Harbour Drive at the foot of Ayre's Cove (June to mid-Sept daily 8.30am–5.30pm; ☎576-8514). Both outlets have bucketfuls of free literature, most usefully a *St John's Visitor Guide*, which lists everything from accommodation and events through to church services and radio station frequencies. They also have free city and provincial maps, the tourism department's comprehensive *Newfoundland and Labrador Travel Guide* and a variety of specialist leaflets detailing local sights, guesthouses and B&Bs.

Accommodation

St John's has a handful of convenient downtown **hotels**, but their charges are fairly high and, with the exception of the *Hotel Newfoundland*, they're of precious little distinction. The town's **motels** also tend to the mundane and most of them are inconveniently located on the main roads into town, with charges that start at about $60 per double. On the other hand, several of the city's **B&Bs – hospitality homes –** are outstanding with the best located in some of the fine nineteenth-century houses and villas that are spread across the centre. Reckon on $60–70 per double, including breakfast. Far cheaper, **Memorial University** offers rooms throughout the summer and, although Newfoundland's weather is too wet and windy for most campers, there is a city **campground**.

Hotels

Delta St John's Hotel, 120 New Gower St (☎739-6404 or 1-800-268-1133, fax 570-1622). Luxurious downtown tower block with over 250 rooms, a swimming pool, whirlpool, saunas and gym. ⑥.

Hotel Newfoundland, Cavendish Square (☎726-4980 or 1-800-441-1414, fax 726-2025). Convenient location near the northern end of Water Street. Grand and slightly stuffy, but most of the three hundred rooms have great views over the harbour and to Signal Hill; swimming pool, sauna and whirlpool; two restaurants. Weekend and off-season discounts of up to thirty percent. ⑥.

Quality Hotel by Journey's End, 2 Hill O'Chips (☎754-7788 or 1-800-228-5151, fax 754-5209). Standard-issue, modern hotel overlooking the waterfront at the north end of Water Street. ④–⑤.

Motels

Best Western Travellers Inn, 199 Kenmount Rd (☎722-5540 or 1-800-261-5540, fax 722-1025). About 5km southwest of the centre, along the Trans-Canada Highway. Comfortable singles and doubles; pool, dining room and cocktail lounge. ④.

Center City Motel, 389 Elizabeth Ave (☎726-0092, fax 726-5921). Three kilometres west of the centre; basic and a bit tatty. ②–③.

1st City Motel, 479 Kenmount Rd (☎722-5400, fax 722-1030). Reasonably priced motel with about thirty rooms, 6km from the city centre. ②–③.

Bed and Breakfasts

Avalon House, 22 Holloway St (☎ & fax 579-4393). In a lovely Victorian home, with views of the harbour. All rooms are non-smoking and with private bath and shower. ②–③.

Bird Island Guest Home, 150 Topsail Rd (☎753-4850 or 722-1675, fax 753-3140). In a semi-detached former railway company house. Two rooms attractively furnished with hardwood floors and antiques. O'Brien's Whale and Bird Tours (see p.398) have their offices here. From the city cen-

<hr>

SIGHTSEEING TOURS

Several tour companies operate in the city, but the best land-based sightseeing tours of St John's and its environs are by McCarthy's Party Tours, Topsail, Conception Bay (May to early Sept daily; ☎781-2244, 781-2266 or 1-888-660-6060). They charge $25 for a three-hour trip that includes all the main sights, but it's the historical gossip that makes it worth the money. They also do tours to Cape Spear and Petty Harbour ($25), plus other excursions, including ones to Bay Bulls and Conception Bay ($35–50). There's also one particularly good boat trip organized by Adventure Tours, on the *Scademia* (May–Oct daily 10am, 1pm, 4pm & 7pm; 2hr–2hr 30min; $30; ☎726-5000 or 1-800-77-WHALE), a refurbished two-masted schooner that sails to Cape Spear and offers a chance to see some whales and icebergs; it leaves from Harbour Drive, just near the railcar tourist information booth. Similar and slightly cheaper sea trips are organized by J&B Schooner Tours, departing from the waterfront at Pier 6 (mid-May to mid-Oct daily 9am, noon, 3pm & 6pm, 2hr, $28.75; 9pm moonlight cruise with live entertainment, 1hr, $15; ☎753-7245).

There are also several walking tours that give you a feel for the city's historic past. St John's Historic Walking Tours (Mon, Tues, Thurs & Fri 11am & 2pm; 1hr 30min; $20; ☎738-3781) organizes a thorough walk around the city, including diversions down lanes and back alleys; departure point is *Le Petit Paris Restaurant*, 73 Duckworth St. Legend Tours (☎753-1497) does a Signal Hill Walk (daily 2pm; 2hr 30min; $25) and a tour of historic locations in the city centre (daily 9.30am, 1.30pm & 4.30pm; 2hr 30min–3hr; $25). A self-guided Women's History Walking Tour (2hr), beginning at Cavendish Square, covers the homes and workplaces of several eighteenth- to twentieth-century St John's women who have contributed to the history of the city and Newfoundland. There's also a highly recommended Haunted St John's Tour (Aug Tues & Thurs 9.30pm; $5), departing from the west entrance of the Anglican cathedral, Cathedral Street; the local historian points out the scenes of murders and ghost sightings, accompanied by dramatic readings and re-enactments.

If your feet are sore, you can take a ride through the city in a horse-drawn coach, driven by a coachman in eighteenth-century dress (daily 10am–midnight; 30min for $30, 1hr for $50; ☎738-6999), departing from beside the *Hotel Newfoundland* or from Kilometre 0 beside City Hall. (Kilometre 0 is where the Trans-Canada begins its long trek across the country.) Double-decker buses also take people around the city centre and to outlying areas such as Quidi Vidi Village (daily 9.30am & 1.30pm; 3hr; $20; ☎738-8687) buses depart from the Newfoundland Museum on Duckworth Street, the *Delta St John's Hotel* on New Gower Street or the *Holiday Inn* on Portugal Cove Road (free pickup at other hotels and some B&Bs).

<hr>

tre, take bus #5 along Topsail Road and Craigmiller Avenue and then walk down the steep gravel path across from the church. ②.

Bonne Esperance, 20 Gower St (☎726-3835, fax 739-0496). Attractive and central Victorian mansion, built by a fishing captain; serves huge breakfasts. ③.

Compton House, 26 Waterford Bridge Rd (☎739-5789). Delightful old home surrounded by an English garden. Five doubles, plus six en-suites with fireplaces and whirlpools. About 2km south of the centre, straight along Water Street. ③–⑤.

Gower House, 180 Gower St (☎754-0047 or 1-800-563-3959, fax 754-0047). Central B&B in a terraced row; four comfortable rooms, all with private bath. ④.

Monkstown Manor, 51 Monkstown Rd (☎754-7324, fax 722-8557). Two large, attractive rooms filled with photos and memorabilia of musician Rufus Guinchard (see box on p.399) and Newfoundland writer Ted Russell. Jacuzzi, garden and patio; also two housekeeping units next door. ②–③.

Oh What a View, 184 Signal Hill Rd (☎576-7063). Four comfortable rooms, en suite and shared-bath, in a modern home, with possibly the best views of the city and harbour. Open mid-May to mid-Oct only. ③.

Prescott Inn, 19 Military Rd (☎753-7733, fax 753-6036). Relaxed and easy-going B&B; very popular and friendly, with comfortable and spacious doubles; gourmet breakfasts; cable TV in all rooms; private bath or shower. Highly recommended ③–④.

The Roses, 9 Military Rd (☎726-3336, fax 726-3483). Another old house converted into a four-bedroom B&B, with a convenient location near downtown. Breakfast served in the balconied rooftop kitchen, which has harbour views. ③.

Winterholme Heritage Inn, 79 Rennie's Mill Rd (☎739-7979 or 1-800-599-7829, fax 753-9411). Seven en-suite rooms, four with Jacuzzis, fireplaces and king-sized beds. In a 1905 Queen Anne mansion, declared a National Historic Site. More like a luxury resort than a B&B. ④–⑥.

Hostel and college rooms

Catherine Booth House Travellers' Hostel, 18 Springdale St (☎738-2804). On the southern edge of downtown; a Salvation Army hostel, with spartan singles and doubles. ①.

Memorial University of Newfoundland, off Elizabeth Avenue (☎737-7590). Pleasant basic rooms 3km west of the centre. Discount for students; reservations advised. Mid-May to mid-Aug. ②.

Campground

C.A. Pippy Park Trailer Park and Campground, in C.A. Pippy Park (☎737-3669). About 4km west of the city centre, near the Confederation Building; turn off Elizabeth Avenue at Allandale Road, then turn left along Nagle's Place. May–Sept daily 7am–10pm. Unserviced sites $14, serviced $19.35, tents $8.60.

The City

Running the length of the town centre, **Water Street** has long been the commercial hub of St John's, though the higgledy-piggledy storefronts of the chandlers and tanners, ship

---

SEALING

The Newfoundland seal hunt has always been dependent on the **harp seal**, a gregarious animal that spends the summer feeding around the shores of Greenland, Baffin Island and northern Hudson Bay. In the fall they gather in a gigantic herd that surges south ahead of the arctic ice pack, passing the coast of eastern Labrador before dividing into two – one group pushing down the Strait of Belle Isle into the Gulf of St Lawrence to form the **Gulf herd**, the other continuing south as far as Newfoundland's northeast coast, where they congregate as the **Front herd**. From the end of February to early March, the seals of the Front herd start to breed, littering the ice with thousands of helpless baby seals or **whitecoats**, as they're known. It's just two or three weeks before the pups begin to moult and their coats turn a shabby white and grey.

From early days, the Front herd provided the people of northeast Newfoundland with fresh meat during the winter, but it was the value of the whitecoats' fur that spawned a clutch of hunting centres – such as Bonavista, Trinity and Twillingate – and thousands of jobs: in 1853, the seal fleet consisted of 4000 ships manned by 15,000 sailors, who combined to kill no fewer than 685,000 harps. However, in the 1860s **steamers** made the old sailing ships obsolete and provoked a drastic restructuring of the industry. The new vessels were too expensive for the shipowners of the smaller ports and control of the fleet fell into the hands of the wealthy traders of St John's. By 1870, the bulk of the fleet was based in the capital and hundreds of Newfoundlanders were obliged to travel here for work every winter.

For those "lucky" enough to get a berth, conditions on board were appalling: as a government report noted, a captain could "take as many men as he could squeeze onto his ship. . . When the seal pelts began to come aboard, the crew had to make way until, by the end of a successful voyage, the men would be sleeping all over the deck, or amongst the skins piled on the deck, even in the most savage weather conditions." All this hardship was endured on a basic diet of "hardtack", hard bread or ship's biscuit, and "switchel", black unsweetened tea, enlivened by the odd plate of "duff", a boiled-up mixture of old flour and water. "Small wonder", as one of the sealers – or **swilers** – recalled, that "most of us learned to eat raw seal meat. The heart, when it was cut out and still

suppliers and fish merchants have mostly been replaced by a series of ill-considered redevelopments. In the architectural gloom, look out for the odd elegant stone and brick facade or take a peek at the old **courthouse**, a monumental Romanesque Revival building of 1904 that overlooks the harbour from Water Street at Baird's Cove.

The Newfoundland Museum to Murray Premises

It's the briefest of walks up the hill from the courthouse to the rather small **Newfoundland Museum** (June–Aug Mon–Wed & Fri–Sun 10am–6pm, Thurs 10am–9pm; Sept–May Tues, Wed & Fri 9am–5pm, Thurs 9am–9pm, Sat & Sun 10am–6pm; free), housed in a sturdy stone edifice on Duckworth Street at Cathedral Street. Here, the second floor is devoted to the prehistoric peoples of Newfoundland and Labrador, beginning with the few bits and bobs that are the sole traces of the Maritime Archaic Indians and their successors, the Dorset Eskimos. This is pretty dull stuff, but the series of displays on the **Beothuks** are more diverting. These Algonquian-speaking people reached Newfoundland in about 200 AD and were semi-nomadic, spending the summer on the coast catching fish, seals and sea birds, and moving inland during the winter to hunt caribou, beaver and otter. They were also the first North American natives to be contacted by British explorers, who came to describe them as **Red Indians** – from their habit of covering themselves with red ochre, perhaps as some sort of fertility ritual. (The term then came to apply to all Indian groups.) The initial contacts between the two cultures were quite cordial, but the whites soon began to encroach on the ancient hunting grounds, pushing the natives inland; their tactics were summarized

---

warm, was as good as steak to we fellows." There were two compensations: money and status – as it left for the Front the seal fleet was cheered on its way and the men of the first ship back, the **highliner**, dispensed seal flippers, an island delicacy, and got free drinks all round.

In the early 1900s, the wooden-walled steamships were, in their turn, replaced by **steel steamers**. Once again, the traders of St John's invested heavily, but the shrinking seal population reduced their profit margins. Increasingly, they began to cut corners, which threatened the safety of the swilers. The inevitable result was a string of disasters that culminated in 1914 in the loss of the *Southern Cross* with all 173 hands. Shortly afterwards, a further 78 men from the *Newfoundland* died on the ice as a consequence of the reckless greed of one of the captains. These twin catastrophes destroyed the hunt's communal popularity, and a decade later the economics of the industry collapsed during the Great Depression. By 1935 most of the sealing firms of St John's had gone broke.

After World War II sealing was dominated by the ships of Norway and Nova Scotia, with the Newfoundlanders largely confining their activities to an inshore cull of between 20,000 and 40,000 whitecoats per year – enough work for about four thousand people. Thus, sealing remained an important part of the island's bedraggled economy up until the 1960s, when various conservationist groups, spearheaded by **Greenpeace**, started a campaign to have it stopped. Slowly but surely, the pressure built up on the Canadian government until it banned all the larger sealing ships and closely restricted the number of seals the islanders were allowed to kill. This remains the position today.

The **conservationists** have always objected to the cruelty of the cull and it's certainly true that the killing of a hapless whitecoat is a brutal act. Yet the furore has much to do with the doleful eyes and cuddly body of the baby seal, an anthropomorphism that doesn't wash with an island people whose way of life has been built on the killing of animals, and who are convinced that the increasing number of seals has damaged the fisheries. Nothing angers many Newfoundlanders more than the very mention of Greenpeace, whose supporters are caricatured as well-heeled, urban outsiders who have no right to meddle in their traditional hunting practices.

by Joseph Banks, a contemporary observer: "the English fire at the Indians whenever they meet them, and if they happen to find their houses or wigwams, they plunder them immediately". The last of the tribe, a young woman by the name of **Shanadithit**, died at age 29 of tuberculosis in 1829. She had spent the last years of her life in the protective custody of the attorney general in St John's, and it was here that she built a small model of a Beothuk canoe and made ten simple drawings of her people and their customs. Copies of the drawings are on display in the museum, a modest memorial to a much-abused people.

Below, the first floor accommodates a **Natural History** collection, where there are models of the fauna of Newfoundland and Labrador, including rare and extinct species; there's also a cliff-top diorama showing the various sea birds that breed and nest along the shores of the province. The third floor houses displays dealing with the daily life of the **fishermen**, including a reconstruction of a "stage" (a wharf building used for gutting, cleaning and salting cod), and a "store" (a workshop shed where fishermen made boats, furniture and barrels). Another section on this floor shows various **Newfoundland furnishings** and fittings, as part of a display recalling the kitchen and parlour of a house in a remote outport village around 1900. Many of the outports remained beyond the cash economy right up until the 1940s, and consequently much of their furniture was made from packing cases and driftwood. The kitchen furniture was painted in bright, primary colours, as seen in the blue balsam-fir sideboard loaded with crockery, but much of the rest was stained dark brown to imitate a decorative graining; this is especially noticeable in the furniture of the rather sombre parlour, whose walls are lined with stitched samplers in frames. Also on the third floor is a small stage where free **performances** of folk and Irish music are held year-round.

As you walk south along Duckworth Street from the museum, the next major building on the left is the imposing 1904 **courthouse**. Duckworth Street veers left down steep McBride's Hill, flanked by murals, and merges with Water Street, where, after a five-minute walk, you'll come to the **Murray Premises**, sandwiched between Water Street and Harbour Drive. The building was formerly an 1840s warehouse that luckily survived the fire of 1892 that destroyed much of St John's; in 1979 it was renovated to house restaurants and shops, and bits of the original brick and timber walls have been sensitively incorporated into the reconstruction.

Military Road

Military Road and adjacent **Kings Bridge Road** boast St John's finest old buildings, a handful of elegant structures beginning near the *Hotel Newfoundland* with the clapboard and elongated chimneys of the **Commissariat House** (1818–20) on Kings Bridge Road (mid-June to mid-Oct daily 10am–5.30pm; free), whose interior has been restored to its appearance circa 1830. Costumed staff provide entertaining guided tours of the building, which was the home and offices of the assistant commisariat general, in charge of supplying the British military with their non-military goods. The most intriguing room is the clerk's office, into which the soldiers entered by a side door to collect their wages. Upstairs, the small sewing room has two tiny paintings by Turner. At the back of the house is a coach house, housing an 1830s coach and an interpretive display. Close by, the trim black and white painted clapboard of the Anglican **Church of St Thomas** (1836) completes the ensemble (guided tours late June to Aug Mon–Sat 2.30pm, Sun 10.30am; 2hr; free).

Continuing along Military Road, it's a couple of minutes' walk to the impressively stylish Palladian-influenced **Government House** (1827–31), the governor's residence until 1949 (grounds open only; for tours of the house, call ☎729-4494). Just across Bannerman Road from Government House, the imperial pomposity of the **Colonial Building** (1846–50), fronted by a large portico of Ionic columns (Mon–Fri 9am–4.15pm, also Wed 6.30–9.45pm; first Tues of each month 2–4.15pm only; free), once housed the provincial assembly and now contains the island's historical archives. From here, it's a further five minutes along Military Road to the grandest of the town's churches, the mid-nineteenth-century Catholic **Basilica of St John the Baptist** (Mon–Fri 8am–4.30pm, Wed until 8pm, Sat 8am–6.30pm, Sun 8.30am–12.30pm), whose twin-towered limestone and granite mass overlooks the harbour from the crest of a hill. The Basilica is fronted by a magnificently unsuccessful entry arch placed much too far in front of the building, but otherwise it's a reasonable attempt to mimic the Romanesque churches of Italy. It's at its best inside, where the crudely coloured stained glass illuminates a delightfully ornate maroon and deep green ceiling. Guided tours are available from mid-June to August (Mon–Sat 10am–5pm; $15). The **cemetery** alongside the Basilica has headstones dating from the eighteenth century, and the grey-stone **museum** to the church's left has a small but splendid collection of sacred objects (Mon–Sat 10.30am–4.30pm, Sun 11.30am–4pm; $2).

From the Basilica it takes about ten minutes to walk back down the hill to Water Street, passing the Anglican **Cathedral of St John the Baptist**, designed in Gothic Revival style by the English architect Sir George Gilbert Scott. Begun in 1847, much of it burnt down in 1892 but was rebuilt to his plans by his son. The lofty interior is an impressive sight, with wooden ceilings and an array of stained glass of exceptionally high quality. Tours are given by knowledgeable guides (June–Aug Mon–Wed & Fri 10am–5pm, Thurs & Sat 10.30am–5pm, Sun 12.30–4pm; free), and there's a tearoom in the crypt (June–Aug Mon–Fri 2.30–4.30pm). The streets in the vicinity of the two churches constitute the oldest residential part of town, with rows of simple, brightly painted clapboard (or vinyl imitation) houses spilling down steep hills and festooned by a quaint cobweb of power and telephone cables – there's nothing of special interest here, but it's a beguiling district that maintains the flavour of old St John's.

Signal Hill

Soaring high above The Narrows, **Signal Hill National Historic Site** (open daily 24hr; free) is a massive, grass-covered chunk of rock with views that are dramatic enough to warrant the strenuous half-hour walk up from the northern end of Duckworth Street – there's no city bus transport up here. Known originally as the Lookout, Signal Hill took its present name in the middle of the eighteenth century, when it became common practice for flags to be hoisted here to notify the merchants of the arrival of a vessel – giving them a couple of hours to prepare docking facilities and supplies. The hill was also an obvious line of defence for the garrison of St John's, and the simple fortifications that were first established during the Napoleonic Wars were restructured every time there was a military emergency, right up until World War II. Since then, it's become a popular place for young Newfoundlanders to try a bit of alfresco fraternization – a 1970s folk song suggested that most of the town's babies should be rechristened in its honour.

Signal Hill is bare and treeless – though speckled with seagull-filled ponds – but there's the odd diversion as you clamber up the approach road. The first is the **Interpretive Centre** (daily: mid-May to Aug 8.30am–8pm; Sept to mid-May 8.30am–4.30pm; ☎772-5367), which has rather overworked staff but which entertainingly explores the history of the city and the island ($2.50 fee for exhibit only). **Gibbet Hill**, beside the centre, was where the bodies of hanged criminals, wrapped in chains, were put on public display in the nineteenth century. Close by, the antiquated guns of the **Queen's Battery** peer over the entrance to the harbour directly above **Chain Rock**, which was used to anchor the chain that was dragged across The Narrows in times of danger. Near the battery, a military tattoo (mid-July to mid-Aug Wed, Thurs, Sat & Sun 3pm & 7pm; 45min; $2.50, or presentation of exhibit ticket), is performed by costumed guards, accompanied by their mascot, a large web-footed Newfoundland dog. From the battery you can look directly across The Narrows to the remains of Fort Amherst (1760s), with a lighthouse. Right on the top of Signal Hill, the squat and ugly **Cabot Tower** was built between 1897 and 1900 to commemorate both John Cabot's landing of 1497 and Queen Victoria's Diamond Jubilee (daily: early June to Aug 8.30am–9pm; Sept to early June

9am–5pm; free). The tower features a small display on electronic signalling, and outside there's a plaque in honour of Guglielmo Marconi, who confirmed the reception of the first transatlantic radio signal here in December 1901. From the top you can walk down to the rocky headland below, a wild and windswept route on all but the balmiest of days.

Guided **tours** of Signal Hill leave from the Interpretive Centre or from the Cabot Tower parking lot (daily 2pm; $2.50, or presentation of exhibit ticket).

Quidi Vidi Village

Quidi Vidi (pronounced "kiddy-viddy") is one of the province's most photographed scenes: several fishing shacks and drying-racks flanked by sharp-edged cliffs, about 3km from the city centre – take Kings Bridge Road and turn first right down Forest Road, or take #15 bus from downtown. The scenery's great, with cliffs sticking out from the deep-blue waters of a tiny inlet that's connected to the sea by the prettiest of narrow channels. It's well worth the trip out here to visit **Mallard Cottage**, right in the centre of the village (June–Oct daily 10am–7pm; Nov–May daily except Tues 10.30am–6pm; 50¢), built about 1750 and considered to be the oldest existing cottage in North America. You can also visit the **Quidi Vidi Brewery**, in a large green and white fish plant on the water's edge. Frequent tours (20min; $1) are given daily in July and August, and tastings of their three beers are included. After visiting here, you can walk round the coast to the nearby **Quidi Vidi gun battery**, reconstructed to its original 1812 appearance (mid-June to mid-Oct daily 10am–5.30pm; free). At nearby **Quidi Vidi Lake**, the annual Royal St John's Regatta canoe race, the oldest continuous sporting event in North America, is held every August.

Memorial University, C.A. Pippy Park and Rennie's River

Overlooking the city from the heights above Elizabeth Avenue are the scattered buildings of **Memorial University**. The principal building of interest here is the modern **Arts and Culture Centre**, on Allandale Road, housing an auditorium and several other smaller theatres where concerts and theatrical and dance performances are held (call ☎729-3900 for information and tickets). The **Art Gallery of Newfoundland and Labrador** (Tues, Wed & Sun noon–5pm, Thurs–Sat noon–5pm & 7–10pm; free) is also in the complex and has a fairly good collection of works by artists from the province.

Behind the university is **C.A. Pippy Park**, home to the **Botanical Gardens** at Oxen Pond (May, June & Sept–Nov Wed–Sun 10am–5pm; July & Aug daily same hours; $1), but the major attraction in the park is the **Fluvarium** in the Newfoundland Freshwater Resource Centre (mid-June to Aug daily 9am–6pm; tours hourly 9am–3pm & 5pm; Sept to mid-June daily except Wed; tours only at 11am, 1pm & 3pm; $4, tour included in price of ticket), in a modern building on Nagle's Place across from the campground. From the third, uppermost, level, housing a reception area, you descend to level 2, where there are displays mainly on the **geology** of freshwater bogs, rivers, ponds and streams, and the fish and plants that live in them. There's also an intriguing model of one of Newfoundland's many **icebergs** – massive chunks of frozen fresh water that break off from glaciers in Greenland and drift south on the Labrador Current in the summer, then float along the Newfoundland coast, often into small bays and coves, where they remain until they melt. At level 3, a dank, fishy aroma indicates that you are now below the level of the brook outside the building. Three areas of the brook – a **shallow pool**, a **fast-flowing stream** and a **deep pool** – can be seen through the glass, and eels, brook trout, rainbow trout and salmon swim by. The best time to be here is at 4pm, when the hungry fish put on a show at **feeding time**. Be aware, though, that the water becomes rather murky after a rain, so plan to visit the Fluvarium only on a fine day. Just to the north of the Fluvarium, at 155 Ridge Rd, you can continue your aquatic investigations at the **Marine Institute** (tours only July & Aug Mon–Fri 1.30pm & 3pm; free), which is given over more to interactive scientific exhibits. You can **get to** the Fluvarium and Marine Institute by bus #10 from Water Street.

From the Fluvarium and the university you can follow some of the course of **Rennie's River** through the south part of C.A. Pippy Park to Elizabeth Avenue along a partly boardwalked footpath – the most pleasant **walking trail** in St John's. Purple thistles, ferns, wildflowers and partridgeberry bushes grow profusely along the path and on the rocky banks of the river, which drops in a series of cascades.

Eating, drinking and entertainment

In the last few years, St John's **restaurant** scene has changed beyond recognition, breaking free of its rather humdrum traditions with the opening of a dozen or so bistros featuring good-quality seafood or ethnic cuisines. Slightly cheaper are a number of central **café-restaurants** catering for the city's office workers, while many of the downtown pubs also sell reasonably appetizing **bar food** at lunch time and sometimes at night. There's also a clutch of inexpensive **snack bars**, usually fish and chip shops, the best of which serve hearty meals for as little as $5. For **drinking**, St John's has dozens of **bars** – it's said to have more drinking places per square kilometre than any other city in North America – though many of them get rowdy late at night: as a general rule, stick to the pubs where there's **folk music**, which you shouldn't miss in any case. You'll find a number of Newfoundland **beers** worth trying, such as Red Dog and Black Horse, but the best is 1892 Traditional Ale, a dark golden ale with a rich, tart flavour, brewed in Quidi Vidi Village (see opposite).

There are some half-dozen pubs and bars dotted around the centre that regularly showcase island musicians, who vary enormously in quality and the type of music they play, ranging from what sounds like C&W with an eccentric nautical twist, through to traditional unaccompanied ballads. If you're content to take pot luck, follow the crowds along George Street, but otherwise ask for advice at **O'Brien's Music Store**, 278 Water St (☎753-8135), where you can also get a comprehensive list of future gigs. Another good contact is the St John's Folk Arts Council, 155 Water St (☎576-8508), which organizes regular folk music concerts and a monthly folk dance at various locations where you can learn the dances and join in a "real Newfoundland time". At the end of July, **George Street** comes alive for a few days with a **street festival** featuring lots of good folk music. The best of the island's dozen folk festivals, the **Newfoundland and Labrador Folk Festival**, is held in Bannerman Park in St John's on the first weekend in August. For a more sedate evening, you could attend a performance during the **Shakespeare by the Sea Festival**, held in July and August in the courtyard of Murray Premises and at other venues around town (tickets around $15).

The Friday and Saturday editions of the local newspaper, the *Evening Telegram*, have arts and entertainment listings. The *Express* publishes comprehensive listings on Wednesdays, and *What's Happening* is a monthly arts and entertainment magazine available at hotels; the latter two are free.

Cafés and restaurants

Bianca's, 178 Water St (☎726-9016). One of St John's most elegant eating places. An attractive bistro specializing in Mediterranean-style cuisine. Reservations recommended. Closed Sun.

Ches's, 9 Freshwater Rd at LeMarchant Road. 15min walk from the *Hotel Newfoundland*, along Military Road and then Harvey Road, *Ches's* is one of the best fish-and-chip shops in town. Seafood platters for $7.49. They also do takeaways. Also a location at 655 Topsail Rd.

Chucky's Fish 'n' Ships, 10 King's Rd. Great place with friendly owner and staff that serves freshly caught snow crab, as well as scallops and salmon, to a background of piped-in Newfoundland sea shanties. Be sure to look at the map on the wall pinpointing all the shipwrecks from the 1830s to the present day.

Classic Café, 364 Duckworth St. An atmospheric 24hr place serving traditional Newfoundland main courses and desserts from $6. A bit noisy, and tables are crowded together.

Crooked Crab Café and Savage Lobster Restaurant, 98 Duckworth St. A small café downstairs (non-smoking) and more formal restaurant upstairs (smoking), serving excellent food prepared with fresh, wholesome ingredients. Friendly and obliging staff. Not licensed and no BYO.

The Galley Fish and Chips, 288 Water St at George Street. Cod, clams, squid and scallops fried with not a hint of grease. Order at the counter.

Heritage Bakeshop & Delicatessen, 320 Duckworth St. Busy snack bar-restaurant. Not much to look at from outside, but serves big juicy sandwiches and tasty salads.

International House, 124 Duckworth St. Cheap tasty, food featuring "dishes from around the world".

Leo's, 27 Freshwater Rd. Superb fish and chips; try cods' tongues and, in season, seal flipper pie. Closed Sun.

Nautical Nellie's, 201 Water St. Pasta, pizza and seafood main courses from $8. Model ships fill the dining area.

Newfie Scoff, 160 Water St. Home-made traditional Newfoundland food; also takeaway. Service is a bit lackadaisical, but the food's tasty, with main courses from $6; try pea soup with doughboys, or partridgeberry tart. Not licensed and no BYO.

Stella's, 183 Duckworth St. Imaginative and well-conceived menu with a health-food slant; excellent lunches for around $8, main evening courses from $12. Short opening hours, but the food's well worth it.

Stone House, 8 Kenna's Hill (☎753-2380). Located near the west end of Quidi Vidi Lake, this expensive place serves traditional Newfoundland game and seafood dinners; reservations advised.

Zachary's Restaurant, 71 Duckworth St. Close to the *Hotel Newfoundland*, this restaurant serves good seafood dishes, though the main courses are overpriced. Best to stick with their lunches and fishcake breakfasts.

Music bars, pubs and clubs

Blarney Stone Irish Pub, corner of George and Adelaide streets. Good live folk acts, with rather a boisterous atmosphere after about 10pm. Foot-tapping Newfoundland Irish and traditional music nightly. $3–5 cover charge Thursday to Saturday. The place is a bit hard to find: at the street corner, look for the *Holdsworth Court* sign, go to the end of the court and up the steps.

Corner Stone Video Dance Bar, 16 Queen St. In a historic stone building that was a fisherman's hall and later a Roman Catholic girls' school. Live rock, folk or disco on Thursday only.

Duke of Duckworth Pub, 325 Duckworth St (down the steps south to Water Street). Serves a wide range of traditional Newfoundland ales and lagers and their own brew, plus daily lunch.

The Edge, above the *Rob Roy* pub, 8a George St. Rock and alternative music – absolutely no folk or Celtic. Live bands Wednesday to Saturday. $3 cover charge.

Erin's Pub, 184 Water St. Popular and well-established bar, showcasing the best of folk acts six nights a week. No cover charge.

Fat Cat Blues Bar, 5 George St. Lively venue, playing R&B and jazz through to folk. Live music nightly. Ten draught beers on tap.

Jungle Jim's Bar and Eatery, corner of George and Holdsworth streets. The food's nothing to write home about, but this lively bar is always good fun and features some of the best folk acts around. $3 cover charge Friday and Saturday.

Ship Inn, down the steps (Solomon's Lane) south off Duckworth Street. Dark, sea captain's pub with pool tables. Jazz, blues, reggae, folk and rock. A mix of grizzled old-timers and arty, black-clad young people.

Sundance Saloon, 33a New Gower St at George Street. Thumping music at a crowded/almost-heaving disco bar. $4 cover charge Friday and Saturday.

Trapper John's, 2 George St. Earthy bar with occasional live Newfoundland folk acts.

Zone 216, 216 Water St. St John's liveliest gay bar. Dark, cramped and sweaty.

Listings

Airlines International and domestic flights: Air Alliance, (Québec City to Wabush), (☎1-800-363-7050); Air Canada in the *Hotel Newfoundland*, Cavendish Square, and Scotia Centre, Water Street (both ☎726-7880, rest of Canada ☎1-800-4-CANADA, USA ☎1-800-776-3000); Air Labrador (within Newfoundland ☎753-5593 or 1-800-563-3042, outside Newfoundland ☎896-3387); Air Nova (an Air Canada partner) in the *Hotel Newfoundland*, Cavendish Square (☎726-7880 or 1-800-563-5151); Air St-Pierre (in St-Pierre ☎508/414718, in Halifax ☎902/873-3566, in Sydney ☎902/562-3140); Canadian Airlines in the *Hotel Newfoundland*, Cavendish Square (☎576-0274 or 1-800-665-1177, in USA 1-800-426-7000). Local flights: Air Atlantic (a Canadian Airlines partner), St John's airport (☎576-0274 or 1-800-665-1177); Interprovincial Airlines, St John's Airport (within Newfoundland ☎1-800-563-2800, outside Newfoundland ☎576-1666).

Bike rental Canary Cycles, 294 Water St (☎579-5972), rents bikes for $20 per day.

Bookshops Afterwords, 245 Duckworth St, has a good secondhand selection; Breakwater Books, 100 Water St, and Wordplay, 221 Duckworth St, have a large range of Newfoundland titles – Wordplay also has a coffee bar and art gallery.

Bus companies There are several minibus companies connecting St John's with the towns and villages across the island, but the biggest and most reliable is DRL Coachlines (☎738-8088), which has daily departures from the airport and the Education Building at Memorial University for towns along the Trans-Canada: principal stops are Clarenville ($28), Gander ($42), Grand Falls–Windsor ($52), Deer Lake ($69), Corner Brook ($73), Stephenville ($79) and Channel-Port aux Basques ($90). DRL also goes to the Burin Peninsula, departing daily from St John's and arriving in Grand Bank and Fortune ($20 one way to both places). For complete details check at their desk at the airport (☎738-8088). Newhook's Transportation, 13 Queen St (☎726-4876), has frequent services to Argentia ($18), connecting with the ferry to Nova Scotia. For services to Trinity and Bonavista villages, call Catalina Taxi (☎682-9977), whose minibuses go to the Lockston intersection, 6km from Trinity, for $20, and to Bonavista for $24. To get to Harbour Grace and the Conception Bay area, take Fleetline Buses (1 Mon–Sat; $10; ☎722-2608) from the *Delta St John's Hotel*, 120 New Gower St. You can also get to the north shore of the Bonavista Peninsula with Bonavista North Transportation, 1 Macklin Place (☎579-3188). Cheeseman's (☎753-7022) goes daily to the Burin Peninsula, picking up door-to-door and charging $20 one way.

Camping equipment The Scout Shop, 5 Terra Nova Rd.

Car rental Budget, at St John's Airport, behind the *Hotel Newfoundland* and at 954 Topsail Rd (all ☎747-1234 or 1-800-268-8900); Discount, 350 Kenmount Rd (☎722-6699 or 1-800-263-2355); Rent-a-Wreck, 43 Pippy Place (☎753-2277 or 1-800-327-0116); Thrifty, 39 Airport Heights Drive (☎576-4351) and 685 Topsail Rd (☎576-4352).

Consulates Netherlands, 55 Kenmount Rd (☎737-5616 or 722-6436); UK, 113 Topsail Rd (☎579-2002 or 579-0475).

Dental emergencies Village Dental Office, Village Shopping Centre, corner of Topsail Road and Columbus Drive (☎364-2453).

Disabled visitors For information on disabled-accessible facilities and accommodation in St John's, call ☎576-8455; for the rest of the province and Labrador, call ☎1-800-563-5363.

Emergencies ☎911 for police, fire and ambulance.

Hospitals Grace General Hospital, 241 LeMarchant Rd (☎778-6222); St Clare's Mercy Hospital, 154 LeMarchant Rd (☎778-3111).

Laundry Mighty White's, 150 Duckworth St, near the *Hotel Newfoundland* (daily 7.30am–9.30pm).

Lost property (☎722-9400 or 570-2064).

Pharmacy Shopper's Drug Mart, 193 LeMarchant Rd (Mon–Sat 9am–10pm, Sun 10am–10pm).

Police (☎772-4546 or 772-5400).

Post office The main central post office is at the corner of Water and Queen streets (Mon–Fri 8am–5pm).

Rape crisis and information line (☎726-1411).

Shopping The best places to purchase genuine Newfoundland handicrafts, knitwear and jewellery are The Cod Jigger, 245–247 Duckworth St; Devon House Craft Shop and Gallery, 59 Duckworth St; the Newfoundland Heritage Gift Shop, Murray Premises, Harbour Drive; Newfoundland Reflections, 202 Water St; Nonia Handicrafts, 286 Water St; and The Salt Box, 194 Duckworth St.

Swimming Aquarena, Memorial University complex, corner of Prince Philip Drive and Westerland Road; Olympic-sized pool.

Taxis Bugden's, 266 Blackmarsh Rd (☎726-4400); Co-op, Churchill Park (☎753-5100); Jiffy Cabs, Avalon Mall, Kenmount Road (☎722-2222); plus ranks outside the *Hotel Newfoundland*.

Travel agencies Harvey's Travel, 92 Elizabeth Ave (☎726-4115 or 726-4715); St-Pierre Tours, 116 Duckworth St (☎722-3892, 722-4103 or 1-888-959-8214); Travel Management, 162 Water St (☎726-9200).

Weather For up-to-date bulletins, call ☎772-5534.

Women's contacts St John's Status of Women Council, 83 Military Rd (☎753-0220).

Around St John's: Cape Spear, Bay Bulls and the eastern shore

It's a twenty-minute drive along Route 11 from St John's – take the signposted turning off Pitts Memorial Drive, the southward continuation of New Gower Street – to the rocky headland that makes up **Cape Spear National Historic Site**, often visited because it's nearer Europe than any other part of mainland North America. To cater for the tourists, the cape is encircled by a winding walkway, from which there are superb views along the coast and of The Narrows, which lead into St John's harbour. In spring and early summer, the waters off the cape are a good place to see both passing whales and the blue-tinged icebergs that have cracked away from the Arctic pack ice and drifted south. If you're keen to see more whales, ask a park ranger at the Visitor Centre (see below). In early summer, when the capelin (smelt) roll onto the Avalon Peninsula's sandier coves to spawn, they're often pursued by shoals of whales devouring hundreds of fish at a gulp. It's a remarkable sight, but there's no way of knowing which cove and when; again the park rangers may be able to point you in the right direction.

The park walkway winds round the cape, connecting its incidental attractions: a **Visitor Centre** (daily: mid-May to June & Sept to mid-Oct 10am–6pm; July & Aug 9am–8pm; ☎772-4862); the remains of a World War II gun emplacement where musical concerts by local performers are held each Thursday during August (2pm & 9pm; $10); a modern lighthouse; and an **old lighthouse** (mid-May to mid-Oct daily 10am–6pm; $2.50), which has been returned to its 1830s appearance with a keeper's residence inside. Guides give the lowdown on lighthouse life.

From Cape Spear it's a fifteen-minute drive south to the village of **PETTY HARBOUR**, where a dramatic headland dotted with houses looms over the community. For **accommodation**, the *Orca Inn Hospitality Home* (☎747-9676; ②), in the south part of town, offers four rooms in an attractive white clapboard house.

Another enjoyable excursion is to the straggling village of **BAY BULLS**, 30km south of St John's along Route 10, sitting at the head of a deep and pointed bay that witnessed the surrender of one of the last active German U-boats in 1945 – much to the amazement of the local inhabitants, who watched from the shoreline. There's nothing much to the place itself, although the **Catholic church**, on Northside Road, is interesting for its iron gate flanked by statues of saints perched on cannons for pedestals. However, the village is the base for two excellent **boat-tour** operators: O'Brien's Whale and Bird Tours, beside the waterfront on Southside Road (tours 9.30am, 11am, 2pm, 5pm & 6.30pm; ☎334-2355 in Bay Bulls or ☎753-4850 in St John's), and Gatheralls Puffin and Whale Watch, on Northside Road (tours 10am, 11.30am, 1pm, 2.30pm, 4pm & 6.30pm; ☎334-2887 or 1-800-419-4253). Both companies run sea trips to the **Witless Bay Ecological Reserve**, four sea-bird-covered islets just south of Bay Bulls (May–Oct 5–6 daily; 2hr 30min; $28–30). Reservations are recommended and O'Brien's will also provide transport from St John's for $13 return. The best time to visit is between mid-June, and mid-July, when over five

NEWFOUNDLAND FOLK MUSIC

The musical culture of Newfoundland was defined by the early settlers from England and Ireland, whose evenings would typically begin with step dances and square sets performed to the accompaniment of the **fiddle** and the **button accordion**, followed by the unaccompanied **singing** of locally composed and "old country" songs. The music was never written down, so as it passed from one generation to another a distinctive **Newfoundland style** evolved, whose rhymes and rhythms varied from village to village – though its Irish and English roots always remained pronounced.

Newfoundland's musical fabric began to unravel in the 1930s and 1940s with the arrival of thousands of American soldiers during World War II and the advent of radio and television. A multitude of influences became interwoven with the indigenous forms, none more pronounced than C&W, whose introduction has produced a hybrid in which an old story or ballad is given a C&W melody and rhythm, the accordion supported by lead and bass guitar and drum. The unadulterated style of folk music is becoming increasingly hard to find, especially after the deaths in the 1980s of the island's most famous fiddlers, **Rufus Guinchard** and **Émile Benoit**, the latter from the Port au Port Peninsula on the island's west coast. Nevertheless, marginally modified versions of Newfoundland's traditional songs are regularly performed by younger generations of **revivalists**: singer-songwriters such as Jim Payne and Ron Hynes, musician-producers such as Kelly Russell, and groups such as **Figgy Duff** have all played important roles in this process. Other important musicians include **Dermot O'Reilly**, **Phyllis Morrissey**, **Pamela Morgan**, **Anita Best**, and the groups **Great Big Sea** and the **Irish Descendants**, who are among the most popular on the island today.

More than 350 recordings of the island's music are available at two principal St John's outlets: **O'Brien's Music Store**, 278 Water St, and **Fred's**, 198 Duckworth St. The **Pigeon Inlet Productions** label is the one to look out for: the company is run by Kelly Russell, and you can get a comprehensive brochure or the recordings themselves direct from him at Pigeon Inlet Productions, 51 Monkstown Rd, St John's A1C 3T4 (☎754-7324, fax 722-8557). Pigeon Inlet also organizes **Dance-Up**, where you're given lessons in the various traditional Newfoundland folk dances.

million birds gather here – the reserve has the largest puffin colony in eastern Canada and there are also thousands of storm petrels, kittiwakes, razorbills, guillemots, cormorants and herring gulls. The waters of Bay Bulls and Witless Bay are home to the largest population of **humpback whales** in the world, and finback and minke whales are also often spotted in the area between June and August. Just north of Bay Bulls is **The Spout**, a wave-driven geyser that shoots water at tremendous speed through a tiny opening in the rock; the boat tours will sometimes include it on their itinerary.

If you decide to **stay** in Bay Bulls, *Gatherall's Hospitality Home*, Northside Road (☎334-2887 or 1-800-419-4253; ②; mid-May to mid-Oct), has three double rooms. Or you can try O'Brien's Bed & Breakfast, across the road (☎334-2007; ②), which has two simple rooms, and at breakfast you'll have the company of the owner's large Newfoundland dog, a web-footed breed that's becoming quite rare. Places to **eat** are limited: try the modern *O'Brien's Restaurant* on the main wharf (open until 8pm only) or the *Riverside* on Northside Road, which has average food but serves a $4 seafood chowder and – better still – you eat in an arcaded area looking out onto a community-hall dance floor that seems like a holdover from the 1950s.

It's worth continuing on to **FERRYLAND**, 40km south of Bay Bulls, to see the remains of the "Colony of Avalon" established by George Calvert in 1621 (see p.400) and the first continuous settlement in Canada. Archeologists are still unearthing traces of the short-lived settlement (destroyed by the French in 1696), including several stone buildings, a **cobblestone street** and a stone **privy** (the earliest-known flush toilet in

North America, allegedly). A new **Visitor Centre** (daily: June–Aug 9am–7pm; Sept to mid-Oct 9am–5pm; $2; ☎432-3200) gives you an insight into the establishment of the colony. Price of admission includes a guided tour of the site, or if you don't have time you can do it on your own. Much of the **excavations** are carried out around the houses of the local inhabitants, and it's amusing to listen to the banter between archeologists and the townspeople, who keenly observe what's being dug up from their streets and gardens. For **food**, the spacious *Irish Loop Drive Restaurant*, on the main road overlooking the village, has shrimp or scallops and chips for $4.95 – the best seafood bargain around.

The newly opened **East Coast Trail**, a three-hundred-kilometre walking trail, consisting of backcountry routes and hunting paths, extends the full length of the Avalon Peninsula's east coast, passing through Cape Spear, Petty Harbour, Bay Bulls, Ferryland and thirty other fishing communities, ending at Cape Race; the trail system is divided into seven paths of various degrees of difficulty, each comprising ten or eleven shorter walks.

The Avalon Peninsula

St John's lies on the eastern shore of the **Avalon Peninsula**, a jagged, roughly rectangular slab of land that's connected to the rest of Newfoundland by a narrow isthmus only 4km wide. Concentrated around **Conception Bay**, whose eastern shoreline lies 15km west of the capital, the Avalon's settlements stick resolutely to the coast, hiding from a bare and rocky interior that received its inappropriate name when **George Calvert**, later Lord Baltimore, received a royal charter to colonize the region in 1621. Calvert subsequently became the victim of a confidence trick: the settlers he dispatched sent him such wonderful reports that he decided to move there himself. He only lasted one winter, writing to a friend – "I have sent [my family] home after much sufferance in this woful country, where with one intolerable wynter were wee almost undone. It is not to be expressed with my pen what wee have endured."

Harbour Grace

Conception Bay's prettiest settlement is **HARBOUR GRACE** on its western shore, tucked in against Route 70, 100km from the capital and reached by Fleetline Buses (see "Listings", p.397). This elongated village – originally called "Havre de Grace" by the French – stretches out along another Water Street, which is at its most attractive near the northern end, where a handful of elegant clapboard houses, the handsome silver and green-spired Church of the Immaculate Conception, and the pretty stone St Paul's Anglican church, are set against a slender, rock-encrusted inlet. The old red-brick Customs House has been turned into a mildly entertaining **museum** (June–Sept Mon–Fri 10am–6pm; free), featuring photos of the village and its Victorian inhabitants, and an outdoor plaque commemorating **Peter Easton**, the so-called "Pirate Admiral" who was based here at the beginning of the seventeenth century. Easton's phenomenally successful fleet was run by five thousand islanders, who made their leader rich enough to retire to a life of luxury in the south of France. Next door, the tiny park has a further plaque in honour of the early aviators who flew across the Atlantic from the Harbour Grace area, including **Amelia Earhart** in 1932, the first woman to complete the journey solo.

There's no reason to spend more than a couple of hours here, but if you decide to **stay** there's the *Hotel Harbour Grace* on Water Street (☎596-5156 or 596-5157; ③), which has an excellent fish restaurant, or the cosier *Garrison House Inn*, 16 Water St (☎596-3658; ③), a historic 1811 house.

Heart's Content

In the middle of the nineteenth century, **HEART'S CONTENT**, 30km northwest of Harbour Grace on the eastern shore of Trinity Bay, was packed with engineers attempting to connect North America with Britain by **telegraph cable**, a project that had begun when the USS *Niagara* hauled the first transatlantic line ashore here in 1858. However, after Queen Victoria and the American president James Buchanan had swapped inaugural jokes, the cable broke and it was eight years before an improved version, running from Valentia in Ireland, could be installed. Heart's Content became an important relay station to New York, a role it performed until technological changes made it obsolete in the 1960s. Squatting by the waterfront, in the centre of the village, the old **Cable Station** (mid-June to mid-Oct daily 10am–5.30pm; mid-Oct to mid-June Mon–Fri 9am–4.30pm; free) boasts an intriguing cable operating room in pristine condition, and houses a series of displays on the history of telecommunications, including a replica of the original Victorian cable office and details of the problems encountered during the laying of the first telegraph lines.

Heart's Content is approached from Harbour Grace along route 74 or from the Trans-Canada Highway, 60km to the south, via route 80. About 2km from the village is the junction of routes 74 and 80, where *Legge's Motel* (☎583-2929; ②) has basic double rooms and its attached restaurant does reasonable fish and chips.

Castle Hill National Historic Site and Cape St Mary's

The thumb-shaped promontory filling out the southwest corner of the Avalon Peninsula is a foggy wilderness of marsh and rock trimmed by St Mary's and Placentia bays. Its northern section is crossed by **Route 100**, branching off the Trans-Canada Highway at Whitbourne, 80km from St John's, and as this is the main road to the ferry terminal at Argentia most people drive straight past the turning for the tiny **Castle Hill National Historic Site**, just 5km short of the port (daily: mid-June to Aug 8.30am–8pm; Sept to mid-June 8.30am–4.30pm; $2.25). This is a pity, because Castle Hill is magnificently located overlooking a watery web of harbour, channel and estuary that combine to connect the fjord-like inlets of the South East Arm and North East rivers with Placentia Bay.

The topography makes **Placentia Harbour** one of Newfoundland's finest anchorages, and its sheltered waters attracted the French, who in 1662 established Plaisance, their regional headquarters, here. Castle Hill was the area's key defensive position and so, as the fortunes of war seesawed, it was successively occupied and refortified by the British and the French. Today, little remains of these works – just a few stone walls and ditches – but make the trip for the views and drop into the trim **Visitor Information Centre** (mid-May to Oct same times as Site; ☎227-2401) for a useful account of the district's history.

Seen from the top of Castle Hill, the village of **Placentia**, at the start of the road leading to Cape St Mary's, looks pretty enough, a ribbon of buildings sandwiched between the green of the hills and the blue of the bay. However, on closer inspection, the village is the most miserable of places and you're better off quickly continuing south for the fifty-kilometre drive to the tiny community of **St Bride's**. From here, it's a further 5km to the start of the fifteen-kilometre gravel track leading down to the lighthouse and interpretive centre (May–Oct daily 9am–7pm; ☎682-9024) of **Cape St Mary's Ecological Reserve**. The reserve is best visited between May and early August, when hundreds of thousands of sea birds, principally gannets, kittiwakes, murres and razorbills, congregate on the rocky cliffs and stumpy sea stacks along the shore. The main vantage point, Bird Rock, is about half an hour's walk from the lighthouse. St Bride's is the nearest village to Cape St Mary's and has three **places to stay**: the dramatically sited *Bird Island Resort* (☎337-2450 or 1-888-337-2450; ③); the slightly cheaper *Atlantica Inn* (☎337-2860; ②), which has a fairly standard restaurant; and the *Capeway Motel* (☎337-

2163 or 337-2028; ②), about midway between the two others in comfort and price range. **Boat tours** of the reserve can be arranged in St Bride's with Cape St Mary's Charters and Boat Tours (April–Oct 4 daily; ☎337-2614).

The Burin Peninsula

The 230-kilometre-long, bony **Burin Peninsula** juts south into the Atlantic between Fortune and Placentia bays from the west side of the isthmus connecting the Avalon Peninsula with the rest of Newfoundland. It's crossed by Route 210, a turning off the Trans-Canada about 160km from St John's, a road that starts promisingly with the melodramatic scenery of the **Piper's Hole River** estuary, where there's excellent salmon fishing and hiking trails in the small park ($2 entry). After that, the journey becomes tedious, a long and dismal trip across an interior bog-filled plateau of intimidating harshness. The main reason for travelling the Burin is to catch the ferry to St-Pierre et Miquelon (see opposite) from **Fortune** (for services to Fortune, see p.405).

Grand Bank
Spreading out beside the sea 200km south of the Trans-Canada, the older streets of **GRAND BANK** incorporate a charming assortment of late nineteenth-century timber houses, a few of which are equipped with the so-called "widow's walks", rooftop galleries where the women watched for their returning menfolk. Some of these houses are splendid, reflecting a time when the village's proximity to the Grand Banks fishing grounds brought tremendous profits to the shipowners, if not to the actual fishermen. Nowadays the fishery is in an acute state of decline, much to the frustration of local people, who apportion blame amongst a number of old enemies: foreigners who overfish, big marketing corporations who are indifferent to their interests, and a government that imposes unrealistic quotas. With many of its fishermen out of work, the future of Grand Bank looks grim, especially as many feel an inflexible affinity to the fishing that it's hard for outsiders to understand: as one of their representatives declared, "Without fish there is no soul, no pride, no nothing."

To see something of this tradition, visit the **Southern Newfoundland Seamen's Museum** (mid-June to Aug daily 10am–6pm, Thurs until 9pm; Sept to mid-June Mon–Fri 9am–5pm, Sat & Sun 2–5pm; free), situated off Marine Drive on the edge of the village in a modern building shaped like the sails of a schooner. It has all sorts of models, paintings and photographs of different types of fishing boats, and a relief model of Newfoundland and the surrounding ocean that shows where the illustrious "Banks" actually are. There's a self-guided **walking tour** of the scenic architecture of the town, as well as marine and nature walks; pick up descriptive brochures at the Brumac Building, 15 Water St (☎832-1574).

Grand Bank has a **B&B**, the *Thorndyke*, a stately old sea captain's house at 33 Water St (☎832-0820; ②; May–Oct), and a **motel**, *Granny's*, on Grandview Boulevard (☎832-2180 or 832-2355; ③). For **food**, the only option is the unexciting *Manuel's Restaurant*, 3 Main St – the service and decor are indifferent, but the seafood platter is a bargain at only $10. *Foote's Taxi* (☎364-1377 in St John's, ☎832-0491 in Grand Bank) operates a daily service to Grand Bank from St John's ($30), departing at 4pm.

Fortune
FORTUNE, perched on the seashore a couple of kilometres from Grand Bank, is a slightly smaller village, whose 2500 inhabitants are mostly employed in the fish-processing plant and the inshore fishery. A modest and sleepy little place, it has one reasonable **motel**, the *Fair Isle*, just back down the main road towards Grand Bank (☎832-1010; ③); there are no B&Bs in town. The *Fair Isle* serves superb **seafood**, at about $12 for a main course; the only

other decent eating place is the *Central Restaurant*, near the ferry terminal at 17 Bayview St, where the usual fried seafood fare is dished up. For **campers** there's the *Horsebrook Trailer Park* (☎832-2090; May–Sept) on Eldon Street on the outskirts of the village, with unserviced sites for $4. The only **public transport** to the Fortune ferry is provided by a local operator, Oceanview Taxi, in Grand Bank (☎832-2311). St-Pierre Tours, 116 Duckworth St, St John's (☎722-3892, 722-4103 or 1-888-959-8214 in St John's, ☎832-0429 in Fortune), also offers a minibus service from St John's to Fortune on most days throughout July and August, as part of their St-Pierre vacation package; it adds an extra $100 to the cost of the trip. If you're planning to go to St-Pierre et Miquelon – and that's probably the reason why you've come to Fortune anyway – keep in mind that you're not allowed to take your car over; however, you can **park** it in Fortune in a secure, fenced-off and patrolled compound near the ferry terminal ($8 flat fee) and pick it up when you return.

St-Pierre et Miquelon

The tiny archipelago of **St-Pierre et Miquelon**, 25km off the coast of the Burin Peninsula, became a fully fledged *département* of mainland France in 1976 and a *collectivité territoriale* in 1985, giving a legalistic legitimacy to the billing of the islands as "a little bit of France at your doorstep" – a phrase that attracts several thousand visitors each year and manages to gloss over the lack of actual attractions and the wetness of the climate. Yet the islands are still worth a day or two for the francophone atmosphere of the main settlement, **St-Pierre**, whose fine restaurants and simple guesthouses have a genuinely European flavour. All but 700 of the 6500 islanders live in the town of St-Pierre, with the remainder – mainly of Acadian and Basque descent – marooned on **Miquelon** to the north. The third and middle island, **Langlade**, has just a scattering of houses and is inhabited only in summer.

The three islands of St-Pierre et Miquelon were first discovered by the Portuguese in 1520 and claimed for the French king by **Jacques Cartier** in 1536. Subsequently settled by fishermen from the Basque provinces, Normandy and Brittany, they were alternately occupied by Britain and France until the French finally lost their North American colonies in 1763, whereupon they were allowed to keep the islands as a commercial sop. St-Pierre et Miquelon soon became a vital supply base and safe harbour for the French fishing fleet, and provided France with a yearly harvest of salted cod.

After World War I, the French colonial authorities wanted to expand the local fishing industry, but their efforts became irrelevant with **Prohibition** in 1920. Quite suddenly, St-Pierre was transformed from a maritime backwater into a giant transit centre for booze smuggling – even the main fish-processing plant was stacked high with thousands of cases of whisky destined for Boston and Long Island; some of the Prohibition warehouses still line the waterfront. It was an immensely lucrative business, but when Prohibition ended thirteen years later the St-Pierre economy dropped through the floor. Those were desperate days, but more misery followed during World War II, when the islands' governor remained controversially loyal to the collaborationist **Vichy** regime. Both the Canadians and the Americans considered invading, but it was a **Free French** naval squadron that got there first, crossing over from their base in Halifax and occupying the islands in late 1941 without a shot being fired.

There was further trouble in 1965 when a **stevedores' strike** forced the administration to resign. De Gaulle promptly dispatched the Navy, who occupied the islands for no less than nine years. Perhaps surprisingly, the St-Pierrais remained largely loyal to France, and they certainly needed the support of Paris when the Canadians extended

The St-Pierre et Miquelon telephone code is ☎508.

the limit of their territorial waters to 200 nautical miles in 1977. The ensuing wrangle between Canada and France over the islands' claim to a similar exclusion zone remains unresolved, although the tightening of controls on foreign vessels has largely ended St-Pierre's role as a supply centre.

St-Pierre

The tidy, narrow streets of the town of **ST-PIERRE** edge back from the harbour fronted by a string of tall, stone buildings of quintessentially French demeanour. However, although the central area makes for an enjoyable stroll, there's nothing particular to aim for, with the possible exception of the early twentieth-century **cathedral**, which does at least attempt to look imposing, although its bell tower, made of grey stone from Alsace, is greatly at odds with the rest of the church's exterior, painted an unappealing yellow. Nearby, on Rue Gloanec, a 1906 **fronton** (a court on which the game of *pelote*, or *jai alai*, is played) proclaims the island's predominantly Basque heritage; behind it is a typically French *pétanque* field, frequented mainly by older men. The new **museum**, perched on a slope above the harbour in the west part of town, is a striking building whose upswept roof emulates the curves of a ship's hull; the displays here include just about everything relating to the islands' colourful history. To the rear of the building is the flamboyant Baroque-style **war memorial**, honouring the dead of the two world wars. The airy concrete and glass-walled **Francoforum**, at the foot of the hill where the museum is, is where the purity of the French language is preserved through a wide variety of French-language courses offered to Canadian and American students and businesspeople. From the compact town centre it's easy to walk out into the surrounding countryside, passing bare hillocks and marshy ponds to reach the rugged cliffs of the northern shore, just 8km away.

The tiny **Ile aux Marins**, across the harbour from St-Pierre's quayside, can only really be seen on a tour (see opposite), but it's worth it, and is the most enjoyable excursion to be made while in St-Pierre. The island, originally settled by people from Normandy but totally abandoned by 1964, comprises a collection of weather-beaten buildings, including a lighthouse, town hall, school (incorporating a museum) and washhouse, plus stone Stations of the Cross leading to a small cemetery perched on the windiest of promontories. Across the cove from the cemetery is the rusted hulk of the German ship *Transpacific*, which was wrecked there in 1971. The most fascinating building on the island, however, is the 1874 **church**, its isolation having prevented it from being altered over the years in any way; the late nineteenth-century furnishings, brought from Brittany, remain intact, including a large black-wrapped catafalque, used for carrying coffins.

Miquelon and Langlade

At the north end of the archipelago, the dumpy-looking island of **Miquelon** is comprised of a peat bog, marsh and a couple of isolated hills, sloping west from its only village, which bears the same name. The tiny **tourist office** on Rue Antoine Soucy (Mon, Wed, Thurs & Sat 8.30am–noon & 2–5pm; Tues, Fri & Sun 8.30am–noon & 2–7.30pm) can provide you with details of what to see on the island, and you can rent a *rosalie* (bicycle) from them to do some touring of your own (F50 for 1hr). Miquelon's 1865 **church**, on Rue Sourdeval (daily 9am–noon & 2–6pm) is a delight, filled with *faux-marbre* columns and containing a good copy of a Murillo *Virgin* (donated by Napoléon III) on the altar. Just down the street from the church, the cramped **museum** (Mon 10–11.30am & 2–4pm, Tues & Fri 10am–noon & 2–5pm, Wed & Sun 10–11.30am, Thurs 10am–noon & 2–4pm; F10) features a collection of artefacts salvaged from the island's shipwrecks, plus a curious reconstruction of a 1913–14 photography laboratory set up by a local doctor.

The island's pride and joy is the **Dune of Langlade**, a sweeping ten-kilometre sandy isthmus that connects with the archipelago's middle island, Langlade. The dune began to appear above the ocean two hundred years ago as a result of sand collecting around shipwrecks, and it has continued to grow to its current width of up to 2500m. Although there's a **road** along the Dune connecting Miquelon and Langlade, in heavy seas parts of the Dune can be engulfed by seawater, so stick to the guided tours (see below), which stop at the **Grand Barachois**, a large saltwater pool at the northern end of the isthmus that's a favourite haunt of breeding seals. You'll also probably see herds of wild ponies running along the Dune.

Langlade itself has a more varied landscape than Miquelon – high hills, deciduous forests and rushing brooks – and is at its liveliest in summer, when the St-Pierrois arrive in droves and open up their summer homes.

Practicalities

The cheapest **flights** to the islands are on Air St-Pierre from St John's (April–Oct 3 weekly; 45min; $97; ☎709/722-4103) and from Sydney, Nova Scotia (April–Oct 1–3 weekly; 45min; $106; ☎902/562-3140), but there are also regular connections on other airlines with Halifax and Montréal. St-Pierre **airport**, with its startlingly pink terminal, is located just south of the town across the harbour, and is connected by taxi to the centre. A new airport, better able to handle air traffic, is being constructed nearby and will be opened in 1999.

Flights here are often delayed by fog and the **ferries** plying between Fortune and the town of St-Pierre are more dependable and far cheaper, though the crossing can get mighty rough. If you come by ferry (May–Sept daily; 2.45pm 1hr 10min; $37.95 one way, $59.95 return for a solo traveller; Oct to early Dec Fri & Sat only, same times and fees; reservations/information from Lake's Travel, Fortune ☎709/832-2006 or 1-800-563-2006), you usually have to stay the night. There is no same-day return ferry, except about nine times on designated days during July and August – usually one weekly (departing from Fortune 9am, returning from St-Pierre 4.30pm; $46.95). Ferry services are often subject to change with little advance notice, so it's best to check with Lake's Travel before arriving in Fortune.

To clear St-Pierre et Miquelon's **customs control**, Canadians and citizens of the United States need only present an identity document such as a driver's licence or social security card; EU visitors need a passport. On the return journey to Newfoundland, Canadian customs officials examine the baggage of about every fourth person, looking for excess purchases of alcohol and foodstuffs. St-Pierre et Miquelon's currency is the French franc, but Canadian dollars are widely accepted; however, you'll usually be given back small change in francs. Also, when you're shopping remember that virtually all shops and public buildings close between noon and 2pm, in keeping with French tradition.

The **Agence Régionale du Tourisme de St-Pierre et Miquelon**, on Place du Général de Gaulle on the waterfront (May–Sept Mon–Sat 8.30am–noon & 1–6pm, Sun 8.30–11.30am & 1–6pm; ☎1-800-565-5118), has the timetables of the **ferries** that run from the town of St-Pierre to the village of Miquelon (mid-April to mid-June Tues, Fri & Sun 1–2 daily; mid-June to Sept same days 2 daily; Oct to mid-April same days 1–2 daily; 1hr 10min; F120 return), plus details of the excellent **day-trips by bus and boat**: the all-day Miquelon trip includes the village of Miquelon and the lagoon of the Grand Barachois (mid-June to Sept Tues, Fri & Sun; 11hr; F195); the bus tour around St-Pierre takes in all the sights of town, as well as the rocky south coast (July–Sept daily 10.30am & 6pm; 2hr; F35); the zodiac tour goes along the coasts of St-Pierre and Langlade, where you can examine at close range the prolific birdlife, seals and whales (mid-June to mid-Sept daily 9am & 2pm; 3hr; F170); and the tour to Ile aux Marins (mid-June to Sept daily 9.30am & 2.30pm; 3hr; F53).

Accommodation

St-Pierre has a good selection of hotels and pensions, though reservations are strongly recommended from July to early September. The easiest solution is to book on a package: Lake's Travel in Fortune (see p.405) offers overnight excursions from $136 and two-night stays from $209; St-Pierre Tours in St John's (☎709/722-3892 722-4103 or 1-888-959-8214) has a two-night deal from $248. The town's deluxe **hotels** include the *Hôtel Île de France*, 6 Rue Maître Georges-Lefèvre (☎41 28 36 or 41 20 22; ⑤), and the *Hôtel/Motel Robert*, 10–12 Rue du 11 novembre (☎41 24 19; ⑤), which was where Al Capone stayed during Prohibition (a small museum off the foyer has one of his straw hats and other memorabilia from that period). For **pensions**, which charge a fixed rate per double including breakfast, try the comfortable *Chez Marcel Hélène*, 15 Rue Beaussant (☎41 31 08; ②; April–Dec); *Chez Roland Vigneau*, 12 Rue des Basques (☎41 38 67; ②; April–Sept); or *L'Arc-en-Ciel*, 26 Rue Jacques-Cartier (☎41 25 69; ②). The village of **Miquelon** has one hotel, one motel and two pensions: the *Hôtel l'Escale*, 30 Rue Victor Briand (☎41 64 56; ③); *Motel de Miquelon*, on the sea at 42 Rue Sourdeval (☎41 63 10; ④); *Chez Paulette*, 8 Rue Victor-Briand (☎41 62 15; ②); and *Chez Monique*, 3 Rue Ernest Petitpas (☎41 61 75; ②; May–Sept).

Eating and drinking

St-Pierre's **restaurants** are splendid, combining the best of French cuisine with local delicacies such as *tiaude*, a highly seasoned cod stew. Prices are quite high – reckon on about F80 for a main dish – but it really is worth splashing out at *La Ciboulette*, 2 Rue Marcel-Bonin, for *nouvelle cuisine* at its fanciest; at *Le Caveau*, 2 Rue Maître Georges-Lefèvre, for the Basque fish and lamb specialities; at *Chez Dutin*, 20 Rue Amiral-Muselier, for the salmon; or at *L'Outre-Mer*, 29 Rue Boursaint, for any of their local specialities. If you're on a tight budget, stick to the **snack bars** such as *Le Marine Bar* on Place du Général de Gaulle, or drop into *Le Maringouin'fre*, 16 Rue Général-Leclerc, for excellent-quality crêpes. On Miquelon, some good traditional food is available at the *Snack Bar-à-Choix*, 2 Rue Sourdeval.

The Bonavista Peninsula

The thickly wooded **Bonavista Peninsula**, crossed by route 230 – which leaves the Trans-Canada 190km west of St John's at Clarenville – is trimmed by lots of little outports that were first settled by the English in the seventeenth century. With Trinity Bay on its south coast and Bonavista Bay on its north, the peninsula juts out into the Atlantic, which pounds its wild and remote shores. Dotted along its rocky headlands are attractive fishing villages such as **Trouty** and **Dunfield**, as well as the historic settlement of **Trinity**.

If you want to find out about the attractions when doing a circuit of the peninsula, call the **Discovery Trail Tourism Association** in Clarenville (☎466-3845) and the staff will help you plan your route. Otherwise, stop in at the **tourist information office** on the Trans-Canada Highway near Clarenville (daily: May to mid-Sept 9am–9pm; mid-Sept to mid-Oct 10am–5pm; ☎466-3100).

Trinity

TRINITY, 70km along the peninsula off the main road on Route 239, is the most enchanting of the peninsula's villages, a gem of a place whose narrow lanes are lined by delightfully restored white and pastel-coloured clapboard houses that reflect its importance as a supply centre during the nineteenth century. Sandwiched between a ring of hills and a deep and intricate bay, it also boasts the island's finest wooden church, **St Paul's Anglican Church** (1892), whose graceful and dignified interior has a ceiling built to resemble an upturned boat. There's a modest and overcrowded **Community Museum** (daily: mid-May to mid-June & mid-Sept to mid-May 10am–noon & 1–5pm; mid-June to mid-Sept 10am–7.30pm; $2), in the saltbox house on Church Road near St Paul's, with an eccentric collection of bygones, such as an old shoemaker's kit, an early cooperage and an 1811 fire engine, thought to be the oldest existing one in North America. Nearby, on Ash's Lane, is the green-trimmed **Holy Trinity Catholic Church** (1835) serving a congregation of only three people. The orange and green **Hiscock House** on Dock Lane (June to mid-Oct daily 10am–5.30pm; free) has been returned to its appearance circa 1910 when it served as a widow's mercantile home; as ever, costumed guides give the background. Closer to the harbour, on West Street, is a **Blacksmith's Museum**, in an old forge (same hours and price as the Community Museum), and an **interpretive centre** (mid-June to mid-Oct daily 10am–5.30pm; free; ☎464-2042) that displays material related to the community's three-hundred-year-old history. Next door to the centre is Trinity's newest historic attraction, the **Lester-Garland Premises** (mid-June to mid-Oct daily 10am–5pm; free), a three-storey brick home that belonged to a prominent family of merchants and politicians, which has been reconstructed to its appearance in the 1830s. An early twentieth-century **general store** and old accounting office next to it completes the ensemble. The most striking building in town, however, is the brown and yellow **Parish Hall**, on Dandy Lane, its elegance accentuated by the roof and cupola.

The **Trinity Pageant**, a combination of live theatre and audience participation, is one of Newfoundland's most famous theatrical events. It's performed on various days throughout June, July and August, when the costumed actors walk you through the town while enacting some of the community's most historic and colourful moments. Tickets are $7.70; for information about performance dates, call ☎464-3232 or 1-888-464-1100 (Trinity), or ☎738-3256 (St John's).

Practicalities

Trinity has half a dozen charming **B&Bs**, foremost of which is the *Campbell House*, on High Street (☎464-3377; ③–④; mid-May to mid-Oct), a handsome early Victorian house perched on a hill in the west part of town. The owners also have two cottages just down the hill, and they serve excellent breakfasts featuring such local delicacies as partridgeberry crêpes. The *Beach B&B*, nearby on Church Road (☎464-3695; ②–③; mid-May to mid-Oct), is another pleasant, if more modest spot. The best place to **eat** is at the *Heritage Tea Rooms*, in the *Eriksen Premises B&B* on West Street, which serves gourmet seafood dinners, or the cheaper *Polly's Pantry*, in the same building, which has chowder, stuffed croissants and thick sandwiches. Afterwards, you can stroll up the hill to *Rocky's Place* for a drink. Good food is also available at the *Dock Marina Restaurant* on Dock Lane.

WHALE-WATCHING

Based at the *Village Inn* in Trinity, Ocean Contact (☎464-3269) runs an extensive programme of **whale-watching** excursions, or rather, as they insist, whale "contact" trips designed to encourage close encounters between whales and humans. They can't guarantee contact, of course, but there is an excellent chance of sighting minke, finbacks and humpbacks, particularly between mid-June and early August. Expertly run, these excursions take place daily during the peak whale season, and prices begin at $44 for a half-day trip (departures 10am, 2pm & 6pm; 3hr, preceded by an introductory talk). If the sea is too rough for a boat trip, Ocean Contact provides escorted whale-watching walks along the nearby cliffs at half the price.

You can **get to** Trinity from St John's with Catalina Taxi (☎682-9977), which, for $20, will take you to the Lockston intersection, a few kilometres away. Alternatively, DRL Coachlines drops passengers at the Irving petrol station on the edge of Clarenville, and the waiting taxis charge about $30 for the onward trip. There are historical **tours** of Trinity's harbour (May–Sept daily 10am, 1.30pm & 5pm; $16; ☎464-3355 or 464-3400) departing from near the *Dock Marina Restaurant*.

Trinity Bay and Cape Bonavista

Exploring the serrated shoreline of **Trinity Bay** is a fine way to spend a day or two, with Route 239 twisting its way south from Trinity through a string of remote outports. **Dunfield** occupies a dramatic setting, straggling along a jutting promontory, whilst tiny **TROUTY**, just 6km from Trinity, is tucked into the rockiest of coves, whose steep and bare cliffs rise lumpily all around. This delightful village, with its tumbling brook and rickety wooden jetties, has a real hideaway, the *Riverside Lodge* (☎464-3780; ②; April–Oct), an unpretentious hotel-cum-B&B. A few kilometres on, **Old** and **New Bonaventure** circle another rocky bay at the end of the road – on a rainy day it seems like the end of the world. Heading north from Trinity, via route 230, is the ribbon village of **TRINITY EAST**, home to the reputedly haunted *Peace Cove Inn* (☎464-3738 or 464-3419; ②–③; May–Oct), whose owners run excellent coastal excursions – Atlantic Adventures – on a motorsailer (May–Oct daily 10am & 2pm, 2hr 30min, $30; 6.30pm, 1hr 30min, $20; ☎464-2133).

Cape Bonavista

Some 55km north of Trinity, the red-and-white-striped lighthouse on **Cape Bonavista** looks out over a violent coastline of dark grey rock and pounding sea. This beautifully desolate headland, populated by hundreds of puffins, is supposed to be the spot where the English-sponsored Genoese explorer **John Cabot** first clapped eyes on the Americas in 1497. The tourist literature claims he exclaimed, "O buona vista!" ("O, happy sight") – whatever the truth of the matter, a statue has been built here in his honour.

The **lighthouse** (mid-June to mid-Oct daily 10am–5.30pm; free), now a Provincial Historic Site, has been restored to its appearance in 1870 when it was occupied by an 80-year-old lighthouse keeper, Jeremiah White, and his family; costumed guides give the background. Close to the lighthouse are the **Dungeons**, huge rock caves formed by collapsing sedimentary rock.

The cape is 5km from the expansive fishing village of **BONAVISTA**, which spreads out across the flattish headlands surrounding its double harbour. Here you'll find another historic site, the plain white clapboard **Mockbeggar Property** on Roper Street (same times as lighthouse; free), once the home of F. Gordon Bradley, one of the island's first representatives in the Canadian Senate. Most of the house is 1940s-style, but has the surprising addition of heavily ornate, English-made Victorian and Edwardian furniture, plus a large library and conference room featuring a stained-glass window of Cabot's landing. On Ryan's Hill, at the other end of town, is the **Ryan Premises National Historic Site**, opened in 1997 (mid-June to mid-Oct daily 10am–6pm; $3.25), a group of plain, solid buildings that replicates a nineteenth-century fish-processing factory and retail store and effectively evokes the importance of the fish industry to the local economy. Several imaginatively designed exhibits explain the significance of the North Atlantic fisheries in a surprisingly engaging manner – tanks of live cod and barrels of highly pungent actual salted cod are strategically placed to appeal to the senses. Close by, at the docks, you can board a replica of **Cabot's ship**, the *Matthew*, and visit the new interpretive centre (for information on hours and fees for the *Matthew*, call the centre on ☎468-1493 or 468-7747).

Bonavista has a handful of **B&Bs** perched among the rocks, all charging about the same price and all open year-round. You could try *Butler's by the Sea*, 15 Butler Crescent (☎468-2445; ③), or *White's Bed & Breakfast* (☎468-7018; ③), which rents out bikes and is just 2.5km from the lighthouse. There's a meagre assortment of **restaurants**; your best option is to eat at the *Baie-Vista*, on John Cabot Drive, right in the town centre. No bus service runs to Bonavista from St John's, but Catalina Taxi (☎682-9977) has a speedy and efficient **minibus** service that will get you there for $24.

Terra Nova National Park to Corner Brook

The **Trans-Canada Highway** is the only major road running along Newfoundland's central northern shore, slicing through **Terra Nova National Park** (mid-May to mid-Oct $3.25 entry fee; mid-Oct to mid-May free) before connecting the towns of the interior – **Gander**, **Grand Falls–Windsor** and **Deer Lake** – a distance of about 450km. Heading north from Clarenville along the Trans-Canada, it's about 40km to the southern entrance of the Terra Nova National Park, whose coniferous forests, ponds and marshes border the indented coastline of southwest Bonavista Bay. A **Visitor Information Centre** (late June to Aug daily 10am–6pm; ☎533-2801, same number for all facilities) is at Twin Rivers, right on the southern edge of the park. It's about 30km further to the **park administration building** and the park's principal **campground** ($12–16; year-round), which has a convenience store, snack bar, laundry, gift shop and bike-rental shop. A few kilometres further up the Trans-Canada there's a turnoff onto a gravel road that will take you to the shore of Newman Sound, where you'll find the newly opened **Marine Interpretation Centre** (daily: June–Aug 9am–9pm; Sept to mid-Oct 9am–5pm; admission with park entry fee), which has aquariums, interactive displays, videos and murals dealing with the mysteries of the sea. The main **Visitor Information Centre** (same hours as Marine Centre) is in the same building. Also from Newman Sound, the reputable Ocean Watch (☎ & fax 533-6024) runs daily **boat trips** (mid-May to Oct daily 9am, 12.30pm, 3pm & 7pm) around the fjord (2hr 30min; $25) and out into the Atlantic (3hr; $28); boats depart from Saltons Wharf. Whales are a common sight, but the best part of the trip is where you get to handle such things as jellyfish, plankton and lobster.

Several excellent **walking trails** begin from Newman Sound, most notably the strenuous Outport Trail, an eighteen-kilometre (5hr) walk along the south shore of the fjord to the rugged slopes of Mount Stamford and beyond. On the way there are a couple of primitive **campgrounds** for $8 per night, plus some semi-serviced ones close to the Trans-Canada ($14–16) – wilderness camping permits are available from the main information centre. For a less strenuous way of seeing the countryside, Ocean Watch will drop passengers out near the end of the Outport Trail, and you can either walk back or wait for the boat to collect you. If you're not content to camp – or the weather turns foul – the village of **CHARLOTTETOWN**, inset into park property 13km south of Newman Sound along the Trans-Canada, has a **motel**, the *Clode Sound* (☎664-3146; ③; May–Oct), with a reasonable restaurant known for its apple pies and apple crisps.

If you have the time, a worthwhile detour can be made off the Trans-Canada at the northern edge of the park, 20km along Hwy 310 to the tiny community of **EASTPORT**, hub of a small peninsula known for its artists' colonies and sandy beaches. **Burnside**, 8km north of Eastport, is the departure point for most tours. Close by the site of **Bloody Bay Cove**, one of the principal settlements of the Beothuks; the largest and richest archeological finds from this ill-fated culture have been unearthed here (tours summer only Mon–Fri 9am–5pm, Sat & Sun noon–6pm; ☎677-2221 or 677-2474). Basing yourself in Eastport, you can thread your way through islands and past abandoned outports on a tour with Smokey Hole Wilderness Tours (late May to mid-Oct daily; 2–4hr; $25; ☎677-

2743, 677-2036 or 579-7888); they'll even pick you up at your hotel or B&B in St John's and take you to Eastport. If you want to **stay** overnight in Eastport, your best bets are *Pinsent's Bed & Breakfast*, 17 Church St (☎677-3021; ②), a quaint saltbox house surrounded by rose gardens and lilac bushes, or *Laurel Cottage*, 41 Bank Rd (☎677-3138; ③).

Gander

The Trans-Canada Highway leaves Terra Nova National Park to sprint 60km to **GANDER**, an inconsequential town built around an airport, whose site was chosen by the British in the 1930s – they considered it ideal because it was far enough inland to escape Newfoundland's coastal fogs and near enough to Europe to facilitate the introduction of regular transatlantic flights. During World War II, the airport was a major staging point for American planes on their way to England and later developed into an important air-traffic control centre for much of the northwest Atlantic. Since the 1960s the airport has been a major stopover destination for incoming flights from Europe. In the 1970s and 1980s several eastern European airlines used Gander as a refuelling stop on the flight to Cuba, and hundreds of passengers decamped here to ask for political asylum. There's no reason to stop – unless you're tired from the long drive – but in emergencies the *Cape Cod Inn*, 66 Bennett Drive (☎651-2269; ③), situated not far from the **tourist chalet** on the Trans-Canada (June–Sept daily 9am–9pm; ☎256-7110), has pleasant double rooms. For standard highway **motel** accommodation, the pick of the bunch is the *Comfort Inn*, on the Trans-Canada (☎256-3535 or 1-800-4-CHOICE; ③–④). If you're **hungry**, try either the *Viscount Restaurant*, 58 McCurdy Drive, or the *Highlight Restaurant*, 342 Elizabeth Drive, both of which serve unexciting, but passable, meals.

Twillingate and around

The myriad headlands and inlets around the northern outport of **TWILLINGATE**, 100km north of Gander along routes 330, 331 and 340, on an island linked by a bridge to the mainland, ensnare dozens of **icebergs** as they drift down from the Arctic between May and July. Tinted by reflections from the sea and sun, they can be wondrously beautiful and, if you're particularly lucky, you might witness the moment when one of them rolls over and breaks apart, accompanied by a tremendous grating, wheezing explosion. Twillingate Island Boat Tours, South Side, Twillingate, runs excellent two-hour **iceberg-watching tours** from mid-May to September, daily at 9.30am, 1pm and 4pm for $25 per person. You can book at the Iceberg Shop (☎884-2242 or 884-2317), an arts and crafts shop and interpretive centre in an old barn in Durrell, a couple of kilometres north of Twillingate.

At the end of July Twillingate hosts the four-day **Fish, Fun and Folk Festival**; folk dancers and musicians gather here from all over the province. The best of the **accommodation** is the *Hillside Bed and Breakfast*, 5 Young's Lane (☎884-5761; ②; June–Sept), and the quaint *Toulinguet Inn Bed & Breakfast*, 56 Main St (☎884-2080 or 884-2028; ②). For **food**, try the simple *R&J Restaurant*.

To find out more about Newfoundland's mysterious extinct native people, it's worth a visit to the **Interpretation Centre** at Boyd's Cove, 35km south of Twillingate along Hwy 340 (May–Aug daily 10am–5.30pm; free). A major Beothuk village existed here in the seventeenth and eighteenth century, and an archeological site and well-designed displays bring the history of these people alive to the visitor.

Lewisporte

Mundane **LEWISPORTE**, west of Gander and just 16km from the Trans-Canada along Route 340, is the terminal for the twice-weekly **ferry** to Goose Bay, in Labrador. DRL Coachlines from St John's drops you at the Irving petrol station, on the Trans-Canada

16km from the dock, and Cyril's Taxis (☎535-8100) will come and collect you, but the times of the buses don't tally with those of the boats, leaving you with several hours to kill, if you're catching the 10pm boat, or an overnight stay, for the 4pm sailing. For overnight **accommodation**, stick to the *Northgate Bed and Breakfast*, close to the ferry at 106 Main St (☎535-2258; ②; May–Oct).

Grand Falls and Windsor

GRAND FALLS, 96km west of Gander, sits in the middle of some of the island's best stands of timber, an expanse of forest that's been intensively exploited ever since Alfred Harmsworth, later Lord Northcliffe, had a paper mill built here in 1905. Harmsworth, the founder of Britain's *Daily Mirror* and the *Daily Mail*, funded the project to secure a reliable supply of newsprint well away from Europe, which he believed was heading towards war. It was an immensely profitable venture, which also established the first Newfoundland community sited, as one contemporary put it, "out of sight and sound of the sea". For many of the employees, recruited from the outports, it was the first time they had ever received a cash wage, though this particular pleasure was countered by some bitter management–union disputes. The worst was in 1959, when the Mounties broke a well-supported strike with appalling barbarity, at the behest of Newfoundland's premier Joey Smallwood.

Grand Falls remains a company town, a singularly unprepossessing place built up around the hulking mass of the paper mill that towers over the Exploits River. Nevertheless, there is one interesting surprise, the **Mary March Museum** at 24 St Catherine St (May–Aug daily 10am–6pm; Sept & Oct Mon–Fri 9am–5pm, Sat & Sun 10am–6pm; free), just to the south of the Trans-Canada where the highway separates Grand Falls from the adjacent drab township of **WINDSOR**. The museum has a good section on the history of the town and an intriguing series of displays on the **Beothuks**, including an explanation about one of the last of the Beothuks, Mary March, or Demasduit, who was captured near here in March 1819. A reconstructed **village** (late May to Aug daily 10am–6pm; $2) stands next to the museum. There's also a **tourist information booth**, on the Trans-Canada just west of the twin towns (daily: June–Aug 8.30am–9pm; Sept–May 9am–5pm; ☎489-6332).

If you're coming by **bus**, DRL Coachlines drops you off at the *Highliner Inn* on the Trans-Canada just west of town. For lower-priced **accommodation**, the *Poplar Inn Bed and Breakfast*, 22 Poplar Rd (☎489-2546; ②), is a good choice. If that's full, try the slightly more luxurious *Robin Hood Inn*, 78 Lincoln Rd (☎489-5324; ③), or the large, comfortable *Mount Peyton Hotel*, just off the Trans-Canada at 214 Lincoln Rd (☎489-2251 or 1-800-563-4894; ④). There are few good **restaurants** in town; the *Peyton Corral Steakhouse*, in the *Mount Peyton Hotel*, is by far the best choice.

Deer Lake

DEER LAKE, 210km west of Grand Falls, lies at the start of Route 430, the only road up to L'Anse aux Meadows, and has the nearest airport to Gros Morne National Park (see p.412), so if you fly in and rent a car at the airport you miss the long trek across the island. There are regular reasonably priced flights in from St John's (from $290 return) and a clutch of **car rental** offices inside the terminal building: try Budget (☎635-3211), Tilden (☎635-3282) or Avis (☎635-3252). DRL Coachlines' service from St John's stops at the Irving petrol station in Deer Lake daily at 5.12pm. From here you can take the only bus service up the Northern Peninsula, operated by Viking Express (☎634-4710), running to Rocky Harbour (Mon–Fri 5.40pm; $13) and St Anthony for L'Anse aux Meadows (Mon, Wed & Fri 5pm; $40). If you want more information about Deer Lake and surrounding area, stop in at the **tourist information booth** on the Trans–Canada, just east of town (daily: June–Aug 8.30am–9pm; Sept & Oct 10am–7pm; ☎635-2202).

If you get stuck in Deer Lake, there's fairly convenient **accommodation** at the *Deer Lake Motel* (☎635-2108 or 1-800-563-2144; ③), just 2km from the airport; alternatively, the *Driftwood Inn* (☎635-5115 or 635-5116; ③), on Nicholsville Road, is a ten-minute drive east of the airport. There are no decent **restaurants** in Deer Lake itself, so you'd best stick to the dining rooms of the motels or grab a snack at the convenience places on the Trans-Canada, which cuts through the town.

Corner Brook

CORNER BROOK, 50km south of Deer Lake, is magnificently sited, surrounded by steep wooded hills dropping down to the blue waters of the Humber Arm. However – although it's Newfoundland's second largest city – there's not really a lot to do or see, as it's essentially a **pulp-and-paper** producing town supplying newsprint to much of the world, and a large mill on the waterfront pours out smoke from its stack. DRL Coachlines stops at the Robertson's Irving petrol station near the Trans-Canada, some 3km from the centre. From here, City Cabs (☎634-6565) or Star Taxi (☎634-4343) will take you down into town. The Millbrook Shopping Mall on Herald Avenue stands near the main stop for the Viking Express **bus** up to St Anthony; always call ahead to confirm schedules and connecting services.

To find out what's on in the town and area, visit the **tourist information centre**, on Confederation Drive, just off the Trans-Canada (May–Aug daily 9am–5pm; Sept–April Mon–Fri same hours; ☎634-5831 or 639-9792). The only attraction that will cause you to linger for a while is the **Captain James Cook Memorial**, in the west part of the city at the end of Hill Road, which honours the British navigator who explored and charted the nearby coastline and inlets of the Bay of Islands in 1767.

If you're stranded in Corner Brook, two good **accommodation** stand-bys are the basic *Hotel Corner Brook*, at 47 Main St (☎634-8211 or 1-800-738-8211; ②–③), and the *Bide-a-Nite Hospitality Home*, centrally located at 11 Wellington St (☎634-7578; ②). The best places to **eat** are *Maggie's Restaurant*, 26 Caribou Rd, specializing in pastries and pies; *Lynn's Café*, 37 Broadway, offering traditional Newfoundland meals; and the *Carriage Room* in the *Glynmill Inn* on Cobb Lane, where you can enjoy a buffet in a 1920s Tudor-style former hotel.

The Northern Peninsula

Stretching between Deer Lake and the township of St Anthony, a distance of about 450km, the **Northern Peninsula** is a rugged and sparsely populated finger of land whose interior is dominated by the spectacular **Long Range Mountains**, a chain of flat-topped peaks that are some of the oldest on earth, punctuated by the starkest of glacier-gouged gorges above the bluest of lakes – or "ponds" as the locals incongruously call them. Most of the region remains inaccessible to all except the most experienced of mountaineers, but **Route 430** – whose bus services are so poor that it's hard to manage without a car – trails along the length of the western part of the peninsula, connecting the small fishing villages of the narrow coastal plain with the remains of the Norse colony at **L'Anse aux Meadows**.

Gros Morne National Park

The southern section of the Long Range Mountains, beginning about 35km from Deer Lake and bordering the Gulf of St Lawrence, has been set aside as the **GROS MORNE NATIONAL PARK** (mid-May to mid-Oct $3.25 entry fee; mid-Oct to mid-May free), a UNESCO World Heritage Site, some 1800 square kilometres of the peninsula's finest and most approachable scenery. The bays, scrawny beaches, straggling villages and sea stacks of the littoral are set against bare-topped, fjord-cut mountains, whose forested lower slopes are home to moose, woodland caribou and snowshoe hare.

The best place to start a tour is the **Visitor Information Centre** (daily: mid-June to Aug 9am–10pm; Sept to mid-June 9am–5pm; ☎458-2066 or 458-2417), situated beside Route 430 as it approaches Rocky Harbour just 70km from Deer Lake. The centre has a series of excellent displays on the geology, botany, biology and human history of the park, and its efficient and helpful staff issue free maps, brochures on Gros Morne's key hiking trails and boat excursions; they also run a programme of guided walks. If you intend to use one of the park's basic **campgrounds** ($10 per night), which are dotted along the longer trails, then you have to register here first.

Rocky Harbour

It's a couple of minutes' drive from the Visitors' Centre to **ROCKY HARBOUR**, the park's largest and prettiest village, which curves around a long and sweeping bay with the mountains lurking in the background. Although there's nothing special to do or see here, the long walk round to the **Lobster Cove Head Lighthouse** is a pleasant way to spend an afternoon. Rocky Harbour is also near several of Gros Morne's **hiking trails**, notably the lung-bursting, sixteen-kilometre James Callaghan Trail, curiously named after the former British prime minister. The trail – for experienced hikers only – begins beside Route 430, just 7km east of the village, and climbs to the top of Gros Morne Mountain where, at 806m above sea level, the views are stupendous. If you decide to stay on the mountain overnight, there's a primitive **campground** on the way down from the summit ($10 per night; July–Oct).

Rocky Harbour is the best place to stay in the park, not least because it's relatively compact and has a reasonable range of tourist facilities. **Accommodation** includes the comfortable *Ocean View Motel*, beside the waterfront (☎458-2730 or 1-800-563-9887; ③); *Bottom Brook Cottages*, on Main Street (☎458-2236; ②–③), consisting of six fully equipped individual housekeeping units; and *Parson's Harbour View Cabins*, also near the waterfront (☎458-2544; ②). In all cases, advance bookings are recommended in July and August. The nearest **campground** is *Juniper Campground*, on Pond Road in the village (☎458-2917; $9–12; late May to Sept), which also has a six-bed hostel (①); or try the more attractive sites at **Berry Hill**, 4km north of Rocky Harbour along Route 430 (no phone; $15.25 per night; June to mid-Oct).

For **food**, the restaurant of the *Ocean View Motel* serves excellent seafood dishes for around $12; the nearby *Fisherman's Landing Restaurant* is a mundane second best.

Bonne Bay, Woody Point and the Tablelands

BONNE BAY, just along the coast from Rocky Harbour, lies at the mouth of a great gash that slices inland from the Gulf of St Lawrence framed by the severest of mountains. Most of the park's villages lie on the shore of the fjord and it's possible to drive right round, but you have to take a long detour on Route 431, which branches off from Route 430 at Wiltondale, at the park's south entrance. Unfortunately, the ferry, which connected with Woody Point across the bay and which shortened the distance considerably, no longer runs. Minuscule **WOODY POINT** has a pleasant guesthouse, the *Victorian Manor* (☎453-2485; ③–⑤), and the small and basic *Woody Point Youth Hostel* (☎453-7254; ①; May–Oct). If you want to see the mountains from the water, **tours** of Bonne Bay are available with Bontours (mid-June to early Sept daily 10am & 2pm; 2hr; $20; ☎458-2730 or 1-800-563-9887); boats depart from Government Wharf at Norris Point.

The **Lookout Trail** (5km return) begins about 1km from Woody Point and has the best panoramic views in the park. Heading further west from the village along Route 431, it's 3km to the start of the **Tablelands Hiking Trail**, a four-kilometre circular track that cuts across a forbidding area of bare and barren rock. Another 8km along Route 431 leads to the sixteen-kilometre loop of the **Green Gardens Trail**, which twists its way to some secluded coves, caves and sea stacks and is equipped with three primitive campgrounds (each $10 per night). Continuing down the road, it's a further 4km to **Trout River Pond**, sandwiched by the yellowed bareness of the Tablelands and the massive cliffs bordering the Gregory Plateau – this is one of the places where you really notice the tremendous uplifts of land caused by the collision of the North American and European continents 450 million years ago. The views here are splendid and the best way to see the lake is on the **Tablelands Boat Tour** (daily: mid- to late June & early to mid-Sept 1pm; July & Aug 10am, 1pm & 4pm; 2hr; $25; ☎451-2101). For **accommodation**, there are simple lodgings at **Crocker Cabins** in Trout River (☎451-3236; units ③; mid-May to mid-Sept).

Western Brook Pond and Broom Point

Western Brook Pond, reached by just one access point, 25km north of Rocky Harbour beside route 430, is one of eastern Canada's finest landscapes, 16km of deep, dark-blue water framed by mighty mountains and huge waterfalls. The whole ensemble is a view rivalling the fjords of Norway. This freshwater fjord is one of the most remote spots in eastern Canada and until the 1970s very few people knew of its existence outside of the hunting and fishing fraternity.

From the access point car park it's a forty-minute walk on a well-maintained trail through forest and over bog land to the edge of the lake's gorge along the **Western Brook Pond Trail**, which crosses the narrow coastal plain. When you get to the end, don't skimp on the two-hour **boat trip** – weather permitting, they run three times daily (10am, 1pm & 4pm) from mid-June to early September, and once daily (1pm) from early to mid-June and early September to mid-October, with an additional evening tour (6.15pm) from mid-July to mid-August, depending on numbers (☎458-2730 or 1-800-563-9887; $27). The boat takes you between the cliffs right to the extreme eastern end of the lake, past several huge rockslides, dramatic **hanging valleys** and former sea caves high up in the cliff faces; at one point you are taken virtually underneath a large waterfall. Western Brook Pond also boasts a couple of extremely difficult hiking trails, the 27-kilometre **Snug Harbour–North Rim** route, which branches off from the main path between the road and the pond, and the 35-kilometre **Long Range Mountains** trail at the eastern end of the pond. Both these tracks have rudimentary campgrounds at $35 per night – obtain advice and permits from the information centre at Rocky Harbour. If you're without a car, Pittman's Taxis in Norris Point (☎458-2486) will take you from Rocky Harbour to the access point for $35, or Gros Morne Adventure Tours (☎458-2250) will get you there on its shuttle bus for roughly the same price.

At **Broom Point**, 6km north of Western Brook Pond, there's a **fisherman's cabin** and store restored to its appearance in the 1940s, when it was an important station for local fishermen (mid-June to Sept daily 10am–6pm; admission with park pass). It's an evocative place, surrounded by **tuckamores** – clumps of balsam firs and spruce stunted by constant exposure to wind.

Port au Choix

The tiny fishing village of **PORT AU CHOIX**, 160km from Rocky Harbour, sits on a bleak headland beside the **Port au Choix National Historic Site** (daily: June–Aug 9am–8pm; Sept to mid-Oct 9.30am–4.30pm; $2.75), established where a mass of prehistoric bones, tools and weapons were accidentally discovered in the 1960s. The ensuing archeological dig unearthed three ancient cemeteries, confirming the area as a centre of settlement for the **Maritime Archaic People**, hunters and gatherers who lived here around 2000 BC. The nearby **Visitor Reception Centre** (same times) provides the background on this culture and on that of the later **Groswater** and **Dorset Eskimos**, whose scant remains in the area confirm that about two or three thousand years ago Port au Choix was their most southerly settlement. Among the centre's exhibits are an actual excavated Dorset house and a collection of shamanistic amulets, some in the shape of newborn babies and killer whales. From the centre it's a twenty-minute walk around the tip of a peninsula to a **lighthouse**, where there are a few uninspiring remains of a Dorset settlement. A further twenty minutes will bring you to **Phillip's Garden**, which has more Eskimo sites. In the rather unattractive village itself, opposite the fish-processing plant, is the site of the Maritime Archaic **burial ground** – although it's nothing more than a grassy mound.

The Port au Choix area has a handful of **places to stay**: try the *Sea Echo Motel*, right in the centre of town (☎861-3777 or 861-3778; ③), or the *Point Riche Inn*, on Point Riche Road (☎861-3773 or 861-2112; ②), which is conveniently near the reception centre and lighthouse. For **food**, the choices are limited: there's the *Anchor Café*, beside the burial ground, or the *Point Riche Room*, in the *Sea Echo Motel*, where for $12.95 you'll get a plate heaped with a halibut steak, salmon steak and fresh **shrimp** – the latter a speciality of the Port au Choix area.

St Barbe and St Anthony

Pressing on from Port au Choix, it's about 80km to the hamlet of **ST BARBE**, where there's a **car ferry** service on the *Northern Princess* (May–Dec 1–3 daily; 1hr 30min; $9 passengers, $18.50 vehicles; ☎726-0015 or 722-4000) across the Strait of Belle Isle to **Blanc-Sablon**, on the Québec–Labrador boundary (see p.421); vehicles are taken on a first-come, first-served basis. If you're waiting for the ferry, the only place to **eat** is in the dining room of the *Dockside Motel*, just up the road from the terminal.

From St Barbe, route 430 slips through a handful of fishing villages before cutting east across the peninsula for the fishing and supply centre of **ST ANTHONY**. With a population of about four thousand, this is the region's largest settlement, but it's not much more than a humdrum port stretched out around the wide sweep of its harbour, the main recompense being the remains of the Norse village at L'Anse aux Meadows, 42km north along route 430 (see p.416).

In town, the one worthwhile attraction is the **Grenfell House Museum** (daily: June–Aug 9am–8pm; Sept 9am–1pm & 2–5pm; $2), tucked behind the Charles S. Curtis Hospital. The building, a dark-green shingled house in New England cottage style, is the restored home of the pioneering missionary doctor, Sir Wilfred Grenfell, an Englishman who first came here on behalf of the Royal National Mission to Deep Sea Fishermen in 1892. He never moved back home and, during his forty-year stay, he established the region's first proper hospitals, nursing stations, schools and cooperative stores. Behind the house, there's a pleasant woodland path that leads to the top of a hill, where the ashes of Grenfell and his wife are kept.

Practicalities

There are daily **flights** to St Anthony from most of Newfoundland's larger settlements and from several of eastern Canada's main cities. The **airport** is near Seal Bay, a rather distant 55km west of town on Hwy 430, and onward transport to the centre is by taxi only – reckon on $40. If flying is out of your price range, Viking Express runs a **bus** service to St Anthony from Deer Lake (see p.411). For central **accommodation**, there's *Howell's Tourist Home*, 1 Spruce Lane (☎454-3402 or 454-8494; ①; April–Nov); the *St Anthony Haven Inn*, 14 Goose Cove Rd (☎454-9100; ③); and the *Vinland Motel*, 19 West St (☎454-8843 or 1-800-563-7578; ③). Most attractive of the lot is *Lynn's Bed & Breakfast*, 340 West St (☎454-2677; ②), a house surrounded by colourful flowerbeds. Good seafood **meals** are available at the *Lightkeeper's Café*, at Fishing Point at the end of West Street, although the service can be a bit unfriendly. However, it's a good place to watch for the numerous icebergs that drift by.

Unfortunately, there are no public transport connections between St Anthony and L'Anse aux Meadows, and the return taxi fare will cost you about $60. Alternatively, Tilden at Woodward Motors on West Street (☎454-4000), and at the airport (☎454-8522), has reasonably priced, short-term car rental deals.

L'Anse aux Meadows: the Norse village

L'Anse aux Meadows National Historic Site (daily: mid-June to Aug 9am–8pm; Sept to mid-Oct 9.30am–4.30pm; $5; hourly 45min guided tours), a UNESCO World Heritage Site comprising the scant remains of the earliest verified European settlement in the Americas, is a tribute to the obsessive drive of **Helge Ingstad**, a Norwegian writer and explorer who from 1960 hunted high and low to find Norse settlements on the North Atlantic seaboard. His efforts were inspired by two medieval Icelandic sagas, which detailed the establishment of the colony of **Vinland** somewhere along this coast in about 1000 AD.

At L'Anse aux Meadows, Ingstad was led by a local to a group of grassed-over bumps and ridges beside Epaves Bay. This unremarkable area, next to a peat bog, contained the remnants of the only **Norse village** ever to have been discovered in North America – the foundations of eight turf and timber buildings and a ragbag of archeological finds, including a cloak pin, a stone anvil, nails, pieces of bog iron, an oil lamp, and a small spindle whorl. Ingstad concluded that these were left behind by a group of about one hundred sailors, carpenters and blacksmiths who probably remained at the site for only one or two years and used it as a base for further exploration of the area.

The site was thoroughly excavated between 1961 and 1968 and there followed an acrimonious academic debate about whether it was actually "Vinland". The geographical clues provided in the sagas are extremely vague, so the argument is essentially linguistic, hinging on the various possible interpretations of the old Icelandic word "Vinland", with one side insisting that it means "Wine-land" and therefore cannot refer to anywhere in Newfoundland, the other suggesting the word means "fertile land" and therefore it could.

Whatever the truth of the matter, hundreds of tourists come here every summer and begin their tour at the **Visitor Reception Centre** (same hours as site; ☎623-2601), where the Norse artefacts and changing exhibitions on Viking life and culture are beefed up by an excellent if somewhat melodramatic thirty-minute film entitled *The Vinland Mystery*. From here it's a few minutes' walk to the cluster of gentle mounds that make up what's left of the original village, and another short stroll to a group of full-scale replicas of a **long house**, storage shed, workshop and a *faering*, a small boat used for coastal hunting. A full-scale replica of a square-masted **Viking ship** dominates the village just a few hundred metres away.

Most people use St Anthony as a base for visiting L'Anse aux Meadows, but if you're travelling by car it's also worth considering a **stay** at the *Tickle Inn* (☎452-4321, reservations essential; ②; June–Sept), an attractive late nineteenth-century house located on the shores of a secluded cove at remote **Cape Onion**. The Cape is approached along Route 437, a 25-kilometre-long paved road that branches off from Route 436, the main highway between St Anthony and L'Anse aux Meadows. If the *Tickle Inn* is full, try the closer community of **Gunner's Cove**, 10km from L'Anse aux Meadows on Route 436; it's where the American author E. Annie Proulx stayed when she was researching and writing her best-selling novel, *The Shipping News*.

Channel-Port aux Basques and the south

CHANNEL-PORT AUX BASQUES sits by the ocean right in the southwest corner of Newfoundland, serving as the region's fishing and transportation centre, with regular ferry connections to North Sydney in Nova Scotia (see p.346), and a daily bus ser-

VINLAND AND THE VIKINGS

The first **Viking** voyages, in the eighth century, had no wider purpose than the plunder of their Scandinavian neighbours, but by the start of the ninth century overpopulation at home had pushed them towards migration and colonization. By 870 they had settled on the shores of Iceland, and by the start of the eleventh century there were about three thousand Norse colonists established in Greenland. As good farmland became scarce, so it was inevitable that there would be another push west.

The two **Vinland sagas** – the *Graenlendinga* and *Eirik's Saga* – give us the only extant account of these further explorations, recounting the exploits of Leif Eiriksson the Lucky and Thorfinn Karlsefni, his merchant brother-in-law, who founded a colony they called **Vinland** in North America around 1000 AD. Although eventually forced to abandon Vinland by relentless threats from the local peoples – whom they called *skraelings*, literally "wretches" – the Norse settlers continued to secure resources from the region for the next few decades, and it seems likely that the site discovered at **L'Anse aux Meadows** is the result of one of these foragings.

The Norse carried on collecting timber from Labrador up until the fourteenth century, when a dramatic deterioration in the climate made the trip from Greenland too dangerous. Attacks from the Inuit and the difficulties of maintaining trading links with Scandinavia then took their toll on the main Greenland colonies. All contact between Greenland and the outside world was lost around 1410 and the last of the half-starved, disease-ridden survivors died out towards the end of the fifteenth century – when Christopher Columbus was eyeing up his "New World".

vice to St John's, about thirteen hours' drive away. The town is divided into two distinct sections, an older part stuck on a bare and bumpy headland behind the ferry terminal, and a newer section spread out around Grand Bay Road, about 2km to the west.

Apart from the ferries, there's no possible reason to come here, but in emergencies it's useful to know that the place has a clutch of reasonably priced **accommodation**. Walking out of the ferry port, turn left towards the old part of town, along Caribou Street, where you'll find the *Heritage Home*, 11 Caribou St (☎695-3240; ②; May–Oct), and *Walker's Motel*, just off Caribou Road on Marine Drive (☎695-7355; ③). Alternatively, in the newer part of town, there's the *Caribou Bed and Breakfast*, 30 Grand Bay Rd (☎695-3408; ②; May–Oct), which is near the *Hotel Port aux Basques* (☎695-2171; ③). The *Harbour Restaurant*, on Caribou Road, is the best place in town to **eat**, but for a taste of real home-cooked food in a typical outport community, drive 10km east on Hwy 470 to **Margaree**, where you'll find the reasonably priced and friendly *Seashore Restaurant*.

The only tourist attraction in Channel-Port aux Basques is the **Gulf Museum**, 118 Main St (mid-June to mid-Aug daily 1–8pm; $2.50), which has a collection of marine artefacts, all of which are rather unexciting, save for an early seventeenth-century astrolabe. The **tourist information chalet**, overlooking the town about 1km north along the Trans-Canada (daily: mid-May to Aug 6am–11pm; Sept & Oct 7am–8pm; ☎695-2262), has a range of literature dealing with the whole of Newfoundland.

The south coast

The submerged rocks and jutting headlands of Newfoundland's **south coast** have witnessed the shipwreck of hundreds of vessels as they attempted to steer round the island into the Gulf of St Lawrence, some running aground in a fog bank, others driven ashore by tremendous gales. Such was the frequency of these disasters that many outports came to rely on washed-up timber for firewood and building materials, a bonus for communities all too dependent on the trade price of fish. The flotsam and jetsam days are long gone, but the south coast remains one of the poorer parts of Newfoundland, an isolated region where most of the tiny villages remain accessible only by sea. If you're after seeing a slice of traditional outport life, then this is the nearest you'll come, though it's difficult to select one place over another. Most of the outports have simple **guesthouses** (usually in price category ②, including all meals), but unfortunately there's no central agency that has lists of which families in which outports take in guests. It's best to check the phone book for each community to see if there's a chamber of commerce – or at least a town office – and give them a call. If you express interest in a particular outport, you won't have any problem finding accommodation there – the townsfolk will be only too pleased that you're coming and, with true Newfoundland hospitality, will set you up for a couple of days or a week.

At one time you could travel the entire length of the south coast by **boat** from Channel-Port aux Basques to Terrenceville, 260km away, but this is no longer possible; visiting the outports now requires more advance planning, with careful attention given to ferry schedules. You have to travel 40km east to Rose Blanche, where the road ends, or take Strickland's Taxi (☎695-3333; $45). From Rose Blanche (the turnoff for the ferry is just a few kilometres west of town) you can get as far as Hermitage–Sandyville, about 180km east, but this involves several changes of ferries and several overnight stays of two or three days, as boats run to very irregular schedules. **ROSE BLANCHE** itself is not to be missed, a picturesque village with the steepest roads and the most brightly coloured houses you'll encounter anywhere in Newfoundland. The Department of Works, Services and Transportation Boat Service (☎635-4100) leaves for Grand Bruit Monday, Wednesday, Friday and Saturday at 3pm (2hr 30min; $3.50), where you have to change for Burgeo (Thurs 9.15am; 3hr; $4.25). In **GRAND BRUIT**, the only approved lodgings are the *Blue Mountain Cabins* (☎492-2753; ②; June–Sept). In **BURGEO**, a much larger community, you can **stay** either at *Gillett's Motel*, on Inspiration Road (☎886-1284; ②), or the *Haven Bed and Breakfast*, right on the harbour (☎886-2544; ②), but be sure to book ahead.

Two of the outports on the south coast are **accessible by road** – Burgeo and Harbour Breton. Devin's Bus Line (5 weekly; ☎886-2955 or 886-2576) links Burgeo with Corner Brook along Hwy 480, and Hickey's (3 weekly; ☎885-2523 or 885-2167) connects Harbour Breton with Grand Falls along Hwy 360. Besides private guesthouses, the only place to **stay** in **HARBOUR BRETON** is the *Southern Port Hotel* (☎885-2283 or 885-2505; ②–③), which has only ten rooms. In all cases, reserve and confirm onward transport before you set out.

One of the prettier outports is **RAMEA**, perched on a tiny island stuck out in the ocean near Burgeo, 83 nautical miles from Channel-Port aux Basques. To **get there**, take the ferry from Burgeo (mid-May to mid-Oct Mon & Wed 2 daily, Tues & Thurs 1 daily, Fri & Sun 3 daily; mid-Oct to mid-May Mon, Wed, Sat & Sun 2 daily, Tues & Thurs 1 daily, Fri 3 daily; 1hr 20min; $2.50). There's one **B&B**, the *Four Winds Tourist Home* (☎625-2002; ②); for bookings at guesthouses call the Town of Ramea (town office) (☎625-2280). A second attractive spot is **FRANÇOIS**, forty nautical miles further east, an ancient settlement sitting precariously under the steep slopes of "The Friar", a startling rocky outcrop. In this truly isolated community of 175 people, there are no automobiles, no locked doors and no policemen. For **lodgings**, contact the François Tourism and Development Committee (☎842-4112).

LABRADOR

Labrador, 293,347 square kilometres of sub-arctic wilderness on the northeastern edge of the Canadian Shield, is a place so desolate that it provoked Jacques Cartier to remark "I am rather inclined to believe that this is the land God gave to Cain." The adjacent towns of **Happy Valley–Goose Bay**, located on the westernmost tip of the huge

Hamilton Inlet, have an average maximum temperature of –16°C/3°F in January and an annual snowfall of 445cm, much of which remains on the ground for half the year. Further inland and up north the climate is even worse. Just thirty thousand people live in Labrador, concentrated in coastal villages that are linked by a ferry service from early July to mid-October, and inland mining areas that have only received road access in the last ten years – the road from **Labrador City** to Happy Valley–Goose Bay was completed in 1991.

This desolate terrain has long been a bone of contention between Québec and Newfoundland, whose current **common border** was set in the 1920s by the Privy Council when it ordained that Newfoundland had jurisdiction not just over the undisputed northern shore – the traditional domain of Newfoundland fishermen – but also over the central Labrador plateau, from which the north shore's rivers drained. Newfoundland's territory was expanded by some 293,000 square kilometres, more than twice the size of the island itself, whilst Québec was left ranting about anglophone imperialism. The border again became a problem in 1961, when it was decided to develop the hydro-electric potential of Labrador's **Churchill Falls**, a project that required Québec's participation, as Québec would have to buy some of the electricity if it were to be a viable scheme, and the power lines would encroach on its land as well. Eventually a compromise was reached whereby Newfoundland could receive Labrador's power via a toll-free route through Québec, in return for which Québec could tap the headwaters of five rivers in southern Labrador. However, the Québécois remain indignant about their loss of territory and the issue is likely to be debated again as they move towards separation.

The original owners of this land, the Naskapi, Innu and Inuit, who collectively number around five thousand, were more or less left alone until the last few decades, when the economic potential of Labrador was realized. Dams and mines have disrupted the local ecology – the Labrador Trough in western Labrador has the highest concentration of **iron ore** in North America, and in August 1997 Inuit and Innu set up blockades in an attempt to disrupt the construction of a **nickel mine** and mill at Voisey Bay, in northern Labrador. Even more destructive is the use of the area by Dutch, British and German air forces to practise wartime drills and bombing raids. Inuits have been imprisoned for staging sit-ins and chaining themselves to the gates of the Goose Bay air base, which is built on their land, and do not intend to halt the protests until the low-level sorties (up to ten thousand a year) and bombings are halted.

Information and tours

Labrador is one of Canada's most forbidding areas, so any trip needs a fair amount of organization, and a great deal if you are heading for the hinterland. It is perhaps best to opt for one of the various **tours** available (see box on p.423) which, though expensive, make the exploration of Labrador's wilds as trouble-free as possible. Whichever way you go, it's important to take the strongest fly ointment you can find (workers in Labrador carry emergency syringes of the stuff) and heavy winter clothing, as even in the height of summer savage snowstorms can occur.

Maps, timetables and other **information** are available in advance from the **Department of Tourism, Culture and Recreation**, PO Box 8730, St John's, Newfoundland A1B 4K2 (☎729-2830 or 1-800-563-6353, fax 729-1965), or **Destination Labrador**, 118 Humphrey Rd, Bruno Plaza, Labrador City A2V 2J8 (☎944-7788, fax 944-7787).

The Newfoundland and Labrador telephone code is ☎709.

Getting there

Labrador has **airports** at Happy Valley–Goose Bay, Wabush and Churchill Falls, with scheduled services by Air Alliance (☎1-800-363-7050) from various points in Québec, and regular flights by Air Nova (☎726-7880 or 1-800-563-5151), Canadian Airlines (☎576-0274 or 1-800-665-1177) and Air Labrador (☎753-5593 or 1-800-563-3042) from Newfoundland. Expect to pay $610 for a return Québec City–Wabush flight and $690 for a return Montréal–Wabush flight; it's half that for a flight from St John's and Deer Lake in Newfoundland.

Less expensive are the **ferries from Newfoundland**. Puddister Trading Company runs a service from St Barbe, about 80km north of Port au Choix, across the Strait of Belle Isle to Blanc-Sablon in Québec, on the southern border of Labrador (May–Dec 1–3 daily; 1hr 30min; adult $18 return, car $37 return; ☎726-0015 or 722-4000 for information). To get to the heart of Labrador, Marine Atlantic runs the *Sir Robert Bond* from Lewisporte in Newfoundland to Happy Valley–Goose Bay (mid-June to mid-Sept 2 weekly; 33hr; adults $97 one way, cars $160, single cabins $37.50 per night, doubles $75; Lewisporte terminal reservations ☎535-6876, Happy Valley–Goose Bay ☎896-5072, USA toll-free ☎1-800-341-7981). Marine Atlantic also runs a foot-passenger steamship, the

Northern Ranger, from St Anthony, which visits numerous coastal settlements in Labrador from early July to mid-October, usually travelling as far north as Nain. Sailing on ten designated days, it takes twelve days to complete a return journey from St Anthony to Nain, and it's possible to travel just a segment of the journey; rates are 25¢ per nautical mile plus the cost of a bunk in a cabin, which starts at $27.50 per night; for your own double cabin, reckon on $77 per night. It's expected that by 1998 this particular Marine Atlantic service will be taken over by the provincial government, resulting in a possible change in schedules; call ☎1-800-341-7981 to find out the latest developments.

The 416-kilometre **rail** line that links Sept-Îles in Québec with Labrador City and Schefferville is primarily an industrial link, but there is limited space for passengers and the journey is an exhilarating ride over high bridges, through dense forest and stunted tundra, past seventy-metre-high waterfalls, deep gorges and rocky mountains – a special dome car allows passengers to appreciate the awesome views. Trains for Labrador City leave Sept-Îles every Tuesday at 7pm and Thursday at 9am, and take around eight hours ($115 return); trains run to Schefferville from Sept-Îles on Thursday at 9am (11hr; $156 return). Contact the Québec North Shore and Labrador Railway (☎709/944-8205 or 418/968-7805) for reservations.

It's possible to **drive** to Labrador from Québec via the 580-kilometre route 389 from Baie-Comeau to Labrador City and Wabush; the road is partly paved and partly gravel and has fuel, food and accommodation services along much of its length. There are rumours of a planned bus service – contact the station in Baie-Comeau for the latest (☎418/296-2593).

Getting around

With the exception of the rail line that terminates at Schefferville, there is no land-based public transport in Labrador, and the unpaved 526-kilometre road linking Happy Valley–Goose Bay to Labrador City via Churchill Falls can only be used with ease in summer and takes, on average, ten hours to traverse. (From mid-May to mid-June, when there's the greatest chance of rain and the road becomes muddy, the Happy Valley–Goose Bay to Churchill Falls section is closed altogether.) The only other road is the 81-kilometre Route 510, which runs north from Blanc-Sablon in Québec to Red Bay. For non-drivers, or for those who want to reach the far-off outposts, there are **internal flights** run by Air Labrador in Happy Valley–Goose Bay (☎896-3387); the flight to Nain (daily except Sat) costs $437 return. Alternatively, but more expensive, is the coastal service of the *Northern Ranger* steamship (see above).

Blanc-Sablon to Red Bay

The car ferry from St Barbe in Newfoundland across the Strait of Belle Isle to Blanc-Sablon makes it possible to explore the coastal settlements along an 81-kilometre road (Route 510) to Red Bay, then return to Newfoundland on the second boat of the day – a possibility that more tourists exploit every year. The trip over is an experience in itself, with the vessel dwarfed by icebergs floating down the strait from Greenland, and minke and humpback whales a constant sight.

This coast has been inhabited for over nine thousand years, first by caribou-hunters and then by Basque whalers, but permanent settlements did not evolve until the turn of the eighteenth century, when fishermen from Newfoundland began summer migrations to these well-stocked waters. Those who chose to live here all year were known in Newfoundland as "livyers" and led terribly harsh lives under the control of the English merchants' corrupt truck system and the supplies of alcohol that kept them in a constant state of debt. Their standard of living was greatly improved by Wilfred Grenfell, the superintendent of the Mission to Deep Sea Fishermen from 1892, who established hospitals, orphanages and nursing stations all along the coast, and succeeded in bringing the truck system to an end (see p.415). The livyers, incidentally, were the first to train **Labrador retrievers** to catch any fish that fell off the hook.

Along Route 510

Villages such as L'Anse-au-Loup, Capstan Island and West St Modeste are the descendants of the fishing camps that huddled against eastern Labrador's cliffs. The only sights that might detain you are the 7500-year-old **burial mound** of a 12-year-old Indian boy at L'Anse-Amour, which is the oldest-known funeral monument in North America; a 33-metre mid-nineteenth-century **lighthouse** at Point Amour (June–Oct daily 10am–5.30pm; free); and the **Labrador Straits Museum** (July to mid-Sept daily 10am–6pm; $1.50) between Forteau and L'Anse-au-Loup, which traces the area's history, with particular emphasis on the important contributions made by Labrador women.

There are also several **places to stay** along this stretch of the 510: the *Beachside Hospitality Home* (☎931-2662 or 1-800-563-8999; ②) and the *Northern Light Inn* (☎931-2332 or 931-2708; ③–④) are both in L'Anse-au-Clair, only 8km from the ferry terminal; the *Seaview Motel* (☎931-2840; ③) is in Forteau, the next settlement northeast; and *Barney's Bed & Breakfast* (☎927-5634; ②) is in L'Anse-au-Loup, 3km northeast of Forteau.

Red Bay

RED BAY, 80km from Blanc-Sablon and at the end of Route 510, was the largest **whaling port** in the world in the late sixteenth century and is the most worthwhile place to visit on Labrador's east coast. At its peak, over a thousand men lived here during the whaling season, producing half a million gallons of whale oil to be shipped back on a month-long voyage to Europe. Whale oil was used for light, lubrication and as an additive to drugs, soap and pitch, and one 55-gallon barrel could fetch a price equal to $10,000 today – so for the **Basques** the discovery of Labrador's right whale stocks was equivalent to striking oil. However, as well as the treacherous journey from Spain to what they knew as Terranova, the Basques withstood terrible hardships to claim their rich booty. Once in Labrador, they rowed fragile wooden craft called *chalupas* into these rough seas and then attached drogues to the whales to slow them down. It was then a matter of following their prey for hours until the whale surfaced and could be lanced to death. Three factors brought the whale boom to an end: first, the Basques were so successful that within thirty years they had killed off more than 15,000 whales; second, the industry became more hazardous with early freeze-ups in the 1570s; and finally, the Basque ships and men were absorbed into the ill-fated Spanish Armada of 1588.

Serious study of this fascinating area began in 1977, when marine archeologists discovered the remains of three Basque galleons and several *chalupas*. Most notable of these vessels was the *San Juan* galleon, which was split in half by an iceberg in 1565, with the loss of one black rat – its bones were found in a wicker basket with a scattering of codfish bones, which showed that the heading and splitting techniques were identical to those used by the Labrador fishermen today. On land, excavations uncovered try-works (where the whale blubber was boiled down into oil), personal artefacts and, in 1982, a cemetery on Saddle Island where the remains of 160 young men were found. Many were lying in groups, indicating that they died as crew members when chasing the whales, but some had not been buried – which suggests that the community had died of starvation when an early freeze dashed their chances of getting home.

New objects are constantly being discovered and a **Visitors' Centre** (mid-June to Sept Mon–Sat 9am–6.30pm, Sun noon–6.30pm; $2; ☎920-2197) at the **Red Bay National Historic Site** allows you to explore the archeological sites. An excellent hour-long documentary film at the centre shows footage of the discovery that revealed so much

---

SPECIALIST TOUR COMPANIES

BreakAway Adventures, c/o Larry Bradley, 4 Cook St, Happy Valley–Goose Bay, Labrador A0P 1E0 (☎896-9343). Guided or unguided wilderness river trips in a kayak at $40–60 per day. April–Oct.

Labrador Adventure Treks, c/o Jim Learning, PO Box 163, Happy Valley–Goose Bay, Labrador A0P 1E0 (☎896-5720). Camping, canoeing, tours, white-water canoeing and kayak trips in central Labrador. One day to two weeks. July–Sept.

Labrador Scenic Limited, PO Box 233, North West River, Labrador A0P 1M0 (☎ & fax 497-8326). Wilderness tours lasting up to two weeks and costing from around $180 per day. Also canoe and kayak rentals. March–Oct. Winter snowmobile tours (half-day $90; full day $180).

Nunatsuak Limited, c/o Tom Goodwin, PO Box 10, Nain, Labrador A0P 1L0 (☎922-2910). Weekly scheduled boat tour offering excursions to sights north of Nain, including the Torngat Mountains and Saglek fjord. $600 per day. April–Oct.

T&R Marina, 1 Hamilton River Rd, Happy Valley–Goose Bay, Labrador A0P 1E0 (☎896-2766). Boat tours on the Churchill River to Muskrat Falls or Mud Lake. Half-day (4hr; $40), full day (12hr; $60) or evening (3hr; $25). May–Oct.

Wilderness Excursions, c/o Mr Lindo Watkins, 322 Curtis Crescent, Labrador City, Labrador A2V 2B9 (☎944-5341). Day and overnight dogsled excursions in Labrador West. Mid-Feb to early April.

---

about Canada's early history. If you're feeling adventurous you can also take a boat trip to Saddle Island (Mon–Sat 3 daily 9am–4pm; $2), where you can roam around the whaler's cemetery.

Red Bay's *Whaling Station Cabins*, 61 East Harbour Drive (☎920-2156; ③), offers en-suite rooms with cable TV, and has the best **restaurant** in the area, while more basic **accommodation** is available at the *Basinview Bed & Breakfast*, 145 Main Highway (☎920-2002; ①–②), run by friendly owners with a knowledge of the town's Basque whaling history.

Northern Labrador

So far, the north is the most untouched area of Labrador, a region where the nomadic Inuit and Naskapi have managed to escape the clutches of modern Canadian society – though the production of souvenirs such as the soapstone carvings available all over Canada is now an intrinsic part of their economy. Few visitors venture this far: once you've reached Happy Valley–Goose Bay from Lewisporte on the *Sir Robert Bond*, it takes a further four or five days for the coastal boats to reach their northerly limit of Nain – and a sudden storm can leave you stranded for days in one of the tiny settlements.

Most of the coastal villages beyond Happy Valley–Goose Bay began as fur-trading posts in the nineteenth century, though some date back to the eighteenth-century establishment of missions by the **Moravian Brethren**, a small German missionary sect. Their old mission – consisting of a church, residence, store, storehouse and small huts to house visiting native peoples – still stands at **Hopedale**, 150km south of Nain (July–Sept by appointment; $5; ☎933-3777 or 623-2601), and at **NAIN** the mission has been converted into a museum called **Piulimatsivik** – Inuit for "place where we keep the old things" (July–Sept by appointment; donation; ☎922-2327 or 922-2158). From Nain you can travel onwards to the flat-topped **Torngat Mountains**, the highest range east of the Rockies; contact Nunatsuak *Limited* at the *Atsanik Lodge* (☎922-2910; ④), whose owners charter boats for up to five people at $600 per day. They will take you wherever you want to go and pick you up when you've finished exploring, but you need all your own equipment. An astounding trip is to the **Nachvak Fjord**, near Labrador's northernmost extremity, where the razorback mountains soar out of the sea at an angle of nearly eighty degrees to a height of 915m. En route you're likely to spot grey seals, whales, peregrine falcons and golden eagles.

Happy Valley–Goose Bay and around

GOOSE BAY, located on the broad Churchill River as it opens into Hamilton Inlet along with the adjacent former trapping community of **HAPPY VALLEY**, is Labrador's principal air-transport hub. Goose Bay itself has, since World War II, been primarily a **military base** for American, Canadian and NATO forces; it's now home to large contingents of British, German and Dutch troops. Happy Valley, by contrast, is where most of the shops and restaurants are located.

The Town

The town is a fairly quiet laid-back place, with sandy paths instead of sidewalks, which peter out into dirt and gravel at the edges of town. However, the stillness is frequently punctuated by the roar of **low-flying military aircraft**, the thunderous noise swelling up when you least expect it, and lasting for about ten seconds at a time. There are few sights to occupy your visit here, but if you're here in late July or early August the **Labrador Canoe Regatta** is the area's most important festival; the hectic, carnival-like event is held on a weekend and features canoe races, musical performances and pavilions serving traditional food. There are also two museums: the **Northern Lights Military Museum**, 170 Hamilton River Rd (Mon–Wed & Sat 9am–5.30pm, Thurs & Fri 9am–9pm; free), an eclectic collection of military memorabilia, stuffed wildlife displays and model trains; and the **Labrador Military Museum**, in a large hangar on C Street on the base (June–Aug Mon–Fri 10am–5pm, Sat & Sun 2–4pm; Sept–May by appointment; ☎896-6900 ext 2177), where the history of the British, American, Dutch and German – as well as Canadian – military presence is documented through displays such as flags, insignia and radar apparatus. Particularly poignant are the references to the all too-frequent fatal **air crashes** that have occurred here in the past forty years.

Practicalities

The tiny **airport** is located on the base, just a few kilometres north of town. As there's no shuttle bus or public transport, you'll have to rely on renting a **car**. Tilden and Budget have booths at the airport and both charge about $40 per day, with the first 100km per day free. To get to town, take C Street and Loring Drive and turn right at the traffic lights (the only ones in town) onto Hamilton River Road. On the way into Goose Bay, notice the metal **chain-link fence** indicating that you've left the base and entered civilian territory. **Taxis** cost about $7.50 to Goose Bay, $10 to Happy Valley.

The helpful staff at the **Visitor Centre**, 365 Hamilton River Rd (June–Aug daily 9am–9pm; Sept–May Mon–Fri 9am–5pm; ☎896-8787) will provide you with brochures and help you plan your trips out of town to places such as North West River (see opposite). Some of the staff will even act as your tour guides. Happy Valley–Goose Bay, as befits its status as a transport hub, has a reasonable range of **accommodation**. The three best choices – all fairly standard motel-type lodgings with the usual facilities – are the large, prefabricated *Aurora Hotel*, 382 Hamilton River Rd (☎896-3398 or 1-800-563-3066; ④–⑤), and the impersonal *Labrador Inn* next door (☎896-3351; ④), both in Goose Bay; and the *Royal Inn*, 3 Royal St (☎896-2456; ③–④), in Happy Valley. The best places to **eat** are *Tricia Dee's*, 96 Hamilton River Rd, specializing in steaks and ribs, and the *Midway Gardens Restaurant*, 350 Hamilton River Rd. At *Trappers Cabin Bar and Grill*, 1 Aspen Rd, you cook your steak yourself on their grill. Happy Valley–Goose Bay is a hard-drinking town, so there are plenty of places to quench your thirst: liveliest are *Mulligan's Pub*, 368 Hamilton River Rd, and *Maxwell's II/Bentley's*, 97 Hamilton River Rd, the town's main nightspot.

Around Happy Valley–Goose Bay

Although Happy Valley–Goose Bay is an isolated town, there are still some excursions to be made beyond its boundaries. The furthest you can go on paved road is about 40km to Sheshatsheits and North West River, passing the turnoff for the Lewisporte ferry and then a large ski hill. Be sure and stop to see **Simeon Falls**, a forest waterfall in the middle of a dense, moss-covered thicket. It's easy to miss: watch for a sign on the road that says "Waterfall 600ft" and then walk along a short winding trail over a tangle of tree roots.

NORTH WEST RIVER itself is a small former fur-trading community picturesquely sited on a broad isthmus between two vast bodies of water: Grand Lake, a deep freshwater lake to the west, and Lake Melville, an inland sea with tides and long sandy beaches to the east. For a panoramic **view**, drive the 2km up to **Sunday Hill** on a rather rough, potholed road; you'll be rewarded with sweeping vistas of both lakes and the Mealy and Mokami ranges in the distance. In the village the main attraction is the home and **studio of John Goudie**, on River Road (Mon–Fri 8am–5pm, Sat & Sun 10am–5pm), a local artist who makes furniture and jewellery out of Labradorite, a lustrous crystallized stone. He'll show you his studio where he and his assistants craft the stone and then take you into his house to see the furniture he's made, as well as a huge Labradorite-studded fireplace.

The newly opened **Labrador Interpretation Centre**, located on Hillview Drive above the town (daily 1–4pm; free), has displays of Innu and Inuit crafts, quilts and sculpture, as well as ancient artefacts found in nearby graves. There's also a display relating to the tragic **Hubbard expedition** in 1903, when three ill-equipped men set out from the town by canoe to explore the interior, resulting in one death. Directions to the centre are poor: take the road sharp left immediately after crossing the bridge and continue driving up the hill to the end of the road.

The Innu village of **SHESHATSHEITS** (pronounced "shesh-ah-shee"), across the small harbour is worth a stroll as long as you don't linger too long; it's a traditional village and doesn't really encourage tourists.

To experience the Labrador countryside at its most awe-inspiring, make a trip to **Muskrat Falls**, a thunderous falls on the Churchill River, which is as close to a safari trek as you'll get in Labrador without going too far from civilization. To get there, drive out of Happy Valley on the Trans-Labrador Route 500. After about 40km, watch for a rather small sign on the left indicating a narrow dirt road, down which you drive about 10km and then park your car. From there it's another twenty-minute hike on a rough unmarked trail down to the bank of the river, where you can view the falls from a spray-covered rocky outcrop. There are no facilities along the way, so be sure to take good walking shoes, plenty of drinking water and insect repellent.

Western Labrador

From Happy Valley–Goose Bay it's also possible in the summer months to drive across to **Labrador City** and adjacent **Wabush** via **Churchill Falls** on the Trans-Labrador Highway (Route 500) – one of the least frequented stretches of road in eastern Canada, so take all necessary supplies, including fuel, with you, as there are no services along the route.

Churchill Falls

Rising from a spring high on the Labrador plateau, the **Churchill River** plunges through the Beaudoin Canyon and in a space of 32k drops 300m – 75m of which are accounted for by the **Churchill Falls**, about 300km west of Happy Valley–Goose Bay.

In order to exploit the massive power of this tumult, an area three and a half times the size of Lake Ontario was dammed for the incredible Churchill Falls hydroelectric development, a project conceived by the premier, Joey Smallwood, in 1952 as part of a drive to save Newfoundland's economy, whose only industrial plant at that time was a small copper mine on the northeast coast. Wrangling with possible US backers and then with the Québec government delayed its commencement until 1967, when a workforce of thirty thousand finally began the largest civil engineering project in North America. The town of **CHURCHILL FALLS** is simply an outgrowth of the power plant; if you want to stay here for a long look at the falls – which are half as high again as Niagara – **accommodation** and **food** are available at the *Churchill Falls Inn* (☎925-3211 or 1-800-229-3269; ④). **Tours** of the plant are offered daily (9am, 1pm & 7pm; 2hr–2hr 30min; free; for further information, call the *Churchill Falls Inn*).

Labrador City

A further 260km west it's a shock to come across **LABRADOR CITY** and neighbouring **Wabush**, two planned mining communities of wide streets and a couple of malls in the middle of nowhere; both were established in the 1950s and, with 10,500 people, make up the largest concentration of people in Labrador. Labrador City, as a terminus of the **rail line** from Sept-Îles, is a convenient gateway into Labrador's hinterland, but little else will bring you here. If you want to stay, **accommodation** is available at the *Carol Inn*, 215 Drake Ave (☎944-7736; ④), and the *Two Seasons Inn* on Avalon Drive (☎944-2661 or 1-800-670-7667; ④). The best choices for **eating** are the *Terrace Dining Room* in the *Two Seasons Inn*, and the *Cornelius Restaurant* in Bruno Plaza, 118 Humphrey Rd. **Duley Lake Park**, 10km from town, is a large **camping** area with over one hundred sites (day use $4; overnight $9; late June to early Sept) and excellent facilities for swimming and boating.

Schefferville

When the IOC mining operation opened the first Labrador iron-ore mine in the 1950s at **SCHEFFERVILLE** – the other rail terminus, 190km beyond Labrador City – they recruited a band of migratory Naskapi as cheap labour, so beginning a particularly woeful episode in the history of Canada's native peoples. In 1978 the natives signed an agreement giving them compensation for their lost land and exclusive hunting and fishing rights, but by that time the majority were so debilitated by alcohol that a return to their former existence was impossible. When the mine closed in the late 1980s, the Naskapi were left to fend for themselves while the white workers moved on to employment in other mines. Schefferville is now a run-down, blackfly-ridden reserve where houses can be bought for less than $10. Lying just over the border in Québec, the town is essentially a dead-end spot and only worth visiting as the terminus of the spectacular rail journey from Sept-Îles (there's no vehicular access); the only **accommodation** is the *Hôtel-Motel Royal*, 182 Rue Montagnais (☎585-2605; ③).

travel details

Trains
Labrador City to: Sept-Îles (2 weekly; 8hr).
Schefferville to: Sept-Îles (1 weekly; 11hr).

Buses
St John's to: Channel-Port aux Basques (1 daily; 12hr 35min); Clarenville (1 daily; 3hr); Corner Brook (1 daily; 10hr 25min); Grand Falls (1 daily; 6hr 45min); Lewisporte (1 daily; 5hr 55min).

Ferries
Argentia to: North Sydney, Nova Scotia (mid-June to Aug 3 weekly; early Sept to mid-Sept 2 weekly; 14hr).

Channel-Port aux Basques to: North Sydney, Nova Scotia (early Jan to mid-Jan 1–2 daily except Mon & Tues; mid-Jan to mid-June & mid-Sept to Dec 1–2 daily; mid-June to mid-Sept 1–3 daily; 5–7hr).

Lewisporte to: Happy Valley-Goose Bay (mid-June to mid-Sept 2 weekly; 33hr).

St Anthony to: Nain, via Labrador north shore ports (early July to mid-Oct weekly; 5–6 days).

St Barbe to: Blanc-Sablon (May–Dec 1–3 daily; 1hr 30min).

Flights

Happy Valley–Goose Bay to: Charlottetown (2 daily; 3hr 45min); Churchill Falls (3 weekly; 45min); Deer Lake (4 daily; 1hr 20min); Halifax (4 daily; 3hr 10min); Montréal (4 daily; 4hr); Québec City (4 daily; 3hr 25min); St John's (4 daily; 2hr–2hr 20min); Wabush (1 daily; 1hr 15min).

St John's to: Charlottetown (4–6 daily; 2hr 50min); Churchill Falls (3 weekly; 4hr 20min); Corner Brook (2–4 daily; 1hr 10min); Deer Lake (2–4 daily; 50min); Gander (3–6 daily; 40min); Halifax (4–6 daily; 1hr 10min); Happy Valley–Goose Bay (4 daily; 2hr–2hr 20min); Montréal (3–6 daily; 2hr 55min); Ottawa (4–5 daily; 3hr 35min); Québec City, no direct flights; (3–5 daily; 4hr 40min); St Anthony (1–2 daily except Sat; 1hr 15min); St Pierre (3 weekly; 1hr 15min); Toronto (5–7 daily; 3hr 25min); Wabash (1–2 daily; 3hr 15min).

Wabush to: Deer Lake (6 weekly; 1hr 55min–2hr 15min); Happy Valley–Goose Bay (1–2 daily; 1hr 5min); Montréal (1–2 daily; 3hr 10min); Ottawa (1 daily; 3hr 45min); Québec City (1–2 daily; 2hr 20min); Sept-Îles (6 weekly; 55min); St John's (1–2 daily; 3hr 15min).

CHAPTER FIVE

MANITOBA AND SASKATCHEWAN

The provinces of **Manitoba** and **Saskatchewan**, a vast tract bounded by the Ontario border to the east and the Rocky Mountains in Alberta to the west, together comprise a region commonly called "the prairies". In fact, flat treeless plains are confined to the southern part of **central Canada** and even then they are broken up by the occasional river valley and range of low-lying hills, which gradually raise the elevation from sea level at Hudson Bay to nearly 1200m near the Rockies. Furthermore, the plains themselves are divided into two broad geographical areas: the semi-arid short **grasslands** that border the United States in Alberta and Saskatchewan, and the **wheat-growing belt**, a crescent-shaped expanse to the north of the grasslands. In turn, this wheat belt borders the low hills, mixed farms and sporadic forests of the **aspen parkland**, a transitional zone between the plains and the **boreal forest**, whose trees, rocky outcrops, rivers and myriad lakes cover well over half of the entire central region, stretching to the Northwest Territories in Saskatchewan and Alberta and as far as the treeless **tundra** beside Hudson Bay in Manitoba.

If you're here in the winter, when the temperature can fall to –30°C or –40°C, and the wind rips down from the Arctic, it's hard to imagine how the European pioneers managed to survive, huddled together in remote log cabins or even sod huts. Yet survive they did, and between about 1895 and 1914 the great swathe of land that makes up the wheat belt and the aspen parkland had been turned into one of the most productive wheat-producing areas in the world. By any standards, the development of this farmland was a remarkable achievement, but the price was high: the nomadic culture of the **Plains Indians** was almost entirely destroyed and the disease-ravaged, half-starved survivors were dumped in a string of meagre reservations. Similarly, the **Métis**, descendants of white fur traders and native women who for more than two centuries had acted as intermediaries between the two cultures, found themselves overwhelmed, their desperate attempts to maintain their independence leading to a brace of futile rebellions under the leadership of Louis Riel in 1869–70 and 1885.

With the Métis and the Indians out of the way, thousands of European immigrants concentrated on their wheat yields, but they were the victims of a one-crop economy, their prosperity dependent on the market price of grain and the freight charges imposed

---

ACCOMMODATION PRICE SYMBOLS

All the accommodation prices in this book have been coded using the symbols below, corresponding to Canadian dollar rates. Prices are for the least expensive double room in each establishment in high season, excluding special offers. For a full explanation, see p.38 in Basics.

① up to $40	③ $60–80	⑤ $100–125	⑦ $175–240
② $40–60	④ $80–100	⑥ $125–175	⑧ $240+

by the railroad. Throughout this century, the region's farmers have experienced alarming changes in their fortunes as bust has alternated with boom, a situation that continues to dominate the economies of Saskatchewan and eastern Alberta today.

Central Canada is not the most popular tourist destination in the country, its main cities caricatured as dull and unattractive, its scenery considered flat and monotonous. To some extent, these prejudices stem from the route of the **Trans-Canada Highway**, which contrives to avoid nearly everything of interest on its way from Winnipeg to Calgary, a generally boring and long drive that many Canadians prefer to do at night when, they say, the views are better. However, on the Trans-Canada itself, busy **Winnipeg** – easily the largest city in central Canada – is well worth a visit for its museums, restaurants and nightlife, while, just to the south of the highway on the Saskatchewan–Alberta border, there are the delightful wooded ridges of the **Cypress Hills Interprovincial Park**, which incorporates the restored Mountie outpost of **Fort Walsh**. It has to be said, though, that the **Yellowhead Route** from Winnipeg – Hwy 16 – makes a far more agreeable journey, with pleasant stops at **Saskatoon** and the **Battlefords**. This road is also within easy reach of central Canada's two outstanding parks, **Riding Mountain National Park** in Manitoba and **Prince Albert National Park** in Saskatchewan, both renowned for their lakes, forest-hiking and canoeing routes.

Most of central Canada's boreal forest is inaccessible except by private float plane, but all the major cities and the region's tourist offices have lists of tour operators and suppliers who run or equip a whole variety of trips into the more remote regions – from white-water rafting and canoeing, through to hunting, fishing and bird-watching. It's also possible to fly or travel by train to **Churchill**, a remote and desolate settlement on the southern shore of Hudson Bay that's one of the world's best places to see polar bears. One word of warning: the boreal forests swarm with voracious insects such as blackflies and mosquitoes, so don't forget your insect repellent.

WINNIPEG

With 650,000 inhabitants, **WINNIPEG** accounts for roughly two-thirds of the population of Manitoba, and lies at the geographic centre of the country, sandwiched between the American frontier to the south and the infertile Canadian Shield to the north and east. The city has been the gateway to the prairies since 1873, and became the transit point for much of the country's transcontinental traffic when the railroad arrived twelve years later. From the very beginning, Winnipeg was described as the city where "the West began", and its polyglot population, drawn from almost every country in Europe, was attracted by the promise of the fertile soils to the west. But this was no classless pioneer town: as early as the 1880s the city had developed a clear pattern of residential segregation, with leafy prosperous suburbs to the south, along the Assiniboine River, while to the north lay "Shanty Town". The long-term effects of this division have proved hard to erase, and today the dispossessed still gather round the cheap dorms just to the north of the business district, a sad rather than dangerous corner near the main intersection at Portage Avenue and Main Street. Winnipeg's skid row is only a tiny part of the downtown area, but its reputation has hampered recent attempts to reinvigorate the city centre as a whole: successive administrations in the last twenty years have refurbished warehouses and built walkways along the Red and

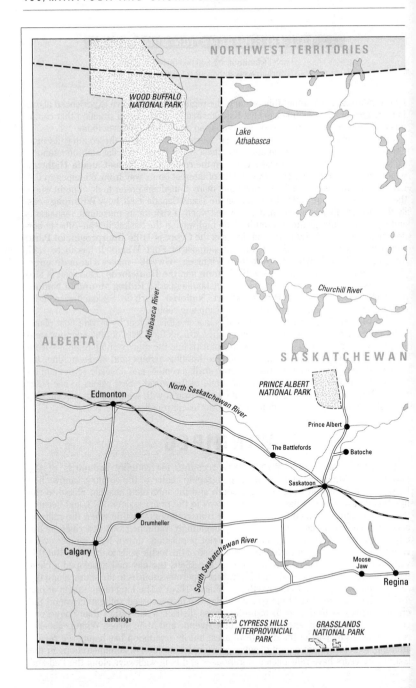

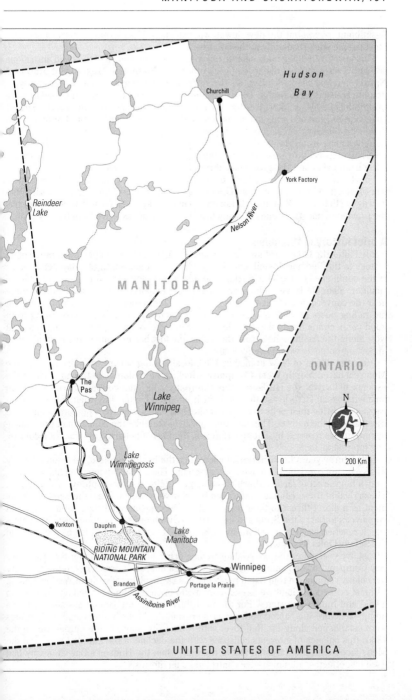

Assiniboine rivers, but the new downtown apartment blocks remain hard to sell, and most people stick resolutely to the suburbs.

That apart, Winnipeg makes for an enjoyable stopover, and all of the main attractions are within easy walking distance of each other. The **Manitoba Museum of Man and Nature** has excellent displays on the history of the province and its various geographic areas; the **Exchange District** features some good examples of Canada's early twentieth-century architecture; the **Winnipeg Art Gallery** has the world's largest collection of Inuit art; and, just across the Red River, the suburb of **St Boniface** has a delightful museum situated in the house and chapel of the Grey Nuns, who arrived here by canoe from Montréal in 1844. Winnipeg is also noted for the excellence and diversity of its **restaurants**, while its flourishing performing-arts scene features everything from ballet and classical music through to C&W and jazz.

Finally, the city makes a useful base for exploring the area's attractions, the most popular of which – chiefly **Lower Fort Garry** – are on the banks of the Red River as it twists its way north to Lake Winnipeg, 60km away. On the lake itself, **Grand Beach Park** has the province's finest stretches of sandy beach, just two hours' drive from the city centre.

A brief history of Winnipeg

Named after the Cree word for murky water ("win-nipuy"), Winnipeg owes much of its history to the Red and Assiniboine rivers, which meet just south of today's city centre at the confluence called **The Forks**. The first European to reach the area was Pierre Gaultier, Sieur de la Vérendrye, an enterprising explorer who founded **Fort Rouge** near the convergence of the two rivers in 1738. This settlement was part of a chain of fur-trading posts he built to extend French influence into the west. Prospering from good connections north along the Red River to Lake Winnipeg and Hudson Bay, and west along the Assiniboine across the plains, the fort became one of the region's most important outposts within twenty years.

After the defeat of New France in 1763, local trading activity was absorbed by the Montréal-based **North West Company**, which came to dominate the fur trade at the expense of its rival, the **Hudson's Bay Company**. The latter continued to operate from fortified coastal factories staffed by British personnel, expecting their Indian trading partners to bring their pelts to them – unlike their rivals, who were prepared to live and travel among the natives. This inflexible policy looked like the ruination of the company until it was rescued by Thomas Douglas, the Earl of Selkirk, who bought a controlling interest in 1809.

In the three years **Lord Selkirk** took to turn the business round, he resettled many of his own impoverished Scottish crofters around The Forks, buying from his own company a huge tract of farmland, which he named the **Red River Colony**, or Assiniboia. The arrival of these colonists infuriated the Nor'Westers, who saw the Scottish settlement as a direct threat to their trade routes. They encouraged their Métis allies and employees to harry the Scots and for several years there was continuous skirmishing, which reached tragic proportions in 1816, when 21 settlers were killed by the Métis in the **Seven Oaks Massacre**.

Just five years later the two rival fur-trading firms amalgamated under the "Hudson's Bay Company" trade name, bringing peace and a degree of prosperity to the area. Yet the colony remained a rough-and-ready place, as a chaplain called John West lamented: "Almost every inhabitant we passed bore a gun upon his shoulder and all appeared in a wild and hunter-like state." For the next thirty years, the colony sustained an economic structure that suited both the farmers and the Métis hunters, and trade routes were established along the Red River with Minnesota, south of the border. But in the 1860s this balance of interests collapsed with the decline of the buffalo herds, and the Métis faced extreme hardship just at the time when the Hudson's Bay Company had itself lost effective administrative control of its territories.

The Manitoba telephone code is ☎204.

At this time of internal crisis, the politicians of eastern Canada agreed the federal union of 1867, opening the way for the transfer of the Red River Colony from British to Canadian control. The Métis majority – roughly 6000 compared to some 1000 whites – were fearful of the consequences and their resistance took shape round **Louis Riel**, under whose dextrous leadership they captured the Hudson's Bay Company's Upper Fort Garry and created a provisional government without challenging the sovereignty of the crown. A delegation went to Ottawa to negotiate the terms of their admission into the Dominion, but their efforts were handicapped by the execution by Métis of an English settler from Ontario, **Thomas Scott**. The subsequent furore pushed prime minister John A. Macdonald into dispatching a military force to restore "law and order"; nevertheless, the **Manitoba Act** of 1870, which brought the Red River into the Dominion, did accede to many of the demands of the Métis, at the price of Riel's exile, and guaranteed the preservation of the French culture and language in the new province – although in practice this was not effectively carried out.

The eclipse of the Métis and the security of Winnipeg – as it became in 1870 – were both assured when the **Canadian Pacific Railway** routed its transcontinental line through The Forks in 1885. With the town's commodity markets handling the expanding grain trade and its industries supplying the vast rural hinterland, its population was swelled by thousands of immigrants, particularly from the Ukraine, Germany and Poland. In 1872 Winnipeg had a population of 1500 and by 1901 it had risen to 42,000. In the period just before World War I Winnipeg had become the third largest city in Canada and the largest grain-producing centre in North America. By 1921 the population had reached 192,000. More recently, the development of other prairie cities, such as Regina and Saskatoon, has undermined something of Winnipeg's pre-eminence, but the city is still the economic focus and transport hub of central Canada.

Arrival, information and transport

Winnipeg **airport** is some 7km west of the city centre. There's a **tourist information desk** inside the airport concourse at the north end of the main level (daily 8am–9.45pm; ☎774-0031), which has a good range of leaflets on the city and its principal attractions, along with accommodation listings. Close by, a display board advertising the city's grander hotels is attached to a free phone for on-the-spot hotel reservations. From outside the terminal building, Winnipeg Transit **bus** #15 (daily: every 20–30min 6.15am–12.45am; flat fare $1.50) runs downtown, dropping passengers at or near most of the larger hotels; tickets are bought from the driver. **Taxis** charge around $15 for the same journey, but are cheaper if you're prepared to share; **limos** cost $30 per person, $11 shared.

The **Mall Centre bus station** is on the west side of the downtown area at Portage Avenue and Memorial Boulevard (daily 6.30am–midnight). **Union Station**, the city's **train station**, is on Main Street, just south of Portage, and has connecting trains to Churchill, Toronto, and Saskatoon for Vancouver. For bus and train enquiries, see "Listings" on p.447.

Information

Tourism Winnipeg has an **information office** on the third floor of the Johnston Terminal at The Forks (Mon–Fri 8.30am–4.30pm; ☎943-1970 or 1-800-665-0204, fax 942-4043), as well as at the airport (see above). A comprehensive range of leaflets on both the city and province is available at the **Manitoba Travel Ideas Centre** adjacent to the Johnston Terminal (Mon–Thurs, Sat & Sun 10am–6pm, Fri 10am–8pm; ☎945-1715), where travel counsellors can also plan your itinerary. All outlets provide free city maps, a Winnipeg Transit bus plan, accommodation listings, a restaurant guide, an historic and architectural guide to the downtown area and the free *Where* magazine, Winnipeg's bimonthly listings of activities and attractions. You can also call ☎942-2535 (24hr) for information on events and sights in the city.

If you're heading off to one of the provincial parks, you should visit the **Manitoba Natural Resources Department**, 200 Saulteaux Crescent (Mon–Fri 8am–4.30pm; ☎945-6784 or 1-800-214-6497). It has a comprehensive range of maps and will provide specialist advice on anything from weather conditions to details of suitable outfitters and guides. The **Parks Canada Information Office,** in the Manitoba Children's Museum at The Forks (Mon–Fri 8.30am–4.30pm; ☎983-2290), offers a similar service for the region's national parks.

Orientation and city transport

Winnipeg's main north–south artery is **Main Street**, which runs roughly parallel to the adjacent Red River. The principal east–west drag is **Portage Avenue**, which begins at its junction with Main. The downtown core falls on either side of Portage, beginning at Main and ending at Memorial Boulevard; it's bounded by Broadway to the south and Logan Avenue to the north. A twenty-minute stroll takes you from end to end, whilst the suburbs and the more outlying attractions are easy to reach by **bus**.

Winnipeg Transit has an excellent range of city-wide services (flat fare $1.50 per journey), with tickets and transfers for trips involving more than one bus available from the driver – exact fare only. The **Transit Service Centre**, in the underground concourse at Portage and Main (Mon–Fri 9.30am–5.30pm) – in a hard to find location in the Scotiabank concourse – sells a book of ten tickets for $14.50. Free route maps are available here, as well as at the tourist offices, and details of services are printed at the back of the Winnipeg telephone directory. There's also a Transit Service Booth (Mon–Thurs 10am–6pm, Fri & Sat 10am–5pm, Sun 1–5pm) in the foyer of the Winnipeg Centennial Library, 251 Donald St. If you want to cover a lot of the downtown attractions in a short space of time, you'll find the #99 Downtown Flyer Service handy. For 25¢ you can get on or off at 22 bus stops in an area bounded roughly by Portage Avenue, Memorial Boulevard, Broadway, Pioneer Boulevard (for The Forks) and Main Street (service Mon–Fri 11am–3.30pm, Sat 11am–5pm, Sun noon–5pm). **Bike rental** is available at the youth hostel (see "Accommodation" below); for details of **car rental** agencies and **taxi** companies, see "Listings", p.447.

Winnipeg also has a transit **information service** (Mon–Sat 6am–10pm, Sun 6.30am–10pm; ☎986-5700) and a **Handi-Transit** door-to-door minibus facility for disabled visitors (Mon–Fri 6.30am–midnight, Sat 7.30am–midnight, Sun 8.30am–10pm; information on ☎986-5722).

Accommodation

Most of Winnipeg's **hotels** are within walking distance of the bus and train stations, and there's rarely any difficulty in finding somewhere to stay. The modern hotels are standard-issue skyscrapers that concentrate on the business clientele; most of these start at ⑨, but some of them offer weekend discounts and up to twenty percent reductions if you stay for three or four nights. The smaller and older downtown hotels start at ①, but at this price the rooms are basic and often grimy – a more comfortable place is likely to be in ②–③. (Avoid the "flophouses", the cheap dorms calling themselves "hotels" on Main Street, just north of Portage Avenue.) Breakfast is extra almost everywhere.

TOURS IN AND AROUND WINNIPEG

Bus and boat tours of the city leave from the dock beside Provencher Bridge at The Forks (see p.441). There are walking tours of the Exchange District (July & Aug daily except Mon 11am & 1.30pm; $5; ☎986-6937 or 986-6927) and Selkirk Avenue in the North End (June–Aug Tues–Sat 10am & 2pm; 1hr; ☎586-2720 or 586-3445). Sites Unseen Tours (☎889-4424 or 284-6373) offers hourly, daily and weekly guided tours of Winnipeg and surrounding areas. Wild-Wise Wilderness Adventures (☎663-1481, fax 663-1659) organizes historical canoe excursions for groups of ten people, where you paddle along the Red and Assiniboine rivers in the spirit of the pioneer voyageur guides and furtraders.

Companies operating half-day, day-, overnight and week-long tours out of Winnipeg include Anishinabe Camp and Cultural Tours (May–Sept; ☎636-2571 or 848-2815, fax 925-2027) to Riding Mountain National Park to experience Native Canadian culture, sleeping in tepees and participating in traditional ceremonies and powwow dancing; Aurora Canada Tours Ltd (Nov–April; ☎942-6617, fax 943-1971), for one-day to two-week tours observing bird and plant life and viewing the Northern Lights; Experience Tours (☎477-4609), for historic, cultural and outdoor adventure tours, including canoeing and cycling; Overland Canada Adventure Expeditions (☎ & fax 866-3075), for day- and overnight trips, including canoeing, horseback riding and hot-air balloon rides.

The major approach roads are dotted with **motels** (from ① up to ③–④), of which the largest concentrations are along the Pembina Highway, which runs south from the city centre as Route #42, and along Portage, which runs west forming part of the Trans-Canada Highway (Route #1). Two recommended motels on these routes are the *Comfort Inn South by Journey's End*, 3109 Pembina Highway (☎269-7390 or 1-800-228-5150; ③), and the *Village Inn Motor Hotel*, 3254 Portage Ave (☎837-5871; ②–④)

Tourism Winnipeg has the details of some thirty **B&B** addresses (mostly in ②), with breakfasts that vary from frugal continental to a complete meal. Most of these are affiliated to Bed and Breakfast of Manitoba, 434 Roberta Ave (☎661-0300), an agency that makes reservations upon payment of a deposit equivalent to one night's stay. Unfortunately, most of their places are far from central, but some of the more convenient locations are given below. The **youth hostel**, within easy walking distance of the bus station, is supplemented in summer by less conveniently located rooms at the University of Manitoba.

The tourist offices will help arrange hotel and B&B accommodation and there's also a free phone number for **reservations** (☎1-800-665-0040). For hostel information, call Hostelling International (☎784-1131). Manitoba Natural Resources has a toll-free reservation service for campgrounds in 35 provincial parks (Mon–Fri 9am–8pm, Sat 10am–5pm; ☎1-888-482-2267). There's a $6.75 booking fee.

Hotels

Balmoral Motor Hotel, 621 Balmoral St at Notre Dame Avenue (☎943-1544). In the northwest corner of downtown, with good services and a coffee shop. ②.

Carlton Inn, 220 Carlton St (☎942-0881 or 1-800-528-1234, fax 943-9312). One of the more agreeable cheap hotels, centrally located near the Convention Centre, with motel-style rooms, restaurant and pool. ③.

Charter House, 330 York Ave at Hargrave Street (☎942-0101 or 1-800-782-0175, fax 956-0665). Central location; all rooms with balcony. ③.

Crowne Plaza Winnipeg Downtown, 350 St Mary Ave at Hargrave Street (☎942-0551 or 1-800-465-4329). Adjoins the city's Convention Centre; tasteful, opulent rooms and includes restaurants and pools. ⑥.

Delta Winnipeg, 288 Portage Ave at Smith Street (☎956-0410 or 1-800-268-1133). One of the city's largest and most modern hotels, with a gym, swimming pool, plus baby-sitting services. There are fine views from the top floors; big discounts at weekends. ⑥.

Gordon Downtowner, 330 Kennedy St at Ellice Avenue (☎943-5581). Probably Winnipeg's most comfortable cheap hotel with restaurant and bar. ②.

Hotel Fort Garry, 222 Broadway (☎942-8251 or 1-800-665-8088). Near the train station. Built in neo-Gothic style between 1911 and 1914 and lavishly refurbished, with an elegant, balconied foyer leading to 250 rooms. ③.

Osborne Village Motor Inn, 160 Osborne St (☎452-9824). Basic accommodation in the heart of lively Osborne Village. Bands often play downstairs and the rooms are not soundproofed. ①.

St Regis, 285 Smith St (☎942-0171 or 1-800-663-7344, fax 943-3077). A historic turn-of-the-century hotel in the downtown area. Tastefully furnished with dining room and coffee shop. ②.

Travelodge Downtown Winnipeg, 360 Colony St at Portage Avenue (☎786-7011 or 1-800-578-7878, fax 772-1443). Next to the bus station. Has big comfortable rooms and is within walking distance of most attractions. ③.

Bed and Breakfasts

Bob Andrews & Margaret Day, 950 Palmerston Ave (☎774-0767). A 15min bus ride on #10 from downtown with a riverside location. Rooms are en suite. Bikes and canoes can be rented. ②.

Butterfly Bed and Breakfast, 226 Walnut St (☎783-6664). Central location, just off Portage Avenue. Has cosy rooms with shared bathroom. ②.

Eugenia & Peter Ellie, 77 Middle Gate (☎772-5832). In the historic Armstrong Point area near the Assiniboine River, with good access to downtown; hearty home-cooked breakfasts. Open April–Nov. ②.

Gîte de la Cathédrale Bed and Breakfast, 581 Rue Langevin, St Boniface (☎233-7792). Enjoy Franco-Manitoban hospitality in the heart of St Boniface. Five bedrooms with shared bathroom. ②.

Mary Jane's Place, 144 Yale Ave (☎453-8104). A gracious Georgian-style home which is only 10min by bus #29 from Portage Avenue. ②.

West Gate Manor, 71 West Gate (☎772-9788, fax 943-8371). Pleasant rooms with Victorian period furnishings in Armstrong Point, within walking distance of downtown. ②.

Hostel and college rooms

Guest House International, 168 Maryland St (☎772-1272 or 1-800-743-4423, fax 772-4117). Bus #17 from Vaughan Street. Dorms and four doubles, with laundry and kitchen. Reservations recommended in summer. Check-in daily 8am–midnight. ①.

Ivey House International Youth Hostel, 210 Maryland St at Broadway (☎772-3022). Bus #17 from Vaughan Street. Rooms for between two and four people, with laundry, kitchen and bike rental. In summer it's often full. Check-in daily 8–10am & 11am–midnight. ①.

University of Manitoba, Fort Garry campus (☎474-9942). Double rooms and dorm beds available from mid-May to mid-August, 10km south of the city centre. ①.

Campgrounds

Conestoga Campsite, St Anne's Road at Perimeter Highway (☎257-7363). 13km southeast of town with most sites having electricity and water. Mid-May to Sept. $12–17.

Jones Campground, 588 Trans-Canada Highway, St François Xavier (☎864-2721). In a small town on the Assiniboine River, 15km west of Winnipeg, this campsite has 44 unreserved sites, most with water and electricity as well as toilets, showers and a BBQ area. May–Sept. $10–15.

Traveller's RV Resort, Murdoch Road (☎256-2186). The nearest campground, some 14km southeast of the centre, just off the Trans-Canada, with over fifty unreserved sites and facilities that include showers, toilets and drinking water. May–Sept. From $15–22 per site

The City

The traditional centre of Winnipeg is the intersection of **Portage Avenue and Main Street** just north of **The Forks**, close to the Red River at the start of what was once the main Métis cart track (the Portage Trail) west across the prairies to the Hudson's Bay Company posts, and the principal trail north to Lake Winnipeg linking the river-

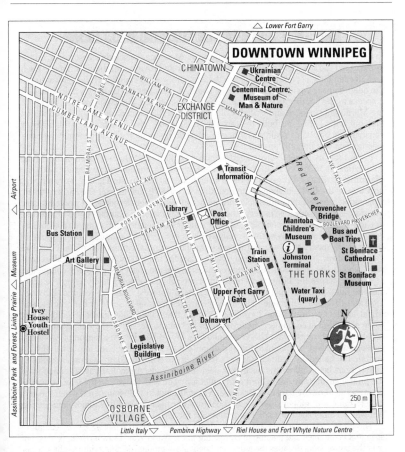

side farm lots and Lower and Upper Fort Garry. Main Street was, in fact, called the Garry Road until the mid-1870s. Despite its historic associations, in 1979 the city council closed most of the junction to pedestrians in return for the construction of an underground shopping concourse, Winnipeg Square. While you're here, have a look at the grand Neoclassical **Bank of Montréal** on the southeast side of the intersection, its fussily carved capitals in stark contrast to the sharp, clean lines of its skyscraper neighbours. The intersection is also known as being the windiest of any city or town in Canada.

The Exchange District

Just to the north of the Portage and Main intersection, the **Exchange District** is a rough rectangle of old warehouses, former commodity exchanges and commercial buildings that are the best-preserved group of any city in Canada. Many of them were converted, from the late 1970s onwards, into art galleries, boutiques, antique shops and restaurants. The effective centre of the district is the **Old Market Square** at King and Albert streets and Bannatyne Avenue, with its weekend produce market, flea

THE HISTORY OF THE RAILWAY IN CANADA

Even before Confederation in 1867, Sir John A. Macdonald, Canada's first prime minister, grasped the need physically to link the disparate provinces of the new nation. Each area needed lines of communication to the east and west to counteract the natural tug of the neighbouring parts of the USA to the south. It was clear the country would fall apart if access to the south was easier than access to the other Canadian provinces, and both the Maritime Provinces and British Columbia joined the Confederation on the condition that rail links would be built to transport their goods throughout the land. Railway construction on such a scale was a huge undertaking for such a young country and outside finance was the only answer.

From 1855, lines were constructed in eastern Ontario and Québec, culminating in the completion in 1876 of the Intercolonial Railway, which linked central Canada with the Maritime Provinces. Progress of the transcontinental line to the Pacific, however, was impeded by the Riel rebellion at the Red River in 1869–70, and in 1871 the Parliamentary Opposition labelled the entire scheme "an act of insane recklessness". Two years later Macdonald's Conservative government fell after implication in scandals involving the use of party funds in railway contracts, and Alexander Mackenzie's subsequent Liberal ministry proceeded so slowly with the railway plans that British Columbia openly spoke of secession if construction was not speeded up. The eventual completion of the Canadian Pacific Railway (CPR) in 1885 finally made Canada "more than a geographical expression", and by the early twentieth century another coast-to-coast line had been completed.

Passage across the hitherto virtually impenetrable Canadian Shield was now feasible and the full agricultural potential of the prairies to the west could be realized. Between 1896 and 1913 more than one million people arrived by train to settle in the prairies, and wheat production rose from 20 million to more than 200 million bushels. Additionally, some of the first major mineral finds in northern Ontario were brought to light during the construction of the railway. The years following World War I were a period of economic consolidation, which culminated in the union of various smaller lines into a nationwide system: the Canadian National Railways (CNR), a government-controlled organization.

What has been called "the bizarre project" of the Hudson Bay Railway stemmed from the prairie farmers' desire to create an outlet for trade with the rest of the world that was not dependent on the bankers back east. A first attempt in 1886 foundered when the promoters ran out of money after the first 65km. After many delays this major engineering feat was accomplished in 1929, just in time for the Great Depression.

The impact of the Depression on Canadian railways was particularly severe, leading to stringent economies and pooling of competing lines. World War II saw a rise in profits, but over the subsequent decades the story has been one of gradual decline, with freight increasingly travelling by road and air, and passenger services pruned almost to extinction on some lines. By 1992, passengers could no longer cross Canada on the CPR, and one of the world's great train rides had gone for ever. Grain and minerals are still moved by train, however, and the privately owned CPR is now exclusively a freight line. VIA, the passenger branch of CNR, operates virtually all Canada's passenger services, with the exception of the Toronto–Cochrane route, the Algoma Canyon line between Sault Ste Marie and Hearst in Ontario, and the British Columbia Railway from Prince George to Vancouver. Other than on the corridor line from Windsor to Québec City, services are slow and often infrequent, though occasionally the scenic views from the window make up for this; the "dome cars", with their glass roofs, are one of the best ways to see the Rockies. In roadless northern Manitoba, the Hudson Bay line to Churchill serves a genuine social need and is probably the only rail route in North America still to exist primarily as a passenger service, see "Contexts" p.896.

markets and buskers. This part of town was built during Winnipeg's boom, a period of frenzied real-estate speculation and construction that peaked in 1882, but only lasted until the outbreak of World War I. The standard architectural design, used for most of the office buildings and nearly all the warehouses, was simple and symmetrical, the plain brick walls topped off by decorative stone cornices. However, one or two companies financed extravagant variations, notably the **Electric Railway Chambers Building** at 213 Notre Dame Ave, an imaginative blend of Italian Renaissance and early twentieth-century motifs, its terracotta facade lined with a magnificent dazzle of 6000 electric lights. The district is also one of the city's principal cultural centres, home to such buildings as the **Manitoba Museum of Man and Nature**, the **Ukrainian Cultural and Educational Centre** and the artist-run **Artspace**.

The Manitoba Museum of Man and Nature

In the heart of the Exchange District, at 190 Rupert Ave, the **Centennial Centre** incorporates the **Manitoba Museum of Man and Nature** (mid-May to mid-Sept daily 10am–6pm; mid-Sept to mid-May Tues–Fri 10am–4pm, Sat & Sun 10am–5pm; $4), an excellent introduction to the province's geographical regions and the history of its peoples. Highlights of the natural history galleries include an imposing polar bear diorama, a well-illustrated explanation of the Northern Lights, and a disconcerting section devoted to the more malicious insects of Manitoba – starring the "no-see-um", a deer fly that specializes in burrowing into the nostrils of caribou. In the evocative **Boreal Forest** gallery you walk past a waterfall, a family of moose, and a diorama of Cree indians gathering food and painting sacred designs on rocks. The museum's most popular exhibit, moored in a massive display area that reproduces a seventeenth-century River Thames dockside, is a full-scale working replica of the **Nonsuch**, the ship whose fur-collecting voyage to Hudson Bay in 1668 led to the creation of the Hudson's Bay Company. The museum's **Grasslands Gallery** has a small display of Assiniboine Indian artefacts, along with a reconstruction of a tepee and a copy of a pioneer log cabin. There's also an example of the sod houses that the pioneers were forced to build in many parts of the treeless southern plains, and a replica of the odd-looking Red River cart, the Métis's favourite form of land transportation, with massive wheels that could tackle the prairie mud and mire. The final part of the museum is the **Urban Gallery**, which re-creates the Winnipeg of the early 1920s, a street complete with pharmacy, barber shop, dentist, promenade and cinema showing period films.

Big changes are planned for the museum by 1999, when a new wing will open to display the **Hudson's Bay Company Museum Collection**, which was donated by the Company in 1994. This major acquisition comprises more than 6000 artefacts and documents amassed by the Company, which form a record of its links with Manitoba. These include early maps and artefacts from the Franklin expedition and archeological materials, as well as a huge number of Indian and Inuit artworks. The wing will also house a research facility. Also, an additional gallery, the **Parklands Gallery**, with displays and dioramas dealing with the largest region of the province, will be ready for the public by the year 2000.

Also in the Centennial Centre are the **planetarium** (summer daily; except Mon winter; $3.50) and the "Touch the Universe" **science centre** (mid-May to mid-Sept daily 10am–9pm; mid-Sept to mid-May Tues–Fri 10am–4pm, Sat & Sun 10am–5pm; $3.50), where more than sixty interactive exhibits focus on the way the universe is perceived by the five senses. A **combined ticket** for the museum, planetarium and science centre costs $9.

Next door is the **Centennial Concert Hall** (☎949-3999), where performances of the Manitoba Opera, Winnipeg Symphony Orchestra and Royal Winnipeg Ballet are held. Just across the street from the Concert Hall is the modern **City Hall**.

The Ukrainian Centre, Artspace and Chinatown

Two blocks north of the Centennial Centre, the **Ukrainian Cultural and Educational Centre (Oseredok)**, 184 Alexander Ave East at Main Street (Tues–Sat 10am–4pm, Sun 2–5pm; $2), occupies a 1930s office building on the edge of the Exchange District.

The second largest ethnic group in Manitoba, the Ukrainians arrived here around the turn of the twentieth century, a peasant people united by language and custom, but divided by religion and politics – Orthodox against Catholic, nationalist against socialist. By 1940, the various factions managed to amalgamate to create the Ukrainian Canadian Committee, a loose coalition committed to the country's institutions and the promotion of Ukrainian interests. Their collection of folk arts in the fifth-floor **museum** of the complex is an excellent introduction to their strongly maintained traditions, with delightful examples of embroidery, weaving, woodcarving and the exquisite designs of *pysanky*, Easter egg painting. There's also an art gallery, library and gift shop.

Artspace, in a warehouse building at the corner of Arthur Street and Bannatyne Avenue, is the largest artist-run centre in Canada and houses a cinema (see p. 446), several galleries, and offices for art groups. To see the best of contemporary local and Canadian **art**, check out the Site Gallery, 2nd Floor, 55 Arthur St (Tues–Sun 11am–4pm), and Plug In, 70 Arthur St (Tues–Sat 11am–5pm). Canada's Finest Arts and Crafts, 217 McDermot Ave (Tues–Sat 10am–6pm), has an excellent selection of clothing, jewellery, sculpture and paintings by prairie and west coast Native Canadian and Inuit artists.

Possibly the most gracious building in the Exchange District is the former **Winnipeg Grain Exchange**, opposite the *Lombard Hotel* on Lombard Avenue. It was built between 1906 and 1928 and was the largest building of its type in Canada; grain offices still occupy some of the floors. Other imposing buildings are the ten-storey **Confederation Life Building**, 457 Main St, which has a curved facade of white terracotta, and the massive **Royal Bank Building** at the corner of Main Street and William Avenue.

Adjacent to the Exchange District, north of Rupert Street and west of Main Street, is **Chinatown**, originally settled in the 1920s by immigrants brought to Manitoba to help build the railway into the west. The area has many good restaurants and groceries, as well as shops selling silk fabrics and exotic herbs and spices – though, other than that, not much in the way of sights.

The Forks

South of Portage Avenue along Main Street rises the ponderous dome of the Beaux-Arts-style **Union Station** designed by the same architect who did Grand Central Station in New York; it has an indoor market and a train museum upstairs (mid-May to early Sept Thurs–Sun & holidays noon–6pm; early Sept to mid-May Sat, Sun & holidays noon–4pm; free). Immediately south of the station is the present headquarters of the Hudson's Bay Company. Across the street, in a small park is the stone gate that's the sole remnant of **Upper Fort Garry**, a Hudson's Bay Company fort from 1837 to 1870 and thereafter the residence of Manitoba's lieutenant governors until 1883, when the fort was dismantled. The pointed dormers and turrets behind belong to the **Hotel Fort Garry**, a chateau-like structure built for the Grand Trunk Railroad.

Behind the station, the chunk of land bordering the Red River as it curves round to **The Forks** was, until recently, one of the country's largest railway yards – you can still see CN freight cars and cabooses dotted around the grounds. In the last seven years or so it's been redeveloped and is now Winnipeg's most-visited sight due to its **Manitoba Travel Ideas Centre** (see p.434), half tourist information point, half museum, with six reasonably interesting themed displays covering the province's tourist areas. It's worth a quick visit, if only to pick the brains of the very helpful staff, and admire the magnificent stuffed polar bear from Churchill, a persistent and dangerous marauder of the town's dump who came to a sticky end. Just east along the river from here, a piece of land has been set aside as **The Forks National Historic Site**, with plaques celebrating the role of the fur traders and pioneers who first settled here. One area is an archeological excavation site, which welcomes volunteer diggers from July to October (advance registration required; for further information, call ☎944-8325). Nearby, the 1888–89 rail-maintenance shed houses the **Manitoba Children's Museum** (July & Aug Mon–Thurs 9.30am–5pm, Fri 9.30am–8pm, Sat 11am–8pm, Sun 11am–5pm; Sept–June Mon, Tues & Thurs 9.30am–5pm, Wed noon–5pm, Fri 9.30am–8pm, Sat 11am–8pm, Sun 11am–5pm; $4), a hands-on, state-of-the-art enterprise that appeals equally to adults. Five different sections cover aspects of history, science, nature and technology. A vintage steam-engine with a couple of Pullman carriages and a mail office is equipped with tickets, luggage, uniforms and mail; close by, bear, lynx and raccoon costumes are on hand for kids to don while they explore a huge model of an oak tree and its ecosystem. Visitors to the museum can be filmed and have their activities displayed simultaneously on two huge video screens, with added optical effects. For older kids, the highlight is probably the fully functioning TV studio where they can experiment with lights and cameras; at certain times, staff conduct interviews with them on their views of current events, which are relayed by one of the local stations.

A couple of minutes' walk away, **The Forks Market** and the **Johnston Terminal**, both old railway buildings, house shops, food stalls, bars, restaurants and (in the Johnston Terminal) the **Manitoba Sports Hall of Fame** (Tues, Wed & Sat 10am–6pm, Thurs & Fri 10am–9pm, Sun noon–6pm; free). **Canoes** can be rented at the Johnston Terminal for the Red and Assiniboine rivers. Paths from the two buildings lead down to the Assiniboine River via an outdoor amphitheatre, where buskers entertain the gathered crowds with anything from hard rock to bagpipe music. Nearby is **The Wall Through Time**, a curving brick barricade covered with plaques and inscriptions recording the historic events of the area. On the banks of the Red River there's a quay beside Provencher Bridge where you can take **boat trips**, which run parallel to the attractive **riverwalk path**, back along the Assiniboine River as far as the Legislative Building on Broadway and in the opposite direction up the Red River (May–Sept daily 2pm, 2hr, $10.75; evening dinner and dance cruise daily 7pm, 3hr, $11.75; moonlight dance cruise Fri & Sat 10pm, 3hr, $11.75). One of the boats is a replica paddlewheel vessel. **Water taxis** also leave every ten minutes from a quay closer to the market (May–Oct daily 11am–10pm; 30min; $6) and run along the same route. **Tours** of the city on a double-decker bus also leave from the dock beside the bridge (3hr 30min; basic tour $17). For boat and bus tour enquiries, call ☎944-8000 (reservations ☎942-4500). For information on all programmes and activities at The Forks, call the hotline (☎957-7618). To get to The Forks from Portage Avenue, take bus #38 or #99.

Downtown

Lined by department stores and offices, downtown **Portage Avenue** is the city's main shopping street, with a web of underground passageways and glass-enclosed overhead walkways linking the various malls and large stores and providing welcome relief from the summer heat and winter cold. The largest complex is the ugly postmodern architecture of **Portage Place**, on the north side of the avenue, with its main entrance at Kennedy Street (daily: Mon–Wed & Sat 10am–6pm, Thurs & Fri 10am–9pm, Sun noon–5pm). There are over 160 shops and services here, plus a giant screen IMAX cinema on the third level (☎956-IMAX). Across from Portage Place, at 266 Edmonton St, is **The Upstairs Gallery** (Mon–Sat 9.30am–5.30pm), Winnipeg's largest gallery of Inuit art. Among the many modern buildings that line Portage are some earlier ones that are architecturally attractive: the **Paris Building** at no. 259, with a splendid piered facade and delicate cornice, and the **Boyd Building** at no. 388, with cream and bronze terracotta decoration.

The uncompromisingly modern **Winnipeg Art Gallery**, a wedge-shaped building at 300 Memorial Blvd and Portage Avenue (Tues & Thurs–Sun 11am–5pm, Wed 11am–9pm; mid-June to Aug opens daily at 10am; $3, free on Wed), is the home of the most comprehensive collection of Inuit art in the world, a large collection of Gothic and Renaissance paintings and a reasonable assortment of modern European art, including work by Miró, Chagall and Henry Moore. The problem is that little of these collections are on display at any one time – much of the available space is taken up by offices while the main display area, on the third floor, is given over to temporary (and often dire) exhibitions of modern Canadian art. The mezzanine level is devoted to the Inuits, each temporary display developing a particular theme – from the symbolic significance of different animals to the role of women sculptors in the isolated communities. The gallery also has an open-air sculpture court and a rooftop restaurant.

The Legislative Building, Osborne Village, Little Italy and Dalnavert
A few minutes' walk south of the Art Gallery, along Memorial Boulevard, is the **Manitoba Legislative Building** (daily 8am–8pm), built between 1913 and 1919 and surrounded by trim lawns and flower borders. The building, made of local Tyndall stone embedded with fossils, has a central pediment decorated with splendidly pompous sculptures representing the ideals of Canadian nationhood. A half-kneeling figure, symbolizing progress, beckons his lazy neighbour to come to the land of promise, whilst a muscular male figure, with a team of powerful horses, idealizes the pioneer spirit. High above, a central square tower rises to a copper-green dome that's topped by the **Golden Boy**, a four-metre-high gold-plated bronze figure that's supposed to embody the spirit of enterprise and eternal youth. Inside (mid-May to early Sept tours every 30min 9am–6pm; free), the marble columns and balconies of the foyer house two magnificent life-size buffalo bronzes by the French sculptor Charles Gardet, framing a staircase of brown-veined Carrara marble. The mural over the entrance to the legislative chamber depicting World War I scenes is by the English artist Frank Brangwyn.

Just behind the Legislative Building, across the Assiniboine, lies **Osborne Village**, the trendy part of town, whose inexpensive bars, restaurants and music joints – strung along Osborne Street – are favourites with the city's students. West off Osborne Street is Corydon Avenue, whose several blocks and sidestreets comprise **Little Italy**, known for its cappuccino bars and restaurants.

A couple of blocks east of the Legislative Building, **Dalnavert**, at 61 Carlton St (guided tours every 30min, Jan & Feb Sat & Sun noon–5pm; March–May & Sept–Dec Tues–Thurs, Sat & Sun noon–5pm; June–Aug Tues–Thurs, Sat & Sun 10am–6pm; $3), was the home of Hugh John Macdonald, the son of Canada's first prime minister and, briefly, premier of Manitoba. Built in 1895 in Queen Anne Revival style, the house has been painstakingly restored, its simple red-brick exterior engulfed by a fanciful wooden veranda, the interior all heavy, dark-stained woods and strong deep colours. Macdonald's conservatism, reflected in the decor, was mellowed by a philanthropic disposition – he even reserved part of his basement for some of the city's destitute.

St Boniface

The suburb of **St Boniface**, a ten-minute walk east of the downtown area just across the Red River (or by bus #10 or #56 from Portage Avenue), was a centre of early French-Canadian and Métis settlement. Founded by two French-Canadian Catholic priests in 1818, it retains something of its distinctive character and even today, 27 years after its incorporation into the city of Winnipeg, roughly 25 percent of its population speaks French as a first language. **Walking tours** of St Boniface run from June to August (Mon–Fri 10am, 1pm & 3pm; 1hr; free); for information, call ☎235-1406 or 945-1715.

St Boniface's principal historic sights are situated beside the river, along avenue Taché. Walking south from the Provencher Bridge, the massive white-stone facade on the left is all that remains of **St Boniface Cathedral**, a huge neo-Romanesque structure built in 1908 and largely destroyed by fire in 1968. Its replacement, just behind, was designed with an interior in the style of a giant tepee. The large silver-domed building immediately to the east is the **Collège Universitaire de Saint-Boniface**, formerly a

Jesuit college and now the French-speaking campus of the University of Manitoba. Here you'll see a controversial modern statue of Louis Riel, in a style that portrays him as naked and deformed. Its original location was on the grounds of the Legislative Building, but it caused such a storm of protest that it was removed to here in 1994. In front of the cathedral is the cemetery containing the grave of **Louis Riel**, whose modest tombstone gives little indication of the furore surrounding his execution in Regina on November 16, 1885. Only after three weeks had passed did the authorities feel safe enough to move the body, which was then sent secretly by rail to St Boniface. The casket lay overnight in Riel's family home in the suburb of St Vital (see below) before its transfer to the cathedral, where a Requiem Mass was attended by most of the Métis population. That same evening, across the river, Riel's enemies burnt his effigy on a street corner, a symptom of a bitter divide that was to last well into the twentieth century.

The **St Boniface Museum** (June–Sept Mon–Thurs 9am–8pm, Fri 9am–5pm, Sat 10am–5pm, Sun 10am–8pm; Oct–May Mon–Fri 9am–5pm; $2; guided tours available by reservation on ☎237-4500) is housed in an attractive whitewashed building across from the cathedral. The oldest building in Winnipeg and the largest squared-oak log building in North America, it was built between 1846 and 1851 as a convent for the Grey Nuns, a missionary order whose four-woman advance party had arrived by canoe from Montréal in 1844. Subsequently, the building was adapted for use as a hospital, a school and an orphanage. Inside, a series of cosy rooms are devoted to the Red River Colony, notably an intriguing collection of Métis memorabilia that includes examples of the colourful sashes that were the most distinctive feature of Métis dress. You can also see the battered wooden casket that was used to transport Riel's body from Regina to St Boniface. There's also a lovely little chapel, whose papier-mâché Virgin was made from an old newspaper that one of the original Grey Nuns found outside Upper Fort Garry when she walked across the frozen river to buy food.

South of the centre: the Riel House and the Fort Whyte Nature Centre

The **Riel House National Historic Site** (mid-May to early Sept daily 10am–6pm; donation; ☎257-1783) is at 330 River Rd in the suburb of St Vital, about 10km south of the city centre, and is just about worth the trip – by bus #16 from the Portage Place Mall. The main feature of the site is a tiny clapboard house that was built by the Riels in 1880–81 and stayed in their possession until 1968. Louis Riel never actually lived here, but this was where his body was brought after his execution in 1885, and the house has been restored to its appearance at that time, complete with black-bordered photographs and a few artefacts left by his wife, Marguerite.

Other period furnishings and fittings give a good idea of the life of a prosperous Métis family in the 1880s. The railway had reached St Boniface in 1877 and this was a time when the simple products of the Red River could be supplemented by manufactured goods from the east with relative ease – the iron stove, the most obvious import, improved the quality of the Riels' life immeasurably. Costumed guides provide an enjoyable twenty-minute tour of the house and the garden, the sole remnant of the once sizable Riel landholdings.

Across the Red River from St Vital, at the city's southern limits, is the **Fort Whyte Nature Centre**, 1961 McCreary Rd (summer Mon & Tues 9am–5pm, Wed–Fri 9am–9pm, Sat, Sun & holidays 10am–9pm; rest of the year Mon–Fri 9am–5pm, Sat, Sun & holidays 10am–5pm; $3.50), an environmental education centre that gives you a better understanding of the diversity of plants and animals that make up the prairie ecosystem. It's a real outdoors experience, incorporating a wildlife observation tower, deer enclosure and a maze of self-guiding trails through woodlands and marsh, plus an interpretive centre. There's no public transport to Fort Whyte.

West of the centre: Assiniboine Park and the Living Prairie Museum

Some 8km west of the city centre, to the south of Portage Avenue, a great chunk of land has been set aside as **Assiniboine Park** (daily 9am–sunset; free; bus #66 from Broadway at Smith Street), whose wooded lawns attract hundreds of visitors every summer weekend. The park's best-known feature is a large half-timbered **pavilion** in mock-Tudor style – a favourite meeting place for Winnipeggers at the weekend and the backdrop of outdoor plays in the summer. The **zoo** (daily 10am–sunset; $3) has over 1200 animals and a giant tropical conservatory, while the most developed part of the park has a full range of amenities, from a miniature train and a cricket pitch to a formal flower garden, a sculpture garden and restaurants. Adjoining the park to the south, the 700-acre nature reserve of **Assiniboine Forest** (sunrise–sunset; free), the largest in Canada, is home to deer, ruffled grouse and waterfowl.

A couple of kilometres further west, the **Living Prairie Museum** at 2795 Ness Ave (late April to June Sat & Sun 10am–5pm; July & Aug daily 10am–5pm; free; bus #24 along Portage) is worth a brief visit, its thirty acres of land forming the largest area of unploughed tall-grass prairie in Manitoba. A small visitor centre provides a wealth of background information on the indigenous plants, whose deep-root systems enable them to withstand both the extreme climate and prairie fires. There's a daily programme of half-hour guided walks, or you can pick up a brochure and stroll alone. Come prepared with insect repellent; the native bugs that thrive among the grass and wildflowers are particularly vicious.

Eating and drinking

Winnipeg boasts literally dozens of good, inexpensive **places to eat**, though many of them are long on quantity but short on finesse. The wide variety of ethnic restaurants are the exception, ranging from deluxe establishments serving fine French and Italian delicacies, through to Ukrainian and French-Canadian restaurant-bars that cater mainly for their own communities. In the more expensive places it's possible to pay upwards of $50 per person for a full dinner, but $20 per head is a reasonable average elsewhere. Many of Winnipeg's more staid **restaurants** and **restaurant-bars** are concentrated in and around the **downtown** shopping malls, but there's a cluster of more interesting ones in **Osborne Village** and the **Exchange District**, and several other good places dotted around the edges of the centre, notably the Jewish delis and Ukrainian restaurants in the **North End**, around Selkirk Avenue. For **drinking**, many of the city's bars are cheerless places and it's best to stick to the restaurant-bars.

Restaurants and restaurant-bars

Alycia's, 559 Cathedral Ave at McGregor Street. A long-established Ukrainian restaurant, 4km north of the centre, which also serves as an informal social centre with cheap, filling food, including borscht and *holubchi* (stuffed cabbage rolls); about $12 for three courses. Mon–Sat 8am–8pm.

Baked Expectations, 161 Osborne St. Delicious burgers and salads, but especially known for its cheesecakes. Dishes between $3 and $8.

Le Beaujolais, 131 blvd Provencher, St Boniface (☎237-6306). Winnipeg's premier French restaurant, with prices to match; reservations recommended. Mon–Fri lunch time, also Sat & Sun evenings.

Between Friends, in the *Crowne Plaza Winnipeg Downtown*, 350 St Mary Ave. Popular restaurant serving imaginatively prepared French and Californian cuisine. From $16.

Le Café Jardin, at **Centre Culturel Franco-Manitobain**, 340 blvd Provencher at Rue des Meurons, St Boniface. A large cultural complex housing an attractive open-air restaurant featuring traditional French-Canadian food – try the meat pies (*tourtière*) and the bread pudding. Open Mon–Fri 11.30am–2pm. A full meal costs around $15.

Carlos & Murphy's, 129 Osborne St. Huge portions of Mexican food from $8, and a raucous and dingy bar.

D'8 Schtove, 1842 Pembina Hwy (☎275-2294). Out of town, but worth tracking down to sample Mennonite cooking, which includes dishes such as borscht, strudel and *kjielkje* (egg noodles in creamy onion gravy). Main courses from $7. Book ahead.

Earl's, 191 Main St. Lively place with a huge menu, including ribs, chicken and stir-fries. Meals from $6.

Edohei, 355 Ellice Ave. Good Japanese meals from $14 plus fifteen varieties of sushi. Closed Tues.

Forks Market, The Forks. A converted railway shed incorporating some cheap, pleasant snack bars; try *Yudyta's* for Ukrainian and *Tavola Calda* for Italian food. For a taste of the prairies, head for *Prairie Oyster Café and Steak House*, on the second level, a mock cowboy ranch which serves wild rice pudding and wood-grilled rabbit. Also try *Branigan's* on the ground level, which has an outdoor patio.

Grapes, 180 Main St at York Avenue. Big burgers, grilled pickerel and cheesecake. Main courses from $8.

Hy's Steak Loft, 216 Kennedy St. Right downtown, this Winnipeg institution serves every cut of steak imaginable. Evenings only.

Kelekis, 110 Main St between Aberdeen and Redwood avenues. Popular restaurant established in 1931 and offering quality sandwiches and soups from $7. Closes 10pm.

Marigold, 245 King St. Fine Chinese cuisine within the medium price range.

Nibbler's Nosh, 973 Corydon Ave at Stafford Street (☎284-0310). A wide selection of Jewish food, ribs, burgers and delicious desserts (mains from $8) and a coffee bar attached; try their special hot dog smothered in fried sauerkraut. A lively Winnipeg institution performing jazz and blues on Saturday night.

Paradise Resturant, 662 Leila Ave and 789 Portage Ave at Beverley Street. Best pizza and baby back ribs in town.

Pasquale's, 109 Marion St, St Boniface. Delightful, busy little place with well-prepared Italian dishes from $6.

Rae & Jerry's Steakhouse, 1405 Portage Ave. Although 5km west of the city centre, this is the choice of Winnipeggers for large, succulent steaks.

Sevala's, 390a blvd Provencher, St Boniface. A plain, sparse, family-style restaurant serving Ukrainian specialities from $5 – best choices are perogies with various fillings (cabbage, mashed potato). All-you-can-eat buffet for $6.49.

Sofia's Caffè, 635 Corydon Ave. In the heart of Little Italy, this restaurant, with outdoor patio, serves large portions of veal, and pasta dishes from $7.

Velvet Glove, in the *Lombard Hotel*, 2 Lombard Place (☎985-6255). Elegant dining in plush surroundings. Four-course menu from $24.

Nightlife and entertainment

Winnipeg tries hard to be the cultural centre of the prairies, and generous sponsorship arrangements support a good range of **theatre, ballet, opera** and **orchestral music**. The city also has some lively **nightspots**, featuring the best of local and national **rock** and **jazz** talent. For **listings**, consult the Thursday edition of the *Winnipeg Free Press* newspaper or the free news sheet *Uptown*, available from self-serve kiosks all over the city. The free magazine *Where*, from tourist offices, also has listings, but their reports are never critical.

These venues are supplemented by an ambitious summer programme of open-air concerts, notably the week-long **Jazz Winnipeg Festival** towards the end of June, and the **Winnipeg Folk Festival**, a four-day extravaganza featuring over two hundred concerts, held in mid-July at Birds Hill Provincial Park, 25km northeast of the city. Apart from the music festivals, the biggest event is **Folklorama**, held during the first two weeks in August. This celebrates Winnipeg's multiethnic population with over forty pavilions spread out over town, each devoted to a particular ethnic group. The **Winnipeg Fringe Festival** is a ten-day event of theatrical productions, held in mid-July in the Exchange District. St Boniface's French-Canadian heritage is honoured annually in the **Festival du Voyageur** – ten days of February fun, whose events lead up to a torchlit procession and the Governor's Ball, where everyone dresses up in period costume.

Music venues and clubs

Centre Culturel Franco-Manitobain, 340 blvd Provencher, St Boniface (☎233-8972). Hosts weekly concerts by French-Canadian musicians. Free jazz sessions on Tuesday at 9pm.

Club 200, 190 Garry St. A popular gay and lesbian club.

Die Maschine, 2nd Floor, 108 Osborne St. Ever so slightly louche; rock, techno, 60s and soul. Closed Sun.

Gio's Room, 272 Sherbrook St. One of Winnipeg's better-known gay and lesbian bars. Closed Sun.

Ice Works Cabaret, 165 McDermot Ave. A hot spot in the Exchange District featuring live entertainment and chart hits.

Jazz on the Rooftop, Winnipeg Art Gallery, 300 Memorial Blvd (☎786-6641 ext 232). Frequent performances by some of Canada's best-known jazz musicians.

Mustang Sally's, 114 Market Ave. Winnipeg's most popular dance club, playing R&B, 70s and 80s hits and techno, and featuring mainstream rock bands; $4 cover charge. Closed Mon–Tues & Sun.

Pyramid Cabaret, 176 Fort St. Best new bands perform rockabilly, Celtic, alternative and reggae music. Closed Sun.

Times Change Blues Bar, 234 Main St. Rough-and-ready jazz and blues place. Live entertainment Thursday to Sunday.

Toad in the Hole, 112 Osborne St. A mix of rock, C&W and Irish fiddle.

The West End Cultural Centre, 586 Ellice Ave (☎783-6918). Everything from jazz and folk to reggae and salsa.

Wise Guys, 65 Rorie St. Packed with students, who come to bop to live mainstream rock. Closed Mon.

Classical music, opera and ballet

Major performances by the **Winnipeg Symphony Orchestra** (☎949-3999) and the **Manitoba Opera** (☎957-7842) take place at the Centennial Concert Hall, 555 Main St, in the Exchange District (☎949-3950); tickets are $11–25. The **Royal Winnipeg Ballet**, (☎956-2792) – the finest dance company in Canada – also performs at the Concert Hall and has an extensive programme of traditional and contemporary ballets; tickets are $8–41, with student and senior citizen discounts of up to twenty percent.

Cinema and theatre

Winnipeg's largest mainstream **cinema** is the Cineplex-Odeon, 234 Donald St, while Cinema 3, 585 Ellice Ave at Sherbrook Street, shows foreign and second-run films, and Cinémathèque, 100 Arthur St, in the Artspace building, concentrates on Canadian releases.

The city has several professional **theatre** groups: principally the Popular Theatre Alliance of Manitoba, whose modern and imaginative plays are performed at the Gas Station, Osborne Street and River Avenue (☎284-9477); and the Prairie Theatre Exchange, Portage Place (☎942-5483), who perform traditional and avant-garde comedy and drama. The Manitoba Theatre Centre, 174 Market Ave (☎ 942-6537), and the Warehouse Theatre, 140 Rupert Ave (☎942-6537), feature local talent, though Winnipeg's main theatrical events are performed by international touring companies in the Centennial Concert Hall.

Listings

Airlines Air Canada, 355 Portage Ave (☎943-9361); Canadian Airlines, 570 Ferry Rd, Winnipeg Airport (☎632-1250).

American Express 200 Graham Ave.

Bike rental Corydon Cycle and Sports, 753 Corydon Ave at Cockburn Street, $15 per day; Olympia Cycle and Ski, 1813 Portage Ave, $12–20 per day; Portage Cycle and Sports, 1841 Portage Ave, $15 per day.

Bookshops Mary Scorer, 389 Graham St at Edmonton Street, is the city's best bookshop, with an excellent range of titles on the Canadian West. The Global Village, 167 Lilac St, is a map and travel shop with a comprehensive selection of specialized maps. Heaven Art and Book Café, 659 Corydon Ave, has a good selection of titles by Manitoban writers and hosts readings.

Bus enquiries Greyhound, 487 Portage Ave. (information ☎1-800-661-8747, reservations 260-4678); Grey Goose, 301 Burnell St (☎784-4500).

Camping equipment United Army Surplus Sales, 460 Portage Ave at Colony Street, sells a wide range of camping and wilderness gear.

Car rental The following firms will collect customers at no extra charge: Discount, at the airport (☎775-2282); Budget, at the airport (☎989-8510), and downtown at Ellice Avenue and Sherbrook Street (☎989-8505); and Thrifty, at the airport (☎949-7608), and downtown at 112 Garry St (☎949-7620).

Consulates UK, 229 Athlone Drive (☎896-1380).

Dental emergencies Broadway Dental Centre, 640 Broadway (☎772-3523).

Disabled visitors *Access Winnipeg Guide* is a free publication that lists hotels, motels, restaurants and points of interest which have disabled-accessible entrances and parking. It can be obtained from Disability International, 101–07 Evergreen Place, Winnipeg, Manitoba R3L 2T3 (☎287-8010, fax 453-1367).

Emergencies ☎911 for police, fire and ambulance.

Gay and lesbian Winnipeg Gay and Lesbian Resource Centre, 1-222 Osborne St (☎284-5208).

Hospital and medical centre Grace General Hospital, 300 Booth St; (outpatient emergencies on ☎837-0157); Health Sciences Centre, 820 Sherbrook St (☎787-3167).

Laundries Shop N Wash Food and Laundromat, 189 Isabel St at Portage Avenue; Zip-Kleen, 110 Sherbrook St at Westminster Avenue.

Left luggage 24hr coin-operated lockers at the train and bus stations.

Lost property VIA baggage information on ☎949-7481; Winnipeg Transit, at the Portage and Main office (☎986-5054).

Newspapers Dominion News, 263 Portage Ave, has a wide variety of international papers.

Pharmacies Shoppers Drug Mart, 471 River Ave and Osborne Street; open 24hr.

Post office The main office is at 266 Graham Ave at Smith Street (☎1-800-267-1177); Mon–Fri 8am–5.30pm.

Sexual Assault Crisis Line ☎786-8631.

Swimming Kildonan Park Swimming Pool, 2021 Main St (☎986-6988); Pan-Am Swimming Pool, 25 Poseidon Bay (☎986-5890 or 986-5891).

Taxis Duffy's, 871 Notre Dame Ave (☎775-0101); Unicity, 340 Hargrave Place (☎925-3131).

Train enquiries VIA Rail ticket office, 123 Main St, for arrival and departure information (☎944-8780, for fares and reservations ☎1-800-561-8630).

Travel agents Apollo Travel, 560 Sargent Ave (☎786-8558); Travel CUTS, 499 Portage Ave (☎783-5353).

Weather ☎983-2050.

Women's contacts Women's Resource Centre, 290 Vaughan St (☎989-4140).

Around Winnipeg

As Winnipeg's dreary suburbs fade into the seamless prairie landscape, the only major interruption is provided by the course of the **Red River** to the north. The sixty-kilometre stretch from the city to Lake Winnipeg – the **Red River Corridor** – was once a tiny part of the supply route that connected the Red River Colony to Hudson Bay, and nowadays it harbours the region's most absorbing tourist attractions, notably a couple of elegant nineteenth-century houses and the refurbished **Lower Fort Garry**. Ornithologists might want to make the trip to the **Oak Hammock Marsh Wildlife Area**, 40km north of Winnipeg, home to thousands of migrating birds, particularly snow- and Canada geese between April and September. In the opposite direction, about 60km southeast of the city in **Steinbach**, the **Mennonite Heritage Village** is worth a peek for its pleasant reconstruction of a nineteenth-century pioneer settlement. Finally, a drive through the **area southwest of Winnipeg** towards the North Dakota border will reward you with some of Manitoba's finest and most typical prairie scenery and take you through neat, tidy Mennonite towns such as **Altona** and **Winkler**.

The Red River Corridor

The trip along the **Red River Corridor** is easily the best day out from Winnipeg, a pleasing diversion along the gentle hills that frame the wide and sluggish river. Driving out from the city on Main Street, which becomes Hwy 9, it's about 10km to the turning for the **River Road Heritage Parkway** (Provincial Road 238), a rough, twisting gravel track that leads to some of the Corridor's lesser attractions. Alternatively, you can keep on the main road for **Selkirk** and **Lower Fort Garry**.

The Beaver **bus** company (☎989-7007) runs a regular service from the bus station on Portage Avenue in Winnipeg to Lower Fort Garry and Selkirk, but there's no public transport along the Parkway and the road's too rough to cycle.

The Heritage Parkway

Turning off the main road, down the **River Road Heritage Parkway**, it's a few minutes' drive to **Twin Oaks**, which was built in the 1850s as part of a girls' school for the daughters of Hudson's Bay Company employees, before curving round to **St Andrew's Rectory** (mid-May to Aug daily 10am–6pm; Sept Sat & Sun 10am–6pm; free), containing exhibits on the role of the Anglican Church in helping to settle the prairies and on its early occupants – stern-looking Victorians determined to save the Métis from themselves. Just opposite, the tidy mid-Victorian **St Andrew's Church** has a number of benches still partly covered by buffalo hide, and stained-glass windows brought here from England packed in barrels of molasses.

A couple of minutes' drive further north, the pretty **Kennedy House** (mid-May to Aug Mon–Sat 10.30am–5pm, Sun & holidays 10.30am–6pm; free) was once the home of Captain William Kennedy, an English-speaking Métis who resigned his Hudson's Bay Company commission because of its increasing involvement with the debilitating liquor trade. The house's three main-floor rooms are furnished in the style of the 1870s, the gardens are a delight, and there's a twee little glassed-in tearoom overlooking the river.

Lower Fort Garry

A few minutes' drive further north, on Hwy 9, 32km from Winnipeg, stands **Lower Fort Garry** (mid-May to Aug daily 10am–6pm; Sept Sat & Sun 10am–6pm; grounds daily until sunset; $5.50, family pass $14), built as the new headquarters of the Hudson's Bay Company between 1830 and 1847. It was the brainchild of **George Simpson**, governor of the company's northern department, an area bounded by the Arctic and Pacific oceans, Hudson Bay and the Missouri River Valley. Nicknamed the "Little Emperor" for his autocratic style, Simpson selected the site because it was downriver from the treacherous waters of the St Andrew's Rapids and was not prone to

Tundra near Churchill, Manitoba

Polar bear

Grain elevator

Mounties

Native Canadian dancer

Moraine Lake, Alberta

Lake Louise, Alberta

Prairies

CHRIS COE, AXIOM

Mount Rundle, Alberta

HEATHER ELTON

The Columbia Icefield, Alberta

CHRIS COE, AXIOM

Bow Lake, Alberta

flooding, as Upper Fort Garry had been. However, the settlers round The Forks were reluctant to cart their produce down to the new camp and when the governors of Assiniboia refused to move here his scheme collapsed.

Sandwiched between Hwy 9 and the Red River, the **Lower Fort Garry National Historic Site** begins at the visitor reception centre, where there's a comprehensive account of the development of the fort and its role in the fur trade. A couple of minutes' walk away, the low thick limestone walls of the fort protect reconstructions of several company buildings, including the retail store, where a small museum is devoted to Inuit and Indian crafts. Several of the exhibits here are exquisite, particularly the decorated skin pouches and an extraordinary necklace fringed by thin strips of metal cut from a sardine can. Next door, the combined sales shop and clerk's quarters has a fur loft packed with pelts, while the middle of the compound is dominated by the Big House with its low sloping roof, built for Governor Simpson in 1832. People in period costume stroll the grounds, ensuring the right atmosphere.

Selkirk and Netley Marsh

About 8km north of the fort, along Hwy 9A, the township of **SELKIRK** was originally chosen as the point where the proposed transcontinental railway was to cross the Red River. Realizing the importance of the railway, the business leaders of Winnipeg – Selkirk's great trade rival – launched a campaign to have the route changed. Their efforts were successful, not least because one of the leading lights of the CPR syndicate, Donald Smith, was a key shareholder in the Hudson's Bay Company, which owned five hundred acres of land around The Forks. Bypassed by the trains, Selkirk slipped into relative obscurity, though it did achieve a degree of prosperity through its shipyards, and apparently retains the dubious title of "Catfish Capital of the World".

Selkirk's only real attraction is the **Marine Museum of Manitoba** (May–Aug daily 9am–6pm; Sept Mon–Fri 9am–3pm, Sat & Sun noon–6pm; $3.50), situated on the edge of Selkirk Park at Eveline and Queen streets. The museum consists of seven passenger and freight ships, dragged out of the water and parked on a lawn, as well as a lighthouse, plus a mildly interesting video on the history of Lake Winnipeg's shipping and fishing industries. **Tour boats** ply the Red River south as far as **Lockport** three times daily from the Marine Museum (☎1-888-204-5008 for details). In the park there's a bird sanctuary and a 6.5-metre-high **oxcart**, which is apparently the world's largest.

If you're in Selkirk in early July, you could take in the Manitoba Highland Gathering, a Scottish festival honouring the original settlers. Places to **stay** include the *Daerwood Motor Inn*, 162 Main St (☎482-7722 or 1-800-930-3888; ②–③) and the *Evergreen Gate B&B*, 1138 River Rd (☎482-6248; ②). You can **camp** at the *Willow Springs Campground*, 13km north of Selkirk on Hwy 320 ($8–10; ☎482-5138; May–Oct). For **food**, try *Barney Gargles*, 185 Main St, which has delicious main courses from $6.

From the Marine Museum, Provincial Road 320 continues north 16km to the edge of **Netley Marsh**, a huge swampy delta formed by the Red River as it seeps into Lake Winnipeg. At the end of the road, there's a small **recreation park** with a snack bar, an observation tower and a series of plaques that detail the way of life of the area's native peoples. The marsh is an impenetrable maze for the inexperienced, but you can hire a boat and guide at the park for about $90 a day. On the lake side of the delta, the **Bird Refuge** is one of North America's largest waterfowl nesting areas and there are lots of good fishing spots; the pickerel, or wall-eye, are delicious.

The Tree House Bed and Breakfast (☎941-0920; ②), on the edge of the marsh, near the village of Matlock, is a relaxing **place to stay** and absorb the tranquil charms of the wetlands area. Go north on Hwy 9 and turn onto the gravel Route 202.

Oak Hammock Marsh

The **Oak Hammock Marsh Wildlife Area** (daylight hours all year; $3.75; no camping) is all that remains of the wetlands that once stretched from St Andrews, near the Red River, up to the village of Teulon, to the west of Netley Creek. Most of this wetland was drained and farmed around the turn of the century, but in the 1960s some of the area was restored to its original state and protected by a series of retaining dykes. In addition, a number of islands were built to provide marshland birds a safe place to nest.

To get there from Winnipeg take Hwy 7 north, turn east along Hwy 67, and follow the signs to the Main Mound Area, where there's an **information and conservation centre**, a picnic site and a couple of observation decks, all connected by a system of dykes and boardwalk trails. The best time to come is in spring or fall, when the grebes, coots and other residents are joined by thousands of migrating birds, from falcons through to Canada geese. Another part of the Wildlife Area has been returned to tall-grass prairie, carpeted from mid-June to August with the blooms of wildflowers such as the purple Blazing Star and the speckled red Prairie Lily.

The Mennonite Heritage Village

A spruce reconstruction of a pioneer settlement of the late 1800s is to be found just 2km north of the township of **Steinbach**, which is an hour's drive southeast from Winnipeg along Hwys 1 and 12 (2 buses daily). In and around the main street of the **Mennonite Heritage Village** (May & Sept Mon–Sat 10am–5pm, Sun noon–5pm; June–Aug Mon–Sat 10am–7pm, Sun noon–7pm; Oct–April Mon–Fri 10am–4pm; $4), there's a church, a windmill and a couple of stores and farmhouses, but it's the general flavour of the place that appeals rather than any particular structure. The Mennonites, a Protestant sect, were founded in the Netherlands under the leadership of Menno Symons in the early sixteenth century. Subsequently the movement divided into two broad factions, with one group refusing to have anything to do with the secular state and sustaining a hostile attitude to private property, and the more "liberal" clans being inclined to compromise. Many of the former – the **Ammanites** – moved to the United States and then Ontario, settling in and around Kitchener-Waterloo, while the more liberal **Untere** migrated to Russia and then Manitoba in the 1870s. There are about 100,000 in Canada today. Few of the Manitoba Mennonites, who congregated in and around Steinbach, wear the traditional black and white clothes or live on communal farms, but like all Mennonite communities they maintain a strong pacifist tradition. Costumed guides at the Heritage Village provide an intriguing account of their history, augmented by displays in the tiny museum and the interpretive centre, which sets the scene at the start of your visit.

The best **accommodation** in the area is to be found in Steinbach. Try the *Frantz Motor Inn*, Hwy 52, just east of town (☎326-9831; ②). For a Mennonite meal, **eat** at the Heritage Village, or in Steinbach at the *Dutch Connection*, 88 Brandt St (evenings only). In keeping with the strict Mennonite beliefs, you'll find that virtually all the restaurants in the area serve no alcohol.

Southwest of Winnipeg

A pleasant day's outing from Winnipeg can be had by making a loop through various towns and villages **southwest of the city**. It's here that you'll encounter the quintessential prairie town – squat false-gabled buildings lining a wide main street, parked half-ton trucks filled with bales of hay, sacks of horsefeed, or a sleeping dog, and quiet sidestreets bordered by tall Manitoba oaks or trembling aspen. The drive takes you along part of the Red River and across vast golden wheatfields punctuated only by

grain elevators, huge storage silos situated at the edge of almost every town, usually with the town's name painted high up in large white letters. You can reach some of these communities, from Winnipeg, with Grey Goose **bus** lines, departing from their terminal at 301 Bunnell St.

ROSENORT, 50km south of Winnipeg on Route 205, off Hwy 75, is the first place of any interest. A Mennonite town, its chief attraction – and a good place to stop for lunch – is the *Rose Lane Heritage House and Tea Room*, 31 Rose Lane, where cracked wheat and cornmeal bread are baked on the premises. **MORRIS**, 15km further on Hwy 75, is home to the annual **Manitoba Stampede and Exhibition**, one of Canada's largest, which takes place in and around a huge recreational complex dominating the town in the third week of July. The area where the Morris River joins the Red River is great for catching wall-eye and catfish, and a Catfish Derby is held here in August. **ST JEAN BAPTISTE**, a bit further south, is an attractive French-speaking community known for its production of the type of pea that's used in French-Canadian pea soup. **EMERSON**, 30km south, is right on the border with Minnesota and North Dakota. Sights here include the log customs house, Fort Dufferin (the original site of the North West Mounted Police), and the 1917–18 **town hall and courthouse**, at the corner of Church Street and Winnipeg Avenue (Mon–Fri 9am–4pm; free), is a good example of Neoclassical prairie architecture in Canada. For a **lunch** or afternoon tea, the place to visit is *Aunt Maud's Tea Room*, 57 4th St (closed Mon–Wed), housed in a historic 1880s home. **GRETNA**, 25km west of Emerson, is another Mennonite community, as is **WINKLER**, to the northwest, which has several arts and crafts shops, a farmer's market (July–Sept Fri eve), and the August Harvest Festival. It's also a great place to sample genuine **Mennonite food**, served in almost all the cafés and restaurants; try *platz*, a rhubarb dessert.

West of Winkler, you pass through the large town of **MORDEN**, site of the annual Corn and Apple Festival in August, and **DARLINGFORD**, 20km further west, where a large granite boulder marks the route taken by the eighteenth-century French explorer Sieur de la Vérendrye on his way west in search of a reputed vast "western sea". The land to the south and west begins to descend into the **Pembina River Valley**, which offers magnificent sweeping views. **Kaleida**, a tiny village about 15km southwest of Darlingford, has a charming pioneer stone church and attractive, yet melancholy, cemetery.

AROUND MANITOBA

Manitoba is distinguished principally by its **parks**, thousands of acres of wilderness, lake, river and forest that boast wonderful scenery, great hikes and hundreds of kilometres of canoe routes. One of the best is **Riding Mountain National Park**, 250km northwest of Winnipeg, which derives its name from the fur trappers who changed from canoe to horseback to travel across its wooded highlands. On the southern edge of the park, the tourist village of **Wasagaming** is a useful base for exploring the surrounding countryside, which incorporates areas of deciduous and mixed forest, lake and grassland. Manitoba's **provincial parks** include the dramatic landscapes and difficult whitewater canoe routes of the remote **Atikaki Wilderness Park**, the lakeside marshes and forests of **Hecla Park**, and yet more canoe routes in **Duck Mountain Park**, which is also noted for its fishing.

Other than the parks and lakeshores, most of Manitoba's significant attractions are concentrated in and around Winnipeg, and many of the province's smaller villages and towns are not really tourist destinations. The notable exceptions are **Brandon** and **Souris**, and remote **Churchill**, a weird and wild outpost on the shores of Hudson Bay that's a great place for seeing beluga whales and polar bears. Elsewhere, **Dauphin, Neepawa** and **Minnedosa** are three of the more agreeable prairie towns, but almost

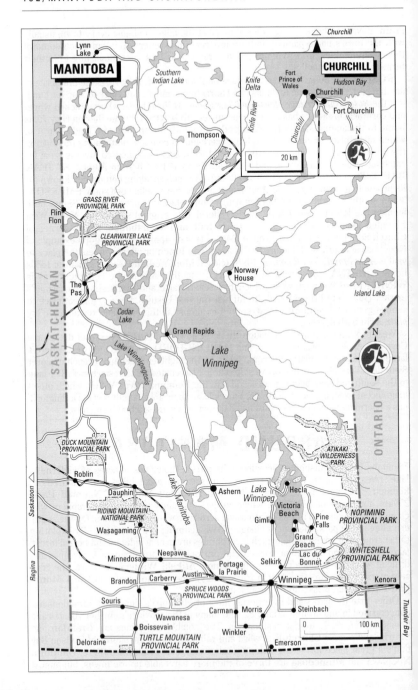

all the other settlements are virtually indistinguishable, even though the European immigrants who cleared and settled Manitoba in the late nineteenth century came from a wide range of backgrounds. Most of them were rapidly and almost entirely assimilated, but the villages around Dauphin are still dominated by the onion domes of the Ukrainians' Orthodox churches, and **Gimli**, on the west side of Lake Winnipeg, has a pleasant museum tracing the history of its Icelandic settlement.

There are reasonably regular **bus** services that run between Manitoba's main settlements, and most of the village bus stops are within relatively comfortable walking distance of at least one hotel. However, nearly all of Manitoba's parks are difficult to reach and impossible to tour by bus, with the exception of **Riding Mountain Park**, where the service from Winnipeg stops right in the centre of Wasagaming; **Whiteshell Park**, where a bus passes through on the Trans-Canada on its way east; and **Spruce Woods Park**, close to the bus routes from Carberry and Brandon. VIA Rail operates just two **train** services to and from Winnipeg, each running three times weekly: the main east–west line connects Winnipeg with Toronto, Saskatoon, Jasper and Vancouver, and a northern line runs to Churchill, via The Pas, well beyond the reach of the road.

Southeast Manitoba

The great slice of Manitoban wilderness that extends north from the Trans-Canada Highway between Lake Winnipeg and the Ontario border is set on the rock of the Canadian Shield, an inhospitable and sparsely inhabited region of lake, river and forest that's home to three of the province's largest parks. To the south, **Whiteshell Park** is the oldest and most developed, with a relatively extensive road system, fifteen campgrounds and one-quarter of Manitoba's holiday and fishing lodges. Just to the north, **Nopiming Park** is more isolated, with a handful of lakeside campgrounds that can be reached along two bumpy gravel roads, while the **Atikaki Wilderness Park** is the most remote of the three, accessible only by canoe or float plane. The Atikaki's mile upon mile of rugged forest and granite outcrop are connected to the east shore of Lake Winnipeg by the Bloodvein and Leyond rivers, two of Manitoba's wildest white-water canoe routes.

The Canadian Shield ends at **Lake Winnipeg**, a giant finger of water some 400km long that connects the Red River with the Nelson River and subsequently Hudson Bay to the north. It's a shallow lake, subject to violent squalls, and, apart from the odd Indian reservation, the only settlement has been around its southern rim. Here, on the east shore, Winnipeg's wealthy have built their cottages in and around **Victoria Beach** and **Hillside Beach**, but **Grand Beach Provincial Park** has the lake's finest bathing and long lines of sand dune stretching as far as the eye can see. The beaches of the west shore are poor by comparison, and the old fishing and farming villages that trail up the coast from Winnipeg Beach to Riverton are not of major interest. Immediately to the north of Riverton, **Hecla Provincial Park** is slightly more agreeable, the developed facilities of Gull Harbour Resort supplemented by unspoilt marsh and forest.

Known as the **Interlake**, the marginal farmland that lies between Lake Winnipeg to the east and lakes Manitoba and Winnipegosis to the west is as flat as a pancake and one of the most boring parts of the prairies. The only significant attraction is at the **Narcisse Wildlife Management Area**, 90km north of Winnipeg on Hwy 17, where thousands of red-sided garter snakes gather to mate in April and May, writhing around the bottom of a series of shallow pits in slithering heaps. It's not for the squeamish.

From Winnipeg, there's a once-daily **bus** service to Rennie and West Hawk Lake in the Whiteshell; three buses a day (Mon, Wed, Thurs & Sun) to Lac du Bonnet, the nearest point to Nopiming Park; a once-daily service to Doris's Grocery Store, 2km from Grand Beach; and one bus daily to **Gimli**, and **Gull Harbour**, on Hecla Island in Hecla Park.

Whiteshell Provincial Park

Whiteshell Provincial Park takes its name from the small, white seashell, the *megis*, that was sacred to the Ojibwa, who believed the Creator blew through the shell to breathe life into the first human being. These shells, left by the prehistoric lake that covered the entire region, were concentrated along the park's two main rivers, the **Whiteshell** to the south and the **Winnipeg** to the north, the latter an important part of the canoe route followed by the voyageurs of the North West Company on their way from Montréal to the Red River.

Most of the park's visitors head for **FALCON LAKE** and **WEST HAWK LAKE**, two well-developed tourist townships situated on either side of the Trans-Canada Highway, near the Ontario border. Crowded throughout the summer, neither site has much to recommend it, though both have a full range of facilities from serviced campgrounds ($10–15), resort hotels – try the *Penguin Resort* at Falcon Lake (☎349-2218; ②–④) – gas stations, grocery stores and minature golf through to boat and watersports equipment rental. Because of its depth, West Hawk Lake is particularly good for scuba diving.The best places to **eat** are in West Hawk Lake are the *Nite Hawk Café*, for home-made burgers, and the *Landing Steak House*, which serves juicy steaks and prime rib. For daytrippers, there's a $5 entrance fee (valid for 3 days). On the south side of West Hawk Lake, formed by a meteorite and the deepest lake in Manitoba, the sixteen-kilometre loop of the **Hunt Lake Hiking Trail** passes through cedar and white pine forests, across sticky aromatic bogs and over rocky outcrops, all in the space of about eight hours. There's a primitive campground on the trail at Little Indian Bay, but be sure to register at the West Hawk Lake **park office** (☎349-2245) if you're planning to stay overnight.

From West Hawk Lake, Route 44 cuts north towards **CADDY LAKE** (campgrounds and two holiday lodges), the starting point for one of the area's most beautiful **canoe routes**, the 160-kilometre journey along the Whiteshell River to Lone Island Lake, in the centre of the park. Experienced walkers could tackle the sixty-kilometre loop of the **Mantario Hiking Trail** just to the east of Caddy Lake, along Provincial Road 312; for beginners, there are the **Bear Lake** (8km) and **McGillivray trails** (4km), clearly signposted walks from Hwy 44 to the west of Caddy Lake; they reveal a good sample of the topography of the park – dry ridges dominated by jack pine, bogs crammed with black spruce, and two shallow lakes brown from algae and humic acid. Opposite the start of the Bear Lake Trail, the **Frances Lake** canoe route makes for a pleasant overnight excursion, a twenty-kilometre trip south to the Frances Lake campground, with three portages past the rapids, and twelve hauls round beaver dams.

Further west, 32km from West Hawk, the village of **RENNIE** is home to the **park headquarters** (Mon–Fri 8.30am–4.30pm; July & Aug also Sat & Sun 9am–4.30pm; ☎369-5426), which has a comprehensive range of information on local trails and canoe routes. The nearby **Alf Hole Goose Sanctuary** (late May to mid-Oct Mon–Fri 10am–5pm, also Sat & Sun until early Sept 10.30am–6pm; free) is best visited in spring or fall, when the Canada geese pass through on their migration. If you need to **stay** in Rennie as a base for excursions into the park, your choices are the rather primitive *Rennie Hotel* (☎369-5261; ①) or the *Rocky Ridge Campground* (☎369-5507; $15; May–Sept). From Rennie, the eighty-kilometre stretch of Route 307 passes most of the park's other campgrounds, lodges, trails and canoe routes.

Nopiming Provincial Park

Separated from the Whiteshell by the Winnipeg River, **Nopiming Provincial Park** is a remote rocky area whose granite shoreline cliffs spread out above black spruce bogs and tiny sandy beaches – the name is Ojibwa for "entrance to the wilderness". The park's four campgrounds (all open May–Sept) lie close to its two gravel roads: Route 314, which meanders across the 80km of its western edge, and the far shorter Route

315, a thirty-kilometre track that cuts east below Bird Lake to the Ontario border. Nopiming Park is crossed by the **Oiseau** and **Manigotagan** waterways, whose creeks and rivers trickle or rush from lake to lake, forming no less than 1200km of possible canoe route. Towards the south of the park, **BIRD LAKE** makes for a useful base, with a main settlement on the south shore that's equipped with a campground, a grocery store and the cabins of the *Nopiming Lodge* (☎884-2281; ③; year-round). There's also motorboat rental, as well as canoe and guide rental for excursions to Snowshoe Lake, around falls and over rapids (55km). Near **BISSETT**, in the north of the park, there are several abandoned **gold-mining shafts** from the 1930s.

Atikaki Provincial Wilderness Park

Accessible by float plane from Winnipeg and Lac du Bonnet, the **Atikaki Provincial Wilderness Park** has half a dozen holiday and fishing lodges dotted across some of the finest Canadian Shield scenery in the province. There are no campgrounds or roads through the park, but the rough gravel track that makes up most of Route 304 does reach Wallace Lake, at the park's southern tip, via the east shore of Lake Winnipeg or Nopiming Park's Route 314. The Atikaki is crisscrossed by canoe routes that give glimpses of the region's ancient pictograph sites, but they all include difficult whitewater stretches that should only be attempted by experienced canoeists.

The park's more popular canoe routes include the dramatic journey down the **Bloodvein River** to Lake Winnipeg, its rapids, falls and wild twistings balanced by peaceful drifts past quiet lakes and wild rice marshes, and the **Kautunigan Route**, a 500-kilometre excursion that starts at Wallace Lake and threads its way to the mouth of the Berens River on Lake Winnipeg, well to the north of the park. Both routes pass stands of white birch, black spruce, jack pine, elm, oak and maple, and you may catch sight of moose, timber wolves, coyotes and black bears.

Maps are available from the Manitoba Department of Natural Resources, 1007 Century St, Winnipeg, Manitoba R3H OW4 (☎945-6666); file trip plans with the Lac du Bonnet Natural Resource Office, Box 850, Lac du Bonnet (☎345-1454). Alternatively, several of the outfitters in Winnipeg and Lac du Bonnet organize guided excursions; details are available from the Manitoba Natural Resources Office, 200 Saulteaux Crescent, Winnipeg, Manitoba R3J 3W3 (☎945-6784 or 1-800-214-6497). To obtain information on canoe routes, call the Manitoba Recreational Canoeing Association (☎925-5078). Three-, five- and ten-day **canoeing** and **white-water rafting** excursions in the park are offered by Wilderness Odysseys (☎412/329-0436 or 1-800-443-6199). An invaluable walking guide is Ruth Marr's *The Manitoba Walking and Hiking Guide*, which details more than two hundred routes of varying degrees of difficulty.

Lake Winnipeg

Approached along Hwy 59, the southeast shore of **Lake Winnipeg** has one major attraction, **Grand Beach Provincial Park**, whose long stretch of powdery white sand, high grass-crowned dunes and shallow bathing water make it the region's most popular day-trip. The beach, a favourite swimming spot with Winnipeggers since the 1920s, is divided into two distinct parts, separated by a narrow channel that drains out of a knobbly lagoon, set just behind the lakeshore. The channel is spanned by a tiny footbridge, but the two parts of the beach are very different: to the west there are privately owned cottages, sports facilities, motor- and rowboat rental, grocery stores and a restaurant; the eastern section is less developed, although it does have a large **campground** (☎754-3759 or 754-2212; $12–14; May–Sept) tucked away amongst the dunes. Both parts of the beach get very crowded on summer weekends, when it seems that all of Winnipeg is stretched out on the sands. By the campground office, the **Ancient Beach Trail** follows the line of the prehistoric lake that dominated southern Manitoba in the last ice age; allow about an hour for the walk. At **GRAND MARAIS**, just outside the park, you'll find an array of motels, beachside cottages and cabins (②–④; most May–Sept). The *Grand Beach Road Café* is famous for its thick hot beef sandwiches.

Roughly 20km north of Grand Beach, the twin townships of **HILLSIDE BEACH** and prettier **VICTORIA BEACH** have good sandy beaches, but their well-heeled inhabitants avoid catering for outsiders. There are no campgrounds and the only **motel** is the recently renovated *Birchwood* (☎754-2596; ②) on the highway, 6km south of Victoria Beach at Traverse Bay; the motel's star facility is the huge patio overlooking the bay.

Gimli and Hecla Provincial Park

In 1875, some two hundred Icelanders moved to the southwestern shore of Lake Winnipeg, where they had secured exclusive rights to a block of land that stretched from today's Winnipeg Beach to Hecla Island, named after a volcano in their homeland. The next year the colonists were struck by a smallpox epidemic, yet they managed to survive and founded the **Republic of New Iceland**, a large self-governing and self-sufficient settlement with its own Icelandic-language school, churches and newspaper. Their independence lasted just twenty years, for in 1897 they acquiesced in the federal government's decision to open their new homeland to other ethnic groups. An identifiable Icelandic community had ceased to exist by the 1920s, but this part of Manitoba still has the largest number of expatriates of Icelandic descent outside Iceland. The residents celebrate their heritage during the *Islendingadagurinn* (Icelanders' Day) festival, on the first weekend in August, when they dress up in Viking helmets and organize beauty pageants, concerts and firework displays. This rather commercial festival – not to everyone's taste – is held in the largest township, **GIMLI** (literally "paradise"). There's little else to attract visitors to this part of the lake, though Gimli's newly refurbished harbourside, with a fibreglass Viking statue and a massive wharf, is modestly attractive. The **Heritage Museum**, at 62 2nd Ave (May, June & Sept Sat & Sun 10am–5pm; July & Aug daily 10am–6pm; donation), chronicles the history of New Iceland. The **tourist office** is located downtown on 7th Avenue (May–Aug Mon–Fri 9am–5pm, Sat & Sun 9am–9pm; ☎642-7974). Two large **festivals** – Sun Country in July and Sun Fest in August – also liven up the town in summer.

Gimli doesn't have a lot of **places to stay**, but the best of the lot is the *Country Resort by Carlson*, 10 Centre St (☎642-8565 or 1-800-456-4000; ③–⑤), which has attractive suites with balconies. More affordable is the bayside **B&B** accommodation at *Ondvik*, on North Drive, 4km south of town (☎642-7031; ②), run by Icelandic descendants. There's also a **campground** near the beach, 8km south of town, *Idle-Wheels Tent & Trailer Park* (☎642-5676; $11–13; May to mid-Oct). *Brennivins*, 70 1st Ave (summer Wed–Sun lunch & dinner; winter Wed–Sun dinner only), serves good **food**, washed down with potent Icelandic schnapps.

Roughly 100km to the north, **Hecla Provincial Park** consists of several islands and a slender peninsula that jut out into Lake Winnipeg, almost touching the eastern shore. The park is approached along Hwy 8, which runs across a narrow causeway to the largest of the islands, **Hecla**, where the tourist township of **GULL HARBOUR** has a comprehensive range of facilities. Nearby, on the east side of the island, the original **Hecla Village** (☎279-2056 or 378-2945 for hours) has a number of old houses, a church and a school dating from the early years of Icelandic settlement; a short heritage trail covers the highlights (guided tours available in summer), or you can strike out on one of the island's hiking trails through forest and marsh.

For **accommodation**, there's the luxurious *Gull Harbour Resort* at Riverton (☎279-2041 or 1-800-267-6700; ④), the *Solmundson Gesta Hus*, in Hecla Village (☎279-2088; ③), a **B&B** offering home-cooked dinners, and a medium-size **campground** (☎378-2945; $18; May–Sept) on the neck of land between Gull Harbour and the lake.

Southwest Manitoba

West of Winnipeg, the Trans-Canada Highway slices across the prairies, past brilliant yellow canola (rapeseed) fields, on its way to Regina, 600km away in Saskatchewan. Dotted with campgrounds and fast-food joints, the Trans-Canada follows the route of the original transcontinental railroad, passing a series of charmless towns that are at the heart of the province's most fertile farming region. **Brandon**, the province's second largest city, has a handful of Victorian mansions, a lively arts centre and lies not too far from **Spruce Woods Provincial Park**, a mixed area of forest and desert. Before you get to Brandon, however, immediately to the west of **Portage la Prairie**, the Yellowhead Highway cuts northwest from the Trans-Canada to form a more attractive route across the prairies, passing through the pretty little villages of **Neepawa** and **Minnedosa** before running south of **Riding Mountain National Park**.

West along the Trans-Canada and points south

The first major settlement west of Winnipeg is **PORTAGE LA PRAIRIE**, Manitoba's third largest city, located in the richest agricultural land in the province. You'll find the **tourist bureau** at 11 2nd St NE (Mon–Fri 9am–5pm; ☎857-7778), which has a good range of free literature on the area. Portage is a food-processing centre with only one mildly interesting attraction, the **Fort la Reine Museum and Pioneer Village** (May, June & Sept daily 9am–6pm; July & Aug Mon, Tues, Sat & Sun 9am–6pm, Wed–Fri 9am–8pm; $2), located on the outskirts of town at the junction of Hwys 1A and 26. The original fort served as the headquarters of Pierre Gaultier, Sieur de la Vérendrye, during his explorations in the 1740s; the present complex depicts life in the nineteenth century, and includes a trading post, a log homestead, a trapper's cabin, a schoolhouse and a railway caboose.

The large **Island Park**, in the city centre, is also worth a stroll. It's almost completely surrounded by Crescent Lake – not actually a lake but an **oxbow** of the Assiniboine River, formed when a river cuts across the narrow end of a loop in its course and creates an isolated body of water. The limestone **city hall**, on Saskatchewan Avenue, is the most attractive building in town; it was built in the 1890s by the same architect who designed the Parliament Buildings in Ottawa. On the same street is the **Portage Arts Centre and Gallery** (Tues–Sat 11am–5pm; free), featuring frequent exhibitions.

Annually in mid-July a **strawberry festival** is held here honouring the red berry and serving it up in all its variations. For **accommodation**, your best bet is the 250-room *Westward Village Inn*, 2401 Saskatchewan Ave West (☎857-9745 or 1-800-817-7855; ③), or the cheaper *Westgate Inn Motel*, 1010 Saskatchewan Ave East (☎239-5200; ②). The unique *Red Roof House*, 102 1st St SW (☎857-7109; ②), is a seventeen-room home where you are pampered with a champagne breakfast – Clark Gable and Carole Lombard once stayed here. There's a well-equipped **campground** 16km east of the city on the Trans-Canada (☎267-2191; $12–17; mid-April to Sept), with a playground, store and hiking trails. The range of good **restaurants** in Portage is limited; your best bets are *Spriggs'*, 1609 Saskatchewan Ave West, which has a weekday lunch buffet for $6.50, and *Franco's*, 1109 Saskatchewan Ave West, which has a similar deal for $5.95.

Delta Marsh, 25km north of the city on Provincial Road 240, is a wetland extending for some 40km along the southern shore of Lake Manitoba, and is one of the largest waterfowl marshes in North America. From May to September, Delta Marsh Canoe Trips (☎243-2009) arranges guided **tours** of the marsh.

Further west, near **AUSTIN**, 3km south of the Trans-Canada on Hwy 34, the **Manitoba Agricultural Museum** (mid-May to Sept daily 9am–5pm; $5) has an exhaustive collection of early twentieth-century farm machinery, from gigantic steam tractors through to threshing machines and balers. The site also includes a **homesteaders' village**, which simulates village life of the late nineteenth century and has the province's largest collection of pioneer household articles. The immensely popular **Manitoba Threshermen's Reunion and Stampede** is held here every year in mid-July, featuring all things "western" – four days of rodeo riding, threshing displays, ploughing competitions, square dancing, jigging and a Fiddlers' Festival. You can camp in the grounds of the museum (☎637-2354; $8.50–10.50; mid-May to Oct); otherwise, B&B **accommodation** is available at *The Oak Tree* (☎637-2029; ②), near the museum.

Spruce Woods Provincial Park

Between Austin and Brandon, about 15km south of the Trans-Canada along Hwy 5, **Spruce Woods Provincial Park** falls on either side of the Assiniboine River, whose confused loops twist slowly south and west. The park has a number of walking trails that begin beside or near the road. To the north, the **Epinette Creek Trails** run through woodland and marsh, the longest being the 25-kilometre Newfoundland Trail. There are a number of unserviced campgrounds along the various paths.

Roughly 5km south of the Epinette Creek Trails, the **Spirit Sands Trails** cross an area of mixed-grass prairie before entering the shifting sand dunes and pots of quicksand that constitute Manitoba's only **desert**. These "Spirit Sands" were of great religious significance to the Ojibwa who, according to one of the earliest fur traders, Alexander Henry, told "of the strange noises heard in its bowels, and its nightly apparitions". Hire a guide or, if it's too hot to walk, try one of the horse-drawn wagon tours that leave from the start of the trail throughout the summer (mid-May to June Mon–Fri by appointment, Sat & Sun noon; July & Aug daily 10am, noon & 2pm; 1hr 30min; $8; ☎827-2800 or 827-2415). The park is filled with strange, bluish-green ponds formed by the action of underground streams, and has some rare animals, notably the hognose snake and the prairie skink (a lizard); there's also a lot of poison ivy about, so take precautions.

A kilometre or so south of the start of the Spirit Sands, there's a full range of tourist facilities at **Kiche Manitou Lake**, including a large campground (☎827-2458; May–Sept), a caravan park, grocery stores, restaurants, a beach, canoe rental and a visitor services centre (mid-May to early Sept daily; summer ☎827-2543, rest of the year ☎834-3223).

CARBERRY is the nearest community of any size to Spruce Woods, and you can use it as a base to explore the park. Other than the **Seton Centre**, 116 Main St (June to early Sept Tues–Sat 1–5pm; $1), displaying the artwork and memorabilia of the naturalist Ernest Thompson Seton, and the local history **Carberry Plains Museum** (mid-June to mid-Sept daily 1–6pm; donation), there's not much to see. You can **stay** at the *4-Way Motel* (☎834-2878; ①) or the more comfortable *Carberry Motor Inn* (☎834-2197; ②).

Brandon and around

In 1881, when the CPR decided to route the transcontinental railroad through Winnipeg, it was clear that they would need a refuelling depot in the western part of the province. The ideal location was on the east bank of the Assiniboine River, opposite today's **BRANDON**, 160km from Winnipeg, but a certain Dugald McVicar was already established here. The sudden arrival of all sorts of speculators encouraged McVicar to overreach himself, and he attempted to sell his farm and sod hut to the CPR for around $60,000, prompting a railway negotiator to exclaim, "I'll be damned if a town of any kind is built here." It wasn't, and Brandon was founded 4km to the west. Nowadays, the city is a major agricultural centre, home to several research institutions, Manitoba's largest livestock show, the professional rodeo competitions of the Provincial Ex held in mid-June, and the Brandon Film Festival in mid-March.

If you're in Brandon between September and mid-May and want to know what's going on, contact the **Chamber of Commerce**, 1043 Rosser Ave (Mon–Fri 8.30am–4.30pm; ☎728-3287 or 1-888-799-1111). There's also a **tourist information kiosk** (Mon–Sat 11.30am–9.30pm) at the Brandon Gallery Shopping Centre, corner of Rosser Avenue and 8th Street. During summer the Brandon **tourist office** on the Trans-Canada Highway (mid-May to Aug daily 9am–7pm; ☎725-3315) has a glossy brochure detailing an **architectural walking tour** of the town, highlighting the historic buildings for which the city is known, some of which are on the south side of Rosser Avenue. Here, a terrace in the Romanesque Revival style includes the former Mutter Brothers Grocery Store, whose interior has been removed to the **Daly House Museum**, 122 18th St (daily 10am–noon & 1–5pm; $2), the restored home of Brandon's first mayor. The highlight of the house, however, is an illuminated, four-storey doll's house, in one of the upstairs bedrooms – complete with minuscule mice and mousetraps.

Other imposing late nineteenth-century residences are located on the stretch of **Louise Avenue** as you walk west to **Brandon University** – note especially the yellow-brick house with the corner turret at no. 1036, and the **Paterson–Matheson House** directly across the street at no. 1039, with a spindle-and-spool carved wooden porch painted bright yellow and green. **Moreland Manor**, the low-slung, red-brick and brown-shingled house, on the corner of Louise Avenue and 14th Street, is as close to a Frank Lloyd Wright design as you'll get in Manitoba. The university itself has a small campus dotted with a mix of old and new buildings, most impressive of which is the original college building, with its ragged silhouette facing you to the right as you approach from Louise Avenue; climb the creaky stairs inside to the attic. The university also houses the **B.J. Hales Museum of Natural History** in McMaster Hall (Mon, Wed & Fri 10am–noon & 1–4pm, Tues & Thurs 1–4pm; free), with a large botanical and geological collection and interactive exhibits. The former courthouse, topped by an octagonal cupola, at 11th Street and Princess Avenue – is Brandon's grandest building.

The **Art Gallery of Southwestern Manitoba**, 638 Princess Ave (July & Aug Mon & Thurs 10am–9pm, Tues, Wed & Fri 10am–5pm; Sept–June Mon & Thurs 10am–9pm, Tues, Wed, Fri & Sat 10am–5pm; donation), has changing exhibitions concentrating on the work of Manitoba artists and craftspeople.

The city has two **bus terminals**: the main one, at 141 6th St, handles Greyhound buses running to Winnipeg, Regina and Saskatoon, as well as smaller places in southwest Manitoba; the smaller one, at 140 12th St, is the depot for Grey Goose Lines which has buses travelling south on Hwy 10.

Brandon has lots of good places to **stay** in all price ranges. The *Super 8 Motel*, 1570 Highland Ave, just off the Trans-Canada (☎729-8024; ②), is perhaps the best value; a free continental breakfast is provided, and facilities include a pool and a hot tub. Other recommended places are the *Royal Oak Inn*, 3130 Victoria Ave (☎728-5775 or 1-800-852-2709; ③–④), the city's most reputable accommodation, with a 1930s-theme restaurant, and the *Victoria Inn*, 3550 Victoria Ave West (☎725-1532 or 1-800-852-2710; ③–④), which has saunas, a hot tub and swimming pool. For a personalized touch, check out *Casa Maley*, 1605 Victoria Ave (☎728-0812; ②), a **B&B** in a 1912 Tudor-style home; the owners have a baby-sitting service and pick you up from the station. There are two **campgrounds** just outside town and a smaller one 8km west on the Trans-Canada there's *Thunder Mountain* (mid-May to early Sept; ☎727-1056; $11–12), which has the popular attraction of the largest waterslide in Manitoba.

Brandon's best-known **restaurant** is *Kokonas*, 1011 Rosser Ave, specializing in prime rib and Greek dishes. Other places along Rosser include *The Green Olive*, at no. 612, which serves cheap pasta and slightly dearer chicken dishes, and the expensive *Jerry's Bistro* (☎727-7781), at no. 926, which serves up such exotic fare as emu and ostrich. Also on Rosser is the favourite meeting place of Brandon's sophisticates, the *Chocolatier and Cappuccino Bar*, at no. 908, where people sip coffee in minimalist splendour.

Souris

SOURIS, 40km southwest, is probably the most interesting village around Brandon and easily reached by Greyhound. A pretty tree-shaded town on the steep banks of the Souris River, its main attraction is the vertigo-inducing **suspension bridge**. Beside the bridge is the charming local history **Hillcrest Museum** (late May & June Sun 2–5pm; July to ealy Sept daily 10am–6pm; $1). If you're feeling active you can prospect for agates, jaspers and other **semi-precious stones** at the pits outside town. The staff at The Rock Shop, at 8 1st St South, which sells some of the stones and also sells the permit ($10.70), will direct you to the pit. You can take away as much as you can carry.

Turtle Mountain Provincial Park

About 25km further south, you come to **Turtle Mountain Provincial Park**, a mixed area of marsh, rolling hills and deciduous forest, whose four hundred shallow lakes form an ideal habitat for the western painted turtle, after which the park takes its name. There's also a substantial moose population, most visible in late September. Turtle Mountain's main facilities are beside the main road at **Adam Lake**, where there's a large campground (☎534-2578; $13–15; May–Sept), a beach, a store, a **park office** (Mon–Thurs 10am–noon & 1–6pm, Fri & Sat 10am–10pm, Sun 1–4pm; ☎534-2578) and a number of walking and cross-country skiing trails. Nearby, the landscaped shrub and formal flower garden of the **International Peace Garden** spans the border between Canada and the USA, at the southeast corner of the park. The dubious attractions on offer here, include a Peace Chapel (built right on the border), the starkly modern Peace Tower and a large, floral clock. You can also take one of three self-guided **walking tours**. The garden costs $7 per vehicle (useful if you want to drive around the outlying trails) or $3 per pedestrian (better value if you just want to see the main sights and the flowerbeds); just park your car by the road immediately outside the entrance.

There's a smaller, prettier campground at **Max Lake** (☎534-2578; May–Sept) on Provincial Road 446. This campground gives easy access to the **Oskar Lake Canoe Route**, a nineteen-kilometre paddle and portage excursion across ten of the park's lakes. Best in the spring or fall, the route should be tackled in an anticlockwise direction to eliminate the need to climb steep hills, and can be completed in one or two days. There's an overnight cabin at James Lake – register at the district office in **BOISSEVAIN**, 40km north (☎534-7204) if you intend to use it. Oddly enough there are no canoe rental facilities in the park.

The Yellowhead Highway and North

Highway 16, one of central Canada's most appealing long-distance drives, is better known as the **Yellowhead Route** – taking its name from a light-haired Iroquois explorer and guide who was called *Tête Jaune* by the voyageurs, the French-speaking boatmen who plied the waterways transporting people, furs and supplies. About 90km along the road from Portage la Prairie lies one of Manitoba's more pleasant townships, tiny **NEEPAWA**, whose streets are lined with elms and cottonwoods. The town's oldest buildings are spread along and around the principal drag, Mountain Avenue – notably the cosy neo-Romanesque **Knox Presbyterian Church** at Mill Street and First Avenue, with an unusual thick, turreted bell tower, and the tidy, late Victorian County Court House, close to Mountain Avenue and Hamilton Street. Also in the centre, in the old CN station at the west end of Hamilton Street, the **Beautiful Plains Museum** (mid-May to Aug Mon–Fri 9am–5pm; July & Aug also Sat & Sun 1–5pm; otherwise by appointment; $1; ☎476-3896) has fairly diverting displays on the life of the district's pioneers. Margaret Laurence, one of Canada's best-known writers, lived in Neepawa in her early years and used the town as a setting for many of her novels. You can visit her home, now a **museum**, at 312 1st Ave North (May–Sept daily 10am–6pm; $2). She is buried in the Riverside Cemetery, in the north of town.

More varieties of **lilies** grow in the area around Neepawa than any other part of the world. If you want to see the flowers in bloom – July to mid-August – you can visit the **Lily Nook**, 4km south of town on Hwy 5 (July to mid-Aug daily 9am–6pm; donation; ☎476-3225). There's also a Lily Festival in Neepawa in the third week of July.

The Yellowhead Highway doubles as Neepawa's Main Street, marking the southern perimeter of the town centre. The **tourist office** (June–Aug Mon & Thurs–Sun 11am–7pm, Tues & Wed 11am–5pm; ☎476-5292) is on the Yellowhead just east of town, beside the Whitemud River. The **bus station** is attached to the Petro Canada gas station at 52 Main St. For **accommodation**, there's a central riverside **campground** on Hamilton Street, the *Lions Riverbend Park* ($8–10; May–Oct) with fishing, a playground and a pool, and two convenient **hotels**, the down-at-heel *Hamilton* at Mountain Avenue and Mill Street (☎476-2368; ②), and the equally rudimentary *Vivian*, 236 Hamilton Ave at 1st Avenue (☎476-5089; ②). You'd do better at the two **motels**, both west of town on Hwy 16: the *Neepawa* (☎476-2331; ③) and the large, spotlessly clean *Westway Inn* (☎476-2355 or 1-800-448-0994; ②, breakfast included). Or try the *Gordon Path B&B*, 536 2nd Ave at Main Street (☎476 3184; ②), in a beautiful 1903 former lumber merchant's home. If you want to avoid the unappealing **restaurants** downtown, head for Hwy 16 (Main Street), where the best of the lot is the busy *Chicken Corral*, which offers dinners from $5.40.

The approach to **MINNEDOSA**, 28km further west, is stunning, as the attractive town sits on the flat of a long valley that slowly rises up at each end. The relaxing small-town atmosphere of the place is most appealing and, as it's about halfway between Winnipeg and the Saskatchewan border, it's a good stopping point for lunch or a night. It's also only thirty minutes from Riding Mountain National Park (see p.462). Again there's not much to see except for a bison compound near the Little Saskatchewan River (March–Oct; free). To get to the compound cross the swinging bridge over the river or turn off Main Street on to 2nd Ave SE, and then drive five minutes along Beach Road – you can view the bison from a platform in a public car park. A **tourist information centre** (daily 11am–7pm; ☎867-2741), incorporating a 1920s CP caboose and diesel engine, is located at 26 Main St South beside the boulder-strewn river. The centre is a museum of its own, filled with old railway memorabilia.

Minnedosa has a handful of acceptable **motels**, the best being the *Minnedosa Inn*, 138 Main St (☎867-2777; ②). *The Castle*, 149 2nd Ave SW (☎867-2830; ②–③), a Queen

Anne-style house on the banks of the Little Saskatchewan River, is thought to be one of the most attractive B&Bs in western Manitoba. Delicious German and French **food** is available at *Brede's*, 121 Main St South (Wed–Sun dinner), but otherwise the choice is limited to nondescript places along Main Street.

Riding Mountain National Park and Wasagaming

Bisected by Hwy 10 on its way from Brandon to Dauphin, **Riding Mountain National Park** (park entry fee $3.25 per person, $7.50 per group) is a vast expanse of wilderness, roughly 50km long and 100km wide, which provides some of Manitoba's finest hiking trails and most beautiful scenery. Its eastern perimeter is formed by a 400-metre-high ridge studded with a dense evergreen forest of spruce, pine, balsam fir and tamarack. This soon gives way to a highland plateau whose mixed forests and lakes form the central, and most scenic, part of the park, bordered to the west by an area of aspen woodland, meadow and open grassland – the habitat of moose, elk and a carefully tended herd of buffalo near Lake Audy (45min drive northwest of Wasagaming on a gravel road; no public transport; open year-round; free).

The only settlement of any significance is the tacky tourist centre of **WASAGAMING**, beside the main highway on the southern edge of the park, adjoining Clear Lake. The village has a campground, motels and restaurants, grocery stores, gas stations, a 1930s log theatre, and boat and canoe rental, but the narrow, scrawny beach is desperately overcrowded in July and August, while the lake is infested with a parasitic flatworm that can cause the painful skin irritation called "Swimmer's Itch".

Beside the beach, the park's **visitors' information centre** (mid-May to mid-June Mon–Thurs 10am–5pm, Fri–Sun 10am–8pm; mid-June to early Sept daily 10am–8pm; early Sept to mid-Oct daily 10am–5pm; ☎848-PARK or 1-800-707-8480) incorporates a collection of stuffed animals and environmental displays, and publishes the *Bugle*, a free broadsheet guide to the park's amenities. The staff here organize a programme of summer events that features free day-long **walks** and **hikes**; reservations are necessary for the more infrequent overnight excursions that take place from July to early September. The centre also issues **fishing permits** and free **backcountry permits**, which are compulsory for overnight stays in the bush. From mid-October to mid-May, when the centre is closed, the adjacent **administration office** (Mon–Fri 8am–noon & 1–4.30pm; ☎848-7208) provides a similar service. Most of the trails that begin in or near Wasagaming are short and easy; the most testing is the eighteen-kilometre **Grey Owl Trail** to Beaver Lodge Lake, where Grey Owl (see p.170) lived for six months in 1931. This trail connects with the nearest of the overnight routes, the **Cowan Lake Trail**, which branches off to pass through a region of dense forest, small lakes and meadows. All the overnight trails have primitive **campgrounds**. To really experience the rugged beauty of the park, contact Riding Mountain Nature Tours (☎636-2968), who offer a variety of longer **tours**, including horseback riding, hiking, bird-watching and wildlife safaris. To learn more about the history of the park – including Grey Owl's stay here – visit the **Pinewood Museum** at 154 Wasagaming Drive (July & Aug daily 2–4pm; free).

Served by daily buses from Winnipeg, Brandon and Dauphin, Wasagaming's main **bus stop** is by the Chamber of Commerce on Mooswa Drive. For **accommodation**, the *Mooswa Resorts*, Mooswa Drive (☎848-2533; ③), has delightfully designed modern chalets, motel rooms and bungalows; basic bungalows and log cabins at *Johnson Cabins*, 109 Ta-Wa-Pit Drive (☎848-2524; ②), are a bit cheaper. *Clear Lake Lodge*, at Ta-Wa-Pit Drive and Columbine Street (☎848-2345; ③–④), is a comfortable, non-smoking hotel, but if you want to save money head for the *Manigaming Resort*, 137 Ta-Wa-Pit Drive (☎848-2459; ②–③), or the *Southgate Motor Hotel* in Onanole, 5km south of Wasagaming (☎848-2158; ②). All accommodation in the park is open from May to September or October only, with the exception of the year-round *New Chalet*, 116

Wasagaming Drive (☎848-2892; ②–④). There's only one **campground**, *Wasagaming Campground*, in the village just beyond the main park gate (☎1-800-707-8480; $8–16; May to mid–Oct; reservations advised).

Wasagaming's **restaurants** are poor, with the notable exception of the *Mooswa*, where a delicious fresh fish meal will set you back about $20. The best of the cheaper establishments is the mundane *Danceland/Cinnamon Bun*, at the corner of Wasagaming and Buffalo drives. The Tempo gas station opposite rents out **bikes** (☎1-800-816-2524; $5-6 an hour), while **canoe** and **powerboat** rentals ($10–24 an hour) are available from the jetty on Clear Lake. **Horseback riding** is available at the riding stables at Triangle Ranch (hourly rides $15; ☎848-4583).

Dauphin

DAUPHIN was founded as a fur-trading post by the French in 1739 and is now a pleasant town that straggles across the flat prairie landscape just to the east of the Vermilion River. Its long **Main Street** features some good examples of early twentieth-century Canadian architecture, but there's only one real attraction, the **Fort Dauphin Museum** (May to Aug daily 9am–5pm; $3). This is a tidy wooden replica of a North West Company trading outpost, located by the river at the end of 4th Ave SW, fifteen minutes' walk from Main Street. Inside the stockade, there are reconstructions of several sorts of pioneer building, including a trapper's cabin. Sights in town include the huge, chateau-like CNR **railway station** on 1st Avenue NW and a modest **arts centre** and gallery at 104 1st Avenue NW (Mon–Fri noon–5pm; free) in a striking Romanesque Revival building. At the corner of 1st Street SW and 11th Avenue SW is the Ukrainian **Church of the Resurrection**, with its distinctive clustered domes (guided tours 30min; donation; ☎638-4659 or 638-5511).

The fertile river valley that runs west of Dauphin towards Roblin was a centre of **Ukrainian** settlement between 1896 and 1925, and its village skylines are still dominated by the onion-domed spires of their Orthodox and Catholic churches. There's a modest collection of Ukrainian pioneer artefacts and traditional handicrafts in Dauphin at the **Selo Ukraina Office**, 119 Main St South (Tue–Sat 10am–5pm), but their main task is to organize the **National Ukrainian Festival**, which takes place on the first weekend of August at a purpose-built complex 12km south of Dauphin, just off Hwy 10 on the edge of Riding Mountain Park. The complex has a tiny heritage village dedicated to the early Ukrainian settlers (daily 10am–5pm; free) and a splendid amphitheatre built into a hillside, ideal for the festival's music and dance performances.

Dauphin's **bus station** is at 4th Avenue NE and Main Street, a couple of minutes' walk from the town centre at Main and 1st Avenue NE. The **Chamber of Commerce**, 21 3rd Ave NE (Mon–Fri 8.30am–4.30pm; ☎638-4838), provides tourist information. There's also a **tourist bureau** (mid-May to Aug daily 10am–6pm; ☎638-5295), 2km away on the southern edge of town on Hwy 10, beside the airport.

For **accommodation**, the *Boulevard Motor Hotel*, 28 Memorial Blvd (☎638-4410; ①), the *Dauphin Inn*, 35 Memorial Blvd (☎638-4430; ①), and the *Dauphin Community Inn*, 104 Main St North (☎638-4311; ①), are all (fairly seedy) downtown **hotels**. The *Rodeway Inn Motel* (☎638-5102; ③), roughly 4km south of town near the junction of Hwys 5 and 10, has a pool, a sauna and more appealing rooms. Or for a more personal atmosphere you could try the *Edgar House B&B*, 703 Main St North (☎ & fax 638-7857; ②). The *Vermilion Trailer Park & Campground* (☎638-3740; $11–15; mid-May to mid-Sept) is ten minutes' walk north of Main Street at 21 2nd Ave NW. You can **eat** at *Irving's Steak House & Lounge*, 26 1st Ave NW, which has a real honky-tonk feel, or *Zamrykut's Ukrainian Family Restaurant*, 119 Main St North, a plain establishment that has delicious home-made food, from borscht through to *pierogies* and *kielbossa* (sausage).

If you want to absorb still more Ukrainian ambience, visit the **Wasyl Negrych Pioneer Farmstead**, near the village of Gilbert Plains, 30km west of Dauphin. Here you'll find the largest assembly of historic Ukrainian buildings in the province (June–Aug daily 1–5pm; rest of year by appointment; $2; ☎548-2326).

Duck Mountain Provincial Park

Duck Mountain Provincial Park, some 100km northwest of Dauphin, is a large slice of the Manitoba Escarpment, comprising several thousand acres of thickly wooded rolling hills punctuated by meadows, bogs, streams and hundreds of tiny lakes. Most of the park is **boreal forest**, a mixture of white spruce, jack pine, balsam fir, aspen and birch, but many of its eastern slopes are covered by maple, bur oak and elm, which are usually found further south. It's not unusual to hear the cry of coyotes at night amongst the dense woodland. The park is noted for its fishing, with pickerel, pike and trout in most of its lakes, and the delicious arctic char to the north.

Access to Duck Mountain Park is along two partly paved roads: Route 367, which branches off Hwy 10 just north of Garland and cuts across the middle from east to west, connecting Hwy 10 with Hwy 83, a distance of 80km; and Route 366, which crosses from south to north, connecting the town of Grandview, on Hwy 5 just 45km west of Dauphin, with the village of Minitonas, 130km away. Approached along Route 366, the best part of the park is its southeast corner, where **Baldy Mountain** (831m) is the highest point in Manitoba, complete with an observation tower which provides good views over the forest. A few kilometres to the north, the twin **West** and **East Blue Lakes** are among the park's finest lakes – curving strips of clear water fed by underground springs. Situated beside the road between the lakes is the **Blue Lakes Campground** (☎542-3482; May to mid-Sept), close to both the Blue Lakes Trail, a six-kilometre cross-country hike, and the Shining Stone Trail, a short path along the peninsula that juts out into West Blue Lake. The campground has a beach, a grocery store and gas station; the camp office advises on boat rental and fishing. There are only unserviced sites here. For serviced sites, try *Childs Lake Campground* (☎546-2463; May to mid-Sept), with similar facilities; it's on Route 367 on the west edge of the park.

Great West Trails (☎734-2321) organizes **horseback riding** excursions through the park, including camping and fishing. High Mountain Outfitters (☎967-2077), based in Kelwood, on the east edge of the park, can also arrange a variety of one- to seven-day camping trips.

Northern Manitoba

Running east from the northern end of Lake Winnipegosis and across through the isolated community of Grand Rapids, the 53rd parallel was Manitoba's boundary until 1912, when it was moved up to the 60th parallel on Hudson Bay. This tripled the size of the province and provided its inhabitants with new resources of timber, minerals and hydroelectricity as well as a direct sea Route to the Atlantic Ocean. Today's **northern Manitoba** is a vast and sparsely populated tract mostly set on the Canadian Shield, whose shallow soils support a gigantic coniferous forest broken up by a complex pattern of lakes and rivers. It's a hostile environment, the deep cold winter alternating with a brief, bright summer, when the first few centimetres of topsoil thaw out above the permafrost to create millions of stagnant pools of water, ideal conditions for mosquitoes and blackflies. There are compensations: out in the bush or along the shores of Hudson Bay, there is a sense of desolate wilderness that's hard to find elsewhere, and a native wildlife that includes caribou, polar bear and all sorts of migratory birds.

Most of the region is inaccessible and its limited **highway system** was built to service the resource towns just to the north of lakes Winnipeg and Winnipegosis. One of these, the paper-and-pulp complex at **The Pas**, is served by buses from Dauphin and Winnipeg and provides a convenient base for the region's two main parks, **Clearwater Lake** and **Grass River**. Northern Manitoba's key tourist centre, however, is **Churchill**, a remote and windswept township on the southern shore of Hudson Bay where the main attractions are the **polar bears** that congregate along the Bay shore from late June to early November.

Churchill is well beyond the reach of Manitoba's highways, but it is connected to Winnipeg and The Pas by **train** along one of the longest railway lines in the world. The trip from Winnipeg takes about 34 hours, but if you haven't the time there are regular excursion flights from Winnipeg (see "Travel details", p.510).

The Pas and around

Situated 400km north of Dauphin on Hwy 10, on the southern bank of the Saskatchewan River, **THE PAS** – a former fur-trading and missionary centre founded in 1750 – is a town with no specific sights. However, it does host the annual **Northern Manitoba Trappers' Festival** in the third week of February, four days of revelling that features competitions in a number of traditional pioneer skills, like tree-felling, trap-setting, ice-fishing and muskrat-skinning. The highlight is the World Championship Sled Dog Race, which features three daily races of 50km. If you're in town in mid-August, you can join in the Native Canadian celebrations during Opasquiak Indian Days, honouring the Cree people.

The town's **bus** and **train stations** are right in the centre, a few minutes' walk from the **Municipal Offices** (Mon–Fri 9am–1pm; ☎623-7256), at 320 Ross Ave, which will provide basic tourist information. There's also a **tourist booth** (June–Aug daily 9am–5pm) about 1km south of town on Hwy 10, beside the tiny *Devon Park and Kinsmen Kampground* (☎623-2233; $11–18; May–Sept) and close to two **motels** on Gordon Avenue: the *Golden Arrow* at no. 1313 (☎623-5451; ②) and the *La Verendrye* at no. 1326 (☎623-3431; ②–③); there's also the *Rupert House Hotel* (☎623-3201; ①–②) and the fourstar *Kikiwak Inn* (☎623-1800 or 1-888-545-4925; ③). Back in the centre, near the train station, the comfortable *Wescana Inn*, at 439 Fischer Ave (☎623-5446 or 1-800-665-9468; ③), is also a good **place to eat**.

Clearwater Lake Provincial Park

Just 19km north of The Pas, the square-shaped lake and adjoining strip of coniferous forest that constitute **Clearwater Lake Park** are a favourite haunt of the region's anglers, who come here to catch northern pike, whitefish and highly prized lake trout. The park's amenities are concentrated along Route 287, a turning off Hwy 10, which runs along the lake's southern shore past The Pas airport. Beside the road there are four summer **campgrounds**, and a couple of **hunting lodges** (④–⑤) that can be booked at the tourist booth in The Pas. If you're after a **wilderness excursion**, Clearwater Canoe Outfitters (☎624-5606 or 624-5467) rents out a full range of equipment and organizes canoe trips from $25 per day.

Grass River

A further thirty minutes' drive north up Hwy 10 brings you to the channels and lakes of the **Grass River** water system, which were first charted in the 1770s by **Samuel Hearne**, an intrepid employee of the Hudson's Bay Company who became the first European to reach the Arctic Ocean by land. Hearne witnessed both the development of the Grass River's fur trade and the cataclysmic effects of the smallpox epidemic that followed. He estimated that about ninety percent of the local Chipewyan population were wiped out in the space of a decade; an indication of the scale of a tragedy whose results were compounded by other European diseases, particularly whooping cough and measles. On this and other matters, Hearne was an acute observer of Indian culture and customs. His *Journey to the Northern Ocean* records, for example, the comments of his Chipewyan guide concerning the importance of women:

" 'Women,' added he, 'were made for labour; one of them can carry, or haul, as much as two men can do. They also pitch our tents, make and mend our clothing, keep us warm at night; and, in fact, there is no such thing as travelling any considerable distance in this country without their assistance. Women,' he said again, 'though they do everything, are maintained at trifling expense; for as they always stand to cook, the very licking of their fingers, in scarce times, is sufficient for their subsistence.' "

Grass River Provincial Park

Grass River Provincial Park is made up of several thousand square kilometres of evergreen forest, lake and river interspersed by the granite outcrops of the Canadian Shield. It's noted for its **canoe routes**, the most popular of which runs 180km from the Cranberry Lakes, on the park's western perimeter, to its eastern boundary, where the southern tip of Tramping Lake is located near Hwy 39. It's an excursion of about ten days – all of the route's portages are short and fairly easy and there are lots of basic campgrounds on the way.

At the start of the canoe route, the first of the three Cranberry Lakes is situated close to **CRANBERRY PORTAGE**, a straggling township on Hwy 10, which runs along the western edge of the park. The settlement has its own park **information kiosk**; a small **campground** 1km west of Hwy 10 (☎472-3219; $18; mid-May to Sept) with its own beach; a couple of **hotels**, including the *Northern Inn* (☎472-3231; ①), 112 Portage Rd; and a handful of holiday **lodges** along its lakeshore, such as the *Viking Lodge* (☎ & fax 472-3337; ④–⑤) and the *Caribou Lodge* (☎472-3351; ④–⑤). Most of the lodges (May–October only) have boat and canoe rentals, and can arrange guided trips and flights to the remoter lakes.

There are other access points to Grass River Park along Hwy 39, which runs along its southern boundary. This hundred-kilometre stretch of road passes three small summer **campgrounds** – *Simonhouse Lake (Gyles)* (24km east of Hwy 10), *Iskwasum Landing* (40km) and *Reed Lake* (56km) – where park entry points lead to circular canoe trips that can be accomplished within one day.

A worthwhile side-trip can be made from the park to **Wekusko Falls**, about 35km beyond the east boundary of the park along Hwy 39 and then south along a short stretch of gravel road (Hwy 596). Here the Mitishto River drops dramatically in a series of falls and rapids. You can view the spectacle from two suspension footbridges or along the walking trails below.

Flin Flon

At the northern end of Hwy 10, about 60km from Cranberry Portage, the mining township of **FLIN FLON**, on the Saskatchewan border, gouges copper, gold, lead and zinc from a massive seam that was discovered in 1914. A stark, rough-looking town, full of precipitously steep streets, where the houses are built on sheer rock in a barren landscape, Flin Flon takes its unusual name from the hero of an obscure novel entitled *The Sunless City*, which one of the first prospectors was reading at the time of the discovery. In the book, Josiah Flintabbatey Flonatin builds a submarine and enters the bowels of the earth, where he discovers that everything is made of gold. The nearest you'll come to his trip is on the free guided tours of the town's **Hudson Bay Mining and Smelting Plant** (June–Aug Mon, Wed & Fri 8.30am; 2hr; reservations ☎687-2050; over-16s only). Surprisingly, you'll see greenhouses in the depths of the mine, the warm and humid conditions being perfect for growing flowers such as orchids. The liveliest month of the year is July, when the town hosts the Trout Festival, featuring a parade, a Queen Mermaid Pageant, the Great Northern Duck Race – and the tantalizing smell of frying fish.

The town's **bus station** is right in the centre at 63 3rd Ave. About 1km to the east, along Hwy 10A, the **tourist office** (June to mid-Sept daily 9am–9pm; ☎687-7674) adjoins the main **campground** (☎687-7674; $8.60–10.70; May–Sept) with a large statue of the intrepid Flintabbatey Flonatin opposite. There are six **places to stay**, including two cheap and central hotels on Main Street: the *Royal*, at no. 93 (☎687-3437; ②), and the *Flin Flon*, at no. 140 (☎687-7534; ②). If you're feeling the pinch of the north's high prices, try the *Friendship Centre Hostel*, 57 Church St (☎687 3900; ①), which offers basic dorm accommodation. For a similarly basic **meal**, try *Mary's Place*, 111 Main St, or the *Victoria Inn*'s restaurant, 160 Hwy 10.

Churchill

Sitting on the east bank of the Churchill River where it empties into Hudson Bay, **CHURCHILL** has the neglected appearance of many of the settlements of the far north, its ill-kempt open spaces dotted with the houses of its mixed Inuit, Cree and white population. These grim buildings are heavily fortified against the biting cold of winter and the insects of the summer – ample justification for a local T-shirt featuring a giant mosquito above the inscription "I gave blood in Churchill". That said, the town has long attracted a rough-edged assortment of people with a taste for the wilderness, and nowadays tourists flock here for the wildlife – a lifeline, now that Churchill's grain-handling facilities are underused.

In 1682, the Hudson's Bay Company established a fur-trading post at **York Factory**, a marshy peninsula some 240km southeast of today's Churchill (see p.470). The move was dictated by the fact that the direct sea Route here from England was roughly 1500km shorter than the old Route via the St Lawrence River, while the Hayes and Nelson rivers gave access to the region's greatest waterways. Within a few years, a regular cycle of trade had been established, with the company's Cree and Assiniboine go-betweens heading south in the fall to **hunt and trade** for skins, and returning in the spring laden with pelts they could exchange for the company's manufactured goods. Throughout the eighteenth century, before the English assumed control of all facets of the trade and laid off their native intermediaries, both sides seem to have benefited economically, and the reports of the company's traders are sprinkled with bursts of irritation at the bargains forced on them by the natives. The company was always keen to increase its trade and it soon expanded its operations to Churchill, building the first of a series of forts here in 1717.

In the nineteenth century the development of faster trade routes through Minneapolis brought decline, and by the 1870s both York Factory and Churchill had become remote and unimportant. Then the development of agriculture on the prairies brought a reprieve. Many of the politicians and grain farmers of this new west were determined to break the trading monopoly of Sault Ste Marie in northern Ontario and campaigned for the construction of a new port facility on Hudson Bay, connected by rail to the south through Winnipeg. In the 1920s the Canadian National Railway agreed to build the line, and it finally reached Churchill in April 1929. Unfortunately, despite all the effort of the railway workers in the teeth of the ferocious climate, the port has never been very successful, largely because the bay is ice-free for only about three months a year.

The town centre

On the northern side of town, the unprepossessing Bayport Plaza is a good place to start a visit, as it incorporates the **Parks Canada Visitors' Reception Centre** (mid-May to mid-Nov daily 1–9pm; rest of year Mon–Fri 8am–4.30pm; ☎675-8863; free), where displays on the history of the fur trade and the Hudson's Bay Company are jazzed up by films dealing with arctic wildlife, **Prince of Wales' Fort** and the

CHURCHILL'S FAUNA AND FLORA

Churchill occupies a transitional zone where the stunted trees of the taiga (subarctic coniferous forest) meet the mosses of the tundra. Blanketed with snow in the winter and covered by thousands of bogs and lakes in the summer, this terrain is completely flat until it reaches the sloping banks of the Churchill River and the ridge around Hudson Bay, whose grey quartzite boulders have been rubbed smooth by the action of the ice, wind and water.

This environment harbours splendid **wildlife**, including Churchill's premier attraction, the **polar bears**, who start to come ashore when the ice melts on the bay in late June. They must then wait for the ice to form again to support their weight before they can start their seal hunt; a polar bear can detect scent from 32km away and can pick up the presence of seals under a metre of snow and ice. The best months to spot bears are September, October and early November, just before the ice re-forms completely.

In mid-June, as the ice breaks on the Churchill River, the spreading patch of open water attracts schools of white **beluga whales**. As many as 3000 of these intelligent, inquisitive and vocal mammals spend July and August around the mouth of the river, joining the **seals**, who arrive in late March for five months. The area around the town is also on one of the major migration routes for **birds** heading north from April to June and returning south in August or early September. Nesting and hatching take place from early June until early July. A couple of hundred species are involved, including gulls, terns, loons, Lapland longspurs, ducks and geese. The star visitor is the rare Ross's Gull, a native of Siberia, which has nested in Churchill for the past decade. The *Birder's Guide to Churchill* ($7) by Bonnie Chartier lists them all and is available in the town and at the Eskimo Museum.

Churchill is also a great place to see the **aurora borealis** (northern lights), whose swirling curtains of blue, green and white are common in the skies between late August and April; occasionally it's seen all year round, and is at its best from January to March. Finally, in spring and fall the tundra is a colourful sheet of moss, lichens, flowers and miniature shrubs and trees that include dwarf birch, spruce and cranberry.

LOCAL TOUR OPERATORS

Local wildlife tour operators have proliferated over the past few years, offering everything from diving with the whales to viewing the polar bears from helicopters.

One of the best-value is Churchill Wilderness Encounter (☎675-2248 or 1-800-265-9458), whose bus meets the train. They offer beluga whale and Prince of Wales' Fort boat trips (July & Aug; $43), a six-day beluga whale-watching adventure ($1625); afternoon nature tours (July–Sept; $43), involving a drive through the taiga, a walk in the Akudlik Marsh and a trip into the boreal forest region; and bird-watching tours (late May to July; $95).

Based in the Bayport Plaza, North Star Tours (☎675-2629 or 1-800-665-0690) operates a similar package of excursions, along with iceberg trips in the middle of June from around $70. Sea North Tours, 39 Franklin St (☎675-2195), concentrates on whales, using stereo hydrophones to listen to their wide range of sounds (tours 2hr 30min; $40). Tundra Buggy Tours (July–Oct; ☎675-212, Nov–June; ☎1-800-544-5049) has a range of excursions in vehicles specially designed to avoid damaging the tundra (starting from $162) – some trips offer overnight lodge accommodation in the heart of the wilderness wildlife area. Midwest Helicopters (☎675-2576) operates helicopter sightseeing tours ($400 for 30min) with guaranteed polar-bear sightings. Northern Expedition Tours (same phone as Tundra Buggy Tours) is a specialist aurora borealis operator, while B&B Scuba (☎257-3696) will take you diving amongst the whales for up to a week at a time (July & Aug only).

construction of the railway. Opposite the plaza, the **Town Centre Complex** offers a good view over Hudson Bay and several recreational facilities, including a curling rink, hockey rink, swimming pool, bowling alley and a cinema.

Just down the road, the **Eskimo Museum**, 242 La Vérendrye Ave (June–Aug Mon 1–5pm, Tues–Sat 9am–noon & 1–5pm; Sept–May Mon & Sat 1–4.30pm, Tues–Fri 10.30am–noon & 1–4.30pm; donation), houses the Inuit collection of the Oblate Fathers of Mary Immaculate, whose missionary work began around here at the turn of the century. The museum's one large room is dominated by two animal-hide canoes and several stuffed Arctic animals, with Inuit art arranged in cases round the walls. It's a fine range of material, from caribou-antler pictographs and highly stylized soapstone figurines through to walrus-tooth scrimshaws and detailed ivory and stone carvings. The sculptures fall into two distinct periods. Up until the 1940s, the artistic work of the local Inuit was essentially limited to the carving of figurines in walrus ivory, modelled on traditional designs. However, in 1949 a Canadian painter, James Houston, travelled the east coast of Hudson Bay in Québec, encouraging the Inuit to vary their designs and experiment with different materials – which led, in particular, to the development of larger and more naturalistic sculptures carved in soapstone.

One corner of the museum functions as a **gift shop** selling a wide range of prints and carvings, plus a good collection of books on the north. Northern Images, a five-minute walk south on Kelsey Boulevard, sells similar work at higher prices – but its profits go back to the producers.

Cape Merry and Prince of Wales' Fort

A couple of minutes' walk from the town centre, Churchill's grain elevators and silos stand at the base of a narrow peninsula that sticks out into the mouth of the Churchill River. At the tip, approached along a gravel track, **Cape Merry National Historic Site** (guided tours June to Aug daily 8am–noon & 5–9pm; donation) has the remains of an eighteenth-century gun emplacement and a cairn commemorating the Danish explorer Jens Munck, who led an expedition that was forced to winter here in 1619; most of the crew died from cold and hunger.

On the other side of the estuary, **Prince of Wales' Fort National Historic Site** (free tours daily July & Aug, times dependent on tides and weather conditions – ask at the visitors' centre or phone the Canadian Parks Service; ☎675-8863) is a partly restored eighteenth-century stone fortress that was built to protect the trading interests of the Hudson's Bay Company from the French. Finished in 1771, this massive structure took forty years to complete, but even then it proved far from impregnable. When a squadron of the French fleet appeared in the bay in 1782 the fort's governor, Samuel Hearne, was forced to surrender without firing a shot because he didn't have enough men to form a garrison. The French spiked the cannon and undermined the walls, and after this fiasco the Company never bothered to repair the damage. The Fort is only accessible as part of a guided tour of the Churchill River organized by Churchill Wilderness Encounter (see box opposite).

East of the centre: the Bay Shore Road

East of town, a rough road runs behind the shoreline past a series of rather eccentric attractions. Near the airport, the **polar bear "prison"** is a large hangar-like compound where dangerous bears are kept until they can be released safely. The problem is that some of the beasts wander into town in search of food and, although most can be scared off quite easily, a handful return. These more persistent specimens are shot with tranquillizers and transported to the compound. It's a necessary precaution, as polar bears can run and swim faster than humans and there are occasional horror stories. In the last one, the owner of a fire-damaged house returned to empty his freezer, whereupon a bear trapped and killed him. Persistent bear offenders have three chances; after that they are humanely destroyed.

Practicalities

Churchill can only be reached by **plane** or **train**. VIA Rail (☎1-800-561-8630) runs a summer service five times a week from Winnipeg (rest of the year thrice weekly; from $231 return, if booked seven days in advance). Canadian Airlines (☎632-1250) operates a service (daily except Sat; $900 return, $497 with two weeks' advance booking), and Calm

Air (☎778-6471 or 1-800-839-2256) runs at least four weekly flights from Winnipeg. The town's **airport** is 7km from the centre, and each flight attracts the minibuses of the main tour operators, who will provide onward transport for about $10. Alternatively, Churchill Taxi, 31 Thompson St (☎675-2345), charges about $12 for the same service. The **train station** is right in the town centre, a few metres from the **Visitor Information Bureau** on Kelsey Boulevard (July & Aug Tues–Fri 8am–1.30pm, Sat 8am–3.30pm; ☎675-2022 or 1-888-389-2327) and a five-minute walk from the Bayport Plaza, where there's a **Parks Canada Visitor Reception Centre** (mid-May to mid-Nov daily 1–9pm; rest of the year Mon–Fri 8.30am–4.30pm; ☎675-8863).

There are no campgrounds or hostels in Churchill, so visitors are dependent on the town's **hotels**, which are so uniformly drab it's hard to see why they vary in price. All are within easy walking distance of the train station, and all should be booked in advance no matter what the time of year. The full list is as follows: *Churchill Motel*, corner of Kelsey Boulevard and Franklin Street (☎675-8853; ③–④); *Northern Lights Lodge*, 101 Kelsey Blvd (☎675-2403; ③); *Tundra Inn*, 34 Franklin St (☎675-8831 or 1-800-265-8563; ④); the recently renovated *Polar Inn*, 15 Franklin St (☎675-8878; ③–④); the ugly *Seaport Hotel*, corner of Kelsey Boulevard and Munck Street (☎675-8807; ④); the *Bear Country Inn*, 126 Kelsey Blvd (☎675-8299; ③); and the *Aurora Inn*, 24 Bernier St (☎675-2071 or 1-800-265-8563; ④–⑤). Vera Gould runs a **B&B** at 87 Hearne St (☎675-2544; ③), as does her daughter, Anne, at *La Peruse*, 100 Button St (☎675-2254; ③).

Churchill's handful of **restaurants** leaves a lot to be desired, with the exception of the expensive *Trader's Table*, 141 Kelsey Blvd, where you can sample caribou burgers, or try the local speciality, arctic char, for around $18. The best snack bar is in the Town Centre Complex, which has burgers from $5; all the hotels also have their own restaurants.

York Factory

The remote **York Factory National Historic Site** (June to mid-Sept daily 8am–5pm, depending on river conditions) lies 240km southeast of Churchill, at the mouth of the Hayes and Nelson rivers. This was the central storehouse of the northwestern fur trade throughout the eighteenth century, its wooden palisades the temporary home of soldiers and explorers, travellers and traders, and settlers bound for the Red River Colony at present-day Winnipeg. With the amalgamation of the North West and Hudson's Bay companies in 1821, it was here that the new governor **George Simpson** set about the delicate task of reconciling the feuds stirred by a generation of inter-company rivalry. In October he arranged his first formal joint banquet, 73 traders facing each other across two long and narrow tables. It was, according to a contemporary, "dollars to doughnuts [whether it would be] a feed or fight", but Simpson's diplomatic skills triumphed, leading to a successful reorganization of trading operations. In its heyday, there were some fifty buildings within the stockade, including a guesthouse, fur stores, trading rooms, living quarters and shops, but they were all destroyed in the 1930s, with the exception of the **main warehouse** (1832), a sturdy wooden building that serves as a reminder of the fort's earlier significance. Wandering around the desolate site today, it's hard to imagine that it was once the largest community in western Canada. Guided tours of the site are available (contact the Parks Canada Visitor Reception Centre in Churchill; $5).

This remote spot can only be reached by **charter flight** – weather permitting – from Thompson, Churchill or Gillam, a hydroelectric centre on the rail line between Winnipeg and Churchill. Or you can get there by **canoe** along the Hayes River from Norway House on the north shore of Lake Winnipeg – an arduous journey of 600km, which should not be undertaken without advice from the Manitoba Parks Department in Winnipeg (☎945-6784 or 1-800-214-6497). Because of the disturbance to polar bears in the area, camping is not allowed at York Factory. The only place to stay is the *Silver Goose*

Lodge, and this must be arranged in advance with the owners (☎652-2776). There are no services, and all supplies must be brought in.

The Seal River

The wild rivers that drain into Hudson Bay constitute some of the most challenging **canoe routes** in Canada, their long stretches of white water demanding considerable planning, experience and skill. One of the more popular is the **Seal River**, whose principal canoe Route begins at the tiny Chipewyan village of Tadoule, and then passes through regions of boreal forest and tundra before emptying into Hudson Bay, just 45km west of Churchill. In the summer the estuary is a gathering place for several thousand beluga whales, an amazing sight to witness. There's float-plane transportation to the start of the canoe Route and from the mouth of the river at the end, which can take between two and four weeks to reach. For details, contact Dymond Air Services, 23 Selkirk St, Churchill (☎675-8875). For something a bit shorter, you can stay at the *Seal River Heritage Lodge* (☎675-8875 or 1-888-326-7325) on a three-day ($1450) or six-day package ($2300) including all meals, services of a guide, whale-watching expeditions, canoeing trips and wildlife tours.

SASKATCHEWAN

"You'd marry anyone to get out of Moose Jaw, Saskatchewan", Susan Sarandon tells Burt Lancaster in Louis Malle's film *Atlantic City*, and the whole province is regarded with similar disdain by many Canadians. It's certainly not one of the country's glamour regions, remaining as dependent on agriculture as it was when the province was established in 1905, and today producing 42 percent of Canada's wheat, 39 percent of its canola, 35 percent of its rye and 20 percent of its barley. Saskatchewan's farmers often struggle to make ends meet when international prices fall, and consequently they have formed various **Wheat Pools**, which attempt to control freight charges and sell the grain at the best possible time. The political spin-off has been the evolution of a strong socialist tradition, built on the farmers' mistrust of the market. For many years Saskatchewan was a stronghold of the **Cooperative Commonwealth Federation (CCF)**, the forerunner of the New Democratic Party (NDP), and in 1944 the CCF formed the country's first leftist provincial government, pushing through bills to set up state-run medical and social security schemes.

However underprivileged Saskatchewan might have been in the past, its image as a featureless zone is grossly unfair. Even the dreariest part of the province, to the south of the Yellowhead Highway, has some splendid diversions, notably **Regina**'s intriguing Royal Canadian Mounted Police Museum, and the coulees and buttes of the **Grasslands National Park**. On the Yellowhead itself, **Saskatoon**, Saskatchewan's largest city, has an attractive riverside setting and boasts good restaurants, plus a complex devoted to the culture of the Northern Plains Indians. Further west, **Battleford** has a splendidly restored Mountie stockade, while to the north **Batoche National Historic Park**, occupying a fine location beside the South Saskatchewan River, commemorates the Métis rebellion of 1885. Not far away from Batoche, **Prince Albert National Park** marks the geographical centre of the province, where the aspen parkland of the south meets the boreal forests and lakes of the north. There are some wonderful walks and canoe routes here, even though the park's tourist village, **Waskesiu Lake**, is rather commercialized.

The Saskatchewan telephone code is ☎306.

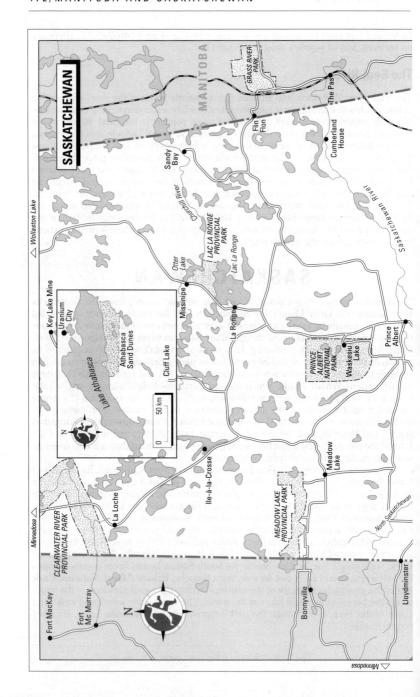

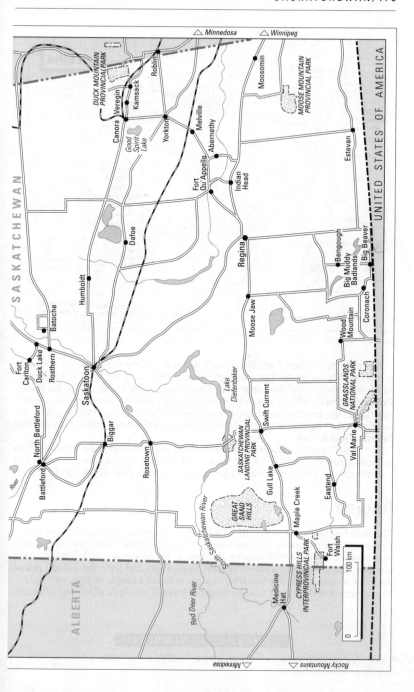

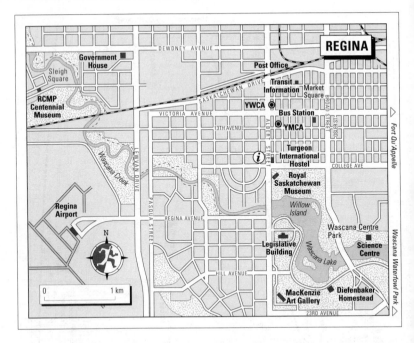

North of Prince Albert Park, the desolate wilderness of the Canadian Shield is mostly inaccessible except by float plane; the main exception is the town of **La Ronge**, which is on the edge of the canoe routes and good fishing waters of **Lac La Ronge Provincial Park** and the **Churchill River**. By comparison, the area bordering eastern Alberta has less to offer, though the desultory prairie landscape that makes up its south and centre does incorporate some of the hills, forests and ravines of the **Cypress Hills Interprovincial Park**.

The region's **public transport** system is limited, but there are regular scheduled **bus** services between most of the major towns, and a useful, once-daily summertime bus from the town of Prince Albert to Waskesiu Lake, in Prince Albert Park, and La Ronge.

Regina

The capital city of Saskatchewan **REGINA** is the commercial and administrative centre of one of the more densely populated parts of central Canada, its services anchoring a vast network of agricultural villages and towns. Yet despite its capital status, brash shopping malls and population of 195,000, Regina acts and feels like a small prairie town. It's a comfortable if unremarkable place to spend a couple of days, with the offbeat attraction of the Royal Canadian Mounted Police Training Academy and Museum,

INFORMATION NUMBERS

Tourism Saskatchewan ☎306-787-2300 or 1-800-667-7191.

PROVINCIAL PARKS

All **provincial parks** in Saskatchewan have the same **entrance fees**: daily $5, three-day entry $12, annual $30. Between late June and mid-August you can **reserve** a site in advance at seven of the parks for a $5 fee: phone numbers at **Candle Lake** (☎929-4544 or 929-4440); **Cypress Hills** (☎662-4411); **Duck Mountain** (☎542-3479); **Greenwater Lake** (☎278-2389); **Lac La Ronge** (☎425-4234 or 1-800-772-4064); **Meadow Lake** (☎236-7690); and **Moose Mountain** (☎577-2611).

and the opportunity to explore some of southern Saskatchewan's less familiar destinations – such as the Big Muddy Badlands and the Grasslands National Park. If you want to improve your suntan, incidentally, you've also come to the right place – Regina gets more hours of **sunshine** than any other major city in Canada.

In 1881 the Indian Commissioner **Edward Dewdney** became lieutenant-governor of the Northwest Territories, a vast tract of land that spread west from Ontario as far as the Arctic and Pacific oceans. Almost immediately, he decided to move his capital south from the established community of Battleford to **Pile O'Bones**, an inconsequential dot on the map that took its name from the heaps of bleached buffalo bones left along its creek by generations of native hunters. The reason for Dewdney's decision was the routing of the Canadian Pacific transcontinental railroad across the southern plains: the capital city was renamed Regina after Queen Victoria, and Dewdney petitioned for it to be expanded on land to the north of the creek, a plot coincidentally owned by him. The site was terrible: the sluggish creek provided a poor water supply, the clay soil was muddy in wet weather and intolerably dusty in the summer, and there was no timber for building. Accordingly, the railway board refused to oblige, and the end result was farcical: Government House and the Mounted Police barracks were built where Dewdney wanted them, but the train station was a three-kilometre trek to the south.

In 1905 Regina became the capital of the newly created province of **Saskatchewan**, and settlers flocked here from the United States and central Europe. At the heart of an expanding wheat-growing district, the city tripled its population during its first fifteen years. It also overcame its natural disadvantages by an ambitious programme of tree-planting, which provided shade and controlled the dust, and by damming the creek to provide a better source of water. However, the city's success was based on the fragile prosperity of a one-crop economy, and throughout this century boom has alternated with bust.

Arrival, information and transport

Regina's **airport** is about 5km west of the centre; the taxi trip costs roughly $12. A ten-minute walk east of the airport brings you to Regina Transit's **buses** #11 or #13 which leave for the city centre from the junction of Regina Avenue and Pasqua Street (Mon–Sat every 25min 6am–12.30am; Sun 11am–6pm hourly). The **bus station** is downtown at 2041 Hamilton St, just south of Victoria Avenue; the train station is now a casino.

The **Tourism Saskatchewan Office** (Mon–Fri 8am–5pm; ☎787-2300 or 1-800-667-7191), at 500-1900 Albert St, has a comprehensive range of leaflets and booklets on Regina and the province as a whole. In addition, Tourism Regina operates a **tourist bureau** east of town on Hwy 1, only really accessible if you have a car (late May to early Sept Mon–Fri 8am–7pm, Sat & Sun 10am–6pm; early Sept to late May Mon–Fri 8.30am–4.30pm; ☎789-5099 or 1-800-661-5099).

The best way to see the centre is on **foot**, though the area around McIntyre Street and Saskatchewan Drive, and sections of Osler Street, six blocks east, are run-down neighbourhoods that are best avoided. Similarly accessible is the **Wascana Centre**, a large multipurpose park and recreational area, whose northern boundary is a few minutes' stroll south of the centre. For longer journeys within the city, **Regina Transit** runs bus services with a standard single fare of $1.20 (exact fare payable to driver), or $12 for a book of ten available at the Tourism Saskatchewan Office or the transit information centre, located at 2124 11th Ave (Mon–Fri 7am–9pm, Sat 9am–4pm; ☎777-7433).

Accommodation

Central Regina has a reasonable range of moderately priced and convenient **hotels**, as well as an excellent **youth hostel**. There's rarely any difficulty in finding a room, but most of the very cheapest places listed by the Tourism Saskatchewan office are effectively grim and cheerless establishments. There's a cluster of reasonably priced, standard **motels** east of the town centre along Hwy 1, which doubles as Victoria Avenue East, and another group of motels south of the centre, along Albert Street. The remaining budget accommodation is provided by a few tiny **B&B** places and three **campgrounds**.

Hotels and motels

Chelton Suites Hotel, 1907 11th Ave (☎569-4600 or 1-800-667-9922, fax 569-3531). In a plain building in the heart of downtown, this has pleasant, large double rooms with bar, fridge and microwave. ③–⑥.

Coachman Inn, 835 Victoria Ave (☎522-8525, fax 757-5984). An excellent budget choice which is close to Wascana Centre Park and major shopping and sights. ②.

Howard Johnson Hotel, 1717 Victoria Ave at Broad Street (☎569-4656 or 1-800-446-4656, fax 569-4977). A good downtown bargain, with comfortable rooms. Check out the occasional weekend discounts. ③.

Ramada Plaza Hotel, 1919 Saskatchewan Drive at Hamilton Street (☎525-5255 or 1-800-272-6232, reservations 1-800-209-3555, fax 781-7188). One of Regina's most luxurious hotels, but located in a slightly dodgy part of town. Facilities include cable and satellite TV, pool, and a three-storey waterslide. ③–⑦.

Regina Inn Hotel, 1975 Broad St (☎525-6767 or 1-800-667-8162, fax 525-3630). Top-quality high-rise hotel in the centre of downtown. All rooms are non-smoking and there are one-bedroom and Jacuzzi suites available. ④–⑤.

Regina Travelodge Hotel, 4177 Albert St South (☎586-3443 or 1-800-578-7878, fax 586-9311). A large, newly upgraded hotel offering a wide range of facilities, including free coffee in rooms and free local calls. There's also a restaurant, pub and gift shop on the premises. ③–④.

Sands Hotel and Resort, corner of Victoria Avenue and Broad Street (☎569-1666 or 1-800-667-6500, fax 525-3550). One of the most attractive and well-equipped of Regina's hotels, including comfortable, spacious singles, doubles and en-suites with all amenities and a large recreation complex. ③–⑦.

Hotel Saskatchewan Radisson Plaza, corner of Victoria Avenue and Scarth Street (☎522-7691 or 1-800-333-3333, fax 522-8988). This large hotel, overlooking Victoria Park, was sensitively restored in 1992 to a luxurious standard and provides a full range of facilities, including a fitness centre and pool. Complimentary pick-up at airport. ④.

West Harvest Inn, 4025 Albert St (☎586-6755 or 1-800-853-1181, fax 584-1345). One of the best bargains in the Regina area. Newly refurbished singles, doubles and en-suites all complete with free in-room coffee and local calls. Health spa and gym. ②–③.

Bed and Breakfasts

B and J's, 2066 Ottawa St (☎522-4575). Situated just south of the city centre and near the General Hospital. Free coffee and pastries in the evening; free parking. ①.

Daybreak B&B, 316 Habkirk Drive (☎586-0211). In the south of the city, east of Albert Street, near the Trans-Canada. Two rooms with a nice old-fashioned feel and the owners offer free pick-up and delivery to airport or bus station. ①.

Morning Glory Manor, corner of Broad Street and College Avenue (☎525-2945). A charming 1920s home, minutes from downtown and Wascana Centre Park. Off-street parking. ②.

Hostels

Turgeon International Hostel, 2310 McIntyre St (☎791-8165 or 1-800-467-8357, fax 721-2667). HI hostel in a restored heritage house, immediately south of the downtown core, with cooking and laundry facilities. In conjunction with local bus companies, it runs a bus fare system whereby HI members can travel anywhere within Saskatchewan for just $21.50 return. Reservations 7–10am & 5pm–midnight. Closed Jan. ①.

YMCA, 2400 13th Ave (☎757-9622). Small budget rooms with weekly rates available. Pool and cafeteria. ①.

YWCA, 1940 McIntyre St (☎525-2141). Budget rooms available, including weekly rates, but about twice as much as at the *YMCA*. ①.

Campgrounds

Buffalo Lookout Campground, south of Hwy 1, 5km east of town (☎525-1448). Store, shower house, phones and indoor recreation facilities. 24hr on-site manager. Open May to mid-Sept. $13–17.

Kings' Acres Campground, 1km east of town on Hwy 1, behind the Tourism Regina Bureau (☎522-1619). A full range of serviced and unserviced sites on a spacious property, with store, phone, pool, and TV and games room. $12–17.Open March–Oct.

Sherwood Forest Country Club, 8km west of the centre on Dewdney Avenue, then 4km north (☎545-0330 or 543-8842). Attractive location in the Wascana Creek Valley. Full range of serviced and unserviced sites. $10–15. Open May–Oct.

The City

Fifteen minutes' walk from end to end, Regina's downtown business and shopping core is known as the **Market Square**, a simple gridiron bounded by Saskatchewan Drive and 13th Avenue to the north and south, Osler and Albert streets to the east and west. The rather mundane **Regina Plains Museum** (April–Sept daily 10am–4pm; Oct–March Mon–Fri 10am–4pm; $2), is within Market Square, on the fourth floor of the mall at 1801 Scarth St and 11th Avenue – its modest displays on the city's history are less diverting than the stories of the elderly volunteers who staff the museum. Exhibitions of innovative, and often controversial, contemporary art can be seen at the **Dunlop Art Gallery**, in the Public Library, west of the museum at 2311 12th Ave (daily: Mon–Thurs 9.30am–9pm, Fri 9.30am–6pm, Sat 9.30am–5pm, Sun 1.30–5pm; free). If the museum and gallery has whetted your appetite you should visit the **Antique Mall**, the largest in western Canada, located beyond the railway tracks north of Market Square, at 1175 Rose St (Mon, Tues, Fri & Sat 10am–6pm, Wed & Thurs 10am–9.30pm, Sun 1.30–5pm; free).

Immediately to the west of the Market Square district, across Albert Street, is **Cathedral Village**, with 13th Avenue as its heart. It's an old area with an eclectic mix of boutiques, coffee shops, craft shops and classy restaurants.

Wascana Centre Park

Roughly eight times the size of the Market Square, Regina's most distinctive feature is **Wascana Centre Park**, which begins three blocks south of 13th Avenue and extends southeast to the city limits, following the curves of **Wascana Lake**, which was created as part of a work project for the unemployed in the 1930s. The city's main recreation area, the park is equipped with a bandstand (performances Sun 2–4pm), barbecue pits, snack bars, boating facilities and waterfowl ponds, but for the most part it's a cheerless combination of reed-filled water and bare lawn.

In the northwest corner of the park, near College Avenue and Albert Street, the **Royal Saskatchewan Museum** (daily: May–Aug 9am–5.30pm; Sept–April 9am–4.30pm; free) is devoted to the province's geology and wildlife, starring a giant animated dinosaur called Megamunch. The museum's highlights are the informative dioramas showing aspects of Native Canadian life in the First Nations Gallery; one shows a grizzled grandfather recounting stories to several rapt youths. A couple of minutes' walk to the east is the swimming pool (June–Aug daily 11am–8pm), and close by there's a ferry boat to **Willow Island** (mid-May to Aug Mon–Fri noon–4pm; $2), a favourite picnic spot. Boat tours are available, departing from the observation deck, near the swimming pool (mid-June to Aug Sun & holidays 1–5pm; 20min; $2; ☎522-3661).

Further east, reached by the winding Wascana Drive, is perhaps Regina's main tourist attraction, the **Saskatchewan Science Centre** (daily: May–Sept Mon–Fri 9am–6pm, Sat & Sun 11am–6pm; Oct–April Mon–Fri 9am–4pm, Sat & Sun noon–6pm; $5.50; hours and admission subject to change, call ☎522-4629 or 1-800-667-6300 for confirmation). The open, airy building houses more than one hundred interactive scientific exhibits, live stage shows and demonstrations; of particular interest is a display on uranium mining and a room which has a direct video link to NASA space headquarters in Houston, enabling you to watch the live proceedings when a mission is under way. A newly opened gallery is devoted to the soils and weather of Saskatchewan, and here you can learn about what's involved in running a farm. Also on the premises is an IMAX cinema ($6.75). A ticket admitting you to both the centre and the cinema costs $11.

On the other side of the lake, accessible from Albert Street, is the grand **Legislative Building** (daily: late May to Sept 8am–9pm; Sept to late May 8am–5pm; free tours every 30min; 2hr), a self-confident cross-shaped structure of Manitoba limestone with an impressive domed tower at its centre. Guided tours take in the oak-and-marble-panelled Legislative Chamber and six small art galleries, the best of which houses Edmund Morris's portraits of local Indian leaders, presented to the province in 1911. A neighbouring corridor is occupied by the paintings of the **Native Heritage Foundation**, some thirty canvases featuring the work of contemporary Métis and native artists, notably Allen Sapp from North Battleford, who has won some international acclaim for his softly coloured studies of life on Saskatchewan's Indian reserves as he remembers them from the 1930s.

A few minutes' walk south of the Legislative Building, just off Albert Street at 23rd Avenue, the **MacKenzie Art Gallery** (daily: 11am–6pm, Wed & Thurs to 10pm; free) has several spacious modern galleries devoted to temporary exhibitions by modern Canadian artists, plus a good permanent collection. It's also the stage for the city's principal theatrical event, **The Trial of Louis Riel** (Aug only Wed–Fri 8pm; $10; for reservations, call ☎584-8890 or 525-1185), whose text is based on the transcripts of the trial in Regina in September 1885. No other single event in Canada's past has aroused such controversy: at the time, most of English-speaking Canada was determined he should hang as a rebel, whereas his French-Canadian defenders saw him as a patriot and champion of a just cause. Though Riel was subject to visions and delusions, the court rejected the defence of insanity on the grounds that he knew what he was doing. As he exclaimed – "No one can say that the North-West was not suffering last year . . . but what I have done, and risked, rested certainly on the conviction [that I was] called upon to do something for my country." The jury found him guilty, but the execution was delayed while prime minister John A. Macdonald weighed the consequences; in the end, he decided against clemency.

The **Diefenbaker Homestead** (mid-May to Aug daily 10am–8pm; free), about 1km east of the gallery but still within the park, was the boyhood home of John Diefenbaker, Conservative prime minister of Canada from 1957 to 1963. Moved from the township of Borden, Saskatchewan, in 1967, the tiny wooden house has been decked out with original and contemporary furnishings and memorabilia reflecting both Diefenbaker's homespun philosophies and the immense self-confidence that earned him the nickname "Dief the Chief".

In the extreme southeast corner of the park, reached by buses #10 or #12 or by car along Arcola Ave East and Prince of Wales Drive from the city centre, is the **Wascana Waterfowl Park** (May–Nov daily 9am–9pm; free; bookings and info ☎522-3661), a

group of ponds that's a habitat for ducks, pelicans and Canada geese. Birds are identified by a number of display panels on boardwalks, and guided tours are given Monday
to Friday between 9am and 4pm.

The Royal Canadian Mounted Police Training Academy

All Mounties do their basic training at the **Royal Canadian Mounted Police Training
Academy**, 4km west of the city centre at Dewdney Ave West, accessible by bus #8 from
11th Avenue at Cornwall Street. Beside the main parade ground of Sleigh Square – site
of the closely choreographed Sergeant Major's parade (Mon–Fri 12.45pm) and Sunset
Retreat Ceremony (July to mid-Aug Tues 6.45pm) – the RCMP **Centennial Museum**
(daily: June to mid-Sept 8am–6.45pm, July & Aug also Tues till 8.45pm; mid-Sept to June
10am–4.45pm; tours Mon–Fri 9am (summer only), 10am, 11am, 1.30pm, 2.30pm &
3.30pm; free) traces the history of the force from early contacts with the Plains Indians
and Métis, through to its present role as an intelligence-gathering organization.

Inside the museum, a series of contemporary quotations illustrates the **Long March**
that first brought the Mounties to the west from Ontario in 1874. Their destination was
Fort Whoop-up, near present-day Lethbridge, Alberta, where they intended to expel the
American whiskey traders. However, by the time they arrived they were in a state of complete exhaustion, and it was fortunate that the Americans had already decamped. Another small section deals with **Sitting Bull**, who crossed into Canada after his victory at the
Battle of the Little Big horn in 1876. Fearing reprisals from the furious American army,
Sitting Bull spent four years in and around the Cypress Hills, where he developed a
friendship with Police Inspector James Walsh. A picture of the chief and his braves, taken
at Fort Walsh in 1877, shows an audience of curious Mounties in their pith helmets.

Throughout the museum you'll note the large collection of Mounties' **uniforms**,
which show how the style of dress constantly changed throughout the force's history –
from the early days of the North West Mounted Police with their jaunty little pillbox hats,
through to the first women's uniforms of 1974 (the year women were admitted to the
force). Their immediately identifiable scarlet-red tunics, accompanied by royal-blue jodh-
purs with a vertical gold stripe down each leg, are worn – surprisingly – only on ceremonial occasions. The more mundane workaday uniform is a brown serge jacket with
straight trousers. But to reinforce the romantic Hollywood image of the Mounties, a free
cinema, decorated with old movie posters, has continuous runnings of such glorified
interpretations as *Rose Marie* (1936), starring Nelson Eddy and Jeanette MacDonald.

On the **tour** of the grounds you're shown the various buildings, including mock-ups
of houses where recruits practise family arrests, search warrants and surveillance techniques; the drill hall where new recruits are put through their paces; and the 1883
chapel – Regina's oldest building – a splendid structure furnished in dark, polished oak
where you can escape the intense training activity outside.

Government House

Government House, a couple of kilometres west of the city centre at 4607 Dewdney
Ave and Lewvan Drive (guided tours every 30min Tues–Sun 1–4pm; free; bus #8), was
the residence of the lieutenant-governors of the Northwest Territories and subsequently Saskatchewan from 1891 to 1945. A stolid yellow-brick building, it has been
delightfully restored to its appearance at the end of the last century, with offices and
reception areas downstairs and a splendid, balconied staircase leading up to the first-
floor bedrooms. The men's billiards room is decorated with an enormous bison head
and a lemon-water stand, where the governor and his cronies would dip their fingers to
hide the smell of the cigars. There are also a couple of mementos of one of the more
eccentric governors, Amédée Forget, whose specially designed "salesman's chair",
beside the entrance, was meant to be uncomfortable, with protruding gargoyles

---

THE MOUNTIES

The heroes of a hundred adventure stories, from *Boys' Own* yarns to more eccentric epics such as the movie *Canadian Mounties versus the Atomic Invaders*, the **Mounties** have been the continent's most charismatic good guys ever since Inspector James Morrow Walsh rode into Chief Sitting Bull's Canadian encampment to lay down the law. Coming straight after the Sioux's victory at the battle of the Little Big horn in 1876, this was an act of extraordinary daring, and it secured the future of the Mounties. The **North West Mounted Police**, as the Mounties were originally called, had been created in Ottawa during the fall of 1873, simply in order to restore law and order to the "Whoop-up Country" of southern Saskatchewan and Alberta in the aftermath of the Cypress Hills Massacre (see box on p.492). There was no long-term strategy: the force's areas of responsibility were undecided, and even their uniforms had been slung together from a surplus supply of British army tunics that happened to be handy. However, they did a brilliant job of controlling the whiskey traders who had created pandemonium through the unscrupulous sale of liquor to the Plains Indians, and it was soon clear – after Walsh's dealings with Sitting Bull – that they were to become a permanent institution.

The Mounties came to perform a vital role in administering the west on behalf of the federal government, acting both as law enforcement officers and as justices of the peace. From the 1880s their patrols diligently crisscrossed the territory, their influence reinforced by a knowledge of local conditions that was accumulated in the exercise of a great range of duties – from delivering the mail to providing crop reports. Despite this level of autonomy, the Mounties saw themselves as an integral, if remote, part of the British Empire, their actions and decisions sanctioned by the weight of its authority. In this sense, they despised the individualism of the American sheriff and marshal, for the Mounties expected obedience because of the dignity of their office, not because of their speed with a firearm.

The officer corps, most of whom were recruited from the social elite of the eastern provinces, became respected for an even-handedness that extended, remarkably for the period, to their dealings with the Plains Indians. **Crowfoot**, the Blackfoot leader, was even moved to remark, "If the police had not come to the country, where would we all be now? They have protected us as the feathers of a bird protect it from the frosts of winter." Yet the officers' class prejudices had a less positive influence on their approach to law and order – socially disruptive crimes of violence were their main priority, whereas prostitution and drunkenness were regarded as predictable and inevitable nuisances that were confined to the "lower orders". They had a cohesive view of the society they wanted to create, a Waspish patriarchy where everyone knew their place.

After 1920, when the force lost its exclusively western mandate to become the **Royal Canadian Mounted Police**, this conservative undertow became more problematic. Time and again the RCMP supported reactionary politicians who used them to break strikes – like prime ministers Bennett in Saskatchewan in 1933 and 1934, and Joey Smallwood in Newfoundland during 1959 – and they have often been accused of bias in their dealings with the Québécois. That said, although the Mounties are seen by some as a bastion of reaction at odds with multicultural definitions of Canada, for the most part they remain a potent symbol of nationality. And, for Labatts' brewery, the endorsement of Malcolm the Mountie is a sure-fire way to sell beer.

---

sticking into the visitor's spine, legs shorter at the front than the back and a flesh-pinching crack cut across the middle of the seat. The rocking horse in the office was for Forget's pet monkey. High tea, complete with finger sandwiches and fragile china cups, is served in the ballroom one weekend each month between 1.30pm and 4pm.

Eating, drinking and nightlife

Regina has a clutch of good downtown **restaurants**, lively places whose prices are usually very reasonable. However, many of them close early and don't open at all on Sundays; in emergencies try the big hotels whose standard-issue snack bars are nearly always open daily to 9.30pm. The city's **nightlife** is hardly inspiring, but the university students provide a little stimulation for the couple of downtown clubs, whilst local roustabouts and government workers alike tend to stick to C&W. As a general rule, avoid the downtown **bars**, which are really not very pleasant, and try one of Regina's **brewpubs**, though most are a bit far from the centre: *Brewster's*, 1832 Victoria Ave East, has the largest selection of beers; *Bonzinni's*, 4364 Albert St, in South Regina, also serves good Italian food; *The Bushwakker*, 2206 Dewdney Ave, has twelve types of beer, plus a large selection of single-malt Scotches; *The Barley Mill*, 6807 Rochdale Blvd, is an English-style pub.

For **theatre**, call the Regina Performing Arts Centre, 1077 Angus St (☎525-9999 or 1-800-667-8497), to find out what's being put on there by the two principal groups, the Saskatchewan Community Theatre and the Regina Little Theatre. The Regina Symphony Orchestra performs at the Saskatchewan Centre of the Arts, 200 Lakeshore Drive (☎586-9555).

Restaurants and cafés

Alfredo's Fresh Pasta and Grill, 1801 Scarth St at 11th Avenue. Specializes in home-made pasta dishes and combines a tasty and imaginative menu with good-value main courses from $8. Closed Sun.

Classic Buffet Co, 100 Albert St. Help yourself to the table laid out with pizza, roast beef and fifteen other hot dishes. Early closing.

The Copper Kettle, 1953 Scarth St at 11th Avenue. A run-down place, but a great Greek-Canadian menu. Fabulous spinach and feta pizza. Open daily to midnight.

Fuddruckers, 211 Albert St North. The best place to go for hamburgers in all their variations.

Grabbajabba, 1881 Scarth St, in the McCallum-Hill Centre. European-style coffee house, with cheap soups, sandwiches, salads and desserts plus an astounding array of coffees. Live jazz Friday 8–11pm.

Heliotrope, 2204 McIntyre St. A wholefood vegetarian restaurant with an emphasis on East Indian and Middle Eastern food. Closed Mon & Sun.

The Keg, 4371 Albert St. Good chicken and seafood dishes from $12.

Magellan's Global Coffee House, 1800 College Ave. This place is a Regina institution. A wide range of coffees and desserts served in a trendy setting.

Maria's, 1810 Smith St. Excellent Greek dishes from $7. Closed Sun.

Marquee, 2903 Powerhouse Drive, at the Saskatchewan Science Centre. Inventively presented contemporary cuisine, with an emphasis on game.

Neo Japonica, 2167 Hamilton St. Voted best Japanese restaurant in Canada. Excellent tempura and sushi.

Nicky's Café and Bake Shop, 1005 8th Ave. Good Canadian menu at reasonable prices, especially their breakfasts, Saskatoon berry pie and bread. Fresh turkey served daily. Closed Sun.

Orleans, 1822 Broad St (☎525-3636). Authentic, spicy Cajun food for $10–15; their jambalaya is terrific. Centrally located. Reservations recommended.

Roca Jack's Coffee House, 1939 Scarth St. Coolest coffee house in town.

The Thirteenth Avenue Coffee House, 3136 13th Ave. This coffee house, in Cathedral Village, offers the best cappuccino and espresso in town. Daily 11am–11pm.

Discos and venues

Bricks and **Oscar's**, 1422 Scarth St. Two lively gay bars, the latter with an Oscar Wilde theme.

Checkers and **Scotland Yard**, in the *Landmark Inn*, 4150 Albert St. The places, to be seen in, catering mainly to the fashionable, twentysomething crowd. $2 cover charge.

Good Time Charlie's, in the *Plains Hotel*, 1965 Albert St. Best blues club in Regina. Jam sessions Thursday, Saturday and Sunday night, plus Saturday afternoons. $3–5 cover charge.

Long Branch Saloon, 1400 McIntyre St. A rip-roarin' hoedown-style C&W club with the usual line dancing.

The Manhattan Club, 2300 Dewdney Ave. Disco with a chaotic combo of Top 40 and dance mix. $2.25 cover charge on Saturday. Closed Sun & Mon.

The Pump, 641 Victoria Ave East. C&W venue with a huge dance floor. $4 cover charge. Closed Sun.

The State, 1326a Hamilton St. Alternative rap, pop, 1980s hits – all on a heaving multilevel dance floor. Great live bands most nights. $6 cover charge on Fridays. Closed Sun.

Listings

Airlines Air Canada (reservations ☎525-4711, arrivals and departures ☎1-888-422-7933); Air Sask (☎359-9757); Athabaska Airways (☎1-800-667-9356); Canadian Regional (reservations ☎569-2307, arrivals and departures ☎565-0090); Northwest Airlines (☎1-800-225-2525 or 1-800-441-1818).

Airport enquiries ☎777-0898.

Bike rental Joe's Cycle, 2255 Albert St (☎347-7711); Western Cycle, 1745 Hamilton St (☎522-5678); Wascana Centre Authority, 2900 Wascana Drive (☎522-3661); all charge about $20 per day.

Bookshops Book and Brier Patch, 4065 Albert St, has the biggest selection of books in the province; Canada Book, at 1861 Scarth St, off 11th Avenue, has a good range of titles.

Buses Regina Transit, at 333 Winnipeg St (☎777-7433). The city bus station, 2041 Hamilton St, just south of Victoria Avenue, has Greyhound (☎352-1745) for long-distance services, and a provincial carrier, the Saskatchewan Transportation Company (☎787-3340).

Camping equipment Fresh Air Experience, 532 Victoria Ave, for most outdoor supplies; Great Northern Rod & Reel, 1121 11th Ave, for fishing gear; Surplus Plus, 2415 11th Ave, for backpacking, canoeing and camping supplies.

Car rental Avis, 2010 Victoria Ave (☎757-1653), and at the airport (☎352-9596); Budget, at the airport (☎791-6814), and 505 McIntyre St (☎791-6810 or 1-800-267-6810); Dollar Rent-a-Car, 1975 Broad St (☎569-8000); Tilden, Saskatchewan Drive and Elphinstone Street (☎522-3696).

Dental emergencies Cathedral Dental Clinic, 3032 13th Ave (☎352-9966); Prairie Dental Clinic, 2109 Retallack St (☎359-7707).

Emergency ☎911 for fire, police and ambulance.

Festivals *Buffalo Days* is a week-long festival held at the end of July and the beginning of August; it begins with the "Pile O' Bones" picnic in Wascana Centre Park on a Sunday, followed by several days of craft and livestock exhibitions and music shows that culminate in a fireworks display. The *Kinsmen Big Valley Jamboree*, held in Craven, a 20min drive north of town, is a four-day C&W shindig in the middle of July; it's the largest outdoor country music festival in Canada and attracts international performers. The mid-June *Folk Festival* is held in Victoria Park; and the *Mosaic – Festival of Cultures*, held in early June at various locations throughout the city, is a multiethnic celebration, featuring folk dancing and pavilions serving food and drink. For complete information on these and other festivals, call 1-800-667-7191 ext 791.

Gay and lesbian Regina Gay Community, 1422 Scarth St (☎522-7343 or information line 525-6046).

Hospital Regina General Hospital, 1440 14th Ave (☎766-4444).

Laundries Cathedral Laundromat, 2911 13th Ave (☎525-2665); Cheap Charlie's Laundry, 515 Broad St (☎545-1070).

Left luggage Coin-operated lockers at the bus station.

Lost property ☎777-7433.

Pharmacy Shopper's Drug Mart, 4602 Albert St, is open 24hr.

Police ☎569-3333.

Post office Main office at 2200 Saskatchewan Drive, opposite the Cornwall Centre.

Sexual assault crisis line ☎352-0434.

Shopping Cowtown Western Wear, at Western Feed Mills, 745 Park St, for western clothing, boots, hats and accessories; Gourmet Pantry, upper level, Scotia Centre Galleria, 1783 Hamilton St, for Saskatchewan foods, such as Saskatoon berry products; Painted Buffalo, 2741 Dewdney Ave, for Native Indian arts and crafts; The Prairie Peddlar, 2206 Dewdney Ave, and Keepsakes Gallery, 2227 14th Ave, for local handicrafts.

Swimming Maple Leaf Pool, 1101 14th St; Wascana Pool, 2211 College Ave.

Taxis Capital Cab, 1358 Cornwall St (☎791-2222); Co-op Taxi, Regina Inn Mall, 1975 Broad St (☎525-2727); Regina Cabs, 3405 Saskatchewan Drive (☎543-3333).

Tours *i*, 41 Wesley Rd (☎584-3555) do tours of the city (2hr 30 min & 5hr; $15 & $25), as well as to Moose Jaw (5–6hr; $25) and the Qu'Appelle Valley (5–6hr; $30). Heritage Regina Tours (☎585-4214) have free guided walking tours of the city from July to mid-September. RC Tours (☎545-0555) have tours of the Legislative Building, Royal Canadian Mounted Police Museum and Government House (11am and 3pm, departing from the *Ramada Plaza Hotel*; 3hr). The Saskatchewan History & Folklore Society, 1860 Lorne St (☎780-9204), organizes one- to four-day tours of the province's historic sites.

Travel agents Marlin Travel, Cornwall Centre, 2102 11th Ave (☎525-3500); Sinfonia, 1801 Scarth St (☎584-9220 or 1-800-667-9220).

Weather ☎780-5744.

Women's contacts Regina Women's Community Centre, 1919 Rose St (☎522-2777).

Northeast of Regina

The slow-moving **Qu'Appelle River** flows 350km from Lake Diefenbaker – 160km west of Regina – to the border with Manitoba, its lush, deep and wide valley a welcome break from the prairies. Punctuated by a series of narrow lakes, and home to half a dozen modest provincial parks, this is one of the province's more popular holiday areas.

Fort Qu'Appelle and around

The river's most pleasant township is **FORT QU'APPELLE**, which sits beside Hwy 10 an hour's drive northeast of Regina, its centre sandwiched between the road and the grooved escarpments of the neighbouring lakes. Roughly ten minutes' walk from end to end, its leafy gridiron streets fall on either side of Broadway Street, the main drag, whose attractively restored red-brick **Hudson's Bay Company store**, on the corner of Company Avenue, dates from 1897 – the oldest original Hudson's Bay store in Canada. Nearby, at the top end of Bay Avenue, the **museum** (June–Aug daily 10am–noon & 1–5pm; other times by appointment; ☎332-6443 or 332-5941; $2) has a small display on the area's European pioneers and the North West Mounted Police and is joined to the Hudson's Bay Company trading post of 1864. Three blocks to the south, the stone **obelisk** at Fifth Street and Company Avenue commemorates the signing of Treaty Number 4 between the Ojibwa, Cree and Assiniboine of the southern prairies and Lieutenant-Governor Morris in 1874. It was a fractious process. The Ojibwa insisted that the Hudson's Bay Company had stolen "the earth, trees, grass, stones, all that we see with our eyes", hectoring Morris to the point where he finally snapped. He confined the more militant Indian leaders to their tents, an authoritarian manoeuvre that undermined the unity of the Indians, who then signed the treaty in return for various land grants, pensions and equipment.

Near Fort Qu'Appelle, the river bulges into a chain of eight little lakes known collectively as the **Fishing Lakes**. It's possible to drive alongside all of them, but the pick of the bunch is the nearest, **Echo Lake**, which affords pleasant views over the river valley. Between this lake and Pasqua Lake is the scenic **Echo Valley Provincial Park** (open year-round; visitor centre and Parks office mid-May to Aug ☎332-3215; $5 entry fee), while **Katepwa Point Provincial Park**, an even tinier park (mid-May to Sept; free), sits at the southernmost point of the chain of lakes.

An early-morning bus (daily 8.45am) makes the seventy-kilometre journey from Regina to Fort Qu'Appelle, where there are three **motels**. The most central is the modern *Country Square Inn* (☎332-5603; ①–②), beside Hwy 10 at the bottom end of Bay Street. There's also an attractive **B&B** in the town: *Company House*, 172 Company Ave (☎332-6333 or 332-7393; ②), which serves up hearty home-cooked breakfasts and is near beaches, and fishing, hiking and canoeing areas. On the north side of town, beside Echo Lake and near the golf course, the *Fort* **campground** (☎332-4614; mid-May to

THE DOUKHOBORS

The first **Doukhobors** developed their dissenting beliefs within the Russian Orthodox Church during the eighteenth century, rejecting both the concept of a mediatory priesthood and the church's formal hierarchy. Later they established an independent sect, but their pacifist and protocommunist views made them unpopular with the tsars, who subjected them to periodic persecution. In the late 1890s they fled Russia for Saskatchewan under the leadership of **Peter Verigin**, a keen advocate of communal labour and the collective ownership of property. Verigin maintained his authority until 1907, when the Canadian government insisted that all Doukhobor homesteads be registered as private property. The colonists were divided, with over one-third accepting the government's proposals despite the bitter opposition of the collectivists, who showed their contempt for worldly possessions by destroying their belongings; some even burnt their clothes and organized Canada's first nude demonstrations. Irretrievably divided, Verigin and his supporters left for British Columbia, but the rest stayed behind to create a prosperous, pacifist and Russian-speaking community, which remained separate and distinct until the 1940s.

mid-Sept) has an unimaginative setting and sites from $10. There are several **restaurants** on Broadway Street, including the Chinese *Jade Palace* at no. 215, and *Bubba's* next door. For more imaginative food, there's the *Off Broadway Bistro*, 12 Boundary Ave, where you can dine on turkey lasagne or *tourtière*. The **tourist information centre** is in the old CNR station at the junction of Boundary Avenue and Hwy 10 (June–Aug daily 9am–7pm; ☎332-4426).

If all accommodation in the popular Qu'Appelle Valley and lakes region is full, head for the small village of **Qu'Appelle**, 20km south of Fort Qu'Appelle on Hwy 35, where you'll find the charming fieldstone *Bluenose Country Vacation Farm* (☎ & fax 699-7192; ②) just north of town; you can also dine in the lovely tearoom, in an enclosed veranda.

About 35km east of Fort Qu'Appelle is the **Motherwell Homestead National Historic Site**, just off Hwy 22 south of the village of Abernethy (daily: May & June 9am–5pm; July & Aug 10am–6pm; $4). The large square house, with its odd assortment of multicoloured fieldstones embedded in the exterior walls, and lacy wrought-iron "widow's walk" on the roof, was built in 1898 for W.R. Motherwell, a local farmer and politician who moved to Saskatchewan from Ontario in 1882. He brought with him his knowledge of domestic architecture, for the six-bedroom building is similar to the gracious stone farmhouses of southern Ontario – and actually looks a bit incongruous in its prairie surroundings. Just behind the house, which is restored to its 1912–14 appearance, there's a large red 1907 barn, with farm equipment and roaming farm animals to complete the rustic setting.

Yorkton

Beyond Fort Qu'Appelle, the only town of any note on Hwy 10 before you hit Dauphin (see p.463) is **YORKTON**, which was founded as an agricultural community in the 1880s by farmers from Ontario, although – as with so many other places – it's the Ukrainian community that features most strongly in the town and the surrounding area. The silver-painted dome and barrel roof of the nave of the white-brick **St Mary's Ukrainian Catholic Church**, at 155 Catherine St (summer daily; rest of the year on request; ☎783-4594), is the town's most distinctive feature. Inside, there's a large illusionistic painting of the *Coronation of the Virgin* (1939–41) on the surface of the dome – about as close as you'll get in western Canada to the Baroque painted domes in Italian and German churches. The Ukrainian community features strongly in Yorkton's branch of the **Western Development Museum** (May to mid-Sept daily 9am–6pm; $4.50), devoted to the various ethnic groups who have settled in the region. You'll also find a replica of the interior of a 1902 Catholic church and a superb collection of early twentieth-century Fords and Buicks. However, the most startling sights are the bright-red, huge-wheeled early fire trucks, looking entirely too fragile for their function. If you want to see farmworkers and their fierce-looking machines in action, you could attend the **Threshermen's Show**, held on the grounds of the museum in early August. Also in the city, at the corner of Smith Street and Third Avenue is the **Godfrey Dean Cultural Centre** (Tues–Fri 1–5pm, Sat & Sun 2–5pm; free), which has a small but striking permanent collection of the work of Saskatchewan artists, plus several galleries which display temporary exhibitions; the Sports Hall of Fame, located in the older part of the building (same hours; free), is also part of the centre. After the long winter, the town is ready to host the **Yorkton Short Film and Video Festival** in May, the oldest festival of its kind in North America (1947).

Just south of the city, on the Yellowhead Hwy near Rokeby, is the **Parkland Heritage Centre** (mid-May to Sept Mon–Fri 1–8pm, Sat 1–5pm; $2.50), a modest but interesting group of nineteenth-century pioneer buildings brought here from other parts of Saskatchewan.

The **Visitors' Information Centre** is located at the junction of Hwys 9, 10 and 16 (June–Aug Mon–Fri 8am–6pm, Sat & Sun 10am–5pm; ☎783-8707) and can supply a good range of information and maps on attractions in Yorkton and the area. If you'll want to stay in Yorkton there are several reasonably priced central **hotels**, including the *Holiday Inn*, 100 Broadway St East (☎783-9781 or 1-800-667-1585; ②–④); the *Imperial 400 Motel*, 207 Broadway St East (☎783-6581 or 1-800-781-2268; ③); and the basic *City Limits Inn*, off Broadway Street at 8 Betts Ave (☎782-2435; ①). A pleasant **B&B** is the *Lazy Maples*, 111 Darlington St West (☎783-7078; ②); the owner is an excellent cook and can serve you Ukrainian perogies for breakfast.

You can camp in town at the well-shaded City Park of Yorkton **campground** (☎786-1757 or 786-1750; $12–15; mid-May to mid-Oct), on Hwy 16A near the Western Development Museum. For **food**, the *Gladstone Inn*, corner of Broadway Street and Gladstone Avenue, is the place to go – it has excellent prime rib. Yorkton's **bus station**, served by three buses daily from Saskatoon, is located downtown on 1st Avenue.

Duck Mountain Provincial Park and around

Duck Mountain Provincial Park, on the Manitoba border some 100km northeast of Yorkton on Hwys 9 and 5, is a rugged continuation of the Manitoba Escarpment (see p.464). One of the more attractive smaller parks in Saskatchewan, it's a paradise for hikers, with an extensive system of walking trails – including one that's fully disabled-accessible – and is open year-round. In winter, the park has some of the best snowmobiling and cross-country skiing in the province. The **parks office** near the lake (year-round; ☎542-3482) has all the information on dates and times of the various activities. One of the most popular attractions are the various **horseback-riding** excursions organized by Coyote Creek Stables, located on Lakeshore Drive, just inside the park's main entrance (call ☎542-3439 for times and fees).

The park centres on the roughly circular **Madge Lake**, ringed with aspens, where you'll find a beach, several stores, canteens, recreational and picnic areas, and places that rent canoes, paddleboats and ski equipment. The chalet-style *Duck Mountain Lodge*, overlooking the lake (☎ & fax 542-3466; ②–④), is a relaxing **place to stay**; you can sleep in the large lodge, the two-bedroom town-house units with fireplaces, or the woodland cabins nearby. There's also a **campground** at Pickerel Point, 4km east of the main Saskatchewan entrance (☎542-3479; $9–17; mid-May to Aug).

KAMSACK, a small town about 10km west of Duck Mountain, is the best place to **stay** if you want to explore the park. The *Woodlander Inn*, corner of Railway Avenue and 3rd Street (☎542-2125 or 542-7646; ①–②), and the *Duck Mountain Motel*, 335 Queen Elizabeth Blvd East (☎542-2656; ②), are the only two in town and are fairly basic, or there's the more costly *Vintage Country Vacation Farm,* on a rough gravel road 4km south of Norquay off Hwy 49, 40km northwest of the park (✆ & fax 594-2629; ③), an attractive parkland country property incorporating a farmstead, a rustic wooden cabin, and a three-bedroom country cottage furnished with period antiques.

Another attractive area is **Good Spirit Lake Provincial Park**, off the Yellowhead Hwy 48km northwest of Yorkton, noted for its ecologically fragile sand dunes and the warm, shallow lake itself, which has exceptionally clear water. Here you'll find fine sandy beaches on the south shore, a gas station, miniature golf course, tennis courts, riding stables, dining and snacking facilities, plus a **campground** (✆792-2110 or 786-1463; $9–17; mid-May to Sept).

Veregin

An hour's drive northeast of Yorkton, the tiny town of **VEREGIN** is named after Peter Verigin, the leader of the pacifist Doukhobor sect whose seven thousand members migrated to Saskatchewan at the end of the last century. The town is home to the **National Doukhobor Heritage Village** (mid-May to mid-Sept daily 10am–6pm; mid-Sept to mid-May Mon–Fri 10am–4pm; $3), where a modest museum traces the history of the sect and a large, square refurbished two-storey prayer home contains the living quarters of their leader, complete with many original furnishings. The building, with its encircling veranda and wrought-iron adornment on both levels, dominates a large green lawn and faces the other buildings of the village, most of which were moved here from Doukhobor colonies in other parts of the province. Lined up in a neat row are a farmhouse, blacksmith's shop, granary, bakery, and bathhouse equipped with dried oak leaves that were used to cleanse the skin and make it fragrant. Another smaller prayer home features a Russian library and a display on Tolstoy, whose financial support helped them to migrate. On the grounds is an imposing bronze statue of Tolstoy, donated by the Soviet Union.

Southern Saskatchewan

The 600-kilometre drive across **southern Saskatchewan** on the **Trans-Canada Highway** is crushingly boring, and apart from Regina the only town worth a stopover is **Moose Jaw**, once a Prohibition hangout of American gangsters, including Al Capone. Otherwise the rest of southern Saskatchewan is mostly undulating farmland, broken up by a handful of lakes and rivers, stretches of arid semi-desert and the odd range of wooded hills. In the southeast corner of the province, the lakes, hillocks and aspen, birch and poplar forests of **Moose Mountain Provincial Park** come complete with campgrounds, nature trails and a resort village. Further west, just south of Regina and near the US border, it's possible to drive across the **Big Muddy Badlands**, but these weathered buttes and conical hills are best explored on the tours that leave the tiny town of **Coronach** throughout the summer. Directly west of here, the **Grasslands National Park** is still being developed and extended, two separate slices of prairie punctuated by coulees and buttes that add a rare touch of drama to the landscape. Some 200km further, straddling the Alberta border, **Cypress Hills Interprovincial Park** is also well worth a visit, its heavily forested hills and ridges harbouring a restored Mountie outpost, **Fort Walsh**. Further west, the area to the northwest of the small city of **Swift Current** is home to the **Great Sand Hills**, a starkly beautiful desert landscape. Directly south of that is **Maple Creek**, a quintessentially cowboy town with **Hutterite colonies** nearby.

Apart from the daily bus services along the Trans-Canada, the region's **public transport** system is abysmal – to see the parks, you'll need a car.

Moose Mountain Provincial Park

Moose Mountain Provincial Park, just 60km south of the Trans-Canada on Route 9, 230km from Regina, is a rough rectangle of wooded hill and lake whose main resort, **KENOSEE LAKE**, is packed with holiday-makers throughout the season. There's a full range of amenities here, including a **parks office** (Mon–Fri 8am–5pm; ☎577-2131), restaurants, bars, sports facilities and canoe and paddleboat rental, but it's still easy enough to escape the crowds and wander off into the surrounding poplar and birch groves. For **accommodation**, *Kenosee Condos and Gardens* (☎ & fax 577-2211), in the resort village, has luxurious two-bedroom units (⑤), and there are also a number of **campgrounds** spread out around the lake. Hotel rooms and cabin rentals are also available through the *Kenosee Inn* (☎577-2099; ③–④), which is near two golf courses, tennis courts and waterslides. The *Fish Creek* and *Lynwood* **campgrounds** (☎577-2611; $13–17; mid-May to early Sept) have the advantage of being right on the western edge of the developed area, a good 2km from the busiest part of the park. If you're **hungry**, try the *Moose Head Dining Room*, on the lake, which serves pizza, pasta, steaks and Saskatoon berry pie.

A short-lived experiment in transplanting English social customs to the prairies is the subject of the **Cannington Manor Provincial Historic Park** (mid-May to Aug daily except Tues 10am–5pm; $2), a partly rebuilt Victorian village about 30km east of Kenosee Lake. Founded in 1882 by Edward Pierce, the would-be squire, the village attracted a number of British middle-class families determined to live as "gentlemen farmers", running small agricultural businesses, organizing tea and croquet evenings and even importing a pack of hounds to stage their own hunts. Their efforts failed when the branch rail line was routed well to the south of Cannington Manor, and by 1900 the settlement was abandoned.

Moose Jaw

MOOSE JAW, 70km west of Regina, was founded as a railway depot in 1882 and is now Saskatchewan's third largest city, with 35,000 inhabitants. It achieved some notoriety during Prohibition in the 1920s, when liquor was smuggled south by car or by train along the Soo Line, which ran from Moose Jaw to Chicago. For most locals this period of bootleggers, gangsters, gamblers and "boozoriums" – liquor warehouses – was not a happy one, and various schemes to attract tourists by developing the "Roaring Twenties" theme have met with considerable opposition from the substantial portion of the population that actually experienced them. As for the town's curious name, it may have come from an Indian word for "warm breezes", or the jaw-like turn the river takes just outside town, or even the repairs made to a cartwheel by an early pioneer with the assistance of a moose's jawbone.

The **downtown** area is bisected by Main Street, running from north to south, and Manitoba Street, the east–west axis, which is adjacent to the railway line and the river. The central area is for the most part dispiriting, though a string of **murals** of early pioneer days, concentrated along 1st Avenue NW between Manitoba and Hochelaga streets, do their best to cheer things up. That apart, some of the streets look like they haven't changed much since the 1920s, the wide treeless avenues framed by solemn brick warehouses and hotels and porticoed banks. One block north of Manitoba, the best example is **River Street**, whose rough-and-ready *Royal* and *Brunswick* hotels were once favourite haunts of the gangsters. There's a network of **tunnels** running underneath River Street from their basements, but their extent and purpose remain obscure – most likely they were built in the late nineteenth century by Chinese railway workers to hide illegal immigrants or simply to escape discrimination, and were later used by gangsters to smuggle liquor. To relive the wild days of Prohibition the city has a **Tunnels of Little Chicago tour** (daily: summer 10am–8pm; winter 1–5pm; $6), where guides in period costume lead you through the network of secret tunnels beneath Main Street, stopping at a gambler's den, Chinese laundry and Turkish bath. Tours begin at the corner of Main and River streets.

The chief sight in Moose Jaw is the huge **Western Development Museum** (Jan–March daily except Mon 9am–6pm; April–Dec daily 9am–6pm; $4.50), about 4km from the centre on bus #1A, beside the Trans-Canada as it loops around the northern edge of town. Divided into sections covering air, land, water and rail transport, its exhibits include a replica of a steamship, several Canadian Pacific railway coaches, a number of fragile old planes, and a 1934 Buick car converted to carry the chief superintendent up and down the rail line.

Practicalities

Moose Jaw's **bus station**, 63 High St East, is a couple of minutes' walk from Main Street and two blocks north of Manitoba Street, and is served by four to six buses daily from Regina; there are no trains. The **tourist bureau** (mid-May to mid-Sept daily 10am–8pm; ☎692-0555) is next to a giant concrete moose near the Western Development Museum. There's also **Tourism Moose Jaw** (Mon–Fri 9am–5pm; ☎693-8097) at 88 Saskatchewan St East in downtown.

The town has several reasonably priced, central **hotels** and **motels**, including the good-value *Midtown Motor Hotel*, centrally located at 132 Athabasca St East (☎692-0601; ①–②); the *Super 8 Motel*, 1706 Main St North (☎692-8888 or 1-800-800-8000; ②–③), Moose Jaw's newest lodging; and the four-star *Temple Gardens Mineral Spa*, 24 Fairford St East (☎694-5055 or 1-800-718-7727; ③–⑦), a complete resort, with over forty luxurious rooms (each with its own Jacuzzi) and 25 spa suites, indoor and outdoor hot geothermal pools, and facilities for reflexology and hydrotherapy treatments. The *River Park Campground* (☎692-5474; mid-April to mid-Oct) is 2km southeast of the centre at 300 River Drive, with sites from $13–18 per night.

Moose Jaw's restaurants would never win any culinary awards, but there are a few worthwhile places to fill your stomach. *Houston Pizza and Steak House*, 117 Main St North, has Italian dishes from $6; the *National Café*, 20 Main St, has a good-value daily smorgasbord; the *Prairie Oasis Restaurant*, junction of Hwy 1 East and Thatcher Drive, specializes in freshly baked pies; and the *Hopkins Dining Parlour*, 65 Athabasca St West, located in a pleasant Victorian house, is a more formal affair with a wide-ranging menu and main courses from $18. At *Charlotte's*, 16 Main St North, which serves good fish and chips and cabbage rolls, you can visit Al Capone's tunnels after your meal. For something more exotic, try the well-recommended but unappealingly named *Nit's Thai Food*, 124 Main St North, which has main courses from $6.

The Big Muddy Badlands

At the end of the last ice age, torrents of meltwater produced a massive gash in the landscape to the south of the site of Moose Jaw, near the US frontier. Edged by rounded hills and flat-topped buttes that rise up to 200m above the valley floor, the **Big Muddy Valley** can best be explored with organized tours, the best of which are the five-and-a-half-hour minibus trips from dreary **CORONACH**, about 200km from Regina (late June to Aug Sat & Sun; $20; ☎267-3312 or 267-2150). The tours include: visits to Indian burial cairns; the dramatic **Castle Butte**, a sandstone formation rising above the plains that resembles the backdrop for an American Western movie; and a couple of outlaw caves, the refuge of American rustlers and robbers like Butch Cassidy and Dutch Henry. Cassidy and his gang, the Wild Bunch, established an outlaw trail that connected the Big Muddy with Mexico via a series of safe houses; their antics were curtailed by the arrival of a detachment of Mounties in 1904 led by a certain Corporal Bird, known ruefully as the "man who never sleeps". The **tourist information** centre in town (mid-June to Aug 9am–5pm; ☎267-3312) can provide information on the history and geography of the area. If you **stay** in Coronach there's the *Country Boy Motel* at the junction of Hwys 18 and 36 (☎267-3267; ①–③), the *South Country Inn* on Main Street (☎267-5666; ①), and the *Coronach Campground* on the south side of town (☎267-4481: May–Sept), with sites from $11. The only places worth **eating** at are the coffee shop in the Coronach Mall, 111 Centre St, and the Chinese *Chopsticks* restaurant at 341 Railway Ave East.

Grasslands National Park and the Eastend area

Directly west of the Big Muddy, accessible along Hwy 18, the **Grasslands National Park** is predominantly mixed-grass prairie, a flat, bare badlands landscape broken up by splendid coulees, buttes and river valleys – notably the wide ravine edging the Frenchman River in the western block. Far from the moderating influence of the oceans, the area has a savage climate, with an average low in January of –22°C and temperatures that soar to 40°C in summer. Even so, this terrain is inhabited by many species that are adapted to cope with the shortage of water, from flora such as prairie grasses, greasewood, rabbit brush, sagebrush and different types of cacti, to fauna like the graceful pronghorn antelope, the rattlesnake and Canada's only colonies of black-tailed prairie dog.

The park made news recently when one of only twelve Tyrannosaurus Rex skeletons in the world was discovered there. The almost complete skeleton is on view at the **Fossil Research Station** in the town of **EASTEND**, 150km west of the park, 118 Maple Ave South (late May to Sept daily 9am–6pm; Oct to late May Mon–Fri 9am–noon & 1–5pm, Sat & Sun 1–4pm; $3; ☎295-4144). You can also see the bones of plesiosaurs (marine reptiles) and brontotheres (plant-eating rhino-like mammals). If you're keen on the prehistory of the area, you may want to join one of the tours run by the Eastend Community Tourism Authority (☎295-4144), which visit a **fossil quarry** where you can watch paleontologists unearthing fossils (July & Aug daily at 9am, noon & 3pm; 2hr 30min). For a more hands-on approach there's an **archeological site** for dinosaur bones near Eastend, where you can dig yourself (Aug daily; $50; ☎295-4009 or 295-4702). In the town itself there's a **museum and cultural centre**, located in the old theatre (May & June daily 9am–5pm; July & Aug daily 10am–8pm; rest of the year by appointment; $1), featuring paleontological exhibits and a late nineteenth-century pioneer log house.

If you want to base yourself in Eastend for a more thorough exploration of the park and the Frenchman River Valley, you could **stay** at the *Riverside Motel*, just west of town on Hwy 13 (☎295-3630 or 295-3773; ①–②), which also has **camping** on its grounds for $8.

At present, Grasslands National Park consists of east and west sections separated by private ranches and farms, which the federal government eventually intends to buy, creating a single park stretching from Hwy 4 in the west to Hwy 2/18 in the east. The **west** section is both more scenic and accessible, its limited system of gravel tracks and roads cutting off from Hwys 18 and 4, south and east of **VAL MARIE**. This tiny township houses the **Grasslands National Park Reception Centre**, at the junction of Hwy 4 and Centre Street (mid-May to Aug daily 8am–6pm; Sept to mid-May Mon–Fri 8am–noon & 1–4.30pm; ☎298-2257 or 298-2217), whose rangers provide advice on weather and road conditions, hand out maps, arrange for self-guided ecotours, issue camping permits and give tips on animal-spotting and hiking. There are no **campgrounds** within the park, but camping is allowed within 1km of its roads – take a good supply of water, a stout pair of walking shoes, and a stick to sweep in front of you in tall grass or brush as a warning to rattlesnakes. Animal activity is at its height at dawn and dusk and during spring and fall; whatever the season, you'll need a pair of binoculars.

The only places to **stay** in town are the *Val Marie Hotel*, 221 Centre St (☎298-9080 or 298-2003; ①), with seven basic rooms, and a centrally located **campground** (☎298-2022; May–Nov), at which sites cost $5. It won't take you long to find the town's only **restaurant**, the antiquated *Rusty's Café* at 217 Centre St.

Swift Current, Maple Creek and around

Driving west from Moose Jaw along the Trans-Canada Highway, it's about 180km to **SWIFT CURRENT**, a small industrial city and farm research centre that's mostly a convenient stopoff on the long journey on the Trans-Canada between Regina and Calgary, in Alberta. It has limited attractions for the visitor, but if you decide to stay here drop into the helpful **tourist office**, at the junction of Hwys 1 and 4 (May–Sept daily 9am–7pm; Oct–April Mon–Fri 9am–noon & 1–5pm; ☎773-7642); it's also worth calling in at the expert HorseShoe Tourism Association (Mon–Fri 8.30am–5.30pm; ☎773-1881 or 1-800-670-1093). The **bus** station is at 143 4th Ave NW, serviced by four buses daily from Regina and one from Saskatoon.

Swift Current has a few modest attractions, the best of which are in **Kinetic Park**, at 17th Avenue and South Railway St East, where you'll find a **Mennonite Heritage Village** (Fri–Sun 2–8pm; other times by appointment on ☎773-7685 or 773-6068; free), consisting of a long rectangular house and adjoining barn built in 1911–15 and six buildings comprising **Doc's Town** (Fri–Sun 1–9pm; other times by appointment on ☎773-2944; $2), a replica of an early twentieth-century prairie village – highlights are a fully functioning windmill, a one-room prairie schoolhouse, and an old dance hall (now a tearoom), transported here from a rural Saskatchewan town. The only other worthwhile stopoff is the **Art Gallery of Swift Current**, 411 Herbert St East (Mon–Thurs 2–5pm & 7–9pm, Fri–Sun 1–5pm; July & Aug closed Sun; free), where you'll see changing exhibitions of paintings, sculpture and ceramics by artists from Saskatchewan and elsewhere in Canada.

Strung out along the Trans-Canada as it skirts the north of the city, and along Hwy 4 south towards the Montana border, are several comfortable **motels**, the best of which are the new, deluxe *Best Western Inn*, just off the Trans-Canada on George Street (☎773-4660 or 1-800-528-1234; ③–⑤), and the less expensive *Imperial* 400, near the Trans-Canada at 1150 Begg St East (☎773-2033; ②–③). Just north of the Trans-Canada there's a small but convenient **campground**, *Trail Campground* (☎773-8088; $10–12; May to mid-Oct). For **restaurants**, try *Carol's Diner*, 914 Central Ave North, specializing in Belgian waffles, or *Humpty's*, at the junction of Hwys 1 and 4 East, which does a cheap all-day breakfast.

Perhaps the best reason for stopping at Swift Current is its proximity to the **Great Sand Hills**, over 1900 square kilometres of giant active sand dunes, which is home to hordes of hopping kangaroo rats as well as mule deer and antelope. The best place to view the dunes is 1.5km south off Hwy 32, at the village of **SCEPTRE**, to the north of the hills. A small **museum** on Hwy 32 (summer Mon–Sat 10am–noon & 1–4pm, Sun 1–5pm; $2) has displays on the ecology of the hills and can provide information about tours.

About 50km further east from the Great Sand Hills, reached by Hwy 32 (or Hwy 4 north from Swift Current), is the pretty little **Saskatchewan Landing Provincial Park**, situated on both banks of the South Saskatchewan River, where it emerges from razorback hills and opens out into the large, finger-like man-made **Lake Diefenbaker**, created in 1967. The park area was once an important river crossing for Native Canadians and early white settlers, and the staff at the **Goodwin House** Visitors' Centre (☎375-5525 or 375-5527), a beautiful turn-of-the-century stone house built by the North West Mounted Police, located in the park, can organize nature trail hikes through coulees and explain the significance of the crossing, once one of the most difficult river crossings in western Canada. There are remains of several ancient tepee encampments in the area. You can **camp** in the park at the *Bear Paw–Nighthawk Riverside Campground* (☎375-5525; $12; mid-May to Oct).

THE HUTTERITES

The **Hutterites**, the only prairie community to have maintained a utopian communal ideal, are members of an Anabaptist sect that takes its name from their first real leader, Jacob Hutter. Originating in the Tyrol and Moravia in the sixteenth century, they gradually moved east across central Europe, ending up in Russia, which they abandoned for South Dakota in the 1870s. It was fifty years before they felt obliged to move again, their pacifism recoiling from the bellicosity that gripped their American neighbours during World War I. They moved north between 1918 and 1922, and established a series of **colonies** where they were allowed to educate their own children, speak their own language and have no truck with military service. In these largely self-sufficient communities tasks are still divided according to ability and skill, property is owned communally, and social life is organized around a common dining room and dormitories. Economically prosperous, they continue to multiply, a new branch community being founded whenever the old one reaches a secure population of between one hundred and two hundred. Apart from the occasional skirmish with the outside world when they buy new land, the Hutterites have been left in peace and have resisted the pressures of assimilation more staunchly than their kindred spirits, the Mennonites and the Doukhobors.

From Swift Current it's another 130km to **MAPLE CREEK**, situated just 8km to the south of the Hwy on the way to the Cypress Hills. Nicknamed "old cow town", Maple Creek lies at the heart of ranching country, and its streets are full of pick-up trucks, cowboy boots and stetsons. Some of the late nineteenth-century brick storefronts have survived, and the trim and tidy **Old Timers' Museum** at 218 Jasper St (June–Sept daily 9am–5pm; April, May & Oct Mon–Fri 1–4pm; other times by appointment; $2) has pleasant displays on pioneer life and the Mounties. The place is also the market town for a number of **Hutterite colonies**, whose the women stand out with their floral dresses and headscarves (see box above).

The Cypress Hills

South of the Trans-Canada Highway, between Maple Creek and Irvine, in Alberta, the wooded ridges of the **Cypress Hills** rise above the plains in a 130-kilometre-long plateau that in places reaches a height of 1400m – the highest point in Canada between Labrador and the Rockies. Because of its elevation, this area was untouched by glaciers as they moved south during the ice age, scouring the land bare of vegetation, and the Cypress Hills are an anomaly in the landscape of the prairies, having a wetter and milder climate than the treeless plains that surround them, creating a rich variety of woodland, wetland and grassland. In turn, this comparatively lush vegetation supports a wealth of wildlife, from the relatively rare elk, lynx, bobcat and coyote through to the more common gopher and raccoon, plus about two hundred species of bird, over half of whom breed in the hills. (Watch out for the colonies of long-necked wild turkeys, as well as the sage grouse, whose bizarre courting rituals involve the male swelling out his chest and discharging air with a sound akin to a gunshot.) One surprise – considering the name – is the absence of cypress trees: the early French voyageurs seem to have confused the area's predominant lodgepole pines with the jack pines of Québec, a species they called *cyprès*. Literal-minded translation did the rest.

Cypress Hills Interprovincial Park

In amongst the cattle ranches two separate sections of the Hills have been set aside to form the **Cypress Hills Interprovincial Park** (entry fee $5): Saskatchewan's Centre Block lies to the south of Maple Creek along Hwy 21, and the larger West Block spans the Saskatchewan–Alberta border, accessible from Maple Creek along Hwy 271 in the

THE CYPRESS HILLS MASSACRE

From the mid-eighteenth century, the Cypress Hills lay in a sort of neutral zone between the **Blackfoot** and the **Cree**, whose intermittent skirmishing was small-scale until the 1860s, when the failure of the Crees' traditional hunting grounds forced them to move west. Some three thousand Cree reached the Cypress Hills in 1865 and the violence began just four years later with the murder of the Cree peacemaker, Maskepetoon. The ensuing war was overshadowed by the Red River rising of 1869–70 in Manitoba, but casualties were high and its effects were compounded by two smallpox epidemics. In 1871 the Cree sued for peace, but both sides were exhausted, their morale, health and social structures further undermined by the whiskey traders who had moved into the region.

These **whiskey traders**, who were mostly American, brought their liquor north in the fall, returning south in late spring laden with furs and buffalo robes. Though it was illegal to supply the Indians with booze, the traders spread out across the southern plains, aptly nicknamed **Whoop-up Country**, establishing dozens of trading posts whose occupants were protected from their disorderly customers by log stockades. (They needed to be, as the stuff they sold was adulterated with such substances as red ink, gunpowder and strychnine.) In the spring of 1873, there were two such outposts beside **Battle Creek**, deep in the Cypress Hills, owned by a certain Abel Farwell and his rival Moses Solomon. For reasons that remain obscure, though the prevailing drunkenness played a part, this was the scene of a violent confrontation between a group of white wolf-hunters, whiskey traders and a band of Assiniboine. Equipped with the latest fast-action rifles, the hunters riddled an Assiniboine camp with bullets, killing up to seventy (according to some sources) before returning to the trading posts to celebrate. News of the incident, known as the **Cypress Hills Massacre**, filtered back to Ottawa, and this speeded up the recruitment of the newly formed **North West Mounted Police**, who in the fall received their first posting west as a detachment to Fort MacLeod, near today's Lethbridge, Alberta. They reached it in early 1874, where they set about suppressing the whiskey trade and establishing law and order.

To consolidate their control of the area, the Mounties built **Fort Walsh**, near Battle Creek, the following year. An unpopular posting, the fort was considered "unhealthy, isolated and indefensible", but it could not be abandoned until 1883, when the last of the restless Indian bands were moved to reservations further north. It was during this period that the fort's first inspector, **James Morrow Walsh**, was faced with an extremely delicate situation. In 1876, **Chief Sitting Bull's** Sioux had exterminated General Custer's army at the battle of the Little Bighorn. Fearing reprisals, five thousand Sioux moved north, establishing their camp at Wood Mountain, 350km east of Fort Walsh. Aware of the danger, Walsh rode into the Sioux encampment with just four other constables to insist that they obey Canadian law. This act of bravery established a rough rapport between the two leaders, and by his tactful dealings with the Sioux Walsh enhanced the reputation of the Mounties, whose efficiency ensured there were no more massacres in the Canadian west.

east and via Alberta's Hwy 41, off the Trans-Canada, in the west. The Saskatchewan part of the West Block is also attached to Fort Walsh National Historic Park, incorporating a partly refurbished Mountie station and a replica of one of the Battle Creek trading posts. The three north–south access highways present no problems, but it's difficult to drive across the park from east to west as the paved road, known as the Gap Road, is interrupted by two long stretches of gravel and clay track that are positively dangerous in wet weather.

Just 30km south of Maple Creek on Hwy 21, a paved sideroad heads into the park's **Centre Block**, a rough rectangle of hilly land dominated by a forest of lodgepole pines. At the centre, a pleasant tourist resort surrounds tiny **Loch Leven**, complete with canoe and bike rental facilities, shops and a gas station. There's also a modest nature centre adjoining the park's **administration office** (Mon–Thurs 8am–8pm, Fri–Sun 8am–10pm;

☎662-4411), which has useful maps and trail brochures. The resort is a popular holiday destination, but it's easy to escape the crowds along the half-dozen hiking trails. For **accommodation**, there's one **hotel**, the modern *Cypress Four Seasons Resort* (☎662-4477), with rooms and cabins (both ②–③) and apartments (③–⑥). Close by, there are several summer **campgrounds** (all $9–17), which have to be booked at the campground office on Pine Avenue, to the west of the centre (mid-May to Aug daily 8.30am–10pm; ☎662-4411; $11). Don't **eat** at the resort; instead, head for the *Cypress Park Café*, right on the lake, where tasty home-cooked meals can be had for as little as $6.

The eastern side of the park's **West Block** has alternating areas of thick forest and open grassland broken up by steep hills and deep, sheltered ravines. Hwy 271 enters this section from the east and becomes increasingly bumpy as it twists south towards the **Fort Walsh National Historic Park** and **Visitors' Information Centre** (mid-May to Sept daily 9am–5.30pm; ☎662-3590 or 662-2645), which has excellent displays on the Plains Indians, the history of the fort and the development of the RCMP.

A five-minute walk behind the information centre, **Fort Walsh** (mid-May to Sept daily 9.30am–6pm; $6) sits in a wide, low-lying valley, its trim stockade framed by pine forests. Built in 1875, the fort was abandoned in favour of Maple Creek just eight years later; in 1942 the RCMP acquired the land, and most of the present buildings date from that decade. Guides in period costumes enliven a tour of whitewashed log buildings, the whole site having returned to its 1880s appearance. Close to the fort is a cemetery containing the tombstones of several North West Mounted Police officers. Every 45 minutes a minibus makes the trip from the information centre over the hills to Battle Creek, where Abel Farwell's **trading post** has been reconstructed and staffed with costumed guides to act out the parts of Farwell and his entourage (mid-May to Aug; cost included in ticket to fort). The guides will also take you to the actual site of the Massacre (see box).

The main **accommodation** in this part of the park is the *West Block Campground* (☎662-3606; $11; May to mid-Nov), 5km north of Fort Walsh, in a dense stand of spindly lodgepole pines and with a babbling brook running through it. It's in an isolated spot, so take your own food and drink. From the campground you can make an expedition to the **Conglomerate Cliffs**, a few kilometres to the northeast near Adams Lake. These are strange-looking walls of rock, some 150m high, composed of multicoloured cobblestones glued together.

There are a variety of guided **tours** of both the Centre and West blocks that will help you to better appreciate the rugged beauty of the area and the high-altitude flora and fauna – much of which is found nowhere else in western Canada except the Rocky Mountains. A tour of the Centre Block (2hr; $60) includes trips to Lookout Point and Bald Butte on the edge of the park, where there are panoramic views north down into the valleys and plains. The more rugged West Block can be experienced on longer tours (4hr, $120; 6hr, $180) that take you over the bone-rattling Gap Road to points of interest such as Fort Walsh and the Conglomerate Cliffs. All tours are led by trained, local guides; to book, call ☎662-4411 (Mon–Fri 8am–5pm).

The lodgepole forests and deep coulees of the **Alberta section** of the park are centred on the tourist resort of **ELKWATER**, 34km south of the Trans-Canada on Hwy 41. Curving round the southern shore of Elkwater Lake, the village has a comprehensive range of facilities, from boat and bike rental through to a sandy beach and sauna baths. There's also a **park office** (Mon–Fri 8.15am–noon & 1–4.30pm; ☎403-893-3777) and a **visitors' centre** (mid-May to early Sept Mon–Fri 10am–6pm; ☎403-893-3833), which has maps and hiking brochures and runs guided walks throughout the summer. For **accommodation**, there's the *Green Tree Motel* (☎403-893-3811; ②–③), while the *Elkwater Campground* is relatively luxurious, with both simple and hooked-up sites.

Southwest of Elkwater, a paved road leads to Horseshoe Canyon and **Head of the Mountain**, where there are striking views over the hills towards Montana; other roads lead east to Reesor Lake and Spruce Coulee Reservoir. Beside the roads there are twelve other **campgrounds**, bookable through the visitors' centre.

Saskatoon

Set on the wide South Saskatchewan River at the heart of a vast wheat-growing area, **SASKATOON** is a commercial, manufacturing and distribution centre with a population of around 215,000 – making it Saskatchewan's largest city and, in the opinion of many of its inhabitants, a better claimant to the title of provincial capital than Regina. Ontario Methodists founded the town as a temperance colony in 1883 and named it after the purple berry that grows in the region, but in spite of their enthusiasm the new settlement made an extremely slow start, partly because the semi-arid farming conditions were unfamiliar to them and partly because the Northwest Rebellion of 1885 raised fears of Indian hostility. Although the railroad reached Saskatoon in 1890, there were still only 113 inhabitants at the turn of the century. In the next decade, however, there was a sudden influx of European and American settlers and, as the agricultural economy of the prairies expanded, so the city came to be dominated by a group of entrepreneurs nicknamed **boomers**, under whose management Saskatoon became the economic focus of the region. This success was underpinned by the development of a particularly sharp form of municipal loyalty – people who dared criticize any aspect of the city, from the poor quality of the water to tyrannical labour practices, were dubbed **knockers**, and their opinions were rubbished by the press. The boomers established a city where community solidarity overwhelmed differences in income and occupation, a set of attitudes that palpably still prevails, making this a pleasant, well-groomed place, albeit one with just a trio of principal tourist attractions – the **Mendel Art Gallery**, a branch of the **Western Development Museum** and, on the outskirts, **Wanuskewin**, a complex dedicated to the Plains Indians.

Arrival, information and transport

Saskatoon **airport**, 7km northwest of the city centre, is connected to downtown by taxi (roughly $12); otherwise, the nearest bus service is #21, which leaves from the junction of Airport Drive and 45th Street, a five-minute walk from the terminal building. The **train station** is 7km west of the town centre, on Chappell Drive, a five-minute walk from the Route of bus #3 on Dieppe Street; a taxi to the downtown core costs about $13. Far more convenient is the city's **bus station**, in the centre at 23rd St East and Pacific Avenue.

The main office of **Tourism Saskatoon** (mid-May to Aug Mon–Fri 8.30am–7pm, Sat & Sun 10am–7pm; Sept to mid-May Mon–Fri 8.30am–5pm; ☎242-1206 or 1-800-567-2444) is in the old CP train station at 6-305 Idylwyld Drive North. In addition to maps and brochures, it has copies of *The Broadway Theatre*, a free bimonthly news sheet that carries details of cultural events. There's also an information centre at the corner of Avenue C North and 47th Street (mid-May to Aug daily 10am–7pm; ☎242-1206). The local newspaper, *The Star Phoenix*, has bland reviews and nightlife listings at the weekend.

Saskatoon's compact city centre is best explored on **foot**, though it takes a little time to work out the street plan, due to the fact that most streets and avenues are given numbers, not names; streets run east–west; avenues, north–south. Edged to the south and east by the river and the adjacent strip of city park, the **downtown core** is bounded by 25th St East to the north and 1st Avenue to the west. Numbered sequentially, these central **streets** are all "East", with their western extensions starting at either 1st Avenue or Idylwyld Drive. However, the **avenues** change from "South" to "North" right in the centre at 22nd St East. For the suburbs, **Saskatoon Transit** (☎975-3100) operates an efficient and fairly comprehensive bus transport system, with a standard adult fare of $1.25 (pay on board; call ☎975-3100 for routes and times).

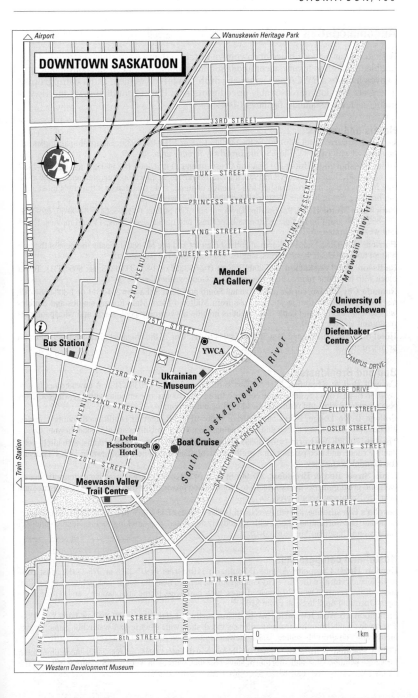

DOWNTOWN SASKATOON

△ Airport △ Wanuskewin Heritage Park

N

33RD STREET

DUKE STREET

PRINCESS STREET

KING STREET

QUEEN STREET

IDYLWYLD DRIVE

2ND AVENUE

SPADINA CRESCENT

Meewasin Valley Trail

Mendel Art Gallery

University of Saskatchewan

Diefenbaker Centre

CAMPUS DRIVE

25TH STREET

YWCA

Bus Station

23RD STREET

Ukrainian Museum

South Saskatchewan River

1ST AVENUE

22ND STREET

COLLEGE DRIVE

ELLIOTT STREET

OSLER STREET

TEMPERANCE STREET

Delta Bessborough Hotel

Boat Cruise

SASKATCHEWAN CRESCENT

20TH STREET

Meewasin Valley Trail Centre

△ Train Station

15TH STREET

CLARENCE AVENUE

11TH STREET

BROADWAY AVENUE

LORNE AVENUE

MAIN STREET

8th STREET

0 1km

▽ Western Development Museum

Accommodation

Saskatoon has a good choice of downtown **hotels** with prices starting at around $40 per double, through to luxury accommodation for about $160. Cheap and convenient alternatives include a YWCA and summer **youth hostel** for women, and a **campground**. There are also lots of reasonably priced **motels** on Hwy 11 south of town and Hwy 16 going east, with standard facilities (②–④).

Hotels and motels

Colonial Square Motel, 1301 8th St East (☎343-1676 or 1-800-667-3939). Eighty simple singles and doubles, all with cable TV. Close to the Broadway Avenue area. ②.

Delta Bessborough Hotel, 601 Spadina Crescent and 21st St East (☎244-5521 or 1-800-268-1133, fax 653-2458). Built for the CNR in 1931, the *Bessborough* is an enormous turreted and gabled affair that has been tastefully refurbished in a "French chateau" style that makes it the city's most striking building. Set in Kiwanis Memorial Park, beside the river. ④–⑦.

Park Town Motor Hotel, 924 Spadina Crescent and 25th St East (☎244-5564 or 1-800-667-3999, fax 665-8698). Pleasant budget place. Rooms have king- and queen-sized beds, TV and movies. Excellent weekend rates. ②.

Patricia Hotel, 345 2nd Ave North at 25th St East (☎ and fax 242-8861). Easily the best of the low-budget hotels – clean, basic dorms, singles and doubles. Free parking. ①.

Radisson Hotel Saskatoon, 405 20th St East (☎665-3322 or 1-800-333-3333, fax 665-5531). Tower block with luxurious rooms. Fourteen en-suites. Good weekend rates. ③–⑤.

Ramada City Centre, corner of 1st Avenue South and 22nd St East (☎244-2311 or 1-800-668-4442, fax 664-2234). Downtown location, across from Midtown Plaza Mall. Roomy singles and doubles with air conditioning and cable TV. Facilities include a swimming pool, sauna and whirlpool, plus restaurant and bar. ③–④.

Hotel Senator, 3rd Ave and 21st St East (☎244-6141). One of the cheapest places in town, but with primitive rooms. ②.

Bed and Breakfasts

Caswell Bed & Breakfast, 31st St West and Idylwyld Drive (☎933-2249). A down-home, family-style B&B, on a quiet residential street, with three cosy rooms, one en suite with bay window. They also provide pick-up and return to the airport or bus station. ②.

College Drive Lodge, 1020 College Drive (☎665-9111). Budget air conditioned rooms; laundry, kitchen, complimentary coffee and tea; free parking. Close to University of Saskatchewan. ①.

The Inn, 702 8th Ave North (☎975-3959). Large, comfortable, non-smoking rooms, with kitchenette and TV room, and free parking. In a pretty residential area close to the Meewasin Valley Trail and the Mendel Art Gallery. ②.

Ninth Street Bed & Breakfast, 227 9th St East (☎224-3754). Three attractive suites with shared bath and great gourmet breakfasts. Bike rental is also provided. In the historic Nutana district and near the Broadway Avenue area. ②.

Savelia's Guesthouse, 330 6th Ave North (☎653-4646, fax 653-2017). In a cottage-style white wooden house. Old-world atmosphere, with attractively decorated, non-smoking rooms. Near Mendel Art Gallery and Ukrainian Museum. ①–②.

Hostel and campgrounds

Gordon Howe Campsite, Avenue P South, off 11th Street (☎975-3328 or 975-3331). Most comfortable and central of the three city campgrounds, located near the South Saskatchewan River, 4km south of the centre. Over 130 serviced sites, with barbecue, picnic area, laundry and on-site manager. Open mid-April to Sept. From $16.

Saskatoon 16 West RV Park, Hwy 16, 1.5km northwest of the city (☎931-8905 or 1-800-478-7833). Twenty-five pull-through sites, plus fifty serviced sites with electric and water hook-ups. Convenience shop on grounds selling Saskatchewan crafts. Open April–Oct. $13–18.

YWCA Residence, 510 25th St East, at 5th Ave North (☎244-0944, fax 653-2468). Accommodation for single women; long- and short-term stays possible, with good weekly and monthly rates. At the same address, the *YWCA Summer Youth Hostel* offers dormitory beds (①) from June to August for women only. ③.

The City

Most of Saskatoon's principal sights are on or near the **Meewasin Valley Trail**, a circular, nineteen-kilometre walking and cycle Route that follows the narrow strip of park along both banks of the river between the Idylwyld Drive and Circle Drive bridges. At the start of the trail, the **Meewasin Valley Centre**, 3rd Ave South at 19th St East (Mon–Fri 9am–5pm, Sat & Sun 10.30am–5pm; free; ☎665-6888), provides a useful introduction to the region's history and geography with the aid of maps, old photographs and a video film; a well-stocked gift shop is part of the centre, and there's also a tourist information office (same hours as centre).

A few minutes' walk from the Valley Centre, along the west bank, the **Ukrainian Museum of Canada**, 910 Spadina Crescent East at 24th St East (Tues–Sat 10am–5pm, Sun 1–5pm; $2), is the more interesting of the city's two Ukrainian museums, representing the Orthodox as distinct from the Catholic tradition. Displays cover the history of Ukrainian migration, traditional textile design, festivals and Easter-egg painting, the most appealing Ukrainian folk art.

The **Mendel Art Gallery**, overlooking the river from Spadina Crescent, just north of 25th St East (daily: late May to mid-Oct 9am–9pm; mid-Oct to late May noon–9pm; free), features temporary shows of modern Canadian and international art and a rotating exhibition drawn from the possessions of local magnate Fred Mendel. His collection includes paintings by many of the country's best artists – Emily Carr, Lawren Harris and David Milne – and a good selection of Inuit sculpture, a small sample of which is always on display. The gallery is also well-known for its collection of German Expressionist prints and paintings. Other parts of the building contain a snack bar, a delightful conservatory and an excellent gift shop.

Across the river from the Mendel Art Gallery, over University Bridge, the campus of the **University of Saskatchewan**, with a number of dignified greystone buildings in Gothic-Revival style, occupies a prime river-bank site just to the north of College Drive. Departmental collections include a dull **Museum of Natural Sciences**, in the Biology complex (Mon–Fri 8am–9pm, Sat 10am–5pm, Sun noon–5pm; free), and a similar **Museum of Antiquities**, in the Murray Building (May–Aug Mon–Fri 9am–4pm; Sept–April 9am–noon; closed mid-Dec to mid-Jan; free); and the small **Kenderdine Gallery** (Mon–Fri 11.30am–4pm, Sun 12.30–5pm; donation). None of these draws as many visitors as the **Diefenbaker Centre**, a museum, archive and research centre at the west end of the campus, beside the river (Mon & Fri 9.30am–4.30pm, Tues–Thurs 9.30am–8pm, Sat & Sun 12.30–5pm; donation). Prime minister from 1957 to 1963, John Diefenbaker was a caricaturist's dream with his large flat face, protruding teeth and wavy white hair, and the museum's high point is its assortment of newspaper cartoons. He was buried just outside the centre in 1979. One of the finest **views** of the city, across the river, is from the grounds of the centre.

Cruises along the South Saskatchewan River, with its weir, sand bars and fast-flowing currents, are organized by Shearwater Boat Cruises on its ship, the *Saskatoon Delta Lady* (May–Oct daily at 10.30am, 12.10pm, 1.30pm, 3pm, 4.30pm, 6pm, 7.30pm & 9pm; 1hr; $8; ☎934-7642); the boat departs from behind the *Delta Bessborough Hotel*.

Western Development Museum

On the south side of the river, 8km from the centre, is the Saskatoon branch of the **Western Development Museum**, 2610 Lorne Ave South (Jan–March Tues–Sun 9am–5pm; April–Dec daily same hours; $4.50), a few minutes' walk from the Route of bus #1 from 2nd Avenue in downtown. The principal exhibit here is **Boomtown**, an ambitious reconstruction of a typical Saskatchewan small-town main street circa 1910, complete with boardwalk sidewalks and parked vehicles. More like a film set than a museum, its mixture of replica and original buildings includes a school, a general store, a church, a theatre, a train station and a combined pool hall and barbershop. There's a shop with a range of unusual gifts, and the *Boomtown Café* serves delicious home-cooked meals with a pioneer flavour.

Wanuskewin Heritage Park

Wanuskewin Heritage Park, 405 3rd Ave South (May to mid-Sept daily 9am–9pm; mid-Sept to Oct daily 9am–5pm; Nov to April Wed–Sun 9am–5pm; $6), twenty minutes' drive north of the city centre along Warman Road, is designed to be Saskatoon's principal tourist attraction, a lavish tribute to the culture of the Northern Plains Indians – and it's well worth the trip out here, as the commercial aspect is played down in favour of a sensitive interpretation of the Indians' spiritual relationship to the land and to living creatures. Bordering the South Saskatchewan River in the attractive wooded Opamihaw Valley, the park embraces a string of marshy creeks and wooded ridges that have been used by native peoples for more than six thousand years. All along the trails are ecologically fragile plants and flowers that must not be picked. The nineteen sites are fully wheelchair-accessible and are connected by trails and walkways to a visitor centre that features reconstructions of tepees, a buffalo pound and a buffalo jump as well as displays on traditional skills as diverse as tool-making and storytelling. For about $40 per person, the park can also arrange for overnight camping in tepees (June–Sept), plus longer sessions of two or three nights (book on ☎931-6767 or 1-800-665-4600). There are also dance demonstrations at the centre (daily 1.30pm & 3.30pm), as well as demonstrations of tepee-raising and spear-throwing. The attached **restaurant** specializes in indigenous foodstuffs such as buffalo meat, bannock bread and pemmican, a mixture of fat, berries and dried meat that's supposed to last for years; a gift shop has a full range of authentic arts and crafts by native people. Wanuskewin has been developed with the cooperation of local native peoples, who provide most of the interpretive staff. There is no public transport to Wanuskewin.

Around Saskatoon

Redberry Lake, about 100km northwest of Saskatoon via Hwys 16, 340 and 40 (☎549-2400 or 549-2258), is one of the province's best areas to view over two hundred species of birds. The sanctuary (mid-May to mid-Sept daily 10am–6pm; free), on the north shore of the lake, is home to several rare species, including piping plovers and white pelicans. There are trails around the lakeshore, and an interpretive centre, which has videos and dioramas on the lake's fragile ecosystem. Boat tours and guided walking tours ($2.50 per person) can also be booked at the centre.

In the opposite direction, some 120km east of Saskatoon via Hwys 16 and 2, is **Little Manitou Lake**. Set in a rather arid landscape, it looks like just any other lake, until you submerge yourself in its murky waters – or rather try to, for it has a saline content three times saltier than ocean water and denser than that of the Dead Sea. You'll find yourself literally floating on the surface, feet up. It's long been known for its healing properties, even by the Indians in the eighteenth and nineteenth centuries, who camped on its shores and called it "lake of the healing waters". You can reach the lake from Saskatoon by bus (Mon, Wed & Fri 5.15pm), which stops in the town of Watrous, 6km south of the lake. From there you can get to tiny **Manitou Beach** on the south shore, where there's the largest and one of the oldest mineral **spas** in Canada (☎946-2233 or 1-800-667-7672; ②–④). For $6.50 per swim, or $9.75 for a whole day, you can relax in their mineral pools, reputedly good for rheumatic and arthritic pains.

Eating, drinking and entertainment

Saskatoon has a useful assortment of **restaurants** clustered in and around the downtown core and along the first couple of blocks of **Broadway Avenue**, which lies just across the river via the bridge at 4th Ave South and 19th St East. Broadway is the nearest thing the city has to a "cultural centre", the home of the Broadway Theatre and a handful of vaguely "alternative" shops and cafés. While you're in town, try a bottle of **Great Western Beer** (especially the Brewhouse brand), the product of a local factory whose future was threatened by the merger of two of Canada's giant brewing companies, Molson and Carling O'Keefe. The workers bought the factory themselves and can barely keep up with demand. It's also customary, while in town, to try a slice of **Saskatoon berry pie**, made with a local berry that has a taste similar to that of a blueberry.

Snack bars and restaurants

Amigos Cantina, 632 10th St East. Mexican specialities with a background of live music. Closed Sun.

The Berry Barn, 830 Valley Rd, 11km southwest of town (☎382-7036). It's worth the journey to sample the home-made soups, waffles and pies that are made on this huge berry farm. Late May to Sept daily 10am–9pm; Oct–Dec Mon–Thurs 10am–5pm, Fri–Sun 10am–9pm.

Broadway Café, 814 Broadway Ave. Wholesome meals from $7–8.

Café Browse, 269b 3rd Ave South. Vaguely alternative place where you can read their newspapers and books in a "library" setting while eating their tempting cakes and pies and drinking fruit and herbal teas.

The Cage, 120 2nd Ave North. Known for its mammoth breakfasts. Open 24hr; closed Sun.

Calories Bakery & Restaurant, 721 Broadway Ave. An atmospheric French-style bistro, with main courses around $8.

Cousin Nik's, 1110 Grosvenor Ave (☎374-2020). Main courses from $14 with especially good pork dishes, plus live entertainment Thursday to Saturday. Reservations recommended.

Earl's, 610 2nd Ave North and Queen Street. Trendy place with an imaginative menu; vegetarian and other dishes between $5 and $15.

Grainfields Pancake and Waffle House, 20th St West at Avenue P. Huge, mouthwatering selections of pancakes, waffles with a multitude of toppings.

John's Cookie & Sandwich Bar, 133 21st St East. Good for sandwiches and hamburgers from about $6. Closed Sat & Sun.

John's Prime Rib and Steakhouse, 401 21st St East. Probably the best steaks in town – done any way you want them. Closed Sun.

The Keg, 301 Ontario Ave North. Popular chain serving standard steak and seafood dishes for between $10 and $20.

La Curry Place, 727 22nd St West. To satisfy your curry, tikka and tandoori cravings. Closed Mon.

Lo-Fat Lloyd's, 129 3rd Ave North. A fast-food takeaway where all items have less than thirty percent calories from fat. An oddity, but the food is surprisingly tasty. No dish over $4.

Morley's, Westgate Plaza, 2410 22nd St West. Gourmet burgers from $4. Breakfast served to 2pm.

Nino's, 801 Broadway Ave. Cosy place with filling pizzas and Greek dishes from as little as $8.

Saigon II, 96 33rd St East. Cheap and filling Vietnamese and Chinese food.

Saskatoon Station Place, corner of Idylwyld Drive and 23rd Street. Eat in Pullman cars in a converted train station. Great Sunday brunches.

Tomas Cook, 5–305 Idylwyld Drive North. A wide variety of weekly specials including filling portions of steaks, ribs (their Greek ribs are best) and chicken from $10.

Bars and clubs

The Artful Dodger, in the Army and Navy Mall, 119 4th Ave South. English pub with occasional live music. Closed Sun.

The Bassment, 245 3rd Ave South. Live jazz Saturday night. Open Sept–June only Sat.

The Black Duck Freehouse, 154 2nd Ave South. Biggest selection of Scotch and beer in Saskatchewan.

Buds, 817 Broadway Ave. Rough-and-ready bar with nightly R&B acts, plus jam sessions Saturday afternoon. $3–5 cover charge.

Cheers Brew Pub, 2105 8th St East. Beer brewed on the premises and large portions of ribs and Cajun food for about $10.

Long Branch, in the *Sands Hotel*, 806 Idylwyld Drive North. A large, noisy C&W nightspot. Lots of tassels, sequins and stetsons. Thursday to Saturday $1 cover charge.

Sharkey's, 302 Pacific Ave. Hot subterranean dance club with different music on different nights. Friday and Saturday $2 cover charge after 9pm. Closed Sun.

Film, theatre and classical music

The Broadway Theatre, 715 Broadway Ave (☎652-6556), has the best of foreign and domestic **films**, while the Midtown Plaza Cinema, 1st Ave South and 21st St East, has mainstream releases. For **theatre**, the Persephone, 2802 Rusholme Rd (☎384-7727), is the best known of the city's professional companies, with performances featuring mostly modern plays; their season runs from October to May. The Twenty-Fifth Street Theatre Centre, 420 Duchess St (☎664-2239), performs more occasionally and concentrates on local work. Visiting ballet, theatre and opera stars appear at the Saskatoon Centennial Auditorium, 35 22nd St East (☎938-7800).

Festivals

Saskatoon's biggest and best shindig is the **SaskTel Saskatchewan Jazz Festival** in the last week in June or first week in July; over five hundred musicians perform jazz, gospel and blues across the city, mostly for free (call ☎652-1421 or 1-800-638-1211 for tickets and information). The **Shakespeare on the Saskatchewan Festival**, where the bard's plays are performed in tents on the river bank by the Mendel Art Gallery, is held on various days from early July to mid-August; call ☎653-2300 for tickets and information. The Twenty-Fifth Street Theatre Company organizes **The Saskatoon International Fringe Festival**, a week of alternative performances held at the end of July and the beginning of August, featuring some fifty theatre groups from all over the world, performing on stages dotted along Broadway Avenue; tickets are all under $8 (☎664-2239). **Folkfest**, a large ethnic festival held in mid-August at various venues around the city, rounds out the summer's activities (☎931-0100 for information).

Listings

Airlines Air Canada (reservations ☎652-4181, arrivals and departures 244-1337; 1-800-361-5373); Air Sask (☎1-800-665-7275); Athabaska Airways (☎665-2700 or 1-800-667-9356) serves Saskatchewan and southern Manitoba; Canadian Regional Airlines, at the airport (reservations ☎665-7688; for arrivals 664-1180; departures 1-800-665-1177); Northwest (☎1-800-225-2525).

Bike rental Bike Doctor, 623 Main St; also from the *Ramada* and *Bessborough* hotels.

Buses Greyhound and the Saskatchewan Transportation Company (both ☎933-8000).

Car rental Avis, 2130 Airport Drive (☎652-3434); Dollar Rent-a-Car, 2130 Airport Drive (☎244-8000); Thrifty, 471 Circle Place (☎664-7740); Tilden, 321 21st St East (☎652-3355), 2–625 Airport Drive (☎665-7703) and 2301 Ave C North (☎664-8771).

Hospitals City Hospital, 701 Queen St (☎655-8000); St Paul's, 1702 20th St West (☎665-5000).

Laundries Broadway Laundromat, 835b Broadway Ave at Main Street (daily 8am–9pm); The Idylwyld, 1715 Idylwyld Drive North (daily: Mon–Fri 8am–10pm, Sat & Sun 9am–9pm).

Left luggage Coin-operated machines at the bus station.

Police 130 4th Ave North (☎975-8300).

Post office Main post office at 202 4th Ave North.

Royal Canadian Mounted Police ☎975-5173.

Taxis Radio Cabs (☎242-1221); United Cabs (☎652-2222).

Train enquiries ☎384-5665 (arrivals and departures) or 1-800-561-8630 (reservations).

Weather ☎975-4266.

Central Saskatchewan

North of Saskatoon you have a choice of two routes. Following the Yellowhead northwest towards Edmonton, you'll come to the **Battlefords**, consisting of grimy and impoverished **North Battleford** and, on the opposite bank of the North Saskatchewan River, the trim riverside streets and refurbished Mountie stockade of **Battleford**. Due north of Saskatoon, the road shadows the South Saskatchewan River on its way to the town of Prince Albert, a distance of 140km, passing the **Batoche National Historic Site**, where the Métis rebellion of 1885 reached its disastrous climax (see box on p.502). Further north still, the lakes and wooded hills of **Prince Albert National Park** are among the region's finest, with innumerable canoe and hiking routes into the wilderness. Central Saskatchewan's **public transport** is poor, but there are reasonably regular **buses** between the major towns and a once-daily summertime service to Waskesiu Lake.

Saskatoon to Prince Albert Park

From Saskatoon, Hwy 11 cuts across the narrow slice of prairie that separates the final stretches of the North and South Saskatchewan rivers, before they flow together further to the northeast. There's nothing to see on the road itself, but on the way the briefest of detours will take you to one of the province's more interesting attractions, **Batoche National Historic Site**.

Batoche National Historic Site

The site of the Métis's last stand – and the last place where Canadians fought against Canadians – **Batoche National Historic Site** (daily: mid-May to June & Sept to mid-Oct 9am–5pm; July & Aug 10am–6pm; $4) occupies a splendid site beside the east bank of the South Saskatchewan River, 90km from Saskatoon just off Provincial Hwy 225. At the entrance to the park, a **visitor reception centre** (☎423-6227) has displays on the culture of the Métis and provides a detailed account of the rebellion, supplemented by a glossy brochure and an excellent 45-minute audiovisual presentation combining slides, spoken narration, music and tableaux of realistic mannequins.

Behind the centre, the main footpath leads to a refurbished Catholic church and adjacent rectory, all that's left of the original village. A few minutes' walk away, in the cemetery perched above the river bank, memorials inscribed with the hoary commendation "a credit to his race" contrast with the rough chunk of rock that commemorates Riel's commander-in-chief **Gabriel Dumont**. A stern and ferocious man, Dumont insisted that he be buried standing up, so that he could enjoy a good view of the river.

The church and cemetery are at the centre of the park's **walking trails**, which extend along the river bank in both directions. Roughly 1km to the south, there's a military graveyard, a Métis farmhouse and the remains of some rifle pits; about the same distance to the north, there's the site of the old ferry crossing, more rifle pits and the foundations of several Métis buildings. With a knowledge of the history, the park becomes an extremely evocative spot.

Duck Lake and Fort Carlton

Back on Hwy 11, on the west side of the South Saskatchewan, the tiny farming community of **DUCK LAKE** – many of whose buildings have outdoor murals depicting local history – is home to a **Regional Interpretive Centre** at 5 Anderson Ave (mid-May to mid-Sept daily 10am–5.30pm; $4; ☎467-2057), with displays on Indian, Métis and pioneer society from 1870 to 1905. Prize exhibits include some elaborate Cree costumes; an outfit that belonged to the Sioux chief Little Fox, an adviser to Sitting Bull; and Gabriel Dumont's gold watch, presented to him in New York where he was appearing in Buffalo Bill's Wild West Show.

THE NORTHWEST REBELLION

The 1869–70 Red River rebellion in Manitoba, led by Louis Riel, won significant concessions from the Canadian government but failed to protect the Métis's way of life against the effects of increasing white settlement. Many **Métis** moved west to farm the banks of the **South Saskatchewan**, where the men worked as freighters, traders, horse breeders and translators, acting as intermediaries between the Indians and the Europeans. In itself, the development of these homesteads was a recognition by the Métis that the day of the itinerant buffalo hunter was over. However, when the government surveyors arrived here in 1878, the Métis realized, as they had on the Red River twenty years before, that their claim to the land they farmed was far from secure.

Beginning with the Métis, a general sense of instability spread across the region in the early 1880s, fuelled by Big Bear's and Poundmaker's increasingly restless and hungry **Cree** and by the discontent of the white settlers at the high freight charges levied on their produce. The leaders of the Métis decided to act in June 1884, when they sent a delegation to Montana, where **Louis Riel** was in exile. Convinced that the Métis were God's chosen instrument to purify the human race, and he their Messiah, Riel was easily persuaded to return to Canada, where he spent the winter unsuccessfully petitioning the Ottawa government for confirmation of Métis rights.

In March 1885, Riel and his supporters declared a provisional government at Batoche and demanded the surrender of the nearest Mountie outpost, **Fort Carlton**, just 35km to their west on the North Saskatchewan. The police superintendent refused, and the force he dispatched to re-establish order was badly mauled at **Duck Lake**. When news of the uprising reached Big Bear's Cree, some 300km away, they attacked the local Hudson's Bay Company store and killed its nine occupants in the so-called **Frog Lake Massacre**. Within a couple of weeks, no fewer than three columns of militia were converging on Big Bear's Cree and the meagre Métis forces at Batoche. The total number of casualties – about fifty altogether – does not indicate the full significance of the engagement, which for the Métis marked the end of their independence and influence. Riel's execution in Regina on November 16, 1885 was bitterly denounced in Québec and remains a potent symbol of the deep divide between English- and French-speaking Canada. In Ontario there was a mood of unrepentant triumphalism, the military success – however paltry – stirring a deep patriotic fervour that excluded Métis and Indian alike.

Continuing 26km west along Hwy 212, you'll reach **Fort Carlton Provincial Historic Park** (mid-May to early Sept daily 10am–6pm; $2.50), a reconstruction of a Hudson's Bay Company trading post circa 1860. Founded in 1810, the river-bank station was fortified in successive decades and became an important centre of the fur and pemmican trade, until the demise of the buffalo brought an end to its success. Reduced to a warehouse facility in the early 1880s, the fort was garrisoned by the Mounties during the Northwest Rebellion (see box), but it was finally burnt down and abandoned in 1885.

The **visitors' centre** (☎467-4512) provides a historical introduction to the fort, whose stockade shelters replicas of the clerk's quarters, a sail and harness shop, a fur and provisions store with piles of colourfully striped Hudson's Bay Company blankets and bottles of bright Indian trading beads and a trading shop, where the merchandise included gunpowder – which meant the clerks were forbidden to light a stove here, no matter what the temperature. Just outside the walls of the stockade are three tepees, neatly aligned along a path. Guided **trail walks** are also offered by the centre, which allow you to see the remains of rutted wagon trails made by carts carrying supplies to and from the fort. There's also an on-site **campground** (☎467-4512; mid-May to early Sept). Take care when hiking or camping, as the wooded gullies of the North Saskatchewan River are home to a large number of **black bears**.

Prince Albert

Founded as a Presbyterian mission in 1866, **PRINCE ALBERT** has a thriving timber industry and is a major transport centre, but its a dull spot, its long main drag, **Central Avenue** (Hwy 2), lined with fast-food joints, gas stations and shopping malls. The only conceivable attractions are the **Historical Museum** at River Street and Central Avenue (mid-May to Aug Mon–Sat 10am–6pm, Sun 10am–9pm; $1), given over chiefly to the area's first farmers and loggers, and the **Museum of Police and Corrections**, 3700 2nd Ave West (mid-May to Aug daily 10am–8pm; free), in an old North West Mounted Police guardroom, where the rather sobering displays relate to the history of law enforcement in northern Saskatchewan.

The appeal of the place is that it has the only **bus** to Prince Albert National Park and La Ronge, the service leaving from the **station** at 20 14th St East and Central Avenue daily at 5pm. The **tourist information office** (June–Aug daily 8am–10pm; Sept–May Mon–Fri 8am–5pm; ☎953-4786 or 953-4385), in the south of town beside the police museum, provides free town maps and brochures. You can get to Prince Albert by **bus** direct from Saskatoon each Friday, departing at 4.30pm.

There's no real reason to stay here, but the town has several central **hotels**, including the *Avenue Motor Hotel*, 1015 Central Ave (☎763-6411; ①–②), whose rooms are grim and basic; the better *Marlboro Inn*, 67 13th St East (☎763-2643 or 1-800-661-7666; ②–④); and the *Prince Albert Inn*, 3680 2nd Ave West (☎922-5000 or 1-800-922-5855; ②) – although the latter can be noisy, as there's a nightclub on the premises. At the south end of Hwy 2 there's the comfortable *Coronet Motor Inn* (☎764-6441; ②). For **campers**, the *Mary Nisbit Campground* (☎953-4800 or 953-4880; $13–15; mid-May to mid-Sept) is situated about 2km north of town, on the other side of the river, beside Hwy 2.

There's not much choice for good **eating** places, but *Amy's on Second*, 2990 2nd Ave West, has three-course lunches from $15, and serves local fish such as pickerel, and *WK Kitchen*, 2840 2nd Ave West, dishes up big Chinese buffets at reasonable prices.

Prince Albert National Park and Waskesiu

Some 230km north of Saskatoon, **Prince Albert National Park** is a great tract of wilderness where the aspen parkland of the south meets the boreal forest of the north, a transitional landscape that incorporates a host of rivers and creeks, dozens of deep lakes, pockets of pasture and areas of spruce bog. The shift in vegetation is mirrored by the wildlife, with prairie species such as coyote and wild bison giving way to black bear, moose, wolf, caribou, osprey and eagle further north. There's an entry fee of $4 to the park, with a variety of reductions and special prices for groups and at weekends.

The tourist village of **WASKESIU**, approached from the south by Hwy 263 and from the east by Hwys 2 and 264, is the only settlement in the park. Spread out along the southern shore of Waskesiu Lake, it has all the usual facilities, a narrow sandy beach that gets ridiculously overcrowded in summer, and the park's **nature centre**, on Lakeview Drive (late June to Aug daily 10am–5pm), which has a new, hands-on display on the region's habitats. In the centre of Waskesiu, at the junction of Lakeview Drive and Waskesiu Drive, the park's main **information office** (mid-May to Aug daily 8am–10pm; Sept to mid-Oct daily 8am–5pm; mid-Oct to mid-May Mon–Sat 8am–4pm; ☎663-4522) gives advice on wildlife and the condition of the hiking trails, along with weather forecasts – particularly important if you intend to use one of the canoe routes. The information office also runs a programme of **guided walks** in July and August and issues camping permits ($3), which allow visitors to use the primitive, seasonal **campgrounds** dotted along most of the more substantial trails. Neo-Watin Marine runs **boat** trips on the lake (July to mid-Sept daily 1pm, 3pm, 5pm & 7pm; 1hr; $8; ☎663-5253). Whatever you do in the park, remember to take insect repellent.

Several of the park's easier **hiking trails** begin in or near Waskesiu, most notably the thirteen-kilometre Kingfisher Trail, which loops through the forest just to the west of the resort. However, the best trails and **canoe routes** begin roughly 15km further north at the bottom end of Kingsmere Lake, accessible by boat or car from Waskesiu. They include a delightful week-long canoe trip that skirts the west shore of Kingsmere Lake before heading through a series of remote lakes amidst dense boreal forest. There's also a twenty-kilometre hike or canoe paddle to **Grey Owl's Cabin** (May–Sept), situated beside tiny Ajawaan Lake, near the northern shore of Kingsmere Lake. Grey Owl (see p.170) lived in this cabin from 1931 until 1937, the year before his death, and it was here that he wrote one of his better books, *Pilgrims of the Wild*. For further information on the trip to the cabin, and on other canoe routes in the park, call the park information office, or the offices of the Saskatchewan Canoe Association (☎653-5568).

Connected by bus to La Ronge to the north and Prince Albert to the south, Waskesiu's **bus stop** is right in the centre, beside a **tourist kiosk** (mid-May to Aug), which provides free maps of the town. Waskesiu's main street, Waskesiu Drive, runs roughly parallel to and just south of the lake, its western section curving round behind Lakeview Drive. Almost all the **hotels** and **motels** are on or near these two streets, including the *Lakeview Hotel*, Lakeview Drive (☎663-5311; ③); *MacKenzie Inn*, Waskesiu Drive (☎663-5377; ②–③); *Skyline Motel & Cedar Village*, Waskesiu Drive (☎663-5461 or 763-1112; ②–⑥); and the *All Season Waskesiu Lake Lodge*, Lakeview Drive (☎663-6161; ④–⑤). **Bungalow** and **cabin** accommodation tends to be block-booked from May to mid-October, but you could try the *Armstrong Hillcrest Cabins*, corner of Lakeview Drive and Willow Street (☎663-5481 or 922-2599; ②–⑤; May to mid-Oct), or *Baker's Bungalows*, Waskesiu Drive (☎663-5211 or 763-2198; mid-May to mid-Sept; ②–④). *Kapasiwin Bungalows* (☎663-5225 or 975-0627; ③–④; May to mid-Oct;), 2km round the lake to the east of the resort, has cabins which form a quiet mini-resort with its own private beach. Waskesiu has two **campgrounds**: the centrally situated *Waskesiu Trailer Park* (mid-May to Sept; $18), and *Beaver Glen* ($13–16; mid-May to Sept), just to the east of the centre. The basic, unserviced *Kingsmere Lake Campgrounds* (permit necessary from park office; May–Oct; $3) is near Grey Owl's Cabin. For reservations at all campgrounds, call ☎1-800-333-7267.

There are several cheap **restaurants** and **snack bars** in the centre, including the *Park Centre Café* opposite the information office, the neighbouring *Mike's Place*, and *Pizza Pete's* at 829 Lakeview Drive. For more expensive dining, try the restaurant of the *Hawood Inn*, 851 Lakeview Drive, where main courses start at around $15.

Waskesiu's stores sell a full range of outback **equipment**, but no one rents out camping gear. **Boat rentals** are available at the marina, a five-minute drive from the village.

The Battlefords and westward

Roughly 150km northwest of Saskatoon, the twin townships of **NORTH BATTLEFORD** and **BATTLEFORD** face each other across the wide valley of the North Saskatchewan River; the former a rough-and-ready industrial settlement, the latter a more sedate little place. From the middle of the eighteenth century, this stretch of the North Saskatchewan River near today's Battlefords formed a natural boundary between the **Blackfeet** to the south and the **Cree** to the north. These two groups were temporary trading partners, the Cree and their Ojibwa allies controlling the flow of European goods, the Blackfeet providing the horses. However, with the arrival of white traders at the start of the nineteenth century, the Blackfeet developed a flourishing trade direct with the Europeans, and by 1870 the Cree and Blackfeet were waging war across the entire length of their frontier, from the Missouri River to Fort Edmonton.

In the 1870s, apprehensive after the Cypress Hills Massacre and the arrival of Sitting Bull and his warriors (see box on p.492), the government speeded its policy of containment and control, determined to push the Plains Indians into reservations and

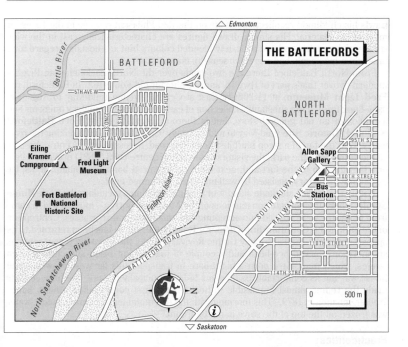

thereby open the area for European settlers. Their chosen instrument was the North West Mounted Police, who in 1876 established a post at Battleford, which then became the regional capital.

With the virtual extinction of the buffalo herds in the late 1870s, the Plains Indians began to starve and Lieutenant-Governor Dewdney used his control of emergency rations to force recalcitrant Indians onto the reservations. Several bands of Cree resisted the process, fighting a series of skirmishes at the same time as the Métis rebellion in Batoche, but by the mid-1880s their independence was over. Meanwhile, Battleford had lost its pre-eminence when the Canadian Pacific Railway routed its transcontinental line through Regina, which became the new capital in 1883. Twenty years later, its prospects were further damaged by the Canadian Northern Railway, which laid its tracks on the other side of the river, creating the rival town of North Battleford. Since then, Battleford has stagnated and shrunk, while its rival has become a moderately successful industrial and distribution centre, with a population of around fourteen thousand.

The townships

Situated on the east side of the river valley, North Battleford's downtown core is arranged into streets running north–south and avenues running west–east, forming a central gridiron that intersects with Railway Avenue, which runs southeast to northwest. Across the river, some 5km away, Battleford sprawls next to Hwy 4, its streets running from west to east and avenues from north to south.

The old municipal library in the centre of **North Battleford**, at 1091 100th St at 11th Avenue, now houses the **Allen Sapp Gallery** (May–Aug daily 1–5pm; Sept–April Wed–Sun same hours; free), showcase for the work of Allen Sapp, a local Cree who is often in attendance dressed in flamboyant cowboy boots, a wide-brimmed stetson and long braids. Perhaps the best known of Canada's contemporary native artists, Sapp trawls his childhood recollections of life on the Red Pheasant reserve in the 1930s for most of his material. His simply drawn figures are characteristically cast in the wide spaces of the prairies, whose delicately blended colours hint at a nostalgic regard for a time when his people had a greater sense of community.

From North Battleford there are two roads over the North Saskatchewan River: a modern flyover that's part of Hwy 16, and the shorter old Route 16A. In Battleford, the **Fred Light Museum**, at 11 20th St East at Central Avenue (mid-May to Aug daily 9am–8pm; free), has a substantial collection of early firearms and military uniforms and a replica of an old general store, but is thoroughly upstaged by **Fort Battleford National Historic Site** (mid-May to mid-Oct daily 9am–5pm; $3), overlooking the river valley from the top of a steep bluff just down the road, accessed from Central Avenue. At the entrance to the park, the visitors' information centre (☎937-2621) provides a general introduction to the fort and, next door, the restored barracks contains a display explaining its history, assisted by well-informed, costumed guides.

Within the replica stockade stand four original buildings, including the **Sick Horse Stable**, where the delicate constitutions of the Mounties' horses – most of which came from Ontario – were coaxed into accepting the unfamiliar prairie grasses. Centrepiece of the park is the **Commanding Officer's Residence**, which has been returned to its appearance in the 1880s. Broadly Gothic Revival in style, the hewn-log house contains an enormous carved bed-head and a couple of magnificent black and chrome oven ranges, which must have been a nightmare to transport this far west. However, the house was not as comfortable as it seems today, principally because the high ceilings made the rooms almost impossible to heat. As the first commanding officer, James Walker, moaned in 1879, "This morning with the thermometer 37 degrees below, water was frozen on the top of the stove in my bedroom."

Practicalities

All long-distance and local bus services use **North Battleford bus station**, located on the edge of the town centre at 75 East Railway Ave; there's a daily service leaving Saskatoon for North Battleford at 5.15pm (4.30pm on Sat). The **Tourist Information Centre** (June–Aug daily 8am–8pm; ☎445-6226) is on the outskirts 2km away, at the junction of Hwys 16 and 40 East, and there's also one (same hours; ☎445-2000) in Battleford, at the junction of Hwys 4 and 40. City buses connect the two towns, and there's also one **taxi** firm, Crown Cab (☎445-8155), which charges about $10 for the trip from the bus station to Fort Battleford.

Most of **North Battleford's** central **hotels** are dispiriting, the haunt of the drunk and the dispossessed. Better alternatives include the *Beaver Brook Lodge Motel*, Hwy 16 bypass (☎445-7747; ②), with reasonably comfortable rooms, and the pleasant *Tropical Inn*, on Hwy 16 (☎446-4700 or 1-800-219-5244; ②–④), about 1km east along the Yellowhead from the bus station. North Battleford is short on good **restaurants** – and none would win any culinary awards – but there are several cheap and central places with filling menus. Try the *Dragon Palace*, 1292 101st St at 13th Avenue, where simple Chinese dishes start at $6; the *Bonanza Steak House*, 11906 Railway Ave East, which has an all-you-can-eat buffet; or *O'Grady's*, 2491 99th St, serving up standard steak-and-rib fare. Alternatively, *Smitty's Family Restaurant*, just outside the town centre in the *Tropical Inn*, has good, basic dishes from $8, and *Da Vinci's*, also in the *Inn*, features some Saskatchewan specialities on its menu.

Battleford has just one **motel**, the popular *Five Star*, 322 22nd St West (☎937-2651; ①–③), with simple, clean air-conditioned rooms, plus large family units with kitchenettes. The town also has a splendid **campground** – the *Eiling Kramer Campground* (☎937-6212 or 937-6216; $10–12; mid-May to Aug) – overlooking the river valley from beside Fort Battleford. For **food**, *Pennydale Junction*, in a converted 1908 CN train station at 92 22nd St and Main Street, has great seafood, pizzas and steaks from $10.

The **Saskatchewan Handcraft Festival**, held in the town each mid-July, is one of the largest and best for crafts in the province.

On from the Battlefords: Lloydminster

Some 140km northwest of the Battlefords you hit the Alberta–Saskatchewan border, and the drab city of **LLOYDMINSTER**, which was founded in 1903 by a group of two thousand British pioneers known as the Barr colonists. A major attraction is the **Barr Colony Heritage Cultural Centre**, located beside the Yellowhead at 44th Street and 45th Avenue (mid-May to early Sept daily 10am–8pm; early Sept to mid-May Wed–Fri noon–5pm, Sat & Sun 1–5pm; $2.75), and even this is scarcely pulse-racing – a small display on the founders, together with a couple of art galleries and a wildlife exhibition. Perhaps the most interesting aspect of the city is its **geographical location**: the 4th Meridian runs right down 50th Avenue, the main street. Thirty-metre-high metal border markers, shaped like the survey stakes used by the original surveyors when they laid out the border between the two provinces, line Hwy 16 on the north and south sides, and smaller markers line the main street.

Yet Lloydminster is a popular town for a break in the journey, and has lots of **hotels** and **motels** along its two main streets, 44th Street (the Yellowhead) and 50th Avenue (Hwy 17). The pick of these are the *Cedar Inn Motel*, 4526 44th St (☎306/825-6155; ①); the *Imperial 400 Motel*, 4320 44th St (☎306/825-4400 or 1-800-781-2268; ③); the *West Harvest Inn*, 5620 44th St (☎403/875-6113 or 1-800-661-7221; ③); and the *Wayside Inn*, a sprawling complex just west of the city on Hwy 16 on the Alberta side (☎403/875-4404 or 1-800-658-4404; ③). For **camping**, *Weaver Park Campground* (☎306/825-3726, 825-6184 or 1-800-825-3726; mid-April to Oct), next door to the heritage centre, has sites from $11 and a full range of facilities, including showers and a playground. There are limited options if you're **eating** out, but the less mundane establishments are *David's Steak House*, 5501 44th St; *Grainfield's*, in the *West Harvest Inn*, 5620 44th St; or any of the pizza chains around town.

The Lloydminster Tourism and Convention Authority has a **tourist office** at 5001 50th Ave (Mon–Fri 8am–5pm; ☎403/875-9013 or 1-800-825-6180). Both Tourism Saskatchewan and Alberta Tourism run seasonal **visitor reception centres** on either side of the border. The bus station is on the Alberta side at 50th Street and is served by four buses daily from Saskatoon.

Northern Saskatchewan

Stretching from Prince Albert National Park to the border with the Northwest Territories on the 60th parallel, the inhospitable and largely uninhabited expanse of **northern Saskatchewan** accounts for almost half the province. The region divides into two slightly different areas, the marginally richer flora and fauna of the **Interior Plains** lying south of the more spartan landscapes of the **Canadian Shield**, whose naked rock stretches north of a rough curve drawn between La Loche, La Ronge and Flin Flon, on the Manitoba border.

Northern Saskatchewan's shallow soils are unable to support any form of agriculture, and its native peoples, the **Woodland Cree**, have traditionally survived by hunting, trapping and fishing. In recent times, this precarious and nomadic existence has been replaced by a more settled and restricted life on the reservations which are concentrated around **Lake Athabasca** in the extreme northwest corner of the province. Nearly all the other settlements in the north are **mining towns**, the result of the discovery of uranium in the 1950s. The main exception is the tourist-resort-cum-mining-centre of **La Ronge**, situated on the edge of the lakes and forests of **Lac La Ronge Provincial Park**. La Ronge is also near a section of the **Churchill River**,

WILDERNESS CANOEING

Northern Saskatchewan has an abundance of **canoe routes** sprinkled across its thousands of lakes. However, it's important that prospective canoeists come fully prepared both in terms of equipment and knowledge of the proposed route. For independent and experienced wilderness travellers, the **Saskatchewan Parks Department** issues a comprehensive range of free material that includes route descriptions, lists of outfitters, details of campgrounds and information on climate, wildlife and potential hazards. Some park offices also sell detailed local maps. The department has **offices** in a number of towns, but its **headquarters** are at 3211 Albert St, Regina (Mon–Fri 8am–5pm; ☎787-2700). This office also operates a **toll-free advice line** in summer on ☎1-800-66-PARKS. You can also get information on canoe routes and canoe outfitters from the Saskatchewan Outfitter Association (☎763-5434) or the Saskatchewan Canoe Association (☎653-5568).

Saskatchewan has a host of **tour operators** running hunting, fishing and canoe excursions into the north of the province from the middle of May to September. A full list of hunting and fishing outfitters is provided in the *Saskatchewan Fishing and Hunting Guide*, while the *Saskatchewan Vacation Book* lists operators offering canoeing, bird-watching and wildlife-viewing excursions throughout the province. Both books are available through Tourism Saskatchewan (☎787-2300 or 1-800-667-7191) or at most tourist offices.

For a complete range of topographic maps and canoe route charts and booklets, plus secondary road maps, contact the Central Survey and Mapping Office, 2151 Scarth St, Regina, Saskatchewan S4P 3V7 (☎787-2799).

whose remote waters boast some of the north's best canoe routes. Finally, **Clearwater River Provincial Park**, near the Alberta border, provides some of the region's most challenging white-water canoeing.

Although northern Saskatchewan attracts hundreds of hunters, anglers and canoeists throughout the summer, it has an extremely poor public transport system. There's just one really useful **bus**, a daily service connecting Saskatoon, Prince Albert, Waskesiu (mid-May to mid-Sept only) and La Ronge.

La Ronge and around

About 240km north of Prince Albert, readily accessible along Hwy 2/102, the scrawny, straggling resort of **LA RONGE** is sandwiched between the road and the western edge of Lac La Ronge. It was home to an isolated Cree community until the road reached here in 1948. Since then, gold mines and forestry operations have started just to the north of town and the area's lakes and rivers have proved popular with visiting canoeists and anglers.

Falling either side of Boardman Street, the town is fronted by La Ronge Avenue, which runs parallel to the waterfront, the location of the **bus depot**. A few minutes' walk away, in Mistasinihk Place, there's the office of the **Saskatchewan Parks Department** (Mon–Fri 8am–noon & 1–5pm; ☎425-4245 or 1-800-772-4064) and an interpretive centre (same days and hours; ☎425-4350) with exhibits on northern lifestyles, crafts and history. The nearest **visitor reception centre** (mid-May to mid-Sept Mon–Fri 8am–9pm, Sat & Sun 10am–8pm; ☎425-5311) is 2km south of town beside Hwy 2.

A good base for exploring the region, La Ronge has several reasonably priced and central **hotels** and **motels**. These include the *Drifters Motel*, at the entrance to town, beside Hwy 2 (☎425-2224; ②–③); *La Ronge Motor Hotel*, 1120 La Ronge Ave (☎425-2190 or 1-800-332-6735; ②); and the *Harbour Inn*, overlooking the lake at 1327 La Ronge Ave (☎425-3262 or 1-800-667-4097; ③–④). There's a series of **campgrounds** strung along

Hwy 102 north of town, the nearest of which is *Nut Point* (☎425-4234 or 1-800-772-4064; $9–17; mid-May to early Aug), 1km north via La Ronge Avenue. The only places to **eat** that are not run-of-the-mill are the vaguely Greek *Kostas II*, 707 La Ronge Ave, and *Willow's Café*, 322 Husky Ave, which has fairly tasty home-cooking and pastries.

La Ronge is on the western edge of **Lac La Ronge Provincial Park**, which incorporates all 1300 square kilometres of Lac La Ronge and extends north to encompass a number of smaller lakes and a tiny section of the **Churchill River**, once the main Route into the northwest for the voyageurs. The Churchill swerves across the width of the province, from west to east, before heading on into Manitoba, its waterways providing some of the region's longest canoe routes. The parks department in La Ronge (☎425-4245 or 1-800-772-4064) provides a detailed description of the river and its history in their booklet entitled *Saskatchewan's Voyageur Highway: A Canoe Trip*. Less strenuously, these waters are also good for fishing – the walleye, pike and lake trout are delicious.

A number of La Ronge **tour operators** and **outfitters** run and equip fishing and canoeing trips into the park, most of them using its web of lakeside holiday **lodges** and **cabins**; the parks department office has the details. There are also several **campgrounds** along Hwy 102 including the *Missinipe* (☎425-4234 or 1-800-772-4064; $9–17; mid-May to Aug) on Otter Lake, where the Hwy crosses the Churchill River.

North of La Ronge, Hwy 102 deteriorates long before it reaches **MISSINIPE**, 80km away, the home of Horizons Unlimited, Box 1110, La Ronge, Saskatchewan S0J 1L0 (☎635-4420), one of the best wilderness holiday companies. Beyond here, the road joins Route 905, a bumpy 300-kilometre track that leads to the uranium mines around Wollaston Lake.

Clearwater River Provincial Park

Apart from Hwy 2/102, the only other paved road running into the heart of northern Saskatchewan is Hwy 155, which extends as far as the tiny town of **LA LOCHE**, near the Alberta border. From here, a rough, gravel track, Route 955 (the Semchuk Trail), passes through **Clearwater River Provincial Park** before continuing on to the uranium mines of Cluff Lake. The park's main feature is the rugged **Clearwater River Valley**, whose turbulent waters are recommended only to the experienced white-water canoeist – you have to navigate 28 sets of rapids. There's a small and simple free **campground** (☎822-1700; May to mid-Nov) where the river meets the road, but otherwise the nearest accommodation is back in La Loche, 60km to the south. The town has one **motel**, the *Pines Motel* (☎822-2600; ②), located beside the highway, and a parks department office (Mon–Fri 8am–5pm; ☎822-1700). Clearwater Raft Tours, PO Box 2828, Meadow Lake, Saskatchewan S0M 1V0 (☎236-3684 or 1-800-661-7275) offers an exciting five-day white-water rafting adventure, including transportation by float plane, services of a guide, tenting accommodation, fishing and all meals. Call for costs.

Lake Athabasca

A particular favourite of the hook-and-bullet brigade – and in recent years, ecotourists – wild and remote **Lake Athabasca**, close to the 60th parallel, can be reached only by private **float plane**. This is the region's largest lake, and much of its southern shore is protected as the **Athabasca Sand Dunes Provincial Wilderness Park**, the most northerly sand dunes in the world. Several companies organize excursions to the area that include flights, food, accommodation and boat rental; if you can afford $3000–4000 for a six-day trip, try *Athabasca Camps*, Box 7800, Saskatoon (☎653-5490 or 1-800-667-5490), or TourQuest, Box 26038, Regina (☎731-2377). If you want to take an **ecotour** of this remote northern region, Athabasca Eco Expeditions, Box 7800, Saskatoon S7K 4R5 (☎653-5490 or 1-800-667-5490) does one- or two-week summer tours led by Native-Canadian guides who know the area well. Call for costs.

travel details

Trains

Winnipeg to: Brandon (3 weekly; 2hr 20min); Churchill (5 weekly summer, 3 weekly rest of the year; 33hr 30min); Dauphin (3 weekly; 3hr 55min); Edmonton (3 weekly; 14hr 30min); Portage La Prairie (3 weekly; 1hr); Saskatoon (3 weekly; 7hr 20min); Sioux Lookout (3 weekly; 6hr 20min); Sudbury (3 weekly; 24hr 40min); The Pas (3 weekly; 11hr 20min); Toronto (3 weekly; 31hr 40 min); Vancouver (3 weekly; 38hr 35min).

Buses

Prince Albert to: La Ronge (1 daily; 3hr 15min); Waskesiu (mid-May to mid-Sept 1 daily; 1hr 10min).

Regina to: Coronach (1 daily; 4hr 40min); Moose Jaw (3 daily; 1hr); Prince Albert (2 daily; 7hr 10min); Saskatoon (3 daily; 3hr); Swift Current (3 daily; 4hr 15min); Yorkton (5 weekly; 4hr 55min).

Saskatoon to: North Battleford (1 daily; 1hr 30min); Prince Albert (1 daily; 2hr 30min); Yorkton (1 daily; 5hr 5 min).

Winnipeg to: Brandon/Regina/Moose Jaw/ Calgary/Vancouver (3 daily; 3hr/7hr/8hr/17hr/ 32hr);

Gimli (1 daily; 1hr 45min); Grand Beach Provincial Park (1 daily; 1hr 40min); Kenora (4 daily; 2hr 30min); Lac du Bonnet (Mon, Wed, Thurs & Sun 3 daily; 2hr); Portage La Prairie/ Neepawa/Dauphin/Flin Flon/The Pas (1–3 daily; 1hr/2hr 30min/6hr 30min/11hr 30 min/14hr 30min); Rennie/West Hawk Lake (1 daily; 2hr/2hr 30min); Saskatoon/North Battleford/Vancouver (3 daily; 19hr/20hr/30hr); Thunder Bay/Sault Ste Marie/Sudbury/Toronto (3 daily; 14hr/18hr/ 23hr/26hr).

Flights

Regina to: Calgary (7 daily; 1hr 20min); Saskatoon (9 daily; 40min); Toronto (5 daily; 3hr); Vancouver (3 daily; 2hr 30min).

Saskatoon to: Calgary (3 daily; 1hr); Regina (8 daily; 40min); Toronto (5 daily; 4hr); Vancouver (4 daily; 2hr 10min).

Winnipeg to: Calgary (3 daily; 2hr 20min); Churchill (Mon–Fri 2 daily; 3hr 40min); Flin Flon (Mon–Fri 1 daily; 2hr 25min); Regina (4 daily; 1hr 10min); Saskatoon (4 daily; 1hr 20min); The Pas (Mon–Fri 2 daily; 1hr 30min); Toronto (8 daily; 2hr 20min); Vancouver (3 daily; 4hr).

CHAPTER SIX

ALBERTA AND THE ROCKIES

Alberta is Canada at its best. For many people the beauty of the **Canadian Rockies**, which rise with awesome majesty from the rippling prairies, is one of the main reasons for coming to the country. Most visitors confine themselves to the four contiguous national parks – **Banff, Jasper, Yoho** and **Kootenay** – enclaves that straddle the southern portion of the range, a vast area whose boundaries spill over into British Columbia. Two smaller parks, **Glacier** and **Mount Revelstoke**, lie firmly in BC and not, technically, in the Rockies, but scenically and logistically they form part of the same region. Managed with remarkable efficiency and integrity, all the parks are easily accessible segments of a much wider wilderness of peaks and forests that extend from the Canada–US border northwards before merging into the ranges of the Yukon and Alaska.

If you're approaching the Rockies from the east or the States, you have little choice but to spend time in either Edmonton or Calgary, the transport hubs for northern and southern Alberta respectively. Poles apart in feel and appearance, the two cities are locked in an intense rivalry, in which **Calgary** comes out top in almost every respect. Situated on the **Trans-Canada Highway**, less than ninety minutes from Banff National Park, it is more convenient whether you plan to take in Yoho, Kootenay, Glacier or Revelstoke, or push on to southern British Columbia and the west coast. It also has far more going for it in its own right: the weather is kinder, the Calgary Stampede is one of the country's rowdiest festivals, and the vast revenues from the oil and natural gas have been spent to good effect on its downtown skyscrapers and civic infrastructure.

Edmonton is a bleaker city, on the edge of an immense expanse of boreal forest and low hills that stretches to the border of the Northwest Territories and beyond. Bypassed by the Canadian Pacific Railway, which brought Calgary its early boom, Edmonton's main importance to travellers is as a gateway to the Alaska Highway and the Arctic extremities of the Yukon, as well as to the more popular landscapes of northern British Columbia. The **Yellowhead Highway** and Canada's last transcontinental **railway** link Edmonton to the town of Jasper and its national park in about four hours.

ACCOMMODATION PRICE CODES

All the accommodation prices in this book have been coded using the symbols below, corresponding to Canadian dollar rates. Prices are for the least expensive double room in each establishment in high season, excluding special offers. For a full explanation, see p.38 in Basics.

① up to $40	③ $60–80	⑤ $100–125	⑦ $175–240
② $40–60	④ $80–100	⑥ $125–175	⑧ $240+

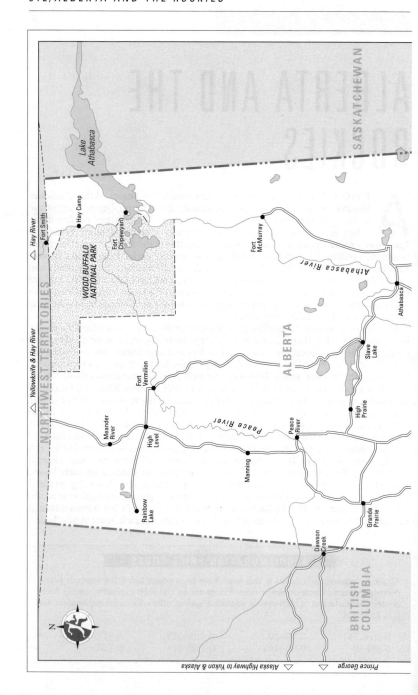

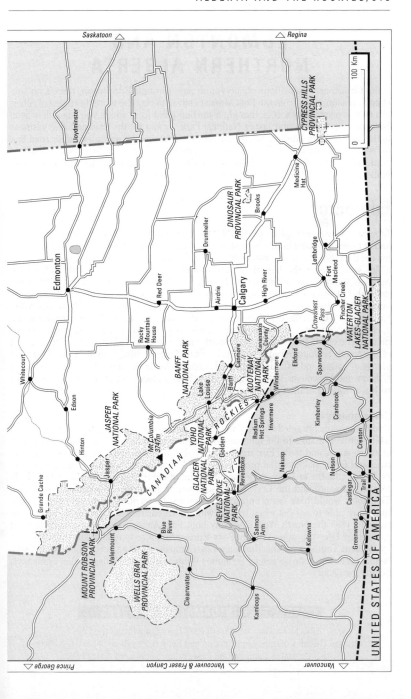

EDMONTON AND
NORTHERN ALBERTA

Unless transport connections oblige you to pass through **Edmonton**, there's no substantial reason, apart from the Folk Music Festival, to visit the more downbeat of Alberta's pair of pivotal cities. It is, though, a starting point from which you can either head west into the Rockies and Jasper National Park, or aim for the unimaginable vastness of the far northern interior. **Northern Alberta** contains the only all-weather road link to Yellowknife, capital of the Northwest Territories, but other than **Wood Buffalo National Park** – the largest protected area in Canada – and a surfeit of fishing possibilities, the region has almost nothing to waylay most casual visitors.

Edmonton

Alberta's provincial capital, **EDMONTON** is among Canada's most northerly cities, and at times – notably in the teeth of its bitter winters – it can seem a little too far north for comfort. Sat above the waters of the North Saskatchewan River, whose park-filled valley winds below the high-rises of downtown, the city tries hard with its festivals, parks, restaurants and urban renewal projects. With a downtown area that still has the unfinished feel of a frontier town, however, it's perhaps appropriate that the premier attraction for seventy percent of visitors is a shopping centre, the infamous **West Edmonton Mall**. This certainly has curiosity value, but not really enough to merit a special journey here. Downtown has a handful of modest sights, though most enjoyment in the city is to be had in **Old Strathcona**, a rejuvenated "historic" district south of the North Saskatchewan River filled with heritage buildings, modest museums and plenty of eating and drinking venues. Edmonton lacks the big set-piece museums of Calgary and Vancouver, but – in the outlying **Space and Science Centre** – has a sight within a whisker of the first rank.

Some history

Edmonton's site attracted Native Canadians for thousands of years before the arrival of white settlers, thanks to the abundance of local **quartzite**, used to make sharp-edged stone weapons and tools. **Fur traders** arrived in the eighteenth century, attracted by river and forest habitats that provided some of Canada's richest fur-producing territory. Better still, the area lay at the meeting point of the territory patrolled by the Blackfoot to the south and the Cree and Assiniboine to the north. Normally these Native Canadians would have been implacable enemies, but around Edmonton's future site they were able to coexist when trading with intermediaries like the North West Company. In 1795 the North West Company built Fort Augustus on Edmonton's present site, joined later the same year by **Fort Edmonton**, a redoubtable log stockade built by William Tomison for the Hudson's Bay Company (and named in fine sycophantic fashion after an estate owned by Sir James Winter Lake, the Hudson's Bay Company's deputy governor).

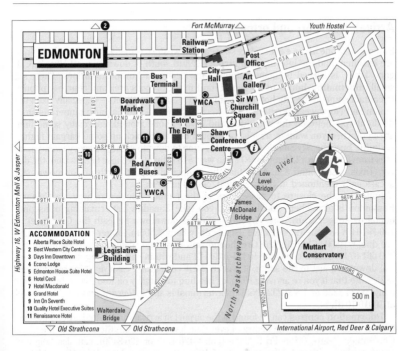

Though the area soon became a major trading district, **settlers** arrived in force only after 1870, when the HBC sold its governing right to the Dominion of Canada. The decline of the fur trade in around 1880 made little impact, as the settlement continued to operate as a staging point for travellers heading north. Worldwide demand for grain also attracted settlers to the region, now able to produce crops despite the poor climate thanks to advances in agricultural technology. Crucially, though, the first trans-Canada railway was pushed through Calgary at Edmonton's expense, and when a spur was built by the Edmonton Railway Company in 1891 it finished south of the town at Strathcona, where a new settlement developed. The city only became firmly established with the Yukon gold rush of 1897, and only then through a scam of tragic duplicity. Prompted by the city's outfitters, newspapers lured prospectors with the promise of an "All Canadian Route" to the gold fields that avoided Alaska and the dreaded Chilkoot Trail (see p.818). In the event, this turned out to be a largely phantom trail across 3000km of intense wilderness. Hundreds of men perished as they pushed north; many of those who survived, or who never set off, ended up settling in Edmonton. World War II saw the city's role reinforced by its strategic position relative to Alaska, while its postwar growth was guaranteed by the **Leduc oil strike** in 1947. By 1956 some 3000 wells were in production within 100km of the city. If Edmonton has achieved any fame since, it has been in the field of **sports**, as the home of Wayne Gretzky, the greatest player in ice-hockey history. Oil money continues to bankroll all sorts of civic improvements, though never quite manages to disguise the city's rather rough-and-ready pioneer roots.

The telephone code for Alberta is ☎403.

Arrival, transport and orientation

Edmonton is one of the easiest places to reach in western Canada. Its road and rail links are excellent and the international **airport**, 29km south of downtown off Hwy 2 (Calgary Trail), is served by many national, American and European airlines. There's a small **information booth** (daily 7am–11pm) in the arrivals area and courtesy phones to contact some of the city hotels. The majority of internal flights – especially from the Yukon and Northwest Territories – fly here in preference to Calgary; numerous shuttle flights ply between the two cities, and if you phone around, especially some time ahead of when you want to travel, you should be able to pick up some bargain flights. A shuttle **bus**, the *Sky Shuttle* (☎465-8515), runs to downtown hotels every twenty minutes from 5.15am to 12.15am, for $11 one way, $18 return; purchase tickets from the driver. Taxis cost around $35. Note that the municipal airport north of downtown, still occasionally mentioned in visitors' blurb, closed in 1996.

Following the closure to passengers of the famous Rockies railway via Calgary, Edmonton is also where you'll arrive if you take Canada's last remaining transcontinental passenger **train**. The VIA Rail station is downtown beneath the CN Tower at 10004-104th Avenue (ticket office usually daily 8am–3.30pm, longer hours when trains are due; ☎1-800-561-8630); the Greyhound **bus terminal** (daily 5.30am–midnight; ☎1-800-661-8747) is also central at 10324-103rd St and within easy walking distance of central downtown just to the south. It has an *A&W* restaurant, cash machine and lockers ($2). Note that if you're arriving from, or heading to Calgary on Red Arrow buses (four daily; ☎424-3339 or 1-800-232-1958) their terminal is at the *Howard Johnson Plaza* hotel at 10010-104th St.

Information centres can be found at the airport in arrivals and dotted around the city, but the most central, on the Pedway Level (one level down from the street) in the Shaw Conference Centre (Mon–Fri 8.30am–4pm; ☎426-4715 or 496-8400), can also help find accommodation. **Travel Alberta**, at 10015-102nd St (summer Mon–Fri 8.15am–4.30pm; ☎427-4321 or 1-800-661-8888), has material on the rest of the province. In Old Strathcona, the restaurant and nightlife district is located south of downtown across the river. Visit the **Caboose Tourist Information Centre** on corner of Whyte Avenue and 103rd Street, adjacent to the Old Strathcona Foundation (summer Wed–Sun 10am–6pm).

The downtown area is easily negotiated on foot. Unless you have a car, longer journeys have to be made using **Edmonton Transit**, an integrated bus and light-rail (LRT) system. Interchangeable tickets for bus and LRT cost $1.35 off-peak and $1.60 during peak times (5–9am & 3–6pm); day passes cost $4.25. Exact money is required to buy tickets on buses. Transfers are available from drivers on boarding for use on other services for ninety minutes. The LRT is free between Grandin and Churchill stations Monday to Friday 9am to 3pm and Saturday 9am to 6pm. Call ☎496-1611 for route and timetable **information** or visit the Customer Services Outlet at Church LRT Station, 99th Street (Mon–Fri 8.30am–4.30pm). For details of taxi companies, see "Listings" on p.524.

Addresses are easy to decipher if you remember that avenues run east–west, with numbers increasing as you travel further north, while streets run north–south, the numbers increasing as you move westwards. Building numbers tend to be tacked onto the end of street numbers, so that 10021-104th Avenue is 21 100th Street, at the intersection with 104th Avenue.

Accommodation

As Edmonton sees fewer tourists than Calgary, its budget **accommodation** is more available but also less salubrious than that of its southern neighbour. There are plenty of reasonably priced beds in the big middle-ranking hotels – especially out of season.

Motels can be found in the bleak outskirts of the city, the main concentrations being along Stony Plain Road (northwest of downtown) and on the Calgary Trail (south). For details of **B&B** lodgings, contact either Edmonton Bed and Breakfast, 13824-110th Ave (☎ 455-2297) or the Gem B&B Reservation Agency, 11216-48th Ave (☎ & fax 434-6098).

Hotels and motels

Alberta Place Suite Hotel, 10049-103rd St (☎423-1565 or 1-800-661-3982, fax 426-6260). Suite or "apartment" hotels provide kitchens and extra facilities, making them good value if you're in town for a few days and aim to self-cater; 86 large and well-equipped suites. Weekly rates available. ③–④.

Best Western City Centre Inn, 11310-109th St (☎479-2042 or 1-800-666-5026, fax 474-2204). Typical property of this reliable mid-priced chain. ④.

Hotel Cecil, 10406-Jasper Ave (☎428-7001). Extremely cheap, central and convenient for the bus terminal, but you're probably taking your life into your hands here. ①.

Days Inn Downtown, 10041-106th St (☎423-1925 or 1-800-267-2191, fax 424-5302). Mid-sized and newly renovated central motel with parking. ③–④.

Econo Lodge, 10209-100th Ave (☎428-6442 or 1-800-613-7043, fax 428-6467). Reliable downtown motel with covered parking, TV, phone and usual facilities. ③–④.

Edmonton House Suite Hotel, 10205-110th Ave (☎420-4000 or 1-800-661-6562, fax 420-40080). Bigger (299 suites) and more expensive than the *Alberta Place*, but rooms have balconies and views; also an indoor pool and a free shuttle to the West Edmonton Mall. ⑤–⑥.

Grand Hotel, 10266-103rd St (☎422-6365, fax 425-9070). Handily located almost next to the bus terminal, this hotel is anything but grand. Clean but knocked about, it's used mainly by long-stay residents; 76 rooms, 26 with private bathroom, the rest with washbasin and possibly toilet. ①.

Inn on Seventh, 10001-107th St (☎429-2861 or 1-800-661-7327, fax 426-7225). Modern, quiet and civilized high-rise, with variously priced rooms; probably the best of the middle-range hotels. ③–⑦.

Hotel Macdonald, 10065-100th St (☎424-5181 or 1-800-441-1414, fax 429-648). One of the big historic "railway" hotels run by Canadian Pacific, and undoubtedly the first choice if you want to stay in Edmonton in traditional style. Some rooms a little small for the price, but lots of facilities including pool and health club. Prices are high, but enquire about weekend and other deals. ⑥–⑦.

Quality Hotel Executive Suites, 10815-Jasper Ave (☎423-1650 or 1-800-463-7666, fax 425-6834). This modern city-centre hotel has 75 low-priced suites and self-catering apartments. ③.

Renaissance Hotel, 10155-105th St (☎423-4811 or 1-800-HOTELS1, fax 423-3204). Edmonton's top-of-the-pile 300-room hotel is worth considering if you want modern facilities rather than the *Macdonald*'s old-world charm. ⑥.

Hostels and student accommodation

Edmonton Youth Hostel, 10422-91st St off Jasper Ave (☎429-0140, fax 421-0131). A friendly 58-bed place a few blocks east of downtown with views south over the city. Women walking here alone at night should take care. Mountain bike rentals. Midnight curfew. Members $13, non-members $18. ①.

St Joseph's College, 114th St and 89th Ave (☎492-7681). Small, cheap and popular student rooms; reservations required in summer. Out of the centre but well served by buses, including the #43. ①.

University of Alberta, 97th Ave between 112th and 114th (☎492-4281). Basic institutional student rooms available in summer. ②.

YMCA, 10030-102nd Ave (☎421-9622). Men and women are welcomed in this clean, sprightly, refurbished building in an excellent downtown location. Simple three-bunk dorms (2 nights maximum), small private singles and doubles are available. ①–②.

YWCA, 10305-100th Ave (☎429-8707). Quiet and pleasant women-only accommodation offering free use of swimming pool and cheap cafeteria (open to all). Dorm bunks and singles are available. ①.

Campgrounds

Androssan Campground. Located 18km east of downtown on Hwy 16; 24 free sites, but no water or facilities other than fire pits.

Half Moon Lake Resort, Sherwood Park (☎922-3045, fax 922-3646). A large private campground with extensive facilities and outdoor activities, 29km east of town on Hwy 14 and then 4km down a signposted sideroad. May to early Oct. $14.

Rainbow Valley Campground, 14340-56th Ave (☎434-5531). The only site within the city limits: 85 sites off the Whitemud Freeway at 119th Street and 45th Avenue in Whitemud Park. It's full by afternoon in summer, so arrive early or be sure to book. Mid-April to mid-Oct. $13.

Shakers Acres Tent and Trailer Park, 21530-103rd Ave (☎447-3564, fax 447-3924). A rather exposed 177-site ground northwest of the city north of Stony Plain Road; exit Hwy 16 at Winterburn Road. March–Nov.

The City

Edmonton feels oddly dispersed, even in the six-block **downtown** area around Sir Winston Churchill Square and along the main east–west drag, **Jasper Avenue** (101st Avenue). Bounded to the south by the North Saskatchewan River, this grid holds a few assorted points of interest, though much of cosmopolitan Edmonton, such as it is, resides south of the river in **Old Strathcona** (see also "Eating and drinking"). For the **West Edmonton Mall** and the **Space and Science Centre**, the city's two big draws, and the more lacklustre **Provincial Museum**, you need to take transport out west. To stretch your legs, wander up and down the big string of parks that protects the river, or cross the Low Level Bridge to the **Muttart Conservatory**, another worthwhile sight consisting of four space-age pyramids filled with flora and natural history displays.

Downtown

Downtown Edmonton only really comes alive as a place to wander on sunny days when office workers pour out for lunch; otherwise it's really not much of a place to linger. However, with time to kill the following low-key sites would keep you occupied. The **Edmonton Art Gallery** (Mon–Wed 10.30am–5pm, Thurs & Fri 10.30am–8pm, Sat, Sun & holidays 11am–5pm; $3, free Thurs 4–8pm; ☎422-6223), part of the Civic Centre on 99th Street and 102nd Avenue on the north edge of Sir Winston Churchill Square, deals mainly in modern Canadian artists, though it also hosts many visiting exhibitions. To get here if you're not already downtown, take the #2 bus or LRT to Churchill station. More satisfyingly offbeat is the **Edmonton Police Museum and Archives** on the third floor of the central police station at 9620-103A Avenue (Mon–Sat 9am–3pm, closed public holidays; free; ☎421-2274), which traces the long arm of Albertan law enforcement from the formation of what would become the RCMP (Royal Canadian Mounted Police) in 1873 to the city's current flatfoots. Marvel at handcuffs, old jail cells, and a stuffed rat that served time as an RCMP mascot.

Walk across the Low Level Bridge to the distinctive glass pyramids of the **Muttart Conservatory** (Mon–Wed & Sun 11am–9pm, Thurs–Sat 11am–6pm; $4.25; ☎496-8755), just south of downtown and the river at 9626-96A Street. Three hi-tech greenhouses reproduce tropical, temperate and arid climates, complete with the trees and plants (and occasional exotic birds) which flourish in them; a fourth houses a potpourri of experimental botanical projects and temporary exhibitions. If you don't want to walk, take **bus** #51 (Capilano) travelling south on 100th Street just south of Jasper Avenue as far as 98th Avenue and 97A Street, then walk one block south.

Finally, you might stop by for a guided tour of the domed sandstone **Alberta Legislative Building** south of Jasper Avenue on 97th Avenue and 107th Street (the nearest LRT station is Grandin). Set in the manner of a medieval cathedral over an ancient shrine, it was built in 1912 on the original site of Fort Edmonton. Topped by a vaulted dome, it's a big city landmark, its interior reflecting the grandiose self-importance of the province's early rulers, who imported wood for their headquarters from as far afield as Belize: the marble came from Québec, Pennsylvania and Italy, the granite from rival British Columbia. Just to the north, amidst 57 acres of parkland that flanks the building, stands the new **Alberta Legislative Assembly Interpretive Centre**, where you can learn more than you probably want to know about Alberta's political history and the building in which much of it took place (Mon–Fri 9am–4.30pm, Sat & Sun noon–5pm; closed Sat Nov–Feb; free tours hourly winter to March 1 Mon–Fri noon-3.30pm, from March 1 Mon–Fri 9am–3.30pm, Sat & Sun noon–5pm; ☎427-2826 for general information on the Legislative Building, ☎427-7362 for tour information and booking).

Old Strathcona

The **Strathcona** district south of the North Saskatchewan River grew up at the end of the nineteenth century, thanks to a decision by the Calgary and Edmonton Railway Company (C&E) to avoid the expense of a bridge across the North Saskatchewan River by concluding a rail spur from Calgary south of the river and Edmonton proper. In 1912, when its population had reached about 7500, the new town was incorporated into the city. Today the streets and many of the older buildings have been spruced up in a manner typical of urban renewal projects – lots of new pavements and fake period street furniture. This said, it's still the city's best-preserved old quarter, and the nicest to wander around on a sunny day. Plenty of buses run here from downtown, or you can walk across the river via the Walterdale or High Level bridges. The best approach is to take the LRT to University station and board buses #8, #43 or #46 to 104th Street and 82nd Avenue and then walk a block south.

The area centres on **Whyte Avenue** (82nd Street) to the south, 109th Street to the west and 103rd to the east. Most of the cafés, restaurants and shops are on or just off Whyte or 103rd, which makes the **Old Strathcona Foundation** office (summer Mon–Fri 8.30am–4.30pm; rest of the year Tues & Wed 8.30am–4.30pm; ☎433-5866), at 401-10324 Whyte Ave, on the corner of these two thoroughfares, a sensible first port of call. Here you can pick up pamphlets detailing walks and drives that take in the area's historic buildings. Just to the north, on 83rd Avenue, is the **Old Strathcona Farmers' Market** (summer Tues noon–5pm, Thurs 4–8pm, Sat 8am–3pm; rest of the year Sat 8am–3pm), a happy hunting ground for picnic supplies and craft goods.

If you tire of wandering or sitting in cafés, you can give a little structure to your exploration by heading for one or more of the area's three small museums. Rail buffs should check out the **C&E Railway Museum**, 10447-86th Ave (summer Tues–Sat 10am–4pm; donation; ☎433-9739), a collection of railway memorabilia, costumes and photos housed in a replica of Strathcona's original 1891 station. Technology freaks might make for the **Telephone Historical Information Centre**, 10437-83rd Ave (Mon–Fri 10am–4pm, Sat noon–4pm; $2; ☎441-2077), a collection of exhibits and displays connected with telecommunications in Edmonton past, present and future housed in Strathcona's original 1912 telephone exchange. It's North America's largest museum of its kind. Finally there's the eccentric little **Old Strathcona Model and Toy Museum**, McKenzie Residence, 8603-104th St (Wed–Sat noon–5pm, Sun 1–5pm, but check latest times; donation; ☎433-4512), supposedly the world's only toy museum where all the exhibits are made from paper, card or kits collected from around the world. The exhibits include a model railway, models of famous boats, historic sites, historical figures and famous buildings.

The Provincial Museum of Alberta

Housed in a drab building well out in the western suburbs at 12845-102nd Ave, the mostly dated displays of the **Provincial Museum of Alberta** (mid-May to early Sept Mon & Wed–Sun 9am–5pm, Tues 9am–9pm; early Sept to mid-May Tues–Sun 9am–5pm; $8, $4 on Tues; ☎453-9100) make a reasonable introduction to the history, culture, flora and fauna of western Canada if Edmonton is your first stop in the region. There's no getting round the fact, though, that Calgary, Victoria and Vancouver all have vastly superior museums on similar themes. To reach it by **bus**, take the #1 (Jasper Place) west on Jasper Avenue downtown, or the #21 (West Jasper Place) west on 102nd Avenue at 102nd Street.

Natural history exhibits include painted dioramas and stuffed animals, taxidermy being the stock in trade of virtually all western Canada's museums; by far the best section concerns the region's bison herds and their virtual extinction. Other displays include a humdrum collection of domestic appliances, a couple of beautiful chrome stoves and vintage jukeboxes and a rundown of the **native peoples** of the province. The latter collection used to be pretty workaday, though the new Aboriginal Peoples Gallery promises better things: hopefully it'll still include the wonderful "Self Torture" section and its harrowing exhibits – the nipple-stretching implements are especially eye-watering.

Fort Edmonton Park

Located southwest of the city on a deep-cut bend of the North Saskatchewan River, the 158-acre **Fort Edmonton Park** (daily mid-May to late June Mon–Fri 10am–4pm, Sat & Sun 10am–6pm; late June to early Sept daily 10am–6pm; $6.75; ☎496-8787) undertakes to re-create the history of white settlement in Edmonton during the nineteenth century. Everything has been built from scratch and, while you can't fault the attention to detail, the pristine woodwork of the supposedly old buildings hardly evokes period authenticity (though the carpentry methods are apparently those used around 1846). To get here take the LRT to University station and there pick up buses #32, #39 or #139 (or take these services from downtown) to Fox Drive, Whitemud Drive and Keillor Road, about ten minutes' walk from the site, which is off the Whitemud Freeway near the Quesnell Bridge.

The heart of the complex is a facsimile of **Fort Edmonton**, a fur-trading post dominated by the Big House, former home of the Chief Factor, John Rowland, head of the (then) ill-defined Saskatchewan District between 1828 and 1854. Arranged around the house are the quarters of the 130 or so people who called the fort home and who are now represented by appropriately dressed guides pretending to be blacksmiths, shopkeepers and schoolteachers from the era. Edmonton's later, pre-railway age is represented by a rendition of Jasper Avenue as it appeared in 1885, while two other streets simulate 1905 and 1920, complete with rides on steam engines and tramcars to bolster the period effect.

Edmonton Space and Science Centre

The splendid **Edmonton Space and Science Centre** opened in Coronation Park, 11211-142nd St, in 1984, since when it's evolved into one of the city's principal attractions (Tues–Sun 10am–10pm, closed Mon except for public holidays; day pass $7 includes Zeidler Star Shows, exhibits and scientific demonstrations or one IMAX film presentation; ☎451-3344 or 452-9100). The complex has two main attractions: the **Margaret Zeidler Star Theatre** (daily 11am–7pm) houses Canada's largest planetarium dome, several galleries and presents different laser and star shows hourly; and the **IMAX Theatre**, housed with a café and shop in the so-called Lower Gallery, is a large-screen cinema with special-format films and laser shows (prices and times vary according to shows). Elsewhere, the Middle Gallery features a range of temporary exhibitions on scientific and technological themes, while the Upper Gallery contains the **Challenger Centre** and its "Astronaut Missions", designed to allow you to make simulated space missions. There are also assorted displays on advanced communications technology, and a selection of the various science demonstrations you can expect to see around the centre throughout the day. Computers are dealt with in the Dow Computer Lab, while budding astronomers can check in to the centre's **Observatory** (weather allowing Fri 8pm–midnight, Sat & Sun 1–5pm & 8pm–midnight). To **get here** on public transport take a #5 (Westmount) bus travelling west on 102nd Avenue or #22 **bus** west along Jasper Avenue to the Westmount Transfer Centre. Once there, either walk two blocks west through Coronation Park or transfer to bus #96.

West Edmonton Mall

"Your Adventure Awaits", announces the brochure to **West Edmonton Mall** (☎444-5200 or 1-800-661-8890), preparing you for a place that gets eleven mentions in the *Guinness Book of Records*, including its main claim to fame as the "largest shopping mall in the world". Built at a total cost of $1.1 billion, the complex extends over the equivalent of 115 American football fields (or 48 city blocks) and boasts more than 800 shops – of which some 110 are restaurants – plus 19 cinemas, and 11 department stores. The mall's effect on Edmonton has been double-edged: it employs 15,000 people but has captured thirty percent of the city's retail business, thus crippling the downtown shopping area, though it has also succeeded, to everyone's surprise, in attracting twenty million visitors a year (or 55,000 a day).

Funnily enough, many of the shops are rather downmarket, though the sheer size of the place is enough to keep you browsing all day. There's almost a queue of superlatives. Its car park is the world's largest, with room for 20,000 cars; it has the world's largest water park (50 million litres of water); it uses enough power to run a town of 50,000 people; and features the world's only indoor bungee jump (jumps from about $60, to $90 if you want the full video and T-shirt package). The world's largest indoor lake (122m long), part of a cluster of attractions known as **Deep Sea Adventure**, contains a full-sized replica of Columbus's *Santa Maria*, and four working submarines – more than are owned by the Canadian navy – offering an underwater trip past some 200 different species of marine life ($12). Other distractions here include dolphin shows, canoe rentals, scuba diving and an underwater aquarium ($2 on its own) laced with the inevitable sharks.

Then there's the world's largest indoor **amusement arcade**, the Galaxyland (day pass $22.95), which features such attractions as the "Drop of Doom", a thirteen-storey "free-fall experience", and the fourteen-storey "Mindbender" triple-loop roller coaster. The latter, it comes as no surprise to learn, is the world's largest indoor roller coaster. The **World Waterpark**, by contrast, is a superb collection of vast swimming pools, immense water slides and wave pools (day pass $22.95, cheaper after 5pm). If you've still any energy, you can also ice-skate on an National Hockey League-size skating rink ($4.50 a session, skate rentals $3). You could round off the day in one of the mall's many **cinemas** or clubs and, if you want to go the whole hog spend the night, in the 354-room **Fantasyland Hotel** (☎444-3000 or 1-800-661-6454; ⑥–⑦) where 118 of the rooms are intricately equipped and decorated to fulfil various assorted fantasies: Roman, Hollywood, Arabian, Victorian Coach, African, Igloo, Canadian Rail and, most intriguing of all, Truck. Cheaper rooms are available without Jacuzzis and mirrored ceilings.

The #10 **bus** goes straight to the mall, heading west out of town along Jasper Avenue west of 101st Street: buses #12 and #115 are also useful. The monster's location, so far as it has an address (it has five different postal codes), is 170th Street and 87th Avenue. Maps are available throughout the main building at information booths, where you can also get **information** and any number of facts and figures. If you get tired, scooters can be rented from about $6 an hour. **Hours** of attractions, bars, restaurants and nightclubs vary, but retail hours are usually Monday to Friday 10am to 9pm, Saturday 10am to 6pm and Sunday noon to 5pm. For more information, call ☎444-5200 or 1-800-661-8890.

Eating and drinking

Few places stand out among Edmonton's 2000-odd **restaurants**, but if you want a bit of nocturnal zip to go with your meal you'd do best to head out to **Old Strathcona**, a vibrant district of café culture, nightlife and alternative arts located along 82nd (Whyte) Avenue between 102nd and 105th streets – any bus marked "University Transit Centre" from 100th Street will get you there. Ethnic options – notably restaurants serving Edmonton's populations of Ukrainian and Eastern European origin – complement the standard steak-and-salmon offerings. Otherwise, the stalls in the Eaton's mall and downtown streetfront snack bars are lively at lunch time, and all the usual fast-food, snack and breakfast options are available, the best of which are the *YWCA* and *YMCA* cafés. **Beer** drinkers should be sure to try the local real ale, Big Rock.

Cafés, snacks and bars

Café La Gare, 10308a-81st Ave. Small tea-and-coffee joint in Old Strathcona; the sort of place where you can read a book or paper for hours. Occasional evening poetry readings.

Grabbajabba, 82nd Avenue and 104th Street. Coffee, cake and the works at this very popular non-smoking café in the heart of Old Strathcona; other outlets around the city.

Hot Pastrami, 1044-108th St. Office-worker favourite for its deli-style food (from 6.30am) and home of the $2.50 breakfast.

Ninth Street Bistro, 9910-109th St. Relaxed and cosy hangout – generous helpings, imaginative soups and good desserts.

Village Café, 11223 Jasper Ave. Good and easy-going place downtown for very cheap breakfasts, lunches, snacks and sandwiches.

Zenari's, Manulife Building, 10180-101 St (☎444-2202). This is a great downtown Italian deli/house-ware shop with a tremendous lunch counter for soups, salads, sandwiches, pasta, pizza and other Italian staples.

Restaurants

Bistro Praha, 10168-100A St (☎424-4218). A good opportunity to sample eastern European cuisine, Edmonton style, is the city's oldest European-style restaurant. Slightly highbrow and expensive, though – better for lunch or late at night.

Da-De-O, 10548A–82nd (Whyte) Ave (☎433-0930). A bright, brash and popular Old Strathcona 1950s-style bistro-diner that claims "loud food and spicy music": this may sound off-putting, but the mostly Cajun food is actually pretty good.

Earl's, 11830 Jasper Ave (☎448-5822). This invariably excellent chain of relaxed and popular mid-range restaurants has no fewer than eight Edmonton outlets serving modern North American cuisine. This branch, known as the *Tin Palace*, is the most central.

Jack' Grill, 5842-111 St (☎434-1113). Probably a tad too south of the city centre unless you have a car, but this is one of the top-rated places in Edmonton for modern, innovative Pacific Rim cuisine.

Mandarin, 11044-82nd Ave (☎433-8494). In a poll for the *Edmonton Journal*, Edmonton's city's leading newspaper, readers voted this the best Chinese restaurant: located on the western side of the Old Strathcona district.

River City Grill, 14218-96th Ave (☎451-0096). This serious bistro, with a regularly changing menu, wins a lot of plaudits for its food, which draws on a wide range of culinary influences from Cajun to Pacific Rim.

The Select, 10018-106th St (☎423-0419). An excellent, intimate place, trendy without being intimidating. Serving fine simple food, it's downtown's best choice for a late-night treat; book ahead.

Silk Hat, 10251 Jasper Ave (☎428-1551). First choice among Edmonton's cheaper restaurants – and also a fine place to knock back a Molson (the brewery's up the road) – this is a city institution whose dim, diner interior hasn't altered in forty years. It's best known for the 1950s jukeboxes at each booth, but the inexpensive, basic food is as good as the ambience. However, it's very popular, so book ahead.

Vi's, 9712-111th St (☎482-6402). Housed in an old residence just outside the city centre with great river valley views, an excellent place for a special occasion; book ahead.

Nightlife and entertainment

Edmonton's enthusiastic self-promotion as Canada's "Festival City" may have something to do with its relative shortage of indigenous **nightlife**. There are any number of small-time nightspots, especially in Old Strathcona, putting on live music, but larger clubs capable of attracting big names are thin on the ground. Such big-name acts as do appear – as well as theatre companies, **Alberta Ballet** (☎428-6839), **Edmonton Opera** (☎429-1000) and the **Edmonton Symphony Orchestra** (☎428-1414) – tend to use the University of Alberta's Jubilee Auditorium, 87th Avenue and 114th Street, and the Citadel Theatre, 9828-101A Ave (☎426-4811 or 425-1820): the latter, with five performance spaces, is Canada's largest theatre complex. The season for most of the city's dozen or more theatre companies runs from May to September. For revivals, foreign films and art-house **cinema**, try the old Princess Theatre, 10337-82nd Ave (☎433-0979), or the Metro Cinema in Canada Place, 10136-100th St (☎425-9212).

The best **listings** sources are the free monthlies, *Something Entertaining* and the alternative *Edmonton Bullet*, as well as the entertainment sections of the city's main newspapers, the *Edmonton Journal* and the *Sun*. **Tickets** for most classical music, dance, opera, theatre and other events – including Edmonton Oilers **ice-hockey** games, which are played in the Northlands Coliseum, 118th Avenue and 74th Street – are available from Ticketmaster outlets (☎451-8000) around the city.

Clubs, discos and live music

Blues on Whyte at the *Commercial Hotel*, 10329-82nd Ave (☎439-5058). Widely acknowledged as one of the city's best live music clubs; live bands most nights, with Saturday jam sessions.

Club Malibu, 10310-85th Ave (☎432-7300). Chart-topping disco very popular with the under-25s housed in a converted armoury. Has another club at the West Edmonton Mall.

Chase Nightclub, Scotia Centre (downstairs), 10060 Jasper Ave (☎426-0728). Predictable Top 40 music, but still one of the city's current favourites.

Cook Country Saloon, 8010-103rd St (☎432-2665). Popular, old Strathcona C&W venue that's been cited as Canada's best country nightclub for five years running by the Canadian Country Music Association. Free dance lessons Thurs 7.30pm to 9pm.

Sidetrack Café, 10323-112th St (☎421-1326). Despite its disconcertingly bombed-out surroundings, this is the city's best live music venue and where you're most likely to see hugely varied international and local acts of some standing.

Yardbird Suite, 10203-86th Ave (☎432-0428). Live groups nightly (10pm–2am) in the city's top jazz venue; admission is lower for the Tuesday night jam session. Non-smoking rule enforced on Friday.

Yuk Yuk's, Bourbon St, Entrance 6, West Edmonton Mall (☎481-9857). Assorted comedy acts every night, featuring well-known US and Canadian names. Wednesday is amateur night; Tuesday, hypnotist night.

Festivals

Hardly any area of entertainment goes uncelebrated by a festival at some time of the year in Edmonton, the self-proclaimed "Festival City". One of the few to merit a special pilgrimage here is the **Edmonton Folk Music Festival** (☎488-3378), rated the best in North America by *Rolling Stone*: it's held at Gallagher Park (near the Muttart Conservatory) at the end of the first week in August. Also well regarded are the **Dreamspeakers Festival** (☎439-3456) on the last weekend of May, devoted to the art and culture of Canada's First Peoples; the **International Street Performers Festival** (☎425-5162), which attracts over 1000 street performers in early July; the **International Jazz City Festival** (☎432-7166) at the end of June; and the increasingly popular August **Fringe Festival**, or Fringe Theatre Event (☎448-9000), a ten-day theatrical jamboree that's turned into the largest festival of its kind in North America.

The more contrived and commercial **Klondike Days** (☎471-4653) is less compelling, a blowout that claims to be the continent's largest "outdoor entertainment" but has rather too obviously been cobbled together to steal some of Calgary's Stampede thunder. Held for ten days during July, this popular outing revolves around a re-creation of the 1890s' gold-rush era, with plenty for kids, and events along the lines of the Fun Tub Race and the Hairiest Chest Competition.

Listings

Airlines Air Canada and Air BC (☎423-1222 or 1-800-332-1080); American (☎1-800-433-7300); Canada 3000 (☎890-4592 or 429-3420); Canadian Airlines International (☎421-1414 or 1-800-665-1177); Canadian Airlines Regional (☎452-9444); Delta (☎426-5990, 890-4410 or 1-800-221-1212); NWT Air (☎423-1222 or 1-800-661-0789); Northwest Airlines (☎1-800-225-2525).

Airport information ☎890-8382.

Ambulance ☎911 or 496-3800.

Bike rental River Valley Cycle and Sports, 9701-100A St (☎421-9125); Campus Outdoor Centre, University of Alberta, 116th Street and 87th Avenue (☎492-2767).

Bookshops Greenwood's (☎439-2005) in Strathcona on 82nd Avenue between 103rd and 104th, is one of the city's best; Athabasca Books (☎431-1776) on 105th Street north of 82nd Avenue, is a quality secondhand outlet.

Bus enquiries Greyhound (☎421-4242 or 1-800-661-8747); bus terminal (☎421-4211). Red Arrow: for Calgary, Red Deer and Fort McMurray (☎424-3339 or 1-800-232-1958). Sky Shuttle/Airporter to and from the airport (☎465-8515).

Car rental Avis (☎423-2847 or 1-800-879-2847); Budget (☎448-2000); Hertz (☎423-3431 or 1-800-263-0600); Rent-a-Wreck (☎448-1234 or 1-800-327-0116); Thrifty (☎428-8555 or 1-800-367-2277); Tilden (☎422-6097 or 1-800-387-4747).

Dentist Contact the Alberta Dental Association (☎432-1012).

Directory enquiries Telephone information (☎411).

Emergency ☎911.

Exchange Thomas Cook, ManuLife Place, 10165-102nd St (☎448-3660).

Hospitals Edmonton General Hospital, 1111 Jasper Ave (☎268-9111). Emergency departments at Royal Alexandra Hospital, 10240 Kingsway; Misericordia Health Centre, 16940-87 Ave (☎484-8811); and University of Alberta Hospital, 8440-112 St (☎492-8822).

Library Centennial Library, 7 Sir Winston Churchill Square (Mon–Fri 9am–9pm, Sat 9am–6pm, Sun 1–5pm; ☎496-7000).

Maps and guides Map Town, 10815-100th Ave (Mon–Fri 9am–6pm, Sat 10am–2pm; ☎429-2600); Audrey's, 10702 Jasper Ave (Mon–Fri 9am–9pm, Sat 9.30am–5.30pm, Sun noon–5pm; ☎423-3487).

Outdoor equipment Budget Sports Rentals, 10344-63rd St (☎434-3808); Track and Trail, 10148-82nd, Strathcona (☎432;1707).

Police ☎423-4567, 421-3333 or 945-5330.

Post office 9808-103A Ave (☎495-3100).

Public transport ☎496-1611 for all city transit.

Taxis Alberta Co-op (☎425-8310 or 425-2525); Checker Cabs (☎484-8888); Skyline (☎468-4646); Yellow Cabs (☎462-3456).

Tickets For tickets to most events, call Ticketmaster ☎451-8000.

Time ☎449-4444.

Tourist information ☎496-8400, 1-800-463-4667 or 1-800-661-8888.

Tours Nite Tours (☎453-2134); Royal Tours (☎488-9040).

Train information VIA Rail (☎422-6032 or 1-800-561-8630).

Travel agent Travel Cuts, 12304 Jasper Ave (☎488-8487).

Weather information ☎468-4940.

Northern Alberta

North of Edmonton stretches an all-but-uninhabited landscape of rippling hills, rivers, lakes, lonely farms, open prairie and the unending mantle of the northern forests. Compared to the spectacular mountain scenery to the west, northern Alberta is more akin to the monotony of the central plains of Saskatchewan and Manitoba. Unless you're fishing or boating, or just into sheer untrammelled wilderness, little here is worth detouring for, with the possible exception of the huge **Wood Buffalo National Park** on the border with the Northwest Territories.

The two great north-flowing waterways – the **Peace River** and **Athabasca River** – were the area's traditional arteries, but they have now been superseded by three main roads. The most travelled is **Hwy 16** (the Yellowhead Highway), which runs due west from Edmonton to Jasper and onwards through the Rockies to Prince George and Prince Rupert (both in BC); **Hwy 43–Hwy 2** heads to Grande Prairie and Dawson Creek (BC) – Mile Zero of the Alaska Highway; and **Hwy 43–Hwy 35** (the Mackenzie Highway) bisects northern Alberta and provides its only road link to the Northwest Territories.

Direct long-haul Greyhound **buses** run on all these routes from Edmonton, supplemented by the **VIA Rail** service from Edmonton to Jasper (with connections on to Vancouver or Prince Rupert). Few roads merit travelling for their own sake, particularly for trips to Wood Buffalo National Park or Hay River (NWT). **Flying** can be a valuable time-saving option, but it's going to be very expensive unless you've organized internal flights before coming to Canada (see "Basics", p.30).

Highway 16 towards Jasper

Highway 16, or the Yellowhead Highway, is, as Edmonton's Chamber of Commerce likes to call it, "the other Trans-Canada Highway"; the second and less-travelled transcontinental route and – by comparison to the Calgary–Banff route – a longer and duller way of making for the Rocky Mountain national parks. Jasper lies 357km west of Edmonton on the highway, an easy journey by car, **bus** (4–5 daily; $47) or **train**, whose tracks run parallel to the highway (Tues, Fri & Sun; $81).

Numerous **campgrounds** and **motels** service the road at regular intervals, the main concentrations being at **Edson**, halfway to Jasper, and **Hinton**. Edson's ten or so motels are all much of a muchness if you're breaking your journey, the cheapest being the *Cedars*, 5720-4th Ave (☎723-4436; ②). Two nearby sites provide camping: the *Lions Club Campground* (☎723-3169; $12; May–Sept) on the east side of town, and the *Willmore Recreation Park* (☎723-4401; $10; May–Oct), 6km south on 63rd Street. The **tourist office** is in RCMP Centennial Park, 5433 3rd Ave (summer daily 8am–6pm; rest of the year Mon–Fri 9am–5pm; ☎723-3339). For **food**, try *Ernie O's*, 4320 2nd Ave (☎723-3600), good for breakfast, or the smarter *Mountain Pizza & Steakhouse*, 5102 4th Ave (☎723-3900).

Highway 43–Highway 2 towards Dawson Creek (BC)

Highway 43 out of Edmonton to Grande Prairie, and **Hwy 2** thereafter, ambles through terminally unexceptional towns, hills and prairie scenery on its way west to Dawson Creek (p.813). It's a mind-numbing day's journey by car or **bus** (2 daily; $68): bus connections run via Grande Prairie (2–4 daily; $52), 463km from Edmonton, where you may wash up if you're forced to break your journey.

Failing dismally to live up to its evocative name, **GRANDE PRAIRIE**'s unfocused sprawl is a legacy of having the luxury of unlimited space in which to build (the centre is a little nicer). The **infocentre** is by Bear Creek Reservoir, off the main highway, which bypasses the main part of town. Most of Grande Prairie's many **motels** are on the strip known as Richmond Avenue (100th Avenue), which links the southern part of the highway bypass to downtown. All are vast affairs with bargain prices – the top-of-the-line is the *Golden Inn Hotel*, 11201-100th Ave (☎539-6000 or 1-800-661-7954; ③), and one of the cheapest is the *Lodge Motor Inn*, 10909-100th Ave (☎539-4700 or 1-800-661-7874; ③). For **food**, head for the *Trax Dining Room*, 11001-100th Ave

(☎532-0776), open early until late for breakfast, lunch and dinner. The bus depot is at 9918-121st St (☎539-1111), the Chamber of Commerce for **information** at 10011-103rd Ave (Mon–Fri 8.30am–4.30pm; ☎532-5340).

One of Canada's ultimate **cowboy bars**, incidentally, has to be *Kelly's Bar* in the *Sutherland Inn* at **Clairmont**, immediately north of Grande Prairie. Owned by a Calgary Stampede chuck-wagon champion, it's the sort of place that has saddles for bar stools and serves up shooters in bull-semen collection tubes.

Along Highway 35: Peace River country

Alberta's northern reaches are accessible only from **Hwy 35**, still a route for the adventurous and one which, according to Albertans, shows the real side of the province: a world of redneck homesteads, buffalo burgers, and the sort of genuine C&W bars where strangers on a Friday night meet silent stares but wind up being invited to the hoedown anyway. You'll find such spots more or less everywhere along the route, but very little in the way of motels, garages or campgrounds, so come prepared. The road itself is well kept and straight, allowing healthier progress than on the more serpentine Alaska Highway to the west. Two Greyhound **buses** run daily from Edmonton to Peace River, and one all the way to Hay River (NWT), where you can make connections for Yellowknife and Fort Smith.

Peace River

If you're travelling under your own steam you'll probably have to stay overnight in **PEACE RIVER**, 486km from Edmonton and the starting point of Hwy 35. The largest town in the region, it has three standard **motels**: the *Peace Valley Inn,* 9609-101st St (☎624-2020 or 1-800-661-5897; ②–④), alongside a 24-hour *Smitty's Restaurant,* the central *Crescent Motor Inn*, 9810-98th St (☎624-2586 or 1-800-461-9782; ②), and – probably the best choice – the large *Traveller's Motor Hotel*, on the northern edge of downtown at 9510-100th St (☎624-3621 or 1-800-661-3227; ②–③). There's also the 84-site *Peace River Lion's Club* **campground** with showers (☎624-2120; $12; May–Oct) at Lion's Club Park on the west side of the river. The Greyhound bus depot is downtown at 9801-97th Ave (☎624-1777) – the *Crescent Motor Inn* is two blocks south of here – while the **tourist office** operates out of the log building at 9309-100th St (summer daily 8.30am–4.30pm; ☎624-2044) on the northern edge of the downtown core; the *Peace Valley Inn* and *Traveller's Motor Hotel* are both close by.

Manning

Modern **MANNING**, 50km north of Peace River, is the last sizable community and services centre for another 200km, making its pair of **motels** vital and often very busy as a result. The sixteen-unit *Garden Court* (☎836-3399; ③) has kitchenettes and is smaller and a shade cheaper than the 42-unit *Manning Motor Inn* (☎836-2801; ③). For the tiny nine-site municipal **campground** (☎836-3606; free; May–Sept) on the Notikewin River, turn east at the summer-only **infocentre** (summer daily 9am–5pm; ☎836-3875) on the highway. Camping is also sometimes available on the golf course, north of town ($7–10).

Only a couple of basic campgrounds and the odd windblown store disturb the peace **north of Manning**, though if you're **camping** it's as well to know you can expect the unwelcome nocturnal attention of bears in these parts. Official tenting spots are *Notikewin River* (☎836-2628; $9; May–Sept), a short way off the road at the junction with Hwy 692, 37km north of Manning, and *Twin Lakes Campground* (☎836-2628; $9; May–Sept), another 15km up the road. The latter is close to the *Twin Lakes* **motel** (☎554-1348; ②), whose eight rooms are the only ones available between Manning and High Level.

High Level and beyond

As with all the larger settlements hereabouts, you're only going to stop in **HIGH LEVEL**, 199km north of Manning, if you want a place to bed down. Room rates begin to creep up the further north you go, and most of the town's five **motels** charge around $70. Book ahead, as rooms are often filled with away from home workers. The ritziest are the 75-unit *Four Winds Hotel* (☎926-3736; ③) and the *Our Place Apartment Hotel* (☎926-2556; ③), which has 20 two-bedroom suites with kitchenettes. Then come the *Sunset Motel* (☎926-2272; ②) and *Stardust Motor Inn* (☎926-4222; ②). The best option for **campers** is to splash out for the private facilities of the 40-site *Aspen Ridge Campground* (April–Oct; ☎926-4540; $14), 3km south of the centre on the main road (Hwy 35). The **tourist office** (summer daily 9am–5pm, rest of the year Mon–Fri 9am–5pm; ☎926-4811) is at the southern end of town.

Between High Level, the Alberta/NWT Border (191km) and Hay River (NWT), a string of campgrounds provides the only **accommodation**, and three native hamlets – Meander River, Steen River and Indian Cabins – offer only food and petrol.

Wood Buffalo National Park

Straddling the border between Alberta and the Northwest Territories, **WOOD BUFFALO NATIONAL PARK** covers an area larger than Switzerland, making it Canada's largest national park (45,000 square kilometres) and the world's second-largest protected environment (the largest is in Greenland). Primarily famous as home on the range for the world's largest free-roaming bison herd, it's also the last refuge of the critically endangered whooping crane – first discovered in a remote part of the park as late as 1954 – and the world's only river rookery of rare white pelicans, which usually nest on lakes. It also embraces North America's finest karst (limestone) scenery, classic swaths of boreal forest and rare salt plain habitats.

In addition to the park's 46 species of mammals, including black and grizzly bear and lynx, the Peace–Athabasca river delta in the park's southeast corner boasts 227 species of wildfowl – no fewer than four major migration routes overfly the area. The **whooping cranes**, majestic birds with a 2.4-metre wingspan, numbered just 21 when they were discovered. Today there are over 130, about half the total world population (most of the others are in captivity). They nest far from any human contamination on the park's northern fringes. If its wildlife is spectacular, however, the park's topography, though wild and vast in its extent, is limited to low hills, lakes, grasslands, boreal forest, salt plains and marsh. These drain into the Peace and Athabasca rivers and then into Lake Claire, forming one of the world's largest freshwater deltas in the process. To the casual visitor the landscape is likely to be a disappointment – there are no real "sights" or scenic set pieces to compare with the Rockies – and this is really a park for dedicated naturalists or those who are prepared to spend time (and money) allowing the landscapes under their skin.

The first refuge here was created in 1922 to protect an estimated 1500 **wood buffalo**, a longer-legged, darker and more robust relative of the plains buffalo. At the time they were being hunted to the edge of extinction, much in the manner of the plains bison in the preceding century. Six years later the federal government moved some 6000 plains buffalo to the park from the now nonexistent Buffalo National Park near Wainright, Alberta, when their grazing lands were appropriated for a firing range. Most of the present herd, now down to some 2500 members, is probably a hybrid strain, and has become the subject of considerable controversy (see box, p.529). At present you'll still see plenty at the roadsides, more often than not wallowing in dust to escape the region's ferocious mosquitoes. The presence of the bisons, not to mention that of the cranes and the various rare and unspoiled habitats, saw the park declared a UNESCO World Heritage Site in 1983.

Access and getting around

Most practicalities and **information** regarding the park are available in Fort Smith (see below). **Getting to** the park by road can be a slow business, and is possible only along a 280-kilometre stretch of Hwy 5 from Hay River (NWT) to Fort Smith. Frontier Coachlines, 16-102 Street, Hay River (☎874-2566, fax 874-2388), runs **buses** from Hay River to Fort Smith (3 weekly; $47 one way), with services timed to connect with the daily Greyhound from Edmonton. You can also easily **fly** to Fort Smith on scheduled flights from Edmonton (daily except Sun; from around $350 one way or $360 APEX seven-day return) on Canadian North (☎872-2057 or 1-800-665-1177), Hay River, Yellowknife and Vancouver, as well as on any number of wing-and-a-prayer charter planes.

Unless you're prepared to backpack or fly into the interior, the only reliable **access** to the park proper is along the 150-kilometre stretch of Hwy 5, which runs through the park's northeastern quadrant and provides its only all-weather road. A 298-kilometre summer-only loop branches off Hwy 5, 8km south of Fort Smith, through the park's southeast corner; some stretches of this are impassable after heavy rain, so check conditions with the park centre in Fort Smith (see below). The west leg of the loop leads to three developed **trails** – Salt River (after 15km), Rainbow Lakes (after 20km) and Pine Lake (after 65km), the last with a nearby **campground**. Backwoods camping is allowed anywhere as long as it's at least 1500m from Pine Lake or any road or trail. **Canoeing** is wide open: the Athabasca and Peace river system was once the main route for trade from the south, and still offers limitless paddling options.

The park's most-visited backcountry destination is the meadowland and delta habitat at **Sweetgrass Station**, 12km south of the Peace River. Built in 1954 to cull and vaccinate diseased bison (see box), the area is a prime spot from which to watch bison and admire the wildlife of the Claire Lake region. You can stay in the cabin (bunks) here free of charge, but must first register with the park visitor centre in Fort Smith (see p.530). Drinking water comes from the river and needs to be boiled and treated. To get here you'll need to canoe or hand over around $350 (for two people and their equipment) for air transport courtesy of Loon Air (☎872-3030) or Northwestern Air (☎872-2216). If this is too much, Northwestern Air runs **flights** over the region for around $60 per person.

Fort Smith

Though it's actually just in the Northwest Territories, **FORT SMITH** (population 2500) is the only conceivable base for exploring Wood Buffalo National Park. Virtually the last settlement for several hundred kilometres east and north, the town developed along one of the major water routes to the north. Its site was particularly influenced by the need to avoid a violent set of rapids, an interruption to waterborne transport that required a 25-kilometre portage (a stretch of water where canoes had to be carried on land). The Dene natives' name for the area, not surprisingly, was Thebacha, meaning "along the rapids". In 1872 the Hudson's Bay Company built a post, Fort Fitzgerald, at the rapids' southern end. Two years later Fort Smith was established at their northern limit. In time the settlement became the administrative capital of the NWT (despite being only a kilometre from Alberta), a function it fulfilled until as recently as 1967, the year the Canadian federal government promoted Yellowknife to the role.

The disappearance of government jobs has left its mark on the town, as has the opening of the all-weather road between Hay River and Yellowknife, which captured a lot of the freight that used to pass through the region by boat. Nonetheless it's a reasonable enough base, with a handful of things to see around town before visiting the park or pressing on towards Yellowknife. The **Northern Life Museum**, 110 King St (mid-May to early Sept Mon–Fri 9am–5pm, Sat & Sun 1–5pm), is worth a few minutes to enjoy an excellent collection of traditional artefacts, crafts, fur-trading memorabilia

BUFFALO KILL

Clean-living Canada rarely causes international environmental outrage, but since 1990 the federal government has been at the heart of a long-simmering row with conservationists. Wood Buffalo's herd of wood buffalo (a unique subspecies of the plains buffalo) is partially infected with apparently highly contagious tuberculosis and brucellosis, and government scientists on the Environmental Advisory Board claim the only way to prevent the spread of the diseases to Alberta's valuable beef herds is to kill it off. Scientists opposed to the government plan point out that the herd has been infected for years (since they were brought here 75 years ago in fact), has kept the disease to itself, and has survived by internal regulation and natural balance (animals show no outward signs of the diseases or of suffering). Furthermore there has never been an instance of disease transferring itself to humans. Most locals, who are largely opposed to the cull, argue that killing or inoculating every animal would be a daunting task, given the immensity of the animals' range, and that, if even a few were missed, the whole cull would be fruitless as disease would presumably erupt afresh when the herd regenerated. The last partial cull occurred in 1967, following on from a large-scale slaughter in the 1950s.

The restocking issue has opened another can of worms, for at last count there were just eighteen pure-bred, disease-free wood buffalo kept in captivity, and it is from these that the government intends to restart the herd. Most experts argue that the resultant weak, inbred group would compare badly with the large and long-evolved gene pool of the present herd. Other scientists take a completely different line, maintaining that wood buffalo aren't genetically different from their plains cousins and so it wouldn't matter if they were wiped out.

The dispute quickly became extremely messy, reflecting fundamental changes in Canadian attitudes towards the rival claims of business and the environment in a tough financial climate. Some see the hand of Canada's powerful beef lobby guiding the government's actions, while others view it as part of a move to relax the powerful injunctions protecting Canada's national parks and open the way for economic growth in what are, almost by definition, regions of depression and high unemployment. This has already started, with Alberta's government taking plains buffalo off the protected list and putting it onto restaurant menus by promoting buffalo farming to boost its northern economy.

In the saga's most ironic twist, tuberculosis and brucellosis have turned up in farmed game animals (mainly elk), and a huge increase in game farming has led to an explosion in the very diseases a cull of the wild herds would seek to eradicate. Animals bred in captivity are more susceptible to such diseases, and escaping farmed elk are spreading them to areas far beyond the range of Wood Buffalo's supposed culprits. The federal government appointed a committee of interested parties to review the affair. No action was taken, and in 1995 a five-year Research and Containment programme was instigated to review long-term management; at the time of writing the park's buffalo, now around 2500 in all, are still nibbling contentedly as the debate continues.

and archive photographs. You might also want to glance at the old **Fort Smith Mission Historic Park**, on the corner of Mercredi Avenue and Breynat Street, former home to the region's bishop, who for years took on many of Fort Smith's bureaucratic responsibilities. To have a chance of seeing the area's famous white pelicans, head for the **Slave River Lookout** on Marine Drive, where there's a telescope trained on their nesting site.

Practicalities and activities

The easiest **access** to Fort Smith and the park is by plane, but isn't cheap: the airport is 5km west of town on McDougal Road, while thrice-weekly Frontier Coachlines (☎872-2031, fax 872-4297 in Fort Smith) **buses** run here from Hay River or Yellowknife. If you need a taxi from the airport or around town call Slave River Cabs (☎872-3333), and for **car rental** contact J & M Enterprises, on Portage Avenue (Mon–Sat 8am–6pm; ☎872-2221, fax 872-5111). Fort Smith's summer-only **infocentre** on Portage Road near the corner with McDougal Road (June–Sept daily 10am–10pm; ☎872-2512) supplies information on the town and Wood Buffalo National Park. The **park visitor centre** and headquarters is a short distance west at 126 McDougal Rd (summer Mon–Fri 8.30am–5pm, Sat & Sun 10am–5pm; rest of the year Mon–Fri 8.30am–5pm only; ☎872-7900 or 872-2349). For advance information, write to Wood Buffalo National Park, Box 750 (EG), Fort Smith NT, X0E 0P0 (☎872-7961, Hotline ☎872-7962, fax 872-3910). Excellent **maps and guides** can be obtained from North of 60 Books (☎872-2606, fax 872-4802), just opposite the town infocentre, or by writing to Box 1050, Fort Smith NT, X0E 0P0.

It's essential to prebook **accommodation** in summer. The cheapest of the town's three hotels is the 24-room *Pinecrest Hotel*, 163 McDougal Rd (☎403/872-2320; ③), but it's worth paying a bit more to stay in the *Pelican Rapids Inn* almost across the road at 152 McDougal Rd (☎403/872-2789; ⑤), which has kitchenettes in most of its fifty units. The *Portage Inn*, 72 Portage Rd (☎872-2276; ⑤), has two doubles, five singles and a suite. Lower prices can be found in one of a handful of **B&Bs**: try the three-roomed *Whispering Pines Cottage* (☎872-2628; ④; weekly, monthly and group rates available) or the similarly priced *Thebacha Guest Home* (☎872-2060; ④), which has two doubles and two singles (no smoking and no alcohol). There's a public **campground** alongside the Slave River on the northern edge of town and the *Queen Elizabeth* site 4km east towards the airport.

Most of Fort Smith's stores and its few **restaurants** are clustered in a tiny two-block area of downtown. Many locals make for the *Old Skillet Restaurant* in the *Pinecrest Hotel*; for snacks and light meals, try the *J-Bell Bakery* almost opposite the park information office on the corner of McDougal Road and Portage Avenue.

For most people the best way to see the park and its wildlife is to sign up for **tour**. Fort Smith has plenty of operators: one of the longest-established is Subarctic Wilderness Adventures (☎403/872-2467 or 872-2126), who offer nine-day sub-arctic "Wildlife Explorer" tours in the park and Peace-Athabasca delta region, and twelve- or fourteen-day Arctic/sub-arctic "Wildlife Explorer" tours in Wood Buffalo and the Slave River Rapids area before continuing to the *Bathurst Inlet Lodge* for tundra scenery, musk ox, caribou, birds, wildlife and Inuit culture. They also offer six-hour rafting trips on the Slave River and day bus trips into the park. River Trails North (☎872-2060) and Res Delta Tours (☎394-3141, fax 394-3413) specialize in two- to seven-day river tours on the Slave River delta, as well as a three-day trip from Fort Resolution to Fort Smith.

CALGARY AND SOUTHERN ALBERTA

Perfectly placed where the prairies buckle suddenly into the Rockies, **Calgary** is the obvious focus of **southern Alberta**, and is the best point from which to strike out west into the mountains. Yet, with some of the continent's most awesome mountains practically on its doorstep, it takes some self-restraint to give the city the couple of days it deserves. Within day-tripping distance lie two unexpected gems: the dinosaur exhibits of the **Royal Tyrrell Museum**, near Drumheller in the strange badlands country to the east; and the **Head-Smashed-In Buffalo Jump**, a Native Canadian site in the heart of Alberta's cowboy country to the south. The latter is most easily visited if you're following the southern route of Hwy 3 across the province, as is **Waterton Lakes National Park**, isolated well to the south of the other Canadian Rockies parks.

Calgary

Cities in North America don't come much more glittering than **CALGARY**, a likeable place whose downtown skyscrapers soared almost overnight on the back of an oil boom in the 1970s to turn it into something of a Canadian Dallas. The tight high-rise core is good for wandering, and contains the prestigious **Glenbow Museum**, while the wooden houses of the far-flung suburbs recall the city's pioneering frontier origins. These are further celebrated in the annual **Calgary Stampede**, a hugely popular cowboy carnival in which the whole town – and hordes of tourists – revel in a boots-and-stetson image that's still very much a way of life in the surrounding cattle country. Year-round you can dip into the city's lesser museums and historic sites, or take time out in its scattering of attractive city parks.

Some history

Modern Calgary is one of the West's largest and youngest cities, its 600,000-strong population having grown from almost nothing in barely 125 years. Long before the coming of outsiders, however, the area was the domain of the **Blackfoot**, who ranged over the site of present-day Calgary for several thousand years. More recently – about 300 years ago – they were joined by **Sarcee** and **Stoney**, tribes forced south by war from their northern heartlands. Traces of old campgrounds, buffalo kills and pictographs from all three tribes lie across the region, though these days tribal lands locally are confined to a few reserves.

Whites first began to gather around the confluence of the Bow and Elbow rivers at the end of the eighteenth century. Explorer **David Thompson** wintered here during his peregrinations, while the Palliser expedition spent time nearby en route for the Rockies. Settlers started arriving in force around 1860, when hunters moved into the region from the United States, where their prey, the buffalo, had been hunted to the edge of extinction. Herds still roamed the Alberta grasslands, attracting not only hunters but also **whiskey traders**, who plied their dubious wares among whites and Native Canadians alike. Trouble inevitably followed, leading to the creation of the West's first North West Mounted Police stockade at Fort Macleod (see p.551). Soon after, in 1875, a second fort was built further north to curb the lawlessness of the whiskey traders. A year later it was christened **Fort Calgary**, taking its name from the Scottish birthplace of its assistant commissioner. The word *calgary* is the Gaelic for "clear running water", and it was felt that the ice-clear waters of the Bow and Elbow rivers were reminiscent of the "old country".

By 1883 a station had been built close to the fort, part of the new trans-Canadian **railway**. The township laid out nearby quickly attracted **ranchers** and British gentlemen farmers to its low, hilly bluffs – which are indeed strongly reminiscent of Scottish moors and lowlands – and cemented an enduring Anglo-Saxon cultural bias. Ranchers from the US – where pasture was heavily overgrazed – were further encouraged by an "open grazing" policy across the Alberta grasslands. Despite Calgary's modern-day cowboy life – most notably its famous annual **Stampede** – the Alberta cattle country has been described as more "mild West" than Wild West. Research suggests that there were just three recorded gunfights in the last century, and poorly executed ones at that.

By 1886 fires had wiped out most of the town's temporary wooded and tented buildings, leading to an edict declaring that all new buildings should be constructed in sandstone (for a while Calgary was known as "Sandstone City"). The fires proved no more than a minor historical hiccup and within just nine years of the railway's arrival Calgary achieved official city status, something it had taken rival Edmonton over 100 years to achieve. Edmonton was to have its revenge in 1910, when it was made Alberta's provincial capital.

Cattle and the coming of the railway generated exceptional growth, though the city's rise was nothing compared to the prosperity that followed the discovery of **oil**. The first strike, the famous Dingman's No. 1 Well, took place in 1914 in the nearby Turner Valley. An

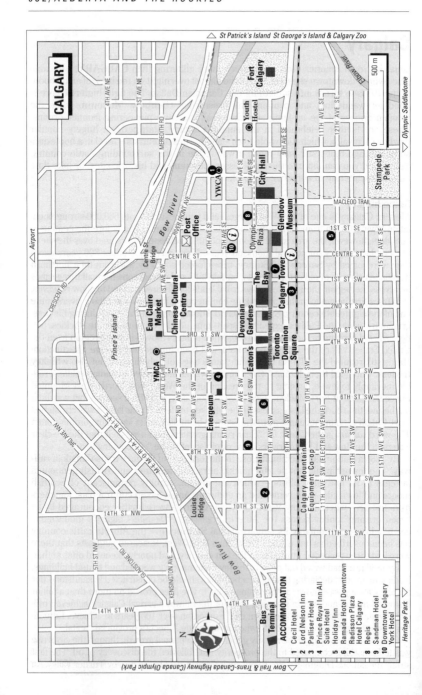

oil refinery opened in 1923, since when Calgary has rarely looked back. In the 25 years after 1950, its population doubled. When oil prices soared during the oil crisis of the 1970s the city exploded, becoming a world energy and financial centre. Calgary became headquarters for some four hundred oil and related businesses, had more American inhabitants than any other Canadian city, and for a while boasted the highest per capita income in Canada.

Falling commodity prices subsequently punctured the city's ballooning economy, but not before the city centre had been virtually rebuilt and acquired improved and oil-financed cultural, civic and other facilities. Better was to come when Calgary attracted the 1988 Winter Olympics, two weeks of much-remembered glory which – like the legacy of its oil and cattle riches – continue to lend the city the air of a brash, self-confident and apparently prospering boom town. Today the optimism is tempered, as elsewhere in Canada, by the notion of **federal disintegration**, much of Alberta and BC – with Calgary at the forefront – declaring their opposition to Québec's separatist ambitions. Much of the West, which still harbours a sense of a new frontier, is increasingly impatient with the "old" East, and happy – if election results are anything to go by – for an increasingly self-sufficient and Western-orientated role.

Arrival

Approaching Calgary **by air** in the right weather you're rewarded with a magnificent view of the Rockies stretching across the western horizon. **Calgary International Airport** (YYC), a modern, often half-deserted strip, is within the city limits about 10km northeast of downtown – a $30 taxi ride. The widely advertised free hotel coaches tend to be elusive, but the reliable **Airporter Bus** (☎531-3909) shuttle into the city departs every thirty minutes and drops at eight downtown hotels: the *Delta Bow, International, Westin, Prince Royal, Ramada, Sandman, Palliser* and *Calgary Plaza* (first bus 6.30am, last bus 11.30pm; $8.50 one way, $15 return). If you're headed for the city bus terminal (see p.534), the nearest drop-off is the *Sandman*: from here, walk south a block to 9th Avenue and turn right (west) and the terminal's a fifteen-minute walk. Buy Airporter **tickets** from one of a bank of bus ticket desks lined up in Arrivals (Level 1) by the exit doors: buses depart from Bay 3 immediately outside the terminal.

Over the last couple of years, **direct services to Banff** and Lake Louise have proliferated, allowing you to jump off the plane, leap into a bus and be in Banff

---

CHINOOKS

Winters in Calgary are occasionally moderated by **chinooks**, sudden warming winds that periodically sweep down from the eastern flanks of the Rockies. Often heralded by a steely cloud band spreading from the mountains over the city, a chinook can raise the temperature by as much as 10°C in a couple of hours and evaporate a foot of snow in a day. Chinooks are the result of a phenomenon that occurs on leeward slopes of mountains all over the world, but nowhere more dramatically than in the plains of southwestern Alberta. The effect has to do with the way prevailing westerly winds are forced to rise over the Rockies, expanding and cooling on the way up and compressing and warming up again on the way back down. On the way up the cooling air, laden with Pacific moisture, becomes saturated – in other words, clouds form – and drops much of its rain and snow on the windward (western) side of the mountains. All this condensation releases latent heat, causing the rising air to cool more slowly than usual; but on the leeward descent the air, now relieved of much of its moisture, warms up at the normal rate. By the time it reaches Calgary it's both drier and warmer than it was to start with.

The name comes from the tribe that traditionally inhabited the area around the mouth of the Columbia River in Washington and Oregon, from where the winds seem to originate; the Chinook tribe also gives us the name of the largest species of Pacific salmon.

National Park in a couple of hours. Brewster Transportation (☎762-6767 or 1-800-661-1152) used to be the only service and is still the only carrier that continues to Jasper (2 daily; $34 to Banff, $39 to Lake Louise, $68 to Jasper). Now they've been joined by Greyhound (3 daily; $20 to Banff, $25 to Lake Louise; ☎260-0877 or 1-800-6618747), Laidlaw (2 daily; $32 to Banff, $37 to Lake Louise) and the Banff Airporter (3 daily; $30 to Banff; 762-3330 or 1-888-449-2901). **Tickets** are available from separate desks adjacent to the Airporter desk in Arrivals. Services leave from Bay 4 outside the terminal.

There's a small **information centre** disguised as a stagecoach (daily 10am–10pm) in Arrivals and another in Departures (6am–midnight). The Arrivals level also offers courtesy phones to hotels and car rental agencies, though most of the hotels are well away from the centre.

Calgary's smart Greyhound **bus terminal** (☎265-9111 or 1-800-661-8747) is comfortable but not terribly convenient. It's located west of downtown at 8th Avenue SW and 850-16th Street, a somewhat uninspiring thirty-minute walk to the city centre. Fortunately free transit buses operate to the C-Train at 7th Avenue SW and 10th Street, the key to the city's central transit system (free from this point through the downtown area). The shuttles leave from Gate 4 within 20 minutes of every bus arrival to the terminal and are announced over the tannoy: keep your ears open. Shuttles return from the same point more or less hourly on the half hour. Alternatively, six-dollar **taxis** for the short run to downtown are plentiful outside the terminal. Left luggage lockers inside the terminal cost $2 for 24hr, $4 for larger lockers. For airport enquiries and bus and rail travel information, see "Listings" (p.545).

If you're arriving **by car**, the Trans-Canada (Hwy 1) passes through the city to the north of downtown. During its spell in the city limits it becomes 16th Avenue. The major north to south road through the city, Highway 2, is rechristened the Deerfoot Trail, while the main route south from the US and Waterton Lakes is known as the Macleod Trail, much of which is a fairly grim strip of malls, motels and fast food joints.

Information and orientation

The main **Visitor Information Services**, part of the Calgary Convention and Visitors Bureau, is on the main floor of the Calgary Tower Centre in the Calgary Tower, 139 Tower Centre, 101-9th Ave SW (daily: mid-May to mid-Sept 8am–8pm; mid-Sept to mid-May 8.30am–5pm; ☎263-8510 in Calgary, ☎1-800-661-1678 elsewhere in North America; recorded information ☎262-2766). It doles out huge amounts of information and provides a free accommodation-finding service. You can also access the bureau on the Internet (*http://www.discoveralberta.com/ATP/*). Minor offices operate at the airport (Arrivals level), the Canada Olympic Park, and on the westbound side of the Trans-Canada Highway between 58th and 62nd St NE. The informative monthly *Where Calgary* is free from shops, hotels and the Visitors Bureau.

For all its rapid expansion, Calgary is a well-planned and straightforward city engineered around an inevitable **grid**. The metropolitan area is divided into **quadrants** (NW, NE, SE and SW) with the Bow River separating north from south, Centre Street–Macleod Trail east from west. Downtown – and virtually everything there is to see and do – is in a small area in or close to the SW quadrant. Streets run north–south, avenues east–west, with numbers increasing as you move out from the centre. As with Edmonton, the last digits of the first number refer to the house number – thus 237-8th Ave SE is on 2nd Street at no. 37, close to the intersection with 8th Avenue. It's easy to overlook the quadrant, so check addresses carefully.

City transport

Almost everything in Calgary, barring Stampede locations and a few minor diversions, is a comfortable walk away – except in winter, when temperatures can make any excursion an ordeal. The city's much-vaunted **Plus 15 Walking System**, a labyrinthine network of enclosed walkways 4.5m above ground, is designed to beat the freeze. It enables you to walk through downtown without setting foot outside, but is too confusing to bother with when the weather's fine.

Calgary's **public transit system** is cheap, clean and efficient, comprising an integrated network of buses and the **C-Train**, the latter a cross between a bus and a train, which is free for its downtown stretch along the length of 7th Avenue SW between 10th Street and City Hall at 3rd St SE. An on-board announcement tells you when the free section is coming to an end. For route information, call ☎276-7801.

Tickets, valid for both buses and C-Train, are available from machines on C-Train stations, shops with a Calgary Transit sticker, and from the main Information and Downtown Sales Centre, also known as the **Calgary Transit Customer Service Centre**, 240-7th Ave SW (Mon–Fri 8.30am–5pm), which also has free schedules and route planners. The one-way adult fare is $1.60 (free for under-6s, $1 for 6–14s); books of five tickets cost $7.25, ten tickets $13.50; day passes $5 adults, $3 children. You can pay on the bus if you have the exact change. Request a transfer from the driver (valid for 90min) if you're changing buses. The sales centre also provides timetables and an invaluable **information line** (Mon–Fri 6am–11pm, Sat & Sun 8am–9.30pm; ☎262-1000): tell them where you are and where you want to go, and they'll give you the necessary details.

You can easily get a **taxi** from outside the bus terminal, or see "Listings" (p.546) for a list of cab companies. Meters currently start at $2.25.

Accommodation

Budget **accommodation** in Calgary is not plentiful, but the little that exists is rarely at a premium except during Stampede (mid-July) when prepaid reservations, in central locations at least, are essential months in advance. Remember that even smart hotels are likely to offer vastly reduced rates on Friday nights and over the weekend, when their business custom drops away. In addition to the recommendations given below, motels abound, mostly well away from the centre along Macleod Trail heading south and on the Trans-Canada Highway heading west. Recently, an unofficial designation, "Motel Village", has sprung up to describe a cluster of a dozen or so cheap motels (all in the $60–70 a night bracket) grouped together at the intersection of 16th Ave NW and Crowchild Trail: if you're not driving, a taxi ride out here costs about $10.

If you run into difficulties, try Visitor Information Services in the Calgary Tower (see opposite), which is primed to hunt out rooms at short notice, or consult the Alberta Hotel Association's ubiquitous *Accommodation Guide*. The Bed & Breakfast Association of Calgary, Box 1462, Station M, Calgary (☎543-3900, fax 543-3901) has some forty **B&B** options on its books. Other agencies to try include the Bed & Breakfast Association of Alberta (☎277-8486) and the Bed & Breakfast Inns of Calgary and Alberta (☎246-4064).

Hotels and motels

Cecil, corner of 4th Avenue and 3rd St SE (☎266-2982). Clean and cheap, but a pretty grim place on a busy junction (the airport road); its bar has a rough reputation. No phones, TV or private baths. Rock-bottom budgets and emergencies only. ②.

Holiday Inn, 119-12th Ave SW (☎266-4611 or 1-800-661-9378, fax 237-0978). An amenity-loaded hotel, but a few blocks off the centre of town. ⑥.

Lord Nelson Inn, 1020-8th Ave SW (☎269-8262 or 1-800-661-6017, fax 269-4868). A newish ten-storey block close to the *Sandman*, to which it is minimally inferior (but cheaper) as a mid-range choice; each room with TV and fridge, and just a block from the free C-Train. ③.

Palliser, 133-9th Ave SW (☎262-1234 or 1-800-441-1414, fax 260-1260). This is the hotel royalty chooses when it comes to Calgary. Built in 1914, and part of the smart Canadian Pacific chain that owns the *Banff Springs* and *Chateau Lake Louise* hotels. ⑥.

Prince Royal Inn All Suite Hotel, 618-5th Ave SW (☎263-0520 or 1-800-661-1592, fax 298-4888). A mixture of 300 studio, one- and two-room suites with full facilities and continental breakfast included. ⑥.

Radisson Plaza Hotel Calgary, 110-9th Ave SE (☎266-7331 or 1-800-648-7776, fax 262-8442). Not the most expensive of Calgary's smart hotels, but probably the best outside the *Palliser* if you want to stay in some style. ⑦.

Ramada Hotel Downtown, 708-8th Ave SW (☎263-7600 or 1-800-661-8684 in Canada, fax 237-6127). A large, comfortable hotel with 200 newly renovated rooms and a swimming pool at the heart of downtown. ⑤.

Regis, 124-7th Ave SE (☎262-4641). A dingy old hotel, but just two blocks from the Calgary Tower. Bathroom facilities are all shared and rooms only have washbasins; beware the rather rough bar. ③.

Sandman Hotel Downtown Calgary, 888-7th Ave SW (☎237-8626 or 1-800-726-3626, fax 290-1238). An excellent and first-choice mid-range hotel, with 300 totally dependable clean, modern rooms with private bathrooms in high-rise block: extremely handy for the free C-Train. ⑤.

Travelodge, 2750 Sunridge Blvd NE (☎291-1260 or 1-800-578-7878, fax 291-9170), 2304-16th Ave (☎289-0211 or 1-800-578-7878, fax 282-6924), and 9206 Macleod Trail (☎253-7070 or 1-800-578-7878, fax 253-2879). Three chain motels; the least expensive out-of-town choices. The first is convenient for the airport. All ③.

York Hotel, 636 Centre St SE (☎262-5581). Central, with good-sized rooms with TVs and baths and laundry service. ③.

Hostels and student accommodation

Calgary International Youth Hostel, 520-7th Ave SE (☎269-8239, fax 266-6227; email: *chostel@HostellingIntl.ca*). Close to downtown and two blocks east of City Hall and the free section of the C-Train. If you're coming from the airport on the Airporter Shuttle (see p.533) get off at the *Delta Bow Valley Inn* stop, which is two blocks from the hostel. Laundry, six- and eight-bed dorms (110 beds in total), four double/family rooms, cooking facilities, bike storage, snack bar. Closed 10am–5pm; midnight curfew. Members $14–15, non-members $18–19; family rooms/doubles add $4 per person. ①.

Calgary YWCA, 320-5th Ave SE (☎263-1550). Hotel comfort for women and children only in quiet safe area; food service, pool, gym, health club and squash courts; book in summer. Singles and dorm beds available; sleeping bag space is sometimes provided in summer. ①–②.

University of Calgary, 3330-24th Ave NW (☎220-3203). Way out in the suburbs, but cheap with a huge number of rooms in the summer. Take the C-Train or bus #9. The 24hr room rental office (call first) is in the Kananaskis Building on campus; 33 percent discount for student ID holders. ②.

Campgrounds

Bow Bend, 5227-13th Ave NW (☎288-2161). RVs only – no tents. Alongside parkland and the Bow River – leave the Trans-Canada at Home Road and follow 13th Avenue. Showers and laundry facilities. Mid-May to Sept. $18.

KOA Calgary West, off the south side of Hwy 1 at the western end of the city, close to Canada Olympic Park (☎288-0411 or 1-800-KOA-0842, fax 286-1612). 224 sites, laundry, store and outdoor pool. Shuttle services to downtown. Mid-April to mid-Oct. $19.

The City

Downtown Calgary lies in a self-evident cluster of mirrored glass and polished granite facades bounded by the Bow River to the north, 9th Avenue to the south, Centre Street to the east and 8th Street to the west. A monument to oil money, the area is about as sleek as an urban centre can be: virtually everything is brand-new, and the modern architecture is easy on the eye. In fact the whole thing looks so modern that it's been used as a setting for several films, most notably *Superman III*. The **city centre**, so far as it has one, is traditionally 8th Avenue between 1st St SE and 3rd St SW, a largely pedestrianized area known as **Stephen Avenue Mall**.

Any city tour, though, should start with a trip to the **Glenbow Museum**, while a jaunt up the **Calgary Tower**, across the street, gives a literal overview of the Calgarian hinterland. Thereafter a good deal of the city lends itself to wandering on foot, whether around the mall-laden main streets or to **Prince's Island**, the nearest of many parks, and **Kensington**, the heart of Calgary's small alternative scene. The appeal of attractions further afield – **Fort Calgary**, **Heritage Park** and the **Calgary Zoo** – will depend on your historical and natural history inclinations. These sights, together with a crop of special interest **museums**, can be easily reached by bus or C-Train.

The Glenbow Museum

The excellent and eclectic collection of the **Glenbow Museum** is, the Stampede apart, the only sight for which you'd make a special journey to Calgary (mid-May to mid-Sept daily 9am–5pm; mid-Sept to mid-May Tues–Sun 9am–5pm; $8, free winter Thurs; ☎268-4100). Although it's opposite the Calgary Tower at 130-9th Ave SE, the main entrance is hidden alongside the Skyline Plaza complex a short way east down the street (there's another entrance from the Stephen Avenue Mall). Built in 1966, the no-expense-spared museum is a testament to sound civic priorities and the cultural benefits of booming oil revenues. Its three floors of displays make a fine introduction to the heritage of the Canadian west.

The permanent collection embraces the eclectic approach, starting with a section devoted to ritual and **sacred art** from around the world and an **art gallery** tracing the development of western Canadian indigenous art. Better still is the Images of the Indian section, an objective and fascinating look at the art that flowed back to Europe after white contact with native peoples. Two outlooks prevail – the romantic nineteenth-century image of the Indian as "noble savage", and the more forward-looking analysis of artists such as Paul Kane, a painter determined to make accurate representations of a people and culture before their assimilation by white expansion.

The second floor runs the gamut of western Canadian history and heritage, including an outstanding exhibit on First Nations or **Native Canadian peoples**. In the treaties section, hidden in a corner almost as if in shame, the museum text skates over the injustices with a glossary of simple facts. The original treaties are on display, and provide some eye-opening examples of incomprehensible jargon and legal gobbledegook. Many chiefs believed they were signing simple peace treaties, when in fact they were signing away land rights. All facets of **native crafts** are explored, with stunning displays of carving, costumes and jewellery and, whilst their emphasis is on the original inhabitants of Alberta, the collection also forays into the Inuit and the Métis – the latter being the offspring of native women and white fur traders, and the most marginalized group of all.

Following a historical chronology, the floor moves on to exhibits associated with the fur trade, Northwest Rebellion, the Canadian Pacific, pioneer life, ranching, cowboys, oil and wheat – each era illustrated by interesting and appropriate artefacts of the time – adding up to a glut of period paraphernalia that includes a terrifying exhibit of frontier dentistry, an absurdly comprehensive display of washing machines, and a solitary 1938 bra.

The eccentric top floor kicks off with a pointless display of Calgary Stampede merchandising, before moving on to a huge collection of **military paraphernalia** and a dazzling display of **gems and minerals**, said to be among the world's best. These exhibits are mainly for genre enthusiasts, though the gems are worth a look if only to see some of the extraordinary and beautiful things that come out of the drab mines that fuel so much of western Canada's economy.

Other downtown sights

The **Calgary Tower** (daily: mid-May to mid-Sept 7.30am–midnight; mid-Sept to mid-May 8am–11pm; $5.50), the city's favourite folly, is a good deal shorter and less imposing than the tourist material would have you believe. An obligatory tourist traipse, the 190-metre-tall salt cellar (762 steps if you don't take the lift) stands in a relatively dingy area at the corner of Centre Street–9th Ave SW, somewhat overshadowed by downtown's more recent sprouting, notably the nearby Petro-Canada towers, which stole its thunder in 1985. As a long-term landmark, however, it makes a good starting point for any tour of the city, the Observation Terrace offering outstanding views, especially on clear days, when the snowcapped Rockies fill the western horizon, with the ski-jump towers of the 1988 Canada Olympic Park in the middle distance. Up on the observation platform after your one-minute elevator ride you'll find a snack bar (reasonable), cocktail bar and revolving restaurant (expensive).

Any number of shopping malls lurk behind the soaring high-rises, most notably Toronto Dominion Square (8th Ave SW between 2nd and 3rd streets), the city's main shopping focus and the unlikely site of **Devonian Gardens** (daily 9am–9pm; free; ☎268-3888). Like something out of an idyllic urban Utopia, the three-acre indoor gardens support a lush sanctuary of streams, waterfalls and full-sized trees, no mean feat given that it's located on the fourth floor of a glass and concrete glitter palace (access by elevator). Around 20,000 plants round off the picture, comprising some 138 local and tropical species. Benches beside the garden's paths are perfect for picnicking on food bought in the takeaways below, while impromptu concerts are held on the small stages dotted around.

Calgary pays homage to its oil industry in the small but oddly interesting **Energeum** plonked in the main lobby of the Energy Resources Building between 5th St and 6th St SW at 640-5th Ave SW (June–Aug daily except Sat 10.30am–4.30pm; Sept–May Mon–Fri same hours; free; ☎297-4293). Its audiovisual and presentational tricks take you through the formation, discovery and drilling for coal and oil. Alberta's peculiar and problematic oil sands are explained – granite-hard in winter, mud-soft in summer – and there are dollops of the stuff on hand for some infantile slopping around.

The **Alberta Science Centre** and **Centennial Planetarium** is located one block west of the 10th St SW C-Train at 701 at 11th Street and 7th Ave SW (daily: late May to early Sept 10am–8pm; early Sept to late May 10am–5pm; $8 for one show and exhibits or a double-feature evening dome show; ☎221-3700). Here you can look through the telescopes of its small observatory, which are trained nightly on the moon, planets and stars (weather permitting). Other daytime highlights here include the interactive exhibits of the Discovery Hall (these change regularly) and the planetarium, or **Discovery Dome**, North America's first multimedia theatre, complete with cinema picture images, computer graphics, slide-projected images and a vast speaker system. The on-site **Pleiades Theatre** offers a series of "mystery and murder plays" throughout the year. For details of current shows and exhibitions, call ☎221-3700. To get here, either walk the five blocks west from 6th Street if you're near the Energeum, or take the C-Train along 7th Ave SW and walk the last block.

Prince's Island, the Bow River and Kensington

Five minutes' walk north of downtown via a footbridge, **Prince's Island** is a popular but peaceful retreat offering plenty of trees, flowers, a snack bar, kids' playground and enough space to escape the incessant stream of joggers pounding the walkways. Between the island and downtown, at the north end of 3rd St SW (six blocks north of the free C-Train), the wonderful **Eau Claire Market** (☎264-6450, or 264-6460 for information) is a bright and deliberately brash warehouse mix of food and craft market, cinemas (including a 300-seat IMAX large-screen complex; $7 a show), buskers, restaurants, walkways and panoramic terraces. All in all it brings some heart to the concrete and glass of downtown – the large communal eating area, in particular, is a good place to people-watch and pick up bargain takeaway Chinese, Japanese, wholefood and burger snacks. The food market is open from 9am to 6pm, but the complex and restaurants are open until late. Note that the tremendous **YMCA** (☎269-6701) opposite the market at 101-3rd St SW has no rooms, though the superb Olympic-size swimming pool, Jacuzzi, sauna, squash courts, running track and weights room are open to all (Mon–Fri 5.30am–10.30pm, weekends 7am–7.30pm; $8; increased admission Mon–Fri 11am–1.30pm and daily 4–6.30pm). Swimmers might be tempted by the broad, fast-flowing **Bow River** nearby, but it's for passive recreation only – the water is just two hours from its icy source in the Rockies – its dangers underlined by lurid signs on the banks. The river is the focus for Calgary's civilized and excellent 210-kilometre system of recreational **walkways**, asphalt paths (also available to cyclists) that generally parallel the main waterways: maps are available from the visitor centre.

Just east of the market and five blocks north of the C-Train at 197-1st St SW lies the **Calgary Chinese Cultural Centre** (centre daily 9am–9pm, museum daily 11am–5pm; ☎262-5071), its big central dome modelled on the Temple of Heaven in Beijing and it claims to be one of the largest Chinese centres in Canada. It forms the focus for Calgary's modest Chinatown and 2,000-strong Chinese-Canadian population, most of whom are descendants of immigrants who came to work on the railways in the 1880s. It contains a small museum and gallery, and a gift shop and restaurant.

A twenty-minute jaunt along the walkway system from Prince's Island in the other direction from the market, **Kensington** is a lively nightlife centre of bars and restaurants focused on 10th St NW and Kensington Road. As alternative as Calgary gets, this is the city's self-proclaimed "People's Place", and the whiff of patchouli and counter-culture hangs in the air despite a tide of encroaching gentrification. Shops here sell healing crystals and advertise yoga and personal-growth seminars, though the older cafés, bookshops and wholefood stores are beginning to give way to trinket shops. As an eating area, though, Kensington is gradually being superseded by the increasingly trendy section of 4th St SW, beyond 17th Avenue.

Fort Calgary

Fort Calgary, the city's historical nexus, stands at 750-9th Ave SE (daily 9am–5pm; shorter hours possible in winter; site free; interpretive centre $3; ☎290-1875), a manageable eight-block walk east of downtown; you could also take bus #1 to Forest Lawn, bus #14 (East Calgary) from 7th Avenue, or the C-Train free to City Hall and walk the remaining five blocks. Built in under six weeks by the North West Mounted Police in 1875, the fort was the germ of the present city, and remained operative as a police post until 1914, when it was sold – inevitably – to the Canadian Pacific Railway. The whole area remained buried under railway tracks and derelict warehouses until comparatively recently.

Period photographs in the adjoining interpretive centre provide a taste of how wild Calgary still was in 1876. Even more remarkable was the ground that men in the fort were expected to cover: the log stockade was a base for operations between Fort Macleod, 160km to the south, and the similar post at Edmonton, almost 400km to the north. It's not as if they had nothing to do: Crowfoot, most prominent of the great Blackfoot chiefs of the time, commented, "If the Police had not come to the country, where would we all be now? Bad men and whiskey were killing us so fast that very few of us indeed would have been left. The Police have protected us as the feathers of a bird protect it from the winter."

Only a few forlorn stumps of the original building remain, much having been torn down by the developers, and what survives is its site, now a pleasant forty-acre park contained in the angled crook of the Bow and Elbow rivers. Moves have recently been made to begin construction of an exact replica of the original log stockade. The interpretive centre traces Calgary's development with the aid of artefacts, audiovisual displays and "interpretive walks" along the river. Among the kinkier things on offer – and you may never get the chance again – is the opportunity to dress up as a Mountie.

Across the river to the east is **Hunt House**, built in 1876 for a Hudson's Bay official and believed to be Calgary's oldest building on its original site. Close by, at 750-9th Ave

THE CALGARY STAMPEDE

An orgy of all things cowboy and cowgirl, the annual **Calgary Stampede** brings around a quarter of a million spectators and participants to the city for ten days during the middle two weeks of July. This is far more than a carefully engineered gift to Calgary's tourist industry, however, for the event is one of the world's biggest rodeos and comes close to living up to its billing as the "The Greatest Outdoor Show on Earth". During "The Week", as it's known by all and sundry, the city loses its collective head; just about everyone turns out in white stetsons, bolo ties, blue jeans and hand-tooled boots, addressing one another in a bastardized cowboy C&W slang. Nightlife is sensational (indoor and out), and away from the huge Stampede Park (see opposite), the venue for the rodeo and a host of other events, there's plenty of fringe activity across the city.

For all its heavily worked visitor appeal, the competition end of things is taken very seriously. Most of the cowboys are for real, as are the injuries – the rodeo is said to be North America's roughest – and the combined prize money is a very serious $500,000. Even the first show in 1912, masterminded by entrepreneur Guy Weadick, put up $100,000 (raised from four Calgary businessmen) and attracted 60,000 people to the opening parade, a line-up that included 2000 natives in full ceremonial rig and Pancho Villa's bandits in a show erroneously billed as a swan song for the cowboy of the American West ("The Last and Best Great West Frontier Days"). Around 40,000 daily attended the rodeo events (today's figure is 100,000), not bad considering Calgary's population at the time was only 65,000. In the event the show didn't mark the end of the west – people had believed the coming of wheat would sound the death knell of traditional ranching life – but it wasn't until 1919, following the interruption caused by World War I, that Weadick was able to repeat his success.

Nowadays the ten days of events kick off on Thursday evening at Stampede Park with **Sneek-a-peek** [sic], which despite being nothing more than a preview of what's to come still attracts 40,000 people. Next day there's the traditional **parade**, timed to begin at 9am, though most of the 250,000 people on the streets are in place by 6am. Leave it until 7am and you'll be at the back of the ten-deep phalanx that lines the parade route (which is west along 6th Avenue from 2nd St SE, south on 10th St SW and east along 9th Avenue). The march past takes two hours, and involves around 150 entries, 4000 participants and some 700 horses. For the rest of the Stampede the **Olympic Plaza** in downtown (known as Rope Square for the duration) offers free pancake breakfasts daily (8.30–11.30am) and entertainment every morning. Typical events include bands, mock gunfights, square dances, native dancing and country bands. Square dancing also fills parts of Stephen Avenue Mall at 10am every morning. **Nightlife** is a world unto itself, with Stampede locations giving way to music, dancing and mega-cabarets, which involve casts of literally thousands. There's also lots of drinking, gambling, fireworks and general partying into the small hours. Barbecues are the norm, and even breakfast is roped

SE, on the same side of the Elbow River, is the renovated **Deane House Historic Site and Restaurant** (☎269-7747), built in 1906 by Mountie supremo Superintendent Richard Deane (free tours daily 11am–2pm). It subsequently served time as the home of an artists' cooperative, a boarding house and a stationmaster's house. Today it's a teahouse and restaurant.

St George's Island

St George's Island is home to Calgary's most popular attraction, the **Calgary Zoo, Botanical Gardens and Prehistoric Park,** all at 1300 Zoo Rd (daily 9am–dusk; Prehistoric Park open June–Sept only; May–Sept $9.50, Oct–April $8; ☎232-9300). It can be reached from downtown and Fort Calgary by riverside path, by C-Train northeast towards Whitehorn, or by car (take Memorial Drive East to just west of Deerfoot Trail). Founded in 1920, this is now Canada's largest zoo (and one of North America's top ten

into the free-for-all – outdoor bacon, pancake and flapjack feasts being the traditional way to start the day. "White hatter stew" and baked beans – inevitably – are other staples.

Stampede's real action, though – the rodeo and allied events – takes place in **Stampede Park**, southeast of downtown and best reached by C-Train (every 10min) to Victoria Park–Stampede Station. This vast open area contains an amusement park, concert and show venues, bars and restaurants and a huge range of stalls and shows that take the best part of day to see. Entrance is $8, which allows you to see all the **entertainments** except the rodeo and chuck-wagon races. Things to see include the Native Village at the far end of the park, where members of the Five Nations tribes (Blackfoot, Blood, Sarcee, Stoney and Piegan) set up a tepee village (tours available); the John Deere Show Ring, scene of the World Blacksmith Competition; the Centennial Fair, which hosts events for children; the Agricultural Building, home to displays of cattle and other livestock; the outdoor Coca-Cola Stage, used for late-night country shows; and the Nashville North, an indoor country venue with bar and dancing until 2am.

If you want to see the daily **rodeo** competition – bronco riding, bull riding, native-buffalo riding, branding, calf-roping, steer-wrestling, cow-tackling, wild-cow milking and the rest – you need another ticket ($8 on the day), though unless you've bought these in advance (see below) it's hardly worth it: you'll probably be in poor seats miles from the action and hardly see a thing. Rodeo heats are held each afternoon from 1.30pm for the first eight days, culminating in winner-takes-all finals on Saturday and Sunday (prize money for the top honcho is $50,000). If you want to watch the other big event, the ludicrously dangerous but hugely exciting **chuck-wagon** races (the "World Championship") you need yet another ticket ($8) on the day, though again you need to buy these in advance to secure anything approaching decent seats. The nine heats are held once-nightly at 8pm, the four top drivers going through to the last-night final, where another $50,000 awaits the winner.

It's worth planning ahead if you're coming to Calgary for Stampede. **Accommodation** is greatly stretched – be certain to book ahead – and prices for most things are hiked for the duration. **Tickets** for the rodeo and chuck-wagon races go on sale anything up to a year in advance. They're sold for the Stampede Park grandstand, which is divided into sections. "A" is best and sells out first; "B" and "C" go next. Then comes the smarter Clubhouse Level (D–E are seats; F–G are Clubhouse Restaurant seats, with tickets sold in pairs only). This is enclosed and air-conditioned, but still offers good views and the bonus of bars, lounge area and restaurants. The top of the stand, or Balcony (J–K) is open, and provides a good vantage point for the chuck-wagon races as you follow their progress around the length of the course. Rodeo tickets range from about $17 to $35, chuck-wagon races from $17 to $40; tickets for the finals of both events are a few dollars more in all seats. For ticket order forms, **advance sales** and general information, write to Calgary Exhibition and Stampede, Box 1860, Station M, Calgary, AB T2P 2L8 (☎261-0101, elsewhere in Alberta or North America ☎1-800-661-1260) or call in person at Stampede Headquarters, 1410 Olympic Way SE, or the visitor centre. Tickets are also available from Ticketmaster outlets (☎270-6700).

zoos), with 850,000 annual visitors and some 1200 animals, 400 species and innovative and exciting displays in which the animals are left as far as possible in their "natural" habitats. There are underwater viewing areas for polar bears and sea creatures, darkened rooms for nocturnal animals, a special Australian section, greenhouses for myriad tropical birds, and any number of pens for the big draws like gorillas, tigers, giraffes and African warthogs. Check out the extended North American and Canadian Wilds, Aspen Woodlands and Rocky Mountains sections for a taste of a variety of fauna. Also worth a look are the Tropical, Arid and Butterfly gardens in the conservatory. There is a fast-food concession, and picnic areas if you want to make a day of it.

The **Botanical Gardens** are dotted throughout the zoo, while the **Prehistoric Park** annexe – a "recreated Mesozoic landscape" – is accessible by suspension bridge across the Bow River (daily June–Sept; free with general admission). Its nineteen life-size dinosaur models, none too convincing in their incongruous settings, are a poor substitute for the superb site and museum at Drumheller (see p.547), and only the fossils in two adjoining buildings are of more than fleeting interest.

Natural history enthusiasts might also want to visit the **Inglewood Bird Sanctuary**, on the Bow River's forested flats at 9th Avenue and 20A St SE, 3km downstream of the zoo and east of downtown. Some 230 species are present year-round – more during migratory cycles, around 266 species having been recorded across the sanctuary, a portion of land once owned by Colonel James Walker, one of Calgary's original North West Mounted Police. Some of the birds you might see include bald eagles, Swainson's hawks, ring-necked pheasants, warblers, grey partridges and great horned owls. Numerous duck, geese and other waterfowl are also present, and you may also catch sight of muskrats, beavers, white-tailed and mule deer, foxes and long-tailed weasels. A new visitor centre opened recently (May–Sept daily 9am–5pm; free; ☎269-6688), offering information, details of the year-round walking trails, and occasional natural history courses to guide non-experts. To get here, follow 9th Ave SE to Sanctuary Road and follow signs to the parking area on the river's south bank. On weekdays the #14 bus (East) turns off 9th Avenue at 17th St SE, leaving you just a short walk from the Sanctuary.

Heritage Park Historical Village

A sixty-acre theme park centred on a reconstructed frontier village 16km southwest of downtown, **Heritage Park** (☎259-1900) replicates life in the Canadian West before 1914 and panders relentlessly to the myth of the "Wild West" (mid-May to early Sept daily 9am–5pm; early Sept to mid-Oct weekends and holidays 9am–5pm; $16 admission with rides, $10 without rides; free pancake breakfast with admission 9–10am). Full of family-oriented presentations and original costumes, this "heritage" offering – the largest of its type in Canada – is thorough enough for you never to feel obliged to see another.

The living, working museum comprises more than 150 **restored buildings**, all transported from other small-town locations. Each has been assigned to one of several communities – fur post, native village, homestead, farm and turn-of-the-century town – and most fulfil their original function. Thus you can see a working blacksmith, buy fresh bread, buy a local paper, go to church, even get married. Transport, too, is appropriate to the period – steam trains, trams, horse-drawn bus, stagecoaches and, the highlight, the restored paddlesteamer **SS Moyie**, which runs trips across the local reservoir. If you're here for the day you can pick up cakes and snacks from the traditional Alberta Bakery, or sit down to a full meal in the old-style *Wainwright Hotel*.

To get there by car, take either Elbow Drive or Macleod Trail south and turn right on Heritage Drive (the turnoff is marked by a huge, maroon steam engine); **bus** #53 makes the journey from downtown, or you can take the C-Train to Heritage Station and then bus #20 to Northmount.

Eating, drinking and nightlife

Calgary's cuisine is heavily meat-oriented; Alberta claims, with some justification, to have some of the best **steaks** in the world. With its particular immigration history the city lacks the Ukrainian influences that grace cooking to the north, and often prefers instead to rehash so-called "Californian cuisine". Most bars and cafés – even the live music venues – double up as restaurants and invariably serve perfectly good food.

The Toronto Dominion Square and Stephen Avenue malls, on 8th Ave SW between 1st and 3rd, are riddled with ethnic **takeaways** and café-style restaurants – hugely popular and perfect for lunch or snacks on the hoof. The nicest thing to do is buy food and eat it – with half of Calgary – either in the superb **Eau Claire Market**, which is packed with food stalls and restaurants, or amid the greenery of Devonian Gardens. Elsewhere, the city has an impressive range of middle- to upper-bracket restaurants, where prices are low by most standards.

Calgary is rarely a party town, except during Stampede and a brief fling in summer when the weather allows barbecues and night-time streetlife. Nonetheless, its **bars and clubs** are all you'd expect of a city of this size, the vast majority of them found in five distinct areas: **Kensington**, with its varied cafés, restaurants and clubs, and good summer-evening wandering possibilities; "**Electric Avenue**", as 11th Ave SW between 5th and 6th streets is called, all Identikit pubs and bars – bright, brash and very popular with the very young and trashy (although less popular in the light of recent petty crime and rowdiness); **17th Ave SW**, a quieter and more varied collection of pubs, bars, speciality shops and ethnic eating; **4th St SW**, a similarly more refined restaurant area; and **downtown**, fine during the day but fairly desolate in the evening.

In the specialist clubs the quality of live music is good – especially in jazz, blues and the genre closest to cowtown Calgary's heart, C&W. The Country Music Association has details of local gigs (☎233-8809). For details of the annual Jazz Festival (third week in June) and for daily information on who's playing where, call the Jazz Line (☎265-1321). Prince's Island is the venue for a folk festival at the end of July.

Tickets for virtually all events are available on ☎270-6700, and through several Marlin Travel offices around the city. You'll find events listings in Calgary's main dailies, the *Herald* (especially in Friday's *What's Up* supplement) and the *Sun*.

Cafés

Bagels and Buns, 807-17th Ave SW near 7th Street. Informal and popular for breakfast and lunch.

Divino's, 1st Street and 9th Ave SW. Café and wine bar opposite the *Palliser* hotel with rather *faux* mahogany-Tiffany chandelier interior, but good Californian-Italian food and particularly noteworthy desserts.

Entre Nous Café, 2206-4th St SW (☎228-5551). Small, lively and congenial, big mirrors and burgundy decor giving a genuine bistro feel. Good French food; booking recommended.

Good Earth Café. The original wholefood store and café, known for great home-made food, at 1502-11th St (☎228-9543) was so successful it has spawned five other outlets: the Eau Claire Market (☎237-8684) – with good outside patio – the Central Library and elsewhere.

Nellie's Kitchen, 17th Avenue and 6th St SW. Laid-back, popular and informal, but busy at breakfast. Open for breakfast and lunch only.

The Roasterie, 314-10th St NW near Kensington Road. Nice hangout and café – no meals, but newspapers, notice board and twenty kinds of coffee and snacks.

Scooza-Mi Eaterie, 1324 Centre St North. Daft name – and more than a café – but excellent Italo-Californian food (including pizzas). See also the out-of-town *Scooza-Mi II* at 6913 Macleod Trail.

Restaurants

Bistro Jo Jo, 917-17th Ave SW (☎245-2382). If you want to eat good French food, but balk at *La Chaumière* prices (see below), try this marble-tiled and red-banquette-filled restaurant.

La Chaumière, 139-17th Ave SW (☎228-5690). Probably too formal (jackets for men) and expensive for most tastes, but if you want what is probably the city's best French food this is the place.

Chianti Café and Restaurant, 1438-17th Ave SW (☎229-1600). A favourite local spot for years: dark, noisy, well priced and extremely popular (try to book), with pasta basics and the odd fancy dish. Patio for summer alfresco dining. Recommended.

Da Paolo, 121-17th Ave and 5th St SW (☎228-5556). Rather upmarket Italian, near *The Ship and Anchor* with tasteful apricot pastel interior and original art on the walls.

Earl's. This ever-reliable mid-range chain, serving North American food, has several outlets around Calgary, the most central of which is on 8th Avenue just up the street from *The Unicorn Pub* (see p.544).

Fourth St Rose, 2116 4th St SW (☎228-5377). Big, busy place in business for over fifteen years with good cocktails and healthy Californian cuisine, in the new trendy restaurant zone on 4th Street.

River Café, Prince Island Park (☎261-7670). Along with *La Chaumière* and *Bistro Jo Jo* this is one of the more highly rated of Calgary's restaurants: it has the advantage of a nice setting on Prince's Island Park across the bridge from the Eau Claire Market. Offers Canadian "Northwestern" cuisine, which includes caribou.

Bars

Barley Mill Eatery & Pub, 201 Barclay Parade, Eau Claire Market (☎290-1500). Busy neighbourhood pub in good location with an outside patio and 100-year-old bar imported from Scotland inside: 24 draught beers, 40 bottled brews and lots of whiskies.

The Fox and Firkin, 11th Ave SW between 5th and 6th. You may have to queue for one of the biggest and most popular of the numerous "Electric Avenue" bars which, like many Calgary bars, affects the atmosphere of a British pub – noisy, crowded, tatty and fun.

Mission Bridge Brewing Company, 2417-4th St (☎228-0100). The owners of *The Ship and Anchor*, emboldened by their success, have opened this impressive state-of-the-art bar and restaurant, with excellent Californian-cross cuisine and beers and lagers from their own Seattle market-style microbrewery.

Rose and Crown, 1503-4th St SW. A Calgary institution, round the corner from *The Ship and Anchor*, though the pub atmosphere is a tad laboured and the clientele can be grating.

The Ship and Anchor, 17th Ave SW on the corner of 5th Street. Long-established and popular pub which is the best bar in Alberta, if not in western Canada; friendly and laid-back but jumping "neighbourhood" pub, with special Anglo-Canadian connections, darts, fine music and excellent pub food. Recommended.

The Unicorn Pub, 304-8th Ave SW, on the corner of 2nd Street, downstairs in the mall (☎233-2666). Well-known downtown pub whose cheap food brings in lunch-time punters and office workers for an after-work drink.

Live music venues

Crazy Horse, 1311-1st St SW (☎266-3339). Popular dance venue with live music on Thursday nights. Small dance floor.

Dusty's Saloon, 1088 Olympic Way (☎263-5343). One of the city's legendary C&W spots (jam sessions on Monday). Claims Calgary's largest dance floor. Free two-step lessons on Tuesday and Wednesday nights. Live C&W bands every night.

Kaos Jazz and Blues Bistro, 718-17th Ave (☎228-9997). Best location in the city for jazz, with blues, acoustic and soul also on offer.

The King Edward Hotel, 438-9th Ave SE. Much-loved, down-at-heel location, with consistently good C&W and R&B bands. The Saturday jam session is renowned and invariably packed – the blues event of the city.

Ranchman's Steak House, 9615 Macleod Trail South (☎253-1100). A classic honky-tonk and restaurant, known throughout Canada, and often packed, due to the live and happening C&W. Free dance lessons at 7.30pm Monday to Thursday. Free admission before 8pm on Thursday. Closed Sun.

Republik, 219-17th Ave SW. After several years still the weirdest, most alternative and probably the most likeable nightclub in the city.

Senor Frog's, 739-2nd Ave SW (☎264-5100). Three blocks west of the Eau Claire Market. New and popular upbeat restaurant and club, with the club taking precedence Thursday to Saturday from 9pm.

Performing arts, cinema and entertainment

Calgary might come on as a redneck cow town, but it has ten or more professional theatre companies, a ballet company, an opera company and a full-blown symphony orchestra. Much of the city's highbrow cultural life focuses on the **Centre for the Performing Arts**, a dazzling modern downtown complex with five performance spaces close to the Glenbow Museum, at 205-8th Ave SE, (☎294-7455). It's also the base for the acclaimed Calgary Philharmonic Orchestra (☎571-0270), Theatre Calgary (☎294-7440) and the well-known Alberta Theatre Project (☎294-7475), which usually produces five fairly avant-garde plays annually. More modest classical concerts include the Music at Noon offerings in the Central Library (Sept–April), and the sessions – planned and impromptu – on the small stages in Devonian Gardens. The long-running and well-known **Lunchbox Theatre**, 2nd Floor, Bow Valley Square, 205-5th Ave SW (☎265-4292 or 265-4293), offers a popular and wildly varied programme aimed at downtown shoppers and passers-by; performances run from September to May and are somewhat irregular, but tend to start daily at noon (except Sun) in the Bow Valley Square on the corner of 6th Avenue and 1st St SW.

Calgary's **ballet** world is dominated by the young and excellent Alberta Ballet Company (☎245-4222), who perform at various locations around the city. **Opera** is the preserve of Calgary Opera (☎262-7286), whose home base is the Jubilee Auditorium at 1415-14th Ave NW. The season runs from October to April.

For repertory, arthouse, classic and foreign **films**, try the newly restored **Uptown Stage & Screen**, 612-8th Ave (☎265-0120) or Plaza Theatre at 1113 Kensington Rd NW; the National Film Board Theatre, 222-1st St SE, puts on free lunch-time shows. The **Museum of Movie Art** at the University of Calgary, 9-3600-21st St NE (Tues–Sat 9.30am–5.30pm), is home to the world's largest collection of cinema posters (4000 of them, dating back to 1920). For first-run mainstream films, head for the downtown malls – most have a cinema complex.

Listings

Airlines Air BC (☎298-9227 or 265-9555); Air Canada, 530-8th Ave SW (☎265-9555, 298-9201 or 1-800-372-9500); Alaska Airlines (☎1-800-426-0333); American (☎254-6331 or 1-800-433-7300); America West (☎1-800-247-5692); British Airways (☎1-800-668-1080 or 1-800-247-9297); Canadian Airlines (☎235-1161 or 1-800-665-1177; airbus to Edmonton ☎235-8154; schedules and reservations ☎248-4888); Canada 3000 (☎266-8095); Cathay Pacific (☎269-3388); Continental (☎1-800-525-0280); Delta (☎265-7610, 263-0177 or 1-800-221-1212); Eastern (☎236-2833); Horizon (☎1-800-547-9308); KLM (☎236-2600, 1-800-361-1887 or 1-800-665-8608); Northwest (☎1-800-225-2525); NWT Air (☎265-9555 or 1-800-661-0789); Qantas (☎1-800-663-3411 or 1-800-221-1212); Time Air (☎235-1161); United (☎1-800-241-6522); West-Jet (☎266-8086).

Airport enquiries ☎292-8400 or 735-1372.

Ambulance ☎261-4000.

American Express 421-7th Ave SW (☎261-5982 or 1-800-221-7282).

Bike and blades rental RnR Tech Shop, Eau Claire Market (☎266-3609), or Sports Rent (☎292-0077). Mountain bikes from $20 per day, blades $10 per day.

Bookshops Canterbury's Bookshop, 513-8th Ave SW, is the best general bookshop. For maps and travel books, check out Mountain Equipment Co-op, 830-10 Ave SW (☎269-2420), or Map Town, 640-6th Ave SW (☎266-2241).

Bus enquiries Airporter (☎531-3909); Brewster Transportation for airport/Banff/Jasper (☎762-6767, 260-0719 or 1-800-661-1152); Greyhound (☎265-9111 or 1-800-661-8747 in Canada); Laidlaw for airport/Banff/Lake Louise (☎762-9102 or 1-800-661-4946); Red Arrow Express, for Edmonton (☎531-0350 or 1-800-232-1958).

Car rental Avis, 211-6th Ave SW (☎291-1475, 269-6166 or 1-800-879-2847); Budget, 140-6th Ave SE (☎226-1550, 263-0505 or 1-800-268-8900); Economy Car Rentals (☎291-1640); Hertz (☎221-1300 or 1-800-263-0600 in Canada); Rent-a-Wreck, 3716-2nd St NE (☎284-0755); Thrifty, 123-5th Ave SE (☎262-4400; airport 221-1806; also 1-800-367-2277); Tilden, 114-5th Ave (☎263-2541 or 1-800-387-4747 in Canada).

Consulates Australian (☎1-604-684-1177); UK (☎1-604-683-4421); US, 1000-615 Macleod Trail SE (☎266-8962).

Disabled visitors Information on wheelchair-accessible transport services (☎262-1000); Calgary Handi-Bus (☎276-8028).

Emergencies ☎911.

Exchange Calgary Foreign Exchange, 307-4th Ave SW; Royal Bank, 339-8th Ave SW (☎292-3938).

Hospital Calgary General Hospital, 841 Centre Ave East (☎268-9111).

Internet U*Wanna*What daily-updated info and listings on Calgary (*http://www.uwannawhat.com*).

Left luggage Facilities at the bus terminal, 850-16th St SW; $2 per 24hr.

Library Central Library, 616-Macleod Trail SE (☎260-2600).

Lost property ☎268-1600.

Maps and guides Map Town, 640-6th Ave SW (☎266-2241).

Outdoor gear Mountain Equipment Co-op, 830-10 Ave SW (☎269-2420); Calgary's newest and largest camping and outdoor store that includes excellent books, guides and maps.

Pharmacy ☎253-2605 (24hr).

Police 316-7th Ave SE (☎266-1234); RCMP (☎230-6483).

Post office 220-4th Ave SE (☎292-5434 or Canada Post 1-800-267-1177).

Public transport Calgary Transit (☎262-1000); public transport information.

Train information VIA Rail (☎1-800-561-8630 in Canada; 1-800-561-3949 in the US); Rocky Mtn Railtours Calgary–Banff–Vancouver (☎1-800-665-7245).

Taxis Associated Cabs (☎299-1111); Calgary Cab Co (☎777-2222); Checker (☎299-9999); Metro Cabs (☎250-1800); Prestige (☎974-1100); Yellow Cab (☎974-1111).

Time ☎263-3333.

Tourist information ☎263-8510 or 1-800-661-8888.

Travel agent Travel Cuts, 1414 Kensington Rd NW (☎531-2070).

Tickets Tickets for events, shows, etc (☎270-6700).

Weather ☎263-3333.

The Alberta Badlands

Formed by the meltwaters of the last ice age, the valley of the Red Deer River cuts a deep gash through the dulcet prairie about 140km east of Calgary, creating a surreal landscape of bare, sunbaked hills and eerie lunar flats dotted with sagebrush and scrubby, tufted grass. On their own, the **Alberta Badlands** – strangely anomalous in the midst of lush grasslands – would repay a visit, but what makes them an essential detour is the presence of the **Royal Tyrrell Museum of Paleontology**, amongst the greatest museums of natural history in North America. The museum is located 8km outside the old coal-mining town of **Drumheller**, a dreary but obvious base if you're unable to fit the museum into a day-trip from Calgary. Drumheller is also the main focus of the **Dinosaur Trail**, a road loop that explores the Red Deer Valley and surrounding badlands; you'll need your own transport for this circuit, and for the trip to the **Dinosaur Provincial Park**, home to the Tyrrell Museum Field Station and the source of many of its fossils.

Drumheller

Whatever way you travel, you'll pass through **DRUMHELLER**, a downbeat town in an extraordinary setting roughly ninety minutes' drive northeast of Calgary. As you approach it from the west, the town is hidden until you come to a virulent red water tower and the road suddenly drops into a dark, hidden canyon. The otherworldliness of the gloomy, blasted landscape is spookily heightened by its contrast to the vivid colours of the earlier wheat and grasslands.

Drumheller sits at the base of the canyon, surrounded by the detritus and spoil heaps of its mining past – the Red Deer River having exposed not only dinosaur fossils but also (now exhausted) coal seams. The coal attracted the likes of Samuel Drumheller, an early mining pioneer after whom the town is named. The first mine opened in 1911, production reaching a peak after the opening of a rail link to Calgary two years later. In less than fifty years it was all over, coal's declining importance in the face of gas and oil sounding the industry's death knell. These days Drumheller is sustained by agriculture, oil – there are some 3000 wells dotted around the surrounding farmland – and tourism, the **Tyrrell Museum** ranking as Alberta's biggest draw after Calgary, Edmonton and the Rockies.

The town is best reached by taking Hwy 2 north towards Edmonton and branching east on Hwy 72 and Hwy 9. It's an easy day-trip with your own transport, and most people make straight for the Tyrrell Museum, signposted from Drumheller on Hwy 838 (or

"North Dinosaur Trail"). Using one of the two **Greyhound buses** daily from Calgary to Drumheller (figure on around $20 one way) makes a day-trip more of a squeeze. The depot (☎823-7566) is some way out of the town centre at the Suncity Mall on Hwy 9. It's definitely too far to walk from here or the town centre to the museum, particularly on a hot day, but Badlands Taxis (☎823-6552) or Jack's Taxi (☎823-2220) will run you there from the bus depot for about $10. Failing that you could rent a car: Tilden (☎823-3371 or 1-800-387-4747) is the only agency in town.

There's not much to do in the town itself, despite the best efforts of its two **infocentres**: one is run by the Chamber of Commerce at the corner of Riverside Drive and 2nd Street West (daily: May–Oct 9am–9pm; Nov–April 9am–4.30pm; ☎823-1331); the other is a private concern in the Suncity Mall on Hwy 9 (daily 9am–9pm; ☎823-7566). For all its half million visitors a year, Drumheller has just 350 or so beds, and if truth be told you don't really want to spend a night here. If you have no choice, be sure to book well in advance: virtually everything's gone by mid-afternoon in high season. A limited selection of **accommodation** lies a block from the bus terminal, the best of the downtown hotels being the slightly overpriced *Lodge at Drumheller* (☎823-3322; ③) opposite the youth hostel on Railway Avenue. Other central options include the *Rockhound Motor Inn*, South Railway Drive (☎823-5302; ③); the top-of-the-pile *Inn at Heartwood Manor*, 320 Railway Drive (☎823-6495 or 1-800-823-6495; ④–⑤); *Drumheller Inn* (☎823-8400; ④), a modern motel on a bluff at 100 South Railway Ave (Hwy 9) off the Hwy 56 approach from the west; and the tasteful log cabins and good adjoining pancake house of the pleasanter *Badlands Motel* (☎823-5155; ②), 1km out of town on Hwy 838. The **youth hostel** is at the *Alexander International Hostel*, 30 Railway Ave (☎823-6337), and offers beds in eight-person dorms (①).

Of the town's two well-situated and neighbouring **campgrounds**, the better option is the *Dinosaur Trailer Court* (☎823-3291; $14; April–Oct), across the river north of downtown at the junction of Hwy 56 and Hwy 838. *Shady Grove Campground* (☎823-2576; $10; May–Oct) is a few hundred metres south, on the other side of the bridge at 25 Poplar St – closer to the town's tatty confines but with boating and swimming possibilities. The visitor infocentre has lists of the many other private and provincial campgrounds (*Little Fish Provincial Park* being the best) up and down the valley.

The tucked-away All West **supermarket** on 1st Street behind the main drag stocks picnic supplies. For cheap eating, the *Diana* on Main Street is half-diner, half-Chinese restaurant, and the *Bridge Greek Restaurant*, 71 Bridge St North, has a relaxed ambience and good food. Better-quality **restaurants** have a reputation of going broke once the tourists have gone home, but currently the two best places to eat are *Jack's Bistro*, 70 Railway Ave (☎823-8422), and the reasonably priced and little-known *Sizzling House*, 160 Centre St (☎823-8098), reckoned to be one of Alberta's best Chinese restaurants. The cafeteria at the museum also makes a reasonable eating option.

The Royal Tyrrell Museum of Paleontology

Packed with high-tech displays, housed in a sleek building and blended skilfully into its desolate surroundings, the **Royal Tyrrell Museum of Paleontology** is an object lesson in museum design (mid-May to early Sept daily 9am–9pm; early Sept to mid-Oct daily 10am–5pm; mid-Oct to mid-May Tues–Sun 10am–5pm; $6.50; ☎823-7707). It attracts half a million plus visitors a year, and its wide-ranging exhibits are likely to appeal to anyone with even a hint of scientific or natural curiosity. Although it claims the world's largest collection of complete dinosaur skeletons (fifty full-size animals and 80,000 miscellaneous specimens), the museum is far more than a load of old bones, and as well as tracing the earth's history from the year dot to the present day it's also a leading centre of study and academic research. Its name comes from Joseph Tyrrell, who in 1884 discovered the Albertosaurus, first of the dinosaur remains to be pulled from the Albertan badlands.

Laid out on different levels to suggest layers of geological time, the open-plan exhibit guides you effortlessly through a chronological progression, culminating in a huge central hall of over two hundred dinosaur specimens. If there's a fault, it's that the hall is visible early on and tempts you to skip the lower-level displays, which place the dinosaurs in context by skilfully linking geology, fossils, plate tectonics, evolution and the like with Drumheller's own landscape. You also get a chance to peer into the preparation lab and watch scientists working on fossils in one of the world's best-equipped paleontology centres.

By far the most impressive exhibits are the **dinosaurs** themselves. Whole skeletons are immaculately displayed against three-dimensional backgrounds that persuasively depict the swamps of sixty million years ago. Some are paired with full-size plastic dinosaurs, which appear less macabre and menacing than the free-standing skeletons. Sheer size is not the only fascination: Xiphactinus, for example, a four-metre specimen, is striking more for its delicate and beautiful tracery of bones. Elsewhere the emphasis is on the creatures' diversity or on their staggeringly small brains, sometimes no larger than their eyes.

The museum naturally also tackles the problem of the dinosaurs' extinction, pointing out that around ninety percent of all plant and animal species that have ever inhabited the earth have become extinct. Leave a few minutes for the wonderful **paleoconservatory** off the dinosaur hall, a collection of living prehistoric plants, some unchanged in 180 million years, selected from fossil records to give an idea of the vegetation that would have typified Alberta in the dinosaur age.

The Dinosaur Trail

The **Dinosaur Trail** is a catch-all circular road route of 51km from Drumheller embracing some of the viewpoints and lesser historic sights of the badlands and the Red Deer Valley area. The comprehensive *Visitor's Guide to the Drumheller Valley* (free from the Drumheller infocentre) lists thirty separate stopoffs, mostly on the plain above the valley, of which the key ones are: the **Little Church** (6km west of Drumheller), the "Biggest Little Church in the World" (capacity six); **Horsethief Canyon** (17.6km west of the museum) and **Horseshoe Canyon** (19km southwest of the museum on Hwy 9), two spectacular viewpoints of the wildly eroded valley, the latter with good trails to and along the canyon floor; the **Hoodoos**, slender columns of wind-sculpted sandstone, topped with mushroom-like caps (17km southeast of Drumheller on Hwy 10); the still largely undeveloped **Midland Provincial Park**, site of the area's first mines and crisscrossed by badland trails, now home to an interpretive centre (daily 9am–6pm; free); and the **Atlas Coal Mine** (guided tours mid-May to mid-Oct daily 9am–6pm; $3; ☎822-2220), dominated by the teetering wooden "tipple", once used to sort ore and now a beautiful and rather wistful piece of industrial archeology.

Dinosaur Provincial Park

Drivers can feasibly fit in a trip to **Dinosaur Provincial Park** the same day as the Tyrrell Museum, a 174-kilometre journey from Drumheller to the park, and then head back to Calgary on the Trans-Canada, which runs just south of the park. The nearest town is Brooks on the Trans-Canada, 48km west of the **Royal Tyrrell Museum Field Station**, the park's obvious hub (May to early Sept daily 8.15am–9pm; early Sept to mid-Oct daily 8.15am–4.30pm; mid-Oct to April Mon–Fri 8.15am–4.30pm; $2; ☎378-4342, reservation line ☎378-4344). The excellent provincial **campground** in the park besides Little Sandhill Creek is open year-round, but only serviced from May to September ($13). Booking is advisable, on ☎378-3700. Otherwise the nearest **accommodation** is the basic and (with bar downstairs) potentially rowdy *Patricia Hotel* (☎378-4647) in Patricia, 15km from the park.

Nestled among some of the baddest of the badlands, the region's landscape is not only one of the most alien in Canada, but also one of the world's richest fossil beds, a superb medley of prairie habitats and ecosystems and (since 1979) a listed UN World Heritage Site. Over 300 complete skeletons have been found and dispatched to museums across the world, representing 35 (or ten per cent) of all known dinosaur species. The field station has five self-guided **trails**, the Badlands Trail and Cottonwood Flats Trail being the most worthwhile, and giving a good taste of this extraordinary region. The centre also has a small museum that goes over the same ground as its parent in Drumheller, leaving the real meat of the visit to the **Badlands Bus Tour**, an excellent ninety-minute guided tour of the otherwise out-of-bounds dinosaur dig near the centre of the park (May–Sept Mon–Fri tours twice-daily, Sat–Sun 7 times daily; $4.50). A few exposed skeletons have been left *in situ*, and panels give background information on the monsters. The station also organizes two-hour guided **hikes**, most notably the Centrosaurus Bone Bed Hike (Tues, Thurs, Sat & Sun 9.15am; $4.50), which visits a restricted area where some 300 centrosaurus skeletons have been uncovered. All tours fill up quickly, so it's worth trying to book ahead by calling ☎378-4344.

Highway 3

The most travelled route across southern Alberta is the Trans-Canada, direct to Calgary; **Hwy 3**, branching off at **Medicine Hat**, takes a more southerly course across the plains before finally breaching the Rockies at Crowsnest Pass. This quieter and less spectacular route into the mountains holds a trio of worthwhile diversions: the new **Carriage Centre** near Cardston, the marvellously monikered **Head-Smashed-In Buffalo Jump** heritage site, and **Waterton Lakes National Park**, a cross-border reserve that links with the United States' Glacier National Park.

Medicine Hat

Though **MEDICINE HAT** is barely a hundred years old, the origin of its wonderful name has already been confused. The most likely story has to do with a Cree medicine man who lost his headdress while fleeing a battle with the Blackfoot; his followers lost heart at the omen, surrendered, and were promptly massacred. These days you rarely see the town mentioned without the adage that it "has all hell for a basement", a quotation from Rudyard Kipling coined in response to the huge reserves of natural gas that lurk below the town. Discovered by railway engineers drilling for water in 1883, the gas fields now feed a flourishing petrochemical industry which blots the otherwise park-studded downtown area on the banks of the South Saskatchewan River.

Medicine Hat may claim that its 1440 hours of summer sunshine make it Canada's sunniest city, but its main function is as a major staging post on the Trans-Canada. The world's **tallest tepee** (twenty storeys tall on the Trans-Canada) and the nightmare **Riverside Waterslide** at Hwy 1 and Powerhouse Road (mid–May to early Sept daily 10am–8pm; $10.75) are the only attractions of note. If you're pulling off the road for a break, the best place to **eat** is *Barney's*, 665 Kingsway Ave SE (☎529-5663), but it's a little expensive and standard North American fare. The least expensive of its many **motels** is the *Bel-Aire*, 633-14th St (☎527-4421; ①), conveniently situated at the junction of the Trans-Canada and Hwy 3, though the *Best Western Inn*, on the Trans-Canada at 722 Redcliff Drive (☎527-3700 or 1-800-528-1234; ③), is more appealing. The best place around is the *Medicine Hat Lodge*, 1051 Ross Gleen Drive (☎529-2222 or 1-800-661-8095; ④). The only downtown accommodation is the *Inn on 4th*, 530 4th St SE (☎526-1313 or 1-800-730-3887; ③).

Lethbridge

Alberta's third city, **LETHBRIDGE** is booming on the back of oil, gas and some of the province's most productive agricultural land; none of which is of much consequence to people passing through, whom the city attempts to sidetrack with the **Nikka Yuko Centennial Gardens** (mid-May to June & Sept daily 9am–5pm; July–Aug daily 9am–8pm; closed Oct–April; $3; ☎328-3511) in its southeastern corner at 7th Avenue and Mayor Macgrath Drive in Henderson Lake Park. Built in 1967 as a symbol of Japanese and Canadian amity, the gardens were a somewhat belated apology for the treatment of Japanese-Canadians during World War II, when 22,000 were interned – 6000 of them in Lethbridge. Four tranquil Japanese horticultural landscapes make up the gardens, along with a pavilion of cypress wood handcrafted in Japan perpetually laid out for a tea ceremony.

Far removed from the gardens' decorum is **Fort Whoop-Up** (June–Aug Mon–Sat 10am–6pm, Sun noon–5pm; Sept–May Tues–Fri 10am–4pm, Sun 1–4pm; $2.50; ☎329-0444) at Indian Battle Park (Scenic Drive at 3rd Avenue), a reconstruction of the wild whiskey trading post set up in 1869 by American desperadoes from Fort Benton, Montana (the first of several in the region). It became the largest and most lucrative of the many similar forts which sprang up illegally all over the Canadian prairies, and led directly to the arrival of the North West Mounted Police in 1874. Natives came from miles around to trade anything – including the clothes off their backs – for the lethal hooch, which was fortified by grain alcohol and supplemented by ingredients such as red peppers, dye and chewing tobacco. The fort was also the scene of the last armed battle in North America between Native American tribes (fought between the Cree and Blackfoot nations in 1870).

Lethbridge's third significant sight is the **Sir Alexander Galt Museum** (July & Aug Mon–Thurs 9am–8pm, Fri 9am–4pm, Sat & Sun 1–8pm; Sept–June Mon–Fri 10am–4pm except Wed 10am–8pm, Sat & Sun 1–4pm; donation; ☎320-3898) at the western end of 5th Ave South off Scenic Drive, widely regarded as one of Canada's leading small-town museums. It's named after a Canadian high commissioner who in 1882 financed a mine that led to the foundation of Lethbridge. Revamped at vast expense in 1985, the museum offers an overview of the city's history, with displays that cover coal mining, irrigation, immigration and the shameful internment episodes during the 1940s. There are also a couple of galleries devoted to art and other temporary exhibitions.

Practicalities

Four Greyhound **buses** operate daily from Calgary to the Lethbridge bus terminal (☎327-1551) at 411-5th St South. Two buses run daily to Fort Macleod, and two to Medicine Hat and the US border for connections to Great Falls and Helena in Montana. The **tourist office** is at 2805 Scenic Drive at the corner of Hwy 4 and Hwy 5 (summer daily 9am–8pm; winter Mon–Sat 9am–5pm; ☎320-1222 or 1-800-661-1222 from western Canada and northwestern US).

Most of the city's **motels** are on a single strip, Mayor Macgrath Drive; the top-of-the-pile *Sandman Hotel Lethbridge*, at no. 421 (☎328-1111 or 1-800-726-3626; ④), and the less expensive *Chinook Motel*, at no. 1303 (☎328-0555 or 1-800-791-8488; ②), are typical. Women alone can stay at the *YWCA*, 604-8th St South (☎329-0088; ①). The *Henderson Lake Campgrounds* (☎328-5452; $11; May–Oct) are near Henderson Lake alongside the Nikka Yuko Centennial Gardens. The best downtown **eating** is to be found in the *Lethbridge Lodge Hotel* at 320 Scenic Drive (☎328-1123 or 1-800-661-1232), which boasts *Anton's*, an upmarket restaurant with modern American food, and the cheaper but pleasant *Garden Café*. For downtown coffee and snacks, make for *The Penny Coffee House*, 331 5th St South, or the *Union Coffee House*, 222 5th St.

Fort Macleod and around

FORT MACLEOD catches traffic coming up from the States and down from Calgary on Hwy 2, which eases around the town centre via the largely rebuilt wooden palisade of the **Fort Museum** at 219 25th St (daily: May, June & Sept to mid-Oct 9am–5pm; July & Aug 9am–8.30pm; mid-Oct to Dec 23 & March–May Mon–Fri 10am–4pm; $4; ☎553-4703). One for die-hard Mountie fans, this was the first fort established in Canada's Wild West by the North West Mounted Police, who got lost after being dispatched to raid Fort Whoop-Up in Lethbridge, allowing the whiskey traders to flee; finding Whoop-Up empty, they continued west under Colonel James Macleod to establish a permanent barracks here on Oldman Island on the river in 1874. The RCMP "musical ride", a display of precision riding, is performed four times daily in July and August by students in replica dress.

Two daily **buses** serve the town from Lethbridge and between three and five from Calgary, the latter continuing west to Cranbrook, Nelson and eventually to Vancouver in British Columbia. The depot's at 2302 2nd Ave (☎553-3383). The **tourist office** is at the east end of town on 24th Street (mid-May to Aug daily 9am–8pm; ☎553-4955). The town has seven similarly priced **motels**, the most central being the *Fort Motel* on Main Street (☎553-3606; ②). Top choice is the *Sunset Motel* (☎553-4448; ③–④), located on Hwy 3 at the western entrance to town. All motels fill up quickly in summer, so arrive early or call ahead.

Head-Smashed-In Buffalo Jump

The image of Indians trailing a lone buffalo with bow and arrow may be Hollywood's idea of how Native Americans foraged for food, but the truth, while less romantic, was often far more effective and spectacular. Over a period of more than 6000–10,000 years, Blackfoot hunters perfected a technique of luring buffalo herds into a shallow basin and stampeding them to their deaths over a broad cliff, where they were then butchered for meat (dried to make pemmican, a cake of pounded meat, berries and lard), bone (for tools) and hide (for clothes and shelter). Such "jumps" existed all over North America, but the **Head-Smashed-In Buffalo Jump**, in the Porcupine Hills 18km northwest of Fort Macleod on Hwy 785, is the best preserved (daily: May–Aug 9am–8pm; Sept–April 9am–5pm; $6.50; ☎553-2731). Its name, which alone should be enough to whet your appetite, is a literal description of how a nineteenth-century Blackfoot met his end after deciding the best spot to watch the jump was at the base of the cliff, apparently unaware he was about to be visited by some five hundred plummeting buffalo.

The modern **interpretive centre**, a seven-storeyed architectural *tour de force*, is built into the ten-metre-high and 305-metre-wide cliff near the original jump. Below it, a ten-metre-deep bed of ash and bones accumulated over millennia is protected by the threat of a $50,000 fine for anyone foolish enough to rummage for souvenirs. All manner of artefacts and objects have been discovered amidst the debris, among them knives, scrapers and sharpened stones used to skin the bison. Metal arrowheads in the topmost layers, traded with white settlers, suggest the jump was used until comparatively recently. Nothing can have changed much here over millennia bar the skilfully integrated centre and some modest excavations. The multilevelled facility delves deep into the history of the jump and native culture in general, its highlight being a film, *In Search of the Buffalo*, which attempts to re-create the thunderous death plunge using a herd of buffalo, which were slaughtered, frozen and then somehow made to look like live animals hurtling to their deaths (shown half-hourly on Level Four). Around the centre the jump is surrounded by a couple of kilometres of **trails**, the starting point for tours conducted by Blackfoot native guides. No public transport serves the site; taxis from Fort Macleod cost about $20.

Remington-Alberta Carriage Centre

Alberta is hoping that the glittering new **Remington-Alberta Carriage Centre** (daily: mid-May to early Sept 9am–8pm; early Sept to mid-May 9am–5pm; $6.50, carriage rides June–Aug $3; ☎653-1000 or 653-5139). Although brilliantly executed, its appeal is perhaps more limited, centring on horse-drawn vehicles and evoking the atmosphere of their nineteenth-century heyday. The main hall boasts around sixty working carriages – the core of a private collection begun by Don Remington in the 1950s – and around 140 in passive display, the exhibits cleverly integrated with 25 "stories" that place the carriages in their social and cultural context. Additionally there's the chance to ride the carriages (usually for free), see working stables and admire the magnificent Quarters and Clydesdales that make up the centre's horse herd. Guides are often in period dress, and you can watch craftspeople in the process of building and renovating various carriages. Free guided tours run regularly around the site. The centre lies immediately south of **Cardston** at 623 Main St (across the river from the town centre), just off Hwy 2 about 50km south of Fort Macleod, and is handily placed for Waterton Lakes National Park.

Waterton Lakes National Park

WATERTON LAKES NATIONAL PARK, about 55km south of Fort Macleod, appears at first glance to be simply an addendum to the much larger Glacier National Park, which joins it across the United States border. Despite its modest acreage, however (just 523 square kilometre), it contains scenery – and trails – as stupendous as any of the bigger Canadian Rockies parks. In particular this is a great place to come for day-hikes, most of which – unlike equivalent walks in Banff and Jasper – can be easily accessed from the park's principal focus, **Waterton Townsite** (or Waterton). Founded in 1895, the park was relaunched in 1932 as an "International Peace Park" to symbolize the understated relationship between Canada and its neighbour. The two parks remain separate national enclaves. Though backpackers can cross the border without formalities, to drive from one to the other you have to exit the park and pass through immigration controls, as stringent as anywhere if you're not a national of either country. In a change to the practice of past years, a **park permit** is required between April and the end of September for all who enter the park: a day pass is $4 and group passes (2–10 people) cost $12 daily (see box on p.567 for more details concerning park entry fees).

Some history

These days Waterton is on the road pretty much to nowhere – if you're down this way you're here to see the park or on your way to or from the US. It was a different story in the past, for the region provided a happy hunting ground for **Ktunaxa** (Kootenai) First Peoples, whose home base was across the Continental Divide in the Kootenay region of present-day British Columbia. Around 200 archeological sites betraying their presence have been found in the park. Anything up to 9000 years ago tribespeople crossed the mountains to fish and hunt bison on the prairie grasslands fringing the Waterton region, foodstuffs denied to them in their own tribal heartlands. By about 1700 the diffusion of the horse across North America (introduced by the Spanish) allowed rival tribes, namely the Blackfoot, to extend their sphere of influence from central Alberta into the area around Waterton. Their presence and increased mobility made it increasingly difficult for the Ktunaxa to make their habitual incursions, though Blackfoot supremacy in turn was to be cut short by the arrival of pioneer guns and white homesteads. By the mid-nineteenth century the Blackfoot had retreated eastwards, leaving the Waterton area virtually uninhabited. The region was named by Lieutenant Thomas Blakiston, a member of the famous Palliser expedition, in honour of the eighteenth-century British naturalist Charles Waterton.

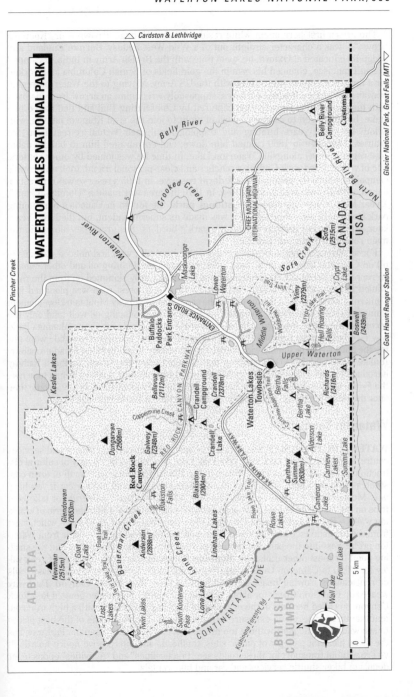

WATERTON LAKES NATIONAL PARK

△ Cardston & Lethbridge

△ Pincher Creek

Belly River

Crooked Creek

Waterton River

Kesler Lakes

Dungarvan (2566m)

Galwey (2348m)

RED ROCK CANYON PARKWAY

Red Rock Canyon

Coppermine Creek

Blakiston Falls

Blakiston (2904m)

Bauerman Creek

Lone Creek

Glendowan (2653m)

Goat Lake

Goat Lake Trail

Newman (2515m)

Tamarack Trail

Anderson (2698m)

Lineham Lakes

Rowe Lake Trail

Rowe Lakes

Lost Lakes

Twin Lakes

Lone Lake

South Kootenay Pass

Akamina Pass Trail

Kishinena Forestry Rd

CONTINENTAL DIVIDE

ALBERTA

BRITISH COLUMBIA

Wall Lake

Forum Lake

N

5 km

0

Maskinonge Lake

Lower Waterton

Park Entrance

Buffalo Paddocks

ENTRANCE ROAD

Bellevue (2112m)

Crandell (2378m)

Crandell Campground

Crandell Lake

AKAMINA PARKWAY

Waterton Lakes Townsite

Middle Waterton

Wishbone Trail

Crypt Lake Trail

Vimy Trail

Bertha Lake Trail

Carthew-Alderson Trail

Bertha Falls

Bertha Lake

Alderson Lake

Carthew Summit (2630m)

Carthew Lakes

Summit Lake

Cameron Lake

Sofa Creek

Sofa (2515m)

Vimy (2379m)

Hell Roaring Falls

Crypt Lake (2515m)

Upper Waterton

Richards (2416m)

Boswell (2439m)

CHIEF MOUNTAIN INTERNATIONAL HIGHWAY

Belly River Campground

North Belly River

Customs

CANADA

USA

△ Glacier National Park, Great Falls (MT)

▽ Goat Haunt Ranger Station

The area's first permanent white resident, **John George Brown** – or "Kootenai Brown" – was a character straight out of a Wild West fantasy. Born in England and allegedly educated at Oxford, he spent time with the British Army in India, decamped to San Francisco, chanced his arm in the gold fields of British Columbia and worked for a time as a pony express rider with the US Army. Moving to the Waterton region he was attacked by Blackfoot natives, supposedly wrenching an arrow from his back with his own hands. He was then captured by Chief Sitting Bull and tied naked to a stake, but managed to escape at dead of night to join the rival Ktunaxa natives, with whom he spent years hunting and trapping, until their virtual retreat from the prairies. Marriage in 1869 calmed him down, and encouraged him to build a cabin (the region's first) alongside Waterton Lake. In time he was joined by other settlers, one of whom, Frederick Godsal, a rancher and close personal friend, took up Brown's campaign to turn the region into a **federal reserve**. In 1895 a reserve was duly established, with Brown as its first warden. In 1910 the area was made a "Dominion Park"; a year later it was designated a **national park**, the fourth in Canada's burgeoning park system. Brown, then aged 71, was made its superintendent, but died four years later, still lobbying hard to extend the park's borders. His grave lies alongside the main road into Waterton Townsite.

For all Brown's environmental zeal it was he, ironically, who first noticed globules of **oil** on Cameron Creek, a local river, a discovery that would bring oil and other mineral entrepreneurs to ravage the region. Brown himself actually skimmed oil from the river, bottled it, and sold it in nearby settlements. In 1901 a forest road was ploughed into Cameron Creek Valley. In September of the same year the Rocky Mountain Development Company struck oil, leading to western Canada's first producing oil well (and only the second in the entire country). The oil soon dried up, a monument on the Akamina Parkway (see below) now marking the well's original location. Tourists meanwhile were giving the park a conspicuously wide berth, thanks mainly to the fact that it had no railway (unlike Banff and Jasper), a situation that changed when the Great Northern Railway introduced a bus link here from its Montana to Jasper railway. Visitors began to arrive, the *Prince of Wales* hotel was built, and the park's future was assured. In 1995, some time after the other big parks, UNESCO declared Waterton a World Heritage Site.

Waterton Townsite

WATERTON TOWNSITE, the park's only base, accommodation source and services centre, is beautifully set on Upper Waterton Lake, but offers little by way of cultural distraction: the small herd of Plains Bison in the **Bison Paddock** just north of town constitutes the only "sight" – don't get too close and don't get out of your car if you have one. Most people are here to walk (see box, p.560), windsurf, horseride or take boat trips on the lake (see below). There are also a handful of town trails, and a trio of cracking walks – Bertha Lake, Crypt Lake and the Upper Waterton Lakeshore – which start from the townsite (see box on p.560). Two wonderfully scenic access roads from Waterton probe west into the park interior and provide picnic spots, viewpoints and the starting point for most other trails: the **Akamina Parkway** follows the Cameron Creek valley for 20km to Cameron Lake, a large subalpine lake where you can follow easy trails or rent canoes, rowing boats and paddleboats. The **Red Rock Canyon Parkway** weaves up Blakiston Creek for about 15km to the mouth of the water-gouged Red Rock Canyon, so called because of the oxidation of local argillite, a rock with a high iron content that turns rust-red on exposure to the elements. The road's one of the best places to see wildlife in the park without too much effort and, like the Akamina Parkway, has the usual pleasant panoply of picnic sites, trailheads and interpretive notice boards. If you're without transport for these roads see "Practicalities" and "Activities" opposite for details of hiker shuttle services and car and bike rentals.

The third named road in the park, the **Chief Mountain International Highway** (25km) runs east from the park entrance at Maskinonge Lake along the park's eastern border. After 7km it reaches a fine **viewpoint** over the mountain-backed Waterton Valley and then passes the park-run *Belly River Campground* (see p.558) before reaching the US–Canadian **border crossing** (open June to late Sept 7am–10pm). When this crossing's closed, depending on your direction of travel, you have to use the crossings on Alberta's Hwy 2 south of Cardston or Hwy 89 north of St Mary in Montana.

Practicalities

Canadian **access** to Waterton is from Fort Macleod via either Hwy 3 west and Hwy 6 south (via Pincher Creek) or on Hwy 2 south to Cardston and then west on Hwy 5. Calgary is 264km and three hours' drive away; Lethbridge, 130km (75min); and St Mary, Montana, 60km (45min). More than other Rockies' parks this is somewhere you really need your own transport to reach. A small taxi-bus service, the Shuttleton Services (usually three times daily, but ring for services; ☎627-2157) runs between Waterton and the nearest Greyhound depot at Pincher Creek 50km away ($15 one way, $25 return); a cab from Crystal Taxi (☎627-4262) will cost around $50 for the same run; otherwise there's no public transport to the town or within the park.

Everything you need to explore the park centres on Waterton Townsite. All accommodation is here, bar the campgrounds, while the national park **visitor centre** is on Entrance Road at the road junction just to the north (May & early Sept 9am–5pm; June–Aug 8am–9pm; ☎859-2445 or 859-2224). Further information is available from the Chamber of Commerce (☎859-2303) and at the park's administration office at 215 Mount View Rd outside the visitor centre's summer hours (Mon–Fri 8am–4pm; ☎859-2477, 859-2224 or 859-2275). The free weekly **newspaper**, the *Waterton-Glacier Views* (☎627-2370), also contains visitor information. Be sure to buy the Canadian Parks Service 1:50,000 **map** *Waterton Lakes National Park* ($9.50), if you're going to do any serious walking. It's usually available from the visitor centre and the **Waterton Heritage Centre** in the old firehall at 117 Waterton Ave (May–Oct 1–5pm, longer hours July & Aug; admission to museum by donation; ☎859-2267 or 859-2624). The latter is a combined art gallery, small natural history museum, bookshop and another useful source of information. For advance information on the park, write to the Superintendent, Waterton Lakes National Park, Waterton Park, AB T0K 2M0.

Pat's Convenience Store, a gas station and camping store on the corner of Mount View Road and Waterton Avenue (☎859-2266), rents out **bikes** and **scooters** by the hour or day and also sells bikes and spares. For **currency exchange**, try the Royal Bank in Tamarack Mall on Waterton Avenue or the Alberta Treasury Branch Agency upstairs at Caribou Clothing on Waterton Avenue (☎859-2604). The Itussististukiopi Coin-Op **laundry** is at 301 Windflower Ave (mid-June to mid-Sept daily 8am–10pm). Waterton Sports and Leisure in Tamarack Mall stocks maps, fishing licences, and camping, walking, fishing and mountain-biking equipment and accessories. The **post office** is alongside the fire station on Fountain Avenue. The nearest **hospitals** are in Cardston (☎653-4411) and Pincher Creek (☎627-3333). For the **police**, call ☎859-2244. There's also a 24-hour park emergency number, but it really *is* for emergencies only (☎859-2636).

Activities

If you want to **cruise the lakes**, the most popular summer activity round these parts, contact Waterton Inter-Nation Shoreline Cruises at the marina (☎859-2362). They run scenic two-hour cruises (June–Aug 5 daily; fewer in May & Sept; $17 or $10 one way) up and down the lake across the US–Canadian border to Goat Haunt in Montana, little more than a quayside and park ranger station, where there is scheduled thirty-minute stop before the return to Waterton (note that after the ranger station closes in mid-September boats no longer stop at Goat Haunt). No immigration procedures are required, but if you

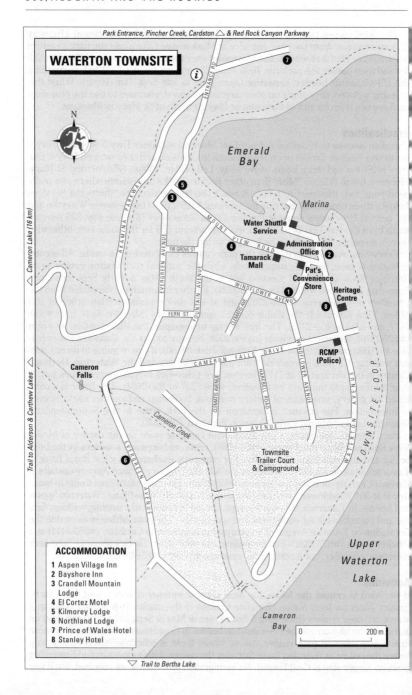

WATERTON TOWNSITE

i

7

N

Emerald
Bay

Marina

5

3

Water Shuttle
Service

MOUNT VIEW ROAD

Administration
Office

2

4

Tamarack
Mall

Pat's
Convenience
Store

1

Heritage
Centre

8

RCMP
(Police)

CAMERON FALLS DRIVE

Cameron
Falls

Cameron Creek

6

EVERGREEN AVENUE

CLEMATIS AVENUE

HARBELL ROAD

VIMY AVENUE

WATERTON AVENUE

TOWNSITE LOOP

Townsite
Trailer Court
& Campground

Upper
Waterton
Lake

Cameron
Bay

0   200 m

ENTRANCE RD

AKAMINA PARKWAY

EVERGREEN AVENUE

FIR GROVE ST

FOUNTAIN AVENUE

WINDFLOWER AVENUE

FERN ST

CLEMATIS AVE

Cameron Lake (16 km) △

Trail to Alderson & Carthew Lakes △

▽ Trail to Bertha Lake

ACCOMMODATION

1 Aspen Village Inn
2 Bayshore Inn
3 Crandell Mountain
   Lodge
4 El Cortez Motel
5 Kilmorey Lodge
6 Northland Lodge
7 Prince of Wales Hotel
8 Stanley Hotel

wish to camp overnight in the backcountry you need to register with the ranger station. You can take an early boat to Goat Haunt and then return on foot to Waterton on the **Waterton Lakeshore Trail**, an easy four-hour walk (13km one way). The same company also provides the **Hikers' Water Shuttle Service**, a ferry to various trails around the lake, most notably a passage ($9 return) to the trailhead of the famed Crypt Lake walk (see box, p.560) and the myriad longer hikes from Goat Haunt in the US. Park Transport in Tamarack Mall on Mount View Road (☎859-2378) organizes two-hour tours round the park ($20), but will also lay on a **taxi** shuttle ($7) to trails on the area's two Parkways: the most popular drop-off is the beginning of the Carthew-Alderson trail (see box, p.560).

Windsurfing is also surprisingly popular locally, thanks to the powerful winds – anything up to 70kph – which often roar across the lakes (Waterton is wetter, windier and snowier than much of Alberta). Winds generally gust south to north, making the beach at Cameron Bay on Upper Waterton Lake a favourite spot for surfers to catch the breeze. The water's cold and deep, though, so you'll need a wet suit. If you want to **swim**, head for the cheap outdoor heated pool on Cameron Falls Drive. **Fishing** is good on the lakes, but remember to pick up the compulsory national park permit ($6 a week) from the visitor centre or park administration office. Off the water, **horseriding** is available from the Alpine Stables, PO Box 53, Waterton Park, AB (☎859-2462), located just east off the highway about 1km north of the Visitor Centre. On offer are one-hour outings (hourly on the hour; from $15) and two-hour, daily and overnight treks. Canadian Wilderness Adventures (☎859-2334, fax 859-2342) offer a range of guided walks and tours long and short. Four kilometres north of town on the main highway is the beautiful eighteen-hole **Waterton Lakes Golf Course** (☎859-2383): green fees are around $30 (cheaper after 5pm) and club rental from $7.50.

Hotels and motels

Aspen Village Inn, Windflower Avenue (☎859-2255, fax 859-2033). Quiet spot with mountain views opposite the municipal pool; 38 motel rooms, twelve bungalows and eight-person suites, some with kitchenettes. April to mid-Oct. ⑤.

Bayshore Inn, 111 Waterton Ave (☎859-2211, fax 859-2291). Just south of the marina; very comfortable hotel, 49 of whose seventy units are on the lakefront; two-unit and deluxe suites available. Mid-April to mid-Oct. ⑤.

Crandell Mountain Lodge, 102 Mount View Rd, corner of Evergreen Avenue (☎859-2288 or 1-888-859-2288, fax 859-2288). Just seventeen nicely finished rooms (two with special wheelchair access), so more intimate than some of the town's hotels; kitchenette and fireplace units available. Easter–Oct. ④–⑥.

El Cortez Motel, next to the Tamarack Mall at 208 Mount View Rd (☎859-2366, fax 859-2605). One of the less expensive places in town; 35 rooms including two- and three-room family units; some rooms with kitchenettes. May to mid-Oct. ④.

Kilmorey Lodge, 117 Evergreen Ave (☎859-2334, fax 859-2342). At the northern entrance to town on Emerald Bay; 23 antique-decorated rooms with a lakefront setting and historic old-fashioned feel. Some rooms have good views (book in advance for these); there's also an excellent restaurant and nice *Gazebo Café on the Bay* with outdoor waterfront deck for snacks and light meals (open to non-residents). Open all year. ④–⑤.

The Lodge At Waterton Lakes, (☎859-2151 or 1-888-985-6343, fax 859-2229). Smart new resort hotel, which opened in the summer of 1997; health spa with indoor pool, rooms with kitchenettes, recreational centre and lots of extra facilities. ⑥–⑦.

Northland Lodge, Evergreen Avenue (☎859-2353). Eight cosy rooms, six with private bathroom, east of the townsite in the lee of the mountains one block south of Cameron Falls; some kitchenettes. Mid-May to mid-Oct. ②.

Prince of Wales Hotel, Waterton Lake (☎859-2231, 236-3400 or 602/207-6000, fax 859-2630). Famous and popular old hotel – the best in town – whose 1927 Gothic outline is in almost every picture of Waterton; worth it if you can afford it. Lakeside rooms with those with views are pricier, but some are rather small, so check what you're getting. Mid-May to mid-Sept. ⑥–⑦.

Stanley Hotel, 112b Waterton Ave (☎859-2345). Old-fashioned and often full nine-roomed hotel. Mid-May to Sept. ③.

GEOLOGY, FLORA AND FAUNA

The Waterton area's unique **geological history** becomes obvious on the ground once you've been able to compare its scenery with the strikingly different landscapes of Banff and Jasper national parks to the north (see pp.565–600 and pp.600–610). Rock and mountains in Waterton moved eastward during the formation of the Rockies (see p.566), but unlike the ruptured strata elsewhere it travelled as a single vast mass known as the Lewis Thrust. Some 6km thick, this monolith moved over 70km along a 300-kilometre front, the result being that rocks over 1.5 billion years old from the Rockies' "sedimentary basement"– now the oldest surface rocks in the range – finally came to rest undisturbed on *top* of the prairies' far more recent 60-million-year-old shales. Scarcely any zone of transition exists between the two, which is why the park is often known as the place where the "peaks meet the prairies", and its landscapes as "upside-down mountains". The effect was to produce not only slightly lower peaks than to the north, but also mountains whose summits are irregular in shape and whose sedimentary formations are horizontal (very different from the steeply tilted strata and distinctive sawtooth ridges of Banff National Park).

The classic glacial U-shaped Waterton Valley and Upper Waterton Lake (at 150m, the Rockies' deepest lake) are more recent phenomena, gouged out 1.9 million years ago by ice age **glaciers** as they carved their way northwards through the present Waterton valley before expiring on the prairies. Upper Waterton Lake and the other two Waterton lakes are residual depressions left after the ice's final retreat 11,000 years ago. Cameron Lake, by contrast, was created when a glacial moraine (debris created by a glacier) dammed the waters of Cameron Creek. The flat townsite area has different origins again, consisting of deposits of silt, mud and gravel washed down from the mountains over the millennia and deposited as an alluvial "fan" across Upper Waterton Lake.

The huge variety of altitude, habitats and climate within the park – a combination of prairie, montane and alpine – mean that plants and wildlife from prairie habitats co-mingle with the species of the purely montane, sub-alpine and alpine regions found elsewhere. The result is the greatest diversity of **flora and fauna** of any of the western national parks: 1200 plant species – well over half of all that grown in Alberta – and 250 species of birds. The variety is immediately noticeable. As you approach the park on Hwy 5 from the north, a route almost as scenic as the park, you pass through dry prairie **grasslands**. This is home to native grasses such as grama and rough fescue, local species now rapid-

Campgrounds

In addition to the private and three Canadian Parks Service park-run campgrounds that are detailed below, the national park has provided thirteen designated **backcountry campgrounds**, where you'll find dry toilets and a surface water supply; a few of them also have shelters and cooking facilities. To use any, you need a backcountry camping permit, issued on a first-come, first-served basis by the Visitor Centre or Administration Office. A quota system is operated to prevent overcrowding. For information on these and other park campgrounds, call ☎859-2224, fax 859-2650. Unrestricted camping within the park is usually permitted only at Lineham Lakes, reached by a 4.2-kilometre trail off the north side of the Akamina Parkway 9.5km from Waterton. Note that at park sites you can pay an optional $3 to use the firewood provided.

Belly River Campground, 29km from the townsite, 1km off Chief Mountain Parkway on Hwy 6 (☎859-2224). Smallest (24 sites) and simplest of the park-operated campgrounds. Self-registration; tap water; kitchen shelters; fireplaces, chemical and pit toilets. Mid-May to Sept. $10 plus optional $3 firewood permit

Crandell Mountain Campground, 8km west of Waterton on the Red Rock Canyon Parkway of Hwy 5 (☎859-2224). Semi-serviced park-run campground with 129 sites. Tap water; fireplaces; no showers. Mid-May to late Sept. $13.

Homestead Campground, 3km north of Waterton Park Gateway on Hwy 6 (☎859-2247). Large private 260-site campground with services, showers, store, video games, laundry, heated outdoor pool, dance floor and many other distractions. May to mid-Sept. $12.

ly disappearing, displaced over the years by cultivated crops. Here, too, you should see the prickly wild rose, Alberta's floral emblem, sagebrush, buckbrush (yellow rose) and pincushion cactus. Entering the park you pass the **wetlands** of Maskinonge Lake on your left, while in the Blakison Valley and around *Belly River Campground* you are in the realms of **aspen parkland**, a transitional zone between prairie and forest habitats dominated by aspen, willow, white spruce, balsam poplar and flowers such as prairie crocus, snowberry and lily of the valley. Higher up you encounter **montane forest** and sub-alpine zones, fecund zones rich in plant and animal life easily explored on hikes such as the Bertha Lake and Carthew Lakes trails (see p.560). On the eastern slopes above Cameron Lake are copses of 400-year-old sub-alpine trees (lodgepole pine, larch, fir, whitebark pine and Engelmann spruce), the oldest forest growth in the park. Here, too, you'll see vast spreads of so-called bear grass, a bright flower-topped grass which can grow up to a metre in height. Trees largely give out in the **alpine zone**, an area of which the park's Crypt Lake is a good example. It is the preserve of heathers, hardy lichens, flower-strewn meadows and rarer high-altitude alpine plants. See "Contexts" p.876 for more on these various habitats.

If you want to see **fauna**, enquire at the park centre for likely locations and times – autumn days at dawn and dusk are usually best. **Birds** are best seen on Maskinonge and Lower Waterton lakes, Linnet Lake, Cameron Lake and along the easy 45-minute Wishbone Trail off Chief Mountain Highway. The best time to look is during the migratory season between September and November, as the park lies under two major migration routes. Ospreys also nest close to Waterton Townsite. Maskinonge Lake is also the place to sit in the hope of seeing mink and muskrats. As for **mammals**, beavers can be seen on the Belly River, and Golden-mantled ground squirrels around Cameron Lake and on the Bear's Hump above town; Columbian ground squirrels are ubiquitous. The park has about fifty black bears, but you'll be lucky to see them: your best bet is to scan the slopes of Blakison Valley in July and August as they forage for berries in readiness for hibernation. Grizzlies, moose and cougars are also prevalent, but rarely seen. White-tailed deer nibble up and down the Red Rock Canyon Parkway, while elk and mule deer often wander in and around Waterton town itself. Mountain goats are shy and elusive, but you may glimpse one or two in the rocky high ground above Bertha, Crypt and Goat lakes. Bighorn sheep congregate above the Visitor Centre and the northern flanks of the Blakison Valley.

Riverside Campground, 5km east of Waterton Park Gateway (☎653-2888). Private; seventy sites with showers, services, breakfasts and live entertainment and barbecue suppers every Saturday. Mid-May to mid-Sept. $10.

Waterton Townsite Campground, off Vimy Avenue (☎859-2224). 238-site serviced park-run campground in town. First-come, first-served basis, and fills up by mid-afternoon in summer. Showers; no open fires; wheelchair-accessible. Self-registration after Labour Day (early Sept). May to Thanksgiving (early Oct). $17.

Eating

Fast Eddy's Gourmet Take-Out, Tamarack Mall. Sandwiches, ice cream, good cappuccino and special hikers' lunch packs (reserve the night before for the last).

Lakeside Kootenai Brown Dining Room, Waterton Avenue at the *Bayshore Inn* (☎859-2211). Along with the *Prince of Wales'* dining rooms, one of the better and more elegant spots in town to treat yourself; the dining room overlooks the lake. Open all day for breakfast, lunch and dinner.

Lamp Post Dining Room, 117 Evergreen Ave at the *Kilmorey Lodge* (☎859-2334). Same sort of old-world appeal and tempting good food as the *Prince of Wales'* dining rooms but without the stuffiness; the prices are lower too (7.30am–10pm). The hotel's *Gazebo* café on the waterfront is also good for snacks (10am–10pm).

New Frank's Restaurant, 106 Waterton Ave (☎859-2240). This recently renovated restaurant serves cheap, odd combinations of breakfasts, burgers, a Chinese buffet plus lunch and six-course buffet specials.

HIKING IN WATERTON LAKES PARK

Waterton Lakes Park's 255km of trails have a reputation as not only the best constructed in the Canadian Rockies, but also among the most easily graded, well marked and scenically routed. Like Moraine Lake in Banff National Park – and unlike Banff and Jasper – you can also access superb walks easily without a car. Bar one or two outlying hikes, three key areas contain trails and trailheads: the **townsite** itself, which has two magnificent short walks; the **Akamina Parkway**; and the **Red Rock Canyon Parkway**. Most walks are day hikes, climaxing at small alpine lakes cradled in spectacular hanging valleys. Options for backpacking are necessarily limited by the park's size, though the 36-kilometre **Tamarack Trail**, following the crenellations of the Continental Divide between the Akamina Parkway (trailhead as for Rowe Lakes – see opposite) and Red Rock Canyon, is rated as one of the Rockies' greatest high-line treks (maximum elevation 2560m); the twenty-kilometre Carthew–Alderson Trail from Cameron Lake to Waterton (maximum elevation 2311m), a popular day's outing, can be turned into a two-day trip by overnighting at the Alderson Lake campground. To do it in a day, take advantage of the hiker shuttle service to the trailhead offered by Park Transport (☎859-2378) based in the Tamarack Mall on Mount View Road (see p.555).

In summary, this is a great park in which to base yourself for a few days' hiking: details of hikes are given below, but as a general guide to do the cream of the hikes you'd first stroll the **Bear's Hump** for views of Waterton town and the lakes; then walk all or part of the **Bertha Lake Trail** (day or half-day) from the townsite. Next day take a boat to Goat Haunt and walk back on the **Waterton Lakeshore Trail**. Then try the **Crypt Lake Trail** from the townsite and/or the **Rowe Lake–Lineham Ridge Trail**, both ranked among the best day walks in the Rockies. Finally gird your loins for the longer **Carthew–Alderson Trail**, possible in a day.

Walks from the townsite

In and around the town, there are various short loops: stroll to Cameron Falls, try the Prince of Wales from the Visitor Centre (2km; 45min) or climb the more demanding **Bear's Hump**, also from the centre (1.2km; 200m vertical; 40min one way); the latter is one of the park's most popular short walks, switchbacking up the slopes to a rocky outcrop with great views of the Waterton Valley. More surprisingly good views can be had from the easily reached viewpoint near the Bison Paddock. Another obvious, and very simple walk from the town is the Waterton Lakeshore Trail (13km one way; 100m ascent; 4hr), which follows Upper Waterton Lake's west shore across the US border to Goat Haunt; regular lake ferries sail back to the townsite, completing a lovely round trip (ferry details from the marina or call ☎859-2362; see main text). Alternatively, catch an early boat and walk back so as not to worry about making a boat connection.

The single most popular half-day or day's walk from the townsite, however, is the classic **Bertha Lake Trail** from Waterton, 5.8km each way with an ascent of 460m (allow 3–4hr for the round trip). It's a short, steep hike beginning on Evergreen Drive to a busy but remarkably unsullied mountain-ringed lake and there's an easy trail that runs right round the lakeshore (adding about another 5km to the trip). If you're not up to this, you can just do the first part of the trail and break off at Lower Bertha Falls (2.9km from the townsite; 150m ascent; 1hr): this deservedly popular section corresponds to the route of the *Bertha Falls Self-Guiding Nature Trail* pamphlet available from the Visitor Centre.

Pearl's Patio Café and Deli, 305 Windflower Ave (☎859-2284). Fresh baking; great first choice for breakfast, lunch, coffee, deli meats, picnic provisions and hikers' takeaway lunches. Indoor and outdoor tables.

Pizza of Waterton, 103 Fountain Ave (☎859-2660). Dough made daily on the premises; good pizzas to eat in or take away. Open daily 4.30–10pm.

Windsor Lounge, *Prince of Wales Hotel* (☎859-2231). One of several lounges, bars and dining rooms in this posh hotel open for non-patrons to enjoy afternoon tea, a good breakfast or a refined hour with a drink and great lake views. Dress the part, and don't come here straight off the trail. The *Garden Court* is the *really* smart restaurant here (reservations required).

Another excellent walk out of Waterton is the unique **Crypt Lake Trail**, often touted as one of the best in Canada. The 8.7-kilometre hike (one way; 675m ascent) involves a boat trip ($9 round trip) across Upper Waterton Lake to the trailhead on the east side of the lake, a (perfectly safe) climb up a ladder, a crawl through a rock tunnel and a section along a rocky ledge with cable for support. The rewards are the crashing waterfalls and the great glacial amphitheatre containing Crypt Lake (1955m); rock walls tower 600m on three sides, casting a chill shadow that preserves small icebergs on the lake's surface throughout the summer. Allow time to catch the last boat back to Waterton (again, ferry details are on ☎859-2362), and note that it's a good idea to make reservations in summer. Campers should be aware that the site here is one of the most heavily used in the park's backcountry.

Trails from the Akamina Parkway

Most of the trails accessed by the Akamina Parkway leave from the road's end near Cameron Lake. To stretch your legs after the drive up, or if you just want a stroll, try either the Akamina Lake (0.5km; 15min) or Cameron Lakeshore (1.6km; 30min) trails. The best of the longer walks is to Carthew Summit (7.9km one-way; 660m ascent), a superb trail that switchbacks through forest to Summit Lake (4km), a good target in itself, before opening out into sub-alpine meadow and a final climb to a craggy summit (2310m) and astounding viewpoint. The trail can be continued all the way back to Waterton Townsite (another 12km) – it's then the **Carthew–Alderson Trail** (see opposite), most of whose hard work you've done in getting up to Carthew Summit; from the summit it's largely steeply downhill via Carthew and Alderson lakes (1875m) to Cameron Falls and the townsite (1295m).

Another highly rated trail from the Akamina Parkway is equally appealing – the Rowe Lakes Trail (5.2km one way; 555m ascent), which is accessed off the Parkway about 5km before Cameron Lake (it is also the first leg of the Tamarack Trail – see opposite). Most people make their way to the Rowe Basin (where there's a backcountry campground) and then, rather than pushing on towards the Upper Rowe Lakes (1.2km beyond), either camp, turn around or – for stronger walkers – take the trail that branches right from the Upper Rowe path to walk to Lineham Ridge (another 3.4km and 540m ascent). This **Rowe Lake-Lineham Ridge** combination has been cited as some as one of the top five day hikes in the Rockies. The stiffish walk is rewarded by Lineham Lake, sapphire blue in the valley far below, and a vast sea of mountains stretching to the horizon. Only come up here in good weather, as it's particularly hazardous when visibility's poor and the winds are up.

Trails from the Red Rock Canyon Parkway

Most trails on the Red Rock Canyon Parkway, such as the short Red Rock Canyon Trail (700m loop) and Blackiston Falls (1km; 30min), leave from Red Rock Canyon at the end of the road. The most exhilarating option from the head of the road, however, is the Goat Lake Trail (6.7km; 550m ascent), which follows Bauerman Creek on an old fire road (flat and easy, but a little dull) before peeling off right at the 4.3-kilometre mark for the climb to tranquil Goat Lake and ever-improving views (there's a backcountry campground at the lake). If you ignore the lake turnoff and follow the fire road for another 4km, you come to a junction: one trail leads north to Lost Lake (2km), the other south to the spectacular Twin Lakes area (3.2km). This latter option will bring you to the long-distance Tamarack Trail (see opposite). Walk south on this from Twin Lakes (3.1km) and you can pick up the Blackiston Creek Trail, which will take you back to the head of the Red Rock Canyon. Parkway.

Crowsnest Pass

The 1382-metre **Crowsnest Pass** is the most southerly of the three major routes into the Rockies and British Columbia from Alberta, and far less attractive than the Calgary and Edmonton approaches. In its early stages as Hwy 3 pushes west out of Fort Macleod across glorious windblown prairie, it augurs well: the settlements are bleaker and more backwoods in appearance, and the vast unbroken views to the mountain-filled horizon appear much as they must have to the first pioneers. As the road climbs towards the pass, however, the grime and dereliction of the area's mining heritage make themselves increasingly felt. Hopes a century ago that Crowsnest's vast coal deposits might make it the "Pittsburgh of Canada" were dashed by disasters, poor-quality coal, complicated seams, cheaper coal from British Columbia and rapid obsolescence. Today much of the area has been declared an Historic District and turned into Alberta's only "ecomuseum", a desperate attempt to bring life and tourist cash back to economically blighted communities (many people commute to work in British Columbia's mines over the Pass or have left altogether). To some extent they've succeeded, though you have to pick your mining-related stopoffs carefully round here. If mines and disaster sites don't appeal, the Crowsnest route west is of most use as a direct route if you're hurrying to Vancouver or aim to explore the Kootenays in southern British Columbia. After breasting the pass, Hwy 3 drops into BC and follows the often spectacular Elk River Valley to join Hwy 95 at Cranbrook (see p.772).

Bellevue and the Frank Slide

Sleepy **BELLEVUE** is the first village worthy of the name after Fort Macleod; an oddball and close-knit spot with an old-world feel unusual in these parts. It's distinguished by a church the size of a dog kennel and a wooden tepee painted lemon yellow, as well as the claim to have "the best drinking water in Alberta". Nonetheless, it supports a small **info-centre** by the campground (see below) and provides visitors with the opportunity to explore – complete with hard hat and miner's lamp – a wonderfully dark and dank 100m or so of the old **Bellevue Mine** (tours every half-hour mid-May to early Sept daily 10am–5.30pm; $5.50 tickets from Jeanies Gifts on 213th St; ☎564-4700). The only mine open to the public locally, it ceased production in 1962, but remains infamous for an explosion in 1910 that destroyed the ventilator fan. Thirty men died in the disaster, though not from the blast, but by breathing so-called "afterdamp", a lethal mixture of carbon dioxide and carbon monoxide left after fire has burnt oxygen from the atmosphere. As if this wasn't enough, Canada's worst mining disaster ever had occurred five years earlier at **HILL-CREST**, a village immediately to the south of Bellevue (signed from Hwy 3), when 189 men were killed by an explosion and the effects of "afterdamp". All were buried together a few centimetres apart in mass graves, now the **Hillcrest Cemetery** on 8th Avenue.

Bellevue has a quaint **campground**, the *Bellecrest Community Association Campground* (☎564-4696; donation), located just off the highway just east of the village: it's open May to October and has 22 "random" sites, toilets, tap water and an on-site tenseat church with recorded sermons. The site is also handy for the **Leitch Collieries Provincial Historic Site**, just off the main road to the north before the campground. This was once the region's largest mining and coking concern; it was also the first to close (in 1915). Today there's little to see in the way of old buildings, but displays and boardwalk interpretive trails past "listening posts" fill you in on mining techniques. The overgrown site is also enthusiastically described by interpretive staff (mid-May to mid-Sept daily 10am–4pm; winter site unmanned; $2; ☎562-7388).

The Crowsnest Pass trail of destruction, death and disaster continues beyond Bellevue. Dominating the skyline behind the village are the crags and vast rock fall of the **Frank Slide**, an enormous landslide that has altered the contours of Turtle Mountain, once riddled with the galleries of local mines. On April 29, 1903 an estimated 100 million tonnes of rock on a front stretching for over 1km and 700m high trundled down the mountain, burying 68 people and their houses in less than two minutes. Amazingly none of the miners working locally were killed – they dug themselves out after fourteen hours of toil. The morbidly interesting **Frank Slide Interpretive Centre**, situated 1.5km off the highway about 1km north of the village, highlights European settlement in the area, the coming of the Canadian Pacific Railway to Alberta and the technology, attitudes and lives of local miners (daily June to early Sept 9am–8pm; early Sept to May 10am–4pm; $4; ☎562-7388). It's well worth wandering around the site and slide area –

there's a 1.5-kilometre trail or you can walk up the ridge above the car park for good views and an idea of the vast scale of the earth movement: no one to this day quite understands the science of how boulders travelled so far from the main slide (several kilometres in many cases). "Air lubrication" is the best theory, a device by which the cascading rock compressed the air in front of it, creating a hovercraft-like cushion of trapped air on which it "rode" across the surface.

Blairmore, Coleman and the Pass

BLAIRMORE, 2km beyond the slide, is a scrappy settlement redeemed only by the walks and four winter and night ski runs on the hill above it (Pass Powder Keg Ski Hill: ☎562-8334 for information). Largest of the Crowsnest towns (population around 1800), it has a handful of "historic" buildings, notably the *Cosmopolitan Hotel* – built in 1912 – at 13001-20th Ave (☎562-7321; ②), but neither town or hotel are places to linger. **COLEMAN** is the place to spend the night if you absolutely have to, especially if you've always wanted to be able to say you've seen "the biggest piggy bank in the world", made from an old steam engine once used to pull coal cars in local mines. The town, battered and bruised by mine closures, amounts to little – the small Crowsnest Museum in the old schoolhouse at 7701-18th Ave (mid-May to Oct daily 10am–4pm; Nov to mid-May Mon–Fri 10am–noon & 1–4pm; $2; ☎563-5434), a single road, a dilapidated strip of houses, three garages and a battered **motel**, the 24-unit *Stop Inn* (☎562-7381; ②), a place favoured by loggers. Almost as knocked about, though apparently recently smartened up a touch by the Southern Alberta Hostelling Association, is a **youth hostel**, the *Grand Union International Hostel*, 7719-17th Ave (☎563-3433; ①). More appealing is the dubiously named ten-unit *Kozy Knest Kabins Triple K Motel* (☎563-5155; ②), open from May to October and more scenically situated 8km west of Coleman on Hwy 3 beside Crowsnest Lake.

Beyond Coleman the road climbs towards **Crowsnest Pass** itself (1382m) and, after a rash of sawmills, the natural scenery finally takes centre stage in a reassuring mix of lakes, mountains and trees protected by **Crowsnest Provincial Park**. A rustic provincial **campground** overlooks the lake at Crowsnest Creek, about 15km west of Coleman ($5).

THE CANADIAN ROCKIES

Few North American landscapes come as loaded with expectation as the **Canadian Rockies**, and it's a relief to find that the superlatives are scarcely able to do credit to the region's immensity of forests, lakes, rivers and snowcapped mountains. Although most visitors confine themselves to visiting just a handful of **national parks**, the range spans almost 1500km as far as the Yukon border, forming the vast watershed of the Continental Divide, which separates rivers flowing to the Pacific, Arctic and Atlantic oceans. Landscapes on such a scale make a nonsense of artificial borderlines, and the major parks are national creations that span both Alberta and British Columbia. Four of the parks – Banff, Jasper, Yoho and Kootenay – share common boundaries, and receive the attention of most of the millions of annual visitors to the Rockies.

There's not a great deal to choose between the parks in terms of scenery – they're all fairly sensational – and planning an itinerary that allows you to fit them all in comfortably is just about impossible. Most visitors start with **Banff National Park**, then follow the otherworldly **Icefields Parkway** north to the larger and much less busy **Jasper National Park**. From there it makes sense to continue west to **Mount Robson Provincial Park**, which protects the highest and most dramatic peak in the Canadian Rockies. Thereafter you're committed to leaving the Rockies unless you double back from Jasper to Banff – no hardship, given the scenery – to pick up the Trans-Canada Highway through the smaller **Yoho**, **Glacier** and **Revelstoke** national parks. Finally, **Kootenay National Park** is more easily explored than its neighbours, though you'll have to backtrack towards Banff or loop down from Yoho to pick up the road that provides its only access. The more peripheral, but no less impressive Waterton Lakes National Park, hugging the US border, is covered on pp.552–560.

Though you can get to all the parks by **bus**, travelling by **car** or **bike** is the obvious way to get the most out of the region. Once there, you'd be foolish not to tackle some of the 3000km of trails that crisscross the mountains, the vast majority of which are well worn and well signed. We've highlighted the best short walks and day hikes in each area, and you can get more details from the **park visitor centres**, which sell 1:50,000 topographical maps and usually offer small reference libraries of trail books; *The Canadian Rockies Trail Guide*, by Brian Patton and Bart Robinson, is invaluable for serious hiking or backpacking. Other activities – fishing, skiing, canoeing, white-water rafting, cycling, horseriding, climbing and so on – are comprehensively dealt with in visitor centres, and you can easily **rent equipment** or sign up for organized tours in the bigger towns.

A word of warning: don't underestimate the Rockies. Despite the impression created by the summer throngs in centres like Banff and Lake Louise, excellent roads and sleek park facilities, the vast proportion of parkland is wilderness and should be respected and treated as such. See Basics, pp.50–53, for more.

Where to go in winter

Six major winter resorts are found in the Rockies – two in Kananaskis Country, two around Banff, and one each near Lake Louise and Jasper. Along with Whistler in British Columbia, these are some of the best, the most popular and the fastest-growing areas in Canada – and not only for downhill and cross-country skiing but also for dogsledding, ice climbing, skating, snowmobiling, snowshoeing, canyon crawling and ice fishing. At most resorts, the season runs from mid-December until the end of May; conditions are usually at their best in March, when the days are getting warmer and longer, and the snow is deepest. Resort accommodation is hardest to come by during Christmas week, the mid-February school holidays and at Easter.

Nakiska, 25km south of the Trans-Canada Highway in Kananaskis Country, is Canada's newest resort. Developed for the 1988 Winter Olympics, it's one of the most user-friendly on the continent, with state-of-the-art facilities; it has snowmaking on all its varied terrain and plenty of fine cross-country skiing. Fortress Mountain, 15km south of Nakiska on Hwy 40, is a much smaller area, where you're likely to share the slopes with school groups and families.

Banff's resorts are invariably the busiest and most expensive, and heavily patronized by foreigners (especially Japanese). Mount Norquay (see p.582) has long been known as an advanced downhill area – "steep and deep" in local parlance – but has recently expanded its intermediate runs, and also boasts the Canadian Rockies' only night skiing. Higher and more exposed, Sunshine Village (see p.582) has even better scenery but few advanced runs.

Lake Louise's three big hills (see p.592) add up to Canada's most extensive resort, with downhill skiing, plus cross-country trails crisscrossing the valley and the lake area. Jasper's Marmot Basin is a more modest downhill area, but it's quieter and cheaper than those further south, and the park, particularly around Maligne Lake, has almost limitless cross-country skiing possibilities.

Kananaskis Country

Most first-time visitors race straight up to Banff, ignoring the verdant foothill region southwest of Calgary. **Kananaskis Country**, a protected area created out of existing provincial parks to take pressure off Banff, remains almost the exclusive preserve of locals, most of whom come for skiing. Kananaskis embraces a huge tract of the Rockies and has all the mountain scenery and outdoor pursuit possibilities of the parks, without the people or the commercialism. It is, however, an area without real focus, much of it remote wilderness; nothing in the way of public transport moves out here, and the only fixed accommodation is in expensive, modern lodges – though it's idyllic camping country.

Minor roads from Calgary lead to such smaller foothill areas of the east as Bragg Creek, but the most obvious approach is to take Hwy 40, a major turn off the Trans-Canada Highway, which bisects Kananaskis's high mountain country from north to south and provides the ribbon to which most of the trails, campgrounds and scattered service centres cling. About 3km down the highway is the Barrier Lake Information Centre (daily 9am–5pm), where you can get a full breakdown on outdoor activities. Another 40km south of the centre is a short spur off Hwy 40 to Upper Kananaskis Lake, probably the biggest concentration of accessible boating, fishing, camping and hiking possibilities in the region. Popular short hikes include the Expedition Trail (2.4km); it and many others are detailed in the definitive *Kananaskis Country Trail Guide* by Gillean Daffern, which is widely available in Calgary.

Banff National Park

BANFF NATIONAL PARK is the most famous of the Canadian Rockies' parks and Canada's leading tourist attraction – so be prepared for the crowds that throng its key centres, **Banff** and **Lake Louise**, as well as the best part of its 1500km of trails, most of which suffer a continual pounding during the summer months. That said, it's worth putting up with every commercial indignity to enjoy the sublime scenery – and if you're camping or are prepared to walk, the worst of the park's excesses are fairly easily left behind. The best plan of attack if you're coming from Calgary or the US is to make straight for Banff, a busy and commercial town where you can pause for a couple of days to soak up the action and handful of sights, or stock up on supplies and make for somewhere quieter as quickly as possible. Then head for nearby Lake Louise, a much smaller but almost equally busy centre with some unmissable landscapes plus good and readily accessible short trails and day hikes if you just want a quick taste of the scenery. Two popular highways within the park offer magnificent vistas – the **Bow Valley Parkway** from Banff to Lake Louise – a far preferable route to the parallel **Hwy 1** (Trans-Canada) road – and the much longer **Icefields Parkway** from Lake Louise to Jasper. Both are lined with trails long and short, waterfalls, lakes, canyons, viewpoints, pull-offs and a seemingly unending procession of majestic mountain, river, glacier and forest scenery.

Some history

The modern road routes in the park provide transport links that have superseded the railway that first brought the park into being. The arrival of the **Canadian Pacific** at the end of the nineteenth century brought to an end some 10,000 years of native presence in the region, an epoch which previously had been disturbed only by trappers and the prodigious exploits of explorers like Mackenzie, Thompson and Fraser, who had sought to breach the Rockies with the help of native guides earlier in the century. Banff itself sprang to life in 1883 after three railway workers stumbled on the present town's Cave and Basin hot springs, its name coined in honour of Banffshire, Scottish birthplace of two of the Canadian Pacific's early financiers and directors. Within two years the government had set aside the Hot Springs Reserve as a protected area, and in 1887 enlarged it to form the **Rocky Mountains Park**, Canada's first national park. However, the purpose was not entirely philanthropic, for the new government-sponsored railway was in desperate need of passengers and profit, and spectacular scenery backed up by luxurious hotels was seen – rightly – as the best way to lure the punters. Cars were actually banned from the park until 1916.

THE CREATION OF THE CANADIAN ROCKIES

About 600 million years ago the vast granite mountains of the Canadian Shield covered North America from Greenland to Guatemala (today the Shield's eroded remnants are restricted largely to northeast Canada). For the next 400 million years, eroded debris from the Shield – mud, sand and gravel – was washed westward by streams and rivers and deposited on the offshore "continental slope" (westward because the Shield had a very slight tilt). Heavier elements such as gravel accumulated close to the shore, lighter deposits like sand and mud were swept out to sea or left in lagoons. The enormous weight and pressure of the sediment, which built up to a depth of 20km, converted mud to shale, sand to sandstone and the natural debris of the reefs and sea bed – rich in lime-producing algae – into limestone. Two further stages were necessary before these deposits – now the strata so familar in the profile of the Rockies – could be lifted from the sea bed and left several thousand metres above sea level to produce the mountains we see today.

The mountain-building stage of the Rockies took just 100 million years, with the collision of the North American and Pacific continental plates (gigantic 50-kilometre-thick floating platforms of the earth's crust). About 200 million years ago, two separate strings of volcanic Pacific islands, each half the size of British Columbia, began to move eastward on the Pacific Plate towards the North American coast. When the first string arrived off the coast, the heavier Pacific Plate slid beneath the edge of the North American Plate and into the earth's molten interior. The lighter, more buoyant rock of the islands stayed "afloat", detaching itself from the plate before crashing into the continent with spectacular effect. The thick orderly deposits on the continental slope were crumpled and uplifted, their layers breaking up and riding over each other to produce the coast's present-day interior and Columbia Mountains. Over the next 75 million years the aftershock of the collision moved inland, bulldozing the ancient sedimentary layers still further to create the Rockies' Western Main Ranges (roughly the mountain edge of Yoho and Kootenay national parks), and then moving further east, where some 4km of uplift created the Eastern Main Ranges (the mountains roughly on a line with Lake Louise). Finally the detached islands "bonded" and mingled with the new mainland mountains (their "exotic" rocks can be found in geological tangles as far east as Salmon Arm in BC).

Behind the first string of islands the second archipelago had also now crashed into the continent, striking the debris of the earlier collision. The result was geological chaos, with more folding, rupturing and uplifting of the earlier ranges. About 60 million years ago, the aftershock from this encounter created the Rockies' easternmost Front Ranges (the distinct line of mountains that rears up so dramatically from the prairies), together with the foothills that spill around Kananaskis and Waterton lakes. The third stage of the Rockies' formation, erosion and glaciation, was relatively short-lived, at least three ice ages over the last 240,000 years turning the mountains into a region resembling present-day Antarctica. While only mountain summits peeked out from ice many kilometres thick, however, glaciers and the like were applying the final touches, carving sharp profiles and dumping further debris.

Today the park is not quite at crisis point, but some hard decisions are having to be made. Around four million visitors come to Banff every year and another four million pass through. Together they pump a staggering $750 million a year into the local economy (the park's 1996 budget, by contrast, was just $17.8 million). Such figures, despite the best efforts and intentions of the park authorities, inevitably have an effect on the environment. It's now believed, for example, that the black and grizzly bear populations are dying out (combined numbers of both types of bear here are probably just 100 to 130), while numbers of wolves are declining at only a slightly lower rate than in areas where they have no protection at all (the park has just 35 or 40). Conversely, elk numbers – you'll see them nibbling contentedly on Banff's verges and garden lawns – have exploded beyond internally sustainable limits (to about 3200), almost entirely because

---

PARK ENTRY FEES

For more than eighty years motorists and motorcyclists had to buy permits to enter Canada's mountain national parks. Since 1996 a new system has been introduced. Now fees and permits are based on a per-person per-day principle, and **everyone entering any of the Rockies national parks, regardless of mode of entry, must buy a permit**. The new system is based on the premise that people – not vehicles – use parks, in much the same way as they enter art galleries or museums. Fees are ploughed directly back into the parks, unlike in the past where they were returned to a central revenue pool. The **cost** of a **Day Pass** valid for all four of the Rocky national parks (Banff, Jasper, Yoho and Kootenay) is $5 per day per person. Or you may buy a **Great Western Annual Pass** for $35, valid for unlimited entry to all eleven national parks in western Canada for a year. "Group" day passes are available for anything between two and ten people at a flat rate: $10 daily, $70 annual. Thus four people in a car, for example, are charged just $10.

Passes can be bought in advance with credit cards by phoning 1-800-748-PARK or email *natlparks-ab@pch.gc.ca*. Passes are also sold at participating Husky gas stations or at the Mountain Equipment Co-op shops in Calgary and Vancouver. Permits can be bought at the road entrances to all parks (compulsory for people in cars or on bikes), park information centres, some park campgrounds and (in summer) at automated pass machines within parks. If you buy a couple of day passes and decide you want to stay on, then you can redeem their cost against a year's pass at park centres on presentation of receipts. Great Western Annual passes are valid for a year from the date of purchase. There's no fee to enter provincial parks.

A separate **backcountry Wilderness Pass** ($6 per person per night to a maximum of $30 per person per trip, vaild in all four national parks – Banff, Jasper, Yoho and Kootenay), available from any park visitor centre or infocentre, is required for all overnight backcountry use. Reservations can made up to three months in advance by phone or in person for some of the more backcountry campgrounds, but *not* for the major park-run campgrounds. There is a $10 non-refundable booking fee.

---

they've realized the town offers food (tasty surburban grass) and total safety from their natural predators. There have been 120 (usually provoked) elk attacks on humans in Banff in the last two years. Studies are in hand and a cull may well result. These are just a handful of symptoms of a greater ecological malaise. In response a ceiling of 10,000 has been put on Banff's human population (it's currently around 7600), building is strictly controlled, areas are being closed to the public (even the famous Bow Valley Parkway may be closed to traffic for parts of the year) and there are plans to close the airport, which – like much of Banff town and the Bow River Valley – lies right in the path of major wildlife routeways. Many of the big mammals require large areas to survive, larger even than the park's 6641 square kilometres. Experts suggest that Banff's ecosystem is on a knife edge: it may be saved and previous damage restored only if action is taken now.

Banff Townsite

BANFF TOWNSITE (or just **BANFF**) is the unquestioned capital of the Canadian Rockies, and with its intense summer buzz it can be a fun, bustling and likeable base – but if you've come to commune with nature, get out as soon as possible. Although the town is quite small, it handles an immense amount of tourist traffic, much of it of the RV and mega-coach-tour variety. Anything up to 50,000 visitors daily flock here in high season, making this the largest and busiest urban focus of any national park anywhere in the world. Backpackers are abundant in summer, and the Japanese presence is also conspicuous, with a huge number of Japanese signs and menus in shops and restaurants. The Japanese also own a third of the town's accommodation, including two of the three largest hotels, and their investment here is an ongoing bone of contention. What's rather odd, given all the people, however, is that there's next to nothing to do or see, save a couple of small museums, a cable-car ride and the chance to gawp at the crowds on **Banff Avenue**, the town's long main street, a thoroughfare lined with probably more souvenir stores and upmarket outdoor shops than anywhere in North America. Whether or not your main aim is to avoid the crowds, however, some contact with the town is inevitable, as it contains essential shops and services almost impossible to come by elsewhere in the park. Many of the more rewarding walks locally are some way from the town – you'll need a car or have to hire a bike to explore properly – but some surprisingly good strolls start just minutes from the main street.

Arrival

Banff is just ninety minutes' **drive** and 128km west of Calgary on a fast, four-laned stretch of the Trans-Canada. Speed limits outside the park are 100kph, inside 90kph, but watch your speed, as countless animals are killed on the road every year (one reason for the big roadside fences). Lake Louise is 58km away, Jasper 288km and Edmonton 424km. The approach from the west is more winding, the total journey time from Vancouver (952km) being about twelve hours. From the States the quickest access is from Spokane (600km away via Hwy 95) or Kalispell in Montana (Hwy 93).

Six daily Greyhound **buses** from Calgary (1hr 40min; $18.19 one-way), and five from Vancouver (via either Kamloops or Cranbrook, all via Lake Louise), arrive at the joint Greyhound–Brewster Transportation **bus terminal** at 100 Gopher St (7.30am–10.45pm, otherwise opens 5min before the departure of night buses; ☎762-6767). Increasingly, popular services are provided between Calgary airport and Banff–Lake Louise by Greyhound, the cheapest option at $20 one way to Banff (3 daily); Laidlaw (2 daily; $32 to Banff, $37 to Lake Louise; ☎762-9102 or 1-800-661-4946); the Banff Airporter 3 daily; $30 to Banff; ☎762-3330 or 1-888-449-2901); and Brewster Transportation (2 daily; $34 to Banff; ☎762-6767 in Banff, ☎221-8242 in Calgary). Given the surfeit of operators, some of the services may well go out of business, so check at the airport. Brewster run the only service between Banff and Jasper (May–Oct 1 daily, $49): it's heavily used. There's no VIA Rail passenger service – a private company runs luxury **trains** once a week between Calgary and Vancouver via Banff, but tickets for the two-night trip are a prohibitive $850 plus.

Banff is small enough **to get around** on foot, but to reach the hostel and campground (some 3km distant) you might need the small town **shuttle bus**, colloquially known as the *Happy Bus*, operated by Banff Transit (June–Sept 8am–9pm; $1; information ☎762-1200). It runs twice-hourly on two routes: the Banff Springs Hotel–Spray Avenue–YWCA–Banff Avenue–Trailer RV Parking (leaving the *Banff Springs Hotel* on the hour and half-hour, the RV Parking on the quarter hour) and Village I Campground–Tunnel Mountain Road–Otter Street–Banff Avenue–Luxton Museum (leaving Village I on the hour and half-hour and the Luxton Museum on the quarter hour). **Taxis** start at $2.30 and then charge around $1.25 a kilometre: from the bus terminal to the hostel or the *Banff Springs Hotel* should cost around $6. For details of taxi firms and **car rentals**, for which bookings should be made well in advance, see "Listings" on p.581.

Information

Banff's showpiece **Banff Information Centre** is an excellent joint park/Chamber of Commerce venture at 224 Banff Ave (daily: late June to end Aug 8am–8pm; Sept & May to late June 8am–6pm; Oct to April 9am–5pm; park information ☎762-1550: Chamber of Commerce, town and accommodation information ☎762-8421, recorded message ☎762-4256). It has information on almost any park-related or town-related subject you care to

The telephone code for the Banff and Jasper parks is ☎403.

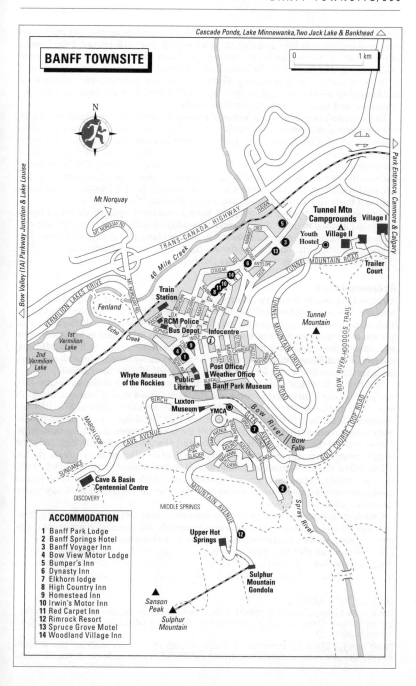

Cascade Ponds, Lake Minnewanka, Two Jack Lake & Bankhead △

BANFF TOWNSITE

0   1 km

N

Park Entrance, Canmore & Calgary

△ Bow Valley (1A) Parkway Junction & Lake Louise

Mt Norquay

TRANS-CANADA HIGHWAY

MT NORQUAY RD

40 Mile Creek

VERMILION LAKES DRIVE

HAWK

MARMOT CRES

BADGER

LYNX

ANTELOPE

COUGAR

DEER

Tunnel Mtn Campgrounds

△

Village II

Village I

Youth Hostel

Trailer Court

TUNNEL MOUNTAIN ROAD

5

3

13

6

14

11 10

8 9

Fenland

1st Vermilion Lake

2nd Vermilion Lake

Echo Creek

MT NORQUAY RD

RAILWAY

SQUIRREL

MARTEN

OTTER

MOOSE

GRIZZLY

WOLVERINE

TUNNEL MOUNTAIN DRIVE

BOW RIVER-HOODOOS TRAIL

Tunnel Mountain

▲

Train Station

ELK

BEAR

RABBIT

GOPHER

RCM Police Bus Depot

WOLF

Infocentre
ℹ

CARIBOU

BEAVER

MUSKRAT

LYNX

Post Office/ Weather Office

4 1

BOW AVE

B

Whyte Museum of the Rockies

Public Library

BUFFALO

Banff Park Museum

Luxton Museum

YMCA ◉

Bow River

BIRCH

CAVE AVENUE

MARSH LOOP

SUNDANCE

DISCOVERY

PARK AVENUE

JASPER

GLACIER

TUNNEL MTN

SPRAY AVENUE

GLEN AVENUE

NAHANNI

KOOTENAY

MOUNT

KLUANE

RUNDLE

7

Bow Falls

Spray River

GOLF COURSE LOOP ROAD

Cave & Basin Centennial Centre

MIDDLE SPRINGS

MOUNTAIN AVENUE

2

Upper Hot Springs

12

Sulphur Mountain Gondola

Sanson Peak

▲

Sulphur Mountain

ACCOMMODATION

1 Banff Park Lodge
2 Banff Springs Hotel
3 Banff Voyager Inn
4 Bow View Motor Lodge
5 Bumper's Inn
6 Dynasty Inn
7 Elkhorn lodge
8 High Country Inn
9 Homestead Inn
10 Irwin's Motor Inn
11 Red Carpet Inn
12 Rimrock Resort
13 Spruce Grove Motel
14 Woodland Village Inn

name, including bear sightings, trails and the weather, and all manner of commercial tours and outdoor activities. It is also the place to pick up a **park permit** if you haven't already done so (see box on p.567). Among their many free handouts, make a point of asking for the *Banff and Vicinity Drives and Walks* and *The Icefields Parkway* for maps of park facilities, the *Backcountry Visitors' Guide* for an invaluable overview of **backpacking trails** and campgrounds, and *Trail Bicycling in the National Parks* for conditions and a full list of **mountain bike trails**.

To the centre's rear there is a selection of maps and guides you can consult free: excellent **topographical maps** can be bought from the "Friends of Banff National Park" shop at the other end of the information centre, but note that many of the shorter and more popular trails are well worn and signed, so you won't really need detailed maps unless you're venturing into the backcountry. This is also the place to pick up details or book a place on the various **events** offered by the "Friends", which in past years have included free guided walks daily in the summer to Vermilion Lakes (2hr), a Discovery Tour of the Cave and Basin Hot Springs (45min) and a Park Museum Wildlife Tour (45min).

Staff will help with room-hunting, and keep a constantly updated vacancies board (but aren't allowed to make specific recommendations), with a free courtesy phone to call accommodation. The central reservation service offers a fee-paying alternative (see below). Information on the national park is also available on the Web (*http://www.worldweb.com/ParksCanada-Banff/*).

Accommodation

It's almost impossible to turn up after midday in Banff during July and August and find a relatively reasonably priced bed; preplanning is absolutely vital. Anything that can be booked has usually been snapped up – and Banff has over 3500 beds at its disposal nightly – and many visitors are forced to accept top-price places ($150 plus) or backtrack as far as Canmore or even Calgary to find space. The information centre or the **Banff-Lake Louise Central Reservations** service may be able to dig something out at short notice, the latter for a fee (☎762-5561 for information, ☎1-800-661-1676 for reservations).

The Bed & Breakfast and Private Home accommodation list at the infocentre lists thirty-plus places with **private rooms** and **B&Bs** and has a map of locations, but don't expect too much – they're usually cheapish by Banff standards (around $75–100) but among the first places to go each day. Note, too, that "breakfast" usually means continental – just toast, coffee and cereal. Most of the town's **motels** are on the busy strip-cum-spur from the Trans-Canada into town, and charge uncommonly high rates for basic lodgings – typically around $140 and up for doubles. Bar one or two treats, the list below offers accommodation at around the $100 threshold. Off season (Oct–May), rates are usually considerably lower. Note that some of the best-value, least-known and most conveniently located double rooms are offered by the excellent *YWCA* (see under "Hostels", p.572).

Campgrounds are not quite as bad (the town offers over 1000 pitches), but even these generally fill up by 2pm or 3pm in summer – especially the excellent government campgrounds, which do not take reservations except for group bookings. In addition to the places listed below, remember that there are lovely and less-developed park-run sites available along both the Bow and Icefields parkways to the north. The *Banff International Youth Hostel* (see p.572) can book you into most of the park's smaller hostels (see box, p.573).

HOTELS AND MOTELS

Banff Park Lodge, 222 Lynx St (☎762-4433 or 1-800-661-9266, fax 762-3553). If you want comfort, but not at *Banff Springs* or *Rimrock Resort* prices, this highly rated hotel is the best downtown upmarket choice. ⑦–⑧.

Banff Springs Hotel, Spray Avenue (☎762-2211 or 1-800-441-1414, fax 762-5755). One of North America's biggest and most famous hotels, but invariably full in summer, despite having 825 rooms and a current starting rate of $239: book ahead and ensure you have a room with a mountain view in the old building. ⑧.

Banff Voyager Inn, 555 Banff Ave (☎762-3301 or 1-800-372-9288, fax 762-4131). Standard 88-unit motel with pool and sauna. ⑤.

Bow View Motor Lodge, 228 Bow Ave (☎762-2261 or 1-800-661-1565, fax 762-8093). Good views from some of the rooms. Two-room family units available. ⑤–⑥.

Bumper's Inn, Banff Avenue and Marmot Crescent (☎762-3386 or 1-800-661-3518, fax 762-8842). Not central, but well priced; with 37 units (some with kitchenettes), you'll have a reasonable chance of finding space. ⑤.

Dynasty Inn, 501 Banff Ave (☎762-8844, 762-8077 or 1-800-667-1464, fax 762-4418). A newish 99-unit motel with a range of rooms, some with fireplaces. ⑤–⑥.

Elkhorn Lodge, 124 Spray Ave (☎762-2299, fax 762-0646). Eight rooms, four with kitchens and fireplaces, at the southern end of the townsite. ③.

High Country Inn, 419 Banff Ave (☎762-2236 or 1-800-661-1244, fax 762-5084). Large seventy-unit mid-range motel with some luxury suites. ⑤.

Holiday Inn Lodge, 311 Marten St (☎762-3648). Three reasonable rooms, two cabins. ④.

Homestead Inn, 217 Lynx St (☎762-4471 or 1-800-661-1021, fax 762-8877). Mid-priced 27-room motel with standard fittings. ⑥.

Irwin's Motor Inn, 429 Banff Ave (☎762-4566 or 1-800-661-1721, fax 762-8220). A variety of rooms with some at the lower end of the price category. ⑤–⑥.

Red Carpet Inn, 425 Banff Ave (☎762-4184 or 1-800-563-4609, fax 762-4894). No-frills 52-unit motel. ⑤.

Rimrock Resort, Mountain Avenue (☎762-3356 or 1-800-661-1587, fax 762-4132). Forget the *Banff Springs Hotel* if you want to do Banff in a modern style; come instead to this superlative and magnificently situated 351-room modern hotel – probably the finest in the Rockies. ⑦–⑧.

Spruce Grove Motel, 545 Banff Ave (☎762-2112, fax 760-5043). The least expensive motel in town; it has 36 units, some with family and kitchenette facilities. ③.

Woodland Village Inn, 449 Banff Ave (☎762-5521, fax 762-0385). The 24 rooms include some with lofts for up to eight people. ⑥.

BED AND BREAKFASTS

A. Roth, 419 Beaver St (☎762-2789). At $45 a night this is the town's cheapest B&B, except there's a two-night minimum stay and no breakfast: the one cabin (sleeps 3–4) has cooking facilities instead. Three blocks from downtown. ②.

L'Auberge des Rocheurs, 402 Squirrel St (☎762-9269 or 1-800-266-4413, fax 762-9269). Three quiet central rooms with private bathrooms, nice views with and French ownership and hospitality. ④.

Banff Squirrel's Nest, 332 Squirrel St (☎762-4432, fax 762-5167). Two pleasant and well-situated rooms with private bathrooms and sitting room for guests' use. ④.

Blue Mountain Lodge, 137 Muskrat St (☎762-5134, fax 762-8086). Ten rooms and two cabins with private or shared bathrooms and a shared kitchen in very central turn-of-the-century Banff landmark building. Non-smoking. ③–④.

Cascade Court, 2 Cascade Court (☎762-2956, fax 762-5653). Two smart non-smoking rooms across the river from downtown and minutes from the town centre. ④.

Eleanor's House, 125 Kootenay Ave (☎760-2457, fax 762-3852). One of the better but more expensive ($125) B&Bs in town: location-wise it's not perfect – across the river in a quiet sidestreet. Both rooms (twin and double) are en suite and there's a library for idle browsing on rainy days. Open Feb to mid-Oct. ④–⑤.

The Holiday Lodge, 311 Marten St (☎762-3648, fax 762-8813). Seven central good-value rooms (two more expensive en-suite rooms); two cabins with kitchenettes are available in summer. ②–③.

Rocky Mountain B&B, 223 Otter St (☎ & fax 762-4811). Ten well-priced B&B rooms with kitchenettes and shared or private baths just three blocks from downtown; laundry service also available. ②–④.

Tan-y-Bryn, 118 Otter St (☎762-3696). Eight simple and extremely reasonable B&B rooms (and one cheap "emergency" room) with private or shared bathrooms and continental breakfast. Quiet residential district three blocks from downtown. ①–②.

HOSTELS

Banff International Youth Hostel, Tunnel Mountain Road (HI ☎762-4122, or 237-8282 direct from Calgary, email *banff@mail.agt.net*). Modern 154-bed place, a 3km slog from downtown – take the Banff *Happy Bus* from Banff Avenue in summer. Friendly staff and excellent facilities, which include big kitchen, laundry, lounge area with fireplace and a bike and ski workshop. The infoboard is a good source of advice and ride offers. Good meals available all day in the self-service *Café Alpenglow* (open to the public). Two-, four- or six-bed dorms cost $18 for members, $22 for non-members ($1 dollar less in both cases mid-Oct to April). For family or couple (double) rooms, add $4 per person. Open all day. Reservations a month or more in advance are virtually essential in July and August. ①.

Banff YWCA, 102 Spray Ave (☎762-3560 or 1-800-813-4138, fax 762-2602). More convenient than the youth hostel. Open to men and women, with plenty of clinically clean rooms, but they're extremely good value and go quickly, so book ahead (at least a week in August); 300 dorm bunks ($19 plus refundable $5 key deposit) available, but bring your own sleeping bag, or rent blankets ($10 refundable deposit, $5 fee). Also forty private singles and doubles ($39, $45 with private bathroom), rooms with two double beds ($49, $55 with bathroom) and family rooms with three double beds ($65 with private bathroom). Downstairs café has good food and there's a kitchen, laundry and showers ($2.50 for non-residents) open to all. Prices drop October to May except for dorms. Dorms ②, private doubles ③.

CAMPGROUNDS

Tunnel Mountain Village I, 4.3km from town and 1km beyond the hostel on Tunnel Mountain Road. Huge 622-pitch government-run campground ($16 plus optional $3 for firewood and fire permit), the nearest to downtown, on the Banff *Happy Bus* bus from Banff Ave. Electricity and hot showers. The nearby *Tunnel Mountain Trailer Court* ($22) is only for RVs. Mid-May to Sept.

Tunnel Mountain Village II, 2.4km from town and close to *Village I* site. In the summer, available for group camping and commercial tenting only. However, after *Tunnel I* shuts (Sept 30) this government-run 189-pitch site becomes available for general walk-in winter camping ($19 plus optional $3 fire permit). Electricity and hot showers. The two sites are set amid trees, with lovely views, plenty of space and short trails close at hand. Bighorn sheep, elk and even the odd bear may drop in. Year-round.

Two Jack Lakeside, 12km northeast of town on the Lake Minnewanka Road. Fully serviced eighty-site park-run campground ($16 plus optional $3 fire permit) with showers. Open May to mid-Sept.

Two Jack Main, 13km northeast of town on Lake Minnewanka Road. Semi-serviced 381-site park campground ($13 plus optional $3 fire permit); no showers. Open mid-June to mid-Sept.

Waterfowl Lake, 57km north of Banff on Hwy 93. Simple 116-pitch park campground ($13) with water, no showers, cooking shelter and flush toilets. Open mid-June to mid-Sept.

The museums

With some of the world's most spectacular mountains on your doorstep, sightseeing in Banff might seem an absurd undertaking, yet it's good to have some rainy-day options. The downtown **Banff Park Museum** at 93 Banff Ave on the right before the bridge bulges with two floors of stuffed animals, many of which are indigenous to the park (daily: June–Sept 10am–6pm; Oct–May Mon–Fri 1–5pm, Sat & Sun 10am–6pm; $2.25; ☎762-1558). In many ways the museum chronicles the changes of attitudes to wildlife in the park over the years. Many Victorians wanted to see the park's animals without the tiresome business of having to venture into the backcountry: what better way to satisfy the whim than by killing and stuffing the beasts for permanent display? The hunting of game animals was eventually banned in the park in 1890, but not before populations of moose, elk, sheep, goats and grizzlies had been severely depleted. Game wardens only arrived to enforce the injunction in 1913, and even then they didn't protect the "bad" animals – wolves, coyotes, foxes, cougars, lynx, eagles, owls and hawks – which were hunted until the 1930s as part of the park's "predator-control program". Many of the stuffed victims in the museum date from this period. Sixty years ago a hapless polar bear was even displayed in the park behind the museum, one of sixty species of animals kept in the Banff Zoo and Aviary between 1904 and 1937. Until as recently as twenty years ago, hotels were organizing trips to the town's rubbish dumps to view foraging bears.

HOSTEL RESERVATIONS

Hostel reservations by phone, fax and credit card can be made for the following Banff National Park and area hostels by calling ☎403/762-4122 (fax 403/762-3441) or writing to *Banff International Youth Hostel*, PO Box 1358, Banff, AB T0L 0C0: *Banff International, Castle Mountain, Hilda Creek, Mosquito Creek, Rampart Creek, Ribbon Creek* and *Whiskey Jack*. For reservations at Lake Louise *International*, contact the hostel directly.

Oddly enough, the museum – a fine building whatever your views on what's inside it – might have gone the same way as the animals. In the 1950s, changing attitudes saw the exhibits condemned as dated, and plans were mooted for the museum's demolition. In the event, it survived as a fine piece of frontier Edwardiana, distinguished, in particular, by its preponderance of skylights, essential features at a time when Banff was still without electricity. The lovely wood-panelled **reading room** – a snug retreat, full of magazines and books on nature and wildlife – makes a perfect spot to while away a cold afternoon. In summer, by contrast, the **riverside park** behind the museum is ideal for a snooze or picnic (people also sleep here unofficially at night – you might get away with a sleeping bag, but certainly not a tent).

Nearby, the excellent **Whyte Museum of the Canadian Rockies** (mid-May to mid-Oct daily 10am–6pm, except July & Aug till 9pm; mid-Oct to mid-May Tues–Sun 1–5pm, Thurs till 9pm; ☎762-2291; $3), next to the library at 111 Bear St, contents itself, among other things, with a look at the Rockies' emergence as a tourist destination through paintings and photographs, and at the early expeditions to explore and conquer the interior peaks. Pictures of bears foraging in Banff rubbish bins and of park rangers grinning over a magnificent lynx they've just shot give some idea of how times have changed. The museum, which opened in 1968, forms part of the Whyte Foundation, created in the 1950s by artists Peter and Catherine Whyte to collate and preserve as great a range of material as possible relating to the Rockies. The gleaming complex is also home to the 2075-volume Alpine Club of Canada library and the 4000-volume Archives of the Canadian Rockies – the largest collection of artistic and historical material relating to the mountains. The museum also hosts temporary exhibitions by local, national and international artists, as well as presenting lectures and walking, nature and gallery tours.

The **Natural History Museum**, in the Clock Tower Mall at 112 Banff Ave (daily: summer 10am–10pm; winter 10am–6pm; free; ☎762-4747), is a rather throwaway venture that concentrates on the Rockies' geological history, with a sketchy account of its forests, flowers and minerals.

Across the river, dated displays of native history, birds and animals fill the **Luxton Museum**, a Native Canadian-run enterprise attractively housed in a huge wooden stockade (mid-May to mid-Oct daily 9am–7pm; mid-Oct to mid-May Wed–Sun 1–5pm; $5; ☎762-2388; entrance on Birch). The museum takes its name from Norman Luxton, a local who ran a trading post here and forged a close relationship with Banff's Stoney native population over the course of sixty years. Today the museum shop is probably the best reason for coming here.

The Banff Springs Hotel

At around $880 a night for some suites – $1500 for the presidential ensemble and its personal glass-sided elevators – plus $20 for any pets, the **Banff Springs Hotel** may be way out of your league, but you can't spend much time in town without coming across at least one mention of the place, and it's hard to miss its landmark Gothic superstructure. Initiated in 1888, it got off to a bad start, when the architect arrived to find the place being built 180 degrees out of kilter: while the kitchens enjoyed magnificent views over the river the guest rooms looked blankly into thick forest. When it finally opened, with 250 rooms and a rotunda to improve the views, it was the world's largest hotel. The thinking behind the project was summed up by William Cornelius Van Horne, the larger-than-life vice-president of the Canadian Pacific Railway, who said of the Rockies, "if we can't export the scenery we'll import the tourists". One of the best ways to make the railway pay, he decided, was to sell people the idea of superb scenery and provide a series of jumbo hotels from which to enjoy it: the *Banff Springs* was the result, soon followed by similar railway-backed accommodation at Lake Louise and Yoho's Emerald Lake. Horne was also the man who, when he discovered the *Banff Springs* was being built back to front, pulled out a piece of paper and quickly sketched a veranda affair, which he decided would put things to rights: he was no architect, but such was his overbearing managerial style that his ad hoc creation was built anyway.

Today the 828-room luxury pile, largely rebuilt between 1911 and 1928, costs around $90,000 a day just to run, but boasts an extraordinary 100 percent occupancy – or over 1700 guests nightly – for half of the year. It largely makes ends meet from busloads of Japanese tourists, the hotel's appearance in a famous Japanese soap having apparently boosted its already rampant popularity. The influx has prompted further rebuilding, including a spa centre being talked of as one of North America's best and a ballroom for 1600 people. The "Building of Banff" trips depart daily at 5pm from the main lobby and cost $5 if you are interested: call ☎762-2211 for further details. Unless you're a fan of kilted hotel staff or Victorian hotel architecture and its allied knick-knacks you can easily give the organized tours a miss. A voyeuristic hour or so can be spent looking around the hotel's first three floors on your own (pick up a map in reception, it's almost a mini-village) or taking a coffee, beer or afternoon tea ($15) in the second-floor café and Sunroom off the main reception; prices for anything else in most of the sixteen various eating places are ludicrous. It's also worth walking out onto the terrace beyond the Sunroom for some truly spectacular views. You can get out here either by walking along the south bank of the Bow River (taking in Bow Falls) or picking up the *Happy Bus* from downtown ($1). Walking up or down Spray Avenue is very dull.

The Gondolas

Banff is rightly proud of its two prize **gondolas** (known elsewhere as cable cars). High-price tickets buy you crowds, great views and commercialized summits, but also the chance to do some high-level hiking without the slog of an early-morning climb; they'll also give you a glimpse of the remote high country if you're short of time or unable to walk the trails. The best times to take a ride are early morning or evening, when wildlife sightings are more likely, and when the play of light gives an added dimension to the views.

Sulphur Mountain Gondola

The **Sulphur Mountain Gondola** on Mountain Avenue some 5km south of town trundles 700m skywards at a stomach-churning 51 degrees to immense 360-degree views from two observation terraces and an ugly but surprisingly good-value summit restaurant, Canada's highest (daily: mid-May to late June & mid-Aug to early Sept 8.30am–8pm; late June to mid-Aug 7.30am–9pm; early Sept to early Oct 8.30am–6pm; rest of the year 9am–4pm; $12; ☎762-2523 or 762-5438 for 24-hour recording of opening times, which change from year to year). If you're without transport the only options for getting here are to walk (dull and tiring) or take a taxi from downtown. In summer Brewster Transportation (☎762-6700) run a short **tour shuttle** to the gondola from the town centre: the price includes the cost of the gondola ticket.

It takes just eight minutes for the glass-enclosed four-passenger cars to reach the 2255-metre high point: eleven million people have come up here on the gondola over the years. From the restaurant a one-kilometre path, the **Summit Ridge Trail**, has been blazed to take you a bit higher, while the short **Vista Trail** leads to the restored weather station and viewpoint on Sanson Peak. Norman Betheune "NB" Sanson was a meteorological buff and first curator of the Banff Park Museum, who between 1903 and 1931 made around 1000 ascents of the mountain – that's before the gondola was built – to take his weather readings. Note that if, like him, you slog the 5.5km up from the car park (see box, p.581) you can ride the gondola down for free. Far too much of the food from the summit restaurant, unfortunately, ends up being eaten by bighorn sheep which, protected within the parks and unafraid of humans, gather here for handouts. Don't encourage them – feeding wildlife is against park regulations and can land you with a stiff fine.

Sunshine Gondola

The newer **Sunshine Gondola**, 18km southwest of town, once whisked you 4km from the Sunshine car park lot in the Bourgeau Valley to the Sunshine Village Resort at 2215m and some staggering views. At no extra cost, the **Standish Chairlift** led on from the resort to the Continental Divide (2430m) and a post marking the BC–Alberta border, but at the time of writing both have been completely closed for the summer (hours in the past, should it reopen, were July & Aug Mon–Thurs 8.30am–7.30pm, Fri–Sun 8.30am–10.30pm; $12). At present White Mountain Adventures run a shuttle bus (with optional guided walks) from Banff to the Sunshine Parking Lot in place of the gondola (departs 8.45am, returns 3pm & 5pm) and four shuttles from here upwards (9.30am, 10.30am, 11.30am and 1.30pm, returns 1pm, 2pm, 3pm & 5pm): numbers are limited so you should book a place on the bus (☎678-4099). Two connecting gravel trails can be followed once you're up the mountain through **Sunshine Meadows**, a beautiful and unusually large tract of alpine grassland. The **Rock Isle Trail** loop starts at the Sunshine Meadows Nature Centre. After 1km, branch right to pass Rock Isle Lake on the left (take the left fork and you'd eventually come to Lake Assiniboine). Around 600m after the branch right you come to a fork: turn left and you loop around the Garden Path Trail (3.8km) past Larix Lake, the Simpson Viewpoint and Grizzly Lake back to the fork. From here it's 500m to a 1.2-kilometre detour to the right to Standish Viewpoint (a dead end). Otherwise head straight on and after 2.8km you come to a junction and the Monarch Viewpoint, where a 1.6-kilometre walk takes you back to the Nature Centre (11.5km total with all loops and detours). Ask for a sketch map of this area from the information centre.

Cave and Basin Hot Springs

Banff also boasts eight **hot springs**, and the next stop after the gondola ride on the standard itinerary is to plunge into the only one of these that's currently commercialized. Today's immersions are usually for pleasure, but in their early days these springs were vital to Banff's rise and popularity, their reputedly therapeutic effects being of great appeal to Canada's ailing Victorian gentry.

Dr R.G. Brett, chief medical officer to the Canadian Pacific Railway, used his position to secure an immensely lucrative virtual monopoly on the best springs. In 1886 he constructed the Grandview Villa, a money-spinning sanitorium promising miracle cures and wonders such as "ice cold temperance drinks". Its handrails were reinforced by crutches abandoned by "cured" patients, though the good doctor reputedly issued crutches to all comers whether they needed them or not.

There may be quieter places in western Canada to take the waters, but hot springs always make for a mildly diverting experience, and even if the crowds are a pain the prices are hardly going to cripple you. On the face of it, the springs at the recently renovated **Cave and Basin Centennial Centre** (mid-June to Aug daily 9am–6pm; Sept–mid-June Mon–Thurs 11am–4pm, Fri–Sun 9.30am–5pm; $2.25; guided tours free with admission summer daily 11am; ☎762-1566 or 762-1557), southwest of downtown at the end of Cave Avenue, are the best place to indulge. The original cave and spring here are what gave birth to the national park, discovered on November 8 1883 by three railway navvies prospecting for gold on their day off. Having crossed the Bow River by raft they discovered a warm-watered stream, which they proceeded to follow to a small eddy of sulphurous and undergrowth-clogged water. Close by lay a small hole, the water's apparent source, which on further exploration turned out to be the entrance to an underground cave and warm mineral pool. The government quickly bought the three out, setting about promoting travel to the springs as a means of contributing to the cost of the railway's construction. A 25-square-kilometre reserve was established in 1885, from which the present park eventually evolved.

The first bathhouse was built in 1887, but over the years succumbed to the corrosive effects of chlorine and the pool's natural minerals. The pools finally closed in 1975, were restored (at a cost of $12 million), opened in 1985 and closed again in 1993 (again because of corrosion and falling numbers). Today the pools are still shut to bathers, leaving a popular **interpretive centre**(☎762-1566) to delve into their history and geology. You can walk here in a few minutes from town. From the foyer, where the faint whiff of sulphur is unmistakable, a short tunnel leads to the original cave, where the stench becomes all but overpowering. Smell aside, it's still a rather magical spot, with daylight shining in from a little hole in the roof and the limpid water inviting but tantalizingly out of bounds. Back down the tunnel and up the stairs brings you to a few rooms of interpretative displays, with a film show, some illuminating old photographs and several pertinent quotations, among which is the acid comment of an early travel writer, Douglas Sladen: "though it consists of but a single street", he grumbled about Banff in 1895, "it is horribly overcivilized", an observation not too far off the mark today. Down the stairs from the displays at the rear brings you to the "basin", a small outdoor hot spring that's separate from the cave spring system, but no less inviting. Alongside is a wooden hut theatre with a half-hour film show.

Immediately outside the centre, the short Discovery Trail (15min) heads up the hill for a view over the site, together with the nearby start of the excellent **Sundance Canyon** surfaced path (see box, p.580). Just below the centre is the **Marsh Loop Trail** (2km; 25min), a treat for naturalists, and **bird-watching** enthusiasts in particular. The area's low-elevation wetlands teem with waterfowl during the winter and spring migrations, with the chance to see – among others – Barrow's goldeneye and all three species of teal: cinnamon, blue-winged and green-winged. The warm microclimate produced here by the springs' warm waters supports mallards over the winter, as well as attracting seasonal rarities such as killdeer, common snipe and rusty blackbird. During the summer you might see belted kingfisher, common yellowthroat, willow flycatcher and red-winged blackbird. Just across the river from here on Vermilion Lakes is the single most important area for bird-watching in the entire park, accessed via trails (see box, p.580) and the Vermilion Lakes Road. Ospreys and bald eagles both nest here, and other highlights include tundra swan, hooded merganser and northern shoveler.

Upper Hot Springs

Unlike the Cave and Basin, there's no problem with swimming in the **Upper Hot Springs**, 4.5km from the town centre on Mountain Avenue, and easily visited after a trip on the Sulphur Mountain Gondola (mid-May to mid-Sept daily 9am–11pm; mid-Sept to mid-May Mon–Thurs & Sun 10am–10pm, Fri & Sat 10am–11pm; $7 mid-May to mid-Sept, $5 mid-Sept to mid-May; lockers, towel and swimming costumes – 1920 or 1990 style – rental extra; ☎762-1515 or 762-2500 for spa bookings). First developed in 1901, the springs were laid out in their present form in 1932 and completely renovated in 1996. At 38°C, the water in the outdoor pool provides a steamy temptation, but it receives a lot of traffic from people coming off the Sulphur Mountain Gondola. They also leave a fairly pungent sulphurous aftersmell. You can sign up for relaxing therapeutic massages ($17) to complement your swim, while adults can make use of the Hot Springs Spa for aromatherapy, steam room, massage, plunge pool and body wraps (from $30). Call for details and appointments. If you don't want all this pampering there's a good poolside restaurant with outside terrace, fresh juice bar and hot and cold snacks.

Lake Minnewanka

Lake Minnewanka lies a few kilometres north of the town centre, and is easily accessed by bike or car from the Trans-Canada and the northern end of Banff Avenue on Lake Minnewanka Road. The largest area of water in the national park, its name means "Lake of the Water Spirit", and with the peaks of the Fairholme Range as backdrop it provides a suitably scenic antidote to the bustle of downtown. Various dams augmented the lake in 1912, 1922 and 1941 to provide Banff with hydroelectric power, though they've done little to spoil the views, most of which are best enjoyed from the various **boat trips** that depart regularly from the quay in summer (the lake's the only one in the park where public motorboats are allowed). Trips last an hour and a half and travel a fair distance up and down the lake (mid-May to Oct daily at 10.30am, 12.30am, 3pm and 5pm; July & Aug sunset cruise at 7pm; $22; ☎762-3473). Brewster Transportation offer an inclusive bus tour and cruise from Banff for around $40. Confirm current sailing times and arrive a good thirty minutes before sailing to pick up tickets. If you have to kill time waiting for a place there are some easy walking trails along the lake's western side.

Eating and drinking

Banff's 100-plus **restaurants** – more per head of population than anywhere else in Canada – run the gamut from Japanese and other ethnic cuisines to nouvelle-frontier grub. If your funds are limited, the *Banff Youth Hostel* and the *YWCA* cafeterias, plus any number of fast-food and take-out options, are probably the best value, while Banff Avenue is lined with good little spots for coffee and snacks, many with pleasant outdoor tables. As for bars and nightlife, given Banff's huge number of summer travellers and large seasonal workforce, there are plenty of people around in summer looking for night-time action.

To stock up if you're camping, use either the big Safeway **supermarket** at 318 Marten St and Elk (daily 9am–10pm), just off Banff Avenue a block down from Wolf Street, or the newly opened and less frenetic Kellers (daily 7am–midnight), opposite the Whyte Museum at 122 Bear St on the corner of Lynx.

Baker Creek Bistro, *Baker Creek Chalets*, Bow Valley Parkway (☎522-2182). As a break from town it's definitely worth driving out here for a meal in a restaurant cited by locals as one of the park's best-regarded. The lounge bar is also nice for a drink, especially later in the year when the fire's lit.

Balkan Village, 120 Banff Ave (☎762-3454). Greek outlet, known for big portions and belly dancing on Tuesday in the winter to whip things up; in summer the place turns raucous on its own, with frequent impromptu navel displays from well-oiled customers.

Barbary Coast, upstairs at 119 Banff Ave (☎762-4616). Excellent, if obvious, food – pizza, steaks, burgers and salads – at good prices: the restaurant is full of sporting memorabilia, and the separate popular bar at the front, open till 2am, also does food (with occasional live music).

Le Beaujolais, 212 Banff Ave at Buffalo St (☎762-2712). Known for almost twenty years as one of western Canada's better, smarter and more expensive restaurants. A choice of set-price menus between $40 and $66 help keep tabs on spending. Reservations recommended.

Bistro, corner of Wolf and Bear next to the Lux Cinema (☎762-8900). A cheaper sister restaurant of *Le Beaujolais*, this is a pleasantly calm place a block or so off Banff Avenue where you can enjoy first-rate food in intimate surroundings.

Bumper's, 603 Banff Ave (☎762-2622). A little out of the centre, but this excellent-value steakhouse – one of the town's busiest – still draws in Banff residents and visitors alike. There's a good lounge upstairs, a locals' favourite, for a drink before or after dinner.

Cilantro Mountain Café, *Buffalo Mountain Lodge*, Tunnel Mountain Road (☎762-2400). A good café-restaurant, with the usual North American fare, that's ideal if you're staying at the hostel or campground and want a modest treat; has a nice outside terrace for the summer.

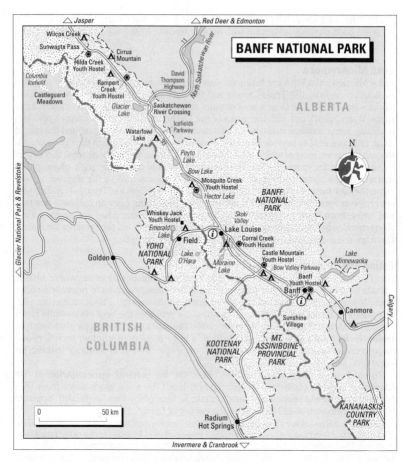

BANFF NATIONAL PARK

Earl's, upstairs at the corner of Banff Avenue and Wolf Street (☎762-4414). You can rarely go wrong at restaurants in this mid-priced Canada-wide chain. Lively, friendly service, plenty of room and consistently good food.

Evelyn's, 201 Banff Ave (corner of Caribou). One of the best places on the strip for breakfast; excellent range of coffees.

Joe Btfspk's [sic] **Diner**, 221 Banff Ave (☎762-5529). Tries too hard to evoke a period feel – red vinyl chairs and black and white floors – but does good, if slightly overpriced, food; often busy at peak times.

Melissa's, 218 Lynx St (☎762-5511). Probably Banff's most popular daytime destination, set in an old log cabin: big breakfasts, superb mignon steaks, salads and burgers, plus an upstairs bar for a leisurely drink, and a summer patio for food and beer in the sun. Recommended, particularly for lunch.

Outabounds, 137 Banff Ave (☎762-8434). Banff's other major bar and nightclub: rather soulless basement bar, food, pool, dancing and occasional music.

Rose and Crown, upstairs at 202 Banff Ave (☎762-2121). Part of a chain, combining a moderately successful pub atmosphere good for a quiet pint (darts, mock-Victorian interior) with a family-oriented restaurant. Food is of the pub-lunch variety and later on you can shake a leg in the adjoining nightclub and disco – occasional live music.

Silver City, 110 Banff Ave (☎762-3337). Very popular bar and nightclub (cheap drinks) with dancing nightly until 2am and live music, usually Friday and Saturday evenings; it attracts younger crowd than the *Rose and Crown* and *Outabounds* and has a reputation as something of a "meat market".

Wild Bill's Legendary Saloon, upstairs at 203 Banff Ave (☎762-0333). Serves good Tex-Mex and vegetarian food (family-oriented until 8pm); doubles as a lively bar with live bands (usually country) Wednesday to Sunday; pool hall and games room.

Activities and entertainment

The information centre carries extensive lists and contact information for guides and outfitters for all manner of **outdoor activities**. Indoor entertainment is limited to **billiards** upstairs at the *King Edward Hotel*, 137 Banff Ave (☎762-4629; $8 an hour), and new-release **films** at the Lux Cinema, 229 Bear St (☎762-8595). You can work out or **swim** for a fee in the pools at the *Banff Rocky Mountain Resort* (☎762-5531) and the Sally Borden Recreation Building at the Banff Centre (☎762-6461). For general bus tours, contact Brewster Transportation (☎762-8400), who've been running trips for decades.

For something just a little more demanding there's **golf** at the stunning Banff Springs Golf Course (☎762-6801; from $30 for nine holes, $75 for eighteen holes, club rental from $25). You'll need to book well in advance. Free shuttles run to the clubhouse from the *Banff Springs Hotel*. **Boat trips** on Lake Minnewanka are almost as relaxing (see p.577), as is **fishing**, which can be arranged through the Upper Bow Fly Fishing Company (☎760-7668, fax 762-8263), Monod Sports, 129 Banff Ave (☎762-4571), and Minnewanka Tours (☎762-3473): the latter company rent out fishing boats ($20 for the first hour, $10 for each additional hour). Tackle can be hired from Performance Ski and Sports, 208 Bear St (☎762-8222). Remember you need a national park licence to fish, available for $6 a week from tackle shops or the information centre.

Mountain biking is big in the park, with plenty of rental places around town (see "Listings", overleaf): one of the best and cheapest, Bactrax Bike Rentals, *Banff Ptarmigan Inn*, 337 Banff Ave (daily 8am–8pm; ☎762-8177), also offers easy guided bike tours for around $20. Rentals here work out at $5 an hour or $19 a day for normal bikes, $7 an hour or $25–32 a day for high-performance bikes: rates include helmet, lock and water bottle. They're also one of two places in town who currently rent out **rollerblades** (the paved Sundance Canyon Trail near the Cave and Basin centre is a popular run); the other rental outlet is Ski Stop at the *Banff Springs Hotel* (☎762-3725). If you're exploring on a bike under your own steam, pick up the *Trail Bicycling Guide* from the infocentre, which outlines some of the dedicated cycling trails: the best known are Sundance (3.7km one way); Rundle Riverside (8km one way); Cascade Trail (9km one way); and the Spray River Loop (4.3km).

Horseriding is equally easy to organize, with anything from one-hour treks to two-week backcountry expeditions available. The leading in-town outfitters are Holiday on Horseback – Warner Guiding and Outfitting, Trail Rider Store, 132 Banff Ave (☎762-4551). One-, two- and three-hour rides start at about $25, while a six-hour trip up the Spray River Valley costs about $100. You can also take overnight trips to the *Sundance Lodge* from around $290 including all meals. Martin Stables, off Cave Avenue across the river from downtown, rent horses by the hour from $22. The Corral (☎762-4551) at the *Banff Springs Hotel* lets them out for $26 and offers a three-hour ride from the hotel to Spray River, Sulphur Mountain and Mount Rundle.

Top of the adrenaline-rush activities is **white-water rafting** on the Kicking Horse, located a few kilometres up the road in Yoho but accessed by several companies in Banff and Lake Louise. For full-day trips with lunch from about $95, contact Wildwater Adventures (☎678-5058 or 522-2211). They also run two half-day trips daily from Lake Louise for about $65, as do Hydra River Guides, 209 Bear St (☎762-4554 or 1-800-644-8888, fax 760-3196). Rocky Mountain Raft Tours offer more sedate one- and three-hour rides ($21–40) down the Bow River. Most operators provide all gear and transportation to and from the rivers. If you want to **rent canoes** for paddling on the Vermilion Lakes or quiet stretches of the Bow River, contact Rocky Mountain Raft Tours ($14 an hour, $40 a day; ☎762-3632); the dock is on the river at Wolf Street.

WALKS AROUND BANFF

Walks from downtown

Banff Townsite is one of two obvious bases for walks in the park (the other is Lake Louise), and trails around the town cater to all levels of fitness. The best short stroll from downtown – at least for flora and fauna – is the **Fenland Trail**, a 1.5-kilometre loop west through the montane wetlands near the First Vermilion Lake (there are three Vermilion lakes, fragments of a huge lake that once probably covered the whole Bow Valley at this point; all can be accessed off Vermilion Lakes Drive). Marsh here is slowly turning to forest, creating habitats whose rushes and grasses provide a haven for wildlife, birds in particular. Ospreys and bald eagles nest around the lake, together with a wide range of other birds and waterfowl, and you may also see beaver, muskrat, perhaps even coyote, elk and other deer. You can walk this and other easy local trails in the company of the "Friends of Banff" – see under "Information" on p.570 for more details.

For a shorter walk, and a burst of spectacular white water, pound the Bow Falls Trail (1km) from beneath the bridge on the south side of the river, which follows the river bank east to a powerful set of waterfalls and rapids just below the *Banff Springs Hotel*. The Hoodoos Trail on the other side of the river (starting at the eastern end of Buffalo Street) offers similar views with fewer people, linking eventually to Tunnel Mountain Road if you walk it all the way, which make this a good way to walk into town for the youth hostel and campgrounds.

The **Marsh Loop Trail** (2km) from Cave Avenue leads along a boardwalk through a marshy habitat renowned for its flora and birds (see p.576): warm waters from the Cave and Basin hot springs immediately above have created a small, anomalous area of lush vegetation. In winter Banff's own wolf pack has been known to hunt within sight of this trail. The **Sundance Canyon Trail** (3.7km), an easy and deservedly popular stroll along a paved path (also popular with cyclists, and rollerbladers – be warned) to the picnic area at the canyon mouth, also starts from close to the springs; you can extend your walk along the 2.1-kilometre loop path up through the canyon, past waterfalls, and back down a peaceful wooded trail. Finally, the most strenuous walk near town is to the summit of Tunnel Mountain. It's approached on a windy track (300m ascent) from the southwest from Tunnel Mountain Drive, culminating in great views over the townsite, Bow River and flanking mountains.

Day hikes near Banff

Day hikes from the town centre are limited – you need transport and usually have to head a few kilometres along the Trans-Canada or to the Sunshine Village gondola

Listings

Ambulance ☎762-2000.

American Express 130 Banff Ave (☎762-3207).

Bike rental Bactrax, 337 Banff Ave at the *Ptarmigan Inn* (☎762-8177); Banff Adventures Unlimited, 209 Bear St (☎762-4554); Park'n'Pedal, 229 Wolf St (☎762-3190); Performance Ski and Sport, 2nd Floor, 208 Bear St (☎762-8222); Ski Stop outlets at 203a Bear St and *Banff Springs Hotel* (☎760-1650 or 762-5333).

Bookshop Banff Book & Art Den, Clock Tower Mall, 110 Banff Ave (daily: summer 10am–9pm; winter 10am–7pm; ☎762-3919).

Bus information 100 Gopher St (Greyhound ☎762-6767 or 1-800-661-8747; Brewster Transportation ☎762-6700); Banff Airporter Banff–Calgary Airport services (☎762-3330 or 1-888-449-2901); Laidlaw Chateau Lake Louise–Lake Louise–Banff–Calgary Airport (☎762-9102 or 1-800-661-4946); Banff Transit/*Happy Bus* town shuttle (☎762-8400).

Camping equipment Tents, outdoor gear and ski equipment to rent from Mountain Magic Equipment, 224 Bear St (tents $20, boots $5, sleeping bag $8 per day; ☎762-2591); Outdoor Access, 201 Banff Ave; and Performance Ski and Sport, 208 Bear St (☎762-8222).

Car rental Avis, Cascade Plaza, Wolf Street (☎762-3222 or 1-800-879-2847); Banff Rent-a-Car, 230 Lynx St (☎762-3352), for low-priced used-car rentals; Budget, 230 Lynx St (☎762-4546 or 1-800-268-8900); Hertz, at the *Banff Springs Hotel* (☎762-2027 or 1-800-263-0600); Sears (☎762-4575); Tilden, corner of Caribou and Lynx (☎762-2688 or 1-800-387-4747).

area to reach trailheads that leave the flat valley floor for the heart of the mountains. Only a couple of longish ones strike out directly from town: the **Spray River Circuit**, a flat, thirteen-kilometre round trip past the *Banff Springs Hotel* up the Spray River; and the Sulphur Mountain Trail, a 5.5-kilometre switchback that climbs 655m up to the Sulphur Mountain gondola terminal at 2255m (you're better off simply taking the gondola).

Park wardens at the infocentre seem unanimous in rating the **Cory Pass Trail** (5.8km; 915m ascent), combined with the Edith Pass Trail to make a return loop, as the best day hike close to Banff. The trailhead is signed 6km west of the town off the Bow Valley Parkway, 500m after the junction with the Trans-Canada. The stiff climbing involved, and a couple of scree passages, mean that it's not for the inexperienced or faint-hearted. The rewards are fantastic, with varied walking, a high mountain environment and spine-tingling views. From the pass itself at 2350m, you can return on the Edith Pass Trail (whose start you'll have passed 1km into the Cory Pass walk), to make a total loop of a demanding 13km.

Another popular local day hike, the trail to **Cascade Amphitheatre** (2195m), starts at Mount Norquay Ski Area, 6km north of the Trans-Canada up Mount Norquay Road. This offers a medley of landscapes, ranging from alpine meadows to deep, ice-scoured valleys and a close view of the knife-edge mountains that loom so tantalizingly above town. Allow about three hours for the 7.7-kilometre (610-metre ascent) walk. For the same amount of effort, you could tackle **Elk Lake** (2165m) from the ski area, though at 13.5km each way it's a long day's hike; some people turn it into an overnight hike by using the campground 2.5km short of Elk Lake. Shorter, but harder on the lungs, is the third of Banff's popular local walks, **C Level Cirque** (1920m), reached by a four-kilometre trail from the Upper Bankhead Picnic Area on the Lake Minnewanka road east of Banff. Elsewhere, the Sunshine Meadows area has five high trails of between 8km and 20km, all possible as day hikes and approached either from the Sunshine Gondola (if running) or its parking area, 18km southwest of Banff. There are also some good short trails off the Bow Valley Parkway, most notably the **Johnston Canyon** path (see box, p.585).

The best backpacking options lie in the Egypt Lake area west of Banff Townsite, with longer trails radiating from the lake's campground. Once you're in the backcountry around Banff, however, the combination of trails is virtually limitless. The keenest hikers tend to march the routes that lead from Banff to Lake Louise – the Sawback Trail and Bow Valley Highline, or the tracks in the Upper Spray and Bryant Creek Valley south of the townsite.

Foreign exchange CTM Currency Exchange at 108 Banff Ave (Clock Tower Mall), 317 Banff Ave (Cascade Plaza) and the *Banff Springs Hotel*. VISA advances at CIBC, 98 Banff Ave; Mastercard advances at Bank of Montréal, 107 Banff Ave.

Hospital Mineral Springs Hospital, 301 Lynx St (☎762-2222).

Laundries Cascade Plaza Coin Laundry, Lower Level, Cascade Plaza, 317 Banff Ave; Laundry Company, 203 Caribou St.

Library 101 Bear St (Mon, Wed, Fri & Sat 11am–6pm, Tues & Thurs 11am–9pm, Sun 1–5pm; ☎762-2661).

Parks Canada Administration ☎762-1500; campground info ☎762-1550. Park wardens ☎762-1470. 24hr emergency number only ☎762-4506.

Pharmacy Cascade Plaza Drug, Lower Level, Cascade Plaza, 317 Banff Ave; Gourlay's, 229 Bear St (Wolf and Bear Mall); Harmony Drug, 111 Banff Ave.

Police ☎762-2226.

Post office 204 Buffalo St at the corner of Bear Street (Mon–Fri 9am–5.30pm). Stamps and other basic postal services also at Cascade Plaza Drug, Lower Level, Cascade Plaza, 317 Banff Ave.

Road conditions ☎762-9233.

Taxis Alpine (☎762-3727); Banff Taxi & Tours (☎762-4444); Mountain (☎762-3351); Taxi-Taxi (☎762-3111).

WINTER IN BANFF

Banff National Park is as enticing in winter as it is the rest of the year. If you're a skier or snowboarder then it's a virtual paradise, for **skiing** here is some of the best and most varied in North America. Yet the park offers the full gamut of winter activities, embracing everything from skating, ice-fishing and toboggan trips to dog-sledding, snowshoeing and sleigh rides. Skiing or snowboarding, though, are the big draws, and of Alberta's six world-class resorts, three are in the park, one in Lake Louise (see p.586) and two close to Banff – **Mount Norquay** and **Sunshine Village**. On top of great snow and pristine runs, you get crisp air, monumental mountains, sky-high forests, and prices and space that make a mockery of Europe's crowded and exorbitant winter playgrounds. You're also pretty certain of snow, sensational views, comfortable hotels and plenty of nightlife. However, what the brochures don't tell you is that here – as in Lake Louise – it can be bitterly cold for virtually all of the skiing season.

Mount Norquay
Mount Norquay is the closest resort to Banff, just 6km and ten minutes' drive from downtown. Skiing started on the mountain's steep eastern slopes in the 1920s. In 1948 it gained Canada's first ever chair lift, immediately gaining a reputation as an experts-only resort – "steep and deep" in local parlance – thanks largely to horrors like the famous double-black diamond Lone Pine run. This reputation has only recently disappeared, the result of a complete revamp and the opening of a new network of lifts on and around Mystic Ridge to provide access to intermediate terrain and 25 **runs** suitable for all levels of skiers and borders alike. An express quad chair was installed in 1990, together with a surface lift, two double chairs and a quad chair.

As a result Norquay is now equally renowned for its uncrowded beginners' slopes as for its expert runs, the **terrain** breaking down as follows: Novice (11 percent); Intermediate (45 percent); Advanced (28 percent); and Expert (16 percent). The average snowfall is 300cm, and there's snowmaking on ninety percent of the terrain. The season runs from early December to mid-April. The highest elevation is 2133m, giving a vertical drop of 497m to the resort's base elevation at 1636m. **Amenities** include a visitor centre, ski school, rental shop, day care and – on Wednesdays – the promise of **night skiing**. Lift tickets are around $35 a day. Accommodation is in Banff, with a free shuttle bus making the tour of local hotels for the short trip to the hill. For more **information** on the resort write, call or fax Mystic Ridge and Norquay, Box 1258, Banff, Alberta T0L 0C0 (☎762-4421, fax 762-8133).

Sunshine Village
Sunshine Village is a stunning resort, situated way up in the mountains at 2160m 18km southwest of Banff. If anything the scenery's better than at Norquay – you're higher – and you have the plus of the national park's only on-hill accommodation. There's also an incredible 10m of snow a year – so there's no need for snowmaking machines – with superb powder that *Snow Country* magazine recently voted "The Best Snow in Canada".

Tickets For info, tickets and reservations for events, call Tickets, 304 Caribou St (☎762-5385).
Tourist information ☎762-1550 for park information or 762-8421 for town and accommodation.
Trail conditions ☎762-1550.
Weather ☎762-4707 or 762-2088 (24hr recording).

Highway 1 and the Bow Valley Parkway

Two roads run parallel through the Bow Valley from Banff to Lake Louise (58km): the faster **Hwy 1** (the Trans-Canada); and the quieter **Bow Valley Parkway**, on the other (north) side of the river, opened in 1989 as a special scenic route. After Banff, there's

Skiing started here in 1929 when two locals got lost on Citadel Pass and came back with tales of fantastic open bowls and dream slopes just made for skiing. In 1938 the Canadian National Ski Championships were held here, and by 1942 a portable lift had been installed on site. The biggest change in the area's fortunes came in 1980, when a gondola (cable car) was built to carry skiers (and occasionally summer walkers) the 6km from the Bourgeau Valley parking area to the self-contained Sunshine Village resort.

Today some 62 uncrowded **runs** can be accessed on the gondola, an express quad chair, a triple chair, four double chairs, 3 T-bars and two beginner rope tows. There's less here for the advanced skier than at Norquay, but plenty for the beginner and competent intermediate. **Terrain** breaks downs as follows: Novice (20 percent); Intermediate (60 percent) and Expert (20 percent). The top elevation is an incredible 2730m at Lookout Mountain, with a drop to base level of 1070m: all runs ultimately converge on the village itself. Lift tickets are around $45 a day. **Amenities** include a day lodge, day care, outdoor hot pool, ski school, rental shop and overnight **rooms** in the Village at the 85-room *Sunshine Inn*, the Rockies' only on-slope accommodation (☎762-4581 or 1-800-661-1272 in Alberta, 1-800-661-1363 in the rest of North America; ⑤–⑥). Ski packages are available here for anything between one and seven nights (mid-Nov to late May) beginning at around $90 a night with two days' skiing: basic overnight charges are between $115 and $170. If you're staying in Banff, shuttle buses run round the hotels and cost around $15 for the round trip. For more **information** on the resort, write, call or fax Sunshine Village, Box 1510, Banff, Alberta T0L 0C0 (☎762-6500, fax 762-6513).

Winter activities

Many of Banff's myriad walking trails are groomed for winter **cross-country skiing**, details of which can be obtained in the *Nordic Trails in Banff National Park* pamphlet available from the town's visitor centre. Favourite destinations include Sundance Canyon, Spray River, Johnson Lake (above Lake Minnewanka) and around Lake Minnewanka itself. You can hire specialist gear from several outlets around town (see "Listings" on p.580). At a more expensive level, Banff has no **heli-skiing** of its own, but is the base for the world's largest heli-ski operator, Hans Gmoser's CMH Heli-Skiing, PO Box 1660 (☎762-7100), who offers package tours to various BC destinations. Other operators include RK Heli-Ski (☎762-3771), who'll take you out to the Panorama area of the Purcell Mountains in BC and Mike Wiegele Helicopter Skiing, PO Box 249 (☎762-5548), will take you further afield in BC to the Monashee and Cariboo mountains.

If you want to **ice-skate**, check out the rinks at Banff High School (Banff Avenue), on the Bow River (off Bow Street) and the *Banff Springs Hotel*; skates can be hired from The Ski Shop, also located in the hotel (☎762-5333). Thrill-seeking **dog-sledders** need to contact Mushers (☎762-3647), who for a rather steep fee (reckon on $100 an hour) will take you on a spin around the Banff Springs Golf Course. For less adrenaline-filled **sleigh rides** on the frozen Bow River, contact Holiday on Horseback (☎762-4551). Hotels often provide sledges for **toboggan** runs, of which there are several unofficial examples around town. **Ice-fishing** can be arranged through Banff Fishing Unlimited (☎762-4936, fax 678-8895).

only one link between the two roads, at Castle Junction, 30km from Lake Louise. Both routes, needless to say, are staggeringly beautiful, as the mountains start to creep closer to the road. For the entire run the **Bow River**, broad and emerald green, crashes through rocks and forest, looking as close to one's image of a "mighty river" as it's possible to get. Despite the tarmac and heavy summer traffic, the surroundings are pristine and suggest the immensity of the wilderness to come. Sightings of elk and deer are common, particularly around dawn and sundown, and occasionally you'll spot moose. Both offer some good **trails**: if you want a short walk, make for the Johnston Canyon on the Parkway; if you want to tackle one of the most highly rated day walks in Banff National Park, make for the Bourgeau Lake Trail off Hwy 1 (see box, p.585).

Highway 1

Most people tend either to cruise Hwy 1's rapid stretch of the Trans-Canada without stopping – knowing that the road north of Lake Louise is more spectacular still – or leap out at every trail and rest stop, overcome with the grandeur of it all. On Greyhound or Brewster **buses** you're whisked through to Lake Louise in about forty minutes; if you're driving, try for the sake of wildlife to stick to the 90kph speed limit. The vast fences that march for kilometre after kilometre along this section of the road are designed to protect animals, not only from traffic but from the brainless visitors who clamber out of their cars to get close to the bears occasionally glimpsed on the road. You won't have to be in the Rockies long during the summer before you're caught in a **bear jam**, when people – contrary to all park laws, never mind common sense – abandon their cars helter-skelter on the road to pursue hapless animals with cameras and camcorders.

The Bow Valley Parkway

If anything the **Bow Valley Parkway** boasts more scenic grandeur than the Trans-Canada – which is saying something – and offers more distractions if you're taking your time: several trails, campgrounds, plus plenty of accommodation choices and one excellent eating option. The largest concentration of sightseers is likely to be found at the Merrent turnoff, enjoying fantastic views of the Bow Valley and the railway winding through the mountains.

If you have the time, therefore, the Parkway is the preferable route, and you should budget some time to walk one of the **trails** en route, in particular the easy but impressive **Johnston Canyon Trail** (see box opposite). En route, some of the various viewpoints and signed pull-offs deserve more attention than others. Around 8km down the highway, look out for the **Backswamp Viewpoint**, where views one way extend to the mountains and the other across a river swamp area where you might see beaver, muskrat, ospreys and other birds (see below), as well as the common butterwort, a purple-flowered carnivorous plant whose diet consists largely of marsh insects. In winter Backswamp Viewpoint is also known locally as one of the most likely areas to spot wolves; at other times of the year you might also see bighorn sheep or mountain goats on the mountain slopes above. Three kilometres further on you come to **Muleshoe Picnic Area**, also noted for its birds and wildfowl (see below). Some of the area around shows signs of having been burnt in forest fires, though these areas were deliberately torched by the park authorities to encourage fresh undergrowth and the return of wildlife excluded from more mature forests (for more on this see the "Vermilion Pass" on p.635). Eleven kilometres on, a 400-metre trail takes you to a lovely little lake once known as Lizard Lake after the long-toed salamanders that once thrived here. These were eaten when the lake was stocked with trout, and the name's now been changed to Pilot Lake. Three kilometres beyond is the trailhead for the **Johnston Canyon Trail** (see box opposite), deservedly the most popular in the area, and three kilometres beyond that **Moose Meadows**, where – name notwithstanding – you'll be mighty lucky to see any moose: habitat changes have forced them out.

If you're a **bird-watcher**, the Parkway is also the route for you. Johnston Canyon is one of only two known breeding sites in Alberta of the black swift – you may see the birds flitting back to their nests at dusk – and is also a breeding place for American dippers, buxom grey birds that have the ability to walk along stream beds underwater and habitually nest below waterfalls. Elsewhere on the Parkway the various pull-offs give you the opportunity to spot species associated with montane forest and meadow zones, notably at the Muleshoe Picnic Area, 21km southeast of Castle Junction, where you might spot western tanagers, pileated woodpeckers and orange-crowned warblers. At various points on the Bow River along the entire run from Banff to Lake Louise you may spot harlequin ducks on the river's islands and gravel bars, as well as spotted sandpipers and common mergansers.

If you want to stay, the road's **accommodation** possibilities make a more rural alternative to Banff and Lake Louise, and are close enough to both to serve as a base if you have transport; as ever, you should book rooms well in advance. Four **lodges** are spaced more or less equally en route and, though expensive, they *may* have room when Lake Louise's hotels are stretched. First is the *Johnston Canyon Resort*, 26km west of Banff and close to the trail that leads to the canyon (☎762-2971; ③–⑤; mid-May to late Sept), which consists of rustic cabins (some with fireplaces and some with kitchenettes), a shop, garage, tennis court and basic groceries. Next come the chalets, laundry and grocery store of Castle Mountain Village, 32km west of Banff near Castle Junction (☎762-3868; ⑥; year-round): the log chalets for four with kitchenettes and fireplaces are more expensive, but the best options of all here are the delightful and newly built deluxe cabins for four, five or six people (complete with full kitchens, dishwashers and Jacuzzis). Some 5km south of Hwy 1 on Hwy 93 to Radium (27km from Banff) is *Storm Mountain Lodge* (☎762-4155; ⑥; end of May to late Sept) with highly appealing log cabins. Finally there's *Baker Creek Chalets*, 12km east of Lake Louise (☎522-3761; ⑥–⑦; year-round), with one- and two-room log cabins for between one and six people: there's also an excellent **restaurant** here that comes with local recommendations and new annexe with eight smart motel-type rooms. By far the least expensive possibility is the Parkway's charming **youth hostel**, *Castle Mountain Hostel*, 1.5km east of Castle Junction (☎762-2367; members $11, non-members $15; ①; year-round but closed Wed). You should call in advance, or better still book ahead through the hostel at Banff (☎762-4122).

Three national park **campgrounds** provide excellent camping retreats: the very popular 132-pitch *Johnston Canyon* ($16; mid-May to mid-Sept), 25km from Banff is the best equipped, and has full facilities including showers and wheelchair access; after that comes the 43-pitch *Castle Mountain*, 32km from Banff near Castle Junction ($13; late June to early Sept), and the 89-pitch *Protection Mountain*, 5km north of Castle Junction (same details). An additional $3 fee is payable at all three if you wish to use firewood.

BOW VALLEY TRAILS

Five major trails branch off the Bow Valley Parkway. The best short walk by a long way is the **Johnston Canyon Trail** (2.7km each way), 25km from Banff, an incredibly engineered path to a series of spray-veiled waterfalls. The Lower Falls are 1.1km, the Upper Falls 2.7km from the trailhead on the Parkway. From the upper falls you can continue on to the seven cold-water springs of the Ink Pots, which emerge in pretty open meadows, to make a total distance of 5.8km (215m ascent). Another short possibility is the **Castle Crags Trail** (3.7km each way; 520m ascent) from the signed turnoff 5km west of Castle Junction. Short but steep, and above the treeline, this walk offers superb views across the Bow Valley and the mountains beyond. Allow ninety minutes one way to take account of the stiff climb.

The best day hike is to **Rockbound Lake** (8.4km each way), a steepish climb to 2210m with wild lakeland scenery at the end; allow at least two and a half hours one way, due to the 760m ascent. Another fifteen minutes' walk beyond Rockbound and Tower lakes at the end of the trail lies the beautiful Silverton waterfall. The other Parkway trails – **Baker Creek** (20.3km) and **Pulsatilla Pass** (17.1km) – serve to link backpackers with the dense network of paths in the Slate Range northeast of Lake Louise.

The two outstanding trails along Hwy 1 are the trek to **Bourgeau Lake** (7.5km one way), considered by many among the top five day hikes in Banff: it starts from a parking area 10km west of Banff – allow two and a half to three hours for the 725-metre ascent – and the long day hike to **Shadow Lake** (14.3km each way), where the lakeside campground (at 1840m), in one of the Rockies' more impressive sub-alpine basins, gives access to assorted onward trails. The main trail starts from the **Redearth Creek** parking area 20km west of Banff (440m ascent; allow 4hr).

Lake Louise

The Banff park's other main centre, **Lake Louise**, is very different to Banff – less a town than two distinct artificial resorts. The first is a small mall of shops and hotels just off the Trans-Canada known as **Lake Louise Village**. The second is the lake itself, the self-proclaimed "gem of the Rockies" and – despite its crowds and monster hotel – a sight you have to see. A third area, **Moraine Lake**, 13km south of the village, has almost equally staggering scenery and several magnificent and easily accessed trails. Lake Louise is 4.5km from the village (and 200m higher) on the winding Lake Louise Drive – or, if you're walking, 2.7km on the uphill Louise Creek Trail, 4.5km via the Tramline Trail. You're better off saving the walking for around the lake, however, and taking a taxi (around $10) from the village (if anything, save the two linking trails for coming down from the lake). All three areas are desperately busy in summer as well as in winter, when people pile in for some of Canada's best powder **skiing** (see box, p.592).

You may find staying near the lakes appealing but very pricey, though if you do want to splash out, the lodge at Moraine Lake makes a dream treat. Nonetheless, the mountains around offer almost unparalleled **hiking country** and the park's most popular day-use area. You'll have to weigh awesome scenery against the sheer numbers, for these are some of the most heavily used trails on the continent – 50,000-plus people in summer – though longer backpacking routes lead quickly away to the quieter spots. If you do intend to hike – and the trails are all a little more accessible and manageable than at Banff – then in an ideal world you'd have two or three days here: one to walk the loop around above Lake Louise (Lake Agnes–Big Beehive–Plain of the Six Glaciers–Lake Louise Shoreline) or the more demanding Saddleback (at a push you could do both in a day if you were fit and keen). Then you'd bike, taxi or drive to Moraine Lake (if you're not staying there), where in a day you could easily walk to Consolation Lake, return to Moraine Lake and then tackle the Moraine Lake–Larch Valley–Sentinel Pass or Moraine Lake–Larch Valley–Eiffel Lake trail. A third day could be spent in Paradise Valley between Lake Louise and Moraine Lake.

If, on the other hand, you merely want to take in the scenery and enjoy **modest strolls** in the course of a day, then cruise up to Lake Louise, walk up and down the shore, then drive the twenty minutes or so to Moraine Lake and do the same.

Lake Louise Village

LAKE LOUISE VILLAGE doesn't amount to much, but it's an essential supply stop, with more or less everything you need in terms of food and shelter (at a price). Most of it centres round a single mall, Samson Mall, and car park, with a smart youth hostel and a few outlying motels dotted along the service road to the north. There's almost nothing to do in the village, and unless you have a vehicle to take you to the lakes (or rent a bike) you're likely to be bored. The impressive **Lake Louise Information Centre**, a few steps from the car park, offers not only information but also hi-tech natural history exhibits (daily: mid-June to early Sept 8am–8pm; early Sept to late Sept & mid-June 8am–6pm; Oct–May 9am–5pm; ☎522-3833). Almost as useful is the excellent Woodruff and Blum bookshop (☎522-3842) in the mall, which has a full range of maps, guides and background reading. A couple of doors down, Wilson Mountain Sports (☎522-3636) is good for **bike rental** (from $8 per hour, $29 a day), rollerblade rentals (from $5 per hour), fishing tackle for sale or rent (fly rod $11, spin rod $7 and waders $10) and **equipment rental** (stoves $7, pack $9 and tent $19). They'll also fill you in on the possiblity of **canoe rentals** for trips downstream on the Bow River to Banff.

A short way from the village, the **Lake Louise Gondola** (the "Friendly Giant") runs thirteen minutes to 2042m, partway up Mount Whitehorn (2669m). To reach it, pick up the free shuttle which operates from some village hotels or return to and cross over the Trans-Canada, and follow the road towards the ski area; the gondola is signed left after about 1km (daily: mid-June to Aug 9am–9pm; early to mid-June & early to mid-Sept 9am–6pm; $9.50; ☎522-3555). Depending on your susceptibility to either vertigo or claustrophobia you can choose between enclosed gondola cars, open chairs, or chairs with bubble domes. At the top (2034m) are the usual sensational views – rated some of the best in the Rockies – a self-service restaurant, sun decks, picnic areas, souvenir shops and several trailheads through the woods and meadows. One track takes you to the summit of Mount Whitehorn, a stiff 600m above the gondola station.

TRANSPORT AND FACILITIES

Four Greyhound **buses** a day link Banff and Lake Louise (50min) and stop in the Samson Mall car park at the little office known as The Depot (☎522-2080); three continue to Vancouver and the west. Four buses a day return from Lake Louise to Banff and Calgary.

HIKES AROUND LAKE LOUISE

All the Lake Louise trails are busy in summer, but they're good for a short taste of the scenery. The're also well worn and well marked, so you don't need to be a seasoned hiker or skilled map-reader. The two most popular end at teahouses – mountain chalets selling welcome, but rather pricey, snacks. The signed Lake Agnes Trail (3.4km), said to be the most-walked path in the Rockies (but don't let that put you off), strikes off from the right (north) shore of the lake immediately past the hotel. It's a gradual, 400-metre climb, relieved by ever more magnificent views, and a teahouse beautifully situated beside mountain-cradled Lake Agnes (2135m); allow one to two hours. Beyond the teahouse, if you want more of a walk things quieten down considerably. You can continue on the right side of the lake and curve left around its head to climb to an easily reached pass. Here a 200-metre stroll to the left brings you to Big Beehive (2255m), an incredible eyrie, 1km from the teahouse. Almost as rewarding is the trail, also 1km from the teahouse, to Little Beehive, a mite lower, but still privy to full-blown panoramas over the broad sweep of the Bow Valley.

Keener walkers can return to the pass from Big Beehive and turn left to follow the steep trail down to intersect another trail; turning right leads west through rugged and increasingly barren scenery to the second teahouse at the Plain of the Six Glaciers (2100m). Alternatively, the more monotonous Six Glaciers Trail (leaving out the whole Lake Agnes–Big Beehive section) leads from the hotel along the lakeshore to the same point (5.3km to the teahouse; 365m ascent). However, a better option is to follow the Lake Agnes and Big Beehive route to the Plain, then use the Six Glaciers Trail for the return to *Chateau Lake Louise*, which neatly ends the day's loop with a downhill stroll and an easy but glorious finale along the shore of Lake Louise (see "Lake Louise Village" map to make sense of what is a pretty straightforward and very well-worn loop).

The main appeal of the last local walk, the less-used Saddleback Trail (3.7km one way), is that it provides access to the superlative viewpoint of Fairview Mountain. Allow from one to two hours to Saddleback itself (2330m; 595m ascent); the trail to the summit of Fairview (2745m) strikes off right from here. Even if you don't make the last push, the Saddleback views – across to the 1200-metre wall of Mount Temple (3544m) – are staggering. Despite the people, this is one of the park's top short walks.

The Skoki Valley

The Skoki Valley region east of Lake Louise offers fewer day hikes; to enjoy it you'll need a tent to overnight at any of the six campgrounds. The main access trail initially follows a gravel road forking off to the right of the Lake Louise Ski Area, off Hwy 1. Many people hike as far as Boulder Pass (2345m), an 8.6-kilometre trek and 640-metre ascent from the parking area, as a day-trip, and return the same way instead of pushing on to the *Lodge*, 8km beyond. Various well-signposted long and short trails from the *Lodge* or the campgrounds are documented in the *Canadian Rockies Trail Guide*.

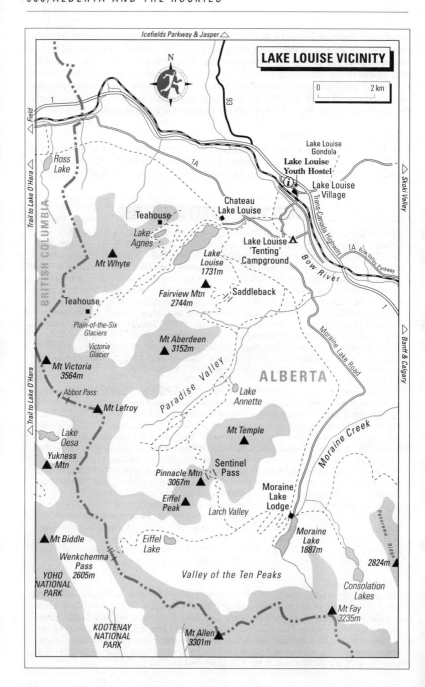

LAKE LOUISE VICINITY

0   2 km

Icefields Parkway & Jasper

N

Field

1

BRITISH COLUMBIA

Trail to Lake O'Hara

Ross Lake

1A

93

Lake Louise Gondola

Lake Louise Youth Hostel

Lake Louise Village

Trans-Canada Highway

Skoki Valley

Teahouse

Lake Agnes

Chateau Lake Louise

Mt Whyte

Lake Louise 'Tenting' Campground

1A

Bow Valley Parkway

Banff & Calgary

Lake Louise 1731m

Bow River

Teahouse

Fairview Mtn 2744m

Saddleback

Plain-of-the-Six Glaciers

Victoria Glacier

Mt Aberdeen 3152m

ALBERTA

Trail to Lake O'Hara

Mt Victoria 3564m

Abbot Pass

Mt Lefroy

Paradise Valley

Lake Annette

Moraine Lake Road

Lake Oesa

Yukness Mtn

Mt Temple

Moraine Creek

Pinnacle Mtn 3067m

Sentinel Pass

Eiffel Peak

Larch Valley

Moraine Lake Lodge

Mt Biddle

Eiffel Lake

Moraine Lake 1887m

Panorama Ridge

Wenkchemna Pass 2605m

YOHO NATIONAL PARK

Valley of the Ten Peaks

2824m

Consolation Lakes

Mt Fay 3235m

KOOTENAY NATIONAL PARK

Mt Allen 3301m

Brewster Transportation (☎762-6700) also runs three buses a day from Banff, also continue to the Chateau Lake Louise. Note that there are also direct Greyhound and Brewster connections to and from Lake Louise and Calgary airport (see p.533 for details). Brewster also run one daily service to Jasper as well as bus tours on the Icefields Parkway. If you need a taxi to ferry you to the lakes, call Lake Louise Taxi & Tours (☎522-2020). The only **car rental** agency is Tilden at The Depot (☎522-3870 or 1-800-387-4747), but you're better off renting in Banff as elsewhere as their cars go quickly.

The Samson Mall takes care of most practical considerations including a **post office** (daily 6.30am–7pm; ☎522-3870). Behind The Depot, which doubles up as a bag storage, and booking office for coach tours and river rafting trips, are a laundrette (☎522-2143) and (downstairs) public washrooms with showers. The general store is good and has a **money exchange**. There's also a currency exchange at the *Chateau Lake Louise* hotel (see p.591). For the **police**, call ☎522-3811. The nearest hospital is in Banff.

Excellent basic **food** – snacks and coffee – can be had at the always busy *Laggan's Mountain Bakery* (daily 6am–7pm) on the corner of the mall opposite the general store. For something more substantial, wander to the relaxed and reasonably priced *Bill Peyto's Café* (daily 7am–9pm; ☎522-2200), within the youth hostel but open to all; in summer the nice outdoor eating area makes a good place to meet people. A unique sort of place with an improving reputation is the restored *Lake Louise Station Restaurant* (☎522-2600), though some of the best (and pricier) meals can be found in the *Post Hotel* (daily 7am–2pm & 5–9.30pm; ☎522-3989) – reservations are essential for dinner. Locals also swear by the hotel's *Outpost Lounge*, a snug **bar** that serves light meals from late afternoon. Other drinking spots include the *Lake Louise Bar and Grill*, upstairs in the mall, and the lively *Charlie's Pub* in the *Lake Louise Inn*, 210 Village Rd.

ACTIVITIES

As for **activities**, most operators are based in Banff or elsewhere (see p.579), though many offer pick-ups in Lake Louise; a handful operate trips directly out of Lake Louise itself. Companies actually based in or near the village include Wildwater Adventures (☎678-5058, 522-2211 or 1-888-771-9453) who run half- or full-day white-water rafting trips on the Kicking Horse River in nearby Yoho National Park (half-day trips at 8.30am and 1.30pm, from $63). If you don't want to hike alone, or wish to know more about what you're walking past, the national park run **guided walks** three or four times a week in summer: the Lake Louise Lakeshore Stroll (Mon, Wed, Thurs & Sat 10am; 2hr; $6) and the Plain of the Six Glaciers (Tues, Thurs & Sun 9am; 6hr; $12). Drop by the visitor centre to confirm latest timings and to buy a ticket, or call ☎522-3833. Cyclists can rent bikes from Wilson Mountain Sports in the mall (see p.586), or sign up for **cycling tours** (from $49 for half a day, $83 full day) and transfers that'll take you up to Bow Summit on the Icefields Parkway so you can pedal downhill or freewheel all the way back to Lake Louise. Serious canoeists can rent canoes from Wilson for trips on the Bow River, while more sedate paddlers can **rent canoes** and kayaks (from $22 per hour) at Chateau Lake Louise to dabble on Lake Louise itself (☎522-3511).

Good **trout fishing** is possible on the Bow River between Lake Louise and Banff, with support and advice available at the *Castle Mountain Lodge* on the Bow Valley Parkway (see p.584). Rental equipment is again on offer at Wilson Mountain Sports. Compulsory fishing permits ($6 weekly) are available from the visitor centre. If you fancy **horseriding**, contact Brewster Stables at the *Chateau Lake Louise* hotel (☎522-3511 ext 1210, or 762-5454) and enquire about their ninety-minute trip along the shores of Lake Louise ($30), half-day tours ($45) to the Lake Agnes or Plain of the Six Glaciers (see box, p.587) or full-day treks to Paradise Valley and Horseshoe Glacier ($80 including lunch). Timberline Tours (☎522-3743) run similar if slightly cheaper treks from the Lake Louise Corral behind the *Deer Lodge* hotel; all-day trips to the Skoki Valley east of Lake Louise; one- and three-hour trips at Bow Lake on the Icefields Parkway from the *Num-Ti-Jah Lodge* (see p.595).

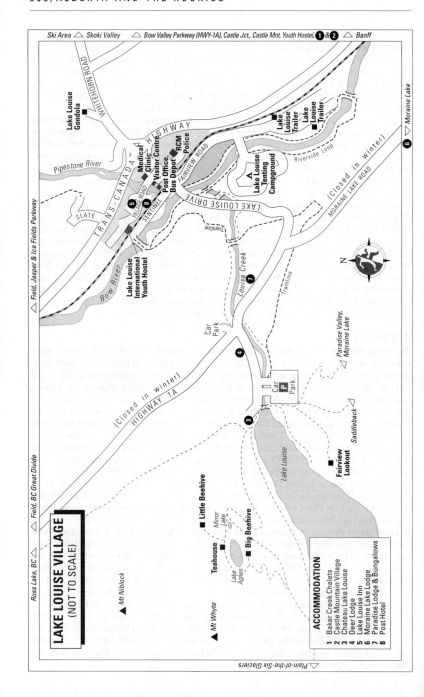

LAKE LOUISE VILLAGE
(NOT TO SCALE)

Ski Area △ Skoki Valley   △ Bow Valley Parkway (HWY-1A), Castle Jct., Castle Mnt. Youth Hostel, ❶ & ❷ △ Banff

△ Field, Jasper & Ice Fields Parkway
△ Field, BC Great Divide
Ross Lake, BC △

Lake Louise Gondola

WHITEHORN ROAD

Pipestone River

TRANS-CANADA   HIGHWAY

SLATE

Medical Clinic
Visitor Centre
Post Office
Bus Depot
RCM Police
FAIRVIEW ROAD

VILLAGE ROAD
SENTINEL

Lake Louise Trailer
Lake Louise Trailer

Riverside Loop

Lake Louise Tenting Campground

LAKE LOUISE DRIVE

(Closed in winter)

MORAINE LAKE ROAD

⑥ ▽ Moraine Lake

N

Bow River

Lake Louise International Youth Hostel

Tramline

Louise Creek

⑦

Tramline

Car Park

⑤
⑧

Paradise Valley, Moraine Lake ▽

Saddleback ▽

Car P Park

④

(Closed in winter)

HIGHWAY 1A

③

Fairview Lookout

Lake Louise

▲ Mt Niblock

Little Beehive

Teahouse

Mirror Lake

Big Beehive

Lake Agnes

▲ Mt Whyte

▽ Plain-of-the-Six Glaciers

ACCOMMODATION
1 Baker Creek Chalets
2 Castle Mountain Village
3 Chateau Lake Louise
4 Deer Lodge
5 Lake Louise Inn
6 Moraine Lake Lodge
7 Paradise Lodge & Bungalows
8 Post Hotel

ACCOMMODATION

Hotel accommodation in or near Lake Louise Village is pricey all year round, and almost certain to be full in summer. Bookings are virtually essential everywhere (you can make them through Banff's **central reservations** on ☎1-800-661-1676, for a fee); at the excellent youth hostel, reservations six months in advance are not unusual. The various options on the Bow Valley Parkway, covered in the preceding section, are all within easy driving or cycling distance.

The lovely 220-site park-run **Lake Louise Campground**, close to the village – follow the signs off Fairview Road up to the lake – gets busy in summer. It's open between mid-May and early October, is partially serviced, and sites cost $14; no fires. Sites are close together, though the trees offer some privacy, and with the railway close by, it can be noisy. There are also no showers – you have to use the ones in the mall below The Depot.

Canadian Alpine Centre and International Youth Hostel, on Village Road just north of the mall across the river (☎522-2200, fax 522-2253; email *llouise@HostellingIntl.ca*). A new, magnificent and popular 150-bed year-round hostel run jointly with the Canadian Alpine Club. Reservations by phone, fax or email are virtually essential in summer and winter ski weekends up to six months in advance, and require the first night's fee as a deposit (credit card bookings accepted). Twenty percent of beds are for walk-ins each day (be there very early). Its dorm beds cost $19.55 for members, $23.55 non-members and it has a selection of more expensive double rooms and four-bed dorms/family rooms at $6 more per person. Daily 7am–9pm. ①.

Castle Mountain Youth Hostel, 1.5km east of Castle Junction on Hwy 93 South (☎762-4122). Well-situated for the Bow Valley Parkway and its trails. Sleeps just 36, with bookings possible through the Banff hostel. Dorm beds $11 for members, $15 for non-members. Closed Wed March–May & Oct–Dec. ①.

Chateau Lake Louise (☎522-3511 or 1-800-441-1414, fax 522-3834) has a monopoly on lakeside accommodation: doubles among its 511 rooms and suites cost up to $550, though in low season (Oct–Dec) some are available for as little as $95, making it one of the least expensive off-season places in the area. If it's beyond your budget, look inside anyway to check out its bizarre appeal. Booking essential. ⑤–⑧.

Deer Lodge, on Lake Louise Drive (☎522-3747 or 1-800-661-1595, fax 522-3883). Cheaper of two alternatives to *Chateau Lake Louise*, with a good restaurant and within walking distance of the lake. ⑤–⑥.

Lake Louise Inn, 210 Village Rd, just north of the village mall to the right (☎522-3791 or 1-800-661-9237, fax 522-2018). The least expensive of the village hotels with a variety of rooms, some with self-catering facilities. ③–⑥.

Paradise Lodge and Bungalows, on the Lake Louise Drive a short walk from Lake Louise (☎522-3595, fax 522-3987). Pricier of the near-lake options, but with reasonable off-season rates for its 21 self-contained bungalows and 24 one- and two-bedroom suites (some with kitchens). Mid-May to mid-Oct. ⑥–⑧.

Post Hotel, Village Road (☎522-3989 or 1-800-661-1586, fax 522-3966). The top hotel in the village, with a noted restaurant and bar – see p.589. ⑦–⑧.

The Lake

Before you see **Lake Louise** you see the hotel: *Chateau Lake Louise*, a 1924 monstrosity that would never get planning permission today. Yet this fades into insignificance beside the immense beauty of its surroundings. The lake is Kodachrome turquoise, the mountains sheer, the glaciers vast; the whole ensemble is utter natural perfection. Outfitter Tom Wilson, the first white Canadian to see Lake Louise when he was led here by a local native in 1882, wrote, "I never, in all my explorations of these five chains of mountains throughout western Canada, saw such a matchless scene . . . I felt puny in body, but glorified in spirit and soul."

You can't help wishing you could have been Tom Wilson, and seen the spot unsullied by the hotel and before the arrival of the tourists and general clutter. Around 10,000 daily in peak season come here to gawp (car parks often fill by noon), while notice boards on

WINTER IN LAKE LOUISE

In a region already renowned for its **skiing** Lake Louise stands out, regarded by many as among the finest winter resorts in North America. In addition to skiing and snowboarding, there are hundreds of kilometres of cross-country trails, numerous other winter activities, and landscape that's earned the area the title of "North America's Most Scenic Ski Area" from *Snow Country* magazine. It's also Canada's largest ski area, with over forty square kilometres of trails, plenty of mogul fields, lots of challenging chutes, vast open bowls and some of the best "powder" on the continent.

Skiing started here in the 1920s. The first chalet was built in 1930, the first lift in 1954. The resort's real birth can be dated to 1958, when a rich Englishman, Norman Watson – universally known as the "Barmy Baronet" – ploughed a large part of his inheritance into building a gondola up Mount Whitehorn. Further lifts and other developments followed. More would have materialized had it not been for environmental lobbying. Further protests forestalled a bid for the 1968 Winter Olympics and put an end to a plan for a 6500-bed mega-resort in 1972. Even so, the resort has grown, and now regularly hosts World Cup skiing events. The only drawback are the phenomenally low temperatures during January and February.

The **ski area** divides into four distinct faces, served by two express quad chairs, one quad chair, two triple chairs, three double chairs, a T-bar, a platter lift and a children's tow rope. The huge **terrain** – some of the bowls are the size of entire European resorts – divides as follows: Novice (25 percent), Intermediate (45 percent) and Expert (30 percent). Most of the bowls are above the tree line, but you can also ski on areas known as Larch and Ptarmigan, whose varied terrain allows you to follow the sun or duck into the trees when the wind's up. Average seasonal snowfall (early Nov to mid-May) is 360cm, and snowmaking is available over much of the area. The top elevation is 2637m, giving a 1000m drop to the base elevation at 1645m. Lift tickets are around $45 a day, but bear in mind that you can invest in the Ski Banff/Lake Louise **three area pass**, which allows you six days' skiing in Lake Louise, Mount Norquay and Sunshine Village (see p.582).

Facilities in the ski area include three day lodges, each of which has a restaurant and bar, a ski school, ski shop, rental shop, day care, nursery and lockers. Free shuttles run from Lake Louise, while transfers from Banff cost around $15 return. Free tours of the mountain are also available three times daily. For further **information**, contact Skiing Louise, Suite 505, 1550-8th St SW, Calgary AB T2R 1K1 or Box 5, Lake Louise, AB T0L 1E0 (☎522-3555, fax 522-2095). Reservations can be made by calling ☎2-LOUISE (☎256-8473), or toll-free in North America 1-800-258-7669.

Cross-country skiing in Lake Louise is also phenomenal, with plenty of options around the lake itself, on Moraine Lake Road and in the Skoki Valley area north of the village. For **heli-skiing**, contact RK Heli-Ski (☎342-3889) who have a desk in the *Chateau Lake Louise* hotel (winter daily 4–9pm); one of their shuttle buses leaves from the hotel daily for the two-hour drive to the Purcell Mountains in BC (the region's nearest heli-skiing). The hotel is also the place to hire skates (at Monod Sports) for **ice-skating** on the lake, probably one of the most sublime spots imaginable to indulge in the activity (the lake is floodlit after dark to allow night skating). If you want a **sleigh ride** on the lake shore, contact Brewster Lake Louise Sleigh Rides (☎522-3511 or 762-5454). Rides are reasonably priced and last an hour, but reservations are essential: sleighs depart hourly from 11am on weekends, 3pm on weekdays.

the waterfront seem obsessed with the profoundly dull dispute over how the lake came by its name – was it named in honour of the governor's wife, or after the fourth daughter of Queen Victoria? The native name translates as the "Lake of the Little Fishes". Wilson, showing precious little wit, originally called it Emerald Lake, for obvious reasons (clearly lacking in any imagination, he coined exactly the same name for the lake he discovered in Yoho; see p.625). More interesting is the account of Hollywood's discovery of the lake in the 1920s, when it was used to suggest "exotic European locations". After

Wilson's "discovery" all access was by rail or trail – the station, then known as Laggan, was 6km away. The first hotel appeared in 1890, a simple two-bedroom affair which replaced a tumbledown cabin on the shore. Numerous fires, false starts and additions followed until the present structure made its unwelcome appearance (the final wings were added as recently as 1988). The first road was built in 1926. Be sure to walk here, despite the paths' popularity (see box, p.587). Alternatively, escape the throng – two million people come here each year – by renting an old-style canoe from the office to the left as you face the lake (June–Sept daily 10am–8pm; $22 per hour). Don't think about swimming: the water's deep and cold – top temperature in summer is a numbing 4°C.

Moraine Lake

Not quite so many people as visit Lake Louise make the thirteen-kilometre road journey to **Moraine Lake**, which is smaller than its neighbour although in many ways its scenic superior. If you're without your own transport, you'll have to rely on a bike or taxi ($35) to get here, but it's one of the great landscapes of the region and has some cracking trails into the bargain (see box, p.596). It also holds one of the most enticing and magnificently executed hotels in the entire Rockies: if you're on honeymoon, or just want to push the boat out once, splash out on a night or two in the *Moraine Lake Lodge* (☎522-3733; ⑦–⑧; June–Sept), a sympathetically landscaped collection of high-quality cabins plus lodge rooms and six units designed by eminent architect Arthur Erickson (also responsible for Vancouver's UBC Museum of Anthropology and the Canadian Embassy in Washington DC). It boasts a friendly staff and great privacy, for prices on a par with decidedly more lacklustre hotels in the village and near Lake Louise.

Bar the *Lodge*, with its good little café and topnotch restaurant, nothing disturbs the lake and its matchless surroundings. Until recently the scene graced the back of Canadian $20 bills, though the illustration did little justice to the shimmering water and the jagged, snow-covered peaks on the eastern shore that inspired the nickname "Valley of the Ten Peaks". The peaks are now officially christened the Wenkchemna, after the Stoney native word for "ten".

The lake itself, half the size of Lake Louise, is the most vivid **turquoise** imaginable. Like Lake Louise and other big Rockies lakes (notably Peyto on the Icefields Parkway), the peacock blue is caused by fine particles of glacial silt, or till, known as rock flour. Meltwater in June and July washes this powdered rock into the lake, the minute but uniform particles of flour absorbing all colours of incoming light except those in the blue–green spectrum. When the lakes have just melted in May and June – and are still empty of silt – their colour is a more normal sky blue. You can admire the lake by walking along the east shore, from above by clambering over the great glacial moraine dam near the lodge (though the lake was probably created by a rock fall rather than glaciation), or from one of the **canoes for rent** on the right just beyond the *Lodge* and car park. For the best overall perspective, tackle the switchback trail through the forest on the east shore (see box, p.596).

The Icefields Parkway

The splendour of the **Icefields Parkway** (Hwy 93) can hardly be overstated: a 230-kilometre road from Lake Louise to Jasper through the heart of the Rockies, it ranks as one of the world's ultimate drives. Its unending succession of huge peaks, immense glaciers, iridescent lakes, wildflower meadows, wildlife and forests – capped by the stark grandeur of the Columbia Icefield – is absolutely overwhelming. Fur traders and natives who used the route as far back as 1800 reputedly christened it the "Wonder Trail", though in practice they tended to prefer the Pipestone River Valley to east, a route that avoided the swamps and other hazards of the Bow Valley. Jim Brewster made the first recorded complete trek along the road's future route in 1904. The present highway was only completed in 1939 and opened in 1940 as part of a Depression-era public-works programme. Although about a million people a year make the journey to experience what the park blurb calls a "window on the wilderness", for the most part you can go your own way in relative serenity.

After 122km, at about its midway point, the Icefields Parkway crosses from Banff into Jasper National Park (about a 2hr drive); you might turn back here, but the divide is almost completely arbitrary, and most people treat the Parkway as a self-contained journey, as we do here. Distances in brackets are from Lake Louise, which is virtually the only way to locate places on the road, though everything mentioned is clearly marked off the highway by distinctive brown-green national park signs. You could drive the whole highway in about four hours, but to do so would be to miss out on the panoply of short (and long) trails, viewpoints and the chance just to soak up the incredible scenery.

Access, transport and accommodation

Tourist literature often misleadingly gives the impression that the Icefields Parkway is highly developed. In fact, the wilderness is extreme, with snow often closing the road from October onwards, and there are only two points for **services**, at Saskatchewan Crossing (the one place campers can stock up with groceries, 77km from Lake Louise), where the David Thompson Highway (Hwy 11) branches off for Red Deer, and at the Columbia Icefield (127km).

Brewster Transportation runs several tours and a single scheduled bus daily in both directions between Banff and Jasper from late May to mid-October ($42 one way), though services at either end of the season are often weather-affected. A word with the driver will usually get you dropped off at hostels and trailheads en route. If you're **cycling** – an increasingly popular way to tackle the journey – note that the grades are far more favourable if you travel from Jasper to Banff (Jasper's 500m higher than Banff) and that bikes can be rented in Jasper for one-way trips (see p.609 for details of rental outlets).

Five youth hostels (four open year-round) and twelve excellent park campgrounds (two year-round) are spaced along the Parkway at regular intervals. If you want more comfort, you'll have to overnight at Banff, Lake Louise or Jasper, as the only other accommodation – invariably booked solid – are hotels at Bow Lake, Saskatchewan Crossing, the Columbia Icefield and Sunwapta Falls.

Between Lake Louise and the Columbia Icefield

One of the biggest problems in the Rockies is knowing what to see and where to walk among the dozens of possible trails and viewpoints. The Parkway is no exception. The following are the must-sees and must-dos along the 122-kilometre stretch of the Parkway from Lake Louise to the Columbia Icefield: best view – Peyto Lake (unmissable); best lake walk – Bow Lake; best waterfalls – Panther–Bridal Falls; best quick stroll – Mistaya Canyon; best short walk – Parker Ridge; best walk if you do no other – Wilcox Pass. Temptations for longer walks are numerous, and the difficulty, as ever, is knowing which to choose.

The first **youth hostel** north of Lake Louise is *Mosquito Creek* (28km), four log cabins which sleep 38 and have basic food supplies, a kitchen, large common room and a wood-fired sauna (no phone, reservations ☎762-4122; $11 members, $15 non-members; year-round, closed Tues). Slightly beyond is the first park **campground**, *Mosquito Creek* ($10: mid-June to mid-Sept; 32 sites) and one of the Parkway's two winter campgrounds (free after mid-Sept; twenty walk-in sites only). You're near the Bow River flats here, and the mosquitoes, as the campground name suggests, can be a torment. Two hikes start from close to the site: **Molar Pass** (9.8km; 535-metre ascent; 3hr), a manageable day trip with good views, and **Upper Fish Lake** (14.8km; 760-metre ascent; 5hr), which follows the Molar Pass trail for 7km before branching off and crossing the superb alpine meadows of North Molar Pass (2590m).

On the *Num-Ti-Jah Lodge* access road just beyond (37km), a great short trail sets off from besides the lodge to **Bow Lake** and **Bow Glacier Falls** (4.3km; 155-metre ascent; 1–2hr), taking in the flats around Bow Lake – one of the Rockies' most beautiful – and climbing to some immense cliffs and several huge waterfalls beyond (the trail proper ends at the edge of the moraine after 3.4km, but it's possible to pick your way through the boulders to reach the foot of the falls 900m beyond). If you don't want to walk, take a break instead at the picnic area on the waterfront at the southeast end of the lake. The *Num-Ti-Jah Lodge* itself, just off the road, is one of the most famous old-fashioned lodges in the Rockies, built in 1920 by legendary guide and outfitter Jimmy Simpson (who lived here until 1972); be sure to book well in advance to have any chance of securing a room (☎522-2167; ⑤; May–Sept). There's a **coffee shop** here if you need a break, or want to admire the *Lodge*'s strange octagonal structure, forced on Jimmy because he wanted a large building but only had access locally to short timbers. You can take dinner here, too, or sign up for **horseriding** with Timberline Tours (☎522-3743), available to residents and non-residents alike: rides include a one-hour trip to Bow Lake; a three-hour ride to Peyto Lake (see below); and a full-day excursion to Helen Lake.

Another 3km up the Parkway comes the pass at Bow Summit, source of the Bow River, the waterway that flows through Banff, Lake Louise and Calgary. (At 2069m, this is the highest point crossed by any Canadian highway.) Just beyond is the unmissable twenty-minute stroll to **Peyto Lake Lookout** (1.4km; elevation loss 100m) one of the finest vistas in the Rockies (signed from the road). The quite beautiful panorama only unfolds in the last few seconds, giving a genuinely breathtaking view of the vivid emerald lake far below; mountains and forest stretch away as far as you can see. Another 3km along the Parkway lies a viewpoint for the Peyto Glacier, part of the much larger Wapta Icefield.

After 57km you reach the *Waterfowl Lake* **campground** (116 sites; $13; mid-June to mid-Sept) and the **Chephren Lake Trail** (3.5km; 80m ascent; 1hr), which leads to quietly spectacular scenery with a minimum of effort. The next pause, 14km further on, is the **Mistaya Canyon Trail**, a short but interesting 300-metre breather of a stroll along a river-gouged "slot" canyon: *mistaya*, incidentally, is a Cree word meaning "grizzly bear". **SASKATCHEWAN CROSSING** (77km) is the lowest point on the road before the icefields; the 700-metre descent from Bow Summit brings you from the high sub-alpine ecoregion into a montane environment with its own vegetation and wildlife. Largely free of snow, the area is a favourite winter range for mountain goats, bighorn sheep and

HOSTEL SHUTTLE SERVICE

The Alberta Hostel Shuttle (mid-June to Sept) runs an extremely useful daily shuttle service, connecting twelve youth hostels between (and including) Calgary, Banff and Jasper – as well as all the places on the Icefields Parkway and beyond. Typical fares are $59 for Calgary to Maligne Canyon (Jasper), the longest possible journey, and $20 for the trip between Lake Louise and *Hilda Creek* hostel near the Columbia Icefield. Banff to Lake Louise is $14, Banff to *Jasper International Hostel* $44, and Lake Louise to Jasper $36. Extra fees are payable for bikes, canoes and other cargo.

For information, call ☎283-5551 or 1-800-248-3837. To make bookings for the shuttle, contact *Banff International* (☎762-4122), *Calgary* (☎269-8239) or *Lake Louise* (☎522-2200). For hostels book no later than 6pm the day before your desired departure with full details of your journey. Once the hostel has confirmed your booking, buy a ticket from any participating Alberta hostel, confirming the shuttle's departure time at the time of purchase. From hostels with phones, use the toll-free number to make enquiries; at those without, reservations can usually be made through the manager. Stand-by tickets may be bought from the van driver at departure, subject to availability. All passengers must have reservations at their destination hostel.

MORAINE LAKE AND PARADISE VALLEY

Moraine Lake

Each of the four basic routes in the **Moraine Lake** area is easily accomplished in a day or less, two with sting-in-the-tail additions if you want added exertion; all start from the lake, which lies at the end of thirteen-kilometre Moraine Lake Road from just outside Lake Louise Village.

The easiest is the one-kilometre amble along the lakeshore – hardly a walk at all – followed by the three-kilometre stroll to Consolation Lake, an hour's trip that may be busy but can provide some respite from the frenzy at Moraine Lake itself. This almost level walk ends with lovely views of a small mountain-circled lake, its name coined by an early explorer who thought it a reward and "consolation" for the desolation of the valley which led up to it. If you're tenting, fairly fit, or can arrange a pick-up, the highline Panorama Ridge Trail (2255m) branches off the trail (signed "Taylor Lake") to run 22km to the Banff–Radium highway 7km west of Castle Junction.

The most popular walk (start as early as possible) is the Moraine Lake–Larch Valley–Sentinel Pass Trail, one of the Rockies' premier hikes, which sets off from the lake's north shore 100m beyond the lodge. A stiffish hairpin climb through forest on a broad track, with breathtaking views of the lake through the trees, brings you to a trail junction after 2.4km and some 300m of ascent. Most hikers branch right, where the track levels off to emerge into Larch Valley, broad alpine upland with stands of larch (glorious in late summer and fall) and majestic views of the encircling peaks. If you have the energy, push on to Sentinel Pass ahead, in all some two hours' walk and 720m above Moraine Lake. At 2605m, this, along with the Wenkchemna Pass, is the highest point reached by a major trail in the Canadian Rockies. You can see what you're in for from the meadows – but not the airy views down into Paradise Valley from the crest of the pass itself. You could even continue down into Paradise Valley, a tough, scree-filled descent, and complete a exceptional day's walk by picking up the valley loop (see below) back to the Moraine Lake Road. Otherwise return to the 2.4-kilometre junction and, if legs are still willing – you'll

---

members of the deer family. The bleak settlement itself offers expensive food (restaurant and cafeteria), gas, a spectacularly tacky gift shop and a 66-room **hotel-restaurant**, *Crossing*, that is surprisingly comfy (early March to mid-Nov; ☎761-7000; ④).

Twelve kilometres north are the *Rampart Creek* thirty-bed **youth hostel**, with two cabins and the "the best sauna in the Rockies" (☎439-3139 or through Banff, Lake Louise or Calgary hostels; $10 members, $14 non-members; June–Oct daily; Nov–May Sat & Sun only with reservations), with a basic food store, and a fifty-pitch park-run **campground** ($10; late June to early Sept). Apparently this area is one of the best black bear habitats close to the road anywhere in the park. The last of the Banff National Park campgrounds is the tiny sixteen-pitch *Cirrus Mountain* site at the 103-kilometre mark ($10; late June to early Sept), but its position is precarious, so check it's open before planning a stay (☎762-1550).

Shortly before the spectacular **Panther Falls** (113.5km) the road makes a huge hairpin climb (the so-called "Big Hill"), to open up yet more panoramic angles on the vast mountain spine stretching back towards Lake Louise. The unmarked and often slippery one-kilometre trail to the falls starts from the lower end of the second of two car parks on the right. Beyond it (117km) is the trailhead to **Parker Ridge** (2.4km one way; elevation gain 210m; allow 1hr one way, less for the return), which, at 2130m, commands fantastic views from the summit ridge of the Saskatchewan Glacier (at 9km, the Rockies' longest). If you're only going to do one walk after the Peyto Lake Lookout (see p.595), make it this one: it gets cold and windy up here, so bring extra clothing. Ideally placed for this area and the Columbia Icefield 9km north is the busy *Hilda Creek* **youth hostel** (☎439-3139 or 762-4122; $10 members, $14 non-members) 1km beyond. The setting is stunning, and accommodation (for 21) is in cosy log cabins. Nearby Sunwapta Pass (2023m) marks the border between Banff and Jasper national parks and

have done most of the hard climbing work already – think about tagging on the last part of the third Moraine Lake option.

This third option, the less-walked Moraine Lake–Eiffel Lake–Wenkchemna Pass Trail, follows the climb from the lake as for the Larch Valley path before branching off left instead of right at the 2.4-kilometre junction. It's equally sound, virtually level, and if anything has the better scenery (if only because less barren than Sentinel Pass) in the stark, glaciated grandeur to be found at the head of the Valley of the Ten Peaks. It's also much quieter once you're beyond the trail junction. At 2255m, Eiffel Lake is a 5.6-kilometre hike and 370-metre climb in total (allow 2–3hr) from Moraine Lake, and you don't need to go much further than the rock pile and clump of trees beyond the lake to get the best out of the walk. Ahead of you, however, a slightly rougher track continues through bleak terrain to Wenkchemna Pass (2605m), clearly visible 4km beyond. Having got this far, it's tempting to push on; the extra 350-metre climb is just about worth it, if lungs and weather are holding out, for the still broader views back down the Valley of the Ten Peaks. The views beyond the pass itself, however, over the Great Divide into Yoho and Kootenay parks, are relatively disappointing.

Paradise Valley

In 1894, the mountaineer Walter Wilcox deemed **Paradise Valley** an appropriate name for "a valley of surpassing beauty, wide and beautiful, with alternating open meadows and rich forests". North of Moraine Lake, it's accessed via Moraine Lake Road about 3km from its junction with Lake Louise Drive. The walk here is a fairly straightforward hike up one side of the valley and down the other, a loop of 18km with a modest 385m of vertical gain. Most people take in the Lake Annette diversion for its unmatched view of Mount Temple's 1200-metre north face (unclimbed until 1966), and many overnight at the campground at the head of the valley (9km from the parking area), though this is one of the busiest sites in the park. Others toughen the walk by throwing in the climb up to Sentinel Pass on the ridge south of the valley, which gives the option of continuing down the other side to connect with the Moraine Lake trails (see above).

the watershed of the North Saskatchewan and Sunwapta rivers: the former flows into the Atlantic, the latter into the Arctic Ocean. From here it's another 108km to Jasper.

The Columbia Icefield

Covering an area of 325 square kilometres, the **Columbia Icefield** is the largest collection of ice and snow in the entire Rockies, and the largest glacial area in the northern hemisphere south of the Arctic Circle. It's also the most accessible of some seventeen glacial areas along the Parkway. Meltwater flows from it into the Arctic, Atlantic and Pacific oceans, forming a so-called "hydrological apex" – the only other one in the world is in Siberia. This is fed by six major glaciers, three of which – the Athabasca, Dome and Stutfield – are partially visible from the highway. The busy and newly opened **Icefield Centre** (daily: May to early June & Sept to mid-Oct 9am–5pm; early June to Aug 9am–6pm; ☎852-6560) provides an eerie viewpoint for the most prominent of these, the Athabasca Glacier, as well as offering the Parks Canada Exhibit Hall and information and slide shows on the glaciers and Canada's most extensive cave system – the Castleguard Caves, which honeycomb the ice but are inaccessible to the public.

You can walk up to the toe of the **Athabasca Glacier** from the parking area at Sunwapta Lake, noting en route the date-markers, which illustrate just how far the glacier has retreated (1.5km in the last 100 years). You can also walk onto the glacier, but shouldn't, as it's riddled with crevasses. Fall in one of these and you probably won't be climbing out. People are killed and injured every year on the glacier: even a slip can rip off great slivers of skin; the effect of sediment frozen into the ice is to turn the glacier surface into a vast and highly abrasive piece of sandpaper. Full-scale expeditions are the preserve of experts but you can join an **organized trip**. Brewster's special "Snocoach-

BEARS

Two types of **bears** roam the Rockies – black bears and grizzlies – and you don't want to meet either. They're not terribly common in these parts (sightings are all monitored and posted at park centres) and risks are pretty low on heavily tramped trails, but if you're camping or walking it's still essential to be vigilant, obey basic rules, know the difference between a black bear and a grizzly (the latter are bigger and have a humped neck), know how to avoid dangerous encounters, and understand what to do if confronted or attacked. Popular misconceptions about bears abound – that they can't climb trees, for example (they can, and very quickly) – so it's worth picking up the parks service's pamphlet *You are in Bear Country*, which cuts through the confusion and lays out some occasionally eye-opening procedures. Be prepared, and if you don't want your scalp pulled off, follow the cardinal rules: **store food and garbage properly, make sure bears know you're there, don't approach or feed bears, don't scream and don't run**.

When hiking, walk in a group – bears rarely attack more than four in a group – and make **noise**, lots of it, as bears are most threatened if surprised. Many people shout, rattle cans with stones in or carry a whistle; the widely touted small bells, be warned, are not loud enough. Be especially alert and noisy when close to streams, in tall vegetation, crossing avalanche slopes or when travelling into the wind, as your scent won't carry to warn bears of your approach: move straight away from dead animals and berry patches, which are important food sources. Watch for bear signs – get out quick if you see fresh tracks, diggings and droppings – and keep in the open as much as possible.

Camp away from rushing water, paths and animal trails, and keep the site scrupulously clean, leaving nothing hanging around in the open. Lock food and rubbish in a car, or hang it well away from a tent between two trees at least 4m above ground (many campgrounds have bear poles or steel food boxes). Take all rubbish away – don't bury it (bears'll just dig it up) and certainly don't store it in or near the tent. Avoid smelly foods, all fresh, dried or tinned meat and fish, and **never store food, cook or eat in or near the tent** – lingering smells may invite unwanted nocturnal visits. Aim to cook at least 50m downwind of the tent: freeze-dried meals and plastic-bag-sealed food is best. Likewise, keep food off clothes and sleeping bags, and sleep in clean clothes at night. Bears have an acute sense of smell, so **avoid *anything* strongly scented** – cosmetics, deodorant, shampoo, gel, lip balm, insect repellents, toothpaste, sun screen – and may be attracted to women during menstruation, so dispose of tampons in an airtight container. They're also attracted by the smell of sex, so watch what you do in your tent if you don't want a rather drastic coitus interruptus.

Bears are unpredictable, and experts simply can't agree on best tactics: there's no guaranteed life-saving way of coping with an aggressive bear. Calm behaviour, however, has proved to be the most successful strategy in preventing an attack after an encounter. Bears don't actually want to attack; they simply want to know you're not a threat. Mothers with cubs are particularly dangerous and prone to suspicion. A bear moving towards you can be considered to have it in for you, other signs being whoofing noises, snapping jaws, and the head down and ears back. A bear raised on its hind legs and sniffing is try-

es" run ninety-minute, five-kilometre rides over the glacier with a chance to get out and walk safely on the ice (daily: every 15min: early May to Sept 9am–5pm; Oct 10am–4pm depending on weather; $22.50; ☎762-6767 or 762-6735 in Banff, 522-3544 in Lake Louise, 852-3544 in Jasper). They're heavily subscribed, so aim to avoid the peak midday rush by taking a tour before 10.30am or after 3pm. More dedicated types can sign up for the Athabasca Glacier ice walks (3hr walks mid-June to early Sept daily at 12.30pm, $16; 5hr walks Thurs & Sun 11.30am; $21), led by licensed guides. Call ☎852-4242 for details, or sign up on the spot at the front desk of the Icefields Centre – be sure to bring warm clothes, boots and provisions.

The new 32-room *Columbia Icefields Chalet* (☎852-6550; ⑤–⑥) provides excellent but much-sought-after **accommodation** in the Icefields Centre between May and mid-ing to identify you: if it does it frequently, though, it's getting agitated; ideally, on first encounter you want first to stand stock still, never engage in direct eye contact (perceived as aggressive by the bear) and – absurd as it sounds – start speaking to it in low tones.

Whatever you do, **don't run**, which simply sets off an almost inevitable predator-prey response in the bear (a bear can manage 61kph – that's easily faster than a racehorse or the fastest Olympic sprinter). Never scream or make sudden movements as surprising the animal is the surest way to provoke an attack. Unfortunately bears often bluff, and will charge and veer at the last moment, so, though it's a fairly tall order, resist the urge to turn and run on an initial charge. **Back away quietly and slowly at the first encounter, speaking gently to the bear**. Don't throw anything and do everything as gradually and calmly as possible. If things look ominous, put your pack on the ground as a distraction. If the backing off seems to be working, then make a wide detour, leave the area or wait for the bear to do so – and always leave it an escape route.

Forget about **trees**, as black bears can climb them better than you (30m trees are no problem). Grizzlies are not inclined to climb and usually get bored after about 4m; though this is also the height they can reach simply by standing on their hind legs. In any case, the chances are the bear will be too close for you to get up a tree in time – and pines aren't the easiest things to climb. If you do manage to get up a tree, climb as high as possible, keep your legs tucked up (bears have pulled people down by their legs in the past) and – another tall order – try to take your pack with you: if you drop it then a bear may hang around for hours trying to figure it out. Dump the pack if leaving it is going to distract the animal long enough to get you up a tree.

If you're **attacked**, things are truly grim, and quack tactics are unlikely to help you. With grizzlies, **playing dead** – curling up in a ball, protecting face, neck and abdomen – may be effective. Fighting back will only increase the ferocity of a grizzly attack, and there's usually no way you're going to win, though in a few cases attacking has caused a bear to leave. Most people who've survived an aggressive attack have had brave companions who walloped the bear with a very large stick or rock. Keep your elbows in to prevent the bear rolling you over, and be prepared to keep the position for a long time until the bear gets bored. You may get one good cuff and a few minutes' attention and that's it – injuries may still be severe but you'll probably live. With a black bear the playing dead routine won't wash, though they're not as aggressive as grizzlies, and a good bop to the nose or sufficient frenzy on your part will sometimes send a black bear running: it's worth a try. **Don't play dead** with either species if the bear stalks or attacks while you're sleeping: this is more dangerous, as bears are often after food. Instead, try and get away or intimidate.

Chemical repellents are available, but of unproven efficacy, and in a breeze you're likely to miss or catch the spray yourself. Another innovation is exploding firecrackers, which could scare the bear off *in extremis*, though these and sprays are last-chance options, and no substitute for vigilance and precautions. If this all sounds too scary to make you even contemplate walking or camping, remember that attacks are very rare – none at all had been recorded between 1995 and 1997.

October (note that lower rates apply in May and October). Brewster bus services between Jasper and Banff stop here: it's possible to take a Banff-bound Brewster bus out of Jasper in the morning, see the Icefield, and pick up the evening Jasper-bound bus later the same day.

Two unserviced but very popular **campgrounds** lie 2km and 3km south of the Icefield Centre respectively: the tent-only 33-site *Columbia Icefield* ($10; mid-May to mid-Oct, or until the first snow), and the 46-site *Wilcox Creek*, which takes tents and RVs ($10; early June to mid-Sept). This latter is also the trailhead for one of the very **finest hikes** in the national park, never mind the highway: the **Wilcox Pass Trail** (4km one way; 335m ascent; allow 2hr round trip), highly recommended by the park centres and just about every trail guide going. The path takes you steeply through thick spruce and alpine fir forest before emerging suddenly onto a ridge that offers vast views over the Parkway and the high peaks of the icefield (including Mount Athabasca). Beyond, the trail enters a beautiful spread of meadows, tarns and creeks, an area many people choose to halt at or wander all day without bothering to reach the pass itself. You could extend the walk to 11km by dropping from the pass to Tangle Creek further along the parkway.

Beyond the Columbia Icefield

If there's a change **beyond the Columbia Icefield**, it's a barely quantifiable lapse in the scenery's awe-inspiring intensity over the 108-kilometre stretch towards Jasper. As the road begins a gradual descent the peaks retreat slightly, taking on more alpine and less dramatic profiles in the process. Yet the scenery is still magnificent, though by this point you're likely to be in the advanced stages of landscape fatigue. It's worth holding on, though, for two good short trails at Sunwapta and Athabasca falls.

Seventeen kilometres beyond the icefield is the 24-berth, two-cabin *Beauty Creek* **youth hostel** (reservations through Jasper International Hostel ☎852-3215; $9 members, $14 non-members; May–Sept; partial closure Oct–April). Nine kilometres further is the unserviced 25-site *Jonas Creek* **campground** ($10; mid-May to first snowfall).

A one-kilometre gravel spur leads off the highway to **Sunwapta Falls** (175km from Banff, 55km from Jasper), fifteen minutes' walk through the woods from the road: they're not terribly dramatic unless in spate, but are interesting for the deep canyon they've cut through the surrounding valley. A short trail along the river bank leads to more rapids and small falls downstream. If you want to put up nearby, the 35-pitch *Honeymoon Lake* **campground** with kitchen shelter, swimming and dry toilets is 4km further along the parkway ($10; mid-June to first snowfall).

The last main stop before you're in striking distance of Jasper Townsite, **Athabasca Falls** (30km from Jasper) are impressive enough, but the platforms and paths show the strain caused by thousands of feet, making it hard to feel you're any longer in wilderness. One kilometre away, however, is the excellent *Athabasca Falls* **youth hostel** (☎852-5959, reservations through *Jasper International Hostel* ☎852-3215; $10 members, non-members $15, $1 cheaper outside of June–Sept; year-round; Oct–April closed Tues), with forty beds in three cabins. Three kilometres back down the road is the 42-site *Mount Kerkeslin* **campground**, with swimming, kitchen shelter and dry toilets, spread over a tranquil riverside site ($10; mid-May to early Sept).

Highway 93A, the route of the old Parkway, branches off the Icefields Parkway at Athabasca Falls and runs parallel to it for 30km. This alternative route has less dramatic views than the Parkway, as dense trees line the road, but the chances of spotting wildlife are higher.

Jasper National Park

Although traditionally viewed as the second-ranking of the Rockies' big four parks after Banff, **JASPER NATIONAL PARK** covers an area greater than Banff, Yoho and Kootenay combined (10,878 square kilometres), and looks and feels far wilder and less commercialized than its southern counterparts. Its backcountry is more extensive and less travelled, and **Jasper Townsite** (or Jasper), the only settlement, is more relaxed and far less of a resort than Banff and has just half Banff's population. Most pursuits centre on Jasper and the **Maligne Lake** area about 50km southeast of the townsite. Other key zones are **Maligne Canyon**, on the way to the lake; the Icefields Parkway (covered in the previous section); and the **Miette Hot Springs** region, an area well to the east of Jasper and visited for its springs and trails.

The park's **backcountry** is a vast hinterland scattered with countless rough camp-grounds and a thousand-kilometre trail system considered among the best in the world for backpackers. Opportunities for day and half-day hikes are more limited and scattered than in other parks. Most of the shorter strolls from the townsite are just low-level walks to forest-circled lakes; the best of the more exciting day hikes start from more remote points off the Maligne Lake road, Icefields Parkway (Hwy 93) and Yellowhead Highway (Hwy 16).

Jasper Townsite

JASPER's small-town feel comes as a relief after the razzmatazz of Banff: its streets still have the windswept, open look of a frontier town and, though the mountains don't ring it with quite the same majesty as Banff, you'll probably feel the town better suits its wild surroundings. Situated at the confluence of the Miette and Athabasca rivers, its core centres around just two streets: **Connaught Drive**, which contains the bus and train terminal, restaurants, motels and park information centre, and – a block to the west – the parallel **Patricia Street**, lined with more shops, restaurants and the odd hotel. The rest of the central grid consists of homely little houses and the fixtures of small-town life: the post office, library, school and public swimming pool. Apart from the **Yellowhead Museum & Archives** at 400 Pyramid Rd, with its fur trade and railroad displays (mid-May to early Sept daily 10am–9pm; early Sept to Oct daily 10am–5pm; Nov to mid-May Thurs–Sun 10am–5pm; $2.50 or donation; ☎852-3013) and a cable car (see p.610), nothing here even pretends to be a tourist attraction; this is a place to sleep, eat and stock up. If you're interested in getting to know a little more about the town or park from the locals, contact the "Friends of Jasper National Park" (☎852-4767), who offer guided walks between July and August, or pick up *Jasper: A Walk in the Past* from local bookshops. If you're still itching for something to do and have a car, a lot of people head 58km northeast of town for a dip in Miette Hot Springs (see hiking box on p.602).

Though Jasper doesn't get as crowded as Banff, it still receives around three million visitors annually, so accommodation, especially in summer, can be extremely tight, though there are numerous B&B options. You are also especially stuck if you don't have a vehicle; trailheads and the best scenery are a long way from downtown. Bikes can be rented at several places and intermittent shuttle services and organized tours can run you out of town to **Maligne Lake**, to various trailheads and to some of the more obvious attractions.

Some history

Permanent settlement first came to the Jasper area in the winter of 1810–11. The great explorer and trader David Thomson left **William Henry** at Old Fire Point (just outside the present townsite), while he and his companions pushed on up the valley to blaze a trail over the Athabasca Pass that would be used for more than fifty years by traders crossing the Rockies. In the meantime, Henry established **Henry House**, the first permanent European habitation in the Rockies (though its exact location has been lost). Two years later the North West Company established Jasper House at the eastern edge of the park's present boundary. Named after Jasper Hawes, a long-time company clerk there, it moved closer to Jasper Lake in 1829, when the North West and Hudson's Bay companies were amalgamated. By 1880, and the collapse of the fur trade, the post had closed. At the turn of the century the entire region boasted just seven homesteads.

Like other parks and their townsites, Jasper traces its real origins to the coming of the railway at the turn of the century. The Canadian Pacific had brought boom to Banff and Yoho in 1885 when it spurned a route through the Jasper region in favour of a more

HIKING IN JASPER NATIONAL PARK

Day hikes

If you haven't travelled to Jasper on the Icefields Parkway, remember that several of the national park's top trails can be accessed from this road: the Wilcox Pass Trail in particular, is one finest of the half-day hikes anywhere in the Rockies. If you just want a simple stroll closer to town, then think about walking the Old Fort Point Loop (see p.613), the Maligne Canyon (see p.613) and the easy path on the eastern shore of Maligne Lake (see p.614). If you're at Maligne Lake and want a longer walk, one of Jasper's best day hikes, the Opal Hills Circuit (8.2km round trip, 460m vertical ascent), starts from the picnic area to the left of the uppermost Maligne Lake car park, 48km east of Jasper. After a heart-pumping haul up the first steep slopes, the trail negotiates alpine meadows and offers sweeping views of the lake before reaching an elevation of 2160m; the trip takes about four hours, but you could easily spend all day loafing around the meadows. The Bald Hills Trail (5.2km one way; 480m ascent) starts with a monotonous plod along a fire road from the same car park, but ends with what Mary Schaffer, one of the area's first white explorers, described as "the finest view any of us had ever beheld in the Rockies"; allow four hours for the round trip, which goes as high as 2170m.

To get to the trailhead for another outstanding day hike, Cavell Meadows (3.8km one way; 370m ascent), which is named after a British nurse who was executed for helping the Allies during World War I, drive, cycle or taxi 7.5km south on the Icefields Parkway, then 5km along Hwy 93A and finally 14km up Mount Edith Cavell Road; there's a daily shuttle bus from Jasper and it takes bikes so you can ride back down. Note that if you're driving, an alternating one-way system has been instigated to reduce traffic flow up Mount Edith Cavell Road every day between 10am to 9.30pm between mid-June and mid-October: contact the park information centre for latest timings. The walk's scenery is mixed and magnificent – but the hike is popular, so don't expect solitude. As well as Cavell's alpine meadows, there are views of Angel Glacier and the dizzying north wall of Mount Edith Cavell. Allow two hours for the round trip; the maximum elevation reached is a breathless 2135m.

Further afield – you'll need transport – another superlative short, sharp walk starts from Miette Hot Springs, 58km northeast of Jasper. The Sulphur Skyline (4km one way, 700m ascent) offers exceptional views of knife-edged ridges, deep gorges, crags and remote valleys. Be sure to take water with you, and allow two hours each way for the steep climb to 2070m. The trailhead is signed from the Miette Hot Springs complex,

southerly route. (See "Field", p.618–623). The **Grand Trunk Pacific Railway** hoped for similar successes in attracting visitors when it started to push its own route west in 1902, and the Jasper Forest Park was duly created in 1908. The government bought up all land locally except for the homestead of Lewis Swift, which remained in stubborn private hands until 1962: the town is now "run" by Parks Canada. By 1911 a tent city known as **Fitzhugh**, named after the company's vice president, had grown up on Jasper's present site, and the name "Jasper" was adopted when the site was officially surveyed. Incredibly, a second railway, the **Canadian Northern** (CNR), was completed almost parallel to the Grand Trunk line in 1913, the tracks at some points running no more than a few metres apart. Within just three years, the line's redundancy became obvious and consolidation took place west of Edmonton, with the most favourably graded portions of the two routes being adopted. The ripped-up rails were then shipped to Europe and used in World War I and Jasper became a centre of operations for the lines in 1924, greatly boosting its importance and population. The first tourist accommodation here was ten tents on the shores of Lac Beauvert, replaced in 1921 by the first *Jasper Lake Lodge*, forerunner of the present hotel. The first road link from Edmonton was completed in 1928. Official national park designation came in 1930. Today Jasper's still a rail town, with around a third of the population employed by the CNR.

reached from Jasper by heading 41km east on Hwy 16 and then 17km south; in the past the Jasper Area Shuttle has made the trip in summer – check latest timetables. More soothing, and a good way to round off a day, are the springs themselves, the hottest in the Rockies – so hot in fact they have to be cooled for swimming; there's one pool for soaking, another for swimming, with massages by appointment and not included in pass price (mid-June to early Sept daily 8.30am–10.30pm, $5 or $9.50 day pass; early Sept to mid-Oct daily 10.30am–9pm, $4 or $7.50 day pass; ☎866-3939). You can hire bathing suits, towels and lockers for an extra $2–3. Other trails from the springs make for the Fiddle River (4.3km one way; 275m ascent) and Mystery Lake (10.5km one way; 475m ascent).

Backpacking trails

Jasper's system of backpacking trails and 111 backcountry campgrounds makes it one of the leading areas for backcountry hiking in North America. To stay overnight in the backcountry, pick up a permit ($6) within 24 hours of your departure, from the park information centre in Jasper Townsite or at the Columbia Icefield. Many popular trails operate quota systems; contact the park information office for details and book yourself a place within 21 days of departure. The office staff offer invaluable advice, and issue excellent low-price strip maps of several trails. Overnight hikes are beyond the scope of this book – talk to staff or get hold of a copy of *The Canadian Rockies Trail Guide* – but by general consent the finest long-distance trails are the Skyline (44km; 820m ascent) and Jonas Pass (19km; 555km ascent), with the latter often combined with the Nigel and Poboktan passes (total 36km; 750m ascent) to make a truly outstanding walk. Not far behind come two hikes in the Tonquin Valley – Astoria River (19km; 445m ascent) and Maccarib Pass (21km; 730m ascent) and the Fryat Valley (3–4 days). Others to consider are Maligne Pass and the long-distance North and South Boundary trails (the latter both over 160km). To summarize, a quick guide to the best walks in Jasper at a glance:

- Best stroll: Maligne Canyon
- Best short walk: Wilcox Pass (see p.599)
- Best day hike (easy): Cavell Meadows
- Best day hike (moderate) Opal Hills
- Best day hike (strenuous): Sulphur Skyline
- Best backpacking trail: Skyline Trail

Arrival

Where Banff's strength is its convenience from Calgary, Jasper's is its ease of **access** from Edmonton, with plenty of transport options and approaches, as well as a wide range of onward destinations. **Driving** time from Edmonton (362km) or Banff (287km) is around four hours; from Kamloops (443km) and Calgary (414km) it's about five hours. Greyhound (☎852-3926 or 1-800-661-8747) runs four **buses** daily from Edmonton (4hr 45min; $49 one way) along the Yellowhead Highway (Hwy 16), plus onward services to Kamloops/Vancouver via scenic Hwy 5 (4 daily) and Prince George (2 daily). Brewster Transportation (☎852-3332 or 1-800-661-1152) operates services to Banff (1 daily), Calgary (1 daily) and Calgary Airport (1 daily, additional connections at Banff), and also runs daytrips to Banff, taking in sights on the Icefields Parkway; note, however, that weather can play havoc with Brewster's schedules in October and April (services finish for the year with the first bad snows). Both companies share the same **bus terminal** (summer open 24hr daily; rest of the year Mon–Sat 7.30am–10.30pm, Sun 7.30–11am & 6.30–10.30pm), located in the train station building at 314 Connaught Drive. There are also left-luggage lockers here and a Tilden **car rental** office (☎852-4972 or 1-800-387-4747).

VIA Rail **trains** operate to Jasper from Winnipeg and Edmonton and continue to Vancouver (via Kamloops) or Prince Rupert (via Prince George). Coach (second-) class tickets currently cost $88.81 including taxes; Jasper to Vancouver, a stunning trip, will

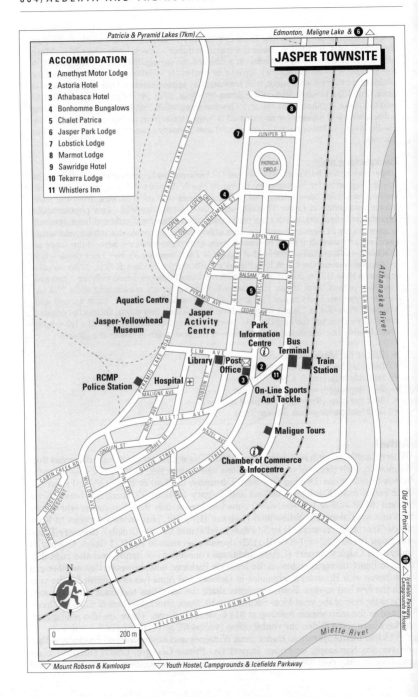

JASPER TOWNSITE

ACCOMMODATION

1 Amethyst Motor Lodge
2 Astoria Hotel
3 Athabasca Hotel
4 Bonhomme Bungalows
5 Chalet Patrica
6 Jasper Park Lodge
7 Lobstick Lodge
8 Marmot Lodge
9 Sawridge Hotel
10 Tekarra Lodge
11 Whistlers Inn

Patricia & Pyramid Lakes (7km)

Edmonton, Maligne Lake & 6

JUNIPER ST

PATRICIA CIRCLE

PYRAMID LAKE ROAD

ASPEN CRES

ASPEN CLOSE

BONHOMME ST

ASPEN AVE

CONNAUGHT DRIVE

COLIN CRES

GEIKIE STREET

PATRICIA STREET

BALSAM AVE

PYRAMID AVE

CEDAR AVE

Aquatic Centre

Jasper-Yellowhead Museum

Jasper Activity Centre

Park Information Centre

Bus Terminal

Train Station

ELM AVE

Library

Post Office

RCMP Police Station

Hospital

MALIGNE AVE

PYRAMID LAKE ROAD

ROBSON ST

MIETTE AVE

On-Line Sports And Tackle

BIRCH AVE

TURRET ST

GEIKIE STREET

PINE AVE

HAZEL AVE

PATRICIA STREET

Maligue Tours

Chamber of Commerce & Infocentre

TONQUIN ST

WILLOW AVE

LODGE POLE CRESCENT

CABIN CREEK RD

ASH AVE

CONNAUGHT DRIVE

HIGHWAY 93A

YELLOWHEAD HIGHWAY 16

Miette River

YELLOWHEAD HIGHWAY 16

Athabaska River

Old Fort Point

Icefields Parkway, Campgrounds & Hostel 10

N

0   200 m

Mount Robson & Kamloops

Youth Hostel, Campgrounds & Icefields Parkway

set you back $151.94. As this is the only scheduled rail route through the Rockies, summer places are hard to come by, but at other times there's little need to book a seat. Fares are considerably more than those of equivalent buses, and journey times considerably longer. Trains run Edmonton–Jasper (currently Mon, Thurs & Sat; 5hr 30min); Jasper–Edmonton (Tues, Fri & Sun); Jasper–Kamloops–Vancouver (Mon, Thurs & Sat; 15hr 30min); Jasper–Prince George (Wed, Fri & Sun; 5hr 15min; $67) and Prince George–Prince Rupert (Mon, Thurs & Sat; 12hr 15min; $85.60). The **ticket office** is open on train days only (☎852-4102 or 1-800-561-8630).

Information

Both the main **Travel Alberta** office (Mon–Fri 9am–noon & 1–5pm; ☎852-3858), and the town's Chamber of Commerce **visitor centre** (May Mon–Fri 9am–5pm; June–Sept daily 8am–8pm; ☎852-4919) are at 632 Connaught Drive on the western edge of town. Both have full lists of accommodation and campgrounds in the area, but do not make advance bookings. The excellent Canadian Parks Service **park information centre**, whose amiable staff sell maps and have all relevant information on the park (don't go here for accommodation unless you're interested in park campgrounds), is at the other end of town at 500 Connaught Drive – 50m east of the station, back from the road on the left (daily: mid-May to mid-June 8am–5pm; mid-June to early Sept 8am–7pm; early Sept to mid-May Mon–Fri 9am–5pm, Sat & Sun 8am–5pm; ☎852-6176; *http://www.worldweb.com/ParksCanada-Jasper*). Apply here for compulsory **national park permits** ($5 daily, $35 annual; see box, p.567) backcountry camping permits ($6) and to register for backpacking trails. If you're hiking seriously you might also want to contact the park's Trail Office (May–Oct; ☎852-6177). Out of season, apply to the Park Administration Office at PO Box 10, 623 Patricia St (Mon–Fri 8am–4.30pm; ☎852-6162 or 852-6220). The Park Warden Office is 2km away on the Maligne Road (Mon–Fri 8am–4.30pm; ☎852-6155). For weather reports, call Environment Canada (☎852-3185). The Reader's Choice **bookshop**, 610 Connaught Drive (☎852-4028), has a good selection of maps and guides. The local **public library** on Elm Avenue (Mon–Thurs 2–5pm & 7–9pm, Fri 2–5pm, Sat 10am–3pm; ☎852-3652) also has a huge number of books on the park. The **post office** is at 502 Patricia St; the **hospital** at 518 Robson St (☎852-3344). For the **police**, call ☎852-4848.

Accommodation

Beds in Jasper are not as expensive or elusive as in Banff, but are still almost unobtainable in July and August. The Chamber of Commerce has a free phone for local hotel and B&B calls, and will call around for private rooms. Jasper had around seventy private homes offering such rooms at the last count, which are virtually all priced between $50 and $60 a double (up to a maximum of around $75 for the most expensive), sometimes with a continental breakfast thrown in (note that virtually all are non-smoking). These rooms also fill up fast. If you can afford more, or are desperate, Banff and Jasper Central Reservations (☎1-800-661-1676) and the office at 622 Connaught Drive (☎852-4242) may come up with something – for a fee. Alternatively, you could try the cheaper, local agencies, Reservations Jasper (☎852-5488) and Jasper Travel (☎852-4400).

Most **motels** are spaced out along Connaught Drive on the eastern edge of town – there's relatively little right in the middle of town – and most charge well over $125 for a basic double room, though prices drop sharply off season. An often cheaper and in many ways more pleasant option is to plump for motels made up of collections of **cabins**; most are within a few kilometres of town. The four park-run **campgrounds** close to the townsite and the three local hostels (joint reservations on ☎439-3139) all fill up promptly in summer, but don't forget the hostels and campgrounds strung along the Icefields Parkway.

HIKER'S WHEELS

An inexpensive transport service, **Hiker's Wheels**, links Jasper with trailheads for hikers, mountain bikers and canoeists. All routes cost under $25: to the Nigel Pass via the Icefield infocentre and the Athabasca and Beauty Creek hostels; to Mount Robson Provincial Park; to the Tonquin Valley (for popular backpack trails); to Maligne Lake; and to the 93A Loop, via the *Cavell* youth hostel, Tonquin trailheads, *Wabasso* campground, Geraldine, *Athabasca* hostel and Wabasso Lake. The eventual aim is to serve all major trails in Jasper National Park and Mount Robson Provincial Park.

All rides must be prebooked (☎852-2188), and depart from the *Hava Java Café*, 407 Patricia St. A daily bus to the *Mount Edith Cavell Hostel* departs at 5pm.

HOTELS, MOTELS AND CHALETS

Alpine Village, 2.5km south of town on Hwy 93A (☎852-3285). An assortment of 41 serene one- and two-room cabins, including twelve deluxe cabins and lodge suites, most with great mountain views; big outdoor tub. May to mid-Oct. ⑤–⑦.

Amethyst Motor Lodge, 200 Connaught Drive (☎852-3394 or 1-800-661-9935, fax 852-5198). Almost 100 rooms two blocks from downtown. ⑥.

Astoria Hotel, Patricia Street (☎852-3351 or 1-800-661-7343, fax 852-5472). Adequate central "alpine" hotel, one block from the train station and bus terminal. ⑥.

Athabasca Hotel, 510 Patricia St (☎852-3386 or 1-800-563-9859, fax 852-4955). Central, if rather forbidding hotel, near the station, where the nightly entertainment and *O'Shea's Lounge Bar* may keep you awake. Choice of suites, newly renovated rooms, en suite or with sinks only and shared facilities. ③–⑤.

Becker's Roaring River Chalets, 5km south of Jasper on Hwy 93 and Athabasca River (☎852-3779, fax 852-7202). Ninety-six of the best (and newest) local one-, two-, three- and four-bedroom log cabins, most with wood-burning stoves and kitchenettes. May to mid-Oct. ③–⑦.

Bonhomme Bungalows, 100 Bonhomme St (☎852-3209, 852-3099). Thirty-seven simple-looking but comfortable bungalows, suites, chalet and lodge units, in the townsite but in a pleasant wooded setting. Mid-April to late Oct. ④–⑥.

Jasper Park Lodge, 5km from townsite on Lac Beauvert (☎852-3301, 1-800-465-7547 in Alberta or 1-800-441-1414 elsewhere in North America). The upmarket, luxury option, with all the facilities and trimmings of a top-class hotel; Jasper's equivalent of the *Banff Springs* or *Chateau Lake Louise*. ⑧.

Lobstick Lodge, 1200 Geikie at Juniper (☎852-4431 or 1-800-661-9317, fax 852-4142). If you're going to pay in-town, east-end motel rates, this big and recently renovated place is probably the best all-round choice. ⑥.

Marmot Lodge, 92 Connaught Drive (☎852-4471 or 1-800-661-6521, fax 852-3280). One of the biggest and least expensive of the east-end motels. ⑥.

Patricia Lake Bungalows, 5km northwest of downtown (☎852-3560, fax 852-4060). Motel or cabin out-of-town base; 35 recently updated units on the Pyramid Lake Road, some with fine views over Patricia Lake; fishing and rentals of boats, canoes and paddle boats available. May to mid-Oct. ③–⑤.

Pine Bungalows, 2km east of Jasper on the Athabasca River (☎852-3491, fax 852-3432). Some 85 good-looking wooden cabins in forest setting, 41 with wood-burning stoves and 72 with kitchenettes. Grocery shop on site. Three-day minimum stay from mid-June to Mid-Sept. May to mid-Oct. ③.

Sawridge Hotel Jasper, 82 Connaught Drive (☎852-5111 or 1-800-661-6427, fax 852-5942). Plush 154-room hotel on the eastern edge of town. The in-house disco may not be to all tastes. ⑦.

Tekarra Lodge (☎852-3058 or 1-800-661-6562, fax 852-4636). Forty-two quiet, nicely kitsch wood cabins with wood-burning stoves, located 1km south of town on the Athabasca River off Hwy 93A. Open May–Oct. ⑤.

Whistlers Inn, 105 Miette Ave (☎852-3361 or 1-800-282-9919, fax 852-4993). Central 41-room motel, opposite the station. ③–⑤.

BED AND BREAKFASTS

A-1 Tourist Rooms, 804 Connaught Drive (☎852-3325). Three rooms with shared bathroom on main street close to bus and train. ①.

Aspen Lodge, 8 Aspen Crescent (☎852-5908, fax 852-5910). Two clean, comfortable rooms with private bathrooms on a quiet street 10min walk from downtown. ③.

Bowen, Reine 228 Colin Crescent (☎852-4532). One well-priced room with two double beds and private bathroom: smoking permitted. ②.

Creekside Accommodation, 1232 Patricia Crescent (☎852-3530, fax 852-2116). Two bright, clean rooms (shared bath) near *Cabin Creek* and trails. ②.

Kennedy's Mountain Holiday Rooms, 1115 Patricia Crescent (☎852-3438). Pair of rooms that share bath, patio, living room and great views. ②.

Marchand, Yves and Caroline, 809 Patricia St (☎852-3609). Three double rooms with shared bathroom in a quiet location 5min from the town centre. A full cooked breakfast is available at extra cost. ②.

Perperidis, Litsa, 719 Geikie St (☎852-3221 or 852-3920, fax 852-5386). Three rooms with a choice of shared or private bathroom. Smoking permitted. ②.

Pooli's Suite, 824 Geikie St (☎852-4379). A one-bedroom suite with two double beds and a pull-out in the living room (sleeps up to six): $60 for two people, $4 for each additional person: private bathroom and use of kitchen for an additional $8. ②–③.

Rainee's Rooms, 6 Aspen Crescent (☎852-5181). Just north of the town centre comprising three rooms with and without private baths. ②.

The Rocky Mountain Retreat, 400 Pyramid Ave (☎852-4090). A new home offering two rooms with private bathrooms a block from downtown close to the Aquatic Centre. ③.

711 Miette Avenue, 711 Miette Ave (☎852-4029, fax 852-4021). A double room plus private living room and bathroom two blocks from downtown. ③.

Worobec, Wayne and Joan, 1215 Patricia Crescent (☎852-5563). A choice of double room with private bathroom at $45 or a suite of bedroom, living room and food preparation area for family for two to four people at $75. ②–③.

HOSTELS

Jasper International Youth Hostel (HI; ☎852-3215). Jasper's principal youth hostel, formerly known as *Whistlers Hostel*, lies 7km south of town (500m south of the gondola terminal) on Skytram Road (Whistlers Mountain Road), accessed from the Icefields Parkway (Hwy 93). The 4km uphill walk from Hwy 93 is a killer, but shuttles run from downtown, as do taxis ($12–15). A modern place with reports that suggest rather overefficient management, its eighty beds fill up quickly in summer, so arrive early or book. Members $15, non-members $20. Facilities include laundry, store and bike rentals. ①.

Maligne Canyon Hostel (HI; ☎852-3584 or 852-3215). Two cabins with beds for 24 in six-bed rooms 11km east of town near Maligne Canyon; the Maligne Lake Shuttle from downtown or Alberta Hostel Shuttle (see p.595) drop off here daily in summer; members $9 ($10 June–Sept), non-members $14 ($15 June–Sept). Open all day, year-round but Oct–April closed Wed. ①.

Mount Edith Cavell Hostel, Edith Cavell Road, 13km off Hwy 93A, 26km south of Jasper (HI; reservations ☎852-3215). Cosier than the Jasper International Hostel (see below), close to trails and with great views of the Angel Glacier. Sleeps 32 in two cabins; outdoor wood-burning sauna. Members $10, non-members 15. Mid-June to Oct. Occasionally opens up with key system for skiers in winter. ①.

HOSTEL RESERVATIONS

For reservations at *Jasper International, Maligne Canyon, Edith Cavell, Beauty Creek* and *Athabasca Falls* hostels, call ☎403/852-3215 or email: *jihostel@telusplanet.net*

CAMPGROUNDS

Pocahontas, 45km east of Jasper and 1km off Hwy 16 on Miette Road. The other simple park campground east of Jasper; 130 pitches, hot and cold water and flush toilets but no showers. Mid-May to mid-Oct. $13 plus $3 for use of firewood.

Snaring River, 16km east of Jasper on Hwy 16. Simple 66-site park-run facility, one of two to the northeast of Jasper on this road; tap water, kitchen shelter, dry toilets only and no showers. Mid-May to early Sept. $10 plus $3 for use of firewood.

Wabasso, 16km south of Jasper on Hwy 93A. 232-pitch riverside park-run site with flush toilets, hot water but no showers. Wheelchair-accessible. Mid-May to early Sept. $13 plus $3 for use of firewood.

Wapiti, 4km south of the townsite and 1km south of *Whistlers* campground (see below) on Hwy 93. Big 322-pitch park-run place with flush toilets and coin showers that accepts tents but also caters for up to forty RVs. Wheelchair-accessible. Forty sites remain open for winter camping from October – the park's only year-round serviced campground. $15–18 in summer plus $3 for use of firewood; winter $14–16 plus $3 for use of firewood.

Whistlers, 3km south of Jasper just west off Hwy 93. Jasper's main 781-site park-run campground is the largest in the Rockies, with three sections, and prices depending on facilities included. Wheelchair-accessible. If you're coming from Banff, watch for the sign; Brewster buses also usually stop here if you ask the driver. Taxis and shuttles run from Jasper. Early May to early Oct. $15, $18 and $22, plus $3 for use of firewood.

Eating

Options for **eating** out are a little restricted in Jasper, but then the town's ambience doesn't suit fine dining (most motels and hotels have dining rooms). Perhaps the best place for a basic budget meal in no-nonsense surroundings is *Mountain Foods and Café*, opposite the station at 606 Connaught Drive (☎852-4050). The menu is cheap and varied (including vegetarian courses), the food is excellent, the staff friendly, and it's a good place to meet people; there's also a wholefood shop at the back. Also popular is the lively and far more carnivorous *Villa Caruso*, 628 Connaught Drive (☎852-3920), where vast steaks sizzle over open grills in the windows to tempt passing trade; there's seafood plus pasta and pizzas if you can't face the steaks. Best of the mid-range places is the ever-reliable *Earl's*, newly opened on the second floor at 600 Patricia St on the corner of Miette Avenue. For pizzas cooked in a wood-burning oven, head to the big and bustling *Jasper Pizza Place* (☎852-3225), 402 Connaught Drive, with a rooftop patio for nice days, and for a locals' favourite try *Papa George's*, 406 Connaught Drive (☎852-3351), one of the town's oldest restaurants (opened in 1924). If you're going for broke, the *Jasper Park Lodge*, Jasper's premier hotel, 5km from town on Lac Beauvert, boasts two outstanding restaurants: *Becker's* is rated by Canadian foodie guides as one of the best in Alberta (☎852-3535; May–Oct; dinner only) – reckon on $115 for a gourmet blowout for two – while the *Edith Cavell Room* is only marginally less renowned. Both places have dining rooms with cracking views.

Cafés and nightlife

The best of the **cafés** is the small, non-smoking *Coco's Café* at 608 Patricia St: inexpensive and vaguely trendy, with newspapers and magazines to pass the time over excellent snacks and coffees. Coffee fiends might also head to the *Soft Rock Café* in Connaught Square at 622 Connaught Drive. In similar vein, but still more laid-back, the *Hava Java Café* behind the national park information centre at 407 Patricia St has tables out on the lawn during summer, while the inside resembles a cosy front room (they also run the Hiker's Wheels service – see box on p.606). Turn left after the station for *Smitty's Restaurant*, where you can drink coffee and write postcards all day. *Nutters* at the west end of Patricia Street is a supermarket with a wholefood bias.

Most **drinking** goes on in the lounge at the *Athabasca Hotel*, 510 Patricia St, where the "nightclub" annexe has dancing and live music most nights. The unpretentious and locals' hangout *Astoria* and its *De'd Dog Bar* at 404 Connaught Drive attracts more of a thirtyish crowd, with big-screen TV, music, darts and food. *The Pub* in Whistlers Inn opposite the station has an old-style wooden bar and lots of memorabilia. The *Tent City* bar C&W evening on Friday nights is also pretty lively at the *Jasper Park Lodge* on Lac Beauvert. If you want a more smoochy evening, the Bonhomme Lounge at the *Chateau Jasper*, 96 Geikie St, has a harpist most nights. The Chaba Theatre is a **cinema** directly opposite the station. Nightlife generally is low-key: most of the campgrounds and motels are too far out of town for people to get in, and the fun is generally of the makeyour-own variety out at hostels or campgrounds.

Local transport

To get around locally, try the Hiker's Wheels service (see box on p.606) or the pricier summer-only Jasper Park Shuttle Service, which runs regularly in summer from the offices of Maligne Tours, 626 Connaught Drive (☎852-3370), to Maligne Lake ($12 one-way) via the canyon ($7), hostel and Skyline trailheads (May, June & mid-Sept to mid-Oct 3 daily; July to mid-Sept 4 daily). You can **rent bikes** at the *Jasper International Youth Hostel*, at Beauvert Boat & Cycles; at *Jasper Park Lodge* on the shore of Lac Beauvert ($8 an hour, $20 for 4hr or $35 a day for bikes; ☎852-5708); from On-Line Sport & Tackle, 600 Patricia St ($5 an hour, $18 a day; ☎852-3630), or from Freewheel Cycles at 618 Patricia St (☎852-3898), with the last offering a one-way rental from Jasper to Banff to let you ride the Icefields Parkway. For a **taxi**, call Heritage Cabs (☎852-5558) or Jasper Taxi (☎852-3146 or 852-3600). Cars can be rented through Avis (☎852-3970 or 1-800-879-2847), from Tilden in the bus and train terminal at 607 Connaught Drive (☎852-4972), or Budget, 638 Connaught Drive (☎852-3222 or 1-800-268-8900).

Activities

The presence of the Athabasca and other rivers around Jasper makes the town a focus of **white-water** and other rafting trips (see box on pp.618–619). If the idea of water appeals, but in much gentler context, the town's **Aquatic Centre** at 401 Pyramid Lake Rd (☎852-3663; $5) is very popular, and provides a large **swimming** pool, whirlpool, wading pool, steam room and showers. You can rent towels and costumes if you've come unprepared. Other tours and activities can be accessed through several operators around town, amongst whom the most wide-ranging is probably the ubiquitous Maligne Tours at 626 Connaught Drive (☎852-3370, fax 852-3405), who, among other things, run boat cruises on Maligne Lake, guided hiking and fishing trips, "Snocoach"

WINTER IN JASPER

Jasper's winter sports tend to be overshadowed by the world-class ski resorts in nearby Banff and Lake Louise. This said, the park has plenty of winter activities and a first-rate ski area in **Marmot Basin** (20min drive from the townsite), a resort with the advantages of cheaper skiing and far less crowded runs than its southern rivals. Skiing in the region began in the 1920s, though the first lift – a 700-metre rope tow – was only introduced in 1961, just a few years after the first road. Today there are a total of seven **lifts**: two T-bars, three double chair lifts, one triple chair lift and one high-speed quad chair lift; few are likely to be crowded in winter. The terrain is a balanced mixture of Novice (35 percent), Intermediate (35 percent) and Expert (30 percent). The drop from the resorts's top elevation at 2601m to the base level is 701m: the longest run is 5.6km and there are a total of 52 named trails. Lift passes cost around $35. The season runs from early December to late April. You can rent equipment at the resort or from several outlets in Jasper itself. To get here, jump aboard one of the three daily buses ($5 one way, $9 return) from downtown hotels, whose rates, incidentally, tumble dramatically during the winter. For more **information** on the resort, contact Marmot Basin Ski-Lifts, PO Box 1300, Jasper AB T0E 1E0 (☎852-3816, fax 852-3533).

Where Jasper rates as highly, if not more so, than Banff National Park is in the range and quality of its **cross-country skiing**, for its summer backcountry trails lend themselves superbly to winter grooming. Pick up the *Cross-Country Skiing in Jasper National Park* leaflet from the park information centre: the key areas are around the *Whistlers campground*, Maligne Lake, around Athabasca Falls, and along Pyramid Lake Road. Ski and cross-country ski equipment can be **bought or rented** from Totem Ski Rentals, 408 Connaught Drive (☎852-3078), and the Sports Shop, 414 Connaught Drive (☎852-3654). **Ice-skating** takes place on parts of Pyramid Lake and Lac Beauvert, and there are the usual sleigh rides around Jasper and its environs.

tours of the Columbia Icefield (summer 1 daily 8.30am), canoe rentals and rafting trips. All manner of short or strenuous and generally cheap **guided hiking** or **wildlife tour** are widely available: contact the Chamber of Commerce for details of the various oper ators. For the free walking tours run by the "Friends of Jasper National Park" in the summer, contact the park visitor centre.

More specifically, bike rental is easy if you want to **cycle** (see "Local transport", p.609) or you can sign up to trips with Wheel Fun Cycles at Freewheel Cycles, 618 Patricia S (☎852-3898) for their Maligne Valley Downhill Interpretive Cycle Tour (daily in summe: 9am; $75). The five-hour tours, which include two hours on bikes, take you by shuttle to Maligne Lake and then let you ride (mostly) downhill to Maligne Canyon. The tours are suitable for all ages and abilities, with a van following the group if you want to bale out.

If you want **fishing** tours or tackle for rent, contact On-Line Sport & Tackle, 600 Patri ca St (☎852-3630) for trips to Maligne Lake for trout, Talbot Lake for trout or various other lake and river-fishing destinations. (They also organize rafting and horseriding tours, and sell and hire a wide range of **camping gear**.) Currie's Guiding, 414 Connaugh Drive, offer similar trips on the rivers and over twenty lakes, with fly-fishing lessons also available. **Golf** on an eighteen-hole course is available at the *Jasper Park Lodge* (green fees from $69, cheaper twilight fees available; ☎852-6090). You can rent clubs and carts

Horseriding enthusiasts should contact Pyramid Stables, 4km from Jasper on Pyra mid Lake Road (see above), who run day treks and one-, two- and three-hour trip (from $18) around Patrician and Pyramid lakes. Ridgeline Riders at Maligne Tours, 62(Connaught Drive (☎852-3370) offer a ride above the treeline at Maligne Lake to the Bald Hills Fire Lookout at 2134m with great views of the lake (3hr 30min; $55). Skyline Trail Rides (see above) at *Jasper Park Lodge* have a more varied programme which includes a one-hour ride to Lake Annette ($23), ninety-minute rides along the Athabas ca River ($30), two-hour "Valley View" treks ($35) and four-hour rides to Maligne Canyon ($65). They can also organize overnight trips and anything up to 21-day expe ditions using a variety of backcountry lodges.

Jasper Tramway and the lakes

With little on offer in town you need to use a bike, car or the shuttle services to get any thing out of the area. The obvious trip is on Canada's longest and highest tramway, the **Jasper Tramway**, 7km south of town on Whistlers Mountain Road, off the Icefields Park way (daily: May–Aug 8.30am–10pm; Sept 9.30am–9pm; Oct 9.30am–4.30pm; shorter hour rest of the year; $14.95 return; ☎852-3093). In peak season you may well have a long wait in line for the 2.5-kilometre cable-car ride, whose two thirty-person cars take seven minutes to make the 1000-metre ascent (often with running commentary from the conductor). I leaves you at an interpretive centre, expensive restaurant, and an excellent viewpoin (2285m) where you can take your bearings on much of the park. A steep trail plough: upwards and onwards to the Whistlers summit (2470m), an hour's walk that requires warn clothes year-round and reveals even more stunning views. A tough but rather redundan ten-kilometre trail follows the route of the tramway from *Jasper International Youth Hoste* if you walk up, you can ride back down for next to nothing.

Also near the town, a winding road wends north to **Patricia** and **Pyramid lakes** popular and pretty moraine-dammed lakes about 5km from Jasper and racked full c rental facilities for riding, boating, canoeing, windsurfing and sailing. Food and drink i available locally, but if you're thinking about staying here as a more rural alternative to the townsite the two lakefront lodges are usually heavily booked (the one at Pyramic Lake is open year-round). Short trails, generally accessible from the approach road include the Patricia Lake Circle, a 4.8-kilometre loop by the Cottonwood slough and creek offering good opportunities for seeing birds and small mammals, like beavers during early morning and late evening. The island on Pyramid Lake, connected by a

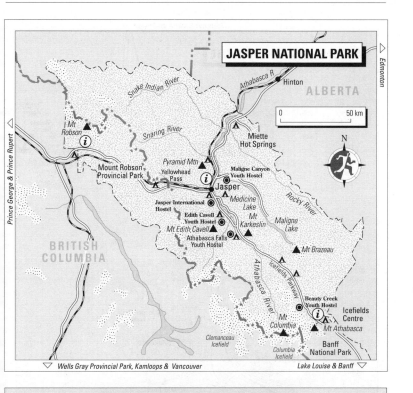

JASPER NATIONAL PARK

ALBERTA

0   50 km

N

Snake Indian River

Snaring River

Mt Robson ⓘ

Prince George & Prince Rupert ◁

Miette Hot Springs

Mount Robson Provincial Park

Pyramid Mtn

Yellowhead Pass ⓘ

Maligne Canyon Youth Hostel

Jasper

Jasper International Hostel ◎

Medicine Lake

Edith Cavell Youth Hostel ◎

Mt Edith Cavell

Mt Karkeslin

Maligne Lake

Athabasca Falls Youth Hostel ◎

BRITISH COLUMBIA

▲ Mt Brazeau

Rocky River

Athabasca River

Icefields Parkway

Beauty Creek Youth Hostel ⓘ

Icefields Centre

Mt Columbia

Mt Athabasca

Clemanceau Icefield

Columbia Icefield

Banff National Park ▽

▽ Wells Gray Provincial Park, Kamloops & Vancouver

Lake Louise & Banff ▽

OPERATION HABBAKUK

Behind every triumph of military ingenuity in World War II, there were probably dozens of spectacular and deliberately obfuscated failures. Few have been as bizarre as the one witnessed by Jasper's Patricia Lake. By 1942, Allied shipping losses in the North Atlantic had become so disastrous that almost anything was considered that might staunch the flow. One Geoffrey Pike, institutionalized in a London mental hospital, put forward the idea of a vast aircraft carrier made of ice, a ship that would be naturally impervious to fire when torpedoed, and not melt from under its seamen in the icy waters of the North Atlantic.

Times were so hard that the scheme was given serious consideration. Louis Mountbatten, one of the Allied Chiefs of Staff, went so far as to demonstrate the theories with ice cubes in the bath in front of Winston Churchill at 10 Downing St. It was decided to build a thousand-tonne model somewhere very cold – Canada would be ideal – and **Operation Habbakuk** was launched. Pike was released from his hospital on special dispensation and dispatched to the chilly waters of Patricia Lake. Here a substance known as pikewood was invented, a mixture of ice and wood chips (spruce chips were discovered to add more buoyancy than pine). It soon became clear, however, that the 650-metre-long and twenty-storey-high boat stood little chance of ever being seaworthy (never mind what the addition of 2000 crew and 26 aircraft would do for its buoyancy). Pike suggested filling the ice with air to help things along. Further complications arose when the labourers on the project, mostly pacifist Doukhobors (see p.484), became aware of the boat's proposed purpose and refused to carry on working. Spring thaws brought the project to a halt. The following season, with $75 million budgeted for the scheme, it was moved to Newfoundland, where it died a quiet death.

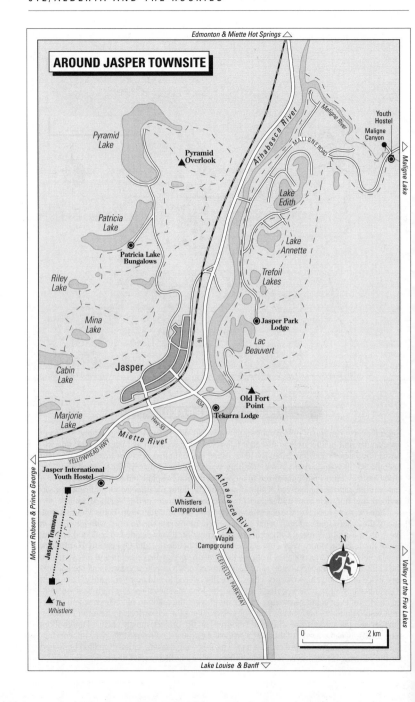

AROUND JASPER TOWNSITE

Edmonton & Miette Hot Springs △

Athabasca River

Maligne River

Youth Hostel
Maligne Canyon

Maligne Lake ▷

MALIGNE ROAD

Pyramid Lake

Pyramid Overlook ▲

Lake Edith

Patricia Lake

Lake Annette

● **Patricia Lake Bungalows**

Trefoil Lakes

Riley Lake

Mina Lake

● **Jasper Park Lodge**

Lac Beauvert

Cabin Lake

Jasper

16

▲ **Old Fort Point**

● **Tekarra Lodge**

Marjorie Lake

93A

Hwy 93

Miette River

YELLOWHEAD HWY

Mount Robson & Prince George ◁

Jasper International Youth Hostel ■●

Athabasca River

Jasper Tramway

▲ Whistlers Campground

△ Wapiti Campground

ICEFIELDS PARKWAY

Valley of the Five Lakes ▷

N

■ ▲ The Whistlers

0   2 km

Lake Louise & Banff ▽

bridge to the shore, is an especially popular destination for a day out: continue on the lake road to the end of the lake and you'll find everything a little quieter. Slightly closer to town on the east side of the Athabasca River, **Lake Edith** and **Lake Annette** are the remains of a larger lake that once extended across the valley floor. Both are similarly busy day-use areas. Their waters are surprisingly warm – in fact they're the warmest in the park, thanks to the lakes' shallow depth. In summer you can lie out on sandy beaches or grassy areas. A clutch of picnic sites are the only development, and the wheelchair-accessible Lee Foundation Trail meanders around Lake Annette (2.4km).

Few other hikes from town are spectacular, but the best of the bunch, the Old Fort Point Loop (6.5km round trip), is recommended. Despite being just thirty minutes out of town, it's remarkably scenic, with 360-degree views and lots of quiet corners. To reach the trailhead (1.6km from town) use the Old Fort Exit, following Hwy 93A across the railway and Hwy 16 until you come to the Old Fort Point–Lac Beauvert turnoff; then turn left and follow the road to the parking lot beyond the bridge. The Valley of the Five Lakes Trail (4.6km) is also good, but the path starts 10km south of town off the Icefields Parkway. For full details of all park walks, ask at the information centre for the free *Day Hiker's Guide to Jasper*.

Maligne Lake Road

Bumper to bumper with cars, campers and tour buses in the summer, the **Maligne Lake Road** runs east from Jasper for 48km, taking in a number of beautiful but rather busy and overdeveloped sights before reaching the sublime Maligne Lake (pronounced "Maleen"), the Rockies' largest glacier-fed lake (and the world's second largest). If you have time to spare, and the transport, you could set aside a day for the trip, white-water raft the Maligne River (see below), or walk one of the trails above Maligne Lake itself. Maligne Tours, 626 Connaught Drive (☎852-3370), books boat tours on the lake (advance booking is highly recommended) and rents out any equipment you may need for canoeing, fishing and so forth (note that rental reservations are also essential in summer). The company also runs a **bus**, the Maligne Lake Shuttle, to the lake eight times daily ($10), with drop-offs (if booked) at *Maligne Canyon* youth hostel ($6) and the northern ($6) and southern ends ($10) of the Skyline Trail, one of the park's three top backpacking trails (see box, p.603). Joint tickets are offered for the shuttle and other activities organized by the company, notably the cruises, raft trips and horse rides on and around Maligne Lake.

The often rather crowded **Maligne Canyon** is a mere 11km out of Jasper, with an oversized car park and a tacky café/souvenir shop. This heavily sold excursion promises one of the Rockies' most spectacular gorges: in fact the canyon is deep (50m), but almost narrow enough to jump across – many people have tried and most have died in the attempt. In the end the geology is more interesting than the scenery; the violent erosive forces that created the canyon are explained on the main trail loop, an easy twenty-minute amble that can be extended to 45 minutes (few people do this, so the latter part of the trail is often quiet), or even turned into a hike back to Jasper. In winter, licensed guides lead tours (more like crawls) through the frozen canyon – contact Maligne Tours, 626 Connaught Drive, Jasper (details above).

Next stop is picture-perfect **Medicine Lake**, 32km from Jasper, which experiences intriguing fluctuations in level. Its waters have no surface outlet: instead the lake fills and empties through lake-bed sink holes into the world's largest system of limestone caves. They re-emerge some 17km away towards Jasper (and may also feed some of the lakes around Jasper Townsite). When the springs freeze in winter, the lake drains and sometimes disappears altogether, only to be replenished in the spring. The lake's strange behaviour captivated local natives, who believed spirits were responsible, hence the name. Few people spend much time at the lake, preferring to press on to Maligne Lake, so it makes a quietish spot to escape the headlong rush down the road.

At the end of the road, 48km from Jasper, is the stunning **Maligne Lake**, 22km long and 92m deep, and surrounded by snow-covered mountains. The largest lake in the Rockies, its name comes from the French for "wicked", and was coined in 1846 by a Jesuit missionary, Father de Smet, in memory of the difficulty he had crossing the **Maligne River** downstream. The road peters out at a warden station, three car parks and a restaurant flanked by a picnic area and the start of the short, self-explanatory Lake Trail along the lake's east side to the Schäffer Viewpoint (3.2km loop; begin from Car Park 2). A small waterfront area is equipped with berths for glass-enclosed boats that run ninety-minute narrated **cruises** on the lake to Spirit Island: the views are sensational (daily hourly: mid-May to late June 10am–4pm; late June to early Sept 10am–5pm; early Sept to late Sept 10am–3pm; $35). The boats are small, however, and reservations are vital during peak times, especially as tour companies often block-book entire sailings: again, contact Maligne Tours. Riding, fishing, rafting and guided hiking tours are also available, as are fishing tackle, rowing boat and canoe rentals ($35 per day, $12 per hour, $6 each additional hour). There are no accommodation or camping facilities here, but two backcountry campgrounds on the lakeshore can be reached by canoe (details from Jasper's information centre).

Mount Robson Provincial Park

The extensive **MOUNT ROBSON PROVINCIAL PARK** borders Jasper National Park to the west and protects Mount Robson which, at 3954m, is the highest peak in the Canadian Rockies. Its scenery equals anything anywhere else in the Rockies, and **Mount Robson** itself is one of the most staggering mountains you'll ever encounter. Facilities are thin on the ground, so stock up on food and fuel before entering the park. Around 16km beyond the park's western boundary Hwy 16 comes the Tête Jaune Cache, where you can pick up one of two immensely scenic roads: the continuation of Hwy 16 north to Prince George (for routes to Prince Rupert, northern BC and the Yukon), or Hwy 5, which heads south past Wells Gray Provincial Park to Kamloops and a whole range of onward destinations: the latter route is dealt with on p.746.

Both road and rail links to the park from Jasper climb through **Yellowhead Pass**, long one of the most important native and fur-trading routes across the Rockies. The pass, 20km west of Jasper Townsite, marks the boundary between Jasper and Mount Robson parks, Alberta and British Columbia, and Mountain and Pacific time zones – set your watch back one hour. This stretch of road is less dramatic than the Icefields Parkway, but then most roads are, given over to mixed woodland – birch interspersed with firs – and mountains that sit back from the road with less scenic effect. The railway meanders alongside the road most of the way, occasionally occupied by epic freight trains hundreds of wagons long – alien intrusions in the usual beguiling wilderness of rocks, river and forest. Just down from the pass, **Yellowhead Lake** is the park's first landmark. Look for moose around dawn and dusk at aptly named **Moose Lake**, another 20km further west.

Mount Robson

Even if the first taste of the park seems relatively tame, the first sight of **Mount Robson** is among the most breathtaking in the Rockies. The preceding ridges creep up in height hiding the massive peak itself from view until the last moment. The British explorer W.B. Cheadle described the mountain in 1863: "On every side the mighty

HIKING IN MOUNT ROBSON PARK

Starting 2km from the park visitor centre, the **Berg Lake Trail** (22km one way; 795m ascent) is perhaps the most popular short backpacking trip in the Rockies, and the only trail that gets anywhere near Mount Robson. You can do the first third or so as a comfortable and highly rewarding day walk, passing through forest to lovely glacier-fed Kinney Lake (6.7km; campground at the lake's northeast corner). Many rank this among the Rockies best day hikes and it's particularly good for naturalists. Trek the whole thing, however, and you traverse the stupendous Valley of a Thousand Waterfalls – the most notable being sixty-metre Emperor Falls (14.3km; campgrounds 500m north and 2km south) – and eventually enjoy the phenomenal area around Berg Lake itself (17.4km to its nearest, western shore). Mount Robson rises an almost sheer 2400m from the lakeshore, its huge cliffs cradling two creaking rivers of ice, Mist Glacier and Berg Glacier – the latter, one of the Rockies' few "living" or advancing glaciers, is 1800m long by 800m wide and the source of the great icebergs that give the lake its name. Beyond the lake you can pursue the trail 2km further to Robson Pass (21.9km; 1652m ascent; campground) and another 1km to Adolphus Lake in Jasper National Park. The most popular campsites are the *Berg Lake* (19.6km) and *Rearguard* (20.1km) campgrounds on Berg Lake itself; but if you've got a Jasper backcountry permit you could press on to Adolphus where there's a less-frequented site with more in the way of solitude.

Once you're camped at Berg Lake, a popular day-trip is to Toboggan Falls, which starts from the southerly *Berg Lake* campground and climbs the northeast (left) side of Toboggan Creek past a series of cascades and meadows to eventual views over the lake's entire hinterland. The trail peters out after 2km, but you can easily walk on and upward through open meadows for still better views. The second trail in the immediate vicinity is Robson Glacier (2km), a level walk that peels off south from the main trail 1km west of Robson Pass near the park ranger's cabin. It runs across an outwash plain to culminate in a small lake at the foot of the glacier; a rougher track then follows the lateral moraine on the glacier's east side, branching east after 3km to follow a small stream to the summit of Snowbird Pass (9km total from the ranger's cabin).

Two more hikes start from Yellowhead Lake, at the other (eastern) end of the park. To get to the trailhead for **Yellowhead Mountain** (4.5km one way; 715m ascent), follow Hwy 16 9km down from the pass and then take a gravel road 1km on an isthmus across the lake. After a steep two-hour climb through forest, the trail levels out in open country at 1830m, offering sweeping views of the Yellowhead Pass area. The **Mount Fitzwilliam Trail** (13km one way; 945m ascent), which leaves Hwy 16 about 1km east of the Yellowhead Mountain Trail (but on the other side of the highway), is a more demanding walk, especially over its last half, but if you don't want to backpack to the endpoint – a truly spectacular basin of lakes and peaks – you could easily walk through the forest to the campground at Rockingham Creek (6km).

heads of snowy hills crowded round, whilst, immediately behind us, a giant among giants, and immeasurably supreme, rose Robson's peak . . . We saw its upper portion dimmed by a necklace of light, feathery clouds, beyond which its pointed apex of ice, glittering in the morning sun, shot up far into the blue heaven above."

The overall impression is of immense size, thanks mainly to the colossal scale of Robson's south face – a sheer rise of 3100m – and to the view from the road, which frames the mountain as a single mass isolated from other peaks. A spectacular glacier system, concealed on the mountain's north side, is visible if you make the popular backpacking hike to the Berg Lake area (see box above). The source of the mountain's name has never been agreed on, but could be a corruption of Robertson, a Hudson's Bay employee who was trapped in the region in the 1820s. Local natives called the peak *Yuh-hai-has-hun* – the

"Mountain of the Spiral Road", an allusion to the clearly visible layers of rock that resemble a road winding to the summit. Not surprisingly, this monolith was one of the last major peaks in the Rockies to be climbed (1913), and is still considered a dangerous challenge.

Practicalities

Trains don't stop anywhere in the park, but if you're travelling by bus you can ask to be let off at Yellowhead Pass or the **Mount Robson Travel Infocentre** (May to early Sept; ☎566-9174, fax 566-9777), located at the Mount Robson viewpoint near the western entrance to the park. Most of the park's few other facilities are found near the info-centre: a **café/garage** (May–Sept) and three fully serviced commercial **campgrounds** – *Emperor Ridge* (☎566-8438; $13.50; June–Sept), 300m north of Hwy 16 on Kinney Lake Road; *Mount Robson Guest Ranch*, with just ten sites (☎566-4370; $10; June–Sept), on Hargreaves Road 2km south of the highway (also with ten **cabins** for rent; ④); and *Robson Shadows Campground* (☎566-4821; $12.50; mid-May to mid-Oct), 25 nice sites on the Fraser River side of Hwy 16, 5km west of the park boundary. The 144-site *Mount Robson Provincial Park Campground* (☎566-4325; $14.50; April–Oct) comprises two closely adjacent campgrounds – *Robson River* and *Robson Meadows* – and is situated further afield on Hwy 16, 22km north of Valemount. It offers hots showers and flush toilets and reservations can be made in advance (see box, p.621). Another park campground with the same name (which has no reservations, dry toilets only and no showers; $9.50; May–Sept) is situated 10km west of the Alberta border on Hwy 16, just west of the eastern boundary of the Mount Robson Provincial Park. The only other beds in or near the park are the eighteen log-sided riverfront units (some with kitchens: $5 extra) at *Mount Robson Lodge* (☎566-4821 or 566-4879; ④; May–Oct) near *Robson Shadows Campground* (meals, river rafting, helicopter tours and horseriding are available nearby); and the cabins belonging to Mount Robson Adventure Holidays (☎566-4351; ③; June–Sept), 16km east of the infocentre (towards Jasper), though preference for these may go to people signed up for the company's canoeing and hiking day-trips.

Backcountry camping in the park is only permitted at seven wilderness campgrounds dotted along the Berg Lake Trail (see box on p.615): to use these you have to register and pay an overnight fee at the infocentre. Mount Robson Adventure Holidays **rent equipment** – complete outfits start at $22 per day.

Yoho National Park

Wholly in British Columbia on the western side of the Continental Divide, **YOHO NATIONAL PARK**'s name derives from a Cree word meaning "wonder" – a fitting testament to the awesome grandeur of the region's mountains, lakes and waterfalls. At the same time it's a small park, whose intimate scale makes it perhaps the finest of the four parks and the one favoured by Rockies' connoisseurs. The Trans-Canada divides Yoho neatly in half, climbing from Lake Louise over the **Kicking Horse Pass** to share the broad, glaciated valley bottom of the Kicking Horse River with the old Canadian Pacific Railway. The only village, **Field**, has the park centre, services and limited accommodation (the nearest full-service towns are Lake Louise, 28km east, and **Golden**, 54km west). Other expensive accommodation is available at the central hubs, **Lake O'Hara** the **Yoho Valley** and **Emerald Lake**, from which radiate most of the park's stunning and well-maintained trails – **hiking** in Yoho is magnificent – and a couple of lodges just off the Trans-Canada. Thus these areas – not Field – are the focal points of the park, and get very busy in summer. Sideroads lead to Emerald Lake and the Yoho Valley, so if you choose you can drive in, do a hike and then move on at night.

Access to Lake O'Hara is far more difficult, being reserved for those on foot, or those with lodge or campground reservations, who must book for a special bus (full details

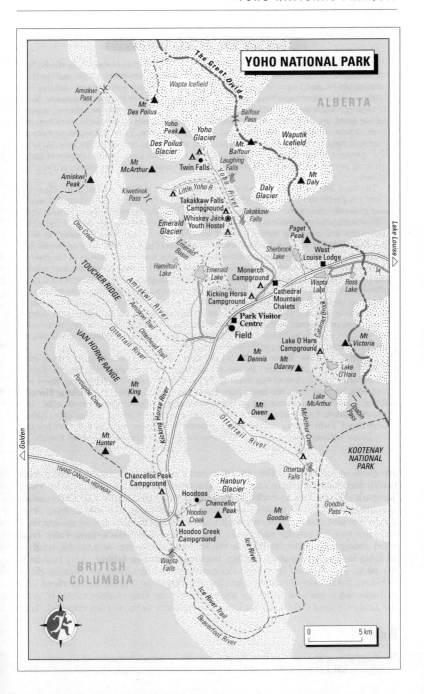

YOHO NATIONAL PARK

RAFTING IN THE ROCKIES

If lazing around Maligne Lake in Jasper, or walking the odd trail elsewhere in the Rockies, sounds a bit tame, think about **white-water rafting** – currently all the rage in the national parks, and Jasper in particular. Many operators are springing up, notably in Jasper, Golden (near Yoho National Park) and in Banff to cater to growing demand. Not all trips are white-knuckle affairs. Depending on the river and trip you choose, some rafting tours are just that – gentle rafting for all the family down placid stretches of river. Others require that you be fit and a strong swimmer. Trips last anything from a couple of hours to a couple of days. Operators will point to the right trips (see "Activities" sections under national park headings for Banff and Lake Louise operators) and, while no previous experience is required for most tours, one or two things are worth knowing.

The most important is how rivers are **graded**. White water is ranked in six classes: Class 1 is gentle and Class 6 is so close to a waterfall as to make no difference. The **season** generally runs from May to mid-September, with the "biggest" water in June and July, when glacial meltwater is coursing down rivers. Operators are licensed by the park authorities and invariably supply you with everything you need, from the basics of helmet and life jacket to wet suits, wool sweaters and spray jackets depending on the likely severity of the trip. They also provide shuttle services from main centres to the rivers themselves, and many on longer trips include lunch, snack or barbecue in the tour price. Bigger operators may also have on-site shower and changing facilities if you're on a run where you're likely to get seriously wet. On any trip it's probably a good idea to have a change of clothes handy for when you finish, wear training shoes or something you don't mind getting wet, and have a towel and bag for any valuables. Many people sport swimming costumes beneath clothing. Often you can choose between trips – gentle or severe – where you sit back and hang on while others do the work in oared boats, or you join a trip where everyone gets a paddle who wants one.

At Banff the **Bow River** has no major rapids, and gentle one-hour float trips are offered through pretty scenery by several operators. Most companies in Banff or Lake Louise offer trips on one of two rivers to the west of the park. The **Kootenay River** in Kootenay National Park, two hours from Banff, is a Class 2–3 river. The **Kicking Horse River**, a premier destination just an hour from Banff, is a much more serious affair. In and just outside Yoho National Park, it has Class 4 sections (Cable Car, Man Eater Hole, Goat Rapid, Twin Towers and the Roller Coaster) in its upper sections and stretches in the Lower Kicking Horse Canyon, which give even seasoned rafters pause for thought.

are given on pp.624–625). The other five park-run campgrounds are all much more readily accessible, and there's a single road-accessible youth hostel in the Yoho Valley. The park also operates six backcountry campgrounds (see p.622). The Trans-Canada also gives direct access to short but scenic trails; as these take only an hour or so, they're the best choice if you only want a quick taste of the park before moving on. If you have time for one day walk, make it the **Iceline–Whaleback–Twin Falls Trail**, rated among the top five day hikes in the Rockies (see the box on p.622 for details of all hikes in the park). If you're cycling, note that **mountain biking** – very popular in the park – is restricted to several designated trails only: these are Kicking Horse (19.5km); the Amiskwi Trail to the Amiskwi River crossing (24km); the Otterhead Trail to Toche Ridge junction (8km); Ice River to Lower Ice Ridge warden cabin (17.5km); the Talley-Ho Trail (3km); and the Ottertail Trail as far as the warden cabin (14.7km).

Field

No more than a few wooden houses, and backed by an amphitheatre of sheer-dropped mountains, **FIELD** looks like an old-world pioneer settlement, little changed from its 1884

Jasper has perhaps the most possibilities on its doorstep. The Class 2 **Athabasca River** (from Athabasca Falls, 35km south of the town) is scenic and provides gentle rafting for families or those who just want a quiet river trip from May to October, but it also has one or two harmless white-water sections. The **Sunwapta River** nearby, 55km south of Jasper, is a Class 3 river with some thrilling stretches of water, magnificent scenery and good chances to spot wildlife. The **Maligne River**, 45km from town, is Class 2–3+, offering a wide variety of trips between July and September for the many operators who use this river (including a lively 1.6-kilometre stretch of rapids). Yet the most riotous local river is the **Fraser**, accessed an hour west of Jasper in Mount Robson Provincial Park. This is Class 4 in places, but also has some gentle sections where the chance to watch salmon spawning at close quarters from mid-August to September provides an added attraction.

Operators in Jasper include Maligne River Adventures, 626 Connaught Drive (☎852-3370, fax 852-3405), who run some of the wildest trips in the park twice-daily down 11km of the Maligne River in six- and eight-passenger rafts from the chalet at Maligne Lake (2hr; $55). All equipment is supplied and they also lay on changing rooms and hot showers. They also offer gentler two-hour raft trips on the Athabasca River suitable for families and children, as well as a three-day wilderness trip to the Kakwa and Smoky rivers. Jasper Raft Tours at *Jasper Park Lodge* (☎852-6091) offer good trips for first-timers: two- to three-hour jaunts twice daily in summer on the Athabasca River in comfortable oar rafts. Tickets cost $40, including shuttle to and from the river, with possible pick-ups from your hotel by prior arrangement; tickets are also available from the Brewster office in the train station. Another long-established company offers similar trips at similar prices (from about $40 for 3hr trips) to suit all ages and courage levels on several rivers: White Water Rafting (Jasper) Ltd (☎852-7238 or 1-800-557-7328, fax 852-3623), with advance reservations from Avalanche Esso, 702 Connaught Drive – they claim to run trips in all weathers and make special provisions for visitors with disabilities.

If you want the real **rough stuff** on the Fraser contact Sekani Mountain Tours, Work World Store, 618 Patricia St (☎852-5211), for twenty Class 3 and 4 rapids along the fourteen-kilometre "Rearguard Run" (6hr 30min; $70 including lunch). If you're experienced you can join the 16km of continuous Class 4 and 4+ rapids on the "Canoe River" (8hr; $100) or put these together with the Rearguard in a two-day camping trip for $160. At the other extreme, the same company runs quiet punt-like trips to admire Mount Robson and see the salmon on the Fraser (10km; 5hr 30min; $35), as do Mount Robson Adventure Holidays (2hr; $35; ☎1-800-882-9921), whose twice-daily raft departures are complemented by an evening run during August. They also offer three-hour guided trips by canoe ($42) to Moose Marsh to spot birds and wildlife, with no experience necessary for this or their rafting trips.

origins as a railroad-construction camp (named after Cyrus Field, sponsor of the first transatlantic communication cable, who visited Yoho that year). As in other national parks, it was the railway that first spawned tourism in the area: the first hotel in Field was built by Canadian Pacific in 1886, and within a few months sixteen square kilometres at the foot of Mount Stephen (the peak to Field's east) had been set aside as a special reserve. National park status arrived in 1911, making Yoho the second of Canada's national parks.

Passenger services (other than private excursions) no longer come through Field, but the **railway** is still one of the park "sights", and among the first things you see whether you enter the park from east or west. That it came this way at all was the result of desperate political and economic horse trading. The Canadian Pacific's chief surveyor, Sandford Fleming, wrote of his journey over the proposed Kicking Horse Pass route in 1883: "I do not think I can forget that terrible walk; it was the greatest trial I ever experienced." Like many in the company he was convinced the railway should take the much lower and more amenable Yellowhead route to the north (see "Mount Robson Provincial Park"). The railway was as much a political as a transportational tool, and designed to unite the country and encourage settlement of the prairies. A northerly route would have ignored great tracts of valuable prairie near the

US border (around Calgary), and allowed much of the area and its resources (later found to include oil and gas) to slip from the Dominion into the hands of the US. Against all engineering advice, therefore, the railway was cajoled into taking the Kicking Horse route, and thus obliged to negotiate four percent grades, the greatest of any commercial railway of the time.

The result was the infamous **Spiral Tunnels**, two vast figure-of-eight galleries within the mountains; from a popular viewpoint about 7km east of Field on Hwy 1, you can watch the front of goods trains emerge from the tunnels before the rear wagons have even entered. Still more notorious was the **Big Hill**, where the line drops 330m in just 6km from Wapta Lake to the flats east of Field (the 4.5 percent grade was the steepest in North America). The very first construction train to attempt the descent plunged into the canyon, killing three railway workers. Runaways became so common that four blasts on a whistle became the standard warning for trains careering out of control (the rusted wreck of an engine can still be seen near the main *Kicking Horse Park Campground*). Lady Agnes MacDonald, wife of the Canadian prime minister, rode down the Big Hill on the front cowcatcher (a metal frame in front of the locomotive to scoop off animals) in 1886, remarking that it presented a "delightful opportunity for a new sensation". She'd already travelled around 1000km on her unusual perch: her lily-livered husband, with whom she was meant to be sharing the symbolic trans-Canada journey to commemorate the opening of the railway, managed just 40km on the cowcatcher. Trains climbing the hill required four locomotives to pull a mere fifteen coaches: the ascent took over an hour, and exploding boilers (and resulting deaths) were recurrent.

The Burgess Shales

Yoho today ranks as highly among geologists as it does among hikers and railway buffs, thanks to the world-renowned **Burgess Shales**, an almost unique geological formation situated close to Field village. The shales – layers of sediamentary rock – lie on the upper slopes of Mount Field and consist of the fossils of some 120 types of soft-bodied marine creatures from the Middle Cambrian period (515–530 million years ago), one of only three places in the world where the remains of these unusual creatures are found. Soft-bodied creatures usually proved ill-suited to the fossilization process, but in the Burgess Shales the fossils are so well preserved and detailed that in some cases scientists can identify what the creatures were eating before they died. Plans are in hand to open a major new museum in Field devoted to the Shales, but in the meantime access is restricted to protect the fossils, and fossil-hunting, needless to say, is strictly prohibited. The area can only be seen on two rather strenuous guided hikes to Walcott's Quarry and the Trilobite beds. The walks are led by qualified guides, limited to fifteen people and run between late June and October. For details and reservations, contact the Yoho Burgess Shale Foundation (☎1-800-343-3006).

Practicalities

Yoho's **park information centre**, marked by a distinctive blue roof about 1km east of Field (daily: mid-May to late June & Sept 9am–5pm; late June to Aug 9am–7pm; variable reduced hours the rest of the year; ☎343-6783 or 343-6433; *http://www.world.web.com.ParksCanada-Yoho*), sells park permits (see p.567), makes backcountry registrations, takes bookings for Lake O'Hara (see p.624), has displays, lectures and slide shows (notably on the famous Burgess Shales), and advises on trail and climbing conditions. It also gives out a useful *Backcountry Guide* with full details of all trails and sells 1:50,000 **maps** of the park. Backcountry camping requires a permit, and if you intend to camp at Lake O'Hara (see below) it's essential to make **reservations** at the information centre. The Park Administration Office in Field offers similar help and services in and out of season (Mon–Fri 8am–4.30pm; ☎343-6324).

PROVINCIAL CAMPGROUNDS

Tent and RV sites at certain public campgrounds in British Columbia's provincial parks can now be reserved in advance. To make reservations, call Discover Camping (March to mid-Sept Mon–Fri 7am–7pm, Sat & Sun 9am–5pm Pacific Standard Time; ☎1-800-689-9025, in Vancouver ☎689-9025). Reservations can be made up to three months in advance and no later than 48 hours before the first day of arrival. Cancellations can be made after 7pm by following the recorded instructions. A non-refundable booking fee of $6 per night up to a maximum of three nights ($18) is charged. You can stay in BC Provincial Parks for up to a maximum of fourteen days. Payment is via VISA or MasterCard only (payment for extra nights once at a campground is by cash only). For more information on the service and parks generally, call ☎250/387-4550 or obtain a toll-free transfer to this number by calling ☎660-2421 (from Greater Vancouver) or 1-800-663-7867 from elsewhere in BC.

Whatever other literature may say, there are now no VIA Rail passenger trains to Field. The village is, however, a flag stop for Greyhound **buses** (5 daily in each direction) – wave them down from the Petro-Canada just east of the turnoff from the highway to the village, though most stop anyway to drop packages.

Yoho's popularity and accessibility mean huge pressure on **accommodation** in late July and August: if you're really stuck, you can always make for one of the motels in Golden (see p.626). The only officially listed **rooms** in Field itself, a fine base if you have transport, are at the excellent *Kicking Horse Lodge and Café*, 100 Centre St (café open summer only; ☎343-6303 or 1-800-659-4944; ⑤–⑥), though you may strike lucky with private rooms. Alternatively, try one of the new so-called B&B "kitchens" – fully furnished suites in private homes – of which there were seven dotted around the village at last count: *Yoho Accommodation* (☎343-6444 or 343-6445); *Mount Burgess Bungalow* (☎343-6480); *Bear's Den Guesthouse* (☎343-6439); *Alpenglow Guesthouse* (☎343-6356); *Otterhead Guesthouse* (☎343-6034); *Mount Stephen Guesthouse* (☎343-6441); and *Van Horne Guesthouse* (☎343-6380) – all ③–④. All are similarly and reasonably priced, and all are easily found in the tiny village – call for precise directions – most lying on the central 1st Avenue or Kicking Horse Avenue.

Away from the village, but on or just off the Trans-Canada (Hwy 1), the twenty units of *Cathedral Mountain Chalets* (☎343-6442; off season call or fax 403/762-0514; ⑤–⑥; mid-May to mid-Oct), 4km east of Field and fifteen minutes' drive from Lake Louise (leave the highway at the Takakkaw Falls turn-off), and the budget fifty-room *West Louise Lodge* (☎343-6311; ④), just inside the park boundary, 11km west of Lake Louise (with café, restaurant and indoor pool). There's also the **youth hostel** in the Yoho Valley (see p.625), perfectly situated for many superb walks, and an expensive lodge at Emerald Lake.

The most central of the five park-run **campgrounds**, the 86-site *Kicking Horse* ($7; mid-May to early Oct), lies 5km east of Field just off the Trans-Canada (Hwy 1) near the junction with Yoho Valley Road for Takakkaw Falls. It's fully serviced (coin showers) and pleasingly forested, though it echoes somewhat with goods trains rumbling through day and night. In summer a separate overflow site is often opened (no showers), but even this fills up and you should aim to arrive early. A short distance east up Yoho Valley Road is the second of the park's major campgrounds, the 46-site *Monarch* ($12; late June to early Sept): the third, *Takakkaw Falls*, lies at the end of the same road by the eponymous falls and is the best-placed for local hikes (see box overleaf). The remaining two sites are both close to the park's western border, lying just north and south of the Trans-Canada: the 106-site *Hoodoo Creek* (no showers; $14; late June to early Sept) and 64-site *Chancellor Peak* (no showers; $12; early May to late Sept). An additional fee of $3 is charged at all campgrounds for use of firewood.

HIKES IN YOHO NATIONAL PARK

Hikes from Lake O'Hara

For walking purposes the Lake O'Hara region divides into five basic zones, each of which deserves a full day of exploration: Lake Oesa, the Opabin Plateau (this area and others are often closed to protect their grizzlies), Lake McArthur, the Odaray Plateau and the Duchesnay Basin.

If you have time to do only one day hike, the classic (if not the most walked) trails are the Wiwaxy Gap (12km; 495m ascent), rated by some among the top five day walks in the Canadian Rockies, or the Opabin Plateau Trail (3.2km one way; 250m ascent), from the *Lake O'Hara Lodge* to Opabin Lake. Despite the latter's brevity, you could spend hours wandering the plateau's tiny lakes and alpine meadows on the secondary trails that crisscross the area. Most people return to O'Hara via the East Circuit Trail, but a still more exhilarating hike – and a good day's outing – is to walk the Yukness Ledge, a section of the Alpine Circuit (see below) that cuts up from the East Circuit just 400m after leaving Opabin Lake. This spectacular high-level route leads to the beautiful Lake Oesa, from where it's just 3.2km down to Lake O'Hara. Oesa is one of many beautiful lakes in the region, and the Lake Oesa Trail (3.2km one way; 240m ascent) from Lake O'Hara is the single most walked path in the O'Hara area. Close behind comes the Lake McArthur Trail (3.5km one way; 310m ascent) which leads to the largest and most photographed of the lakes in the Lake O'Hara area. The Odaray Plateau Trail (2.6km one way; 280m ascent) is another highly rated, but rather overpopular hike.

The longest and least-walked path is the Linda Lake–Cathedral Basin trip, past several lakes to a great viewpoint at Cathedral Platform Prospect (7.4km one way; 305m ascent). The most challenging hike is the high-level Alpine Circuit (11.8km), taking in Oesa, Opabin and Schaffer lakes. This is straightforward in fine weather, and when all the snow has melted; very fit and experienced walkers should have little trouble, though there's considerable exposure, and some scrambling is required. At other times it's best left to climbers, or left alone completely.

Yoho Valley and Emerald Lake hikes

Most trails in the Yoho Valley area start from the Takakkaw Falls campground and car park at the end of the Yoho Valley Road. Many of the area's trails connect, and some run over the ridge to the Emerald Lake region, offering numerous permutations. We've tried to highlight the very best. If you want a stroll from the main trailhead at the campground after a drive or cycle, then walk to Point Lace Falls (1.9km one way; minimum ascent) or Laughing Falls (3.8km one way; 60m gain). Another shortish, extremely popular walk from the same car park is the Yoho Pass (10.9km; 310m ascent, 510m height loss), which links to Emerald Lake and its eponymous lodge (though you'll need transport arranged at the lake). A southern branch from this hike will take you over the Burgess Pass and down into Field, another manageable day-trip with fine overviews of the entire area.

If you want to follow the most tramped path in the Yoho Valley, however, take the Twin Falls Trail (8.5km one way; 290m ascent) from the Takakkaw Falls car park. This easy six-hour return journey passes the Laughing Falls (see above) and has the reward of the Twin Falls cataract at the end, plus fine scenery and other lesser waterfalls en route. Stronger walkers could continue over the highly recommended Whaleback Trail (4.5km one way; 1hr 30min) to give some quite incredible views of the glaciers at the

The six **backcountry campgrounds** (see maps p.624 and p.626) are *McArthur Creek* (ten sites); *Float Creek* (four sites); *Yoho Lake* (eight sites); *Laughing Falls* (eight sites); *Twin Falls* (eight sites); and *Little Yoho* (ten sites): the only facilities are privies (except *Float Creek*) and bear poles. All of these campgrounds are popular, but unlike the front-country campgrounds (where it's first-come, first-served) between one and

valley head. A complete circuit returning to Takakkaw Falls with the Whaleback is 20.1km.

If you're allowing yourself just one big walk in Yoho it's going to be a hard choice between the Takakkaw Falls–Twin Falls–Whaleback Trail just described or the Iceline–Little Yoho Valley–(Whaleback)–Twin Falls combination. The latter is often cited as one of the top five day walks in the Rockies, and on balance might be the one to go for, though both options duplicate parts of one another's route. The Iceline (695m vertical gain), specially built in 1987, also starts close to the Takakkaw Falls car park at the *Whiskey Jack* youth hostel, climbing west through a large avalanche path onto a level bench with jaw-dropping views of the Emerald Glacier above and the Daly Glacier across the valley. It contours above Lake Celeste (a trail drops to this lake, making a shorter 17km circuit in all back to the car park) and then drops to the Little Yoho Valley and back to Takakkaw Falls for a 19.8-kilometre circuit. If you're very fit (or can camp overnight to break the trip), tagging on the Whaleback before returning to Takakkaw Falls makes a sensational 27-kilometre walk with 1000m of ascent.

Most people will want to do this as a backpacking option (there are four backcountry sites up here) – and they don't come much better – though the Iceline–Little Yoho walk coupled with the trek west to the Kiwetinok Pass (30km; 1070m) is also in many people's list of top five day/backpacking Rocky Mountain walks. Juggling further with the permutations brings the Whaleback into this last combination to make one of *the* best backpacking routes in the Rockies: Iceline–Little Yoho Valley–Kiwetinok Pass–Whaleback (35.5km, 1375m ascent), a route up there with the Rockwall Trail in Kootenay, Skyline in Jasper and Berg Lake in Mount Robson Provincial Park.

From Emerald Lake, if you just want a stroll, then follow the self-guided and wheelchair-accessible nature trail (4.6km circuit; minimal ascent) around the lake from the parking area to the bridge at the back of the lake. Even shorter is the trail from the entrance to the parking area to Hamilton Falls (1.6km return; minimal ascent). The best day-trip is the comparatively underused but interesting Hamilton Lake Trail (5.5km one way; 850m vertical; 2–3hr), again leaving from the parking area at the end of Emerald Lake Road. It's demanding and steep in places, and confined to forest for the first hour or so – thereafter it's magnificent, culminating in a classic alpine lake. The more modest climb to Emerald Basin, which you could manage in half a day (4.3km one way; 300m vertical; 1–2hr), also gives relative peace and quiet, following the lakeshore before climbing through a forest of yew and hemlock, and ending in a small, rocky amphitheatre of hanging glaciers and avalanche paths.

Hikes from the Trans-Canada

Five short walks can be accessed off the Trans-Canada Highway as it passes through Yoho. From east to west these are: Ross Lake (1.3km), a stunning little walk given the loveliness of the lake and the ease with which you reach it (accessed 1km south of the Great Divide picnic area); Sherbrooke Lake (3.1km), a peaceful sub-alpine lake accessible from the Wapta Lake picnic area (5km west of the Great Divide), where stronger walkers can peel off after 1.4km to Paget Lookout for huge views of the Kicking Horse Valley (3.5km; 520m ascent); Mount Stephen Fossil Beds (2.7km), a short but very steep trail, for fossil lovers only, from 1st St East in Field; Hoodoo Creek (3.1km), on the western edge of the park (22km west of Field), accessed from the 600-metre gravel road from the *Hoodoo Creek* campground (the steep path leads to the weirdly eroded hoodoos themselves, pillars of glacial debris topped by protective capping stones), and finally Wapta Falls (2.4km), an excellent and almost level forty-minute walk on a good trail to Yoho's largest waterfalls (by volume of water), accessed via a 1.6-kilometre dirt road 25km west of Field.

---

three sites at each campground can be reserved up to 21 days in advance through the park centre at Field. **Random camping** is allowed in the Amiskwi, Otterhead, Lower Ice River and Porcupine valleys, but check current closures: you must be at least 3km from any road, 100m from water, 50m from a trail and purchase the usual $6 backcountry pass.

Lake O'Hara

Backed up against the Continental Divide at the eastern edge of the park, **Lake O'Hara** is one of the Rockies' finest all-round enclaves – staggering scenery, numerous lakes, and an immense diversity of alpine and sub-alpine terrain. It's a great base for concentrated hiking: you could easily spend a fortnight exploring the well-constructed trails that strike out from the central lodge and campground. The setting is matchless, the lake framed by two of the peaks that also overlook Lake Louise across the ridge – mounts Lefroy (3423m) and Victoria (3464m). The one problem is **access**, which is severely restricted to safeguard the mountain flora and fauna.

To get there, turn off the Trans-Canada onto Hwy 1A (3.2km west of the Continental Divide), cross the railway and turn right onto the gravel road leading to the parking area (1km). This fire road continues all the way up to the lake (13km), but it's not open to general traffic (or bikes – *no* bikes are allowed on the road or anywhere else in the Lake O'Hara region). Getting up here, therefore, is quite a performance, but worth it if you want to hike some of the continent's most stunning scenery. Anybody can walk the 13km up the road, or the more picturesque **Cataract Brook Trail** (12.9km), which runs roughly parallel to the road, but a quota system applies for the bus up here and the campground at the end; and, after 13km, of course, you'd need to be superfit to get in any meaningful walking in the area where it matters. Aim instead for the special **bus** from the car park up to the lake, but note that priority is given to those with reservations or those with reservations for the lodge, campground or Alpine Club huts. Reservations for bus and campground can be made three months in advance by telephone only (March 20–April 18 Mon–Fri 8am–noon; April 19 to mid-June Mon–Fri 8am–4pm; mid-June to Aug daily 8am–4pm; Sept reduced hours; ☎343-6433). If you're going **for the**

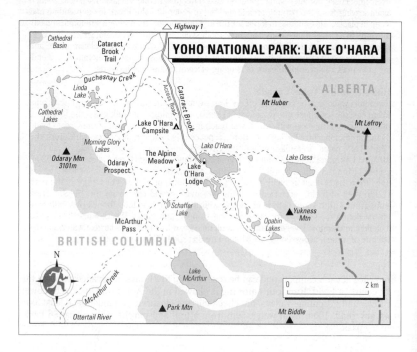

day, your only feasible buses leave at 8.30am and 10.30am, and the maximum number in a party is six. If you want to use the campground you have to have dates ready (up to a maximum of four nights), state the number of people, the number of campsites required (maximum of two per party, one tent per site) and your preferred bus time (first and second choices from 8.30am, 10.30am, 4.30pm or 7.30pm). The reservation fee for bus (day use or campground) is $10 and the return bus fare $12, payable by credit card over the phone. Cancellation must be made to an answering machine (☎343-6344); you forfeit your booking fee, and you can't just cancel the first day of several you booked to camp and expect to come later. Cancellations made less than three days in advance mean you lose the booking fee, half the bus fare and, if you're camping, the first night's campground fee. Cancel after 4pm on the day before your trip and you lose everything.

If all this sounds like Kafka has hit the Rockies, remember the park does merit attention, but if you don't manage to plan in advance there are arrangements for **stand-bys**: six day-use places are available daily and five campsites are kept available each night. You must reserve at the Field park information centre in person the day *before* you wish to take the bus and/or camp: these places are *not* available over the phone, and you'll have to get to the centre early. To stay in one of the 23 rooms at *Lake O'Hara Lodge* (☎343-6418; ⑨; mid-June to late Sept & Feb to mid-April), you need to reserve weeks in advance and be prepared to part with a very large amount of money. Out of season you can make bookings by post to Box 55, Lake Louise, Alberta T0L 1E0, or call ☎403/678-4110.

The Yoho Valley and Emerald Lake

Less compact an area than Lake O'Hara, the **Yoho Valley** and nearby **Emerald Lake** are far more accessible for casual visitors, and offer some great sights – the Takakkaw Falls in particular – and a variety of topnotch trails. Both areas were formerly used by the Cree to hide their women and children while the men crossed the mountains into Alberta to trade and hunt buffalo. The eradication of the buffalo herds, and the arrival of the railway in 1884, put paid to such ways. The lake was "discovered" by Tom Wilson, the same Canadian Pacific employee who first saw Lake Louise. He named it Emerald Lake after its colour. Now the lake and valley combine to form one of the Rockies' most important backpacking zones. Though popular and easily reached – access roads head north from the Trans-Canada up both the Emerald and Yoho valleys – the region is not, however, quite as crowded as its counterpart to the south. The scenery is equally mesmerizing, and if fewer of the trails are designed for day hikes, many of them interlock so that you can tailor walks to suit your schedule or fitness (see box on pp.622–623).

Most trails (see box) start from the end of the Yoho Valley Road at the **Takakkaw Falls** parking area; the road leaves the Trans-Canada about 5km east of Field (signed from the *Kicking Horse* campground), a narrow and switchbacking route unsuitable for trailers and RVs and open in the summer only. It's 14km from the Trans-Canada to the parking area. The cascades' total 254-metre drop make them among the most spectacular road-accessible falls in the mountains: *takakkaw* is a Cree word roughly meaning "it is wonderful". The *Whiskey Jack* **youth hostel**, ideally placed just beyond the end of the Yoho Valley Road, 500m south of Takakkaw Falls, has room for 27 in three dorms (☎762-4122, reservations ☎237-8282 or 762-4122; ①; mid-June to mid-Sept). Close by is the park-run *Takakkaw Falls* **campground** with 35 unserviced sites ($12; mid-June to mid-Sept). Trails to the north (see box, p.622–623) lead to four further backcountry campgrounds, while the Alpine Club of Canada operates a members-only trail hut 8.5km north of Takakkaw Falls ($15); reservations are required – write to Box 1026, Banff, Alberta T0L 0C0, or call ☎403/762-4481.

The Emerald Lake Road leaves the Trans-Canada about 2km west of Field and ends, 8km on, at the *Emerald Lake Lodge* (☎343-6321 or 1-800-663-6336; ⑧), which has a

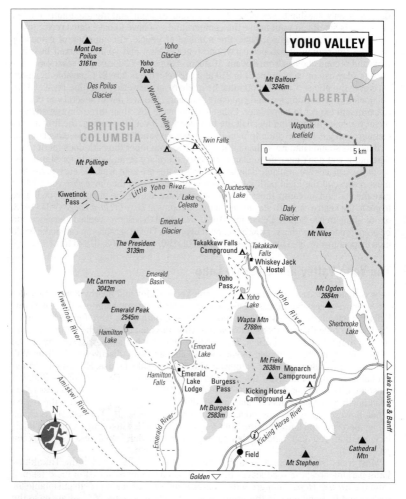

YOHO VALLEY

Mont Des Poilus 3161m

Yoho Peak

Yoho Glacier

Des Poilus Glacier

Waterfall Valley

Mt Balfour 3246m

ALBERTA

BRITISH COLUMBIA

Waputik Icefield

Twin Falls

0   5 km

Mt Pollinge

Little Yoho River

Duchesnay Lake

Kiwetinok Pass

Lake Celeste

Daly Glacier

Mt Niles

Emerald Glacier

The President 3139m

Takakkaw Falls Campground

Takakkaw Falls

Whiskey Jack Hostel

Emerald Basin

Yoho Pass

Mt Carnarvon 3042m

Kiwetinok River

Emerald Peak 2545m

Yoho Lake

Wapta Mtn 2788m

Mt Ogden 2684m

Sherbrooke Lake

Hamilton Lake

Amiskwi River

Emerald Lake

Hamilton Falls

Emerald Lake Lodge

Burgess Pass

Mt Field 2638m

Monarch Campground

Kicking Horse Campground

Emerald River

Mt Burgess 2583m

Kicking Horse River

N

Field

Mt Stephen

Cathedral Mtn

Lake Louise & Banff

Golden

restaurant where walking boots are certainly not in order, and a less formal **bar** for drinks and snacks. If you want to stay, advance reservations are essential, as is a willingness to part with a fair wedge of cash. Like the Yoho Valley Road, this road offers access to easy strolls and a couple of good day or half-day hikes (see box, p.622).

Golden

GOLDEN, 54km west of Field and midway between Yoho and Glacier national parks, is the nearest town to either. Despite its name and mountain backdrop, the part of Golden most people see amounts to little more than an ugly ribbon of motels and garages at the junction of Hwy 1 and Hwy 95. The town proper occupies a semi-scenic site down by the Columbia River, way below the highway strip, but only if you use the municipal campground or book onto one of the many rafting and other **tours** based here will you do anything but look down on it from above. The town has a small **museum** at 1302-11th St (July & Aug daily 9am–5pm; $3; ☎344-5169). The main **infocentre** is at 500-10th Ave North (year-round; ☎344-7125, fax 344-6688), but a small infocentre also sits at the strip's southern end disguised as a plastic and wood tepee (June–Sept). Two hundred metres north is the **bus terminal**, next to the Chinese-Canadian *Golden Palace Restaurant* – open 24 hours a day, like several of the local joints. All the many **motels** on the strip such as the *Swiss Village* (☎344-2276; ③) and the *Selkirk Inn*, Hwy 1 (☎ 344-6315 or 344-5153; ③), are much of a muchness, looking over the road or onto the backs of garages opposite. None has anything you could call a view of the mountains, but at least the *Sportsman*, 1200-12th St North (☎344-2915 or 344-2277; ③), is off the road.

Campgrounds have prettier settings, particularly the *KOA Campground* (☎344-6464; $12), 3km east of the strip on Hwy 1. The town's own site, the *Golden Municipal Campground* (☎344-5412; $12; May–Sept), is on the banks of the river on 10th Avenue, three blocks east of the main street. It has flush toilets, hot showers, wash houses, firewood and is adjacent to a swimming pool and tennis courts.

Glacier National Park

Strictly speaking, **GLACIER NATIONAL PARK** is part of the Selkirk and Columbia Mountains rather than the Rockies, but on the ground little sets it apart from the magnificence of the other national parks, and all the park agencies include it on an equal footing with its larger neighbours. It is, however, to a great extent the domain of ice, rain and snow; the weather is so atrocious that locals like to say that it rains or snows four days out of every three, and in truth you can expect a soaking three days out of five. As the name suggests, **glaciers** – 422 of them – form its dominant landscape, with fourteen percent of the park permanently blanketed with ice or snow. Scientists have identified 68

HIKING IN GLACIER

Glacier's primary renown is among serious climbers, but day hikers and backpackers have plenty of options. Some of the park's 21 trails (140km of walking in all) push close to glaciers for casual views of the ice – though only two spots are now safe at the toe of the Illecillewaet – and the backcountry is noticeably less busy than in the Big Four parks to the east.

The easiest short strolls off the road are the Abandoned Rails Trail (1.2km one way; 30min), along old rail beds to abandoned snowsheds betweeen the Rogers Pass centre and the Summit Monument (suitable for wheelchairs); the Loop Trail (1.6km) from the viewpoint just east of the Loop Brook campground, full of viewpoints and features relating to the building of the railway; the Hemlock Grove Boardwalk (400m), a stroll through old growth stands of Western Hemlock trees, some more than 350 years old (wheelchair-accessible; trailhead midway between Loop Brook campground and the park's western boundary); and the Meeting of the Water Trail (30min) from the Illecillewaet campground, the hub of Glacier's trail network. Six manageable day hikes from the campground give superb views onto the glaciers, particularly the Great Glacier, Avalanche Crest and Abbott's Ridge trails. Other hikes, not centred on the campground, include Bostock Creek (9km) and Flat Creek (9km), a pair of paths on the park's western edge heading north and south respectively from the same point on the Trans-Canada.

Among the backpacking routes, the longest is the Beaver River Trail (30km-plus), which peels off from the highway at the Mount Shaughnessy picnic area on the eastern edge (also a favourite mountain-bike route). The single best long-haul trail, however, is the Copperstain Creek Trail (16km), which leaves the Beaver River path after 3km, and climbs to meadows and bleak alpine tundra from where camping and onward walking options are almost endless.

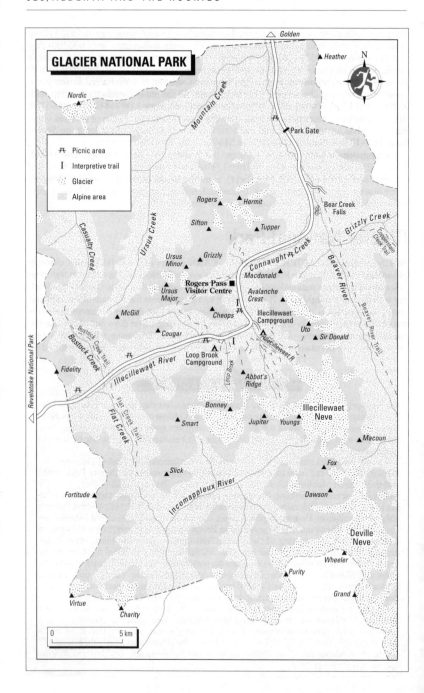

GLACIER NATIONAL PARK

⚲ Picnic area
I Interpretive trail
Glacier
Alpine area

Golden

Heather

N

Nordic

Mountain Creek

Park Gate

Bear Creek Falls

Grizzly Creek

Rogers ▲ Hermit

Sifton ▲ Tupper

Connaught Creek

Ursus Creek

Grizzly

Ursus Minor

Macdonald

Rogers Pass Visitor Centre

Avalanche Crest

Beaver River

Casualty Creek

Ursus Major

Illecillewaet Campground

Uto

Sir Donald

McGill

Cheops

Beaver River Trail

Cougar

Bostock Creek Trail

Illecillewaet R.

Bostock Creek

Illecillewaet River

Loop Brook Campground

Revelstoke National Park

Fidelity

Flat Creek Trail

Loop Brook

Abbot's Ridge

Illecillewaet Neve

Flat Creek

Bonney

Smart

Jupiter Youngs

Macoun

Slick

Fox

Fortitude ▲

Incomappleux River

Dawson

Deville Neve

Wheeler

Purity

Grand

Virtue

Charity

0   5 km

new glaciers forming on the sites of previously melted ice sheets in the park – a highly uncommon phenomenon. The main ice sheet, the still-growing **Illecillewaet Neve**, is easily seen from the Trans-Canada Highway or from the park visitor centre.

The Columbia range's peaks are every bit as imposing as those of the Rockies – Glacier's highest point, **Mount Dawson**, is 3390m tall – and historically they've presented as much of a barrier as their neighbours. Native Canadians and then railwaymen shunned the icefields and the rugged interior for centuries until the discovery of **Rogers Pass** (1321m) in 1881 by Major A.B. Rogers, the chief engineer of the Canadian Pacific. Suffering incredible hardships, navvies drove the railway over the pass by 1885, paving the way for trains which, until 1916, helped to open the region both to settlers and tourists. Despite the railway's best efforts the pounding of repeated avalanches eventually forced the company to bore a tunnel under the pass, and the flow of visitors fell to almost nothing.

In the 1950s the pass was chosen as the route for the Trans-Canada Highway, whose completion in 1962 once again made the area accessible. This time huge snowsheds were built, backed up by the world's largest **avalanche-control system**. Experts monitor the slopes year-round, and at dangerous times they call in the army, who blast howitzers into the mountains to dislodge potential slips.

Glacier is easy enough to get to, but it doesn't tie in well with a circuit of the other parks; many people end up traversing it at some point simply because the main route west passes this way, but comparatively few stop, preferring to admire the scenery from the road. The visitor centre is a flag stop for Greyhound **buses**, which zip through up to seven times a day in each direction. Entering Glacier you pass from Mountain to Pacific time – remember to set your watch back an hour.

Practicalities

The **Rogers Pass visitor centre** (daily: mid-June to early Oct 9am–9pm; rest of year 9am–5pm; ☎837-6274), 1km west of Rogers Pass, is a draw in itself, attracting some 160,000 visitors annually. It houses a variety of hi-tech audiovisual aids, including a fun video on avalanche control called *Snow Wars*. In summer, staff run **guided walks** featuring flowers, wildlife and glaciers, some of them fairly strenuous and lasting up to five hours. Also ask about trips to the **Nakimu Caves**, some of the largest in Canada: they were opened to the public (in the company of experienced guides only) in 1995. If you're heading for the backcountry, pick up *Footloose in the Columbias*, a hiker's guide to Glacier and Revelstoke national parks; you can also buy good walking **maps**. Next to the visitor centre, a **garage** and a **shop** are the only services on the Trans-Canada between Golden and Revelstoke, an hour's drive east and west respectively.

Accommodation is best sought in Golden (see p.626). The sole in-park **hotel**, the excellent fifty-room *Best Western Glacier Park Lodge* (☎837-2126; ⑥), located just east of the visitor centre, tends to be full in season. If you're passing through, it has a useful 24-hour service and cafeteria. Other places close to Glacier's borders are the ten-unit *Purcell Lodge* (mid-June to mid-Oct; mid-Dec to April; two-night minumum stay; ☎344-2639; ⑥), a remote lodge at 2180m on the eastern border accessible only by hiking trail, scheduled helicopter flights or winter ski trails; *Canyon Hot Springs Resort Campground*, 35km east of Revelstoke (☎837-2420; $15–19; May–Sept), which has mineral hot and warm springs, secluded sites, café, firewood and cabins with B&B deals available; *Hillside Lodge*, 1740 Seward Front Rd (☎344-7281; ④) – nine cosy cabins set in sixty acres 13km west of Golden at Blaeberry River with breakfast included; and *Big Lake Resort*, Kinbasket Lake (no phone; rooms ②, tents $12; May–Oct), 25km west of Golden off Hwy 1 at Donald Station.

The park-run **campgrounds** are the 57-site *Illecillewaet* ($13; mid-June to early Oct; also winter camping), 3.4km west of the visitor centre just off the Trans-Canada (and the trailhead for eight walks), and the twenty-site *Loop Brook*, 2km further west ($13; mid-June to early Sept; self-serve check-in), which provides the luxuries of wood, water and flush toilets only on a first-come, first-served basis. If you don't manage to get into these, or want more facilities, there are three commercial campgrounds west of the park on the Trans-Canada towards Revelstoke. Wilderness camping is allowed anywhere if you register with the visitor centre, pay for a nightly backcountry camping permit ($6) and pitch more than 5km from the road.

Mount Revelstoke National Park

The smallest national park in the region, **MOUNT REVELSTOKE NATIONAL PARK** is a somewhat arbitrary creation, put together at the request of local people in 1914 to protect the Clachnacudainn Range of the Columbia Mountains. The lines on the map mean little, for the thrilling scenery in the 16km of no-man's-land between Glacier and Revelstoke is largely the same as that within the parks. The mountains here are especially steep, their slopes often scythed clear of trees by avalanches. The views from the Trans-Canada, as it peeks out of countless tunnels, are of forests and snowcapped peaks aplenty and, far below, the railway and the Illecillewaet River crashing through a twisting, steep-sided gorge.

The main access to the park interior is the very busy **Summit Road**, or **Summit Parkway** (generally open June–Oct), which strikes north from the Trans-Canada at the town of Revelstoke and winds 26km almost to the top of Mount Revelstoke (1938m) through forest and alpine meadows noted for glorious displays of wildflowers (best during July and Aug). You can also walk this stretch on the **Summit Trail** (10km one way;

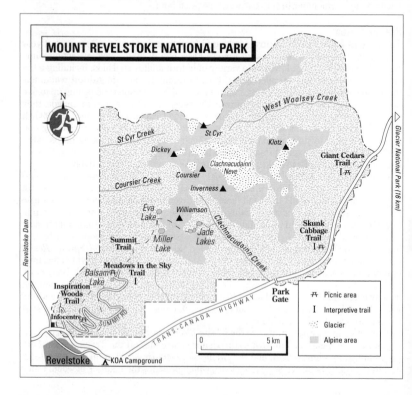

4hr) from the car park at the base of Summit Road. Recent damage to the delicate ecosystem has prompted park authorities to rethink, and often the last 1.5km of the road is closed to cars, leaving the choice of a walk or regular shuttle bus to the summit from a car park at Balsam Lake.

Most of the longer of the park's ten official **trails** start from the top of Summit Road; serious backpackers prefer to head to **Eagle Lake**, off Summit Road, rather than take the more popular **Miller Lake Trail** (6km one way). The award-winning **Giant Cedars Trail** is a wooded one-kilometre jaunt with ten interpretive exhibits off the road on the park's eastern edge, its boardwalks negotiating a tract of ancient forest crammed with 800-year-old Western Red Cedars and rough-barked Western Hemlock (the trailhead begins at the Giant Cedars Picnic Area). You could also try the **Skunk Cabbage Boardwalk** (1.2km), an easy trail through temperate forest and wetland inhabited by muskrat, beaver, numerous birds and the eponymous skunk cabbage. **Meadows in the Sky Trail**, by contrast, is a quick one-kilometre paved loop through alpine meadows at the top of Summit Road. Look out for the so-called Icebox, a shaded rock cleft that contains what is reputedly the world's smallest glacier. The *Footloose in the Columbias* booklet, available from Glacier's Rogers Pass visitor centre, has further trail information.

Revelstoke

REVELSTOKE, the only community within striking range of the park, sits just outside the western boundary, but in its promotional pitch chooses to ignore its scenic appeal in favour of a somewhat unimpressive claim to be "Home of the World's Largest Sculpted Grizzly Bears" (they stand at Mackenzie Avenue at the entrance to downtown). Like many mountain towns, it's divided between a motel-and-garage strip along the Trans-Canada and a dispersed, frontier-type collection of houses to the rear. The river and rugged scenery round about redeem it, and the downtown area also has a nice feel, having been spruced up as a placatory measure following the disaster at the dam site (see overleaf). If you're without your own vehicle, it's a good twenty-minute walk from the strip. In downtown you might want to drop into the **Revelstoke Piano Keep Gallery**, 117 Campbell Ave (July & Aug Tues–Sat 10am–10pm; rest of the year provisionally 10am–5.30pm; $4.50; ☎837-6554), a seventeen-room 1905 period building that houses one of North America's finest piano collections. Also dip into the small but polished **Revelstoke Railway Museum** (May, June, Sept & Oct Mon–Sat 9am–5pm; July & Aug daily 9am–8pm; $5; ☎837-6060), which has a steam engine, snowploughs and assorted memorabilia relating to the building of the stretch of the CPR between Field and Kamloops. If you want to relax close to town, try warm-watered **Williamson Lake**, a favourite swimming spot for locals with mini-golf and campground 4km south of town east of Airport Way.

Seven daily Greyhound **buses** stop at the town of Revelstoke between Kamloops and Calgary; the terminal is at the west end of the strip, immediately after the big blue Columbia River bridge (☎837-5874). The **infocentre** is 200m beyond on the left at 204 Campbell Ave (daily: May & June 10am–6pm; July & Aug 8am–8pm; ☎837-5345, fax 837-4223). Get park information there, or call in on the **Park Administration Office** at 301 Campbell Ave-3rd St West (Mon–Fri 8am–4.30pm; ☎837-7500, fax 837-7536) or the Rogers Pass visitor centre.

Accommodation

A far more amenable place to stay than Golden, the town of Revelstoke has plenty of **accommodation** – fifteen-plus motels and half a dozen campgrounds.

Best Western Wayside Inn, 1901 Laforme Blvd (☎837-6161 or 1-800-528-1234, fax 837-5460). The priciest and probably the best of the town's hotels. ⑤.

Columbia Motel, 301 Wright St-2nd St West (☎837-2191 or 1-800-663-5303). With 54 rooms, one of the larger places in town; air-conditioned and heated pool in season as an extra draw. ③.

Frontier Motel and Restaurant, 122 North Nakusp Hwy (☎837-5512 or 1-800-382-7763, fax 837-6604). On the main Trans-Canada away from the town centre; good motel and first-rate food. ②.

Nelles Ranch Bed and Breakfast, Hwy 23 South (☎ & fax 837-3800). Just six units on a working horse and cattle ranch 2km off the Trans-Canada Highway. ②–③.

Peaks Lodge, 5km west of Revelstoke off Hwy 1 (☎837-2176 or 1-800-668-0330, fax 837-2133). Nice small place (twelve units) in a reasonably rustic setting convenient for hikes, bird-watching and the like. Open mid-May to mid-Oct & mid-Nov to mid-April. ③.

Revelstoke Traveller's Hostel and Guest House, 400-2nd St West (☎837-4050, fax 837-5600). Cheap private, semi-private and dorm beds convenient for local restaurants and supermarkets. ①.

'R' Motel, 1500 1st St (☎837-2164, fax 837-6847). One of the cheapest motels in town. ②.

Sandman Inn, 1821 Fraser St (☎837-5271 or 1-800-726-3626). Part of a usually reliable mid-range hotel chain. Has 83 rooms, so a good chance of finding space. ④.

CAMPGROUNDS

Revelstoke has no park-run sites. **Backcountry** camping in the park is free, with tent-pads, outhouses and food-storage poles provided at Eva and Jade lakes, but no camping is allowed in the Miller Lake area or anywhere within 5km of the Trans-Canada and Summit Road. Registration at the Park Administration Office is obligatory. The park is so small, however, that you might be better off at some of the area's more developed private **campgrounds**.

Highway Haven Motel and Campground, Three Valley Lake (☎837-2525). 20km west of Revelstoke, near the lake for swimming and boating. Thirty pitches and hot showers. April–Nov. $10.

KOA Revelstoke, 5km east of Revelstoke (☎837-2085). The best of the area's campgrounds. Free showers, plus shop and swimming pool. May–Oct. $20.50.

Lamplighter Campground, off Hwy 1 before the Columbia River bridge; take Hwy 23 south towards Nakusp and turn into Nixon Road (first left) (☎837-3385, fax 837-5856). A peaceful, fully serviced tent and RV site within walking distance of downtown. Fifty fully serviced sites. April–Oct. $14.50.

Williamson Lake Campground, 1818 Williamson Lake Rd (☎837-5512 or 1-800-676-2267 for toll-free reservations). Nice forty-site lakeside campground 4km south of the town centre. Free hot showers, canoe and rowboat rentals, flush toilets and beach. Mid-April to Oct. $13.

Eating and drinking

Eating possibilities include the *Frontier Restaurant* on the Trans-Canada, part of the eponymous motel near the infocentre, which serves up superior steak-and-salad meals at reasonable prices, with friendly service and a genuine cow-poke atmosphere. In town, the *One-Twelve Restaurant* at 112 Victoria Rd is a favourite, with a pub and dance floor.

Revelstoke Dam

A trip to Canada's largest dam may sound dull, but the **Revelstoke Dam** (daily: mid-March to mid-June & early Sept to late Oct 9am–5pm; mid-June to early Sept 8am–8pm; free; ☎837-6515) makes an interesting outing. Four kilometres north of the town on Hwy 23, the 175-metre-tall barrier holds back the waters of the Columbia River, around 500km from its source. Its sleek, space-age **visitor centre** offers a well-put-together two-hour self-guided tour, which omits to tell you that insufficient mapping during the construction caused a landslide that threatened to swamp Revelstoke: millions had to be spent or it would have been curtains for the town. The boring bits of the tour can be skipped in favour of a lift to the top for a great view of the dam and surrounding valley.

Kootenay National Park

KOOTENAY NATIONAL PARK, lying across the Continental Divide from Banff in British Columbia, is the least known of the four contiguous parks of the Rockies, and the easiest to miss out – many people prefer to follow the Trans-Canada through Yoho rather than commit themselves to the less enthralling westward journey on Hwy 3

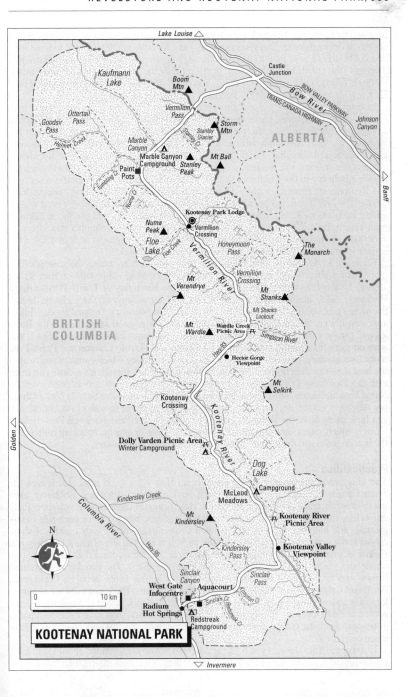

KOOTENAY NATIONAL PARK

imposed by Kootenay. The park's scenery, however, is as impressive as that of its neighbours – it draws three million visitors a year – and if you're not determined to head west you could drive a neat loop from Banff through Kootenay on Hwy 93 to **Radium Hot Springs** (the only town in this area), north on Hwy 95, and back on the Trans-Canada through Yoho to Lake Louise and Banff. You could drive this in a day and still have time for a few short walks and a dip in Radium's hot springs to boot.

In many ways the park's mountains seem closer at hand and more spectacular than on the Icefields Parkway, partly because the road climbs higher over the Continental Divide, and partly because the park's origins guaranteed it an intimate link with the highway. In 1910 Randolph Bruce, a local businessman, persuaded the Canadian government and Canadian Pacific to push a road from Banff through the Rockies to connect the prairies with western seaports (prompted by the hope of promoting a fruit-growing industry in the Columbia Valley). Previously the area had been the reserve of the Kootenai or Ktunaxa natives (*Kootenay* is a native word meaning "people from beyond the hills") and had been explored by David Thompson, but otherwise it was an all but inviolate mountain fastness. The project began in 1911 and produced 22km of road before the money ran out. To wangle more cash British Columbia was forced to cede 8km of land on each side of the highway to the government and, in 1920, 1406 square kilometres of land were established as a national park.

Kootenay lends itself to admiration from a car, bus or bike, mainly because it's little more than a sixteen-kilometre-wide ribbon of land running either side of Hwy 93 for around 100km (the highway here is known as the **Kootenay** or **Banff–Windermere Parkway**). All its numerous easy **short walks** start immediately off the highway, though the scenery, of course, doesn't simply stop at the park boundary. Options for **day hikes** are more limited, though the best of the longer walks are as good as anything in the Rockies and can be extended into outstanding two-day (or more) backpacking options If you want no more than a stroll from a car or bike follow the **Marble Canyon** and **Paint Pots** trails: for something longer but not too long go for the **Stanley Glacier** walk; if you're after the best day hike the choice is the **Kindersley Pass Trail**, though it's a close-run thing with the Floe Lake Trail to Floe Lake and its possible continuation northwest over the Numa Pass and down Numa Creek back to the highway. If you have time do both of these two day hikes – if you do, you'll have done two of the top ten or so walks in the Rockies. If you have more time, the Rockwall Trail (Floe Lake–Numa Pass–Rockwell Pass–Helmet Falls) is widely considered among the Rockies' top three or four backpacking routes. See the box on p.636 and the map on p.637 to make sense of these routes.

Practicalities

The only practicable access to Kootenay is on Hwy 93, a good road that leaves the Trans-Canada at Castle Junction (in Banff National Park), traverses Kootenay from north to south, and joins Hwy 95 at Radium Hot Springs at the southern entrance. Radium offers the only practical accommodation options, bar a trio of park-run campgrounds and handful of rooms at Vermilion Crossing, a summer-only huddle of shop, cabins and gas station midway through the park. It is also the site of a new privately run **visitor centre** (currently summer Mon–Thurs & Sun 9am–5pm, Fri & Sat 9am–8pm; phone and winter hours not established at time of writing). The two daily Greyhound **buses** east and west on the southern British Columbia route between Cranbrook, Banff and Calgary stop at Vermilion Crossing and Radium. **Park permits** are required for entry unless you already have a valid permit from Banff, Jasper or Kootenay: $5 per person per day, valid for all four parks, or $35 for an annual pass valid for eleven parks in western Canada: group passes for two to ten people cost $10 (see box on p.567 for more on passes).

If you come from the east you'll hit the Marble Canyon campground about 15km from Castle Junction, where occasionally in summer there's a simple information kiosk (mid-

June to early Sept Mon & Fri–Sun 8.30am–8pm, Tues–Thurs 8.30am–4.30pm; no phone); coming the other way, the main park visitor centre, the **West Gate Information Centre**, park warden station and ticket booth are at the southern/western end of the highway at the Radium Hot Springs Pools (daily: late June to mid-Sept 9am–7pm; May–June & Sept–Oct 9am–5pm; ☎347-9505; Nov–April call ☎347-9615 Mon–Fri 8.30am–4.30pm only). The latter can sell you a topographical map of the park, but the West Gate and Vermilion centres both distribute the free *Backcountry Guide to Kootenay National Park*, all you need walk-wise if you're not planning anything too ambitious.

Park staff are also usually on hand at the park's only two roadside serviced **campgrounds**: the 98-site *McLeod Meadows*, 25km north of Radium ($13; mid-May to mid-Sept; no showers), and the 61-site *Marble Canyon*, near the Information Centre ($13; mid-June to early Sept; no showers). If you want more comforts (including hot showers) and easier access use the big 240-site *Redstreak* campground, Kootenay's major park campground. It's located 3km north of Radium Hot Springs ($16–21; May–Sept; ☎347-9567); the turnoff for the site is a minor road (Redstreak Road) signed off Hwy 95 from the village, close to the RCMP station, and not off the main Hwy 93, which branches north 200m to the west for the hot springs and the park proper. If you're staying at the campground, incidentally, note that the Redstreak Campground Trail (2.2km) takes you from the northwest corner of the site to the Radium Hot Springs Pools. The Valleyview Trail (1.4km) takes you from the campground entrance into Radium village, avoiding Redstreak Road.

A dozen or more **backcountry sites** with pit toilets and firewood are scattered within easy backpacking range of the highway, for which you need a **permit** from the info-centres ($6). The small seven-site *Dolly Varden* park campground just north of McLeod Meadows opens for **winter camping** (Sept–May; flush toilets only).

The only indoor **accommodation** in the heart of the park is ten rustic cottages at Vermilion Crossing (☎762-9196; ④; May–Sept). You'll need to book these well in advance; similarly the twelve cabins at *Mount Assiniboine Lodge* (☎344-2639; ⑥; Feb–April & late June to mid-Oct; reservations obligatory; two-night minimum stay). Located at 2195m within the Assiniboine Provincial Park, this lodge is accessible only by helicopter, skiing or hiking trail. The other listed hotels within the park borders are so close to Radium as to make little difference (see "Radium Hot Springs", p.639).

Vermilion Pass

Vermilion Pass (1637m) marks the northern entrance to the park, the Great Divide's watershed and the border between Alberta and British Columbia. Little fanfare, however, accompanies the transition – only the barren legacy of a huge forest fire (started by a single lightning bolt) which ravaged the area for four days in 1968, leaving a 24-square-kilometre blanket of stark, blackened trunks. Take the short **Fireweed Trail** (1km) through the desolation from the car park at the pass to see how nature deals with such disasters, indeed how it seems to invite lightning fires to promote phoenix-like regeneration. The ubiquitous lodge-pole pine, for example, specifically requires the heat of a forest fire to crack open its resin-sealed cones and release its seeds. Strange as it seems, forests are intended to burn, at least if a healthy forest is to be preserved: in montane regions the natural "fire return cycles" are a mere 42–46 years; in lower sub-alpine habitats, 77–130 years; and in upper sub-alpine areas, 180 years. Forests any older are actually in decline, providing few species and poor wildlife habitats. Ironically, as a result of the national parks' success in preventing forest fires over the last fifty years, many woods are now over-mature and the need for controlled burning is increasingly being addressed. At Vermilion Pass a broad carpet of lodge-pole pines have taken root among the blasted remnants of the earlier forest, while young plants and shrubs ("doghair forest") are pushing up into the new clearings. Birds, small mammals and deer, elk and moose are being attracted to new food sources and, more significantly, black and grizzly bears are returning to the area.

DAY AND BACKPACKING HIKES IN KOOTENAY

If you have time and energy for only one long walk in Kootenay, make it the Kindersley Pass Trail, a strenuous 9.8-kilometre trail that climbs to Kindersley Pass and then cuts northeast for the steep final push to Kindersley Summit (2210m). Here you can enjoy the sublime prospect of an endless succession of peaks fading to the horizon away to the northeast. Rather than double back down through the open tundra, many people push on another 2km (trail vague) and contour around the head of the Sinclair Creek valley before dropping off the ridge (the Kindersley–Sinclair Coll) to follow the well-defined Sinclair Creek Trail (6.4km) down to meet the highway 1km from the starting point (be sure to do the hike this way round – the Sinclair Creek Trail is a long, dull climb).

Most of Kootenay's other longish day walks are in the park's northern half, accessed on the west side of the highway from the Marble Canyon, Paint Pots, Numa Creek and Floe Lake parking areas. The Rockwall Trail, an incredible thirty-kilometre (54km including approach trails; 1450m ascent), backpacking high-level trail, follows the line of the mountains on the west side of the highway, and can be joined using four of the six trails described below. You could walk it in two days, but could easily spend longer, particularly as there are five backcountry campgrounds en route.

From north to south on the highway, the trails start with the Kaufmann Lake Trail (15km one way; 570m ascent; allow 4–6hr one way), which climbs to one of the park's loveliest high mountain lakes (there's also a campground here). A trail from the Paint Pots runs for 2km before dividing to provide three onward options: the first to the dull Ottertail Pass, the second up Tumbling Creek (10.3km; 440m ascent to the intersection with the Rockwall Trail), and the third and best option the Helmet Creek Trail (14.3km; 310m ascent), a long day hike to the amazing 365-metre Helmet Waterfalls (another intersection with the Rockwall Trail). The best of the day hikes after Kindersley Pass is the easier Floe Lake Trail (10.5km; 715m ascent), up to a spellbinding lake edged by a 1000-metre sheer escarpment and a small glacier. There are campgrounds on the route, and another tie-in to the Rockwall Trail. The Numa Creek Trail (6.4km; 115m ascent) to the north is less enthralling – though you could use it as a downhill leg to add to the Floe Lake Trail (see map opposite) – as are the series of fire-road walks advertised in the park: unless you're mountain biking, therefore, ignore the Simpson River, West Kootenay, Honeymoon Pass and East Kootenay trails.

Stanley Glacier and Marble Canyon

About 3km south of Vermilion Pass, the small, well-defined **Stanley Glacier Trail** (4.2km; 365m ascent; 1hr 30min) strikes off up Stanley Creek from a parking area on the eastern side of the highway. In its first 2km the trail provides you with a hike through the Vermilion Pass Burn (see above), but more to the point pushes into the beautiful hanging valley below Stanley Peak. Here you can enjoy close-up views of the Stanley Glacier and its surrounding recently glaciated landscapes. The area is also known for its fossils, and for the chance to see marmots, pikas and white-tailed ptarmigan.

Marble Canyon, 8km south of Vermilion Pass, the site of a park-run **campground**, has an easy trail (800m) that's probably the most heavily trafficked of Kootenay's shorter hikes. The track crosses a series of log bridges over Tokumm Creek, which has carved through a fault in the limestone over the last 8000 years, to produce a 600-metre-long and 37-metre-deep gorge. In cold weather this is a fantastic medley of ice and snow, but in summer the climax is the viewpoint from the top of the path onto a thundering waterfall as the creek pounds its way through the narrowest section of the gorge. The rock here was once mistakenly identified as marble – hence the canyon's name; the white marble-like rock is actually dolomite limestone.

One of the park's better longer hikes also starts from the Marble Canyon car park – the **Kaufmann Lake Trail** (15km one way; 570m ascent; 4–6hr), which follows Tokumm Creek towards the head of the valley at Kaufmann Lake (see box above).

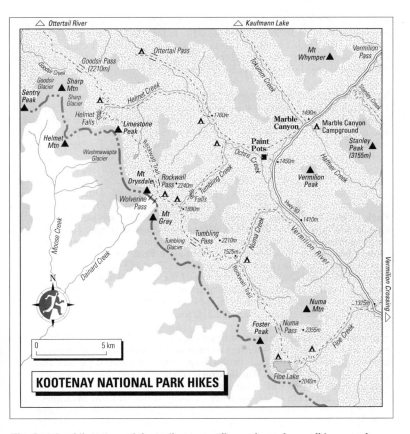

The first few kilometres of the trail – easy valley and meadow walking – make an appealing hour or so's stroll.

The Paint Pots

You could extend the Marble Canyon walk by picking up the Paint Pots Trail south, which puts another 2.7km onto your walk, or drive 2km south and stroll 1km to reach the same destination. Either way you come first to the Ochre Beds (after 800m) and then (1.5km) to the **Paint Pots**, one of the Rockies' more magical spots: red, orange and mustard-coloured pools prefaced by damp, moss-clung forest and views across the white water of the Vermilion River to the snowcapped mountains beyond. The pools' colours are created by iron-laden water bubbling up from three mineral springs through clay sediments deposited on the bed of an ancient glacial lake.

Natives from all over North America collected the coloured clays from the ponds and ochre beds to make into small cakes, which they baked in embers. The fired clay was then ground into powder – **ochre** – and added to animal fat or fish oil to use in rock, tepee or ceremonial body painting. Ochre has always had spiritual significance for North American natives, in this case the Stoney and Ktunaxa, who saw these oxide-stained pools and their yellow-edged surroundings as inhabited by animal and thunder spirits. Standing in the quiet, rather gloomy glade, particularly on overcast days, it's easy to see why – not that the atmosphere or sanctity of the place stopped European speculators in the 1920s from mining the ochre to manufacture paint in Calgary.

The car park is the trailhead for three longer (day or backpack) trails, all of which kick off along the Ochre Creek Valley: Tumbling Creek Trail, Ottertail Pass Trail and the Helmet Creek–Helmet Waterfalls Trail (see box on p.636).

Vermilion Crossing and Kootenay Crossing

VERMILION CROSSING, 20km south of the Paint Pots Trail, is gone in a flash, but it's the only place, in summer at least, to find lodgings, petrol and food in the park. It also has a new visitor centre (see p.634), built on the site of a 1920 CPR railway camp. You can also stop to walk the **Vérendrye Creek Trail** (2.1km), accessed west off the highway, an easy stroll, but forest-enclosed, and with only limited views of Mount Verendrye as a reward. One of the Rockies' tougher walks heads east from the Crossing, up over Honeymoon Pass and Redearth Pass to Egypt Lake and the Trans-Canada Highway in Banff National Park, while to the south equally demanding trails provide the only westside access into the wilderness of **Mount Assiniboine Provincial Park**. Sandwiched between Kootenay and Banff, this wilderness park was created in honour of Mount Assiniboine (3618m), a sabre-tooth-shaped mountain with one of the most dramatic profiles imaginable, whose native Stoney name means "those who cook by placing hot rocks in water". The **Simpson Road Trail** (8.2km) leads to the park boundary, and then divides into two paths (20km and 32km) to Lake Magog in the heart of Assiniboine. Some 8.5km beyond the Crossing look out for the Animal Lick, a spot where animals come down to lick nutrients from a natural mineral source: with luck you may see elk, mule deer and even moose here. Over the next few kilometres, for similar reasons, you might also see mountain goats by banks at the side of the road.

Kootenay Crossing is no more than a ceremonial spot – it was where the ribbon was cut to open Hwy 93 in 1923 – though a clutch of short trails fan out from its park warden station, and the nearby *Dolly Varden* campground (see p.635) is the park's only specific site for winter camping. **Wardle Creek** nearby is a good place to unpack a picnic if you're determined to stick to the road.

Around 11km south of the Kootenay Crossing is the **McLeod Meadows** campground (see p.635), and immediately behind it to the east the easy **Dog Lake Trail** (2.7km), much tramped as an after-dinner leg-stretcher by campers (the trail can also be accessed from the highway at the picnic area 500m south). The path offers glimpses of the Kootenay Valley through the trees, and ends in a marsh-edged lake whose temperate microclimate makes it ideal for nature study. You may see deer, elk and coyotes, and – if you're lucky – bears and moose. Several types of orchid also bloom here in early summer (June & July), including white bog, round-leafed, calypso and sparrow's egg. About 11km further on, the **Kootenay Valley Viewpoint** offers one of the broadest views on the highway, with great vistas of the Mitchell and Vermilion mountain ranges, and with them the inevitable hordes in search of a photo opportunity.

Sinclair Pass

For its final rundown out of the park, the highway doglegs west through the **Sinclair Pass**, a red-cliffed gorge filled with the falling waters of Sinclair Creek and the start of the **Kindersley Pass Trail**, possibly the most scenic day hike in the park (see box on p.636). If this seems too much of a slog, Sinclair Pass offers three far easier short trails, all marked off the highway to the west. The best is the **Juniper Trail** (3.2km), accessed just 300m inside the park's West Gate. The trail drops to Sinclair Creek and over the next couple of kilometres touches dry canyon, arid forest slopes of juniper and Douglas fir, and thick woods of Western Red Cedar, before emerging at the hot springs, or Aquacourt (see below), 1.4km up the road from the start. The **Redstreak Creek Trail** (2.7km), 4.5km east of the West Gate, starts off as a good forest walk, but tails off into dullness subsequently, as does the **Kimpton Creek Trail** (4.8km), also on the south side of the road and canyon, accessed 7.5km east of the West Gate.

Radium Hot Springs

RADIUM HOT SPRINGS is far less attractive than its evocative name suggests but, as the service centre for Kootenay, its tacky motels and garages are likely to claim your attention and money. The town spreads across the flats of the Columbia Valley, 3km from the southern/western entrance at the junction of Hwy 93 and Hwy 95.

The **hot springs** (or Aquacourt) themselves (plus park visitor centre) are nicely away from the settlement, 2km north of town off the Banff–Windermere Parkway (Hwy 93) and are administered by the park authorities (daily: mid-May to mid-Oct 9am–10.30pm; mid-Oct to mid-May noon–10pm; $5 and $4.50 respectively; ☎347-9485). Native Canadians used the springs for centuries, and commercial white development started as early as 1890 when Roland Stuart bought the area for $160. Traces of supposedly therapeutic radium found in the water turned Stuart's investment into a recreational gold mine. When the government appropriated the springs for inclusion in the national park, it paid him $40,000 – a small fortune, but considerably less than what they were worth, which at the time was estimated to be $500,000. The pools today are outdoors, but serviced by a large, modern centre. In summer, 4000 people per day take the plunge into the odourless 45°C waters – enough to discourage any idea of a quiet swim, though in late evening or off season (when the hot pool steams invitingly) you can escape the bedlam and pretend more easily that the water is having some sort of soothing effect. The radium traces sound a bit worrying, but 300,000 visitors a year don't seem to mind.

If you have the choice, aim to stay in one of the new **motels** creeping up the Sinclair Valley around the hot springs area away from downtown – they're more expensive, but far more attractively sited than the thirty-odd mirror-image motels in town (where there are any number of rooms in the $40–60 bracket). Try the big 120-room *Radium Hot Springs Resort*, 1km south of the springs at 8100 Golf Course Rd (☎347-9311 or 1-800-667-6444; ⑥), for all the trimmings (including swimming pool and massage therapist); *Addison's Bungalows* (☎347-9545; ③; April–Oct), a mix of 31 motel and cabin rooms nearby with units offering anything up to five bedrooms and kitchenettes; or the adjacent *Mount Farnham Bungalows* (☎347-9515; ③–④). Almost alongside the park entrance are the fourteen-room *Alpen Motel* (☎347-9823; ③), and the sixteen-room *Kootenay* (☎347-9490; ③) and nine-room *Crescent* (☎347-9570; ③) motels. Most of the motels along the main drag in town are smaller – the cheapest are the *Tuk-In* (☎347-9464 or 1-800-641-4959; ②) and the *Sunset* (☎347-9863 or 1-800-214-7413; ②).

travel details

Trains

Calgary to: Vancouver with private Rocky Mountain Railtours (July–Sept 2 weekly; $465 one-way; 36hr).

Edmonton to: Prince Rupert via Jasper and Prince George (3 weekly; 30hr); Vancouver (3 weekly; 24hr); Winnipeg via Saskatoon (3 weekly; 24hr).

Jasper to: Edmonton (3 weekly; 5hr 30min); Prince Rupert via Prince George (3 weekly; 20hr); Vancouver (3 weekly).

Buses

Calgary to: Banff (6 daily; 1hr 40min); Coutts (US; connections for Las Vegas and Los Angeles) via Fort Macleod and Lethbridge (1 daily; 4hr 30min); Creston via Banff, Radium Hot Springs and Cranbrook (1 daily; 7hr 30min); Dawson Creek (2 daily; 7hr 15min); Drumheller (2 daily; 1hr 50min); Edmonton (14 daily; 3hr 30min); Fort St John (2 daily; 9hr 15min); Lake Louise (6 daily; 2hr 35min); Prince George (2 daily; 14hr); Saskatoon (2 daily; 9hr); Vancouver via Fort Macleod, Cranbrook, Nelson, Osoyoos and Hope (2 daily; 24hr); Vancouver via Kamloops (7 daily; 13hr); Vancouver via Vernon, Kelowna and Penticton (3 daily; 16hr); Winnipeg via Lethbridge, Medicine Hat and Regina (2 daily; 24hr).

Edmonton to: Calgary (14 daily; 3hr 30min); Drumheller (1 daily; 4hr 45min); Grande Prairie (4 daily; 6hr); Hay River via Peace River (1 daily; 17hr); Jasper (6 daily; 4hr 30min); Peace River (3 daily; 6hr 30min); Saskatoon (4 daily; 5hr); Vancouver (6 daily; 14hr); Whitehorse (mid-May to mid-Oct 1 daily; rest of the year 3 weekly; 28hr); Winnipeg (2 daily; 21hr).

Flights

Calgary to: Edmonton (every 30min; 50min); Montréal (12 daily; 5hr); Toronto (14 daily; 4hr); Vancouver (every 30min; 1hr 20min).

Edmonton to: Calgary (every 30min; 50min); Montréal (9 daily; 5hr); Toronto (10 daily; 4hr 10min); Vancouver (every 30min; 1hr 25min).

CHAPTER SEVEN

SOUTHERN BRITISH COLUMBIA

The often pristine scenery of **British Columbia** more than lives up to most people's image of the wilds of Canada. What may come as a surprise, however, is the region's sheer natural diversity: between the expected extremes of the mountainous, forested interior and the fjord-cut mountains of the coast lies a jigsaw of landscapes, including genteel farmland, ranching country, immense lakes and even a patch of genuine desert. British Columbia contains both Canada's wettest and its driest climates, and more species of flora and fauna than the rest of the country put together. The range of recreational possibilities is equally impressive: the country's biggest ski area, its warmest lakes and some of its best beaches are all here, not to mention hot springs and hiking, sailing and canoeing galore, as well as some of the best salmon fishing in the world. Interior towns may not always be terribly interesting – **Nelson** is a notable exception – but from almost anywhere in the region you can be sure that secluded and peaceful countryside and myriad outdoor pursuits lie just a few kilometres away.

Culturally and logistically, southern British Columbia stands apart from the northern half of the province, containing most of the roads, towns and accessible sights. Ninety-five percent of the population lives in the south, mainly in **Vancouver**, Canada's third largest city. A cosmopolitan, sophisticated and famously hedonistic place, Vancouver gives the lie to the stereotype of the Canadian west as an introverted, cultural wasteland, its combination of glittering skyline and generous open spaces standing as a model of urban planning. The province's modest capital is **Victoria**, a considerably smaller city on the southern tip of Vancouver Island, which affects a somewhat English ambience to lure more tourists than it probably deserves.

If you're making a circuit of the interior, or even just cutting across it as part of a transcontinental route, you'll want to set aside time for the mountain-hemmed lakes and tidy mining towns of the **Kootenays**, or – if you're into wine tasting or rowdy lakeside resorts – the **Okanagan**. For big wilderness and waterfalls, **Wells Gray Provincial Park** stands out, though exhilarating hikes and camping are possible in dozens of other parks. Variety is also the byword for **Vancouver Island**, by far the largest of an archipelago of islets off BC's coast, where in a short time you can move from wild seascapes and rainforest to jagged, glaciated peaks. Vancouver Island can also be used as a springboard for the ferry up to the famed **Inside Passage** to Prince Rupert and beyond, or the new Discovery Coast Passage to Bella Coola; inland, roads and rail lines converge to follow a single route north through the endless expanse of the **Cariboo** region of the interior plateau.

TOLL-FREE INFORMATION AND HOTEL RESERVATIONS NUMBER

Tourism British Columbia ☎ 1-800-663-6000.

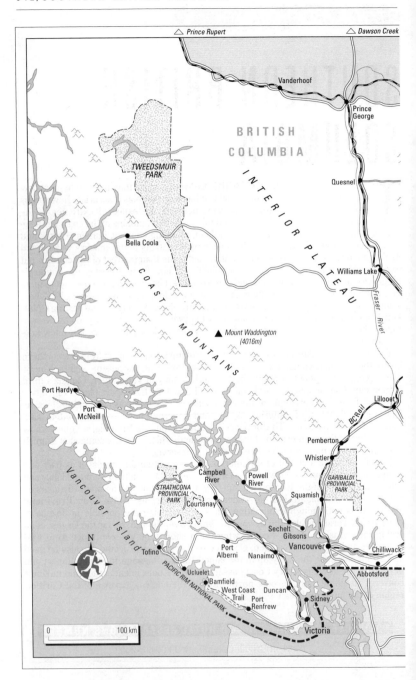

△ Prince Rupert   △ Dawson Creek

Vanderhoof

Prince
George

BRITISH
COLUMBIA

INTERIOR PLATEAU

Quesnel

TWEEDSMUIR
PARK

Bella Coola

Williams Lake

Fraser River

COAST

MOUNTAINS

▲ Mount Waddington
(4016m)

Port Hardy

Port
McNeill

Lillooet

BC Rail

Pemberton

Whistler

GARIBALDI
PROVINCIAL
PARK

Campbell
River

Powell
River

STRATHCONA
PROVINCIAL
PARK

Squamish

Courtenay

Sechelt
Gibsons

Vancouver

Vancouver Island

Chilliwack

Tofino

Port
Alberni

Nanaimo

Abbotsford

PACIFIC RIM NATIONAL PARK

Ucluelet

Bamfield

West Coast
Trail

Duncan

Port
Renfrew

Sidney

Victoria

N

0   100 km

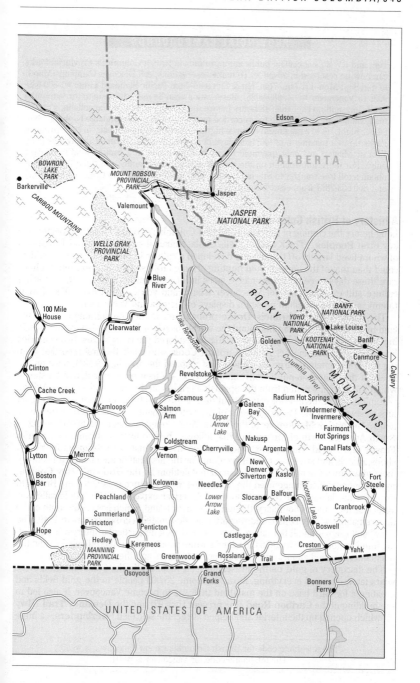

PROVINCIAL CAMPGROUNDS

Tent and RV sites at certain public campgrounds in British Columbia's Provincial Parks can now be reserved in advance. To make reservations, call Discover Camping (March to mid-Sept Mon–Fri 7am–7pm, Sat & Sun 9am–5pm Pacific Standard Time; ☎1-800-689-9025 or Vancouver ☎604/689-9025). Reservations can be made from up to three months in advance and no later than 48 hours before the first day of arrival. Cancellations can be made after 7pm by following the recorded instructions. A non-refundable booking fee of $6 per night, up to a maximum of three nights, is charged. You can stay in BC Provincial Parks up to a maximum of fourteen days in any single park. Payment in advance is by Visa or MasterCard only (payment for extra nights once at a campground is by cash only). For more information on the service and parks generally, call ☎250/387-4550 or obtain a toll-free transfer to this number by calling ☎660-2421 (from Greater Vancouver) or 1-800-663-7867 from elsewhere in BC.

A history of British Columbia

Long before the coming of Europeans, British Columbia's coastal region supported five key **First Peoples** – The Kwakiutl, Bella Coola, Nuu-chah-nulth, Haida and Tlingit – all of whom lived largely off the sea and developed a culture in many ways more sophisti-cated than that of the nomadic and hunting-oriented tribes of the interior. Although it's rare these days to come across native faces in interior southern BC, villages of living culture still exist on parts of Vancouver Island, and you can find examples of their totemic art in the excellent museum displays of Victoria and Vancouver.

The British explorer **Francis Drake** probably made the first sighting of the main-land by a European, during his round-the-world voyage of 1579. Spanish explorers sail-ing from California and Russians from Alaska explored the coast almost two centuries later, though it was another Briton, **Captain Cook**, who made the first recorded land-ing in 1778. Captain George Vancouver first mapped the area in 1792–94, hard on the heels of the Nuu-chah-nulth Convention of 1790 – a neat piece of colonial bluster in which the British wrested from the Spanish all rights on the mainland as far as Alaska.

Exploration of the interior came about during the search for an easier way to export furs westwards to the Pacific (instead of the arduous haul eastwards across the conti-nent). **Alexander Mackenzie** of the North West Company made the first crossing of North America north of Mexico in 1793, followed by two further adventurers, **Simon Fraser** and **David Thompson**, whose names also resonate as sobriquets for rivers, shops, motels and streets across the region. For the first half of the nineteenth century most of western Canada was ruled as a virtual fiefdom by the **Hudson's Bay Compa-ny**, a monopoly that antagonized the Americans, which in turn persuaded the British to formalize its claims to the region to forestall American expansion. The 49th Parallel was agreed as the national boundary, though Vancouver Island, which lies partly south of the line, remained wholly British and was officially designated a crown colony in 1849. The "Bay" still reigned in all but name, however, and took no particular interest in promot-ing immigration; as late as 1855 the island's white population numbered only 774 and the mainland remained almost unknown except to trappers and the odd prospector.

The discovery of **gold** on the Fraser River in 1858, and in the Cariboo region three years later, changed everything, attracting some 25,000 people to the gold fields and creating a forward base on the mainland that was to become Vancouver. It also led to the building of the **Cariboo Road** (the present Hwy 97) and the **Dewdney Trail** (Hwy 3), which opened up the interior and helped attract the so-called **Overlanders** – a huge

The telephone code for British Columbia except Vancouver is ☎250.
The telephone code for Vancouver is ☎604.

straggle of pioneers that tramped from Ontario and Québec in the summer of 1862. Britain declared mainland British Columbia a crown colony in 1858 to impose imperial authority on the region and, more importantly, to lay firm claim to the huge mineral wealth that was rightly believed to lie within it. When Canada's eastern colonies formed the Dominion in 1867, though, British Columbia dithered over joining until it received the promise of a railway to link it to the east in 1871 – though the Canadian Pacific didn't actually arrive for another fifteen years.

While British Columbia no longer dithers over its destiny, it still tends to look to itself – and increasingly to the new economic markets of the Pacific Rim – rather than to the rest of Canada. The francophone concerns of the east are virtually nonexistent here – for years, for example, there was just one French school in the entire province. For the most part British Columbians are well off, both financially and in terms of quality of life, and demographically the province is one of the Canada's youngest. If there are flies in the ointment, they're the environmental pressures thrown up by an economy that relies on primary resources for its dynamism: British Columbia supplies 25 percent of North America's commercial timber and exports significant amounts of hydroelectric power, fish, zinc, silver, oil, coal and gypsum. Few of these can be exploited without exacting a toll on the province's natural beauty: British Columbians may be well off, but they're increasingly aware of the environmental price being paid for their prosperity.

VANCOUVER

Cradled between the ocean and snowcapped mountains, Vancouver's dazzling downtown district fills a narrow peninsula bounded by Burrard Inlet to the north, English Bay to the west and False Creek to the south, with greater Vancouver sprawling south to the Fraser River. Edged around its idyllic waterfront are fine beaches, a dynamic port and a magnificent swath of parkland, not to mention the mirror-fronted ranks of skyscrapers that look across Burrard Inlet and its bustling harbour to the residential districts of North and West Vancouver. Beyond these comfortable suburbs, the Coast Mountains rise in steep, forested slopes to form a dramatic counterpoint to the downtown skyline and the most stunning of the city's many outdoor playgrounds. Small wonder, given Vancouver's surroundings, that Greenpeace was founded in the city.

Vancouver's 1.8 million residents exploit their spectacular natural setting to the hilt, and when they tire of the immediate region can travel a short distance to the unimaginably vast wilderness of the BC interior. Whether it's sailing, swimming, fishing, hiking, skiing, golf or tennis, locals barely have to move to indulge in a plethora of **recreational** whims. Summer and winter the city oozes hedonism and healthy living – it comes as no surprise to find that you can lounge on beaches downtown – typically West Coast obsessions that spill over into its sophisticated **arts and culture**. Vancouver claims a world-class museum and symphony orchestra, as well as opera, theatre and dance companies at the cutting edge of contemporary arts. Festivals proliferate

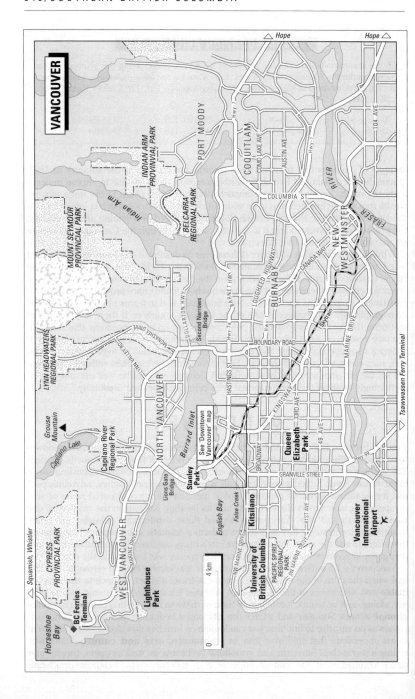

throughout its mild, if occasionally rain-soaked summer, and numerous music venues provide a hotbed for up-and-coming rock bands and a burgeoning jazz scene.

Vancouver is not all pleasure, however. Business growth continues apace in Canada's third largest and fastest-growing city, much of its prosperity stemming from a **port** so laden with the raw materials of the Canadian interior – lumber, wheat and minerals – that it now outranks New York as North America's largest port, handling more dry tonnage than the West Coast ports of Seattle, Tacoma, Portland, San Francisco and San Diego put together. The port in turn owes its prominence to Vancouver's much-trumpeted position as a **gateway to the Far East**, and its increasingly pivotal role in the new global market of the Pacific Rim. This lucrative realignment is strengthened by a two-way flow in traffic: in the past decade Vancouver has been inundated with Hong Kong Chinese (the so-called "yacht people"), an influx which has pushed up property prices and slightly strained the city's reputation as an ethnically integrated metropolis.

Much of the city's earlier immigration focused on Vancouver's extraordinary **Chinatown**, just one of a number of ethnic enclaves – Italian, Greek, Indian and Japanese in particular – which lend the city a refreshingly gritty quality that belies its sleek, modern reputation. So too do the city's semi-derelict eastern districts, whose worldly lowlife characters, addicts and hustlers are shockingly at odds with the glitzy lifestyles pursued in the lush residential neighbourhoods. Low rents and Vancouver's cosmopolitan young have also nurtured an unexpected **counterculture**, at least for the time being, distinguished by varied restaurants, secondhand shops, avant-garde galleries, clubs and bars – spots where you'll probably have more fun than in many a Canadian city. And at the top of the scale there are restaurants as good – and as varied – as any in North America.

These days Vancouver is more **dynamic** than ever, its growth and energy almost palpable as you walk the streets. In just five years, between 1987 and 1992, the city's population increased by an extraordinary seventeen per cent. Over the next decade it's expected to grow by as much as fifty per cent. The downtown population, currently around 521,000, is the fastest-growing on the continent. In response the downtown area is spreading – visibly – to the older and previously run-down districts to the southeast of the old city core. Recent development is symbolized by a superb library and performing arts complex which constitutes the most expensive capital project ever undertaken in the city. Real estate here is now more expensive than Toronto, and in 1990 the city became North America's largest film and TV production centre after Los Angeles and New York; *The X Files* is just the most famous of the many movies and programmes now being made here. Yet, in the peculiar way that seems second nature to Canadians, the boom is being handled in a manner that's enhancing rather than compromising the city's beguiling combination of pleasure, culture, business and natural beauty.

A brief history of Vancouver

Vancouver in the modern sense has existed for a little over 110 years. Over the course of the previous 9000 years the Fraser Valley was home to the Tsawwassen, Musqueam and another twenty or so native tribes, who made up the Stó:lo Nation, or "people of the river". The fish, particularly salmon, of this river was the Stó:lo lifeblood. Over the millennia these people ventured little into the mountainous interior, something that remains true to this day. One of the things that makes modern Vancouver so remarkable is how wild and empty British Columbia remains beyond the Fraser's narrow corridor. The Stó:lo inhabited about ten villages on the shores of Vancouver's Burrard Inlet before the coming of the Europeans. A highly developed culture, the Stó:lo were skilled carpenters, canoe-makers and artists, though little in the present city – outside its museums – pays anything but lip service to their existence. Vancouver Island is the nearest best bet if you're in search of latter-day tokens of Native Canadian culture.

Europeans appeared on the scene in notable numbers during the eighteenth century, when **Spanish** explorers charted the waters along what is now southwestern British

The telephone code for Vancouver is ☎604.

Columbia. In 1778 **Captain James Cook** reached nearby Nootka Sound while searching for the Northwest Passage, sparking off immediate British interest in the area. In 1791 José Maria Narvaez, a Spanish pilot and surveyor, glimpsed the mouth of the Fraser from his ship, the *Santa Saturnia*. This led to wrangles between the British and Spanish, disputes quickly settled in Britain's favour when Spain became domestically embroiled in the aftermath of the French Revolution. **Captain George Vancouver** officially claimed the land for Britain in 1792, but studying the Fraser from a small boat decided that it seemed too shallow to be of practical use. Instead he rounded a headland to the north, sailing into a deep natural port – the future site of Vancouver – which he named Burrard after one of his companions. He then traded briefly with several Squamish tribespeople at X'ay'xi, a village on the inlet's forested headland – the future Stanley Park. Afterwards the Squamish named the spot Whul-whul-Lay-ton, or "place of the white man". Vancouver sailed on, having spent just a day in the region – scant homage to an area that was to be named after him a century later.

Vancouver's error over the Fraser was uncovered in 1808, when Scottish-born Simon Fraser made an epic 1368-kilometre journey down the river from the Rockies to the sea. In 1827 the Hudson's Bay Company set up a fur-trading post at **Fort Langley**, 48km east of the present city, bartering not only furs but also salmon from the Stó:lo, the latter being salted and then packed off to company forts across Canada. The fort was kept free of homesteaders, despite being the area's first major white settlement, their presence deemed detrimental to the fur trade. Major colonization of the area only came after the Fraser River and Cariboo gold rushes in 1858, when **New Westminster** bustled with the arrival of as many 25,000 hopefuls, many of whom were refugees from the 1849 Californian rush. Many also drifted in from the US, underlining the fragility of the national border and the precarious nature of British claims to the region. These claims were consolidated when British Columbia was declared a crown colony, with New Westminster as its capital. Both were superseded by Fort Victoria in 1868, by which time the gold rush had dwindled almost to nothing.

In 1862, meanwhile, three British prospectors, unable to find gold in the interior, bought a strip of land on the southern shore of Burrard Inlet and – shortsightedly, given the amount of lumber around – started a brickworks. This soon gave way to the Hastings Sawmill and a shantytown of bars which by 1867 had taken the name of **Gastown**, after "Gassy" – as in loquacious – Jack Leighton, proprietor of the site's first saloon. Two years later Gastown became incorporated as the town of **Granville** and prospered on the back of its timber and small coal deposits. The birth of the present city dates to 1884, when the **Canadian Pacific Railway** decided to make it the terminus of its transcontinental railway. In 1886, on a whim of the CPR president, Granville was renamed Vancouver, only to be destroyed on June 13 that year when fire razed all but half a dozen buildings. The setback proved short-lived, and since the arrival of the first train from Montréal in 1887 the city has never looked back.

Arrival and information

Vancouver Airport
Vancouver International Airport is situated on Sea Island, 13km south of the city centre. Its often-used coded abbreviation is YVR. International flights arrive at the majestic new main terminal; domestic flights at the smaller and linked old Main Terminal. As an international passenger you'll find a **tourist information** desk as you exit customs and immigration and before entering the terminal's public spaces (daily

---

DEPARTURE TAX

All passengers departing from Vancouver International Airport must pay (cash or credit card) an Airport Improvement Fee – $5 within BC, $10 within North America (including Mexico and Hawaii) and $15 outside North America.

7am–midnight; ☎688-5515). On the right just before this is a desk where you can book taxis, limousines (only a little more expensive) and also buy tickets or obtain information for the bus shuttles to downtown (see below) and direct bus services from the airport to Victoria, Whistler, Bellingham Airport (Seattle) and Sea-Tac Airport in the US. There are also plenty of **foreign exchange** and other facilities, along with free phone lines to several upmarket hotels. Domestic passengers also have a tourist information desk just before the terminal exit

The best way to get into Vancouver is on the private **Airporter bus** (6.45am–1.10am; $9 single, $15 return; ☎946-8866), which leaves from a bay immediately outside the main door of the international arrivals; domestic arrivals can walk here if you need information or wait at the domestic arrivals pick-up outside the terminal. You can buy **tickets** from the desk inside international arrivals or from the stand set up by the bus stop at the international terminal departure point. Helpful staff and a pamphlet with a useful map help you figure out which drop-offs are most useful. Note that if you're headed straight for the bus depot (see below) you need to transfer to another Airporter service closer to downtown. Returning to the airport, buses run round the same pick-up points, including the bus depot.

Taxis into town cost about $25, limos a few dollars more. **Public transport** is cheaper, but slower and involves a change of bus – take the BC Metro Transit bus #100 to the corner of 70th Street and Granville (it leaves the domestic terminal roughly every 30min), then change to the #20 or #21 which drops off downtown on Granville Street. Tickets cost $2.25 rush hour, $1.50 off-peak, and exact change is required to buy tickets on board: make sure you get a transfer if the driver doesn't automatically give you one (see "City transport" below for more on transfers).

It's also useful to know that you can pick up direct **buses** to Victoria from the airport: ask for details at the bus desk in international arrivals, or go straight to the hotel shuttle bus stop outside the international terminal and take the Delta Hotels Shuttle, (every 15min, $4), which runs 5km to the Delta Pacific Resort and Conference Centre. In the Delta lobby, look to the left for the Tour and Transportation desk where you can purchase a Pacific Coach Lines (☎662-8074) ticket, inclusive of ferry crossing, for the next Victoria-bound coach (hourly in summer, twice-hourly in winter; 3hr 30min; $25). Perimeter buses (☎266-5386) run two direct daily services – currently departing 10am and 7.30pm – to Whistler (2hr 15min; $45), with pick-ups outside the domestic and international terminals. Quick Shuttle (☎940-4428 or 1-800-665-2122) run eight daily departures from outside the domestic terminal to Bellingham Airport (1hr 20min; $19), downtown Seattle (2hr 40min; $31) and Sea-Tac Airport (3hr 10min; $38). Tickets are available from the information desk in the domestic terminal.

Bus terminal

Vancouver's new main **bus terminal**, which is used by Pacific Coach Lines (for Victoria, Vancouver Island), Maverick Coach Lines (Whistler, Sunshine Coast and Nanaimo) and all Greyhound services, is in a slightly dismal area alongside the VIA Rail Pacific Central train station at 1150 Station St; ticket offices for all companies are on the inside on the left as you face the station entrance. It's too far to walk to downtown from here, so bear left from the station through a small park, to the Science World–Main St SkyTrain station and it's a couple of stops to downtown (take a train

---

ONWARDS FROM VANCOUVER

Vancouver is at the hub of transport links to many parts of western Canada. Deciding where to move **onward from the city** – and how to go – presents a wealth of possibilities. We've listed the basic alternatives, together with cross-references to more detailed accounts of the various options.

Alaska and the Yukon You can fly to Whitehorse (see p.820) in the Yukon directly from Vancouver, but there are no non-stop flights to Alaska from the city: all go via Seattle in the US. You can fly to Seattle or take a bus to Sea-Tac Airport in around three hours from Vancouver Airport or the city bus depot (see "Arrival and information" above for details). You can **drive** to Alaska through southern British Columbia to Dawson Creek, where you can pick up the Alaska Hwy (see p.815) which runs through the Yukon to Fairbanks. Alternatively drive to Prince George, head west towards Prince Rupert and then strike north up the more adventurous Cassiar Hwy (see p.809) to connect with the Alaska Hwy in the Yukon. Using **public transport** you could take either a BC Rail train (see "Arrival and information") or Greyhound bus to Prince George, connecting with another Greyhound to Dawson Creek and Whitehorse. Alaskon Express buses link Whitehorse with Alaskan destinations. There is also a two-day bus service from Prince Rupert (see p.798) to the Yukon via the Cassiar Hwy.

To travel to Alaska by **boat** from Vancouver you need to go via Bellingham (in the US), Prince Rupert, or Port Hardy on Vancouver Island (see p.738).

British Columbia Two main **road** routes strike east from Vancouver towards Alberta and the Canadian Rockies – the Trans-Canada Highway and Hwy 3, both served by regular Greyhound **buses**. Both give access to the Okanagan, known for its warm-watered lakes

---

marked "Waterfront"); tickets ($1.50) are available from platform machines. Alternatively, you could take a taxi downtown from the station for about $6. There are **left-luggage** facilities here and a useful **hotel board**, whose free phone line connects to some of the city's genuine cheapies (but check locations) – some of whom will deduct the taxi fare from the terminal from your first night's bill.

Trains

The skeletal **VIA Rail** services also operate out of Pacific Central Station (☎669-3050 or 1-800-561-8630); they run to and from Jasper ($152), where there are connections for Prince George and Prince Rupert, and on to Edmonton ($212) and the east (3 weekly Mon, Thurs & Sat). There is a chance that the closed VIA–Amtrak service between Vancouver and Seattle will be reopened – contact the Infocentre for the latest. At present the train has been replaced by bus services: the Quick Shuttle operates from the airport (see p.649) to and from Sea-Tac Airport, downtown Seattle and Bellingham Airport. Greyhound in Seattle (☎214/789-7000) and Trailways in Vancouver (☎604/875-1307) run one daily service each between Vancouver and Seattle.

A second train station, belonging to the provincial **BC Rail**, at 1311 W 1st St, in North Vancouver (☎984-5246 or 1-800-339-8752 in BC, 1-800-663-8238 from the rest of Canada and US), provides passenger services to and from Whistler (1 daily; 2hr 35min; $29), Lillooet (1 daily; 5hr 35min; $63), and Prince George (3 weekly; 13hr 30min; $185) via 100 Mile House, Williams Lake and Quesnel. Note that in the summer they also run very popular **excursion trips** to Squamish aboard the *Royal Hudson* steam train, sometimes combined with a sea cruise (train $45 return, train/boat $78 return). For more on this, see the "North of Vancouver" section on p.778.

Information

The **Vancouver Travel Infocentre** is in the Waterfront Centre at 200 Burrard St, at the corner of Canada Place Way (June–Aug daily 8am–6pm; Sept–May Mon–Fri

and summer resorts, and to the beautiful mountain and lakes enclave of the Kootenays (see p.762). VIA **trains** run through the region via Kamloops to Jasper (for the Rockies) and Edmonton three times weekly. Buses and BC Rail trains also serve the **Cariboo** region, the duller central part of the province. Several mouthwatering itineraries can be put together by combining car or public transport journeys in the BC interior with BC Ferries' connections from Port Hardy on Vancouver Island (see below) to either Bella Coola or Prince Rupert.

Calgary and the Canadian Rockies It takes between ten and twelve hours to drive to Calgary on the Trans-Canada Highway, and about ninety minutes less to reach the heart of the Canadian Rockies, Banff. Special express service Greyhound buses operate over the same route. There is no longer a VIA Rail passenger service to Calgary. Very frequent one-hour flights connect Vancouver and Calgary, and charter operators such as Canada 3000 offer highly competitive rates on this route.

Seattle Regular fifty-minute flights connect Vancouver with Seattle in the US. Greyhound or Quick Shuttle buses offer a less expensive alternative from Vancouver Airport or the city bus depot.

Vancouver Island Numerous **ferries** ply between Vancouver and three points on its eponymous island – Swartz Bay (for Victoria), Nanaimo and Comox. Most leave from Tsawwassen and Horseshoe Bay, terminals about thirty minutes' drive south and west of downtown respectively. As a foot passenger you can buy inclusive bus and ferry tickets from Vancouver to Victoria or Nanaimo. Car drivers should make reservations well in advance for all summer crossings (see pp.686–687 for full details of getting to Vancouver Island). **Public transport** connects to the Pacific Rim National Park, the island's highlight, and to Port Hardy on the island's northern tip for ferry connections to Prince Rupert and Bella Coola.

8.30am–5pm, Sat 9am–5pm; ☎683-2000 or 1-800-663-6000). Besides information on the city and much of southeastern British Columbia, the office provides **foreign exchange** facilities, BC Transit tickets and information, and tickets to sports and entertainment events. It's also got one of the most comprehensive **accommodation services** imaginable, backed up by bulging photo albums of hotel rooms and B&Bs. Smaller kiosks open in the summer (July & Aug) in Stanley Park and outside Eaton's Department Store on the corner of Georgia and Granville (daily 9.30am–5.30pm, Thurs & Fri till 9pm).

City transport

Vancouver's **public transport** system is an efficient, integrated network of bus, light-rail (SkyTrain), SeaBus and ferry services which are operated by BC Transit (daily 6.30am–11.30pm; call ☎521-0400 for information).

Tickets are valid across the system for bus, SkyTrain and SeaBus. Generally they cost $1.50 for journeys in the large central Zone 1 ($2.25 or $3 for longer two- and three-zone journeys – though you're unlikely to go out of Zone 1 – and the SeaBus during peak hours). They are valid for transfers throughout the system for ninety minutes from the time of issue; on buses you should ask for a transfer ticket if the driver doesn't automatically give you one. Otherwise, you can buy tickets individually (or in books of ten for $13.75) at station offices or machines, 7-Eleven stores, or any other shop displaying a blue and red BC Transit sticker (so-called "Faredealer" outlets). You must carry tickets with you as proof of payment. Probably the simplest and cheapest deal if you're going to be making three or more journeys in a day is to buy a **Day Pass** ($4.50), valid after 9.30am Monday to Friday, all day Saturday and Sunday; monthly passes are $54. If you buy these over the counter at stores or elsewhere (not in machines) they're "Scratch & Ride" – you scratch out the day and month before travel. If you lose anything on the transit system go to the **lost property** office at the SkyTrain

Stadium Station (Mon–Fri 8.30am–5pm; ☎682-7887 or 985-7777 for items left on West Van buses). If you don't want to use public transport, **car and bicycle rental** and **taxis** are easy to come by – see "Listings" on p.680 for details.

Buses

The invaluable *BC Transit Guide* ($1.50) is available from the Infocentre and Faredealer shops, while free **bus** timetables can be found at the Infocentre, 7–Eleven stores and the central library. The free *Discover Vancouver on the Transit* pamphlet from the Infocentre is also extremely useful. You can buy tickets on the bus, but make sure you have the right change (they don't carry any) to shovel into the box by the driver; ask specially if you want a transfer ticket. If you have a pass or transfer, simply show the driver. Normal buses stop running around midnight, when a rather patchy "Night Owl" service comes into effect on major routes until about 4am. Note that blue **West Van** buses (☎985-7777) also operate (usually to North and West Vancouver destinations) in the city and BC Transit tickets are valid on these buses as well. The box below shows some of Vancouver's more useful routes.

SeaBuses

The **SeaBuses** ply between downtown and Lonsdale Quay in North Vancouver, a ride definitely worth taking for its own sake: the views of the mountains across Burrard Inlet, the port and the downtown skyline are superb. The downtown terminal is Waterfront Station in the old Canadian Pacific station buildings at the foot of Granville Street. There is no ticket office, only a ticket machine, but you can get a ticket from the small newsagent immediately on your left as you face the long gallery that takes you to the boats. Two 400-seat catamarans make the thirteen-minute crossing every fifteen or thirty minutes (6.30am–12.30am). Arrival in North Vancouver is at Lonsdale Quay, where immediately to the left is a bus terminal for connections to Grouse Mountain and other North Vancouver destinations. Bicycles can cross free during off-peak periods; otherwise you need an extra ticket for them.

BUS ROUTES

Some of the more important Vancouver **bus routes** are:

#1 Gastown – English Bay loop.

#3 & #8 Gastown – Downtown – Marine Drive.

#4 & #10 Granville Street – University of British Columbia–Museum of Anthropology.

#23, #35, #123 & #135 – Downtown (Pender and Burrard) – Stanley Park.

#50 – Gastown – False Creek – Broadway.

#51 SeaBus Terminal – Downtown – Granville Island.

#19 Pender Street (Downtown) – Stanley Park (Stanley Park Loop).

#20 & #17 Downtown – Marine Drive; transfer to #100 for the airport at Granville and 70th Street.

#236 Lonsdale Quay terminal (North Vancouver) – Capilano Suspension Bridge–Grouse Mountain.

Some **scenic routes** are worth travelling for their own sakes:

#250 Georgia Street (Downtown) – North Vancouver – West Vancouver – Horseshoe Bay.

#52 "Around the Park" service takes 30min through Stanley Park (April–Oct Sat, Sun & holidays only); board at Stanley Park Loop (connections from #23, #35 or #135) or Denman Street (connections from #1, #3 or #8).

#351 Howe Street – White Rock – Crescent Beach (1hr each way).

#210 Pender Street – Phibbs Exchange; change there for the #211 (mountain route) or #212 (ocean views) to Deep Cove.

Ferries

The city also has a variety of small **ferries** – glorified bathtubs – run over similar routes by two rival companies: Aquabus (☎689-5858) and False Creek Ferries (☎684-7781). These provide a useful, very frequent and fun service. If you wish to reach Granville Island from downtown ($1.75), Aquabus, from the foot of Hornby Street, is the most convenient – or the Vanier Park museum complex from downtown ($1.75) or Granville Island ($3). You buy **tickets** on board. Both companies also offer what amount to mini-cruises up False Creek, with hourly connections from Granville Island to Science World ($3) and the Plaza of Nations ($2). You can pick up the Aquabus boat at the Arts Club Theatre on Granville Island, the foot of Hornby Street downtown or – with False Creek Ferries – below the Aquatic Centre at the northern end of Burrard Bridge on Granville Island or below the spit and small harbour near the Maritime Museum in Vanier Park.

SkyTrain

Vancouver's single light-rail line – **SkyTrain** – is a model of its type: driverless, completely computerized and magnetically propelled, half underground and half on raised track. It covers 22km between the downtown Waterfront Station (housed in the CPR building with the SeaBus terminal) and the southeastern suburb of New Westminster. Only the first three or four stations – Waterfront, Burrard, Granville and Stadium – are of any practical use to the casual visitor, but the 39-minute trip along the twenty-station line is worth taking if only to see how the Canadians do these things – spotless interiors and Teutonic punctuality.

Accommodation

Vancouver has a surprisingly large number of **inexpensive hotels**, but some – mainly in the area east of downtown – are of a dinginess at odds with the city's highly polished image. Gastown, Chinatown and the area between them hold the cheaper places, often on top of a bar where live bands and late-night drinking will keep you awake till the small hours. These areas are not safe for women at night, and everyone needs to avoid the backstreets. If you really need to stick to the rock-bottom price bracket, you're better off in the hostels, *YWCA* or one of the invariably dodgy hotels north of the Granville Street Bridge, a tame but tacky red-light area. **Mid-range hotels** are still reasonable ($65–90), but Vancouver is a tourist city and things can get tight in summer – book ahead for the best and most popular places such as the *Sylvia* and *Kingston*. A lot of the nicer options (including the *Sylvia*) are in the West End, a quiet residential area bordering Vancouver's wonderful Stanley Park, only five or ten minutes' walk from downtown. Out of season, hotels in all categories offer reductions, and you can reckon on thirty percent discounts on the prices below. Remember, too, that the prices below are for doubles, though even the smartest hotels will introduce an extra bed into a double room at very little extra cost if there are three of you.

B&B accommodation can be booked through agencies, but most of them operate as a phone service only and require two days' notice – it's better to try the Infocentre's accommodation service first. Though seldom central or cheap – reckon on $70 plus for a double – B&Bs are likely to be relaxed and friendly, and if you choose well you can have beaches, gardens, barbecues and as little or as much privacy as you want. The following **B&B agencies** have accommodation throughout the city: A Home Away from Home (☎873-4888); Best Canadian (☎738-7207); Born Free (☎298-8815) Canada West Accommodations (☎929-1424); and Town and Country (☎731-5942).

In addition to the **hostels**, budget accommodation is available in summer at the **University of British Columbia**, though this is a long way from downtown, and most rooms go to convention visitors – enquire at the Walter Gage Residence in the Student

Union Mall (☎822-1010). Vancouver is not a camper's city – the majority of the in-city **campgrounds** are for RVs only and will turn you away if you've only got a tent. We've listed the few places that won't.

Hotels

Barclay Hotel, 1348 Robson and Jervis (☎688-8850, fax 688-2534). One of the nicer of several hotels at the north end of Robson, with ninety rooms, a chintzy French rustic ambience, and rated as one of the city's bargains. ②–④.

Buchan Hotel, 1906 Haro, near Robson and Denman (☎685-5354 or 1-800-668-6654, fax 685-5367). Some smallish rooms, past their best, but still a genuine bargain given the peaceful residential location, only a block from Stanley Park and English Bay Beach. ③–④.

Burrard Motor Inn, 1100 Burrard near Helmcken (☎663-0366 or 1-800-663-0366, fax 681-9753). A fairly central and pleasantly dated motel with standard fittings: some rooms look onto a charming garden courtyard, and some have kitchens. ④.

Days Inn Vancouver Downtown, 921 W Pender and Burrard (☎681-4335 or 1-800-329-7466). Rather a city institution, this old seventy-room, seven-storey block in the financial district has more character than most and lots of original Art Deco touches, but looks tatty, and streetfront rooms are likely to be noisy. ⑥.

Hotel Dakota, 654 Nelson St on the corner of Granville (☎605-4333 or 1-888-605-5333, fax 605-4334). The location is not pleasant, but this is the exception to the rule among the grim hotels at the lower end of Granville Street; clean, cheap and newly renovated rooms in big, bright-looking building. ④.

Dominion Hotel, 210 Abbott and Water (☎681-6666, fax 681-5855). A nice, newly decorated old hotel on the edge of Gastown – ask for a new room with private bathroom, preferably well away from the live music. ③–⑤.

Canadian Pacific Hotel Vancouver, 900 West Georgia (☎684-3131 or 1-800-701-9070, fax 662-1929). This traditional old hotel, recently given a multimillion-dollar face-lift, is the city's most famous and prestigious. The place to stay if money's no object and you want old-world style and downtown location. Doubles among the 550 rooms range from $215 to $415. ⑧.

Canadian Pacific Waterfront Central Hotel, 900 Canada Place Way (☎691-1991). Another prestigious *Canadian Pacific* hotel, this time a new multistorey affair on the dazzling downtown waterfront. ⑧.

Granville Island Hotel and Marina, 1253 Johnson St (☎683-7373 or 1-800-663-1840, fax 683-3061). You're away from central downtown, but on the other hand you're at the heart of one of the city's trendiest and most enjoyable little enclaves. You pay a premium for this and for the spectacular waterfront setting. ⑥–⑦.

Holiday Inn Downtown, 1110 Howe St (☎684-2151, 1-800-465-4329 or hotel direct 1-800-663-9151, fax 684-4736). Central, large and – unlike the dingier hotels – you'll know what to expect, though at this price there's plenty of alternative choice around town. ⑥–⑦.

Kingston Hotel, 757 Richards and Robson (☎684-9024, fax 684-9917). This well-known bargain is handily sited for downtown and its clean and well-decorated interior affects the spirit of a "European-style" hotel. Rooms with or without private bathroom plus a modest but free breakfast to start the day. With the *Sylvia*, by far the best at its price in the city. Book ahead. Long-stay terms available. ②–③.

Pacific Palisades, 1277 Robson St (☎688-0461 or 1-800-663-1815, fax 688-4374). Not quite up there in the luxury bracket with the *Canadian Pacific* hotels, but still one of the city's best-known top-price hotels. ⑦.

Patricia Budget Hotel, 403 East Hastings (☎255-4301, fax 254-7154). A well-known and widely advertised budget choice with 24 rooms, but rather far from downtown in the heart of Chinatown: an exciting or grim location, depending on your point of view, though women have reported feeling distinctly unsafe in the area. Clean and newly renovated, it's the best of the many in this district. ②–③.

Riviera Motor Inn, 1431 Robson St (☎685-1301). Reasonably priced central motels such as this place are rare; the one- and two-room suites have kitchenettes. ④–⑥.

Sandman Inn, 180 West Georgia and Homer (☎681-2211 or 1-800-726-3626). Flagship of a mid-price chain with hotels all over western Canada and well placed at the eastern edge of downtown. Rooms are bland but fine and spacious as far as chain hotels go, which makes this first choice if you want something one up from the *Kingston*. ⑥.

Shatto Inn at Stanley Park, 1825 Comox St (☎681-8920). A small, quiet, family-run place two blocks from the park and the beach. Some of the rooms have balconies and/or kitchen units. ④.

Sunset Inn Apartment Hotel, 1111 Burnaby between Davie and Thurlow (☎684-8763 or 1-800-786-1997, fax 669-3340). One of the best West End "apartment" hotels and a good spot for a longer stay – spacious rooms (all with kitchens and balconies), laundry, nearby shops. 10min walk to downtown. ③–⑤.

Sylvia Hotel, 1154 Gilford St (☎681-9321). A local landmark located in a "heritage" building, this is a popular place with a high reputation, making reservations essential. It's by the beach two blocks from Stanley Park, and its snug bar, quiet, old-world charm and sea views make it one of Vancouver's best. ④–⑥.

West End Guest House, 1362 Haro near Jervis (☎681-2889). A wonderful small guesthouse with an old-time parlour and bright rooms, each with private bathroom; expensive, but you still need to book well in advance. Full breakfast included. No smoking. ⑥.

Hostels

Cambie International Hostel, 300 Cambie St at Cordova (☎684-6466). Private hostel just off Gastown's main streets, so a much better position than the *Backpacker* places (see below). ②–③.

Globetrotter's Inn, 170 West Esplanade, North Vancouver (☎988-5141). Less convenient than the central hostels, though still only 5min and two blocks from Lonsdale Quay and the SeaBus terminal. Laid-back and a little battered. Dorm beds, singles and doubles available. ②.

Vancouver Downtown Hostel (HI), 1114 Burnaby St (☎684-4565, fax 684-4540). The newly opened and more central of the city's two official HI hostels is located in the city's West End, with 223 beds in shared and private rooms (maximum of four per room). Bike rental and storage as well as laundry. To get here from downtown, take bus # 1 or # 8 along Davies Street to Thurlow and walk one block south. ①–②.

Vancouver Jericho Beach Hostel (HI), 1515 Discovery St (☎224-3208, fax 224-4852). Canada's biggest youth hostel has a superb position by Jericho Beach south of the city – take bus #4 from Granville Street to the Jericho Park stop on 4th Avenue. It fills up quickly, occasionally leading to a three-day limit in summer; open all day, with an excellent cafeteria, but the 2am curfew and lights out are rigidly enforced. There are dorm beds and a few private rooms, with reductions for members and free bunks occasionally offered in return for a couple of hours' work. ①.

Vincent's Backpacker's Hostel, 927 Main St (☎682-2441). Well-known backpackers' retreat, with no curfew, but recent reports suggest that its cleanliness and organization have deteriorated. Seedy eastern edge of downtown location but convenient for SkyTrain station; 150 rooms, but you should still book or arrive early (office open 8am–midnight). Another similar *Backpacker's Hostel* has opened at 347 West Pender St (☎688-0112). Both have dorm beds, singles and doubles. ①.

YWCA Hotel/Residence, 733 Beatty St (☎895-5830 or 1-800-663-1424, fax 681-2550). An excellent new place in a perfect east downtown location close to the stunning central library. Top-value rooms (especially for small groups) spread over eleven floors with a choice of private, shared or hall bathrooms. TVs in all rooms, and; there are sports and cooking facilities as well as a cheap cafeteria. Open to men, women and families. Singles ($49), doubles ($61, $77 or $99), triples ($89) four-($119) or five-person ($134) rooms available; long-term rates offered in winter. ③–④.

Camping

Burnaby Cariboo RV Park, 8765 Cariboo Place, Burnaby (☎420-1722 or 1-800-667-9901, fax 420-4782). This site has luxurious facilities (indoor pool, Jacuzzi, laundry, free showers) and a separate tenting area away from the RVs. Take Cariboo exit from Hwy 1. Free shuttle bus to various sights. $21–32.95.

Capilano Mobile Park, 295 Tomahawk, West Vancouver (☎987-4722, fax 987-2015). The most central site for trailers and tents, beneath the north foot of the Lion's Gate Bridge. Reservations (with deposit) essential June to August. $18–32.

Mount Seymour Provincial Park, North Vancouver (☎986-2261). Lovely spot, with full facilities, but only a few tent sites alongside car parks 2 and 3. July–Sept. $12.

Richmond RV Park and Campground, Hollybridge and River Road, Richmond (☎270-7878 or 1-800-755-4905, fax 244-9713). Best of the RV outfits, with the usual facilities; take Hwy 99 to the Westminster Highway and follow signs. April 15–Oct 15. $16–23.

The City

Vancouver is not a city which offers or requires lots of relentless sightseeing. Its breathtaking physical beauty makes it a place where often it's enough just to wander and watch the world go by – "the sort of town", wrote Jan Morris, "nearly everyone would want to live in." In summer you'll probably end up doing what the locals do, if not actually sailing, hiking, skiing, fishing or whatever, then certainly going to the beach, lounging in one of the parks or spending time in waterfront cafés.

In addition to the myriad leisure activities, however, there are a handful of sights that make worthwhile viewing by any standards. You'll inevitably spend a good deal of time in the **downtown** area and its Victorian-era equivalent, **Gastown**, now a renovated and less than convincing pastiche of its past. **Chinatown**, too, could easily absorb a morning, and contains more than its share of interesting shops, restaurants and rumbustiously busy streets. For a taste of the city's sensual side, hit **Stanley Park**, a huge area of semi-wild parkland and beaches that crowns the northern tip of the downtown peninsula. Take a walk or a bike ride here and follow it up with a stroll to the **beach**. Be certain to spend a morning on **Granville Island**, by far the city's most tempting spot for wandering and people-watching. If you prefer a cultural slant on things, hit the formidable **Museum of Anthropology** or the other museums of the Vanier Park complex, the latter easily accessible from Granville Island.

At a push, you could cram the city's essentials into a couple of days. If you're here for a longer stay, though, you'll want to venture further out from downtown: trips across Burrard Inlet to **North Vancouver**, worth making for the views from the SeaBus ferry alone, lend a different panoramic perspective of the city, and lead into the mountains and forests that give Vancouver its tremendous setting. Most popular trips here are the to Capilano Suspension Bridge, something of a triumph of PR over substance, and to the more worthwhile cable-car trip up **Grouse Mountain** for some staggering views of the city.

Downtown

You soon get the hang of Vancouver's **downtown** district, an arena of streets and shopping malls centred on **Robson Street**. On hot summer evenings it's like a latter-day vision of la dolce vita – a dynamic meeting place crammed with bars, restaurants, late-night stores, and bronzed youths preening in bars or cafés ostentatiously cruising in open-topped cars. At other times a more sedate class hangs out on the steps of the Vancouver Art Gallery or glides in and out of the two big department stores, Eaton's and The Bay. Downtown's other principal thoroughfares are **Burrard Street** – all smart shops, hotels and offices – and **Granville Street**, partly pedestrianized with plenty of shops and cinemas, but curiously seedy in places, especially at its southern end near the Granville Street Bridge. New development, however, is taking downtown's reach further east, and at some point in your stay you should try to catch the new **public library** at 350 West Georgia, a focus of this growth and a striking piece of modern architecture to boot.

For the best possible introduction to Vancouver, though, you should walk down to the waterfront and **Canada Place**, the Canadian pavilion for Expo '86 and another architectural *tour de force* that houses a luxury hotel, cruise-ship terminal and two glitzy convention centres. For all its excess, however, it makes a superb viewpoint, with stunning vistas of port, mountains, sea and buzzing boats, helicopters and float planes. The port activity, especially, is mesmerizing. North America's busiest, the **port** began by exporting timber (inevitably) in 1864 in the shape of fence pickets to Australia. Today it handles seventy million tonnes of cargo annually, turns over $40 billion

VANCOUVER'S BEACHES

Vancouver, it's rather surprising to find, has **beaches**. Perhaps not of Malibu or Bondi standard, but beaches just the same, and ones that look and feel like the real thing, even if much of the sand comes from Japan in container ships. All are clean and well kept: the clarity of the water is remarkable given the size of the city's port – and the majority have lifeguards during the summer months. The best face each other across False Creek and English Bay, starting with Stanley Park's three adjacent beaches: **English Bay Beach**, ranged along Beach Avenue; **Second Beach**, to the north, which also features a shallow onshore swimming pool; and **Third Beach**, further north still, least crowded of the three and the one with the best views of West Vancouver and the mountains. English Bay at the southern end of Denman is the most readily accessible, and easily visited after seeing Stanley Park.

Across the water to the south and west of the Burrard Bridge, **Kitsilano Beach**, or "Kits", is named – like the district behind it – after Chief Khahtsahlano, a Squamish chieftain of a band who once owned the area. Walk here from Vanier Park and the museums (30min) on the coast path or, from downtown, take a #22 **bus** southbound on Burrard Street. Kits is a city favourite and the busiest and most self-conscious of the beaches. It's especially popular with the university, volleyball and rippling torso crowd, and the more well-heeled locals. Families also come here, though, to take advantage of the warm and safe swimming area, while sunbathers can take up a position on the grass to the rear. Vancouver's largest and most popular outdoor heated pool is the **lido** at Yew and Cornwall (mid-May to early Sept only daily; $3.70), while the **shoreline path** is a lovely place for an evening stroll, cycle or time out on a bench to watch the streetlife. Follow the path all the way east and it takes you to Granville Island by way of Vanier Park and the museums. A former hippie and alternative-lifestyle hang-out, Kits still betrays shades of its past and, with nearby bars and restaurants to fuel the party spirit, there's always plenty going on (though there's also sometimes a vaguely meat-market sort of atmosphere).

Jericho Beach, west of Kits and handy for the youth hostel, is a touch quieter and serves as a hang-out for the windsurfing crowd. Still further west, Jericho blurs into **Locarno Beach** and **Spanish Banks**, progressively less crowded, and the start of a fringe of sand and parkland that continues round to the University of British Columbia (UBC) campus. Locals rate Spanish Banks the most relaxed of the city's beaches, while Locarno is one of its most spectacular, especially at low tide, when the sand seems to stretch for ever. Bikers and walkers use the dirt track at the top of Locarno, beyond which a broad sward of grass with picnic tables and benches runs to the road. You can rent canoes at Jericho from Ecomarine Ocean Kayak, 1688 Duranleau St (☎689-7575).

At low tide the more athletically inclined could walk all the way round to UBC (otherwise take the bus as for the Museum of Anthropology; see p.666), where the famous clothing-optional **Wreck Beach** lies just off the campus area below NW Marine Drive – ask any student to point you towards the half-hidden access paths. It's inevitably aroused a fair bit of prudish criticism in the past, but at the moment attitudes seem more relaxed. The atmosphere is generally laid-back – though women have been known to complain of voyeurs – and nude peddlers are often on hand to sell you anything from pizza and illegal smokeables to (bona fide) massage and hair-braiding. Finally, **Ambleside**, west of the Park Royal Mall along Marine Drive (turn south at 13th St West), is the most accessible beach if you're in North or West Vancouver.

in trade and processes 3000 ships a year from almost a hundred countries. Canada Place's design, and the manner in which it juts into the port, is meant to suggest a ship, and you can walk the building's perimeter as if "on deck", stopping to read the boards that describe the immediate cityscape and the appropriate pages of its history. Inside are expensive shops, a restaurant and an IMAX cinema (☎682-6422 for programme); most of the films shown – often on boats, rock concerts and obscure wildlife – are a waste of a good screen.

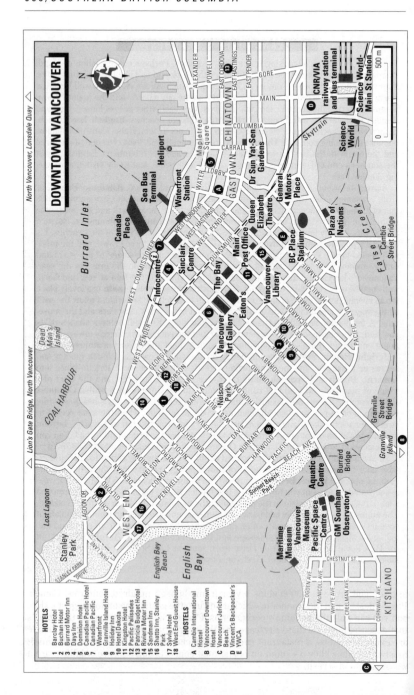

DOWNTOWN VANCOUVER

North Vancouver, Lonsdale Quay

Lion's Gate Bridge, North Vancouver

Dead Man's Island

Burrard Inlet

Stanley Park

Lost Lagoon

COAL HARBOUR

WEST END

English Bay Beach

English Bay

Sunset Beach Park

Aquatic Centre

Burrard Bridge

Maritime Museum

Vancouver Museum

Pacific Space Centre

GM Southam Observatory

KITSILANO

Granville Island

Granville Street Bridge

False Creek

Cambie Street Bridge

Plaza of Nations

Science World

Skytrain

Science World–Main St Station

CNR/VIA railway station and bus terminal

CHINATOWN

GASTOWN

Dr Sun Yat-Sen Gardens

General Motors Place

BC Place Stadium

Vancouver Library

Post Office

Queen Elizabeth Theatre

The Bay

Eaton's

Vancouver Art Gallery

Sinclair Centre

Infocentre

Waterfront Station

Sea Bus Terminal

Canada Place

Heliport

Mapletree Square

Streets labelled: ALEXANDER, POWELL, EAST CORDOVA, EAST HASTINGS, EAST PENDER, GORE, MAIN, COLUMBIA, CARRALL, ABBOTT, WATER, WEST CORDOVA, WEST HASTINGS, WEST PENDER, DUNSMUIR, WEST COMMISSIONER, WEST PENDER, GEORGIA, ALBERNI, ROBSON, BARCLAY, HARO, NELSON Park, SMITHE, NELSON, HELMCKEN, DAVIE, BURNABY, HARWOOD, PACIFIC, BEACH AVE, PENDRELL, COMOX, DENMAN, BIDWELL, CARDERO, NICOLA, BROUGHTON, JERVIS, BUTE, THURLOW, BURRARD, HORNBY, HOWE, GRANVILLE, SEYMOUR, RICHARDS, HOMER, HAMILTON, MAINLAND, CAMBIE, BEATTY, PACIFIC BLVD

PARK LANE, LAGOON DR, CHILCO, GILFORD, STANLEY PARK DRIVE

OGDEN AVE, McNICOL AVE, WHYTE AVE, CREELMAN AVE, CORNWALL AVE, CHESTNUT ST

N

500 m
0

HOTELS
1 Barclay Hotel
2 Buchan Hotel
3 Burrard Motor Inn
4 Days Inn
5 Dominion Hotel
6 Canadian Pacific Hotel
7 Canadian Pacific Waterfront
8 Granville Island Hotel
9 Holiday Inn
10 Hotel Dakota
11 Kingston Hotel
12 Pacific Palisades
13 Patricia Budget Hotel
14 Riviera Motor Inn
15 Sandman Inn
16 Shatto Inn, Stanley Park
17 Sylvia Hotel
18 West End Guest House

HOSTELS
A Cambie International Hostel
B Vancouver Downtown Hostel
C Vancouver Jericho Beach
D Vincent's Backpacker's
E YWCA

An alternative to Canada Place's vantage point, the nearby **Harbour Centre Building** at 555 West Hastings, is one of the city's tallest structures, and is known by locals either as the "urinal" or, more affectionately, the "hamburger", after its bulging upper storeys. On a fine day it's definitely worth paying to ride the stomach-churning, all-glass, SkyLift elevators that run up the side of the tower – 167m in a minute – to the fortieth-storey observation deck, or "The Lookout!", with its staggering 360°-degree, views (daily: May–Sept 8.30am–10.30pm; Oct–April 9am–9pm; $8; ☎689-0421). Admission is valid all day so you can return and look out over the bright lights of Vancouver at night.

Much of the **Expo site** here and to the east has been levelled or is undergoing rigorous redevelopment, and to see its remaining sights requires a long walk from central downtown (take the SkyTrain or ferries from Granville Island instead). The geodesic dome is the main survivor, and has become a striking city landmark – but the museum it now houses, **Science World** at Québec St–Terminal Avenue near Science World–Main St SkyTrain station – is something of a disappointment (Mon–Fri 10am–5pm, Sat & Sun 10am–6pm; $9 or $12 with Omnimax film; add $1.50 for Laser Theatre; ☎268-6363). Probably only children, at whom the place seems largely aimed, will be satisfied by the various hi-tech, hands-on displays, which include the opportunity to make thunderous amounts of noise on electronic instruments and drum machines. Three galleries deal with three basic themes – physics, biology and music – with a fourth devoted to temporary exhibitions, but probably the best things here are the building itself and the vast screen of the Omnimax Cinema at the top of the dome.

Another remnant of the Expo is the 60,000-seat **BC Place Stadium** at 1 Robson St (☎669-2300), the world's largest air-inflated dome; unless you're there for a sporting event, the "mushroom" or "marshmallow in bondage", in popular parlance, isn't worth the bother. To visit, take the SkyTrain to Stadium station or buses #15 east on Robson or #17 on Burrard. Its thunder has also been slightly stolen by the new **General Motors Place**, a big new 20,000-seat stadium (known locally as "The Garage") that's home to the Vancouver Canucks ice-hockey team and Vancouver Grizzlies NBA basketball team.

The Vancouver Art Gallery

Centrally located in the imposing old city courthouse is the rather exorbitant **Vancouver Art Gallery**, located at the corner of Howe and Robson (June–Sept Mon–Wed & Fri 10am–6pm, Thurs 10am–9pm, Sat 10am–5am, Sun noon–5pm; Oct–May Wed–Fri 10am–6pm, Sat 10am–5pm, Sun noon–5pm, closed Mon & Tues; $9.50, "pay what you wish" June–Sept Thurs 5–9pm; ☎662-4700). It looks as if it ought to contain a treasure trove of art, but too much space is given to dud works of the sort that give modern art a bad name. What redeems the place are its temporary exhibitions and the powerful and almost surreal works of Emily Carr, who was born on Vancouver Island in 1871 and whose paintings – characterized by deep greens and blues – evoke something of the scale and intensity of the West Coast and its native peoples. A sparse international collection offers Warhol and Lichtenstein, with token rooms of half a dozen Italian, Flemish and British paintings. The **gallery café** is excellent, with a suntrap of a terrace if you want to sit outside.

Gastown

An easy walk east of downtown – five minutes from Canada Place and concentrated largely on Water Street – **Gastown** is a determined piece of city rejuvenation aimed fair and square at the tourist, distinguished by new cobbles, fake gas lamps, *Ye Olde English Tea Room*-type cafés and a generally overpolished patina. The name derives from "Gassy" Jack Leighton, a retired sailor turned publican and self-proclaimed "mayor", who arrived on site by canoe with his native wife and a mangy yellow dog in 1867, quickly opening a bar to service the nearby lumber mills, whose bosses banned drinking on or near the yards. Leighton's statue stands in **Maple Tree Square**, Gastown's heart, focus of its main streets and reputed site of this first tavern. Trade was brisk, and a second bar opened, soon followed by a village of sorts – "Gassy's Town" – which, though swept away by fire in 1886, formed in effect the birthplace of modern Vancouver. Over the years, the downtown focus moved west and something of Gastown's boozy beginnings returned to haunt it, as its cheap hotels and warehouses turned into a skid row for junkies and alcoholics. By the 1970s the area was declared a historic site – the buildings are the city's oldest – and an enthusiastic beautification programme was set in motion.

The end product never quite became the dynamic, city-integrated spot the planners had hoped, and was slated for years by locals as something of a tourist trap, though recent signs suggest that interesting cafés, clubs and restaurants are slowly beginning to make themselves felt. It's certainly worth a stroll for its buskers, Sunday crowds and occasional points of interest. These do not include the hype-laden two-tonne **steam-powered clock**, the world's first and hopefully last, at the west end of Water Street. It's invariably surrounded by tourists armed with cocked cameras, all awaiting the miniature Big Ben's toots and whistles every fifteen minutes, and bellowing performances on the hour that seem to presage imminent explosion. The steam comes from an underground system that also heats surrounding buildings. Nearby you'll find the **Inuit Gallery**, a large commercial showcase of Inuit art at 345 Water St (Mon–Sat 9.30am–5.30pm). Interesting and eye-openingly informative is the **Western Canadian Wilderness Committee** shop and office, 20 Water St (☎683-8220 or 1-800-661-9453) – if you thought BC was people, trees and nature in peace and harmony, this leading conservation group will soon disabuse you.

Probably the most surprising aspect of Gastown, however, is the contrast between its manicured pavements and the down-at-heel streets immediately to the south and east. The bustling hub of **alternative Vancouver**, the area between Gastown and Chinatown is both a skid row and a haven for secondhand clothes shops, bookshops, galleries, new designers and cheap five-and-dimes. In places, however, this area recalls Gastown's bad old days: unpleasantly seedy, pocked with the dingiest of dingy bars and hotels, and inhabited by characters to match.

Chinatown

Vancouver's vibrant **Chinatown** – clustered mainly on Pender Street from Carrall to Gore and on Keefer Street from Main to Gore (buses #22 or #19 east from Pender, or #22 north from Burrard) – is a city apart. Vancouver's 100,000 Chinese are expected soon to surpass San Francisco's as the largest Chinese community outside the Far East, and are the city's oldest and largest ethnic group after the British-descended majority. Many crossed the Pacific in 1858 to join the Fraser Valley gold rush; others followed under contract to help build the Canadian Pacific Railway. Most stayed, and found themselves treated appallingly. Denied citizenship and legal rights until as late as 1947, they sought safety and familiarity in a ghetto of their own, where clan associations and societies provided for new arrivals and the local poor – and helped build the distinctive houses of recessed balconies and ornamental roofs that have made the area a protected historic site.

Unlike Gastown's gimmickry, Chinatown is all genuine – shops, hotels, markets, tiny restaurants and dim alleys vie for attention amidst an incessant hustle of jammed pavements and the buzz of Chinese conversation. Virtually every building replicates an Eastern model without a trace of self-consciousness, and written Chinese characters feature everywhere in preference to English. Striking and unexpected after downtown's high-rise glitz, the district brings you face to face with Vancouver's oft-touted multiculturalism, and helps explain why Hong Kong immigrants continue to be attracted to the city. There's an edge to Chinatown, however, especially at night and, though central districts are fine, lone tourists are better off avoiding Hastings and the back streets.

Apart from the obvious culinary temptations (see "Eating and drinking"), Chinatown's main points of reference are its **markets**. Some of the best boast fearsome butchery displays and such edibles as live eels, flattened ducks, hundred-year-old eggs and other stuff you'll be happy not to identify. Check out the new open-air **night market** at Main and Keefer streets (summer 6pm–midnight). Keefer Street is **bakery** row, with lots of tempting stickies on offer like moon cakes and *bao*, steamed buns with a meat or sweet bean filling. On the corner of Keefer and Main is the Ten Ren Tea and Ginseng Company, with a vast range of teas, many promising cures for a variety of ailments (free tastings). In a similar vein, it's worth dropping into one of the local **herbalists** to browse amongst their panaceas: snakeskins, reindeer antlers, buffalo tongues, dried sea horses and bears' testicles are all available if you're feeling under the weather. Ming Wo, 23 East Pender, is a fantastic cookware shop, with probably every utensil ever devised, while China West, 41 East Pender, is packed with slippers, jackets, pens, cheap toys and the like. Most people also flock dutifully to the 1913 **Sam Kee Building**, at the corner of Carrall and Pender; at just 1.8m across, it's officially the world's narrowest building.

Chinatown's chief cultural attraction is the small **Dr Sun Yat-Sen Garden**, at 578 Carrall St near Pender, a 2.5-acre park billed as the first authentic, full-scale classical Chinese garden ever built outside China (May to mid-June 10am–6pm; mid-June to mid-Sept 10am–7pm; mid-Sept to April 10am–4.30pm; $5.25; ☎689-7133). Named after the founder of the first Chinese Republic, who was a frequent visitor to Vancouver, the park was created for the Expo '86 and cost $5.3 million, $500,000 of which came from the People's Republic accompanied by 52 artisans and 950 crates of materials. The latter included everything from limestone rocks from Taihu – whose jagged shapes are prized in this sort of garden – to the countless tiny pebbles that make up the intricate courtyard pavements. The whole thing is based on classical gardens developed in the city of Suzhou during the Ming dynasty (1368–1644). China's horticultural emissaries, following traditional methods that didn't allow use of a single power tool, spent thirteen months in the city replicating a Suzhou Ming garden to achieve a subtle balance of Yin and Yang: small and large, soft and hard, flowing and immovable, light and dark. Every stone, pine and flower was carefully placed and has symbolic meaning. Hourly free guided tours on the half-hour explain the Taoist philosophy behind the carefully placed elements. At first glance it all seems a touch small and austere, and isn't helped by the preponderance of sponsors' nameplates and glimpses of the road, pub and highrise outside. After a time, though, the chances are you'll find the garden working its calm and peaceful spell.

Alongside the entrance to the gardens, the **Chinese Cultural Centre**, Chinatown's community focus and a sponsor of New Year festivities, offers classes and hosts changing exhibitions. Next to the gardens and centre is a small and slightly threadbare Dr Sun Yat-Sen Park (free) which, though less worked than the Dr Sun Yat-Sen Garden, is still a pleasant place to take time out from Chinatown. Hours are the same as for the garden, and there's an alternative entrance on Columbia Street and Keefer.

Stanley Park

One of the world's great urban spaces, **Stanley Park** is Vancouver's green heart, and one of the things that lends the city its particular character. At nearly 1000 acres, it's the largest urban park in North America – less a tame collection of lawns and elms than a semi-wilderness of dense rainforest, marshland and beaches. Ocean surrounds it on three sides, with a road and parallel cycleway/pedestrian promenade following the sea wall right the way round the peninsula for a total of 10.5km. From here, views of the city and across the water to the mountains are particularly worthwhile. Away from the coastal trail network and main draw – the aquarium – the interior is nearly impenetrable scrub and forest, with few paths and few people. At the same time there are plenty of open, wooded or flower-decorated spaces to picnic, snooze or watch the world go by.

The peninsula was partially logged in the 1860s, when Vancouver was still a twinkle in "Gassy" Jack Leighton's eye, but in 1886 the newly formed city council – showing typical Canadian foresight and an admirable sense of priorities – moved to make what had become a military reserve into a permanent park. Thus its remaining first-growth forest of cedar, hemlock and Douglas fir, and the swamp now known as Lost Lagoon, were saved for posterity in the name of Lord Stanley, Canada's governor general from 1888 to 1893, who dedicated the park "to the use and enjoyment of people of all colours, creeds and customs for all time".

A neat **itinerary** would be to walk or take the bus to the park, stroll or cycle all or part of the sea wall – there's a slew of bike and rollerblade rental places nearby – and then walk back to Denman Street. Here you can grab some food or pause at one of several cafés – the *Bread Garden* midway down Denman on the left is good – and then sit on the grass or sand at English Bay Beach at the foot of the street. The park is a simple though rather dull **walk** from most of downtown, if a fairly lengthy one from the eastern districts. Beach Avenue to the south and Georgia to the north are the best approaches if you're on foot, leading to the southern and northern starts of the sea wall respectively. Walking all the way round the sea-wall path takes about two hours at a brisk lick. Perhaps a better approach is to take a Stanley Park **bus** #23, #35 or #135 from the corner of Burrard and Pender downtown, which drop you near the so-called Stanley Park Loop just inside the park by Lost Lagoon and in summer continue deeper into the park to the Upper Zoo Loop (though the zoo's now closed). Other buses which will take you close to the park are the #1 (Beach) to Davie and Beach Avenue and the #3 (Robson) to Denman Street.

If you want to rent a bike, go to the corner of Denman and Georgia, where there's a cluster of **bike rental** outlets. Spokes, 1798 West Georgia (☎688-5141), is a big, busy place established in 1938 (one-speed bikes $3.90 an hour, $11.70 half-day or $15.60 a day; mountain bike $9.35/$16.83/$22.44; tandems $9.35/$28.05/$37.40). You need to leave ID, $40 cash or Visa or MasterCard as a deposit. Helmets, which are compulsory in BC, and locks are included in the rental. If this place looks too frenetic you might be better advised to walk a few metres up the street, where Bikes 'n' Blades (☎602-9899) is smaller, less busy and rents **rollerblades** as well. Directly opposite is Bayshore Rentals (☎688-2453). From Denman it's just a minute's pedalling to the park, but watch the traffic.

If you don't want to walk, cycle or blade, then there's a special "Around the Park" **bus service** (bus #52), which runs hourly in summer (April–Oct 10am–7pm) at weekends and on holidays only (but not if it's raining). You can transfer to the service from the #1 and #3 buses on Denman (the bus journeys down the street before looping the park) or the #23, #35 and #135 at Stanley Park or Upper Zoo Loops. Remember you won't need an extra ticket if you've taken a transfer from the driver and make the onward journey round the park within ninety minutes (see "City transport" on p.651). Driving a **car** here is foolish, especially at weekends, when parking is just about impossible.

Taking time in the park, however you do it, especially on a busy Sunday, gives a good taste of what it means to live in Vancouver. The first thing you see is the **Lost Lagoon**, a fair-sized lake that started life as a tidal inlet, and got its name because its water all but disappeared at low tide. Dozens of waterfowl species inhabit its shoreline. Just east are the pretty Rose Garden and Vancouver Rowing Club, before which stands a statue of Scottish poet Robbie Burns. From here, or the Upper Zoo Loop, you can follow the sea wall path all the way, or make a more modest loop past the **totem poles** and round Brockton Point.

Moving around the sea wall anticlockwise, odd little sights dot the promenade, all signed and explained, the most famous being the *Girl in a Wetsuit* statue, a rather lascivious update of Copenhagen's *Little Mermaid*. If you want a more focused walk, the **Cathedral Trail**, northwest of the Lost Lagoon, takes you past some big first-growth cedars. **Beaver Lake**, carpeted green with water lilies, is a peaceful spot for a sleep or a stroll. **Lumberman's Arch**, near the aquarium (see below) was raised in 1952 to honour those in the lumber industry, an odd memorial given that the industry in question would probably give its eyeteeth to fell the trees in Stanley Park. Its meadow surroundings are a favourite for families and those after a siesta. **Prospect Point**, on the park's northern tip, is a busy spot but worth braving for its beautiful view of the city and the mountains rising behind West Vancouver across the water. There's a café-restaurant here, popular for its outdoor deck and sweeping views. West of here lies **Siwash Rock**, an outcrop which has defied the weather for centuries, attracting numerous native legends in the process, and which is distinguished by its solitary tree (not visible from the road, but quickly reached by path). Further around the wall there are various places to eat and drink, the best being the *Teahouse Restaurant* at Ferguson Point, about a kilometre beyond Siwash Rock.

Though people do swim in the sea at beaches around the park's western fringes, most bathers prefer the **swimming pool** next to Second Beach (see box on p.657). Facilities of all sorts – cafés, playgrounds, golf, outdoor dancing – proliferate near the downtown margins. Guided **nature walks** are also occasionally offered around the park; ask at the Infocentre for details.

Vancouver Aquarium

Stanley Park zoo and its all too obviously distressed animals has now thankfully closed, leaving the **Vancouver Aquarium** as the park's most popular destination (daily: July to early Sept 9.30am–7pm; early Sept to June 10am–5.30pm; $9.50; ☎268-9900). At its entrance stands a vast killer whale in bronze, the work of celebrated Haida artist Bill Reid, whose famous *Raven and the Beast* sculpture forms the centrepiece of the Museum of Anthropology (see p.666). The aquarium is ranked among North America's best, and with over a million visitors a year claims to be the most visited sight in Canada west of the Toronto CN Tower. It contains over 8000 living exhibits representing some 600 different species, though in truth this is a relatively modest summation of the eighty percent of the world's creatures that live in water. Like the zoo before it, the complex has been targeted by animal rights campaigners for its treatment of performing beluga and killer whales, not to mention cooped-up seals and otters. Given the aquarium's reputation as a tourist attraction, however, as well as its claims as a research centre, the campaigners have a long, uphill battle. The whales in particular – Bjossa and Finna – are huge draws, but you can't help but feel they should really be in the sea, for all the hoopla surrounding their $14-million marine mammal area.

The aquarium has four key areas to see. The **Arctic Canada** section concerns itself with the surprisingly fragile world of the Canadian north, with a chance to see whales face to face through glass and hear the sounds of whales, walruses, seals and other creatures in this icy domain. The **Amazon Gallery** displays the vegetation, fishes, iguanas, sloths and other creatures of the rainforest in a climate-controlled environment, while the **Pacific Northwest Habitat** performs a similar role for otters, beavers and other creatures of the waters of BC. The **Ducks Unlimited Wetlands** displays are fairly self-explanatory.

Granville Island

Granville Island, huddled under the Granville Street Bridge south of downtown, is the city's most enticing "people's place" – the title it likes for itself – and pretty much lives up to its claim to be the "heart of Vancouver". Friendly, easy-going and popular, its shops, markets, galleries, marina and open spaces are juxtaposed with a light-industrial setting whose faint whiff of warehouse squalor saves the area from accusations of pretentiousness. The island was reclaimed from swampland in 1917 as an ironworks and shipbuilding centre, but by the 1960s the yards were derelict and the place had become a rat-infested dumping ground for the city's rubbish. In 1972 the federal government agreed to bankroll a programme of residential, commercial and industrial redevelopment that retained the old false-fronted buildings, tin-shack homes, sea wall and rail sidings. The best part of the job had been finished by 1979 – and was immediately successful – but work continues unobtrusively today, the various building projects only adding to the area's sense of change and dynamism. Most people come here during the day, but there are some good restaurants, bars and the Arts Club Theatre, which are all enough to keep the place buzzing at night.

The most direct approach is to take **bus** #50 from Gastown or Granville Street. The walk down Granville Street and across the bridge is deceptively long, not terribly salubrious, and so probably only worthwhile on a fine day when you need the exercise. Alternatively and more fun, regular bathtub-sized private **ferries** ($1.75, pay on board) ply back and forth almost continuously between the island and little quays at the foot of Hornby Street or the Aquatic Centre at the foot of Thurlow Street (see "Ferries" on p.653). They also connect from Granville Island to Science World (hourly) and, more significantly, to Vanier Park (half-hourly), a much nicer way than bus to get to the park's Vancouver Museum, Maritime Museum and Space Centre (see opposite). A logical and satisfying day's **itinerary** from downtown, therefore, would take you to Granville Island, to the museums and back by ferry. You might also choose to **walk** from the Island along the False Creek sea wall (east) or west to Vanier Park (see opposite) and Kits Beach.

There's a good **infocentre** at the heart of the Island for Island-related information only (☎666-5784), with a **foreign exchange** facility in the same building and ATM machines on the wall outside. Stamps are available from the LottoCentre inside the Public Market Building. Note that many of the Island's shops and businesses close on Mondays, and that if you want a **bus back** to downtown you should *not* take the #51 from the stop opposite the infocentre: walk out of the Island complex's only road entrance, and at the junction the #50 stop is immediately on your right.

Virtually the first building you see on the Island walking from the bus stop augurs well: the **Granville Island Brewery**, a small outfit run by a German brewmaster which offers guided tours that include tastings of its additive-free beers (tours only June–Sept Mon–Fri on the hour noon–5pm, Sat & Sun on the half-hour 11.30am–5pm; $6). Dominant amongst the maze of shops, galleries and businesses, the **Granville Island Public Market** (daily 9am–6pm; closed Mon in winter) is the undisputed highlight of the area. On summer weekends it's where people go to see and be seen and it throngs with arts-and-crafts types, and a phalanx of dreadful, but harmless buskers. The quality and variety of **food** is staggering, with dozens of kiosks and cafés selling ready-made titbits and potential picnic ingredients. Parks, patios and walkways nearby provide lively areas to eat and take everything in. Other spots to look out for include Blackberry Books, the Water Park and Kids Only Market (a kids-only playground with hoses to repel intruders) and the bright-yellow *Bridges* pub/restaurant/wine bar, which has a nice outdoor drinking and eating area. You can also rent **canoes** (single $22 for two hours, double $32) for safe and straightforward paddling in False Creek and English Bay from Ecomarine Ocean Kayak on the island at 1688 Duranleau St (☎689-7575).

Vanier Park museum complex

A little to the west of Granville Island, **Vanier Park** conveniently collects all but one of the city's main museums: the **Vancouver Museum**, the **Maritime Museum** and the newly renovated **Pacific Space Centre** (combining the old planetarium and observatory). The complex sits on the waterfront at the west end of the Burrard Bridge, near Kitsilano Beach and the residential-entertainment centres of Kitsilano and West 4th Avenue, and Vanier Park itself is a fine spot to while away a summer afternoon. You could easily incorporate a visit to the museums with a trip to Granville Island using the **ferry** (see above), which docks just below the Maritime Museum. Coming from downtown, take the #22 Macdonald **bus** south from anywhere on Burrard or West Pender – get off at the first stop after the bridge and walk down Chester Street to the park. The park's pleasant but open – there's little shade – and has a few nice patches of sandy beach on its fringes if you don't want to trek all the way to Kits and Jericho beaches (see p.657).

The Vancouver Museum

Canada's largest civic museum, the **Vancouver Museum**, 1100 Chestnut St (June–Aug daily 10am–5pm; Sept–April Tues–Sun 10am–5pm; $5; ☎736-4431), traces the history of the city and the lower British Columbian mainland, and invokes the area's past in its very form – the flying-saucer shape is a nod to the conical cedar-bark hats of the Northwest Coast natives, former inhabitants of the area. The fountain outside, looking like a crab on a bidet, recalls the animal of native legend that guards the port entrance.

Though it's the main focus of interest at Vanier Park, the museum is not as captivating as you'd expect from a city like Vancouver. It claims 300,000 exhibits, but it's hard to know where they all are, and a visit needn't take more than an hour or so. A patchy collection of baskets, tools, clothes and miscellaneous artefacts of Native Canadians – including a huge whaling canoe, the only example in a museum – homes in on the 8000 years before the coming of white settlers. After that, the main collection, weaving in and out of Vancouver's history up to World War I, is full of offbeat and occasionally memorable insights if you have the patience to read the material – notably the accounts of early explorers' often extraordinary exploits, the immigration section (which re-creates what it felt like to travel steerage) and the forestry displays. The twentieth-century section is disappointing, most of the time looking more like an antique shop than a museum.

The Pacific Space Centre

The **Pacific Space Centre** (hours and price not fixed at time of writing: call for details ☎738-2855) incorporates the Macmillan Planetarium, downstairs from the museum, and a range of displays and shows recently spruced up in a programme of works designed to turn the old planetarium into a "new" space centre (currently June–Sept daily 9am–10pm; Oct–May Tues–Sun same times; $5.50). It's likely to continue twining its star shows with rock and laser extravaganzas (most evenings at 8.30pm), the latter for fans of the genre only. Also on display in the past – and accorded almost the status of a national shrine – was the favourite piano of cult classical pianist Glenn Gould (see p.76), though it may well find a new home. The **Gordon Southam Observatory**, nearby, is usually open for public stargazing on clear weekend nights; astronomers are on hand to show you the ropes and help you position your camera for a "Shoot the Moon" photography session of the heavens (summer daily 7–11pm; winter Fri–Sun only; free).

The Maritime Museum

The **Maritime Museum**, 1905 Ogden Ave (May–Sept daily 10am–5pm; Oct–April Tues–Sun 10am–5pm; $6; ☎257-8300) is a short 150-metre walk from the Vancouver Museum and features lovely early photographs evoking turn-of-the-century Vancouver, though the rest of the presentation hardly does justice to the status of the city as one of the world's leading ports. The shabbier displays, however, are redeemed by the renovated *St Roch*, a two-masted schooner that was the first vessel to navigate the famed Northwest Passage in a single season (see p.854); it now sits impressively in its own wing of the museum, where it can be viewed by guided tour only. Special summer shows spice things up a little, with activities such as hornpipe dancing and shanty-song sing-alongs (July & Aug Wed 5–9pm; free) and an annual mid-July open period. Outside, just below the museum on **Heritage Harbour** (quay for ferries to and from Granville Island), you can admire, free of charge, more restored old-fashioned vessels.

The Museum of Anthropology

Located well out of downtown on the University of British Columbia campus, the **Museum of Anthropology**, 6393 NW Marine Drive, is far and away Vancouver's most important museum (mid-May to early Sept daily 10am–5pm, Tues 10am–9pm; early Sept to mid-May Tues 11am–9pm, Wed–Sun 11am–5pm, closed Mon; $6; ☎822-3825). Emphasizing the art and culture of the natives of the Pacific Northwest, and the Haida in particular, its collection of carvings, totem poles and artefacts is unequalled in North America.

To get there by bus, catch the #10 or #4 bus south from Granville Street and stay on until the end of the line. The campus is huge and disorientating – to find the museum, turn right from the bus stop, walk along the tree-lined East Mall to the very bottom (10min), then turn left on NW Marine Drive and walk till you see the museum on the right (another 5min). In the foyer pick up a free mini-guide or the cheap larger booklet – a worthwhile investment, given the exhibits' almost total lack of labelling, but still pretty thin.

Much is made of the museum's award-winning layout, a cool and spacious collection of halls designed by Arthur Erickson, the eminent architect also responsible for converting the city art gallery. Particularly outstanding is the huge **Great Hall**, inspired by native cedar houses, which makes as perfect an artificial setting for its thirty-odd **totem poles** as you could ask for. Huge windows look out to more poles and Haida houses, which you're free to wander around, backed by views of Burrard Inlet and the distant mountains. Most of the poles and monolithic carvings, indoors and out, are taken from the coastal tribes of the Haida, Salish, Tsimshian and Kwakiutl, all of which share cultural elements. The suspicion – though it's never confessed – is that scholars really don't know terribly much of the arcane mythology behind the carvings, but the best guess as to their meaning is that the various animals correspond to different clans or the creatures after which the clans were named. To delve deeper into the complexities, it's worth joining an hour-long, all-year **guided walk**.

One of the museum's great virtues is that none of its displays are hidden away in basements or back rooms; instead they're jammed in overwhelming numbers into drawers and cases in the galleries to the right of the Great Hall. Most of the permanent collection revolves around **Canadian Pacific** cultures, but the **Inuit** and **Far North** exhibits are also outstanding. So, too, are the jewellery, masks and baskets of Northwest native tribes, all markedly delicate after the blunt-nosed carvings of the Great Hall. Look out especially for the argillite sculptures, made from a jet-black slate found only on BC's Haida Gwaii or Queen Charlotte Islands. The **African** and **Asian** collections are also pretty comprehensive, if smaller, but appear as something of an afterthought alongside the indigenous artefacts. A small, technical archeological section rounds off the smaller galleries, along with a new three-gallery wing designed to house the Koerner Collection, an assortment of six hundred European ceramics dating from the fifteenth century onwards.

The museum saves its best for last. Housed in a separate rotunda, **The Raven and the Beast**, a modern sculpture designed by Haida artist Bill Reid, is the museum's pride and joy and has achieved almost iconographic status in the city. Carved from a 4.5-tonne block of cedar and requiring the attention of five people over three years, it describes the Haida legend of human evolution with stunning virtuosity, depicting terrified figures squirming from a half-open clam shell, overseen by an enormous and stern-faced raven. However, beautiful as the work is, its rotunda setting makes it seem oddly out of place – almost like a corporate piece of art.

Around the museum

There are any number of odds and ends dotted around the museum, but they amount to little of real interest. For the exception, turn right out the front entrance and a five-minute walk leads to the **Nitobe Memorial Garden**, a small Japanese garden that might be good for a few minutes of peace and quiet (April–Sept daily 10am–6pm; Oct–March Mon–Fri 10am–3pm; $2.50 or $5.75 with the Botanical Garden; ☎822-9666). It's considered the world's most authentic Japanese garden outside Japan (despite its use of many non-Japanese species), and is full of gently curving paths, trickling streams and waterfalls, as well as numerous rocks, trees and shrubs placed with Oriental precision.

Beyond the garden, lies the greater seventy-acre area of the university's **Botanical Garden**, 16th Avenue and SW Marine Drive (daily 10am–6pm; $4.50 or $5.75 with Nitobe Memorial Garden), established in 1916, making it Canada's oldest such garden. Non-gardeners will probably be interested only in the macabre poisonous plants of the Physick Garden, a recreated sixteenth-century monastic herb garden – though most plants here are actually medicinal rather than lethal – and the swaths of shrubs and huge trees in the Asian Garden. If you're more curious or green-fingered, you'll take time to look at all five component parts of the garden. The Asian Garden is cradled amidst a swath of second-growth forest of fir, cedar and hemlock, home to 400 varieties of rhododendrons, roses, flowering vines and floral rarities such as blue Himalayan poppy and giant Himalayan lily. The BC Native Garden shelters some 3500 plants and flowers found across British Columbia in a variety of bog, marsh and other habitats, while the Alpine Garden conjures rare alpine varieties from five continents at around 2000m lower than their preferred altitude. The Food Garden produces a cornucopia of fruit and vegetables from a remarkably restricted area, the entire crop being donated to the Salvation Army.

While you're out at the university, you might also take advantage of the **University Endowment Lands**, on the opposite, west side of the museum. A huge tract of wild parkland – as large as Stanley Park, but used by a fraction of the number of people – the endowment lands boast 48km of trails and abundant wildlife (blacktail deer, otters, foxes and bald eagles). Best of all, there are few human touches – no benches or snack bars, and only the occasional signpost.

North Vancouver

Perhaps the most compelling reason to visit **North Vancouver** (known colloquially as North Van) is the trip itself – preferably by SeaBus – which provides views of not only the downtown skyline but also the teeming port area, a side of the city that's otherwise easily missed. Most of North Van itself is residential, as is neighbouring West Vancouver, whose cosseted citizens boast the highest per capita income in Canada. You'll probably cross to the north shore less for these leafy suburbs than to sample the outstanding areas of natural beauty here: **Lynn Canyon**, **Grouse Mountain**, **Capilano Gorge** (the most popular excursion), **Mount Seymour** and **Lighthouse Park**. All nestle in the mountains that rear up dramatically almost from the West Van waterfront, the proximity of Vancouver's residential areas to genuine wilderness being one of the city's most remarkable aspects. Your best bet if you wish to **hike**, and want the wildest scenery close to downtown, is Mount Seymour (see p.669).

Most of North Vancouver is within a single bus ride of **Lonsdale Quay**, the north shore's SeaBus terminal. **Buses** to all points leave from two parallel bays immediately in front of you as you leave the boat – blue West Van buses are run by an independent company but accept BC Transit tickets. If you've bought a ticket to come over on the SeaBus, remember you have ninety minutes of transfer time to ride buses from the time of purchase, which should be long enough to get you to most of the destinations below.

The **Lonsdale Quay Market**, to the right of the buses, is worth making the crossing for whether or not you intend to explore further. While not as vibrant as Granville Island Market, it's still an appealing place, with great food stalls and takeaways, plus walkways looking out over the port, tugs and moored fishing boats.

Grouse Mountain

The trip to **Grouse Mountain**, named by hikers in 1894 who stumbled across a blue grouse, is a popular one. This is mainly due to the Swiss-built **cable cars** – North America's largest cable cars – which run from the 290-metre base station at 6400 Nancy Greene Way to the mountain's 1250-metre summit (daily 9am–10pm; $17). A favourite among people learning to **ski** after work, the mountain's brightly illuminated slopes and dozen or so runs are a North Vancouver landmark on winter evenings. In summer, the cable car is an expensive way of getting to the top. It's possible to walk up on the aptly named Grouse Grind Trail from the base station, but it's not a great hike, so settle instead into the inevitable queue for the ticket office (get here early if you can). After two stomach-churning lurches over the cables' twin towers you reach the summit, which, with its restaurants and allied tourist paraphernalia, is anything but wild. The views, though, are stunning, sometimes stretching as far as the San Juan Islands 160km away in Washington State. Have a quick look at the interpretative centre off to the right when you leave the cable car. A 3-D quality film is shown in the theatre downstairs (admission is included in your cable-car ticket) and there are a couple of cafés and a smarter restaurant if you need fortifying after your ascent. The first of the cafés, *Bar 98*, has panoramic views, but it fills up quickly. If you're interested in the *Grouse Restaurant* (☎986-6378 for reservations), note that you can come here in the evening for dinner, accompanied by a fine prospect of the sunset and city lights below. Rides up on the cable car are free with a restaurant booking. Ask at the centre, or small information desk just beyond the centre, about easy **guided walks** (summer daily 11am–5pm): the *Tribute to the Forest* (30min) leaves on the hour, the *Walk in the Woods* every hour on the half hour (35min).

Walk up the paved paths away from the centre for about five minutes – you can't get lost – and you pass a cabin office offering guided "gravity assisted" (read downhill) **bike tours** from the summit (May–Oct 3 daily; 20km trips cost $70, 30km $90 including cable-car fee): behind the office you can sign up for expensive helicopter tours. On the left up the path lies the scene of the "Logging Sports" shows (twice daily; free), involving various crowd-pleasing sawing and wood-chopping displays. Just beyond this is the **Peak Chairlift** (also included in your ticket), which judders upwards for another eight minutes to the mountain's summit: views of the city and Fraser delta are even better, only slightly spoilt by the worn paths and odd buildings immediately below you. Check with the office at the lower cable-car base station for details of long **hikes** – many are down below rather than up at the summit proper. The best easy stroll is to **Blue Grouse Lake** (15min); the Goat Ridge Trail is for experienced hikers. More rugged paths lead into the mountains of the West Coast Range, but for these you'll need maps.

To get directly to the base station of the cable car from Lonsdale Quay, take the special #236 Grouse Mountain **bus** from Bay 8 to the left of the SeaBus terminal. You can also take a #246 Highland bus from Bay 7 and change to the #232 Grouse Mountain at Edgemount Village.

Lynn Canyon Park

Among the easiest targets for a quick taste of backwoods Vancouver is **Lynn Canyon Park** (open all year dawn to dusk), a quiet, forested area with a modest ravine and suspension bridge which, unlike the more popular Capilano Suspension Bridge (see below), you don't have to pay to cross. Several walks of up to ninety minutes take you through fine scenery – cliffs, rapids, waterfalls and naturally the eighty-metre-high bridge over Lynn Creek – all just twenty minutes from Lonsdale Quay. Take bus #228 from the quay to its penultimate stop at Peters Street, from where it's a ten-minute walk to the gorge; alternatively, take the less-frequent #229 Westlynn bus from Lonsdale Quay, which drops you about five minutes closer. Before entering the gorge, it's worth popping into the **Ecology Centre**, 3663 Park Rd, off Peters Road (☎981-3103 or 987-5922), a friendly and informative place where you can pick up maps and pamphlets on park trails and wildlife (daily 10am–5pm).

Capilano River Regional Park

Lying just off the approach road to Grouse Mountain, **Capilano River Park**'s most publicized attraction is the inexplicably popular seventy-metre-high and 137-metre-long **suspension bridge** – the world's longest pedestrian suspension bridge – over the vertiginous Capilano Gorge (daily: May–Sept 8.30am–dusk; Oct–April 9am–5pm; $8.95; ☎985-7474). The first bridge here was built in 1889, making this Vancouver's oldest "attraction", though the present structure dates from 1956. Although part of the park, the footbridge is privately run as a money-making venture. Stick to the paths elsewhere in the park and avoid the $8.95 pedestrian toll, which buys you miscellaneous tours, forestry exhibits and trails, and a visit to a native carving centre; frankly they don't amount to much, especially when you can have much the same sort of scenery for free up the road. More interesting, is the **salmon hatchery** just upstream (usually April–Oct daily 9am–5pm; Nov–March 8am–4pm but phone to confirm ☎666-1790; free), a provincial operation dating from 1977 designed to help salmon spawn and thus combat declining stocks: it nurtures some two million fish a year, and was the first of many similar schemes across the province. The building is well designed and the information plaques interesting, but it's a prime stop on city coach tours, so the place can often be packed.

Capilano is probably best visited on the way back from Grouse Mountain – from the cable-car station it's an easy downhill walk (1km) to the north end of the park, below the Cleveland Reservoir, source of Vancouver's often disconcertingly brown drinking water. From there, marked trails – notably the **Capilano Pacific Trail** – follow the eastern side of the gorge to the hatchery (2km). The area below the hatchery is worth exploring, especially the Dog's Leg Pool (1km), which is along a swirling reach of the Capilano River, and if you really want to stretch your legs you could follow the river the full 7km to its mouth on the Burrard Inlet. Alternatively, you could ride the #236 Grouse Mountain bus to the Cleveland Dam or the main park entrance – the hatchery is quickly reached by a sideroad (or the Pipeline Trail) from the signed main entrance left off Nancy Greene Way. This comes not far after the busy roadside entrance to the Capilano Suspension Bridge (on the bus, ring the bell for the stop after the Bridge).

Mount Seymour Provincial Park

Mount Seymour Provincial Park is the biggest (8668 acres) of the North Vancouver parks, the most easterly and the one that comes closest to the flavour of high mountain scenery. It's 16km north of Vancouver and named after the short-serving BC provincial governor, Frederick Seymour (1864–69). For **information**, call ☎924-2200 or ask at the city Infocentre for the blue *BC Parks* pamphlet on the park. To get there by **bus**, take the #239 from Lonsdale Quay to Phibbs Exchange and then the #215 to the Mount Seymour Parkway (1hr) – from there you'll have to walk or cycle up the thirteen-kilometre road to the heart of the park. The road climbs to over 1000m and ends at a car park where boards spell out clearly the trails and mountaineering options available. Views are superb on good days, particularly from the popular **Vancouver Lookout** on the parkway approach road, where a map identifies the city landmarks below. There's also a café, toilets, a small infocentre (summer only), while in the past the winter skiing **chair lift** has operated in summer to take you up to 1200m: check with the infocentre that it's operating before setting out(July & Aug daily 11am–5pm; Sept & Oct Sat & Sun only; $3; weather allowing). In winter this is the most popular family and learners' **ski area** near Vancouver.

Four major **trails** here are manageable in a day, but be aware that conditions can change rapidly and snow lingers as late as June. The easiest hikes go out to Goldie Lake, a half-hour stroll, and to **Dog Mountain**, an hour from the parking area (one way), with great views of the city below. Still better views, requiring more effort, can be had on the trails to First and Second Pump. The wildest and most demanding hike bypasses Mount Seymour's summit and runs by way of an intermittently marked trail to the forest- and mountain-circled Elsay Lake.

Adjacent to the park to the northwest is the **Seymour Demonstration Forest** (☎987-1273), a big, 14,000-acre area of mostly temperate rainforest, nestled in the lower part of a glacier-carved valley. It's situated at the northern end of Lillooet Road and, if going by public transport, you need to take the #229 Lynn Valley bus to Dempsey Road and Lynn Valley Road. From here it's a ten-minute walk over Lynn Creek via the bridge on Rice Lake Road. You're far better off, however, coming up here on a bike, for the 40km of trails in the area offers some of the best **mountain biking** close to downtown. Forestry education is the area's chief concern, as the area's name suggests, and you can follow various sixty- and ninety-minute marked **hiking trails** that will top up your general knowledge about local trees, soils, fish and wildlife.

Cypress Provincial Park

Cypress Provincial Park, most westerly of the big parks that part-cover the dramatic mountains and forest visible from Vancouver's downtown, is perhaps among BC's most visited day-use parks and probably the most popular of the north shore's protected areas. It takes its name from the huge old red and yellow cedars that proliferate here. Something of a hit with locals who prefer their wilderness just slightly tamed, its trails can be rugged and muddy, but they're always well marked, and even just a few minutes from the parking area you can feel in the depths of the great outdoors. There are several good trails, including the three-kilometre **Yew Lake Trail** – wheelchair-accessible – and the main park trail, which climbs through forest and undergrowth, occasionally opening up to reveal views. The trail also shadows part of Cypress Creek, a torrent that has cut a deep and narrow canyon. For more **information**, ask for the relevant *BC Parks* pamphlet at the infocentre or call ☎926-6007. To get here, take the #253 Caulfield/Park Royal **bus**.

Lighthouse Park

Lighthouse Park, just west of Cypress, offers a seascape semi-wilderness at the extreme western tip of the north shore, 8km from the Lion's Gate Bridge. Smooth granite rocks and low cliffs line the shore, backed by huge Douglas firs up to 1500 years old, some of the best virgin forest in southern BC. The rocks make fine sun beds, though the water out here is colder than around the city beaches. A map at the car park shows the two trails to the 1912 Point Atkinson **lighthouse** itself – you can take one out and the other back, a return trip of about 5km which involves about two hours' walking. Although the park has its secluded corners (no camping allowed), it can be disconcertingly busy during summer weekends. For more **information** on the park, contact the infocentre or call ☎925-7200 or 925-7000. The West Van #250 **bus** makes the journey all the way from Georgia Street in downtown.

Eating and drinking

Vancouver's ethnic restaurants are some of Canada's finest, and span the price spectrum from budget to blowout. **Chinese** and **Japanese** cuisines have the highest profile (though the latter tend to be expensive), followed by **Italian**, **Greek** and other European imports. **Vietnamese**, **Cambodian**, **Thai** and **Korean** are more recent arrivals and can often provide the best starting points if you're on a tight budget. Specialist seafood restaurants are surprisingly thin on the ground, but those that exist are of high quality and often remarkably cheap. Seafood, however, crops up on most menus – salmon is ubiquitous in all its forms. **Vegetarians** are well served by a number of specialist places – *Naam*, *Bread Garden* and *O-Tooz* being the best – though less so by the restaurants serving so-called West Coast or Californian cuisine, the *nouvelle cuisine*-based hybrid which has replaced Japanese as Vancouver's current culinary fad.

Restaurants are spread around the city – check locations carefully if you don't want to travel too far from downtown – though are naturally thinner on the ground in North and West Vancouver. Places in Gastown are generally tourist- and expense-account-oriented, in marked contrast to Chinatown's bewildering plethora of genuine and reasonably priced options. Downtown also offers plenty of chains and choice, particularly with fast-food fare: the *White Spot* chain – glorified fast food – is good if time and money are tight; the branch at 1616 West Georgia St is the most central downtown outlet. Superior chains like *Earl's* and *Milestones* are highly commendable, and a reliable choice for downtown eating right on Robson (see "West Coast restaurants").The old warehouse district of **Yaletown**, part of downtown's new southeasterly spread, is also a developing eating and nightlife area. Similar places line 4th Avenue in Kitsilano and neighbouring West Broadway, though these require something of a special journey if you're based in or around downtown. Perhaps try them for lunch if you're at the beach (see feature on p.657) or visiting the nearby Vanier Park museum complex.

Cafés are found mainly around the beaches, in parks, along downtown streets, and especially on Granville Island. Many sell light meals as well as the coffee and snack staples. **Little Italy**, the area around Commercial Drive (between Venables and Broadway), is the city's latest hip spot for cheap, cheerful and downright trendy cafés and restaurants, though as new waves of immigrants fill the area Little Italy is increasingly becoming "Little Vietnam" and "Little Nicaragua". Yaletown and the heavily residential **West End**, notably around Denman and Davie streets – Vancouver's "gay village" – is also booming, the latter having recently lost its seedy reputation and gained a selection of interesting shops and restaurants.

The city also has a commendable assortment of **bars**, many a cut above the functional dives and sham pubs found elsewhere in BC. Note, however, that the definitions of bar, café, restaurant and nightclub can be considerably blurred: food in some form – usually substantial – is available in most places, while daytime cafés and restaurants also operate happily as night-time bars. In this section we've highlighted places whose main emphasis is food and drink; entertainment venues are listed in the next section. Note, too, that Vancouver has a handful of places that stay open all night or until the small hours.

Cafés and snacks

Benny's Bagels, 2503 West Broadway and Larch (☎688-8018). Snacks available 24hr at this highly popular and laid-back bagel joint – good for spending late nights or sunny afternoons. There's also one at Yaletown, 1095 Hamilton St, which is still relatively untried.

Bread Garden, 1040 Denman St (☎685-2996). Also at 1880 West 1st at Cypress and 812 Bute, downtown, off Robson. Locals love to moan about the slow service, but food in these hyper-trendy deli-cafés is some of the best – and best looking – in the city. Great for people-watching – and most branches are open 24hr. There are now ten branches in the Vancouver area. Recommended.

Café Calabria, 1745 Commercial Drive (☎253-7017). Very popular café, known to locals as *Franks*, and tucked away from downtown in "Little Italy". Probably as close as you can get in Vancouver to a genuine Italian bar.

Café S'Il Vous Plaît, 500 Robson St and Richards St. Young, casual and vaguely alternative with good sandwiches, basic home-cooking and local art displays. It is close to the *Kingston Hotel* and central library. Open till 10pm.

Doll and Penny's, 1167 Davie St (☎685-5080). Fun West End place with big servings, large gay clientele (but all welcome), and daily drinks specials. Comes alive when the clubs close and stays open to the wee small hours.

Flying Pizza, 3499 Cambie St (☎874-8284). If you want pizza this is the place; cheap, thin-crust pizza by the slice (but no alcohol) at five outlets, including Library Square (lunch only), Cornwall Avenue (for Kits beach) and just south of the Burrard Street Bridge.

Gallery Café, Vancouver Art Gallery, 750 Hornby St (☎688-2233). Relaxed, stylish and pleasantly arty place at the heart of downtown for coffee, good lunches and healthy, high-quality food (especially desserts); also has a popular summer patio. Recommended.

Hamburger Mary's, 1202 Davie St (☎687-1293). These may well be the best burgers in the city, though there are plenty of other things on the menu. Lots of people end the evening for a snack at this former West End diner that's had a recent face-lift. Open all night, or "22 hours out of 24" according to the sign. Recommended.

Joe's Café, 1150 Commercial Drive and William Street. Lively hang-out which is popular with students, pool sharks, local intellectuals and old hippies. Open daily 9.30am–1pm.

The Only Café, 20 East Hastings and Carrall. One of Vancouver's most famous institutions, founded in 1912, and worth the trip to the less than salubrious part of town to sample the food and old-world atmosphere. This counter-seating greasy spoon has little more than seafood (but the best in town) and potatoes on its menu; no toilets, no credit cards, no licence, and no messing with the service. Closed Sun.

O-Tooz the Energie Bar, 1068 Davie St. Began as a juice bar and now probably serves the healthiest food in the city (good hotpot specials, soups and rice wraps) in brisk, modern surroundings. Recommended.

Sophie's Cosmic Diner, 2095 West 4th Ave (☎732-6810). This excellent 1950s-style diner is a Kits institution and is packed out for weekend breakfasts and weekday lunch; renowned for its vast, spicy burgers, milkshakes and whopping breakfasts. Recommended.

Starbucks, 1100 Robson and Thurlow; 748 Thurlow near Robson; 811 Hornby near Robson; 102-700 W Pender at Granville, and at the SeaBus terminal. Outlets of this chain are ubiquitous, and the hip and sleek espresso bars are downtown's best cups of coffee.

Taf's Café and Gallery, 829 Granville St (☎684-8900). Popular, smoky and street-cred spot that attracts punks-and-their-dogs clientele. Serves adequate food in a surround of jukebox music and local art. Open till the small hours.

Water Street Café, 300 Water St (☎689-2832). The café of choice if you wind up in Gastown (located close to the famous steam clock). An airy and casual atmosphere that offers a short but well-chosen menu; consider booking an outside table if you're going to be here for lunch.

Chinese

Hon's Wun Tun House, 108-268 Keefer at Gore (☎688-0871). Started life as a cheap, basic and popular place known for the house specialities, "potstickers" – fried meat-filled dumplings – and ninety-odd soups (including fish ball and pig's feet). Success has spawned other branches and a slight smartening-up, but the encouraging queues, good food and low prices are mercifully unchanged. No alcohol or credit cards.

Imperial Chinese Seafood Restaurant, 355 Burrard St (☎688-8191). A grand and opulent spot in the old Marine Building with good views and busy atmosphere, serving fine, but pricey, food.

Kirin Mandarin, 1166 Alberni near Bute (☎682-8833). Among the first of the city's smart Chinese arrivals with an elegant, postmodern decor that's a world away from old-fashioned Chinatown. The superior food is at top-dollar prices but you're repaid with great views of the mountains.

Landmark Hotpot House, 3338 Cambie St at 17th Street (☎873-3338). Choose the ingredients and base sauces and then make up food on a personal gas burner at your table; their Duo Soup Base (satay and chicken) is great. This fun place set a trend for hotpot restaurants in the city – it's still the best.

Moutai Mandarin, 1710 Davie St (☎681-2288). Intimate place with striking modern decoration producing good food at average prices. It's perfectly placed if you're staying in the West End, or are down here after seeing Stanley Park or English Bay Beach.

Pink Pearl, 1132 E Hastings near Glen (☎253-4316). Big, bustling and old-fashioned with highly authentic feel but in a dingy part of town. The food has a Cantonese slant, strong on seafood and great for dim sum. It frequently emerges as the city's top Chinese restaurant in dining polls. Recommended.

Shanghai Chinese Bistro, 1128 Alberni St (☎683-8222). A modern-looking but less ostentatious and more reasonably priced alternative to the *Imperial,* if you want to eat Chinese downtown. The handmade noodles are a must. Open very late (2–3am).

Sun Wong Kee, 4136 Main St (☎879-7231). Some of the city's best and cheapest Chinese food and popular with Chinese families, so get here early. Over 225 items on the menu, yet deep-fried seafood remains a winner.

Italian

CinCin, 1154 Robson St (☎688-7338). A celebrity haunt downtown, with food that merits the high prices and includes top-grade home-made pastas and desserts. It has a pleasant ambience with wood-burning oven and view over the open kitchen.

Da Pasta Bar, 1232 Robson St (☎688-1288). Deservedly popular mid-priced spot, with varied clientele, in a visually brash place downtown on Robson. You can pick and mix from six pastas and around fourteen inventive sauces and blend to taste. Good for lunch.

Il Giardino, 1382 Hornby St (☎669-2422). Sublime food with pasta and game bias served to a trendy and casually smart thirty-something clientele. Weekend reservations are essential, especially for the superlative vine-trailed outside terrace.

The Old Spaghetti Factory, 55 Water St. Part of a chain and hardly *alta cucina*, but a standby if you're in Gastown and better than the tourist trap it appears from the outside, with its spacious 1920s Tiffany interior.

Piccolo Mondo, 850 Thurlow and Smithe (☎688-1633). Pricey but excellent food and an award-winning selection of Italian wines. A nicely restrained dining room, just off Robson Street, that's not as formal as it first appears. The clientele are expense accounts at lunch and smoochy couples in the evenings. Recommended.

Quattro on Fourth, 2611 West 4th Ave (☎734-4444). Currently the Italian restaurant of choice if you're in Kitsilano. Comfortable, casual but still upmarket in feel, with mosaic floors and pseudo-Roman Etruscan decoration.

Spumante's, 1736 Commercial Drive (☎253-8899). If you're prepared to make the trek to "Little Italy", this is the restaurant to go for: good pasta and main-course combination choices for around $10 at lunch, $15 at dinner.

Villa del Lupo, 869 Hamilton St (☎688-7436). Authentic, high-quality food in a renovated country house – unfussy and elegant – on the eastern edge of downtown midway between the new library and Yaletown: there's not a better osso bucco in Vancouver. It has been called Vancouver's best restaurant. Recommended for a treat.

Greek

Le Grec, 1447 Commercial Drive (☎253-1253). Popular restaurant with a big range of titbits at reasonable prices, though you'll have to travel out of downtown to enjoy them. Casual and lively later on, especially at weekends.

Orestes, 3116 West Broadway (☎738-1941). Good, basic food in one of the city's oldest Greek restaurants. Belly dancers shake their stuff Thurday to Saturday and there's live music on Sunday.

Ouzeri, 3189 West Broadway (☎739-9995). A friendly and fairly priced restaurant that is the first port of call if you're at the hostel or beach in Kitsilano.

Stepho's, 1124 Davie St (☎683-2555). This West End restaurant has simple interior, fine food, efficient service and is very popular. Recommended.

Vassilis, 2884 West Broadway near Macdonald (☎733-3231). Family-run outfit with a high reputation; serves a mean roast chicken. Closed weekend lunch times.

West Coast

Bishop's, 2183 West 4th near Yew (☎738-2025). Almost universally recognized as Vancouver's best restaurant. Although there's a frequent film-star and VIP presence, the welcome's as warm for everyone. The light and refined "contemporary home cooking" – Italy meets the Pacific Rim – commands high prices but is worth it. First choice for the big, one-off splurge but booking is essential.

Bridges, 1696 Duranleau, Granville Island (☎687-4400). Unmissable big, yellow restaurant upstairs, pub and informal bistro (the best option), downstairs, with a large outdoor deck. A reliable and very popular choice for a drink or meal on Granville Island.

Earl's On Top, 1185 Robson St, corner of Bute. Come here first if you don't want to mess around scouring downtown for somewhere to eat. The mid-priced, and often innovative, high-quality food is served in a big, open and casual dining area, with outside terrace in the summer. Recommended.

Ferguson Point Teahouse, Ferguson Point, Stanley Park (☎669-3281). A very pretty and romantic spot, and the best place for a lunch or brunch during a walk or ride round Stanley Park. Be sure to book.

Isadora's, 1540 Old Bridge St, Granville Island (☎681-8816). Popular Granville Island choice for a beer or a meal, though *Bridges* is probably a shade better. Fine breakfasts, weekend brunches and light meals with plenty of good veggie/wholefood options. Lots of outdoor seating, but expect queues and slower service at weekends, particularly Sunday brunch.

Liliget Feast House, 1724 Davie St (☎681-7044). This West End Native Canadian restaurant serves types of food you'll get nowhere else in the city: seaweed, roast caribou, barbecued juniper duck.

Milestone's, 1145 Robson St (☎682-4477) and 1210 Denman St (☎662-3431). Popular mid-market chain restaurants with cheap drinks and food (especially good breakfasts) in very generous portions at the heart of downtown (fast and noisy) and the English Bay Beach end of Denman Street (more laid-back).

Raku, 4422 West 10th near Trimble (☎222-8188). Eclectic cuisine (Middle East, California, Asia and Caribbean) served in tiny, exquisite portions in an austere setting. Popular but not cheap.

Tomato Fresh Food Café, 3305 Cambie St (☎874-6020). This high-energy place serves good simple food, with a fresh, health-conscious bias. It's way south of downtown, so it's a good place to stop en route for the airport Vancouver Island or the ferry terminal at Tsawwassen. Eat in or take away.

Other ethnic restaurants

Akbar's Own, 3629 West Broadway (☎739-8411). Reasonably priced Indian food, with plenty of vegetarian choices.

Chiyoda, 1050 Alberni at Burrard (☎688-5050). Everything here, down to the beer glasses, was designed in Japan. Chic but convivial – the emphasis is on grilled food (*robata*) rather than sushi – and draws in Japanese visitors and businesspeople at lunch and the fashionable in the evenings.

Ezoggiku Noodle Café, 1329 Robson St (☎685-8608). This tiny Japanese noodle house is a perfect place for quick food downtown. The queues are prohibitive, but the turnover's speedy.

Kamei-Sushi, 1030 West Georgia (☎687-8588). Superlative sushi, but at stratospheric prices. Large and bright, and a menu as long as your arm.

Le Crocodile, 100-909 Burrard St (☎669-4298). Plush, French-Alsace establishment that pushes *Bishop's* close for the title of the city's best restaurant and, unlike its rival, it's located downtown. A memorable meal is guaranteed – but check your credit limit first.

Le Gavroche, 1616 Alberni St (☎685-3924). *Le Crocodile* may just take the culinary plaudits, but this other top French restaurant (with a West Coast twist) is not far behind. A formal but amiable place and rated as one of the most romantic places in the city.

Mescalero's, 1215 Bidwell (☎669-2399). Very popular Mexican-Latin restaurant in the West End with appropriately rustic atmosphere and fit young punters.

Phnom-Penh, 244 East Georgia near Gore (☎682-5777) and 955 West Broadway (☎734-8988). Excellent, cheap Vietnamese cuisine, especially seafood, in a friendly, family-oriented restaurant. Recommended.

Pho Hoang, 3610 Main at 20th (☎874-0810) and 238 East Georgia (☎682-5666). The first and perhaps friendliest of the many Vietnamese *pho* (beef soup) restaurants now springing up all over the city. Choose from thirty soup varieties with herbs, chillies and lime at plate-side as added seasoning. Open for breakfast, lunch and dinner. The new Chinatown branch is right by the *Phnom-Penh* (see above).

Tojo's, 777 West Broadway at Willow (☎872-8050). Quite simply the best Japanese food in the city.

Topanga Café, 2904 West 4th Ave near Macdonald (☎733-3713). A small but extremely popular Mexican restaurant and Vancouver institution.

Vegetarian

Bodai Vegetarian Restaurant, 337 East Hastings (☎682-2666). Over 130 menu items, prepared to a unique style of cuisine created by fourth-century monks. Consistently voted the city's best vegetarian restaurant. Sit down with Chinese Buddhists from the temple next door and study the Buddhist riddles on the wall.

The Naam, 2724 West 4th Ave near Stephens (☎738-7151). The oldest and most popular health-food and vegetarian restaurant in the city. Comfortable and friendly ambience with folk music and outside eating some evenings. Open 24hr. Recommended.

Sweet Cherubim, 1105 Commercial Drive (☎253-0969). Good organic and vegetarian restaurant/shop; serves no meat, fish, eggs, nor chemical additives.

Pubs and bars

The Arts Club, 1585 Johnston on Granville Island (☎687-1354). The Arts Club's popular Backstage Lounge, part of the theatre complex, has a waterfront view, easy-going atmosphere, decent food and puts on blues, jazz and other live music Friday and Saturday evenings. Recommended.

Bar None, 1222 Hamilton St (☎689-7000). Busy, reasonably smart and hip New York-style Yaletown bar and club where you can eat, drink, watch TV, smoke cigars (walk-in humidor) and play backgammon or shoot pool and listen to taped music.

Blarney Stone, 216 Carrall (☎687-4322). A lively Irish pub and restaurant, in Gastown, complete with live Irish music and dance floor. Closed Sun.

La Bodega, 1277 Howe near Davie. One of the city's best and most popular places, with *tapas* and excellent main courses, but chiefly dedicated to lively drinking. It's packed later on, so try to arrive before 8pm. Recommended. Closed Sun.

Darby D. Dawes, 2001 Macdonald St and 4th Avenue (☎731-0617). A pub handy for Kits Beach and the youth hostel. People often start the evening here, meals are served 11.30am–7pm, snacks till 10pm, and then move on to the Fairview for live blues (see p.676). Live music is only played on Friday and Saturday evenings with jam sessions on Saturday afternoons.

Gerard's, 845 Burrard (☎682-5511). The smooth wood-panelled lounge and piano bar with leather chairs and tapestries, all make this very elegant downtown drinking. Also, the place to spot the stars currently filming in town.

Rose and Thorne, 757 Richards near Georgia. Popular, comfortable place next to the *Kingston Hotel* and very close to the look and feel of an English pub.

Shark Bar & Grill, 180 West Georgia (☎687-4275). The best and busiest of several sports bars in the city. There are 30 screens, a 180-seat oak bar, 22 beers on tap, Italian food from the kitchen, and lots of testosterone.

Sylvia Hotel, 1154 Gilford and Beach (☎688-8865). This nondescript but easy-going hotel bar is popular for quiet drinks and superlative waterfront views, and pleasant after a stroll on English Bay Beach.

Yaletown Brewing Company, 1111 Mainland St (☎681-2739). An extremely large bar and restaurant with their own six-beer on-site brewery. Currently very popular, and leading the way in the funky Yaletown revival.

Nightlife and entertainment

Vancouver gives you plenty to do come sunset, laying on a varied and cosmopolitan blend of **live music** and **comedy**. Clubs are more adventurous than in many a Canadian city, particularly the fly-by-night alternative dives in the Italian quarter on Commercial Drive and in the backstreets off Gastown and Chinatown. There's also a choice of smarter and more conventional clubs, a handful of discos and a smattering of **gay** and **lesbian** clubs and bars. Summer nightlife often takes to the streets in West Coast fashion, with outdoor bars and (to a certain extent) beaches becoming venues in their own right. Fine weather also allows the city to host a range of **festivals**, from jazz to theatre, and the **performing arts** are as widely available as you'd expect in a city as culturally self-conscious as Vancouver.

The most comprehensive **listings** guide to all the goings-on is *Georgia Straight*, a free weekly published on Thursday; the monthly *Night Moves* concentrates more on live music. For detailed information on **gay and lesbian** events, check out *X*, a free monthly magazine aimed specifically at the gay and lesbian community, which is available at clubs, bookshops and many of the *Georgia Straight* distribution points. Many other free magazines devoted to different musical genres and activities are available at the same points, but they come and go quickly. **Tickets** for many major events are sold through Ticketmaster, based at 1304 Hornby St and with forty outlets round the city (☎280-4444); they'll sometimes unload discounted tickets for midweek and matinee performances.

Live music and clubs

Vancouver's live-music venues showcase a variety of local bands. Mainstream **rock** groups are the most common bill of fare and the city is also a fertile breeding ground for **heavy-metal** bands, with particularly vocal fans. **Jazz** is currently hot news in Vancouver, with a dozen spots specializing in the genre (ring the Jazz Hot Line at ☎682-0706 for current and upcoming events). And, while Vancouver isn't as cowpoke as, say, Calgary, it does have several clubs dedicated to **country music**, though many are in the outer suburbs.

Many venues also double as clubs and discos, and as in any city with a healthy alternative scene there are also plenty of fun, one-off clubs that have an irritating habit of cropping up and disappearing at speed. Cover charges are usually nominal, and tickets are often available (sometimes free) at record shops. At the other end of the spectrum, the 60,000-seat Pacific Coliseum is on the touring itinerary of most international acts.

Rock venues

Big Bam Boo, 1236 West Broadway near Oak (☎733-2220). Sports on TV, pool and sushi upstairs; dancing downstairs to safe Top 40 stuff and 1980s throwbacks. Smart place with a strict dress code and generally queues Thursday to Saturday. Wednesday and Saturday are two of the best "Ladies" nights in the city.

Commodore Ballroom, 870 Granville and Smithe (☎681-7838). Recently given a $1 million face-lift – but retaining its renowned 1929 sprung dance floor – the city's best mid-sized venue. There is an adventurous music policy and they feature a new DJ every two to three weeks.

The Rage, 750 Pacific Blvd and Cambie (☎685-5585). Loud and young, progressive dance and live music club with huge, packed dance floor. It mainly caters for up-and-coming bands: as one critic puts it – "if you've heard it before, you won't hear it here".

Railway Club, 579 Dunsmuir and Seymour (☎681-1625). Long-established favourite with excellent bookings, wide range of music (folk, blues, jazz) and a casual atmosphere. Has a separate "conversation" lounge, so it's ideal for a drink (and weekday lunches). Arrive before 10pm at weekends – the place is tiny – and be prepared to pay private-club membership fee.

Roxy, 932 Granville and Nelson (☎684-7699). Nightly live bands with emphasis on retro 1950s to 1970s music. Casual and fun place for college crowd and people in from the 'burbs.

Starfish Room, 1055 Homer at Nelson (☎682-4171). Intimate, smoke-filled and loud place known for top local bands, smaller touring bands, occasional bigger names and AOR music at other times.

Town Pump, 66 Water and Abbott (☎683-6695). Vancouver's best-known music venue, with live bands nightly. Convenient mid-Gastown location attracts a varied clientele – it's also known as something of a pick-up spot. Bar food and piano lounge until 9pm, when the band strikes up.

Jazz and blues

Arts Club Theatre Backstage Lounge, 1585 Johnston, Granville Island (☎687-1354). The lounge is a nice spot to hear R&B, jazz and blues, or watch the boats and sunset on False Creek.

Casbah Jazzbah, 175 West Pender South (☎669-0837). Smooth restaurant-club with live traditional and swing jazz cabaret Thurday to Saturday.

Fairview, 898 West Broadway at the *Ramada Inn* (☎872-1262). Good local blues and 1950s rock-'n'roll in a pub atmosphere, so only a small dance floor. Snacks are served during the day and good-value meals in the evening. Open Mon–Sat.

Glass Slipper, 2714 Prince Edward St (☎877-0066). Home of the Coastal Jazz and Blues Society; contemporary and improvised sessions, often provided by the house band, the New Orchestra Workshop. Fri–Sun only.

Hot Jazz, 2120 Main St and 5th (☎873-4131). Oldest and most established jazz club in the city. Mainly trad – swing, Dixieland and New Orleans, both local and imported bands. A good dance floor and big bar ensures this place swings past midnight. Wednesday is jam night. Closed Mon & Sun.

Purple Onion Cabaret, 15 Water St (☎602-9442). Casual club right in the heart of Gastown: topnotch jazz and live Latin music upstairs, dance floor, cigars, oysters and cabaret downstairs. Currently, a very popular choice, so expect to wait in line on Friday and Saturday.

Yale, 1300 Granville and Drake (☎681-9253). An outstanding venue: *the* place in the city to hear hardcore blues and R&B. Relaxed air, big dance floor and occasional outstanding international names. Often jam sessions with up to 50 players at once, on Saturday (3–8pm) and Sunday (3pm–midnight). Recommended. Closed Mon & Tues.

C&W

Boone County Cabaret, 801 Brunette Ave, Coquitlam (☎523-3144). Just off the Trans-Canada – take bus #151 – this is suburbia's favourite C&W club and it shows – raucous and crowded. There's no cover Monday to Thursday, and free dance lessons on Monday, Tuesday & Thursday at 8pm. Closed Sun.

Cheyenne Social Club, *Lynnwood Hotel*, 1515 Barrow St, North Vancouver. Local C&W Thursday to Saturday.

JR Country Club, *Sandman Inn*, 180 West Georgia near Cambie. Downtown's main C&W venue highlights top Canadian bands in Old West setting; no cover Monday to Thursday. Closed Sun.

Discos and clubs

Graceland, 1250 Richards between Davie and Drake (☎688-2648). Bizarre warehouse-sized venue for the art and fashion crowd. Current dance music (different genre most nights) is occasionally enlivened by live shows with the avant-garde art rounding off the experience. Closed Sun.

Luv-a-Fair, 1275 Seymour and Davie (☎685-3288). This old-timer is probably the city's top club and boasts an excellent dance floor and sound system, plenty of imported videos and cutting-edge dance music. The occasional theme nights and live bands have to compete with the everyday madcap, eclectic crowd, ranging from punks to drag queens. Recommended. Closed Sun.

Mars, 1320 Richards (☎662-7707). Huge and technically astonishing dance club and restaurant on the edge of Yaletown. *Mars* clubs are opening in New York and LA. Well worth a look.

Richard's on Richards, 1036 Richards and Nelson (☎687-6794). A well-known club and disco, but pretentious and aimed at the BMW set. Long waits and dress code. Open Thurs–Sat.

The World, 1369 Richards St (☎688-7806). Currently one of the city's most popular place to retire after clubbing: music, food and non-alcoholic drinks. Open Fri & Sat midnight–5am only.

Comedy club

Yuk Yuk's Plaza of Nations, 750 Pacific Blvd and Cambie (☎687-LAFF). Top US and Canadian stand-up acts and the usual scary amateur night on Wednesday. Shows at 9pm, plus Sat & Sun 11.30pm. Closed Mon & Tues.

Gay clubs and venues

Celebrities Night Club, 1022 Davie and Burrard (☎689-3180). A big and popular playing Top 40, funk and techno disco every night, plus occasional drag and other shows for a mixed, mostly gay crowd between 20 and 30.

Denman Station, 860 Denman off Robson (☎669-3488). A friendly basement bar with game shows, karaoke, darts and the like every night for a largely gay and lesbian clientele in an area increasingly becoming a gay "village".

Ms T's Cabaret, 339 West Pender near Richards (☎682-8096). Popular club for men and women, with live music. Fri is currently theme night and Sat for cross-dressers and friends. Mon–Sat.

Numbers Cabaret, 1042 Davie and Burrard (☎685-4077). Good, cruisy disco, movies and pool tables upstairs, mixed downstairs but with very few women. Open nightly.

Odyssey, 1251 Howe near Davie (☎689-5256). A young gay and bisexual club with techno disco most nights (expect to queue Fri & Sat), and caged dancers alongside the dance floor. There's a garden in the rear to cool off.

Shaggy Horse, 818 Richards and Robson. Hip gay club patronized by an older crowd, with Thurs being hetero night.

Performing arts and cinema

Vancouver serves up enough highbrow culture to suit the whole spectrum of its cosmopolitan population, with plenty of unusual and avant-garde performances to spice up the more mainstream fare you'd expect of a major North American city. The main focus for the city's performing arts is the **Queen Elizabeth Theatre** (☎299-9000) at 600 Hamilton St at Georgia, which plays host to a steady procession of visiting theatre, opera and dance troupes, and even the occasional big rock band. Recently it's been joined by the new **Ford Centre for the Performing Arts** opposite the central library at 777 Homer St (☎280-2222 or 602-0616). For information on the Vancouver arts scene, call the Arts Hotline (☎684-ARTS or 684-2787) or visit their office at 938 Howe St. The refurbished **Orpheum Theatre**, 884 Granville at Smithe (☎665-3050 for information, 280-4444 for tickets), is Vancouver's oldest theatre and headquarters of the Vancouver Symphony Orchestra. There's also a special line for information relating to dance (☎872-0432).

The western capital of Canada's film industry, Vancouver is increasingly favoured by Hollywood studios in their pursuit of cheaper locations and production deals. It's therefore no surprise that the spread of **cinemas** is good. Home-produced and Hollywood first-run films play in the downtown cinemas on "Theatre Row" – the two blocks of Granville between Robson and Nelson – and other big complexes, and there's no shortage of cinemas for more esoteric productions.

Classical music

Early Music Vancouver (☎732-1610). Early music with original instruments where possible; concerts all over the city, and at the UBC during the Early Music Festival in July & August.

Festival Concert Society (☎736-3737). The society often organizes cheap Sunday morning concerts (jazz, folk or classical) at the Queen Elizabeth Playhouse.

Music in the Morning Concert Society, 1270 Chestnut, Vanier Park (☎873-4612). This began modestly in someone's front room a decade ago but now organizes innovative and respected concerts of old and new music with local and visiting musicians.

Vancouver Bach Choir (☎921-8012). The city's top non-professional choir performs three major concerts yearly at the Orpheum Theatre.

Vancouver Chamber Choir (☎738-6822). One of two professional, internationally renowned choirs in the city. They perform at the Orpheum and on some Sunday afternoons at the *Hotel Vancouver*.

Vancouver New Music Society (☎874-6200 or 606-6440). Responsible for several annual concerts of cutting-edge twentieth-century music, usually at the East Cultural Centre (see "Drama" below).

Vancouver Opera Association (☎682-2871). Four operas are produced annually at the Queen Elizabeth Theatre and productions currently enjoy an excellent reputation.

Vancouver Recital Society (☎736-6034). Hosts two of the best and most popular cycles in the city: the summer Chamber Music Festival (at St George's School) and the main Vancouver Playhouse recitals (Sept–April). Catches up-and-coming performers plus a few major international names each year.

Vancouver Symphony Orchestra (☎684-9100). Presents most concerts at the Orpheum or new Chan Shun Hall on Crescent Road off NW Marine Drive, but also sometimes gives free recitals in the summer at beaches and parks, culminating in a concert on the summit of Whistler Mountain.

Drama

Arts Club Theatre (☎687-1644). A leading light in the city's drama scene, performing at three venues: the main stage, at 1585 Johnston St on Granville Island, offers mainstream drama, comedies and musicals; the next-door bar presents small-scale revues and cabarets; and a third stage, at

1181 Seymour and Davie, focuses on avant-garde plays and Canadian dramatists – a launching pad for the likes of Michael J. Fox. The theatre has cult status for its "theatre sports", in which teams of actors compete for applause with improvisation. Beware, as audience participation features highly!

Firehall Arts Centre, 280 East Cordova and Gore (☎689-0926). The leader of Vancouver's community and avant-garde pack, presenting mime, music, video and visual arts.

Theatre Under the Stars (TUTS), Malkin Bowl, Stanley Park (☎687-0174). Summer productions here are fun and lightweight, but can suffer from being staged in one of Canada's rainiest cities.

Vancouver East Cultural Centre, 1895 Venables and Victoria (☎254-9578). Renowned performance space housed in an old church, used by a highly eclectic mix of drama, dance, mime and musical groups.

Vancouver Playhouse Theatre Company, Hamilton at Dunsmuir (☎873-3311). One of western Canada's biggest companies. It usually presents six top-quality shows with some of the region's premier performers and designers during its October to May season.

Waterfront Theatre, 1405 Anderson St (☎685-6217). Home to three resident companies that also hold workshops and readings.

Dance

Anna Wyman Dance Theatre (☎662-8846). Although their repertoire is wide, this group specializes in contemporary dance. As well as standard shows, they occasionally put on free outdoor performances at Granville Island and at Robson Square near the Art Gallery.

Ballet British Columbia (☎669-5954). The province's top company performs – along with major visiting companies – at the Queen Elizabeth Theatre.

EDAM (☎876-9559). Experimental Dance and Music present modern mixes of dance, film, music and art.

Karen Jamieson Dance Company (☎872-5658). Award-winning company and choreographer that often uses Canadian composers and artists, and incorporates native cultural themes.

Cinema

Cineplex, in the lower level of the Royal Centre at Georgia and Burrard. This ten-screen complex is the biggest first-run venue in town.

Fifth Avenue Cinemas, 2110 Burrard. Fiveplex cinema run by the founder of the Vancouver Film Festival. It is one of the better in the city for arthouse films.

Pacific Cinémathèque, 1131 Howe near Helmcken (☎688-FILM). Best of the arthouses. The programmes are hit-and-miss, but any film buff will find something to tempt them.

Ridge Theatre, 3131 Arbutus and 16th Ave (☎738-6311). New releases, European films and classic reruns all play here.

Festivals

Warm summers, outdoor venues and a culture-hungry population combine to make Vancouver an important festival city. Recognized as one of the leading beanos of its kind, Vancouver's annual **International Jazz Festival** (late June to early July; call ☎682-0706 for information) is organized by the Coastal Jazz and Blues Society. Past line-ups have featured such luminaries as Wynton Marsalis, Youssou N'Dour, Ornette Coleman, Carla Bley and John Zorn. Some 800 international musicians congregate annually, many offering workshops and free concerts in addition to paid-admission events.

Other music festivals include the **Vancouver Folk Festival** (☎602-9798), a bevy of international acts centred on Jericho Park and the Centennial Theatre for three days during the third week of July. In July, Vancouver loses its collective head over the **Sea Festival** (☎684-3378) – nautical fun, parades and excellent fireworks around English Bay. Further afield in Whistler (see p.782), there's a **Country & Bluegrass Festival** held in mid-July.

Theatre festivals come thick and fast, particularly in the summer. The chief event – and one that's growing in size and reputation – is the **Fringe Festival**, modelled on the Edinburgh equivalent. It currently runs to 550 shows, staged by ninety companies at ten venues. There's also an annual **Shakespeare Festival** (June–Aug) in Vanier Park and an **International Comedy Festival** (☎683-0883) in early August on Granville Island. Many of the city's arthouse cinemas join forces to host the **Vancouver International Film Festival** (☎685-0260), an annual showcase for more than 150 films running from late September to mid-October. Canada's largest independent dance festival, **Dancing on the Edge**, runs for ten days in September at the Firehall Arts Centre, featuring the work of fifty of Canada's hottest (and weirdest) choreographers.

Listings

Airlines Air BC (☎360–9074); Air Canada, 300-1177 West Hasting St (☎279-6112, 270-5211 or 688-5515); American Airlines, 507-1030 W Hastings St (☎222-2532 or 1-800-433-7300); British Airways (☎270-8131); Canadian Airlines (☎279-6112 or 279-6611); Canadian Regional (☎604/279-6611); Central Mountain Air (☎847-4780); Continental (☎1-800-525-0280); Delta (☎1-800-345-3400); Harbour Air Seaplanes: services to Victoria Inner Harbour (☎688-1277 or 1-800-665-0212); Helijet Airways: helicopter service to Victoria (☎273-1414 or 1-800-665-4354); KLM (☎303-3666); North Vancouver (☎604/278-1608); United (☎1-800-241-6522).

American Express, Park Place Building, 666 Burrard St, enter at Hornby and Dunsmuir (☎669-2813), and is open Mon–Fri 8.30am–5.30pm, Sat 10am–4pm. There's another office on the fourth floor of the The Bay department store, 674 Granville and Georgia (☎687-7688), which is open Mon–Fri 9.30am–5pm.

Bike rental Bayshore Bicycles, 1876 West Georgia near Denman (☎688-2453); Granville Island Bike Rentals, 1496 Cartwright, Granville Island (☎669-2453); Robson Cycles, 1810 Fir at 2nd (☎731-5552) and 1463 Robson St near Broughton (☎687-2777); Spokes, 1798 Georgia at Denman (☎688-5141).

Bookshops Duthie Books, 919 Robson St (☎684-4496), is the best mainstream bookshop. World Wide Books and Maps, 1247 Granville St, is adequate for maps, guides and travel.

Buses Airporter (☎946-8866 or 1-800-668-3141) for shuttle from Vancouver Airport to bus depot and downtown; Greyhound (☎662-3222 or 1-800-661-8747) for BC, Alberta, Yukon and long-haul destinations including Seattle and the US; Maverick Coach Lines (☎662-8051 or 1-800-972-6300) for the Sunshine Coast, Powell River, Whistler, Pemberton and Nanaimo on Vancouver Island; Pacific Coach Lines (☎662-8074) for Victoria, Vancouver Island; Perimeter (☎266-5386) for services between Whistler and Vancouver Airport; Quick Shuttle (☎940-4428 or 1-800-665-2122) for Bellingham Airport, downtown Seattle and SeaTac Airport.

Car rental Avis, airport and 757 Hornby near Georgia (☎606-2847); Budget, airport 450 West Georgia St (☎668-7000 or 1-800-268-8900 in Canada, 1-800-527-0700 in US); Exotic Car and Motorcycle Rentals, 1820 Burrard at West 2nd (☎736-9130); Hertz, 1128 Seymour St (☎688-2411 or 1-800-263-0600); Rent-a-Wreck (☎606-1672).

Consulates Australia, 602-999 Canada Place (☎684-1177); New Zealand, 1200-888 Dunsmuir (☎684-7388); UK, 800-1111 Melville (☎683-4421); US, 1095 West Pender (☎685-4311).

Crisis Centre Crisis Line (☎733-4111); Rape Relief (☎872-8212).

Dentists For your nearest dentists, call ☎736-3621. Drop-in dentist, Dentacare (Mon–Fri only; ☎669-6700), is in the lower level of the Bentall Centre at Dunsmuir and Burrard.

Doctors The College of Physicians provides names of three doctors near you (☎733-7758). Drop-in service at Medicentre (☎683-8138) in the Bentall Centre (see "Dentists" above).

Directory enquiries ☎411.

Emergencies ☎911.

Exchange Custom House Currency, 375 Water St, Gastown (☎482-6000); International Securities Exchange, 1169 Robson St near Thurlow (☎683-9666); Thomas Cook, 1016 West Georgia St (☎641-1229).

Ferries BC Ferries for services to Vancouver Island, the Gulf Islands, the Sunshine Coast, Prince Rupert, the Inside Passage and the Queen Charlotte Islands; reservations and information ☎1-888-223-3779 (in BC); Victoria (☎250/386-3431 or recorded information 250/381-5335); Vancouver (☎277-0277 recorded information). Aquabus (☎689-5858) and False Creek Ferries (☎684-7781) for services between downtown, Granville Island and Vanier Park.

Gay and lesbian switchboard 1-1170 Bute St (☎684-6869).

Hospitals St Paul's Hospital is the closest to downtown at 1081 Burrard St (☎682-2344). The city hospital is Vancouver General at 855 West 12th near Oak, south of Broadway (☎875-4111).

Laundry Scotty's One Hour Cleaners, 834 Thurlow near Robson (☎685-7732).

Left luggage At the bus station ($2 per 24hr).

Lost property BC Transit (☎682-7887); West Vancouver Transit (☎985-7777); police (☎665-2232); airport (☎276-6104).

Maps Geological Survey of Canada, 101-605 Robson near Richards (Mon–Fri 8.30am–4.30pm; ☎666-0529). Superb source of official survey maps, including *all* 1:50,000 maps of BC and Yukon.

Newspapers and magazines US, UK and other European editions at Manhattan Books and Magazines, 1089 Robson near Thurlow (☎681-9074).

Optician Same-day service Granville Mall Optical, 807 Granville and Robson (☎683-4716).

Parking Main downtown garages are at The Bay (entrance on Richards near Dunsmuir), Robson Square (on Smithe and Howe), and the Pacific Centre (on Howe and Dunsmuir) – all are expensive and fill up quickly. A better idea might be to leave your car at the free Park'n'Ride in New Westminster (off Hwy 1).

Pharmacies Shopper's Drug Mart, 1125 Davie and Thurlow (☎669-2424), is open 24hr and has five other outlets open Mon–Sat 9am–midnight, Sun 9am–9pm. Carson Midnite Drug Store, 6517 Main at 49th, is open daily until midnight.

Police RCMP (☎264-3111); Vancouver City Police (☎665-3535).

Post office Main office at 349 West Georgia and Homer (Mon–Fri 8am–5.30pm; ☎662-5725); branch in Eaton's department store. Post office infomation (☎1-800-267-1177).

Taxis Black Top (☎731-1111 or 681-2181); Vancouver Taxi (☎255-5111 or 874-5111); Yellow Cab (☎681-3311 or 681-1111).

Tourist information 200 Burrard St (☎683-2000).

Train enquiries VIA Rail (☎669-3050 or toll-free in Canada only ☎1-800-561-8630, 1-800-561-3949 in the US); BC Rail (reservations and info ☎984-5246 or 1-800-663-8238 in North America; recorded info ☎631-3501); Amtrak (☎1-800-872-7245); Rocky Mountain Railtours (☎606-7200 or 1-800-665-7245) for expensive rail tours through the Rockies.

Weather ☎664-9010.

VANCOUVER ISLAND

VANCOUVER ISLAND's proximity to Vancouver makes it one of western Canada's premier tourist destinations, though its popularity is slightly out of proportion to what is, in most cases, a pale shadow of the scenery on offer on the region's mainland. The largest of North America's west coast islands, it stretches almost 500km from north to south, but has a population of around only 500,000, mostly concentrated around **Victoria**, whose small-town feel belies its role as British Columbia's second metropolis and provincial capital. It is also the most British of Canadian cities in feel and appearance, something it shamelessly plays up to attract its two million – largely American – visitors annually. While Victoria makes a convenient base for touring the island – and, thanks to a superlative museum, merits a couple of days in its own right – little else here, or (for that matter) in any of the island's other sizable towns, is enough to justify an overnight stop.

For most visitors Vancouver Island's main attraction is the great outdoors and – increasingly – **whale-watching**, an activity which can be pursued from Victoria, **Tofino**, **Ucluelet** and several other places up and down the island. The scenery is a mosaic of landscapes, principally defined by a central spine of snowcapped mountains which divide it decisively between the rugged and sparsely populated wilderness of the west coast and the more sheltered lowlands of the east. Rippling hills characterize the northern and southern tips, and few areas are free of the lush forest mantle that supports one of BC's most lucrative logging industries. Apart from three minor east–west roads (and some rough logging and gravel roads), all the urban centres are linked by a single recently upgraded and widened highway running along almost the entire length of the east coast.

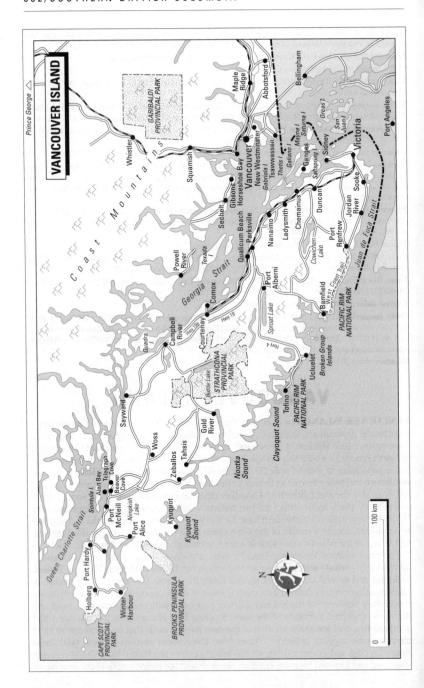

VANCOUVER ISLAND

Prince George

GARIBALDI PROVINCIAL PARK

Coast Mountains

Maple Ridge
Abbotsford
Bellingham

Whistler

Squamish

Vancouver
New Westminster
Tsawwassen
Port Angeles

Gibsons
Horseshoe Bay

Sidney
Victoria

Sechelt

Powell River

Texada

Qualicum Beach
Parksville
Nanaimo
Gabriola I
Orcas I
Mayne I
Saturna I
Galiano I
San Juan I

Georgia Strait

Comox

Hwy 19

Port Alberni

Ladysmith
Chemainus
Ganges
Saltspring
Thetis I

Duncan

Powell River

Campbell River
Courtenay

Quadra

Cowichan Lake
Port Renfrew
Jordan River
Sooke

Sproat Lake
Sproat Lake
Hwy 4

Battle Lake

STRATHCONA PROVINCIAL PARK

Bamfield
West Coast Trail
PACIFIC RIM NATIONAL PARK

Juan de Fuca Strait

Sayward

Woss

Gold River

Ucluelet
Broken Group Islands

Tahsis

Zeballos

Clayoquot Sound
Tofino
PACIFIC RIM NATIONAL PARK

Nootka Sound

Kyuquot

Sointula I.
Alert Bay
Telegraph Cove
Beaver Cove
Port McNeill
Nimpkish Lake
Port Alice

Kyuquot Sound

Queen Charlotte Strait

Holberg
Port Hardy

Winter Harbour

CAPE SCOTT PROVINCIAL PARK

BROOKS PENINSULA PROVINCIAL PARK

N

100 km

0

Once beyond the main towns of **Duncan** and **Nanaimo**, the northern two-thirds of the island is distinctly underpopulated. Locals and tourists alike are lured by the beaches at **Parksville** and **Qualicum**, while the stunning seascapes of the unmissable **Pacific Rim National Park**, protecting the central portion of the island's west coast, and **Strathcona Provincial Park**, which embraces the heart of the island's mountain fastness, are the main destinations for most visitors. Both of these parks offer the usual panoply of outdoor activities, with hikers being particularly well served by the national park's **West Coast Trail**, which is a tough and increasingly popular long-distance path. Shuttle buses and once-daily scheduled bus services from Victoria to points in the park, together with a wonderful approach by **boat** from Port Alberni, offer a choice of beguiling alternative itineraries for exploring the region. Another **boat trip** on a smaller working vessel from the tiny settlements of Tahsis and Gold River to the north is also becoming deservedly popular.

For a large number of travellers, however, the island is little more than a necessary pilgrimage on a longer journey north. Thousands annually make the trip to **Port Hardy**, linked by bus to Victoria, at the northern tip, to pick up the ferry that follows the so-called **Inside Passage**, a breathtaking trip up the British Columbia coast to Prince Rupert. More are likely to pick up on the new scenic ferry service, the **Discovery Coast Passage**, from Port Hardy to Bella Coola, south of Prince Rupert. You'll probably meet more backpackers plying these routes than anywhere else in the region, many of them en route to the far north, taking the ferries that continue on from Prince Rupert to Skagway and Alaska.

Victoria

VICTORIA has a lot to live up to. Leading travel magazine *Condé Nast Traveler* recently voted it one of the world's top ten cities to visit, and world number one for ambience and environment. And it's not named after a queen and an era for nothing. Victoria has gone to town in serving up lashings of fake Victoriana and chintzy commercialism – tearooms, Union Jacks, bagpipers, pubs and ersatz echoes of empire confront you at every turn. Much of the waterfront area has an undeniably quaint and likeable English feel – "Brighton Pavilion with the Himalayas for a backdrop", as Kipling remarked – and Victoria has more British-born residents than anywhere in Canada, but its tourist potential is exploited chiefly for American visitors who make the short sea journey from across the border. Despite the seasonal influx, and the sometimes atrocious attractions designed to part tourists from their money, it's a small, relaxed and pleasantly sophisticated place, worth lingering in if only for its inspirational museum. It's also rather genteel in parts, something underlined by the number of gardens around the place and some 900 hanging baskets that adorn much of the downtown area during the summer. Though often damp, the weather here is extremely mild: Victoria's meteorological station has the distinction of being the only one in Canada to record a winter in which the temperature never fell below freezing.

A brief history of Victoria

Victoria's site was originally inhabited by **Salish natives**, and in particular by the Lekwammen, who had a string of some ten villages in the area. From here they cultivated camas bulbs – vital to their diet and trade – and applied their advanced salmon-fishing methods to the shoals of migrating salmon in net-strung reefs offshore. At the time the region must have been a virtual paradise. Captain George Vancouver, apparently mindless of the native presence, described his feelings on first glimpsing this part of Vancouver Island: "The serenity of the climate, the innumerable pleasing landscapes, and the abundant fertility that nature puts forth, require only to be enriched by the industry of man with villages, mansions, cottages and other buildings, to render it the most lovely

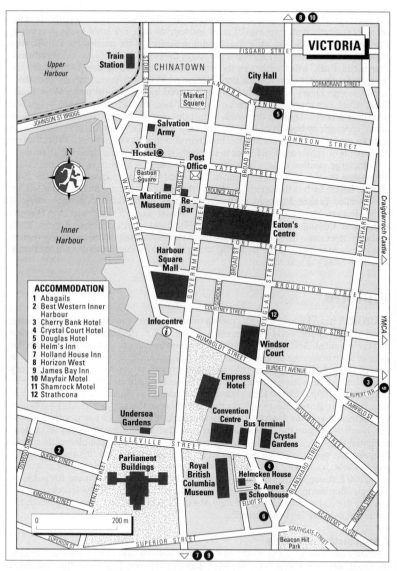

country that can be imagined." The first step in this process began in 1842, when Victoria received some of its earliest **white visitors**, when James Douglas disembarked during a search for a new local headquarters for the Hudson's Bay Company. One look at the natural harbour and its surroundings was enough: this, he declared, was a "perfect Eden", a feeling only reinforced by the friendliness of the indigenous population, who helped him build Fort Camouson, named after an important native landmark (the name was later changed to Fort Victoria to honour the British queen). The native peoples from up and down the island settled near the fort, attracted by the new trading opportunities it offered. Soon they were joined by British pioneers, brought in to settle the land by a Bay subsidiary, the Puget Sound Agricultural Company, which quickly built several large company farms as a focus for immigration. In time, the harbour became the busiest west coast port north of San Francisco and a major base for the British navy's Pacific fleet, a role it still fulfils for the bulk of Canada's present navy.

Boom time came in the 1850s following the mainland gold strikes, when Victoria's port became an essential stopoff and supplies depot for prospectors heading across the water and into the interior. Military and bureaucratic personnel moved in to ensure order, bringing Victorian morals and manners with them. Alongside there grew a rumbustious shantytown of shops, bars and brothels, one bar run by "Gassy" Jack Leighton, soon to become one of Vancouver's unwitting founders.

Though the gold-rush bubble soon burst, Victoria carried on as a military, economic and political centre, becoming capital of the newly created British Columbia in 1866 – years before the foundation of Vancouver. British values were cemented in stone by the Canadian Pacific Railway, which built the *Empress Hotel* in 1908 in place of a proposed railway link that never came. Victoria's planned role as Canada's western rail terminus was surrendered to Vancouver, and with it any chance of realistic growth or industrial development. These days the town survives – but survives well – almost entirely on the backs of tourists (four million a year), the civil service bureaucracy, and – shades of the home country – retirees in search of a mild-weathered retreat. Its population today is around 330,000, almost exactly double what it was just thirty years ago.

Arrival and information

Victoria International Airport is 20km north of downtown on Hwy 17. The Airporter shuttle bus heads downtown (where it stops at major hotels) every half-hour between 4.30am and 1am; a single fare for the thirty-minute journey is $13 (☎386-2525 or 386-2526 for information). Leaving the city for flights, you should call to arrange pick-ups. Otherwise contact West Coast Air, 1000 Wharf St (☎1-800-347-2222), who operate float planes between Vancouver's port and Victoria's downtown Inner Harbour. The **bus terminal** is downtown at 700 Douglas and Belleville, close to the Royal British Columbia Museum; the central VIA Rail **station** is at 450 Pandora St, about seven blocks north of the *Empress Hotel*, but you'll only arrive there if you've managed to get a seat on the lone daily train from Courtenay and Nanaimo.

Victoria's busy **infocentre** is 812 Wharf St, in front of the *Empress Hotel* on the harbour (daily: May–Sept 8.30am–8pm; Oct–April 9am–5pm; ☎953-2033, for accommodation reservations ☎1-800-663-3883 in North America, 250/953-2022 from outside North America). It offers help finding accommodation and can book you onto whale-watching and other tours (see box, p.696), while its huge range of information – on both Victoria and Vancouver Island as a whole – makes as good a reason as any for starting a tour of the island from the city. Also, there's a separate desk for concert, theatre and other tickets. It's also worth checking out the notice board at the **HI youth hostel** (see p.690), which has lots of current practical information likely to be of use to independent travellers.

The best in-town means of transport are the tiny Inner Harbour **ferries**, worth taking just for the ride: try an $8 evening "mini-cruise" around the harbour (tickets on Inner Harbour or book at the infocentre). You're unlikely to need to take a local **bus** anywhere, but if you do, most services run from the corner of Douglas and Yates. The fare within the large central zone is $1.50 – tickets and the DayPass ($5) are sold at the infocentre, 7-Eleven stores and other marked outlets, or you can pay on board if you have the exact fare. For 24-hour recorded information on city transit, call ☎382-6161. Other potentially useful private bus lines for **onward travel** from Victoria include Laidlaw (☎385-4411 or 1-800-318-0818) at the bus terminal, responsible for scheduled services across the island

GETTING TO VANCOUVER ISLAND

There are three ways to reach Vancouver Island – by bus and ferry, car and ferry, or air. Most people travelling under their own steam from Vancouver use the first means, which is a simple matter of buying an all-inclusive through-ticket to Victoria. More involved crossings to other points on the island, however, whether from the Canadian or US mainlands, are worth considering if you wish to skip Victoria and head as quickly as possible to Port Hardy for the Inside Passage ferry connections, or to Strathcona or the Pacific Rim parks. You can also reach Victoria directly from Vancouver Airport by inclusive coach and ferry arrangements (see pp.649 for details).

Foot passengers from Vancouver
If you're without your own transport, the most painless way to Victoria from Vancouver is to buy a Pacific Coach Lines (PCL; ☎604/662-8074 or 250/385-4411 in Victoria, 604/662-8074) ticket at the Vancouver bus terminal at 1150 Station St, which takes you, inclusive of the ferry crossing and journeys to and from ferry terminals at both ends, to Victoria's central bus station at 700 Douglas St. Buses leave hourly in the summer (first bus 5.45am), every two hours in the winter: total journey time is about three hours thirty minutes and a single ticket costs $25 ($47 return). No bookings are necessary or taken: overflow passengers are simply put on another coach. The ferry crossing takes 95 minutes, and offers some stunning views as the boat navigates the narrow channels between the Gulf Islands en route. Be sure to keep your ticket stub for reboarding the bus after the crossing. Coach drivers give you all the practical details en route. It's also worth stocking up on food on board, as subsidized ferry meals are famously cheap (queues form instantly). You can save yourself about $13 by using public transport at each end and buying a ferry ticket ($8) separately, but for the extra hassle and time involved it hardly seems worth it. A similar all-inclusive bus/ferry arrangement also operates from Vancouver to Nanaimo on Vancouver Island via the Horseshoe Bay Terminal, about fifteen minutes north of West Vancouver on Hwy 1. You can reach the Horseshoe Bay Terminal under your own steam by taking bus #250 or #257 from Georgia Street. The ferry charges $8 for foot passengers.

By car from British Columbia
BC Ferries operates four routes to the island across the Georgia Strait from mainland British Columbia (☎1-888-223-3779 from anywhere in BC; otherwise ☎604/669-1211 in Vancouver, ☎250/386-3431 in Victoria or for recorded timetable information 604/277-0277 in Vancouver, 250/656-0757 in Victoria and 250/753-6626 in Nanaimo). Reservations on all routes are essential in summer if you want to avoid long waits. The most direct and heavily used by Victoria–Vancouver passengers is the Tsawwassen–Swartz Bay connection, the route used by Pacific Coach Lines' buses. Tsawwassen is about a forty-minute drive south of downtown Vancouver; Swartz Bay is the same distance north of Victoria. Ferries ply the route almost continuously from 7am to 9pm (sixteen sailings daily in summer, minimum of eight daily in winter). Car tickets cost $30 at weekends and $28 on weekdays in high season ($23 and $21.75 in low season); bicycles cost $2.50. The Mid-Island Express from Tsawwassen to Nanaimo, midway up the island, has ten or more departures daily on the two-hour crossing (and a minimum of eight in the winter). More boats cover the Horseshoe Bay–Nanaimo route, a 95-minute journey from a terminal about fifteen minutes' drive from West Vancouver. Note that a new ferry terminal, Discovery Point, has been opened at Nanaimo. Fares for both these routes are the same as for Tsawwassen to Swartz Bay. The fourth route is Powell River–Comox, Powell River being some 160km northwest of Vancouver on the Sunshine Coast.

Ferries from the United States

Travellers from the United States have several options. Coach and ferry inclusive arrangements are offered by Gray Lines of Seattle, who operate a once-daily service in each direction between Seattle and Victoria (currently leaves 5.30am; $39 one way, $70 return; ☎250/344-5248, 206/624-3079 or 1-800-426-7562). Washington State Ferries, 2499 Ocean Ave, Sidney (in Victoria ☎250/381-1551 or 250/656-1531 in Sidney, in Seattle ☎206/464-6400, statewide 1-800-84-FERRY) runs ferries from Anacortes, ninety minutes north of Seattle, to Sidney, thirty minutes (and 30km) north of Victoria (summer 2 daily in each direction, winter 1 daily; 3hr–3hr 30min) via Friday Harbor on the San Juan Islands. Passenger fares are US$6.90 (US$1.75 from the San Juan Islands), a car and driver US$35.65 (US$15 from the San Juan Islands). Car reservations are required from Orcas and Friday Harbor and can be made by calling at least a day in advance (☎360/378-4777 in Friday Harbor).

Black Ball Transport, 430 Belleville St, Victoria (in BC ☎250/386-2202, in Washington ☎360/457-4491 or 1-800/633-1589) operates a ferry across the Juan de Fuca Strait between Port Angeles on Washington's Olympic Peninsula right to Victoria's Inner Harbour (1–4 daily; 95min). Passenger fares are around US$7 and US$30 for cars. Reservations are not accepted. Car drivers should call ahead in summer to have some idea of how long they'll have to wait.

For foot passengers, and day-trippers in particular, a speedier option is Victoria Express's service from Port Angeles (2 daily late May to late June & Sept to mid-Oct; late June to Aug 3 daily; 55min) to Victoria's Inner Harbour. The fare is US$10 one way, US$20 return, except July, August and September when it's US$25. Ferries run only from mid-May to mid-Oct. For information and reservations, call ☎250/361-9144 (Canada), ☎360/452-8088 (Port Angeles) or ☎1-800-633-1589 (Washington). Alternatively, the 300-passenger-only Victoria Clipper catamaran travels between Pier 69 in downtown Seattle and Victoria's Inner Harbour in three hours or two hours if you take the more "Turbojet" departures (250 Bellevue St, Victoria, ☎250/382-8100 in Victoria, ☎206/448-5000 in Seattle or 1-800-888-2535 outside Seattle and BC). There is one sailing daily in each direction from January to March and mid-September to December; two sailings daily in the first half of May and second half of Sept; and four sailings daily from mid-May to mid-September. Tickets prices vary according to season – US$54 single, US$88 return off season, about US$58/94 for three-hour crossings and US$66/109 for the Turbojet in summer. The Victoria Line, 185 Dallas Rd, Victoria (☎1-800-668-1167 or 250/480-5555 for reservations) also runs a similar service (May–Oct 1 daily in each direction) from Seattle's Pier 48 to Ogden Point in Victoria. The journey time is slower (4hr 30 min), but fares are cheaper (around US$25 single, US$49 return).

By air

Several provincial airlines as well as the big two – Air Canada and Canadian Airlines – fly to Victoria, though it's an expensive way to make the journey if you're only coming from Vancouver or Washington State. Open return fares from Vancouver typically run to around $115, excursion fares around $75. Air BC, 1000 Wharf St, Victoria (☎688-5515), flies the most frequent shuttles between Vancouver and Victoria airports. If you are going to fly, however, it's more fun and more direct to fly from Vancouver harbour to Victoria harbour by helicopter or float plane: West Coast Air (☎1-800-347-2222) fly from the Tradewinds Marina just west of Canada Place in Vancouver. Helijet Airways (☎604/273-1414) fly from the helipad to the east. Kenmore Air, 6321 NE 175th, Seattle (☎206/486-1257), runs scheduled seaplane services (45 min) between downtown Seattle and Victoria's Inner Harbour.

to Duncan, Nanaimo, Port Alberni, Tofino, Ucluelet, Campbell River, Port Hardy and points in between (no reservations are necessary or taken for Laidlaw services). Also useful are Gray Lines of Seattle for a once-daily service to Seattle inclusive of ferry (leaves 10am; $39; ☎250/344-5248, 206/624-3079 or 1-800-426-7562). The West Coast Trail Connector, 767 Audley St (☎475-2010), is a shuttle service for connections to Port Renfrew and the southern trailhead of the West Coast Trail (see pp.729–730) and points off Hwy 14. For the trail's northern head, and access to Bamfield in the Pacific Rim National Park (see p.728), take the daily *West Coast Trail Express*, 3954 Bow Rd (☎477-8700; $50).

Accommodation

Victoria fills up quickly in the summer, and most of its budget **accommodation** is well-known and heavily patronized. Top-price hotels cluster around the Inner Harbour area; **hostels** and more downmarket alternatives are scattered all over, though the largest concentration of cheap **hotels** and **motels** is around the Gorge Road and Douglas Street areas northwest of downtown. Reservations are virtually obligatory in all categories, though the infocentre's accommodation service will root out a room if you're stuck (☎1-800-663-3883 in North America, 250/953-2022 from outside North America). They are more than likely to offer you **B&B**, of which the town has a vast selection, though prices for many are surprisingly elevated; many owners of the more far-flung places will pick you up from downtown. Some B&Bs are also real treats – romantic hideaways or housed in lovely old houses. In desperation it's worth consulting one of the specialist B&B agencies such as Canada-West (☎388-4620).

Victoria's commercial **campgrounds** are full to bursting in summer, with most space given over to RVs. Few of these are convenient for downtown anyway – given that you'll have to travel, you might as well head for one of the more scenic provincial park sites. Most are on the Trans-Canada Highway to the north, or on Hwy 14 east of Victoria.

Hotels and motels

Abagail's, 960 McClure St (☎388-5363). A classy, small hotel in a fine building with log fires, voluminous duvets, Jacuzzis and a good breakfast. Situated on the corner of Quadra Street, a block east of Blanshard and easy walking distance from the centre. ⑥–⑧.

Best Western Inner Harbour, 412 Quebec St (☎384-5122 or 1-800-528-1234). Very convenient, central and comfortable, but pricey. ⑥.

Cherry Bank Hotel, 825 Burdett Ave (☎385-5380 or 1-800-998-6688). Reservations are essential at this deservedly popular and pleasantly eccentric 26-room budget hotel (note rotating mermaid on the roof); excellent rooms and breakfast included. ③.

Crystal Court Motel, 701 Belleville St (☎384-0551, fax 384-5125). Large, functional and fairly priced motel well located just one block from the Inner Harbour, though it fronts a fairly busy road. ③.

Douglas Hotel, 1450 Douglas and Pandora (☎383-4157 or 1-800-332-9981, fax 383-2279). Clean, no-frills and slightly rough-edged big hotel. It is opposite the city hall, close to downtown, and on bus routes #1, #6, #14 and #30. ③–④.

Helm's Inn, 600 Douglas St (☎385-5767). Popular if gaudily decorated hotel on the main road just half a block from the Royal BC Museum. One-bedroom and studio suites with kitchens available. Cheaper rates off season. ⑤–⑥.

Holland House Inn, 595 Michegan St near Government (☎384-6644). A comfortable and smart, small hotel located a couple of blocks south of the BC Museum. ⑤–⑦.

Horizon West, 1961 Douglas (☎382-2111 or 1-800-830-2111). Reasonably central hotels in this price range are unusual in Victoria, so call ahead to secure one of its eighty rooms. ③–④.

James Bay Inn, 270 Government and Toronto (☎384-7151 or 1-800-836-2649, fax 385-2311). Vying with the *Cherry Bank* as Victoria's best reasonably low-cost option, this Edwardian building was the home of painter Emily Carr. Simple rooms at varying prices, with a restaurant and pub in the basement. Two blocks south of the Government Buildings (buses #5 or #30 to Government and Superior Street). ④–⑤.

Mayfair Motel, 650 Speed Ave and Douglas (☎388-7337). This small motel 2km north of downtown is ideal if you want to be away from the centre. ③.

Shamrock Motel, 675 Superior St (☎385-8768 or 1-800-294-5544, fax 385-1837). Has just fifteen units, but (with the *Crystal Court*), one of the best-value motels or hotels in the central area. ④.

Strathcona, 919 Douglas St (☎383-7137 or 1-800-663-7476, fax 383-6893). Large, modern hotel where rooms include baths and TVs. There's a "British pub" and restaurant downstairs with booming live and DJ music and the nightly dancing may not be to all tastes. ④–⑤.

Bed and Breakfasts

Ambleside, 1121 Faithful St (☎388-9948 or 1-800-916-9948, fax 383-9317). Expensive as B&Bs go, but you get a 1919 "craftsman heritage home", a full breakfast and a choice of two tasteful rooms in a pleasant neighbourhood due east of Beacon Hill Park (so a long but pleasant walk to downtown). ⑤–⑥.

Anderson House, 301 Kingston St (☎388-4565). Another pricey and tasteful two-room heritage home (built 1891) with private baths and even CD players. ⑥.

At Craig House, 52 San Jose Ave (☎383-0339, fax 383-0349). Three reasonably priced rooms in a residential neighbourhood. ③–④.

Craigmyle Guest House, 1037 Craigmyle Rd (☎595-5411, fax 370-5276). By Craigdarroch Castle this friendly antique-furnished home has seventeen rooms, but is 1.5km from downtown. Buses #11 or #14 run from the corner of Fort Street and Joan Crescent. ④.

Heathergate House, 122 Simcoe St (☎383-0068, fax 383-4320). Four rooms within walking distance of the Inner Harbour and the sights. ⑤.

Prior House, 620 St Charles St (☎592-8847). Pretty swanky for a B&B; once the home of Victoria's lieutenant governor – ask for his suite, complete with bathroom and chandelier. Out east in smart Rockland area, so better if you have transport. ⑤–⑧.

Ryan's, 224 Superior St (☎389-0012). A very pretty 1892 heritage building south of the BC Museum and 5min walk to downtown; all nicely decorated rooms with private bathrooms. ⑥.

Hostels and student accommodation

Beverley Lodge, 1729 Oak Bay Ave (☎598-7323). Hostel with non-smoking bunk rooms for two, four and six people. A 20min walk from downtown: follow Fort Street until it intersects Oak Bay Avenue; turn right and the newly renovated four-storey heritage house is four roads down on the right. or you can catch buses #1 or #2 from opposite *MacDonalds* on Douglas Street, which drop you virtually outside. Self-serve kitchen and outside deck available. $18–20. ①.

Renouf House, 2010 Stanley Ave (☎595-4774, fax 598-1515). A 30min walk east from downtown or catch #10 (Haultain) bus from the corner of Douglas and View and ask to be dropped at Fernwood and Stanley. Then walk a block east on Gladstone to Stanley, turn left at the corner store and the hostel is the white house next door. The owners are great kayaking and sailing experts, so well worth staying here if this is what you want to do on Vancouver Island. Choice of bunk rooms ($19.75), singles/doubles with shared bathroom ($33.25/50) or singles/doubles with private bathroom ($55/70). ①–④.

Salvation Army Men's Hostel, 525 Johnson St (☎384-3396). Better than it sounds, being clean and modern, but for men only. Rooms are given on a first-come, first-served basis, with doors open at 4pm. Dorm beds, private rooms and weekly and monthly rates are available. ①.

University of Victoria (☎721-8395 or 721-8396). The nicely situated campus is 20min northeast of downtown near Oak Bay and reached on buses #7 or #14. Ring for the University Housing and Conference Services, or register on site at the Housing Office, near the campus Coffee Gardens. Offers single and double private rooms with shared bath including breakfast. May–Sept. ①.

Victoria Backpackers' Hostel, 1418 Fernwood Rd (☎386-4471). Battered and laid-back but less convenient than the youth hostel: take bus #1, #10, #11, #14, #27 or #28 towards Fernwood: the #10 to Haultain from the corner of Douglas and Fort is the best bet. Dorm beds, private singles and doubles available with one bunk room reserved for women only. No curfew. Dorm beds $18 summer, $10 winter. ①.

Victoria YM-WCA Women's Residence, 880 Courtney and Quadra (☎386-7511). A short stroll from downtown and on the #1 bus route. Mixed cafeteria and sports facilities, including pool, but rooms are for women only. Singles and doubles available; discounts October to May. ②.

Victoria Youth Hostel (HI), 516 Yates and Wharf (Mon–Thurs 7.30am to midnight, Fri–Sun 7am–2am; ☎385-4511, fax 385-3232). Large, modern, welcoming and extremely well-run place just a few blocks north of the Inner Harbour. The bunk rooms, though, can be noisy: the reception, rather ominously, sells earplugs. The notice boards are packed with useful information. Members $15.50, non-members $19.50. Just two private doubles are available at $35 for members, $43 for non-members. ①–②.

Campgrounds
Fort Victoria RV and Park Campground, 340 Island Hwy 1A (☎479-8112, fax 479-5806). Closest site to downtown, located 6km north of Victoria off the Trans-Canada. Take bus #14 (for Craigflower) from the city centre. Large (250-pitch) site with free hot showers. $24–26 per two persons.

Goldstream Provincial Park, 2930 Trans-Canada Highway (☎387-4363). Although 20km north of the city, this is Victoria's best camping option, with plenty of hiking, swimming and fishing opportunities.

McDonald Provincial Park. A government site with limited facilities, 32km from Victoria, but only 3km from the Swartz Bay Ferry Terminal, so useful for boat travellers.

Thetis Lake, 1938 Trans-Canada Highway (☎478-3845). Runs a close second to *Goldstream Park* for the pleasantness of its setting, and is only 10km north of downtown. Family-oriented, with 100 sites, laundry and coin-operated showers.

Weir's Beach Resort, 5191 Williams Head Rd (☎478-3323). Enticing beachfront location 24km east of Victoria on Hwy 14.

The City

The Victoria that's worth bothering with is very small: almost everything worth seeing, as well as the best shops and restaurants, is within walking distance in the **Inner Harbour** area and the Old Town district behind it. On summer evenings this area is alive with strollers and buskers, and a pleasure to wander as the sun drops over the water. Foremost amongst the daytime diversions are the **Royal British Columbia Museum** and the **Empress Hotel**. Most of the other trumpeted attractions are dreadful, and many charge entry fees out of all proportion to what's on show. If you're tempted by the Royal London Wax Museum, the Pacific Undersea Gardens, Miniature World, English Village, Anne Hathaway's Thatched Cottage or any of Victoria's other dubious commercial propositions, details are available from the infocentre. Otherwise you might drop by the modest **Maritime Museum** and think about a trip to the celebrated **Butchart Gardens**, some way out of town, but easily accessed by public transport or regular tours from the bus terminal. If you're around for a couple of days you should also find time to walk around **Beacon Hill Park**, a few minutes' walk from downtown to the south.

The best of the area's beaches are well out of town on Hwy 14 and Hwy 1 (see pp.705–706), but for idling by the sea drop down to the pebble shore along the southern edge of Beacon Hill Park. For some local swimming, the best option by far is **Willows Beach** on the Esplanade in Oak Bay, 2km east of Victoria; take bus #1 to Beach and Dalhousie Road. Other good stretches of sand can be found on Dallas Road and at Island View Beach.

The Royal British Columbia Museum
The **Royal British Columbia Museum**, 675 Belleville St (daily: mid-May to Sept 9am–5pm; $7; Oct to mid-May $5.35; ☎387-3701 or 1-800-661-5411), founded in 1886, is perhaps the best museum in Canada, and regularly rated, by visitors, as one of North America's top ten. All conceivable aspects of the province are examined, but the **First Peoples** section is probably the definitive collection of a much-covered genre, while the natural history sections – huge re-creations of natural habitats, complete with sights, sounds and smells – are mind-boggling in scope and imagination. Allow at least two trips to take it all in.

From the word go – a huge stuffed mammoth and sculpture of a tweedy Brit and his chiffon-swathed wife taking tea – you can tell that thought, wit and a lot of money have gone into the museum. Much of the cash must have been sunk into its most popular display, the **Open Ocean**, a self-contained, in-depth look at the sea and the deep-level ocean. Groups of ten are admitted into a series of tunnels, dark rooms, lifts and mock-ups of submarines at thirty-minute intervals. You take a time-coded ticket and wait your turn, so either arrive early or reckon on seeing the rest of the museum first. Though rather heavy-handed in its "we're-all-part-of-the-cosmic-soup" message, it's still an object lesson in presentation and state-of-the-art museum dynamics. It's also designed to be dark and enclosed, and signs wisely warn you to stay out if you suffer even a twinge of claustrophobia.

The first floor contains **dioramas**, full-scale reconstructions of some of the many natural habitats found in British Columbia. The idea of re-creating shorelines, coastal rainforests and Fraser Delta landscapes may sound far-fetched, yet all are incredibly realistic, down to dripping water and cool, dank atmospheres. Audiovisual displays and a tumult of information accompany the exhibits (the beaver film is worth hunting down), most of which focus attention on the province's 25,600km of coastline, a side of British Columbia usually overlooked in favour of its interior forests and mountains.

Upstairs on the second floor is the mother of all the tiny museums of bric-a-brac and pioneer memorabilia in BC. Arranged eccentrically from the present day backwards, it explores every aspect of the province's **social history** over two centuries in nit-picking detail. Prominently featured are the best part of an early twentieth-century town, complete with cinema and silent films, plus comprehensive displays on logging, mining, the gold rush, farming, fishing and lesser domestic details, all the artefacts and accompanying information being presented with impeccable finesse.

Up on the mezzanine third floor is a superb collection of **Native Canadian art, culture and history** (see box, overleaf). It's presented in gloomy light, against muted wood walls and brown carpet – precautions intended to protect the fragile exhibits, but which also create a solemn atmosphere in keeping with the tragic nature of many of the displays. The collection divides into two epochs – before and after the coming of Europeans – tellingly linked by a single native carving of a white man, starkly and brilliantly capturing the initial wonder and weirdness of the new arrivals. Alongside are shamanic displays and carvings of previously taboo subjects, subtly illustrating the first breakdown of the old ways. The whole collection reflects this thoughtful and oblique approach, taking you to the point where smallpox virtually wiped out in one year a culture that was eight millennia in the making. A section on land and reservations is left for last – the issues are contentious even today – and even if you're succumbing to museum fatigue, the arrogance and duplicity of the documents on display will shock you. The highlights in this section are many, but try to make a point of seeing the short film footage *In the Land of the War Canoes* (1914), the **Bighouse** and its chants, and the audiovisual display on native myths and superstition. Outside the museum, there's also **Thunderbird Park**, a strip of grass with a handful of totem poles.

Helmcken House

Helmcken House (daily: May–Oct 10am–5pm; Nov–April noon–4pm; $4) stands strangely isolated in Thunderbird Park directly adjacent to the museum, a predictable heritage offering that showcases the home, furnishings and embroidery talents of the Helmcken family. Built in 1852, it is the oldest surviving standing home on the island. Dr John Helmcken was Fort Victoria's doctor and local political bigwig, and his house is a typical monument to stolid Victoria values. Upstairs it also contains various attic treasures and some of the good doctor's fearsome-looking medical tools. It's probably only of interest, however, if you've so far managed to avoid any of Canada's many thousands of similar houses. If you do visit, pick up the free guided tapes and listen to "voices from history" (actors and actresses) that give a more personalized slant to the building: listen, for example, to "Aunt Dolly" as she tells why she left the good doctor's

THE NATIVE CULTURES OF THE NORTHWEST COAST

Of all Canada's native peoples, the numerous linguistic groups that inhabit the northwest coast of British Columbia have the most sophisticated artistic tradition and the most lavish of ceremonials. Traditionally their social organization stemmed from a belief in a mythical time when humans and animals were essentially the same: each tribe was divided into **kin groups** who were linked by a common supernatural animal ancestor and shared the same names, ritual dances, songs and regalia. Seniority within each kin group was held by a rank of chiefs and nobles, who controlled the resources of private property such as house sites, stands of cedar, and fishing, gathering and hunting territories.

Such privileges, almost unique among Canadian native groups, led to the accumulation of private wealth, and thus great emphasis was placed on their inheritance. Central to the power structure was the ceremonial **potlatch**, which was held in the winter village, a seasonal resting place for these otherwise nomadic people, located where the supernatural forces were believed to be most accessible. The potlatch marked every significant occasion from the birth of an heir to the raising of a carved pole, and underscored an individual's right to his or her inherited status. Taking its name from the Chinook word for "gift", the potlatch also had the function of **redistributing wealth**. All the guests at the potlatch acted as witnesses to whatever event or object was being validated, and were repaid for their services with gifts from the host chief. Though these gifts often temporarily bankrupted the host, they heightened his prestige and ensured that he would be repaid in kind at a subsequent potlatch.

The most important element of potlatches were the **masked dances** that re-enacted ancestral encounters with supernatural beings, and were the principal means of perpetuating the history and heritage of each kin group. Created by artists whose innovative ideas were eagerly sought by chiefs in order to impress their guests, the dramatic masks were often elaborate mechanisms that could burst open to reveal the wearer or – like the well-known Cannibal Bird – could produce loud and disconcerting noises.

The **Kwakiutl** produced the most developed potlatches, featuring highly ranked dances like the *hamatsa* or **"cannibal dance"**, whose performers had served a long apprenticeship as participants in less exalted dances. Before the *hamatsa* the initiate was sent to the "Cannibal at the North End of the World", a long period of seclusion and instruction in the snowbound woods. On returning to the village he would seem to be in a complete cannibalistic frenzy and would rush around biting members of the audience. These apparent victims were all paid for their role, which usually involved cutting themselves with knives to draw a flow of blood – and the *hamatsa* would burst blood-filled

room untouched as a shrine after his death. Just behind the house there's another old white wood building, the **St Anne's Pioneer Schoolhouse** ($2), originally purchased by a Bishop Demers for four sisters of the Order of St Ann, who in 1858 took it upon themselves to leave their Québec home to come and teach in Victoria. Built between 1843 and 1858, it's believed to be the oldest building in Victoria still in use.

The Parliament Buildings

The huge Victorian pile of the **Parliament Buildings**, at 501 Belleville St (June–Sept daily 9am–noon & 1–5pm; free; guided tours every 20min), is old and imposing in the manner of a large and particularly grand British town hall. Beautifully lit at night by some three hundred tiny bulbs (though locals grumble about the cost), the domed building is fronted by the sea and well-kept gardens – a pleasant enough ensemble, though it doesn't really warrant the manic enthusiasm visited on it by hordes of summer tourists. You're more likely to find yourself taking time out on the front lawns, distinguished by a perky statue of Queen Victoria and a giant sequoia, a gift from California. Designed by the 25-year-old Francis Rattenbury, who was also responsible for the

bladders in his mouth to add to the carnage, while relatives shook rattles and sang to tame him. A fantastic finale came with the arrival of the loudly clacking "Cannibal Birds", dancers dressed in long strips of cedar bark and huge masks, of which the most fearsome was the "Cannibal Raven", whose long straight beak could crush a human skull. The *hamatsa* would then return in ceremonial finery completely restored to his human state.

As elsewhere in Canada, **European contact** was disastrous for the coastal peoples. The establishment of fur-trading posts in the early nineteenth century led to the abandonment of traditional economic cycles, the loss of their creative skills through reliance on readily available European goods, the debilitation from alcohol and internecine wars. Though most of BC remains non-treaty, lands on Vancouver Island were surrendered to become the "Entire property of the White people forever" in return for small payments – the whole Victoria area was obtained for 371 blankets. Infectious disease, the greatest of all threats, reached its peak with the 1862 smallpox epidemic, which spread from Victoria along the entire coast and far into the interior, killing probably a third of BC's native population.

In this period of decline, potlatches assumed an increased significance as virtually the only medium of cultural continuity, with rival chiefs asserting their status through ever more extravagant displays – even going as far as to burn slaves who had been captured in battle. Excesses such as these and the newly adopted "whiskey feasts" were seen by the **missionaries** as a confirmation that these peoples were enveloped in the "dark mantle of degrading superstition". With BC's entry into confederation the responsibility for the natives fell to the federal government in faraway Ottawa, much of whose knowledge of the indigenous peoples came from the missionaries – the subsequent **Indian Act**, passed in 1884, prohibited the potlatch ceremony.

For a while the defiant native groups managed to evade detection by holding potlatches at fishing camps rather than the winter villages, and there were few successful prosecutions until the 1920s. Things came to a head in 1922 with the conviction of 34 Kwakiutl from Alert Bay – all were sentenced to jail terms but a deal was struck whereby all those who surrendered their potlatch regalia were freed. Thirty years later, when potlatching was again legalized, native pressure began to mount for return of these treasures from the collections into which they had been dispersed, but it took a further twenty years for the federal government to agree to return the goods on condition that they be put on public display. Though the masks totally lose their dramatic emphasis in static exhibitions, many of the more local museums have a dual function as community centres, and as such are vital to the preservation of a dynamic native culture.

Empress Hotel opposite, the building was completed in 1897, at a cost of $923,000, in time for Queen Victoria's jubilee. Figures from Victoria's grey bureaucratic past are duly celebrated, the main door guarded by statues of Sir James Douglas, who chose the site of the city, and Sir Matthew Baillie Begbie (aka the "Hanging Judge"), responsible for law and order during the heady days of gold fever. Sir George Vancouver keeps an eye on proceedings from the top of the dome. Free tours start to the right of the main steps. Guides are chirpy and full of anecdotes. Look out for the dagger which killed Captain Cook, and the gold-plated dome, painted with scenes from Canadian history.

Beacon Hill Park

The best park within walking distance of the town centre is **Beacon Hill Park**, south of the Inner Harbour and a few minutes' walk up the road behind the museum. Victoria is sometimes known as the "City of Gardens", and at the right times of the year this park shows why. Victoria's biggest green space, it has lots of paths, ponds, big trees and quiet corners, and plenty of views over the Juan de Fuca Strait to the distant Olympic Mountains of Washington State (especially on its southern side). These pretty straits, incidentally, are the focus of some rather bad feeling between Victoria and its US neighbour, for the city has a (literally) dark secret: it dumps raw sewage into the strait, excusing itself by claiming it's quickly broken up by the sea's strong currents. Washington State isn't so sure, and there have been plenty of arguments over the matter and, more to the point for city elders, economically damaging convention boycotts by US companies. Either way, it's pretty bad PR for Victoria and totally at odds with its image. Gardens in the park are alternatively tended and wonderfully wild and unkempt, and were a favoured retreat of celebrated Victorian artist, Emily Carr. They also claim the world's tallest totem pole, Mile Zero of the Trans-Canada Highway, and – that ultimate emblem of Englishness – a cricket pitch. Some of the trees are massive old-growth timbers that you'd normally only see on the island's west coast. Come here in spring and you'll catch swaths of daffodils and blue camas flowers, the latter a floral monument to Victoria's earliest native inhabitants, who cultivated the flower for its edible bulb. Some 30,000 other flowers are planted out annually.

Crystal Gardens and Butchart Gardens

The heavily advertised **Crystal Gardens**, behind the bus terminal at 713 Douglas St (daily July & Aug 9am–8pm; Sept–June 10am–4.30pm; $7; ☎381-1213), was designed on the model of London's destroyed Crystal Palace and was billed on opening in 1925 as housing the "Largest Saltwater Swimming Pool in the British Empire". Now much restored, the greenery-, monkey- and bird-filled greenhouse makes for an unaccountably popular tourist spot; only the exterior has any claims to architectural sophistication, and much of its effect is spoilt by the souvenir shops on its ground-floor arcade. Once the meeting place of the town's tea-sipping elite, it still plays host to events such as the Jive and Ballroom Dance Club and the People Meeting People Dance. The daytime draws are the conservatory-type tearoom and tropical gardens. Inhumanely enclosed birds and monkeys, though, are liable to put you off your scones.

If you're into things horticultural you'll want to make a trek out to the heavily over-advertised but deservedly celebrated **Butchart Gardens**, 22km north of Victoria at 800 Benvenuto, Brentwood Bay on Hwy 17 towards the Swartz Bay ferry terminal (daily: mid-June to Aug 9am–10.30pm; first half of June & Sept 9am–9pm; rest of the year 9am–sunset; $14.50; ☎652-4422 or 652-5256 for recorded information). They're also renowned amongst visitors and locals alike for the stunning **firework displays** that usually take place each Saturday evening in July and August. There is also a restaurant and various other commercial enterprises, with musical entertainments well to the fore. The gardens are also illuminated during the late evening opening hours between mid-June and the end of September. To get here by public transport take bus #75 for "Central Sahnich" from downtown. Otherwise there are regular summer **shuttles** (May–Oct daily hourly in the morning, half-hourly in the afternoon; ☎388-5248) from the main bus terminal, where tickets are obtainable not from the main ticket office but from a separate Gray Lines desk: ticket prices include garden entrance. Internationally, the gardens were started in 1904 by Mrs Butchart wife of a mine-owner and pioneer of Portland Cement in Canada and the US. The initial aim was to landscape one of her husband's quarries, and now cover fifty breathtaking acres, comprising rose, Japanese and Italian gardens and lots of decorative details. About half a million visitors a year tramp through the foliage, which includes over a million plants and seven hundred different species.

The Empress Hotel

A town is usually desperate when one of its key attractions is a hotel, but in the case of Victoria the **Empress Hotel**, 721 Government St (☎384-8111), is so physically overbearing and plays such a part in the town's tourist appeal that it demands some sort of attention. You're unlikely to be staying here – rooms start at around $200 and are largely snapped up by Japanese visitors – but it's worth wandering through the huge lobbies and palatial dining areas for a glimpse of well-restored colonial splendour. In a couple of lounges there's a fairly limp "Smart Casual" dress code – no dirty jeans, running shoes, short shorts or backpacks – but elsewhere you can wander at will. If you want **take tea**, which is why most casual visitors are here, enter the Tea Lounge by the hotel's side entrance (the right, or south side): there you can enjoy scones, biscuits, cakes and, of course, tea over six courses costing $29 but you have to abide by the dress code. In other lounges like the Bengal (see below) you can ask for just tea and scones. At the last count the hotel was serving 1.6 million cups of tea a year.

The hotel's **Crystal Lounge** and its lovely Tiffany-glass dome forms the most opulent part of the hotel on view, but the marginally less ornate entrance lounge is *the* place for the charade of afternoon tea, and indulging can be a bit of a laugh. There's also a reasonable bar and restaurant downstairs, **Kipling's**, and the so-called **Bengal Lounge** where you can have a curry and all the trimmings for about $10 (the hotel also boasts Victoria's best-appointed toilets). For a splurge, try the London clubland surroundings – chesterfields and aspidistras – and the champagne-and-chocolate-cake special ($8.50) on offer in the lounge to the left of the entrance lobby.

The old town

The oldest part of Victoria focuses on **Bastion Square**, original site of Fort Victoria, from which it's a short walk to Market Square, a nice piece of old town rejuvenation, and the main downtown shopping streets. Bastion Square's former saloons, brothels and warehouses have been spruced up to become offices, cafés and galleries. The modest **Maritime Museum** at 28 Bastion Square (daily 9.30am–4.30pm; $5; ☎385-4222) is of interest mainly for the lovely chocolate-and-vanilla-coloured building in which it's housed, the former provincial courthouse. Recently updated displays embrace old charts, uniforms, ships' bells, period photographs, lots of models and a new BC Ferries section on the second floor. On the top floor is the restored vice-admiralty courtroom, once the main seat of justice for the entire province. Note the old open elevator built to reach it, commissioned by Chief Justice Davie in 1901, supposedly because he was too fat to manage the stairs. Just to the north lies **Market Square**, the old heart of Victoria but now a collection of some 65 speciality shops and cafés around a central courtyard (bounded by Store, Pandora and Johnson streets). This area erupted in 1858 following the gold rush, providing houses, saloons, opium dens, stores and various salacious entertainments for thousands of chancers and would-be immigrants. On the Pandora side of the area was a ravine, marked by the current sunken courtyard, beyond which lay **Chinatown** (now centred slightly further north on Fisgard) the American west coast's oldest. Here, among other things, 23 factories processed 90,000 pounds of opium a year for what was then a legitimate trade and – until the twentieth century – one of BC's biggest industries. As for the downtown **shopping streets**, it's worth looking out for E.A. Morris, a wonderful old cigar and tobacco shop next to *Murchie's* coffee shop at 1110 Government St, and Roger's Chocolates, 913 Government St, whose whopping Victoria creams (among other things) are regularly dispatched to Buckingham Palace for royal consumption.

Other attractions

Outside the Inner Harbour Victoria has a scattering of minor attractions that don't fit into any logical tour of the city – and at any rate are only short-stop diversions. Most have a pioneer slant, though if you want old buildings the best is **Craigdarroch Castle**, nestled on a hilltop in Rockland, one of Victoria's more prestigious neighbourhoods, at 1050 Joan Crescent (daily: summer 9am–7pm; winter 10am–4.30pm; $7.50; ☎592-5323; bus #11 or #14-University from downtown). It was built by Robert Dunsmuir, a caricature Victorian politician, strike-breaker, robber baron and coal tycoon – the sort of man who could change a community's name on a whim (Ladysmith near Nanaimo) – and who was forced to put up this gaunt Gothic

WHALE-WATCHING TRIPS

The waters around Victoria are not as whale-rich as those around Tofino (see pp.719–720), but there's still a very good chance of spotting the creatures. Three pods of orcas (killer whales) live in the seas around southern Vancouver Island, around a hundred creatures in all, so you may see these, though minke are the most common whale spotted, with occasional greys and humpbacks also present. Bar one or two companies, few outfits offer guaranteed sightings, and many cover themselves by preparing you for the fact that if you don't see whales you stand a good chance of seeing Harbour of Dall's porpoises, harbour or elephant seals and California and Steller sea lions.

Day- or half-day trips from the city are becoming massively popular. A couple of years ago there were just two or three companies running trips: now you can hardly move for them. Most offer almost identical trips at identical prices, typically around $55 for a two-hour trip, $80 for a three-hour outing. Most offer full protective gear, and towels and gloves when required, and all offer life jackets and other safety essentials. Most have a naturalist, or at least a knowledgeable crew member, to fill you in on what you're seeing (or not). The only real variables are the **boats** used, so you need to decide whether you want rigid hull cruisers (covered or uncovered), which are more comfortable and sedate, or the high-speed aluminium hull inflatables known as "zodiacs", which are infinitely more exhilarating, but can offer a fast and sometimes bumpy ride that makes them unsuitable for pregnant women, young children or people with back problems. They won't have toilets on board either. You might also want to find out whether your chosen company has hydrophone equipment that enables you to listen to the whales' underwater vocalizing.

Note that morning trips can be less choppy than afternoon excursions (bad weather will halt tours), and be sure to take sunglasses, sun block, a tight-fitting hat, good soft-soled footwear, a sound plastic bag for camera and films and a warm sweater. Smoking is invariably not allowed on boats. If you're here just for the day and travelling on zodiacs you might want to bring a change of clothing. Trips often run a little over the scheduled time, so don't make any hard-and-fast plans for catching buses or ferries.

Drop by the **Victoria Infocentre** for details of the tours and options. Its pamphlet racks are stuffed with brochures if you want to compare companies' PR material. Staff can book you a place on any tour, and if you call in early morning they'll probably have the lowdown from the companies on whether whales have been found that day. Companies tend to pool their information, and dash headlong to any sighting. The question of whether the upsurge in boat activity is disturbing the whales or changing their habits seems not to have been addressed. Rules are in place regarding the distance boats must remain from the creatures, but even some of the companies' own photographs seem to suggest boats are getting in extremely close. It can only be a matter of time before the whole issue blows up. All the companies claim to offer top professional services: the two below have been around longer than most.

Seacoast Expeditions are located across the Inner Harbour at the Boardwalk Level, Oceane Pointe Resort, 45 Songhees Rd (☎383-4383). It's ten minutes' walk across the Johnson Street bridge or take the three-minute harbour ferry crossing to Seacoast: they also have a shuttle bus pick-up from downtown hotels. Victoria's founding whale-watching company, they've been in the business over a decade and offer four three-hour trips daily in May, June and September, six daily in July and August, and one daily in April and October. They also offer a guaranteed sighting deal (May–Aug only) whereby you carry a pager that tells you to turn up at the office for a tour only when whales have been spotted.

Five Star Charters, located in the *Empress Hotel* (☎386-3253 or 388-7223), has in the past claimed the highest percentage of whale sightings out of all the tour operators (thanks to spotter boats and a good network of contacts). It runs six daily three-hour trips in the summer as well as an all-day trip on its spotter boat.

pastiche to lure his wife away from Scotland. Only the best was good enough, from the marble, granite and sandstone of the superstructure to the intricately handworked panels of the ceilings over the main hall and staircase. Unfortunately for him the dastardly Dunsmuir never enjoyed his creation – he died before it was finished. There's the usual clutter of Victoriana and period detail, in particular some impressive woodwork and stained and leaded glass.

Much the same goes for the Victorian-Italianate **Point Ellice House & Gardens**, 2616 Pleasant St (mid-May to early Oct daily 10am–5pm; $4; ☎387-4697; bus #14 from downtown), magnificently re-created but less enticing because of its slightly shabby surroundings. These can be overcome, however, if you make a point of arriving by sea, taking one of the little Harbour Ferry services to the house (10min) from the Inner Harbour. The restored Victorian-style gardens here are a delight on a summer afternoon. The interior – one of the best of its kind in western Canada – retains its largely Victorian appearance thanks partly to the reduced circumstances of the O'Reilly family, whose genteel slide into relative poverty over several generations (they lived here from 1861 to 1974) meant that many furnishings were simply not replaced. Tea, inevitably, is served on the lawns in the summer: it's a good idea to book ahead (Thurs–Sun 4pm).

Similar reservations apply to the **Craigflower Manor & Farmhouse** about 9km and fifteen minutes' drive from downtown on Admiral's Road, or take the #14-Craigflower bus from downtown (July & Aug daily noon–4pm; $5; ☎387-4697). In its day the latter was among the earliest of Victoria's farming homesteads, marking the town's transition from trading post to permanent community. It was built in a mock-Georgian style in 1856, apparently from timbers salvaged from the first four farmhouses built in the region. Its owner was Kenneth McKenzie, a Hudson's Bay Company bailiff, who recruited fellow Scottish settlers to form a farming community on Portage Inlet. The house was to remind him of the old country (Scotland), and soon became the foremost social centre in the fledgling village – mainly visited by officers because McKenzie's daughters were virtually the only white women on the island.

The **Art Gallery of Greater Victoria**, 1040 Moss St, just off Fort Street (Mon–Sat 10am–5pm, Thurs till 9pm, Sun 1–5pm; $5; bus #10-Haultain, #11 or #14-Uvic from downtown), is a long way to come and of little interest unless you're partial to contemporary Canadian paintings and the country's best collection of Japanese art: the building, housed in the 1890 Spencer Mansion, boasts the only complete Shinto shrine outside Japan. It does, however, have a small permanent collection of Emily Carr's work, and you may catch an interesting temporary exhibition that changes every six weeks.

Eating and drinking

Although clearly in Vancouver's culinary shadow, Victoria still has a plethora of **restaurants**, some extremely good, offering greater variety – and higher prices – than you'll find in most other BC towns. **Pubs** tend to be plastic mock-ups of their British equivalents, with one or two worthy exceptions, as do the numerous **cafés** that pander to Victoria's self-conscious afternoon tea ritual. Good snacks and pastry shops abound, while at the other extreme there are budget-busting establishments if you want a one-off treat or a change from the standard Canadian menus that await you on much of the rest of the island. As a quick guide to the best, *Rebecca's* and *Dilettante's* are good for lunch or dinner at mid-price; the *Herald Street Café* or *Water Club* for a pricier but not exorbitant dinner. *Earl's* is part of a reliable mid-price chain, as is *Milestone's*, the latter giving you harbour views from some tables. The slightly wacky *Reebar* serves what may well be the healthiest food and drinks in North America.

Cafés, tea and snacks

Barb's Fish and Chips, 310 St Lawrence, Fisherman's Wharf off Kingston. Much-loved floating shack that offers classic home-cut chips, fish straight off the boat and oyster burgers and chowder to boot: the small bathtub ferries from the Inner Harbour drop you close by.

Blethering Place, 2250 Oak Bay Ave. Along with the *Empress*, known as a place to indulge in the tea-taking custom. Scones, cakes and dainty sandwiches are served up against the background of hundreds of toby jugs and royal family memorabilia. Perhaps a tad overrated – try the *Windsor House* as an alternative.

C'est Bon Croissant, 10 Bastion Square. A nice place to sit out on the old town square, with coffees and plain and filled croissants to eat in or take away.

Demitasse Coffee Bar, 1320 Blanshard St near Pandora. Popular, elegantly laid-back hole-in-the-wall café with excellent coffee, salads, bagels, lunch-time snacks, and an open fire in season. Recommended.

Dutch Bakery & Coffee Shop, 718 Fort St. An institution in Victoria serving pastries and chocolate to take away, or you can eat in the popular if plain coffee shop at the back.

Empress Hotel, 721 Government St. Try tea in the lobby ($29), with tourists and locals alike on their best behaviour amidst the chintz and potted plants. A strict dress code allows no dirty jeans, anoraks or sportswear.

Java, 543 Johnson St. Young, cool but relaxed café with bright-red-and-yellow vinyl sofas and lots of broken-mirror decoration. Live acoustic or semi-acoustic music some nights, and drag shows or club-DJ dance sessions other nights. Don't miss the tables out back. Handy for the youth hostel just up Waddington Alley.

Murchie's Tea and Coffee, 1110 Government St. The best place for basic tea, coffee and cakes in the centre of Victoria's shopping streets.

Reebar, 50 Bastion Square–Langley Street. A great place that serves teas, coffees (charcoal-filtered water) and health food at lunch (usually organically grown), but most remarkable for its extraordinary range of fresh-squeezed juices in strange combinations, smoothies, "power tonics" and frighteningly healthy wheatgrass drinks ("Astro Turf" – carrot, beet, garlic and wheatgrass).

Sally's, 714 Cormorant St, near corner of Douglas Street. Funky little café and very popular with locals and local office workers despite its location on the northern edge of downtown. Drop by if you're up this way, but don't come specially.

Windsor House Tea Room, 2450 Windsor Rd. If you're making the effort to come out of town for tea at the famous *Blethering Place*, you could stay on the bus (the #2 Oak Bay) to have your cuppa by the sea here instead.

Restaurants

Dilettante's Café, 787 Fort St near Blanshard. Although a little north of the central core, so few outsiders, this only vaguely decadent and relaxed single-room restaurant is deservedly popular at lunch.

Earl's, 1703 Blanshard St. You'll find an *Earl's* in many Canadian towns, but the restaurants are none the worse for being part of a chain: good – not fast – food, with a lively, pleasant interior and friendly service.

La Terrazza, 555 Johnson St, Waddington Alley (passageway). Smooth, laid-back ambience with lots of red brick and plants and a summer patio that provides the setting for good North American versions of Italian food.

Green Cuisine, Courtyard Level, Market Square, 560 Johnson St. Vegetarian restaurant and bakery in pleasant off-street setting with a good hot buffet and salad bar.

Herald Street Café, 546 Herald St. A sister restaurant to the *Water Club* and an excellent old favourite which rivals *Rebecca's* for Italian food with a Northwest twist. Pricey, but good value and relaxed atmosphere with lots of art on the walls, and well worth the walk from the Inner Harbour.

Marina Restaurant, 1327 Beach Drive (☎598-8555). An upscale restaurant with great marine views and a reputation for some of the best fish and seafood in the city.

Milestone's, 812 Wharf St (☎381-2244). Popular mid-priced place slap-bang on the Inner Harbour beneath the infocentre, so lots of bustle, passing trade and good views, but not the place for a quiet meal.

Pagliacci's, 1011 Broad St between Fort and Broughton. Best restaurant in Victoria if you want a fast, furious atmosphere, live music, good Italian food and excellent desserts. A rowdy throng begins to queue almost from the moment the doors are open.

Rebecca's, 1127 Wharf St (☎380-6999). One of Victoria's nicest restaurants with first-rate Pacific Northwest food, an easy-going atmosphere, and a wooden bar. It gets crowded at dinner, so book ahead. Also has a take-out counter for lunch snacks.

Water Club, 703 Douglas St (☎388-4200). Recently opened on the back of the successful and co-owned *Herald Street Café*, but bigger, smoother and more ambitious than its sister restaurant, serving up superb food in a plum location.

Ethnic cuisine

Da Tandoor, 1010 Fort St. Tandoori specialist that is, with the *Taj Mahal*, the best of Victoria's half-dozen or so Indian restaurants offering good food and definitely an over-the-top interior.

Le Petit Saigon, 1010 Langley St, off Fort Street (☎386-1412). A byword for good downtown Vietnamese food.

Ming's, 1321 Quadra St (☎385-4405). Regularly voted Victoria's best Chinese restaurant.

Periklis, 531 Yates St. Greek restaurant opposite the youth hostel, often with belly dancers, plate-spinning and good (if predictable) Greek food.

Taj Mahal, 679 Herald St. Housed in a mini Taj Mahal, a bit of a walk from the centre, this restaurant serves good Indian food with chicken, lamb and tandoori specialities.

Tomoe, 726 Johnson St (☎381-0223). Victoria's best Japanese restaurant with a comfortable, low-key atmosphere. Fresh produce is flown in daily from Tsukiji, the world's largest fish market.

Bars

Big Bad John's, next to the *Strathcona Hotel* at 919 Douglas St. Victoria's most atmospheric bar by far with bare boards, a fug of smoke, and authentic old banknotes and IOUs pasted to the walls.

Charles Dickens Pub, 633 Humboldt St. One of Victoria's hideously mocked-up British pubs but good for a laugh.

Spinnakers Brew Pub, 308 Catherine St near Esquimalt Road. Thirty-eight beers, including several home-brewed options, restaurant, live music, occasional tours of the brewery and good harbour views draw a mixed and relaxed clientele. Take bus #23 to Esquimalt Road.

Swan's Pub, 506 Pandora Ave at Store Street. This pretty and highly popular hotel-café-brewery, housed in a 1913 warehouse, is the place to watch Victoria's young professionals at play. Several foreign and six home-brewed beers on tap, with a nightclub in the basement.

Nightlife

Nocturnal diversions in Victoria are tame compared to Vancouver's, but there's more to the town than its tearooms and chintzy shops initially suggest. Highbrow tastes are surprisingly well catered for, and there's a smattering of **live music** venues and **discos** to keep you happy for the limited time you're likely to spend in the city. **Jazz** is particularly popular – for information on the city's jazz underground, contact the Victoria Jazz Society, 250-727 Johnson St (☎388-4423).

Listings appear in the main daily newspaper, the *Times-Colonist*; in the *Monday Magazine*, a free weekly tabloid printed on Wednesday despite its title; and in the fortnightly *Arts Victoria*. **Tickets** for most offerings are available from the city's main performance space, the McPherson Playhouse, 3 Centennial Square, Pandora and Government (☎386-6121).

Clubs and live music

Bartholomew's Bar and Grill, *Executive House Hotel*, 777 Douglas St (☎388-5111). An upbeat pub with a steady diet of local bands.

Esquimalt Inn, 856 Esquimalt Rd. Long-established venue with C&W seven nights a week and a 3pm jam session on Saturday and Sunday. Take the #23 bus.

FESTIVALS IN VICTORIA

Summer brings out the buskers and **free entertainment** in Victoria's people-places – James Bay, Market Square and Beacon Hill Park in particular. Annual highlights include:

Terrifvic Dixieland Jazz Festival, April (☎953-2011). A showcase for about a dozen top international bands held over four days.

Jazz Fest, June (☎386-6121 for information). More than a hundred assorted lesser bands perform in Market Square.

Victoria International Festival, July and August (☎736-2119). Victoria's largest general arts jamboree.

Folk Fest, last week of July (☎388-5322). Extravaganza of folk.

First People's Festival, early August (☎387-2134). Celebration of the cultures of Canada's native peoples.

Classic Boat Festival, August 30–September 1 (☎385-7766). Dozens of wooden antique boats on display.

Fringe Festival, September (☎383-2663). Avant-garde performances of all kinds.

House of the Blues, 1417 Government St (☎386-1717). Victoria's "House of the Blues" at the *Victoria Plaza Hotel* has disco some nights and local blues, and R&B bands most others. Wednesday is showcase and jam night.

Hermann's Jazz Club, 753 View St. Dimly lit club thick with 1950s atmosphere which specializes in Dixieland but has occasional excursions into fusion and blues. Open Mon–Fri 11.30am–2am, Sat 3pm–2am.

Legends, 919 Douglas St. Biggest, best and noisiest of the hard-rock venues, this club occupies the garish, neon-lit basement of the *Strathcona Hotel*. Music and dancing nightly.

Pagliacci's, 1011 Broad St. Live music (jazz, blues, rock and R&B) starting at 9pm Tuesday to Saturday, in packed and popular restaurant.

Planet Harpo's, 15 Bastion Square. Easily Victoria's best live-music venue, which has hosted an eclectic mix of names including Robert Cray, Billy Bragg and the Wailers. Cover from $5. Closed Sun.

Victoria Folk Music Society, Norway House, 1110 Hillside Ave. Hosts weekly live music at 8pm.

Discos

Euphoria, 858 Yates St near Quadra Street. Expensive club popular with under-20s. Wed–Sat until midnight.

Heaven, 1417 Government St (☎386-1717). Standard disco housed in the *Victoria Plaza*: some nights doubles as live venue for the "House of the Blues" (see above).

Millennium, 1605 Store St at Pandora Avenue. You may well have to queue to join the slightly older crew who frequent the basement disco of *Swan's Pub*. 1960s and 1970s classics generally rule as well as current Top 40 fodder. Open Tues–Sat.

Sweetwaters Niteclub, Market Square off Store Street (☎383-7844). Central, upmarket and elegant spot with queues seven days a week and a reputation as a singles club.

Drama

Belfry Theatre, 1291 Gladstone St and Fernwood (☎385-6815). Foremost of Victoria's companies, with a nationally renowned five-play season in its own playhouse. Although it concentrates on contemporary Canadian dramatists, the repertoire runs the gamut of twentieth-century playwrights.

Intrepid Theatre Company, 510 Fort St (☎383-2663 or 1-888-FRINGE2). Responsible for the nine-day September Fringe Festival, featuring some 200 highly varied shows.

Kaleidoscope Theatre, 520 Herald St (☎475-4444). Theatre troupe known particularly for its work with young audiences.

Victoria Theatre Guild, 805 Langham Court Rd (☎384-2142). A good company performing lightweight musicals, dramas and comedies.

Classical music, opera and dance

Pacific Opera Victoria, 1316b Government St (☎382-1641). Highly acclaimed company which usually produces three operas yearly in February, April and September at the McPherson Playhouse, 3 Centennial Square (box office ☎386-6121).

Victoria Operatic Society, 798 Fairview Rd (☎381-1021). Year-round performances of lightweight operatic fare.

Victoria Symphony Orchestra, 846 Broughton Rd (☎385-9771). Numerous concerts annually, usually performed at the nearby Royal Theatre.

Listings

Airlines Air BC (☎273-2464 or 1-800-663-9826); Air Canada, 20 Centennial Square (☎360-9074 or 360-4088); Canadian, 901 Gordon St (☎382-6111 or 1-800-665-1177); Helijet: helicopter service to Vancouver harbour (☎382-6222 or 1-800-665-4354); Horizon–Alaska Airlines (☎1-800-547-9308 or 206/431-4513); Kenmore Air: seaplane service Seattle–Victoria (☎1-800-543-9595 or 206/486-1257); West Coast Air: direct float-plane service Vancouver–Victoria, 1000 Wharf St (☎388-4521 or 1-800-347-2222).

American Express 1203 Douglas St (☎385-8731 or 1-800-669-3636); open Mon, Wed & Sat 9.30am–5.30pm, Tues & Fri 9.30am–9pm.

Bike rental Sports Rent, 611 Discovery St, on the corner of Government and Discovery (☎385-7368). Mountain bikes from $22 daily, $85 weekly (compulsory helmets $5/12); tandems $35/60.

BC Transit City buses (☎382-6161 or 385-2551).

Bookstores Chapters, 1212 Douglas St near corner with View: huge modern bookshop; Munro's Books, 1108 Government St (☎382-2424), is more traditional.

Bus information Airporter shuttle bus from Victoria Airport (☎386-2525). For services to Vancouver, Pacific Coast Lines (☎604-662-8074 in Vancouver or 250/385-4411 at the Victoria bus terminal); for services on the island, Laidlaw (☎385-4411 or 1-800-318-0818). Both operate from the bus terminal at 700 Douglas and Belleville, which also has an office for Greyhound (☎388-5248). Gray Line of Seattle service to Seattle (☎206-626-6090 or 1-800-544-0739). For West Coast Trail Connector to Port Renfrew, call ☎475-2010, and for the West Coast Trail Express to Bamfield, call ☎477-8700.

Car rental ABC Rent a Car, 2507 Government St (☎381-3153 or 388-5248); Avis, 62b-1001 Douglas St (☎386-8468 or 1-800-879-2847) and Victoria Airport (☎656-6033); Budget, 757 Douglas St (☎953-5300 or 1-800-668-9833); Island Auto Rentals, 837 Yates St (☎384-4881), guarantee "lowest rates"; Rent-a-Wreck, 2634 Douglas St (☎384-5343).

Dentist Cresta Dental Centre (☎384-1154) or Family Dental Centre (☎384-7711).

Doctors' directory ☎383-1193.

Equipment rental Sports Rent, 611 Discovery St, on corner of Government and Discovery (☎385-7368). Rents bikes, rollerblades, all camping, hiking, climbing and diving gear. Tents (two-person) $15 daily, $50 weekly; sleeping bags $9/27; blades $17/70; canoe or kayak $35/135.

Exchange Currencies International, 724 Douglas St (☎384-6631 or 1-800-706-6656); Custom House Currency, 815 Wharf St (☎389-6001).

Ferries BC Ferries (☎386-3431 or 1-888-223-3779); Black Ball Transport (☎386-2202 or 360/457-4491); Victoria Clipper (☎382-8100, 206/448-5000 or 1-800-888-2535); Victoria Express (☎1-800-633-1589); Washington State Ferries (☎656-1831 or 1-800-542-7052).

Gay and lesbian information ☎361-4900.

Hospitals Fairfield Health Centre, 841 Fairfield Rd (☎389-6300), three blocks from the *Empress Hotel*; Victoria General Hospital, 35 Helmcken Rd (☎727-4212).

Laundry 812 Wharf St, below the infocentre.

Left luggage At bus terminal; $1.25 per 24hr.

Lost property Contact Victoria police (☎384-4111) or BC Transit's lost-and-found line (☎382-6161).

Maps Crown Publications Inc, 521 Fort St (☎386-4636). Also see "Bookstores" above.

Pharmacies Shopper's Drug Mart, 1222 Douglas St, open daily 8am–9pm; Save-On Food & Drugs, 3510 Blanshard St (☎384-2333); 362 days a year open daily until midnight.

Post office 1230 Government and Yates (☎388-3575). Mon–Fri 8.30am–5pm.

Royal Canadian Mounted Police 625 Fisgard and Government (☎384-4111).

Taxis Blue Bird Cabs (☎384-1155 or 382-3611); Empire Taxi (☎381-2222); Victoria Taxi (☎383-7111 or 383-1515). Preferred Cab (☎380-3022) has wheelchair-adapted cabs.

Tourist information ☎953-2033. Accommodation reservations ☎953-2022 outside North America or 1-800-663-3883 in North America.

Train information VIA Rail, 450 Pandora Ave (☎383-4324 or 1-800-561-8630 in Canada and 1-800-561-3949 in USA).

Weather ☎656-3978.

Wildlife The Field Naturalist, 1126 Blanshard St (☎388-41744). Specialist books, equipment, information and field course.

Women's Victoria Contact Every Woman's Books, 641 Johnson St (☎388-9411), for books on and by women, and for feedback on what's happening in Victoria's women's and lesbian communities.

The Southern Gulf Islands

Scattered between Vancouver Island and the mainland lie several hundred tiny islands, most no more than lumps of rock, a few large enough to hold permanent populations and warrant a regular ferry service. Two main clusters are accessible from Victoria: the **Southern Gulf Islands** and the San Juan Islands, both part of the same archipelago, except that the San Juan group is in the United States.

You get a good look at the Southern Gulf Islands on the ferry from Tsawwassen – twisting and threading through their coves and channels, the ride sometimes seems even a bit too close for comfort. The coastline makes for superb **sailing**, and an armada of small boats crisscross between the islands for most of the year. Hikers and campers are also well served, and **fishing**, too, is good, with some of the world's biggest salmon having met their doom in the surrounding waters. The climate is mild, though hardly "Mediterranean" as claimed in the tourist blurbs, and the vegetation is particularly lush. There's also an abundance of marine wildlife (sea lions, orcas, seals, bald eagles, herons, cormorants). All this has made the Gulf Islands the dream idyll of many people from Washington State and BC, whether they're artists, writers, pensioners or dropouts from the mainstream. For full details of what they're all up to, grab a copy of the local listings, the *Gulf Islander*, distributed on the islands and the ferries.

Getting to the islands

BC Ferries (☎250/386-3431) sails to five of the Southern Gulf Islands – **Saltspring, Pender, Saturna, Mayne** and **Galiano** – from Swartz Bay, 33km north of Victoria on Hwy 17 (a few others can be reached from Chemainus and Nanaimo, for which see those sections on p.710 and pp.711–714). Reckon on at least two crossings to each daily, but be prepared for all boats to be jammed solid during the summer. Pick up the company's *Southern Gulf Islands* timetable, widely available on boats and in the mainland infocentres, which is invaluable if you aim to exploit the many inter-island connections. If you just want a quick, cheap cruise, BC Ferries runs a daily four-hour jaunt from Swartz Bay around several of the islands. All the ferries take cars, bikes and motorbikes, though with a car you'll need to make a **reservation** (in Vancouver ☎604/669-1211, in Victoria ☎386-3431). Bear in mind that there's next to no public transport on the islands, so what few taxis there are can charge more or less what they wish.

For the San Juans you obviously have to pass through US and Canadian immigration, but you can get good stopover deals on ferries between Sidney on Vancouver Island and Anacortes on the Washington mainland, and foot passengers travel free between the four main San Juan islands.

Aim to have your **accommodation** worked out well in advance in summer. **Campers** should have few problems finding sites, most of which are located in the islands' provincial parks, though at peak times you'll want to arrive before noon to ensure a pitch – there are reservations in some parks (see p.644 for details of booking places). For help with B&Bs, use the *BC Accommodations* guide, or contact the Victoria infocentre.

Saltspring Island

SALTSPRING (pop. 7871), or Salt Spring, is the biggest, most populated and most visited of the islands, though if you're without transport it's as well to think twice about coming here on a day-trip as getting around's pretty tough. It's served by three ferry terminals: **Fulford Harbour**, from Victoria's Swartz Bay (ten sailings daily, more in summer; 35min; foot passengers $5 return, cars $17.25) and **Vesuvius Bay** (from Crofton, near Duncan on Vancouver Island; 13 daily; 20min; same fares) provide links to Vancouver Island; **Long Harbour** connects to points on the BC mainland via other islands. In the past the Saltspring Island Bus service has connected the ferry terminals with **GANGES**, the island's main village, but check with the Victoria infocentre for the latest. For more complicated journeys, call up the 24-hour Saltspring Taxi (☎537-9712) or consider **renting a bike** from Island Spoke Folk (☎537-4664) in Ganges (for a few dollars they can deliver bikes to be waiting for you at the ferry terminal). Locals are a particularly cosmopolitan bunch, the island having been colonized not by whites but by pioneer black settlers seeking refuge from prejudice in the US. If you're here to slum it on a **beach**, the best strips are on the island's more sheltered west side (Beddis Beach in particular, off the Fulford to Ganges road), at Vesuvius Bay and at Drummond Park near Fulford.

Ganges, close to Long Harbour, is armed with a small **infocentre** at 121 Lower Ganges Rd (daily 8am–6pm; ☎537-5252 or 537-4223) and a rapidly proliferating assortment of galleries, tourist shops and holiday homes. Community high spirits reach a climax during the annual **Artcraft**, a summer crafts fair that displays the talents of the island's many dab-handed creatives.

Ganges' infocentre is the place to check out the island's relatively plentiful **accommodation**. A lot of independent travellers are lured here by the prospect of the offical HI-affiliated **youth hostel**, the lovely *Salt Spring Island Hostel*, set amidst ten peaceful acres on the eastern side of the island at 640 Cusheon Lake Rd (☎537-4149; ①–③). Under your own steam from Victoria, take the #70 Pat Bay Hwy bus ($2.50) to the Swartz Bay ferry terminal. Catch the ferry to Fulford Harbour ($5 return) and ask car drivers disembarking the ferry if they're headed past the hostel on Cusheon Lake Road: if they're locals, most say yes. You can choose between dorm rooms, tepees, tents, tree house and private family room ($8–50). It's just a short walk to Cusheon Lake or the ocean at Beddis Beach. Otherwise you can choose from the multitudinous (but often exorbitant) B&B option (owners can arrange to pick you up from the ferry) or one of the so-called "resorts" dotted round the island – usually a handful of houses with camping, a few rooms to rent, and little else. Each of the ferry terminals also has a range of mid-price motels. Some of the more reasonable include the twelve-unit *Beachcomber Motel* at 770 Vesuvius Bay Rd at Vesuvius Bay 7km from Ganges (☎537-5415; ③); the *Harbour House Hotel*, 121 Upper Ganges Rd, Ganges (☎537-5571; ③), and the 28-unit *Seabreeze Inn* in a park-like setting above Ganges harbour at 101 Bittancourt Rd (☎537-4145; ③). For a different sort of experience, try the nineteen-bed HI *Saltspring Island* **youth hostel**, 640 Cusheon Rd (☎537-4149; ①), where you can choose between sleeping indoors, in a tent ($8) or in a tepee.

One of the island's better-known places to **eat** is *The Vesuvius Inn* (☎537-2312) alongside the ferry at Vesuvius Bay, blessed with live music nightly and a great **bar** deck overlooking the harbour. In Ganges, try the Saltspring Nature Works, 158

Fulford–Ganges roads, for healthy picnic supplies, or the popular *Sweet Arts Patisserie Café* at 112 Lower Ganges Rd (opposite the fire station), for high-quality sandwiches.

The island's best hiking and its top **campground** are to be found in Ruckle Provin-cial Park. The camp ($9.50; March–Oct) at Beaver Point, is reached by following Beaver Point Road from the Fulford Harbour ferry terminal (9km). There's further walking and good views on and around Mount Maxwell.

Galiano Island

Long and finger-shaped, **Galiano** (pop. 909) is one of the more promising islands to visit if you want variety and a realistic chance of finding somewhere to stay. There are two ferry terminals: **Sturdies Bay**, which takes boats from the mainland, and **Montague Harbour**, which handles the Vancouver Island crossings. The **infocentre** is in the former (May–Sept daily 8am–6pm; ☎539-2233), which also has bike, boat and canoe rentals, motels, B&B, and an excellent **campground** at Montague Harbour Provincia Marine Park, 10km from the ferry terminal on the west side of the island (☎250/391-2300; $12; March–Oct; 15 reservable tent sites). (See box on p.644 for details of provin cial park campground reservations.)

Galiano Gables operates as a **mini hostel** (☎539-2594) and is located on Warbler Road 3.5km from Sturdies Bay; turn left up Burrill Road off the main road after the Burrill Bros store. The island's only pub, the *Hummingbird Inn* (☎539-5472; ③), has **rooms** and is conveniently close to the ferry on Sturdies Road (a bus meets boats and also runs out to the provincial park). **Food** is reasonable at the *Hummingbird*, likewise at *La Berengerie* near Montague Harbour on the corner of Montague and Clanton roads (☎539-5392; ③) a genteel restaurant that also has four B&B rooms upstairs.

For a downy and comfortable stay in peaceful and elegant surroundings (close to Montague Harbour Provincial Marine Park), try the excellent but expensive *Woodstone Country Inn* (☎539-2022; ⑤–⑦) on Georgeson Bay Road, 4km from the ferry: breakfas and afternoon tea are included in the price. For a special treat book well in advance to secure one of the seven well-priced rooms at the *Sutil Lodge*, Montague Harbour (☎539-2930; ③). A restored 1928 fishing lodge, this place is on the beach and surrounded by twenty acres of forested seclusion with lovely views, great sunsets and general all round old-style delights. You can even take a four-hour nature cruise aboard a catama ran, and there's free ferry and canoe pick-up. Not surprisingly it's received glowing reviews in the *LA Times*, *New York Times* and the *Globe and Mail*.

A less exalted but still good choice on the island's quieter northern end are the sever log cabins of the *Bodega Resort*, at 120 Monastery Rd off Porlier Pass Drive and Cook Drive (☎539-2677; ③), complete with kitchens and wood-burning stoves and set in acres of woods and meadows with sea views.

If you're **canoeing**, stick to the calmer waters, cliffs and coves off the west coast **Hikers** can walk almost the entire length of the east coast, or climb Mount Sutil (323m) or Mount Galiano (342m) for views of the mainland mountains. The locals' favourite **beach** is at Coon Bay at the island's northern tip.

North and South Pender

The bridge-linked islands of **North** and **South Pender** can muster about a thousand people between them, many of whom will try to entice you into their studios to buy loca arts and crafts. Ferries come here from Swartz Bay and Tsawwassen. The **infocentre** is at the ferry terminal in **Otter Bay**, 2332 Otter Bay Rd (mid-May to early Sept daily 8am–6pm; no phone) on North Pender, home of the Otter Bay Marina, where you can rent **bikes** and buy maps for a tour of the islands' rolling, hilly interior. The best **beach es** are at Hamilton (North Pender) and Mortimer Spit (South Pender).

Accommodation-wise there are plenty of B&Bs, and a small wooded **campground** at Prior Centennial Provincial Park, 6km south of the Otter Bay ferry terminal (☎250/391-2300 for reservations; March–Oct). For the only **hotel**-type rooms, as opposed to B&Bs, try the *Inn on Pender Island* prettily situated in 7.5 acres of wooded country near Prior Park at 4709 Canal Rd, North Pender (☎629-3353 or 1-800-550-0172; ③; April–Sept); or the *Bedwell Harbour Island Resort*, 9801 Spalding Rd, South Pender (☎629-3212 or 1-800-663-2899; ④), which has a pool, pub, restaurant, store, tennis, harbour views, canoe, boat and bike rentals, and a choice of rooms or cabins; or the four fully equipped self-catering cottages of *Pender Lodge*, 1325 MacKinnon Rd, North Pender (☎629-3221; ⑤–⑥), with tennis court, outdoor pool and private decks.

Mayne and Saturna islands

Mayne is the first island to your left if you're crossing from Tsawwassen to Swartz Bay – which is perhaps as close as you'll get, since it's the quietest and most difficult to reach of the islands served by ferries, and has few places to stay; fix up accommodation before you arrive. That may be as good a reason as any for heading out here, however, particularly if you have a bike to explore the web of quiet country roads. Best of several **beaches** is Bennett Bay, a sheltered strip with warm water and good sand. It's reached by heading east from Miner's Bay (5min from the ferry terminal at Village Bay) to the end of Fernhill Road and then turning left onto Wilks Road. Village Bay has a summer-only **infocentre** (daily 8am–6pm) which should be able to fill you in on the limited (currently around six) but expanding number of **B&B** possibilities – though the island is small enough to explore as a day-trip. Alternatively, try the three-unit *Root Seller Inn*, a kilometre south of the ferry terminal at 478 Village Bay Rd (☎539-2621; ③; March–Oct), or the *Blue Vista Resort*, eight fully-equipped cabins overlooking Bennett Bay on Arbutus Drive 6km from the ferry terminal (☎539-2463; ③), with handy sandy beach, park-like setting and bike rental. The *Tinkerer's B&B* on Georgina Point Road (☎539-2280; ③–④; mid-April to mid-Oct), 2km from the Village Bay ferry terminal, is offbeat: it rents bikes, provides hammocks and offers "demonstrations of medicinal herb and flower gardens". For a real treat, the best **food** around is to be found at the Oceanwood, 630 Dinner Bay Rd (☎539-5074).

Saturna, to the south, is another **B&B** hideaway: try the seven-room waterfront *Saturna Lodge* (☎539-2254; ④–⑤), a couple of kilometres from the ferry at 130 Payne Rd in Saturna Point, home to a pub, a shop and the **infocentre** (May–Sept daily 8am–6pm; no phone) which will rent you boats and bicycles. Another relatively large place to stay is the *East Point Resort*, East Point Road (☎539-2975; ③–④), situated in a park-like setting near a gradually sloping sandy beach; the six cabins are fully equipped and you can choose between one- and two-bedroom units – note that in July and August there's a minimum stay of a week. The best local **beach** is at Winter Cove Marine Park (no campground) and there's walking, wildlife and good views to the mainland from Mount Warburton Pike.

Highway 14: Victoria to Port Renfrew

Highway 14 runs west from **Victoria** to **Port Renfrew** and is lined with numerous beaches and provincial parks, most – especially those close to the city – heavily populated during the summer months. The 107-kilometre route is covered in summer by the Port Renfrew Connector (☎475-2010), a twice-daily private bus service intended for hikers walking the West Coast Trail (see pp.729–730), but popular for the ride alone. Victoria city buses go as far as **SOOKE** (38km; take #50 to Western Exchange and transfer to a #61), best known for its **All Sooke Day** in mid-July, when lumberjacks from all over the island compete in various tests of forestry expertise. The **infocentre** lies across the Sooke River Bridge at 2070 Phillips and Sooke (daily 10am–6pm; ☎ 642-6351). This is the last place of any size, so stock up on supplies if you're continuing west. It also has a surfeit of **accommodation**, with a bias towards B&B, if you're caught short. Check out the small **Sooke Region Museum** (daily 10am–5pm) if you want to bone up on the largely logging-dominated local history. Quite a few people make the trip here just for the **food** at *Sooke Harbour House*, 1528 Whiffen Spit (☎642-3421; ⑦), one of the finest restaurants on the West Coast and frequently lauded as one of the best in the Northwest; it's expensive, but has a surprisingly casual atmosphere. It also has a few topnotch **rooms**.

Beaches beyond Sooke are largely grey pebble and driftwood, the first key stop being **French Beach Provincial Park**, 20km from Sooke. An infoboard here fills in the natural history background, and there are maps of trails and the highlights on the road further west. There's good walking on the fairly wild and windswept beach, and a provincial park campground (☎391-2300; $9.50; March–Oct) on the grass immediately away from the shore. Sandy, signposted trails lead off the road to beaches over the next 12km to **Jordan River**, a one-shop, one-hamburger-stall town known for its good surf. Just beyond is the best of the beaches on this coast, part of **China Beach Provincial Park**, reached after a fifteen-minute walk from the road through rainforest.

There's a campground if you're staying over; otherwise you can push on – the road is gravel from here on – past Mystic and Sombrio beaches to **PORT RENFREW**, a logging community that's gained recently from being the western starting point of the West Coast Trail. Accommodation, however, is still limited to the four cottages at *Gallaugher's West Coast Fish Camp* on Beach Road (☎647-5535; ③; May–Oct); the four beachfront rooms of the *Arbutus Beach Lodge*, 5 Queesto Drive (☎647-5458; ③–④); the *Orca II B&B* on San Juan Bay one block from the beach at 44 Tsonoquay Rd (☎647-5528; ②); and the 124-site *Port Renfrew RV Park and Marina* on Gordon River Road (☎647-5430; $12–14; April–Oct), with a separate tenting area across the bridge on the northern side of the village. South of the village on a logging road (6km) is **Botanical Beach**, a sandstone shelf and tidal pool area that reveals a wealth of marine life at low tide.

If you're driving and don't want to retrace your steps, think about taking the gravel logging roads from the village on the north side of the San Juan River to either Shawnigan Lake or the Cowichan Valley. They're marked on most maps, but it's worth picking up the detailed map of local roads put out by the Sooke Combined Fire Organization (ask at the Victoria infocentre); heed all warnings about logging trucks.

Highway 1: Victoria to Nanaimo

If you leave Victoria with high hopes of Vancouver Island's lauded scenery, **Hwy 1** – the final western leg of the Trans-Canada – will come as a disappointing introduction to what you can expect along most of the island's southeast coast. After a lengthy sprawl of suburbs, blighted by more billboards than you'd see in supposedly less scenic cities, the landscape becomes suddenly wooded and immensely lush; unfortunately the beauty is constantly interrupted by bursts of dismal motels, highway junk, and huge swathes of destruction where the road is being widened into a dual carriageway. **Buses** operated by Laidlaw make the trip between Victoria and Nanaimo (6 daily). One **train** a day also covers this route, and beyond to Courtenay, but it's a single-carriage job and gets booked solid in summer; it stops at every stump.

Goldstream Provincial Park

Thetis Lake Regional Park, appearing on the right 11km out of the city, is good for swimming, with forested trails and sandy beaches on two lakes backed by high cliffs;

there's a busy beach near the car park, which is quieter round the shore, or beyond at the bottom of the hill at Prior Lake. Prettier still is **Goldstream Provincial Park**, 5km beyond Langford and 20km from the city centre, where you'll find an ancient forest of Douglas fir and western red cedar and a large provincial park **campground** with good facilities and a visitor centre (☎391-2300 $15.00; reservations accepted). There's also a network of marked **trails**, to hilltops and waterfalls designed for anything between five minutes and an hour's walking. Try the paths towards Mount Finlayson (three hour's hard walk if you go all the way to the summit) for views of the ocean – views you also get if you carry on up the highway, which soon meets Saanich Inlet, a bay with a lovely panorama of wooded ridges across the water. Look out for the Malahat Summit (31km from Victoria) and Gulf Islands (33km) viewpoints. To **stay**, the small *Malahat Oceanview Motel* (☎478-9213; ③), 35km north of Victoria, is best sited to catch the sea and island vistas.

A scenic diversion off the main road takes you 7km to **Shawnigan Lake**, fringed by a couple of provincial parks: West Shawnigan Park on the lake's northwest side has a safe beach and swimming possibilities. If you're biking or are prepared to tackle pretty rough roads, note the logging road that links the north end of the lake to Port Renfrew on the west coast (check access restrictions at the Victoria infocentre).

Duncan

DUNCAN, 60km north of Victoria, begins inauspiciously, with a particularly scrappy section of highway spoiling what would otherwise be an exquisitely pastoral patch of country. Still, the town's native centre merits a stop – unlike the Glass Castle, a messy affair made from glass bottles off the road to the south, and the even sillier "World's Largest Hockey Stick", arranged as a triumphal arch into the town centre. It was bought at an auction by Duncan, in competition with dozens of other cities.

Duncan's **infocentre** is at 381 Trans-Canada Hwy opposite the Overwaitea supermarket on the main road (Mon–Fri 8.30am–5pm; ☎746-4636), close to the **bus station**, which has six daily connections to and from Victoria (1hr 10min). Duncan is not a place you want even to consider staying in, but for **meals** you could try the excellent *Arbutus*, 195 Kenneth St, and *Jubilee* (☎746-5443), which is much-frequented by locals. Just east of town, the *Quamichan Inn*, 1478 Maple Bay Rd (☎746-7028), also has its devotees. You could also visit one of several local vineyards: one of the best is the **Vigneti Zenatta Winery**, 5039 Marshall Rd (call for tour details on ☎748-4981 or 748-2338), which has been in business for over forty years; as well as their wine, you can also buy meals here.

Three kilometres south of town on Hwy 1, the *Pioneer House Restaurant* has a rustic log-cabin feel helped by a genuine **saloon bar** transplanted from a period building in Montana. Alternatively, head 10km north of Duncan to the *Red Rooster Diner* (by the Mount Sicker gas station), reputed to be the greasy spoon immortalized by Jack Nicholson in *Five Easy Pieces*. It's still a classic – good, cheap food, vinyl booths and all the authentic tacky trimmings you'd expect.

Cowichan Native Village

The first real reason to pull over out of Victoria is Duncan's **Cowichan Native Village**, 200 Cowichan Way (daily: mid-May to mid-Oct 9.30am–5pm; mid-Oct–mid-May 10am–4.30pm; $9.50), on your left off the highway in the unmissable wooden buildings next to Malaspina College.

Duncan has long been the self-proclaimed "City of Totems", reference to a rather paltry collection of poles – arranged mostly alongside the main road – that belong to the local Cowichan tribes, historically British Columbia's largest native group. The tribes, about 3000 strong locally, still preserve certain traditions, and it's been their energy – along with cash from white civic authorities, attuned as ever to potentially lucrative

OLD-GROWTH FORESTS: GOING, GOING, GONE

While Vancouver Island isn't the only place in North America where environmentalists and the forestry industry are at loggerheads, some of the most bitter and high-profile confrontations have taken place here. The island's wet climate is particularly favourable to the growth of thick **temperate rainforest**, part of a belt that once stretched from Alaska to northern California. The most productive ecosystem on the planet, **old-growth** virgin Pacific rainforest contains up to ten times more biomass per acre than its more famous tropical counterpart – and, though it covers a much smaller area, it is being felled at a greater rate and with considerably less media outrage. Environmentalists estimate that British Columbia's portion of the Pacific rainforest has already been reduced by two thirds; all significant areas will have been felled, they predict, within fifteen years. The powerful logging industry claims two-thirds survive, but even the Canadian government – largely in thrall to and supportive of the industry – concedes that only a small percentage of the BC rainforest is currently protected.

What is clear is that the government wants a very firm lid kept on the whole affair. In 1990 it commissioned a report into **public opinion** on the issue in the United Kingdom, which takes half of all British Columbia's plywood exports, three-quarters of all its lumber shipments to Europe, and a third of all Canada's paper pulp output. It observed that "UK public opinion appears to be highly uncritical of Canadian forestry, largely because awareness of the subject is low . . . [there is] a reassuringly romantic and simplistic image of Canadian forestry based on a lumberjack in a checked shirt, felling a single tree." The report concluded that "media attention and coverage of Canadian forestry management issues should not be sought".

No such apathy exists in British Columbia, however. The controversy over logging often pits neighbour against neighbour, for 270,000 in the province depend directly or

tourist attractions – that have put up the poles and pulled the project together. Much of the heavily worked commercial emphasis is on shifting native crafts, especially the ubiquitous lumpy jumpers for which the area is famous, but you can usually expect to find historical displays and demonstrations of dancing, knitting, carving, weaving and even native cooking.

British Columbia Forestry Museum

Vancouver Island is one of the most heavily logged areas in Canada, and the **British Columbia Foresty Museum**, 1km north of town on Hwy 1 (May–Sept Mon–Fri 8.30am–4.30pm, Sat & Sun 9.30am–6pm; $7), is run by the province to preserve artefacts from its lumbering heritage; but with industry bigwigs as museum trustees, you can't help feeling it's designed to be something of a palliative in the increasingly ferocious controversy between loggers and environmentalists. Nonetheless, it does a thorough job on trees, and if the forestry displays in Victoria's museum have whetted your appetite, you'll have a good couple of hours rounding off your arboreal education. The entrance is marked by a small black steam engine and a massive piece of yellow logging machinery.

Ranged over a hundred-acre site next to a scenic lake, the well-presented displays tell everything you want to know about trees and how to cut them down. The narrow-gauge steam train round the park is a bit gimmicky (10am–5.30pm only), but a good way of getting around; check out the forest dioramas and the artefacts and archive material in the **Log Museum** in particular. There's also the usual array of working blacksmiths, sawmills, a farmstead, an old logging camp, and a few as-yet-underforested patches where you can take time out.

indirectly on the industry, and multinationals like McMillan Bloedel and Fletcher Challenge dominate the scene. **Employment** is a major rallying cry here, and the prospect of job losses through industry regulation is usually enough to override objections. The trend towards **automation** only adds fuel to the argument: by volume of wood cut, the BC forestry industry provides only half as many jobs as in the rest of Canada, which means, in effect, that twice as many trees have to be cut down in BC to provide the same number of jobs.

Some **environmental groups** have resorted to such tactics as fixing huge nails in trees at random – these ruin chainsaws and lumber-mill machinery, but also endanger lives. Countless people have been arrested in recent years for obstructing logging operations. The most level-headed and impressive of the conservation groups, the **Western Canada Wilderness Committee** (WCWC), condemns these acts of environmental vandalism, and instead devotes its energies to alerting the public to the landslide damage and destruction of salmon habitats caused by logging, and the dioxin pollution from pulp mills that in the past has closed 220,000 acres of offshore waters to fishing for shellfish. They point out that the battle is over what they call "the last cookies in the jar", for only eight of the island's 91 watersheds over 12,000 acres have escaped logging; the old-growth bonanza is nearly over, they argue, and the industry might as well wean itself over to sustainable practices now, before it's too late.

In the meantime, however, ninety percent of timber is still lifted from the rainforest instead of from managed stands, clear-cutting of old-growth timber is blithely described by McMillan as "a form of harvesting", and independent audits suggest that companies are failing to observe either their cutting or replanting quotas. Things may change following the election of a centrist provincial government, which has pledged to improve forestry practices and protect at least twelve percent of the province within reserves.

The complex forms part of the **Cowichan and Chemainus Valleys Ecomuseum**, a vaguely defined park that takes in much of the surrounding area intended to preserve the logging heritage of the area – a curiously ill-defined concept that appears to be largely a PR exercise on the part of the logging companies. Ask for details of tours and maps from the Duncan infocentre, or the Ecomuseum office, 160 Jubilee St (☎748-7620).

The Cowichan Valley

Striking west into the hills from Hwy 1 north of Duncan, Hwy 18 enters the **Cowichan Valley** and fetches up at Cowichan Lake, the largest freshwater lake on the island. Rather than drive, however, the nicest way up the valley is to walk the eighteen-kilometre **Cowichan Valley Footpath**, following the river from Glenora (a hamlet southwest of Duncan at the end of Robertson Road) to Lake Cowichan Village on the lake's eastern shore. You could do the trip in a day, camp en route, or turn around at Skutz Falls and climb up to the Riverbottom Road to return to Duncan which would be a half-day walk.

A road, rough in parts, circles **Cowichan Lake** (allow 2hr) and offers access to a gamut of outdoor pursuits, most notably fishing – the area is touted, with typical smalltown hyperbole, as the "Fly-Fishing Capital of the World". The water gets warm enough for summer swimming, and there's also ample hiking in the wilder country above. At Youbou on the north shore you can visit the **Heritage Mill**, a working sawmill (tours May–Sept): this area boasts some of the most productive forest in Canada, thanks to the lake's mild microclimate, and lumber is the obvious mainstay of the local economy. On the road up to the lake from Duncan you pass the **Valley**

Demonstration Forest, another link in the industry's public-relations weaponry, with signs and scenic lookouts explaining the intricacies of forest management.

For details of the area's many tours, trails and outfitters contact the **infocentre** at Lake Cowichan village, 125c South Shore Rd (May–Sept daily 9am–8pm; ☎749-3244). Good, cheap **campgrounds** line the shore, which despite minimal facilities can be quite busy in summer – don't expect to have the place to yourself. The biggest and best is at Gordon Bay Provincial Park ($14.50; ☎391-2300; March–Oct) on the south shore 14km from Lake Cowichan village, a popular family place but with a quiet atmosphere and a good sandy **beach**. There are also plenty of hotels, motels and the like in all the lakeside settlements, plus a non-HI **hostel**, the *River's Edge Guest House*, 160 Lake Cowichan (☎749-6994).

Chemainus

CHEMAINUS is the "Little Town That Did", as the billboards for miles around never stop telling you. Its mysterious achievement was the creation of its own tourist attraction, realized when the closure of the local sawmill – once amongst the world's largest – threatened the place with almost overnight extinction. In 1983 the town's worthies commissioned an artist to paint a huge **mural** – *Steam Donkey at Work* – recording the area's local history. This proved so successful that more panels quickly followed (33 at last count), drawing some 300,000 visitors annually to admire the artwork and tempting them to spend money in local businesses as they did. As murals go, these are surprisingly good, and if you're driving it's worth the short, well-signed diversion off Hwy 1. You might also want to drop in the **Mechanical Music Museum**, 2853 Oak St, home to a collection of old working music machines. Ironically enough, a new sawmill has now opened, though this has done nothing to deter the welcome influx of resident painters and craftspeople attracted by the murals, a knock-on effect that has done much to enliven the village's pleasant commuity feel.

Buses also detour here on the run up to Nanaimo (☎246-3354 for details), and the train drops you slap-bang next to a mural. You can also pick up a ferry from Chemainus to the small islands of **Kuper** and **Thetis**. There's a summer-only **infocentre** in town at 9758 Chemainus Rd in the red caboose by Heritage Square (mid-May to early Sept daily 9am–6pm; ☎246-3944 or 246-4701). If you fancy **staying** – the village's cosy waterside setting is nicer than either Duncan or Nanaimo – it's worth booking ahead, as the village's increasing popularity means the two local **hotels** and half a dozen B&Bs are in heavy demand in summer. For motel accommodation, try the *Horseshoe Bay Inn*, 9576 Chemainus Rd (☎246-3425 or 1-800-828-3030; ②–③), in the village 1km off the main highway, or the *Fuller Lake Chemainus Motel*, 9300 Trans-Canada Hwy (☎246-3282; ②). The best **B&B** is *Bird Song Cottage*, 9909 Maple St (☎246-9910; ④), followed by the cheaper two-room *Hummingbird House*, a modern waterfront building with good ocean and mountain views at 11120 Chemainus Rd (☎245-8412; ③), or the two-room *Laughing Gull Guest House*, 9836 Willow St (☎246-4068; ③), a short stroll from the beach and murals. There's also a small **hostel**, the *Chemainus Hostel*, three minutes' walk from the bus and train stations at 9694 Chemainus Rd (☎246-2809; $15; April–Oct). There's also a tiny **youth hostel** at 3040 Henry Rd (☎246-4407; ①; year-round), about 2km north of town off the Ladysmith road (they can pick you up from the village); there's a kitchen and showers, but you're supposed to bring your own sleeping bag. The choice of **campgrounds** is between the *Chemainus Gardens RV Park*, 3042 River Rd, 1km east of Hwy 1, set in 37 acres of natural forest with separate tenting area, laundry and showers (☎246-3569 or 1-800-341-5060; $20), or the larger *Country Maples Campground*, 9010 Trans-Canada Hwy (☎246-2078; $15; May–Oct) in sixty acres of open and treed parkland above the Chemainus River with showers, laundry and pool. All manner of dinky little cafés, shops and tearooms are springing up across the village: for **food**, try the *Upstairs Downstairs Café*, 9745 Willow St, with cheap, varied dishes including several good vegetarian options, or the *Waterford Inn & Restaurant*, five minutes north of the village centre at 9875 Maple St (☎246-1046).

Ladysmith

LADYSMITH's claim to fame is based solely on an accident of geography, as it straddles the 49th Parallel, the latitude that divides mainland Canada and the US. Canada held onto Vancouver Island only after some hard bargaining, even though the boundary's logic ought to put much of it in the States. It was originally named Oyster Bay, but was renamed by Dunsmuir, a Nanaimo coal baron, at the time of the Boer War battle for Ladysmith (many streets bear the name of Boer War generals). There's little to the place other than the usual motels and garages, though a recent attempt to spruce up the older buildings won it a Western Canada Award of Excellence. Ladysmith's scenic profile, it has to be said, would be considerably higher were it not for a huge sawmill and a waterfront hopelessly jammed with lumber. The **infocentre** at the Black Nugget Museum, 12 Gatacre St (summer only; ☎245-8544), has walking maps of the "heritage centre". The **museum** itself (daily noon–4pm; $2) is a restored 1881 hotel stuffed with predictable memorabilia of coal mining and pioneers. If you stop off, check out **Transfer Beach Park** on the harbour, where the water's said to be the warmest in the Pacific north of San Francisco.

For **accommodation**, make for the fourteen-unit *Holiday House Motel*, 540 Esplanade St (☎245-2231; ②), overlooking Ladysmith's waterfront, the *Seaview Marine Resort*, 1111 Chemainus Rd (☎245-3768 or 1-800-891-8832; ③), just off the highway 6km south of town (and 8km north of Chemainus) with fully equipped self-catering one- and two-bedroom cottages on the ocean (two-night minimum stay), or the *Inn of the Sea*, 3600 Yellow Point Rd (☎245-2211; ⑤), 13km northeast on the seafront and a popular bolt hole for weekending Victorians. The best **food** option is the oldest "English-style pub" in BC, the *Crow and Gate* just off the main road 19km north of the town. For campers, the most central site is the *Sea-RRA RV Park and Campground* in Transfer Beach Park overlooking the port (☎245-5344; $14).

Nanaimo

With a fast-growing population of about 72,000, **NANAIMO**, 113km from Victoria, is Vancouver Island's second biggest city, the terminal for ferries from Horseshoe Bay and Tsawwassen on the mainland, and a watershed between the island's populated southeastern tip and its wilder, more sparsely peopled countryside to the north and west. In BC, only Vancouver and Kelowna are expanding faster. This said, the town is unexceptional, though the setting, as ever in BC, is eye-catching – particularly around the harbour, which bobs with yachts and rusty fishing boats and, if you've come from Victoria, allows the first views across to the big mountains on the mainland. If you are going to stop here, more than likely it'll be for **Petroglyph Park** or the town's increasingly famous **bungee-jumping** zone. If not, the new Nanaimo Parkway provides a 21-kilometre bypass around the town.

Coal first brought white settlers to the region, many of whom made their fortunes here, including the Victorian magnate Robert Dunsmuir, who was given £750,000 and almost half the island in return for building the Victoria–Nanaimo railway – an indication of the benefits that could accrue from the British government to those with the pioneering spirit. Five bands of Salish natives originally lived on the site, which they called **Sney-ne-mous**, or "meeting place", from which the present name derives. It was they who innocently showed the local black rock to Hudson's Bay agents in 1852. The old mines are now closed, and the town's pockets are padded today by forestry, deep-sea fishing, tourism and – most notably – by six deep-water docks and a booming port.

The Town

In downtown Nanaimo itself, only two other sights warrant the considerable amount of energy used to promote them. The **Nanaimo District Museum**, just off the main harbour area at 100 Cameron St by the Harbour Park Mall (May–Sept Mon–Fri 9am–6pm, Sat & Sun 10am–6pm; Oct–April Tues–Sat 9am–5pm; $2; ☎753-1821), houses a collection that runs the usual historical gamut of pioneer, logging, mining, native peoples and natural history displays. The best features are the reconstructed coal mine and the interesting insights into the town's cosmopolitan population – a mix of Polish, Chinese, Native Canadians and British citizens – who all see themselves today as some of the island's "friendliest folk". The **Bastion**, close by at the corner of Bastion and Front streets, is a wood-planked tower built by the Hudson's Bay Company in 1853 as a store and a stronghold against native attack, though in the event it was never used in anger. It's the oldest (perhaps the only) such building in the west. These days it houses a small **museum** of Hudson's Bay memorabilia (summer only 10am–5pm; donation); its silly tourist stunt, without which no BC town would be complete, is "the only ceremonial cannon firing west of Ontario" (summer only, daily at noon). This is marginally more impressive than the town's claim to have the most retail shopping space per capita in the country.

Nanaimo's outskirts are not pretty, nor, if you keep to the road through town, is the main strip of malls and billboards on and around downtown. Big efforts are being made to spruce the place up, however, not least in the town's 25 or so gardens and small parks. Many of these hug the shore, perfectly aligned for a seafront breath of air. With the completion of the **Harbourfront Walkway**, you can now stroll 3km along the seafront. Also popular is the new Swyalana Lagoon, an artificial tidal lagoon built on a renovated stretch of the downtown harbour in Maffeo Sutton Park. It's become a popular swimming, snoozing and picnic area. Further afield, **Piper's Lagoon Park** offers a windblown, grassy spit, with lots of trails, flowers, rocky bluffs and good sea views; it's off Hammond Bay Road north of the city centre. For **beaches** you could head for **Departure Bay**, again north of the centre off Stewart Avenue. Plenty of local shops rent out a range of marine gear, as well as bikes and boats.

For the wildest of the local parks, head due west of town to **Westwood Lake Park**, good for a couple of hours' lonely hiking and some fine swimming. Tongue-twisting **Petroglyph Provincial Park**, off Hwy 1 3km south of downtown, showcases Native Canadian carvings of the sort found all over BC (particularly along coastal waterways), many of them thousands of years old. Often their meaning is vague, but they appear to record important rituals and events. There are plenty of figures – real and mythological – carved into the local sandstone here, though their potential to inspire wonder is somewhat spoilt by more recent graffiti and the first thin edge of Nanaimo's urban sprawl.

Nanaimo's only other major claim to fame is as home of North America's first legal public bungee-jumping site. The **Bungee Zone Adrenalin Centre** is 13km south of the town at 35 Nanaimo River Rd (April–Oct daily 9.30am–dusk; ☎753-5867 or 1-800-668-7874; jumps from around $95): look out for the signed turn off Hwy 1. To date it has played host to more than 60,000 safe bungee jumps, including night jumps. So popular has it become that three variations have been added to the standard 42-metre plunge off the bridge, all slightly less breakfast-revisitingly terrifying than the bungee. The "Flying Fox" is a line to which you are fixed extending in a deep arc along the canyon – expect to hit speeds of 100kph; "Rap Jumping" involves a rapid mountaineering rappel straight down from the bridge; while the "Ultimate Swing" lets you jump off the bridge and swing in a big arc at speeds of up to 140kph. The last innovation was described by the safety engineer who inspected it – a man with twenty years' experience of fairground and other rides – as "the best ride I've ever ridden, and I've ridden them all". There is provision for **camping** here (with showers, laundry and tents for rent), and if you call in advance you should be able to book free shuttles to the site from Victoria and Nanaimo.

Nanaimo, like any self-respecting BC town, also lays on a fair few festivals, best known of which is the annual **Bathtub Race** or **Silly Boat Race**, in which bathtubs are raced (and sunk, mostly) across the 55km to Vancouver. The winner, who gets to Vancouver, takes the silver Plunger Trophy from the Loyal Nanaimo Bathtub Society. It's all part of the Marine Festival held in the second week of July. More highbrow is the May to June **Nanaimo Festival**, a cultural jamboree that takes place in and around Malaspina College, 900 Fifth St. The town's other minor claim to fame is the Nanaimo bar, a glutinous chocolate confection made to varying recipes and on sale everywhere.

Newcastle and Gabriola islands

Barely a stone's throw offshore from Nanaimo lies **Newcastle Island**, and beyond it the larger bulk of **Gabriola Island**, both incongruously graced with palm trees: they're beneficiaries of what is supposedly Canada's mildest climate. Ferries make the crossing every hour on the hour (10am–9pm; foot passengers $4 return, cars $10.75) from Maffeo Sutton Park (the wharf behind the Civic Arena) to **Newcastle Island Provincial Park**, which has a fine stretch of sand, tame wildlife, no cars, and lots of walking and picnic possibilities. It'll take a couple of hours to walk the 7.5-kilometre trail that encircles the island. There are about fifteen daily crossings to Gabriola Island (20min), a much quieter place that's home to about 2000 people, many of them artists and writers. Author Malcolm Lowry, he of *Under the Volcano* fame, immortalized the island in a story entitled *October Ferry to Gabriola Island* (characters in the tale never actually reach the island). Gabriola also offers several **beaches** – the best are Gabriola Sands' Twin Beaches at the island's northwest end and Drumbeg Provincial Park – and lots of scope for scuba diving, bird-watching (eagles and sea birds), beachcombing and easy walking, plus the added curiosity of the **Malaspina Galleries**, a series of caves and bluffs near Gabriola Sands sculpted by wind, frost and surf.

Both islands have numerous **B&Bs** and several **campgrounds**, though if you're thinking of staying the night it's as well to check first with the Nanaimo infocentre. You can buy snacks on Newcastle from various concessions, notably the newly restored 1931 Pavilion building, but if you're camping take supplies with you.

Information and transport

Nanaimo's **bus terminal** (☎753-4371) is some way from the harbour on the corner of Comox and Terminal (behind the *Tally-Ho Inn*), with six daily runs to Victoria, two to Port Hardy and three or four to Port Alberni, for connections to Tofino and Ucluelet. **BC Ferries** (☎386-3431 or 1-888-223-3779) sail to and from Departure Bay, 2km north of downtown (take the Hammond Bay bus #2 to the north end of Stewart Avenue), to Tsawwassen (south of Vancouver) and more frequently to Horseshoe Bay on the mainland (summer hourly 7am–9pm; off season every 2hr; foot passengers $8 one way, cars $30; cheaper in low season). Another terminal, Duke Point, which will take increasing numbers of ferries, opened recently just to the south of the town. The town lies on the Victoria–Courtenay line and sees two trains daily, northbound around 11am and southbound at 3pm: the station is in the centre of downtown.

You'll find a typically overstocked **infocentre** at Beban House, 2290 Bowen Rd (May–Sept daily 8am–8pm; Oct–April Mon–Fri 9am–5pm; ☎756-0106 or 1-800-663-7337). They'll phone around and help with **accommodation** referrals, and shower you with pamphlets on the town and the island as a whole. There are also details of the many boat rides and tours you can make to local sawmills, canneries, nature reserves and fishing research stations.

Accommodation

Nanaimo's cheapest beds are at the central, private **mini-hostel**, the *Nicol Street Hostel*, 65 Nicol St (☎753-1188, reservations ☎754-9697; ①; open year-round), located seven blocks south of the bus terminal and one block south of the Harbour Park Shopping Centre off Hwy 1. A handful of camping spots on the lawn (with ocean views) are also available, plus bike rental.

Numerous **motels** are clustered on the city limits, the best-known cheapies being the small *Colonial*, 950 Terminal Ave on Hwy 1 (☎754-4415; ②), and the *Diplomat Motel*, 333 Nicol St (☎753-3261; ②), three blocks south of the centre in the downtown area. For more tasteful lodgings, try the big *Tally-Ho Island Inn*, 1 Terminal Ave (☎753-2241 or 1-800-663-7322; ③–⑤), convenient for the bus terminal, or the *Schooner Cove Resort Hotel and Marina* (☎468-7691 or 1-800-663-7060; ⑤), 26km north of town near Nanoose Bay.

If you're **camping**, by far the best choice is Newcastle Island Provincial Park (see p.713), which has the only pitches within walking distance of town. Other sites are spread along the main road to the north and south. The best of these – a rural, watery retreat – is *Brannan Lake Campsites*, 6km north of the ferry terminal off Hwy 19 on a 150-acre working farm at 4228 Biggs Rd (☎756-0404; $14–16). The forestry bigwigs have set up a free site at lovely Nanaimo Lake on Nanaimo Lake Road about ten minutes south of the town.

Where **eating** is concerned, have your obligatory Nanaimo bar, or other cheap edibles at the food stands in the **Public Market**, which is near the ferry terminal on Stewart Avenue (daily 9am–9pm). The big Overwaitea supermarket is 2km north of town on Hwy 19. For meals try *Gina's*, 47 Skinner St, an unmissable Mexican outfit perched on the edge of a cliff and painted bright pink with an electric blue roof. The town's best **seafood** choice is the *Bluenose Chowder House*, 1340 Stewart Ave (closed Mon), also party to a nice outside terrace. Up the road near the BC Ferry terminal, *The Grotto*, 1511 Stewart Ave, is another reliable choice (closed Sun & Mon). A more recent arrival, and worth a look, is *Missoula's*, on the highway near the Rutherford Mall.

From Nanaimo to Port Alberni

North of Nanaimo Hwy 1 is replaced by **Hwy 19**, a messy stretch of road spotted with billboards and a rash of motels, marinas and clapboard houses. Almost every last centimetre of the coast is privately owned, this being the chosen site of what appears to be every British Columbian's dream holiday home. Don't expect, therefore, to be able to weave through the houses, wooden huts and boat launches to reach the tempting beaches that flash past below the highway. For sea and sand you have to hang on for **Parksville**, 37km north of Nanaimo, and its quieter near-neighbour **Qualicum Beach**.

Parksville marks a major parting of the ways: while Hwy 19 continues up the eastern coast to Port Hardy, **Hwy 4**, the principal trans-island route, pushes west to **Port Alberni** and on through the tremendously scenic Mackenzie Mountains to the Pacific Rim National Park. Laidlaw (☎385-4411 or 388-5248) runs three **buses** daily from Nanaimo to Port Alberni, where there are connecting services for Ucluelet and Tofino in the national park.

Parksville

The approach to **PARKSVILLE** from the south is promising, heralded by a lonely **infocentre** 6km south of town alongside the entrance to Craig's Camping. Thereafter the road takes you through lovely wooded dunes, with lanes striking off eastwards to hidden beaches and a half-dozen secluded **campgrounds**. Four kilometres on is the best of the beaches, stretched along 2km of **Rathtrevor Beach Provincial Park**. In summer this area is madness – there's more beach action here than just about anywhere in the country, and if you want to lay claim to some of the park's camping space expect to start, queueing first thing in the morning or take advantage of the provincial park reservations service ($9.50–15.50; ☎954-4600). The public sand here stretches for 2km and sports all the usual civilized facilities of Canada's tamed outdoors: cooking shelters, picnic spots and walking trails.

The dross starts beyond the bridge into **Parksville** and its eight blocks of motels and garages. The worst of the development has been kept off the promenade, however, which fronts **Parksville Beach**, whose annual **Sandfest** draws 30,000 visitors a day in July to watch the World Sandcastle Competition. The beach offers lovely views across to the mainland and boasts Canada's warmest sea water – up to 21°C in summer. Though busy, it's as immaculately kept as the rest of the town – a tidiness that bears witness to the reactionary civic pride of Parksville's largely retired permanent population. You'll see some of these worthy burghers at play during August, when the town hosts the World Croquet Championships.

For local **information**, Parksville's Chamber of Commerce is clearly signed off the highway in downtown at 1275 East Island Hwy (daily 8am–6pm; ☎248-3613). Ask especially for details of the many **hiking** areas and other nearby refuges from the beaches' summer maelstrom, and **fishing**, which is naturally another of the region's big draws.

If you must **stay**, camping offers the best locations. There are a multitude of cheapish Identikit **motels** in town and "resort complexes" out along the beaches, though summer vacancies are few and far between. South of Rathtrevor Beach Provincial Park, try a pair of cottage resorts that look onto the sea: the big *Tigh-Na-Mara Resort Hotel*, 1095 East Island Hwy (☎248-2072 or 1-800-663-7373; ④–⑥), with log cottages and oceanfront condos, forest setting, beach, indoor pool and self-catering units; or the smaller and slightly cheaper *Graycrest Seaside Resort*, 1115 East Island Hwy (☎248-6513 or 1-800-663-2636; ⑤–⑥). More upmarket still is the *Beach Acres Resort*, 1015 East Island Hwy (☎248-3424 or 1-800-663-7309; ⑤–⑦), set in 57 acres of woodland with its own pool, sandy beach, and forest or ocean-view cabins. Much cheaper, the large *Island Hall Beach Resort*, 181 West Island Hwy (☎248-3225 or 1-800-663-7370; ②–⑤), is one of the smarter and better-known downtown establishments, though you'd be just as well off in the nearby and similarly priced *Sea Edge Motel*, 209 West Island Hwy (☎248-8377 or 1-800-667-3382; ④–⑤), which shares the *Island Hall*'s beach. If you're after one of the cheapest motels, try the *Skylite*, 459 East Island Hwy (☎248-4271 or 1-800-667-1886; ②–③).

Qualicum Beach

QUALICUM BEACH, says its Chamber of Commerce, "is to the artist of today what Stratford-on-Avon was to the era of Shakespeare" – a Bohemian enclave of West Coast artists and writers that has also been dubbed the "Carmel of the North" after the town in California. Both estimations obviously pitch things ridiculously high, but compared to Parksville the area has more greenery and charm, and it's infinitely less commercialized, though it probably has just as many summer visitors.

More a collection of dispersed houses than a town, Qualicum's seafront is correspondingly wilder and more picturesque, skirted by the road and interrupted only by an **infocentre** at 2711 West Island Hwy, the obvious white building midway on the strand (daily 9am–6pm, open longer in summer; ☎752-9532), and a couple of well-sited **hotels**: the *Sand Pebbles Inn* (☎752-6974; ④–⑤) and the small *Captain's Inn* (☎752-6743; ③). A cluster of **motels** sit at its northern end, where the road swings inland, the best being the *Shorewater Resort Condos* (☎752-6901; ④–⑤). There's plenty of other local accommodation and B&Bs and campgrounds: contact the infocentre for details. Keep heading north and the road becomes quieter and edged with occasional **campgrounds**, amongst which the *Qualicum Bay* and *Spider Lake Provincial Park* sites stand out (both from $9.50).

Twenty-four kilometres north of the Qualicum is the area's only half-decent sight, the **Big Qualicum River Fish Hatchery**, a so-called "enhancement centre" which encourages salmon to spawn and thus bolster dwindling stocks. A tour of the government-run concern will fill you in on as much as you ever wanted to know about salmon.

Highway 4 to Port Alberni

If you've not yet ventured off the coastal road from Victoria, the short stretch of **Hwy 4 to Port Alberni** offers the first real taste of the island's beauty. The cheapest place to stay along here is the log-cabin-style **mini-hostel** (☎248-5694; $12) at 2400 Hwy 4 in Coombs, about 10km west of Parksville – take the third entrance past the school on the south side of the main road. Buses will stop here on request, but there are only half a dozen beds – and no cooking facilities – so call in advance.

The first worthwhile stop is **Englishman River Falls Provincial Park**, 3km west of Parksville and then another 8km south off the highway. Named after an early immigrant who drowned here, the park wraps around the Englishman River, which tumbles over two main sets of waterfalls. A thirty-minute trail takes in both falls, with plenty of swimming and fishing pools en route. The popular year-round provincial park **campground** ($12; April–Oct) is on the left off the approach road before the river, nestled amongst cedars, dogwoods – BC's official tree – and lush ferns.

Back on the main highway, a further 8km brings you to the **Little Qualicum Hatchery**, given over to chum, trout and chinook salmon, and just beyond it turn right for the **Little Qualicum Falls Provincial Park**, on the north side of Hwy 4 19km west of Parksville, which is claimed by some to be the island's loveliest small park. A magnificent forest trail follows the river as it drops several hundred metres through a series of gorges and foaming waterfalls. A half-hour stroll gives you views of the main falls, but for a longer **hike** try the five-hour Wesley Ridge Trail. There's a sheltered provincial park **campground** ($12; April–Oct) by the river and a recognized **swimming area** on the river at its southern end.

Midway to Port Alberni, the road passes **Cameron Lake** and then an imperious belt of old-growth forest. At the lake's western end, it's well worth walking ten minutes into **McMillan Provincial Park** (no campground) to reach the famous **Cathedral Grove**, a beautiful group of huge Douglas firs, some of them reaching 70m tall, 2m thick and up to a thousand years old. The park is the gift of the vast McMillan timber concern, whose agents have been responsible for felling similar trees with no compunction over the years. Wandering the grove will take only a few minutes, but just to the east, at the Cameron Lake picnic site, is the start of the area's main **hike**. The well-maintained trail was marked out by railway crews in 1908 and climbs to the summit of **Mount Arrowsmith** (1817m), a long, gentle twenty-kilometre pull through alpine meadows that takes between six and nine hours. The mountain is also one of the island's newer and fast-developing ski areas. To stay locally, head for the *Cameron Lake Resort* (☎752-6707; ②; April–Oct), based in a park-like setting on the lake: it has seven cottages and a campground ($15).

Port Alberni

Self-proclaimed "Gateway to the Pacific" and – along with half of Vancouver Island – "Salmon Capital of the World", **PORT ALBERNI** is a mostly ugly town overdominated by the sights and smells of its huge lumber mills. It's also a busy fishing port, situated at the end of the impressive fjord-like Alberni Inlet, Vancouver Island's longest inlet. Various logging and pulp-mill tours are available, but the town's main interest to travellers is as a forward base for the Pacific Rim National Park. If you've ever wanted to hook a salmon, though, this is probably one of the easier places to do so – there are any number of boats and guides ready to help out.

The only conventional sight is the **Alberni Valley Museum**, 4255 Wallace St and 10th Avenue, home to a predictable but above-average logging and Native Canadian collection, a waterwheel and small steam engine (summer Tues, Wed, Fri & Sat 10am–5pm, Thur 10am–9pm; free; ☎723-2181). For hot-weather swimming, locals head out to **Sproat Lake Provincial Park**, 8km north of town on Hwy 4. It's a hectic scene in summer, thanks to a fine beach, picnic area and a pair of good campgrounds – one on the lake, the other north of the highway about 1km away. Of peripheral interest, you can take a guided tour of the world's largest fire-fighting planes or follow the short trails that lead to a few ancient petroglyphs on the park's eastern tip.

Sproat Lake marks the start of the superb scenery that unfolds over the 100km of Hwy 4 west of the town. Only heavily logged areas detract from the grandeur of the Mackenzie Range and the majestic interplay of trees and water. Go prepared, however, as there's no fuel or shops for about two hours of driving.

Practicalities

Laidlaw (☎385-4411 or 1-800-318-0818) runs four **buses** daily to and from Nanaimo, with the terminal on Victoria Quay at 5065 Southgate (though the bus company are based at 4541 Margaret St). Jump off at the 7–Eleven, one stop earlier, to be nearer the centre of town. The same company runs connections from here on to Ucluelet and Tofino in Pacific Rim National Park. Western Coach Lines (☎723-3341) run two services weekly to Bamfield (Mon & Fri; $17 one way) as does the Pacheenaht First Nation Bus Service (☎647-5521). Several other companies from Victoria (see p.688) make connections to Bamfield for the West Coast Trail (see pp.729–730). For help and information on fishing charters, hiking options, minor summer events, or tours of the two local pulp mills, call in at the **infocentre**, unmissable as you come into town at 2533 Redford St, RR2, Site 215 Comp 10 (daily 9am–6pm; ☎724-6535), off Hwy 4 east of town – look out for the big yellow mural. Also on the way into town, off Hwy 4, is the fine Curious Coho **bookstore**, 4841 Johnston Rd (☎724-2141), whose staff should be able to give you advice on good places to eat and drink (see below).

Given the 8am departure of the MV *Lady Rose* (see p.718), there's a good chance you may have to stay overnight in the town. For **accommodation** there are the usual motel choices, though for a good central hotel you might be better off with the *Coast Hospitality Inn*, 3835 Redford St (☎723-8111 or 1-800-663-1144; ⑤), probably the town's best bet. *The Barclay*, 4277 Stamp Ave (☎724-7171 or 1-800-563-6590; ③), with outdoor pool and the smaller *Somass Motel and RV*, 5279 River Rd (☎724-3236 or 1-800-927-2217; ③), are also both reliable choices. Cheaper, and 14km west of town on the lakefront off Hwy 4, is the *Westbay Hotel on Sproat Lake* (☎723-2811 or 1-800-358-2811; ③). The infocentre has a list of the constantly changing **B&B** outlets. For **camping**, you can try the small, reasonably central and wooded *Dry Creek Public Campground*, 6230 Beaver Creek Rd at 4th Avenue and Napier Street: ask at the infocentre for directions – it's hard to find (☎723-6011; $8–19; May–Sept). Further afield is the bigger 250-site *China Creek Marina and Campground*, Bamfield Road (☎723-2657; $12–25), 15km south of the town on Alberni Inlet, which has a wooded, waterside location and sandy, log-strewn beach. Camping at Sproat Lake (see above) is excellent, but busy in the summer.

Eating possibilities are numerous. For coffee down by the dock before jumping aboard the MV *Lady Rose*, use the *Blue Diner*. For lunch, make for the *Swale's Rock*, 5328 Argyle St (☎723-0777), and for **seafood** try the new waterfront *Clockworks*, Harbour Quay (☎723-2333), or the more basic fish and chips of *Friar John's*, 4726 Johnston Rd (a few blocks up from Victoria Quay). The *Canal*, 5093 Johnson St, serves good Greek food, and for cheap lunches there's the *Paradise Café*, 4505 Gertrude St, and several deli-bakeries, of which the best is probably *Mountain View*, 3727 10th Ave (takeout only).

The MV Lady Rose

The thing you'll probably most want to do in Port Alberni is to leave it, preferably on the **MV Lady Rose**, a small, fifty-year-old Scottish-built freighter that plies between Kildonan, Bamfield, Ucluelet and the Broken Group Islands (see p.727). Primarily a conduit for freight and mail, it also takes up to a hundred passengers, many of whom use it as a drop-off for canoe trips or the West Coast Trail at Bamfield. You could easily ride it simply for the exceptional scenery – huge cliffs and tree-covered mountains – and for the abundant wildlife (sea lions, whales, eagles, depending on the time of year). Passengers started as something of a sideline for the company that runs the boat, but such has been the boat's popularity that another boat has been added to the "fleet" – the 200-passenger MV *Frances Barkley* – and reservations for trips are now virtually essential. Remember to take a sweater and jacket and wear sensible shoes, for these are still primarily working boats, and creature comforts are few.

The basic year-round **schedule** is as follows and has remained basically unchanged for a few years: the boat leaves at 8am from the Argyle Pier, 5425 Argyle St at the Alberni Harbour Quay (year-round Tues, Thurs & Sat). It arrives in **Bamfield** ($20 one way, $40 return) via Kildonan ($12/$24), at 12.30pm and starts its return journey an hour later, reaching Port Alberni again at 5.30pm. From October to May the boat stops on request in advance at the Broken Group Islands ($20/$40). From July 1 to Labour Day only (early Sept) there are additional sailing on this route (same times) on Fridays and Sundays.

From June to late September, there are additional sailings on Monday, Wednesday and Friday to **Ucluelet** and the Broken Group Islands, departing 8am and arriving at Ucluelet at 1pm via the islands, where the boat docks at 11am at Sechart, site of the new *Sechart Whaling Station Lodge* (☎723-8313; ③), the only place to stay if you're not wilderness camping on the archipelago. The return journey starts from Ucluelet at 2pm, calling at Sechart again (3.30pm) before arriving back at Port Alberni (7pm).

Contact Barkley Sound Service for information and reservations (☎723-8313 or 1-800-663-7192; April–Sept only). They also offer canoe and kayak rentals and transportation of the same to the Broken Group Islands (canoe and single kayak rental $30, double kayak $40 daily including lifejackets, paddles, pumps and spray skirts). Note that smaller boats running more irregular services to the same destinations can occasionally be picked up from Tofino and Ucluelet.

Pacific Rim National Park

The **Pacific Rim National Park** is the single best reason to visit Vancouver Island, a stunning amalgam of mountains, coastal rainforest, wild beaches, and unkempt marine landscapes that stretches intermittently for 130km between the towns of Tofino in the north and Port Renfrew to the south. It divides into three distinct areas: **Long Beach**, which is the most popular; the **Broken Group Islands**, hundreds of islets only really accessible to sailors and canoeists; and the **West Coast Trail**, a tough but increasingly popular long-distance footpath. The whole area has also become a magnet for surfing and **whale-watching** enthusiasts, and dozens of small companies run charters out from the main centres to view the migrating mammals. By taking the MV *Lady Rose* from Port Alberni (see above) to Bamfield or Ucluelet or back, and combining this with shuttle buses or Laidlaw buses from Victoria, Port Alberni and Nanaimo, a wonderfully varied combination of itineraries is possible around the region.

Lying at the north end of Long Beach, **Tofino**, once essentially a fishing village, is now changing in the face of tourism, but with its natural charm, scenic position and plentiful accommodation still makes the best base for general exploration. **Ucluelet** to the south is comparatively less attractive, but almost equally geared to providing tours and accommodating the park's 800,000 or so annual visitors. **Bamfield**, a tiny and picturesque community with a limited amount of in-demand accommodation, lies still further south and is known mainly as the northern trailhead of the West Coast Trail and a fishing, marine research and whale-watching centre. Unless you fly in, you enter the park on Hwy 4 from Port Alberni, which means the first part you'll see is Long Beach (Hwy 4 follows its length en route for Tofino), so if you're dashing in by car for a day-trip, cut straight to the section dealing with this area on p.725. Long Beach, rather than Tofino, is also the site of the park's main **information centre** and the nearby Wickaninnish Centre, an interpretive centre. Remember that a **park fee** – $8 per vehicle per day – is payable at the park entrance.

Weather in the park is an important consideration, because it has a well-deserved reputation for being appallingly wet, cold and windy – and that's the good days. An average of 300cm of rain falls annually, and in some places it buckets down almost 700cm, well over ten times what falls on Victoria. So don't count on doing much swimming or sunbathing (though **surfing**'s a possibility): think more in terms of spending your time admiring crashing Pacific breakers, hiking the backcountry and maybe doing a spot of beachcombing. Better still, time your visit to coincide with the worst of the weather off season – **storm-watching** is an increasingly popular park pastime.

Tofino

TOFINO, most travellers' target base in the park, is beginning to show the adverse effects of its ever-increasing tourist influx, but it clearly realizes it has a vested interest in preserving the salty, waterfront charm that brings people here in the first place. Crowning a narrow spit, the village is bounded on three sides by tree-covered islands and water, gracing it with magnificent views and plenty of what the tourist literature refers to as "aquaculture". As a service centre it fulfils most functions, offering food, accommodation and a wide variety of boat and sea-plane tours, most of which have a **whale-watching** or fishing angle or provide a means to get out to **islands and hot springs** close by (see overleaf). Sleepy in off season, the place erupts into a commercial frenzy during the summer (unreconstructed hippies, surfer types and easy-going family groups being the most visible visitors), though there's little to do in town other than walk its few streets, enjoy the views and soak up the casual atmosphere.

You might drop into the small **West Coast Maritime Museum** and **Whale Centre** at 411 Campbell St (May–Sept daily 9am–8.30pm; free; ☎725-2132), one of many places to book whale-watching tours, but also home to exhibits and artefacts devoted to local seafaring and trading history, whales and Native Canadian culture. Another notable place around town is the **Eagle Aerie Gallery**, 350 Campbell St (☎725-3235), a gallery belonging to noted Tsimshian artist Roy Vickers and housed in a traditional long-house-style building with a beautiful cedar interior. Two fine beaches also lie within walking distance to the southeast of the town: **Mackenzie Beach** and **Chesterman's Beach**, the former one of the warmer spots locally, the latter home to a fair number of out-of-town accommodation possibilities (see p.721). Beyond Chesterman lies Frank Island, a tempting proposition at low tide, but (sadly) private property. The quietest beach around these parts, though, is **Templar**, a miniature strip of sand: ask at the infocentre for directions.

Tofino's easily reached by Laidlaw **bus** (☎385-4411 or 1-800-318-0818) from Port Alberni (2 daily; 3hr) and Nanaimo (1 daily; 4hr 30min), with a single early-morning connection from Victoria, changing at Nanaimo (6hr 30min; $45.60 one way, $88.90 return). The bus depot is on 1st Street near the junction with Neil Street. For **flights**, the excellent North Vancouver Air (☎604/278-1608 or 1-800-228-6608) operates to here from Vancouver (1hr flight) and Victoria (45min), for around $200 return if tickets are booked fourteen days in advance. Baxter Aviation (☎250/754-1066, 604/683-6525 in Vancouver or 1-800-661-5599) also run connecting flights to Tofino and Ucluelet (see below) from Vancouver harbour, Victoria, Seattle and many other smaller centres. The **infocentre** at

380 Campbell St (March–Sept daily 9am–8pm; ☎725-3414) can give you the exhaustive lowdown on all the logistics of boat and plane tours.

Trips from Tofino

Once they've wandered Tofino's streets, most people head south to explore Long Beach, or put themselves at the mercy of the boat and plane operators. Their playground is the stretch of ocean and landscapes around Tofino known as **Clayoquot Sound**. The name has gained tremendous resonance over the last few years, largely because it has been the focus for some of the most bitterly fought battles against loggers by environmentalists and Native Canadian campaigners. It stretches for some 65km from Kennedy Lake to the south of Tofino to the Hesquiat Peninsula 40km to the north, embracing three major islands – Meares, Vargas and Flores – and numerous smaller islets and coastal inlets. More importantly, it is the largest surviving area of low-altitude temperate **rainforest** in North America. Quite incredibly the BC government gave permission to logging companies in 1993 to fell two-thirds of this irreplaceable and age-old forest. The result was the largest outbreak of **civil disobedience** in Canadian history, resulting in eight hundred arrests, as vast numbers congregated at a peace camp in the area and made daily attempts to stop the logging trucks. The standoff resulted in partial victory, with the designation of new protected areas and limited recognition of the Nuu-chah-nulth tribes moral and literal rights to the land. The region remains precarious, however, and if it's happened once you can be pretty sure that, where forestry interests are concerned, it'll happen again.

There are five main destinations in this region for boat and float-plane trips. The nearest is **Meares Island**, easily visible to the east of Tofino and just fifteen minutes away by boat. A beautiful island swathed in lush temperate rainforest, this was one of the area's earmarked for the lumberjack's chainsaw, despite its designation as Nuu-chah-nulth tribal park in 1985. At present its ancient cedars and hemlock are safe, and visible on the Meares Island Big Cedar Trail (3km), which meanders among some of the biggest trees you'll ever see, many of them more than a thousand years old and up to 6m across – big enough to put a tunnel through. **Vargas Island**, the next nearest target, lies just 5km from Tofino to the north, and is visited for its beauty, beaches, kayaking and swimming possibilities. **Flores Island**, 20km to the northwest, is accessed by boat or plane and, like Vargas Island, is partly protected by partial provincial park status. At the Native Canadian community of Ahousaht you can pick up the Ahousaht Wild Side Heritage Trail, which runs for 16km through idyllic beach and forest scenery to the Mount Flores viewpoint (886m). This is also a chance to encounter Native Canadian culture and people at first hand, with **tours** accompanied by local guides available: see the Tofino infocentre or call ☎725-3309 for details and information on trail conditions.

Perhaps the best, and certainly one of the most popular trips from Tofino, is the 37-kilometre boat or plane ride to **Hot Springs Cove**, site of one of only a handful of hot springs on Vancouver Island (1hr by boat, 15min by float plane). A thirty-minute trek from the landing stage brings you to the springs, which emerge at a piping 43°C and run, as a creek, to the sea via a small waterfall and four pools, becoming progressively cooler. Be prepared for something of a crowd in summer when swimming costumes can be optional. Primitive camping is probably possible, but certainly not encouraged, and an expensive new hotel, the *Hot Springs Lodge* – a way to beat other punters by getting in an early-morning or late-night dip – has opened on the cove near the landing stage (see "Accommodation" opposite). Finally, a forty-kilometre trip north takes you to **Hesquiat Peninsula**, where you land at or near Refuge Cove, site of a Hesquiaht Native Canadian village. Locals offer tours here and some lodgings: ask for the latest details at the Tofino infocentre. The infocentre is also the place to pick up information on **tours**: otherwise, contact Seaside Adventures, 300 Main St (☎725-2292 or 1-800-222-3588), Chinook Charters, 450 Campbell St (☎725-3431 or 1-800-665-3646), or the whale-watching companies listed under "Activities" on p.722, most of whom also offer boat tours to the above destinations.

Accommodation

The infocentre (see p.719) may be able to get you into one of the village's ever-expanding roster of **hotels**, **motels** and **B&B**, should you be unwise enough to turn up in Tofino without reservations in high summer. There are two main concentrations of accommodation options: in Tofino itself or a couple of kilometres out of town to the east en route for Long Beach on or near Lynn Road, which overlooks Chesterman Beach. Bed and breakfast options, in particular, tend to be out of town near Chesterman Beach. You might also want to check whether they offer full or continental breakfasts. Note that out of town but across the water (access by water taxi) there's also the desirable but expensive self-contained units at the *Hot Springs Lodge* (☎724-8570; ⑤–⑥), the only accommodation at Hot Springs Cove (see opposite), but book early.

Otherwise you can try one of many **campgrounds** or the **private hostels** that now seem to spring up overnight here and disappear just as quickly, though local reports suggest some of these places can be pretty unsalubrious, home to a sprinkling of the untrustworthy sort of beach-bum year-round drifters that get travellers a bad name. Current good hostels include the *Tofino Backpackers Hostel*, 241 Campbell St (☎725-2288; ①), and *Vargas Island Inn & Hostel* (☎725-3309; ①), the latter in a good position out on an island north of the town (see "Trips from Tofino" opposite).

HOTELS AND MOTELS

Cable Cove Inn, 201 Main St (☎725-4236 or 1-800-663-6449). Stay in high style in one of six smart rooms at the westernmost edge of town that comes complete with Jacuzzis, fireplaces and four-poster beds. ④–⑥.

Dolphin Motel, 1190 Pacific Rim Hwy (☎725-3377, fax 725-3374). Rooms with coffee-maker and fridge or self-catering units 3km south of town; 5min walk to Chesterman Beach. ②–③.

Duffin Cove and Resort, 215 Campbell St (☎725-3448 or 1-800-222-3588). Thirteen nice cabins and suites (for one to eight people) with kitchens and sea view balconies just south of the *Cable Cove Inn* at the western edge of town overlooking the Clayoquot Sound. ⑤–⑥.

Maquinna Lodge, 120 First St (☎725-3261 or 1-800-665-3199, fax 725-3433). Central town location at the corner of Main and First street, containing renovated rooms, some overlooking Tofino Harbour and Meares Island. ④.

Middle Beach Lodge, 400 Mackenzie Beach (☎725-2900). Extremely nice, secluded place south of town and west of Chesterman Beach with big stone fireplace, deep old chairs and the gentle splash of waves on tiny Templar Beach to lull you to sleep. ⑦.

Ocean Village Beach Resort, 555 Hellesen Drive (☎725-3755). A resort just north of Long Beach, 2km from town on the main road, with "Gothic" accommodation, ocean views, kitchen units and indoor pool. ④–⑥.

Schooner Motel, 311 Campbell St (☎725-3478, fax 725-3499). Overlooking Tofino Inlet and Meares Island in the town centre, this motel has some rooms complete with kitchen. ③–⑤.

Tofino Motel, 542 Campbell St (☎725-2055). Newish motel on the eastern edge of town including rooms with balconies offering views of the sea and neighbouring islands. ④–⑤.

Tofino Swell Lodge, 340 Olsen Rd (☎725-3274). On the eastern edge of town near Crab Dock, this excellent lodge on the waterfront looking out to Meares Island has kitchen or plain sleeping units. ③–④.

Wickaninnish Inn, Osprey Lane at Chesterman Beach (☎725-3100 or 1-800-333-4604, fax 725-3110). If you really want to push the boat out shell, out for this superb $8.5-million 45-room inn, situated on a rocky promontory at the western end of Chesterman Beach. All rooms are large and have ocean views, fireplaces and baths big enough for two. As well as the obvious local attractions, storm-watching here is a growing wintertime activity. ⑦–⑧.

BED AND BREAKFASTS

Beach Retreat, 1217 Lynn Rd (☎725-2441). A peaceful out of town option at the western end of Lynn Road near Chesterman Beach with great ocean views and good, wholesome breakfasts. ④.

Brimar, 1375 Thornberg Crescent (☎725-3410). At the south end of Chesterman Beach, off Lynn Road, these three rooms have good Pacific Ocean views and come with a full breakfast. ④.

Christa's B&B, 1367 Chesterman Beach (☎725-2827, fax 725-4416). You can walk from your room with its ocean view and private bathroom onto Chesterman Beach. ④.

Crab Dock, 310 Olsen Rd (☎725-2911). Situated a little east of the town at Crab Dock, these three newly built rooms all have private bathroom. A full breakfast is offered but you can also use the guest kitchen, as well as the living room. ④–⑤.

Gull Cottage, 1254 Lynn Rd (☎725-3177). A few minutes' walk to the beach, at the west end of Lynn Road, this Victorian-era home has three rooms (private bathrooms) and a hot tub in the woods. ④–⑤.

Paddler's Inn, 320 Main St (☎725-4222). A recommended spot on the waterfront right in the middle of town; non-smoking. ④–⑤.

Penny's Place, 565 Campbell St (☎725-3457). A choice of rooms on the east edge of the small downtown with and without private bathrooms offering a full breakfast but non-smoking. ④–⑤.

The Tide's Inn B&B, 160 Arnet Rd (☎725-3765). An easy walk south of town (walk down First Avenue and turn right) on the waterfront with good views of Clayoquot Sound. ④.

Village Gallery B&B, 321 Main St (☎725-4229). Quiet upper room and living room in a heritage building in the centre of town with good ocean view and full breakfast.

West Beach Manor, 1314 Lynn Rd (☎725-3483). Self-contained suites close to Chesterman Beach with kitchens and separate bedrooms with space for up to four people. ④–⑤.

Wilp Gybuu (*Wolf House*), 311 Leighton Way (☎725-2330). Three rooms in a walkable location south of town close to *The Tide's Inn*. Sea views, good breakfast and private en-suite bathroom. ④.

CAMPGROUNDS

Bella Pacifica Resort and Campground (☎725-3400, fax 725-2400). Sites with hot showers, flush toilets and laundry 2km south of town, with wilderness and oceanfront sites, private nature trails to Templar Beach and walk-on access to Mackenzie Beach. Reservations recommended. March–Oct. $22–27.

Crystal Cove Beach Resort (☎725-4213, fax 725-4219). Sites with flush toilets, laundry and showers and some cabins; 3km south of town and also close to Mackenzie Beach with one- and two-bedroom smart log cabins. Reservations recommended. $22–35; cabins ⑥.

Eating and drinking

For **food**, just about everyone in town clusters around the heaving tables of the *Common Loaf Bake Shop* behind the bank at 180 First St (☎725-3915), deservedly the most popular choice for coffee and snacks. In the evening the home-made dough is turned into pizzas instead of bread and rolls. In similar vein is the *Alley Way Café*, also behind the bank at Campbell and First Street, a friendly locals type of place with newspapers to read and cheap, wholesome food where everything down to the mayonnaise is home-made. The *Crab Bar*, 601 Campbell St, near the corner of Gibson Street (☎725-3733) is something of a local institution, selling little more than crab, seafood, beer, bread and some imaginative salads. One of the best views in town is available at the *Sea Shanty*, 300 Main St (☎725-2902), a Native Canadian-run restaurant which offers **outdoor dining** overlooking the harbour and the chance of some tremendous sunsets on fine evenings. For a real treat, head out of town to *The Pointe Restaurant* at the *Wickaninnish Inn* (☎725-3100; see hotel listings above), which for most people's money has superseded the *Orca Lodge*, 1254 Pacific Hwy (☎725-2323), as the area's best upmarket restaurant, mainly on account of its views.

Activities

Ucluelet to the south may claim to be "whale-watching capital of the world", but **whales** – the main reason a lot of people are here – are just as easily seen from Tofino. As in Victoria (see p.696), you have plenty of operators, most costing about the same and offering similar **excursions**: all you have to do is decide what sort of boat you want to go out on – zodiacs (inflatables), which are bouncier, more thrilling and potentially wetter (but not recommended for pregnant women or people with back problems) or rigid hull cruisers (covered or uncovered), which are more sedate. Remember that if you take tours to Meares Islands, Hot Springs Cove and elsewhere, especially in spring or fall (best times to see whales), you stand a good chance of seeing whales en route anyway – some operators try to combine whale-watching and excursions. Operators to try include: Cypre Prince Tours midway down the main street at 430 Campbell St (☎725-2202 or 1-800-787-2202); Chinook Charters, 450 Campbell St (☎725-3431 or 1-800-665-3646), who offer trips (2hr 30min) on rigid or zodiac boats; and Jamie's Whaling Station, 606 Campbell St (☎725-3919 or 1-800-667-9913), who also offer a choice of zodiac boats or the twenty-metre *Lady Selkirk,* which comes with heated cabin, no small consideration on cold days, of which Tofino has a few.

Many of these companies double up as **fishing** charters, though for more specialist operators contact Bruce's Smiley Seas Charters, based at the 4th Street Dock/Fisherman's Wharf (May–Sept; ☎725-2557), who're quite happy to have novices aboard; or the Weigh West Marine Resort (☎725-3238, 725-3277 or 1-800-665-8922), who have a restaurant and lodgings just above the marina at 634 Campbell St. Still on the water, Tofino is quickly becoming the **surfing** capital of Canada, thanks to some enormous Pacific waves, though floating driftwood and big lumps of lumber caught up in the waves can be a hazard. For information, board rental and all other equipment, contact Live to Surf east of the town centre at 1180 Tofino Hwy (☎725-

---

WHALES

The Pacific Rim National Park is amongst the world's best areas for **whale-watching**, thanks to its location on the main migration routes, food-rich waters and numerous sheltered bays. People come from five continents for the spectacle, and it's easy to find a boat going out from Tofino, Ucluelet or Bamfield, most charging around $50–70 a head for the trip depending on duration (usually 2–3hr). Regulations prohibit approaching within 100m of an animal but, though few locals will admit it, there's no doubt that the recent huge upsurge in boat tours has begun to disrupt the **migrations**. The whales' 8000-kilometre journey – the longest known migration of any mammal – takes them from their breeding and calving lagoons in Baja, Mexico, to summer feeding grounds in the Bering and Chukchi seas off Siberia. The northbound migration takes from February to May, with the peak period of passage between March and April. A few dozen animals occasionally abort their trip and stop off the Canadian coast for summer feeding (notably at Maquinna Marine Park, 20min by boat from Tofino). The return journey starts in August, hitting Tofino and Ucluelet in late September and early October. **Mating** takes place in Mexico during December, after which the males turn immediately northwards, to be followed by females and their young in February.

Although killer whales (orcas) are occasionally seen, the most commonly spotted type are **grey whales**, of which some 19,000 are thought to make the journey annually. Averaging 14m in length and weighing 35 to 50 tonnes, they're distinguished by the absence of a dorsal fin, a ridge of lumps on the back, and a mottled blue-grey colour. Females have only one offspring, following a gestation period of thirteen months, and, like the males, cruise at only two to four knots – perfect for viewing and, sadly, for capture.

Even if you don't take a boat trip, you stand a faint chance of seeing whales from the coast as they dive, when you can locate their tails, or during fluking, when the animals surface and "blow" three or four times before making another five-minute dive. There are telescopes at various points along Long Beach, the best-known viewpoints being Schooner Cove, Radar Hill, Quistis Point and Combers Beach near Sea Lion Rocks.

4464). If you want to go out in a **kayak** (no experience required) contact Remote Passages Sea Kayaking, 71 Wharf St (☎725-3330 or 1-800-666-9833), who provide day or evening paddles, or Tofino Sea Kayaking, 320 Main St (☎725-4222 or 1-800-863-4664), who offer day-trips or longer **tours** with lodge accommodation or wilderness camping. Nine holes of **golf** are available at the local course near the airport (☎725-3332), while **guided hikes** and easy nature rambles in the forest and along the seashore are offered by several companies: try Raincoast Communications (☎725-2878). Tofino Kite & Bike, 441a Campbell St (☎725-121), offer guided **bike tours** and **bike rentals**.

Long Beach

The most accessible of the park's components, **LONG BEACH** is just what it says: a long tract of wild, windswept sand and rocky points stretching for about 30km from Tofino to Ucluelet. Around 19km can be hiked unbroken from Schooner Bay in the west to Half Moon Bay in the east. The snow-covered peaks of the Mackenzie Range rise up over 1200m as a scenic backdrop, and behind the beach grows a thick, lush canopy of coastal rainforest. The white-packed sand itself is the sort of primal seascape that is all but extinct in Europe, scattered with beautiful, sea-sculpted driftwood, smashed by surf, broken by crags, and dotted with islets and rock pools oozing with marine life. It's worth realizing that Long Beach, while a distinct beach in itself, also rather loosely refers to several other beaches to either side, the relative merits of which are outlined below. If you haven't done so already, driving or biking Hwy 4 along the beach area is the best time to call in at the Pacific Rim National Park **Information Centre** (May to mid-Oct daily; ☎762-4212), located right off Hwy 4 3km northwest of the Ucluelet–Tofino–Port Alberni road junction.

Scenery aside, Long Beach is noted for its **wildlife**, the BC coastline reputedly having more marine species than any other temperate area in the world. As well as the smaller stuff in tidal pools – starfish, anemones, snails, sponges and suchlike – there are large mammals like whales and sea lions, as well as thousands of migrating birds (especially in Oct & Nov), notably pintails, mallards, black brants and Canada geese. Better weather brings out lots of beachcombers (Japanese glass fishing floats are highly coveted), clam diggers, anglers, surfers, canoeists, windsurfers and divers, though the water is usually too cold to venture in without a wet suit, and rip currents and rogue lumps of driftwood crashed around by the waves can make swimming dangerous. Surf guards patrol the Long Beach day-use area in July and August. By the way, try to resist the temptation to pick up shells as souvenirs – it's against park regulations.

The beaches

As this is a national park, some of Long Beach and its flanking stretches of coastline have been very slightly tamed for human consumption, but in the most discreet and tasteful manner. The best way to get a taste of the area is to walk the beaches or forested shorelines themselves – there are plenty of hidden coves – or to follow any of nine very easy and well-maintained **hiking trails** (see box). If you're driving or biking along Hwy 4, which backs the beaches all the way, there are distinct areas to look out for. Moving west, the first of these is the five-kilometre **Florencia Beach** (1.5km from the Hwy: access by trails 1, 2, 3 and 5; see box), also known as Wreck Beach and formerly the home of hippie beach dwellers in driftwood shacks before the park's formation. This is something of a locals' favourite, with relatively few people and good rock pools.

Further along Hwy 4 you come to a turnoff (Long Beach Road) for the **Wickaninnish Centre**, on a headland at the start of Long Beach, not to be confused with the similarly named well-known hotel and restaurant closer to Tofino (confusingly, the centre also has a restaurant). Wickaninnish was a noted nineteenth-century Native Canadian chief, and arbitrator between Europeans and native fur traders. His name left no doubt

LONG BEACH WALKS

With an eye on the weather and tide, you can walk more or less anywhere on and around Long Beach. Various trails and roads drop to the beach from the main Hwy 4 road to Tofino. At the same time there are nine official trails, most of them short and very easy, so you could tackle a few in the course of a leisurely drive or cycle along the road. All the paths are clearly marked from Hwy 4, but it's still worth picking up a *Hiker's Guide* from the infocentre. From east to west you can choose from the following. The linked trails **1** and **2**, the **Willowbrae Trail** (2.8km round trip), are accessed by turning left at the main Hwy 4 junction and driving or biking 2km towards Ucluelet. A level wooded trail then leads from the trailhead towards the beach, following the steps of early pioneers who used this route before the building of roads between Tofino and Ucluelet. Just before the sea it divides, dropping steeply via steps and ramps, to either the tiny Half Moon Bay or the larger, neighbouring Florencia Bay to the north.

All other walks are accessed off Hwy 4 to Tofino, turning right (north) at the main Hwy 4 junction. The gentle **3 Gold Mine Trail** (3km round trip), signed left off the road, leads along Lost Shoe Creek, a former gold-mining area (look out for debris), to Florencia Beach. For walks **4**, **5** and **6**, take the turn left off the highway for the Wickaninnish Centre. The **4 South Beach Trail** (1.5km round trip) leaves from behind the centre, leading above forest-fringed shores and coves before climbing to the headlands for a view of the coast and a chance to climb down to South Beach, famous for its big rock-crashing breakers and the sound of the water ripping noisily through the beach pebbles. The **5 Wickaninnish Trail** (5km) follws the South Beach Trail for a while and then at the top of the first hill is signed left, passing through rainforest – once again this is the route of the old pioneer trail – before ending at the parking area above Florencia Beach to the east. The **6 Shorepine Bog Trail** (800m) is a wheelchair-accessible boardwalk trail (accessed on the left on the access road to the centre) that wends through the fascinating stunted bog vegetation; trees which are just a metre or so tall here can be hundreds of years old.

Moving further west towards Tofino along Hwy 4, the **7 Rain Forest Trails** are two small loops (1km each round trip), one on each side of the road, that follow a boardwalk through virgin temperate rainforest: each has interpretive boards detailing forest life cycle and forest "inhabitants" respectively. Further down the road on the right at the Combers Beach parking area, a road gives access to the gentle **8 Spruce Fringe Trail** (1.5km loop). This graphically illustrates the effects of the elements on spruce forest, following a log-strewn beach fringe edged with bent and bowed trees before entering more robust forest further from the effects of wind and salt spray. It also crosses willow and crab-apple swamp to a glacial terrace, the site of a former shoreline, past the airport turnoff. The final walk, the **Schooner Beach Trail** (1km one way), leads left off the road through superb tranches of rainforest to an extremely scenic beach at Schooner Cove. This might be the end of the official trails, but don't fail to climb to the viewpoint on **Radar Hill** off to the right as you get closer to Tofino.

as to his number-one status, as it means "having no one in front of him in the canoe". The centre is the departure point for several trails (see box), has telescopes for whale-spotting and a variety of films, displays and exhibits relating to the park and ocean. Around 8km beyond the Long Beach Road turnoff is the entrance to the Greenpoint park **campground** and further access to Long Beach, while 4km beyond that lies the turnoff on the right to Tofino's small airstrip. Around here the peninsula narrows, with **Grice Bay** coming close to the road on the right (north side), a shallow inlet known in winter for its countless wildfowl. Beyond the airstrip turnoff comes a trail to Schooner Cove (see box) and 3.5km beyond that a 1.5-kilometre turn-off to Kap'yong, or **Radar Hill** (96m), the panoramic site of a wartime radar station. By now Tofino is getting close, and 4.5km further on (and a couple of kilometres outside the park boundary) you come to **Cox Bay Beach**, **Chesterman Beach** and **Mackenzie Beach**, all accessed from Hwy 4. Cox and Chesterman are known for their breakers; Mackenzie for its relative warmth if you want to chance a dip.

Practicalities

Long Beach's **Pacific Rim National Park Information Centre** is just off Hwy 4, 3km north of the T-junction for Tofino and Ucluelet. It provides a wealth of material on all aspects of the park, and in summer staff offer guided walks and interpretative programmes (mid-March to early Oct daily 9am–7pm; ☎726-4212). For year-round information, call the Park Administration Office (☎726-7721). For more Long Beach information, viewing decks with telescopes and lots of well-presented displays, head for the **Wickaninnish Centre**, Long Beach Road (mid-March to early Oct daily 10.30am–6pm; ☎726-4212).

There is one park **campground**, the *Greenpoint*, set on a lovely bluff overlooking the beach ($13; drive-in; washrooms but no showers; firewood available; $13). However, it's likely to be full every day in July and August, and it's first-come, first-served, so you may have to turn up for several days before getting a spot. There's usually a waiting-list system, however, whereby you're given a number and instructions as to when you should be able to return. The nearest commercial sites and conventional accommodation are in Tofino and Ucluelet.

Ucluelet

UCLUELET (pop. 1747), 8km south of the main Hwy 4 Port Alberni junction, means "People of the Sheltered Bay", from the native word *ucluth* – "wind blowing in from the bay". It was named by the Nuu-chah-nulth, who lived here for centuries before the arrival of whites who came to exploit some of the world's richest fishing grounds immediately offshore. Today the port is still the third largest in BC by volume of fish landed, a trade that gives the town a slightly dispersed appearance and an industrial fringe – mainly lumber and canning concerns – and makes it a less appealing, if nonetheless popular base for anglers, whale-watchers, watersports enthusiasts and tourists headed for Long Beach to the north. If you want a breath of air in town, the nearest trails are at **Terrace Beach**, just east of the town off Peninsula Road before the lighthouse.

Buses and **boats** call here from Port Alberni and Tofino – a Laidlaw bus makes the road trip twice a day en route to and from Tofino and Port Alberni, with one connection daily from Port Alberni to Nanaimo and Victoria. Boats from Port Alberni usually dock here three days a week (see p.716). There's plenty of accommodation (though less than Tofino), much of it spread on or just off Peninsula Road, the main approach to and through town from Hwy 4 (see below). A car or bike is useful here, as there's relatively little in the small central area, though location isn't vital unless you want to be near the sea. For full details visit the **infocentre**, off Peninsula Road at the centre of town at 227 Main St (July–Sept daily 9am–6pm; Oct–June Tues–Sat 9am–5pm; ☎726-4641 or 726-7289).

Practicalities

The most unusual **hotel** is the *Canadian Princess Resort* (☎726-7771 or 1-800-663-7090; ②–⑥) on Peninsula Road just west of the centre, a hotel with on-shore rooms or one- to six-berth cabins in a 1932 west coast steamer moored in the harbour. You can also book upmarket whale-watching and fishing trips here in big, comfortable cabin cruisers and it has a restaurant open to non-residents. The two key central choices are the *Pacific Rim Motel*, 1755 Peninsula Rd (☎726-7728; ③–④), a place between the harbour and small centre near the corner of Bay Street, and the *Peninsula Motor Inn*, a short way east across the road at 1648 Peninsula Rd (☎726-7751; ③). Also convenient is the *Island West Fishing Resort* overlooking the boat basin and marina at 160 Hemlock St

(☎726-4624; ③–④): it has a pub on site for drinks and food and also organizes fishing charters and tours. Moving east away from the centre to prettier outskirts try *Four Cedar Cottages* (☎726-4284; ④–⑤), 1183 Eber Rd (take Alder St, off Peninsula Road), which is very close to seafront piers and the *Little Beach Resort*, 1187 Peninsula Rd (☎726-4202; ③), with quiet self-contained one- and two-bedroom suites with kitchenettes and just a few steps from Little Beach with great views to the south. Right at the end of Peninsula Road up by the lighthouse are two good **B&B** options: *Spring Cove B&B*, 963 Peninsula Rd (☎726-2955; ③), a quiet oceanfront place with two rooms (shared bathroom), and *Ocean's Edge B&B*, 855 Barkley Crescent (☎726-7099; ③), a new building in old growth forest with views and private entrance and bathroom.

The **public campground** (☎726-4355; $12–20; March–Oct) overlooks the harbour at 260 Seaplane Base Rd (first right off Peninsula Road after the *Canadian Princess*) to the west of the centre and has washroom and shower facilities. The central *Island West Resort* (see above) also has a campground.

Seafood here is as fresh as it comes, and is best sampled at *Smiley's* just a little west from the *Canadian Princess* at 1992 Peninsula Rd (☎726-4213): a no-frills, no-decor diner popular with locals (eat in or take out), and to work off the waffles there's five-pin bowling and billiards here as well. For coffee and snacks head for *Blueberries Café* (☎726-7707) on the strip in town at 1627 Peninsula Road. It also serves breakfast, lunch and dinner, is licensed, and has an outdoor patio with sea views.

Many companies are on hand to offer whale-watching, fishing and sightseeing **tours**. The longest-established outfit in the region is here, Subtidal Adventures, 1950 Peninsula Rd at the corner of Norah Road (☎726-7336). They run all the usual boat trips in zodiacs or a ten-metre former coastguard rescue vessel, and do a nature tour to the Broken Group Islands with a beach stop.

The Broken Group Islands

The only way for the ordinary traveller to approach these hundred or so islands, speckled across Barkley Sound between Ucluelet and Bamfield, is by sea plane, chartered boat or boat tours from Port Alberni or Ucluelet (see p.716 & p.726); boats dock at Sechart. Immensely wild and beautiful, the islands have the reputation for tremendous wildlife (seals, sea lions and whales especially), the best **canoeing** in North America, and some of the continent's finest **scuba diving**. You can hire canoes and gear – contact the *Lady Rose* office in Port Alberni or Sea Kayaking at 320 Main St, Tofino; ☎725-

---

NUU-CHAH-NULTH WHALE HUNTS

All the peoples of the Northwest coast are famed for their skilfully constructed canoes, but only the **Nuu-chah-nulth** – whose name translates roughly as "all along the mountains" – used these fragile cedar crafts to pursue whales, an activity that was accompanied by elaborate ritual. Before embarking on a whaling expedition the whalers had not only to be trained in the art of capturing these mighty animals but also had to be purified through a rigorous programme of fasting, sexual abstinence and bathing. Whalers also visited forest shrines made up of a whale image surrounded by human skulls or corpses and carved wooden representations of deceased whalers – the dead were thought to aid the novice in his task and to bring about the beaching of dead whales near the village.

When the whaler was on the chase, his wife would lie motionless in her bed; it was thought that the whale would become equally docile. His crew propelled the canoe in total silence until the moment of the harpooning, whereupon they frantically back-paddled to escape the animal's violent death throes as it attempted to dive, only to be thwarted by a long line of floats made from inflated sea-lion skins. After exhausting itself, the floating whale was finally killed and boated back to the village, where its meat would be eaten and its blubber processed for its highly prized oil.

4222), and then take them on board the *Lady Rose* to be dropped off en route (check current arrangements). You need to know what you're doing, however, as there's plenty of dangerous water and you should pick up the relevant marine chart (*Canadian Hydrographic Service Chart: Broken Group* 3670), available locally. Divers can choose from among fifty shipwrecks claimed by the reefs, rough waters and heavy fogs that beset the aptly named islands.

Recently opened is the *Sechart Whaling Station Lodge* (☎723-8313 or 1-800-663-7192; ③), a potentially magical base for exploring and the only place to **stay** if you're not wilderness camping on the archipelago. Access is via the MV *Lady Rose*, which docks nearby (see p.718 for detailed schedule to the islands). Eight rough **campgrounds** also serve the group, but water is hard to come by; pick up the park leaflet on camping and freshwater locations. A park warden patrols the region from Nettle Island; otherwise the islands are as pristine as the day they rose from the sea.

Bamfield

BAMFIELD (pop. 256) is a quaint spot, half-raised above the ocean on a wooden boardwalk, accessible by unpaved road from Port Alberni 102km to the north, by boat – the MV *Lady Rose* – or gravel road from Lake Cowichan 113km to the east. Shuttle **buses** run along the Port Alberni road route if you're without transport and don't want to take the boat: for details, see the "West Coast Trail" opposite. If you can't get aboard the MV *Lady Rose*, or miss it, you can take the far speedier but more expensive Bamfield Express Water Taxi (☎728-3001), from Port Alberni. The village is best known as the northern starting point of this trail, but its population jumps to well over 2000 in the summer with the arrival of divers, canoeists, kayakers and fishermen, the last attracted by its suitability as a base for salmon fishing in the waters of Alberni Inlet and Barkley Sound. Plenty of services have sprung up to meet visitors' demands, with lots of tours, fishing charters, stores and galleries, but only relatively limited accommodation (see below).

Despite the influx the village retains its charm, with the boardwalk accessing one side of Bamfield Inlet (the open sea, the other), so that the bay below the boardwalk is a constant hum of activity as boats ply across the water. Trails lead down from the boardwalk to a series of nice small beaches. The village is a good place to join in the activities, bird-watch, walk, beachcomb, sit in cafés or simply relax in a quiet corner with a book. For a short stroll, wander to **Brady's Beach** or the Cape Beale Lighthouse some way beyond. And if you just want to tackle the stage to the trailhead of the West Coast Trail and return to Bamfield in a day, you can walk the 11km (round trip) to the **Pachena Lighthouse**, starting from the Ross Bible Camp on the Ohiaht First Nation campground at Pachena Beach. After that, the route becomes the real thing.

Accommodation

Bamfield has only limited and mainly expensive **accommodation**. If you think you'll need a bed, definitely make reservations, especially at the small *Seabeam Fishing Resort and Campground* overlooking Grappler Inlet, which runs as a campground and a small hostel-like hotel – bring bedding (☎728-3286; ①, tent and RV sites $15–20; May–Oct) and phone for directions or for a taxi pick-up. The setting is tranquil, and the resort has a small kitchen, common room with open fire and sixteen beds arranged as one-, two- or three-bed dorms. Otherwise try the *Bamfield Inn*, Customs House Lane, a **lodge** built in 1923 overlooking Bamfield Harbour, Barkley Sound and the islands (☎728-3354; ④–⑤; Feb–Oct). The modest *McKay Bay Lodge* (☎728-3323; ④; May–Oct) also overlooks the harbour and is good for families and fishing enthusiasts. The biggest place locally is the new *Bamfield Trails Motel* overlooking Bamfield Inlet at Frigate

Road (☎728-3231 or 728-3215; ③–④). Final choice, unless you plump for one of a trio of more remote lodges, is the excellent *Woods End Landing Cottages*, 168 Wild Duck Rd, which has six secluded and high-quality self-contained log cottages on a two-acre water-front site with great opportunities for outdoor activities, bird-watching, scuba diving and kayaking (☎728-3383; ④–⑦). More **B&B** options are opening each year but try the two-room *Sherry's*, Regent Street (☎728-2323; ③), overlooking Bamfield Harbour, which offers a free pick-up by boat from the dock: showers are shared, but an outoor hot tub and free canoe use are available to residents. If you're **camping**, try the Ohiaht First Nation campground at Pachena Beach.

The West Coast Trail

One of North America's classic walks, the **West Coast Trail** starts 5km south of Bam-field (see opposite) and traverses exceptional coastal scenery for 77km to Port Ren-frew. It's no stroll, and though becoming very popular – quotas operate to restrict num-bers – it still requires experience of longer walks, proper equipment and a fair degree of fitness. Many people, however, do the first easy stage as a day-trip from Bamfield. Reckon on five to eight days for the full trip; carry all your own food, camp where you can, and be prepared for rain, landslips, treacherous stretches, thick soaking forest, and almost utter isolation.

As originally conceived, the trail had nothing to do with promoting the great out-doors. Mariners long ago dubbed this area of coastline the "graveyard of the Pacific", and when the SS *Valencia* went down with all hands here in 1906 the government was persuaded that constructing a trail would at least give stranded sailors a chance to walk to safety along the coast (trying to penetrate the interior's rainforest was out of the question). The path followed a basic telegraph route that linked Victoria with outlying towns and lighthouses, and was kept open by linesmen and lighthouse keepers until the 1960s, when it fell into disrepair. Early backpackers re-blazed the old trail; many thousands now make the trip annually, and the numbers, so far as quotas allow, are ris-ing (see below). The trail passes through the land of the Pacheenaht First Nation near Port Renfrew, passing through Ditidaht First Nation country before ending at Bamfield in the traditional territory of the Ohiaht First Nation. Wardens from each of these tribes works in association with Parks Canada to oversee the trail's management and the care of traditional native villages and fishing areas.

Weather is a key factor in planning any trip; the trail is really only passable between June and September (July is the driest month), which is also the only period when it's patrolled by wardens and the only time locals are on hand to ferry you (for a fee) across some of the wider rivers en route. However, you should be prepared for dreadful weath-er and poor trail conditions at all times. Take cash with you to pay for ferries and nom-inal fees for camping on native land.

Practicalities

Pre-planning is essential if you wish to walk the trail, as Parks Canada have introduced a **quota system** and reservation-registration procedure to protect the environment. Numbers are limited to around 8000 a year while the path is open (mid-April to end Sept). A total of 52 people are allowed onto the trail each day: 26 starting at Port Ren-frew, 26 at Bamfield. **Reservations** can made from March of the year you wish to walk, and the phones start ringing on the first of the month, so move fast. To make bookings, call ☎1-800-663-6000 (Mon & Tues 7am–6pm, Wed–Fri 7am–9pm, Sat & Sun 8am–6pm). Be ready to nominate the location from which you wish to start, the date of departure and the number in your party. July and August are clearly the most popular months. It currently **costs** $25 to make a reservation (payment by Visa or Master-

Card). This is non-refundable, though you may change your date of departure if spaces are available on another day. Another $70 per person is payable as a user fee, paid in person at the beginning of the trail. Allow about another $25 to pay for ferry crossings along the route. You must then register in person at the park centre at Bamfield or Port Renfrew between 9am and 12.30pm on the day you have booked to start your walk. (You may want to arrive the night before – if so, be sure to book accommodation in Bamfield if you're starting there: see below.) If you miss this deadline your place is forfeited and will be given to someone on the **waiting list**.

Of the 52 places available each day, twelve (six at each departure point) are available on a first-come, first-served basis. Unless you're very lucky this still doesn't mean you can just turn up and expect to start walking. You must first register in person at either the Port Renfrew or Bamfield centre. Here you'll be given a waiting-list number and told when to come back, which could be anything between two and ten days.

Further **information** regarding the trail, path conditions and pre-planning can be obtained from the Parks Canada offices in Port Renfrew (☎647-5434) and Ucluelet (☎726-7211), or from the infocentres in Tofino, Ucluelet, Long Beach or Port Alberni. An increasing amount of literature and **route guides** are appearing on the trail every year, available directly or by mail order from most BC bookshops (see "Listings" for Vancouver and Victoria). Two of the best are *The West Coast Trail* by Tim Leaden (Douglas and McIntyre, seventh edition; $12.95) and the more irreverent *Blisters and Bliss: A Trekker's Guide to the West Coast Trail* by Foster, Aiteken and Dewey (B&B Publishing Victoria; $10.95). The recommended **trail map** is the 1:50,000 *West Coast Trail, Port Renfrew–Bamfield*, complete with useful hints for walking the trail, available locally or direct from the Ministry of the Environment, 553 Superior St, Victoria (☎387-1441).

Access to and from the trailheads is also an important consideration. Several small shuttle-bus companies have sprung up to run people to the trailheads, mostly from Victoria to Bamfield via Nanaimo, not all of which are likely to survive (consult the Victoria infocentre for latest updates). For the northern trailhead at Bamfield, the most exhilarating and reliable access is via the MV *Lady Rose* or other boats from Port Alberni (see p.718 for full details). Otherwise the West Coast Trail Express, 3954 Bow Rd, Victoria (May to early Oct; ☎477-8700) runs a single daily shuttle bus in each direction between Victoria (currently from outside the Royal BC Museum at 7am) and Pachena Bay/Bamfield ($50) via Duncan, Nanaimo ($35) and Nitinat ($25). Pick-ups are possible from these points, but reservations are essential to secure a seat from any departure point. They also have a daily service to Port Renfrew ($50). Other operators worth contacting include: the long-established West Coast Trail Connector, which runs two daily services in each direction between Victoria and Port Renfrew for access to the southern trailhead (2hr 30min; ☎475-2010); Western Bus Lines, 4521 10th Ave, Port Alberni (☎723-3341), also run a service on Monday and Friday along the 100-kilometre gravel road from Port Alberni to the *Tides and Trails Café* in Bamfield; and the Pacheenaht First Nation Service, 4521 10th Ave, Port Alberni (around $35: ☎647-5521), which operates a summer-only bus service along the same route.

North Vancouver Island

It's a moot point where the **north of Vancouver Island** starts, but if you're travelling on Hwy 19 the landscape's sudden lurch into more unspoilt wilderness after Qualicum Beach makes as good a watershed as any. The scenery north of Qualicum Beach is uneventful but restful on the eye, and graced with ever-improving views of the mainland. Along Hwy 19 is the hamlet Buckley Bay, which consists of a single B&B and the ferry terminal to **Denman** and **Hornby islands** (16 sailings daily; 10min).

Few of the towns along Hwy 19 amount to much, and you could bus, drive or hitch the length of the Vancouver Island to Port Hardy and take the **Inside Passage** ferry up to Prince Rupert – the obvious and most tantalizing itinerary – without missing a lot. Alternatively, you could follow the main highway only as far as **Courtenay**, and from there catch a ferry across to the mainland. If you have the means, however, try to get into the wild, central interior, much of it contained within **Strathcona Provincial Park**.

Denman and Hornby islands

Denman and **Hornby Islands** are two outposts that have been described, with some justification, as the "undiscovered Gulf Islands". Big-name celebrities have recently bought property here, complementing a population made up of artists, craftspeople and a laid-back (if wary) mishmash of alternative types. Ferries drop you on Denman, with an **infocentre** clearly marked on the road from the terminal (☎335-2293). To get to Hornby you need to head 11km across Denman to another terminal, where a fifteen-minute crossing drops you at Hornby's Shingle Spit dock. Most of what happens on Hornby, however, happens at **Tribune Bay** on the far side of the island, 10km away – try hitching a lift from a car coming off the ferry if you're without transport. There's no public transport on either island, so you'll need a car or bike to explore: **bikes** can be rented from the Bike Shoppe on Denman, 4696 Lacon Rd (☎335-0638).

Highlights on Denman, the less retrogressive of the islands, are the beaches of the Sandy Island Marine Park and the trails of Boyle Point Park to the Chrome Island Lighthouse. On Hornby you want to be looking at the **Hellivel Provincial Park** and its trails, the best a six-kilometre (1hr–1hr 30min) loop to Hellivel Bluffs, offering plenty of opportunities to see eagles, herons, spring wildflowers and lots of aquatic wildlife. Whaling Station Bay and Tribune Bay Provincial Park have good beaches (and there's a nudist beach at Little Tribune Bay).

Accommodation and food

Accommodation is in short supply on both islands, and it's virtually essential in summer to have prebooked rooms. On Denman the main options are the *Sea Canary Bed & Breakfast*, 3375 Kirk Rd (☎335-0905; ③), a restored 1904 heritage building close to the ferry terminal with three guest **rooms**, and the *Hawthorn House Bed and Breakfast*, 3305 Kirk Rd (☎335-2949; ③), also with three rooms. There's a small, rural provincial park **campground** at Fillongley Provincial Park, close to old-growth forest and pebbly beach 4km across the island from the ferry on the east shore facing the Lambert Channel (information ☎954-4600; $9.50). Hornby has many more **rooms** and **campgrounds**: *Sea Breeze Lodge*, Fowler Road (☎335-2321; ⑤, weekly $635–700), with twelve waterfront cottages with sea views; *Hornby Island Resort*, Shingle Spit Road (☎335-0136; ③, tents $12–18), with waterfront cabins and camp sites, tennis court, boat rental, pub, waterfront restaurant and sandy beach; *Bradsdadsland Country Camp Resort*, 1980 Shingle Spit Rd (☎335-0757; tents $16–19; May–Oct); *Ford's Cove Marina* at Ford's Cove, 12km from the ferry at Government Wharf (☎335-2169; ③, weekly rates only $440–465, tents $14–20), with six fully equipped cottages, grocery store and camp and RV sites; and the big *Tribune Bay Campsite*, Shields Road (☎335-2359; $16–23; April-Oct), a treed site close to a sandy beach and with hot showers, restaurant and bike rental.

Eating places on Denman are concentrated near the ferry, the most notable being the *Denman Island Store and Café*. At the ferry dock on Hornby is *The Thatch*, a tourist-oriented restaurant and deli with great views. Across at Tribune Bay the *Co-op* is the hub of island life, with virtually everything you'll need in the way of food and supplies (☎335-1121).

Courtenay

Back along Hwy 19 beyond Buckley Bay is a short stretch of wild, pebbly beach, and then the Comox Valley, open rural country that's not as captivating as the brochures might lead you to expect. Of three settlements here – Comox, Cumberland and **COURTENAY** – only the last is of real interest for all but the most committed Vancouver Island devotee, and only then as a ferry link to Powell River on the mainland. The terminal is a good twenty minutes' drive from the town down back roads – hitching is almost impossible, so you have to take a taxi or hold out for the minibus shuttle that leaves the bus depot twice on Tuesday and Friday to connect with sailings. Courtenay is connected to Nanaimo and Victoria by **bus** (4 daily), and is the terminus for **trains** from Victoria (1 daily). If you get stranded in town, there are plenty of **motels** along the strip on the southern approach, close to the black steam engine and **infocentre** at 2040 Cliffe Ave (daily 9am–5pm, longer hours in summer; ☎334-3234). The best **camping** is 20km north of Courtenay at Miracle Beach Provincial Park – a vast, but very popular, tract of sand.

The **Comox Valley** scores higher inland, on the eastern fringes of Strathcona Provincial Park (see p.734) and the new **skiing** areas of Forbidden Plateau and Mount Washington. There's plenty of **hiking** in summer, when the Forbidden Plateau lifts operate at weekends from 11am to 3pm. A great day hike on Mount Washington is the five-hour walk on well-marked trails from the ski area across Paradise Meadows to Moat Lake or Circlet Lake. For details of tougher walks (Battleship Lake, Lady Lake), ask at the infocentre. Access to the trailheads is by minor road from Courtenay.

Campbell River

Of the hundred or so Canadian towns that claim to be "Salmon Capital of the World", **CAMPBELL RIVER**, 46km north of Courtenay, is probably the one that comes closest to justifying the boast. Fish and fishing dominate the place to a ludicrous degree, and you'll soon be heartily sick of pictures of grinning anglers holding impossibly huge chinook salmon. Massive shoals of these monsters are forced into the three-kilometre channel between the town and the mainland, making the job of catching them little more than a formality. The town grew to accommodate fishermen from the outset, centred on a hotel built in 1904 after word spread of the colossal fish that local Cape Mudge natives were able to pluck from the sea. Today about sixty percent of all visitors come to dangle a line in the water. Others come for the scuba diving, while for the casual visitor the place serves as the main road access to the wilds of Strathcona Provincial Park or an overnight stop en route for the morning departures of the MV *Uchuck III* from Gold River (see p.735).

If you want to **fish**, hundreds of shops and guides are on hand to help out and hire equipment. It'll cost about $20 a day for the full kit, and about $60 for a morning's guidance. Huge numbers of people, however, fish from the new 200-metre **Discovery Pier**, Canada's first saltwater fishing pier (small fee). **Diving** rentals come more expensive; try Beaver Aquatics near the Quadra ferry dock in Discovery Bay Marina (☎287-7652). If you merely want to know something about salmon before they end up on a plate, drop in on the **Quinsam Salmon Hatchery**, 5km west of town on the road to Gold River (daily 8am–4pm).

Campbell River's well-stocked **infocentre** is at 1235 Shoppers' Row (daily 9am–6pm; ☎287-4636). Four Laidlaw **buses** run daily to Victoria, but there's only one, occasionally two, a day north to Port Hardy and towns en route. Airlines big and small also **fly** here, including Air BC, Canadian Regional, Central Mountain Air and North Vancouver Air (see Vancouver "Listings" on p.680 for details). The **bus terminal** is on the corner of Cedar and 13th near the Royal Bank (☎287-7151). **Accommodation** is no problem, with numerous motels, Campbell River being a resort first and foremost: try the *Super 8 Motel*,

340 South Island Hwy, on the main road south of town (☎286-6622 or 1-800-800-8000; ③), or the carving-stuffed *Campbell River Lodge and Fishing Resort*, a kilometre north of the town centre at 1760 North Island Hwy (☎287-7446 or 1-800-663-7212; ②–④). You won't be able to escape the fishing clutter common to all hotels unless you head for a **B&B**. Contact the infocentre for listings, or try *Pier House B&B*, 670 Island Hwy (☎287-2943; ③), a five-room 1920s antique-filled heritage home in downtown right by the fishing pier.

Cheap **places to eat** abound, mainly of the fast-food variety, and in the pricier restaurants there's no prize for spotting the main culinary emphasis. The best burger joint is *Del's Drive-In & Diner*, 1423 Island Hwy, a place with plenty of local colour. For beer and snacks, try the *Royal Coachman*, 84 Dogwood St, popular with tourists and locals alike. For a **seafood** treat, head for the *Anchor Inn*, 261 Island Hwy (good views), or the *Gourmet by the Sea* on the main road about 15km south of town at Bennett's Point.

Quadra Island

Quadra Island and its fine beaches and museum are fifteen minutes away from Campbell River and makes nice respite from the fish, though the famous fishing lodge here has been host to such big-name fisherfolk over the years as John Wayne, Kevin Costner and Julie Andrews. Ferries run roughly hourly from the well-signed terminal out of town (foot passenger $3.50 return, car $9.50). The main excuse for the crossing is the **Kwagiulth Museum and Cultural Centre**, home to one of the country's most noted collections of Native Canadian regalia (July to early Sept daily 10am–4.30pm; closed Sun & Mon off season; $2; ☎285-3733). As elsewhere in Canada, the masks, costumes and ritual objects were confiscated by the government in 1922 in an attempt to stamp out one of the natives' most potent ceremonies, and only came back in the 1980s on condition they would be locked up in a museum. The museum has around three hundred articles, and you should also ask directions to the petroglyphs (rock drawings) in the small park across the road.

While on the island you could also laze on its beaches, walk its coastal **trails**, or climb Chinese Mountain for some cracking views. There's swimming in a warm, sheltered bay off a rocky beach at **Rebecca Spit Provincial Park**, a 1.5-kilometre spit near Drew Harbour 8km east of the ferry terminal, but the water's warmer still and a trifle sandier at the more distant **Village Bay Park**. Around ten places offer **accommodation**, including the *Heriot Bay Inn* on Heriot Bay Road (☎285-3322; ③, camping from $10–16.75), which has cottages, camping and RV sites, and the *Whiskey Point Resort Motel*, by the ferry dock at 725 Quathioski Cove Rd (☎285-2201 or 1-800-622-5311; ③). The main **campground** is the *We Wai Kai Campsite*, Rebecca Spit Road (☎285-3111; $15–16; mid-May to mid-Sept), 16km northeast of the ferry terminal.

Cortes Island

If you've taken the trouble to see Quadra Island, then you should push on to the still quieter **Cortes Island**, 45 minutes from Quadra on a second ferry (5 daily; foot passenger $4.50 return, car $11.75 single), an island with a deeply indented coastline at the neck of Desolation Sound, among North America's finest sailing and kayaking areas. Boating aside, it's known for its superlative clams and oysters, exported worldwide, and for one of Canada's leading holistic centres, the Hollyhock Seminar Centre on Highland Road (☎1-800-933-6639), where you can sign up for all manner of body- and soul-refreshing courses and stay in anything from a tent, dorm or private cottage. Other **accommodation** includes *The Blue Heron B&B* (☎935-6584), while you should aim to eat at the *Old Floathouse* (☎935-6631) at the Gorge Marina Resort on Hunt Road, where you can also rent boats and scooters. Places to make for around the island include the small **Smelt Bay Provincial Park**, which has a campground and opportunities to swim, fish, canoe and walk, and the **Hague Lake Provincial Park**, signed from Mansons Landing, with

---

HIKING IN STRATHCONA

Hiking, it hardly needs saying, is superb in Strathcona, with a jaw-dropping scenic combination of jagged mountains – including Golden Hinde (2220m), the island's highest point – lakes, rivers, waterfalls and all the trees you could possibly want. Seven marked **trails** fan out from the Buttle Lake area, together with six shorter nature walks, most less than 2km long, amongst which the Lady Falls and Lupin Falls trails stand out for their waterfall and forest views. All the longer trails can be tramped in a day, though the most popular, the **Elk River Trail** (10km), which starts from Drum Lake on Hwy 28, lends itself to an overnight stop. Popular with backpackers because of its gentle grade, the path ends up at Landslide Lake, an idyllic camping spot. The other highly regarded trail is the **Flower Ridge** walk, which starts at the southern end of Buttle Lake. In the Forbidden Plateau area, named after a native legend that claimed evil spirits lay in wait to devour women and children who entered its precincts, the most popular trip is the **Forbidden Plateau Skyride** to the summit of Wood Mountain where there's a two-kilometre trail to a viewpoint over Boston Canyon. Backcountry camping is allowed throughout the park, and the backpacking is great once you've hauled up onto the summit ridges above the tree line. For serious exploration, buy the relevant topographic maps at MAPS BC, Ministry of Environment and Parks, Parliament Buildings, Victoria.

several looped trails accessible from different points on the road. If you're in a canoe or boat then you can also make for a couple of marine parks (Von Donop and Mansons Landing) and any number of delightful small bays, lagoons and beaches.

Strathcona Provincial Park

Vancouver Island's largest protected area, and the oldest park in British Columbia, **Strathcona Provincial Park** (established in 1911) is one of the few places on the island where the scenery approaches the grandeur of the mainland mountains. The island's highest point, Golden Hinde (2220m) is here, and it's also a place where there's a good chance of seeing rare indigenous wildlife (the Roosevelt elk, marmot and black-tailed deer are the most notable examples). Only two areas have any sort of facilities for the visitor – **Forbidden Plateau**, approached from Courtenay, and the more popular **Buttle Lake** region, accessible from Campbell River via Hwy 28. The Gold River Minibus will drop you at the head of Buttle Lake, about 40km west of Campbell River (Tues, Thurs & Sun). The rest of the park is unsullied wilderness, but fully open to backpackers and hardier walkers. Be sure to pick up the blue *BC Parks* pamphlet (available from the info-centre at Campbell River and elsewhere): it has a good general map and gives lots of information, such as the comforting fact that there are no grizzly bears in the park.

You'll see numerous pictures of **Della Falls**, around Campbell River, which (at 440m) are Canada's highest (and amongst the world's highest), though unfortunately it'll take a two-day trek and a canoe passage if you're going to see them.

The approach to the park along Hwy 28 is worth taking for the scenery alone; numerous short trails and nature walks are signposted from rest stops, most no more than twenty minutes' stroll from the car. **Elk Falls Provincial Park**, noted for its gorge and waterfall, is the first stop, ten minutes out of Campbell River. It also has large provincial park **campground**.

Park practicalities
The **Park Visitor Centre** is located at the junction of Hwy 28 and the Buttle Lake road (May–Sept only); fifteen information shelters around the lake also provide some trail and wildlife information. Buttle Lake has two provincial **campgrounds** (both $9.50–12) with basic facilities – one alongside the park centre, the other at Ralph River on the

extreme southern end of Buttle Lake, accessed by the road along the lake's eastern shore. Both have good **swimming** areas nearby.

The park's only commercial **accommodation** is provided by the *Strathcona Park Lodge* (☎286-8206 or 286-3122; ③–⑤), just outside the Buttle Lake entrance, a mixture of hotel and outdoor pursuits centre. You can **rent canoes**, **bikes** and other outdoor equipment, and sign up for any number of organized tours and activities.

Gold River and Tahsis

There's not a lot happening at **GOLD RIVER,** a tiny logging community 89km west of Campbell River – founded in 1965 in the middle of nowhere to service a big pulp mill 12km away at Muchalat Inlet. The place only has a handful of hotels and a couple of shops – but the ride over on Hwy 28 is superb, and there's the chance to explore the sublime coastline by boat, the main reason for the settlement's increasing number of visitors. Year-round, the **MV Uchuck III**, a converted World War II US minesweeper, takes mail, cargo and passengers to logging camps and settlements up and down the surrounding coast on a variety of routes. Like the MV *Lady Rose* out of Port Alberni, what started as a sideline has recently become far more of a commercial enterprise, with glossy pamphlets and extra summer sailings, though it's none the worse for that – you just have to book to make sure of a place. For information and **reservations**, contact Nootka Sound Service Ltd (☎283-2325 or 283-2515).

There are **three basic routes**, all of them offering wonderful windows onto the wilderness and wildlife (whales, bears, bald eagles and more) of the region's inlets, islands and forested mountains. The dock is at the end of Hwy 28, about 15km southwest of Gold River. The **Tahsis Day Trip** ($45) departs at 9am every Tuesday year-round for Tahsis (see p.736) (arriving at 1pm), returning after a one-hour stopover to Gold River at 6pm. The shorter **Nootka Sound Day Trip** ($38) leaves Gold River every Wednesday at 10am July to mid-September only (returning at 4.30pm), with longer stops at Resolution Sound and Kyuquot (the native word for "Friendly Cove"), the latter involving a $7 landing fee, proceeds from which go to the Mowachaht Band for the redevelopment of the Native Canadian site. During the ninety-minute halt you are offered a guided tour by Native Canadian guides around their ancestral home. The previous stop, at Friendly Cove, is equally historic, for it was here that Captain Cook made his first-known landing on the west coast in 1778, from which, among other things, was to spring the important sea-otter fur trade. Whites named the area and people here "Nootka", though locals today say *nootka* was merely a word of warning to Cook and his crew, meaning "circle around" to avoid hitting offshore rocks. If you're equipped with provisions and wish to stay over, there are **cabins** and a **campground** here, but call first to confirm arrangements (☎283-2054). The third trip, the **Kyuquot Adventure** ($165), is a two-day overnight cruise, departing every Thursday year-round (April–Oct 7am, Nov–March 6am). It takes you much further north up the coast, returning to Gold River at 5pm on Friday afternoon: accommodation is included, as is breakfast – though you make it yourself from food supplied – and you can buy Thursday's evening meal on board or onshore at Kyuquot. A 25 percent deposit is required for these trips, refundable in full up until two weeks before departure. People on all trips should bring warm and waterproof clothing. There's a coffee shop on board for drinks and hot snacks. **Kayakers** should note that they can be deposited by lift into the sea at most points en route by prior arrangement.

Boat aside, one of the area's two minor attractions is **Quatsino Cave**, the deepest vertical cave in North America, parts of which are open to the public – for details ask at the infocentre; the other is the **Big Drop**, a stretch of Gold River white water known to kayakers worldwide. The local **infocentre** is at Hwy 28 and Muchalat Drive (mid-May to mid-Sept; ☎283-2418). **Accommodation** is in short supply: the only large place is the *Ridgeview Motel,* located in a panoramic spot above the village at 395 Donner

Court (☎283-2277 or 1-800-989-3393; ③) – but the *Peppercorn Trail Motel and Camp-ground* on Mill Road (☎283-2443; ②) also has rooms to as well as a **campground** ($18). Otherwise there's currently just one listed **B&B** – the *Valley View*, 408 Donner Rd (☎283-7532; ②) – and a basic campground run by the local Lions Club.

Note that there are also two beautiful roads north from Gold River, both rough, but worth the jolts for the scenery. One provides an alternative approach to **TAHSIS**, anoth-er logging community 70km northwest of Gold River, which has two **motels**, both with restaurants if you need to break your journey: advance summer reservations are need-ed at both the *Tahsis Motel*, Head Bay Road (☎934-6318; ③), and the larger *Maquinna Resort*, 1400 South Maquinna Rd (☎934-6367; ⑤). For more background on a lovely part of the coast, with plenty of fishing, boating and hiking opportunities, contact the **info-centre** on Rugged Mountain Road (late June to early Sept Mon–Sat 10am–4.30pm; ☎934-6667) or the Village Office (Mon–Fri 9am–noon & 1–5pm; ☎934-6622).

North to Port McNeill, Telegraph Cove and Alert Bay

The main highway north of Campbell River cuts inland and climbs through increasingly rugged and deserted country, particularly after Sayward, the one main community en route. Near Sayward is the marvellously oddball **Valley of a Thousand Faces**: 1400 famous faces painted onto cedar logs, the work of a Dutch artist, and more interesting than it sounds (May–Aug daily 10am–4pm; donation). Almost alongside, west of Hwy 19 at Sayward Junc-tion, is a RV and tent **campground**, the *White River Court* (☎282-3265; sites $8). With a car, you could strike off south from here to **Schoen Lake Provincial Park**, located 12km off Hwy 19 on a rough road south of Woss village and featuring a couple of forest trails and a well-kept campground (free). **PORT McNEILL**, 180km north of Campbell River and the first real town along Hwy 19, is little more than a motel and logging centre and not some-where to spend longer than necessary. If you get stuck here, the infocentre's on Broughton Boulevard in the new museum building dedicated to pioneering days (☎956-3131).

Telegraph Cove

By contrast, tiny **TELEGRAPH COVE**, 8km south of Port McNeill and reached by a rough sideroad, is an immensely likeable place and the best of BC's so-called "board-walk villages": the whole community is raised on wooden stilts over the water, a sight that's becoming ever more popular with tourists. It was built as the terminus of a tree-strung telegraph line from Victoria, and it comes as a surprise to discover that its char-acter is threatened by plans for a massive waterfront development of houses, lodge and restaurant. As an added bonus, the village has become one of the island's premier **whale-watching** spots, the main attraction here being the pods of orcas (killer whales) that calve locally. Some nineteen of these families live or visit Robson Bight, 20km down the Johnstone Strait, which was established as an ecological reserve in 1982 (the whales like the gravel beaches, where they come to rub). This is the world's most accessible and predictable spot to see the creatures – around a ninety percent chance. The best outfit for a trip to see them is Stubbs Island Charters at the dock at the end of the boardwalk through the old village (☎928-3185, 928-3117 or 1-800-665-3066). The first whale-watching company in BC, they run up to five three- or five-hour trips daily (June–Oct), but they're very popular, so call well in advance to be sure of a place.

In summer you can buy food at a small café, but otherwise the only provision for vis-itors is an incongruous new building with shop, ice-cream counter and coffee bar. The only **accommodation** is the large wooded *Telegraph Cove Resort Campground* (☎928-3131 or 1-800-200-4665; $17.25–21.25; May–Sept), a short walk from the village and one of the best-located sites on Vancouver Island, a reputation that makes reservations essential in summer. It has showers, laundry, restaurant, boat rentals and access to

Vancouver skyline, British Columbia

The mountains over Vermillion Lakes, Alberta

B&C ALEXANDER

Brown bear with sushi

CHRIS COE, AXIOM

Okanagan Valley, British Columbia

Cowichan Bay, British Columbia

Totem pole

The Bank at Dawson City, The Yukon

Inuit seal hunters, Baffin Island

...and don't forget the milk

The Dempster Highway

guides, charters and whale-watching tours. The *Hidden Cove Lodge* (☎956-3916; ⑤; May–Nov) at Lewis Point, a secluded cove on Johnstone Strait 7km from Telegraph Cove, has superb lodge units, but they go very quickly. The big *Alder Bay Campsite* 6km off Hwy 19 en route for Telegraph Cove from Port McNeill provides grassy tent sites with ocean views (☎956-4117; reservations recommended; $12; May–Sept).

Alert Bay

The breezy fishing village of **ALERT BAY**, on Cormorant Island, is reached by numerous daily ferries from Port McNeill just 8km away (foot passenger $4.50 return, car $11.75). The fifty-minute crossing in the migrating season provides a good chance of seeing whales en route. Despite the predominance of the non-native industries (mainly fish processing), half the population of the island are native 'Namgis, and a visit here offers the opportunity to get to grips with something of their history and to meet those who are keeping something of the old traditions alive. Be sure to have pre-booked accommodation (see below) before heading out here in high season. The **infocentre** (June–Sept daily; Oct–May Mon–Fri; ☎974-5213) is at 116 Fir St to your right as you come off the ferry. Also off to the right from the terminal are the totems of a 'Namgis Burial Ground: you're asked to view from a respectful distance.

Bear left from the terminal out of the main part of the village to reach the excellent **U'Mista Cultural Centre** on Front Street (mid-May to early Sept daily 9am–5pm; Oct–mid-May Mon–Fri 9am–5pm; $5; ☎974-5403), a modern building based on old models, which houses a collection of potlatch items and artefacts confiscated in 1921 and returned by the government in 1979. It also shows a couple of award-winning films, and you might also come across local kids being taught native languages, songs and dances. More local artefacts are on show in the library and small museum, open most summer afternoons, at 199 Fir St. For years the village also claimed the world's tallest fully carved **totem pole** (other contenders, say knowing villagers, are all pole and no carving), though much to local chagrin Victoria raised a pole in 1994 that the *The Guinness Book of Records* has recognized as 2.1m taller. Also worth a look is the wildlife and weird swamp habitat at **Gator Gardens** behind the bay, accessible via several trails and boardwalks.

Most people come over for the day, but **accommodation** options include: the six-room *Orca Inn*, 291 Fir St, ten minutes' walk from the ferry terminal (☎974-5322 or 1-800-672-2466; ②), with steak and seafood restaurant and café overlooking Broughton Strait and the sea; the *Ocean View Cabins*, 390 Poplar St, 1km from the ferry terminal overlooking Mitchell Bay (☎974-5457; ③); the *Bayside Inn Hotel*, overlooking the harbour, at 81 First St (☎974-5857; ②); and the *Oceanview Camping and Trailer Park* on Alder Road (☎974-5213; $10–15).

Sointula

SOINTULA village is a wonderful aberration. It's located on Malcolm Island, accessible by ferry en route from Port McNeill to Alert Bay (25min; foot passenger $4.50 return car $11.75) and directly from Alert Bay (35min; foot passenger $2.50 one way, car $4.50). The fishing village would be a good place to wander at any time, thanks to its briney maritime appeal, but what gives added lustre is the fact that it contains a tiny fossil Finnish settlement. An early cult community, it was founded with Finnish pioneers as a model cooperative settlement in 1901 by Matti Kurrika, a curious mixture of guru, dramatist and philosopher. In 1905 the experiment collapsed, but 100 Finns from the original settlement stayed on. Their descendants survive to this day, and you'll still hear Finnish being spoken on the streets. You can wander local beaches, explore the island interior by logging road, or spend a few minutes in the **Sointula Finnish Museum**, which is located on 1st Street just to the left after disembarking the ferry: you'll probably need to call someone (☎973-6353 or 973-6764) to come and open up and show you around.

THE INSIDE PASSAGE

One of Canada's great trips, the **Inside Passage** aboard BC Ferries' *Queen of the North*, between Port Hardy and Prince Rupert on the British Columbia mainland, is a cheap way of getting what people on the big cruise ships are getting: 274 nautical miles of mountains, islands, waterfalls, glaciers, sea lions, whales, eagles and some of the grandest coastal scenery on the continent. By linking up with the Greyhound bus network or the VIA Rail terminal at Prince Rupert, it also makes a good leg in any number of convenient itineraries around British Columbia. Some travellers will have come from Washington State, others will want to press on from Prince Rupert to Skagway by boat and then head north into Alaska and the Yukon (see p.800 for details on the Alaska Marine ferries). A lot of people simply treat it as a cruise, and sail north one day and return south to Port Hardy the next. If nothing else, the trip's a good way of meeting fellow travellers and taking a break from the interminable trees of the BC interior.

The boat carries 750 passengers and 160 cars and runs every two days, departing at 7.30am on **even-numbered days** in August, **odd-numbered days** in June, July, September and the first half of October. The journey takes around fifteen hours, arriving in Prince Rupert about 10.30pm, sometimes with a stop at Bella Bella. Be aware that from about October 15 to May 25 the sailings in both directions are predominantly at night (they leave Port Hardy in the late afternoon), which rather defeats the sightseeing object of the trip. On board there are cafeterias, restaurants and a shop (among other services): at the last, pick up the cheap and interesting *BC Ferries Guide to the Inside Passage* for more on the trip.

The cost from June to September is $102 single for a foot passenger (May & Oct $75, Nov–April $55), $210 for a car (May & Oct $154, Nov–April $114); reservations are **essential** throughout the summer season if you're taking a car or want a cabin. Bookings can be made by phone (☎1-888-223-3779 anywhere in BC, ☎250/386-3431 in Victoria, ☎604/669-1211 in Vancouver), fax (☎381-5452 in Victoria) or by post to BC Ferry Corporation, 1112 Fort St, Victoria, BC V8V 4V2. Include name and address; number in party; length, height and type of car; choice of day-room or cabin; and preferred date of departure and alternatives. Full payment is required up front. **Day cabins** can be reserved by foot passengers, and range from $22 for two berths with basin, to $43 on the Promenade with two berths, basin and toilet. If you are making the return trip only you can rent **cabins overnight**, saving the hassle of finding accommodation in Port Hardy, but if you do you are obliged to take the cabin for the following day's return trip as well: cabins are not available as an alternative to rooms in town, so don't think you can rent a cabin overnight and then disappear next morning at Prince Rupert. Two-berth overnight cabins range from $49 with basin only, to $117 for shower, basin and toilet. Reports suggest BC Ferries are not happy for passengers to roll out sleeping bags in the lounge area. If you're making a return trip and want to leave your car behind, there are several supervised lock-ups in Port Hardy: try Daze Parking (☎949-7792) or the *Sunny Sanctuary RV Park* (☎949-8111) just five minutes from the terminal (the town shuttle bus will pick you

Port Hardy

Dominated by big-time copper mining, a large fishing fleet and the usual logging concerns, **PORT HARDY**, a total of 485km from Victoria and 230km from Campbell River, is best known among travellers as the departure point for ships plying one of the more spectacular stretches of the famous **Inside Passage** to Prince Rupert (and thence to Alaska) and the newly introduced **Discovery Coast Passage** (see box). If you have time to kill waiting for the boat you could drop into the occasionally open **town museum** at 7110 Market St or visit the **Quatse River Salmon Hatchery** on Hardy Bay Road, just off Hwy 19 across from the *Pioneer Inn*.

up from here). You can leave vehicles at the ferry terminal, but there have been incidents of vandalism in recent years: neither BC Ferries nor the Port Hardy infocentre seem to recommend the practice. Note, again, that it is vital to book accommodation at your final destination before starting your trip; both Port Hardy and Prince Rupert hotels get very busy on days when the boat arrives.

THE DISCOVERY COAST PASSAGE
The huge success of the Inside Passage sailing amongst visitors has led BC Ferries to introduce the new **Discovery Coast Passage**, a trip they candidly admit will only pay as a result of tourists. The route offers many of the scenic rewards of the Inside Passage, but over a shorter and more circuitous route between Port Hardy and **Bella Coola**, where you pick up the occasionally steep and tortuous road (Hwy 20) through the Coast Mountains to Williams Lake (see p.787) – it goes nowhere else. En route, the boat, the *Queen of Chilliwack*, stops at Namu, McLoughlin Bay, Shearwater, Klemtu and Ocean Falls (Namu is a request stop and must be booked in advance). If the route takes off as BC Ferries hope, you can expect visitor facilities to mushroom at these places – you can disembark at all of them – but at present the only places to stay overnight are campgrounds at McLoughlin Bay and a resort, hotels, cabins and B&B at Shearwater. Bella Coola is better-equipped, and will probably become more so as the route becomes better known. BC Ferries is offering inclusive ferry and accommodation **packages** – even renting fishing tackle so you can fish over the side – and these too may mature as the service finds its feet.

Currently there are **departures** roughly every couple of days between late May and the end of September, leaving at 6.30am, 7.30am or 10pm depending on the day of departure. There's a slight catch, however, for while the early morning departures offer you plenty of scenery, some arrive at McLoughlin Bay at 8.30pm and Bella Coola at 5.30am in the morning, meaning that the very best bit of the trip – along the inlet to Bella Coola – is in the middle of the night. The 6.30am departures are quicker (they only stop once, at Ocean Falls) and make Bella Coola the same day, arriving at 10pm, so the problem is lessened. Alternatively take the 10pm departures and wake at McLoughlin Bay at 8am with a further daylight trip to Bella Coola, arriving at 7.30pm – read the timetables carefully. Making the trip southbound from Bella Coola gets round the problem, though there are similar staggered departure and arrival times, with overnight and same-day journeys. Unlike the Inside Passage, there are **no cabins**: you sleep in aircraft-style reclining seats and – for the time being – sleeping bags seem ok on the floor: check for the latest on freestanding tents on the decks.

Reservations can be made through BC Ferries (see Inside Passage above for details). **Prices** for a foot passenger are $110 one way to Bella Coola, $55 to Namu and $70 to all other destinations. If you want to camp or stop over and hop on and off, the boat fares between any two of McLoughlin Bay, Ocean Falls, Klemtu and Namu are $22 and $40 from any of these to Bella Coola. Cars cost $220 from Port Hardy to Bella Coola, $140 to all other destinations ($45 and $80 respectively for the single-leg options). To take a **canoe** or **kayak** costs $40.75 stowage from Port Hardy to Bella Coola, $30.75 to points en route.

If possible, though, time your arrival to coincide with one of the Inside Passage **sailings** (see box) which leave every other day in summer and twice-weekly in winter. **Bus** services aren't really scheduled to do this for you, with a Laidlaw bus meeting each *incoming* sailing from Prince Rupert. A Laidlaw bus (☎949-7532 in Port Hardy, ☎385-4411 or 388-5248 in Victoria) also leaves Victoria daily (currently 11.45am), sometimes with a change in Nanaimo, arriving at the Port Hardy ferry terminal in the evening to connect with the ferry next morning (currently 9.50pm); in summer an extra service departs from Victoria on the morning before ferry sailings. Maverick Coach Lines (☎250/753-4371 in Nanaimo, ☎604/662-8051 in Vancouver) runs an early-morning bus from Vancouver to Nanaimo (inclusive of ferry), connecting with the daily Laidlaw bus to Port Hardy. You can **fly** from Vancouver International Airport to Port Hardy or Air BC (☎1-800-663-3721 in BC, 1-800-776-3000 in the States, 604/688-5515 in Vancouver, 250/360-9074 in Victoria).

The Port Hardy **ferry terminal** is visible from town but is actually 8km away at Bear Cove, where buses stop before carrying on to terminate opposite the **infocentre**, 7250 Market St (year-round Mon–Fri 9am–5pm, early June to late Sept 8am–8pm; ☎949-7622). The infocentre can give you all the details about Port Hardy's tiny but free **museum** (see p.738), and the immense wilderness of **Cape Scott Provincial Park**, whose interior is accessible only by foot and which is supposed to have some of the most consistently bad weather in the world. As a short taster you could follow the forty-minute hike from the small campground and trailhead at San Josef River to some sandy beaches. Increasingly popular, but demanding (allow eight hours plus), is the historic **Cape Scott Trail**, part of a complex web of trails hacked from the forest by early Danish pioneers. Around 28km has been reclaimed from the forest, opening a trail to the cape itself.

If you stay in town overnight, leave plenty of time to reach the ferry terminal – sailings in summer are usually around 7.30am. North Island Transportation provides a shuttle-bus service between the ferry and the town's airport, main hotels and the **bus station** at Market Street, whence it departs ninety minutes before each sailing (☎949-6300 for information or to arrange a pick-up from hotel or campground); otherwise call a **taxi** (☎949-8000).

Many travellers to Port Hardy are in RVs, but there's still a huge amount of pressure on hotel **accommodation** in summer, and it's absolutely vital to call ahead if you're not camping or haven't worked your arrival to coincide with one of the ferry sailings. Note that the ferry from Prince Rupert docks around 10.30pm, so you don't want to be hunting out rooms late at night with dozens of others. The cheaper **rooms** are out of town at the *Airport Inn*, 4030 Byng Rd (☎949-9424; ③–④), but you'd be better off in one of the slightly more upmarket central choices like the *North Shore Inn*, 7370 Market St (☎949-8500; ③), at the end of Hwy 19, where all units have ocean views, or the *Thunderbird Inn*, 7050 Rupert St and Granville (☎949-7767; ④). The former has nice views of the harbour but sometimes has noisy live music. Five minutes south of town at 4965 Byng Rd, in a park-like setting near the river, is the *Pioneer Inn* (☎949-7271 or 1-800-663-8744; ③–⑤), which has rooms, RV sites and a campground ($17–25). The only other hotel is the *Glen Lyon Inn* by the marina at 6435 Hardy Bay Rd (☎949-7115; ③–④): otherwise contact the infocentre for details of the town's five or so B&B options. The *Wildwoods* **campground** (☎949-6753; $5–15; May–Oct) is a good option, being within walking distance (3km) of the ferry, though reports suggest it's not too comfy for tenting – or try the *Quatse River Campground* at 5050 Hardy Rd (☎949-2395; $14), with lots of spruce-shaded sites opposite the *Pioneer Inn*, 5km from the ferry dock.

Food here is nothing special, but there's a bevy of budget outlets, so you should be able to fill up for well under $10. Granville and Market streets have the main restaurant concentrations: try *Snuggles*, next to the *Pioneer Inn*, which aims at a cosy English pub atmosphere with live music, theatre (Friday-nights) and steaks, salads and salmon grilled over an open fire. The cafeteria-coffee shop in the *Pioneer* does filling breakfasts and other snacks.

THE INTERIOR

It says something about the magnificence of British Columbia's **interior** that you can enter it from Vancouver or the Rockies and find a clutch of landscapes every bit as spectacular as those you've just left. Some people will travel inland from Vancouver, others across country from the Rockies or the US. Unfortunately, whatever your approach, both major routes through the region confine you to some of its least interesting areas. The most obvious and quickest line east or west, the **Trans-Canada Highway**, isn't worth considering in its entirety unless you're keen to cross the region in a hurry – little west of Revelstoke compares to what you might find further north or south. Nor does **Hwy 3**, rumbling along just north of the US border, offer a convincing reason for sticking to it religiously.

The best option would be to take a meandering course towards the outstanding **Kootenay** region in the province's southeastern corner – an idyllic assortment of mountains and lakes and several towns that are fun to stay in – perhaps by way of the **Okanagan**, an almost Californian enclave of orchards, vineyards, warm lakes and resort towns, whose beaches and scorching summers suck in hordes of vacationers from all over Canada and the western United States. From here you could push north to **Kamloops**, a far from exciting town, but the transport hub of the region and a jumping-off point for the magnificent **Wells Gray Provincial Park** or the Yukon. The other major option would be to head south to take in the better parts of Hwy 3 west of Osoyoos, also reasonably easily reached directly from Vancouver, and which includes a corner of **desert** and the spectacular ridges of the **Cascades** and **Coast Mountains**.

Vancouver to Kamloops

Two major routes **connect Vancouver and Kamloops**, the latter an unexceptional town but almost unavoidable as the junction of major routes in the region. These days most cars, buses and anyone in any sort of hurry take the **Coquihalla Highway** (Hwy 5). The scenery is unexceptional in the early part, but things look up considerably in the climb to the Coquihalla Pass (1244m), when forests, mountains and crashing rivers make a dramatic reappearance – compromised somewhat by old mines, clear-cuts (hillsides completely cleared of trees) and recent road-building scars. There's only a single exit, at the supremely missable town of Merritt, and literally no services for the entire 182km from **Hope** to Kamloops. Come stocked up with fuel and food, and be prepared to pay a toll (about $15) at the top of the pass – a wind- and snow-whipped spot that must offer amongst the loneliest employment opportunities in the province.

The older, slower (and more scenic) route from Vancouver is on the **Trans-Canada Highway** or by VIA Rail, both of which follow a more meandering course along the Thompson River and then the lower reaches of the Fraser River. The remainder of this section details this route.

Hope

Reputedly christened by prospectors with a grounding in Dante, **HOPE** – as in "Abandon all hope . . ." – is a pleasant mountain-ringed town and the last port of call before all scenic splendour is abandoned in the flat run of meadows and small towns en route for Vancouver. It also achieved a certain fame as the town wasted in spectacular fashion by Sylvester Stallone at the end of *First Blood*, the first Rambo movie. Despite the number of roads that converge here – the Trans-Canada, Hwy 3 and the Coquihalla – it remains a remarkably unspoilt stopover. In the past it was rivers, not roads, that accounted for the town's growth: the Fraser and two of its major tributaries, the Skagit and Coquihalla, meet at the townsite. The Native Canadian villages here were forced to move when a Hudson's Bay Post was established in 1848, the status quo being further disturbed when the gold rush hit in 1858. The bust that followed boom in neighbouring places was averted in Hope, largely because its situation made it an important station stop on the Canadian Pacific. Today its pretty location, which catches visitors slightly unawares, is turning it into something of a sight in its own right.

The **infocentre** (daily: summer 8am–8pm; rest of year 9am–5pm; ☎604-869-2021) is the building next to the artfully dumped pile of antique farm machinery at 919 Water

Ave. The town **museum** is in the same building, and offers the usual hand-me-downs of Hope's erstwhile old-timers. Across the road, the lovely view over the Fraser as it funnels out of the mountains is one of the town's best moments. Drop by **Memorial Park** in downtown, where trees ravaged by rot have been given a new lease of life by a local chainsaw sculptor. Nearby, the Christ Church National Historic Site, built in 1861, is one of BC's oldest churches still on its original site. Another one-off novelty is the "H" tree at the corner of 5th Street and Hudson's Bay Street, two trees cleverly entwined as saplings to grow together in the form of an "H" for Hope.

Fishing, canoeing, even gold-panning are all popular time-wasters around the hundreds of local lakes, rivers and creeks, details of which are available from the infocentre, which also prints a summary of local hikes. Of these, the **Rotary Trail** (3km) to the confluence of the Fraser and Coquihalla rivers is popular, as is the more demanding clamber over gravel paths to the top of **Thacker Mountain** (5km). Another walking expedition worth pursuing is the dark jaunt through the **tunnels** of the abandoned Vancouver–Nelson railway, reached by a short trail from the **Coquihalla Canyon Provincial Park**, 6km northeast of town off Coquihalla Highway. This was one of the backcountry locations used during the filming of *First Blood*, and offers spectacular views over the cliffs and huge sand bars of the Coquihalla Gorge. **Kawkawa Lake Provincial Park**, 3km northeast of Hope off Hwy 3, is another popular mountain retreat, endowed with plenty of hiking, relaxing and swimming opportunities. The latest big thrill hereabouts, though, is **gliding**, or soaring, the prevailing westerly winds funnelling suddenly into the valley above Hope creating perfect thermals for the sport. The Vancouver Soaring Association (☎521-5501), at Hope airport, offer twenty-minute unpowered flights (no experience necessary).

Practicalities

Most of what happens in Hope happens on its single main street, Water Avenue. The Greyhound **bus terminal** is here, and is a critical juncture for bus travellers because you'll have to transfer depending on whether you're going west to Vancouver, north to Kamloops or east to Penticton and the Okanagan. Cheap **motels** proliferate along Hwy 3 as you leave town heading east, and though most are much of a muchness, the *Flamingo* (☎604/869-9610; ①), last on the strip, has a nice piney setting. Closer in on the same road, the *Heritage* (☎604/869-7166; ②), a lovely grey-wood building smothered in flowers, is also excellent, but slightly more expensive. In the town itself the *Best Continental Motel*, 860 Fraser Ave (☎604/869-9726; ③), lies a block back from the main highway and is handy for the bus depot; or there are the *City Centre Motel*, 455 Wallace St (☎604/869-5411; ②), the *Park Motel*, 832-4th Ave (☎604/869-5891; ②–③), and the *Windsor Motel* overlooking the park at 778-3rd Ave (☎604/869-9944; ②). **Campgrounds**, too, are numerous, but most are some way from downtown. The town site is at *Coquihalla Campground* (☎604/869-7119; $15–20; April–Oct), in a treed park setting off Hwy 3 and reached via 7th Avenue. The top of the pile is the *KOA Campground*; 5km west of town on Flood Hope Road (☎604/869-9857; $17.50; March–Oct).

Food facilities and late-night entertainment are limited in what is, despite Vancouver's proximity, still a small-time Canadian town. For snacks, try the bakery on the main street, or the rock-bottom café in the Greyhound station. For more ambitious fare, try the *Hope Hotel* and *Lee's Kettle Valley Restaurant*, both on Wallace Street.

The Fraser Canyon

Veering north from Hope, the Trans-Canada runs up the famous Fraser River valley, squeezed here by the high ridges of the Cascade and Coast ranges into one of British Columbia's grandest waterways. Though it's now a clear-cut transport corridor – the Canadian Pacific Railway also passes this way – the **Fraser Canyon** was long regarded as impassable; to negotiate it, the Trans-Canada is forced to push through tunnels, hug the Fraser's banks, and at times cling perilously to rock ledges hundreds of metres above the swirling waters.

The river is named after **Simon Fraser** (1776–1862), one of North America's most remarkable early explorers, who as an employee of the North West Company established western Canada's first white settlements: Fort McCleod (1805), Fort St James (1806), Fort Fraser (1806) and Fort George (1807–present-day Prince George). Having traced the route taken by fellow explorer Alexander Mackenzie across the continent, he set out in 1808 to establish a route to the Pacific and secure it for Britain against the rival claims of the US. Instead he travelled the entire 1300-kilometre length of a river – the Fraser – under the mistaken impression he was following the Columbia. "We had to pass where no man should venture", he wrote, making most of the journey on foot guided by local natives, pushing forward using ladders, ropes and improvised platforms to bypass rapids too treacherous to breach by boat. Some 35 days were needed to traverse the canyon alone. Reaching the river's mouth, where he would have glimpsed the site of present-day Vancouver, he realized his error and deemed the venture a commercial failure, despite the fact he had successfully navigated one of the continent's greatest rivers for the first time. Few people, needless to say, felt the need to follow Fraser's example until the discovery of **gold** near Yale in 1858; prospectors promptly waded in and panned every tributary of the lower Fraser until new strikes tempted them north to the Cariboo.

Yale

YALE, about 15km north of Hope, opens the canyon with a ring of plunging cliffs. Sitting at the river's navigable limit, it was once a significant Native Canadian site, providing an important point of departure for the canoes of the Stó:lo ("People of the River"). Tribespeople would come from as far afield as Vancouver Island to plunder the rich salmon waters just above the present townsite. A Hudson's Bay Company post, The Falls, appeared here in the 1840s, later renamed in honour of James Murray Yale, commander of the HBC post at Fort Langley, then one of the predominant white outposts on the BC mainland. Within a decade it became the largest city in North America west of Chicago and north of San Francisco: during the 1858 gold rush, when it marked the beginning of the infamous Cariboo Wagon Road, its population mushroomed to over 20,000, a growth only tempered by the end of the boom and the completion of the Canadian Pacific. Today it's a small lumber town of about 170, though a visit to the **Yale Museum** (June–Sept daily 9am–6pm) in a building of 1868 on Hwy 1, known here as Douglas Street, offers an exhaustive account of the town's golden age. The **infocentre** is also in the museum on Douglas Street (June–Sept daily 9am–6pm; ☎863-2324). The trilingual monument in front of the building is dedicated to the countless Chinese navvies who helped build the Canadian Pacific, one of only a handful of such memorials. You might also want to pay homage at **Lady Franklin Rock**, the vast river boulder which blocked the passage of steamers beyond Yale. It takes its name from Lady Franklin, wife of Sir John Franklin, the Arctic explorer who vanished on a voyage in July 1845. Numerous expeditions set out to find him (with no luck), and it's said that Lady Franklin, on her own personal odyssey, came as far as Yale and its big boulder. Ask locals or at the museum for directions. If you fancy a longer walk, take Hwy 1 a kilometre south out of the village for the trailhead of the Spirit Cave Trail, a one-hour walk with fine views of the mountains. For **rooms**, you can't do much better than the *Fort Yale Motel* (☎604/863-2216; ①) at the entrance to the Canyon. Some 11km north of Yale on Hwy 1, the *Colonial Inn* (☎604/863-2277; ②) has cabins and pitches (tents $12). If you're **camping**, though, you might want to push on 10km towards Hope on Hwy 1 to the *Emory Creek Provincial Park*, a large, peaceful wooded site with river walks and camping sites (☎824-2300; reservations possible).

Hell's Gate and Boston Bar

Around 10km north of Yale is the famous **HELL'S GATE**, where – in a gorge almost 180m deep – the huge swell of the Fraser is squeezed into a 38-metre channel of foaming water that crashes through the rocks with awe-inspiring ferocity. The water here is up to 60m deep and as fast-flowing as any you're likely to see, but to get down to the river there's a certain amount of resort-like commercialism to negotiate and an "Air-Tram" (cable car) to pay for (daily: April 10am–4pm; May to mid-June & early Sept to Oct 9am–5pm; mid-June to early Sept 9am–6pm; $9.50; ☎867-9277). Close by there are also displays on the various provisions made to help migrating **salmon** complete their journeys, which have been interrupted over the years by the coming of the road and railway beside the Fraser. The river is one of the key runs for Pacific salmon, and every summer and fall they fill the river as they head for tributaries and upstream lakes to spawn (see p.750). The biggest obstacle to their passage came in 1913, when a landslide occured during the construction of the Canadian Pacific Railway, yet it wasn't until 1945 that ladders were completed to bypass the fall. The numbers of salmon have never fully recovered. For other good views of the canyon, travel around 8km south of Hell's Gate on Hwy 1 to the **Alexander Bridge Provincial Park**, where an old section of the highway drops to the Alexander Bridge for some startling panoramas.

To **stay** locally, make for the *Blue Lake Lodge* (☎604-867-9624; ③), located a kilometre east on Blue Lake Road off the highway 15km north of Boston Bar (see below). The only local **campground**, the *Canyon Alpine RV Park & Campground* (☎604-867-9734 or 1-800-644-7275; $12–20), 5km north of Boston Bar, has treed tenting sites and restaurant.

BOSTON BAR, 20km north of Yale, boasts a trio of motels and is also the main centre for **white-water** raft trips down the Fraser as far as Yale. Various companies run several trips a week from May to August; contact Frontier River Adventure for details (☎604-867-9244). The village's name, apparently, was coined by locals in villages nearby amazed at the number of American prospectors who seemed to hail from Boston. A "bar", by contrast, was the name given to places where miners stopped to make camp en route for the goldfields.

Cache Creek

CACHE CREEK has a reputation as a hitchhiker's black hole and indeed is the sort of sleepy place you could get stuck in for days. Locals also say it didn't help that an infamous child murderer, Charles Olsen, was captured nearby in 1985 – since then they've been understandably wary of picking up strangers. The town's name is accounted for by a variety of legends, the most romantic version concerning a couple of prospectors who buried a hoard of gold and never returned to pick it up. Sadly, it's likelier to derive from early trappers' more prosaic habit of leaving a cache of supplies at points on a trail to be used later.

Cache Creek is known as the "Arizona of Canada" for its baking summer climate, which settles a heat-wasted somnolence on its dusty streets. The parched, windswept mountains roundabout are anomalous volcanic intrusions in the regional geology, producing a legacy of hard rock and semi-precious stones – including jade – that attract climbers and rock hounds. There's not much else to do here – you can watch semi-precious stones being worked at several places – but for local insights visit the **infocentre** on the northwest side of town at 1340 Hwy 97 near the main road junction (summer daily 9am–6pm; ☎457-5306). If you're stranded, try one of half a dozen **motels**, the most interesting of which is the bizarrely built *Castle Inn* (☎457-9547 or 1-800-457-9547; ②). Less eccentric are the *Bonaparte* on Hwy 97 North (☎457-9693; ②), with large heated pool, and the central *Sage Hills Motel*, 1390 Hwy 97 North (☎457-6451; ②), also with pool. The nearest **campground** is the *Brookside* (☎457-6633; $10–13; April–Oct), with laundry, free hot showers and heated outdoor pool 1km east of town on the main highway.

Kamloops

Almost any trip in southern British Columbia brings you sooner or later to **KAMLOOPS**, a town which has been a transport centre from time immemorial – its name derives from the Shuswap word for "meeting of the rivers" – and which today marks the meeting point of the Trans-Canada and Yellowhead (South) highways, the region's principal transcontinental roads, as well as the junction of the Canadian Pacific and Canadian National railways. The largest interior town in southern British Columbia (pop. 75,000), it's fairly unobjectionable, except when the wind blows from the uptown sawmills – which makes it smell as if something's been dead for a week. If you're on public transport, there's no particular need to spend any time here; if you're camping or driving, however, it makes a convenient provisions stop, especially for those heading north on Hwy 5 or south on the Coquihalla Hwy, neither of which has much in the way of facilities.

Kamloops is determinedly functional and not a place to spend a happy day wandering, but all the same the **Kamloops Museum** (Sept–June Tues–Sat 9.30am–4.30pm; July–Aug Mon–Fri 9am–8pm, Sat 10am–5pm, Sun 1–5pm; free) is one of the more interesting provincial offerings, with illuminating archive photographs (especially the one of the railway running down the centre of the main street) artefacts, bric-a-brac, period set pieces and a particularly well-done section on the Shuswap. The stuffed-animal display, without which no BC museum is complete, has a fascinating little piece on the life cycle of the tick presented without any noticeable irony. For a more complete picture of local native history and traditions, call at the **Secwepemec Museum**, just over the bridge on Hwy 5 (summer daily 9am–5pm; winter Mon–Fri 8.30am–4.30pm; $5).

Perhaps the most interesting thing about Kamloops is its surroundings, dominated by strange, bare-earthed brown hills that locals like to say represent the northernmost point of the Mohave Desert. There's no doubting the almost surreal touches of near-desert, which are particularly marked in the bare rock and clay outcrops above the bilious waters of the Thompson River and in the bleached scrub and failing stands of pines that spot the barren hills. Most scenic diversions lie a short drive out of town, and the infocentre has full details of every last local bolt hole, with a special bias towards the two hundred or so trout-stuffed lakes that dot the hinterland. The nearest and most popular on a hot summer's day is **Paul Lake Provincial Park**, 17km northeast of town on a good paved road, with swimming and a provincial campground.

Practicalities

The **infocentre**, 1290 West Trans-Canada Hwy (June–Sept daily 9am–6pm; Oct–May Mon–Fri 9am–5pm; ☎374-3377 or 1-800-662-1994) is well out of downtown across from the Aberdeen Mall close to the Greyhound depot (see below). They have full accommodation and recreational details for the town and much of the province, and a particularly useful book of B&Bs. They're also keen to emphasize that Kamloops has *no fort*, this for some reason being something most people come expecting to see. The **Greyhound terminal** (☎374-1212) is in the Aberdeen Mall off Hwy 1, a good 6km west of the centre, and is a crucial interchange for buses to all parts of the province; the #3 bus into town leaves from immediately outside. Kamloops is also served by three weekly **trains** in each direction to Edmonton (via Jasper) and Vancouver. The VIA Rail office is at 95 3rd Ave, behind Landsdowne Street, but is open only on days trains are running (☎372-5858).

Kamloops's huge volume of accommodation is aimed fair and square at the motorist and consists of thick clusters of **motels**, most of which blanket the town's eastern margins on Hwy 1 or out on Columbia Street West. The *Thrift Inn* (☎374-2488 or 1-800-661-7769; ①) is probably the cheapest of all, but it's about the last building on eastbound Hwy 1 out of town. You pay a slight premium for central beds, most of which are on Columbia Street: here the *Casa Marquis Motor Inn*, 530 Columbia St (☎372-7761 or 1-

800-533-9233; ②) is reasonably priced, or you can try the always reliable *Sandman*, 550 Columbia St (☎374-1218 or 1-800-726-3626; ②), part of a chain, or the *Fountain Motel*, 506 Columbia (☎374-4451 or 1-888-253-1569; ②). If you want top-of-the-range comfort after a long journey, make for the central *Stockmen's Hotel*, 540 Victoria St (☎372-2281 or 1-800-663-2837; ⑤). The offical **youth hostel** is housed downtown in a restored court house building at 7 West Seymour St (☎828-7991; ①): it has dorm beds and a few private rooms. There's also a clutch of motels around the bus terminal, in case you arrive late and have no need to drop into town. The nearest **campground** is the *Silver Sage Tent and Trailer Park* at 771 Athabasca St East (☎828-2077; $15–18), but if you've got a car aim for the far more scenic facilities at Paul Lake Provincial Park (see p.745). Snack **food** is cheap and served in generous portions at the popular *Steiger's Pastry Café*, 359 Victoria St, which really is run by Swiss people and does good muesli, cappuccino, lots of sticky buns, and excellent bread. For supermarket stock-ups, the Safeway is on the corner of Seymour and 5th Avenue. If you're splashing out on a proper meal, on the other hand, the best restaurant is the upmarket *Deja Vu*, 172 Battle St (☎374-3227), where Thai meets France and Japan, though locals also rate *Pete's Pasta* at 149 Victoria St highly for a good mid-priced meal.

Highway 5: Clearwater and Wells Gray Park

Northbound **Hwy 5** (here known as the Yellowhead South Hwy) heads upstream along the broad North Thompson River as it courses through high hills and rolling pasture between Kamloops and **Clearwater** and beyond. It is one of the most scenically astounding road routes in this part of the world, and follows the river as it carves through the Monashee Mountains from its source near **Valemount**, to the final meeting with the main Yellowhead Hwy (Hwy 16) at Tête Jaune Cache, a total distance of 338km. The entire latter half of the journey is spent sidestepping the immense **Wells Gray Provincial Park**, one of the finest protected areas in British Columbia.

Greyhound **buses** cover the route on their run between Kamloops and Prince George via Clearwater (2 daily in each direction), as do VIA **trains**, which connect Kamloops with Jasper via Clearwater (3 weekly). To get into Wells Gray without your own transport, however, you'd have to hitch from Clearwater up the 63-kilometre main access road – a feasible proposition at the height of summer, but highly unlikely at any other time. This access road will be enough for most casual visitors to get a taste of the park – you could run up and down it and see the sights in a day – but note that there are some less-travelled gravel roads into other sectors of the park from **Blue River**, 112km north of Clearwater on Hwy 5, and from the village of **100 Mile House**, on Hwy 97 west of the park.

Clearwater

CLEARWATER is a dispersed farming community that's invisible from Hwy 5, and unless you arrive by rail there's no need to drop down to it at all. Everything you need apart from the odd shop is on or just off the junction between the highway and the slip road to the village, including the **bus stop** and the excellent **infocentre** (daily: June–Aug 8am–8pm; Sept–May 9am–5pm; ☎674-2646), a model of the genre that has immensely useful information on all aspects of Wells Gray Provincial Park. If you're planning on staying locally or doing any walking or canoeing, take time to flick through its reference books devoted to accommodation, trails and paddling routes.

Unless you're camping, Clearwater is the most realistic place **to stay** along Hwy 5 if you're planning on doing Wells Gray. By far the best prospect, thanks to its lovely views over Dutch Lake, is the *Jasper Way Inn Motel*, 57 East Old North Thompson Hwy (☎674-3345; ②–④), 1km off the highway to the west and well signed from the infocentre; some rooms have cooking facilities. If it's full, try the big *Wells Gray Inn* (☎674-2214 or 1-800-567-4088; ③), close by on the main road; the doubles here are more comfortable, but lack the view. The latter is virtually the only place to **eat** locally. As the park becomes more popular, so more places are opening on its fringes: the big new *Clearwater Adventures Resort*, 373 Clearwater Valley Rd (☎674-3909; ②–⑤) on the corner of the Yellowhead Hwy and the Wells Grey Park Road, is one such, a combination of motel and camping and RV sites ($18–32; March–Oct). If you've come for wilderness you probably won't want to be in such a place, but it does also have three restaurants, endless facilities and a whole host of equipment rental possibilities and organized tours.

Three other **campgrounds** lie more or less within walking distance of the infocentre: the best – again, on the lake – is the *Dutch Lake Resort and RV Park* (☎674-3351; $14–24; May–Oct). Don't forget, though, that there are three simple provincial park campgrounds within the park (see p.748). If you want to be slightly away from Clearwater, stop at the *Birch Island Campground* (☎587-6567; $12.50–19; May to mid-Oct), a treed seventy-acre area with tent sites overlooking the Thompson River 8km north of the village on Hwy 5.

Blue River and Valemount

Clearwater is by far the best base locally, but you may find the **accommodation** options at Blue River and Valemount (a whopping 225km north of Clearwater on Hwy 5) useful. **BLUE RIVER**, a slip of a place, has far fewer possibilities, with its cheapest option being the *Blue River Motel* with one- and two-bedroom units two blocks off the highway on Spruce Street (☎673-8387; ②). For a few dollars more you could try the *Mountain View Motel* on 3rd Avenue and Spruce Street (☎673-8366; ②) and, top-of-the-pile, but on the highway, is the fine *Venture Lodge* (☎673-8384; ②–③). The only **campgrounds** for miles are the *Eleanor Lake Campsite and Trailer Park* on Herb Bilton Way (☎673-8316; $10–14; May to mid-Oct), with free showers, store and canoe rentals, and the *Blue River Campground and RV Park*, Myrtle Lake Road and Cedar Street (☎673-8203; $10-14; May to mid-Oct), with showers, canoe rentals and a variety of fishing, canoeing and horseriding tours.

In **VALEMOUNT** there's a seasonal infocentre at 98 Gorse St on Hwy 5 (mid-May to mid-Sept daily 9am–5pm; ☎566-4846) and around ten motels and two campgrounds. One block off the highway on 5th Avenue are a bunch of **motels**, of which the cheapest is the *Yellowhead* (☎566-4411; ③); there's little to choose between the other two, the *Chalet Continental*, 1470 5th Ave (☎566-9787; ③–④), and the *Alpine*, 1470 5th Ave (☎566-4471; ③). On Swift Creek adjoining the village is one of two local **campgrounds**, the *Yellowhead Campsite and Trailer Park* (☎566-4227; $12; June–Aug), The wooded *Valemount Campground* is off the highway (☎566-4141; $19; April–Oct).

Wells Gray Provincial Park

WELLS GRAY PROVINCIAL PARK is the equal of any of the Rocky Mountain national parks to the east: if anything, its wilderness is probably more extreme – so untamed, in fact, that many of its peaks remain unclimbed and unnamed. Wildlife sightings are common – especially if you tramp some of the wilder trails, where encounters with black bears, grizzlies and mountain goats are a possibility, not to mention glimpses of smaller mammals such as timber wolves, coyotes, weasels, martens, minks, wolverines and beavers. Seeing the park is straightforward, at least if you have transport and only want a superficial – but still rewarding – glimpse of the interior. A 63-kilometre access road strikes into the park from Hwy 5 at Clearwater, culminating in Clearwater Lake – there's no further wheeled access. Various trails long and short, together with campgrounds, viewpoints and easily seen waterfalls, are dotted along the road, allowing you to see just about all the obvious scenic landmarks with a car in a day.

With some 250km of maintained trails and dozens of other lesser routes, the park is magnificent for **hiking**. Short walks and day hikes from the park access road are described below, but serious backpackers can easily spend a week or more tramping the Murtle River (14km) and Kostal Lake (26km) trails. Make sure you pick up a free *BC Parks* map-pamphlet at the Clearwater infocentre, and if you're thinking of doing any backcountry exploration you'll want to invest in their more detailed maps and guides. **Cross-country skiing** is also possible, but there are only a few groomed routes in the park: again, details from the infocentre.

Another of the park's big attractions is **canoeing** on Clearwater and Azure lakes, the former at the end of the access road, which can be linked with a short portage to make a 100-plus-kilometre dream trip for paddlers; you can rent canoes for long- or short-haul trips from Clearwater Lake Tours (☎674-3052). White-water rafting down the Clearwater River is also extremely popular and recommended, and half-day to full-week tours can be arranged through the Clearwater infocentre or at the two accommodation options below. Several local operators run shorter commercial boat trips around Clearwater Lake, as well as full-scale **tours** featuring horseriding, camping, trekking, fishing, boating, and even float-plane excursions around the park – the Clearwater infocentre has the inside story on all of these.

The only indoor **accommodation** in or near the park is in the log cabins at *Wells Gray Ranch* (☎674-2792; ⑤; mid-May to mid-Oct) just before the park entrance (26km from Hwy 5), or the slightly larger, slightly more expensive but equally lonely *Helmcken Falls Lodge* (☎674-3657; ④–⑤; Jan–March & May–Oct) at the entrance itself (35km from Hwy 5), which offers similar facilities at slightly higher prices. You'll be lucky to find vacancies in summer, however. Both of these also have tent pitches, but there's far better roadside **camping** along the park access road at *Spahats Creek Provincial Park* ($9.50; April–Oct) a small forested site only 16km from Hwy 5 at Clearwater. Within the park border itself are three provincial campgrounds: the *Dawson Falls*, 5km from the park entrance; *Falls Creek*, 30km from the entrance; and *Clearwater Lake*, 31km from the entrance (information ☎851-3000; $9.50; all May–Sept). All fill up promptly in summer. Many backpackers' campsites dot the shores of the park's major lakes; Clearwater Lake Tours operates a water-taxi service, which can drop you off at any site on Clearwater Lake and pick you up at a prearranged time.

Sights and hikes along the access road

Even if you're not geared up for the backcountry, the access road to the park from Clearwater opens up a medley of waterfalls, walks and viewpoints that make a day or more's detour extremely worthwhile. The road's paved for the first 30km to the park boundary, but the remaining 33km to Clearwater Lake is gravel. Most of the sights are well signed.

About 8km north of Clearwater, a short walk from the car park at **Spahats Creek Provincial Park** brings you to the 61-metre Spahats Falls, the first of several mighty cascades along this route. You can watch the waters crashing down through layers of pinky-red volcanic rock from a pair of observation platforms, which also provide an impressive and unexpected view of the Clearwater Valley way down below. A few hundred metres further up the road, a fifteen-kilometre gravel lane peels off into the **Wells Gray Recreation Area**; a single trail from the end of the road strikes off into alpine meadows, feeding four shorter day trails into an area particularly known for its bears. This is also the site of a juvenile correction centre, which must rank as possibly the most beautiful but godforsaken spot to do time in North America. About 15km further up the main access road, a second four-wheel-drive track branches east to reach the trailhead for **Battle Mountain** (2369m; 19km), with the option of several shorter hikes like the Mount Philip Trail (5km) en route.

Green Mountain Lookout, reached by a rough, winding road to the left just after the park entrance, offers one of the most enormous roadside panoramas in British Columbia, and it's a sight that will help you grasp the sheer extent of the Canadian wilderness: as far as you can see, there's nothing but an almighty emptiness of primal forest and mountains. Various landscape features are picked out on plaques, and the immediate area is a likely place to spot moose.

The next essential stop is **Dawson Falls**, a broad, powerful cascade (91m wide and 18m high) just five minutes' walk from the road – signed "Viewpoint". Beyond, the road crosses an ugly iron bridge and shortly after meets the start of the **Murtle River Trail** (14km one way), a particularly good walk if you want more spectacular waterfalls.

Immediately afterwards, a dead-end sideroad is signed to **Helmcken Falls**, the park's undisputed highlight. The site is heavily visited, and it's not unknown for wedding parties to come up here to get dramatic matrimonial photos backed by the luminous arc of water plunging into a black, carved bowl fringed with vivid carpets of lichen and splintered trees, the whole ensemble framed by huge plumes of spray wafting up on all sides. At 137m, the falls are two and a half times the height of Niagara – or, in the infoboard's incongruous comparison, approximately the same height as the Vancouver skyline.

Continuing north, the park access road rejoins the jade-green Clearwater River, passing tastefully engineered picnic spots and short trails that wend down to the bank for close-up views of one of the province's best white-water-rafting stretches. The last sight before the end of the road is **Ray Farm**, home to John Bunyon Ray, who in 1912 was the first man to homestead this area. Though it's not much to look at, the farm offers a sobering insight into the pioneer mentality – Ray's struggle to scrape a living and raise a family in this harsh environment beggars belief – and the picturesquely ruined, wooden shacks are scattered in a lovely, lush clearing. The park road ends at **Clearwater Lake**, where there are a couple of boat launches, a provincial campground and a series of short trails clearly marked from the trailhead.

Salmon Arm and the Shuswap

Given the variety of routes across southern BC there's no knowing when you might find yourself in **SALMON ARM**, 108km east of Kamloops, though that's not something that need concern you in planning an itinerary, because the town – the largest of the somewhat bland resorts spread along **Shuswap Lake**'s 1000km of navigable waterways – has relatively little to recommend it. This said, if you fancy time fishing, swimming, water-skiing or houseboating, you could do worse than relax for a couple of days in one of the 32 provincial parks or small lakeside villages – Chase, Sorrento, Eagle Bay and others. Depending on the season, you can also watch one of Canada's most famous salmon-spawning runs, or indulge in a little **bird-watching**, for the bay at Salmon Arm is one of the world's last nesting area of the Western Grebe. As ever in Canada, Salmon Arm and its satellites are much smaller places than their bold label on most maps would suggest. Many of the settlements are oddly dispersed and a touch scrappy and haphazard in appearance, but if you're driving they make a natural break along one of the Trans-Canada's more monotonous stretches. To get anything out of Salmon Arm proper, you'll have to pull off the main drag, which is formed by the Trans-Canada itself, a settlement known as Canoe, and head to the village itself a little to the south. In Canoe, head one block to the lakeside and, barring a huge sawmill and plywood works, you find a pleasant open area with a view of distant hazy hills.

The lake and the surrounding region take their name from the Shuswap natives, the northernmost of the great Salishan family and the largest single tribe in British Columbia. The name of the town harks back to a time when it was possible to spear salmon straight from the lake, and fish were so plentiful that they were shovelled onto the land

SPAWN TO BE WILD

At times it seems impossible to escape the **salmon** in British Columbia. Whether it's on restaurant menus, in rivers, or in the photographs of grinning fishermen clutching their catch, the fish is almost as much a symbol of the region as its mountains and forests. Five different species inhabit the rivers and lakes of western Canada: **pink, coho, chum, chinook** and, most important of all, the **sockeye**.

Though they start and finish their lives in fresh water, salmon spend about four years in the open sea between times. Mature fish make their epic migrations from the Pacific to **spawn** in the BC rivers of their birth between June and November, swimming about 30km a day; some chinook travel more than 1400km up the Fraser beyond Prince George, which means almost fifty days' continuous swimming upstream. Though the female lays as many as 4000 eggs, only about six percent of the offspring survive: on the Adams River near Salmon Arm, for example, it's estimated that of four billion sockeye eggs laid in a typical year, one billion survive to become fry (hatched fish about 2cm long), of which 75 percent are eaten by predators before becoming smolts (year-old fish), and only five percent of these then make it to the ocean. In effect each pair of spawners produces about ten mature fish: of these, eight are caught by commercial fisheries and only two return to reproduce.

These are returns that clearly put the salmon's survival and British Columbia's lucrative **fishing industry** on a knife edge. Caught, canned and exported, salmon accounts for two-thirds of BC's $1 billion annual revenues from fishing – the largest of any Canadian province, and its third-ranking money-earner after forestry and energy products. Commercial fishing suffered its first setback in British Columbia as long ago as 1913, when large rock slides at Hell's Gate in the Fraser Canyon disrupted many of the spawning runs. Although fish runs were painstakingly constructed to bypass the slides, new pressures have subsequently been heaped on the salmon by mining, logging, urban and agricultural development, and the dumping of industrial and municipal wastes. An increasingly important line of defence, **hatcheries** have been built on rivers on the mainland and Vancouver Island to increase the percentage of eggs and fry that successfully mature. Meanwhile, overfishing, as the above figures suggest, remains a major concern, particularly as the **drift nets** of Japanese and Korean fleets, designed for neon squid, have over the past decade taken numerous non-target species, including BC and Yukon salmon. Under intense lobbying from Canada and the US, both nations agreed to a moratorium on large-scale drift nets as from June 30, 1992.

as fertilizer. Shuswap still provides an important sanctuary for hatched salmon fry before they make their long journey down the Thompson and Fraser rivers to the sea – the abundance of such lakes, together with ideal water temperatures, free-flowing, well-oxygenated and silt-free tributaries, and plenty of sand and gravel beds for egg-laying, make the Fraser River system the continent's greatest salmon habitat.

One of the few reasons you might make a special journey to the Salmon Arm area is to watch the huge migrations of **spawning salmon** that take place around October. Anything up to two million fish brave the run from the Pacific up to their birthplace in the Adams River – one of the most famous spawning grounds in the province – which during the peak week of the run attracts around 250,000 visitors. This short stretch of river is protected by **Roderick Haig-Brown Provincial Park**, reached from Salmon Arm by driving 46km west on the Trans-Canada to Squilax and then 5km north on a sideroad. If you're thinking of dangling a line, pick up the *Fishing in Shuswap* leaflet from the infocentre in Salmon Arm, and don't forget to get a licence at the same time.

The best chance of a leg-stretch around here if you're just passing through is at **Herald Provincial Park** on the shore opposite Salmon Arm (turn right off Hwy 1 at Tappen, 6km west of town). There's good swimming from a sandy beach, a provincial **campground**, and a lovely fifteen-minute walk culminating at Margaret Falls.

Practicalities

Greyhound **buses** serve Salmon Arm from Vancouver and Calgary (5 daily in each direction) and Kelowna, Vernon and Penticton (2 daily). The bus terminal is at the West Village Mall on Hwy 1, and the **infocentre** (year-round Mon–Sat 8.30am–5.30pm; ☎832-2230) is at 751 Marine Park Drive. You might also contact Tourism Shuswap (☎832-5200 or 1-800-661-4800).

One of the most convenient of Salmon Arm's many **motels** is the *Village Motel* (☎832-3955; ②) at 620 Trans-Canada Hwy. More upmarket, and still close to the highway, is the Best Western Villager West Motor Inn, 61 10th St (☎832-9793 or 1-800-528-1234; ③). There is also a HI-affiliated **youth hostel**, the *Squilax General Store and Caboose Hostel* (☎675-2977; ①) in Chase on the waterfront just off the Trans-Canada. Of several **campgrounds**, the obvious first choice is the *Salmon Arm KOA*, 3km east of town in a big wooded site, whose excellent facilities include a heated swimming pool (☎832-6489 or 1-800-562-9389; $22; May–Oct). For beds or tent space, the *Salmon River Motel and Campground*, 1km west of downtown at 910 40th Street SW (☎832-3065; ③; year-round), is also good with tent pitches between $16.50 and $19.

For a decidedly alternative form of accommodation, head east along the Trans-Canada to **SICAMOUS**, a pleasant but very busy waterfront village which, though crammed with motels and campgrounds, is better known for its many upmarket **houseboats**. A few rent by the night, but most tend to be let weekly by about half a dozen local agencies scattered around the village. Agencies you might try include Bluewater Houseboats (April–Oct; ☎836-2255), Sicamous Creek Marina (☎836-4611) or the Shuswap Lake Houseboat Association (☎836-2450). The village is also the place to pick up a boat for a sightseeing **cruise** on the lake, one of the best ways of enjoying a scenic slice of the region: contact the Shuswap Ferry Lake Service for details of daily summer sailings (☎836-2200). To **eat** locally, head for the *Mara Lake Inn* on the lakeshore 3km south of the village and the Trans-Canada on Hwy 97, and for a **drink** try the *Brothers Pub*, 420 Main St.

Highway 97 to the Okanagan

Passing through landscapes of Eden-like clarity and beauty, **Hwy 97** is a far better exit from (or entrance to) the Okanagan than the dreary road to Salmon Arm (see p.749). The grass-green meadows, grazing cattle and low wooded hills here are the sort of scenery pioneers must have dreamed of: most of the little hamlets en route make charming spots to stay, and if you have time and transport any number of minor roads lead off to small lakes, each with modest recreational facilities.

The highway peels off the Trans-Canada 26km east of Kamloops, its first good stops being **MONTE LAKE**, served by the excellent *Heritage Campsite and RV Park* (☎375-2478; $12–15; April–Oct) and the equally well-tended and unspoilt public campground at **Monte Lake Provincial Park**. Both places make good spots to overnight. **WESTWOLD**, 5km beyond, is a dispersed ranching community of clean, old wooden houses and large pastures that present a picture of almost idyllic rural life. **FALKLAND**, 13km beyond, is an unassuming place whose **motel** blends easily into its rustic village atmosphere. The central *Big Highland Motel* (☎379-2249; ②) is on Adelphi Street, but you might also drop into the infant infocentre (summer only) for lists of local B&B. There are also a couple of well-signposted, quiet **campgrounds** ($12–15). Country lanes lead north and east from here to **Bolean Lake** (10km) at 1437m, served by a lodge and campground: *Bolean Lake Lodge*, Bolean Lake Road (May–Oct; ☎558-9008; rooms ②, tents $12); to **Pillar Lake** (13km) and the *Pillar Lake Resort* (☎379-2623; ①–③; May–Oct), which provides cabins and campsites from $12; and to **Pinaus Lake** (10km) and its adjacent cabins and campground, *Pinaus Lake Camp* (☎549-8060; cabins ②–③; sites $12; April–Oct).

The O'Keefe Ranch

Twelve kilometres short of Vernon, near the junction with the west-side Okanagan Lake road, stands the **O'Keefe Ranch**, a collection of early pioneer buildings and a tidy little museum that's well worth a half-hour's pause (daily; May, June, Sept & Oct 9am–5pm; July & Aug 9am–6.30pm; $5.50). In addition to a proficient summary of nineteenth-century frontier life, the museum contains an interesting section on Native Canadians' role in the two world wars. Some 25 percent of eligible men immediately volunteered for service – a tour of duty that did little to resolve their national dilemma, which the museum sums up pithily with the observation that they belong to that "unhappy group who lost the old but are unable to obtain the new". Outside, a complete period street includes a persuasively detailed general store where you can buy oddments from staff in old-time dress – a twee conceit, but one that fails to take the edge off the place's surprisingly successful evocation of an era. You feel the past most strongly in the church and graveyard, where the lovely building and its poignant handful of graves – three generations of O'Keefes, who first settled here in 1867 – capture the isolation and close-knit hardship of pioneer life.

The Okanagan

The vine- and orchard-covered hills and warm-water lakes of the **Okanagan** are in marked contrast to the rugged beauty of British Columbia's more mountainous interior, and have made the region not only one of Canada's most favoured fruit-growing areas but also one of its most popular summer holiday destinations. However, unless you want (occasionally) rowdy beach life or specifically enjoy mixing with families on their annual vacation, you'll probably want to ignore the area altogether in summer, despite its high word-of-mouth reputation. Few things can be as disorientating as stumbling onto one of the brash towns of the Okanagan after lazing through BC's mountain emptiness. Three main centres – **Vernon**, **Kelowna** and **Penticton**, ranging from north to south along 100-kilometre **Okanagan Lake** – together contain the lion's share of the province's interior population, and all lay on an array of accommodation and mostly tacky attractions for the summer hordes. As ever in BC, however, things improve immeasurably if you can slip away from the towns and head for the hills or quieter stretches of lakeshore.

On the plus side, the almost year-round Californian lushness that makes this "the land of beaches, peaches, sunshine and wine" means that, in the relative peace of **off season**, you can begin to experience the region's considerable potential charms: fruit trees in blossom, quiet lakeside villages and free wine tastings in local vineyards. Not only that – you can also expect room rates to be up to fifty percent less in off season. Kelowna is the biggest and probably best overall base at any time of the year, but local **buses** link all the towns and Greyhounds ply Hwy 97 on their way between Osoyoos and Kamloops or Salmon Arm.

Vernon

The beach scene is less frenetic in **VERNON** than elsewhere in the Okanagan. Located at the junction of Hwys 6 and 97 near the northern edge of Okanagan Lake, the town attracts fewer of the bucket-and-spade brigade, though the emphasis on fruit and the great outdoors is as strong as ever, and the main highway through town is bumper-to-bumper with motels, fast-food joints and ever more garish neon signs. On the whole it's easier to find a place to stay here than in Kelowna (see opposite) – but there are fewer reasons for wanting to do so.

Downtown Vernon centres on 32nd Avenue (Hwy 97) and leaves a far more gracious impression than the town's outskirts by virtue of its elegant tree-lined streets and five hundred listed buildings. The locals are an amenable and cosmopolitan bunch made up of British, Germans, Chinese and Salish natives, plus an abnormally large number of Jehovah's Witnesses, whose churches seem to have a virtual monopoly on religious observance in the town. The local **museum**, by the clock tower at 3009 32nd Ave, does the usual job on local history (Mon–Sat 10am–5pm; winter closed Mon; donation). At the southern entrance to town, **Polson Park** makes a green sanctuary from the crowds, but for beaches you have to head further afield to **Kalamalka Beach** on Kalamalka Lake, south of Vernon, or to **Kin Beach** on Okanagan Lake west on Okanagan Landing Road – both places have adjoining campgrounds.

Other outdoor recreation (but not camping) is on hand at **Silver Star Recreation Area**, a steep 22-kilometre drive to the northeast on 48th Avenue off Hwy 97, where in summer a **ski lift** (late June to mid-Oct daily 10am–5pm; $7.50) trundles to the top of Silver Star Mountain (1915m) for wide views and meadow-walking opportunities; the most-used trail wends from the summit back to the base area.

Practicalities

Vernon's **infocentre** is at 6326 Hwy 97 North (June–Aug daily 8am–6pm; Sept–May Mon–Fri 9am–5pm; ☎542-1415 or 1-800-665-0795 for reservations only), along with seasonal offices north and south of town on the main highway. The **Greyhound station** is on the corner of 30th Street and 31st Avenue (☎545-0527).

Local motels may well have **rooms** when nearby towns are full: a sound if bland choice is the *Sandman* at 4201 32nd St (☎542-4325 or 1-800-726-3626; ③). The *Polson Park Motel* (☎549-2231 or 1-800-480-2231; ②), opposite the eponymous park on 24th Avenue, is one of the cheapest options. The *Schell Motel*, 2810 35th Ave (☎545-1351; ②), tempts clients with a pool and sauna. **Campgrounds** near town all get busy, and you may have to trek along the lakeshore for some way to strike lucky; try *Dutch's Tent and Trailer Court* (☎545-1023; $16–20; May–Sept) at 15408 Kalamalka Rd, 3km south of Vernon near Kalamalka Beach. Much more rural is *Ellison Provincial Park*, 16km off to the southwest on Okanagan Lake (March–Nov; ☎494-6500; reservations accepted). To the north, 5km south of the O'Keefe Ranch (see opposite), is *Newport Beach Recreational Park* (☎542-7131; $15–20; mid-May to mid-Oct), situated at Westside Road on Okanagan Lake.

In the **food** department, there's plenty of cosmopolitan choice, especially amongst the many cafés and sandwich places. Downtown, try the *Café Belabasso* on the main street at 2921 30th Ave, or *The Italian Kitchen*, 3006 30th Ave. *Sir Winston's*, 2705 32nd St, is the downtown **pub** of choice.

Kelowna

If you're continuing south from Vernon, be sure to take the minor road on the western shore of Okanagan Lake – a quiet detour that offers something of the beauty for which the area is frequently praised, but which can be somewhat obscured by the commercialism of towns to the south. From the road, weaving through woods and small bays, the lake looks enchanting. The shore is often steep and there are few places to get down to the water – though at a push you might squeeze a tent between the trees for some unofficial camping.

If you want a summer suntan and cheek-by-jowl nightlife – neither of which you'd readily associate with the British Columbian interior – then **KELOWNA** ("grizzly bear" in the Salish dialect) – is probably the place to come. People had such a good time here in the summer of 1988 that the annual **Kelowna Regatta** turned into a full-blown and very un-Canadian **riot** in which the police were forced to wade in with truncheons and tear gas. The following year people from as far away as Vancouver responded to invitations to a showdown in similar vein, arriving with truckloads of rocks to hurl at the enemy; the main event has since been cancelled in its original format, but the beach and downtown bars remain as busy as ever. That this modest city should have fostered such an urban-style mêlée isn't all that surprising. Compared to other interior towns, Kelowna (pop. 92,000) ranks as a sprawling metropolis, and to the unsuspecting tourist its approaches come as an unpleasant surprise – particularly the appalling conglomeration of motels, garages and fast-food outlets on Hwy 97 at the north end of town.

That said, the lakefront and beaches, though heavily developed, aren't too bad, and off season Kelowna's undeniably pretty **downtown** can make a good couple of days' respite from mountains and forests. Its attractions are increasingly well-known across BC – a leading magazine rated it one of the top ten places to live in Canada – and quite remarkable jumps in population have taken place over the last few years: 35,000 people have moved here since 1990, creating something of a development nightmare for local planners. A full quarter of the population are retired. Main attractions are the public beach off **City Park**, a lovely green space that fronts downtown, and the strips along Lakeshore Road south of Kelowna's famed pontoon bridge, which tend to attract a younger, trendier crowd – **Rotary Beach** here is the windsurfers' hang-out, and **Boyce Gyro Park**, just north, is where the town's teenagers practise their preening and petting. Across the bridge and 2km up the lake's west bank, **Bear Creek Provincial Park** is a lovely spot with another great beach and campground, but it's also horrendously popular.

Kelowna owes its prosperity primarily to one man, Father Pandosy, a French priest who founded a mission here in 1859 and planted a couple of apple trees two years later. Much of Canada's **fruit** is now grown in the area – including virtually all the apricots, half the pears and plums, and thirty percent of the apples. The infocentre (see below) can point you to dozens of juice, fruit, food and forestry tours, but if you feel like sampling the more hedonistic fruits of Father Pandosy's labours, consider visiting one of the local **vineyards**, all of them known for their open-handed generosity with free samples after a tour of the premises. **Calona Wines** is Canada's second biggest winery and the Okanagan's oldest (founded 1932), and lies just six blocks off Hwy 97 at 1125 Richter Ave (summer daily 9am–4pm; tours every 30min; ☎762-9144), but the infocentre can provide a full rundown of smaller, more far-flung estates – almost every local winery is open to the public. All of them join together in early October to lay on the region's annual **wine festival**.

Getting away from Kelowna's crowds isn't easy, but the closest you come to shaking them off is by climbing **Knox Mountain**, the high knoll that overlooks the city to the north, just five minutes' drive (or 30min walk) from downtown. It offers lovely views over the lake and town, particularly at sunset, and there's a wooden observation tower to make the most of the panorama. RVs are kept out of the area by a barrier dropped at dusk, but if you took a sleeping bag up there – though perhaps not a tent – you might get away with an undisturbed night.

Practicalities

The **bus terminal** is at the east end of town at 2366 Leckie Rd on the corner of Harvey (Hwy 97), and sees off two buses daily to Calgary, Banff, Cache Creek and Kamloops respectively (☎860-3835). The **infocentre** (daily: June–Aug 8am–8pm; Sept–May 10am–4pm; ☎861-1515), five blocks back from the lake at 544 Harvey, has all the information you could possibly need. To **rent a bike**, go to Sports Rent, 3000 Pandosy St.

As in Penticton, there's an enormous number of motels and campgrounds in and around town. However, **accommodation** can still be a major headache in the height of summer unless you can get to one of the **motels** on northbound Hwy 97 early in the morning, but it's a neon- and traffic-infested area well away from downtown and the lake (prices drop the further out you go). The HI-affiliated **youth hostel**, the *SameSun Hostel*, is at 730 Bernard Ave (☎763-9800; ③). There's also an unofficial hostel downtown, the *Kelowna Backpackers' Hostel*, 2343 Pandosy St (☎763-6024): both hostels fill quickly in summer. Remarkably, there's only one central downtown **hotel**, the perfect-ly placed and very comfortable *Willow Inn* at 235 Queensway (☎762-2122 or 1-800-268-1055; ③) – ring or book very early for summer vacancies, and don't be deterred by the adjoining bar, which appears to be the headquarters of the Kelowna chapter of the Hell's Angels. As ever, the chain hotels also come up trumps: the reasonably central *Sandman Hotel*, 2130 Harvey Ave (☎860-6409 or 1-800-726-3626; ③), is a good mid-range bet. As a change from motels you might try for a room in one of two highly rated B&B places: the *Casa Rio Lakeside*, 485 Casa Rio Drive, turn off Hwy 97 at Campbell Road (☎769-0076 or 1-800-313-1033; ④), which has a private sandy beach; or the outly-ing *Grapevine*, 2621 Longhill Rd (☎860-5580; ④; phone for directions).

If you're camping, all sites are pretty expensive, and in high season some places may only accept reservations for three days or more: mosquitoes can also be a problem. If you want to stay reasonably close to the action, three **campgrounds** conveniently back onto Lakeshore Road: the *Willow Creek Family Campground*, 3316 Lakeshore Rd (☎762-6302; $15–20; April–Oct), which has free showers and a grassy tenting area flanking a sandy beach; the *Hiawatha RV Park*, 3787 Lakeshore Rd, with separate tent-ing area, laundry, heated pool and free hot showers (☎861-4837; $27–35; mid-March to mid-Oct), and the *Lakeside*, 654 Cook Rd (☎860-4072; $25–32; year-round) with free hot showers, pool and laundry near Rotary Beach. To be sure of camping space, arrive early at the *Bear Creek Provincial Park*, 9km west of town on Westside Road off Hwy 97 on the west side of the lake (March–Nov; ☎494-6500; showers and most facilities; $15.50): reservations are accepted (see box on p.644). Most of the other campgrounds are on the other side of the lake at Westbank, a left turn off Hwy 97 on Boucherie Road just over the pontoon bridge (but really only accessible by car) – try *West Bay Beach*, 3745 West Bay Rd (☎768-3004; $14–27.50; April–Oct).

Most **eating** places are crammed into the small downtown area. The variety is large, and a short walk should offer something to suit most tastes and budgets. Many trav-ellers and young locals head for *Kelly O'Brian's* on Bernard Street, opposite the cine-ma, which has an "Irish" bar atmosphere and reasonable food. Despite its rather slick cocktail-lounge ambience, *Earl's Hollywood on Top*, 211 Bernard Ave at the corner of Abbott (☎763-2777 or 763-3121), is good for ribs, seafood and steaks; go early to get a table on the upstairs patio. At the top of the tree you could splurge at *De Montreuil*, 368 Bernard Ave (☎860-5508), widely considered the best restaurant in the Okanagan. Also good in the top range is the *Williams Inn*, 526 Laurence Ave (☎763-5136).

Penticton

PENTICTON is a corruption of the Salish phrase *pen tak tin* – "a place to stay forever" – but this is not a sobriquet the most southerly of the Okanagan's big towns even remotely deserves. Its summer daily average of ten hours of sunshine ranks it higher than Honolulu, making tourism its biggest industry after fruit (this is "Peach City"). That, along with Penticton's proximity to Vancouver and the States, keeps prices well over the odds and ensures that the town and beaches are swarming with watersports jocks, cross-country travellers, RV skippers and lots of happy families. Off the beaches there's some festival or other playing virtually every day of the year to keep the pun-ters entertained, the key ones being the spring-celebrating **Blossom Festival** in April and the **Peach Festival** at the end of July.

Most leisure pastimes in Penticton – water-orientated ones in particular – take place on or near Okanagan Lake, just ten blocks from the town centre. **Okanagan Beach** is the closest sand to downtown and is usually covered in oiled bodies for most of its one-kilometre stretch; **Skaha Beach**, 4km south of town on Skaha Lake, is a touch quieter and trendier – both close at midnight, and sleeping on them is virtually out of the ques-tion. If the beaches don't appeal, you can take your sun from a cruise on the lake aboard the *Casabella Princess*, which departs from 45 East Lakeshore Drive (call ☎493-5551 for times and prices).

If you're determined to sightsee, the **museum** at 785 Main St has a panoply of predictable Canadiana (Mon–Fri 10am–5pm; admission by donation) and you can take tours around the SS *Sicamous*, a beached **paddlesteamer** off Lakeshore Drive on the Kelowna side of town (take in the lovely rose gardens alongside the boat while you're here). Just off Main Street there's the **South Okanagan Art Gallery**, 11 Ellis St, which often carries high-quality shows, and apparently qualifies as the "world's first solar-powered art gallery" (Tues–Fri 10am–5pm, Sat & Sun 1–5pm). More tempting perhaps, and an ideal part of a day's stopover – possibly to fit in before a sprawl on the beach – is a trip to the **Tin Whistle Brewery**, 954 West Eckhardt Ave (drop-in tours and tastings year-round), which offers three English-type ales and a celebrated Peaches and Cream beer (summer only). If your taste is for wine rather than beer, head for the **Blue Mountain Vineyard**, Oliver Ranch Road (☎497-8224), or **Casobello Wines Vineyard**, 2km south of town off Hwy 97 on Skaha Lake Road, both of which offer tours and tastings. Otherwise, Penticton's main diversions are the curse of all Canadian tourist towns – the water slides.

Practicalities

Arriving by Greyhound, you'll pull into the **bus depot** just off Main Street between Robinson and Ellis streets (☎493-4101); Penticton is a major intersection of routes, with buses bound for Vancouver (5 daily), Kamloops (2 daily), Nelson and points east (2 daily), and Wenatchee/Spokane (WA) in the States (1 daily; change at Osoyoos). The downtown area is small and easy to negotiate, particularly after a visit to the big **infocentre** at 185 Lakeside Drive (daily 9am–5pm, stays open later in summer; ☎493-4055 or 1-800-663-5052); if it's shut there's a big map and notice board outside, plus smaller summer offices north and south of town on Hwy 97. All three concentrate on recreational pursuits, and dozens of specialist shops around town rent out equipment for every conceivable activity. For **bikes**, try Riverside Bike Rental at 75 Riverside Drive on the west side of the lakefront (May–Sept daily).

Although Penticton boasts a brimful of **accommodation**, it doesn't make finding a room in summer any easier. In high season it's best to head straight for the infocentre and ask for help, and if this fails there are so many **motels** you can easily walk from one to the next in the hope of striking lucky; most of the cheaper fall-backs line the messy southern approach to the town along Hwy 97. Two of the best and more central choices – though you have to pay for them – are the *Tiki Shores Condominium Beach Resort* on the lake at 914 Lakeshore Drive (☎492-8769; ④–⑥), with luxurious doubles, and the big *Penticton Inn*, 333 Martin St (☎492-3600 or 1-800-665-2221; ③–⑥). Dropping down to mid-range places there's the *Sandman Hotel*, part of a reliable chain opposite the Convention Centre at 939 Burnaby Ave (☎493-7151 or 1-800-726-3626; ③–④). If you're after somewhere cheap and location doesn't matter too much, try the *Plaza Motel*, 1485 Main St (☎492-8631; ②–③), halfway between the town's two lakes; the *Waterfront Inn*, 3688 Parkview St (☎492-8228 or 1-800-563-6006; ②–③); and the *Valley Star Motel*, 3455 Skaha Lake Rd (☎492-7205; ②–③), a couple of blocks from Skaha Lake. The HI-affiliatd **youth hostel** is at 464 Ellis St (☎492-3992; ①).

Most **campgrounds** have their full-up signs out continuously in summer, and you may well have trouble if you arrive without a reservation. The best and therefore busiest sites are along the lake, and the bulk of the second-rank spots near the highway on the southern approaches. Recommended are the *South Beach Gardens*, 3815 Skaha Lake Rd (☎492-0628; $17–22; April–Oct), or *Wright's Beach Camp*, south of town on Hwy 97 on Lake Skaha (☎492-7120; $20–30; May–Sept). If you want to be away from town make for the *Camp-Along Tent and Trailer Park*, 6km south of the town off Hwy 97 in an apricot orchard overlooking Skaha Lake (☎497-5584 or 1-800-968-5267; $17–25).

Budget **eating** choices don't extend much beyond the fast-food joints and cafés bunched largely around Main Street: try *Taco Grande*, 452 Main St, for Mexican and cheap breakfasts, or the *Elite*, 340 Main St, the best overall for basic burgers, soup and salads. *Theo's* at 687 Main St is a friendly, crowded and highly rated Greek place that does big portions, while *Earl's*, part of a reliable chain, is at 101 1848 Main St (☎493-7455). For something different and more upmarket, search out *Salty's Beach House*, 988 Lakeshore Drive, a restaurant that's eccentric in all departments – setting, service and menu – but delivers excellent food.

Highway 3: the border towns

Unless you're crossing the US/Canada border locally, British Columbia's faintly tawdry necklace of border towns between Hope and the Albertan border along **Hwy 3** is as good a reason as any for taking a more northerly route across the central part of the province. None amounts to much, and you'd be advised to whisk through by car or Greyhound; if you have to break the journey, aim to do it in **Salmo** or **Castlegar**, towns on which some of the Kootenays' charm has rubbed off. Things are more interesting around **Osoyoos** and **Keremeos**, where the road enters a parched desert landscape after climbing from Hope (see p.741) through the gripping mountain scenery of the Coastal Ranges, passing en route through **Manning Provincial Park**.

If you're crossing over **the border** hereabouts, incidentally, don't be lulled by the remote customs posts into expecting an easy passage: if you don't hold a Canadian or US passport you can expect the sort of grilling you'd get at major entry points.

Manning Provincial Park

One of the few parks in the Coast and Cascade ranges, **Manning Provincial Park** parcels up a typical assortment of mountain, lake and forest scenery about 60km south of Princeton and is conveniently bisected by Hwy 3. Even if you're just passing through it's an idea to walk at least one of the short **trails** off the road, the best of which is the flower-festooned Rhododendron Flats path at the park's western edge. The most popular drive within the park is the fifteen-kilometre sideroad to **Cascade Lookout**, a viewpoint over the Similkameen Valley and its amphitheatre of mountains; a gravel road carries on another 6km from here to **Blackwall Peak**, the starting point for the **Heather Trail** (10km one way), renowned for its swaths of summer wildflowers. Other manageable day hikes leave the south side of the main highway, the majority accessed from a rough road to Lightning Lake just west of the park visitor centre.

The **park visitor centre**, 1km east of the resort (daily May–Sept 9am–8pm), is good for trail leaflets and has history and natural history exhibitions. **Accommodation** at the *Manning Park Resort* (☎840-8822; ④), on Hwy 3 almost exactly midway between Princeton and Hope (64km), runs to cabins and chalets, but all these go quickly in summer. There are also four provincial **campgrounds** ($9.50–15.50) on and off the highway, the best close to the road being *Hampton* and *Mule Deer*, 4km and 8km east of the visitor centre respectively.

Highway 3 from Princeton

Lacklustre low hills ripple around **PRINCETON**'s dispersed collection of drab, rather jerry-built houses. The **motels** – of which there are plenty – group around a large and grim lumber mill on the east side of town, but in many ways you're better off hanging on for Keremeos. If circumstances dump you in town overnight, try the *Riverside Motel*

(☎295-6232; ①–②) at 307 Thomas Ave, three blocks north of the town centre, with fifteen nice individual log cabins. The **bus depot** is at the west end of town by the good-value, cheap-and-cheerful *Village Kitchen Restaurant*, not so far from the virtually redundant **infocentre** (year-round daily 9am–5pm; ☎295-3103), which is housed in an old Canadian Pacific rail wagon at 195 Bridge St.

HEDLEY, an old gold-mining hamlet is these days just a single street with great scenery and a couple of motels. Try the *Colonial Inn Bed & Breakfast* (☎292-8131; ④), an historic 1930s house built by the Kelowna Exploration Gold Mining Company to wine and dine potential investors; it has just five rooms, so book ahead. Beyond Hedley, off the highway, lies **Bromley Rock**, a lovely if oversanitized picnic stop looking down on the white water of the Similkameen River. Also west of the village is the *Stemwinder Provincial Park* **campground** ($9.50; April–Oct).

West of Keremeos (see below), Hwy 3 retraces the historic **Dewdney Trail**, a 468-kilometre mule track used in the 1860s to link Hope (p.741) with the Kootenay gold-fields. Another of British Columbia's extremely picturesque patches of road, for much of the way it follows the ever-narrowing Similkameen Valley, backed by ranks of pines and white-topped mountains. To explore some of the backcountry off the highway, take the 21-kilometre gravel road (signed just west of Keremeos) south into the heart of **Cathedral Provincial Park**, a spectacular upland enclave with an unserviced camp-ground and 32km of marked trails.

Keremeos

Highway 3 meanders eventually to pretty little **KEREMEOS**, whose native name sup-posedly means "to cut across the flats from the creek". The local landscape lurches sud-denly into a more rural mode, thanks mainly to a climate that blesses the region with the longest growing season in the country – hence the tag, "Fruit Stand Capital of Canada". Keremeos, whose attractive situation rivals Nelson's, spreads over a dried-up lake bed, with hills and mountains rising from the narrow plain on all sides. Lush, irrigated orchards surround the town, offset in spring by huge swaths of flowers across the val-ley floor, and depending on the season you can pick up fruit and veg from stands dotted more or less everywhere: cherries, apricots, peaches, pears, apples, plums – even grapes – all grow in abundance. If you're not tempted by the food, however, you may be by the **wine tastings** at St Laszlo Vineyards (☎499-2856), 1km east of town on Hwy 3.

Keremeos itself is a rustic, two-street affair that's almost unspoilt by neon or urban clut-ter. A few shopfronts are oldish, and several make a stab at being heritage houses – the *Old Fish and Chipper* on Main Street, for example – and though there's little to see or do (bar the inevitable small-town museum), it's a pleasant spot to spend the night. The central **info-centre** is at 415 7th Ave near Memorial Park (June–Sept daily 9am–5pm; ☎499-5225). There are a couple of **motels** locally: the nicest is the *Similkameen* (☎499-5984; ②; April to mid-Oct), 1km west of the centre in open country surrounded by lawns and orchards.

Osoyoos

Beyond Keremeos the road climbs from some 46km, eventually unfolding a dramatic view, far below, of **OSOYOOS** – meaning "gathered together" – and a sizable lake sur-rounded by bare, ochre hills. Descending, you enter one of Canada's strangest land-scapes – a bona fide desert of half-bare, scrub-covered hills, sand, lizards, cactus, snakes, and Canada's lowest average rainfall (around 25cm per year). Temperatures here are regularly 10°C higher than in Nelson, less than a morning's drive away, enabling exotic fruit like bananas and pomegranates to be grown and prompting Osoy-oos to declare itself the "Spanish Capital of Canada". The houses here are supposed to have been restyled to give the place an Iberian flavour to match its climate, but on the ground it's almost impossible to find any trace of the conversion.

The town is otherwise distinguished only by its position beside **Lake Osoyoos** in the Okanagan Valley – Hwy 97, which passes through the town, is the main route into the Okanagan region. In summer the place comes alive with swimmers and boaters, drawn to some of the warmest waters of any lake in Canada, and with streams of American RVs slow-tailing their way northwards to where the real action is. The relative lack of crowds and strange scenery might persuade you to do your beach-bumming in Osoyoos, though you may be pushed to find space in any of the town's twenty or so **hotels** and **motels** during high season: cheap choices include the *Avalon* 9106 Main St (☎495-6334 or 1-800-264-5999; ②) and *Falcon*, 7106 Main St (☎495-7544; ③). Most of the motels are across the causeway on the southeastern shore of the lake, alongside the **bus stop** and the vivid-pink Pay 'n' Save. For more choice and help, contact the **infocentre** at the junction of Hwys 3 and 97 (☎495-7142 or 1-888-676-9667). You're more likely to get a place in one of the half-dozen local **campgrounds** – try the *Cabana Beach* (☎495-7705; $17–25; April–Oct) at 2231 Lakeshore Drive.

Moving on from Osoyoos involves a major decision if you're travelling by car or bike, the choices being to continue east on Hwy 3, or to strike north on Hwy 97 through the Okanagan to the Trans-Canada Highway. If you're on a Greyhound, the bus heads north and the decision can be deferred until Penticton, the major parting of the ways for services in this part of BC.

Midway, Greenwood and Grand Forks

At **MIDWAY**, some 65km east of Osoyoos, something of the desert atmosphere lingers, the hills strange, broad whalebacks cut by open valleys and covered in coarse scrub and brown-baked grass. The hamlet's handful of scattered homes are like a windblown and wistful ghost town, making an evocative backdrop for the overgrown train tracks and tiny **railway museum** housed alongside a rusted minuscule steam engine. It's a fascinating little spot. Two other railway museums have recently opened locally: one next to the old CPR railway station, the other next to the Kettle Valley Railway station 3km out of the village. For more background, contact the **infocentre** on Hwy 3 (June–Sept 9am–6pm; ☎449-2614). To **stay**, check in to the *Midway Motor Inn*, 622 Palmerston St, (☎449-2662; ②) or put up a tent at the *Riverfront Municipal Campground* three blocks off Hwy 3 or the small *Midway Mobile Home and RV Park*, located on the north side of the highway at 925 13th Ave (☎449-2618; ①; May–Oct).

East out of town, the scenery along Hwy 3 begins to change from a flatter, drier landscape of bleached grass and sagebrush to rather more bland meandering hills. At **GREENWOOD**, however, the pines reappear, heralding a wild, battered brute of a village, which has suffered from the closure of its mines and can't muster much more than a handful of old buildings and some abandoned workings. The all-but-redundant **infocentre** is housed on the main road at 214 South Copper St (mid-June to mid-Sept daily; ☎455-6355). You're pretty sure of a welcome in any of the local **motels**, cheapest of which is the *Evening Star*, 798 North Government St (☎445-6733; ①–②), at the eastern entrance to town. For **camping** there are a couple of small provincial park sites: *Jewel Lake* ($6; June–Sept), 12km east of Greenwood off Hwy 3; and *Boundary Creek* ($9.50; April–Oct), just west of town off Hwy 3.

GRAND FORKS is not grand at all – it's very small and very dull and little more than a perfunctory transit settlement built on a river flat. Several Greyhound **buses** drop in daily, probably the biggest thing to happen to the place, stopping at *Stanley's*, which is the spot for sustenance unless you shop at the big Overwaitea supermarket alongside. The small **museum** by the traffic lights is the standard small-town model and can be seen in about the time it takes for the lights to change. The **infocentre** is close by (☎442-

2833). Just north of town, **Christina Lake** – which claims BC's warmest water – is a modestly unspoilt summer resort with lots of swimming, boating and camping opportunities (two other BC lakes make similar claims for their waters). A dozen or so motels and campgrounds sprout along its shore, with about the same number in and around the town itself, but it's doubtful that you'd want to use them except in an emergency. For information on the area, contact the Chamber of Commerce on Hwy 3 (☎447-6161).

Trail and Rossland

TRAIL is home to the world's largest lead and zinc smelter, a vast industrial complex whose chimneys cast a dismal shadow over the village's few houses. There's no reason to stop here and you'll probably want to head straight on to **ROSSLAND**, 10km west, which also relies on Trail's smelter for employment, and which also has a mining foundation – gold this time, some $125 million-worth of which was gouged from the surrounding hills around the turn of the century (that's $2 billion-worth at today's prices). If you're into mining heritage, a tour of the **Le Roi Gold Mine** – once one of the world's largest, with 100km of tunnels – and the adjoining **Rossland Historical Museum** will entertain you with fascinating technical and geological background (mid-May to mid-Sept daily 9am–5pm; $7).

The **infocentre** (May–Oct daily 9am–8pm; ☎362-7722), in the museum at the junction of the town's two main roads, is most useful for details of the **Nancy Greene Provincial Park** northwest of town. Though the park and recreation area is best known for its world-class skiing – its **Red Mountain Ski Area** is a training ground for the Canadian national team – it's also excellent for hiking, an outdoor commodity that isn't easy to come by in these parts. There's an HI-affiliated **youth hostel**, the *Mountain Shadow Hostel* at 2125 Columbia Ave (☎362-7160); a provincial park **campground** ($7) at the junction of Hwys 3 and 3B; and several resort hotels; or try the upmarket twelve-unit *Ram's Head Inn*, 3km west of Rossland on Hwy 3B (☎362-9577; ③–⑥), with hot tubs and bike rental.

Castlegar

CASTLEGAR is a strange, diffuse place with no obvious centre, probably because roads and rivers – this is where the Kootenay meets the Columbia – make it more a transport hub than a community. In its time it was famous for its immigrant **Doukhobor** or "Spirit Wrestler" population, members of a Russian sect who fled religious persecution in 1899 from Russia and brought their pacifist-agrarian lifestyle to western Canada. By the 1920s BC had around ninety Doukhobor settlements, each with a cooperative, communal population of around sixty. They arrived in Castlegar in 1908, establishing at least 24 villages in the area, each with Russian names meaning things like "the beautiful", "the blessed" or "consolation". Accomplished farmers, they laboured under the motto "Toil and a Peaceful Life", creating highly successful orchards, farms, sawmills and packing plants. Although their way of life waned after the death of their leader Peter Verigin in 1924, killed by a bomb planted in his railway carriage, the Doukhobors' considerable industry and agricultural expertise transformed the Castlegar area; many locals still practise the old beliefs – Doukhobor numbers are around 5000 across the region – and Russian is still spoken and taught in local schools. These days there's also a breakaway radical sect, the Freedomites, or Sons of Freedom, infamous for their eye-catching demonstrations – of which fires and nude parades are just two – against materialism and other morally dubious values.

Much of the community's heritage has been collected in the **Doukhobor Village Museum** (May–Sept daily 9am–5pm; $3; ☎365-6622), just off the main road on the right after you cross the big suspension bridge over the Kootenay River. A Doukhobor descendant is on hand to take you through the museum, which houses a winsome display of farm machinery, handmade tools and traditional Russian clothing that's intriguing as much for its alien context as for its content. If you've built up a massive appetite, try the Doukhobor *Spinning Wheel* **restaurant** alongside. The ambience is bizarrely austere – the walls are bare but for a few crafts and jumble-sale notices – and the menu an exercise in strait-laced cuisine: Doukhobor chefs face something of a daily creative challenge, given that they can't use meat, fish or alcohol in cooking. To meet it they produce just two set dinners daily. One menu brings you borscht, bread, tart and coffee, and the other delivers tasty and shudderingly stodgy things called *varenyky, galoopsie, pyrogy* and *nalesnici*. For a further taste of Doukhobor culture, visit the evocative **Zuckerburg Island Heritage Park** off 7th Avenue, named after a local Doukhobor teacher who built a log Russian Orthodox Chapel House here: it was bought and restored by the town in 1981, and is reached by a ninety-metre pedestrian suspension bridge.

Castlegar's **infocentre** (year-round; ☎365-6313) is at 1995 6th Ave off the main road as you leave town for Grand Forks over the Columbia bridge. There are some half-dozen motels in and around town: the best **motel** – small, and with a nice view – is the *Cozy Pines* on Hwy 3 on the western edge of town at 2100 Crestview Crescent (☎365-5613; ②). Closer in, the modern and attractive *Best Western Fireside Motor Inn*, 1810 8th Ave at the junction of Hwys 3 and 22 (☎365-2128 or 1-800-499-6399; ③), is a touch more expensive. Three kilometres out of town to the west on Hwy 3 is the *Castlegar RV Park and Campground*, 1725 Mannix Rd (☎365-2337; $12–18; May–Oct), with rural setting, separate tenting area, free hot showers, laundry and restaurant. There are also a regional and two provincial park **campgrounds** in the vicinity: *Champion Lakes* (no showers; $12; May–Oct), 10km from Hwy 3B, just west of the junction with Hwy 3; *Pass Creek Regional Park*, with a sandy beach, ($9; May–Sept), 2km west off Hwy 3A at the Kootenay River Bridge; and the *Syringa Provincial Park* ($12; April–Oct), 19km north of Hwy 3 at Castelgar on the east side of Lower Arrow Lake.

Salmo

A classic stretch of scenic road, Hwy 3 climbs from Salmo to the fruit-growing plains around Creston via **Kootenay Pass** (1774m) – though the views are less of spectacular mountains than of a pretty tracery of creeks and rivers crashing down through forest on all sides. This is one of the highest main roads in the country – it's frequently closed by bad weather – and it has no services for 70km after Creston, so check your petrol before setting out. If you're cycling, brace yourself for a fifty-kilometre uphill slog, but the reward is an unexpected and stunning lake at the pass, where there's a pull-off picnic area and views of high peaks in the far distance.

Despite the large volume of traffic converging on it along Hwy 3 and Hwy 6, tiny **SALMO** somehow manages to retain a pioneer feel with most of its tidy wooden buildings are fronted by verandas, decked with baskets of flowers in summer. The **infocentre** (mid-June to mid-Sept; ☎357-9332) is on the corner of Hwy 6 and 4th Street, but it doesn't have a lot to promote apart from the "World's Smallest Telephone Box", next to the *Salcrest Motel* on the south side of town, and the **museum** (May–Sept Mon–Fri 10am–4pm), a more credible attraction housed in a picturesque white-painted building at 4th Street and Railway Avenue, which charts the vicissitudes of pioneer life and hosts the odd travelling exhibition. In winter there's **skiing** at the Salmo ski area, 2km east of town.

Buses usually pull in here for a long rest stop at the terminal by the Petro-Canada garage on the north side of the village. If you need to overnight, use either of the two central motels: the *Reno*, 123 Railway Ave (☎357-9937; ①), one block east of the bus terminal, or the *Salcrest*, 110 Motel Ave (☎357-9557; ②), at the junction of Hwys 3 and 6. The nearest **campground** is the *Hidden Creek Guest Ranch* (☎357-2266; $7–12; May–Oct), 6km north of town on Hwy 6.

For **food**, try *Charlie's Pizza and Spaghetti House*, an old-style diner on 4th Street. Just up the road, the *Silver Dollar Pub* is the town's favourite **bar**, with pool tables, a jukebox and lots of good ol' boys in an atmospheric wooden interior. Salmo Foods, opposite the bar, is the best supermarket for stocking up.

Creston

Don't stop in **CRESTON** unless you're a bird-watcher, want a taste of the terminally bland or such sightseeing frippery as "Canada's best mural" (the original, in McDowell's department store, had spawned another nine pictures around town at last count). The **infocentre** is in a log cabin (one of the town's few buildings of interest) on the east side of town at 1711 Canyon St (☎428-4342): use it if by mischance you need **accommodation**, though with twenty or so motels and campgrounds to choose from you probably won't be fighting for a bed. The cheapest and most central spot is the *Hotel Creston*, 1418 Canyon St (☎428-9321; ①); motels on the town's fringes offer more salubrious, if slightly costlier alternatives. As well as Greyhounds passing through along Hwy 3, Empire Bus Lines runs an early-morning service from here to Spokane, WA (Mon & Thurs–Sun). If you're passing through, you want to pause for the **Creston Valley Museum and Archives**, 219 Devon St (daily summer 9am–6pm, by appointment the rest of the year; ☎428-9262), known for its replica Kuntenai (Ktunaxa) canoe. Similar canoes, with their downpointed ends, are only found elsewhere in the world in parts of eastern Russia, underlining the fact that millennia ago migrations took place across the Bering Straits into North America.

Probably the best reason to spend time locally is the **Creston Valley Wildlife Management Area**, located 10km northwest of town off Hwy 3. Creston overlooks a broad section of valley and lowlands – relatively rare commodities in BC, home to the idly meandering Kootenay River. Over the years the river has repeatedly burst its banks, creating a rich alluvial plain beloved by farmers, and producing the lush medley of orchards and verdant fields that fringe Creston. Much of the flood plain and its wetlands, however – the so-called "Valley of the Swans" – have been preserved in their original state, creating a haven for birds and waterfowl. This is one of the world's largest nesting osprey populations, while a total of 250 species have been recorded in the confines of the Creston Management Area (not to mention otters, moose and other animals). Birds can be seen from several points, but for full details of the area visit the sanctuary's Wildlife Centre, which provides telescopes and lookouts, a library and theatre, and a wide range of guided walks and canoe trips through the area's forest, marsh and grasslands habitats.

The Kootenays

The Kootenays is one of the most attractive and unvisited parts of British Columbia, and one of the most loosely defined. It consists essentially of two major north–south valleys – the Kootenay and the Columbia, which are largely taken up by **Kootenay Lake** and **Upper** and **Lower Arrow Lakes** – and three intervening mountain ranges – the Purcells, Selkirks and Monashees, whose once-rich mineral deposits formed the kernel of the province's early mining industry. **Nelson** is the key town, slightly peripheral to the Kootenays' rugged core, but a lovely place, and one of the few provincial towns that holds out real attractions in its own right. Scattered lakeside hamlets, notably **Kaslo** and **Nakusp**, make excellent bases for excursions into mountain scenery which has a pristine quality not found outside the Kootenays. Watery activities – canoeing and fishing in particular – are excellent, and you can also explore the ramshackle mining heritage of near-ghost towns like **Sandon** and **New Denver**, or wallow in the hot springs at Nakusp. Many of these towns and villages also have more than their fair share of artists, painters and writers, lending the region considerable cultural lustre.

Getting around the region is tricky without private transport, for there are next to no public services, which is a shame because the roads here are amongst the most scenic in a province noted for its scenery. Even with your own car, there's no way to do the Kootenays justice without retracing your steps at times. You can dip in and out of the region from the Trans-Canada Highway (to the north) or Hwy 3 (to the south), but any trans-Kootenay route is more attractive than either of these main highways: the most **scenic routes** are Hwy 31A from Kaslo to New Denver, and Hwy 6 from New Denver to Vernon. Given no time constraints, your best strategy would be to enter from Creston and exit via Vernon, which sets you up for the Okanagan.

Highway 3A to Kootenay Bay

Starting from just north of Creston, **Hwy 3A** picks a slow, twisting course up the eastern shore of **Kootenay Lake** to the free car ferry at Kootenay Bay. Apart from the ample scenic rewards of the lake and the mountains beyond it, the highway is almost completely empty for all of its 79km, and none of the villages marked on maps amount to anything more than scattered houses hidden in the woods. The only noteworthy sight is the **Glass House** (daily May, June, Sept & Oct 9am–5pm; July & Aug 8am–8pm; $5), midway up the lake 7km south of **BOSWELL**, which ranks highly in the list of Canada's more bizarre offerings. Constructed entirely from embalming bottles, the house was built by a Mr David Brown in 1955 after 35 years in the funeral business – "to indulge", so the wonderfully po-faced pamphlet tells you, "a whim of a peculiar nature". The retired mortician travelled widely, visiting friends in the funeral profession until he'd collected 500,000 bottles – that's 250 tonnes' worth – to build his lakeside retirement home. The family continued to live here until curious tourists took the upper hand. Nearby **accommodation** is provided by the four-unit *Heidelburg Inn* (☎223-8263; ②) overlooking the lake and the lakeside *Mountain Shores Resort and Marina* (☎223-8258; ③; April–Sept), a combination of ten motel-type rooms, cottages and **campground** ($14–23) with store, hot showers and heated outdoor pool. There's another smaller campground, *Kootenay Kampsites* (☎223-8488; $16–20; May–Oct), 39km north of Creston with rustic, well-treed sites, laundry and hot showers.

At **GRAY CREEK**, a few kilometres onward, check out the superb Gray Creek Store, which boasts the once-in-a-lifetime address of 1979 Chainsaw Avenue and claims, with some justification, to be "The Most Interesting Store You've Ever Seen". The shop basically *is* Gray Creek – it's the sort of place you go to get your chainsaw fixed and where real lumberjacks come for their red-checked shirts. There are two lakeside **campgrounds** nearby: the *Old Crow* (☎227-9495; $12; May–Oct) and the small *Lockhart Beach* provincial park campground ($9.50; April–Oct) with RV and tent sites 13km south of Gray Creek and 20km south of Kootenay Bay (see below).

CRAWFORD BAY and **KOOTENAY BAY** are names on the map that refer in the flesh to the most fleeting of settlements, the latter also being the **ferry terminal** for boats to Balfour on the west shore. Crawford Bay, 3.5km from the terminal, boasts the Kootenay Forge, an old-world forge, where in summer you can often watch blacksmiths working. The area has also long been famous for the Yasodhara Ashram (☎227-9224), a spiritual retreat established over thirty years ago. As a place to stay, this side of the crossing is a touch brighter, and there's an **infocentre** (June–Sept daily 9am–5pm; ☎227-9267) just off the road at Crawford Bay, which can help you find some of the nicer accommodation tucked away in the woods nearby. The cheapest **motel** is the *Last Chance Swiss* (☎227-9477; ②), near the ferry dock, which includes a restaurant (Easter to mid-Oct). The more expensive *Wedgewood Manor Country Inn* (☎227-9233 or 1-800-862-0022; ④–⑤; April to mid-Oct), a 1910 heritage building set amidst fifty acres of gardens and estate, is upmarket and extremely pleasant, but you'll have to book well in advance. The better of two **campgrounds** here is the nicely wooded *Kokanee Chalets, Motel, Campground & RV Park* on Hwy 3A (☎227-9292 or 1-800-448-9292; mid-April to mid-Oct): as well as tent and RV sites ($16–22) it also has motel and chalet rooms around seven minutes' walk from the beach (③–④); note, however, that there's also a choice of three reasonable campgrounds across the water in Balfour.

The nine-kilometre, forty-minute **ferry crossing** – purportedly the longest free ferry crossing in the world – is beautiful. Boats leave every fifty minutes from June to September, and every two hours the rest of the year, but it's a first-come, first-served affair, and in high summer unless you're a pedestrian or bike passenger it may be a couple of sailings before your turn comes round.

Balfour and Ainsworth Hot Springs

Not quite the fishing village it's billed as, **BALFOUR** is a fairly shoddy and dispersed collection of motels, garages and cafés – albeit in verdant surroundings – designed to catch the traffic rolling on and off the Kootenay Lake ferry. RV **campgrounds** line the road to Nelson for about 2km, the quietest being those furthest from the terminal, but a much better option is the campground at Kokanee Creek Provincial Park, about 10km beyond Balfour ($12 fee May–Sept; reservations possible – see box on p.644; April–Oct) with a sandy beach. The handiest **motel** for the ferry is the *Balfour Beach Inn and Motel* (☎229-4235; ③; April–Nov), with heated indoor pool but convenient also for the small pebbly beach just north of the terminal.

About 15km north of Balfour on Hwy 31 – look out for the telegraph poles wearing ties – **AINSWORTH HOT SPRINGS** is home to some one hundred residents – a town by local standards. The tasteful *Ainsworth Hot Springs Resort* (☎229-4212 or 1-800-668-1171; ④–⑥) is ideal if you want to stay over while taking in the scalding water of the **mineral springs** (daily 8.30am–9.30pm; day pass $10, single visit $6), though the chalets are expensive and, despite the lovely views and the health-giving properties of the waters, local opinion rates the Nakusp Hot Springs (see p.768) rather more highly. Note that you don't need to stay in the resort to sample the springs. The nicest local **motel** is the cheaper and smaller eight-room *Mermaid Lodge and Motel* (☎229-4969 or 1-888-229-4963; ②) alongside the springs and pools. Cave enthusiasts might want to take a guided tour of **Cody Caves Provincial Park**, 12km up a rough, well-signposted gravel sideroad off Hwy 3 3km north of town. From the end of a road it's a twenty-minute walk to the caves, whose kilometre or more of galleries can be seen by tour only: contact HiAdventure Corporation (☎353-7425).

A touch further up the increasingly beautiful Hwy 31 comes the self-contained **Woodbury Resort and Marina** (☎353-7177; ②–③; year-round), a collection of motel, cottages, campground ($15–18), restaurant, pub, store, heated pool, boat rentals and watersport facilities; pitched on the lakeshore with lovely views and a small beach, it makes an attractive long-term accommodation prospect if you're tenting. Directly opposite is the **Woodbury Mining Museum** (July–Sept daily 9am–6pm; $4; ☎354-4470), a quaint pioneer building crammed with mining regalia and the entrance to a thirty-minute underground tour of the old lead, zinc and silver workings.

Kaslo and around

KASLO must rate as one of British Columbia's most attractive and friendliest little villages. Huddled at the edge of Kootenay Lake and dwarfed by towering mountains, its half-dozen streets are lined with picture-perfect wooden homes and flower-filled gardens. It started life as a sawmill in 1889 and turned into a boom town with the discovery of silver in 1893; diversification, and the steamers that plied the lakes, saved it from the cycle of boom and bust that ripped the heart out of so many similar towns. Today Kaslo remains an urbane and civilized community whose thousand or so citizens work hard at keeping it that way, supporting a cultural centre, art galleries, rummage sales – even a concert society.

The **town hall**, a distinctive green and white wooden building dating from 1898, is an architectural gem by any standards, as is the church opposite. Yet Kaslo's main attraction is the SS *Moyie*, the oldest surviving **paddlesteamer** in North America (daily tours May to mid-Sept 9am–7pm; $5), which ferried men, ore and supplies along the mining routes from 1897 until the relatively recent advent of reliable roads. Similar steamers were the key to the Kootenays' early prosperity, their shallow draught and featherweight construction allowing them to nose into the lakes' shallowest waters and unload close to the shore. They were, in local parlance, "able to float on dew". Canada claims just six of the 24 paddlesteamers left in North America, but in the *Moyie* it has the oldest, launched in 1898 and only mothballed in 1957. Inside is a collection of antiques, artefacts and photographs from the steamer's heyday. Look for the small hut alongside it, the "world's smallest post office" (closed since 1970), and drop in on Kaslo's thriving **arts centre**, the Langham Cultural Society, on A Avenue opposite the post office (☎353-2661), for theatrical performances and art exhibitions. The building, which dates from 1893, began life as hotel-cum-brothel for miners.

Kaslo makes an ideal base for tackling two of the region's major parks – Kokanee Glacier Provincial Park and the Purcell Wilderness Conservancy – and for pottering around some of the charming lakeshore communities. People at the arts centre can advise on getting to **ARGENTA** (pop. 150), 35km north, a refugee settlement of Quakers who in 1952 came from California, alienated by growing militarism, to start a new life; it's also the western trailhead for the difficult sixty-kilometre **Earl Grey Pass Trail** over the Purcell Mountains to Invermere (p.777). It's a beautiful area, but has no services and only the occasional B&B if you want to stay: ask at the Kaslo infocentre for latest details. This area, incidentally, offers a good chance of seeing **ospreys**: the Kootenays' hundred or so breeding pairs represent the largest concentration of the species in North America.

Practicalities

Finding your way round Kaslo is no problem, nor is getting information – everyone is disarmingly helpful – and there's also a **Chamber of Commerce** (mid-May to late Sept daily 9am–6pm; ☎ & fax 353-2525) at 324 Front St.

The best and virtually only central **accommodation** is the *Kaslo Motel*, 330 D Ave (☎353-2431; ①). For most other alternatives head towards the marina just north of the centre where en route you'll find, amongst others, the *Sunny Bluffs Cabins & Camp*, 434 North Marine Drive (☎353-2277; ①–③), offering cabins and camping sites ($10–12) overlooking Kaslo Bay Park. For **B&B** try the *Morningside*, 670 Arena Ave off Hwy 31 at West Kootenay Power Office (☎353-7681; ②; no credit cards). More interesting accommodation possibilities are available further up the lake, many with private lakeside beaches and lovely settings. The most notable are the combined hotel and campground *Lakewood Inn* (☎353-2395; ③–④, tent and RV sites $13–17; April–Oct), lakeside log cabins with fully equipped kitchens and camping sites with private beach and boat rentals; it's 6km north of Kaslo on Kohle Road. There are also the *Wing Creek Cabins* (☎353-2475; ②), 7km north at 9114 Hwy 31, and two B&Bs at Argenta – *Earl Grey Pass* (☎366-4472; ①) or *Place Cockaigne* (☎366-4394; ②).

Kaslo has a free municipal **campground** on the flat ground by the lake at the end of Front Street, past the SS *Moyie* on the right. *Mirror Lake Campground* (☎353-7102; mid-April to mid-Oct), beautifully situated 2km south of town on the main road to Ainsworth, has more facilities and charges $10 per site. North of the village on the lake are combined campground and motel or cabin lodgings (see above), as well as the

Kootenay Lake Provincial Park campground (☎825-3500; April–Oct), two small camp-grounds ($7–9.50) 25km north of the village on Hwy 31 with access to sandy beaches.

For **food** and **drink** in Kaslo try the town's social hub – the excellent *Treehouse Restaurant* on Front Street, a warm and cosy place where you can eat superbly and easily strike up conversations. The nearby *Mariner Inn and Motel* has a beer hall, and is more of a downmarket hang-out.

Kokanee Glacier Provincial Park

Kaslo is one of several possible jumping-off points for **Kokanee Glacier Provincial Park**, straddling the Slocan Range of the Selkirk Mountains to the southwest, as the access road from here – signed off Hwy 31A 6km northwest of town – offers the best views and choice of trails. However, the 24-kilometre drive up Keen Creek that follows from the turnoff degenerates in poor weather from compacted gravel to a severely rutted dirt road: this really only makes it suitable for four-wheel-drive vehicles. If you do make it, the road cuts to the heart of the park, reaching the Joker Millsite parking area set amidst spectacular glacier-ringed high country. Of the eleven fine trails in the area, the most obvious **hike** from the car park runs up to Helen Deane and Kaslo lakes (8km round trip), an easy morning amble. If you're staying overnight you can choose from the usual undeveloped campgrounds (you're supposed to camp in designated sites only) and three basic summer-only **cabins** ($10 nightly) – the main one, *Slocan Chief*, is past Helen Deane Lake alongside a park ranger office. If you're outdoors, be warned about the rubber-chewing (and -eating) porcupines: you'll need a full wrap of chicken wire to protect equipment.

An easier approach to the park is to drive south of Kaslo on Hwy 3A for around 40km and then follow the road up Kokanee Creek for 16km to park at Lake Gibson. Though further from Kaslo it usually gets you into the park quicker. Other approaches are from Hwy 31 10km north of Ainsworth, driving 13km up Woodbury Creek into the park; from Hwy 6 some 14km north of Slocan, where you drive 13km up Enterprise Creek; and from Hwy 6 14km south of Slocan, where you follow a road up Lemon Creek for 16km. For more **information** on the park, call ☎825-4421 or pick up the blue *BC Parks* pamphlet from local infocentres.

Highway 31A and the Slocan Valley

After Kaslo you can either rattle north along a gravel road to link with the Trans-Canada Highway at Revelstoke, a wild and glorious 150-kilometre drive with a free ferry crossing at **GALENA BAY**, or you can stay in the Kootenays and shuffle west on **Hwy 31A** through the Selkirk Mountains to the **Slocan Valley**. The latter road ascends from Kaslo alongside the Kaslo River, a crashing torrent choked with branches and fallen trees and hemmed in by high mountains and cliffs of dark rock, whose metallic sheen suggests the mineral potential that fired the early growth of so many of the settlements in the region. Near its high point the road passes a series of massively picturesque lakes: **Fish Lake** is deep green and has a nice picnic spot at one end; **Bear Lake** is equally pretty; and **Beaver Pond** is an amazing testament to the beaver's energy and ingenuity.

Sandon

The ghost town of **SANDON**, one of five in the region, is located 13km south of Hwy 31A, up a signed gravel sideroad that climbs through scenery of the utmost grandeur. Unfortunately, nowadays Sandon is too much ghost and not enough town to suggest how it might have looked in its silver-mining heyday, when it had 24 hotels, 23 saloons, an opera house, thriving red-light district and 5000 inhabitants (it even had electric light, well before Victoria or Vancouver). Its dilapidated, rather than evocative, state is due mainly to a flood, which swept away the earlier boardwalk settlement in 1955, leaving a partly inhabited rump that clutters around a café, small museum and summer-only **info-centre** immediately past the salmon-pink wooden building at the top of the town.

The trip is enhanced, however, if you manage a couple of local **hikes**. Idaho Peak is a must from Sandon, being one of the most accessible and spectacular walks in the area. A reasonable twelve-kilometre gravel access road leads into Alpine pastures and a car park: from there it's five-kilometre round trip to the summit of Mount Idaho and back, with emerging views all the way to the breathtaking panorama at the Forest Service lookout point. Or follow all or part of the **KNS Historic Trail** (6km each way) from the site, which follows the course of the 1895 Kaslo–New Denver–Slocan ore-carrying railway, past old mine works and eventually to fine views of the New Denver Glacier across the Slocan Valley to the west. Coupled with leaflets from the infocentre, the walk vividly documents the area's Wild West mining history, harking back to an era when the district – known as "Silvery Slocan" – produced the lion's share of Canada's silver. "Silver, lead, and hell are raised in the Slocan," wrote one local newspaper in 1891, "and unless you can take a hand in producing these articles, your services are not required." The immense vein of silver-rich galena that started the boom was discovered by accident in 1891 by two colourful prospectors, Eli Carpenter and Jack Seaton, when they got lost on the ridges returning to Ainsworth from Slocan Lake. Back in the bar they fell out over the find, and each raced out with his own team to stake the claim. Seaton won, and was to become a vastly wealthy silver baron who travelled in his own train carriage across Canada, condemning Carpenter to return to his earlier profession as a tightrope walker and to an ultimately penurious death.

New Denver

After the Sandon turnoff Hwy 31A drops into the **Slocan Valley**, a minor but still spectacular lake-bottomed tributary between the main Kootenay and Columbia watersheds, and meets Hwy 6 at **NEW DENVER**. Born of the same silver-mining boom as Kaslo, and with a similarly pretty lakeside setting and genuine pioneer feel, New Denver is, if anything, quieter than its neighbour. The clapboard houses are in peeling, pastel-painted wood, and the tree-lined streets are mercifully free of neon, fast food and most evidence of tourist passage. The **Silvery Slocan Museum**, housed in the old wooden Bank of Montréal building at the corner of 6th Street and Marine Drive (July & Aug 10.30am–4.30pm; admission by donation; ☎358-2201), is good for twenty minutes on the background and artefacts of the area's mining heritage. There's no official **infocentre**, but local bookstores or a business, Nuru Designs (summer daily 10am–4pm; ☎358-2733), are the places to contact for specific information on the surrounding valley.

As a stopover it's appealing but not quite as enticing as Kaslo; its **accommodation** possibilities include a single beach-hut-type motel, the *Valhalla Inn*, 509 Slocan Ave (☎358-2228; ③); the lake-view *Sweet Dreams Guest House* (☎358-2415; ③), a restored heritage home on Slocan Lake; and the simple *New Denver Municipal Campground* (☎358-2316; mid-May to late Sept; $12–15) on the south side of the village. Four kilometres north of town on Hwy 6 is the *Rosebury Provincial Park* campground ($9.50) on the banks of Wilson Creek, a lightly forested site with lake and mountain views. For **food** in the village try Main Street: the *Apple Tree Sandwich Shop* or the *Reco Mountain* restaurant at the top of the same street. There's more accommodation and a campground at Silverton, another tiny former mining village just 4.5km south of New Denver on Hwy 6.

Slocan and the Slocan Valley

Southbound out of New Denver, Hwy 6 follows the tight confines of the **Slocan Valley** for another 100km of ineffable mountain and lake landscapes. Be certain to stop at the **Slocan Lake Viewpoint**, 6km out of New Denver, where a short path up a small cliff provides stupendous views. The 125,000-acre **Valhalla Provincial Park** (☎825-3500) wraps up the best of the landscapes on the eastern side of Slocan Lake; a wilderness area with no developed facilities, most of it is out of reach unless you can boat across the water, though there are two trails that penetrate it from the hamlet of **SLOCAN**, another former mining village, at the south end of the lake. For a taste of the local outdoors, the canter up the old railway bed from Slocan is a popular short hike, and there's more fresh air and good picnicking spots at the nearby Mulvey Basin and Cove Creek **beaches**. Note, too, that gravel roads lead up from Hwy 6 to the more accessible heights of **Kokanee Glacier Provincial Park** to the east (p.766). For more on the area, notably tours into the Valhalla park, contact Slocan's **infocentre**, 704 Arlington St (year-round; ☎355-2277) or drop by the village office at Delaney Avenue and Slocan Street.

If you need **accommodation** en route south there are about half a dozen options, all in rustic settings with mountain or lake views. Try either *Lemon Creek Lodge* (☎355-2403; cabins ③, campground $15), 7km south of Slocan on Kennedy Road, or the *Slocan Motel* (☎355-2344; ②), at 801 Harold St in Slocan itself off Hwy 6. In addition to provincial **campgrounds** at Mulvey Basin and Cove Creek ($9.50; both May–Oct), there's the unserviced *Silverton Municipal Campground* (free; May–Oct), just south of New Denver.

Along Highway 6

Highway 6 may not be the most direct east–west route through British Columbia, but it's certainly one of the most dramatic, and the one to think about if you're heading across country towards Revelstoke to the north or the Okanagan to the west. From New Denver it initially strikes north and after 30km passes **Summit Lake**, a perfect jewel of water, mountain and forest that's served by the *Three Islands Resort* **campground** (☎265-3023; $14.50; May–Sept). A rough road ("Take at Your Own Risk") runs south from here into the mountains and a small winter ski area.

Nakusp and onwards

Sixteen kilometres beyond Summit Lake, lakefront **NAKUSP** is, like Kaslo and Nelson, a rare thing in British Columbia: a town with enough charisma to make it worth visiting for its own sake. The setting is par for the course in the Kootenays, with a big lake – **Upper Arrow Lake**, part of the Columbia River system – and the snowcapped Selkirk Mountains to the east to provide a majestic backdrop. Its name is supposed to mean "closed in", suggesting a secure landfall for canoes. The nearby hot springs are the main attraction, but you could happily wander around the town for a morning, or boat or swim off the public **beach**. The only actual sight in town is the **Nakusp Museum** in the village hall at 6th Avenue and 1st Street, full of the usual archive material, logging displays and Victorian bric-a-brac (May–Sept Tues–Thur 12.30–4.30pm, Mon & Fri–Sun 11am–5pm; free or donation). The helpful **infocentre**, based in the fake paddlesteamer building next door at 92 West St and 6th Avenue just off the main street (summer daily 9am–5pm; winter Mon–Fri 10am–4pm; ☎265-4234 or 1-800-909-8819), can provide details on local fishing, boating and hiking possibilities, and – for those driving onwards – timings for the Galena Bay and Fauquier ferries. Also ask about the possibility of renting houseboats on the lake if you're staying for a few days.

If you're only going to try the hot springs experience once, **Nakusp Hot Springs**, a well-signposted complex 13km northeast of town, is the place to do it (daily: June–Sept 9.30am–10pm; Oct–May 11am–9.30pm; $5, day pass $7): it's not unusual for late-night informal parties to develop around the two outdoor pools. Unlike many similar enterprises, the natural pools are cleaned each night and are backed up by nice changing facilities, but bear in mind they're very popular in the summer. Note that there are some undeveloped springs within striking distance of here if you have a car: take Hwy 23 north out of Nakusp for 24km and then turn down the logging road after the second bridge for 10km to the trailhead; the piping hot springs are 100m away by the river.

For a place to **stay** in Nakusp, try the *Selkirk Inn*, 210 6th Ave West (☎265-3666 or 1-800-661-8007; ②), or *Kuskanax/Tenderfoot Lodge*, 515 Broadway (☎265-3618 or 1-800-663-0100; ②–④), which is equally central but more upmarket and has a **restaurant** – though not as good as the pricier *Lord Minto*, Nakusp's top eatery.

Campers would do best to aim for the lovely *Nakusp Hot Springs* **campground**, near the hot springs at 1701 Canyon Rd (☎265-4528; $12–14; mid-May to mid-Oct); non-campers could try the adjoining *Cedar Chalets* (☎352-4034; ③), but reservations are essential in summer. Another out-of-town campground is the *McDonald Creek Provincial Park* site ($9.50; April-Oct), 10km south of Nakusp on Hwy 6 with lakeside beaches.

From Nakusp, you can either continue along Hwy 6 or or branch off up Hwy 23, which heads 99km north to Revelstoke (see p.631), a lonely and spectacular journey involving a free ferry crossing halfway at **Galena Bay** (hourly sailings each way).

Fauquier

Highway 6 doglegs south from Nakusp for 57 delightful kilometres to the ferry crossing at **FAUQUIER**. This hamlet consists of a handful of buildings including a garage, a store, the *Mushroom Addition* **café** for coffee and meals, and the only **motel** for kilometres – the *Alpine Lake Motel and Restaurant* (☎269-7622; ②), bang on the lakeside near the ferry at 101 Oak St. There's a **campground** 2km back towards Nakusp, *Plum Hollow Camping*, Needles Road North (☎269-7669; $6–12; March–Nov), marked by two big arrows sticking in the ground. Some 3km beyond that the *Goose Downs* **B&B** (☎265-3139; ②) is signed off Hwy 6.

Onwards from Needles

The free **ferry** across **Lower Arrow Lake** to Needles takes about five minutes, departs half-hourly from 5.15am to 9.45pm and operates an intermittent shuttle throughout the night. **NEEDLES** amounts to no more than a ramp off the ferry on the other side. There's an unofficial **campground** at Whatshan Lake, 3km off the highway just after Needles, but otherwise Hwy 6 is a gloriously empty ribbon as it burrows through the staggering Monashee Mountains – though some of the time it's too hemmed in by forest for you to catch anything but trees. After cresting Monashee Pass (1198m), the highway begins the long descent through the **Coldstream Valley** towards the Okanagan. Snow dusts the mountains here almost year-round, crags loom above the meadows that increasingly break the forest cover, and beautiful flower-filled valleys wind down to the highway. The first sign of life in over 100km is the *Gold Panner* **campground** (☎547-2025; $12–14; April–Oct), a good spot to overnight or to explore the utter wilderness of **Monashee Provincial Park** to the north. The park is reached by rough road from the hamlet of **CHERRYVILLE**, 10km further west, which despite its cartographic prominence is just three houses, a garage and Frank's General Store.

LUMBY, another 20km beyond, is scarcely more substantial, although **rooms** at the *Twin Creeks Motel* (☎547-9221; ②) might be worth considering if it's late, given that the Okanagan lodgings ahead could well be packed. The village also boasts a simple riverside **campground** run by the local Lions Club (☎547-9504; $7; May–Oct) and there's a seasonal **infocentre** at 2400 Vernon St (July & Aug; ☎547-8844). Beyond the village, the road glides through lovely pastoral country, with orchards, verdant meadows, low, tree-covered hills, and fine wooden barns built to resemble inverted longboats.

Nelson

NELSON is one of British Columbia's best towns, and one of the few interior settlements you could happily spend two or three days in – longer if you use it as a base for touring the Kootenays by car (there's plenty of accommodation). It's home to more than its share of baby-boomers and refugees from the 1960s, a hangover that's nurtured a friendly, civilized and close-knit community, a healthy cultural scene and a liveliness – manifest in alternative cafés, nightlife and secondhand clothes shops – that you'll be hard pushed to find elsewhere in the province outside Vancouver. There are, apparently, more artists and craftspeople here per head of the 9000 population than any other town in Canada. At the same time it's a young place permeated with immense civic pride, which was given a further boost by the filming here of *Roxanne*, Steve Martin's spoof version of *Cyrano de Bergerac* (there's a *Roxanne* walk around location sites). Producers chose the town for its idyllic lakeside setting and 350-plus turn-of-the-century homes, factors which for once live up to the Canadian talent for hyperbole – in this case a claim to be "Queen of the Kootenays" and "Heritage Capital of Western Canada".

Located 34km west of Balfour on Hwy 3A, the town forms a tree-shaded grid of streets laid over the hilly slopes that edge down to the westernmost shores of Kootenay Lake. Most homes are immaculately kept and vividly painted, and even the commercial **buildings** along the parallel main streets – Baker and Vernon – owe more to the vintage architecture of Seattle and San Francisco than to the drab Victoriana of much of eastern Canada. If you want to add purpose to your wanderings, pick up the *Heritage Walking Tour* pamphlet from the **infocentre**, 225 Hall St (June–Aug daily 8am–8pm; Sept–May Mon–Fri 8.30am–4.30pm; ☎352-3433 or 354-4636), which takes you around the sort of houses that many Canadians dream of retiring to, and only occasionally oversells a place – notably when it lands you in front of the old jam factory and the electricity substation. Better bets are the courthouse and city hall, both designed by F.M. Rattenbury, also responsible for Victoria's *Empress Hotel* and Parliament Buildings. Free tours with a costumed guide are available from the infocentre in summer. You could even go out of your way for some of the town's **shops**, particularly those of its many artists and craftspeople, who in summer club together to present **Artwalk**, a crawl round many of the town's little galleries. Most of these have regular openings and wine-gorging receptions, making for numerous free-for-all parties. If you don't want to walk, take the restored streetcar that runs the length of the town's waterfront from near to the infocentre. Oliver's Books on Baker Street is excellent for maps, guides and general reading, with a bias towards the sort of New Age topics that find a ready market here.

For the most part the area owes its development to the discovery of copper and silver ore on nearby Toad Mountain at the turn of the century, and though the mines declined fairly quickly Nelson's diversification into gold and lumber, and its roads, railway and waterways, saved it from mining's usual downside. Today mining is back on the agenda as old claims are re-explored, and even if the idea of the town's **Museum of Mines** (daily 9am–5pm; free; ☎352-5242), next to the infocentre, leaves you cold, it's worth meeting the curator, an old prospector who talks at length – and interestingly – on the quest for silver, copper and gold, past and present.

It's probably less worthwhile to trek over to the **Nelson Museum**, about twenty minutes' walk from the centre, which offers a rather haphazard display that's obviously the work of enthusiastic amateurs, though none the worse for that (summer daily 1–6pm; winter Mon–Sat 1–4.30pm; $1). There are, however, odd points of interest, notably a chronicle of the original 1886 Silver King Mine that brought the town to life, as well as tantalizingly scant details on the Doukhobor, a Russian religious sect whose members still live in self-contained communities around the Kootenays (see p.762). Better instead to walk to **Lakeside Park** near the Nelson Bridge, where there are surprisingly good sandy **beaches** and picnic areas, boat rentals and waterfront paths.

Practicalities

Nelson is served by Greyhound **buses** (☎352-3939) that run west to Penticton (for connections to Vancouver, the Okanagan and Kamloops) and east to Cranbrook (connections to Calgary via Banff or Fort Macleod). In the past there have also been infrequent minibus services to Kaslo (☎353-2492 for details) and Nakusp (☎265-3511), but check with the infocentre before building a trip around these. The depot is almost on the lakeshore, just below the town proper.

There's a reasonable spread of **accommodation**, but comparatively little in the downtown area: among the central choices are *Queen's*, 621 Baker St (☎352-5351; ①), the cheapest and dingiest, and the similarly priced and equally central *Dancing Bear Inn*, 171 Baker St (☎352-7573; ①), a nicely renovated HI-affiliated **youth hostel**. For something around twice the price you could try downtown **B&B** options such as the four-room *Emory House*, 811 Vernon St (☎352-7007; ④), or the highly regarded *Inn the Garden*, a restored Victorian home one block south of Baker St at 408 Victoria St (☎352-3226; ④–⑤). Most of the **motels** are on Hwy 31A at the north end of town or over the miniature Forth Road bridge on the north side of the lake. Here you can try the *Villa Motel*, 655 Hwy 3A (☎352-5515 or 1-888-352-5515; ③–⑤), with the use of an indoor pool, or the *North Shore Inn*, 687 Hwy 3A (☎352-6606 or 1-800-593-6636; ③–④), where rates include a coffee and muffin breakfast. The nearest **campground** is the *City Tourist Park*, on the corner of High Street and Willow (☎352-9031; $13–16; mid-May to early Oct). If this is full, head east towards Balfour and the three or more sites near the ferry terminal (see p.764).

The choice of **restaurants** is broad, and you can't go far wrong wandering around and choosing something that looks tempting. *Stanley Baker's*, a locals' place on Baker Street next to the Nelson Shopping Company mall, is good for cappuccino, snacks and big, cheap breakfasts. The *Vienna*, an alternative café and bookshop just off Baker Street opposite the Bank of Montréal, is also worth a try, though the *Book Garden Café* 556 Josephine St (☎352-1812), is probably the best of several in-house bookstore cafés around town. For lunch or evening meals, downtown residents head to the *Main Street Diner*, 616 Baker St (closed Sun), or the top-flight *All Seasons Café*, The Alley, 620 Herridge Lane, which also has a nice patio dining area. Newly opened and also worth a look is *Max Irma's*, 515a Kootenay St, while for novelty value you could do worse than spoil your breath at the *Outer Clove*, 353 Stanley St (☎354-1667), where everything from decor to dessert features garlic (it's better than it sounds). For **drinking**, make for *Mike's Bar* round the side of the *Heritage Inn*, 422 Vernon St, which sells the full range of Nelson Brewing Company beers (the brewery was founded in 1893): top tipple is the flagship Old Brewery Ale (OBA). If you're shopping for your own meals, the big **supermarkets** are in or near the mall alongside the bus depot.

North to Radium Hot Springs

Heading north from Creston and the Kootenays, Hwy 95 travels through scenery as spectacular as anything in the big Rockies parks to the north. The route follows the broad valley bottom of the **Columbia River**, bordered on the east by the Rockies and on the west by the marginally less breathtaking **Purcell Mountains**, though for the most part access to the wilderness here is limited and you'll have to be content with enjoying it from the highway. It's a fast run if you're driving, except where the road hugs the river's dramatic bluffs and sweeping meanders. Hwys 93 and 95 meet near **Cranbrook**, where you can make for either of two US border crossings, double back eastwards on Hwy 3 to Crowsnest Pass and Alberta, or head north for Radium Hot Springs and the entrance to Kootenay National Park (see p.632). Greyhound **buses** ply all these routes, with most connections at Cranbrook.

East from Creston

Some forty kilometres east of Creston, buses drop off at the small Shell garage in unspoilt **YAHK**, no more than a few houses nestled amidst the trees; a good, quiet stopover here is the single **motel**, *Bob's* (☎424-5581; ②). Hwy 95 branches off from Hwy 3 here and heads south for the US border (11km). Incidentally, the highway crosses a **time zone** between Moyie and Yahk – clocks go back one hour.

Following Hwy 3 northbound you reach the tiny community of **MOYIE** on the edge of lovely **Moyie Lake**, which provides a welcome visual relief after the unending tree-covered slopes hereabouts. Though there's no motel accommodation, there is a **B&B**, the *Long Shadows House* on Barclay Road just north of the village (☎829-0650; ②). There are also three local **campgrounds**, including the excellent one at **Moyie Lake Provincial Park** ($14.50; May–Oct) – reach it by taking Munro Lake Road west off Hwy 3/95 for a kilometre from the northernmost point of Moyie Lake. Alternatively, you could try the private *Green River Campground,* on the lakeshore, signed about 1km off Hwy 3/95 (☎426-4154; $10–13.50; May–Oct). Another excellent site is the *Moyie River Campground*, 18km south of Cranbrook on Hwy 3/95 (☎489-3047; $9–13.50; April–Nov).

Cranbrook

The ex-mining town of **CRANBROOK**, despite a location that marks it out as a trans-port hub, is one of the most dismal in the province, its dreariness hardly redeemed by the surrounding high mountains. A long strip of motels, neon clutter and marshalling yards dominates a downtown area otherwise distinguished only by thrift shops and closing-down sales. Local lifeblood, such as it is, flows from the motels, this being an obvious place to eat, sleep and drive away from the next morning.

The only sight to speak of is the **Canadian Museum of Rail Travel**, a smallish affair that centres on the restored carriages of an old trans-Canada luxury train (daily: July & Aug 8am–8pm; rest of the year 10am–6pm; $6). The period buildings pushed by the **infocentre**, 2279 Cranbrook St (year-round 9am–5pm; ☎426-5914 or 489-5261), aren't interesting enough to justify the trawl round the streets.

You may have to stay in Cranbrook, as there's little in the way of **accommodation** on the roads north and south; there are a dozen or more motels that fit the bill. The top of the range in town is the *Inn of the South* at 803 Cranbrook (☎489-4301 or 1-800-663-2708; ③–④), a large, modern motel on the main road. Cheaper and more intimate is the *Heritage Estate Motel* (☎426-3862 or 1-800-670-1001; ②), near the southern edge of town at 362 Van Horne St SW and therefore removed from some of the bleaker corners. The same can be said of a nice **B&B**, the *Singing Pines*, 5180 Kennedy Rd (☎426-5959 or 1-800-863-4969; ③), situated off Hwy 95A 3km north of town in a quiet location with mountain views. The town has a municipal **campground** at Baker Park on 14th Avenue and 1st Street (☎426-2162; $14–20; March–Nov 1), though it's a good deal less appeal-ing than the *Jimsmith Lake Provincial Park*, 4km southwest of town, but which has no showers (May–Oct; $9.50).

The strip offers plenty of cheap **eating** options: for something more welcoming make for the *ABC Family Restaurant* at 1601 Cranbrook St North. The Greyhound **bus ter-minal** (☎426-3331) is hidden in a jungle of neon behind *McDonald's* and the Mohawk gas station. Bus services run east to Fernie, Sparwood and southern Alberta (2 daily); west to Nelson, Castlegar and Vancouver (3 daily); north to Kimberley, Radium, Banff and Calgary (1 daily); and south to Spokane in the US (1 daily).

East from Cranbrook

Highway 93 leaves Hwy 95 between Fort Steele (see p.774) and Cranbrook, following Hwy 3 as far as Elko before branching off south for the United States border (91km). An unsullied hamlet of around half a dozen homes, **ELKO** is gone in a flash, but you might want to stop and eat at *Wendy's Place*, a cosy backwoods spot, or to camp at the excellent *Kikomun Creek Provincial Park* **campground** (☎529-7484; $9.50–14;

May–Sept), on the eastern shore of the artificial Lake Koocanusa signed off Hwy 93 3km west of town. The only other local **accommodation** is the *West Crow Motel and Campground* at the entrance to the Elk Valley (☎529-7349; ②, tents and RVs $14; May–Oct), with a secluded tenting area. Hwy 3 offers colossal views of the Rockies and the fast-flowing, ice-clear Elk River, before hitting **FERNIE**, 32km north of Elko, a pleasant place of tree-lined streets, a few motels and small wooden houses, surrounded by a ring of knife-edged mountains. The *Cedar Lodge* (☎423-4622; ②–③) is the place to stay here or, failing that, the HI-affiliated official **youth hostel**, the *Sundown Budget Motel and International Hostel*, 802 6th Ave (☎423-6811; motel ①, hostel $12). The **infocentre** (daily 9am–5pm; ☎423-6868) stands alongside a reconstructed wooden oil derrick 2km north of town on Hwy 3 at Dicken Road. **Mount Fernie Provincial Park** has plenty of hiking trails, picnic areas and a campground just west of town off Hwy 3 ($9.50; May–Sept). **Fernie Snow Valley**, 5km west of town and 2km off the main highway, boasts what is reputedly the longest ski season in the BC Rockies (Nov–May); it also has few typical resort-type accommodation possibilities.

Hwy 3 leaves the Elk Valley at **SPARWOOD**, 29km beyond Fernie, where signs of the area's coal-mining legacy begin to appear. Close to the town – but barely visible – is Canada's largest open-cast **coal mine**, capable of disgorging up to 18,000 tonnes of coal daily. Tours of the mine (July & Aug Mon–Fri 1.30pm) leave from the local **infocentre** (daily 9am–6pm; ☎425-2423), at the junction of Hwy 3 and Aspen Drive – look for the big miner's statue. The town itself is surprisingly neat and clean, and the obvious *Black Nugget Motor Inn*, Hwy 3 at Red Cedar Drive (☎425-2236 or 1-800-663-2706; ②), makes a convenient place to stay.

Elkford

The remainder of Hwy 3 in British Columbia is despoiled by mining; the road crests the Continental Divide 19km east of Sparwood at **Crowsnest Pass** (see p.561). Far more scenic is the drive north from Sparwood on Hwy 43, which heads upstream beside the Elk River for 35km to **ELKFORD**. Nestled against a wall of mountains to the east and more gentle hills to the west, the village claims to be the "wilderness capital of British Columbia" – a high-pitched punt, but close to the mark if you're prepared to carry on up either of two rough gravel roads to the north. The more easterly road follows the Elk a further 80km to **Elk Lakes Provincial Park** close to the Continental Divide, one of the wildest road-accessible spots in the province. The slightly better route to the west heads 55km into the heart of unbeatable scenery below 2792-metre **Mount Armstrong**. Both areas offer excellent chances of spotting wildlife like cougars, deer, moose, elk or members of North America's largest population of bighorn sheep.

Before entering either area, however, it's essential to pick up maps and information at the Elkford **infocentre** (year-round daily 9am–5pm; ☎865-4362), located at the junction of Hwy 43 and Michel Road. It can also give directions to nearby **Josephine Falls**, a few minutes' walk from the parking area on Fording Mine Road. Whether you're staying here or pushing on north, a tent is helpful: the only accommodation options are the *Elkford Motor Inn*, 808 Michel Rd, next to the shopping centre (☎865-2211; ②); Elkford's municipal **campground** (☎865-2241; $10; April–Oct); and wilderness campgrounds around Elk Lakes.

Kimberley

KIMBERLEY, a few kilometres from Cranbrook on Hwy 95A, is British Columbia's highest town (1117m), and in many ways one of its silliest, thanks to a tourist-tempting ruse to transform itself into a Bavarian village, after the imminent closure of the local mine in the 1970s threatened it with economic oblivion. The result is a masterpiece of kitsch that's almost irresistible: buildings have been given a plywood-thin veneer of authenticity, piped Bavarian music dribbles from shops with names like The Yodelling Woodcarver, and even the fire hydrants have been painted to look like miniature replicas of Happy Hans, Kimberley's lederhosened mascot. The ploy might seem absurd to many Europeans, but there's no doubting the energy and enthusiasm that have gone into it, nor the economic rewards that have accrued from the influx of tourists and European immigrants – Germans included – who've provided an authentic range of cafés and restaurants and a variety of family-orientated summer activities. Most of the Teutonic gloss is around the **Bavarian Platzl** on Spokane Street in the small downtown area, whose fake houses compare poorly with the authentic wooden buildings and more alpine surroundings on the outskirts. Recently the wisdom of the drive to attract tourists has been underlined, for the news from Cominco, which owns the big local mine, is that it's to close permanently by 2001.

If nothing else, you can leave Kimberley safe in the knowledge that you have seen the "**World's Biggest Cuckoo Clock**", a fraudulent affair which amounts to little more than a large wooden box that twitters inane and incessant music. The dreaded contraption performs on being fed small change, and people oblige often enough so that Happy Hans (rather than a cuckoo) makes his noisy appearance almost continuously; when he doesn't, the council often employs some unfortunate to play the accordion morning, noon and night to keep up the musical interludes.

Apart from the clock, and a small **museum** upstairs in the library down the road, other minor local sights include the **Sullivan Mine**, pre-Bavarian Kimberley's main employer and one of the world's biggest lead and zinc mines, which is occasionally open to tourists in the summer (ask at the infocentre). The Bavarian City Mining Railway is a 2.5-kilometre ride from downtown on a train salvaged from a local mine, while at Marysville, a couple of kilometres south of town on Hwy 95A, you can take a twenty-minute amble to see the **Marysville Waterfalls**, a series of small falls in verdant surroundings.

Practicalities

If you need **accommodation**, try the central *Inn of the Rockies*, 300 Wallinger Ave (☎427-2266 or 1-800-661-7559; ③), or the smaller *North Star Motel* (☎427-5633 or 1-800-663-5508; daily 8am–8pm; ②) at the northern edge of town: for an extra $5 you have access to a kitchen. The nearest **campground**, the inevitably named *Happy Hans Campground and RV Park* (☎427-2929; $14.50–18; May-Oct), is 2km northwest of the town centre on Ski Hill Road and has good facilities. Drop into the twee but excellent *Chef Bernard* café and **restaurant** opposite the clock, where the owner – heartily sick of Bavaria – often plays Irish fiddle music as a mark of defiance. He's also known as one of the best local chefs, and people come from miles for his fondue evenings. A favourite cheap place for lunch and breakfast is *Our Place*, 290 Spokane St, just down from the post office on the main crossroads. For more refined culinary offerings, make for *Pepper's*, 490 Wallinger Ave, a chicken, ribs and pasta place a couple of minutes' walk from the main plaza. Further afield is the *Old Barn House*, about fifteen minutes' walk or a short drive from the town centre towards the ski area. For full details of Kimberley's many summer events, call in on the **infocentre** (daily 9am–6pm; ☎427-3666) at 350 Ross St, just off the main crossroads past the *Inn of the Rockies*. The key draw is **Julyfest**, which concludes with a one-week beer festival and – almost inevitably – an international accordion championship.

Fort Steele Heritage Town

If you stick to Hwy 93/95 rather than detouring to Kimberley, you'll come to **FORT STEELE HERITAGE TOWN** (daily 9.30am–dusk; $5.50), an impressively reconstructed turn-of-the-century village of some 55 buildings in a superb mountain-ringed setting. It suffers somewhat by comparison with the similar reconstruction at Barkerville (125 buildings), but that's far further from civilization deep in Cariboo country (see p.787). The settlement started life in the 1860s as a provisions stop and river crossing for gold prospectors heading east to the seams on Wildhorse Creek, 6km beyond the present town site. Then it was known as Galbraith's Ferry or Galbraith's Landing, after John Galbraith, who built the cableway which ferried miners across the Kootenay River. Its subsequent history contains episodes and injustices that must have been played out across much of the west at the time.

On one side of the river lived the area's Ktunaxa tribe, ancient custodians of the land. On the other stood Colonel James Baker, property owner, businessman and a member of the provincial government. Baker soon got into an argument with Chief Isadore, the Ktunaxa chieftain, over a piece of disputed land a few kilometres to the southwest known as Joseph's Prairie. In 1884, two miners were murdered, two Ktunaxa being arrested for the crime – on highly suspect evidence – two years later. Isadore, convinced of their innocence, forcibly released them from jail, at the same time throwing Baker's surveyor off Ktunaxa grazing land as he attempted to fence it off. In 1887 the uproar led the settlers to call 75 North West Mounted Police under the leadership of Inspector Sam Steele. The police resolved the dispute up to a point – the Ktunaxa were exonerated – but Baker managed to get his hands on Joseph's Prairie. The force then spent a winter at Galbraith's Landing, named Fort Steele ever after, but left within the year. Baker, meanwhile, named his new piece of land Cranbrook. Over the next few years Fort Steele boomed on the expectation of Canadian Pacific Railway's arrival in town, a not unnatural expectation given its superb setting and situation near the confluence of the Kootenay and St Mary rivers. The population reached 4000, bolstered by the discovery in 1893 of silver, lead and zinc to the north (at modern-day Kimberley). Much of the ore was moved to Fort Steele and loaded onto riverboats, and this trade was another good reason to expect the railway. Locals, though, had reckoned without Baker, who with his money and political clout was able to persuade the rail barons to push their line through Cranbrook, a damp, low-lying and generally inferior spot sunk between two modest creeks. By 1910, with money, railway and people now in Cranbrook, Fort Steele's population had shrunk to 150.

Though the site was never completely abandoned, there was still much to do when restoration began in 1961. Staffed by volunteers in period dress, the town now consists of numerous buildings, some replicas, some original (1860s), some from the period of Steele's tenure, others brought from elsewhere and rebuilt. Among them are an old-time music hall, a blacksmiths', bakery, printers', general store and many more, with the added novelty of being able to watch people shoe horses, bake bread, make quilts and so forth. More spookily, there's also a restored Masonic Lodge, where a couple of funny-handshakers let you in on various selected "secrets" of masonic life. You can also nab a ride on a steam engine and, if you really must, take a turn on a wagon pulled by the massive Clydesdale horses that are reared in the village. These foibles notwithstanding, proceedings are all under the auspices of the provincial government, so generally lack the commercial frenzy that often characterizes such places. It's also a delight to see a village as it appeared in 1897, the scenery at the boardwalks' end unsullied by malls, fast-food joints and the like. At 8pm most summer evenings the village reopens for a old-time variety show and cabaret.

A couple of ranches and B&Bs aside, there's little accommodation in the immediate vicinity, though there are two **campgrounds**: the *Fort Steele Resort and RV Park* across from the village (☎489-4268; $16–22), which has all the usual facilities, and the smaller and cheaper *Original Fort Steele* campground (☎426-5117; $14–19; May to mid-Sept), 2km south of the village and with similar facilities. Just east of Fort Steele there's also the *Norbury Lake Provincial Park* campground (☎422-3212; $9.50; April–Oct) with tent and RV sites. If you can get in, the *Wild Horse Farm* (☎426-6000; ④; May–Oct), with only three **rooms**, is an attractive log-faced "manor house" surrounded by eighty acres of meadows, woods and park-like estate across from the village.

To Fairmont Hot Springs

Back on Hwy 93/95, the Columbia Valley's scenery begins to pick up as the Rockies begin to encroach and the blanket of trees opens up into pastoral river meadows. First stop is **Wasa**, whose lake, protected by the Wasa Lake Provincial Park, is warm enough for summer swimming; so warm, in fact, that many claim it has BC's warmest waters (Christina and Osoyoos lakes further west make similar claims: see p.760 and p.759). The lake also has a sizable provincial park **campground** (reservations possible; see p.644). A couple of kilometres away is the Wasa Slough Wildlife Sanctuary, partly visible from the main highway, which shelters ospreys, eagles, herons and a wide variety of other waterfowl. **Skookumchuck** ("strong water"), marked as a town on most maps, is in fact little more than a pulp mill whose chimneys belch out unpleasantness that spreads for kilometres downwind.

After a few kilometres the road curves around the **Dutch Creek Hoodoos**, fantastically eroded river bluffs, according to Ktunaxa legend created when a vast wounded fish crawling up the valley expired at this point: as its flesh rotted, the bones fell apart to create the hoodoos. Close by is **Columbia Lake** – not one of the area's most picturesque patches of water, though the *Mountain Village*, a fine wooden **restaurant** crammed with hundreds of old bottles, makes a good meal stop and is just short of a colossal lumber yard that blights **Canal Flats** at the head of the lake. This little area resonates to the history of the wonderful William Adolph Baillie-Grohman, a man whose life was littered with glorious and wonderfully eccentric catastrophes. Here, in the 1880s, he planned to build a canal to link the Columbia and Kootenay rivers, also intending to drain virtually all of the Kootenay into the Columbia to prevent flooding (residents up and down the Columbia, not to mention the Canadian Pacific Railway, quickly prevented the latter plan). The canal, however, was completed in 1889, but proved so tortuous and perilous that only two boats ever made it all the way through (in 1894 and 1902). Even then the second boat only made it through by demolishing virtually all of the locks en route. In this instance Baille-Grohman had the last laugh, for completing the canal – useless as it was – earned him a provincial land grant of some 30,000 acres. Head to Canal Flats Provincial Park, 3km north of Canal Flats, if you want to view the remnants of the doomed project.

Just to the south of the Canal Flats mill is the Whiteswan Lake Road turnoff for **Whiteswan Lake Provincial Park**, a handkerchief-sized piece of unbeatable scenery at the end of a twenty-kilometre gravel logging road (caution needed); the park has four **campgrounds** but few trails, as its main emphasis is on boating and trout fishing. Three of the campgrounds are at Whiteswan Lake itself, the other at Alces Lake: also keep an eye open for some undeveloped hot springs, Lussier Hot Springs, at the entrance ot the park (after 17.5km from the main road). The same access road, now called the Lussier River Road, continues another 30km to **Top of the World Provincial Park**, a far wilder and very beautiful alpine region where you need to be completely self-sufficient – the five walk-in campgrounds, reached by trail from the parking area at the end of the road, offer only water and firewood. Hiking in the park is good, an obvious shortish jaunt being the trail from the parking area along the Lussier River to Fish Lake (7km one way; 2hr), where there's an unserviced campground and a cabin (summer only). Mount Morro (3002m), the peak that looms over the region, is believed to have had great spiritual significance for the Ktunaxa, who came here to mine chert, a hard flinty quartz used to make tools and weapons.

FAIRMONT HOT SPRINGS spills over the Columbia's flat flood plain, less a settlement than an ugly modern upmarket resort that feeds off the appeal of the hot springs themselves. The pools were commandeered from the Ktunaxa (Kootenay) in 1922 for exploitation as a tourist resource; the calcium springs (daily 8am–10pm; $4) were particularly prized by the whites because they lack the sulphurous stench of many

BC hot dips. However, the locals have now got their own back by opening some cheaper, makeshift pools above the resort, which are proving very popular with tourists. If you don't fancy coughing up around $117–233 to stay in a room at the swish resort, you could try its big **campground** (☎345-6311; $15–35), one minute from the pools but only if you're in an RV – they don't want tents – or the *Spruce Grove Resort* (☎345-6561; ③, tents $15; May-Oct), near the river 2km south of Fairmont with cheap rooms and a lovely riverside campground with outdoor pool.

Invermere

Windermere, 13km south of Radium, is little more than a supermarket, gas station and campground immediately off the highway, and hardly hints at the presence of **INVERMERE**, about 1km beyond on the western shore of Windermere Lake. White settlement of the region can almost be said to have begun here, for explorer David Thompson passed this way in 1807 as he travelled up the Columbia River. With his Native Canadian wife, several children and eight companions, he built Kootenay House, the area's first trading post. Its site is marked by a cairn on Westside Road. A feel-good summer resort with the usual range of aquatic temptations, Invermere today makes a nicer accommodation prospect than Radium. However, droves of anglers, boaters and beach bums mean summer vacancies may be in short supply, in which case call the central **infocentre** at 5A Street and 7th Avenue (late July to early Sept daily 8am–8pm; ☎342-6316 or 342-2844) for B&B possibilities or head for one of the town's four **motels** – the *Lee-Jay*, 1015 13th St (☎342-9227; ③), is the most reasonable; the *Best Western Invermere Inn* at the heart of downtown at 1310 7th Ave is smarter (☎342-9246 or 1-800-661-8911; ④). The nearest provincial **campground**, with vehicle and tent sites, is 7km back towards Radium at Dry Gulch Provincial Park (☎422-3212; $9.50; May-Oct), but the private *Coldstream Lakeside Campground* (☎342-6793; $23–25 per vehicle; May–Sept) is on the lake and has a sandy beach. For **food**, try the popular *Myrtle's* on 7th Avenue, *Huckleberry's* on Laurier Street or the *Blue Dog Café* on 7th Avenue, the last being particularly good for vegetarians and wholefood aficionados. For highly regarded Pacific Northwest cuisine make for *Strand's Old House*, 818 12th St (☎342-6344). If you want a break from eating, drinking or lazing on beaches, spend a few minutes with the mining, railway and other displays in the **Windermere Valley Museum**, 622 3rd St (June–Sept Tues–Sun 9.30am–4pm; $2; ☎342-9769), housed in a heritage building at the top of the hill and to the right on entering the village.

From Invermere a minor road (Toby Creek Road) climbs west into the mountains to the burgeoning **Panorama Ski Resort** (18km), whose slick facilities include only limited and rather expensive accommodation. At over 1000m, the big 250-room *Panorama Resort* (☎342-6941 or 1-800-663-2929; ⑤) is also open in summer for tennis, riding, white-water rafting and fishing. In summer the chief appeal of the area is hiking, particularly if you continue up the road to the less tainted **Purcell Wilderness Conservancy**, one of the few easily accessible parts of the Purcell Mountains. If you have a tent and robust hiking inclinations, you could tackle the 61-kilometre **trail** through the area to Argenta (see p.765) on the northern end of Kootenay Lake, an excellent cross-country route that largely follows undemanding valleys except when crossing the Purcell watershed at Earl Grey Pass (2256m).

If you're continuing from Invermere into the **Kootenay National Park** and the Rockies, our account of the park begins on p.632. See p.561 if you're crossing the Crowsnest Pass into southern Alberta for **Waterton Lakes National Park**.

NORTH OF VANCOUVER

Apart from Vancouver Island, two other excursions from Vancouver stand out, each of which can easily be extended to embrace longer itineraries out of the city. The first is the 150-kilometre **Sunshine Coast**, the only stretch of accessible coastline on mainland British Columbia, and a possible springboard to Vancouver Island and the Inside Passage ferry to Prince Rupert. Ferries depart from Powell River at the Sunshine Coast highway to Comox on Vancouver Island (see p.732). The second is the inland route to **Garibaldi Provincial Park**, containing by far the best scenery and hiking country within striking distance of Vancouver, and the famous world-class ski resort of **Whistler**; the road becomes a summer-only route beyond Whistler, but train passengers can forge on through wilder parts all the way to Prince George. En route to Whistler you'll pass through **Squamish**, nothing to rave over scenically, but rapidly emerging as one of North America's premier destinations for windsurfing, climbing and – in season – eagle-watching.

The Sunshine Coast

A mild-weathered stretch of sandy beaches, rugged headlands and quiet lagoons backed by forested hills, the **Sunshine Coast** receives heavy promotion – and heavy tourist traffic as a result – though in truth its reputation is overstated and the scenic rewards are slim compared to the grandeur of the BC interior. In summer, however, this area offers what are reputedly some of Canada's best diving, boating and fishing opportunities, all of which stoke a string of busy villages eager to provide accommodation, run tours and rent anything from bikes to full-sized cruisers.

Highway 101 runs the length of the coast, but it's interrupted at two points by sizable inlets that entail lengthy ferry crossings. Motorists face enormous queues to get on the boats in summer, but the crossings present no problems for bus or foot passengers – indeed, they're the best bits of the trip. Given that the area is hardly worth full-scale exploration by car anyway, you might as well go by **bus**; it's perfectly feasible to get to **Powell River** and back in a day, though (ferry rides aside), it's not the first day-trip you'd want to make from Vancouver. Maverick Coach Lines (☎662-8051) runs two buses daily to Powell River (5hr) and a third as far as **Sechelt** (2hr).

Along Highway 101

Soon reached and well signposted from North Vancouver, **HORSESHOE BAY** is the departure point for the first of the Hwy 101 **ferry** crossings, a half-hour passage through the islands of fjord-like Howe Sound (regular sailings year-round). Ferries also ply from here to Nanaimo on Vancouver Island, with hourly sailings in summer and every other hour off season. For information on either of these services, contact BC Ferries in Vancouver (☎669-1211), or pick up a timetable from the Vancouver infocentre.

GIBSONS, the terminal on the other side of Howe Sound, is a scrappy place spread widely over a wooded hillside – the nicest area is around the busy marina, where you'll find the **infocentre** at 668 Sunny Crest Rd (daily 9am–6pm; ☎886-2325). Motels abound, but for decent camping hold out for **Roberts Creek Provincial Park**, 8km northwest of the terminal on Hwy 101.

The telephone code for the Sunshine Coast, Squamish and Whistler is ☎604.

Beyond, the service and supplies centre of **SECHELT** panders to tourists less than Gibsons, and ongoing development lends the town a messy air which isn't helped by its drab, flat location. Just 4km north, however, **Porpoise Bay Provincial Park** has a campground, a sandy beach, good swimming and a few short woodland trails. The main road beyond Sechelt is very pretty, and offers occasional views to the sea when it's not trapped in the trees.

Pender Harbour comprises a collection of small communities, of which **MADEIRA PARK** is the most substantial; whales occasionally pass this section of coast – which, sadly, is the source of most of the whales in the world's aquariums – but the main draws are fishing and boating.

Earl's Cove is nothing but the departure ramp of the second **ferry** en route, a longer crossing (45min), which again offers fantastic views of sheer mountains plunging into the sea. A short trail (4km) from the adjacent car park leads to a viewpoint for the **Skookumchuck Narrows**, where the Sechelt Inlet constricts to produce boiling rapids at the turn of each tide. On board the ferry, look north beyond the low wooded hills – devoid of all human trace – to the immense waterfall that drops off a "Lost World"-type plateau into the sea.

From Jervis Bay, the opposite landing stage, the country is comparatively less travelled. A couple of kilometres up the road is the best of all the provincial parks in this region, **Saltery Bay Provincial Park**. Everything here is discreetly hidden in the trees between the road and the coast, and the campground – beautifully sited – is connected by short trails to a couple of swimming beaches. The main road beyond is largely enclosed by trees, so there's little to see of the coast, though various **campgrounds** give onto the sea, notably the big *Oceanside* site, 4km short of Powell River, which sits on a superb piece of shoreline (☎485-2435 or 1-888-889-2435; ①). Although it's given over mainly to RVs, there are a few sites for tents ($12–14) and cheap cabins.

Powell River and beyond

Given its seafront location, **POWELL RIVER** inevitably has its scenic side, but like many a BC town its unfocused sprawl and nearby sawmill slightly dampen the overall appeal. The main road cruises past almost 4km of box-like retirement bungalows before reaching the town centre, which at first glance makes it a not terribly captivating resort. If you're catching the **ferry** to Courtenay on Vancouver Island (4 daily; 75min), you might not even see the town site, as the terminal is 2km to the east at Westview, and some of the **buses** from Vancouver are timed to coincide with the boats; if your bus doesn't connect, you can either walk from the town centre or bus terminal or call a taxi (☎483-3666). The local **infocentre** (daily 9am–5pm; ☎485-4701), which is immediately at the end of the wooden ferry pier, can supply a visitor's map with detailed coverage of the many trails leading inland from the coast hereabouts; they can also advise on boat trips on Powell Lake, immediately inland, and tours to Desolation Sound further up the coast.

In the event of having to stay overnight locally, you can choose from a dozen or so **motels** in town and a couple near the terminal itself. The most central of several **campgrounds** is the *Willingdon Beach* on the seafront off Marine Avenue at 6910 Duncan St (☎485-2242; $11–18).

The northern end point of Hwy 101 – which, incidentally, starts in Mexico City, making it one of North America's longest continuous routes – is the hamlet of **LUND**, 28km up the coast from Powell River. It has a single **hotel**, the *Lund Hotel* (☎604-483-3187; ③), an interesting combination of pub, laundry, post office, store, water taxis, helicopter pad and waterfront units. **Desolation Sound Marine Provincial Park**, about 10km north of Lund, offers some of Canada's best boating and scuba diving, plus fishing, canoeing and kayaking. There's no road access to the park, but a number of outfitters in Powell River run tours to it and can hire all the equipment you could possibly need – try Westview Live Bait Ltd, 4527 Marine Ave, for **canoes**; Coulter's Diving, 4557 Willingdon Ave, for **scuba gear**; and Spokes, 4710 Marine Drive, for **bicycles**. The more modest **Okeover Provincial Park**, immediately north of Lund, has an unserviced campground.

The Sea to Sky Highway

A fancy name for Hwy 99 between North Vancouver and Whistler, the **Sea to Sky Highway** has a slightly better reputation than it deserves, mainly because Vancouver's weekend hordes need to reassure themselves of the grandeur of the scenery at their doorstep. It undoubtedly scores in its early coastal stretch, where the road clings perilously to an almost sheer cliff and mountains come dramatically into view on both sides of Howe Sound. Views here are better than along the Sunshine Coast, though plenty of campgrounds, motels and minor roadside distractions fill the route until the mountains of the Coast Range rear up beyond **Squamish** for the rest of the way to Whistler.

If you've a **car** you're better off driving the highway only as far as **Garibaldi Provincial Park** – the summer-only section between Pemberton and Lillooet is very slow-going. Six daily Maverick Coach Lines **buses** (☎662-8051 or 932-5031) connect Vancouver and Whistler (3 daily continue to Pemberton), which you can easily manage as a day-trip (it's 2hr 30min one way to Whistler from Vancouver by bus), though a far more interesting and popular way of covering this ground is by **train**. BC Rail operates a daily passenger service between North Vancouver and Lillooet, calling at Whistler and other minor stations; the train arrives in Lillooet at 1pm and sets off back for Vancouver at 3.30pm, making for an excellent day-trip. Another train continues on to Prince George daily between mid-June and late September, and on Sunday, Wednesday and Friday the rest of the year; this is a much better way to make the journey than by bus via Hope and Cache Creek. Reservations are required if you're travelling beyond Lillooet (☎984-5246 or 1-800-663-8238).

Britannia Beach

Road and rail lines meet with some squalor at tiny **BRITANNIA BEACH**, 53km from Vancouver, whose **BC Museum of Mining** is the first reason to take time out from admiring the views (mid-May to June, Sept & Oct Wed–Sun 10am–4.30pm; July & Aug daily 10am–4.30pm; $8.50). Centring around what was, in the 1930s, the largest producer of copper in the British empire, the museum is housed in a huge, derelict-looking white building on the hillside and is chock-full of hands-on displays, original working machinery and archive photographs. You can also take guided underground tours around the mine galleries on small electric trains. If you need refreshment at this point make for *Jane's Coffee House* or *Twin Gables Tearoom* for snacks, and *Mountain Woman's* for something more substantial.

Beyond Britannia Beach a huge, chimney-surrounded lumber mill hoves into view across Howe Sound to spoil the scenic wonder along this stretch, though **Petgill Lake** makes a nice picnic spot. This is but one of several small coastal reserves, the most striking of which is **Shannon Falls Provincial Park**, 7km beyond Britannia Beach, signed right off the road and worth a stop for its spectacular 335-metre **waterfall**. Six times the height of Niagara, you can see them from the road, but it's only five minutes' walk to the viewing area at the base, where the proximity of the road, plus some commercial fuss and bother, detract a touch.

Squamish

The sea views and coastal drama end 11km beyond Britannia Beach at **SQUAMISH**, not a pretty place, whose houses spread out over a flat plain amidst warehouses, logging waste and old machinery. Scenery is not the be-all and end-all, however, for if you want to climb, windsurf or watch bald eagles, there's nowhere better in Canada to do so. At first glance all the town has by way of fame is the vast granite rock literally overshadowing it, "The Stawamus Chief", which looms into view to the east just beyond Shannon Falls and is claimed to be the world's "second-biggest free-standing rock" (after Gibraltar, apparently). Over the last few years, however, the rock has caused the town's stock to rise considerably, for it now rates as one of Canada's top – if not *the* top – spot for **rock climbing**. If all you want to do is watch this activity from below, the pull-off beyond the falls is a good spot. Around 160,000 climbers from around the world come here annually, swarming over more than 280 routes pioneered over the 625-metre monolith: the University Wall and its culmination, the Dance Platform, is rated Canada's toughest climb, which is saying something in a country with Canada's countless mountains. Other simpler but highly rated climbs include Banana Peel, Sugarloaf and Cat Crack, and other more varied routes on the adjacent Smoke Bluffs and outcrops in Murrin Provincial Park.

The rock is sacred to the local Squamish, whose ancient tribal name – which means "place where the wind blows" – gives a clue as to the town's second big activity. **Windsurfing** here is now renowned across North America, thanks to some truly extraordinary winds, most drummed up by the vast rock walls around the town and its inlet – which are then funnelled along the inlet's narrow corridor to Squamish at its head. There are strong, consistent winds here to suit all standards, from beginner to world-class, but the water is cold, so a wet suit's a good idea if you're still at the falling-off-frequently stage (there are rental outlets around town). Most people head for the artificial Squamish Spit, a dyke separating the waters of the Howe Sound from the Squamish River, a park area run by the Squamish Windsurfing Society (☎926-WIND or 892-2235). It's around 3km from town (ask at the infocentre for directions) and a small fee is payable to the Society to cover rescue boats, insurance and washroom facilities.

The town has one more unexpected treat, for the Squamish River, and the tiny hamlet of Brackendale in particular (10km to the north on Hwy 99), is – literally – the world's **bald-eagle** capital. In winter – drop by on the way to ski at Whistler – around 2000 eagles regularly congregate here, attracted by the chance to pick off the salmon that migrates upriver to spawn. In 1994, 3769 eagles were counted locally. The best place to see them is the so-called Eagle Run behind the Sunwolf Outdoor Centre, and on the river in the Brackendale Eagle Reserve. The birds largely winter on the river's west bank, with the viewing area on the east – eagles will stop feeding if approached within about 150m, so the river provides an invaluable buffer zone. For more information and details of guided walks in the area, contact the Brackendale Art Gallery on Government Road (winter Mon–Fri noon–5pm, Sat & Sun noon–10pm; ☎898-3333).

If Squamish's outdoor activities leave you cold, then you might want to look in on the new **West Coast Railway Heritage Park**, Centennial Way (mid-May to early Sept daily 9am–6pm; $4.50 plus a small fee to ride the miniature railway; ☎1-800-722-1233), signed off Hwy 99 about 3km north of town. The twelve-acre park contains 58 fine old railway carriages and locomotives in a pretty natural setting.

Practicalities

Most of the relevant parts of the town are concentrated on Cleveland Avenue, including the **infocentre** (daily 9am–6pm, longer hours in summer; ☎892-9244), the big Overwaitea supermarket and the most central **accommodation** if you're not at the hostel, the *August Jack Motor Inn* on Cleveland Avenue (☎892-3504; ③). If you're in town in

August, incidentally, Squamish shows it has not forgotten its lumbering roots by holding what it deems to be the World Lumberjack Competition. If you want to **stay**, or want the inside knowledge on the climbing or wildlife, be certain to stay at the superlative new **Squamish Hostel** (the only hostel in town). The hostel's clean and friendly, and offers a kitchen, common room and private room as well as shared accommodation. If you're here to climb, there are two key **guides**, which you should be able to order in advance from bookstores in Vancouver (see "Listings" on p.680): *The Rockclimbers' Guide to Squamish* by Kevin McLane (Merlin Productions; $30) and *New Climbs 1992–95* (same details; $19).

Garibaldi Provincial Park

The road north of Squamish continues to be a mess, but after about 5km begins to enter the classic river, mountain and forest country redolent of the BC interior. The journey thereafter is a joy, with only the march of electricity pylons and big road-widening schemes to take the edge off an idyllic drive.

Unless you're skiing, **Garibaldi Provincial Park** is the main incentive for heading this way. As you'd expect, it's a huge and unspoilt area which combines all the usual breathtaking ingredients of lakes, rivers, forests, glaciers and the peaks of the Coast Mountains (Wedge Mountain, at 2891m, is the park's highest point). Four rough roads access the park from points along the highway between Squamish and Whistler, but you'll need transport to reach the trailheads at the end of them. Pick up the excellent BC Parks pamphlet for Garibaldi from the Vancouver tourist office for a comprehensive rundown on all trails, campgrounds and the like. Unless you're camping, the only accommodation close to the park is at Whistler, though with an early start from Vancouver you could feasibly enjoy a good walk and return the same day.

There are five main areas with trails, of which the **Black Tusk/Garibaldi Lake** region is the most popular and probably most beautiful. Try the trail from the parking area at Rubble Creek to Garibaldi Lake (9km; 3hr one-way) or to Taylor Meadows (7km; 2hr 30min return). Further trails then fan out from Garibaldi Lake, including one to the huge basalt outcrop of **Black Tusk** (2316m), a rare opportunity to reach an alpine summit without any rock climbing. The other hiking areas from south to north are **Diamond Head**, **Cheakamus Lake**, **Singing Pass** and **Wedgemount Lake**. Access to each is clearly signed from the highway, and all have wilderness campgrounds and are explored by several trails of varying lengths. Outside these small defined areas, however, the park is untrammelled wilderness. Bear in mind there are also hiking possibilities outside the park from Whistler (see below), where in summer you can get a head start on hikes by riding up the ski lifts.

Whistler

WHISTLER, 56km beyond Squamish, is Canada's finest four-season resort, and frequently ranks among most people's world top five winter ski resorts. In 1996, for the first time ever, *Ski, Snow Country* and *Skiing* magazines were unanimous in voting it North America's top skiing destination. Skiing is clearly the main activity, but all manner of other winter sports are possible – snowboarding is particularly big – and in summer the lifts keep running to provide supreme highline hiking and other outdoor activities (not to mention North America's finest summer skiing). Standards are high, and for those raised on the queues and waits at European resorts, the ease with which you can get onto the slopes here will come as a pleasant surprise.

The resort consists of two adjacent but separate mountains – **Whistler** (2182m) and **Blackcomb** – each with their own extensive lift and chair systems, and each covered in a multitude of runs. Both lift systems are accessed from the resort's heart, the purpose-built and largely pedestrianized **Whistler Village**, the tight-clustered focus of many hotels, shops, restaurants and aprés-ski activity. Around this core are two other "village" complexes, Upper Village (also known as Blackcomb Resort) and the recently completed Village North. Around 6km to the south of Whistler Village is **Whistler Creek**, a cheaper alternative base (also with a gondola and lift base), though in truth the whole ribbon of land on and just off the main Hwy 99 from Whistler Creek to Whistler Village is gradually being developed – Whistler is the single fastest-growing municipality in BC.

Whistler Village

WHISTLER VILLAGE is the key to the resort, a newish and – in summer at least – a rather characterless and pastel-shaded conglomeration of hotels, restaurants, mountain-gear shops and more loud people in fluorescent clothes than are healthy in one place at the same time. Its name is said to derive from the piercing whistle of the marmot, a small and rather chubby mammal, which emits its distinctive shriek as a warning call. Others say the name comes from the sound of the wind whistling through Singing Pass up in the mountains. Whatever its origins, the village has all the facilities of any normal village, with the difference that they all charge more than what you'd pay anywhere else. At the same time it's a somewhat soulless place, very much a resort complex than an organic village, though for most people who are here to indulge on the slopes, character is a secondary consideration. Huge amounts of money have been invested here and elsewhere in the area since the resort opened in 1980, with the result that services, food, lifts and the resort's general overall polish are almost faultless. More money's on the way – another $35 million – and Whistler's challenge is now seen as being able to rein in development before it spoils the scenery – one of the resort's many attractions – and kills the goose laying the golden egg: at present the area is about 75 percent of the way to its target ceiling of an incredible 80,000 visitor beds.

Whistler Mountain

Winter sports enthusiasts can argue long and late over the relative merits of **WHISTLER MOUNTAIN** and its near rival, Blackcomb Mountain, both accessed from Whistler Village's lifts. Together they have over 200 runs, thirty lifts, three major glaciers and twelve vast, high-alpine bowls. Both are great mountains, and both offer great skiing or boarding: Whistler Mountain hosts the Men's World Cup Downhill events and Blackcomb World Freestyle Championships. Each has a distinctive character, however, at least for the time being, for major injections of money are on the way to upgrade Whistler Mountain's already impressive facilities. Traditionally this has been seen as the more intimate and homely of the two mountains, somewhere you can ski or board for days on end and never have to retrace your steps. **Highlight runs** for intermediates or confident novices are Hwy 86 or Burnt Stew Basin, with Franz's Run the best of the bunch generally, a high-velocity cruiser that drops virtually from the tree line right down to Whistler Creek. Real thrill-seekers should head to three above-tree-line swaths of snow: Harmony Bowl, Symphony Bowl and the steep Glacier Bowl.

Facts and figures to help you sort out your priorities include area – 3657 acres of skiing, of which 20 percent is beginner, 55 percent intermediate and 25 percent expert. There are over a hundred marked **trails**, one glacier and seven major bowls. **Lifts** include two high-speed gondolas, three express quads, three triple and one double chair lift, two T-bars, two handle tows and one platter lift. Total vertical drop is 1530m. For general **information** on Whistler Mountain, call ☎932-3434 (☎664-5614 in Vancouver) and for snow conditions on the hill, call ☎932-4191 (☎687-6761 in Vancouver).

ACTIVITIES

Outdoor activities aside, there's not a lot else to do in Whistler save sit in the cafés and watch the world go by. In summer, though, the chances are you'll be here to walk or mountain bike, the latter a big summer activity. If you're **walking**, remember you can ride the ski lifts way up onto both mountains for tremendous views and easy access to high-altitude trails. **Mountain bikers** can also take bikes up and ride down. Pick up the duplicated sheet of biking and hiking trails from the infocentre or from the smaller kiosks in the Village (see p.783), or better yet buy the 1:50,000 *Whistler and Garibaldi Region* map. The two most popular shorter walks are the **Rainbow Falls** and the six-hour **Singing Pass** trails. Other good choices are the four-kilometre trail to Cheakamus Lake or any of the high alpine hikes accessed from the Upper Gondola station (1837m) on Whistler Mountain or the Seventh Heaven lift on Blackcomb: you can, of course, come here simply for the view. Among the walks from Whistler Mountain gondola station, think about the **Glacier Trail** (2.5km round trip; 150m ascent; 1hr) for views of the snow and ice in Glacier Bowl – snowshoe rental and tours are possible to let you cross some of the safer snow fields ($5 for the first hour, then $3 an hour; tours from $14). Or go for the slightly more challenging **Little Whistler Trail** (3.8km round trip; 265m ascent; 1hr 30min–2hr), which takes you to the summit of Little Whistler Peak (2115m) and grand views of Black Tusk in Garibaldi Provincial Park. Remember to time your hike to get back to the gondola station for the last ride down (times vary according to season).

If the high-level stuff seems too daunting (it shouldn't be – the trails are good) – then there are plenty of trails (some surfaced) for bikers, walkers and rollerbladers around the Village. There are also numerous operators offering guided walks and bike rides to suit all abilities, as well as numerous **rental outlets** for bikes, blades and other equipment around the Village. If you want to go **horseriding**, contact the resort info-numbers (☎932-3141 for Blackcomb Mountain, ☎932-3434 for Whistler Mountain) or Whistler Outdoor Experience (☎932-3389). This last company will also set you up with **jet boating**, white-water and float **rafting**, as will Whistler River Adventures (☎932-3532) and Whistler Jet Boating (☎932-3389). You can play tennis at several public courts, or play squash or **swim** at the Meadow Park Sports Centre (☎938-PARK). If you're a **golfer** the area has four great courses, including one designed by Jack Nicklaus – *Golf* magazine called Whistler "one of the best golf resorts in the world". The cheapest to play on is the Whistler Golf Club course (from $65 weekdays, $80 weekends; ☎1-800-376-1777), while the others, including Nicklaus North (☎604-938-9898), all cost from about $95 during the week and $115 at weekends.

Blackcomb Mountain

BLACKCOMB MOUNTAIN, the "Mile-High Mountain", is a ski area laden with superlatives: the most modern resort in Canada or the US, North America's finest (only) summer skiing (on Horstman Glacier), the continent's longest unbroken fall-line skiing and the longest *and* second longest lift-serviced vertical falls in North America (1609m and 1530m). In shape, its trail and run-system resembles an inverted triangle, with ever more skiing and boarding possibilities branching off the higher you go. The most famous run is the double black diamond Couloir Extreme, the first such run in Canada, one of several precipitous chutes in the Rendezvous Bowl. Three other **runs** are also particularly renowned: the Zig-Zag, a long, winding cruise; Blackcomb Glacier, one of North America's longest above-tree-line runs; and Xhiggy's Meadow on the Seventh Heaven Express. If you're here to board or ski in summer, two T-bars take you up to the wide open cruising terrain on Horstman Glacier.

Blackcomb is slightly smaller than Whistler, at 3341 acres, but has the same break-down of **terrain** (20 percent beginner, 55 percent intermediate and 25 percent expert). **Lifts** are one high-speed gondola, six express quads, three triple chair lifts, two T-bars, three handle tows and one platter lift. There are over a hundred marked trails, two glaciers and five bowls. For general **information** on Blackcomb Mountain, call ☎938-7747 or 932-3141, and for snow conditions call ☎932-4211 (☎687-7507 in Vancouver). Even if you're not skiing, come up here (summer or winter) on the ski lifts to walk, enjoy the **view** from the top of the mountain, or to eat in the *Rendezvous* or new *Glacier Creek* restaurants. If you want some **cross-country skiing** locally, the best spots are 22km of groomed trails around Lost Lake and the Chateau Whistler golf course, all easily accessible from Whistler Village.

Arrival, information and accommodation

There are several ways of **getting to** Whistler. If you're flying to Vancouver on a skiing package (or otherwise) and want to get straight to the resort, then Perimeter (☎266-536 or 905-0041 from Whistler) run a direct **bus shuttle** from the airport to Whistler, with drop-offs at Whistler Creek and several major hotels in and around Whistler Village. Reservations are required for the service, with prepayment by credit card and cancellations allowed up to 24 hours in advance (2 daily; $45 one way). Maverick Coach Lines (☎662-8051) run six daily **bus** services (more in winter) from Vancouver bus depot (see p.649) to the Village via Britannia Beach, Whistler Creek and other stops en route. You can also travel by BC Rail **train** (☎984-5246 or 1-800-339-8752 in BC or 1-800-663-8238 in the rest of North America) from the station in North Vancouver (1 daily; $29; 1hr 35min). If you need taxis to get around locally, try Sea to Sky (☎932-3333) or Whistler Taxi (☎932-5455).

Many people in winter are likely to be on a package. If not, or if you're here in summer, all local **accommodation** can be booked through **Whistler Central Reservations** (☎664-5625 or 1-800-944-7853), who can help find a room or a condo for you in an appropriate price bracket. If you're booking for winter, note that reservations should be made well in advance. Such is demand that many hotels have a thirty-day cancellation window and may insist on a minimum of three days' stay. If money's no object, the summer **information kiosks** in the Village (at the central Village Square and Village Gate) can also help with to masses of comfortable chalet and lodge accommodation (remember that chalets can put extra beds in double rooms at nominal rates). Whistler Creek is home to the main **infocentre**, 2097 Lake Placid Rd (daily 9am–5pm, longer hours in summer; ☎932-5528), but not terribly useful as a base unless you have transport and are skiing. Note that the resort and mountains have their own information numbers (see above).

If you're going to do Whistler in style, the top resort hotel is the $75-million *Chateau Whistler* (☎938-8000). Best budget choice is the **youth hostel** on Alta Lake at 5678 Alta Lake Rd, one of the nicest hostels in BC (☎932-5492; ①), a signposted forty-minute walk from the infocentre or ten-minute drive to the village centre; note that BC Rail trains may sometimes stop alongside the hostel if you ask the conductor. As it's popular year-round, reserve ahead. All beds are in shared rooms ($17.50–22.50). Another reasonable choice is the *Fireside Lodge* (☎932-4545; ②) at Nordic Estates, 3km south of the village. Finally, you could try the *Whistler Lodge* (☎932-6604 or 228-5851; ①), also in Nordic Estates, which is owned by the University of British Columbia but lets non-students stay; check-in time is from 4pm to 10pm. Best of the **campgrounds** is the *Whistler KOA*, 1km north of the village off Hwy 99 to the right (☎932-5181; $17).

Eating, drinking and nightlife

As for **food and drink**, Whistler Village and its satellites are loaded with cafés and some ninety restaurants, though none really have an "address" as such. These can come and go at an alarming rate, but the top-rated restaurants of long standing are

Araxi's Restaurant and Antipasto Bar (☎932-4540), the *Rim Rock Café & Oyster Bar* (☎932-5565) – excellent for seafood – and the much-praised *Il Caminetto di Umberto* (☎932-4442): in winter and busy summer evenings you'll probably need to book at all three, and especially the last. If you want to get away from the Village, the *Thai One On* (☎932-4822) in the Upper Village is good, as is *Caramba!* (☎938-1879) in Village North. In Whistler Creek (6km) the no-nonsense *South Side Deli* is a popular local hang-out for breakfast and cheap meals and snacks throughout the day. If you're shopping for supplies the Village offers the Grocery Store, though locals tend to head for Nester's up on the main highway.

Winter or summer Whistler enjoys a lot of **nightlife** and aprés-ski activity, visitors being bolstered by the large seasonal workforce – Whistler needs over four thousand people just to keep the show on the road – among which a vocal Antipodean presence figures large. If you want relative peace and quiet, or a cosy nook for a nightcap, the key spot is the smartish *Mallard Bar* (☎938-8000) in the *Chateau Whistler* hotel. If you're just off Whistler Mountain, the aprés-ski haunt is the *Longhorn Pub* (☎932-5999) in the Village at the *Carleton Lodge*, with the lively beer-heavy *Merlin's* (☎932-3141) in the *Blackcomb Daylodge* performing the same function for Blackcomb. As evening draws on, make for *Buffalo Bill's* (☎932-5211) at the *Timberline Lodge*, a good bar with dance floor and occasional **live music** (some of it pretty good). A younger set, snowboarding hipsters among them, make for bars and **clubs** like *Tommy Africa's* (☎932-6090) and the *Savage Beagle Club* (☎932-4540), both in the village.

North of Whistler

Hwy 99 funnels down to two slow lanes at **PEMBERTON** and, beyond, you're treated to some wonderfully wild country in which Vancouver and even Whistler seem a long way away. Patches of forest poke through rugged mountainsides and scree slopes, and a succession of glorious lakes culminate in Sefton Lake, whose hydroelectric schemes feed power into the grid as far south as Arizona, accounting for the pylons south of Whistler.

At the lumber town of **LILLOOET** the railway meets the Fraser River, which marks a turning point in the scenery as denuded crags and hillsides increasingly hint at the *High Noon*-type ranching country to come. In July and August, the rocky banks and bars of the sluggish, mud-coloured river immediately north of town are dotted with vivid orange and blue tepees and tarpaulins. These belong to Native Canadians who still come to catch, dry and smoke salmon as the fish make their way upriver to spawn. It's one of the few places where this tradition is continued and is well worth stopping to watch. The town boasts four central **motels** if you need to stay: best are the *Mile 0 Motel*, 616 Main St (☎256-7511 or 1-888-766-4530; ②–④), downtown, overlooking the river and mountains (kitchenettes available in some units for self-catering), and the *4 Pines Motel* on the corner of 8th Avenue and Russell Street at 108 8th Ave, also with kitchenettes (☎256-4247; ①). The **infocentre** is at 790 Main St (late May to Oct daily 9am–6pm; ☎250-256-4308). The nearest **campground** is the riverside *Cayoosh Creek* on Hwy 99 within walking distance of downtown (☎256-4180; $13; mid-April to mid-Oct).

Over the next 100km the **Fraser Valley** is more than enough to justify the price of a train ticket to Prince George. The alpine profile of the Coast Range flattens out into the high, table-topped ridges of the Cariboo Plateau, and the railway looks down to the dry, dust-bowl gullies and cliffs of the vast canyon from a vantage point some 1000m above the river. The views are some of the grandest and strangest in the province, taking in huge horizons of bleached ochre soil and deserts of lonely scrubby pasture that once belonged to the so-called "**remittance men**": the off-beam, half-mad or just plain dangerous sons of nineteenth-century English aristocrats dispatched here on a monthly remittance, or allowance, and encouraged not to get in touch. There were many such errant offspring locally, and several ranches here – some of the biggest in Canada – were long owned by Britons, amongst them the ranch bought in 1912 by the Marquis of Exeter and run by his son, Lord Martin Cecil, who used it as a base for the Emissaries of Divine Light, a religious group, until his death.

The Cariboo

The Cariboo is the name given to the broad, rolling ranching country and immense forests of British Columbia's interior plateau, which extend north of Lillooet between the Coast Mountains to the west and Cariboo Mountains to the east. The region contains by far the dullest scenery in the province, and what little interest it offers – aside from fishing and boating on thousands of remote lakes – comes from its **gold-mining** heritage. Initially exploited by fur traders to a small degree, the region was fully opened up following the discovery of gold in 1858 in the lower Fraser Valley by prospectors who had made their way north from the Californian gold fields. The building of the **Cariboo Wagon Road**, a stagecoach route north out of Lillooet, spread gold fever right up the Fraser watershed as men leapfrogged from creek to creek, culminating in the big finds at Williams Creek in 1861 and Barkerville a year later.

Much of the old Wagon Road is today retraced by lonely **Hwy 97** – the Cariboo Hwy – and **VIA Rail**, which run in tandem through hour after hour of straggling pine forests and past the occasional ranch and small, marsh-edged lake – scenery that strikes you as pristine and pastoral for a while but which soon leaves you in a tree-weary stupor. If you're forced to stop over, there are innumerable lodges, ranches and motels on or just off the highway, and you can pick up copious material on the region at the Vancouver tourist office or infocentres en route.

Clinton and Williams Lake

A compact little village surrounded by green pastures and tree-covered hills, **CLINTON** – named after a British duke – marks the beginning of the heart of Cariboo country. The town has a couple of **motels** and a couple of lodges, the most central being the *Nomad* (☎459-2214 or 1-888-776-6623; ②). The three tiny settlements beyond Clinton at 70, 100, and 150 Mile House are echoes of the old roadhouses built by men who were paid by the mile to blaze the Cariboo Wagon Road – which is doubtless why 100 Mile House is well short of a 100 miles from the start of the road. 100 Mile House has a year-round **infocentre** at 422 Cariboo Hwy 97 South (☎250-395-5353) for details of the fishing, ranch stays, riding and other local outdoor pursuits. There are also a handful of **motels** in or a few kilometres away from town, the biggest in-town choice being the *Red Coach Inn*, 170 Hwy 97 North (☎250-395-2266 or 1-800-663-8422; ③–④). The central *Imperial* is smaller and cheaper (☎250-395-2471; ③).

WILLIAMS LAKE, 14km north of 150 Mile House and still 238km south of Prince George, is a busy and drab transport centre that huddles in the lee of a vast crag on terraces above the lake of the same name. It has plenty of motels, B&Bs, boat launches and swimming spots south of the town – but it's hardly a place you'd want to spend any time, unless you're deadbeat after driving or around on the first weekend in July for its famous **rodeo**. The year-round **infocentre** is at 1148 Broadway South (☎250-392-5025).

Bella Coola

Highway 20 branches west from Williams Lake, a part-paved, part-gravel road that runs 455km to **BELLA COOLA**, a village likely to gain an ever greater tourist profile in the wake of the new visitor-oriented ferry service from Port Hardy on Vancouver Island (see p.739). Most of the road ploughs through the interminable forest of the Cariboo Plateau, but the last 100km or so traverses the high and stunningly spectacular peaks of the Coast Mountains and Tweedsmuir Provincial Park. Just outside the park you encounter the notorious "Hill", a hugely winding and precipitous stretch of highway barely tamed by the various upgradings over the years. Until 1953 there was no road link here at all. For years there was a sixty-kilometre gap in the mountain stretch, a missing link the state refused to bridge. In response the locals of Bella Coola took it upon themselves to build the road on their own, completing their so-called Freedom Road in three years. Previously the settlement was the domain of the Bella Coola, or Nuxalk Native Canadians, a group visited by George Vancouver as early as 1793. In 1869 the Hudson's Bay Company opened a trading post. One house belonging to a company clerk is now all that remains. Besides a small museum and glorious scenery, Bella Coola is hardly stacked with sights. Norwegian settlers, however, perhaps drawn by the fjord-like scenery nearby, were notable early pioneers, and language, heritage and buildings – notably the square-logged barns – all show a Scandinavian touch. **Hagensborg**, a village 18km east of Bella Coola, preserves a particularly strong Nordic flavour. About 10km from the village, roughly midway to Bella Coola, are the **Thorsen Creek Petroglyphs**, a hundred or so rock drawings: the infocentre (see below) should be able to fix you up with a guide to explore the site.

If you're without a car, Chilcotin Stage Lines, based at 27 7th Ave South in Williams Lake (☎392-6170), have in the past run **buses** all the way to Bella Coola – check the service is still running. Beyond the village there is no onward road route: unless you fly out, you'll have to either head back the way you came or pick up the new **Discovery Coast Passage** boats to Port Hardy that stop off at the port. Boats leave every couple of days or so at 6.30am or 8.15am, arriving in Port Hardy at around 8.30pm that evening or 6.15am the following morning depending on the number of stops en route (see p.739 for full details of the service). If you want to indulge in a plane in or out of town, contact Wilderness Airlines (☎982-2225 or 1-800-665-9453).

Bella Coola's **infocentre** is on the Mackenzie Hwy near town (☎799-5919). The new ferry service will probably lead to the opening of new hotels and restaurants: currently **accommodation** is provided by the *Cedar Inn* (☎799-5316; ③–④), closest hotel to the ferry terminal, and the *Bella Coola Motel* (☎799-5323; ②) at the corner of Burke and Clayton – both places are downtown. There's also the *Bay Motor Hotel* on Hwy 20 14km east of the town and 1km from the airport (☎982-2212 or 1-888-982-2212; ③–④).

Along Hwy 97: north of Williams Lake

North of Williams Lake on Hwy 97, the **Fraser River** re-enters the scenic picture and, after a dramatic stretch of canyon, reinstates more compelling hills and snatches of river meadows. This also marks the start, however, of some of the most concerted **logging operations** in all British Columbia, presaged by increasing numbers of crude pepper-pot kilns used to burn off waste wood. By **QUESNEL**, home of the "world's largest plywood plant", you're greeted with scenes out of an environmentalist's nightmare: whole mountainsides cleared of trees, piles of sawdust the size of small hills, and unbelievably large lumber mills surrounded by stacks of logs and finished timber that stretch literally as far as the eye can see. If you're stuck for accommodation (there are a dozen or so hotels) or tempted by any of the many mill tours, contact the **infocentre** in Le Bourdais Park at 703 Carson Ave (year-round; ☎992-8716 or 1-800-992-4922).

Barkerville

Most people who take the trouble to drive this route detour from Quesnel to **Barkerville Provincial Historic Park**, 90km to the east in the heart of the Cariboo Mountains, the site of the Cariboo's biggest gold strike and an invigorating spot in its own right, providing a much-needed jolt to the senses after the sleepy scenery to the south (June–Sept daily 8am–8pm; $5.50). In 1862 a Cornishman named Billy Barker idly staked a claim here and after digging down a metre or so was about to pack up and head north. Urged on by his mates, however, he dug another couple of spadefuls and turned up a cluster of nuggets worth $600,000. Within months Barkerville, as it was later dubbed, had become the largest city in the region, and rode the boom for a decade until the gold finally ran out. Today numerous buildings have been restored, and the main administrative building has displays on mining methods and the gold rush, together with propaganda on their importance to the province.

If you want to **stay** under cover up here, there are just three options, all at **WELLS**, 8km west of the park: the *Hub Motel* (☎994-3313; ②); the *Wells Hotel*, 2341 Pooley St (☎250-994-3427 or 1-800-860-2299; ③–⑤), a newly restored 1933 heritage country inn with licensed café and breakfast included; and the *White Cap Motor Inn* (☎994-3489 or 1-800-377-2028; ③) – the last also has RV and camping spaces for $9.50. Failing this you can **camp** at the three-way campground at Barkerville Provincial Park adjacent to the old town (reservations accepted; ☎250-398-4414; $9.50–12; May–Oct). Wells has an **infocentre** on Pooley Street, part of a small museum (summer only; ☎994-3237).

travel details

Trains

Vancouver to: Edmonton (3 weekly; 25hr); Jasper (June–Sept daily except Wed; Oct–May 3 weekly; 19hr); Lillooet (mid-June to Oct 1 daily; rest of year 4 weekly; 5hr 30min); Prince George (mid-June to Oct 1 daily; rest of year 3 weekly; 13hr 30min); Whistler (1 daily; 3hr); Winnipeg via Edmonton and Saskatoon (3 weekly; 40hr).

Victoria to: Courtenay via Nanaimo (1 daily; 4hr 35min).

Buses

Nanaimo to: Port Alberni (4 daily; 1hr 20min); Port Hardy (1 daily; 6hr 50min); Tofino (1–2 daily; 4hr 30min); Ucluelet (1–2 daily; 3hr 10min); Victoria (7 daily; 2hr 20min).

Penticton to: Prince George via Kamloops and Cache Creek (2 daily; 13hr).

Port Alberni to: Nanaimo (4 daily; 1hr 20min); Tofino via Ucluelet (1–2 daily; 3hr).

Vancouver to: Bellingham (8–10 daily; 1hr 45min); Calgary via Kamloops (6 daily; 13hr); Calgary via Penticton, Nelson and Cranbrook (2 daily; 24hr); Calgary via Princeton and Kelowna (2 daily; 18hr); Edmonton via Jasper (3 daily; 16hr 30min); Nanaimo (8 daily; 5hr); Pemberton (3 daily; 3hr 10min); Powell River (2 daily; 5hr 10min); Prince George via Cache Creek and Williams Lake (2 daily; 13hr); Seattle, US (8–10 daily; 3hr 15min);

Sea-Tac Airport, US (8–10 daily; 4hr 10min); Vernon (6 daily; 6hr); Victoria (8 daily; 5hr); Whistler (6 daily; 2hr 30min).

Victoria to: Bamfield (1–3 daily; 6–8hr); Campbell River (5 daily; 5hr); Nanaimo (7 daily; 2hr 20min); Port Hardy (1 daily; 9hr 45min); Port Renfrew (2 daily; 2hr 30min); Vancouver (8–10 daily; 4hr); Vancouver Airport direct (3 daily; 3hr 30min).

Ferries

Courtenay to: Powell River (4 daily; 1hr 15min).

Powell River to: Courtenay (4 daily; 1hr 15min).

Vancouver to: Nanaimo (16 daily; 1hr 35min–2hr); Victoria (hourly 7am–9pm; 1hr 35min).

Victoria to: Anacortes and San Juan Islands, US (1–2 daily; 2hr 30min); Seattle, US (1–2 daily; 2hr 30min); Vancouver (hourly 7am–10pm; 1hr 35min).

Flights

Vancouver to: Calgary (20 daily; 1hr 15min); Edmonton (14 daily; 1hr 30min); Montréal (8 daily; 5hr 35min); Ottawa (10 daily; 4hr 40min); Toronto (15 daily; 4hr 55min); Victoria (14 daily; 25min); Winnipeg (8 daily; 2hr 40min).

Victoria to: Calgary (4 daily; 1hr 40min); Vancouver (14 daily; 25min).

CHAPTER EIGHT

THE NORTH

A lthough much of western Canada still has the flavour of the "last frontier", it's only when you embark on the mainland push north to the Yukon that you know for certain you're leaving the mainstream of North American life behind. In the popular imagination, **the north** figures as a perpetually frozen wasteland blasted by ferocious gloomy winters, inhabited – if at all – by hardened characters beyond the reach of civilization. In truth, it's a region where months of summer sunshine offer almost limitless opportunities for outdoor activities and an incredible profusion of flora and fauna; a country within a country, the character of whose settlements has often been forged by the mingling of white settlers and **native peoples**. The indigenous hunters of the north are as varied as in the south, but two groups predominate: the **Dene**, people of the northern forests who traditionally occupied the Mackenzie River region from the Albertan border to the river's delta at the Beaufort Sea; and the Arctic **Inuit** (literally "the people"), once known as the Eskimos or "fish eaters", a Dene term picked up by early European settlers and now discouraged.

The north is as much a state of mind as a place. People "north of 60" – the 60th Parallel – claim the right to be called **northerners**, and claim a kinship with Alaskans, but those north of the Arctic Circle look with light-hearted disdain on these "southerners". All mock the inhabitants of the northernmost corners of Alberta and such areas of the so-called Northwest, who, after all, live with the luxury of being able to get around their backcountry by road. To any outsider, however, in terms of landscape and spirit of place the north begins well south of the 60th Parallel. Accordingly, this chapter includes not just the provinces of the "true north" – **Yukon Territory** and parts of the **Northwest Territories** – but also northern **British Columbia**, a region more stark and extreme than BC's southern reaches.

Northern British Columbia

The two roads into the Yukon strike through northern British Columbia: the **Alaska Highway**, connecting **Dawson Creek** to Fairbanks in Alaska, and the adventurous **Cassiar Highway**, from near **Prince Rupert** to **Watson Lake**, on the Yukon border. Though the Cassiar's passage through the Coast Mountains offers perhaps the better landscapes, it's the Alaska Highway – serviced by daily Greyhound **buses** and plentiful motels and campgrounds – that is more travelled, starting in the rolling wheatlands of the Peace River country before curving into the spruce forests and sawtooth ridges of the northern Rockies. While the scenery is superb, most towns on both roads are battered and perfunctory places built around lumber mills, oil and gas plants and mining camps, though increasingly they are spawning motels and restaurants to serve the surge of summer visitors out to capture the thrill of driving the frontier highways. Equally popular are the **sea journeys** offered by northern British Columbia, among the most breathtaking trips in all Canada. Prince Rupert, linked by ferry to Vancouver Island, is the springboard for boats to the magnificent **Haida Gwaii**, or **Queen Charlotte Islands** – home of the Haida people – and a vital way-station for boats plying the Inside Passage up to Alaska.

The telephone code for British Columbia is ☎250.

The Yukon

The Cassiar and Alaska highways converge at **Watson Lake**, a weather-beaten junction that straddles the 60th Parallel and marks the entrance to the **Yukon Territory** (YT), perhaps the most exhilarating and varied destination in this part of the world. Taking its name from a Dene word meaning "great", it boasts the highest mountains in Canada, wild sweeps of forest and tundra, and the fascinating nineteenth-century relic, **Dawson City**. The focus of the Klondike gold rush, Dawson was also the territory's capital until that role shifted south to **Whitehorse**, a town booming on tourism and the ever-increasing exploitation of the Yukon's vast mineral resources.

Road access is easier than you might think. In addition to the Alaska Highway, which runs through the Yukon's southern reaches, the **Klondike Highway** strikes north to link Whitehorse with Dawson City. North of Dawson the recently completed **Dempster Highway** is the only road in Canada to cross the Arctic Circle, offering an unparalleled direct approach to the northern tundra and to several remote communities in the Northwest Territories. The Yukon's other major road is the short spur linking the Alaskan port of Skagway to Whitehorse, which shadows the **Chilkoot Trail**, a treacherous track taken by the poorest of the 1898 prospectors that is now a popular long-distance footpath.

Combining coastal ferries with the Chilkoot Trail makes an especially fine itinerary. Following the old gold-rush trail, the route begins at Skagway – reached by ferry from Prince Rupert – then follows the Chilkoot to Whitehorse, before heading north to Dawson City. From there you could continue up the Dempster Highway, or travel on the equally majestic **Top of the World** road into the heart of Alaska. However, many people coming up from Skagway or plying the mainland routes from British Columbia head to Alaska directly on the Alaska Highway, to enjoy views of the extraordinary and largely inaccessible mountain fastness of **Kluane National Park**, which contains Canada's highest peaks and most extensive glacial wilderness.

Nunavut and the Northwest Territories

If the Yukon is the far north at its most accessible, the **Northwest Territories** (NWT) is the region at its most uncompromising. Just three roads nibble at the edges of this almost unimaginably vast area, which occupies a third of Canada's landmass – about the size of India – but contains only 60,000 people, almost half of whom live in or around **Yellowknife**, the territories' peculiarly overblown capital. Unless you're taking the adventurous and rewarding **Dempster Highway** from Dawson City across the tundra to **Inuvik**, Yellowknife will probably feature on any trip to the NWT, as it's the hub of the (rather expensive) flight network servicing the area's widely dispersed communities.

Otherwise most visitors are here to fish or canoe, to hunt or watch wildlife, or to experience the Inuit native cultures and ethereal landscapes. More for convenience than any political or geographical reasons, the NWT was formally divided into **eight regions**, each with its own tourist association. From 1999 a new two-way division will

---

TOLL-FREE INFORMATION NUMBERS

Tourism British Columbia ☎1-800-663-6000.
NWT Arctic Tourism (Western NWT) ☎1-800-661-0788.

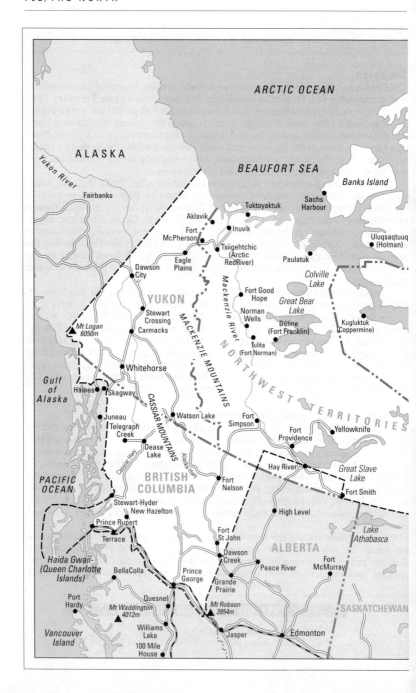

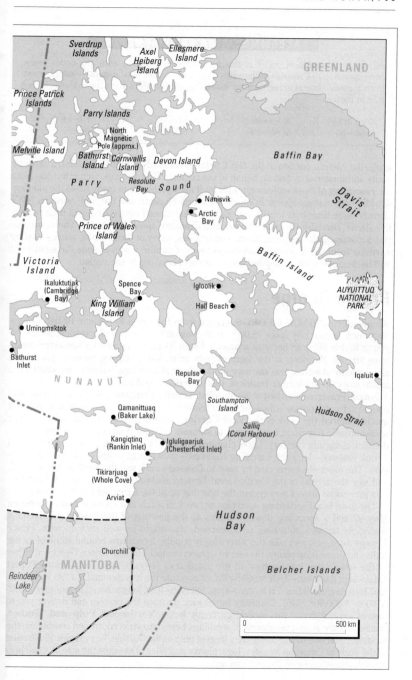

Sverdrup Islands

Axel Heiberg Island

Ellesmere Island

GREENLAND

Prince Patrick Islands

Parry Islands

Melville Island

North Magnetic Pole (approx.)

Bathurst Island

Cornwallis Island

Devon Island

Baffin Bay

Davis Strait

P a r r y   S o u n d

Resolute Bay

Nanisvik

Arctic Bay

Prince of Wales Island

Baffin Island

Victoria Island

AUYUITTUQ NATIONAL PARK

Ikaluktutiak (Cambridge Bay)

Spence Bay

Igloolik

Umingmaktok

King William Island

Hall Beach

Bathurst Inlet

Iqaluit

N U N A V U T

Repulse Bay

Southampton Island

Hudson Strait

Qamanittuaq (Baker Lake)

Salliq (Coral Harbour)

Kangiqtinq (Rankin Inlet)

Igluligaarjuk (Chesterfield Inlet)

Tikirarjuag (Whale Cove)

Arviat

Hudson Bay

Churchill

MANITOBA

Belcher Islands

Reindeer Lake

0   500 km

ACCOMMODATION PRICE SYMBOLS

All the accommodation prices in this book have been coded using the codes below, corresponding to Canadian dollar rates. Prices are for the least expensive double room in each establishment in high season, excluding special offers. For a full explanation, see p.38 in Basics.

① up to $40   ③ $60–80   ⑤ $100–125   ⑦ $175–240
② $40–60   ④ $80–100   ⑥ $125–175   ⑧ $240+

---

apply, the eastern portion of the NWT being renamed Nunavut (see p.838), a separate entity administered by and on behalf of the region's First Peoples. One effect has been the **renaming** of most settlements with Inuit names, though in many cases the old English-language names appear in much literature. Nunavut and the "old" western NWT already issue their own tourist material, and you should obtain a copy of their respective *Arctic Traveller Vacation Planner* and *Explorers' Guide* brochures. These summarize accommodation options, airline connections, many of the available tours – costing anything from $50 to $5000 – and the plethora of outfitters who provide the equipment and backup essential for any but the most superficial trip to the region.

Prince George

Rough-edged **PRINCE GEORGE**, carved from the forest to become British Columbia's sixth largest city (pop. 78,000), is the region's services and transport centre, so you're highly likely to become acquainted with its dispersed and half-deserted downtown streets. Forestry, in the form of pulp mills, kilns, planers, plywood plants and allied chemical works, is at the core of its industrial landscape – if you ever wanted the inside story on the lumber business, this is where to find it.

Simon Fraser established a North West Trading Company post here in 1805, and named it **Fort George** in honour of the reigning George III. As a commercial nexus it quickly altered the lives of the local **Carrier Sekani** natives, who abandoned their semi-nomadic migration from winter to summer villages in favour of a permanent settlement alongside the fort. Little changed until 1914 when the arrival of the Grand Trunk Railway – later the Canadian National – spawned an influx of pioneers and loggers. The town was connected by road to Dawson Creek and the north as late as 1951, and saw the arrival of the Pacific Great Eastern Railway in 1958 – two developments that give some idea of how recent the opening up of the Canadian north has been.

The town is a disorienting open-plan network of roads and sporadic houses between Hwy 97 and a sprawling downtown area at the junction of the Fraser and Nechako rivers. As far as sightseeing is concerned, you might as well stick to what Prince George does best and take the surprisingly popular free **tours** around some of its big mills and processing plants; to reserve a place, contact Tourism Prince George at either of the town's two **infocentres**: at the junction of Hwys 97 and 16 to Prince Rupert (May–Sept daily 9am–8pm; ☎563-5493), or opposite the bus terminal at 1198 Victoria St and 15th Avenue (Mon–Fri 8.30am–4pm, Sat 9am–4pm, longer hours in summer; ☎562-3700 or 1-800-668-7646). Company buses pick up from the centres and deliver you to one of several firms, the biggest currently being **Northwood Pulp and Timber**, where you are shown thousands of seedlings being grown in controlled conditions, the sawmills, and one of the continent's largest pulp mills. Outside, in a graphic illustration of the scale of Canadian forestry, logs, planks and piles of sawdust the size of small hills stretch almost as far as the eye can see.

Practicalities

Air BC (☎561-2905) and Canadian (☎563-0521) serve Prince George by air: the airport is 18km east of downtown and linked by regular shuttles. The town is linked by BC Rail to Vancouver (via the Cariboo region), and by VIA Rail to Jasper, Edmonton and beyond eastbound, and Prince Rupert westbound (for the Haida Gwaii/Prince Charlotte Islands and Inside Passage ferries). Only VIA Rail drops you downtown at 1300 1st Ave (☎564-5223); if you're heading for motels or the bus terminal use a taxi from either Prince George Taxi (☎564-4444); or Emerald Taxi Ltd (☎563-3333). The **BC Rail** (☎564-9080) trains arrive 5km south of downtown on Hwy 97 at the end of Terminal Boulevard, but there's a free connecting bus service to various points, including the motels at the bus terminal and on Hwy 97 for a quick getaway the following day.

The town is also a staging post for **Greyhound** routes to the north (and thus Alaska), and integral to the main road routes to Dawson Creek (for the Alaska Highway) and Prince Rupert (for the Cassiar Highway). The Greyhound **bus terminal**, well south of downtown at 1566 12th Ave (☎564-5454), is close to a handful of the town's many hotels and motels.

The best **motel** on the Hwy 97 strip is the big *Spruceland Inn* (☎563-0102 or 1-800-663-3295; ②), at 1391 Central St at the junction of Hwy 97 and 15th Avenue. At the near-

THE AURORA BOREALIS

The **aurora borealis**, or "Northern Lights", is a beautiful and ethereal display of light in the upper atmosphere that can be seen over large parts of northern Canada. The night sky appears to shimmer with dancing curtains of colour, ranging from luminescent monotones – most commonly green or a dark red – to fantastic veils that run the full spectrum. The display becomes more animated as it proceeds, twisting and turning in patterns called "rayed bands". As a finale, a corona sometimes appears, in which rays seem to flare in all directions from a central point.

Named after the Roman goddess of dawn, the aurora was long thought to be produced by sunlight reflected from polar snow and ice, or refracted light produced in the manner of a rainbow. Certain Inuit tribes believed the lights were the spirits of animals or ancestors; others thought they represented wicked forces. Old-time gold prospectors thought they might be vapours given off by ore deposits. The Japanese believed a marriage would be particularly successful if consummated beneath them. Research still continues into the phenomenon, but it seems the aurora is caused by radiation emitted as light from atoms in the upper atmosphere as they are hit by fast-moving electrons and protons. The earth's geomagnetic field certainly plays some part in the creation of the aurora, but its source would appear to lie with the sun – auroras become more distinct and are seen spread over a larger area two days after intense solar activity, the time it takes the "solar wind" to arrive. This wind is composed of fast-moving electrically charged ions. When these hit the earth's atmosphere they respond to the earth's magnetic field and move towards the poles (the reason they are seen at northern latitudes). En route they strike atoms and molecules of gas in the upper atmosphere, causing them to become temporarily charged or ionized. These molecules then release the charge, or energy, usually in the form of light. Different colours are emitted depending on the gases involved: oxygen produces a green colour (or orange at higher altitudes), nitrogen an occasionally violet colour.

You should see the northern lights as far south as Prince George in British Columbia, over parts of northern Alberta (where on average they're visible some 160 nights a year) and over much of the Northwest Territories, Nunavut and northern Manitoba. They are at their most dazzling from **December to March**, when nights are longest and the sky darkest, though they are potentially visible all year round. Look out for a faint glow on the northeastern horizon after dusk, and then – if you're lucky – for the full show as the night deepens.

by *Esther's Inn* (☎562-4131 or 1-800-663-6844; ③), one block off the highway at 1151 Commercial Drive (10th Avenue), the price includes a swimming pool and Jacuzzi. Closer to downtown are the *Downtown Motel*, 650 Dominion St at 6th Avenue (☎563-9241 or 1-800-663-5729 in BC; ②); the comfortable *Ramada Hotel Downtown Prince George*, 444 George St (☎563-0055 or 1-800-272-6232; ⑥); and the *Connaught Motor Inn*, opposite the bus terminal at 1550 Victoria St (☎562-4441 or 1-800-663-6620; ②). All the campgrounds are some way out, the best being the big *Blue Spruce RV & Campground* about 5km west at Kimball Road on Hwy 16 (☎964-7272 or 964-4060; $13; April–Oct), which includes a heated outdoor pool. The municipal campground is at at 4188 18th Ave ($12–17).

With **food**, don't expect much in the way of culinary sophistication and stick to good chains like *Earl's*, 1440 East Central St; otherwise treat yourself at *Da Moreno*, 1493 3rd Ave (☎564-7922), probably the best restaurant in town. **Moving on**, three VIA Rail trains run weekly to Prince Rupert and to Edmonton via Jasper; BC Rail runs daily trains to Vancouver in summer (3 weekly in winter) and it's well worth making a reservation on one of the more scenic of Canada's rail journeys (☎561-4033 or 1-800-561-8630), but note, however, that this line is currently under threat of closure. Greyhound runs one bus daily to Whitehorse in the Yukon, two daily to Vancouver, and two daily to Prince Rupert.

Prince George to Prince Rupert

There are two ways to make the 735-kilometre journey west from **Prince George to Prince Rupert**: using Hwy 16 or the parallel VIA Rail railway, neither of them terribly scenic by BC standards until they reach the glorious river and mountain landscapes of the **Skeena Valley** 150km before Prince Rupert. Most people make this trip as a link in a much longer journey, either to reach Prince Rupert to pick up **ferries** north to Alaska or south to Port Hardy on Vancouver Island, or to pick up the start of the Cassiar Highway, a rough wilderness road that cuts north from the Skeena Valley to meet the Alaska Highway at Watson Lake over the Yukon border. Unless you fly, it's also the only way to reach the Haida Gwaii/Queen Charlotte Islands, accessible by ferry or plane from Prince Rupert. The best place to pause during the journey is near **Hazelton**, where you can visit a little cluster of **native villages**.

Vanderhoof to Smithers

Riding out of Prince George you're confronted quickly with the relentless monotony of the Interior Plateau's rolling forests, an arboreal grind broken only by the occasional lake and the grey silhouettes of distant low-hilled horizons. At **VANDERHOOF**, 98km down the highway, gentler patches of pasture begin to poke through the tree cover, but these do little to soften the impact of the town itself. An abrupt grid of garages and motels, it's best known for its July airshow and the more graceful aerial dynamics of thousands of Canadian geese at the nearby **Nechako Bird Sanctuary**. Before pushing on, grab a coffee at the *OK Café*, part of a fine collection of half-timbered heritage houses at the town's western end. If you get stuck, or would prefer to stay in the village rather than Prince George, there are cheap **motels**: the largest of them is the *Grand Trunk Inn*, 2351 Church Ave (☎567-3188; ②); or you could try the *Siesta Motel* downtown on Hwy 16 (☎567-2365 or 1-800-914-3388; ②). There's a small municipal **campground** off the main highway at Stony Creek (☎567-9393; $9; May–Sept) and the *Riverside Park Campground*, overlooking the bird sanctuary at 3100 Burrard Ave (☎567-4710; $13; May–Sept). The **infocentre** is at 2353 Burrard Ave (year-round; ☎567-2124).

Beyond here the ride becomes more verdant still, making the **accommodation** possibilities of **FORT FRASER**, 50km beyond, more attractive than those of Vanderhoof itself; try the quaint wooden cabins of the *Northgate Motel* (☎690-7414; ②) on the ham-let's eastern edge. If you're **camping**, hold out for the *Piper's Glen Resort* (☎690-7565; $10–12; May–Sept) 5km to the west, whose meadow site falls away gently to Fraser Lake. The lake has a seasonal **infocentre** at 65 Endako Ave (June–Sept; ☎699-8941).

Beyond Burn's Lake the scenery picks up still more, as if preparing for the mountains in the distance, though the run of villages continues to offer little but places to fill either the tank or the stomach. If you're going as far as to **stay** in this region, aim for the excellent new *Douglas Motel* (☎846-5679; ③), on the banks of the Bulkley River, just 150m out of the unspoilt hamlet of **TELKWA**, 10km east of Smithers. Next day take a few minutes to stroll up the riverfront street of heritage buildings and its handsome brown-and-white wood-planked **pioneer museum**.

SMITHERS, the largest place after Prince George (370km to the east), is focused on a crossroads, with an **infocentre** on one corner at 1425 Main St (year-round; ☎847-9854 or 1-800-542-6673) and a big Super-Valu **supermarket** for supplies on the other. If you're overnighting here – and there's plenty of **accommodation** – ignore the brace of motels on the road and settle for the big white-timbered *Hudson Bay Lodge* (☎847-4581 or 1-800-663-5040; ④) outside the village as you enter from the east. If this is out of your budget, try the *Florence Motel* (☎847-2678; ②) on the west side of town, or the *Sandman Inn* on Hwy 16, part of an invariably trustworthy chain (☎847-2637 or 1-800-726-3626; ③).

The Skeena Valley

Hard on the heels of industrial Terrace, the **Skeena River** (the "River of the Mists") carves a beautiful valley through the Coast Mountains, an important trade route for natives and stern-wheelers before the coming of the railway in 1912. For a couple of hours the road and railway run past a huge backdrop of snowcapped peaks half-reflected in the mist-wraithed estuary. Out on the water there's a good chance of seeing the ripples of beavers and sea otters, not to mention bald eagles perched on the river's immense log jams. Dark valleys peel off the main river's majestic course, suggestive of a deep, untrodden wilderness and repeatedly pierced by delicate threads of waterfalls half visible though the trees.

Shortly after Hwy 16 meets the river crashing down from the north near Hazelton and New Hazelton, a couple of minor roads strike off to four nearby **Gitxsan native villages**, places where something of the culture of the area's indigenous Gitxsan peoples has been preserved, along with new examples of totem carving and other crafts. 'Ksan and Kispiox, home to the best totems and long houses, are a few kilometres off Hwy 16 on the minor High Level Road (Hwy 62) out of New Hazelton ; just north of 'Ksan a road links west to Gitwangak and Gitanyow (formerly Kitwancool), or they can be reached by continuing west on Hwy 16 a few kilometres and heading north on Hwy 37 (the Cassiar Highway).

The most easterly of the west coast aboriginal tribes, the Gitxsan – "people of the river of the mists" – traditionally lived off fish and game rather than agriculture, and were consummate artists and carvers. Many of their traditions were eroded by the coming of whites, and by missionaries in particular, but in the 1950s the tribe's elders made a determined decision to resurrect as much of their dying culture as possible, re-creating an entire 1870 settlement at **'KSAN**. Although there's a good deal of commercialism, this is the village to concentrate on – native women act as guides around several long houses, giving a commentary on the carvings, clothes, buildings and masks on show, as well as offering accounts of local history (tours mid-May to mid-Oct daily 9am–5pm; $5.50). The **Northwest Coast Exhibition Centre** (summer daily 9am–6pm; rest of the year closed Tues & Wed; ☎842-5544) has information, more exhibits, a gift shop and carving shed, and presents displays of native dancing and other performances.

KISPIOX, 13km north of Hazelton, is the ancient Gitxsan home of the Frog, Wolf and Fireweed clans, and was given its name by the old Department for Indian Affairs. It means "place of loud talkers" but locals not surprisingly prefer the traditional name, which is Anspayaxw, meaning "the hidden place". The highlights here are fifteen riverside totems. **GITWANGAK** to the west, just 500m north of the Hwy 16 and Hwy 37 junction, means "the place of rabbits", and was the traditional village home of the Eagle, Wolf and Frog. It, too, has some impressive totems, as does **GITANYOW** – "people of a small village" – 21km north on Hwy 37, whose eighteen poles include the 140-year-old "Hole in the Ice" or "Hole in the Sky" totem. You can sometimes watch poles being repaired at one of two carving sheds around the village.

The nearest **infocentre** for the villages is near New Hazelton at the junction of Hwys 16 and 62 (mid-May to mid-Sept; ☎842-6071 or 842-6571 year-round), but you should also spend a few minutes looking round the evocative old Victorian streets of old **HAZELTON** 6km to the northwest on Hwy 62. **Accommodation** at 'Ksan is limited to the pretty *'Ksan Campground*, located on the banks of the Skeena and Bulkley rivers (☎842-5940; $9–12; May–Oct) and New Hazelton has a trio of motels. Kispiox also has a few rooms and campgrounds: the *Sportsman's Kispiox Lodge* (☎842-6455 or 1-800-KISPIOX; ②–④), the *Steelhead Camp* (☎842-5435; ①) and the *Kispiox River Resort and Campground* (☎842-6182; ②; camping $10–16; May–Oct).

Prince Rupert

There's a bracing tang of salt and fish on the air in **PRINCE RUPERT**, a distinctive port that comes as an invigorating relief after the run of characterless villages out of Prince George. A good-looking place, similar in appearance to a Scottish fishing town, it looks out over an archipelago of islands and is ringed by mountains that tumble to the sea along a beautiful fjord-cut coastline. A crowd of cars, backpackers and RVs washes daily through its streets off the **Alaska**, **Queen Charlotte** and **Port Hardy ferries**, complementing the seafront's vibrant activity, and adding to the coffers of a town that's quite clearly on the up and up. There's nothing much to do, but if you're waiting for a boat it's an amiable enough spot and you'll probably bump into more fellow travellers here than almost anywhere else in northern BC.

Arrival and accommodation

The **Greyhound station** is in the centre of town at 822 3rd Ave and 8th Street (daily 8.30am–8.30pm; ☎624-5090) and handles two buses daily (morning and evening) for the twelve-hour ride to Prince George ($84.74 one way). The **VIA Rail tran station** is on the waterfront at 1st Avenue and the foot of 2nd Street (open 2hr either side of departures and arrivals; ☎627-7589, 627-7304 or 1-800-561-8630). Trains to Prince George ($85.60) for connections from Prince George to Edmonton ($155.15) via Jasper currently leave on Wednesday, Friday and Sunday at 8am, arriving in Prince George at 8.10pm. If you're thinking of taking the train right through, note that you have to overnight in Prince George as there are no through-trains to Jasper or Edmonton. The local **airport** is on Digby Island just across the harbour, with ferry connections to the BC and Alaska Marine ferry terminals (see box on p.800) and shuttle bus connections to downtown. Canadian Regional (☎624-6292 or 1-800-665-1177) currently flies three times daily to Vancouver via Terrace and has a check-in at the Rupert Square Mall on 2nd Avenue between 3rd and 6th streets. Air BC (☎624-4554 or 1-800-663-3721) also flies to Vancouver and has a base in town at 112 6th St. Canadian Regional also fly to Sandspit on the Queen Charlotte Islands (see p.801), but you might get better deals and flights to smaller centres on the islands (and elsewhere up and down the coast) with local firms Inland Air (☎627-1351, fax 627-1356) and Harbour Air (☎627-1341).

Many people reach **Prince Rupert** by ferry. For details of how to reach downtown from the **ferry terminal**, which is 2km from town, see the "Ferries from Prince Rupert" feature on p.800. For car rentals, contact Tilden (☎624-5318) or Budget (☎627-4700) in the Rupert Mall. In planning onward itineraries, however, don't overlook a new **bus service** from Prince Rupert to Whitehorse via the Cassiar Highway (see p.809), a two-day trip operated by Rival Highway Tours, Suite 1, Berner Heritage Building, 342 3rd Ave West, Prince Rupert (☎624-6124 in Prince Rupert, ☎667-7896 in Whitehorse; check availability).

Finding **accommodation** in Prince Rupert shouldn't present problems outside July and August, when places fill up quickly on days when the ferries come in: book ahead to be on the safe side. If there's nothing in town, you can always backtrack along Hwy 16 to the villages beyond the Skeena Valley. The town's only decent budget option, with basic hostel-type rooms and shared bathrooms, is the quickly filled *Pioneer Rooms*, around the corner from the museum and infocentre at 167 3rd Ave (☎624-6259; ①). The nearest motel to the ferry terminals is the *Totem Lodge Motel*, 1335 Park Ave (☎624-6761 or 1-800-550-0178; ③): Park Avenue is a continuation of 2nd Avenue that runs south to the terminals from downtown. Perhaps the best all-round central choice, especially if you can secure a room with a sea view, is the *Inn on the Harbour*, 720 1st Ave (☎624-9107 or 1-800-663-8155; ③), while most reasonable of the many mid-range establishments is the *Aleeda*, 900 3rd Ave (☎627-1367; ③). *Slumber Lodge Motor Inn*, 909 3rd Ave West (☎627-1711; ③), is a good-value, middling motel, but if you want to go top-of-the-range try the big *Crest Motor Hotel*, 222 1st Ave (☎624-6771 or 1-800-663-8150; ⑥) or more reasonable mini-skyscraper *Best Western Highliner Inn*, 815 1st Ave West (☎624-9060 or 1-800-668-3115; ④–⑤). Further afield, the *Parkside Resort*, 101 11th Ave (☎624-9131; ②), is a smart lurid-green hotel about a kilometre out of town and more likely to have room when downtown places are full.

The only big local **campground** is the *Park Avenue Campground*, 1750 Park Ave (☎624-5861; $9–16; year-round), 1km west of town and 1km from the ferry terminals: it has tent sites but is usually full of RVs. Otherwise the *Parkside Resort* (see above) has some sites ($15) that few people know about, and there's also the rural *Prudhomme Lake* provincial campground (☎798-2277; $9.50; April–Nov), with forested lakeside sites, 16km east of town on Hwy 16.

The Town

Although you wouldn't know to look at it, the port is one of the world's largest deep-water terminals, and handles a huge volume of trade (grain, coal and fish in particular). In the past the region was the focal point of trade between tribes to the north and south, one reason why the Hudson's Bay Company built a post at Fort Simpson, 30km north of the present townsite. It was also the reason why the old Hudson's Bay post was chosen as the terminus of Canada's second **transcontinental rail link**. Work began in 1906, but as time went by it was decided there was a better harbour to the south, a national competition being launched to decide on a name for the new railhead: $250 was paid for "Prince Rupert", named after the company's royal founding member, a label that was duly grafted onto the ramshackle collection of tents that constituted the settlement in 1909. A year later the first town lot was sold for around $500; within twelve months it was worth $17,000. The Grand Trunk Railway chairman, Charles M. Hays, hoped to turn Prince Rupert into a port to rival Vancouver. In 1912 he set off for Britain to raise stock for the venture, but unfortunately booked a return passage on the *Titanic*. Although he went down, the railway was finished two years later – too late, in the event, to steal a march on Vancouver. By 1919 the Grand Trunk was bankrupt, though its restructuring as the Canadian National in 1923 and the magnificence of the port has allowed the town to prosper to this day. For more on the railway and its history, visit the **Kwinitsa Station Railway Museum** just across from the VIA Rail sta-

FERRIES FROM PRINCE RUPERT

Ferry terminals for both BC Ferries (for Port Hardy and the Queen Charlotte Islands) and the Alaska Marine Highway (for Skagway and Alaska Panhandle ports) are at **Fairview Dock** 2km southwest of town at the end of Hwy 16. Walk-on tickets for foot passengers are rarely a problem at either terminal, but advance reservations are essential if you're taking a car or want a cabin for any summer crossing. A town bus passes the terminal every two or three hours for incoming sailings, but for outbound sailings it's probably best to grab a **taxi** from downtown. A shuttle bus ($3.50) meets BC (but not Alaska Marine) ferries. Alternatively walk a kilometre to the corner of Pillsbury and Kootenay, where the local #52 bus passes roughly every half an hour (Mon–Sat 7.30am–5.30pm). The *Park Avenue Campground* is about a kilometre from the terminal.

BC Ferries operate the MV *Queen of Prince Rupert* **to Skidegate** on the Queen Charlotte Islands six times a week from July to September at 11am (except Mon 9pm), four times a week the rest of the year (Mon, Tues, Thurs & Fri), a crossing that takes between 6hr 30min and 8hr (depending on weather) and costs $23 one way for foot passengers (plus $87 for cars and $6 for bikes). Return ferries from Skidegate operate on the same days, leaving at 11pm and arriving at 7.30am except on some summer Fridays and Saturdays, when the boat docks earlier to provide a connection with the Inside Passage boat to Port Hardy on Vancouver Islands (see below). For **reservations** or timetable information, contact Prince Rupert's infocentre or BC Ferries direct on ☎386-3431, 669-1211, or 1-888-223-3779 anywhere in BC).

Ferries **to Port Hardy** leave every other day in summer at 7.30am (even-numbered days in June, July, Sept and first half of Oct, odd-numbered days in Aug) and once a week in winter for a stunning fifteen-hour cruise that costs $102 one way for drivers or walk-on passengers. Bikes cost $6.50. To take on a car ($210) you'll need to have booked at least two months in advance (see also Port Hardy, p.738). Note that fares drop by around forty percent between November and April.

The **Alaska Marine Highway** (☎627-1744 or 1-800-642-0066) ferries run **to Skagway** (via some or all of Ketchikan, Wrangell, Petersburg, Sitka, Hyder, Stewart, Juneau, Haines and Hollis) almost daily in July and August, four times a week for the rest of the summer and in spring and fall, and twice a week in winter (to Ketchikan, passengers US$38, vehicles US$75; to Juneau, pasengers US$104, vehicles US$240; to Haines, passengers US$118, vehicles US$273). They stop frequently en route, with the chance to go ashore for a short time, though longer stopovers must be arranged when buying a through-ticket. For all Alaskan sailings turn up at least an hour before departure to go through US customs and immigration procedures if you're a foot passenger, and three hours if you have a car, and note that though the journey takes two days there are various restrictions on the fresh food you can take on board. You may find you can't make telephone or credit card bookings, and have to pay in person for tickets at the terminal ticket office (May–Sept daily 9am–4pm and 2hr either side of sailings; on days of sailings the rest of the year). Fares are 25 percent lower between October and April.

tion near the waterfront (early June to early Sept daily 9am–6pm; donation; ☎627-1915 or 627-3207).

Prince Rupert's excellent little **Museum of Northern British Columbia** (June–Sept Mon–Sat 9am–8pm, Sun 9am–5pm; Oct–May Mon–Sat 10am–5pm; $3) is annexed to the **infocentre** (same hours; ☎624-5637 or 1-800-667-1994 in BC) on 1st Avenue and McBride Street at the northern end of the town's tight downtown zone. Note that there are plans to transfer the museum to Chatham Village just down the street. It's particularly strong on the culture and history of the local **Tsimshian**, and has a clutch of wonderful silent archive films on topics ranging from fishing to the building of the railway – ideal ways to whittle away a wet afternoon, of which storm-lashed Prince Rupert ("City of Rainbows") has plenty. There's also a small art gallery with a few native works, a well-stocked bookshop and a carving shed outside where you can sometimes see totems being crafted.

While you're here, check out some of the local **tours** or **boat trips**, many of which are inexpensive and a good way to see the offshore islands and wildlife. Seashore Charters (☎624-5645) are a good outfit, with two-hour harbour tours, among others, starting at around $50. For an inexpensive ($2.50) look at the harbour you could jump aboard the Rupert Water Taxi, which leaves for Digby Island from the dock at the bottom of McBride Street (check times at the infocentre; departures vary according to school runs). A trip fast becoming famous locally is to **Khuzeymateen Provincial Park** (☎847-7320 for information), a remote coastal valley 45km to the north of Prince Rupert created in 1994 to protect BC's largest-known coastal population of **grizzly bears**. This is the first park of its kind in the world, but there will certainly be more, especially in BC, where the damage done to declining grizzly habitats by logging, mining, hunting and other concerns – notably the slaughter of the animals for body parts in quack Oriental remedies – is rapidly becoming one of the keenest environmental issues in the province.

A little out of town, beyond the museum, the gondola ride to **Mount Hays** once gave a bird's-eye view of the harbour and the chance to spot bald eagles. It was also the most popular attraction in town, which makes you wonder why it had to close: check with the infocentre to see if there's news of its reopening. To reach it, or the steep track that currently provides the only route to the top, take the Wantage Road turn off by the *McDonald's* on Hwy 16. It's three hours to the top but you get fairly good views after clambering just a short way up the track. Details of less energetic **walks** can be obtained from the infocentre.

Eating and drinking

Fresh **fish** is the obvious thing to **eat** locally, preferably at the *Green Apple*, a shack (and town institution) that serves a mean halibut and chips for $6; it's at 301 McBride just before Hwy 16 turns into town. For something a touch more upmarket, locals flock to the *Smile's Seafood Café*, at 113 George Hills Way (about 300m north of the infocentre), which has been doing a roaring trade since 1934. The *Breakers Pub* next door is a popular hostelry. The **bar** under the *Coast Prince Rupert* high-rise hotel on 2nd Avenue, between 6th and 7th streets, also does decent food, and seems to be one of the few places prepared to open for breakfast. Just a little to the north of the town centre the *Cow Bay Café*, 205 Cow Bay (☎627-1212; closed Mon), pushes *Smile's* close for the best food in town. Also here is *Cowpuccinos*, a good café that's the centre of Prince Rupert's alternative scene.

Haida Gwaii – The Queen Charlotte Islands

Ranged in an arc some 150km off the Prince Rupert coast, the **Haida Gwaii**, until recently better known as the **Queen Charlotte Islands**, consist of a triangular-shaped archipelago of about 200 islets that make an enticing diversion from the heavily travelled sea route up the BC. The islands have become something of a cult amongst travellers and environmentalists – partly for their scenery, flora and fauna and almost legendary remoteness from the mainstream, but also because they've achieved a high profile in the battle between the forestry industry and ecology activists. At the forefront of the battle are the **Haida**, widely acknowledged as one of the region's most advanced native groups, and who have made the islands their home for over 10,000 years (see

The telephone code for the Haida Gwaii-Queen Charlotte Islands is ☎250.

box opposite). Their culture, and in particular the chance to visit their many **deserted villages**, form an increasing part of the Charlottes' attraction, but many people also come here to sample the islands' immensely rich **flora and fauna**, a natural profusion that's earned them the title of the "Canadian Galapagos".

The Haida Gwaii were one of only two areas in western Canada to escape the last ice age, which elsewhere altered the evolutionary progress, and which has resulted in the survival of many so-called **relic species**. Species unique to the islands include a fine yellow daisy, the world's largest **black bears**, and subspecies of pine marten, deer mouse, hairy woodpecker, saw-whet owl and Stellar's jay. There are also more **eagles** here than anywhere else in the region, as well as the world's largest population of Peale's peregrine falcons and the elusive **black-footed albatross** – whose wingspan exceeds that of the largest eagles. Fish, too, are immensely plentiful, and there's a good chance of spotting whales, otters, sea lions and other aquatic mammals.

Practicalities

Access to the islands is by air or ferry from Prince Rupert. Ferries from Prince Rupert dock at tiny Skidegate near Queen Charlotte City on **Graham Island**, the northern of the group's two main collections of islands (see p.800 for details of ferries from Prince Rupert). Most of the archipelago's 6000 inhabitants live either in Queen Charlotte City or at Masset to the north, leaving the southern cluster of islands across Skidegate Channel – known for convenience as **Moresby Island** – a virtually deserted primal wilderness, but for the small community at Sandspit (see p.807). Regular twenty-minute ferry crossings connect Moresby Island to Skidegate (twelve sailings daily year-round). You can also **fly** to the islands from Prince Rupert, landing at Sandspit, which has the islands' only airstrip (float planes can land elsewhere). Canadian Regional (☎1-800-665-1177) and Air BC (☎1-800-663-372) fly here daily from Vancouver, but you might get better deals out of carriers with offices in Prince Rupert, such as Inland Air (☎627-1351) and the larger Harbour Air (☎627-1341). Harbour Air, for example, fly here twice daily from Prince Rupert and also fly small planes from Rupert to Masset on the north of Graham Island. It also has other flights around the islands, as do South Moresby Air Charters (☎559-4222) in Queen Charlotte City, who'll take you out to the deepest of the backwoods.

Accommodation is available only at Sandspit (on Moresby) and Queen Charlotte City, Tl'ell, Masset and Port Clements (on Graham) and should be prebooked. The only **public transport** at the time of writing is the Evergreen Bus Line, based at General Delivery, Masset (☎626-5678), which links Port Clements and Queen Charlotte City. Budget (☎637-5688) have **car rental** offices in Queen Charlotte City, Masset and Sandspit, but in summer you'll need to have booked in advance to secure a car. Rates at Rustic Car Rentals (☎559-4641) in Queen Charlotte City are a touch lower. Car rental rates here are among the world's highest, and unless you have a car, bike or canoe it's as well to know that you could be in for a long and expensive trip that shows you very little of what you came for. To see the **Haida villages**, in any case, virtually all of which are on inaccessible parts of Moresby, you'll need to take to a boat, and more probably a pricey tour by float plane.

Graham Island

Most casual visitors stick to **Graham Island**, where the bulk of the islands' roads and accommodation are concentrated along the eastern side of the island, between **Queen Charlotte City** in the south and **Masset** some 108km to the north. These settlements and the villages in between – Skidegate, Tl'ell and Port Clements – lie along Hwy 16,

THE HAIDA

The **Haida** are widely considered to have the most highly developed culture and sophisticated art tradition of British Columbia's Native Canadians. Extending from the Haida Gwaii (Queen Charlotte Islands) to south Alaska, their lands included major stands of red cedar, the raw material for their huge dug-out **canoes**, intricate **carvings** and refined **architecture**. Haida trade links were built on the reputation of their skill, other BC tribes considering the ownership of a Haida canoe, for example, as a major status symbol. Renowned as traders and artists, the Haida were also feared **warriors**, paddling into rival villages and returning with canoes laden with goods, slaves and the severed heads of anyone who had tried to resist. Their skill on the open sea has seen them labelled the "Vikings" of the Pacific Northwest. This success at warfare was due, in part, to their use of wooden slat armour, which included a protective face visor and helmets topped with terrifying images.

Socially the Haida divided themselves into two main groups, the **Eagles** and the **Ravens**, which were further divided into hereditary kin groups named after their original village location. Marriage within each major group – or *moiety* – was considered incestuous, so Eagles would always seek Raven mates and vice versa. Furthermore, descent was traced through the **female line**, which meant that a chief could not pass his property onto his sons because they would belong to a different *moiety* – instead his inheritance passed to his sister's sons. Equally, young men might have to leave their childhood village to claim their inheritance from their maternal uncles.

Haida **villages** were an impressive sight, their vast cedar-plank houses dominated by fifteen-metre totem poles displaying the kin group's unique animal crest or other mythical creatures, all carved in elegantly fluid lines. Entrance to each house was through the gaping mouth of a massive carved figure; inside, supporting posts were carved into the forms of the crest animals and most household objects were similarly decorative. Equal elaboration attended the many Haida ceremonies, one of the most important of which was the **mortuary potlatch**, serving as a memorial service to a dead chief and the validation of the heir's right to succession. The dead individual was laid out at the top of a carved pole near the village entrance, past which the visiting chiefs would walk wearing robes of finely woven and patterned mountain-goat wool and immense headdresses fringed with long sea-lion whiskers and ermine skins. A hollow at the top of each headdress was filled with eagle feathers, which floated down onto the witnesses as the chiefs sedately danced.

After **European contact** the Haida population was devastated by smallpox and other epidemics. In 1787, when Captain George Dixon named the Queen Charlotte Islands after his boat, the *Queen Charlotte*, there were probably around 8000 Haida scattered across the archipelago. Their numbers were then reduced from around 6000 in 1835 to 588 by 1915. Consequently they were forced to abandon their traditional villages and today gather largely at two sites, Old Masset (pop. 650) and Skidegate (Haida population 550). At other locations the homes and totems fell into disrepair, and only at **Sgan Gwaii**, a remote village at the southern tip of the Queen Charlottes, has an attempt been made to preserve an original Haida settlement; it has now been declared a World Heritage Site by UNESCO.

These days the Haida number around 2000, and are highly regarded in the Canadian art world; Bill Reid, Freda Diesing and Robert Davidson are amongst the best-known figures, and scores of other Haida craftspeople produce a mass of carvings and jewellery for the tourist market. They also play a powerful role in the islands' social, political and cultural life, having been vocal in the formation of sites such as the Gwaii Haanas National Park Reserve (p.808), South Moresby's Haida Heritage Site and Duu Guusd Tribal Park (p.807), the last established to protect old tribal villages on Graham Island's northwest coast.

the principal road, and shelter in the lee of the islands, away from a mountainous and indented rocky west coast that boasts the highest combined seismic, wind and tidal energy of any North American coastline (producing treacherous seas and a tidal range of 8m). Much of the east coast consists of beautiful half-moon, driftwood-strewn beaches and a string of provincial parks where you can appreciate the milder climes produced by the Pacific's Japanese Current, a warming stream that contributes to the islands' lush canopy of thousand-year-old spruce and cedar rainforests. On the downside, though, it drenches both sides of the islands with endless rainstorms, even in summer. Make sure you pack a raincoat.

Queen Charlotte City

It would be hard to imagine anywhere less like a city than the islands' second largest settlement, **QUEEN CHARLOTTE CITY** (pop. 1200), a picturesque fishing village and frontier administrative centre about 5km west of the Skidegate terminal for ferries to and from Prince Rupert and Moresby Island (see opposite). It takes its name – like the islands – from the ship of Captain George Dixon, the British explorer who sailed to the Haida Gwaii in 1787, thirteen years after first European contact was probably made by the Spaniard Juan Perez. Most of its residents squeeze a living from the McMillan Bloedel timber giant, whose felling exploits have cleared most of the hills around the port, and who have a veto on access to many of the islands' 2000km of backcountry logging roads. For a fine overview of the place, try the stroll to the top of **Sleeping Beauty Mountain**, which is reached by a rough track from Crown Forest Road near Honna Road. The village **dump** south of the houses rates as another sight for the black bears and forty-plus bald and golden eagles that often gather there at dusk. Further afield you may be able to watch salmon and other wildlife at the **Skidegate Band Salmon Project** on the Honna Forest Service Road 3km west of town: contact the Band Council for information (☎559-4496). Further away still, you can drive to **Rennell Sound**, a west coast inlet with shingle beaches accessed by a logging road: take the main logging road north from the town for 22km and then turn left and follow the steep gravel road for 14km, but contact McMillan Bloedel or the infocentre before setting out (see below). At the Sound, the **Rennell Sound Recreation Site** offers paths through stands of primal rainforest to isolated sandy beaches and a couple of campgrounds with a total of ten beachfront wilderness pitches.

Otherwise the town is the major place to sign up for any number of outdoor activities; contact the **infocentre**, 3220 Wharf St (May to early Sept daily 9am–5pm, longer hours July & Aug; ☎559-8316). The staff are incredibly knowledgeable, and there's a good selection of detailed guides and maps to the area: be sure to pick up the invaluable *Guide to the Queen Charlotte Islands*. The centre is also the place to pick up brochures and organize **tours** of the island, with some forty or more fishing, sailing, sightseeing, canoeing and other operators being based in Queen Charlotte City. There's also a **Canadian Parks Service** office for information on Moresby Island's Gwaii Haanas National Park Reserve and Haida Heritage Site (see p.808), west of town along Hwy 33 (Mon–Fri 8am–noon & 1–4.30pm; ☎559-8818). The **Ministry of Forests**, in the obvious new blue building on 3rd Avenue (☎559-8447), has information on the free primitive campgrounds run by the Forest Service on Graham and Moresby islands. If you're planning to drive logging roads, you must call **McMillan Bloedel** (☎559-4224 or 557-4212) – which controls most of these roads on Graham Island – for latest access details. Enquire, too, about their free weekly forestry tours (departs from the infocentre and Port Clements museum – see p.806).

ACCOMMODATION AND FOOD

Accommodation is scarce and demand is high in summer, so definitely call ahead to make bookings. The first-choice hotel is probably the *Premier Creek Lodging*, 3101 3rd

Ave (☎559-8451 or 1-888-322-3388; ④), a splendidly restored 1910 heritage building overlooking the harbour and Bearskin Bay. Then there's the unique *Gracie's Place*, 3113 3rd Ave (☎559-4262 or 1-888-244-4262; ③), with ocean-view rooms, antique furniture and rustic decor; and the *Spruce Point Lodging*, 609 6th Ave (☎559-8234; ③), which offers rooms and breakfast overlooking Skidegate Inlet opposite the Chevron garage at the west end of town. Similarly intimate is *Dorothy and Mike's Guest House*, 3125 2nd Ave (☎559-8439; ②), with central rooms and full cooking facilities (note there's no smoking allowed here and credit cards aren't accepted). Or try the *Hecate Inn*, 321 3rd Ave (☎559-4543 or 1-800-665-3350; ③), which has units with full use of kitchen on the corner of 3rd Avenue and 4th Street. A touch closer to the ferry terminal, overlooking Bearskin Bay, is the *Sea Raven Motel*, 3301 3rd Ave (☎559-4423 or 1-800-665-9606; ③). If you're **camping**, try the *Haydn Turner Park*, in a community park at the western end of town (simply follow the main street), or the *Kagan Bay Forest Service Campground*, a handful of lovely beachfront campsites on Honna Forest Service Road 5km west of the town.

For **food**, locals make for the *Hummingbird Café*, which has no known address, but is located straight up the main road from the dock. There are also *Margaret's Café*, 3223 Wharf St, on the east side of town, or *Claudette's Place*, 233 3rd Ave (on the west of downtown), which has a nice patio and is well-known for its good breakfasts.

Skidegate

There's not much doing at **SKIDEGATE** (pop. 550), other than the ferries docking at Skidegate Landing 2km away to the south and the chance to browse through the more accessible aspects of Haida culture at the **Haida Gwaii Museum**, located near Second Beach at Qay'llnagaay around 500m east of the ferry terminal (Oct–April Mon & Wed–Fri 10am–noon & 1–5pm, Sat 1–5pm; May & Sept Mon–Fri 9am–5pm, Sat 1–5pm, closed Sun; June–Aug Mon–Fri 9am–5pm, Sat & Sun 1–5pm; $2.50; ☎559-4643). Among other things, this contains the world's largest collection of the Haida's treasured argillite carvings (you may have seen such carvings in Vancouver's UBC Museum of Anthropology). Argillite is a form of black slate-like rock found only on the Haida Gwaii, and only in one site whose location is kept a closely guarded secret. Also check out the platform here for viewing grey whales during their migrations (April & May) and the **Haida Gwaii Watchmen** in the longhouse office alongside the museum. Bands of Haida "watchmen" were formed in the 1970s to protect native sites from vandalism and theft, and survive to this day. Ask at the office about seeing the famous *Loo Taas* ("Wave Eater") canoe, which is generally on show here on weekdays. When it's not out on hire to rich tourists – for a mere $1500, or thereabouts – you're very occasionally able to take a six-hour tour in the huge vessel. It was made for the '86 Expo, the first Haida canoe carved since 1909. You can obtain a permit to visit some of the five hundred or more abandoned tribal villages and sites on the southern islands from the long house, or alternatively from the nearby **Skidegate Mission** or Band Council Office close to Skidegate proper – a Haida village 2.5km from the ferry terminal. There's also a carving long house here, where you may be able to watch craftspeople at work. In summer the Mission usually hosts a 6pm Thursday **seafood feast**, open to all-comers for around $20 (check latest details at the Queen Charlotte City infocentre). If you're here to catch the boat across the channel to Moresby Island and Sandspit, the MV *Kuvuna* **ferry** runs twelve times daily year-round (7.30am–10.30pm; 20min; $3).

Tl'ell and Port Clements

If you blink you'll miss the ranching community of **TL'ELL** (pop. 138), 36km north of Skidegate, first settled by outsiders in 1904 and home to the Richardson Ranch, the island's oldest working ranch. Stop here and walk down to the sea, where you can stroll for hours on deserted wind-sculpted dunes. It's a community favoured by craftspeople and alternative types – pop into the little café or gallery – and in the past there's been a **hostel** here, the intermittently open *Bellis Lodge* (☎557-4434; ①) – check before turning up. Nearby is the small *Weavers Inn Motel* (☎557-4491; ③), in a lovely rural setting, whose rates include breakfast, and the use of a kitchen for an extra $10. A touch larger is the *Tl'ell River House*, off Hwy 16 overlooking Tl'ell River and Hecate Strait: offers a licensed lounge and a restaurant (☎557-4211 or 1-800-667-8906; ③). Or try the pleasantly rustic *Cacilia's B&B* just north of Richardson Ranch on the main road (☎557-4664; ③), a newly renovated log house set behind the dunes on Hecate Strait 2km from the Naikoon Park (see below). **Bikes** and **kayaks** are available for rent here.

As the road cuts inland for **PORT CLEMENTS** (pop. 577), 21km to the northwest of Tl'ell, it forms the southern border of the **Naikoon Provincial Park**, an enclave that extends over Graham Island's northeast corner designed to protect fine beach, dune and dwarf woodland habitats. There's a small **park centre** on the road 2km north of Tl'ell (enquire about beach and other walks and drives). **Campers** should head for the *Misty Meadows Campground* ($9.50; May–Oct), just south of the Tl'ell River Bridge and 500m north of the park centre (☎557-4390) to the north of Tl'ell (backcountry camping is allowed across the park). About 8km beyond, look out for the picnic site and trails at the southern tip of **Mayer Lake**, one of the nicer spots to pull over. Port Clements itself has a small museum (summer daily 1–5pm; donation) of forestry and pioneer-related offerings, but in the past was most famous for the world's only **Golden Spruce** tree, a 300-year-old bleached albino tree – sacred to the Haida – which puzzled foresters by refusing to produce anything but ordinary green-leafed saplings; in 1997 a vandal chopped it down. A rare genetic mutation allowed the tree's needles to be bleached by sunlight. Geneticists and foresters are desperately trying to produce another tree.

Port Clements' little **infocentre** booth is just out of the village, and there's a small **museum** at 45 Bayview Drive on the main road into the town (June–Sept Tues–Sun 2–5pm, winter hours according to availability of volunteers; donation). The one listed **hotel** is the *Golden Spruce*, 2 Grouse St (☎557-4325; ②), but it's worth asking around for B&B possibilities, such as the *Islands North Tours and Lodging* (☎557-2005; ③; May–Sept), which overlooks Masset Inlet at 197 Bayview Drive: it has one guest room, a fully equipped beachfront cabin, and offers bird-watching, fishing charters, sightseeing tours and canoes. For **food and drink**, the main option is the *Yakoun River Inn* on Bayview Drive. About 20km north of town on the road for Masset, look out for the signed **Pure Lake Provincial Park**, where on summer days the waters of Pure Lake should be warm enough for swimming.

Masset

MASSET, 40km north of Port Clements, is the biggest place on the islands, a scattered town of some 1490 people (though the population's falling), half of whom are employed by a military base built in 1971 (earmarked for closure), the other half by fishing and crab-canning. Many visitors are here to bird-watch at the **Delkatla Wildlife Sanctuary**, a saltwater marsh north of the village that supports 113 bird species, or to walk the trails around Tow Hill 26km to the east (see opposite). Most come to wander the neighbouring village of **HAIDA**, or "Old Massett", 2km to the west, the administrative centre for the Council of the Haida First Nation and where some six hundred natives still live and work. Visitors should show respect when visiting totem sites, craft houses and community homes. Many locals are involved in producing crafts for tourists, or organizing wilderness tours, but some are restoring and adding to the few totems still standing locally (it's possible to visit various canoe and carving sheds) and there's a small museum giving some context. For more **information** on where to see carving and on the village in general, visit the Old Masset Council office on Eagle Road (☎626-3337), where you should also enquire about permission to visit the **Duu Guusd Tribal Park**, established by the Haida to protect villages on the coast to the northwest. Two villages here are still active, and the park is used as a base for the Haida Gwaii Rediscovery Centre, which offers courses to children on Haida culture and history.

The Masset **infocentre**, at 1455 Old Beach Rd (July & Aug daily 9am–5pm; ☎626-3995 or 626-3982), has full details of wildlife and bird-watching possibilities. The Masset Village Office on Main Street also provides invaluable background (☎626-3995). Sadly they can't do much about the village's limited **accommodation** prospects, other than point you to the *Singing Surf Inn*, 1504 Old Beach Rd (☎626-3318; ④), the *Harbourview Lodging*, overlooking the harbour at 1608 Delkatla Rd (☎626-5109 or 1-800-661-3314; ②), or to a handful of intermittently open B&Bs. The only nearby **campground** is the *Masset-Haida Lions RV Site and Campground* ($8; no reservations) on Tow Hill Road, 2km north of town alongside the wildlife sanctuary. Further afield there's a provincial park site near trails and sandy beaches, the *Agate Beach* ($9.50; May–Sept) in Naikoon Park, which is located 26km northeast of Masset off the secondary road towards Tow Hill (see below). To get around, call a **taxi** (☎626-5017) or **rent a car** from Tilden, 1504 Old Beach Rd (☎626-3318). There are a couple of pizza and takeaway places to **eat**, and one **bar** on Collision Avenue and Main Street, with live music most nights.

Heading away from the village, follow Tow Hill Road to **Tow Hill**, 26km to the east, where you can pick up trails into the Naikoon Park: three begin by the Heillen River at the foot of Tow Hill itself. The easiest is the one-kilometre **Blow Hole Trail**, which drops down to striking rock formations and basalt cliffs by the sea. From here you can follow another path to the top of Tow Hill (109m) for superb views of deserted sandy beaches stretching into the hazy distance. The third track, the **Cape Fife Trail**, is a longer (10km) hike to the east side of the island. Naikoon means "point", a reference to Rose Spit, the twelve-kilometre spit that extends from the park and Graham Island's northeasterly tip. Today it's an ecological and wildlife reserve of beaches, dunes, marsh and stunted forest, but it's also a sacred Haida site, for it was here, according to legend, that the Haida's Raven clan were first tempted from a giant clamshell by a solitary raven.

Moresby Island

Moresby Island is all but free from human contact except for deserted Haida villages, one of which contains the world's largest stand of totems, forestry roads and the small logging community of **Sandspit** (pop. 202). The last lies 15km from the **Alliford Bay** terminal for the inter-island ferry link with Skidegate on Graham Island (12 daily; 20min crossing; $3 passengers, cars $8.50). Canadian Regional and minor local airlines fly from Prince Rupert to a small airstrip near the village. Budget (☎637-5688) and Thrifty (☎637-2299) have **car rental** offices at the airport and Twin Service shuttles ($6) meet flights to take passengers to Queen Charlotte City across the water.

Most locals here and on Graham Island work in Moresby's forests, and the **forestry issue** has divided the community for years between the Haida and ecologists – "hippies" in the local parlance – and the lumber workers (the "rednecks" as the environmentalists call them). At stake are the islands' temperate rainforests and the traditional sites of the Haida, themselves politically shrewd media manipulators, who've sent representatives to Brazil to advise local tribes there on their own rainforest programmes. They've also occasionally provided the muscle to halt logging on the islands, and to prove a point in the past they've blocked access to **Hot Spring Island**, whose thermal pools are a favourite tourist target. On the other hand the forests provide jobs and some of the world's most lucrative timber – a single good sitka trunk can be worth up to $60,000. Currently a compromise has been reached and most of Moresby has National Park Reserve status (established in 1987), though stiff lobbying from the logging companies leaves its position perilous. If you're intending to drive any of the logging roads, however – and most of the handful of roads here *are* logging roads – note that generally they're open to the public at weekends and after 6pm on weekdays: otherwise check for latest details with TimberWest (☎637-5323 or 637-5436).

Sandspit's only **accommodation**, apart from a couple of B&Bs, is the *Sandspit Inn* on Airport Road near the airstrip (☎637-5334; ④) – also the area's only bar and restaurant – and the *Moresby Island Guest House* at 385 Alliford Bay Rd overlooking the ocean at Shingle Bay, 1km south of the airport (☎637-5300; ②); an airport pick-up is included. The *Seaport B&B*, 371 Alford Bay Rd (☎637-5698; ②), offers accommodation in a waterfront mobile home with self-serve breakfast included. Many people choose to sleep on the spit's beaches: Gray Bay, 21km southeast of Sandspit, has primitive and peaceful **campsites** near gravel and sand beaches (for more details, contact the Timber West forestry offices on Beach Road; ☎637-5436). For **car rental**, Budget have offices at the airport and Sandspit at Beach and Blaine Shaw roads (☎637-5688). If you fancy going into the interior by plane under your own steam, contact South Moresby Air Charters (☎559-4222) for details of charter flights.

Gwaii Haanas National Park Reserve

If you're determined enough you can canoe, mountain bike or backpack the interior of northern Moresby Island, but you need to know what you're doing – the seas here are especially treacherous for canoeists – and be prepared to lug plenty of supplies. You must, however, join a tour if you want to visit the **Gwaii Haanas National Park Reserve**, a ninety-kilometre archipelago that embraces 138 islands, some 500 Haida archeological sites, five deserted Haida villages and some 1500km of coastline across the south of the island group. Treaties signed with the federal government in Ottawa in 1990 gave the Haida joint control of this region, and afforded protection to their ancient villages, but most land claims to the region remain unresolved. You need money, time and effort to see the park. There are no roads, and access is by boat or chartered planes only. Not only must you make reservations for tours, but you also have to undergo a compulsory "orientation" session at the Queen Charlotte City or Sandspit **infocentres** (held daily each morning in the summer).

Visits to a variety of **Haida sites** are possible, described here in order of distance (and therefore time and expense) from Sandspit. Closest are **Hlkenul** (Cumshewa) and **K'una** (Skedans) just outside the park, both accessible on day-trips by boat from Moresby Camp on Cumshewa Inlet, 46km south of Sandspit (access to the Camp by logging road). Further afield, and in the park proper, are T'anuu, Hlk'waah – one of the main battlegrounds in the fight to protect the region in the 1980s – and **Gandla K'in** (Hot Spring Island), whose hot springs make it one of the most popular destinations. The finest site of all, of course, is the one that's furthest away: **Sgan Gwaii** (Ninstints) lies close to the southern tip of the archipelago, and was abandoned by the Haida around 1880 in the wake of smallpox epidemics introduced by outsiders. Today it contains the most striking of the ruined Haida villages, its long houses and countless totems declared a UNESCO World Heritage Site in 1981.

The **Canadian Parks Service** offices at Sandspit off Beach Road at the north end of town (May–Sept daily 8.30am–6pm; ☎637-5362), the Gwaii Haanas office in Sandspit Mall (☎559-8818) and the infocentre at Queen Charlotte City (see p.804) all provide information on the park. Sandspit's **infocentre** in the airport terminal building (June–Sept daily 9am–6pm; ☎637-5436) has details of the many tours to the park and the limited facilities on the whole southern half of the archipelago.

The Cassiar Highway

The 733km of the **Cassiar Highway** (Hwy 37) from the Skeena Valley east of Prince Rupert to Watson Lake just inside Yukon Territory are some of the wildest and most beautiful on any British Columbian road. Though less famous than the Alaska Highway, the road is increasingly travelled by those who want to capture some of the adventure that accompanied the wilder reaches of its better-known neighbour in the 1950s and 1960s. A two-day **bus service** has recently been introduced along the road by Rival Highway Tours, Suite 1, Berner Heritage Building, 342 3rd Ave West, Prince Rupert (☎624-6124 in Prince Rupert, 667-7896 in Whitehorse), a potentially excellent way of seeing the scenery for independent travellers. It connects Prince Rupert to Whitehorse ($210 single, $398 return) in two stages: Prince Rupert–Dease Lake (currently departs on Tues 8am, arrives 6.15pm) and Dease Lake–Watson Lake–Whitehorse (Wed 8am, arrives Whitehorse 6pm). The cost of a hotel in **Dease Lake** is not included in the price.

Most people, however, will probably be tackling the road by **car**. Stretches are still gravel (124km at the time of writing), and the gas and repair facilities, let alone food and lodgings, are extremely patchy: don't contemplate the journey unless your vehicle's in top condition, with two spare tyres and spare fuel containers. Currently the longest stretch without fuel is the 240km between Meziadin Lake and Eddontenajon, but you'll probably want to fill up wherever possible. The road also provides a shorter route from Prince George to the Yukon than the Alaska Highway, and as more of it is paved the number of big trucks and logging vehicles using it is on the increase, creating more potential hazards. British Columbia's North by Northwest Tourist Association puts out complete lists of facilities, which are vital accompaniments to any journey and are available from the infocentres in Prince Rupert and Terrace.

If you're ready to drive the distances involved, you'll also probably be prepared to explore the highway's two main sideroads to **Stewart** and to **Telegraph Creek**, and possibly the rough roads and trails that lead into two wilderness parks midway up the highway – the **Mount Edziza Provincial Park** and the **Spatsizi Plateau Wilderness Park**. If you can't face the highway's entire length, the side-trip to Stewart offers exceptional sea and mountain **scenery**, as well as the chance to cross into Alaska at **Hyder** to indulge in its vaunted alcoholic border initiation (see p.811).

Stewart

The Cassiar Highway starts near Kitwanga, one of several native villages off Hwy 16 (see p.797), and a crossroads of the old "grease trail", named after the candlefish oil which was once traded between Coast and Interior tribes. Some hint of the sense of adventure required comes when you hit a section (47km beyond Cranberry Junction), where the road doubles up as an airstrip – planes have right of way. Another 27km on, there's another stretch used as an airstrip in emergencies. Almost immediately you leave Hwy 16, though, the road pitches into the mesmerizing high scenery of the Coast Ranges, a medley of mountain, lake and forest that reaches a crescendo after about 100km and the side turn to **STEWART**, Canada's most northerly ice-free port. Here a series of immense glaciers culminates in the dramatic appearance of the unmissable **Bear Glacier**, a vast sky-blue mass of ice that comes down virtually to the highway and has the strange ability to glow in the dark. Stewart itself, 37km west of the glacier, is a shrivelled mining centre (pop. 2200) that sits at the end of the Portland Canal, the world's fourth longest fjord, a natural boundary between British Columbia and Alaska that lends the town a superb peak-ringed location (the ferry ride in from Prince Rupert through some of the west coast's wildest scenery is sensational). Dominating its rocky amphitheatre is **Mount Rainey**, whose cliffs represent one of the greatest vertical rises from sea level in the world.

Stewart's **history**, together with that of nearby Hyder (see opposite), might have marked it out as a regional player were it not quite so remote and apparently doomed to ultimate disappointment in every venture ever tried in the town. In the distant past it was an important trading point, marking the meeting point of territories belonging to the Nisga'a and Gitxsan interior tribes to the south, the Thaltan to the north, the interior Tsesaut and the Tlingit to the east. Captain George Vancouver, searching for the Northwest Passage in 1793, spoke for many who came after him when, having spent an eternity working his way inland up the Portland Canal, he declared himself "mortified with having devoted so much time to so little purpose". Almost exactly a century later the area welcomed its first settlers: in 1896 Captain Gilliard of the US Army Corps built four storehouses here – Alaska's first stone buildings – and Stewart was named after two of its earliest settlers (Robert and John Stewart). For a time it looked as if the terminus of the trans-Canadian railway might materialize in Stewart, a hope that brought in 10,000 fortune-seeking pioneers. The railway never came, and Stewart's local line was abandoned after a few kilometres. As slump set in, gold was discovered – almost inevitably – and until 1948, when it closed, the Premier Gold and Silver Mine was North America's largest gold mine. Then came a copper mine, its eighteen-kilometre gallery apparently the longest tunnel ever built by boring from just one end. This closed in 1984, but not before 27 men were killed in a mine accident in 1965. All manner of new mining ventures have since been promised. None have materialized, leaving Stewart's scenery its main money-spinner: visitors and B-movie location scouts alike having been lured by the region's cliffs, mountains and glaciers – the *Iceman* and *The Thing* are two of the films to have used the local landscape as scenographic backdrop.

Scenery aside, the main thing to see in town is the **Stewart Historical Museum** housed in the former fire hall at Columbia and 6th Avenue (summer Mon–Fri 1–4pm, Sat & Sun noon–5pm; or by appointment on ☎636-2568). A fine little provincial museum, it exhibits are devoted largely to stuffed wildlife and the town's logging and mining heritage. You might also want to journey out 5km beyond Hyder (see opposite) to Fish Creek, where from the special viewing platform above the artificial spawning channel you may be lucky enough to see **black bears** catching some of the world's largest chum salmon. Around town there are also a handful of enticing trails, some along old mining roads: for details, contact the infocentre (see below) or visit the British Columbia Forest Service (☎636-2663) office at 8th and Brightwell.

PRACTICALITIES

The town's **infocentre** is housed at 222 5th Ave near Victoria (mid-May to mid-Sept daily; 9am–8pm; ☎636-9224). If you want to sleep over, there are two **hotels**: the *King Edward Hotel*, 5th and Columbia (☎636-2244 or toll-free in BC 1-800-663-3126; ③), and the *King Edward Motel*, Columbia Avenue (same details): the latter has basic housekeeping units and is $12 more expensive. The *King Edward Hotel* is virtually the town's only **pub**, **restaurant** and **coffee shop** – it's where the locals eat, while visitors prefer the pleasantly polished *Bitter Creek Café* (a block west of the *King Edward*), which offers an eclectic mix of food and an outside deck for warm days. For bread and baked snacks, duck into *Brothers Bakery* next door to the *Bitter Creek*. There's also a late-opening Chinese restaurant, *Fong's Garden*, at 5th and Conway. The nearest **campground** is the *Stewart Lions Campground* on the edge of town on 8th Avenue (☎636-2537; $12–15; May–Sept): it also offers nature trails and glacier tours; the tenting area (as opposed to RVs) is located across Raine Creek, a pleasant little stream. One of the easiest local trails starts here: the **Raine Creek Nature Walk**, shadowing the creek for 2.5km to the northern end of town (return to the centre on Railway Street).

In summer Stewart is added to the itinerary of certain sailings of the Alaska Marine Highway ferry service, albeit infrequently (double-check details of latest sailings), so with careful planning you could travel overland to Stewart, or ride a boat to Ketchikan and thence to either Skagway or Prince Rupert, to complete a neat circular itinerary.

Hyder

Most people come to **HYDER** (pop. 70–100), Stewart's oddball twin, simply to drink in one or both of its two bars. It's a ramshackle place – barely a settlement at all – 3km from Stewart across the **border in Alaska** with none of the usual formalities, there being nothing beyond the end of the road but 800km of wilderness. People use Canadian currency, the police are of the Mountie variety and the phone system and code – 250 – are also Canadian. At the *Glacier Inn* the tradition is to pin a dollar to the wall in case you return broke and need a drink, and then toss back a shot of hard liquor in one and receive an "I've Been Hyderized" card. The result is many thousands of tacked dollars and the "world's most expensive wallpaper". There's a penalty (or two) if you fail the test, the little card if you pass. It sounds a bit of a tourist carry-on, but if you arrive out of season there's a genuine amiability about the place that warrants its claims to be the "The Friendliest Ghost Town in Alaska". The town's two bars are often open 23 hours a day and a couple of **motels** are on hand if you literally can't stand any more: the *Sealaska Inn*, Premier Avenue (☎636-9003; ③), and the preferable *Grand View Inn* (☎636-9174; ③). They're both cheaper than their Stewart equivalents, and as you're in Alaska there's no room tax to pay on top. If you want something to soak up the alcohol, make for the *Border Café* (☎636-2379) or the *Sealaska Inn Restaurant* (☎636-2486): both serve no-nonsense food. For caffeine the morning after, try the *Salmon River Outpost* (☎636-9019). The community's little **infocentre**, if you need it, is on the right as you come into town (June to early Sept daily except Wed 9am–1pm).

Dease Lake and Iskut

For several hundred kilometres beyond the Stewart junction there's nothing along the Cassiar other than the odd garage, rest area, campground, trailhead and patches of burnt or clear-cut forest etched into the Cassiar and Skeena mountains. In places, though, you can still see traces of the incredible 3060-kilometre Dominion Telegraph line that used to link the Dawson City gold fields with Vancouver, and glimpses of a proposed railway extension out of Prince George that was abandoned as late as 1977.

DEASE LAKE, the first place of any size, has a single **motel**, the *Northway Motor Inn* on Boulder Avenue (☎771-5341; ③), still 246km from the junction with the Alaska Highway to the north. Close by lies **ISKUT**, a native village offering tours into the adjacent wilderness parks, which are also accessible by float plane from Dease Lake itself. For **information**, contact the Iskut Band Office (☎234-3331) or local stores and garages. The village has the most **accommodation** options for a fair way: on the highway there's the *Black Sheep Motel* (☎234-3141; ③). The *Mountain Shadow Guest Ranch*, at Kluachon Lake 3km north of the village, has just three rooms, tent/RV sites and offers canoe rentals (☎234-3333; ②, tents $14–20; May–Sept). There's also an official HI-affiliated **youth hostel**, the *Red Goat Lodge* (☎234-3261 or 1-888-733-4628; ④, tents $9.35; late May to mid-Sept), and *Iskutine Lodge* (☎234-3456; ①, tents $10) on Eddontenajon Lake, 9km south of the village, both of which have rooms and campgrounds combined. In the other direction, near Stikine Grand Canyon 8km north of the village, is the *Bear Paw Ranch* (radio phone only; ③) with cabins or rooms in the adjacent *Alpine Hotel*.

The road from Dease Lake is wild and beautiful, the 240km up to the Yukon border from here passing through some of the most miraculous scenery of what is already a superb journey. Around 28km north of Dease Lake is a rest area, unremarkable except for its wonderful name – the Rabid Grizzly Rest Area. Some 84km north of Dease Lake is the *Moose Meadows Resort* (radio phone only; ①, tents $10; May to mid-Oct) which has cabins, tent and RV sites, a convenience store and canoe rentals. Much of this area was swamped with gold-hungry pioneers during the **Cassiar Gold Rush** of 1872–80, when the region got its name – possibly from a white prospector's corruption of *kaskamet*, the dried beaver meat eaten by local Kaska tribes. In 1877 Alfred Freedman plucked one of the world's largest pure gold nuggets – a 72-ounce monster – from a creek east of present-day **CASSIAR** (133km from the junction with the Alaska Highway to the north) though these days the mining has a less romantic allure, being concentrated in an open-pit **asbestos mine** 5km from the village. Most of the world's high-grade asbestos once came from here, and poisonous-looking piles of green chrysotile asbestos tailings are scattered for kilometres around. The mine closed in 1992, transforming the community into a virtual ghost town at a stroke. Equipment has been sold and sites cleared, and the area is off limits to the pubic until reclamation is complete.

Telegraph Creek

For a taste of what is possibly a more remarkable landscape than you see on the Cassiar, it's worth driving the potentially treacherous 113-kilometre sideroad from Dease Lake to **TELEGRAPH CREEK** (allow 2hr in good conditions), a delightful river-bank place whose look and feel can scarcely have changed since the turn of the century, when it was a major telegraph station and trading post for the gold-rush towns to the north. The road from the Cassiar navigates some incredible gradients and bends, twisting past canyons, old lava beds and touching on several **native villages**, notably at Tahltan River, where salmon are caught and cured in traditional smokehouses and sold to passing tourists. If you're lucky you might see a Tahltan bear dog, a species now virtually extinct. Only ankle high, and weighing less than fifteen pounds, these tiny animals were able to keep a bear cornered by barking and darting around until a hunter came to finish it off. Telegraph Creek itself is an object lesson in how latter-day pioneers live on the north's last frontiers: it's home to a friendly mixture of city exiles, hunters, trappers and ranchers, but also a cloistered bunch of **religious fundamentalists** who have eschewed the decadent mainstream for wilderness purity. Such groups are growing in outback British Columbia, an as-yet undocumented phenomenon that's creating friction with the easy-going types who first settled the backwoods. Gold has recently been discovered 100km, attracting mining companies, so ways of life may be about to change here for all concerned.

Much of the village and village life revolves around the General Delivery – a combined café (the *Riversong*), grocery and garage – and small adjoining **motel**, the *Stikine River Song Lodge* (☎235-3196; ②), whose rooms include kitchenettes. No one here, except perhaps the Bible brigade, minds if you pitch a tent – but ask around first. Also enquire at the café for details of rafting and other local trips into the backcountry.

Prince George to Dawson Creek

Dawson Creek is the launching pad for the Alaska Highway. While it may not be somewhere you'd otherwise stop, it's almost impossible to avoid a night here whether you're approaching from Edmonton and the east or **from Prince George** on the scenically more uplifting **John Hart Highway** (Hwy 97). Named after a former BC premier, this seemingly innocuous road is one of the north's most vital highways. Completed in 1952, it linked at a stroke the road network of the Pacific Coast with that of the northern interior, cutting 800km off the journey from Seattle to Alaska, for example, a trip that previously had to take in a vast inland loop to Calgary. The route leads you out of British Columbia's upland interior to the so-called Peace River country, a region of slightly ridged land that belongs in look and spirit to the Albertan prairies. There's some 409km of driving, and two daily Greyhound **buses** make the journey.

Out of Prince George the road bends through mildly dipping hills and mixed wood-land, passing small lakes and offering views to the Rockies, whose distant jagged sky-line keeps up the spirits as you drive through an otherwise unbroken tunnel of conifers. About 70km on, **Bear Lake** and the **Crooked River Provincial Park** are just off the road, and it's well worth taking the small lane west of the park entrance to reach an idyllic patch of water fringed on its far shore by a fine sickle of sand. There's a free **campground** at the park, and the *Grizzly Inn* **motel** just beyond (☎972-4436; ③), with the road's first services after Prince George.

Both Mackenzie Junction, 152km from Prince George, and Mackenzie, 29km off the highway, are scrappy, unpleasant places, easily avoided and soon forgotten as the road climbs to **Pine Pass** (933m), one of the lower road routes over the Rockies, but spectacular all the same. The **Bijoux Falls Provincial Park**, just before it, is good for a picnic near the eponymous falls, and if you want to **camp** plump for the *Pine Valley Park Lodge* ($8; May–Oct), an immensely scenic lakeside spot that looks up to crags of massively stratified and contorted rock just below the pass. Thereafter the road drops steeply through Chetwynd (three motels and a campground) to the increasingly flatter country that heralds Dawson Creek.

Dawson Creek

Arrive in **DAWSON CREEK** (pop. 11,500) late and leave early: except for a small museum next to the town's eye-catching red grain hopper, and the obligatory photograph of the cairn marking **Mile Zero** of the Alaska Highway, there's nothing to do here except eat and sleep. Contact the **infocentre** at the museum, 900 Alaska Ave (daily 9am–6pm, longer hours in summer; ☎782-9595), for details of the **motels** – and there are plenty, mostly concentrated on the Alaska Highway northeast of town. If you've climbed off a Greyhound at the **bus terminal**, 1201 Alaska Ave, try the newish *Northwinds Lodge* (☎782-9181 or 1-800-665-1759; ③) beyond the Co-op Mall east of the Mile Zero cairn at 832 103rd Ave. One of the nicer places is the *Trail Inn*, 1748 Alaska Ave (☎782-8595 or 1-800-663-2749; ③), with views of countryside rather than tarmac. None of the three local **campgrounds** and RV parks are places you'd want to linger, but the most attractive is the *Mile 0 RV Park and Campground* (☎782-2590; $10–16; May to mid-Sept), about a kilometre west of the town centre and junction of Hwy 97 N and Hwy 97 S opposite 20th Street on the Alaska Highway.

For something to **eat**, call at the excellent *Alaska Café* on 10th Street, an attractive old wooden building completely at odds with the rest of the town. The food and ambience are good – though prices aren't the cheapest – and the bar's not bad either.

Dawson Creek to Whitehorse

The best part of the **Alaska Highway** – a distance of about 1500km – winds through northern British Columbia from Dawson Creek to Whitehorse, the capital of the Yukon (only 320km of the Alaska Highway is actually in Alaska). Don't be fooled by the string of villages emblazoned across the area's maps, for there are only two towns worthy of the name en route, **Fort St John** and **Fort Nelson** – the rest are no more than a garage, a store and perhaps a motel. **Watson Lake**, on the Yukon border, is the largest of these lesser spots, and also marks the junction of the Alaska and Cassiar highways. All the way down the road, though, it's vital to book accommodation during July and August.

Driving the Alaska Highway is no longer the adventure of days past – that's now provided by the Cassiar and Dempster highways. Food, fuel and lodgings are found at between forty- and eighty-kilometre intervals, though cars still need to be in good shape. You should drive with headlights on at all times, and take care when passing or being passed by heavy trucks. It also goes without saying that wilderness – anything up to 800km of it each side – begins at the edge of the highway and unless you're very experienced you shouldn't contemplate any off-road exploration. Any number of guides and pamphlets are available to take you through to Fairbanks, but *The Milepost*, the road's bible, now into its fiftieth edition, is for all its mind-numbing detail the only one you need buy.

From mid-May to mid-October daily (except Sun) a **Greyhound bus** leaves Dawson Creek in the morning and plies the road all the way to Whitehorse; it runs on Tuesday, Thursday and Saturday the rest of the year. The twenty-hour trip finishes at 5am, with only occasional half-hour meal stops, but covers the road's best scenery in daylight.

Dawson Creek to Fort Nelson

You need to adapt to a different notion of distance on a 2500-kilometre drive: on the Alaska Highway points of interest are a long way apart, and pleasure comes in broad changes in scenery, in the sighting of a solitary moose, or in the passing excitement of a lonely bar. Thus it's forty minutes before the benign ridged prairies around Dawson Creek prompt attention by dropping suddenly into the broad, flat-bottomed valley of the Peace River, a canyon whose walls are scalloped with creeks, gulches and deep muddy scars. Just across the river **FORT ST JOHN**, which, until the coming of the highway (when it was the field headquarters of the road's eastern construction gangs), was a trading post for local Sikanni and Beaver natives, which had remained little changed since its predecessor sank into the mud of the Peace River (there have been a total of six "Fort St Johns" in various incarnations in the area). The shantytown received a boost when the province's largest oilfield was discovered nearby in 1955, and it's now a functional settlement with all the services you need – though at just 75km into the highway it's unlikely you'll be ready to stop. If you are, there's a small museum at 93rd and 100th Street and a dozen **motels**: solid choices are the big *Alexander Mackenzie Inn*, 9223 100th St (☎785-8364 or 1-800-663-8313; ③), and the *Four Seasons Motor Inn*, 9810 100th St (☎785-6647 or 1-800-523-6677; ②). The **infocentre** is at 9323 100th St (☎785-6037 or 785-3033).

The next stop is **WONOWON** (pop. 84), a military check point in the war, and at 161km from Dawson typical of the bleak settlements all the way up the road: alongside the wooden and corrugated iron shacks, it has a couple of **motels** – the *Blueberry* (☎772-3322; ②) and *Pine Hill* (☎772-3340; ②) – a few wires strung between poles, rusting oil and gas storage tanks, and some concrete blocks laid out as a nominal attempt at a kerb, as if to impose a semblance of civic order on the wilderness.

PINK MOUNTAIN (pop. 19), 226km on from Dawson, is much the same, with *Mae's Kitchen* (☎772-3215; ②) the only listed accommodation (other places open and close here regularly). There's also a **restaurant** favoured by truckers (but run by hatchet-faced staff) with a reasonable campground across the road (☎772-3226; $8–20; May–Oct). Thirty kilometres on, however, is one of the better of the campgrounds on this section of the road, the fully serviced *Sikanni River RV Park* (☎774-1028; $10). It also has a couple of cabins (②). Thereafter the road offers immense **views** of utter wilderness in all directions, the trees as dense as ever, but noticeably more stunted than further south and nearing the limit of commercial viability. Look out for the bright "New Forest Planted" signs, a token riposte from the loggers to the ecology lobby, as they are invariably backed by a graveyard of sickly looking trees. If you're **camping**, look out for two provincial sanctuaries over the remaining 236km to Fort Nelson. Around 60km north of Pink Mountain is the Buckinghorse River Provincial Park campground; another 69km further is the Prophet River Provincial Recreation Area, with a campground overlooking the river: this is good bird-watching country, but it's also good bear country, so be careful (see pp.598–599).

Fort Nelson

One of the highway's key stopoffs, **FORT NELSON** greets you with a large poster proclaiming "Jail is only the beginning – don't drink and drive", a sobering sign that hints
at the sort of extremes to which people hereabouts might go to relieve the

THE ALASKA HIGHWAY

The **Alaska Highway** runs northeast from Mile Zero at Dawson Creek through the
Yukon Territory to Mile 1520 in Fairbanks, Alaska. Built as a military road, it's now an
all-weather highway travelled by daily bus services and thousands of tourists out to
recapture the thrill of the days when it was known as the "junkyard of the American automobile". It's no longer a driver's Calvary, but the scenery and the sense of pushing
through wilderness on one of the continent's last frontiers remain as alluring as ever.
Around 360,000 people a year make the journey.

As recently as 1940 there was no direct land route to the Yukon or Alaska other than
trails passable only by experienced trappers. When the Japanese invaded the Aleutian
Islands during World War II, however, they both threatened the traditional sea routes to
the north and seemed ready for an attack on mainland Alaska – the signal for the building of the joint US-Canadian road to the north. A proposed coastal route from Hazelton
in British Columbia was deemed too susceptible to enemy attack (it's since been built as
the Cassiar Highway), while an inland route bypassing Whitehorse and following the
Rockies would have taken five years to build. This left the so-called **Prairie Route**,
which had the advantage of following a line of air bases through Canada into Alaska – a
chain known as the **Northwest Staging Route**. In the course of the war, some 8000
planes were ferried from Montana to Edmonton and then to Fairbanks along this route,
where they were picked up by Soviet pilots and flown into action on the Siberian front.

Construction of the highway began on **March 9, 1942**, the start of months of misery
for the 20,000 mainly US soldiers shanghaied to ram a road through mountains, mud,
mosquito-ridden bog, icy rivers and forest during some of the harshest extremes of
weather. Incredibly, crews working on the eastern and western sections met at Contact
Creek, British Columbia, in September 1942, and completed the last leg to Fairbanks in
October – an engineering triumph that had taken less than a year but cost around $140
million. The first full convoy of trucks to make Fairbanks managed an average 25kph
during one of the worst winters in memory.

By 1943 the highway already needed virtual rebuilding, and for seven years workers
widened the road, raised bridges, reduced gradients, bypassed swampy ground and started
to remove some of the vast bends that are still being ironed out – the reason why it's now only
1488 miles (2394km), for example, to the old Mile 1520 post in Fairbanks. All sorts of ideas
have been put forward to explain the numerous curves – that they were to stop Japanese
planes using the road as a landing strip, that they simply went where bulldozers could go at
the time, or even at one point that they followed the trail of a rutting moose. Probably the chief
reason is that the surveying often amounted to no more than a pointed finger aimed at the
next horizon. Canada took over control of the road in 1946, but civilian traffic was barred until
1948. Within months of its opening so much traffic had been lost that it was closed for a year.

Although the road is now widely celebrated, there are sides to the story that are still
glossed over. Many of its toughest sections, for example, were given to black GIs, few of
whom have received credit for their part in building the highway – you'll look in vain for
black faces amongst the white officers in the archive photos of ribbon-cutting ceremonies. Another tale is the road's effect on natives on the route, scores of whom died
from epidemics brought in by the workers. Yet another was the building of the controversial "Canadian Oil" or **Canol pipeline** in conjunction with the road, together with
huge dumps of poisonous waste and construction junk. Wildlife en route was also devastated by trigger-happy GIs taking recreational pot shots as they worked: the virtual
eradication of several species was part of the reason for the creation of the Kluane Game
Sanctuary, the forerunner of the Yukon's Kluane National Park (see p.827).

tedium of winter's long semi-twilight. Everything in town, except a small **museum** devoted to the highway's construction, speaks of a frontier supplies depot, the last in a long line of trading posts attracted to a site that is fed by four major rivers and stands in the lee of the Rockies. Dour buildings stand in a battered sprawl around a windswept grid, only a single notch up civilization's ladder from the time in the late 1950s when this was still a community without power, phones, running water or doctors. Life's clearly too tough here to be geared to anything but pragmatic survival and exploitation of its huge natural gas deposits – the town has the world's second largest gas-processing plant and the huge storage tanks to prove it. Natives and white trappers live as they have for centuries, hunting beaver, wolf, wolverine, fox, lynx and mink, as well as the ubiquitous moose, which is still an important food source for many natives.

The town does, however, have an extraordinary claim to fame, namely that it's home to the **world's largest chopstick factory**, located south of the town off the highway behind the weigh scales at Industrial Park Chopstick Road (☎774-4448 for details of tours). This has nothing to do with gargantuan demand for Chinese food in Fort Nelson – at last count there were only three Chinese restaurants in town – but more to do with the region's high-quality aspen, a wood apparently perfectly suited to producing the dream chopstick. The Canadian Chopstick Manufacturing Company produces an incredible 7.5 million pairs of chopsticks a *day*, or 1.95 billion a year.

The town's many **motels** are much of a muchness and you'll be paying the inflated rates – about $70 for doubles worth half that – which characterize the north. The *Mini Price Inn* a block off the highway at 5036 51st Ave West (behind the CIBC bank) is central and inexpensive (☎774-2136; ②) – though location's not terribly important here – and on the town's southern approaches the *Bluebell Inn*, 3907 50th Ave South (☎774-6961 or 1-800-663-5267; ③), is better looking than many of the run-of-the-mill places. If you're completely exhausted and want the best the town has to offer as a treat, the choice is the *Best Western Woodlands Inn*, 3995 50th Ave South (☎774-6669 or 1-800-528-1234; ⑤), at the southern approach to town. There's a big central **campground** beside the museum, the *Westend* (☎774-2340; $11–17; April–Nov) with a full range of services. The **infocentre** is at Mile 300.5 of the Alaska Highway (☎774-6400; rest of the year for information, call ☎774-2541; May–Sept).

Fort Nelson to Liard Hot Springs

This is the highway at its best. Landscapes divide markedly around **Fort Nelson**, where the highway arches west from the flatter hills of the Peace River country to meet the **northern Rockies** above the plains and plateau of the Liard River. Within a short time – once the road has picked up the river's headwaters – you're in some of the most grandiose scenery in British Columbia. The area either side of the road is some of the world's wildest – 20 million acres of nothing – experts say that only parts of Africa surpass the region for the variety of mammals present and the pristine state of its ecosystems. Services and motels become scarcer, but those that exist – though often beaten-up looking places – make atmospheric and often unforgettable stops. The first worthwhile stopoff, a kilometre off the highway on a gravel road, is **Tetsa River Provincial Park**, about 90km from Fort Nelson, which has a nice and secluded **campground** and appealing short hikes through the trees and along the river. Next up is **Stone Mountain Provincial Park**, with a campground which gives access to a short trail (10min) to two hoodoos claimed by myth to be the heads of two devils; a longer trail, the Flower Springs Lake Trail (6km), leads to a delightful upland tarn. Other **accommodation** and services include the *Summit Lake Motel*, 150km west of Fort Nelson, near the highway's highest point (1295m) – the *Rocky Mountain Lodge* (☎232-5000; ②), 15km on, is if anything more dilapidated, but has an astounding position and an adjacent **campground** ($10).

Toad River, 60km beyond (a total of 195km from Fort Nelson), has perhaps the best motel of all on this lonely stretch, the *Toad River Lodge* (☎232-5401; ②), giving superlative views of thickly forested and deeply cleft mountains on all sides. Note that it also has a grocery, gas station and sites for RVs ($10). About 3km to its north is the *Poplars Campground & Café*, with log cabins and fully serviced tent and RV sites (☎232-5465; ②, tent sites $12–16; May to late Sept); it's an equally attractive spot despite its disconcerting claims to be "Home of the Foot-Long Hot Dog".

Muncho Lake, the next big natural feature, sits at the heart of a large provincial park whose ranks of bare mountains are a foretaste of the barren tundra of the far north. There's a small **motel** and **campground** at the lake's southern end, but it's worth hanging on for the popular *Flats Provincial Campground* ($9.50, free in Oct; May–Oct), midway up the lake on its eastern side, or the fine *Northern Rockies Lodge-Highland Glen Lodge and Campground* (☎776-3481 or 1-800-663-5269; ③) for a choice of log cabins or camping sites ($16–25). A little way beyond is the cheaper *Muncho Lake Lodge*, again with rooms and campground (☎776-3456; ②, tent sites $10; May–Oct). Two kilometres north of the Muncho Lake settlement there is the small *MacDonald Provincial Campground*.

About 70km beyond the lake is the excellent *Lower Liard River Lodge* (☎776-7341; ③), a wonderfully cosy and friendly spot for food and rooms. (*Liard* comes from the French for "poplar" or "cottonwood tree", a ubiquitous presence in these parts.) It also has RV and tent sites ($8–10) and lies close to one of the most popular spots on the entire Alaska Highway, the **Liard Hot Springs**, whose **two thermal pools** (Alpha and Beta) are amongst the best and hottest in BC. Road crews loved these during the construction of the highway, or rather the men did: women in the teams were allowed a soak just once a week. They're reached by a short wooden boardwalk across steaming marsh, and are otherwise unspoilt apart from a wooden changing room and the big high-season crowds (aim to be here early in the day for a dip ahead of the rush). As the marsh never freezes, it attracts moose and grizzlies down to drink and graze, and some 250 plant species grow in the mild microhabitat nearby, including fourteen species of orchid, lobelias, ostrich ferns and other rare boreal forest plants. The nearby *Liard River Hotsprings Provincial Park* **campground** is one of the region's most popular, and fills up early in July and August: bookings are possible through the provincial park central reservation line ($7–12); see box on p.644.

The telephone code for the Yukon is ☎867.

Watson Lake to Whitehorse

Beyond Liard Hot Springs the road follows the Liard River, settling into about 135km of unexceptional scenery before **WATSON LAKE**, just over the Yukon border (though the road's tripped back and forth across the border seven times before hitting the town). Created by the coming of the highway and air base, it's neither attractive nor terribly big, but shops, motels and garages have sprung up here to service the traffic congregating off the Cassiar and Campbell highways to the north and south. In the past the region was the preserve of Kaska natives, people whose centuries-old way of life was altered in the 1870s by the Cassiar gold rush. Another gold rush, the Klondike, gave the settlement its present name, when Frank Watson, an English prospector gave up on his attempts to reach the northern gold fields and stopped here instead. If you're just passing through it's well worth pulling off to look at the **Alaska Highway Interpretive Centre** (May–Sept daily 9am–9pm; ☎536-7469), which as well as providing information on the Yukon also describes the high-

THE CHILKOOT TRAIL

No single image better conjures the human drama of the 1898 gold rush than the lines of prospectors struggling over the **Chilkoot Trail**, a 53-kilometre path over the Coast Mountains between **Dyea**, north of Skagway in Alaska, and **Bennett Lake** on the British Columbian border south of Whitehorse. Before the rush Dyea was a small village of Chilkat Tlingit, a native tribe who made annual trade runs over the trail to barter fish oil, clamshells and dried fish with the Tutchone, Tagish and other interior Dene tribes in exchange for animal hides, skin clothing and copper. The Chilkat jealously guarded access to the **Chilkoot Pass** (1122m), the key to the trail and one of only three glacier-free routes through the Coast Mountains west of Juneau. Sheer weight of numbers and a show of force from a US gunboat, however, opened the trail to stampeders, who used it as a link between the ferries at the Pacific Coast ports and the Yukon River, which they then rode to the goldfields at Dawson City.

For much of 1897 the pass and border were disputed by the US and Canada until the Canadian NWMP (Northwest Mounted Police) established a storm-battered shack at the summit and enforced the fateful "ton of goods" entry requirement. Introduced because of chronic shortages in the gold fields, this obliged every man entering the Yukon to carry a ton of provisions – and had appalling consequences for the stampeders. Weather conditions and the trail's fifty-degree slopes proved too severe even for horses or mules, so that men had to carry supplies on their backs over as many as fifty journeys to move their "ton of goods". Many died in avalanches or lost everything during a winter when temperatures dropped to –51°C and 25m of snow fell. Even so, the lure of gold was enough to drag some 22,000 prospectors over the pass.

These days most people off the **ferries from Prince Rupert and the Alaska Pan-handle** make the fantastic journey across the mountains by car or Gray Line bus on Hwy 2 from **Skagway to Whitehorse**, a route that parallels the old trail at a distance. More affluent tourists take the restored White Pass & Yukon Railway (WP & YR), originally built to supersede the Chilkoot Trail (May 18–Sept 24 2 daily; Skagway–White Pass by train then connecting bus to Whitehorse; around $95). Increasing numbers, however, are

---

way's construction through archive photos and audiovisual displays. It's situated on the highway next to the Chevron garage, close to the famous **Sign Post Forest**. This bit of gimmickry was started by homesick GI Carl K. Lindley in 1942, who erected a sign pointing the way and stating the mileage to his home in Danville, Illinois. Since then the signs have just kept on coming, and at last count numbered around thirty thousand. You might also want to dip briefly into the new **Northern Lights Centre** (June–Aug daily 2–10pm; $6–12; ☎536-7522), a planetarium and science centre that explores the myths, folklore and science behind phenomena such as the aurora borealis (see p.795).

It's still 441km from Watson Lake to Whitehorse. After the long haul on the Alaska Highway, a lot of people ignore the settlement's rather unlovely appearance and wisely stop overnight here to recuperate. If you're camping there are no problems, for countless small Yukon government-run **campgrounds** are dotted along the length of the highway beyond the village. If not, you have to think more carefully to avoid being stranded. If you decide to **stay in town** the cheapest options are the *Gateway Motor Inn* (☎536-7744; ③), open 24 hours a day, and the *Cedar Lodge Motel* (☎536-7406; ③). If these are full you may have to plump for one of the smarter hotels, all of which have rooms for around $90 – the best is the *Belvedere Hotel* (☎536-7712; ④), followed by the *Watson Lake Hotel* (☎536-7781; ④). Both have dining rooms if you're after food, though the *Watson Lake Hotel* and *Gateway* have some rooms with kitchenettes if you're cooking for yourself. The nearest **campground** is

walking the old trail (fifty hikers a day set off daily in summer), which has been laid out and preserved by the Canadian Parks Service as a **long-distance footpath**. Its great appeal lies not only in the scenery and natural habitats – which embrace coastal rainforest, tundra and sub-alpine boreal woodland – but also in the numerous artefacts like old huts, rotting boots, mugs and broken bottles still scattered where they were left by the prospectors.

The trail is well marked, regularly patrolled and generally fit to walk between about June and September. Although it only takes about four days, you shouldn't launch into it lightly. There are dangers from bears, avalanches, drastic changes of weather and exhaustion – there's one twelve-kilometre stretch, for example, for which you're advised to allow twelve hours. Excellent maps, guides and information are available from Skagway's Visitor Information Bureau at 2nd and Broadway, and at the Canadian Parks Service office at the SS *Klondike* in Whitehorse.

If, like most people, you walk the path from south to north, you must first pre-clear **Canadian customs** at Fraser on Hwy 2, 25km north of Skagway. This you can do, however, by calling ☎867/821-411 (it's easier to call from Skagway, not Dyea, which has few phones). You are given a time limit to complete the trail, after which you must report to the Customs and Immigration Office in Whitehorse at 101 Main St (daily 8.30am–4.30pm; ☎667-6471). Immigration controls are no less lax than elsewhere: you should have money (at least $150), a credit card and valid passport and photo-ID to ease your way across the border.

Walk or take a taxi the 15km from Skagway to the trailhead at Dyea to start the hike, and then be prepared to camp, for although there are three cabins on the trail the chances of finding space are almost zero. There are eight approved **campgrounds** at intervals along the trail, but these too become busy, though it's unlikely you'll be turned away. Note that no rough camping is allowed. At Bennett Lake at the end of the trail you can either take a **boat** to Carcross and pick up a Gray Line bus to Whitehorse, or take a minibus to **Log Cabin** on Hwy 2 136km south of Whitehorse and pick up a bus to either Whitehorse or Skagway. For a short taste of the White Pass railway, you can take the train from Bennett Lake to Fraser, 8km south of Log Cabin ($17), and catch the Gray Line from there.

the rustic Yukon government site, 4km west of the Sign Forest (May–Oct; $8), but for full services use the *Gateway to Yukon RV Park and Campground* near the Husky garage (☎536-7448; $12; year-round).

West of Watson Lake the road picks up more fine mountain scenery, running for hour after hour past apparently identical combinations of snowcapped peaks and thick forest. The next **accommodation**, campgrounds apart, is the *Rancheria Hotel* (☎851-6456; ③), 122km on from Watson: it's open 24 hours and has gas, groceries and a campground. About 10km before unlovely **TESLIN**, 263km to the west of Watson, look out for the *Dawson Peaks Northern Resort* (☎390-2310; ③; mid-May to mid-Sept), which not only has cabins and a campground, but also boasts one of the highway's better restaurants; fishing and boat rentals are also available. Teslin itself was founded as a trading post in 1903 and now has one of the region's largest Native Canadian populations, many of whom still live by hunting and fishing. The **George Johnston Museum** (June–Sept daily 9am–7pm; $2.50; ☎390-2550) is on the right on the way into the village and has a good collection of local Tlingit artefacts as well as the photos of Johnston, a Tlingit who recorded his culture on film between 1910 and 1940. If you get stuck overnight – it's 179km to Whitehorse – there are two **motels**: the *Northlake Motel* (☎390-2571; ②) is cheapest; the *Yukon Motel* (☎390-2575; ②) has a restaurant, newly renovated rooms and a serviced RV park and **campground** on the bay by the bridge ($12); and *Halstead's Teslin Lake Resort* (☎390-2608; ②; May–Sept), just out of the village, has a few rooms and a good **campground**.

Whitehorse

WHITEHORSE is the likeable capital of the Yukon, home to two-thirds of its population (23,000 people), the centre of its mining and forestry industries, and a bustling, welcoming stopoff for thousands of summer visitors. Whilst roads bring in today's business, the town owes its existence to the **Yukon River**, a 3000-kilometre artery that rises in BC's Coast Mountains and flows through the heart of the Yukon and Alaska to the Bering Sea. The river's flood plain and strange escarpment above the present town were long a resting point for Dene natives, but the spot burgeoned into a full-blown city with the arrival of thousands of stampeders in the spring of 1898. Having braved the Chilkoot Pass (see feature on p.818) to meet the Yukon's upper reaches,

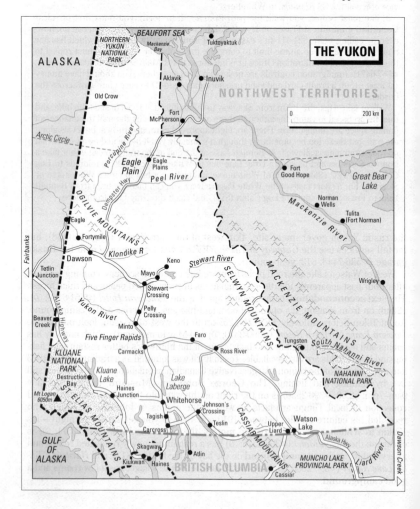

men and supplies then had to pause on the shores of Lineman or Bennett Lake before navigating the **Mile's Canyon** and White Horse rapids southeast of the present town. After the first few boats through had been reduced to matchwood, the Mounties laid down rules allowing only experienced boatmen to take craft through – writer Jack London, one such boatman, made $3000 in the summer of 1898, when more than seven thousand boats left the lakes. After a period the prospectors constructed an eight-kilometre wooden tramway around the rapids, and in time raised a shantytown settlement at the canyon and tramway's northern head to catch their breath before the river journey to Dawson City.

The completion of the White Pass and Yukon Railway (WP & YR) to Whitehorse (newly named after the rapids) put this tentative settlement on a firmer footing – almost at the same time as the gold rush petered out. In the early years of the twentieth century the town's population dwindled quickly from about 10,000 to about 400; for forty years the place slumbered, barely sustained by copper mining and the paddle-wheelers that plied the river carrying freight and the occasional tourist. The town's second boom arrived with the construction of the Alaska Highway, a kick-start that swelled the town's population from 800 to 40,000 almost overnight, and has stood it in good stead ever since.

Arrival, information and accommodation

Whitehorse's **airport** is on the bluff above the town, 5km west of downtown; taxis (around $8) and shuttle buses connect with downtown: the Whitehorse Transit Hillcrest bus ($1.25) runs past the airport hourly or so. The Greyhound **bus terminal** is at 3211 3rd Ave (☎667-2223) at the extreme eastern end of downtown, ten minutes' walk from Main Street – you turn left out of the terminal for the town centre, something it's as well to know if you stagger off the six-times-weekly Greyhound from Dawson Creek, which arrives at 5am. Alaskon Express buses, or Gray Line of Yukon (☎668-3225) from Fairbanks, Anchorage, Tok and Skagway, also stop here and at the *Westmark Whitehorse* hotel downtown.

Whitehorse's new downtown **Yukon Visitor Reception Centre** is on 2nd Avenue and Hanson Street (daily: mid-May to Sept 8am–8pm; Oct to mid-May 8.30am–5pm; ☎667-2915). Note that the "reception centre" up on the Alaska Highway still mentioned in some literature is now the Beringia Centre (see p.824). The Canadian Parks Service information office alongside the SS *Klondike* (May–Sept daily 9am–6pm; ☎667-4511) is the place to pick up information on the Chilkoot Trail. Almost as useful as these is Mac's Fireweed, 203 Main St (Mon–Sat 9am–9pm, Sun 10am–7pm), which has a full range of Yukon books, guides and pamphlets you won't find elsewhere. For an outstanding selection of **maps** visit Jim's Toy and Gifts, 208 Main St.

Car rental agencies have desks or courtesy phones at the airport: Avis (☎667-2847); Budget (☎667-6200), Rent-a-Wreck (☎668-7554) and Norcan (668-2137) are companies to try, but remember some have restrictions on taking cars on gravel roads if you're thinking of heading north on the Dempster Highway (see p.836). For **bike rental**, contact Wheels and Brakes Cyclery, 4168 4th Ave (☎663-3760). **Canoes**, paddles and life-jackets can be rented from the Kanoe People, Strickland Street and 1st Avenue (☎668-4899), who can also set you up with everything you need to paddle to Dawson (700km but lots of people do it): they also organize guided day-trips (from $50) and two-week expeditions on the river.

Accommodation

Whitehorse has a surprising amount of **accommodation** but in summer it gets booked up well in advance. If you arrive cold, contact the visitor centre or try the string of six hotels on Main Street between 1st and 5th avenues. For **B&B**, try the information centre's B&B list, or contact the recommendations below, but note that places open and close with some regularity. The *Robert Service* **campground**, about 2km and twenty minutes' walk down South Access Road, is set out on the banks of the Yukon River specifically for tents and backpackers (☎668-3721; $11; mid-May to mid-Sept). It gets very busy in summer; if it's full try the woods above the lake down past the dam beyond the campground or along the bluff above town by the airport. The heavily advertised *Trail of 98 RV Park* at 117 Jasper Rd (☎668-3768), on the road between the Alaska Highway and downtown, is for RVs and is not really suitable for tents.

HOTELS

98 Hotel, 110 Wood St (☎667-2641 or 667-2656). Cheap, fairly grim and occasionally with live bands to serenade you through the small hours. ②.

Airline Inn, 16 Burns Rd (☎668-4400, fax 668-2641). If you arrive late at the airport, or need an early getaway, this is the airstrip's nearest hotel – serviceable enough for its purposes. ③.

Capital Hotel, 103 Main St (☎667-2565, fax 668-4651). This is the place to stay if you want one of the town's more lively, historic and boisterous hotels, complete with fine rooms. ③.

Edgewater Hotel, 101 Main St (☎667-2572, fax 668-3014). Good, middle-priced hotel in downtown area. ④.

High Country Inn, 4051 4th Ave, at the far western end, a 10min walk from downtown (☎667-4471, fax 667-6457). An easy-going hotel with a wide variety of excellent room deals and weekly rates. ②.

Roadhouse Inn, 2163 2nd Ave (☎667-2594, fax 668-7291). Of a similar standard, but marginally better than the *98 Hotel* and near the bus terminal. ②.

Stratford Motel, 401 Jarvis St (☎667-4243 or 1-800-661-0539, fax 668-7432). Spotlessly clean, newly renovated rooms (some with kitchenettes) and with a friendly staff. Three blocks from downtown. Weekly rates available. ④.

Town & Mountain Hotel, 401 Main St (☎668-7644 or 1-800-661-0522, fax 668-5822) Another good middle-priced place. ④.

Westmark Klondike Inn, 2288 2nd Ave (☎668-4747, 1-800-999-2570 or 1-800-544-0970, fax 667-7639) One of two top-of-the-range, comfortable hotels belonging to the northern *Westmark* chain. ⑥.

Westmark Whitehorse Hotel, 201 Wood St (☎668-4700 or 1-800-478-1111, fax 668-2789; ⑥). If you want to see Whitehorse in style, this is the smartest and most expensive hotel in town.

BED AND BREAKFAST

Baker's, 84 11th Ave (☎633-2308). Two rooms in a quiet area 5km from downtown. Long-established, and patrons are longtime Yukon residents. ③.

Four Seasons, 18 Tagish Rd (☎667-2161, fax 667-2171). Centrally located, about 10min walk from downtown and offering full breakfast and snacks. ③.

Garland's, 4 11th Ave (☎633-2173, fax 633-4313). Close to downtown this place has a pleasant setting with nice views over the trees. ③.

Haeckel Hill, 1501 Birch St (☎633-5625, fax 633-5630). On a bus route to downtown but amidst a quiet setting overlooking the Yukon River Valley close to hiking trails. Full breakfast. ③.

Hawkins House, 303 Hawkins St (☎668-7638, fax 668-7632). Old Victorian home in downtown; laundry and private bathrooms available. No smoking.

Highland Home, 1 11th Ave (☎633-5804, fax 668-5705). Located in a quiet residential area, facilities here include an outdoor hot tub and sun room, as well as home-cooking, complimentary tea, coffee and snacks. ④–⑤.

International House, 17 14th Ave (☎633-5490, fax 668-4751). A quiet residential location with friendly and relaxed atmosphere created by hosts who have been 36 years in the Yukon. Two blocks off the Alaska Highway, 10min from downtown: hosts will pick up from airport or bus depot. ③.

Town & Country, 338 Klukshu Ave (☎633-3523, fax 667-6442). Not as central as some places, but the views of the Yukon River Valley are hard to beat. ③.

Downtown

Although greater Whitehorse spills along the Alaska Highway for several kilometres, the old **downtown** core is a forty-block grid centred on Main Street and mostly sandwiched between 2nd and 4th avenues. Though now graced only with a handful of pioneer buildings, the place still retains the dour integrity and appealing energy of a frontier town, and at night the baying of timber wolves and coyotes is a reminder of the wilderness immediately beyond the city limits. Nonetheless, the tourist influx provides a fair amount of action in the bars and cafés, and the streets are more appealing and lively than in many northern towns.

The main thing to see is the **SS Klondike** (May–Sept daily tours every half-hour 9.30am–7pm; $3.50; ☎667-4511), one of only two surviving paddlesteamers in the Yukon, now rather sadly beached at the western end of 2nd Avenue at 300 Main St, though it has been beautifully restored to the glory of its 1930s heyday. More than 250 stern-wheelers once plied the river, taking 36 hours to make the 700-kilometre journey to Dawson City, and five days to make the return trip against the current. The SS *Klondike* was built in 1929, sank in 1936, and was rebuilt in 1937 using the original remnants. The largest of all the river's steamers, it then battled against the river until 1955, ferrying 300 tons of cargo a trip and making some fifteen round trips a season. Bridges built on the improved road to Dawson increasingly hampered river traffic, though the SS *Klondike*'s end came when an inexperienced pilot ran her aground and condemned her to museum status. Beached at Whitehorse in 1960, the boat is visitable by a 25-minute guided tour only. Before or after a tour, take in the twenty-minute documentary film on the riverboat story in the theatre alongside. Note that you can still make the week-long journey by boat to Dawson by joining a **tour**: for details call Youcon Voyage Inc, 1 Morely Rd, Whitehorse (☎668-2927 or 668-1252).

Elsewhere in town you could pop into the **MacBride Museum**, housed in a sod-roofed log cabin at 1st Avenue and Wood Street (May to late Sept daily 10am–6pm; $4; ☎667-2709), for the usual zoo of stuffed animals, an old WP & YR engine, pioneer and gold-rush memorabilia, as well as hundreds of marvellous **archive photos** and a display on the Asiatic tribes who crossed the Bering Straits to inhabit the Americas. Another in-town sight is the **Old Log Church Museum**, 3rd Avenue and Elliot Street (late May to early Sept Mon–Sat 9am–6pm, Sun 12.30–4pm; $2.50; ☎668-2555), a modest museum devoted to the pre-contact life of the region's Native Canadians, whaling, missionaries, children's toys and music, the gold rush and early exploration. You may find it easy to resist the widely touted *Frantic Follies* **stage shows**, however – a pair of expensive ($18) vaudeville acts of the banjo-plucking and frilly-knickered-dancing variety that have been playing in town for close to thirty years; if this sort of thing does appeal, however, call ☎668-2042 for details of "music, mirth and magic, gay Nineties songs, cancan dances and humorous renditions".

The rest of town

Your money's better spent taking one of the **river tours** that shoot the **Miles Canyon** 9km south of the town, otherwise reached off the Alaska Highway, or from the South Access Road, which hugs the river edge beyond the SS *Klondike*. Whitehorse Transit buses ($1.25) run along the South Access Road from town every hour daily except Sunday. The building of a hydroelectric dam has tamed the rapids' violence and replaced them with **Schwatka Lake**, but the two-hour narrated trip on the MV *Schwatka* (June–Sept daily 2pm & 7pm; $17; ☎668-4716) gives a better view of the river's potential ferocity and the canyon's sheer walls than the viewpoints off the road. Book tickets through Atlas Tours in town at the Westmark Hotel Mall (☎668-3161), or go straight to the dock above the dam about 3km down Canyon Road. A Taste of '98 Yukon River Tours (☎633-4767) runs similar three-hour sightseeing tours, as well as extended four- to 21-day guided or fully equipped tours to Dawson City and elsewhere.

If you fancy a **walk** or a picnic, you can stroll from the main canyon car park some of the 11km to Canyon City, the all-but-vanished site of the initial stage of the stampeders' tramway at the southern end of the old rapids. You could also walk all the way round Schwatka Lake from Whitehorse, beginning from the bridge by the SS *Klondike*. Pick up details of this and other self-guiding trail booklets from the visitor reception centre (see p.821). If you don't fancy embarking on walks on your own, join the downtown walk offered by the Whitehorse Heritage Buildings Walking Tours, which departs four times daily in high summer from Donnenworth House, 3126 3rd Ave (☎667-4704; $2). Or try the variety of free summer strolls organized by the Yukon Conservation Society, 302 Hawkins St (July & Aug daily; ☎668-5678), two- to six-hour walks that delve into local and natural history, and the Yukon's geology, flora and fauna. If flora interests you, visit the rather overpriced **Yukon Gardens** at the intersection of the Alaska Highway and the South Access Road (April–Sept daily 9am–9pm; shorter hours at the beginning and end of the season; $10; ☎668-7972), filled with around a thousand species of wild and domestic flowers, trees and shrubs. These are the only botanical gardens north of Vancouver, the fact that anything survives here through the Yukon winter – never mind the gardens' 250,000 annuals – being something of a miracle. The town enjoys only 72 frost-free days a year – Vancouver has 216.

There is another trio of attractions just outside the downtown area, two of the most tempting up on the bluff above the town on the Alaska Highway close to the airport. One is the excellent **Yukon Transportation Museum** (mid-May to mid-Sept daily 9am–6pm; $3.50; ☎668-4792), one of the region's best museums. Devoted to the area's transportation history, its displays, murals, superb historical videos, memorabilia and vehicles embrace everything from dog-sledding, early aviation and the construction of the Alaska Highway to the Canol pipeline, the gold rush and the White Pass and Yukon Railway. Among the things on show are old army jeeps, bicycles, bulldozers, a stage-coach and – suspended from the ceiling – the *Queen of the Yukon*, the territory's first commercial plane. Right next door is the dynamic new **Yukon Beringia Interpretive Centre** (mid-May to mid-Sept daily 8am–9pm; $6; ☎667-5340), Beringia being the vast subcontinent that existed some 24,000 years ago when the Yukon and Alaska were joined by a land bridge across the Bering Sea to Arctic Russia. The centre's interactive exhibits, film shows and other displays explore the native history of the time, the people who crossed this land bridge having ultimately colonized the most distant reaches of present-day North and South America. It also looks at the flora, fauna and geology of the time with the help of paleontological and archeological exhibits, among which the skeletal remains of a 12,000-year-old mammoth figure large.

On a totally different tack, if you fancy total relaxation make for the topnotch **Takhini Hot Springs** ($9; ☎633-2706), located 31km from Whitehorse off the Klondike Highway to Dawson. The water in the large pool is a piping-hot 36°C, there's no sulphurous aftersmell, and the pool is emptied daily. You can camp here ($7) and if you resent paying for the privilege of a hot soak the locals have built a public pool at the outflow point in the stream below.

Eating

Of several friendly laid-back **eating** places, the best overall is the *Talisman Café*, 2112 2nd Ave (Mon–Sat 6am–11pm), which serves a range of full meals, and is also a spot to while away time over a cup of coffee. The *Chocolate Claim* at 305 Strickland is a good, welcoming café for coffee, cakes and great chocolate. The *No Pop Sandwich Shop*, 312 Steele St, is altogether less cosy, but it's popular all the same and the food's fine. Along the avenue, at 4123 2nd Ave, there's the excellent and rather hippie *Alpine Bakery* (Thurs–Sat 10am–5.30pm), which is often crammed with campers and whose counter greets you with the Shakespearean sentiment "one feast, one house, one mutual happiness". If you're feeling flush, look out for *Pandas*, 212 Main St (☎667-2632), widely celebrated as the best restaurant in town, though there have to be doubts whether a place with these sorts of prices will survive once the visitors have gone home.

Onward from Whitehorse

Whitehorse provides the main **transport** links not only to most other points in the territory, but also to Alaska and the Northwest Territories. In summer there are thrice-daily Canadian North (☎668-4466 or 1-800-665-1177) **flights** to and from Edmonton and Vancouver (both from $500 return): the airline has an office at 4th Avenue and Elliot Street (☎668-3535). In this part of the world, however, it's also worth knowing the various smaller airline options. Air North (☎668-2228 or 1-800-661-0407 in BC and the Yukon, fax 668-6224) operates alarmingly old-fashioned looking but totally reliable scheduled planes (usually four weekly) between Whitehorse, Dawson City, Old Crow, Mayo, Juneau and Fairbanks, and issues a Klondike Explorer pass ($550 plus tax) for travel between all six destinations. Alkan Air (☎668-2107 or 1-800-661-6117, fax 667-6117) offers flights to and from Dawson City, Faro, Ross River, Old Crow, Watson Lake and a handful of BC destinations – most enable you to make same-day connections to flights from Whitehorse to Vancouver and Edmonton; it also flies to Norman Wells and Inuvik in the NWT. There are also any number of small charter companies who fly into the backcountry (notably Kluane National Park) for sightseeing, wildlife-watching, fishing and photography trips. Contact the visitor centre for details.

Whitehorse is the end of the line for Greyhound **buses** in Canada (☎667-2223). For **Alaska and Yukon stops west of Whitehorse**, the expensive Gray Lines' **Alaskon Express** (☎667-2223) runs from Skagway to Whitehorse's bus terminal and *Westmark Whitehorse* hotel (late May to mid-Sept daily; around $55) and then on to Anchorage and Fairbanks three times a week (days of departure vary from year to year so check current times). Note that the bus sometimes stops overnight at Beaver Creek (YT) en route for Alaska, so you either have to camp or to find the price of accommodation ($40 single, $80 double prepaid through Alaskon). Gray Lines' Whitehorse office is at the *Westmark Whitehorse* hotel, 2nd Avenue and Wood Street (☎668-3225 or 1-800-544-2206 winter only). Currently, a more ramshackle and much cheaper service, **Alaska Direct** (☎668-4833 or 1-800-780-6652), operates from Whitehorse to Skagway (and vice versa) and three times weekly to Fairbanks, Anchorage, Tok, Haines Junction, Burwash Landing and Beaver Creek. Unlike Alaskon, it does not overnight at Beaver Creek en route for Alaska, so you sleep (or otherwise) on the bus.

Norline buses at 34 MacDonald Rd (☎668-3864, fax 633-3849) operate out of the main bus terminal and run **to Dawson City** at 9am, arriving at Dawson around 3.30pm (March, April, Sept & Oct Tues & Thurs; summer Mon, Wed & Fri; weekly in winter on varied days according to the weather; $68). If you want to take the **White Pass & Yukon Railway** to Skagway, buses currently leave Whitehorse at 8.15am and arrive at Frasier (BC) at 10.20am, where you pick up the railway at its northern terminus: you arrive in Skagway at noon ($95 inclusive one way). Check current timings by calling ☎907/983-2217 or 1-800-343-7373, fax 907/983-2734 (see also "The Chilkoot Trail" feature on p.818).

For **car rental**, try Hertz, 4158 4th Ave (☎667-2505), Budget Car and Truck, 4178 4th Ave (☎667-6200), or Norcan, Mile 917 Alaska Highway (☎668-2137 or 1-800-661-0445, fax 633-7596), which unlike its competitors might rent you a car or truck suitable for gravel roads like the Dempster and Cassiar highways.

Kluane Country

Kluane Country is the pocket of southwest Yukon on and around a scenically stunning 491-kilometre stretch of the Alaska Highway from Whitehorse to **Beaver Creek** at the border with Alaska. *Kluane* comes from the Southern Tutchone native word meaning a "place of many fish" after the area's teeming waters, and of **Kluane Lake** in particular, the Yukon's highest and largest stretch of water. These days, though, the name's associated more with the all-but-impenetrable wilderness of Canada's largest mountain park, the **Kluane National Park** – a region that contains the country's highest mountains, the most extensive non-polar icefields in the world, and the greatest diversity of plant and animal species in the far north. The park's main centre is **Haines Junction** at the intersection of the Alaska Highway and the Haines Road. Although motels and campgrounds regularly dot the Alaska Highway, the only other settlements of any size are **Destruction Bay** and **Burwash Landing** on Kluane Lake. Gray Line's **Alaskon Express** and **Alaska Direct** buses (see p.825) ply the length of the Alaska Highway, which is also very popular with hitchhikers.

Haines Junction

A blunt and modern place 160km from Whitehorse, with a fine mountain-circled setting, **HAINES JUNCTION** (pop. 796) mushroomed into life in 1942 during the building of the Alaska Highway as a base for the US Army Corps of Engineers during construction of the Haines Road – a highway that connects with Skagway's sister port at Haines, 174km to the southeast. Today it's the biggest service centre between Whitehorse and Tok in Alaska, boasting plenty of shops, a handful of accommodation possibilities (contact the visitor centre for B&B details) and lots of **tour and rental companies** for river-rafting, canoeing, fishing, cycling, horseriding and glacier flights in the Kluane National Park. It's the national park's eastern headquarters – the park covers a vast tract west of the Alaska Highway well to the north and south of the village. The combined Canadian Parks Service and Yukon government **Visitor Reception Centre** is on Logan Street just off the north side of the Alaska Highway (daily: May–Sept 8.30am–9pm; Oct–April 9am–5pm; ☎634-2345 or 634-7201). The village also has its own information line (☎634-2386).

The cheapest of the **motels** is the *Gateway* (open 24hr; ③; ☎634-2371) on the junction of Haines Road and the Alaska Highway; it has rooms with kitchenettes, laundry and café and a few serviced **campsites** to the rear. Or try the *Kluane Park Inn* (☎634-2261; ③; open 24hr) or the new non-smoking *Raven Motel* (☎634-2500, fax 634-2517; ④), an eye-catching central place with a decent restaurant that includes breakfast in its room rate. The *Cozy Corner Motel & Restaurant* (☎634-2511; ③) lies just down the Alaska Highway on the corner of Bates Road. The simple *Pine Lake* **campground** ($8; May–Oct) is 7km east of the village signed off the Alaska Highway, or there's the bigger and more central *Kluane RV Kampground* in town (☎634-2709; $10; May–Sept) which has wooded RV and tent sites, laundry and a grocery store.

The best general place **to eat** is the popular *Village Bakery & Deli* (7.30am–9pm daily) on Logan Street across from theVisitor Reception Centre. Foodie guides rate *The Raven* (☎634-2500) as the best restaurant in the Yukon and Alaska, but you're looking at around $70 a head to test the chef. A good place to **shop** is Madley's General Stores, which proclaims, with little exaggeration, that "We've Got it All". There's also a good municipal **swimming pool** just across from the visitor centre.

WALKING IN KLUANE NATIONAL PARK

Kluane's **trail system** is still in its infancy, though experienced walkers will enjoy wilderness routes totalling about 250km, most of which follow old mining roads or creek beds and require overnight rough camping. A few more manageable walks start from seven distinct trailheads, each signed from the highways and mapped on pamphlets available from Haines's Reception Centre, where enthusiastic staff also organize popular guided day walks during the summer.

Three trails start from points along a twenty-kilometre stretch of Haines Road immediately south of Haines Junction. The path nearest to the town, and the most popular walk, is the nineteen-kilometre round trip **Auriol Trail**; nearby, the **Rock Glacier Trail** is a twenty-minute jaunt to St Elias Lake; the third and longest trek is the **Mush Lake Road** route (21.6km one way). North of Haines Junction, most people walk all or part of two paths that strike out from the Sheep Mountain information kiosk on Kluane Lake – either the **Sheep Mountain Ridge** (11.5km), with good chances of seeing the area's Dall sheep, or the longer **Slim's River West Trail** (28.4km one way), which offers a relatively easy way to see the edges of the park's icefield interior.

Kluane National Park

Created in 1972 using land from the earlier Kluane Game Sanctuary, the **KLUANE NATIONAL PARK** contains some of the Yukon's greatest but most inaccessible scenery, and for the most part you must be resigned to seeing and walking its easterly margins from points along the Alaska Highway (no road runs into the park). Together with the neighbouring Wrangell-St Elias National Park in Alaska the park protects the **St Elias Mountains**, though from the highway the peaks you see rearing up to the south are part of the subsidiary Kluane Range. Beyond them, and largely invisible from the road, are St Elias's monumental **Icefield Ranges**, which contain Mount St Elias (5488m), **Mount Logan** (5950m) – Canada's highest point – and Mount McKinley (6193m) in Alaska, the highest point in North America. These form the world's second highest coastal range (the Andes are the highest). Below them, and covering half the park, is a huge base of mile-deep glaciers and icefields, the world's largest nonpolar icefield and just one permanent resident, the legendary ice worm. Unless you're prepared for full-scale expeditions, this interior is off limits, though from as little as $90 you can take plane and helicopter **tours** over the area with companies such as Trans North Helicopters, based on the Alaska Highway (Mile 1056/Km 1698) between Silver City and the Sheep Mountain Reception Centre (☎841-5809 or 668-2177), or Glacier Air Tours at Burwash Landing (May 24–Sept 1; ☎841-5171); details of these and other guided tours are available from the Haines Junction Reception Centre.

On the drier, warmer ranges at the edge of the icefields a green belt of meadow, marsh, forest and fen provides sanctuary for a huge variety of **wildlife** such as grizzlies, moose, mountain goats and a 4000-strong herd of white **Dall sheep**, the last being the animals the park originally set out to protect. These margins also support the widest spectrum of **birds** in the far north, some 150 species in all, including easily seen raptors such as peregrine falcons, bald eagles and golden eagles, together with smaller birds like arctic terns, mountain bluebirds, tattlers and hawk owls.

Limited **trails** (see feature above) offer the chance to see some of these creatures, but the only **campground** within the park is at the *Kathleen Lake*, on the Haines Road 16km southeast of Haines Junction ($8) – though there is plenty of hotel and camping accommodation along the Alaska Highway.

Kluane Lake

The Kluane region might keep its greatest mountains out of sight, but it makes amends by laying on the stunning **Kluane Lake** along some 60km of the Alaska Highway. About 75km northwest of Haines Junction, and hot on the heels of some magnificent views of the St Elias Mountains, the huge lake (some 400 square kilometres in area) is framed on all sides by snow-covered peaks whose sinister glaciers feed its ice-blue waters. It's not part of the national park, but there's still a second park kiosk at its southern tip, the **Sheep Mountain Information Kiosk** (daily: mid-May to end of June & first fortnight of Sept 10am–6pm; July & Aug 9am–7pm;☎ 841-5161). About 5km before the kiosk is the *Kluane Bed & Breakfast* (no phone; ③), with four cabins on the lakeshore. A kilometre beyond it lies the *Bayshore Motel and Restaurant* (☎841-4551; ③), open 24 hours a day from May to October; as well as rooms it offers sites for tents and RVs.

If you want to boat or fish there are rental facilities at the two main settlements along the shores, Destruction Bay and Burwash Landing, each of which also has a small selection of **accommodation** to supplement the odd lodges and campgrounds along the Alaska Highway. In the smaller **DESTRUCTION BAY** (pop. 44), named when a previous road construction camp was destroyed by a storm in 1942, bed down at the *Talbot Arm Motel* with restaurant, café, store and Chevron garage (☎841-4461; ③); it also has a partly serviced **campground** ($10). The best overall campground locally, however, is the lovely Yukon government-run *Congdon Creek* ($8) site off the Alaska Highway, 12km south of Destruction Bay which ($8) also offers the start of hiking trails.

At **BURWASH LANDING**, 15km beyond, there's a tiny 1944 Oblate mission church and museum, Our Lady of the Holy Rosary, and the *Burwash Landing Resort* (☎841-4441; ③), with restaurant, store, glacier flights, fishing trips, gold-panning and a big unserviced campground (May–Oct). Five kilometres further south the *Cottonwood Park Campground*, a private outfit, offers rather more facilities (☎634-2739; $12; mid-May to mid-Oct). Moving on from Burwash, there are just two more major indoor accommodation possibilities before Beaver Creek: 85km east of Burwash is the *Pine Valley Motel & Café* (☎862-7407; ③) and, 36km beyond that, the white *River Motor Inn* (☎862-7408; ③), with café and gas.

Beaver Creek

BEAVER CREEK, Canada's westernmost settlement (pop. 145), is the last stop before Alaska. Following concerted lobbying from its inhabitants, however, it no longer houses the customs post – this has been moved a couple of kilometres up the road in response to complaints from the locals about the flashing lights and sirens that used to erupt whenever a tourist forgot to stop. Though the border is open 24 hours a day, you may have to stay here, particularly if you're catching the Alaskon **bus** service from Skagway and Whitehorse, which stops overnight at Beaver Creek on trans-Alaskan routes. The bus company can book you into the large and expensive *Westmark Inn* (☎862-7501; ⑥; May–Sept): if that's too steep you've got the choice of arranging things for yourself at the eccentric twenty-room *Ida's Motel and Restaurant* (☎862-7223; ④; summer 6am–2am, winter 8am–10pm), a distinctive pink and beige building across the highway or, failing that, at the *Motor Inn* (☎862-7600 or 1-800-661-0540 in the Yukon; ④).

The *Westmark* has a large serviced **campground** ($18), though they're happier to see RVs than backpackers (try free camping in the woods). There's a good but small Yukon government-run site located 10km south at the *Snag Junction* ($8; May–Oct). Also be warned that if US Customs take against you or your rucksack, they can insist on seeing at least $400 cash, and won't be swayed by any number of credit cards. For full details on border crossing, and what to expect on the other side, visit the **Yukon Visitor Information Centre** (mid-May to early Sept daily 9am–9pm; ☎862-7321).

Dawson City

Few episodes in Canadian history have captured the imagination like the **Klondike gold rush,** and few places have remained as evocative of their past as **DAWSON CITY,** the stampede's tumultuous capital. For a few months in 1898 this former patch of moose pasture became one of the wealthiest and most famous places on earth, as something like 100,000 people struggled across huge tracts of wilderness to seek their fortunes in the richest gold field of all time.

Most people approach the town on the Klondike Highway from Whitehorse, a wonderful road running through almost utter wilderness, and knowing the background to the place it's hard not to near the road's end without high expectations. Little at first, however, distinguishes its surroundings. Some 500km from Whitehorse the road wanders through low but steeply sided hills covered in spruce, aspen and dwarf firs, and then picks up a small ice-clear river – the **Klondike.** Gradually the first small spoil heaps appear on the hills to the south, and then suddenly the entire valley bottom turns into a devastated landscape of vast boulders and abandoned workings. The desolate tailings continue for several kilometres until the Klondike flows into the much broader **Yukon** and the town, previously hidden by hills, comes suddenly into view.

An ever-increasing number of tourists and backpackers come up here, many drawn by the boardwalks, rutted dirt streets and dozens of false-fronted wooden houses, others to canoe the Yukon or travel down the Dempster or Top of the World highways into Alaska and the Northwest Territories. After decades of decline the Canada Parks Service is restoring the town, now deservedly a National Historic Site, a process that is bringing about increased commercialism, increased population (2000 and rising), new hotels and a sense that some of the town's character may be about to be lost. That said, in a spot where permafrost buckles buildings, it snows in August, and temperatures touch –60°C during winters of almost perpetual gloom, there's little real chance of Dawson losing the gritty, weather-battered feel of a true frontier town. More to the point, small-time prospecting still goes on, and there are one or two rough-and-ready bars whose hardened locals take a dim view of sharing their beers, let alone their gold, with coachloads of tourists.

You could easily spend a couple of days here: one exploring the town, the other touring the old Klondike creeks to the east. If at all possible prime yourself beforehand with the background to one of the most colourful chapters in Canada's history: Pierre Berton's widely available bestseller, *Klondike – The Last Great Gold Rush 1896–1899,* is a superbly written introduction both to the period and to the place.

The Town

You should start any wander on **Front Street,** the leading edge of a street grid that runs parallel to the Yukon River and is home to the impressive **Visitor Reception Centre** (mid-May to mid-Sept daily 8am–8pm; ☎993-5566). Loaded with a huge amount of material, the place also shows good introductory archive and contemporary films throughout the day, as well as letting you leave your bag or pack ($1) while you explore. It also organizes walking tours (June to mid-Sept several daily; $5) of the town's **heritage buildings** – though these are easily seen on your own, as are the cabins that belonged to two chroniclers of the gold rush, poet **Robert Service** and the better-known **Jack London.** The local **museum** is also good for an hour, and you might want to dabble in the **casino,** though when all's said and done it's the atmospheric streets of Dawson that are most compelling.

THE KLONDIKE GOLD RUSH

Gold rushes in North America during the nineteenth century were nothing new, but none generated quite the delirium of the **Klondike gold rush** in 1898. Over a million people are estimated to have left home for the Yukon gold fields, the largest single one-year mass movement of people in the century. Of these, about 100,000 made it to the Yukon, about 20,000 panned the creeks, 4000 found something and a couple of dozen made – and invariably lost – huge fortunes.

The **discovery of gold in 1896** on the Klondike, a tributary of the Yukon River, was the culmination of twenty years of prospecting in the Yukon and Alaska. A Hudson's Bay fur trader first noticed gold in 1842, and the first substantial report was made by an English missionary in 1863, but as the exploitation of gold was deemed bad for trade in both furs and religion neither report was followed up. The first mining on any scale took place in 1883 and gradually small camps sprang up along almost 3200km of river at places like Forty Mile, Sixty Mile and Circle City. All were established before the Klondike strike, but were home to only a few hundred men, hardened types reared on the earlier Californian and British Columbian gold rushes.

The discovery of the gold that started the stampede is inevitably shrouded in myth and countermyth. The first man to prospect near the Klondike River was **Robert Henderson**, a dour Nova Scotian and the very embodiment of the lone pioneer. In early 1896 he found 8¢ worth of gold in a pan scooped from a creek in the hills above present-day Dawson City. This was considered an excellent return at the time, and a sign to Henderson that the creek would make worthwhile yields. He panned out about $750 with four companions and then returned downriver to pick up supplies.

Henderson then set about finding a route up the Klondike to meet the creek he'd prospected, and at the mouth of the Klondike met **George Washington Carmack** and a couple of his native friends, Skookum Jim and Tagish Charley. Henderson told Carmack of his hopes for the area, and then – with a glance at the natives – uttered the phrase that probably cost him a fortune, "There's a chance for you George, but I don't want any damn Siwashes [natives] staking on that creek." Henderson wandered off into the hills, leaving Carmack, rankled by the remark, to prospect a different set of creeks – the right ones, as it turned out. On the eve of August 16, Skookum Jim found $4 of gold in a pan on Bonanza Creek, a virtually unprecedented amount at the time. Next day Carmack staked the first claim, and rushed off to register the find leaving Henderson prospecting almost barren ground on the other side of the hills.

By the end of August all of Bonanza had been staked by a hundred or so old-timers from camps up and down the Yukon. Almost all the real fortunes had been secured by the winter of 1896, when the snows and frozen river effectively sealed the region from the outside world. The **second phase** occurred after the thaw when a thousand or so miners from the West Coast arrived drawn by vague rumours of a big find, emanating

The heritage buildings

Fuelled by limitless avarice, Dawson between 1898 and 1900 exploded into a full-blown metropolis of 30,000 people – the largest city in the Canadian West and the equal of places like Seattle and San Francisco in its opportunities for vice, decadence and good living. There were opera houses, theatres, cinemas (at a time when motion-picture houses were just three years old), steam heating, three hospitals, restaurants with French chefs, and bars, brothels and dance halls which generated phenomenal business – one Charlie Kimball took $300,000 in a month from his club, and spent the lot within days. Show girls charged miners $5 – payable in gold – for a minute's dance; slow dances were charged at a higher rate. Cleaners panning the bars' sawdust floors after hours were clearing $50 in gold dust a night. Rules of supply and demand also made Dawson an expensive town, with a single two-metre frontage

from the north. The headlong rush that was to make the Klondike unique, however, followed the docking in **July 1897** of the *Excelsior* in San Francisco and the *Portland* in Seattle. Few sights could have been so stirring a proof of the riches up for grabs as the battered Yukon miners who came down the gangplanks dragging bags, boxes and sacks literally bursting with gold. The press were waiting for the *Portland*, which docked with two tons of gold on board, all taken by hand from the Klondike creeks by just a few miners. The rush was now on in earnest.

Whipped up by the media and the outfitters of Seattle and San Francisco, thousands embarked on trips that were to claim hundreds of lives. The most common route – the "poor man's route" – was to take a boat from a West Coast port to Skagway, climb the dreaded **Chilkoot Pass** to pick up the Yukon River at Whitehorse and then boat the last 500 miles to Dawson City. The easiest and most expensive route lay by boat upstream from the mouth of the Yukon in western Alaska. The most dangerous and most bogus were the "All Canadian Route" from Edmonton and the overland trails through the northern wilderness.

The largest single influx came with the melting of the ice on the Yukon in May 1898 – 21 months after the first claim – when a vast makeshift armada drifted down the river. When they docked at Dawson City, the boats nestled six deep along a two-mile stretch of the waterfront. For most it was to have been a fruitless journey – every inch of the creeks having long been staked – yet in most accounts of the stampede it is clear that this was a rite of passage as much as a quest for wealth. Pierre Berton observed that "there were large numbers who spent only a few days in Dawson and did not even bother to visit the hypnotic creeks that had tugged at them all winter long. They turned their faces home again, their adventure over . . . It was as if they had, without quite knowing it, completed the job they had set out to do and had come to understand that it was not the gold they were seeking after all."

As for the gold, it's the smaller details that hint at the scale of the Klondike: the miner's wife, for example, who could wander the creek by her cabin picking nuggets from the stream bed as she waited for her husband to come home; or the destitutes during the Great Depression who could pan $40 a day from the dirt under Dawson's boardwalks; or the $1000 panned during rebuilding of the Orpheum Theatre in the 1940s, all taken in a morning from under the floorboards where it had drifted from miners' pockets half a century before; or the $200 worth of dust panned nightly from the beer mats of a Dawson saloon during 1897.

By about 1899 the rush was over, not because the gold had run out, but because the most easily accessible gold had been taken from the creeks. It had been the making of Alaska; Tacoma, Portland, Victoria and San Francisco all felt its impact; Edmonton sprang from almost nothing; and Vancouver's population doubled in a year. It was also the first of a string of mineral discoveries in the Yukon and the far north, a region whose vast and untapped natural resources are increasingly the subject of attention from multinationals as rapacious and determined as their grizzled predecessors.

fetching as much in rent in a month as a four-bedroom apartment in New York cost for two years.

Only a few of the many intact **heritage buildings** around the town date from the earliest days of the rush, dozens having been lost to fire and to permafrost, whose effects are seen in some of the most appealing of the older buildings: higgledy-piggledy collapsing ruins of rotting wood, weeds and rusting corrugated iron. Most of these, thankfully, have been deliberately preserved in their tumbledown state. Elsewhere, almost overzealous restoration projects are in full flow, partly financed by profits from the town casino. Permafrost precluded the construction of brick buildings with deep foundations, so restoration has had to work doubly hard to save what are generally all-wood buildings, most notably the **Palace Grand Theatre** on King Street (1899). The theatre was originally built from the hulks of two beached paddlesteamers, and but for the intervention of the Klondike Visitors Association would have been pulled down for scrap timber in 1960. Tours run daily in summer ($5) and every night in summer except Tuesday. There's a performance of *Gaslight Follies* (8pm; $13–16), a predictable medley of cancan, frilly knickers and gold-rush cabaret, though if you're tempted this is among the best of several such shows around the region.

Nearby on the corner of King Street and 3rd Avenue there's the working 1901 **Post Office** (daily June–Sept noon–6pm); opposite is **Madame Tremblay's Store**; **Harrington's Store** on 3rd Avenue and Princess Street has a "Dawson as They Saw It" exhibition of photos arranged by Canadian Parks (June–Aug daily 9am–5pm; free); near the same junction stands **Billy Bigg's Blacksmith Shop**; elsewhere are the cream-and-brown clapboard **Anglican Church**, built in 1902 with money collected from the miners. At 4th Avenue and Queen Street is **Diamond Tooth Gertie's Gambling House**, founded by one of the town's more notorious characters, and still operating as the first legal **casino** in Canada (opened after restoration in 1971) – it's also the world's northernmost casino (mid-May to mid-Sept daily 7pm–2am; $4.75); you need to be over 19 to gamble and all proceeds go to the restoration of Dawson. Also check out the **Firefighters Museum** at 5th Avenue and King Street (summer Mon–Sat 11am–5pm; $5), where a guide takes you on a tour of old fire tenders, water pumps and other old firefighting equipment. In a town built almost entirely of wood these were once vital to Dawson's survival: the town all but burnt to the ground twice in the space of a year in 1898–99. So far you can't visit one of the town's more obvious old wooden constructions, the **SS Keno** riverboat, moored on the river just down from the visitor centre. Currently being restored for use as a museum, it was built in 1922 and ran up and down the Stewart River carrying ore from the mines around Mayo. At the Yukon River the ore was unloaded for collection by larger boats and the journey to Whitehorse and the railway.

The Dawson City Museum

The **Dawson City Museum**, 5th Avenue and Church Street (June–Sept daily 10am–6pm; $3.50 for a day pass; ☎993-5291), has an adequate historical run-through of the gold rush from the first finds, though you get more out of the displays if you have some background to the period. Fascinating old diaries and newspaper cuttings vividly document the minutiae of pioneer life and events such as the big winter freeze of 1897–98 when temperatures reputedly touched –86°C, and of the summer heat wave of 1898 when the sun shone unbroken for almost 23 hours daily, bringing temperatures up to the upper thirties centigrade. The museum also shows some of the hundreds of old films that were discovered under some Dawson floorboards a few years back. Its highlight – in fact, one of Dawson's highlights – is the wistful award-winning black and white film, *City of Gold*, a wonderful documentary which first drew the attention of the federal government to Dawson's decline in the 1950s. The museum also holds interesting touring exhibitions in the wood-framed rooms upstairs that once housed the council offices. You might also take a **tour** of the museum building (summer daily 11am, 1pm & 5pm), the former Territorial Administration Building (1901), during which you're shown the old court chambers (still occasionally used), the resource library and archive, the Visible Storage area (with some 6000 of the museum's 30,000 artefacts) and (outside) a view of the Victory Gardens (1910). The obvious **locomotives** outside the museum, incidentally, ran to Dawson from the gold fields between 1906 and 1914.

The Robert Service and Jack London cabins

The cabins of Dawson's two literary lions are only about 100m apart on 8th Avenue, about ten minutes' walk from Front Street. Most Canadians hold **Robert Service** in high esteem and he rightly has his place in the pantheon of Canadian literature. Verses like *The Shooting of Dan McGrew* and *The Cremation of Sam McGee* (see "Contexts", p.895) combine strong narrative and broad comedy to successfully evoke the myth of the North. Born in Preston, England, in 1874, the poet wrote most of his gold-rush verse before he'd even set foot in the Yukon – he was posted by his bank employers to Whitehorse in 1904 and only made Dawson in 1908. He retired a rich man on the proceeds of his writing – he outsold Kipling and was one of the biggest-selling poets of his time – spending his last years mainly in France, where he died in 1958. His **cabin** (June–Sept daily 9am–noon & 1–5pm; $2) is probably cosier and better decorated than it was, but it still gives an idea of how most people must have lived once Dawson was reasonably established. During the summer people flock here to hear poetry recitals in front of the cabin from a bearded eccentric – Irish-born actor Tom Byrne – dressed and mannered as the "Bard of the Yukon" (July & Aug daily 10am & 3pm; $6 for cabin and recital).

Jack London's Cabin home is an unpersuasive piece of reconstruction, little more than a bleak, blank-walled and incomplete hut (logs from the original were separated and half of them used to build a cabin in Jack London Square in Oakland, California). London knew far more than Service of the real rigours of northern life, having spent time in 1897 as a ferryman on Whitehorse's Miles Canyon before moving north to spend about a year holed up on Henderson's Creek above the Klondike River. He returned home to California penniless, but loaded with a fund of material that was to find expression in books like *The Call of the Wild*, *White Fang* and *A Daughter of the Snows*. Alongside the hut there's a good little museum of pictures and memorabilia, presided over by an amiable and knowledgeable curator (hut and museum June to mid-Sept daily 10am–6pm; free). Readings of London's work are given here in summer, currently at noon and 2.15pm.

Practicalities

Dawson City's **airport**, 19km southeast of the town on the Klondike Highway, is used by scheduled Alkan Air (☎668-2107 or 1-800-661-0432) services to Inuvik (NWT), Old Crow, Mayo and Whitehorse, and by Air North (☎668-2228 or 1-800-661-0407 in BC and the Yukon) services to Fairbanks (4 weekly), Whitehorse, Watson Lake and Juneau. Norline **buses** (☎993-6010 or 993-5331) to and from Whitehorse arrive and depart from the Chevron garage on Princess and 5th (Mon, Wed & Fri; 2 weekly in winter). Tickets for all air services, Alaska and BC ferries, sightseeing **tours** of the gold fields (see p.835), and for the Dempster Highway bus to Inuvik, can be arranged at the excellent Gold City Travel on Front Street opposite the SS *Keno* (☎993-5175, fax 993-5261).

Another way of moving on from Dawson is to take a Gray Line **cruise** on the *Yukon Queen*, which in summer runs daily on the Yukon River between Dawson and Eagle, just over the Alaskan border (from $80 one way, including meal). Standby, round trip and one-way tickets are available from Yukon Queen River Cruise on Front Street (☎668-3225, fax 667-4494). Shorter and cheaper ninety-minute river trips are available on the *Yukon Lou* from the dock behind the Birch Cabin ticket office close to the SS *Keno* (☎993-5482). Trans North Helicopters (☎993-5494) run helicopter trips over the gold fields, the Klondike Valley and Midnight Dome: for further details of tours and general information, contact the **Visitor Reception Centre** on Front Street (☎993-5566). Information is also available from the **public library** on 5th and Queen (Tues, Wed & Fri noon–7pm, Thurs noon–8pm, Sat 11am–5pm). **Currency exchange** facilities exist at the CIBC bank on Queen Street. between Front and 2nd, while **maps** are available from the mining recorder's office alongside the **post office** on 5th between Queen and Princess. For **showers** (there are none at the campgrounds), the most central are the tight-fit bathrooms at the laundry behind the Chief Isaac Hale building alongside the visitor centre. There are also showers at the municipal **swimming pool** by the museum.

Accommodation

More and more accommodation is opening in Dawson, but the increased competition isn't bringing the prices down. The two hostels are likely to be heavily oversubscribed, as are the B&Bs options, though calls to the latter a couple of days in advance should secure a room. Rates are high in the half-dozen or so mid-range places, most of which look the part of old-fashioned wood- and false-fronted hotels. If you arrive without a room, check the lodging scrapbook at the visitor centre which keeps an updated record of accommodation availability: hotels often offer cheap last-minute deals in the book to fill empty rooms.

The main town **campground** for tents is the government-run *Yukon River Campground* ($8), which is on the west bank of the Yukon on the right about 500m after the free *George Black* ferry crossing from the top of Front Street. Black, incidentally, made one of the first journeys to Dawson by car from Whitehorse in 1912 in the (then) record-breaking time of 33 hours. If you're really roughing it there is a "squatters' tent city" just past the site: every now and again there's talk of charging for this site, but currently nobody seems to know who's responsible for collecting the $2 fee. The *Gold Rush Campground* in town at 5th and York is a bleak, fully serviced but busy place designed for RVs (☎993-5247; $20; May–Sept).

Beer Creek B&B, 11km south of Dawson by Bear Creek Historical Site (☎993-5605, fax 993-6532). A Native Canadian family-run guesthouse with four rooms in a peaceful natural setting away from town. ③.

Bonanza House B&B, near the museum on 7th Avenue and Grant (☎993-5772, fax 993-6509). Offers a two- or three-bedroom suite with shared sitting rooms and TV. ③.

Dawson City B&B, 451 Craig St (☎993-5649, fax 993-5648). Located near the junction of the Yukon and Klondike rivers and arranges pick-ups from the airport or even offers car rentals. ④.

Dawson City Bunkhouse, corner of 2nd and Princess (☎993-6164). An excellent brand-new hostel-type place with a choice between rooms with shared bathrooms or private facilities. ②–④.

Dawson City River Hostel, across the river from downtown; first left after you jump the free ferry (☎993-6823). A new HI-affiliated collection of bunks in smart log cabins with a good view of Dawson and the river. There are family rooms, a sweat lodge and canoe and bike rentals available. Open May to mid-Sept. ①.

Downtown Hotel, 2nd and Queen (☎993-5346 or 1-800-764-0514 in BC and the Yukon, fax 993-5076). One of the town's plusher wooden-fronted hotels, and – unlike some – open year-round. ⑤.

Eldorado, 3rd and Princess (☎993-5451 or 1-800-661-0518, fax 993-5256). Much the same as the *Downtown*, and also open 24hr year-round. ⑤.

Fifth Ave B&B, on 5th Ave near the museum (☎ & fax 993-5941). New and spacious house with shared kitchen, and optional en suites. ③.

Klondike Kate's Cabins & Rooms, 3rd and King (June–Aug; ☎993-6257, fax 993-6044). Old-fashioned and simple, but clean and warm, offering some of the cheapest rooms in town as well as cabins. Open May–Sept. ③.

Northern Comfort, 6th and Church (☎993-5271). A centrally located B&B that provides bike rentals. ③.

Trail of '98 Mini-Golf, 5km out of town at the junction of the Klondike Highway and Bonanza Creek Road (☎993-6101). The best budget deal around if you can get four people together for one of the simple $40 cabins. No power or running water, but washrooms are available nearby. ②.

Triple J Hotel, 5th and Queen (☎993-5323 or 1-800-661-0405, fax 993-5030). Some 47 rooms or cabins in old-fashioned-style hotel next to *Diamond Tooth Gertie's*. May–Oct. ⑤.

Westmark Inn Dawson, 5th and Harper (☎993-5542 or 1-800-544-0970, fax 993-5623). Part of an upmarket northern chain, and the town's swishest hotel: look out for frequent cut-price promotions to fill empty rooms. ⑥.

Westminster Hotel, 3rd and Queen (☎993-5463, fax 993-6029). Despite the tempting old false-fronted exterior and the clean and cheap rooms, this is a rough-house spot where the miners come in to drink long and noisily into the night. April–Sept. ③.

White Ram B&B, 7th and Harper (☎993-5772, fax 993-6509). A distinctive pink house that has a hot tub and outside deck. Pick-up from bus on request. ③.

Whitehorse Motel, Front Street (☎993-5576). Six cabins with kitchenettes on the waterfront at the northern end of the street beyond the *George Black* ferry. Mid-May to mid-Sept. ③.

Food and nightlife

For **eating** there are a couple of good snack places on Front Street – the *River West Food & Health* (☎993-6339), a health-food store with café, and the rather austere *Nancy's Restaurant* for German and Canadian home-made snacks (summer daily 7am–midnight; ☎993-5633). The excellent *Klondike Kate's* (May–Sept daily 7am–11pm; ☎993-6527), at 3rd and King, is the friendliest and most laid-back place in town for staples like breakfasts and straightforward dinners (and has an outdoor patio); the popular *Marina's*, 5th and Harper (☎993-6800), is the best place for something a touch more special, with pizzas and wonderful dinners for up to about $25. For ice cream and frozen yoghurts, make for *Madame Zoom's* at 2nd and King. For picnic goodies and **self-catering** supplies, there's the Dawson General Store on Front Street and the Farmer's Market on 2nd near Princess.

Nightlife revolves around drinking in the main hotel bars, or an hour or so at *Diamond Tooth Gertie's* at 4th and Queen, Canada's only legal gambling hall. You can also catch the almost equally touristy period-costume melodramas and vaudeville acts held at the Palace Grand Theatre (June–Sept nightly except Tues at 8pm; $13–16).

Around Dawson

While in Dawson, make a point of seeing the two creeks where it all started and where most of the gold was mined – **Bonanza and Eldorado**, both over 20km away from the town site along rough roads to the southeast. These days no big working mine survives in the region, though most of the claims are still owned and definitely out of bounds to amateurs. However, it's still possible to see some of the huge dredges that supplanted the individual prospectors, once the easily reached gold had been taken out. Another popular local excursion is to **Midnight Dome**, the gouged-out hill behind the town, while further afield numerous RVs, cyclists and hitchhikers follow the **Top of the World Highway**, which runs on beyond the Alaskan border to link with the Alaska Highway at Tetlin Junction.

Bonanza and Eldorado creeks

To reach **Bonanza Creek**, follow the Klondike Highway – the continuation of Front Street – for 4km to the junction with Bonanza Creek Road. The road threads through scenes of apocalyptic piles of boulders and river gravel for some 12km until it comes to a simple cairn marking **Discovery Claim**, the spot staked by George Carmack after pulling out a nugget the size of his thumb, or so the story goes. Every 150m along the creek in front of you – the width of a claim – was to yield some 3000kg of gold, or about $25 million worth at 1900 prices. Exact amounts of gold taken out are difficult to establish because it was in miners' interests to undervalue their takings to the authorities, but most estimates suggest that around $600-million worth left the creeks between 1897 and 1904. Given a claim's huge value they were often subdivided and sold as "fractions": one miner pulled out over 100kg of gold in eight hours from a fraction – almost $1 million worth.

At Discovery Claim the road forks again, one spur running east up **Eldorado Creek**, if anything richer than Bonanza; the other following Upper Bonanza Road to the summit of **King Solomon's Dome**, where you can look down over smaller scarred rivulets like Hunker and Dominion creeks, before returning in a loop to the Klondike Highway via Hunker Road.

As time went by and the easily reached gold was exploited, miners increasingly consolidated claims, or sold out to large companies who installed dredges capable of clawing out the bedrock and gravel. Numerous examples of these industrial dinosaurs litter the creeks, but the largest and most famous is the 1912 **No. 4 Dredge** at Claim 17 BD ("Below Discovery") off Bonanza Creek Road, an extraordinary piece of industrial archeology that from the start of operations in 1913 until 1966 dug up as much as 25kg of gold a day. Modern mines are lucky to produce a quarter of that amount in a week.

Without a car you'll have to rent a bike or join up with one of the various **gold-field tours** run by Gold City Tours, on Front Street (☎993-5175), either to see the dredges and creeks or to **pan for gold** yourself, at a price. Only three small fractions on Claim 6 can currently be panned free of charge – but enquire at the reception centre for latest locations: for $5 you can pan with a guarantee of finding gold (because it's been put there) on Claim 33.

Midnight Dome and Top of the World Highway

The **Midnight Dome** is the distinctive hill that rears up behind Dawson City, half-covered in stunted pines and half-eaten away by landslips. It's named because from its summit at midnight on June 21 you can watch the sun dip to the horizon before rising again straight away – Dawson being only 300km south of the Arctic Circle. The Midnight Dome Road runs 8km to its summit (884m) from the Klondike Highway just out of the town proper. Without a car it's an extremely steep haul (ask at the visitor centre for details of the well-worn and partially signed trail), but more than worth the slog for the massive views over Dawson, the gold fields, the Yukon's broad meanders and the ranks of mountains stretching away in all directions. At the summer solstice there's a race to the top and lots of drink-sodden and fancy-dress festivities down in Dawson. Gold City Tours also run regular daytime and evening tours up here.

You can snatch further broad vistas from the **Top of the World Highway** (Hwy 9), a good summer-only gravel road reached by ferry from Front Street across the Yukon (mid-May to mid-Sept daily 24hr except Wed 5–7am; mid-Sept to mid-May 7am–11pm depending on weather; every 45min; free; ☎667-5644). After only 5km the road unfolds a great panorama over the area, and after 14km another **viewpoint** looks out over the Yukon Valley and the **Ogilvie Mountains** straddling the Arctic Circle. Thereafter the road runs above the tree line as a massive belvedere and can be seen switchbacking over barren ridges way into the distance. It hits the **Alaska border** 108km from Dawson, where you can cross only when the customs post is open (May–Sept 9am–9pm). Unlike the Dempster Highway (see below), there's no **bus** on this route, but you should be able to hitch easily in summer because it's much-travelled as a neat way of linking with the Alaska Highway at Tok for the roads to Fairbanks and Anchorage or the loop back to Whitehorse. Be prepared to do only about 50kph, and enquire about local difficulties and fuel availability at the Dawson Visitor Reception Centre.

The Dempster Highway

Begun in 1959 to service northern oilfields, and completed over twenty years later – by which time all the accessible oil had been siphoned off – the 741-kilometre **Dempster Highway** between Dawson City and Inuvik in the Northwest Territories is the only road in Canada to cross the **Arctic Circle**, offering a tremendous journey through a superb spectrum of landscapes. An increasingly travelled route – which locals say means four cars an hour – it crosses the **Ogilvie Mountains** just north of Dawson before dropping down to **Eagle Plains** and almost unparalleled access to the sub-arctic tundra. Shortly before meeting the NWT border after 470km it rises through the **Richardson Mountains** and then drops to the drab low hills and plain of the Peel Plateau and Mackenzie River. For much of its course the road follows the path of the dog patrols operated by the Mounties in the first half of the century, taking its name from a Corporal W.J.D. Dempster, who in March 1922 was sent to look for a patrol lost between **Fort McPherson** (NWT) and Dawson. He found their frozen bodies just 26 miles from where they had set off. They were buried on the banks of the Peel River and there's a monument to their memory at Fort McPherson.

> The telephone code for the NWT is ☎867.

Practicalities

The Dempster is a gravel road and the 741-kilometre journey by **car** takes anything between twelve and fifteen hours in good conditions. It is not, however, a journey to be undertaken lightly. If you're **cycling** or motorbiking, both increasingly popular ways of doing the trip, you need to be prepared for rough camping, and should call at the **NWT Information Centre** on Front Street in Dawson City (May–Sept 9am–7pm; ☎993-6456, 993-6167 or 1-800-661-0752) for invaluable practical as well as anecdotal information from the staff. If you're without your own transport you might pick up a **lift** here, or take the twelve-hour **Dempster Highway Bus Service** run by the Arctic Tour Company (☎979-4100 or 1-800-661-0721). Departures leave from Dawson to Inuvik at 8am on Tuesday and Thursday between June and mid-September (with returns from Inuvik on the same days), and an additional Wednesday service between late June and mid-August. **Tickets** cost $198 one way to Inuvik ($350 return), and $99 to Eagle Plains/Arctic Circle ($175 same-day return). If you're driving or biking it's also worth checking that the two ferry services (☎1-800-661-0752) on the route at Peel River and Tsiigehtchic (formerly Arctic Red River) are running when bad weather threatens, and that you have sufficient fuel in a car to make the long stretches.

In the Dempster's Yukon section there is **accommodation** only at *Eagle Plains Hotel* (☎979-4187; ⑤, camping $10; year-round), 363km north of Dawson. There are also three rudimentary Yukon government **campgrounds** at *Tombstone Mountain*, 72km north of Dawson; at *Engineer Creek* (194km); and at *Rock River* (447km). In July and August there's a trailer information kiosk at Tombstone Mountain with details of good trails from the campground. Fort McPherson also has a small summer-only visitor centre in the log building by the monument to Dempster's "Lost Patrol".

Currently the only other **hotel** – but check it's still open – is the small *Tet'lit Service Co-op-Inns North* (☎952-2417 or 952-2339; ⑤) in the NWT at the tiny Gwich'in Dene village of **Fort McPherson**, 115km south of Inuvik soon after crossing the Peel River. It also offers food and gas and is open all year. There's also the unserviced NWT government *Nutuiluie Territorial Campground* (547km from Dawson) 10km south of Fort McPherson ($10; June–Sept). For tours from the village, contact the local Dempster Patrol (☎952-2053), which runs interesting trips such as visits to the Shildii Rock, a spot sacred to the Tet'lit Gwich'in, trips to an abandoned Gwich'in camp, and themed day tours by boat such as "On the Trail of the Lost Patrol".

The even tinier settlement of **Tsiigehtchic** (formerly Arctic Red River), 80km south of Inuvik, also *sometimes* has gas and a three-roomed B&B, *Sundog Enterprises* (☎953-3003; ⑤). The settlement was founded as a mission in 1868 – a red-roofed mission church from 1931 still stands – acquiring a Hudson's Bay post soon after. Since 1996 it has been known by its Dene native name, which means "mouth of the red-coloured river".

Dawson City to the Arctic Circle

Having come this far north it's hard to resist the temptation of crossing the **Arctic Circle** 403km north of **Dawson City**, a journey that takes you over the most captivating

---

NUNAVUT

"Apparently we have administered these vast territories in an almost continuous state of absence of mind."

Prime Minister Louis S St Laurent to the Canadian parliament in 1953

Long an amorphous political entity administered not as a semi-autonomous province but by central government, the **Northwest Territories** are set to be formally superseded on April 1, 1999 by a land treaty which will divide the territories in two and create a new eastern Arctic territory called **Nunavut** (meaning "Our Land"). A preliminary division took place on January 1, 1996, and the name Nunavut is already widely used, not least in information for visitors, with the new region putting out its own heavyweight brochure, *The Arctic Traveller Nunavut Vacation Planner*, full of all the information you are likely to need for casual visits or fully fledged expeditions with tour operators and outfitters (all of whom are listed). The remainder of the "old" NWT, the clumsily titled Western Northwest Territories (though this may change), currently puts out an equally detailed *Explorers' Guide*. Both can be obtained from Canadian state tourist offices abroad or from the telephone numbers in the box at the beginning of this chapter (see p.791).

The new $1.15-billion land deal – the largest in Canadian history – will give back their homeland to the Inuit, who in return will renounce their claim to the remainder of the NWT. The new Nunavut territory will cover a fifth of Canada's land surface, an area five times the size of California and twice the size of Ontario. It will be home to some 17,500 Inuit, about eighty percent of the new region's population, with the capital at Iqaluit on Baffin Island. The deal follows fifteen years of low-profile but effective talking and campaigning, and makes the Inuit the single largest private landowners in the world.

However, **Ovide Mercredi**, the former grand chief of the Assembly of First Nations, representing 500,000 natives, is on record as saying the Inuit are giving away too much and receiving too little. He seems to have a point. Of the 136,000 square miles in question, the Inuit provisionally had mineral rights to only 14,000, though this should be extended, and they now have unrestricted rights to hunt, fish and trap over a far greater area. More crucially, however, the region will probably still have a centrally appointed government along the lines of the present Yukon and NWT administrations, and this lack of native self-government may well provide a stumbling block to complete agreement.

---

stretch of the highway. At the very least you should take a short ride out of the mixed deciduous spruce woods of the boreal forests for a look at the tundra which starts beyond the **North Fork Pass** (1370m), just 79km north of Dawson. All distances given below are from Dawson City, almost the only way to locate things on the road.

After the millions of lodgepole pines in this part of the world, it's almost time for a celebration when you pass what are reputedly Canada's most northerly pines (8km). Beyond them you'll see occasional trappers' cabins: the hunting of mink, wolverine and lynx is still lucrative, providing the Yukon's 700 or so full-time trappers with a $1.5-million annual income. At **Hart River** (80km) you may see part of the 1200-strong Hart River Woodland **caribou herd**; unlike the barren-ground herds further north these caribou have sufficient fodder to graze one area instead of making seasonal migrations. **Golden eagles** and **ptarmigan** are also common on willow-lined streams like Blackstone River (93km), as are **tundra birds** like Lapland longspurs, lesser golden plovers, mew gulls and long-tailed jaegers. At Moose Lake (105km), **moose** (needless to say) can often be seen feeding, along with numerous species of waterfowl such as northern shoveller, American widgeon and the **arctic tern**, whose Arctic to Antarctic migration is the longest of any bird.

Chapman Lake (120km) marks the start of the northern Ogilvie Mountains, a region that has never been glaciated and so preserves numerous relic species of plant and insect, as well as providing an important early wintering range for the **Porcupine**

Caribou Herd; as many as 40,000 caribou cross the highway in mid-October – they take four days and have right of way. Unique **butterfly** species breed at Butterfly Ridge (155km), close to some obvious caribou trails which cross the region, and it should also be easy to spot Dall sheep, cliff swallows and bald eagles.

The **Arctic Circle** (403km) is marked on the Dempster by a battered roadside cairn, and the occasional summer home of one of the north's premier eccentrics, one Harry Waldron, the self-proclaimed "Keeper of the Arctic Circle". In his late 60s, Harry was wont to sit in a rocking chair in a tuxedo with a glass of champagne and regale all-comers with snippets of Robert Service, facts about the Arctic and some fairly unim-peachable views on the environment. An ex-highway worker, he started his act of his own accord, but proved so popular that he was paid by the Yukon government to sit and do his spiel. After here, the road climbs into the Richardson Mountains to meet the bor-der of the NWT (470km) before the less arresting flats of the Mackenzie River and the run to Inuvik.

Delta-Beaufort

The **Delta-Beaufort** region centres on the planned government-built town of **Inuvik**, embracing the mighty delta of the **Mackenzie River**, North America's second longest river, and reaching across the Beaufort Sea to Banks Island, the most westerly of Cana-da's Arctic islands. The delta ranks as one of the continent's great **bird** habitats, with swans, cranes and big raptors amongst the many hundreds of species that either nest or overfly the region during the spring and fall migration cycles. It also offers the chance of seeing pods of **beluga whales** and other big sea mammals, while Native Canadian guides on Banks Island should be able to lead you to possible sightings of musk ox, white fox and polar bears.

After Inuvik and the two villages on the short NWT section of the Dempster – Fort McPherson and Tsiigehtchic – the area's other four settlements are **fly-in communi-ties** reached from Inuvik. Two of them, **Aklavik** and **Tuktoyaktuk**, are near – at least, by NWT standards – and are the places to fly out to if you want a comparatively acces-sible taste of aboriginal northern culture. **Sachs Harbour** (on Banks Island) and **Paulatuk** lie much further afield, and are bases for more arduous tours into the delta and Arctic tundra. Inuvik, along with Yellowknife and Fort Smith, is one of the key cen-tres of the accessible north, and one of the main places from which to make, take or plan tours further afield. Two major – and several minor – **tour companies** run a wide variety of boat and plane tours to all four destinations (see p.841), varying from rea-sonably priced day-trips to full-on expeditions. Having come this far it's well worth tak-ing one of the shorter tours for a taste of Arctic life, and to enjoy the superb bird's-eye view of the delta and surrounding company from the air.

Inuvik

INUVIK – "the place of man" – is the furthest north you can drive on a public highway in North America, unless, that is, you wait for the winter freeze and follow the ice road carved across the frozen sea to the north. Canada's first planned town north of the Arc-tic Circle, Inuvik was begun in 1954 as an administrative centre to replace Aklavik, a settlement to the west wrongly thought to be doomed to envelopment by the Macken-zie's swirling waters and shifting mud flats. Finished in 1961, it's a strange melting pot of around 3000 people, with native Dene, Métis and Inuvialuit living alongside the trap-pers, pilots, scientists and frontier entrepreneurs drawn here in the 1970s when a boom followed the oil exploration in the delta. Falling oil prices and the rising cost of exploita-tion, however, soon toppled the delta's vast rigs and it seems the oil is destined to remain largely untapped until the next century. Today the local economy also relies on government jobs, services and the town's role as a supply and communication centre for much of the western Arctic.

Wandering the town provides an eye-opening introduction to the vagaries of northern life, from the strange stilted buildings designed to prevent their heat melting the permafrost (which would have disastrous effects on foundations, assuming any could be dug), to the strange pipes, or *utilidors*, which snake round the streets carrying water, power and sewage lines – again, to prevent problems with permafrost. There are also the all-too-visible signs of the **alcoholism** that affects this and many northern communities – a problem rarely alluded to outside them, partly because the region's native groups seem to be disproportionately afflicted: suicides here are four times the national average for Native Canadian groups.

On a happier note, the influence of Inuvialuit people in local political and economic life has increased, to the extent that the **Western Claims Settlement Act** of 1984 saw the government cede titles to various lands in the area, returning control that had been lost to the fur trade, the church, oil companies and national government. A potent symbol of the church's local role in particular resides in the town's most-photographed building, the **Igloo Church**, or Our Lady of Victory, a rather incongruous yoking of a native icon and foreign religion. It's on Mackenzie Road, the main street which runs west to east through town, but isn't always open: ask at the rectory for a glimpse inside and for the paintings of local Inuvialuit artist, Mona Thrasher. Much further west on Mackenzie Road you might also want to take a look at the **Ingamo Hall**, a three-storey building built almost entirely from 1000 white spruce logs brought up the Mackenzie River (local trees, such as there are, don't grow sufficiently to provide the timber required for building).

Practicalities

Canadian North (☎979-2951 or 1-800-665-1177) has daily scheduled **flights** to Inuvik's **Mike Zubko airport** (12km south of town) from Edmonton, usually via Yellowknife, Fort Smith or Hay River. Several regional companies also run regular services from Yellowknife (NWT Air; ☎979-2341 or 1-800-661-0789), Whitehorse (Alkan Air; ☎979-3999 or 1-800-661-0432), Dawson City and numerous smaller destinations in the NWT. A **taxi** (☎979-2525 or 979-2121) from the airport should cost around $25–30. As elsewhere in Canada and the NWT, the cheapest way of getting to Inuvik may be to buy a Canadian or Air Canada pass before arriving in Canada (see "Basics", p.30). When talking to airlines about onward flights to the fly-in communities or elsewhere, remember that local tour companies often use their scheduled flights, and may be able to offer better flight-only deals than the airlines (see tour company details below). In summer a **bus** service operates from Dawson (see p.837) – its Inuvik office is at 181 Mackenzie Rd (☎979-4100 or toll-free in northern BC and the Yukon 1-800-661-0721); the **Dempster Highway** is open year-round except for brief periods during the November freeze and April thaw.

For **information** on Inuvik and the region, contact the new **Western Arctic Visitor Centre** (June–Sept daily 9am–8pm; ☎979-4321), located near the entrance to town at the eastern end of Mackenzie Road at the junction with Spruce Hill Drive (10min walk from the centre). In town you can dig out more background to the area at the **Inuvik Centennial Library** (Mon & Fri 2–5pm, Tues–Thurs 10am–9pm; ☎979-2749) on Mackenzie Road west of the Igloo church, and pick up **maps**, **guides**, books and charts at the Boreal Bookstore (☎979-3748), located almost opposite the church at the Arctic Tour Company office, 181 Mackenzie Rd. The **post office** is at 187 Mackenzie Rd, and the **hospital** (☎979-2955) is at the eastern end of town close to the visitor centre. For the **police**, call ☎979-2935.

ACCOMMODATION

There are only three **hotels** in town, and all are almost identically pricey: the big *Eskimo Inn* (☎979-2801 or 1-800-661-0725; ⑤), in central downtown; the *Finto Motor Inn* (☎979-2647 or 1-900-661-0843; ⑤), to the east next door to the Western Arctic Visitor Centre, with a good restaurant; and the central *Mackenzie Hotel* (☎979-2861; ⑥), which is probably the smartest of the three. *Robertson's Bed and Breakfast*, 41 Mackenzie Rd (☎979-3111; ④), has non-smoking rooms, which need to be booked well in advance during summer. So, too, do the *East Branch Bed and Breakfast* (☎979-4529; ④), which has non-smoking rooms close to downtown, and the central *Polar Bed and Breakfast* (☎979-2554 or 979-3636; ④). The *Arctic Chalet Bed and Breakfast* (☎979-3535; ② sharing, otherwise ④), which is 3km from town, has a log house and cabins. The best local **campground**, the *Happy Valley*, overlooks the delta; the simple and peaceful *Chuk Park* site is out of town on the way to the airport.

EATING

Eating possibilities are largely confined to *To Go's*, a cheap takeout with a handful of tables at 71 Mackenzie Rd, or the expensive hotel dining rooms – where at a price you can gorge on char, caribou and musk ox: the best is probably *The Peppermill* at the *Finto Motor Inn*, 288 Mackenzie Rd (☎979-2647), followed by the *Green Briar Dining Room* (☎979-2414) in the *Mackenzie Hotel*, whose coffee shop is also a good place for breakfast. The *Back Room*, 108 Mackenzie Rd, is famed for its stuffed polar bear, and serves the usual steaks, fish, fries, and won't break the bank. For the best and busiest **bar**, head for the infamous *Zoo* in the *Mackenzie Hotel*, a gathering place for an eclectic mix of locals, backpackers and assorted out-of-towners. The *Sly Fox* (in the *Eskimo Inn*) and the *Trapper Pub* opposite are locals' hangouts.

CAR AND EQUIPMENT RENTAL, TOUR OPERATORS

Inuvik may be the best place to **rent a car** for the far north, because southern firms tend not to rent vehicles for rough roads, and make hefty charges if you return a car that's obviously been over gravel: Delta Auto Body (☎979-3793), Avis (☎979-4571), Budget (☎979-2888) and Tilden (☎979-3383) rent out suitably robust trucks and pick-ups. To **rent outdoor equipment**, contact Arctic Chalet Outfitting, 25 Carn St (☎979-3535, fax 979-4443), and Beaufort Delta Tours (☎979-4881, fax 979-4898) for canoes and kayaks, and Western Arctic Adventures & Equipment (☎979-4542) for general camping and recreational gear.

Most people who come to Inuvik take a tour of some description. The town's two big **tour operators** are both well worth investigating, as each runs a selection of affordable daily boat and plane tours as well as longer fully blown tours and expeditions: contact the Arctic Tour Company (☎979-4100 or 1-800-661-0721, fax 979-2259), almost opposite the Igloo Church at 181 Mackenzie Rd. Day-trips include tours to the tundra, to Hershel Island, to a traditional bush camp, boat tours on the Mackenzie River, beluga whale-watching and trips to Aklavik by boat or plane; longer tours include three- to five-day trips to Bank's Island and Sachs Harbour to watch wildlife (notably musk ox); whale-watching trips and a nine-day Mackenzie River trip to Yellowknife. Arctic Nature Tours (☎979-3300, fax 979-3400), with forty years' experience of the region, run similar trips, but – as their name suggests – have a special bias towards wildlife: trips include tours to view Dall's Sheep in the Richardson Mountains, Arctic safaris, Barrenlands photography tours, boat and plane trips to view the Porcupine Caribou Herd, and bird and wildlife visits to Hershel Island. Both these and other companies also run trips to all the fly-in communities below.

The fly-in communities

Accessible only by air except in winter, when incredible snow roads are ploughed across the frozen delta, Delta-Beaufort's four **fly-in communities** are close to some fascinating and relatively accessible Arctic landscapes and cultures. All are served by Inuvik-based Aklak Air, Box 1190, Inuvik (☎979-3377 or 979-3555, fax 979-3388) or Arctic Wings, Box 1159, Inuvik (☎979-2220, fax 979-3440). All also have simple stores, though their prices make it wise to take in at least some of your own supplies. Some have hotels, but you should be able to camp close to all four: ask permission first at the village head office. The best way to see them is with a tour company from Inuvik (see p.841), but even if you're going under your own steam it's still worth checking with the tour companies for discounted flight-only deals.

AKLAVIK (pop. 800), 50km west of Inuvik on the western bank of the Mackenzie delta, means "Place of the Barren Lands Grizzly Bear". A Hudson's Bay post aimed at the trade in muskrat fur was established here in 1918, though for generations before the region had been the home of Inuvialuit families who once traded and frequently clashed with the Gwich'in of Alaska and the Yukon. Today both live together in a town that melds modern and traditional, and whose inhabitants are proud not to have jumped ship when they were invited to leave their sinking town for Inuvik in the 1950s. Most are happy to regale you with stories of the mysterious "Mad Trapper of Rat River", a crazed drifter (supposedly a former Chicago gangster) who reputedly killed trappers for the gold in their teeth. Questions should really have been asked when he arrived in Fort McPherson and purchased – with suspiciously vast amounts of cash – unusually large numbers of guns and ammunition. He then built a cabin-cum-fortress on the delta and shot the constable sent to figure out what was going on. A seven-man posse armed with guns and fistfuls of dynamite were then forced to retreat after a fifteen-hour siege. After fleeing and shooting a Mountie, he grabbed world headlines briefly in 1931 as he managed to elude capture for forty days in the dead of a brutal winter. To this day no one knows who he was, where he came from or why he embarked on his killing spree. He was eventually shot on the Eagle River, surrounded by seventeen men and buzzed by a bomb-carrying light plane: he's buried in town in unconsecrated ground. The Hudson's Bay post is still around, together with a former mission church, now a small museum, but there's no restaurant and only one shop, but two **places to stay**: the *Daadzaii Lodge* (☎978-2252; ④) and *Bessie's Boarding and Room Rentals* (☎978-2215; ④). Arctic Wings and Aklak Air **flights** from Inuvik operate daily except Sunday. A one-day tour with stunning twenty-minute flight and an hour in town from either of Inuvik's big tour companies should cost around $120: for a few dollars more you can fly in and boat out, probably the best way of doing things. If you want a more intimate local-based tour of the village, including a visit to the Mad Trapper gravesite with tea and cakes to conclude, contact Ruth Elanik at the Mad Trapper Touring Company (☎978-2548).

TUKTOYAKTUK, or simply Tuk (pop. 1000), sits on a sandspit on the Beaufort coast about 137km north of Inuvik, and acts as a springboard for oil workers and tourists, both considered outsiders who have diluting the traditional ways of the whale-hunting Karngmalit (or Mackenzie Inuit), who have lived and hunted in small family groups on this fascinating but inhospitable shore for centuries. Half the families were wiped out earlier this century by an influenza epidemic introduced by outsiders. The Hudson's Bay Company, inevitably, arrived in 1937. Many locals still hunt, fish and trap, but government, tourism and the oil business now pay most wages. This is the most popular tour outing from Inuvik, with trips starting at about $130, a sum worth paying just to enjoy the scenic low-altitude flight up here. Most casual visitors come to see pods of beluga and great bowhead whales, or to look at the world's largest concentration of **pingoes**, 1400 volcano-like hills thrown up by frost heaves across the delta's otherwise treeless flats. This is among the world's largest grouping of these strange features, and includes the world's largest pingo, Ibyuk, a mound 30m high and 1.5km in circumference visible from the village.

Tuk's only **hotels** – booking is essential – are the *Hotel Tuk Inn* (☎977-2381; ⑥), on the main street near the ocean, and the *Pingo Park Lodge* (☎977-2155; ⑥): both have dining rooms open to non-residents. The Northern supermarket sells groceries. You should be able to **camp** near the beach, but ask first. **Flights** from Inuvik operate daily (around $200 return). Inuvik's main tour companies come out here, but if you want a local operator contact *Rendezvouz Lake Outpost Camp* (☎977-2406) for naturalist, fishing, camping, hiking or wildlife-watching tours in the Anderson River area.

PAULATUK (pop. 110), 400km east of Inuvik, is one of NWT's smallest permanent communities. Situated on a spur between the Beaufort and an inland lake, the settlement was started by the Roman Catholic Mission in 1935 as a communal focus for the semi-nomadic Karngmalit, who despite such paternalism have fought off the adverse effects of missionaries and trader-introduced alcoholism to hang onto some of their old ways. Hunting, fishing and trapping still provide their economic staples, along with handicrafts aimed at the tourists out here mainly for the chance to watch or hunt big game. Key sites for the former activity are the cliffs of the Cape Parry Bird Sanctuary and the **Tuktut National Park** on the Parry Peninsula to the west, a gathering place for the migrating Bluenose caribou herd. Local operators will take you out to both areas, and in spring run trips to look for polar bears on the Amundsen Gulf. The village's name means "place of coal", a reference to the coal seams to the northeast, where the (literally) Smoking Hills take their name from the smouldering coal ignited years ago and still burning. The *Paulatuk Hotel* provides pricey **accommodation** (☎580-3860; ⑧), together with a small restaurant. Otherwise there's the *Paulaken Services Bed and Breakfast* (☎580-3531 or 580-3532; ⑤), with use of kitchen, laundry and living room. Aklak Air **flights** operate twice weekly from Inuvik.

The only settlement on Bank's Island is **SACHS HARBOUR** (pop. 150–200), situated 520km northeast of Inuvik. It was only permanently settled in the late 1920s, and only then by just three Inuvialuit families. Today it supports a handful of self-sufficient Inuit families who survive largely by outfitting hunters and trapping musk ox for food and underfur (*qiviut*), which is spun and woven into clothes on sale locally. For generations the island has been known as one of the north's finest trapping areas, the abundance of white foxes in particular having long attracted the Inuit and other hunters. Today there's still an abundance of wildlife, including the world's largest grouping of musk ox.

Rooms are available at the *Kuptana's Guest House* (☎690-4151; ⑦ including meals), with shared facilities, or the small *Wolkie's Bed and Breakfast* (☎690-3451; ⑦ including meals). Ask first and you should be able to **camp** by the beach. Be warned: there is no restaurant in the town, just a small grocery store. Two Aklak Air **flights** operate from Inuvik weekly (from $350 one way), though for a little more you can join an all-inclusive Arctic Nature Tours trip from Inuvik. Alternatively, contact a local outfit such as Kuptana's Outfitters and Nature Tours (☎690-4151) for one-day or longer birdwatching, fishing and wildlife-watching tours by boat or snowmobile.

The Sahtu

The **Sahtu** embraces the Mackenzie River south of its delta as far as Fort Norman and the tranche of land across to and including **Great Bear Lake** to the east, the world's eighth largest lake. There's no year-round road access: you either fly in here, canoe the Mackenzie – no mean feat – or sign up with **fishing** and hunting charters that boat or fly you into the backcountry, home to some of North America's finest fishing lodges and lakes. Great Bear Lake, to name but one, holds world records for most classes of arctic char and for *every* class of lake trout going (top trout overall – weighing in at 30kg – was caught in 1991). In 1994 a road was built to Wrigley, 225km northwest of Fort Simpson, with plans to push it through to Inuvik, but it'll be a long while before this becomes reality. In the meantime, most tours operate out of the area's nominal capital at **Norman Wells**, or its near neighbour **Tulita** (formerly Fort Norman), both on the Mackenzie in the lee of the Franklin Mountains, which separate the river and Great Bear Lake. The area has just three other lonely communities: **Fort Good Hope** on the Mackenzie north of Norman Wells; **Déline** (formerly Fort Franklin) on Great Bear Lake, a self-sufficient Dene community of hunters and trappers; and **Colville Lake**, north of Great Bear Lake, a spot which amounts to little more than a few log cabins in the woods.

Canadian North (☎873-5533 or 1-800-661-1505 in the western Arctic, 1-800-426-7000 in the US) flies daily to Norman Wells from Inuvik, Yellowknife and Edmonton, and within the area Williams Aero/Arctic Airlines (☎587-2243, fax 587-2335) and North-Wright Air link all five communities from Norman Wells and fly to Inuvik (☎587-2333, 587-2288 or 1-800-661-0702, fax 587-2962) as well as offering sightseeing flights and two- or three-day tasters of hiking the Canol footpath (see below). For general **information** on the area, write to or call Sahtu Tourism Association, Box 115, Norman Wells, NWT (☎873-2122 or 1-800-661-0788).

Norman Wells and Tulita

Ramshackle **NORMAN WELLS** (pop. 550) once owed its economic well-being to **oil** – the local Dene long knew this region as *Le Gohlini* – "where the oil is". The black gold was first noticed by an outsider as a yellow liquid seeping from the rocks by the explorer Alexander Mackenzie as early as 1789, but only rediscovered in 1919 after Dene natives had led geologists to the same spot. Production began in 1932 and was boosted during World War II when the American government sponsored the building of the **Canol Pipeline** to supply the Alaska Highway – now long abandoned, though for a while the town continued to pump about 30,000 barrels a day through a pipeline to Zama, Alberta. At one time 160 wells pushed out 10 million barrels a year from the field. Economic disaster struck the region in 1996, when it was announced the wells and refinery were to close. The only glimmer of hope is that the works and wells are likely to remain intact for a possible new lease of life sometime in the future. You can follow the oil and Canol story in the **Norman Wells Historical Centre** (summer daily 10am–10pm, but check current opening; ☎587-2415), filled with photographs, modest displays and oddments of memorabilia. Alongside, the settlement's uniquely ecumenical **church** does double duty: Catholics sit on one side, Protestants on the other. These days the Canol's old route is becoming an increasingly popular **long-distance footpath**, a tough three- or four-week 372-kilometre wilderness trail from Norman Wells to the Canol Road above Ross River (YT). Logistics are a problem, but if you want one of the world's tougher treks, this one's up there with the toughest. The mountains east of the town contain some of the NWT's bleaker and more spectacular ranges, but good outdoor skills are a must unless you sign up for a tour.

As for **practicalities**, the airport is a twenty-minute walk from the centre of the village, which runs to a bank, post office, a trio of motels, Northern supermarket and plenty of tumbledown housing. The local **visitor centre** is on the corner of Forestry Road and Mackenzie Drive (☎587-2054). There are three **hotels** in town: the *Mackenzie Valley Hotel* (☎587-2511; ⑥), the *Yamouri Inn* (☎587-2744; ⑤) and the *Rayuka Inn* (☎587-2354; ⑤). A touch cheaper is the intermittently open *Log Home B&B* (c/o John Plowman), 5km out of town, with a 160-kilometre view from its front porch and weekly and monthly room deals (☎587-2784; ④).

If you want to spend time on the river, Mountain River Outfitters (☎587-2324 or 587-2285) runs day-trips to Fort Good Hope and the Arctic Circle (mid-June to mid-Sept) and also **rents canoes** and other outdoor equipment. Another good operator offering a wide variety of tours is West to North Tours (☎587-3043, fax 587-2312). For details of the many fishing charter companies, enquire locally or obtain the *Canada Western Northwest Ter-*

ritories' Explorers' Guide from Canadian national tourist offices before you leave home.

TULITA (pop. 300), formerly known as Fort Norman, some 60km to the south, owes its long history to a strategic position at the junction of the Mackenzie and Great Bear rivers (its Dene name means "where the two rivers meet"). Long a Dene native settlement, it first acquired a trading post in 1810. Today it's an ethnically mixed community that looks to trapping and fishing for its livelihood: many houses have tepees out back for drying and smoking fish. It boasts just a riverfront mid-nineteenth-century church and old Hudson's Bay Company post as "attractions". Most visitors use the settlement to outfit canoe and boat trips downstream to Norman Wells or the Great Bear Lake, the latter lying 128km away on the easily navigable Great Bear River, a popular canoe trip with one simple portage. The *Fort Norman Lodge* (☎588-4311; ⑨) is the only **accommodation** base; reservations are essential and meals can be arranged.

Nahanni-Ram

The **Nahanni-Ram** area in the southwestern corner of the NWT centres on **Fort Simpson**, which is accessible by two long gravel roads: from the west, the **Liard Highway** follows the Liard Valley from close to Fort Nelson (BC) on the Alaska Highway; from the east, the **Mackenzie Highway** follows the Mackenzie Valley from close to Fort Providence and Hay River. Both roads offer drives through a fairly mundane wilderness of boreal forest and muskeg bog, and neither penetrates beyond Fort Simpson to offer ordinary travellers access to the Nahanni National Park, the area's jewel.

With gorges deeper than the Grand Canyon and waterfalls twice the height of Niagara, the 4766 square kilometres of the **NAHANNI NATIONAL PARK** rank as one of the finest national parks in North America and one of the most sensational wilderness areas anywhere in the world. Located close to the Yukon border in the heart of the Mackenzie Mountains, it surrounds the **South Nahanni River**, a renowned 322-kilometre stretch of water whose white-water torrents, pristine mountains and 1200-metre-deep canyons have attracted the world's most eminent explorers and the ultimate thrill-seeking canoeists (the river ranks as one of the best white-water runs in the world). Unless you fit one of these categories, however, or can afford to fork out for guided boat trips or sightseeing by air – well worth the money, even if you're only out in the wilderness for a short time – there's no way of getting close to the best areas, even by backpacking: the park is totally roadless and totally wild. Operators in Fort Simpson cater to all levels of demand, from day-trippers wanting air tours of the big set pieces to self-contained canoeists and walkers off on month-long expeditions who require no more than a drop-off or pick-up by air. Even self-sufficient explorers should note that it can still save considerable time, hassle and money to take a three- or four-week tour with a licensed outfitter in Fort Simpson. Also note that the popularity of trips means that a reservation and fee system have been instigated for people wishing to use the river: details from the tourist and park offices in Fort Simpson.

Fort Simpson

All means of access and facilities – including tour operators and outfitters – for the park reside in busy **FORT SIMPSON** (pop. 1000), a perfect base 150km to the east at the confluence of the Liard and Mackenzie, two of North America's greatest rivers. This spot has been inhabited for 9000 years by the Slavey native peoples and their ancestors, making this the longest continually inhabited region in the NWT. The North West Company established a fur post here in 1804 at the so-called "Fort of the Forks" (after the river junction). This was renamed Fort Simpson in 1821, but the settlement became as important as much for its role as a staging point for supply boats using the Mackenzie as for its fur-trading potential. Later the inevitable missions arrived – in 1858 and 1894 – so often the bane of indigenous communities. Latterly the area has been an important base for oil exploration projects up and down the Mackenzie, a major regional administrative centre, and a bustling summer base for visitors hiring **camping equipment** or booking onto **tours and charter flights** to the interior.

Most of what you want in town is situated along the main street, **100th Street**, effectively a continuation of the main road through the town. Before this highway was built the main street was the almost parallel Mackenzie Drive on the lake waterfront, at the southern end of which you'll find the site of the old Hudson's Bay Company post and an area known as the "Flat" or the Papal Grounds, the latter an area whose tepee and other development dates from the papal visit here on September 20, 1987 (this area was inhabited until disastrous floods in 1963). A light plane and float-plane airstrip lies just to the northwest of the downtown area, while the bulk of the outfitters' offices are gathered north of the strip at the top of Mackenzie Drive; the main **airport** is 12km south of town.

Practicalities

You can get to Fort Simpson by **bus** using Frontier Coachlines (☎874-2566), which currently runs once weekly between Hay River, Fort Simpson and Yellowknife. By **air** you need to take connecting flights from Yellowknife with Buffalo Airways (☎874-3333 or 873-6112) or from Whitehorse or Yellowknife with Ptarmigan Airways (☎873-4461 or 1-800-661-0808). The **visitor centre** (mid-May to early Sept daily 8am–8pm; ☎695-3182) lies at the south entrance to town close to the intersection of Antoine Drive and 93rd Avenue (which leads to the Papal Grounds) with 100th Street. Don't confuse this with the **Tourist Service Centre** opposite across the street, which provides coin showers, a laundry and car wash. For extra information on the Nahanni National Park, contact the **Nahanni National Park Reserve Office**, Box 348 EX, Fort Simpson (☎695-2310 or 695-3151). There are also summer **infocentres** at Fort Liard (☎770-4141) and Wrigley (☎581-3321).

If you're hoping to **stay** in town, be sure to book ahead. In town there are two major hotels on or just off 100th Street. The more northerly, on the junction with 101st Avenue, is the *Nahanni Inn* (☎695-2201, 695-2202, 695-2203 or 695-2204; ⑤–⑥), which also has a coffee shop; a couple of blocks south is the smaller *Maroda Motel* (☎695-2602; ⑤–⑥), half of whose units have fully equipped kitchenettes. Other possibilities are the *Check Point* (☎695-2953; ⑤), with a restaurant at the junction of Hwy 1 and Hwy 7, and two **B&B** options: the *Mac-View* (☎695-2724; ④) and the *Bannock Land Resorts* (☎695-3337; ④). The local **campground** is just to the southwest of the Papal Grounds with lots of space and firewood, charging $5 nightly.

As for **tours**, the sky's the limit, and you should be able to organize just about any sort and length of trip into the National Park or elsewhere. For day-trips to the spectacular **Virginia Falls**, one of the most popular day outings in the park (usually with 2 or 3hr on the ground), contact Deh Cho Air (☎770-4103), who also rent canoes, plan fishing charters and organize all manner of other flights and canoe or hiking drop-offs and pick-ups. For trips on the rivers, including day-trips and overnight trips or trips by traditional wooden scows (native canoes), contact North Nahanni River Tours (☎695-2116 or 695-2042, fax 695-2118). Another outfit that caters to day and half-day visitors wanting to sightsee in the National Park is Nahanni Mountain Lodge (☎695-2505, fax 695-2925). Most of the town's other operators offer full-scale expeditions that run into thousands of dollars: full details are available in Fort Simpson or from the *Canada's Western Northwest Territories Explorers' Guide*, which you can obtain from national tourist offices before you leave.

Big River

BIG RIVER covers the country stretching north from Alberta to the south shore of the Great Slave Lake, and embraces several rivers, including large parts of the Mackenzie and Slave watersheds, and several of the territories' most accessible towns. **Hay River**, near the head of the Mackenzie Highway from Alberta, is the area's hub and provides a gateway both to the **Great Slave Lake**, the third largest in North America, and to Fort Smith and the upper reaches of the mainly Albertan Wood Buffalo National Park. Unless you're headed for the park, however, or are prepared to drive east to **Fort Resolution** to see one of the most southerly examples of living Dene culture, most of this region and its seemingly limitless ridges of boreal forest is not the most rewarding zone of the north. However, if you do want to explore, it's relatively easy to get around under your own steam: Greyhound **buses** run daily except Saturday to Hay River – contact the Greyhound office in Hay River on ☎873-6966 or 1-800-661-8747. Here they connect three times weekly with Frontier Coachlines, 16 102nd St (☎874-2566, fax 874-2388), which runs buses to Fort Providence, Yellowknife and connections to Fort Smith. For more information on the whole area, contact the Big River Tourism Association, Box 185, Hay River (☎874-2422).

Hay River

HAY RIVER (pop. 3100) is a typical no-nonsense northern town designed for practicalities rather than sightseeing self-indulgence. Long a strategic site, it's been inhabited for thousands of years by Slavey Dene natives attracted by its position on Great Slave Lake at the mouth of the Hay River. White settlers had put it on the map by 1854, but the inevitable Hudson's Bay Company trading post arrived only in 1868, and it wasn't until recently – with the completion of the Mackenzie Highway, oil and gas exploration, and the arrival of a railway to carry zinc ore from local mines – that the town became an important transport centre. It's now also one of the most important **ports** in the north, shipping freight up the Mackenzie in huge barges to provide a precarious lifeline for High Arctic communities as far away as Inuvik and Tuktoyaktuk. If you're stuck in town, the best way to kill time is to wander the wharves where piles of supplies compete for space with tugs, barges, huge dredges and the town's big fishing fleet.

The town divides into the New Town on the west bank of the Hay River – home to most of the motels, restaurants and key buildings – and the somewhat moribund Vale Island across a bridge to the north: in the latter, which centres on Mackenzie Drive, you'll find the wharves, airport, the remnants of the old town (badly damaged by flooding in 1963), the campground and a series of passable and popular **beaches** (the last a total of 7km from the centre of New Town). The best sand is near the campground on the northeast side of the island at the end of 106th Avenue. The **bus depot** is on the right immediately over the bridge: cross back over for the New Town.

The **Visitor Centre** (mid-May to mid-Sept daily 9am–9pm; ☎874-3180) is on Hwy 2 south of the New Town centre. There's ample **accommodation**, much of it cheaper than elsewhere in the north. Most reasonable is the pretty downbeat *Cedar Rest Motel* (☎874-3732; ②) on the main Hwy 2 south of the New Town downtown area (rooms have kitchenettes). Just north of downtown, on the right between New Town and the Vale Island bridge, is the *Migrator Motel* (☎874-6792; ④), five minutes' walk from the town centre. The best if you want comfort after a long haul is the downtown *Ptarmigan Inn*, 10 J. Gagnier St (☎874-6781 or 1-800-661-0842; ⑤): the **restaurant** at the *Ptarmigan*, *The Keys*, is popular, or you can try the excellent *Back Eddy's* (☎874-6680) on Capital Crescent, one block back from the river in downtown. You can **camp** near the beach on Vale Island at the *Hay River Campground* ($12; mid-May to mid-Sept) or to the south of the New Town off Hwy 2 at the private *Paradise Gardens Campground* ($8.50).

The Northern Frontier

The **Northern Frontier** is the broad sweep of lake-spotted barren land between the Great Slave and Great Bear lakes, and is largely the playground of canoeists and naturalists, or of hunters on the trail of the region's 400,000-strong herd of caribou. At its heart lies **Yellowknife**, Canada's most northerly big town and until 1999 the capital of the NWT (see feature on "Nunavut", p.838). Despite its surreal inappropriateness in a region of virtual wilderness, it's not worth making a special trip to see – though you may find yourself passing through, as it's the main transport hub for movement throughout the territories. **Buses** run here from Edmonton via Hay River, and there are regular Canadian North and NWT Air **flights** from all major Canadian cities, as well as numerous smaller airline connections from most NWT destinations. For **information** and useful brochures on the region, contact the NWT Arctic Tourism, Box 1320, Yellowknife (☎873-7200 or 1-800-661-0788, fax 873-0294).

Yellowknife

Nothing about **YELLOWKNIFE** – named after the copper knives of Slavey natives – can hide the fact that it's a city that shouldn't really be here. Its high-rise core of offices and government buildings exists to administer the NWT and support a workforce whose service needs keep a population of some 18,500 occupied in a region whose resources should by rights support only a small town. Even the Hudson's Bay Company closed its trading post here as early as 1823 on the grounds of economics, and except for traces of gold found by prospectors on the way to the Klondike in 1898, the spot was a forgotten backwater until the advent of commercial gold and uranium mining in the 1930s. This prompted the growth of the **Old Town** on an island and rocky peninsula on Great Slave Lake, and then in 1947 the **New Town** on the sandy plain behind it. In 1967, the year a road to the outside world was completed (Edmonton is 1524km away by car), Yellowknife replaced Ottawa as the seat of government for the NWT. Oiled by bureaucratic profligacy and the odd gold mine, the city has blossomed ever since, if that's the word for so dispersed and unprepossessing a place.

Arrival and information

If you're arriving by **air**, Yellowknife's airport is 5km west of the city on Hwy 3. **Car rental** companies at the airport include Budget (☎873-3366): elsewhere try Avis, c/o Arctic Frontier Carriers, 328 Old Airport Rd (☎873-5648); Tilden, c/o The Sportsman, 5118 50th St (☎873-2911, 920-2970 or 1-800-387-4747); and Yellowknife Motors (☎873-4414). **Taxis** to downtown from the airport cost around $12: call City Cab (☎873-4444) if you need a ride. Three **buses** are run weekly by Frontier Coachlines (328 Old Airport Rd, Yellowknife; ☎873-4892) and shuttle from Hay River via Fort Smith (around $70 one way).

The **Northern Frontier Regional Visitors Centre** is on the edge of Frame Lake just north of the Northern Heritage Centre at 4807 49th St (mid-June to late Aug daily 10am–6pm; ☎873-4262). The **post office** is at 4902 50th St, and the **Stanton Yellowknife Hospital** is on Old Airport Road at Range Lake Road (☎920-4111). For the **police**, call ☎669-1111. To rent camping gear, canoes, snowmobiles, fishing tackle and other **outdoor equipment**, contact Snowcraft Cruises (☎873-6160), Narwhal Northern Adventures, 101, 5103-51st Ave (☎873-6443, fax 873-0516), the latter canoe trip and rental experts for 25 years. For **bike rentals**, visit Sports Traders, 5 Old Airport Rd (☎893-9030).

Accommodation

Hotels in the city have plenty of rooms, but prices are high, and it can be worth looking up one of the dozen or so **B&Bs** if you're on a tight budget: try *Barb's B&B* on Latham Lake at 31 Morrison Drive (☎873-4786), where the host will give bird-watching tips; the non-smoking *Cranberry House B&B*, 87 Lanky Court (☎873-5076; ③), which offers a free pick-up from the airport for pre-booked guests; the lakeshore *Captina Ron's B&B* near the *Wild-cat Café* in the Old Town at 8, Lessard Drive (☎873-3746; ③); or the *Blue Raven B&B*, 37b Otto Drive (☎873-6328; ③). The *Igloo Inn* (☎873-8511 or 873-5547; ④) at 4115 Franklin Ave between the Old Town and downtown, is the cheapest of the hotels proper (pay a bit more and you can have a kitchenette), closely followed by the downtown *Northern Lites Motel* (☎873-6023). If you want something more salubrious try the simply appointed *Discovery Inn*, 4701 Franklin Ave (☎873-4151; ⑥), recently renovated; the facility-laden *Explorer*, 49th Avenue and 48th Street (☎873-3531 or 1-800-661-0892; ⑥); or the *Yellowknife Inn*, 50th Street and 49th Street (☎873-2601 or 1-800-661-0580; ⑥), which has a health club and com-plimentary airport shuttle. The only **campground** is the *Fred Henne Territorial Park* (☎920-2472; $10) by Long Lake off Hwy 3 north of the airport. Trails run to town from here via Frame Lake: allow an hour – or you can follow the Prospectors' Trail north from the site, a good way to get a taste of the wilderness that encircles Yellowknife.

The City

Visitors are steered carefully down the main street, Franklin Avenue (50th Avenue), and the long hill from the New Town to quaint Old Town cabins such as the still-oper-ating **Wildcat Café**, 3904 Wiley Rd (June–Sept daily), an atmospheric and endlessly busy little café opened in 1937. Elsewhere the old town is a shakedown of pitted and buckled roads (the result of permafrost) and a few quaintly battered buildings on the aptly named Ragged Ass Road and Willow Road. These are more or less the only rem-nants of the old times – though if you venture to the outskirts you'll find native shanty settlements and scenes of poverty that take the lustre off the high-rises of the city cen-tre. This lends some irony to the city's promotional tag – "Where Yesterday Rubs Shoul-ders with Tomorrow" – coined to underline the city's undeniably striking juxtaposition of the old and new.

Just west of New Town's core lies the **Prince of Wales Northern Heritage Centre** (summer daily 9am–5pm; winter Tues–Sun same hours; free; ☎873-7551), three blocks from downtown on Frame Lake. Yellowknife's key sight, the modern centre peddles a more sanitized view of northern history and native culture than is on offer in parts of the Old Town, offering extensive displays of northern artefacts, Inuit carvings and per-suasive dioramas of local wildlife and habitats. Shops around town also sell a variety of northern native crafts, still expensive, but cheaper than you'll find in southerly cities; most are beautiful products of a living culture – even if the culture is not at its healthi-est in the city itself. The centre's South Gallery deals with native displays, the North Gallery with life in the north after the arrival of Europeans; there's also an Aviation Gallery, devoted to the planes and pilots who for years played (and play) a vital part in keeping the north alive. The centre also houses the NWT Archives, a collection of maps, books, photographs and documents devoted to the region. Just northwest of the centre, also on Frame Lake, stands the $25-million **Northwest Territories Legislative Assembly**, opened in 1993 to house the Territories' 24-strong Legislative Assembly. It's an impressive piece of architecture, much of it open to public view (tours 2 daily Mon–Fri, 1 daily Sun; free; ☎669-2200).

Otherwise the only things to do close to town are walk the trails around Frame Lake and from the campground on Long Lake (see below). Or you look round Canada's largest **gold mine** (☎873-6301), or drive out on the **Ingraham Trail**, an 81-kilometre highway that was to be the start of a major NWT "Road to Resources" but which was abandoned in the 1960s. There are plenty of boat launches, picnic sites and campgrounds en route,

THE INUIT

"They be like to Tartars, with long blacke haire, broad faces, and flatte noses, and tawnie in colour, wearing Seale skinnes . . .The women are marked in the faces with blewe streakes downe the cheekes, and round about the eies".

An officer on Frobisher's 1576 search for the Northwest Passage

Distinct from all other Canadian natives by virtue of their culture, language and Asiatic physical features, the **Inuit** are the dominant people of a **territory** that extends all the way from northern Alaska to Greenland. Nowadays increasingly confined to reserves, they once led a **nomadic** existence in one of the most hostile environments on earth, dwelling in domed **igloos** during the winter and **skin tents** in the summer, and moving around using **kayaks** (*umiaks*) or **dog sleds** (*komatik*). The latter were examples of typical Inuit adaptability – the runners were sometimes made from frozen fish wrapped in sealskin and, in the absence of wood, caribou bones were used for crossbars.

Their prey – caribou, musk ox, seals, walruses, narwhals, beluga whales, polar bears, birds and fish – provided oil for heating and cooking, hides for clothing and tents, harpoon lines, ivory and dog harnesses. Using harpoons, bows and arrows and spears, ingenious hunting methods were devised: to catch caribou, for example, huge **inuksuits**, piles of rocks resembling the human form, were used to steer the herd into a line of armed hunters.

The Inuit **diet** was composed totally of flesh, and every part of the animal was eaten, usually raw, from eyeballs to the heart. Delicacies included the plaited and dried intestines of seals and whole sealskins stuffed with small birds and left to putrefy until the contents had turned to the consistency of cheese. All food was **shared** and the successful hunter had to watch his catch being distributed amongst other families in the group, in accordance with specific relationships, before his own kin were allowed the smallest portion. **Starvation** was common – it was not unusual for whole villages to perish in the winter – and consequently **infanticide**, particularly of females, was employed to keep population sizes down. Elderly people who could not keep up with the travelling group were abandoned, a fate that also befell some **offenders** against the social code, though the usual way of resolving conflict was the **song-duel**, whereby the aggrieved would publicly ridicule the behaviour of the other, who was expected to accept the insults with good grace.

Making **clothes**, most often of caribou hide, was a task assigned to **women** and was as essential to survival as a man's ability to hunt. Older women also **tattooed** the faces of the younger ones by threading a sinew darkened with soot through the face to make lines that radiated from the nose and mouth. Women were usually betrothed at birth and married at puberty, and both polygamy and polyandry were frequent – though female infanticide made it rare for a man to have more than two spouses.

as well as short walking trails like the **Cameron River Falls** (48km from Yellowknife) and lakeside beaches where the hardier of the city's population brave the water.

Food, nightlife and festivals

For **food**, join the locals and curious sightseers in the Old Town's *Wildcat Café* (see p.849) or the *Old Town Pub* across the road. The basement cafeteria in the Yellowknife Centre Mall is cheap, plastic and popular with office workers at breakfast and lunch. *Mr Mike's* downstairs in the Scotia Mall is big and busy, with a good salad bar and plenty of steak and burger basics. For more of a treat, head for the *Bistro on Franklin*, 4910 Franklin Ave (☎873-3991), or slightly less intimate but gastronomic *Office*, 4915 50th St (☎873-3750), an excellent place to sample northern specialities such as arctic char. If you hit a warm summer's day, the *Sweetgrass Café*, 5022 47th St (☎873-9640), has an outside terrace for alfresco eating and drinking. Most of the hotels have good dining

Communion with supernatural spirits was maintained by a **shaman** or *angakok*, who was often a woman, and the deity who features most regularly in Inuit myth is a goddess called **Sedna**, who was mutilated by her father. Her severed fingers became seals and walruses and her hands became whales, while Sedna lived on as the mother and protector of all sea life, capable of withholding her bounty if strict **taboos** were not adhered to. These taboos included keeping land and sea products totally separate – and so seals could never be eaten with caribou and all caribou clothing had to be made before the winter seal hunt.

Although sporadic **European contact** dates back to the Norse settlement of Greenland and some Inuit were visited by early missionaries, it wasn't until the early nineteenth century that the two cultures met in earnest. By 1860 commercial **whalers** had begun wintering around the north of Hudson Bay, employing Inuit as crew members and hunters for their food in return for European goods. Even then, the impact on the Inuit was not really deleterious until the arrival of **American whalers** in Canadian waters in 1890, when the liberal dispensing of alcohol and diseases such as smallpox and VD led to a drastic **decline in population**.

By the early decades of this century **fur traders** were encouraging the Inuit to stop hunting off the coast and turn inland using firearms and traps. The accompanying **missionaries** brought welcome medical help and schools, but put an end to multiple marriages, shamanism and other traditional practices. More changes came when Inuits were employed to build roads, airfields and other military facilities during World War II and to construct the line of radar installations known as Distant Early Warning during the Cold War era. As well as bringing **new jobs**, this also focused **government attention** on the plight of the Inuit.

The consequent largesse was not wholly beneficial: subsidized housing and welfare payments led many Inuit to abandon their hunting camps and settle in **permanent communities**, usually located in places strategic to Canada's sovereignty in the Arctic. Without knowledge of the English and French languages, these Inuit were left out of all decision-making and often lived in a totally separate part of towns that were administered by outsiders. Old values and beliefs were all but eroded by television and radio, and high levels of depression, alcoholism and violence became the norm. The 1982 ban on European imports of sealskins created mass **unemployment**, and although hunting still provides the basics of subsistence, the high cost of ammunition and fuel makes commercial-scale hunting uneconomical.

All is not gloom, however. Inuit cooperatives are increasingly successful and the production of **soapstone carvings** – admittedly a commercial adulteration of traditional Inuit ivory art – is very profitable. Having organized themselves into politically active groups and secured such **land claims** as Nunavut, the Inuit are slowly rebuilding an ancient culture that was shattered in under half a century.

rooms – the *Red Apple* in the *Discovery* is popular – and much of the nightlife revolves around their lounges, notably the plush nightclub at the *Explorer* – though you'll meet far more interesting and dubiously harmless types at the *Gold Range Hotel*, 5010 50th St (☎873-4441). This is one of *the* great northern **bars**, and claims to sell the second largest amount of beer per customer of any bar in Canada.

You'll also have an interesting time if you can contrive to be in town during one of Yellowknife's **festivals**: one of the most intriguing (check it's still running) is the **Caribou Carnival** in March, whose attractions include dog-sled racing, bingo on ice, igloo-building, flour packing and – best of all – "ugliest truck" competitions. Midsummer on June 21 is celebrated in Raven Mad Daze, with lots of street events, drinking and high spirits all through 24 hours of daylight. More cerebral and fascinating is **Folk on the Rocks** (third weekend of July), when folk singers from across Canada and the US meet Inuit and Dene folk singers, folk dancers and the famous Inuit "throat singers" in an amazing medley of world music.

Yellowknife is, along with Inuvik and Fort Smith, the headquarters of most of the far north's **outfitters and tour operators**. Many outfits run fishing, wildlife, Arctic sightseeing, canoeing, kayaking, boating and other trips, most ranging from one- or two-day outings up to full-blown three-week mini-expeditions to unimaginably wild areas. The best bet is to go forewarned, obtain the comprehensive listing in *Canada's Western Northwest Territories Explorers' Guide*, which should be obtainable from national tourist offices before you go. If you decide you want adventure on the spur of the moment, contact the regional visitors centre (see p.848).

Keewatin

The **Keewatin** stretches a vast distance west from Hudson Bay north of Churchill into the great so-called "Barrenlands" of the NWT interior. Along with the Arctic islands to the north, it forms the bulk of **Nunavut**, Canada's new territory (see box on p.838), belated recognition for a region that contains the majority of NWT's indigenous Inuit. This is the land of vast caribou migrations, musk oxen, polar bears (see them at Wager Bay) and endless empty kilometres of fish-filled lakes and rivers. Most of the region's communities lie on the arc of Hudson Bay's western coast, from **Arviat** in the south through **Whale Cove** (Tikirarjuaq), **Rankin Inlet** (Kangiqtinq) – the area's main transport and administrative centre – to **Chesterfield Inlet** (Igluligaarjuk) and **Coral Harbour** (Salliq) in the north. In all of these you will find an almost unchanged way of life – the local arts and handicrafts are outstanding, and in places you can hear the old drummers and "throat singers" traditionally responsible for handing down the stories and myths of the Inuit.

The region's two major centres are covered below, but it's as well to know rough **flight details** and where **accommodation** is available in the smaller communities. Note that hotel prices in the north are invariably per person, not per room, so double all rates if you are two people sharing a double room. Rates sometimes include meals, so are not as steep as they first appear. **Coral Harbour** (pop. 500), the only settlement on Southampton Island, has the small *Leonie's Place* (☎867/925-9751 or 925-8810; ⑦ with all meals per person). There are Calm Air flights here three times weekly and one First Air flight weekly from Iqualut via Rankin Inlet. **ARVIAT** (pop. 1300), 240km southwest of Rankin Inlet (connected by daily Calm Air flights from Rankin Inlet), only offers *Padlei Inns North* (☎867/857-2919; ⑤ per person) and *Ralph's* B&B (☎857-2653; ⑥); rates at the latter include three meals a day. At **WHALE COVE** (pop. 200), 80km south of Rankin Inlet, there's *Tavani Inns North* (☎896-9252; ⑦ per person with all meals). **CHESTERFIELD INLET** (pop. 290) has daily flights from Rankin Inlet to the south, and one hotel, the *Tangmavik*, (☎898-9975; ⑦ per person with all meals).

For more **information** on the region, contact Nunavut Tourism, PO Box 1450, Iqaluit (☎979-6551 or 1-800-491-7910), or Travel Keewatin, Dept Eg, Box 328, Rankin Inlet (☎645-2618).

Kangiqtinq (Rankin Inlet)

Although you'll find an old way of life and sublime Arctic scenery in the region, don't expect much in the way of prettiness in the villages: communities are often poor, roads pitted, houses strung out and battered, and the streets festooned with telephone and electric cables. The region currently has just one paved road – from the airport at **KANGIQTINQ** to the settlement's "downtown". And remember that villages often aren't communities at all in the accepted sense: Rankin Inlet, for example, was only founded in 1955 when the North Rankin Nickel Mine opened. Three years later the government, shocked at conditions of local Inuit, "moved" people here from their nomadic homes in the wilderness: the resulting settlement, **Itivia** (now all but vanished), a kilometre from Rankin, was a disaster, that was made worse by the closure of the nickel mine in 1962. Only a craft-producing initiative and recent tourism saved the day.

NWT Air (☎920-2500 or 1-800-661-0789) runs five flights weekly to Rankin Inlet from Yellowknife for around $525 Apex return. First Air (☎613/839-3340, fax 839-5690) has direct **flights** to Rankin Inlet from Iqaluit via Coral Harbour for around $560 return, and connecting services from Ottawa and Montréal via Iqualuit on Baffin Island. Calm Air (☎204/778-6471, fax 778-6954) flies scheduled services from Churchill in Manitoba to Rankin Inlet and most other Keewatin villages. Outfitters and small charter firms here and in all the communities are available to fly or guide you into the interior or out into Hudson Bay for fishing and naturalist trips. Rankin Inlet boasts the small regional **Kivalliq Regional Visitor Centre**, housed – along with the post office – at the *Siniktarvik Hotel* (☎645-5091 or 645-5067 for the Regional Tourism office). As in much of the far north, prices in **hotels** tend to be per person whether you're in a double or single: thus for two people sharing you need to *double* our given rate. Rankin Inlet has three accommodation possibilities: the *Siniktarvik Hotel* (☎645-2807 or 645-2949; ⑥ per person); the *Nanuq Inn* (☎645-2513; ⑤ per person); and the smallest, *Keewatin Guest Lodge* (☎645-2839; ⑤), though check that the last remains open. The first two hotels both have dining rooms.

Qamanittuaq (Baker Lake)

Some 260km west of Rankin Inlet at the mouth of the Thelon River lies **Qamanittuaq** (formerly Baker Lake), population 1000, the Arctic's only inland Inuit community (*Qamanittuaq* means "far inland"), which marks both Canada's geographic centre – it has long been a meeting place for members of different Inuit groups – and provides a point of access into the **tundra** that characterizes the vastness of the region. This is a subtle landscape that's worth more than its "Barrenland" label suggests, particularly in summer, when the thaw brings to life thousands of tiny streams and lakes, and some three hundred species of wildflowers amidst the lichens and grasses that provide fodder for huge herds of musk ox and caribou. Millions of wildfowl can also be seen, and the huge skies and flat horizons are also one of the best places in Canada to see the **aurora borealis** (see feature p.795). Also be sure to take in the **Traditional Inuit Camp**, a demonstration by Inuit families of the activities, such as hunting, trapping and weaving, that might have taken place in a Caribou Inuit camp.

For **accommodation** there's the *Iglu Hotel* (☎793-2801; ⑥ per person) and the *Baker Lake Lodge* (☎793-2965; ⑤ per person), a group of cabins sleeping a total of twenty. The summer Akumalik **visitors centre** (☎793-2456) occupies a reconstructed 1936 Hudson's Bay Company post in the original building, successor to the 1916 post that originally brought about the settlement's development. Calm Air has daily flights here from Rankin Inlet for around $220 one way.

The Arctic Coast

Canada's last frontier, the **Arctic Coast** encompasses the country's northern mainland coast from the Mackenzie to Baffin Island, and – as "coast" is a relative term in a region where the sea is often frozen – numerous islands too, most notably Victoria and King William Island. It is barren, ice-carved country, comprising a wind-scoured landscape of chill lakes and low hills with not a tree to be seen: it's also nearly completely dark and frozen for nine months of the year, yet still boasts a permanent population of a few hundred. It is home to **Inuit** (see pp.850–851) who as recently as fifty years ago had known little or no contact with the outside world. Few explorers encountered them, and even the most determined of western agencies – the church and the trading companies

THE NORTHWEST PASSAGE

Traversed in its entirety fewer than fifty times, the fabled **Northwest Passage** around the American continent exerts a continuing romantic allure – and, in the wake of oil discoveries in the far north, an increasing economic attraction too. The world's severest maritime challenge, it involves a 1500-kilometre traverse from north of Baffin Island to the Beaufort Sea above Alaska. Some 50,000 icebergs constantly line the eastern approaches and thick pack ice covers the route for nine months of the year, with temperatures rising above freezing only in July and August. Perpetual darkness reigns for four months of the year, and thick fog and blizzards can obscure visibility for the remaining eight months. Even with modern technology navigation is almost impossible: a magnetic compass is useless as the magnetic north lies in the passage, and a gyro compass is unreliable at high latitudes; little is known of Arctic tides and currents; sonar is confused by submerged ice; and the featureless tundra of the Arctic islands provides the only few points of visual or radar reference.

John Cabot can hardly have been happy with his order from Henry VII in **1497** to blaze the northwest trail, the first recorded instance of such an attempt. The elusive passage subsequently excited the imagination of the world's greatest adventurers, men such as Sir Francis Drake, Jacques Cartier, Sir Martin Frobisher, James Cook and **Henry Hudson** – cast adrift by his mutinous crew in 1611 when the Hudson Bay turned out to be an icebound trap rather than the passage.

Details of a possible route were pieced together over the centuries, though many paid with their lives in the process, most famously **Sir John Franklin**, who vanished into the ice with 129 men in 1845. Many rescue parties set out to find Franklin's vessels, *HMS Erebus* and HMS *Terror*, and it was one searcher, **Robert McClure**, who – in the broadest sense – made the first northwest passage in 1854. Entering the passage from the west, he was trapped for two winters, and then sledged to meet a rescue boat coming from the east. The **first sea crossing**, however, was achieved by the Norwegian **Roald Amundsen**, his success in 1906 coming after a three-year voyage. The first single-season traverse was made by a Canadian Mountie, **Henry Larsen**, in 1944 – his schooner, the *St Roch*, is now enshrined in Vancouver's Maritime Museum. More recently huge icebreakers have explored the potential of cracking a commercial route through the ice mainly for the export of oil from the Alaskan and new Beaufort fields and for the exploitation of minerals in Canada's Arctic north.

– have failed to compromise a people who are still extraordinarily isolated by climate, distance and culture. Today, however, few of the native Inuit live according to the ways of popular myth. Except on the odd trapping party, for example, igloos have been replaced by government-built homes, and the bone tools, sledges and kayaks of a generation ago have been superseded by rifles, snow bikes and light aircraft.

You still have to be fairly determined, however, to reach any of the region's **eight communities** (five on the coast, three on islands), let alone explore the hauntingly beautiful icefields and tundra. People up here are usually looking to spot wildlife, fish, or, more dubiously, to hunt for musk ox, caribou and for polar bears, a practice the government defends by claiming "It's done the Inuit way, using dog teams, on a demanding safari over land and sea ice": it also provides much-needed income for the Inuit, who have the right to sell the limited number of permits. Most visitors base themselves either at **Kugluktuk** (formerly **Coppermine**) or at Victoria Island's **Ikaluktutiak** (formerly **Cambridge Bay**), the transport and service capital. Each main Arctic coast community, remarkably, has **accommodation**, but reservations are vital and prices predictably steep. You need to come prepared: in some cases meals must be booked in advance. Basic groceries are usually available at stores, but there are no banks. As ever, various **tour operators** run trips to and from the main centres: for information, send for the *Arctic Traveller Nunavut Vacation Planner* before you go.

Ikaluktutiak (Cambridge Bay)

IKALUKTUTIAK, formerly known as **Cambridge Bay**, lies to the north of the Arctic Circle on the barren southern shore of **Victoria Island**, which at a monster 212,688 square kilometres is Canada's second largest island. As ever in the high Arctic, you need a special reason to come here, for accommodation, food and flights are all hideously expensive. Today it's the regional centre for the Kitikmeot communities and an important staging point for visitors making tours or heading still deeper into the hinterland. Once Nunavut is up and running (see p.838), it will also operate as the administrative focus for the region's western lands, despite a location a full 1300km from Nunavut's capital at Iqaluit. Over the centuries the region was a summer gathering place for the Copper Inuit (so-called by the whites because they made many of their tools and weapons from copper), attracted here by the abundance of good hunting, notably seals, caribou and arctic char. The last two are local staples to this day, and still provide work and income, Kitikmeot Meats processing caribou and musk for export, Ikaluktutiak Co-op running a fishery that supplies arctic char nationwide (both concerns are open to the public for direct sales). The Hudson's Bay Company arrived in 1921, late by Canadian standards, and purchased the *Maud*, explorer Roald Amundsen's schooner, for use as a supplies and trading ship. This little piece of Arctic history was used for years before being left to sink into disrepair and ultimately into the harbour, where its hulk can still be seen in the bay.

Practicalities

The region's main **tourist office** is the Arctic Coast Tourism Association, Box 91, Omingmak Street and Tigiganiak Road, Cambridge Bay (☎983-2224). It's located in an attractive modern building overlooking the bay, and features displays on the art, history and culture of the Copper and Netsilik Inuit, as well as exhibits of maps and documents that sheds light on the age-old search for the Northwest Passage. A library of northern books and videos is also available, and there are pamphlets on self-guided walks around the community. **Scheduled flights** serve Cambridge Bay on Canadian North (☎983-2435 in Cambridge Bay, 1-800-665-1177 in the eastern Arctic, 1-800-426-7000 elsewhere) from Calgary and Edmonton; NWT Air (983-2591 or 1-800-661-0789)and Aklak Air (☎979-3777) from Inuvik and Delta-Beaufort towns; and First Air (☎873-6884 in Yellowknife, or 983-2919 or 1-800-267-1247) from Yellowknife and Baffin Island. Within the Arctic Coast area itself, First Air flies between all the settlements except Bathurst Inlet and Umingmaktok, which can be reached by charter aircraft only.

As regards **accommodation**, there's the *Inns North* or *Ikaluktutiak Co-op Hotel* (☎983-2215; ⑤ per person), where meals – which you're almost bound to have to buy – cost around $50 a head. There are also one- and two-bedroom apartments, a coffee shop and restaurant. Then there is the smaller and slightly more expensive *Enokhok Inn* (☎983-2444; ⑤ per person), which has seven self-contained suites, kitchenettes and provides deals on longer stays. The *Arctic Islands Lodge* (☎983-2345; ⑥) has luxury rooms at $150 per person a night single or $190 per double room a night. It, too, has a restaurant, coffee shop and laundry, and also offers weekly and monthly rates. You can **camp** at Freshwater Creek, 5km away, and – if you're self-catering – buy supplies at the Northern store. You should also be able to camp on the shoreline of the bay, but ask first, and make sure you are well away and out of sight of any houses.

Kugluktuk (Coppermine)

KUGLUKTUK (pop. 1000) lies to the west of Cambridge Bay in the Canadian "mainland", sitting astride the **Coppermine River** close to the westernmost point of

Nunavut (the river lends Kugluktuk its name, which means "place of rapids"). Yellowknife lies 600km away to the south. A relatively narrow sea passage, the Coronation Gulf, separates the mainland coast from Victoria Island at this point, a vital through-route on the Northwest Passage. The river has long been of primary importance in the region. Copper Inuit, so called because they fashioned tools and weapons from copper, converged at its mouth for a millennium to fish and hunt. In the twentieth century, as the numbers of caribou in the interior have declined, the Inuit have increasingly abandoned their semi-nomadic ways to settle on the coast. Today hunting and fishing still play a part in generating local income, though latterly tourism and oil and gas exploration have also contributed to local coffers. The river, which rises in the wilderness 360km north of Yellowknife, has also provided a "convenient" way of accessing the far north. It was used by Samuel Hearne, for example, the first white to reach the region, who paddled here on the orders of the Hudson's Bay Company to seek out the source of the copper being traded by the Inuit at company posts to the south. Today the river provides one of the continent's great **canoe trips**, most canoeists (or rafters) joining tours or chartering a plane from Yellowknife to the river's headwaters. The 325-kilometre trip downstream takes around ten days. The trip, among other things, offers sensational opportunities for watching wildlife, but you should also strike lucky with wildlife by walking or taking short tours from Kugluktuk itself. The most popular walk (20km one way) is to the **Bloody Falls**, so called because a party of Inuit were massacred here following an argument with a group of Dene guides accompanying Hearne (relations between the two native groups were traditionally poor). If you don't fancy the walk – and it's tough going in places – you can pick up a boat trip up the river to the same point.

Practicalities

Access by **air** is provided through First Air (☎982-3208 or 1-800-267-1247) from Yellowknife and other "local" communities. As far as accommodation is concerned there are two options. The central *Coppermine Inn* (☎982-3333; ⑥) charges $125 per person per night for motel rooms or self-contained units; breakfast, lunch and dinner together are an extra $65 and should be reserved in advance (you can also take meals individually). The smaller *Enokhok Inn* (☎982-3197) charges $160 per person per night inclusive of meals. **Camping** is possible at Kukluktuk Park. As for **eating**, non-residents can use the *Coppermine Inn*, but you need to book meals a day in advance.

Uluqsaqtuuq (Holman)

One of the region's more northerly communities, **ULUQSAQTUUQ**, or **Holman** (pop. 300), lies across Coronation Gulf on Victoria Island from Cambridge Bay. Most people are here to fish for trout and arctic char or, remarkably, for the novelty of playing golf on one of the world's most northerly courses. The settlement is situated in a scenic open cove, the half-moon Queen's Bay, backed by massive two-metre bluffs and escarpments. It developed almost by default, when a Hudson's Bay Company post was moved here from Prince Albert Sound in 1939. Inuit had previously summered here in the search for caribou, but the post encouraged some to settle and sell white fox furs with the Hudson's Bay traders. Today two groups of Inuit – the Copper and Inuvialuit – live here, the region forming part of a designated Inuvialuit settlement area. The community has become particularly well-known for its crafts, notably clothing and traditional tools, but most particularly prints and silk-screened items, a tradition that goes back fifty years, when an Oblate missionary, the Reverend Henri Tardi, came here and taught locals various printing techniques.

You can buy crafts around the settlement, or at the gift shop in the hamlet's only **accommodation**, the *Arctic Char Inn* (☎396-3501 or 396-3531; ⑥), which has just eight rooms at $130 per person per night. You can **camp** at Okpilik Lake, but should be able to pitch a tent just about anywhere if you ask at the hamlet office. The *Arctic Char Inn* is the only place to **eat**, but there is a Northern groceries store almost opposite for supplies.

Baffin Island

Baffin Island comprises half a million square kilometres of Arctic vastness, whose main attraction is **Auyuittuq National Park Reserve** on the Cumberland Peninsula, Canada's northernmost accessible national park. With a treeless landscape, mountains towering over 1500m, icy glacial streams and 24-hour daylight from May to July, hiking in Auyuittuq offers one of the most majestic experiences in Canada. However, with temperatures rising to a mere 6°C from June to August, it's a brutal environment that will appeal only to the truly adventurous; expensive though they are, package tours are definitely recommended if this is your first venture into such a forbidding place. Be sure to bring all necessary gear with you, as the island supplies arrive just once a year.

The main gateway to Baffin Island is **IQALUIT** (formerly Frobisher Bay), whose population of 4000-plus is dominated by Inuits, and will serve as the capital of Nunavut (see p.838). The Baffin Regional Visitors Centre is here (☎979-4636, fax 979-1261), as are many of the tour operators who run trips into the interior.

Practicalities

Getting to Baffin Island is only feasible by **air**. First Air (☎1-800-267-1247, or 979-5810 in Iqaluit) and Canadian North (☎1-800-665-1430 in Keewatin, or 1-800-665-1177 in Nunavut and the eastern Arctic or 979-5331) make the trip from Montréal (1–2 daily; 3hr) and from Ottawa (4 weekly; 4hr). Ticket **prices** can get as low as $400 return, but are usually nearer $700. First Air and Northwest Territorial Airways (☎920-2500 or 1-800-661-0789) also link Yellowknife to Iqaluit (5 weekly; 3hr 50min) for around $700 return. Remember to ask about cheap pass deals and other prebooked flight deals if you're making international flights into Canada: these are often much cheaper bought beforehand in conjunction with the carrier you're using to fly to the country.

Within the island, there is a daily one-hour First Air flight during the summer from Iqaluit to **PANGNIRTUNG**, the gateway to Auyuittuq National Park. There are also scheduled flights to the various small communities and chartered sightseeing flights.

Consult the *Arctic Traveller Vacation Planner* or contact the Iqaluit visitor centre for details of flights and other **information** on outfitters, guides and accommodation. However, hiking maps should be bought in advance from The Canada Map Office, 615 Booth St, Ottawa, ON K1A 0E9. Information on the Auyuittuq park is available from Auyuittuq National Park Reserve, Pangnirtung, NWT XOA 0R0 (☎473-8828).

In summer the Inuit families of Iqaluit abandon their homes in favour of tents, and your best **accommodation** option is to join them, although there are no fixed campgrounds. Iqaluit's five **motels** charge more or less similar rates – around $140 per person per night – for similar facilities: *The Navigator* (☎979-6201; ⑥), *Discovery Lodge* (☎979-4433; ⑥), *Frobisher Inn* (☎979-2222 or 979-0427; ⑥), *Bayshore Inn* (☎979-6733; ⑥), and *Toonoonik* (☎979-6733; ⑥).

In Pangnirtung there is an established free **campground**, *Pisuktinee Tungavik*, and a church that will let you sleep on the floor for a donation if you are desperate. The only commercial **accommodation** is the *Auyuittuq Lodge* (☎473-8955; ⑥). The lodge has good but expensive meals and they usually allow exhausted hikers to use their showers for a few dollars. Each of the following remoter settlements have single and highly expensive hotels: Arctic Bay, Broughton Island, Cape Dorset, Clyde River, Grise Ford, Hall Beach, Igloolik, Lake Harbour, Pond Inlet, Resolute Bay and Sanikiluak.

Auyuittuq National Park Reserve

Straddling the Arctic Circle in the northeast of Baffin Island, **Auyuittuq National Park Reserve** is one of the most spectacular destinations in the Canadian north. The heart of the park is the massive **Penney Ice Cap**, a remnant of the ice sheet that extended over most of Canada east of the Rockies about 18,000 years ago, and the major **hiking route** is the 110-kilometre Pangnirtung/Aksayuk Pass, which cuts through the mountains between Cumberland Sound and the Davis Strait. *Auyuittuq* is Inuit for "the land that never melts", but despite the unrelenting cold there is abundant life here: in summer the sparse tundra plants burst into green, the wildflowers are blooming and the amazing array of wildlife includes lemmings, polar bears, caribou, arctic hares and foxes, snow geese, peregrines, narwhals, walruses, bowhead and beluga whales, as well as harp, ringed and bearded seals.

The only transport for the 25km from Pangnirtung to the south entrance of the park is by **freighter canoe**, which the Inuit also charter for fishing, whale-watching and sightseeing trips. The rates on these "canoes" – which are like small fishing boats with outboard motors – are set by the Inuit cooperative, and work out at around $125 for two people one way, plus $35–60 for each additional person. The boats can only pass through the Pangnirtung Fjord after the ice break-up in July – at other times you have to walk. Arrangements for a canoe pick-up should be possible by radio from the few emergency shelters in the park, but be warned that one summer all the batteries were stolen, so you may have to arrange your pick-up before being dropped off.

Services within the park are extremely limited and the weather is highly unpredictable. Snowstorms, high wind and rain occur frequently, and deaths from hypothermia have been known even in the height of summer. All-weather hiking gear is essential, and a walking stick or ski pole is necessary to assist you with the ice-cold stream crossings which occur every 200–300m and can still be waist-high in July. There is no wood for fuel, as the park is located kilometres north of the tree line, so a camping stove is also essential.

travel details

Trains

Prince George to: Edmonton via Jasper (3 weekly; 8hr 15min); Prince Rupert (3 weekly; 13hr); Vancouver (mid-June to Oct 1 daily; rest of year 3 weekly; 13hr 30min).

Buses

Dawson City to: Inuvik (mid-June to early Sept 2–3 weekly; 12hr); Whitehorse (late June–Sept 3 weekly; Oct & March to early June 2 weekly; rest of year 1 weekly; 7hr 30min).

Dawson Creek to: Edmonton (2 daily; 9hr); Prince George (2 daily; 6hr 30min); Whitehorse (mid-May to mid-Oct 1 daily except Sun; rest of year 3 weekly; 21hr).

Hay River to: Fort Resolution (3 weekly; 6hr); Fort Smith (3 weekly; 7hr); Peace River (daily except Mon; connections for Edmonton and Grande Prairie; 8hr); Yellowknife (3 weekly; 12hr).

Prince George to: Dawson Creek (2 daily; 6hr 30min); Edmonton via Jasper (2 daily; 9hr 45min); Prince Rupert (2 daily; 11hr); Vancouver via Williams Lake and Cache Creek (2 daily; 13hr).

Whitehorse to: Dawson City (June–Sept 3 weekly; Oct & March to early June 2 weekly; rest of year 1 weekly; 7hr 30min); Dawson Creek (mid-

May to mid-Oct 1 daily except Sun; rest of year 3 weekly; 21hr); Skagway (mid-May to mid-June 1 daily except Wed & Sun; 4hr).

Flights

Listed below are only the main direct scheduled flights operated by the big carriers; for details on the vast range of small provincial companies operating within the north, see the town entries in the Guide.

To Inuvik from: Yellowknife (1 daily; 2hr 35min).

To Iqaluit from: Montréal (1–2 daily; 3hr); Ottawa (4 weekly; 4hr); Yellowknife (5 weekly; 3hr 50min).

To Whitehorse from: Vancouver (3 daily; 2hr 20min).

To Yellowknife from: Cambridge Bay (1 weekly; 1hr 30min); Edmonton (3 daily; 1hr 35min); Fort Smith (1 daily; 1hr 30min); Inuvik (1 daily; 2hr 35min); Norman Wells (1 daily; 1hr 15min); Resolute (2 weekly; 3hr 20min).

PART THREE

THE

CONTEXTS

THE HISTORICAL FRAMEWORK

Fully unified only since 1949, and still plagued by the Québec imbroglio, Canada is a country of intertwining histories rather than a single national evolution. Not only does each of its provinces maintain a high degree of autonomy, but each grouping of native peoples can claim a heritage that cannot be fully integrated into the story of white Canada. Such a complex mosaic militates against generalization – although Canadians themselves continue to grapple with the nature of their own identity – but nonetheless what follows attempts to identify key events and themes.

THE BEGINNINGS

The ancestors of the **native peoples** of North America first entered the continent around 25,000 years ago, when vast glaciers covered most of the northern continents, keeping the sea level far beneath that of today. It seems likely that North America's first human inhabitants crossed the land bridge linking Asia with present-day Alaska – they were probably Siberian hunter-nomads travelling in pursuit of mammoths, hairy rhinos, bison, wild horses and sloths, the ice-age animals that made up their diet. These people left very little to mark their passing, apart from some simple graves and the grooved, chipped stone spear-heads which

earned them the name **Fluted Point People**. In successive waves the Fluted Point People moved down through North America, across the isthmus of Panama, until they reached the southernmost tip of South America. As they settled, so they slowly developed distinctive cultures and languages, whose degree of elaboration depended on the resources of their environment.

About **3000 BC** another wave of migration passed over from Asia to North America. This wave was made up of the first group of **Inuit** migrants who – because the sea level had risen and submerged the land bridge under the waters of today's Bering Strait – made their crossings either in skin-covered boats or on foot over the winter ice. Within the next thousand years the Inuit occupied the entire northern zone of the continent, moving east as far as Greenland and displacing the earlier occupants. These first Inuits – called the **Dorset Culture** after Cape Dorset, on Baffin Island in the Northwest Territories, where archeologists first identified their remains in the 1920s – were assimilated or wiped out by the next wave of Inuit, who, crossing into the continent 3000 years ago, created the **Thule** culture – so-called after the Greek word for the world's northernmost extremity. The Thule people were the direct ancestors of today's Inuit.

THE NATIVE PEOPLES

Before the Europeans arrived, the native peoples – numbering around 300,000 – were divided into three main language groups: Algonkian, Athapascan (principally in the north and west) and Inuktitut (Inuit). Within these groups existed a multitude of cultures. None of these people had a written language, the wheel was unknown to them and their largest draught animal, prior to the introduction of the horse, was the dog. However, over the centuries, each of the tribes developed techniques that enabled them to cope with the problems of survival posed by their environments.

THE NORTHERN PEOPLES

Immediately prior to the arrival of the Europeans, Canada was divided into a number of cultural zones. In the extreme north lived the nomadic **Inuit** (see. p.850), whose basic unit was the family group, small enough to survive in the precarious conditions. The necessarily small-scale nature of Inuit life meant that they developed no political structures and gathered together in larger groups only if the supply of food required it – when, for example, the Arctic char were running upriver from the sea to spawn, or the caribou were migrating.

Immediately to the south of the Inuit, in a zone stretching from the Labrador coast across the Canadian Shield to northern British Columbia, lived the tribes of the **northern forests**. This was a harsh environment, too, and consequently these peoples spent most of their time in small nomadic bands following the game on which they depended. Indeed, variations between the tribes largely resulted from the type of game they pursued: the **Naskapi** fished and hunted seals on the Labrador coast; the **Chipewyan**, occupying the border country between the tundra and forest to the west of Hudson Bay, mainly hunted caribou; the **Wood Cree**, to the south of the Chipewyan, along the Churchill River, hunted deer and moose; and the **Tahltan** of British Columbia combined hunting with seasonal fishing. Like the Inuit, the political structures of these tribes were rudimentary and, although older men enjoyed a certain respect, there were no "chiefs" in any European sense of the term. In fact, decisions were generally made collectively with the opinions of successful hunters – the guarantors of survival – carrying great weight, as did those of their shaman, whose main function was to satisfy the spirits that they believed inhabited every animate and inanimate object around them.

THE IROQUOIS

The southern zone of Canada, stretching from the St Lawrence River along the northern shores of the Great Lakes to southern British Columbia was climatically much kinder, and it's in this region that Canada's native peoples developed their most sophisticated cultures. Here, along the banks of the St Lawrence and the shores of the Great Lakes, lived the **Iroquois-speaking** peoples, divided into three tribal confederacies: the **Five Nations**, the **Huron** (see p.122–123) and the **Neutrals**.

All three groups cultivated corn (maize), beans and squash in an agricultural system that enabled them to lead a settled life – often in communities of several hundreds. Iroquois society was divided into matriarchal clans, whose affairs would be governed by a female elder. The clan shared a longhouse and when a man married (always outside his own clan), he would go to live in the longhouse of his wife. Tribal chiefs (*sachems*) were male, but they were selected by the female elders of the tribe and they also had to belong to a lineage through which the rank of *sachem* descended. Once selected a *sachem* had to have his rank confirmed by the federal council of the inter-tribal league: in the case of the Five Nations this consisted of *sachems* from the Seneca, Cayuga, Onondaga, Oneida and Mohawk tribes. Iroquoian society had its nastier side, too. An assured winter supply of food enabled the Iroquois to indulge in protracted inter-tribal warfare: in particular, the Five Nations were almost always at war with the Hurons.

THE OJIBWA AND BLACKFOOT PEOPLES

To the west of the Iroquois, between lakes Superior and Winnipeg, lived the **Ojibwa**, forest hunters who learned to cultivate maize from the Iroquois and also harvested the wild rice that grew on the fringes of the region's lakes.

Further west still, on the prairies, lived the peoples of the **Blackfoot Confederation**: the **Piegan**, **Blackfoot** and **Blood** tribes. The economy of this grouping was based on the buffalo (or bison): its flesh was eaten; its hide provided clothes and shelter; its bones were made into tools; its sinews provided bow strings; and its hooves were melted down to provide glue. In the late seventeenth century, the hunting techniques of these prairie peoples were transformed by the arrival of the horse, which had made its way – either wild or by trade – from Mexico, where it had been introduced by the Spanish conquistadors. The horse made the bison easy prey and, as with the Iroquois, a ready food supply spawned the development of a militaristic culture centred on the prowess of the tribes' young braves.

THE PACIFIC PEOPLES

On the **Pacific coast**, tribes such as the **Tlingit** and **Salish** were dependent on the ocean, which provided them with a plentiful supply of food. There was little cohesion within tribes and people from different villages – even though of the same tribe – would at times be in conflict with each other. Yet these tribes had a rich ceremonial and cultural life, as exemplified by the excellence of their woodcarvings, whose most conspicuous manifestations were the **totem poles**, which reached colossal sizes in the nineteenth century.

THE COMING OF THE EUROPEANS

The first recorded contact between Europeans and the native peoples of North America occurred in around 1000 AD, when a **Norse** expedition sailing from Greenland landed somewhere on the Atlantic seaboard. It was a fairly short-lived stay – according to the Icelandic sagas, the Norse were forced to withdraw from the area they called Vinland due to the hostility of the natives (see p.417 for more details).

In 1492 Ferdinand and Isabella of Spain were finally persuaded to underwrite **Christopher Columbus**'s expedition in search of the westward route to Asia. Columbus bumped into the West Indies instead, but his "discovery" of islands that were presumed to lie off India encouraged other European monarchs to sponsor expeditions of their own. In 1497 **John Cabot**, supported by the English king Henry VII, sailed west and sighted Newfoundland and Cape Breton. On his return, Cabot reported seeing multitudes of cod off Newfoundland, and his much-publicised comments effectively started the **Newfoundland** cod fishery. In less than sixty years, up to four hundred **fishing** vessels from Britain, France and Spain were making annual voyages to the Grand Banks fishing grounds around the island. Soon some of the fishermen established shore bases to cure their catch in the sun, and then they started to overwinter here – which was how settlement of the island began.

By the end of the sixteenth century the cod trade was largely controlled by the British and French, and Newfoundland became an early cockpit of English-French rivalries, a colonial conflict that continued until England secured control of the island in the 1713 Treaty of Utrecht.

NEW FRANCE

Meanwhile, in 1535, **Jacques Cartier**, on a voyage paid for by the French crown, made his way down the St Lawrence, also hoping to find Asia. Instead he stumbled upon the Iroquois, first at Stadacona, on the site of Québec City,

and later at Hochelaga, today's Montréal. At both places the Frenchman had a friendly reception, but the Iroquois attitude changed after Cartier seized one of their *sachems* and took him to France. For a time the Iroquois were a barrier to further exploration up the St Lawrence, but subsequently they abandoned their riverside villages, enabling French traders to move up the river buying **furs**, an enterprise pioneered by seasonal fishermen.

The development of this trade aroused the interest of the French king, who in 1603 commissioned **Samuel de Champlain** to chart the St Lawrence. Two years later Champlain founded **Port Royal** in today's Nova Scotia, which became the capital of **Acadie** (Acadia), a colony whose agricultural preoccupations were soon far removed from the main thrust of French colonialism along the St Lawrence. It was here, on a subsequent expedition in 1608, that Champlain established the settlement of Québec City at the heart of **New France**, and, to stimulate the fur trade, allied the French with those tribes he identified as likely to be his principal suppliers. In practice this meant siding with the Huron against the Five Nations, a decision that intensified their traditional hostility. Furthermore, the fur trade destroyed the balance of power between the tribes: first one and then another would receive, in return for their pelts, the latest type of musket as well as iron axes and knives, forcing enemies back to the fur trade to redress the military balance. One terrible consequence of such European intervention was the **extermination of the Huron people** in 1648 by the Five Nations, armed by the Dutch merchants of the Hudson River.

As pandemonium reigned among the native peoples, the pattern of life in **New France** was becoming well established. On the farmlands of the St Lawrence a New World feudalism was practised by the land-owning seigneurs and their *habitant* tenants, while the fur territories – entered at Montréal – were extended deep into the interior. Many of the fur traders adopted native dress, learnt aboriginal languages, and took wives from the tribes through which they passed, bringing into existence the mixed-race people known as the **Métis**. The furs they brought back to Montréal were shipped downriver to Québec City whence they were shipped to France. But the white population in the French colony remained relatively small – there were only 18,000 New French in 1713. In the context of a growing British presence, it represented a dangerous weakness.

THE RISE OF THE BRITISH

In 1670 Charles II of England had established the **Hudson's Bay Company** and given it control of a million and a half square miles adjacent to the Bay, a territory named Rupert's Land, after the king's uncle. Four years later the British captured the Dutch possessions of the Hudson River Valley – thereby trapping New France. Slowly the British closed the net: in 1713, they took control of Acadia, renaming it **Nova Scotia** (New Scotland), and in 1755 they deported its French-speaking farmers. When the Seven Years' War broke out in 1756, the French attempted to outflank the British by using the Great Lakes route to occupy the area to the west of the British colonies and then, with the help of their native allies, pin them to the coast. In the event the British won the war by exploiting their naval superiority: a large force under the command of **General James Wolfe** sailed up the St Lawrence in 1759 and, against all expectations, successfully scaled the Heights of Abraham to capture Québec City. Montréal fell a few months later – and at that point the French North American empire was effectively finished, though they held onto Louisiana until Napoleon sold it off in 1803.

For the native peoples the ending of the Anglo-French conflict was a mixed blessing. If the war had turned the tribes into sought-after allies, it had also destroyed the traditional inter-tribal balance of power and subordinated native to European interests. A recognition of the change wrought by the end of the war inspired the uprising of the Ottawas in 1763, when **Pontiac**, their chief, led an unsuccessful assault on Detroit, hoping to restore the French position and halt the progress of the English settlers.

Moved largely by a desire for a stable economy, the response of the British Crown was to issue a proclamation which confirmed the legal right of the natives to their lands and set aside the territory to the west of the Appalachian Mountains and the Great Lakes as "**Indian Territory**". Although colonial governors were given instructions to remove trespassers on "Indian Land", in reality the proclamation had little practical effect until the twentieth century,

when it became a cornerstone of the native peoples' attempts to seek compensation for the illegal confiscation of their land.

The other great problem the British faced in the 1760s was how to deal with the French-speaking **Canadiens** of the defunct New France – the term *Canadiens* used to distinguish local settlers from those born in France, most of whom left the colony after the British conquest. Initially the British government hoped to anglicize the province, swamping the French-speaking population with English-speaking Protestants. In the event large-scale migration failed to materialize immediately, and the second English governor of Québec, **Sir Guy Carleton**, realized that – as discontent grew in the American colonies – the loyalty of the *Canadiens* was of vital importance.

Carleton's plan to achieve this was embodied in the 1774 **Québec Act**, which made a number of concessions to the region's French speakers: Catholics were permitted to hold civil appointments, the seigneurial system was maintained, and the Roman Catholic Church allowed to collect tithes. Remarkably, all these concessions were made at a time when Catholics in Britain were not politically emancipated.

THE MIGRATIONS

The success of this policy was seen during the **American War of Independence** (1775–83) and the Anglo-American War of 1812: the *Canadiens* refused to volunteer for the armed forces of the Crown, but equally they failed to respond to the appeals of the Americans – no doubt calculating that their survival as a distinctive cultural group was more likely under the British than in an English-speaking United States.

In the immediate aftermath of the American War of Independence, the population of what was left of British North America expanded rapidly, both in "Canada" – which then covered the present-day provinces of Québec and Ontario – and in the separate colonies of New Brunswick, Nova Scotia, Prince Edward Island and Newfoundland. The first large wave of migration came from the United States as 40,000 **United Empire Loyalists** made their way north to stay within British jurisdiction. Of these, all but 8000 moved to Nova Scotia and New Brunswick, the rest going to the western edge of Québec, where they laid the foundations of the future province of Ontario. Between 1783 and 1812 the population of Canada, as defined at the time, trebled to 330,000, with a large part of the increase being the product of *revanche du berceau* (revenge of the cradle) – an attempt, encouraged by the Catholic clergy, to outbreed the ever increasing English-speaking population.

However, tensions between Britain and the United States still deterred potential colonists, a problem resolved by the **War of 1812**. Neither side was strong enough to win, but by the Treaty of Ghent in 1814 the Americans recognized the legitimacy of British North America, whose border was established along the **49th parallel** west from Lake of the Woods to the Rockies. Immigration now boomed, especially in the 1840s, when economic crises and shortages in Great Britain, as well as the Irish famine, pushed it up to levels that not even the fertile *Canadiens* could match. Between 1815 and 1850, over 800,000 immigrants entered British North America. Most headed for "Upper Canada", later called Ontario, which received 66,000 in the year of 1832 alone.

Frenetically the surveyors charted new townships, but could not keep pace with demand. The result was that many native peoples were dispossessed in direct contravention of the 1763 proclamation. By 1806 the region's native peoples had lost 4.5 million acres.

THE DIVISION AND UNION OF CANADA

During this period economic expansion was principally generated by the English-speaking merchants who now controlled the Montréal-based fur trade, organized as the **North West Company**. Seeking political changes that would enhance their economic power, they wanted their own legislative assembly and the universal application of English law, which of course would not have been acceptable to the French-speakers.

In 1791, through the **Canada Act**, the British government imposed a compromise, dividing the region into **Upper** and **Lower Canada**, which broadly separated the ethnic groups along the line of the Ottawa River. In Lower Canada, the French-based legal system was retained, as was the right of the Catholic Church to collect tithes, while in Upper Canada, English common law was introduced. Each of the new

provinces had an elective assembly, though these shared their limited powers with an appointed assembly, whilst the executive council of each province was responsible to the appointed governor, not the elected assembly. This arrangement allowed the assemblies to become the focal points for vocal opposition, but ultimately condemned them to impotence. At the same time, the plutocrats built up chains of influence and power around the appointed provincial governments: in Upper Canada this grouping was called the "**Family Compact**", in Lower Canada the "**Château Clique**".

By the late 1830s considerable opposition had developed to these cliques. In Upper Canada the **Reform Movement** led by **William Lyon Mackenzie** demanded a government accountable to a broad electorate, and the expansion of credit facilities for small farmers. In 1837 both Mackenzie and **Louis-Joseph Papineau**, the reform leader in Lower Canada, were sufficiently frustrated to attempt open rebellion. Neither was successful and both were forced into exile in the United States, but the rebellions did bring home to the British Government the need for effective reform, prompting the **Act of Union** of 1840, which united Lower and Upper Canada with a single assembly.

The rationale for this arrangement was the racist belief that the French-Canadians were incapable of handling elective government without Anglo-Saxon guidance. Nevertheless, the assembly provided equal representation for Canada East and West – in effect the old Lower and Upper Canadas. A few years later, this new assembly achieved **responsible government** almost accidentally. In 1849 the Reform Party, which had a majority of the seats, passed an Act compensating those involved in the 1837 rebellions. The Governor-General, Lord Elgin, disapproved, but he didn't exercise his veto – so, for the first time, a Canadian administration acted on the vote of an elected assembly, rather than imperial sanction.

The Reform Party, which pushed through the compensation scheme, included both French- and English-speakers and mainly represented small farmers and businessmen opposed to the power of the cliques. In the 1850s it became the Canadian **Liberal Party**, but this French-English coalition fell apart with the emergence of "Clear Grit" Liberals in Canada West in the

1860s. This group argued for "Representation by Population" – in other words, instead of equal representation for the two halves of Canada, they wanted constituencies based on the total population. As the English-speakers outnumbered the French, the "Rep by Poppers" rhetoric seemed a direct threat to many of the institutions of French Canada. As a consequence many French-Canadians transferred their support to the **Conservative Party**, while the radicals of Canada East, the **Rouges**, developed a nationalist creed.

The Conservative Party represented the fusion of a number of elements, including the rump of the business cliques who had been so infuriated by their loss of control that they burnt the Montréal parliament building to the ground in 1849. Some of this group campaigned to break the imperial tie and join the United States, but, when the party fully emerged in 1854, the old "Compact Tories" were much less influential than a younger generation of moderate conservatives, such as **John A. Macdonald**, who was to form the first federal government in 1868. Such moderates sought, by overcoming the democratic excesses of the "Grits" and the nationalism of the "Rouges", to weld together an economic and political state that would not be absorbed into the increasingly powerful United States.

CONFEDERATION

In the mid-1860s "Canada" had achieved responsible party government, but British North America was still a collection of **self-governing colonies**. In the east, Newfoundland was almost entirely dependent on its cod fishery, Prince Edward Island had a prosperous agricultural economy, and both Nova Scotia and New Brunswick had boomed on the backs of the shipbuilding industry. Far to the west, on the Pacific coast, lay fur-trading British Columbia, which had just beaten off American attempts to annex the region during the Oregon crisis, finally resolved in 1846, when the international frontier was fixed along a westward extension of the original 49th parallel. Not that this was the end of British Columbia's problems: in 1858 gold was discovered beside the Fraser River and, in response to the influx of American prospectors, British Columbia was hastily designated a Crown Colony – a process that was repeated in 1895 when gold was discovered in the Yukon's

Klondike. Between Canada West and British Columbia stretched thousands of miles of prairie and forest, the old Rupert's Land that was still under the extremely loose authority of the Hudson's Bay Company.

The American Civil War raised fears of a US invasion of the incoherently structured British North America, at the same time as "Rep by Poppers" agitation was making problematic the status of the French-speaking minority. These issues prompted a series of conferences to discuss the issue of **Confederation**, and after three years of debate the British Parliament passed the British North America Act of 1867. In effect this was a constitution for the new **Dominion of Canada**, providing for a federal parliament to be established at Ottawa; for Canada East and West to become the provinces of Québec and Ontario respectively; and for each province to retain a regional government and assembly. All of the existing colonies joined the Confederation except British Columbia, which waited until 1871; Prince Edward Island, till 1873; and Newfoundland, which remained independent until 1949.

THE CONSOLIDATION OF THE WEST

Having apparently settled the question of a constitution, the Dominion turned its attention to the west. In 1869, the territory of the Hudson's Bay Company was bought for £300,000; the **Northwest Territories**, as the area then became known, reverted to the Crown until Canada was ready to administer them, irrespective of the wishes of its population, the Plains Indians and the 7000-odd settlers, of whom 5000 were **Métis**. The Métis, whose main settlement was near the site of modern-day Winnipeg, were already alarmed by the arrival of Ontario expansionists and were even more alarmed when government land surveyors arrived to divide the land into lots that cut right across their holdings. Fearful of their land rights, the Métis formed a provisional government under the leadership of **Louis Riel** and prepared to resist the federal authorities (see p.502).

In the course of the rebellion, Riel executed a troublesome Ontario Orangeman by the name of Thomas Scott, an action which created uproar in Ontario. Despite this, the federal government negotiated with a Métis delegation and appeared to meet all their demands, although Riel was obliged to go into exile in the States. As a result of the negotiations, Ottawa created the new province of **Manitoba** to the west of Ontario in 1870, and set aside 140 acres per person for the Métis – though land speculators and lawyers ensured that fewer than twenty percent of those eligible actually got their land.

Dispossession was also the fate of the **Plains Indians**. From 1871 onwards a series of treaties were negotiated, offering native families 160-acre plots and a whole range of goods and services if they signed. By 1877 seven treaties had been agreed (eventually there were eleven), handing over to the government all of the southern prairies. However, the promised aid did not materialize; instead the native peoples found themselves confined to small, infertile reservations.

The federal government's increased interest in the area – spurred by the **Cypress Hills Massacre** of Assiniboine natives in 1873 (see p.492) – was underlined by the arrival in 1874 of the first 275 members of the newly formed Northwest Mounted Police, the **Mounties** (for more, see p.480). One of their first actions was to expel the American whiskey traders who had earned the region the nickname Whoop-up Country. Once the police had assumed command, Ottawa passed the **Second Indian Act** of 1880, making a Minister of Indian Affairs responsible for the native peoples. The minister and his superintendents exercised a near dictatorial control, so that almost any action that a native person might wish to take, from building a house to making a visit off the reservation, had to be approved by the local official, and often the ministry in Ottawa too. The Act laid down that an applicant for "enfranchisement" as an ordinary Canadian citizen had to pass through a three-year probation period and was to be examined to see if the applicant had attained a sufficient level of "civilization". If "enfranchised", such people became so-called "non-status Indians", as opposed to the "status Indians" of the reservations.

Meanwhile, during the 1870s, most of the **Métis** had moved west into the territory that would become the province of **Saskatchewan** in 1905. Here they congregated along the Saskatchewan River in the vicinity of Batoche, but once again federal surveyors caught up with

them and, in the 1880s, began to divide the land into the familiar gridiron pattern. In 1885, the Métis again rose in **revolt** and, after the return of Riel, formed a provisional government. In March they successfully beat off a detachment of Mounted Police, encouraging the neighbouring Cree people to raid a Hudson's Bay Company Store. It seemed that a general native insurrection might follow, born of the desperation that accompanied the treaty system, the starvation which went with the disappearance of the buffalo, and the ravages of smallpox. The government dispatched a force of 7000 with Gatling guns and an armed steamer, and after two preliminary skirmishes the Métis and the Cree were crushed. Riel, despite his obvious insanity, was found guilty of treason and hanged in November 1885.

The defeat of the Métis opened a new phase in the development of the west. In 1886 the **first train ran from Montréal to Vancouver** and settlers swarmed onto the prairies, pushing the population up from 250,000 in 1890 to 1,300,000 in 1911. Clifford Sifton, Minister of the Interior, encouraged the large-scale immigration from Eastern Europe of what he called "stalwart peasants in sheepskin coats". These Ukrainians, Poles, Czechs and Hungarians ploughed up the grasslands and turned central Canada into a vast granary, leading the Dominion into the "wheat boom" of the early twentieth century.

NATIVE PEOPLES IN THE TWENTIETH CENTURY

For the **native peoples** the opening of the twentieth century ushered in a far from happy time. Herded onto small reservations under the authoritarian paternalism of the ministry, they were subjected to a concerted campaign of Europeanization – ceremonies such as the sun dance and the potlatch were banned, and they were obliged to send their children to boarding schools for ten months of the year. Deprived of their traditions and independence, they lapsed into poverty, alcoholism and apathy. In the late 1940s, the academic Frederick Tisdall estimated that no fewer than 65,000 reservation aboriginals were "chronically sick" from starvation. The Inuit were drawn into increasing dependence on the Hudson's Bay Company, who encouraged them to concentrate on hunting for furs rather than food, while the twin agencies of the Christian missions and the Royal Canadian

Mounted Police worked to incorporate the Inuit into white culture. All over Canada, a major consequence of the disruption of the traditional way of life was the spread of disease, especially TB, which was fifteen to twenty times more prevalent amongst the aboriginal population than amongst whites.

In 1951 a new **Indian Act** increased the autonomy of tribal bands, but despite this and increased federal expenditure, aboriginal people remained well behind the rest of Canadian society: in 1969 the average income of a Canadian family was $8874, whilst 88 percent of aboriginal families earned $3000 or less, with fifty percent earning less than $1000.

In recent years, however, native peoples have begun to assert their identity. "Status Indians" are now represented by the **Assembly of First Nations** (AFN), which has, since its foundation in the early 1980s, sponsored a number of legal actions over treaty rights, many of the cases being based on breaches of the 1763 proclamation, whose terms stated that native land rights could only be taken away by direct negotiation with the Crown. The last Grand Chief of the AFN, **Ovide Mercredi** – a lawyer and former human rights commissioner – announced that the objective of the AFN was to secure an equal status with the provincial governments, a stance indicative of the growth in native self-confidence, despite the continuing impoverishment of the reservations. The political weight of the AFN was made clear in the constitutional talks that took place over the **Inuit homeland** in the Northwest Territories, a complex negotiation resulting in an agreement to create two self-governing territories in 1999 (see p.838). But not all of Canada's natives see negotiation as their salvation: the action of armed Mohawks to prevent a golf course being built on tribal burial grounds at **Oka** in Québec (p.235) displayed an almost uncontainable anger against the dominant whites, and divided sympathies across the country. Elected in 1997, the new leader of the AFN, **Phil Fontaine**, has a reputation for conciliation and it was perhaps this that secured his success, representing a reaction to the brinksmanship of the Oka militants.

QUÉBEC AND THE FUTURE OF CANADA

Just as Canada's native peoples drew inspiration from the national liberation movements of the late 1950s and 1960s, so too did the **Québécois**. Ever since the conquest of 1760, francophones had been deeply concerned about *la survivance*, the continuation of their language and culture. Periodically this anxiety had been heightened, notably during both world wars, when the Québécois opposed the introduction of conscription because it seemed to subordinate their interests to those of Britain. Nevertheless, despite these difficulties, the essentially conservative Québécois political-religious establishment usually recommended accommodation with the British and later the federal authorities. This same establishment upheld the traditional values of Catholic rural New France, a consequence of which was that Québec's industry and commerce developed under anglophone control. Thus, in early twentieth-century Montréal, a francophone proletariat worked in the factories of anglophone owners, an anglophone dominance that was compounded by the indifference of Canada's other provinces to French-Canadian interests, spurring the development of a new generation of Québec **separatists**.

Expo '67, held in Montréal, was meant to be a confirmation of Canada's arrival as an industrial power of the first rank, but when President de Gaulle of France used the event as a platform to announce his advocacy of a "free Québec", it turned into the catalyst for a political row that has dominated the country ever since. That same year, **René Lévesque** formed the **Parti Québécois** (PQ), with the ultimate goal of full independence and the slogan *Maîtres chez nous* ("masters in our own house"). Yet 1968 also witnessed the election as prime minister of **Pierre Trudeau**, a French-Canadian politician dedicated to the maintenance of the federation, highlighting the increasing polarization of francophone opinion.

The PQ represented the constitutional wing of a social movement which at its most militant extreme embraced the activities of the short-lived **Front de la Libération du Québec** (FLQ). In 1970 the FLQ kidnapped and murdered Pierre Laporte, the province's Minister of Labour, an action which provoked Trudeau into putting the troops onto the streets of Montréal. This reaction was to benefit the PQ, a modernizing party of the social-democratic left, which came to power in 1976 and set about using state resources to develop economic interests such as the Québec hydroelectric plant on James Bay. It also reformed education – including controversial legislation to make Québec unilingual – and pressed ahead with plans for a referendum on secession. But when the referendum came, in 1980, sixty percent of Québec's electorate voted "*non*" to separation, partly because the 1970s had witnessed a closing of the opportunity gap between the francophone and anglophone communities. This did not, however, end the affair.

In 1985, Québec's PQ government was defeated by **Robert Bourassa**'s Liberals, not so much reflecting a shift in francophone feeling but more Bourassa's espousal of the bulk of the nationalist agenda and what many felt to be the PQ's poor economic track record. The Liberals held power in Québec until 1994, when the PQ bounced back into office, promising to hold another independence referendum. They seemed well set. Polls regularly rated support at around sixty percent, but in 1995 the PQ lost again in a **second referendum** that rejected independence by just 50,000 votes. Despite all the subsequent bluster, this was a political disaster for the PQ, and, with the momentum lost, subsequent polls have seemed to suggest that the separatist bubble may well have burst. If this is the case, one of the key reasons is the PQ's failure to define the precise nature of Québec sovereignty and how future relations with the rest of Canada would be conducted.

THE PRESENT

To say that the rest of Canada has become exasperated by the interminable discussions over the future of Québec would be an understatement; this has never been more true than in 1990 when the **Meech Lake** conference conspicuously failed to agree a new decentralized constitution. The conference was convened by the Conservative **Brian Mulroney**, who became the country's premier in 1984. Mulroney had other pressing problems, too, though nothing as fractious as Québec. The free trade agreement (NAFTA) between the US and Canada, which Mulroney pushed through parliament, came into effect in 1989, destroying the country's protective tariffs and thereby exposing its industries to undercutting and causing the loss of thousands of jobs; the collapse of the North Atlantic cod fishery brought Nova Scotia and Newfoundland to the brink of economic ruin; and the wheat-producing areas of the west complained that Ottawa failed to secure adequate prices for its produce. Efforts were made to deal with these issues, but few were satisfied and during Mulroney's second term (1988–93), the premier became a byword for incompetence, his party commonly accused of large-scale corruption. As a result, the **federal elections of November 1993** almost wiped out the Conservatives and, equipped with a huge majority, the new Liberal administration, under **Jean Chrétien**, once Trudeau's Minister of Finance, set about rebuilding federal prestige. A cautious politician, Chrétien had some success, his pragmatic approach to politics proving sufficiently popular to see him re-elected for a second term in June 1997 albeit with a reduced majority. These federal elections also witnessed the balkanization of the Canadian political scene: the Liberals, for example, swept Ontario but were locked out of Nova Scotia, whilst in the west the Right-Wing Reform Party made substantial gains. The fiasco of Mulroney's second term and the distinct failure to solve the Québec issue are probable reasons for this scenario. The future is open to the prospect of further turbulence.

CANADIAN WILDLIFE

Canada has just about every natural habitat going, from ice-bound polar islands in the far north to sun-drilled pockets of desert along the United States border. Between these extremes the country's mountains, forests and grasslands support an incredible variety and profusion of wildlife – any brief account can only scratch the surface of what it's possible to see.

National and provincial parks offer the best starting places, and we've listed some of the outstanding sites for spotting particular species. However, don't expect to see the big attractions like bears and wolves easily – despite the enthusiasm of guides and tourist offices, these are encountered only rarely.

EASTERN FORESTS

Canada's **eastern forests** divide into two main groups – the Carolinian forest of southwestern Ontario, and the Great Lakes-St Lawrence forest extending from the edge of the Carolinian forest to Lake Superior and the Gulf of St Lawrence.

CAROLINIAN FOREST

The **Carolinian forest** forms a narrow belt of largely deciduous hardwood trees similar to the broad-leaved woodlands found over much of the eastern United States. Trees are often typical of more southerly climes – Kentucky coffee tree, tulip tree, sassafras, sycamore, chinquapin oak,

shagbark hickory and more ordinary staples like beech, sugar maple, basswood and swamp oak. None of these is rare in the States, but in Canada they grow only here, thanks to the region's rich soils and relatively warm, sheltered climate.

A good deal of the Carolinian flora and fauna is coming under increasing threat from southern Ontario's urban and agricultural sprawl. These days much of the original forest has shrunk to a mosaic of fragments protected by national and provincial parks. The forests are most often visited by tourists for the astounding October colours, but if you're looking for **wildlife** you might also catch Canada's only marsupial, the **opossum**; or other southern species like the **fox squirrel** (introduced on Lake Erie's Pelee Island); the **eastern mole**, which occurs only in Essex County on Lake Erie's north shore; and the **eastern vole**, found only in a narrow band around Lake Erie.

Naturalists are equally drawn here for the **birds**, many of which are found nowhere else in Canada, especially during seasonal migrations, when up to one hundred species can easily be seen in a day. Most noteworthy of the more unusual species is the golden swamp warbler, a bird of almost unnaturally colourful plumage. More common visitors are hooded and Kentucky warblers, blue-winged and golden-winged warblers, gnatcatchers and virtually every species of eastern North American hawk. Sharp-shin hawks are common, and during autumn migrations of up to 70,000 broad-winged hawks might be seen in a single day near Port Stanley on Lake Erie's north shore.

In the wetlands bordering the forests, particularly at Long Point on Lake Erie, you can search out **reptiles** found nowhere else in the country. Most impressive is the water-loving fox snake, a harmless animal that reaches often well over a metre in length, but is often killed because of its resemblance to the rattlesnake and venomous copperhead – neither of which is found in the region. Also present, but in marked decline, are several **turtle** species, especially Blanding's, wood, spotted and spiny softshell.

GREAT LAKES-ST LAWRENCE FOREST

Occurring in one of the most densely populated parts of Canada, the mixed conifer forests of the **Great Lakes-St Lawrence** area have been

WILDLIFE CHECKLIST

This is by no means an exhaustive list of all Canada's wildlife species and their habitats – it should be treated simply as an indication of the places and the times that you are most likely to see certain species and types of wildlife.

Beluga, fin, humpback, blue and **minke whales**: near Tadoussac, north of Québec City; summer.

Bison: Wood Buffalo National Park (Alberta).

Black bears: Glacier National Park (BC); Banff and Jasper national parks (BC); Kananaskis Country (Alberta); summer.

Butterfly migrations: Point Pelee and Long Point, Lake Erie (Ontario); spring and autumn.

Caribou: Dempster Highway north of Dawson City (Yukon); autumn.

Cranes and pelicans: Last Mountain Lake, northwest of Regina (Saskatchewan); late August.

Dall's sheep: Sheep Mountain, Kluane National Park (Yukon); summer.

Desert species: Cacti, sagebrush, rattlesnakes and kangaroo rats around Osoyoos (BC); summer.

Eagles and owls: Boundary Bay, 20km south of Vancouver (BC); winter.

Elk: Banff and Jasper national parks (BC); Kananaskis Country (Alberta); summer.

Grey whales: Pacific Rim National Park, Vancouver Island (BC); spring and summer.

Grizzly bears: Glacier National Park and at Khutzeymateen Estuary, north of Prince Rupert (BC); August.

Killer whales: Robson Bight in Johnstone Strait, Vancouver Island (BC); summer.

Orchids: Bruce Peninsula National Park (Ontario); spring and summer.

Polar bears: near Churchill, Manitoba; autumn.

Prairie species: Hawks, coyotes and rattlesnakes in the Milk River region (Alberta); May and June.

Salmon: Adams River sockeye salmon run near Salmon Arm (BC); October.

Sea birds: Gannets, murres and black kittiwakes around Cape St Mary's (Newfoundland); water-fowl, sea birds and seals in the Queen Charlotte Islands (BC); northern gannets on Bonaventure Island, Gaspé Peninsula (Québec); June and July.

Sea otters and sea lions: off Pacific Rim National Park, Vancouver Island (BC); spring and summer.

Snow geese: Cap-Tourmente, north of Québec City; autumn.

Wild flowers: Numerous woodland species on Vancouver Island and the Gulf Islands, and at Mount Revelstoke National Park (BC); late spring to summer.

---

heavily logged and severely affected by urbanization. Most of the trees are southern species – beech and sugar maple, red and white pines – but are mixed with the eastern hemlock, spruce, jack pine, paper birch and balsam fir typical of more northerly forests.

Ironically, widespread human disturbance has, if anything, created a greater diversity of forest types, which makes this region second only to southern British Columbia in the number of bird species it supports. It also provides for large numbers of **white-tailed deer**, a rare beneficiary of logging as it prefers to browse along the edges of clearings. In the evergreen stands on the north shore of the St Lawrence there are also large numbers of Canada's smallest mammal, the **pygmy shrew**. These tiny animals must eat their own weight in food daily and can't rest for more than an hour or so – they'd starve to death if they tried to sleep through the night.

GRASSLAND

Contrary to the popular image of Canada's interior as a huge prairie of waving wheat, true grassland covers only ten percent of the country. Most is concentrated in the southernmost reaches of Alberta and Saskatchewan, with tiny spillovers in Manitoba and British Columbia – areas which lie in the Rockies' rain shadow and are too dry to support forest.

Two grassland belts once thrived in the region, tall-grass prairie in the north and short-grass in the south. Farming has now not only put large areas of each under crops, but also decimated most of the large mammals that roamed the range – pronghorns, mule deer, white-tailed deer and elk – not to mention their predators, such as wolves, grizzlies, coyotes, foxes, bobcats and cougars.

The most dramatic loss from the grasslands, though, has been **bison** (or buffalo), the continent's largest land mammal. Once numbering an estimated 45 million, bison are now limited to just a few free-roaming herds in Canada. They're extraordinarily impressive animals – the average bull stands six feet at the shoulder and weighs over a ton – and early prairie settlers were so struck with their size that they believed bison, not the climate, had been responsible for clearing the grasslands.

Once almost as prevalent as the bison, but now almost as rare, is the **pronghorn**, a beautiful tawny-gold antelope species. Capable of speeds of over 100kph, it's the continent's swiftest land mammal, so you'll generally see nothing but distinctive white rump disappearing at speed. Uniquely adapted for speed and stamina, the pronghorn has long legs, a heart twice the size of similar-sized animals, and an astonishingly wide windpipe. It also complements its respiratory machinery by running with its mouth open to gulp maximum amounts of air. Though only the size of a large dog, it has larger eyes than those of a horse, a refinement that spots predators several kilometres away. These days, however, wolves and coyotes are more likely to be after the prairie's new masters – countless small rodents such as gophers, ground squirrels and jackrabbits.

Birds have had to adapt not only to the prairie's dryness but also, of course, to the lack of extensive tree cover, and most species nest on the ground; many are also able to survive on reduced amounts of water and rely on seed-centred diets. Others confine themselves to occasional ponds, lakes and "sloughs", which are important breeding grounds for ducks, grebes, herons, pelicans, rails and many more. Other birds typical of the grassland in its natural state are the marbled godwit, the curlew, and raptors such as the **prairie falcon**, a close relation of the peregrine falcon that's capable of diving speeds of up to 290kph.

BOREAL FOREST

The **boreal forest** is Canada's largest single ecosystem, bigger than all the others combined. Stretching in a broad belt from Newfoundland to the Yukon, it fills the area between the eastern forests, grasslands and the northern tundra, occupying a good slice of every province except British Columbia. Only certain **trees** thrive in

this zone of long, cold winters, short summers and acidic soils: although the cover is not identical countrywide, expect to see billions of white and black spruce (plus red spruce in the east), balsam fir, tamarack (larch) and jack pine, as well as such deciduous species as birch, poplar and aspen – all of which are ideal for wood pulp, making the boreal forest the staple resource of the country's **lumber industry**.

If you spend any time in the backcountry you'll also come across **muskeg**: neither land nor water, this porridge-like bog is the breeding ground of choice for pestilent hordes of mosquitoes and blackflies – and Canada has 1.3 million square kilometres of it. It also harbours mosses, scrub willow, pitcher plant, leatherleaf, sundew, cranberry and even the occasional orchid.

The boreal forest supports just about every animal recognized as distinctively Canadian: moose, beaver, black bear, wolf and lynx, plus a broad cross section of small mammals and creatures such as deer, caribou and coyote from transitional forest-tundra and aspen-parkland habitats to the north and south.

Wolves are still numerous in Canada, but hunting and harassment has pushed them to the northernmost parts of the boreal forest. Their supposed ferocity is more myth than truth; intelligent and elusive creatures, they rarely harm humans, and it's unlikely you'll see any – though you may well hear their howling if you're out in the sticks.

Lynx are even more elusive. One of the northern forest's most elegant animals, this big cat requires a 150- to 200-square-kilometre range, making Canada's northern wilderness one of the world's few regions capable of sustaining a viable population. Nocturnal hunters, lynx feed on deer and moose but favour the hare, a common boreal creature that is to the forest's predators what the lemming is to the carnivores of the tundra.

Beavers, on the other hand, are commonly seen all over Canada. You may catch them at dawn or dusk, heads just above the water as they glide across lakes and rivers. Signs of their legendary activity include log jams across streams and ponds, stumps of felled saplings resembling sharpened pencils, and dens which look like domed piles of mud and sticks.

Lakes, streams and marshy muskeg margins are all favoured by **moose**. A lumbering animal with magnificent spreading antlers, it is the largest member of the deer family and is found over most of Canada, but especially near swampy ground, where it likes to graze on mosses and lichens. It's also a favourite with hunters, and few northern bars are without their moose head – perhaps the only place you'll see this solitary and reclusive species.

Forest wetlands also offer refuge for **ducks and geese**, with loons, grebes and songbirds attracted to their surrounding undergrowth. Canada's three species of ptarmigan – willow, rock and white-tailed – are also common, and you'll see plenty of big **raptors**, including the great grey owl, Canada's largest owl. Many boreal birds migrate, and even those that don't, such as hawks, jays, ravens and grouse, tend to move a little way south, sometimes breaking out into southern Canada in mass movements known as "irruptions". Smaller birds, like chickadees, waxwings and finches, are particularly fond of these sporadic forays.

MOUNTAIN FORESTS

Mountain forests cover much of western Canada and, depending on location and elevation, divide into four types: West Coast, Columbia, montane and sub-alpine.

WEST COAST FOREST

The **West Coast**'s torrential rainfall, mild maritime climate, deep soils and long growing season produce Canada's most impressive forests and its biggest trees. Swathes of luxuriant temperate **rainforest** cover much of Vancouver Island and the Pacific coast, dominated by Sitka spruce, western red cedar, Pacific silver fir, western hemlock, western yew and, biggest of all, **Douglas fir**, some of which tower 90 metres high and are 1200 years old. However, these conifers make valuable timber, and much of this forest is under severe threat from logging. Some of the best stands – a fraction of the original – have been preserved on the Queen Charlotte Islands and in Vancouver Island's Pacific Rim National Park.

Below the luxuriant, dripping canopy of the big trees lies an **undergrowth** teeming with life. Shrubs and bushes such as salal, huckleberry, bunchberry, salmonberry and twinberry thrive alongside mosses, ferns, lichens, liverworts, skunk cabbage and orchids. All sorts of animals can be found here, most notably the **cougar** and its main prey, the Columbian blacktail **deer**, a subspecies of the mule deer. **Birds** are legion, and include a wealth of woodland species such as the Townsend's warbler, Wilson's warbler, orange-crowned warbler, junco, Swainson's thrush and golden-crowned kinglet. Rarer birds include the rufous **hummingbird**, which migrates from its wintering grounds in Mexico to feed on the forest's numerous nectar-bearing flowers.

COLUMBIA FOREST

The **Columbia forest** covers the lower slopes (400–1400m) of British Columbia's interior mountains and much of the Rockies. **Trees** here are similar to those of the West Coast's warmer and wetter rainforest – western red cedar, western hemlock and Douglas fir – with Sitka spruce, which rarely thrives away from the coast, the notable exception. The undercover, too, is similar, with lots of devil's club (a particularly vicious thorn), azaleas, black and red twinberry, salmonberry and redberry alder. Mountain lily, columbine, bunchberry and heartleaf arnica are among the common flowers.

Few mammals live exclusively in the forests with the exception of the **red squirrel**, which makes a meal of conifer seeds, and is in turn preyed on by hawks, owls, coyotes and weasels, among others. Bigger predators roam the mountain forest, however, most notably the **brown bear**, a western variant of the ubiquitous **black bear**. Aside from the coyote, the tough, agile black bear is one of the continent's most successful carnivores and the one you're most likely to see around campgrounds and rubbish dumps. Black bears have adapted to a wide range of habitats and food sources, and their only natural enemies – save wolves, which may attack young cubs – are hunters, who bag some 30,000 annually in North America.

Scarcer but still hunted is the famous **grizzly bear**, a far larger and potentially dangerous creature distinguished by its brownish fur and the ridged hump on its back. Now extinct in many of its original habitats, the grizzly is largely confined to the remoter slopes of the Rockies and West Coast ranges, where it feeds mainly on berries and salmon. Like other bears, grizzlies are unpredictable and readily provoked –

see p.598 for tips on minimizing unpleasant encounters.

MONTANE FOREST

Montane forest covers the more southerly and sheltered reaches of the Rockies and the dry plateaux of interior British Columbia, where spindly Douglas fir, western larch, ponderosa pine and the **lodgepole pine** predominate. Like its eastern counterpart, the jack pine, the lodgepole requires intense heat before opening and releasing its seeds, and huge stands of these trees grew in the aftermath of the forest fires which accompanied the building and running of the railways.

Plentiful voles and small rodents attract **coyotes**, whose yapping – an announcement of territorial claims – you'll often hear at night close to small towns. Coyotes are spreading northwards into the Yukon and Northwest Territories and eastwards into Ontario and Québec, a proliferation that continues despite massive extermination campaigns, prompted by the coyotes' taste for livestock.

Few predators have the speed to keep up with coyotes – only the stealthy **cougar**, or wolves hunting in tandem, can successfully bring them down. Cougars are now severely depleted in Canada, and the British Columbia interior and Vancouver Island are the only regions where they survive in significant numbers. Among the biggest and most beautiful of the carnivores, they seem to arouse the greatest bloodlust in hunters.

Ponderosa and lodgepole pines provide fine cover for **birds** like goshawks, Swainson's hawks and lesser species such as ruby-crowned kinglets, warblers, pileated woodpeckers, nuthatches and chickadees. In the forest's lowest reaches the vegetation and birds are those of the southern prairies – semi-arid regions of sagebrush, prickly pear and bunch grasses, dotted with lakes full of common **ducks** such asmallard, shoveler and widgeon. You might also see the cinnamon teal, a red version of the more common green-wing teal, a bird whose limited distribution draws bird-watchers to British Columbia on its own account.

SUB-ALPINE FOREST

Sub-alpine forest covers mountain slopes from 1300m to 2200m throughout the Rockies and much of British Columbia, supporting lodgepole, whitebark and limber pines, alpine fir and Engelmann spruce. It also contains a preponderance of **alpine larch**, a deciduous conifer whose vivid autumnal yellows dot the mountainsides to beautiful effect.

One of the more common animals of this zone is the **elk**, or **wapiti**, a powerful member of the deer family which can often be seen summering in large herds above the tree line. Elk court and mate during the autumn, making a thin nasal sound called "bugling". Respect their privacy, as rutting elk have notoriously unpredictable temperaments.

Small herds of **mule deer** migrate between forests and alpine meadows, using small glands between their hooves to leave a scent for other herd members to follow. They're named after their distinctive ears, designed to provide early warning of predators. Other smaller animals which are also attracted to the sub-alpine forest include the golden-mantled ground squirrel, and birds such as Clark's nutcracker, both tame and curious creatures which often gather around campgrounds in search of scraps.

ALPINE ZONES

Alpine zones occur in mountains above the tree line, which in Canada means parts of the Rockies, much of British Columbia and large areas of the Yukon. Plant and animal life varies hugely between summer and winter, and according to terrain and exposure to the elements – sometimes it resembles that of the tundra, at others it recalls the profile of lower forest habitats.

In spring, alpine meadows are carpeted with breathtaking displays of **wild flowers**: clumps of Parnassus grass, lilies, anemones, Indian paintbrushes, lupins and a wealth of yellow flowers such as arnica, cinquefoil, glacier lily and wood betony. These meadows make excellent pasture, attracting elk and mule deer in summer, as well as full-time residents such as **Dall's sheep**, the related **bighorn** and the incredible **mountain goat**, perhaps the hardiest of Canada's bigger mammals. Staying close to the roughest terrain possible, mountain goats are equipped with short, stolid legs, flexible toes and non-skid soles, all designed for clambering over near-vertical slopes, grazing well out of reach of their less agile predators.

Marmots, resembling hugely overstuffed squirrels, take things easier and hibernate through the worst of the winter and beyond. In a good year they can sleep for eight months, prey only to grizzly bears, which are strong enough and have the claws to dig down into their dens. In their waking periods they can be tame and friendly, often nibbling contentedly in the sunnier corners of campgrounds. When threatened, however, they produce a piercing and unearthly whistle. (They can also do a lot of damage: some specialize in chewing the radiator hoses of parked cars.) The strange little **pika**, a relative of the rabbit, is more elusive but keeps itself busy throughout the year, living off a miniature haystack of fodder which it builds up during the summer.

Birds are numerous in summer, and include rosy finches, pipits and blue grouse, but few manage to live in the alpine zone year-round. One which does is the white-tailed **ptarmigan**, a plump, partridge-like bird which, thanks to its heavily feathered feet and legs, is able to snowshoe around deep drifts of snow; its white winter plumage provides camouflage. Unfortunately, ptarmigans can be as slow-moving and stupid as barnyard chickens, making them easy targets for hunters and predators.

COASTLINES

Canada has three coastlines: the Atlantic, the Pacific and the Arctic (dealt with under "Tundra"). Each boasts a profusion of maritime, dunal and intertidal life; the Pacific coast, warmed by the Japanese current, actually has the greatest number of species of any temperate shore. Few people are very interested in the small fry, however – most come for the big mammals, and **whales** in particular.

Grey whales are most common in the Pacific, and are often easily spotted from mainland headlands in the February to May and September to October periods as they migrate between the Arctic and their breeding grounds off Mexico. Once hunted close to the point of extinction, they've now returned in large numbers, and most West Coast harbours have charter companies offering whale-watching tours.

Humpback whales are another favourite, largely because they're curious and follow sightseeing boats, but also because of their surface acrobatics and long, haunting "songs". They too were hunted to near-extinction, and though protected by international agreement since 1966 they still number less than ten percent of their original population.

Vancouver Island's inner coast supports one of the world's most concentrated populations of **killer whales** or **orcas**. These are often seen in family groups or "pods" travelling close to shore, usually on the trail of large fish – which on the West Coast means **salmon**. The orca, however, is the only whale whose diet also runs to warm-blooded animals – hence the "killer" tag – and it will gorge on walrus, seal and even minke, grey and beluga whales.

Another West Coast inhabitant, the **sea otter**, differs from most marine mammals in that it keeps itself warm with a thick soft coat of fur rather than with blubber. This brought it to the attention of early Russian and British fur traders, and by the beginning of this century it was virtually extinct. Re-introduced in 1969 to Vancouver Island's northwest coast, they are now breeding successfully at the heart of their original range. With binoculars, it's often easy to spot these charming creatures lolling on their backs, cracking open sea urchins or mussels with a rock and using their stomachs as anvils; they often lie bobbing asleep, entwined in kelp to stop them floating away.

Northern **fur seals** breed on Alaska's Pribilof Islands but are often seen off the British Columbian coast during their migrations. Like their cousin, the northern **sea lion**, a year-round resident, they are "eared seals", who can manage rudimentary shuffling on land thanks to short rear limbs which can be rotated for forward movement. They also swim with strokes from front flippers, as opposed to the slithering, fishlike action of true seals.

The **Atlantic**'s colder waters nurture fewer overall species than the Pacific coast, but many birds and larger mammals – especially **whales** – are common to both. One of the Atlantic region's more distinctive creatures is the **harp seal** (or saddleback), a true seal species that migrates in late winter to breeding grounds off Newfoundland and in the Greenland and White seas. Most pups are born on the pack ice, and for about two weeks sport fluffy white coats that have been highly prized by the fur trade for centuries. Until the late-1960s tens of thousands of young seals died annually in an unsupervised slaughter whose methods – clubbing and skinning alive – brought about outrage on an international scale (see p.390–391).

TUNDRA

Tundra extends over much of northern Yukon and the Northwest Territories, stretching between the boreal forest and the polar seas. Part grassland and part wasteland, it's a region distinguished by high winds, bitter cold and **permafrost**, a layer of perpetually frozen subsoil which covers over thirty percent of Canada. The tundra is not only the domain of ice and emptiness, however: long hours of summer sunshine and the melting of topsoil nurture a carpet of wild flowers and many species of birds and mammals have adapted to the vagaries of climate and terrain.

Vegetation is uniformly stunted by poor drainage, acidic soils and permafrost, which prevents the formation of deep roots and locks nutrients in the ice. **Trees** like birch and willow can grow, but they spread their branches over a wide area, rarely rising over a metre in height. Over 99 percent of the remaining vegetation consists of perennials like **grasses** and sedges, small flowering annuals, mosses, lichens and shrubs. Most have evolved ingenious ways of protecting themselves against the elements: Arctic cotton grass, for example, grows in large insulated hummocks in which the interior temperature is higher than the air outside; others have large, waxy leaves to conserve moisture or catch as much sunlight as possible. **Wild flowers** during the short, intense spring can be superlative, covering seemingly inert ground in a carpet of purple mountain saxifrage, yellow Arctic poppy, indigo clusters of Arctic forget-me-not and the pink buds of Jacob's ladder.

Tundra grasses provide some of the first links in the food chain, nourishing mammals such as white **Arctic ground squirrels**, also known as parkas, as their fur is used by the Inuit to make parka jackets. Vegetation also provides the staple diet of **lemmings**, amongst the most remarkable of the Arctic fauna. Instead of hibernating these creatures live under the snow, busily tucking away on shoots in order to double their weight daily – the intake they need merely to survive. They also breed almost continuously, which is just as well for they are the mainstay of a long list of predators. Chief of these are **Arctic white foxes**, ermines and weasels, though birds, bears and Arctic wolves may also hunt them in preference to larger prey.

Because they provide a staple diet to so many, lemming populations have a marked effect on the life cycles of numerous creatures.

A notable exception is the **caribou**, a member of the reindeer family and the most populous of the big tundra mammals. Caribou are known above all for their epic migrations, frequently involving thousands of animals, which start in March when the herds leave their wintering grounds on the fringes of the boreal forest for calving grounds to the north. The exact purpose of these migrations is still a matter of conjecture. They certainly prevent the overgrazing of the tundra's fragile mosses and lichens, and probably also enable the caribou to shake off some of the wolves that would otherwise shadow the herd (wolves have to find southerly dens at this time to bear their own pups). The timing of treks also means that calving takes place before the arrival of biting insects, which can claim as many calves as predators – an adult caribou can lose as much as a litre of blood a week to insects.

The tundra's other large mammal is the **musk ox**, a vast, shaggy herbivore and close cousin of the bison. The musk ox's Achilles' heel is a tendency to form lines or circles when threatened – a perfect defence against wolves, but not against rifle-toting hunters, who until the introduction of conservation measures threatened to be their undoing. Canada now has some of the world's largest free-roaming herds, although – like the caribou – they're still hunted for food and fur by the Inuit.

Tundra **birds** number about a hundred species and are mostly migratory. Three quarters of these are waterfowl, which arrive first to take advantage of streams, marshes and small lakes created by surface meltwater: Arctic wetlands provide nesting grounds for numerous swans, geese and ducks, as well as the loon, which is immortalized on the back of the Canadian dollar coin. The red-necked **phalarope** is a particularly specialized visitor, able to feed on aquatic insects and plankton, though not as impressive in its abilities as the migratory **Arctic tern**, whose 32,000-kilometre round trip from the Antarctic is the longest annual migration of any creature on the planet. The handful of non-migratory birds tend to be scavengers like the raven, or predators like the **gyrfalcon**, the world's largest falcon, which preys on Arctic hares and ptarmigan. Jaegers, gulls, hawks and owls largely depend on the lemming: the snowy owl, for example, synchronizes its returns to southern Canada with four-year dips in the lemming population.

Fauna on the Arctic **coast** has a food chain that starts with plankton and algae, ranging up through tiny crustaceans, clams and mussels, sea cucumbers and sea urchins, cod, ringed and bearded seals, to beluga whales and **polar bears** – perhaps the most evocative of all tundra creatures, but still being killed in their hundreds for "sport" despite almost thirty years of hunting restrictions. Migrating **birds** are especially common here, notably near Nunaluk Spit on the Yukon coast, which is used as a corridor and stopover by millions of loons, swans, geese, plovers, sandpipers, dowitchers, eagles, hawks, guillemots and assorted songbirds.

CANADA'S ABORIGINAL PEOPLES

Nearly a million Canadians can claim at least partial aboriginal ancestry. Aboriginal populations continue to increase, and interest in their cultural heritage, by aborigines and non-aborigines alike, continues to grow. However, the term "aborigine" does not indicate a common or shared culture, only descent from groups of people who arrived on the continent long before Europeans. Canada's constitution specifies three categories of "aboriginal peoples": Indian, Inuit and Métis.

The term "**Indian**" is now recognized as a misnomer, but other attempts to be more specific, such as "Amerindians" or "Native Canadians", have been no more successful and you're likely to hear several different terms on your travels. The terms "First Nations" and "aboriginals" are in vogue but again there is the possibility of more change. Treated as wards of the federal government since the birth of Canada, the Indians were put in a different legal category from all other Canadians by the Indian Acts in the nineteenth century. Modern legal distinctions divide this group further into those who are recognized as "Indian" by the federal government – a status bestowed on more than 800,000 Canadians – and those who are denied this recognition, the so-called "non-status Indians". Amongst status Indians there are 633 aboriginal bands (the term "tribe" has also become outmoded) across Canada. Some communities number fewer than 100 inhabitants and others more than 5000. Status enables rights to fishing, hunting and living on a reservation, while non-status denies these rights but allows a person to vote, buy property and alcohol. Status can be lost and gained through marriage, an act of parliament or even a band taking a vote on the matter.

Later, as Canada's attention turned to its vast nothern regions, the **Inuit** were also recognized as falling under federal jurisdiction. The Inuit have a separate origin, arriving much later to North America and inhabiting the inhospitable lands of Arctic Canada. The term Inuit totally replaced use of the derogatory term "Eskimo" in the 1970s. Eskimo is an Algonkian word for "eaters of raw meat". The Inuit share a common origin and a single language and at present number around 27,000.

With a current population of 400,000, the **Métis** are the product of the unions between male fur traders, usually French-Canadians, and native women, particularly Cree. For centuries they were not recognized as Canadians or aborigines, and with no rights they wandered the country, unable to settle. After a failed rebellion in 1885, they almost disappeared from social and political life and became "the forgotten people", largely poverty-stricken squatters on Crown land. Finally, in 1982, they were recognised as a First Nation in the Constitution.

Because of the distances separating them, each nation and even each community has its own characteristics. Their personality and cul-

ABORIGINAL POPULATION		
Population in Canada defining itself as aboriginal: number of individuals and percentage of local population of each region (1996)		
		Percentage
Atlantic	30,300	1.3
Québec	76,400	1.0
Ontario	159,500	1.4
Manitoba	119,500	10.6
Saskatchewan	105,300	10.5
Alberta	137,500	4.9
British Columbia	135,500	3.6
Yukon	6,200	18.2
Northwest Territories	41,200	62.0
Total	811,400	2.7

ture are fashioned by history, the environment and by their surrounding neighbours. A large part of the aboriginal people live in relatively close contact with non-aboriginal people and interact on a daily basis with cultures that have a determining influence on their way of life.

If there is any thread linking these groups, it is the cultural revival experienced over the last forty years. Under the banner of national political movements, all of these groups have renewed their commitment to organizing their social world, to re-establishing legal relationships to the land, and to maintaining and revitalizing their cultures and languages.

COLONIZATION

When Europeans first arrived in northern North America they saw it as a *terra nullius* – empty land – but in reality it was a complex environment containing many cultures and communities. On the west coast the peoples had built societies of wealth and sophistication with plentiful resources from the sea and forest; in the prairies and northern tundra, the aborigines lived off the vast herds of buffalo and caribou; in central Canada the forests were home to peoples who harvested wild rice from the marshes and grew corn, squash and beans by the rivers, supplementing their harvest with fishing and hunting; on the east coast and in the far north, the sea and land supplied their needs, and with incredible ingenuity enabled the inhabitants to survive harsh conditions.

Encounters between aboriginal and non-aboriginal people began to increase in number and complexity in the 1500s. There was an increased exchange of goods, trade deals, friendships and intermarriage as well as military and trade alliances. For at least two hundred years, the newcomers would not have been able to survive the rigours of the climate, succeed in their businesses (fishing, whaling, fur trading), or dodge each other's bullets, without aboriginal help.

Meanwhile **diseases** (typhoid, influenza, diptheria, plague, measles, tuberculosis, venereal disease and scarlet fever) killed tens of thousands – it is estimated that within a 200-year period aboriginal populations were reduced by as much as 95 percent.

As the fur trade intensified, the animal populations were wiped out in certain areas. This not only removed the traditional hunting practices but sparked off **inter-tribal wars**, all the more bloody now firearms were involved.

During this period, the French and British were few in number, the land seemed inhospitable and they feared attack from the aboriginal nations surrounding them. They were also fighting wars for trade and dominance – they needed alliances with Indian nations, so many **treaties** were consequently negotiated. The treaties seemed to recognize the nationhood of aboriginal peoples and their equality but also demanded the authority of the monarch and, increasingly, the ceding of large tracts of land (particularly to British control for settlement and protection from seizure by the French and Americans). Usually what was agreed orally differed from what actually appeared in the treaties. The aborigines did accept the monarch, but only as a kind of kin figure, a distant "protector" who could be called on to safeguard their interests and enforce treaty agreements. They had no notion of giving up their land, a concept foreign to aboriginal cultures:

In my language, there is no word for "surrender". There is no word. I cannot describe "surrender" to you in my language, so how do you expect my people to [have] put their X on "surrender"?

Chief François Paulette.

In 1763, the **Royal Proclamation** was a defining document in the relationship between the natives and the newcomers. Issued in the name of the king, it summarized the rules and regulations that were to govern British dealings with the aboriginal peoples – especially in relation to the question of land. It stated that aboriginal people were not to be "molested or disturbed" on their lands. Transactions involving aboriginal land were to be negotiated properly between the Crown and "assemblies of Indians". Aboriginal lands were to be acquired only by fair dealing: treaty, or purchase by the Crown. The aboriginal nations were portrayed as autonomous political entities, with their own internal political authority. Allowing for British settlement, it still safeguarded the rights of the aborigines.

By the 1800s, the relationship between aboriginal and non-aboriginal people began to tilt on its foundation of rough equality. Through immigration the number of settlers was swelling, while disease and poverty continued to diminish aboriginal populations – by 1812, whites outnumbered indigenous people in Upper Canada by ten to one. The fur trade, which was established on a solid economic partnership between traders and trappers, was a declining industry. The new economy was based on timber, mining and agriculture and it needed land from the natives, who began to be seen as "impediments to progress". Colonial governments in Upper and Lower Canada no longer needed military allies, the British were victors in Canada, and the USA had won its independence. There was also a new attitude of European superiority over all other peoples and policies of domination and assimilation slowly replaced those of partnership.

Ironically, the transformation from respectful co-existence to **domination** by non-aboriginal laws and institutions began with the main instruments of the partnership: the treaties and the Royal Proclamation of 1763. These documents offered aboriginal people not only peace and friendship, respect and approximate equality, but also "protection". Protection was the leading edge of domination. At first, it meant preservation of aboriginal lands and cultural integrity from encroachment by settlers. Later, it meant "assistance", a code word implying an encouragement to stop being a part of aboriginal society and merge into the settler society.

Protection took the form of compulsory education, economic adjustment programmes, social and political control by federal agents, and much more. These policies, combined with missionary efforts to civilize and convert, tore wide holes in aboriginal cultures, autonomy and identity.

RESERVES

In 1637, with a Jesuit settlement at Sillery in New France, the establishment of "**reserves**" of land for aboriginals (usually of inadequate size and resources) began. Designed to "protect", they instead led to isolation and impoverishment. In 1857 the Province of Canada passed an act to "Encourage the Gradual Civilization of the Indian tribes" – Indians of "good character" could be declared "non-Indian" by a panel of whites. Only one man, a Mohawk, is known to have accepted the invitation.

Confederation in 1867 was negotiated without reference to aboriginal nations. Indeed, newly elected Prime Minister John A. Macdonald announced that it would be his government's goal to "do away with the tribal system, and assimilate the Indian people in all respects with the inhabitants of the Dominion."

The **British North America Act**, young Canada's new constitution, made "Indians, and Lands reserved for the Indians" a subject for government regulation, like mines or roads. Indians became wards of the federal government and Parliament took on the job with vigour – passing laws to replace traditional aboriginal governments with band councils who had insignificant powers, taking control of valuable resources located on reserves, taking charge of reserve finances, imposing an unfamiliar system of land tenure, and applying non-aboriginal concepts of marriage and parenting.

These and other laws were codified in the main **Indian Acts** of 1876, 1880 and 1884. The Department of the Interior (later, Indian Affairs) sent Indian agents to every region to see that the laws were obeyed. In 1884, the **potlatch ceremony**, central to the cultures of west coast aboriginal nations, was outlawed. A year later the **sun dance**, central to the cultures of prairie aboriginal nations, was outlawed. Participation was a criminal offence.

In 1885, the Department of Indian Affairs instituted a **pass system**. No outsider could come onto a reserve to do business with an aboriginal resident without permission from the Indian agent (a sort of government official with law enforcement powers). Occasionally all aboriginal person could not *leave* the reserve without permission from the Indian agent, either. Reserves were beginning to resemble prisons.

In 1849, the first of what would become a network of residential schools for aboriginal children was opened in Alderville, Ontario. Church and government leaders had come to the conclusion that the problem (as they saw it) of aboriginal independence and "savagery" could be solved by taking children from their families at an early age and instilling the ways of the dominant society during eight or nine years of residential schooling far from home. Attendance was compulsory. Aboriginal languages, customs and native skills were suppressed. The bonds between many hundreds of aboriginal children, their families and whole nations were broken.

During this stage Canadian governments moved aboriginal communities from one place to another at will. If aboriginal people were thought to have too little food, they could be relocated where game was more plentiful or jobs might be found. If they were suffering from illness, they could be sent to new communities where health services, sanitary facilities and permanent housing might be provided. If they were in the way of expanding agricultural frontiers, or in possession of land needed for settlement, they could be removed "for their own protection". If their lands contained minerals to be mined, forests to be cut, or rivers to be dammed, they could be displaced "in the national interest".

The result of centuries of mistreatment is that by almost every statistical indicator the aboriginal population is highly **disadvantaged** compared to all other Canadians. The problems affecting native peoples are grim, as alcoholism, drug use and sexual abuse continue to plague reserves. Infant mortality is twice as high among natives than non-natives, suicide rates among young people are five times higher among Indians than other Canadians, and life expectancy is seven years less for natives. Native peoples are also vastly over-represented in jails across the country.

RESURGENCE

The **1940s** were the beginning of a new era. Around 3000 aborigines and unrecorded numbers of Métis and non-status Indians had fought for their country in both **World Wars**, and although accepted on the battlefield they were still badly treated at home. Aboriginal leaders emerged, forcefully expressing their people's desire to gain their rightful position of equality with other Canadians and maintain their cultural heritage, and in British Columbia, Alberta, Saskatchewan and Ontario, aboriginals formed provincially based organizations to protect and advance their interests. The Canadian public became more aware of the shocking way native society was being treated and how far their living standards had fallen behind all other groups of citizens. The **1951 Indian Act** rescinded the laws banning the potlatch and other ceremonies and aboriginal members were given the freedom to enter public bars to consume alcohol. But, on the whole, government oppression remained formidable. The **right to vote** in federal elections was granted only in 1960.

The rebirth of Canada's indigenous people can be traced to 1969, when a federal "**white paper**" proposed the elimination of Indian status. The result was a native backlash that forced the Trudeau Government to retreat and led to the creation of the **National Indian Brotherhood**, the forerunner of today's **Assembly of First Nations.**

Also in 1969, all Indian agents were withdrawn from reserves, and aboriginal political organizations started receiving government funding. Increasingly, these organizations focused on the need for full recognition of their aboriginal rights and renegotiation of the treaties. They believed that only in this way could they rise above their disadvantaged position in Canadian society. By 1973, aboriginals had local control of education and today more than half of all aboriginal students who live on reserves attend their own community schools.

RECLAIMING THE LAND

Land reserved for aboriginal people was steadily whittled away after its original allocation. Almost two-thirds of it has "disappeared" by various means since Confederation. In some cases, the government failed to deliver as much land as specified in a treaty. In other cases, it expropriated or sold reserved land, rarely with aboriginals as willing vendors. Once in a while, outright fraud took place. Even when aboriginals were able to keep hold of reserved land, the government sometimes sold its resources to outsiders. Some aboriginal nations have gone to court to force governments to recognize their rights to land and resources, and some have been successful. A series of court decisions in the 1970s confirmed that aboriginal peoples have more than a strong moral case for redress on land and resource issues – they have legal rights.

In recent years, Canada has come to a few new treaty-like **agreements**. The Inuit and Cree took Québec to court in 1973, to stop a major hydro-electric project that threatened to decimate their traditional hunting grounds. The consequent **James Bay and Northern Québec Agreement**, signed in 1975, gave Inuit and Crees (and later the Naskapi) $225 million over 20 years in return for 981,610 square kilometres of territory. They were also given lands with exclusive hunting and trapping rights, native-controlled education and health authorities. With their funds the Cree have set up successful businesses such as Air Creebec and the Cree Construction Company. The **Cree-Naskapi Act**, passed in 1984, followed and enabled the Cree and Naskapi to establish their own forms of self-government – the first such legislation in Canada.

In 1973, the Supreme Court of Canada's decision on the Haida Indians led the federal government to establish a negotiating process to resolve **land claims** by recognizing two broad classes of claims – comprehensive and specific. Comprehensive claims are based on the recognition that there are continuing aboriginal rights to lands and natural resources and have a wide scope including such things as land title, fishing and trapping rights, financial compensation and other social and economic benefits. Specific claims deal with specific grievances that aborigines may have regarding the fulfilment of treaties.

In 1982, the government's recognition of land claims was renewed by a constitutional change, which touched off further favourable court decisions leading to new treaties with the Inuit of the Northwest Territories (1984 and 1993), the Yukon First Nations (1993) and the Nisga'a in BC (1996).

From the early 1970s to March 1996, the government provided aboriginal groups with approximately $380 million for work on their claims. This money enabled aboriginal peoples to conduct research into **treaties and rights** and to research, develop and negotiate their claims. But the negotiations are notoriously long and painstaking, and until 1990 there was a limit of no more than six comprehensive claims at one time. Since 1973, aboriginal peoples have submitted more than 700 specific claims to the federal government. By early 1996, the government had concluded 392 claims – 151 had resulted in settlement agreements, 76 were rejected, 40 were before the courts, 98 were closed at the request of aborigines and 27 were referred to other areas of Department of Indian Affairs and Northern Development (DIAND) for settlement. At the same time, an additional 354 specific claims were being processed – 94 were in negotiation and 259 were under review.

THE NINETIES

The ownership of land and control over funding have brought opportunities for economic self-sufficiency and expansion previously unavailable to aboriginal groups. This last decade has seen the rapid growth of a **free-enterprise** economy among Canada's aboriginals, especially in the cities. In 1995 there were an estimated 18,000 aboriginal-owned businesses across Canada. About 66 percent of aboriginal businesses were in the service sector; 13 percent were in construction and related sectors. Another 12 percent were in the primary industries such as mining and forestry, and 9 percent were businesses related to food processing, clothing, furniture, publishing and other manufacturing. One fast-growing area is aboriginal tourism, where an insight is given into culture and environment. However, employment and subsequent social problems (particularly among the growing young population) are still rampant.

Each year the oil-rich aborigines get $32 million in petroleum revenues. This upsurge in revenue would seem to bode well, but migration from the still impoverished reserves to the city (which began three decades ago) is on the increase, resulting in an unskilled and impoverished underclass of aborigines in Canadian cities and a subsequent increase in social fragmentation, greater unrest and increased crime. Most of the aborigine newcomers to the cities are young, and they are increasingly angry with the federal government and their own leaders. With 60 percent of aboriginal populations now city-based, there has also been the formation of young **street gangs**. Such gangs have made a mark in Winnipeg, which has the nation's biggest aboriginal urban population.

The **anger** that the street gangs epitomize has risen across native communities. Gang members complain about financial and political corruption by their leaders; young people, who make up more than half of the native population, say they are being ignored by an uncaring federal government and ineffectual elders. As a young native activist said recently, "Most of us have nothing to lose, so we will do what we have to to have our voices heard..." **Violence** is inevitable, and flared up most notoriously with an armed standoff between Mohawk militants and the Canadian military at Oka in 1990 see p.235). Five years later there was trouble again at Gustafsne Lake in the British Columbia interior and Ipperwash Provincial Park on the shores of Lake Huron. Meanwhile, the white attitude to militancy has hardened. Tough prison sentences are passed out to native protesters who break the law, yet there is little punishment for police officers who overstep the mark – in 1997, an Ontario Provincial policeman was given two years of community service after he was found guilty of criminal negligence in the fatal shooting of an aborigine demonstrator at Ipperwash Provincial Park.

The showdowns attracted much media attention and after Oka the government funded a $60 million exhaustive **Royal Commission on Aboriginal Peoples**, which was finally published in November 1996 and called for fundamental change and self-government for aboriginals. Unbelievably, its recommendations seem to have been totally ignored by the present Liberal government – they've made it clear that broad structural change, particularly anything connected with the Constitution, is simply not on their agenda. Weary of constitutional issues, particularly those raised by Québec, the Canadian public has shown little enthusiasm for aboriginal affairs.

For their part the fractured **Assembly of First Nations** have just elected a new national chief, Phil Fontaine, who has called for unity and a need to cement relations with government. He follows Ovide Mercredi, who led the AFN from 1991 to 1997 and whose hardline, "all or nothing" approach to aboriginal sovereignty alienated the federal government and diminished his credibility within the aboriginal community. Phil Fontaine has quite a task before him, particularly as the AFN is $1.6 million in debt and Ottawa has threatened to withdraw the annual core fund of $2 million unless they clean up their finances. The longed-for self-government still seems a long way off.

THE FUTURE

Beyond this gloomy scenario there have been dramatic improvements secured since World War II that have led to a revival of interest in their own culture for many aboriginal people. Ceremonies, like the summer pow-wow celebrations, and art forms that have been almost forgotten, are being revived through research and reconstruction. There are aboriginal theatre groups that reinterpret the legends for modern audiences, aboriginal authors and poets who are publishing works that present unique and indigenous viewpoints; and aboriginal painters and sculptors who are using a mix of traditional and modern techniques to produce vivid and exciting works of art. It is questionable how far this revival is one of a living culture but there is definitely a cultural optimism that has never been felt before. As George Erasmus, leader of the AFN in 1986, said, "Native people will have much to contribute over the next century. It's our turn."

BOOKS

Most of the following books should be readily available in the UK, US or Canada. We have given publishers for each title in the form UK/US publisher, unless the book is published in one country only; o/p means out of print. Note that virtually all the listed books published in the US will be stocked by major Canadian bookshops; we've indicated those books published only in Canada.

TRAVEL

Hugh Brody *Maps and Dreams* (Faber/Waveland, both o/p). Brilliantly written account of the lives and lands of the Beaver natives of northwest Canada. For further acute insights into the ways of the far north see also the same author's *Living Arctic* (Faber, o/p/University of Washington Press) and *The People's Land: Eskimos and Whites in the Eastern Arctic* (Douglas & McIntyre in US, o/p).

P. Browning *The Last Wilderness* (Hutchinson in UK and Great West Books in US, o/p). An engrossing description of a harsh and lonely canoe journey through the Northwest Territories.

Ranulph Fiennes *The Headless Valley* (Hodder & Stoughton in UK, o/p). Tales of derring-do from noted adventurer, white-water rafting down the South Nahanni and Fraser rivers of British Columbia and the old NWT.

Barry Lopez *Arctic Dreams: Imagination and Desire in a Northern Landscape* (Picador/Bantam). Extraordinary, award-winning book combining natural history, physics, poetry, earth sciences and philosophy in a dazzling portrait of the far north.

Duncan Pryde *Nununga: Ten Years of Eskimo Life* (Eland/Hippocrene). Less a travel book than a social document from a Glaswegian who left home at eighteen to spend ten years with the Inuit.

Gary and Joannie McGuffin *Canoeing Across Canada* (Diadem in UK, o/p). Reflections on a 6000-mile journey through the country's rivers and backwaters.

Susanna Moodie *Roughing it in the Bush: or Forest Life in Canada* (McClelland & Stewart). Wonderful narrative written in 1852, describing an English couple's slow ruin as they attempt to create a new life in southeastern Ontario.

Jan Morris *O Canada: Travels in an Unknown Country* (Robert Hale, o/p/HarperCollins, o/p) Musings from this well-known travel writer after a coast-to-coast Canadian trip.

CULTURE AND SOCIETY

David Cruise & Alison Griffiths *The Great Adventure: How the Mounties conquered the West* (St Martin's Press, US). Contemporary accounts of the Mounties' first major expedition into the West from the strange assortment of men who made up this legendary force.

Beatrice Culleton *April Raintree* (Pemmican in Canada/Peguis in US). Heart-rending account of the enforced fostering of Métis children in Manitoba during the 1950s.

Don Dumond *The Eskimos and Aleuts* (Thames & Hudson in UK and US). Anthropological and archeological tour de force on the prehistory, history and culture of northern peoples: backed up with fine maps, drawings and photographs.

Christian F. Feest *Native Arts of North America* (Thames & Hudson, US & UK). This attractively illustrated book covers every aspect of North American native art in revealing detail. Everything you've ever wanted to know – and probably a good bit more.

Paul Fleming *The North American Indians in Early Photographs* (Phaidon/HarperCollins, o/p in US). Stylized poses don't detract from a plaintive record of a way of life that has all but vanished.

Glenn Gould *The Solitude Trilogy* (CBC PSCD 2003–3). These CDs comprise three extraordinary sound documentaries made by Gould for CBC (who also recorded his music) concerning life in the extreme parts of Canada. A fascinating insight into harsh lifestyles in the words of the people themselves.

Alan D. McMillan *Native Peoples and Cultures of Canada* (Orca in US). Comprehensive account of Canada's native groups from prehistory to current issues of self-government and land claims. Well-written, though more an academic textbook than a leisure-time read.

Dennis Reid *A Concise History of Canadian Painting* (Oxford University Press in UK and US). Not especially concise, but a thorough trawl through Canada's leading artists, with bags of biographical detail and lots of black and white (and a few colour) illustrations of major works.

Mordecai Richler *Oh Canada! Oh Québec!* (Chatto & Windus/Knopf). A satirical chronicle of the hysteria, zeal and chicanery surrounding Québec's independence movement.

The True North – Canadian Landscape Painting 1896–1939 (Lund Humphries in UK and US). A fascinating and well-illustrated book exploring how Canadian artists have treated the country's challenging landscapes.

BIOGRAPHY

Anahareo *Grey Owl and I: a New Autobiography* (Davies in Canada). The story of Grey Owl's Iroquois wife, their fight to save the beaver from extinction and her shock at discovering that her husband was in fact an Englishman. Good insights into the changing life of Canada's natives in this century.

Grey Owl *The Men of the Last Frontier; Pilgrims of the Wild; The Adventures of Sajo and Her Beaver People; Tales of an Empty Cabin* (all o/p). First published in the 1930s, these books romantically describe life in the wilds of Canada at the time when exploitation was changing the land forever. Grey Owl's love of animals and the wilderness are inspiring and his forward-thinking, ecological views are particularly startling.

Richard Gwyn *Smallwood: the Unlikely Revolutionary* (McClelland & Stewart in Canada). Detailed biography of Joey Smallwood, the Newfoundland premier who pushed his island into Confederation in 1949. Gwyn's exploration of island corruption and incompetence is incisive and intriguing in equal measure.

Paul Kane *Wanderings of an Artist among the Indians of North America* (Dover in UK & US). Kane, one of Canada's better-known landscape artists, spent two and a half years travelling from Toronto to the Pacific Coast and back in the 1840s. His witty, racy account of his wanderings makes a delightful read.

James MacKay *Robert Service: Vagabond of Verse* (Mainstream, UK). Not the first, but certainly the most substantial biography discussing this prominent Canadian poet's life and work.

Peter F. Ostwald *Glenn Gould: The Ecstasy and Tragedy of Genius* (W. W. Norton & Co). A biography by a psychiatrist (100 percent Freud-free) of Canada's most famous musician. The eccentric pianist comes across as a rather inhuman egotist but with a talent to make this sufferable to many of his followers.

Constance Rooke, *Writing Home: a PEN Anthology* (McClelland & Stewart). A handful of Canada's leading contemporary authors muse on the idea of home. Though more an insight into the inner workings of writers' minds than Canadian culture, this book's "sampler" style makes it a welcome partner on cross-country journeys.

HISTORY

Owen Beattie and John Geiger *The Fate of the Franklin Expedition 1845–48* (Bloomsbury/NAL-Dutton, o/p). An account both of the doomed expedition to find the Northwest Passage and the discovery of artefacts and bodies still frozen in the northern ice; worth buying for the extraordinary photos.

Pierre Berton *Klondike: the Last Great Goldrush 1896–1899* (McClelland & Stewart in US). Exceptionally readable account from one of Canada's finest writers of the characters and epic episodes of the Yukon gold rush. Other Berton titles include *The Arctic Grail* (Viking, o/p/Penguin), describing the quest for the North Pole and the Northwest Passage from 1818 to 1919; *The Last Spike* (Penguin in US), an account of the history and building of the transcontinental railway; *The Mysterious North: Encounters with the Canadian Frontier 1947–1954* (McClelland & Stewart in Canada); *Flames across the Frontier* (Penguin in US), episodes from the often uneasy relationship between Canada and the US; and *Vimy*, an account of the World War I battle fought mainly by Canadians which Berton sees as a turning point in the nation's history.

Gerald Friesen *The Canadian Prairies: a History* (University of Toronto Press in UK and US). Stunningly well-researched and detailed account of the development of Central Canada. A surprisingly entertaining book that's particularly good on the culture of the Métis and Plains Indians.

Kenneth McNaught *The Penguin History of Canada* (Penguin in UK and US). Recently revised and concise analysis of the country's economic, social and political history.

Peter Neary and Patrick O'Flaherty *Part of the Main: an Illustrated History of Newfoundland and Labrador* (Breakwater in Canada). Lively text and excellent illustrations make this the best account of the province's history, though it's short of contemporary information.

Peter C. Newman *Caesars of the Wilderness* (Penguin in UK and US, o/p). Highly acclaimed and readable account of the rise and fall of the Hudson's Bay Company.

George Woodcock *A Social History of Canada* (Penguin in UK and US, o/p). Erudite and incisive book about the peoples of Canada and the country's development. Woodcock is the most perceptive of Canada's historians and his work has the added advantage of being very readable. Also by the author is *The Canadians* (Harvard University Press, US, o/p), a lavishly illustrated and brilliantly lucid attempt to summarize the Canadian experience.

NATURAL HISTORY

Richard Chandler *The Macmillan Field Guide to North Atlantic Shorebirds* (Macmillan in UK, o/p). Well-illustrated and comprehensive handbook.

The Pocket Guide Series (Dragon's World in UK). Clearly laid-out and well-illustrated, the Pocket Book series are excellent basic handbooks for general locations of species, identification and background. Individual titles are: *The Pocket Guide to Mammals of North America* (John Burton); *The Pocket Guide to Birds of Prey of North America* (Philip Burton); *The Pocket Guide to Wild Flowers of North America* (Pamela Forey); *The Pocket Guide to Trees of North America* (Alan Mitchell); *The Pocket*

Guide to Birds of Western North America (Frank Shaw).

Lyall Watson *Whales of the World* (Hutchinson/NAL-Dutton, both o/p). Encyclopedic and lavishly illustrated guide to the whale.

FICTION

Margaret Atwood *Surfacing* (Virago/Fawcett). Canada's most eminent novelist is not always easy reading, but her analysis, particularly of women and society, is invariably witty and penetrating. In *Surfacing* (Virago/Fawcett), the remote landscape of northern Québec plays an instrumental part in an extreme voyage of self-discovery. Regeneration through exploration of the past is also the theme of *Cat's Eye* (Virago/Doubleday) and *Lady Oracle* (Virago/Doubleday), while the collection of short stories *Wilderness Tips* (Virago/Bantam) sees women ruminating over the bastards in their lives. Atwood's latest offering, *Alias Grace* (Virago/Doubleday) is a dark and sensual tale centred around the true story of one of Canada's most notorious female criminals of the 1840's.

Robertson Davies For many years the leading figure of Canada's literary scene, Davies died in 1995 at the age of 82. Amongst his considerable output are big, dark and complicated webs of familial and social history which include wonderful evocations of the semi-rural Canada of his youth. A good place to start is *What's Bred in the Bone,* part of *The Cornish Trilogy*, whose other titles are *The Rebel Angels* and *The Lyre of Orpheus* (All by Penguin in UK and US). Similarly intriguing is *Fifth Business* (Penguin in UK and US), the first part of *The Deptford Trilogy.*

Lovat Dickson *Wilderness Man* (Abacus in UK, o/p). The fascinating story of Archie Belaney, the Englishman who became famous as his adopted persona, Grey Owl. Written by his English publisher and friend, who was one of many that did not discover the charade until after Grey Owl's death.

William Gibson *Virtual Light* (Penguin/Bantam Spectra) and *Idoru* (Penguin/Berkeley) are the best recent books from the master of cyberdom. The impact of technologies on human experience and the overlapping of artifice and reality are his significant themes.

Hammond Innes *Campbell's Kingdom* (Pan/Addison-Wesley). A melodrama of love and oil-drilling in the Canadian Rockies – though the landscape's less well evoked than in *The Land God Gave Cain* (Pan/Carroll & Graf, o/p), the story of one man's search for "gold and truth" in Labrador.

Margaret Laurence *A Jest of God*; *The Stone Angel*; *The Diviners* (all Virago/University of Chicago Press). Manitoba-born Laurence epitomized the new vigour that swept through the country's literature during the Sixties – though the best of her fiction was written in England. Most of her books are set in the fictional prairie backwater of Manawaka, and explore the loneness and frustration of women within an environment of stifling small-town conventionality. Always highly revered at home, Laurence's reptation is on the increase abroad.

Stephen Leacock *Sunshine Sketches of a little Town* (McClelland & Stewart/New Canadian Library). Whimsical tale of Ontario small-town life; the best of a series based on the author's summertime stays in Orillia.

Jack London *The Call of the Wild; White Fang and Other Stories* (Penguin in UK and US). London spent over a year in the Yukon gold fields during the Klondike gold rush. Many of his experiences found their way into his vivid if sometimes overwrought tales of the northern wilderness, but he left behind a burning evocation of the North.

Malcolm Lowry *Hear Us O Lord from Heaven thy Dwelling Place* (Carroll & Graf). Lowry spent almost half his writing life (1939–54) in log cabins and beach houses he built for himself round Vancouver. *Hear Us O Lord* is a difficult read to say the least: a fragmentary novella which, amongst other things, describes a disturbing sojourn on Canada's wild Pacific coast.

Ann-Marie MacDonald. *Fall on Your Knees* (Vintage/Simon & Schuster). Entertaining, epic-style family saga from this young, Toronto-based writer with an astute eye for characters and a fine story-telling touch. The novel follows the fortunes of four sisters from Halifax, against a backdrop which sweeps from World War II to the New York jazz scene.

Anne Michaels *Fugitive Pieces* (Bloomsbury/Knopf). This debut novel from an award-winning poet concerns survivors from the Nazis who emigrate to Canada. Their relationship deepens but memory and the past are never far away. A beautiful work.

W. O. Mitchell *Who Has Seen the Wind* (Canongate/Little, Brown). Canada's equivalent of *Huckleberry Finn* is a folksy story of a young boy coming of age in small-town Saskatchewan, with great offbeat characters and fine evocations of prairie life. Mitchell's *The Vanishing Point* (Macmillan in US), though witty and fun to read, is a moving testimony to the complexities of native assimilation in a country dominated by "immigrants".

L. M. Montgomery *Anne of Green Gables* (Puffin/Pengiun). Growing pains and bucolic bliss in a children's classic from 1908. Bound to appeal to little girls of all ages.

Brian Moore *Black Robe* (Flamingo/NAL-Dutton). Moore emigrated to Canada from Ireland in 1948 and stayed long enough to gain citizenship before moving on to California. *Black Robe* – the story of a missionary's journey into native territory – is typical of the author's preoccupations with Catholicism, repression and redemption.

Alice Munro *Lives of Girls and Women* (Penguin/NAL-Dutton); *The Progress of Love* (Vintage/Penguin); *The Beggar Maid* (Penguin in UK and US); *Friend of my Youth* (Vintage in UK and US); *Dance of the Happy Shades* (Penguin/Vintage); *Who Do You Think you Are?* (Penguin); *Something I've Been Meaning to Tell You* (Penguin/Plume); *The Moons of Jupiter* (Penguin). Amongst the world's finest living short-story writers, Munro deals primarily with the lives of women in the semi-rural and Protestant backcountry of southwest Ontario. Unsettling emotions are never far beneath the surface. Among her more recent works, *Open Secrets* (Vintage in UK and US) focuses on stories set in two small Ontario towns from the days of the early settlers to the present.

New Oxford Book of Canadian Short Stories in English (ed. Margaret Atwood & Robert Weaver; OUP in UK and US). A broad selection which delves beyond the better-known names of Alice Munro and Margaret Atwood, with space being given to diaspora writers. While the intention is to celebrate Canadian writing, some of the works offer a stangely negative view of the country.

Michael Ondaatje *In the Skin of a Lion* (Picador/McKay) Highly charged work with intriguing insights into the essence of Toronto and its people.

Oxford Book of Canadian Ghost Stories (OUP in US, o/p). Over twenty stories, including W. P. Kinsella's *Shoeless Joe Jackson Comes to Iowa* – the inspiration for the fey *Field of Dreams*.

Oxford Companion to Canadian Literature (OUP in UK and US, both o/p). At almost 900 pages, this is the last word on the subject, though it is more useful as a work of reference than as a primer for the country's literature.

E. Annie Proulx *The Shipping News* (Fourth Estate/Simon & Schuster). The 1994 Pulitzer Prize-winner is a rambling, inconclusive narrative of a social misfit who finds love and happiness of sorts in small-town Newfoundland. Superb descriptions of sea, weather and all things fishy (as distinct from some very average characterization) make it an essential primer for any visitor to the province.

Mordecai Richler French-Canadian, working-class and Jewish – Yiddishkeit is Richler's bag. He is the laureate of the minority within a minority within a minority. All his novels explore this relation with broad humour and pathos. *The Apprenticeship of Duddy Kravitz* (Penguin in UK and US). Richler uses his early experiences of Montréal's working-class Jewish ghetto in many of his novels, especially in this, his best-known work, an acerbic and slick cross-cultural romance built around the ambivalent but tightly drawn figure of Kravitz. Richler's pushy and ironic prose is not to all tastes, but you might also try *Solomon Gursky Was Here* (Vintage/DIANE) or his latest book, *Barney's Version* (Chatto & Windus/Knopf) – a rip-roaring comic portrait of a reckless artist *manqué*.

Carol Shields *Happenstance*; *The Stone Diaries*; *Larry's Party* (all Fourth Estate/Penguin US). Winner of the Pulitzer Prize, Shields is much lauded for the detail she finds in the everyday. There are moments of great beauty and sensitivity in these books which chronicle frankly the experiences of bourgeois North American suburbia.

Elizabeth Smart *By Grand Central Station I Sat Down and Wept* (Flamingo/Vintage). A cult masterpiece which lyrically details the writer's love affair with the English poet George Barker.

Audrey Thomas *The Wild Blue Yonder* (Fourth Estate). A collection of witty tales about male/female relationships by a renowned Canadian short-story writer.

Jane Urquhart *The Underpainter* (Bloomsbury/Viking). A painful book concerning the life of a narcissistic painter who uses and leaves his muse but ultimately finds the demands of art destroy his humanity.

John Wyndham *The Chrysalids* (Penguin/Carroll & Graf). A science-fiction classic built around a group of telepathic children and their adventures in post-Holocaust Labrador.

POETRY

Elizabeth Bishop *The Complete Poems* (Chatto & Windus/Farrar, Straus & Giroux). Though American by birth, Bishop spent much of her youth in Nova Scotia. Many of her early poems feed off her Canadian childhood and her fascination with the country's rough landscapes.

Leonard Cohen *Poems: 1956–1968* (Cape/Penguin, o/p). A fine collection from Sixties survivor who enjoyed high critical acclaim as a poet before emerging as a husky-throated crooner of bedsit ballads. See also his *Beautiful Losers*, one of the most aggressively experimental Canadian novels of the Sixties (Black Spring Press/Vintage).

New Oxford Book of Canadian Verse (ed Margaret Atwood; OUP in UK and US). Canadian poets are increasingly finding a distinctive voice, but few except this collection editor have made much impact outside their native country. Atwood's own sharp, witty examinations of nationality and gender are among the best in this anthology – more of her verse is published in the UK by Virago.

Robert Service *The Best of Robert Service* (A & C Black/Running Press). Service's Victorian ballads of pioneer and gold-rush life have a certain charm and they capture the essence of the gold-rush period amongst which the *Songs of Sourdough* collection of 1907 is perhaps the most memorable.

SPECIALIST GUIDES

Don Beers *The Wonder of Yoho* (Rocky Mountain Books in Canada). Good photos and solid text extolling the delights of Yoho National Park in the Rockies.

Darryl Bray *Kluane National Park Hiking Guide* Travel Vision in Canada). A much-needed guide to long and short walks in a park where the trail network is still in its infancy.

Neil G. Carey *A Guide to the Queen Charlotte Islands* (Northwest Books in US). An authoritative guide to islands which are difficult to explore and ill-served by back-up literature.

Ron Dalby *The Alaska Highway: an Insider's Guide* (Fulcrum in UK and US). Less detailed but less dry than its main competitor, the better-known and encyclopedic *Milepost* (Northwest Books).

John Dodd and Gail Helgason *The Canadian Rockies Access Guide* (London Pine in US). Descriptions of 115 day hikes, with degrees of difficulty, time needed, sketch maps of routes, wildlife descriptions and numerous photos.

David Dunbar *The Outdoor Traveller's Guide to Canada* (Stewart, Tabori & Chang in UK and US). Too bulky to be a useful guide in the field, but a lavishly illustrated introduction to the outdoor pursuits, wildlife and geology of 37 of the country's best national and provincial parks.

Heather Elton *Banff's Best Day Hikes* (Lone Pine, US & Canada). Good selection of walks in and around Banff town and national park with adequate maps and tempting photos.

Ben Gadd *A Handbook of the Canadian Rockies* (Corax). Widely available in western Canada's larger bookshops, this is a lovingly produced and painstakingly detailed account of walks, flora, fauna, geology and anything else remotely connected with the Rockies.

The Lost Moose Catalogue (Lost Moose Publishing in Canada). Highly entertaining and iconoclastic magazine-style guide and commentary on the contemporary mores of the Yukon and far north.

Teri Lydiard *The British Columbia Bicycling Guide* (Gordon Soules in US). Small but extremely detailed pointer to some tempting routes, backed up with good maps.

Janice E. Macdonald *Canoeing Alberta* (Macdonald in Canada). A canoeist's Bible, with many detailed accounts of the province's waterways, and especially good on routes in the Rockies.

Ken Madsen and Graham Wilson *Rivers of the Yukon* (Primrose Publishing in Canada). An invaluable guide to some of the country's best canoeing rivers.

Linda Moyer and Burl Willes *Unexplored Islands of the US and Canadian West Coast* (John Muir in UK and US). A generous portion of the guide is devoted to an intimate but rather homely run through some of British Columbia's lesser-known islands.

Bruce Obee *The Pacific Rim Explorer* (Whitecap in UK). A good overall summary of the walks, wildlife and social history of the Pacific Rim National Park and its nearby towns. The same writer's *The Gulf Islands Explorer* and, in the same series, Eliane Jones's *The Northern Gulf Islands Explorer*, are also useful.

Brian Patton and Bart Robinson *The Canadian Rockies Trail Guide* (Summerthought in Canada). An absolutely essential guide for anyone wishing to do more than simply scratch the surface of the Rockies' walking possibilities.

Betty Pratt-Johnson series (Adventure Publishing in Canada). The author has produced five separate books whose 157 canoeing routes provide the definitive account of how and where to canoe the lakes and rivers of British Columbia.

Archie Shutterfield *The Chilkoot Trail: a Hiker's Historical Guide* (Northwest Books in US). A pithy accompaniment to the Chilkoot Trail that should be read in conjunction with Pierre Berton's *Klondike*.

Sierra Club of West Canada *The West Coast Trail* (Douglas & McIntyre in Canada). Now in its sixth edition, this is probably the best of several guides to Vancouver Island's popular but demanding long-distance footpath.

CANADIAN LITERATURE

Getting to grips with the vastness of the country is what most Canadian literature is about. Until recently nature made its mark on man rather than man on nature. The first piece amply describes the conditions most homesteaders suffered. The pioneering Susanna Moodie left a comfortable England in the mistaken belief of finding a tame nature to control and oblige her. The second piece is from the Klondike boom which acted as a beacon for young dreamers and bored office workers worldwide. Robert Service left his home, like many at the time, in search of adventure, but also discovered the pitiless conditions that destroy people yet still cannot dissuade them from the love of gold. The last piece describes the most crucial part of Canadian history. When the trains speeded their way west, their importance in holding the country together was readily valued. But with the arrival of the train, and the homesteaders, came the end of the frontier for many, leaving only the North as the last unknown.

SUSANNA MOODIE (1803–1885)

Born in Suffolk, England, to a genteel family, Moodie emigrated to Canada in 1832. She and her husband, J. W. Dunbar Moodie, a lieutenant in the British army, hoped to create a new life in the new world. By 1834 they had settled on a farm in Douro, Ontario. Susanna was shocked by the rude democracy of Upper Canada and the realities of being a frontierswoman.

Arriving in a leaky hut, an "untenable tenement", with a wagon loaded with lace gloves and silver cutlery, she had to survive the landscape, the weather and the bugs – "the prospect was indeed dreary". Roughing It In The Bush (1852) is the frank and humorous autobiography of her arrival and settlement in Canada. It created an international sensation when it was published as it punctured the illusions land agents were circulating about the good life in Canada. She made clear that life in the new world was one of hardship, both physical and psychological, and that Canada was a hostile place of wild

animals, wild people and very few decent cups of tea. In time, Susanna grew to be reconciled to "this noble country", and eventually loved it, "feeling a deep interest in its welfare, and the fair prospect of its future greatness".

Susanna also contributed to the Montréal Literary Garland and created the Victoria Magazine with her husband. Together they had two sons and five daughters. She was widowed in 1869, when she moved to Toronto where she died at the age of 81.

ROUGHING IT IN THE BUSH

I had a great desire to visit our new location, but when I looked out upon the cheerless waste, I gave up the idea, and contented myself with hoping for a better day on the morrow; but many morrows came and went before a frost again hardened the road sufficiently for me to make this attempt.

The prospect from the windows of my sister's log hut was not very prepossessing. The small lake in front, which formed such a pretty object in summer, now looked like an extensive field covered with snow, hemmed in from the rest of the world by a dark belt of sombre pine woods. The clearing round the house was very small, and only just reclaimed from the wilderness, and the greater part of it covered with piles of brushwood, to be burnt the first days of spring. The charred and blackened stumps on the few acres that had been cleared during the preceding year were anything but picturesque; and I concluded, as I turned, disgusted, from this prospect before me, that there was very little beauty to be found in the backwoods. But I came to this decision, during a Canadian thaw, be it remembered, when one is wont to view every object with jaundiced eyes.

Moodie had only been able to secure sixty-six acres of his government grant upon the Upper Kutchawanook Lake, which, being interpreted, means in English, the "Lake of the Waterfalls", a very poetical meaning, which most Indian names have. He had, however, secured a clergy reserve of two hundred acres adjoining: and he afterwards purchased a fine lot, which likewise formed part of the same block, one hundred acres, for £150. This was an enormously high price for wild land; but the prospect of opening the Trent and Otonabee for the navigation of steamboats and other small craft, was at that period a favourite speculation and its practicability, and the great advantages to be derived from it, were so widely believed as to raise the value of the wild lands along these remote waters to an enormous price; and settlers in the vicintiy were eager to secure lots, at any sacrifice, along their shores.

Our government grant was upon the lake shore, and Moodie had chosen for the site of his log house a bank that slipped gradually from the edge of the water, until it attained to the dignity of a hill. Along the top of this ridge; the forest-road ran, and midway down the hill, our humble home, already nearly completed, stood, surrounded by the eternal forest. A few trees had been cleared in the immediate vicinity, just sufficient to allow the workmen to proceed, and to prevent the fall of any tree injuring the building, or the danger of its taking fire during the process of burning the fallow.

A neighbour had undertaken to build this rude dwelling by contract, and was to have it ready for us by the first week in the new year. The want of boards to make the divisions in the apartments alone hindered him from fulfilling his contract. Those had lately been procured, and the house was to be ready for our reception in the course of a week. Our trunks and baggage had already been conveyed by Mr D— hither: and in spite of my sister's kindness and hospitality, I longed to find myself once more settled in a home of my own.

The day after our arrival, I was agreeably surprised by a visit from Monaghan, whom Moodie had once more taken into his service. The poor fellow was delighted that his nurse-child, as he always called little Katie, had not forgotten him, but evinced the most lively satisfaction at the sight of her dark friend.

Early every morning, Moodie went off to the house; and the first fine day, my sister undertook to escort me through the wood, to inspect it. The proposal was joyfully accepted; and although I felt *rather* timid when I found myself with only my female companion in the vast forest, I kept my fears to myself, lest I should be laughed at. This foolish dread of encountering wild beasts in the woods, I never could wholly shake off, even after becoming a constant resident in their gloomy depths, and accustomed to follow the forest path, alone, or attended, with little children, daily. The cracking of an old bough, or the hooting of the owl, was enough to fill me with alarm, and try my strength in a precipitate flight.

Often have I stopped and reproached myself for want of faith in the goodness of Providence, and repeated this text, "The wicked are afraid when we man pursueth: but the righteous are as bold as a lion," as if to shame myself into courage. But it would not do: I could not overcome the weakness of the flesh. If I had one of our infants with me, the wish to protect the child from any danger which might beset my path gave me for a time a fictitious courage; but it was like love fighting with despair.

It was in vain that my husband assured me that no person had ever been attacked by wild animals in the woods, that a child might traverse them even at night in safety; whilst I knew that wild animals existed in these woods, I could not believe him, and my fears on this head rather increased than diminished.

The snow had been so greatly decreased by the late thaw, that it had been converted into a coating of ice, which afforded a dangerous and slippery footing. My sister, who had resided for nearly twelve months in the woods, was provided for her walk with Indian moccasins, which rendered her quite independent: but I stumbled at every step. The sun shone brightly, the air was clear and invigorating, and, in spite of the treacherous ground and my foolish fears, I greatly enjoyed my first walk in the woods. Naturally of a cheerful, hopeful disposition, my sister was enthusiastic in her admiration of the woods. She drew such a lively picture of the charms of a summer residence in the forest that I began to feel greatly interested in her descriptions, and to rejoice that we, too, were to be her near neighbours and dwellers in the woods; and this circumstance not a little reconciled me to the change.

Hoping that my husband would derive an income equal to the one he had parted with from the investment of the price of his commission in the steam-boat stock, I felt no dread of want. Our legacy of £700 had afforded us means to purchase land, build our house, and give out a large portion of land to be cleared, and, with a considerable sum of money still in hand, our propects for the future were in no way discouraging.

When we reached the top of the ridge that overlooked our cot, my sister stopped, and pointed out a large dwelling among the trees "There, S—," she said, "is your home. When that black cedar swamp is cleared away, that now hides the lake from us, you will have a very pretty view." My conversation with her had quite altered the aspect of the country, and predisposed me to view things in the most favourable light. I found Moodie and Monaghan employed in piling up heaps of bush near the house, which they intended to burn off by hand previous to firing the rest of the fallow, to prevent any risk to the building from fire. The house was made of cedar logs, and presented a superior air of comfort to most dwellings of the same kind. The dimensions were thirty-six feet in length, and thirty-two in breadth, which gave us a nice parlour, a kitchen, and two small bedrooms, which were divided by plank partitions. Pantry or store-room there was none; some rough shelves in the kitchen, and a deal cupboard in a corner of the parlour, being the extent of our accommodations in that way.

Our servant, Mary Tate, was busy scrubbing out the parlour and bedroom; but the kitchen and the sleeping room off it, were still knee-deep in chips and filled with the carpenter's bench and tools, and all our luggage. Such as it was, it was a palace when compared to Old Satan's log hut, or the miserable cabin we had wintered in during the severe winter of 1833, and I regarded it with complacency as my future home.

While we were standing outside the building, conversing with my husband, a young gentleman, of the name of Morgan, who had lately purchased land in that vicinity, went into the kitchen to light his pipe at the stove, and, with true backwood carelessness, let the hot cinder fall among the dry chips that strewed the floor. A few minutes after, the whole mass was in a blaze, and it was not without great difficulty that Moodie and Mr R— succeeded in putting out the fire. Thus were we nearly deprived of our home before we had taken up our abode in it.

The indifference to the danger of fire in a country where most of the dwellings are composed of inflammable materials, is truly astonishing. Accustomed to see enormous fires blazing on every hearth-stone, and to sleep in front of those fires, his bedding often riddled with holes made by hot particles of wood flying out during the night, and igniting beneath his very nose, the sturdy backwoodsman never dreads an enemy in the element that he is used to regard as his best friend. Yet what awful accidents, what ruinous calamities arise, out of this criminal negligence, both to himself and others!

A few days after this adventure, we bade adieu to my sister, and took possession of our new dwelling; and commenced "a life in the woods".

The first spring we spent in comparative ease and idleness. Our cows had been left upon our old place during the winter. The ground had to be cleared before it could reserve a crop of any kind, and I had little to do but to wander by the lake shore, or among the woods, and amuse myself.

These were halcyon days of the bush. My husband had purchased a very light cedar canoe, to which he attached a keel and a sail: and most of our leisure hours, directly the snows melted, were spent upon the water.

These fishing and shooting excurions were delightful. The pure beauty of the Canadian water, the sombre but august grandeur of the vast forces that hemmed us in on every side and shut us out from the rest of the world, soon cast a magic spell upon our spirits, and we began to feel charmed with the freedom and solitude around us. Every object was new to us. We felt as if we were the first discoverers of every beautiful flower and stately tree that attracted our attention, and we gave names to fantastic rocks and fairy isles, and raised imaginary houses and bridges on every picturesque spot which we floated past during our aquatic excursions. I learned the use of the paddle, and became quite a proficient in the gentle craft.

From Roughing it in the Bush
(Virago/Beacon, both o/p)

ROBERT SERVICE (1874–1958)

Born in Preston and raised in Glasgow, Service emigrated to Canada and worked as a bank clerk, ending up in Whitehorse during the tailend of the Klondike gold rush. This opportunity was the impetus for his first book, Songs of a Sourdough *(1907), and what followed was a stream of popular, melodramatic ballads, that made his name ("the Canadian Kipling") and his fortune. One poem alone, "The Shooting of Dan McGrew", allegedly made him half a million* dollars. He worked as a labourer, and as a reporter on the Toronto Star and he served as a stretcher-bearer in World War I, after which he resided in the south of France, writing poetry, novels and volumes of autobiography. Although enjoying the high life and regular royalties, he frequently took menial jobs to fuel his imagination. As he said: "The only society I like, is that which is rough and tough – and the tougher the better. That's where you get down to bedrock and meet human people."

Below is one of his most famous ballads which disguises, with a rough wit, the cruelty of the Yukon experience.

THE CREMATION OF SAM MCGEE

There are strange things done in the midnight sun

By the men who moil for gold;
The Arctic trails have their secret tales
That would make your blood run cold;
The Northern Lights have seen queer sights,
But the queerest they ever did see
Was that night on the marge of Lake Lebarge
I cremated Sam McGee.

Now Sam McGee was from Tennessee, where the cotton blooms and blows.

Why he left his home in the South to roam round the Pole God only knows.

He was always cold, but the land of gold seemed to hold him like a spell;

though he'd often say in his homely way that he'd "sooner live in hell".

On a Christmas Day we were mushing our way over the Dawson trail.

Talk of your cold! through the parka's fold it stabbed like a driven nail.

If our eyes we'd close, then the lashes froze, till sometimes we couldn't see;

It wasn't much fun, but the only one to whimper was Sam McGee.

And that very night as we lay packed tight in our robes beneath the snow,

And the dogs were fed, and the stars o'erhead were dancing heel and toe,

He turned to me, and, "Cap," says he, " I'll cash in this trip, I guess;

And if I do, I'm asking that you won't refuse my last request."

Well, he seemed so low that I couldn't say no: then he says with a sort of moan:

"It's the cursed cold, and it's got right hold till I'm chilled clean through to the bone.

Yet 'taint being dead, it's my awful dread of the icy grave that pains:

So I want you to swear that, foul or fair, you'll cremate my last remains."

A pal's last need is a thing to heed, so I swore I would not fail;

And we started on at the streak of dawn, but God! he looked ghastly pale.

He crouched on the sleigh, and he raved all day of his home in Tennessee;

And before nightfall a corpse was all that was left of Sam McGee.

There wasn't a breath in that land of death, and I hurried, horror driven,

With a corpse half-hid that I couldn't get rid because of a promise given;

It was lashed to the sleigh, and it seemed to say: "You may tax your brawn and brains,

But you promised true, and it's up to you to cremate those last remains."

Now a promise made is a debt unpaid, and the trial has its own stern code.

In the days to come, though my lips were dumb, in my heart how I cursed that load.

In the long, long night, by the lone firelight, while the huskies, round in a ring,

Howled out their woes to the homeless snows – O God I how I loathed the thing!

And every day that quiet clay seemed to heavy and heavier grow;

And on I went, though the dogs were spent and the grub was getting low;

The trail was bad, and I felt half mad, but I swore I would not give in;

And I'd often sing to the hateful thing, and it hearkened with a grin.

Till I came to the marge of Lake Lebarge, and a derelict there lay;

It was jammed in the ice, but I saw in a trice it was called the "Alice May".

And I looked at it, and I thought a bit, and I looked at my frozen chum:

Then, "Here," said I, with a sudden cry, "is my cre-ma-tor-eum."

Some planks I tore from the cabin floor, and I lit the boiler fire;
Some coal I found that was lying around, and I heaped the fuel higher;
The flames just soared, and the furnace roared – such a blaze you seldom see;
And I burrowed a hole in the glowing coal, and I stuffed in Sam McGee.

Then I made a hike, for I didn't like to hear him sizzle so;
And the heavens scowled, and the huskies howled, and the wind began to blow.
It was icy cold, but the hot sweat rolled down my cheeks, and I don't know why;
And the greasy smoke in an inky cloak went streaking down the sky.

I do not know how long in the snow I wrestled with grisly fear;
But the stars came out and they danced about ere again I ventured near;
I was sick with dread, but I bravely said: "I'll just take a peep inside.
I guess he's cooked, and it's time I looked," then the door I opened wide.

And there sat Sam, looking cool and calm, in the heart of the furnace roar;
And he wore a smile you could see a mile, and he said: "Please close that door.
It's fine in here, but I greatly fear you'll let in the cold and storm –
Since I left Pluntree, down in Tennessee, it's the first time I've been warm."

There are strange things done in the midnight sun
By the men who moil for gold;
The Arctic trails have their secret tales
That would make your blood run cold;
The Northern Lights have seen queer sights,
But the queerest they ever did see
Was that night on the marge of Lake Lebarge
I cremated Sam McGee.

From The Best of Robert Service
(A & C Black/Putnam).
Reprinted with the kind permission of the
estate of Robert Service.

THE RAILWAYS

More than anything else, it was the **railway** *that welded Canada into a coherent nation. By the middle of the nineteenth century it was obvious that the haphazard land, river and sea routes linking the self-governing colonies of British North America were entirely inadequate if Canadian* **Confederation** *was to be achieved – and the pressure for some form of union had become intense by the 1860s. The British North America Act of 1867 effectively provided a con-stitution for the new Dominion of Canada and almost as soon as the ink was dry the Canadians set about building railroads. Every political leader saw their importance and indeed the representatives of British Columbia insisted as a condition of their joining that a transcontinental railroad be constructed within ten years. A 700-mile railroad linking Ontario, Québec and the Maritimes was completed in 1876 and, after extraordinary endeavours, the last spike of a transcontinental line was ham-mered in during November 1885. Thus, Canadian communications were transformed and the foundations were laid for that great movement of people which was to settle the furthest reaches of this enormous country. For several decades it was the railway that provid-ed many Canadians with their only contact with the outside world and inevitably it became a rich store of folklore and anecdote – everything from trains battling through mammoth snow-falls to drunken squabbles and romantic encounters.*

BRINGING IN THE SHEAVES

Every August and September for more than thir-ty years, the Harvest Excursion trains journeyed to the prairies from eastern Canada carrying contingents of temporary labourers. The number of men travelling west to help bring in the crops was awesome –nearly 350,000 between 1920 and 1928; 45,000 in 1924 alone. The majority of the farm hands were Canadian by birth, but each year there was a large influx of foreigners. The federal government enticed them with cheap boat fares and the glamorous posters it distributed throughout the British Isles and Continental Europe after the first Harvest Excursion in 1896 – posters of brawny, deliri-ously happy males stacking sheaves of golden wheat on glorious, sunlit fields.

The posters tactfully avoided showing the less inviting realities of harvesting: the dawn-to-dusk labour for meagre wages that, at times, took place under a scorching sun. Many farm hands were treated like members of the family and slept in comfortable guest rooms. Others lived in barns, tarpaper shacks, or tents. Despite hardships, more than half of the workers made the Harvest Excursion an annual event: some eventually married farm girls and settled permanently on the prairies.

Bill Morris was one of them. His trips west were motivated equally by a youthful yearning for fresh experiences and the need to help his parents keep the family farm at Cobourg, Ontario, financially stable. Morris and his wife, Betty, now have their own small farm in northern Alberta, which they bought after he retired from the civil service. At 81, Morris still plants twenty acres of oats every spring, just to keep his hand in. He was a neighbour of mine for many years but, as so often happens when you're doing research, I tried a dozen different sources looking for someone who had been on a harvest special before a local storekeeper said, "Why don't you talk to Bill Morris? I'm sure he was on one of those things."

"Yes, sir, I was on the Harvest Excursions, all right. Six years. From the month I became sixteen till I married and went into the post office. Come August, I'd haul myself to Union Station and climb onto the first special heading west. They had a cheap rate. In the 1920s, you could travel to Winnipeg from Ontario and Québec for fifteen bucks, twenty-five from the Maritimes. Return fare, you'd add on another five bucks. Each train had five, maybe six, hundred men on it.

"It's hard to say which was the worst, the sleeping or eating. You'd lie on slatted seats, without pillows, without blankets, and another guy sharing it with you. When you needed food it was the lunch counter and corned beef or the cafés near the stations. Those cafés were sure sleazy. So sleazy you'd wonder if it was chicken on your plate or alley cat. Plenty of whisky on the Excursions. Whisky, some dice, and at least one fight per trip. I heard of guys wrecking a colonist car. Smashed the windows and lights because a trainman threw a fella off for peeing wherever he felt like — on the floor, against walls, on somebody's seat. No one sided with the filthy pig, but they didn't like the trainman so they had an excuse for running wild.

"I don't recall anybody special. No faces, names. It was a long time ago. I do remember that they were from different backgrounds. Salesmen, penpushers, farm boys, lumberjacks, everything under the sun. Hold on. There was a painter once. He did these little drawings night and day. Of the men in the cars. The government hiring agents were in Winnipeg. You'd get a look-over and if you weren't too puny or old, you'd be assigned to a region. The painter and me were sent on to towns in southern Saskatchewan. The fare from Winnipeg was maybe a dollar. The painter got off at this one-elevator town. The farmer who was supposed to hire him saw the drawings and said he should get back on the train. He wanted a real man, used to real work. The last memory I have of them is the painter and the farmer arguing beside the track as the train moved away.

"Those farmers were the pharaohs, we were the slaves. Take it from me, it felt like we were building the bloody pyramids. Backbusting work. Sweat running down your face and your whole body aching with pain. Oh, the farmers fed you good. You bet they did. And nobody beat you with a stick. But they expected the harvesters to be in the fields from sunup to sundown. Machines didn't do the stooking in those days. You'd run behind the binder, picking up sheaves, one under each arm, and stacking them in cone-shaped stooks. The binder was your enemy. It was noisy and dusty and it was cutting and spitting the sheaths out so fast you nearly died trying to keep up.

"Then there was the threshing gangs. Weeks, sometimes months, after the stooking was done, the threshers were on the fields to take the grain from the sheaves. Most farmers wouldn't hack the price of a machine and they contracted out to roaming gangs. A dozen or more men travelled with the thresher. Some gangs had their own kitchens and old railway cars on wheels for bunkhouses; others slept in tents and ate when farm wives brought their meals to the fields. Everything was hurry, hurry, hurry. The big rush was to do the crops before bad weather set in. I saw men collapse, fall right over, from exhaustion. I saw some give up; walk right over to the farmer, demand their pay, and then walk to the closest train.

"Jeez, it was rough slogging. Big money? Ha, that's a laugh. Three bucks a day was the average and, no matter how hard you laboured, five bucks a day was the most you could pull down. But, you know, we took pride in what we did. Riding the train to the East, a man could look at the levelled fields and know he did his bit to feed the country. The government was proud of its harvesters. Pictures in railway stations showed men bringing in crops. In Regina, I saw real stooks of wheat in the concourse and a banner praising the harvesters. It said, Thanks For A Job Well Done, or something.

"Going home, a fella had to keep his wits sharp. Pickpockets and card sharks and floozies. The pickpockets and card sharks rode the colonist cars, dressed like us. The ones you spotted straight off were the ones with white skin. They couldn't have been harvesting if they weren't burnt brown or didn't have calloused hands. Some were really cute. They had tans and rough hands and talked farming and mixed real well. A good pickpocket could steal hundreds of dollars on a single trip. The floozies were at the city depots. Some stupid clods jumped off to buy a newspaper and ended up wasting their money in a flea-bag hotel with a degenerate woman.

"Bigger and better machines killed the Harvest Excursions. The final one rumbled west, I believe, around 1930. It got so a farmer and his family could do a crop all by themselves. Now the combines have radios and air-conditioning and fairly soon they'll be remote-controlled and the farmer won't have to leave his bed. I'm glad for them that they've got things easier but I'm sorry they're missing the companionship we had. The feeling of sharing and accomplishing you get when a gang of men work hard together."

A SCHOOL OUTING

I was in Grade Eleven at Govan High School in 1946. Govan's in southern Saskatchewan, a farm town. The kids from Nokomis invited us up for a day and everyone in our school went, sixty kids. It was only thirteen miles to Nokomis but that was a big deal, going so far by train. The gals wore their nicest saddle shoes and bobbysox and the fellows drowned their hair in Wildroot Cream Oil. We were a pretty tame lot. One brave guy smoked a cigarette and two other brave guys sipped a beer in the washroom. The girls huddled and giggled and whispered about which nifty guys from

Nokomis they'd seen at the last track meet. When we got to Nokomis, we had a skating party and a dance in the school gymnasium and then we trundled down to the station. Going home, the talk was of new Nokomis romances started and old Govan romances ended. The following summer, the Nokomis kids came by train to Govan. For a treasure hunt. I don't doubt they did and said the same things that we did and said coming and going on the railway. Just like our mothers and fathers had and, maybe, some of our grandmothers and grandfathers, too.

EIGHT HOURS OF DIGGING

Late in the winter of 1948 south Saskatchewan was clobbered by a blizzard that didn't want to quit. Three months of wind, snow, and bitter cold — 30 and 40 below. The snow drifted as high as telephone poles in open country and was hard as marble; so hard, farmers rode horses to the tops of the mounds without breaking through. No man in his right mind wanted to venture out in that weather. I know I sure as hell didn't. But I was a railroader and when I got the call, I went.

You see, the railway was the lifeline for the small towns. Should the roads be plugged and planes couldn't drop supplies, they relied upon us to help them survive. Some folks on the line south of Swift Current needed coal desperately. A train hadn't been by for twelve days. We had three engines and a plough when we left Swift Current. Eighty diggers too. The railway recruited men in beer parlours, cafés, and hotel lobbies and paid them 75 cents an hour for shovelling.

Heavens, it was storming that day. I'd been a trainman since 1918 and an engineer since '46 and that was the most wicked weather, bar none. You couldn't see ten feet in front of you. Quick as the plough cleared a rough section, and our train moved over it, the snow started filling it in again. They were really hard-up for coal at Neville. The local citizens heard the engine whistles and rushed to the station, despite the fact that it was 40 below that day. They anxiously watched us crack through the drifts north of town. They had sacks and buckets and anything you could carry coal in.

We didn't disappoint them. We got to Neville, all right. But what a battle. We ran smack into a 25-foot-high drift. The plough barged into it and got stuck halfway through. So the diggers went to work. Eighty men shovelled as fast as they could. Eighty hungry men, I might add. We hadn't brought any food with us, and working that hard at that temperature without eating was a terrible ordeal. Eight hours they dug. The poor souls were bone-tired.

We unloaded coal and ran for Vanguard, forty miles down the line. The diggers could eat and rest there. My fireman, Ed Sadler, and I were terribly worried. What if we hit more big drifts like the 25-footer? The shovelling might be too much for some of the men. Travelling behind a plough wasn't very relaxing either. All you could see was a blur of flying snow, and you had to be constantly ready for the tremendous jolt when the equipment made contact. You could be pitched against the boiler head and into valves and gauges and be badly hurt.

We were lucky. We got to Vanguard safe and sound. Make no mistake, that was a murderous winter for the railways.

Chic Cane's a retired engineer. He says that in February of '48 the Broadview–Moose Jaw run, normally a three-hour trip, took 68 hours. He remembers a train being held at Indian Head for two and a half days. Beside a coal shack and a water tank. The crew laboured round the clock so the engine didn't die and there'd be heat in the coaches.

Things were worse over at Expanse. Six engines with a plough on each end were ordered to clear track and got snowed-in. Including diggers, there were ninety men aboard. The people of Expanse contributed what food they could but they had precious little themselves. The men were trapped nine days. On the tenth day, the company hired planes when the storm eased and dropped them food.

The weather was tough on everybody. Harry Taylor, the CPR'S general manager for Saskatchewan, slept on a cot in his office for months so he'd be ready for new problems. Another official, Jack Miller, rode out on a plough and came back cut and bruised. How come? The hard snow. When the plough battered it, brick-sized pieces of snow flew in the cab and struck him. Those walls of snow were as solid as the Parthenon. The arrowpoints broke on some ploughs, others were derailed, and a few had caved-in roofs.

The only creatures that didn't mind the weather were the gophers. They hibernated and slept through it all.

Reprinted with the kind permission of Doubleday. From Sentimental Journey: an Oral history of Train Travel in Canada *by Tom Ferguson (Doubleday, 1985; ISBN 0-385-23252-7).*

LANGUAGE

Canada has two official languages – **English** and **French** – but there are numerous native tongues as well. Tensions between the two main groups play a prominent part in the politics of Canada, but the native languages are more or less ignored except in the country's most remote areas, particularly in the Northwest Territories, where **Inuktitut**, the language of the Inuit, is spoken widely. The Inuit are the only native population with their own-language TV channel; the only group afforded comparable attention are the Montagnais – Montagnais-Naskapi translations appear in northern Québec and Labrador official publications.

In a brief glossary such as this there is no space to get to grips with the complexities of aboriginal languages, and very few travellers would have any need of them anyway – most natives (including those in Québec) have a good knowledge of English, especially if they deal with tourists in any capacity. If you plan to be spending much time in French-speaking Canada, consider investing in **the Rough Guide to French** (Penguin, UK/US), a pocket-guide, in a handy A–Z format.

FRENCH IN QUÉBEC

Québec's official language differs from its European source only as far as North American English differs from British English. Yet while the Québécois French vocabulary, grammar and syntax may not constitute a separate language, the speech of Québec can pose a few problems. Tracing its roots back to seventeenth-century popular French, the Québécois language has preserved features that disappeared long ago in France itself and it has also been affected by its close contact with English. The end result is a dialect that is – frankly – a source of amusement to many French people and bafflement for those educated in the French language back in Europe. Within Québec itself there are marked regional differences of pronunciation, so much so that Montréalers find it hard to understand northern Québécois.

However, the Québécois are extremely sympathetic when visiting English-speakers make the effort to speak French – and most Québécois are much more forthcoming with their knowledge of English when talking to a Briton or American than to a Canadian. Similarly easy-going is the attitude towards the formal *vous* (you), which is used less often in Québec – you may even be corrected when saying *S'il vous plaît* with the suggestion that *S'il te plaît* is more appropriate. Another popular phrase that you are likely to come across is *pas de tout* ("not at all") which in Québec is pronounced *pan toot*, completely different from the French *pa du too*. The same goes for *c'est tout?* ("is that all?" pronounced *say toot*), which you'll hear every time you buy something in a shop.

With **pronunciation** there's little point trying to mimic the local dialect – generally, just stick to the classic French rules. Consonants at the ends of words are usually silent and at other times are much as in English, except that **ch** is always sh, **ç** is s, **h** is silent, **th** is the same as t, **ll** is like the y in yes and **r** is growled.

FRENCH WORDS AND PHRASES

BASICS

Good morning/ afternoon/Hello	*Bonjour*	Today	*Aujourd'hui*
Good evening	*Bonsoir*	Tomorrow	*Demain*
Good night	*Bonne nuit*	Day after tomorrow	*après-demain*
Goodbye	*Au revoir*	Yesterday	*Hier*
Yes	*Oui*	Now	*Maintenant*
No	*Non*	Later	*Plus tard*
Please	*S'il vous/te plaît*	Wait a minute!	*Un instant!*
Thank you (very much)	*Merci (beaucoup)*	In the morning	*Le matin*
You're welcome	*Bienvenue/de rien/ Je vous en prie*	In the afternoon	*L'après-midi*
		In the evening	*Le soir*
OK	*D'accord*	Here/there	*Ici/là*
How are you?	*Comment allez-vous?/Ça va?*	Good/bad	*Bon/mauvais*
Fine, thanks	*Très bien, merci*	Big/small	*Grand/petit*
Do you speak English?	*Parlez-vous anglais?*	Cheap/expensive	*Bon marché/cher*
		Early/late	*Tôt/Tard*
I don't understand	*Je ne comprends pas*	Hot/cold	*Chaud/froid*
I don't know	*Je ne sais pas*	Near/far	*Près (pas loin)/loin*
Excuse me	*Je m'excuse*	Vacant/occupied	*Libre/occupé*
Excuse me (in a crowd)	*Excusez-moi*	Quickly/slowly	*Vite/lentement*
		Loudly/quietly	*Bruyant/tranquille*
Sorry	*Pardon/désolé(e)*	With/without	*Avec/sans*
I'm English/ Scottish/Welsh/ Irish/American	*Je suis anglais(e)/ écossais(e)/gallois(e)/ irlandais(e)/américain(e)*	More/less	*Plus/moins*
		Enough/no more	*Assez/ça suffit*
		Mr	*Monseiur*
I live in . .	*Je demeure à*	Mrs	*Madame*
		Miss	*Mademoiselle*

QUESTIONS AND DIRECTIONS

Where?	*Où?*	Can you give me a lift to . . . ?	*Pouvez-vous me conduire jusqu'à . . . ?*
When?	*Quand?*	Can you tell me when to get off?	*Pouvez-vous me dire quand descendre?*
What? (what is it?)	*Quoi? (qu'est-ce que c'est?)*	What time is it?	*Quelle heure est-il?*
How much/many?	*Combien?*	What time does it open?	*À quelle heure ça ouvre?*
Why?	*Pourquoi?*	How much does it cost	*Combien cela coûte-t-il?*
It is/there is (is it/is there . . . ?)	*C'est/Il y a (est-ce/Y a-t-il . . . ?)*	How do you say it in French?	*Comment ça se dit en français?*
How do I get to . . . ?	*Où se trouve . . . ?*		
How far is it to . . . ?	*À quelle distance est-il à . . . ?*		

NUMBERS

1	*un/une*	11	*onze*	21	*vingt-et-un*	101	*cent-et-un*
2	*deux*	12	*douze*	22	*vingt-deux*	110	*cent-dix*
3	*trois*	13	*treize*	30	*trente*	200	*deux cents*
4	*quatre*	14	*quatorze*	40	*quarante*	500	*cinq cents*
5	*cinq*	15	*quinze*	50	*cinquante*	1000	*mille*
6	*six*	16	*seize*	60	*soixante*	2000	*deux milles*
7	*sept*	17	*dix-sept*	70	*soixante-dix*	1,000,000	*un million*
8	*huit*	18	*dix-huit*	80	*quatre-vingts*		
9	*neuf*	19	*dix-neuf*	90	*quatre-vingt-dix*		
10	*dix*	20	*vingt*	100	*cent*		

ACCOMMODATION

Is there a campsite nearby?	*Y a-t-il un camping près d'ici?*	with a shower/bath	*avec douche/ salle de bain*
Tent	*Tente*	hot/cold water	*eau chaude/froide*
Cabin	*Chalet*	How much is it?	*C'est combien?*
Youth hostel	*Auberge de jeunesse*	It's expensive	*C'est chère*
Do you have anything cheaper?	*Avez-vous quelque chose de meilleur marché?*	Is breakfast included?	*Est-ce que le petit déjeuner est compris?*
Full board	*Tout compris*	Hotel	*Hôtel*
Can I see the room?	*Je peux voir la chambre?*	Is there a room nearby?	*Y a-t-il une chambre près d'ici?*
I'll take this one	*Je vais prendre celle-ci*	Do you have a room . . .	*Avez-vous une chambre . . .*
I'd like to book a room	*J'aimerais réserver une chambre*	for one/two/ three people	*pour une/deux/ trois personne(s)*
I have a booking	*J'ai une réservation*	for one/two/ three nights	*pour une/deux/ trois nuit(s)*
Can we camp here?	*Pouvons-nous camper ici?*	for one/two weeks	*pour une/deux semaine(s)*
with a double bed	*avec un lit double*		

TRAVELLING

Aeroplane	*Avion*	Can I book a seat?	*Puis-je réserver un siège?*
Bus	*Autobus*	What time does it leave?	*Il part à quelle heure?*
Train	*Train*	When is the next bus/train/ ferry to . . .	*Quand est le prochain bus/train/ traversée pour . . . .*
Car	*Voiture*		
Taxi	*Taxi*		
Bicycle	*Vélo*		
Ferry	*Traverse*	Do I have to change?	*Ai-je à transférer?*
Ship	*Bâteau*	Where does it leave from?	*D'où est-ce qu'il part?*
Hitch-hiking	*Faire du pouce*		
On foot	*À pied*	How many kilometres?	*Combien de kilomètres?*
Bus station	*Gare routière/ gare des autobuses*	How many hours?	*Combien d'heures?*
		What number bus is it to . . . ?	*Quel autobus dois-je prendre pour aller à/au . . .?*
Railway station	*Gare centrale*		
Ferry terminal	*Terminus*		
Port	*Port*	Where's the road to . . . ?	*Où est la route pour . . .?*
A ticket to . . .	*Un billet pour . . .*		
One-way/return	*Aller simple/aller-retour*	Next stop	*Le prochain arrêt*

SOME SIGNS

Entrance/Exit	*Entrée/Sortie*	Platform	*Voie*
Free entrance	*Entrée Libre*	Cash desk	*Caisse*
Gentlemen/Ladies	*Messieurs/Dames*	Go/Walk	*Marchez*
WC	*Toilette*	Stop	*Arrêtez*
Vacant/Engaged	*Libre/Occupé*	Customs	*Douanes*
Open/Closed	*Ouvert/Fermé*	Do not touch	*Défense de toucher*
Arrivals/Departures	*Arrivées/Départs*	Danger	*Danger*
Closed for holidays	*Fermé pour les vacances*	Beware	*Attention*
Pull/Push	*Tirez/Poussez*	First aid	*Premiers soins*
Out of order	*Hors d'usage/Brisé*	Ring the bell	*Sonnez*
To let	*A loué*	No smoking	*Défense de fumer*

DRIVING

Left/right	*Gauche/droite*	No overtaking	*Défenser de dépasser*
Straight ahead	*Tout droit*	Passing lane only	*Voie réservée au depassement*
Turn to the left/right	*Tournez à gauche/droite*		
Car park	*Le terrain de stationnement*	Speed	*Vitesse*
		Self-service	*Libre-service*
No parking	*Défense de stationner/ stationnement interdit*	Full service	*Service complet*
		Fill the tank with	*Faites le plein avec de*
Tow-away zone	*Zone de remorquage*	regular . . . super	*l'essence ordinaire . . . du*
Cars towed at owner's expense	*Remorquage à vos frais*	. . . unleaded	*super . . . du sans plomb*
		Check the oil . . .	*Vérifiez l'huile . . .*
One-way street	*Sens unique*	battery . . .	*la batterie . . .*
No entry	*Défenser d'entrer*	radiator . . .	*le radiateur . . .*
Slow down	*Ralentir*	tyre pressure . . .	*pression des pneus/ tires . . .*
Proceed on flashing green light	*Attendez sur le feu vert clignotant*		
Turn on headlights	*Allumez vos phares*	plugs	*bougies*
No through road	*Cul-de-sac*	Blow up the tyres	*Soufflez les tires*

INDEX

Stay in touch with us!

ROUGH*NEWS* is Rough Guides' free newsletter. In three issues a year we give you news, travel issues, music reviews, readers' letters and the latest dispatches from authors on the road.

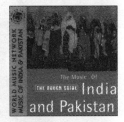
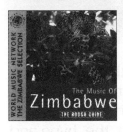

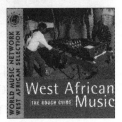

¿Qué pasa?

WHAT'S HAPPENING?
A ROUGH GUIDES SERIES –
ROUGH GUIDES PHRASEBOOKS

Rough Guide Phrasebooks
represent a complete shakeup of
the phrasebook format.
Handy and pocket sized, they
work like a dictionary to get you
straight to the point. With clear
guidelines on pronunciation,
dialogues for typical situations,
and tips on cultural issues, they'll
have you speaking the language
quicker than any other
phrasebook.

Czech, French, German, Greek,
Hindi & Urdu, Italian, Indonesian,
Mandarin Chinese, Mexican
Spanish, Polish, Portuguese,
Russian, Spanish, Thai, Turkish,
Vietnamese
Further titles coming soon...

the perfect getaway vehicle

low-price holiday car rental.

rent a car from holiday autos and you'll give yourself real freedom to explore your holiday destination. with great-value, fully-inclusive rates in over 4,000 locations worldwide, wherever you're escaping to, we're there to make sure you get excellent prices and superb service.

what's more, you can book now with complete confidence. our £5 undercut* ensures that you are guaranteed the best value for money in holiday destinations right around the globe.

drive away with a great deal, call holiday autos now on **0990 300 400** and quote ref RG.

holiday autos
miles ahead

*in the unlikely event that you should see a cheaper like for like pre-paid rental rate offered by any other independent uk car rental company before or after booking but prior to departure, holiday autos will undercut that price by a full £5. we truly believe we cannot be beaten on price.